W9-AND-658

A NEW CONCORDANCE

TO THE

HOLY BIBLE

King James Version

•

CONTAINING A NEW SELECTION OF WORDS, AND
SOME 70,000 CONTEXT LINES AS GUIDES TO
OFTEN-SOUGHT PASSAGES

AMERICAN BIBLE SOCIETY
NEW YORK

A New Concordance
King James Version

Copyright © 1960, American Bible Society

ISBN 1-58516-468-2
Printed in the United States of America
Eng. Concordance KJV743-101758
ABS-9/02-1,500-155,500–RRD25

How to use a Concordance

The Nature of a Concordance

A concordance serves much the same purpose as the index of a book in helping a person locate some specific name, word, or idea in that book. In addition, a concordance serves a broader purpose in giving both the name or the word sought and the passage in which it is found. Brief selections or *context lines* are printed, along with the references, and arranged in Biblical order under one or more of the leading *key words* in the line. A person may vaguely recall some phrase and want to find the exact quotation and reference; or, a person may be looking for what the Bible says about a given topic or theme. A concordance is designed to help one locate such references quickly and accurately. The references include the name or abbreviation of the Biblical book, chapter number, and verse number: *e.g.,* Is. 52:7 means Isaiah, chapter 52, verse 7.

The Key Words

The clue to quick location of a desired passage is the choice of the best word in the phrase which one recalls. Is there an unusual, vivid word which stands out in one's mind? It may be a name, a place, a color, a kind of action or a quality. The key words, especially chosen for their vividness, ease of remembering, and colorful associations, are given in bold type. In this concordance, there are about 4,700 key words, such as **Adoption, Adversary, Charity, Forgiveness, Love,** and **Martyr.** Listed in Biblical order under the key words are a selection of context lines in which the key word is found. In order to save space in the context lines, the key words are there represented by the first letter of the word in italics. Included in parentheses after the key words are alternative forms (such as **Knife (Knives), Less (Lesser),** or **Lie (Lay, Lain)**) which may be found in some of the context lines in that section.

Parallel Passages

Many passages in the Bible are actually quoted almost identically elsewhere either in the Old or the New Testament. The concordance gives many such cross-references in parentheses beside the first occurrence. Thus, context lines for **Bring** include Is. 52:7 (Nah. 1:15; Rom. 10:15) "that *b* good tidings." Context lines for **Poor** include Mt. 26:11 (Mk. 14:7; Jn. 12:8) "the *p* always with you." This listing of parallel passages helps show the inter-relatedness of Scripture and also serves to limit the number of context lines through which one must search.

Biographical Paragraphs

When looking for information about leading characters in the Bible, check the biographical summary immediately under the key word which gives the name of the person. It contains a summary of the main events in the person's life, along with the accompanying references. In addition, context lines are also provided for many persons in the Bible. Where the name occurs elsewhere with a different spelling, this is given too: *e.g.,* **Abraham (Abram), Elisha (Eliseus).** Where two or more persons have the same name, the persons are listed separately, such as **James** the son of Zebedee, **James** the son of Alpheus, and **James** the brother of Jesus.

The major geographical names and personal names are included in the concordance in alphabetical order. A name may be followed by an alternative spelling, an alternate name, or a cross-reference such as **Agar** *See* Hagar. Along with the name are either references or select context lines in which the name occurs.

Text Used in This Concordance

This concordance is not exhaustive but does contain about 70,000 context lines from the passages which most Bible readers will be seeking. Since the concordance is based on the American Bible Society English Reference Bible edition, there are a few differences of spelling from some other editions of the King James Version of the Bible. *E.g.,* "labour" is spelled "labor" and "an hungered" is spelled "a hungered." However, these differences in spelling will not affect the use of this concordance with other editions of the King James Version.

Alphabetical List of Biblical Books and Abbreviations

Acts	Acts	Jas.	James	Neh.	Nehemiah
Amos	Amos	Jer.	Jeremiah	Num.	Numbers
Chr., 1	1 Chronicles	Job	Job	Obad.	Obadiah
Chr., 2	2 Chronicles	Joel	Joel	Pet., 1	1 Peter
Col.	Colossians	Jn.	John	Pet., 2	2 Peter
Cor., 1	1 Corinthians	Jn., 1	1 John	Phlm.	Philemon
Cor., 2	2 Corinthians	Jn., 2	2 John	Phil.	Philippians
Dan.	Daniel	Jn., 3	3 John	Prov.	Proverbs
Deut.	Deuteronomy	Jon.	Jonah	Ps.	Psalms
Eccl.	Ecclesiastes	Josh.	Joshua	Rev.	Revelation
Eph.	Ephesians	Jude	Jude	Rom.	Romans
Esth.	Esther	Judg.	Judges	Ruth	Ruth
Ex.	Exodus	Kgs., 1	1 Kings	Sam., 1	1 Samuel
Ezek.	Ezekiel	Kgs., 2	2 Kings	Sam., 2	2 Samuel
Ezra	Ezra	Lam.	Lamentations	Song	Song of Solomon
Gal.	Galatians	Lev.	Leviticus	Thes., 1	1 Thessalonians
Gen.	Genesis	Lk.	Luke	Thes., 2	2 Thessalonians
Hab.	Habakkuk	Mal.	Malachi	Tim., 1	1 Timothy
Hag.	Haggai	Mk.	Mark	Tim., 2	2 Timothy
Heb.	Hebrews	Mt.	Matthew	Tit.	Titus
Hos.	Hosea	Mic.	Micah	Zech.	Zechariah
Is.	Isaiah	Nah.	Nahum	Zeph.	Zephaniah

Order and Abbreviations of Biblical Books

OLD TESTAMENT

Gen.	Genesis	2 Chr.	2 Chronicles	Dan.	Daniel
Ex.	Exodus	Ezra	Ezra	Hos.	Hosea
Lev.	Leviticus	Neh.	Nehemiah	Joel	Joel
Num.	Numbers	Esth.	Esther	Amos	Amos
Deut.	Deuteronomy	Job	Job	Obad.	Obadiah
Josh.	Joshua	Ps.	Psalms	Jon.	Jonah
Judg.	Judges	Prov.	Proverbs	Mic.	Micah
Ruth	Ruth	Eccl.	Ecclesiastes	Nah.	Nahum
1 Sam.	1 Samuel	Song	Song of Solomon	Hab.	Habakkuk
2 Sam.	2 Samuel	Is.	Isaiah	Zeph.	Zephaniah
1 Kgs.	1 Kings	Jer.	Jeremiah	Hag.	Haggai
2 Kgs.	2 Kings	Lam.	Lamentations	Zech.	Zechariah
1 Chr.	1 Chronicles	Ezek.	Ezekiel	Mal.	Malachi

NEW TESTAMENT

Mt.	Matthew	Eph.	Ephesians	Heb.	Hebrews
Mk.	Mark	Phil.	Philippians	Jas.	James
Lk.	Luke	Col.	Colossians	1 Pet.	1 Peter
Jn.	John	1 Thes.	1 Thessalonians	2 Pet.	2 Peter
Acts	Acts	2 Thes.	2 Thessalonians	1 Jn.	1 John
Rom.	Romans	1 Tim.	1 Timothy	2 Jn.	2 John
1 Cor.	1 Corinthians	2 Tim.	2 Timothy	3 Jn.	3 John
2 Cor.	2 Corinthians	Tit.	Titus	Jude	Jude
Gal.	Galatians	Phlm.	Philemon	Rev.	Revelation

A Concordance to The Holy Bible

KING JAMES VERSION

A

Aaron

Brother of Moses, Ex. 4:14; 7:1; commended for his eloquence, Ex. 4:14; chosen to assist Moses, Ex. 4:16, 27; co-leader with Moses, Ex. 5:1; 8:25; supported Moses' arms, Ex. 17:12; set apart as priest, Ex. 28; Heb. 5:4; made a golden calf, Ex. 32; Acts 7:40; found fault with Moses, Num. 12; his rod budded, Num. 17; Heb. 9:4.

Abana 2 Kgs. 5:12

Abarim Num. 27:12 (Deut. 32:49)

Abase *See also* Humble

Job 40:11 behold every one that is proud, and *a* him
Is. 31:4 he will not be afraid..nor *a* himself for
Ezek. 21:26 exalt..low, and *a* him that is high
Dan. 4:37 those that walk in pride he is able to *a*
Mt. 23:12 (Lk. 14:11; 18:14) exalt himself shall be *a*
2 Cor. 11:7 in *a* myself that ye might be exalted
Phil. 4:12 know both how to be *a*, and..to abound

Abate *See also* Decrease, Diminish

Gen. 8:3 hundred and fifty days the waters were *a*
Deut. 34:7 eye..not dim, nor his natural force *a*

Abba

Mk. 14:36 he said, *A*, Father..take away this cup
Rom. 8:15 the Spirit..whereby we cry, *A*, Father
Gal. 4:6 into your hearts, crying, *A*, Father

Abed-nego Dan. 1:6–3:30

Abel Gen. 4:2–10

Mt. 23:35 (Lk. 11:51) from the blood of righteous *A*
Heb. 11:4 by faith *A* offered..a more excellent
12:24 that speaketh better things than that of *A*

Abhor *See also* Contemn, Despise, Detest, Disdain, Hate, Loathe

Ex. 5:21 our savor to be *a* in the eyes of Pharaoh
Lev. 26:11 among you: and my soul shall not *a* you
Deut. 7:26 utterly *a* it; for it is a cursed thing
1 Sam. 27:12 hath made his people..utterly to *a* him
Job 19:19 all my inward friends *a* me
42:6 wherefore I *a* myself, and repent in dust
Ps. 5:6 Lord will *a* the bloody and deceitful man
10:3 and blesseth the covetous, whom the Lord *a*
36:4 he deviseth mischief..he *a* not evil
78:59 heard..he was wroth, and greatly *a* Israel
89:38 thou hast cast off and..thine anointed
106:40 insomuch that he *a* his own inheritance
107:18 their soul *a* all manner of meat
119:163 I hate and *a* lying..thy law do I love
Prov. 22:14 is *a* of the Lord shall fall therein
24:24 the people curse, nations shall *a* him
Is. 7:16 the land that thou *a* shall be forsaken

Is. 66:24 they shall be an *a* unto all flesh
Jer. 14:21 do not *a* us, for thy name's sake
Lam. 2:7 he hath *a* his sanctuary, he hath given up
Ezek. 16:25 and hast made thy beauty to be *a*
Amos 5:10 and they *a* him that speaketh uprightly
6:8 I *a* the excellency of Jacob, and hate his
Rom. 12:9 *a* that which is evil; cleave to..good

Abiathar

1 Sam. 22:20 *A*, escaped, and fled after David
1 Kgs. 2:27 Solomon thrust out *A* from being priest
Mk. 2:26 he went..in the days of *A* the high priest

Abib Ex. 13:4 (Deut. 16:1)

Abide (Abode) *See also* Dwell, Inhabit, Lodge, Sojourn

Gen. 19:2 but we will *a* in the street all night
44:33 let thy servant *a* instead of the lad
49:24 but his bow *a* in strength, and the arms
Ex. 16:29 the sabbath..*a* ye every man in his place
24:16 the glory of the Lord *a* upon mount Sinai
Num. 20:1 the people *a* in Kadesh; and Miriam died
24:2 he saw Israel *a* in his tents according to
31:19 *a* without the camp seven days: whosoever
35:25 *a* in it unto the death of the high priest
Judg. 5:16 why *a* thou among the sheepfolds
21:2 the people..*a* there till even before God
Ruth 2:8 go not..but *a* here fast by my maidens
1 Sam. 5:7 the ark of..God..shall not *a* with us
7:2 the ark *a* in Kirjath-jearim..twenty years
Job 24:13 know not..nor *a* in the paths thereof
Ps. 15:1 Lord, who shall *a* in thy tabernacle?
55:19 and afflict them, even he that *a* of old
61:4 I will *a* in thy tabernacle for ever
91:1 shall *a* under the shadow of the Almighty
125:1 shall be as mount Zion, which..*a* for ever
Prov. 15:31 ear that heareth the reproof of life *a*
19:23 he that hath it shall *a* satisfied; he shall
Eccl. 1:4 one generation..but the earth *a* for ever
Jer. 42:10 if ye will still *a* in this land, then
49:18 (49:33; 50:40) no man shall *a* there, neither
Hos. 3:3 thou shalt *a* for me many days
Joel 2:11 great and very terrible..who can *a* it?
Mic. 5:4 they shall *a*: for now shall he be great
Mal. 3:2 but who may *a* the day of his coming?
Mt. 10:11 (Mk. 6:10; Lk. 9:4) *a* till ye go thence
Lk. 1:56 and Mary *a* with her about three months
2:8 shepherds *a* in the field, keeping watch over
19:5 come down; for today I must *a* at thy house
24:29 *a* with us: for it is toward evening
Jn. 1:32 the Spirit descending..and it *a* upon him
1:39 they came..and *a* with him that day
3:36 not see life; but the wrath of God *a* on him
5:38 and ye have not his word *a* in you
8:44 he was a murderer..and *a* not in the truth
14:16 another Comforter, that he may *a* with you

Jn. 15:4 *a* in me, and I in you . . except ye *a* in me
  15:7 if ye *a* in me, and my words *a* in you, ye
  15:10 keep my commandments . . shall *a* in my love
Acts 14:3 long . . *a* they speaking boldly in the Lord
  16:15 besought us . . come into my house, and *a*
  18:3 same craft, he *a* with them, and wrought
  27:31 except these *a* in the ship, ye cannot be
1 Cor. 3:14 if any man's work *a* . . receive a reward
  7:24 wherein he is called, therein *a* with God
  13:13 now *a* faith, hope, charity, these three
Phil. 1:24 to *a* in the flesh is more needful for you
1 Tim. 1:3 I besought thee to *a* still at Ephesus
2 Tim. 2:13 if we believe not, yet he *a* faithful
1 Pet. 1:23 by the word of God, which . . *a* for ever
1 Jn. 2:6 he that saith he *a* in him ought himself
  2:14 are strong, and the word of God *a* in you
  2:17 he that doeth the will of God *a* for ever
  2:28 and now, little children, *a* in him
  3:6 whosoever *a* in him sinneth not

Abigail 1 Sam. 25:3–42

Abihu Lev. 10:1

Abijah son of Jeroboam 1 Kgs. 14:1–18

Abijah (Abijam) king of Judah
1 Kgs. 15:1–8 (2 Chr. 13:1–22)

Ability
Lev. 27:8 according to his *a* that vowed shall the
Ezra 2:69 gave after their *a* unto the treasure of
Neh. 5:8 after our *a*, have redeemed our brethren
Dan. 1:4 *a* in them to stand in the king's palace
Mt. 25:15 to every man according to his several *a*
Acts 11:29 according to his *a* . . to send relief unto
1 Pet. 4:11 minister . . as of the *a* which God giveth

Abimelech king of Gerar
Gen. 20:2–18; 21:22–32; 26:1–31

Abimelech son of Gideon
Judg. 9:1–57; 2 Sam. 11:21

Abinadab of Kirjath-jearim
1 Sam. 7:1 (2 Sam. 6:4)

Abinadab son of Jesse 1 Sam. 16:8
Abinadab son of Saul
1 Sam. 31:2 (1 Chr. 10:2)

Abiram the Levite Num. 16:1–32; Ps. 106:17

Abiram son of Hiel 1 Kgs. 16:34

Abishag 1 Kgs. 1:3; 2:17

Abishai
Sought to kill Saul, 1 Sam. 26:5–9; pursued Abner,
2 Sam. 2:18, 24; desired to kill Shimei, 2 Sam. 16:9–
11; 19:21; slew the Edomites, 1 Chr. 18:12.

Abject
Ps. 35:15 *a* gathered themselves together against

Able
Ex. 18:25 and Moses chose *a* men out of all Israel
Num. 13:30 go up . . for we are well *a* to overcome it
Deut. 16:17 every man shall give as he is *a*
Josh. 23:9 no man hath been *a* to stand before you
1 Sam. 6:20 *a* to stand before this holy Lord God?
1 Kgs. 3:9 who is *a* to judge . . so great a people?
2 Chr. 2:6 but who is *a* to build him a house

2 Chr. 25:9 Lord is *a* to give thee much more than
Prov. 27:4 but who is *a* to stand before envy?
Dan. 3:17 our God whom we serve is *a* to deliver us
  6:20 O Daniel . . is thy God . . *a* to deliver thee
Amos 7:10 the land is not *a* to bear all his words
Mt. 3:9 (Lk. 3:8) God is *a* of these stones to raise
  9:28 saith . . Believe ye that I am *a* to do this?
  20:22 are ye *a* to drink of the cup . . We are *a*
  22:46 and no man was *a* to answer him a word
Lk. 12:26 be not *a* to do that thing which is least
  13:24 will seek to enter in, and shall not be *a*
Jn. 10:29 and no man is *a* to pluck them out of my
Acts 6:10 not *a* to resist the wisdom and . . spirit
Rom. 4:21 had promised, he was *a* also to perform
  8:39 be *a* to separate us from the love of God
1 Cor. 10:13 to be tempted above that ye are *a*
2 Cor. 3:6 us *a* ministers of the new testament
  9:8 God is *a* to make all grace abound toward
Eph. 3:20 is *a* to do exceeding abundantly above all
Phil. 3:21 he is *a* even to subdue all things unto
2 Tim. 1:12 am persuaded that he is *a* to keep that
Heb. 2:18 he is *a* to succor them that are tempted
  7:25 he is *a* also to save them to the uttermost
Jas. 1:21 word, which is *a* to save your souls
  4:12 lawgiver, who is *a* to save and to destroy
Jude 24 unto him that is *a* to keep you from falling
Rev. 5:3 no man . . was *a* to open the book, neither
  6:17 day . . is come; and who shall be *a* to stand?

Abner
Captain of the host, 1 Sam. 14:50; made Ish-bosheth
king, 2 Sam. 2:8–11; fought David's forces, 2 Sam.
2:12–32; made a league with David, 2 Sam. 3:6–21;
slain by Joab, 2 Sam. 3:22–30; mourned by David, 2
Sam. 3:31–39.

Abode *See also* Dwelling, Habitation, House
2 Kgs. 19:27 (Is. 37:28) I know thy *a* . . thy going out
Jn. 14:23 we will come . . and make our *a* with him

Abolish *See also* Destroy
Is. 2:18 and the idols he shall utterly *a*
  51:6 for ever . . my righteousness shall not be *a*
Ezek. 6:6 be cut down, and your works may be *a*
2 Cor. 3:13 look to the end of that which is *a*
Eph. 2:15 having *a* in his flesh the enmity
2 Tim. 1:10 Jesus Christ, who hath *a* death

Abominable *See also* Base, Loathsome, Vile, Wicked
Lev. 7:21 that shall touch . . any *a* unclean thing
  18:30 ye commit not any one of these *a* customs
Deut. 14:3 thou shalt not eat any *a* thing
Job 15:16 how much more *a* and filthy is man
Ps. 14:1 (53:1) are corrupt, they have done *a* works
Is. 14:19 cast out of thy grave like an *a* branch
  65:4 and broth of *a* things is in their vessels
Jer. 16:18 with the carcases of their . . *a* things
  44:4 saying, Oh, do not this *a* thing that I hate
Mic. 6:10 and the scant measure that is *a*?
Tit. 1:16 but in works they deny him, being *a*
1 Pet. 4:3 past . . when we walked in . . *a* idolatries
Rev. 21:8 the fearful, and unbelieving, and the *a*

Abominably
1 Kgs. 21:26 and he did very *a* in following idols

Abomination *See also* Evil, Shame
Gen. 46:34 shepherd is an *a* unto the Egyptians
Ex. 8:26 shall we sacrifice the *a* of the Egyptians

Lev. 11:10 have not fins and scales. . shall be an *a*
18:22 thou shalt not lie with mankind. . it is *a*
Deut. 7:26 neither. . bring an *a* into thine house
17:1 bullock, or sheep, wherein is blemish. . is an *a*
18:9 learn to do after the *a* of those nations
24:4 may not take her again. . for that is *a*
25:16 and all that do unrighteously, are an *a*
27:15 maketh any graven or molten image, an *a*
1 Sam. 13:4 Israel. . had in *a* with the Philistines
1 Kgs. 14:24 according to all the *a* of the nations
Prov. 3:32 for the froward is *a* to the LORD
6:16 these six. . yea, seven are an *a* unto him
8:7 speak truth. . wickedness is an *a* to my lips
11:1 a false balance is *a* to the LORD
12:22 lying lips are *a* to the LORD
15:9 way of the wicked is an *a* unto the LORD
15:26 the thoughts of the wicked are an *a* to
20:23 divers weights are an *a* unto the LORD
21:27 the sacrifice of the wicked is *a*
28:9 turneth away. . even his prayer shall be *a*
Is. 1:13 vain oblations; incense is an *a* unto me
41:24 of nought: an *a* is he that chooseth you
44:19 shall I make the residue thereof an *a*?
66:3 and their soul delighteth in their *a*
66:17 gardens. . eating swine's flesh, and the *a*
Jer. 2:7 defiled my land. . made mine heritage an *a*
4:1 if thou. . put away thine *a* out of my sight
6:15 (8:12) ashamed when they had committed *a*?
Ezek. 5:11 defiled my sanctuary. . with all thine *a*
7:3 and will recompense upon thee all thine *a*
7:20 but they made the images of their *a* and of
8:9 go in. . behold the wicked *a* that they do here
11:18 they shall take away. . all the *a* thereof
16:2 son of man, cause Jerusalem to know her *a*
16:51 but thou hast multiplied thine *a* more
18:13 hath done all these *a*; he shall surely die
33:29 and most desolate, because of all their *a*
Dan. 9:27 for the overspreading of *a* he shall make
11:31 (12:11) place the *a* that maketh desolate
Hos. 9:10 and their *a* were according as they loved
Mal. 2:11 an *a* is committed in Israel. . for Judah
Mt. 24:15 (Mk. 13:14) shall see the *a* of desolation
Lk. 16:15 which is highly esteemed among men is *a*
Rev. 21:27 in no wise enter. . whatsoever worketh *a*

Abound *See also* Overflow

Prov. 28:20 a faithful man shall *a* with blessings
Mt. 24:12 because iniquity shall *a*, the love of
Rom. 3:7 truth of God hath more *a* through my lie
5:20 but where sin *a*, grace did much more *a*
15:13 peace in believing, that ye may *a* in hope
1 Cor. 15:58 always *a* in the work of the Lord
2 Cor. 1:5 sufferings. . *a*. . our consolation also *a*
8:2 joy and their deep poverty *a* unto the riches
8:7 as ye *a* in everything. . ye *a* in this grace
9:8 God is able to make all grace *a* toward you
Eph. 1:8 *a* toward us in all wisdom and prudence
Phil. 4:12 how to be abased, and I know how to *a*
4:17 I desire fruit that may *a* to your account
Col. 2:7 in the faith. . *a* therein with thanksgiving
1 Thes. 3:12 and *a* in love one toward another
2 Pet. 1:8 for if these things be in you, and *a*

Above

Deut. 28:13 shalt be *a* only, and. . not be beneath
2 Sam. 22:17 (Ps. 18:16) he sent from *a*, he took me
Job 31:2 for what portion of God is there from *a*?
Ps. 10:5 thy judgments are far *a* out of his sight
Prov. 15:24 the way of life is *a* to the wise
Mt. 10:24 (Lk. 6:40) disciple is not *a* his master
Jn. 3:31 he that cometh from *a* is *a* all: he that
8:23 ye are from beneath; I am from *a*
19:11 no power. . except it were given thee from *a*

Rom. 14:5 one man esteemeth one day *a* another
1 Cor. 4:6 to think of men *a* that which is written
Gal. 4:26 but Jerusalem which is *a* is free
Eph. 4:6 one God and Father of all, who is *a* all
Phil. 2:9 given him a name which is *a* every name
Col. 3:2 set your affection on things *a*, not on
Jas. 1:17 every good. . and. . perfect gift is from *a*

Abraham (Abram)

Born, Gen. 11:26; married Sarai, Gen. 11:29; migrated from Ur to Haran, Gen. 11:31; called by God, Gen. 12:1–5; went to Egypt, Gen. 12:10–20; separated from Lot, Gen. 13:7–11; rescued Lot, Gen. 14: 13–16; God's covenant with him, Gen. 15:18; 17:1–22; entertained angels, Gen. 18:1–21; interceded for Sodom, Gen. 18:22–33; banished Hagar and Ishmael, Gen. 21:9–21; offered Isaac, Gen. 22:1–14; buried Sarah in Machpelah, Gen. 23; married Keturah, Gen. 25:1; death and burial, Gen. 25:8–9.

Is. 41:8 thou, Israel. . the seed of *A* my friend
Mt. 3:9 (Lk. 3:8) of these stones. . children unto *A*
8:11 sit down with *A*, and Isaac, and Jacob
Lk. 13:28 see *A*. . Isaac, and Jacob. . in the kingdom
16:22 was carried by the angels into *A*'s bosom
Jn. 8:39 *A*'s children, ye would do the works of *A*
8:58 Jesus said unto them. . Before *A* was, I am
Acts 7:2 God of glory appeared unto our father *A*
Rom. 4:3 (Gal. 3:6; Jas. 2:23) *A* believed God
4:16 faith of *A*; who is the father of us all
9:7 neither. . seed of *A*, are they all children
Gal. 3:7 which are of faith. . are the children of *A*
Heb. 11:8 by faith *A*, when he was called. . obeyed
Jas. 2:21 was not *A* our father justified by works

Absalom

Third son of David, 2 Sam. 3:3; avenged Tamar and fled, 2 Sam. 13:21–39; returned to Jerusalem, 2 Sam. 14:23–33; conspired against David, 2 Sam. 15:1–12; slain by Joab, 2 Sam. 18:9–17; mourned by David, 2 Sam. 18:33.

Absent

Gen. 31:49 watch. . when we are *a* one from another
1 Cor. 5:3 as *a* in body, but present in spirit
2 Cor. 5:6 at home in the body. . *a* from the Lord
10:1 in presence am base. . but being *a* am bold
Col. 2:5 be *a* in the flesh. . with you in the spirit

Abstain

Acts 15:20 (15:29) they *a* from pollutions of idols
1 Thes. 4:3 that ye should *a* from fornication
5:22 *a* from all appearance of evil
1 Tim. 4:3 commanding to *a* from meats, which God
1 Pet. 2:11 *a* from fleshly lusts, which war against

Abstinence

Acts 27:21 but after long *a*, Paul stood forth

Abundance *See also* Fulness, Plenty

Deut. 28:47 with gladness. . for the *a* of all things
1 Sam. 1:16 out of the *a* of my complaint and grief
2 Sam. 12:30 forth the spoil of the city in great *a*
1 Kgs. 18:41 for there is a sound of *a* of rain
1 Chr. 29:21 and sacrifices in *a* for all Israel
Job 36:31 by them judgeth he. . he giveth meat in *a*
Ps. 52:7 but trusted in the *a* of his riches
72:7 *a* of peace so long as the moon endureth
Eccl. 5:12 *a* of the rich will not suffer him to sleep
Is. 60:5 the *a* of the sea shall be converted unto
66:11 and be delighted with the *a* of her glory
Jer. 33:6 will reveal. . the *a* of peace and truth
Ezek. 16:49 fulness of bread, and *a* of idleness

Mt. 12:34 (Lk. 6:45) of the *a* of the heart. . speaketh
13:12 (25:29) shall be given. . shall have more *a*
Mk. 12:44 (Lk. 21:4) they did cast in of their *a*
Lk. 12:15 a man's life consisteth not in the *a* of
Rom. 5:17 much more they which receive *a* of grace
2 Cor. 8:2 *a* of their joy and their deep poverty
8:14 your *a* may be a supply for their want
12:7 exalted. . through the *a* of the revelations
Rev. 18:3 rich through the *a* of her delicacies

Abundant *See also* Plenteous, Rich

Ex. 34:6 the LORD God. . *a* in goodness and truth
Is. 56:12 shall be as this day, and much more *a*
1 Cor. 12:23 upon these we bestow more *a* honor
2 Cor. 4:15 *a* grace. . redound to the glory of God
9:12 is *a* also by many thanksgivings unto God
11:23 in labors more *a*, in stripes above measure
1 Tim. 1:14 the grace of our Lord was exceeding *a*
1 Pet. 1:3 according to his *a* mercy hath begotten

Abundantly

Gen. 1:20 God said, Let the waters bring forth *a*
Job 36:28 the clouds do drop and distil upon man *a*
Is. 55:7 and to our God, for he will *a* pardon
Jn. 10:10 might have life, and. . have it more *a*
1 Cor. 15:10 but I labored more *a* than they all
2 Cor. 10:15 be enlarged. . according to our rule *a*
Eph. 3:20 able to do exceeding *a* above all that
Tit. 3:6 he shed on us *a* through Jesus Christ our
Heb. 6:17 wherein God, willing more *a* to show unto
2 Pet. 1:11 an entrance shall be ministered unto you *a*

Abuse

Judg. 19:25 they knew her, and *a* her all the night
1 Sam. 31:4 (1 Chr. 10:4) these uncircumcised. . *a* me
1 Cor. 7:31 they that use this world, as not *a* it
9:18 charge, that I *a* not my power in the gospel

Accept *See also* Receive, Take

Gen. 4:7 if thou doest well, shalt thou not be *a*?
32:20 the present. . peradventure he will *a* of me
Ex. 28:38 upon his forehead, that they may be *a*
Lev. 10:19 if I had eaten. . should it have been *a*
Deut. 33:11 bless. . and *a* the works of his hands
1 Sam. 18:5 was *a* in the sight of all the people
2 Sam. 24:23 Araunah said. . The LORD thy God *a*
Esth. 10:3 and *a* of the multitude of his brethren
Job 13:8 will ye *a* his person? will ye contend for
32:21 let me not, I pray you, *a* any man's person
34:19 to him that *a* not the persons of princes
42:8 Job shall pray for you: for him will I *a*
Ps. 20:3 thy offerings, and *a* thy burnt sacrifice
82:2 ye judge. . and *a* the persons of the wicked?
119:108 *a* . . the freewill offerings of my mouth
Prov. 18:5 not good to *a* the person of the wicked
Jer. 14:12 and when they offer. . I will not *a* them
37:20 let my supplication, I pray thee, be *a*
42:2 let, we beseech thee, our supplication be *a*
Ezek. 20:40 in mine holy mountain. . will I *a* them
43:27 your peace offerings; and I will *a* you
Amos 5:22 though ye offer me. . I will not *a* them
Mal. 1:13 offering: should I *a* this of your hand?
Lk. 4:24 no prophet is *a* in his own country
Acts 10:35 worketh righteousness, is *a* with him
Rom. 15:31 that my service. . may be *a* of the saints
2 Cor. 5:9 present or absent, we may be *a* of him
8:12 it is *a* according to that a man hath
Gal. 2:6 no matter to me: God *a* no man's person

Acceptable

Lev. 22:20 hath a blemish. . shall not be *a* for you
Ps. 19:14 meditation of my heart, be *a* in thy sight
69:13 prayer is unto thee, O LORD, in an *a* time

Prov. 10:32 lips of the righteous know what is *a*
Eccl. 12:10 the Preacher sought to find out *a* words
Is. 49:8 (2 Cor. 6:2) in an *a* time have I heard thee
61:2 (Lk. 4:19) proclaim the *a* year of the LORD
Jer. 6:20 your burnt offerings are not *a*, nor your
Rom. 12:1 a living sacrifice, holy, *a* unto God
12:2 that good, and *a*, and perfect will of God
14:18 in these things serveth Christ is *a* to God
15:16 offering up of the Gentiles might be *a*
Eph. 5:10 proving what is *a* unto the Lord
1 Pet. 2:20 take it patiently, this is *a* with God

Acceptably

Heb. 12:28 serve God *a* with reverence and. . fear

Acceptation

1 Tim. 1:15 (4:9) faithful saying, and worthy of all *a*

Accepted *See also* Accept

2 Cor. 6:2 in a time *a* . . behold, now is the *a* time
Eph. 1:6 wherein he hath made us *a* in the beloved

Access

Rom. 5:2 also we have *a* by faith into this grace
Eph. 2:18 both have *a* by one Spirit unto the Father
3:12 we have boldness and *a* with confidence by

Accompany

Acts 10:23 and certain brethren from Joppa *a* him
20:38 no more. And they *a* him unto the ship
Heb. 6:9 better things. . and things that *a* salvation

Accomplish *See also* Do, Execute, Fulfil, Perform, Work

Lev. 22:21 offerings unto the LORD to *a* his vow
1 Kgs. 5:9 thou shalt *a* my desire, in giving food
Job 14:6 till he shall *a*, as a hireling, his day
Ps. 64:6 out iniquities; they *a* a diligent search
Prov. 13:19 the desire *a* is sweet to the soul
Is. 40:2 cry unto her, that her warfare is *a*
55:11 void, but it shall *a* that which I please
Jer. 25:34 for the days. . of your dispersions are *a*
39:16 my words. . shall be *a* in that day before
44:25 ye will surely *a* your vows, and. . perform
Dan. 9:2 by books. . that he would *a* seventy years
Lk. 9:31 decease which he should *a* at Jerusalem
12:50 and how am I straitened till it be *a*!
18:31 all. . concerning the Son of man shall be *a*
22:37 this that is written must yet be *a* in me
Jn. 19:28 knowing that all things were now *a*
1 Pet. 5:9 same afflictions are *a* in your brethren

Accord

Lev. 25:5 which groweth of its own *a* of thy harvest
Acts 1:14 all continued with one *a* in prayer and
2:1 come, they were all with one *a* in one place
2:46 continuing daily with one *a* in the temple
4:24 lifted up their voice to God with one *a*
8:6 the people with one *a* gave heed unto those
Phil. 2:2 same love, being of one *a*, of one mind

Account *See also* Count, Reckon, Record

Job 33:13 he giveth not *a* of any of his matters
Ps. 144:3 son of man, that thou makest *a* of him!
Mt. 12:36 that every idle word. . they shall give *a*
18:23 king, which would take *a* of his servants
Lk. 16:2 give an *a* of thy stewardship
20:35 shall be *a* worthy to obtain that world
21:36 be *a* worthy to escape all these things
22:24 which of them should be *a* the greatest
Rom. 8:36 we are *a* as sheep for the slaughter

Rom. 14:12 every one. . shall give *a* of himself to God
Gal. 3:6 and it was *a* to him for righteousness
Phil. 4:17 desire fruit that may abound to your *a*
Phlm. 18 oweth thee aught, put that on mine *a*
Heb. 11:19 *a* that God was able to raise him up
    13:17 for they watch. . as they that must give *a*
1 Pet. 4:5 give *a* to him that is ready to judge
2 Pet. 3:15 *a* that the long-suffering of our Lord

Accursed *See also* Anathema, Cursed

Deut. 21:23 for he that is hanged is *a* of God
Josh. 6:18 any wise keep yourselves from the *a* thing
    7:1 Israel committed a trespass in the *a* thing
Is. 65:20 sinner. . a hundred years old shall be *a*
Rom. 9:3 wish that myself were *a* from Christ for
1 Cor. 12:3 by the Spirit of God calleth Jesus *a*
Gal. 1:8 (1:9) preach any other gospel. . let him be *a*

Accusation *See also* Charge

Ezra 4:6 wrote. . an *a* against. . Judah and Jerusalem
Mt. 27:37 (Mk. 15:26) over his head his *a* written
Lk. 6:7 that they might find an *a* against him
    19:8 taken any thing from any man by false *a*, I
Jn. 18:29 said, What *a* bring ye against this man?
Acts 25:18 none *a* of such things as I supposed
1 Tim. 5:19 against an elder receive not an *a*
2 Pet. 2:11 bring not railing *a* against them before
Jude 9 durst not bring against him a railing *a*

Accuse *See also* Condemn, Judge

Prov. 30:10 *a* not a servant unto his master, lest
Dan. 3:8 Chaldeans came near, and *a* the Jews
Mt. 12:10 (Mk. 3:2) sabbath. . that they might *a* him
    27:12 (Mk. 15:3; Lk. 23:10) *a* of the chief priests
Lk. 3:14 neither *a* any falsely; and be content with
    11:54 out of his mouth, that they might *a* him
    16:1 was *a* unto him that he had wasted his goods
Jn. 5:45 that I will *a* you. . there is one that *a*
Acts 24:2 called forth, Tertullus began to *a* him
    25:16 before that he which is *a* have the accuser
    26:7 for which hope's sake. . I am *a* of the Jews
Rom. 2:15 their thoughts the mean while *a* or else
Tit. 1:6 having faithful children not *a* of riot or
1 Pet. 3:16 that falsely *a* your good conversation
Rev. 12:10 *a* them before our God day and night

Accuser

Jn. 8:10 woman, where are those thine *a*? hath no
Acts 23:30 gave commandment to his *a* also to say
    25:16 which is accused have the *a* face to face
2 Tim. 3:3 trucebreakers, false *a*, incontinent
Tit. 2:3 not false *a*, not given to much wine
Rev. 12:10 for the *a* of our brethren is cast down

Aceldama Acts 1:19

Achaia

Acts 18:27 when he was disposed to pass into *A*
Rom. 15:26 hath pleased them of Macedonia and *A*
1 Cor. 16:15 Stephanas, that it is the firstfruits of *A*
2 Cor. 9:2 I boast. . that *A* was ready a year ago
    11:10 me of this boasting in the regions of *A*

Achan (Achar) Josh. 7:1–26

Josh. 22:20 did not *A*. . commit a trespass in the
1 Chr. 2:7 *A*, the troubler of Israel, who transgressed

Achish

1 Sam. 21:10 (27:2) David. . went to *A* the king of
    29:2 David. . passed on in the rearward with *A*
1 Kgs. 2:39 servants of Shimei ran away unto *A*

Achor Josh. 7:24; Hos. 2:15

Achsah (Achsa) Josh. 15:16 (Judg. 1:12)

Acknowledge *See also* Confess

Deut. 33:9 neither did he *a* his brethren, nor
Ps. 32:5 I *a* my sin unto thee, and mine iniquity
    51:3 I *a* my transgressions: and my sin is ever
Prov. 3:6 in all thy ways *a* him, and he shall
Is. 33:13 and, ye that are near, *a* my might
    63:16 art our Father, though. . Israel *a* us not
Jer. 3:13 only *a* thine iniquity, that thou hast
    14:20 we *a*, O LORD, our wickedness. . for we have
    24:5 like these good figs, so will I *a* them
Dan. 11:39 with a strange god, whom he shall *a*
Hos. 5:15 I will go. . till they *a* their offense
1 Cor. 14:37 him *a* that the things that I write
2 Cor. 1:13 none other. . than what ye read or *a*
1 Jn. 2:23 he that *a* the Son hath the Father also

Acknowledging

2 Tim. 2:25 repentance to the *a* of the truth
Tit. 1:1 *a* of the truth which is after godliness
Phlm. 6 become effectual by the *a* of every good

Acknowledgment

Col. 2:2 to the *a* of the mystery of God, and of

Acquaint

Job 22:21 *a* now thyself with him, and be at peace
Ps. 139:3 lying down, and art *a* with all my ways
Eccl. 2:3 unto wine, yet *a* mine heart with wisdom
Is. 53:3 a man of sorrows, and *a* with grief: and

Acquaintance *See also* Companion, Friend

Job 19:13 and mine *a* are verily estranged from me
Ps. 31:11 I was a reproach. . and a fear to mine *a*
    55:13 a man mine equal, my guide, and mine *a*
    88:8 thou hast put away mine *a* far from me
Lk. 2:44 they sought him among their kinsfolk and *a*
    23:49 and all his *a*. . stood afar off, beholding
Acts 24:23 forbid none of his *a* to. . come unto him

Acquit

Job 10:14 thou wilt not *a* me from mine iniquity
Nah. 1:3 the LORD. . will not at all *a* the wicked

Act *See also* Deed, Doing

Deut. 11:7 your eyes have seen all the great *a*
Judg. 5:11 rehearse the righteous *a* of the LORD
Ps. 103:7 known. . his *a* unto the children of Israel
    106:2 who can utter the mighty *a* of the LORD?
    145:6 speak of the might of thy terrible *a*
    150:2 praise him for his mighty *a*: praise him
Is. 28:21 and bring to pass his *a*, his strange *a*

Action

1 Sam. 2:3 God of knowledge. . by him *a* are weighed

Activity

Gen. 47:6 men of *a* among them. . make them rulers

Adam *See also* Man Gen. 1:26–5:5

Gen. 2:19 unto *A* to see what he would call them
    2:21 God caused a deep sleep to fall upon *A*
    3:9 the LORD God called unto *A*. . Where art thou?
    3:17 unto *A*. . cursed is the ground for thy sake
    5:2 and blessed them, and called their name *A*
Deut. 32:8 the Most High. . separated the sons of *A*
Job 31:33 if I covered my transgressions as *A*
Rom. 5:14 death reigned from *A* to Moses, even over
1 Cor. 15:22 for as in *A* all die, even so in Christ

1 Cor. 15:45 the first man *A* was made a living soul
1 Tim. 2:14 *A* was not deceived, but the woman being

Adamant

Ezek. 3:9 as an *a* harder than flint have I made
Zech. 7:12 they made their hearts as an *a* stone

Adar Esth. 9:21

Add

Gen. 30:24 the LORD shall *a* to me another son
Deut. 4:2 ye shall not *a* unto the word which I
5:22 spake. . with a great voice; and he *a* no more
29:19 of mine heart, to *a* drunkenness to thirst
1 Kgs. 12:11 (12:14; 2 Chr. 10:14) heavy yoke, I will *a*
Ps. 69:27 *a* iniquity unto their iniquity: and let
Prov. 3:2 long life, and peace, shall they *a* to
10:22 maketh rich, and he *a* no sorrow with it
Is. 30:1 a covering. . that they may *a* sin to sin
Mt. 6:27 (Lk. 12:25) *a* one cubit unto his stature?
6:33 (Lk. 12:31) these things shall be *a* unto you
Acts 2:41 *a* unto them about three thousand souls
2:47 Lord *a* to the church daily such as should
5:14 and believers were the more *a* to the Lord
11:24 faith: and much people was *a* unto the Lord
Gal. 2:6 somewhat in conference *a* nothing to me
3:19 it was *a* because of transgressions, till
Phil. 1:16 supposing to *a* affliction to my bonds
2 Pet. 1:5 *a* to your faith virtue; and to virtue
Rev. 22:18 shall *a* unto these things, God shall *a*

Adder *See also* Asp

Gen. 49:17 a serpent by the way, an *a* in the path
Ps. 58:4 like the deaf *a* that stoppeth her ear
91:13 thou shalt tread upon the lion and *a*
140:3 a serpent; *a'* poison is under their lips
Prov. 23:32 like a serpent, and stingeth like an *a*

Addict

1 Cor. 16:15 have *a* themselves to the ministry of

Adjure *See also* Charge, Command, Swear

Josh. 6:26 Joshua *a* them at that time, saying
1 Sam. 14:24 for Saul had *a* the people, saying
1 Kgs. 22::16 (2 Chr. 18:15) how many times shall I *a*
Mt. 26:63 I *a* thee by the living God, that thou
Mk. 5:7 I *a* thee by God, that thou torment me not
Acts 19:13 we *a* you by Jesus whom Paul preacheth

Admah Deut. 29:23; Hos. 11:8

Administer

2 Cor. 8:19 with this grace, which is *a* by us to

Administration

1 Cor. 12:5 differences of *a*, but the same Lord
2 Cor. 9:12 *a* of this service not only supplieth

Admiration

Jude 16 swelling words, having men's persons in *a*
Rev. 17:6 when I saw her, I wondered with great *a*

Admire

2 Thes. 1:10 and to be *a* in all them that believe

Admonish *See also* Enjoin, Rebuke, Reprove, Warn

Eccl. 4:13 foolish king, who will no more be *a*
12:12 and further, by these, my son, be *a*
Jer. 42:19 know certainly that I have *a* you this
Acts 27:9 when much time was spent. . Paul *a* them
Rom. 15:14 knowledge, able also to *a* one another

Col. 3:16 teaching and *a* one another in psalms and
1 Thes. 5:12 are over you in the Lord, and *a* you
2 Thes. 3:15 as an enemy, but *a* him as a brother
Heb. 8:5 Moses was *a* of God when he was about to

Admonition

1 Cor. 10:11 they are written for our *a*, upon whom
Eph. 6:4 bring them up in the nurture and *a* of the
Tit. 3:10 after the first and second *a*, reject

Ado

Mk. 5:39 why make ye this *a*, and weep? the damsel

Adoni-bezek Judg. 1:5–7

Adonijah 1 Kgs. 1:5–2:28

Adoniram (Adoram, Hadoram)

1 Kgs. 4:6; 12:18 (2 Chr. 10:18)

Adoni-zedek Josh. 10:1–3

Adoption

Rom. 8:15 but ye have received the Spirit of *a*
8:23 waiting for the *a*. . the redemption of our
9:4 who are Israelites; to whom pertaineth the *a*
Gal. 4:5 that we might receive the *a* of sons
Eph. 1:5 predestinated us unto the *a* of children by

Adoram *See* Adoniram

Adorn *See also* Deck, Garnish

Is. 61:10 as a bride *a* herself with her jewels
Lk. 21:5 how it was *a* with goodly stones and gifts
1 Tim. 2:9 women *a* themselves in modest apparel
Tit. 2:10 that they may *a* a doctrine of God our
1 Pet. 3:3 whose *a*, let it not be that outward *a*
3:5 women. . who trusted in God, *a* themselves
Rev. 21:2 prepared as a bride *a* for her husband

Adullam 1 Sam. 22:1

Adulterer

Lev. 20:10 the *a*. . shall surely be put to death
Job 24:15 eye. . of the *a* waiteth for the twilight
Jer. 23:10 the land is full of *a*; for because of
Hos. 7:4 all *a*, as an oven heated by the baker
Mal. 3:5 I will be a swift witness. . against the *a*
Lk. 18:11 I am not as other men are. . unjust, *a*, or
1 Cor. 6:9 shall not inherit the kingdom. . nor *a*
Heb. 13:4 but whoremongers and *a* God will judge
Jas. 4:4 ye *a* and adulteresses, know ye not that

Adulteress *See also* Harlot, Whore

Hos. 3:1 a woman beloved of her friend, yet an *a*
Rom. 7:3 married to another. . shall be called an *a*

Adulterous

Mt. 12:39 (16:4) *a* generation seeketh after a sign
Mk. 8:38 ashamed. . in this *a* and sinful generation

Adultery

Ex. 20:14 (Deut. 5:18; Mt. 5:27; 19:18; Mk. 10:19; Lk. 18:20; Rom. 13:9; Jas. 2:11) thou shalt not commit *a*
Lev. 20:10 committeth *a*. . surely be put to death
Prov. 6:32 whoso committeth *a* with a woman
Jer. 3:8 whereby backsliding Israel committed *a*
5:7 fed them to the full, they then committed *a*
13:27 I have seen thine *a*, and thy neighings
Ezek. 16:32 as a wife that committeth *a*
23:37 committed *a*, and blood is in their hands
Hos. 2:2 put away. . her *a* from between her breasts

Mt. 5:28 woman to lust after her hath committed *a*
5:32 (19:9; Mk. 10:11; Lk. 16:18) marry her that is
divorced committeth *a*
15:19 (Mk. 7:21) of the heart proceed. . murders, *a*
Jn. 8:3 brought unto him a woman taken in *a*
Gal. 5:19 the works of the flesh. . *A*, fornication
2 Pet. 2:14 having eyes full of *a*, and that cannot
Rev. 2:22 that commit *a* . . into great tribulation

Advance

1 Sam. 12:6 it is the Lord that *a* Moses and Aaron
Esth. 3:1 Ahasuerus promote Haman. . and *a* him

Advantage *See also* Gain, Profit

Job 35:3 thou saidst, What *a* will it be unto thee?
Lk. 9:25 what is a man *a*, if he gain the whole world
Rom. 3:1 what *a* then hath the Jew? or what profit
1 Cor. 15:32 what *a* it me, if the dead rise not?
2 Cor. 2:11 lest Satan should get an *a* of us
Jude 16 men's persons in admiration because of *a*

Adventure

Acts 19:31 he would not *a* himself into the theatre

Adversary *See also* Enemy, Foe, Satan

Ex. 23:22 obey. . then I will be. . an *a* unto thine *a*
Num. 22:22 stood in the way for an *a* against him
Deut. 32:43 and will render vengeance to his *a*
1 Sam. 1:6 her *a* also provoked her sore
2:10 the *a* of the Lord shall be broken to pieces
1 Kgs. 5:4 there is neither *a* nor evil occurrent
11:14 and the Lord stirred up an *a* unto Solomon
Ezra 4:1 when the *a* of Judah and Benjamin heard
Job 31:35 desire is. . that mine *a* had written a book
Ps. 38:20 that render evil for good are mine *a*
69:19 my dishonor: mine *a* are all before thee
74:10 O God, how long shall the *a* reproach?
89:42 thou hast set up the right hand of his *a*
109:29 let mine *a* be clothed with shame
Is. 1:24 I will ease me of mine *a*, and avenge me
9:11 Lord shall set up the *a* of Rezin against him
11:13 and the *a* of Judah shall be cut off
50:8 who is mine *a*? let him come near to me
59:18 accordingly he will repay, fury to his *a*
64:2 to make thy name known to thine *a*, that
Jer. 30:16 all thine *a* . . shall go into captivity
46:10 a day. . that he may avenge him of his *a*
Amos 3:11 an *a* there shall be even round about
Mic. 5:9 hand shall be lifted up upon thine *a*
Nah. 1:2 the Lord will take vengeance on his *a*
Mt. 5:25 agree with thine *a* quickly, while thou
Lk. 12:58 thou goest with thine *a* to the magistrate
13:17 said these things, all his *a* were ashamed
18:3 came unto him, saying, Avenge me of mine *a*
21:15 all your *a* shall not be able to gainsay
1 Cor. 16:9 opened unto me, and there are many *a*
Phil. 1:28 in nothing terrified by your *a*
1 Tim. 5:14 give none occasion to the *a* to speak
Heb. 10:27 indignation, which shall devour the *a*
1 Pet. 5:8 your *a* the devil, as a roaring lion

Adversity *See also* Affliction, Anguish, Calamity, Distress, Grief, Misery, Sorrow, Suffering, Tribulation, Trouble

1 Sam. 10:19 himself saved you out of all your *a*
2 Sam. 4:9 who hath redeemed my soul out of all *a*
2 Chr. 15:6 for God did vex them with all *a*
Ps. 10:6 not be moved: for I shall never be in *a*
31:7 my trouble; thou hast known my soul in *a*
35:15 but in mine *a* they rejoiced, and gathered
94:13 mayest give him rest from the days of *a*
Prov. 17:17 at all times, and a brother is born for *a*

Prov. 24:10 faint in the day of *a*, thy strength is small
Eccl. 7:14 joyful, but in the day of *a* consider
Is. 30:20 though the Lord give you the bread of *a*
Heb. 13:3 remember. . them which suffer *a*, as being

Advertise

Num. 24:14 will *a* thee what this people shall do
Ruth 4:4 and I thought to *a* thee, saying, Buy it

Advice *See also* Counsel, Instruction

Judg. 19:30 consider of it, take *a*, and speak your
1 Sam. 25:33 blessed be thy *a*, and blessed be thou
2 Sam. 19:43 that our *a* should not be first had
2 Chr. 10:9 what *a* give ye that we may return answer
Prov. 20:18 by counsel: and with good *a* make war
2 Cor. 8:10 herein I give my *a* . . this is expedient

Advise *See also* Counsel

2 Sam. 24:13 (1 Chr. 21:12) now *a* . . see what answer
1 Kgs. 12:6 do ye *a* that I may answer this people?
Prov. 13:10 but with the well *a* is wisdom
Acts 27:12 the more part *a* to depart thence also

Advocate *See also* Comforter

1 Jn. 2:1 if any man sin, we have an *a* with the

Aeneas (Eneas) Acts 9:33-35

Aenon Jn. 3:23

Afar Off

Gen. 22:4 lifted up his eyes. . saw the place *a o*
Ex. 24:1 the elders of Israel; and worship *a o*
Ps. 138:6 the lowly: but the proud he knoweth *a o*
139:2 thou understandest my thought *a o*
Jer. 23:23 am I a God at hand. . and not a God *a o*?
46:27 Israel. . behold, I will save thee from *a o*
Mt. 26:58 (Mk. 14:54; Lk. 22:54) Peter followed. . *a o*
Acts 2:39 your children, and to all that are *a o*
Eph. 2:17 preached peace to you which were *a o*
Heb. 11:13 having seen them *a o*, and were persuaded
2 Pet. 1:9 lacketh. . is blind, and cannot see *a o*

Affair

1 Chr. 26:32 pertaining to God, and *a* of the king
Ps. 112:5 he will guide his *a* with discretion
Dan. 2:49 over the *a* of the province of Babylon
Phil. 1:27 may hear of your *a*, that ye stand fast
2 Tim. 2:4 entangleth himself with the *a* of this life

Affect

Lam. 3:51 mine eye *a* mine heart, because of all
Acts 14:2 their minds evil *a* against the brethren
Gal. 4:17 they zealously *a* you, but not well

Affection *See also* Love

1 Chr. 29:3 have set my *a* to the house of my God
Rom. 1:26 this cause God gave them up unto vile *a*
1:31 (2 Tim. 3:3) without natural *a*
12:10 be kindly *a* one to another with brotherly
2 Cor. 7:15 his inward *a* is more abundant toward
Gal. 5:24 crucified the flesh with the *a* and lusts
Col. 3:2 set your *a* on things above, not on things
3:5 fornication, uncleanness, inordinate *a*, evil

Affinity

1 Kgs. 3:1 Solomon made *a* with Pharaoh king of
2 Chr. 18:1 now Jehoshaphat. . joined *a* with Ahab
Ezra 9:14 *a* with the people of these abominations?

Affirm

Lk. 22:59 of one hour after another confidently *a*

Acts 12:15 but she constantly *a* that it was even so
25:19 which was dead, whom Paul *a* to be alive
1 Tim. 1:7 what they say, nor whereof they *a*
Tit. 3:8 things I will that thou *a* constantly

Afflict *See also* Oppress, Persecute

Gen. 15:13 they shall *a* them four hundred years
Ex. 1:11 did set over them taskmasters to *a* them
22:22 shall not *a* any widow, or fatherless child
Lev. 16:29 (16:31; 23:27, 32; Num. 29:7) *a* your souls
Num. 11:11 wherefore hast thou *a* thy servant?
Judg. 16:5 prevail . . that we may bind him to *a* him
Ruth 1:21 Naomi, seeing . . the Almighty hath *a* me?
2 Sam. 7:10 shall . . *a* them any more, as beforetime
1 Kgs. 8:35 (2 Chr. 6:26) their sin, when thou *a* them
11:39 I will for this *a* the seed of David
Ezra 8:21 that we might *a* ourselves before our God
Job 30:11 because he hath loosed my cord, and *a*
37:23 and in plenty of justice: he will not *a*
Ps. 44:2 thou didst *a* the people, and cast them out
55:19 God shall hear, and *a* them, even he that
90:15 glad according to the days . . thou hast *a* us
94:5 they break in pieces . . and *a* thine heritage
107:17 fools . . because of their iniquities, are *a*
119:67 before I was *a* I went astray: but now
119:71 it is good for me that I have been *a*
119:75 and that thou in faithfulness hast *a* me
129:1 many a time have they *a* me from my youth
143:12 destroy all them that *a* my soul
Prov. 26:28 lying tongue hateth those that are *a*
Is. 9:1 when at the first he lightly *a* the land
51:23 put it into the hand of them that *a* thee
53:7 he was oppressed, and he was *a*, yet he
63:9 in all their affliction he was *a*
64:12 thou hold thy peace, and *a* us very sore?
Lam. 1:12 sorrow . . wherewith the LORD hath *a* me
3:33 for he doth not *a* willingly, nor grieve
Amos 5:12 they *a* the just, they take a bribe
Mic. 4:6 and I will gather . . her that I have *a*
Nah. 1:12 though I have *a* . . I will *a* thee no more
Zeph. 3:19 that time I will undo all that *a* thee
Mt. 24:9 then shall they deliver you up to be *a*
2 Cor. 1:6 we be *a*, it is for your consolation

Afflicted *See also* Afflict, Poor

2 Sam. 22:28 (Ps. 18:27) the *a* people thou wilt save
Job 6:14 to him that is *a* pity should be showed
34:28 unto him, and he heareth the cry of the *a*
Ps. 25:16 mercy upon me; for I am desolate and *a*
82:3 fatherless: do justice to the *a* and needy
140:12 the LORD will maintain the cause of the *a*
Prov. 15:15 all the days of the *a* are evil
22:22 poor: neither oppress the *a* in the gate
31:5 and pervert the judgment of any of the *a*
Is. 49:13 the LORD . . will have mercy upon his *a*
51:21 hear now this, thou *a*, and drunken
53:4 esteem him stricken, smitten of God, and *a*
54:11 O thou *a*, tossed with tempest, and not
58:10 satisfy the *a* soul; then shall thy light
Zeph. 3:12 the midst of thee an *a* and poor people
1 Tim. 5:10 if she have relieved the *a*, if she
Heb. 11:37 wandered . . being destitute, *a*, tormented
Jas. 4:9 be *a*, and mourn, and weep: let your
5:13 is any among you *a*? let him pray

Affliction *See also* Adversity, Anguish, Calamity, Distress, Grief, Misery, Sorrow, Suffering, Tribulation, Trouble

Gen. 16:11 because the LORD hath heard thy *a*
29:32 surely the LORD hath looked upon my *a*
41:52 me to be fruitful in the land of my *a*

Ex. 3:7 (Acts 7:34) I have . . seen the *a* of my people
Deut. 16:3 unleavened bread . . even the bread of *a*
1 Sam. 1:11 indeed look on the *a* of thine handmaid
2 Sam. 16:12 be that the LORD will look on mine *a*
1 Kgs. 22:27 (2 Chr. 18:26) bread of *a* . . water of *a*
2 Chr. 20:9 and cry unto thee in our *a*, then thou
33:12 when he was in *a*, he besought the LORD
Neh. 9:9 didst see the *a* of our fathers in Egypt
Job 5:6 although *a* cometh not forth of the dust
10:15 I am full of confusion . . see thou mine *a*
30:16 the days of *a* have taken hold upon me
36:15 delivereth the poor in his *a*, and openeth
36:21 for this hast thou chosen rather than *a*
Ps. 22:24 nor abhorred the *a* of the afflicted
25:18 look upon mine *a* and my pain; and forgive
34:19 many are the *a* of the righteous
66:11 into the net; thou laidst *a* upon our loins
106:44 nevertheless he regarded their *a*, when he
107:39 brought low through oppression, *a*, and
119:50 this is my comfort in my *a*: for thy word
119:153 consider mine *a*, and deliver me: for I
132:1 LORD, remember David, and all his *a*
Is. 30:20 bread of adversity, and the water of *a*
48:10 I have chosen thee in the furnace of *a*
63:9 in all their *a* he was afflicted
Jer. 16:19 my fortress . . my refuge in the day of *a*
30:15 why criest thou for thine *a*? thy sorrow is
Lam. 3:1 I am the man that hath seen *a* by the rod
3:19 remembering mine *a* and my misery
Hos. 5:15 in their *a* they will seek me early
Jon. 2:2 cried by reason of mine *a* unto the LORD
Nah. 1:9 shall not rise up the second time
Zech. 8:10 neither . . any peace . . because of the *a*
10:11 and he shall pass through the sea with *a*
Mk. 4:17 afterward, when *a* or persecution ariseth
13:19 in those days shall be *a*, such as was not
Acts 20:23 witnesseth . . that bonds and *a* abide me
2 Cor. 2:4 out of much *a* and anguish of heart I
4:17 for our light *a*, which is but for a moment
6:4 in much patience, in *a*, in necessities
8:2 that in a great trial of *a*, the abundance
Phil. 1:16 supposing to add *a* to my bonds
4:14 well . . that ye did communicate with my *a*
Col. 1:24 that which is behind of the *a* of Christ
1 Thes. 1:6 having received the word in much *a*
3:3 that no man should be moved by these *a*
3:7 we were comforted over you in all our *a*
2 Tim. 1:8 be thou partaker of the *a* of the gospel
3:11 *a*, which came unto me at Antioch
4:5 but watch thou in all things, endure *a*
Heb. 10:32 ye endured a great fight of *a*
11:25 rather to suffer *a* with the people of God
Jas. 1:27 the fatherless and widows in their *a*
5:10 the prophets . . for an example of suffering *a*
1 Pet. 5:9 that the same *a* are accomplished in

Affrighted *See also* Afraid, Terrify

Deut. 7:21 thou shalt not be *a* at them
Job 39:22 he mocketh at fear, and is not *a*
Mk. 16:5 saw a young man sitting . . and they were *a*

Afoot

Mk. 6:33 many knew him, and ran *a* thither out of
Acts 20:13 take in Paul . . minding himself to go *a*

Afraid *See also* Affrighted, Dismayed

Gen. 3:10 I heard thy voice . . and I was *a*, because
28:17 he was *a*, and said, How dreadful is this
31:31 Jacob . . said to Laban, Because I was *a*
32:7 then Jacob was greatly *a* and distressed
42:28 their heart failed them, and they were *a*
Ex. 3:6 Moses hid his face; for he was *a* to look
14:10 marched after them; and they were sore *a*
15:14 the people shall hear, and be *a*: sorrow

Lev. 26:6 shall lie down, and none shall make you *a*
Josh. 1:9 be not *a*, neither be thou dismayed
Judg. 7:3 whosoever is fearful and *a*, let him return
1 Sam. 18:29 and Saul was yet the more *a* of David
   21:1 and Ahimelech was *a* at the meeting of David
2 Sam. 22:46 (Ps. 18:45) be *a* out of their close places
Neh. 6:9 they all made us *a*, saying, Their hands
Job 3:25 that which I was *a* of is come unto me
   9:28 I am *a* of all my sorrows, I know that thou
   11:19 shalt lie down, and none shall make thee *a*
   21:6 even when I remember I am *a*, and trembling
   39:20 canst thou make him *a* as a grasshopper?
Ps. 3:6 I will not be *a* of ten thousands of people
   18:45 the strangers shall fade away, and be *a*
   27:1 strength of my life; of whom shall I be *a*?
   56:3 what time I am *a*, I will trust in thee
   56:11 I will not be *a* what man can do unto me
   65:8 dwell in the uttermost parts are *a* at thy
   77:16 O God, the waters saw thee; they were *a*
   83:15 persecute . . and make them *a* with thy storm
   91:5 thou shalt not be *a* for the terror by night
   112:7 he shall not be *a* of evil tidings
Is. 8:12 neither fear ye their fear, nor be *a*
   10:24 saith the Lord . . be not *a* of the Assyrians
   12:2 I will trust, and not be *a*: for the Lord
   13:8 they shall be *a*: pangs and sorrows shall
   40:9 lift up thy voice . . lift it up, be not *a*
   41:5 ends of the earth were *a*, drew near, and
   51:7 of men, neither be ye *a* of their revilings
   51:12 shouldest be *a* of a man that shall die
Jer. 1:8 be not *a* of their faces: for I am with
Mic. 4:4 (Zeph. 3:13) none shall make them *a*
Mal. 2:5 he feared me, and was *a* before my name
Mt. 14:27 (Mk. 6:50; Jn. 6:20) it is I; be not *a*
   17:6 (Mk. 9:6) they fell . . and were sore *a*
   28:10 then said Jesus unto them, Be not *a*: go
Mk. 5:36 unto the ruler . . Be not *a*, only believe
   9:32 they understood not . . and were *a* to ask him
   10:32 amazed; and as they followed, they were *a*
Lk. 2:9 round about them; and they were sore *a*
   12:4 be not *a* of them that kill the body
Jn. 14:27 heart be troubled, neither let it be *a*
   19:8 when Pilate . . heard that . . he was the more *a*
Acts 9:26 they were all *a* of him, and believed not
   10:4 and when he looked on him, he was *a*
   18:9 be not *a*, but speak, and hold not thy peace
Rom. 13:3 wilt thou then not be *a* of the power?
Gal. 4:11 I am *a* of you, lest I have bestowed upon
Heb. 11:23 were not *a* of the king's commandment
2 Pet. 2:10 are not *a* to speak evil of dignities

Afresh

Heb. 6:6 crucify to themselves the Son of God *a*

Agabus Acts 11:28; 21:10

Agag 1 Sam. 15:8–33

Again

Jn. 3:3 except a man be born *a*, he cannot see
   14:3 I will come *a*, and receive you unto myself
1 Pet. 1:23 being born *a*, not of corruptible seed

Against

Gen. 16:12 *a* every man, and every man's hand *a* him
Lev. 20:3 I will set my face *a* that man, and will
Mt. 12:30 (Lk. 11:23) he that is not with me is *a* me
Mk. 9:40 (Lk. 9:50) that is not *a* us is on our part
Lk. 2:34 and for a sign which shall be spoken *a*
Acts 13:45 *a* those things which were spoken by Paul
   19:36 then that these things cannot be spoken *a*
   28:22 we know that every where it is spoken *a*
Rom. 4:18 who *a* hope believed in hope, that he
   8:31 if God be for us, who can be *a* us?

2 Cor. 13:8 for we can do nothing *a* the truth
Rev. 2:4 have somewhat *a* thee, because thou hast

Agar *See* Hagar

Agate

Is. 54:12 make thy windows of *a*, and thy gates of

Age *See also* Day, Generation, Life, Time, World

Gen. 18:11 Abraham and Sarah . . well stricken in *a*
Josh. 23:1 that Joshua waxed old and stricken in *a*
1 Sam. 2:33 shall die in the flower of their *a*
Job 5:26 thou shalt come to thy grave in a full *a*
   11:17 thine *a* shall be clearer than the noonday
Ps. 39:5 mine *a* is as nothing before thee
Is. 38:12 mine *a* is departed, and is removed from
Lk. 3:23 Jesus . . began to be about thirty years of *a*
Jn. 9:21 we know not: he is of *a*; ask him
Eph. 2:7 that in the *a* to come he might show
   3:5 which in other *a* was not made known unto
   3:21 be glory . . by Christ Jesus throughout all *a*
Col. 1:26 the mystery which hath been hid from *a*
Heb. 5:14 strong meat . . to them that are of full *a*

Aged *See also* Ancient, Old

2 Sam. 19:32 now Barzillai was a very *a* man
Job 12:20 taketh away the understanding of the *a*
   15:10 are both the grayheaded and very *a* men
   29:8 men saw me . . and the *a* arose, and stood up
   32:9 neither do the *a* understand judgment
Tit. 2:2 that the *a* men be sober, grave, temperate
Phlm. 9 beseech thee, being such a one as Paul the *a*

Agony

Lk. 22:44 being in an *a* he prayed more earnestly

Agree

Amos 3:3 can two walk together, except they be *a*?
Mt. 5:25 *a* with thine adversary quickly, while
   18:19 if two of you shall *a* on earth as touching
   20:2 had *a* with the laborers for a penny a day
Mk. 14:56 against him, but their witness *a* not
Lk. 5:36 piece . . out of the new *a* not with the old
Acts 5:9 ye have *a* together to tempt the Spirit
   15:15 and to this *a* the words of the prophets
   23:20 the Jews have *a* to desire thee that thou
1 Jn. 5:8 bear witness . . and these three *a* in one
Rev. 17:17 to *a*, and give their kingdom unto

Agreement

2 Kgs. 18:31 (Is. 36:16) an *a* with me by a present
Is. 28:15 with death, and with hell are we at *a*
   28:18 and your *a* with hell shall not stand
2 Cor. 6:16 *a* hath the temple of God with idols?

Agrippa Acts 25:13–26:32

Ague

Lev. 26:16 burning *a*, that shall consume the eyes

Agur Prov. 30:1

Ahab 1 Kgs. 16:29–22:40

Ahasuerus king of Persia

   Ezra 4:6; Esth. 1:1–10:3

Ahava Ezra 8:21

Ahaz

   2 Kgs. 16:1–20 (2 Chr. 28:1–27); Is. 7:1–12

Ahaziah king of Israel
1 Kgs. 22:51–2 Kgs. 1:18

Ahaziah king of Judah
2 Kgs. 8:25–9:29 (2 Chr. 22:1–9)

Ahiah 1 Sam. 14:3, 18

Ahijah 1 Kgs. 11:29–30; 14:2–18

Ahikam Jer. 26:24

Ahimaaz son of Zadok
2 Sam. 15:27, 36; 17:17–21; 18:19–30

Ahimelech 1 Sam. 21:1–22:16

Ahinoam 1 Sam. 25:43; 30:5

Ahio 2 Sam. 6:3–4 (1 Chr. 13:7)

Ahithophel 2 Sam. 15:12–17:23

Aholah Ezek. 23:4–44

Aholiab Ex. 31:6; 35:34–36:2; 38:23

Aholibah Ezek. 23:4–44

Ahungered

Mt. 4:2 forty days . . forty nights, he was afterward *a*
12:1 disciples were *a*, and began to pluck
25:35 I was *a*, and ye gave me meat

Ai

Josh. 7:2 and Joshua sent men from Jericho to *A*
8:1 go up to *A*: see, I have given into thy hand
8:28 Joshua burnt *A*, and made it a heap for ever

Aid

Judg. 9:24 *a* him in the killing of his brethren

Ail

Gen. 21:17 what *a* thee, Hagar? fear not; for God
Judg. 18:23 what *a* thee, that thou comest with such
1 Sam. 11:5 Saul said, What *a* the people that they
Ps. 114:5 what *a* thee, O . . sea, that thou fleddest?

Air

Job 41:16 so near . . no *a* can come between them
1 Cor. 9:26 fight . . not as one that beateth the *a*
14:9 is spoken? for ye shall speak into the *a*
Eph. 2:2 prince of the power of the *a*, the spirit
1 Thes. 4:17 caught up . . to meet the Lord in the *a*
Rev. 9:2 sun and the *a* were darkened by . . the smoke
16:17 seventh angel poured . . his vial into the *a*

Ajalon Josh. 10:12

Alabaster

Mt. 26:7 (Mk. 14:3; Lk. 7:37) an *a* box of . . ointment

Alarm

Num. 10:5 when ye blow an *a*, then the camps that
2 Chr. 13:12 priests with sounding trumpets to cry *a*
Jer. 4:19 the sound of the trumpet, the *a* of war
Joel 2:1 sound an *a* in my holy mountain: let all
Zeph. 1:16 a day of the trumpet and *a* against the

Alas

Num. 12:11 *a*, my lord . . lay not the sin upon us
24:23 *a*, who shall live when God doeth this!
2 Kgs. 6:5 he cried . . *A*, master! for it was borrowed
6:15 unto him, *A*, my master! how shall we do?
Jer. 30:7 *a*! for that day is great, so that none

Joel 1:15 *a* for the day! for the day of the LORD
Amos 5:16 shall say in all the highways, *A*! *a*!
Rev. 18:10 (18:16, 19) *a*, *a*, that great city Babylon

Alexander

Acts 19:33 drew *A* out of the multitude, the Jews
1 Tim. 1:20 Hymeneus and *A*; whom I have delivered
2 Tim. 4:14 *A* the coppersmith did me much evil

Alexandria Acts 18:24; 27:6

Algum *See also* Almug

2 Chr. 2:8 fir trees, and *a* trees, out of Lebanon
9:11 the king made of the *a* trees terraces

Alien *See also* Foreigner, Sojourner, Stranger

Ex. 18:3 said, I have been an *a* in a strange land
Deut. 14:21 or thou mayest sell it unto an *a*
Job 19:15 for a stranger: I am an *a* in their sight
Ps. 69:8 am become . . *a* unto my mother's children
Is. 61:5 the sons of the *a* shall be your plowmen
Lam. 5:2 is turned to strangers, our houses to *a*
Eph. 2:12 being *a* from the commonwealth of Israel
Heb. 11:34 turned to flight the armies of the *a*

Alienate

Ezek. 23:17 polluted . . her mind was *a* from them
48:14 nor *a* the firstfruits of the land
Eph. 4:18 being *a* from the life of God through
Col. 1:21 you, that were sometime *a* and enemies

Alike

Job 21:26 they shall lie down *a* in the dust
Ps. 33:15 he fashioneth their hearts *a*
139:12 darkness and the light are both *a* to thee
Eccl. 9:2 all things come *a* to all: there is one
11:6 or whether they both shall be *a* good
Rom. 14:5 another esteemeth every day *a*

Alive *See also* Living, Quick

Gen. 7:23 Noah only remained *a*, and they that were
Ex. 1:17 the midwives . . saved the men children *a*
Lev. 14:4 to take for him . . two birds *a* and clean
16:10 to be the scapegoat, shall be presented *a*
Num. 16:33 went down *a* into the pit, and the earth
21:35 smote him . . until there was none left him *a*
Deut. 4:4 did cleave unto the LORD your God are *a*
32:39 is no god with me: I kill, and I make *a*
1 Sam. 2:6 the LORD killeth, and maketh *a*
2 Kgs. 5:7 am I God, to kill and to make *a*
Ps. 30:3 thou hast kept me *a*, that I should not go
Jer. 49:11 thy . . children, I will preserve them *a*
Ezek. 13:18 ye save the souls *a* that come unto you?
18:27 lawful and right, he shall save his soul *a*
Dan. 5:19 he slew; and whom he would he kept *a*
Mt. 27:63 that deceiver said, while he was yet *a*
Mk. 16:11 they, when they had heard that he was *a*
Lk. 15:24 (15:32) this my son was dead, and is *a* again
24:23 vision of angels, which said that he was *a*
Acts 1:3 he showed himself *a* after his passion by
25:19 of one Jesus . . whom Paul affirmed to be *a*
Rom. 6:11 be dead indeed unto sin, but *a* unto God
6:13 unto God, as those that are *a* from the dead
1 Cor. 15:22 even so in Christ shall all be made *a*
1 Thes. 4:17 are *a* and remain shall be caught up
Rev. 1:18 dead; and, behold, I am *a* for evermore
2:8 first and the last, which was dead, and is *a*
19:20 these both were cast *a* into a lake of fire

Allege

Acts 17:3 *a*, that Christ must needs have suffered

Allegory
Gal. 4:24 an *a*: for these are two covenants

Alleluia
Rev. 19:1 voice of much people in heaven, saying, *A*
   19:4 fell down and worshipped . . saying, Amen; *A*

Allow
Lk. 11:48 that ye *a* the deeds of your fathers
Acts 24:15 have hope . . which they themselves also *a*
Rom. 7:15 for that which I do, I *a* not: for what I
   14:22 condemneth not . . in that thing which he *a*
1 Thes. 2:4 as we were *a* of God to be put in trust

Allure
Hos. 2:14 behold, I will *a* her, and bring her into
2 Pet. 2:18 they *a* through the lusts of the flesh

Almighty
Gen. 17:1 I am the *A* God; walk before me, and be
Ex. 6:3 and unto Jacob, by the name of God *A*
Num. 24:4 which saw the vision of the *A*, falling
Ruth 1:20 the *A* hath dealt very bitterly with me
Job 5:17 despise not thou the chastening of the *A*
   11:7 canst thou find out the *A* unto perfection?
   22:25 yea, the *A* shall be thy defense, and thou
   29:5 when the *A* was yet with me . . my children
   32:8 and the inspiration of the *A* giveth them
   37:23 touching the *A*, we cannot find him out
Ps. 91:1 shall abide under the shadow of the *A*
Is. 13:6 (Joel 1:15) come as a destruction from the *A*
Ezek. 10:5 the voice of the *A* God when he speaketh
Rev. 1:8 which was, and which is to come, the *A*
   4:8 saying, Holy, holy, holy, Lord God *A*
   11:17 saying, We give thee thanks, O Lord God *A*
   15:3 and marvelous are thy works, Lord God *A*
   16:7 even so, Lord God *A*, true and righteous are
   21:22 God *A* and the Lamb are the temple of it

Almond
Gen. 43:11 honey, spices and myrrh, nuts and *a*
Ex. 25:33 (37:19) bowls made like unto *a*, with a
Num. 17:8 rod . . bloomed blossoms, and yielded *a*
Eccl. 12:5 the way, and the *a* tree shall flourish
Jer. 1:11 and I said, I see a rod of an *a* tree

Almost
Ex. 17:4 this people? they be *a* ready to stone me
Ps. 73:2 but as for me, my feet were *a* gone
   94:17 my help, my soul had *a* dwelt in silence
   119:87 they had *a* consumed me upon earth; but I
Acts 13:44 came *a* the whole city together to hear
   26:28 *a* thou persuadest me to be a Christian
   26:29 were both *a*, and altogether such as I am
Heb. 9:22 *a* all things are by the law purged with

Alms
Mt. 6:1 take heed that ye do not your *a* before men
Lk. 11:41 rather give *a* of such things as ye have
   12:33 sell that ye have, and give *a*; provide
Acts 3:2 ask *a* of them that entered into the temple
   10:2 gave much *a* to the people, and prayed to God
   24:17 now after many years I came to bring *a* to

Almug *See also* Algum
1 Kgs. 10:11 from Ophir great plenty of *a* trees

Aloes
Ps. 45:8 all thy garments smell of myrrh, and *a*
Prov. 7:17 I have perfumed my bed with myrrh, *a*
Jn. 19:39 brought a mixture of myrrh and *a*

Alone
Gen. 2:18 it is not good that the man should be *a*
   32:24 Jacob was left *a*; and there wrestled a man
   42:38 for his brother is dead, and he is left *a*
Ex. 18:18 thou art not able to perform it thyself *a*
   24:2 Moses *a* shall come near the LORD
Num. 11:14 (Deut. 1:9) not able to bear all this . . *a*
Deut. 32:12 the LORD *a* did lead him
1 Kgs. 11:29 and they two were *a* in the field
2 Kgs. 23:18 let him *a*; let no man move his bones
Job 1:15 (1:16, 17, 19) I only am escaped *a* to tell thee
   31:17 or have eaten my morsel myself *a*, and the
Ps. 136:4 to him who *a* doeth great wonders
   148:13 of the LORD: for his name *a* is excellent
Eccl. 4:8 there is one *a*, and there is not a second
   4:10 woe to him that is *a* when he falleth
Is. 2:11 the LORD *a* shall be exalted in that day
   44:24 that stretcheth forth the heavens *a*
   51:2 for I called him *a*, and blessed him
Hos. 4:17 Ephraim is joined to idols: let him *a*
Mt. 4:4 (Lk. 4:4) man shall not live by bread *a*
   14:23 (Mk. 6:47) evening was come, he was there *a*
   18:15 tell him his fault between thee and him *a*
Mk. 4:34 when they were *a*, he expounded all things
Lk. 9:18 as he was *a* praying, his disciples were
   9:36 when the voice was past, Jesus was found *a*
   13:8 let it *a* this year also, till I shall dig
Jn. 6:15 departed again into a mountain himself *a*
   8:9 Jesus was left *a*, and the woman standing
   8:16 (16:32) I am not *a*, but I and the Father
   12:24 fall into the ground and die, it abideth *a*
   17:20 neither pray I for these *a*, but for them
Heb. 9:7 went the high priest *a* once every year
Jas. 2:17 if it hath not works, is dead, being *a*

Aloof
Ps. 38:11 my friends stand *a* from my sore

Alpha
Rev. 1:8 (21:6; 22:13) I am *A* and Omega

Already
Eccl. 1:10 this is new? it hath been *a* of old times
   6:10 that which hath been is named *a*, and it is
Mal. 2:2 I will curse . . yea, I have cursed them *a*
Mk. 15:44 and Pilate marveled if he were *a* dead
Jn. 3:18 but he that believeth not is condemned *a*
2 Cor. 12:21 bewail many which have sinned *a*
Phil. 3:12 though I had *a* attained . . were *a* perfect

Altar *See also* Offering, Sacrifice, Sanctuary, Temple, Worship
Gen. 8:20 and Noah builded an *a* unto the LORD
   12:7 appeared unto Abram . . there builded he an *a*
   13:4 unto the place of the *a*, which he had made
   13:18 which is in Hebron, and built there an *a*
   22:9 Abraham built an *a* there, and laid the wood
   26:25 he builded an *a* there, and called upon
   33:20 there an *a*, and called it El-Elohe-Israel
   35:1 go up to Bethel . . make there an *a* unto God
Ex. 17:15 Moses built an *a*, and called the name
   20:24 an *a* of earth thou shalt make unto me
   20:25 if thou wilt make me an *a* of stone, thou
   27:1 (38:1) thou shalt make an *a* of shittim wood
   29:12 (Lev. 8:15) put it upon the horns of the *a*
   30:1 (37:25) thou shalt make an *a* to burn incense
   34:13 (Deut. 7:5) destroy their *a*, break . . images
Lev. 1:5 sprinkle the blood round about upon the *a*
   1:9 burn all on the *a*, to be a burnt sacrifice
   9:7 go unto the *a*, and offer thy sin offering
Num. 23:1 (23:29) Balak, Build me here seven *a*
Deut. 12:27 the flesh and the blood, upon the *a*

Deut. 27:5 there shalt thou build an *a* . . an *a* of stones
Josh. 8:30 then Joshua built an *a* . . in mount Ebal
22:10 built there an *a* by Jordan, a great *a*
Judg. 6:24 Gideon built an *a* there unto the LORD
1 Sam. 14:35 Saul built an *a* . . the first *a* that he
2 Sam. 24:25 (1 Chr. 21:26) David built there an *a*
1 Kgs. 1:50 and caught hold on the horns of the *a*
3:4 (2 Chr. 1:6) did Solomon offer upon that *a*
13:1 Jeroboam stood by the *a* to burn incense
16:32 he reared up an *a* for Baal in the house
18:30 repaired the *a* of the LORD that was broken
19:10 (19:14; Rom. 11:3) thrown down thine *a*
2 Kgs. 16:10 Ahaz . . saw an *a* that was at Damascus
18:22 (Is. 36:7) worship before this *a* in Jerusalem?
21:3 (2 Chr. 33:3) reared up *a* for Baal, and made
23:12 *a* which Manasseh had made . . beat down
23:15 the *a* that was at Bethel . . he brake down
2 Chr. 4:1 he made an *a* of brass, twenty cubits
14:3 for he took away the *a* of the strange gods
28:24 he made him *a* in every corner of Jerusalem
31:1 threw down the high places and the *a* out of
33:16 repaired the *a* of the LORD, and sacrificed
Ezra 3:2 and builded the *a* of the God of Israel
Neh. 10:34 the wood offering . . to burn upon the *a*
Ps. 26:6 in innocency: so will I compass thine *a*
43:4 then will I go unto the *a* of God, unto God
84:3 where she may lay her young, even thine *a*
118:27 with cords, even unto the horns of the *a*
Is. 6:6 had taken with the tongs from off the *a*
19:19 in that day shall there be an *a* to the LORD
65:3 and burneth incense upon *a* of brick
Jer. 11:13 have ye set up *a* to that shameful thing
Lam. 2:7 the Lord hath cast off his *a*, he hath
Ezek. 6:4 your *a* shall be desolate, and your images
43:13 measures of the *a* after the cubits
Hos. 8:11 because Ephraim hath made many *a* to sin
10:1 according to . . fruit he hath increased the *a*
Joel 1:13 ye priests: howl, ye ministers of the *a*
Amos 9:1 I saw the Lord standing upon the *a*
Mal. 1:7 ye offer polluted bread upon mine *a*
2:13 covering the *a* of the LORD with tears
Mt. 5:23 if thou bring thy gift to the *a*, and there
23:18 shall swear by the *a*, it is nothing
23:35 (Lk. 11:51) slew between the temple and . . *a*
Lk. 1:11 an angel . . on the right side of the *a*
Acts 17:23 *a* with this inscription, TO THE UNKNOWN
1 Cor. 9:13 wait at the *a* are partakers with the *a*?
10:18 eat of the sacrifices partakers of the *a*?
Heb. 7:13 of which no man gave attendance at the *a*
13:10 we have an *a*, whereof they have no right
Rev. 6:9 I saw under the *a* the souls of them that
8:3 the golden *a* which was before the throne
9:13 a voice from the four horns of the golden *a*
11:1 measure the temple of God, and the *a*, and
14:18 and another angel came out from the *a*
16:7 I heard another out of the *a* say, Even so

Alter *See also* Change

Lev. 27:10 he shall not *a* it, nor change it, a good
Ps. 89:34 *a* the thing that is gone out of my lips
Dan. 6:8 law of the Medes and Persians, which *a* not
Lk. 9:29 the fashion of his countenance was *a*

Alway (Always)

Gen 6:3 my Spirit shall not *a* strive with man
Deut. 14:23 learn to fear the LORD thy God *a*
1 Chr. 16:15 be ye mindful *a* of his covenant
Job 7:16 I would not live *a*: let me alone
27:10 in the Almighty? will he *a* call upon God?
Ps. 9:18 for the needy shall not *a* be forgotten
103:9 he will not *a* chide: neither will he keep
119:112 mine heart to perform thy statutes *a*
Is. 57:16 neither will I be *a* wroth

Mt. 26:11 (Mk. 14:7; Jn. 12:8) ye have the poor *a*
28:20 lo, I am with you *a*, even unto the end
Lk. 18:1 men ought *a* to pray, and not to faint
21:36 watch ye therefore, and pray *a*, that ye
Jn. 8:29 for I do *a* those things that please him
18:20 in the temple, whither the Jews *a* resort
Acts 24:16 to have *a* a conscience void of offence
Eph. 6:18 praying *a* with all prayer . . in the Spirit
Phil. 4:4 rejoice in the Lord *a*: and again I say
Col. 4:6 let your speech be *a* with grace, seasoned
Heb. 9:6 priests went *a* into the first tabernacle

Am

Ex. 3:14 and God said unto Moses, I *A* THAT I *A*
Jn. 8:58 I say unto you, Before Abraham was, I *a*

Amalek

Ex. 17:8 then came *A*, and fought with Israel
17:16 LORD will have war with *A* from generation
Num. 24:20 *A* was the first of the nations; but his
Deut. 25:17 remember what *A* did unto thee by the
Judg. 3:13 gathered . . the children of Ammon and *A*
1 Sam. 15:3 go and smite *A*, and utterly destroy
28:18 nor executedst his fierce wrath upon *A*

Amalekite

Num. 13:29 the *A* dwell in the land of the south
14:43 *A* and the Canaanites are there before you
Judg. 6:3 the Midianites came up, and the *A*, and
1 Sam. 14:48 he gathered a host, and smote the *A*
30:1 *A* had invaded the south . . and smitten Ziklag
30:13 I am a young man of Egypt, servant to an *A*
2 Sam. 1:13 I am the son of a stranger, an *A*

Amariah 2 Chr. 19:11

Amasa 2 Sam. 17:25–20:13

Amazed *See also* Astonished

Ex. 15:15 then the dukes of Edom shall be *a*
Ezek. 32:10 I will make many people *a* at thee
Mt. 19:25 disciples . . were exceedingly *a*, saying
Mk. 1:27 (Lk. 4:36) were all *a* . . that they questioned
2:12 (Lk. 5:26) were all *a*, and glorified God
14:33 began to be sore *a*, and to be very heavy
Lk. 9:43 they were all *a* at the mighty power of God
Acts 9:21 but all that heard him were *a*, and said

Amazement *See also* Astonishment, Wonder

Acts 3:10 they were filled with wonder and *a* at
1 Pet. 3:6 do well, and are not afraid with any *a*

Amaziah king of Judah
2 Kgs. 14:1–20 (2 Chr. 25:1–28)

Amaziah the priest Amos 7:10–14

Ambassador *See also* Apostle, Disciple, Messenger, Minister, Prophet

Josh. 9:4 and went and made as if they had been *a*
2 Chr. 32:31 the *a* of the princes of Babylon
35:21 sent *a* to him, saying, What have I to do
Prov. 13:17 mischief: but a faithful *a* is health
Is. 18:2 sendeth *a* by the sea, even in vessels
33:7 the *a* of peace shall weep bitterly
Jer. 49:14 (Obad. 1) an *a* is sent unto the heathen
Ezek. 17:15 rebelled . . in sending his *a* into Egypt
2 Cor. 5:20 we are *a* for Christ, as though God did
Eph. 6:20 for which I am an *a* in bonds; that therein

Ambassage
Lk. 14:32 he sendeth an *a*, and desireth conditions

Amber
Ezek. 1:4 of the midst thereof as the color of *a*

Ambush
Josh. 8:19 and the *a* arose quickly out of their place
Jer. 51:12 set up the watchmen, prepare the *a*

Ambushment
2 Chr. 13:13 Jeroboam caused an *a* to come about
    20:22 sing and to praise, the Lord set *a* against

Amen
Num. 5:22 to rot. And the woman shall say, *A, a*
Deut. 27:15 all the people shall answer and say, *A*
1 Chr. 16:36 (Ps. 106:48) and all the people said, *A*
Ps. 41:13 (89:52) blessed be the Lord . . *A*, and *A*
    106:48 all the people say, *A*. Praise ye the Lord
1 Cor. 14:16 say *A* at thy giving of thanks, seeing
2 Cor. 1:20 all the promises . . are yea, and in him *A*
Rev. 3:14 these things saith the *A*, the faithful
    22:20 surely I come quickly: *A*. Even so, come

Amend
Lev. 5:16 make *a* for the harm that he hath done
Jer. 7:3 *a* your ways and your doings, and I will
    26:13 now *a* your ways . . obey the voice
Jn. 4:52 inquired he . . the hour when he began to *a*

Amiable
Ps. 84:1 how *a* are thy tabernacles, O Lord of hosts!

Amiss
2 Chr. 6:37 we have sinned, we have done *a*
Dan. 3:29 which speak any thing *a* against the God
Lk. 23:41 deeds: but this man hath done nothing *a*
Jas. 4:3 ye ask, and receive not, because ye ask *a*

Ammon
Gen. 19:38 same is the father of the children of *A*
Deut. 2:19 the children of *A*, distress them not
Judg. 3:13 he gathered unto him the children of *A*
    11:4 the children of *A* made war against Israel
1 Sam. 14:47 Moab, and against the children of *A*
2 Sam. 10:1 (1 Chr. 19:1) king of the children of *A*
    11:1 (1 Chr. 20:1) they destroyed the children of *A*
    12:31 (1 Chr. 20:3) did he unto all the cities . . of *A*
2 Kgs. 24:2 Lord sent . . bands of the children of *A*
2 Chr. 20:1 children of *A* . . against Jehoshaphat
Is. 11:14 and the revilings of the children of *A*
Zeph. 2:8 and the revilings of the children of *A*

Ammonite
Deut. 23:3 (Neh. 13:1) *A* or Moabite shall not enter
1 Sam. 11:11 slew the *A* until the heat of the day
2 Chr. 26:8 the *A* gave gifts to Uzziah
    27:5 he fought also with the king of the *A*
Jer. 41:10 Ishmael . . departed to go over to the *A*
    49:1 concerning the *A*, thus saith the Lord
Ezek. 25:2 son of man, set thy face against the *A*

Amnon
2 Sam. 3:2 (1 Chr. 3:1) firstborn was *A*, of Ahinoam
    13:1 Tamar; and *A* the son of David loved her
    13:22 for Absalom hated *A*, because he had forced
    13:39 comforted concerning *A*, seeing he was dead

Amon governor of Samaria
1 Kgs. 22:26 (2 Chr. 18:25)

Amon king of Judah
2 Kgs. 21:19–26 (2 Chr. 33:21–25)

Amorite
Gen. 15:16 the iniquity of the *A* is not yet full
    48:22 I took out of the hand of the *A* with my
Ex. 34:11 behold, I drive out before thee the *A*
Num. 21:25 Israel dwelt in all the cities of the *A*
Josh. 5:1 when all the kings of the *A*, which were
    10:12 the day when the Lord delivered up the *A*
    24:15 the gods of the *A*, in whose land ye dwell
Judg. 1:34 the *A* forced the children of Dan into
    11:21 so Israel possessed all the land of the *A*
1 Sam. 7:14 was peace between Israel and the *A*
Ezek. 16:3 (16:45) thy father was an *A* . . thy mother
Amos 2:9 yet destroyed I the *A* before them

Amos Amos 1:1–9:15

Amram Ex. 6:20

Amraphel Gen. 14:1

Anak Num. 13:33; Josh. 15:14

Anakim
Deut. 9:2 great and tall, the children of the *A*
Josh. 11:21 and cut off the *A* from the mountains
    14:12 heardest in that day how the *A* were there

Ananias of Jerusalem Acts 5:1–5

Ananias of Damascus Acts 9:10–17 (22:12)

Ananias the high priest Acts 23:2; 24:1

Anathema *See also* Accursed, Cursed
1 Cor. 16:22 love not the Lord Jesus . . let him be *A*

Anathoth
1 Kgs. 2:26 get thee to *A*, unto thine own fields
Jer. 1:1 Jeremiah . . of the priests that were in *A*
    11:21 the men of *A*, that seek thy life, saying
    32:7 saying, Buy thee my field that is in *A*

Anchor
Acts 27:29 they cast four *a* out of the stern
Heb. 6:19 which hope we have as an *a* of the soul

Ancient *See also* Aged, Old
2 Kgs. 19:25 (Is. 37:26) *a* times that I have formed it?
Ezra 3:12 *a* men, that had seen the first house
Job 12:12 with the *a* is wisdom . . in length of days
Ps. 119:100 I understand more than the *a*, because
Prov. 22:28 remove not the *a* landmark, which thy
Is. 3:5 shall behave himself proudly against the *a*
    3:14 enter into judgment with the *a* of his people
    23:7 joyous city, whose antiquity is of *a* days?
    45:21 who hath declared this from *a* time?
    46:10 from *a* times the things that are not yet
    47:6 the *a* hast thou very heavily laid thy yoke
    51:9 awake, as in the *a* days, in the generations
Jer. 18:15 stumble in their ways from the *a* paths
Ezek. 8:11 stood before them seventy men of the *a*
    36:2 the *a* high places are ours in possession
Dan. 7:9 the *A* of days did sit, whose garment was

Andrew
Mt. 4:18 (Mk. 1:16) and *A* his brother, casting a net
    10:2 (Lk. 6:14) called Peter, and *A* his brother
Jn. 1:40 heard John speak, and followed him, was *A*
    6:8 *A*, Simon Peter's brother, saith unto him
    12:22 telleth *A* . . again *A* and Philip tell Jesus

Angel *See also* Cherub, Cherubim, Messenger, Minister

Gen. 16:7 a of the LORD found her by a fountain
19:15 then the a hastened Lot, saying, Arise
21:17 the a of God called to Hagar out of heaven
22:11 a of the LORD called . . Abraham, Abraham
24:7 he shall send his a before thee, and thou
28:12 a of God ascending and descending on it
31:11 and the a of God spake unto me in a dream
32:1 went on his way, and the a of God met him
48:16 the a which redeemed me from all evil
Ex. 3:2 a of the LORD appeared unto him in a flame
14:19 the a of God, which went before the camp
23:20 behold, I send an a before thee, to keep
Num. 20:16 he heard our voice, and sent an a
22:23 the ass saw the a of the LORD standing in
Judg. 2:1 an a of the LORD came up from Gilgal to
6:11 came an a of the LORD, and sat under an oak
13:3 the a of the LORD appeared unto the woman
13:20 the a of the LORD ascended in the flame
1 Sam. 29:9 thou art good in my sight, as an a of God
2 Sam. 14:20 according to the wisdom of an a of God
19:27 but my lord the king is as an a of God
24:16 (1 Chr. 21:15) a stretched out his hand upon
1 Kgs. 13:18 a spake unto me by . . word of the LORD
19:5 as he lay and slept . . then an a touched him
2 Kgs. 1:3 but the a of the LORD said to Elijah
19:35 (Is. 37:36) a of the LORD went out, and smote
Ps. 8:5 (Heb. 2:7) made him a little lower than the a
34:7 the a of the LORD encampeth round about
35:5 and let the a of the LORD chase them
68:17 the chariots of God . . even thousands of a
78:25 man did eat a' food: he sent them meat
91:11 (Mt. 4:6; Lk. 4:10) give his a charge over thee
103:20 bless the LORD, ye his a, that excel
104:4 (Heb. 1:7) maketh his a spirits; his ministers
148:2 praise ye him, all his a: praise ye him
Eccl. 5:6 neither say thou before the a, that it
Is. 63:9 a of his presence saved them: in his love
Dan. 3:28 sent his a, and delivered his servants
6:22 my God hath sent his a, and hath shut
Hos. 12:4 he had power over the a, and prevailed
Zech. 1:9 (4:5) a that talked with me said unto me
3:1 standing before the a of the LORD, and Satan
Mt. 1:20 (2:13, 19) a of the Lord appeared unto him
4:11 (Mk. 1:13) a came and ministered unto him
13:41 the Son of man shall send forth his a
16:27 (Mk. 8:38) the glory of his Father with his a
18:10 in heaven their a do always behold the face
22:30 (Mk. 12:25; Lk. 20:36) as the a of God in
24:31 (Mk. 13:27) send his a . . they shall gather
24:36 (Mk. 13:32) no man, no, not the a of heaven
25:31 in his glory, and all the holy a with him
25:41 fire, prepared for the devil and his a
26:53 give me more than twelve legions of a?
28:2 the a of the Lord . . rolled back the stone
Lk. 1:11 there appeared unto him an a of the Lord
1:26 the a Gabriel was sent from God unto a city
2:9 and, lo, the a of the Lord came upon them
12:8 Son of man also confess before the a of God
15:10 joy in the presence of the a of God over
16:22 was carried by the a into Abraham's bosom
20:36 die any more: for they are equal unto the a
22:43 a unto him from heaven, strengthening him
24:23 that they had also seen a vision of a
Jn. 1:51 the a of God ascending and descending upon
5:4 an a went down . . into the pool, and troubled
12:29 thundered: others said, An a spake to him
20:12 seeth two a in white sitting, the one at
Acts 5:19 a of the Lord by night opened the prison
6:15 his face as it had been the face of an a
7:53 received the law by the disposition of a

Acts 8:26 the a of the Lord spake unto Philip, saying
10:3 in a vision . . an a of God coming in to him
12:7 the a of the Lord . . smote Peter on the side
12:15 was even so. Then said they, It is his a
23:8 no resurrection, neither a, nor spirit
23:9 but if a spirit or an a hath spoken to him
27:23 there stood by me this night the a of God
Rom. 8:38 that neither death, nor life, nor a, nor
1 Cor. 4:9 a spectacle unto the world, and to a
6:3 know ye not that we shall judge a? how much
11:10 to have power on her head because of the a
13:1 I speak with the tongues of men and of a
2 Cor. 11:14 Satan . . transformed into an a of light
Gal. 1:8 though we, or an a from heaven, preach
Col. 2:18 voluntary humility and worshipping of a
2 Thes. 1:7 revealed from heaven with his mighty a
1 Tim. 3:16 seen of a, preached unto the Gentiles
5:21 I charge thee before God . . and the elect a
Heb. 1:4 being made so much better than the a
1:6 saith, And let all the a of God worship him
2:2 for if the word spoken by a was steadfast
2:16 verily he took not on him the nature of a
12:22 Jerusalem . . to an innumerable company of a
13:2 thereby some have entertained a unawares
1 Pet. 1:12 which things the a desire to look into
3:22 a and authorities and powers . . made subject
2 Pet. 2:4 for if God spared not the a that sinned
2:11 a . . bring not railing accusation against them
Jude 6 and the a which kept not their first estate
Rev. 1:1 sent and signified it by his a unto his
1:20 seven stars are the a of the seven churches
5:2 saw a strong a proclaiming with a loud voice
5:11 the voice of many a round about the throne
7:1 I saw four a standing on the four corners
7:2 and I saw another a ascending from the east
7:11 all the a stood round about the throne
8:2 and I saw the seven a which stood before God
9:14 loose the four a which are bound in the
10:1 another mighty a come down from heaven
12:7 Michael and his a fought against the dragon
14:6 I saw another a fly in the midst of heaven
15:1 seven a having the seven last plagues
15:6 the seven a came out of the temple
16:5 I heard the a of the waters say, Thou art
18:1 I saw another a . . having great power
18:21 a took up a stone like a great millstone
19:17 saw an a standing in the sun; and he cried
20:1 an a . . having the key of the bottomless pit
21:12 twelve gates, and at the gates twelve a
22:8 to worship before the feet of the a which
22:16 I Jesus have sent mine a to testify unto

Anger *See also* Indignation, Passion, Rage, Wrath

Gen. 27:45 until thy brother's a turn away
30:2 and Jacob's a was kindled against Rachel
44:18 let not thine a burn against thy servant
49:7 cursed be their a, for it was fierce
Ex. 4:14 a of the LORD was kindled against Moses
11:8 and he went out from Pharaoh in a great a
32:19 Moses' a waxed hot, and he cast the tables
Num. 11:1 the LORD heard it; and his a was kindled
12:9 the a of the LORD was kindled against them
22:22 and God's a was kindled because he went
24:10 and Balak's a was kindled against Balaam
25:3 the a of the LORD was kindled against Israel
Deut. 4:25 and shall do evil . . to provoke him to a
13:17 LORD may turn from the fierceness of his a
29:20 a of the LORD and his jealousy shall smoke
31:17 then my a shall be kindled against them
32:21 (Rom. 10:19) to a with a foolish nation
Josh. 7:1 the a of the LORD was kindled against
23:16 the a of the LORD be kindled against you

Judg. 2:12 other gods . . and provoked the LORD to *a*
  6:39 Gideon said . . Let not thine *a* be hot against
1 Sam. 20:30 Saul's *a* was kindled against Jonathan
2 Sam. 6:7 (1 Chr. 13:10) *a* of the LORD . . Uzzah
  12:5 David's *a* was greatly kindled against
  24:1 the *a* of the LORD was kindled against Israel
1 Kgs. 15:30 provoked the LORD God of Israel to *a*
  21:22 provoked me to *a*, and made Israel to sin
Neh. 4:5 provoked thee to *a* before the builders
  9:17 to pardon, gracious and merciful, slow to *a*
Job 9:5 mountains . . which overturneth them in his *a*
  9:13 if God will not withdraw his *a*, the proud
  21:17 God distributeth sorrows in his *a*
Ps. 6:1 O LORD, rebuke me not in thine *a*, neither
  21:9 them as a fiery oven in the time of thine *a*
  27:9 far from me; put not thy servant away in *a*
  30:5 his *a* endureth but a moment; in his favor
  37:8 cease from *a*, and forsake wrath: fret not
  38:3 no soundness in my flesh because of thine *a*
  69:24 and let thy wrathful *a* take hold of them
  74:1 why doth thine *a* smoke against the sheep
  78:58 provoked him to *a* with their high places
  85:4 turn us . . cause thine *a* toward us to cease
  90:7 are consumed by thine *a*, and by thy wrath
  90:11 who knoweth the power of thine *a*?
  103:8 (145:8) slow to *a*, and plenteous in mercy
  106:32 they *a* him also at the waters of strife
Prov. 15:1 but grievous words stir up *a*
  15:18 but he that is slow to *a* appeaseth strife
  16:32 that is slow to *a* is better than the mighty
  19:11 the discretion of a man deferreth his *a*
  20:2 provoketh him to *a* sinneth against his own
  21:14 a gift in secret pacifieth *a*: and a reward
  27:4 wrath is cruel, and *a* is outrageous
Eccl. 7:9 for *a* resteth in the bosom of fools
Is. 1:4 have provoked the Holy One of Israel unto *a*
  5:25 therefore is the *a* of the LORD kindled
  10:5 the rod of my *a*, and the staff in their
  12:1 wast angry with me, thine *a* is turned away
  13:9 cometh, cruel both with wrath and fierce *a*
  30:27 LORD cometh from far, burning with his *a*
  48:9 for my name's sake will I defer mine *a*
  65:3 a people that provoketh me to *a* continually
Jer. 2:35 I am innocent, surely his *a* shall turn
  3:5 will he reserve his *a* for ever? will he keep
  3:12 I will not cause mine *a* to fall upon you
  4:8 the fierce *a* of the LORD is not turned back
  7:19 do they provoke me to *a*? saith the LORD
  8:19 provoked me to *a* with their graven images
  10:24 in thine *a*, lest thou bring me to nothing
  23:20 the *a* of the LORD shall not return, until
  25:6 provoke me not to *a* with the works of your
  33:5 bodies of men, whom I have slain in mine *a*
  44:6 wherefore my fury and mine *a* was poured
Lam. 1:12 afflicted me in the day of his fierce *a*
  2:1 the daughter of Zion with a cloud in his *a*
  2:22 in the day of the LORD's *a* none escaped nor
Ezek. 5:13 thus shall mine *a* be accomplished
  5:15 execute judgments in thee in *a* and in fury
  7:3 will send mine *a* upon thee, and will judge
  16:26 increased . . whoredoms, to provoke me to *a*
Dan. 9:16 let thine *a* and thy fury be turned away
Hos. 8:5 mine *a* is kindled against them: how long
  11:9 I will not execute the fierceness of mine *a*
  14:4 love them freely: for mine *a* is turned away
Jon. 3:9 repent, and turn away from his fierce *a*
Mic. 5:15 I will execute vengeance in *a* and fury
Nah. 1:3 the LORD is slow to *a*, and great in power
Zeph. 2:2 before the day of the LORD's *a* come upon
  3:8 pour . . mine indignation, even all my fierce *a*
Zech. 10:3 mine *a* was kindled against the shepherds
Mk. 3:5 he had looked round about on them with *a*
Eph. 4:31 let all bitterness, and wrath, and *a*

Col. 3:8 also put off all these; *a*, wrath, malice
  3:21 fathers, provoke not your children to *a*

Angle

Is. 19:8 that cast *a* into the brooks shall lament

Angry *See also* Wroth

Gen. 18:30 let not the Lord be *a*, and I will speak
Lev. 10:16 and he was *a* with Eleazar and Ithamar
Deut. 1:37 (4:21) LORD was *a* with me for your sakes
Ps. 2:12 kiss the Son, lest he be *a*, and ye perish
  7:11 and God is *a* with the wicked every day
  76:7 may stand in thy sight when once thou art *a*?
  79:5 (85:5) wilt thou be *a* for ever? shall thy
  80:4 thou be *a* against the prayer of thy people?
Prov. 14:17 he that is soon *a* dealeth foolishly
  21:19 than with a contentious and *a* woman
  22:24 make no friendship with an *a* man
  25:23 doth an *a* countenance a backbiting tongue
  29:22 an *a* man stirreth up strife . . a furious man
Eccl. 7:9 be not hasty in thy spirit to be *a*
Song 1:6 my mother's children were *a* with me
Is. 12:1 though thou wast *a* with me, thine anger
Jon. 4:4 (4:9) said the LORD, Doest thou well to be *a*?
Mt. 5:22 whosoever is *a* with his brother without
Lk. 14:21 then the master of the house being *a* said
Jn. 7:23 *a* at me, because I have made a man . . whole
Eph. 4:26 be ye *a*, and sin not: let not the sun go
Tit. 1:7 a bishop . . not self-willed, not soon *a*
Rev. 11:18 nations were *a*, and thy wrath is come

Anguish *See also* Adversity, Calamity, Distress, Grief, Misery, Sorrow, Suffering, Tribulation, Trouble

Gen. 42:21 in that we saw the *a* of his soul, when
Ex. 6:9 hearkened not unto Moses for *a* of spirit
Deut. 2:25 tremble, and be in *a* because of thee
2 Sam. 1:9 slay me: for *a* is come upon me, because
Job 7:11 I will speak in the *a* of my spirit
  15:24 trouble and *a* shall make him afraid
Ps. 119:143 trouble and *a* have taken hold on me
Jn. 16:21 she remembereth no more the *a*, for joy
Rom. 2:9 tribulation and *a*, upon every soul of man
2 Cor. 2:4 out of much affliction and *a* of heart

Anise

Mt. 23:23 ye pay tithe of mint and *a* and cummin

Anna Lk. 2:36

Annas

Lk. 3:2 *A* and Caiaphas being the high priests
Jn. 18:13 and led him away to *A* first; for he was
  18:24 now *A* had sent him bound unto Caiaphas
Acts 4:6 *A* the high priest, and Caiaphas, and John

Anoint *See also* Consecration, Dedication, Oil, Ointment

Gen. 31:13 God of Bethel, where thou *a* the pillar
Ex. 28:41 (30:30) shalt *a* them, and consecrate them
  29:7 oil, and pour it upon his head, and *a* him
  30:26 shalt *a* the tabernacle of the congregation
  40:9 *a* the tabernacle, and all that is therein
Deut. 28:40 thou shalt not *a* thyself with the oil
Ruth 3:3 wash thyself therefore, and *a*
1 Sam. 9:16 thou shalt *a* him to be captain over
  10:1 LORD hath *a* thee to be captain over
  15:1 LORD sent me to *a* thee to be king over his
  16:13 Samuel took the horn of oil, and *a* him
2 Sam. 2:4 *a* David king over the house of Judah
  12:7 I *a* thee king over Israel, and I delivered

2 Sam. 14:2 *a* not thyself with oil, but be as a woman
1 Kgs. 1:39 Zadok the priest took . . and *a* Solomon
  19:16 Jehu . . *a* to be king . . Elisha . . to be prophet
2 Kgs. 9:3 thus saith the LORD, I have *a* thee king
  11:12 (2 Chr. 23:11) they made him king, and *a* him
2 Chr. 28:15 them to eat and to drink, and *a* them
Ps. 23:5 thou *a* my head with oil; my cup runneth
  45:7 (Heb. 1:9) hath *a* thee with the oil of gladness
Is. 21:5 arise, and *a* the shield
  61:1 (Lk. 4:18) hath *a* me to preach good tidings
Dan. 9:24 to seal up the vision . . *a* the Most Holy
Mic. 6:15 tread the olives, but . . not *a* thee with oil
Mt. 6:17 but thou, when thou fastest, *a* thine head
Mk. 6:13 *a* with oil many that were sick, and healed
  14:8 come aforehand to *a* my body to the burying
  16:1 spices, that they might come and *a* him
Lk. 7:38 kissed his feet, and *a* them with the ointment
Jn. 9:6 *a* the eyes of the blind man with the clay
  11:2 (12:3) Mary which *a* the Lord with ointment
Acts 4:27 thy holy child Jesus, whom thou hast *a*
  10:38 *a* Jesus of Nazareth with the Holy Ghost
2 Cor. 1:21 stablisheth us . . and hath *a* us, is God
Jas. 5:14 *a* him with oil in the name of the Lord
Rev. 3:18 *a* thine eyes with eyesalve, that thou

Anointed *See also* Anoint

1 Sam. 2:10 his king, and exalt the horn of his *a*
  2:35 and he shall walk before mine *a* for ever
  12:3 witness . . before the LORD, and before his *a*
  16:6 and said, Surely the LORD's *a* is before him
  24:10 against my lord; for he is the LORD's *a*
  26:9 stretch forth his hand against the LORD's *a*
2 Sam. 1:14 not afraid . . to destroy the LORD's *a*?
  22:51 (Ps. 18:50) mercy to his *a*, unto David
1 Chr. 16:22 (Ps. 105:15) touch not mine *a*, and do my
2 Chr. 6:42 (Ps. 132:10) not away the face of thine *a*
Ps. 2:2 against the LORD, and against his *A*, saying
  20:6 now know I that the LORD saveth his *a*
  28:8 the LORD . . is the saving strength of his *a*
  84:9 behold . . and look upon the face of thine *a*
  89:38 but . . thou hast been wroth with thine *a*
  132:17 I have ordained a lamp for mine *a*
Is. 45:1 thus saith the LORD to his *a*, to Cyrus
Ezek. 28:14 thou art the *a* cherub that covereth
Hab. 3:13 thy people . . for salvation with thine *a*
Zech. 4:14 these are the two *a* ones, that stand by

Anointing *See also* Anoint

Ex. 30:25 (37:29) apothecary: it shall be a holy *a* oil
Lev. 10:7 for the *a* oil of the LORD is upon you
Is. 10:27 yoke shall be destroyed because of the *a*
1 Jn. 2:27 but the *a* which ye have received of him

Another

Gen. 4:25 God, said she, hath appointed me *a* seed
1 Sam. 10:9 turned his back . . God gave him *a* heart
Job 19:27 and mine eyes shall behold, and not *a*
Is. 42:8 my glory will I not give to *a*, neither my
Mt. 11:3 (Lk. 7:19) art thou he . . or do we look for *a*?
Rom. 7:23 but I see *a* law in my members, warring
2 Cor. 11:4 *a* Jesus . . or if . . *a* spirit . . or *a* gospel
Gal. 1:6 from him that called you . . unto *a* gospel

Answer

Gen. 30:33 so shall my righteousness *a* for me
  41:16 God shall give Pharaoh an *a* of peace
Deut. 20:11 if it make thee *a* of peace, and open
1 Kgs. 18:24 the God that *a* by fire, let him be God
  18:29 there was neither voice, nor any to *a*
Job 11:2 should not the multitude of words be *a*?
  19:16 I called my servant, and he gave me no *a*
  31:35 my desire is, that the Almighty would *a* me
  32:3 had found no *a*, and yet had condemned Job

Job 34:36 be tried . . because of his *a* for wicked men
  35:12 there they cry, but none giveth *a*, because
  38:1 then the LORD *a* Job out of the whirlwind
  38:3 for I will demand of thee, and *a* thou me
Ps. 27:7 I cry . . have mercy also upon me, and *a* me
  65:5 by terrible things . . wilt thou *a* us, O God
  86:7 I will call upon thee: for thou wilt *a* me
  138:3 in the day when I cried thou *a* me
Prov. 1:28 then shall they call . . but I will not *a*
  15:1 a soft *a* turneth away wrath: but grievous
  16:1 the *a* of the tongue, is from the LORD
  18:13 he that *a a* matter before he heareth it
  26:4 *a* not a fool according to his folly, lest
  29:19 for though he understand he will not *a*
Eccl. 10:19 maketh merry: but money *a* all things
Song 5:6 I called him, but he gave me no *a*
Is. 65:12 because when I called, ye did not *a*
  65:24 before they call, I will *a*; and while they
Jer. 23:35 to his brother, What hath the LORD *a*?
  33:3 call unto me, and I will *a* thee, and show
Mic. 3:7 cover their lips; for there is no *a* of God
Mt. 15:23 but he *a* her not a word
  22:46 no man was able to *a* him a word, neither
Lk. 2:47 astonished at his understanding and *a*
  12:11 no thought how or what thing ye shall *a*
  21:14 not to meditate before what ye shall *a*
  23:9 questioned with him . . but he *a* him nothing
Jn. 1:22 that we may give an *a* to them that sent us
  19:9 whence art thou? But Jesus gave him no *a*
1 Cor. 9:3 mine *a* to them that do examine me is
2 Cor. 5:12 that ye may have somewhat to *a* them
Col. 4:6 ye may know how ye ought to *a* every man
2 Tim. 4:16 at my first *a* no man stood with me
Tit. 2:9 please . . well in all things; not *a* again
1 Pet. 3:15 ready always to give an *a* to every man
  3:21 but the *a* of a good conscience toward God

Ant

Prov. 6:6 go to the *a*, thou sluggard; consider her
  30:25 the *a* are a people not strong, yet they

Antichrist

1 Jn. 2:18 *a* shall come, even now are there many *a*
  4:3 is that spirit of *a*, whereof ye have heard
2 Jn. 7 in the flesh. This is a deceiver and an *a*

Antioch of Syria

Acts 11:19 as far as Phenice, and Cyprus, and *A*
  11:26 disciples . . called Christians first in *A*
  13:1 now there were in the church that was at *A*
  14:26 thence sailed to *A*, from whence they had
  15:22 send chosen men of their own company to *A*
  15:35 Paul also and Barnabas continued in *A*
  18:22 and saluted the church, he went down to *A*

Antioch of Pisidia

Acts 13:14 from Perga, they came to *A* in Pisidia
  14:19 there came thither certain Jews from *A*
2 Tim. 3:11 afflictions, which came unto me at *A*

Antipas Rev. 2:13

Antipatris Acts 23:31

Apart

Ex. 13:12 set *a* unto the LORD all that openeth
Ps. 4:3 LORD . . set *a* him that is godly for himself
Zech. 12:12 the land shall mourn, every family *a*
Mt. 14:13 departed . . by ship into a desert place *a*
  14:23 he went up into a mountain *a* to pray
  17:1 (Mk. 9:2) them up into a high mountain *a*
  17:19 came the disciples to Jesus *a*, and said
  20:17 took the twelve disciples *a* in the way

Mk. 6:31 come ye yourselves *a* into a desert place
Jas. 1:21 lay *a* all filthiness and superfluity of

Aphek

1 Sam. 4:1 to battle . . the Philistines pitched in *A*
29:1 Philistines gathered . . all their armies to *A*
1 Kgs. 20:26 went up to *A*, to fight against Israel
2 Kgs. 13:17 for thou shalt smite the Syrians in *A*

Apollos

Acts 18:24 certain Jew named *A*, born at Alexandria
19:1 while *A* was at Corinth, Paul having passed
1 Cor. 1:12 (3:4) saith, I am of Paul; and I of *A*
3:6 I have planted, *A* watered; but God gave the
4:6 in a figure transferred to myself and to *A*
16:12 touching our brother *A*, I greatly desired
Tit. 3:13 Zenas the lawyer and *A* on their journey

Apostle *See also* Ambassador, Disciple, Messenger, Minister, Prophet

Mt. 10:2 now the names of the twelve *a* are these
Mk. 6:30 (Lk. 9:10) *a* gathered . . unto Jesus, and told
Lk. 6:13 he chose twelve, whom also he named *a*
11:49 I will send them prophets and *a*, and some
22:14 he sat down, and the twelve *a* with him
24:10 women . . which told these things unto the *a*
Acts 1:2 had given commandments unto the *a* whom
1:26 Matthias . . was numbered with the eleven *a*
2:42 continued steadfastly in the *a'* doctrine
4:33 and with great power gave the *a* witness of
4:35 and laid them down at the *a'* feet
5:12 by the hands of the *a* were many signs
5:18 laid their hands on the *a*, and put them in
6:6 whom they set before the *a*: and when they
8:1 they were all scattered abroad . . except the *a*
8:18 saw that through laying on of the *a'* hands
9:27 Barnabas took him, and brought him to the *a*
11:1 the *a* and brethren that were in Judea heard
15:2 unto the *a* and elders about this question
15:22 the *a* and elders, with the whole church
16:4 the decrees . . ordained of the *a* and elders
Rom. 1:1 (1 Cor. 1:1; 2 Cor. 1:1; Gal. 1:1; Eph. 1:1; Col. 1:1; 1 Tim. 1:1; 2 Tim. 1:1; Tit. 1:1) Paul . . called to be an *a*
11:13 inasmuch as I am the *a* of the Gentiles
16:7 who are of note among the *a*, who also were
1 Cor. 4:9 that God hath set forth us the *a* last
9:1 am I not an *a*? am I not free? have I not
12:28 God hath set some in the church, first *a*
15:7 he was seen of James; then of all the *a*
15:9 I am the least of the *a*, that am not meet
2 Cor. 11:5 (12:11) behind the very chiefest *a*
11:13 for such are false *a*, deceitful workers
12:12 the signs of an *a* were wrought among you
Gal. 1:17 neither went . . to them which were *a* before
Eph. 2:20 the foundation of the *a* and prophets
3:5 as it is now revealed unto his holy *a* and
4:11 gave some, *a*; and some, prophets; and some
1 Thes. 2:6 been burdensome, as the *a* of Christ
1 Tim. 2:7 (2 Tim. 1:11) ordained a preacher, and an *a*
Heb. 3:1 the *A* and High Priest of our profession
1 Pet. 1:1 (2 Pet. 1:1) Peter, an *a* of Jesus Christ
2 Pet. 3:2 the commandment of us the *a* of the Lord
Rev. 2:2 them which say they are *a*, and are not
18:20 rejoice over her . . ye holy *a* and prophets
21:14 the names of the twelve *a* of the Lamb

Apostleship

Acts 1:25 he may take part of this ministry and *a*
Rom. 1:5 by whom we have received grace and *a*
1 Cor. 9:2 the seal of mine *a* are ye in the Lord
Gal. 2:8 in Peter to the *a* of the circumcision

Apparel

2 Sam. 12:20 then David arose . . and changed his *a*
Esth. 6:11 took Haman the *a* . . and arrayed Mordecai
Zeph. 1:8 all such as are clothed with strange *a*
Lk. 7:25 gorgeously *a*, and live delicately, are in
Acts 1:10 behold, two men stood by them in white *a*
1 Tim. 2:9 that women adorn themselves in modest *a*
Jas. 2:2 a man with a gold ring, in goodly *a*
1 Pet. 3:3 wearing of gold, or of putting on of *a*

Appeal

Acts 25:11 no man may deliver me . . *a* unto Caesar

Appear

Gen. 1:9 and let the dry land *a*: and it was so
Ex. 16:10 the glory of the Lord *a* in the cloud
23:15 month Abib . . none shall *a* before me empty
Ps. 42:2 when shall I come and *a* before God?
90:16 let thy work *a* unto thy servants, and thy
Song 2:12 the flowers *a* on the earth; the time of
Is. 1:12 when ye come to *a* before me, who hath
Jer. 31:3 the Lord hath *a* of old unto me, saying
Ezek. 21:24 that in all your doings your sins do *a*
Mt. 6:16 faces, that they may *a* unto men to fast
23:28 so ye also outwardly *a* righteous unto men
24:30 then shall *a* the sign of the Son of man
Mk. 16:9 he *a* first to Mary Magdalene, out of whom
16:12 he *a* in another form unto two of them
16:14 he *a* unto the eleven as they sat at meat
Lk. 19:11 the kingdom of God should immediately *a*
Acts 7:2 God of glory *a* unto our father Abraham
Rom. 7:13 sin, that it might *a* sin, working death
2 Cor. 5:10 we must all *a* before the judgment seat
Col. 3:4 when Christ, who is our life, shall *a*
1 Tim. 4:15 that thy profiting may *a* to all
Tit. 2:11 for the grace of God . . hath *a* to all men
Heb. 9:24 now to *a* in the presence of God for us
9:26 hath he *a* to put away sin by the sacrifice
9:28 and unto them that look for him shall he *a*
11:3 seen were not made of things which do *a*
1 Pet. 4:18 shall the ungodly and the sinner *a*?
1 Jn. 2:28 when he shall *a*, we may have confidence
3:2 doth not yet *a* . . we know . . when he shall *a*

Appearance

Num. 9:15 the tabernacle as it were the *a* of fire
1 Sam. 16:7 for man looketh on the outward *a*, but
Ezek. 1:5 and this was their *a*; they had the likeness
1:26 the likeness as the *a* of a man above
Jn. 7:24 judge not according to the *a*, but judge
2 Cor. 5:12 which glory in *a*, and not in heart
10:7 do ye look on things after the outward *a*?
1 Thes. 5:22 abstain from all *a* of evil

Appearing

1 Tim. 6:14 until the *a* of our Lord Jesus Christ
2 Tim. 1:10 by the *a* of our Saviour Jesus Christ
4:1 shall judge the quick and the dead at his *a*
4:8 but unto all them also that love his *a*
Tit. 2:13 glorious *a* of the great God and our Saviour
1 Pet. 1:7 honor and glory at the *a* of Jesus Christ

Appease

Gen. 32:20 he said, I will *a* him with the present
Esth. 2:1 when the wrath of king Ahasuerus was *a*
Prov. 15:18 but he that is slow to anger *a* strife
Acts 19:35 and when the townclerk had *a* the people

Appetite

Job 38:39 lion? or fill the *a* of the young lions
Prov. 23:2 thy throat, if thou be a man given to *a*
Eccl. 6:7 his mouth, and yet the *a* is not filled
Is. 29:8 behold, he is faint, and his soul hath *a*

Apphia Phlm. 2

Appii Forum Acts 28:15

Apple

Deut. 32:10 he kept him as the *a* of his eye
Ps. 17:8 keep me as the *a* of the eye; hide me
Prov. 7:2 and my law as the *a* of thine eye
  25:11 is like *a* of gold in pictures of silver
Song 2:3 as the *a* tree among the trees of the wood
  2:5 comfort me with *a*: for I am sick of love
Lam. 2:18 let not the *a* of thine eye cease
Zech. 2:8 toucheth you, toucheth the *a* of his eye

Apply

Ps. 90:12 that we may *a* our hearts unto wisdom
Prov. 2:2 and *a* thine heart to understanding
  22:17 and *a* thine heart unto my knowledge
  23:12 *a* thine heart unto instruction, and thine
Eccl. 7:25 I *a* mine heart to know, and to search
  8:9 and *a* my heart unto every work that is done
  8:16 when I *a* mine heart to know wisdom . . to see

Appoint *See also* Ordain

Gen. 4:25 hath *a* me another seed instead of Abel
  30:28 said, *A* me thy wages, and I will give it
Lev. 26:16 even *a* over you terror, consumption, and
Num. 35:6 *a* for the manslayer, that he may flee
2 Sam. 6:21 *a* me ruler over the people of the LORD
  17:14 *a* to defeat the good counsel of Ahithophel
1 Kgs. 20:42 a man whom I *a* to utter destruction
Job 14:5 thou hast *a* his bounds that he cannot pass
Ps. 79:11 preserve thou those that are *a* to die
  102:20 to loose those that are *a* to death
  104:19 *a* the moon for seasons: the sun knoweth
Prov. 8:29 when he *a* the foundations of the earth
  31:8 cause of all such as are *a* to destruction
Is. 26:1 salvation will God *a* for walls and bulwarks
  44:7 declare it . . since I *a* the ancient people?
  61:3 to *a* unto them that mourn in Zion, to give
Mt. 24:51 (Lk. 12:46) *a* him . . with the hypocrites
Lk. 10:1 the Lord *a* other seventy also, and sent
  22:29 *a* unto you a kingdom, as my Father hath *a*
Acts 1:23 and they *a* two, Joseph . . and Matthias
  6:3 seven men . . whom we may *a* over this business
  17:31 hath *a* a day, in the which he will judge
1 Thes. 5:9 for God hath not *a* us to wrath, but to
Heb. 1:2 Son, whom he hath *a* heir of all things
  3:2 faithful to him that *a* him, as also Moses
  9:27 as it is *a* unto men once to die, but after
1 Pet. 2:8 disobedient: whereunto also they were *a*

Appointed *See also* Appoint

Judg. 18:11 six hundred men *a* with weapons of war
1 Sam. 19:20 and Samuel standing as *a* over them
Job 7:1 is there not an *a* time to men upon earth?
  14:14 all the days of my *a* time will I wait
  30:23 to death . . to the house *a* for all living
Ps. 44:11 thou hast given us like sheep *a* for meat
Is. 1:14 new moons and your *a* feasts my soul hateth
1 Cor. 4:9 apostles last, as it were *a* to death

Apprehend

Acts 12:4 when he had *a* him, he put him in prison
2 Cor. 11:32 with a garrison, desirous to *a* me
Phil. 3:12 I may *a* that for which also I am *a* of

Approach

Num. 4:19 when they *a* unto the most holy things
Deut. 31:14 behold, thy days *a* that thou must die
2 Sam. 11:20 wherefore *a* ye so nigh unto the city
Ps. 65:4 thou choosest, and causest to *a* unto thee
Is. 58:2 of justice; they take delight in *a* to God

Jer. 30:21 and he shall *a* unto me: for who is this
Lk. 12:33 where no thief *a*, neither moth corrupteth
1 Tim. 6:16 in the light which no man can *a* unto
Heb. 10:25 so much the more, as ye see the day *a*

Approve

Ps. 49:13 yet their posterity *a* their sayings
Rom. 2:18 and *a* the things that are more excellent
2 Cor. 6:4 *a* ourselves as the ministers of God
Phil. 1:10 that ye may *a* things that are excellent

Approved

Acts 2:22 a man *a* of God among you by miracles
Rom. 14:18 is acceptable to God, and *a* of men
2 Tim. 2:15 study to show thyself *a* unto God

Apron

Gen. 3:7 sewed fig leaves . . and made themselves *a*

Apt

2 Kgs. 24:16 all that were strong and *a* for war
1 Tim. 3:2 bishop . . given to hospitality, *a* to teach
2 Tim. 2:24 be gentle unto all men, *a* to teach

Aquila Acts 18:2–26

Rom. 16:3 Priscilla and *A*, my helpers in Christ
1 Cor. 16:19 *A* and Priscilla salute you much
2 Tim. 4:19 salute Prisca and *A*, and the household

Arabia

1 Kgs. 10:15 (2 Chr. 9:14) and of all the kings of *A*
Is. 21:13 the burden upon *A*. In the forest in *A*
Gal. 1:17 I went into *A*, and returned again unto
  4:25 Agar is mount Sinai in *A*, and answereth to

Arabian Is. 13:20; Jer. 3:2

Arad Num. 21:1 (33:40)

Ararat Gen. 8:4

Araunah *See also* Ornan 2 Sam. 24:18

Archangel

1 Thes. 4:16 with a shout, with the voice of the *a*
Jude 9 Michael the *a* . . contending with the devil

Archelaus Mt. 2:22

Archer

Gen. 21:20 dwelt in the wilderness, and became an *a*
  49:23 the *a* have sorely grieved him, and shot at
1 Sam. 31:3 (1 Chr. 10:3) he was . . wounded of the *a*
2 Chr. 35:23 *a* shot at king Josiah; and the king
Job 16:13 his *a* compass me round about, he cleaveth

Archippus Col. 4:17; Phlm. 2

Arcturus Job 9:9; 38:32

Areopagus Acts 17:19

Aretas 2 Cor. 11:32

Arguing

Job 6:25 words! but what doth your *a* reprove?

Argument

Job 23:4 order my cause . . and fill my mouth with *a*

Ariel Is. 29:1

Aright

Ps. 50:23 to him that ordereth his conversation *a*
  78:8 a generation that set not their heart *a*
Prov. 15:2 tongue of the wise useth knowledge *a*
  23:31 color in the cup, when it moveth itself *a*

Jer. 8:6 hearkened and heard, but they spake not *a*

Arioch Dan. 2:14

Arise (Arose) *See also* Rise

Gen. 13:17 *a*, walk through the land in the length
  31:13 *a*, get thee out from this land, and return
Ex. 1:8 (Acts 7:18) there *a* up a new king over Egypt
Josh. 1:2 now therefore *a*, go over this Jordan
Judg. 5:7 I.Deborah *a*, that I *a* a mother in Israel
1 Kgs. 18:44 there *a* a little cloud out of the sea
1 Chr. 22:16 *a* therefore, and be doing, and the LORD
Neh. 2:20 we his servants will *a* and build: but ye
Ps. 3:7 *a*, O LORD; save me, O my God: for thou hast
  12:5 for the sighing of the needy, now will I *a*
  44:26 *a* for our help . . redeem us for thy mercies'
  68:1 let God *a*, let his enemies be scattered
  88:10 shall the dead *a* and praise thee?
  102:13 thou shalt *a*, and have mercy upon Zion
Is. 26:19 together with my dead body shall they *a*
  60:1 *a*, shine; for thy light is come
Jer. 2:27 trouble they will say, *A*, and save us
Amos 7:2 by whom shall Jacob *a*? for he is small
Mic. 7:8 O mine enemy: when I fall, I shall *a*
Mal. 4:2 Sun of righteousness *a* with healing in
Mt. 9:6 (Mk. 2:11; Lk. 5:24) *a*, take up thy bed . . go
  9:25 and took her by the hand, and the maid *a*
  24:24 shall *a* false Christs, and false prophets
  27:52 many bodies of the saints which slept *a*
Mk. 5:41 (Lk. 8:54) and said unto her . . . Damsel . . *a*
Lk. 7:14 he said, Young man, I say unto thee, *A*
  15:18 I will *a* and go to my father, and will say
Jn. 11:29 as soon as she heard that, she *a* quickly
Acts 9:6 (22:10) *a*, and go into the city, and it shall
  9:40 turning him to the body said, Tabitha, *a*
  22:16 *a*, and be baptized, and wash away thy sins
Eph. 5:14 thou that sleepest, and *a* from the dead
2 Pet. 1:19 until . . the day-star *a* in your hearts

Aristarchus

Acts 19:29 caught Gaius and *A*, men of Macedonia
  20:4 and of the Thessalonians, *A* and Secundus
  27:2 one *A*, a Macedonian of Thessalonica, being
Col. 4:10 *A* my fellow prisoner saluteth you
Phlm. 24 *A*, Demas, Lucas, my fellow laborers

Ark

Gen. 6:14 make thee an *a* of gopher wood
  7:1 come thou and all thy house into the *a*
  7:15 went in unto Noah into the *a*, two and two
  8:16 go forth of the *a*, thou, and thy wife, and
Ex. 2:3 she took for him an *a* of bulrushes
  25:10 (37:1) shall make an *a* of shittim wood
  31:7 the *a* of the testimony, and the mercy seat
  40:3 *a* of the testimony, and cover the *a* with
Num. 3:31 their charge shall be the *a*
  10:33 *a* of the covenant of the LORD went before
Deut. 31:9 the sons of Levi, which bare the *a*
Josh. 3:3 ye see the *a* of the covenant of the LORD
  4:5 pass over before the *a* of the LORD your God
  6:4 priests shall bear before the *a* seven trumpets
  8:33 stood on this side the *a* and on that side
Judg. 20:27 the *a* of the covenant of God was there
1 Sam. 4:3 fetch the *a* of the covenant of the LORD
  4:11 *a* of God was taken; and the two sons of Eli
  4:18 made mention of the *a* of God, that he fell
  5:2 Philistines took the *a* . . and set it by Dagon
  5:10 therefore they sent the *a* of God to Ekron
  6:2 what shall we do to the *a* of the LORD? tell us
  6:11 they laid the *a* of the LORD upon the cart
  6:19 smote . . because they had looked into the *a*
  7:1 the men of Kirjath-jearim . . fetched up the *a*
  14:18 and Saul said . . Bring hither the *a* of God

2 Sam 6:2 (1 Chr. 13:5) to bring up . . the *a* of God
  6:17 (1 Chr. 16:1) brought in the *a* of the LORD
  15:29 carried the *a* of God again to Jerusalem
1 Kgs. 2:26 because thou barest the *a* of the Lord
  8:1 (2 Chr. 5:2) bring up the *a* of the covenant
  8:21 (2 Chr. 6:11) I have set there a place for the *a*
1 Chr. 13:3 let us bring again the *a* of our God to
  15:1 David . . prepared a place for the *a* of God
  28:2 heart to build a house of rest for the *a*
2 Chr. 6:41 (Ps. 132:8) thou, and the *a* of thy strength
  35:3 the holy *a* in the house which Solomon
Jer. 3:16 shall say no more, The *a* of the covenant
Mt. 24:38 (Lk. 17:27) day that Noe entered into the *a*
Heb. 9:4 golden censer, and the *a* of the covenant
  11:7 prepared an *a* to the saving of his house
1 Pet. 3:20 while the *a* was a preparing, wherein
Rev. 11:19 in his temple the *a* of his testament

Arm (noun) *See also* Might, Power, Strength

Gen. 49:24 *a* of his hands were made strong by the
Ex. 6:6 I will redeem you with a stretched out *a*
  15:16 by the greatness of thine *a* they shall be
Deut. 33:27 and underneath are the everlasting *a*
Job 22:9 the *a* of the fatherless have been broken
  40:9 hast thou an *a* like God? or canst thou
Ps. 10:15 break thou the *a* of the wicked and the
  44:3 neither did their own *a* save them: but thy
  77:15 thou hast with thine *a* redeemed thy people
  89:13 thou hast a mighty *a*: strong is thy hand
  89:21 my hand . . mine *a* also shall strengthen him
  98:1 and his holy *a*, hath gotten him the victory
Is. 33:2 for thee: be thou their *a* every morning
  40:10 strong hand, and his *a* shall rule for him
  49:22 and they shall bring thy sons in their *a*
  51:5 mine *a* shall judge the people
  52:10 LORD hath made bare his holy *a* in the eyes
  53:1 (Jn. 12:38) is the *a* of the LORD revealed?
  63:5 mine own *a* brought salvation unto me
  63:12 by the . . hand of Moses with his glorious *a*
Jer. 21:5 will fight against you . . with a strong *a*
  27:5 I have made the earth . . by my outstretched *a*
Mk. 10:16 took them up in his *a* . . and blessed them
Lk. 1:51 he hath showed strength with his *a*
Acts 13:17 with a high *a* brought he them out of it

Arm (verb)

Gen. 14:14 he *a* his trained servants, born in his
1 Sam. 17:5 and he was *a* with a coat of mail
  17:38 Saul *a* David with his armor
Lk. 11:21 when a strong man *a* keepeth his palace
1 Pet. 4:1 *a* yourselves likewise with the same mind

Armageddon Rev. 16:16

Armenia 2 Kgs. 19:37 (Is. 37:38)

Armor

1 Sam. 17:38 Saul armed David with his *a*
  17:54 to Jerusalem; but he put his *a* in his tent
1 Kgs. 22:38 washed his *a*; according unto the word
Is. 22:8 look . . to the *a* of the house of the forest
Lk. 11:22 from him all his *a* wherein he trusted
Rom. 13:12 and let us put on the *a* of light
2 Cor. 6:7 power of God, by the *a* of righteousness
Eph. 6:11 put on the whole *a* of God, that ye may

Armor-bearer

1 Sam. 31:4 Saul unto his *a-b*, Draw thy sword

Army *See also* Host, Soldier

Ex. 7:4 hand upon Egypt, and bring forth mine *a*
  12:17 I brought your *a* out of the land of Egypt

Num. 33:1 with their *a* under the hand of Moses
1 Sam. 4:16 the *a*, and I fled today out of the *a*
  17:10 I defy the *a* of Israel this day; give me
1 Kgs. 20:19 city, and the *a* which followed them
2 Kgs. 25:5 (Jer. 39:5; 52:8) *a* of the Chaldees
2 Chr. 25:7 let not the *a* of Israel go with thee
  25:9 which I have given to the *a* of Israel?
Job 25:3 is there any number of his *a*?
Ps. 44:9 cast off . . and goest not forth with our *a*
Song 6:4 (6:10) terrible as an *a* with banners
  6:13 Shulamite? As it were the company of two *a*
Jer. 37:5 Pharaoh's *a* was come forth out of Egypt
Ezek. 37:10 upon their feet, an exceeding great *a*
Dan. 3:20 the most mighty men that were in his *a*
  4:35 according to his will in the *a* of heaven
Mt. 22:7 he sent forth his *a*, and destroyed those
Lk. 21:20 when ye . . see Jerusalem compassed with *a*
Acts 23:27 then came I with an *a*, and rescued him
Heb. 11:34 turned to flight the *a* of the aliens
Rev. 19:14 *a* which were in heaven followed him
  19:19 kings of the earth, and their *a*, gathered

Arnon

Num. 21:13 pitched on the other side of *A* . . for *A*
  21:24 and possessed his land from *A* unto Jabbok
Deut. 2:24 rise ye up . . and pass over the river *A*
Josh. 12:1 from the river *A* unto mount Hermon
Is. 16:2 the daughters of Moab . . at the fords of *A*

Aroer Is. 17:2; Jer. 48:19

Arose *See* Arise

Arphaxad Gen. 11:10

Array *See also* Clothe

Judg. 20:20 the men of Israel put themselves in *a*
1 Sam. 17:2 battle in *a* against the Philistines
2 Sam. 10:9 (1 Chr. 19:10) in *a* against the Syrians
Job 6:4 the terrors of God do set themselves in *a*
  40:10 and *a* thyself with glory and beauty
Jer. 43:12 shall *a* himself with the land of Egypt
Mt. 6:29 (Lk. 12:27) Solomon . . was not *a* like . . these
Acts 12:21 Herod, *a* in royal apparel, sat upon his
1 Tim. 2:9 not with . . gold, or pearls, or costly *a*
Rev. 7:13 are these which are *a* in white robes?
  17:4 the woman was *a* in purple and scarlet color
  19:8 granted that she should be *a* in fine linen

Arrogancy *See also* Conceit, Haughtiness, Pride

1 Sam. 2:3 let not *a* come out of your mouth
Prov. 8:13 pride, and *a*, and the evil way . . I hate
Is. 13:11 I will cause the *a* of the proud to cease
Jer. 48:29 his loftiness, and his *a*, and his pride

Arrow

Num. 24:8 and pierce them through with his *a*
Deut. 32:23 I will spend mine *a* upon them
1 Sam. 20:20 I will shoot three *a* on the side thereof
2 Sam. 22:15 (Ps. 18:14) sent out *a* . . scattered them
2 Kgs. 13:17 the *a* of the *a* of the LORD's deliverance
Job 6:4 for the *a* of the Almighty are within me
  41:28 the *a* cannot make him flee: sling stones
Ps. 11:2 they make ready their *a* upon the string
  38:2 for thine *a* stick fast in me, and thy hand
  45:5 thine *a* are sharp in the heart of the King's
  76:3 there brake he the *a* of the bow, the shield
  91:5 by night; nor for the *a* that flieth by day
  127:4 as *a* are in the hand of a mighty man
Prov. 25:18 is a maul, and a sword, and a sharp *a*
  26:18 man who casteth firebrands, *a*, and death
Jer. 9:8 their tongue is as an *a* shot out

Jer. 51:11 make bright the *a*; gather the shields
Lam. 3:12 his bow, and set me as a mark for the *a*
Ezek. 5:16 send upon them the evil *a* of famine
  39:3 cause thine *a* to fall out of thy right hand
Zech. 9:14 his *a* shall go forth as the lightning

Artaxerxes Ezra 4:7–11; 7:1–26

Artemas Tit. 3:12

Artificer

Gen. 4:22 instructor of every *a* in brass and iron
1 Chr. 29:5 of work to be made by the hands of *a*
2 Chr. 34:11 to the *a* and builders gave they it
Is. 3:3 the cunning *a*, and the eloquent orator

Artillery

1 Sam. 20:40 and Jonathan gave his *a* unto his lad

Asa 1 Kgs. 15:9–24 (2 Chr. 14:1–16:14); Jer. 41:9

Asahel 2 Sam. 2:18–32

Asaph 1 Chr. 6:39; 16:5, 7, 37

Ascend *See also* Mount

Gen. 28:12 angels of God *a* and descending on it
Num. 13:22 *a* by the south, and came unto Hebron
Josh. 6:5 shall *a* up every man straight before him
1 Sam. 28:13 Saul, I saw gods *a* out of the earth
Ps. 24:3 who shall *a* into the hill of the LORD?
  68:18 (Eph. 4:8) *a* on high . . led captivity captive
  139:8 if I *a* up into heaven, thou art there
Is. 14:13 I will *a* into heaven, I will exalt my
Lk. 19:28 he went before, *a* up to Jerusalem
Jn. 1:51 *a* and descending upon the Son of man
  3:13 no man hath *a* up to heaven, but he that
  6:62 the Son of man *a* up where he was before?
  20:17 touch me not . . I am not yet *a* to my Father
Rom. 10:6 in thine heart, Who shall *a* into heaven?
Rev. 8:4 the smoke of the incense . . *a* up before God
  11:7 (17:8) beast that *a* out of the bottomless pit
  11:12 they *a* up to heaven in a cloud

Ascribe

Deut. 32:3 the LORD: *a* ye greatness unto our God
Ps. 68:34 *a* ye strength unto God: his excellency

Asenath Gen. 41:45

Ashamed

Gen. 2:25 they were both naked . . and were not *a*
Ezra 9:6 I am *a* and blush to lift up my face to
Job 11:3 thou mockest, shall no man make thee *a*?
Ps. 6:10 let all mine enemies be *a* and sore vexed
  25:3 none that wait on thee be *a*: let them be *a*
  31:1 LORD, do I put my trust; let me never be *a*
  31:17 let me not be *a* . . let the wicked be *a*
  34:5 were lightened: and their faces were not *a*
  119:6 then shall I not be *a*, when I have respect
  119:78 proud be *a*; for they dealt perversely
Prov. 12:4 maketh *a* is as rottenness in his bones
Is. 30:5 *a* of a people that could not profit them
  45:17 not be *a* nor confounded world without end
  65:13 servants shall rejoice, but ye shall be *a*
Jer. 2:26 as the thief is *a* . . so is the house of Israel *a*
  2:36 be *a* of Egypt, as thou wast *a* of Assyria
  6:15 (8:12) *a* when they . . committed abomination?
  12:13 they shall be *a* of your revenues because
  14:4 plowmen were *a*, they covered their heads
Joel 2:26 ye shall eat . . my people shall never be *a*
Zech. 13:4 the prophets shall be *a* . . of his vision
Mk. 8:38 (Lk. 9:26) whosoever . . shall be *a* of me

Lk. 13:17 these things, all his adversaries were *a*
16:3 shall I do? . . I cannot dig; to beg I am *a*
Rom. 1:16 for I am not *a* of the gospel of Christ
5:5 hope maketh not *a*; because the love of God
9:33 (10:11) believeth on him shall not be *a*
Phil. 1:20 my hope, that in nothing I shall be *a*
2 Tim. 1:8 be not thou. . *a* of the testimony of our
1:12 I am not *a*; for I know whom I have believed
2:15 a workman that needeth not to be *a*, rightly
Heb. 2:11 he is not *a* to call them brethren
11:16 God is not *a* to be called their God
1 Pet. 3:16 may be *a* that falsely accuse your good
4:16 suffer as a Christian, let him not be *a*
1 Jn. 2:28 and not be *a* before him at his coming

Ashdod

1 Sam. 5:1 ark. . brought it from Eben-ezer unto *A*
2 Chr. 26:6 wall of *A*, and built cities about *A*
Is. 20:1 Tartan came unto *A* . . and fought against *A*
Amos 1:8 and I will cut off the inhabitant from *A*
Zeph. 2:4 they shall drive out *A* at the noonday
Zech. 9:6 a bastard shall dwell in *A*, and I will

Asher

Gen. 30:13 happy am I . . and she called his name *A*
49:20 out of *A* his bread shall be fat
Deut. 33:24 of *A* . . Let *A* be blessed with children
Judg. 5:17 *A* continued on the seashore, and abode
6:35 he sent messengers unto *A*, and unto Zebulun

Ashes *See also* Dust

Gen. 18:27 me to speak . . which am but dust and *a*
Num. 19:9 shall gather up the *a* of the heifer
2 Sam. 13:19 Tamar put *a* on her head, and rent
1 Kgs. 20:38 disguised himself with *a* upon his face
Esth. 4:1 Mordecai . . put on sackcloth with *a*
Job 2:8 a potsherd . . and he sat down among the *a*
30:19 the mire, and I am become like dust and *a*
42:6 I abhor myself, and repent in dust and *a*
Ps. 102:9 I have eaten a like bread, and mingled
Is. 44:20 he feedeth on *a*: a deceived heart hath
58:5 and to spread sackcloth and *a* under him?
61:3 beauty for *a*, the oil of joy for mourning
Jon. 3:6 covered him with sackcloth, and sat in *a*
Mt. 11:21 (Lk. 10:13) repented . . in sackcloth and *a*
Heb. 9:13 the *a* of a heifer sprinkling the unclean
2 Pet. 2:6 the cities of Sodom and Gomorrah into *a*

Ashkelon (Askelon)

Judg. 1:18 Judah took . . *A* with the coast thereof
14:19 went down to *A*, and slew thirty men of them
1 Sam. 6:17 for Gaza one, for *A* one, for Gath one
2 Sam. 1:20 publish it not in the streets of *A*
Jer. 47:5 *A* is cut off with the remnant of their
Amos 1:8 and him that holdeth the sceptre from *A*
Zeph. 2:4 Gaza . . be forsaken, and *A* a desolation
Zech. 9:5 *A* shall see it, and fear; Gaza also

Ashpenaz Dan. 1:3

Ashtaroth *See also* Ashtoreth

Judg. 2:13 forsook the LORD, and served Baal and *A*
1 Sam. 7:3 then put away the strange gods and *A*
12:10 have served Baalim and *A*: but now deliver
31:10 and they put his armor in the house of *A*

Ashtoreth *See also* Ashtaroth 1 Kgs. 11:5

Asia

Acts 2:9 dwellers in Mesopotamia. . in Pontus, and *A*
6:9 Cilicia and of *A*, disputing with Stephen
16:6 were forbidden . . to preach the word in *A*
19:10 all they which dwelt in *A* heard the word

Acts 19:27 whom all *A* and the world worshippeth
20:18 from the first day that I came into *A*
21:27 the Jews which were of *A*, when they saw
24:18 certain Jews from *A* found me purified in
2 Cor. 1:8 of our trouble which came to us in *A*
2 Tim. 1:15 all they which are in *A* be turned away
Rev. 1:4 (1:11) to the seven churches which are in *A*

Aside

Ex. 3:3 Moses said, I will now turn *a*, and see
Ruth 4:1 ho, such a one! turn *a*, sit down here
2 Sam. 3:27 Joab took him *a* in the gate to speak
2 Kgs. 4:4 and thou shalt set *a* that which is full
Ps. 14:3 they are all gone *a* . . all together become
Song 6:1 whither is thy beloved turned *a*?
Mt. 2:22 he turned *a* into the parts of Galilee
Mk. 7:8 laying *a* the commandment of God, ye hold
7:33 he took him *a* from the multitude, and put
Acts 26:31 and when they were gone *a*, they talked
Heb. 12:1 let us lay *a* every weight, and the sin
1 Pet. 2:1 laying *a* all malice, and all guile

Ask *See also* Beg, Beseech, Entreat, Inquire, Petition, Plead, Pray, Question, Request, Seek

Gen. 32:29 is it that thou dost *a* after my name?
Deut. 4:32 for *a* now of the days that are past
32:7 *a* thy father, and he will show thee
1 Sam. 1:20 saying, Because I have *a* him of the LORD
1 Kgs. 3:5 (2 Chr. 1:7) *a* what I shall give thee
2 Chr. 20:4 Judah gathered . . to *a* help of the LORD
Neh. 1:2 and I *a* them concerning the Jews
Ps. 2:8 *a* of me, and I shall give thee the heathen
21:4 he *a* life of thee, and thou gavest it him
Is. 7:11 *a* thee a sign of the LORD thy God; *a* it
45:11 *a* me of things to come concerning my sons
65:1 (Rom. 10:20) sought of them that *a* not for me
Jer. 6:16 *a* for the old paths, where is the good
50:5 they shall *a* the way to Zion with their
Dan. 2:10 that *a* such things at any magician
6:12 that shall *a* a petition of any God or man
Mic. 7:3 prince *a*, and the judge *a* for a reward
Zech. 10:1 *a* ye of the LORD rain in the time of
Mt. 5:42 (Lk. 6:30) give to him that *a* thee
6:8 what things ye have need of, before ye *a* him
7:7 (Lk. 11:9) *a*, and it shall be given you; seek
7:11 give good things to them that *a* him?
14:7 (Mk. 6:22) give her whatsoever she would *a*
16:13 (Mk. 8:27; Lk. 9:18) *a* his disciples. . Whom
20:22 (Mk. 10:38) ye know not what ye *a*. Are ye
21:22 *a* in prayer, believing, ye shall receive
Lk. 11:13 give the Holy Spirit to them that *a* him?
12:48 committed much, of him they will *a* the more
15:26 servants, and *a* what these things meant
Jn. 4:9 thou, being a Jew, *a* drink of me, which am
14:13 whatsoever ye shall *a* in my name, that will
15:7 ye shall *a* what ye will, and it shall be
15:16 that whatsoever ye shall *a* of the Father
16:24 hitherto have ye *a* nothing in my name: *a*
21:12 none of the disciples durst *a* him, Who art
1 Cor. 10:25 eat, *a* no question for conscience' sake
14:35 let them *a* their husbands at home
Eph. 3:20 abundantly above all that we *a* or think
Jas. 1:5 any of you lack wisdom, let him *a* of God
4:2 war, yet ye have not, because ye *a* not
1 Pet. 3:15 to every man that *a* you a reason of
1 Jn. 3:22 and whatsoever we *a*, we receive of him
5:14 if we *a* any thing according to his will, he
5:16 he shall *a*, and he shall give him life for

Askelon *See* Ashkelon

Asleep

Judg. 4:21 and smote . . for he was fast *a* and weary
Song 7:9 the lips of those that are *a* to speak
Jon. 1:5 of the ship; and he lay, and was fast *a*
Mt. 8:24 (Mk. 4:38; Lk. 8:23) the waves: but he was *a*
    26:40 unto the disciples, and findeth them *a*
Acts 7:60 and when he had said this, he fell *a*
1 Cor. 15:6 part remain . . but some are fallen *a*
    15:18 which are fallen *a* in Christ are perished
1 Thes. 4:13 concerning them which are *a*
2 Pet. 3:4 since the fathers fell *a*, all things

Asnapper Ezra 4:10

Asp *See also* Adder

Deut. 32:33 their wine is . . the cruel venom of *a*
Job 20:14 his meat . . is the gall of *a* within him
Is. 11:8 child shall play on the hole of the *a*
Rom. 3:13 the poison of *a* is under their lips

Ass

Gen. 22:5 abide ye here with the *a* . . I and the lad
    49:14 Issachar is a strong *a* couching down
Ex. 13:13 firstling of an *a* thou shalt redeem with
    23:4 meet thine enemy's ox or his *a* going astray
Num. 22:23 the *a* saw the angel . . the *a* turned aside
Deut. 22:10 not plow with an ox and an *a* together
Judg. 10:4 thirty sons that rode on thirty *a* colts
    12:14 that rode on threescore and ten *a* colts
1 Sam. 9:3 the *a* of Kish Saul's father were lost
    10:16 he told us plainly that the *a* were found
    25:20 she rode on the *a* . . David and his men came
Job 1:14 the oxen were plowing, and the *a* feeding
    39:5 who hath sent out the wild *a* free? or who
Prov. 26:3 whip for the horse, a bridle for the *a*
Is. 1:3 his owner, and the *a* his master's crib
Jer. 22:19 shall be buried with the burial of an *a*
Dan. 5:21 and his dwelling was with the wild *a*
Hos. 8:9 up to Assyria, a wild *a* alone by himself
Zech. 9:9 (Mt. 21:5; Jn. 12:15) riding upon an *a*
Mt. 21:2 a tied, and a colt with her
Lk. 13:15 loose his ox or his *a* from the stall
    14:5 shall have an *a* or an ox fallen into a pit
Jn. 12:14 Jesus, when he had found a young *a*, sat
2 Pet. 2:16 the dumb *a* speaking with man's voice

Assault

Acts 14:5 was an *a* made both of the Gentiles, and

Assay

Deut. 4:34 hath God *a* to go and take him a nation
1 Sam. 17:39 sword upon his armor, and he *a* to go
Acts 9:26 he *a* to join himself to the disciples
    16:7 they *a* to go into Bithynia: but the Spirit
Heb. 11:29 the Egyptians *a* to do were drowned

Assemble *See also* Bring, Gather

Num. 1:18 they *a* all the congregation together
    10:3 shall *a* themselves to thee at the door
1 Sam. 2:22 lay with the women that *a* at the door
    14:20 Saul and all the people . . *a* themselves
2 Sam. 20:4 *a* me the men of Judah within three days
1 Kgs. 8:1 (2 Chr. 5:2) Solomon *a* the elders of Israel
1 Chr. 15:4 David *a* the children of Aaron
2 Chr. 30:13 there *a* at Jerusalem much people
Ezra 10:1 *a* unto him . . a very great congregation
Neh. 9:1 *a* with fasting, and with sackclothes
Esth. 9:18 Jews that were at Shushan *a* together
Ps. 48:4 for, lo, the kings were *a*, they passed by
Is. 11:12 *a* the outcasts of Israel, and gather
    43:9 and let the people be *a*: who among them can
    45:20 *a* yourselves and come; draw near together
Jer. 4:5 *a* yourselves . . go into the defensed cities

Jer. 21:4 I will *a* them into the midst of this city
Ezek. 11:17 *a* you out of the countries where ye
Dan. 6:6 these presidents and princes *a* together
    11:10 and shall *a* a multitude of great forces
Joel 2:16 sanctify the congregation, *a* the elders
Amos 3:9 *a* yourselves upon . . mountains of Samaria
Mic. 2:12 I will surely *a*, O Jacob, all of thee
    4:6 in that day . . will I *a* her that halteth
Mt. 26:3 then *a* together the chief priests
Jn. 20:19 the disciples were *a* for fear of the Jews
Acts 1:4 being *a* together with them, commanded
    11:26 *a* themselves with the church, and taught
    15:25 good unto us, being *a* with one accord, to
Heb. 10:25 forsaking the *a* of ourselves together

Assembly *See also* Church, Company, Congregation, Synagogue

Ex. 12:6 the whole *a* of the congregation of Israel
    16:3 us forth . . to kill this whole *a* with hunger
Lev. 4:13 the thing be hid from the eyes of the *a*
    8:4 the *a* was gathered together unto the door
    23:36 solemn *a*; and ye shall do no servile work
Num. 14:5 fell on their faces before all the *a*
    20:6 went from the presence of the *a* unto the door
Deut. 10:4 midst of the fire, in the day of the *a*
    16:8 on the seventh day shall be a solemn *a*
2 Kgs. 10:20 said, Proclaim a solemn *a* for Baal
2 Chr. 30:23 and the whole *a* took counsel to keep
Ps. 22:16 the *a* of the wicked have inclosed me
    86:14 *a* of violent men have sought after my soul
    89:7 greatly to be feared in the *a* of the saints
    107:32 and praise him in the *a* of the elders
    111:1 praise the LORD . . in the *a* of the upright
Is. 1:13 new moons and sabbaths, the calling of *a*
    4:5 upon her *a*, a cloud and smoke by day
Jer. 6:11 and upon the *a* of young men together
    9:2 be all adulterers, an *a* of treacherous men
    15:17 I sat not in the *a* of the mockers, nor
    50:9 *a* of great nations from the north country
Lam. 1:15 he hath called an *a* against me to crush
Ezek. 44:24 my laws and my statutes in all mine *a*
Joel 1:14 (2:15) sanctify ye a fast, call a solemn *a*
Acts 19:39 it shall be determined in a lawful *a*
Heb. 12:23 general *a* and church of the firstborn
Jas. 2:2 come unto your *a* a man with a gold ring

Assent

2 Chr. 18:12 declare good to the king with one *a*
Acts 24:9 Jews also *a*, saying that these things

Asshur *See also* Assyria

Gen. 10:11 of that land went forth *A*, and builded
Num. 24:22 until *A* shall carry thee away captive
Ps. 83:8 *A* also is joined with them
Ezek. 32:22 *A* is there and all her company
Hos. 14:3 *A* shall not save us; we will not ride

Assign

2 Sam. 11:16 *a* Uriah unto a place where he knew

Associate

Is. 8:9 *a* yourselves, O ye people, and ye shall be

Assos Acts 20:13

Assuage

Gen. 8:1 to pass over the earth, and the waters *a*
Job 16:5 the moving of my lips should *a* your grief
    16:6 though I speak, my grief is not *a* . . though I

Assurance *See also* Confidence, Faith, Trust

Deut. 28:66 and shalt have none *a* of thy life

Is. 32:17 the effect . . quietness and *a* for ever
Acts 17:31 whereof he hath given *a* unto all men
Col. 2:2 all riches of the full *a* of understanding
1 Thes. 1:5 and in the Holy Ghost, and in much *a*
Heb. 6:11 to the full *a* of hope unto the end
   10:22 with a true heart in full *a* of faith

Assure

Jer. 14:13 I will give you *a* peace in this place
2 Tim. 3:14 thou hast learned and hast been *a* of
1 Jn. 3:19 know . . and shall *a* our hearts before him

Assuredly

Acts 2:36 let all the house of Israel know *a*, that
   16:10 *a* gathering that the Lord had called us

Assyria *See also* Asshur

Gen. 2:14 is it which goeth toward the east of *A*
2 Kgs. 15:29 king of *A* . . carried them captive to *A*
   17:6 took Samaria, and carried Israel away into *A*
Is. 7:18 and for the bee that is in the land of *A*
   19:23 shall there be a highway out of Egypt to *A*
   20:4 the king of *A* lead away the Egyptians
   30:31 shall the *A* be beaten down, which smote
Jer. 2:18 or what hast thou to do in the way of *A*
Hos. 7:11 they call to Egypt, they go to *A*
   8:9 for they are gone up to *A*, a wild ass alone
Mic. 5:6 shall waste the land of *A* with the sword
Nah. 3:18 thy shepherds slumber, O king of *A*
Zeph. 2:13 he will stretch out his hand . . destroy *A*
Zech. 10:11 the pride of *A* shall be brought down

Assyrian

2 Kgs. 19:35 (Is. 37:36) smote in the camp of the *A*
Is. 10:5 O *A*, the rod of mine anger, and the staff
   14:25 I will break the *A* in my land, and upon my
   30:31 voice of the LORD shall the *A* be beaten down
   31:8 then shall the *A* fall with the sword
Ezek. 31:3 the *A* was a cedar in Lebanon with fair
Hos. 11:5 but the *A* shall be his king, because
Mic. 5:5 shall be the peace, when the *A* shall come

Astonished *See also* Amazed

Ezra 9:3 and plucked off . . my beard, and sat down *a*
Job 17:8 upright men shall be *a* at this
   21:5 mark me, and be *a*, and lay your hand upon
   26:11 pillars of heaven . . are *a* at his reproof
Is. 52:14 as many were *a* at thee; his visage was
Jer. 2:12 be *a*, O ye heavens, at this, and be
Ezek. 3:15 remained there *a* among them seven days
Dan. 3:24 then Nebuchadnezzar the king was *a*
   4:19 Daniel . . was *a* for one hour, and his thoughts
   5:9 king . . greatly troubled . . and his lords were *a*
   8:27 I was *a* at the vision, but none understood
Mt. 7:28 (22:33; Mk. 1:22; 11:18; Lk. 4:32) the people
   were *a* at his doctrine
   13:54 (Mk. 6:2) they were *a*, and said, Whence
Mk. 5:42 and they were *a* with a great astonishment
Lk. 2:47 were *a* at his understanding and answers
   5:9 for he was *a* . . at the draught of the fishes
   24:22 certain women . . of our company made us *a*
Acts 9:6 he trembling and *a* said, Lord, what wilt
   12:16 opened the door, and saw him, they were *a*
   13:12 deputy . . believed, being *a* at the doctrine

Astonishment *See also* Amazement, Wonder

Deut. 28:28 madness, and blindness, and *a* of heart
   28:37 shalt become an *a*, a proverb, and a byword
2 Chr. 7:21 house, which is high, shall be an *a*
   29:8 delivered . . to trouble, to *a*, and to hissing
Ps. 60:3 thou hast made us to drink the wine of *a*

Jer. 8:21 I am black; *a* hath taken hold on me
   25:9 destroy . . and make them an *a*, and a hissing
   51:41 is Babylon become an *a* among the nations!
Ezek. 5:15 instruction and an *a* unto the nations
   23:33 filled . . with the cup of *a* and desolation
Mk. 5:42 and they were astonished with a great *a*

Astray *See also* Wander

Ps. 58:3 the wicked . . go *a* as soon as they be born
   119:67 before I was afflicted I went *a*: but now
   119:176 I have gone *a* like a lost sheep: seek
Prov. 28:10 whoso causeth the righteous to go *a*
Is. 53:6 all we like sheep have gone *a*; we have
Mt. 18:12 hundred sheep, and one of them be gone *a*
1 Pet. 2:25 ye were as sheep going *a*; but are now
2 Pet. 2:15 forsaken the right way, and are gone *a*

Astrologer

Is. 47:13 let now the *a* . . stand up, and save thee
Dan. 2:2 to call the magicians, and the *a*, and the

Asunder

Lev. 1:17 shall cleave . . but shall not divide it *a*
2 Kgs. 2:11 horses of fire, and parted them both *a*
Ps. 2:3 let us break their bands *a*, and cast away
Mt. 19:6 (Mk. 10:9) hath joined . . let not man put *a*
Mk. 5:4 and the chains had been plucked *a* by him

Athaliah 2 Kgs. 11:1–20 (2 Chr. 22:10–23:15); 2 Chr. 24:7

Athens

Acts 17:22 ye men of *A*, I perceive that in all things
   18:1 Paul departed from *A*, and came to Corinth
1 Thes. 3:1 thought it good to be left at *A* alone

Athirst

Judg. 15:18 he was sore *a*, and called on the LORD
Ruth 2:9 when thou art *a*, go unto the vessels
Mt. 25:44 Lord, when saw we thee ahungered, or *a*
Rev. 21:6 give unto him that is *a* of the fountain
   22:17 and let him that is *a* come. And whosoever

Atonement *See also* Blood, Propitiation, Reconciliation, Sacrifice

Ex. 29:33 shall eat those things wherewith the *a*
   30:10 Aaron shall make an *a* upon the horns of it
   32:30 peradventure I shall make an *a* for your sin
Lev. 1:4 be accepted for him to make *a* for him
   4:20 the priest shall make an *a* for them
   9:7 make an *a* for thyself . . make an *a* for them
   10:17 given . . to make a for them before the LORD?
   12:7 offer it before the LORD, and make an *a* for
   14:18 the priest shall make an *a* for him before
   16:6 make an *a* for himself, and for his house
   16:30 that day shall the priest make an *a* for you
   16:34 to make an *a* for the children of Israel
   17:11 is the blood that maketh an *a* for the soul
   23:27 the tenth day . . there shall be a day of *a*
   25:9 in the day of *a* shall ye make the trumpet
Num. 5:8 ram of the *a*, whereby an *a* shall be made
   8:12 unto the LORD, to make an *a* for the Levites
   15:25 shall make an *a* for all the congregation
   25:13 and made an *a* for the children of Israel
   28:22 for a sin offering, to make an *a* for you
   31:50 to make an *a* for our souls before the LORD
2 Sam. 21:3 wherewith shall I make the *a*, that ye
2 Chr. 29:24 altar, to make an *a* for all Israel
Neh. 10:33 sin offerings to make an *a* for Israel
Rom. 5:11 by whom we have now received the *a*

Attain

Gen. 47:9 have not *a* unto the days . . of my fathers

2 Sam. 23:19 (1 Chr. 11:21) *a* not unto the first three
Ps. 139:6 it is high, I cannot *a* unto it
Prov. 1:5 a man of understanding shall *a* unto wise
Hos. 8:5 long will it be ere they *a* to innocency?
Rom. 9:31 hath not *a* to the law of righteousness
Phil. 3:11 might *a* unto the resurrection of the dead
 3:16 whereto we have already *a*, let us walk
1 Tim. 4:6 of good doctrine, whereunto thou hast *a*

Attalia Acts 14:25

Attend *See also* Ear, Hearken, Wait

Esth. 4:5 whom he had appointed to *a* upon her
Ps. 17:1 hear the right, O LORD, *a* unto my cry
 55:2 *a* unto me, and hear me: I mourn in my
 61:1 hear my cry, O God; *a* unto my prayer
 86:6 and *a* to the voice of my supplications
 142:6 *a* unto my cry; for I am brought very low
Prov. 4:1 ye children . . and *a* to know understanding
 4:20 my son, *a* to my words; incline thine ear
 5:1 my son, *a* unto my wisdom, and bow thine ear
Acts 16:14 she *a* unto the things which were spoken
Rom. 13:6 *a* continually upon this very thing
1 Cor. 7:35 *a* upon the Lord without distraction

Attendance

1 Tim. 4:13 give *a* to reading, to exhortation
Heb. 7:13 of which no man gave *a* at the altar

Attentive

Neh. 1:6 let thine ear now be *a*, and thine eyes
Ps. 130:2 let thine ears be *a* to the voice of my
Lk. 19:48 all the people were very *a* to hear him

Attire

Lev. 16:4 and with the linen mitre shall he be *a*
Prov. 7:10 met him a woman with the *a* of a harlot
Jer. 2:32 forget her ornaments, or a bride her *a*?
Ezek. 23:15 exceeding in dyed *a* upon their heads

Audience

Gen. 23:10 in the *a* of the children of Heth
Ex. 24:7 covenant, and read in the *a* of the people
1 Sam. 25:24 let thine handmaid . . speak in thine *a*
1 Chr. 28:8 in the *a* of our God, keep and seek for
Neh. 13:1 the book of Moses in the *a* of the people
Lk. 20:45 then in the *a* of all the people he said
Acts 13:16 Israel, and ye that fear God, give *a*
 15:12 silence, and gave *a* to Barnabas and Paul

Augustus Lk. 2:1; Acts 25:25

Austere

Lk. 19:21 I feared thee, because thou art an *a* man

Author

1 Cor. 14:33 for God is not the *a* of confusion
Heb. 5:9 became the *a* of eternal salvation unto all
 12:2 unto Jesus the *a* and finisher of our faith

Authority *See also* Dominion, Power, Reign, Right, Rule, Strength

Prov. 29:2 when the righteous are in *a*, the people
Mt. 7:29 (Mk. 1:22) he taught them as one having *a*
 8:9 (Lk. 7:8) I am a man under *a*, having soldiers
 20:25 (Lk. 22:25) they that are great exercise *a*
 21:23 (Mk. 11:28; Lk. 20:2) by what *a* doest thou
Mk. 1:27 (Lk. 4:36) for with *a* commandeth he even
 13:34 left his house, and gave *a* to his servants
Lk. 9:1 and gave them power and *a* over all devils
 19:17 good servant . . have thou *a* over ten cities
Jn. 5:27 hath given him *a* to execute judgment also
Acts 8:27 a eunuch of great *a* under Candace queen

Acts 9:14 hath *a* from the chief priests to bind all
1 Cor. 15:24 down all rule, and all *a* and power
2 Cor. 10:8 I should boast somewhat more of our *a*
1 Tim. 2:2 for kings, and for all that are in *a*
 2:12 woman to teach, nor to usurp *a* over the man
Tit. 2:15 speak, and exhort, and rebuke with all *a*
1 Pet. 3:22 *a* and powers being made subject unto
Rev. 13:2 dragon gave him . . his seat, and great *a*

Avail

Esth. 5:13 yet all this *a* me nothing, so long as I
Gal. 5:6 (6:15) neither circumcision *a* any thing, nor
Jas. 5:16 fervent prayer of a righteous man *a* much

Avenge *See also* Recompense, Revenge, Vengeance

Gen. 4:24 if Cain shall be *a* sevenfold, truly
Lev. 19:18 thou shalt not *a*, nor bear any grudge
 26:25 that shall *a* the quarrel of my covenant
Deut. 32:43 he will *a* the blood of his servants
Josh. 10:13 until the people had *a* themselves upon
Judg. 15:7 have done this, yet will I be *a* of you
1 Sam. 24:12 the LORD *a* me of thee: but mine hand
 25:26 and from *a* thyself with thine own hand
2 Sam. 22:48 (Ps. 18:47) it is God that *a* me
Esth. 8:13 Jews should be ready . . to *a* themselves
Is. 1:24 ah, I will ease . . and *a* me of mine enemies
Jer. 5:29 (5:29) shall not my soul be *a* on such a nation
Lk. 18:3 a widow . . saying, *A* me of mine adversary
 18:7 shall not God *a* his own elect, which cry
Rom. 12:19 dearly beloved, *a* not yourselves
Rev. 6:10 dost thou not judge and *a* our blood
 18:20 rejoice over her . . God hath *a* you on her
 19:2 *a* the blood of his servants at her hand

Avenger *See also* Revenger

Num. 35:12 (Josh. 20:3) cities for refuge from the *a*
Deut. 19:6 the *a* of the blood pursue the slayer
Ps. 8:2 thou mightest still the enemy and the *a*
 44:16 blasphemeth; by reason of the enemy and *a*
1 Thes. 4:6 the Lord is the *a* of all such

Avoid

1 Sam. 18:11 and David *a* out of his presence twice
Prov. 4:15 *a* it, pass not by it, turn from it, and
Rom. 16:17 them which cause divisions . . and *a* them
1 Cor. 7:2 to *a* fornication, let every man have
2 Cor. 8:20 *a* this, that no man should blame us
1 Tim. 6:20 *a* profane and vain babblings
2 Tim. 2:23 but foolish and unlearned questions *a*
Tit. 3:9 but *a* foolish questions, and genealogies

Avouch

Deut. 26:17 hast *a* the LORD this day to be thy God

Awake (Awoke) *See also* Wake

Gen. 28:16 Jacob *a* out of his sleep, and he said
Judg. 5:12 *a*, *a*, Deborah: *a*, *a*, utter a song: arise
 16:20 he *a* out of his sleep, and said, I will go
1 Sam. 26:12 no man saw it, nor knew it, neither *a*
2 Kgs. 4:31 told him, saying, The child is not *a*
Job 14:12 not *a*, nor be raised out of their sleep
Ps. 3:5 and slept; I *a*; for the LORD sustained me
 17:15 be satisfied, when I *a*, with thy likeness
 57:8 (108:2) *a* up, my glory; *a*, psaltery and harp
 59:5 God of Israel, *a* to visit all the heathen
 73:20 dream when one *a*; so, O Lord, when thou *a*
 78:65 then the Lord *a* as one out of sleep
 139:18 when I *a*, I am still with thee
Prov. 23:35 when shall I *a*? I will seek it yet
Song 2:7 (3:5; 8:4) that ye stir not up, nor *a* my love
Is. 51:9 (52:1) *a*, *a*, put on strength

Dan. 12:2 sleep in the dust of the earth shall *a*
Joel 1:5 *a*, ye drunkards, and weep; and howl, all
Zech. 13:7 *a*, O sword, against my shepherd
Mt. 8:25 (Mk. 4:38; Lk. 8:24) *a* him, saying, Lord
Lk. 9:32 and when they were *a*, they saw his glory
Jn. 11:11 but I go, that I may *a* him out of sleep
Acts 16:27 keeper of the prison *a* out of his sleep
Rom. 13:11 now it is high time to *a* out of sleep
1 Cor. 15:34 *a* to righteousness, and sin not
Eph. 5:14 *a* thou that sleepest, and arise from

Aware *See also* Ware

Song 6:12 or ever I was *a*, my soul made me like
Mt. 24:50 (Lk. 12:46) in an hour that he is not *a*
Lk. 11:44 that walk over them are not *a* of them

Awe

Ps. 4:4 stand in *a*, and sin not: commune with your
33:8 inhabitants of the world stand in *a* of him
119:161 but my heart standeth in *a* of thy word

Awoke *See* Awake

Axe

Deut. 19:5 his hand fetcheth a stroke with the *a*
1 Sam. 13:20 to sharpen . . his coulter, and his *a*
1 Kgs. 6:7 so that there was neither hammer nor *a*
2 Kgs. 6:5 a beam, the *a* head fell into the water
Ps. 74:5 famous according as he had lifted up *a*
Is. 10:15 *a* boast itself against him that heweth
Jer. 10:3 cutteth a tree out of the forest . . with the *a*
Mt. 3:10 (Lk. 3:9) *a* is laid unto the root of the trees

Azariah king of Judah *See also* Uzziah
2 Kgs. 14:21–15:7

Azariah the prophet 2 Chr. 15:1

Azariah the priest 2 Chr. 26:17–20; 31:10, 13

Azekah

Josh. 10:10 and smote them to *A*, and unto Makkedah
1 Sam. 17:1 and pitched between Shochoh and *A*
Jer. 34:7 fought . . against Lachish, and against *A*

Azotus Acts 8:40

B

Baal *See also* Baalim

Num. 22:41 brought him up into the high places of *B*
Judg. 2:13 they forsook the LORD, and served *B*
6:25 throw down the altar of *B* that thy father
6:31 will ye plead for *B*? will ye save him?
1 Kgs. 16:31 went and served *B*, and worshipped him
18:19 the prophets of *B* four hundred and fifty
19:18 (Rom. 11:4) knees . . not bowed unto *B*
22:53 for he served *B*, and worshipped him
2 Kgs. 3:2 put away the image of *B* that his father
10:18 Ahab served *B* a little; but Jehu shall
10:27 image of *B*, and brake down the house of *B*
11:18 (2 Chr. 23:17) house of *B*, and brake it down
17:16 made them molten images . . and served *B*
21:3 he reared up altars for *B*, and made a grove
23:4 all the vessels that were made for *B*
Jer. 2:8 the prophets prophesied by *B*, and walked
7:9 and swear falsely, and burn incense unto *B*
11:13 even altars to burn incense unto *B*
12:16 as they taught my people to swear by *B*
19:5 they have built also the high places of *B*
23:13 they prophesied in *B*, and caused my people
Hos. 2:8 silver and gold, which they prepared for *B*

Hos. 13:1 but when he offended in *B*, he died
Zeph. 1:4 cut off the remnant of *B* from this place

Baalim *See also* Baal

Judg. 3:7 forgat the LORD their God, and served *B*
8:33 turned again, and went a whoring after *B*
10:10 have forsaken our God, and also serve *B*
1 Sam. 7:4 Israel did put away *B* and Ashtaroth
2 Chr. 33:3 he reared up altars for *B*, and made
34:4 brake down the altars of *B* in his presence
Jer. 2:23 am not polluted, I have not gone after *B*?
Hos. 2:13 and I will visit upon her the days of *B*
2:17 take away the names of *B* out of her mouth
11:2 they sacrificed unto *B*, and burned incense

Baal-peor

Num. 25:3 and Israel joined himself unto *B*
Deut. 4:3 have seen what the LORD did because of *B*
Ps. 106:28 joined themselves also unto *B* and ate
Hos. 9:10 went to *B*, and separated themselves unto

Baal-perazim 2 Sam. 5:20 (1 Chr. 14:11)

Baal-zebub *See also* Beelzebub 2 Kgs. 1:2

Baal-zephon Ex. 14:2

Baanah 2 Sam. 4:2–12

Baasha 1 Kgs. 15:16–16:13

Babbler

Eccl. 10:11 serpent will bite . . and a *b* is no better
Acts 17:18 some said, What will this *b* say?

Babbling

Prov. 23:29 who hath contentions? who hath *b*?
1 Tim. 6:20 avoiding profane and vain *b*, and
2 Tim. 2:16 but shun profane and vain *b*: for they

Babe

Ex. 2:6 she saw the child: and, behold, the *b* wept
Ps. 8:2 (Mt. 21:16) out of . . mouth of *b* and sucklings
17:14 leave the rest of their substance to their *b*
Is. 3:4 their princes, and *b* shall rule over them
Mt. 11:25 (Lk. 10:21) and hast revealed them unto *b*
Lk. 1:41 salutation of Mary, the *b* leaped in her womb
2:12 find the *b* wrapped in swaddling clothes
Rom. 2:20 instructor of the foolish, a teacher of *b*
1 Cor. 3:1 as unto carnal, even as unto *b* in Christ
Heb. 5:13 is unskilful in the word . . for he is a *b*
1 Pet. 2:2 as newborn *b*, desire the sincere milk

Babel *See also* Babylon

Gen. 10:10 and the beginning of his kingdom was *B*
11:9 called *B* . . the LORD did there confound

Babylon *See also* Babel

2 Kgs. 17:24 king of Assyria brought men from *B*
20:14 (Is. 39:3) from a far country, even from *B*
24:16 (2 Chr. 36:10) king of *B* brought captive to *B*
25:7 (Jer. 39:7; 52:11) with fetters . . carried . . to *B*
Ezra 1:11 were brought up from *B* unto Jerusalem
7:6 Ezra went up from *B* . . a ready scribe in the law
Ps. 87:4 mention of Rahab and *B* to them that know
137:1 by the rivers of *B*, there we sat down, yea
137:8 O daughter of *B*, who art to be destroyed
Is. 13:1 the burden of *B*, which Isaiah . . did see
13:19 *B*, the glory of kingdoms, the beauty of
14:4 take up this proverb against the king of *B*
21:9 answered and said, *B* is fallen, is fallen
47:1 and sit in the dust, O virgin daughter of *B*
48:14 he will do his pleasure on *B*, and his arm
Jer. 25:11 shall serve the king of *B* seventy years
27:22 be carried to *B*, and there shall they be

Jer. 34:3 mouth to mouth, and thou shalt go to *B*
  50:1 the word that the LORD spake against *B*
  51:1 will raise up against *B* . . a destroying wind
Dan. 4:30 is not this great *B*, that I have built
Mic. 4:10 shalt go even to *B*; there shalt thou be
Zech. 2:7 Zion, that dwellest with the daughter of *B*
1 Pet. 5:13 the church that is at *B* . . saluteth you
Rev. 14:8 (18:2) *B* is fallen, is fallen, that great city
  16:19 great *B* came in remembrance before God
  17:5 *B* THE GREAT, THE MOTHER OF HARLOTS
  18:10 alas, that great city *B*, that mighty city!

Babylonish Josh. 7:21

Baca Ps. 84:6

Back

Gen. 19:26 but his wife looked *b* from behind him
Ex. 33:23 and thou shalt see my *b* parts; but my face
Josh. 7:8 turneth their *b* before their enemies!
2 Sam. 19:10 ye not a word of bringing the king *b*?
Neh. 9:26 cast thy law behind their *b*, and slew
Ps. 21:12 shalt thou make them turn their *b*
  78:41 they turned *b* and tempted God, and limited
  129:3 the plowers plowed upon my *b*: they made
Prov. 10:13 a rod is for the *b* of him that is void
  19:29 for scorners, and stripes for the *b* of fools
  26:3 bridle for the ass, and a rod for the fool's *b*
Is. 38:17 thou hast cast all my sins behind thy *b*
  50:6 I gave my *b* to the smiters, and my cheeks
Jer. 2:27 for they have turned their *b* unto me
Mt. 28:2 came and rolled *b* the stone from the door
Lk. 9:62 put his hand to the plow, and looking *b*
Jn. 6:66 many of his disciples went *b*, and walked
Rom. 11:10 may not see, and bow down their *b* alway
Heb. 10:38 if any man draw *b*, my soul shall have no

Backbite

Ps. 15:3 he that *b* not with his tongue, nor doeth
Prov. 25:23 so doth an angry countenance a *b* tongue
2 Cor. 12:20 debates, envyings, wraths, strifes, *b*

Backbiter

Rom. 1:30 *b*, haters of God, despiteful, proud

Backslider

Prov. 14:14 *b* in heart . . filled with his own ways

Backsliding

Jer. 2:19 thy *b* shall reprove thee: know therefore
  3:6 hast thou seen that which *b* Israel hath done?
  3:22 return, ye *b* children, and I will heal your *b*
  8:5 is this people . . slidden back by a perpetual *b*?
  14:7 for our *b* are many; we have sinned against
  31:22 long wilt thou go about, O thou *b* daughter?
Hos. 4:16 for Israel slideth back as a *b* heifer
  11:7 my people are bent to *b* from me
  14:4 I will heal their *b*, I will love them freely

Backward

Gen. 49:17 heels, so that his rider shall fall *b*
1 Sam. 4:18 fell from off the seat *b* by the side
2 Kgs. 20:10 (Is. 38:8) shadow return *b* ten degrees
Job 23:8 go forward . . *b*, but I cannot perceive him
Ps. 40:14 (70:2) be driven *b* and put to shame
Is. 59:14 judgment is turned away *b*, and justice
Jer. 7:24 evil heart, and went *b*, and not forward
Jn. 18:6 they went *b*, and fell to the ground

Bad See also Worse

Gen. 24:50 we cannot speak unto thee *b* or good
  31:24 thou speak not to Jacob either good or *b*
Lev. 27:10 change it, a good for a *b*, or a *b* for

Lev. 27:12 shall value it, whether it be good or *b*
Num. 13:19 they dwell in, whether it be good or *b*
  24:13 to do either good or *b* of mine own mind
2 Sam. 13:22 spake unto . . Amnon neither good nor *b*
  14:17 so is my lord the king to discern good and *b*
1 Kgs. 3:9 that I may discern between good and *b*
Jer. 24:2 figs . . could not be eaten, they were so *b*
Mt. 13:48 good into vessels, but cast the *b* away
  22:10 all as many as they found, both *b* and good
2 Cor. 5:10 he hath done, whether it be good or *b*

Bade See Bid

Bag

Deut. 25:13 shalt not have in thy *b* divers weights
1 Sam. 17:40 stones . . and put them in a shepherd's *b*
2 Kgs. 5:23 bound two talents of silver in two *b*
Job 14:17 my transgression is sealed up in a *b*
Prov. 7:20 he hath taken a *b* of money with him
  16:11 all the weights of the *b* are his work
Is. 46:6 they lavish gold out of the *b*, and weigh
Mic. 6:11 pure . . with the *b* of deceitful weights?
Hag. 1:6 wages to put it into a *b* with holes
Lk. 12:33 provide yourselves *b* which wax not old
Jn. 12:6 (13:29) had the *b*, and bare what was put

Bahurim

2 Sam. 3:16 husband went . . weeping behind her to *B*
  16:5 king David came to *B* . . thence came out
  17:18 came to a man's house in *B*, which had a well

Bake

Gen. 19:3 did *b* unleavened bread, and they did eat
Ex. 16:23 *b* that which ye will *b* today, and seethe
Lev. 24:5 thou shalt take fine flour . . *b* twelve cakes
  26:26 ten women shall *b* your bread in one oven
Num. 11:8 and *b* it in pans, and made cakes of it
1 Sam. 28:24 kneaded it, and did *b* unleavened bread
Is. 44:15 yea, he kindleth it, and *b* bread

Baker

Gen. 40:1 the butler . . and his *b* had offended
1 Sam. 8:13 he will take your daughters . . to be *b*
Jer. 37:21 a piece of bread out of the *b*' street
Hos. 7:4 as an oven heated by the *b*, who ceaseth

Balaam Num. 22:5–24:25

Num. 31:8 (Josh. 13:22) *B* . . the son of Beor they slew
  31:16 counsel of *B*, to commit trespass against
Deut. 23:4 (Neh. 13:2) they hired against thee *B*
Josh. 24:9 called *B* the son of Beor to curse you
Mic. 6:5 and what *B* the son of Beor answered him
2 Pet. 2:15 gone astray, following the way of *B*
Jude 11 greedily after the error of *B* for reward
Rev. 2:14 that hold the doctrine of *B*, who taught

Balak (Balac) Num. 22:2–24:25

Josh. 24:9 then *B* . . arose and warred against Israel
Judg. 11:25 now art thou any thing better than *B*
Mic. 6:5 remember . . what *B* king of Moab consulted
Rev. 2:14 taught *B* to cast a stumblingblock before

Balance

Lev. 19:36 just *b*, just weights . . shall ye have
Job 6:2 and my calamity laid in the *b* together!
  31:6 let me be weighed in an even *b*, that God
Ps. 62:9 to be laid in the *b*, they are altogether
Prov. 11:1 a false *b* is abomination to the LORD
  16:11 a just weight and *b* are the LORD'S
Is. 40:12 mountains in scales, and the hills in a *b*?
  40:15 and are counted as the small dust of the *b*
  46:6 weigh silver in the *b*, and hire a goldsmith
Jer. 32:10 and weighed him the money in the *b*

Ezek. 5:1 then take thee *b* to weigh, and divide
45:10 ye shall have just *b*, and a just ephah
Dan. 5:27 weighed in the *b*, and art found wanting
Hos. 12:7 *b* of deceit are in his hand: he loveth
Amos 8:5 shekel great and falsifying the *b* by deceit?
Mic. 6:11 shall I count them pure with the wicked *b*
Rev. 6:5 he that sat on him had a pair of *b* in his

Bald

Lev. 13:40 whose hair is fallen off his head, he is *b*
2 Kgs. 2:23 go up, thou *b* head; go up, thou *b* head
Jer. 48:37 every head shall be *b*, and every beard
Ezek. 27:31 they shall make themselves utterly *b*
29:18 every head was made *b*, and every shoulder
Mic. 1:16 make thee *b* . . for thy delicate children

Baldness

Lev. 21:5 they shall not make *b* upon their head
Deut. 14:1 any *b* between your eyes for the dead
Is. 3:24 instead of well set hair *b*; and instead
15:2 on all their heads shall be *b*, and every beard
22:12 call to weeping, and to mourning, and to *b*
Ezek. 7:18 all faces, and *b* upon all their heads
Amos 8:10 upon all loins, and *b* upon every head
Mic. 1:16 enlarge thy *b* as the eagle

Balm

Gen. 37:25 camels bearing spicery and *b* and myrrh
43:11 a present, a little *b*, and a little honey
Jer. 8:22 no *b* in Gilead? is there no physician
46:11 go up into Gilead, and take *b*, O virgin
51:8 *b* for her pain, if so be she may be healed
Ezek. 27:17 in thy market . . honey, and oil, and *b*

Band

Gen. 32:7 Jacob . . divided the people . . into two *b*
Lev. 26:13 and I have broken the *b* of your yoke
1 Sam. 10:26 *b* of men, whose hearts God . . touched
2 Kgs. 6:23 *b* of Syria came no more into the land
Job 38:31 canst thou bind . . or loose the *b* of Orion?
Ps. 2:3 let us break their *b* asunder, and cast
73:4 no *b* in their death: but their strength
107:14 brought them out . . brake their *b* in sunder
119:61 the *b* of the wicked have robbed me
Eccl. 7:26 whose heart is snares . . and her hands as *b*
Is. 58:6 to loose the *b* of wickedness, to undo
Hos. 11:4 them with cords of a man, with *b* of love
Zech. 11:7 called Beauty, and the other I called *B*
Mt. 27:27 (Mk. 15:16) gathered . . *b* of soldiers
Lk. 8:29 he brake the *b*, and was driven of the devil
Jn. 18:3 having received a *b* of men and officers
Acts 10:1 centurion of the *b* called the Italian *b*
16:26 were opened, and every one's *b* were loosed
23:12 certain of the Jews *b* together, and bound
Col. 2:19 from which all the body by joints and *b*

Bank

Gen. 41:17 behold, I stood upon the *b* of the river
2 Sam. 20:15 and they cast up a *b* against the city
2 Kgs. 2:13 went back, and stood by the *b* of Jordan
19:32 (Is. 37:33) not come . . nor cast a *b* against it
Ezek. 47:7 at the *b* of the river were very many trees
Dan. 8:16 heard a man's voice between the *b* of Ulai
Lk. 19:23 then gavest not thou my money into the *b*

Banner

Ps. 20:5 the name of our God we will set up our *b*
60:4 thou hast given a *b* to them that fear thee
Song 2:4 banqueting house . . his *b* over me was love
6:4 (6:10) terrible as an army with *b*
Is. 13:2 lift ye up a *b* upon the high mountain

Banquet

Esth. 5:4 (7:1) king and Haman come . . unto the *b*
Job 41:6 shall the companions make a *b* of him?
Song 2:4 he brought me to the *b* house, and his
Dan. 5:10 now the queen . . came into the *b* house
Amos 6:7 the *b* of them that stretched themselves
1 Pet. 4:3 lusts, excess of wine, revelings, *b*

Baptism

Mt. 3:7 the Pharisees and Sadducees come to his *b*
20:22 (Mk. 10:39) baptized with the *b* that I am
21:25 (Mk. 11:30; Lk. 20:4) *b* of John, whence was
Mk. 1:4 (Lk. 3:3; Acts 13:24; 19:4) *b* of repentance
Lk. 7:29 being baptized with the *b* of John
12:50 I have a *b* to be baptized with; and how am
Acts 1:22 from the *b* of John, unto that same day
18:25 and taught . . knowing only the *b* of John
Rom. 6:4 (Col. 2:12) buried with him by *b* into death
Eph. 4:5 one Lord, one faith, one *b*
Heb. 6:2 doctrine of *b*, and of laying on of hands
1 Pet. 3:21 whereunto even *b* doth also now save us

Baptize

Mt. 3:6 (Mk. 1:5) *b* of him in Jordan, confessing
3:11 (Mk. 1:8; Lk. 3:16; Jn. 1:26) *b* you with water
3:13 (Mk. 1:9) Jesus . . unto John, to be *b* of him
20:22 (Mk. 10:39) *b* with the baptism . . I am *b* with
28:19 teach all nations, *b* them in the name of
Mk. 1:4 John did *b* in the wilderness, and preach
16:16 he that believeth and is *b* shall be saved
Lk. 7:29 justified God, being *b* with the baptism of
12:50 have a baptism to be *b* with; and how am I
Jn. 1:25 why *b* thou then, if thou be not that
1:33 the same is he which *b* with the Holy Ghost
3:23 and John also was *b* in Aenon near to Salim
4:1 Jesus made and *b* more disciples than John
10:40 into the place where John at first *b*
Acts 1:5 (11:16) *b* with water; but ye shall be *b*
2:38 be *b* every one of you in the name of Jesus
8:12 believed Philip . . were *b* . . men and women
8:16 only they were *b* in the name of the Lord
8:36 here is water; what doth hinder me to be *b*?
9:18 received sight forthwith . . arose, and was *b*
10:47 forbid water, that these should not be *b*
16:15 was *b*, and her household, she besought us
16:33 and was *b*, he and all his, straightway
18:8 Corinthians hearing believed, and were *b*
19:3 said unto them, Unto what then were ye *b*?
22:16 arise, and be *b*, and wash away thy sins
Rom. 6:3 *b* into Jesus Christ were *b* into his death
1 Cor. 1:13 or were ye *b* in the name of Paul?
1:17 for Christ sent me not to *b*, but to preach
10:2 *b* unto Moses in the cloud and in the sea
12:13 by one Spirit are we all *b* into one body
15:29 what shall they do which are *b* for the dead
Gal. 3:27 as have been *b* into Christ have put on

Bar

Ex. 26:26 (36:31) shalt make *b* of shittim wood
Judg. 16:3 Samson . . went away with them, *b* and all
Job 17:16 they shall go down to the *b* of the pit
38:10 it my decreed place, and set *b* and doors
Ps. 107:16 he hath . . cut the *b* of iron in sunder
Is. 45:2 I will . . cut in sunder the *b* of iron
Ezek. 38:11 safely . . having neither *b* nor gates

Barabbas Mt. 27:15–26 (Mk. 15:6–15; Lk. 23:17–25; Jn. 18:39–40)

Barak Judg. 4:6–5:12; Heb. 11:32

Barbarian

Acts 28:4 when the *b* saw the venomous beast hang
Rom. 1:14 debtor both to the Greeks, and to the *B*
1 Cor. 14:11 I shall be unto him that speaketh a *b*
Col. 3:11 neither .. *B*, Scythian, bond nor free

Barbarous

Acts 28:2 the *b* people showed us no little kindness

Barber

Ezek. 5:1 take thee a *b*'s razor, and cause it to

Bare (adjective)

Is. 52:10 the LORD hath made *b* his holy arm
1 Cor. 15:37 *b* grain, it may chance of wheat, or

Bare (verb) *See* Bear (verb)

Barefoot

2 Sam. 15:30 had his head covered, and he went *b*
Is. 20:3 my servant Isaiah hath walked naked and *b*

Bar-jesus Acts 13:6

Bar-jona Mt. 16:17

Bark

Is. 56:10 they are all dumb dogs, they cannot *b*
Joel 1:7 laid my vine waste, and *b* my fig tree

Barley

Ex. 9:31 the flax and the *b* was smitten: for the *b*
Deut. 8:8 a land of wheat, and *b*, and vines, and
Ruth 1:22 Bethlehem in the beginning of *b* harvest
2 Kgs. 7:1 (7:18) two measures of *b* for a shekel
Jn. 6:9 is a lad here, which hath five *b* loaves
Rev. 6:6 and three measures of *b* for a penny

Barn

Job 39:12 thy seed, and gather it into thy *b*?
Prov. 3:10 so shall thy *b* be filled with plenty
Joel 1:17 are laid desolate, the *b* are broken down
Hag. 2:19 is the seed yet in the *b*? yea, as yet
Mt. 6:26 (Lk. 12:24) neither .. reap, nor gather into *b*
   13:30 burn them: but gather the wheat into my *b*
Lk. 12:18 I will pull down my *b*, and build greater

Barnabas

Sold his possessions, Acts 4:36–37; introduced Saul
to the apostles, Acts 9:26–27; preached at Antioch,
Acts 11:22–24; sought out Saul from Tarsus, Acts
11:25–26; took relief to Judea, Acts 11:29–30; accompanied Paul, Acts 13:1–14:28; Gal. 2:1–13;
attended the Council of Jerusalem, Acts 15:1–31;
separated from Paul, Acts 15:36–41.

Barrel

1 Kgs. 17:14 the *b* of meal shall not waste, neither
   18:33 fill four *b* with water, and pour it on

Barren

Gen. 11:30 but Sarai was *b*; she had no child
   25:21 entreated .. for his wife, because she was *b*
   29:31 he opened her womb: but Rachel was *b*
Ex. 23:26 cast their young, nor be *b*, in thy land
Deut. 7:14 shall not be male or female *b* among you
Judg. 13:2 Manoah .. his wife was *b*, and bare not
2 Sam. 2:19 the water is naught, and the ground *b*
Job 24:21 evil entreateth the *b* that beareth not
Ps. 113:9 he maketh the *b* woman to keep house
Is. 54:1 (Gal. 4:27) sing, O *b*, thou that didst not bear
Lk. 1:7 had no child, because that Elisabeth was *b*
   23:29 say, Blessed are the *b*, and the wombs that

2 Pet. 1:8 ye shall neither be *b* nor unfruitful

Barrenness

Ps. 107:34 fruitful land into *b*, for the wickedness

Barsabas (Justus) Acts 1:23

Barsabas (Judas) Acts 15:22

Bartholomew Mt. 10:3 (Mk. 3:18; Lk. 6:14)

Bartimeus Mk. 10:46

Baruch Jer. 32:12–16; 36:4–32

Jer. 43:3 but *B* the son of Neriah setteth thee on
   45:1 word that Jeremiah the prophet spake unto *B*

Barzillai 2 Sam. 17:27–29; 19:31–39

Base (Baser, Basest) *See also* Abominable, Loathsome, Vile, Wicked

2 Sam. 6:22 thus, and will be *b* in mine own sight
Job 30:8 children of fools, yea, children of *b* men
Is. 3:5 ancient, and the *b* against the honorable
Ezek. 17:14 that the kingdom might be *b*, that it
Dan. 4:17 and setteth up over it the *b* of men
Mal. 2:9 have I also made you contemptible and *b*
Acts 17:5 took .. certain lewd fellows of the *b* sort
1 Cor. 1:28 *b* things of the world .. hath God chosen
2 Cor. 10:1 who in presence am *b* among you, but

Bashan

Num. 21:33 (Deut. 3:1) and went up by the way of *B*
Deut. 3:13 the rest of Gilead, and all *B* .. gave I
   32:14 fat of lambs, and rams of the breed of *B*
Ps. 22:12 strong bulls of *B* have beset me round
   68:15 the hill of God is as the hill of *B*
Is. 2:13 the cedars of Lebanon .. all the oaks of *B*
Jer. 22:20 lift up thy voice in *B*, and cry from
   50:19 shall feed on Carmel and *B*, and his soul
Ezek. 27:6 the oaks of *B* have they made thine oars
   39:18 of bullocks, all of them fatlings of *B*
Amos 4:1 hear this word, ye kine of *B*, that are in
Mic. 7:14 feed in *B* and Gilead, as in the days of
Nah. 1:4 *B* languisheth, and Carmel, and the flower
Zech. 11:2 howl, O ye oaks of *B*; for the forest of

Basin

Ex. 12:22 dip it in the blood that is in the *b*
1 Chr. 28:17 the golden *b* .. by weight for every *b*
Jn. 13:5 poureth water into a *b*, and began to wash

Basket

Gen. 40:16 behold, I had three white *b* on my head
Deut. 28:5 blessed shall be thy *b* and thy store
Jer. 24:1 showed me, and, behold, two *b* of figs
Amos 8:1 and behold a *b* of summer fruit
Mt. 14:20 (Mk. 6:43; Lk. 9:17; Jn. 6:13) fragments
   that remained twelve *b* full
   15:37 (Mk. 8:8) meat that was left seven *b*
   16:9 (Mk. 8:19) five loaves .. how many *b* ye took
Acts 9:25 (2 Cor. 11:33) let him down .. wall in a *b*

Bastard

Deut. 23:2 *b* shall not enter into the congregation
Heb. 12:8 then are ye *b*, and not sons

Bat

Lev. 11:19 (Deut. 14:18) the lapwing, and the *b*
Is. 2:20 cast his idols .. to the moles and to the *b*

Bathe

Lev. 16:26 *b* his flesh in water, and afterward

Lev. 17:15 wash his clothes, and *b* himself in water
Num. 19:7 the priest . . shall *b* his flesh in water
Is. 34:5 for my sword shall be *b* in heaven

Bath-sheba

Taken by David, 2 Sam. 11:1–5; became the mother
of Solomon, 2 Sam. 12:24; interceded for Solomon's
succession, 1 Kgs. 1:15–31; petitioned for Adonijah,
1 Kgs. 2:12–25.

Battle *See also* Fight, Strife, War

Gen. 14:8 they joined *b* . . in the vale of Siddim
Num. 31:21 unto the men of war which went to the *b*
Deut. 20:1 goest out to *b* against thine enemies
　20:5 return to his house, lest he die in the *b*
Josh. 4:13 passed over before the LORD unto *b*
　22:33 did not intend to go up against them in *b*
Judg. 8:13 Gideon . . returned from *b* before the sun
　20:20 of Israel went out to *b* against Benjamin
1 Sam. 4:1 went out against the Philistines to *b*
　7:10 Philistines drew near to *b* against Israel
　8:20 king may . . go out before us, and fight our *b*
　14:20 assembled themselves, and . . came to the *b*
　17:1 the Philistines gathered . . their armies to *b*
　17:20 forth to the fight, and shouted for the *b*
　17:47 the *b* is the LORD's, and he will give you
　18:17 be thou valiant . . and fight the LORD's *b*
　25:28 because my lord fighteth the *b* of the LORD
　26:10 or he shall descend into *b*, and perish
　29:4 not go down with us to *b*, lest in the *b* he
　31:3 (1 Chr. 10:3) the *b* went sore against Saul
2 Sam. 2:17 a very sore *b* that day; and Abner was
　10:8 (1 Chr. 19:9) of Ammon . . put the *b* in array
　11:1 (1 Chr. 20:1) the time when kings go forth to *b*
　11:15 Uriah in the forefront of the hottest *b*
　17:11 and that thou go to *b* in thine own person
　18:8 the *b* was there scattered over the face of
　21:17 thou shalt go no more out with us to *b*
　22:40 (Ps. 18:39) hast girded me with strength to *b*
1 Kgs. 8:44 thy people go out to *b* against their
　20:14 who shall order the *b*? . . he answered, Thou
　22:4 wilt thou go with me to *b* to Ramoth-gilead?
2 Kgs. 3:7 wilt thou go with me against Moab to *b*?
1 Chr. 5:20 for they cried to God in the *b*
2 Chr. 20:1 Moab . . came against Jehoshaphat to *b*
　20:15 not afraid . . the *b* is not yours, but God's
　25:8 if thou wilt go, do it, be strong for the *b*
Job 39:25 he smelleth the *b* afar off, the thunder
Ps. 24:8 strong and mighty, the LORD mighty in *b*
　55:18 hath delivered my soul in peace from the *b*
　76:3 bow, the shield, and the sword, and the *b*
　140:7 thou hast covered my head in the day of *b*
Eccl. 9:11 to the swift, nor the *b* to the strong
Jer. 50:22 a sound of *b* is in the land, and of
Zech. 9:10 and the *b* bow shall be cut off
　14:2 gather all nations against Jerusalem to *b*
1 Cor. 14:8 who shall prepare himself to the *b*?
Rev. 9:7 locusts . . like unto horses prepared unto *b*
　16:14 to gather them to the *b* of that great day
　20:8 Gog and Magog, to gather them together to *b*

Battle-axe

Jer. 51:20 thou art my *b-a* and weapons of war

Battlement

Deut. 22:8 thou shalt make a *b* for thy roof
Jer. 5:10 go ye up upon her walls . . take away her *b*

Bay

Ps. 37:35 spreading himself like a green *b* tree
Zech. 6:3 the fourth chariot grizzled and *b* horses

Beacon

Is. 30:17 left as a *b* upon the top of a mountain

Beam

Judg. 16:14 and went away with the pin of the *b*
1 Sam. 17:7 staff of his spear was like a weaver's *b*
2 Kgs. 6:2 take thence every man a *b*, and let us
Ps. 104:3 the *b* of his chambers in the waters
Hab. 2:11 the *b* out of the timber shall answer it
Mt. 7:3 (Lk. 6:41) the *b* that is in thine own eye?

Bear (noun)

1 Sam. 17:34 came a lion, and a *b*, and took a lamb
2 Sam. 17:8 be chafed . . as a *b* robbed of her whelps
2 Kgs. 2:24 came forth two she *b* out of the wood
Prov. 17:12 a *b* robbed of her whelps meet a man
　28:15 as a roaring lion, and a ranging *b*; so is
Is. 11:7 the cow and the *b* shall feed; their young
　59:11 we roar all like *b*, and mourn sore like
Dan. 7:5 another beast, a second, like to a *b*
Hos. 13:8 meet them as a *b* that is bereaved of her
Amos 5:19 did flee from a lion, and a *b* met him
Rev. 13:2 and his feet were as the feet of a *b*

Bear (Bare, Borne) (verb)

See also Carry

Gen. 4:13 my punishment is greater than I can *b*
　13:6 the land was not able to *b* them, that they
　17:17 shall Sarah, that is ninety years old, *b*?
　21:7 for I have *b* him a son in his old age
　36:7 could not *b* them because of their cattle
Ex. 19:4 I *b* you on eagles' wings, and brought you
　20:16 (Deut. 5:20; Mt. 19:18; Mk. 10:19; Lk.
　　18:20; Rom. 13:9) thou shalt not *b* false witness
　25:14 (37:5) staves . . that the ark may be *b*
　28:12 Aaron shall *b* their names before the LORD
　28:38 Aaron . . *b* the iniquity of the holy things
Lev. 24:15 curseth his God shall *b* his sin
Num. 11:14 am not able to *b* all this people alone
　13:23 and they *b* it between two upon a staff
　14:27 shall I *b* with this evil congregation
Deut. 1:9 I am not able to *b* you myself alone
　1:31 thy God *b* thee, as a man doth *b* his son
　31:9 priests . . which *b* the ark of the covenant
1 Chr. 15:15 children of the Levites *b* the ark of God
Job 34:31 I have *b* chastisement, I will not offend
Ps. 55:12 was not an enemy . . then I could have *b* it
　69:7 because for thy sake I have *b* reproach
　75:3 the earth . . I *b* up the pillars of it
　91:12 (Mt. 4:6; Lk. 4:11) *b* thee up in their hands
　126:6 he that goeth forth . . *b* precious seed
Prov. 18:14 but a wounded spirit who can *b*?
Is. 1:14 a trouble unto me; I am weary to *b* them
　52:11 clean, that *b* the vessels of the LORD
　53:4 surely he hath *b* our griefs, and carried
　53:11 for he shall *b* their iniquities
　53:12 *b* the sin of many, and made intercession
　63:9 and he *b* them . . all the days of old
Jer. 10:19 truly this is a grief, and I must *b* it
　17:21 *b* no burden on the sabbath day, nor bring
　31:19 because I did *b* the reproach of my youth
　44:22 LORD could no longer *b*, because of the evil
Lam. 3:27 is good . . that he *b* the yoke in his youth
　5:7 have sinned . . and we have *b* their iniquities
Ezek. 16:54 that thou mayest *b* thine own shame
　23:49 ye shall *b* the sins of your idols
Zech. 6:13 he shall *b* the glory, and shall sit
Mt. 3:11 whose shoes I am not worthy to *b*
　8:17 took our infirmities, and *b* our sicknesses
　20:12 have *b* the burden and heat of the day
　23:4 (Lk. 11:46) heavy burdens and grievous to be *b*

Mt. 27:32 (Mk. 15:21; Lk. 23:26) to *b* his cross
Mk. 14:13 (Lk. 22:10) a man *b* a pitcher of water
Lk. 11:27 blessed is the womb that *b* thee, and the
  14:27 whosoever doth not *b* his cross, and come
  18:7 not God avenge . . though he *b* long with them
Jn. 2:8 draw . . and *b* unto the governor of the feast
  12:6 and had the bag, and *b* what was put therein
  15:2 every branch in me that *b* not fruit he
  16:12 to say unto you, but ye cannot *b* them now
  19:17 and he *b* his cross went forth into a place
Acts 9:15 to *b* my name before the Gentiles
  21:35 he was *b* of the soldiers for the violence
  27:15 when the ship . . could not *b* up into the wind
Rom. 13:4 he *b* not the sword in vain: for he is
  15:1 ought to *b* the infirmities of the weak
1 Cor. 3:2 for hitherto ye were not able to *b* it
  10:13 way to escape, that ye may be able to *b* it
  13:7 *b* all things, believeth all things, hopeth
  15:49 and as we have *b* the image of the earthy
2 Cor. 4:10 always *b* about in the body the dying
Gal. 6:2 *b* ye one another's burdens, and so fulfil
  6:17 I *b* in my body the marks of the Lord Jesus
Heb. 9:28 was once offered to *b* the sins of many
  13:13 unto him without the camp, *b* his reproach
Jas. 3:12 can the fig tree . . *b* olive berries?
1 Pet. 2:24 *b* our sins in his own body on the tree
Rev. 2:2 how thou canst not *b* them which are evil
  2:3 hast *b*, and hast patience, and for my name's
  22:2 tree of life, which *b* twelve manner of fruits

Beard

Lev. 13:29 have a plague upon the head or the *b*
  19:27 neither shalt . . mar the corners of thy *b*
  21:5 neither . . shave off the corner of their *b*
1 Sam. 17:35 I caught him by his *b*, and smote him
  21:13 and let his spittle fall down upon his *b*
2 Sam. 10:4 and shaved off the one half of their *b*
  10:5 (1 Chr. 19:5) tarry . . until your *b* be grown
  20:9 and Joab took Amasa by the *b* . . to kiss him
Ps. 133:2 that ran down upon the *b*, even Aaron's *b*
Jer. 41:5 fourscore men, having their *b* shaven
Ezek. 5:1 to pass upon thine head and upon thy *b*

Beast

Gen. 1:24 and *b* of the earth after his kind
  1:30 and to every *b* of the earth . . I have given
  2:19 the LORD God formed every *b* of the field
  3:1 now the serpent was more subtile than any *b*
  7:2 of every clean *b* thou shalt take . . by sevens
  37:20 (37:33) say, Some evil *b* hath devoured him
Ex. 11:5 shall die . . and all the firstborn of *b*
  13:12 every firstling that cometh of a *b*
  22:5 put in his *b*, and shall feed in another
  22:19 whosoever lieth with a *b* . . be put to death
Lev. 11:2 (Deut. 14:4) are the *b* which ye shall eat
  18:23 neither shalt thou lie with any *b* to defile
  27:9 a *b*, whereof men bring an offering unto the
Job 12:7 ask now the *b*, and they shall teach thee
  18:3 wherefore are we counted as *b*, and reputed
Ps. 8:7 all sheep and oxen . . and the *b* of the field
  36:6 O LORD, thou preservest man and *b*
  49:12 abideth not: he is like the *b* that perish
  73:22 and ignorant: I was as a *b* before thee
  80:13 the wild *b* of the forest doth devour it
  104:20 wherein all the *b* of the forest do creep
  147:9 giveth to the *b* his food, and to the young
Prov. 12:10 righteous man regardeth the life of his *b*
Eccl. 3:18 they might see that they themselves are *b*
  3:19 a man hath no preeminence above a *b*
Is. 13:21 (Jer. 50:39) wild *b* of the desert shall lie there
Dan. 4:12 the *b* of the field had shadow under it
  4:25 dwelling shall be with the *b* of the field
  7:3 four great *b* came up from the sea, diverse

Mic. 1:13 bind the chariot to the swift *b*
Mk. 1:13 forty days . . and was with the wild *b*
Lk. 10:34 set him on his own *b*, and brought him to
Acts 10:12 (11:6) were all manner of fourfooted *b*
  28:4 saw the venomous *b* hang on his hand
Rom. 1:23 and four-footed *b*, and creeping things
1 Cor. 15:32 if . . I have fought with *b* at Ephesus
  15:39 kind of flesh of men, another flesh of *b*
Tit. 1:12 the Cretians are always liars, evil *b*
Jas. 3:7 every kind of *b* . . been tamed of mankind
2 Pet. 2:12 as natural brute *b*, made to be taken
Jude 10 but what they know naturally, as brute *b*
Rev. 4:6 and round about the throne, were four *b*
  11:7 (17:8) *b* . . ascendeth out of the bottomless pit
  13:1 and saw a *b* rise up out of the sea
  13:11 another *b* coming up out of the earth
  13:17 he that had the mark, or the name of the *b*
  15:2 them that had gotten the victory over the *b*
  17:3 I saw a woman sit upon a scarlet-colored *b*
  19:4 and the four *b* fell down and worshipped God
  19:20 the *b* was taken, and . . the false prophet
  20:10 where the *b* and the false prophet are

Beat

Ex. 5:14 and the officers . . were *b*, and demanded
Ps. 89:23 I will *b* down his foes before his face
Prov. 23:14 *b* him with the rod . . deliver his soul
Is. 2:4 (Mic. 4:3) *b* their swords into plowshares
  3:15 what mean ye that ye *b* my people to pieces
Joel 3:10 *b* your plowshares into swords, and your
Mic. 4:13 and thou shalt *b* in pieces many people
Mt. 7:25 (Lk. 6:48) winds blew . . *b* upon that house
  21:35 (Mk. 12:3; Lk. 20:10) his servants . . *b* one
Mk. 13:9 in the synagogues ye shall be *b*
Lk. 12:47 which knew . . shall be *b* with many stripes
Acts 16:37 they have *b* us openly uncondemned
1 Cor. 9:26 so fight I, not as one that *b* the air
2 Cor. 11:25 thrice was I *b* with rods, once was I

Beautiful

Gen. 29:17 but Rachel was *b* and well-favored
2 Sam. 11:2 and the woman was very *b* to look upon
Esth. 2:7 that is, Esther . . the maid was fair and *b*
Ps. 48:2 *b* for situation . . city of the great King
Eccl. 3:11 he hath made every thing *b* in his time
Song 6:4 thou art *b*, O my love, as Tirzah, comely
  7:1 how *b* are thy feet with shoes, O prince's
Is. 4:2 that day shall the branch of the LORD be *b*
  52:1 O Zion; put on thy *b* garments, O Jerusalem
  52:7 (Rom. 10:15) how *b* . . are the feet of him that
  64:11 our holy and our *b* house . . is burned up
Jer. 13:20 flock that was given thee, thy *b* flock?
Ezek. 16:12 and I put . . a *b* crown upon thine head
Mt. 23:27 sepulchres, which indeed appear *b* outward
Acts 3:2 the gate of the temple which is called *B*

Beautify

Ps. 149:4 the LORD . . will *b* the meek with salvation

Beauty

Ex. 28:2 garments for Aaron . . for glory and for *b*
2 Sam. 1:19 *b* of Israel is slain upon thy high places
  14:25 none . . so much praised as Absalom for his *b*
1 Chr. 16:29 (Ps. 29:2; 96:9) in the *b* of holiness
2 Chr. 3:6 the house with precious stones for *b*
  20:21 and that should praise the *b* of holiness
Job 40:10 and array thyself with glory and *b*
Ps. 27:4 to behold the *b* of the LORD, and to
  39:11 makest his *b* to consume away like a moth
  45:11 so shall the king greatly desire thy *b*
  49:14 and their *b* shall consume in the grave
  50:2 out of Zion, the perfection of *b*, God hath
  90:17 let the *b* of the LORD our God be upon us

Ps. 96:6 strength and *b* are in his sanctuary
110:3 *b* of holiness from the womb of the morning
Prov. 6:25 lust not after her *b* in thine heart
20:29 and the *b* of old men is the gray head
31:30 favor is deceitful, and *b* is vain; but a woman
Is. 3:24 there shall be . . burning instead of *b*
28:1 whose glorious *b* is a fading flower
33:17 thine eyes shall see the King in his *b*
53:2 there is no *b* that we should desire him
61:3 give unto them *b* for ashes, the oil of joy
Lam. 1:6 and from . . Zion all her *b* is departed
2:15 the city that men call The perfection of *b*
Ezek. 7:20 as for the *b* of his ornament, he set it
16:14 thy renown . . among the heathen for thy *b*
16:25 hast made thy *b* to be abhorred, and hast
27:3 O Tyrus, thou hast said, I am of perfect *b*
28:7 their swords against the *b* of thy wisdom
28:17 thine heart was lifted up because of thy *b*
32:19 whom dost thou pass in *b*? go down, and be
Hos. 14:6 and his *b* shall be as the olive tree
Zech. 9:17 how great is his goodness, and . . his *b*!
11:7 took unto me two staves; the one I called *B*

Beckon

Lk. 1:22 he *b* unto them, and remained speechless
5:7 *b* unto their partners . . in the other ship
Jn. 13:24 Simon Peter therefore *b* to him, that he
Acts 12:17 he, *b* unto them with the hand to hold
21:40 Paul . . *b* with the hand unto the people

Become

Ps. 93:5 holiness *b* thine house, O LORD, for ever
Prov. 17:7 excellent speech *b* not a fool: much less
Mt. 3:15 thus it *b* us to fulfil all righteousness
Rom. 16:2 ye receive her in the Lord, as *b* saints
Eph. 5:3 not once be named among you, as *b* saints
Phil. 1:27 your conversation be as it *b* the gospel
1 Tim. 2:10 which *b* women professing godliness
Tit. 2:3 aged women . . in behavior as *b* holiness

Bed

2 Sam. 4:5 of Ish-bosheth, who lay on a *b* at noon
2 Kgs. 4:10 set for him there a *b*, and a table
Job 7:13 say, My *b* shall comfort me, my couch
17:13 I have made my *b* in the darkness
33:15 in a dream . . in slumberings upon the *b*
Ps. 4:4 commune with your own heart upon your *b*
41:3 strengthen him upon the *b* of languishing
63:6 I remember thee upon my *b*, and meditate
139:8 if I make my *b* in hell . . thou art there
Song 3:7 behold his *b*, which is Solomon's
Is. 28:20 *b* is shorter than that a man can stretch
57:2 into peace: they shall rest in their *b*
Amos 3:12 dwell in Samaria in the corner of a *b*
Mt. 9:6 (Mk. 2:11) arise, take up thy *b*, and go
Mk. 4:21 (Lk. 8:16) put under a bushel, or under a *b*
Lk. 11:7 my children are with me in *b*; I cannot rise
17:34 that night there shall be two men in one *b*
Jn. 5:8 (5:11, 12) take up thy *b*, and walk
Acts 9:33 Aeneas, which had kept his *b* eight years
Heb. 13:4 marriage is honorable . . the *b* undefiled
Rev. 2:22 I will cast her into a *b*, and them that

Bedstead

Deut. 3:11 his *b* was a *b* of iron . . nine cubits was

Bee

Deut. 1:44 and the Amorites . . chased you, as *b* do
Judg. 14:8 a swarm of *b* and honey in the carcase
Ps. 118:12 they compassed me about like *b*; they are
Is. 7:18 for the *b* that is in the land of Assyria

Beelzebub (Beelzebul) *See also* Baal-
zebub Mt. 10:25; 12:24 (Mk. 3:22; Lk. 11:15)

Beer Num. 21:16

Beer-lahoi-roi Gen. 16:14

Beer-sheba

Gen. 21:14 Hagar . . wandered in the wilderness of *B*
21:32 thus they made a covenant at *B*
22:19 went together to *B*; and Abraham dwelt at *B*
28:10 Jacob went out from *B* . . went toward Haran
46:1 Israel took his journey . . and came to *B*
Judg. 20:1 gathered together . . from Dan even to *B*
1 Kgs. 19:3 arose, and went for his life, and came to *B*

Befall (Befallen) *See also* Happen

Gen. 42:4 said, Lest peradventure mischief *b* him
49:1 that which shall *b* you in the last days
Lev. 10:19 and such things have *b* me: and if I had
Deut. 31:17 many evils and troubles shall *b* them
31:29 and evil will *b* you in the latter days
Judg. 6:13 why then is all this *b* us? and where be
Ps. 91:10 there shall no evil *b* thee, neither shall
Eccl. 3:19 that which *b* the sons of men *b* beasts
Dan. 10:14 shall *b* thy people in the latter days
Acts 20:22 not knowing the things that shall *b* me

Beg *See also* Beseech, Entreat, Petition, Request

Ps. 37:25 righteous forsaken, nor his seed *b* bread
Prov. 20:4 therefore shall he *b* in harvest
Mt. 27:58 (Lk. 23:52) to Pilate . . *b* the body of Jesus
Mk. 10:46 (Lk. 18:35) sat by the highway side *b*
Lk. 16:3 shall I do? . . I cannot dig; to *b* I am ashamed
Jn. 9:8 said, Is not this he that sat and *b*?

Beget (Begat, Begotten) *See also* Begotten

Gen. 5:3 Adam . . *b* a son in his own likeness
Num. 11:12 have I *b* them, that thou shouldest say
Deut. 4:25 when thou shalt *b* children, and children's
Job 38:28 or who hath *b* the drops of dew?
Ps. 2:7 (Acts 13:33; Heb. 1:5; 5:5) this day have I *b*
Prov. 17:21 that *b* a fool doeth it to his sorrow
23:24 he that *b* a wise child shall have joy
Eccl. 6:3 if a man *b* a hundred children, and live
Is. 45:10 woe unto him that saith . . What *b* thou?
49:21 who hath *b* me these, seeing I have lost
1 Cor. 4:15 I have *b* you through the gospel
Phlm. 10 Onesimus, whom I have *b* in my bonds
Jas. 1:18 of his own will *b* he us with the word
1 Pet. 1:3 hath *b* us again unto a lively hope
1 Jn. 5:1 loveth him that *b* loveth him . . that is *b*
5:18 but he that is *b* of God keepeth himself

Beggar *See also* Destitute, Needy, Poor, Poverty

1 Sam. 2:8 and lifteth up the *b* from the dunghill
Lk. 16:20 there was a certain *b* named Lazarus

Beggarly

Gal. 4:9 turn ye again to the weak and *b* elements

Begin (Began, Begun)

Gen. 4:26 *b* men to call upon the name of the LORD
Deut. 3:24 God, thou hast *b* to show thy servant
Josh. 3:7 this day will I *b* to magnify thee
1 Sam. 3:12 when I *b*, I will also make an end
2 Chr. 29:27 offering *b*, the song of the LORD *b*
Ezek. 9:6 *b* at my sanctuary. Then they *b* at the

Lk. 24:27 and *b* at Moses and all the prophets, he
24:47 preached . . among all nations, *b* at Jerusalem
Jn. 9:32 since the world *b* was it not heard that
Acts 1:22 *b* from the baptism of John, unto that
8:35 Philip . . *b* at the same Scripture, and preached
Rom. 16:25 which was kept secret since the world *b*
2 Cor. 3:1 do we *b* again to commend ourselves?
8:6 as he had *b*, so he would also finish in you
Gal. 3:3 having *b* in the Spirit, are ye now made
Phil. 1:6 he which hath *b* a good work in you will
1 Tim. 5:11 have *b* to wax wanton against Christ
2 Tim. 1:9 given us in Christ . . before the world *b*
1 Pet. 4:17 judgment must *b* at the house of God

Beginning *See also* Creation, First

Gen. 1:1 in the *b* God created the heaven and the
1 Chr. 17:9 waste them any more, as at the *b*
Job 8:7 though thy *b* was small, yet thy latter end
42:12 blessed the latter end of Job more than his *b*
Ps. 111:10 (Prov. 9:10) fear of the LORD is the *b* of
119:160 thy word is true from the *b*: and every
Prov. 1:7 fear of the LORD is the *b* of knowledge
8:22 the LORD possessed me in the *b* of his way
8:23 set up . . from the *b*, or ever the earth was
Eccl. 3:11 that God maketh from the *b* to the end
7:8 better is the end of a thing than the *b*
10:13 *b* of the words of his mouth . . foolishness
Is. 48:3 declared the former things from the *b*
Mt. 19:8 (Mk. 10:6) but from the *b* it was not so
24:8 (Mk. 13:8) all these are the *b* of sorrows
Mk. 1:1 the *b* of the gospel of Jesus Christ
Jn. 1:1 in the *b* was the Word, and the Word was
2:11 this *b* of miracles did Jesus in Cana
6:64 for Jesus knew from the *b* who they were
15:27 because ye have been with me from the *b*
Eph. 3:9 from the *b* of the world hath been hid
Col. 1:18 is the *b*, the firstborn from the dead
2 Thes. 2:13 from the *b* chosen you to salvation
Heb. 1:10 Lord, in the *b* hast laid the foundation
3:14 we hold the *b* of our confidence steadfast
7:3 having neither *b* of days, nor end of life
2 Pet. 2:20 end is worse with them than the *b*
Rev. 1:8 (21:6; 22:13) I am . . the *b* and the ending
3:14 the Amen . . the *b* of the creation of God
22:13 the *b* and the end, the first and the last

Begotten *See also* Beget

Jn. 1:14 the glory as of the only *b* of the Father
1:18 the only *b* Son . . he hath declared him
3:16 God so loved . . that he gave his only *b* Son
Heb. 11:17 Abraham . . offered up his only *b* son
1 Jn. 4:9 God sent his only *b* Son into the world
Rev. 1:5 Jesus Christ . . the first-*b* of the dead

Beguile

Gen. 3:13 said, The serpent *b* me, and I did eat
29:25 for Rachel? wherefore then hast thou *b* me?
Num. 25:18 their wiles, wherewith they have *b* you
Josh. 9:22 wherefore have ye *b* us, saying, We are
2 Cor. 11:3 the serpent *b* Eve through his subtilty
Col. 2:4 any man should *b* you with enticing words
2:18 let no man *b* you of your reward
2 Pet. 2:14 full of adultery . . *b* unstable souls

Behave *See also* Live, Walk

Deut. 32:27 adversaries should *b* themselves strangely
1 Sam. 18:5 David went out . . and *b* himself wisely
1 Chr. 19:13 *b* ourselves valiantly for our people
Ps. 101:2 I will *b* myself wisely in a perfect way
131:2 I have *b* and quieted myself, as a child
Is. 3:5 the child shall *b* himself proudly against
Mic. 3:4 have *b* themselves ill in their doings
1 Cor. 13:5 doth not *b* itself unseemly, seeketh not

1 Thes. 2:10 how holily . . we *b* ourselves among you
1 Tim. 3:15 oughtest to *b* thyself in the house

Behavior *See also* Manner

1 Sam. 21:13 he changed his *b* before them
1 Tim. 3:2 bishop then must be . . sober, of good *b*
Tit. 2:3 aged women . . be in *b* as becometh holiness

Behead

Deut. 21:6 the heifer that is *b* in the valley
Mt. 14:10 (Mk. 6:27) sent, and *b* John in the prison
Mk. 6:16 said, It is John, whom I *b*: he is risen
Lk. 9:9 John have I *b*; but who is this, of whom
Rev. 20:4 that were *b* for the witness of Jesus

Behemoth

Job 40:15 behold now *b*, which I made with thee

Behold (Beheld) *See also* Look,
Observe, See

Num. 21:9 when he *b* the serpent of brass, he lived
24:17 not now: I shall *b* him, but not nigh
Deut. 3:27 *b* it with thine eyes . . thou shalt not go
Job 19:27 and mine eyes shall *b*, and not another
24:18 he *b* not the way of the vineyards
Ps. 11:4 in heaven: his eyes *b* . . the children of men
17:2 let thine eyes *b* the things that are equal
17:15 for me, I will *b* thy face in righteousness
27:4 to *b* the beauty of the LORD, and to inquire
33:13 looketh from heaven; he *b* all the sons of men
37:37 mark the perfect man, and *b* the upright
46:8 *b* the works of the LORD, what desolations
66:7 his power for ever; his eyes *b* the nations
91:8 shalt thou *b* and see the reward of the wicked
113:6 who humbleth himself to *b* the things that
119:18 I may *b* wondrous things out of thy law
119:37 turn away mine eyes from *b* vanity
Prov. 15:3 in every place, *b* the evil and the good
Eccl. 8:17 then I *b* all the work of God, that a man
Is. 40:9 say unto the cities of Judah, *B* your God
65:1 I said, *B* me, *b* me, unto a nation that
Hab. 1:3 why dost thou . . cause me to *b* grievance?
1:13 thou art of purer eyes than to *b* evil
Mt. 18:10 their angels do always *b* the face of
19:26 but Jesus *b* them, and said unto them
Mk. 10:21 then Jesus *b* him loved him, and said
12:41 Jesus . . *b* how the people cast money into
16:6 not here: *b* the place where they laid him
Lk. 10:18 I *b* Satan as lightning fall from heaven
19:41 come near, he *b* the city, and wept over it
22:56 a certain maid *b* him as he sat by the fire
24:12 *b* the linen clothes laid by themselves
Jn. 1:14 we *b* his glory, the glory as of the only
1:29 *b* the Lamb of God, which taketh away the
17:24 that they may *b* my glory, which thou hast
19:5 and Pilate saith unto them, *B* the man!
19:14 and he saith unto the Jews, *B* your king!
19:26 saith unto his mother, Woman, *b* thy son!
Acts 1:9 while they *b*, he was taken up
4:14 and *b* the man which was healed standing
23:1 and Paul, earnestly *b* the council, said
2 Cor. 3:7 not steadfastly *b* the face of Moses
3:18 *b* as in a glass the glory of the Lord
Jas. 1:23 a man *b* his natural face in a glass
1 Pet. 3:2 while they *b* your chaste conversation
Rev. 5:6 I *b*, and, lo, in the midst of the throne
7:9 after this I *b*, and, lo, a great multitude
11:12 they ascended . . and their enemies *b* them

Behoove

Lk. 24:46 thus it *b* Christ to suffer, and to rise
Heb. 2:17 *b* him to be made like unto his brethren

Being

Acts 17:28 in him we live, and move. and have our *b*

Bel

Is. 46:1 *B* boweth down, Nebo stoopeth; their idols
Jer. 50:2 say, Babylon is taken, *B* is confounded
51:44 and I will punish *B* in Babylon, and I will

Belial

Deut. 13:13 men, the children of *B*, are gone out
Judg. 19:22 certain sons of *B*, beset the house
1 Sam. 1:16 not thine handmaid for a daughter of *B*
2:12 sons of Eli were sons of *B*; they knew not
10:27 children of *B* said, How shall this man
25:17 such a son of *B*, that a man cannot speak
30:22 answered all the wicked men, and men of *B*
2 Sam. 16:7 thou bloody man, and thou man of *B*
20:1 there a man of *B*, whose name was Sheba
1 Kgs. 21:10 set two men, sons of *B*, before him
2 Cor. 6:15 and what concord hath Christ with *B*?

Belief

2 Thes. 2:13 sanctification . . and *b* of the truth

Believe *See also* Assurance, Confidence, Faith, Trust

Gen. 15:6 *b* in the LORD; and he counted it to him
Ex. 4:1 they will not *b* me, nor hearken unto my
4:5 may *b* that the LORD God of their fathers
4:31 people *b*: and when they heard that the LORD
14:31 people . . *b* the LORD, and his servant Moses
19:9 the people may hear . . and *b* thee for ever
Num. 14:11 and how long will it be ere they *b* me
20:12 because ye *b* me not, to sanctify me in the
Deut. 1:32 yet in this thing ye did not *b* the LORD
9:23 ye *b* him not, nor hearkened to his voice
2 Kgs. 17:14 that did not *b* in the LORD their God
2 Chr. 20:20 *b* in the LORD your God . . *b* his prophets
32:15 neither yet *b* him: for no god of any nation
Job 9:16 yet would I not *b* that he had hearkened
15:22 *b* not that he shall return out of darkness
29:24 if I laughed on them, they *b* it not
39:12 wilt thou *b* him, that he will bring home
Ps. 27:13 I had fainted, unless I had *b* to see
78:22 because they *b* not in God, and trusted not
116:10 (2 Cor. 4:13) I *b*, therefore have I spoken
119:66 teach me . . for I have *b* thy commandments
Prov. 14:15 simple *b* every word; but the prudent
26:25 when he speaketh fair, *b* him not
Is. 7:9 if ye will not *b* . . not be established
28:16 (Rom. 9:33; 10:11; 1 Pet. 2:6) he that *b* shall
43:10 I have chosen; that ye may know and *b* me
53:1 (Jn. 12:38; Rom. 10:16) who hath *b* our report
Jer. 12:6 *b* them not, though they speak fair words
Lam. 4:12 would not have *b* that the adversary
Dan. 6:23 and no . . hurt . . because he *b* in his God
Jon. 3:5 so the people of Nineveh *b* God
Hab. 1:5 (Acts 13:41) a work . . which ye will not *b*
Mt. 8:13 as thou hast *b*, so be it done unto thee
9:28 *b* ye that I am able to do this?
18:6 (Mk. 9:42) these little ones which *b* in me
21:22 (Mk. 11:24) ask in prayer, *b*, ye shall receive
21:25 (Mk. 11:31; Lk. 20:5) why . . ye not then *b*
21:32 ye *b* him not; but the publicans . . *b* him
24:23 (Mk. 13:21) here is Christ, or there; *b* it not
27:42 (Mk. 15:32) down from the cross . . we will *b*
Mk. 1:15 is at hand: repent ye, and *b* the gospel
5:36 he saith: Be not afraid, only *b*
9:23 all things are possible to him that *b*
9:24 Lord, I *b*; help thou mine unbelief
16:11 they had heard that he was alive . . *b* not

Mk. 16:16 he that *b* and is baptized shall be saved
Lk. 1:1 things which are most surely *b* among us
1:20 shalt be dumb . . because thou *b* not my words
1:45 blessed is she that *b*: for there shall be
8:12 lest they should *b* and be saved
8:13 these have no root, which for a while *b*
8:50 *b* only, and she shall be made whole
22:67 unto them, If I tell you, ye will not *b*
24:11 unto them as idle tales, and they *b* them not
24:25 O fools, and slow of heart to *b* all that
Jn. 1:7 that all men through him might *b*
1:12 even to them that *b* on his name
2:11 forth his glory; and his disciples *b* on him
2:22 they *b* the Scripture, and the word which
2:23 many *b* in his name, when they saw
3:12 how shall ye *b*, if I tell you of heavenly
3:16 whosoever *b* in him should not perish
3:18 he that *b* on him is not condemned . . *b* not is
3:36 he that *b* on the Son hath everlasting life
4:21 woman, *b* me, the hour cometh, when ye shall
4:39 many of the Samaritans of that city *b*
4:42 now we *b*, not because of thy saying: for we
4:48 except ye see signs and wonders, ye will not *b*
4:53 and himself *b*, and his whole house
5:24 *b* on him that sent me, hath everlasting life
5:46 for had ye *b* Moses, ye would have *b* me
6:29 this is the work of God, that ye *b* on him
6:35 and he that *b* on me shall never thirst
6:36 that ye also have seen me, and *b* not
6:64 but there are some of you that *b* not
6:69 we *b* and are sure that thou art that Christ
7:5 for neither did his brethren *b* in him
7:31 and many of the people *b* on him, and said
7:38 that *b* on me . . out of his belly shall flow
7:48 any of the rulers or . . Pharisees *b* on him?
8:24 for if ye *b* not that I am he, ye shall die
8:30 as he spake these words, many *b* on him
8:45 because I tell you the truth, ye *b* me not
9:18 Jews did not *b* . . that he had been blind
9:35 unto thee, Dost thou *b* on the Son of God?
10:26 ye *b* not, because ye are not of my sheep
10:38 though ye *b* not me, *b* the works
10:42 and many *b* on him there
11:15 I was not there, to the intent ye may *b*
11:25 he that *b* in me, though he were dead, yet
11:27 I *b* that thou art the Christ, the Son of
11:40 if thou wouldest *b*, thou shouldest see
11:45 of the Jews which came to Mary . . *b* on him
11:48 if we let him thus alone, all men will *b*
12:11 many of the Jews went away, and *b* on Jesus
12:36 while ye have light, *b* in the light
12:37 had done so many miracles . . yet they *b* not
12:42 among the chief rulers also many *b* on him
12:44 he that *b* on me, *b* not on me, but on him
12:47 if any man . . *b* not, I judge him not
13:19 come to pass, ye may *b* that I am he
14:1 be troubled: ye *b* in God, *b* also in me
14:10 *b* thou not that I am in the Father
14:12 he that *b* on me, the works that I do
14:29 that, when it is come to pass, ye might *b*
16:9 of sin, because they *b* not on me
16:27 and have *b* that I came out from God
17:8 and they have *b* that thou didst send me
17:20 but for them also which shall *b* on me
17:21 that the world may *b* that thou hast sent me
19:35 that he saith true, that ye might *b*
20:8 that other disciple . . and he saw, and *b*
20:25 except I shall see . . I will not *b*
20:29 because thou hast seen me, thou hast *b*
20:31 these are written that ye might *b*
Acts 2:44 *b* were together, and had all things common
4:4 howbeit many of them which heard the word *b*
4:32 that *b* were of one heart and of one soul

Acts 8:12 when they *b* Philip preaching the things
8:37 I *b* that Jesus Christ is the Son of God
9:26 all afraid . . and *b* not that he was a disciple
9:42 throughout all Joppa; and many *b* in the Lord
10:43 *b* in him shall receive remission of sins
11:17 the like gift as he did unto us, who *b*
11:21 a great number *b*, and turned unto the Lord
13:12 the deputy, when he saw what was done, *b*
13:39 by him all that *b* are justified from all
13:48 as many as were ordained to eternal life *b*
14:1 both of the Jews and also of the Greeks *b*
15:5 rose up certain . . of the Pharisees which *b*
15:7 the Gentiles by my mouth should hear . . and *b*
15:11 we *b* that . . we shall be saved, even as they
16:1 a certain woman, which was a Jewess, and *b*
16:31 *b* on the Lord Jesus Christ, and thou shalt
17:4 some of them *b*, and consorted with Paul
17:34 howbeit certain men clave unto him, and *b*
18:8 Crispus . . *b* on the Lord with all his house
19:2 have ye received the Holy Ghost since ye *b*?
19:4 should *b* on him which should come after him
21:20 many thousands of Jews there are which *b*
22:19 I imprisoned and beat . . them that *b* on thee
24:14 *b* all things which are written in the law
26:27 King Agrippa, *b* thou the prophets? I know
27:11 the centurion *b* the master . . of the ship
27:25 I *b* God, that it shall be even as . . told me
Rom. 1:16 unto salvation to every one that *b*
3:3 what if some did not *b*? shall their unbelief
3:26 and the justifier of him which *b* in Jesus
4:3 (Gal. 3:6; Jas. 2:23) Abraham *b* God, and it was
4:5 but to him that worketh not, but *b* on him
4:18 who against hope *b* in hope, that he might
4:24 imputed, if we *b* on him that raised up Jesus
6:8 we *b* that we shall also live with him
9:33 (10:11) *b* on him shall not be ashamed
10:4 is the end of the law . . to every one that *b*
10:9 shalt *b* in thine heart that God . . raised him
10:14 they call on him in whom they have not *b*?
11:30 as ye in times past have not *b* God, yet
13:11 now is our salvation nearer than when we *b*
14:2 one *b* that he may eat all things: another
1 Cor. 1:21 of preaching to save them that *b*
3:5 but ministers by whom ye *b*
7:12 if any brother hath a wife that *b* not
10:27 any of them that *b* not bid you to a feast
13:7 *b* all things, hopeth all things, endureth
14:24 come in one that *b* not, or one unlearned
15:2 preached unto you, unless ye have *b* in vain
2 Cor. 4:4 blinded the minds of them which *b* not
6:15 what part hath he that *b* with an infidel?
Gal. 2:16 even we have *b* in Jesus Christ
3:22 the promise . . might be given to them that *b*
Eph. 1:13 after that ye *b*, ye were sealed with
1:19 greatness of his power to us-ward who *b*
Phil. 1:29 not only to *b* on him, but also to suffer
1 Thes. 1:7 that ye were ensamples to all that *b*
2:13 the word of God . . worketh also in you that *b*
4:14 for if we *b* that Jesus died and rose again
2 Thes. 1:10 and to be admirèd in all them that *b*
2:11 strong delusion, that they should *b* a lie
2:12 all might be damned who *b* not the truth
1 Tim. 3:16 *b* on in the world, received up into
4:3 received . . of them which *b* and know the truth
5:16 if any man or woman that *b* have widows
2 Tim. 1:12 I know whom I have *b*, and am persuaded
2:13 if we *b* not, yet he abideth faithful
Heb. 3:18 to whom sware he . . but to them that *b* not
4:3 for we which have *b* do enter into rest
10:39 of them that *b* to the saving of the soul
11:6 for he that cometh to God must *b* that he is
11:31 Rahab perished not with them that *b* not
Jas. 2:19 *b* that there is one God . . devils also *b*

1 Pet. 1:8 now ye see him not, yet *b*, ye rejoice
1:21 who by him do *b* in God, that raised him up
2:7 unto you therefore which *b* he is precious
1 Jn. 3:23 that we should *b* on the name of his Son
4:1 *b* not every spirit, but try the spirits
4:16 we have known and *b* the love that God hath
5:1 whosoever *b* that Jesus is the Christ is
5:10 that *b* on the Son of God hath the witness
5:13 unto you that *b* on the name of the Son
Jude 5 Lord . . afterward destroyed them that *b* not

Believing *See also* Believe

Jn. 20:27 and be not faithless, but *b*
1 Tim. 6:2 they that have *b* masters, let them not

Belly

Gen. 3:14 *b* shalt thou go, and dust shalt thou eat
Num. 5:21 thy thigh to rot, and thy *b* to swell
25:8 man of Israel, and the woman through her *b*
Judg. 3:21 took the dagger . . and thrust it into his *b*
Job 15:2 wise man . . fill his *b* with the east wind?
15:35 vanity, and their *b* prepareth deceit
20:20 he shall not feel quietness in his *b*
32:19 behold, my *b* is as wine which hath no vent
Ps. 44:25 to the dust; our *b* cleaveth unto the earth
Song 7:2 thy *b* is like an heap of wheat set about
Jer. 1:5 before I formed thee in the *b* I knew thee
51:34 he hath filled his *b* with my delicates
Ezek. 3:3 cause thy *b* to eat . . this roll that I give
Jon. 1:17 Jonah was in the *b* of the fish three days
2:2 out of the *b* of hell cried I, and thou
Mt. 12:40 as Jonas was . . in the whale's *b*; so shall
15:17 (Mk. 7:19) goeth into the *b*, and is cast out
Lk. 15:16 fain have filled his *b* with the husks
Jn. 7:38 out of his *b* shall flow rivers of living
Rom. 16:18 serve not our Lord . . but their own *b*
1 Cor. 6:13 meats for the *b*, and the *b* for meats
Phil. 3:19 whose God is their *b*, and whose glory
Tit. 1:12 the Cretians are . . evil beasts, slow *b*
Rev. 10:9 eat it up; and it shall make thy *b* bitter

Beloved

Deut. 21:15 two wives, one *b*, and another hated
33:12 *b* of the LORD shall dwell in safety by him
Neh. 13:26 no king like him, who was *b* of his God
Ps. 60:5 (108:6) that thy *b* may be delivered
127:2 for so he giveth his *b* sleep
Prov. 4:3 and only *b* in the sight of my mother
Song 1:14 my *b* is unto me as a cluster of camphire
2:3 as the apple tree . . so is my *b* among the sons
2:16 (6:3) my *b* is mine, and I am his: he feedeth
4:16 let my *b* come into his garden, and eat
5:2 it is the voice of my *b* that knocketh
6:1 whither is thy *b* gone, O thou fairest among
8:5 who is this that cometh . . leaning upon her *b*?
Is. 5:1 sing . . a song of my *b* touching his vineyard
Jer. 12:7 I have given the dearly *b* of my soul
Dan. 9:23 thou art greatly *b*: therefore understand
10:11 O Daniel, a man greatly *b*, understand the
10:19 O man greatly *b*, fear not: peace be unto
Mt. 3:17 (17:5; Mk. 1:11; 9:7; Lk. 3:22; 9:35; 2 Pet.
1:17) this is my *b* Son, in whom I am well pleased
12:18 my *b*, in whom my soul is well pleased
Lk. 20:13 what shall I do? I will send my *b* son
Acts 15:25 unto you with our *b* Barnabas and Paul
Rom. 1:7 to all that be in Rome, *b* of God, called
9:25 I will call . . her *b*, which was not *b*
11:28 but as touching the election, they are *b*
1 Cor. 4:14 shame you, but as my *b* sons I warn you
2 Cor. 12:19 we do all things, dearly *b*, for your
Eph. 1:6 wherein he hath made us accepted in the *b*
Phil. 4:1 my brethren dearly *b* and longed for
Col. 3:12 put on . . as the elect of God, holy and *b*

Col. 4:9 with Onesimus, a faithful and *b* brother
4:14 Luke, the *b* physician, and Demas, greet
1 Tim. 6:2 they are faithful and *b*, partakers of
2 Tim. 1:2 to Timothy, my dearly *b* son: Grace
Phlm. 2 to our *b* Apphia, and Archippus our fellow
16 above a servant, a brother *b*, specially to me
Heb. 6:9 *b*, we are persuaded better things of you
Jas. 1:16 do not err, my *b* brethren
1 Pet. 2:11 dearly *b*, I beseech you as strangers
2 Pet. 3:15 even as our *b* brother Paul . . hath written
1 Jn. 3:2 *b*, now are we the sons of God, and it
4:1 *b*, believe not every spirit, but try the
4:7 *b*, let us love one another: for love is of God
4:11 *b*, if God so loved us, we ought also to love
3 Jn. 11 *b*, follow not that which is evil, but
Jude 20 but ye, *b*, building up yourselves on your
Rev. 20:9 and compassed the camp . . and the *b* city

Belshazzar Dan. 5:1–30

Belteshazzar *See also* Daniel Dan. 1:7

Bemoan *See also* Mourn

Job 42:11 they *b* him, and comforted him over all
Jer. 22:10 weep ye not for the dead, neither *b* him
31:18 I have surely heard Ephraim *b* himself
Nah. 3:7 Nineveh is laid waste: who will *b* her?

Benaiah 1 Kgs. 1:8–2:46

2 Sam. 8:18 (20:23) *B* . . over both the Cherethites
23:20 (1 Chr. 11:22) *B* . . slew two lionlike men

Ben-ammi Gen. 19:38

Bend

Ps. 11:2 the wicked *b* their bow, they make ready
58:7 when he *b* his bow to shoot his arrows, let
64:3 *b* their bows to shoot their arrows, even
Is. 60:14 afflicted thee shall come *b* unto thee
Jer. 9:3 *b* their tongues like their bow for lies
50:14 all ye that *b* the bow, shoot at her, spare
51:3 against him that *b* let the archer *b* his bow
Ezek. 17:7 this vine did *b* her roots toward him

Beneath

Deut. 28:13 be above only, and thou shalt not be *b*
Jn. 8:23 ye are from *b*; I am from above: ye are of

Benefactor

Lk. 22:25 that exercise authority . . are called *b*

Benefit *See also* Blessing, Gift

2 Chr. 32:25 rendered not again according to the *b*
Ps. 68:19 be the Lord, who daily loadeth us with *b*
103:2 bless the LORD . . and forget not all his *b*
116:12 shall I render . . for all his *b* toward me?
Jer. 18:10 good, wherewith I said I would *b* them
2 Cor. 1:15 to come . . that ye might have a second *b*
1 Tim. 6:2 faithful and beloved, partakers of the *b*
Phlm. 14 that thy *b* should not be . . of necessity

Benevolence

1 Cor. 7:3 the husband render unto the wife due *b*

Ben-hadad

Bribed by Asa, 1 Kgs. 15:18–22 (2 Chr. 16:2–6);
warred against Ahab, 1 Kgs. 20:1–34; besieged Samaria, 2 Kgs. 6:24–25; consulted Elisha, 2 Kgs.
8:7–14; killed by Hazael, 2 Kgs. 8:15; "palaces of
Ben-hadad," Jer. 49:27 (Amos 1:4).

Benjamin

Born, Gen. 35:16–18; brought to Egypt, Gen. 43; accused of theft, Gen. 44; blessed by Jacob, Gen. 49:27.
Tribe of Benjamin: blessed by Moses, Deut. 33:12;

allotted its territory, Josh. 18:11–28; punished, Judg.
20; procured wives, Judg. 21; Paul from this tribe,
Phil. 3:5.

Berachah 2 Chr. 20:26

Berea Acts 17:10–14

Bereave

Gen. 42:36 have ye *b* of my children: Joseph is not
43:14 if I be *b* of my children, I am *b*
Eccl. 4:8 for whom do I labor, and *b* my soul
Jer. 15:7 I will *b* them of children, I will
18:21 let their wives be *b* of their children
Lam. 1:20 abroad the sword *b*, at home there is as
Ezek. 5:17 and evil beasts, and they shall *b* thee
36:12 shalt no more henceforth *b* them of men
Hos. 9:12 bring up their children, yet will I *b*
13:8 meet them as a bear that is *b* of her whelps

Berith Judg. 9:46

Bernice Acts 25:13, 23; 26:30

Berodach-baladan (Merodach-baladan) 2 Kgs. 20:12 (Is. 39:1)

Beseech (Besought) *See also* Ask, Beg, Petition, Plead, Request

Gen. 42:21 when he *b* us, and we would not hear
Ex. 3:18 let us go, we *b* thee, three days' journey
32:11 Moses *b* the LORD his God, and said, LORD
33:18 and he said, I *b* thee, show me thy glory
Deut. 3:23 and I *b* the LORD at that time, saying
2 Sam. 16:4 I humbly *b* thee that I may find grace
1 Kgs. 13:6 man of God *b* the LORD, and the king's
2 Kgs. 13:4 Jehoahaz *b* the LORD . . LORD hearkened
2 Chr. 33:12 in affliction, he *b* the LORD his God
Ezra 8:23 so we fasted and *b* our God for this
Esth. 8:3 Esther . . fell down . . and *b* him with tears
Ps. 80:14 return, we *b* thee, O God of hosts: look
116:4 O LORD, I *b* thee, deliver my soul
118:25 save now, I *b* thee . . I *b* thee, send now
119:108 accept, I *b* thee, the freewill offerings
Jon. 1:14 we *b* thee, let us not perish for this
Mal. 1:9 *b* God that he will be gracious unto us
Mt. 8:5 (Lk. 7:3) unto him a centurion, *b* him
8:31 (Mk. 5:12; Lk. 8:32) devils *b* him . . If thou
8:34 (Lk. 8:37) they *b* him that he would depart
Mk. 1:40 and there came a leper to him, *b* him
5:23 and *b* him greatly . . My little daughter lieth
7:26 *b* him that he would cast forth the devil
7:32 and they *b* him to put his hand upon him
Lk. 5:12 seeing Jesus fell on his face, and *b* him
7:3 *b* him that he would come and heal his servant
8:38 the man . . *b* him that he might be with him
9:38 Master, I *b* thee, look upon my son
Jn. 4:40 they *b* him that he would tarry with them
4:47 *b* him that he would come down, and heal his
19:31 *b* Pilate that their legs might be broken
19:38 *b* Pilate that he might take away the body
Acts 27:33 Paul *b* them all to take meat, saying
Rom. 12:1 I *b* you therefore, brethren, by the
1 Cor. 4:16 I *b* you, be ye followers of me
2 Cor. 5:20 as though God did *b* you by us: we pray
6:1 *b* you also that ye receive not . . in vain
10:1 now I Paul myself *b* you by the meekness and
12:8 for this thing I *b* the Lord thrice, that it
Gal. 4:12 brethren, I *b* you, be as I am; for I am
Eph. 4:1 *b* you that ye walk worthy of the vocation
Phil. 4:2 I *b* Euodias, and *b* Syntyche, that they
1 Tim. 1:3 as I *b* thee to abide still at Ephesus
Phlm. 9 yet for love's sake I rather *b* thee

Heb. 13:19 but I *b* you the rather to do this, that
1 Pet. 2:11 I *b* you . . abstain from fleshly lusts

Beset

Judg. 19:22 the men of the city . . *b* the house round
Ps. 22:12 strong bulls of Bashan have *b* me round
  139:5 thou hast *b* me behind and before
Hos. 7:2 now their own doings have *b* them about
Heb. 12:1 and the sin which doth so easily *b* us

Beside

Mk. 3:21 lay hold . . for they said, He is *b* himself
Acts 26:24 Festus said . . Paul, thou art *b* thyself
2 Cor. 5:13 whether we be *b* ourselves, it is to

Besiege

Deut. 20:12 war against thee, then thou shalt *b*
  28:52 and he shall *b* thee in all thy gates, until
1 Kgs. 8:37 (2 Chr. 6:28) if their enemy *b* them
  20:1 Ben-hadad . . and he went up and *b* Samaria
2 Kgs. 6:24 king of Syria . . went up, and *b* Samaria
  25:2 (Jer. 39:1; 52:5) and the city was *b*
Eccl. 9:14 came a great king against it, and *b* it

Besieged *See also* Besiege

2 Kgs. 19:24 (Is. 37:25) I dried up . . rivers of *b* places
Is. 1:8 the daughter of Zion is left . . as a *b* city

Besom

Is. 14:23 will sweep it with the *b* of destruction

Besought *See* Beseech

Best *See also* Better, Good, Well

Gen. 43:11 take of the *b* fruits in the land
  47:6 in the *b* of the land make thy father
Deut. 23:16 he shall dwell . . where it liketh him *b*
1 Sam. 15:9 spared Agag, and the *b* of the sheep
2 Sam. 18:4 what seemeth you *b* I will do
Ps. 39:5 every man at his *b* state is . . vanity
Lk. 15:22 bring forth the *b* robe, and put it on
1 Cor. 12:31 but covet earnestly the *b* gifts

Bestow *See also* Give, Pay

Ex. 32:29 he may *b* upon you a blessing this day
Deut. 14:26 *b* that money for whatsoever thy soul
1 Chr. 29:25 *b* upon him such royal majesty as had
Ezra 7:20 *b* it out of the king's treasure house
Is. 63:7 great goodness . . which he hath *b* on them
Lk. 12:17 I have no room where to *b* my fruits
Jn. 4:38 sent you to reap that whereon ye *b* no labor
1 Cor. 12:23 upon these we *b* more abundant honor
  13:3 though I *b* all my goods to feed the poor
  15:10 and his grace . . *b* upon me was not in vain
Gal. 4:11 lest I have *b* upon you labor in vain
1 Jn. 3:1 what manner of love the Father hath *b*

Bethabara Jn. 1:28

Bethany

Mt. 21:17 (Mk. 11:11) went out of the city into *B*
  26:6 (Mk. 14:3) Jesus was in *B*, in the house
Mk. 11:1 (Lk. 19:29) came . . unto Bethphage and *B*
Lk. 24:50 he led them out as far as to *B*, and he
Jn. 11:1 Lazarus, of *B*, the town of Mary and her
  12:1 Jesus six days before the Passover came to *B*

Bethel

Gen. 28:19 and he called the name of that place *B*
  31:13 I am the God of *B*, where thou anointedst
  35:1 Jacob, Arise, go up to *B*, and dwell there
Judg. 1:22 the house of Joseph . . went up against *B*
1 Kgs. 12:29 the one in *B*, and the other . . in Dan
  13:1 came a man of God out of Judah . . unto *B*

2 Kgs. 2:3 the sons of the prophets that were at *B*
  2:23 he went up from thence unto *B*: and as he
  17:28 one of the priests . . came and dwelt in *B*
  23:15 the altar that was at *B* . . he brake down
Jer. 48:13 as the house of Israel was ashamed of *B*
Hos. 12:4 he found him in *B*, and there he spake
Amos 3:14 I will also visit the altars of *B*
  4:4 come to *B*, and transgress; at Gilgal multiply
  5:5 but seek not *B* . . *B* shall come to nought
  7:13 prophesy not again any more at *B*: for it is

Bethesda Jn. 5:2

Beth-horon

  Josh. 10:10–11; 1 Kgs. 9:17 (2 Chr. 8:5)

Bethlehem

Gen. 35:19 died . . in the way to Ephrath, which is *B*
Ruth 1:22 to *B* in the beginning of barley harvest
1 Sam. 16:4 and Samuel did that . . and came to *B*
2 Sam. 23:15 (1 Chr. 11:17) drink of . . the well of *B*
Mic. 5:2 (Mt. 2:6) thou, *B* . . though thou be little
Mt. 2:1 now when Jesus was born in *B* of Judea
  2:16 and slew all the children that were in *B*
Lk. 2:4 unto the city of David, which is called *B*
  2:15 let us now go even unto *B*, and see this
Jn. 7:42 that Christ cometh . . out of the town of *B*

Bethphage Mt. 21:1 (Mk. 11:1; Lk. 19:29)

Bethsaida

Mt. 11:21 (Lk. 10:13) woe unto thee, *B*! for if
Mk. 6:45 to go to the other side before unto *B*
  8:22 he cometh to *B*; and they bring a blind man
Lk. 9:10 into a desert place belonging to . . *B*

Beth-shan (Beth-shean)

  Josh. 17:16; 1 Sam. 31:10, 12

Beth-shemesh

  1 Sam. 6:9–13; 2 Kgs. 14:11 (2 Chr. 25:21)

Betray

1 Chr. 12:17 if ye be come to *b* me to mine enemies
Mt. 17:22 (20:18) the Son of man shall be *b* into
  24:10 many be offended, and shall *b* one another
  26:2 and the Son of man is *b* to be crucified
  26:16 (Mk. 14:11; Lk. 22:6) sought . . to *b* him
  26:21 (Mk. 14:18; Jn. 13:21) one of you shall *b* me
  26:24 (Mk. 14:21; Lk. 22:22) woe unto that man
    by whom the Son of man is *b*!
  26:45 (Mk. 14:41) is *b* into the hands of sinners
  26:48 (Mk. 14:44) he that *b* him gave them a sign
  27:4 sinned in that I have *b* the innocent blood
Mk. 13:12 the brother shall *b* the brother to death
Lk. 21:16 shall be *b* both by parents, and brethren
  22:21 hand of him that *b* me is with me on the
  22:48 Judas, *b* thou the Son of man with a kiss?
Jn. 6:64 knew from the beginning . . who should *b* him
  13:2 now put into the heart of Judas . . to *b*
  13:21 I say unto you, that one of you shall *b* me
  18:2 and Judas also, which *b* him, knew the place
  21:20 and said, Lord, which is he that *b* thee?
1 Cor. 11:23 same night in which he was *b*, took

Betroth *See also* Espouse, Marry

Ex. 21:8 she please not her master, who hath *b* her
Deut. 20:7 what man is there that hath *b* a wife
Hos. 2:19 I will *b* thee unto me for ever

Better *See also* Best, Good, Well

Gen. 29:19 it is *b* that I give her to thee, than
1 Sam. 1:8 am not I *b* to thee than ten sons?
  15:22 behold, to obey is *b* than sacrifice

1 Kgs. 19:4 for I am not *b* than my fathers
Ps. 37:16 a little that a righteous man hath is *b*
  63:3 because thy loving-kindness is *b* than life
  84:10 a day in thy courts is *b* than a thousand
  118:8 it is *b* to trust in the LORD than to put
  119:72 the law of thy mouth is *b* unto me than
Prov. 3:14 it is *b* than the merchandise of silver
  8:11 wisdom is *b* than rubies; and all the things
  8:19 my fruit is *b* than gold, yea, than fine
  15:16 *b* is little with the fear of the LORD
  16:16 how much *b* is it to get wisdom than gold!
  19:22 and a poor man is *b* than a liar
Eccl. 2:24 nothing *b* for a man, than that he. .eat
  4:9 two are *b* than one; because they have a good
  7:1 a good name is *b* than precious ointment
  7:3 sorrow is *b* than laughter
  7:10 that the former days were *b* than these?
Song 1:2 kiss me. . for thy love is *b* than wine
Dan. 1:20 he found them ten times *b* than all the
Jon. 4:3 (4:8) it is *b* for me to die than to live
Mt. 6:26 the fowls. . Are ye not much *b* than they?
  12:12 how much then is a man *b* than a sheep?
  18:6 (Mk. 9:42; Lk. 17:2) *b* for him that a millstone
Mk. 5:26 and was nothing *b*, but rather grew worse
Lk. 5:39 desireth new; for he saith, The old is *b*
Rom 3:9 are we *b* than they? No, in no wise
1 Cor. 9:15 it were *b* for me to die, than that any
Phil. 1:23 and to be with Christ; which is far *b*
  2:3 let each esteem other *b* than themselves
Heb. 1:4 being made so much *b* than the angels
  7:19 but the bringing in of a *b* hope did
  7:22 was Jesus made a surety of a *b* testament
  8:6 of a *b* covenant. . established upon *b* promises
  9:23 the heavenly. . with *b* sacrifices than these
  10:34 in heaven a *b* and an enduring substance
  11:16 desire a *b* country, that is, a heavenly
  11:40 God having provided some *b* thing for us
  12:24 that speaketh *b* things than that of Abel
2 Pet. 2:21 had been *b* for them not to have known

Beulah Is. 62:4

Bewail

Lev. 10:6 but let your brethren. . *b* the burning
Deut. 21:13 *b* her father and her mother a full month
Judg. 11:38 and *b* her virginity upon the mountains
Jer. 4:31 of the daughter of Zion, that *b* herself
Lk. 8:52 wept, and *b* her: but he said, Weep not
  23:27 of women, which also *b* and lamented him
2 Cor. 12:21 that I shall *b* many which have sinned
Rev. 18:9 and the kings of the earth. . shall *b* her

Beware

Gen. 24:6 *b* thou that thou bring not my son thither
Ex. 23:21 *b* of him, and obey his voice, provoke
Deut. 6:12 then *b* lest thou forget the LORD
  15:9 *b* that there be not a thought in thy wicked
Judg. 13:4 *b*, I pray thee, and drink not wine nor
Job 36:18 lest he take thee away with his stroke
Prov. 19:25 smite a scorner, and the simple will *b*
Mt. 7:15 *b* of false prophets, which come to you in
  10:17 but *b* of men: for they will deliver you up
  16:6 (Mk. 8:15; Lk. 12:1) *b* of the leaven of the
Mk. 12:38 *b* of the scribes, which love to go in
Lk. 12:15 take heed, and *b* of covetousness
Phil. 3:2 *b* of dogs, *b* of evil workers, *b* of the
Col. 2:8 *b* lest any man spoil you through philosophy

Bewitch

Acts 8:9 Simon. . used sorcery, and *b* the people
Gal. 3:1 O foolish Galatians, who hath *b* you

Bewray

Prov. 27:16 ointment of his right hand, which *b* itself

Prov. 29:24 he heareth cursing, and *b* it not
Is. 16:3 the outcasts; *b* not him that wandereth
Mt. 26:73 art one of them; for thy speech *b* thee

Bezaleel Ex. 31:2 (35:30); 36:1

Bezek Judg. 1:4–5

Bid (Bade, Bidden)

Gen. 27:19 I have done according as thou *b* me
Josh. 6:10 day I *b* you shout; then shall ye shout
  11:9 and Joshua did unto them as the LORD *b* him
Jon. 3:2 and preach. . the preaching that I *b* thee
Zeph. 1:7 prepared a sacrifice, he hath *b* his guests
Mt. 1:24 then Joseph. .did as the angel. .had *b* him
  14:28 *b* me come unto thee on the water
  22:9 as many as ye shall find, *b* to the marriage
  23:3 whatsoever they *b* you observe, that observe
Lk. 10:40 *b* her therefore that she help me
  14:8 when thou art *b* of any man to a wedding, sit
  14:16 man made a great supper, and *b* many
Acts 11:12 Spirit *b* me go. . nothing doubting
2 Jn. 11 he that *b* him God-speed is partaker of

Bier

2 Sam. 3:31 and king David himself followed the *b*
Lk. 7:14 and he came and touched the *b*

Bildad Job 2:11; 8:1–22; 18:1–21; 25:1–6

Bilhah Gen. 29:29; 30:3–7

Bill

Deut. 24:1 (Mk. 10:4) write her a *b* of divorcement
Lk. 16:6 take thy *b*, and sit down quickly, and write

Billow

Ps. 42:7 all thy waves and thy *b* are gone over me
Jon. 2:3 all thy *b* and thy waves passed over me

Bind (Bound)

Gen. 44:30 that his life is *b* up in the lad's life
Num. 30:2 swear an oath to *b* his soul with a bond
Judg. 15:13 and they *b* him with two new cords
  16:7 if they *b* me with seven green withes
  16:21 to Gaza, and *b* him with fetters of brass
Job 26:8 he *b* up the waters in his thick clouds
  38:31 thou *b* the sweet influences of Pleiades
Ps. 118:27 *b* the sacrifice with cords, even unto the
  147:3 the broken in heart, and *b* up their wounds
Prov. 3:3 mercy and truth. . *b* them about thy neck
  6:21 *b* them continually upon thine heart
  7:3 *b* them upon thy fingers, write them upon the
  22:15 foolishness is *b* in the heart of a child
  26:8 as he that *b* a stone in a sling, so is he
Is. 8:16 *b* up the testimony, seal the law among
  30:26 in the day that the LORD *b* up the breach
  61:1 he hath sent me to *b* up the broken-hearted
Ezek. 34:16 and will *b* up that which was broken
Hos. 4:19 the wind hath *b* her up in her wings
  6:1 he hath smitten, and he will *b* us up
  7:15 though I have *b* and strengthened their arms
Mt. 12:29 (Mk. 3:27) except he first *b* the strong man?
  16:19 (18:18) shalt *b* on earth shall be *b* in heaven
  22:13 *b* him hand and foot, and take him away
  23:4 *b* heavy burdens and grievous to be borne
  27:2 (Mk. 15:1) they had *b* him, they led him away
Mk. 5:3 no man could *b* him, no, not with chains
Lk. 13:16 whom Satan hath *b*, lo, these eighteen years
Acts 9:14 authority. . to *b* all that call on thy name
  21:11 he took Paul's girdle, and *b* his own hands
  22:4 and delivering unto prisons both men and
  22:25 and as they *b* him with thongs, Paul said
Rev. 20:2 Satan, and *b* him a thousand years

Bird *See also* Fowl

Gen. 7:14 after his kind, every *b* of every sort
Lev. 14:4 to take for him. . two *b* alive and clean
Deut. 14:11 of all clean *b* ye shall eat
22:6 if a *b*'s nest chance to be before thee
2 Sam. 21:10 neither the *b*. . to rest on them by day
Ps. 11:1 how say ye. . Flee as a *b* to your mountain
104:17 where the *b* make their nests: as for the
124:7 soul is escaped as a *b* out of the snare
Prov. 1:17 net is spread in the sight of any *b*
6:5 and as a *b* from the hand of the fowler
27:8 as a *b* that wandereth from her nest, so is
Eccl. 10:20 a *b* of the air shall carry the voice
Song 2:12 the time of the singing of *b* is come
Jer. 12:9 mine heritage is unto me as a speckled *b*
Amos 3:5 can a *b* fall in a snare. . where no gin is
Mt. 8:20 (Lk. 9:58) the *b* of the air have nests
13:32 so that the *b* of the air come and lodge
Jas. 3:7 every kind of beasts, and of *b*. . is tamed
Rev. 18:2 a cage of every unclean and hateful *b*

Birth

2 Kgs. 19:3 (Is. 37:3) children are come to the *b*
Eccl. 7:1 the day of death than the day of one's *b*
Is. 66:9 shall I bring to the *b*, and not cause to
Mt. 1:18 the *b* of Jesus Christ was on this wise
Lk. 1:14 and many shall rejoice at his *b*
Jn. 9:1 he saw a man which was blind from his *b*
Gal. 4:19 of whom I travail in *b* again until

Birthday

Gen. 40:20 the third day, which was Pharaoh's *b*
Mt. 14:6 (Mk. 6:21) but when Herod's *b* was kept

Birthright

Gen. 25:31 (Heb. 12:16) sell me this day thy *b*
27:36 he took away my *b*; and, behold, now he
43:33 they sat. . the firstborn according to his *b*
1 Chr. 5:1 his *b* was given unto the sons of Joseph

Bishop *See also* Deacon, Elder

Phil. 1:1 at Philippi, with the *b* and deacons
1 Tim. 3:1 if a man desire the office of a *b*
3:2 (Tit. 1:7) a *b* then must be blameless
1 Pet. 2:25 unto the Shepherd and *B* of your souls

Bishopric

Acts 1:20 dwell therein: and, His *b* let another take

Bit

Ps. 32:9 mouth must be held in with *b* and bridle
Jas. 3:3 behold, we put *b* in the horses' mouths

Bite (Bit, Bitten)

Gen. 49:17 be a serpent. . that *b* the horse heels
Num. 21:6 sent fiery serpents. . and they *b* the people
Prov. 23:32 at the last it *b* like a serpent
Eccl. 10:8 breaketh a hedge, a serpent shall *b* him
Jer. 8:17 will send serpents. . and they shall *b* you
Amos 5:19 hand on the wall, and a serpent *b* him
9:3 I command the serpent, and he shall *b* them
Mic. 3:5 that *b* with their teeth, and cry, Peace
Gal. 5:15 but if ye *b* and devour one another, take

Bithynia Acts 16:7

Bitter

Gen. 27:34 cried with a great and exceeding *b* cry
Ex. 1:14 they made their lives *b* with hard bondage
12:8 bread; and with *b* herbs they shall eat it
15:23 of the waters of Marah, for they were *b*
Num. 5:18 the *b* water that causeth the curse
2 Kgs. 14:26 the affliction of Israel. . was very *b*

Job 13:26 for thou writest *b* things against me
23:2 even today is my complaint *b*: my stroke is
Ps. 64:3 bows to shoot their arrows, even *b* words
Prov. 5:4 but her end is *b* as wormwood, sharp as
27:7 to the hungry soul every *b* thing is sweet
Is. 5:20 that put *b* for sweet, and sweet for *b*
24:9 strong drink shall be *b* to them that drink it
Jer. 2:19 see that it is an evil thing and *b*
31:15 heard in Ramah, lamentation, and *b* weeping
Hab. 1:6 the Chaldeans, that *b* and hasty nation
Col. 3:19 love your wives, and be not *b* against them
Jas. 3:11 at the same place sweet water and *b*?
Rev. 8:11 of the waters, because they were made *b*
10:9 eat it up; and it shall make thy belly *b*

Bitterly

Ruth 1:20 for the Almighty hath dealt very *b* with me
Is. 22:4 said I, Look away from me; I will weep *b*
Mt. 26:75 (Lk. 22:62) Peter. . went out, and wept *b*

Bittern

Is. 14:23 also make it a possession for the *b*
34:11 the cormorant and the *b* shall possess it

Bitterness

1 Sam. 1:10 and she was in *b* of soul, and prayed
15:32 Agag said, Surely the *b* of death is past
Job 21:25 and another dieth in the *b* of his soul
Prov. 14:10 the heart knoweth his own *b*
17:25 a foolish son is. . *b* to her that bare him
Lam. 3:15 he hath filled me with *b*, he hath made
Zech. 12:10 as one that is in *b* for his firstborn
Acts 8:23 perceive that thou art in the gall of *b*
Rom. 3:14 whose mouth is full of cursing and *b*
Eph. 4:31 let all *b*, and wrath. . be put away from
Heb. 12:15 any root of *b* springing up trouble you

Black

1 Kgs. 18:45 the heaven was *b* with clouds and wind
Song 1:5 I am *b*, but comely, O ye daughters of
5:11 his locks are bushy, and *b* as a raven
Jer. 8:21 I am *b*; astonishment hath taken hold on
Lam. 4:8 their visage is *b* than a coal; they are not
Zech. 6:2 and in the second chariot *b* horses
Mt. 5:36 thou canst not make one hair white or *b*
Rev. 6:5 opened the third seal. . and lo a *b* horse
6:12 and the sun became *b* as sackcloth of hair

Blackness

Joel 2:6 be much pained: all faces shall gather *b*
Nah. 2:10 and the faces of them all gather *b*
Heb. 12:18 nor unto *b*, and darkness, and tempest
Jude 13 is reserved the *b* of darkness for ever

Blade

Judg. 3:22 and the haft also went in after the *b*
Job 31:22 let mine arm fall from my shoulder *b*
Mt. 13:26 when the *b* was sprung up, and brought
Mk. 4:28 first the *b*, then the ear, after that the

Blame *See also* Accuse, Charge

Gen. 43:9 then let me bear the *b* for ever
2 Cor. 6:3 no offense. . that the ministry be not *b*
8:20 that no man should *b* us in this abundance
Gal. 2:11 I withstood him. . because he was to be *b*
Eph. 1:4 be holy and without *b* before him in love

Blameless *See also* Guiltless

Gen. 44:10 shall be my servant; and ye shall be *b*
Mt. 12:5 priests. . profane the sabbath, and are *b*?
Lk. 1:6 walking in all the. . ordinances of the Lord *b*
1 Cor. 1:8 *b* in the day of our Lord Jesus Christ
Phil. 2:15 may be *b* and harmless, the sons of God

Phil. 3:6 the righteousness which is in the law, *b*
1 Thes. 5:23 be preserved *b* unto the coming of our
1 Tim. 3:2 (Tit. 1:7) a bishop then must be *b*
  3:10 use the office of a deacon, being found *b*
  5:7 things give in charge, that they may be *b*
2 Pet. 3:14 found. . in peace, without spot, and *b*

Blaspheme

Lev. 24:11 the Israelitish woman's son *b* the name
  24:16 he that *b* the name of the LORD, he shall
2 Sam. 12:14 occasion to the enemies of the LORD to *b*
1 Kgs. 21:10 saying, Thou didst *b* God and the king
2 Kgs. 19:6 (Is. 37:6) of the king of Assyria have *b*
Ps. 74:10 shall the enemy *b* thy name for ever?
Is. 52:5 (Rom. 2:24) name continually every day is *b*
  65:7 burned incense. . and *b* me upon the hills
Ezek. 20:27 yet in this your fathers have *b* me
Mt. 9:3 scribes said within themselves, This man *b*
Mk. 3:29 (Lk. 12:10) shall *b* against the Holy Ghost
Jn. 10:36 say ye him. . Thou *b*; because I said
Acts 13:45 the Jews. . spake. . contradicting and *b*
  18:6 and when they opposed themselves, and *b*
  26:11 I punished. . oft. . and compelled them to *b*
1 Tim. 1:20 that they may learn not to *b*
  6:1 the name of God and his doctrine be not *b*
Tit. 2:5 obedient. . that the word of God be not *b*
Jas. 2:7 do not they *b* that worthy name
Rev. 13:6 to *b* his name, and his tabernacle, and
  16:9 men were scorched. . and *b* the name of God

Blasphemer

Acts 19:37 robbers. . nor yet *b* of your goddess
1 Tim. 1:13 who was before a *b*, and a persecutor
2 Tim. 3:2 men shall be. . proud, *b*, disobedient

Blasphemous

Acts 6:11 heard him speak *b* words against Moses

Blasphemously

Lk. 22:65 other things *b* spake they against him

Blasphemy

2 Kgs. 19:3 (Is. 37:3) this. . is a day. . of rebuke, and *b*
Ezek. 35:12 heard all thy *b* which thou hast spoken
Mt. 12:31 (Mk. 3:28) sin and *b* shall be forgiven
  15:19 (Mk. 7:22) out of the heart proceed. . *b*
  26:65 (Mk. 14:64) behold, now ye have heard his *b*
Mk. 2:7 (Lk. 5:21) why doth this man thus speak *b*?
Jn. 10:33 good work we stone thee not; but for *b*
Col. 3:8 also put off all these. . wrath, malice, *b*
Rev. 2:9 I know the *b* of them which say they are
  13:1 crowns, and upon his heads the name of *b*
  13:5 a mouth speaking great things and *b*
  17:3 a scarlet-colored beast, full of names of *b*

Blast

Gen. 41:6 seven thin ears and *b* with the east wind
Josh. 6:5 they make a long *b* with the ram's horn
2 Sam. 22:16 (Ps. 18:15) *b* of the breath of his nostrils
2 Kgs. 19:7 (Is. 37:7) I will send a *b* upon him
Job 4:9 by the *b* of God they perish, and by the
Is. 25:4 the *b* of the terrible ones is as a storm
Amos 4:9 I have smitten you with *b* and mildew

Blastus Acts 12:20

Blaze

Mk. 1:45 began. . to *b* abroad the matter, insomuch

Bleating

Judg. 5:16 abodest. . to hear the *b* of the flocks?
1 Sam. 15:14 what meaneth then this *b* of the sheep

Blemish *See also* Spot

Ex. 12:5 your lamb shall be without *b*, a male of
Lev. 1:3 let him offer a male without *b*
  21:17 that hath any *b*, let him not approach
  22:19 offer at your own will a male without *b*
Deut. 17:1 any bullock, or sheep, wherein is *b*
2 Sam. 14:25 to the crown. . there was no *b* in him
Dan. 1:4 children in whom was no *b*, but well-favored
Eph. 5:27 that it should be holy and without *b*
1 Pet. 1:19 of a lamb without *b* and without spot
2 Pet. 2:13 spots they are and b, sporting

Bless *See also* Praise

Gen. 1:22 and God *b* them, saying, Be fruitful
  1:28 God *b* them. . God said unto them, Be fruitful
  2:3 (Ex. 20:11) *b* the seventh day, and sanctified
  9:1 God *b* Noah and his sons, and said unto them
  12:2 and I will *b* thee, and make thy name great
  12:3 I will *b* them that *b* thee, and curse him
  12:3 (18:18; Gal. 3:8) in thee shall all. . be *b*
  17:16 I will *b* her, and give thee a son also
  17:20 and as for Ishmael. . Behold, I have *b* him
  22:17 (Heb. 6:14) that in blessing I will *b* thee
  22:18 (26:4; 28:14; Acts 3:25) in thy seed shall all
    the nations of the earth be *b*
  33:1 wherewith Moses the man of God *b*. . Israel
Josh. 17:14 forasmuch as the LORD hath *b* me hitherto
  22:6 so Joshua *b* them, and sent them away
Judg. 5:9 the governors of Israel. . *B* ye the LORD
  13:24 and the child grew, and the LORD *b* him
Ruth 2:4 and they answered him, The LORD *b* thee
2 Sam. 6:11 (1 Chr. 13:14) the LORD *b* Obed-edom
  6:20 (1 Chr. 16:43) returned to *b* his household
  7:29 (1 Chr. 17:27) please thee to *b* the house
1 Kgs. 2:45 Solomon shall be *b*, and the throne
  8:55 and *b* all the congregation of Israel
1 Chr. 4:10 oh that thou wouldest *b* me indeed
  29:10 wherefore David *b* the LORD before all
  29:20 David said to all. . Now *b* the LORD your God
2 Chr. 20:26 Berachah; for there they *b* the LORD
  30:27 priests the Levites arose and *b* the people
Neh. 8:6 and Ezra *b* the LORD, the great God
  9:5 stand up and *b* the LORD your God for ever
  24:1 and the LORD had *b* Abraham in all things
  24:48 and *b* the LORD God of my master Abraham
  25:11 God *b* his son Isaac; and Isaac dwelt by
  26:3 and I will be with thee, and will *b* thee
  27:4 that my soul may *b* thee before I die
  27:23 and he discerned him not. . so he *b* him
  28:1 Isaac called Jacob, and *b* him, and charged
  30:30 and the LORD hath *b* thee since my coming
  32:26 I will not let thee go, except thou *b* me
  39:5 *b* the Egyptian's house for Joseph's sake
  47:7 set him before Pharaoh: and Jacob *b* Pharaoh
  48:9 bring them. . unto me, and I will *b* them
  48:20 he blessed them. . saying, In thee shall Israel *b*
  49:25 Almighty, who shall *b* thee with blessings
Ex. 12:32 your flocks. . and be gone; and *b* me also
  20:24 I will come unto thee, and I will *b* thee
  23:25 and he shall *b* thy bread, and thy water
Lev. 9:22 Aaron lifted up his hand. . and *b* them
Num. 6:24 the LORD *b* thee, and keep thee
  22:6 for I wot that he whom thou *b* is blessed
  23:20 received commandment to *b*: and he hath *b*
  24:1 saw that it pleased the LORD to *b* Israel
Deut. 7:13 will love thee, and *b* thee, and multiply
  7:14 thou shalt be *b* above all people
  8:10 and art full, then thou shalt *b* the LORD
  15:4 the LORD shall greatly *b* thee in the land
  26:15 look down. . from heaven, and *b* thy people
  27:12 stand upon mount Gerizim to *b* the people
  29:19 he *b* himself in his heart, saying, I shall
  30:16 the LORD thy God shall *b* thee in the land

Job 1:10 thou hast *b* the work of his hands
31:20 if his loins have not *b* me, and if he were
42:12 so the LORD *b* the latter end of Job more
Ps. 5:12 for thou, LORD, wilt *b* the righteous
10:3 and *b* the covetous, whom the LORD abhorreth
16:7 will *b* the LORD, who hath given me counsel
29:11 the LORD will *b* his people with peace
34:1 I will *b* the LORD at all times: his praise
45:2 therefore God hath *b* thee for ever
62:4 *b* with their mouth, but they curse inwardly
63:4 thus will I *b* thee while I live
66:8 O *b* our God, ye people, and make the voice
67:1 God be merciful unto us, and *b* us
68:26 *b* ye God in the congregations, even the
100:4 be thankful unto him, and *b* his name
103:1 *b* the LORD, O my soul: and all that is
103:20 *b* the LORD, ye his angels, that excel
107:38 *b* them also, so that they are multiplied
115:13 he will *b* them that fear the LORD, both
128:5 the LORD shall *b* thee out of Zion
134:1 *b* ye the LORD, all ye servants of the LORD
135:19 *b* the LORD, O house of Israel, *b* the LORD
145:1 and I will *b* thy name for ever and ever
147:13 he hath *b* thy children within thee
Prov. 3:33 but he *b* the habitation of the just
22:9 he that hath a bountiful eye shall be *b*
30:11 a generation that. .doth not *b* their mother
Is. 51:2 for I called him alone, and *b* him
61:9 they are the seed which the LORD hath *b*
65:16 who *b* himself in the earth shall *b* himself
Jer. 4:2 and the nations shall *b* themselves in him
Dan. 2:19 then Daniel *b* the God of heaven
Hag. 2:19 from this day will I *b* you
Mt. 5:44 (Lk. 6:28) *b* them that curse you
14:19 (Mk. 6:41; Lk. 9:16) he *b*, and brake, and
26:26 (Mk. 14:22) Jesus took bread, and *b* it
Mk. 10:16 put his hands upon them, and *b* them
Lk. 2:28 took he him up in his arms, and *b* God
14:14 thou shalt be *b*; for they cannot recompense
24:50 and he lifted up his hands, and *b* them
24:53 in the temple, praising and *b* God
Acts 3:26 God. .sent him to *b* you, in turning away
Rom. 12:14 *b* them which persecute you: *b*, and
1 Cor. 4:12 being reviled, we *b*; being persecuted
10:16 the cup of blessing which we *b*, is it not
Eph. 1:3 hath *b* us with all spiritual blessings
Heb. 7:1 Melchisedec. .met Abraham. .and *b* him
11:20 by faith Isaac *b* Jacob and Esau concerning
Jas. 3:9 therewith *b* we God. .and therewith curse

Blessed *See also* Bless, Glad, Happy, Joyful

Gen.14:19 said, *B* be Abram of the most high God
24:27 *b* be the LORD God of my master Abraham
24:31 come in, thou *b* of the LORD; wherefore
27:29 and *b* be he that blesseth thee
30:13 happy. .for the daughters will call me *b*
Num. 24:9 *b* is he that blesseth thee, and cursed
Deut. 28:3 *b* shalt thou be in the city, and *b* shalt
Ruth 2:19 *b* be he that did take knowledge of thee
4:14 *b* be the LORD, which hath not left thee
1 Sam. 15:13 Saul said. .*B* be thou of the LORD
25:33 and *b* thy advice, and *b* be thou
26:25 *b* be thou, my son David: thou shalt both
2 Sam. 22:47 (Ps. 18:46) LORD liveth. .*b* be my rock
1 Kgs. 5:7 (2 Chr. 2:12) *b* be the LORD this day
1 Chr. 16:36 (Ps. 106:48) *b* be the LORD God
Ezra 7:27 *b* be the LORD God of our fathers
Job 1:21 taken away; *b* be the name of the LORD
Ps. 1:1 *b* is the man that walketh not in the
2:12 *b* are all they that put their trust in him
32:1 (Rom. 4:7) *b*. .whose transgression is forgiven

Ps. 33:12 *b* is the nation whose God is the LORD
34:8 is good: *b* is the man that trusteth in him
40:4 *b* is that man that maketh the LORD his trust
41:1 *b* is he that considereth the poor
65:4 *b* is the man whom thou choosest, and causest
68:19 *b* be the Lord, who daily loadeth us with
72:18 *b* be the LORD God, the God of Israel
84:4 *b* are they that dwell in thy house
89:52 *b* be the LORD for evermore. Amen, and
94:12 *b* is the man whom thou chastenest, O LORD
106:3 *b* are they that keep judgment, and he that
112:1 *b* is the man that feareth the LORD
118:26 (Mt. 21:9; Mk. 11:9; Lk. 19:38; Jn. 12:13)
b be he that cometh in the name of the LORD
119:1 *b* are the undefiled in the way, who walk
124:6 *b* be the LORD, who hath not given us as a
Prov. 8:32 for *b* are they that keep my ways
31:28 her children arise up, and call her *b*
Is. 19:25 *b* be Egypt my people, and Assyria
30:18 *b* are all they that wait for him
56:2 *b* is the man that doeth this, and the son
Jer. 17:7 *b* is the man that trusteth in the LORD
Dan. 3:28 *b* be the God of Shadrach, Meshach, and
12:12 *b* is he that waiteth, and cometh to the
Mal. 3:12 and all nations shall call you *b*: for ye
Mt. 5:3 (Lk. 6:20) *b* are the poor in spirit
11:6 (Lk. 7:23) *b*. .whosoever shall not be offended
13:16 (Lk. 10:23) *b* are your eyes, for they see
16:17 *b* art thou, Simon Bar-jona: for flesh and
24:46 (Lk. 12:43) *b* is that servant, whom his lord
25:34 ye *b* of my Father, inherit the kingdom
Mk. 14:61 art thou the Christ, the Son of the *B*?
Lk. 1:28 Lord is with thee; *b* art thou among women
1:42 *b* art thou. .and *b* is the fruit of thy womb
1:45 *b* is she that believed: for there shall be
1:48 henceforth all generations shall call me *b*
1:68 *b* be the Lord God of Israel; for he hath
11:28 *b* are they that hear the word of God, and
12:37 *b* are those servants, whom the Lord when
Jn. 20:29 *b* are they that have not seen, and yet
Acts 20:35 it is more *b* to give than to receive
Rom. 1:25 more than the Creator, who is *b* for ever
4:8 *b* is the man to whom the Lord will not impute
2 Cor. 1:3 (Eph. 1:3; 1 Pet. 1:3) *b* be God. .the Father
11:31 Jesus Christ, which is *b* for evermore
1 Tim. 6:15 *b* and only Potentate, the King of kings
Tit. 2:13 looking for that *b* hope, and the glorious
Jas. 1:12 *b* is the man that endureth temptation
Rev. 1:3 *b* is he that readeth, and they that hear
14:13 *b* are the dead which die in the Lord
16:15 *b* is he that watcheth, and keepeth his
19:9 *b* are they. .called unto the marriage supper
20:6 *b* and holy is he that hath part in the first
22:7 *b* is he that keepeth the sayings of the

Blessedness

Rom. 4:9 cometh this *b*. .upon the circumcision only
Gal. 4:15 where is then the *b* ye spake of? for I

Blessing

Gen. 12:2 I will bless thee. .and thou shalt be a *b*
22:17 (Heb. 6:14) that in *b* I will bless thee
27:12 I shall bring a curse upon me, and not a *b*
27:35 said, Thy brother. .hath taken away thy *b*
28:4 give thee the *b* of Abraham, to thee, and to
33:11 take, I pray thee, my *b* that is brought
39:5 the *b* of the LORD was upon all that he had
49:25 with *b* of heaven above, *b* of the deep
49:28 every one according to his *b* he blessed
Ex. 32:29 that he may bestow upon you a *b* this day
Lev. 25:21 then I will command my *b* upon you in
Deut. 11:26 before you this day a *b* and a curse
16:17 shall give. .according to the *b* of the LORD

Deut. 23:5 (Neh. 13:2) God turned the curse into a *b*
  28:2 and all these *b* shall come on thee
  28:8 command the *b* upon thee in thy storehouses
  30:19 set before you life and death, *b* and cursing
  33:1 and this is the *b*, wherewith Moses. . blessed
Josh. 8:34 read all the words. . the *b* and cursings
  15:19 (Judg. 1:15) give me a *b*; for thou hast given
2 Sam. 7:29 with thy *b* let the house. . be blessed
Neh. 9:5 name. . is exalted above all *b* and praise
Job 29:13 the *b* of him that was ready to perish
Ps. 3:8 unto the LORD: thy *b* is upon thy people
  21:3 thou preventest him with the *b* of goodness
  24:5 he shall receive the *b* from the LORD
  109:17 as he delighted not in *b*, so let it be
  129:8 the *b* of the LORD be upon you: we bless
  133:3 there the LORD commanded the *b*, even life
Prov. 10:6 *b* are upon the head of the just: but
  10:22 the *b* of the LORD, it maketh rich, and he
  11:11 by the *b* of the upright the city is exalted
  24:25 delight, and a good *b* shall come upon them
  28:20 a faithful man shall abound with *b*: but he
Is. 19:24 Israel be. . a *b* in the midst of the land
  44:3 I will pour. . my *b* upon thine offspring
  65:8 destroy it not; for a *b* is in it: so will I
Ezek. 34:26 season; there shall be showers of *b*
  44:30 he may cause the *b* to rest in thine house
Joel 2:14 knoweth if he will. . leave a *b* behind him
Zech. 8:13 so will I save you, and ye shall be a *b*
Mal. 2:2 I will curse your *b*. . because ye do not
  3:10 and pour you out a *b*, that there shall not
Rom. 15:29 in the fulness of the *b* of the gospel
1 Cor. 10:16 the cup of *b* which we bless, is it
Gal. 3:14 *b* of Abraham might come on the Gentiles
Eph. 1:3 with all spiritual *b* in heavenly places
Heb. 6:7 for the earth. . receiveth *b* from God
  12:17 when he would have inherited the *b*, he was
Jas. 3:10 the same mouth proceedeth *b* and cursing
1 Pet. 3:9 railing for railing: but contrariwise *b*
Rev. 5:13 *b*, and honor, and glory. . be unto him

Blind

Ex. 23:8 (Deut. 16:19) for the gift *b* the wise
Lev. 19:14 nor put a stumblingblock before the *b*
  22:22 *b*, or broken. . ye shall not offer these
Deut. 27:18 cursed be he that maketh the *b* to wander
1 Sam. 12:3 have I received any bribe to *b* mine eyes
Job 29:15 I was eyes to the *b*. . feet. . to the lame
Ps. 146:8 the LORD openeth the eyes of the *b*
Is. 29:18 eyes of the *b* shall see out of obscurity
  35:5 then the eyes of the *b* shall be opened
  42:7 to open the *b* eyes, to bring out the prisoners
  42:16 bring the *b* by a way that they knew not
  42:19 who is *b*, but my servant? or deaf, as my
  43:8 bring forth the *b* people that have eyes
  56:10 his watchmen are *b*: they are all ignorant
Zeph. 1:17 they shall walk like *b* men, because
Mal. 1:8 offer the *b* for sacrifice, is it not evil?
Mt. 9:27 Jesus departed. . two *b* men followed him
  11:5 (Lk. 7:22) *b* receive their sight, and the lame
  12:22 that the *b* and dumb both spake and saw
  15:14 be *b* leaders of the *b*. . if the *b* lead the *b*
  15:31 saw. . the lame to walk, and the *b* to see
  20:30 behold, two *b* men sitting by the wayside
  23:16 woe unto you, ye *b* guides, which say
Mk. 8:22 bring a *b* man unto him, and besought him
  10:46 Lk. 18:35) *b* Bartimeus. . sat by the highway
Lk. 4:18 to preach. . recovering of sight to the *b*
  6:39 can the *b* lead the *b*? shall they not both
  14:13 call the poor, the maimed, the lame, the *b*
Jn. 9:1 he saw a man which was *b* from his birth
  9:25 I know, that, whereas I was *b*, now I see
  9:39 and that they which see might be made *b*
  9:41 if ye were *b*, ye should have no sin: but

Jn. 12:40 *b* their eyes, and hardened their heart
Acts 13:11 thou shalt be *b*, not seeing the sun for
Rom. 2:19 that thou thyself art a guide of the *b*
  11:7 hath obtained it, and the rest were *b*
2 Cor. 3:14 their minds were *b*: for until this day
  4:4 the god of this world hath *b* the minds of
2 Pet. 1:9 but he that lacketh these things is *b*
1 Jn. 2:11 because that darkness hath *b* his eyes
Rev. 3:17 that thou art. . poor, and, *b*, and naked

Blindfold

Lk. 22:64 when they had *b* him, they struck him

Blindness *See also* Darkness, Evil, Ignorance

Gen. 19:11 they smote the men. . at the door. . with *b*
Deut. 28:28 shall smite thee with madness, and *b*
2 Kgs. 6:18 smite this people, I pray thee, with *b*
Zech. 12:4 smite every horse of the people with *b*
Rom. 11:25 that *b* in part is happened to Israel
Eph. 4:18 because of the *b* of their heart

Blood *See also* Atonement, Life

Gen. 4:10 voice of thy brother's *b* crieth unto me
  9:4 flesh with. . the *b* thereof, shall ye not eat
  9:6 whoso sheddeth man's *b*, by man shall his *b* be
  37:22 shed no *b*, but cast him into this pit
  37:31 killed a kid. . and dipped the coat in the *b*
Ex. 4:9 water. . shall become *b* upon the dry land
  7:20 the waters. . in the river were turned to *b*
  12:7 take of the *b*, and strike it on the two
  12:13 and when I see the *b*, I will pass over you
  22:2 a thief. . there shall no *b* be shed for him
  23:18 (34:25) not offer the *b* of my sacrifice with
  24:8 took the *b*, and sprinkled it on the people
  29:12 (Lev. 8:15) take of the *b* of the bullock
  29:16 (Lev. 1:5; 8:19) take his *b*, and sprinkle it
  30:10 the *b* of the sin offering of atonements
  34:25 thou shalt not offer the *b*. . with leaven
Lev. 3:17 statute. . that ye eat neither fat nor *b*
  4:7 put. . of the *b* upon the horns of the altar
  7:26 ye shall eat no manner of *b*, whether it be
  12:4 then continue in the *b* of her purifying
  14:14 some of the *b* of the trespass offering
  16:14 *b* of the bullock. . upon the mercy seat
  16:15 his *b* within the veil, and do with that *b*
  17:4 *b* shall be imputed unto that man; he hath
  17:11 for it is the *b* that maketh an atonement
  17:14 for the life of all flesh is the *b* thereof
  19:26 ye shall not eat any thing with the *b*
  20:9 he hath cursed. . his *b* shall be upon him
  20:18 she hath uncovered the fountain of her *b*
Num. 35:19 the revenger of *b* himself shall slay
  35:33 not pollute. . for *b* it defileth the land
Deut. 12:16 only ye shall not eat the *b*; ye shall
  19:10 that innocent *b* be not shed in thy land
  21:9 put away the guilt of innocent *b* from among
  32:43 for he will avenge the *b* of his servants
Josh. 2:19 his *b* shall be upon his head, and we
  20:3 shall be your refuge from the avenger of *b*
1 Sam. 14:32 the people did eat them with the *b*
  19:5 wherefore wilt thou sin against innocent *b*
2 Sam. 1:16 thy *b* be upon thy head; for thy mouth
  16:8 LORD hath returned upon thee all the *b* of
  23:17 (1 Chr. 11:19) *b* of the men. . in jeopardy
1 Kgs. 2:32 shall return his *b* upon his own head
  21:19 place where dogs licked the *b* of Naboth
2 Kgs. 9:7 that I may avenge the *b* of my servants
  21:16 Manasseh shed innocent *b* very much, till
1 Chr. 22:8 thou hast shed *b*. . thou shalt not build
  28:3 hast been a man of war, and hast shed *b*
2 Chr. 29:24 they made reconciliation with their *b*

Job 16:18 O earth, cover not thou my *b*, and let my
Ps. 16:4 drink offerings of *b* will I not offer
  30:9 what profit is there in my *b*, when I go
  72:14 and precious shall their *b* be in his sight
  78:44 and had turned their rivers into *b*
  79:3 have they shed like water round about
  105:29 he turned their waters into *b*, and slew
  106:38 shed innocent *b*, even the *b* of their sons
Prov. 1:11 come with us, let us lay wait for *b*
  6:17 proud look. . and hands that shed innocent *b*
Is. 1:11 I delight not in the *b* of bullocks, or of
  1:15 I will not hear: your hands are full of *b*
  4:4 shall have purged the *b* of Jerusalem from
  9:5 confused noise, and garments rolled in *b*
  33:15 that stoppeth his ears from hearing of *b*
  49:26 and they shall be drunken with their own *b*
  59:3 for your hands are defiled with *b*, and your
  59:7 (Rom. 3:15) haste to shed innocent *b*
  63:3 their *b* shall be sprinkled upon my garments
  66:3 an oblation, as if he offered swine's *b*
Jer. 2:34 the *b* of the souls of the poor innocents
  19:4 filled this place with the *b* of innocents
Lam. 4:13 have shed the *b* of the just in the midst
Ezek. 3:18 (33:8) his *b* will I require at thine hand
  5:17 pestilence and *b* shall pass through thee
  9:9 the land is full of *b*, and the city full of
  16:6 saw thee polluted in thine own *b*, I said
  18:13 shall surely die; his *b* shall be upon him
  22:4 become guilty in thy *b* that thou hast shed
  33:4 him away, his *b* shall be upon his own head
  33:5 took not warning; his *b* shall be upon him
  33:25 ye eat with the *b*. . and shed *b*: and shall
  35:5 hast shed the *b* of the children of Israel
  39:17 gather. . that ye may eat flesh, and drink *b*
  44:7 when ye offer my bread, the fat and the *b*
  45:19 shall take of the *b* of the sin offering
Hos. 1:4 avenge the *b* of Jezreel upon the house
Joel 2:31 (Acts 2:20) into darkness. . the moon into *b*
Jon. 1:14 and lay not upon us innocent *b*: for thou
Mic. 3:10 they build up Zion with *b*, and Jerusalem
Hab. 2:12 woe to him that buildeth a town with *b*
Zeph. 1:17 their *b* shall be poured out as dust
Zech. 9:11 by the *b* of thy covenant I have sent
Mt. 9:20 (Mk. 5:25; Lk. 8:43) with an issue of *b*
  16:17 flesh and *b* hath not revealed it unto thee
  23:30 partakers with them in the *b* of the prophets
  23:35 (Lk. 11:51) of. . Abel. . the *b* of Zacharias
  26:28 (Mk. 14:24; Lk. 22:20; 1 Cor. 11:25) this is
    my *b* of the new testament
  27:4 in that I have betrayed the innocent *b*
  27:6 is not lawful. . because it is the price of *b*
  27:24 I am innocent of the *b* of this just person
  27:25 said, His *b* be on us, and on our children
Lk. 13:1 *b* Pilate had mingled with their sacrifices
  22:44 his sweat was as it were great drops of *b*
Jn. 1:13 born, not of *b*, nor of the will of the flesh
  6:53 except ye. . drink his *b*, ye have no life
  6:55 is meat indeed, and my *b* is drink indeed
  19:34 and forthwith came there out *b* and water
Acts 1:19 Aceldama, that is to say, The field of *b*
  5:28 and intend to bring this man's *b* upon us
  15:20 (15:29; 21:25) things strangled, and from *b*
  17:26 and hath made of one *b* all nations of men
  18:6 your *b* be upon your own heads; I am clean
  20:26 that I am pure from the *b* of all men
  20:28 which he hath purchased with his own *b*
Rom. 3:25 to be a propitiation through faith in his *b*
  5:9 being now justified by his *b*, we shall be
1 Cor. 10:16 not the communion of the *b* of Christ?
  11:27 be guilty of the body and *b* of the Lord
  15:50 flesh and *b* cannot inherit the kingdom of
Gal. 1:16 I conferred not with flesh and *b*
Eph. 1:7 (Col. 1:14) have redemption through his *b*

Eph. 2:13 far off are made nigh by the *b* of Christ
  6:12 for we wrestle not against flesh and *b*, but
Col. 1:20 made peace through the *b* of his cross
Heb. 2:14 children are partakers of flesh and *b*
  9:7 priest alone once every year, not without *b*
  9:12 the *b* of goats and calves, but by his own *b*
  9:22 and without shedding of *b* is no remission
  10:4 is not possible that the *b* of bulls and of
  10:19 enter into the holiest by the *b* of Jesus
  10:29 hath counted the *b* of the covenant. . unholy
  12:4 ye have not yet resisted unto *b*, striving
  12:24 and to the *b* of sprinkling, that speaketh
  13:12 might sanctify the people with his own *b*
  13:20 through the *b* of the everlasting covenant
1 Pet. 1:2 unto obedience and sprinkling of the *b*
  1:19 with the precious *b* of Christ, as of a lamb
1 Jn. 1:7 the *b* of Jesus Christ his Son cleanseth
  5:6 that came by water and *b*, even Jesus Christ
Rev. 1:5 washed us from our sins in his own *b*
  5:9 redeemed us to God by thy *b* out of every
  6:12 the sun became black. . the moon became as *b*
  7:14 washed their robes. . in the *b* of the Lamb
  8:8 and the third part of the sea became *b*
  11:6 have power over waters to turn them to *b*
  12:11 they overcame him by the *b* of the Lamb
  16:3 the sea. . became as the *b* of a dead man
  16:4 rivers and fountains of waters. . became *b*
  16:6 shed the *b* of saints. . given them *b* to drink
  17:6 the woman drunken with the *b* of the saints
  19:2 avenged the *b* of his servants at her hand

Bloodguiltiness

Ps. 51:14 deliver me from *b*, O God

Blossom

Gen. 40:10 though it budded, and her *b* shot forth
Num. 17:8 rod of Aaron. . was budded. . bloomed *b*
Is. 27:6 Israel shall *b* and bud, and fill the face
  35:1 the desert shall rejoice, and *b* as the rose
Ezek. 7:10 the rod hath *b*, pride hath budded
Hab. 3:17 although the fig tree shall not *b*

Blot

Ex. 32:32 if not, *b* me, I pray thee, out of thy book
Deut. 9:14 and *b* out their name from under heaven
  25:19 thou shalt *b* out the remembrance of Amalek
  29:20 LORD shall *b* out his name from under heaven
2 Kgs. 14:27 not. . he would *b* out the name of Israel
Job 31:7 and if any *b* hath cleaved to mine hands
Ps. 51:1 tender mercies *b* out my transgressions
  51:9 from my sins, and *b* out all mine iniquities
  69:28 them he *b* out of the book of the living
Prov. 9:7 rebuketh a wicked man getteth himself a *b*
Is. 43:25 I, am he that *b* out thy transgressions
  44:22 *b* out, as a thick cloud, thy transgressions
Jer. 18:23 neither *b* out their sin from thy sight
Acts 3:19 converted, that your sins may be *b* out
Col. 2:14 *b* out the handwriting of ordinances that
Rev. 3:5 I will not *b* out his name out of the book

Blow (Blew, Blown)

Ex. 15:10 thou didst *b* with thy wind, the sea
Num. 10:5 when ye *b* an alarm, then the camps
  10:9 if ye go to war. . then ye shall *b* an alarm
Josh. 6:9 the priests that *b* with the trumpets
Ps. 78:26 caused an east wind to *b* in the heaven
  147:18 he causeth his wind to *b*, and the waters
Song 4:16 awake, O north wind. . *b* upon my garden
Is. 27:13 that the great trumpet shall be *b*
  40:7 because the spirit of the LORD *b* upon it
  40:24 also *b* upon them, and they shall wither
Hag. 1:9 when ye brought it home, I did *b* upon it
Mt. 7:25 floods came, and the winds *b*, and beat

Jn. 3:8 wind *b* where it listeth, and thou hearest
Rev. 7:1 that the wind should not *b* on the earth

Blueness

Prov. 20:30 the *b* of a wound cleanseth away evil

Blush

Ezra 9:6 I am ashamed and *b* to lift up my face
Jer. 6:15 (8:12) ashamed, neither could they *b*

Boanerges Mk. 3:17

Boar

Ps. 80:13 the *b* out of the wood doth waste it

Board

Ex. 27:8 (38:7) hollow with *b* shalt thou make it
Acts 27:44 some on *b*, and some on broken pieces

Boast *See also* Glory, Vaunt

1 Kgs. 20:11 girdeth on his harness *b* himself as
2 Chr. 25:19 and thine heart lifteth thee up to *b*
Ps. 10:3 for the wicked *b* of his heart's desire
34:2 my soul shall make her *b* in the LORD
44:8 in God we *b* all the day long, and praise
49:6 *b* themselves in the multitude of their riches
52:1 why *b* thou thyself in mischief, O mighty
94:4 all the workers of iniquity *b* themselves?
Prov. 20:14 but when he is gone his way, then he *b*
25:14 whoso *b* himself of a false gift is like
27:1 *b* not thyself of tomorrow . . thou knowest not
Is. 10:15 axe *b* itself against him that heweth
Acts 5:36 rose up Theudas, *b* himself to be somebody
Rom. 2:17 restest in the law, and makest thy *b* of God
2:23 thou that makest thy *b* of the law, through
11:18 *b* not against the branches. But if thou *b*
2 Cor. 10:8 though I should *b* somewhat more of our
10:16 not to *b* in another man's line of things
11:16 as a fool . . that I may *b* myself a little
Eph. 2:9 not of works, lest any man should *b*
Jas. 3:5 tongue is a little member, and *b* great things

Boaster

Rom. 1:30 haters of God, despiteful, proud, *b*
2 Tim. 3:2 for men shall be . . covetous, *b*, proud

Boasting

Rom. 3:27 where is *b* then? It is excluded
2 Cor. 7:14 our *b*, which I made before Titus, is
8:24 show ye . . the proof . . of our *b* on your behalf
9:3 lest our *b* of you should be in vain in this
11:10 no man shall stop me of this *b* in the
11:17 as it were foolishly, in this confidence of *b*
Jas. 4:16 but now ye rejoice in your *b*

Boat *See also* Ship

Jn. 6:22 went not with his disciples into the *b*
Acts 27:16 we had much work to come by the *b*
27:30 when they had let down the *b* into the sea

Boaz Ruth 2:1–4:13

Bochim Judg. 2:1–5

Bodily

Lk. 3:22 descended in a *b* shape like a dove upon
2 Cor. 10:10 powerful; but his *b* presence is weak
Col. 2:9 dwelleth all the fulness of the Godhead *b*
1 Tim. 4:8 for *b* exercise profiteth little: but

Body *See also* Flesh

Gen. 47:18 aught left . . but our *b*, and our lands
Ex. 24:10 the *b* of heaven in his clearness
Lev. 21:11 neither shall he go in to any dead *b*

Num. 9:6 who were defiled by the dead *b* of a man
19:11 he that toucheth the dead *b* of any man
Deut. 21:23 (Jn. 19:31) *b* shall not remain . . upon the
28:4 blessed shall be the fruit of thy *b*
1 Sam. 31:12 the *b* of Saul, and the *b* of his sons
2 Kgs. 8:5 how he had restored a dead *b* to life
Neh. 9:37 they have dominion over our *b*, and over
Job 13:12 are like unto ashes, your *b* to *b* of clay
19:26 though . . worms destroy this *b*, yet in my
Ps. 79:2 dead *b* of thy servants have they given to
132:11 of the fruit of thy *b*. . set upon thy throne
Prov. 5:11 when thy flesh and thy *b* are consumed
Is. 10:18 of his fruitful field, both soul and *b*
26:19 together with my dead *b* shall they arise
51:23 thou hast laid thy *b* as the ground, and as
Jer. 33:5 is to fill them with the dead *b* of men
34:20 dead *b* shall be for meat unto the fowls
36:30 his dead *b* shall be cast out in the day
Ezek. 1:11 two wings of every one . . covered their *b*
10:12 their whole *b* . . full of eyes round about
Dan. 3:27 men, upon whose *b* the fire had no power
4:33 (5:21) his *b* was wet with the dew of heaven
10:6 his *b* also was like the beryl, and his face
Amos 8:3 there shall be many dead *b* in every place
Mic. 6:7 the fruit of my *b* for the sin of my soul
Hag. 2:13 if one that is unclean by a dead *b* touch
Mt. 5:29 that thy whole *b* should be cast into hell
6:22 (Lk. 11:34) the light of the *b* is the eye
6:25 (Lk. 12:22) for your *b*, what ye shall put on
10:28 (Lk. 12:4) fear not them which kill the *b*
14:12 and his disciples came, and took up the *b*
26:12 (Mk. 14:8) ointment on my *b* . . for my burial
26:26 (Mk. 14:22; Lk. 22:19; 1 Cor. 11:24) and said,
    Take, eat, this is my *b*
27:52 and many *b* of the saints which slept arose
27:58 (Mk. 15:43; Lk. 23:52; Jn. 19:38) he went to
    Pilate, and begged the *b* of Jesus
Lk. 17:37 wheresoever the *b* is . . will the eagles be
24:3 and found not the *b* of the Lord Jesus
Jn 2:21 but he spake of the temple of his *b*
19:31 that the *b* should not remain upon the cross
20:12 two angels . . where the *b* of Jesus had lain
Acts 9:40 Peter . . turning him to the *b* said, Tabitha
19:12 that from his *b* were brought unto the sick
Rom. 1:24 gave them up . . to dishonor their own *b*
4:19 he considered not his own *b* now dead, when
6:6 that the *b* of sin might be destroyed
6:12 let not sin therefore reign in your mortal *b*
7:4 become dead to the law by the *b* of Christ
7:24 shall deliver me from the *b* of this death?
8:10 Christ be in you, the *b* is dead because of sin
8:11 also quicken your mortal *b* by his Spirit
8:13 mortify the deeds of the *b*, ye shall live
8:23 for the adoption . . the redemption of our *b*
12:1 that ye present your *b* a living sacrifice
12:5 (1 Cor. 10:17) being many, are one *b* in Christ
1 Cor. 5:3 as absent in *b*, but present in spirit
6:13 *b* is . . for the Lord; and the Lord for the *b*
6:15 not that your *b* are the members of Christ?
6:18 fornication sinneth against his own *b*
6:19 that your *b* is the temple of the Holy Ghost
6:20 a price: therefore glorify God in your *b*
7:4 the wife hath not power of her own *b*, but
7:34 she may be holy both in *b* and in spirit
9:27 keep under my *b*, and bring it into subjection
10:16 is it not the communion of the *b* of Christ?
10:17 for we being many are one bread, and one *b*
11:27 be guilty of the *b* and blood of the Lord
12:12 for as the *b* is one, and hath many members
12:27 now ye are the *b* of Christ, and members
13:3 though I give my *b* to be burned, and have
15:35 raised up? and with what *b* do they come
15:40 are also celestial *b*, and *b* terrestrial

1 Cor. 15:44 is sown a natural *b* . . raised a spiritual *b*
2 Cor. 4:10 bearing about in the *b* the dying of
    5:6 are at home in the *b* . . absent from the Lord
    5:10 may receive the things done in his *b*
    12:3 whether in the *b*, or out of the *b*, I cannot
Gal. 6:17 bear in my *b* the marks of the Lord Jesus
Eph. 1:23 which is his *b*, the fulness of him that
    2:16 reconcile both unto God in one *b* by the cross
    3:6 should be fellow heirs, and of the same *b*
    4:4 there is one *b*, and one Spirit, even as ye
    4:16 maketh increase of the *b* unto the edifying
    5:23 as Christ. . and he is the saviour of the *b*
    5:28 men to love their wives as their own *b*
Phil. 1:20 also Christ shall be magnified in my *b*
    3:21 change our vile *b* . . like unto his glorious *b*
Col. 1:18 and he is the head of the *b*, the church
    2:11 putting off the *b* of the sins of the flesh
    2:23 in. . humility, and neglecting of the *b*
1 Thes. 5:23 spirit and soul and *b* be preserved
Heb. 10:5 but a *b* hast thou prepared me
    10:10 through the offering of the *b* of Jesus
    10:22 and our *b* washed with pure water
Jas. 2:26 for as the *b* without the spirit is dead
    3:2 perfect man. . able also to bridle the whole *b*
1 Pet. 2:24 bare our sins in his own *b* on the tree
Jude 9 the devil he disputed about the *b* of Moses
Rev. 11:8 and their dead *b* shall lie in the street

Boil

Ex. 9:9 shall be a *b* breaking forth with blains
2 Kgs. 20:7 (Is. 38:21) on the *b*, and he recovered
Job 2:7 so went Satan. . and smote Job with sore *b*
Ezek. 24:5 and make it *b* well, and let them seethe

Bold

Prov. 28:1 but the righteous are *b* as a lion
Acts 13:46 then Paul and Barnabas waxed *b*
2 Cor. 10:1 but being absent am *b* toward you
    11:21 whereinsoever any is *b* . . I am *b* also
Phil. 1:14 are much more *b* to speak the word
1 Thes. 2:2 were *b* in our God to speak unto you
Phlm. 8 might be much *b* in Christ to enjoin thee

Boldly

Gen. 34:25 Simeon and Levi. . came upon the city *b*
Jn. 7:26 lo, he speaketh *b*, and they say nothing
Acts 9:27 and how he had preached *b* at Damascus
    14:3 therefore abode they speaking *b* in the Lord
    18:26 and he began to speak *b* in the synagogue
    19:8 and spake *b* for the space of three months
Rom. 15:15 I have written the more *b* unto you
Heb. 4:16 let us. . come *b* unto the throne of grace
    13:6 so that we may *b* say, The Lord is my helper

Boldness

Eccl. 8:1 and the *b* of his face shall be changed
Acts 4:13 when they saw the *b* of Peter and John
    4:31 and they spake the word of God with *b*
2 Cor. 7:4 great is my *b* of speech toward you
Eph. 3:12 we have *b* and access with confidence
1 Tim. 3:13 good degree, and great *b* in the faith
Heb. 10:19 having. . *b* to enter into the holiest
1 Jn. 4:17 we may have *b* in the day of judgment

Bond *See also* Bondage, Yoke

Num. 30:2 swear an oath to bind his soul with a *b*
Ps. 116:16 I am thy servant. . thou hast loosed my *b*
Jer. 5:5 altogether broken the yoke, and burst the *b*
Ezek. 20:37 bring you into the *b* of the covenant
Lk. 13:16 loosed from this *b* on the sabbath day?
Acts 8:23 that thou art. . in the *b* of iniquity
    20:23 saying that *b* and afflictions abide me
    23:29 laid to his charge worthy of death or of *b*
    26:29 altogether such as I am, except these *b*

1 Cor. 12:13 Jews or Gentiles, whether. . *b* or free
Gal. 3:28 neither Jew nor Greek. . neither *b* nor free
Eph. 4:3 the unity of the Spirit in the *b* of peace
    6:20 for which I am an ambassador in *b*
Phil. 1:13 so that my *b* in Christ are manifest
    1:16 preach. . supposing to add affliction to my *b*
Col. 3:14 charity, which is the *b* of perfectness
    4:3 mystery of Christ, for which I am also in *b*
    4:18 remember my *b*. Grace be with you. Amen
2 Tim. 2:9 wherein I suffer trouble. . even unto *b*
Phlm. 13 ministered unto me in the *b* of the gospel
Heb. 10:34 for ye had compassion of me in my *b*
    11:36 others had trial. . of *b* and imprisonment
    13:3 remember them that are in *b*, as bound with

Bondage *See also* Captivity, Yoke

Ex. 1:14 they made their lives bitter with hard *b*
    2:23 children of Israel sighed by reason of the *b*
    6:5 of Israel, whom the Egyptians keep in *b*
    13:14 out from Egypt, from the house of *b*
    20:2 (Deut. 5:6) brought. . out of the house of *b*
Jn. 8:33 were never in *b* to any man: how sayest
Acts 7:6 and that they should bring them into *b*
Rom. 8:15 ye have not received the spirit of *b*
    8:21 shall be delivered from the *b* of corruption
Gal. 2:4 spy out. . that they might bring us into *b*
    4:3 were in *b* under the elements of the world
    4:9 whereunto ye desire again to be in *b*
    5:1 be not entangled again with the yoke of *b*
Heb. 2:15 were all their lifetime subject to *b*
2 Pet. 2:19 overcome, of the same is he brought in *b*

Bondmaid

Gal. 4:22 Abraham had two sons, the one by a *b*

Bondman

Gen. 43:18 and take us for *b*, and our asses
Deut. 6:21 we were Pharaoh's *b* in Egypt
    7:8 and redeemed you out of the house of *b*
    15:15 remember that thou wast a *b* in. . Egypt
1 Kgs. 9:22 but of. . Israel did Solomon make no *b*
Ezra 9:9 we were *b*; yet our God hath not forsaken

Bondwoman

Gen. 21:10 (Gal. 4:30) cast out this *b* and her son

Bone

Gen. 2:23 and Adam said, This is now *b* of my *b*
    50:25 (Ex. 13:19) shall carry up my *b* from hence
Ex. 12:46 (Num. 9:12; Jn. 19:36) neither. . break a *b*
    13:19 and Moses took the *b* of Joseph with him
1 Kgs. 13:2 and men's *b* shall be burnt upon thee
2 Kgs. 13:21 touched the *b* of Elisha, he revived
    23:14 and filled their places with the *b* of men
Job 19:20 my *b* cleaveth to my skin and to my flesh
    20:11 his *b* are full of the sin of his youth
    33:21 and his *b* that were not seen stick out
    40:18 his *b* are as strong pieces of brass; his *b*
Ps. 22:17 I may tell all my *b*: they look and stare
    31:10 my strength faileth. . my *b* are consumed
    34:20 (Jn. 19:36) all his *b*: not one. . is broken
    51:8 the *b* which thou hast broken may rejoice
    53:5 hath scattered the *b* of him that encampeth
    141:7 our *b* are scattered at the grave's mouth
Prov. 14:30 but envy the rottenness of the *b*
Jer. 8:1 bring out the *b* of the kings of Judah
Ezek. 6:5 scatter your *b* round about your altars
    37:1 the midst of the valley which was full of *b*
    37:7 shaking, and the *b* came together, *b* to his *b*
Zeph. 3:3 they gnaw not the *b* till the morrow
Mt. 23:27 but are within full of dead men's *b*
Lk. 24:39 a spirit hath not flesh and *b*, as ye see
Eph. 5:30 of his body, of his flesh, and of his *b*
Heb. 11:22 and gave commandment concerning his *b*

Bonnet

Ex. 28:40 *b* shalt thou make for them, for glory
  39:28 a mitre. . and goodly *b* of fine linen
Is. 3:20 the *b*, and the ornaments of the legs
Ezek. 44:18 shall have linen *b* upon their heads

Book

Gen. 5:1 this is the *b* of the generations of Adam
Ex. 17:14 Moses, Write this for a memorial in a *b*
  24:7 and he took the *b* of the covenant, and read
  32:32 if not, blot me, I pray thee, out of thy *b*
Num. 5:23 priest shall write these curses in a *b*
  21:14 is said in the *b* of the wars of the LORD
Deut. 17:18 write him a copy of this law in a *b*
  28:58 to do all the words. . written in this *b*
  29:20 all the curses that are written in this *b*
  30:10 statutes. . written in this *b* of the law
  31:26 this *b* of the law, and put it in. . the ark
Josh. 1:8 this *b* of the law shall not depart out
  8:31 it is written in the *b* of the law of Moses
  23:6 do all that is written in the *b* of the law
  24:26 Joshua wrote these words in the *b*
1 Sam. 10:25 Samuel. . wrote it in a *b*, and laid it
2 Kgs. 14:6 written in the *b* of the law of Moses
  22:8 (2 Chr. 34:15) found the *b* of the law
  22:13 (2 Chr. 34:21) concerning the words of this *b*
  23:2 (2 Chr. 34:30) read. . all the words of the *b*
2 Chr. 17:9 the *b* of the law of the LORD with them
Ezra 4:15 search may be made in the *b* of the records
Neh. 8:3 people were attentive unto the *b* of the law
  9:3 they stood up. . and read in the *b* of the law
Job 19:23 oh that my words. . were printed in a *b*!
  31:35 and that mine adversary had written a *b*
Ps. 40:7 (Heb. 10:7) in the volume of the *b* it is
  69:28 be blotted out of the *b* of the living
  139:16 in thy *b* all my members were written
Eccl. 12:12 of making many *b* there is no end
Is. 29:11 as the words of a *b* that is sealed
  29:18 shall the deaf hear the words of the *b*
  30:8 and note it in a *b*. . for the time to come
  34:16 seek ye out of the *b* of the LORD, and read
Jer. 25:13 this *b*, which Jeremiah hath prophesied
  30:2 all the words that I have spoken. . in a *b*
  32:12 that subscribed the *b* of the purchase
  36:2 take thee a roll of a *b*, and write therein
  36:10 read Baruch in the *b* the words of Jeremiah
  36:32 words of the *b* which Jehoiakim. . had burned
  51:60 so Jeremiah wrote in a *b* all the evil that
Ezek. 2:9 and lo, a roll of a *b* was therein
Dan. 7:10 (Rev. 20:12) and the *b* were opened
  9:2 understood by *b* the number of the years
  12:1 that shall be found written in the *b*
Mal. 3:16 *b* of remembrance was written before him
Mt. 1:1 the *b* of the generation of Jesus Christ
Lk. 4:17 unto him the *b* of the prophet Esaias
Jn. 20:30 many other signs. . not written in this *b*
  21:25 the world itself could not contain the *b*
Acts 19:19 brought their *b* together, and burned them
Gal. 3:10 in all things which are written in the *b*
Phil. 4:3 whose names are in the *b* of life
2 Tim. 4:13 the *b*, but especially the parchments
Heb. 9:19 sprinkled both the *b* and all the people
Rev. 1:11 what thou seest, write in a *b*, and send
  3:5 not blot out his name out of the *b* of life
  5:1 saw. . a *b* written within and on the back side
  5:2 who is worthy to open the *b*, and to loose
  10:2 he had in his hand a little *b* open
  13:8 (17:8; 20:15) not written in the *b* of life
  20:12 and another *b* was opened. . the *b* of life
  21:27 which are written in the Lamb's *b* of life
  22:7 the sayings of the prophecy of this *b*
  22:19 take away his part out of the *b* of life

Booth

Gen. 33:17 to Succoth. . and made *b* for his cattle
Lev. 23:42 ye shall dwell in *b* seven days
Neh. 8:14 the children of Israel should dwell in *b*
Job 27:18 his house. . as a *b* that the keeper maketh
Jon. 4:5 so Jonah. . made him a *b*, and sat under it

Border

Ex. 34:24 cast out the nations. . and enlarge thy *b*
Num. 34:4 *b* shall turn from the south to the ascent
Deut. 12:20 when the LORD. . shall enlarge thy *b*
Josh. 22:10 when they came unto the *b* of Jordan
2 Sam. 8:14 he went to recover his *b*
1 Kgs. 7:29 on the *b*. . between the ledges were lions
2 Kgs. 16:17 king Ahaz cut off the *b* of the bases
  19:23 (Is. 37:24) enter into the lodgings of his *b*
Ps. 74:17 thou hast set all the *b* of the earth
  78:54 brought them to the *b* of his sanctuary
  147:14 he maketh peace in thy *b*, and filleth
Song 1:11 make thee *b* of gold with studs of silver
Is. 37:24 I will enter into the height of his *b*
Jer. 31:17 children shall come again to their own *b*
Ezek. 47:13 this shall be the *b*, whereby ye shall
Amos 6:2 or their *b* greater than your *b*?
Mk. 6:56 (Lk. 8:44) touch. . the *b* of his garment

Born

Gen. 17:17 child be *b* unto him that is a hundred
Ex. 1:22 every son that is *b* ye shall cast into
Josh. 5:5 the people that were *b* in the wilderness
2 Sam. 12:14 child. . *b* unto thee shall surely die
1 Kgs. 13:2 a child shall be *b* unto the house
Job 3:3 let the day perish wherein I was *b*
  5:7 yet man is *b* unto trouble, as the sparks fly
  14:1 man that is *b* of a woman is of few days
  25:4 how can he be clean that is *b* of a woman?
Ps. 22:31 declare. . unto a people that shall be *b*
  58:3 the wicked. . go astray as soon as they be *b*
  87:5 be said, This and that man was *b* in her
Prov. 17:17 and a brother is *b* for adversity
Eccl. 3:2 a time to be *b*, and a time to die
Is. 9:6 unto us a child is *b*, unto us a son is
  66:8 in one day? or shall a nation be *b* at once?
Mt. 1:16 of whom was *b* Jesus, who is called Christ
  2:1 now when Jesus was *b* in Bethlehem of Judea
  2:2 where is he that is *b* King of the Jews?
  2:4 he demanded of them where Christ should be *b*
  11:11 (Lk. 7:28) among them that are *b* of women
  26:24 (Mk. 14:21) that man if he had not been *b*
Lk. 2:11 unto you is *b* this day in the city of David
Jn. 1:13 were *b*, not of blood, nor of the will of
  3:3 (3:7) except a man be *b* again, he cannot see
  3:6 *b* of the flesh is flesh. . *b* of the Spirit is
  16:21 for joy that a man is *b* into the world
1 Cor. 15:8 me also, as of one *b* out of due time
Gal. 4:29 *b* after the flesh. . *b* after the Spirit
1 Pet. 1:23 being *b* again, not of corruptible seed
1 Jn. 3:9 (5:18) is *b* of God doth not commit sin
  4:7 and every one that loveth is *b* of God
  5:1 believeth that Jesus is the Christ is *b* of God
  5:4 whatsoever is *b* of God overcometh the world

Borne *See* Bear

Borrow

Ex. 3:22 but every woman shall *b* of her neighbor
  11:2 (12:35) every man *b* of his neighbor. . jewels
  22:14 if a man *b* aught of his neighbor, and it
Deut. 15:6 thou shalt lend. . but thou shalt not *b*
2 Kgs. 4:3 go, *b* thee vessels abroad. . *b* not a few
  6:5 and he cried. . Alas, master! for it was *b*
Neh. 5:4 we have *b* money for the king's tribute

Ps. 37:21 the wicked *b*, and payeth not again: but
Mt. 5:42 from him that would *b* of thee turn not

Borrower

Prov. 22:7 and the *b* is servant to the lender

Bosom

Ex. 4:6 unto him, Put now thine hand into thy *b*
Job 31:33 as Adam, by hiding mine iniquity in my *b*
Ps. 35:13 and my prayer returned into mine own *b*
89:50 how I do bear in my *b* the reproach of all
129:7 nor he that bindeth sheaves his *b*
Prov. 6:27 can a man take fire in his *b*, and his
19:24 a slothful man hideth his hand in his *b*
Eccl. 7:9 for anger resteth in the *b* of fools
Is. 40:11 the lambs. .and carry them in his *b*
Lk. 6:38 good measure. .shall men give into your *b*
16:22 was carried by the angels into Abraham's *b*
Jn. 1:18 Son, which is in the *b* of the Father
13:23 leaning on Jesus' *b* one of his disciples

Botch

Deut. 28:27 will smite thee with the *b* of Egypt

Bottle

Gen. 21:15 the water was spent in the *b*, and she cast
Josh. 9:4 and wine *b*, old, and rent, and bound up
Judg. 4:19 opened a *b* of milk, and gave him drink
Job 32:19 my belly. .is ready to burst like new *b*
Ps. 56:8 put thou my tears into thy *b*: are they
119:83 for I am become like a *b* in the smoke
Jer. 19:1 go and get a potter's earthen *b*
Hab. 2:15 that puttest thy *b* to him, and makest
Mt. 9:17 (Mk. 2:22; Lk. 5:37) new wine into old *b*

Bottomless

Rev. 9:1 to him was given the key of the *b* pit
11:7 (17:8) beast that ascendeth out of the *b* pit
20:3 cast him into the *b* pit, and shut him up

Bough

Gen. 49:22 Joseph is a fruitful *b*. .by a well
Lev. 23:40 *b* of goodly trees. .and *b* of thick trees
Deut. 24:20 thou shalt not go over the *b* again
Judg. 9:49 likewise cut down every man his *b*
2 Sam. 18:9 went under the thick *b* of a great oak
Job 14:9 will bud, and bring forth *b* like a plant
Ps. 80:10 *b* thereof were like the goodly cedars
Is. 17:9 his strong cities be as a forsaken *b*
Ezek. 31:3 and his top was among the thick *b*
Dan. 4:12 the fowls of the heaven dwelt in the *b*

Bought *See* Buy

Bound (adjective, adverb)

Ps. 107:10 being in affliction and iron
Is. 61:1 opening of the prison to them that are *b*
Lk. 8:29 he was kept *b* with chains and in fetters
Jn. 11:44 forth, *b* hand and foot with graveclothes
Acts 20:22 I go *b* in the spirit unto Jerusalem
2 Thes. 1:3 (2:13) we are *b* to thank God always
2 Tim. 2:9 but the word of God is not *b*
Heb. 13:3 remember them. .in bonds, as *b* with them

Bound (noun)

Ex. 23:31 I will set thy *b* from the Red sea even
Deut. 32:8 he set the *b* of the people according to
Hos. 5:10 princes. .were like them that remove the *b*

Bound (verb) *See* Bind

Bountiful

Prov. 22:9 he that hath a *b* eye shall be blessed
Is. 32:5 liberal, nor the churl said to be *b*

Bountifully

Ps. 13:6 sing. .because he hath dealt *b* with me
116:7 for the LORD hath dealt *b* with thee
119:17 deal *b* with thy servant, that I may live
142:7 for thou shalt deal *b* with me
2 Cor. 9:6 and J he which soweth *b* shall reap also *b*

Bountifulness

2 Cor. 9:11 enriched in every thing to all *b*

Bounty

1 Kgs. 10:13 which Solomon gave her of his royal *b*
2 Cor. 9:5 make up beforehand your *b*, whereof ye

Bow (noun)

Gen. 9:13 I do set my *b* in the cloud. .for a token
48:22 which I took. .with my sword and with my *b*
Josh. 24:12 but not with thy sword, nor with thy *b*
1 Sam. 2:4 the *b* of the mighty men are broken
18:4 stripped. .even to his sword, and to his *b*
2 Sam. 1:18 he bade them teach. . the use of the *b*
1:22 the *b* of Jonathan turned not back
1 Kgs. 22:34 (2 Chr. 18:33) man drew a *b* at a venture
2 Kgs. 9:24 Jehu drew a *b* with his full strength
13:15 Elisha said unto him, Take *b* and arrows
Ps. 7:12 he hath bent his *b*, and made it ready
44:6 for I will not trust in my *b*, neither shall
46:9 he breaketh the *b*, and cutteth the spear in
78:57 they were turned aside like a deceitful *b*
Jer. 9:3 bend their tongues like their *b* for lies
Lam. 2:4 he hath bent his *b* like an enemy
Ezek. 1:28 as the appearance of the *b*. . in the cloud
Hos. 1:5 I will break the *b* of Israel in. .Jezreel
1:7 will not save them by *b*, nor by sword, nor
2:18 and I will break the *b* and the sword
7:16 they are like a deceitful *b*: their princes
Rev. 6:2 white horse: and he that sat on him had a *b*

Bow (verb)

Gen. 27:29 serve thee, and nations *b* down to thee
37:10 indeed come to *b* down ourselves to thee
47:31 and Israel *b* himself upon the bed's head
Ex. 4:31 then they *b* their heads and worshipped
12:27 and the people *b* the head and worshipped
20:5 (Deut. 5:9) shalt not *b* down thyself to them
23:24 thou shalt not *b* down to their gods, nor
Josh. 23:7 serve them, nor *b* yourselves unto them
Judg. 7:5 that *b* down upon his knees to drink
16:30 Samson. .*b* himself with all his might
1 Sam. 24:8 his face to the earth, and *b* himself
2 Sam. 22:10 (Ps. 18:9) *b* the heavens also, and came
1 Kgs. 19:18 (Rom. 11:4) which have not *b* unto Baal
2 Kgs. 5:18 and I *b* myself in the house of Rimmon
Ps. 95:6 O come, let us worship and *b* down: let us
144:5 *b* thy heavens, O LORD, and come down
Prov. 14:19 evil *b* before the good; and the wicked
22:17 *b* down thine ear, and hear the words
Is. 45:23 (Rom. 14:11) unto me every knee shall *b*
Mic. 6:6 come. .and *b* myself before the high God?
Mt. 27:29 (Mk. 15:19) *b* the knee before him
Jn. 19:30 and he *b* his head, and gave up the ghost
Eph. 3:14 I *b* my knees unto the Father of our Lord
Phil. 2:10 the name of Jesus every knee should *b*

Bowels

Gen. 43:30 for his *b* did yearn upon his brother
2 Chr. 21:15 great sickness by disease of thy *b*
Job 30:27 my *b* boiled, and rested not: the days
Ps. 22:14 my heart. .is melted in the midst of my *b*
Is. 63:15 the sounding of thy *b*. .toward me?
Jer. 4:19 my *b*, my *b*! I am pained at my very heart
31:20 therefore my *b* are troubled for him
Acts 1:18 burst asunder. .and all his *b* gushed out

2 Cor. 6:12 but ye are straitened in your own *b*
Phil. 1:8 after you all in the *b* of Jesus Christ
  2:1 if there be therefore. . any *b* and mercies
Col. 3:12 put on therefore. . *b* of mercies, kindness
Phlm. 7 the *b* of the saints are refreshed by thee
  12 therefore receive him, that is, mine own *b*
  20 let me have joy. . refresh my *b* in the Lord
1 Jn. 3:17 shutteth up his *b* of compassion from

Bowl *See also* Vial

Eccl. 12:6 be loosed, or the golden *b* be broken
Amos 6:6 drink wine in *b*, and anoint themselves
Zech. 4:2 candlestick. . with a *b* upon the top of it

Bozrah Jer. 49:13; Mic. 2:12

Bracelet

Gen. 38:18 she said, Thy signet, and thy *b*, and thy

Brake *See* Break

Bramble

Judg. 9:14 said all the trees unto the *b*, Come
Is. 34:13 come up. . nettles and *b* in the fortresses
Lk. 6:44 figs, nor of a *b* bush gather they grapes

Branch

Gen. 40:10 in the vine were three *b*: and it was
Num. 13:23 thence a *b* with one cluster of grapes
Job 8:16 and his *b* shooteth forth in his garden
  14:7 that the tender *b* thereof will not cease
  15:32 his time, and his *b* shall not be green
Ps. 80:11 she sent out. . her *b* unto the river
Prov. 11:28 the righteous shall flourish as a *b*
Is. 4:2 shall the *b* of the Lord be beautiful
  9:14 cut off from Israel head and tail, *b* and rush
  11:1 Jesse, and a *B* shall grow out of his roots
  18:5 he shall. . take away and cut down the *b*
  25:5 *b* of the terrible ones shall be brought low
  60:21 the *b* of my planting, the work of my hands
Jer. 23:5 (33:15) raise unto David a righteous *B*
Ezek. 19:11 stature was exalted among the thick *b*
Hos. 14:6 his *b* shall spread, and his beauty shall
Zech. 3:8 I will bring forth my servant the *B*
  6:12 saying, Behold the man whose name is The *B*
Mal. 4:1 it shall leave them neither root nor *b*
Mt. 13:32 (Lk. 13:19) birds. . come and lodge in the *b*
  21:8 (Mk. 11:8) *b* from the trees, and strewed them
  24:32 Mk. 13:8) fig tree; When his *b* is yet tender
Jn. 12:13 took *b* of palm trees, and went forth
  15:2 every *b* in me that beareth not fruit he
  15:5 I am the vine, ye are the *b*. He that abideth
Rom. 11:16 and if the root be holy, so are the *b*
  11:21 if God spared not the natural *b*, take heed

Brand

Judg. 15:5 when he had set the *b* on fire, he let
Zech. 3:2 is not this a *b* plucked out of the fire

Brass

Gen. 4:22 instructor of every artificer in *b*
Ex. 25:3 (35:5) offering. . gold, and silver, and *b*
  30:18 (38:8) thou shalt also make a laver of *b*
Lev. 26:19 heaven as iron, and your earth as *b*
Num. 21:9 Moses made a serpent of *b*, and put it
Deut. 8:9 out of whose hills thou mayest dig *b*
  28:23 heaven that is over thy head shall be *b*
Judg. 16:21 Gaza, and bound him with fetters of *b*
1 Sam. 17:5 he had a helmet of *b* upon his head
  17:6 and he had greaves of *b*. . and a target of *b*
1 Kgs. 7:14 (2 Chr. 2:14) man of Tyre, a worker in *b*
1 Chr. 15:19 appointed to sound with cymbals of *b*
Job 6:12 strength of stones? or is my flesh of *b*?

Job 41:27 esteemeth. . as straw, and *b* as rotten wood
Ps. 107:16 for he hath broken the gates of *b*
Is. 45:2 I will break in pieces the gates of *b*
  48:4 thy neck is an iron sinew, and thy brow *b*
  60:17 for *b* I will bring gold, and for iron
Dan. 2:32 of silver, his belly and his thighs of *b*
  2:39 and another third kingdom of *b*, which shall
Mic. 4:13 make thine horn iron, and. . thy hoofs *b*
Zech. 6:1 and the mountains were mountains of *b*
Mt. 10:9 gold, nor silver, nor *b* in your purses
1 Cor. 13:1 as sounding *b*, or a tinkling cymbal
Rev. 1:15 his feet like unto fine *b*, as if they

Brawler

1 Tim. 3:3 but patient, not a *b*, not covetous
Tit. 3:2 to speak evil of no man, to be no *b*, but

Brawling

Prov. 21:9 (25:24) with a *b* woman. . in a wide house

Bray

Job 6:5 doth the wild ass *b* when he hath grass?
  30:7 among the bushes they *b*; under the nettles
Prov. 27:22 thou shouldest *b* a fool in a mortar

Brazen

Ex. 39:39 the *b* altar, and his grate of brass
1 Kgs. 14:27 king. . made in their stead *b* shields
2 Kgs. 18:4 brake in pieces the *b* serpent that Moses
Jer. 1:18 and *b* walls against the whole land
  15:20 make thee unto this people a fenced *b* wall
Mk. 7:4 washing of cups, and pots, *b* vessels

Breach

Lev. 24:20 *b* for *b*, eye for eye, tooth for tooth
Num. 14:34 and ye shall know my *b* of promise
Judg. 21:15 because that the Lord had made a *b*
Neh. 6:1 the wall. . there was no *b* left therein
Job 16:14 he breaketh me with *b* upon *b*; he runneth
Ps. 60:2 thou hast broken it: heal the *b* thereof
  106:23 had not Moses. . stood before him in the *b*
Prov. 15:4 but perverseness. . is a *b* in the spirit
Is. 30:26 the Lord bindeth up the *b* of his people
  58:12 shalt be called, The repairer of the *b*
Jer. 14:17 of my people is broken with a great *b*
Lam. 2:13 thy *b* is great like the sea: who can
Amos 4:3 ye shall go out at the *b*, every cow at
  6:11 and he will smite the great house with *b*

Bread

Gen. 3:19 the sweat of thy face shalt thou eat *b*
  14:18 and Melchizedek. . brought forth *b* and wine
  47:19 buy us and our land for *b*, and we and our
Ex. 16:4 (Jn. 6:31) I will rain *b* from heaven for you
  23:25 the Lord. . shall bless thy *b*, and thy water
Num. 15:19 when ye eat of the *b* of the land, ye
  21:5 is no *b*. . and our soul loatheth this light *b*
Deut. 8:3 (Mt. 4:4; Lk. 4:4) doth not live by *b* only
Ruth 1:6 had visited his people in giving them *b*
1 Sam. 21:4 there is no common *b* under mine hand
1 Kgs. 17:6 the ravens brought him *b* and flesh
  22:27 (2 Chr. 18:26) feed him with *b* of affliction
2 Kgs. 4:42 the man of God *b* of the firstfruits
Neh. 9:15 gavest them *b* from heaven for their hunger
Job 22:7 thou hast withholden *b* from the hungry
  33:20 so that his life abhorreth *b*, and his soul
Ps. 14:4 (53:4) who eat up my people as they eat *b*
  41:9 (Jn. 13:18) eat of my *b*. . hath lifted up his
  80:5 thou feedest them with the *b* of tears
  105:40 and satisfied them with the *b* of heaven
  127:2 to sit up late, to eat the *b* of sorrows
  132:15 provision: I will satisfy her poor with *b*
Prov. 4:17 they eat the *b* of wickedness, and drink

Prov. 9:17 sweet, and *b* eaten in secret is pleasant
12:11 tilleth his land shall be satisfied with *b*
20:17 *b* of deceit is sweet to a man; but afterward
22:9 blessed; for he giveth of his *b* to the poor
28:21 for a piece of *b* that man will transgress
31:27 household, and eateth not the *b* of idleness
Eccl. 9:7 eat thy *b* with joy, and drink thy wine
11:1 cast thy *b* upon the waters: for thou shalt
Is. 33:16 *b* shall be given him; his waters shall
55:2 do ye spend money for that which is not *b*?
55:10 (2 Cor. 9:10) to the sower . . *b* to the eater
58:7 is it not to deal thy *b* to the hungry
Lam. 4:4 young children ask *b*, and no man breaketh
Hos. 9:4 their sacrifices . . as the *b* of mourners
Amos 4:6 given you . . want of *b* in all your places
Mt. 4:3 (Lk. 4:3) command . . these stones be made *b*
6:11 (Lk. 11:3) give us this day our daily *b*
7:9 (Lk. 11:11) if his son ask *b* . . give him a stone?
15:26 (Mk. 7:27) not meet to take the children's *b*
15:33 (Mk. 8:4) whence should we have so much *b*
16:5 (Mk. 8:14) they had forgotten to take *b*
26:26 (Mk. 14:22; Lk. 22:19; 1 Cor. 11:23) Jesus
took *b* . . and said . . this is my body
Mk. 6:8 (Lk. 9:3) no scrip, no *b*, no money in their
6:37 (Jn. 6:7) buy two hundred pennyworth of *b*
Lk. 7:33 John the Baptist came neither eating *b*
14:15 he that shall eat *b* in the kingdom of God
15:17 hired servants of my father's have *b* enough
24:35 how he was known of them in breaking of *b*
Jn. 6:5 whence shall we buy *b*, that these may eat?
6:32 my Father giveth you the true *b* from
6:35 (6:48) Jesus said . . I am the *b* of life
6:51 am the living *b* which came down from heaven
21:13 cometh, and taketh *b*, and giveth them
Acts 2:42 continued steadfastly . . in breaking of *b*
2:46 and breaking *b* from house to house, did eat
20:7 when the disciples came together to break *b*
1 Cor. 5:8 the unleavened *b* of sincerity and truth
10:16 *b* which we break, is it not the communion
11:26 as often as ye eat this *b*, and drink this
2 Thes. 3:8 did we eat any man's *b* for nought
3:12 quietness they work, and eat their own *b*

Breadth

Job 37:10 and the *b* of the waters is straitened
Hab. 1:6 shall march through the *b* of the land
Eph. 3:18 the *b*, and length, and depth, and height
Rev. 20:9 they went up on the *b* of the earth
21:16 the length and the *b* and the height . . equal

Break (Brake, Broken)

Gen. 17:14 the uncircumcised . . hath *b* my covenant
27:40 thou shalt *b* his yoke from off thy neck
Ex. 9:25 and the hail . . *b* every tree of the field
12:46 (Num. 9:12; Jn. 19:36) neither . . ye *b* a bone
32:19 (Deut. 9:17) cast the tables . . and *b* them
34:1 (Deut. 10:2) in the first tables, which thou *b*
34:13 (Deut. 7:5) their altars, *b* their images
Num. 30:2 if a man vow . . he shall not *b* his word
Judg. 7:19 blew the trumpets, and *b* the pitchers
1 Sam. 4:18 he fell . . and his neck *b*, and he died
2 Kgs. 11:18 (2 Chr. 23:17) house of Baal . . *b* it down
23:14 *b* in pieces the images, and cut down
25:4 (Jer. 39:2; 52:7) and the city was *b* up
Ezra 9:14 should we again *b* thy commandments
Job 13:25 wilt thou *b* a leaf driven to and fro?
16:12 I was at ease, but he hath *b* me asunder
17:11 my days are past, my purposes are *b* off
19:2 how long will ye . . *b* me in pieces with words?
34:24 he shall *b* in pieces mighty men without
Ps. 2:3 let us *b* their bands asunder, and cast
2:9 thou shalt *b* them with a rod of iron
10:15 *b* thou the arm of the wicked and the evil

Ps. 18:34 so that a bow of steel is *b* by mine arms
34:20 (Jn. 19:36) his bones: not one of them is *b*
44:19 hast sore *b* us in the place of dragons
58:6 *b* their teeth, O God, in their mouth: *b* out
69:20 reproach hath *b* my heart; and I am full of
76:3 there *b* he the arrows of the bow, the shield
89:31 if they *b* my statutes, and keep not my
89:34 my covenant will I not *b*, nor alter
107:14 them out . . and *b* their bands in sunder
119:20 my soul *b* for the longing that it hath
Prov. 15:13 by sorrow of the heart the spirit is *b*
Song 2:17 (4:6) until the day *b*, and the shadows
Is. 9:4 for thou hast *b* the yoke of his burden
14:5 the LORD hath *b* the staff of the wicked
24:5 they have . . *b* the everlasting covenant
28:24 doth he open and *b* the clods of his ground?
30:14 shall *b* it as the breaking of the potter's
42:3 (Mt. 12:20) a bruised reed shall he not *b*
Jer. 4:3 (Hos. 10:12) *b* up your fallow ground
11:10 and the house of Judah have *b* my covenant
14:21 remember, *b* not thy covenant with us
19:11 I *b* this people . . as one *b* a potter's vessel
23:9 mine heart within me is *b* because of the
28:10 yoke from off . . Jeremiah's neck, and *b* it
31:32 my covenant they *b* . . I was a husband unto
33:21 then may also my covenant be . *b* with David
51:21 I *b* in pieces the horse and his rider
Ezek. 17:16 oath he despised . . whose covenant he *b*
29:7 when they leaned upon thee, thou *b*
34:16 will bind up that which was *b*, and will
Dan. 6:24 the lions . . *b* all their bones in pieces
Hos. 5:11 Ephraim is oppressed and *b* in judgment
10:2 he shall *b* down their altars, he shall spoil
Mic. 2:13 have *b* up . . have passed through the gate
Zech. 11:10 might *b* my covenant which I had made
Mt. 5:19 shall *b* one of these least commandments
6:20 where thieves do not *b* through nor steal
9:17 wine into old bottles: else the bottles *b*
14:19 (Mk. 6:41; Lk. 9:16) *b*, and gave the loaves
21:44 (Lk. 20:18) fall on this stone shall be *b*
Mk. 14:3 she *b* the box, and poured it on his head
Lk. 5:6 great multitude of fishes: and their net *b*
Jn. 5:18 he not only had *b* the sabbath, but said
10:35 and the Scripture cannot be *b*
19:31 besought Pilate that their legs might be *b*
Acts 2:46 *b* bread from house to house, did eat
21:13 what mean ye to weep and to *b* mine heart?
27:41 the hinder part was *b* with the violence of
1 Cor. 11:24 this is my body, which is *b* for you
Eph. 2:14 hath *b* down the middle wall of partition
Rev. 2:27 of a potter shall they be *b* to shivers

Breast

Gen. 49:25 blessings of the *b*, and of the womb
Lev. 7:30 the *b* may be waved for a wave offering
Is. 60:16 thou shalt also . . suck the *b* of kings
66:11 ye may suck . . the *b* of her consolations
Dan. 2:32 his *b* and his arms of silver, his belly
Lk. 18:13 the publican . . smote upon his *b*, saying
23:48 the people . . smote their *b*, and returned
Jn. 13:25 (21:20) he then lying on Jesus' *b* saith
Rev. 15:6 their *b* girded with golden girdles

Breastplate

Ex. 28:15 (39:8) the *b* of judgment with cunning work
Is. 59:17 for he put on righteousness as a *b*
Eph. 6:14 stand . . having on the *b* of righteousness
1 Thes. 5:8 putting on the *b* of faith and love
Rev. 9:9 and they had *b*, as it were *b* of iron
9:17 *b* of fire, and of jacinth, and brimstone

Breath

Gen. 2:7 breathed into his nostrils the *b* of life

Gen. 6:17 destroy all flesh, wherein is the *b* of life
2 Sam. 22:16 (Ps. 18:15) blast of the *b* of his nostrils
1 Kgs. 17:17 sore, that there was no *b* left in him
Job 4:9 by the *b* of his nostrils are they consumed
12:10 in whose hand is. . the *b* of all mankind
17:1 my *b* is corrupt, my days are extinct
27:3 all the while my *b* is in me, and the spirit
33:4 the *b* of the Almighty hath given me life
37:10 by the *b* of God frost is given
Ps. 33:6 the host of them by the *b* of his mouth
104:29 thou takest away their *b*, they die
146:4 *b* goeth forth, he returneth to his earth
150:6 let every thing that hath *b* praise the LORD
Eccl. 3:19 they have all one *b*; so that a man hath
Is. 2:22 from man, whose *b* is in his nostrils
11:4 with the *b* of his lips shall he slay
30:28 and his *b*, as an overflowing stream, shall
42:5 he that giveth *b* unto the people upon it
Lam. 4:20 the *b* of our nostrils, the anointed of
Ezek. 37:5 behold, I will cause *b* to enter into you
37:10 so I prophesied. . and the *b* came into them
Dan. 5:23 the God in whose hand thy *b* is, and whose
Acts 17:25 seeing he giveth to all life, and *b*

Breathe

Gen. 2:7 *b* into his nostrils the breath of life
Josh. 11:11 smote all. . there was not any left to *b*
Ps. 27:12 false witnesses. . such as *b* out cruelty
Ezek. 37:9 *b* upon these slain, that they may live
Jn. 20:22 *b* on them. . Receive ye the Holy Ghost
Acts 9:1 Saul, yet *b* out threatenings and slaughter

Breeches

Ex. 28:42 thou shalt make them linen *b* to cover
Lev. 16:4 he shall have linen *b* upon his flesh
Ezek. 44:18 shall have linen *b* upon their loins

Brethren *See also* Brother

Gen. 13:8 Lot, Let there be no strife. . for we be *b*
27:29 be lord over thy *b*. . thy mother's sons bow
37:11 his *b* envied him, but his father observed
42:8 Joseph knew his *b*, but they knew not him
45:1 while Joseph made himself known unto his *b*
48:22 have given to thee one portion above thy *b*
49:8 Judah, thou art he whom thy *b* shall praise
Ex. 2:11 (Acts 7:23) Moses. . went out unto his *b*
4:18 let me go. . and return unto my *b*. . in Egypt
Lev. 25:46 but over your *b*. . ye shall not rule
25:48 he is sold. . one of his *b* may redeem him
Num. 8:26 minister with their *b* in the tabernacle
25:6 and brought unto his *b* a Midianitish woman
27:9 ye shall give his inheritance unto his *b*
32:6 your *b* go to war, and shall ye sit here?
Deut. 1:16 hear the causes between your *b*, and judge
10:9 Levi hath no part nor inheritance with his *b*
15:7 be among you a poor man of one of thy *b*
17:15 one from among thy *b* shalt thou set king
18:15 (Acts 3:22) a Prophet. . of thy *b*, like unto me
24:14 poor and needy, whether he be of thy *b*, or
25:5 if *b* dwell together, and one of them die
Josh. 2:13 ye will save alive my father. . and my *b*
17:4 an inheritance among the *b* of their father
Judg. 9:5 slew his *b* the sons of Jerubbaal
14:3 never a woman among the daughters of thy *b*
Ruth 4:10 name. . be not cut off from among his *b*
1 Sam. 16:13 anointed him in the midst of his *b*
17:17 ten loaves, and run to the camp to thy *b*
2 Sam. 19:12 ye are my *b*. . my bones and my flesh
1 Kgs. 12:24 (2 Chr. 11:4) nor fight against your *b*
1 Chr. 5:2 Judah prevailed above his *b*
Neh. 5:1 was a great cry. . against their *b* the Jews
5:8 and will ye even sell your *b*?
Job 6:15 my *b* have dealt deceitfully as a brook

Job 19:13 he hath put my *b* far from me, and mine
Ps. 22:22 (Heb. 2:12) declare thy name unto my *b*
122:8 for my *b* and companions' sakes, I will now
133:1 good. . for *b* to dwell together in unity!
Prov. 6:19 and he that soweth discord among *b*
19:7 all the *b* of the poor do hate him: how much
Mic. 5:3 then the remnant of his *b* shall return
Mt. 5:47 if ye salute your *b* only, what do ye more
12:46 (Mk. 3:31; Lk. 8:19) and his *b* stood without
12:49 (Mk. 3:34) behold my mother and my *b*!
13:55 and his *b*, James. . Joses. . Simon, and Judas?
20:24 moved with indignation against the two *b*
22:25 (Mk. 12:20; Lk. 20:29) were with us seven *b*
23:8 for one is your Master. . and all ye are *b*
25:40 unto one of the least of these my *b*, ye
28:10 go tell my *b* that they go into Galilee
Lk. 21:16 shall be betrayed both by parents, and *b*
22:32 when thou art converted, strengthen thy *b*
Jn. 2:12 his mother, and his *b*, and his disciples
7:5 for neither did his *b* believe in him
Acts 1:14 Mary the mother of Jesus, and with his *b*
11:1 the apostles and *b* that were in Judea heard
11:29 relief unto the *b* which dwelt in Judea
14:2 their minds evil affected against the *b*
15:1 which came down from Judea taught the *b*
15:36 Paul said. . Let us go and visit our *b*
21:17 come to Jerusalem, the *b* received us gladly
28:14 where we found *b*, and were desired to tarry
Rom. 8:29 he might be the firstborn among many *b*
9:3 myself were accursed from Christ for my *b*
1 Cor. 6:5 that shall be able to judge between his *b*?
8:12 but when ye sin so against the *b*, and wound
9:5 a wife. . as the *b* of the Lord, and Cephas?
15:6 he was seen of above five hundred *b* at once
2 Cor. 11:9 *b* which came from Macedonia supplied
11:26 perils in the sea, in perils among false *b*
Gal. 2:4 because of false *b* unawares brought in
Eph. 6:23 peace be to the *b*, and love with faith
Phil. 1:14 many of the *b*. . waxing confident by my
4:1 my *b*, dearly beloved and longed for, my joy
Col. 1:2 to the saints and faithful *b* in Christ
1 Thes. 5:27 this epistle be read unto all the holy *b*
1 Tim. 4:6 thou put the *b* in remembrance of these
5:1 him as a father; and the younger men as *b*
6:2 not despise them, because they are *b*; but
Heb. 2:11 cause he is not ashamed to call them *b*
2:17 to be made like unto his *b*, that he might
1 Pet. 1:22 Spirit unto unfeigned love of the *b*
3:8 having compassion one of another; love as *b*
5:9 accomplished in your *b* that are in the world
1 Jn. 3:14 death unto life, because we love the *b*
3:16 we ought to lay down our lives for the *b*
Rev. 12:10 for the accuser of our *b* is cast down
19:10 of thy *b* that have the testimony of Jesus
22:9 am thy fellow servant. . of thy *b* the prophets

Bribe

1 Sam. 8:3 his sons. . took *b*, and perverted judgment
12:3 of whose hand have I received any *b* to blind
Ps. 26:10 and their right hand is full of *b*
Is. 33:15 that shaketh his hands from holding of *b*
Amos 5:12 they afflict the just, they take a *b*

Bribery

Job 15:34 fire shall consume the tabernacles of *b*

Brick

Gen. 11:3 let us make *b*, and burn them thoroughly
Ex. 1:14 with hard bondage, in mortar, and in *b*
5:7 shall no more give the people straw to make *b*
Is. 9:10 the *b* are fallen down, but we will build

Bride

Is. 61:10 as a *b* adorneth herself with her jewels
Jer. 2:32 forget her ornaments, or a *b* her attire?
Jn. 3:29 he that hath the *b* is the bridegroom
Rev. 21:2 prepared as a *b* adorned for her husband
21:9 I will show thee the *b*, the Lamb's wife
22:17 the Spirit and the *b* say, Come. And let him

Bridechamber

Mt. 9:15 (Mk. 2:19; Lk. 5:34) children of the *b* mourn

Bridegroom

Ps. 19:5 which is as a *b* coming out of his chamber
Is. 61:10 as a *b* decketh himself with ornaments
62:5 as the *b* rejoiceth over the bride, so shall
Mt. 9:15 (Mk. 2:19; Lk. 5:34) as the *b* is with them?
25:1 their lamps, and went forth to meet the *b*
Jn. 2:9 the governor of the feast called the *b*
3:29 that hath the bride is the *b*: but the friend

Bridle

2 Kgs. 19:28 (Is. 37:29) I will put. .my *b* in thy lips
Ps. 32:9 whose mouth must be held in with bit and *b*
39:1 I will keep my mouth with a *b*, while the wicked
Prov. 26:3 a whip for the horse, a *b* for the ass
Is. 30:28 shall be a *b* in the jaws of the people
Jas. 1:26 to be religious, and *b* not his tongue
3:2 perfect man, and able also to *b* the whole body
Rev. 14:20 blood came out. .even unto the horse *b*

Brier *See also* Thorn

Is. 5:6 (32:13) there shall come up *b* and thorns
27:4 who would set the *b* and thorns against me
55:13 instead of the *b* shall come up the myrtle
Ezek. 2:6 afraid. .though *b* and thorns be with thee
28:24 no more a pricking *b* unto the house of Israel
Heb. 6:8 which beareth thorns and *b* is rejected

Brightness *See also* Light

2 Sam. 22:13 (Ps. 18:12) through the *b* before him
Is. 59:9 we wait. .for *b*, but we walk in darkness
60:3 to thy light, and kings to the *b* of thy rising
60:19 neither for *b* shall the moon give light
62:1 the righteousness thereof go forth as *b*
Ezek. 10:4 was full of the *b* of the LORD's glory
Amos 5:20 day of the LORD. .very dark, and no *b* in it
Hab. 3:4 and his *b* was as the light; he had horns
Acts 26:13 light. .above the *b* of the sun, shining
2 Thes. 2:8 shall destroy with the *b* of his coming
Heb. 1:3 the *b* of his glory, and the express image

Brimstone

Gen. 19:24 rained upon Sodom and. . Gomorrah *b*
Deut. 29:23 the whole land thereof is *b*, and salt
Job 18:15 *b* shall be scattered upon his habitation
Ps. 11:6 wicked he shall rain snares, fire and *b*
Is. 30:33 breath of the LORD, like a stream of *b*
34:9 turned into pitch, and the dust thereof into *b*
Lk. 17:29 Sodom it rained fire and *b* from heaven
Rev. 14:10 he shall be tormented with fire and *b*
19:20 alive into a lake of fire burning with *b*

Bring (Brought) *See also* Gather

Gen. 28:15 and will *b* thee again into this land
Ex. 3:12 thou hast *b* forth the people out of Egypt
33:12 see, thou sayest unto me, *B* up this people
Deut. 26:8 the LORD *b* us forth out of Egypt with
30:12 go up for us to heaven and *b* it unto us
Judg. 19:22 *b*. . the man that came into thine house
2 Sam. 7:18 (1 Chr. 17:16) thou hast *b* me hitherto?
22:20 (Ps. 18:19) *b* me forth also into a large place
1 Kgs. 8:1 (2 Chr. 5:2) that they might *b* up the ark
1 Chr. 13:3 let us *b* again the ark of our God to us

Job 30:23 for I know that thou wilt *b* me to death
33:30 to *b* back his soul from the pit
Ps. 43:3 let them *b* me unto thy holy hill
66:12 but thou *b* us out into a wealthy place
105:43 he *b* forth his people with joy, and his
107:12 *b* down their heart with labor; they fell
126:6 with rejoicing, *b* his sheaves with him
Prov. 27:1 thou knowest not what a day may *b* forth
Is. 1:13 *b* no more vain oblations; incense is an
42:3 he shall *b* forth judgment unto truth
46:13 I *b* near my righteousness; it shall not
52:7 (Nah. 1:15; Rom. 10:15) that *b* good tidings
52:8 eye to eye, when the LORD shall *b* again Zion
58:7 *b* the poor that are cast out to thy house?
60:9 ships of Tarshish. .to *b* thy sons from far
60:11 may *b* unto thee the forces of the Gentiles
66:8 the earth be made to *b* forth in one day?
Ezek. 34:16 *b* again that which was driven away
Hos. 2:14 allure her, and *b* her into the wilderness
9:12 though they *b* up their children, yet will I
Mal. 3:10 *b* ye all the tithes into the storehouse
Mt. 1:21 (Lk. 1:31) *b* forth a son, and thou shalt
3:8 (Lk. 3:8) *b* forth. .fruits meet for repentance
5:23 if thou *b* thy gift to the altar, and there
7:18 (Lk. 6:43) a good tree cannot *b* forth evil
10:18 (Mk. 13:9; Lk. 21:12) be *b* before. .kings
13:23 (Mk. 4:20; Lk. 8:15) *b* forth. .hundredfold
19:13 (Mk. 10:13; Lk. 18:15) *b* unto him. .children
Mk. 12:15 why tempt ye me? *b* me a penny, that I
Lk. 2:10 behold, I *b* you good tidings of great joy
Jn. 12:24 but if it die, it *b* forth much fruit
15:5 and I in him, the same *b* forth much fruit
Acts 5:19 opened the prison doors, and *b* them forth
22:3 *b* up in this city at the feet of Gamaliel
27:24 fear not, Paul; thou must be *b* before Caesar
Rom. 10:6 that is, to *b* Christ down from above
1 Cor. 1:28 are not, to *b* to nought things that are
6:12 but I will not be *b* under the power of any
Gal. 3:24 was our schoolmaster to *b* us unto Christ
Col. 1:6 and *b* forth fruit, as it doth also in you
1 Thes. 4:14 sleep in Jesus will God *b* with him
1 Tim. 6:7 we *b* nothing into this world, and it is
Tit. 2:11 the grace of God that *b* salvation hath
Heb. 7:19 but the *b* in of a better hope did
13:20 that *b* again from the dead our Lord Jesus
1 Pet. 1:13 for the grace that is to be *b* unto you
3:18 suffered for sins. .that he might *b* us to God
Rev. 12:5 she *b* forth a man child, who was to rule
21:26 shall *b* the glory and honor of the nations

Broad

Neh. 3:8 they fortified Jerusalem unto the *b* wall
Job 36:16 thee out of the strait into a *b* place
Ps. 119:96 but thy commandment is exceeding *b*
Is. 33:21 unto us a place of *b* rivers and streams
Jer. 5:1 seek in the *b* places thereof, if ye can
Mt. 7:13 for wide is the gate, and *b* is the way
23:5 they make *b* their phylacteries, and enlarge

Broken *See also* Break

Ps. 34:18 is nigh unto them that are of a *b* heart
51:17 are a *b* spirit: a *b* and a contrite heart
147:3 he healeth the *b* in heart, and bindeth up
Prov. 17:22 but a *b* spirit drieth the bones
25:19 is like a *b* tooth, and a foot out of joint
Eccl. 12:6 golden bowl be *b*, or the pitcher be *b* at
Is. 36:6 thou trustest in the staff of this *b* reed
Jer. 2:13 and hewed them out cisterns, *b* cisterns

Broken-hearted

Is. 61:1 (Lk. 4:18) hath sent me to bind up the *b-h*

Brook *See also* River, Stream

Deut. 8:7 into a good land, a land of *b* of water
1 Kgs. 17:5 for he went and dwelt by the *b* Cherith
Ps. 42:1 as the hart panteth after the water *b*, so
110:7 shall drink of the *b* in the way

Brother *See also* Brethren

Gen. 4:9 LORD said unto Cain, Where is Abel thy *b*?
Deut. 25:5 perform. . duty of a husband's *b* unto her
Ps. 50:20 thou sittest and speakest against thy *b*
Prov. 17:17 all times, and a *b* is born for adversity
18:9 slothful. . is *b* to him that is a great waster
18:19 a *b* offended is harder to be won than a
18:24 is a friend that sticketh closer than a *b*
Eccl. 4:8 hath neither child nor *b*: yet is there no
Jer. 9:4 trust ye not in any *b*: for every *b* will
Amos 1:11 Edom. . did pursue his *b* with the sword
Mal. 1:2 was not Esau Jacob's *b*? saith the LORD
Mt. 5:22 angry with his *b* without a cause shall be
10:21 (Mk. 13:12) the *b* shall deliver up the *b*
12:50 (Mk. 3:35) the same is my *b*, and sister
18:15 *b* shall trespass against thee, go and tell
18:21 how oft shall my *b* sin against me, and I
22:24 (Mk. 12:19; Lk. 20:28) *b* shall marry his wife
Lk. 15:32 thy *b* was dead and is alive again
Jn. 11:21 (11:32) been here, my *b* had not died
Rom. 14:10 thou judge thy *b*?. . set at nought thy *b*?
14:21 nor any thing whereby thy *b* stumbleth
1 Cor. 6:6 *b* goeth to law with *b*, and that before
8:11 through thy knowledge shall the weak *b* perish
2 Cor. 8:18 have sent with him the *b*, whose praise
2 Thes. 3:15 as an enemy, but admonish him as a *b*
Phlm. 16 not now as a servant, but. . a *b* beloved
Jas. 2:15 if a *b* or sister be naked, and destitute
1 Jn. 2:10 that loveth his *b* abideth in the light
3:10 not of God, neither he that loveth not his *b*
3:17 seeth his *b* have need, and shutteth up his
4:20 if a man say, I love God, and hateth his *b*
Rev. 1:9 I John, who also am your *b*, and companion

Brotherhood

Zech. 11:14 break the *b* between Judah and Israel
1 Pet. 2:17 honor all men. Love the *b*. Fear God

Brotherly

Amos 1:9 and remembered not the *b* covenant
Rom. 12:10 affectioned one to another with *b* love
1 Thes. 4:9 as touching *b* love ye need not that I
Heb. 13:1 let *b* love continue
2 Pet. 1:7 *b* kindness; and to *b* kindness, charity

Brought *See* Bring

Bruise *See also* Hurt, Wound

Gen. 3:15 *b* thy head, and thou shalt *b* his heel
2 Kgs. 18:21 trustest upon the staff of this *b* reed
Is. 1:6 is no soundness in it; but wounds, and *b*
42:3 (Mt. 12:20) *b* reed shall he not break
53:5 was *b* for our iniquities: the chastisement
53:10 yet it pleased the LORD to *b* him; he hath
Jer. 30:12 thy *b* is incurable, and thy wound is
Ezek. 23:8 and they *b* the breasts of her virginity
Nah. 3:19 there is no healing of thy *b*; thy wound
Lk. 4:18 blind, to set at liberty them that are *b*

Brutish

Ps. 92:6 a *b* man knoweth not; neither doth a fool
94:8 understand, ye *b* among the people: and ye
Prov. 12:1 but he that hateth reproof is *b*
30:2 surely I am more *b* than any man
Jer. 10:8 but they are altogether *b* and foolish
10:21 pastors are become *b*, and have not sought
Ezek. 21:31 and deliver thee into the hand of *b* men

Buckler *See also* Shield

2 Sam. 22:31 (Ps. 18:30) a *b* to all them that trust
Ps. 18:2 my *b*, and the horn of my salvation
91:4 his truth shall be thy shield and *b*
Prov. 2:7 he is a *b* to them that walk uprightly
Jer. 46:3 order ye the *b* and shield, and draw

Bud

Num. 17:8 rod of Aaron for the house of Levi was *b*
Ps. 132:17 there will I make the horn of David to *b*
Is. 18:5 afore the harvest, when the *b* is perfect
Ezek. 29:21 horn of the house of Israel to *b* forth
Hos. 8:7 *b* shall yield no meal: if so be it yield

Buffet

Mt. 26:67 (Mk. 14:65) spit in his face, and *b* him
1 Cor. 4:11 and thirst, and are naked, and are *b*
2 Cor. 12:7 the messenger of Satan to *b* me, lest I
1 Pet. 2:20 if, when ye be *b* for your faults, ye

Build (Built) *See also* Edify

Gen. 11:4 go to, let us *b* us a city, and a tower
2 Sam. 7:5 (1 Chr. 17:4) *b* me a house for me to dwell
1 Kgs. 5:5 I purpose to *b* a house unto the name of
8:17 (2 Chr. 6:7) to *b* a house for the name
1 Chr. 22:10 he shall *b* a house for my name
28:6 Solomon. . shall *b* my house and my courts
2 Chr. 2:6 but who is able to *b* him a house, seeing
36:23 (Ezra 1:2) me to *b* him a house in Jerusalem
Ezra 4:1 the children of the captivity *b* the temple
Neh. 2:17 and let us *b* up the wall of Jerusalem
4:6 so *b* we the wall. . people had a mind to work
Ps. 51:18 unto Zion: *b* thou the walls of Jerusalem
127:1 *b* the house, they labor in vain that *b* it
147:2 the LORD doth *b* up Jerusalem: he gathereth
Prov. 9:1 wisdom hath *b* her house, she hath hewn
14:1 wise woman *b* her house: but the foolish
24:3 through wisdom is a house *b*
Eccl. 2:4 I *b* me houses; I planted me vineyards
3:3 a time to break down, and a time to *b* up
Is. 9:10 fallen down, but we will *b* with hewn stones
58:12 be of thee shall *b* the old waste places
61:4 shall *b* the old wastes, they shall raise up
66:1 (Acts 7:49) where is the house. . ye *b* unto me?
Jer. 22:14 I will *b* me a wide house and large
24:6 I will *b* them, and not pull them down
31:4 again I will *b* thee, and thou shalt be *b*
33:7 to return, and will *b* them, as at the first
42:10 still abide in this land, then will I *b* you
Dan. 4:30 I have *b* for the house of the kingdom
Amos 9:11 will raise up his ruins, and I will *b* it
Mic. 3:10 they *b* up Zion with blood, and Jerusalem
Hag. 1:2 the time that the LORD's house should be *b*
Zech. 6:12 and he shall *b* the temple of the LORD
Mal. 1:4 return and *b*. . They shall *b*, but I will throw
Mt. 7:24 (Lk. 6:48) which *b* his house upon a rock
16:18 upon this rock I will *b* my church
23:29 (Lk. 11:47) ye *b* the tombs of the prophets
26:61 (Mk. 14:58) destroy. . and to *b* it in three days
Lk. 12:18 I will pull down my barns, and *b* greater
14:30 began to *b*, and was not able to finish
Jn. 2:20 forty and six years was this temple in *b*
Acts 20:32 his grace, which is able to *b* you up
Rom. 15:20 should *b* upon another man's foundation
1 Cor. 3:10 but let every man take heed how he *b*
Gal. 2:18 if I *b* again the things which I destroyed
Eph. 2:20 are *b* upon the foundation of the apostles
2:22 also are *b* together for a habitation of God
Col. 2:7 rooted and *b* up in him, and stablished in
Heb. 3:4 house is *b* by some man; but he that *b* all
1 Pet. 2:5 lively stones, are *b* up a spiritual house
Jude 20 *b* up yourselves on your most holy faith

Builder

1 Kgs. 5:18 Solomon's *b* and Hiram's *b* did hew them
Ezra 3:10 the *b* laid the foundation of the temple
Ps. 118:22 (Mt. 21:42; Mk. 12:10; Lk. 20:17; Acts 4:11; 1 Pet. 2:7) the stone which the *b* refused is
Heb. 11:10 foundations, whose *b* and maker is God

Building *See also* Build

Ezra 6:8 these Jews for the *b* of this house of God
Eccl. 10:18 by much slothfulness the *b* decayeth
Mk. 13:1 what manner of stones and what *b* are here!
1 Cor. 3:9 ye are God's husbandry, ye are God's *b*
2 Cor. 5:1 we have a *b* of God, a house not made
Eph. 2:21 in whom all the *b* fitly framed together
Heb. 9:11 not made with hands, that is. . not of this *b*

Bull

Ps. 22:12 *b* have compassed me: strong *b* of Bashan
Heb. 9:13 blood of *b* and of goats, and the ashes
10:4 it is not possible that the blood of *b*

Bulrush

Ex. 2:3 took for him an ark of *b*, and daubed it

Bulwark

Deut. 20:20 thou shalt build *b* against the city
Ps. 48:13 mark ye well her *b*, consider her palaces
Is. 26:1 salvation will God appoint for walls and *b*

Bundle

Gen. 42:35 every man's *b* of money was in his sack
1 Sam. 25:29 bound in the *b* of life with the LORD
Song 1:13 a *b* of myrrh is my well-beloved unto me
Mt. 13:30 bind them in *b* to burn them: but gather
Acts 28:3 when Paul had gathered a *b* of sticks

Burden

Ex. 2:11 unto his brethren, and looked on their *b*
18:22 be easier. . they shall bear the *b* with thee
Num. 11:11 layest the *b* of all this people upon me?
2 Kgs. 9:25 how that. . the LORD laid this *b* upon him
Job 7:20 as a mark. . so that I am a *b* to myself?
Ps. 38:4 as a heavy *b* they are too heavy for me
55:22 cast thy *b* upon the LORD. . he shall sustain
Eccl. 12:5 grasshopper shall be a *b*, and desire
Is. 9:4 for thou hast broken the yoke of his *b*
10:27 *b* shall be taken away from off thy shoulder
13:1 the *b* of Babylon, which Isaiah. . did see
14:25 and his *b* depart from off their shoulders
15:1 *b* of Moab. Because in the night Ar of Moab
17:1 *b* of Damascus. Behold, Damascus is taken
19:1 *b* of Egypt. Behold, the LORD rideth upon
21:1 *b* of the desert of the sea. As whirlwinds
22:1 *b* of the valley of vision. What aileth thee
23:1 the *b* of Tyre. Howl, ye ships of Tarshish
58:6 undo the heavy *b*, and to let the oppressed
Jer. 17:21 and bear no *b* on the sabbath day
23:34 say, The *b* of the LORD, I will even punish
Nah. 1:1 *b* of Nineveh. The book of the vision of
Hab. 1:1 the *b* which Habakkuk the prophet did see
Zeph. 3:18 to whom the reproach of it was a *b*
Zech. 12:1 the *b* of the word of the LORD for Israel
Mt. 11:30 for my yoke is easy, and my *b* is light
20:12 which have borne the *b* and heat of the day
23:4 (Lk. 11:46) heavy *b* and grievous to be borne
Acts 15:28 no greater *b* than these necessary things
2 Cor. 5:4 are in this tabernacle do groan, being *b*
8:13 I mean not that other men be eased, and ye *b*
12:16 I did not *b* you: nevertheless, being crafty
Gal. 6:2 bear ye one another's *b*, and so fulfil the
6:5 for every man shall bear his own *b*
Rev. 2:24 I will put upon you none other *b*

Burdensome

Zech. 12:3 will I make Jerusalem a *b* stone for all
2 Cor. 11:9 have kept myself from being *b* unto you
12:13 except it be that I myself was not *b* to you?
1 Thes. 2:6 we might have been *b*, as the apostles

Burial

Eccl. 6:3 not filled with good, and. . he have no *b*
Is. 14:20 thou shalt not be joined with them in *b*
Jer. 22:19 he shall be buried with the *b* of an ass
Mt. 26:12 ointment on my body, she did it for my *b*
Acts 8:2 devout men carried Stephen to his *b*

Burn (Burned, Burnt)

Gen. 44:18 not thine anger *b* against thy servant
Ex. 3:2 the bush *b* with fire, and the bush was not
32:20 took the calf which they had made, and *b* it
Lev. 1:3 *b* sacrifice of the herd, let him offer a male
Deut. 32:22 anger, and shall *b* unto the lowest hell
Josh. 11:6 hough their horses, and *b* their chariots
2 Kgs. 23:4 vessels. . he *b* them without Jerusalem
25:9 (Jer. 52:13) he *b* the house of the LORD
Ps. 39:3 while I was musing the fire *b*: then spake
46:9 cutteth the spear. . *b* the chariot in the fire
74:8 they have *b* up all the synagogues of God
80:16 it is *b* with fire, it is cut down
89:46 for ever? shall thy wrath *b* like fire?
97:3 fire goeth before him, and *b* up his enemies
Prov. 6:28 can one go up hot coals. . feet not be *b*?
Is. 1:31 they shall both *b* together, and none shall
9:18 wickedness *b* as the fire: it shall devour
27:4 I would go through them, I would *b* them
40:16 Lebanon is not sufficient to *b*, nor the
Jer. 36:25 to the king that he would not *b* the roll
Lam. 2:3 and he *b* against Jacob like a flaming fire
Mal. 4:1 the day cometh, that shall *b* as an oven
Mt. 3:12 (Lk. 3:17) *b* up the chaff with. . fire
13:30 tares, and bind them in bundles to *b* them
Lk. 24:32 did not our heart *b* within us, while he
Acts 19:19 books together, and *b* them before all men
1 Cor. 3:15 if any man's work shall be *b*, he shall
7:9 for it is better to marry than to *b*
13:3 though I give my body to be *b*, and have not
2 Cor. 11:29 who is offended, and I *b* not?
Heb. 6:8 nigh unto cursing; whose end is to be *b*
12:18 that might be touched, and that *b* with fire
13:11 bodies of those beasts. . *b* without the camp
2 Pet. 3:10 works that are therein shall be *b* up
Rev. 8:7 trees was *b* up, and all green grass was *b* up
17:16 shall eat her flesh, and *b* her with fire
18:8 she shall be utterly *b* with fire: for strong

Burning

Ex. 21:25 *b* for *b*, wound for wound, stripe for
Prov. 26:21 coals are to *b* coals, and wood to fire
26:23 *b* lips and a wicked heart are like a
Is. 4:4 spirit of judgment, and by the spirit of *b*
33:14 among us shall dwell with everlasting *b*?
Jer. 20:9 his word was in mine heart as a *b* fire
Amos 4:11 were as a firebrand plucked out of the *b*
Lk. 12:35 loins be girded about, and your lights *b*
Rev. 4:5 seven lamps of fire *b* before the throne
19:20 alive into a lake of fire *b* with brimstone

Burnt Offering *See also* Sacrifice

Gen. 8:20 Noah builded an altar. . and offered *b o*
22:7 the wood: but where is the lamb for a *b o*?
Ex. 18:12 Jethro. . took a *b o* and sacrifices for God
29:42 (Num. 28:3) this shall be a continual *b o*
Lev. 6:9 this is the law of the *b o*
1 Sam. 7:9 sucking lamb, and offered it for a *b o*
13:12 I forced myself therefore, and offered a *b o*
15:22 hath the LORD as great delight in *b o*

2 Sam. 24:24 neither will I offer *b o* unto the LORD
1 Chr. 16:40 offer *b o* unto the LORD upon the altar
2 Chr. 29:27 Hezekiah commanded to offer the *b o*
Ezra 3:4 offered the daily *b o* by number, according
Job 1:5 offered *b o* according to the number of them
Ps. 40:6 (Heb. 10:6) *b o* and sin offering hast thou
   51:16 would I give it: thou delightest not in *b o*
   66:13 I will go into thy house with *b o*
Is. 1:11 I am full of the *b o* of rams, and the fat
   40:16 nor the beasts thereof sufficient for a *b o*
   56:7 *b o* and their sacrifices shall be accepted
   61:8 I hate robbery for *b o*; and I will direct
Jer. 6:20 your *b o* are not acceptable, nor your
   7:21 put your *b o* unto your sacrifices, and eat
Ezek. 45:17 it shall be the prince's part to give *b o*
Hos. 6:6 and the knowledge of God more than *b o*
Amos 5:22 though ye offer me *b o* and your meat
Mic. 6:6 shall I come before him with *b o*
Mk. 12:33 is more than all whole *b o* and sacrifices

Burst

Job 32:19 my belly. . is ready to *b* like new bottles

Bury

Gen. 23:4 that I may *b* my dead out of my sight
   25:9 *b* him in the cave of Machpelah, in the field
   47:29 deal kindly. . *b* me not, I pray thee, in Egypt
   49:29 *b* me with my fathers in the cave that is in
   50:13 *b* him in the cave of the field of Machpelah
Ruth 1:17 diest, will I die, and there will I be *b*
Ps. 79:3 and there was none to *b* them
Eccl. 8:10 saw the wicked *b*, who had come and gone
Ezek. 39:11 shall they *b* Gog and all his multitude
Mt. 8:21 (Lk. 9:59) me first to go and *b* my father
   27:7 bought. . potter's field, to *b* strangers in
Mk. 14:8 (Jn. 12:7) to anoint my body to the *b*

Bush

Ex. 3:2 *b* burned with fire, and. . was not consumed
Deut. 33:16 good will of him that dwelt in the *b*
Mk. 12:26 (Lk. 20:37) Moses, how in the *b* God spake
Acts 7:30 an angel. . in a flame of fire in a *b*

Bushel

Mt. 5:15 (Mk. 4:21; Lk. 11:33) put it under a *b*, but on

Business

1 Sam. 21:8 because the king's *b* required haste
Lk. 2:49 not that I must be about my Father's *b*?
Acts 6:3 seven men. . we may appoint over this *b*
1 Thes. 4:11 study to be quiet, and to do your own *b*

Busybody

2 Thes. 3:11 some. . working not at all, but are *b*
1 Tim. 5:13 not only idle, but tattlers also and *b*
1 Pet. 4:15 a thief, or as an evildoer, or as a *b*

Butler

Gen. 40:9 and the chief *b* told his dream to Joseph
   41:9 then spake the chief *b* unto Pharaoh, saying

Butter

Gen. 18:8 he took *b*, and milk, and the calf
Judg. 5:25 she brought forth *b* in a lordly dish
Job 29:6 I washed my steps with *b*, and the rock
Ps. 55:21 words of his mouth were smoother than *b*
Prov. 30:33 the churning of milk bringeth forth *b*
Is. 7:15 *b* and honey shall he eat, that he may know
   7:22 eat *b*: for *b* and honey shall every one eat

Buy (Bought)

Gen. 42:2 corn in Egypt: get you down. . and *b* for us
   43:20 came indeed down at the first time to *b* food
   47:19 *b* us and our land for bread

Ex. 21:2 if thou *b* a Hebrew servant, six years he
Deut. 32:6 is not he thy father that hath *b* thee?
Ruth 4:9 that I have *b* all that was Elimelech's
2 Sam. 24:24 (1 Chr. 21:24) I will surely *b* it of thee
Neh. 10:31 would not *b* it of them on the sabbath
Prov. 23:23 *b* the truth. . sell it not; also wisdom
Is. 55:1 he that hath no money; come ye, *b*, and eat
Jer. 32:7 *b* thee my field that is in Anathoth
Hos. 3:2 I *b* her to me for fifteen pieces of silver
Amos 8:6 that we may *b* the poor for silver
Mt. 13:44 selleth all that he hath, and *b* that field
   13:46 one pearl. . sold all that he had, and *b* it
   14:15 (Mk. 6:36) and *b* themselves victuals
   21:12 (Mk. 11:15; Lk. 19:45) Jesus. . cast out all
      them that sold and *b* in the temple
   27:7 and *b* with them the potter's field, to bury
Mk. 15:46 he *b* fine linen, and took him down
   16:1 had *b* sweet spices, that they might. . anoint
Lk. 14:18 I have *b* a piece of ground, and I must
   17:28 they did eat, they drank, they *b*, they sold
   22:36 sword, let him sell his garment, and *b* one
Acts 7:16 and laid in the sepulchre that Abraham *b*
1 Cor. 6:20 (7:23) for ye are *b* with a price
2 Pet. 2:1 even denying the Lord that *b* them
Rev. 18:11 no man *b* their merchandise any more

Byword *See also* Parable, Proverb

Deut. 28:37 an astonishment, a proverb, and a *b*
1 Kgs. 9:7 and Israel shall be a proverb and a *b*
2 Chr. 7:20 will make it to be a proverb and a *b*
Job 17:6 he hath made me also a *b* of the people
   30:9 and now am I their song, yea, I am their *b*
Ps. 44:14 thou makest us a *b* among the heathen

C

Cabul 1 Kgs. 9:13

Caesar

Mt. 22:17 (Mk. 12:14; Lk. 20:22) give tribute unto *C*
   22:21 (Mk. 12:17; Lk. 20:25) render. . unto *C*
Lk. 2:1 there went out a decree from *C* Augustus
   3:1 fifteenth year of the reign of Tiberius *C*
   23:2 forbidding to give tribute to *C*, saying
Jn. 19:12 let this man go, thou art not *C*'s friend
   19:15 priests answered, We have no king but *C*
Acts 11:28 came to pass in the days of Claudius *C*
   17:7 these all do contrary to the decrees of *C*
   25:8 temple, nor yet against *C*, have I offended
   25:11 no man may deliver me. . I appeal unto *C*
   27:24 Paul; thou must be brought before *C*
Phil. 4:22 chiefly they that are of *C*'s household

Caesarea

Acts 8:40 Philip. . preached. . till he came to *C*
   9:30 brought him down to *C*, and sent him forth
   10:1 man in *C* called Cornelius, a centurion of
   18:22 had landed at *C*. . and saluted the church
   21:8 the next day we. . departed, and came unto *C*
   23:23 make ready two hundred soldiers to go to *C*
   25:4 Festus answered, that Paul should be kept at *C*

Caesarea Philippi Mt. 16:13 (Mk. 8:27)

Cage

Jer. 5:27 as a *c* is full of birds. . their houses
Rev. 18:2 a *c* of every unclean and hateful bird

Caiaphas

Served as the high priest, Mt. 26:3, 57; Lk. 3:2; Jn.
18:13; "prophesied that Jesus should die," Jn. 11:49–

53; 18:14; took part in the trial of Jesus, Mt. 26:62–66 (Mk. 14:60–64; Jn. 18:19–24, 28); present at examination of Peter and John, Acts 4:6–21.

Cain Gen. 4:1–25

Heb. 11:4 offered. . more excellent sacrifice than *C*
1 Jn. 3:12 *C*, who was of that wicked one, and slew
Jude 11 gone in the way of *C*, and ran greedily

Cake

Gen. 18:6 knead it, and make *c* upon the hearth
Ex. 12:39 they baked unleavened *c* of the dough
    29:23 (Lev. 8:26) *c* of oiled bread, and one wafer
Lev. 2:4 a meat offering. . shall be unleavened *c*
Josh. 5:11 did eat. . unleavened *c*, and parched corn
Judg. 6:19 made ready a kid, and unleavened *c* of
    7:13 a *c* of barley bread tumbled into the host
1 Kgs. 17:13 but make me thereof a little *c* first
1 Chr. 23:29 offering, and for the unleavened *c*
Ezek. 4:12 eat it as barley *c*. . bake it with dung
Hos. 7:8 Ephraim is a *c* not turned

Calamity See also Affliction, Anguish, Distress, Grief, Misery, Sorrow, Suffering, Tribulation, Trouble

Deut. 32:35 for the day of their *c* is at hand
2 Sam. 22:19 (Ps. 18:18) they prevented me in. . my *c*
Job 6:2 and my *c* laid in the balances together!
Ps. 57:1 my refuge, until these *c* be overpast
    141:5 yet my prayer also shall be in their *c*
Prov. 1:26 I also will laugh at your *c*; I will
    6:15 therefore shall his *c* come suddenly
    17:5 that is glad at *c* shall not be unpunished
    19:13 a foolish son is the *c* of his father
    24:22 for their *c* shall rise suddenly; and who
    27:10 thy brother's house in the day of thy *c*
Jer. 46:21 the day of their *c* was come upon them
    48:16 the *c* of Moab is near to come, and his
Obad. 13 gate of my people in the day of their *c*

Caldron

1 Sam. 2:14 struck it into the pan. . or *c*, or pot
Job 41:20 smoke, as out of a seething pot or *c*
Ezek. 11:3 this city is the *c*, and we be the flesh
Mic. 3:3 chop them in pieces. . as flesh within the *c*

Caleb

Sent with the spies, Num. 13:1–6; exhorted the people, Num. 13:30; 14:6–10; was promised entrance into Canaan, Num. 14:22–38 (32:10–12; Deut. 1:34–36); Num. 26:65; received Hebron as inheritance, Josh. 14:6–15; 15:13–19; Judg. 1:20.

Calf (Calves)

Gen. 18:7 Abraham. . fetched a *c* tender and good
Ex. 32:8 made them a molten *c*, and have worshipped
    32:24 into the fire, and there came out this *c*
Lev. 9:2 take thee a young *c* for a sin offering
Deut. 9:16 had sinned. . and had made you a molten *c*
1 Sam. 6:7 tie the kine. . and bring their *c* home
1 Kgs. 12:28 king took counsel. . made two *c* of gold
Neh. 9:18 yea, when they had made them a molten *c*
Ps. 29:6 he maketh them also to skip like a *c*
    106:19 they made a *c* in Horeb, and worshipped
Is. 11:6 the *c* and the young lion and the fatling
Jer. 34:18 they cut the *c* in twain, and passed
Hos. 8:5 thy *c*, O Samaria, hath cast thee off
    14:2 so will we render the *c* of our lips
Mic. 6:6 burnt offerings, with *c* of a year old?
Mal. 4:2 go forth, and grow up as *c* of the stall
Lk. 15:23 (15:30) hither the fatted *c*, and kill it

Acts 7:41 they made a *c*. . and offered sacrifice
Heb. 9:12 neither by the blood of goats and *c*, but
    9:19 took the blood of *c* and of goats, with water

Call

Gen. 2:19 whatsoever Adam *c* every living creature
    4:26 began men to *c* upon the name of the LORD
    21:12 (Rom. 9:7; Heb. 11:18) Isaac. . thy seed be *c*
    22:11 angel of the LORD *c* unto him out of heaven
Ex. 2:7 and *c* to thee a nurse of the Hebrew women
    3:4 God *c* unto him out of the midst of the bush
    19:20 LORD *c* Moses up to the top of the mount
Deut. 4:26 I *c* heaven and earth to witness against
    30:19 I *c* heaven and earth to record this day
Judg. 16:25 *c* for Samson out of the prison house
1 Sam. 3:4 LORD *c* Samuel. . he answered, Here am I
    3:6 thou didst *c* me. And he answered, I *c* not
2 Sam. 22:4 (Ps. 18:3) *c* on the LORD, who is worthy
    22:7 (Ps. 18:6) in my distress I *c* upon the LORD
1 Kgs. 17:18 *c* my sin to remembrance, and to slay
    18:26 *c* on the name of Baal from morning even
2 Kgs. 4:12 *c* this Shunammite. And when he had *c*
1 Chr. 16:8 (Ps. 105:1) the LORD, *c* upon his name
2 Chr. 7:14 if my people, which are *c* by my name
Job 13:22 then *c* thou, and I will answer: or let
    14:15 thou shalt *c*, and I will answer thee
Ps. 4:1 hear me when I *c*, O God of my righteousness
    14:4 (53:4) of iniquity. . *c* not upon the LORD
    17:6 I have *c* upon thee, for thou wilt hear me
    31:17 me not be ashamed. . for I have *c* upon thee
    49:11 they *c* their lands after their own names
    50:4 he shall *c* to the heavens from above
    50:15 *c* upon me in the day of trouble: I will
    55:16 as for me, I will *c* upon God; and the LORD
    80:18 quicken us, and we will *c* upon thy name
    86:5 in mercy unto all them that *c* upon thee
    86:7 in the day of my trouble I will *c* upon thee
    99:6 they *c* upon the LORD, and he answered them
    102:2 in the day when I *c* answer me speedily
    116:2 will I *c* upon him as long as I live
    118:5 I *c* upon the LORD in distress: the LORD
    145:18 LORD is nigh unto all them that *c* upon him
Prov. 1:24 because I have *c*, and ye refused
    1:28 shall they *c* upon me, but I will not answer
    8:4 unto you, O men, I *c*; and my voice is to
Is. 5:20 woe unto them that *c* evil good. . good evil
    41:9 *c* thee from the chief men thereof, and said
    41:25 rising of the sun shall he *c* upon my name
    42:6 I the LORD have *c* thee in righteousness
    43:1 I have *c* thee by thy name; thou art mine
    45:4 mine elect, I have even *c* thee by thy name
    49:1 the LORD hath *c* me from the womb
    51:2 look unto Abraham your father. . for I *c* him
    55:5 thou shalt *c* a nation that thou knowest not
    55:6 be found, *c* ye upon him while he is near
    56:7 (Mt. 21:13; Mk. 11:17) be *c* a house of prayer
    58:13 *c* the sabbath a delight. . holy of the LORD
    64:7 there is none that *c* upon thy name, that
    65:12 (66:4) when I *c*, ye did not answer; when
    65:24 before they *c*, I will answer; and while
    66:4 when I *c*, none did answer; when I spake
Jer. 33:3 *c* unto me, and I will answer thee, and show
    35:17 *c* unto them, but they have not answered
Ezek. 21:23 he will *c* to remembrance the iniquity
Dan. 9:19 thy city and thy people are *c* by thy name
Hos. 7:7 there is none among them that *c* unto me
    11:1 (Mt. 2:15) loved him. . *c* my son out of Egypt
Joel 1:14 (2:15) sanctify. . fast, *c* a solemn assembly
    2:32 (Acts 2:21; Rom. 10:13) whosoever shall *c* on
    the. . LORD shall be delivered
Amos 9:12 (Acts 15:17) heathen. . *c* by my name
Jon. 1:6 what meanest thou. . arise, *c* upon thy God
Zech. 13:9 they shall *c* on my name, and I will hear

Mal. 3:12 all nations shall *c* you blessed
Mt. 4:21 (Mk. 1:20) mending their nets; and he *c* them
  5:9 for they shall be *c* the children of God
  5:19 be *c* the least. . be *c* great in the kingdom
  9:13 (Mk. 2:17; Lk. 5:32) to *c* the righteous
  10:1 (Mk. 6:7; Lk. 9:1) *c* unto him his twelve
  11:16 (Lk. 7:32) markets, and *c* unto their fellows
  18:2 Jesus *c* a little child unto him, and set him
  19:17 (Mk. 10:18; Lk. 18:19) why *c* thou me good?
  20:16 first last: for many be *c*, but few chosen
  20:32 Jesus stood still, and *c* them
  22:3 to *c* them that were bidden to the wedding
  22:14 for many are *c*, but few are chosen
  27:47 (Mk. 15:35) said, This man *c* for Elias
Mk. 10:49 commanded him to be *c*. . they *c* the blind
Lk. 1:48 behold. . all generations shall *c* me blessed
  6:46 and why *c* ye me, Lord, Lord, and do not the
  14:13 when thou makest a feast, *c* the poor
  15:6 he *c* together his friends and neighbors
  16:5 so he *c* every one of his lord's debtors
Jn. 2:2 was *c*, and his disciples, to the marriage
  10:3 he *c* his own sheep by name, and leadeth them
  15:15 *c* you not servants. . but I have *c* you friends
Acts 2:21 *c* on the name of the Lord shall be saved
  2:39 even as many as the Lord our God shall *c*
  9:14 authority. . to bind all that *c* on thy name
  10:5 (11:13) to Joppa, and *c* for one Simon
  10:15 (11:9) cleansed, that *c* not thou common
  13:2 Saul for the work whereunto I have *c* them
  16:10 assuredly gathering that the Lord had *c* us
  19:40 to be *c* in question for this day's uproar
  28:17 Paul *c* the chief of the Jews together
  28:20 for this cause therefore have I *c* for you
Rom. 4:17 *c* those things which be not as though they
  8:30 whom he did predestinate, them he also *c*
  9:25 I will *c* them my people, which were not my
  9:26 they be *c* the children of the living God
  10:12 over all is rich unto all that *c* upon him
  10:13 *c* upon the name of the Lord shall be saved
  10:14 how then shall they *c* on him in whom they
1 Cor. 1:24 but unto them which are *c*, both Jews
  1:26 not many wise men. . not many noble, are *c*
  7:15 not under bondage. . God hath *c* us to peace
  7:20 abide in the same calling wherein he was *c*
Gal. 1:15 who separated me. . and *c* me by his grace
  5:13 for, brethren, ye have been *c* unto liberty
Eph. 4:1 worthy of the vocation wherewith ye are *c*
  4:4 even as ye are *c* in one hope of your calling
1 Thes. 2:12 walk worthy of God, who hath *c* you
  4:7 God hath not *c* us unto uncleanness, but unto
2 Thes. 2:14 whereunto he *c* you by our gospel
2 Tim. 1:9 saved us, and *c* us with a holy calling
Heb. 2:11 he is not ashamed to *c* them brethren
  5:4 but he that is *c* of God, as was Aaron
  11:8 by faith Abraham, when he was *c*. . obeyed
1 Pet. 1:15 he which hath *c* you is holy, so be ye
  2:9 *c* you out of darkness into. . marvelous light
  5:10 hath *c* us unto his eternal glory by Christ
1 Jn. 3:1 that we should be *c* the sons of God
Rev. 19:9 which are *c* unto the marriage supper of

Called *See also* Call

Rom. 1:1 (1 Cor. 1:1) Paul. . *c* to be an apostle
  1:6 among whom are ye also the *c* of Jesus Christ
  8:28 them who are the *c* according to his purpose

Calling *See also* Call, Election

Rom. 11:29 gifts and *c* of God are without repentance
1 Cor. 1:26 ye see your *c*, brethren, how that not
  7:20 abide in the same *c* wherein he was called
Eph. 1:18 ye may know what is the hope of his *c*
  4:4 even as ye are called in one hope of your *c*
Phil. 3:14 prize of the high *c* of God in Christ
2 Thes. 1:11 God would count you worthy of this *c*

2 Tim. 1:9 saved us, and called us with a holy *c*
Heb. 3:1 holy brethren, partakers of the heavenly *c*
2 Pet. 1:10 to make your *c* and election sure

Calm

Ps. 107:29 maketh the storm a *c*, so that the waves
Jon. 1:11 what shall we do. . that the sea may be *c*
Mt. 8:26 (Mk. 4:39; Lk. 8:24) there was a great *c*

Calvary Lk. 23:33

Calve

Job 21:10 their cow *c*, and casteth not her calf
Ps. 29:9 voice of the Lord maketh the hinds to *c*
Jer. 14:5 hind also *c* in the field, and forsook it

Came *See* Come

Camel

Gen. 12:16 he had sheep, and oxen. . she asses, and *c*
  24:10 servant took ten *c* of the *c* of his master
  24:19 she said, I will draw water for thy *c* also
  24:64 when she saw Isaac, she lighted off the *c*
  37:25 Ishmaelites came from Gilead, with their *c*
Ex. 9:3 hand of the Lord is. . upon the *c*, upon the
Lev. 11:4 (Deut. 14:7) *c*, because he cheweth the cud
Esth. 8:10 horseback, and riders on mules, *c*, and
Job 1:17 made out three bands, and fell upon the *c*
Is. 60:6 the multitude of *c* shall cover thee
Mt. 3:4 (Mk. 1:6) John had his raiment of *c*'s hair
  19:24 (Mk. 10:25; Lk. 18:25) it is easier for a *c*
  23:24 which strain at a gnat, and swallow a *c*

Camp

Ex. 14:19 angel of God, which went before the *c*
  16:13 the quails came up, and covered the *c*
  19:2 Sinai. . and there Israel *c* before the mount
Lev. 6:11 and carry forth the ashes without the *c*
  13:46 without the *c* shall his habitation be
Num. 1:52 pitch their tents, every man by his own *c*
  4:5 when the *c* setteth forward, Aaron shall come
  5:2 that they put out of the *c* every leper
  11:26 but. . two of the men. . prophesied in the *c*
  12:15 Miriam was shut out from the *c* seven days
Deut. 23:10 then shall he go abroad out of the *c*
  23:14 thy God walketh in the midst of thy *c*
  29:11 stranger that is in thy *c*, from the hewer
1 Sam. 4:6 great shout in the *c* of the Hebrews?
  4:7 afraid; for they said, God is come into the *c*
Ps. 78:28 he let it fall in the midst of their *c*
  106:16 they envied Moses also in the *c*, and Aaron
Is. 29:3 and I will *c* against thee round about
Jer. 50:29 all ye that bend the bow, *c* against it
Ezek. 4:2 cast a mount against it; set the *c* also
Heb. 13:13 go forth therefore unto him without the *c*
Rev. 20:9 and compassed the *c* of the saints about

Camphire

Song 1:14 my beloved is unto me as a cluster of *c*

Cana Jn. 2:1; 4:46

Canaan

Gen. 9:25 cursed be C; a servant of servants shall
  12:5 land of C; and into the land of C they came
  13:12 Abram dwelt in the land of C, and Lot dwelt
  17:8 I will give unto thee. . all the land of C
  28:1 shalt not take a wife of the daughters of C
  36:2 Esau took his wives of the daughters of C
  36:6 substance, which he had got in the land of C
  37:1 Jacob dwelt in the land. . in the land of C
Ex. 15:15 all the inhabitants of C shall melt away

Num. 13:2 men, that they may search the land of *C*
Is. 19:18 cities in. . Egypt speak the language of *C*

Canaanite

Gen. 10:18 the families of the *C* spread abroad
13:7 *C* and the Perizzite dwelt then in the land
Josh. 17:12 (Judg. 1:27) *C* would dwell in that land
Judg. 1:9 Judah went down to fight against the *C*

Candace Acts 8:27

Candle *See also* Lamp, Light

Job 18:6 and his *c* shall be put out with him
21:17 how oft is the *c* of the wicked put out!
29:3 when his *c* shined upon my head, and when
Ps. 18:28 thou wilt light my *c*: the LORD my God
Prov. 20:27 the spirit of man is the *c* of the LORD
24:20 the *c* of the wicked shall be put out
31:18 her *c* goeth not out by night
Zeph. 1:12 will search Jerusalem with *c*, and punish
Mt. 5:15 (Mk. 4:21; Lk. 8:16; 11:33) light a *c*, and put
Lk. 15:8 light a *c*, and sweep the house, and seek
Rev. 18:23 light of a *c* shall shine no more at all
22:5 they need no *c*, neither light of the sun

Candlestick

Ex. 25:31 (37:17) shalt make a *c* of pure gold
Lev. 24:4 he shall order the lamps upon the pure *c*
Num. 8:2 lamps shall give light over against the *c*
2 Kgs. 4:10 bed, and a table, and a stool, and a *c*
Zech. 4:2 I have looked, and behold a *c* all of gold
Mt. 5:15 (Mk. 4:21; Lk. 8:16; 11:33) put it. . on a *c*
Heb. 9:2 first, wherein was the *c*, and the table
Rev. 1:12 and being turned, I saw seven golden *c*
1:20 *c* which thou sawest are the seven churches
2:5 will remove thy *c* out of his place, except

Canker

2 Tim. 2:17 and their word will eat as doth a *c*
Jas. 5:3 your gold and silver is *c*; and the rust

Cankerworm

Joel 1:4 *c* eaten; and that which the *c* hath left
2:25 the years that the locust hath eaten, the *c*

Capernaum

Mt. 4:13 leaving Nazareth, he came and dwelt in *C*
8:5 (Lk. 7:1) when Jesus was entered into *C*
11:23 (Lk. 10:15) *C*, which art exalted unto heaven
17:24 were come to *C*, they that received tribute
Mk. 1:21 (Lk. 4:31) into *C*; and. . on the sabbath
Jn. 4:46 certain nobleman, whose son was sick at *C*
6:17 into a ship, and went over the sea toward *C*

Caphtor *See also* Crete

Deut. 2:23; Jer. 47:4; Amos 9:7

Captain

Gen. 21:22 Phichol the chief *c* of his host spake
37:36 Potiphar, an officer. . and *c* of the guard
Ex. 15:4 chosen *c* also are drowned in the Red sea
Num. 14:4 make a *c*, and let us return into Egypt
Josh. 5:14 nay; but as *c* of the host of the LORD
Judg. 11:6 said unto Jephthah, Come, and be our *c*
2 Kgs. 9:5 he said, I have an errand to thee, O *c*
2 Chr. 13:12 God himself is with us for our *c*
Neh. 9:17 appointed a *c* to return to their bondage
Jer. 51:27 appoint a *c* against her; cause the
Ezek. 21:22 divination for Jerusalem, to appoint *c*
Dan. 3:2 to gather together the princes. . and the *c*
Mk. 6:21 Herod. . made a supper to his lords, high *c*
Lk. 22:4 communed with the chief priests and *c*, how
22:52 the chief priests, and *c* of the temple
Jn. 18:12 *c* and officers of the Jews took Jesus

Acts 4:1 *c* of the temple, and the Sadducees, came
28:16 centurion delivered the prisoners to the *c*
Heb. 2:10 to make the *c* of their salvation perfect
Rev. 19:18 the flesh of kings, and the flesh of *c*

Captive *See also* Prisoner

Gen. 14:14 Abram heard that his brother was taken *c*
34:29 little ones, and their wives took they *c*
Ex. 12:29 the firstborn of the *c*. . in the dungeon
Num. 24:22 until Asshur shall carry thee away *c*
2 Kgs. 5:2 brought away *c*. . of Israel a little maid
15:29 Tiglath-pileser. . carried them *c* to Assyria
24:16 the king of Babylon brought *c* to Babylon
2 Chr. 28:11 which ye have taken *c* of your brethren
Ps. 68:18 (Eph. 4:8) thou hast led captivity *c*
137:3 carried us away *c* required of us a song
Is. 14:2 they shall take them *c*, whose *c* they were
20:4 Egyptians prisoners, and the Ethiopians *c*
49:25 even the *c* of the mighty shall be taken
51:14 *c* exile hasteneth that he may be loosed
52:2 the bands of thy neck, O *c* daughter of Zion
61:1 (Lk. 4:18) sent. . to proclaim liberty to the *c*
Jer. 13:19 Judah shall be carried away *c* all of it
20:4 carry them *c* into Babylon, and shall slay
29:14 whence I caused you to be carried away *c*
52:30 Nebuzar-adan. . carried away *c* of the Jews
Dan. 2:25 found a man of the *c* of Judah, that will
Amos 6:7 shall they go *c* with the first that go *c*
Lk. 21:24 and shall be led away *c* into all nations
2 Tim. 2:26 who are taken *c* by him at his will
3:6 creep into houses, and lead *c* silly women

Captivity *See also* Bondage

Deut. 30:3 then the LORD thy God will turn thy *c*
Judg. 5:12 arise, Barak, and lead thy *c* captive
2 Kgs. 24:15 carried he into *c* from Jerusalem to
1 Chr. 5:22 they dwelt in their steads until the *c*
Ezra 1:11 the *c* that were brought up from Babylon
2:1 (Neh. 7:6) province that went up out of the *c*
8:35 the children. . which were come out of the *c*
Neh. 4:4 and give them for a prey in the land of *c*
Esth. 2:6 carried away from Jerusalem with the *c*
Job 42:10 LORD turned the *c* of Job, when he prayed
Ps. 14:7 (53:6) bringeth back the *c* of his people
68:18 (Eph. 4:8) on high, thou hast led *c* captive
85:1 LORD. . thou hast brought back the *c* of Jacob
126:1 when the LORD turned again the *c* of Zion
126:4 turn again our *c*, O LORD, as the streams
Is. 5:13 therefore my people are gone into *c*, because
46:2 burden, but themselves are gone into *c*
Jer. 15:2 and such as are for the *c*, to the *c*
20:6 thou, Pashur. . shall go into *c*
22:22 pastors, and thy lovers shall go into *c*
29:14 I will turn away your *c*, and I will gather
30:3 (Amos 9:14) bring again the *c* of my people
32:44 (33:26) for I will cause their *c* to return
33:7 cause the *c* of Judah and the *c* of Israel to
43:11 such as are for *c* to *c*; and such as are
Lam. 1:3 Judah is gone into *c* because of affliction
Ezek. 3:15 then I came to them of the *c* at Tel-abib
12:4 shalt go forth. . as they that go forth into *c*
12:7 I brought forth my stuff. . as stuff for *c*
39:23 house of Israel went into *c* for their
Amos 1:6 they carried away captive the whole *c*
5:27 cause you to go into *c* beyond Damascus
Zeph. 2:7 shall visit them, and turn away their *c*
3:20 when I turn back your *c* before your eyes
Rom. 7:23 bringing me into *c* to the law of sin
2 Cor. 10:5 into *c* every thought to the obedience
Rev. 13:10 he that leadeth into *c* shall go into *c*

Carcass

Judg. 14:8 of bees and honey in the *c* of the lion
1 Kgs. 13:24 *c* was cast in the way, and the ass

Is. 14:19 art cast out. . as a c trodden under feet
  66:24 go forth, and look upon the c of the men
Jer. 7:33 (16:4; 19:7) c of this people shall be meat
Mt. 24:28 wheresoever the c is. . will the eagles be
Heb. 3:17 sinned, whose c fell in the wilderness?

Carchemish 2 Chr. 35:20 (Jer. 46:2)

Care

1 Sam. 10:2 thy father hath left the c of the asses
2 Sam. 18:3 if we flee away, they will not c for us
2 Kgs. 4:13 been careful for us with all this c
Ps. 142:4 refuge failed me; no man c for my soul
Jer. 49:31 wealthy nation, that dwelleth without c
Ezek. 4:16 shall eat bread by weight, and with c
Mt. 13:22 (Mk. 4:19) the c of this world, and the
Mk. 4:38 Master, c thou not that we perish?
Lk. 8:14 choked with c and riches and pleasures
  10:34 brought him to an inn, and took c of him
  10:40 not c that my sister hath left me to serve
  21:34 surfeiting. . drunkenness. . c of this life
Jn. 10:13 is a hireling, and c not for the sheep
  12:6 this he said, not that he c for the poor
Acts 18:17 and Gallio c for none of those things
1 Cor. 7:21 called being a servant? c not for it
  7:32 unmarried c for the things that belong to
  9:9 treadeth. . the corn. Doth God take c for oxen?
  12:25 the members should have the same c one for
2 Cor. 7:12 that our c for you in the sight of God
  8:16 the same earnest c into the heart of Titus
  11:28 upon me daily, the c of all the churches
Phil. 2:20 no man likeminded, who will naturally c
  4:10 at the last your c of me hath flourished
1 Tim. 3:5 how shall he take c of the church of God?
1 Pet. 5:7 casting all your c upon him; for he c

Careful

2 Kgs. 4:13 hast been c for us with all this care
Jer. 17:8 shall not be c in the year of drought
Dan. 3:16 O Nebuchadnezzar, we are not c to answer
Lk. 10:41 Martha, thou art c and troubled about
Phil. 4:6 be c for nothing; but in every thing by
  4:10 ye were also c, but ye lacked opportunity
Tit. 3:8 in God might be c to maintain good works

Carefully

Phil. 2:28 I sent him therefore the more c, that
Heb. 12:17 though he sought it c with tears

Carefulness

Ezek. 12:18 thy water with trembling and with c
1 Cor. 7:32 I would have you without c
2 Cor. 7:11 a godly sort, what c it wrought in you

Careless

Judg. 18:7 came to Laish, and saw. . how they dwelt c
Is. 32:9 hear my voice, ye c daughters; give ear

Carmel

1 Sam. 15:12 told Samuel, saying, Saul came to C
  25:2 possessions. . in C. . shearing his sheep in C
1 Kgs. 18:19 gather to me all Israel unto mount C
2 Kgs. 4:25 came unto the man of God to mount C
  19:23 (Is. 37:24) enter. . into the forest of his C
Is. 33:9 and Bashan and C shake off their fruits
  35:2 shall be given unto it, the excellency of C
Jer. 50:19 to his habitation, and he shall feed on C
Amos 1:2 shall mourn, and the top of C shall wither

Carnal

Rom. 7:14 law is spiritual: but I am c, sold under sin
  8:7 because the c mind is enmity against God
  15:27 is also to minister unto them in c things
1 Cor. 3:1 as unto c, even as unto babes in Christ

1 Cor. 3:3 divisions, are ye not c, and walk as men?
  9:11 great thing if we shall reap your c things?
2 Cor. 10:4 the weapons of our warfare are not c
Heb. 7:16 not after the law of a c commandment, but
  9:10 and c ordinances, imposed on them until

Carnally

Rom. 8:6 to be c minded is death. . to be spiritually

Carpenter

2 Sam. 5:11 (1 Chr. 14:1) sent messengers. . and c
2 Chr. 24:12 and c to repair the house of the LORD
Is. 41:7 so the c encouraged the goldsmith, and he
  44:13 the c stretcheth out his rule; he marketh
Jer. 24:1 had carried away captive. . c and smiths
Zech. 1:20 and the LORD showed me four c
Mt. 13:55 not this the c's son? is not his mother
Mk. 6:3 is not this the c, the son of Mary

Carpus 2 Tim. 4:13

Carriage

1 Sam. 17:22 David left his c. . and ran into the army
Is. 10:28 at Michmash he hath laid up his c
  46:1 your c were heavy laden; they are a burden
Acts 21:15 took up our c, and went up to Jerusalem

Carried See also Carry

1 Cor. 12:2 Gentiles, c away unto these dumb idols
Eph. 4:14 c about with every wind of doctrine
Heb. 13:9 c about with divers and strange doctrines
Jude 12 clouds. . without water, c about of winds

Carry See also Bear

Gen. 31:18 c away all his cattle, and all his goods
  31:26 thou hast stolen. . and c away my daughters
  43:11 c down the man a present, a little balm
  50:25 (Ex. 13:19) shall c up my bones from hence
Ex. 33:15 thy presence go not with me, c us not up
Num. 11:12 c them in thy bosom, as a nursing father
Deut. 14:24 so that thou art not able to c it
1 Sam. 17:18 c these ten cheeses unto the captain
2 Sam. 19:18 ferryboat to c. . the king's household
1 Kgs. 18:12 the Spirit of the LORD shall c thee
2 Kgs. 17:6 took Samaria. . c Israel away into Assyria
  20:17 (Is. 39:6) shall be c unto Babylon
  25:7 (Jer. 39:7; 52:11) and c him to Babylon
Ezra 8:35 children of those that had been c away
  9:4 transgression of those that had been c away
Ps. 46:2 though the mountains be c into the midst
  49:17 for when he dieth he shall c nothing away
  90:5 thou c them away as with a flood; they are
  137:3 that c us away captive required of us a song
Eccl. 5:15 nothing of his labor, which he may c
Is. 40:11 with his arm, and c them in his bosom
  46:4 and even to hoar hairs will I c you
  53:4 he hath borne our griefs, and c our sorrows
  63:9 bare them, and c them all the days of old
Jer. 13:17 the LORD's flock is c away captive
  24:5 I acknowledge them that are c away captive
  28:6 to bring again. . all that is c away captive
Ezek. 22:9 men that c tales to shed blood
Mk. 6:55 to c about in beds those that were sick
  11:16 suffer that any man should c any vessel
  15:1 bound Jesus, and c him away, and delivered
Lk. 10:4 c neither purse, nor scrip, nor shoes
  16:22 the beggar died, and was c by the angels
  24:51 was parted from them, and c up into heaven
Jn. 5:10 it is not lawful for thee to c thy bed
  21:18 and another shall gird thee, and c thee
Acts 5:6 wound him up, and c him out, and buried
  8:2 devout men c Stephen to his burial, and made

Acts 21:34 he commanded him to be *c* into the castle
1 Tim. 6:7 and it is certain we can *c* nothing out
2 Pet. 2:17 clouds that are *c* with a tempest
Rev. 17:3 so he *c* me away in the spirit into the
   21:10 he *c* me away in the spirit to a great

Cart

1 Sam. 6:7 make a new *c*, and take two milch kine
2 Sam. 6:3 (1 Chr. 13:7) ark of God upon a new *c*
Is. 5:18 vanity, and sin as it were with a *c* rope
Amos 2:13 *c* is pressed that is full of sheaves

Carve

1 Kgs. 6:35 he *c* thereon cherubim ar.d palm trees

Carved

Judg. 18:18 Micah's house, and fetched the *c* image
Ps. 74:6 now they break down the *c* work thereof
Prov. 7:16 I have decked my bed. . with *c* works

Cassia

Ps. 45:8 garments smell of myrrh, and aloes, and *c*

Cast *See also* Throw

Gen. 21:10 (Gal. 4:30) *c* out this bondwoman and her
Ex. 32:24 I *c* it into the fire. . came out this calf
   34:24 for I will *c* out the nations before thee
Lev. 18:24 the nations are defiled which I *c* out
Deut. 7:1 and hath *c* out many nations before thee
1 Kgs. 19:19 Elijah passed. . and *c* his mantle upon
2 Chr. 25:8 God hath power to help, and to *c* down
Neh. 9:26 *c* thy law behind their backs, and slew
Esth. 3:7 they *c* Pur, that is, the lot, before
Job 27:22 for God shall *c* upon him, and not spare
Ps. 5:10 *c* them out in the multitude of their
   22:10 I was *c* upon thee from the womb: thou art
   22:18 (Mt. 27:35; Mk. 15:24; Lk. 23:34; Jn. 19:24)
     part my garments. . *c* lots upon my vesture
   36:12 are *c* down, and shall not be able to rise
   37:24 he fall, he shall not be utterly *c* down
   42:5 (42:11; 43:5) why art thou *c* down, O my soul?
   44:9 but thou hast *c* off, and put us to shame
   51:11 *c* me not away from thy presence; and take
   55:22 *c* thy burden upon the LORD, and he shall
   62:4 consult to *c* him down from his excellency
   76:6 chariot and horse are *c* into a dead sleep
   77:7 will the Lord *c* off for ever? and will he
   78:49 he *c* upon them the fierceness of his anger
   80:8 thou hast *c* out the heathen, and planted it
   88:14 LORD, why *c* thou off my soul? why hidest
   94:14 for the LORD will not *c* off his people
   102:10 for thou hast lifted me up, and *c* me down
Prov. 16:33 lot is *c* into the lap; but the whole
   26:18 mad man who *c* firebrands, arrows, and death
Is. 2:20 that day a man shall *c* his idols of silver
   16:2 as a wandering bird *c* out of the nest, so
   25:7 the face of the covering *c* over all people
   34:3 their slain also shall be *c* out, and their
   38:17 thou hast *c* all my sins behind thy back
   41:9 I have chosen thee, and not *c* thee away
   66:5 that *c* you out for my name's sake, said
Jer. 7:15 *c* you out of my sight, as I have *c* out
   16:13 therefore will I *c* you out of this land
   31:37 I will also *c* off all the seed of Israel
Ezek. 11:16 have *c* them far off among the heathen
   18:31 *c* away from you all your transgressions
Dan. 3:6 be *c* into the midst of a. . fiery furnace
   6:7 O king, he shall be *c* into the den of lions
Hos. 8:3 Israel hath *c* off the thing that is good
   14:5 as the lily, and *c* forth his roots as Lebanon
Jon. 1:15 took up Jonah, and *c* him forth into the sea
   2:4 then I said, I am *c* out of thy sight
Mic. 7:19 thou wilt *c* all their sins into the depths

Mt. 3:10 (Lk. 3:9) hewn down, and *c* into the fire
   4:6 (Lk. 4:9) be the Son of God, *c* thyself down
   5:29 (18:9) offend thee, pluck it out, and *c* it
   5:30 (18:9) thy whole body should be *c* into hell
   6:30 (Lk. 12:28) and tomorrow is *c* into the oven
   7:5 (Lk. 6:42) hypocrite, first *c* out the beam
   7:6 neither *c* ye your pearls before swine, lest
   8:12 children of the kingdom shall be *c* out into
   8:16 (Mk. 1:34) *c* out the spirits with his word
   9:34 said, He *c* out devils through the prince of
   10:1 (Mk. 3:15) unclean spirits, to *c* them out
   12:24 (Mk. 3:22; Lk. 11:15) this fellow doth not *c*
     out devils, but by Beelzebub
   12:26 (Mk. 3:23) and if Satan *c* out Satan, he is
   13:42 (13:50) shall *c* them into a furnace of fire
   13:47 like unto a net, that was *c* into the sea
   13:48 gathered the good. . but *c* the bad away
   15:26 (Mk. 7:27) children's bread. . to *c* it to dogs
   17:19 (Mk. 9:28) why could not we *c* him out?
   17:27 *c* a hook, and take up the fish that first
   21:12 (Mk. 11:15; Lk. 19:45) *c* out all. . that sold
   21:21 (Mk. 11:23) and be thou *c* into the sea
   21:39 (Mk. 12:8; Lk. 20:15) *c* him out of. . vineyard
   27:5 *c* down the pieces of silver in the temple
Mk. 1:34 of divers diseases, and *c* out many devils
   9:22 and ofttimes it hath *c* him into the fire
   9:38 (Lk. 9:49) saw one *c* out devils in thy name
   9:42 (Lk. 17:2) neck, and he were *c* into the sea
   9:45 than having two feet to be *c* into hell
   12:43 (Lk. 21:3) this poor widow hath *c* more in
   16:17 in my name shall they *c* out devils
Lk. 1:29 *c* in her mind what manner of salutation
   4:29 unto the brow. . that they might *c* him down
Jn. 6:37 that cometh to me I will in no wise *c* out
   8:7 without sin. . let him first *c* a stone .
   12:31 shall the prince of this world be *c* out
   21:6 *c* the net on the right side of the ship
Acts 27:26 we must be *c* upon a certain island
   27:29 they *c* four anchors out of the stern
Rom. 11:1 I say then, Hath God *c* away his people?
   13:12 therefore *c* off the works of darkness
2 Cor. 4:9 not forsaken; *c* down, but not destroyed
   7:6 God, that comforteth those that are *c* down
1 Tim. 5:12 they have *c* off their first faith
Heb. 10:35 *c* not away therefore your confidence
2 Pet. 2:4 angels that sinned, but *c* them down to
1 Jn. 4:18 but perfect love *c* out fear: because
3 Jn. 10 forbiddeth. . and *c* them out of the church
Rev. 2:10 devil shall *c* some of you into prison
   4:10 *c* their crowns before the throne, saying
   19:20 these both were *c* alive into a lake of fire
   20:10 and the devil. . was *c* into the lake of fire

Castaway

1 Cor. 9:27 preached to others, I. .should be a *c*

Casting

Mic. 6:14 thy *c* down shall be in the midst of thee
2 Cor. 10:5 *c* down imaginations. .every high thing
1 Pet. 5:7 *c* all your care upon him; for he careth

Castle

Num. 31:10 burnt. .all their goodly *c*, with fire
1 Chr. 11:5 nevertheless David took the *c* of Zion
Prov. 18:19 contentions are like the bars of a *c*
Acts 21:34 commanded him to be carried into the *c*
   22:24 commanded him to be brought into the *c*

Catch (Caught)

Gen. 22:13 behold behind him a ram *c* in a thicket
Ex. 4:4 and *c* it, and it became a rod in his hand
Judg. 21:21 and *c* you every man his wife of the
1 Sam. 17:35 I *c* him by his beard, and smote him

2 Sam. 18:9 his head *c* hold of the oak, and he was
1 Kgs. 2:28 Joab . . *c* hold on the horns of the altar
11:30 Ahijah *c* the new garment that was on him
2 Kgs. 7:12 out of the city, we shall *c* them alive
Ps. 10:9 he lieth in wait to *c* the poor: he doth *c*
35:8 and let his net that he hath hid *c* himself
Prov. 7:13 so she *c* him, and kissed him, and with
Ezek. 19:3 lion, and it learned to *c* the prey
Hab. 1:15 they *c* them in their net, and gather
Mt. 13:19 *c* away that which was sown in his heart
14:31 Jesus stretched forth his hand, and *c* him
21:39 (Mk. 12:3) *c* him . . cast . . out of the vineyard
Mk. 12:13 of the Herodians, to *c* him in his words
Lk. 5:10 fear not . . henceforth thou shalt *c* men
11:54 seeking to *c* something out of his mouth
Jn. 10:12 wolf *c* them, and scattereth the sheep
21:3 into a ship . . and that night they *c* nothing
Acts 8:39 the Spirit of the Lord *c* away Philip
16:19 they *c* Paul and Silas, and drew them into
2 Cor. 12:2 such a one *c* up to the third heaven
12:4 *c* up into paradise, and heard unspeakable
12:16 being crafty, I *c* you with guile
1 Thes. 4:17 are alive and remain shall be *c* up
Rev. 12:5 child was *c* up unto God, and to his throne

Caterpillar

Ps. 78:46 he gave also their increase unto the *c*
105:34 he spake, and the locusts came, and *c*
Joel 1:4 the cankerworm hath left hath the *c* eaten
2:25 cankerworm, and the *c*, and the palmerworm

Cattle

Gen. 1:25 God made . . *c* after their kind
8:1 and all the *c* that was with him in the ark
13:2 Abram was very rich in *c*, in silver, and
30:32 from thence all the speckled and spotted *c*
30:43 man increased exceedingly, and had much *c*
46:32 for their trade hath been to feed *c*
Ex. 9:4 between the *c* of Israel and the *c* of Egypt
10:26 our *c* also shall go with us; there shall
20:10 (Deut. 5:14) not do any work . . nor thy *c*
Deut. 2:35 the *c* we took for a prey unto ourselves
3:7 but all the *c*, and the spoil of the cities
Josh. 8:2 the *c* thereof, shall ye take for a prey
1 Kgs. 1:9 Adonijah slew sheep and oxen and fat *c*
Ps. 50:10 is mine, and the *c* upon a thousand hills
104:14 he causeth the grass to grow for the *c*
107:38 and suffereth not their *c* to decrease
Ezek. 34:17 I judge between *c* and *c*, between the
Jon. 4:11 great city, wherein are . . also much *c*?
Zech. 13:5 man taught me to keep *c* from my youth
Lk. 17:7 having a servant plowing or feeding *c*
Jn. 4:12 the well, and drank thereof . . and his *c*?

Caught *See* Catch

Caul

Is. 3:18 ornaments about their feet, and their *c*
Hos. 13:8 and will rend the *c* of their heart

Cause *See also* Occasion, Reason

Num. 27:5 Moses brought their *c* before the Lord
Deut. 1:17 *c* that is too hard for you, bring it
2 Chr. 19:10 what *c* soever shall come to you of
Job 5:8 unto God would I commit my *c*
13:18 behold now, I have ordered my *c*; I know
Ps. 25:3 be ashamed which transgress without *c*
35:1 plead my *c*, O Lord, with them that strive
35:7 without *c* have they hid for me their net
35:19 wink with the eye that hate me without a *c*
69:4 (Jn. 15:25) they that hate me without a *c*
109:3 hatred; and fought against me without a *c*
119:78 they dealt perversely with me without a *c*

Ps. 140:12 Lord will maintain the *c* of the afflicted
Prov. 18:17 he that is first in his own *c* seemeth just
31:9 and plead the *c* of the poor and needy
Is. 41:21 produce your *c*, saith the Lord; bring
51:22 thy God that pleadeth the *c* of his people
Jer. 5:28 judge not the *c*, the *c* of the fatherless
20:12 for unto thee have I opened my *c*
22:16 he judged the *c* of the poor and needy
Jon. 1:7 that we may know for whose *c* this evil is
Mt. 5:22 angry with his brother without a *c* shall
19:3 for a man to put away his wife for every *c*?
19:5 for this *c* shall a man leave father and
Lk. 23:22 I have found no *c* of death in him
Jn. 12:27 but for this *c* came I unto this hour
18:37 born, and for this *c* came I into the world
Acts 25:14 Festus declared Paul's *c* unto the king
1 Cor. 11:30 for this *c* many are weak and sickly
2 Cor. 4:16 for which *c* we faint not; but though
5:13 or whether we be sober, it is for your *c*
9:11 which *c* through us thanksgiving to God
Eph. 3:1 for this *c* I Paul, the prisoner of Jesus
3:14 for this *c* I bow my knees unto the Father
1 Tim. 1:16 howbeit for this *c* I obtained mercy
Heb. 2:11 for which *c* he is not ashamed to call
1 Pet. 4:6 for this *c* was the gospel preached also

Cave

Gen. 19:30 dwelt in a *c*, he and his two daughters
23:19 buried Sarah his wife in the *c* of . . Machpelah
25:9 buried him in the *c* of Machpelah
49:29 bury me with my fathers in the *c* that is
50:13 in the *c* of the field of Machpelah
Josh. 10:16 kings fled, and hid themselves in a *c*
1 Sam. 13:6 the people did hide themselves in *c*
22:1 departed thence . . escaped to the *c* Adullam
24:10 delivered thee . . into mine hand in the *c*
2 Sam. 23:13 (1 Chr. 11:15) unto the *c* of Adullam
1 Kgs. 18:4 prophets, and hid them by fifty in a *c*
19:9 he came thither unto a *c*, and lodged there
Is. 2:19 *c* of the earth, for fear of the Lord
Ezek. 33:27 in the *c* shall die of the pestilence
Jn. 11:38 himself cometh to the grave. It was a *c*
Heb. 11:38 wandered in deserts . . and in dens and *c*

Cease

Gen. 8:22 winter, and day and night shall not *c*
Deut. 15:11 the poor shall never *c* out of the land
1 Sam. 7:8 to Samuel, *C* not to cry unto the Lord
Ezra 4:23 and made them to *c* by force and power
Neh. 6:3 why should the work *c*, whilst I leave it
Job 3:17 there the wicked *c* from troubling
Ps. 12:1 help, Lord; for the godly man *c*; for the
37:8 *c* from anger, and forsake wrath: fret not
46:9 maketh wars to *c* unto the end of the earth
77:2 sore ran in the night, and *c* not: my soul
85:4 turn . . and cause thine anger toward us to *c*
Prov. 19:27 *c*, my son, to hear the instruction
20:3 it is an honor for a man to *c* from strife
22:10 go out; yea, strife and reproach shall *c*
23:4 labor not to be rich: *c* from thine own wisdom
26:20 where there is no talebearer, the strife *c*
Eccl. 12:3 and the grinders *c* because they are few
Is. 1:16 wash ye, make you clean . . *c* to do evil
2:22 *c* ye from man, whose breath is in his
10:25 the indignation shall *c*, and mine anger in
Jon. 1:15 cast him . . and the sea *c* from her raging
Mt. 14:32 (Mk. 6:51) come into the ship, the wind *c*
Mk. 4:39 the wind *c*, and there was a great calm
Acts 20:31 three years I *c* not to warn every one
1 Cor. 13:8 whether there be tongues, they shall *c*
Gal. 5:11 then is the offense of the cross *c*
Eph. 1:16 *c* not to give thanks for you, making
Col. 1:9 do not *c* to pray for you, and to desire

Heb. 4:10 rest, he also hath *c* from his own works
1 Pet. 4:1 suffered in the flesh hath *c* from sin
2 Pet. 2:14 having eyes. . that cannot *c* from sin

Ceasing

Acts 12:5 prayer was made without *c* of the church
Rom. 1:9 without *c* I make mention of you always
1 Thes. 1:3 remembering without *c* your work of faith
　　2:13 for this cause also thank we God without *c*
　　5:17 pray without *c*
2 Tim. 1:3 without *c* I have remembrance of thee in

Cedar

Lev. 14:4 and *c* wood, and scarlet, and hyssop
Judg. 9:15 bramble, and devour the *c* of Lebanon
2 Sam. 5:11 (1 Chr. 14:1) messengers to David, and *c*
　　7:2 (1 Chr. 17:1) dwell in a house of *c*, but the ark
1 Kgs. 4:33 and he spake of trees, from the *c* tree
　　5:6 command thou that they hew me *c* trees out of
　　6:9 covered the house with beams and boards of *c*
　　7:11 above were costly stones. . and *c*
2 Kgs. 14:9 (2 Chr. 25:18) thistle. . sent to the *c*
　　19:23 (Is. 37:24) will cut down the tall *c* trees
Job 40:17 he moveth his tail like a *c*: the sinews
Ps. 29:5 the voice of the LORD breaketh the *c*
　　80:10 the boughs thereof were like the goodly *c*
　　92:12 righteous. . shall grow like a *c* in Lebanon
　　104:16 full of sap; the *c* of Lebanon, which he
　　148:9 and all hills; fruitful trees, and all *c*
Song 1:17 the beams of our house are *c*
　　5:15 his countenance is. . excellent as the *c*
Is. 2:13 upon all the *c* of Lebanon, that are high
　　9:10 cut down, but we will change them into *c*
　　37:24 I will cut down the tall *c* thereof
　　44:14 heweth him down *c*, and taketh the cypress
Jer. 22:7 shall cut down thy choice *c*, and cast
　　22:15 reign, because thou closest thyself in *c*?
Ezek. 17:3 eagle. . took the highest branch of the *c*
　　27:5 taken *c* from Lebanon to make masts for thee
　　31:3 the Assyrian was a *c* in Lebanon with fair
　　31:8 *c* in the garden of God could not hide him
Amos 2:9 whose height was like the height of the *c*

Cedron Jn. 18:1

Celebrate

Lev. 23:32 even unto even, shall ye *c* your sabbath
　　23:41 feast. . ye shall *c* it in the seventh month
Is. 38:18 cannot praise thee, death cannot *c* thee

Celestial

1 Cor. 15:40 also *c* bodies, and bodies terrestrial

Cenchrea Acts 18:18; Rom. 16:1

Censer

Lev. 10:1 sons of Aaron, took either of them his *c*
　　16:12 he shall take a *c* full of burning coals
Heb. 9:4 which had the golden *c*, and the ark of
Rev. 8:3 and stood at the altar, having a golden *c*

Centurion

Mt. 8:5 (Lk. 7:6) came unto him a *c*, beseeching
　　27:54 (Mk. 15:39; Lk. 23:47) now when the *c*. . saw
Lk. 7:2 *c*'s servant. . was sick, and ready to die
Acts 10:1 Cornelius, a *c* of the band called
　　22:25 Paul said unto the *c* that stood by, Is it
　　27:1 unto one named Julius, a *c* of Augustus' band
　　27:43 but the *c*, willing to save Paul, kept them

Cephas *See also* Peter

Jn. 1:42 the son of Jona: thou shalt be called *C*
1 Cor. 1:12 of Paul; and I of Apollos; and I of *C*
　　9:5 a wife. . as the brethren of the Lord, and *C*?

1 Cor. 15:5 that he was seen of *C*, then of the twelve
Gal. 2:9 James, *C*, and John, who seemed to be pillars

Ceremony

Num. 9:3 according to all the *c* thereof, shall ye

Certainty

Prov. 22:21 know the *c* of the words of truth
Lk. 1:4 know the *c* of those things, wherein thou
Acts 21:34 he could not know the *c* for the tumult
　　22:30 have known the *c* wherefore he was accused

Certify

2 Sam. 15:28 until there come word from you to *c* me
Esth. 2:22 Esther *c* the king. . in Mordecai's name
Gal. 1:11 but I *c* you, brethren, that the gospel

Chaff

Job 21:18 and as *c* that the storm carrieth away
Ps. 1:4 are like the *c* which the wind driveth away
　　35:5 let them be as *c* before the wind: and let
Is. 5:24 stubble, and the flame consumeth the *c*
　　17:13 chased as the *c* of the mountains before
　　33:11 ye shall conceive *c*, ye shall bring forth
　　41:15 them small, and shalt make the hills as *c*
Jer. 23:28 what is the *c* to the wheat? saith the
Dan. 2:35 like the *c* of the summer threshingfloors
Mt. 3:12 (Lk. 3:17) burn up the *c* with unquenchable

Chain

Gen. 41:42 Pharaoh. . put a gold *c* about his neck
Ps. 68:6 bringeth out those which are bound with *c*
　　73:6 pride compasseth them about as a *c*
　　149:8 bind their kings with *c*, and their nobles
Prov. 1:9 ornament of grace. . and *c* about they neck
Song 1:10 rows of jewels, thy neck with *c* of gold
Is. 3:19 *c*, and the bracelets, and the mufflers
Ezek. 19:4 they brought him with *c* unto the land
Mk. 5:3 and no man could bind him, no, not with *c*
Acts 12:7 Peter. . And his *c* fell off from his hands
　　28:20 the hope of Israel I am bound with this *c*
2 Tim. 1:16 Onesiphorus. . was not ashamed of my *c*
2 Pet. 2:4 delivered them into *c* of darkness
Jude 6 reserved in everlasting *c* under darkness

Chalcedony

Rev. 21:19 second, sapphire; the third, a *c*

Chaldean (Chaldea, Chaldees)

Job 1:17 the *C* made out three bands, and fell upon
Is. 23:13 behold the land of the *C*; this people
Jer. 25:12 that I will punish. . the land of the *C*
　　32:24 the city is given into the hand of the *C*
Ezek. 1:3 in the land of the *C* by the river Chebar
Dan. 1:4 teach the learning and the tongue of the *C*
Hab. 1:6 the *C*, that bitter and hasty nation, which

Challenge

Ex. 22:9 lost thing, which another *c* to be his

Chamber

Gen. 43:30 he entered into his *c*, and wept there
2 Kgs. 4:10 let us make a little *c*. . on the wall
Ps. 19:5 as a bridegroom coming out of his *c*
Prov. 24:4 by knowledge shall the *c* be filled with
Song 1:4 King hath brought me into his *c*: we will
Jer. 22:13 by unrighteousness, and his *c* by wrong
Mt. 24:26 he is in the secret *c*; believe it not

Chambering

Rom. 13:13 not in *c* and wantonness, not in strife

Chamberlain

Esth. 1:10 seven *c* that served in the presence of

Acts 12:20 made Blastus the king's *c* their friend
Rom. 16:23 Erastus the *c* of the city saluteth you

Champion

1 Sam. 17:4 a *c* out of the camp of the Philistines
   17:51 when the Philistines saw their *c* was dead

Chance

1 Sam. 6:9 it was a *c* that happened to us
2 Sam. 1:6 as I happened by *c* upon mount Gilboa
Eccl. 9:11 but time and *c* happeneth to them all
Lk. 10:31 by *c* there came down a certain priest
1 Cor. 15:37 bare grain, it may *c* of wheat, or of

Change *See also* Alter

Gen. 45:22 he gave each man *c* of raiment
Job 14:14 appointed time will I wait, till my *c*
   30:18 great force of my disease is my garment *c*
Ps. 15:4 that sweareth to his own hurt, and *c* not
   55:19 they have no *c*, therefore they fear not God
   102:26 (Heb. 1:12) *c* them, and they shall be *c*
Prov. 24:21 and meddle not with them. . given to *c*
Jer. 2:11 my people have *c* their glory for that
   2:36 why gaddest thou about so much to *c* thy way
   13:23 the Ethiopian *c* his skin, or the leopard
Ezek. 5:6 she hath *c* my judgments into wickedness
Dan. 6:15 that no decree nor statute. . may be *c*
Hos. 4:7 therefore will I *c* their glory into shame
Hab. 1:11 then shall his mind *c*, and he shall pass
Zech. 3:4 and I will clothe thee with *c* of raiment
Mal. 3:6 for I am the LORD, I *c* not; therefore ye
Acts 6:14 shall *c* the customs which Moses delivered
Rom. 1:25 who *c* the truth of God into a lie
   1:26 their women did *c* the natural use into that
1 Cor. 15:51 not all sleep, but we shall all be *c*
2 Cor. 3:18 are *c* into the same image from glory to
Phil. 3:21 who shall *c* our vile body, that it may
Heb. 7:12 priesthood being *c*. . a *c* also of the law

Changer

Mt. 21:12 (Mk. 11:15; Jn. 2:14) tables of the money *c*

Channel

2 Sam. 22:16 (Ps. 18:15) the *c* of the sea appeared
Is. 27:12 from the *c* of the river unto the stream

Chant

Amos 6:5 *c* to the sound of the viol, and invent

Chapel

Amos 7:13 at Bethel: for it is the king's *c*

Chapman

2 Chr. 9:14 that which *c* and merchants brought

Charge *See also* Accusation, Command

Gen. 26:5 Abraham obeyed my voice, and kept my *c*
Ex. 6:13 gave them a *c* unto the children of Israel
Num. 5:19 and the priest shall *c* her by an oath
1 Kgs. 2:1 he should die; and he *c* Solomon his son
   11:28 ruler over all the *c* of the house of Joseph
1 Chr. 22:6 *c* him to build a house for the LORD God
2 Chr. 36:23 (Ezra 1:2) *c* me to build him a house
Job 1:22 Job sinned not, nor *c* God foolishly
   4:18 and his angels he *c* with folly
Ps. 35:11 they laid to my *c* things that I knew not
   91:11 (Mt. 4:6; Lk. 4:10) his angels *c* over thee
Song 2:7 I *c* you, O ye daughters of Jerusalem
Ezek. 44:11 ministers in my sanctuary, having *c* at
Mt. 9:30 Jesus straitly *c* them, saying, See that
   17:9 (Mk. 9:9) *c* them. . Tell the vision to no man
Mk. 5:43 he *c* them straitly that no man should

Mk. 10:48 many *c* him that he should hold his peace
Acts 7:60 cried. . Lord, lay not this sin to their *c*
   21:24 and purify thyself. . and be at *c* with them
Rom. 8:33 lay any thing to the *c* of God's elect?
1 Cor. 9:7 goeth a warfare any time at his own *c*?
1 Thes. 2:11 comforted and *c* every one of you, as
1 Tim. 1:3 *c* some that they teach no other doctrine
   5:7 things give in *c*, that they may be blameless
   5:16 relieve them, and let not the church be *c*
   5:21 I *c* thee before God, and the Lord Jesus
   6:13 I give thee *c* in the sight of God
   6:17 *c* them that are rich in this world, that
2 Tim. 4:16 that it may not be laid to their *c*

Chargeable

2 Cor. 11:9 I was *c* to no man: for that which was
1 Thes. 2:9 (2 Thes. 3:8) we would not be *c* unto any

Charger

Num. 7:13 his offering was one silver *c*, the weight
Mt. 14:8 (Mk. 6:25) John Baptist's head in a *c*

Chariot

Gen. 41:43 and he made him to ride in the second *c*
Ex. 14:25 took off their *c* wheels, that they drave
Judg. 1:19 the valley, because they had *c* of iron
1 Sam. 13:5 fight with Israel, thirty thousand *c*
2 Kgs. 2:11 appeared a *c* of fire, and horses of fire
   2:12 (13:14) my father, my father, the *c* of Israel
   6:17 mountain was full of horses and *c* of fire
Ps. 20:7 some trust in *c*, and some in horses: but
   76:6 both the *c* and horse are cast into a dead
   104:3 who maketh the clouds his *c*: who walketh
Song 3:9 Solomon made. . *c* of the wood of Lebanon
Is. 21:9 here cometh a *c* of men, with a couple of
   31:1 stay on horses, and trust in *c*, because they
Jer. 4:13 his *c* shall be as a whirlwind: his horses
Ezek. 27:20 thy merchant in precious clothes for *c*
Hab. 3:8 upon thine horses and thy *c* of salvation?
Zech. 6:1 four *c* out from between two mountains
Acts 8:29 Philip, Go near, and join thyself to this *c*

Charitably

Rom. 14:15 brother be grieved. . walkest thou not *c*

Charity *See also* Love

1 Cor. 8:1 knowledge puffeth up, but *c* edifieth
   13:1 have not *c*, I am become as sounding brass
   13:13 faith, hope, *c*. . the greatest of these is *c*
   14:1 follow after *c*, and desire spiritual gifts
   16:14 let all your things be done with *c*
Col. 3:14 put on *c*, which is the bond of perfectness
2 Thes. 1:3 the *c* of every one of you all toward
1 Tim. 1:5 commandment is *c* out of a pure heart
   2:15 in faith and *c* and holiness with sobriety
Tit. 2:2 aged men be sober. . sound in faith, in *c*
1 Pet. 4:8 have fervent *c* among yourselves: for *c*
   5:14 greet ye one another with a kiss of *c*
2 Pet. 1:7 kindness; and to brotherly kindness, *c*
3 Jn. 6 borne witness of thy *c* before the church
Jude 12 these are spots in your feasts of *c*
Rev. 2:19 I know thy works, and *c*, and service

Charmer

Deut. 18:11 *c*, or a consulter with familiar spirits
Ps. 58:5 which will not hearken to the voice of *c*

Charran *See* Haran

Chase

Lev. 26:7 ye shall *c* your enemies, and they shall
Deut. 1:44 Amorites. . *c* you. . and destroyed you
Josh. 23:10 one man of you shall *c* a thousand

Neh. 13:28 son-in-law to Sanballat. . I *c* him from me
Ps. 35:5 and let the angel of the LORD *c* them
Is. 17:13 the nations. . shall be *c* as the chaff of

Chaste *See also* Clean, Holy, Pure, Virtuous

2 Cor. 11:2 may present you as a *c* virgin to Christ
Tit. 2:5 to be discreet, *c*, keepers at home, good
1 Pet. 3:2 your *c* conversation coupled with fear

Chasten *See also* Correct, Punish

Deut. 8:5 as a man *c* his son. . thy God *c* thee
2 Sam. 7:14 I will *c* him with the rod of men
Job 33:19 he is *c* also with pain upon his bed
Ps. 6:1 (38:1) neither *c* me in thy hot displeasure
   94:12 blessed is the man whom thou *c*, O LORD
   118:18 the LORD hath *c* me sore: but he hath not
Prov. 13:24 his son: but he that loveth him *c* him
   19:18 *c* thy son while there is hope, and let not
Dan. 10:12 and to *c* thyself before thy God
1 Cor. 11:32 we are judged, we are *c* of the Lord
2 Cor. 6:9 as dying. . we live; as *c*, and not killed
Heb. 12:6 whom the Lord loveth he *c*, and scourgeth
   12:7 for what son is he whom the father *c* not?
Rev. 3:19 as many as I love, I rebuke and *c*

Chastening. *See also* Correction, Punishment

Job 5:17 despise not thou the *c* of the Almighty
Prov. 3:11 (Heb. 12:5) despise not the *c* of the LORD
Is. 26:16 poured out a prayer when thy *c* was upon
Heb. 12:7 if ye endure *c*, God dealeth with you as
   12:11 no *c* for the present seemeth to be joyous

Chastise *See also* Chasten, Punish

Lev. 26:28 I, will *c* you seven times for your sins
Deut. 22:18 that city shall take that man and *c* him
1 Kgs. 12:11 (2 Chr. 10:11) my father hath *c* you with
Ps. 94:10 that *c* the heathen, shall not he correct?
Jer. 31:18 thou hast *c* me, and I was *c*, as a bullock
Hos. 7:12 I will *c* them, as their congregation hath
   10:10 it is in my desire that I should *c* them
Lk. 23:16 I will therefore *c* him, and release him

Chastisement *See also* Chastening, Punishment

Job 34:31 I have borne *c*, I will not offend any more
Is. 53:5 the *c* of our peace was upon him; and with
Heb. 12:8 but if ye be without *c*, whereof all are

Chatter

Is. 38:14 like a crane or a swallow, so did I *c*

Chebar Ezek. 1:1

Chedorlaomer Gen. 14:1–17

Cheek

1 Kgs. 22:24 (2 Chr. 18:23) smote Micaiah on the *c*
Ps. 3:7 smitten all mine enemies upon the *c* bone
Song 1:10 thy *c* are comely with rows of jewels
   5:13 *c* are as a bed of spices, as sweet flowers
Is. 50:6 my *c* to them that plucked off the hair
Lam. 3:30 he giveth his *c* to him that smiteth him
Mic. 5:1 smite the judge of Israel. . upon the *c*
Mt. 5:39 (Lk. 6:29) smite thee on thy right *c*, turn

Cheer *See also* Mirth, Rejoice

Deut. 24:5 home one year, and shall *c* up his wife

Judg. 9:13 leave my wine, which *c* God and man
Mt. 9:2 be of good *c*; thy sins be forgiven thee
   14:27 (Mk. 6:50) be of good *c*; it is I; be not afraid
Jn. 16:33 be of good *c*; I have overcome the world
Acts 23:11 be of good *c*, Paul: for as thou hast
   27:25 sirs, be of good *c*: for I believe God

Cheerful

Prov. 15:13 a merry heart maketh a *c* countenance
Zech. 9:17 corn shall make the young men *c*
2 Cor. 9:7 necessity: for God loveth a *c* giver

Cheerfulness

Rom. 12:8 diligence; he that showeth mercy, with *c*

Cheese

1 Sam. 17:18 carry these ten *c* unto the captain of

Chemosh Judg. 11:24; 2 Kgs. 23:13

Cherish

1 Kgs. 1:2 stand before the king, and let her *c* him
Eph. 5:29 his own flesh; but nourisheth and *c* it
1 Thes. 2:7 among you, even as a nurse *c* her children

Cherith 1 Kgs. 17:3

Cherub *See also* Angel, Cherubim

2 Sam. 22:11 (Ps. 18:10) rode upon a *c*, and did fly
Ezek. 9:3 glory. . was gone up from the *c*, whereupon

Cherubim *See also* Angel, Cherub

Gen. 3:24 at the east of the garden of Eden *c*
Ex. 25:18 (37:7) thou shalt make two *c* of gold
   26:1 (36:8) with *c* of cunning work shalt thou make
1 Sam. 4:4 of hosts, which dwelleth between the *c*
1 Kgs. 6:23 (2 Chr. 3:10) made two *c* of olive tree
   6:29 round about with carved figures of *c*
   8:7 (2 Chr. 5:8) the *c* spread forth their two wings
2 Kgs. 19:15 (Is. 37:16) which dwellest between the *c*
Ps. 99:1 he sitteth between the *c*; let the earth
Ezek. 10:3 *c* stood on the right side of the house
Heb. 9:5 the *c* of glory shadowing the mercy seat

Chest

2 Kgs. 12:9 the priest took a *c*, and bored
2 Chr. 24:8 at the king's commandment they made a *c*

Chestnut

Gen. 30:37 and *c* tree; and pilled white streaks in

Chicken

Mt. 23:37 as a hen gathereth her *c* under her wings

Chide (Chode)

Gen. 31:36 and Jacob was wroth, and *c* with Laban
Ex. 17:2 Moses said unto them, why *c* ye with me?
Num. 20:3 and the people *c* with Moses, and spake
Judg. 8:1 men of Ephraim. . did *c* with him sharply
Ps. 103:9 he will not always *c*: neither will he

Chief *See also* Chief Priest, Noble, Prince

1 Sam. 15:21 sheep and oxen, the *c* of the things
1 Kgs. 8:1 (2 Chr. 5:2) assembled. . the *c* of the fathers
Ezra 9:2 and rulers hath been *c* in this trespass
Neh. 11:3 *c* of the province that dwelt in Jerusalem
Song 5:10 my beloved is. . the *c* among ten thousand
Mt. 20:27 (Mk. 10:44; Lk. 22:26) whosoever will be *c*
   among you, let him be your servant
   23:6 (Mk. 12:39) the *c* seats in the synagogues
Lk. 11:15 through Beelzebub the *c* of the devils
   14:1 into the house of one of the *c* Pharisees
   14:7 he marked how they chose out the *c* rooms

Lk. 19:2 Zaccheus . . was the *c* among the publicans
19:47 the *c* of the people sought to destroy him
Jn. 12:42 among the *c* rulers also many believed
Acts 14:12 and Paul . . because he was the *c* speaker
17:4 multitude, and of the *c* women not a few
Eph. 2:20 Christ himself being the *c* corner stone
1 Tim. 1:15 came . . to save sinners; of whom I am *c*
1 Pet. 2:6 I lay in Sion a *c* corner stone, elect
5:4 when the *c* Shepherd shall appear, ye shall

Chief Priest *See also* High Priest

Mt. 2:4 he had gathered all the *c p* and scribes
16:21 (Mk. 8:31; Lk. 9:22) suffer . . of the . . *c p*
27:1 (Mk. 15:1) *c p* and elders . . took counsel
27:41 (Mk. 15:31) also the *c p* mocking him, with
Jn. 7:32 Pharisees and the *c p* sent officers
Acts 9:14 he hath authority from the *c p* to bind

Child *See also* Children, Daughter, Son

Gen. 11:30 but Sarai was barren; she had no *c*
17:10 every man *c* among you shall be circumcised
37:30 the *c* is not; and I, whither shall I go?
42:22 do not sin against the *c*; and ye would not
44:20 a *c* of his old age, a little one
Ex. 2:2 when she saw him that he was a goodly *c*
21:22 if men strive, and hurt a woman with *c*
22:22 shall not afflict any widow, or fatherless *c*
Lev. 12:2 borne a man *c*, then she shall be unclean
Deut. 25:5 one of them die, and have no *c*, the wife
Judg. 13:5 the *c* shall be a Nazarite unto God from
Ruth 4:16 Naomi took the *c*, and laid it in her bosom
1 Sam. 1:11 give unto thine handmaid a man *c*, then
1:27 for this *c* I prayed; and the LORD hath given
2 Sam. 12:14 *c* also that is born unto thee shall
12:22 while the *c* was yet alive, I fasted and
1 Kgs. 3:7 I am but a little *c*: I know not how to
3:25 divide the living *c* in two, and give half to
17:21 he stretched himself upon the *c* three times
2 Kgs. 4:18 when the *c* was grown, it fell on a day
Prov. 20:11 even a *c* is known by his doings, whether
22:6 train up a *c* in the way he should go
22:15 foolishness is bound in the heart of a *c*.
23:13 withhold not correction from the *c*
29:15 a *c* left to himself bringeth his mother to
Is. 9:6 unto us a *c* is born, unto us a son is given
11:6 together; and a little *c* shall lead them
65:20 the *c* shall die a hundred years old
66:7 (Rev. 12:5) she was delivered of a man *c*
Jer. 1:6 God! behold, I cannot speak: for I am a *c*
Hos. 11:1 when Israel was a *c*, then I loved him
Mt. 1:18 she was found with *c* of the Holy Ghost
1:23 a virgin shall be with *c*, and shall bring
2:8 search diligently for the young *c*; and when
10:21 deliver up . . to death, and the father the *c*
17:18 and the *c* was cured from that very hour
18:2 (Mk. 9:36; Lk. 9:47) Jesus called a little *c*
24:19 (Mk. 13:17; Lk. 21:23) woe unto . . with *c*
Mk. 10:15 (Lk. 18:17) kingdom of God as a little *c*
Lk. 1:7 had no *c*, because that Elisabeth was barren
1:66 saying, What manner of *c* shall this be?
1:76 thou, *c*, shalt be called the prophet of the
1:80 and the *c* grew, and waxed strong in spirit
2:5 Mary his espoused wife, being great with *c*
2:40 and the *c* grew, and waxed strong in spirit
2:43 the *c* Jesus tarried behind in Jerusalem
9:38 look upon my son; for he is mine only *c*
Jn. 4:49 unto him, Sir, come down ere my *c* die
Acts 4:27 against thy holy *c* Jesus, whom thou hast
4:30 may be done by the name of thy holy *c* Jesus
13:10 thou *c* of the devil, thou enemy of all
1 Cor. 13:11 when I was a *c*, I spake as a *c*
Gal. 4:1 heir, as long as he is a *c*, differeth nothing
2 Tim. 3:15 a *c* thou hast known the holy Scriptures

Heb. 11:11 delivered of a *c* when she was past age
Rev. 12:2 and she being with *c* cried, travailing

Childbearing

1 Tim. 2:15 saved in *c* if they continue in faith

Childhood

Eccl. 11:10 thy flesh: for *c* and youth are vanity

Childish

1 Cor. 13:11 I became a man, I put away *c* things

Childless

Gen. 15:2 what wilt thou give me, seeing I go *c*

Children *See also* Child

Gen. 3:16 in sorrow thou shalt bring forth *c*
18:19 he will command his *c* and his household
25:22 and the *c* struggled together within her
30:1 when Rachel saw that she bare Jacob no *c*
33:5 the *c* which God hath graciously given thy
37:3 now Israel loved Joseph more than all his *c*
46:8 and these are the names of the *c* of Israel
49:8 thy father's *c* shall bow down before thee
Ex. 1:17 midwives feared God . . saved the men *c* alive
20:5 (34:7; Num. 14:18; Deut. 5:9) visiting the
iniquity of the fathers upon the *c* unto the
Deut. 4:10 and that they may teach their *c*
6:7 thou shalt teach them diligently unto thy *c*
14:1 ye are the *c* of the LORD your God: ye shall
24:16 (2 Kgs. 14:6; 2 Chr. 25:4) fathers shall not be
put to death for the *c*, neither shall the *c* be
32:20 froward generation, *c* in whom is no faith
Josh. 4:22 let your *c* know . . Israel came over this
1 Kgs. 9:6 turn from following me, ye or your *c*
2 Kgs. 2:24 she bears . . tare forty and two *c* of them
10:1 and to them that brought up Ahab's *c*
2 Chr. 28:3 and burnt his *c* in the fire, after the
Job 21:11 little ones like a flock, and their *c* dance
Ps. 14:2 looked down from heaven upon the *c* of men
34:11 *c*, hearken unto me: I will teach you
45:16 instead of thy fathers shall be thy *c*
103:13 as a father pitieth his *c*, so the LORD
103:17 fear him, and his righteousness unto *c*'s *c*
107:8 for his wonderful works to the *c* of men!
113:9 keep house, and to be a joyful mother of *c*
127:3 *c* are a heritage of the LORD: and the fruit
128:3 *c* like olive plants round about thy table
144:7 great waters, from the hand of strange *c*
Prov. 4:1 hear, ye *c*, the instruction of a father
14:26 and his *c* shall have a place of refuge
17:6 *c*'s *c* are the crown of old men
31:28 her *c* arise up, and call her blessed
Is. 3:12 as for my people, *c* are their oppressors
8:18 (Heb. 2:13) *c* whom the LORD hath given me
13:16 their *c* also shall be dashed to pieces
30:9 lying *c*, *c* that will not hear the law
54:1 (Gal. 4:27) more are the *c* of the desolate
54:13 all thy *c* shall be taught of the LORD
63:8 they are my people, *c* that will not lie
66:8 as Zion travailed, she brought forth her *c*
Jer. 3:14 turn, O backsliding *c*, saith the LORD
31:15 (Mt. 2:18) Rachel weeping for her *c* refused
31:17 thy *c* shall come again to their own border
31:29 (Ezek. 18:2) the *c*'s teeth are set on edge
Lam. 1:5 her *c* are gone into captivity before the
1:16 *c* are desolate, because the enemy prevailed
Ezek. 2:4 for they are impudent *c* and stiffhearted
23:39 when they had slain their *c* to their idols
Dan. 1:4 *c* in whom was no blemish, but well-favored
Hos. 4:6 law of thy God, I will also forget thy *c*
Joel 1:3 tell ye your *c* . . and let your *c* tell their *c*
Mal. 4:6 (Lk. 1:17) heart of the fathers to the *c*

Mt. 2:16 and slew all the *c* that were in Bethlehem
3:9 (Lk. 3:8) stones to raise up *c* unto Abraham
5:9 peacemakers . . shall be called the *c* of God
5:45 that ye may be the *c* of your Father
7:11 (Lk. 11:13) to give good gifts unto your *c*
8:12 *c* of the kingdom shall be cast out into
9:15 (Mk. 2:19; Lk. 5:34) *c* of the bridechamber
10:21 (Mk. 13:12) *c* shall rise up against . . parents
11:16 (Lk. 7:32) like unto *c* sitting in the markets
13:38 the good seed are the *c* of the kingdom
15:26 (Mk. 7:27) is not meet to take the *c*'s bread
17:26 Jesus saith unto him, Then are the *c* free
18:3 converted, and become as little *c*, ye shall
19:13 (Mk. 10:13) brought unto him little *c*, that
19:14 (Mk. 10:14; Lk. 18:16) *c* . . to come unto me
19:29 (Mk. 10:29; Lk. 18:29) forsaken. . wife, or *c*
22:24 (Mk. 12:19; Lk. 20:28) man die, having no *c*
23:37 (Lk. 13:34) would I have gathered thy *c*
Mk. 9:37 shall receive one of such *c* in my name
Lk. 6:35 ye shall be the *c* of the Highest
14:26 hate not his. . wife, and *c*, and brethren
16:8 *c* of this world. . wiser than the *c* of light
20:36 *c* of God, being the *c* of the resurrection
Jn. 8:39 if ye were Abraham's *c*, ye would do the
12:36 the light, that ye may be the *c* of light
13:33 little *c*, yet a little while I am with you
Acts 2:39 the promise is unto you, and to your *c*
Rom. 8:16 with our spirit, that we are the *c* of God
8:21 into the glorious liberty of the *c* of God
9:8 *c* of the promise are counted for the seed
9:26 shall they be called the *c* of the living God
1 Cor. 7:14 else were your *c* unclean; but now are
14:20 not *c* in understanding. . in malice be ye *c*
Gal. 3:7 of faith, the same are the *c* of Abraham
3:26 ye are all the *c* of God by faith in Christ
4:28 now we. . as Isaac was, are the *c* of promise
Eph. 1:5 us unto the adoption of *c* by Jesus Christ
2:3 were by nature the *c* of wrath, even as others
4:14 be no more *c*, tossed to and fro, and carried
5:1 be ye therefore followers of God, as dear *c*
5:6 the wrath of God upon the *c* of disobedience
5:8 are ye light in the Lord: walk as *c* of light
6:1 (Col. 3:20) *c*, obey your parents in the Lord
6:4 (Col. 3:21) fathers, provoke not your *c* to
1 Thes. 2:11 charged. . you, as a father doth his *c*
5:5 ye are all the *c* of light. . *c* of the day
1 Tim. 3:4 his *c* in subjection with all gravity
5:4 but if any widow have *c* or nephews, let them
Tit. 1:6 having faithful *c* not accused of riot or
2:4 to love their husbands, to love their *c*
Heb. 2:14 as the *c* are partakers of flesh and blood
12:5 exhortation. . speaketh unto you as unto *c*
1 Pet. 1:14 obedient *c*, not fashioning yourselves
1 Jn. 2:1 little *c*, these things write I unto you
3:10 in this the *c* of God are manifest, and the *c*
5:2 we love the *c* of God, when we love God

Chinnereth (Cinneroth)

See also Galilee, Gennesaret, Tiberias

Num. 34:11; 1 Kgs. 15:20

Chisleu Neh. 1:1; Zech. 7:1

Chittim (Kittim) *See also* Cyprus

Num. 24:24; Is. 23:1; Dan. 11:30

Chloe 1 Cor. 1:11

Chode *See* Chide

Choice

Gen. 23:6 in the *c* of our sepulchres bury thy dead

1 Sam. 9:2 was Saul, a *c* young man, and a goodly
2 Sam. 10:9 (1 Chr. 19:10) all the *c* men of Israel
Prov. 8:10 silver; and knowledge rather than *c* gold
10:20 the tongue of the just is as *c* silver
Acts 15:7 God made *c* among us, that the Gentiles

Choke

Mt. 13:7 (Mk. 4:7; Lk. 8:7) thorns sprung up, and *c*
13:22 (Mk. 4:19; Lk. 8:14) of riches, *c* the word
Mk. 5:13 (Lk. 8:33) herd ran. . and were *c* in the sea

Choose (Chose, Chosen) *See also* Elect

Gen. 13:11 then Lot *c* him all the plain of Jordan
Num. 16:7 man whom the LORD doth *c*, he shall be
17:5 man's rod, whom I shall *c*, shall blossom
Deut. 4:37 therefore he *c* their seed after them
7:6 thy God hath *c* thee to be a special people
12:5 the place which the LORD your God shall *c*
17:15 set him king over thee, whom. . God shall *c*
18:5 thy God hath *c* him out of all thy tribes
21:5 LORD thy God hath *c* to minister unto him
30:19 *c* life, that both thou and thy seed may
Josh. 24:15 *c* you this day whom ye will serve
Judg. 5:8 *c* new gods; then was war in the gates
10:14 go and cry unto the gods which ye have *c*
1 Sam. 2:28 *c* him out of all the tribes of Israel
10:24 see ye him whom the LORD hath *c*
17:8 *c* you a man for you, and let him come down
17:40 *c* him five smooth stones out of the brook
2 Sam. 21:6 in Gibeah of Saul, whom the LORD did *c*
24:12 (1 Chr. 21:10) thee three things; *c* thee one
1 Kgs. 3:8 midst of thy people which thou hast *c*
8:16 (2 Chr. 6:5) *c* no city out of all the tribes
11:13 (11:32) for Jerusalem's sake which I have *c*
14:21 (2 Chr. 12:13) city which the LORD did *c*
1 Chr. 28:4 God of Israel *c* me before all the house
2 Chr. 29:11 LORD hath *c* you to stand before him
Neh. 9:7 art the LORD the God, who didst *c* Abram
Ps. 25:12 shall he teach in the way that he shall *c*
33:12 whom he hath *c* for his own inheritance
47:4 he shall *c* our inheritance for us
65:4 blessed is the man whom thou *c*, and causest
78:68 but *c* the tribe of Judah, the mount Zion
119:30 I have *c* the way of truth: thy judgments
Prov. 3:31 the oppressor, and *c* none of his ways
16:16 understanding rather to be *c* than silver!
22:1 good name is rather to be *c* than great riches
Is. 7:15 know to refuse the evil, and *c* the good
14:1 will yet *c* Israel, and set them in their own
41:8 Israel, art my servant, Jacob whom I have *c*
43:10 (Mt. 12:18) my servant whom I have *c*
49:7 the Holy One of Israel, and he shall *c* thee
58:6 is not this the fast that I have *c*?
65:12 and did *c* that wherein I delighted not
66:3 they have *c* their own ways, and their soul
Jer. 8:3 death shall be *c* rather than life by all
33:24 the two families which the LORD hath *c*
Hag. 2:23 make thee as a signet: for I have *c* thee
Zech. 1:17 comfort Zion, and shall yet *c* Jerusalem
Mt. 20:16 (22:14) for many be called, but few *c*
Mk. 13:20 but for the elect's sake, whom he hath *c*
Lk. 6:13 he *c* twelve, whom also he named apostles
10:42 is needful; and Mary hath *c* that good part
14:7 he marked how they *c* out the chief rooms
Jn. 6:70 have not I *c* you twelve, and one of you
13:18 speak not of you all: I know whom I have *c*
15:16 ye have not *c* me, but I have *c* you
15:19 I have *c* you out of the world, therefore
Acts 1:2 unto the apostles whom he had *c*
1:24 Lord. . show whether of these two thou hast *c*
6:5 they *c* Stephen, a man full of faith and of
15:40 Paul *c* Silas, and departed. . recommended
22:14 he said, The God of our fathers hath *c* thee

1 Cor. 1:27 but God hath *c* the foolish things of
2 Cor. 8:19 but who was also *c* of the churches to
Eph. 1:4 according as he hath *c* us in him before
Phil. 1:22 my labor: yet what I shall *c* I wot not
2 Thes. 2:13 from the beginning *c* you to salvation
2 Tim. 2:4 please him who hath *c* him to be a soldier
Heb. 11:25 *c* rather to suffer affliction with the
Jas. 2:5 hath not God *c* the poor of this world rich

Chorazin Mt. 11:21 (Lk. 10:13)
Chosen *See also* Choose, Elect

Ex. 14:7 he took six hundred *c* chariots, and all
  15:4 *c* captains also are drowned in the Red sea
1 Chr. 16:13 (Ps. 105:6) ye children of Jacob, his *c*
Ps. 78:31 and smote down the *c* men of Israel
  89:3 made a covenant with my *c*, I have sworn
  89:19 I have exalted one *c* out of the people
  106:5 that I may see the good of thy *c*, that I
  106:23 destroy them, had not Moses his *c* stood
Dan. 11:15 withstand, neither his *c* people, neither
Lk. 23:35 save himself, if he be Christ the *c* of God
Acts 9:15 he is a *c* vessel unto me, to bear my name
  10:41 but unto witnesses *c* before of God
  15:22 send *c* men of their own company to Antioch
1 Pet. 2:4 disallowed indeed of men, but *c* of God
  2:9 are a *c* generation, a royal priesthood
Rev. 17:14 they that are with him are called, and *c*

Christ *See also* Christ Jesus, Jesus, Jesus Christ, Lord, Lord Jesus, Lord Jesus Christ, Messiah, Saviour

Mt. 16:16 (Mk. 8:29; Lk. 9:20) thou art the *C*, the Son
  22:42 what think ye of *C* ? whose son is he?
  23:8 one is your Master, even *C*; and all ye are
  24:5 (Mk. 13:6; Lk. 21:8) come . . saying, I am *C*
  24:23 (Mk. 13:21) here is *C*, or there; believe it not
  24:24 (Mk. 13:22) arise false *C*, and false prophets
  26:63 (Mk. 14:61; Lk. 22:67) whether thou be the *C*
Mk. 9:41 a cup of water. . because ye belong to *C*
  12:35 (Lk. 20:41) say . . that *C* is the son of David?
Lk. 2:11 of David a Saviour, which is *C* the Lord
  2:26 see death, before he had seen the Lord's *C*
  4:41 devils . . saying, Thou art *C* the Son of God
  23:2 this fellow . . saying that he himself is *C* a king
  23:39 saying, If thou be *C*, save thyself and us
  24:26 ought not *C* to have suffered these things
  24:46 it behooved *C* to suffer, and to rise from
Jn. 1:20 (3:28) but confessed, I am not the *C*
  4:25 know that Messias cometh, which is called *C*
  4:29 all . . that ever I did: is not this the *C*?
  4:42 know that this is indeed the *C*, the Saviour
  6:69 believe and are sure that thou art that *C*
  7:26 rulers know indeed that this is the very *C*?
  7:42 said, That *C* cometh of the seed of David
  10:24 to doubt? If thou be the *C*, tell us plainly
  11:27 yea, Lord: I believe that thou art the *C*
  20:31 that ye might believe that Jesus is the *C*
Acts 2:30 he would raise up *C* to sit on his throne
  2:36 whom ye have crucified, both Lord and *C*
  3:18 of all his prophets, that *C* should suffer
  4:26 together against the Lord, and against his *C*
  8:5 Philip went down . . and preached *C* unto them
  9:20 he preached *C* in the synagogues, that he is
  17:3 this Jesus, whom I preach unto you, is *C*
  18:5 and testified to the Jews that Jesus was *C*
  18:28 showing by the Scriptures that Jesus was *C*
  26:23 *C* should suffer, and . . rise from the dead
Rom. 5:6 in due time *C* died for the ungodly
  5:8 while we were yet sinners, *C* died for us
  6:4 as *C* was raised up from the dead by the glory

Rom. 8:9 have not the Spirit of *C*, he is none of his
  8:10 if *C* be in you, the body is dead because of
  8:11 raised up *C* from the dead shall also quicken
  8:17 heirs of God, and joint-heirs with *C*, if so
  8:34 he that condemneth? It is *C* that died, yea
  8:35 who shall separate us from the love of *C*?
  9:3 myself were accursed from *C* for my brethren
  9:5 and of whom as concerning the flesh *C* came
  10:4 *C* is the end of the law for righteousness
  12:5 we, being many, are one body in *C*, and every
  14:10 all stand before the judgment seat of *C*
  14:18 he that . . serveth *C* is acceptable to God
  15:3 for even *C* pleased not himself
  15:7 receive ye one another, as *C* also received
1 Cor. 1:6 the testimony of *C* was confirmed in you
  1:13 is *C* divided? was Paul crucified for you?
  1:23 but we preach *C* crucified, unto the Jews a
  1:24 the power of God, and the wisdom of God
  2:16 may instruct him? But we have the mind of *C*
  3:23 and ye are *C*'s; and *C* is God's
  5:7 for even *C* our passover is sacrificed for us
  6:15 your bodies are the members of *C*? shall I
  8:12 wound their weak conscience, ye sin against *C*
  10:4 Rock that followed them . . that Rock was *C*
  10:9 neither let us tempt *C*, as some of them also
  11:3 head of every man is *C* . . head of *C* is God
  15:3 *C* died for our sins according to the Scriptures
  15:17 and if *C* be not raised, your faith is vain
  15:18 which are fallen asleep in *C* are perished
  15:20 now is *C* risen from the dead, and become
  15:22 even so in *C* shall all be made alive
  15:23 afterward they that are *C*'s at his coming
2 Cor. 1:5 as the sufferings of *C* abound in us, so
  2:14 God, which always causeth us to triumph in *C*
  3:14 old testament; which veil is done away in *C*
  5:14 for the love of *C* constraineth us
  5:16 though we have known *C* after the flesh
  5:17 if any man be in *C*, he is a new creature
  5:19 God was in *C*, reconciling the world unto
  5:20 we are ambassadors for *C*, as though God did
  6:15 and what concord hath *C* with Belial? or what
  10:5 captivity every thought to the obedience of *C*
  10:7 that, as he is *C* 's, even so are we *C* 's
  11:3 corrupted from the simplicity that is in *C*
  12:10 in persecutions, in distresses for *C*'s sake
Gal. 2:20 crucified with *C* . . not I, but *C* liveth in me
  3:13 *C* hath redeemed us from the curse of the law
  3:27 as have been baptized into *C* have put on *C*
  3:29 and if ye be *C*'s, then are ye Abraham's seed
  4:19 travail in birth . . until *C* be formed in you
  5:1 in the liberty wherewith *C* hath made us free
  5:4 *C* is become of no effect unto you, whosoever
Eph. 1:10 gather together in one all things in *C*
  1:12 praise of his glory, who first trusted in *C*
  2:5 in sins, hath quickened us together with *C*
  2:12 at that time ye were without *C*, being aliens
  3:8 should preach . . the unsearchable riches of *C*
  3:17 that *C* may dwell in your hearts by faith
  4:15 him in all things, which is the head, even *C*
  4:20 but ye have not so learned *C*
  4:32 even as God for *C*'s sake hath forgiven you
  5:2 and walk in love, as *C* also hath loved us
  5:23 wife, even as *C* is the head of the church
  5:25 your wives, even as *C* also loved the church
  6:5 servants, be obedient to them . . as unto *C*
Phil. 1:18 in pretense, or in truth, *C* is preached
  1:20 *C* shall be magnified in my body, whether it
  1:21 for to me to live is *C*, and to die is gain
  1:23 having a desire to depart, and to be with *C*
  1:29 for unto you it is given in the behalf of *C*
  2:16 I may rejoice in the day of *C*, that I have
  3:7 were gain to me, those I counted loss for *C*
  4:13 all things through *C* which strengtheneth me

Col. 1:27 which is *C* in you, the hope of glory
2:20 dead with *C* from the rudiments of the world
3:1 if ye then be risen with *C*, seek those things
3:3 are dead, and your life is hid with *C* in God
3:4 when *C*, who is our life, shall appear, then
3:11 bond nor free: but *C* is all, and in all
3:13 even as *C* forgave you, so also do ye
3:16 let the word of *C* dwell in you richly in all
3:24 receive the reward. . for ye serve the Lord *C*
1 Thes. 4:16 trump of God. . the dead in *C* shall rise
2 Thes. 2:2 as that the day of *C* is at hand
3:5 your hearts. . into the patient waiting for *C*
Heb. 3:6 as a son over his own house; whose house
5:5 so also *C* glorified not himself to be made a
9:28 so *C* was once offered to bear the sins of
1 Pet. 2:21 *C* suffered for us, leaving us an
3:18 *C* also hath once suffered for sins, the just
4:13 as ye are partakers of *C*'s sufferings
1 Jn. 2:22 liar but he that denieth that Jesus is the *C* ?
5:1 believeth that Jesus is the *C* is born of God
Rev. 11:15 the kingdoms of our Lord, and of his *C*
12:10 kingdom of our God, and the power of his *C*
20:4 lived and reigned with *C* a thousand years

Christ Jesus *See also* Christ, Jesus, Jesus Christ, Lord, Lord Jesus, Lord Jesus Christ, Messiah, Saviour

Rom. 3:24 through the redemption that is in *C J*
8:1 now no condemnation to them which are in *C J*
8:2 law of the Spirit of life in *C J* hath made
8:39 the love of God, which is in *C J* our Lord
1 Cor. 1:2 to them that are sanctified in *C J*
1:30 of him are ye in *C J*, who of God is made
2 Cor. 4:5 we preach not ourselves, but *C J* the Lord
Gal. 2:4 spy out our liberty which we have in *C J*
3:26 all the children of God by faith in *C J*
3:28 male nor female: for ye are all one in *C J*
Eph. 2:10 we are his workmanship, created in *C J*
3:11 eternal purpose which he purposed in *C J*
Phil. 2:5 mind be in you, which was also in *C J*
3:12 for which also I am apprehended of *C J*
3:14 the prize of the high calling of God in *C J*
4:19 according to his riches in glory by *C J*
Col. 2:6 received *C J* the Lord, so walk ye in him
1 Thes. 5:18 for this is the will of God in *C J*
1 Tim. 1:15 *C J* came into the world to save sinners
2:5 mediator between God and men, the man *C J*
2 Tim. 3:12 will live godly in *C J* shall suffer
3:15 unto salvation through faith which is in *C J*
Heb. 3:1 and High Priest of our profession, *C J*
1 Pet. 5:10 called us unto his eternal glory by *C J*

Christian

Acts 11:26 disciples were called *C* first in Antioch
26:28 Paul, Almost thou persuadest me to be a *C*
1 Pet. 4:16 if any man suffer as a *C*, let him not

Church *See also* Assembly, Congregation, Sanctuary, Tabernacle, Temple

Mt. 16:18 upon this rock I will build my *c*
18:17 unto the *c*: but if he neglect to hear the *c*
Acts 2:47 Lord added to the *c* daily such as should
5:11 great fear came upon all the *c*, and upon
7:38 in the *c* in the wilderness with the angel
8:3 Saul, he made havoc of the *c*, entering into
9:31 then had the *c* rest throughout all Judea
11:22 the ears of the *c* which was in Jerusalem
11:26 year they assembled themselves with the *c*
12:1 forth his hands to vex certain of the *c*
12:5 but prayer was made without ceasing of the *c*

Acts 13:1 now there were in the *c* that was at Antioch
14:23 they had ordained them elders in every *c*
14:27 gathered the *c* together, they rehearsed all
15:3 brought on their way by the *c*, they passed
15:4 to Jerusalem, they were received of the *c*
16:5 *c* established in the faith, and increased in
19:37 neither robbers of *c*, nor yet blasphemers
20:28 feed the *c* of God, which he hath purchased
Rom. 16:5 greet the *c* that is in their house
1 Cor. 7:17 let him walk. And so ordain I in all *c*
10:32 nor to the Gentiles, nor to the *c* of God
11:18 when ye come together in the *c*, I hear that
11:22 despise ye the *c* of God, and shame them
12:28 God hath set some in the *c*, first apostles
14:4 but he that prophesieth edifieth the *c*
14:35 it is a shame for women to speak in the *c*
15:9 (Gal. 1:13) because I persecuted the *c* of God
16:19 and Priscilla salute you. . with the *c*
2 Cor. 8:1 grace bestowed on the *c* of Macedonia
8:23 they are the messengers of the *c*
11:8 I robbed other *c*, taking wages of them, to
Eph. 1:22 to be the head over all things to the *c*
3:2 L glory in the *c* by Christ Jesus throughout
5:23 wife, even as Christ is the head of the *c*
5:25 Christ also loved the *c*, and gave himself
5:27 might present it to himself a glorious *c*
Phil. 3:6 concerning zeal, persecuting the *c*
Col. 1:18 he is the head of the body, the *c*
4:15 Nymphas, and the *c* which is in his house
1 Tim. 3:5 how shall he take care of the *c* of God?
3:15 which is the *c* of the living God
5:16 relieve them, and let not the *c* be charged
Heb. 2:12 in the midst of the *c* will I sing praise
12:23 general assembly and *c* of the firstborn
Jas. 5:14 call for the elders of the *c*; and let them
3 Jn. 10 that would, and casteth them out of the *c*
Rev. 1:4 (1:11) to the seven *c* which are in Asia
1:20 seven stars are the angels of the seven *c*
2:7 (2:11, 17, 29; 3:6, 13, 22) that hath an ear, let him hear what the Spirit saith unto the *c*
2:23 all the *c* shall know that I am he which
22:16 mine angel to testify. . these things in the *c*

Churlish

1 Sam. 25:3 the man was *c* and evil in his doings

Chushan-rishathaim Judg. 3:8–10

Cilicia Acts 15:41; Gal. 1:21

Circle

Is. 40:22 he that sitteth upon the *c* of the earth

Circuit

1 Sam. 7:16 went from year to year in *c* to Bethel
Job 22:14 and he walketh in the *c* of heaven
Ps. 19:6 the heaven, and his *c* unto the ends of it
Eccl. 1:6 wind returneth again according to his *c*

Circumcise

Gen. 17:10 every man child among you shall be *c*
21:4 (Acts 7:8) Abraham *c* his son Isaac
Deut. 10:16 *c* therefore the foreskin of your heart
Josh. 5:2 *c* again the children of Israel the second
Jer. 4:4 *c* yourselves to the LORD, and take away
Jn. 7:22 and ye on the sabbath day *c* a man
Acts 15:5 it was needful to *c* them, and to command
16:3 took and *c* him. . his father was a Greek
Rom. 4:11 them that believe, though they be not *c*
1 Cor. 7:18 is any man called being *c*? let him not
Gal. 5:2 if ye be *c*, Christ shall profit you nothing
6:12 show in the flesh, they constrain you to be *c*

Phil. 3:5 *c* the eighth day, of the stock of Israel
Col. 2:11 also ye are *c* with the circumcision made

Circumcision

Jn. 7:22 Moses therefore gave unto you *c*
Acts 10:45 of the *c* which believed were astonished
  11:2 they that were of the *c* contended with him
Rom. 2:29 and *c* is that of the heart, in the spirit
  3:1 hath the Jew? or what profit is there of *c*?
  4:11 the sign of *c*, a seal of the righteousness
  4:12 father of *c* to them. .not of the *c* only, but
  15:8 Christ was a minister of the *c* for the truth
1 Cor. 7:19 *c* is nothing. .uncircumcision is nothing
Gal. 2:7 me, as the gospel of the *c* was unto Peter
  5:6 (6:15) in Jesus Christ neither *c* availeth any
Phil. 3:3 we are the *c*, which worship God in the
Col. 2:11 *c* made without hands. .by the *c* of Christ
  3:11 neither Greek nor Jew, *c* nor uncircumcision
Tit. 1:10 and deceivers, specially they of the *c*

Circumspect

Ex. 23:13 all things that I have said unto you be *c*

Circumspectly

Eph. 5:15 that ye walk *c*, not as fools, but as wise

Cistern

2 Kgs. 18:31 (Is. 36:16) every one the waters of his *c*
Prov. 5:15 drink waters out of thine own *c*
Eccl. 12:6 fountain, or the wheel broken at the *c*
Jer. 2:13 hewed them out *c*, broken *c*, that can hold

Citizen

Lk. 15:15 and joined himself to a *c* of that country
  19:14 hated him, and sent a message after him
Acts 21:39 am a Jew of Tarsus. .a *c* of no mean city
Eph. 2:19 foreigners, but fellow *c* with the saints

City *See also* Town, Village

Num. 35:11 ye shall appoint you *c* to be *c* of refuge
Deut. 19:2 shalt separate three *c* for thee in the midst
Josh. 6:3 ye shall compass the *c*, all ye men of war
  20:2 appoint out for you *c* of refuge
2 Sam. 10:12 (1 Chr. 19:13) and for the *c* of our God
  19:37 may die in mine own *c*, and be buried
1 Kgs. 9:11 Solomon gave Hiram twenty *c*
2 Kgs. 25:4 (Jer. 39:2; 52:7) and the *c* was broken up
Ps. 46:4 the streams. .shall make glad the *c* of God
  48:1 greatly to be praised in the *c* of our God
  48:2 (Mt. 5:35) the *c* of the great King
  87:3 glorious things are spoken of thee, O *c* of God
  107:4 solitary way; they found no *c* to dwell in
  122:3 Jerusalem is builded as a *c* that is compact
  127:1 except the LORD keep the *c*, the watchman
Prov. 10:15 the rich man's wealth is his strong *c*
  16:32 ruleth his spirit than he that taketh a *c*
  18:19 offended is harder to be won than a strong *c*
Eccl. 9:14 was a little *c*, and few men within it
Is. 1:21 how is the faithful *c* become an harlot!
  1:26 the *c* of righteousness, the faithful *c*
  33:20 look upon Zion, the *c* of our solemnities
  48:2 for they call themselves of the holy *c*
  52:1 beautiful garments, O Jerusalem, the holy *c*
  60:14 The *c* of the LORD, The Zion of the Holy One
  61:4 and they shall repair the waste *c*
  62:12 be called, Sought out, A *c* not forsaken
Jer. 3:14 take you one of a *c*, and two of a family
  4:7 land desolate; and thy *c* shall be laid waste
  4:29 the whole *c* shall flee. . *c* shall be forsaken
  21:10 have I set my face against this *c* for evil
  29:7 and seek the peace of the *c* whither I have
  32:28 give this *c* into the hand of the Chaldeans
  52:6 the famine was sore in the *c*, so that there

Lam. 1:1 how doth the *c* sit solitary, that was full
Ezek. 26:19 make thee a desolate *c*, like the *c* that
Amos 3:6 shall there be evil in a *c*, and the LORD
  4:8 two or three *c* wandered unto one *c*, to drink
  9:14 they shall build the waste *c*, and inhabit
Zeph. 3:1 filthy and polluted, to the oppressing *c*!
Zech. 8:3 Jerusalem shall be called A *c* of truth
Mt. 5:14 a *c* that is set on a hill cannot be hid
  10:11 into whatsoever *c* or town ye shall enter
  12:25 every *c* or house divided against itself
  21:10 come into Jerusalem, all the *c* was moved
Lk. 2:3 went to be taxed, every one into his own *c*
  2:11 born this day in the *c* of David a Saviour
  8:1 that he went throughout every *c* and village
  19:17 faithful. .have thou authority over ten *c*
Acts 8:8 and there was great joy in that *c*
  9:6 arise, and go into the *c*, and it shall be
  13:44 sabbath day. .almost the whole *c* together
  16:13 sabbath we went out of the *c* by a river
  17:16 when he saw the *c* wholly given to idolatry
Heb. 11:10 he looked for a *c* which hath foundations
  11:16 for he hath prepared for them a *c*
  12:22 *c* of the living God, the heavenly Jerusalem
  13:14 here have we no continuing *c*, but we seek
Rev. 11:2 the holy *c* shall they tread under foot
  16:19 *c* was divided into three parts, and the *c*
  17:18 woman which thou sawest is that great *c*
  18:10 alas, that great *c* Babylon, that mighty *c*!
  20:9 camp of the saints about, and the beloved *c*
  21:2 I John saw the holy *c*, new Jerusalem, coming
  21:18 the *c* was pure gold, like unto clear glass
  22:14 may enter in through the gates into the *c*

Clad *See also* Array, Clothe

1 Kgs. 11:29 he had *c* himself with a new garment
Is. 59:17 clothing, and was *c* with zeal as a cloak

Clamor

Eph. 4:31 *c*, and evil speaking, be put away from

Clap

2 Kgs. 11:12 they *c* their hands. .God save the king
Ps. 47:1 O *c* your hands, all ye people; shout unto
  98:8 let the floods *c* their hands: let the hills
Is. 55:12 trees of the field shall *c* their hands
Lam. 2:15 all that pass by *c* their hands at thee

Claudius Acts 11:28; 18:2

Clave *See* Cleave

Claw

Deut. 14:6 and cleaveth the cleft into two *c*
Dan. 4:33 feathers, and his nails like birds' *c*
Zech. 11:16 of the fat, and tear their *c* in pieces

Clay

Job 10:9 thou hast made me as the *c*; and wilt thou
  13:12 like unto ashes, your bodies to bodies of *c*
  33:6 God's stead: I also am formed out of the *c*
  38:14 it is turned as *c* to the seal
Ps. 40:2 he brought me up also. .out of the miry *c*
Is. 29:16 shall be esteemed as the potter's *c*
  45:9 shall the *c* say to him that fashioneth it
  64:8 we are the *c*, and thou our potter
Jer. 18:6 as the *c* is in the potter's hand, so are
  43:9 and hide them in the *c* in the brickkiln
Dan. 2:33 his feet part of iron and part of *c*
  2:41 the feet and toes, part of potters' *c*
Hab. 2:6 to him that ladeth himself with thick *c*!
Jn. 9:6 spat on the ground, and made *c* of the spittle
Rom. 9:21 hath not the potter power over the *c*

Clean *See also* Chaste, Cleanse, Holy, Pure, Purity

Gen. 7:2 of every *c* beast thou shalt take to thee
35:2 put away the strange gods. .and be *c*
Lev. 7:19 as for the flesh, all that be *c* shall eat
10:10 holy and unholy, and between unclean and *c*
13:6 the skin, the priest shall pronounce him *c*
14:4 to be cleansed two birds alive and *c*
16:30 may be *c* from all your sins before the LORD
22:4 not eat of holy things, until he be *c*
2 Kgs. 5:12 may I not wash in them, and be *c*?
5:14 dipped himself seven times. .and he was *c*
Job 14:4 who can bring a *c* thing out of an unclean?
15:14 what is man, that he should be *c*?
15:15 yea, the heavens are not *c* in his sight
17:9 he that hath *c* hands shall be stronger and
25:4 how can he be *c* that is born of a woman?
33:9 I am *c* without transgression, I am innocent
Ps. 19:9 fear of the LORD is *c*, enduring for ever
24:4 he that hath *c* hands, and a pure heart
51:7 purge me with hyssop, and I shall be *c*
51:10 create in me a *c* heart, O God; and renew
73:1 to Israel, even to such as are of a *c* heart
Prov. 16:2 the ways of a man are *c* in his own eyes
20:9 who can say, I have made my heart *c*, I am
Is. 1:16 wash ye, make you *c*; put away the evil
52:11 be ye *c*, that bear the vessels of the LORD
Jer. 13:27 O Jerusalem! wilt thou not be made *c*?
Ezek. 22:26 difference between the unclean and the *c*
36:25 sprinkle *c* water upon you, and ye shall be *c*
Mt. 8:2 (Mk. 1:40; Lk. 5:12) thou canst make me *c*
23:25 (Lk. 11:39) make *c* the outside of the cup
Lk. 11:41 and, behold, all things are *c* unto you
Jn. 13:10 *c* every whit: and ye are *c*, but not all
15:3 now ye are *c* through the word which I have
Acts 18:6 your blood be upon your own heads; I am *c*
2 Pet. 2:18 those that were *c* escaped from them
Rev. 19:8 arrayed in fine linen, *c* and white

Cleanness

2 Sam. 22:21 (Ps. 18:20) according to the *c* of my
Amos 4:6 given you *c* of teeth in all your cities

Cleanse *See also* Clean, Purify

Lev. 16:19 seven times, and *c* it, and hallow it
Num. 8:21 Aaron made an atonement for them to *c*
35:33 land cannot be *c* of the blood that is shed
2 Chr. 29:15 and came. .to *c* the house of the LORD
34:5 he burnt the bones. *c* Judah and Jerusalem
Job 35:3 profit shall I have, if I be *c* from my sin?
37:21 clouds: but the wind passeth, and *c* them
Ps. 19:12 his errors? *c* thou me from secret faults
51:2 from mine iniquity, and *c* me from my sin
73:13 *c* my heart in vain, and washed my hands
119:9 wherewithal shall a young man *c* his way?
Prov. 20:30 the blueness of a wound *c* away evil
Jer. 33:8 I will *c* them from all their iniquity
Ezek. 22:24 thou art the land that is not *c*
36:25 and from all your idols, will I *c* you
37:23 wherein they have sinned, and will *c* them
Dan. 8:14 then shall the sanctuary be *c*
Mt. 8:3 (Mk. 1:42) and immediately his leprosy was *c*
10:8 heal the sick, *c* the lepers, raise the dead
11:5 (Lk. 7:22) lepers are *c*, and the deaf hear
23:26 *c* first that which is within the cup
Lk. 4:27 and none. .was *c*, saving Naaman the Syrian
17:17 were there not ten *c*? but where are the
Acts 10:15 (11:9) what God hath *c*, that call not
2 Cor. 7:1 let us *c* ourselves from all filthiness
Eph. 5:26 that he might sanctify and *c* it with the
Jas. 4:8 *c* your hands, ye sinners; and purify your

1 Jn. 1:7 blood of Jesus Christ his Son *c* us from
1:9 and to *c* us from all unrighteousness

Clear (Clearer)

Gen. 24:8 (24:41) thou shalt be *c* from this my oath
44:16 how shall we *c* ourselves? God hath found
Ex. 34:7 and that will by no means *c* the guilty
Job 11:17 thine age shall be *c* than the noonday
Ps. 51:4 thou speakest, and be *c* when thou judgest
Amos 8:9 and I will darken the earth in the *c* day
Zech. 14:6 that the light shall not be *c*, nor dark
2 Cor. 7:11 approved yourselves to be *c* in this
Rev. 21:18 city was pure gold, like unto *c* glass
22:1 pure river of water of life, *c* as crystal

Clearly

Mt. 7:5 (Lk. 6:42) thou see *c* to cast out the mote
Rom. 1:20 for the invisible things. .are *c* seen

Cleave (Clave) (to cling) *See also* Join

Gen. 2:24 (Mt. 19:5; Mk. 10:7) shall *c* unto his wife
Deut. 4:4 but ye that did *c* unto the LORD your God
10:20 to him shalt thou *c*, and swear by his name
11:22 to walk in all his ways, and to *c* unto him
13:4 and ye shall serve him, and *c* unto him
30:20 thou mayest *c* unto him: for he is thy life
Josh. 22:5 keep his commandments, and to *c* unto
23:8 *c* unto the LORD your God, as ye have done
Ruth 1:14 her mother-in-law; but Ruth *c* unto her
2 Sam. 23:10 weary, and his hand *c* unto the sword
2 Kgs. 5:27 leprosy. .of Naaman shall *c* unto thee
18:6 he *c* to the LORD, and departed not from
Neh. 10:29 they *c* to their brethren, their nobles
Job 29:10 their tongue *c* to the roof of their mouth
Ps. 22:15 like a potsherd; and my tongue *c* to my jaws
119:25 my soul *c* unto the dust: quicken thou me
Jer. 13:11 to *c* unto me the whole house of Israel
Dan. 11:34 many shall *c* to them with flatteries
Mt. 19:5 (Mk. 10:7) and shall *c* to his wife: and
Lk. 10:11 the very dust of your city, which *c* on us
Acts 11:23 of heart they would *c* unto the Lord
17:34 certain men *c* unto him, and believed
Rom. 12:9 which is evil; *c* to that which is good

Cleave (Clave) (to split)

Gen. 22:3 and *c* the wood for the burnt offering
Num. 16:31 ground *c* asunder that was under them
1 Sam. 6:14 they *c* the wood of the cart, and offered
Job 16:13 he *c* my reins asunder, and doth not spare
Ps. 74:15 thou didst *c* the fountain and the flood
Hab. 3:9 thou didst *c* the earth with rivers

Cleft

Ex. 33:22 that I will put thee in a *c* of the rock
Song 2:14 O my dove, that art in the *c* of the rock
Is. 2:21 to go into the *c* of the rocks, and into
Jer. 49:16 thou that dwellest in the *c* of the rock
Amos 6:11 with breaches, and the little house with *c*
Obad. 3 *c* of the rock, whose habitation is high

Clemency

Acts 24:4 wouldest hear us of thy *c* a few words

Clement Phil. 4:3

Cleopas Lk. 24:18

Climb

1 Sam. 14:13 Jonathan *c* up upon his hands and upon
Jer. 4:29 go into thickets, and *c* up upon the rocks
Joel 2:7 they shall *c* the wall like men of war
Amos 9:2 though they *c* up to heaven, thence will I
Lk. 19:4 *c* up into a sycamore tree to see him; for

Jn. 10:1 the sheepfold, but *c* up some other way

Cloak

Is. 59:17 clothing, and was clad with zeal as a *c*
Mt. 5:40 (Lk. 6:29) away thy coat, let him have thy *c*
Jn. 15:22 but now they have no *c* for their sin
1 Thes. 2:5 nor a *c* of covetousness; God is witness
2 Tim. 4:13 *c* that I left at Troas. . bring with thee
1 Pet. 2:16 your liberty for a *c* of maliciousness

Clod

Job 7:5 flesh is clothed with worms and *c* of dust
21:33 *c* of the valley shall be sweet unto him
Is. 28:24 he open and break the *c* of his ground?
Hos. 10:11 shall plow, and Jacob shall break his *c*

Close (adjective)

Prov. 18:24 friend that sticketh *c* than a brother
Lk. 9:36 kept it *c*, and told no man in those days

Close (verb) *See also* Shut

Gen. 2:21 took one of his ribs, and *c* up the flesh
Is. 29:10 spirit of deep sleep, and hath *c* your eyes
Dan. 12:9 words are *c* up and sealed till the time
Mt. 13:15 (Acts 28:27) their eyes they have *c*; lest

Closet

Joel 2:16 his chamber, and the bride out of her *c*
Mt. 6:6 but. . when thou prayest, enter into thy *c*
Lk. 12:3 spoken in the ear in *c* shall be proclaimed

Cloth

2 Kgs. 8:15 took a thick *c*, and dipped it in water
Mt. 9:16 (Mk. 2:21) no man putteth a piece of new *c*
27:59 the body, he wrapped it in a clean linen *c*

Clothe *See also* Array, Clad, Gird

Gen. 3:21 LORD God make coats of skins, and *c* them
2 Chr. 6:41 let thy priests. . be *c* with salvation
Job 29:14 I put on righteousness, and it *c* me
39:19 hast thou *c* his neck with thunder?
Ps. 35:26 let them be *c* with shame and dishonor
65:13 the pastures are *c* with flocks; the valleys
93:1 *c* with majesty; the LORD is *c* with strength
104:1 O LORD. . thou art *c* with honor and majesty
109:18 he *c* himself with cursing like as with his
109:29 let mine adversaries be *c* with shame
132:9 let thy priests be *c* with righteousness
Prov. 23:21 and drowsiness shall *c* a man with rags
31:21 for all her household are *c* with scarlet
Is. 50:3 I *c* the heavens with blackness, and I make
61:10 he hath *c* me with the garments of salvation
Jer. 4:30 though thou *c* thyself with crimson
Hag. 1:6 ye *c* you, but there is none warm
Mt. 6:30 (Lk. 12:28) God so *c* the grass of the field
11:8 (Lk. 7:25) to see? A man *c* in soft raiment?
25:36 naked, and ye *c* me: I was sick, and ye visited
Mk. 1:6 and John was *c* with camel's hair, and with
5:15 (Lk. 8:35) sitting. . *c*, and in his right mind
15:17 *c* him with purple, and platted a crown
16:5 saw a young man. . *c* in a long white garment
Lk. 16:19 rich man, which was *c* in purple and fine
2 Cor. 5:2 desiring to be *c* upon with our house
1 Pet. 5:5 be *c* with humility: for God resisteth
Rev. 3:18 and white raiment, that thou mayest be *c*
11:3 and they shall prophesy. . *c* in sackcloth
12:1 wonder in heaven; a woman *c* with the sun
19:13 he was *c* with a vesture dipped in blood

Clothes *See also* Clothing, Garment, Raiment, Robe

Gen. 37:29 Joseph was not in the pit; and he rent his *c*
Gen. 37:34 and Jacob rent his *c*, and put sackcloth
49:11 in wine, and his *c* in the blood of grapes
Ex. 19:10 sanctify them. . and let them wash their *c*
Lev. 11:25 shall wash his *c*, and be unclean until
Num. 14:6 that searched the land, rent their *c*
19:7 priest shall wash his *c*, and he shall bathe
Deut. 29:5 your *c* are not waxen old upon you
Judg. 11:35 when he saw her, that he rent his *c*
1 Sam. 19:24 he stripped off his *c* . . and prophesied
Amos 2:8 lay themselves down upon *c* laid to pledge
Mt. 26:65 (Mk. 14:63) the high priest rent his *c*
Mk. 5:28 I may touch but his *c*, I shall be whole
15:20 put his own *c* on him, and led him out to
Lk. 2:7 wrapped him in swaddling *c*, and laid him
8:27 which had devils long time, and ware no *c*
19:36 as he went, they spread their *c* in the way
24:12 (Jn. 20:6) the linen *c* laid by themselves
Jn. 19:40 body of Jesus, and wound it in linen *c*
Acts 7:58 laid down their *c* at a young man's feet
14:14 Barnabas and Paul, heard. . they rent their *c*
22:23 off their *c*, and threw dust into the air

Clothing *See also* Clothes, Garment, Raiment, Robe

Job 22:6 nought, and stripped the naked of their *c*
31:19 if I have seen any perish for want of *c*
Ps. 35:13 when they were sick, my *c* was sackcloth
45:13 King's daughter. . her *c* is of wrought gold
Prov. 27:26 the lambs are for thy *c*, and the goats
31:25 strength and honor are her *c*; and she shall
Is. 3:7 in my house is neither bread nor *c*
23:18 to eat sufficiently, and for durable *c*
59:17 he put on the garments of vengeance for *c*
Mt. 7:15 prophets, which come to you in sheep's *c*
11:8 they that wear soft *c* are in kings' houses
Mk. 12:38 scribes, which love to go in long *c*
Jas. 2:3 respect to him that weareth the gay *c*

Cloud

Gen. 9:13 I do set my bow in the *c*, and it shall
Ex. 13:21 went before them by day in a pillar of a *c*
14:19 pillar of the *c* went from before their face
16:10 the glory of the LORD appeared in the *c*
24:18 Moses went into the midst of the *c*
40:34 (Num. 9:15) a *c* covered the tent
Num. 12:5 LORD came down in the pillar of the *c*
Deut. 4:11 with darkness, *c*, and thick darkness
5:22 out of the midst of the fire, of the *c*, and
31:15 the pillar of the *c* stood over the door
1 Kgs. 18:44 *c* out of the sea, like a man's hand
Neh. 9:19 the *c* departed not from them by day
Job 22:13 can he judge through the dark *c*?
36:32 with *c* he covereth the light
37:11 also by watering he wearieth the thick *c*
Ps. 36:5 and thy faithfulness reacheth unto the *c*
57:10 (108:4) the heavens, and thy truth unto the *c*
68:34 over Israel, and his strength is in the *c*
78:14 in the daytime did he led them with a *c*
105:39 he spread a *c* for a covering; and fire to
Prov. 25:14 false gift is like *c* and wind without
Eccl. 11:4 he that regardeth the *c* shall not reap
Is. 4:5 a *c* and smoke by day, and the shining
44:22 have blotted out. . as a *c*, thy sins
Dan. 7:13 Son of man came with the *c* of heaven
Hos. 6:4 for your goodness is as a morning *c*, and
13:3 they shall be as the morning *c*
Zech. 10:1 the LORD shall make bright *c*, and give
Mt. 17:5 (Mk. 9:7; Lk. 9:34) *c* overshadowed them
24:30 (Mk. 13:26; Lk. 21:27) coming in the *c* of
26:64 (Mk. 14:62) and coming in the *c* of heaven
Acts 1:9 and a *c* received him out of their sight
1 Cor. 10:2 were all baptized unto Moses in the *c*

1 Thes. 4:17 caught up together with them in the *c*
Heb. 12:1 with so great a *c* of witnesses, let us
2 Pet. 2:17 *c* that are carried with a tempest
Jude 12 *c* they are without water, carried about
Rev. 1:7 he cometh with *c*; and every eye shall see
11:12 they ascended up to heaven in a *c*
14:14 upon the *c* one sat like unto the Son of man

Cloudy

Neh. 9:12 leddest them in the day by a *c* pillar
Ps. 99:7 he spake unto them in the *c* pillar

Clout

Josh. 9:5 old shoes and *c* upon their feet, and old
Jer. 38:12 old cast *c* and rotten rags under thine

Cloven

Deut. 14:7 that divide the *c* hoof; as the camel
Acts 2:3 appeared unto them *c* tongues like as of

Cluster

Num. 13:23 thence a branch with one *c* of grapes
Song 1:14 as a *c* of camphire in the vineyards of
Is. 65:8 as the new wine is found in the *c*
Rev. 14:18 gather the *c* of the vine of the earth

Coal

2 Sam. 22:9 (Ps. 18:8) *c* were kindled by it
Job 41:21 his breath kindleth *c*, and a flame goeth
Ps. 140:10 let burning *c* fall upon them: let them
Prov. 6:28 can one go upon hot *c*, and his feet not
25:22 (Rom. 12:20) heap *c* of fire upon his head
Song 8:6 jealousy. . the *c* thereof are *c* of fire
Is. 6:6 seraphim unto me, having a live *c* in his hand
47:14 shall not be a *c* to warm at, nor fire to
Lam. 4:8 their visage is blacker than a *c*
Hab. 3:5 and burning *c* went forth at his feet
Jn. 18:18 had made a fire of *c*. for it was cold
21:9 they saw a fire of *c* there, and fish laid

Coast

Deut. 19:8 if the LORD thy God enlarge thy *c*
1 Chr. 4:10 bless me indeed, and enlarge my *c*
Mt. 8:34 (Mk. 5:17) he would depart out of their *c*

Coat

Gen. 3:21 God make *c* of skins, and clothed them
37:3 loved Joseph. . made him a *c* of many colors
37:31 took Joseph's *c*. . dipped the *c* in the blood
1 Sam. 2:19 his mother made him a little *c*
17:5 armed with a *c* of mail. . the weight of the *c*
Song 5:3 have put off my *c*; how shall I put it on?
Dan. 3:27 neither were their *c* changed, nor the
Mt. 5:40 (Lk. 6:29) take away thy *c*, let him have
10:10 nor scrip for your journey, neither two *c*
Lk. 3:11 two *c* let him impart to him that hath none
Jn. 19:23 also his *c*: now the *c* was without seam
21:7 Simon Peter. . girt his fisher's *c* unto him

Cock

Mt. 26:34 (Mk. 14:30; Lk. 22:34; Jn. 13:38) before
the *c* crow, thou shalt deny me thrice

Cockatrice

Is. 11:8 child shall put his hand on the *c*' den
14:29 of the serpent's root shall come forth a *c*
59:5 they hatch *c*' eggs, and weave the spider's

Cockcrowing

Mk. 13:35 midnight, or at the *c*, or in the morning

Cockle

Job 31:40 instead of wheat, and *c* instead of barley

Coffer

1 Sam. 6:8 the jewels of gold. . in a *c* by the side

Coffin

Gen. 50:26 Joseph. . was put in a *c* in Egypt

Cogitation

Dan. 7:28 as for me Daniel, my *c* much troubled me

Cold

Gen. 8:22 and *c* and heat, and summer and winter
Prov. 20:4 sluggard will not plow by reason of the *c*
25:20 taketh away a garment in *c* weather
25:25 as *c* waters to a thirsty soul, so is good
Mt. 10:42 a cup of *c* water only in the name of a
24:12 shall abound, the love of many shall wax *c*
Acts 28:2 present rain, and because of the *c*
2 Cor. 11:27 in fastings often, in *c* and nakedness
Rev. 3:15 neither *c* nor hot: I would thou wert *c*

Collection

2 Chr. 24:6 out of Jerusalem the *c*, according to
1 Cor. 16:1 now concerning the *c* for the saints

College

2 Kgs. 22:14 (2 Chr. 34:22) in Jerusalem in the *c*

Colony

Acts 16:12 the chief city of. . Macedonia, and a *c*

Color

Gen. 37:3 loved Joseph. . made him a coat of many *c*
Num. 11:7 manna. . the *c* thereof as the *c* of bdellium
Prov. 23:31 when it giveth his *c* in the cup
Dan. 10:6 arms and. . feet like in *c* to polished brass

Colt

Zech. 9:9 (Mt. 21:5; Jn. 12:15) riding upon. . a *c*
Mt. 21:2 (Mk. 11:2; Lk. 19:30) an ass tied, and a *c*

Come (Came)

Gen. 7:1 *c* thou and all thy house into the ark
24:31 *c* in, thou blessed of the LORD; wherefore
Ex. 24:1 Moses, *C* up unto the LORD, thou, and
Num. 10:29 Moses said unto Hobab. . *c* thou with us
24:17 there shall *c* a Star out of Jacob
1 Sam. 13:11 thou *c* not within the days appointed
14:12 *c* up to us, and we will show you a thing
17:45 said David. . Thou *c* to me with a sword
18:13 he went out and *c* in before the people
1 Chr. 29:14 for all things *c* of thee, and of thine
Neh. 6:3 a great work, so that I cannot *c* down
Esth. 4:14 whether thou art *c* to the kingdom for
Job 1:6 (2:1) sons of God *c* to present themselves
13:13 that I may speak, and let *c* on me what will
14:2 he *c* forth like a flower, and is cut down
22:21 be at peace: thereby good shall *c* unto thee
23:10 he hath tried me, I shall *c* forth as gold
28:20 whence then *c* wisdom. . where is the place
Ps. 24:7 and the King of glory shall *c* in
30:5 endure for a night, but joy *c* in the morning
40:7 (Heb. 10:7) lo, I *c*: in the volume of the book
42:2 when shall I *c* and appear before God?
50:3 our God shall *c*, and shall not keep silence
65:2 hearest prayer, unto thee shall all flesh *c*
86:9 (Rev. 15:4) shall *c* and worship before thee
88:2 let my prayer *c* before thee: incline thine
91:7 right hand; but it shall not *c* nigh thee
100:2 *c* before his presence with singing
118:26 (Mt. 21:9; 23:39; Mk. 11:9; Lk. 13:35; 19:
38; Jn. 12:13) blessed be he that *c* in the name
121:1 eyes unto the hills, from whence *c* my help

Eccl. 9:2 all things *c* alike to all: there is one
Is. 11:1 there shall *c* forth a rod out of the stem
35:4 fear not. . your God will *c* with vengeance
55:1 every one that thirsteth, *c* ye to the waters
55:3 incline your ear, and *c* unto me: hear
60:3 and the Gentiles shall *c* to thy light
63:1 who is this that *c* from Edom, with dyed
Jer. 3:22 we *c* unto thee; for thou art the LORD
Ezek. 3:15 then I *c* to them of the captivity at
Dan. 7:13 one like the Son of man *c* with the clouds
Joel 2:31 (Acts 2:20) the terrible day of the LORD *c*
Mic. 5:2 yet out of thee shall he *c* forth unto me
Zech. 9:9 (Mt. 21:5; Jn. 12:15) behold, thy King *c*
Mal. 3:1 the LORD. . shall suddenly *c* to his temple
4:1 the day *c*. . the day that *c* shall burn them up
Mt. 2:6 for out of thee shall *c* a Governor
3:11 (Mk. 1:7; Lk. 3:16; Jn. 1:27; Acts 13:25) he
that *c* after me is mightier than I, whose shoes
5:17 think not that I am *c* to destroy the law
5:37 for whatsoever is more than these *c* of evil
6:10 (Lk. 11:2) thy kingdom *c*. Thy will be done
8:9 (Lk. 7:8) goeth; and to another, *C*, and he *c*
8:11 (Lk. 13:29) shall *c* from the east and west
11:3 (Lk. 7:19) art thou he that should *c*, or do we
11:28 *c* unto me, all ye that labor and are heavy
16:24 (Mk. 8:34; Lk. 9:23) any man will *c* after me
18:7 (Lk. 17:1) it must needs be that offenses *c*
18:11 (Lk. 19:10) is *c* to save that which was lost
19:14 (Mk. 10:14; Lk. 18:16) children. . *c* unto me
19:21 (Mk. 10:21; Lk. 18:22) sell. . *c* and follow me
20:28 (Mk. 10:45) *c* not to be ministered unto, but
22:4 all things are ready: *c* unto the marriage
22:12 how *c* thou in hither not having a wedding
24:5 (Mk. 13:6; Lk. 21:8) many shall *c* in my name
24:14 unto all nations; and then shall the end *c*
24:30 (Mk. 13:26; Lk. 21:27) see the Son of man *c*
24:44 (Lk. 12:40) as ye think not the Son of man *c*
26:64 (Mk. 14:62) and *c* in the clouds of heaven
27:40 (Mk. 15:30) *c* down from the cross
28:6 he is risen, as he said. *C*, see the place
Mk. 1:17 Jesus said unto them, *C* ye after me
1:25 (Lk. 4:35) hold thy peace, and *c* out of him
2:4 they could not *c* nigh unto him for the press
Lk. 10:9 the kingdom of God is *c* nigh unto you
14:23 compel them to *c* in, that my house may be
17:20 the kingdom of God *c* not with observation
18:8 when the Son of man *c*, shall he find faith
19:5 Zaccheus, make haste, and *c* down; for today
Jn. 1:11 he *c* unto his own, and his own received
1:39 saith unto them, *C* and see. They *c* and saw
1:46 can there any good thing *c* out of Nazareth?
1:46 Nazareth? Philip saith unto him, *C* and see
4:35 are yet four months, and then *c* harvest?
4:49 saith unto him, Sir, *c* down ere my child die
5:14 sin no more, lest a worse thing *c* unto thee
5:40 we will not *c* to me, that ye might have life
5:43 I am *c* in my Father's name, and ye receive
6:35 he that *c* to me shall never hunger; and he
6:37 all that the Father giveth me shall *c* to me
6:37 him that *c* to me I will in no wise cast out
6:44 no man can *c* to me, except the Father which
7:8 this feast; for my time is not yet full *c*
7:28 (8:42) I am not *c* of myself, but he that sent
7:34 (7:36; 8:21, 22; 13:33) thither ye cannot *c*
7:37 any man thirst, let him *c* unto me, and drink
10:10 I am *c* that they might have life, and that
11:43 cried with a loud voice, Lazarus, *c* forth
12:27 but for this cause *c* I unto this hour
12:46 I am *c* a light into the world
13:3 and that he was *c* from God, and went to God
14:3 I will *c* again, and receive you unto myself
14:6 no man *c* unto the Father, but by me
14:18 not leave you comfortless: I will *c* to you

Jn. 15:22 if I had not *c* and spoken unto them, they
16:4 when the time shall *c*, ye may remember that
16:28 I *c* forth from the Father, and am *c* into
17:1 Father, the hour is *c*; glorify thy Son, that
21:22 if I will that he tarry till I *c*, what is
Acts 1:11 same Jesus. . shall so *c* in like manner
16:9 *c* over into Macedonia, and help us
Rom. 3:8 let us do evil, that good may *c*?
15:23 desire these many years to *c* unto you
1 Cor. 11:26 ye do show the Lord's death till he *c*
15:24 *c* the end, when he shall have delivered up
15:35 raised up? and with what body do they *c*?
2 Cor. 13:1 this is the third time I am *c* to you
Gal. 4:4 when the fulness of the time was *c*, God
Eph. 4:13 till we all *c* in the unity of the faith
1 Thes. 5:2 (2 Pet. 3:10) day of the Lord so *c* as a thief
1 Tim. 1:15 Jesus *c* into the world to save sinners
2 Tim. 4:9 do thy diligence to *c* shortly unto me
Heb. 4:16 let us therefore *c* boldly unto the throne
7:25 save them to the uttermost that *c* unto God
10:37 he that shall *c* will *c*, and will not tarry
11:6 he that *c* to God must believe that he is
Jas. 1:17 gift is from above, and *c* down from the
2 Jn. 7 confess not that. . Christ is *c* in the flesh
Jude 14 Lord *c* with ten thousands of his saints
Rev. 2:5 or else I will *c* unto thee quickly
3:11 (22:7, 12) behold, I *c* quickly
3:20 I will *c* in to him, and will sup with him
22:17 Spirit and the bride say, *C*. . heareth say, *C*
22:20 surely I *c* quickly: Amen. Even so, *c*, Lord

Comeliness

Is. 53:2 he hath no form nor *c*; and when we shall
Ezek. 16:14 it was perfect through my *c*, which I

Comely

1 Sam. 16:18 a *c* person, and the LORD is with him
Ps. 33:1 rejoice. . for praise is *c* for the upright
Prov. 30:29 go well, yea, four are *c* in going
Song 1:5 I am black, but *c*, O ye daughters of
1 Cor. 7:35 snare upon you, but for that which is *c*
11:13 *c* that a woman pray unto God uncovered?

Comer

Heb. 10:1 continually, make the *c* thereunto perfect

Comfort *See also* Encourage, Exhort

Gen. 5:29 name Noah, saying, This same shall *c* us
37:35 rose up to *c* him; but he refused to be *c*
Job 2:11 to come to mourn with him, and to *c* him
6:10 should I yet have *c*; yea, I would harden
10:20 let me alone, that I may take *c* a little
21:34 how then *c* ye me in vain, seeing in your
Ps. 23:4 with me; thy rod and thy staff they *c* me
71:21 increase my greatness. . *c* me on every side
77:2 and ceased not: my soul refused to be *c*
86:17 thou, LORD, hast helped me, and *c* me
119:50 is my *c* in my affliction: for thy word
Song 2:5 *c* me with apples: for I am sick of love
Is. 12:1 thine anger is turned away, and thou *c* me
40:1 *c* ye, *c* ye my people, saith your God
49:13 for the LORD hath *c* his people, and will
51:3 LORD shall *c* Zion: he will *c* all her waste
51:12 I, even I, am he that *c* you: who art thou
52:9 for the LORD hath *c* his people, he hath
61:2 vengeance of our God; to *c* all that mourn
66:13 as one whom his mother *c*, so will I *c* you
Jer. 31:13 their mourning into joy, and will *c* them
31:15 (Mt. 2:18) Rachel weeping. . refused to be *c*
Lam. 1:2 all her lovers she hath none to *c* her
Ezek. 14:22 and ye shall be *c* concerning the evil
16:54 hast done, in that thou art a *c* unto them
Zech. 1:17 LORD shall yet *c* Zion, and shall yet

Zech. 10:2 have told false dreams; they *c* in vain
Mt. 5:4 blessed are they that mourn . . they shall be *c*
  9:22 (Lk. 8:48) daughter, be of good *c*; thy faith
Mk. 10:49 be of good *c*, rise; he calleth thee
Lk. 16:25 but now he is *c*, and thou art tormented
Jn. 11:19 came . . to *c* them concerning their brother
Acts 9:31 the Lord, and in the *c* of the Holy Ghost
  16:40 they had seen the brethren, they *c* them
Rom. 15:4 through patience and *c* of the Scriptures
1 Cor. 14:31 that all may learn, and all may be *c*
2 Cor. 1:3 Father of mercies, and the God of all *c*
  1:4 who *c* us in all our tribulation, that we may
  7:4 I am filled with *c*, I am exceeding joyful
  7:6 God, that *c* those that are cast down, *c* us by
  7:13 we were *c* in your *c*: yea, and exceedingly
  13:11 be of good *c*, be of one mind, live in peace
Eph. 6:22 (Col. 4:8) and that he might *c* your hearts
Phil. 2:1 if any *c* of love, if any fellowship
Col. 2:2 that their hearts might be *c*, being knit
1 Thes. 3:2 and to *c* you concerning your faith
  3:7 we were *c* over you in all our affliction
  4:18 wherefore *c* one another with these words
  5:11 *c* yourselves together, and edify one another
  5:14 *c* the feebleminded, support the weak
2 Thes. 2:17 *c* your hearts, and stablish you in

Comfortably

Is. 40:2 speak ye *c* to Jerusalem, and cry unto her
Hos. 2:14 into the wilderness, and speak *c* unto her

Comforter *See also* Advocate

Job 16:2 many such things: miserable *c* are ye all
Ps. 69:20 was none; and for *c*, but I found none
Eccl. 4:1 such as were oppressed, and they had no *c*
Nah. 3:7 Nineveh . . whence shall I seek *c* for thee?
Jn. 14:16 Father, and he shall give you another *C*
  14:26 but the *C*, which is the Holy Ghost, whom
  15:26 when the *C* is come, whom I will send unto
  16:7 if I go not away, the *C* will not come unto

Comfortless

Jn. 14:18 will not leave you *c*: I will come to you

Coming *See also* Come

Gen. 30:30 the LORD hath blessed thee since my *c*
Ps. 121:8 thy going out and thy *c* in from this time
Mal. 4:5 send you Elijah the prophet before the *c*
Mt. 24:3 what shall be the sign of thy *c*, and of
  24:27 so shall also the *c* of the Son of man be
  24:48 (Lk. 12:45) shall say . . My lord delayeth his *c*
Lk. 19:23 at my *c* I might have required mine own
1 Cor. 1:7 waiting for the *c* of our Lord Jesus
  15:23 afterward they that are Christ's at his *c*
2 Cor. 7:6 God . . comforted us by the *c* of Titus
Phil. 1:26 rejoicing may be more abundant . . by my *c*
1 Thes. 2:19 in the presence of our Lord . . at his *c*?
  3:13 at the *c* of our Lord Jesus Christ with all
  4:15 are alive and remain unto the *c* of the Lord
2 Thes. 2:1 beseech you, brethren, by the *c* of our
  2:8 shall destroy with the brightness of his *c*
  2:9 him, whose *c* is after the working of Satan
Jas. 5:7 patient therefore . . unto the *c* of the Lord
  5:8 for the *c* of the Lord draweth nigh
2 Pet. 1:16 unto you the power and *c* of our Lord
  3:4 where is the promise of his *c*? for since the
  3:12 and hasting unto the *c* of the day of God
1 Jn. 2:28 and not be ashamed before him at his *c*

Command *See also* Charge, Instruct, Order

Gen. 2:16 God *c* the man, saying, Of every tree of
  6:22 did Noah; according to all that God *c* him

Gen. 18:19 he will *c* his children and his household
Ex. 7:2 thou shalt speak all that I *c* thee
  7:6 Moses and Aaron did as the LORD *c* them
  32:8 (Deut. 9:12) out of the way which I *c* them
  39:32 Israel did according to all that the LORD *c*
Lev. 7:38 LORD *c* Moses in mount Sinai, in the day
  10:1 offered strange fire . . which he *c* them not
  14:4 then shall the priest *c* to take for him that
  25:21 *c* my blessing upon you in the sixth year
Deut. 4:2 ye shall not add unto the word which I *c*
  5:32 observe to do . . as the LORD your God hath *c*
  12:32 what thing soever I *c* you, observe to do it
  17:3 and worshipped them . . which I have not *c*
  26:16 LORD . . hath *c* thee to do these statutes
  28:8 the LORD shall *c* the blessing upon thee in
  30:16 I *c* thee this day to love the LORD thy God
  32:46 ye shall *c* your children to observe to do
  34:9 Israel hearkened . . did as the LORD *c* Moses
Josh. 1:9 have not I *c* thee? Be strong and of a
  1:16 Joshua . . All that thou *c* us we will do
  11:15 as the LORD *c* Moses . . so did Moses *c* Joshua
Judg. 2:20 hath transgressed my covenant which I *c*
1 Sam. 13:14 LORD hath *c* him to be captain over his
2 Sam. 13:28 now Absalom had *c* his servants, saying
1 Kgs. 8:58 his judgments, which he *c* our fathers
  11:10 *c* him . . he kept not that which the LORD *c*
  11:38 thou wilt hearken unto all that I *c* thee
  17:4 and I have *c* the ravens to feed thee there
  17:9 have *c* a widow woman there to sustain thee
2 Chr. 33:16 and *c* Judah to serve the LORD God of
Ezra 7:23 whatsoever is *c* by the God of heaven, let
Ps. 7:6 awake for me to the judgment that thou hast *c*
  33:9 and it was done; he *c*, and it stood fast
  42:8 yet the LORD will *c* his loving-kindness in
  68:28 God hath *c* thy strength: strengthen
  111:9 he hath *c* his covenant for ever: holy and
  119:35 make me to go in the path of thy *c*
  133:3 LORD *c* the blessing, even life for evermore
  148:5 the LORD: for he *c*, and they were created
Is. 13:3 *c* my sanctified ones, I have also called
  34:16 for my mouth it hath *c*, and his spirit it
  45:12 the heavens, and all their host have I *c*
Jer. 1:7 and whatsoever I *c* thee thou shalt speak
  7:23 but this thing *c* I them . . Obey my voice
  11:4 and do them, according to all which I *c* you
  14:14 I sent them not, neither have I *c* them
  26:2 I *c* thee to speak unto them; diminish not
Lam. 3:37 cometh to pass, when the Lord *c* it not?
Mt. 4:3 (Lk. 4:3) *c* that these stones be made bread
  8:4 (Mk. 1:44; Lk. 5:14) offer the gift that Moses *c*
  10:5 these twelve Jesus sent forth, and *c* them
  15:4 God *c*, saying, Honor thy father and mother
  19:7 why did Moses then *c* to give a writing of
  21:6 the disciples went, and did as Jesus *c* them
  28:20 observe all things whatsoever I have *c* you
Mk. 1:27 (Lk. 4:36) he even the unclean spirits
  10:3 and said unto them, What did Moses *c* you?
Lk. 8:25 for he *c* even the winds and water
  9:21 and *c* them to tell no man that thing
  9:54 Lord, wilt thou that we *c* fire to come down
Jn. 15:14 my friends, if ye do whatsoever I *c* you
  15:17 these things I *c* you, that ye love
Acts 1:4 *c* them that they should not depart from
  4:18 *c* them not to speak at all nor teach in the
  10:42 he *c* us to preach unto the people, and to
  13:47 Lord *c* us, saying, I have set thee to be a
  15:5 and to *c* them to keep the law of Moses
  16:18 I *c* thee in the name of Jesus Christ to
  17:30 but now *c* all men every where to repent
  24:23 he *c* a centurion to keep Paul, and to let
1 Cor. 7:10 unto the married I *c*, yet not I, but
2 Cor. 4:6 God, who *c* the light to shine out of
2 Thes. 3:6 we *c* you, brethren, in the name of our

2 Thes. 3:10 this *c* you, that if any would not work
1 Tim. 4:3 to marry, and *c* to abstain from meats
    4:11 these things *c* and teach
Heb. 12:20 they could not endure that which was *c*

Commander

Is. 55:4 I have given him for. .a leader and *c* to

Commandment *See also* Decree, Law, Order, Ordinance, Precept, Statute

Gen. 26:5 Abraham obeyed. . kept my charge, my *c*
Ex. 20:6 (Deut. 5:10) that love me, and keep my *c*
    34:28 wrote. . the words of the covenant, the ten *c*
    34:32 he gave them in *c* all that the LORD had
Lev. 26:14 not hearken. .and will not do all these *c*
Num. 9:18 at the *c* of the LORD. .Israel journeyed
    14:41 now do ye transgress the *c* of the LORD?
    15:31 broken his *c*, that soul shall utterly be
    24:13 I cannot go beyond the *c* of the LORD
Deut. 1:26 but rebelled against the *c* of the LORD
    4:13 he commanded you to perform, even ten *c*
    6:17 (11:22) diligently keep the *c* of the LORD
    10:13 to keep the *c* of the LORD, and his statutes
    11:27 a blessing, if ye obey the *c* of the LORD
    30:11 this *c*. . is not hidden from thee, neither
1 Kgs. 18:18 ye have forsaken the *c* of the LORD
2 Kgs. 17:16 left all the *c* of the LORD their God
Neh. 1:5 for them that love him and observe his *c*
Ps. 19:8 the *c* of the LORD is pure, enlightening
    71:3 thou hast given *c* to save me; for thou art
    89:31 they break my statutes, and keep not my *c*
    103:18 to those that remember his *c* to do them
    111:7 verity and judgment; all his *c* are sure
    111:10 understanding have all they that do his *c*
    112:1 the LORD, that delighteth greatly in his *c*
    119:6 when I have respect unto all thy *c*
    119:47 I will delight myself in thy *c*, which I
    119:86 all thy *c* are faithful. .help thou me
    119:96 but thy *c* is exceeding broad
    119:127 therefore I love thy *c* above gold
    119:151 near, O LORD; and all thy *c* are truth
    119:172 for all thy *c* are righteousness
Prov. 4:4 retain my words: keep my *c*, and live
    6:20 my son, keep thy father's *c*, and forsake not
    6:23 for the *c* is a lamp; and the law is light
    7:2 keep my *c*, and live; and my law as the apple
    10:8 wise in heart shall receive *c*: but a prating
    13:13 but he that feareth the *c* shall be rewarded
    19:16 he that keepeth the *c* keepeth his own soul
Eccl. 12:13 the conclusion. .Fear God, and keep his *c*
Dan. 9:4 that love him, and to them that keep his *c*
Mt. 5:19 shall break one of these least *c*
    15:6 *c* of God of none effect by your tradition
    15:9 (Mk. 7:7) teaching for doctrines the *c* of men
    19:17 if thou wilt enter into life, keep the *c*
    22:38 (Mk. 12:30) this is the first and great *c*
    22:40 on these two *c* hang all the law and the
Mk. 10:19 (Lk. 18:20) thou knowest the *c*, Do not
Lk. 1:6 walking in all the *c* and ordinances of the
    23:56 rested the sabbath day according to the *c*
Jn. 12:49 the Father which sent me, he gave me a *c*
    13:34 (15:12) a new *c*. . That ye love one another
    14:15 if ye love me, keep my *c*
    14:21 that hath my *c*, and keepeth them, he it is
    14:31 and as the Father gave me *c*, even so I do
    15:10 if ye keep my *c*, ye shall abide in my love
Rom. 7:8 sin, taking occasion by the *c*, wrought
    7:12 law is holy, and the *c* holy, and just, and
    13:9 if there be any other *c*, it is briefly
1 Cor. 7:25 now concerning virgins I have no *c*
    14:37 I write unto you are the *c* of the Lord
Eph. 6:2 which is the first *c* with promise

Col. 2:22 after the *c* and doctrines of men?
1 Tim. 1:5 end of the *c* is charity out of a pure
    6:14 keep this *c* without spot, unrebukable, until
Heb. 7:5 of the priesthood, have a *c* to take tithes
    7:16 made, not after the law of a carnal *c*, but
2 Pet. 2:21 to turn from the holy *c* delivered unto
1 Jn. 2:3 know that we know him, if we keep his *c*
    2:7 I write no new *c* unto you, but an old *c*
    3:22 we receive of him, because we keep his *c*
    3:23 this is his *c*, That we should believe on
    4:21 this *c* have we from him, That he who loveth
    5:3 we keep his *c*: and his *c* are not grievous
2 Jn. 4 as we have received a *c* from the Father
    6 love, that we walk after his *c*. This is the *c*
Rev. 14:12 here are they that keep the *c* of God
    22:14 blessed are they that do his *c*, that they

Commend *See also* Commit

Prov. 12:8 man shall be *c* according to his wisdom
Eccl. 8:15 I *c* mirth, because a man hath no better
Lk. 16:8 the lord *c* the unjust steward, because he
    23:46 said, Father, into thy hands I *c* my spirit
Acts 14:23 they *c* them to the Lord, on whom they
    20:32 brethren, I *c* you to God, and to the word
Rom. 3:5 our unrighteousness *c* the righteousness
    5:8 God *c* his love toward us, in that, while we
    16:1 I *c* unto you Phoebe our sister, which is a
1 Cor. 8:8 but meat *c* us not to God: for neither
2 Cor. 3:1 do we begin again to *c* ourselves?
    4:2 *c* ourselves to every man's conscience
    5:12 for we *c* not ourselves again unto you
    10:12 compare. . with some that *c* themselves
    10:18 *c* himself is approved, but whom the Lord *c*

Commission

Ezra 8:36 the king's *c* unto the king's lieutenants
Acts 26:12 I went to Damascus with authority and *c*

Commit *See also* Commend

Ps. 31:5 into thine hand I *c* my spirit: thou hast
    37:5 *c* thy way unto the LORD; trust also in him
Prov. 16:3 *c* thy works unto the LORD, and thy
Lk. 12:48 and did *c* things worthy of stripes
    16:11 who will *c* to your trust the true riches?
Jn. 2:24 but Jesus did not *c* himself unto them
    5:22 no man, but hath *c* all judgment unto the Son
    8:34 whosoever *c* sin is the servant of sin
Acts 27:40 anchors, they *c* themselves unto the sea
Rom. 1:32 which *c* such things are worthy of death
    3:2 because. .unto them were *c* the oracles of God
1 Cor. 9:17 dispensation of the gospel is *c* unto me
2 Cor. 5:19 hath *c* unto us the word of reconciliation
2 Tim. 1:12 he is able to keep that which I have *c*
Tit. 1:3 preaching, which is *c* unto me according
1 Pet. 4:19 *c* the keeping of their souls to him
1 Jn. 3:8 he that *c* sin is of the devil

Common

1 Sam. 21:4 there is no *c* bread under mine hand
Eccl. 6:1 there is an evil. .and it is *c* among men
Jer. 31:5 shall plant, and shall eat them as *c* things
Mt. 27:27 took Jesus into the *c* hall, and gathered
Mk. 12:37 and the *c* people heard him gladly
Acts 2:44 (4:32) all that believed. .had all things *c*
    5:18 the apostles, and put them in the *c* prison
    10:14 (11:8) eaten any thing that is *c* or unclean
    10:28 I should not call any man *c* or unclean
1 Cor. 10:13 temptation taken you but such as is *c*
Tit. 1:4 to Titus, mine own son after the *c* faith
Jude 3 to write unto you of the *c* salvation

Commonwealth

Eph. 2:12 being aliens from the *c* of Israel

Commotion

Jer. 10:22 and a great *c* out of the north country
Lk. 21:9 when ye shall hear of wars and *c*, be not

Commune

Ex. 25:22 meet with thee, and I will *c* with thee
1 Sam. 19:3 and I will *c* with my father of thee
Job 4:2 if we. . *c* with thee, wilt thou be grieved?
Ps. 4:4 *c* with your own heart upon your bed
   77:6 I *c* with mine own heart: and my spirit made
Eccl. 1:16 I *c* with mine own heart, saying, Lo
Zech. 1:14 the angel that *c* with me said unto me
Lk. 6:11 *c* one with another what they might do to
   24:15 while they *c* together and reasoned, Jesus
Acts 24:26 sent for him the oftener, and *c* with him

Communicate

Gal. 2:2 *c* unto them that gospel which I preach
   6:6 let him that is taught in the word *c* unto
Phil. 4:15 no church *c* with me as concerning giving
1 Tim. 6:18 ready to distribute, willing to *c*
Heb. 13:16 but to do good and to *c* forget not: for

Communication

2 Sam. 3:17 Abner had *c* with the elders of Israel
2 Kgs. 9:11 unto them, Ye know the man, and his *c*
Mt. 5:37 but let your *c* be, Yea, yea; Nay, nay
Lk. 24:17 what manner of *c* are these that ye have
1 Cor. 15:33 deceived: evil *c* corrupt good manners
Eph. 4:29 let no corrupt *c* proceed out of your mouth
Col. 3:8 blasphemy, filthy *c* out of your mouth
Phlm. 6 *c* of thy faith may become effectual by the

Communion

1 Cor. 10:16 it not the *c* of the blood of Christ?
2 Cor. 6:14 and what *c* hath light with darkness?
   13:14 love of God, and the *c* of the Holy Ghost

Compact

Ps. 122:3 Jerusalem is builded as a city that is *c*
Eph. 4:16 and *c* by that which every joint supplieth

Companion *See also* Acquaintance, Friend

Judg. 14:20 but Samson's wife was given to his *c*
Ps. 119:63 I am a *c* of all them that fear thee
Prov. 13:20 but a *c* of fools shall be destroyed
   28:7 is a *c* of riotous men shameth his father
Song 8:13 *c* hearken to thy voice: cause me to hear
Mal. 2:14 yet is she thy *c*, and the wife of thy
Phil. 2:25 Epaphroditus, my brother, and *c* in labor
Heb. 10:33 ye became *c* of them that were so used
Rev. 1:9 I John. . your brother, and *c* in tribulation

Company

Num. 14:7 and they spake unto all the *c* of. . Israel
Judg. 7:16 divided the three hundred men into three *c*
1 Sam. 10:5 thou shalt meet a *c* of prophets coming
   11:11 Saul put the people in three *c*
2 Kgs. 5:2 the Syrians had gone out by *c*
Ps. 55:14 and walked unto the house of God in *c*
   68:11 great was the *c* of those that published it
Song 6:13 Shulamite? As it were the *c* of two armies
Is. 57:13 when thou criest, let thy *c* deliver thee
Mk. 6:39 (Lk. 9:14) all sit down by *c* upon the green
Lk. 2:44 they, supposing him to have been in the *c*
Lk. 5:29 a great *c* of publicans and of others that sat
Jn. 6:5 when Jesus. . saw a great *c* come unto him
Acts 10:28 unlawful thing for. . a Jew to keep *c*, or
   17:5 gathered a *c*. . set all the city on an uproar
Rom. 15:24 if first I be somewhat filled with your *c*

1 Cor. 5:11 I have written unto you not to keep *c*
2 Thes. 3:14 note that man, and have no *c* with him
Heb. 12:22 and to an innumerable *c* of angels

Comparable

Lam. 4:2 the precious sons of Zion, *c* to fine gold

Compare *See also* Liken

Ps. 89:6 who in the heaven can be *c* unto the LORD?
Prov. 3:15 canst desire are not to be *c* unto her
Is. 40:18 or what likeness will ye *c* unto him?
   46:5 make me equal, and *c* me, that we may be like?
Rom. 8:18 not worthy to be *c* with the glory which
1 Cor. 2:13 *c* spiritual things with spiritual
2 Cor. 10:12 or *c* ourselves with some that commend

Comparison

Judg. 8:2 what have I done now in *c* of you? Is not
Hag. 2:3 not in your eyes in *c* of it as nothing?
Mk. 4:30 or with what *c* shall we compare it?

Compass

Deut. 2:3 *c* this mountain long enough: turn you
Josh. 6:4 seventh day ye shall *c* the city seven
2 Sam. 5:23 not go up; but fetch a *c* behind them
   22:6 (Ps. 18:5) the sorrows of hell *c* me about
2 Kgs. 11:8 (2 Chr. 23:7) *c* the king round about
Ps. 5:12 the righteous; with favor wilt thou *c* him
   32:10 trusteth in the LORD, mercy shall *c* him
   73:6 therefore pride *c* them about as a chain
   118:11 they *c* me about; yea, they *c* me about: but
   139:3 thou *c* my path and my lying down, and art
   142:7 the righteous shall *c* me about; for thou
Is. 44:13 he marketh it out with the *c*, and maketh
   50:11 fire, that *c* yourselves about with sparks
Jer. 31:22 a new thing. . A woman shall *c* a man
Jon. 2:3 floods *c* me about: all thy billows and
Mt. 23:15 ye *c* sea and land to make one proselyte
Lk. 19:43 a trench about thee, and *c* thee round
Acts 28:13 we fetched a *c*, and came to Rhegium
Heb. 12:1 *c* about with so great a cloud of witnesses

Compassion *See also* Kindness, Love, Loving-kindness, Mercy, Pity

Ex. 2:6 babe wept. And she had *c* on him, and said
Deut. 13:17 show thee mercy, and have *c* upon thee
   30:3 turn thy captivity, and have *c* upon thee
2 Kgs. 13:23 gracious unto them, and had *c* on them
2 Chr. 36:15 *c* on his people, and on his dwelling
Ps. 86:15 but thou, O Lord, art a God full of *c*
   111:4 the LORD is gracious and full of *c*
Is. 49:15 not have *c* on the son of her womb? yea
Jer. 12:15 I will return, and have *c* on them
Lam. 3:22 are not consumed, because his *c* fail not
Mic. 7:19 will turn again, he will have *c* upon us
Zech. 7:9 execute true judgment. . show mercy and *c*
Mt. 9:36 (Mk. 6:34) he was moved with *c* on them
   14:14 (Mk. 6:34) multitude, and was moved with *c*
   15:32 (Mk. 8:2) I have *c* on the multitude, because
   18:27 the lord of that servant was moved with *c*
   20:34 Jesus had *c* on them, and touched their eyes
Mk. 1:41 Jesus, moved with *c*, put forth his hand
   5:19 Lord hath done for thee, and hath had *c* on
Lk. 7:13 when the Lord saw her, he had *c* on her
   10:33 Samaritan. . saw him, he had *c* on him
   15:20 his father saw him, and had *c*, and ran, and
Rom. 9:15 and I will have *c* on whom I will have *c*
Heb. 5:2 who can have *c* on the ignorant, and on
1 Pet. 3:8 all of one mind, having *c* one of another
1 Jn. 3:17 shutteth up his bowels of *c* from him
Jude 22 and of some have *c*, making a difference

Compel

Lev. 25:39 shalt not *c* him to serve as a bondservant
Mt. 5:41 whosoever shall *c* thee to go a mile, go
　27:32 (Mk. 15:21) Simon . . they *c* to bear his cross
Lk. 14:23 highways and hedges, and *c* them to come
Acts 26:11 every synagogue, and *c* them to blaspheme
2 Cor. 12:11 a fool in glorying; ye have *c* me
Gal. 2:3 but neither Titus . . was *c* to be circumcised

Complain

Num. 11:1 when the people *c*, it displeased the LORD
Judg. 21:22 or their brethren come unto us to *c*
Job 7:11 I will *c* in the bitterness of my soul
　31:38 or that the furrows likewise thereof *c*
Ps. 77:3 I *c*, and my spirit was overwhelmed
　144:14 that there be no *c* in our streets
Lam. 3:39 wherefore doth a living man *c*, a man for

Complaint

1 Sam. 1:16 out of the abundance of my *c* and grief
Job 7:13 shall comfort me, my couch shall ease my *c*
　10:1 I will leave my *c* upon myself; I will speak
　21:4 as for me, is my *c* to man?
　23:2 today is my *c* bitter: my stroke is heavier
Ps. 142:2 I poured out my *c* before him; I showed
Acts 25:7 and laid many and grievous *c* against Paul

Complete

Lev. 23:15 shall count . . seven sabbaths shall be *c*
Col. 2:10 ye are *c* in him, which is the head of all
　4:12 stand perfect and *c* in all the will of God

Comprehend *See also* Know, Perceive, Understand

Job 37:5 great things doeth he, which we cannot *c*
Is. 40:12 and *c* the dust of the earth in a measure
Jn. 1:5 light shineth . . and the darkness *c* it not
Rom.13:9 commandment . . is briefly *c* in this saying
Eph. 3:18 may be able to *c* with all saints what is

Conceal *See also* Hide

Gen. 37:26 if we slay our brother, and *c* his blood?
Deut. 13:8 thou spare, neither shalt thou *c* him
Job 27:11 which is with the Almighty will I not *c*
Ps. 40:10 not *c* thy loving-kindness and thy truth
Prov. 11:13 is of a faithful spirit *c* the matter
　12:23 a prudent man *c* knowledge: but the heart
　25:2 it is the glory of God to *c* a thing: but
Jer. 50:2 publish, and *c* not: say, Babylon is

Conceit *See also* Haughtiness, Pride

Prov. 18:11 city, and as a high wall in his own *c*
　26:5 to his folly, lest he be wise in his own *c*
　26:16 sluggard is wiser in his own *c* than seven
　28:11 rich man is wise in his own *c*; but the poor
Rom. 11:25 lest ye should be wise in your own *c*
　12:16 be not wise in your own *c*

Conceive

Gen. 4:1 Adam knew Eve his wife; and she *c*
　21:2 Sarah *c*, and bare Abraham a son in his old
　25:21 entreated of him, and Rebekah his wife *c*
Num. 11:12 I *c* all this people? have I begotten
Job 3:3 night . . it was said, There is a man child *c*
Ps. 51:5 in iniquity; and in sin did my mother *c* me
Is. 7:14 behold, a virgin shall *c*, and bear a son
　33:11 shall *c* chaff, ye shall bring forth stubble
　59:4 they *c* mischief, and bring forth iniquity
　59:13 *c* and uttering from the heart words of
Mt. 1:20 which is *c* in her is of the Holy Ghost
Lk. 1:36 cousin Elisabeth, she hath also *c* a son

Acts 5:4 why hast thou *c* this thing in thine heart?
Jas. 1:15 when lust hath *c*, it bringeth forth sin

Conclude

Acts 21:25 we have written and *c* that they observe
Rom. 3:28 we *c* that a man is justified by faith
　11:32 God hath *c* them all in unbelief, that he
Gal. 3:22 Scripture hath *c* all under sin, that the

Conclusion

Eccl. 12:13 let us hear the *c* of the whole matter

Concord

2 Cor. 6:15 and what *c* hath Christ with Belial? or

Concubine

Judg. 19:1 was a certain Levite . . who took to him a *c*
2 Sam. 3:7 hast thou gone in unto my father's *c*?
　5:13 David took him more *c* and wives out of
　16:22 Absalom went in unto his father's *c*
1 Kgs. 11:3 wives, princesses, and three hundred *c*

Concupiscence

Rom. 7:8 but sin . . wrought in me all manner of *c*
Col. 3:5 *c*, and covetousness, which is idolatry
1 Thes. 4:5 in the lust of *c*, even as the Gentiles

Condemn *See also* Accuse, Judge

Deut. 25:1 justify the righteous, and *c* the wicked
Job 9:20 justify myself, mine own mouth shall *c* me
　40:8 thou *c* me, that thou mayest be righteous?
Ps. 37:33 will not leave him in his hand, nor *c* him
　94:21 soul of the righteous, and *c* the innocent
　109:7 when he shall be judged, let him be *c*
　109:31 to save him from those that *c* his soul
Prov. 12:2 but a man of wicked devices will he *c*
Is. 50:9 God will help me; who is he that shall *c*
　54:17 rise against thee in judgment thou shalt *c*
Amos 2:8 they drink the wine of the *c* in the house
Mt. 12:37 justified, and by thy words thou shalt be *c*
　12:41 (Lk. 11:32) rise in judgment . . and shall *c* it
　20:18 (Mk. 10:33) and they shall *c* him to death
Lk. 24:20 our rulers delivered him to be *c* to death
Jn. 3:17 God sent not his Son into the world to *c*
　8:11 neither do I *c* thee: go, and sin no more
Rom. 8:3 his own Son . . for sin, *c* sin in the flesh
　8:34 who is he that *c*? It is Christ that died
1 Cor. 11:32 we should not be *c* with the world
Tit. 2:8 sound speech, that cannot be *c*
　3:11 subverted, and sinneth, being *c* of himself
Heb. 11:7 the which he *c* the world, and became heir
Jas. 5:9 against another, brethren, lest ye be *c*
1 Jn. 3:20 if our heart *c* us, God is greater than

Condemnation *See also* Damnation, Hell, Punishment

Lk. 23:40 fear God, seeing thou art in the same *c*?
Jn. 3:19 this is the *c*, that light is come into
　5:24 everlasting life, and shall not come into *c*
Rom. 8:1 no *c* to them which are in Christ Jesus
1 Cor. 11:34 at home . . ye come not together unto *c*
2 Cor. 3:9 for if the ministration of *c* be glory
Jas. 3:1 knowing that we shall receive the greater *c*
　5:12 yea; and your nay, nay; lest ye fall into *c*

Condescend

Rom. 12:16 high things, but *c* to men of low estate

Condition

1 Sam. 11:2 on this *c* will I make a covenant with
Lk. 14:32 an ambassage, and desireth *c* of peace

Conduct *See also* Lead

1 Cor. 16:11 despise him: but *c* him forth in peace

Coney

Lev. 11:5 (Deut. 14:7) *c*, because he cheweth the cud
Prov. 30:26 the *c* are but a feeble folk, yet make

Confection

Ex. 30:35 thou shalt make it a perfume, a *c* after

Confectionary

1 Sam. 8:13 he will take your daughters to be *c*

Confederacy

Is. 8:12 say ye not, A *c*. . this people shall say, A *c*
Obad. 7 men of thy *c* have brought thee even to the

Confederate

Gen. 14:13 and these were *c* with Abram
Ps. 83:5 with one consent: they are *c* against thee
Is. 7:2 saying, Syria is *c* with Ephraim

Confer

Gal. 1:16 immediately I *c* not with flesh and blood

Conference

Gal. 2:6 to be somewhat in *c* added nothing to me

Confess *See also* Acknowledge

Lev. 26:40 if they shall *c* their iniquity, and the
Num. 5:7 shall *c* their sin which they have done
Neh. 9:2 *c* their sins, and the iniquities of their
Job 40:14 then will I also *c* unto thee that thine
Ps. 32:5 I will *c* my transgressions unto the LORD
Prov. 28:13 but whoso *c* and forsaketh them shall
Mt. 3:6 baptized of him in Jordan, *c* their sins
10:32 (Lk. 12:8) *c* me before men, him will I *c*
Jn. 1:20 he *c*, and denied not; but *c*, I am not the
9:22 that if any man did *c* that he was Christ, he
12:42 because of the Pharisees they did not *c*
Acts 19:18 many that believed came, and *c*
Rom. 10:9 shalt *c* with thy mouth the Lord Jesus
14:11 to me, and every tongue shall *c* to God
15:9 I will *c* to thee among the Gentiles
Phil. 2:11 every tongue should *c* that Jesus Christ
Jas. 5:16 *c* your faults one to another, and pray
1 Jn. 1:9 if we *c* our sins, he is faithful and just
4:2 every spirit that *c* that Jesus Christ
4:15 *c* that Jesus is the Son of God, God dwelleth
2 Jn. 7 *c* not that Jesus Christ is come in the flesh
Rev. 3:5 but I will *c* his name before my Father

Confession

Josh. 7:19 LORD God of Israel, and make *c* unto him
2 Chr. 30:22 peace offerings, and making *c* to the
Ezra 10:11 now therefore make *c* unto the LORD
Dan. 9:4 prayed unto the LORD. . and made my *c*
Rom. 10:10 with the mouth *c* is made unto salvation
1 Tim. 6:13 who before. . Pilate witnessed a good *c*

Confidence *See also* Assurance, Believe, Faith, Trust

2 Kgs. 18:19 (Is. 36:4) what *c* is this wherein thou
Job 18:14 *c* shall be rooted out of his tabernacle
Ps. 65:5 who art the *c* of all the ends of the earth
118:8 to trust in the LORD than to put *c* in man
Prov. 3:26 LORD shall be thy *c*, and shall keep thy
25:19 *c* in an unfaithful man in time of trouble
Is. 30:15 quietness and in *c* shall be your strength
Mic. 7:5 not in a friend, put ye not *c* in a guide
Acts 28:31 preaching. . with all *c*, no man forbidding
2 Cor. 2:3 having *c* in you all, that my joy is the

2 Cor. 7:16 I rejoice therefore that I have *c* in you
Gal. 5:10 I have *c* in you through the Lord, that ye
Eph. 3:12 boldness and access with *c* by the faith
Phil. 1:25 having this *c*, I know that I shall abide
3:4 though I might also have *c* in the flesh
2 Thes. 3:4 and we have *c* in the Lord touching you
Heb. 3:14 hold the beginning of our *c* steadfast
10:35 cast not away therefore your *c*, which hath
1 Jn. 2:28 that, when he shall appear, we may have *c*
5:14 this is the *c* that we have in him, that, if

Confident

Ps. 27:3 war. . rise against me, in this will I be *c*
Prov. 14:16 but the fool rageth, and is *c*
Rom. 2:19 art *c* that thou thyself art a guide of
2 Cor. 5:6 we are always *c*, knowing that, whilst
Phil. 1:6 *c* of this very thing, that he which hath

Confirm

Ruth 4:7 *c* all things; a man plucked off his shoe
Ps. 68:9 whereby thou didst *c* thine inheritance
Is. 35:3 the weak hands, and *c* the feeble knees
44:26 *c* the word of his servant, and performeth
Dan. 9:27 *c* the covenant with many for one week
Mk. 16:20 Lord working with them, and *c* the word
Acts 14:22 *c* the souls of the disciples, and exhorting
15:32 and Judas and Silas. . exhorted. . and *c* them
15:41 through Syria and Cilicia, *c* the churches
Rom. 15:8 to *c* the promises made unto the fathers
1 Cor. 1:6 as the testimony of Christ was *c* in you
1:8 who shall also *c* you unto the end, that ye
2 Cor. 2:8 that ye would *c* your love toward him
Gal. 3:15 yet if it be *c*, no man disannulleth, or
Heb. 2:3 spoken by the Lord, and was *c* unto us by
6:17 immutability of his counsel, *c* it by an oath

Confirmation

Phil. 1:7 in the defense and *c* of the gospel, ye
Heb. 6:16 oath for *c* is to them an end of all strife

Conflict

Phil. 1:30 having the same *c* which ye saw in me
Col. 2:1 that ye knew what great *c* I have for you

Conformed

Rom. 8:29 predestinate to be *c* to the image of his
12:2 not *c* to this world: but be ye transformed

Conformable

Phil. 3:10 know him. . being made *c* unto his death

Confound

Gen. 11:7 us go down, and there *c* their language
Job 6:20 they were *c* because they had hoped
Ps. 22:5 they trusted in thee, and were not *c*
69:6 let not those that seek thee be *c* for my
83:17 let them be *c* and troubled for ever; yea
97:7 *c* be all they that serve graven images
Is. 50:7 will help me; therefore shall I not be *c*
Jer. 10:14 every founder is *c* by the graven image
17:18 let not me be *c*: let them be dismayed
50:2 Babylon is taken, Bel is *c*. . her idols are *c*
Ezek. 16:54 mayest be *c* in all that thou hast done
Acts 2:6 the multitude came together, and were *c*
9:22 Saul. . *c* the Jews which dwelt at Damascus
1 Cor. 1:27 foolish things of the world to *c* the

Confused

Is. 9:5 every battle of the warrior is with *c* noise
Acts 19:32 and some another: for the assembly was *c*

Confusion

1 Sam. 20:30 to thine own *c*, and unto the *c* of thy

Job 10:15 I am full of c. .see thou mine affliction
Ps. 35:4 them be. .brought to c that devise my hurt
  44:15 my c is continually before me
  70:2 let them be turned backward, and put to c
  71:1 do I put my trust: let me never be put to c
  109:29 let them cover themselves with their own c
Is. 24:10 city of c is broken down: every house is
  30:3 and the trust in the shadow of Egypt your c
  41:29 their molten images are wind and c
  61:7 for c they shall rejoice in their portion
Jer. 3:25 our c covereth us: for we have sinned
Dan. 9:7 but unto us c of faces, as at this day
Acts 19:29 the whole city was filled with c
1 Cor. 14:33 for God is not the author of c, but
Jas. 3:16 where envying and strife is, there is c

Congeal

Ex. 15:8 the depths were c in the heart of the sea

Congratulate

1 Chr. 18:10 inquire of his welfare, and to c him

Congregation *See also* Assembly,
Church

Ex. 12:3 speak ye unto all the c of Israel, saying
  12:19 soul shall be cut off from the c of Israel
  27:21 (Lev. 24:3) in the tabernacle of the c
Lev. 4:13 whole c of Israel sin through ignorance
  4:21 first bullock. .is a sin offering for the c
  8:3 gather thou all the c together unto the door
  9:5 all the c drew near and stood before the LORD
  10:17 iniquity of the c, to make atonement for
  16:17 made an atonement. .for all the c of Israel
  24:14 upon his head, and let all the c stone him
Num. 1:2 take ye the sum of all the c of. .Israel
  14:1 all the c lifted up their voice, and cried
  14:27 with this evil c, which murmur against me?
  15:15 one ordinance. .both for you of the c, and
  16:3 too much upon you, seeing all the c are holy
  16:22 sin, and wilt thou be wroth with all the c?
  20:1 even the whole c, into the desert of Zin in
  27:17 c of the LORD be not as sheep which have no
  35:24 then the c shall judge between the slayer
Josh. 8:35 which Joshua read not before all the c
Judg. 21:5 came not up with the c unto the LORD?
1 Chr. 29:20 David said to all the c, Now bless
2 Chr. 23:3 all the c made a covenant with the king
  29:28 all the c worshipped, and the singers sang
Neh. 5:13 the c said, Amen, and praised the LORD
Job 15:34 the c of hypocrites shall be desolate
Ps. 1:5 nor sinners in the c of the righteous
  7:7 c of the people compass thee about
  22:22 in the midst of the c will I praise thee
  26:5 I have hated the c of evil-doers; and will
  26:12 in the c will I bless the LORD
  74:19 forget not the c of thy poor for ever
  75:2 shall receive the c I will judge uprightly
  82:1 God standeth in the c of the mighty
  89:5 thy faithfulness also in the c of the saints
  107:32 exalt him also in the c of the people
  111:1 the assembly of the upright, and in the c
Prov. 21:16 shall remain in the c of the dead
Jer. 30:20 their c shall be established before me
Joel 2:16 sanctify the c, assemble the elders
Acts 13:43 now when the c was broken up, many of

Conquer *See also* Subdue

Rev. 6:2 unto him: and he went forth c, and to c

Conqueror

Rom. 8:37 are more than c through him that loved

Conscience *See also* Heart, Mind, Soul

Jn. 8:9 being convicted by their own c, went out
Acts 23:1 I have lived in all good c before God
  24:16 have always a c void of offense toward God
Rom. 2:15 their c also bearing witness, and their
  9:1 c also bearing me witness in the Holy Ghost
  13:5 not only for wrath, but also for c sake
1 Cor. 8:7 c of the idol. .c being weak is defiled
  8:12 and wound their weak c, ye sin against
  10:25 that eat, asking no question for c' sake
  10:29 why is my liberty judged of another man's c?
2 Cor. 4:2 commending ourselves to every man's c
  5:11 manifest unto God; and. .manifest in your c
1 Tim. 1:5 and of a good c, and of faith unfeigned
  1:19 holding faith, and a good c; which some
  4:2 having their c seared with a hot iron
Tit. 1:15 but even their mind and c is defiled
Heb. 9:9 service perfect, as pertaining to the c
  9:14 purge your c from dead works to serve the
  13:18 we trust we have a good c, in all things
1 Pet. 2:19 if a man for c toward God endure grief
  3:16 having a good c; that, whereas they
  3:21 but the answer of a good c toward God

Consecrate *See also* Dedicate, Give,
Hallow, Present, Purify, Sanctify

Ex. 29:9 and thou shalt c Aaron and his sons
  29:35 do unto Aaron. .seven days shalt thou c them
  32:29 c yourselves today to the LORD, even every
Lev. 8:33 for seven days shall he c you
Num. 6:12 c unto the LORD the days of his separation
Josh. 6:19 of brass and iron, are c unto the LORD
Judg. 17:5 and the man Micah. .c one of his sons
1 Chr. 29:5 who then is willing to c his service
2 Chr. 29:31 ye have c yourselves unto the LORD
  31:6 tithe of holy things which were c unto the
Ezra 3:5 all the set feasts of the LORD that were c
Ezek. 43:26 purify it; and they shall c themselves
Mic. 4:13 I will c their gain unto the LORD
Heb. 7:28 maketh the Son, who is c for evermore
  10:20 new and living way, which he hath c for us

Consecration *See also* Anoint,
Dedication

Lev. 8:22 he brought the other ram, the ram of c
  8:28 offering: they were c for a sweet savor
  8:33 until the days of your c be at an end
Num. 6:7 because the c of his God is upon his head

Consent

Deut. 13:8 thou shalt not c unto him, nor hearken
1 Sam. 11:7 people, and they came out with one c
Ps. 50:18 thou sawest a thief, then thou c with him
Prov. 1:10 son, if sinners entice thee, c thou not
Dan. 1:14 he c to them in this matter, and proved
Zeph. 3:9 name of the LORD, to serve him with one c
Lk. 14:18 they all with one c began to make excuse
  23:51 the same had not c to the counsel and deed
Acts 8:1 (22:20) Saul was c unto his death
Rom. 7:16 I c unto the law that it is good
1 Cor. 7:5 defraud ye not. .except it be with c for
1 Tim. 6:3 otherwise, and c not to wholesome words

Consider

Ex. 33:13 and c that this nation is thy people
Deut. 4:39 c it in thine heart, that the LORD
  32:7 c the years of many generations: ask thy
  32:29 were wise. .they would c their latter end!
Judg. 18:14 now therefore c what ye have to do
1 Sam. 12:24 c how great things he hath done for
Job 23:15 presence: when I c, I am afraid of him

Job 34:27 from him, and would not *c* any of his ways
  37:14 stand still. . *c* the wondrous works of God
Ps. 5:1 ear to my words, O LORD; *c* my meditation
  8:3 I *c* thy heavens, the work of thy fingers
  9:13 O LORD; *c* my trouble which I suffer of them
  31:7 hast *c* my trouble; thou hast known my soul
  33:15 their hearts alike; he *c* all their works
  41:1 blessed is he that *c* the poor: the LORD will
  45:10 hearken, O daughter, and *c*, and incline
  50:22 *c* this, ye that forget God, lest I tear you
Prov. 6:6 go to the ant, thou sluggard; *c* her ways
  24:32 then I saw, and *c* it well: I looked upon it
  28:22 and *c* not that poverty shall come upon him
  29:7 the righteous *c* the cause of the póor
Eccl. 5:1 fools: for they *c* not that they do evil
  7:13 *c* the work of God: for who can make that
  7:14 be joyful, but in the day of adversity *c*
Is. 5:12 LORD, neither *c* the operation of his hands
  44:19 and none *c* in his heart, neither is there
  52:15 that which they had not heard shall they *c*
Jer. 23:20 the latter days ye shall *c* it perfectly
Hag. 1:5 (1:7) saith the LORD of hosts; *C* your ways
Mt. 6:28 (Lk. 12:27) *c* the lilies of the field, how
Mk. 6:52 they *c* not the miracle of the loaves
Lk. 12:24 *c* the ravens: for they neither sow nor
Jn. 11:50 nor *c* that it is expedient for us, that
Acts 12:12 had *c* the thing, he came to the house
Rom. 4:19 he *c* not his own body now dead, when he
Gal. 6:1 *c* thyself, lest thou also be tempted
2 Tim. 2:7 *c* what I say; and the Lord give thee
Heb. 7:4 *c* how great this man was, unto whom even
  10:24 let us *c* one another to provoke unto love
  12:3 *c* him that endured such contradiction of

Consist

Lk. 12:15 a man's life *c* not in the abundance of
Col. 1:17 before all things, and by him all things *c*

Consolation

Job 15:11 are the *c* of God small with thee?
  21:2 my speech, and let this be your *c*
Is. 66:11 be satisfied with the breasts of her *c*
Jer. 16:7 neither shall men give them the cup of *c*
Lk. 2:25 and devout, waiting for the *c* of Israel
  6:24 that are rich! for ye have received your *c*
Acts 4:36 Barnabas. . being interpreted, The son of *c*
  15:31 when they had read, they rejoiced for the *c*
Rom. 15:5 now the God of patience and *c* grant you
2 Cor. 1:5 so our *c* also aboundeth by Christ
  1:6 be afflicted, it is for your *c* and salvation
  7:7 by the *c* wherewith he was comforted in you
Phil. 2:1 if there be therefore any *c* in Christ
2 Thes. 2:16 given us everlasting *c* and good hope
Phlm. 7 for we have great joy and *c* in thy love
Heb. 6:18 we might have a strong *c*, who have fled

Conspiracy

2 Sam. 15:12 and the *c* was strong; for the people
2 Kgs. 12:20 his servants. . made a *c*, and slew Joash
  15:30 Hoshea the son of Elah made a *c* against
Jer. 11:9 LORD said unto me, A *c* is found among the
Ezek. 22:25 there is a *c* of her prophets in the midst
Acts 23:13 more than forty which had made this *c*

Conspire

Gen. 37:18 they *c* against him to slay him
1 Sam. 22:8 that all of you have *c* against me
1 Kgs. 16:9 Zimri, captain of half his chariots, *c*
Amos 7:10 Amos hath *c* against thee in the midst of

Constantly

Prov. 21:28 but the man that heareth speaketh *c*
Acts 12:15 but she *c* affirmed that it was even so
Tit. 3:8 these things I will that thou affirm *c*

Constrain

2 Kgs. 4:8 great woman; and she *c* him to eat bread
Job 32:18 full of matter; the spirit within me *c* me
Mt. 14:22 (Mk. 6:45) *c* his disciples to get into a ship
Lk. 24:29 but they *c* him, saying, Abide with us
Acts 28:19 I was *c* to appeal unto Caesar; not that
2 Cor. 5:14 love of Christ *c* us; because we thus
Gal. 6:12 in the flesh, they *c* you to be circumcised

Constraint

1 Pet. 5:2 taking the oversight thereof, not by *c*

Consult *See also* Counsel

1 Kgs. 12:6 king Rehoboam *c* with the old men
1 Chr. 13:1 David *c* with the captains of thousands
Ps. 62:4 *c* to cast him down from his excellency
  83:3 thy people, and *c* against thy hidden ones
Ezek. 21:21 *c* with images, he looked in the liver
Mt. 26:4 *c* that they might take Jesus by subtilty
Lk. 14:31 *c* whether he be able with ten thousand
Jn. 12:10 priests *c* that they might put Lazarus

Consume *See also* Devour, Eat

Gen. 41:30 Egypt; and the famine shall *c* the land
Ex. 3:2 burned with fire, and the bush was not *c*
  32:10 wrath. . against them, and that I may *c* them
Num. 16:21 congregation that I may *c* them in a
Deut. 4:24 (Heb. 12:29) LORD thy God is a *c* fire
1 Kgs. 18:38 fell, and *c* the burnt sacrifice, and
2 Kgs. 1:10 from heaven, and *c* thee and thy fifty
Job 1:16 and *c* them; and I only am escaped alone
  7:9 as the cloud is *c* and vanisheth away; so he
Ps. 59:13 *c* them in wrath, *c* them, that they may
  78:33 days did he *c* in vanity, and their years
  78:63 fire *c* their young men; and their maidens
  90:7 we are *c* by thine anger, and by thy wrath
  104:35 let the sinners be *c* out of the earth
Is. 10:18 and shall *c* the glory of his forest
  29:20 brought to nought, and the scorner is *c*
  64:7 and hast *c* us, because of our iniquities
Lam. 3:22 of the LORD's mercies that we are not *c*
Ezek. 4:17 astonished. . and *c* away for their iniquity
Lk. 9:54 we command fire. . from heaven, and *c* them
2 Thes. 2:8 Wicked. . revealed, whom the Lord shall *c*
Jas. 4:3 ye ask. . that ye may *c* it upon your lusts

Consummation

Dan. 9:27 shall make it desolate, even until the *c*

Consumption

Lev. 26:16 I will even appoint over you terror, *c*
Deut. 28:22 the LORD shall smite thee with a *c*
Is. 10:22 *c* decreed shall overflow with righteousness
  28:22 a *c*, even determined upon the whole earth

Contain

1 Kgs. 8:27 (2 Chr. 2:6; 6:18) heavens cannot *c* thee
Jn. 21:25 world itself could not *c* the books that
1 Cor. 7:9 but if they cannot *c*, let them marry

Contemn *See also* Abhor, Despise, Detest, Disdain, Hate, Loathe, Scorn

Ps. 10:13 wherefore doth the wicked *c* God?
  15:4 in whose eyes a vile person is *c*
  107:11 and *c* the counsel of the Most High
Song 8:7 give all. . for love, it would utterly be *c*
Ezek. 21:10 make mirth? it *c* the rod of my son

Contempt *See also* Reproach, Scorn

Ps. 119:22 remove from me reproach and *c*; for I
Prov. 18:3 the wicked cometh, then cometh also *c*
Is. 23:9 bring into *c* all the honorable of the earth

Dan. 12:2 life, and some to shame and everlasting *c*

Contemptible

Mal. 1:7 in that ye say, The table of the LORD is *c*
2:9 have I also made you *c* and base before all
2 Cor. 10:10 bodily presence is weak . . his speech *c*

Contend

Neh. 13:11 then *c* I with the rulers, and said
Job 9:3 if he will *c* with him, he cannot answer him
10:2 show me wherefore thou *c* with me
13:8 ye accept his person? will ye *c* for God?
40:2 he that *c* with the Almighty instruct him?
Prov. 28:4 but such as keep the law *c* with them
Eccl. 6:10 neither . . *c* with him that is mightier
Is. 49:25 I will *c* with him that *c* with thee, and I
50:8 near that justifieth me; who will *c* with me?
57:16 I will not *c* for ever, neither will I be
Jer. 12:5 then how canst thou *c* with horses?
Amos 7:4 behold, the Lord GOD called to *c* by fire
Acts 11:2 that were of the circumcision *c* with him
Jude 3 ye should earnestly *c* for the faith which
9 Michael the archangel, when *c* with the devil

Content *See also* Satisfy

Ex. 2:21 Moses was *c* to dwell with the man
Josh. 7:7 would to God we had been *c*, and dwelt on
2 Kgs. 5:23 and Naaman said, Be *c*, take two talents
Prov. 6:35 rest *c*, though thou givest many gifts
Lk. 3:14 and be *c* with your wages
Phil. 4:11 whatsoever state I am, therewith to be *c*
1 Tim. 6:8 food and raiment, let us be therewith *c*
Heb. 13:5 be *c* with such things as ye have

Contention

Prov. 13:10 only by pride cometh *c*: but with the
18:6 a fool's lips enter into *c*, and his mouth
18:19 and their *c* are like the bars of a castle
19:13 the *c* of a wife are a continual dropping
22:10 cast out the scorner, and *c* shall go out
Jer. 15:10 borne me a man of strife and a man of *c*
Hab. 1:3 and there are that raise up strife and *c*
Acts 15:39 *c* was so sharp between them, that they
1 Cor. 1:11 declared unto me . . are *c* among you
Phil. 1:16 one preach Christ of *c*, not sincerely
1 Thes. 2:2 unto you the gospel of God with much *c*
Tit. 3:9 and *c*, and strivings about the law

Contentious

Prov. 21:19 than with a *c* and an angry woman
26:21 to fire; so is a *c* man to kindle strife
27:15 a very rainy day and a *c* woman are alike
Rom. 2:8 them that are *c*, and do not obey the truth
1 Cor. 11:16 if any man seem to be *c*, we have no

Contentment

1 Tim. 6:6 but godliness with *c* is great gain

Continual

Ex. 29:42 (Num. 28:6) shall be a *c* burnt offering
Prov. 15:15 that is of a merry heart hath a *c* feast
Ezek. 39:14 shall sever out men of *c* employment
Lk. 18:5 lest by her *c* coming she weary me
Rom. 9:2 great heaviness and *c* sorrow in my heart

Continually

Gen. 6:5 the thoughts of his heart was only evil *c*
1 Chr. 16:11 LORD and his strength, seek his face *c*
Ps. 34:1 his praise shall *c* be in my mouth
40:11 loving-kindness and thy truth *c* preserve me
44:15 my confusion is *c* before me, and the shame
52:1 O mighty man? . . goodness of God endureth *c*
71:3 strong habitation, whereunto I may *c* resort
72:15 prayer also shall be made for him *c*

Ps. 73:23 I am *c* with thee: thou hast holden me by
119:44 shall I keep thy law *c* for ever and ever
Prov. 6:21 bind them *c* upon thine heart, and tie
Is. 58:11 LORD shall guide thee *c*, and satisfy thy
Jer. 6:7 before me *c* is grief and wounds
Dan. 6:20 God, whom thou servest *c*, able to deliver
Hos. 12:6 mercy and judgment . . wait on thy God *c*
Lk. 24:53 *c* in the temple, praising and blessing
Acts 6:4 but we will give ourselves *c* to prayer
Heb. 7:3 made like unto the Son . . abideth a priest *c*
10:1 sacrifices, which they offered year by year *c*
13:15 us offer the sacrifice of praise to God *c*

Continuance

Ps. 139:16 were written, which in *c* were fashioned
Is. 64:5 in those is *c*, and we shall be saved
Rom. 2:7 by patient *c* in well doing seek for glory

Continue

Ex. 21:21 *c* a day or two, he shall not be punished
1 Sam. 1:12 she *c* praying before the LORD, that Eli
12:14 that reigneth over you *c* following the LORD
1 Kgs. 2:4 the LORD may *c* his word which he spake
Ps. 36:10 *c* thy loving-kindness unto them that know
Mt. 15:32 they *c* with me now three days, and have
Lk. 6:12 into a mountain to pray, and *c* all night
Jn. 8:31 if ye *c* in my word, then are ye my disciples
15:9 so have I loved you: *c* ye in my love
Acts 1:14 these all *c* with one accord in prayer and
2:42 they *c* steadfastly in the apostles' doctrine
13:43 persuaded them to *c* in the grace of God
14:22 exhorting them to *c* in the faith, and that
20:7 and *c* his speech until midnight
26:22 help of God, I *c* unto this day, witnessing
Rom. 6:1 shall we *c* in sin, that grace may abound?
11:22 goodness, if thou *c* in his goodness
Phil. 1:25 I know that I shall abide and *c* with you
Col. 1:23 if ye *c* in the faith grounded and settled
4:2 *c* in prayer, and watch in the same with
2 Tim. 3:14 *c* thou in the things which thou hast
Heb. 7:24 *c* ever, hath an unchangeable priesthood
8:9 because they *c* not in my covenant
13:1 let brotherly love *c*
13:14 here have we no *c* city, but we seek one to
Jas. 1:25 the perfect law of liberty, and *c* therein
2 Pet. 3:4 fell asleep, all things *c* as they were
1 Jn. 2:19 us, they would no doubt have *c* with us
2:24 also shall *c* in the Son, and in the Father

Contradiction

Heb. 7:7 without all *c* the less is blessed of the
12:3 consider him that endured such *c* of sinners

Contrary

Lev. 26:21 and if ye walk *c* unto me, and will not
Esth. 9:1 turned to the *c*, that the Jews had rule
Mt. 14:24 (Mk. 6:48) with waves: for the wind was *c*
Acts 18:13 persuadeth men to worship God *c* to the
23:3 commandest me to be smitten *c* to the law?
26:9 I ought to do many things *c* to the name of
Rom. 11:24 graffed *c* to nature into a good olive
Gal. 5:17 these are *c* the one to the other
Col. 2:14 handwriting of ordinances . . was *c* to us
1 Tim. 1:10 other thing that is *c* to sound doctrine

Contribution *See also* Gift, Present

Rom. 15:26 make a certain *c* for the poor saints

Contrite

Ps. 34:18 and saveth such as be of a *c* spirit
51:17 broken and a *c* heart, O God, thou wilt not
Is. 57:15 with him also . . of a *c* and humble spirit
66:2 even to him that is poor and of a *c* spirit

Controversy

Deut. 17:8 being matters of *c* within thy gates
  19:17 both the men, between whom the *c* is, shall
  21:5 and by their word shall every *c* . . be tried
  25:1 if there be a *c* between men, and they come
2 Sam. 15:2 had a *c* came to the king for judgment
Jer. 25:31 for the LORD hath a *c* with the nations
Ezek. 44:24 and in *c* they shall stand in judgment
Hos. 4:1 LORD hath a *c* with the inhabitants of the
  12:2 the LORD hath also a *c* with Judah, and will
Mic. 6:2 hear ye, O mountains, the LORD's *c*, and
1 Tim. 3:16 and without *c* great is the mystery of

Convenient

Prov. 30:8 nor riches; feed me with food *c* for me
Jer. 40:4 whither it seemeth good and *c* for thee
Mk. 6:21 *c* day was come, that Herod on his birthday
Acts 24:25 have a *c* season, I will call for thee
Rom. 1:28 mind, to do those things which are not *c*
1 Cor. 16:12 he will come when he shall have *c* time
Eph. 5:4 nor jesting, which are not *c*: but rather
Phlm. 8 in Christ to enjoin thee that which is *c*

Conversation *See also* Behavior

Ps. 37:14 and to slay such as be of upright *c*
  50:23 to him that ordereth his *c* aright will I
2 Cor. 1:12 we have had our *c* in the world
Gal. 1:13 my *c* in time past in the Jews' religion
Eph. 2:3 *c* in times past in the lusts of our flesh
Phil. 1:27 let your *c* be as it becometh the gospel
  3:20 for our *c* is in heaven; from whence also we
1 Tim. 4:12 example of the believers, in word, in *c*
Heb. 13:5 let your *c* be without covetousness
  13:7 faith follow, considering the end of their *c*
Jas. 3:13 let him show out of a good *c* his works
1 Pet. 1:15 so be ye holy in all manner of *c*
  2:12 having your *c* honest among the Gentiles
  3:1 without the word be won by the *c* of the wives
2 Pet. 2:7 just Lot, vexed with the filthy *c* of the
  3:11 ought ye to be in all holy *c* and godliness

Conversion

Acts 15:3 declaring the *c* of the Gentiles

Convert

Ps. 19:7 the law of the LORD is perfect, *c* the soul
  51:13 thy ways; and sinners shall be *c* unto thee
Is. 6:10 (Mt. 13:15; Mk. 4:12; Jn. 12:40; Acts 28:27)
    understand with their heart, and be *c*
  60:5 abundance of the sea shall be *c* unto thee
Mt. 18:3 except ye be *c*, and become as little children
Lk. 22:32 when thou art *c*, strengthen thy brethren
Acts 3:19 repent ye therefore, and be *c*, that your
Jas. 5:20 he which *c* the sinner from the error of

Convict

Jn. 8:9 being *c* by their own conscience, went out

Convince

Job 32:12 behold, there was none of you that *c* Job
Jn. 8:46 which of you *c* me of sin? And if I say
Acts 18:28 mightily *c* the Jews, and that publicly
1 Cor. 14:24 he is *c* of all, he is judged of all
Tit. 1:9 both to exhort and to *c* the gainsayers
Jas. 2:9 sin, and are *c* of the law as transgressors
Jude 15 to *c* all that are ungodly among them

Convocation

Ex. 12:16 in the first day there shall be a holy *c*
Lev. 23:3 the seventh day is the sabbath . . a holy *c*
  23:27 be a day of atonement: it shall be a holy *c*
Num. 28:26 day of the firstfruits . . have a holy *c*

Cook

1 Sam. 8:13 to be confectionaries, and to be *c*, and

Cool

Gen. 3:8 walking in the garden in the *c* of the day
Lk. 16:24 tip of his finger in water, and *c* my tongue

Copy

Deut. 17:18 write him a *c* of this law in a book
Josh. 8:32 wrote there upon the stones a *c* of the
Prov. 25:1 the men of Hezekiah king of Judah *c* out

Corban Mk. 7:11

Cord

Josh. 2:15 let them down by a *c* through the window
Judg. 15:13 bound him with two new *c*, and brought
Job 30:11 he hath loosed my *c*, and afflicted me
Ps. 129:4 he hath cut asunder the *c* of the wicked
Prov. 5:22 shall be holden with the *c* of his sins
Eccl. 12:6 or ever the silver *c* be loosed, or the
Is. 5:18 them that draw iniquity with *c* of vanity
  54:2 spare not, lengthen thy *c*, and strengthen
Jer. 38:11 down by *c* into the dungeon to Jeremiah
Hos. 11:4 I drew them with *c* of a man, with bands
Jn. 2:15 made a scourge of small *c*, he drove them

Core *See* Korah

Corinth

Acts 18:1 Paul departed from Athens, and came to C

Corn

Gen. 27:28 fatness of the earth, and plenty of *c*
  41:5 seven ears of *c* came up upon one stalk
  41:57 came into Egypt to Joseph for to buy *c*
  42:2 (Acts 7:12) heard that there is *c* in Egypt
Deut. 25:4 (1 Cor. 9:9; 1 Tim. 5:18) thou shalt not
    muzzle the ox when he treadeth out the *c*
  33:28 shall be upon a land of *c* and wine
Ruth 2:2 the field, and glean ears of *c* after him
Job 24:6 they reap every one his *c* in the field
Ps. 4:7 time that their *c* and their wine increased
  65:13 the valleys also are covered over with *c*
  72:16 shall be a handful of *c* in the earth upon
  78:24 and had given them of the *c* of heaven
Joel 2:19 behold, I will send you *c*, and wine, and
Zech. 9:17 *c* shall make the young men cheerful
Mt. 12:1 (Mk. 2:23; Lk. 6:1) sabbath . . through the *c*
Mk. 4:28 after that the full *c* in the ear
Jn. 12:24 except a *c* of wheat fall into the ground

Cornelius Acts 10:1

Corner

Ps. 118:22 (Mt. 21:42; Mk. 12:10; Lk. 20:17; Acts
    4:11; 1 Pet. 2:7) is become the head stone of the *c*
Is. 28:16 (1 Pet. 2:6) lay in Zion . . a precious *c* stone
Amos 3:12 in the *c* of a bed, and in Damascus in
Zech. 10:4 out of him came forth the *c*, out of him
Mt. 6:5 *c* of the streets, that they may be seen of
Acts 10:11 (11:5) knit at the four *c*, and let down
  26:26 for this thing was not done in a *c*
Eph. 2:20 Christ himself being the chief *c* stone
Rev. 7:1 angels standing on the four *c* of the earth

Cornet *See also* Trumpet

2 Sam. 6:5 on timbrels, and on *c*, and on cymbals
Ps. 98:6 trumpets and sound of *c* make a joyful noise
Dan. 3:5 (3:7, 10, 15) hear the sound of the *c*

Corpse

2 Kgs. 19:35 (Is. 37:36) behold, they were all dead *c*
Mk. 6:29 and took up his *c*, and laid it in a tomb

Correct *See also* Chasten

Job 5:17 happy is the man whom God *c*
Ps. 39:11 thou with rebukes dost *c* man for iniquity
Prov. 3:12 for whom the LORD loveth he *c*; even as a
29:17 *c* thy son, and he shall give thee rest; yea
29:19 servant will not be *c* by words: for though
Jer. 2:19 thine own wickedness shall *c* thee
10:24 O LORD, *c* me, but with judgment; not in
30:11 (46:28) I will *c* thee in measure
Heb. 12:9 had fathers of our flesh which *c* us

Correction *See also* Chastening,
Chastisement, Punishment

Prov. 3:11 of the LORD; neither be weary of his *c*
15:10 *c* is grievous unto him that forsaketh
23:13 withhold not *c* from the child: for if thou
Jer. 2:30 smitten your children; they received no *c*
5:3 but they have refused to receive *c*: they have
7:28 nation that obeyeth not . . nor receiveth *c*
Hab. 1:12 God, thou hast established them for *c*
Zeph. 3:2 obeyed not the voice; she received not *c*
2 Tim. 3:16 for reproof, for *c*, for instruction in

Corrupt *See also* Debase, Defile,
Pervert, Profane

Gen. 6:11 the earth also was *c* before God
Ex. 32:7 (Deut. 9:12) thy people . . have *c* themselves
Deut. 4:16 *c* yourselves, and make you a graven
31:29 after my death ye will utterly *c* yourselves
32:5 they have *c* themselves, their spot is not
Job 17:1 my breath is *c*, my days are extinct
Ps. 14:1 (53:1) *c*, they have done abominable works
73:8 they are *c*, and speak wickedly concerning
Prov. 25:26 as a troubled fountain, and a *c* spring
Dan. 11:32 as do wickedly . . shall he *c* by flatteries
Hos. 9:9 have deeply *c* themselves, as in the days
Zeph. 3:7 they rose early, and *c* all their doings
Mal. 2:3 I will *c* your seed, and spread dung upon
2:8 ye have *c* the covenant of Levi, saith the LORD
Mt. 6:20 (Lk. 12:33) neither moth nor rust doth *c*
7:18 (Lk. 6:43) *c* tree bring forth good fruit
1 Cor. 15:33 evil communications *c* good manners
2 Cor. 2:17 not as many, which *c* the word of God
11:3 minds should be *c* from the simplicity
Eph. 4:22 is *c* according to the deceitful lusts
4:29 let no *c* communication proceed out of your
1 Tim. 6:5 perverse disputings of men of *c* minds
2 Tim. 3:8 also resist the truth: men of *c* minds
Jas. 5:2 your riches are *c*, and your garments are
Jude 10 beasts, in those things they *c* themselves

Corrupter

Is. 1:4 a seed of evildoers, children that are *c*
Jer. 6:28 they are brass and iron; they are all *c*

Corruptible

Rom. 1:23 into an image made like to *c* man
1 Cor. 9:25 they do it to obtain a *c* crown; but we
15:53 this *c* must put on incorruption, and this
1 Pet. 1:18 ye were not redeemed with *c* things, as
1:23 not of *c* seed, but of incorruptible
3:4 not *c*, even the ornament of a meek and quiet

Corruption

2 Kgs. 23:13 on the right hand of the mount of *c*
Job 17:14 I have said to *c*, Thou art my father
Ps. 16:10 (Acts 2:27; 13:35) thine Holy One to see *c*
Is. 38:17 my soul delivered it from the pit of *c*
Jon. 2:6 yet hast thou brought up my life from *c*
Acts 13:37 but he, whom God raised again, saw no *c*

Rom. 8:21 shall be delivered from the bondage of *c*
1 Cor. 15:42 it is sown in *c*, it is raised in
Gal. 6:8 he that soweth to his flesh shall . . reap *c*
2 Pet. 1:4 the *c* that is in the world through lust
2:12 and shall utterly perish in their own *c*
2:19 they themselves are the servants of *c*

Corruptly

2 Chr. 27:2 and the people did yet *c*
Neh. 1:7 we have dealt very *c* against thee

Cost

2 Sam. 19:42 have we eaten at all of the king's *c*
24:24 (1 Chr. 21:24) which doth *c* me nothing
Lk. 14:28 sitteth not down first, and counteth the *c*

Costly

Jn. 12:3 a pound of ointment of spikenard, very *c*

Cottage

Is. 1:8 daughter of Zion is left as a *c* in a vineyard
24:20 the earth . . shall be removed like a *c*

Couch

Job 7:13 comfort me, my *c* shall ease my complaint
Ps. 6:6 my bed to swim; I water my *c* with my tears
Amos 6:4 stretch themselves upon their *c*, and eat
Lk. 5:19 let him down through the tiling with his *c*
5:24 and take up thy *c*, and go into thine house
Acts 5:15 the streets, and laid them on beds and *c*

Council

Mt. 5:22 brother, Raca, shall be in danger of the *c*
10:17 (Mk. 13:9) they will deliver you up to the *c*
12:14 Pharisees went out, and held a *c* against
26:59 (Mk. 14:55) priests . . and all the *c*, sought
Lk. 22:66 came together, and led him into their *c*
Acts 5:21 called the *c* together, and all the senate
6:12 and caught him, and brought him to the *c*
22:30 chief priests and all their *c* to appear

Counsel *See also* Advice, Advise,
Consult, Instruction

Ex. 18:19 I will give thee *c*, and God shall be with
Num. 31:16 through the *c* of Balaam, to commit
Deut. 32:28 they are a nation void of *c*, neither
Josh. 9:14 asked not *c* at the mouth of the LORD
Judg. 18:5 ask *c*, we pray thee, of God, that we may
20:18 up to the house of God, and asked *c* of God
1 Sam.14:37 Saul asked *c* of God, Shall I go down
2 Sam. 15:31 the *c* of Ahithophel into foolishness
17:7 the *c* that Ahithophel hath given is not good
1 Kgs. 12:8 (2 Chr. 10:8) forsook the *c* of the old men
1 Chr. 10:13 *c* of one that had a familiar spirit
Neh. 4:15 God had brought their *c* to nought
Job 5:13 *c* of the froward is carried headlong
12:13 and strength, he hath *c* and understanding
21:16 the *c* of the wicked is far from me
37:12 it is turned round about by his *c*
38:2 that darkeneth *c* by words without knowledge?
Ps. 1:1 that walketh not in the *c* of the ungodly
16:7 I will bless the LORD, who hath given me *c*
33:10 the LORD bringeth the *c* of the heathen to
55:14 we took sweet *c* together, and walked unto
73:24 guide me with thy *c*, and afterward receive
106:43 but they provoked him with their *c*
107:11 and contemned the *c* of the Most High
Prov. 11:14 where no *c* is, the people fall: but in
12:5 but the *c* of the wicked are deceit
12:15 but he that hearkeneth unto *c* is wise
15:22 without *c* purposes are disappointed: but
19:20 hear *c*, and receive instruction, that thou

Prov. 19:21 the *c* of the LORD, that shall stand
   20:5 *c* in the heart of man is like deep water
   21:30 nor understanding nor *c* against the LORD
   24:6 by wise *c* thou shalt make thy war
   27:9 sweetness of a man's friend by hearty *c*
Is. 7:5 Syria, Ephraim. . taken evil *c* against thee
   8:10 take *c* together, and it shall come to nought
   11:2 the spirit of *c* and might, the spirit of
   19:17 because of the *c* of the LORD of hosts
   25:1 thy *c* of old are faithfulness and truth
   28:29 the LORD of hosts, which is wonderful in *c*
   29:15 seek deep to hide their *c* from the LORD
   30:1 saith the LORD, that take *c*, but not of me
Jer. 7:24 but walked in the *c*. .of their evil heart
   23:18 who hath stood in the *c* of the LORD
Dan. 2:14 then Daniel answered with *c* and wisdom
Mic. 6:16 the house of Ahab, and ye walk in their *c*
Zech. 6:13 *c* of peace shall be between them both
Mt. 22:15 and took *c* how they might entangle him
   27:1 elders of the people took *c* against Jesus
Lk. 7:30 rejected the *c* of God against themselves
Acts 2:23 being delivered by the determinate *c* and
   5:33 cut to the heart, and took *c* to slay them
   5:38 if this *c* or this work be of men, it will
   20:27 to declare unto you all the *c* of God
Eph. 1:11 all things after the *c* of his own will
Heb. 6:17 immutability of his *c*, confirmed it by
Rev. 3:18 I *c* thee to buy of me gold tried in the

Counselor

2 Chr. 22:3 his mother was his *c* to do wickedly
Job 12:17 he leadeth *c* away spoiled, and maketh
Ps. 119:24 testimonies also are my delight, and my *c*
Prov. 11:14 in the multitude of *c* there is safety
   12:20 imagine evil: but to the *c* of peace is joy
Is. 1:26 will restore. . thy *c* as at the beginning
   9:6 his name shall be called Wonderful, *C*
   40:13 (Rom. 11:34) or being his *c* hath taught him?
   41:28 there was no *c*, that, when I asked of them
Mic. 4:9 no king in thee? is thy *c* perished?
Lk. 23:50 Joseph, a *c*; and he was a good man
Rom. 11:34 of the Lord? or who hath been his *c*?

Count *See also* Account

Gen. 15:6 (Rom. 4:3) *c* it to him for righteousness
Job 31:4 not he see my ways, and *c* all my steps?
Ps. 44:22 we are *c* as sheep for the slaughter
   87:6 LORD shall *c*, when he writeth up the people
   139:18 I should *c* them, they are more in number
   139:22 with perfect hatred: I *c* them mine enemies
Prov. 17:28 a fool. .holdeth his peace, is *c* wise
Is. 40:15 are *c* as the small dust of the balance
Hos. 8:12 my law, but they were *c* as a strange thing
Mt. 14:5 because they *c* him as a prophet
Mk. 11:32 for all men *c* John, that he was a prophet
Lk. 14:28 *c* the cost, whether he have sufficient to
Acts 5:41 *c* worthy to suffer shame for his name
   20:24 neither *c* I my life dear unto myself
Rom. 2:26 his uncircumcision be *c* for circumcision?
Phil. 3:7 were gain to me, those I *c* loss for Christ
1 Tim. 1:12 he *c* me faithful, putting me into the
   6:1 *c* their own masters worthy of all honor
Heb. 3:3 was *c* worthy of more glory than Moses
   10:29 hath *c* the blood of the covenant. .an unholy
Jas. 1:2 brethren, *c* it all joy when ye fall into
   5:11 behold, we *c* them happy which endure

Countenance *See also* Face

Gen. 4:5 and Cain was very wroth, and his *c* fell
Ex. 23:3 neither shalt thou *c* a poor man in his
Num. 6:26 LORD lift up his *c* upon thee, and give
1 Sam. 16:7 look not on his *c*, or on the height of
   17:42 was but a youth, and ruddy, and of a fair *c*

Neh. 2:2 why is thy *c* sad, seeing thou art not sick?
Ps. 4:6 lift thou up the light of thy *c* upon us
   21:6 thou hast made him exceeding glad with thy *c*
   42:11 him, who is the health of my *c*, and my God
Prov. 25:23 so doth an angry *c* a backbiting tongue
   27:17 so a man sharpeneth the *c* of his friend
Eccl. 7:3 for by the sadness of the *c* the heart is
Song 5:15 *c* is as Lebanon, excellent as the cedars
Is. 3:9 show of their *c* doth witness against them
Dan. 1:13 then let our *c* be looked upon before thee
Mt. 6:16 be not, as the hypocrites, of a sad *c*
   28:3 his *c* was like lightning, and his raiment
Acts 2:28 thou shalt make me full of joy with thy *c*
2 Cor. 3:7 face of Moses for the glory of his *c*
Rev. 1:16 *c* was as the sun shineth in his strength

Country

Gen. 12:1 (Acts 7:3) Abram, Get thee out of thy *c*
   26:3 and unto thy seed, I will give all these *c*
Josh. 2:2 children of Israel to search out the *c*
   19:51 so they made an end of dividing the *c*
Prov. 25:25 soul, so is good news from a far *c*
Jer. 2:7 I brought you into a plentiful *c*, to eat
Ezek. 11:16 I have scattered them among the *c*, yet
Mt. 2:12 departed into their own *c* another way
   13:54 (Mk. 6:1) when he was come into his own *c*
   13:57 (Mk. 6:4; Lk. 4:24; Jn. 4:44) a prophet is not
      without honor, save in his own *c*
   21:33 (Mk. 12:1; Lk. 20:9) and went into a far *c*
Mk. 15:21 (Lk. 23:26) Simon. .coming out of the *c*
Lk. 15:15 and joined himself to a citizen of that *c*
Heb. 11:9 in the land of promise, as in a strange *c*
   11:16 they desire a better *c*, that is, a heavenly

Countrymen

2 Cor. 11:26 in perils by mine own *c*

Courage

Num. 13:20 be ye of good *c*, and bring of the fruit
Deut. 31:6 good *c*, fear not, nor be afraid of them
Josh. 1:6 be strong and of a good *c*: for unto this
   10:25 be strong and of good *c*: for thus shall
2 Sam. 10:12 (1 Chr. 19:13) be of good *c*, and let us
Ezra 10:4 we also will be with thee: be of good *c*
Ps. 27:14 wait on the LORD: be of good *c*, and he
   31:24 good *c*, and he shall strengthen your heart
Is. 41:6 every one said to his brother, Be of good *c*
Acts 28:15 Paul saw, he thanked God, and took *c*

Courageous *See also* Valiant

Josh. 1:7 only be thou strong and very *c*, that thou
2 Chr. 32:7 be strong and *c*, be not afraid nor
Amos 2:16 *c* among the mighty shall flee away naked

Courageously

2 Chr. 19:11 deal *c*. .the LORD shall be with the good

Course

1 Chr. 23:6 David divided them into *c* among the
2 Chr. 31:2 Hezekiah appointed the *c* of the priests
Ps. 82:5 the foundations of the earth are out of *c*
Jer. 8:6 every one turned to his *c*, as the horse
Acts 20:24 so that I might finish my *c* with joy
1 Cor. 14:27 and that by *c*; and let one interpret
Eph. 2:2 ye walked according to the *c* of this world
2 Thes. 3:1 the word of the Lord may have free *c*
2 Tim. 4:7 finished my *c*, I have kept the faith
Jas. 3:6 and setteth on fire the *c* of nature

Court

Ex. 27:9 (38:9) make the *c* of the tabernacle
1 Kgs. 6:36 he built the inner *c* with three rows of
Ps. 65:4 thou choosest. .that he may dwell in thy *c*
   84:2 yea, even fainteth for the *c* of the LORD

Ps. 100:4 thanksgiving, and into his *c* with praise
  116:19 in the *c* of the LORD's house, in the midst
Is. 62:9 shall drink it in the *c* of my holiness
Jer. 19:14 he stood in the *c* of the LORD's house
Amos 7:13 the king's chapel, and it is the king's *c*
Rev. 11:2 the *c* which is without the temple leave

Courteous

1 Pet. 3:8 love as brethren, be pitiful, be *c*

Covenant *See also* League, Oath, Testament, Testimony

Gen. 6:18 but with thee will I establish my *c*
  9:9 I establish my *c* with you, and with your seed
  15:18 same day the LORD made a *c* with Abram
  17:2 and I will make my *c* between me and thee
  17:21 but my *c* will I establish with Isaac
  26:28 let us make a *c* with thee
  31:44 let us make a *c*, I and thou; and let it be
Ex. 2:24 their groaning, and God remembered his *c*
  6:4 I have also established my *c* with them
  19:5 ye will obey my voice indeed, and keep my *c*
  23:32 make no *c* with them, nor with their gods
  24:8 behold the blood of the *c*, which the LORD
  31:16 to observe the sabbath. . for a perpetual *c*
  34:10 behold, I make a *c*: before all thy people
  34:28 wrote upon the tables the words of the *c*
Lev. 2:13 salt of the *c* of thy God to be lacking
  26:9 multiply you, and establish my *c* with you
Num. 18:19 it is a *c* of salt for ever before the LORD
  25:12 say, Behold, I give unto him my *c* of peace
Deut. 4:23 lest ye forget the *c* of the LORD your
  5:2 the LORD our God made a *c* with us in Horeb
  7:9 the faithful God, which keepeth *c* and mercy
  9:15 two tables of the *c* were in my two hands
  29:1 the words of the *c*. . in the land of Moab
Josh. 24:25 so Joshua made a *c* with the people
Judg. 2:1 I said, I will never break my *c* with you
1 Sam. 18:3 Jonathan and David made a *c*
  20:16 Jonathan made a *c* with the house of David
  23:18 they two made a *c* before the LORD
2 Sam. 23:5 an everlasting *c*, ordered in all things
1 Kgs. 8:23 (2 Chr. 6:14) keepest *c* and mercy with
  19:10 (19:14) children of Israel have forsaken thy *c*
2 Kgs. 11:4 (2 Chr. 23:1) Jehoiada . . made a *c* with
  23:3 (2 Chr. 34:31) made a *c* before the LORD
1 Chr. 16:15 be ye mindful always of his *c*
  16:17 (Ps. 105:10) to Israel for an everlasting *c*
2 Chr. 15:12 *c* to seek the LORD God of their fathers
Ezra 10:3 let us make a *c* with our God to put away
Neh. 9:8 madest a *c* with him to give the land of
  9:38 and because of all this we make a sure *c*
Job 31:1 I made a *c* with mine eyes; why then should
Ps. 25:10 such as keep his *c* and his testimonies
  50:5 that have made a *c* with me by sacrifice
  89:3 I have made a *c* with my chosen, I have sworn
  89:34 my *c* will I not break, nor alter the thing
  105:8 he hath remembered his *c* for ever, the word
  106:45 he remembered for them his *c*, and repented
  111:5 fear him: he will ever be mindful of his *c*
Prov. 2:17 and forgetteth the *c* of her God
Is. 28:18 your *c* with death shall be disannulled
  33:8 broken the *c*, he hath despised the cities
  42:6 give thee for a *c* of the people, for a light
  49:8 give thee for a *c* of the people, to establish
  54:10 neither shall the *c* of my peace be removed
  55:3 I will make an everlasting *c* with you
  59:21 (Rom. 11:27) this is my *c* with them
  61:8 and I will make an everlasting *c* with them
Jer. 11:10 have broken my *c* which I made with their
  31:31 (Heb. 8:8) will make a new *c* with the house
  31:33 (Heb. 10:16) this shall be the *c* that I

Jer. 32:40 I will make an everlasting *c* with them
  33:20 my *c* of the day, and my *c* of the night
  33:21 then may also my *c* be broken with David
  50:5 a perpetual *c* that shall not be forgotten
Ezek. 16:8 and entered into a *c* with thee
  16:60 I will remember my *c* with thee in the
  17:14 by keeping of his *c* it might stand
  34:25 (37:26) I will make with them a *c* of peace
Dan. 9:4 keeping the *c* and mercy to them that love
  9:27 shall confirm the *c* with many for one week
  11:28 his heart shall be against the holy *c*
Hos. 6:7 but they like men have transgressed the *c*
Mal. 2:4 my *c* might be with Levi, saith the LORD
  2:10 against his brother, by profaning the *c*
Mt. 26:15 (Lk. 22:5) *c* with him for thirty pieces
Lk. 1:72 and to remember his holy *c*
Acts 3:25 children of the prophets, and of the *c*
Gal. 3:17 the *c*, that was confirmed before of God
  4:24 are an allegory: for these are the two *c*
Eph. 2:12 and strangers from the *c* of promise
Heb. 8:6 also he is the mediator of a better *c*
  10:29 counted the blood of the *c*. . an unholy thing
  12:24 Jesus the mediator of the new *c*
  13:20 through the blood of the everlasting *c*

Cover

Gen. 7:20 waters prevail; and the mountains were *c*
  24:65 therefore she took a veil, and *c* herself
Ex. 10:5 they shall *c* the face of the earth
  33:22 will *c* thee with my hand while I pass by
  40:3 and *c* the ark with the veil
Deut. 32:15 grown thick, thou art *c* with fatness
  33:12 the LORD shall *c* him all the day long
Neh. 4:5 *c* not their iniquity, and let not their
Job 31:33 if I *c* my transgressions as Adam
Ps. 32:1 (Rom. 4:7) is forgiven, whose sin is *c*
  71:13 let them be *c* with reproach and dishonor
  85:2 of thy people; thou hast *c* all their sin
  91:4 *c* thee with his feathers, and under his wings
  104:2 who *c* thyself with light as with a garment
  139:11 if I say, Surely the darkness shall *c* me
  139:13 thou hast *c* me in my mother's womb
Prov. 10:12 hatred stirreth up. . but love *c* all sins
  12:16 presently known: but a prudent man *c* shame
  17:9 he that *c* a transgression seeketh love
  28:13 he that *c* his sins shall not prosper
Eccl. 6:4 and his name shall be *c* with darkness
Is. 6:2 *c* his face, and with twain he *c* his feet
  11:9 (Hab. 2:14) as the waters *c* the sea
  22:17 a mighty captivity, and will surely *c* thee
  60:2 behold, the darkness shall *c* the earth
Jer. 3:25 our confusion *c* us: for we have sinned
Lam. 3:44 thou hast *c* thyself with a cloud
Ezek. 28:14 thou art the anointed cherub that *c*
Hos. 10:8 (Lk. 23:30) say to the mountains, *C* us
Hab. 3:3 his glory *c* the heavens, and the earth
Mal. 2:13 *c* the altar of the LORD with tears
Mt. 8:24 the ship was *c* with the waves: but he was
  10:26 (Lk. 12:2) nothing *c*, that shall not be
Mk. 14:65 began to spit on him, and to *c* his face
1 Cor. 11:6 woman be not *c*, let her also be shorn
1 Pet. 4:8 charity shall *c* the multitude of sins

Covering

Gen. 8:13 Noah removed the *c* of the ark, and looked
Ex. 26:7 goats' hair to be a *c* upon the tabernacle
Job 26:6 hell is naked. . and destruction hath no *c*
Ps. 105:39 he spread a cloud for a *c*; and fire to
Prov. 31:22 she maketh herself *c* of tapestry
Is. 30:1 that cover with a *c*, but not of my Spirit
  50:3 with blackness, and I make sackcloth their *c*
1 Cor. 11:15 for her hair is given her for a *c*

Covert

Ps. 61:4 I will trust in the *c* of thy wings
Is. 4:6 a place of refuge, and for a *c* from storm
16:4 a *c* to them from the face of the spoiler

Covet *See also* Desire, Wish

Ex. 20:17 (Deut. 5:21; Rom. 7:7; 13:9) shalt not *c*
Josh. 7:21 *c* them, and took them; and. . they are hid
Prov. 21:26 he *c* greedily all the day long
Mic. 2:2 they *c* fields, and take them by violence
Hab. 2:9 woe to him that *c* an evil covetousness to
Acts 20:33 I have *c* no man's silver, or gold, or
1 Cor. 12:31 *c* earnestly the best gifts
14:39 *c* to prophesy, and forbid not to speak
1 Tim. 6:10 root of all evil: which while some *c*

Covetous

Ps. 10:3 blesseth the *c*, whom the LORD abhorreth
Lk. 16:14 Pharisees also, who were *c*, heard all
1 Cor. 5:10 or with the *c*, or extortioners, or with
6:10 thieves, nor *c*, nor drunkards, nor revilers
Eph. 5:5 nor *c* man, who is an idolater, hath any
1 Tim. 3:3 but patient, not a brawler, not *c*
2 Tim. 3:2 lovers of their own selves, *c*, boasters
2 Pet. 2:14 a heart. . exercised with *c* practices

Covetousness *See also* Envy, Jealousy

Ex. 18:21 such as fear God, men of truth, hating *c*
Ps. 119:36 heart unto thy testimonies, and not to *c*
Is. 57:17 for the iniquity of his *c* was I wroth
Jer. 6:13 (8:10) every one is given to *c*
22:17 eyes and thine heart are not but for thy *c*
Ezek. 33:31 but their heart goeth after their *c*
Hab. 2:9 woe to him that coveteth an evil *c* to his
Mk. 7:22 *c*, wickedness, deceit, lasciviousness
Lk. 12:15 take heed, and beware of *c*: for a man's
Rom. 1:29 filled with. . wickedness, *c*, maliciousness
2 Cor. 9:5 as a matter of bounty, and not as of *c*
Col. 3:5 concupiscence, and *c*, which is idolatry
1 Thes. 2:5 nor a cloak of *c*; God is witness
Heb. 13:5 let your conversation be without *c*

Cow *See also* Heifer, Kine

Is. 7:21 man shall nourish a young *c* and two sheep
11:7 and the *c* and the bear shall feed
Amos 4:3 every *c* at that which is before her

Craft *See also* Deceit, Guile, Subtilty

Dan. 8:25 he shall cause a *c* to prosper in his hand
Mk. 14:1 sought how they might take him by *c*
Acts 18:3 because he was of the same *c*, he abode
19:25 ye know that by this *c* we have our wealth

Craftiness

Job 5:13 (1 Cor. 3:19) taketh the wise in their own *c*
Lk. 20:23 perceived their *c*, and said unto them
2 Cor. 4:2 not walking in *c*, nor handling the word
Eph. 4:14 by the sleight of men, and cunning *c*

Craftsman

Acts 19:24 Diana, brought no small gain unto the *c*
Rev. 18:22 no *c*, of whatsoever craft he be, shall

Crafty

Job 5:12 he disappointeth the devices of the *c*
15:5 and thou choosest the tongue of the *c*
Ps. 83:3 have taken *c* counsel against thy people
2 Cor. 12:16 being *c*, I caught you with guile

Create *See also* Fashion, Form, Invent, Make, Shape

Gen. 1:1 beginning God *c* the heaven and the earth

Gen. 1:27 so God *c* man in his own image, in the
2:3 rested from all his work which God *c* and made
Ps. 51:10 *c* in me a clean heart, O God; and renew a
102:18 the people which shall be *c* shall praise
104:30 thou sendest forth thy spirit, they are *c*
148:5 LORD: for he commanded, and they were *c*
Is. 41:20 and the Holy One of Israel hath *c* it
42:5 he that *c* the heavens, and stretched them
43:7 I have *c* him for my glory, I have formed him
45:7 I form the light, and *c* darkness: I make
45:12 I have made the earth, and *c* man upon it
45:18 for thus saith the LORD that *c* the heavens
65:17 behold, I *c* new heavens and a new earth
Jer. 31:22 LORD hath *c* a new thing in the earth
Ezek. 28:13 in thee in the day that thou wast *c*
Amos 4:13 formeth the mountains, and *c* the wind
Mal. 2:10 one father? hath not one God *c* us? why do
1 Cor. 11:9 neither was the man *c* for the woman
Eph. 2:10 *c* in Christ Jesus unto good works
3:9 hid in God, who *c* all things by Jesus Christ
4:24 man, which after God is *c* in righteousness
Col. 1:16 all things were *c* by him, and for him
3:10 knowledge after the image of him that *c* him
1 Tim. 4:3 meats, which God hath *c* to be received
Rev. 4:11 for thou hast *c* all things, and for thy
10:6 who *c* heaven, and the things that therein

Creation *See also* Beginning

Mk. 10:6 from the beginning of the *c* God made them
13:19 such as was not from the beginning of the *c*
Rom. 1:20 invisible things of him from the *c* of the
8:22 the whole *c* groaneth and travaileth in pain
2 Pet. 3:4 as they were from the beginning of the *c*
Rev. 3:14 true witness, the beginning of the *c* of God

Creator

Eccl. 12:1 remember now thy *C* in the days of thy
Is. 40:28 *C* of the ends of the earth, fainteth not
43:15 your Holy One, the *C* of Israel, your King
Rom. 1:25 and served the creature more than the *C*
1 Pet. 4:19 in well doing, as unto a faithful *C*

Creature

Gen. 1:20 bring forth abundantly the moving *c* that
9:16 covenant between God and every living *c*
Ezek. 1:5 came the likeness of four living *c*
Mk. 16:15 and preach the gospel to every *c*
Rom. 1:25 and served the *c* more than the Creator
8:21 the *c* itself also shall be delivered from
8:39 nor any other *c*, shall be able to separate
2 Cor. 5:17 if any man be in Christ, he is a new *c*
Gal. 6:15 any thing, nor uncircumcision, but a new *c*
Col. 1:15 invisible God, the firstborn of every *c*
1:23 preached to every *c* which is under heaven
1 Tim. 4:4 every *c* of God is good, and nothing to
Jas. 1:18 should be a kind of firstfruits of his *c*
Rev. 5:13 and every *c* which is in heaven, and on

Creditor

Deut. 15:2 *c* that lendeth aught unto his neighbor
2 Kgs. 4:1 is come to take unto him my two sons
Is. 50:1 or which of my *c* is it to whom I have sold
Lk. 7:41 a certain *c* which had two debtors

Creep (Crept)

Gen. 1:25 and every thing that *c* upon the earth
2 Tim. 3:6 this sort are they which *c* into houses
Jude 4 certain men *c* in unawares, who were before

Creeping

Gen. 1:24 the living creature. . cattle, and *c* thing
Lev. 11:41 every *c* thing. . shall be an abomination
Acts 10:12 (11:6) wherein were. . *c* things, and fowls
Rom. 1:23 image made like to. . beasts, and *c* things

Crete *See also* Caphtor Acts 27:12; Tit. 1:5

Cretian Tit. 1:12

Crib
Job 39:9 the unicorn be willing to. .abide by thy *c*?
Prov. 14:4 where no oxen are, the *c* is clean: but
Is. 1:3 ox knoweth his owner. .ass his master's *c*

Cried *See* Cry

Crime
Job 31:11 is a heinous *c*; yea, it is an iniquity
Ezek. 7:23 land is full of bloody *c*, and the city
Acts 25:16 to answer for himself concerning the *c*
25:27 not withal to signify the *c* laid against

Crimson
Is. 1:18 though they be red like *c*, they shall be
Jer. 4:30 though thou clothest thyself with *c*

Cripple
Acts 14:8 impotent in his feet, being a *c* from his

Crispus Acts 18:8; 1 Cor. 1:14

Crooked
Deut. 32:5 they are a perverse and *c* generation
Job 26:13 his hand hath formed the *c* serpent
Ps. 125:5 such as turn aside unto their *c* ways
Prov. 2:15 whose ways are *c*, and they froward in
Eccl. 1:15 that which is *c* cannot be made straight
Is. 40:4 (Lk. 3:5) the *c* shall be made straight
45:2 before thee, and make the *c* places straight
59:8 they have made them *c* paths; whosoever
Phil. 2:15 in the midst of a *c* and perverse nation

Cross
Mt. 10:38 (Lk. 14:27) he that taketh not his *c*
16:24 (Mk. 8:34; Lk. 9:23) take up his *c*, and
27:32 (Mk. 15:21; Lk. 23:26) to bear his *c*
27:40 (Mk. 15:30) come down from the *c*
Mk. 10:21 and come, take up the *c*, and follow me
Jn. 19:17 he bearing his *c* went forth into a place
19:19 Pilate wrote a title, and put it on the *c*
1 Cor. 1:17 lest the *c* of Christ should be made of
1:18 preaching of the *c* is to them that perish
Gal. 5:11 then is the offense of the *c* ceased
6:12 should suffer persecution for the *c* of Christ
6:14 I should glory, save in the *c* of our Lord
Eph. 2:16 reconcile both unto God. .by the *c*
Phil. 2:8 obedient unto death. .death of the *c*
3:18 they are the enemies of the *c* of Christ
Col. 1:20 made peace through the blood of his *c*
2:14 took it out of the way, nailing it to his *c*
Heb. 12:2 endured the *c*, despising the shame

Crouch
1 Sam. 2:36 and *c* to him for a piece of silver
Ps. 10:10 he *c*, and humbleth himself, that the poor

Crow
Mt. 26:34 (26:75; Mk. 14:30, 72; Lk. 22:34, 61; Jn. 13:38) before the cock *c*, thou shalt deny me thrice

Crown
2 Sam. 1:10 I took the *c* that was upon his head
2 Kgs. 11:12 (2 Chr. 23:11) king's son, and put the *c*
Esth. 1:11 queen before the king with the *c* royal
2:17 he set the royal *c* upon her head, and made
Job 31:36 and bind it as a *c* to me
Ps. 8:5 and hast *c* him with glory and honor
21:3 thou settest a *c* of pure gold on his head
65:11 thou *c* the year with thy goodness

Ps. 89:39 profaned his *c* by casting it to the ground
103:4 who *c* thee with loving-kindness and tender
Prov. 4:9 a *c* of glory shall she deliver to thee
12:4 a virtuous woman is a *c* to her husband
14:18 but the prudent are *c* with knowledge
14:24 the *c* of the wise is their riches
16:31 the hoary head is a *c* of glory, if it be
27:24 and doth the *c* endure to every generation?
Is. 28:1 woe to the *c* of pride, to the drunkards
28:5 shall the LORD of hosts be for a *c* of glory
62:3 a *c* of glory in the hand of the LORD
Lam. 5:16 *c* is fallen from our head: woe unto us
Ezek. 16:12 and a beautiful *c* upon thine head
Zech. 6:11 *c*, and set them upon the head of Joshua
Mt. 27:29 (Mk. 15:17; Jn. 19:2) platted a *c* of thorns
1 Cor. 9:25 they do it to obtain a corruptible *c*
Phil. 4:1 brethren dearly beloved. .my joy and *c*
1 Thes. 2:19 our hope, or joy, or *c* of rejoicing?
2 Tim. 2:5 is he not *c*, except he strive lawfully
4:8 there is laid up for me a *c* of righteousness
Jas. 1:12 is tried, he shall receive the *c* of life
1 Pet. 5:4 receive a *c* of glory that fadeth not
Rev. 2:10 faithful. .I will give thee a *c* of life
3:11 hold that fast. .that no man take thy *c*
6:2 a *c* was given unto him: and he went forth
12:1 and upon her head a *c* of twelve stars
14:14 having on his head a golden *c*

Crucified *See also* Crucify
1 Cor. 1:23 but we preach Christ *c*, unto the Jews
2:2 know any thing. .save Jesus Christ, and him *c*
Gal. 3:1 hath been evidently set forth, *c* among you?

Crucify
Mt. 20:19 to mock, and to scourge, and to *c* him
23:34 some of them ye shall kill and *c*
26:2 and the Son of man is betrayed to be *c*
27:22 (27:23; Lk. 23:23) let him be *c*
27:26 (Mk. 15:15; Jn. 19:16) delivered him to be *c*
27:38 (Mk. 15:27; Lk. 23:33; Jn. 19:18) then were
there two thieves *c* with him
28:5 (Mk. 16:6) that ye seek Jesus, which was *c*
Mk. 15:13 (15:14; Jn. 19:6, 15) cried out. .*C* him
Lk. 23:33 which is called Calvary, there they *c* him
24:20 to be condemned to death, and have *c* him
Jn. 19:10 knowest thou not that I have power to *c*
Acts 2:23 and by wicked hands have *c* and slain
2:36 Jesus, whom ye have *c*, both Lord and Christ
4:10 whom ye *c*, whom God raised from the dead
Rom. 6:6 our old man is *c* with him, that the body
1 Cor. 1:13 is Christ divided? was Paul *c* for you?
2:8 known it, they would not have *c* the Lord of
2 Cor. 13:4 though he was *c* through weakness, yet
Gal. 2:20 I am *c* with Christ: nevertheless I live
5:24 they that are Christ's have *c* the flesh with
6:14 by whom the world is *c* unto me, and I unto
Heb. 6:6 they *c* to themselves the Son of God afresh
Rev. 11:8 the great city. .where also our Lord was *c*

Cruel
Gen. 49:7 was fierce; and their wrath, for it was *c*
Job 30:21 thou art become *c* to me: with thy strong
Ps. 25:19 and they hate me with *c* hatred
71:4 of the hand of the unrighteous and *c* man
Prov. 5:9 honor unto others. .thy years unto the *c*
11:17 but he that is *c* troubleth his own flesh
12:10 but the tender mercies of the wicked are *c*
17:11 a *c* messenger shall be sent against him
Song 8:6 as death; jealousy is *c* as the grave
Is. 13:9 day of the LORD cometh, *c* both with wrath
Heb. 11:36 and others had trial of *c* mockings and

Cruelty
Gen. 49:5 instruments of *c*. .in their habitations

Ps. 27:12 against me, and such as breathe out *c*
  74:20 dark places. . full of the habitations of *c*
Ezek. 34:4 with force and with *c* have ye ruled

Crumb

Mt. 15:27 (Mk. 7:28) yet the dogs eat of the *c*
Lk. 16:21 fed with the *c* which fell from the rich

Crush

Num. 22:25 and *c* Balaam's foot against the wall
Job 5:4 far from safety, and they are *c* in the gate
Lam. 1:15 an assembly against me to *c* my young men
  3:34 to *c* under his feet all the prisoners
Amos 4:1 which oppress the poor, which *c* the needy

Cry (Cried) *See also* Lament, Mourn, Wail, Weep

Gen. 4:10 voice of thy brother's blood *c* unto me
  18:20 because the *c* of Sodom and Gomorrah is
  27:34 Esau. . *c* with a great and exceeding bitter *c*
Ex. 2:23 and they *c*, and their *c* came up unto God
  3:7 heard their *c* by reason of their taskmasters
  22:23 *c* at all unto me, I will surely hear their *c*
Lev. 13:45 upper lip, and shall *c*, Unclean, unclean
1 Sam. 8:18 *c* out in that day because of your king
2 Sam. 22:7 (Ps. 18:6) in my distress I. . *c* to my God
1 Kgs. 18:27 Elijah mocked them, and said, *C* aloud
2 Chr. 13:12 priests with sounding trumpets to *c*
Job 19:7 I *c* out of wrong, but I am not heard: I *c*
  29:12 because I delivered the poor that *c*
  35:12 they *c*, but none giveth answer, because of
Ps. 3:4 I *c* unto the LORD with my voice, and he
  5:2 hearken unto the voice of my *c*, my King
  9:12 he forgetteth not the *c* of the humble
  17:1 attend unto my *c*; give ear unto my prayer
  34:6 this poor man *c*, and the LORD heard him
  34:17 the righteous *c*, and the LORD heareth
  55:17 morning, and at noon, will I pray, and *c*
  61:2 from the end of the earth will I *c* unto thee
  77:1 I *c* unto God with my voice, even unto God
  86:3 merciful unto me, O Lord: for I *c* unto thee
  88:1 O LORD. . I have *c* day and night before thee
  102:1 prayer, O LORD, and let my *c* come unto thee
  107:6 then they *c* unto the LORD in their trouble
  119:145 I *c* with my whole heart; hear me, O LORD
  120:1 in my distress I *c* unto the LORD, and he
  130:1 out of the depths have I *c* unto thee
  141:1 LORD, I *c* unto thee: make haste unto me
Prov. 8:1 doth not wisdom *c*? and understanding put
  21:13 stoppeth his ears at the *c* of the poor
Is. 5:7 looked for. . righteousness, but behold a *c*
  12:6 *c* out and shout, thou inhabitant of Zion
  15:5 my heart shall *c* out for Moab; his fugitives
  30:19 gracious unto thee at the voice of thy *c*
  40:3 (Mt. 3:3; Mk. 1:3; Lk. 3:4; Jn. 1:23) voice of
    him that *c* in the wilderness, Prepare ye the way
  40:6 voice said, *C*. And he said, What shall I *c*?
  42:2 (Mt. 12:19) he shall not *c*, nor lift up, nor
  58:1 *c* aloud, spare not, lift up thy voice like
Jer. 3:4 *c* unto me, My father, thou art the guide
  7:16 neither lift up *c* nor prayer for them
  11:11 though they shall *c* unto me, I will not
Jon. 1:2 Nineveh, that great city, and *c* against it
  3:8 with sackcloth, and *c* mightily unto God: yea
Hab. 1:2 how long shall I *c*, and thou wilt not hear!
  2:11 for the stone shall *c* out of the wall
Mt. 20:31 (Mk. 10:48; Lk. 18:39) but they *c* the more
  21:15 and the children *c* in the temple
  25:6 at midnight there was a *c*. . the bridegroom
  27:46 (Mk. 15:34) hour Jesus *c* with a loud voice
  27:50 (Mk. 15:37; Lk. 23:46) Jesus, when he had *c*
Lk. 18:7 avenge his own elect, which *c* day and night
  19:40 peace, the stones would immediately *c* out

Jn. 7:37 Jesus stood and *c*, saying, If any man thirst
Acts 19:32 some. . *c* one thing, and some another
  23:9 and there arose a great *c*: and the scribes
Rom. 8:15 (Gal. 4:6) whereby we *c*, Abba, Father
Jas. 5:4 and the *c* of them which have reaped
Rev. 7:10 *c* with a loud voice, saying, Salvation to
  14:18 a loud *c* to him that had the sharp sickle

Crying

Ps. 69:3 I am weary of my *c*: my throat is dried
Heb. 5:7 and supplications with strong *c* and tears
Rev. 21:4 be no more death, neither sorrow, nor *c*

Crystal

Job 28:17 the gold and the *c* cannot equal it
Ezek. 1:22 was as the color of the terrible *c*
Rev. 4:6 there was a sea of glass like unto *c*
  21:11 her light. . like a jasper stone, clear as *c*
  22:1 a pure river of water of life, clear as *c*

Cucumber

Num. 11:5 remember the fish. . the *c*, and the melons
Is. 1:8 as a lodge in a garden of *c*, as a besieged

Cumber

Lk. 10:40 but Martha was *c* about much serving
  13:7 find none: cut it down; why *c* it the ground?

Cummin

Is. 28:25 scatter the *c*, and cast in the principal
Mt. 23:23 for ye pay tithe of mint and anise and *c*

Cunning *See also* Curious, Skilful

Gen. 25:27 Esau was a *c* hunter, a man of the field
Ex. 31:4 to devise *c* works, to work in gold, and
1 Kgs. 7:14 and *c* to work all works in brass
Ps. 137:5 Jerusalem, let my right hand forget her *c*
Is. 3:3 the *c* artificer, and the eloquent orator
Dan. 1:4 *c* in knowledge, and understanding science
Eph. 4:14 by the sleight of men, and *c* craftiness

Cunningly

2 Pet. 1:16 we have not followed *c* devised fables

Cup

Gen. 40:11 and I gave the *c* into Pharaoh's hand
  44:2 put my *c*, the silver *c*, in the sack's mouth
Ps. 11:6 this shall be the portion of their *c*
  23:5 anointest my head with oil; my *c* runneth over
  75:8 in the hand of the LORD there is a *c*
  116:13 I will take the *c* of salvation, and call
Prov. 23:31 red, when it giveth his color in the *c*
Is. 51:17 at the hand of the LORD the *c* of his fury
  51:22 taken out of thine hand the *c* of trembling
Jer. 16:7 give them the *c* of consolation to drink
Hab. 2:16 the *c* of the LORD's right hand shall be
Zech. 12:2 I will make Jerusalem a *c* of trembling
Mt. 10:42 (Mk. 9:41) little ones a *c* of cold water
  20:22 (Mk. 10:38) are ye able to drink of the *c*
  23:25 (Lk. 11:39) make clean the outside of the *c*
  26:27 (Mk. 14:23; Lk. 22:17) he took the *c*
  26:39 (Mk. 14:36; Lk. 22:42) let this *c* pass from
Mk. 7:4 received to hold, as the washing of *c*
Lk. 22:20 (1 Cor. 11:25) this *c* is the new testament
Jn. 18:11 *c* which my Father hath given me, shall I
1 Cor. 10:16 the *c* of blessing which we bless, is
  10:21 the *c* of the Lord, and the *c* of devils
Rev. 16:19 the *c* of the wine of the fierceness

Cupbearer

Neh. 1:11 for I was the king's *c*

Cure *See also* Heal, Restore, Save

Jer. 33:6 bring it health and *c*, and I will *c* them
    46:11 use many medicines; for thou shalt not be *c*
Hos. 5:13 not heal you, nor *c* you of your wound
Mt. 17:16 thy disciples, and they could not *c* him
Lk. 7:21 he *c* many of their infirmities and plagues
    9:1 authority over all devils, and to *c* diseases
    13:32 I do *c* today and tomorrow, and the third

Curious *See also* Cunning, Skilful

Ex. 28:8 *c* girdle of the ephod, which is upon
    35:32 to devise *c* works, to work in gold, and in
Acts 19:19 which used *c* arts brought their books

Curse

Gen. 3:14 done this, thou art *c* above all cattle
    4:11 now art thou *c* from the earth, which hath
    8:21 I will not again *c* the ground any more
    12:3 them that bless thee, and *c* him that *c* thee
    27:13 upon me be thy *c*, my son: only obey my
    27:29 cursed be every one that *c* thee
Ex. 21:17 (Lev. 20:9; Mt. 15:4; Mk. 7:10) *c* his father,
    or his mother, shall surely be put to death
    22:28 the gods, nor *c* the ruler of thy people
Lev. 19:14 thou shalt not *c* the deaf, nor put
    24:15 whosoever *c* his God shall bear his sin
Num. 22:6 *c* me this people; for they are too mighty
Deut. 11:26 before you this day a blessing and a *c*
    27:13 these shall stand upon mount Ebal to *c*
    28:15 that all these *c* shall come upon thee
Josh. 6:18 make the camp of Israel a *c*, and trouble
Judg. 5:23 *c* ye Meroz, said the angel of the LORD
2 Sam. 16:5 he came forth, and *c* still as he came
2 Kgs. 2:24 and *c* them in the name of the LORD
2 Chr. 34:24 even all the *c* that are written in
Job 1:5 sons have sinned, and *c* God in their hearts
    1:11 touch all that he hath, and he will *c* thee
    2:9 still retain thine integrity? *c* God, and die
    3:1 after this opened Job his mouth. . *c* his day
    31:30 I suffered my mouth to sin by wishing a *c*
Ps. 62:4 bless with their mouth. . they *c* inwardly
    109:28 let them *c*, but bless thou
    119:21 thou hast rebuked the proud that are *c*
Prov. 3:33 the *c* of the LORD is in the house of
    20:20 whoso *c* his father or his mother, his
    26:2 so the *c* causeless shall not come
    28:27 he that hideth his eyes shall have many a *c*
    30:11 there is a generation that *c* their father
Eccl. 10:20 *c* not the king, no not in thy thought
Jer. 15:10 yet every one of them doth *c* me
    25:18 astonishment, a hissing, and a *c*
    29:18 to all the kingdoms of the earth, to be a *c*
    29:22 shall be taken up a *c* by all the captivity
Zech. 8:13 that as ye were a *c* among the heathen
Mal. 2:2 a *c* upon you, and I will *c* your blessings
    3:9 ye are *c* with a *c*: for ye have robbed me
    4:6 lest I come and smite the earth with a *c*
Mt. 5:44 (Lk. 6:28) bless them that *c* you, do good
    26:74 (Mk. 14:71) then began he to *c* and to swear
Mk. 11:21 fig tree which thou *c* is withered away
Jn. 7:49 this people who knoweth not the law are *c*
Acts 23:12 and bound themselves under a *c*, saying
Rom. 12:14 which persecute you: bless, and *c* not
Gal. 3:10 of the works of the law are under the *c*
    3:13 from the *c* of the law, being made a *c* for us
Rev. 22:3 there shall be no more *c*: but the throne

Cursed *See also* Curse, Accursed, Anathema

Gen. 3:17 *c* is the ground for thy sake; in sorrow
    9:25 he said, *C* be Canaan; a servant of servants

Gen. 27:29 *c* be every one that curseth thee
Deut. 27:15 *c* be the man that maketh any graven
    27:26 (Gal. 3:10) *c* be he that confirmeth not all
Josh. 6:26 *c* be the man. . that. . buildeth this city
1 Sam. 14:24 *c* be the man that eateth any food
Jer. 11:3 *c* be the man that obeyeth not the words
    17:5 *c* be the man that trusteth in man
    20:14 *c* be the day wherein I was born
    48:10 *c* be he that doeth. . deceitfully, and *c* be
Mt. 25:41 depart from me, ye *c*, into everlasting
Gal. 3:13 *c* is every one that hangeth on a tree
2 Pet. 2:14 with covetous practices; *c* children

Cursing

Deut. 30:19 before you life and death, blessing and *c*
Ps. 10:7 (Rom. 3:14) mouth is full of *c* and deceit
    109:17 as he loved *c*, so let it come unto him
Prov. 29:24 he heareth *c*, and bewrayeth it not
Heb. 6:8 is nigh unto *c*; whose end is to be burned
Jas. 3:10 the same mouth proceedeth blessing and *c*

Curtain

Ex. 26:1 (36:8) ten *c* of fine twined linen, and blue
2 Sam. 7:2 (1 Chr. 17:1) ark of God dwelleth within *c*
Ps. 104:2 who stretchest out the heavens like a *c*

Cush *See also* Ethiopia Is. 11:11

Cushi 2 Sam. 18:21

Custom

Lev. 18:30 commit not any one of these abominable *c*
Jer. 10:3 for the *c* of the people are vain
    32:11 was sealed according to the law and *c*
Mt. 9:9 (Mk. 2:14; Lk. 5:27) at the receipt of *c*
Lk. 4:16 as his *c* was, he went into the synagogue
Jn. 18:39 but ye have a *c*, that I should release
Acts 16:21 teach *c*, which are not lawful for us to
    26:3 because I know thee to be expert in all *c*
Rom. 13:7 *c* to whom *c*; fear to whom fear; honor to
1 Cor. 11:16 to be contentious, we have no such *c*

Cut *See also* Hew

Lev. 19:28 (Deut. 14:1) not make any *c* in your flesh
1 Sam. 24:4 *c* off the skirt of Saul's robe privily
    24:21 that thou wilt not *c* off my seed after me
1 Kgs. 18:28 and *c* themselves after their manner
1 Chr. 20:3 and *c* them with saws, and with harrows
Job 8:14 whose hope shall be *c* off, and whose trust
    14:7 tree, if it be *c* down, that it will sprout
Ps. 12:3 the LORD shall *c* off all flattering lips
    31:22 I am *c* off from before thine eyes
    37:9 for evildoers shall be *c* off: but those
    90:10 labor and sorrow; for it is soon *c* off
    94:23 shall *c* them off in their own wickedness
Prov. 2:22 but the wicked shall be *c* off from the
Is. 9:14 LORD will *c* off from Israel head and tail
    14:22 rise up. . and *c* off from Babylon the name
    53:8 he was *c* off out of the land of the living
    55:13 everlasting sign that shall not be *c* off
Jer. 10:3 one *c* a tree out of the forest
    34:18 when they *c* the calf in twain, and passed
    36:23 he *c* it with the penknife, and cast it
Dan. 9:26 Messiah be *c* off, but not for himself
Amos 3:14 the horns of the altar shall be *c* off
Zech. 11:10 my staff, even Beauty, and *c* it asunder
Mt. 5:30 (18:8; Mk. 9:43) offend thee, *c* it off
    24:51 (Lk. 12:46) *c* him asunder, and appoint him
Mk. 14:47 (Lk. 22:50; Jn. 18:10) and *c* off his ear
Acts 5:33 were *c* to the heart, and took counsel to
    7:54 were *c* to the heart, and they gnashed on him
    27:32 the soldiers *c* off the ropes of the boat
Gal. 5:12 would they were even *c* off which trouble

Cymbal

2 Chr. 5:13 their voice with the trumpets and *c*
29:25 Levites in the house of the LORD with *c*
Ezra 3:10 sons of Asaph with *c*, to praise the LORD
Neh. 12:27 thanksgivings, and with singing, with *c*
Ps. 150:5 praise him upon the loud *c*: praise him
1 Cor. 13:1 as sounding brass, or a tinkling *c*

Cyprus *See also* Chittim (Kittim)

Acts 11:19 traveled as far as Phoenicia, and *C*, and
11:20 some of them were men of *C* and Cyrene
13:4 sent forth by the Holy Ghost. . sailed to *C*
15:39 so Barnabas took Mark, and sailed unto *C*

Cyrene Acts 11:20

Cyrenian Acts 6:9

Cyrenius Lk. 2:2

Cyrus

2 Chr. 36:22 (Ezra 1:1) LORD stirred up. . *C*
Ezra 5:13 king *C* made a decree to build this house
Is. 44:28 that saith of *C*, He is my shepherd
45:1 thus saith the LORD to his anointed, to *C*
Dan. 1:21 continued. . unto the first year of king *C*

D

Dagger

Judg. 3:16 Ehud made him a *d* which had two edges

Dagon

Judg. 16:23 a great sacrifice unto *D* their god
1 Sam. 5:2 took the ark. . into the house of *D*
1 Chr. 10:10 fastened his head in the temple of *D*

Daily

Ex. 5:13 fulfil your works, your *d* tasks, as when
16:5 it shall be twice as much as they gather *d*
Num. 4:16 sweet incense, and the *d* meat offering
28:24 shall offer *d*, throughout the seven days
2 Chr. 31:16 his *d* portion for their service in
Neh. 5:18 which was prepared for me *d* was one ox
Ps. 13:2 sorrow in my heart *d*? how long shall mine
42:10 they say *d* unto me, Where is thy God?
61:8 name for ever, that I may *d* perform my vows
68:19 the Lord, who *d* loadeth us with benefits
Prov. 8:30 I was *d* his delight, rejoicing always
Dan. 1:5 the king appointed them a *d* provision
8:11 and by him the *d* sacrifice was taken away
11:31 and shall take away the *d* sacrifice
12:11 from the time that the *d* sacrifice shall
Mt. 6:11 (Lk. 11:3) give us this day our *d* bread
Lk. 9:23 deny himself, and take up his cross *d*
19:47 he taught *d* in the temple
Acts 2:46 they, continuing *d* with one accord
2:47 and the Lord added to the church *d* such as
5:42 *d* in the temple, and in every house
6:1 widows were neglected in the *d* ministration
16:5 churches established. . increased in number *d*
17:11 searched the Scriptures *d*, whether those
19:9 disputing *d* in the school of one Tyrannus
1 Cor. 15:31 in Christ Jesus our Lord, I die *d*
Heb. 3:13 but exhort one another *d*, while it is
7:27 who needeth not *d*. . to offer up sacrifice
Jas. 2:15 a brother or sister. . destitute of *d* food

Dainty

Gen. 49:20 be fat, and he shall yield royal *d*

Job 33:20 abhorreth bread, and his soul *d* meat
Ps. 141:4 and let me not eat of their *d*
Prov. 23:3 of his *d*: for they are deceitful meat
23:6 evil eye, neither desire thou his *d* meats
Rev. 18:14 *d* and goodly are departed from thee

Dalmanutha Mk. 8:10

Damage *See also* Harm, Hurt, Mischief

Ezra 4:22 should *d* grow to the hurt of the kings?
Esth. 7:4 enemy could not countervail the king's *d*
Prov. 26:6 cutteth off the feet, and drinketh *d*
Dan. 6:2 and the king should have no *d*
Acts 27:10 voyage will be with hurt and much *d*
2 Cor. 7:9 ye might receive *d* by us in nothing

Damaris Acts 17:34

Damascus

2 Sam. 8:6 (1 Chr. 18:6) put garrisons in Syria of *D*
1 Kgs. 20:34 thou shalt make streets for thee in *D*
2 Kgs. 8:7 Elisha came to *D*. . Ben-hadad. . was sick
14:28 acts of Jeroboam. . how he recovered *D*
16:10 king Ahaz went to *D* to meet Tiglath-pileser
Is. 7:8 head of Syria is *D*, and the head of *D* is
8:4 riches of *D* and the spoil of Samaria shall
17:1 the burden of *D*. Behold, *D* is taken away
Jer. 49:23 concerning *D*. Hamath is confounded
Amos 1:3 three transgressions of *D*, and for four
3:12 in the corner of a bed, and in *D* in a couch
Acts 9:2 (22:5) letters to *D* to the synagogues
9:22 Saul. . confounded the Jews which dwelt at *D*
2 Cor. 11:32 in *D* the governor under Aretas the king
Gal. 1:17 into Arabia, and returned again unto *D*

Damnation *See also* Condemnation, Hell, Punishment

Mt. 23:14 (Mk. 12:40; Lk. 20:47) receive. . greater *d*
23:33 vipers, how can ye escape the *d* of hell?
Mk. 3:29 but is in danger of eternal *d*
Jn. 5:29 done evil, unto the resurrection of *d*
Rom. 3:8 evil, that good may come? whose *d* is just
13:2 that resist shall receive to themselves *d*
1 Cor. 11:29 unworthily, eateth and drinketh *d* to
1 Tim. 5:12 having *d*, because they have cast off
2 Pet. 2:3 lingereth not, and their *d* slumbereth not

Damned

Mk. 16:16 but he that believeth not shall be *d*
Rom. 14:23 he that doubteth is *d* if he eat
2 Thes. 2:12 they all might be *d* who believed not

Damsel *See also* Girl, Handmaid, Maid, Maiden, Virgin

Gen. 24:16 and the *d* was very fair to look upon
34:3 loved the *d*, and spake kindly unto the *d*
Deut. 22:15 forth the tokens of the *d*'s virginity
Ruth 2:5 whose *d* is this?
Ps. 68:25 among them. . the *d* playing with timbrels
Mt. 14:11 (Mk. 6:28) in a charger, and given to the *d*
26:69 (Jn. 18:17) a *d* came unto him, saying, Thou
Mk. 5:39 the *d* is not dead, but sleepeth
Acts 12:13 door of the gate, a *d* came to hearken
16:16 a certain *d* possessed with a spirit

Dan son of Jacob

Born, Gen. 30:6; blessed by Jacob, Gen. 49:16–17.
Tribe of Dan blessed by Moses, Deut. 33:22.

Dan the town *See also* Laish

Named, Judg. 18:29; "from Dan even unto Beer-sheba," Judg. 20:1; 2 Sam. 3:10; 17:11; 24:2;

1 Kgs. 4:25; 1 Chr. 21:2; 2 Chr. 30:5; place of idolatry, 1 Kgs. 12:28-30.

Dance

Ex. 15:20 out after her with timbrels and with *d*
Judg. 11:34 meet him with timbrels and with *d*
   21:21 if the daughters of Shiloh come out to *d*
1 Sam. 21:11 of him in *d*, saying Saul hath slain his
2 Sam. 6:14 and David *d* before the LORD with all
Job 21:11 like a flock, and their children *d*
Ps. 149:3 let them praise his name in the *d*
   150:4 praise him with the timbrel and *d*
Eccl. 3:4 a time to mourn, and a time to *d*
Is. 13:21 dwell there, and satyrs shall *d* there
Jer. 31:13 then shall the virgin rejoice in the *d*
Lam. 5:15 is ceased; our *d* is turned into mourning
Mt. 11:17 (Lk. 7:32) piped unto you.. ye have not *d*
   14:6 (Mk. 6:22) daughter of Herodias *d* before

Dancing

Ex. 32:19 saw the calf, and the *d*: and Moses' anger
1 Sam. 18:6 singing and *d*, to meet king Saul
Ps. 30:11 hast turned for me my mourning into *d*
Lk. 15:25 nigh to the house, he heard music and *d*

Dandled

Is. 66:12 upon her sides, and be *d* upon her knees

Danger *See also* Jeopardy, Peril

Mt. 5:21 shall kill shall be in *d* of the judgment
   5:22 say, Thou fool, shall be in *d* of hell fire
Mk. 3:29 blaspheme.. is in *d* of eternal damnation
Acts 19:27 our craft is in *d* to be set at nought

Daniel (Belteshazzar)

Trained in the king's palace, Dan. 1:1-7; abstained from the king's food, Dan. 1:8-16; interpreted Nebuchadnezzar's dreams, Dan. 2; 4; interpreted the handwriting on the wall, Dan. 5:5-29; delivered from the lions' den, Dan. 6; visions and dreams, Dan. 7; 8; 10-12; prayed for his people, Dan. 9.

Ezek. 14:14 (14:20) Noah, and Job, were in it
   28:3 thou art wiser than *D*; there is no secret
Mt. 24:15 (Mk. 13:14) abomination.. spoken of by *D*

Dare

Job 41:10 none is so fierce that *d* stir him up
Rom. 5:7 for a good man some would even *d* to die
   15:18 for I will not *d* to speak of any of those
1 Cor. 6:1 *d* any of you, having a matter against
2 Cor. 10:12 we *d* not make ourselves of the number

Darius the Persian

Ezra 5:5 till the matter came to *D*: and then they
   6:1 then *D* the king made a decree, and search
Hag. 1:1 second year of *D* the king.. came the word
Zech. 1:1 in the second year of *D*, came the word

Darius the Median Dan. 5:31-6:28; 11:1

Dark

Gen. 15:17 and it was *d*, behold a smoking furnace
Num. 12:8 even apparently, and not in *d* speeches
Josh. 2:5 when it was *d*, that the men went out
Job 3:9 let the stars of the twilight thereof be *d*
   12:25 they grope in the *d* without light
   18:6 the light shall be *d* in his tabernacle
   22:13 God know? can he judge through the *d* cloud
   24:16 in the *d* they dig through houses
Ps. 49:4 I will open my *d* saying upon the harp
   74:20 *d* places of the earth are full of.. cruelty

Ps. 78:2 in a parable: I will utter *d* sayings of old
   88:12 shall thy wonders be known in the *d*?
Prov. 1:6 words of the wise, and their *d* sayings
Lam. 3:6 he hath set me in *d* places, as they that
Joel 2:10 the sun and the moon shall be *d*
Amos 5:8 morning, and maketh the day *d* with night
Mic. 3:6 not have a vision; and it shall be *d* unto
Zech. 14:6 the light shall not be clear, nor *d*
Lk. 11:36 be full of light, having no part *d*
Jn. 20:1 Mary Magdalene early, when it was yet *d*
2 Pet. 1:19 a light that shineth in a *d* place

Darken

Ex. 10:15 for they covered.. so that the land was *d*
Job 38:2 that *d* counsel by words without knowledge
Ps. 69:23 (Rom. 11:10) let their eyes be *d*, that
Eccl. 12:2 stars, be not *d*, nor the clouds return
Is. 9:19 wrath of the LORD of hosts is the land *d*
   13:10 (Mt. 24:29; Mk. 13:24) the sun shall be *d*
Ezek. 30:18 at Tehaphnehes also the day shall be *d*
Joel 3:15 sun and the moon shall be *d*, and the stars
Amos 8:9 and I will *d* the earth in the clear day
Lk. 23:45 sun was *d*, and the veil of the temple
Rom. 1:21 and their foolish heart was *d*
Eph. 4:18 understanding *d*, being alienated from
Rev. 8:12 third part of them was *d*, and the day
   9:2 and the sun and the air were *d* by reason of

Darkly

1 Cor. 13:12 for now we see through a glass, *d*

Darkness *See also* Blindness, Evil, Ignorance, Night, Sin

Gen. 1:2 and *d* was upon the face of the deep
   1:4 and God divided the light from the *d*
   15:12 and, lo, a horror of great *d* fell upon him
Ex. 10:21 *d* over.. Egypt, even *d* which may be felt
   14:20 it was a cloud and *d* to them, but it gave
   20:21 Moses drew near unto the thick *d* where
Deut. 4:11 of heaven, with *d*, clouds, and thick *d*
   28:29 at noonday, as the blind gropeth in *d*
Josh. 24:7 he put *d* between you and the Egyptians
1 Sam. 2:9 the wicked shall be silent in *d*
2 Sam. 22:10 (Ps. 18:9) and *d* was under his feet
   22:29 (Ps. 18:28) the LORD will lighten my *d*
1 Kgs. 8:12 (2 Chr. 6:1) would dwell in the thick *d*
Job 3:4 let that day be *d*; let not God regard it
   3:5 let *d* and the shadow of death stain it
   5:14 they meet with *d* in the daytime, and grope
   10:21 to the land of *d* and the shadow of death
   10:22 land of *d*, as *d* itself.. the light is as *d*
   12:22 he discovereth deep things out of *d*
   17:13 I have made my bed in the *d*
   19:8 cannot pass, and he hath set *d* in my paths
   28:3 he setteth an end to *d*, and searcheth out
   29:3 and when by his light I walked through *d*
   30:26 and when I waited for light, there came *d*
   34:22 there is no *d*, nor shadow of death, where
   37:19 we cannot order our speech by reason of *d*
   38:19 where light dwelleth? and as for *d*, where
Ps. 18:11 he made *d* his secret place; his pavilion
   18:28 light my candle.. God will enlighten my *d*
   88:6 thou hast laid me in the lowest pit, in *d*
   91:6 nor for the pestilence that walketh in *d*
   97:2 clouds and *d* are round about him
   104:20 thou makest *d*, and it is night
   107:10 as sit in *d* and in the shadow of death
   112:4 unto the upright there ariseth light in the *d*
   139:12 the *d* hideth not from thee; but the night
   143:3 he hath made me to dwell in *d*
Prov. 2:13 of uprightness, to walk in the ways of *d*
   4:19 way of the wicked is as *d*: they know not
   20:20 his lamp shall be put out in obscure *d*

Eccl. 2:13 wisdom excelleth. .as light excelleth *d*
2:14 eyes are in his head; but the fool walketh in *d*
6:4 he cometh in with vanity, and departeth in *d*
Is. 5:20 that put *d* for light, and light for *d*
5:30 look unto the land, behold *d* and sorrow
9:2 (Mt. 4:16) walked in *d* have seen a great light
29:18 shall see out of obscurity, and out of *d*
42:7 them that sit in *d* out of the prison house
42:16 I will make *d* light before them
45:7 I form the light, and create *d*: I make
49:9 to them that are in *d*, Show yourselves
50:10 that walketh in *d*, and hath no light?
58:10 in obscurity, and thy *d* be as the noonday
60:2 the *d* shall cover the earth, and gross *d*
Jer. 13:16 give glory to. .God, before he cause *d*
Joel 2:2 a day of *d* and of gloominess, a day of
2:31 (Acts 2:20) sun shall be turned into *d*
Amos 5:20 the day of the Lord be *d*, and not light?
Mt. 6:23 (Lk. 11:34) thy whole body shall be full of *d*
8:12 the children of the kingdom. .into outer *d*
10:27 I tell you in *d*, that speak ye in light
22:13 take him away, and cast him into outer *d*
25:30 the unprofitable servant into outer *d*
27:45 (Mk. 15:33; Lk. 23:44) *d* over all the land
Lk. 1:79 to give light to them that sit in *d*
12:3 spoken in *d* shall be heard in the light
22:53 but this is your hour, and the power of *d*
Jn. 1:5 light shineth in *d*; and the *d* comprehended
3:19 condemnation. .men loved *d* rather than light
8:12 he that followeth me shall not walk in *d*
12:35 walk while ye have the light, lest *d* come
12:46 believeth on me should not abide in *d*
Acts 26:18 to turn them from *d* to light, and from
Rom. 2:19 a light of them which are in *d*
13:12 let us therefore cast off the works of *d*
1 Cor. 4:5 bring to light the hidden things of *d*
2 Cor. 4:6 commanded the light to shine out of *d*
6:14 and what communion hath light with *d*?
Eph. 5:8 ye were sometime *d*, but now are ye light
5:11 no fellowship with the unfruitful works of *d*
6:12 against the rulers of the *d* of this world
Col. 1:13 hath delivered us from the power of *d*
1 Thes. 5:4 but ye, brethren, are not in *d*
5:5 we are not of the night, nor of *d*
Heb. 12:18 nor unto blackness, and *d*, and tempest
1 Pet. 2:9 out of *d* into his marvelous light
2 Pet. 2:4 delivered them into chains of *d*, to be
2:17 to whom the mist of *d* is reserved for ever
1 Jn. 1:5 God is light, and in him is no *d* at all
2:8 *d* is past, and the true light now shineth
2:9 hateth his brother, is in *d* even until now
Jude 6 reserved in everlasting chains under *d* unto
13 to whom is reserved the blackness of *d* for ever
Rev. 16:10 beast; and his kingdom was full of *d*

Darling

Ps. 22:20 deliver. .my *d* from the power of the dog

Dart

Job 41:29 *d* are counted as stubble: he laugheth at
Prov. 7:23 till a *d* strike through his liver
Eph. 6:16 to quench all the fiery *d* of the wicked

Dash

Ex. 15:6 thy right hand. .hath *d* in pieces the enemy
2 Kgs. 8:12 and wilt *d* their children, and rip up
Ps. 2:9 *d* them in pieces like a potter's vessel
91:12 (Mt. 4:6; Lk. 4:11) lest thou *d* thy foot
137:9 taketh and *d* thy little ones against
Is. 13:16 their children also shall be *d* to pieces
13:18 bows also shall *d* the young men to pieces
Jer. 13:14 and I will *d* them one against another
Hos. 13:16 their infants shall be *d* in pieces

Dathan

Num. 16:1–33; 26:9–10 (Deut. 11:6; Ps. 106:17)

Daughter *See also* Child

Gen. 6:2 sons of God saw the *d* of men. .were fair
19:30 Lot. .dwelt in a cave, and his two *d*
20:12 *d* of my father, but not the *d* of my mother
24:23 (24:47) whose *d* art thou? tell me, I pray thee
27:46 if Jacob take a wife of the *d* of Heth
Ex. 1:16 but if it be a *d*, then she shall live
2:5 *d* of Pharaoh came down to wash herself
21:7 and if a man sell his *d* to be a maidservant
Num. 27:1 then came the *d* of Zelophehad
27:8 cause his inheritance to pass unto his *d*
36:2 the inheritance of Zelophehad. .unto his *d*
Deut. 28:53 the flesh of thy sons and of thy *d*
Judg. 11:34 Jephthah came. .his *d* came out to meet
Ruth 1:12 turn again, my *d*, go your way; for I am
1 Sam. 8:13 will take your *d* to be confectionaries
2 Sam. 1:20 lest the *d* of the Philistines rejoice
12:3 lay in his bosom, and was unto him as a *d*
1 Kgs. 3:1 and Solomon. .took Pharaoh's *d*
Ps. 45:9 kings' *d* were among thy honorable women
48:11 Zion rejoice, let the *d* of Judah be glad
144:12 that our *d* may be as corner stones
Prov. 30:15 horseleech hath two *d*, crying, Give
31:29 *d* have done virtuously, but thou excellest
Eccl. 12:4 all the *d* of music shall be brought low
Is. 3:16 saith, Because the *d* of Zion are haughty
22:4 of the spoiling of the *d* of my people
Jer. 6:14 (8:11) have healed. .the *d* of my people
8:21 for the hurt of the *d* of my people am I hurt
9:1 weep. .for the slain of the *d* of my people!
31:22 wilt thou go about, O thou backsliding *d*?
Lam. 2:11 the destruction of the *d* of my people
Ezek. 16:44 saying, As is the mother, so is her *d*
Joel 2:28 (Acts 2:17) and your *d* shall prophesy
Mic. 7:6 (Mt. 10:35; Lk. 12:53) *d*. .against. .mother
Zeph. 3:14 sing, O *d* of Zion; shout, O Israel
Zech. 9:9 (Mt. 21:5; Jn. 12:15) rejoice. .O *d* of Zion
Mt. 9:18 (Mk. 5:35; Lk. 8:49) *d* is even now dead
9:22 (Mk. 5:34; Lk. 8:48) *d*, be of good comfort
10:35 (Lk. 12:53) and the *d* against her mother
15:22 (Mk. 7:26) *d* is grievously vexed with a devil
21:5 (Jn. 12:15) *d* of Sion, Behold, thy King
Lk. 8:42 for he had one only *d*, about twelve years
13:16 a *d* of Abraham, whom Satan had bound
Acts 21:9 had four *d*, virgins, which did prophesy
Heb. 11:24 to be called the son of Pharaoh's *d*
1 Pet. 3:6 as Sarah obeyed Abraham. .whose *d* ye are

David

Anointed by Samuel, 1 Sam. 16:1–13; played the harp
for Saul, 1 Sam. 16:14–23; killed Goliath, 1 Sam. 17;
won Jonathan's friendship, 1 Sam. 18:1–4; incurred
Saul's jealousy, 1 Sam. 18:5–9; married Michal, 1
Sam. 18:20–29; fled from Saul, 1 Sam. 19–22;
fought with the Philistines, 1 Sam. 23; spared
Saul at En-gedi, 1 Sam. 24; David and Abigail,
1 Sam. 25; spared Saul at Ziph, 1 Sam. 26; lived
among the Philistines, 1 Sam. 27:1–28:2; 29; defeated the Amalekites, 1 Sam. 30; made king over
Judah, 2 Sam. 2:1–7; made king over Israel, 2 Sam.
5:1–16; brought ark to Jerusalem, 2 Sam. 6; God's
covenant with David, 2 Sam. 7; extended his kingdom, 2 Sam. 8; David and Bath-sheba, 2 Sam. 11:1–
12:25; fled Absalom's revolt, 2 Sam. 15–16; returned
to Jerusalem, 2 Sam. 19; David's song, 2 Sam. 22:1–
23:7; numbered Israel and Judah, 2 Sam. 24; charged
Solomon, 1 Kgs. 2:1–9; died, 1 Kgs. 2:10–12. (*See
also* 1 Chr. 11–29.)

Ps. 78:70 he chose *D* also his servant, and took him
Jer. 23:5 (33:15) raise unto *D* a righteous Branch
  33:21 then may also my covenant be broken with *D*
  33:22 will I multiply the seed of *D* my servant
Ezek. 34:23 he shall feed them, even my servant *D*
Amos 9:11 (Acts 15:16) I raise up the tabernacle of *D*
Zech. 12:8 be as *D*. . the house of *D* shall be as God
Mt. 1:1 generation of Jesus Christ, the son of *D*
  9:27 and saying, Thou Son of *D*, have mercy on us
  12:3 (Mk. 2:25; Lk. 6:3) read what *D* did, when he
  21:9 Hosanna to the Son of *D*: Blessed is he that
  22:43 (Mk. 12:37; Lk. 20:44) *D*. . call him LORD
Lk. 1:32 give unto him the throne of his father *D*
  2:4 the city of *D*, which is called Bethlehem
Jn. 7:42 said, That Christ cometh of the seed of *D*
Acts 2:25 for *D* speaketh concerning him, I foresaw
  4:25 who by the mouth of thy servant *D* hast said
Rom. 1:3 of the seed of *D* according to the flesh
Rev. 5:5 Root of *D*, hath prevailed to open the
  22:16 I am the root and the offspring of *D*

Dawn

Mt. 28:1 the end of the sabbath, as it began to *d*
2 Pet. 1:19 a light that shineth. . until the day *d*

Dawning

Josh. 6:15 they rose early about the *d* of the day
Judg. 19:26 came the woman in the *d* of the day
Job 3:9 neither let it see the *d* of the day
  7:4 I am full of tossings to and fro unto the *d*
Ps. 119:147 I prevented the *d* of the morning

Day *See also* Age, Hour, Judgment, Time

Gen. 1:5 God called the light *D*, and the darkness
  2:2 (Heb. 4:4) rested on the seventh *d* from all
  2:17 the *d* that thou eatest thereof thou shalt
  7:4 will cause it to rain upon the earth forty *d*
  7:24 waters. . upon the earth a hundred and fifty *d*
  8:22 and winter, and *d* and night shall not cease
  32:26 and he said, Let me go, for the *d* breaketh
  35:3 who answered me in the *d* of my distress
Ex. 12:14 this *d* shall be unto you for a memorial
  13:6 (34:18) seven *d* thou shalt eat unleavened
  14:30 thus the LORD saved Israel that *d* out of
  20:9 (Deut. 5:13) six *d* shalt thou labor, and do
  20:12 (Deut. 5:16) that thy *d* may be long
Lev. 25:9 in the *d* of atonement shall ye make the
Deut. 4:10 *d* that thou stoodest before the LORD
  4:32 for ask now of the *d* that are past
  5:24 seen this *d* that God doth talk with man
  11:26 before you this *d* a blessing and a curse
  25:15 just measure. . that thy *d* may be lengthened
  30:15 have set before thee this *d* life and good
  33:25 as thy *d*, so shall thy strength be
Josh. 1:8 thou shalt meditate therein *d* and night
  10:14 was no *d* like that before it or after it
  24:15 choose you this *d* whom ye will serve
1 Sam. 3:1 word of the LORD was precious in those *d*
  10:19 and ye have this *d* rejected your God
  14:23 so the LORD saved Israel that *d*
2 Kgs. 7:9 this *d* is a *d* of good tidings
1 Chr. 11:22 and slew a lion in a pit in a snowy *d*
  29:15 our *d* on the earth are as a shadow
Neh. 8:10 for this *d* is holy unto our LORD
Esth. 9:26 wherefore they called these *d* Purim
Job 3:1 opened Job his mouth, and cursed his *d*
  7:6 my *d* are swifter than a weaver's shuttle
  10:20 are not my *d* few? cease then, and let me
  14:5 seeing his *d* are determined, the number of
  19:25 shall stand at the latter *d* upon the earth
  21:30 wicked is reserved to the *d* of destruction
Ps. 1:2 in his law doth he meditate *d* and night
  2:7 (Acts 13:33; Heb. 1:5) this *d* have I begotten
  19:2 *d* unto *d* uttereth speech, and night unto

Ps. 23:6 mercy shall follow me all the *d* of my life
  25:5 my salvation; on thee do I wait all the *d*
  27:4 the house of the LORD all the *d* of my life
  44:22 (Rom. 8:36) are we killed all the *d* long
  50:15 call upon me in the *d* of trouble: I will
  74:16 the *d* is thine, the night also is thine
  77:2 in the *d* of my trouble I sought the LORD
  84:10 *d* in thy courts is better than a thousand
  90:10 *d* of our years are threescore years and
  90:12 so teach us to number our *d*, that we may
  91:5 nor for the arrow that flieth by *d*
  102:11 my *d* are like a shadow that declineth
  103:15 as for man, his *d* are as grass
  118:24 this is the *d* which the LORD hath made
  119:97 thy law! it is my meditation all the *d*
  121:6 sun shall not smite thee by *d*, nor the moon
  139:12 but the night shineth as the *d*
  145:2 every *d* will I bless thee; and I will
Prov. 3:16 length of *d* is in her right hand
  4:18 shineth more and more unto the perfect *d*
  7:20 and will come home at the *d* appointed
  10:27 the fear of the LORD prolongeth *d*
  11:4 riches profit not in the *d* of wrath
  27:1 thou knowest not what a *d* may bring forth
Eccl. 2:23 all his *d* are sorrows, and his travail
  7:1 and the *d* of death than the *d* of one's birth
  7:10 that the former *d* were better than these?
  7:14 in the *d* of prosperity be joyful
  8:8 neither hath he power in the *d* of death
  12:1 remember. . thy Creator in the *d* of thy youth
Song 4:6 until the *d* break, and the shadows flee
Is. 2:2 (Mic. 4:1) it shall come to pass in the last *d*
  2:12 the *d* of the LORD. . shall be upon every one
  10:3 and what will ye do in the *d* of visitation
  11:10 in that *d* there shall be a root of Jesse
  12:1 in that *d* thou shalt say, O LORD, I will
  13:6 (Joel 1:15; Zeph. 1:7) *d* of the LORD is at hand
  27:3 lest any hurt it, I will keep it night and *d*
  29:18 in that *d* shall the deaf hear the words
  34:8 the *d* of the LORD's vengeance, and the year
  49:8 (2 Cor. 6:2) in a *d* of salvation have I helped
  53:10 he shall prolong his *d*, and the pleasure
  58:13 from doing thy pleasure on my holy *d*
  60:19 the sun shall be no more thy light by *d*
  65:20 shall be no more thence an infant of *d*
Jer. 2:32 people have forgotten me *d* without number
  16:19 and my refuge in the *d* of affliction
  23:6 (33:16) in his *d* Judah shall be saved
  46:10 this is the *d* of the Lord. . *d* of vengeance
Ezek. 12:23 the *d* are at hand, and the effect
  30:2 howl ye, Woe worth the *d*!
  30:3 *d* is near, even the *d* of the LORD is near
  36:33 in the *d* that I shall have cleansed you
Dan. 6:10 he kneeled. . three times a *d*, and prayed
Hos. 3:5 the LORD and his goodness in the latter *d*
Joel 2:11 *d* of the LORD is great and very terrible
  2:31 (Acts 2:20) terrible *d* of the LORD come
Amos 5:18 *d* of the LORD is darkness, and not light
Obad. 15 *d* of the LORD is near upon all the heathen
Jon. 1:17 was in the belly of the fish three *d* and
Nah. 1:7 LORD is. . a stronghold in the *d* of trouble
Zech. 4:10 who hath despised the *d* of small things
  12:3 that *d* will I make Jerusalem a burdensome
  14:1 behold the *d* of the LORD cometh
Mal. 3:2 but who may abide the *d* of his coming?
  3:17 in that *d* when I make up my jewels
  4:1 the *d* cometh that shall burn as an oven
Mt. 4:2 (Lk. 4:2) had fasted forty *d* and forty nights
  6:11 (Lk. 11:3) give us this *d* our daily bread
  6:34 sufficient unto the *d* is the evil thereof
  7:22 many will say to me in that *d*, Lord, Lord
  9:15 (Mk. 2:20; Lk. 5:35) but the *d* will come
  10:15 Sodom and Gomorrah in the *d* of judgment

Mt. 12:36 give account thereof in the *d* of judgment
12:40 as Jonas was three *d* and three nights in
16:21 (Mk. 8:31; Lk. 9:22) be raised . . the third *d*
17:23 (Mk. 9:31) third *d* he shall be raised again
24:22 (Mk. 13:20) except those *d* . . be shortened
24:36 (Mk. 13:32) that *d* and hour knoweth no man
24:37 (Lk. 17:26) as the *d* of Noe were, so shall
26:29 (Mk. 14:25) until that *d* when I drink it new
26:61 (Mk. 14:58) temple . . to build it in three *d*
Lk. 2:11 for unto you is born this *d* in the city
4:21 this *d* is this Scripture fulfilled in your
17:24 so shall also the Son of man be in his *d*
17:30 in the *d* when the Son of man is revealed
21:34 and so that *d* come upon you unawares
24:46 and to rise from the dead the third *d*
Jn. 2:19 temple, and in three *d* I will raise it up
6:39 but should raise it up again at the last *d*
8:56 Abraham rejoiced to see my *d*: and he saw it
11:24 rise . . in the resurrection at the last *d*
12:48 the same shall judge him in the last *d*
14:20 that *d* ye shall know that I am in my Father
Acts 1:3 proofs, being seen of them forty *d*
2:17 shall come to pass in the last *d*, saith God
10:40 him God raised up the third *d*, and showed
17:31 appointed a *d*, in the which he will judge
20:31 to warn every one night and *d* with tears
Rom. 2:5 against the *d* of wrath and revelation of
13:13 let us walk honestly, as in the *d*; not in
14:5 one man esteemeth one *d* above another
1 Cor. 1:8 may be blameless in the *d* of our Lord
15:4 he rose again the third *d* according to the
16:2 upon the first *d* of the week let every one
2 Cor. 6:2 behold, now is the *d* of salvation
Gal. 4:10) ye observe *d*, and months, and times
Eph. 4:30) ye are sealed unto the *d* of redemption
5:16 redeeming the time, because the *d* are evil
6:13 ye may be able to withstand in the evil *d*
Phil. 1:6 will perform it until the *d* of Jesus
1 Thes. 2:9 laboring night and *d*, because we would
3:10 night and *d* praying exceedingly that we
5:2 that the *d* of the Lord so cometh as a thief
5:5 ye are all . . children of the *d*
2 Thes. 2:3 that *d* shall not come, except there
2 Tim. 1:12 have committed unto him against that *d*
3:1 that in the last *d* perilous times shall come
Heb. 1:2 in these last *d* spoken unto us by his Son
4:4 God did rest the seventh *d* from all his works
10:25 but exhorting . . as ye see the *d* approaching
1 Pet. 2:12 glorify God in the *d* of visitation
3:10 for he that will love life, and see good *d*
2 Pet. 1:19 *d* dawn, and the *d*-star arise in your
3:3 that there shall come in the last *d* scoffers
3:8 one *d* is with the Lord as a thousand years
3:10 but the *d* of the Lord will come as a thief
1 Jn. 4:17 may have boldness in the *d* of judgment
Rev. 1:10 I was in the Spirit on the Lord's *d*
4:8 rest not *d* and night, saying, Holy, holy
6:17 for the great *d* of his wrath is come
14:11 they have no rest *d* nor night, who worship
21:25 gates of it shall not be shut at all by *d*

Deacon *See also* Minister, Servant

Phil. 1:1 are at Philippi, with the bishops and *d*
1 Tim. 3:8 must the *d* be grave, not double-tongued
3:10 the office of a *d*, being found blameless
3:12 the *d* be the husbands of one wife, ruling

Dead

Gen. 20:3 Abimelech . . Behold, thou art but a *d* man
23:4 buryingplace with you, that I may bury my *d*
Ex. 12:30 not a house where there was not one *d*
14:30 saw the Egyptians *d* upon the seashore
Lev. 11:31 when they be *d*, shall be unclean until

Num. 16:48 he stood between the *d* and the living
19:11 that toucheth the *d* body . . shall be unclean
Deut. 25:5 wife of the *d* shall not marry without
Josh. 1:2 Moses my servant is *d*; now therefore
Ruth 1:8 as ye have dealt with the *d*, and with me
4:5 raise up the name of the *d* upon his inheritance
1 Sam. 17:51 saw their champion was *d*, they fled
24:14 thou pursue? after a *d* dog, after a flea
28:3 Samuel was *d*, and all Israel had lamented
1 Kgs. 3:20 and laid her *d* child in my bosom
2 Kgs. 4:32 when Elisha was come . . the child was *d*
8:5 how he had restored a *d* body to life
Job 1:19 they are *d*; and I only am escaped alone
Ps. 31:12 I am forgotten as a *d* man out of mind
79:2 *d* bodies of thy servants . . given to be meat
88:10 show wonders to the *d*? shall the *d* arise
115:17 the *d* praise not the LORD, neither any
Prov. 2:18 unto death, and her paths unto the *d*
21:16 shall remain in the congregation of the *d*
Eccl. 9:3 live, and after that they go to the *d*
9:5 they shall die: but the *d* know not any thing
Is. 8:19 unto their God? for the living to the *d*?
14:9 at thy coming: it stirreth up the *d* for thee
26:14 they are *d*, they shall not live; they are
Jer. 16:7 in mourning, to comfort them for the *d*
22:10 weep ye not for the *d*, neither bemoan him
Lam. 3:6 in dark places, as they that be *d* of old
Ezek. 24:17 forbear to cry . . no mourning for the *d*
Mt. 2:19 but when Herod was *d*, behold, an angel
8:22 (Lk. 9:60) let the *d* bury their *d*
9:24 (Mk. 5:39; Lk. 8:52) the maid is not *d*, but
10:8 cleanse the lepers, raise the *d*, cast out
11:5 (Lk. 7:22) the deaf hear, the *d* are raised up
14:2 (Mk. 6:14; Lk. 9:7) John . . is risen from the *d*
17:9 (Mk. 9:9) Son of man be risen again from the *d*
22:31 (Mk. 12:26) touching . . resurrection of the *d*
22:32 (Mk. 12:27; Lk. 20:38) not the God of the *d*
23:27 but are within full of *d* men's bones
27:64 he is risen from the *d*: so the last error
28:7 his disciples that he is risen from the *d*
Mk. 5:35 (Lk. 8:49) thy daughter is *d*; why troublest
15:44 and Pilate marveled if he were already *d*
Lk. 7:12 was a *d* man carried out, the only son of
10:30 wounded him . . departed, leaving him half *d*
15:24 for this my son was *d*, and is alive again
16:30 if one went . . from the *d*, they will repent
24:5 why seek ye the living among the *d*?
Jn. 2:22 when therefore he was risen from the *d*
5:21 for as the Father raiseth up the *d*
5:25 when the *d* shall hear the voice of the Son
8:52 Abraham is *d*, and the prophets; and thou
11:14 said Jesus unto them plainly, Lazarus is *d*
11:25 in me, though he were *d*, yet shall he live
20:9 Scripture, that he must rise again from the *d*
21:14 after that he was risen from the *d*
Acts 2:29 David, that he is both *d* and buried
3:15 Prince of life, whom God . . raised from the *d*
4:2 through Jesus the resurrection from the *d*
5:10 found her *d* . . buried her by her husband
10:41 drink with him after he rose from the *d*
10:42 ordained . . to be the Judge of quick and *d*
13:30 but God raised him from the *d*
14:19 drew him out . . supposing he had been *d*
17:3 have suffered, and risen again from the *d*
23:6 hope and resurrection of the *d* I am called
24:15 a resurrection of the *d*, both of the just
26:8 incredible . . that God should raise the *d*?
Rom. 1:4 by the resurrection from the *d*
4:17 even God, who quickeneth the *d*, and calleth
5:15 for if through the offense of one many be *d*
6:2 that are *d* to sin, live any longer therein?
6:8 now if we be *d* with Christ, we believe that
6:11 to be *d* indeed unto sin, but alive unto God

Rom. 7:2 the husband be *d*, she is loosed from the law
7:4 become *d* to the law by the body of Christ
8:10 body is *d* because of sin; but the Spirit is
10:7 to bring up Christ again from the *d*
14:9 he might be Lord both of the *d* and living
1 Cor. 7:39 if her husband be *d*, she is at liberty
15:12 that there is no resurrection of the *d*?
15:20 now is Christ risen from the *d*, and become
15:29 why are they then baptized for the *d*?
15:32 advantageth it me, if the *d* rise not?
15:35 how are the *d* raised up? and with what
15:52 and the *d* shall be raised incorruptible
2 Cor. 1:9 but in God which raiseth the *d*
5:14 that if one died for all, then were all *d*
Gal. 1:1 God the Father, who raised him from the *d*
2:19 for I through the law am *d* to the law
2:21 come by the law, then Christ is *d* in vain
Eph. 2:1 (Col. 2:13) who were *d* in trespasses
5:14 awake thou that sleepest. . arise from the *d*
Phil. 3:11 attain unto the resurrection of the *d*
Col. 1:18 the beginning, the firstborn from the *d*
2:12 of God, who hath raised him from the *d*
2:20 wherefore if ye be *d* with Christ from
3:3 ye are *d*, and your life is hid with Christ
1 Thes. 4:16 and the *d* in Christ shall rise first
1 Tim. 5:6 liveth in pleasure is *d* while she liveth
2 Tim. 2:8 was raised from the *d*, according to my
2:11 for if we be *d* with him, we shall also live
4:1 Christ, who shall judge the quick and the *d*
Heb. 9:14 purge your conscience from *d* works to
11:4 and by it he being *d* yet speaketh
13:20 brought again from the *d* our Lord Jesus
Jas. 2:20 that faith without works is *d*?
2:26 for as the body without the spirit is *d*, so
1 Pet. 1:21 raised him up from the *d*, and gave him
2:24 *d* to sins, should live unto righteousness
4:5 that is ready to judge the quick and the *d*
4:6 gospel preached also to them that are *d*
Rev. 1:5 witness, and the first-begotten of the *d*
1:17 and when I saw him, I fell at his feet as *d*
1:18 I am he that liveth, and was *d*; and, behold
2:8 first and the last, which was *d*, and is alive
3:1 thou hast a name that thou livest, and art *d*
11:8 and their *d* bodies shall lie in the street
14:13 blessed are the *d* which die in the Lord
16:3 sea; and it became as the blood of a *d* man
20:5 but the rest of the *d* lived not again until
20:12 book of life: and the *d* were judged out of
20:13 and death and hell delivered up the *d*

Deadly

1 Sam. 5:11 there was a *d* destruction throughout
Ps. 17:9 from my *d* enemies, who compass me about
Ezek. 30:24 with the groanings of a *d* wounded man
Mk. 16:18 drink any *d* thing, it shall not hurt
Jas. 3:8 tongue. . is an unruly evil, full of *d* poison
Rev. 13:3 and his *d* wound was healed

Deaf

Ex. 4:11 who maketh the dumb, or *d*, or the seeing
Lev. 19:14 thou shalt not curse the *d*, nor put a
Ps. 38:13 but I, as a *d* man, heard not; and I was
58:4 are like the *d* adder that stoppeth her ear
Is. 29:18 in that day shall the *d* hear the words
35:5 and the ears of the *d* shall be unstopped
42:18 hear, ye *d*; and look, ye blind, that ye
42:19 or *d*, as my messenger that I sent?
43:8 that have eyes, and the *d* that have ears
Mic. 7:16 hand upon their mouth, their ears shall be *d*
Mt. 11:5 (Lk. 7:22) the *d* hear, the dead are raised
Mk. 7:32 and they bring unto him one that was *d*
7:37 he maketh both the *d* to hear, and the dumb
9:25 dumb and *d* spirit, I charge thee, come out

Deal (Dealt)

Gen. 19:9 will we *d* worse with thee than with them
24:49 kindly and truly with my master
32:9 return. . and I will *d* well with thee
Ex. 1:10 come on, let us *d* wisely with them; lest
Lev. 19:11 ye shall not steal, neither *d* falsely
Josh. 2:14 we will *d* kindly and truly with thee
2 Chr. 19:11 *d* courageously, and the LORD shall be
Job 42:8 lest I *d* with you after your folly
Ps. 13:6 because he hath *d* bountifully with me
75:4 I said unto the fools, *D* not foolishly
103:10 hath not *d* with us after our sins; nor
119:17 *d* bountifully with thy servant, that I
119:78 be ashamed; for they *d* perversely with me
142:7 for thou shalt *d* bountifully with me
Prov. 12:22 but they that *d* truly are his delight
13:16 every prudent man *d* with knowledge
Is. 21:2 (24:16) the treacherous dealer *d* treacherously
26:10 in the land of uprightness will he *d* unjustly
33:1 thou shalt make an end to *d* treacherously
52:13 my servant shall *d* prudently, he shall be
58:7 is it not to *d* thy bread to the hungry
Jer. 6:13 (8:10) prophet. . priest every one *d* falsely
Ezek. 16:59 I will even *d* with thee as thou hast
Hos. 5:7 have *d* treacherously against the LORD
Zech. 1:6 to our doings, so hath he *d* with us
Mal. 2:10 why do we *d* treacherously every man
Lk. 1:25 thus hath the Lord *d* with me in the days
Acts 7:19 the same *d* subtilely with our kindred
Rom. 12:3 hath *d* to every man the measure of faith
Heb. 12:7 chastening, God *d* with you as with sons

Dealing

1 Sam. 2:23 hear of your evil *d* by all this people
Ps. 7:16 violent *d* shall come down upon his own pate
Jn. 4:9 for the Jews have no *d* with the Samaritans

Dear *See also* Beloved, Precious

Jer. 31:20 is Ephraim my *d* son? is he a pleasant
Lk. 7:2 servant, who was *d* unto him, was sick
Acts 20:24 neither count I my life *d* unto myself
Eph. 5:1 be ye. . followers of God, as *d* children
Col. 1:13 translated us into the kingdom of his *d* Son
1 Thes. 2:8 own souls, because ye were *d* unto us

Dearth *See also* Drought, Famine

Gen. 41:54 the *d* was in all lands; but in. . Egypt
2 Kgs. 4:38 to Gilgal: and there was a *d* in the land
2 Chr. 6:28 be *d* in the land, if there be pestilence
Neh. 5:3 that we might buy corn, because of the *d*
Jer. 14:1 that came to Jeremiah concerning the *d*
Acts 7:11 *d* over all the land of Egypt and Chanaan
11:28 should be great *d* throughout all the world

Death *See also* Grave, Hell, Sin, Sleep

Gen. 21:16 said, Let me not see the *d* of the child
Ex. 10:17 he may take away from me this *d* only
21:12 so that he die, shall be surely put to *d*
31:14 that defileth it shall surely be put to *d*
35:2 doeth work therein shall be put to *d*
Lev. 20:2 seed unto Molech; he shall. . be put to *d*
20:10 the adulteress shall surely be put to *d*
20:27 that is a wizard, shall surely be put to *d*
Num. 16:29 if these men die the common *d* of all
23:10 let me die the *d* of the righteous
35:16 the murderer shall surely be put to *d*
Deut. 13:5 dreamer of dreams, shall be put to *d*
17:6 shall he that is worthy of *d* be put to *d*
19:6 slay him; whereas he was not worthy of *d*
21:22 sin worthy of *d*, and he be to be put to *d*
24:16 (2 Kgs. 14:6) not be put to *d* for the children
30:15 this day life and good, and *d* and evil
30:19 I have set before you life and *d*, blessing

Josh. 2:13 save. .and deliver our lives from *d*
Judg. 1:1 after the *d* of Joshua it came to pass
  16:30 the dead which he slew at his *d* were more
Ruth 1:17 if aught but *d* part thee and me
1 Sam. 15:32 surely the bitterness of *d* is past
  20:3 there is but a step between me and *d*
2 Sam. 1:23 and in their *d* they were not divided
  22:5 (Ps. 18:4) waves of *d* compassed me, the flood
2 Kgs. 4:40 thou man of God, there is *d* in the pot
  20:1 (2 Chr. 32:24; Is. 38:1) Hezekiah sick unto *d*
2 Chr. 15:13 not seek the LORD. .should be put to *d*
Job 3:5 let darkness and the shadow of *d* stain it
  3:21 which long for *d*, but it cometh not
  5:20 in famine he shall redeem thee from *d*
  7:15 chooseth strangling, and *d* rather than my
  10:21 the land of darkness and the shadow of *d*
  12:22 and bringeth out to light the shadow of *d*
  24:17 morning is to them even as the shadow of *d*
  30:23 for I know that thou wilt bring me to *d*
  38:17 have the gates of *d* been opened unto
Ps. 6:5 in *d* there is no remembrance of thee
  9:13 thou that liftest me up from the gates of *d*
  13:3 mine eyes, lest I sleep the sleep of *d*
  18:4 sorrows of *d* compassed me, and the floods
  23:4 walk through the valley of the shadow of *d*
  33:19 to deliver their soul from *d*, and to keep
  48:14 he will be our guide even unto *d*
  55:4 and the terrors of *d* are fallen upon me
  56:13 for thou hast delivered my soul from *d*
  102:20 to loose those that are appointed to *d*
  116:8 for thou hast delivered my soul from *d*
  116:15 precious. . is the *d* of his saints
  118:18 but he hath not given me over unto *d*
Prov. 2:18 for her house inclineth unto *d*, and her
  5:5 her feet go down to *d*; her steps take hold
  7:27 to hell, going down to the chambers of *d*
  8:36 all they that hate me love *d*
  10:2 but righteousness delivereth from *d*
  12:28 and in the pathway thereof there is no *d*
  13:14 to depart from the snares of *d*
  14:12 but the end thereof are the ways of *d*
  14:32 but the righteous hath hope in his *d*
  18:21 *d* and life are in the power of the tongue
  24:11 to deliver them that are drawn unto *d*
Eccl. 7:1 the day of *d* than the day of one's birth
  8:8 neither hath he power in the day of *d*
Song 8:6 love is strong as *d*; jealousy is cruel as
Is. 9:2 (Mt. 4:16) in the land of the shadow of *d*
  25:8 (1 Cor. 15:54) he will swallow up *d* in victory
  53:9 with the wicked, and with the rich in his *d*
  53:12 because he hath poured out his soul unto *d*
Jer. 8:3 *d* shall be chosen rather than life by all
  21:8 before you the way of life, and the way of *d*
  26:15 if ye put me to *d*, ye shall surely bring
  43:11 deliver such as are for *d* to *d*; and such
Ezek. 18:32 (33:11) I have no pleasure in the *d* of
Hos. 13:14 I will redeem them from *d*: O *d*, I will
Amos 5:8 turneth the shadow of *d* into the morning
Hab. 2:5 enlargeth his desire as hell, and is as *d*
Mt. 10:21 (Mk. 13:12) deliver up the brother to *d*
  10:21 (Mk. 13:12; Lk. 21:16) them to be put to *d*
  14:5 when he would have put him to *d*, he feared
  16:28 (Mk. 9:1; Lk. 9:27) shall not taste of *d*
  20:18 (Mk. 10:33; Lk. 18:33) condemn him to *d*
  26:38 (Mk. 14:34) exceeding sorrowful, even unto *d*
  26:59 (Mk. 14:55) false witness. . to put him to *d*
  26:66 (Mk. 14:64) said, He is guilty of *d*
Mk. 5:23 little daughter lieth at the point of *d*
  14:1 might take him by craft, and put him to *d*
Lk. 1:79 sit in darkness and in the shadow of *d*
  2:26 he should not see *d*, before he had seen the
Jn. 5:24 but is passed from *d* unto life
  8:51 (8:52) keep my saying, he shall never see *d*

Jn. 11:4 sickness is not unto *d*, but for the glory
  12:10 priests consulted. .put Lazarus also to *d*
  12:33 he said, signifying what *d* he should die
  18:31 is not lawful for us to put any man to *d*
  21:19 signifying by what *d* he should glorify God
Acts 2:24 raised up, having loosed the pains of *d*
  8:1 (22:20) and Saul was consenting unto his *d*
  13:28 and though they found no cause of *d* in him
  23:29 laid to his charge worthy of *d* or of bonds
  28:18 go, because there was no cause of *d* in me
Rom. 1:32 which commit such things are worthy of *d*
  5:10 were reconciled to God by the *d* of his Son
  5:12 and *d* by sin; and so *d* passed upon all men
  5:14 nevertheless *d* reigned from Adam to Moses
  6:3 into Jesus Christ were baptized into his *d*?
  6:5 planted together in the likeness of his *d*
  6:9 dieth no more; *d* hath no more dominion over
  6:16 whether of sin unto *d*, or of obedience unto
  6:23 wages of sin is *d*; but the gift of God
  7:5 in our members to bring forth fruit unto *d*
  7:13 sin, working *d* in me by that which is good
  7:24 shall deliver me from the body of this *d*?
  8:2 hath made me free from the law of sin and *d*
  8:6 carnally minded is *d*; but to be spiritually
  8:38 I am persuaded, that neither *d*, nor life
1 Cor. 3:22 or life, or *d*, or things present, or
  11:26 ye do show the Lord's *d* till he come
  15:21 since by man came *d*, by man. .resurrection
  15:26 last enemy that shall be destroyed is *d*
  15:55 O *d*, where is thy sting? O grave, where is
  15:56 the sting of *d* is sin; and the strength of sin
2 Cor. 1:9 we had the sentence of *d* in ourselves
  2:16 to the one we are the savor of *d* unto *d*
  4:11 are alway delivered unto *d* for Jesus' sake
  7:10 but the sorrow of the world worketh *d*
Phil. 1:20 my body, whether it be by life, or by *d*
  2:8 obedient unto *d*, even the *d* of the cross
  3:10 know him. . made conformable unto his *d*
Col. 1:22 in the body of his flesh through *d*
2 Tim. 1:10 Christ, who hath abolished *d*, and hath
Heb. 2:9 the suffering of *d*. . taste *d* for every man
  2:14 through *d*. .destroy. .that had the power of *d*
  2:15 through fear of *d* were. .subject to bondage
  9:15 that by means of *d*, for the redemption of
  11:5 Enoch was translated. .he should not see *d*
Jas. 1:15 sin, when. .finished, bringeth forth *d*
  5:20 error of his way shall save a soul from *d*
1 Pet. 3:18 put to *d* in the flesh, but quickened
1 Jn. 3:14 that we have passed from *d* unto life
  5:16 his brother sin a sin which is not unto *d*
Rev. 1:18 and have the keys of hell and of *d*
  2:10 be thou faithful unto *d*, and I will give
  2:11 shall not be hurt of the second *d*
  6:8 and his name that sat on him was *D*, and Hell
  9:6 shall men seek *d*, and shall not find it
  12:11 and they loved not their lives unto the *d*
  20:6 on such the second *d* hath no power
  20:13 and *d* and hell delivered up the dead which
  20:14 *d* and hell were cast into the lake of fire
  21:4 there shall be no more *d*, neither sorrow
  21:8 fire and brimstone: which is the second *d*

Debase *See also* Corrupt

Is. 57:9 and didst *d* thyself even unto hell

Debate

Prov. 25:9 *d* thy cause with thy neighbor himself
Is. 58:4 behold, ye fast for strife and *d*
Rom. 1:29 murder, *d*, deceit, malignity; whisperers
2 Cor. 12:20 lest there be *d*, envyings, wraths

Deborah Rachel's nurse Gen. 35:8

Deborah the prophetess Judg. 4:4–5:15

Debt

1 Sam. 22:2 distress, and every one that was in *d*
2 Kgs. 4:7 said, Go, sell the oil, and pay thy *d*
Neh. 10:31 seventh year, and the exaction of every *d*
Prov. 22:26 strike hands, or . . are sureties for *d*
Mt. 6:12 forgive us our *d*, as we forgive our debtors
 18:27 lord of that servant . . forgave him the *d*
Rom. 4:4 reward not reckoned of grace, but of *d*

Debtor

Ezek. 18:7 but hath restored to the *d* his pledge
Mt. 6:12 forgive us our debts, as we forgive our *d*
 23:16 swear by the gold of the temple, he is a *d*
Lk. 7:41 a certain creditor which had two *d*
 16:5 called every one of his lord's *d* unto him
Rom. 1:14 *d* . . to the Greeks, and to the Barbarians
 8:12 we are *d*, not to the flesh, to live after
 15:27 pleased them verily; and their *d* they are
Gal. 5:3 circumcised . . is a *d* to do the whole law

Decapolis

Mt. 4:25 people from Galilee, and from *D*, and from
Mk. 5:20 publish in *D* how great things Jesus had
 7:31 sea of Galilee, through . . the coasts of *D*

Decay

Lev. 25:35 brother be waxen poor, and fallen in *d*
Neh. 4:10 strength of the bearers of burdens is *d*
Job 14:11 the sea, and the flood *d* and drieth up
Eccl. 10:18 by much slothfulness the building *d*
Is. 44:26 and I will raise up the *d* places thereof
Heb. 8:13 which *d* and waxeth old is ready to vanish

Decease

Is. 26:14 dead, they shall not live; they are *d*
Mt. 22:25 the first, when he had married a wife, *d*
Lk. 9:31 spake of his *d* which he should accomplish
2 Pet. 1:15 that ye may be able after my *d* to have

Deceit *See also* Falsehood, Hypocrisy, Lie

Job 15:35 and their belly prepareth *d*
 27:4 speak wickedness, nor my tongue utter *d*
 31:5 with vanity, or if my food hath hasted to *d*
Ps. 10:7 mouth is full of cursing and *d* and fraud
 36:3 the words of his mouth are iniquity and *d*
 38:12 speak mischievous things, and imagine *d*
 50:19 mouth to evil, and thy tongue frameth *d*
 55:11 *d* and guile depart not from her streets
 72:14 he shall redeem their soul from *d*
 101:7 worketh *d* shall not dwell within my house
 119:118 thy statutes: for their *d* is falsehood
Prov. 12:5 but the counsels of the wicked are *d*
 12:20 *d* is in the heart of them that imagine evil
 20:17 bread of *d* is sweet . . ʾbut afterward his
 26:26 hatred is covered by *d*, his wickedness
Is. 53:9 violence, neither was any *d* in his mouth
Jer. 5:27 of birds, so are their houses full of *d*
 9:6 habitation is in the midst of *d*; through *d* they
 14:14 thing of nought, and the *d* of their heart
Hos. 11:12 lies, and the house of Israel with *d*
 12:7 merchant, the balances of *d* are in his hand
Amos 8:5 and falsifying the balances by *d*?
Zeph. 1:9 masters' houses with violence and *d*
Mk. 7:22 thefts, covetousness, wickedness, *d*
Rom. 1:29 murder, debate, *d*, malignity; whisperers
 3:13 with their tongues they have used *d*
Col. 2:8 spoil you through philosophy and vain *d*
1 Thes. 2:3 for our exhortation was not of *d*, nor

Deceitful

Ps. 5:6 the LORD will abhor the bloody and *d* man

Ps. 35:20 but they devise *d* matters against them
 43:1 O deliver me from the *d* and unjust man
 52:4 lovest all devouring words, O thou *d* tongue
 55:23 *d* men shall not live out half their days
 78:57 they were turned aside like a *d* bow
 109:2 the mouth of the *d* are opened against me
 120:2 LORD, from lying lips, and from a *d* tongue
Prov. 14:25 but a *d* witness speaketh lies
 27:6 but the kisses of an enemy are *d*
 29:13 the poor and the *d* man meet together
 31:30 favor is *d*, and beauty is vain
Jer. 17:9 the heart is *d* above all things
Mic. 6:11 balances, and with the bag of *d* weights?
Zeph. 3:13 neither shall a *d* tongue be found in
2 Cor. 11:13 such are false apostles, *d* workers
Eph. 4:22 is corrupt according to the *d* lusts

Deceitfully

Gen. 34:13 answered Shechem and Hamor . . *d*
Job 6:15 my brethren have dealt *d* as a brook
Ps. 24:4 his soul into vanity, nor sworn *d*
Jer. 48:10 be he that doeth the work of the LORD *d*
2 Cor. 4:2 nor handling the word of God *d*

Deceitfulness

Mt. 13:22 (Mk. 4:19) the *d* of riches, choke the word
Heb. 3:13 of you be hardened through the *d* of sin

Deceive *See also* Betray, Lie

Gen. 31:7 your father hath *d* me, and changed my
Lev. 6:2 away by violence, or hath *d* his neighbor
Deut. 11:16 your heart be not *d*, and ye turn aside
2 Kgs. 19:10 (Is. 37:10) let not thy God . . *d* thee
Job 31:9 if mine heart have been *d* by a woman
Prov. 20:1 and whosoever is *d* thereby is not wise
 24:28 without cause; and *d* not with thy lips
 26:19 so is the man that *d* his neighbor
Jer. 4:10 surely thou hast greatly *d* this people
 9:5 they will *d* every one his neighbor
 20:7 O LORD, thou hast *d* me, and I was *d*
 29:8 let not your prophets and . . diviners . . *d* you
 37:9 *d* not yourselves, saying, The Chaldeans
Lam. 1:19 I called for my lovers, but they *d* me
Ezek. 14:9 I the LORD have *d* that prophet
Obad. 3 the pride of thine heart hath *d* thee
Zech. 13:4 shall they wear a rough garment to *d*
Mt. 24:4 (Mk. 13:5; Lk. 21:8) that no man *d* you
 24:5 (Mk. 13:6) I am Christ; and shall *d* many
 24:24 were possible, they shall *d* the very elect
Lk. 21:8 take heed that ye be not *d*: for many shall
Jn. 7:12 others said, Nay; but he *d* the people
 7:47 answered them the Pharisees, Are ye also *d*?
Rom. 7:11 taking occasion by the commandment, *d*
 16:18 fair speeches *d* the hearts of the simple
1 Cor. 3:18 let no man *d* himself. If any man among
 6:9 be not *d*: neither fornicators, nor idolaters
 15:33 be not *d*: evil communications corrupt good
Gal. 6:7 be not *d*; God is not mocked
Eph. 4:14 craftiness whereby they lie in wait to *d*
 5:6 let no man *d* you with vain words
2 Thes. 2:3 let no man *d* you by any means
1 Tim. 2:14 Adam was not *d*, but the woman being *d*
2 Tim. 3:13 wax worse and worse, *d*, and being *d*
Jas. 1:22 and not hearers only, *d* your own selves
1 Jn. 1:8 say that we have no sin, we *d* ourselves
 3:7 little children, let no man *d* you: he that
Rev. 12:9 Satan, which *d* the whole world
 18:23 for by thy sorceries were all nations *d*
 19:20 miracles before him, with which he *d* them
 20:3 that he should *d* the nations no more, till
 20:10 devil that *d* them was cast into the lake

Deceived *See also* Deceive

Job 12:16 the *d* and the deceiver are his

Is. 44:20 a *d* heart hath turned him aside, that he
Tit. 3:3 disobedient, *d*, serving divers lusts and

Deceiver

Gen. 27:12 feel me, and I shall seem to him as a *d*
Job 12:16 the deceived and the *d* are his
Mal. 1:14 cursed be the *d*, which hath in his flock
Mt. 27:63 we remember that that *d* said, while he
2 Cor. 6:8 as *d*, and yet true
Tit. 1:10 unruly and vain talkers and *d*, specially
2 Jn. 7 this is a *d* and an antichrist

Decently

1 Cor. 14:40 let all things be done *d* and in order

Decision

Joel 3:14 multitudes, multitudes in the valley of *d*

Deck *See also* Adorn, Garnish

Job 40:10 *d* thyself now with majesty and excellency
Prov. 7:16 *d* my bed with coverings of tapestry
Is. 61:10 as a bridegroom *d* himself with ornaments
Jer. 4:30 though thou *d* thee with ornaments of
10:4 they *d* it with silver and with gold
Ezek. 16:11 I *d* thee also with ornaments
16:16 and *d* thy high places with divers colors
Rev. 17:4 and *d* with gold and precious stones and
18:16 and purple, and scarlet, and *d* with gold

Declare *See also* Preach, Proclaim, Prophesy, Publish, Tell

Gen. 41:24 magicians. . none that could *d* it to me
Ex. 9:16 (Rom. 9:17) my name may be *d* throughout
Deut. 1:5 land of Moab, began Moses to *d* this law
Josh. 20:4 *d* his cause in the ears of the elders
Judg. 14:12 a riddle. . if ye can certainly *d* it me
1 Chr. 16:24 (Ps. 96:3) *d* his glory among the heathen
Job 15:17 that which I have seen I will *d*
21:31 who shall *d* his way to his face?
31:37 I would *d* unto him the number of my steps
38:4 the earth? *d*, if thou hast understanding
40:7 I will demand of thee, and *d* thou unto me
Ps. 2:7 I will *d* the decree: the LORD hath said
9:11 sing praises. . *d* among the people his doings
19:1 the heavens *d* the glory of God
22:22 (Heb. 2:12) will *d* thy name unto my brethren
22:31 shall *d* his righteousness unto a people
40:10 have *d* thy faithfulness and thy salvation
50:6 the heavens shall *d* his righteousness
64:9 men shall fear, and shall *d* the work of God
66:16 and I will *d* what he hath done for my soul
75:1 that thy name is near thy wondrous works *d*
75:9 but I will *d* for ever; I will sing praises
77:14 thou hast by thy strength among the people
118:17 but live, and *d* the works of the LORD
145:4 to another, and shall *d* thy mighty acts
145:6 and I will *d* thy greatness
Eccl. 9:1 I considered in my heart even to *d* all
Is. 3:9 *d* their sin as Sodom, they hide it not
12:4 *d* his doings among the people, make mention
21:10 that which I have heard. . have I *d* unto you
41:26 who hath *d* from the beginning, that we may
42:9 are come to pass, and new things do I *d*
43:26 *d* thou, that thou mayest be justified
45:19 righteousness, I *d* things that are right
45:21 who hath *d* this from ancient time?
46:10 *d* the end from the beginning, and from
48:3 have *d* the former things from the beginning
53:8 (Acts 8:33) who shall *d* his generation?
66:19 they shall *d* my glory among the Gentiles
Jer. 38:15 said unto Zedekiah, If I *d* it unto thee
50:2 *d* ye among the nations, and publish

Amos 4:13 and *d* unto man what is his thought
Mic. 1:10 *d* ye it not at Gath, weep ye not at all
3:8 to *d* unto Jacob his transgression
Mt. 13:36 *d* unto us the parable of the tares
Lk. 8:47 she *d* unto him before all the people
Jn. 1:18 in the bosom of the Father, he hath *d* him
17:26 I have *d* unto them thy name, and will *d* it
Acts 13:32 and we *d* unto you glad tidings, how that
15:4 *d* all things that God had done with them
15:12 Barnabas and Paul, *d* what miracles
17:23 ye ignorantly worship, him *d* I unto you
20:27 not shunned to *d* unto you all the counsel
21:19 *d* particularly what things God had wrought
Rom. 1:4 and *d* to be the Son of God with power
3:25 to *d* his righteousness for the remission of
1 Cor. 2:1 *d* unto you the testimony of God
3:13 be made manifest: for the day shall *d* it
15:1 I *d* unto you the gospel which I preached
2 Cor. 3:3 ye are manifestly *d* to be the epistle
Heb. 11:14 they that say such things *d* plainly that
1 Jn. 1:3 we have seen and heard *d* we unto you

Decline

Ex. 23:2 to *d* after many to wrest judgment
Deut. 17:11 thou shalt not *d* from the sentence
2 Chr. 34:2 *d* neither to the right hand, nor. . left
Job 23:11 his way have I kept, and not *d*
Ps. 44:18 neither have our steps *d* from thy way
102:11 my days are like a shadow that *d*
109:23 I am gone like the shadow when it *d*
119:51 yet have I not *d* from thy law
119:157 yet do I not *d* from thy testimonies
Prov. 4:5 neither *d* from the words of my mouth
7:25 let not thine heart *d* to her ways

Decrease *See also* Abate, Diminish

Gen. 8:5 the waters *d* continually until the tenth
Ps. 107:38 and suffereth not their cattle to *d*
Jn. 3:30 he must increase, but I must *d*

Decree *See also* Commandment, Law, Ordain, Order, Ordinance, Precept, Statute

2 Chr. 30:5 established a *d*. . to keep the passover
Ezra 6:1 Darius the king made a *d*, and search was
Esth. 2:8 king's commandment and his *d* was heard
3:15 and the *d* was given in Shushan the palace
9:32 decree of Esther confirmed these matters of Purim
Job 22:28 *d* a thing, and it shall be established
28:26 when he made a *d* for the rain, and a way
Ps. 2:7 I will declare the *d*: the LORD hath said
148:6 he hath made a *d* which shall not pass
Prov. 8:15 by me kings reign, and princes *d* justice
8:29 he gave to the sea his *d*, that the waters
Is. 10:1 woe unto them that *d* unrighteous *d*
Jer. 5:22 bound of the sea by a perpetual *d*
Dan. 2:9 unto me the dream, there is but one *d* for
2:13 *d* went forth that the wise men should be slain
3:10 thou, O king, hast made a *d*, that every man
4:6 made I a *d* to bring in all the wise men of
4:24 and this is the *d* of the Most High
6:8 now, O king, establish the *d*, and sign the
6:13 regardeth not thee, O king, nor the *d* that
6:15 no *d*. . the king establisheth may be changed
6:26 I make a *d*. . fear before the God of Daniel
Jon. 3:7 published through Nineveh by the *d* of the
Lk. 2:1 *d* from Caesar Augustus, that all the world
Acts 16:4 they delivered them the *d* for to keep
17:7 these all do contrary to the *d* of Caesar
1 Cor. 7:37 so *d* in his heart that he will keep

Dedan Jer. 49:8–12; Ezek. 25:13; 27:15, 20

Dedicate *See also* Consecrate, Give, Present

Num. 7:10 princes offered for *d* of the altar
Deut. 20:5 built a new house, and hath not *d* it?
Judg. 17:3 I had wholly *d* the silver unto the LORD
2 Sam. 8:11 (1 Chr. 18:11) David did *d* unto the LORD
1 Kgs. 7:51 (2 Chr. 5:1) which David his father had *d*
    8:63 (2 Chr. 7:5) Israel *d* the house of the LORD
1 Chr. 26:27 *d* to maintain the house of the LORD
2 Chr. 2:4 name of the LORD my God, to *d* it to him
Heb. 9:18 the first testament was *d* without blood

Dedicated *See also* Dedicate

2 Kgs. 12:4 all the money of the *d* things that is
Ezek. 44:29 every *d* thing in Israel shall be theirs

Dedication *See also* Consecration

Num. 7:84 this was the *d* of the altar, in the day
2 Chr. 7:9 they kept the *d* of the altar seven days
Ezra 6:17 offered at the *d* of this house of God
Neh. 12:27 at the *d* of the wall of Jerusalem
Dan. 3:2 the *d* of the image which Nebuchadnezzar
Jn. 10:22 it was at Jerusalem the feast of the *d*

Deed *See also* Act, Doing

Gen. 20:9 thou hast done *d* unto me that ought not
    44:15 Joseph said unto them, What *d* is this that
Judg. 19:30 there was no such *d* done nor seen from
2 Sam. 12:14 by this *d* thou hast given great occasion
1 Chr. 16:8 (Ps. 105:1) make known his *d* among the
Ezra 9:13 all that is come upon us for our evil *d*
Neh. 13:14 wipe not out my good *d* that I have done
Ps. 28:4 give them according to their *d*
Is. 59:18 to their, accordingly he will repay
Jer. 5:28 yea, they overpass the *d* of the wicked
    25:14 will recompense them according to their *d*
Lk. 11:48 ye allow the *d* of your fathers
    23:41 we receive the due reward of our *d*
    23:51 not consented to the counsel and *d* of them
    24:19 a prophet mighty in *d* and word before God
Jn. 3:19 loved darkness. . because their *d* were evil
    8:41 ye do the *d* of your father
Acts 4:9 the good *d* done to the impotent man
    7:22 and Moses. . was mighty in words and in *d*
    19:18 came, and confessed, and showed their *d*
    24:2 worthy *d* are done unto this nation by thy
Rom. 2:6 render to every man according to his *d*
    3:20 by the *d* of the law. . no flesh be justified
    8:13 do mortify the *d* of the body, ye shall live
    15:18 make the Gentiles obedient, by word and *d*
1 Cor. 5:3 concerning him that hath so done this *d*
2 Cor. 12:12 in signs, and wonders, and mighty *d*
Col. 3:9 ye have put off the old man with his *d*
    3:17 ye do in word or *d*, do all in the name of
Jas. 1:25 this man shall be blessed in his *d*
2 Pet. 2:8 from day to day with their unlawful *d*
1 Jn. 3:18 not love in word. . but in *d* and in truth
2 Jn. 11 him God-speed is partaker of his evil *d*
Jude 15 ungodly among them of all their ungodly *d*
Rev. 2:6 that thou hatest the *d* of the Nicolaitans
    16:11 their sores, and repented not of their *d*

Deep (Deeper)

Gen. 1:2 and darkness was upon the face of the *d*
    2:21 LORD God caused a *d* sleep to fall upon Adam
    7:11 all the fountains of the great *d* broken up
    8:2 the *d* and the windows of heaven were stopped
Deut. 33:13 and for the *d* that coucheth beneath
Job 11:8 *d* than hell; what canst thou know?
    33:15 night, when *d* sleep falleth upon men
    38:30 and the face of the *d* is frozen
    41:31 maketh the *d* to boil like a pot

Ps. 36:6 thy judgments are a great *d*: O LORD, thou
    42:7 *d* calleth unto *d* at the noise of thy
    64:6 both the inward thought. . and the heart, is *d*
    69:15 neither let the *d* swallow me up
    92:5 are thy works! and thy thoughts are very *d*
    95:4 in his hand are the *d* places of the earth
    104:6 coveredst it with the *d* as with a garment
    107:24 works of the LORD, and his wonders in the *d*
Is. 33:19 of a *d* speech than thou canst perceive
    63:13 that led them through the *d*, as a horse in
Dan. 2:22 he revealeth the *d* and secret things
Jon. 2:3 for thou hadst cast me into the *d*
Hab. 3:10 the *d* uttered his voice, and lifted up
Lk. 5:4 Simon, Launch out into the *d*, and let down
    6:48 which built a house, and digged *d*, and laid
    8:31 would not command them to go out into the *d*
Jn. 4:11 nothing to draw with, and the well is *d*
Acts 20:9 Eutychus, being fallen into a *d* sleep
Rom. 10:7 or, Who shall descend into the *d*?
1 Cor. 2:10 Spirit searcheth. . the *d* things of God
2 Cor. 11:25 night and a day I have been in the *d*

Deepness

Mt. 13:5 sprung up, because they had no *d* of earth

Defame

Jer. 20:10 I heard the *d* of many, fear on every side
1 Cor. 4:13 being *d*, we entreat

Defeat

2 Sam. 15:34 for me the *d* the counsel of Ahithophel
    17:14 LORD had appointed to *d* the good counsel

Defend

2 Kgs. 19:34 (Is. 37:35) I will *d* this city
Ps. 5:11 ever shout for joy, because thou *d* them
    20:1 the name of the God of Jacob *d* thee
    59:1 *d* me from them that rise up against me
    82:3 *d* the poor and fatherless: do justice to
Is. 31:5 LORD of hosts *d* Jerusalem; *d* also he will
Zech. 9:15 LORD of hosts shall *d* them
Acts 7:24 suffer wrong, he *d* him, and avenged him

Defense

Num. 14:9 their *d* is departed from them
Job 22:25 yea, the Almighty shall be thy *d*
Ps. 7:10 my *d* is of God, which saveth the upright
    31:2 my strong rock, for a house of *d* to save me
    59:9 will I wait upon thee: for God is my *d*
    59:16 thou hast been my *d* and refuge in the day
    59:17 for God is my *d*, and the God of my mercy
    62:2 (62:6) is my rock and my salvation; he is my *d*
    89:18 LORD is our *d*; and the Holy One of Israel
    94:22 LORD is my *d*; and my God is the rock of my
Eccl. 7:12 for wisdom is a *d*, and money is a *d*
Is. 4:5 for upon all the glory shall be a *d*
    19:6 brooks of *d* shall be emptied and dried up
    33:16 place of *d* shall be the munitions of rocks
Acts 19:33 Alexander. . would have made his *d* unto
    22:1 men, brethren, and fathers, hear ye my *d*
Phil. 1:7 in the *d* and confirmation of the gospel
    1:17 I am set for the *d* of the gospel

Defer

Prov. 13:12 hope *d* maketh the heart sick
    19:11 the discretion of a man *d* his anger
Eccl. 5:4 vowest a vow unto God, *d* not to pay it
Is. 48:9 for my name's sake will I *d* mine anger
Acts 24:22 Felix heard these things. . he *d* them

Defile *See also* Corrupt, Pollute, Profane

Gen. 34:2 he took her, and lay with her, and *d* her
Ex. 31:14 that *d* it shall surely be put to death

Lev. 11:44 neither shall ye *d* yourselves with any
13:46 plague shall be in him he shall be *d*
15:31 they die not . . when they *d* my tabernacle
18:20 thy neighbor's wife, to *d* thyself with her
18:24 in all these the nations are *d* which I cast
20:3 *d* my sanctuary, and to profane my holy name
21:1 (Ezek. 44:25) shall none be *d* for the dead
21:4 he shall not *d* himself, being a chief man
Num. 5:2 and whosoever is *d* by the dead
6:9 he hath *d* the head of his consecration
19:13 toucheth the dead body . . *d* the tabernacle
19:20 he hath *d* the sanctuary of the LORD
35:33 for blood it *d* the land
35:34 *d* not . . the land which ye shall inhabit
Deut. 21:23 bury him that day . . thy land be not *d*
22:9 lest the fruit of thy seed . . be *d*
2 Kgs. 23:8 *d* the high places where the priests
Neh. 13:29 because they have *d* the priesthood
Ps. 74:7 they have *d* by casting down the dwelling
79:1 thy holy temple have they *d*; they have laid
106:39 thus were they *d* with their own works
Is. 24:5 the earth also is *d* under the inhabitants
30:22 *d* also the covering of thy graven images
59:3 for your hands are *d* with blood
Jer. 2:7 but when ye entered, ye *d* my land
16:18 because they have *d* my land
Ezek. 5:11 because thou hast *d* my sanctuary with
7:22 the robbers shall enter into it, and *d* it
9:7 *d* the house, and fill the courts with the slain
20:7 *d* not yourselves with the idols of Egypt
20:43 all your doings, wherein ye have been *d*
22:3 maketh idols against herself to *d* herself
23:38 they have *d* my sanctuary in the same day
28:7 thy wisdom, and they shall *d* thy brightness
33:26 and ye *d* every one his neighbor's wife
36:17 *d* it by their own way and by their doings
37:23 neither shall they *d* themselves any more
43:8 even *d* my holy name by their abominations
Dan. 1:8 Daniel purposed . . he would not *d* himself
Hos. 5:3 thou committest whoredom, and Israel is *d*
Mt. 15:11 cometh out of the mouth, this *d* a man
15:18 (Mk. 7:23) from the heart . . they *d* the man
Jn. 18:28 the judgment hall, lest they should be *d*
1 Cor. 3:17 if any man *d* the temple of God
8:7 and their conscience being weak is *d*
1 Tim. 1:10 them that *d* themselves with mankind
Tit. 1:15 unto them that are *d* . . is nothing pure
Heb. 12:15 trouble you, and thereby many be *d*
Jas. 3:6 the tongue . . *d* the whole body, and setteth
Jude 8 these filthy dreamers *d* the flesh, despise
Rev. 3:4 in Sardis which have not *d* their garments
21:27 in no wise enter into it any thing that *d*

Defiled *See also* Defile
Ezek. 4:13 eat their *d* bread among the Gentiles
Mk. 7:2 with *d*, that is to say, with unwashen hands

Defraud
Lev. 19:13 thou shalt not *d* thy neighbor
1 Sam. 12:3 whom have I *d*? whom have I oppressed?
Mk. 10:19 do not bear false witness, *D* not, Honor
1 Cor. 6:7 not rather suffer yourselves to be *d*?
6:8 ye do wrong, and *d*, and that your brethren
7:5 *d* ye not one the other, except it be with
2 Cor. 7:2 have corrupted no man, we have *d* no man
1 Thes. 4:6 no man go beyond and *d* his brother in

Defy
1 Sam. 17:10 said, I *d* the armies of Israel this day

Degenerate
Jer. 2:21 how then art thou turned into the *d*

Degree
2 Kgs. 20:10 (Is. 38:8) shadow return backward ten *d*
1 Chr. 17:17 regarded me . . a man of high *d*, O LORD
Ps. 62:9 men of low *d* are vanity . . high *d* are a lie
Lk. 1:52 and exalted them of low *d*
1 Tim. 3:13 purchase to themselves a good *d*
Jas. 1:9 let the brother of low *d* rejoice in that

Delay
Ex. 22:29 thou shalt not *d* to offer the first of
32:1 the people saw that Moses *d* to come down
Ps. 119:60 and *d* not to keep thy commandments
Mt. 24:48: (Lk. 12:45) say . . My lord *d* his coming
Acts 9:38 that he would not *d* to come to them
25:17 without any *d* on the morrow I sat on the

Delectable
Is. 44:9 and their *d* things shall not profit

Delicacy
Rev. 18:3 rich through the abundance of her *d*

Delicate *See also* Gentle, Tender
Deut. 28:56 tender and *d* woman among you
Is. 47:1 thou shalt no more be called tender and *d*
Jer. 51:34 he hath filled his belly with my *d*
Mic. 1:16 bald, and poll thee for thy *d* children

Delicately
Lam. 4:5 did feed *d* are desolate in the streets
Lk. 7:25 appareled, and live *d*, are in kings' courts

Delight *See also* Gladness, Joy, Pleasure
Num. 14:8 if the LORD *d* in us, then he will bring
Deut. 10:15 only the LORD had a *d* in thy fathers
1 Sam. 15:22 LORD as great *d* in burnt offerings
2 Sam. 15:26 if he thus say, I have no *d* in thee
22:20 (Ps. 18:19) delivered me, because he *d* in me
Esth. 6:6 unto the man whom the king *d* to honor?
Job 22:26 shalt thou have thy *d* in the Almighty
27:10 will he *d* himself in the Almighty?
34:9 nothing that he should *d* himself with God
Ps. 1:2 but his *d* is in the law of the LORD
16:3 and to the excellent, in whom is all my *d*
22:8 let him deliver him, seeing he *d* in him
37:4 *d* thyself also in the LORD; and he shall
37:11 *d* themselves in the abundance of peace
40:8 I *d* to do thy will, O my God: yea, thy law
51:16 thou *d* not in burnt offering
62:4 they *d* in lies: they bless with their mouth
94:19 thy comforts *d* my soul
112:1 that *d* greatly in his commandments
119:16 I will *d* myself in thy statutes
119:24 thy testimonies also are my *d*, and my
119:47 and I will *d* myself in thy commandments
119:77 that I may live: for thy law is my *d*
119:92 unless thy law had been my *d*, I should
119:143 yet thy commandments are my *d*
119:174 salvation, O LORD; and thy law is my *d*
Prov. 1:22 scorners *d* in their scorning, and fools
2:14 and *d* in the frowardness of the wicked
3:12 even as a father the son in whom he *d*
8:30 I was daily his *d*, rejoicing always before
8:31 and my *d* were with the sons of men
11:1 is abomination . . but a just weight is his *d*
11:20 such as are upright in their way are his *d*
12:22 but they that deal truly are his *d*
15:8 but the prayer of the upright is his *d*
16:13 righteous lips are the *d* of kings
18:2 a fool hath no *d* in understanding
19:10 *d* is not seemly for a fool; much less for
29:17 yea, he shall give *d* unto thy soul
Song 2:3 I sat down under his shadow with great *d*

Is. 1:11 I *d* not in the blood of bullocks, or of
42:1 I uphold; mine elect, in whom my soul *d*
55:2 and let your soul *d* itself in fatness
58:2 they seek me daily, and *d* to know my ways
58:13 call the sabbath a *d*, the holy of the LORD
62:4 LORD *d* in thee, and thy land shall be married
66:3 and their soul *d* in their abominations
Jer. 6:10 word of the LORD . . they have no *d* in it
Mic. 7:18 anger for ever, because he *d* in mercy
Mal. 3:1 messenger of the covenant, whom ye *d* in
Rom. 7:22 *d* in the law of God after the inward man

Delightsome
Mal. 3:12 for ye shall be a *d* land, saith the LORD

Delilah Judg. 16:4–20

Deliver *See also* Redeem, Rescue, Rid, Save

Gen. 14:20 God, which hath *d* thine enemies into
32:11 *d* me, I pray thee . . from the hand of Esau
40:13 thou shalt *d* Pharaoh's cup into his hand
Ex. 2:19 an Egyptian *d* us out of the hand of the
3:8 (Acts 7:34) I am come down to *d* them
18:4 help, and *d* me from the sword of Pharaoh
22:26 (Deut. 24:13) pledge, thou shalt *d* it unto him
Num. 21:2 if thou wilt indeed *d* this people into
35:25 congregation shall *d* the slayer out of the
Deut. 1:27 to *d* us into the hand of the Amorites
2:30 that he might *d* him into thy hand
3:2 (Num. 21:34) fear him not: for I will *d* him
7:16 people which the LORD thy God shall *d* thee
32:39 is there any that can *d* out of my hand
Josh. 2:13 and *d* our lives from death
21:44 LORD *d* all their enemies into their hand
Judg. 4:7 Sisera . . and I will *d* him into thine hand
5:11 they that are *d* from the noise of archers
10:14 gods which ye have chosen; let them *d* you
13:5 and he shall begin to *d* Israel out of the
1 Sam. 4:8 woe unto us! who shall *d* us out of the
17:37 *d* me out of the hand of this Philistine
17:46 this day will the LORD *d* thee into mine
23:12 and the LORD said, They will *d* thee up
23:20 part shall be to *d* him into the king's hand
28:19 the LORD will also *d* Israel with thee into
2 Sam. 22:20 (Ps. 18:19) *d* me, because he delighted
22:49 (Ps. 18:48) hast *d* me from the violent man
2 Kgs. 18:32 (Is. 36:18) saying, The LORD will *d* us
19:10 Jerusalem shall not be *d* into the hand of
19:12 (Is. 37:12) have the gods of the nations *d*
20:6 (Is. 38:6) I will *d* thee and this city out of
1 Chr. 16:7 David *d* first this psalm to thank the
2 Chr. 28:11 *d* the captives . . which ye have taken
Neh. 9:28 many times didst thou *d* them according
Job 5:19 he shall *d* thee in six troubles: yea, in
10:7 there is none that can *d* out of thine hand
16:11 God hath *d* me to the ungodly, and turned
29:12 I *d* the poor that cried, and the fatherless
33:28 he will *d* his soul from going into the pit
36:18 then a great ransom cannot *d* thee
Ps. 6:4 return, O LORD, *d* my soul: oh save me for
17:13 cast him down: *d* my soul from the wicked
18:17 he *d* me from my strong enemy
22:4 they trusted, and thou didst *d* them
22:8 (Mt. 27:43) trusted . . that he would *d* him
27:12 *d* me not . . unto the will of mine enemies
31:2 *d* me speedily: be thou my strong rock
33:16 a mighty man is not *d* by much strength
33:19 to *d* their soul from death, and to keep
34:4 and he heard me, and *d* me from all my fears
37:40 *d* them: he shall *d* them from the wicked
39:8 *d* me from all my transgressions: make me

Ps. 41:1 considereth the poor: the LORD will *d* him
51:14 *d* me from bloodguiltiness, O God
54:7 for he hath *d* me out of all trouble
55:18 he hath *d* my soul in peace from the battle
56:13 thou hast *d* my soul from death: wilt not
59:1 *d* me from mine enemies, O my God: defend
69:18 redeem it: *d* me because of mine enemies
71:2 *d* me in thy righteousness, and cause me to
72:12 for he shall *d* the needy when he crieth
78:42 nor the day when he *d* them from the enemy
81:7 thou calledst in trouble, and I *d* thee
82:4 *d* the poor and needy: rid them out of the
91:3 shall *d* thee from the snare of the fowler
106:43 did he *d* them; but they provoked him with
107:6 and he *d* them out of their distresses
116:8 for thou hast *d* my soul from death
119:134 *d* me from the oppression of man
119:170 me according to thy word
140:1 *d* me, O LORD, from the evil man: preserve
143:9 *d* me, O LORD, from mine enemies: I flee
144:10 who *d* David his servant from the hurtful
Prov. 2:12 to *d* thee from the way of the evil man
6:5 *d* thyself . . from the hand of the hunter
11:8 the righteous is *d* out of trouble, and the
23:14 with the rod, and shalt *d* his soul from hell
24:11 if thou forbear to *d* them that are drawn
28:26 but whoso walketh wisely, he shall be *d*
Eccl. 8:8 neither shall wickedness *d* those that
9:15 and he by his wisdom *d* the city; yet no man
Is. 19:20 saviour, and a great one . . shall *d* them
38:17 hast in love to my soul *d* it from the pit
43:13 there is none that can *d* out of my hand
44:17 and saith, *D* me; for thou art my god
50:2 cannot redeem? or have I no power to *d*?
Jer. 1:8 I am with thee to *d* thee, saith the LORD
15:9 the residue of them will I *d* to the sword
20:5 I will *d* all the strength of this city
39:17 I will *d* thee in that day, saith the LORD
43:11 *d* such as are for death to death; and such
51:6 out of . . Babylon, and every man his soul
Lam. 5:8 is none that doth *d* us out of their hand
Ezek. 3:19 in his iniquity; but thou hast *d* thy soul
7:19 gold shall not be able to *d* them in the day
14:14 (14:20) they should *d* but their own souls
33:12 righteous shall not *d* him in the day
34:10 I will *d* my flock from their mouth
Dan. 3:17 our God whom we serve is able to *d* us
3:29 is no other God that can *d* after this sort
6:14 the king . . set his heart on Daniel to *d* him
6:20 is thy God . . able to *d* thee from the lions?
8:4 was there any that could *d* out of his hand
12:1 and at that time thy people shall be *d*
Hos. 11:8 how shall I *d* thee, Israel?
Amos 2:14 neither shall the mighty *d* himself
9:1 and he that escapeth of them shall not be *d*
Mic. 6:14 not *d*; and that which thou *d* will I give
Zech. 2:7 *d* thyself, O Zion, that dwellest with
11:6 and out of their hand I will not *d* them
Mal. 3:15 yea, they that tempt God are even *d*
Mt. 5:25 (Lk. 12:58) judge *d* thee to the officer
6:13 (Lk. 11:4) into temptation, but *d* us from evil
10:17 (Mk. 13:9) they will *d* you up to the councils
11:27 (Lk. 10:22) things . . *d* unto me of my Father
18:34 was wroth, and *d* him to the tormentors
20:19 (Mk. 10:33; Lk. 18:32) *d* him to the Gentiles
24:9 shall they *d* you up to be afflicted
25:14 his own servants, and *d* unto them his goods
27:2 (Mk. 15:1) and *d* him to Pontius Pilate
27:43 he trusted in God; let him *d* him now
27:58 then Pilate commanded the body to be *d*
Lk. 19:13 his ten servants, and *d* them ten pounds
20:20 so they might *d* him unto the power and
Acts 2:23 being *d* by the determinate counsel

Acts 7:25 how that God by his hand would *d* them
12:11 hath *d* me out of the hand of Herod
26:17 *d* thee from the people. . from the Gentiles
Rom. 4:25 was *d* for our offenses, and was raised
7:6 but now we are *d* from the law, that being
7:24 who shall *d* me from the body of this death?
8:21 shall be *d* from the bondage of corruption
8:32 spared not his own Son, but *d* him up for us
1 Cor. 5:5 to *d* such a one unto Satan for the
11:23 received of the Lord that which also I *d*
15:3 I *d* unto you first of all that which I also
15:24 when he shall have *d* up the kingdom to God
2 Cor. 1:10 *d* us from so great a death, and doth *d*
4:11 are alway *d* unto death for Jesus' sake
Gal. 1:4 that he might *d* us from this present evil
Col. 1:13 who hath *d* us from the power of darkness
1 Thes. 1:10 which *d* us from the wrath to come
1 Tim. 1:20 Alexander; whom I have *d* unto Satan
2 Tim. 3:11 but out of them all the LORD *d* me
4:18 Lord shall *d* me from every evil work
Heb. 2:15 and *d* them, who through fear of death
2 Pet. 2:4 and *d* them into chains of darkness
2:7 and *d* just Lot, vexed with the filthy
2:9 knoweth how to *d* the godly out of temptation
Jude 3 the faith which was once *d* unto the saints
Rev. 20:13 and death and hell *d* up the dead which

Deliverance *See also* Freedom, Liberty, Redemption, Salvation

Gen. 45:7 sent me. . to save your lives by a great *d*
Judg. 15:18 thou hast given this great *d* into the
2 Kgs. 5:1 by him the LORD had given *d* unto Syria
13:17 arrow of the LORD's *d*, and the arrow of *d*
1 Chr. 11:14 and the LORD saved them by a great *d*
2 Chr. 12:7 I will grant them some *d*; and my wrath
Ezra 9:13 and hast given us such *d* as this
Esth. 4:14 enlargement and *d* arise to the Jews
Ps. 18:50 great *d* giveth he to his king
32:7 thou shalt compass me about with songs of *d*
44:4 art my King, O God: command *d* for Jacob
Is. 26:18 we have not wrought any *d* in the earth
Joel 2:32 mount Zion and in Jerusalem shall be *d*
Obad. 17 but upon mount Zion shall be *d*, and there
Lk. 4:18 preach *d* to the captives, and recovering
Heb. 11:35 others were tortured, not accepting *d*

Deliverer *See also* Redeemer, Saviour

Judg. 3:9 Israel cried. . and the LORD raised up a *d*
2 Sam. 22:2 (Ps. 18:2) rock, and my fortress, and my *d*
Ps. 40:17 (70:5) help and my *d*; make no tarrying
144:2 my *d*; my shield, and he in whom I trust
Acts 7:35 same did God send to be a ruler and a *d*
Rom. 11:26 there shall come out of Sion the *D*

Delusion

Is. 66:4 I also will choose their *d*, and will
2 Thes. 2:11 God shall send them strong *d*

Demand *See also* Require

Job 38:3 (40:7; 42:4) I will *d* of thee, and answer thou
Dan. 4:17 and the *d* by the word of the holy ones
Mt. 2:4 he *d* of them where Christ should be born
Lk. 3:15 the soldiers likewise *d* of him, saying
17:20 was *d* of the Pharisees, when the kingdom
Acts 21:33 and *d* who he was, and what he had done

Demas 2 Tim. 4:10; Phlm. 24

Demetrius the silversmith Acts 19:24–38

Demetrius a Christian 3 Jn. 12

Demonstration

1 Cor. 2:4 but in *d* of the Spirit and of power

Den

Judg. 6:2 Israel made them the *d* which are in the
Job 37:8 then the beasts go into *d*, and remain
Is. 11:8 shall put his hand on the cockatrice' *d*
Jer. 7:11 called by my name, become a *d* of robbers
9:11 make Jerusalem heaps, and a *d* of dragons
Dan. 6:16 Daniel, and cast him into the *d* of lions
Amos 3:4 will a young lion cry out of his *d*, if he
Mt. 21:13 (Mk. 11:17; Lk. 19:46) it a *d* of thieves
Heb. 11:38 and in mountains, and in *d* and caves of
Rev. 6:15 hid themselves in the *d* and in the rocks

Deny *See also* Renounce

Gen. 18:15 then Sarah *d*, saying, I laughed not
Josh. 24:27 a witness unto you, lest ye *d* your God
Job 31:28 I should have *d* the God that is above
Prov. 30:9 lest I be full, and *d* thee, and say
Mt. 10:33 (Lk. 12:9) shall *d* me. . him will I also *d*
16:24 (Mk. 8:34; Lk. 9:23) let him *d* himself
26:34 (26:75; Mk. 14:30, 72; Lk. 22:34, 61; Jn. 13:
38) before the cock crow, thou shalt *d* me thrice
26:70 (Mk. 14:68; Lk. 22:57) he *d* before them all
Lk. 20:27 which *d* that there is any resurrection
Jn. 1:20 *d* not; but confessed, I am not the Christ
18:27 Peter then *d* again; and. . the cock crew
Acts 3:13 and *d* him in the presence of Pilate
3:14 ye *d* the Holy One and the Just, and desired
1 Tim. 5:8 *d* the faith, and is worse than an infidel
2 Tim. 2:12 if we *d* him, he also will *d* us
2:13 he abideth faithful: he cannot *d* himself
3:5 having a form of godliness, but *d* the power
Tit. 1:16 in works they *d* him, being abominable
2:12 *d* ungodliness and worldly lusts, we should
2 Pet. 2:1 in damnable heresies, even *d* the Lord
1 Jn. 2:22 antichrist, that *d* the Father and the Son
2:23 *d* the Son, the same hath not the Father
Jude 4 into lasciviousness, and *d* the only Lord
Rev. 2:13 fast my name, and hast not *d* my faith
3:8 hast kept my word, and hast not *d* my name

Depart *See also* Go, Leave

Gen. 13:9 if thou *d* to the right hand, then I will
49:10 the sceptre shall not *d* from Judah
Num. 12:10 and the cloud *d* from off the tabernacle
14:9 their defense is *d* from them, and the LORD
Deut. 9:7 thou didst *d* out of the land of Egypt
1 Sam. 16:14 the Spirit of the LORD *d* from Saul
2 Sam. 7:15 but my mercy shall not *d* away from him
22:22 (Ps. 18:21) have not wickedly *d* from my God
1 Kgs. 12:16 so Israel *d* unto their tents
Job 7:19 how long wilt thou not *d* from me, nor let
21:14 therefore they say unto God, *D* from us
28:28 and to *d* from evil is understanding
Ps. 6:8 (Mt. 7:23; Lk. 13:27) *d* from me, all ye
34:14 (37:27) *d* from evil, and do good; seek peace
105:38 Egypt was glad when they *d*: for the fear
Prov. 3:7 fear the LORD, and *d* from evil
15:24 the wise, that he may *d* from hell beneath
16:17 highway of the upright is to *d* from evil
22:6 and when he is old, he will not *d* from it
27:22 yet will not his foolishness *d* from him
Is. 52:11 *d* ye, *d* ye, go ye out from thence, touch
54:10 my kindness shall not *d* from thee
Jer. 6:8 Jerusalem, lest my soul *d* from thee
Lam. 4:15 *d* ye; it is unclean; *d*, *d*, touch not
Mic. 2:10 arise ye, and *d*; for this is not your rest
Mt. 7:23 (Lk. 13:27) *d* from me, ye that work iniquity
8:18 gave commandment to *d* unto the other side

Mt. 8:34 (Mk. 5:17; Lk. 8:37) *d* out of their coasts
10:14 (Mk. 6:11) when ye *d* out of that house
14:16 they need not *d*; give ye them to eat
25:41 *d* from me, ye cursed, into everlasting fire
Lk. 2:29 now lettest thou thy servant *d* in peace
4:13 the temptation, he *d* from him for a season
5:8 *d* from me; for I am a sinful man, O Lord
21:21 let them which are in the midst of it *d*
Jn. 13:1 that he should *d* out of this world unto
Acts 13:13 (15:38) in Pamphylia. . John *d* from them
15:39 that they *d* asunder one from the other
16:36 have sent to let you go: now therefore *d*
28:10 when we *d*, they laded us with such things
1 Cor. 7:10 let not the wife *d* from her husband
7:15 but if the unbelieving *d*, let him *d*
2 Cor. 12:8 Lord thrice, that it might *d* from me
Phil. 1:23 having a desire to *d*, and to be with Christ
1 Tim. 4:1 shall *d* from the faith, giving heed to
2 Tim. 2:19 the name of Christ *d* from iniquity
Jas. 2:16 *d* in peace, be ye warmed and filled
Rev. 6:14 heaven *d* as a scroll when it is rolled

Departing

Dan. 9:5 even by *d* from thy precepts and from thy
Acts 20:29 after my *d* shall grievous wolves enter
Heb. 3:12 of unbelief, in *d* from the living God

Departure

Ezek. 26:18 the isles. . shall be troubled at thy *d*
2 Tim. 4:6 and the time of my *d* is at hand

Deprive

Gen. 27:45 why should I be *d* also of you both in
Job 39:17 God hath *d* her of wisdom, neither hath
Is. 38:10 I am *d* of the residue of my years

Depth

Ex. 15:5 the *d* have covered them: they sank into
15:8 were congealed in the heart of the sea
Job 28:14 *d* saith, It is not in me: and the sea
Ps. 33:7 he layeth up the *d* in storehouses
77:16 they were afraid: the *d* also were troubled
106:9 so he led them through the *d*, as through
107:26 the heaven, they go down again to the *d*
130:1 out of the *d* have I cried unto thee
Prov. 8:24 when there were no *d*, I was brought
8:27 he set a compass upon the face of the *d*
25:3 the heaven for height, and the earth for *d*
Is. 7:11 ask it either in the *d*, or in the height
51:10 the *d* of the sea a way for the ransomed
Jon. 2:5 the *d* closed me round about
Mic. 7:19 thou wilt cast all their sins into the *d*
Mt. 18:6 that he were drowned in the *d* of the sea
Mk. 4:5 it sprang up, because it had no *d* of earth
Rom. 8:39 height, nor *d*, nor any other creature
11:33 the *d* of the riches both of the wisdom and
Eph. 3:18 what is the breadth, and length, and *d*
Rev. 2:24 and which have not known the *d* of Satan

Deputy

1 Kgs. 22:47 then no king in Edom: a *d* was king
Esth. 8:9 to the lieutenants, and the *d* and rulers
Acts 13:8 to turn away the *d* from the faith
18:12 when Gallio was the *d* of Achaia, the Jews
19:38 the law is open, and there are *d*: let them

Derbe Acts 14:6, 20–21; 16:1

Deride

Hab. 1:10 they shall *d* every stronghold
Lk. 16:14 Pharisees. . heard all these things. . *d* him
23:35 rulers also with them *d* him, saying, He

Derision *See also* Contempt, Reproach, Scorn

Job 30:1 they that are younger than I have me in *d*
Ps. 2:4 shall laugh: the LORD shall have them in *d*
44:13 (79:4) our neighbors, a scorn and a *d* to them
59:8 thou shalt have all the heathen in *d*
119:51 the proud have had me greatly in *d*
Jer. 20:7 I am in *d* daily, every one mocketh me
20:8 was made a reproach unto me, and a *d*, daily
Lam. 3:14 I was a *d* to all my people
Ezek. 23:32 shalt be laughed to scorn and had in *d*
36:4 a prey and *d* to the residue of the heathen
Hos. 7:16 shall be their *d* in the land of Egypt

Descend *See also* Fall, Light

Gen. 28:12 the angels of God ascending and *d* on it
Ex. 19:18 on a smoke, because the LORD *d* upon it
34:5 the LORD *d* in the cloud, and stood with him
1 Sam. 26:10 or he shall *d* into battle, and perish
Ps. 49:17 his glory shall not *d* after him
133:3 the dew that *d* upon the mountains of Zion
Prov. 30:4 who hath ascended up into heaven, or *d*?
Ezek. 26:20 (31:16) with them that *d* into the pit
Mt. 3:16 (Lk. 3:22; Jn. 1:32) Spirit. . *d* like a dove
7:25 and the rain *d*, and the floods came
28:2 angel of the Lord *d* from heaven, and came
Mk. 1:10 and the Spirit like a dove *d* upon him
15:32 the King of Israel *d* now from the cross
Jn. 1:33 upon whom thou shalt see the Spirit *d*
1:51 angels. . ascending and *d* upon the Son of man
Acts 10:11 (11:5) a certain vessel *d* unto him, as it
Rom. 10:7 or, Who shall *d* into the deep?
Eph. 4:10 he that *d* is the same also that ascended
1 Thes. 4:16 Lord himself shall *d* from heaven with
Jas. 3:15 wisdom *d* not from above, but is earthly
Rev. 21:10 holy Jerusalem, *d* out of heaven from

Descent

Lk. 19:37 even now at the *d* of the mount of Olives
Heb. 7:3 without father, without mother, without *d*
7:6 he whose *d* is not counted from them received

Describe

Josh. 18:4 go through the land, and *d* it according
Judg. 8:14 he *d* unto him the princes of Succoth
Rom. 4:6 David also *d* the blessedness of the man
10:5 for Moses *d* the righteousness. . of the law

Desert *See also* Wilderness

Ex. 3:1 he led the flock to the back side of the *d*
5:3 three days' journey into the *d*, and sacrifice
19:2 come to the *d* of Sinai. . there Israel camped
Deut. 32:10 he found him in a *d* land, and in the
Ps. 78:40 the wilderness, and grieve him in the *d*!
102:6 I am like an owl of the *d*
106:14 and tempted God in the *d*
Is. 13:21 but wild beasts of the *d* shall lie there
34:14 wild beasts of the *d* shall also meet with
35:1 *d* shall rejoice, and blossom as the rose
35:6 waters break out, and streams in the *d*
40:3 make straight in the *d* a highway for our God
43:19 way in the wilderness, and rivers in the *d*
51:3 Eden, and her *d* like the garden of the LORD
Jer. 2:6 through a land of *d* and of pits
17:6 he shall be like the heath in the *d*
25:24 of the mingled people that dwell in the *d*
50:39 wild beasts of the *d* with the wild beasts
Ezek. 13:4 prophets are like the foxes in the *d*
Mt. 14:13 (Mk. 6:32; Lk. 9:10) by ship into a *d*
24:26 behold, he is in the *d*; go not forth
Lk. 1:80 was in the *d* till the day of his showing
Jn. 6:31 our fathers did eat manna in the *d*

Heb. 11:38 they wandered in *d*, and in mountains

Deserve

Ezra 9:13 punished us less than our iniquities *d*
Job 11:6 God exacteth. . less than thine iniquity *d*

Desire *See also* Covet, Purpose, Wish

Gen. 3:6 a tree to be *d* to make one wise
Deut. 7:25 thou shalt not *d* the silver or gold
18:6 and come with all the *d* of his mind unto
1 Sam. 12:13 king whom ye have chosen. . ye have *d*!
2 Sam. 23:5 this is all my salvation, and all my *d*
1 Kgs. 2:20 then she said, I *d* one small petition
2 Chr. 15:15 and sought him with their whole *d*
21:20 eight years, and departed without being *d*
Neh. 1:11 of thy servants, who *d* to fear thy name
Job 13:3 the Almighty, and I *d* to reason with God
14:15 wilt have a *d* to the work of thine hands
31:16 if I have withheld the poor from their *d*
31:35 my *d* is, that the Almighty would answer me
Ps. 10:3 for the wicked boasteth of his heart's *d*
10:17 LORD, thou hast heard the *d* of the humble
19:10 more to be *d* are they than gold, yea, than
21:2 thou hast given him his heart's *d*, and hast
27:4 one thing have I *d* of the LORD, that will I
34:12 what man is he that *d* life, and loveth
37:4 and he shall give thee the *d* of thine heart
38:9 all my *d* is before thee; and my groaning is
40:6 sacrifice and offering thou didst not *d*
45:11 shall the King greatly *d* thy beauty
51:6 behold, thou *d* truth in the inward parts
51:16 thou *d* not sacrifice; else would I give it
54:7 mine eye hath seen his *d* upon mine enemies
59:10 shall let me see my *d* upon mine enemies
73:25 is none upon earth that I *d* besides thee
92:11 my *d* on mine enemies. . my *d* of the wicked
112:10 the *d* of the wicked shall perish
145:16 satisfiest the *d* of every living thing
145:19 will fulfil the *d* of them that fear him
Prov. 3:15 canst *d* are not to be compared unto her
10:24 the *d* of the righteous shall be granted
11:23 the *d* of the righteous is only good
13:4 soul of the sluggard *d*, and hath nothing
13:12 when the *d* cometh, it is a tree of life
13:19 the *d* accomplished is sweet to the soul
21:10 the soul of the wicked *d* evil
21:25 the *d* of the slothful killeth him
Eccl. 6:2 wanteth nothing. . of all that he *d*
6:9 is the sight. . than the wandering of the *d*
12:5 *d* shall fail: because man goeth to his long
Is. 26:8 the *d* of our soul is to thy name
53:2 there is no beauty that we should *d* him
Jer. 22:27 to the land whereunto they *d* to return
Ezek. 24:16 I take away from thee the *d* of thine
Dan. 2:18 that they would *d* mercies of the God of
Hos. 6:6 for I *d* mercy, and not sacrifice
Mic. 7:3 great man, he uttereth his mischievous *d*
Hab. 2:5 enlargeth his *d* as hell, and is as death
Hag. 2:7 *D* of all nations shall come: and I will
Mt. 13:17 (Lk. 10:24) righteous men have *d* to see
16:1 *d* him that he would show them a sign from
20:20 worshipping him, and *d* a certain thing of
Mk. 9:35 man *d* to be first, the same shall be last
10:35 shouldest do for us whatsoever we shall *d*
11:24 things soever ye *d*, when ye pray, believe
15:6 (Lk. 23:25) one prisoner, whomsoever they *d*
Lk. 16:21 *d* to be fed with the crumbs which fell
17:22 *d* to see one of the days of the Son of man
20:46 the scribes, which *d* to walk in long robes
22:15 with *d* I have *d* to eat this passover with
22:31 Simon, behold, Satan hath *d* to have you

Acts 3:14 ye denied the Holy One. . and *d* a murderer
13:7 Sergius Paulus. . *d* to hear the word of God
19:31 *d* him that he would not adventure himself
23:20 said, The Jews have agreed to *d* thee that
Rom. 10:1 *d* and prayer to God for Israel is, that
15:23 great *d* these many years to come unto you
1 Cor. 14:1 after charity, and *d* spiritual gifts
2 Cor. 5:2 we groan, earnestly *d* to be clothed
7:7 he told us your earnest *d*, your mourning
8:6 that we *d* Titus, that as he had begun, so he
Gal. 4:9 whereunto ye *d* again to be in bondage?
4:20 I *d* to be present with you now
4:21 tell me, ye that *d* to be under the law, do
6:12 as *d* to make a fair show in the flesh
Eph. 2:3 fulfilling the *d* of the flesh
3:13 I *d* that ye faint not at my tribulations
Phil. 1:23 having a *d* to depart, and to be with Christ
4:17 not because I *d* a gift: but I *d* fruit that
1 Tim. 1:7 *d* to be teachers of the law
3:1 *d* the office of a bishop, he *d* a good work
Heb. 11:16 *d* a better country, that is, a heavenly
Jas. 4:2 ye kill, and *d* to have, and cannot obtain
1 Pet. 1:12 which things the angels *d* to look into
2:2 babes, *d* the sincere milk of the word
1 Jn. 5:15 we have the petitions that we *d* of him
Rev. 9:6 *d* to die, and death shall flee from them

Desirous

Prov. 23:3 be not *d* of his dainties: for they are
Lk. 23:8 exceeding glad: for he was *d* to see him
Jn. 16:19 Jesus knew that they were *d* to ask him
2 Cor. 11:32 with a garrison, *d* to apprehend me
Gal. 5:26 let us not be *d* of vainglory, provoking
1 Thes. 2:8 so being affectionately *d* of you, we

Desolate *See also* Solitary, Waste

Gen. 47:19 and not die, that the land be not *d*
Lev. 26:33 land shall be *d*, and your cities waste
2 Chr. 36:21 as long as she lay *d* she kept sabbath
Ps. 25:16 mercy upon me; for I am *d* and afflicted
34:22 none of them that trust in him shall be *d*
40:15 let them be *d* for a reward of their shame
69:25 (Acts 1:20) let their habitation be *d*
143:4 spirit overwhelmed. . heart within me is *d*
Is. 1:7 your country is *d*, your cities are burned
24:6 they that dwell therein are *d*
49:8 to cause to inherit the *d* heritages
49:19 for thy waste and thy *d* places
49:21 seeing I have lost my children, and am *d*
54:1 (Gal. 4:27) more are the children of the *d*
59:10 we are in *d* places as dead men
62:4 neither shall thy land any more be termed *D*
Jer. 2:12 afraid, be ye very *d*, saith the LORD
4:7 to make thy land *d*; and thy cities shall be
4:27 the whole land shall be *d*; yet will I not
6:8 my soul depart from thee; lest I make thee *d*
12:10 made my pleasant portion a *d* wilderness
18:16 make their land *d*, and a perpetual hissing
32:43 (33:12) it is *d* without man or beast
46:19 for Noph shall be waste and *d* without an
Ezek. 6:6 waste, and the high places shall be *d*
15:8 I will make the land *d*, because they have
32:15 when I shall make the land of Egypt *d*
33:28 I will lay the land most *d*, and the pomp
Dan. 11:31 place the abomination that maketh *d*
Hos. 13:16 Samaria shall become *d*; for she hath
Joel 2:3 and behind them a *d* wilderness
Mic. 6:13 in making thee *d* because of thy sins
Zech. 7:14 thus the land was *d* after them, that no
Mal. 1:4 but we will return and build the *d* places
Mt. 23:38 (Lk. 13:35) your house is left unto you *d*
1 Tim. 5:5 a widow indeed, and *d*, trusteth in God
Rev. 18:19 great city. . in one hour is she made *d*

Desolation *See also* Destruction, Ruin, Waste

Lev. 26:31 and bring your sanctuaries unto *d*
Josh. 8:28 Joshua burnt Ai, and made it. . even a *d*
2 Kgs. 22:19 they should become a *d* and a curse
Ezra 9:9 repair the *d* thereof, and to give us a wall
Job 30:14 in the *d* they rolled themselves upon me
Ps. 46:8 what *d* he hath made in the earth
    73:19 are they brought into *d*, as in a moment!
    74:3 lift up thy feet unto the perpetual *d*
Prov. 1:27 when your fear cometh as *d*
    3:25 sudden fear, neither of the *d* of the wicked
Is. 17:9 in that day. . there shall be *d*
    47:11 and *d* shall come upon thee suddenly
    61:4 they shall raise up the former *d*
Jer. 25:9 astonishment. . a hissing, and perpetual *d*
    25:11 and this whole land shall be a *d*, and an
    25:12 Chaldeans, and will make it perpetual *d*
    50:23 Babylon become a *d* among the nations!
Lam. 3:47 snare is come upon us, *d* and destruction
Ezek. 23:33 with the cup of astonishment and *d*
    35:9 I will make thee perpetual *d*, and thy cities
Dan. 8:13 sacrifice, and the transgression of *d*
    9:2 would accomplish seventy years in the *d*
    9:18 my God. . open thine eyes, and behold our *d*
    9:26 unto the end of the war *d* are determined
Zeph. 1:15 and distress, a day of wasteness and *d*
Mt. 12:25 (Lk. 11:17) kingdom divided. . brought to *d*
    24:15 (Mk. 13:14) shall see the abomination of *d*
Lk. 21:20 then know that the *d* thereof is nigh

Despair

1 Sam. 27:1 and Saul shall *d* of me, to seek me
Eccl. 2:20 to cause my heart to *d* of all the labor
2 Cor. 1:8 we were pressed. . that we *d* even of life.
    4:8 we are perplexed, but not in *d*

Desperate

Job 6:26 words, and the speeches of one that is *d*
Is. 17:11 heap in the day of grief and of *d* sorrow

Desperately

Jer. 17:9 heart is deceitful. . and *d* wicked

Despise *See also* Abhor, Contemn, Detest, Disdain, Hate, Loathe, Scorn

Gen. 16:4 she had conceived, her mistress was *d* in
    25:34 thus Esau *d* his birthright
Lev. 26:15 if ye shall *d* my statutes, or if your
Num. 11:20 because that ye have *d* the LORD which
    15:31 because he hath *d* the word of the LORD
1 Sam. 2:30 that *d* me shall be lightly esteemed
2 Sam. 6:16 (1 Chr. 15:29) David leaping. . she *d* him
2 Kgs. 19:21 (Is. 37:22) daughter of Zion. . *d* thee
Neh. 4:4 hear, O our God; for we are *d*: and turn
Esth. 1:17 so that they shall *d* their husbands
Job 5:17 *d* not. . the chastening of the Almighty
    12:5 *d* in the thought of him that is at ease
    19:18 yea, young children *d* me
    36:5 behold, God is mighty, and *d* not any
Ps. 22:6 a reproach of men, and *d* of the people
    51:17 a contrite heart, O God, thou wilt not *d*
    53:5 put them to shame, because God hath *d* them
    73:20 thou awakest, thou shalt *d* their image
    102:17 of the destitute, and not *d* their prayer
    119:141 I am small and *d*: yet do not I forget
Prov. 1:7 but fools *d* wisdom and instruction
    1:30 none of my counsel: they *d* all my reproof
    3:11 (Heb. 12:5) *d* not the chastening of the LORD
    5:12 I hated instruction, and my heart *d* reproof
    6:30 do not *d* a thief, if he steal to satisfy

Prov. 11:12 he that is void of wisdom *d* his neighbor
    12:9 he that is *d*, and hath a servant is better
    13:13 whoso *d* the word shall be destroyed
    14:21 he that *d* his neighbor sinneth: but he
    15:5 a fool *d* his father's instruction
    15:20 but a foolish man *d* his mother
    15:32 that refuseth instruction *d* his own soul
    19:16 but he that *d* his ways shall die
    23:22 and *d* not thy mother when she is old
    30:17 mocketh at his father, and *d* to obey his
Eccl. 9:16 poor man's wisdom is *d*, and his words
Is. 5:24 and *d* the word of the Holy One of Israel
    30:12 ye *d* this word, and trust in oppression
    33:15 he that *d* the gain of oppressions
    49:7 thus saith the LORD. . to him whom man *d*
    53:3 is *d* and rejected of men; a man of sorrows
Jer. 4:30 thyself fair; thy lovers will *d* thee
    49:15 I will make thee small. . and *d* among men
Ezek. 20:13 my statutes, and they *d* my judgments
    22:8 hast *d* mine holy things, and hast profaned
Amos 2:4 because they have *d* the law of the LORD
    5:21 I hate, I *d* your feast days, and I will not
Zech. 4:10 for who hath *d* the day of small things?
Mal. 1:6 *d* my name. And ye say, Wherein have we *d*
Mt. 6:24 (Lk. 16:13) hold to the one, and *d* the other
    18:10 *d* not one of these little ones
Lk. 10:16 *d* you *d* me; and he that *d* me *d* him that
    18:9 trusted. . they were righteous, and *d* others
Acts 19:27 temple of. . goddess Diana should be *d*
Rom. 2:4 or *d* thou the riches of his goodness and
    14:3 him that eateth *d* him that eateth not
1 Cor. 1:28 things which are *d*, hath God chosen
    4:10 are strong; ye are honorable, but we are *d*
    11:22 or *d* ye the church of God, and shame them
    16:11 let no man therefore *d* him: but conduct
Gal. 4:14 my temptation. . in my flesh ye *d* not
1 Thes. 4:8 that *d*, not man, but God, who hath
    5:20 *d* not prophesyings
1 Tim. 4:12 let no man *d* thy youth; but be thou an
    6:2 have believing masters, let them not *d* them
Tit. 2:15 with all authority. Let no man *d* thee
Heb. 10:28 he that *d* Moses' law died without mercy
    12:2 endured the cross, *d* the shame, and is set
    12:5 *d* not thou the chastening of the LORD, nor
Jas. 2:6 but ye have *d* the poor
2 Pet. 2:10 lust of uncleanness, and *d* government
Jude 8 *d* dominion, and speak evil of dignities

Despiser

Acts 13:41 behold, ye *d*, and wonder, and perish
2 Tim. 3:3 fierce, *d* of those that are good

Despite

Ezek. 25:6 all thy *d* against the land of Israel
Heb. 10:29 hath done *d* unto the Spirit of grace?

Despiteful

Rom. 1:30 backbiters, haters of God, *d*, proud

Despitefully

Mt. 5:44 (Lk. 6:28) pray for them which *d* use you
Acts 14:5 rulers, to use them *d*, and to stone them

Destitute *See also* Needy, Poor

Gen. 24:27 hath not left *d* my master of his mercy
Ps. 102:17 he will regard the prayer of the *d*
    141:8 in thee is my trust; leave not my soul *d*
Prov. 15:21 folly is joy to him that is *d* of wisdom
Ezek. 32:15 Egypt desolate. . the country shall be *d*
1 Tim. 6:5 of corrupt minds, and *d* of the truth
Heb. 11:37 wandered. . being *d*, afflicted, tormented
Jas. 2:15 naked, and *d* of daily food

Destroy *See also* Kill, Perish, Slay, Waste

Gen. 6:7 and the LORD said, I will *d* man whom I
7:23 every living substance was *d* which was upon
9:11 there any more be a flood to *d* the earth
13:10 before the LORD *d* Sodom and Gomorrah
18:23 thou also *d* the righteous with the wicked?
18:32 he said, I will not *d* it for ten's sake
Ex. 22:20 unto any god . . he shall be utterly *d*
23:27 *d* all the people to whom thou shalt come
34:13 (Deut. 7:5) ye shall *d* their altars, break
Num. 33:52 *d* all their pictures, and *d* all . . images
Deut. 2:21 tall, as the Anakim . . the LORD *d* them
4:31 he will not forsake thee, neither *d* thee
7:2 thou shalt smite them, and utterly *d* them
9:14 let me alone, that I may *d* them, and blot
9:26 I prayed . . and said, O LORD God, *d* not thy
12:2 ye shall utterly *d* all the places, wherein
Josh. 7:12 except ye *d* the accursed from among you
Judg. 21:17 that a tribe be not *d* out of Israel
1 Sam. 15:6 the Amalekites, lest I *d* you with them
2 Sam. 1:14 thine hand to *d* the LORD's anointed?
22:41 (Ps. 18:40) that I might *d* them that hate me
24:16 (1 Chr. 21:15) hand upon Jerusalem to *d*
2 Kgs. 8:19 (2 Chr. 21:7) LORD would not *d* Judah for
10:28 thus Jehu *d* Baal out of Israel
18:25 (Is. 36:10) up against this land, and *d* it
1 Chr. 21:15 sent an angel unto Jerusalem to *d* it
Ezra 6:12 *d* all kings and people, that shall put
Esth. 3:6 wherefore Haman sought to *d* all the Jews
7:4 for we are sold, I and my people, to be *d*
Job 2:3 against him, to *d* him without cause
6:9 even that it would please God to *d* me
9:22 I said it, He *d* the perfect and the wicked
10:8 thine hands have made me . . yet thou dost *d*
14:19 and thou *d* the hope of man
19:10 he hath *d* me on every side, and I am gone
19:26 and though after my skin worms *d* this body
Ps. 5:10 *d* thou them, O God; let them fall by their
9:5 rebuked the heathen, thou hast *d* the wicked
11:3 if the foundations be *d*, what can the
21:10 their fruit shalt thou *d* from the earth
37:38 but the transgressors shall be *d* together
63:9 but those that seek my soul, to *d* it, shall
78:47 he *d* their vines with hail, and their
101:8 I will early *d* all the wicked of the land
145:20 but all the wicked will he *d*
Prov. 1:32 the prosperity of fools shall *d* them
6:32 adultery . . he that doeth it *d* his own soul
13:13 whoso despiseth the word shall be *d*
13:20 but a companion of fools shall be *d*
13:23 there is that is *d* for want of judgment
15:25 LORD will *d* the house of the proud
21:7 the robbery of the wicked shall *d* them
Eccl. 7:7 a wise man mad; and a gift *d* the heart
9:18 but one sinner *d* much good
Is. 9:16 and they that are led of them are *d*
11:9 (65:25) not hurt nor *d* in all my holy mountain
13:9 land desolate: and he shall *d* the sinners
19:3 I will *d* the counsel thereof: and they shall
65:8 saith, *D* it not; for a blessing is in it
Jer. 1:10 to *d*, and to throw down, to build, and to
6:5 let us go by night, and let us *d* her palaces
12:10 many pastors have *d* my vineyard, they have
12:17 pluck up and *d* that nation, saith the LORD
15:7 I will *d* my people, since they return not
17:18 and *d* them with double destruction
23:1 woe be unto the pastors that *d* and scatter
48:42 and Moab shall be *d* from being a people
Lam. 2:8 the LORD hath purposed to *d* the wall
Ezek. 9:8 wilt thou *d* all the residue of Israel in
22:27 and to *d* souls, to get dishonest gain
25:7 I will *d* thee; and thou shalt know that I

Ezek. 26:17 how art thou *d*, that wast inhabited
28:16 and I will *d* thee, O covering cherub, from
34:16 I will *d* the fat and the strong; I will
Dan. 2:44 set up a kingdom, which shall never be *d*
8:24 he shall *d* wonderfully, and shall prosper
Hos. 2:12 and I will *d* her vines and her fig trees
4:6 my people are *d* for lack of knowledge
13:9 O Israel, thou hast *d* thyself; but in me is
Amos 9:8 I will not utterly *d* the house of Jacob
Mt. 2:13 Herod will seek the young child to *d* him
5:17 think not that I am come to *d* the law
10:28 fear him which is able to *d* both soul and
12:14 (Mk. 3:6) against him, how they might *d* him
21:41 (Mk. 12:9; Lk. 20:16) *d* those wicked men
22:7 *d* those murderers, and burned up their city
26:61 (Mk. 14:58) I am able to *d* the temple of God
27:20 that they should ask Barabbas, and *d* Jesus
27:40 (Mk. 15:29) thou that *d* the temple, and
Mk. 1:24 (Lk. 4:34) art thou come to *d* us?
11:18 (Lk. 19:47) and sought how they might *d* him
Lk. 6:9 or to do evil? to save life, or to *d* it?
9:56 the Son of man is not come to *d* men's lives
17:27 and the flood came, and *d* them all
Jn. 2:19 *d* this temple, and in three days I will
Acts 3:23 will not hear that Prophet, shall be *d*
9:21 is not this he that *d* them which called on
Rom. 6:6 that the body of sin might be *d*
14:15 *d* not him with thy meat, for whom Christ
1 Cor. 1:19 I will *d* the wisdom of the wise
3:17 defile the temple of God, him shall God *d*
6:13 belly for meats: but God shall *d* both it
10:9 as some . . tempted, and were *d* of serpents
15:26 the last enemy that shall be *d* is death
2 Cor. 4:9 but not forsaken; cast down, but not *d*
Gal. 1:23 now preacheth the faith which once he *d*
2:18 for if I build again the things which I *d*
2 Thes. 2:8 *d* with the brightness of his coming
Heb. 2:14 through death he might *d* him that had
Jas. 4:12 lawgiver, who is able to save and to *d*
2 Pet. 2:12 brute beasts made to be taken and *d*
1 Jn. 3:8 that he might *d* the works of the devil
Jude 5 afterward *d* them that believed not
Rev. 11:18 and shouldest *d* them which *d* the earth

Destroyer

Ex. 12:23 and will not suffer the *d* to come in
Judg. 16:24 our enemy, and the *d* of our country
Job 15:21 in prosperity the *d* shall come upon him
33:22 near unto the grave, and his life to the *d*
Ps. 17:4 I have kept me from the paths of the *d*
Prov. 28:24 whoso robbeth . . is the companion of a *d*
Is. 49:17 *d* and they that made thee waste shall go
Jer. 22:7 I will prepare *d* against thee, every one
50:11 O ye *d* of mine heritage, because ye are
1 Cor. 10:10 murmured, and were destroyed of the *d*

Destruction *See also* Ruin, Slaughter

Deut. 7:23 and shall destroy them with a mighty *d*
32:24 devoured with . . heat, and with bitter *d*
1 Kgs. 20:42 a man whom I appointed to utter *d*
2 Chr. 22:4 for they were his counselors . . to his *d*
26:16 strong, his heart was lifted up to his *d*
Esth. 8:6 can I endure to see the *d* of my kindred?
Job 5:21 neither shalt thou be afraid of *d* when it
18:12 hunger-bitten, and *d* shall be ready at his
21:17 and how oft cometh their *d* upon them!
21:20 his eyes shall see his *d*, and he shall
21:30 the wicked is reserved to the day of *d*?
26:6 hell is naked before him . . *d* hath no covering
31:3 is not *d* to the wicked?
31:23 for *d* from God was a terror to me
31:29 if I rejoiced at the *d* of him that hated me
Ps. 9:6 thou enemy, *d* are come to a perpetual end

Ps. 35:8 let *d* come upon him at unawares
   55:23 shalt bring them down into the pit of *d*
   73:18 thou castedst them down into *d*
   88:11 in the grave? or thy faithfulness in *d*?
   90:3 thou turnest man to *d*; and sayest, Return
   91:6 nor for the *d* that wasteth at noonday
   103:4 who redeemeth thy life from *d*
Prov. 1:27 and your *d* cometh as a whirlwind
   10:14 but the mouth of the foolish is near *d*
   10:15 the *d* of the poor is their poverty
   10:29 (21:15) *d* shall be to the workers of iniquity
   14:28 the want of people is the *d* of the prince
   15:11 hell and *d* are before the LORD
   16:18 pride goeth before *d*, and a haughty spirit
   17:19 and he that exalteth his gate seeketh *d*
   18:7 a fool's mouth is his *d*, and his lips are
   18:12 before *d* the heart of man is haughty
   24:2 their heart studieth *d*, and their lips talk
   27:20 hell and *d* are never full; so the eyes of
   31:8 the cause of all such as are appointed to *d*
Is. 1:28 *d* of the transgressors and of the sinners
   13:6 it shall come as a *d* from the Almighty
   14:23 and I will sweep it with the besom of *d*
   19:18 one shall be called, The city of *d*
   49:19 thy desolate places, and the land of thy *d*
   59:7 (Rom. 3:16) wasting and *d* are in their paths
   60:18 wasting nor *d* within thy borders
Jer. 4:20 *d* upon *d* is cried: for the whole land is
   17:18 and destroy them with double *d*
   46:20 but *d* cometh; it cometh out of the north
   50:22 of battle is in the land, and of great *d*
Lam. 2:11 (3:48) the *d* of the daughter of my people
   4:10 meat in the *d* of the daughter of my people
Ezek. 7:25 *d* cometh; and they shall seek peace
   32:9 I shall bring thy *d* among the nations
Hos. 13:14 thy plagues; O grave, I will be thy *d*
Obad. 12 children of Judah in the day of their *d*
Zech. 14:11 there shall be no more utter *d*
Mt. 7:13 and broad is the way, that leadeth to *d*
Rom. 3:16 *d* and misery are in their ways
   9:22 endured . . the vessels of wrath fitted to *d*
1 Cor. 5:5 unto Satan for the *d* of the flesh
2 Cor. 10:8 for edification, and not for your *d*
   13:10 hath given me to edification, and not to *d*
1 Thes. 5:3 safety; then sudden *d* cometh upon them
2 Thes. 1:9 shall be punished with everlasting *d*
1 Tim. 6:9 hurtful lusts, which drown men in *d* and
2 Pet. 2:1 and bring upon themselves swift *d*
   3:16 also the other Scriptures, unto their own *d*

Determinate

Acts 2:23 delivered by the *d* counsel . . of God

Determination

Zeph. 3:8 for my *d* is to gather the nations

Determine *See also* Purpose

Ex. 21:22 and he shall pay as the judges *d*
1 Sam. 20:7 then be sure that evil is *d* by him
2 Chr. 2:1 Solomon *d* to build a house for the name
   25:16 I know that God hath *d* to destroy thee
Job 14:5 seeing his days are *d*, the number of his
Is. 19:17 counsel . . which he hath *d* against it
Dan. 9:24 seventy weeks are *d* upon thy people
   11:36 for that that is *d* shall be done
Lk. 22:22 Son of man goeth, as it was *d*: but woe
Acts 3:13 Pilate, when he was *d* to let him go
   4:28 to do whatsoever thy hand and thy counsel *d*
   15:2 they *d* that Paul and Barnabas, and certain
   15:37 Barnabas to take with them John
   17:26 and hath *d* the times before appointed
   19:39 other matters . . be *d* in a lawful assembly
1 Cor. 2:2 for I *d* not to know any thing among you
2 Cor. 2:1 I *d* this with myself, that I would not

Detest *See also* Abhor, Contemn, Despise, Disdain, Hate, Loathe, Scorn

Deut. 7:26 thou shalt utterly *d* it, and thou shalt

Detestable

Jer. 16:18 the carcasses of their *d* and abominable
Ezek. 5:11 defiled my sanctuary with all thy *d*
   11:18 and they shall take away all the *d* things
   37:23 with their idols, nor with their *d* things

Device *See also* Imagination, Invention

2 Chr. 2:14 every *d* which shall be put to him
Esth. 8:3 that he had devised against the Jews
   9:25 he commanded by letters that his wicked *d*
Job 5:12 he disappointeth the *d* of the crafty
   21:27 *d* which ye wrongfully imagine against me
Ps. 10:2 be taken in the *d* that they have imagined
   21:11 they imagined a mischievous *d*, which they
   33:10 maketh the *d* of the people of none effect
   37:7 of the man who bringeth wicked *d* to pass
   140:8 further not his wicked *d*; lest they exalt
Prov. 1:31 own way, and be filled with their own *d*
   12:2 but a man of wicked *d* will he condemn
   19:21 there are many *d* in a man's heart
Eccl. 9:10 there is no work, nor *d*, nor knowledge
Is. 32:7 he deviseth wicked *d* to destroy the poor
Jer. 11:19 they had devised *d* against me, saying
   18:11 I frame evil against you, and devise a *d*
   18:12 no hope: but we will walk after our own *d*
Lam. 3:62 and their *d* against me all the day
Dan. 11:24 forecast his *d* against the strongholds
Acts 17:29 or stone, graven by art and man's *d*
2 Cor. 2:11 for we are not ignorant of his *d*

Devil *See also* Satan, Unclean

Lev. 17:7 no more offer their sacrifices unto *d*
Deut. 32:17 (1 Cor. 10:20) sacrificed unto *d*, not to
2 Chr. 11:15 for the high places, and for the *d*
Ps. 106:37 their sons and their daughters unto *d*
Mt. 4:1 (Lk. 4:2) wilderness to be tempted of the *d*
   4:5 then the *d* taketh him up into the holy city
   4:11 (Lk. 4:13) then the *d* leaveth him
   4:24 and those which were possessed with *d*
   7:22 and in thy name have cast out *d*
   8:31 (Mk. 5:12) *d* besought him, saying, If thou cast
   9:32 (Lk. 11:14) a dumb man possessed with a *d*
   9:34 (12:24; Mk. 3:22; Lk. 11:15) he casteth out *d* through the prince of the *d*
   11:18 (Lk. 7:33) they say, He hath a *d*
   12:24 (Mk. 3:22; Lk. 11:15) doth not cast out *d*, but by Beelzebub the prince of the *d*
   12:28 but if I cast out *d* by the Spirit of God
   13:39 the enemy that sowed them is the *d*
   15:22 (Mk. 7:26) my daughter is . . vexed with a *d*
   17:18 Jesus rebuked the *d*; and he departed out
   25:41 fire, prepared for the *d* and his angels
Mk. 1:34 (Lk. 4:41) and suffered not the *d* to speak
   3:15 power to heal sicknesses, and to cast out *d*
   7:29 unto her . . the *d* is gone out of thy daughter
   9:38 (Lk. 9:49) saw one casting out *d* in thy name
   16:9 Magdalene, out of whom he had cast seven *d*
   16:17 in my name shall they cast out *d*
Lk. 4:33 a man, which had a spirit of an unclean *d*
   4:41 and *d* also came out of many, crying out
   8:12 then cometh the *d*, and taketh away the word
   8:27 a certain man, which had *d* long time
   8:29 and was driven of the *d* into the wilderness
   9:1 and gave them power and authority over all *d*
   9:42 the *d* threw him down, and tare him
   11:20 but if I with the finger of God cast out *d*
Jn. 6:70 chosen you twelve, and one of you is a *d*?
   7:20 thou hast a *d*: who goeth about to kill thee?

Jn. 8:44 ye are of your father the *d*, and the lusts
  8:48 that thou art a Samaritan, and hast a *d*?
  10:20 he hath a *d*, and is mad; why hear ye him?
  13:2 the *d* having now put into the heart of Judas
Acts 10:38 healing all that were oppressed of the *d*
  13:10 mischief, thou child of the *d*, thou enemy
1 Cor. 10:20 they sacrifice to *d*, and not to God
Eph. 4:27 neither give place to the *d*
  6:11 be able to stand against the wiles of the *d*
1 Tim. 3:6 fall into the condemnation of the *d*
  3:7 fall into reproach and the snare of the *d*
  4:1 heed to seducing spirits, and doctrines of *d*
2 Tim. 2:26 themselves out of the snare of the *d*
Heb. 2:14 had the power of death, that is, the *d*
Jas. 2:19 the *d* also believe, and tremble
  4:7 resist the *d*, and he will flee from you
1 Pet. 5:8 your adversary the *d*, as a roaring lion
1 Jn. 3:8 committeth sin is of the *d*; for the *d*
  3:10 are manifest, and the children of the *d*
Jude 9 the archangel, when contending with the *d*
Rev. 2:10 the *d* shall cast some of you into prison
  9:20 that they should not worship *d*, and idols
  12:9 that old serpent, called the *D*, and Satan
  16:14 the spirits of *d*, working miracles, which
  18:2 Babylon. . is become the habitation of *d*
  20:2 the *D*, and Satan, and bound him a thousand
  20:10 and the *d* that deceived them was cast into

Devilish

Jas. 3:15 from above, but is earthly, sensual, *d*

Devise *See also* Device

Ex. 31:4 (35:32) *d* cunning works, to work in gold
2 Sam. 14:14 doth he *d* means, that his banished be
Ps. 31:13 against me, they *d* to take away my life
  35:4 and brought to confusion that *d* my hurt
  36:4 *d* mischief upon his bed; he setteth himself
  41:7 against me: against me do they *d* my hurt
  52:2 thy tongue *d* mischiefs; like a sharp razor
Prov. 3:29 *d* not evil against thy neighbor, seeing
  6:14 *d* mischief continually; he soweth discord
  6:18 heart that *d* wicked imaginations, feet that
  14:22 do they not err that *d* evil? but mercy and
  16:9 heart *d* his way: but the LORD directeth his
Is. 32:7 he *d* wicked devices to destroy the poor
  32:8 but the liberal *d* liberal things
Jer. 18:18 come, and let us *d* devices against
  51:12 for the LORD hath both *d* and done that
Lam. 2:17 LORD hath done that which he had *d*
Ezek. 11:2 these are the men that *d* mischief
Mic. 2:1 woe to them that *d* iniquity
2 Pet. 1:16 have not followed cunningly *d* fables

Devoted

Lev. 27:28 *d* thing is most holy unto the LORD
Num. 18:14 every thing *d* in Israel shall be thine
Ps. 119:38 unto thy servant, who is *d* to thy fear

Devotions

Acts 17:23 and beheld your *d*, I found an altar

Devour *See also* Consume, Destroy, Eat, Waste

Gen. 37:20 we will say, Some evil beast hath *d* him
  41:7 seven thin ears *d* the seven rank and full
  49:27 a wolf: in the morning he shall *d* the prey
Lev. 10:2 went out fire from the LORD, and *d* them
Deut. 32:24 burnt with hunger, and *d* with burning
2 Sam. 2:26 shall the sword *d* for ever?
  11:25 for the sword *d* one as well as another
  22:9 (Ps. 18:8) and fire out of his mouth *d*
Job 18:13 firstborn of death shall *d* his strength

Ps. 21:9 in his wrath, and the fire shall *d* them
  50:3 not keep silence: a fire shall *d* before him
  80:13 and the wild beast of the field doth *d* it
  105:35 and *d* the fruit of their ground
Prov. 19:28 and the mouth of the wicked *d* iniquity
  20:25 snare to the man who *d* that which is holy
  30:14 to *d* the poor from off the earth
Is. 1:7 your land, strangers *d* it in your presence
  1:20 rebel, ye shall be *d* with the sword
  5:24 as the fire *d* the stubble, and the flame
  9:12 and they shall *d* Israel with open mouth
  42:14 will I cry. . I will destroy and *d* at once
Jer. 3:24 shame hath *d* the labor of our fathers
  30:16 therefore all they that *d* thee shall be *d*
Ezek. 15:7 one fire, and another fire shall *d* them
  23:37 pass for them through the fire, to *d* them
  36:14 *d* men no more, neither bereave thy nations
Hos. 7:7 hot as an oven, and have *d* their judges
  8:14 upon his cities, and it shall *d* the palaces
  13:8 and there will I *d* them like a lion
Joel 2:3 a fire *d* before them; and behind them a
Amos 1:4 which shall *d* the palaces of Ben-hadad
  4:9 palmerworm *d* them: yet have ye not returned
  7:4 to contend by fire, and it *d* the great deep
Nah. 1:10 they shall be *d* as stubble fully dry
Hab. 1:13 wicked *d* the man that is more righteous
  3:14 rejoicing was as to *d* the poor secretly
Zeph. 1:18 shall be *d* by the fire of his jealousy
  3:8 all the earth shall be *d* with the fire of my
Zech. 9:4 in the sea; and she shall be *d* with fire
  9:15 they shall *d*, and subdue with sling stones
  12:6 and they shall *d* all the people round about
Mt. 13:4 (Mk. 4:4; Lk. 8:5) fowls came and *d* them up
  23:14 (Mk. 12:40; Lk. 20:47) ye *d* widows' houses
Lk. 15:30 which hath *d* thy living with harlots
2 Cor. 11:20 if a man *d* you, if a man take of you
Gal. 5:15 if ye bite and *d* one another, take heed
Heb. 10:27 indignation, which shall *d* the adversaries
1 Pet. 5:8 walketh about, seeking whom he may *d*
Rev. 20:9 and fire came down from God. . and *d*

Devout

Lk. 2:25 Simeon; and the same man was just and *d*
Acts 2:5 dwelling at Jerusalem Jews, *d* men, out of
  8:2 and *d* men carried Stephen to his burial
  10:2 *d* man, and one that feared God with all his
  10:7 and a *d* soldier of them that waited on him
  13:50 Jews stirred up the *d* and honorable women
  17:4 of the *d* Greeks a great multitude
  17:17 with the Jews, and with the *d* persons
  22:12 one Ananias, a *d* man according to the law

Dew

Gen. 27:28 God give thee of the *d* of heaven
Ex. 16:13 morning the *d* lay round about the host
Num. 11:9 *d* fell upon the camp in the night
Deut. 32:2 my speech shall distil as the *d*
  33:13 for the precious things of heaven, for the *d*
  33:28 also his heavens shall drop down *d*
Judg. 6:37 if the *d* be on the fleece only
2 Sam. 1:21 mountains of Gilboa, let there be no *d*
  17:12 we will light upon him as the *d* falleth on
1 Kgs. 17:1 shall not be *d* nor rain these years
Job 29:19 and the *d* lay all night upon my branch
  38:28 or who hath begotten the drops of *d*?
Ps. 110:3 thou hast the *d* of thy youth
  133:3 of Hermon, and as the *d* that descended
Prov. 3:20 and the clouds drop down the *d*
  19:12 but his favor is as *d* upon the grass
Song 5:2 my head is filled with *d*, and my locks
Is. 18:4 like a cloud of *d* in the heat of harvest
  26:19 for thy *d* is as the *d* of herbs
Dan. 4:15 (4:23) let it be wet with the *d* of heaven

Hos. 6:4 (13:3) and as the early *d* it goeth away
14:5 I will be as the *d* unto Israel: he shall
Mic. 5:7 as a *d* from the LORD, as the showers upon
Hag. 1:10 the heaven over you is stayed from *d*
Zech. 8:12 heavens shall give their *d*; and I will

Diadem

Job 29:14 my judgment was as a robe and a *d*
Is. 28:5 for a *d* of beauty, unto the residue of
62:3 and a royal *d* in the hand of thy God
Ezek. 21:26 thus saith the Lord GOD; Remove the *d*

Dial

2 Kgs. 20:11 (Is. 38:8) gone down in the *d* of Ahaz

Diamond

Ex. 28:18 shall be an emerald, a sapphire, and a *d*
Jer. 17:1 with the point of a *d*: it is graven upon
Ezek. 28:13 sardius, topaz, and the *d*, the beryl

Diana Acts 19:24–35

Dibon Num. 32:34; Is. 15:2; Jer. 48:18, 22

Didymus (Thomas) Jn. 11:16; 20:24; 21:2

Die *See also* Perish

Gen. 2:17 thou eatest thereof thou shalt surely *d*
3:4 said unto the woman, Ye shall not surely *d*
7:21 and all flesh *d* that moved upon the earth
25:8 Abraham . . *d* in a good old age, an old man
27:4 that my soul may bless thee before I *d*
Ex. 2:23 the king of Egypt *d*: and . . Israel sighed
9:4 and there shall nothing *d* of all that is
11:5 the firstborn in the land of Egypt shall *d*
14:11 (Num. 21:5) away to *d* in the wilderness?
16:3 would to God we had *d* by the hand of the
20:19 but let not God speak with us, lest we *d*
21:12 that smiteth a man, so that he *d*, shall be
28:43 that they bear not iniquity, and *d*
30:20 shall wash with water, that they *d* not
Lev. 7:24 the fat of the beast that *d* of itself
10:2 devoured them, and they *d* before the LORD
15:31 that they *d* not in their uncleanness
22:9 lest they bear sin for it, and *d*
Num. 4:15 not touch any holy thing, lest they *d*
14:35 in this wilderness . . and there they shall *d*
16:29 if these men *d* the common death of all men
16:49 they that *d* in the plague were fourteen
17:13 (18:22) near unto the tabernacle . . shall *d*
23:10 let me *d* the death of the righteous
26:65 they shall surely *d* in the wilderness
35:12 the manslayer *d* not, until he stand before
Deut. 5:25 now therefore why should we *d*?
13:10 stone him with stones, that he *d*
14:21 shall not eat of any thing that *d* of itself
18:20 of other gods, even that prophet shall *d*
19:11 smite him mortally that he *d*, and fleeth
25:5 (Mt. 22:24; Mk. 12:19; Lk. 20:28) and one of
them *d*, and have no child, the wife of the dead
34:5 so Moses the servant of the LORD *d* there
Judg. 13:22 surely *d*, because we have seen God
Ruth 1:17 where thou *d*, will I *d*, and there will I
1 Sam. 2:33 the increase of thine house shall *d* in
14:45 shall Jonathan *d*, who hath wrought this
25:38 that the LORD smote Nabal, that he *d*
2 Sam. 3:33 and said, *D* Abner as a fool *d*?
6:7 (1 Chr. 13:10) and there he *d* by the ark of God
12:13 hath put away thy sin; thou shalt not *d*
12:18 on the seventh day, that the child *d*
14:14 we must needs *d*, and are as water spilt on
18:33 my son Absalom! would God I had *d* for thee
1 Kgs. 3:19 and this woman's child *d* in the night
19:4 he requested for himself that he might *d*

2 Kgs. 7:3 to another, Why sit we here until we *d*?
20:1 (Is. 38:1) house in order; for thou shalt *d*
1 Chr. 10:13 so Saul *d* for his transgression which
2 Chr. 25:4 fathers shall not *d* for the children
Job 2:9 retain thine integrity? curse God, and *d*
3:11 why *d* I not from the womb? why did I not
4:21 they *d*, even without wisdom
12:2 are the people, and wisdom shall *d* with you
14:10 man *d*, and wasteth away: yea, man giveth
14:14 if a man *d*, shall he live again?
21:23 one *d* in his full strength, being wholly
21:25 another *d* in the bitterness of his soul
29:18 I shall *d* in my nest, and I shall multiply
36:12 and they shall *d* without knowledge
Ps. 41:5 when shall he *d*, and his name perish?
49:10 seeth that wise men *d*, likewise the fool
49:17 for when he *d* he shall carry nothing away
79:11 preserve . . those that are appointed to *d*
82:7 but ye shall *d* like men, and fall like one
88:15 I am afflicted and ready to *d* from my youth
104:29 thou takest away their breath, they *d*
118:17 I shall not *d*, but live, and declare the
Prov. 10:21 but fools *d* for want of wisdom
11:7 wicked man *d*, his expectation shall perish
15:10 and he that hateth reproof shall *d*
19:16 but he that despiseth his ways shall *d*
Eccl. 2:16 and how *d* the wise man? as the fool
3:2 a time to be born, and a time to *d*; a time
3:19 as the one *d*, so *d* the other; yea, they
7:17 why shouldest thou *d* before thy time?
9:5 living know that they shall *d*: but the dead
Is. 6:1 in the year that king Uzziah *d* I saw also
22:13 (1 Cor. 15:32) for tomorrow we shall *d*
51:6 that dwell therein shall *d* in like manner
65:20 for the child shall *d* a hundred years old
66:24 (Mk. 9:44, 46, 48) for their worm shall not *d*
Jer. 16:6 both the great and the small shall *d*
21:9 abideth in this city shall *d* by the sword
26:11 man is worthy to *d*; for he hath prophesied
27:13 why will ye *d*, thou and thy people
28:16 this year thou shalt *d*, because thou hast
31:30 but every one shall *d* for his own iniquity
34:5 but thou shalt *d* in peace: and with the
38:9 and he is like to *d* for hunger in
44:12 they shall *d*, from the least even unto the
Ezek. 3:18 (33:8) the wicked, Thou shalt surely *d*
3:19 (33:9) wicked way, he shall *d* in his iniquity
13:19 to slay the souls that should not *d*
18:4 (18:20) the soul that sinneth, it shall *d*
18:17 shall not *d* for the iniquity of his father
18:23 pleasure at all that the wicked should *d*?
18:31 (33:11) why will ye *d*, O house of Israel?
18:32 no pleasure in the death of him that *d*
24:18 and at even my wife *d*
33:8 O wicked man, thou shalt surely *d*
Hos. 13:1 but when he offended in Baal, he *d*
Amos 6:9 ten men in one house, that they shall *d*
9:10 sinners of my people shall *d* by the sword
Jon. 4:3 (4:8) it is better for me to *d* than to live
Zech. 11:9 not feed you: that that *d*, let it *d*
Mt. 15:4 (Mk. 7:10) curseth father . . let him *d*
22:27 (Mk. 12:22; Lk. 20:32) last . . the woman *d*
26:35 (Mk. 14:31) *d* with thee, yet will I not deny
Lk. 7:2 centurion's servant . . sick, and ready to *d*
16:22 the rich man also *d*, and was buried
20:36 neither can they *d* any more: for they are
Jn. 4:49 unto him, Sir, come down ere my child *d*
6:50 that a man may eat thereof, and not *d*
8:24 shall *d* in your sins: for if ye believe not
11:16 let us also go, that we may *d* with him
11:21 thou hadst been here, my brother had not *d*
11:26 liveth and believeth in me shall never *d*
11:50 (18:14) expedient . . that one man should *d*

Jn. 11:51 he prophesied that Jesus should *d* for that
12:24 and *d*, it abideth alone: but if it *d*, it
12:33 he said, signifying what death he should *d*
19:7 by our law he ought to *d*, because he made
21:23 that that disciple should not *d*: yet Jesus
Acts 9:37 that she was sick, and *d*: whom when they
21:13 to *d* at Jerusalem for the name of the Lord
25:11 worthy of death, I refuse not to *d*: but if
Rom. 5:6 in due time Christ *d* for the ungodly
5:7 scarcely for a righteous man will one *d*: yet
5:8 while we were yet sinners, Christ *d* for us
6:9 Christ being raised from the dead *d* no more
6:10 for in that he *d*, he *d* unto sin once: but
7:9 the commandment came, sin revived, and I *d*
8:13 if ye live after the flesh, ye shall *d*: but
8:34 that condemneth? It is Christ that *d*, yea
14:7 liveth to himself, and no man *d* to himself
14:8 whether we *d*, we *d* unto the Lord
14:9 to this end Christ both *d*, and rose
14:15 not him with thy meat, for whom Christ *d*
1 Cor. 8:11 weak brother perish, for whom Christ *d*?
9:15 were better for me to *d*, than that any man
15:3 how that Christ *d* for our sins according to
15:22 as in Adam all *d*, even so in Christ shall
15:31 I have in Christ Jesus our Lord, I *d* daily
15:32 let us eat and drink; for tomorrow we *d*
15:36 thou sowest is not quickened, except it *d*
2 Cor. 5:14 if one *d* for all, then were all dead
7:3 ye are in our hearts to *d* and live with you
Phil. 1:21 to live is Christ, and to *d* is gain
1 Thes. 4:14 if we believe that Jesus *d* and rose
5:10 *d* for us, that, whether we wake or sleep
Heb. 7:8 here men that *d* receive tithes; but there
9:27 is appointed unto men once to *d*, but after
10:28 he that despised Moses' law *d* without mercy
11:13 these all *d* in faith, not having received
Rev. 3:2 things which remain, that are ready to *d*
8:9 which were in the sea, and had life, *d*
9:6 desire to *d*, and death shall flee from them
14:13 blessed are the dead which *d* in the Lord
16:3 and every living soul *d* in the sea

Differ

Rom. 12:6 having then gifts *d* according to the grace
1 Cor. 4:7 who maketh thee to *d* from another?
15:41 for one star *d* from another star in glory
Gal. 4:1 he is a child, *d* nothing from a servant

Difference

Ex. 11:7 put a *d* between the Egyptians and Israel
Lev. 10:10 ye may put *d* between holy and unholy
11:47 make a *d* between the unclean and the clean
20:25 put a *d* between clean beasts and unclean
Ezek. 22:26 put no *d* between the holy and profane
Acts 15:9 put no *d* between us and them, purifying
Rom. 3:22 all them that believe; for there is no *d*
10:12 is no *d* between the Jew and the Greek
1 Cor. 7:34 is a also between a wife and a virgin
12:5 are *d* of administrations, but the same Lord
Jude 22 and of some have compassion, making a *d*

Dig

Gen. 21:30 witness unto me, that I have *d* this well
Ex. 21:33 if a man shall *d* a pit, and not cover it
Num. 21:18 princes *d* the well, the nobles . . *d* it
Deut. 6:11 and wells *d*, which thou *d* not
8:9 and out of whose hills thou mayest *d* brass
Job 3:21 and *d* for it more than for hid treasures
6:27 and ye *d* a pit for your friend
24:16 in the dark they *d* through houses
Ps. 7:15 he make a pit, and *d* it, and is fallen
35:7 which without cause they have *d* for my soul
57:6 they have *d* a pit before me, into the midst
94:13 until the pit be *d* for the wicked

Prov. 16:27 ungodly man *d* up evil: and in his lips
26:27 (Eccl. 10:8) whoso *d* a pit shall fall therein
Is. 5:6 it shall not be pruned, nor *d*
51:1 and to the hole of the pit whence ye are *d*
Jer. 18:20 for they have *d* a pit for my soul
Ezek. 8:8 *d* now in the wall: and when I had *d* in
12:5 *d* thou through the wall in their sight
Amos 9:2 though they *d* into hell, thence shall
Mt. 21:33 (Mk. 12:1) *d* a winepress in it, and built
25:18 *d* in the earth, and hid his lord's money
Lk. 6:48 which built a house, and *d* deep, and laid
13:8 till I shall *d* about it, and dung it
16:3 from me the stewardship: I cannot *d*; to beg
Rom. 11:3 *d* down thine altars; and I am left alone

Dignity

Gen. 49:3 the excellency of *d*, and the excellency
Esth. 6:3 honor and *d* hath been done to Mordecai
Eccl. 10:6 folly is set in great *d*, and the rich
Hab. 1:7 their judgment and their *d* shall proceed
2 Pet. 2:10 (Jude 8) not afraid to speak evil of *d*

Diligence

Prov. 4:23 keep thy heart with all *d*; for out of
Lk. 12:58 give *d* that thou mayest be delivered
Rom. 12:8 he that ruleth, with *d*; he that showeth
2 Cor. 8:7 in all *d*, and in your love to us, see
2 Tim. 4:9 (4:21) do thy *d* to come shortly unto me
Heb. 6:11 show the same *d* to the full assurance of
2 Pet. 1:5 giving all *d*, add to your faith virtue
1:10 give *d* to make your calling and election
Jude 3 when I gave all *d* to write unto you of the

Diligent

Deut. 19:18 the judges shall make *d* inquisition
Josh. 22:5 but take *d* heed to do the commandment
Ps. 64:6 they accomplish a *d* search
77:6 mine own heart: and my spirit made *d* search
Prov. 10:4 but the hand of the *d* maketh rich
12:24 the hand of the *d* shall bear rule: but
12:27 but the substance of a *d* man is precious
13:4 but the soul of the *d* shall be made fat
21:5 thoughts of the *d* tend . . to plenteousness
22:29 seest thou a man *d* in his business?
27:23 be thou *d* to know the state of thy flocks
2 Cor. 8:22 *d* in many things, but now much more *d*
2 Pet. 3:14 *d* that ye may be found of him in peace

Diligently

Ex. 15:26 wilt *d* hearken to the voice of the Lord
Deut. 4:9 and keep thy soul *d*, lest thou forget
6:7 thou shalt teach them *d* unto thy children
6:17 (11:22) shall *d* keep the commandments
13:14 thou inquire, and make search, and ask *d*
24:8 plague of leprosy, that thou observe *d*
Ezra 7:23 it be *d* done for the house of the God of
Ps. 37:10 thou shalt *d* consider his place, and it
119:4 hast commanded us to keep thy precepts *d*
Prov. 7:15 *d* to seek thy face, and I have found
11:27 he that *d* seeketh good procureth favor
23:1 eat with a ruler, consider *d* what is before
Is. 55:2 hearken *d* unto me, and eat ye that which
Jer. 2:10 and consider *d*, and see if there be such
12:16 if they will *d* learn the ways of my people
17:24 if ye *d* hearken unto me, saith the Lord
Zech. 6:15 if ye will *d* obey the voice of the Lord
Mt. 2:7 inquired of them *d* what time the star
2:8 go and search *d* for the young child
Lk. 15:8 sweep the house, and seek *d* till she find
Acts 18:25 and taught *d* the things of the Lord
1 Tim. 5:10 if she have *d* followed every good work
2 Tim. 1:17 was in Rome, he sought me out very *d*
Heb. 11:6 he is a rewarder of them that *d* seek him
12:15 looking *d* lest any man fail of the grace

1 Pet. 1:10 prophets have inquired and searched *d*

Dim

Gen. 27:1 when isaac was old, and his eyes were *d*
    48:10 now the eyes of Israel were *d* for age
Deut. 34:7 eye was not *d*, nor his natural force abated
1 Sam. 3:2 (4:15) Eli. . and his eyes began to wax *d*
Job 17:7 mine eye also is *d* by reason of sorrow
Is. 32:3 eyes of them that see shall not be *d*
Lam. 4:1 how is the gold become *d*! how is the most

Diminish *See also* Abate, Decrease

Ex. 5:8 ye shall not *d* aught thereof: for they be
Lev. 25:16 fewness of years thou shalt *d* the price
Deut. 4:2 not add unto the word. . neither shall ye *d*
    12:32 thou shalt not add thereto, nor *d* from it
Prov. 13:11 wealth gotten by vanity shall be *d*
Jer. 26:2 thee to speak unto them; *d* not a word
Ezek. 16:27 and have *d* thine ordinary food
Rom. 11:12 *d* of them the riches of the Gentiles

Dimness

Is. 8:22 behold trouble and darkness, *d* of anguish
    9:1 *d* shall not be such as was in her vexation

Dinah Gen. 30:21; 34:1-31

Dine

Gen. 43:16 for these men shall *d* with me at noon
Lk. 11:37 certain Pharisee besought him to *d* with
Jn. 21:12 Jesus saith unto them, Come and *d*

Dinner *See also* Supper

Prov. 15:17 better is a *d* of herbs where love is
Mt. 22:4 are bidden, Behold, I have prepared my *d*
Lk. 11:38 that he had not first washed before *d*
    14:12 when thou makest a *d* or a supper, call not

Dionysius Acts 17:34

Diotrephes 3 Jn. 9

Dip

Gen. 37:31 and *d* the coat in the blood
Ex. 12:22 a bunch of hyssop, and *d* it in the blood
Lev. 4:6 priest shall *d* his finger in the blood
    14:6 shall *d* them and the living bird in the blood
Num. 19:18 and *d* it in the water, and sprinkle it
Josh. 3:15 feet of the priests. . were *d* in the brim
Ruth 2:14 and *d* thy morsel in the vinegar
1 Sam. 14:27 in his hand, and *d* it in a honeycomb
2 Kgs. 5:14 and *d* himself seven times in Jordan
Ps. 68:23 thy foot may be *d* in the blood of thine
Mt. 26:23 (Mk. 14:20) he that *d* his hand with me
Lk. 16:24 send Lazarus, that he may *d* the tip of
Jn. 13:26 I have *d* it. And when he had *d* the sop

Direct *See also* Guide, Lead, Order

Gen. 46:28 unto Joseph, to *d* his face unto Goshen
Job 32:14 now he hath not *d* his words against me
    37:3 he *d* it under the whole heaven, and his
Ps. 5:3 morning will I *d* my prayer unto thee
    119:5 O that my ways were *d* to keep thy statutes!
Prov. 3:6 acknowledge him, and he shall *d* thy paths
    11:5 righteousness of the perfect shall *d* his
    16:9 deviseth his way: but the LORD *d* his steps
    21:29 but as for the upright, he *d* his way
Eccl. 10:10 but wisdom is profitable to *d*
Is. 40:13 who hath *d* the Spirit of the LORD
    45:13 I will *d* all his ways: he shall build my
    61:8 I will *d* their work in truth, and I will
Jer. 10:23 not in man that walketh to *d* his steps
1 Thes. 3:11 Lord Jesus Christ, *d* our way unto you
2 Thes. 3:5 Lord *d* your hearts into the love of

Dirt

Ps. 18:42 did cast them out as the *d* in the streets

Disallow

Num. 30:5 but if her father *d* her in the day that
    30:8 husband *d* her on the day that he heard it
1 Pet. 2:7 stone which the builders *d*, the same is

Disannul

Job 40:8 wilt thou also *d* my judgment? wilt thou
Is. 14:27 LORD. . hath purposed, and who shall *d* it?
    28:18 your covenant with death shall be *d*
Gal. 3:15 yet if it be confirmed, no man *d*
    3:17 cannot *d*, that it should make the promise
Heb. 7:18 a *d* of the commandment going before

Disappoint

Job 5:12 he *d* the devices of the crafty, so that
Ps. 17:13 O LORD, *d* him, cast him down: deliver my
Prov. 15:22 without counsel purposes are *d*

Discern *See also* Judge, Know, Perceive, See

Gen. 27:23 *d* him not, because his hands were hairy
    31:32 *d* thou what is thine with me, and take it
    38:25 she said, *D*, I pray thee, whose are these
2 Sam. 14:17 is my lord the king to *d* good and evil
    19:35 and can I *d* between good and evil?
1 Kgs. 3:9 that I may *d* between good and bad
Ezra 3:13 so that the people could not *d* the noise
Job 4:16 but I could not *d* the form thereof
    6:30 cannot my taste *d* perverse things?
Prov. 7:7 the simple ones, I *d* among the youths
Eccl. 8:5 and a wise man's heart *d* both time and
Jon. 4:11 cannot *d* between their right hand and
Mal. 3:18 *d* between the righteous and the wicked
Mt. 16:3 (Lk. 12:56) ye can *d* the face of the sky·
1 Cor. 2:14 because they are spiritually *d*
    11:29 damnation to himself, not *d* the Lord's body
    12:10 another prophecy; to another *d* of spirits
Heb. 5:14 senses exercised to *d* both good and evil

Discerner

Heb. 4:12 and is a *d* of the thoughts and intents

Discharge

1 Kgs. 5:9 and will cause them to be *d* there
Eccl. 8:8 and there is no *d* in that war

Disciple *See also* Apostle

Is. 8:16 the testimony, seal the law among my *d*
Mt. 5:1 and when he was set, his *d* came unto him
    8:21 of his *d* said unto him, Lord, suffer me first
    9:14 (Mk. 2:18) fast oft, but thy *d* fast not?
    10:1 (Lk. 9:1) called unto him his twelve *d*
    10:24 (Lk. 6:40) the *d* is not above his master
    10:42 cup of cold water only in the name of a *d*
    11:2 (Lk. 7:19) John had heard. . sent two of his *d*
    12:1 (Mk. 2:23; Lk. 6:1) and his *d* were ahungered
    14:19 (Mk. 6:41; Lk. 9:16; Jn. 6:11) gave the loaves
      to his *d*, and the *d* to the multitude
    14:26 when the *d* saw him walking on the sea
    15:2 (Mk. 7:5) why do thy *d* transgress the tradition
    15:36 (Mk. 8:6) brake them, and gave to his *d*
    16:5 (Mk. 8:14) his *d*. . had forgotten to take bread
    16:13 (Mk. 8:27) Caesarea Philippi, he asked his *d*
    17:6 and when the *d* heard it, they fell on their
    17:16 (Mk. 9:18; Lk. 9:40) I brought him to thy *d*
    19:13 (Mk. 10:13; Lk. 18:15) the *d* rebuked them
    19:25 (Mk. 10:24) *d* heard it, they were. . amazed
    20:17 up to Jerusalem took the twelve *d* apart
    21:1 (Mk. 11:1; Lk. 19:29) then sent Jesus two *d*

Mt. 22:16 out unto him their *d* with the Herodians
    24:3 *d* came unto him privately, saying, Tell us
    26:8 but when his *d* saw it, they had indignation
    26:18 (Mk. 14:14; Lk. 22:11) passover . . with my *d*
    26:56 then all the *d* forsook him
    27:57 (Jn. 19:38) Joseph, who also . . was Jesus' *d*
    27:64 lest his *d* come by night, and steal him
    28:7 (Mk. 16:7) and tell his *d* that he is risen
Mk. 4:34 alone, he expounded all things to his *d*
    9:31 for he taught his *d*, and said unto them
Lk. 6:13 he called unto him his *d*: and . . chose twelve
    10:23 unto his *d*, and said privately, Blessed are
    11:1 his *d* said unto him, Lord, teach us to pray
    14:26 and his own life also, he cannot be my *d*
    14:33 forsaketh not all . . he cannot be my *d*
    19:37 whole multitude of the *d* began to rejoice
Jn. 1:37 two *d* heard him speak, and they followed
    2:11 forth his glory; and his *d* believed on him
    3:25 a question between some of John's *d* and the
    4:1 Jesus made and baptized more *d* than John
    6:66 from that time many of his *d* went back
    8:31 if ye continue in my word, then are ye my *d*
    9:28 said, Thou art his *d*; but we are Moses' *d*
    12:16 these things understood not his *d* at the
    13:5 began to wash the *d*' feet, and to wipe them
    13:23 Jesus' bosom one of his *d*, whom Jesus loved
    13:35 ye are my *d*, if ye have love one to another
    15:8 ye bear much fruit; so shall ye be my *d*
    18:15 Peter followed Jesus, and so did another *d*
    18:17 art not thou also one of this man's *d*?
    19:26 saw his mother, and the *d* standing by
    19:38 being a *d* of Jesus, but secretly for fear
    20:2 (21:7, 20) the other *d*, whom Jesus loved
    20:4 and the other *d* did outrun Peter
    20:18 Mary Magdalene came and told the *d* that
    20:20 were the *d* glad, when they saw the Lord
    21:4 but the *d* knew not that it was Jesus
    21:23 that *d* should not die: yet Jesus said not
Acts 1:15 Peter stood up in the midst of the *d*
    6:1 when the number of the *d* was multiplied
    9:1 threatenings and slaughter against the *d*
    9:10 a certain *d* at Damascus, named Ananias
    9:26 he assayed to join himself to the *d*
    11:26 *d* were called Christians first in Antioch
    13:52 *d* were filled with joy, and with the Holy
    15:10 to put a yoke upon the neck of the *d*
    18:23 Phrygia in order, strengthening all the *d*
    20:7 when the *d* came together to break bread
    20:30 speaking perverse things, to draw away *d*
    21:4 finding *d*, we tarried there seven days
    21:16 with us also certain of the *d* of Caesarea

Discipline

Job 36:10 he openeth also their ear to *d*

Disclose

Is. 26:21 earth also shall *d* her blood, and shall

Discomfit

Ex. 17:13 and Joshua *d* Amalek and his people
Josh. 10:10 Lord *d* them before Israel, and slew
Judg. 4:15 the Lord *d* Sisera, and all his chariots
    8:12 Zebah and Zalmunna, and *d* all the host
1 Sam. 7:10 upon the Philistines, and *d* them
2 Sam. 22:15 (Ps. 18:14) sent . . lightning, and *d* them
Is. 31:8 the sword, and his young men shall be *d*

Discomfiture

1 Sam. 14:20 and there was a very great *d*

Discontented

1 Sam. 22:2 was in debt, and every one that was *d*

Discontinue

Jer. 17:4 shalt *d* from thine heritage that I gave

Discord

Prov. 6:14 mischief continually; he soweth *d*
    6:19 and he that soweth *d* among brethren

Discourage

Num. 32:7 *d* ye the heart of the children of Israel
Deut. 1:28 our brethren have *d* our heart

Discouraged *See also* Afraid, Dismayed

Num. 21:4 the people was much *d* because of the way
Deut. 1:21 said unto thee; fear not, neither be *d*
Is. 42:4 he shall not fail nor be *d*, till he have
Col. 3:21 your children to anger, lest they be *d*

Discover

Lev. 20:18 her nakedness; he hath *d* her fountain
Deut. 22:30 father's wife, nor *d* his father's skirt
1 Sam. 14:8 and we will *d* ourselves unto them
2 Sam. 22:16 (Ps. 18:15) foundations of the world . . *d*
Job 12:22 he *d* deep things out of darkness
    41:13 who can *d* the face of his garment?
Ps. 29:9 the voice of the Lord . . *d* the forests
Prov. 18:2 but that his heart may *d* itself
    25:9 and *d* not a secret to another
Is. 3:17 and the Lord will *d* their secret parts
    22:8 he *d* the covering of Judah, and thou didst
Jer. 13:26 (Nah. 3:5) I *d* thy skirts upon thy face
Lam. 4:22 O daughter of Edom; he will *d* thy sins
Hos. 2:10 now will I *d* her lewdness in the sight
    7:1 then the iniquity of Ephraim was *d*
Acts 21:3 now when we had *d* Cyprus, we left it on
    27:39 they *d* a certain creek with a shore

Discreet

Gen. 41:33 let Pharaoh look out a man *d* and wise
    41:39 there is none so *d* and wise as thou art
Tit. 2:5 to be *d*, chaste, keepers at home, good

Discreetly

Mk. 12:34 when Jesus saw that he answered *d*

Discretion *See also* Prudence

Ps. 112:5 good man . . will guide his affairs with *d*
Prov. 1:4 to the young man knowledge and *d*
    2:11 *d* shall preserve thee, understanding shall
    3:21 keep sound wisdom and *d*
    5:2 thou mayest regard *d*, and that thy lips may
    11:22 so is a fair woman which is without *d*
    19:11 the *d* of a man deferreth his anger
Is. 28:26 his God doth instruct him to *d*
Jer. 10:12 hath stretched out the heavens by his *d*

Disdain *See also* Abhor, Contemn, Despise, Detest, Hate, Loathe, Scorn

1 Sam. 17:42 saw David, he *d* him: for he was but a
Job 30:1 in derision, whose fathers I would have *d*

Disease *See also* Infirmity, Sickness

Ex. 15:26 I will put none of these *d* upon thee
Deut. 7:15 will put none of the evil *d* of Egypt
    28:60 he will bring upon thee all the *d* of Egypt
2 Kgs. 1:2 whether I shall recover of this *d*
    8:8 saying, Shall I recover of this *d*?
2 Chr. 21:18 in his bowels with an incurable *d*
Job 30:18 force of my *d* is my garment changed
Ps. 38:7 my loins are filled with a loathsome *d*
    41:8 an evil *d*, say they, cleaveth fast unto him
    103:3 who healeth all thy *d*
Eccl. 6:2 this is vanity, and it is an evil *d*

Mt. 4:23 (9:35; 10:1) healing. . all manner of *d*
    4:24 that were taken with divers *d* and torments
Lk. 6:17 to hear him, and to be healed of their *d*
    9:1 and authority over all devils, and to cure *d*
Jn. 5:4 was made whole of whatsoever *d* he had
Acts 28:9 had a *d* in the island, came, and were healed

Diseased

1 Kgs. 15:23 (2 Chr. 16:12) Asa. . was *d* in his feet
Ezek. 34:4 the *d* have ye not strengthened, neither
    34:21 and pushed all the *d* with your horns
Mt. 9:20 woman, which was *d* with an issue of blood
    14:35 brought unto him all that were *d*
Mk. 1:32 (Lk. 4:40) brought unto him all that were *d*

Disfigure

Mt. 6:16 they *d* their faces, that they may appear

Disgrace *See also* Reproach, Shame

Jer. 14:21 do not *d* the throne of thy glory

Disguise

1 Sam. 28:8 and Saul *d* himself, and put on other
1 Kgs. 14:2 and *d* thyself, that thou be not known
    20:38 and *d* himself with ashes upon his face
    22:30 (2 Chr. 18:29) *d* myself. . into the battle
2 Chr. 35:22 Josiah. . *d* himself, that he might fight
Job 24:15 saying, No eye shall see me: and *d* his

Dish

2 Kgs. 21:13 wipe Jerusalem as a man wipeth a *d*
Mt. 26:23 (Mk. 14:20) dippeth. . with me in the *d*

Dishonest

Ezek. 22:13 I have smitten mine hand at thy *d* gain

Dishonesty

2 Cor. 4:2 have renounced the hidden things of *d*

Dishonor *See also* Disgrace, Reproach, Shame

Ezra 4:14 was not meet for us to see the king's *d*
Ps. 35:26 let them be clothed with shame and *d*
    69:19 thou hast known. . my shame, and my *d*
    71:13 let them be covered with reproach and *d*
Prov. 6:33 a wound and *d* shall he get
Mic. 7:6 son *d* the father, the daughter riseth up
Jn. 8:49 but I honor my Father, and ye do *d* me
Rom. 1:24 to *d* their own bodies between themselves
    2:23 through breaking the law *d* thou God?
    9:21 one vessel unto honor, and another unto *d*?
1 Cor. 11:4 having his head covered, *d* his head
    15:43 it is sown in *d*, it is raised in glory
2 Cor. 6:8 by honor and *d*, by evil report and good
2 Tim. 2:20 some to honor, and some to *d*

Disinherit

Num. 14:12 with the pestilence, and *d* them

Dismayed *See also* Afraid, Discouraged

Deut. 31:8 fear not, neither be *d*
Josh. 1:9 (8:1; 10:25) not afraid, neither be thou *d*
1 Sam. 17:11 words of the Philistine, they were *d*
1 Chr. 22:13 of good courage; dread not, nor be *d*
2 Chr. 20:17 and Jerusalem: fear not, nor be *d*
    32:7 be not afraid nor *d* for the king of Assyria
Is. 41:10 am with thee: be not *d*; for I am thy God
Jer. 1:17 be not at their faces, lest I confound
    8:9 wise men are ashamed, they are *d* and taken
    10:2 be not *d* at the signs of heaven
    17:18 let them be *d*, but let not me be *d*
    23:4 they shall fear no more, nor be *d*, neither

Jer. 30:10 saith the LORD; neither be *d*, O Israel
    46:5 have I seen them *d* and turned away back?
Ezek. 2:6 nor be *d* at their looks, though they be
Obad. 9 and thy mighty men, O Teman, shall be *d*

Dismiss

2 Chr. 23:8 Jehoiada the priest *d* not the courses
Acts 15:30 when they were *d*, they came to Antioch
    19:41 when he had thus spoken, he *d* the assembly

Disobedience *See also* Rebellion

Rom. 5:19 by one man's *d* many were made sinners
2 Cor. 10:6 having in a readiness to revenge all *d*
Eph. 2:2 that now worketh in the children of *d*
    5:6 (Col. 3:6) wrath of God upon the children of *d*
Heb. 2:2 *d* received a just recompense of reward

Disobedient *See also* Rebellious

1 Kgs. 13:26 who was *d* unto the word of the LORD
Neh. 9:26 they were *d*, and rebelled against thee
Lk. 1:17 to turn. . the *d* to the wisdom of the just
Acts 26:19 I was not *d* unto the heavenly vision
Rom. 1:30 inventors of evil things, *d* to parents
    10:21 my hands unto a *d* and gainsaying people
1 Tim. 1:9 the law is. . for the lawless and *d*
2 Tim. 3:2 blasphemers, *d* to parents, unthankful
Tit. 1:16 they deny him, being abominable, and *d*
    3:3 we ourselves also were sometime foolish, *d*
1 Pet. 2:7 unto them which be *d*, the stone which
    2:8 to them which stumble at the word, being *d*
    3:20 which sometime were *d*, when once

Disobey

1 Kgs. 13:21 as thou hast *d* the mouth of the LORD

Disorderly

2 Thes. 3:6 from every brother that walketh *d*
    3:7 for we behaved not ourselves *d* among you
    3:11 some which walk among you *d*, working not

Dispensation

1 Cor. 9:17 a *d* of the gospel is committed unto me
Eph. 1:10 that in the *d* of the fulness of times
    3:2 ye have heard of the *d* of the grace of God
Col. 1:25 a minister, according to the *d* of God

Disperse *See also* Scatter

1 Sam. 14:34 and Saul said, *D* yourselves among the
Ps. 112:9 (2 Cor. 9:9) he hath *d*, he hath given
Prov. 5:16 thy fountains be *d* abroad, and rivers
    15:7 lips of the wise *d* knowledge: but the heart
Ezek. 22:15 and *d* thee in the countries
    36:19 and they were *d* through the countries
Acts 5:37 all, even as many as obeyed him, were *d*

Dispersed *See also* Disperse, Scattered

Esth. 3:8 a certain people scattered abroad and *d*
Is. 11:12 and gather together the *d* of Judah from
Zeph. 3:10 even the daughter of my *d*, shall bring
Jn. 7:35 will he go unto the *d* among the Gentiles

Dispersion

Jer. 25:34 days of your slaughter and of your *d*

Displease *See also* Provoke, Vex

Gen. 38:10 and the thing which he did *d* the LORD
    48:17 hand upon the head of Ephraim, it *d* him
Num. 11:1 the people complained, it *d* the LORD
    11:10 LORD was kindled greatly; Moses also was *d*
    22:34 if it *d* thee, I will get me back again
1 Sam. 8:6 but the thing *d* Samuel, when they said
    18:8 Saul was very wroth, and the saying *d* him
2 Sam. 6:8 (1 Chr. 13:11) David was *d*, because the

2 Sam. 11:27 the thing that David had done *d* the LORD
1 Kgs. 1:6 his father had not *d* him at any time
1 Chr. 21:7 God was *d* with this thing; therefore
Ps. 60:1 thou hast scattered us, thou hast been *d*
Prov. 24:18 lest the LORD see it, and it *d* him
Is. 59:15 and it *d* him that there was no judgment
Dan. 6:14 then the king. . was sore *d* with himself
Jon. 4:1 it *d* Jonah exceedingly, and he was very
Hab. 3:8 was the LORD *d* against the rivers?
Zech. 1:2 LORD hath been sore *d* with your fathers
   1:15 sore *d* with the heathen that are at ease
Mt. 21:15 to the Son of David; they were sore *d*
Mk. 10:14 but when Jesus saw it, he was much *d*
   10:41 began to be much *d* with James and John
Acts 12:20 Herod was highly *d* with them of Tyre

Displeasure

Deut. 9:19 for I was afraid of the anger and, hot *d*
Judg. 15:3 than the Philistines, though I do them a *d*
Ps. 2:5 in his wrath, and vex them in his sore *d*
   6:1 (38:1) anger, neither chasten me in thy hot *d*

Dispose

Job 34:13 or who hath *d* the whole world?
   37:15 dost thou know when God *d* them
Prov. 16:33 but the whole *d* thereof is of the LORD
1 Cor. 10:27 bid you to a feast, and ye be *d* to go

Disposition

Acts 7:53 have received the law by the *d* of angels

Dispossess

Num. 33:53 ye shall *d* the inhabitants of the land
Deut. 7:17 are more than I; how can I *d* them?
Judg. 11:23 God of Israel hath *d* the Amorites

Disputation

Acts 15:2 had no small dissension and *d* with them
Rom. 14:1 receive ye, but not to doubtful *d*

Dispute

Job 23:7 there the righteous might *d* with him
Mk. 9:33 what was it that ye *d* among yourselves
Acts 6:9 of Cilicia and of Asia, *d* with Stephen
   9:29 *d* against the Grecians: but they went about
   17:17 *d* he in the synagogue with the Jews
   19:8 *d* and persuading the things concerning the
   19:9 *d* daily in the school of one Tyrannus
   24:12 neither found me in the temple *d* with any
Jude 9 with the devil he *d* about the body of Moses

Disputing *See also* Dispute

Acts 15:7 when there had been much *d*, Peter rose
Phil. 2:14 do all things without murmurings and *d*
1 Tim. 6:5 perverse *d* of men of corrupt minds

Disquiet

1 Sam. 28:15 Samuel said to Saul, Why hast thou *d*
Ps. 39:6 surely they are *d* in vain
   42:5 (42:11; 43:5) and why art thou *d* in me?
Prov. 30:21 for three things the earth is *d*
Jer. 50:34 and *d* the inhabitants of Babylon

Dissemble

Josh. 7:11 have also stolen, and *d* also
Prov. 26:24 he that hateth *d* with his lips
Jer. 42:20 for ye *d* in your hearts, when ye sent
Gal. 2:13 other Jews *d* likewise with him

Dissembler

Ps. 26:4 vain persons, neither will I go in with *d*

Dissension *See also* Variance

Acts 15:2 had no small *d* and disputation with them
   23:7 a *d* between the Pharisees and the Sadducees

Dissimulation

Rom. 12:9 let love be without *d*
Gal. 2:13 Barnabas also was carried away with their *d*

Dissolve

Job 30:22 me to ride upon it, and *d* my substance
Ps. 75:3 the earth and all the inhabitants . . are *d*
Is. 14:31 O city; thou, whole Palestina, art *d*
   24:19 utterly broken down, the earth is clean *d*
   34:4 all the host of heaven shall be *d*
Dan. 5:16 canst make interpretations, and *d* doubts
Nah. 2:6 be opened, and the palace shall be *d*
2 Cor. 5:1 earthly house of this tabernacle were *d*
2 Pet. 3:11 then that all these things shall be *d*
   3:12 the heavens being on fire shall be *d*

Distaff

Prov. 31:19 the spindle, and her hands hold the *d*

Distil

Deut. 32:2 my speech shall *d* as the dew
Job 36:28 the clouds do drop and *d* upon man

Distinction

1 Cor. 14:7 give a *d* in the sounds, how shall it

Distinctly

Neh. 8:8 they read in the book in the law of God *d*

Distracted

Ps. 88:15 while I suffer thy terrors I am *d*

Distraction

1 Cor. 7:35 ye may attend upon the Lord without *d*

Distress *See also* Affliction, Anguish, Calamity, Grief, Misery, Sorrow, Suffering, Tribulation, Trouble

Gen. 32:7 then Jacob was greatly afraid and *d*
   35:3 God, who answered me in the day of my *d*
   42:21 therefore is this *d* come upon us
Deut. 2:9 *d* not the Moabites, neither contend with
Judg. 11:7 ye come unto me now when ye are in *d*?
1 Sam. 22:2 every one that was in *d*, and every one
2 Sam. 22:7 (Ps. 18:6) in my *d* I called upon the LORD
1 Kgs. 1:29 hath redeemed my soul out of all *d*
2 Chr. 28:22 in the time of his *d* did he trespass
Neh. 2:17 see the *d* that we are in, how Jerusalem
   9:37 at their pleasure, and we are in great *d*
Ps. 4:1 thou hast enlarged me when I was in *d*
   25:17 are enlarged: O bring thou me out of my *d*
   107:6 (107:13, 19, 28) delivered them out of their *d*
   118:5 I called upon the LORD in *d*: the LORD
Prov. 1:27 when *d* and anguish cometh upon you
Is. 25:4 a strength to the needy in his *d*, a refuge
Lam. 1:20 behold, O LORD; for I am in *d*
Ezek. 30:16 and Noph shall have *d* daily
Obad. 12 have spoken proudly in the day of *d*
Zeph. 1:15 a day of wrath, a day of trouble and *d*
Lk. 21:23 for there shall be great *d* in the land
   21:25 and upon the earth *d* of nations
Rom. 8:35 love of Christ? shall tribulation, or *d*
1 Cor. 7:26 that this is good for the present *d*
2 Cor. 4:8 are troubled on every side, yet not *d*
   6:4 in afflictions, in necessities, in *d*
   12:10 I take pleasure . . in *d* for Christ's sake
1 Thes. 3:7 all our affliction and *d* by your faith

Distribute

Josh. 13:32 the countries which Moses did *d*
1 Chr. 24:3 David *d* them, both Zadok of the sons
Neh. 13:13 office was to *d* unto their brethren
Job 21:17 God *d* sorrows in his anger
Lk. 18:22 sell all that thou hast, and *d* unto the poor
Jn. 6:11 had given thanks, he *d* to the disciples
Rom. 12:13 *d* to the necessity of saints
1 Cor. 7:17 but as God hath *d* to every man
2 Cor. 10:13 which God hath *d* to us, a measure to
1 Tim. 6:18 they be rich in good works, ready to *d*

Distribution

Acts 4:35 *d* was made unto every man according as
2 Cor. 9:13 and for your liberal *d* unto them

Ditch

2 Kgs. 3:16 make this valley full of *d*
Job 9:31 yet shalt thou plunge me in the *d*
Ps. 7:15 and is fallen into the *d* which he made
Prov. 23:27 whore is a deep *d*; and a strange woman
Is. 22:11 ye made also a *d* between the two walls
Mt. 15:14 (Lk. 6:39) blind, both shall fall into the *d*

Divers

Deut. 22:9 shalt not sow thy vineyard with *d* seeds
22:11 thou shalt not wear a garment of *d* sorts
25:13 thou shalt not have in thy bag *d* weights
25:14 shalt not have in thine house *d* measures
Prov. 20:10 *d* weights, and *d* measures, both of
20:23 *d* weights are an abomination unto the LORD
Eccl. 5:7 and many words there are also *d* vanities
Mt. 4:24 people that were taken with *d* diseases
24:7 (Mk. 13:8; Lk. 21:11) earthquakes, in *d* places
Mk. 8:3 by the way: for *d* of them came from far
Acts 19:9 when *d* were hardened, and believed not
1 Cor. 12:10 to another *d* kinds of tongues
2 Tim. 3:6 laden with sins, led away with *d* lusts
Tit. 3:3 deceived, serving *d* lusts and pleasures
Heb. 1:1 God, who at sundry times and in *d* manners
2:4 with *d* miracles, and gifts of the Holy Ghost
9:10 *d* washings, and carnal ordinances, imposed
13:9 carried about with *d* and strange doctrines
Jas. 1:2 all joy when ye fall into *d* temptations

Diversity

1 Cor. 12:4 are *d* of gifts, but the same Spirit
12:6 are *d* of operations, but it is the same God
12:28 healings, helps, governments, *d* of tongues

Divide *See also* Part, Separate

Gen. 1:4 and God *d* the light from the darkness
1:6 and let it *d* the waters from the waters
Ex. 14:16 out thine hand over the sea, and *d* it
14:21 the sea dry land, and the waters were *d*
26:33 the veil shall *d* unto you between the holy
Lev. 11:4 (Deut. 14:7) that *d* the hoof: as the camel
Num. 31:27 *d* the prey into two parts; between them
33:54 *d* the land by lot for an inheritance
Josh. 23:4 I have *d* unto you by lot these nations
Judg. 19:29 and laid hold on his concubine, and *d* her
2 Sam. 1:23 and in their death they were not *d*
1 Kgs. 3:25 king said, *D* the living child in two
2 Kgs. 2:8 and smote the waters, and they were *d*
2 Chr. 35:13 *d* them speedily among all the people
Neh. 9:11 and thou didst *d* the sea before them
Job 26:12 he *d* the sea with his power, and by his
27:17 and the innocent shall *d* the silver
38:25 hath *d* a watercourse for the overflowing
Ps. 29:7 voice of the LORD *d* the flames of fire
68:12 and she that tarried at home *d* the spoil
74:13 thou didst *d* the sea by thy strength

Ps. 78:13 *d* the sea, and caused them to pass through
136:13 to him which *d* the Red sea into parts
Prov. 16:19 than to *d* the spoil with the proud
Is. 9:3 and as men rejoice when they *d* the spoil
53:12 and he shall *d* the spoil with the strong
Lam. 4:16 the anger of the LORD hath *d* them
Ezek. 37:22 be *d* into two kingdoms any more at all
Dan. 5:28 PERES; Thy kingdom is *d*, and given to
Hos. 10:2 their heart is *d*; now shall they be
Amos 7:17 and thy land shall be *d* by line
Mt. 12:25 (Mk. 3:24; Lk. 11:17) kingdom *d* against
12:26 (Mk. 3:26; Lk. 11:18) Satan . . is *d* against
25:32 as a shepherd *d* his sheep from the goats
Lk. 12:13 brother . . he *d* the inheritance with me
12:52 five in one house *d*, three against two
15:12 and he *d* unto them his living
22:17 said, Take this, and *d* it among yourselves
Acts 14:4 city was *d*: and part held with the Jews
23:7 a dissension . . and the multitude was *d*
1 Cor. 1:13 is Christ *d*? was Paul crucified for you?
12:11 selfsame Spirit, *d* to every man
2 Tim. 2:15 ashamed, rightly *d* the word of truth

Divider

Lk. 12:14 who made me a judge or a *d* over you?

Dividing *See also* Divide

Josh. 19:49 an end of *d* the land for inheritance
Dan. 7:25 until a time and times and the *d* of time
Heb. 4:12 piercing even to the *d* asunder of soul

Divination

Num. 22:7 elders . . departed with the rewards of *d*
23:23 neither is there any *d* against Israel
Deut. 18:10 that useth *d*, or an observer of times
Jer. 14:14 prophesy unto you a false vision and *d*
Ezek. 12:24 any vain vision nor flattering *d*
13:6 they have seen vanity and lying *d*, saying
21:21 at the head of the two ways, to use *d*
Acts 16:16 damsel possessed with a spirit of *d* met

Divine (adjective)

Prov. 16:10 *d* sentence is in the lips of the king
Heb. 9:1 ordinances of *d* service, and a worldly
2 Pet. 1:3 as his *d* power hath given unto us all
1:4 ye might be partakers of the *d* nature

Divine (verb)

Gen. 44:5 lord drinketh, and whereby indeed he *d*?
44:15 that such a man as I can certainly *d*?
1 Sam. 28:8 unto me by the familiar spirit
Ezek. 13:9 prophets that see vanity . . that *d* lies
22:28 seeing vanity, and *d* lies unto them
Mic. 3:6 be dark unto you, that ye shall not *d*
3:11 and the prophets thereof *d* for money

Diviner

Jer. 27:9 not ye to your prophets, nor to your *d*
29:8 let not your prophets and your *d* . . deceive

Division

Ex. 8:23 put a *d* between my people and thy people
Judg. 5:15 *d* of Reuben there were great thoughts
1 Chr. 24:1 these are the *d* of the sons of Aaron
2 Chr. 35:5 according to the *d* of the families of
Lk. 12:51 on earth? I tell you, Nay; but rather *d*
Jn. 7:43 was a *d* among the people because of him
9:16 such miracles? And there was a *d* among them
10:19 was a *d* therefore again among the Jews
Rom. 16:17 mark them which cause *d* and offenses
1 Cor. 1:10 that there be no *d* among you
3:3 strife, and *d*, are ye not carnal, and walk
11:18 I hear that there be *d* among you

Divorce

Num. 30:9 vow of a widow, and of her that is *d*
Jer. 3:8 put her away, and given her a bill of *d*
Mt. 5:32 marry her that is *d* committeth adultery

Divorcement

Deut. 24:1 (Mt. 5:31) him write her a bill of *d*
Is. 50:1 where is the bill of your mother's *d*
Mt. 19:7 (Mk. 10:4) command to give a writing of *d*

Do (Did, Done) *See also* Accomplish, Fulfil, Labor, Perform, Work, Wrought

Gen. 18:25 not the Judge of all the earth *d* right?
31:16 whatsoever God hath said unto thee, *d*
Num. 10:29 thou with us, and we will *d* thee good
23:19 hath he said, and shall he not *d* it?
29:39 shall *d* unto the LORD in your set feasts
Deut. 27:26 (Gal. 3:10) words of this law to *d* them
Ruth 3:5 all that thou sayest unto me I will *d*
2 Kgs. 19:31 (Is. 37:32) zeal of the LORD . . shall *d*
2 Chr. 16:9 herein thou hast *d* foolishly: therefore
Neh. 6:3 am *d* a great work, so that I cannot come
Ps. 33:9 he spake, and it was *d*; he commanded
34:14 (37:27; 1 Pet. 3:11) from evil, and *d* good
34:16 (1 Pet. 3:12) is against them that *d* evil
37:3 trust in the LORD, and *d* good; so shalt
109:21 but *d* thou for me, O GOD the Lord
118:6 (Heb. 13:6) not fear: what can man *d* . . me?
125:4 *d* good, O LORD, unto those that be good
126:3 the LORD hath *d* great things for us
Eccl. 3:12 to rejoice, and to *d* good in his life
8:11 heart . . is fully set in them to *d* evil
9:10 thy hand findeth to *d*, *d* it with thy might
Is. 45:7 I the LORD *d* all these things
46:11 I have purposed it, I will also *d* it
Ezek. 33:31 hear thy words, but they will not *d* them
Hos. 6:4 O Ephraim, what shall I *d* unto thee?
Mic. 6:8 require of thee, but to *d* justly, and to love
Mt. 5:44 (Lk. 6:27) *d* good to them that hate you
6:10 (Lk. 11:2) thy will be *d* in earth, as it is
7:12 (Lk. 6:31) that men should *d* to you, *d* ye
7:24 (Lk. 6:47) heareth these sayings . . and *d* them
12:50 (Mk. 3:35) whosoever shall *d* the will of
18:35 shall my heavenly Father *d* also unto you
19:16 (Mk. 10:17; Lk. 18:18) what good thing shall
I *d*, that I may have eternal life?
21:23 (Mk. 11:28; Lk. 20:2) by what authority *d*
thou these things?
21:40 (Mk. 12:9; Lk. 20:15) *d* unto . . husbandmen?
23:3 they bid you observe, that observe and *d*
23:23 (Lk. 11:42) these ought ye to have *d*, and not
24:46 (Lk. 12:43) when he cometh shall find so *d*
25:40 as ye have *d* it unto one of the least of
Mk. 3:4 (Lk. 6:9) is it lawful to *d* good . . or to *d* evil?
Lk. 6:33 if ye *d* good to them which *d* good to you
6:46 why call ye me, Lord, Lord, and *d* not the
10:28 answered right: this *d*, and thou shalt live
10:37 said Jesus . . Go, and *d* thou likewise
22:19 (1 Cor. 11:24) this *d* in remembrance of me
22:42 nevertheless, not my will, but thine, be *d*
23:34 forgive them; for they know not what they *d*
Jn. 2:5 whatsoever he saith unto you, *d* it
5:19 Son can *d* nothing of himself, but what he
6:38 not to *d* mine own will, but the will of him
8:29 for I *d* always those things that please him
10:37 if I *d* not the works of my Father, believe
13:27 said Jesus unto him, That thou *d*, *d* quickly
15:5 for without me ye can *d* nothing
15:7 ask what ye will, and it shall be *d* unto you
15:14 my friends, if ye *d* whatsoever I command
Acts 1:1 all that Jesus began both to *d* and teach

Acts 2:37 men and brethren, what shall we *d*?
9:6 (22:10) Lord, what wilt thou have me to *d*?
10:38 who went about *d* good, and healing all
14:27 they rehearsed all that God had *d* with them
16:30 and said, Sirs, what must I *d* to be saved?
Rom. 7:15 that *d* I not; but what I hate, that *d* I
1 Cor. 10:31 ye *d*, *d* all to the glory of God
2 Cor. 11:12 what I *d*, that I will *d*, that I may
Gal. 5:17 ye cannot *d* the things that ye would
6:10 let us *d* good unto all men, especially unto
Eph. 6:6 *d* the will of God from the heart
Phil. 2:13 to will and to *d* of his good pleasure
2:14 *d* all things without murmurings and
4:13 I can *d* all things through Christ which
Col. 3:17 ye *d* in word or deed, *d* all in the name
3:23 whatsoever ye *d*, *d* it heartily, as to the Lord
Heb. 4:13 the eyes of him with whom we have to *d*
6:3 and this will we *d*, if God permit
13:16 to *d* good and to communicate forget not
Jas. 4:17 knoweth to *d* good, and *d* it not, to him
1 Pet. 3:12 the Lord is against them that *d* evil
4:11 minister, let him *d* it as of the ability
2 Pet. 1:10 ye *d* these things, ye shall never fall
Rev. 19:10 (22:9) he said unto me, See thou *d* it not

Doctor

Lk. 2:46 the temple, sitting in the midst of the *d*
5:17 were Pharisees and *d* of the law sitting by
Acts 5:34 Pharisee, named Gamaliel, a *d* of the law

Doctrine *See also* Teach

Deut. 32:2 my *d* shall drop as the rain, my speech
Job 11:4 for thou hast said, My *d* is pure
Prov. 4:2 I give you good *d*, forsake ye not my law
Is. 28:9 whom shall he make to understand *d*?
29:24 and they that murmured shall learn *d*
Mt. 7:28 (Mk. 1:22; Lk. 4:32) astonished at his *d*
15:9 (Mk. 7:7) for *d* the commandments of men
16:12 *d* of the Pharisees and of the Sadducees
22:33 heard this, they were astonished at his *d*
Mk. 1:27 what new *d* is this? for with authority
4:2 by parables, and said unto them in his *d*
Jn. 7:16 my *d* is not mine, but his that sent me
7:17 will do his will, he shall know of the *d*
18:19 asked Jesus of his disciples, and of his *d*
Acts 2:42 in the apostles' *d* and fellowship
5:28 ye have filled Jerusalem with your *d*
17:19 may we know what this new *d*, whereof thou
Rom. 6:17 that form of *d* which was delivered you
16:17 contrary to the *d* which ye have learned
1 Cor. 14:6 knowledge, or by prophesying, or by *d*?
14:26 every one of you hath a psalm, hath a *d*
Eph. 4:14 and carried about with every wind of *d*
1 Tim. 1:3 charge some that they teach no other *d*
1:10 any other thing that is contrary to sound *d*
4:1 heed to seducing spirits, and *d* of devils
4:6 words of faith and of good *d*, whereunto thou
4:13 attendance to reading, to exhortation, to *d*
4:16 take heed unto thyself, and unto the *d*
5:17 especially they who labor in the word and *d*
6:1 the name of God and his *d* be not blasphemed
6:3 and to the *d* which is according to godliness
2 Tim. 3:10 but thou hast fully known my *d*
3:16 all scripture . . is profitable for *d*
4:2 rebuke, exhort with all long-suffering and *d*
4:3 will come when they will not endure sound *d*
Tit. 1:9 by sound *d* both to exhort and to convince
2:1 speak thou the things which become sound *d*
2:7 in *d* showing uncorruptness, gravity, sincerity
2:10 may adorn the *d* of God our Saviour
Heb. 6:1 leaving the principles of the *d* of Christ
6:2 the *d* of baptisms, and of laying on of hands
13:9 not carried about with divers and strange *d*

2 Jn. 9 abideth not in the *d* of Christ, hath not God
10 bring not this *d*, receive him not into your
Rev. 2:14 hold the *d* of Balaam, who taught Balak

Doeg 1 Sam. 21:7–22:22

Doer

2 Sam. 3:39 the LORD shall reward the *d* of evil
Ps. 31:23 and plentifully rewardeth the proud *d*
101:8 I may cut off all wicked *d* from the city
Prov. 17:4 wicked *d* giveth heed to false lips
Rom. 2:13 but the *d* of the law shall be justified
Jas. 1:22 but be ye *d* of the word, and not hearers

Dog

Ex. 11:7 of Israel shall not a *d* move his tongue
Judg. 7:5 water with his tongue, as a *d* lappeth
1 Sam. 17:43 Philistine said unto David, Am I a *d*
24:14 thou pursue? after a dead *d*, after a flea
2 Sam. 9:8 should look upon such a dead *d* as I
16:9 should this dead *d* curse my lord the king?
1 Kgs. 14:11 dieth of Jeroboam . . shall the *d* eat
21:19 *d* licked the blood of Naboth shall lick
21:23 *d* shall eat Jezebel by the wall of Jezreel
2 Kgs. 8:13 Hazael said . . is thy servant a *d*, that
Job 30:1 have disdained to have set with the *d*
Ps. 22:16 for *d* have compassed me: the assembly of
22:20 deliver . . my darling from the power of the *d*
59:6 they make a noise like a *d*, and go round
Prov. 26:11 (2 Pet. 2:22) a *d* returneth to his vomit
26:17 is like one that taketh a *d* by the ears
Eccl. 9:4 a living *d* is better than a dead lion
Is. 56:10 they are all dumb *d*, they cannot bark
56:11 greedy *d* which can never have enough
Mt. 7:6 give not that which is holy unto the *d*
15:26 (Mk. 7:27) children's bread, and to cast it to *d*
Lk. 16:21 moreover the *d* came and licked his sores
Phil. 3:2 beware of *d*, beware of evil workers
Rev. 22:15 for without are *d*, and sorcerers

Doing *See also* Do, Act, Deed

Lev. 18:3 *d* of the land of Egypt . . shall ye not do
Judg. 2:19 they ceased not from their own *d*
1 Sam. 25:3 Nabal . . was churlish and evil in his *d*
Ps. 9:11 declare among the people his *d*
64:9 for they shall wisely consider of his *d*
66:5 the works of God: he is terrible in his *d*
77:12 will meditate . . thy work, and talk of thy *d*
118:23 (Mt. 21:42; Mk. 12:11) this is the LORD's *d*
Prov. 20:11 even a child is known by his *d*
Is. 1:16 put away the evil of your *d* from before
Jer. 4:4 quench it, because of the evil of your *d*
7:3 amend your ways and your *d*, and I will
26:13 now amend your ways and your *d*, and obey
Mic. 2:7 of the LORD straitened? are these his *d*?
Rom. 2:7 who by patient continuance in well *d* seek
2 Cor. 8:11 therefore perform the *d* of it
Gal. 6:9 let us not be weary in well *d*: for in due
2 Thes. 3:13 ye, brethren, be not weary in well *d*
1 Pet. 2:15 with well *d* ye may put to silence the
3:17 ye suffer for well *d*, than for evildoing
4:19 the keeping of their souls to him in well *d*

Dominion *See also* Authority, Kingdom, Power, Reign, Rule

Gen. 1:26 let them have *d* over the fish of the sea
27:40 come to pass when thou shalt have the *d*
37:8 or shalt thou indeed have *d* over us?
Num. 24:19 of Jacob shall come he that shall have *d*
Judg. 5:13 LORD made me have *d* over the mighty
Neh. 9:37 also they have *d* over our bodies
Job 25:2 *d* and fear are with him; he maketh peace

Job 38:33 canst thou set the *d* thereof in the earth?
Ps. 8:6 thou madest him to have *d* over the works
19:13 sins; let them not have *d* over me
49:14 and the upright shall have *d* over them
72:8 (Zech. 9:10) shall have *d* also from sea to sea
103:22 in all places of his *d*: bless the LORD
114:2 Judah was his sanctuary, and Israel his *d*
119:133 and let not any iniquity have *d* over me
145:13 thy *d* endureth throughout all generations
Is. 26:13 lords besides thee have had *d* over us
Dan. 4:3 his *d* is from generation to generation
4:34 for ever, whose *d* is an everlasting *d*
6:26 and his *d* shall be even unto the end
7:14 was given him, *d*, and glory, and a kingdom
7:27 and the kingdom and *d*, and the greatness of
11:5 and have *d*; his *d* shall be a great *d*
Mt. 20:25 princes of the Gentiles exercise *d* over
Rom. 6:9 death hath no more *d* over him
6:14 for sin shall not have *d* over you
7:1 law hath *d* over a man as long as he liveth?
2 Cor. 1:24 not for that we have *d* over your faith
Eph. 1:21 far above all . . power, and might, and *d*
Col. 1:16 invisible, whether they be thrones, or *d*
1 Pet. 4:11 (5:11; Rev. 1:6) to whom be praise and *d*
Jude 8 filthy dreamers defile the flesh, despise *d*
25 glory and majesty, *d* and power, both now and

Door *See also* Entrance, Gate, Threshold, Way

Gen. 4:7 thou doest not well, sin lieth at the *d*
Ex. 12:23 LORD will pass over the *d*, and will not
33:8 stood every man at his tent *d*, and looked
Num. 12:5 LORD . . stood in the *d* of the tabernacle
Judg. 16:3 took the *d* of the gate of the city
19:22 sons of Belial, beset . . and beat at the *d*
2 Kgs. 9:3 then open the *d*, and flee, and tarry not
Job 31:9 or if I have laid wait at my neighbor's *d*
31:32 but I opened my *d* to the traveler
38:17 seen the *d* of the shadow of death?
41:14 who can open the *d* of his face?
Ps. 24:7 (24:9) and be ye lifted up, ye everlasting *d*
78:23 from above, and opened the *d* of heaven
141:3 before my mouth; keep the *d* of my lips
Prov. 5:8 and come not nigh the *d* of her house
8:3 entry of the city, at the coming in at the *d*
26:14 as the *d* turneth upon his hinges, so doth
Is. 6:4 posts of the *d* moved at the voice of him
26:20 thy chambers, and shut thy *d* about thee
57:8 behind the *d* also and the posts hast thou
Ezek. 8:8 when I had digged in the wall, behold a *d*
41:3 *d*, six cubits; and the breadth of the *d*
Hos. 2:15 and the valley of Achor for a *d* of hope
Amos 9:1 smite the lintel of the *d*, that the posts
Mal. 1:10 you that would shut the *d* for nought?
Mt. 6:6 thou hast shut thy *d*, pray to thy Father
24:33 (Mk. 13:29) that it is near, even at the *d*
25:10 to the marriage: and the *d* was shut
27:60 (Mk. 15:46) stone to the *d* of the sepulchre
28:2 rolled back the stone from the *d*, and sat
Mk. 1:33 the city was gathered together at the *d*
2:2 not so much as about the *d*: and he preached
11:4 and found the colt tied by the *d*
Lk. 13:25 knock at the *d*, saying, Lord, Lord, open
Jn. 10:1 entereth not by the *d* into the sheepfold
10:7 I say unto you, I am the *d* of the sheep
10:9 I am the *d*: by me if any man enter in
18:16 but Peter stood at the *d* without
20:19 the *d* were shut where the disciples were
20:26 then came Jesus, the *d* being shut
Acts 5:9 which have buried thy husband are at the *d*
5:19 opened the prison *d*, and brought them forth
12:13 Peter knocked at the *d* . . a damsel came

Acts 14:27 opened the *d* of faith unto the Gentiles
  16:26 and immediately all the *d* were opened
1 Cor. 16:9 a great *d* and effectual is opened unto
2 Cor. 2:12 and a *d* was opened unto me of the Lord
Col. 4:3 God would open unto us a *d* of utterance
Jas. 5:9 behold, the judge standeth before the *d*
Rev. 3:8 behold, I have set before thee an open *d*
  3:20 behold, I stand at the *d*, and knock
  4:1 *d* was opened in heaven: and the first voice

Doorkeeper

1 Chr. 15:23 Berechiah and Elkanah . . *d* for the ark
Ps. 84:10 had rather be a *d* in the house of my God

Doorpost

Ex. 12:7 posts and on the upper *d* of the houses
Deut. 11:20 and thou shalt write them upon the *d*

Dorcas (Tabitha) Acts 9:36–41

Dothan Gen. 37:17; 2 Kgs. 6:13–19

Double

Gen. 41:32 that the dream was *d* unto Pharaoh twice
  43:12 take *d* money in your hand
Ex. 22:4 ox, or ass, or sheep; he shall restore *d*
  22:7 if the thief be found, let him pay *d*
  22:9 whom the judges shall condemn . . shall pay *d*
Deut. 15:18 been worth a *d* hired servant to thee
2 Kgs. 2:9 a *d* portion of thy spirit be upon me
1 Chr. 12:33 they were not of *d* heart
Job 11:6 wisdom, that they are *d* to that which is!
Ps. 12:2 lips and with a *d* heart do they speak
Is. 40:2 of the LORD's hand *d* for all her sins
  61:7 for your shame ye shall have *d*
Jer. 16:18 first I will recompense . . their sin *d*
  17:18 and destroy them with *d* destruction
Ezek. 21:14 and let the sword be *d* the third time
Zech. 9:12 declare that I will render *d* unto thee
1 Tim. 5:17 rule well be counted worthy of *d* honor
Rev. 18:6 and *d* unto her *d* according to her works

Double-minded

Jas. 1:8 *d-m* man is unstable in all his ways
  4:8 and purify your hearts, ye *d-m*

Double-tongued

1 Tim. 3:8 deacons be grave, not *d-t*

Doubt See also Unbelief

Deut. 28:66 thy life shall hang in *d* before thee
Job 12:2 no *d* but ye are the people, and wisdom
Dan. 5:12 dissolving of *d*, were found in . . Daniel
  5:16 canst make interpretations, and dissolve *d*
Mt. 14:31 of little faith, wherefore didst thou *d*?
  21:21 (Mk. 11:23) have faith, and *d* not, ye shall
  28:17 saw him, they worshipped him: but some *d*
Lk. 11:20 no *d* the kingdom of God is come upon you
Jn. 10:24 how long dost thou make us to *d*?
  13:22 looked one on another, *d* of whom he spake
Acts 2:12 and they were all amazed, and were in *d*
  5:24 they *d* of them whereunto this would grow
  10:17 while Peter *d* in himself what this vision
  10:20 go with them, *d* nothing: for I have sent
  25:20 because I *d* of such manner of questions
Rom. 14:23 he that *d* is damned if he eat, because
Gal. 4:20 change my voice; for I stand in *d* of you
1 Tim. 2:8 up holy hands, without wrath and *d*

Doubtful

Lk. 12:29 ye shall drink, neither be ye of *d* mind
Rom. 14:1 receive ye, but not to *d* disputations

Dove See also Turtledove

Gen. 8:8 he sent forth a *d* from him, to see if the
  8:9 the *d* found no rest for the sole of her foot
Ps. 55:6 oh that I had wings like a *d*! for then
  68:13 yet shall ye be as the wings of a *d*
Song 1:15 (4·1) thou art fair; thou hast *d* ' eyes
  2:14 O my *d*, that art in the clefts of the rock
  5:12 his eyes are as the eyes of *d* by the rivers
Is. 38:14 I did mourn as a *d*: mine eyes fail with
  59:11 mourn sore like *d*: we look for judgment
Jer. 48:28 be like the *d* that maketh her nest in
Hos. 7:11 Ephraim also is like a silly *d* without
Nah. 2:7 voice of *d*, taboring upon their breasts
Mt. 3:16 (Mk. 1:10; Lk. 3:22; Jn. 1:32) Spirit of God
  descending like a *d*
  10:16 be ye . . wise as serpents, and harmless as *d*
  21:12 (Mk. 11:15) seats of them that sold *d*
Jn. 2:14 those that sold oxen and sheep and *d*

Downsitting

Ps. 139:2 thou knowest my *d* and mine uprising

Downward

2 Kgs. 19:30 (Is. 37:31) root *d* . . bear fruit upward
Eccl. 3:21 spirit of the beast that goeth *d* to the

Dowry

Gen. 30:20 God hath endued me with a good *d*
  34:12 ask me never so much *d* and gift, and I
Ex. 22:17 pay money according to the *d* of virgins
1 Sam. 18:25 to David, The king desireth not any *d*

Drag

Hab. 1:15 in their net, and gather them in their *d*
Jn. 21:8 in a little ship . . *d* the net with fishes

Dragon

Deut. 32:33 their wine is the poison of *d*
Neh. 2:13 before the *d* well, and to the dung port
Job 30:29 I am a brother to *d*, and a companion to
Ps. 74:13 thou brakest the heads of the *d* in the
  91:13 lion and the *d* shalt thou trample under
  148:7 praise the LORD . . ye *d*, and all deeps
Is. 13:22 and *d* in their pleasant palaces
  27:1 and he shall slay the *d* that is in the sea
  34:13 be a habitation of *d*, and a court for owls
  43:20 beast . . shall honor me, the *d* and the owls
  51:9 art thou not it that hath . . wounded the *d*?
Jer. 9:11 make Jerusalem heaps, and a den of *d*
  10:22 cities of Judah desolate, and a den of *d*
Ezek. 29:3 Pharaoh king of Egypt, the great *d* that
Mic. 1:8 I will make a wailing like the *d*
Mal. 1:3 laid . . waste for the *d* of the wilderness
Rev. 12:3 behold a great red *d*, having seven heads
  12:9 the great *d* was cast out, that old serpent
  12:17 the *d* was wroth with the woman, and went
  13:2 the *d* gave him his power, and his seat
  13:11 two horns like a lamb, and he spake as a *d*
  16:13 like frogs come out of the mouth of the *d*
  20:2 and he laid hold on the *d*, that old serpent

Drank See Drink

Draught

2 Kgs. 10:27 house of Baal, and made it a *d* house
Mt. 15:17 (Mk. 7:19) and is cast out into the *d*?
Lk. 5:4 and let down your nets for a *d*

Draw (Drew, Drawn)

Gen. 24:11 the time that women go out to *d* water
  37:28 they *d* and lifted up Joseph out of the pit
Ex. 2:10 Moses . . Because I *d* him out of the water
  3:5 *d* not nigh hither: put off thy shoes from

Josh. 8:26 Joshua *d* not his hand back, wherewith
Ruth 4:8 buy it for thee. So he *d* off his shoe
2 Sam. 22:17 (Ps. 18:16) *d* me out of many waters
1 Kgs. 22:34 (2 Chr. 18:33) man *d* a bow at a venture
2 Kgs. 9:24 Jehu *d* a bow with his full strength
2 Chr. 5:9 out the staves of the ark
Esth. 5:2 so Esther *d* near, and touched the top of
Job 21:33 and every man shall *d* after him
    40:23 that he can *d* up Jordan into his mouth
    41:1 canst thou *d* out leviathan with a hook?
Ps. 28:3 *d* me not away with the wicked, and with
    37:14 the wicked have *d* out the sword, and have
    69:18 *d* nigh unto my soul, and redeem it: deliver
    73:28 but it is good for me to *d* near to God
    88:3 and my life *d* nigh unto the grave
Song 1:4 *d* me, we will run after thee
Is. 5:18 woe unto them that *d* iniquity with cords
    12:3 ye *d* water out of the wells of salvation
    29:13 (Mt. 15:8) people *d* near me with their mouth
Jer. 31:3 with loving-kindness have I *d* thee
    38:13 so they *d* up Jeremiah with cords, and took
Lam. 3:57 thou *d* near in the day that I called
Hos. 11:4 I *d* them with cords of a man, with bands
Zeph. 3:2 she *d* not near to her God
Mt. 26:51 (Mk. 14:47; Jn. 18:10) *d* his sword . . struck
Lk. 15:25 *d* nigh to the house, he heard music
    21:8 saying, I am Christ; and the time *d* near
    21:28 lift up your heads . . your redemption *d* nigh
    24:15 Jesus himself *d* near, and went with them
Jn. 2:8 *d* out now, and bear unto the governor of
    4:11 nothing to *d* with, and the well is deep
    4:15 that I thirst not, neither come hither to *d*
    6:44 except the Father which hath sent me *d* him
    12:32 lifted up from the earth, will *d* all men
    21:6 not able to *d* it for the multitude of fishes
Acts 5:37 and *d* away much people after him
    7:17 when the time of the promise *d* nigh
    11:10 and all were *d* up again into heaven
    14:19 having stoned Paul, *d* him out of the city
    20:30 speaking perverse things, to *d* away disciples
Heb. 7:19 hope . . by the which we *d* nigh unto God
    10:22 let us *d* near with a true heart in full
    10:38 if any man *d* back, my soul shall have no
    10:39 are not of them who *d* back unto perdition
Jas. 1:14 when he is *d* away of his own lust
    2:6 oppress you, and *d* you before the judgment
    4:8 *d* nigh to God, and he will *d* nigh to you
    5:8 for the coming of the Lord *d* nigh

Drawer

Deut. 29:11 of thy wood unto the *d* of thy water
Josh. 9:21 hewers of wood and *d* of water unto all

Dread *See also* Fear, Horror, Terror

Gen. 9:2 the *d* of you shall be upon every beast
Ex. 15:16 fear and *d* shall fall upon them
Deut. 1:29 *d* not, neither be afraid of them
    2:25 this day will I begin to put the *d* of thee
    11:25 shall lay . . the *d* of you upon all the land
1 Chr. 22:13 be strong, and of good courage; *d* not
Job 13:21 and let not thy *d* make me afraid
Is. 8:13 LORD of hosts himself . . let him be your *d*

Dreadful

Gen. 28:17 how *d* is this place! this is none other
Job 15:21 a *d* sound is in his ears: in prosperity
Dan. 9:4 the great and *d* God, keeping the covenant
Mal. 4:5 coming of the great and *d* day of the LORD

Dream *See also* Trance, Vision

Gen. 20:3 God came to Abimelech in a *d* by night
    28:12 and he *d*, and behold a ladder set up on
    31:10 saw in a *d*, and, behold, the rams which

Gen. 31:11 angel . . spake . . in a *d*, saying, Jacob
    31:24 and God came to Laban the Syrian in a *d*
    37:5 Joseph *d* a *d*, and he told it his brethren
    37:8 they hated him yet the more for his *d*
    40:5 they *d* a *d* both of them, each man his *d* in
    41:1 Pharaoh *d*: and, behold, he stood by the river
    41:8 Pharaoh told them his *d*; but there was none
Num. 12:6 I the LORD. . will speak unto him in a *d*
Judg. 7:13 I *d* a *d*, and, lo, a cake of barley bread
1 Kgs. 3:5 the LORD appeared to Solomon in a *d*
Job 20:8 he shall fly away as a *d*, and shall not
    33:15 in a *d*, in a vision of the night, when deep
Ps. 73:20 as a *d* when one awaketh; so, O Lord, when
    126:1 captivity of Zion, we were like them that *d*
Eccl. 5:3 *d* cometh through the multitude of business
    5:7 in the multitude of *d*. . are also divers vanities
Is. 29:8 hungry man *d*, and, behold, he eateth
Jer. 23:28 prophet that hath a *d*, let him tell a *d*
Dan. 2:1 Nebuchadnezzar *d d*, wherewith his spirit
    4:19 my lord, the *d* be to them that hate thee
Joel 2:28 (Acts 2:17) your old men shall *d d*
Zech. 10:2 have seen a lie, and have told false *d*
Mt. 1:20 appeared unto him in a *d*, saying, Joseph
    2:12 being warned of God in a *d* that they should
    2:13 appeareth to Joseph in a *d*, saying, Arise
    2:22 being warned of God in a *d*, he turned aside
    27:19 have suffered many things this day in a *d*

Dreamer

Gen. 37:19 one to another, Behold, this *d* cometh
Deut. 13:5 or that *d* of dreams, shall be put to death
Jer. 27:9 nor to your diviners, nor to your *d*, nor
Jude 8 filthy *d* defile the flesh, despise dominion

Dregs

Ps. 75:8 *d* thereof, all the wicked . . drink them
Is. 51:17 drunken the *d* of the cup of trembling
    51:22 *d* of the cup of my fury; thou shalt no more

Dress

Gen. 2:15 garden of Eden to *d* it and to keep it
Ex. 30:7 he *d* the lamps, he shall burn incense
Deut. 28:39 thou shalt plant vineyards, and *d* them
2 Sam. 12:4 but took the poor man's lamb, and *d* it
Heb. 6:7 forth herbs meet for them by whom it is *d*

Drew *See* Draw

Drink (Drank, Drunk)

Gen. 9:21 he *d* of the wine, and was drunken
    19:32 make our father *d* wine, and we will lie
    21:19 the bottle with water, and gave the lad *d*
    24:46 also: so I *d*, and she made the camels *d*
    27:25 did eat: and he brought him wine, and he *d*
Ex. 15:23 they could not *d* of the waters of Marah
    15:24 against Moses, saying, What shall we *d*?
    17:1 and there was no water for the people to *d*
    32:20 and made the children of Israel *d* of it
Lev. 10:9 do not *d* wine nor strong *d*, thou, nor
Num. 5:24 cause the woman to *d* the bitter water
    6:3 separate himself from wine and strong *d*
    20:8 give the congregation and their beasts *d*
Deut. 29:6 neither have ye *d* wine or strong *d*
Judg. 4:19 I pray thee, a little water to *d*
    7:5 one that boweth down upon his knees to *d*
1 Sam. 1:15 I have *d* neither wine nor strong *d*
    30:12 eaten no bread, nor *d* any water, three days
2 Sam. 23:16 (1 Chr. 11:18) David . . would not *d*
1 Kgs. 17:6 in the evening; and he *d* of the brook
2 Kgs. 18:31 (Is. 36:16) *d* ye every one the waters
Neh. 8:10 go your way, eat the fat, and *d* the sweet
Esth. 3:15 the king and Haman sat down to *d*; but

Job 15:16 filthy is man, which *d* iniquity like water?
21:20 he shall *d* of the wrath of the Almighty
40:23 behold, he *d* up a river, and hasteth not
Ps. 36:8 make them *d* of the river of thy pleasures
50:13 flesh of bulls, or *d* the blood of goats?
60:3 hast made us to *d* the wine of astonishment
69:21 and in my thirst they gave me vinegar to *d*
80:5 and givest them tears to *d* in great measure
102:9 like bread, and mingled my *d* with weeping
110:7 shall *d* of the brook in the way
Prov. 4:17 wickedness, and *d* the wine of violence
5:15 *d* waters out of thine own cistern
20:1 wine is a mocker, strong *d* is raging
25:21 (Rom. 12:20) thirsty, give him water to *d*
31:4 kings to *d* wine; nor for princes strong *d*
31:5 they, *d*, and forget the law, and pervert
31:6 strong *d* unto him that is ready to perish
31:7 let him *d*, and forget his poverty
Eccl. 2:24 nothing better for a man, than. . eat and *d*
9:7 and *d* thy wine with a merry heart
Song 5:1 *d*, yea, *d* abundantly, O beloved
Is. 5:11 morning, that they may follow strong *d*
5:22 woe unto them that are mighty to *d* wine
22:13 (1 Cor. 15:32) let us eat and *d*; for tomorrow
24:9 strong *d* shall be bitter to them that *d* it
28:7 and the prophet have erred through strong *d*
32:6 he will cause the *d* of the thirsty to fail
43:20 in the desert, to give *d* to my people
51:22 thou shalt no more *d* it again
65:13 servants shall *d*, but ye shall be thirsty
Jer. 25:17 and made all the nations to *d*, unto whom
35:6 they said, We will *d* no wine: for Jonadab
35:14 unto this day they *d* none, but obey their
Lam. 5:4 we have *d* our water for money; our wood
Ezek. 4:11 thou shalt *d* also water by measure
Dan. 1:5 king's meat, and of the wine which he *d*
5:4 they *d* wine, and praised the gods of gold
Hos. 4:18 *d* is sour: they have committed whoredom
Amos 2:8 *d* the wine of the condemned in the house
6:6 that *d* wine in bowls, and anoint themselves
Obad. 16 for as ye have *d* upon my holy mountain
Mic. 2:11 prophesy unto thee of wine and of strong *d*
Hab. 2:15 woe unto him that giveth his neighbor *d*
Hag. 1:6 ye *d*, but ye are not filled with *d*
Zech. 9:15 and they shall *d*, and make a noise as
Mt. 6:25 (Lk. 12:29) shall eat, or what ye shall *d*
10:42 (Mk. 9:41) give to *d* unto one of these little
11:18 (Lk. 7:33) John came neither eating nor *d*
20:22 (Mk. 10:38) to *d* of the cup that I shall *d*
24:38 (Lk. 17:27) were eating and *d*, marrying and
25:35 I was thirsty, and ye gave me *d*
26:27 (Mk. 14:23) to them, saying, *D* ye all of it
26:29 (Mk. 14:25; Lk. 22:18) not *d*. . of this fruit
26:42 may not pass away from me, except I *d* it
27:34 (Mk. 15:23) they gave him vinegar to *d*
Mk. 2:16 (Lk. 5:30) *d* with publicans and sinners?
16:18 *d* any deadly thing, it shall not hurt them
Lk. 1:15 and shall *d* neither wine nor strong *d*
5:39 no man also having *d* old wine. . desireth new
10:7 eating and *d* such things as they give
Jn. 2:10 good wine; and when men have well *d*, then
4:7 Jesus saith unto her, Give me to *d*
4:13 whosoever *d* of this water shall thirst
4:14 *d* of the water that I shall give him shall
6:55 is meat indeed, and my blood is *d* indeed
7:37 any man thirst, let him come unto me, and *d*
18:11 my Father hath given me, shall I not *d* it?
Rom. 12:20 if he thirst, give him *d*: for in so doing
14:17 the kingdom of God is not meat and *d*
14:21 good neither to eat flesh, nor to *d* wine
1 Cor. 10:4 did all *d* the same spiritual *d*
10:31 ye eat, or *d*. . do all to the glory of God
11:25 as oft as ye *d* it, in remembrance of me

1 Cor. 11:29 *d* unworthily, eateth and *d* damnation
12:13 have been all made to *d* into one Spirit
15:32 let us eat and *d*; for tomorrow we die
Col. 2:16 let no man. . judge you in meat, or in *d*
1 Tim. 5:23 *d* no longer water. . use a little wine
Rev. 14:8 made all nations *d* of the wine of
14:10 shall *d* of the wine of the wrath of God

Drink Offering

Gen. 35:14 pillar of stone: and he poured a *d o*
Ex. 29:40 the fourth part of a hin of wine for a *d o*
Lev. 23:13 the *d o* thereof shall be of wine
Num. 15:5 wine for a *d o* shalt thou prepare
Ps. 16:4 *d o* of blood will I not offer
Jer. 7:18 to pour out *d o* unto other gods
Ezek. 20:28 and poured out there their *d o*

Drive (Drave, Drove, Driven)

Gen. 3:24 so he *d* out the man: and he placed at
4:14 behold, thou hast *d* me out this day from
Ex. 6:1 and with a strong hand shall he *d* them out
14:25 chariot wheels, that they *d* them heavily
23:28 hornets. . which shall *d* out the Hivite, the
Deut. 4:19 heaven, shouldest be *d* to worship them
4:38 to *d* out nations from before thee greater
9:4 for the wickedness. . LORD doth *d* them out
11:23 *d* out all these nations from before you
30:4 if any of thine be *d* out unto the outmost
Josh. 3:10 that he will without fail *d* out from
Judg. 11:24 God shall *d* out from before us, them
2 Kgs. 9:20 driving of Jehu. . for he *d* furiously
Job 6:13 and is wisdom *d* quite from me?
24:3 they *d* away the ass of the fatherless
30:5 they were *d* forth from among men
Ps. 1:4 are like the chaff which the wind *d* away
44:2 thou didst *d* out the heathen with thy hand
68:2 as smoke is *d* away, so *d* them away
114:3 sea saw it, and fled: Jordan was *d* back
Prov. 14:32 the wicked is *d* away in his wickedness
22:15 rod of correction shall *d* it far from him
25:23 north wind *d* away rain: so doth an angry
Is. 8:22 and they shall be *d* to darkness
22:19 I will *d* thee from thy station
Jer. 8:3 (23:3, 8; 29:14, 18; 32:37) whither I have *d*
46:15 stood not, because the LORD did *d* them
Ezek. 4:13 among the Gentiles, whither I will *d*
31:11 I have *d* him out for his wickedness
34:16 and bring again that which was *d* away
Dan. 4:25 (4:32) they shall *d* thee from men
4:33 (5:21) Nebuchadnezzar. . was *d* from men
Hos. 13:3 the chaff that is *d* with the whirlwind
Mic. 4:6 (Zeph. 3:19) I will gather her that is *d* out
Mk. 1:12 the Spirit *d* him into the wilderness
Lk. 8:29 was *d* of the devil into the wilderness
Jn. 2:15 he *d* them all out of the temple
Acts 7:45 whom God *d* out before the face of our

Dromedary

1 Kgs. 4:28 and straw for the horses and *d*
Esth. 8:10 riders on mules, camels, and young *d*
Jer. 2:23 thou art a swift *d* traversing her ways

Drop

Deut. 32:2 my doctrine shall *d* as the rain
33:28 also his heavens shall *d* down dew
2 Sam. 21:10 beginning of harvest until water *d* upon
Job 29:22 and my speech *d* upon them
36:27 he maketh small the *d* of water: they pour
36:28 clouds do *d* and distil upon man abundantly
38:28 or who hath begotten the *d* of dew?
Ps. 65:11 thy goodness; and thy paths *d* fatness
68:8 heavens also *d* at the presence of God

Eccl. 10:18 through idleness of the hands the house *d*
Is. 40:15 the nations are as a *d* of a bucket
   45:8 *d* down, ye heavens, from above, and let the
Ezek. 20:46 and *d* thy word toward the south
Joel 3:18 that the mountains shall *d* down new wine
Amos 9:13 and the mountains shall *d* sweet wine
Lk. 22:44 sweat was as it were great *d* of blood

Dropping

Prov. 19:13 contentions of a wife are a continual *d*
   27:15 a continual *d*. . a contentious woman. . alike

Dropsy

Lk. 14:2 a certain man before him which had the *d*

Dross

Ps. 119:119 all the wicked of the earth like *d*
Prov. 25:4 take away the *d* from the silver
Is. 1:22 thy silver is become *d*, thy wine mixed
   1:25 purge away thy *d*, and take away all thy tin
Ezek. 22:18 house of Israel is to me become *d*

Drought *See also* Dearth, Famine

Gen. 31:40 in the day the *d* consumed me
Ps. 32:4 moisture is turned into the *d* of summer
Is. 58:11 satisfy thy soul in *d*, and make fat thy
Jer. 17:8 shall not be careful in the year of *d*
Hos. 13:5 in the wilderness, in the land of great *d*
Hag. 1:11 I called for a *d* upon the land, and upon

Drove (noun) *See also* Flock, Herd

Gen. 32:16 and put a space betwixt *d* and *d*
   33:8 what meanest thou by all this *d* which I met?

Drove (verb) *See* Drive

Drown

Ex. 15:4 chosen captains also are *d* in the Red sea
Song 8:7 quench love, neither can the floods *d* it
Mt. 18:6 hanged about his neck, and that he were *d*
1 Tim. 6:9 lusts, which *d* men in destruction
Heb. 11:29 the Egyptians assaying to do were *d*

Drowsiness

Prov. 23:21 and *d* shall clothe a man with rags

Drunk (adjective) *See also* Drunken

2 Sam. 11:13 David. . made him *d*
1 Kgs. 16:9 he was in Tirzah, drinking himself *d*
   20:16 but Ben-hadad was drinking himself *d*
Is. 63:6 in mine anger, and make them *d* in my fury
Jer. 46:10 be satiate and made *d* with their blood
Eph. 5:18 be not *d* with wine, wherein is excess
Rev. 17:2 made *d* with the wine of her fornication

Drunk (verb) *See* Drink

Drunkard

Deut. 21:20 he is a glutton, and a *d*
Ps. 69:12 against me; and I was the song of the *d*
Prov. 23:21 *d* and the glutton shall come to poverty
   26:9 as a thorn goeth up into the hand of a *d*
Is. 24:20 the earth shall reel to and fro like a *d*
   28:1 woe to the crown of pride, to the *d* of Ephraim
Joel 1:5 awake, ye *d*, and weep; and howl, all ye
1 Cor. 5:11 or a *d*. . with such a one, no, not to eat
   6:10 nor *d*. . shall inherit the kingdom of God

Drunken *See also* Drunk

Gen. 9:21 he drank of the wine, and was *d*
1 Sam. 25:36 for he was very *d*: wherefore she told
Job 12:25 he maketh them to stagger like a *d* man
Ps. 107:27 reel to and fro, and stagger like a *d* man

Is. 29:9 they are *d*, but not with wine; they stagger
Jer. 23:9 all my bones shake: I am like a *d* man
Lam. 3:15 he hath made me *d* with wormwood
Nah. 1:10 and while they are *d* as drunkards
Hab. 2:15 makest him *d* also, that thou mayest look
Lk. 12:45 shall begin. . to 'eat and drink, and to be *d*
Acts 2:15 these are not *d*, as ye suppose, seeing
1 Cor. 11:21 and one is hungry, and another is *d*
1 Thes. 5:7 and they that be *d* are *d* in the night
Rev. 17:6 the woman *d* with the blood of the saints

Drunkenness

Deut. 29:19 of mine heart, to add *d* to thirst
Eccl. 10:17 eat. . for strength, and not for *d*!
Jer. 13:13 the inhabitants of Jerusalem, with *d*
Ezek. 23:33 thou shalt be filled with *d* and sorrow
Lk. 21:34 overcharged with surfeiting, and *d*, and
Rom. 13:13 not in rioting and *d*, not in chambering
Gal. 5:21 murders, *d*, revelings, and such like

Drusilla Acts 24:24

Dry

Gen. 8:13 behold, the face of the ground was *d*
Josh. 3:17 firm on *d* ground in the midst of Jordan
Judg. 6:37 and it be *d* upon all the earth besides
1 Kgs. 13:4 and his hand, which he put forth. . *d* up
Ps. 107:33 he turneth. . watersprings into *d* ground
Prov. 17:22 but a broken spirit *d* the bones
Is. 19:5 and the river shall be wasted and *d* up
   32:2 as rivers of water in a *d* place
   44:3 and floods upon the *d* ground: I will pour
   44:27 the deep, Be *d*, and I will *d* up thy rivers
   53:2 root out of a *d* ground: he hath no form nor
   56:3 let the eunuch say, Behold, I am a *d* tree
Ezek. 17:24 *d* up the green tree. . made the *d* tree to
   30:12 and I will make the rivers *d*, and sell
   37:4 O ye *d* bones, hear the word of the LORD
Hos. 9:16 Ephraim is smitten, their root is *d* up
Mt. 12:43 (Lk. 11:24) he walketh through *d* places
Mk. 5:29 fountain of her blood was *d* up
   11:20 passed by, they saw the fig tree *d* up
Lk. 23:31 green tree, what shall be done in the *d*?
Rev. 16:12 Euphrates; and the water thereof was *d*

Due

Lev. 10:13 because it is thy *d*, and thy sons' *d*
   26:4 then I will give you rain in *d* season
1 Chr. 16:29 (Ps. 29:2; 96:8) glory *d* unto his name
Ps. 104:27 (145:15) give them their meat in *d* season
Prov. 3:27 withhold not good from. . whom it is *d*
   15:23 a word spoken in *d* season, how good is it!
Mt. 18:34 he should pay all that was *d* unto him
   24:45 (Lk. 12:42) to give them meat in *d* season?
Lk. 23:41 for we receive the *d* reward of our deeds
Rom. 5:6 in *d* time Christ died for the ungodly
   13:7 render therefore to all their *d*: tribute to
1 Cor. 7:3 render unto the wife *d* benevolence
   15:8 of me also, as of one born out of *d* time
Gal. 6:9 well doing: for in *d* season we shall reap
1 Tim. 2:6 ransom for all, to be testified in *d* time
Tit. 1:3 but hath in *d* times manifested his word
1 Pet. 5:6 that he may exalt you in *d* time

Duke

Gen. 36:15 these were *d* of the sons of Esau

Dull

Mt. 13:15 (Acts 28:27) their ears are *d* of hearing
Heb. 5:11 seeing ye are *d* of hearing

Dumb *See also* Speechless

Ex. 4:11 or who maketh the *d*, or deaf, or the seeing

Ps. 38:13 and I was as a *d* man that openeth not
    39:2 I was *d* with silence, I held my peace
Prov. 31:8 open thy mouth for the *d* in the cause
Is. 35:6 then shall. . the tongue of the *d* sing
    53:7 (Acts 8:32) sheep before her shearers is *d*
    56:10 watchmen . . are all *d* dogs, they cannot bark
Ezek. 3:26 roof of thy mouth, that thou shalt be *d*
Dan. 10:15 face toward the ground, and I became *d*
Hab. 2:19 to the *d* stone, Arise, it shall teach!
Mt. 9:32 (Lk. 11:14) a *d* man possessed with a devil
    12:22 that the blind and *d* both spake and saw
    15:30 lame, blind, *d*, maimed, and many others
Mk. 7:37 both the deaf to hear, and the *d* to speak
    9:17 unto thee my son, which hath a *d* spirit
    9:25 *d* and deaf spirit, I charge thee, come out
Lk. 1:20 thou shalt be *d*, and not able to speak
    11:14 he was casting out a devil, and it was *d*
1 Cor. 12:2 carried away unto these *d* idols
2 Pet. 2:16 the *d* ass speaking with man's voice

Dung

Jer. 8:2 shall be for *d* upon the face of the earth
Mal. 2:3 spread *d* upon your faces, even the *d* of
Lk. 13:8 also, till I shall dig about it, and *d* it
Phil. 3:8 count them but *d*, that I may win Christ

Dungeon *See also* Prison

Gen. 40:15 that they should put me into the *d*
    41:14 and they brought him hastily out of the *d*
Jer. 37:16 when Jeremiah was entered into the *d*
    38:6 took they Jeremiah, and cast him into the *d*
Lam. 3:53 they have cut off my life in the *d*
    3:55 upon thy name, O LORD, out of the low *d*

Durable

Prov. 8:18 yea, *d* riches and righteousness
Is. 23:18 to eat sufficiently, and for *d* clothing

Dust *See also* Ashes, Earth, Ground

Gen. 2:7 God formed man of the *d* of the ground
    3:14 *d* shalt thou eat all the days of thy life
    3:19 *d* thou art, and unto *d* shalt thou return
    13:16 I will make thy seed as the *d* of the earth
    18:27 me to speak unto the Lord, which am but *d*
Ex. 8:16 stretch out thy rod, and smite the *d*
Num. 23:10 who can count the *d* of Jacob
Deut. 9:21 as small as *d*: and I cast the *d* thereof
Josh. 7:6 and put *d* upon their heads
Job 2:12 and sprinkled *d* upon their heads toward
    10:9 and wilt thou bring me into *d* again?
    22:24 then shalt thou lay up gold as *d*
    27:16 though he heap up silver as the *d*
    30:19 and I am become like *d* and ashes
    34:15 and man shall turn again unto *d*
    38:38 when the *d* groweth into hardness
    39:14 leaveth her eggs. . warmeth them in the *d*
    42:6 I abhor myself, and repent in *d* and ashes
Ps. 30:9 shall the *d* praise thee? shall it declare
    103:14 our frame; he remembereth that we are *d*
    104:29 they die, and return to their *d*
    119:25 my soul cleaveth unto the *d*: quicken thou
Eccl. 3:20 all are of the *d*, and all turn to *d*
    12:7 then shall the *d* return to the earth
Is. 40:12 and comprehended the *d* of the earth in a
    40:15 are counted as the small *d* of the balance
    47:1 sit in the *d*, O virgin daughter of Babylon
    65:25 *d* shall be the serpent's meat
Lam. 2:10 they have cast up *d* upon their heads
    3:29 he putteth his mouth in the *d*; if so be
Dan. 12:2 sleep in the *d* of the earth shall awake
Mic. 1:10 house of Aphrah roll thyself in the *d*
    7:17 they shall lick the *d* like a serpent
Nah. 1:3 and the clouds are the *d* of his feet

Mt. 10:14 (Mk. 6:11; Lk. 9:5) shake off the *d* of your
Lk. 10:11 the very *d* of your city, which cleaveth
Acts 13:51 but they shook off the *d* of their feet
    22:23 their clothes, and threw *d* into the air

Duty

Ex. 21:10 her *d* of marriage, shall he not diminish
Deut. 25:5 perform the *d* of a husband's brother
2 Chr. 8:14 (Ezra 3:4) as the *d* of every day required
Eccl. 12:13 fear God. . this is the whole *d* of man
Lk. 17:10 we have done that which was our *d* to do
Rom. 15:27 their *d* is also to minister unto them

Dwell (Dwelt) *See also* Abide, Inhabit, Lodge, Remain, Sojourn, Stay

Gen. 4:16 Cain went out. . and *d* in the land of Nod
Ex. 2:21 Moses was content to *d* with the man
Deut. 12:11 choose to cause his name to *d* there
    33:12 beloved of the LORD shall *d* in safety by him
1 Sam. 4:4 of hosts, which *d* between the cherubim
1 Kgs. 8:27 (2 Chr. 6:18) God indeed *d* on the earth?
Neh. 11:1 to bring one of ten to *d* in Jerusalem
Ps. 4:8 for thou, LORD, only makest me *d* in safety
    5:4 neither shall evil *d* with thee
    15:1 who shall *d* in thy holy hill?
    23:6 I will *d* in the house of the LORD for ever
    25:13 his soul shall *d* at ease; and his seed
    27:4 that I may *d* in the house of the LORD all
    37:3 and do good; so shalt thou *d* in the land
    65:4 unto thee, that he may *d* in thy courts
    68:16 this is the hill which God desireth to *d* in
    68:18 that the LORD God might *d* among them
    84:4 blessed are they that *d* in thy house
    84:10 than to *d* in the tents of wickedness
    85:9 that fear him; that glory may *d* in our land
    91:1 that *d* in the secret place of the Most High
    107:4 a solitary way; they found no city to *d* in
    120:6 my soul hath long *d* with him that hateth
    132:14 this is my rest for ever: here will I *d*
    133:1 it is for brethren to *d* together in unity!
Prov. 8:12 I wisdom *d* with prudence, and find out
    21:9 (25:24) better to *d* in a corner of the housetop
Song 8:13 *d* in the gardens, the companions hearken
Is. 11:6 the wolf also shall *d* with the lamb
    33:14 among us shall *d* with the devouring fire?
    33:16 he shall *d* on high; his place of defense
    57:15 I *d* in the high and holy place
Jer. 7:3 and I will cause you to *d* in this place
Hos. 12:9 will yet make thee to *d* in tabernacles
Amos 3:12 that *d* in Samaria in the corner of a bed
Nah. 3:18 Assyria: thy nobles shall *d* in the dust
Mt. 12:45 (Lk. 11:26) they enter in and *d* there
Jn. 1:14 the Word was made flesh, and *d* among us
    1:38 they said unto him, Rabbi. . where *d* thou?
    6:56 drinketh my blood, *d* in me, and I in him
    14:10 Father that *d* in me, he doeth the works
    14:17 ye know him; for he *d* with you, and shall
Acts 7:48 the Most High *d* not in temples made with
    17:26 nations of men for to *d* on all the face of
    28:16 but Paul was suffered to *d* by himself
    28:30 Paul *d* two whole years in his own hired
Rom. 7:17 no more I that do it, but sin that *d* in
    8:9 if so be that the Spirit of God *d* in you
    8:11 mortal bodies by his Spirit that *d* in you
1 Cor. 3:16 and that the Spirit of God *d* in you?
2 Cor. 6:16 as God hath said, I will *d* in them
Eph. 3:17 Christ may *d* in your hearts by faith
Col. 1:19 that in him should all fulness *d*
    2:9 for in him *d* all the fulness of the Godhead
    3:16 let the word of Christ *d* in you richly
1 Tim. 6:16 *d* in. . light which no man can approach
2 Tim. 1:14 keep by the Holy Ghost which *d* in us

Jas. 4:5 the spirit that *d* in us lusteth to envy?
2 Pet. 3:13 a new earth, wherein *d* righteousness
1 Jn. 3:17 how *d* the love of God in him?
　4:12 if we love one another, God *d* in us
　4:13 hereby know we that we *d* in him, and he in
　4:16 he that *d* in love *d* in God, and God in him
2 Jn. 2 for the truth's sake, which *d* in us
Rev. 7:15 sitteth on the throne shall *d* among them
　21:3 he will *d* with them, and they shall be his

Dwelling *See also* Abode, Habitation, Home, House, Lodging

1 Kgs. 8:30 hear thou in heaven thy *d* place
Ps. 90:1 Lord, thou hast been our *d* place in all
　91:10 neither shall any plague come nigh thy *d*
Prov. 24:15 against the *d* of the righteous
Nah. 2:11 where is the *d* of the lions
Zeph. 2:6 the seacoast shall be *d* and cottages

E

Eagle

Ex. 19:4 and how I bare you on *e*' wings
Deut. 28:49 swift as the *e* flieth; a nation whose
　32:11 as an *e* stirreth up her nest, fluttereth
2 Sam. 1:23 Saul and Jonathan . . were swifter than *e*
Job 9:26 as the *e* that hasteth to the prey
　39:27 doth the *e* mount up at thy command
Ps. 103:5 that thy youth is renewed like the *e*'s
Prov. 30:19 the way of an *e* in the air
Is. 40:31 they shall mount up with wings as *e*
Jer. 4:13 his horses are swifter than *e*
　49:16 as high as the *e*, I will bring thee down
Ezek. 1:10 (10:14) they four also had the face of an *e*
　17:3 a great *e* with great wings, long-winged
Dan. 4:33 his hairs were grown like *e*' feathers
Obad. 4 though thou exalt thyself as the *e*
Mic. 1:16 enlarge thy baldness as the *e*
Mt. 24:28 (Lk. 17:37) there will the *e* be gathered
Rev. 4:7 and the fourth beast was like a flying *e*
　12:14 woman were given two wings of a great *e*

Ear (noun)

Gen. 41:5 seven *e* of corn came up upon one stalk
Ex. 10:2 that thou mayest tell in the *e* of thy son
　21:6 (Deut. 15:17) bore his *e* through with an awl
Deut. 23:25 thou mayest pluck the *e* with thine hand
1 Sam. 3:11 both the *e* . . that heareth it shall tingle
2 Sam. 22:7 (Ps. 18:6) my cry did enter into his *e*
2 Kgs. 19:16 (Is. 37:17) bow down thine *e*, and hear
　21:12 heareth of it, both his *e* shall tingle
Neh. 1:6 let thine *e* now be attentive, and thine
Job 12:11 (34:3) doth not the *e* try words?
　13:1 mine *e* hath heard and understood it
　15:21 a dreadful sound is in his *e*
　28:22 we have heard the fame thereof with our *e*
　29:11 when the *e* heard me, then it blessed me
　33:16 he openeth the *e* of men, and sealeth their
　36:15 and openeth their *e* in oppression
　42:5 heard of thee by the hearing of the *e*
Ps. 5:1 give *e* to my words, O Lord; consider my
　10:17 thou wilt cause thine *e* to hear
　17:6 O God: incline thine *e* unto me, and hear my
　31:2 bow down thine *e* to me; deliver me speedily
　34:15 (1 Pet. 3:12) his *e* are open unto their cry
　40:6 mine *e* hast thou opened: burnt offering and

Ps. 45:10 consider, and incline thine *e*; forget also
　58:4 are like the deaf adder that stoppeth her *e*
　78:1 give *e*, O my people, to my law: incline your *e*
　94:9 he that planted the *e*, shall he not hear?
　115:6 (135:17) they have *e*, but they hear not
　116:2 he hath inclined his *e* unto me, therefore
　143:1 prayer, O Lord, give *e* to my supplications
Prov. 2:2 so that thou incline thine *e* unto wisdom
　15:31 *e* that heareth the reproof of life abideth
　17:4 and a liar giveth *e* to a naughty tongue
　18:15 and the *e* of the wise seeketh knowledge
　20:12 hearing *e*, and the seeing eye, the Lord
　21:13 stoppeth his *e* at the cry of the poor
　22:17 bow down thine *e*, and hear the words
　23:9 speak not in the *e* of a fool: for he will
　23:12 apply . . thine *e* to the words of knowledge
　25:12 so is a wise reprover upon an obedient *e*
　26:17 is like one that taketh a dog by the *e*
Eccl. 1:8 nor the *e* filled with hearing
Is. 6:10 make their *e* heavy, and shut their eyes
　35:5 and the *e* of the deaf shall be unstopped
　42:20 opening the *e*, but he heareth not
　48:8 from that time that thine *e* was not opened
　50:4 he wakeneth mine *e* to hear as the learned
　55:3 incline your *e*, and come unto me: hear, and
　59:1 neither his *e* heavy, that it cannot hear
　64:4 (1 Cor. 2:9) nor perceived by the *e*, neither
Jer. 5:21 (Ezek. 12:2) which have *e*, and hear not
　9:20 women, and let your *e* receive the word
Lam. 3:56 hide not thine *e* at my breathing
Amos 3:12 of the lion two legs, or a piece of an *e*
Mt. 10:27 (Lk. 12:3) ye hear in the *e*, that preach
　11:15 (13:9, 43; Mk. 4:9, 23; Lk. 8:8; 14:35) he that
　　　hath *e* to hear, let him hear
　12:1 (Mk. 2:23; Lk. 6:1) to pluck the *e* of corn
　13:15 (Acts 28:27) and their *e* are dull of hearing
　13:16 but blessed are . . your *e*, for they hear
　26:51 (Mk. 14:47; Lk. 22:50; Jn. 18:10) struck a
　　　servant of the high priest, and smote off his *e*
Mk. 4:28 the *e*, after that the full corn in the *e*
　7:33 put his fingers into his *e*, and he spit
　7:35 and straightway his *e* were opened
　8:18 eyes, see ye not? and having *e*, hear ye not?
Lk. 9:44 let these sayings sink down into your *e*
　22:51 and he touched his *e*, and healed him
Acts 7:51 and uncircumcised in heart and *e*, ye do
　17:20 bringest certain strange things to our *e*
Rom. 11:8 not see, and *e* that they should not hear
1 Cor. 2:9 nor *e* heard, neither have entered into
　12:16 *e* shall say, Because I am not the eye
2 Tim. 4:3 to themselves teachers, having itching *e*
Jas. 5:4 cries . . are entered into the *e* of the Lord
Rev. 2:7 (2:11; 2:17; 2:29; 3:6; 3:13; 3:22) hath an *e*,
　let him hear what the Spirit saith unto the churches

Ear (verb)

1 Sam. 8:12 will set them to *e* his ground, and to reap
Is. 30:24 young asses that *e* the ground shall eat

Early

Gen. 19:27 Abraham gat up *e* in the morning to the
Ex. 34:4 Moses rose up *e* in the morning, and went
Judg. 7:3 return and depart *e* from mount Gilead
1 Sam. 15:12 and when Samuel rose *e* to meet Saul
Ps. 46:5 God shall help her, and that right *e*
　57:8 (108:2) I myself will awake *e*
　63:1 O God, thou art my God; *e* will I seek thee
　78:34 and they returned and inquired *e* after God
　90:14 O satisfy us *e* with thy mercy; that we may
Prov. 1:28 they shall seek me, but . . not find me
　8:17 and those that seek me *e* shall find me
Song 7:12 let us get up *e* to the vineyards
Is. 26:9 my spirit within me will I seek thee *e*

Hos. 5:15 in their affliction they will seek me *e*
  6:4 and as the *e* dew it goeth away
Mk. 16:2 (Lk. 24:1) very *e* in the morning, the first
Lk. 24:22 women . . which were *e* at the sepulchre
Jn. 8:2 *e* in the morning he came . . into the temple
  20:1 cometh Mary Magdalene *e* . . it was yet dark
Acts 5:21 entered into the temple *e* in the morning
Jas. 5:7 until he receive the *e* and latter rain

Earnest (adjective)

Rom. 8:19 *e* expectation of the creature waiteth
2 Cor. 7:7 when he told us your *e* desire
Phil. 1:20 my *e* expectation and my hope
Heb. 2:1 we ought to give the more *e* heed to the

Earnest (noun)

2 Cor. 1:22 the *e* of the Spirit in our hearts
  5:5 also hath given unto us the *e* of the Spirit
Eph. 1:14 which is the *e* of our inheritance until

Earnestly

Job 7:2 as a servant *e* desireth the shadow
Jer. 31:20 against him, I do *e* remember him still
Mic. 7:3 that they may do evil with both hands *e*
Lk. 22:44 being in an agony he prayed more *e*
  22:56 he sat by the fire, and *e* looked upon him
Acts 3:12 or why look ye so *e* on us, as though by
  23:1 Paul, *e* beholding the council, said, Men
1 Cor. 12:31 covet *e* the best gifts: and yet show
2 Cor. 5:2 *e* desiring to be clothed upon with our
Jas. 5:17 Elias . . prayed *e* that it might not rain
Jude 3 ye should *e* contend for the faith which was

Earring

Gen. 35:4 they gave unto Jacob . . all their *e*
Ex. 32:2 Aaron said . . Break off the golden *e*
Judg. 8:24 give me every man the *e* of his prey
Prov. 25:12 as an *e* of gold, and an ornament of
Ezek. 16:12 on thy forehead, and *e* in thine ears

Earth *See also* Dust, Ground, Land,
  World

Gen. 1:1 God created the heaven and the *e*
  1:10 and God called the dry land *E*
  1:26 and let them have dominion . . over all the *e*
  6:11 *e* also was corrupt before God; and the *e*
  6:17 bring a flood of waters upon the *e*
  7:10 the waters of the flood were upon the *e*
  8:22 while the *e* remaineth, seedtime and harvest
  9:13 a token of a covenant between me and the *e*
  10:25 (1 Chr. 1:19) in his days was the *e* divided
  11:1 the whole *e* was of one language, and of one
  12:3 in thee shall all families of the *e* be blessed
  18:25 shall not the Judge of all the *e* do right?
Ex. 8:22 that I am the LORD in the midst of the *e*
  9:16 (Rom. 9:17) be declared throughout all the *e*
  9:29 mayest know how that the *e* is the LORD'S
  20:4 (Deut. 5:8) or that is in the *e* beneath
Num. 14:21 the *e* shall be filled with the glory of
  16:30 the *e* open their mouth, and swallow them up
Deut. 28:23 the *e* that is under thee shall be iron
Josh. 3:11 ark . . of the Lord of all the *e* passeth
  23:14 this day I am going the way of all the *e*
1 Sam. 2:8 for the pillars of the *e* are the LORD'S
2 Sam. 22:8 (Ps. 18:7) the *e* shook and trembled
1 Kgs. 8:27 (2 Chr. 6:18) God indeed dwell on the *e*?
2 Kgs. 5:17 to thy servant two mules' burden of *e*?
Job 1:7 (2:2) from going to and fro in the *e*
  7:1 is there not an appointed time to man upon *e*?
  9:6 which shaketh the *e* out of her place
  9:24 the *e* is given into the hand of the wicked
  12:8 or speak to the *e*, and it shall teach thee

Job 19:25 shall stand at the latter day upon the *e*
  26:7 empty place, and hangeth the *e* upon nothing
  38:4 thou when I laid the foundations of the *e*?
  41:33 upon *e* there is not his like, who is made
Ps. 2:8 and the uttermost parts of the *e* for thy
  8:1 (8:9) how excellent is thy name in all the *e*!
  19:4 (Rom. 10:18) line is gone out through all the *e*
  24:1 (1 Cor. 10:26) *e* is the LORD'S, and the fulness
  25:13 and his seed shall inherit the *e*
  33:5 the *e* is full of the goodness of the LORD
  34:16 cut off the remembrance of them from the *e*
  37:9 wait upon the LORD, they shall inherit the *e*
  41:2 and he shall be blessed upon the *e*
  46:2 will not we fear, though the *e* be removed
  46:6 he uttered his voice, the *e* melted
  46:8 what desolations he hath made in the *e*
  46:10 the heathen, I will be exalted in the *e*
  47:7 for God is the King of all the *e*: sing ye
  47:9 the shields of the *e* belong unto God
  48:2 the joy of the whole *e*, is mount Zion
  50:4 and to the *e*, that he may judge his people
  57:5 (108:5) let thy glory be above all the *e*
  58:11 verily he is a God that judgeth in the *e*
  60:2 thou hast made the *e* to tremble; thou hast
  63:9 shall go into the lower parts of the *e*
  65:9 thou visitest the *e*, and waterest it
  67:6 then shall the *e* yield her increase
  71:20 bring me up again from the depths of the *e*
  72:6 the mown grass: as showers that water the *e*
  72:16 there shall be a handful of corn in the *e*
  72:19 let the whole *e* be filled with his glory
  73:9 and their tongue walketh through the *e*
  73:25 is none upon *e* that I desire besides thee
  74:12 working salvation in the midst of the *e*
  74:17 thou hast set all the borders of the *e*
  75:3 *e* and all the inhabitants . . are dissolved
  78:69 the *e* which he hath established for ever
  83:18 JEHOVAH, art the Most High over all the *e*
  85:11 truth shall spring out of the *e*
  89:11 the heavens are thine, the *e* also is thine
  90:2 ever thou hadst formed the *e* and the world
  97:1 the LORD reigneth; let the *e* rejoice
  98:3 the ends of the *e* have seen the salvation
  99:1 between the cherubim; let the *e* be moved
  102:25 (Heb. 1:10) laid the foundation of the *e*
  104:13 the *e* is satisfied with the fruit of thy
  104:24 the *e* is full of thy riches
  112:2 his seed shall be mighty upon *e*
  114:7 tremble, thou *e*, at the presence of the
  115:16 *e* hath he given to the children of men
  119:19 I am a stranger in the *e*: hide not thy
  119:64 the *e*, O LORD, is full of thy mercy
  119:90 thou hast established the *e*, and it abideth
  146:4 breath goeth forth, he returneth to his *e*
  147:8 who prepareth rain for the *e*, who maketh
  148:13 his glory is above the *e* and heaven
Prov. 3:19 the LORD by wisdom hath founded the *e*
  8:26 while as yet he had not made the *e*, nor the
  8:29 when he appointed the foundations of the *e*
  10:30 but the wicked shall not inhabit the *e*
  11:31 righteous shall be recompensed in the *e*
  25:3 the heaven for height, and the *e* for depth
  30:14 to devour the poor from off the *e*
  30:16 the *e* that is not filled with water
  30:21 for three things the *e* is disquieted
Eccl. 1:4 generation cometh: but the *e* abideth for
  5:9 moreover the profit of the *e* is for all
  7:20 not a just man upon *e*, that doeth good
  12:7 then shall the dust return to the *e* as it
Is. 4:2 the fruit of the *e* shall be excellent
  6:3 the whole *e* is full of his glory
  11:9 (Hab. 2:14) *e* shall be full of the knowledge
  13:13 and the *e* shall remove out of her place

Is. 14:7 the whole *e* is at rest, and is quiet
14:16 is this the man that made the *e* to tremble
24:1 LORD maketh the *e* empty . . maketh it waste
24:4 the *e* mourneth and fadeth away, the world
24:19 the *e* is clean dissolved, the *e* is moved
24:20 *e* shall reel to and fro like a drunkard
34:1 let the *e* hear, and all that is therein
40:22 he that sitteth upon the circle of the *e*
40:28 Creator of the ends of the *e*, fainteth not
44:24 that spreadeth abroad the *e* by myself
45:12 I have made the *e*, and created man upon it
45:22 and be ye saved, all the ends of the *e*
49:6 (Acts 13:47) salvation unto the end of the *e*
49:13 joyful, O *e*; and break forth into singing
51:6 and the *e* shall wax old like a garment
52:10 the ends of the *e* shall see the salvation
65:16 who blesseth himself in the *e* shall bless
65:17 (66:22; 2 Pet. 3:13) new heavens and a new *e*
66:1 (Acts 7:49) and the *e* is my footstool
66:8 the *e* be made to bring forth in one day?
Jer. 15:10 a man of contention to the whole *e*!
22:29 O *e*, *e*, *e*, hear the word of the LORD
23:24 do not I fill heaven and *e*? saith the LORD
27:5 I have made the *e*, the man and the beast
31:22 the LORD hath created a new thing in the *e*
51:15 he hath made the *e* by his power
Lam. 2:15 city that men call . . The joy of the whole *e*
Ezek. 9:9 they say, The LORD hath forsaken the *e*
34:27 and the *e* shall yield her increase
43:2 and the *e* shined with his glory
Dan. 7:17 kings, which shall arise out of the *e*
12:2 that sleep in the dust of the *e* shall awake
Hos. 2:22 *e* shall hear the corn, and the wine, and
Joel 2:30 (Acts 2:19) wonders in the heavens and . . *e*
Amos 8:9 and I will darken the *e* in the clear day
Jon. 2:6 the *e* with her bars was about me for ever
Mic. 1:2 hear, all ye people; hearken, O *e*, and all
6:2 ye strong foundations of the *e*: for the LORD
7:2 the good man is perished out of the *e*
7:17 move out of their holes like worms of the *e*
Nah. 1:5 melt, and the *e* is burned at his presence
Hab. 2:20 in his holy temple: let all the *e* keep silence
3:3 heavens, and the *e* was full of his praise
Zeph. 3:8 *e* shall be devoured with the fire of my
Hag. 1:10 and the *e* is stayed from her fruit
2:6 (2:21; Heb. 12:26) shake the heavens, and the *e*
Zech. 4:10 run to and fro through the whole *e*
14:9 LORD shall be King over all the *e*
Mal. 4:6 lest I come and smite the *e* with a curse
Mt. 5:5 are the meek: for they shall inherit the *e*
5:13 ye are the salt of the *e*: but if the salt
5:18 (Lk. 16:17) till heaven and *e* pass, one jot or
5:35 nor by the *e*; for it is his footstool
6:10 (Lk. 11:2) thy will be done in *e*, as it is
6:19 lay not up for yourselves treasures upon *e*
9:6 (Mk. 2:10; Lk. 5:24) power on *e* to forgive
10:34 (Lk. 12:51) not . . come to send peace on *e*
12:40 and three nights in the heart of the *e*
13:5 (Mk. 4:5) where they had not much *e*
16:19 (18:18) bind on *e* shall be bound in heaven
18:19 if two of you shall agree on *e* as touching
23:9 call no man your father upon the *e*
24:35 (Mk. 13:31; Lk. 21:33) heaven . . *e* shall pass
25:18 digged in the *e*, and hid his lord's money
27:51 and the *e* did quake, and the rocks rent
28:18 power is given unto me in heaven and in *e*
Mk. 4:28 the *e* bringeth forth fruit of herself
Lk. 2:14 and on *e* peace, good will toward men
12:49 I am come to send fire on the *e*
18:8 Son . . cometh, shall he find faith on the *e*?
Jn. 3:31 of the *e* is earthly, and speaketh of the *e*
12:32 I, if I be lifted up from the *e*, will draw
17:4 have glorified thee on the *e*: I have finished

Acts 1:8 and unto the uttermost part of the *e*
2:19 wonders in heaven above, and signs in the *e*
8:33 for his life is taken from the *e*
9:4 (26:14) fell to the *e*, and heard a voice saying
10:11 at the four corners, and let down to the *e*
17:24 Lord of heaven and *e*, dwelleth not in
1 Cor. 15:47 first man is of the *e*, earthy
Eph. 3:15 whole family in heaven and *e* is named
4:9 descended . . into the lower parts of the *e*?
Phil. 2:10 and things in *e*, and things under the *e*
Col. 1:16 by him were all things created . . in *e*
3:2 set your affection . . not on things on the *e*
Heb. 6:7 for the *e* . . receiveth blessing from God
8:4 if he were on *e*, he should not be a priest
11:13 they were strangers and pilgrims on the *e*
12:25 who refused him that spake on *e*, much more
Jas. 5:5 ye have lived in pleasure on the *e*
5:7 waiteth for the precious fruit of the *e*
2 Pet. 3:7 but the heavens and the *e*, which are now
3:10 melt with fervent heat, the *e* also and the
3:13 look for new heavens and a new *e*
1 Jn. 5:8 three that bear witness in *e*, the spirit
Rev. 5:10 and we shall reign on the *e*
6:4 power was given . . to take peace from the *e*
7:3 saying, Hurt not the *e*, neither the sea
9:1 and I saw a star fall from heaven unto the *e*
13:11 another beast coming up out of the *e*
14:15 for the harvest of the *e* is ripe
16:1 the vials of the wrath of God upon the *e*
18:1 and the *e* was lightened with his glory
20:9 they went up on the breadth of the *e*
20:11 from whose face the *e* and the heaven fled
21:1 and I saw a new heaven and a new *e*

Earthen

Num. 5:17 shall take holy water in an *e* vessel
Jer. 19:1 go and get a potter's *e* bottle
Lam. 4:2 how are they esteemed as *e* pitchers
2 Cor. 4:7 but we have this treasure in *e* vessels

Earthly

Jn. 3:12 told you *e* things, and ye believe not
3:31 he that is of the earth is *e*, and speaketh
2 Cor. 5:1 if our *e* house of this tabernacle were
Phil. 3:19 glory is in their shame, who mind *e* things
Jas. 3:15 wisdom . . not from above, but is *e*

Earthquake

1 Kgs. 19:11 but the LORD was not in the *e*
Is. 29:6 LORD of hosts with thunder, and with *e*
Amos 1:1 words of Amos . . two years before the *e*
Zech. 14:5 from before the *e* in the days of Uzziah
Mt. 24:7 (Mk. 13:8; Lk. 21:11) and *e*, in divers places
27:54 were with him, watching Jesus, saw the *e*
28:2 behold, there was a great *e*: for the angel
Acts 16:26 suddenly there was a great *e*, so that
Rev. 6:12 sixth seal, and, lo, there was a great *e*
8:5 and thunderings, and lightnings, and an *e*
11:13 in the *e* were slain of men seven thousand
16:18 a great *e*, such as was not since men were

Earthy

1 Cor. 15:47 the first man is of the earth, *e*
15:48 as is the *e*, such are they also that are *e*
15:49 as we have borne the image of the *e*

Ease

Deut. 23:13 when thou wilt *e* thyself abroad
28:65 among these nations shalt thou find no *e*
2 Chr. 10:4 *e* thou somewhat the grievous servitude
Job 12:5 despised in the thought of him that is at *e*
16:6 and though I forbear, what am I *e*?
21:23 dieth in his full strength, being wholly at *e*

Ps. 25:13 his soul shall dwell at *e*; and his seed
   123:4 with the scorning of those that are at *e*
Is. 1:24 ah, I will *e* me of mine adversaries
   32:9 rise up, ye women that are at *e*; hear my
Jer. 46:27 Jacob shall return . . be in rest and at *e*
Amos 6:1 woe to them that are at *e* in Zion
Zech. 1:15 displeased with the heathen that are at *e*
Lk. 12:19 take thine *e*, eat, drink, and be merry
2 Cor. 8:13 that other men be *e*, and ye burdened

East

Gen. 3:24 at the *e* of the garden of Eden cherubim
   13:11 and Lot journeyed *e*: and they separated
   29:1 came into the land of the people of the *e*
   41:6 seven thin ears and blasted with the *e* wind
Ex. 10:13 the LORD brought an *e* wind upon the land
   14:21 the sea to go back by a strong *e* wind
Job 1:3 was the greatest of all the men of the *e*
   27:21 *e* wind carrieth him away, and he departeth
   38:24 which scattereth the *e* wind upon the earth?
Ps. 48:7 the ships of Tarshish with an *e* wind
   75:6 promotion cometh neither from the *e*, nor
   103:12 as far as the *e* is from the west, so far
   107:3 gathered them out of the lands, from the *e*
Is. 27:8 his rough wind in the day of the *e* wind
   43:5 I will bring thy seed from the *e*
Ezek. 8:16 they worshipped the sun toward the *e*
   19:12 and the *e* wind dried up her fruit
   43:2 the glory of the God . . from the way of the *e*
   47:1 forefront of the house stood toward the *e*
   47:8 these waters issue out toward the *e* country
Hos. 12:1 Ephraim . . followeth after the *e* wind
   13:15 an *e* wind shall come, the wind of the LORD
Jon. 4:5 so Jonah . . sat on the *e* side of the city
   4:8 God prepared a vehement *e* wind
Zech. 8:7 I will save my people from the *e* country
Mt. 2:2 we have seen his star in the *e*, and are come
   8:11 (Lk. 13:29) shall come from the *e* and west
   24:27 as the lightning cometh out of the *e*
Rev. 7:2 I saw another angel ascending from the *e*
   16:12 way of the kings of the *e* might be prepared
   21:13 on the *e* three gates; on the north three

Easter Acts 12:4

Easy (Easier)

Ex. 18:22 judge: so shall it be *e* for thyself
Prov. 14:6 knowledge is *e* unto him that
Mt. 9:5 (Mk. 2:9; Lk. 5:23) whether is *e*, to say
   11:30 for my yoke is *e*, and my burden is light
   19:24 (Mk. 10:25; Lk. 18:25) *e* for a camel to go
Lk. 16:17 and it is *e* for heaven and earth to pass
1 Cor. 14:9 by the tongue words *e* to be understood
Jas. 3:17 peaceable, gentle, and *e* to be entreated

Eat (Ate, Eaten) *See also* Consume,
Devour

Gen. 2:17 tree of the knowledge . . thou shalt not *e*
   3:5 God doth know that in the day ye *e* thereof
   3:14 dust shalt thou *e* all the days of thy life
   3:17 in sorrow shalt thou *e* of it all the days
   9:4 which is the blood thereof, shall ye not *e*
   24:33 *e*: but he said, I will not *e* until I have
   25:28 loved Esau, because he did *e* of his venison
   43:32 Egyptians . . not *e* bread with the Hebrews
Ex. 12:16 save that which every man must *e*
   12:43 passover: There shall no stranger *e* thereof
   16:35 children of Israel did *e* manna forty years
   23:11 that the poor of thy people may *e*
   29:34 it shall not be *e*, because it is holy
   32:6 (1 Cor. 10:7) sat down to *e* and to drink
Lev. 10:12 *e* it without leaven beside the altar

Lev. 10:17 wherefore have ye not *e* the sin offering
   19:26 ye shall not *e* any thing with the blood
   25:20 what shall we *e* the seventh year?
Num. 11:13 saying, Give us flesh, that we may *e*
   13:32 a land that *e* up the inhabitants thereof
Deut. 12:16 ye shall not *e* the blood; ye shall pour
   20:6 vineyard, and hath not yet *e* of it?
Josh. 5:12 did *e* of the fruit of the land of Canaan
Judg. 13:4 drink not wine . . *e* not any unclean thing
1 Sam. 14:30 people had *e* freely today of the spoil
   14:34 sin not . . in *e* with the blood
   28:20 no strength in him; for he had *e* no bread
2 Sam. 7:11 . . shall *e* at my table
   19:42 have we *e* at all of the king's cost?
1 Kgs. 17:12 and my son, that we may *e* it, and die
   19:5 touched him, and said unto him, Arise and *e*
2 Kgs. 4:43 give the people, that they may *e*
   6:28 give thy son, that we may *e* him today
   18:31 (Is. 36:16) *e* ye every man of his own vine
Neh. 5:2 corn for them, that we may *e*, and live
   8:10 go your way, *e* the fat, and drink the sweet
Job 3:24 for my sighing cometh before I *e*
   5:5 whose harvest the hungry *e* up, and taketh it
   6:6 can that which is unsavory be *e* without salt
   21:25 of his soul, and never *e* with pleasure
   31:8 let me sow, and let another *e*; yea, let my
   31:17 or have *e* my morsel myself alone
Ps. 14:4 (53:4) who *e* up my people as they *e* bread
   22:26 the meek shall *e* and be satisfied
   69:9 (Jn. 2:17) zeal of thine house hath *e* me up
   78:25 man did *e* angels' food: he sent them meat
   102:9 for I have *e* ashes like bread, and mingled
   106:28 *a* the sacrifices of the dead
   128:2 for thou shalt *e* the labor of thine hands
   141:4 and let me not *e* of their dainties
Prov. 1:31 they *e* of the fruit of their own way
   13:2 man shall *e* good by the fruit of his mouth
   13:25 righteous *e* to the satisfying of his soul
   18:21 and they that love it shall *e* the fruit
   23:1 thou sittest to *e* with a ruler, consider
   24:13 my son, *e* thou honey, because it is good
   25:27 it is not good to *e* much honey: so for men
   31:27 and *e* not the bread of idleness
Eccl. 2:25 for who can *e*, or who else can hasten
   4:5 fool foldeth his hands . . and *e* his own flesh
   5:11 goods increase, they are increased that *e*
   5:12 is sweet, whether he *e* little or much
   5:17 all his days also he *e* in darkness
   5:19 power to *e* thereof . . this is the gift of God
   6:2 not power to *e* thereof, but a stranger *e* it
   10:16 and thy princes *e* in the morning!
Song 5:1 I have *e* my honeycomb with my honey
Is. 1:19 obedient, ye shall *e* the good of the land
   3:10 for they shall *e* the fruit of their doings
   4:1 of one man, saying, We will *e* our own bread
   7:15 butter and honey shall he *e*, that he may
   11:7 (65:25) the lion shall *e* straw like the ox
   22:13 (1 Cor. 15:32) *e* and drink; for tomorrow
   29:8 hungry man dreameth, and, behold, he *e*
   51:8 for the moth shall *e* them up like a garment
   55:1 he that hath no money; come ye, buy, and *e*
   55:2 *e* ye that which is good, and let your soul
   65:4 *e* swine's flesh, and broth of abominable
   65:13 my servants shall *e*, but ye shall be hungry
Jer. 5:17 shall *e* up thine harvest and thy bread
   15:16 thy words were found, and I did *e* them
   19:9 cause them to *e* the flesh of their sons
   24:3 figs . . that cannot be *e*, they are so evil
   29:17 make them like vile figs, that cannot be *e*
   31:29 (Ezek. 18:2) fathers have *e* a sour grape
Ezek. 2:8 open thy mouth, and *e* that I give thee
   3:1 Son of man, *e* that thou findest; *e* this roll
   4:10 meat which thou shalt *e* shall be by weight

Dan. 4:33 Nebuchadnezzar . . did *e* grass as oxen
  10:3 I *a* no pleasant bread, neither came flesh
Hos. 4:10 for they shall *e*, and not have enough
  10:13 ye have *e* the fruit of lies: because thou
Joel 1:4 palmerworm hath left hath the locust *e*
Amos 6:4 upon their couches, and *e* the lambs out
Mic. 6:14 thou shalt *e*, but not be satisfied
  7:1 of the vintage: there is no cluster to *e*
Hag. 1:6 ye *e*, but ye have not enough; ye drink
Mt. 6:25 (Lk. 12:22) no thought . . what ye shall *e*
  9:11 (Mk. 2:16; Lk. 5:30) why *e* your master with
  12:1 (Lk. 6:1) to pluck the ears of corn, and to *e*
  12:4 (Mk. 2:26; Lk. 6:4) and did *e* the showbread
  14:16 (Mk. 6:37; Lk. 9:13) give ye them to *e*
  14:20 (Mk. 6:42; Lk. 9:17) did all *e*, and were filled
  15:20 but to *e* with unwashen hands defileth not
  15:27 (Mk. 7:28) yet the dogs *e* of the crumbs
  15:32 (Mk. 8:2) three days, and have nothing to *e*
  15:38 (Mk. 8:9) that did *e* were four thousand men
  24:38 (Lk. 17:27) were *e*, and drinking, marrying
  24:49 (Lk. 12:45) begin to smite . . to *e* and drink
  26:17 (Mk. 14:12; Lk. 22:8) thee to *e* the passover?
  26:26 (Mk. 14:22; 1 Cor. 11:24) *e*; this is my body
Mk. 1:6 and he did *e* locusts and wild honey
  6:31 and they had no leisure so much as to *e*
  6:44 *e* of the loaves were about five thousand
  7:2 some of his disciples *e* bread with defiled
  11:14 no man *e* fruit of thee hereafter for ever
  14:18 one of you which *e* with me shall betray me
Lk. 5:33 of the Pharisees; but thine *e* and drink?
  7:36 Pharisees desired him that he would *e* with
  10:8 *e* such things as are set before you
  12:19 take thine ease, *e*, drink, and be merry
  13:26 say, We have *e* and drunk in thy presence
  15:2 this man receiveth sinners, and *e* with them
  15:16 belly with the husks that the swine did *e*
  15:23 the fatted calf, and kill it; and let us *e*
  22:30 may *e* and drink at my table in my kingdom
  24:43 and he took it, and did *e* before them
Jn. 4:31 his disciples prayed him, saying, Master, *e*
  4:32 I have meat to *e* that ye know not of
  6:13 remained over . . unto them that had *e*
  6:26 but because ye did *e* of the loaves
  6:52 how can this man give us his flesh to *e*?
  6:57 so he that *e* me, even he shall live by me
  6:58 he that *e* of this bread shall live for ever
Acts 2:46 did *e* their meat with gladness
  9:9 without sight, and neither did *e* nor drink
  10:13 (11:7) rise, Peter; kill, and *e*
  11:3 to men uncircumcised, and didst *e* with them
  12:23 he was *e* of worms, and gave up the ghost
  23:14 we will *e* nothing until we have slain Paul
  27:35 and when he had broken it, he began to *e*
  27:38 had *e* enough, they lightened the ship
Rom. 14:2 may *e* all things: another . . *e* herbs
  14:3 let not him that *e* despise him that *e* not
  14:20 it is evil for that man who *e* with offense
  14:21 good neither to *e* flesh, nor to drink wine
  14:23 damned if he *e*, because he *e* not of faith
1 Cor. 5:11 with such a one, no, not to *e*
  8:7 *e* it as a thing offered unto an idol
  8:8 *e*, are we the better; neither, if we *e* not
  8:13 I will *e* no flesh while the world standeth
  9:4 have we not power to *e* and to drink?
  10:3 and did all *e* the same spiritual meat
  10:27 *e*, asking no question for conscience' sake
  10:31 ye *e*, or drink, or whatsoever ye do
  11:20 this is not to *e* the Lord's supper
  11:26 for as often as ye *e* this bread, and drink
  11:29 unworthily, *e* and drinketh damnation to
  11:34 if any man hunger, let him *e* at home
2 Thes. 3:10 would not work, neither should he *e*
2 Tim. 2:17 and their word will *e* as doth a canker

Heb. 13:10 no right to *e* which serve the tabernacle
Jas. 5:3 and shall *e* your flesh as it were fire
Rev. 2:7 give to *e* of the tree of life
  2:17 will I give to *e* of the hidden manna
  10:10 book out of the angel's hand, and *a* it up
  19:18 that ye may *e* the flesh of kings

Ebal

Deut. 11:29 Gerizim, and the curse upon mount *E*
  27:4 shall set up these stones . . in mount *E*
Josh. 8:30 then Joshua built an altar . . in mount *E*

Ebed-melech the Ethiopian

Jer. 38:7–39:18

Eben-ezer

1 Sam. 4:1 to battle, and pitched beside *E*
  5:1 took the ark of God, and brought it from *E*
  7:12 *E*, saying, Hitherto hath the LORD helped us

Eden *See also* Paradise

Gen. 2:8 God planted a garden eastward in *E*
  3:23 God sent him forth from the garden of *E*
Is. 51:3 he will make her wilderness like *E*
Ezek. 28:13 thou hast been in *E* the garden of God
  36:35 desolate is become like the garden of *E*
Joel 2:3 land is as the garden of *E* before them

Edge

Ps. 89:43 thou hast also turned the *e* of his sword
Eccl. 10:10 iron be blunt, and he do not whet the *e*
Jer. 31:29 (Ezek. 18:2) children's teeth are set on *e*
Rev. 2:12 he which hath the sharp sword with two *e*

Edification

Rom. 15:2 please his neighbor for his good to *e*
1 Cor. 14:3 prophesieth speaketh unto men to *e*
2 Cor. 10:8 our authority . . given us for *e*
  13:10 power which the Lord hath given me to *e*

Edify *See also* Build

Acts 9:31 then had the churches rest . . and were *e*
Rom. 14:19 and things wherewith one may *e* another
1 Cor. 8:1 knowledge puffeth up, but charity *e*
  10:23 are lawful for me, but all things *e* not
  14:4 tongue *e* himself; but he that prophesieth *e*
1 Thes. 5:11 and *e* one another, even as also ye do

Edifying

1 Cor. 14:5 interpret, that the church may receive *e*
  14:12 that ye may excel to the *e* of the church
  14:26 let all things be done unto *e*
2 Cor. 12:19 all things, dearly beloved, for your *e*
Eph. 4:12 for the *e* of the body of Christ
  4:29 that which is good to the use of *e*
1 Tim. 1:4 rather than godly *e* which is in faith

Edom

Gen. 25:30 therefore was his name called *E*
Num. 20:18 *E* said unto him, Thou shalt not pass by
2 Sam. 8:14 (1 Chr. 18:13) and he put garrisons in *E*
2 Kgs. 8:20 (2 Chr. 21:8) *E* revolted from under
  14:7 he slew of *E* in the valley of salt
Is. 63:1 who is this that cometh from *E*, with dyed
Jer. 49:7 (Obad. 1) concerning *E*, thus saith the LORD
  49:17 also *E* shall be desolation: everyone
Ezek. 25:13 will also stretch out mine hand upon *E*
Amos 1:11 three transgressions of *E*, and for four
Mal. 1:4 whereas *E* saith, We are impoverished

Edomite

Deut. 23:7 not abhor an *E*; for he is thy brother
1 Kgs. 11:14 adversary unto Solomon, Hadad the *E*

2 Chr. 21:8 *E* revolted from under the dominion
25:14 come from the slaughter of the *E*
28:17 again the *E* had come and smitten Judah

Effect

Num. 30:8 then he shall make her vow. . of none *e*
2 Chr. 7:11 and in his own house, he prosperously *e*
Ps. 33:10 the devices of the people of none *e*
Is. 32:17 the *e* of righteousness, quietness and
Jer. 48:30 not be so; his lies shall not so *e* it
Mt. 15:6 (Mk. 7:13) commandment of God of none *e*
Rom. 3:3 unbelief make the faith of God without *e*?
4:14 made void, and the promise made of none *e*
9:6 as though the word of God hath taken none *e*
1 Cor. 1:17 lest the cross. . be made of none *e*
Gal. 3:17 it should make the promise of none *e*
5:4 Christ is become of no *e* unto you, whosoever

Effectual

1 Cor. 16:9 a great door and *e* is opened unto me
2 Cor. 1:6 which is *e* in the enduring of the same
Eph. 3:7 unto me by the *e* working of his power
4:16 according to the *e* working in the measure
Phlm. 6 communication of thy faith may become *e*
Jas. 5:16 the *e* fervent prayer of a righteous man

Effectually

Gal. 2:8 wrought *e* in Peter to the apostleship
1 Thes. 2:13 word of God, which *e* worketh also in

Effeminate

1 Cor. 6:9 idolaters, nor adulterers, nor *e*, nor

Egg

Deut. 22:6 upon the *e*, thou shalt not take the dam
Job 6:6 is there any taste in the white of an *e*?
39:14 leaveth her *e* in the earth, and warmeth
Is. 10:14 as one gathereth *e* that are left, have I
59:5 hatch cockatrice' *e*, and weave the spider's
Jer. 17:11 partridge sitteth on *e*, and hatcheth
Lk. 11:12 ask an *e*, will he offer him a scorpion?

Eglon king of Moab Judg. 3:12–30

Egypt

Gen. 12:10 Abram went down into *E* to sojourn there
37:28 and they brought Joseph into *E*
41:57 all countries came into *E* to Joseph
42:3 ten brethren went down to buy corn in *E*
46:6 and came into *E*, Jacob, and all his seed
Ex. 1:8 a new king over *E*, which knew not Joseph
3:7 (Acts 7:34) affliction of my people. . in *E*
7:3 my signs and my wonders in the land of *E*
10:2 son's son, what things I have wrought in *E*
11:1 one plague more upon Pharaoh, and upon *E*
13:14 Lord brought us out from *E*, from the house
13:18 went up harnessed out of the land of *E*
2 Kgs. 18:21 (Is. 36:6) behold, thou trustest. . upon *E*
25:26 (Jer. 43:7) all the people. . came to *E*
Ps. 105:38 *E* was glad when they departed
106:21 saviour, which had done great things in *E*
135:8 who smote the firstborn of *E*, both of man
Is. 19:1 the burden of *E*. Behold, the Lord rideth
19:20 a witness unto the Lord. . in the land of *E*
27:12 channel of the river unto the stream of *E*
30:3 the trust in the shadow of *E* your confusion
31:1 woe to them that go down to *E* for help
Jer. 31:32 (Heb. 8:9) bring them out of the land of *E*
37:5 Pharaoh's army was come forth out of *E*
42:14 but we will go into the land of *E*
44:28 shall return out of the land of *E* into
46:2 against *E*, against the army of Pharaoh-necho
46:13 Nebuchadrezzar. . smite the land of *E*

Ezek. 19:4 brought him with chains unto. . *E*
29:2 prophesy against him, and against all *E*
30:4 the sword shall come upon *E*, and great pain
Dan. 11:8 carry captives into *E* their gods
Hos. 9:3 but Ephraim shall return to *E*
11:1 (Mt. 2:15) and called my son out of *E*
Joel 3:19 *E* shall be a desolation, and Edom shall
Zech. 10:10 out of the land of *E*, and gather them
14:18 if the family of *E* go not up, and come not
Mt. 2:13 child and his mother, and flee into *E*
Acts 7:9 sold Joseph into *E*: but God was with him
Heb. 11:27 by faith he forsook *E*, not fearing
Rev. 11:8 which spiritually is called Sodom and *E*

Egyptian

Gen. 47:20 *E* sold every man his field
Ex. 1:19 Hebrew women are not as the *E* women
2:11 (Acts 7:24) spied an *E* smiting a Hebrew
2:14 (Acts 7:28) kill me, as thou killedst the *E*?
2:19 said, An *E* delivered us out of the hand
3:9 the oppression wherewith the *E* oppress them
3:21 this people favor in the sight of the *E*
7:5 the *E* shall know that I am the Lord, when I
8:26 shall we sacrifice the abomination of the *E*
12:23 Lord will pass through to smite the *E*
14:9 *E* pursued after them, all the horses and
14:27 overthrew the *E* in the midst of the sea
Deut. 23:7 thou shalt not abhor an *E*; because thou
1 Sam. 30:11 and they found an *E* in the field
Is. 31:3 now the *E* are men, and not God
Ezek. 16:26 committed fornication with the *E*
Acts 21:38 not thou that *E*, which. . madest an uproar
Heb. 11:29 which the *E* assaying to do were drowned

Ehud Judg. 3:15–30

Ekron 1 Sam. 5:10–12; 6:16–17; 7:14; 17:52;
Amos 1:8; Zeph. 2:4

Elam Gen. 10:22; 14:1; Is. 11:11; 21:2; 22:6;
Jer. 49:34–39; Ezek. 32:24; Dan. 8:2

Elath (Eloth) Deut. 2:8; 2 Kgs. 14:22; 16:6

Elder *See also* Bishop

Gen. 25:23 (Rom. 9:12) the *e* shall serve the younger
50:7 *e* of his house, and all the *e* of the land
Ex. 3:16 go, and gather the *e* of Israel together
24:1 seventy of the *e* of Israel; and worship ye
Lev. 4:15 and the *e* of the congregation shall lay
Num. 11:16 gather unto me seventy men of the *e*
11:25 spirit. . and gave it unto the seventy *e*
Deut. 21:19 bring him out unto the *e* of his city
Josh. 23:2 called for all Israel, and for their *e*
1 Sam. 15:30 honor me. . before the *e* of my people
16:4 and the *e* of the town trembled
Ezra 5:5 eye of their God was upon the *e*
Job 15:10 very aged men, much *e* than thy father
32:4 Job had spoken, because they were *e* than he
Ps. 107:32 and praise him in the assembly of the *e*
Prov. 31:23 the gates, when he sitteth among the *e*
Jer. 29:1 from Jerusalem unto the residue of the *e*
Ezek. 8:1 and the *e* of Judah sat before me
Mt. 15:2 (Mk. 7:5) transgress the tradition of the *e*?
16:21 (Mk. 8:31; Lk. 9:22) and suffer. . of the *e* and
21:23 (Mk. 11:27; Lk. 20:1) priests and. . *e*. . came
26:59 and *e*, and all the council, sought false
27:41 priests mocking him, with the scribes and *e*
Lk. 15:25 now his *e* son was in the field
Acts 4:5 on the morrow, that their rulers, and *e*
6:12 they stirred up the people, and the *e*, and
11:30 sent it to the *e* by the hands of Barnabas
14:23 they had ordained them *e* in every church
15:4 received of the church, and. . apostles and *e*

Acts 15:6 and the apostles and *e* came together for to
15:23 apostles and *e* and brethren send greeting
16:4 that were ordained of the apostles and *e*
20:17 to Ephesus, and called the *e* of the church
1 Tim. 5:1 rebuke not an *e*, but entreat him as a
5:2 *e* women as mothers; the younger as sisters
5:17 let the *e* that rule well be counted worthy
Tit. 1:5 and ordain *e* in every city
Heb. 11:2 for by it the *e* obtained a good report
Jas. 5:14 sick among you? let him call for the *e*
1 Pet. 5:1 the *e* which are among you I exhort
5:5 ye younger, submit yourselves unto the *e*
2 Jn. 1 the *e* unto the elect lady and her children
3 Jn. 1 the *e* unto the well-beloved Gaius
Rev. 4:4 upon the seats I saw four and twenty *e*
7:11 about the *e* and the four beasts
14:3 new song. . before the four beasts, and the *e*

Eleazar Num. 20:28; 26:1

Elect See also Chosen

Is. 42:1 mine *e*, in whom my soul delighteth
45:4 Jacob my servant's sake, and Israel mine *e*
65:9 my mountains: and mine *e* shall inherit it
65:22 mine *e* shall long enjoy the work of their
Mt. 24:22 (Mk. 13:20) but for the *e*'s sake those days
24:24 (Mk. 13:22) they shall deceive the very *e*
24:31 (Mk. 13:27) gather. . *e* from the four winds
Lk. 18:7 shall not God avenge his own *e*, which cry
Rom. 8:33 lay any thing to the charge of God's *e*?
Col. 3:12 put on therefore, as the *e* of God, holy
1 Tim. 5:21 charge thee before God. . the *e* angels
2 Tim. 2:10 I endure all things for the *e*'s sake
Tit. 1:1 according to the faith of God's *e*
1 Pet. 1:2 *e* according to the foreknowledge of God
2:6 in Sion a chief corner stone, *e*, precious
5:13 church that is at Babylon, *e* together with
2 Jn. 1 the elder unto the *e* lady and her children
13 the children of thy *e* sister greet thee

Election See also Calling

Rom. 9:11 the purpose of God according to *e* might
11:5 is a remnant according to the *e* of grace
11:7 seeketh for; but the *e* hath obtained it
11:28 but as touching the *e*, they are beloved
1 Thes. 1:4 knowing. . your *e* of God
2 Pet. 1:10 to make your calling and *e* sure

Element

Gal. 4:3 were in bondage under the *e* of the world
4:9 how turn ye again to the weak and beggarly *e*
2 Pet. 3:10 the *e* shall melt with fervent heat

Eleven

Gen. 37:9 moon and the *e* stars made obeisance to me
Mt. 28:16 the *e* disciples went away into Galilee
Mk. 16:14 appeared unto the *e* as they sat at meat
Lk. 24:9 and told all these things unto the *e*
Acts 1:26 Matthias; and he was numbered with the *e*

Eli the priest 1 Sam. 1:3–4:18

Elias See Elijah

Elihu Job 32:2–37:24

Elijah (Elias)

Predicted the drought, 1 Kgs. 17:1; fed by ravens, 1
Kgs. 17:2–7; fed by the widow of Zarephath, 1 Kgs.
17:8–16; revived the son of the widow, 1 Kgs. 17:17–
24; met Ahab, 1 Kgs. 18:1–19; contested the prophets
of Baal, 1 Kgs. 18:20–40; prayed for rain, 1 Kgs. 18:
41–46; fled to Mount Horeb, 1 Kgs. 19:1–8; heard

the still small voice, 1 Kgs. 19:9–18; chose Elisha,
1 Kgs. 19:19–21; reproved Ahab, 1 Kgs. 21:17–29;
called fire from heaven, 2 Kgs. 1:3–16; taken up into
heaven, 2 Kgs. 2:1–11.

Mal. 4:5 I will send you *E* the prophet before the
Mt. 11:14 if ye will receive it, this is *E*, which
16:14 (Mk. 8:28; Lk. 9:19) some say. . thou art. . *E*
17:3 (Mk. 9:4; Lk. 9:30) appeared. . Moses and *E*
17:12 (Mk. 9:13) I say unto you, That *E* is come
27:47 (Mk. 15:35) said, This man calleth for *E*
Mk. 6:15 (Lk. 9:8) others said, That it is *E*
Lk. 1:17 before him in the spirit and power of *E*
9:54 heaven, and consume them, even as *E* did?
Jn. 1:21 art thou *E*? And he saith, I am not
Rom. 11:2 the Scripture saith of *E*? how he maketh
Jas. 5:17 *E* was a man subject to like passions as

Elimelech Ruth 1:2; 4:3, 9

Eliphaz Job 2:11; 15:1–35; 22:1–30; 42:7–9

Elisabeth Lk. 1:5–25, 39–45, 56–61

Elisha (Eliseus)

Called, 1 Kgs. 19:19–21; succeeded Elijah, 2 Kgs. 2:
1–15; healed the water, 2 Kgs. 2:19–22; cursed the
children, 2 Kgs. 2:23–25; increased the widow's oil,
2 Kgs. 4:1–7; restored the life of Shunammite's son,
2 Kgs. 4:8–37; purified the pottage, 2 Kgs. 4:38–41;
fed the prophets, 2 Kgs. 4:42–44; healed Naaman's
leprosy, 2 Kgs. 5; caused Syrians' blindness, 2
Kgs. 6:8–23; promised food in time of famine, 2 Kgs.
6:24–7:2; prophesied victory over Syria, 2 Kgs. 13:
14–19; death and burial, 2 Kgs. 13:20; bones of
Elisha, 2 Kgs. 13:21.

Lk. 4:27 lepers were in Israel in the time of *E*

Eloquent

Ex. 4:10 Moses said. . O my Lord, I am not *e*
Is. 3:3 the cunning artificer, and the *e* orator
Acts 18:24 Apollos, born at Alexandria, an *e* man

Embalm

Gen. 50:2 *e* his father: and the physicians *e* Israel
50:26 so Joseph died. . and they *e* him

Embolden

Job 16:3 or what *e* thee that thou answerest?
1 Cor. 8:10 conscience of him which is weak be *e*

Embrace See also Kiss

Gen. 29:13 Laban. . ran to meet him, and *e* him
33:4 Esau ran to meet him, and *e* him, and fell
48:10 and he kissed them, and *e* them
2 Kgs. 4:16 thou shalt *e* a son. And she said, Nay
Job 24:8 and *e* the rock for want of a shelter
Prov. 4:8 bring thee to honor, when thou dost *e* her
5:20 with a strange woman, and *e* the bosom of a
Eccl. 3:5 a time to *e*, and a time to refrain
Lam. 4:5 were brought up in scarlet *e* dunghills
Acts 20:1 Paul called. . the disciples, and *e* them
20:10 Paul went down. . *e* him said, Trouble not
Heb. 11:13 were persuaded of them, and *e* them

Embroider

Ex. 28:39 thou shalt *e* the coat of fine linen

Emerald

Ex. 28:18 (39:11) second row shall be an *e*, a sapphire
Rev. 4:3 about the throne, in sight like unto an *e*

Rev. 21:19 the third, a chalcedony; the fourth, an *e*

Emerod

1 Sam. 5:6 he destroyed them, and smote them with *e*

Eminent

Ezek. 16:24 hast also built unto thee an *e* place
16:39 they shall throw down thine *e* place
17:22 will plant it upon a high mountain and *e*

Emmanuel *See also* Immanuel Mt. 1:23

Emmaus Lk. 24:13

Employ

Deut. 20:19 cut them down. . to *e* them in the siege
1 Chr. 9:33 they were *e* in that work day and night

Empty *See also* Void

Gen. 24:20 and she hasted, and *e* her pitcher into
31:42 surely thou hadst sent me away now *e*
37:24 and cast him into a pit: and the pit was *e*
41:27 seven years; and the seven *e* ears blasted
42:35 as they *e* their sacks, that, behold, every
Ex. 3:21 when ye go, ye shall not go *e*
23:15 and none shall appear before me *e*
Deut. 15:13 thou shalt not let him go away *e*
16:16 they shall not appear before the LORD *e*
Ruth 1:21 LORD hath brought me home again *e*
3:17 said to me, Go not *e* unto thy mother-in-law
1 Sam. 20:25 and David's place was *e*
2 Sam. 1:22 and the sword of Saul returned not *e*
2 Kgs. 4:3 even *e* vessels; borrow not a few
2 Chr. 24:11 priest's officer came and *e* the chest
Job 22:9 thou hast sent widows away *e*
Eccl. 11:3 full of rain, they *e* themselves upon
Is. 24:1 behold, the LORD maketh the earth *e*
24:3 the land shall be utterly *e*
29:8 eateth; but he awaketh, and his soul is *e*
32:6 to make *e* the soul of the hungry
Jer. 48:11 hath not been *e* from vessel to vessel
51:2 shall fan her, and shall *e* her land
51:34 Nebuchadrezzar. . hath made me an *e* vessel
Hos. 10:1 Israel is an *e* vine, he bringeth forth
Nah. 2:2 for the emptiers have *e* them out
2:10 she is *e*, and void, and waste
Zech. 4:12 two golden pipes *e* the golden oil out
Mt. 12:44 when he is come, he findeth it *e*, swept
Mk. 12:3 (Lk. 20:10) beat him, and sent him away *e*
Lk. 1:53 and the rich he hath sent *e* away

Emulation

Rom. 11:14 if by any means I may provoke to *e*
Gal. 5:20 witchcraft, hatred, variance, *e*, wrath

Enable

1 Tim. 1:12 who hath *e* me, for that he counted me

Encamp *See also* Pitch

Ex. 13:20 journey from Succoth, and *e* in Etham
14:2 that they turn and *e* before Pihahiroth
Num. 1:50 and shall *e* round about the tabernacle
10:31 knowest how we are to *e* in the wilderness
Job 19:12 his troops. . *e* round about my tabernacle
Ps. 27:3 though a host should *e* against me
34:7 angel of the LORD *e* round about them that
53:5 scattered the bones of him that *e* against

Enchanter

Deut. 18:10 observer of times, or an *e*, or a witch
Jer. 27:9 nor to your dreamers, nor to your *e*

Enchantment *See also* Witchcraft

Ex. 7:11 they also did in like manner with their *e*

Lev. 19:26 neither shall ye use *e*, nor observe times
Num. 23:23 there is no *e* against Jacob, neither is
24:1 went not, as at other times, to seek for *e*
2 Kgs. 17:17 used divination and *e*, and sold
21:6 (2 Chr. 33:6) observed times, and used *e*
Is. 47:9 and for the great abundance of thine *e*

Encounter

Acts 17:18 Epicureans, and of the Stoics, *e* him

Encourage *See also* Comfort, Exhort

Deut. 1:38 he shall go in thither: *e* him
3:28 charge Joshua, and *e* him, and strengthen
1 Sam. 30:6 David *e* himself in the LORD his God
2 Sam. 11:25 say unto Joab. . and *e* thou him
2 Chr. 31:4 they might be *e* in the law of the LORD
35:2 the priests in their charges, and *e* them
Ps. 64:5 they *e* themselves in an evil matter

End *See also* Finish, Last, Purpose

Gen. 2:2 on the seventh day God *e* his work
6:13 said unto Noah, The *e* of all flesh is come
Ex. 23:16 (34:22) ingathering. . in the *e* of the year
Lev. 8:33 the days of your consecration be at an *e*
Num. 23:10 righteous, and let my last *e* be like his!
Deut. 8:16 to do thee good at thy latter *e*
32:29 that they would consider their latter *e*!
Ruth 3:10 more kindness in the latter *e* than at
Job 6:11 is mine *e*, that I should prolong my life?
8:7 beginning was small, yet thy latter *e* should
16:3 vain words have an *e*? or what emboldeneth
18:2 how long. . ere ye make an *e* of words?
26:10 until the day and night come to an *e*
28:3 he setteth an *e* to darkness, and searcheth
42:12 LORD blessed the latter *e* of Job more than
Ps. 7:9 wickedness of the wicked come to an *e*
9:6 destructions are come to a perpetual *e*
19:4 (Rom. 10:18) words to the *e* of the world
19:6 his going forth is from the *e* of the heaven
22:27 all the *e* of the world shall remember
37:37 upright: for the *e* of that man is peace
37:38 the *e* of the wicked shall be cut off
39:4 to know mine *e*, and the measure of my days
65:5 the confidence of all the *e* of the earth
67:7 and all the *e* of the earth shall fear him
73:17 then understood I their *e*
98:3 the *e* of the earth have seen the salvation
102:27 the same, and thy years shall have no *e*
107:27 a drunken man, and are at their wit's *e*
119:33 statutes; and I shall keep it unto the *e*
119:96 I have seen an *e* of all perfection
Prov. 14:12 (16:25) *e* thereof are the ways of death
17:24 eyes of a fool are in the *e* of the earth
19:20 that thou mayest be wise in thy latter *e*
23:18 there is an *e*; and thine expectation shall
25:8 know not what to do in the *e* thereof
Eccl. 3:11 God maketh from the beginning to the *e*
4:8 yet is there no *e* of all his labor
4:16 there is no *e* of all the people
7:2 for that is the *e* of all men
7:8 better is the *e* of a thing than the beginning
10:13 the *e* of his talk is mischievous madness
12:12 of making many books there is no *e*
Is. 9:7 government and peace there shall be no *e*
16:4 extortioner is at an *e*, the spoiler ceaseth
45:22 be ye saved, all the *e* of the earth
46:10 declaring the *e* from the beginning
49:6 (Acts 13:47) salvation unto the *e* of the earth
52:10 the *e* of the earth shall see the salvation
60:20 and the days of thy mourning shall be *e*
Jer. 4:27 desolate; yet will I not make a full *e*
5:31 and what will ye do in the *e* thereof?
8:20 the summer is *e*, and we are not saved

Jer. 17:11 and at his *e* shall be a fool
  29:11 and not of evil, to give you an expected *e*
  31:17 there is hope in thine *e*, saith the LORD
Lam. 1:9 she remembereth not her last *e*
  4:18 our *e* is near, our days are fulfilled
Ezek. 7:2 an *e*, the *e* is come upon the four corners
  21:25 day is come, when iniquity shall have an *e*
  35:5 in the time that their iniquity had an *e*
Dan. 8:17 at the time of the *e* shall be the vision
  8:19 shall be in the last *e* of the indignation
  9:26 and the *e* thereof shall be with a flood
  11:27 yet the *e* shall be at the time appointed
  11:45 yet he shall come to his *e*, and none shall
  12:4 seal the book, even to the time of the *e*
  12:8 Lord, what shall be the *e* of these things?
  12:13 go thou thy way till the *e* be
Amos 8:2 the *e* is come upon my people of Israel
Hab. 2:3 but at the *e* it shall speak, and not lie
Zech. 9:10 the river even to the *e* of the earth
Mt. 10:22 (24:13; Mk. 13:13) that endureth to the *e*
  13:39 the harvest is the *e* of the world
  24:3 of thy coming, and of the *e* of the world?
  24:6 (Mk. 13:7; Lk. 21:9) but the *e* is not yet
  24:14 unto all nations; and then shall the *e* come
  24:31 from one *e* of heaven to the other
  26:58 Peter. . sat with the servants, to see the *e*
  28:1 the *e* of the sabbath, as it began to dawn
  28:20 I am with you alway, even unto the *e*
Mk. 3:26 he cannot stand, but hath an *e*
Lk. 1:33 and of his kingdom there shall be no *e*
  4:2 and when they were *e*, he afterward hungered
  4:13 when the devil had *e* all the temptation
  22:37 for the things concerning me have an *e*
Jn. 13:1 he loved them unto the *e*
  13:2 supper being *e*, the devil having now put
  18:37 I am a king. To this *e* was I born, and for
Rom. 6:21 for the *e* of those things is death
  6:22 unto holiness, and the *e* everlasting life
  10:4 Christ is the *e* of the law for righteousness
1 Cor. 10:11 upon whom the *e* of the world are come
  15:24 cometh the *e*, when he shall have delivered
Eph. 3:21 throughout all ages, world without *e*
Phil. 3:19 whose *e* is destruction, whose God is
1 Tim. 1:5 now the *e* of the commandment is charity
Heb. 6:8 unto cursing; whose *e* is to be burned
  6:16 confirmation is to them an *e* of all strife
  7:3 neither beginning of days, nor *e* of life
  9:26 once in the *e* of the world hath he appeared
  13:7 considering the *e* of their conversation
Jas. 5:11 of Job, and have seen the *e* of the Lord
1 Pet. 1:9 the *e* of your faith, even the salvation
  1:13 hope to the *e* for the grace that is to be
  4:7 *e* of all things is at hand: be ye therefore
  4:17 what shall the *e* be of them that obey not
2 Pet. 2:20 latter *e* is worse with them than the
Rev. 2:26 keepeth my works unto the *e*, to him will
  21:6 Alpha and Omega, the beginning and the *e*

Endeavor

Ps. 28:4 according to the wickedness of their *e*
Acts 16:10 immediately we *e* to go into Macedonia
Eph. 4:3 *e* to keep the unity of the Spirit in the
1 Thes. 2:17 *e* the more abundantly to see your face
2 Pet. 1:15 will *e* that ye may be able

Endless

1 Tim. 1:4 give heed to fables and *e* genealogies
Heb. 7:16 who is made. . after the power of an *e* life

En-dor 1 Sam. 28:7

Endue

Gen. 30:20 God hath *e* me with a good dowry

2 Chr. 2:12 the king a wise son, *e* with prudence
Lk. 24:49 until ye be *e* with power from on high
Jas. 3:13 wise man and *e* with knowledge among you?

Endure

Gen. 33:14 the cattle. . and the children be able to *e*
1 Chr. 16:34 (Ezra 3:11) for his mercy *e* for ever
Esth. 8:6 how can I *e* to see the evil that shall
Job 8:15 he shall hold it fast, but it shall not *e*
  31:23 by reason of his highness I could not *e*
Ps. 9:7 LORD shall *e* for ever: he hath prepared
  19:9 the fear of the LORD is clean, *e* for ever
  30:5 weeping may *e* for a night, but joy cometh
  52:1 the goodness of God *e* continually
  72:5 fear thee as long as the sun and moon *e*
  72:17 his name shall *e* for ever: his name shall
  89:29 his seed also will I make to *e* for ever
  100:5 and his truth *e* to all generations
  102:12 but thou, O LORD, shalt *e* for ever
  102:26 they shall perish, but thou shalt *e*
  104:31 the glory of the LORD shall *e* for ever
  106:1 (107:1; 118:1; 136:1) his mercy *e* for ever
  111:3 and his righteousness *e* for ever
  111:10 his praise *e* for ever
  119:160 every one of thy righteous judgments *e*
  135:13 thy name, O LORD, *e* for ever
  138:8 thy mercy, O LORD, *e* for ever: forsake not
  145:13 thy dominion *e* throughout all generations
Prov. 27:24 doth the crown *e* to every generation?
Ezek. 22:14 can thine heart *e*, or can thine hands
Mt. 10:22 (24:13; Mk. 13:13) but he that *e* to the end
Mk. 4:17 have no root. . and so *e* but for a time
Jn. 6:27 that meat which *e* unto everlasting life
Rom. 9:22 *e* with much long-suffering the vessels
1 Cor. 13:7 hopeth all things, *e* all things
2 Tim. 2:3 *e* hardness, as a good soldier of Jesus
  2:10 I *e* all things for the elect's sake
  4:3 they will not *e* sound doctrine
  4:5 watch thou in all things, *e* afflictions
Heb. 6:15 had patiently *e*, he obtained the promise
  10:32 ye *e* a great fight of afflictions
  10:34 in heaven a better and an *e* substance
  11:27 for he *e*, as seeing him who is invisible
  12:2 *e* the cross, despising the shame
  12:3 consider him that *e* such contradiction of
  12:7 if ye *e* chastening, God dealeth with you as
Jas. 1:12 blessed is the man that *e* temptation
  5:11 behold, we count them happy which *e*
1 Pet. 1:25 but the word of the Lord *e* for ever
  2:19 if a man for conscience toward God *e* grief

Eneas (Aeneas) Acts 9:33–35

Enemy *See also* Adversary, Foe

Gen. 14:20 God, which hath delivered thine *e* into
  22:17 thy seed shall possess the gate of his *e*
Ex. 15:6 hand, O LORD, hath dashed in pieces the *e*
  23:22 then I will be an *e* unto thine *e*
Lev. 26:8 and your *e* shall fall before you
  26:17 ye shall be slain before your *e*
Num. 10:9 and ye shall be saved from your *e*
  10:35 (Ps. 68:1) let thine *e* be scattered
  14:42 (Deut. 1:42) ye be not smitten before your *e*
  35:23 and was not his *e*, neither sought his harm
Deut. 28:48 therefore shalt thou serve thine *e*
  32:31 even our *e* themselves being judges
  32:41 I will render vengeance to mine *e*
Josh. 7:12 Israel could not stand before their *e*
  23:1 had given rest unto Israel from all their *e*
Judg. 5:31 let all thine *e* perish, O LORD: but let
1 Sam. 12:11 out of the hand of your *e* on every side
  18:29 and Saul became David's *e* continually
  20:15 when the LORD hath cut off the *e* of David

1 Sam. 24:19 if a man find his *e*, will he let him go
2 Sam. 19:6 lovest thine *e*, and hatest thy friends
  22:4 (Ps. 18:3) so shall I be saved from mine *e*
  24:13 wilt thou flee three months before thine *e*
1 Kgs. 21:20 hast thou found me, O mine *e*?
Ezra 8:31 he delivered us from the hand of the *e*
Esth. 7:6 the adversary and *e* is this wicked Haman
  8:13 that day to avenge themselves on their *e*
Job 13:24 thy face, and holdest me for thine *e*?
Ps. 6:10 let all mine *e* be ashamed and sore vexed
  8:2 because of thine *e*. . mightest still the *e* and
  18:48 he delivereth me from mine *e*
  23:5 a table before me in the presence of mine *e*
  27:11 lead me in a plain path, because of mine *e*
  37:20 *e* of the Lord shall be as the fat of lambs
  61:3 a shelter for me. . a strong tower from the *e*
  68:1 let God arise, let his *e* be scattered
  72:9 and his *e* shall lick the dust
  74:4 *e* roar in the midst of thy congregations
  92:9 thine *e*, O Lord, for, lo, thine *e* shall perish
  110:1 (Mt. 22:44; Mk. 12:36; Lk. 20:43; Heb. 1:13)
    my right hand, until I make thine *e* thy footstool
  119:98 hast made me wiser than mine *e*
  127:5 they shall speak with the *e* in the gate
  136:24 and hath redeemed us from our *e*
  139:22 with perfect hatred: I count them mine *e*
Prov. 16:7 he maketh even his *e* to be at peace
  24:17 rejoice not when thine *e* falleth
  25:21 (Rom. 12:20) if thine *e* be hungry, give him
  27:6 but the kisses of an *e* are deceitful
Is. 1:24 mine adversaries, and avenge me of mine *e*
  59:19 when the *e* shall come in like a flood
  63:10 therefore he was turned to be their *e*
Jer. 15:11 I will cause the *e* to entreat thee well
  17:4 I will cause thee to serve thine *e*
  30:14 I have wounded thee with the wound of an *e*
Lam. 2:5 the Lord was as an *e*: he hath swallowed up
Mic. 7:6 a man's *e* are the men of his own house
Mt. 5:44 (Lk. 6:27, 35) I say unto you, Love your *e*
  13:25 slept, his *e* came and sowed tares among
  13:28 he said unto them, An *e* hath done this
  13:39 the *e* that sowed them is the devil
Lk. 19:43 thine *e* shall cast a trench about thee
Acts 13:10 thou *e* of all righteousness, wilt thou
Rom. 5:10 if, when we were *e*, we were reconciled
  11:28 they are *e* for your sakes
  12:20 therefore if thine *e* hunger, feed him
1 Cor. 15:25 reign, till he hath put all *e* under
  15:26 last *e* that shall be destroyed is death
Gal. 4:16 *e*, because I tell you the truth?
Phil. 3:18 they are the *e* of the cross of Christ
Col. 1:21 alienated and *e* in your mind by wicked
2 Thes. 3:15 count him not as an *e*, but admonish
Jas. 4:4 a friend of the world is the *e* of God

Engage
Jer. 30:21 that *e* his heart to approach unto me?

Engine
2 Chr. 26:15 he made in Jerusalem *e*, invented by
Ezek. 26:9 he shall set *e* of war against thy walls

Engrafted
Jas. 1:21 receive with meekness the *e* word

Engrave *See also* Grave
Ex. 28:11 thou *e* the two stones with the names of
Zech. 3:9 I will *e* the graving. . saith the Lord
2 Cor. 3:7 written and *e* in stones, was glorious

Enjoin *See also* Admonish, Rebuke, Reprove, Warn
Job 36:23 who hath *e* him his way? or who can say

Phlm. 8 I might be much bold in Christ to *e* thee
Heb. 9:20 the testament which God hath *e* unto you

Enjoy
Lev. 26:34 then shall the land *e* her sabbaths
Num. 36:8 Israel may *e* every man the inheritance
Deut. 28:41 shalt beget. . but thou shalt not *e* them
Josh. 1:15 the land of your possession, and *e* it
Eccl. 2:1 *e* pleasure: and, behold, this also is vanity
  2:24 he should make his soul *e* good in his labor
  5:18 eat and to drink, and to *e* the good of all
Is. 65:22 and mine elect shall long *e* the work of
Acts 24:2 seeing that by thee we *e* great quietness
1 Tim. 6:17 who giveth us richly all things to *e*
Heb. 11:25 than to *e* the pleasures of sin for a

Enlarge *See also* Flourish, Grow, Increase
Gen. 9:27 God shall *e* Japheth, and he shall dwell
Ex. 34:24 nations before thee, and *e* thy borders
Deut. 12:20 *e* thy border, as he hath promised thee
1 Chr. 4:10 bless me indeed, and *e* my coast
Job 12:23 he *e* the nations, and straiteneth them
Ps. 4:1 thou hast *e* me when I was in distress
  25:17 troubles of my heart are *e*: O bring thou
  119:32 commandments, when thou shalt *e* my heart
Is. 5:14 hell hath *e* herself, and opened her mouth
  54:2 *e* the place of thy tent, and let them
  60:5 thine heart shall fear, and be *e*
Hab. 2:5 who *e* his desire as hell, and is as death
Mt. 23:5 and *e* the borders of their garments
2 Cor. 6:11 mouth is open unto you, our heart is *e*
  6:13 for a recompense in the same. . be ye also *e*
  10:15 that we shall be *e* by you according to our

Enlighten *See also* Illuminate, Lighten, Shine
1 Sam. 14:27 to his mouth; and his eyes were *e*
Job 33:30 to be *e* with the light of the living
Ps. 18:28 the Lord my God will *e* my darkness
  19:8 commandment of the Lord is pure, *e* the eyes
  97:4 his lightnings *e* the world: the earth saw
Eph. 1:18 eyes of your understanding being *e*
Heb. 6:4 impossible for those who were once *e*

Enmity
Gen. 3:15 I will put *e* between thee and the woman
Num. 35:21 or in *e* smite him with his hand
  35:22 but if he thrust him suddenly without *e*
Lk. 23:12 Pilate and Herod. . before they were at *e*
Rom. 8:7 because the carnal mind is *e* against God
Eph. 2:15 having abolished in his flesh the *e*
  2:16 one body by the cross, having slain the *e*
Jas. 4:4 the friendship of the world is *e* with God?

Enoch
Gen. 5:24 *E* walked with God: and he was not
Heb. 11:5 by faith *E* was translated that he should
Jude 14 *E* also, the seventh from Adam, prophesied

Enough *See also* Sufficient
Gen. 33:9 Esau said, I have *e*, my brother
  33:11 I have *e*. And he urged him, and he took it
  45:28 said, It is *e*; Joseph my son is yet alive
Ex. 36:5 bring much more than *e* for the service
Deut. 1:6 ye have dwelt long *e* in this mount
2 Sam. 24:16 (1 Chr. 21:15) is *e*: stay now thine hand
1 Kgs. 19:4 is *e*; now, O Lord, take away my life
2 Chr. 31:10 we have had *e* to eat, and have left
Prov. 28:19 vain persons shall have poverty *e*
  30:15 yea, four things say not, It is *e*

Is. 56:11 are greedy dogs which can never have *e*
Jer. 49:9 they will destroy till they have *e*
Hos. 4:10 for they shall eat, and not have *e*
Obad. 5 would they not have stolen till they had *e*
Hag. 1:6 ye eat, but ye have not *e*; ye drink, but
Mal. 3:10 there shall not be room *e* to receive it
Mt. 10:25 it is *e* for the disciple that he be as
    25:9 not so; lest there be not *e* for us and you
Mk. 14:41 your rest: it is *e*, the hour is come
Lk. 15:17 servants of my father's have bread *e*
    22:38 two swords. And he said unto them, It is *e*

Enrich

1 Sam. 17:25 who killeth him, the king will *e* him
Ps. 65:9 thou greatly *e* it with the river of God
Ezek. 27:33 thou didst *e* the kings of the earth
1 Cor. 1:5 that in every thing ye are *e* by him
2 Cor. 9:11 *e* in every thing to all bountifulness

Ensample *See also* Example

1 Cor. 10:11 these things happened unto them for *e*
Phil. 3:17 which walk so as ye have us for an *e*
1 Thes. 1:7 so that ye were *e* to all that believe
2 Thes. 3:9 but to make ourselves an *e* unto you
1 Pet. 5:3 but being *e* to the flock
2 Pet. 2:6 making them an *e* unto those that after

Ensign

Num. 2:2 with the *e* of their father's house
Ps. 74:4 thine enemies. . set up their *e* for signs
Is. 5:26 he will lift up an *e* to the nations from
    11:10 root of Jesse, which shall stand for an *e*
    11:12 and he shall set up an *e* for the nations
    18:3 when he lifted up an *e* on the mountains
    30:17 flee: till ye be left. . as an *e* on a hill
Zech. 9:16 crown, lifted up as an *e* upon his land

Entangle

Ex. 14:3 they are *e* in the land, the wilderness
Mt. 22:15 counsel how they might *e* him in his talk
Gal. 5:1 be not *e* again with the yoke of bondage
2 Tim. 2:4 no man that warreth *e* himself
2 Pet. 2:20 they are again *e* therein, and overcome

Enter

Gen. 7:13 selfsame day *e* Noah, and Shem, and Ham
    12:11 when he was come near to *e* into Egypt
Ex. 40:35 Moses was not able to *e* into the tent
Num. 20:24 Aaron. . shall not *e* into the land which
Deut. 23:1 shall not *e* into the congregation
    29:12 shouldest *e* into covenant with the LORD
2 Sam. 22:7 and my cry did *e* into his ears
2 Chr. 30:8 and *e* into his sanctuary
Job 22:4 will he *e* with thee into judgment?
Ps. 95:11 (Heb. 3:11) they should not *e* into my rest
    100:4 *e* into his gates with thanksgiving
    118:20 into which the righteous shall *e*
    143:2 *e* not into judgment with thy servant
Prov. 2:10 when wisdom *e* into thine heart
    4:14 *e* not into the path of the wicked
    17:10 a reproof *e* more into a wise man than
    18:6 a fool's lips *e* into contention
Is. 2:10 *e* into the rock, and hide thee in the
    26:2 nation which keepeth the truth may *e* in
    26:20 come, my people, *e* thou into thy chambers
    57:2 he shall *e* into peace: they shall rest
Ezek. 2:2 (3:24) spirit *e* into me. . set me upon my
    16:8 *e* into a covenant with thee, saith the Lord
    44:2 not be opened, and no man shall *e* in by it
Hos. 11:9 and I will not *e* into the city
Mt. 5:20 ye shall in no case *e* into the kingdom
    6:6 thou, when thou prayest, *e* into thy closet
    7:13 (Lk. 13:24) *e* ye in at the strait gate
    7:21 that saith unto me, Lord, Lord, shall *e* into

Mt. 10:11 (Lk. 10:8) whatsoever city. . ye shall *e*
    12:29 (Mk. 3:27) one *e* into a strong man's house
    15:17 whatsoever *e* in at the mouth goeth into
    18:3 become as little children, ye shall not *e*
    18:8 (Mk. 9:43, 45) is better. . to *e* into life halt
    19:17 wilt *e* into life, keep the commandments
    19:24 (Mk. 10:25; Lk. 18:25) than . . a rich man to *e*
    23:13 (Lk. 11:52) suffer ye them that are *e* to go in
    25:21 (25:23) *e* thou into the joy of thy lord
    26:41 (Mk. 14:38; Lk. 22:40) *e* not into temptation
Mk. 1:29 (Lk. 4:38) they *e* into the house of Simon
    4:19 lusts of other things *e* in, choke the word
    5:12 (Lk. 8:32) swine, that we may *e* into them
    6:10 (Lk. 9:4) ye *e* into a house, there abide till
    7:15 without a man, that *e* into him can defile
    16:5 *e* into the sepulchre, they saw a young man
Lk. 7:6 not worthy that thou shouldest *e* under my
    9:34 and they feared as they *e* into the cloud
    24:26 these things, and to *e* into his glory?
Jn. 3:4 *e* the second time into his mother's womb
    3:5 of the Spirit, he cannot *e* into the kingdom
    4:38 other men labored, and ye are *e* into their
    10:1 that *e* not by the door into the sheepfold
Acts 3:2 ask alms of them that *e* into the temple
    5:21 heard that, they *e* into the temple early
    14:22 through much tribulation *e* into the kingdom
    16:40 the prison, and *e* into the house of Lydia
    18:7 *e* into a certain man's house, named Justus
    20:29 shall grievous wolves *e* in among you
Rom. 5:12 as by one man sin *e* into the world
    5:20 law *e*, that the offense might abound
1 Cor. 2:9 neither have *e* into the heart of man
Heb. 4:3 for we which have believed do *e* into rest
    4:6 first preached *e* not in because of unbelief
    4:11 let us labor therefore to *e* into that rest
    6:19 anchor. . which *e* into that within the veil
    6:20 whither the forerunner is for us *e*
    9:12 but by his own blood he *e* in once into the
    9:24 Christ is not *e* into the holy places made
    10:19 *e* into the holiest by the blood of Jesus
2 Jn. 7 for many deceivers are *e* into the world
Rev. 11:11 the Spirit of life from God *e* into them
    15:8 no man was able to *e* into the temple, till
    21:27 no wise *e* into it any thing that defileth
    22:14 may *e* in through the gates into the city

Entertain

Heb. 13:2 *e* strangers. . some have *e* angels unawares

Entice *See also* Tempt

Ex. 22:16 if a man *e* a maid that is not betrothed
Deut. 13:6 *e* thee secretly, saying, Let us go and
Judg. 14:15 said unto Samson's wife, *E* thy husband
    16:5 *e* him, and see wherein his great strength
2 Chr. 18:19 and the LORD said, Who shall *e* Ahab
Job 31:27 and my heart hath been secretly *e*
Prov. 1:10 if sinners *e* thee, consent thou not
    16:29 a violent man *e* his neighbor, and leadeth
Jer. 20:10 peradventure he will be *e*, and we shall
1 Cor. 2:4 and my preaching was not with *e* words
Col. 2:4 any man should beguile you with *e* words
Jas. 1:14 he is drawn away of his own lust, and *e*

Entrance

2 Chr. 12:10 that kept the *e* of the king's house
Ps. 119:130 the *e* of thy words giveth light
2 Pet. 1:11 so an *e* shall be ministered unto you

Entreat *See also* Beg, Beseech, Pray

Gen. 12:16 he *e* Abram well for her sake
    23:8 hear me, and *e* for me to Ephron the son
Ex. 8:8 *e* the LORD, that he may take away the frogs
    8:8 *e* the LORD, that he may take away the frogs
Ruth 1:16 Ruth said, *E* me not to leave thee

1 Sam. 2:25 against the LORD, who shall *e* for him?
2 Sam. 21:14 and after that God was *e* for the land
    24:25 LORD was *e* for the land, and the plague
1 Kgs. 13:6 man of God, *E* now the face of the LORD
Job 24:21 he evil *e* the barren that beareth not
Ps. 45:12 rich among the people shall *e* thy favor
    119:58 I *e* thy favor with my whole heart
Is. 19:22 shall be *e* of them, and shall heal them
Jer. 15:11 I will cause the enemy to *e* thee well
Mt. 22:6 took his servants, and *e* them spitefully
Lk. 15:28 therefore came his father out, and *e* him
    18:32 mocked, and spitefully *e*, and spitted on
    20:11 they beat him also, and *e* him shamefully
Acts 7:6 bring them into bondage, and *e* them evil
    27:3 and Julius courteously *e* Paul, and gave him
1 Cor. 4:13 being defamed, we *e*: we are made as
Phil. 4:3 and I *e* thee also, true yokefellow, help
1 Thes. 2:2 suffered before, and were shamefully *e*
1 Tim. 5:1 rebuke not an elder, but *e* him as a
Heb. 12:19 *e* that the word should not be spoken to
Jas. 3:17 gentle, and easy to be *e*, full of mercy

Entry

1 Chr. 9:19 their fathers. . were keepers of the *e*
Prov. 8:3 she crieth at the gates, at the *e*
Ezek. 8:5 behold. . this image of jealousy in the *e*

Envious

Ps. 37:1 neither be thou *e* against the workers of
    73:3 *e* at the foolish, when I saw the prosperity
Prov. 24:1 be not thou *e* against evil men
    24:19 neither be thou *e* at the wicked

Envy *See also* Covetousness, Jealousy

Gen. 26:14 and the Philistines *e* him
    30:1 bare Jacob no children, Rachel *e* her sister
    37:11 brethren *e* him; but his father observed
Num. 11:29 Moses said unto him, *E*. . for my sake?
Job 5:2 foolish man, and *e* slayeth the silly one
Ps. 106:16 they *e* Moses also in the camp
Prov. 3:31 *e* thou not the oppressor, and choose
    14:30 but *e* the rottenness of the bones
    23:17 let not thine heart *e* sinners; but be thou
    27:4 but who is able to stand before *e*?
Eccl. 4:4 that for this a man is *e* of his neighbor
    9:6 their hatred, and their *e*, is now perished
Is. 11:13 the *e* also of Ephraim shall depart
    26:11 be ashamed for their *e* at the people
Ezek. 31:9 that were in the garden of God, *e* him
Mt. 27:18 (Mk. 15:10) for *e* they had delivered him
Acts 7:9 the patriarchs, moved with *e*, sold Joseph
    13:45 they were filled with *e*, and spake against
    17:5 the Jews which believed not, moved with *e*
Rom. 1:29 maliciousness; full of *e*, murder, debate
1 Cor. 13:4 charity *e* not; charity vaunteth not
Gal. 5:26 provoking one another, *e* one another
Phil. 1:15 preach Christ even of *e* and strife
1 Tim. 6:4 whereof cometh *e*, strife, railings
Tit. 3:3 living in malice and *e*, hateful
Jas. 4:5 spirit that dwelleth in us lusteth to *e*?
1 Pet. 2:1 guile, and hypocrisies, and *e*, and all

Envying

Rom. 13:13 and wantonness, not in strife and *e*
1 Cor. 3:3 there is among you *e*, and strife
2 Cor. 12:20 lest there be debates, *e*, wraths
Gal. 5:21 *e*, murders, drunkenness, revelings
Jas. 3:14 if ye have bitter *e* and strife in your
    3:16 where *e* and strife is, there is confusion

Epaphras Col. 1:7; 4:12; Phlm. 23

Epaphroditus Phil. 2:25; 4:18

Ephah

Zech. 5:6 he said, This is an *e* that goeth forth

Ephesus

Acts 18:19 he came to *E*, and left them there
    19:1 came to *E*; and finding certain disciples
    19:26 not alone at *E*, but almost throughout all
    20:17 sent to *E*. . called the elders of the church
1 Cor. 15:32 I have fought with beasts at *E*
    16:8 but I will tarry at *E* until Pentecost
1 Tim. 1:3 as I besought thee to abide still at *E*
2 Tim. 1:18 many things he ministered unto me at *E*
Rev. 2:1 unto the angel of the church of *E* write

Ephod

Ex. 28:6 (39:2) make the *e* of gold, of blue. . of purple
Lev. 8:7 him with the robe, and put the *e* upon him
Judg. 8:27 Gideon made an *e* thereof, and put it in
1 Sam. 2:18 being a child, girded with a linen *e*
    22:18 and five persons that did wear a linen *e*
2 Sam. 6:14 (1 Chr. 15:27) David. . with a linen *e*

Ephraim

Gen. 41:52 name of the second called he *E*
    48:14 his right hand, and laid it upon *E*'s head
Judg. 1:29 neither did *E* drive out the Canaanites
    7:24 men of *E* gathered themselves together
    8:1 men of *E* said unto him, Why hast thou served
    12:4 men of Gilead, and fought with *E*. . smote *E*
Ps. 78:67 of Joseph, and chose not the tribe of *E*
Is. 7:2 Syria is confederate with *E*
    11:13 *E* shall not envy Judah. . shall not vex *E*
Jer. 7:15 your brethren, even the whole seed of *E*
    31:18 I have surely heard *E* bemoaning himself
    31:20 is *E* my dear son? is he a pleasant child?
Hos. 4:17 *E* is joined to idols: let him alone
    5:3 I know *E*. . O *E*, thou committest whoredom
    5:9 *E* shall be desolate in the day of rebuke
    5:14 I will be unto *E* as a lion, and as a young
    6:4 O *E*, what shall I do unto thee?
    7:1 then the iniquity of *E* was discovered
    7:11 *E* also is like a silly dove without heart
    8:11 because *E* hath made many altars to sin
    9:3 the LORD's land; but *E* shall return to Egypt
    10:6 *E* shall receive shame, and Israel shall be
    11:8 how shall I give thee up, *E*? how shall I
    12:1 *E* feedeth on wind, and followeth after the
    13:12 iniquity of *E* is bound up; his sin is hid
    14:8 *E* shall say, What have I to do any more
Zech. 10:7 they of *E* shall be like a mighty man
Jn. 11:54 to the wilderness, into a city called *E*

Ephratah (Ephrath)

Gen. 35:19; Ruth 4:11; Mic. 5:2

Epicurean Acts 17:18

Epistle *See also* Letter

Acts 15:30 to Antioch. . they delivered the *e*
    23:33 delivered the *e* to the governor, presented
2 Cor. 3:1 need we. . *e* of commendation to you
    3:2 ye are our *e* written in our hearts, known
    3:3 manifestly declared to be the *e* of Christ
    7:8 perceive that the same *e* hath made you sorry
Col. 4:16 and when this *e* is read among you
1 Thes. 5:27 *e* be read unto all the holy brethren
2 Thes. 2:15 taught, whether by word, or our *e*
    3:14 and if any man obey not our word by this *e*
    3:17 which is the token in every *e*: so I write
2 Pet. 3:1 second *e*, beloved, I now write unto you
    3:16 as also in all his *e*, speaking in them

Equal

Ps. 17:2 thine eyes behold the things that are *e*
55:13 but it was thou, a man mine *e*, my guide
Prov. 26:7 the legs of the lame are not *e*
Is. 40:25 (46:5) or shall I be *e*? saith the Holy One
Ezek. 18:25 (18:29; 33:17, 20) way of the Lord is not *e*
18:29 O house of Israel, are not my ways *e*?
33:17 but as for them, their way is not *e*
Mt. 20:12 hour, and thou hast made them *e* unto us
Lk. 20:36 for they are *e* unto the angels
Jn. 5:18 that God was his Father, making himself *e*
Gal. 1:14 in the Jews' religion above many my *e*
Phil. 2:6 thought it not robbery to be *e* with God
Col. 4:1 your servants that which is just and *e*

Equality

2 Cor. 8:14 for your want; that there may be *e*

Equity *See also* Judgment, Justice, Righteousness

Ps. 98:9 judge the world, and the people with *e*
99:4 also loveth judgment; thou dost establish *e*
Prov. 1:3 of wisdom, justice, and judgment, and *e*
2:9 then shalt thou understand . . judgment, and *e*
17:26 nor to strike princes for *e*
Eccl. 2:21 man whose labor is in wisdom . . and in *e*
Is. 11:4 reprove with *e* for the meek of the earth
59:14 fallen in the street, and *e* cannot enter
Mic. 3:9 that abhor judgment, and pervert all *e*
Mal. 2:6 he walked with me in peace and *e*

Erastus

Acts 19:22 sent into Macedonia . . Timotheus and *E*
Rom. 16:23 *E* the chamberlain of the city saluteth
2 Tim. 4:20 *E* abode at Corinth: but Trophimus

Err *See also* Sin, Wander

Lev. 5:18 concerning his ignorance wherein he *e*
Num. 15:22 and if ye have *e*, and not observed all
1 Sam. 26:21 I have played the fool, and have *e*
2 Chr. 33:9 so Manasseh made Judah . . to *e*
Job 6:24 cause me to understand wherein I have *e*
Ps. 95:10 (Heb. 3:10) people that do *e* in their heart
119:21 the proud . . do *e* from thy commandments
119:110 yet I *e* not from thy precepts
Prov. 10:17 but he that refuseth reproof *e*
14:22 do they not *e* that devise evil? but mercy
19:27 causeth to *e* from the words of knowledge
Is. 3:12 they which lead thee cause thee to *e*
9:16 the leaders of this people cause them to *e*
19:14 they have caused Egypt to *e* in every work
28:7 they *e* in vision, they stumble in judgment
29:24 *e* in spirit shall come to understanding
35:8 wayfaring men, though fools, shall not *e*
63:17 why hast thou made us to *e* from thy ways
Jer. 23:13 Baal, and caused my people Israel to *e*
23:32 cause my people to *e* by their lies
Ezek. 45:20 for every one that *e*, and for him that
Hos. 4:12 spirit of whoredoms hath caused them to *e*
Amos 2:4 and their lies caused them to *e*
Mic. 3:5 prophets that make my people *e*, that bite
Mt. 22:29 (Mk. 12:24) *e*, not knowing the Scriptures
Mk. 12:27 ye therefore do greatly *e*
1 Tim. 6:10 they have *e* from the faith
6:21 some professing have *e* concerning the faith
2 Tim. 2:18 concerning the truth have *e*
Jas. 1:16 do not *e*, my beloved brethren
5:19 if any of you do *e* from the truth

Errand

Gen. 24:33 will not eat, until I have told mine *e*
Judg. 3:19 I have a secret *e* unto thee, O king

2 Kgs. 9:5 I have an *e* to thee, O captain

Error *See also* Sin

2 Sam. 6:7 and God smote him there for his *e*
Job 19:4 have erred, mine *e* remaineth with myself
Ps. 19:12 who can understand his *e*? cleanse thou
Eccl. 5:6 thou before the angel, that it was an *e*
10:5 as an *e* which proceedeth from the ruler
Is. 32:6 and to utter *e* against the LORD
Jer. 10:15 they are vanity, and the work of *e*
Dan. 6:4 neither was there any *e* or fault found
Mt. 27:64 the last *e* shall be worse than the first
Rom. 1:27 recompense of their *e* which was meet
Heb. 9:7 for himself, and for the *e* of the people
Jas. 5:20 converteth the sinner from the *e* of his
2 Pet. 3:17 led away with the *e* of the wicked
1 Jn. 4:6 the spirit of truth, and the spirit of *e*
Jude 11 greedily after the *e* of Balaam for reward

Esaias *See* Isaiah

Esar-haddon

2 Kgs. 19:37 (Is. 37:38); Ezra 4:2

Esau

Born, Gen. 25:24–26; sold his birthright, Gen. 25:29–34; married Hittite women, Gen. 26:34; lost Isaac's blessing, Gen. 27:30–40; hated Jacob, Gen. 27:41; married Mahalath, Gen. 28:9; reconciled with Jacob, Gen. 33:1–15.

Jer. 49:8 I will bring the calamity of *E* upon him
Mal. 1:3 I hated *E*, and laid his mountains . . waste
Rom. 9:13 Jacob have I loved but *E* have I hated
Heb. 12:16 profane person, as *E* who for one morsel

Escape *See also* Flee

Gen. 14:13 came one that had *e*, and told Abram
19:17 said, *E* for thy life; look not behind thee
Deut. 23:15 the servant which is *e* from his master
1 Sam. 19:10 and David fled, and *e* that night
1 Kgs. 18:40 prophets of Baal; let not one of them *e*
2 Kgs. 9:15 none go forth nor *e* out of the city
Esth. 4:13 that thou shalt *e* in the king's house
Job 1:15 (1:16, 17, 19) I only am *e* alone to tell thee
11:20 wicked shall fail, and they shall not *e*
19:20 and I am *e* with the skin of my teeth
Ps. 55:8 I would hasten my *e* from the windy storm
56:7 shall they *e* by iniquity? in thine anger
71:2 cause me to *e*: incline thine ear unto me
124:7 our soul is *e* as a bird out of the snare
Prov. 19:5 and he that speaketh lies shall not *e*
Eccl. 7:26 whoso pleaseth God shall *e* from her
Is. 20:6 the king of Assyria: and how shall we *e*?
Ezek. 33:21 had *e* out of Jerusalem came unto me
Dan. 11:41 but these shall *e* out of his hand
Amos 9:1 he that *e* of them shall not be delivered
Mt. 23:33 how can ye *e* the damnation of hell?
Lk. 21:36 that ye may be accounted worthy to *e* all
Jn. 10:39 to take him; but he *e* out of their hand
Acts 27:42 lest any of them should swim out, and *e*
27:44 came to pass, that they *e* all safe to land
28:4 though he hath *e* the sea, yet vengeance
Rom. 2:3 that thou shalt *e* the judgment of God?
1 Cor. 10:13 with the temptation . . make a way to *e*
2 Cor. 11:33 let down by the wall, and *e* his hands
1 Thes. 5:3 woman with child; and they shall not *e*
Heb. 2:3 how shall we *e*, if we neglect so great
11:34 violence of fire, *e* the edge of the sword
12:25 if they *e* not who refused him that spake
2 Pet. 1:4 divine nature, having *e* the corruption
2:20 have *e* the pollutions of the world through

Eschew

Job 1:8 man, one that feareth God, and *e* evil?
1 Pet. 3:11 let him *e* evil, and do good

Eshcol Num. 13:23, 24; 32:9; Deut. 1:24

Especially

Ps. 31:11 mine enemies, but *e* among my neighbors
Gal. 6:10 *e* unto them. . of the household of faith
1 Tim. 5:17 honor, *e* they who labor in the word
2 Tim. 4:13 and the books, but *e* the parchments

Espousal

Song 3:11 mother crowned him in the day of his *e*
Jer. 2:2 kindness of thy youth, the love of thine *e*

Espouse *See also* Betroth, Marry

2 Sam. 3:14 my wife Michal, which I *e* to me
Mt. 1:18 when as his mother Mary was *e* to Joseph
Lk. 1:27 to a virgin *e* to a man whose name was
2:5 to be taxed with Mary his *e* wife
2 Cor. 11:2 for I have *e* you to one husband

Establish *See also* Found, Settle, Stablish

Gen. 6:18 with thee will I *e* my covenant
9:9 I *e* my covenant with you, and with your seed
17:7 I will *e* my covenant between me and thee
17:21 but my covenant will I *e* with Isaac
Deut. 19:15 (Mt. 18:16; 2 Cor. 13:1) the matter be *e*
28:9 the Lord shall *e* thee a holy people
32:6 hath he not made thee, and *e* thee?
2 Sam. 7:12 (1 Chr. 17:11; 28:7) will *e* his kingdom
7:25 (1 Chr. 17:23) *e* it for ever, and do as
1 Kgs. 9:5 then I will *e* the throne of thy kingdom
15:4 his son after him, and to *e* Jerusalem
Ps. 24:2 upon the seas, and *e* it upon the floods
40:2 set my feet upon a rock, and *e* my goings
48:8 the city of our God: God will *e* it for ever
78:69 like the earth which he hath *e* for ever
89:2 thy faithfulness shalt thou *e* in the very
89:4 thy seed will I *e* for ever, and build up
90:17 *e* thou the work of our hands upon us
93:2 thy throne is *e* of old: thou art from
96:10 world also shall be *e* that it shall not be
99:4 thou dost *e* equity, thou executest judgment
112:8 his heart is *e*, he shall not be afraid
Prov. 3:19 by understanding hath he *e* the heavens
4:26 path of thy feet, and let all thy ways be *e*
8:28 he *e* the clouds above: when he strengthened
12:19 the lip of truth shall be *e* for ever
16:12 for the throne is *e* by righteousness
20:18 every purpose is *e* by counsel
24:3 house builded; and by understanding it is *e*
25:5 and his throne shall be *e* in righteousness
Is. 7:9 will not believe, surely ye shall not be *e*
9:7 to *e* it with judgment and with justice
16:5 and in mercy shall the throne be *e*
45:18 he hath *e* it, he created it not in vain
49:8 covenant of the people, to *e* the earth
Jer. 10:12 (51:15) he hath *e* the world by his wisdom
Ezek. 16:60 *e* unto thee an everlasting covenant
Amos 5:15 love the good, and *e* judgment in the gate
Zech. 5:11 be *e*, and set there upon her own base
Acts 16:5 so were the churches *e* in the faith
Rom. 3:31 God forbid: yea, we *e* the law
10:3 going about to *e* their own righteousness
Heb. 8:6 a better covenant. . *e* upon better promises
10:9 away the first, that he may *e* the second
13:9 a good thing that the heart be *e* with grace
2 Pet. 1:12 and be *e* in the present truth

Estate

1 Chr. 17:17 to the *e* of a man of high degree

Ps. 136:23 who remembered us in our low *e*
Eccl. 1:16 heart, saying, Lo, I am come to great *e*
3:18 concerning the *e* of the sons of men
Ezek. 16:55 then thou. . shall return to your former *e*
36:11 I will settle you after your old *e*
Dan. 11:7 of her roots shall one stand up in his *e*
Mk. 6:21 high captains, and chief *e* of Galilee
Lk. 1:48 hath regarded the low *e* of his handmaiden
Acts 22:5 witness, and all the *e* of the elders
Rom. 12:16 but condescend to men of low *e*
Col. 4:8 that he might know your *e*, and comfort
Jude 6 and the angels which kept not their first *e*

Esteem *See also* Regard, Respect

Deut. 32:15 lightly *e* the Rock of his salvation
1 Sam. 2:30 that despise me shall be lightly *e*
18:23 seeing that I am a poor man, and lightly *e*
Job 23:12 I have *e* the words of his mouth more
36:19 will he *e* thy riches? no, not gold
41:27 *e* iron as straw, and brass as rotten wood
Ps. 119:128 I *e* all thy precepts concerning all
Prov. 17:28 that shutteth his lips is *e* a man of
Is. 32:15 fruitful field shall be *e* as a forest?
53:3 he was despised, and we *e* him not
53:4 yet we did *e* him stricken, smitten of God
Lam. 4:2 how are they *e* as earthen pitchers
Lk. 16:15 is highly *e* among men is abomination
Rom. 14:5 *e* one day above another: another *e* every
14:14 but to him that *e* any thing to be unclean
1 Cor. 6:4 to judge who are least *e* in the church
Phil. 2:3 let each *e* other better than themselves
1 Thes. 5:13 *e* them very highly in love for their
Heb. 11:26 *e* the reproach of Christ greater riches

Esther Esth. 2:7-9:32

Estimation

Lev. 27:2 persons shall be for the Lord by thy *e*
27:15 add the fifth part of the money of thy *e*

Estranged

Job 19:13 mine acquaintance are verily *e* from me
Ps. 58:3 the wicked are *e* from the womb
78:30 they were not *e* from their lust
Jer. 19:4 have forsaken me, and have *e* this place
Ezek. 14:5 are all *e* from me through their idols

Eternal *See also* Everlasting

Deut. 33:27 *e* God is thy refuge, and underneath
Is. 60:15 I will make thee an *e* excellency, a joy
Mt. 19:16 (Mk. 10:17; Lk. 18:18) I may have *e* life?
25:46 but the righteous into life *e*
Mk. 3:29 but is in danger of *e* damnation
10:30 and in the world to come *e* life
Lk. 10:25 what shall I do to inherit *e* life?
Jn. 3:15 in him should not perish, but have *e* life
4:36 and gathereth fruit unto life *e*
5:39 Scriptures. . in them ye think ye have *e* life
6:54 flesh, and drinketh my blood, hath *e* life
6:68 shall we go? thou hast the words of *e* life
10:28 I give unto them *e* life; and they shall
12:25 in this world shall keep it unto life *e*
17:2 he should give *e* life to as many as thou
17:3 this is life *e*, that they might know thee
Acts 13:48 as were ordained to *e* life believed
Rom. 1:20 even his *e* power and Godhead
2:7 for glory and honor and immortality, *e* life
5:21 reign through righteousness unto *e* life
6:23 but the gift of God is *e* life through Jesus
2 Cor. 4:17 more exceeding and *e* weight of glory
4:18 but the things which are not seen are *e*
5:1 house not made with hands, *e* in the heavens
Eph. 3:11 *e* purpose which he purposed in Christ

1 Tim. 1:17 unto the King *e*, immortal, invisible
   6:12 the good fight of faith, lay hold on *e* life
2 Tim. 2:10 which is in Christ Jesus with *e* glory
Tit. 1:2 hope of *e* life, which God, that cannot lie
Heb. 5:9 became the author of *e* salvation unto all
   6:2 resurrection of the dead, and of *e* judgment
   9:12 having obtained *e* redemption for us
   9:14 who through the *e* Spirit offered himself
   9:15 might receive the promise of *e* inheritance
1 Pet. 5:10 called us unto his *e* glory by Christ
1 Jn. 1:2 witness, and show unto you that *e* life
   2:25 he hath promised us, even *e* life
   3:15 that no murderer hath *e* life abiding in him
   5:11 God hath given to us *e* life, and this life
   5:13 that ye may know that ye have *e* life
   5:20 this is the true God, and *e* life
Jude 7 example, suffering the vengeance of *e* fire
   21 mercy of our Lord Jesus Christ unto *e* life

Eternity

Is. 57:15 the high and lofty One that inhabiteth *e*

Ethiopia *See also* Cush

Gen. 2:13 that compasseth the whole land of *E*
Esth. 1:1 which reigned from India even unto *E*
Ps. 68:31 *E* shall soon stretch out her hands unto God
Is. 18:1 woe to the land . . beyond the rivers of *E*
   20:3 a sign and wonder upon Egypt and upon *E*
   43:3 Egypt for thy ransom, *E* and Seba for thee
Ezek. 30:4 and great pain shall be in *E*
Nah. 3:9 *E* and Egypt were her strength
Zeph. 3:10 beyond the rivers of *E* my suppliants
Acts 8:27 a man of *E*, a eunuch of great authority

Ethiopian

Num. 12:1 against Moses because of the *E* woman
2 Chr. 14:9 came out against them Zerah the *E*
   14:12 so the LORD smote the *E* before Asa
Jer. 13:23 can the *E* change his skin, or the leopard

Eunice 2 Tim. 1:5

Eunuch

2 Kgs. 9:32 there looked out to him two or three *e*
Is. 56:3 neither let the *e* say . . I am a dry tree
   56:4 the LORD unto the *e* that keep my sabbaths
Jer. 52:25 he took also out of the city a *e*
Dan. 1:3 spake unto Ashpenaz the master of his *e*
Mt. 19:12 *e*, which have made themselves *e* for the
Acts 8:27 man of Ethiopia, a *e* of great authority
   8:38 both Philip and the *e*; and he baptized him

Euphrates

Gen. 2:14 and the fourth river is *E*
   15:18 of Egypt unto the great river, the river *E*
Josh. 1:4 even unto the great river, the river *E*
2 Sam. 8:3 (1 Chr. 18:3) his border at the river *E*
Jer. 13:4 go to *E*, and hide it there in a hole
   51:63 this book . . and cast it into the midst of *E*
Rev. 9:14 which are bound in the great river *E*
   16:12 poured out his vial upon the great river *E*

Eutychus Acts 20:9–12

Evangelist

Acts 21:8 entered into the house of Philip the *e*
Eph. 4:11 prophets; and some, *e*; and some, pastors
2 Tim. 4:5 endure afflictions, do the work of an *e*

Eve

Gen. 3:20 Adam called his wife's name *E*
2 Cor. 11:3 as the serpent beguiled *E* through his
1 Tim. 2:13 for Adam was first formed, then *E*

Evening (Even)

Gen. 1:5 the *e* and the morning were the first day
   8:11 the dove came in to him in the *e*
   30:16 Jacob came out of the field in the *e*
Ex. 12:6 the whole assembly . . shall kill it in the *e*
Judg. 19:9 day draweth toward *e*, I pray you tarry
1 Sam. 14:24 cursed . . that eateth any food until *e*
1 Kgs. 17:6 and bread and flesh in the *e*
   18:29 time of the offering of the *e* sacrifice
Ps. 55:17 *e*, and morning, and at noon, will I pray
   65:8 outgoings of the morning and *e* to rejoice
   90:6 in the *e* it is cut down, and withereth
   104:23 his work and to his labor until the *e*
   141:2 lifting up of my hands as the *e* sacrifice
Eccl. 11:6 in the *e* withhold not thine hand
Jer. 6:4 the shadows of the *e* are stretched out
Zech. 14:7 that at *e* time it shall be light
Mt. 14:23 (Mk. 6:47) *e* was come, he was there alone
   16:2 is *e*, ye say, It will be fair weather
   26:20 (Mk. 14:17) *e* was come, he sat down with
Lk. 24:29 abide with us; for it is toward *e*
Jn. 20:19 same day at *e* . . when the doors were shut

Event

Eccl. 2:14 also that one *e* happeneth to them all
   9:2 is one *e* to the righteous, and to the wicked

Ever *See also* Alway, Everlasting

Gen. 3:22 tree of life, and eat, and live for *e*
   43:9 then let me bear the blame for *e*
Ex. 14:13 ye shall see them again no more for *e*
Lev. 6:13 fire shall *e* be burning upon the altar
Deut. 4:33 did *e* people hear the voice of God
   5:29 with them, and with their children for *e*!
   13:16 and it shall be a heap for *e*; it shall not
   32:40 my hand to heaven, and say, I live for *e*
1 Kgs. 10:9 because the LORD loved Israel for *e*
1 Chr. 16:36 be the LORD God of Israel for *e* and *e*
Job 4:7 who *e* perished, being innocent?
Ps. 9:7 but the LORD shall endure for *e*
   12:7 preserve them from this generation for *e*
   22:26 that seek him: your heart shall live for *e*
   23:6 I will dwell in the house of the LORD for *e*
   25:15 mine eyes are *e* toward the LORD
   29:10 yea, the LORD sitteth King for *e*
   33:11 the counsel of the LORD standeth for *e* .
   37:26 he is *e* merciful, and lendeth
   45:6 (Heb. 1:8) thy throne, O God, is for *e* and *e*
   48:14 this God is our God for *e* and *e*
   49:9 still live for *e*, and not see corruption
   51:3 transgressions: and my sin is *e* before me
   52:8 I trust in the mercy of God for *e* and *e*
   61:4 I will abide in thy tabernacle for *e*
   73:26 strength of my heart, and my portion for *e*
   81:15 but their time should have endured for *e*
   92:7 it is that they shall be destroyed for *e*
   93:5 holiness becometh thine house, O LORD, for *e*
   102:12 but thou, O LORD, shalt endure for *e*
   103:9 neither will he keep his anger for *e*
   105:8 he hath remembered his covenant for *e*
   110:4 (Heb. 5:6; 7:17, 21) thou art a priest for *e*
   119:89 for *e* . . thy word is settled in heaven
   132:14 this is my rest for *e*: here will I dwell
   145:1 and I will bless thy name for *e* and *e*
   146:6 that therein is: which keepeth truth for *e*
   146:10 the LORD shall reign for *e*, even thy God
Prov. 27:24 for riches are not for *e*
Eccl. 1:4 but the earth abideth for *e*
   3:14 whatsoever God doeth, it shall be for *e*
Is. 26:4 trust ye in the LORD for *e*
   32:17 the effect . . quietness and assurance for *e*
   34:10 the smoke thereof shall go up for *e*

Is. 40:8 (1 Pet. 1:25) but the word of our God shall
    stand for *e*
51:6 but my salvation shall be for *e*
51:8 but my righteousness shall be for *e*
57:16 I will not contend for *e*, neither will I
Lam. 3:31 for the Lord will not cast off for *e*
5:19 thou, O LORD, remainest for *e*; thy throne
Dan. 2:20 blessed be the name of God for *e* and
12:3 to righteousness, as the stars for *e* and *e*
Mt. 6:13 and the power, and the glory, for *e*
21:19 (Mk. 11:14) no fruit grow on thee . . for *e*
24:21 the world to this time, no, nor *e* shall be
Lk. 15:31 said unto him, Son, thou art *e* with me
Jn. 4:29 which told me all things that *e* I did
6:51 man eat of this bread, he shall live for *e*
8:35 in the house for *e*: but the Son abideth *e*
10:8 all that *e* came before me are thieves
12:34 out of the law that Christ abideth for *e*
14:16 Comforter, that he may abide with you for *e*
Rom. 9:5 who is over all, God blessed for *e*
Gal. 1:5 to whom be glory for *e* and *e*
Phil. 4:20 unto God and our Father be glory for *e*
1 Thes. 4:17 and so shall we *e* be with the Lord
5:15 but *e* follow that which is good
2 Tim. 3:7 *e* learning, and never able to come to
Heb. 1:8 saith, Thy throne, O God, is for *e* and *e*
7:25 he *e* liveth to make intercession for them
13:8 the same yesterday, and today, and for *e*
1 Pet. 1:23 word of God . . liveth and abideth for *e*
1 Jn. 2:17 doeth the will of God abideth for *e*
Jude 25 dominion and power, both now and *e*
Rev. 4:9 sat on the throne, who liveth for *e* and *e*
5:14 and worshipped him that liveth for *e* and *e*
11:15 his Christ; and he shall reign for *e* and *e*
14:11 of their torment ascendeth up for *e* and *e*
19:3 and her smoke rose up for *e* and *e*
22:5 and they shall reign for *e* and *e*

Everlasting *See also* Eternal, Ever

Gen. 9:16 remember the *e* covenant between God
17:7 an *e* covenant, to be a God unto thee
21:33 called . . on the name of the LORD, the *e* God
48:4 to thy seed after thee for an *e* possession
Ex. 40:15 surely be an *e* priesthood throughout
Lev. 16:34 and this shall be an *e* statute unto you
Num. 25:13 even the covenant of an *e* priesthood
Deut. 33:27 refuge, and underneath are the *e* arms
Ps. 24:7 (24:9) and be ye lifted up, ye *e* doors
90:2 the world, even from *e* to *e*, thou art God
93:2 is established of old: thou art from *e*
100:5 for the LORD is good; his mercy is *e*
103:17 the mercy of the LORD is from *e* to *e*
112:6 the righteous shall be in *e* remembrance
119:142 thy righteousness is an *e* righteousness
139:24 wicked way in me, and lead me in the way *e*
145:13 kingdom is an *e* kingdom, and thy dominion
Prov. 8:23 I was set up from *e*, from the beginning
10:25 but the righteous is an *e* foundation
Is. 9:6 Counselor, The mighty God, The *e* Father
26:4 for in the LORD JEHOVAH is *e* strength
33:14 who among us shall dwell with *e* burnings?
35:10 and come to Zion with songs and *e* joy
40:28 hast thou not heard, that the *e* God
45:17 be saved in the LORD with an *e* salvation
51:11 and *e* joy shall be upon their head
54:8 with *e* kindness will I have mercy on thee
55:13 for an *e* sign that shall not be cut off
56:5 I will give them an *e* name, that shall not
60:19 but the LORD shall be unto thee an *e* light
61:7 *e* joy shall be unto them
63:12 before them, to make himself an *e* name?
Jer. 10:10 he is the living God, and an *e* King
31:3 I have loved thee with an *e* love

Dan. 4:3 his wonders! his kingdom is an *e* kingdom
7:27 Most High, whose kingdom is an *e* kingdom
9:24 to bring in *e* righteousness, and to seal up
12:2 to *e* life, and some to shame and *e* contempt
Mic. 5:2 goings forth have been from of old, from *e*
Hab. 1:12 art thou not from *e*, O LORD my God
3:6 perpetual hills did bow: his ways are *e*
Mt. 18:8 hands or two feet to be cast into *e* fire
19:29 (Lk. 18:30) and shall inherit *e* life
25:41 depart from me, ye cursed, into *e* fire
25:46 these shall go away into *e* punishment
Lk. 16:9 they may receive you into *e* habitations
Jn. 3:16 in him should not perish, but have *e* life
3:36 he that believeth on the Son hath *e* life
4:14 a well of water springing up into *e* life
5:24 believeth on him that sent me, hath *e* life
6:27 for that meat which endureth unto *e* life
6:40 Son, and believeth on him, may have *e* life
6:47 he that believeth on me hath *e* life
12:50 and I know that his commandment is life *e*
Acts 13:46 and judge yourselves unworthy of *e* life
Rom. 6:22 fruit unto holiness, and the end *e* life
16:26 according to the commandment of the *e* God
Gal. 6:8 shall of the Spirit reap life *e*
2 Thes. 1:9 shall be punished with *e* destruction
2:16 hath given us *e* consolation and good hope
Heb. 13:20 through the blood of the *e* covenant
2 Pet. 1:11 the *e* kingdom of our Lord and Saviour
Jude 6 he hath reserved in *e* chains under darkness
Rev. 14:6 having the *e* gospel to preach unto them

Evermore

Deut. 28:29 shalt be only oppressed and spoiled *e*
2 Kgs. 17:37 ye shall observe to do for *e*
Ps. 16:11 thy right hand there are pleasures for *e*
18:50 anointed, to David, and to his seed for *e*
37:27 from evil, and do good; and dwell for *e*
77:8 gone for ever? doth his promise fail for *e*?
86:12 and I will glorify thy name for *e*
89:52 blessed be the LORD for *e*. Amen, and Amen
92:8 but thou, LORD, art most high for *e*
105:4 LORD, and his strength: seek his face *e*
106:31 righteousness unto all generations for *e*
113:2 blessed . . from this time forth and for *e*
121:8 thy coming in from this time . . even for *e*
133:3 commanded the blessing, even life for *e*
Jn. 6:34 unto him, Lord, *e* give us this bread
2 Cor. 11:31 Jesus Christ, which is blessed for *e*
1 Thes. 5:16 rejoice *e*
Heb. 7:28 maketh the Son, who is consecrated for *e*
Rev. 1:18 was dead; and, behold, I am alive for *e*

Every

Deut. 8:3 (Mt. 4:4; Lk. 4:4) but by *e* word that
2 Chr. 30:18 saying, The good LORD pardon *e* one
Ps. 145:2 *e* day will I bless thee; and I will praise
Is. 45:23 (Rom. 14:11) *e* knee shall bow, *e* tongue
Mk. 16:15 and preach the gospel to *e* creature
Acts 2:38 repent, and be baptized *e* one of you
1 Thes. 5:18 in *e* thing give thanks

Evidence *See also* Witness

Jer. 32:10 I subscribed the *e*, and sealed it
Heb. 11:1 hoped for, the *e* of things not seen

Evident *See also* Manifest

Job 6:28 for it is *e* unto you if I lie
Gal. 3:11 no man is justified by the law . . it is *e*
Phil. 1:28 to them an *e* token of perdition
Heb. 7:14 it is *e* that our Lord sprang out of Juda

Evidently

Acts 10:3 he saw in a vision *e*, about the ninth

Gal. 3:1 Jesus Christ hath been *e* set forth

Evil *See also* Abomination, Bad, Iniquity, Sin, Wicked, Wickedness

Gen. 2:9 and the tree of knowledge of good and *e*
3:5 and ye shall be as gods, knowing good and *e*
6:5 thoughts of his heart was only *e* continually
8:21 imagination of man's heart is *e* from his
47:9 few and *e* have the. . years of my life been
48:16 angel which redeemeth me from all *e*
50:20 ye thought *e* against me; but God meant it
Ex. 23:2 thou shalt not follow a multitude to do *e*
32:14 LORD repented of the *e* which he thought to
Num. 14:27 shall I bear with this *e* congregation
Deut. 13:5 so shalt thou put the *e* away from the
28:54 his eye shall be *e* toward his brother
28:56 her eye shall be *e* toward the husband
29:21 LORD shall separate him unto *e* out of all
30:15 this day life and good, and death and *e*
31:29 and *e* will befall you in the latter days
Josh. 24:15 seem *e* unto you to serve the LORD
Judg. 9:23 God sent an *e* spirit between Abimelech
9:57 and all the *e* of the men of Shechem did God
1 Sam. 16:14 *e* spirit from the LORD troubled him
2 Sam. 13:16 this *e* in sending me away is greater
24:16 (1 Chr. 21:15) the LORD repented him of the *e*
1 Kgs. 16:25 Omri wrought *e* in the eyes of the LORD
2 Kgs. 17:13 turn ye from your *e* ways, and keep my
1 Chr. 21:17 I it is that have sinned and done *e*
Ezra 9:13 all that is come upon us for our *e* deeds
Job 1:1 and one that feared God, and eschewed *e*
2:10 hand of God, and shall we not receive *e*?
28:28 and to depart from *e* is understanding
30:26 when I looked for good, then *e* came unto
Ps. 7:4 rewarded *e* unto him that was at peace with
21:11 they intended *e* against thee: they imagined
23:4 I will fear no *e*: for thou art with me
34:13 (1 Pet. 3:10) keep thy tongue from *e*
34:14 (1 Pet. 3:11) depart from *e*, and do good
34:16 (1 Pet. 3:12) LORD is against them that do *e*
34:21 *e* shall slay the wicked
35:12 rewarded me *e* for good to the spoiling
37:27 depart from *e*, and do good; and dwell for
40:12 for innumerable *e* have compassed me about
52:3 thou lovest *e* more than good; and lying
54:5 he shall reward *e* unto mine enemies
91:10 there shall no *e* befall thee
97:10 ye that love the LORD, hate *e*
121:7 the LORD shall preserve thee from all *e*
140:11 let not an *e* speaker be established
141:4 incline not my heart to any *e* thing
Prov. 1:16 their feet run to *e*, and make haste
2:12 deliver thee from the way of the *e* man
3:7 fear the LORD, and depart from *e*
4:14 enter not. . and go not in the way of *e* men
8:13 the fear of the LORD is to hate *e*
12:21 there shall no *e* happen to the just
13:21 *e* pursueth sinners: but to the righteous
14:19 the *e* bow before the good; and the wicked
15:3 every place, beholding the *e* and the good
16:27 ungodly man diggeth up *e*: and in his lips
17:13 whoso rewardeth *e* for good, *e* shall not
21:10 the soul of the wicked desireth *e*
24:8 he that deviseth to do *e* shall be called a
28:72 he that hasteth to be rich hath an *e* eye
Eccl. 6:1 (10:5) an *e* which I have seen under the sun
8:3 stand not in an *e* thing
8:11 sentence against an *e* work is not executed
9:3 heart of the sons of men is full of *e*
12:1 thy youth, while the *e* days come not
Is. 1:16 put away the *e* of your doings from before
5:20 woe unto them that call *e* good, and good *e*
7:15 know to refuse the *e*, and choose the good

Is. 45:7 make peace, and create *e*: I the LORD do all
57:1 righteous is taken away from the *e* to come
59:7 their feet run to *e*, and they make haste
Jer. 2:13 for my people have committed two *e*
2:19 *e* thing and bitter, that thou hast forsaken
4:6 stay not; for I will bring *e* from the north
4:22 they are wise to do *e*, but to do good
6:19 behold, I will bring *e* upon this people
9:3 they proceed from *e* to *e*, and they know not
11:17 pronounced *e* against thee, for the *e*
16:10 pronounced all this great *e* against us?
17:17 thou art my hope in the day of *e*
18:8 turn from their *e*, I will repent of the *e*
18:11 return ye now every one from his *e* way
18:20 shall *e* be recompensed for good?
24:3 the good figs, very good; and the *e*, very *e*
29:11 thoughts of peace, and not of *e*
29:17 figs, that cannot be eaten, they are so *e*
42:6 be good, or whether it be *e*, we will obey
44:11 I will set my face against you for *e*
44:23 therefore this *e* is happened unto you
Ezek. 7:5 an *e*, an only *e*, behold, is come
33:11 turn ye from your *e* ways; for why will ye
Dan. 9:14 LORD watched upon the *e*, and brought it
Amos 3:6 shall there be *e* in a city, and the LORD
5:14 seek good, and not *e*, that ye may live
9:10 the *e* shall not overtake nor prevent us
Jon. 3:10 their *e* way; and God repented of the *e*
Nah. 1:11 that imagineth *e* against the LORD
Hab. 1:13 thou art of purer eyes than to behold *e*
Zeph. 3:15 thou shalt not see *e* any more
Zech. 7:10 none of you imagine *e* against his brother
8:17 none of you imagine *e*. . against his neighbor
Mt. 5:11 say all manner of *e* against you falsely
5:37 whatsoever is more than these cometh of *e*
5:39 ye resist not *e*: but whosoever shall smite
5:45 maketh his sun to rise on the *e* and. . good
6:13 (Lk. 11:4) but deliver us from *e*
6:23 (Lk. 11:34) if thine eye be *e*, thy whole body
6:34 sufficient unto the day is the *e* thereof
7:11 (Lk. 11:13) being *e*, know how to give good
7:18 a good tree cannot bring forth *e* fruit
9:4 said, Wherefore think ye *e* in your hearts?
12:34 how can ye, being *e*, speak good things?
12:35 (Lk. 6:45) *e* man out of the *e* treasure. . *e*
15:19 (Mk. 7:21) of the heart proceed *e* thoughts
20:15 is thine eye *e*, because I am good?
27:23 (Mk. 15:14; Lk. 23:22) what *e* hath he done?
Mk. 3:4 (Lk. 6:9) good on the sabbath days, or to do *e*
9:39 in my name, that can lightly speak *e* of me
Lk. 6:22 reproach you, and cast out your name as *e*
6:35 he is kind unto the unthankful and to the *e*
Jn. 3:19 than light, because their deeds were *e*
3:20 for every one that doeth *e* hateth the light
5:29 done *e*, unto the resurrection of damnation
17:15 that thou shouldest keep them from the *e*
18:23 if I have spoken *e*, bear witness of the *e*
Acts 7:6 and entreat them *e* four hundred years
9:13 *e* hath done to thy saints at Jerusalem
23:5 thou shalt not speak *e* of the ruler of thy
Rom. 1:30 proud, boasters, inventors of *e* things
2:9 anguish, upon every soul of man that doeth *e*
3:8 let us do *e*, that good may come?
7:19 but the *e* which I would not, that I do
12:9 abhor that which is *e*; cleave to that which
12:17 recompense to no man *e* for *e*
12:21 be not overcome of *e*, but overcome *e* with
13:4 but if thou do that which is *e*, be afraid
14:16 let not then your good be *e* spoken of
14:20 is *e* for that man who eateth with offense
1 Cor. 13:5 is not easily provoked, thinketh no *e*
15:33 *e* communications corrupt good manners
2 Cor. 6:8 dishonor, by *e* report and good report

Gal. 1:4 deliver us from this present *e* world
Eph. 4:31 and *e* speaking, be put away from you
   5:16 redeeming the time, because the days are *e*
   6:13 ye may be able to withstand in the *e* day
1 Thes. 5:15 that none render *e* for *e* unto any man
   5:22 abstain from all appearance of *e*
1 Tim. 6:10 the love of money is the root of all *e*
2 Tim. 3:13 *e* men and seducers shall wax worse
   4:14 Alexander the coppersmith did me much *e*
Tit. 3:2 to speak *e* of no man, to be no brawlers
Heb. 5:14 exercised to discern both good and *e*
Jas. 1:13 God cannot be tempted with *e*
   3:8 tongue can no man tame; it is an unruly *e*
   4:11 speak not *e* one of another, brethren
1 Pet. 3:9 not rendering *e* for *e*, or railing for
   3:11 let him eschew *e*, and do good
   3:16 they speak *e* of you, as of evildoers
   4:14 on their part he is *e* spoken of
2 Pet. 2:10 (Jude 8) afraid to speak *e* of dignities
1 Jn. 3:12 because his own works were *e*
2 Jn. 11 him God-speed is partaker of his *e* deeds
3 Jn. 11 but he that doeth *e* hath not seen God
Rev. 2:2 how thou canst not bear them which are *e*

Evildoer *See also* Sinner, Transgressor

Ps. 37:1 fret not thyself because of *e*, neither be
   37:9 for *e* shall be cut off: but those that wait
   94:16 who will rise up for me against the *e*?
   119:115 depart from me, ye *e*: for I will keep
Is. 1:4 a people laden with iniquity, a seed of *e*
   9:17 for every one is a hypocrite and an *e*
   14:20 the seed of *e* shall never be renowned
   31:2 but will arise against the house of the *e*
Jer. 20:13 soul of the poor from the hand of *e*
1 Pet. 3:16 they speak evil of you, as of *e*
   4:15 or as a thief, or as an *e*, or as a busybody

Exact

Deut. 15:2 he shall not *e* it of his neighbor
Neh. 5:7 ye *e* usury, every one of his brother
   5:10 might *e* of them money and corn
   5:11 the wine, and the oil, that ye *e* of them
Job 11:6 God *e* of thee less than thine iniquity
Ps. 89:22 the enemy shall not *e* upon him
Is. 58:3 ye find pleasure, and *e* all your labors
Lk. 3:13 *e* no more than that which is appointed

Exaction

Neh. 10:31 seventh year, and the *e* of every debt
Ezek. 45:9 take away your *e* from my people

Exactor

Is. 60:17 I will also make . . thine *e* righteousness

Exalt *See also* Extol, Lift, Magnify, Praise

Ex. 15:2 my father's God, and I will *e* him
1 Sam. 2:1 mine horn is *e* in the LORD; my mouth is
   2:10 and *e* the horn of his anointed
2 Sam. 22:47 (Ps. 18:46) *e* be the God of the rock
1 Kgs. 1:5 Adonijah the son of Haggith *e* himself
1 Chr. 29:11 O LORD . . thou art *e* as head above all
Neh. 9:5 thy glorious name, which is *e* above all
Job 5:11 that those which mourn may be *e* to safety
   24:24 they are *e* for a little while, but are
   36:22 God *e* by his power: who teacheth like him?
Ps. 12:8 on every side, when the vilest men are *e*
   34:3 magnify the LORD . . let us *e* his name
   46:10 I am God: I will be *e* among the heathen
   57:5 (108:5) be thou *e*, O God, above the heavens
   75:10 but the horns of the righteous shall be *e*
   89:16 and in thy righteousness shall they be *e*
   92:10 but my horn shalt thou *e* like the horn of
   97:9 thou art *e* far above all gods

Ps. 99:5 *e* ye the LORD our God, and worship at his
   107:32 let them *e* him also in the congregation
   118:16 the right hand of the LORD is *e*
   118:28 thou art my God, I will *e* thee
   140:8 his wicked device; lest they *e* themselves
Prov. 4:8 *e* her, and she shall promote thee
   11:11 by the blessing of the upright the city is *e*
   14:29 but he that is hasty of spirit *e* folly
   14:34 righteousness *e* a nation: but sin is a
   17:19 and he that *e* his gate seeketh destruction
Is. 2:2 (Mic. 4:1) and shall be *e* above the hills
   2:11 and the LORD alone shall be *e* in that day
   5:16 LORD of hosts shall be *e* in judgment
   25:1 O LORD, thou art my God; I will *e* thee
   33:5 the LORD is *e*; for he dwelleth on high
   40:4 every valley shall be *e*, and every mountain
   52:13 deal prudently, he shall be *e* and extolled
Ezek. 17:24 that I the LORD . . have *e* the low tree
   21:26 *e* him that is low . . abase him that is high
   29:15 of the kingdoms; neither shall it *e* itself
Obad. 4 though thou *e* thyself as the eagle
Mt. 11:23 (Lk. 10:15) thou, Capernaum, which art *e*
   23:12 (Lk. 14:11; 18:14) *e* himself shall be abased
Lk. 1:52 their seats, and *e* them of low degree
Acts 5:31 him hath God *e* with his right hand to be
2 Cor. 10:5 *e* itself against the knowledge of God
   11:20 if a man *e* himself, if a man smite you on
   12:7 lest I should be *e* above measure through
Phil. 2:9 wherefore God also hath highly *e* him
2 Thes. 2:4 *e* himself above all that is called God
Jas. 1:9 of low degree rejoice in that he is *e*
1 Pet. 5:6 of God, that he may *e* you in due time

Examine *See also* Prove, Try

Ezra 10:16 day of the tenth month to *e* the matter
Ps. 26:2 *e* me, O LORD, and prove me; try my reins
Lk. 23:14 having *e* him before you, have found no
Acts 4:9 if we this day be *e* of the good deed done
   12:19 and found him not, he *e* the keepers
   22:24 he should be *e* by scourging; that he might
   22:29 departed from him which should have *e* him
   24:8 by *e* of whom thyself mayest take knowledge
   28:18 when they had *e* me, would have let me go
1 Cor. 9:3 mine answer to them that do *e* me is
   11:28 let a man *e* himself, and so let him eat of
2 Cor. 13:5 *e* yourselves, whether ye be in the faith

Example *See also* Ensample, Pattern

Mt. 1:19 and not willing to make her a public *e*
Jn. 13:15 given you an *e*, that ye should do as I
1 Cor. 10:6 these things were our *e*, to the intent
1 Tim. 4:12 but be thou an *e* of the believers
Heb. 4:11 man fall after the same *e* of unbelief
   8:5 who serve unto the *e* and shadow of heavenly
Jas. 5:10 for an *e* of suffering affliction
1 Pet. 2:21 suffered for us, leaving us an *e*
Jude 7 set forth for an *e*, suffering the vengeance

Exceed *See also* Pass

Deut. 25:3 not *e*: lest, if he should *e*, and beat
1 Sam. 20:41 wept one with another, until David *e*
1 Kgs. 10:7 (2 Chr. 9:6) *e* the fame which I heard
   10:23 Solomon *e* all the kings of the earth
Job 36:9 and their transgressions that they have *e*
Mt. 5:20 except your righteousness shall *e* the
2 Cor. 3:9 the ministration of righteousness *e* in

Excel

Gen. 49:4 unstable as water, thou shalt not *e*
Ps. 103:20 ye his angels, that *e* in strength
Prov. 31:29 done virtuously, but thou *e* them all
Eccl. 2:13 that wisdom *e* folly, as far as light *e*
Is. 10:10 graven images did *e* them of Jerusalem

1 Cor. 14:12 may *e* to the edifying of the church
2 Cor. 3:10 by reason of the glory that *e*

Excellency

Gen. 49:3 the *e* of dignity, and the *e* of power
Ex. 15:7 and in the greatness of thine *e* thou hast
Job 4:21 doth not their *e* which is in them go away?
 13:11 shall not his *e* make you afraid?
 20:6 though his *e* mount up to the heavens
 37:4 he thundereth with the voice of his *e*
 40:10 deck thyself now with majesty and *e*
Ps. 47:4 our inheritance for us, the *e* of Jacob
 62:4 consult to cast him down from his *e*
 68:34 strength unto God: his *e* is over Israel
Is. 13:19 the beauty of the Chaldees' *e*, shall be
 35:2 the glory of the LORD, and the *e* of our God
 60:15 I will make thee an eternal *e*, a joy of
Ezek. 24:21 my sanctuary, the *e* of your strength
Amos 6:8 abhor the *e* of Jacob, and hate his palaces
 8:7 LORD hath sworn by the *e* of Jacob, Surely I
1 Cor. 2:1 came not with *e* of speech or of wisdom
2 Cor. 4:7 that the *e* of the power may be of God
Phil. 3:8 for the *e* of the knowledge of Christ

Excellent *See also* Glorious, Great, Honorable, Magnificent, Mighty, Noble

Job 37:23 he is *e* in power, and in judgment
Ps. 8:1 Lord, how *e* is thy name in all the earth!
 16:3 and to the *e*, in whom is all my delight
 36:7 *e* is thy loving-kindness, O God!
 76:4 art more glorious and *e* than the mountains
 141:5 let him reprove me; it shall be an *e* oil
 148:13 name of the LORD: for his name alone is *e*
Prov. 8:6 hear; for I will speak of *e* things
 12:26 the righteous is more *e* than his neighbor
 17:7 *e* speech becometh not a fool: much less do
 17:27 a man of understanding is of an *e* spirit
 22:20 written to thee *e* things in counsels
Song 5:15 his countenance is . . *e* as the cedars
Is. 12:5 unto the LORD; for he hath done *e* things
 28:29 is wonderful in counsel, and *e* in working
Dan. 5:12 forasmuch as an *e* spirit, and knowledge
 6:3 preferred . . because an *e* spirit was in him
Lk. 1:3 unto thee in order, most *e* Theophilus
Acts 23:26 Lysias unto the most *e* governor Felix
Rom. 2:18 and approvest the things that are more *e*
1 Cor. 12:31 and yet show I unto you a more *e* way
Phil. 1:10 that ye may approve things that are *e*
Heb. 1:4 by inheritance obtained a more *e* name
 8:6 but now hath he obtained a more *e* ministry
 11:4 Abel offered unto God a more *e* sacrifice
2 Pet. 1:17 such a voice to him from the *e* glory

Except

Ps. 127:1 *e* the LORD build the house, they labor
Is. 1:9 (Rom. 9:29) *e* the LORD . . had left unto us
Amos 3:3 can two walk together, *e* they be agreed?
Mt. 5:20 that *e* your righteousness shall exceed
 18:3 *e* ye be converted, and become as little
 24:22 (Mk. 13:20) *e* those days . . be shortened
 26:42 from me, *e* I drink it, thy will be done
1 Cor. 15:27 he is *e*, which did put all things

Excess

Mt. 23:25 within they are full of extortion and *e*
Eph. 5:18 be not drunk with wine, wherein is *e*
1 Pet. 4:3 in lasciviousness, lusts, *e* of wine
 4:4 ye run not with them to the same *e* of riot

Exchange

Gen. 47:17 Joseph gave . . bread in *e* for horses

Lev. 27:10 it and the *e* thereof shall be holy
Job 28:17 the *e* of it shall not be for jewels
Ezek. 48:14 they shall not sell of it, neither *e*
Mt. 16:26 (Mk. 8:37) a man give in *e* for his soul?

Exchanger

Mt. 25:27 oughtest . . to have put my money to the *e*

Exclude

Rom. 3:27 where is boasting then? It is *e*
Gal. 4:17 they would *e* you, that ye might affect

Excuse

Lk. 14:18 all with one consent began to make *e*
Rom. 1:20 so that they are without *e*
 2:15 thoughts the mean while accusing or else *e*
2 Cor. 12:19 think ye that we *e* ourselves unto you?

Execration

Jer. 42:18 enter into Egypt: and ye shall be an *e*
 44:12 they shall be an *e*, and an astonishment

Execute *See also* Accomplish, Fulfil, Perform, Wrought

Ex. 12:12 the gods of Egypt I will *e* judgment
Num. 8:11 that they may *e* the service of the LORD
Deut. 10:18 doth *e* the judgment of the fatherless
 33:21 he *e* the justice of the LORD
1 Chr. 6:10 he it is that *e* the priest's office
 24:2 Eleazar and Ithamar *e* the priest's office
Ps. 9:16 LORD is known by the judgment which he *e*
 103:6 LORD *e* righteousness and judgment for all
 119:84 when wilt thou *e* judgment on them
 146:7 which *e* judgment for the oppressed
 149:7 to *e* vengeance upon the heathen
Is. 16:3 take counsel, *e* judgment; make thy shadow
Jer. 5:1 if there be any that *e* judgment
 7:5 if ye thoroughly *e* judgment between a man
 21:12 saith the LORD; *E* judgment in the morning
 22:3 LORD; *E* ye judgment and righteousness
Ezek. 25:17 I will *e* great vengeance upon them
Hos. 11:9 will not *e* the fierceness of mine anger
Joel 2:11 for he is strong that *e* his word
Mic. 5:15 and I will *e* vengeance in anger and fury
Zech. 7:9 saying, *E* true judgment, and show mercy
 8:16 *e* the judgment of truth and peace in your
Lk. 1:8 while he *e* the priest's office before God
Jn. 5:27 given him authority to *e* judgment also
Rom. 13:4 revenger to *e* wrath upon him that doeth
Jude 15 to *e* judgment upon all, and to convince all

Executioner

Mk. 6:27 king sent an *e*, and commanded his head to

Exercise

Ps. 131:1 neither do I *e* myself in great matters
Eccl. 1:13 God given to the sons of man to be *e*
Jer. 9:24 I am the LORD which *e* loving-kindness
Ezek. 22:29 have used oppression, and *e* robbery
Mt. 20:25 (Mk. 10:42; Lk. 22:25) Gentiles *e* dominion
Acts 24:16 herein do I *e* myself, to have always a
1 Tim. 4:7 and *e* thyself rather unto godliness
 4:8 for bodily *e* profiteth little: but godliness
Heb. 5:14 senses *e* to discern both good and evil
 12:11 of righteousness unto them which are *e*
2 Pet. 2:14 they have *e* with covetous practices
Rev. 13:12 he *e* all the power of the first beast

Exhort *See also* Advise, Encourage, Warn

Acts 2:40 many other words did he testify and *e*

Acts 11:23 was glad, and *e* them all, that with purpose
   14:22 *e* them to continue in the faith
   18:27 wrote, *e* the disciples to receive him
   27:22 now I *e* you to be of good cheer
Rom. 12:8 or he that *e*, on exhortation
2 Cor. 9:5 thought it necessary to *e* the brethren
1 Thes. 2:11 as ye know how we *e* and comforted
2 Thes. 3:12 we command and *e* by our Lord Jesus
1 Tim. 2:1 I *e* therefore, that, first of all
   6:2 these things teach and *e*
2 Tim. 4:2 *e* with all long-suffering and doctrine
Tit. 1:9 sound doctrine both to *e* and to convince
   2:6 young men likewise *e* to be sober-minded
   2:9 *e* servants to be obedient unto their own
   2:15 speak, and *e*, and rebuke with all authority
Heb. 3:13 *e* one another daily, while it is called
   10:25 *e* one another: and so much the more, as ye
1 Pet. 5:1 the elders which are among you I *e*
   5:12 I have written briefly, *e*, and testifying

Exhortation

Lk. 3:18 many other things in his *e* preached he
Acts 13:15 if ye have any word of *e* for the people
   20:2 had given them much *e*, he came into Greece
1 Cor. 14:3 men to edification, and *e*, and comfort
2 Cor. 8:17 indeed he accepted the *e*; but being
1 Thes. 2:3 for our *e* was not of deceit, nor of
1 Tim. 4:13 give attendance to reading, to *e*, to
Heb. 12:5 ye have forgotten the *e* which speaketh
   13:22 brethren, suffer the word of *e*: for I have

Exile

2 Sam. 15:19 thou art a stranger, and also an *e*
Is. 51:14 the captive *e* hasteneth that he may be

Exorcist

Acts 19:13 certain of the vagabond Jews, *e*, took

Expect

Jer. 29:11 and not of evil, to give you an *e* end
Acts 3:5 heed unto them, *e* to receive something
Heb. 10:13 from henceforth *e* till his enemies be

Expectation *See also* Hope

Ps. 9:18 *e* of the poor shall not perish for ever
   62:5 only upon God; for my *e* is from him
Prov. 10:28 but the *e* of the wicked shall perish
   11:7 when a wicked man dieth, his *e* shall perish
   11:23 but the *e* of the wicked is wrath
   23:18 and thine *e* shall not be cut off
   24:14 a reward, and thy *e* shall not be cut off
Is. 20:5 be afraid and ashamed of Ethiopia their *e*
   20:6 such is our *e*, whither we flee for help
Lk. 3:15 the people were in *e*, and all men mused
Acts 12:11 from all the *e* of the people of the Jews
Rom. 8:19 the earnest *e* of the creature waiteth
Phil. 1:20 according to my earnest *e* and my hope

Expedient

Jn. 11:50 (18:14) it is *e*. . that one man should die
   16:7 it is *e* for you that I go away: for if I go
1 Cor. 6:12 (10:23) but all things are not *e*
2 Cor. 8:10 give my advice: for this is *e* for you
   12:1 it is not *e* for me doubtless to glory

Expel

Josh. 23:5 he shall *e* them from before you
Judg. 11:7 and *e* me out of my father's house?
2 Sam. 14:14 that his banished be not *e* from him
Acts 13:50 against Paul and Barnabas, and *e* them

Expense

Ezra 6:4 the *e* be given out of the king's house

Experience

Gen. 30:27 I have learned by *e* that the LORD hath
Eccl. 1:16 yea, my heart had great *e* of wisdom and
Rom. 5:4 and patience, *e*; and *e*, hope

Expert

Jer. 50:9 their arrows shall be as of a mighty *e*
Acts 26:3 I know thee to be *e* in all customs

Expire

1 Chr. 17:11 when thy days be *e* that thou must go
Acts 7:30 when forty years were *e*, there appeared
Rev. 20:7 and when the thousand years are *e*, Satan

Exploit

Dan. 11:28 shall do *e*, and return to his own land
   11:32 know their God shall be strong, and do *e*

Expound

Judg. 14:14 could not in three days *e* the riddle
Mk. 4:34 alone, he *e* all things to his disciples
Lk. 24:27 he *e* unto them in all the Scriptures the
Acts 11:4 Peter. . *e* it by order unto them, saying
   18:26 *e* unto him the way of God more perfectly
   28:23 to whom he *e* and testified the kingdom of

Express

Heb. 1:3 his glory, and the *e* image of his person

Expressly

1 Sam. 20:21 the arrows. If I *e* say unto the lad
Ezek. 1:3 the word of the LORD came *e* unto Ezekiel
1 Tim. 4:1 Spirit speaketh *e*, that in the latter

Extend

Ps. 16:2 art my Lord: my goodness *e* not to thee
   109:12 let there be none to *e* mercy unto him
Is. 66:12 I will *e* peace to her like a river

Extinct

Job 17:1 my days are *e*, the graves are ready for me
Is. 43:17 not rise: they are *e*, they are quenched

Extol *See also* Exalt, Honor, Magnify, Praise

Ps. 30:1 I will *e* thee, O LORD; for thou hast
   66:17 with my mouth, and he was *e* with my tongue
   68:4 *e* him that rideth upon the heavens
   145:1 I will *e* thee, my God, O King; and I will
Is. 52:13 shall be exalted and *e*, and be very high
Dan. 4:37 I Nebuchadnezzar praise and *e* and honor

Extortion

Ezek. 22:12 greedily gained of thy neighbors by *e*
Mt. 23:25 but within they are full of *e* and excess

Extortioner

Ps. 109:11 let the *e* catch all that he hath
Is. 16:4 the *e* is at an end, the spoiler ceaseth
Lk. 18:11 I am not as other men are, *e*, unjust
1 Cor. 5:10 or with the covetous, or *e*, or with
   6:10 nor *e*, shall inherit the kingdom of God

Extremity

Job 35:15 anger; yet he knoweth it not in great *e*

Eye

Gen. 3:5 eat thereof, then your *e* shall be opened
   6:8 but Noah found grace in the *e* of the LORD
   21:19 and God opened her *e*, and she saw a well
   27:1 when Isaac was old, and his *e* were dim
   49:12 *e* shall be red with wine, and his teeth

Ex. 13:9 and for a memorial between thine *e*
  21:24 (Lev. 24:20; Deut. 19:21; Mt. 5:38) *e* for *e*
Num. 10:31 and thou mayest be to us instead of *e*
  16:14 wilt thou put out the *e* of these men?
  20:12 believed me not, to sanctify me in the *e* of
  24:3 and the man whose *e* are open hath said
Deut. 3:27 of Pisgah, and lift up thine *e* westward
  4:19 lest thou lift up thine *e* unto heaven
  11:12 *e* of the LORD thy God are always upon it
  12:8 every man whatsoever is right in his own *e*
  16:19 for a gift doth blind the *e* of the wise
  19:21 thine *e* shall not pity; but life shall go
  28:32 thine *e* shall look, and fail with longing
  32:10 he kept him as the apple of his *e*
  34:7 when he died: his *e* was not dim, nor his
Judg. 16:21 Philistines took him, and put out his *e*
  17:6 (21:25) that which was right in his own *e*
1 Sam. 18:9 Saul *e* David from that day and forward
  24:10 kill thee: but mine *e* spared thee
1 Kgs. 1:20 O king, the *e* of all Israel are upon
  8:29 (2 Chr. 6:20) *e* may be open toward this house
  20:6 whatsoever is pleasant in thine *e*
2 Kgs. 6:17 the LORD opened the *e* of the young man
  6:20 Elisha said, LORD, open the *e* of these men
  19:16 (Is. 37:17) open, LORD, thine *e*, and see
  22:20 (2 Chr. 34:28) *e* shall not see all the evil
  25:7 (Jer. 39:7) and put out the *e* of Zedekiah
2 Chr. 16: 9 for the *e* of the LORD run to and fro
Ezra 5:5 the *e* of their God was upon the elders
  9:8 God may lighten our *e*, and give us a little
Job 7:8 thine *e* are upon me, and I am not
  10:18 given up the ghost, and no *e* had seen me!
  11:20 *e* of the wicked shall fail, and they shall
  15:12 carry thee away? and what do thy *e* wink at
  19:27 and mine *e* shall behold, and not another
  24:15 twilight, saying, No *e* shall see me
  28:7 a path . . which the vulture's *e* hath not seen
  28:10 and his *e* seeth every precious thing
  29:11 when the *e* saw me, it gave witness to me
  29:15 I was *e* to the blind, and feet was I to
  31:16 or have caused the *e* of the widow to fail
  32:1 Job, because he was righteous in his own *e*
  34:21 for his *e* are upon the ways of man
  42:5 heard of thee . . but now mine *e* seeth thee
Ps. 6:7 mine *e* is consumed because of grief
  11:4 LORD's throne is in heaven: his *e* behold
  15:4 in whose *e* a vile person is contemned
  17:8 keep me as the apple of the *e*; hide me
  19:8 commandment . . is pure, enlightening the *e*
  25:15 mine *e* are ever toward the LORD; for he
  32:8 shalt go: I will guide thee with mine *e*
  33:18 *e* of the LORD is upon them that fear him
  34:15 (1 Pet. 3:12) *e* of the LORD are upon the
  36:1 (Rom. 3:18) is no fear of God before his *e*
  69:3 mine *e* fail while I wait for my God
  77:4 thou holdest mine *e* waking
  91:8 only with thine *e* shalt thou behold and see
  94:9 he that formed the *e*, shall he not see?
  115:5 (135:16) *e* have they, but they see not
  116:8 my soul from death, mine *e* from tears
  118:23 (Mt. 21:42; Mk. 12:11) marvelous in our *e*
  119:18 open thou mine *e*, that I may behold
  119:82 mine *e* fail for thy word, saying, When
  119:123 mine *e* fail for thy salvation, and for
  121:1 I will lift up mine *e* unto the hills
  123:1 unto thee lift I up mine *e*, O thou that
  132:4 will not give sleep to mine *e*, or slumber
  141:8 but mine *e* are unto thee, O GOD the Lord
  145:15 *e* of all wait upon thee; and thou givest
  146:8 the LORD openeth the *e* of the blind
Prov. 3:7 be not wise in thine own *e*: fear the LORD
  10:26 as smoke to the *e*, so is the sluggard to
  12:15 the way of a fool is right in his own *e*

Prov. 15:3 *e* of the LORD are in every place, beholding
  16:2 all the ways of a man are clean in his own *e*
  20:12 ear, and the seeing *e*, the LORD hath made
  21:2 every way of a man is right in his own *e*
  22:9 he that hath a bountiful *e* shall be blessed
  23:26 and let thine *e* observe my ways
  27:20 so the *e* of man are never satisfied
  30:12 a generation that are pure in their own *e*
  30:17 that mocketh at his father, and despiseth
Eccl. 1:8 the *e* is not satisfied with seeing
  2:14 wise man's *e* are in his head; but the fool
  6:9 is the sight of the *e* than the wandering of
  11:7 pleasant thing . . for the *e* to behold the sun
Song 1:15 (4:1) thou art fair; thou hast doves' *e*
Is. 1:15 I will hide mine *e* from you; yea, when ye
  6:5 mine *e* have seen the King, the LORD of hosts
  6:10 (Mt. 13:15; Jn. 12:40; Acts 28:27) shut their *e*
  29:10 (Rom. 11:8) sleep, and hath closed your *e*
  32:3 and the *e* of them that see shall not be dim
  33:17 thine *e* shall see the King in his beauty
  35:5 the *e* of the blind shall be opened
  40:26 lift up your *e* on high, and behold who
  42:7 open the blind *e*, to bring out the prisoners
  51:6 lift up your *e* to the heavens, and look
  52:8 they shall see *e* to *e*, when the LORD shall
  64:4 (1 Cor. 2:9) neither hath the *e* seen
Jer. 5:21 (Ezek. 12:2) which have *e*, and see not
  9:1 were waters, and mine *e* a fountain of tears
  13:17 for your pride; and mine *e* shall weep sore
  13:20 lift up your *e*, and behold them that come
  14:17 let mine *e* run down with tears night and
  16:17 neither is their iniquity hid from mine *e*
  24:6 I will set mine *e* upon them for good
Lam. 2:11 mine *e* do fail with tears, my bowels are
  2:18 let not the apple of thine *e* cease
Ezek. 5:11 neither shall mine *e* spare, neither
  10:12 and the wheels, were full of *e* round about
  24:16 take away from thee the desire of thine *e*
Amos 9:4 I will set mine *e* upon them for evil
  9:8 the *e* of the Lord God are upon the sinful
Hab. 1:13 thou art of purer *e* than to behold evil
Zech. 4:10 the *e* of the LORD, which run to and fro
  8:6 should it also be marvelous in mine *e*?
Mal. 1:5 your *e* shall see, and ye shall say
Mt. 5:29 (18:9; Mk. 9:47) *e* offend thee, pluck it out
  6:22 (Lk. 11:34) light of the body is the *e*
  7:3 (Lk. 6:41) mote that is in thy brother's *e*
  13:16 (Lk. 10:23) blessed are your *e*, for they see
  19:24 (Mk. 10:25; Lk. 18:25) the *e* of a needle
  20:15 is thine *e* evil, because I am good?
  20:33 unto him, Lord, that our *e* may be opened
Mk. 8:18 having *e*, see ye not? and having ears
Lk. 2:30 for mine *e* have seen thy salvation
  4:20 *e* of all them that were in the synagogue
  18:13 not lift up so much as his *e* unto heaven
  19:42 peace! but now they are hid from thine *e*
  24:16 their *e* were holden that they should not
Jn. 4:35 lift up your *e*, and look on the fields
  9:6 he anointed the *e* of the blind man with the
  10:21 can a devil open the *e* of the blind?
  11:37 could not this man, which opened the *e* of
Rom. 3:18 there is no fear of God before their *e*
1 Cor. 12:16 ear shall say, Because I am not the *e*
  15:52 the twinkling of an *e*, at the last trump
Gal. 3:1 before whose *e* Jesus Christ hath been
  4:15 ye would have plucked out your own *e*
Eph. 1:18 the *e* of your understanding . . enlightened
Heb. 4:13 are naked and opened unto the *e* of him
1 Pet. 3:12 *e* of the Lord are over the righteous
2 Pet. 2:14 having *e* full of adultery, and that
1 Jn. 1:1 which we have seen with our *e*
  2:11 because that darkness hath blinded his *e*
  2:16 the lust of the *e*, and the pride of life

Rev. 1:7 cometh with clouds; and every *e* shall see
   1:14 (2:18) and his *e* were as a flame of fire
   4:6 were four beasts full of *e* before and behind
   21:4 God shall wipe away all tears from their *e*

Eyelid

Job 16:16 on my *e* is the shadow of death
   41:18 and his eyes are like the *e* of the morning
Ps. 11:4 his eyes behold, his *e* try, the children
Prov. 4:25 let thine *e* look straight before thee
   6:25 neither let her take thee with her *e*

Eyeservice

Eph. 6:6 (Col. 3:22) not with *e*, as menpleasers

Eyewitness

Lk. 1:2 from the beginning were *e*, and ministers
2 Pet. 1:16 but were *e* of his majesty

Ezekiel Call, Ezek. 2–3. Visions: cherubim, 1;
10; abominations in Jerusalem, 8–9; valley of dry
bones, 37; the temple, 40–48. Prophecies: against
Israel, 4–7; 11–12; 14–24; 33; against false prophets,
13; 34; against other nations, 25–32; 35; 38–39; of
restoration, 11:14–20; 34; 36; 39:23–29.

Ezion-gaber (Ezion-geber)

   Num. 33:35; 1 Kgs. 9:26 (2 Chr. 8:17); 1 Kgs.
   22:48 (2 Chr. 20:36)

Ezra Ezra 7:1–10:16; Neh. 8:1–12:36

F

Fable

1 Tim. 1:4 neither give heed to *f* and endless
   4:7 but refuse profane and old wives' *f*
2 Tim. 4:4 from the truth, and shall be turned unto *f*
Tit. 1:14 not giving to heed to Jewish *f*
2 Pet. 1:16 have not followed cunningly devised *f*

Face *See also* Countenance, Visage

Gen. 3:19 in the sweat of thy *f* shalt thou eat
   4:14 hast driven me out . . from the *f* of the earth
   32:30 for I have seen God *f* to *f*, and my life
Ex. 3:6 Moses hid his *f*; for he was afraid to look
   19:7 Moses . . laid before their *f* all these words
   20:20 and that his fear may be before your *f*
   33:11 the LORD spake unto Moses *f* to *f*, as a man
   33:20 not see my *f*: for there shall no man see me
   34:29 wist not that the skin of his *f* shone
   34:33 speaking with them, he put a veil on his *f*
Lev. 17:10 my *f* against that soul that eateth blood
   19:32 and honor the *f* of the old man
Num. 6:25 the LORD make his *f* shine upon thee
   14:14 that thou LORD art seen *f* to *f*
Deut. 1:17 ye shall not be afraid of the *f* of man
   5:4 the LORD talked with you *f* to *f* in the mount
   25:9 shoe from off his foot, and spit in his *f*
   31:17 I will hide my *f* from them, and they shall
   34:10 like unto Moses, whom the LORD knew *f* to *f*
1 Sam. 5:3 Dagon . . fallen upon his *f* to the earth
2 Sam. 14:24 his own house, and let him not see my *f*
1 Kgs. 19:13 Elijah . . wrapped his *f* in his mantle
2 Kgs. 4:29 lay my staff upon the *f* of the child
   14:8 (2 Chr. 25:17) let us look one another in the *f*
1 Chr. 16:11 (Ps. 105:4) seek his *f* continually
2 Chr. 6:42 (Ps. 132:10) away the *f* of thine anointed
   7:14 if my people . . pray, and seek my *f*, and turn
   30:9 will not turn away his *f* from you
Ezra 9:7 and to a spoil, and to confusion of *f*
Neh. 8:6 worshipped . . with their *f* to the ground
Job 1:11 (2:5) and he will curse thee to thy *f*

Job 4:15 then a spirit passed before my *f*
   13:24 wherefore hidest thou thy *f*, and holdest
Ps. 13:1 how long wilt thou hide thy *f* from me?
   17:15 I will behold thy *f* in righteousness
   27:8 seek ye my *f* . . Thy *f*, LORD, will I seek
   27:9 hide not thy *f* far from me; put not thy
   31:16 (119:135) thy *f* to shine upon thy servant
   34:5 looked unto him . . their *f* were not ashamed
   34:16 (1 Pet. 3:12) *f* of the LORD is against them
   44:24 hidest thou thy *f*, and forgettest our
   51:9 hide thy *f* from my sins, and blot out all
   69:17 hide not thy *f* from thy servant; for I am
   80:3 (80:7, 19) cause thy *f* to shine
   84:9 and look upon the *f* of thine anointed
   88:14 why hidest thou thy *f* from me?
   89:14 mercy and truth shall go before thy *f*
   102:2 hide not thy *f* from me in the day when I
   143:7 hide not thy *f* from me, lest I be like
Prov. 27:19 as in water *f* answereth to *f*, so
Eccl. 8:1 a man's wisdom maketh his *f* to shine
Is. 3:15 and grind the *f* of the poor?
   6:2 had six wings; with twain he covered his *f*
   25:8 God will wipe away tears from off all *f*
   50:7 therefore have I set my *f* like a flint
   53:3 and we hid as it were our *f* from him
   59:2 and your sins have hid his *f* from you
Jer. 1:8 be not afraid of their *f*: for I am with
   2:27 (32:33) their back unto me, and not their *f*
   5:3 they have made their *f* harder than a rock
   16:17 all their ways: they are not hid from my *f*
   30:6 all *f* are turned into paleness?
   50:5 ask the way to Zion with their *f* thitherward
Ezek. 1:15 by the living creatures, with his four *f*
   38:18 my fury shall come up in my *f*
   39:23 trespassed . . therefore hid I my *f* from them
   41:18 and every cherub had two *f*
Dan. 1:10 why should he see your *f* worse liking
   9:3 set my *f* unto the Lord God, to seek by prayer
   9:8 O Lord, to us belongeth confusion of *f*
   10:6 and his *f* as the appearance of lightning
Hos. 5:5 (7:10) pride of Israel doth testify to his *f*
   5:15 acknowledge their offense, and seek my *f*
Joel 2:6 all *f* shall gather blackness
Mt. 6:16 disfigure their *f*, that they may appear
   6:17 fastest, anoint thine head, and wash thy *f*
   11:10 (Mk. 1:2; Lk. 7:27) messenger before thy *f*
   16:3 (Lk. 12:56) ye can discern the *f* of the sky
   17:2 transfigured . . his *f* did shine as the sun
   18:10 angels do always behold the *f* of my Father
Lk. 1:76 go before the *f* of the Lord to prepare
   2:31 hast prepared before the *f* of all people
   9:51 he steadfastly set his *f* to go to Jerusalem
   22:64 they struck him on the *f*, and asked him
   24:5 afraid, and bowed down their *f* to the earth
Acts 2:25 I foresaw the Lord always before my *f*
   6:15 saw his *f* as it had been the *f* of an angel
   20:25 I know that ye all . . shall see my *f* no more
   25:16 which is accused have the accusers *f* to *f*
1 Cor. 13:12 through a glass, darkly; but then *f* to *f*
2 Cor. 3:13 as Moses, which put a veil over his *f*
   3:18 we all, with open *f* beholding as in a glass
   4:6 the glory of God in the *f* of Jesus Christ
   11:20 for ye suffer . . if a man smite you on the *f*
Gal. 1:22 unknown by *f* unto the churches of Judea
   2:11 I withstood him to the *f*
Jas. 1:23 man beholding his natural *f* in a glass
Rev. 9:7 locusts . . and their *f* were as the *f* of men
   11:16 fell upon their *f*, and worshipped God
   20:11 from whose *f* the earth and the heaven fled
   22:4 they shall see his *f*; and his name shall be

Fade

2 Sam. 22:46 (Ps. 18:45) strangers shall *f* away

Is. 1:30 for ye shall be as an oak whose leaf *f*
24:4 the earth mourneth and *f* away, the world
28:1 whose glorious beauty is a *f* flower
40:7 the grass withereth, the flower *f*
64:6 we all do *f* as a leaf; and our iniquities
Jer. 8:13 on the fig tree, and the leaf shall *f*
Ezek. 47:12 trees for meat, whose leaf shall not *f*
Jas. 1:11 shall the rich man *f* away in his ways
1 Pet. 1:4 to an inheritance. . that *f* not away
5:4 receive a crown of glory that *f* not away

Fail

Gen. 42:28 even in my sack: and their heart *f* them
47:16 will give you for your cattle, if money *f*
Deut. 28:32 thine eyes shall look, and *f* with longing
31:6 (Josh. 1:5) will not *f* thee, nor forsake thee
Josh. 21:45 (23:14) *f* not aught of any good thing
Judg. 11:30 if thou shalt without *f* deliver. . Ammon
1 Sam. 17:32 let no man's heart *f* because of him
1 Kgs. 2:4 (2 Chr. 6:16; 7:18) shall not *f* thee. . a man
8:56 hath not *f* one word of all his good promise
17:14 neither shall the cruse of oil *f*, until
1 Chr. 28:20 he will not *f* thee, nor forsake thee
Ezra 4:22 take heed now that ye *f* not to do this
Job 11:20 but the eyes of the wicked shall *f*
14:11 as the waters *f* from the sea
19:14 my kinsfolk have *f*, and my familiar
Ps. 12:1 faithful *f* from among the children of men
31:10 my strength *f* because of mine iniquity
38:10 my heart panteth, my strength *f* me
40:12 therefore my heart *f* me
69:3 mine eyes *f* while I wait for my God
71:9 forsake me not when my strength *f*
73:26 my flesh and my heart *f*: but God is the
77:8 doth his promise *f* for evermore?
89:33 nor suffer my faithfulness to *f*
119:123 mine eyes *f* for thy salvation
142:4 refuge *f* me; no man cared for my soul
143:7 hear me speedily, O LORD; my spirit *f*
Eccl. 10:3 fool walketh by the way, his wisdom *f*
12:5 and desire shall *f*: because man goeth to
Is. 15:6 the grass *f*, there is no green thing
19:3 the spirit of Egypt shall *f* in the midst
19:5 and the waters shall *f* from the sea
31:3 fall down, and they all shall *f* together
32:6 he will cause the drink of the thirsty to *f*
32:10 vintage shall *f*, the gathering shall not
34:16 no one of these shall *f*, none shall want
38:14 mine eyes *f* with looking upward
41:17 their tongue *f* for thirst, I the LORD will
42:4 he shall not *f* nor be discouraged, till he
44:12 yea, he is hungry, and his strength *f*
57:16 for the spirit should *f* before me
58:11 like a spring of water, whose waters *f* not
59:15 yea, truth *f*; and he that departeth
Jer. 14:6 eyes did *f*, because there was no grass
15:18 unto me as a liar, and as waters that *f*?
48:33 caused wine to *f* from the winepresses
Lam. 3:22 because his compassions *f* not
4:17 our eyes as yet *f* for our vain help
Ezek. 12:22 days are prolonged, and every vision *f*?
Hos. 9:2 not feed them, and the new wine shall *f*
Amos 8:4 even to make the poor of the land to *f*
Hab. 3:17 the labor of the olive shall *f*
Lk. 12:33 a treasure in the heavens that *f* not
16:9 that, when ye *f*, they may receive you into
16:17 to pass, than one tittle of the law to *f*
21:26 men's hearts *f* them for fear, and for
22:32 have prayed for thee, that thy faith *f* not
1 Cor. 13:8 charity never *f*; but whether there be
Heb. 1:12 art the same, and thy years shall not *f*
11:32 the time would *f* me to tell of Gideon, and
12:15 lest any man *f* of the grace of God

Fain

Job 27:22 he would *f* flee out of his hand
Lk. 15:16 he would *f* have filled his belly with

Faint

Gen. 25:29 Esau came from the field, and he was *f*
45:26 Jacob's heart *f*, for he believed them not
Deut. 25:18 and smote. . when thou wast *f* and weary
Josh. 2:9 inhabitants of the land *f* because of you
Judg. 8:4 and the three hundred men. . *f*, yet pursuing
2 Sam. 21:15 against the Philistines. . David waxed *f*
Job 4:5 but now it is come upon thee, and thou *f*
Ps. 27:13 I had *f*, unless I had believed to see
84:2 my soul longeth, yea, even *f* for the courts
107:5 hungry and thirsty, their soul *f* in them
119:81 my soul *f* for thy salvation: but I hope
Prov. 24:10 if thou *f* in the day of adversity
Is. 1:5 whole head is sick, and the whole heart *f*
10:18 they shall be as when a standardbearer *f*
13:7 therefore shall all hands be *f*, and every
40:28 Creator of the ends of the earth, *f* not
40:29 he giveth power to the *f*; and to them that
40:30 even the youths shall *f* and be weary
40:31 run, and not be weary. . walk, and not *f*
44:12 he drinketh no water, and is *f*
Jer. 8:18 against sorrow, my heart is *f* in me
45:3 I *f* in my sighing, and I find no rest
Lam. 1:13 hath made me desolate and *f* all the day
1:22 for my sighs are many, and my heart is *f*
5:17 for this our heart is *f*; for these things
Amos 8:13 fair virgins and young men *f* for thirst
Jon. 2:7 when my soul *f* within me I remembered the
4:8 sun beat upon the head of Jonah, that he *f*
Mt. 9:36 with compassion on them, because they *f*
15:32 (Mk. 8:3) away fasting, lest they *f* in the way
Lk. 18:1 men ought always to pray, and not to *f*
2 Cor. 4:1 as we have received mercy, we *f* not
4:16 for which cause we *f* not; but though our
Gal. 6:9 in due season we shall reap, if we *f* not
Eph. 3:13 that ye *f* not at my tribulations for you
Heb. 12:3 lest ye be wearied and *f* in your minds
12:5 nor *f* when thou art rebuked of him

Faint-hearted

Deut. 20:8 what man is there that is fearful and *f-h*?
Is. 7:4 fear not, neither be *f-h* for the two tails
Jer. 49:23 have heard evil tidings: they are *f-h*

Faintness

Lev. 26:36 I will send a *f* into their hearts

Fair (Fairer, Fairest)

Gen. 6:2 saw the daughters of men that they were *f*
12:11 that thou art a *f* woman to look upon
Job 37:22 *f* weather cometh out of the north
Ps. 45:2 thou art *f* than the children of men
Prov. 7:21 much *f* speech she caused him to yield
11:22 so is a *f* woman which is without discretion
26:25 when he speaketh *f*, believe him not
Song 1:8 O thou *f* among women, go thy way forth
2:10 rise up, my love, my *f* one, and come away
4:1 behold, thou art *f*; thou hast doves' eyes
6:10 who is she. . *f* as the moon, clear as the sun
Is. 5:9 houses shall be desolate, even great and *f*
54:11 I will lay thy stones with *f* colors
Jer. 4:30 in vain shalt thou make thyself *f*
12:6 though they speak *f* words unto thee
Dan. 1:15 their countenances appeared *f* and fatter
Zech. 3:5 so they set a *f* mitre upon his head
Mt. 16:2 it will be *f* weather: for the sky is red
Acts 7:20 Moses was born, and was exceeding *f*
Rom. 16:18 words and *f* speeches deceive the hearts
Gal. 6:12 desire to make a *f* show in the flesh

Faith *See also* Assurance, Believe, Confidence, Obedience, Trust

Deut. 32:20 very froward. . children in whom is no *f*
Hab. 2:4 (Rom. 1:17; Gal. 3:11; Heb. 10:38) but the just shall live by his *f*
Mt. 6:30 (Lk. 12:28) clothe you, O ye of little *f*?
8:10 (Lk. 7:9) not found so great *f*. . in Israel
8:26 (Mk. 4:40; Lk. 8:25) fearful, O ye of little *f*?
9:2 (Mk. 2:5; Lk. 5:20) and Jesus seeing their *f*
9:22 (Mk. 5:34; Lk. 8:48) thy *f*. . made thee whole
14:31 O thou of little *f*, wherefore didst thou
15:28 O woman, great is thy *f*: be it unto thee
17:20 (Lk. 17:6) have *f* as a grain of mustard seed
21:21 if ye have *f*, and doubt not, ye shall
23:23 mercy, and *f*: these ought ye to have done
Mk. 10:52 (Lk. 18:42) thy *f* hath made thee whole
11:22 Jesus. . saith unto them, Have *f* in God
Lk. 7:50 said to the woman, Thy *f* hath saved thee
8:25 said unto them, Where is your *f*?
17:5 apostles said unto the Lord, Increase our *f*
17:19 go thy way: thy *f* hath made thee whole
18:8 cometh, shall he find *f* on the earth?
18:42 receive thy sight: thy *f* hath saved thee
22:32 have prayed for thee, that thy *f* fail not
Acts 3:16 through *f* in his name, hath made this
6:5 Stephen, a man full of *f* and of the Holy Ghost
11:24 good man. . full of the Holy Ghost and of *f*
14:9 and perceiving that he had *f* to be healed
14:22 and exhorting them to continue in the *f*
14:27 had opened the door of *f* unto the Gentiles
15:9 purifying their hearts by *f*
16:5 so were the churches established in the *f*
20:21 *f* toward our Lord Jesus Christ
24:24 for Paul, and heard him concerning the *f*
26:18 which are sanctified by *f* that is in me
Rom. 1:5 for obedience to the *f* among all nations
1:8 *f* is spoken of throughout the whole world
1:17 righteousness of God revealed from *f* to *f*
3:3 unbelief make the *f* of God without effect?
3:22 righteousness of God which is by *f* of Jesus
3:25 to be a propitiation through *f* in his blood
3:27 law? of works? Nay; but by the law of *f*
3:28 we conclude that a man is justified by *f*
4:5 his *f* is counted for righteousness
4:14 are of the law be heirs, *f* is made void
4:16 it is of *f*. . of the *f* of Abraham
4:19 being not weak in *f*, he considered not his
5:1 being justified by *f*, we have peace with God
5:2 we have access by *f* into this grace
9:30 even the righteousness which is of *f*
10:6 the righteousness which is of *f* speaketh
10:8 that is, the word of *f*, which we preach
10:17 so then *f* cometh by hearing, and hearing
12:3 hath dealt to every man the measure of *f*
12:6 prophesy according to the proportion of *f*
14:1 him that is weak in the *f* receive ye
14:22 hast thou *f*? have it to thyself before God
14:23 for whatsoever is not of *f* is sin
1 Cor. 2:5 your *f* should not stand in the wisdom
12:9 to another *f* by the same Spirit; to another
13:2 though I have all *f*, so that I could remove
13:13 and now abideth *f*, hope, charity, these three
15:14 (15:17) Christ be not risen. . *f* is also vain
16:13 watch ye, stand fast in the *f*, quit you
2 Cor. 1:24 not. . that we have dominion over your *f*
4:13 we having the same spirit of *f*, according
5:7 for we walk by *f*, not by sight
10:15 but having hope, when your *f* is increased
13:5 examine yourselves, whether ye be in the *f*
Gal. 1:23 preacheth the *f* which once he destroyed
2:16 that we might be justified by the *f* of Christ
2:20 live by the *f* of the Son of God, who loved

Gal. 3:2 works of the law, or by the hearing of *f*?
3:12 and the law is not of *f*: but, The man that
3:14 receive the promise of the Spirit through *f*
3:22 that the promise by *f* of Jesus Christ might
3:23 before *f* came, we were kept under the law
3:26 are all the children of God by *f* in Christ
5:6 uncircumcision; but *f* which worketh by love
5:22 fruit of the Spirit is love. . goodness, *f*
6:10 unto them who are of the household of *f*
Eph. 1:15 (Col. 1:4) I heard of your *f* in the Lord
2:8 for by grace are ye saved through *f*
3:12 and access with confidence by the *f* of him
3:17 that Christ may dwell in your hearts by *f*
4:5 one Lord, one *f*, one baptism
4:13 till we all come in the unity of the *f*
6:16 above all, taking the shield of *f*
Phil. 1:27 striving together for the *f* of the gospel
3:9 the righteousness which is of God by *f*
Col. 1:23 continue in the *f* grounded and settled
2:5 and the steadfastness of your *f* in Christ
2:7 stablished in the *f*, as ye have been taught
1 Thes. 1:3 remembering. . your work of *f*, and labor
1:8 in every place your *f* to God-ward is spread
3:2 and to comfort you concerning your *f*
3:10 perfect that which is lacking in your *f*?
5:8 putting on the breastplate of *f* and love
2 Thes. 1:3 that your *f* groweth exceedingly
1:4 your patience and *f* in all your persecutions
1:11 and fulfil all. . the work of *f* with power
3:2 for all men have not *f*
1 Tim. 1:2 unto Timothy, my own son in the *f*
1:5 and of a good conscience, and of *f* unfeigned
1:19 holding *f*, and a good conscience
2:15 continue in *f* and charity and holiness
3:9 holding the mystery of the *f* in a pure
3:13 great boldness in the *f* which is in Christ
4:1 latter times some shall depart from the *f*
4:12 an example. . in spirit, in *f*, in purity
5:8 provide not for his own. . hath denied the *f*
6:10 coveted after, they have erred from the *f*
6:11 follow after righteousness, godliness, *f*
6:12 fight the good fight of *f*, lay hold on
6:21 some professing have erred concerning the *f*
2 Tim. 1:5 call to remembrance the unfeigned *f*
2:18 and overthrow the *f* of some
2:22 but follow righteousness, *f*, charity, peace
3:8 corrupt minds, reprobate concerning the *f*
3:15 to make thee wise unto salvation through *f*
4:7 I have finished my course, I have kept the *f*
Tit. 1:1 according to the *f* of God's elect
1:4 to Titus, mine own son after the common *f*
1:13 rebuke. . that they may be sound in the *f*
2:2 that the aged men be sober. . sound in *f*
Phlm. 5 hearing of thy love and *f*, which thou hast
Heb. 4:2 not being mixed with *f* in them that heard
6:1 foundation of repentance. . of *f* toward God
6:12 through *f* and patience inherit the promises
10:22 with a true heart in full assurance of *f*
10:23 let us hold fast the profession of our *f*
11:1 now *f* is the substance of things hoped for
11:4 by *f* Abel offered unto God a more excellent
11:5 by *f* Enoch was translated that he should
11:6 without *f* it is impossible to please him
11:7 by *f* Noah, being warned of God of things
11:8 by *f* Abraham, when he was called to go out
11:13 these all died in *f*, not having received
11:17 by *f* Abraham, when he was tried, offered
11:24 by *f* Moses. . refused to be called the son
11:31 by *f* the harlot Rahab perished not with
11:33 who through *f* subdued kingdoms, wrought
11:39 having obtained a good report through *f*
12:2 Jesus the author and finisher of our *f*
13:7 whose *f* follow, considering the end of

Jas. 1:3 the trying of your *f* worketh patience
   1:6 but let him ask in *f*, nothing wavering
   2:1 the *f* of our Lord . . with respect of persons
   2:5 God chosen the poor of this world rich in *f*
   2:14 hath *f*, and have not works? can *f* save him?
   2:18 thy *f* without thy works . . my *f* by my works
   2:20 O vain man, that *f* without works is dead?
   2:22 how *f* wrought . . by works was *f* made perfect
   2:24 by works a man is justified . . not by *f* only
   5:15 and the prayer of *f* shall save the sick
1 Pet. 1:5 are kept by the power of God through *f*
   1:7 trial of your *f* . . more precious than of gold
   1:9 receiving the end of your *f* . the salvation
   5:9 whom resist steadfast in the *f*, knowing that
2 Pet. 1:1 have obtained like precious *f* with us
   1:5 giving all diligence, add to your *f* virtue
1 Jn. 5:4 that overcometh the world, even our *f*
Jude 3 that ye should earnestly contend for the *f*
   20 building up yourselves on your most holy *f*
Rev. 2:13 hast not denied my *f*, even in those days
   2:19 I know thy works . . and service, and *f*
   13:10 is the patience and the *f* of the saints
   14:12 here are they that keep . . the *f* of Jesus

Faithful

Num. 12:7 (Heb. 3:2) Moses . . is *f* in all mine house
Deut. 7:9 the LORD thy God, he is God, the *f* God
1 Sam. 2:35 and I will raise me up a *f* priest
   22:14 so *f* among all thy servants as David
2 Sam. 20:19 that are peaceable and *f* in Israel
Neh. 7:2 charge over Jerusalem: for he was a *f* man
   9:8 foundest his heart *f* before thee, and madest
   13:13 for they were counted *f*, and their office
Ps. 12:1 help, LORD . . for the *f* fail from among
   31:23 the LORD preserveth the *f*, and plentifully
   89:37 as the moon, and as a *f* witness in heaven
   101:6 mine eyes shall be upon the *f* of the land
   119:86 all thy commandments are *f*
   119:138 thy testimonies . . are righteous and very *f*
Prov. 11:13 is of a *f* spirit concealeth the matter
   13:17 but a *f* ambassador is health
   14:5 a *f* witness will not lie: but a false
   20:6 own goodness: but a *f* man who can find?
   27:6 *f* are the wounds of a friend
   28:20 a *f* man shall abound with blessings
Is. 1:21 how is the *f* city become a harlot!
   1:26 The city of righteousness, the *f* city
   8:2 and I took unto me *f* witnesses to record
Jer. 42:5 LORD be a true and *f* witness between us
Hos. 11:12 but Judah yet . . is *f* with the saints
Mt. 24:45 (Lk. 12:42) is a *f* and wise servant
   25:21 well done, thou good and *f* servant
Lk. 16:10 he that is *f* in . . least is *f* also in much
   19:17 because thou hast been *f* in a very little
Acts 16:15 have judged me to be *f* to the Lord
1 Cor. 1:9 God is *f*, by whom ye were called unto
   4:2 required in stewards, that a man be found *f*
   10:13 but God is *f*, who will not suffer you to
Gal. 3:9 they . . of faith are blessed with *f* Abraham
Eph. 6:21 (Col. 4:7) beloved brother and *f* minister
Col. 1:7 Epaphras . . who is for you a *f* minister
1 Thes. 5:24 *f* is he that calleth you, who also
2 Thes. 3:3 the Lord is *f*, who shall stablish you
1 Tim. 1:12 counted me *f*, putting me into the ministry
   1:15 (4:9; Tit. 3:8) this is a *f* saying
   3:11 must their wives be grave . . *f* in all things
2 Tim. 2:2 the same commit thou to *f* men
   2:11 it is a *f* saying: For if we be dead with him
   2:13 if we believe not, yet he abideth *f*
Tit. 1:9 holding fast the *f* word as . . taught
Heb. 2:17 he might be a merciful and *f* high priest
   3:2 *f* to him that appointed him, as . . Moses was *f*

Heb. 10:23 for he is *f* that promised
   11:11 because she judged him *f* who had promised
1 Pet. 4:19 in well doing, as unto a *f* Creator
1 Jn. 1:9 if we confess our sins, he is *f* and just
Rev. 1:5 from Jesus Christ, who is the *f* witness
   2:10 tribulation ten days: be thou *f* unto death
   17:14 with him are called, and chosen, and *f*
   19:11 he that sat upon him was called *F* and True
   21:5 write: for these words are true and *f*
   22:6 said unto me, These sayings are *f* and true

Faithfully

2 Kgs. 12:15 they reckoned not . . for they dealt *f*
   22:7 (2 Chr. 34:12) because they dealt *f*
2 Chr. 19:9 shall ye do in the fear of the LORD, *f*
   31:12 brought . . tithes and the dedicated things *f*
Prov. 29:14 the king that *f* judgeth the poor
Jer. 23:28 hath my word, let him speak my word *f*
3 Jn. 5 beloved, thou doest *f* . . to the brethren

Faithfulness *See also* Truth

1 Sam. 26:23 the LORD render to every man . . his *f*
Ps. 5:9 for there is no *f* in their mouth
   36:5 thy *f* reacheth unto the clouds
   40:10 I have declared thy *f* and thy salvation
   88:11 in the grave? or thy *f* in destruction?
   89:1 will I make known thy *f* to all generations
   89:2 thy *f* shalt thou establish in the . . heavens
   89:8 like unto thee? or to thy *f* round about
   89:24 but my *f* and my mercy shall be with him
   89:33 take from him, nor suffer my *f* to fail
   92:2 to show forth . . thy *f* every night
   119:75 that thou in *f* hast afflicted me
   119:90 thy *f* is unto all generations
   143:1 hear my prayer, O LORD . . in thy *f* answer
Is. 11:5 *f* the girdle of his reins
   25:1 thy counsels of old are *f* and truth
Lam. 3:23 are new every morning: great is thy *f*
Hos. 2:20 I will even betroth thee unto me in *f*

Faithless

Mt. 17:17 (Mk. 9:19; Lk. 9:41) O *f*. . generation
Jn. 20:27 to Thomas . . be not *f*, but believing

Fall (Fell, Fallen) *See also* Descend

Gen. 2:21 God caused a deep sleep to *f* upon Adam
   4:5 Cain was very wroth, and his countenance *f*
   44:14 to Joseph's house . . and they *f* before him
   45:24 see that ye *f* not out by the way
Ex. 15:16 fear and dread shall *f* upon them
   21:33 dig a pit . . and an ox or an ass *f* therein
Lev. 26:36 and they shall *f* when none pursueth
Num. 24:4 vision of the Almighty, *f* into a trance
Josh. 6:20 great shout, that the wall *f* down flat
Judg. 8:21 Zalmunna said, Rise thou, and *f* upon us
Ruth 2:16 let *f* also some of the handfuls . . for her
1 Sam. 3:19 let none of his words *f* to the ground
   4:18 he *f* from off the seat backward by the side
   14:45 there shall not one hair of his head *f*
2 Sam. 1:19 (1:25, 27) how are the mighty *f*!
   14:11 there shall not one hair of thy son *f*
   24:14 (1 Chr. 21:13) let us *f* now into the hand
1 Kgs. 18:38 then the fire of the LORD *f*
   22:20 (2 Chr. 18:19) go up and *f* at Ramoth-gilead?
2 Kgs. 6:5 the axe head *f* into the water
   10:10 shall *f*. . nothing of the word of the LORD
   14:10 (2 Chr. 25:19) shouldest *f*. . Judah with thee?
2 Chr. 25:8 God shall make thee *f* before the enemy
Job 4:4 thy words have upholden him that was *f*
   4:13 visions of the night, when deep sleep *f* on
Ps. 5:10 O God; let them *f* by their own counsels
   16:6 the lines are *f* unto me in pleasant places
   37:24 though he *f*, he shall not be utterly cast
   64:8 make their own tongue to *f* upon themselves

Ps. 69:9 (Rom. 15:3) reproaches of them . . *f* upon me
72:11 yea, all kings shall *f* down before him
78:64 their priests *f* by the sword
91:7 a thousand shall *f* at thy side, and ten
141:10 let the wicked *f* into their own nets
145:14 LORD upholdeth all that *f*, and raiseth up
Prov. 10:8 but a prating fool shall *f*
11:5 the wicked shall *f* by his own wickedness
11:14 where no counsel is, the people *f*
11:28 he that trusteth in his riches shall *f*
13:17 a wicked messenger *f* into mischief
16:18 and a haughty spirit before a *f*
17:20 hath a perverse tongue *f* into mischief
24:16 for a just man *f* seven times, and riseth
24:17 rejoice not when thine enemy *f*
25:26 a righteous man *f* down before the wicked
26:27 whoso diggeth a pit shall *f* therein
29:16 but the righteous shall see their *f*
Eccl. 4:10 if they *f*, the one will lift up his fellow
11:3 place where the tree *f*, there it shall be
Is. 9:10 the bricks are *f* down, but we will build
10:4 without me . . they shall *f* under the slain
22:25 nail that is fastened . . be cut down, and *f*
34:4 all their host shall *f* down, as the leaf *f*
40:30 and the young men shall utterly *f*
Jer. 8:4 shall they *f*, and not arise?
23:19 *f* grievously upon the head of the wicked
37:14 it is false; I *f* not away to the Chaldeans
46:6 they shall stumble, and *f* toward the north
48:44 fleeth from the fear shall *f* into the pit
49:21 the earth is moved at the noise of their *f*
49:26 her young men shall *f* in her streets
Ezek. 6:7 the slain shall *f* in the midst of you
24:6 piece by piece; let no lot *f* upon it
26:15 the isles shake at the sound of thy *f*
31:16 nations to shake at the sound of his *f*
44:12 caused . . house of Israel to *f* into iniquity
Dan. 3:5 (3:7, 10, 15) *f* down and worship the . . image
4:31 there *f* a voice from heaven, saying, O king
11:26 and many shall *f* down slain
Hos. 4:5 and the prophet also shall *f* with thee
4:14 the people that doth not understand shall *f*
10:8 (Lk. 23:30) shall say . . to the hills, *F* on us
14:1 for thou hast *f* by thine iniquity
Joel 2:8 when they *f* upon the sword, they shall not
Amos 9:9 not the least grain *f* upon the earth
Jon. 1:7 they cast lots, and the lot *f* upon Jonah
Mic. 7:8 rejoice not . . when I *f*, I shall arise
Mt. 2:11 they saw . . and *f* down, and worshipped him
4:9 if thou wilt *f* down and worship me
7:25 it *f* not: for it was founded upon a rock
7:27 (Lk. 6:49) it *f*: and great was the *f* of it
10:29 two sparrows . . one of them shall not *f* on
12:11 (Lk. 14:5) sheep, and if it *f* into a pit
13:4 (Mk. 4:4; Lk. 8:5) seeds *f* by the wayside
15:14 (Lk. 6:39) blind, both shall *f* into the ditch
18:29 fellow servant *f* down . . and besought him
21:44 (Lk. 20:18) whosoever shall *f* on this stone
24:29 (Mk. 13:25) the stars shall *f* from heaven
Lk. 2:34 this child is set for the *f* and rising
5:8 Peter saw it, he *f* down at Jesus' knees
8:13 believe, and in time of temptation *f* away
8:47 she came trembling, and *f* down before him
10:18 I beheld Satan as lightning *f* from heaven
10:30 Jerusalem to Jericho, and *f* among thieves
13:4 eighteen, upon whom the tower in Siloam *f*
15:20 his father . . *f* on his neck, and kissed him
Jn. 12:24 except a corn of wheat *f* into the ground
18:6 they went backward, and *f* to the ground
Acts 1:18 and *f* headlong, he burst asunder
1:25 from which Judas by transgression *f*
1:26 their lots; and the lot *f* upon Matthias
9:4 (22:7; 26:14) *f* to the earth, and heard
10:44 (11:15) Holy Ghost *f* on all them which heard

Acts 19:35 the image which *f* down from Jupiter
20:9 with sleep, and *f* down from the third loft
27:17 lest they should *f* into the quicksands
27:34 not a hair *f* from the head of any of you
Rom. 11:11 through their *f* salvation is come unto
11:12 if the *f* of them be the riches of the world
14:4 to his own master he standeth or *f*
14:13 or an occasion to *f* in his brother's way
1 Cor. 10:12 he standeth take heed lest he *f*
14:25 so *f* down on his face he will worship God
15:6 five hundred brethren . . some are *f* asleep
15:18 which are *f* asleep in Christ are perished
1 Tim. 3:6 with pride he *f* into the condemnation
3:7 have a good report . . lest he *f* into reproach
6:9 but they that will be rich *f* into temptation
Heb. 4:11 man *f* after the same example of unbelief
6:6 if they shall *f* away, to renew them again
10:31 fearful thing to *f* into the hands of . . God
11:30 by faith the walls of Jericho *f* down
Jas. 1:2 joy when ye *f* into divers temptations
1:11 (1 Pet. 1:24) and the flower thereof *f*
5:12 swear not . . lest ye *f* into condemnation
2 Pet. 1:10 ye do these things, ye shall never *f*
3:17 lest ye also . . *f* from your own steadfastness
Rev. 1:17 when I saw him, I *f* at his feet as dead
6:16 said to the mountains and rocks, *F* on us
9:1 I saw a star *f* from heaven unto the earth
16:19 and the cities of the nations *f*

Fallen *See also* Fall

Lev. 25:35 brother be waxen poor, and *f* in decay
2 Sam. 3:38 is a prince and a great man *f* this day
Ps. 7:15 and is *f* into the ditch which he made
Is. 14:12 how art thou *f* from heaven, O Lucifer
21:9 (Rev. 18:2) and said, Babylon is, is *f*
Jer. 51:8 Babylon is suddenly *f* and destroyed
Lam. 5:16 crown is *f* from our head: woe unto us
Zech. 11:2 howl, fir tree; for the cedar is *f*
Gal. 5:4 justified by the law; ye are *f* from grace
Rev. 2:5 remember therefore from whence thou art *f*
14:8 (18:2) angel, saying, Babylon is *f*, is *f*

Falling *See also* Fall

Job 14:18 surely the mountain *f* cometh to nought
Ps. 56:13 wilt not thou deliver my feet from *f*
2 Thes. 2:3 except there come a *f* away first
Jude 24 unto him that is able to keep you from *f*

Fallow

Jer. 4:3 (Hos. 10:12) break up your *f* ground

False *See also* Lying, Wrong

Ex. 20:16 (Deut. 5:20; Mt. 19:18; Mk. 10:19; Lk. 18:
20; Rom. 13:9) thou shalt not bear *f* witness
23:1 thou shalt not raise a *f* report
23:7 keep thee far from a *f* matter
Deut. 19:16 if a *f* witness rise up against any man
2 Kgs. 9:12 and they said, It is *f*; tell us now
Job 36:4 for truly my words shall not be *f*
Ps. 27:12 for *f* witnesses are risen up against me
35:11 *f* witnesses did rise up; they laid to my
119:104 therefore I hate every *f* way
120:3 shall be done unto thee, thou *f* tongue?
Prov. 6:19 a *f* witness that speaketh lies
11:1 a *f* balance is abomination to the LORD
12:17 but a *f* witness deceit
17:4 a wicked doer giveth heed to *f* lips
19:5 a *f* witness shall not be unpunished
21:28 a *f* witness shall perish
25:14 whoso boasteth himself of a *f* gift is like
25:18 a man that beareth *f* witness . . is a maul
Jer. 14:14 they prophesy unto you a *f* vision
23:32 I am against them that prophesy *f* dreams

Lam. 2:14 prophets. . have seen for thee *f* burdens
Ezek. 21:23 shall be unto them as a *f* divination
Zech. 8:17 love no *f* oath: for all these. . I hate
    10:2 diviners have seen a lie. . told *f* dreams
Mal. 3:5 be a swift witness. . against *f* swearers
Mt. 7:15 beware of *f* prophets. . in sheep's clothing
    15:19 out of the heart proceed. . thefts, *f* witness
    24:11 *f* prophets shall rise, and shall deceive
    24:24 (Mk. 13:22) arise *f* Christs, and *f* prophets
    26:59 (Mk. 14:56) sought *f* witness against Jesus
Lk. 19:8 have taken. . from any man by *f* accusation
Acts 6:13 set up *f* witnesses, which said, This man
1 Cor. 15:15 and we are found *f* witnesses of God
2 Cor. 11:13 for such are *f* apostles, deceitful
    11:26 perils in the sea, in perils among *f* brethren
Gal. 2:4 because of *f* brethren unawares brought in
2 Tim. 3:3 trucebreakers, *f* accusers, incontinent
Tit. 2:3 the aged women likewise. . not *f* accusers
2 Pet. 2:1 as there shall be *f* teachers among you
1 Jn. 4:1 because many *f* prophets are gone out
Rev. 19:20 beast was taken. . with him the *f* prophet

Falsehood *See also* Deceit, Hypocrisy, Lie, Lying

2 Sam. 18:13 wrought *f* against mine own life
Job 21:34 seeing in your answers there remaineth *f*
Ps. 7:14 conceived mischief, and brought forth *f*
    119:118 from thy statutes: for their deceit is *f*
    144:8 their right hand is a right hand of *f*
Is. 28:15 and under *f* have we hid ourselves
    57:4 children of transgression, a seed of *f*
    59:13 and uttering from the heart words of *f*
Jer. 10:14 (51:17) for his molten image is *f*
    13:25 thou hast forgotten me, and trusted in *f*
Hos. 7:1 wickedness of Samaria: for they commit *f*
Mic. 2:11 man walking in the spirit and *f* do lie

Falsely

Gen. 21:23 swear. . thou wilt not deal *f* with me
Lev. 6:3 and lieth concerning it, and sweareth *f*
    19:12 ye shall not swear by my name *f*
Deut. 19:18 hath testified *f* against his brother
Ps. 44:17 neither have we dealt *f* in thy covenant
Jer. 5:31 the prophets prophesy *f*, and the priests
    6:13 (8:10) unto the priest every one dealeth *f*
    7:9 will ye steal, murder. . and swear *f*
    29:9 for they prophesy *f* unto you in my name
    43:2 saying unto Jeremiah, Thou speakest *f*
Hos. 10:4 swearing *f* in making a covenant
Zech. 5:4 house of him that sweareth *f* by my name
Mt. 5:11 say all manner of evil against you *f*
Lk. 3:14 violence to no man, neither accuse any *f*
1 Tim. 6:20 and oppositions of science *f* so called
1 Pet. 3:16 that *f* accuse your good conversation

Fame *See also* Honor, Praise

Gen. 45:16 *f* thereof was heard in Pharaoh's house
Num. 14:15 nations which have heard the *f* of thee
Josh. 6:27 *f* was noised throughout all the country
    9:9 thy God: for we have heard the *f* of him
1 Kgs. 4:31 his *f* was in all nations round about
    10:1 (2 Chr. 9:1) heard of the *f* of Solomon
1 Chr. 22:5 the house. . magnificent, of *f* and of glory
Job 28:22 death say, We have heard the *f* thereof
Is. 66:19 isles afar off, that have not heard my *f*
Zeph. 3:19 get them praise and *f* in every land
Mt. 4:24 and his *f* went throughout all Syria
    9:26 the *f* hereof went abroad into all that land
    9:31 spread abroad his *f* in all that country
    14:1 Herod the tetrarch heard of the *f* of Jesus
Mk. 1:28 (Lk. 4:37) his *f* spread abroad throughout
Lk. 4:14 a *f* of him through all the region round
    5:15 but so much the more went there a *f* abroad

Familiar

Lev. 19:31 regard not them that have *f* spirits
    20:6 that turneth after such as have *f* spirits
    20:27 hath a *f* spirit. . surely be put to death
1 Sam. 28:3 had put away those that had *f* spirits
    28:7 seek me a woman that hath a *f* spirit
2 Kgs. 21:6 (2 Chr. 33:6) and dealt with *f* spirits
1 Chr. 10:13 counsel of one that had a *f* spirit
Job 19:14 and my *f* friends have forgotten me
Ps. 41:9 yea, mine own *f* friend, in whom I trusted
Is. 8:19 seek unto them that have *f* spirits
    29:4 thy voice. . as of one that hath a *f* spirit
Jer. 20:10 all my *f* watched for my halting

Family *See also* House, Household

Gen. 10:5 divided. . after their *f*, in their nations
    12:3 in thee shall all *f* of the earth be blessed
    28:14 in thy seed shall all the *f* of the earth
Ex. 12:21 and take you a lamb according to your *f*
Lev. 25:10 ye shall return every man unto his *f*
Num. 27:4 name. . be done away from among his *f*
Deut. 29:18 *f*, or tribe, whose heart turneth away
Judg. 1:25 but they let go the man and all his *f*
1 Sam. 9:21 my *f*. . least of all the *f* of. . Benjamin?
    18:18 what is. . my father's *f* in Israel
1 Chr. 4:38 mentioned. . were princes in their *f*
Ps. 68:6 God setteth the solitary in *f*
    107:41 and maketh him *f* like a flock
Jer. 3:14 take you one of a city, and two of a *f*
    10:25 fury. . upon the *f* that call not on thy name
    31:1 will I be the God of all the *f* of Israel
Amos 3:2 you only have I known of all the *f* of the
Zech. 12:12 the land shall mourn, every *f* apart
Eph. 3:15 the whole *f* in heaven and earth is named

Famine *See also* Dearth, Drought

Gen. 12:10 was a *f* in the land: and Abram went
    41:27 the seven empty ears. . seven years of *f*
    41:56 the *f* was over all the face of the earth
    47:13 land of Canaan fainted by reason of the *f*
Ruth 1:1 there was a *f* in the land
2 Sam. 21:1 a *f* in the days of David three years
    24:13 (1 Chr. 21:12) shall seven years of *f* come
1 Kgs. 8:37 if there be in the land *f*, if there be
    18:2 Elijah went. . there was a sore *f* in Samaria
2 Kgs. 6:25 and there was a great *f* in Samaria
    7:4 the *f* is in the city, and we shall die
    8:1 sojourn: for the LORD hath called for a *f*
    25:3 (Jer. 52:6) the *f* prevailed in the city
2 Chr. 20:9 upon us. . judgment, or pestilence, or *f*
Job 5:20 in *f* he shall redeem thee from death
    5:22 at destruction and *f* thou shalt laugh
Ps. 33:19 from death, and to keep them alive in *f*
    37:19 in the days of *f* they shall be satisfied
    105:16 moreover he called for a *f* upon the land
Is. 51:19 desolation, and destruction, and the *f*
Jer. 11:22 sons and their daughters shall die by *f*
    14:15 by sword and *f* shall those prophets be
    15:2 such as are for the *f*, to the *f*
    24:10 send the sword, the *f* and the pestilence
    42:16 the *f*. . shall follow close after you there
Lam. 5:10 skin was black. . because of the terrible *f*
Ezek. 5:12 and with *f* shall they be consumed
    5:16 I shall send upon them the evil arrows of *f*
    6:11 for they shall fall by the sword, by the *f*
    36:29 call for the corn. . and lay no *f* upon you
Amos 8:11 not a *f* of bread, nor a thirst for water
Mt. 24:7 (Mk. 13:8; Lk. 21:11) be *f* and pestilences
Lk. 4:25 when great *f* was throughout all the land
    15:14 there arose a mighty *f* in that land
Rom. 8:35 or *f*, or nakedness, or peril, or sword?
Rev. 18:8 in one day, death, and mourning, and *f*

Famish

Gen. 41:55 when all the land of Egypt was *f*
Prov. 10:3 not suffer the soul of the righteous to *f*
Is. 5:13 their honorable men are *f*
Zeph. 2:11 for he will *f* all the gods of the earth

Famous

Num. 16:2 *f* in the congregation, men of renown
Ruth 4:14 that his name may be *f* in Israel
Ps. 74:5 a man was *f* according as he had lifted up
136:18 and slew *f* kings: for his mercy endureth
Ezek. 23:10 and she became *f* among women

Fan

Is. 41:16 thou shalt *f* them, and the wind shall
Jer. 4:11 of my people, not to *f*, nor to cleanse
15:7 and I will *f* them with a *f* in the gates
51:2 send unto Babylon fanners, that shall *f* her
Mt. 3:12 (Lk. 3:17) whose *f* is in his hand

Far

Gen. 18:25 be *f* from thee to do after this manner
Ex. 23:7 keep thee *f* from a false matter
Deut. 12:21 (14:24) if the place . . be too *f* from thee
30:11 not hidden from thee, neither is it *f* off
1 Sam. 2:30 now the LORD saith, Be it *f* from me
20:9 Jonathan said, *F* be it from thee
2 Sam. 15:17 tarried in a place that was *f* off
20:20 Joab answered and said, *F* be it, *f* be it
23:17 be it *f* from me, O LORD, that I should do
Job 5:4 his children are *f* from safety
11:14 iniquity be in thine hand, put it *f* away
19:13 he hath put my brethren *f* from me
22:23 put away iniquity *f* from thy tabernacles
30:10 they abhor me, they flee *f* from me
Ps. 10:5 judgments are *f* above out of his sight
22:1 why art thou so *f* from helping me
22:11 be not *f* from me; for trouble is near
27:9 hide not thy face *f* from me
35:22 keep not silence: O Lord, be not *f* from me
38:21 forsake me not . . my God, be not *f* from me
73:27 they that are *f* from thee shall perish
97:9 thou art exalted *f* above all gods
103:12 as *f* as the east is from the west, so *f*
Prov. 15:29 the LORD is *f* from the wicked
31:10 a virtuous woman . . price is *f* above rubies
Eccl. 7:23 I will be wise; but it was *f* from me
Is. 29:13 (Mt. 15:8; Mk. 7:6) their heart *f* from me
33:17 behold the land that is very *f* off
43:6 bring my sons from *f*, and my daughters from
46:12 stout-hearted, that are *f* from righteousness
57:19 peace, peace to him that is *f* off
60:9 ships of Tarshish . . to bring thy sons from *f*
Ezek. 7:20 therefore have I set it *f* from them
22:5 near, and . . *f* from thee, shall mock thee
Amos 6:3 ye that put *f* away the evil day
Mt. 16:22 be it *f* from thee, Lord: this shall not be
21:33 (Mk. 12:1; Lk. 20:9) went into a *f* country
25:14 (Lk. 19:12) a man traveling into a *f* country
Mk. 8:3 will faint . . for divers of them came from *f*
12:34 thou art not *f* from the kingdom of God
13:34 Son of man is as a man taking a *f* journey
Lk. 15:13 and took his journey into a *f* country
24:50 and he led them out as *f* as to Bethany
Acts 17:27 though he be not *f* from every one
Rom. 13:12 night is *f* spent, the day is at hand
2 Cor. 4:17 a *f* more exceeding and eternal weight
Eph. 1:21 *f* above all principality, and power
2:13 ye who sometime were *f* off are made nigh
4:10 also that ascended up *f* above all heavens
Phil. 1:23 to be with Christ; which is *f* better
Heb. 7:15 and it is yet *f* more evident

Fare (noun)

Jon. 1:3 ship going to Tarshish: so he paid the *f*

Fare (verb)

1 Sam. 17:18 look how thy brethren *f*, and take
Lk. 16:19 rich man, which . . *f* sumptuously every day

Farewell

Lk. 9:61 but let me first go bid them *f*
Acts 18:21 bade them *f* . . and he sailed from Ephesus
2 Cor. 13:11 finally, brethren, *f*. Be perfect

Farm

Mt. 22:5 went their ways, one to his *f*, another to

Farthing

Mt. 5:26 till thou hast paid the uttermost *f*
10:29 (Lk. 12:6) are not two sparrows sold for a *f*?
Mk. 12:42 poor widow . . two mites, which make a *f*

Fashion

Gen. 6:15 this is the *f* which thou shalt make it
Ex. 26:30 tabernacle according to the *f* thereof
32:4 and *f* it with a graving tool
Job 10:8 (Ps. 119:73) hands have made me and *f* me
31:15 and did not one *f* us in the womb?
Ps. 33:15 he *f* their hearts alike
139:16 written, which in continuance were *f*
Is. 44:12 smith . . *f* it with hammers
45:9 shall the clay say to him that *f* it
Mk. 2:12 saying, We never saw it on this *f*
Lk. 9:29 as he prayed, the *f* of his countenance
Acts 7:44 Moses . . should make it according to the *f*
1 Cor. 7:31 for the *f* of this world passeth away
Phil. 2:8 being found in *f* as a man, he humbled
3:21 it may be *f* like unto his glorious body
Jas. 1:11 and the grace of the *f* of it perisheth
1 Pet. 1:14 not *f* . . according to the former lusts

Fast (adverb)

Gen. 20:18 LORD had *f* closed up all the wombs
Judg. 4:21 he was *f* asleep and weary. So he died
16:11 unto her, If they bind me *f* with new ropes
Job 2:3 my servant Job . . he holdeth *f* his integrity
27:6 my righteousness I hold *f*, and will not let
Ps. 33:9 it was done; he commanded, and it stood *f*
65:6 by his strength settest *f* the mountains
111:8 they stand *f* for ever and ever
Prov. 4:13 take *f* hold of instruction
Mt. 26:48 I . . kiss, that same is he; hold him *f*
Acts 16:24 and made their feet *f* in the stocks
1 Cor. 16:13 watch ye, stand *f* in the faith
Gal. 5:1 stand *f* therefore in the liberty
Phil. 1:27 that ye stand *f* in one spirit
4:1 so stand *f* in the Lord, my dearly beloved
1 Thes. 5:21 prove all . . hold *f* that which is good
Tit. 1:9 holding *f* the faithful word as he hath
Heb. 10:23 hold *f* the profession of our faith
Rev. 3:3 and hold *f*, and repent
3:11 I come quickly: hold that *f* which thou hast

Fast (noun, verb)

Judg. 20:26 and *f* that day until even, and offered
1 Sam. 7:6 *f* on that day, and said . . We have sinned
2 Sam. 1:12 wept, and *f* until even, for Saul
12:16 besought God for the child; and David *f*
12:23 now he is dead, wherefore should I *f*?
1 Kgs. 21:9 proclaim a *f*, and set Naboth on high
2 Chr. 20:3 Jehoshaphat feared . . proclaimed a *f*
Ezra 8:21 I proclaimed a *f* there . . before our God
Esth. 4:16 the Jews . . in Shushan, and *f* ye for me
Is. 58:3 wherefore have we *f* . . and thou seest not?
58:4 behold, ye *f* for strife and debate

Is. 58:5 is it such a *f* that I have chosen?
Jer. 14:12 when they *f*, I will not hear their cry
Joel 1:14 (2:15) sanctify ye a *f*, call a solemn
Jon. 3:5 Nineveh believed God, and proclaimed a *f*
Zech. 7:5 when ye *f*. . did ye at all *f* unto me
　8:19 the *f* of the tenth, shall be to . . Judah joy
Mt. 4:2 when he had *f* forty days and forty nights
　6:16 when ye *f*, be not, as the hypocrites
　6:18 that thou appear not unto men to *f*
　9:14 (Mk. 2:18; Lk. 5:33) but thy disciples *f* not?
Mk. 2:19 (Lk. 5:34) children of the bridechamber *f*
Lk. 18:12 I *f* twice in the week, I give tithes of
Acts 10:30 Cornelius said, Four days ago I was *f*
　13:2 as they ministered to the Lord, and *f*
　27:9 the *f* was now already past, Paul admonished

Fasten

1 Sam. 31:10 *f* his body to the wall of Beth-shan
Job 38:6 are the foundations thereof *f*?
Eccl. 12:11 as nails *f* by the masters of assemblies
Is. 22:23 I will *f* him as a nail in a sure place
Lk. 4:20 eyes. . in the synagogue were *f* on him
Acts 3:4 Peter, *f* his eyes upon him with John
　11:6 which when I had *f* mine eyes, I considered
　28:3 a viper out of the heat, and *f* on his hand

Fasting *See also* Fast (verb)

Neh. 9:1 children of Israel were assembled with *f*
Ps. 35:13 I humbled my soul with *f*; and my prayer
　69:10 when I wept, and chastened my soul with *f*
　109:24 my knees are weak through *f*; and my flesh
Jer. 36:6 read. . in the LORD's house upon the *f* day
Dan. 6:18 to his palace, and passed the night *f*
　9:3 to seek by prayer and supplications, with *f*
Mt. 15:32 (Mk. 8:3) I will not send them away *f*
　17:21 (Mk. 9:29) goeth not out but by prayer and *f*
Lk. 2:37 but served God with *f* and prayers night
Acts 14:23 had prayed with *f*, they commended them
　27:33 and continued *f*, having taken nothing
1 Cor. 7:5 ye may give yourselves to *f* and prayer
2 Cor. 6:5 in labors, in watchings, in *f*
　11:27 in hunger and thirst, in *f* often, in cold

Fat

Gen. 41:20 did eat up the first seven *f* kine
　45:18 and ye shall eat the *f* of the land
　49:20 out of Asher his bread shall be *f*
Ex. 29:13 take all the *f* that covereth the inwards
Lev. 3:16 sweet savor: all the *f* is the LORD's
　3:17 statute. . that ye eat neither *f* nor blood
　7:23 ye shall eat no manner of *f*, of ox, or of
Num. 13:20 what the land is, whether it be *f* or
Deut. 32:15 but Jeshurun waxed *f*, and kicked
Judg. 3:17 and Eglon was a very *f* man
Neh. 8:10 eat the *f*, and drink the sweet, and send
　9:25 and they took strong cities, and a *f* land
　9:35 in the large and *f* land which thou gavest
Ps. 17:10 they are inclosed in their own *f*
　37:20 enemies of the LORD. . be as the *f* of lambs
　92:14 they shall be *f* and flourishing
　119:70 their heart is as *f* as grease
Prov. 11:25 the liberal soul shall be made *f*
　13:4 the soul of the diligent shall be made *f*
　15:30 and a good report maketh the bones *f*
　28:25 his trust in the LORD shall be made *f*
Is. 1:11 I am full of. . the *f* of fed beasts
　6:10 make the heart of this people *f*
　10:16 the Lord. . send among his *f* ones leanness
　25:6 make unto all people a feast of *f* things
　58:11 and satisfy thy soul. . and make *f* thy bones
Jer. 50:11 ye are grown *f* as the heifer at grass
Hab. 1:16 because. by them their portion is *f*

Father *See also* God, Parent

Gen. 2:24 (Mt. 19:5; Mk. 10:7; Eph. 5:31) shall a man
　leave his *f* and his mother, and shall cleave
　4:20 Jabal. . was the *f* of such as dwell in tents
　15:15 and thou shalt go to thy *f* in peace
　17:5 (Rom. 4:17) *f* of many nations. . I made thee
Ex. 13:5 he sware unto thy *f* to give thee, a land
　15:2 is my God. . my *f*'s God, and I will exalt him
　20:5 (34:7; Num. 14:18; Deut. 5:9) visiting the
　iniquity of the *f* upon the children
　20:12 (Deut. 5:16; Mt. 15:4; 19:19; Mk. 7:10; 10:19
　Lk. 18:20; Eph. 6:2) honor thy *f* and thy mother
　21:15 smiteth his *f*. . be surely put to death
　21:17 (Lev. 20:9; Mt. 15:4; Mk. 7:10) curseth his *f*,
　or his mother, shall surely be put to death
Deut. 21:18 which will not obey the voice of his *f*
　24:16 (2 Kgs. 14:6; 2 Chr. 25:4) *f* shall not be put to
　death for the children
Judg. 2:10 generation were gathered unto their *f*
　17:10 Micah said. . be unto me a *f* and a priest
Ruth 2:11 how thou hast left thy *f* and thy mother
2 Sam. 7:14 (1 Chr. 17:13; Heb. 1:5) I will be his *f*
　10:2 (1 Chr. 19:2) sent to comfort him. . for his *f*
2 Kgs. 2:12 Elisha saw it, and he cried, My *f*, my *f*
　13:14 Joash. . said, O my *f*, my *f*! the chariot
　14:6 (2 Chr. 25:4) *f* shall not be put to death
1 Chr. 28:9 Solomon. . know thou the God of thy *f*
2 Chr. 30:7 not ye like your *f*. . which trespassed
Ezra 7:27 blessed be the LORD God of our *f*
Neh. 9:2 their sins, and the iniquities of their *f*
Job 29:16 I was a *f* to the poor: and the cause
　31:18 he was brought up with me, as with a *f*
　38:28 hath the rain a *f*? or who hath begotten
Ps. 22:4 our *f* trusted in thee: they trusted
　27:10 when my *f* and my mother forsake me, then
　39:12 and a sojourner, as all my *f* were
　68:5 a *f* of the fatherless, and a judge of
　95:9 (Heb. 3:9) your *f* tempted me, proved me
　103:13 like as a *f* pitieth his children, so
Prov. 3:12 he correcteth; even as a *f* the son
　4:1 hear, ye children, the instruction of a *f*
　4:3 I was my *f*'s son, tender and only beloved
　6:20 keep thy *f*'s commandment, and forsake not
　10:1 (15:20) a wise son maketh a glad *f*
　13:1 a wise son heareth his *f*'s instruction
　17:21 and the *f* of a fool hath no joy
　17:25 a foolish son is a grief to his *f*
　19:13 a foolish son is the calamity of his *f*
　23:24 *f* of the righteous shall greatly rejoice
Is. 9:6 The everlasting *F*, The Prince of Peace
　14:21 his children for the iniquity of their *f*
　22:21 be a *f* to the inhabitants of Jerusalem
　49:23 and kings shall be thy nursing *f*
　63:16 thou, O LORD, art our *F*, our Redeemer
　64:8 O LORD, thou art our *F*; we are the clay
Jer. 3:4 my *f*, thou art the guide of my youth?
　16:11 because your *f* have forsaken me, saith
　31:9 for I am a *f* to Israel, and Ephraim is my
　31:29 (Ezek. 18:2) the *f* have eaten a sour grape
　31:32 (Heb. 8:9) covenant that I made with their *f*
　32:18 recompensest the iniquity of the *f* into
Ezek. 18:4 all souls are mine; as the soul of the *f*
　18:20 son shall not bear the iniquity of the *f*
　22:7 in thee have they set light by *f* and mother
Mal. 1:6 if then I be a *f*, where is my honor?
　2:10 have we not all one *f*? hath not one God
　4:6 (Lk. 1:17) the heart of the *f* to the children
Mt. 3:9 (Lk. 3:8) we have Abraham to our *f*
　5:16 and glorify your *F* which is in heaven
　5:45 that ye may be the children of your *F*
　5:48 be ye therefore perfect, even as your *F*
　6:6 pray to thy *F* which is in secret; and thy *F*
　6:8 your *F* knoweth what things ye have need of
　6:9 (Lk. 11:2) our *F* which art in heaven

Mt. 6:15 (Mk. 11:26) neither will your *F* forgive your
  7:11 (Lk. 11:13) how much more shall your *F*
  7:21 but he that doeth the will of my *F* which
  8:21 (Lk. 9:59) first to go and bury my *f*
  10:21 (Mk. 13:12) to death, and the *f* the child
  10:32 him will I confess also before my *F*
  10:37 loveth *f* or mother more than me is not
  11:27 (Lk. 10:22) no man knoweth the Son . . the *F*
  12:50 do the will of my *F* . . is my brother
  16:27 (Mk. 8:38; Lk. 9:26) in the glory of his *F*
  18:10 angels do always behold the face of my *F*
  18:14 even so it is not the will of your *F*
  19:5 (Mk. 10:7) shall a man leave *f* and mother
  20:23 be given . . for whom it is prepared of my *F*
  23:9 and call no man your *f*. . for one is your *F*
  24:36 (Mk. 13:32) hour knoweth no man . . my *F*
  25:34 his right hand, Come, ye blessed of my *F*
  26:29 I drink it new with you in my *F*'s kingdom
  26:39 (Lk. 22:42) *F*, if it be possible, let this
  28:19 baptizing them in the name of the *F*
Mk. 14:36 Abba, *F*, all things are possible unto
Lk. 2:49 that I must be about my *F*'s business?
  6:23 like manner did their *f* unto the prophets
  6:36 be ye . . merciful, as your *F* also is merciful
  12:32 it is your *F*'s good pleasure to give you
  15:12 *f*, give me the portion of goods that
  15:18 I will arise and go to my *f*
  16:24 *f* Abraham, have mercy on me, and send
  23:34 then said Jesus, *F*, forgive them
  23:46 *F*, into thy hands I commend my spirit
  24:49 I send the promise of my *F* upon you
Jn. 1:14 glory as of the only begotten of the *F*
  2:16 not my *F*'s house a house of merchandise
  3:35 the *F* loveth the Son, and hath given all
  4:23 shall worship the *F* in spirit and in truth
  5:17 my *F* worketh hitherto, and I work
  5:20 the *F* loveth the Son, and showeth him all
  5:21 for as the *F* raiseth up the dead
  5:22 the *F* judgeth no man, but hath committed
  5:23 honor the Son, even as they honor the *F*
  5:26 for as the *F* hath life in himself; so hath
  5:30 but the will of the *F* which hath sent me
  5:37 the *F* himself . . hath borne witness of me
  6:37 all that the *F* giveth me shall come to me
  6:46 not that any man hath seen the *F*, save he
  6:65 except it were given unto him of my *F*
  8:16 for I am not alone, but I and the *F* that
  8:39 they answered and said . . Abraham is our *f*
  8:44 ye are of your *f* the devil
  8:49 but I honor my *F*, and ye do dishonor me
  10:15 as the *F* knoweth me, even so know I the *F*
  10:29 *F*, which gave them me, is greater than all
  10:30 I and my *F* are one
  12:26 if any man serve me, him will my *F* honor
  12:27 *F*, save me from this hour: but for this
  12:28 *F*, glorify thy name
  12:49 for I have not spoken of myself; but the *F*
  13:1 should depart out of this world unto the *F*
  14:2 in my *F*'s house are many mansions
  14:6 no man cometh unto the *F*, but by me
  14:9 he that hath seen me hath seen the *F*
  14:10 that I am in the *F*, and the *F* in me?
  14:16 I will pray the *F*, and he shall give you
  14:20 I am in my *F*, and ye in me, and I in you
  14:21 he that loveth me shall be loved of my *F*
  14:23 keep my words: and my *F* will love him
  14:24 which ye hear is not mine, but the *F*'s
  14:28 go unto the *F*: for my *F* is greater than I
  15:1 the true vine, and my *F* is the husbandman
  15:8 herein is my *F* glorified, that ye bear much
  15:10 even as I have kept my *F*'s commandments
  15:16 (16:23) ask of the *F* in my name, he may give
  15:23 he that hateth me hateth my *F* also

Jn. 16:3 because they have not known the *F*, nor me
  16:15 all things that the *F* hath are mine
  16:16 ye shall see me, because I go to the *F*
  16:26 I say not . . that I will pray the *F* for you
  16:32 I am not alone, because the *F* is with me
  17:1 *F*, the hour is come; glorify thy Son
  20:17 for I am not yet ascended to my *F*
  20:21 as my *F* hath sent me, even so send I you
Acts 1:4 but wait for the promise of the *F*
  2:33 received of the *F* the promise of the Holy
  24:14 call heresy, so worship I the God of my *f*
Rom. 4:11 might be the *f* of all them that believe
  8:15 Spirit of adoption, whereby we cry, Abba, *F*
  11:28 they are beloved for the *f*' sakes
1 Cor. 4:15 yet have ye not many *f*: for in Christ
  8:6 but to us there is but one God, the *F*
2 Cor. 1:3 *F* of mercies . . the God of all comfort
  6:18 be a *F* unto you, and ye shall be my sons
Gal. 1:14 zealous of the traditions of my *f*
  4:2 governors until the time appointed of the *f*
  4:6 of his Son into your hearts, crying, Abba, *F*
Eph. 2:18 have access by one Spirit unto the *F*
  4:6 one God and *F* of all, who is above all
  6:4 (Col. 3:21) ye *f*, provoke not your children
Phil. 2:11 is Lord, to the glory of God the *F*
  2:22 as a son with the *f*, he hath served with me
1 Thes. 2:11 charged . . you . . as a *f* doth his children
1 Tim. 5:1 rebuke not an elder . . entreat him as a *f*
Heb. 7:3 without *f*, without mother, without descent
  12:7 what son is he whom the *f* chasteneth not?
  12:9 had *f* of our flesh which corrected us
Jas. 1:17 and cometh down from the *F* of lights
1 Pet. 1:17 *F*, who without respect of persons
  1:18 received by tradition from your *f*
2 Pet. 3:4 for since the *f* fell asleep, all things
1 Jn. 1:2 with the *F*, and was manifested unto us
  1:3 and truly our fellowship is with the *F*
  2:1 any man sin, we have an advocate with the *F*
  2:13 (2:14) I write unto you, *f*, because ye have
  2:15 the world, the love of the *F* is not in him
  2:23 denieth the Son, the same hath not the *F*
  3:1 what manner of love the *F* hath bestowed upon
  4:14 that the *F* sent the Son to be the Saviour
  5:7 bear record . . *F*, the Word . . the Holy Ghost
2 Jn. 9 he hath both the *F* and the Son
Rev. 3:5 but I will confess his name before my *F*

Fatherless

Ex. 22:22 shall not afflict any widow, or *f* child
Deut. 10:18 he doth execute the judgment of the *f*
  14:29 and the *f*, and the widow . . within thy gates
  24:17 shalt not pervert the judgment . . of the *f*
Job 6:27 yea, ye overwhelm the *f*, and ye dig a pit
  22:9 and the arms of the *f* have been broken
  24:9 they pluck the *f* from the breast, and take
  29:12 I delivered the poor that cried, and the *f*
  31:17 and the *f* hath not eaten thereof
  31:21 if I have lifted up my hand against the *f*
Ps. 10:14 unto thee; thou art the helper of the *f*
  10:18 to judge the *f* and the oppressed
  68:5 father of the *f*, and a judge of the widows
  82:3 defend the poor and *f*: do justice to the
  94:6 they slay the widow . . and murder the *f*
  109:9 his children be *f*, and his wife a widow
  146:9 he relieveth the *f* and widow
Prov. 23:10 enter not into the fields of the *f*
Is. 1:17 judge the *f*, plead for the widow
  1:23 princes are rebellious . . judge not the *f*
  10:2 be their prey, and that they may rob the *f*!
Jer. 5:28 they judge not . . the cause of the *f*
  7:6 if ye oppress not the stranger, the *f*
  22:3 do no violence to the stranger, the *f*, nor
  49:11 leave thy *f* children, I will preserve them

Ezek. 22:7 in thee have they vexed the *f*
Hos. 14:3 for in thee the *f* findeth mercy
Zech. 7:10 and oppress not the widow, nor the *f*
Mal. 3:5 those that oppress. . the widow, and the *f*
Jas. 1:27 pure religion. . to visit the *f* and widows

Fatling

2 Sam. 6:13 six paces, he sacrificed oxen and *f*
Ps. 66:15 offer unto thee burnt sacrifices of *f*
Is. 11:6 and the young lion and the *f* together
Mt. 22:4 my *f* are killed. . come unto the marriage

Fatness

Gen. 27:28 dew of heaven, and the *f* of the earth
27:39 thy dwelling shall be the *f* of the earth
Deut. 32:15 covered with *f*; then he forsook God
Judg. 9:9 the olive tree said. . Should I leave my *f*
Ps. 36:8 satisfied with the *f* of thy house
63:5 shall be satisfied as with marrow and *f*
65:11 with thy goodness; and thy paths drop *f*
73:7 their eyes stand out with *f*: they have more
Is. 55:2 and let your soul delight itself in *f*
Rom. 11:17 partakest of the. . *f* of the olive tree

Fault

Gen. 41:9 chief butler. . saying, I do remember my *f*
Ex. 5:16 beaten; but the *f* is in thine own people
Deut. 25:2 wicked. . be beaten. . according to his *f*
1 Sam. 29:3 Achish said. . I have found no *f* in him
2 Sam. 3:8 chargest me. . a *f* concerning this woman?
Ps. 19:12 cleanse thou me from secret *f*
Dan. 6:4 but they could find none occasion nor *f*
Mt. 18:15 and tell him his *f* between thee and him
Mk. 7:2 eat. . with unwashen hands, they found *f*
Lk. 23:4 (Jn. 18:38) I find no *f* in this man
Jn. 19:4 that ye may know that I find no *f* in him
Rom. 9:19 say then unto me, Why doth he yet find *f*?
1 Cor. 6:7 a *f* among you, because ye go to law
Gal. 6:1 brethren, if a man be overtaken in a *f*
Heb. 8:8 for finding *f* with them, he saith, Behold
Jas. 5:16 confess your *f* one to another, and pray
1 Pet. 2:20 if, when ye be buffeted for your *f*
Rev. 14:5 they are without *f* before the throne

Faultless *See also* Blameless

Heb. 8:7 for if that first covenant had been *f*
Jude 24 present you *f* before the presence of

Faulty

2 Sam. 14:13 king doth speak. . as one which is *f*
Hos. 10:2 their heart is divided. . they be found *f*

Favor *See also* Grace

Gen. 18:3 Lord, if now I have found *f* in thy sight
39:21 LORD was with Joseph. . and gave him *f* in
Ex. 3:21 people *f* in the sight of the Egyptians
Num. 11:11 have I not found *f* in thy sight
Deut. 33:23 he said, O Naphtali, satisfied with *f*
Ruth 2:13 she said, Let me find *f* in thy sight
1 Sam. 2:26 Samuel. . was in *f* both with the LORD
16:22 let David. . for he hath found *f* in my sight
29:6 upright. . nevertheless the lords *f* thee not
2 Sam. 15:25 shall find *f* in the eyes of the LORD
Esth. 2:15 Esther obtained *f* in the sight of all
5:2 king saw Esther. . she obtained *f* in his sight
Job 10:12 thou hast granted me life and *f*
Ps. 5:12 righteous; with *f* wilt thou compass him
30:5 his anger. . but a moment; in his *f* is life
41:11 by this I know that thou *f* me, because
44:3 save them. . because thou hadst a *f* unto them
45:12 rich among the people shall entreat thy *f*
89:17 and in thy *f* our horn shall be exalted
102:13 upon Zion: for the time to *f* her. . is come

Ps. 106:4 remember me, O LORD, with the *f* that thou
112:5 a good man showeth *f*, and lendeth
Prov. 3:4 shalt thou find *f*. . in the sight of God
8:35 whoso findeth me. . shall obtain *f* of the LORD
11:27 that diligently seeketh good procureth *f*
12:2 a good man obtaineth *f* of the LORD: but
13:15 good understanding giveth *f*
14:9 but among the righteous there is *f*
14:35 the king's *f* is toward a wise servant
16:15 his *f* is as a cloud of the latter rain
18:22 findeth a wife. . obtaineth *f* of the LORD
19:6 many will entreat the *f* of the prince
19:12 but his *f* is as dew upon the grass
21:10 his neighbor findeth no *f* in his eyes
22:1 and loving *f* rather than silver and gold
31:30 *f* is deceitful, and beauty is vain
Eccl. 9:11 nor yet *f* to men of skill; but time and
Song 8:10 was I in his eyes as one that found *f*
Is. 26:10 let *f* be showed to the wicked, yet will
60:10 but in my *f* have I had mercy on thee
Jer. 16:13 I cast you. . where I will not show you *f*
Dan. 1:9 now God had brought Daniel into *f*
2:52 and Jesus increased. . in *f* with God and man
Acts 2:47 praising God, and having *f* with all
7:10 and wisdom in the sight of Pharaoh
7:46 who found *f* before God, and desired to find

Favorable

Judg. 21:22 be *f* unto them for our sakes: because
Job 33:26 pray unto God, and he will be *f* unto him
Ps. 77:7 Lord cast off for ever? and. . be *f* no more
85:1 LORD, thou hast been *f* unto thy land

Fear *See also* Afraid, Dread, Honor, Obey, Quake, Respect, Reverence, Tremble, Trembling, Worship

Gen. 9:2 the *f* of you. . shall be upon every beast
15:1 saying, *F* not, Abram: I am thy shield
20:11 surely the *f* of God is not in this place
22:12 for now I know that thou *f* God, seeing
26:24 *f* not, for I am with thee, and will bless
42:18 this do, and live; for I *f* God
Ex. 1:21 because the midwives *f* God, that he made
9:20 he that *f* the word of the LORD among the
9:30 I know that ye will not yet *f* the LORD God
14:13 and Moses said unto the people, *F* ye not
14:31 and the people *f* the LORD, and believed
15:16 *f* and dread shall fall upon them ·
18:21 shalt provide. . able men, such as *f* God
Lev. 19:14 but shalt *f* thy God: I am the LORD
Num. 14:9 and the LORD is with us: *f* them not
Deut. 1:21 *f* not, neither be discouraged
2:25 to put. . the *f* of thee upon the nations
4:10 hear my words, that they may learn to *f* me
5:29 oh that. . they would *f* me, and keep all my
6:2 thou mightest *f* the LORD thy God, to keep
6:13 thou shalt *f* the LORD thy God, and serve him
10:12 God require of thee, but to *f* the LORD
13:11 (21:21) all Israel shall hear, and *f*
25:18 wast faint and weary; and he *f* not God
28:58 mayest *f* this glorious and fearful name
28:66 and thou shalt *f* day and night, and shalt
Josh. 8:1 Joshua, *F* not, neither be thou dismayed
24:14 now therefore *f* the LORD, and serve him
Judg. 6:10 *f* not the gods of the Amorites
1 Sam. 12:14 if ye will *f* the LORD, and serve him
15:24 I *f* the people, and obeyed their voice
1 Kgs. 18:12 thy servant *f* the LORD from my youth
2 Kgs. 17:28 taught. . how they should *f* the LORD
17:33 they *f* the LORD, and served their own gods
17:38 not forget; neither shall ye *f* other gods

1 Chr. 16:25 (Ps. 96:4) is to be *f* above all gods
16:30 (Ps. 96:9) *f* before him, all the earth
Neh. 5:9 ought ye not to walk in the *f* of our God
Job 1:1 and one that *f* God, and eschewed evil
1:9 Satan answered . . Doth Job *f* God for nought?
4:6 is not this thy *f*, thy confidence, thy hope
11:15 thou shalt be steadfast, and shalt not *f*
28:28 behold, the *f* of the Lord, that is wisdom
39:22 he mocketh at *f*, and is not affrighted
Ps. 2:11 serve the Lord with *f*, and rejoice with
5:7 in thy *f* will I worship toward thy holy temple
14:5 (53:5) there were they in great *f*
15:4 but he honoreth them that *f* the Lord
19:9 *f* of the Lord is clean, enduring for ever
23:4 I will *f* no evil: for thou art with me
25:12 what man is he that *f* the Lord? him shall
25:14 secret of the Lord is with them that *f* him
27:1 my light and my salvation; whom shall I *f*?
27:3 encamp against me, my heart shall not *f*
31:19 thy goodness . . laid up for them that *f* thee
33:8 let all the earth *f* the Lord
33:18 eye of the Lord is upon them that *f* him
34:7 angel of the Lord . . about them that *f* him
34:9 O *f* the Lord, ye his saints: for there is
34:11 I will teach you the *f* of the Lord
36:1 (Rom. 3:18) no *f* of God before his eyes
46:2 will not we *f*, though the earth be removed
52:6 the righteous also shall see, and *f*
56:4 I will not *f* what flesh can do unto me
60:4 hast given a banner to them that *f* thee
61:5 the heritage of those that *f* thy name
66:16 come and hear, all ye that *f* God
72:5 they shall *f* thee as long as the sun and
76:7 thou, even thou, art to be *f*: and who may
85:9 surely his salvation is nigh them that *f* him
86:11 in thy truth: unite my heart to *f* thy name
89:7 God is greatly to be *f* in the assembly
90:11 even according to thy *f*, so is thy wrath
103:11 is his mercy toward them that *f* him
103:13 so the Lord pitieth them that *f* him
111:5 he hath given meat unto them that *f* him
111:10 (Prov. 9:10) *f* of the Lord is the beginning
112:1 blessed is the man that *f* the Lord
115:11 ye that *f* the Lord, trust in the Lord
118:4 let them now that *f* the Lord say, that his
118:6 (Heb. 13:6) Lord is on my side; I will not *f*
119:74 they that *f* thee will be glad when they
128:1 blessed is every one that *f* the Lord
130:4 forgiveness with thee, that thou mayest be *f*
145:19 will fulfil the desire of them that *f* him
147:11 Lord taketh pleasure in them that *f* him
Prov. 1:7 (9:10) *f* of the Lord is the beginning
1:26 I will mock when your *f* cometh
3:7 *f* the Lord, and depart from evil
3:25 be not afraid of sudden *f* . . when it cometh
8:13 the *f* of the Lord is to hate evil
10:27 the *f* of the Lord prolongeth days
14:16 a wise man *f*, and departeth from evil
14:26 in the *f* of the Lord is strong confidence
14:27 the *f* of the Lord is a fountain of life
15:16 better is little with the *f* of the Lord
15:33 *f* of the Lord is the instruction of wisdom
19:23 the *f* of the Lord tendeth to life
23:17 be thou in the *f* of the Lord all the day long
24:21 my son, *f* thou the Lord and the king
29:25 the *f* of man bringeth a snare
31:30 woman-that *f* the Lord, she shall be praised

Eccl. 3:14 God doeth it, that men should *f* before him
5:7 are also divers vanities: but *f* thou God
7:18 he that *f* God shall come forth of them all
8:12 that it shall be well with them that *f* God
12:13 *f* God, and keep his commandments: for this
Is. 2:19 and into the caves . . for *f* of the Lord

Is. 7:4 be quiet; *f* not, neither be faint-hearted
8:12 neither *f* ye their *f*, nor be afraid
8:13 let him be your *f*, and let him be your dread
11:2 of knowledge and of the *f* of the Lord
14:3 the Lord shall give thee rest . . from thy *f*
24:17 *f*, and the pit, and the snare, are upon thee
29:13 their *f* toward me is taught by the precept
35:4 be strong, *f* not: behold, your God will
41:10 *f* thou not; for I am with thee: be not
41:14 *f* not, thou worm Jacob . . I will help thee
43:1 O Israel, *F* not: for I have redeemed thee
43:5 *F* not; for I am with thee: I will bring thy
50:10 who is among you that *f* the Lord
51:7 *f* ye not the reproach of men, neither be
59:19 so shall they *f* the name of the Lord
Jer. 5:22 *f* ye not me? saith the Lord: will ye not
5:24 neither say they . . Let us now *f* the Lord
10:7 who would not *f* thee, O King of nations?
23:4 and they shall *f* no more, nor be dismayed
30:5 we have heard a voice of trembling, of *f*
32:40 but I will put my *f* in their hearts
33:9 shall *f* and tremble for all the goodness
48:44 he that fleeth from the *f* shall fall
Ezek. 3:9 *f* them not, neither be dismayed
Dan. 6:26 tremble and *f* before the God of Daniel
Hos. 3:5 shall *f* the Lord and his goodness in the
Joel 2:21 *f* not, O land; be glad and rejoice
Jon. 1:9 I am a Hebrew; and I *f* the Lord, the God
Zeph. 3:7 I said, Surely, thou wilt *f* me
Hag. 1:12 and the people did *f* before the Lord
Zech. 8:13 *f* not, but let your hands be strong
Mal. 1:6 if I be a master, where is my *f*?
3:16 that *f* the Lord spake often one to another
4:2 but unto you that *f* my name shall the Sun
Mt. 1:20 *f* not to take unto thee Mary thy wife
10:28 (Lk. 12:5) *f* him which is able to destroy
10:31 (Lk. 12:7) *f* ye not . . ye are of more value
14:5 have put him to death, he *f* the multitude
14:26 it is a spirit; and they cried out for *f*
21:26 (Mk. 11:32) say, Of men; we *f* the people
27:54 *f* greatly, saying, Truly this was the Son
28:4 and for *f* of him the keepers did shake
28:5 *f* not ye: for I know that ye seek Jesus
Mk. 4:41 *f* exceedingly and said . . what manner
5:33 but the woman *f* and trembling, knowing what
6:20 Herod *f* John, knowing that he was a just
11:18 how they might destroy him: for they *f* him
Lk. 1:30 *f* not, Mary: for thou hast found favor
1:50 and his mercy is on them that *f* him
2:10 angel said unto them, *F* not: for, behold
7:16 came a *f* on all: and they glorified God
8:50 *f* not: believe only, and she shall be
9:34 and they *f* as they entered into the cloud
12:32 *f* not, little flock; for it is your Father's
18:2 was in a city a judge, which *f* not God
19:21 I *f* thee, because thou art an austere man
21:26 men's hearts failing them for *f*, and for
23:40 rebuked him, saying, Dost not thou *f* God
Jn. 7:13 spake openly of him for *f* of the Jews
12:15 *f* not, daughter of Sion: behold, thy King
19:38 but secretly for *f* of the Jews, besought
20:19 the doors were shut . . for *f* of the Jews
Acts 2:43 *f* came upon every soul: and many wonders
5:11 and great *f* came upon all the church
9:31 were edified . . walking in the *f* of the Lord
10:22 Cornelius . . a just man, and one that *f* God
10:35 in every nation he that *f* him . . is accepted
13:16 Israel, and ye that *f* God, give audience
27:24 *f* not, Paul; thou must be brought before
Rom. 8:15 received the spirit of bondage again to *f*
11:20 be not high-minded, but *f*
13:7 render . . to all their dues . . *f* to whom *f*
1 Cor. 2:3 I was with you in weakness, and in *f*

2 Cor. 7:1 perfecting holiness in the *f* of God
  7:5 without were fightings, within were *f*
  7:11 yea, what indignation, yea, what *f*
  12:20 for I *f*, lest, when I come, I shall not
Eph. 5:21 submitting yourselves . . in the *f* of God
  6:5 servants, be obedient . . with *f* and trembling
Phil. 1:14 more bold to speak the word without *f*
  2:12 work out your own salvation with *f* and
Col. 3:22 but in singleness of heart, *f* God
1 Tim. 5:20 that sin rebuke . . that others also may *f*
2 Tim. 1:7 God hath not given us the spirit of *f*
Heb. 2:15 and deliver them, who through *f* of death
  4:1 let us therefore *f*, lest, a promise being
  5:7 offered up prayers . . was heard in that he *f*
  11:7 Noah . . moved with *f*, prepared an ark
  12:21 Moses said, I exceedingly *f* and quake
  12:28 serve God . . with reverence and godly *f*
1 Pet. 1:17 the time of your sojourning here in *f*
  2:17 love the brotherhood. *F* God. Honor the king
  3:2 your chaste conversation coupled with *f*
  3:15 hope that is in you, with meekness and *f*
1 Jn. 4:18 no *f* in love . . perfect love casteth out *f*
Jude 12 they feast . . feeding themselves without *f*
  23 and others save with *f*, pulling them out
Rev. 1:17 *f* not; I am the first and the last
  2:10 *f* none of those things . . thou shalt suffer
  11:18 to the saints, and them that *f* thy name
  14:7 a loud voice, *F* God, and give glory to him
  15:4 who shall not *f* thee, O Lord, and glorify
  19:5 all ye his servants, and ye that *f* him

Fearful *See also* Horrible, Terrible

Ex. 15:11 like thee . . *f* in praises, doing wonders?
Deut. 20:8 that is *f* and faint-hearted? let him go
  28:58 glorious and *f* name, THE LORD THY GOD
Judg. 7:3 whosoever is *f* and afraid, let him return
Is. 35:4 say to them that are of a *f* heart
Mt. 8:26 (Mk. 4:40) why are ye *f*, O ye of little faith?
Lk. 21:11 *f* sights and great signs shall there be
Heb. 10:27 but a certain *f* looking for of judgment
  10:31 a *f* thing to fall into the hands of . . God
Rev. 21:8 but the *f*. . have their part in the lake

Fearfully

Ps. 139:14 for I am *f* and wonderfully made

Fearfulness

Ps. 55:5 *f* and trembling are come upon me
Is. 21:4 my heart panted, *f* affrighted me
  33:14 *f* hath surprised the hypocrites

Feast

Gen. 19:3 he pressed upon them . . he made them a *f*
Ex. 5:1 people go, that they may hold a *f* unto me
  10:9 for we must hold a *f* unto the LORD
  12:14 and ye shall keep it a *f* to the LORD
  12:17 (23:15; 34:18) observe the *f* of unleavened
  23:14 three times thou shalt keep a *f* unto me
  23:16 (34:22) *f* of harvest . . and the *f* of ingathering
  32:5 proclamation . . Tomorrow is a *f* to the LORD
  34:22 (Deut. 16:10) shalt observe the *f* of weeks
Lev. 23:34 (Deut. 16:13) *f* of tabernacles that ye
Num. 29:39 shall do unto the LORD in your set *f*
Judg. 14:10 and Samson made there a *f*
1 Kgs. 8:65 (2 Chr. 7:8) at that time Solomon held a *f*
2 Chr. 2:4 on the solemn *f* of the LORD our God
Ezra 3:5 offering . . of all the set *f* of the LORD
Esth. 1:3 he made a *f* unto all his princes and
Ps. 35:16 with hypocritical mockers in *f*
Prov. 15:15 is of a merry heart hath a continual *f*
Is. 1:14 your appointed *f* my soul hateth
  25:6 make unto all people a *f* of fat things
Ezek. 45:21 have the passover, a *f* of seven days
  46:9 shall come before the Lord in the solemn *f*

Dan. 5:1 Belshazzar the king made a great *f*
Hos. 2:11 cause all her mirth to cease, her *f* days
  9:5 will ye do . . in the day of the *f* of the LORD?
  12:9 tabernacles, as in the days of the solemn *f*
Amos 5:21 I hate, I despise your *f* days
  8:10 I will turn your *f* into mourning
Nah. 1:15 keep thy solemn *f*, perform thy vows
Zech. 8:19 Judah joy and gladness, and cheerful *f*
Mt. 23:6 (Mk. 12:39; Lk. 20:46) uppermost rooms at *f*
  26:2 (Mk. 14:1; Lk. 22:1) is the *f* of the passover
  27:15 (Mk. 15:6) at that *f* the governor . . release
Lk. 5:29 Levi made him a great *f* in his own house
  14:13 but when thou makest a *f*, call the poor
Jn. 2:8 and bear unto the governor of the *f*
  5:1 there was a *f* of the Jews; and Jesus went up
  7:2 now the Jews' *f* of tabernacles was at hand
  7:37 in the last day, that great day of the *f*
  10:22 was at Jerusalem the *f* of the dedication
1 Cor. 5:8 let us keep the *f*, not with old leaven
  10:27 of them that believe not bid you to a *f*
2 Pet. 2:13 own deceivings while they *f* with you
Jude 12 spots in your *f* of charity, when they *f*

Feasting

Esth. 9:17 and made it a day of *f* and gladness
Eccl. 7:2 mourning, than to go to the house of *f*

Feather

Job 39:13 gavest . . wings and *f* unto the ostrich?
Ps. 68:13 wings of a dove . . her *f* with yellow gold
  91:4 cover thee with his *f*, and under his wings
Ezek. 17:3 great eagle with great wings . . full of *f*
Dan. 4:33 till his hairs were grown like eagles' *f*

Fed *See* Feed

Feeble *See also* Weak

Gen. 30:42 the cattle were *f*, he put them not in
1 Sam. 2:5 she that hath many children is waxed *f*
Neh. 4:2 what do these *f* Jews? will they fortify
Job 4:4 and thou hast strengthened the *f* knees
Ps. 38:8 I am *f* and sore broken: I have roared
  105:37 was not one *f* person among their tribes
Prov. 30:26 conies are but a *f* folk, yet make they
Is. 16:14 the remnant shall be very small and *f*
  35:3 (Heb. 12:12) hands, and confirm the *f* knees
Jer. 6:24 heard the fame thereof: our hands wax *f*
Ezek. 7:17 all hands shall be *f*, and all knees
  21:7 heart shall melt, and all hands shall be *f*
Zech. 12:8 and he that is *f*. . shall be as David
1 Cor. 12:22 seem to be more *f*, are necessary

Feeble-minded

1 Thes. 5:14 comfort the *f-m*, support the weak

Feed (Fed)

Gen. 25:30 Esau said to Jacob, *F* me, I pray thee
  30:36 and Jacob *f* the rest of Laban's flocks
  37:12 went to *f* their father's flock in Shechem
  37:16 my brethren . . where they *f* their flocks
  41:2 seven well-favored kine . . *f* in a meadow
  46:32 for their trade hath been to *f* cattle
  48:15 the God which *f* me all my life long
Ex. 16:32 I have *f* you in the wilderness, when I
Deut. 8:3 (8:16) and *f* thee with manna
2 Sam. 5:2 (1 Chr. 11:2) shalt *f* my people Israel
  7:7 (1 Chr. 17:6) I commanded to *f* my people
  19:33 I will *f* thee with me in Jerusalem
1 Kgs. 17:4 I have commanded the ravens to *f* thee
  22:27 (2 Chr. 18:26) *f* him with bread of affliction
Ps. 28:9 bless thine inheritance: *f* them also
  37:3 trust in the LORD . . verily thou shalt be *f*
  49:14 laid in the grave; death shall *f* on them

Ps. 78:72 so he *f* them according to the integrity of
81:16 he should have *f* them also with the finest
Prov. 10:21 the lips of the righteous *f* many
15:14 but the mouth of fools *f* on foolishness
30:8 *f* me with food convenient for me
Song 1:7 O thou whom my soul loveth, where thou *f*
2:16 (6:3) beloved in mine. . he *f* among the liles
Is. 5:17 then shall the lambs *f* after their manner
11:7 the cow and the bear shall *f*
27:10 like a wilderness: there shall the calf *f*
30:23 shall thy cattle *f* in large pastures
40:11 he shall *f* his flock like a shepherd
44:20 he *f* on ashes: a deceived heart hath
49:9 shall *f* in the ways, and their pastures
58:14 and *f* thee with the heritage of Jacob
61:5 and strangers shall stand and *f* your flocks
65:25 the wolf and the lamb shall *f* together
Jer. 3:15 pastors. . shall *f* you with knowledge
5:7 when I had *f* them to the full, they then
6:3 they shall *f* every one in his place
23:2 against the pastors that *f* my people
23:4 shepherds over them which shall *f* them
50:19 and he shall *f* on Carmel and Bashan
Lam. 4:5 they that did *f* delicately are desolate
Ezek. 34:2 should not the shepherds *f* the flocks?
34:8 shepherds *f* themselves, and *f* not my flock
34:16 I will *f* them with judgment
Dan. 5:21 they *f* him with grass like oxen
Hos. 12:1 Ephraim *f* on wind, and followeth after
Mic. 5:4 stand and *f* in the strength of the LORD
Zeph. 2:7 house of Judah; they shall *f* thereupon
Zech. 11:4 my God; *F* the flock of the slaughter
11:7 and I will *f* the flock of slaughter
11:9 said I, I will not *f* you: that that dieth
Mt. 6:26 (Lk. 12:24) yet your heavenly Father *f* them
8:30 (Mk. 5:11; Lk. 8:32) a herd of many swine *f*
25:37 when saw we thee ahungered, and *f* thee?
Lk. 15:15 sent him into his fields to *f* swine
16:21 desiring to be *f* with the crumbs which
Jn. 21:15 he saith unto him, *F* my lambs
Acts 20:28 you overseers, to *f* the church of God
Rom. 12:20 therefore if thine enemy hunger, *f* him
1 Cor. 3:2 I have *f* you with milk. . not with meat
13:3 though I bestow all my goods to *f* the poor
1 Pet. 5:2 *f* the flock of God which is among you
Jude 12 feast with you, *f* themselves without fear
Rev. 7:17 the Lamb. . shall *f* them, and shall lead
12:6 prepared of God, that they should *f* her

Feel (Felt)

Gen. 27:12 my father peradventure will *f* me
Judg. 16:26 suffer me that I may *f* the pillars
Job 20:20 he shall not *f* quietness in his belly
Eccl. 8:5 whoso keepeth. . shall *f* no evil thing
Acts 17:27 Lord, if haply they might *f* after him
28:5 and he shook off the beast. . and *f* no harm

Feeling

Eph. 4:19 who being past *f* have given themselves
Heb. 4:15 be touched with the *f* of our infirmities

Feet *See also* FOOT

Gen. 49:10 nor a lawgiver from between his *f*
Ex. 3:5 (Acts 7:33) put off thy shoes from off thy *f*
Deut. 2:28 only I will pass through on my *f*
Josh. 3:15 *f* of the priests that bare the ark were
10:24 put your *f* upon the necks of these kings
14:9 the land whereon thy *f* have trodden shall
Ruth 3:4 thou shalt go in, and uncover his *f*
3:14 and she lay at his *f* until the morning
1 Sam. 2:9 he will keep the *f* of his saints
2 Sam. 4:4 (9:3) Jonathan. . had a son. . lame of his *f*
22:34 (Ps. 18:33) maketh my *f* like hinds' *f*

2 Sam. 22:37 (Ps. 18:36) that my *f* did not slip
2 Kgs. 6:32 sound of his master's *f* behind him?
9:35 no more of her than the skull, and the *f*
13:21 he revived, and stood up on his *f*
Neh. 9:21 waxed not old, and their *f* swelled not
Job 12:5 he that is ready to slip with his *f* is as
29:15 eyes to the blind, and *f* was I to the lame
Ps. 8:6 (1 Cor. 15:27; Heb. 2:8) all things under his *f*
22:16 they pierced my hands and my *f*
25:15 for he shall pluck my *f* out of the net
31:8 thou hast set my *f* in a large room
40:2 set my *f* upon a rock, and established
56:13 wilt not thou deliver my *f* from falling
66:9 and suffereth not our *f* to be moved
73:2 as for me, my *f* were almost gone
105:18 whose *f* they hurt with fetters
115:7 *f* have they, but they walk not
116:8 for thou hast delivered. . my *f* from falling
119:59 and turned my *f* unto thy testimonies
119:101 I have refrained my *f* from every evil
119:105 thy word is a lamp unto my *f*. . a light
122:2 our *f* shall stand within thy gates
Prov. 1:16 for their *f* run to evil, and make haste
4:26 ponder the path of thy *f*, and let all thy
5:5 her *f* go down to death; her steps take hold
6:13 he speaketh with his *f*, he teacheth with
6:18 *f* that be swift in running to mischief
6:28 upon hot coals, and his *f* not be burned?
7:11 and stubborn; her *f* abide not in her house
19:2 and he that hasteth with his *f* sinneth
29:5 that flattereth. . spreadeth a net for his *f*
Song 5:3 I have washed my *f*; how shall I defile
7:1 how beautiful are thy *f* with shoes
Is. 3:16 and making a tinkling with their *f*
6:2 and with twain he covered his *f*
23:7 own *f* shall carry her afar off to sojourn
26:6 *f* of the poor, and the steps of the needy
28:3 the drunkards of Ephraim. . trodden under *f*
49:23 bow down. . and lick up the dust of thy *f*
52:7 (Rom. 10:15) how beautiful. . are the *f* of him
59:7 *f* run to evil, and they make haste to shed
60:13 I will make the place of my *f* glorious
Jer. 13:16 your *f* stumble upon the dark mountains
Lam. 3:34 to crush under his *f* all the prisoners
Ezek. 2:1 Son of man, stand upon thy *f*, and I will
2:2 (3:24) spirit entered into me. . set me upon my *f*
24:17 put on thy shoes upon thy *f*, and cover not
25:6 stamped with the *f*, and rejoiced in heart
32:2 troubledst the waters with thy *f*
34:18 ye must foul the residue with your *f*?
Dan. 2:33 (2:41) his *f* part of iron and part of clay
10:6 his *f* like in color to polished brass
Nah. 1:3 and the clouds are the dust of his *f*
1:15 *f* of him that bringeth good tidings
Hab. 3:19 and he will make my *f* like hinds' *f*
Zech. 14:4 and his *f* shall stand in that day upon
Mt. 7:6 lest they trample them under their *f*
10:14 (Mk. 6:11; Lk. 9:5) shake off. . dust of your *f*
15:30 down at Jesus' *f*; and he healed them
18:8 (Mk. 9:45) or two *f* to be cast into. . fire
18:29 and his fellow servant fell down at his *f*
28:9 held him by the *f*, and worshipped him
Lk. 1:79 to guide our *f* into the way of peace
7:38 (Jn. 12:3) wash his *f* with tears, and did wipe
8:35 sitting at the *f* of Jesus, clothed, and in
10:39 Mary. . sat at Jesus' *f*, and heard his word
15:22 put a ring on his hand, and shoes on his *f*
24:39 behold my hands and my *f*, that it is I
Jn. 11:2 (12:3) Mary which. . wiped his *f* with her hair
13:5 began to wash the disciples' *f*
13:9 Lord, not my *f* only, but also my hands
13:10 is washed needeth not save to wash his *f*
20:12 one at the head, and the other at the *f*

Acts 3:7 his *f* and ankle bones received strength
4:35 and laid them down at the apostles' *f*
5:2 certain part, and laid it at the apostles' *f*
5:9 the *f* of them which have buried this husband
7:58 clothes at a young man's *f*, whose name was
13:51 they shook off the dust of their *f* against
14:8 a certain man at Lystra, impotent in his *f*
21:11 girdle, and bound his own hands and *f*
22:3 yet brought up. . at the *f* of Gamaliel
Rom. 3:15 their *f* are swift to shed blood
16:20 shall bruise Satan under your *f* shortly
1 Cor. 12:21 head to the *f*, I have no need of you
15:25 till he hath put all enemies under his *f*
Eph. 6:15 and your *f* shod with the preparation of
1 Tim. 5:10 if she have washed the saints' *f*
Heb. 12:13 make straight paths for your *f*
Rev. 1:15 (2:18) his *f* like unto fine brass
1:17 when I saw him, I fell at his *f* as dead
3:9 make them to come and worship before thy *f*
13:2 the beast. . his *f* were as the *f* of a bear
19:10 I fell at his *f* to worship him

Feign

1 Sam. 21:13 *f* himself mad in their hands
2 Sam. 14:2 I pray thee, *f* thyself to be a mourner
1 Kgs. 14:6 thou wife of Jeroboam; why *f* thou
Neh. 6:8 but thou *f* them out of thine own heart
Ps. 17:1 my prayer, that goeth not out of *f* lips
Lk. 20:20 sent forth spies. . *f* themselves just men
2 Pet. 2:3 they with *f* words make merchandise of

Feignedly

Jer. 3:10 not turned. . with her whole heart, but *f*

Felix the governor Acts 23:24–24:27; 25:14

Fell *See* Fall

Fellow

Gen. 19:9 this one *f* came in to sojourn, and he
Ex. 2:13 wherefore smitest thou thy *f*?
Judg. 7:22 set every man's sword against his *f*
1 Sam. 21:15 brought this *f* to play the madman
29:4 Philistines said. . Make this *f* return, that
2 Sam. 2:16 caught every one his *f* by the head
6:20 who uncovered himself. . as one of the vain *f*
1 Kgs. 22:27 (2 Chr. 18:26) put this *f* in the prison
2 Kgs. 9:11 wherefore came this mad *f* to thee?
Ps. 45:7 (Heb. 1:9) oil of gladness above thy *f*
Eccl. 4:10 they fall, the one will lift up his *f*
Dan. 2:13 they sought Daniel and his *f* to be slain
Zech. 13:7 O sword. . against the man that is my *f*
Mt. 11:16 in the markets, and calling unto their *f*
12:24 this *f* doth not cast out devils, but by
18:28 found one of his *f* servants, which owed
24:49 and shall begin to smite his *f* servants
26:61 *f* said, I am able to destroy the temple
26:71 (Lk. 22:59) this *f* was also with Jesus
Lk. 23:2 we found this *f* perverting the nation
Jn. 9:29 as for this *f*, we know not from whence
Acts 17:5 the Jews. . took unto them certain lewd *f*
18:13 this *f* persuadeth men to worship God
22:22 said, Away with such a *f* from the earth
24:5 for we have found this man a pestilent *f*
2 Cor. 8:23 Titus, he is my partner and *f* helper
Eph. 2:19 but *f* citizens with the saints
3:6 that the Gentiles should be *f* heirs
Phil. 4:3 Clement. . and with other my *f* laborers
Col. 4:11 are my *f* workers unto the kingdom of God
1 Thes. 3:2 Timotheus. . our *f* laborer in the gospel
Phlm. 2 Apphia, and Archippus our *f* soldier
24 Aristarchus, Demas, Lucas, my *f* laborers
3 Jn. 8 that we might be *f* helpers to the truth

Rev. 19:10 (22:9) do it not: I am thy *f* servant

Fellowship *See also* Friendship

Lev. 6:2 which was delivered him to keep, or in *f*
Ps. 94:20 the throne of iniquity have *f* with thee
Acts 2:42 in the apostles' doctrine and *f*
1 Cor. 1:9 ye were called unto the *f* of his Son
10:20 not that ye should have *f* with devils
2 Cor. 6:14 for what *f* hath righteousness with
8:4 the *f* of the ministering to the saints
Gal. 2:9 to me and Barnabas the right hands of *f*
Eph. 3:9 all men see what is the *f* of the mystery
5:11 no *f* with the unfruitful works of darkness
Phil. 1:5 for your *f* in the gospel from the first
2:1 if any *f* of the Spirit, if any bowels and
3:10 I may know him. . and the *f* of his sufferings
1 Jn. 1:3 may have *f* with us. . truly our *f* is with
1:6 if we say that we have *f* with him, and walk
1:7 in the light, we have *f* one with another

Female *See also* Woman

Gen. 1:27 (5:2) male and *f* created he them
6:19 (7:2, 9) two of every sort. . shall be male and *f*
7:16 went in male and *f* of all flesh
Lev. 3:1 male or *f*, he shall offer it without blemish
4:28 goats, a *f* without blemish, for his sin
27:4 if it be a *f*, then thy estimation shall be
Deut. 4:16 graven image. . the likeness of male or *f*
7:14 shall not be male or *f* barren among you
Mt. 19:4 (Mk. 10:6) beginning made them male and *f*
Gal. 3:28 neither male nor *f*. . all one in Christ

Fence

Num. 32:17 little ones shall dwell in the *f* cities
Deut. 3:5 all these cities were *f* with high walls
2 Sam. 23:7 shall touch them must be *f* with iron
Job 10:11 and hast *f* me with bones and sinews
19:8 he hath *f* up my way that I cannot pass
Ps. 62:3 bowing wall shall ye be. . as a tottering *f*
Is. 5:2 and he *f* it, and gathered out the stones

Ferryboat

2 Sam. 19:18 a *f* to carry over the king's household

Fervent

Acts 18:25 *f* in the spirit, he spake and taught
Rom. 12:11 *f* in spirit; serving the Lord
2 Cor. 7:7 your *f* mind toward me; so that I rejoiced
Jas. 5:16 effectual *f* prayer of a righteous man
1 Pet. 4:8 have *f* charity among yourselves
2 Pet. 3:10 (3:12) elements shall melt with *f* heat

Fervently

Col. 4:12 Epaphras. . laboring *f* for you in prayers
1 Pet. 1:22 love one another with a pure heart *f*

Festus Acts 24:27–26:32

Fetch

Gen. 18:7 Abraham ran. . *f* a calf tender and good
Num. 20:10 must we *f* you water out of this rock?
Deut. 24:10 not go into his house to *f* his pledge
1 Sam. 4:3 let us *f* the ark. . out of Shiloh unto us
Job 36:3 I will *f* my knowledge from afar
Is. 56:12 come ye, say they, I will *f* wine, and we
Acts 16:37 let them come themselves and *f* us out
28:13 we *f* a compass, and came to Rhegium

Fetter

Judg. 16:21 Philistines. . bound him with *f* of brass
Ps. 105:18 whose feet they hurt with *f*
149:8 to bind. . their nobles with *f* of iron
Mk. 5:4 (Lk. 8:29) often bound with *f* and chains

Fever

Deut. 28:22 the LORD shall smite thee . . with a *f*
Mt. 8:14 (Mk. 1:30; Lk. 4:38) mother . . sick of a *f*
Jn. 4:52 at the seventh hour the *f* left him
Acts 28:8 the father of Publius lay sick of a *f*

Few (Fewer, Fewest)

Gen. 24:55 let the damsel abide with us a *f* days
   29:20 they seemed unto him but a *f* days, for
   47:9 *f* and evil have the days of . . my life been
Deut. 7:7 for ye were the *f* of all people
1 Sam. 14:6 to the LORD to save by many or by *f*
2 Kgs. 4:3 even empty vessels; borrow not a *f*
1 Chr. 16:19 (Ps. 105:12) ye were but *f*, even a *f*
Neh. 7:4 city was . . great: but the people were *f*
Job 10:20 are not my days *f*? cease then, and let
   14:1 man that is born of a woman is of *f* days
   16:22 when a *f* years are come, then I shall go
Ps. 109:8 let his days be *f*; and let another take
Eccl. 5:2 upon earth: therefore let thy words be *f*
   12:3 and the grinders cease because they are *f*
Mt. 7:14 unto life, and *f* there be that find it
   9:37 (Lk. 10:2) plenteous, but the laborers are *f*
   15:34 (Mk. 8:7) seven, and a *f* little fishes
   20:16 (22:14) many be called, but *f* chosen
   25:21 (25:23) been faithful over a *f* things
Mk. 6:5 save that he laid his hands upon a *f* sick
Lk. 12:48 knew not . . shall be beaten with *f* stripes
   13:23 Lord, are there *f* that be saved?
Heb. 12:10 they verily for a *f* days chastened us
1 Pet. 3:20 ark . . wherein *f* . . were saved by water
Rev. 2:14 (2:20) I have a *f* things against thee
   3:4 thou hast a *f* names even in Sardis

Fidelity

Tit. 2:10 not purloining, but showing all good *f*

Field

Gen. 23:20 *f*, and the cave . . sure unto Abraham
   27:27 the smell of my son is as the smell of a *f*
   33:19 and he bought a parcel of a *f*, where he
Num. 20:17 (21:22) we will not pass through the *f*
Deut. 5:21 covet thy neighbor's house, his *f*
   21:1 if one be found slain . . lying in the *f*
Ruth 2:2 let me now go to the *f* and glean ears of corn
   2:9 thine eyes be on the *f* that they do reap
1 Sam. 22:7 son of Jesse give . . you *f* and vineyards
2 Sam. 14:31 have thy servants set my *f* on fire?
1 Chr. 16:32 (Ps. 96:12) let the *f* rejoice, and all
Prov. 24:30 I went by the *f* of the slothful
   31:16 she considereth a *f*, and buyeth it
Is. 5:8 woe unto them . . that lay *f* to *f*, till there
   32:15 and the wilderness be a fruitful *f*
Jer. 26:18 (Mic. 3:12) Zion shall be plowed like a *f*
   32:7 saying, Buy thee my *f* that is in Anathoth
Ezek. 17:5 and planted it in a fruitful *f*
   29:5 thou shalt fall upon the open *f*
Hab. 3:17 and the *f* shall yield no meat
Mt. 13:38 the *f* is the world; the good seed are
   13:44 kingdom . . is like unto treasure hid in a *f*
   24:18 (Mk. 13:16; Lk. 17:31) him which is in the *f*
   24:40 (Lk. 17:36) two be in the *f*; the one shall
   27:8 (Acts 1:19) that *f* was called, The *f* of blood
Lk. 2:8 same country shepherds abiding in the *f*
   15:25 his elder son was in the *f*: and as he came
Jn. 4:35 look on the *f*; for they are white already
Acts 1:18 this man purchased a *f* with the reward
Jas. 5:4 the laborers who have reaped down your *f*

Fierce (Fiercer)

Gen. 49:7 cursed be their anger, for it was *f*
Ex. 32:12 turn from thy *f* wrath, and repent
Deut. 28:50 a nation of *f* countenance, which shall

2 Sam. 19:43 words of . . Judah were *f* than . . Israel
Ezra 10:14 until the *f* wrath of our God for this
Job 10:16 thou huntest me as a *f* lion
Is. 19:4 Egyptians . . a *f* king shall rule over them
   33:19 thou shalt not see a *f* people, a people
Lam. 1:12 afflicted me in the day of his *f* anger
Dan. 8:23 a king of *f* countenance . . shall stand up
Mt. 8:28 coming out of the tombs, exceeding *f*
Lk. 23:5 were the more *f*, saying, He stirreth up
2 Tim. 3:3 *f*, despisers of those that are good
Jas. 3:4 ships . . great, and are driven of *f* winds

Fierceness

Deut. 13:17 LORD may turn from the *f* of his anger
2 Chr. 30:8 *f* of his wrath may turn away from you
Job 39:24 he swalloweth the ground with *f* and rage
Ps. 78:49 he cast upon them the *f* of his anger
   85:3 thou hast turned . . from the *f* of thine anger
Jer. 25:38 because of the *f* of the oppressor
Rev. 16:19 cup of the wine of the *f* of his wrath
   19:15 of the *f* and wrath of Almighty God

Fiery

Num. 21:6 LORD sent *f* serpents among the people
   21:8 LORD said unto Moses, Make thee a *f* serpent
Deut. 8:15 wilderness, wherein were *f* serpents
   33:2 from his right hand went a *f* law for them
Ps. 21:9 thou shalt make them as a *f* oven
Is. 14:29 his fruit shall be a *f* flying serpent
Dan. 3:6 (3:11, 15) midst of a burning *f* furnace
   7:9 his throne was like the *f* flame
   7:10 *f* stream issued and came forth from before
Eph. 6:16 to quench all the *f* darts of the wicked
Heb. 10:27 and *f* indignation, which shall devour
1 Pet. 4:12 concerning the *f* trial which is to try

Fig

Gen. 3:7 naked; and they sewed *f* leaves together
Deut. 8:8 a land of wheat . . and vines, and *f* trees
Judg. 9:10 trees said to the *f* tree . . reign over us
1 Sam. 30:12 they gave him a piece of a cake of *f*
1 Kgs. 4:25 safely, every man . . under his *f* tree
2 Kgs. 18:31 (Is. 36:16) eat . . every one of his *f* tree
   20:7 (Is. 38:21) Isaiah said, Take a lump of *f*
Prov. 27:18 whoso keepeth the *f* tree shall eat
Song 2:13 the *f* tree putteth forth her green *f*
Is. 34:4 and as a falling *f* from the *f* tree
Jer. 8:13 grapes on the vine, nor *f* on the *f* tree
   24:1 two baskets of *f* were set before the temple
Hos. 9:10 fathers as the first ripe in the *f* tree
Joel 1:7 laid my vine waste, and barked my *f* tree
Mic. 4:4 shall sit every man . . under his *f* tree
Nah. 3:12 thy strongholds shall be like *f* trees
Hab. 3:17 although the *f* tree shall not blossom
Mt. 7:16 (Lk. 6:44) grapes of thorns, or *f* of thistles?
   21:19 (Mk. 11:13) saw a *f* tree in the way
   24:32 (Mk. 13:28; Lk. 21:29) parable of the *f* tree
Lk. 13:6 certain man had a *f* tree planted
Jn. 1:48 thou wast under the *f* tree, I saw thee
Jas. 3:12 can the *f* tree . . bear olive berries?
Rev. 6:13 even as a *f* tree casteth her untimely *f*

Fight (Fought) *See also* Battle, Strife, War

Ex. 1:10 lest they multiply . . and *f* against us
   14:14 the LORD shall *f* for you, and ye shall
   17:8 then came Amalek, and *f* with Israel
Deut. 1:30 the LORD your God . . he shall *f* for you
   1:41 we will go up and *f*, according to all that
Josh. 10:14 (10:42) for the LORD *f* for Israel
   23:10 the LORD your God, he it is that *f* for you
1 Sam. 4:9 quit yourselves like men, and *f*
   8:20 our king may judge us . . and *f* our battles

1 Sam. 17:10 give me a man, that we may *f* together
25:28 because my lord *f* the battles of the LORD
1 Kgs. 12:24 (2 Chr. 11:4) nor *f* against your brethren
22:32 (2 Chr. 18:31) they turned aside to *f*
2 Kgs. 10:3 and *f* for your master's house
2 Chr. 13:12 *f* ye not against the LORD God
35:22 and came to *f* in the valley of Megiddo
Neh. 4:14 *f* for your brethren, your sons, and your
Ps. 35:1 *f* against them that *f* against me
109:3 and *f* against me without a cause
144:1 teacheth my hands to war. . my fingers to *f*
Is. 31:4 so shall the LORD. . *f* for mount Zion
Jer. 1:19 and they shall *f* against thee; but they
21:5 and I myself will *f* against you with
Zech. 10:5 they shall *f,* because the LORD is with
14:14 and Judah also shall *f* at Jerusalem
Jn. 18:36 of this world, then would my servants *f*
Acts 5:39 haply ye be found even to *f* against God
23:9 spoken to him, let us not *f* against God
1 Cor. 9:26 *f* I, not as one that beateth the air
15:32 I have *f* with beasts at Ephesus
1 Tim. 6:12 *f* the good *f* of faith, lay hold on
2 Tim. 4:7 I have *f* a good *f.* . finished my course
Heb. 10:32 ye endured a great *f* of afflictions
11:34 were made strong, waxed valiant in *f*
Jas. 4:2 ye *f* and war, yet ye have not, because ye
Rev. 2:16 repent; or else I. . will *f* against them
12:7 Michael and his angels *f* against the dragon

Fighting

2 Cor. 7:5 without were *f,* within were fears
Jas. 4:1 from whence come wars and *f* among you?

Figure

Deut. 4:16 graven image, the similitude of any *f*
1 Kgs. 6:29 carved *f* of cherubim and palm trees
Is. 44:13 and maketh it after the *f* of a man
Acts 7:43 *f* which ye made to worship them
Rom. 5:14 who is the *f* of him that was to come
1 Cor. 4:6 I have in a *f* transferred to myself
Heb. 9:9 which was a *f* for the time then present
9:24 holy places. . which are the *f* of the true
11:19 from whence also he received him in a *f*
1 Pet. 3:21 the like *f* whereunto even baptism doth

Fill

Gen. 1:22 *f* the waters in the seas, and let fowl
6:13 the earth is *f* with violence through them
42:25 then Joseph commanded to *f* their sacks
Ex. 40:34 the glory of the LORD *f* the tabernacle
Num. 14:21 earth. . be *f* with the glory of the LORD
1 Kgs. 8:11 (2 Chr. 5:14) the glory. . had *f* the house
Job 8:21 till he *f* thy mouth with laughing
16:8 and thou hast *f* me with wrinkles
23:4 and *f* my mouth with arguments
Ps. 71:8 let my mouth be *f* with thy praise
72:19 let the whole earth be *f* with his glory
78:29 so they did eat, and were well *f*
81:10 open thy mouth wide, and I will *f* it
104:28 openest thine hand, they are *f* with good
123:3 for we are exceedingly *f* with contempt
126:2 then was our mouth *f* with laughter
Prov. 1:31 and be *f* with their own devices
3:10 so shall thy barns be *f* with plenty
14:14 backslider. . shall be *f* with his own ways
20:17 afterward his mouth shall be *f* with gravel
30:22 and a fool when he is *f* with meat
Is. 6:1 saw also the Lord. . and his train *f* the temple
65:20 nor an old man that hath not *f* his days
Jer. 23:24 do not I *f* heaven and earth? saith the
46:12 thy shame, and thy cry hath *f* the land
Ezek. 43:5 (44:4) the glory of the LORD *f* the house

Dan. 2:35 a great mountain, and *f* the whole earth
Hab. 2:14 the earth shall be *f* with the knowledge
Hag. 2:7 and I will *f* this house with glory
Zech. 9:13 Judah for me, *f* the bow with Ephraim
Mt. 5:6 after righteousness: for they shall be *f*
23:32 *f* ye up then the measure of your fathers
27:48 (Mk. 15:36; Jn. 19:29) *f* it with vinegar
Mk. 7:27 unto her, Let the children first be *f*
Lk. 1:15 and he shall be *f* with the Holy Ghost
1:53 he hath *f* the hungry with good things
2:40 and waxed strong in spirit, *f* with wisdom
3:5 every valley shall be *f,* and every mountain
6:21 ye that hunger now: for ye shall be *f*
14:23 to come in, that my house may be *f*
15:16 would fain have *f* his belly with the husks
Jn. 2:7 Jesus saith. . F the waterpots with water
6:26 ye did eat of the loaves, and were *f*
16:6 sorrow hath *f* your heart
Acts 2:2 mighty wind, and it *f* all the house where
2:4 (4:31) were all *f* with the Holy Ghost
4:8 then Peter, *f* with the Holy Ghost, said unto
5:3 Ananias, why hath Satan *f* thine heart to lie
5:28 ye have *f* Jerusalem with your doctrine
9:17 receive thy sight. . be *f* with the Holy Ghost
13:9 Saul. . *f* with the Holy Ghost, set his eyes
13:52 the disciples were *f* with joy, and with
14:17 *f* our hearts with food and gladness
Rom. 1:29 *f* with all unrighteousness, fornication
15:13 now the God of hope *f* you with all joy
15:14 are full of goodness, *f* with all knowledge
15:24 if first I be somewhat *f* with your company
Eph. 1:23 the fulness of him that *f* all in all
3:19 ye might be *f* with all the fulness of God
4:10 ascended up. . that he might *f* all things
5:18 be not drunk. . but be *f* with the Spirit
Phil. 1:11 *f* with the fruits of righteousness
Col. 1:9 might be *f* with the knowledge of his will
1:24 *f* up that which is behind of the afflictions
1 Thes. 2:16 to *f* up their sins always
Jas. 2:16 depart in peace, be ye warmed and *f*
Rev. 15:1 for in them is *f* up the wrath of God
18:6 the cup which she hath *f, f* to her double
19:21 and all the fowls were *f* with their flesh

Filth

Is. 4:4 washed away the *f* of the daughters of Zion
Nah. 3:6 and I will cast abominable *f* upon thee
1 Cor. 4:13 we are made as the *f* of the world
1 Pet. 3:21 putting away of the *f* of the flesh

Filthiness

Ezra 9:11 with the *f* of the people of the lands
Is. 28:8 for all tables are full of vomit and *f*
Lam. 1:9 her *f* is in her skirts; she remembereth
Ezek. 36:25 from all your *f.* . will I cleanse you
2 Cor. 7:1 let us cleanse ourselves from all *f* of
Eph. 5:4 neither *f,* nor foolish talking, nor
Jas. 1:21 lay apart all *f* and superfluity of
Rev. 17:4 abominations and *f* of her fornication

Filthy

Job 15:16 how much more abominable and *f* is man
Ps. 14:3 (53:3) they are all together become *f*
Is. 64:6 and all our righteousnesses are as *f* rags
Zeph. 3:1 woe to her that is *f* and polluted
Zech. 3:3 now Joshua was clothed with *f* garments
Col. 3:8 *f* communication out of your mouth
1 Tim. 3:3 (Tit. 1:7) not greedy of *f* lucre
1 Pet. 5:2 not for *f* lucre, but of a ready mind
2 Pet. 2:7 Lot, vexed with the *f* conversation of
Jude 8 these *f* dreamers defile the flesh, despise
Rev. 22:11 and he which is *f,* let him be *f* still

Find (Found)

Gen. 2:20 but for Adam there was not *f* a help meet
4:14 that every one that *f* me shall slay me
6:8 but Noah *f* grace in the eyes of the LORD
8:9 dove *f* no rest for the sole of her foot
27:20 how is it that thou hast *f* it so quickly
37:32 to their father; and said, This have we *f*
44:16 hath *f* out the iniquity of thy servants
Num. 15:32 *f* a man that gathered sticks upon the
32:23 and be sure your sin will *f* you out
Deut. 4:29 shalt seek the LORD thy God, thou shalt *f*
22:14 when I came to her, I *f* her not a maid
32:10 *f* him in a desert land, and in the waste
33:29 thine enemies shall be *f* liars unto thee
Judg. 14:18 my heifer, ye had not *f* out my riddle
1 Sam. 9:20 thine asses that were lost . . they are *f*
1 Kgs. 20:36 departed . . a lion *f* him, and slew him
21:20 and Ahab said to Elijah, Hast thou *f* me
2 Kgs. 22:8 (2 Chr. 34:15) have *f* the book of the law
1 Chr. 28:9 if thou seek him, he will be *f* of thee
2 Chr. 2:14 skilful . . to *f* out every device
15:4 and sought him, he was *f* of them
19:3 there are good things *f* in thee, in that
Neh. 8:14 they *f* written in the law which the LORD
Job 11:7 canst thou by searching *f* out God?
23:3 oh that I knew where I might *f* him!
28:12 but where shall wisdom be *f* ?
33:24 deliver him . . I have *f* a ransom
37:23 touching the Almighty, we cannot *f* him out
Ps. 17:3 thou hast tried me, and shalt *f* nothing
32:6 in a time when thou mayest be *f*
36:2 until his iniquity be *f* to be hateful
37:36 yea, I sought him, but he could not be *f*
69:20 I looked . . for comforters, but I *f* none
83:3 the sparrow hath *f* a house, and the swallow
89:20 I have *f* David my servant
107:4 solitary way; they *f* no city to dwell in
116:3 I *f* trouble and sorrow
Prov. 3:4 shalt thou *f* favor and good understanding
4:22 for they are life unto those that *f* them
8:17 and those that seek me early shall *f* me
8:35 whoso *f* me *f* life, and shall obtain favor
18:22 whoso *f* a wife *f* a good thing
Eccl. 3:11 no man can *f* out the work that God
7:28 one man among a thousand have I *f*
7:29 lo, this only have I *f*, that God hath made
9:10 whatsoever thy hand *f* to do, do it with
11:1 for thou shalt *f* it after many days
Song 3:4 *f* him whom my soul loveth: I held him
5:8 if ye *f* my beloved, that ye tell him
Is. 55:6 seek ye the LORD while he may be *f*
58:13 nor *f* thine own pleasure, nor speaking
65:1 (Rom. 10:20) am *f* of them that sought me not
Jer. 2:5 what iniquity have your fathers *f* in me
2:26 as the thief is ashamed when he is *f*, so is
2:34 in thy skirts is *f* the blood of . . innocents
6:16 ye shall *f* rest for your souls
10:18 will distress them, that they may *f* it so
29:13 ye shall seek me, and *f* me, when ye shall
31:2 people which were left of the sword *f* grace
Lam. 2:9 prophets also *f* no vision from the LORD
Ezek. 22:30 and I sought for a man . . but I *f* none
Dan. 5:27 weighed in the balances, and art *f* wanting
Hos. 14:8 green fir tree. From me is thy fruit *f*
Mal. 2:6 iniquity was not *f* in his lips
Mt. 1:18 she was *f* with child of the Holy Ghost
7:7 (Lk. 11:9) seek, and ye shall *f*; knock, and it
7:8 (Lk. 11:10) receiveth; and he that seeketh *f*
7:14 unto life, and few there be that *f* it
8:10 (Lk. 7:9) I have not *f* so great faith, no
10:39 he that *f* his life shall lose it
11:29 and ye shall *f* rest unto your souls
12:44 (Lk. 11:25) is come, he *f* it empty, swept

Mt. 13:46 when he had *f* one pearl of great price
18:13 that he *f* it . . rejoiceth more of that sheep
20:6 he went out, and *f* others standing idle
21:2 (Mk. 11:2; Lk. 19:30) shall *f* an ass tied
21:19 (Mk. 11:13) *f* nothing thereon, but leaves
22:9 as many as ye shall *f*, bid to the marriage
24:46 (Lk. 12:43) when he cometh shall *f* so doing
26:40 (Mk. 14:37; Lk. 22:45) and *f* them asleep
26:60 (Mk. 14:55) witnesses came, yet *f* they none
Mk. 7:2 eat . . with unwashen hands, they *f* fault
7:30 to her house, she *f* the devil gone out
13:36 lest coming suddenly he *f* you sleeping
Lk. 2:12 ye shall *f* the babe wrapped in swaddling
2:16 and *f* Mary and Joseph, and the babe lying
2:46 after three days they *f* him in the temple
6:7 that they might *f* an accusation against him
7:10 *f* the servant whole that had been sick
8:35 *f* the man . . sitting at the feet of Jesus
15:4 go after that which is lost, until he *f* it?
15:6 rejoice . . I have *f* my sheep which was lost
15:8 sweep . . and seek diligently till she *f* it?
15:24 (15:32) for this my son . . was lost, and is *f*
18:8 Son . . cometh, shall he *f* faith on the earth?
19:48 could not *f* what they might do: for all
23:4 (Jn. 18:38) I *f* no fault in this man
24:2 *f* the stone rolled away from the sepulchre
24:3 and *f* not the body of the Lord Jesus
Jn. 1:41 saith unto him, We have *f* the Messias
1:45 we have *f* him, of whom Moses in the law
7:34 (7:36) shall seek me, and shall not *f* me
10:9 and shall go in and out, and *f* pasture
Acts 7:11 dearth . . and our fathers *f* no sustenance
9:2 that if he *f* any . . he might bring them bound
17:23 I *f* an altar with this inscription
17:27 haply they might feel after him, and *f* him
21:4 *f* disciples, we tarried there seven days
23:9 strove, saying, We *f* no evil in this man
24:5 for we have *f* this man a pestilent fellow
Rom. 7:10 ordained to life, I *f* to be unto death
7:18 how to perform that which is good I *f* not
7:21 I *f* then a law, that, when I would do good
1 Cor. 15:15 and we are *f* false witnesses of God
2 Cor. 12:20 I shall not *f* you such as I would
Gal. 2:17 but if . . we ourselves also are *f* sinners
Phil. 2:8 being *f* in fashion as a man, he humbled
3:9 *f* in him, not having mine own righteousness
1 Tim. 3:10 office of a deacon, being *f* blameless
2 Tim. 1:18 he may *f* mercy of the Lord in that day
Heb. 4:16 we may obtain mercy, and *f* grace to help
11:5 was not *f*, because God had translated him
12:17 rejected: for he *f* no place of repentance
1 Pet. 2:22 neither was guile *f* in his mouth
2 Pet. 3:14 be diligent that ye may be *f* of him
Rev. 3:2 have not *f* thy works perfect before God
9:6 shall man seek death, and shall not *f* it
12:8 neither was their place *f* any more in heaven
16:20 fled away, and the mountains were not *f*
20:15 whosoever was not *f* written in the book

Finding *See also* Find

Job 9:10 which doeth great things past *f* out
Rom. 11:33 his judgments, and his ways past *f* out!

Finger

Ex. 8:19 said unto Pharaoh, This is the *f* of God
31:18 (Deut. 9:10) written with the *f* of God
1 Kgs. 12:10 (2 Chr. 10:10) my little *f* shall be thicker
Ps. 8:3 consider thy heavens, the work of thy *f*
144:1 teacheth my hands to war . . my *f* to fight
Prov. 6:13 he teacheth with his *f*
7:3 bind them upon thy *f*, write them upon the
Is. 2:8 worship . . that which their own *f* have made
17:8 neither . . respect that which his *f* have made

Is. 58:9 putting forth of the *f*, and speaking vanity
  59:3 defiled with blood, and your *f* with iniquity
Dan. 5:5 same hour came forth *f* of a man's hand
Mt. 23:4 (Lk. 11:46) move them with one of their *f*
Lk. 11:20 if I with the *f* of God cast out devils
  16:24 tip of his *f* in water, and cool my tongue
Jn. 8:6 Jesus stooped down, and with his *f* wrote
  20:27 saith he to Thomas, Reach hither thy *f*

Finish *See also* End

Gen. 2:1 thus the heavens and the earth were *f*
Ruth 3:18 will not be in rest, until he have *f*
1 Chr. 28:20 until thou hast *f* all the work
Neh. 6:15 so the wall was *f*
Dan. 5:26 God hath numbered thy kingdom, and *f* it
  9:24 seventy weeks. . to *f* the transgression
Lk. 14:28 whether he have sufficient to *f* it?
Jn. 4:34 my meat is to do. . and to *f* his work
  5:36 works which the Father hath given me to *f*
  17:4 I have *f* the work which thou gavest me
  19:30 had received the vinegar, he said, It is *f*
Acts 20:24 so that I might *f* my course with joy
Rom. 9:28 for he will *f* the work, and cut it short
2 Cor. 8:6 he would also *f* in you the same grace
2 Tim. 4:7 fought a good fight, I have *f* my course
Heb. 4:3 works were *f* from the foundation of
Jas. 1:15 sin, when it is *f*, bringeth forth death
Rev. 10:7 to sound, the mystery of God should be *f*
  11:7 and when they shall have *f* their testimony
  20:5 not again until the thousand years were *f*

Finisher

Heb. 12:2 unto Jesus the author and *f* of our faith

Fir

1 Kgs. 5:10 Hiram gave Solomon cedar trees and *f*
Is. 41:19 I will set in the desert the *f* tree, and
  55:13 instead of the thorn shall come up the *f*
Hos. 14:8 I am like a green *f* tree. From me is thy
Nah. 2:3 and the *f* trees shall be terribly shaken

Fire *See also* Flame, Hell

Gen. 19:24 rained upon Sodom. . brimstone and *f*
  22:7 behold the *f* and the wood: but where is the
Ex. 3:2 behold, the bush burned with *f*
  9:23 hail, and the *f* ran along upon the ground
  13:21 night in a pillar of *f*, to give them light
  19:18 because the LORD descended upon it in *f*
  22:6 kindled the *f* shall surely make restitution
  32:24 I cast it into the *f*. . came out this calf
  35:3 ye shall kindle no *f*. . upon the sabbath day
  40:38 (Num. 9:16) by day, and *f* was on it by night
Lev. 9:24 there came a *f* out from before the LORD
  10:2 went out *f* from the LORD, and devoured them
  18:21 not let any of thy seed pass through the *f*
Num. 11:1 and the *f* of the LORD burnt among them
  16:35 *f* from the LORD, and consumed the. . men
  16:46 Aaron, Take a censer, and put *f* therein
Deut. 4:11 mountain burned with *f* unto the midst
  4:12 spake unto you out of the midst of the *f*
  4:24 (Heb. 12:29) thy God is a consuming *f*
  5:5 for ye were afraid by reason of the *f*
  9:3 as a consuming *f* he shall destroy them
  18:10 son or his daughter to pass through the *f*
  32:22 a *f* is kindled in mine anger, and shall
Josh. 8:19 took it, and hasted and set the city on *f*
Judg. 6:21 *f* out of the rock. . consumed the flesh
  9:15 let *f* come out of the bramble, and devour
  9:49 and set the hold on *f* upon them; so that
  15:5 had set the brands on *f*, he let them go
2 Sam. 22:9 (Ps. 18:8) *f* out of his mouth devoured
1 Kgs. 18:24 that answereth by *f*, let him be God
  18:38 then the *f* of the LORD fell, and consumed

1 Kgs. 19:12 a *f*; but the LORD was not in the *f*
2 Kgs. 1:10 (1:12; Lk. 9:54) *f* come down from heaven
  2:11 appeared a chariot of *f*, and horses of *f*
  17:17 caused their sons. . to pass through the *f*
  21:6 (2 Chr. 33:6) his son pass through the *f*
1 Chr. 21:26 and he answered him from heaven by *f*
2 Chr. 7:1 made an end of praying, the *f* came down
Job 1:16 said, The *f* of God is fallen from heaven
Ps. 39:3 while I was musing the *f* burned
  46:9 he burneth the chariot in the *f*
  66:12 we went through *f* and through water
  74:7 they have cast *f* into thy sanctuary
  97:3 a *f* goeth before him, and burneth up his
  104:4 (Heb. 1:7) his ministers a flaming *f*
  148:8 *f*, and hail; snow, and vapor; stormy wind
Prov. 6:27 can a man take *f* in his bosom, and his
  25:22 (Rom. 12:20) heap coals of *f* upon his head
  26:20 where no wood is, there the *f* goeth out
  26:21 and wood to *f*; so is a contentious man to
  30:16 and the *f* that saith not, It is enough
Is. 4:5 and the shining of a flaming *f* by night
  5:24 therefore as the *f* devoureth the stubble
  9:18 for wickedness burneth as the *f*
  9:19 the people shall be as the fuel of the *f*
  24:15 wherefore glorify ye the LORD in the *f*
  31:9 saith the LORD, whose *f* is in Zion
  33:14 among us shall dwell with the devouring *f*?
  43:2 through the *f*, thou shalt not be burned
  44:16 saith, Aha, I am warm, I have seen the *f*
  64:2 when the melting *f* burneth, the *f* causeth
  65:5 are a smoke in my nose, a *f* that burneth
  66:15 behold, the LORD will come with *f*
  66:16 by *f* and by his sword will the LORD plead
  66:24 (Mk. 9:44, 46, 48) shall their *f* be quenched
Jer. 5:14 I will make my words in thy mouth *f*
  20:9 his word was in mine heart as a burning *f*
  23:29 is not my word like as a *f*? saith the LORD
Lam. 1:13 from above hath he sent *f* into my bones
Ezek. 1:4 a great cloud, and a *f* infolding itself
  36:5 in the *f* of my jealousy have I spoken
  39:10 for they shall burn the weapons with *f*
Dan. 3:22 flame of the *f* slew those men that took
  3:25 men loose, walking in the midst of the *f*
  3:27 upon whose bodies the *f* had no power
Hos. 7:6 in the morning it burneth as a flaming *f*
  8:14 but I will send a *f* upon his cities, and
Joel 2:30 (Acts 2:19) blood, and *f*, and pillars of
Amos 5:6 seek the LORD. . lest he break out like *f*
  7:4 behold, the Lord GOD called to contend by *f*
Nah. 1:6 his fury is poured out like *f*
Zech. 2:5 will be unto her a wall of *f* round
  3:2 is not this a brand plucked out of the *f*?
Mal. 1:10 neither do ye kindle *f* on mine altar
  3:2 for he is like a refiner's *f*
Mt. 3:10 (7:19; Lk. 3:9) hewn down. . cast into the *f*
  3:11 (Lk. 3:16) with the Holy Ghost, and with *f*
  5:22 thou fool, shall be in danger of hell *f*
  13:40 the tares are gathered and burned in the *f*
  13:42 and shall cast them into a furnace of *f*
  17:15 (Mk. 9:22) ofttimes he falleth into the *f*
  18:8 (Mk. 9:43) to be cast into everlasting *f*
  25:41 depart. . ye cursed, into everlasting *f*
Mk. 9:44 worm dieth not, and the *f* is not quenched
  14:54 and Peter. . warmed himself at the *f*
Lk. 9:54 wilt thou that we command *f* to come
  12:49 I am come to send *f* on the earth
  17:29 rained *f* and brimstone from heaven
  22:56 certain maid beheld him as he sat by the *f*
Jn. 15:6 men gather them, and cast them into the *f*
  21:9 saw a *f* of coals. . and fish laid thereon
Acts 2:3 unto them cloven tongues like as of *f*
  28:2 kindled a *f*, and received us every one
Rom. 12:20 thou shalt heap coals of *f* on his head

1 Cor. 3:13 because it shall be revealed by *f*
  3:15 he himself shall be saved; yet so as by *f*
2 Thes. 1:8 in flaming *f* taking vengeance on them
Heb. 11:34 quenched the violence of *f*, escaped the
  12:18 might be touched, and that burned with *f*
  12:29 for our God is a consuming *f*
Jas. 3:5 how great a matter a little *f* kindleth!
  3:6 and the tongue is a *f*, a world of iniquity
1 Pet. 1:7 than of gold. . though it be tried with *f*
2 Pet. 3:7 reserved unto *f* against the day of
  3:12 the heavens being on *f* shall be dissolved
Jude 7 suffering the vengeance of eternal *f*
  23 save with fear, pulling them out of the *f*
Rev. 1:14 (2:18) his eyes were as a flame of *f*
  3:18 to buy of me gold tried in the *f*, that thou
  4:5 seven lamps of *f* burning before the throne
  8:8 as it were a great mountain burning with *f*
  15:2 as it were a sea of glass mingled with *f*
  20:9 *f* came down from God out of heaven
  20:10 the devil. . was cast into the lake of *f*
  20:14 death and hell were cast into the lake of *f*
  21:8 lake which burneth with *f* and brimstone

Firebrand

Prov. 26:18 as a mad man who casteth *f*, arrows
Is. 7:4 for the two tails of these smoking *f*
Amos 4:11 as a *f* plucked out of the burning

Firm

Josh. 3:17 priests. . stood *f* on dry ground
Job 41:24 his heart is as *f* as a stone; yea, as
Ps. 73:4 in their death: but their strength is *f*
Dan. 6:7 a royal statute, and to make a *f* decree
Heb. 3:6 the rejoicing of the hope *f* unto the end

Firmament

Gen. 1:6 God said, Let there be a *f* in the midst
Ps. 19:1 and the *f* showeth his handiwork
  150:1 praise him in the *f* of his power
Ezek. 1:22 the likeness of the *f* upon the heads of
Dan. 12:3 wise. . shine as the brightness of the *f*

First *See also* Beginning, Creation

Gen. 1:5 evening and the morning were the *f* day
Ex. 12:2 shall be the *f* month of the year to you
  12:5 lamb. . without blemish, a male of the *f* year
  22:29 to offer the *f* of thy ripe fruits
  34:1 (Deut. 10:1) tables of stone like unto the *f*
Deut. 26:2 shalt take of the *f* of all the fruit
Is. 41:4 I the LORD, the *f*, and with the last; I am he
  44:6 (48:12) I am the *f*, and I am the last
Jer. 33:7 return, and will build them, as at the *f*
Dan. 6:2 three presidents; of whom Daniel was *f*
Hag. 2:3 that saw this house in her *f* glory?
Mt. 5:24 *f* be reconciled to thy brother, and then
  6:33 but seek ye *f* the kingdom of God, and his
  7:5 (Lk. 6:42) *f* cast out the beam out of thine own
  8:21 (Lk. 9:59) Lord, suffer me *f* to go and bury
  12:29 (Mk. 3:27) except he *f* bind the strong man?
  12:45 (Lk. 11:26) last state. . is worse than the *f*
  17:10 (Mk. 9:11) that Elias must *f* come?
  19:30 (Mk. 10:31) *f* shall be last. . last. . *f*
  20:16 (Lk. 13:30) last shall be *f*, and the *f* last
  22:38 (Mk. 12:30) the *f* and great commandment
  23:26 cleanse *f* that which is within the cup
  27:64 the last error shall be worse than the *f*
  28:1 (Mk. 16:2; Lk. 24:1; Jn. 20:1) *f*. . of the week
Mk. 9:35 desire to be *f*, the same shall be last
  13:10 the gospel must *f* be published among all
Lk. 17:25 but *f* must he suffer many things
  21:9 for these things must *f* come to pass
Jn. 5:4 whosoever then *f* after the troubling of
  8:7 without sin. . let him *f* cast a stone at her

Jn. 20:19 *f* day of the week, when the doors were shut
Acts 3:26 unto you *f* God, having raised up his Son
  11:26 disciples. . called Christians *f* in Antioch
  13:46 word of God. . *f* have been spoken to you
  26:23 be the *f* that should rise from the dead
Rom. 1:16 (2:9, 10) Jew *f*, and also to the Greek
  11:35 or who hath *f* given to him, and it shall
1 Cor. 12:28 *f* apostles, secondarily prophets
  15:3 delivered unto you *f* of all that which I
  15:45 the *f* man Adam was made a living soul
  15:46 howbeit that was not *f* which is spiritual
  16:2 upon the *f* day of the week let every one
2 Cor. 8:5 but *f* gave their own selves to the Lord
  8:12 for if there be *f* a willing mind, it is
Gal. 4:13 I preached the gospel unto you at the *f*
Eph. 1:12 of his glory, who *f* trusted in Christ
  4:9 he also descended *f* into the lower parts of
  6:2 which is the *f* commandment with promise
1 Thes. 4:16 and the dead in Christ shall rise *f*
2 Thes. 2:3 except there come a falling away *f*
1 Tim. 1:16 that in me *f* Jesus Christ might show
  5:4 let them learn *f* to show piety at home
  5:12 because they have cast off their *f* faith
Heb. 4:6 to whom it was *f* preached entered not in
  5:12 be the *f* principles of the oracles of God
  7:27 to offer up sacrifice, *f* for his own sins
  8:7 for if that *f* covenant had been faultless
  9:1 *f* covenant had. . ordinances of divine service
  10:9 he taketh away the *f*, that he may establish
Jas. 3:17 the wisdom that is from above is *f* pure
1 Jn. 4:19 we love him, because he *f* loved us
Jude 6 the angels which kept not their *f* estate
Rev. 1:11 (1:17; 22:13) I am. . the *f* and the last
  2:4 because thou hast left thy *f* love
  20:5 this is the *f* resurrection

First-begotten

Rev. 1:5 Jesus Christ, who is. . the *f-b* of the dead

Firstborn *See also* Firstfruit

Gen. 19:31 *f* said unto the younger, Our father is
  27:19 said unto his father, I am Esau thy *f*
  43:33 the *f* according to his birthright
Ex. 4:22 Israel is my son, even my *f*
  11:5 all the *f* in the land of Egypt shall die
  12:29 LORD smote all the *f* in the land of Egypt
  13:2 sanctify unto me all the *f*. . both of man and
  13:15 but all the *f* of my children I redeem
  22:29 the *f* of thy sons shalt thou give unto me
  34:20 all the *f* of thy sons thou shalt redeem
Num. 3:12 (8:18) the Levites. . instead of all the *f*
  3:13 (8:17) all the *f* are mine; for on the day
  3:40 number all the *f* of the males of the children
Deut. 21:15 if the *f* son be hers that was hated
Josh. 6:26 (1 Kgs. 16:34) lay the foundation. . in his *f*
2 Chr. 21:3 gave. . to Jehoram; because he was the *f*
Job 18:13 the *f* of death shall devour his strength
Ps. 78:51 and smote all the *f* in Egypt
  89:27 also I will make him my *f*, higher than
  105:36 he smote also all the *f* in their land
Is. 14:30 the *f* of the poor shall feed
Jer. 31:9 a father to Israel, and Ephraim is my *f*
Mic. 6:7 shall I give my *f* for my transgression
Mt. 1:25 (Lk. 2:7) had brought forth her *f* son
Rom. 8:29 he might be the *f* among many brethren
Col. 1:15 image of. . God, the *f* of every creature
  1:18 who is the beginning, the *f* from the dead
Heb. 12:23 general assembly and church of the *f*

Firstfruit *See also* Firstborn, Harvest

Ex. 23:16 feast of harvest, the *f* of thy labors
  23:19 (34:26) first of the *f* of thy land
Lev. 2:14 offer for the meat offering of thy *f*. . corn

Lev. 23:10 the *f* of your harvest unto the priest
Num. 18:12 the *f* of them which they shall offer
  28:26 also in the day of the *f*, when ye bring
Deut. 18:4 the *f* also of thy corn, of thy wine
  26:10 behold, I have brought the *f* of the land
2 Chr. 31:5 Israel brought in abundance the *f* of
Neh. 10:35 bring the *f*. . unto the house of the LORD
Prov. 3:9 and with the *f* of all thine increase
Jer. 2:3 unto the LORD, and the *f* of his increase
Rom. 8:23 which have the *f* of the Spirit, even we
  11:16 if the *f* be holy, the lump is also holy
1 Cor. 15:20 and become the *f* of them that slept
  15:23 every man in his own order: Christ the *f*
Jas. 1:18 should be a kind of *f* of his creatures
Rev. 14:4 being the *f* unto God and to the Lamb

Firstling

Lev. 27:26 the LORD's *f*, no man shall sanctify it
Deut. 15:19 *f* males that come of thy herd. . sanctify

Fish

Gen. 1:26 have dominion over the *f* of the sea
Ex. 7:21 and the *f* that was in the river died
Num. 11:5 remember the *f* we did eat in Egypt
Deut. 4:18 likeness of any *f* that is in the waters
Ps. 105:29 waters into blood, and slew their *f*
Eccl. 9:12 as the *f* that are taken in an evil net
Jer. 16:16 saith the LORD, and they shall *f* them
Jon. 1:17 prepared a great *f* to swallow up Jonah
Hab. 1:14 and makest men as the *f* of the sea
Zeph. 1:10 be the noise of a cry from the *f* gate
Mt. 7:10 (Lk. 11:11) ask a *f*, will he give him a serpent
  14:17 (Mk. 6:38; 9:13; Jn. 6:9) loaves, and two *f*
  15:34 (Mk. 8:7) said, Seven, and a few little *f*
  17:27 and take up the *f* that first cometh up
Lk. 5:6 great multitude of *f*: and their net brake
  24:42 and they gave him a piece of a broiled *f*
Jn. 21:6 not able to draw it for the multitude of *f*
  21:9 a fire of coals there, and *f* laid thereon
1 Cor. 15:39 another flesh of beasts, another of *f*

Fisher

Is. 19:8 the *f* also shall mourn, and all they that
Jer. 16:16 I will send for many *f*, saith the LORD
Mt. 4:19 (Mk. 1:17) and I will make you *f* of men

Fishing

Jn. 21:3 Simon Peter saith unto them, I go a *f*

Fit *See also* Meet, Worthy

Lev. 16:21 send him away by the hand of a *f* man
Job 34:18 *f* to say to a king, Thou art wicked?
Prov. 24:27 and make it *f* for thyself in the field
Lk. 9:62 and looking back, is *f* for the kingdom
  14:35 it is neither *f* for the land, nor yet for
Acts 22:22 for it is not *f* that he should live
Col. 3:18 wives, submit. . as it is *f* in the Lord

Fitly

Prov. 25:11 a word *f* spoken is like apples of gold
Eph. 2:21 whom all the building *f* framed together
  4:16 from whom the whole body *f* joined together

Fitted

Rom. 9:22 the vessels of wrath *f* to destruction

Five

Mt. 25:2 *f* of them were wise, and *f* were foolish
Jn. 4:18 for thou hast had *f* husbands; and he whom
1 Cor. 14:19 speak *f* words with my understanding

Fixed

Ps. 57:7 (108:1) my heart is *f*, O God

Ps. 112:7 his heart is *f*, trusting in the LORD
Lk. 16:26 between us and you. . is a great gulf *f*

Flagon

2 Sam. 6:19 (1 Chr. 16:3) of flesh, and a *f* of wine
Song 2:5 stay me with *f*, comfort me with apples
Hos. 3:1 look to other gods, and love *f* of wine

Flame *See also* Fire, Hell

Gen. 3:24 and a *f* sword which turned every way
Ex. 3:2 (Acts 7:30) appeared unto him in a *f* of fire
Judg. 13:20 angel. . ascended in the *f* of the altar
  20:38 that they should make a great *f* with smoke
Job 41:21 and a *f* goeth out of his mouth
Ps. 29:7 voice of the LORD divideth the *f* of fire
  104:4 (Heb. 1:7) his ministers a *f* fire
Is. 5:24 and the *f* consumeth the chaff, so their
  10:17 for a fire, and his Holy One for a *f*
  13:8 shall be amazed. . their faces shall be as *f*
  29:6 and tempest, and the *f* of devouring fire
  43:2 neither shall the *f* kindle upon thee
  66:15 his anger with fury, and his rebuke with *f*
Ezek. 20:47 the flaming *f* shall not be quenched
Dan. 3:22 the *f* of the fire slew those men that
  7:9 his throne was like the fiery *f*
Joel 2:3 before them; and behind them a *f* burneth
Lk. 16:24 my tongue; for I am tormented in this *f*
Rev. 1:14 (2:18) his eyes were as a *f* of fire

Flatter

Ps. 5:9 open sepulchre; they *f* with their tongue
  36:2 for he *f* himself in his own eyes, until his
  78:36 they did *f* him with their mouth
Prov. 2:16 (7:5) stranger which *f* with her words
  20:19 meddle not with him that *f* with his lips
  28:23 rebuketh. . find more favor than he that *f*
  29:5 *f* his neighbor spreadeth a net for his feet

Flattering

Job 32:21 neither let me give *f* titles unto man
Ps. 12:2 with *f* lips and with a double heart do they
  12:3 the LORD shall cut off all *f* lips
Prov. 26:28 and a *f* mouth worketh ruin
1 Thes. 2:5 neither at any time used we *f* words

Flattery

Job 17:5 he that speaketh *f* to his friends
Dan. 11:21 but he shall. . obtain the kingdom by *f*
  11:32 such as do wickedly. . shall he corrupt by *f*
  11:34 but many shall cleave to them with *f*

Flax

Ex. 9:31 and the *f* and the barley was smitten
Josh. 2:6 and hid them with the stalks of *f*
Is. 19:9 that work in fine *f*. . shall be confounded
  42:3 (Mt. 12:20) smoking *f* shall he not quench

Flee (Fled)

Gen. 14:10 and the kings of Sodom and Gomorrah *f*
  16:6 when Sarai dealt hardly with her, she *f*
  19:20 behold now, this city is near to *f* unto
  27:43 arise, *f* thou to Laban my brother to Haran
  39:12 and he left his garment in her hand, and *f*
Ex. 2:15 (Acts 7:29) Moses *f* from the face of Pharaoh
  14:27 sea returned. . the Egyptians *f* against it
Lev. 26:17 and ye shall *f* when none pursueth you
  26:36 they shall *f*, as *f* from a sword
Num. 10:35 (Ps. 68:1) let them that hate thee *f* before
  35:6 for the manslayer, that he may *f* thither
Deut. 19:4 the case of the slayer, which shall *f*
Judg. 7:21 and all the host ran, and cried, and *f*
2 Sam. 10:18 (1 Chr. 19:18) Syrians *f* before Israel
  15:14 let us *f*; for we shall not else escape

2 Kgs. 7:7 wherefore they arose and *f* in the twilight
Neh. 6:11 and I said, Should such a man as I *f*?
Job 14:2 he *f* also as a shadow, and continueth not
27:22 he would fain *f* out of his hand
30:10 they abhor me, they *f* far from me
Ps. 11:1 to my soul, *F* as a bird to your mountain?
31:11 they that did see me without *f* from me
64:8 all that see them shall *f* away
114:3 sea saw it, and *f*: Jordan was driven back
139:7 or whither shall I *f* from thy presence?
143:9 O LORD.. I *f* unto thee to hide me
Prov. 28:1 the wicked *f* when no man pursueth
28:17 man that doeth violence.. shall *f* to the pit
Song 2:17 (4:6) the day break, and the shadows *f*
Is. 22:3 all thy rulers are *f* together
30:16 will *f* upon horses; therefore shall ye *f*
35:10 (51:11) sorrow and sighing shall *f* away
Jer. 6:1 gather yourselves to *f* out of the midst
9:10 fowl of the heavens and the beast are *f*
48:9 give wings unto Moab, that it may *f*
51:6 *f* out of the midst of Babylon, and deliver
Hos. 7:13 woe unto them! for they have *f* from me
Amos 5:19 did *f* from a lion, and a bear met him
9:1 he that *f* of them shall not *f* away
Jon. 1:3 Jonah rose up to *f* unto Tarshish
1:10 that he *f* from the presence of the LORD
4:2 therefore I *f* before unto Tarshish
Zech. 14:5 yea, ye shall *f*, like as ye *f* from
Mt. 2:13 child and his mother, and *f* into Egypt
3:7 (Lk. 3:7) to *f* from the wrath to come?
8:33 (Mk. 5:14; Lk. 8:34) and they that kept them *f*
10:23 persecute you in this city, *f* ye into
24:16 (Mk. 13:14; Lk. 21:21) *f* into the mountains
26:56 (Mk. 14:50) disciples forsook him, and *f*
Mk. 16:8 *f* from the sepulchre; for they trembled
Jn. 10:5 will they not follow, but will *f* from him
10:13 the hireling *f*, because he is a hireling
Acts 14:6 ware of it.. *f* unto Lystra and Derbe
16:27 supposing that the prisoners had been *f*
27:30 shipmen were about to *f* out of the ship
1 Cor. 6:18 *f* fornication. Every sin that a man
10:14 my dearly beloved, *f* from idolatry
1 Tim. 6:11 but thou, O man of God, *f* these things
2 Tim. 2:22 *f* also youthful lusts: but follow
Heb. 6:18 who have *f* for refuge to lay hold upon
Jas. 4:7 resist the devil, and he will *f* from you
Rev. 9:6 desire to die, and death shall *f* from
12:6 the woman *f* into the wilderness, where she
20:11 from whose face the earth and the heaven *f*

Fleece

Judg. 6:37 I will put a *f* of wool in the floor

Flesh *See also* Body

Gen. 2:23 is now bone of my bones, and *f* of my *f*
2:24 (Mt. 19:5; Mk. 10:8; Eph. 5:31) shall be one *f*
6:12 all *f* had corrupted his way upon the earth
6:13 the end of all *f* is come before me
6:17 even I, do bring a flood.. to destroy all *f*
7:15 into the ark, two and two of all *f*
7:21 and all *f* died that moved upon the earth
9:11 neither shall all *f* be cut off any more
17:13 and my covenant shall be in your *f* for an
Ex. 12:8 they shall eat the *f* in that night
Lev. 11:8 (Deut. 14:8) of their *f* shall ye not eat
13:24 *f* that burneth have a white bright spot
17:14 for the life of all *f* is the blood thereof
19:28 any cuttings in your *f* for the dead
Num. 11:4 and said, Who shall give us *f* to eat?
16:22 O God, the God of the spirits of all *f*
1 Kgs. 17:6 the ravens brought him bread and *f*
2 Chr. 32:8 with him is an arm of *f*; but with us
Neh. 5:5 yet now our *f* is as the *f* of our brethren

Job 10:4 hast thou eyes of *f*? or seest thou as man
10:11 thou hast clothed me with skin and *f*
19:26 yet in my *f* shall I see God
34:15 all *f* shall perish together, and man shall
Ps. 16:9 (Acts 2:26) my *f* also shall rest in hope
56:4 will not fear what *f* can do unto me
65:2 hearest prayer, unto thee shall all *f* come
73:26 my *f* and my heart faileth: but God is the
78:39 for he remembered that they were but *f*
84:2 and my *f* crieth out for the living God
119:120 my *f* trembleth for fear of thee
145:21 let all *f* bless his holy name for ever
Prov. 4:22 for they are.. health to all their *f*
5:11 when thy *f* and thy body are consumed
11:17 but he that is cruel troubleth his own *f*
14:30 a sound heart is the life of the *f*
Eccl. 11:10 and put away evil from thy *f*
12:12 and much study is a weariness of the *f*
Is. 40:5 (Lk. 3:6) and all *f* shall see it together
40:6 (1 Pet. 1:24) all *f* is grass, and all the
49:26 all *f* shall know that I.. am thy Saviour
66:23 shall all *f* come to worship before me
Jer. 17:5 cursed be the man that.. maketh *f* his arm
32:27 behold, I am the LORD, the God of all *f*
Ezek. 11:19 (36:26) will give them a heart of *f*
20:48 all *f* shall see that I.. have kindled it
36:26 take away the stony heart out of your *f*
Joel 2:28 (Acts 2:17) pour out my Spirit upon all *f*
Mt. 16:17 for *f* and blood hath not revealed it
19:5 (Mk. 10:8) and they twain shall be one *f*?
24:22 (Mk. 13:20) there should no *f* be saved
26:41 (Mk. 14:38) is willing, but the *f* is weak
Lk. 24:39 a spirit hath not *f* and bones, as ye see
Jn. 1:13 not of blood, nor of the will of the *f*
1:14 the Word was made *f*, and dwelt among us
3:6 that which is born of the *f* is *f*
6:51 the bread that I will give is my *f*
6:54 whoso eateth my *f*, and drinketh my blood
6:55 for my *f* is meat indeed, and my blood is
6:63 that quickeneth; the *f* profiteth nothing
8:15 ye judge after the *f*; I judge no man
17:2 as thou hast given him power over all *f*
Acts 2:30 fruit of his loins, according to the *f*
2:31 neither his *f* did see corruption
Rom. 1:3 of the seed of David according to the *f*
3:20 (Gal. 2:16) shall no *f* be justified in his sight
6:19 because of the infirmity of your *f*
7:5 when we were in the *f*, the motions of sins
7:18 in me (that is, in my *f*,) dwelleth no good
8:1 walk not after the *f*, but after the Spirit
8:3 his own Son in the likeness of sinful *f*
8:5 are after the *f* do mind the things of the *f*
8:8 they that are in the *f* cannot please God
8:9 but ye are not in the *f*, but in the Spirit
8:12 brethren, we are debtors, not to the *f*
8:13 for if ye live after the *f*, ye shall die
9:3 my brethren, my kinsmen according to the *f*
9:5 and of whom as concerning the *f* Christ came
13:14 make not provision for the *f*, to fulfil
1 Cor. 1:29 that no *f* should glory in his presence
6:16 for two, saith he, shall be one *f*
15:39 one kind of *f* of men, another *f* of beasts
15:50 flesh and blood cannot inherit the kingdom
2 Cor. 4:11 might be made manifest in our mortal *f*
5:16 though we have known Christ after the *f*
7:1 let us cleanse.. from all filthiness of the *f*
10:2 as if we walked according to the *f*
12:7 a thorn in the *f*, the messenger of Satan
Gal. 1:16 I conferred not with *f* and blood
2:20 the life which I now live in the *f* I live
3:3 are ye now made perfect by the *f*?
5:13 use not liberty for an occasion to the *f*
5:16 and ye shall not fulfil the lust of the *f*

Gal. 5:17 for the *f* lusteth against the Spirit
  5:24 they that are Christ's have crucified the *f*
  6:8 he that soweth to his *f* shall of the *f* reap
Eph. 2:3 in times past in the lusts of our *f*
  5:30 for we are members of his body, of his *f*
  6:12 for we wrestle not against *f* and blood
Phil. 3:3 and have no confidence in the *f*
Col. 1:22 in the body of his *f* through death
  2:11 putting off the body of the sins of the *f*
1 Tim. 3:16 God was manifest in the *f*, justified
Heb. 2:14 children are partakers of *f* and blood
  5:7 in the days of his *f*, when he had offered
  9:13 sanctifieth to the purifying of the *f*
  10:20 through the veil, that is to say, his *f*
1 Pet. 3:18 being put to death in the *f*, but quickened
  4:1 as Christ hath suffered for us in the *f*
  4:2 the rest of his time in the *f* to the lusts
2 Pet. 2:10 that walk after the *f* in the lust of
1 Jn. 2:16 the lust of the *f*, and the lust of the eyes
  4:2 that Jesus Christ is come in the *f* is of God
2 Jn. 7 not that Jesus Christ is come in the *f*
Jude 8 these filthy dreamers defile the *f*, despise
  23 hating even the garment spotted by the *f*
Rev. 19:18 eat the *f* of kings, and the *f* of captains
  19:21 all the fowls were filled with their *f*

Fleshly

2 Cor. 1:12 not with *f* wisdom, but by the grace
  3:3 of stone, but in *f* tables of the heart
Col. 2:18 vainly puffed up by his *f* mind
1 Pet. 2:11 dearly beloved. . abstain from *f* lusts

Flight

Lev. 26:8 hundred of you shall put ten thousand to *f*
Is. 52:12 nor go by *f*: for the LORD will go before
Amos 2:14 the *f* shall perish from the swift
Mt. 24:20 (Mk. 13:18) that your *f* be not in the winter
Heb. 11:34 turned to *f* the armies of the aliens

Flint

Deut. 8:15 who brought. . water out of the rock of *f*
Ps. 114:8 turned. . the *f* into a fountain of waters
Is. 5:28 horses' hoofs shall be counted like *f*
  50:7 therefore have I set my face like a *f*
Ezek. 3:9 harder than *f* have I made thy forehead

Flock *See also* Church, Congregation, People, Sheep

Gen. 4:4 Abel. . brought of the firstlings of his *f*
  30:40 and Jacob. . put his own *f* by themselves
  33:13 should overdrive them. . all the *f* will die
  37:14 with thy brethren, and well with the *f*
Ex. 3:1 Moses kept the *f* of Jethro
Lev. 1:10 and if his offering be of the *f*
  27:32 the tithe of the herd, or of the *f*
Deut. 7:13 he will also bless. . the *f* of thy sheep
  8:13 and when thy herds and thy *f* multiply
  12:6 the firstlings of your herds and of your *f*
Ps. 65:13 pastures are clothed with *f*; the valleys
  77:20 thou leddest thy people like a *f*
Song 1:7 where thou makest thy *f* to rest at noon
  6:6 thy teeth are as a *f* of sheep which go up
Is. 40:11 he shall feed his *f* like a shepherd
Jer. 10:21 and all their *f* shall be scattered
  13:17 the LORD's *f* is carried away captive
  23:2 against the pastors. . Ye have scattered my *f*
  31:10 and keep him, as a shepherd doth his *f*
Ezek. 24:5 take the choice of the *f*, and burn
  34:3 ye eat the fat. . but ye feed not the *f*
  34:12 as a shepherd seeketh out his *f*. . so will I
  34:31 and ye my *f*, the *f* of my pasture, are men
Mic. 2:12 as the *f* in the midst of their fold

Hab. 3:17 the *f* shall be cut off from the fold
Zeph. 2:14 *f* shall lie down in the midst of her
Zech. 10:2 therefore they went their way as a *f*
Mt. 26:31 the sheep of the *f* shall be scattered
Lk. 2:8 keeping watch over their *f* by night
  12:32 fear not, little *f*; for it is your
Acts 20:28 heed. . unto yourselves, and to all the *f*
  20:29 grievous wolves enter. . not sparing the *f*
1 Pet. 5:2 feed the *f* of God which is among you
  5:3 but being ensamples to the *f*

Flood *See also* Water

Gen. 6:17 I, even I, do bring a *f* of waters
  7:6 Noah was six hundred years old when the *f*
  9:11 any more be a *f* to destroy the earth
Ex. 15:8 the *f* stood upright as a heap
Josh. 24:2 fathers dwelt on the other side of the *f*
2 Sam. 22:5 (Ps. 18:4) *f* of ungodly. . made me afraid
Job 22:16 whose foundation was overflown with a *f*
  28:4 the *f* breaketh out from the inhabitant
  28:11 he bindeth the *f* from overflowing
Ps. 24:2 for he hath. . established it upon the *f*
  29:10 the LORD sitteth upon the *f*
  32:6 in the *f* of great waters they shall not
  66:6 they went through the *f* on foot
  90:5 thou carriest them away as with a *f*
  93:3 O LORD, the *f* have lifted up their voice
Song 8:7 quench love, neither can the *f* drown it
Is. 44:3 for I will pour. . *f* upon the dry ground
  59:19 when the enemy shall come in like a *f*
Jer. 46:8 Egypt riseth up like a *f*, and his waters
Amos 8:8 (9:5) it shall rise up wholly as a *f*
Mt. 7:25 (Lk. 6:48) rain descended, and the *f* came
  24:38 as in the days that were before the *f*
  24:39 (Lk. 17:27) until the *f* came, and took them
2 Pet. 2:5 the *f* upon the world of the ungodly
Rev. 12:15 and the serpent cast out. . water as a *f*

Floor

Judg. 6:37 I will put a fleece of wool in the *f*
Is. 21:10 O my threshing, and the corn of my *f*
Joel 2:24 and the *f* shall be full of wheat
Mic. 4:12 gather them as the sheaves into the *f*
Mt. 3:12 (Lk. 3:17) he will thoroughly purge his *f*

Flour

Lev. 2:1 a meat offering. . shall be of fine *f*
2 Kgs. 7:1 a measure of fine *f* be sold for a shekel

Flourish *See also* Enlarge, Grow, Increase

Ps. 72:7 in his days shall the righteous *f*
  90:6 in the morning it *f*, and groweth up
  92:12 the righteous shall *f* like the palm tree
  92:13 planted in the house of the LORD shall *f*
  103:15 as a flower of the field, so he *f*
  132:18 but upon himself shall his crown *f*
Prov. 11:28 but the righteous shall *f* as a branch
  14:11 but the tabernacle of the upright shall *f*
Eccl. 12:5 and the almond tree shall *f*
Is. 17:11 morning shalt thou make thy seed to *f*
Ezek. 17:24 made the dry tree to *f*: I the LORD
Dan. 4:4 at rest in mine house, and *f* in my palace
Phil. 4:10 your care. of me hath *f* again

Flow

Lev. 20:24 a land that *f* with milk and honey
Job 20:28 goods shall *f* away in the day of his wrath
Ps. 147:18 causeth his wind to blow, and the waters *f*
Prov. 18:4 the wellspring of wisdom as a *f* brook
Song 4:16 that the spices thereof may *f* out
Is. 2:2 (Mic. 4:1) and all nations shall *f* unto it
  48:21 he caused the waters to *f* out of the rock
  60:5 then thou shalt see, and *f* together

Is. 64:1 the mountains might *f* down at thy presence
66:12 glory of the Gentiles like a *f* stream
Jer. 31:12 *f* together to the goodness of the LORD
Joel 3:18 and the hills shall *f* with milk
Jn. 7:38 of his belly shall *f* rivers of living water

Flower

Lev. 15:24 her *f* be upon him, he shall be unclean
1 Sam. 2:33 shall die in the *f* of their age
Job 14:2 he cometh forth like a *f*, and is cut down
15:33 and shall cast off his *f* as the olive
Ps. 103:15 days are as grass: as a *f* of the field
Song 2:12 the *f* appear on the earth; the time of
5:13 his cheeks . . as a bed of spices, as sweet *f*
Is. 18:5 and the sour grape is ripening in the *f*
28:1 whose glorious beauty is a fading *f*
40:6 goodliness thereof is as the *f* of the field
40:8 (1 Pet. 1:24) the grass withereth, the *f* fadeth
Nah. 1:4 and the *f* of Lebanon languisheth
1 Cor. 7:36 virgin, if she pass the *f* of her age
Jas. 1:10 as the *f* of the grass he shall pass
1 Pet. 1:24 all the glory of man as the *f* of grass

Flutter

Deut. 32:11 stirreth up her nest, *f* over her young

Fly (noun)

Ex. 8:21 behold, I will send swarms of *f* upon thee
Ps. 78:45 (105:31) he sent divers sorts of *f*
Eccl. 10:1 dead *f* cause the ointment . . stinking
Is. 7:18 the LORD shall hiss for the *f* that is in

Fly (Flew)

Gen. 1:20 and fowl that may *f* above the earth
1 Sam. 15:19 not obey . . but didst *f* upon the spoil
2 Sam. 22:11 (Ps. 18:10) upon a cherub, and did *f*
Job 5:7 born unto trouble, as the sparks *f* upward
39:26 doth the hawk *f* by thy wisdom, and stretch
Ps. 55:6 wings like a dove! . . then would I *f* away
90:10 for it is soon cut off, and we *f* away
Prov. 23:5 for riches . . *f* away as an eagle
Is. 6:6 then *f* one of the seraphim unto me
11:14 *f* upon the shoulders of the Philistines
31:5 as birds *f*, so will the LORD . . defend
60:8 who are these that *f* as a cloud
Jer. 48:40 behold, he shall *f* as an eagle
Ezek. 13:20 there hunt the souls to make them *f*
Dan. 9:21 man Gabriel . . being caused to *f* swiftly
Hos. 9:11 as for Ephraim, their glory shall *f* away
Hab. 1:8 shall *f* as the eagle that hasteth to eat
Zech. 5:1 lifted up mine eyes . . and behold a *f* roll
Rev. 8:13 an angel *f* through the midst of heaven
19:17 to all the fowls that *f* in the midst

Foal

Gen. 49:11 binding his *f* unto the vine, and his
Zech. 9:9 (Mt. 21:5) upon a colt the *f* of an ass

Foam

Hos. 10:7 king is cut off as the *f* upon the water
Mk. 9:18 (Lk. 9:39) teareth him . . he *f*, and gnasheth
Jude 13 waves of the sea, *f* out their own shame

Foe *See also* Adversary, Enemy

Esth. 9:16 but the other Jews . . slew of their *f*
Ps. 27:2 the wicked, even . . my *f*, came upon me
30:1 and hast not made my *f* to rejoice over me
89:23 and I will beat down his *f* before his face
Mt. 10:36 a man's *f* shall be . . of his own household
Acts 2:35 until I make thy *f* thy footstool

Fold (noun)

Ps. 50:9 no bullock . . nor he goats out of thy *f*
Is. 13:20 neither . . shepherds make their *f* there

Is. 65:10 and Sharon shall be a *f* of flocks
Jer. 23:3 and will bring them again to their *f*
Mic. 2:12 as the flock in the midst of their *f*
Hab. 3:17 the flock shall be cut off from the *f*
Jn. 10:16 other sheep I have, which are not of this *f*

Fold (verb)

Prov. 6:10 (24:33) a little *f* of the hands to sleep
Eccl. 4:5 the fool *f* his hands together
Heb. 1:12 as a vesture shalt thou *f* them up

Follow

Gen. 24:8 the woman will not be willing to *f* thee
Ex. 14:4 harden Pharaoh's heart, that he shall *f*
23:2 thou shalt not *f* a multitude to do evil
Num. 14:24 but my servant Caleb . . hath *f* me fully
32:12 Caleb . . Joshua . . have wholly *f* the LORD
Deut. 12:30 that thou be not snared by *f* them
16:20 which is altogether just shalt thou *f*
Josh. 14:8 but I wholly *f* the LORD my God
Ruth 1:16 or to return from *f* after thee
1 Kgs. 18:21 if the LORD be God, *f* him: but if
2 Kgs. 6:19 Elisha said . . This is not the way . . *f* me
Ps. 23:6 surely goodness and mercy shall *f* me
63:8 my soul *f* hard after thee: thy right hand
68:25 before, the players on instruments *f* after
Prov. 12:11 *f* vain persons . . void of understanding
28:19 *f* after vain persons shall have poverty
Is. 5:11 the morning, that they may *f* strong drink
51:1 hearken . . ye that *f* after righteousness
Jer. 17:16 hastened from being a pastor to *f* thee
Hos. 6:3 shall we know, if we *f* on to know the LORD
Amos 7:15 and the LORD took me as I *f* the flock
Mt. 4:19 *f* me, and I will make you fishers of men
8:19 (Lk. 9:57) I will *f* thee whithersoever thou
8:22 (Lk. 9:59) *f* me; and let the dead bury their
9:9 (Mk. 2:14; Lk. 5:27) *f* me . . he arose, and *f* him
16:24 (Mk. 8:34; Lk. 9:23) take up his cross . . *f* me
19:21 (Mk. 10:21; Lk. 18:22) sell . . come and *f* me
19:27 (Mk. 10:28; Lk. 18:28) forsaken all . . *f* thee
26:58 (Mk. 14:54; Lk. 22:54) Peter *f* him afar off
Mk. 1:18 (Lk. 5:11) forsook their nets, and *f* him
5:37 he suffered no man to *f* him, save Peter
9:38 (Lk. 9:49) forbade him, because he *f* not us
10:32 and as they *f*, they were afraid
16:17 and these signs shall *f* them that believe
16:20 and confirming the word with signs *f*
Lk. 9:61 Lord, I will *f* thee; but let me first go
Jn. 1:43 findeth Philip, and saith unto him, *F* me
8:12 he that *f* me shall not walk in darkness
10:5 a stranger will they not *f*, but will flee
10:27 my sheep hear my voice . . and they *f* me
12:26 if any man serve me, let him *f* me
13:36 whither I go, thou canst not *f* me now
13:37 Peter said . . Lord, why cannot I *f* thee now?
18:15 Peter *f* Jesus, and so did another disciple
20:6 Simon Peter *f* . . and went into the sepulchre
21:22 what is that to thee? . . *f* thou me
Acts 12:9 and he went out, and *f* him; and wist not
13:43 religious proselytes *f* Paul and Barnabas
21:36 the people *f* after, crying, Away with him
Rom. 9:30 Gentiles, which *f* not after righteousness
14:19 *f* after the things which make for peace
1 Cor. 10:4 of that spiritual Rock that *f* them
14:1 *f* after charity, and desire spiritual gifts
Phil. 3:12 were already perfect: but I *f* after
1 Thes. 5:15 but ever *f* that which is good
2 Thes. 3:7 yourselves know how ye ought to *f* us
3:9 make ourselves an ensample unto you to *f* us
1 Tim. 5:24 to judgment; and some men they *f* after
6:11 thou, O man of God . . *f* after righteousness
2 Tim. 2:22 youthful lusts: but *f* righteousness
Heb. 12:14 *f* peace with all men, and holiness

Heb. 13:7 unto you the word of God: whose faith *f*
1 Pet. 1:11 of Christ, and the glory that should *f*
　2:21 us an example, that ye should *f* his steps
2 Pet. 1:16 not *f* cunningly devised fables
　2:2 and many shall *f* their pernicious ways
　2:15 and are gone astray, *f* the way of Balaam
3 Jn. 11 beloved, *f* not that which is evil
Rev. 6:8 on him was Death, and Hell *f* with him
　14:4 virgins. These are they which *f* the Lamb
　14:13 their labors; and their works do *f* them

Follower

1 Cor. 4:16 (11:1; Phil. 3:17) be ye *f* of me
Eph. 5:1 be ye. . *f* of God, as dear children
1 Thes. 1:6 and ye became *f* of us, and of the Lord
　2:14 for ye, brethren, became *f* of the churches
Heb. 6:12 but *f* of them who. . inherit the promises
1 Pet. 3:13 if ye be *f* of that which is good?

Folly

Gen. 34:7 wrought *f* in Israel in lying with
Deut. 22:21 wrought *f* in Israel, to play the whore
Josh. 7:15 and because he hath wrought *f* in Israel
Judg. 20:6 have committed lewdness and *f* in Israel
1 Sam. 25:25 Nabal is his name, and *f* is with him
2 Sam. 13:12 nay, my brother. . do not thou this *f*
Job 4:18 and his angels he charged with *f*
　24:12 crieth out: yet God layeth not *f* to them
　42:8 lest I deal with you after your *f*
Ps. 49:13 this their way is their *f*: yet their
　85:8 but let them not turn again to *f*
Prov. 5:23 greatness of his *f* he shall go astray
　13:16 but a fool layeth open his *f*
　14:8 but the *f* of fools is deceit
　14:18 the simple inherit *f*: but the prudent are
　14:24 but the foolishness of fools is *f*
　14:29 he that is hasty of spirit exalteth *f*
　15:21 *f* is joy to him that is destitute of wisdom
　16:22 but the instruction of fools is *f*
　17:12 meet a man, rather than a fool in his *f*
　26:4 answer not a fool according to his *f*, lest
　26:5 answer a fool according to his *f*, lest he
Eccl. 1:17 to know madness and *f*: I perceived that
　2:13 then I saw that wisdom excelleth *f*, as far
　7:25 and to know the wickedness of *f*, even of
　10:6 *f* is set in great dignity, and the rich sit
Is. 9:17 an evildoer, and every mouth speaketh *f*
Jer. 23:13 have seen *f* in the prophets of Samaria
2 Cor. 11:1 ye could bear with me a little in my *f*
2 Tim. 3:9 their *f* shall be manifest unto all men

Food *See also* Meat, Provision, Victuals

Gen. 2:9 pleasant to the sight, and good for *f*
　3:6 the woman saw that the tree was good for *f*
　6:21 take thou unto thee of all *f* that is eaten
　41:35 gather all the *f* of those good years
　42:7 said, From the land of Canaan-to buy *f*
　42:33 take *f* for the famine of your households
　44:1 fill the men's sacks with *f*, as much as
Ex. 21:10 her *f*, her raiment, and her duty of marriage
Lev. 22:7 of the holy things; because it is his *f*
Deut. 10:18 loveth the stranger, in giving him *f*
1 Sam. 14:24 (14:28) cursed. . that eateth any *f*
Job 23:12 more than my necessary *f*
　24:5 the wilderness yieldeth *f* for them
　38:41 who provideth for the raven his *f*?
Ps. 78:25 man did eat angels' *f*: he sent them meat
　104:14 he may bring forth *f* out of the earth
　136:25 who giveth *f* to all flesh: for his mercy
　146:7 which giveth *f* to the hungry
　147:9 he giveth to the beast his *f*, and to the
Prov. 6:8 and gathereth her *f* in the harvest
　13:23 much *f* is in the tillage of the poor

Prov. 30:8 feed me with *f* convenient for me
Ezek. 48:18 be for *f* unto them that serve the city
Acts 14:17 filling our hearts with *f* and gladness
2 Cor. 9:10 both minister bread for your *f*, and
1 Tim. 6:8 having *f* and raiment. . therewith content
Jas. 2:15 brother or sister. . destitute of daily *f*

Fool

1 Sam. 26:21 then said Saul. . I have played the *f*
2 Sam. 3:33 and said, Died Abner as a *f* dieth?
Job 12:17 and maketh the judges *f*
Ps. 14:1 (53:1) *f*. . said in his heart, There is no God
　75:4 I said unto the *f*, Deal not foolishly
　92:6 neither doth a *f* understand this
　107:17 *f*, because of their transgression
Prov. 1:7 but *f* despise wisdom and instruction
　3:35 but shame shall be the promotion of *f*
　10:8 commandments: but a prating *f* shall fall
　10:21 *f* die for want of wisdom
　10:23 it is as sport to a *f* to do mischief
　11:29 *f* shall be servant to the wise of heart
　12:15 the way of a *f* is right in his own eyes
　13:16 knowledge: but a *f* layeth open his folly
　13:20 but a companion of *f* shall be destroyed
　14:8 but the folly of *f* is deceit
　14:9 *f* make a mock at sin
　14:16 but the *f* rageth, and is confident
　15:2 but the mouth of *f* poureth out foolishness
　15:5 a *f* despiseth his father's instruction
　16:22 but the instruction of *f* is folly
　17:7 excellent speech becometh not a *f*
　17:10 than a hundred stripes into a *f*
　17:12 rather than a *f* in his folly
　17:16 a price in the hand of a *f* to get wisdom
　17:21 that begetteth a *f* doeth it to his sorrow
　17:28 *f*, when he holdeth his peace, is counted wise
　18:2 a *f* hath no delight in understanding
　18:6 a *f*'s lips enter into contention
　18:7 a *f*'s mouth is his destruction
　19:1 he that is perverse in his lips, and is a *f*
　20:3 but every *f* will be meddling
　24:7 wisdom is too high for a *f*: he openeth not
　26:4 answer not a *f* according to his folly, lest
　26:5 answer a *f* according to his folly, lest he
　27:3 but a *f*'s wrath is heavier than them both
　27:22 though thou shouldest bray a *f* in a mortar
　28:26 he that trusteth in his own heart is a *f*
　29:11 a *f* uttereth all his mind: but a wise man
Eccl. 2:14 but the *f* walketh in darkness: and I
　2:16 remembrance of the wise more than of the *f*
　2:19 whether he shall be a wise man or a *f*?
　4:5 the *f* foldeth his hands together, and eateth
　5:1 to hear, than to give the sacrifice of *f*
　5:3 a *f*'s voice is known by multitude of words
　5:4 vow unto God. . for he hath no pleasure in *f*
　7:4 but the heart of *f* is in the house of mirth
　7:9 for anger resteth in the bosom of *f*
　10:2 his right hand; but a *f*'s heart at his left
　10:14 a *f* also is full of words: a man cannot
Is. 35:8 wayfaring men, though *f*, shall not err
Jer. 17:11 getteth riches. . at his end shall be a *f*
Hos. 9:7 Israel shall know it: the prophet is a *f*
Mt. 5:22 say, Thou *f*, shall be in danger of hell
　23:17 ye *f* and blind: for whether is greater
Lk. 11:40 ye *f*, did not he, that made that which
　12:20 but God said unto him, Thou *f*, this night
　24:25 O *f*, and slow of heart to believe all that
Rom. 1:22 professing. . to be wise, they became *f*
1 Cor. 3:18 let him become a *f*, that he may be wise
　4:10 we are *f* for Christ's sake, but ye are wise
　15:36 thou *f*, that which thou sowest is not
2 Cor. 11:16 I say again, Let no man think me a *f*
　11:23 of Christ? (I speak as a *f*,) I am more

2 Cor. 12:6 I would desire to glory, I shall not be a *f*
12:11 I am become a *f* in glorying; ye have
Eph. 5:15 that ye walk circumspectly, not as *f*

Foolish

Deut. 32:6 do ye thus requite the LORD, O *f* people
32:21 (Rom. 10:19) them to anger with a *f* nation
Job 2:10 thou speakest as one of the *f* women
5:2 wrath killeth the *f* man, and envy slayeth
5:3 I have seen the *f* taking root: but suddenly
Ps. 5:5 the *f* shall not stand in thy sight
39:8 make me not the reproach of the *f*
73:3 for I was envious at the *f*, when I saw the
73:22 so *f* was I, and ignorant: I was as a beast
Prov. 9:6 forsake the *f*, and live; and go in the
9:13 a *f* woman is clamorous: she is simple
10:1 but a *f* son is the heaviness of his mother
10:14 but the mouth of the *f* is near destruction
14:1 her house: but the *f* plucketh it down
14:7 go from the presence of a *f* man, when thou
17:25 a *f* son is a grief to his father
19:13 a *f* son is the calamity of his father
Eccl. 4:13 and a wise child, than an old and *f* king
7:17 be not over much wicked, neither be thou *f*
10:15 labor of the *f* wearieth every one of them
Is. 44:25 and maketh their knowledge *f*
Jer. 4:22 my people is *f*, they have not known me
5:4 I said, Surely these are poor; they are *f*
10:8 but they are altogether brutish and *f*
Lam. 2:14 thy prophets have seen vain and *f* things
Ezek. 13:3 woe unto the *f* prophets, that follow
Zech. 11:15 take. . the instruments of a *f* shepherd
Mt. 7:26 shall be likened unto a *f* man, which built
25:2 and then were wise, and five were *f*
Rom. 1:21 and their *f* heart was darkened
2:20 an instructor of the *f*, a teacher of babes
1 Cor. 1:20 God made *f* the wisdom of this world?
Gal. 3:1 O *f* Galatians, who hath bewitched you
3:3 are ye so *f*? having begun in the Spirit
Eph. 5:4 neither filthiness, nor *f* talking, nor
1 Tim. 6:9 into many *f* and hurtful lusts
2 Tim. 2:23 but *f* and unlearned questions avoid
Tit. 3:3 for we ourselves also were sometime *f*
3:9 but avoid *f* questions, and genealogies
1 Pet. 2:15 put to silence the ignorance of *f* men

Foolishly

1 Sam. 13:13 Samuel said to Saul, Thou hast done *f*
2 Sam. 24:10 (1 Chr. 21:8) I have done very *f*
2 Chr. 16:9 herein thou hast done *f*: therefore
Job 1:22 Job sinned not, nor charged God *f*

Foolishness

2 Sam. 15:31 turn the counsel of Ahithophel into *f*
Ps. 69:5 O God, thou knowest my *f*; and my sins
Prov. 12:23 but the heart of fools proclaimeth *f*
15:2 but the mouth of fools poureth out *f*
19:3 the *f* of man perverteth his way
22:15 *f* is bound in the heart of a child
24:9 the thought of *f* is sin: and the scorner
27:22 yet will not his *f* depart from him
Eccl. 7:25 know the wickedness of folly, even of *f*
10:13 beginning of the words of his mouth is *f*
Mk. 7:22 an evil eye, blasphemy, pride, *f*
1 Cor. 1:18 the cross is to them that perish, *f*
1:21 pleased God by the *f* of preaching to save
1:23 preach Christ crucified. . unto the Greeks *f*
1:25 because the *f* of God is wiser than men
2:14 Spirit of God: for they are *f* unto him
3:19 for the wisdom of this world is *f* with God

Foot *See also* Feet, Sole

Gen. 8:9 dove found no rest for the sole of her *f*

Gen. 41:44 no man lift up his hand or *f* in all. . Egypt
Ex. 21:24 (Deut. 19:21) hand for hand, *f* for *f*
40:11 and thou shalt anoint the laver and his *f*
Deut. 8:4 neither did thy *f* swell, these forty years
11:10 thy seed, and wateredst it with thy *f*
32:35 their *f* shall slide in due time
33:24 Asher be blessed. . let him dip his *f* in oil
Josh. 5:15 Joshua, Loose thy shoe from off thy *f*
Job 31:5 or if my *f* hath hasted to deceive
Ps. 26:12 my *f* standeth in an even place
38:16 when my *f* slippeth, they magnify
66:6 they went through the flood on *f*
91:12 (Mt. 4:6; Lk. 4:11) lest thou dash thy *f*
94:18 my *f* slippeth; thy mercy, O LORD, held me
121:3 he will not suffer thy *f* to be moved
Prov. 3:23 safely, and thy *f* shall not stumble
4:27 nor to the left: remove thy *f* from evil
25:17 withdraw thy *f* from thy neighbor's house
Eccl. 5:1 keep thy *f* when thou goest to the house
Is. 1:6 from the sole of the *f* even unto the head
18:7 a nation meted out and trodden under *f*
20:2 and put off thy shoe from thy *f*
26:6 the *f* shall tread it down, even the
41:2 up the righteous man. . called him to his *f*
58:13 if thou turn away thy *f* from the sabbath
Jer. 2:25 withhold thy *f* from being unshod
12:10 many pastors. . trodden my portion under *f*
Lam. 1:15 Lord hath trodden under *f* all my mighty
Mt. 5:13 cast out, and to be trodden under *f* of men
14:13 they followed him on *f* out of the cities
18:8 (Mk. 9:45) thy *f* offend thee, cut them off
Jn. 11:44 bound hand and *f* with graveclothes
Acts 7:5 inheritance. . so much as to set his *f* on
1 Cor. 12:15 if the *f* shall say. . I am not the hand
Heb. 10:29 who hath trodden under *f* the Son of God

Footmen

Jer. 12:5 if thou hast run with the *f*, and they have

Footstep

Ps. 17:5 goings in thy paths, that my *f* slip not
77:19 thy way is in the sea. . thy *f* are not known
89:51 have reproached the *f* of thine anointed

Footstool

1 Chr. 28:2 build a house. . for the *f* of our God
Ps. 99:5 and worship at his *f*; for he is holy
110:1 (Mt. 22:44; Mk. 12:36; Lk. 20:43; Acts 2:35;
Heb. 1:13) until I make thine enemies thy *f*
132:7 his tabernacles: we will worship at his *f*
Is. 66:1 (Acts 7:49) and the earth is my *f*
Mt. 5:35 nor by the earth; for it is his *f*
Heb. 10:13 till his enemies be made his *f*
Jas. 2:3 and say to the poor. . sit here under my *f*

Forbade *See* Forbid

Forbear

Deut. 23:22 if thou shalt *f* to vow. . no sin in thee
2 Chr. 35:21 *f* thee from meddling with God
Neh. 9:30 yet many years didst thou *f* them
Job 16:6 and though I *f*, what am I eased?
Prov. 24:11 if thou *f* to deliver them that are
Jer. 20:9 shut up in my bones. . I was weary with *f*
Ezek. 2:5 (3:11) will hear, or whether they will *f*
3:27 heareth, let him hear. . he that *f*, let him *f*
24:17 *f* to cry, make no mourning for the dead
Zech. 11:12 good, give me my price; and if not, *f*
1 Cor. 9:6 have not we power to *f* working?
2 Cor. 12:6 for I will say the truth: but now I *f*
Eph. 4:2 (Col. 3:13) long-suffering, *f* one another
6:9 *f* threatening: knowing that your Master also
1 Thes. 3:1 wherefore when we could no longer *f*

Forbearance

Rom. 3:25 sins that are past, through the *f* of God

Forbid (Forbade, Forbidden)

Lev. 5:17 commit. . things which are *f* to be done
Num. 11:28 Joshua. . said, My lord Moses, *f* them
Deut. 2:37 nor unto whatsoever is the LORD our God *f*
  4:23 image. . which the LORD thy God hath *f*
Mt. 3:14 but John *f* him, saying, I have need to be
  19:14 (Mk. 10:14; Lk. 18:16) children. . *f* them not
Mk. 9:38 (Lk. 9:49) *f* him, because he followeth not
Lk. 6:29 *f* not to take thy coat also
  23:2 the nation, and *f* to give tribute to Caesar
Acts 10:47 can any man *f* water, that these should
  16:6 were *f* of the Holy Ghost to preach. . in Asia
  24:23 *f* none of his acquaintance to minister
  28:31 preaching the kingdom of God. . no man *f*
1 Cor. 14:39 and *f* not to speak with tongues
Gal. 6:14 but God *f* that I should glory, save in
1 Thes. 2:16 *f* us to speak to the Gentiles
1 Tim. 4:3 *f* to marry, and commanding to abstain
2 Pet. 2:16 dumb ass. . *f* the madness of the prophet

Force *See also* Power, Strength

Gen. 31:31 take by *f* thy daughters from me
Deut. 34:7 eye was not dim, nor his natural *f* abated
Ezra 4:23 the Jews, and made them to cease by *f*
Is. 60:5 *f* of the Gentiles shall come unto thee
Jer. 18:21 out their blood by the *f* of the sword
Ezek. 34:4 with *f* and. . cruelty have ye ruled them
Dan. 11:38 in his estate shall he honor the God of *f*
Amos 2:14 the strong shall not strengthen his *f*
Mt. 11:12 violence, and the violent take it by *f*
Jn. 6:15 and take him by *f*, to make him a king
Acts 23:10 soldiers. . to take him by *f* from among
Heb. 9:17 a testament is of *f* after men are dead

Forcible

Job 6:25 how *f* are right words! but what doth your

Forecast

Dan. 11:24 *f* his devices against the strongholds
  11:25 for they shall *f* devices against him

Forefather

Jer. 11:10 back to the iniquities of their *f*
2 Tim. 1:3 I thank God, whom I serve from my *f*

Forefront

2 Sam. 11:15 Uriah in the *f* of the hottest battle

Forehead *See also* Temple

Ex. 28:38 and it shall be upon Aaron's *f*
1 Sam. 17:49 David. . smote the Philistine in his *f*
Jer. 3:3 thou hadst a whore's *f*, thou refusedst to
Ezek. 3:8 have made. . thy *f* strong against their *f*
  3:9 adamant harder than flint have I made thy *f*
  9:4 set a mark upon the *f* of the men that sigh
  16:12 and I put a jewel on thy *f*, and earrings
Rev. 7:3 sealed the servants of our God in their *f*
  9:4 which have not the seal of God in their *f*
  13:16 a mark in their right hand, or in their *f*
  14:1 having his Father's name written in their *f*
  14:9 his image, and receive his mark in his *f*
  17:5 and upon her *f* was a name written, MYSTERY
  20:4 neither had received his mark upon their *f*
  22:4 and his name shall be in their *f*

Foreigner *See also* Alien, Sojourner, Stranger

Ex. 12:45 a *f* and a hired servant shall not eat

Deut. 15:3 of a *f* thou mayest exact it again
Eph. 2:19 ye are no more strangers and *f*, but

Foreknow (Foreknew)

Rom. 8:29 whom he did *f*, he also did predestinate
  11:2 hath not cast away his people which he *f*

Foreknowledge

Acts 2:23 by the determinate counsel and *f* of God
1 Pet. 1:2 elect according to the *f* of God

Foremost

Gen. 32:17 he commanded the *f*, saying, When Esau
  33:2 he put the handmaids and their children *f*
2 Sam. 18:27 methinketh the running of the *f* is

Foreordain *See also* Predestinate

1 Pet. 1:20 who verily was *f* before the foundation

Forerunner

Heb. 6:20 the *f* is for us entered, even Jesus

Foresee (Foresaw)

Prov. 22:3 (27:12) prudent man *f* the evil, and hideth
Acts 2:25 I *f* the Lord always before my face
Gal. 3:8 *f* that God would justify the heathen

Forest

1 Kgs. 7:2 built also the house of the *f* of Lebanon
Ps. 50:10 for every beast of the *f* is mine
Is. 29:17 (32:15) fruitful field. . esteemed as a *f*?
Jer. 26:18 (Mic. 3:12) as the high places of a *f*
  46:23 they shall cut down her *f*, saith the LORD
Ezek. 15:6 as the vine tree among the trees of the *f*
  20:46 prophesy against the *f* of the south field
Hos. 2:12 vines and her fig trees. . make them a *f*
Amos 3:4 will a lion roar in the *f*, when he hath

Forewarn

Lk. 12:5 but I will *f* you whom ye shall fear
1 Thes. 4:6 as we also have *f* you and testified

Forgat *See* Forget

Forgave *See* Forgive

Forge

Ps. 119:69 the proud have *f* a lie against me

Forget (Forgat, Forgot, Forgotten)

Gen. 27:45 he *f* that which thou hast done to him
  40:23 chief butler remember Joseph, but *f* him
  41:30 the plenty shall be *f* in the land of Egypt
  41:51 God, said he, hath made me *f* all my toil
Deut. 4:9 lest thou *f* the things which thine eyes
  4:23 lest ye *f* the covenant of the LORD your God
  4:31 will not forsake thee. . nor *f* the covenant
  6:12 beware lest thou *f* the LORD, which brought
  8:14 heart be lifted up, and thou *f* the LORD
  24:19 hast *f* a sheaf in the field, thou shalt
  32:18 unmindful, and hast *f* God that formed thee
Judg. 3:7 Israel did evil. . and *f* the LORD
1 Sam. 12:9 when they *f* the LORD their God, he
2 Kgs. 17:38 and the covenant. . ye shall not *f*
Job 8:13 so are the paths of all that *f* God
  19:14 and my familiar friends have *f* me
Ps. 9:12 he *f* not the cry of the humble
  9:17 into hell, and all the nations that *f* God
  9:18 for the needy shall not always be *f*
  10:11 he hath said in his heart, God hath *f*
  10:12 God, lift up thine hand: *f* not the humble
  13:1 how long wilt thou *f* me, O LORD? for ever?
  31:12 I am *f* as a dead man out of mind
  42:9 say unto God my rock, Why hast thou *f* me?

Ps. 44:17 is come upon us; yet have we not *f* thee
  44:20 if we have *f* the name of our God
  44:24 and *f* our affliction and our oppression?
  45:10 *f* also thine own people, and thy father's
  50:22 now consider this, ye that *f* God, lest I
  74:19 *f* not the congregation of thy poor
  77:9 hath God *f* to be gracious? hath he in anger
  78:7 and not *f* the works of God, but keep his
  78:11 *f* his works, and his wonders that he had
  102:4 so that I *f* to eat my bread
  103:2 O my soul, and *f* not all his benefits
  106:13 they soon *f* his works; they waited not
  106:21 they *f* God their saviour, which had done
  119:16 in thy statutes: I will not *f* thy word
  119:61 have robbed me: but I have not *f* thy law
  119:93 I will never *f* thy precepts
  119:141 despised: yet do not I *f* thy precepts
  137:5 if I *f* thee, O Jerusalem, let my right hand
Prov. 2:17 and *f* the covenant of her God
  3:1 my son, *f* not my law; but let thine heart
  4:5 get wisdom, get understanding: *f* it not
  31:5 lest they drink, and *f* the law, and pervert
  31:7 let him drink, and *f* his poverty
Eccl. 2:16 in the days to come shall all be *f*
  8:10 and they were *f* in the city where they had
  9:5 dead know not . . for the memory of them is *f*
Is. 17:10 hast *f* the God of thy salvation
  44:21 O Israel, thou shalt not be *f* of me
  49:14 hath forsaken me, and my Lord hath *f* me
  49:15 can a woman *f* her sucking child
  49:15 yea, they may *f*, yet will I not *f* thee
  51:13 and *f* the LORD thy Maker, that hath
  65:11 forsake the LORD, that *f* my holy mountain
  65:16 because the former troubles are *f*
Jer. 2:32 my people have *f* me days without number
  3:21 and they have *f* the LORD their God
  13:25 thou hast *f* me, and trusted in falsehood
  18:15 because my people hath *f* me, they have
  23:27 think to cause my people to *f* my name
  30:14 all thy lovers have *f* thee
  44:9 have ye *f* the wickedness of your fathers
  50:5 in a perpetual covenant that shall not be *f*
  50:6 they have *f* their resting place
Lam. 2:6 the solemn feasts and sabbaths to be *f*
  3:17 my soul far off from peace: I *f* prosperity
  5:20 wherefore dost thou *f* us for ever
Ezek. 22:12 hast greedily gained . . and hast *f* me
  23:35 because thou hast *f* me, and cast me behind
Hos. 2:13 and she went after her lovers, and *f* me
  4:6 hast *f* the law . . I will also *f* thy children
  8:14 for Israel hath *f* his Maker
  13:6 heart was exalted; therefore have they *f* me
Amos 8:7 surely I will never *f* any of their works
Mt. 16:5 (Mk. 8:14) they had *f* to take bread
Lk. 12:6 sparrows . . not one of them is *f* before God?
Phil. 3:13 I do, *f* those things which are behind
Heb. 6:10 God is not unrighteous to *f* your work
  12:5 ye have *f* the exhortation which speaketh
  13:16 but to do good and to communicate *f* not
Jas. 1:24 straightway *f* what manner of man he was
2 Pet. 1:9 *f* that he was purged from his old sins

Forgetful

Heb. 13:2 be not *f* to entertain strangers
Jas. 1:25 not a *f* hearer, but a doer of the work

Forgetfulness

Ps. 88:12 and thy righteousness in the land of *f* ?

Forgive (Forgave, Forgiven)

Gen. 50:17 Joseph, *F* . . the trespass of thy brethren
Ex. 32:32 yet now, if thou wilt *f* their sin
  34:7 *f* iniquity and transgression and sin
Lev. 4:20 atonement for them, and it shall be *f* them

Lev. 19:22 the sin which he hath done shall be *f* him
Num. 14:18 mercy, *f* iniquity and transgression
  15:25 it shall be *f* them; for it is ignorance
  30:5 the LORD shall *f* her, because her father
Josh. 24:19 he will not *f* your transgressions
1 Sam. 25:28 *f* the trespass of thine handmaid
1 Kgs. 8:30 (2 Chr. 6:21) and when thou hearest, *f*
  8:39 (2 Chr. 6:30) hear thou in heaven . . and *f*
2 Chr. 7:14 hear from heaven, and will *f* their sin
Ps. 25:18 look upon . . my pain; and *f* all my sins
  32:1 (Rom. 4:7) is he whose transgression is *f*
  32:5 and thou *f* the iniquity of my sin
  78:38 being full of compassion, *f* their iniquity
  85:2 thou hast *f* the iniquity of thy people
  86:5 for thou, Lord, art good, and ready to *f*
  99:8 thou wast a God that *f* them, though thou
  103:3 who *f* all thine iniquities; who healeth
Is. 2:9 man humbleth himself: therefore *f* them not
  33:24 dwell therein shall be *f* their iniquity
Jer. 31:34 for I will *f* their iniquity, and I will
Dan. 9:19 O Lord, hear; O Lord, *f*; O Lord, hearken
Amos 7:2 then I said, O Lord GOD, *f*, I beseech
Mt. 6:12 (Lk. 11:4) *f* us our debts, as we *f* our debtors
  6:14 (Mk. 11:25) for if ye *f* men their trespasses,
    your heavenly Father will also *f* you
  9:2 (Mk. 2:5; Lk. 5:20) son . . thy sins be *f* thee
  9:6 (Mk. 2:10; Lk. 5:24) power on earth to *f* sins
  12:31 (Mk. 3:28; Lk. 12:10) be *f* unto men: but the
    blasphemy against the Holy Ghost shall not be *f*
  18:21 against me, and I *f* him? till seven times?
  18:32 wicked servant, I *f* thee all that debt
  18:35 if ye from your hearts *f* not every one
Mk. 2:7 (Lk. 5:21) who can *f* sins but God only?
Lk. 6:37 *f*, and ye shall be *f*
  7:42 had nothing to pay, he frankly *f* them both
  7:47 to whom little is *f*, the same loveth little
  17:3 rebuke him; and if he repent, *f* him
  23:34 Father, *f* them; for they know not what
Acts 8:22 the thought of thine heart may be *f* thee
2 Cor. 2:7 contrariwise ye ought rather to *f* him
  2:10 whom ye *f* any thing, I *f* also: for if I *f*
Eph. 4:32 even as God for Christ's sake hath *f* you
Col. 2:13 quickened . . having *f* you all trespasses
  3:13 even as Christ *f* you, so also do ye
Jas. 5:15 have committed sins, they shall be *f* him
1 Jn. 1:9 he is faithful and just to *f* us our sins
  2:12 your sins are *f* you for his name's sake

Forgiveness *See also* Pardon, Remission

Ps. 130:4 but there is *f* with thee, that thou
Dan. 9:9 to the Lord our God belong mercies and *f*
Mk. 3:29 against the Holy Ghost hath never *f*
Acts 5:31 give repentance to Israel, and *f* of sins
  13:38 is preached unto you the *f* of sins
  26:18 unto God, that they may receive *f* of sins
Eph. 1:7 (Col. 1:14) through his blood . . *f* of sins

Form *See also* Create, Fashion, Invent, Make, Shape

Gen. 1:2 and the earth was without *f*, and void
  2:7 LORD God *f* man of the dust of the ground
  2:19 of the ground the LORD God *f* every beast
Deut. 32:18 and hast forgotten God that *f* thee
1 Sam. 28:14 he said unto her, What *f* is he of ?
2 Sam. 14:20 to fetch about this *f* of speech
2 Kgs. 19:25 (Is. 37:26) not heard . . that I have *f* it?
Job 4:16 but I could not discern the *f* thereof
  26:5 dead things are *f* from under the waters
  26:13 his hand hath *f* the crooked serpent
  33:6 God's stead: I also am *f* out of the clay
Ps. 90:2 or ever thou hadst *f* the earth and the
  94:9 he that *f* the eye, shall he not see?
  95:5 he made it: and his hands *f* the dry land

Prov. 26:10 the great God that *f* all things both
Is. 43:1 and he that *f* thee, O Israel, Fear not
43:7 for my glory, I have *f* him; yea, I have
43:10 before me there was no God *f*, neither
43:21 this people have I *f* for myself
44:2 that made thee, and *f* thee from the womb
44:10 who hath *f* a god, or molten a graven image
44:21 thou art my servant: I have *f* thee
45:7 I *f* the light, and create darkness
45:18 God himself that *f* the earth and made it
49:5 LORD that *f* me from the womb to be his
52:14 and his *f* more than the sons of men
53:2 he hath no *f* nor comeliness
54:17 no weapon that is *f* against thee shall
Jer. 1:5 before I *f* thee in the belly I knew thee
4:23 earth, and, lo, it was without *f*, and void
Ezek. 8:3 he put forth the *f* of a hand, and took
10:8 in the cherubim the *f* of a man's hand
43:11 be ashamed. . show them the *f* of the house
Dan. 3:19 the *f* of his visage was changed against
3:25 the *f* of the fourth is like the Son of God
Amos 4:13 he that *f* the mountains, and createth
7:1 behold, he *f* grasshoppers in the beginning
Zech. 12:1 and *f* the spirit of man within him
Mk. 16:12 appeared in another *f* unto two of them
Rom. 2:20 hast the *f* of knowledge. . in the law
6:17 that *f* of doctrine which was delivered you
9:20 shall the thing formed say to him that *f* it
Gal. 4:19 travail. . until Christ be *f* in you
Phil. 2:6 who, being in the *f* of God, thought it
2:7 took upon him the *f* of a servant
1 Tim. 2:13 for Adam was first *f*, then Eve
2 Tim. 1:13 hold fast the *f* of sound words
3:5 having a *f* of godliness, but denying the

Former (adjective)

Gen. 40:13 the *f* manner when thou wast his butler
Ruth 4:7 this was the manner in *f* time in Israel
Job 8:8 for inquire, I pray thee, of the *f* age
30:3 into the wilderness in *f* time desolate
Ps. 79:8 O remember not against us *f* iniquities
89:49 Lord, where are thy *f* loving-kindnesses
Eccl. 1:11 there is no remembrance of *f* things
7:10 that the *f* days were better than these?
Is. 41:22 let them show the *f* things, what they be
42:9 behold, the *f* things are come to pass
43:18 remember ye not the *f* things, neither
46:9 remember the *f* things of old: for I am God
48:3 declared the *f* things from the beginning
65:7 I measure their *f* work into their bosom
65:16 because the *f* troubles are forgotten
Jer. 5:24 giveth rain, both the *f* and the latter
36:28 write in it all the *f* words that were in
Dan. 11:13 a multitude greater than the *f*
Hos. 6:3 as the latter and *f* rain unto the earth
Joel 2:23 he hath given you the *f* rain moderately
Hag. 2:9 latter house shall be greater than of the *f*
Zech. 1:4 unto whom the *f* prophets have cried
7:7 which the LORD hath cried by the *f* prophets
7:12 hath sent in his Spirit by the *f* prophets
8:11 residue of this people as in the *f* days
Mal. 3:4 be pleasant unto the LORD. . as in *f* years
Acts 1:1 the *f* treatise have I made, O Theophilus
Eph. 4:22 put off concerning the *f* conversation
1 Pet. 1:14 fashioning. . according to the *f* lusts
Rev. 21:4 for the *f* things are passed away

Former (noun)

Jer. 10:16 (51:19) he is the *f* of all things

Fornication

2 Chr. 21:11 inhabitants of Jerusalem to commit *f*
Ezek. 16:29 multiplied thy *f* in the land of Canaan
Mt. 5:32 (19:9) wife, saving for the cause of *f*

Mt. 15:19 (Mk. 7:21) proceed evil thoughts. . *f*, thefts
Jn. 8:41 we be not born of *f*; we have one Father
Acts 15:20 (15:29; 21:25) from . idols, and from *f*
Rom. 1:29 being filled with all unrighteousness, *f*
1 Cor. 5:1 reported. . that there is *f* among you
6:13 now the body is not for *f*, but for the Lord
6:18 flee *f*. Every sin that a man doeth is
7:2 to avoid *f*, let every man have his own wife
2 Cor. 12:21 not repented of the uncleanness and *f*
Gal. 5:19 works of the flesh are manifest. . *f*
Eph. 5:3 but *f*. . let it not be once named among you
Col. 3:5 *f*, uncleanness, inordinate affection
1 Thes. 4:3 will of God. . ye should abstain from *f*
Jude 7 even as Sodom. . giving themselves over to *f*
Rev. 2:14 (2:20) unto idols, and to commit *f*
14:8 drink of the wine of the wrath of her *f*
17:2 the kings of the earth have committed *f*
18:3 drunk of the wine of the wrath of her *f*
19:2 which did corrupt the earth with her *f*

Fornicator

1 Cor. 5:9 in an epistle not to company with *f*
6:9 be not deceived: neither *f*, nor idolaters

Forsake (Forsook, Forsaken)

See also Leave

Deut. 4:31 he will not *f* thee, neither destroy
12:19 take heed. . that thou *f* not the Levite
28:20 of thy doings, whereby thou hast *f* me
29:25 because they have *f* the covenant of
31:6 fear not. . he will not fail thee, nor *f* thee
31:16 will *f* me, and break my covenant
31:17 I will *f* them, and I will hide my face
32:15 then he *f* God which made him, and lightly
Josh. 1:5 (Heb. 13:5) will not fail thee, nor *f* thee
Judg. 2:12 they *f* the LORD God of their fathers
6:13 but now the LORD hath *f* us, and delivered
9:11 fig tree said. . Should I *f* my sweetness
10:13 yet ye have *f* me, and served other gods
1 Sam. 8:8 they have *f* me, and served other gods
12:10 sinned, because we have *f* the LORD
1 Kgs. 9:9 (2 Chr. 7:22) because they *f* the LORD
12:8 (2 Chr. 10:8) *f* the counsel of the old men
18:18 ye have *f* the commandments of the LORD
2 Kgs. 21:14 *f* the remnant of mine inheritance
1 Chr. 28:9 if thou *f* him, he will cast thee off
2 Chr. 12:1 *f* the law of the LORD, and all Israel
13:11 we keep the charge. . but ye have *f* him
15:2 but if ye *f* him, he will *f* you
24:20 ye have *f* the LORD, he hath also *f* you
Ezra 8:22 his wrath is against all them that *f* him
9:10 for we have *f* thy commandments
Neh. 9:19 yet thou. . *f* them not in the wilderness
10:39 and we will not *f* the house of our God
Job 6:14 but he *f* the fear of the Almighty
20:13 though he spare it, and *f* it not, but keep
20:19 he hath oppressed and hath *f* the poor
Ps. 9:10 LORD, hast not *f* them that seek thee
22:1 (Mt. 27:46; Mk. 15:34) why hast thou *f* me?
27:10 father and my mother *f* me, then the LORD
37:8 cease from anger, and *f* wrath: fret not
37:28 LORD loveth judgment, and *f* not his saints
71:11 God hath *f* him: persecute and take him
89:30 if his children *f* my law, and walk not in
94:14 neither will he *f* his inheritance
119:8 I will keep thy statutes: O *f* me not
119:53 because of the wicked that *f* thy law
119:87 consumed me. . but I *f* not thy precepts
Prov. 1:8 (6:20) and *f* not the law of thy mother
2:17 which *f* the guide of her youth
3:3 let not mercy and truth *f* thee: bind them
4:6 *f* her not, and she shall preserve thee
9:6 *f* the foolish, and live; and go in the way

Prov. 27:10 own friend. . thy father's friend, *f* not
    28:13 confesseth and *f* them shall have mercy
Is. 1:4 ah sinful nation. . they have *f* the LORD
    1:28 and they that *f* the LORD shall be consumed
    2:6 thou hast *f* thy people the house of Jacob
    6:12 be a great *f* in the midst of the land
    7:16 the land. . shall be *f* of both her kings
    32:14 because the palaces shall be *f*
    49:14 but Zion said, The LORD hath *f* me
    54:7 for a small moment have I *f* thee
    55:7 let the wicked *f* his way
    58:2 and *f* not the ordinance of their God
Jer. 1:16 who have *f* me, and have burned incense
    2:13 have committed two evils; they have *f* me
    4:29 every city shall be *f*, and not a man dwell
    5:7 thy children have *f* me, and sworn by them
    5:19 as ye have *f* me, and served strange gods
    15:6 thou hast *f* me, saith the LORD
    16:11 because your fathers have *f* me
    17:13 because they have *f* the LORD, the fountain
    18:14 or shall the cold flowing waters. . be *f*?
    22:9 they have *f* the covenant of the LORD
    23:33 I will even *f* you, saith the LORD
Ezek. 8:12 (9:9) the LORD hath *f* the earth
Jon. 2:8 observe lying vanities *f* their own mercy
Mt. 19:27 behold, we have *f* all, and followed thee
    19:29 every one that hath *f* houses, or brethren
    26:56 (Mk. 14:50) the disciples *f* him, and fled
    27:46 (Mk. 15:34) my God, why hast thou *f* me?
Mk. 1:18 (Lk. 5:11) *f* their nets, and followed him
Lk. 14:33 that *f* not all. . he cannot be my disciple
2 Tim. 4:10 Demas hath *f* me, having loved this
    4:16 no man stood with me, but all men *f* me
Heb. 10:25 not *f* the assembling of ourselves
    11:27 by faith he *f* Egypt, not fearing the wrath
2 Pet. 2:15 which have *f* the right way

Forsaken *See also* Forsake

Neh. 13:11 contended. . Why is the house of God *f*?
Ps. 37:25 yet have I not seen the righteous *f*
Is. 17:9 shall his strong cities be as a *f* bough
    54:6 for the LORD hath called thee as a woman *f*
    62:4 thou shalt no more be termed *F*
    62:12 shalt be called, Sought out, A city not *f*
Ezek. 36:4 saith the LORD. . to the cities that are *f*
Amos 5:2 virgin of Israel. . she is *f* upon her land
2 Cor. 4:9 persecuted, but not *f*; cast down, but

Forswear

Mt. 5:33 thou shalt not *f* thyself, but shalt

Fortress

2 Sam. 22:2 (Ps. 18:2) LORD is my rock, and my *f*
Ps. 31:3 for thou art my rock and my *f*
    91:2 he is my refuge and my *f*; my God
    144:2 my goodness, and my *f*; my high tower
Jer. 16:19 O LORD, my strength, and my *f*

Forty

Gen. 7:17 the flood was *f* days upon the earth
Ex. 16:35 children of Israel did eat manna *f* years
    24:18 (Deut. 9:9) in the mount *f* days and *f* nights
Num. 13:25 from searching of the land after *f* days
    14:33 shall wander in the wilderness *f* years
Deut. 25:3 *f* stripes he may give him, and not exceed
Judg. 3:11 and the land had rest *f* years
    8:28 the country was in quietness *f* years
1 Sam. 17:16 Philistine. . presented himself *f* days
1 Kgs. 19:8 went. . *f* days and *f* nights unto Horeb
Ps. 95:10 *f* years long was I grieved with this
Ezek. 4:6 shalt bear the iniquity. . of Judah *f* days
    29:11 neither shall it be inhabited *f* years
Jon. 3:4 yet *f* days, and Nineveh shall be overthrown
Mt. 4:2 and when he had fasted *f* days and *f* nights

Mk. 1:13 he was there in the wilderness *f* days
Lk. 4:2 being *f* days tempted of the devil
Acts 1:3 being seen of them *f* days, and speaking
2 Cor. 11:24 five times received I *f* stripes

Forward

Ex. 14:15 speak unto. . Israel, that they go *f*
Ezra 3:8 set *f* the work of the house of the LORD
Job 23:8 behold, I go *f*, but he is not there
Jer. 7:24 but they. . went backward, and not *f*
Ezek. 1:9 they went every one straight *f*
Zech. 1:15 and they helped *f* the affliction
Mk. 14:35 and he went *f* a little. . and prayed that
2 Cor. 8:17 but being more *f*, of his own accord
Gal. 2:10 the same which I also was *f* to do
3 Jn. 6 whom if thou bring *f* on their journey

Forwardness

2 Cor. 8:8 but by occasion of the *f* of others
    9:2 for I know the *f* of your mind, for which I

Fought *See* Fight

Foul

Job 16:16 my face is *f* with weeping
Mt. 16:3 it will be *f* weather today: for the sky
Mk. 9:25 he rebuked the *f* spirit, saying unto him
Rev. 18:2 of devils, and the hold of every *f* spirit

Found *See also* Find

Ps. 24:2 for he hath *f* it upon the seas
Prov. 3:19 the LORD by wisdom hath *f* the earth
Is. 14:32 that the LORD hath *f* Zion
Mt. 7:25 (Lk. 6:48) fell not: for it was *f* upon a rock

Foundation

Josh. 6:26 (1 Kgs. 16:34) lay the *f*. . in his firstborn
2 Sam. 22:8 (Ps. 18:7) *f* of heaven moved and shook
    22:16 (Ps. 18:15) *f* of the world were discovered
1 Kgs. 7:10 and the *f* was of costly stones
Ezra 3:10 when the builders laid the *f* of the temple
    5:16 and laid the *f* of the house of God
Job 4:19 houses of clay, whose *f* is in the dust
    22:16 whose *f* was overflown with a flood
    38:4 wast thou when I laid the *f* of the earth?
Ps. 11:3 *f* be destroyed, what can the righteous do?
    18:7 *f* also of the hills moved and were shaken
    82:5 all the *f* of the earth are out of course
    87:1 his *f* is in the holy mountains
    102:25 (Heb. 1:10) of old hast thou laid the *f*
    104:5 who laid the *f* of the earth
    137:7 who said, Rase it, rase it, even to the *f*
Prov. 8:29 when he appointed the *f* of the earth
    10:25 but the righteous is an everlasting *f*
Is. 24:18 and the *f* of the earth do shake
    28:16 behold, I lay in Zion for a *f* a stone
    40:21 not understood from the *f* of the earth?
    51:13 thy Maker, that. . laid the *f* of the earth
    54:11 behold, I will. . lay thy *f* with sapphires
    58:12 shalt raise up the *f* of many generations
Jer. 50:15 her *f* are fallen, her walls are thrown
Mic. 6:2 hear ye. . ye strong *f* of the earth
Zech. 12:1 layeth the *f* of the earth, and formeth
Mt. 13:35 kept secret from the *f* of the world
    25:34 prepared for you from the *f* of the world
Lk. 6:48 built a house. . and laid the *f* on a rock
    11:50 which was shed from the *f* of the world
    14:29 lest haply, after he hath laid the *f*
Jn. 17:24 lovedst me before the *f* of the world
Acts 16:26 that the *f* of the prison were shaken
Rom. 15:20 lest I should build upon another man's *f*
1 Cor. 3:10 I have laid the *f*, and another buildeth
    3:11 other *f* can no man lay than that is laid
Eph. 1:4 chosen us in him before the *f* of the world

Eph. 2:20 are built upon the *f* of the apostles and
1 Tim. 6:19 a good *f* against the time to come
2 Tim. 2:19 the *f* of God standeth sure
Heb. 4:3 works were finished from the *f* of the world
  6:1 not laying again the *f* of repentance from
  11:10 city which hath *f,* whose builder. . is God
1 Pet. 1:20 foreordained before the *f* of the world
Rev. 13:8 the Lamb slain from the *f* of the world
  21:14 and the wall of the city had twelve *f*
  21:19 *f* of the wall of the city were garnished

Fountain *See also* Spring, Well

Gen. 7:11 all the *f* of the great deep broken up
  8:2 the *f* also of the deep. . were stopped
  16:7 found her by a *f* of water in the wilderness
Num. 33:9 and in Elim were twelve *f* of water
Deut. 8:7 a land of brooks of water, of *f*
2 Chr. 32:3 took counsel. . to stop the waters of the *f*
Neh. 2:14 then I went on to the gate of the *f*
Ps. 36:9 for with thee is the *f* of life
  68:26 bless ye. . the Lord, from the *f* of Israel
  114:8 which turned. . the flint into a *f* of waters
Prov. 5:16 thy *f* be dispersed abroad, and rivers
  5:18 let thy *f* be blessed. . rejoice with the wife
  8:24 when there were no *f* abounding with water
  13:14 the law of the wise is a *f* of life
  14:27 the fear of the LORD is a *f* of life
  25:26 is as a troubled *f,* and a corrupt spring
Eccl. 12:6 or the pitcher be broken at the *f*
Song 4:12 my spouse; a spring shut up, a *f* sealed
  4:15 a *f* of gardens, a well of living waters
Jer. 2:13 (17:13) forsaken me the *f* of living waters
  6:7 as a *f* casteth out her waters, so she
  9:1 mine eyes a *f* of tears, that I might weep
Hos. 13:15 and his *f* shall be dried up
Joel 3:18 a *f* shall come forth of the house of the
Zech. 13:1 be a *f* opened to the house of David
Mk. 5:29 straightway the *f* of her blood was dried
Jas. 3:11 doth a *f* send. . sweet water and bitter?
Rev. 7:17 shall lead them unto living *f* of waters
  14:7 him that made heaven. . and the *f* of waters
  21:6 I will give. . of the *f* of the water of life

Four

Ezek. 1:5 came the likeness of *f* living creatures
  10:10 their appearances, they *f* had one likeness
Dan. 7:3 *f* great beasts came up from the sea
  8:22 *f* kingdoms shall stand up out of the nation
Mt. 24:31 (Mk. 13:27) his elect from the *f* winds
Rev. 4:6 round about the throne, were *f* beasts

Fourfold

2 Sam. 12:6 he shall restore the lamb *f,* because
Lk. 19:8 and if I have taken any. . I restore him *f*

Fourscore

Ex. 7:7 Moses was *f* years old. . spake unto Pharaoh
2 Sam. 19:32 now Barzillai was. . even *f* years old
Ps. 90:10 if by reason of strength they be *f* years

Foursquare

Ex. 28:16 (39:9) *f* it shall be being doubled
Ezek. 48:20 ye shall offer the holy oblation *f*
Rev. 21:16 and the city lieth *f,* and the length is

Fowl *See also* Bird

Gen. 1:21 every winged *f* after his kind
  7:3 of *f* also of the air by sevens. . to keep seed
  15:11 when the *f* came down upon the carcasses
Lev. 1:14 sacrifice for his offering. . be of *f*
  11:20 *f* that creep. . shall be an abomination
Deut. 4:17 likeness of any winged *f* that flieth
Job 12:7 *f* of the air, and they shall tell thee
  28:7 there is a path which no *f* knoweth

Ps. 50:11 I know all the *f* of the mountains
  78:27 he rained flesh. . and feathered *f* like as
  104:12 the *f* of the heaven have their habitation
  148:10 cattle; creeping things, and flying *f*
Is. 18:6 and the *f* shall summer upon them
Ezek. 39:17 Lord GOD; Speak unto every feathered *f*
Mt. 6:26 behold the *f* of the air: for they sow not
  13:4 (Mk. 4:4; Lk. 8:5) *f* came and devoured them
Mk. 4:32 (Lk. 13:19) *f* of the air may lodge under
Lk. 12:24 how much more are ye better than the *f*?
Acts 10:12 (11:6) were all manner of. . *f* of the air
Rev. 19:21 all the *f* were filled with their flesh

Fowler

Ps. 91:3 deliver thee from the snare of the *f*
  124:7 as a bird out of the snare of the *f*
Prov. 6:5 and as a bird from the hand of the *f*
Hos. 9:8 prophet is a snare of a *f* in all his ways

Fox

Judg. 15:4 Samson went and caught three hundred *f*
Neh. 4:3 if a *f* go up, he shall even break down
Ps. 63:10 they shall be a portion for *f*
Song 2:15 take us the *f,* the little *f,* that spoil
Lam. 5:18 the mountain of Zion. . the *f* walk upon it
Ezek. 13:4 O Israel, thy prophets are like the *f*
Mt. 8:20 (Lk. 9:58) *f* have holes, and the birds
Lk. 13:32 go ye, and tell that *f,* Behold, I cast

Fragment

Mt. 14:20 (Mk. 6:43; Lk. 9:17; Jn. 6:13) they took up
  of the *f* that remained twelve baskets full
Mk. 8:19 how many baskets full of *f* took ye up?

Frail

Ps. 39:4 know mine end. . I may know how *f* I am

Frame

Judg. 12:6 he could not *f* to pronounce it right
Ps. 50:19 mouth to evil, and thy tongue *f* deceit
  94:20 throne of iniquity. . *f* mischief by a law?
  103:14 for he knoweth our *f;* he remembereth that
Is. 29:16 the thing framed say of him that *f* it
Jer. 18:11 the LORD; Behold, I *f* evil against you
Ezek. 40:2 was as the *f* of a city on the south
Hos. 5:4 they will not *f* their doings to turn unto
Eph. 2:21 in whom all the building fitly *f* together
Heb. 11:3 the worlds were *f* by the word of God

Frankincense

Ex. 30:34 Moses, Take. . sweet spices with pure *f*
Lev. 2:1 offer a meat offering. . put *f* thereon
  24:7 and thou shalt put pure *f* upon each row
Song 3:6 who is this. . perfumed with myrrh and *f*
  4:6 the mountain of myrrh, and to the hill of *f*
Mt. 2:11 unto him gifts; gold, and *f,* and myrrh
Rev. 18:13 odors, and ointments, and *f,* and wine

Fraud

Ps. 10:7 mouth is full of cursing and deceit and *f*
Jas. 5:4 which is of you kept back by *f*

Fray

Deut. 28:26 (Jer. 7:33) no man shall *f* them away
Zech. 1:21 but these are come to *f* them, to cast

Free *See also* Liberty

Ex. 21:2 (Deut. 15:12; Jer. 34:14) he shall go out *f*
  21:11 then shall she go out *f* without money
  36:3 and they brought yet unto him *f* offerings
Deut. 15:13 when thou sendest him out *f* from thee
  24:5 a new wife. . he shall be *f* at home one year
Josh. 9:23 none of you be *f* from being bondmen
1 Sam. 17:25 make his father's house *f* in Israel

2 Chr. 29:31 as were of a *f* heart, burnt offerings
Job 3:19 and the servant is *f* from his master
Ps. 51:12 and uphold me with thy *f* Spirit
  88:5 *f* among the dead, like the slain that lie
Is. 58:6 and to let the oppressed go *f*
Jer. 34:9 let his manservant. . being a Hebrew. . go *f*
Amos 4:5 and proclaim and publish the *f* offerings
Mt. 15:6 (Mk. 7:11) honor not his father. . shall be *f*
  17:26 Jesus saith. . Then are the children *f*
Jn. 8:32 and the truth shall make you *f*
  8:36 Son. . shall make you *f*, ye shall be *f* indeed
Rom. 5:15 not as the offense, so also is the *f* gift
  6:7 for he that is dead is *f* from sin
  6:18 being then made *f* from sin, ye became
  6:20 servants of sin, ye were *f* from righteousness
  8:2 hath made me *f* from the law of sin and death
1 Cor. 9:1 am I not an apostle? am I not *f*?
  9:19 for though I be *f* from all men, yet have I
  12:13 Jews or Gentiles, whether we be bond or *f*
Gal. 3:28 is neither Jew nor Greek. . bond nor *f*
  4:22 one by a bondmaid, the other by a *f* woman
  4:26 but Jerusalem which is above is *f*
  5:1 liberty wherewith Christ hath made us *f*
Eph. 6:8 shall he receive. . whether he be bond or *f*
Col. 3:11 Barbarian, Scythian, bond nor *f*
2 Thes. 3:1 the word of the Lord may have *f* course
1 Pet. 2:16 as *f*, and not using your liberty for a
Rev. 13:16 *f* and bond, to receive a mark in their
  19:18 and the flesh of all men, both *f* and bond

Freeborn

Acts 22:28 and Paul said, But I was *f*

Freedom *See also* Deliverance, Liberty

Lev. 19:20 nor *f* given her; she shall be scourged
Acts 22:28 with a great sum obtained I this *f*

Freely

Gen. 2:16 tree of the garden thou mayest *f* eat
Num. 11:5 the fish, which we did eat in Egypt *f*
1 Sam. 14:30 had eaten *f* today of the spoil
Ezra 2:68 offered *f* for the house of God to set it
  7:15 have *f* offered unto the God of Israel
Ps. 54:6 I will *f* sacrifice unto thee
Hos. 14:4 I will love them *f*: for mine anger is
Mt. 10:8 *f* ye have received, *f* give
Rom. 3:24 being justified *f* by his grace
  8:32 with him also *f* give us all things?
1 Cor. 2:12 things that are *f* given to us of God
2 Cor. 11:7 preached to you the gospel of God *f*?
Rev. 21:6 of the fountain of the water of life *f*
  22:17 let him take the water of life *f*

Freeman

1 Cor. 7:22 being a servant, is the Lord's *f*

Freewill

Lev. 22:18 his vows, and for all his *f* offerings
Deut. 16:10 tribute of a *f* offering of thine hand
  23:23 perform; even a *f* offering. . thou hast vowed
Ezra 3:5 offered a *f* offering unto the LORD
  7:16 with the *f* offering of the people
  8:28 the silver and the gold are a *f* offering
Ps. 119:108 accept. . the *f* offerings of my mouth

Fresh (Fresher)

Num. 11:8 taste of it was as the taste of *f* oil
Job 29:20 my glory was *f* in me, and my bow was
  33:25 his flesh shall be *f* than a child's
Jas. 3:12 no fountain both yield salt water and *f*

Fret

1 Sam. 1:6 provoked her sore, for to make her *f*

Ps. 37:1 *f* not thyself because of evildoers
  37:8 *f* not thyself in any wise to do evil
Prov. 19:3 and his heart *f* against the LORD
  24:19 *f* not thyself because of evil men
Is. 8:21 when. . hungry, they shall *f* themselves
Ezek. 16:43 but hast *f* me in all these things

Friend

Ex. 33:11 unto Moses. . as a man speaketh unto his *f*
Deut. 13:6 or thine *f*. . entice thee secretly, saying
2 Sam. 15:37 so Hushai David's *f* came into the city
  19:6 lovest thine enemies, and hatest thy *f*
2 Chr. 20:7 gavest it to the seed of Abraham thy *f*
Job 2:11 when Job's three *f* heard of all this evil
  6:14 afflicted pity should be showed from his *f*
  6:27 and ye dig a pit for your *f*
  16:20 my *f* scorn me: but mine eye poureth out
  19:14 my and familiar *f* have forgotten me
  42:10 captivity of Job, when he prayed for his *f*
Ps. 35:14 I behaved. . as though he had been my *f*
  38:11 lovers and my *f* stand aloof from my sore
  41:9 mine own familiar *f*. . lifted up his heel
  88:18 lover and *f* hast thou put far from me
Prov. 6:1 my son, if thou be surety for thy *f*
  14:20 poor is hated. . but the rich hath many *f*
  16:28 and a whisperer separateth chief *f*
  17:17 a *f* loveth at all times, and a brother
  18:24 a *f* that sticketh closer than a brother
  19:4 wealth maketh many *f*; but the poor is
  27:6 faithful are the wounds of a *f*; but the
  27:10 own *f*, and thy father's *f*, forsake not
Song 5:1 eat, O *f*; drink, yea, drink abundantly
Is. 41:8 I have chosen, the seed of Abraham my *f*
Jer. 20:4 I will make thee a terror. . to all thy *f*
  38:22 women shall say, Thy *f* have set thee on
Lam. 1:2 her *f* have dealt treacherously with her
Mic. 7:5 trust ye not in a *f*, put ye not confidence
Zech. 13:6 I was wounded in the house of my *f*
Mt. 11:19 (Lk. 7:34) a *f* of publicans and sinners
  20:13 but he answered. . *F*, I do thee no wrong
  22:12 *f*, how camest thou in hither not having
  26:50 Jesus said. . *F*, wherefore art thou come?
Mk. 3:21 when his *f* heard of it, they went out to
  5:19 Jesus. . saith unto him, Go home to thy *f*
Lk. 11:5 and say unto him, *F*, lend me three loaves
  11:8 rise and give him, because he is his *f*
  12:4 I say unto you my *f*, Be not afraid of them
  14:10 he may say unto thee, *F*, go up higher
  14:12 when thou makest a dinner. . call not thy *f*
  15:6 he cometh home, he calleth together his *f*
  16:9 make. . *f* of the mammon of unrighteousness
  21:16 shall be betrayed both by parents. . and *f*
  23:12 the same day Pilate and Herod were made *f*
Jn. 3:29 but the *f* of the bridegroom. . rejoiceth
  11:11 our *f* Lazarus sleepeth: but I go, that I
  15:13 that a man lay down his life for his *f*
  15:14 my *f*, if ye do whatsoever I command you
  15:15 not servants. . but I have called you *f*
  19:12 let this man go, thou art not Caesar's *f*
Acts 27:3 and gave him liberty to go unto his *f*
Jas. 2:23 Abraham. . and he was called the *F* of God
  4:4 will be a *f* of the world is the enemy of God

Friendly

Prov. 18:24 that hath friends must show himself *f*

Friendship *See also* Fellowship

Prov. 22:24 make no *f* with an angry man
Jas. 4:4 the *f* of the world is enmity with God?

Fringe

Num. 15:38 *f* in the borders of their garments
Deut. 22:12 shalt make thee *f* upon. . thy vesture

Frog

Ex. 8:2 I will smite all thy borders with *f*
Ps. 78:45 he sent. . *f*, which destroyed them
  105:30 their land brought forth *f* in abundance
Rev. 16:13 and I saw three unclean spirits like *f*

Frontlet

Ex. 13:16 and for *f* between thine eyes
Deut. 6:8 (11:18) shall be as *f* between thine eyes

Frost

Gen. 31:40 drought consumed me, and the *f* by night
Ex. 16:14 round thing, as small as the hoar *f*
Job 37:10 by the breath of God *f* is given
  38:29 hoary *f* of heaven, who hath gendered it?
Ps. 147:16 he scattereth the hoar *f* like ashes

Froward

Deut. 32:20 for they are a very *f* generation
2 Sam. 22:27 (Ps. 18:26) with the *f* thou wilt show
Job 5:13 the counsel of the *f* is carried headlong
Ps. 101:4 a *f* heart shall depart from me
Prov. 2:12 from the man that speaketh *f* things
  2:15 ways are crooked, and they *f* in their paths
  3:32 for the *f* is abomination to the LORD
  4:24 put away from thee a *f* mouth
  6:12 a wicked man, walketh with a *f* mouth
  8:8 there is nothing *f* or perverse in them
  8:13 the evil way, and the *f* mouth, do I hate
  10:31 but the *f* tongue shall be cut out
  11:20 of a *f* heart are abomination to the LORD
  16:28 a *f* man soweth strife: and a whisperer
  17:20 he that hath a *f* heart findeth no good
  21:8 the way of man is *f* and strange
  22:5 thorns and snares are in the way of the *f*
1 Pet. 2:18 not only to the. . gentle, but also to the *f*

Frowardly

Is. 57:17 he went on *f* in the way of his heart

Frowardness

Prov. 6:14 *f* is in his heart, he deviseth mischief

Fruit *See also* Firstfruit, Harvest

Gen. 1:11 and the *f* tree yielding *f* after his kind
  3:3 but of the *f* of the tree. . Ye shall not eat
  4:3 Cain brought of the *f* of the ground
  30:2 hath withheld from thee the *f* of the womb?
  43:11 take of the best *f* in the land in your
Ex. 23:10 (Lev. 25:3) six years. . gather in the *f*
Lev. 19:23 count the *f* thereof as uncircumcised
Num. 13:26 and showed them the *f* of the land
Deut. 1:25 and they took of the *f* of the land
  7:13 he will also bless the *f* of thy womb
  22:9 lest the *f* of thy seed. . be defiled
  26:2 thou shalt take of the first of all the *f*
  28:4 blessed shall be the *f* of thy body
  33:14 the precious *f* brought forth by the sun
Ps. 1:3 that bringeth forth his *f* in his season
  72:16 the *f* thereof shall shake like Lebanon
  92:14 they shall still bring forth *f* in old age
  107:37 vineyards, which may yield *f* of increase
  127:3 and the *f* of the womb is his reward
  132:11 (Acts 2:30) *f* of thy body will I set upon
Prov. 1:31 they eat of the *f* of their own way
  8:19 my *f* is better than gold, yea, than fine
  10:16 the *f* of the wicked to sin
  11:30 the *f* of the righteous is a tree of life
  12:14 satisfied with good by the *f* of his mouth
Song 2:3 and his *f* was sweet to my taste
  4:16 into his garden, and eat his pleasant *f*
Is. 3:10 for they shall eat the *f* of their doings
  27:6 and fill the face of the world with *f*

Is. 28:4 as the hasty *f* before the summer
  33:9 and Bashan and Carmel shake off their *f*
  57:19 I create the *f* of the lips; Peace, peace
  65:21 plant vineyards, and eat the *f* of them
Jer. 6:19 this people, even the *f* of their thoughts
  12:2 they grow, yea, they bring forth *f*
  17:8 neither shall cease from yielding *f*
  17:10 give. . according to the *f* of his doings
  21:14 punish. . according to the *f* of your doings
Ezek. 36:11 and they shall increase and bring *f*
Hos. 10:13 ye have eaten the *f* of lies
Amos 7:14 a herdman, and a gatherer of sycamore *f*
  8:1 and behold a basket of summer *f*
Mic. 6:7 of my body for the sin of my soul?
  7:1 my soul desired the first ripe *f*
  7:13 be desolate. . for the *f* of their doings
Hab. 3:17 neither shall *f* be in the vines
Hag. 1:10 and the earth is stayed from her *f*
Mt. 3:8 (Lk. 3:8) bring forth. . *f* meet for repentance
  7:16 (Lk. 6:44) shall know them by their *f*
  7:17 every good tree bringeth forth good *f*
  12:33 either make the tree good, and his *f* good
  13:8 (Mk. 4:8; Lk. 8:8) and brought forth *f*
  21:19 no *f* grow on thee henceforward for ever
  21:34 (Mk. 12:2; Lk. 20:10) might receive the *f*
  26:29 (Mk. 14:25; Lk. 22:18) of this *f* of the vine
Mk. 4:28 the earth bringeth forth *f* of herself
  11:14 no man eat *f* of thee hereafter for ever
Lk. 1:42 and blessed is the *f* of thy womb
  12:17 I have no room where to bestow my *f*?
  13:6 came and sought *f* thereon, and found none
Jn. 4:36 and gathereth *f* unto life eternal
  12:24 but if it die, it bringeth forth much *f*
  15:2 branch. . that beareth not *f* he taketh away
  15:4 as the branch cannot bear *f* of itself
  15:5 I in him, the same bringeth forth much *f*
  15:8 my Father glorified, that ye bear much *f*
  15:16 that ye should go and bring forth *f*
Rom. 1:13 that I might have some *f* among you also
  6:21 what *f* had ye then in those things
  6:22 ye have your *f* unto holiness, and the end
  7:4 that we should bring forth *f* unto God
1 Cor. 9:7 planteth a vineyard, and eateth not of the *f*
2 Cor. 9:10 increase the *f* of your righteousness
Gal. 5:22 but the *f* of the Spirit is love, joy
Eph. 5:9 the *f* of the Spirit is in all goodness
Phil. 1:11 filled with the *f* of righteousness
  4:17 I desire *f* that may abound to your account
Col. 1:6 bringeth forth *f*, as it doth also in you
2 Tim. 2:6 laboreth must be first partaker of the *f*
Heb. 12:11 afterward it yieldeth the peaceable *f*
  13:15 *f* of our lips, giving thanks to his name
Jas. 3:17 to be entreated, full of mercy and good *f*
  3:18 the *f* of righteousness is sown in peace
  5:7 the husbandman waiteth for the precious *f*
Jude 12 trees whose *f* withereth, without *f*
Rev. 22:2 tree of life, which bare twelve manner of *f*

Fruitful

Gen. 1:22 God blessed them, saying, Be *f*, and
  9:1 and God blessed Noah. . Be *f*, and multiply
  17:6 I will make thee exceeding *f*, and I will
  35:11 I am God Almighty: be *f* and multiply
  41:52 for God hath caused me to be *f* in the land
Ex. 1:7 children of Israel were *f*, and increased
Lev. 26:9 have respect unto you, and make you *f*
Ps. 107:34 a *f* land into barrenness
  148:9 and all hills; *f* trees, and all cedars
Is. 5:1 hath a vineyard in a very *f* hill
  10:18 shall consume the glory. . of his *f* field
  29:17 Lebanon shall be turned into a *f* field
  32:15 Spirit be poured. . wilderness be a *f* field
Jer. 4:26 and, lo, the *f* place was a wilderness

Jer. 23:3 the remnant . . shall be *f* and increase
Ezek. 17:5 the seed . . and planted it in a *f* field
19:10 she was *f* and full of branches by reason
Hos. 13:15 though he be *f* among his brethren
Acts 14:17 gave us rain from heaven, and *f* seasons
Col. 1:10 all pleasing, being *f* in every good work

Frustrate

Ezra 4:5 to *f* their purpose, all the days of Cyrus
Is. 44:25 that *f* the tokens of the liars
Gal. 2:21 I do not *f* the grace of God

Fuel

Is. 9:5 this shall be with burning and *f* of fire
Ezek. 15:4 behold, it is cast into the fire for *f*
21:32 thou shalt be for *f* to the fire

Fugitive

Gen. 4:12 a *f* and a vagabond shalt thou be in the
Judg. 12:4 said, Ye Gileadites are *f* of Ephraim
2 Kgs. 25:11 *f* that fell away to the king of Babylon
Is. 15:5 for Moab; his *f* shall flee unto Zoar
Ezek. 17:21 and all his *f*. . shall fall by the sword

Fulfil *See also* Accomplish, Perform

Gen. 25:24 when her days to be delivered were *f*
Ex. 5:13 saying, *F* your works, your daily tasks
23:26 the number of thy days I will *f*
2 Sam. 7:12 thy days be *f*. . I will set up thy seed
14:22 the king hath *f* the request of his servant
1 Chr. 22:13 if thou takest heed to *f* the statutes
Ezra 1:1 word . . by the mouth of Jeremiah might be *f*
Ps. 20:4 to thine own heart, and *f* all thy counsel
20:5 the LORD *f* all thy petitions
145:19 will *f* the desire of them that fear him
148:8 snow, and vapor; stormy wind *f* his word
Dan. 10:3 till three whole weeks were *f*
Mt. 1:22 now all this was done, that it might be *f*
3:15 thus it becometh us to *f* all righteousness
5:17 I am not come to destroy, but to *f*
5:18 in no wise pass from the law, till all be *f*
24:34 (Lk. 21:32) pass, till all these things be *f*
26:54 but how then shall the Scriptures be *f*
27:35 might be *f* which was spoken by the prophet
Mk. 1:15 the time is *f*. . kingdom of God is at hand
13:4 the sign when all these things shall be *f*?
Lk. 1:20 my words, which shall be *f* in their season
21:22 that all things which are written may be *f*
21:24 until the times of the Gentiles be *f*
22:16 until it be *f* in the kingdom of God
24:44 all things must be *f*, which were written
Jn. 3:29 this my joy therefore is *f*
17:13 they might have my joy *f* in themselves
19:28 the Scripture might be *f*, saith, I thirst
Acts 13:22 found David . . which shall *f* all my will
13:25 and as John *f* his course, he said, Whom
13:33 God hath *f* the same unto us their children
Rom. 2:27 uncircumcision . . if it *f* the law, judge
8:4 righteousness of the law might be *f* in us
13:8 for he that loveth another hath *f* the law
13:14 provision for the flesh, to *f* the lusts
Gal. 5:14 for all the law is *f* in one word
5:16 and ye shall not *f* the lust of the flesh
6:2 burdens, and so *f* the law of Christ
Eph. 2:3 in times past . . *f* the desires of the flesh
Phil. 2:2 *f* ye my joy, that ye be likeminded
Col. 1:25 given to me for you, to *f* the word of God
4:17 hast received in the Lord, that thou *f* it
2 Thes. 1:11 calling, and *f* all the good pleasure
Jas. 2:8 if ye *f* the royal law according to the
Rev. 15:8 seven plagues of the seven angels were *f*
17:17 God hath put in their hearts to *f* his will
20:3 till the thousand years should be *f*

Fulfilling *See also* Fulfil

Rom. 13:10 therefore love is the *f* of the law

Full

Gen. 15:16 iniquity of the Amorites is not yet *f*
Ex. 22:3 for he should make *f* restitution
Lev. 2:14 meat offering . . corn beaten out of *f* ears
19:29 and the land become *f* of wickedness
Num. 22:18 (24:13) give me his house *f* of silver
Deut. 6:11 houses *f* of all good things, which thou
8:12 lest when thou hast eaten and art *f*
34:9 and Joshua . . was *f* of the spirit of wisdom
Ruth 1:21 I went out *f*, and the LORD hath brought
2 Kgs. 3:16 LORD, Make this valley *f* of ditches
4:6 when the vessels were *f*, that she said unto
6:17 the mountain was *f* of horses and chariots
10:21 the house of Baal was *f* from one end to
1 Chr. 21:22 shalt grant it me for the *f* price
Esth. 5:9 he was *f* of indignation against Mordecai
Job 5:26 thou shalt come to thy grave in a *f* age
10:15 I am *f* of confusion; therefore see thou
11:2 and should a man *f* of talk be justified?
14:1 man . . is of few days, and *f* of trouble
20:11 his bones are *f* of the sin of his youth
21:23 one dieth in his *f* strength, being wholly
32:18 for I am *f* of matter; the spirit within me
Ps. 10:7 (Rom. 3:14) mouth is *f* of cursing and deceit
29:4 the voice of the LORD is *f* of majesty
48:10 thy right hand is *f* of righteousness
65:9 with the river of God, which is *f* of water
73:10 waters of a *f* cup are wrung out to them
74:20 earth are *f* of the habitations of cruelty
88:3 for my soul is *f* of troubles: and my life
104:16 the trees of the LORD are *f* of sap
119:64 the earth, O LORD, is *f* of thy mercy
127:5 happy is the man that hath his quiver *f*
144:13 that our garners may be *f*, affording all
Prov. 27:7 the *f* soul loatheth a honeycomb
27:20 hell and destruction are never *f*
30:9 lest I be *f*, and deny thee, and say, Who
Eccl. 1:7 run into the sea; yet the sea is not *f*
4:6 both the hands *f* with travail and vexation
10:14 a fool also is *f* of words: a man cannot
11:3 if the clouds be *f* of rain, they empty
Is. 1:11 I am *f* of the burnt offerings of rams
2:8 their land also is *f* of idols; they worship
6:3 the whole earth is *f* of his glory
11:9 shall be *f* of the knowledge of the LORD
28:8 all tables are *f* of vomit and filthiness
Jer. 6:11 therefore I am *f* of the fury of the LORD
Lam. 1:1 city sit solitary, that was *f* of people!
Ezek. 28:12 thou sealest up the sum, *f* of wisdom
37:1 midst of the valley which was *f* of bones
Amos 2:13 a cart is pressed that is *f* of sheaves
Mic. 3:8 I am *f* of power by the Spirit of the LORD
Hab. 3:3 and the earth was *f* of his praise
Zech. 8:5 streets of the city shall be *f* of boys
Mt. 6:22 (Lk. 11:34) whole body shall be *f* of light
Mk. 4:37 beat into the ship, so that it was now *f*
Lk. 6:25 woe unto you that are *f*! for ye shall
11:39 but your inward part is *f* of ravening
Jn. 1:14 and dwelt among us . . *f* of grace and truth
15:11 have I spoken . . that your joy might be *f*
16:24 ye shall receive, that your joy may be *f*
Acts 2:13 said, These men are *f* of new wine
6:3 seven men . . *f* of the Holy Ghost and wisdom
6:5 and they chose Stephen, a man *f* of faith
7:55 but he, being *f* of the Holy Ghost, looked
9:36 Dorcas: this woman was *f* of good works
11:24 good man . . *f* of the Holy Ghost and of faith
Rom. 15:14 brethren, that ye also are *f* of goodness
1 Cor. 4:8 now ye are *f*, now ye are rich
Phil. 2:26 he longed after you all . . *f* of heaviness

Phil. 4:12 instructed both to be *f* and to be hungry
  4:18 but I have all, and abound: I am *f*, having
2 Tim. 4:5 make *f* proof of thy ministry
Heb. 5:14 strong meat . . to them that are of *f* age
  6:11 to the *f* assurance of hope unto the end
  10:22 with a true heart in *f* assurance of faith
1 Pet. 1:8 with joy unspeakable and *f* of glory
1 Jn. 1:4 write we unto you, that your joy may be *f*
Rev. 15:7 seven golden vials *f* of the wrath of God
  16:10 beast; and his kingdom was *f* of darkness
  21:9 seven vials *f* of the seven last plagues

Fuller

2 Kgs. 18:17 (Is. 36:2) highway of the *f*'s field
Mal. 3:2 like a refiner's fire, and like *f*' soap
Mk. 9:3 so as no *f* on earth can white them

Fully *See also* Wholly

Num. 14:24 my servant Caleb . . hath followed me *f*
1 Kgs. 11:6 Solomon . . went not *f* after the LORD
Eccl. 8:11 of men is *f* set in them to do evil
Nah. 1:10 they shall be devoured as stubble *f* dry
Acts 2:1 and when the day of Pentecost was *f* come
Rom. 4:21 *f* persuaded, that what he had promised
  14:5 every man be *f* persuaded in his own mind
  15:19 I have *f* preached the gospel of Christ
2 Tim. 3:10 but thou hast *f* known my doctrine
  4:17 that by me the preaching might be *f* known
Rev. 14:18 and gather . . for her grapes are *f* ripe

Fulness *See also* Abundance, Plenty

Num. 18:27 as though it were . . the *f* of the winepress
1 Chr. 16:32 (Ps. 96:11) sea roar, and the *f* thereof
Ps. 16:11 in thy presence is *f* of joy
  24:1 (1 Cor. 10:26) earth is the LORD's, and the *f*
Jn. 1:16 of his *f* have all we received, and grace
Rom. 11:12 of the Gentiles; how much more their *f*?
  11:25 until the *f* of the Gentiles be come in
  15:29 in the *f* of the blessing of the gospel
Gal. 4:4 when the *f* of the time was come, God sent
Eph. 1:23 the *f* of him that filleth all in all
  3:19 ye might be filled with all the *f* of God
  4:13 measure of the stature of the *f* of Christ
Col. 1:19 that in him should all *f* dwell
  2:9 in him dwelleth all the *f* of the Godhead

Furious

Prov. 22:24 and with a *f* man thou shalt not go
  29:22 and a *f* man aboundeth in transgression
Ezek. 5:15 execute judgments in thee . . in *f* rebukes
Nah. 1:2 the LORD revengeth, and is *f*

Furiously

2 Kgs. 9:20 driving of Jehu . . for he driveth *f*
Ezek. 23:25 and they shall deal *f* with thee

Furnace *See also* Fire, Flame, Hell

Gen. 15:17 and it was dark, behold a smoking *f*
  19:28 the smoke . . went up as the smoke of a *f*
Deut. 4:20 and brought you forth out of the iron *f*
1 Kgs. 8:51 Egypt, from the midst of the *f* of iron
Ps. 12:6 as silver tried in a *f* of earth
Prov. 17:3 fining pot is for silver . . *f* for gold
  27:21 the *f* for gold; so is a man to his praise
Is. 31:9 fire is in Zion, and his *f* in Jerusalem
  48:10 I have chosen thee in the *f* of affliction
Ezek. 22:18 iron, and lead, in the midst of the *f*
Dan. 3:6 (3:11, 15) into the midst of a burning fiery *f*
  3:17 able to deliver us from the burning fiery *f*
Mt. 13:42 and shall cast them into a *f* of fire
Rev. 1:15 fine brass, as if they burned in a *f*
  9:2 out of the pit, as the smoke of a great *f*

Furnish *See also* Provide

Ps. 78:19 can God *f* a table in the wilderness?
Is. 65:11 *f* the drink offering unto that number
Mt. 22:10 and the wedding was *f* with guests
2 Tim. 3:17 thoroughly *f* unto all good works

Furniture

Gen. 31:34 Rachel had . . images . . in the camel's *f*

Furrow

Ps. 65:10 thou settlest the *f* thereof: thou makest
  129:3 the plowers . . made long their *f*
Ezek. 17:7 water it by the *f* of her plantation
Hos. 10:4 as hemlock in the *f* of the field
  10:10 they shall bind themselves in their two *f*

Further

Ezra 8:36 they *f* the people, and the house of God
Job 38:11 hitherto shalt thou come, but no *f*
  40:5 yea, twice; but I will proceed no *f*
Ps. 140:8 *f* not his wicked device; lest they exalt
Mt. 26:39 went a little *f*, and fell on his face
Mk. 5:35 why troublest thou the Master any *f*?
Lk. 24:28 he made as though he would have gone *f*
Acts 4:17 but that it spread no *f* among the people
2 Tim. 3:9 but they shall proceed no *f*: for their

Furtherance

Phil. 1:12 rather unto the *f* of the gospel
  1:25 with you all for your *f* and joy of faith

Fury *See also* Anger, Indignation, Passion, Rage, Wrath

Gen. 27:44 tarry . . until thy brother's *f* turn away
Job 20:23 God shall cast the *f* of his wrath upon
Is. 27:4 *f* is not in me: who would set the briers
  42:25 he hath poured upon him the *f* of his anger
  51:13 because of the *f* of the oppressor
  51:20 they are full of the *f* of the LORD
  59:18 he will repay, *f* to his adversaries
  63:3 in mine anger, and trample them in my *f*
  63:5 salvation unto me; and my *f*, it upheld me
Jer. 6:11 therefore I am full of the *f* of the LORD
  21:5 will fight against you . . in anger, and in *f*
  23:19 whirlwind of the LORD is gone forth in *f*
  25:15 take the winecup of this *f* at my hand
Lam. 4:11 the LORD hath accomplished his *f*
Ezek. 20:8 (20:13, 21) I will pour out my *f* upon them
  21:17 will cause my *f* to rest: I the LORD
Dan. 3:13 then Nebuchadnezzar in his rage and *f*
  8:6 and ran unto him in the *f* of his power
  9:16 let thine anger and thy *f* be turned away
  11:44 he shall go forth with great *f* to destroy
Zech. 8:2 and I was jealous for her with great *f*

G

Gabriel

Dan. 8:16 *G*, make this man to understand the vision
  9:21 in prayer, even the man *G* . . touched me
Lk. 1:19 I am *G*, that stand in the presence of God
  1:26 the angel *G* was sent from God unto a city

Gad the son of Jacob

Gen. 30:11 troop cometh: and she called his name *G*
  49:19 *G*, a troop shall overcome him: but he
Num. 32:1 children of *G* had a . . multitude of cattle
Deut. 33:20 said, Blessed be he that enlargeth *G*
Josh. 13:28 the inheritance of the children of *G*

Gad the prophet

1 Sam. 22:5 prophet *G* said unto David, Abide not

2 Sam. 24:11 (1 Chr. 21:9) the prophet *G*, David's seer
1 Chr. 29:29 written . . in the book of *G* the seer
2 Chr. 29:25 the commandment . . of *G* the king's seer

Gad (verb)

Jer. 2:36 why *g* thou about so much to change thy

Gadarene *See also* Gergesene

Mk. 5:1–17 (Lk. 8:26–37)

Gain *See also* Advantage, Profit

Judg. 5:19 of Megiddo; they took no *g* of money
Job 22:3 is it *g* to him, that thou makest thy ways
27:8 though he hath *g*, when God taketh away his
Prov. 1:19 ways of every one that is greedy of *g*
3:14 of silver, and the *g* thereof than fine gold
15:27 greedy of *g* troubleth his own house
28:8 that by usury and unjust *g* increaseth his
Is. 33:15 he that despiseth the *g* of oppressions
Ezek. 22:12 thou hast greedily of thy neighbors
22:13 have smitten mine hand at thy dishonest *g*
22:27 and to destroy souls, to get dishonest *g*
Dan. 11:39 and shall divide the land for *g*
Mic. 4:13 I will consecrate their *g* unto the Lord
Mt. 16:26 (Mk. 8:36; Lk. 9:25) *g* the whole world, and
18:15 shall hear thee, thou hast *g* thy brother
25:17 that had received two, he also *g* other two
Lk. 19:15 how much every man had *g* by trading
Acts 16:16 her masters much *g* by soothsaying
16:19 hope of their *g* was gone, they caught Paul
19:24 brought no small *g* unto the craftsmen
1 Cor. 9:19 servant unto all, that I might *g* the more
9:20 I became as a Jew, that I might *g* the Jews
2 Cor. 12:17 did I make a *g* of you by any of them
12:18 did Titus make a *g* of you? walked we not
Phil. 1:21 to live is Christ, and to die is *g*
3:7 things were *g* to me, those I counted loss
1 Tim. 6:5 supposing that *g* is godliness
6:6 but godliness with contentment is great *g*
Jas. 4:13 a year, and buy and sell, and get *g*

Gainsay

Lk. 21:15 your adversaries shall not be able to *g*

Gainsayer

Tit. 1:9 both to exhort and to convince the *g*

Gainsaying

Acts 10:29 therefore came I unto you without *g*
Rom. 10:21 hands unto a disobedient and *g* people
Jude 11 for reward, and perished in the *g* of Core

Gaius Acts 19:29; Rom. 16:23; 3 Jn. 1

Galatia

Acts 16:6 throughout Phrygia and the region of *G*
18:23 went over all the country of *G* and Phrygia
1 Cor. 16:1 have given order to the churches of *G*
Gal. 1:2 which are with me, unto the churches of *G*

Galilean

Mk. 14:70 for thou art a *G*, and thy speech agreeth
Lk. 13:2 that these *G* were sinners above all the *G*
22:59 this fellow also was with him; for he is a *G*
Jn. 4:45 was come into Galilee, the *G* received him
Acts 2:7 behold, are not all these which speak *G* ?

Galilee *See also* Gennesaret, Tiberias

1 Kgs. 9:11 Solomon gave Hiram twenty cities in . . *G*
Is. 9:1 (Mt. 4:15) beyond Jordan, in *G* of the nations
Mt. 2:22 he turned aside into the parts of *G*
4:12 (Mk. 1:14; Lk. 4:14) he departed into *G*
4:18 (Mk. 1:16) walking by the sea of *G*, saw two
4:23 (Mk. 1:39; Lk. 4:44) Jesus went about all *G*
4:25 (Mk. 3:7) great multitudes of people from *G*

Mt. 26:32 (Mk. 14:28) I will go before you into *G*
27:55 (Mk. 15:41; Lk. 23:49) women . . from *G*
28:7 (Mk. 16:7) he goeth before you into *G*
28:16 then the eleven disciples went away into *G*
Lk. 3:1 Herod being tetrarch of *G*
4:14 returned in the power of the Spirit into *G*
23:5 all Jewry, beginning from *G* to this place
24:6 how he spake unto you when he was yet in *G*
Jn. 4:43 he departed thence, and went into *G*
6:1 went over the sea of *G*, which is . . Tiberias
7:41 but some said, Shall Christ come out of *G* ?
7:52 art thou also of *G* ? . . of *G* ariseth no prophet
Acts 1:11 ye men of *G*, why stand ye gazing up into
10:37 Judea, and began from *G*, after the baptism

Gall

Deut. 29:18 a root that beareth *g* and wormwood
32:32 are grapes of *g*, their clusters are bitter
Job 16:13 he poureth out my *g* upon the ground
20:14 is turned, it is the *g* of asps within him
Ps. 69:21 they gave me also *g* for my meat
Jer. 8:14 given us water of *g* to drink, because we
9:15 (23:15) and give them water of *g* to drink
Lam. 3:5 and compassed me with *g* and travail
3:19 and my misery, the wormwood and the *g*
Amos 6:12 for ye have turned judgment into *g*
Mt. 27:34 gave him vinegar to drink mingled with *g*
Acts 8:23 thou art in the *g* of bitterness

Gallery

Song 7:5 like purple; the King is held in the *g*

Gallio Acts 18:12–17

Gallows

Esth. 5:14 let a *g* be made of fifty cubits high
6:4 unto the king to hang Mordecai on the *g*
7:10 so they hanged Haman on the *g* that he had
9:13 let Haman's ten sons be hanged upon the *g*

Gamaliel Acts 5:34–40; 22:3

Gap

Ezek. 13:5 ye have not gone up into the *g*, neither
22:30 and stand in the *g* before me for the land

Gape

Job 16:10 they have *g* upon me with their mouth
Ps. 22:13 they *g* upon me with their mouths, as a

Garden

Gen. 2:8 the Lord God planted a *g* eastward in Eden
2:15 and put him into the *g* of Eden to dress it
3:23 God sent him forth from the *g* of Eden
13:10 and Gomorrah, even as the *g* of the Lord
Deut. 11:10 not as the land of Egypt . . a *g* of herbs
1 Kgs. 21:2 vineyard, that I may have it for a *g*
2 Kgs. 9:27 he fled by the way of the *g* house
Song 4:12 a *g* inclosed is my sister, my spouse
4:16 let my beloved come into his *g*, and eat his
5:1 I am come into my *g*, my sister, my spouse
8:13 thou that dwellest in the *g*, the companions
Is. 1:8 a lodge in a *g* of cucumbers, as a besieged
1:30 leaf fadeth, and as a *g* that hath no water
51:3 Eden, and her desert like the *g* of the Lord
58:11 thou shalt be like a watered *g*, and like a
61:11 as the *g* causeth the things that are sown
65:3 that sacrificeth in *g*, and burneth incense
Jer. 29:5 (29:28) and plant *g*, and eat the fruit
31:12 their soul shall be as a watered *g*
Ezek. 28:13 thou hast been in Eden the *g* of God
31:8 cedars in the *g* of God could not hide him
36:35 was desolate is become like the *g* of Eden
Joel 2:3 the land is as the *g* of Eden before them

Amos 4:9 when your *g* . . increased, the palmerworm
 9:14 they shall also make *g*, and eat the fruit
Jn. 18:1 over the brook Cedron, where was a *g*
 18:26 did not I see thee in the *g* with him?
 19:41 a *g*; and in the *g* a new sepulchre, wherein

Gardener

Jn. 20:15 she, supposing him to be the *g*, saith

Garment *See also* Clothes, Clothing, Raiment, Robe, Vesture

Gen. 25:25 came out red, all over like a hairy *g*
 39:12 and he left his *g* in her hand, and fled
 49:11 he washed his *g* in wine, and his clothes
Ex. 28:2 (28:4; 39:1) shalt make holy *g* for Aaron
 29:29 and the holy *g* of Aaron shall be his sons'
Lev. 13:47 *g* also that the plague of leprosy is in
 19:19 (Deut. 22:11) *g* mingled of linen and woolen
Num. 20:28 Moses stripped Aaron of his *g*, and put
Deut. 22:5 neither shall a man put on a woman's *g*
Josh. 7:21 among the spoils a goodly Babylonish *g*
 9:5 clouted upon their feet, and old *g* upon them
Judg. 14:12 thirty sheets and thirty change of *g*
1 Kgs. 11:30 Ahijah caught the new *g* that was on
2 Kgs. 5:26 is it a time to receive money, and . . *g*
 7:15 lo, all the way was full of *g* and vessels
Job 13:28 consumeth, as a *g* that is moth-eaten
 37:17 thy *g* are warm, when he quieteth the earth
Ps. 22:18 (Mt. 27:35; Mk. 15:24) they part my *g*
 45:8 thy *g* smell of myrrh, and aloes, and cassia
 69:11 I made sackcloth also my *g*; and I became a
 102:26 (Heb. 1:11) shall wax old like a *g*
 104:2 coverest thyself with light as with a *g*
 104:6 coveredst it with the deep as with a *g*
 109:18 clothed . . with cursing like as with his *g*
Prov. 20:16 (27:13) take his *g* that is surety for a
 25:20 that taketh away a *g* in cold weather
 30:4 who hath bound the waters in a *g* ? who hath
Eccl. 9:8 let thy *g* be always white; and let thy
Is. 9:5 with confused noise, and *g* rolled in blood
 50:9 (Heb. 1:11) they all shall wax old as a *g*
 51:6 earth shall wax old like a *g*, and they that
 51:8 the moth shall eat them up like a *g*
 52:1 O Zion; put on thy beautiful *g*, O Jerusalem
 59:17 he put on the *g* of vengeance for clothing
 61:3 the *g* of praise for the spirit of heaviness
 61:10 he hath clothed me with the *g* of salvation
 63:1 cometh from Edom, with dyed *g* from Bozrah
 63:3 their blood shall be sprinkled upon my *g*
Jer. 36:24 they were not afraid, nor rent their *g*
Ezek. 44:17 they shall be clothed with linen *g*
Dan. 7:9 Ancient of days did sit, whose *g* was white
Joel 2:13 and rend your heart, and not your *g*
Zech. 3:3 Joshua was clothed with filthy *g*
 13:4 neither shall they wear a rough *g* to deceive
Mt. 9:16 (Mk. 2:21; Lk. 5:36) new cloth unto an old *g*
 9:20 (Mk. 5:27; Lk. 8:44) touched the hem of his *g*
 14:36 (Mk. 6:56) only touch the hem of his *g*
 21:8 (Mk. 11:8) multitude spread their *g* in the way
 22:11 there a man which had not on a wedding *g*
 23:5 enlarge the borders of their *g*
Mk. 11:7 (Lk. 19:35) colt to Jesus, and cast their *g* on
 13:16 not turn back again for to take up his *g*
 16:5 saw a young man . . clothed in a long white *g*
Lk. 22:36 no sword, let him sell his *g*, and buy
 24:4 behold, two men stood by them in shining *g*
Jn. 13:4 laid aside his *g*; and took a towel
 19:23 crucified Jesus, took his *g*, and made four
Acts 9:39 coats and *g* which Dorcas made, while she
Jas. 5:2 are corrupted, and your *g* are moth-eaten
Jude 23 hating even the *g* spotted by the flesh
Rev. 3:4 in Sardis which have not defiled their *g*
 16:15 blessed . . that watcheth, and keepeth his *g*

Garner

Ps. 144:13 our *g* may be full, affording all manner
Joel 1:17 the *g* are laid desolate, the barns are
Mt. 3:12 (Lk. 3:17) gather his wheat into the *g*

Garnish *See also* Adorn, Deck

2 Chr. 3:6 he *g* the house with precious stones for
Job 26:13 by his Spirit he hath *g* the heavens
Mt. 12:44 (Lk. 11:25) findeth it empty, swept, and *g*
 23:29 and *g* the sepulchres of the righteous
Rev. 21:19 *g* with all manner of precious stones

Garrison

1 Sam. 10:5 where is the *g* of the Philistines
 13:3 and Jonathan smote the *g* of the Philistines
2 Sam. 8:6 (1 Chr. 18:6) David put *g* in Syria
Ezek. 26:11 and thy strong *g* shall go down to the
2 Cor. 11:32 with a *g*, desirous to apprehend me

Gate *See also* Door, Entrance, Way

Gen. 19:1 at even; and Lot sat in the *g* of Sodom
 22:17 seed shall possess the *g* of his enemies
 28:17 house of God, and this is the *g* of heaven
 34:20 and Shechem . . came unto the *g* of their city
Ex. 32:26 then Moses stood in the *g* of the camp
Deut. 6:9 (11:20) them upon the posts . . and on thy *g*
 22:15 unto the elders of the city in the *g*
Judg. 5:8 chose new gods; then was war in the *g*
 16:3 Samson . . took the doors of the *g* of the city
Neh. 13:19 I commanded that the *g* should be shut
Job 38:17 the *g* of death been opened unto thee?
Ps. 9:13 that liftest me up from the *g* of death
 24:7 lift up your heads, O ye *g*
 69:12 they that sit in the *g* speak against me
 100:4 enter into his *g* with thanksgiving
 107:18 and they draw near unto the *g* of death
 118:19 open to me the *g* of righteousness: I will
 118:20 *g* of the LORD, into which the righteous
 122:2 feet shall stand within thy *g*, O Jerusalem
Prov. 14:19 the wicked at the *g* of the righteous
 17:19 he that exalteth his *g* seeketh destruction
 31:23 husband is known in the *g*, when he sitteth
Is. 26:2 open ye the *g*, that the righteous nation
 38:10 my days, I shall go to the *g* of the grave
 45:2 I will break in pieces the *g* of brass
 60:11 therefore thy *g* shall be open continually
 60:18 call thy walls Salvation, and thy *g* Praise
 62:10 go through the *g*; prepare ye the way of
Jer. 7:2 stand in the *g* of the LORD's house
Ezek. 44:2 the LORD unto me; This *g* shall be shut
 46:3 shall worship at the door of this *g*
Dan. 2:49 but Daniel sat in the *g* of the king
Mic. 1:9 he is come unto the *g* of my people
Nah. 2:6 the *g* of the rivers shall be opened
Mt. 7:13 (Lk. 13:24) enter ye in at the strait *g*
 16:18 the *g* of hell shall not prevail against it
Acts 3:2 they laid daily at the *g* of the temple
 3:10 for alms at the Beautiful *g* of the temple
 12:10 came unto the iron *g* that leadeth unto
 12:14 she opened not the *g* for gladness, but ran
Heb. 13:12 Jesus also . . suffered without the *g*
Rev. 21:12 twelve *g*, and at the *g* twelve angels
 21:21 *g* were twelve pearls; every several *g* was
 21:25 *g* of it shall not be shut at all by day
 22:14 may enter in through the *g* into the city

Gath

1 Sam. 5:8 let the ark . . be carried about unto *G*
 27:4 it was told Saul that David was fled to *G*
2 Sam. 1:20 tell it not in *G*, publish it not in
Amos 6:2 then go down to *G* of the Philistines

Gather *See also* Assemble, Bring

Gen. 1:9 the waters under the heaven be *g* together
41:49 Joseph *g* corn as the sand of the sea
49:2 *g* yourselves together, and hear, ye sons
Ex. 5:7 let them go and *g* straw for themselves
9:19 send therefore now, and *g* thy cattle
16:16 *g* of it every man according to his eating
16:18 (2 Cor. 8:15) he that *g* much had nothing
23:10 (Lev. 25:3) shalt *g* in the fruits thereof
Lev. 8:3 *g* thou all the congregation together unto
19:9 (23:22) neither shalt thou *g* the gleanings
Num. 15:32 man that *g* sticks upon the sabbath day
Deut. 28:30 a vineyard, and shalt not *g* the grapes
28:38 carry much seed out . . shalt *g* but little in
30:3 will return and *g* thee from all the nations
Josh. 24:1 Joshua *g* all the tribes of Israel to Shechem
Judg. 1:7 kings . . *g* their meat under my table
2 Sam. 14:14 water spilt . . cannot be *g* up again
1 Kgs. 18:19 *g* to me all Israel unto mount Carmel
2 Kgs. 22:20 (2 Chr. 34:28) *g* thee unto thy fathers
1 Chr. 16:35 (Ps. 106:47) and *g* us . . from the heathen
Job 11:10 or *g* together, then who can hinder him?
24:6 field: and they *g* the vintage of the wicked
Ps. 26:9 *g* not my soul with sinners, nor my life
33:7 *g* the waters of the sea together as a heap
39:6 up riches, and knoweth not who shall *g* them
41:6 his heart . *g* iniquity to itself; when he
50:5 *g* my saints together unto me; those that
104:28 that thou givest them they *g*
107:3 and *g* them out of the lands, from the east
147:2 he *g* together the outcasts of Israel
Prov. 6:8 summer, and *g* her food in the harvest
10:5 he that *g* in summer is a wise son
13:11 but he that *g* by labor shall increase
Eccl. 2:8 I *g* me also silver and gold
Is. 11:12 *g* together the dispersed of Judah from
27:12 ye shall be *g* one by one, O ye children
40:11 he shall *g* the lambs with his arm
49:5 though Israel be not *g*, yet shall I be
54:7 but with great mercies will I *g* thee
56:8 GOD which *g* the outcasts of Israel saith
62:10 cast up the highway; *g* out the stones
Jer. 9:22 carcasses of men shall fall . . and none shall *g*
23:3 I will *g* the remnant of my flock out of all
29:14 and I will *g* you from all the nations
31:8 *g* them from the coasts of the earth
31:10 he that scattered Israel will *g* him
32:37 behold, I will *g* them out of all countries
51:11 make bright the arrows; *g* the shields
Ezek. 11:17 I will even *g* you from the people
22:19 I will *g* you into the midst of Jerusalem
36:24 *g* you out of all countries, and will bring
Mic. 2:12 I will surely *g* the remnant of Israel
Zech. 14:2 I will *g* all nations against Jerusalem
Mt. 3:12 (Lk. 3:17) *g* his wheat into the garner
6:26 neither do they reap, nor *g* into barns
7:16 (Lk. 6:44) do men *g* grapes of thorns, or figs
12:30 (Lk. 11:23) he that *g* not with me scattereth
13:29 lest while ye *g* up the tares, ye root up
13:41 they shall *g* out of his kingdom all things
13:47 was cast into the sea, and of every kind
18:20 where two or three are *g* together in my
23:37 (Lk. 13:34) *g* thy children . . even as a hen *g*
24:28 (Lk. 17:37) there will the eagles be *g*
24:31 (Mk. 13:27) *g* together his elect from the
25:24 sown, and *g* where thou hast not strewed
25:32 before him shall be *g* all nations
Mk. 1:33 all the city was *g* together at the door
Lk. 11:29 when the people were *g* thick together
Jn. 4:36 and *g* fruit unto life eternal
6:12 disciples, *G* up the fragments that remain
11:52 *g* together in one the children of God
15:6 and men *g* them, and cast them into the fire

Acts 4:26 rulers were *g* together against the Lord
14:27 *g* the church together, they rehearsed all
16:10 assuredly *g* that the Lord had called us
Eph. 1:10 *g* together in one all things in Christ
Rev. 14:18 *g* the clusters of the vine of the earth
20:8 Gog and Magog, to *g* them together to battle

Gatherer

Amos 7:14 was a herdman, and a *g* of sycamore fruit

Gathering *See also* Assembly

Gen. 49:10 unto him shall the *g* of the people be
Is. 32:10 vintage shall fail, the *g* shall not come
1 Cor. 16:2 that there be no *g* when I come
2 Thes. 2:1 Christ, and by our *g* together unto him

Gave *See* Give

Gay

Jas. 2:3 him that weareth the *g* clothing, and say

Gaza

Josh. 10:41 smote . . from Kadesh-barnea . . unto *G*
Judg. 16:1 Samson to *G*, and saw there a harlot
2 Kgs. 18:8 he smote the Philistines, even unto *G*
Jer. 47:1 Philistines, before that Pharaoh smote *G*
Amos 1:6 three transgressions of *G*, and for four
Zeph. 2:4 for *G* shall be forsaken, and Ashkelon a
Zech. 9:5 *G* also shall see it, and be very sorrowful
Acts 8:26 that goeth down from Jerusalem unto *G*

Gaze

Acts 1:11 Galilee, why stand ye *g* up into heaven?

Gazingstock

Nah. 3:6 make thee vile, and will set thee as a *g*
Heb. 10:33 a *g* both by reproaches and afflictions

Gedaliah 2 Kgs. 25:22–25; Jer. 39:14–43:6

Gehazi 2 Kgs. 4:12–5:27; 8:4–5

Gender

Lev. 19:19 not let thy cattle *g* with a diverse kind
Job 21:10 their bull *g*, and faileth not; their cow
38:29 the hoary frost of heaven, who hath *g* it?
Gal. 4:24 Sinai, which *g* to bondage, which is Agar
2 Tim. 2:23 avoid, knowing that they do *g* strifes

Genealogy

1 Tim. 1:4 neither give heed to fables and endless *g*

Generation *See also* Age, Time

Gen. 2:4 are the *g* of the heavens and of the earth
6:9 Noah was a just man and perfect in his *g*
7:1 have I seen righteous before me in this *g*
Ex. 3:15 and this is my memorial unto all *g*
12:14 a feast to the LORD throughout your *g*
20:5 (34:7; Num. 14:18; Deut. 5:9) upon the children unto the third and fourth *g* of them that
Deut. 1:35 not one of these men of this evil *g* see
7:9 and keep his commandments to a thousand *g*
32:5 children: they are a perverse and crooked *g*
32:20 for they are a very froward *g*, children in
Ps. 14:5 for God is in the *g* of the righteous
22:30 it shall be accounted to the Lord for a *g*
24:6 this is the *g* of them that seek him
45:17 make thy name to be remembered in all *g*
48:13 that ye may tell it to the *g* following
61:6 the king's life: and his years as many *g*
72:5 the sun and moon endure, throughout all *g*
78:6 that the *g* to come might know them
78:8 a stubborn and rebellious *g*; a *g* that set
79:13 we will show forth thy praise to all *g*

Ps. 89:1 will I make known thy faithfulness to all *g*
　90:1 thou hast been our dwelling place in all *g*
　95:10 (Heb. 3:10) forty years . . grieved with this *g*
　100:5 his truth endureth to all *g*
　102:18 this shall be written for the *g* to come
　112:2 the *g* of the upright shall be blessed
　145:4 one *g* shall praise thy works to another
　145:13 thy dominion endureth throughout all *g*
Prov. 27:24 and doth the crown endure to every *g*?
　30:12 is a *g* that are pure in their own eyes
Eccl. 1:4 one *g* passeth away, and another *g* cometh
Is. 34:10 from *g* to *g* it shall lie waste
　41:4 done it, calling the *g* from the beginning?
　53:8 (Acts 8:33) who shall declare his *g*?
　60:15 an eternal excellency, a joy of many *g*
Jer. 2:31 O *g*, see ye the word of the LORD
Lam. 5:19 remainest for ever; thy throne from *g* to *g*
Dan. 4:3 kingdom, and his dominion is from *g* to *g*
Mt. 3:7 (Lk. 3:7) O *g* of vipers, who hath warned you
　11:16 (Lk. 7:31) liken this *g*? It is like unto
　12:34 *g* of vipers, how can ye, being evil, speak
　12:39 (16:4; Mk. 8:12; Lk. 11:29) *g* seeketh . . sign
　12:41 (Lk. 11:32) rise in judgment with this *g*
　17:17 (Mk. 9:19; Lk. 9:41) faithless and perverse *g*
　23:33 serpents, ye *g* of vipers, how can ye escape
　24:34 (Mk. 13:30; Lk. 21:32) this *g*. . not pass
Lk. 1:48 henceforth all *g* shall call me blessed
　16:8 children of this world are in their *g* wiser
　17:25 suffer many things . . be rejected of this *g*
Acts 2:40 save yourselves from this untoward *g*
　13:36 David, after he had served his own *g*
Col. 1:26 been hid from ages and from *g*, but now
1 Pet. 2:9 ye are a chosen *g*, a royal priesthood

Gennesaret *See also* Galilee

Mt. 14:34 (Mk. 6:53); Lk. 5:1

Gentile *See also* Greek, Heathen, Nation

Gen. 10:5 by these were the isles of the *G* divided
Is. 11:10 (Rom. 15:12) to it shall the *G* seek
　42:1 (Mt. 12:18) bring forth judgment to the *G*
　42:6 a covenant of the people . . a light of the *G*
　49:6 (Acts 13:47) give thee for a light to the *G*
　49:22 behold, I will lift up mine hand to the *G*
　54:3 thy seed shall inherit the *G*, and make the
　60:3 the *G* shall come to thy light, and kings to
　60:5 the forces of the *G* shall come unto thee
　61:6 ye shall eat the riches of the *G*
　61:9 their seed shall be known among the *G*
　62:2 the *G* shall see thy righteousness, and all
　66:19 they shall declare my glory among the *G*
Jer. 16:19 *G* shall come unto thee from the ends of
Hos. 8:8 now shall they be among the *G* as a vessel
Joel 3:9 proclaim ye this among the *G*; Prepare war
Mic. 5:8 the remnant of Jacob shall be among the *G*
Zech. 1:21 to cast out the horns of the *G*
Mal. 1:11 same, my name shall be great among the *G*
Mt. 6:32 for after all these things do the *G* seek
　10:5 go not into the way of the *G*, and into any
　12:21 and in his name shall the *G* trust
　20:19 (Mk. 10:33; Lk. 18:32) deliver him to the *G*
　20:25 (Mk. 10:42; Lk. 22:25) *G* exercise dominion
Lk. 2:32 a light to lighten the *G*, and the glory
　21:24 until the times of the *G* be fulfilled
Jn. 7:35 dispersed among the *G*, and teach the *G*?
Acts 4:27 Herod, and Pontius Pilate, with the *G*
　9:15 chosen vessel . . to bear my name before the *G*
　10:45 on the *G* also was poured out the gift of
　11:18 hath God also to the *G* granted repentance
　13:42 the *G* besought that these words might be
　13:46 yourselves unworthy . . lo, we turn to the *G*
　14:2 but the unbelieving Jews stirred up the *G*
　14:27 he had opened the door of faith unto the *G*

Acts 15:3 declaring the conversion of the *G*
　15:7 the *G* by my mouth should hear the word
　15:14 how God at the first did visit the *G*
　18:6 from henceforth I will go unto the *G*
　22:21 I will send thee far hence unto the *G*
Rom. 1:13 fruit among you. . even as among other *G*
　2:10 to the Jew first, and also to the *G*
　2:14 *G*, which have not the law, do by nature the
　2:24 the name of God is blasphemed among the *G*
　3:9 both Jews and *G*, that they are all under sin
　3:29 is he not also of the *G*? Yes, of the *G* also
　9:24 not of the Jews only, but also of the *G* ?
　11:11 their fall salvation is come unto the *G*
　11:12 diminishing of them the riches of the *G*
　11:13 *G*, inasmuch as I am the apostle of the *G*
　11:25 until the fulness of the *G* be come in
　15:9 that the *G* might glorify God for his mercy
　15:11 praise the Lord, all ye *G*; and laud him
　15:27 if the *G* have been made partakers of their
1 Cor. 5:1 as is not so much as named among the *G*
　12:2 ye know that ye were *G*, carried away unto
　12:13 one body, whether we be Jews or *G*
Gal. 2:14 a Jew, livest after the manner of *G*
　3:14 the blessing of Abraham might come on the *G*
Eph. 2:11 ye being in time past *G* in the flesh
　3:6 that the *G* should be fellow heirs
　3:8 given, that I should preach among the *G*
　4:17 ye henceforth walk not as other *G* walk
Col. 1:27 of the glory of this mystery among the *G*
1 Thes. 4:5 lust of concupiscence, even as the *G*
1 Tim. 2:7 (2 Tim. 1:11) apostle. . a teacher of the *G*
1 Pet. 2:12 your conversation honest among the *G*
Rev. 11:2 for it is given unto the *G*

Gentle *See also* Gracious, Kind, Meek, Merciful, Tender

1 Thes. 2:7 we were *g* among you, even as a nurse
2 Tim. 2:24 must not strive; but be *g* unto all men
Tit. 3:2 but *g*, showing all meekness unto all men
Jas. 3:17 above is first pure, then peaceable, *g*
1 Pet. 2:18 not only to the good and *g*, but also

Gentleness *See also* Kindness, Meekness

2 Sam. 22:36 (Ps. 18:35) thy *g* hath made me great
2 Cor. 10:1 you by the meekness and *g* of Christ
Gal. 5:22 joy, peace, long-suffering, *g*, goodness

Gently

2 Sam. 18:5 deal *g* for my sake with the young man
Is. 40:11 shall *g* lead those that are with young

Gergesene *See also* Gadarene Mt. 8:28-34

Gerizim

Deut. 11:29 blessing upon mount *G*, and the curse
　27:12 these shall stand upon mount *G* to bless
Josh. 8:33 half of them over against mount *G*

Get (Gotten)

Gen. 4:1 I have *g* a man from the LORD
　12:1 (Acts 7:3) *g* thee out of thy country
Ps. 119:104 through thy precepts I *g* understanding
Prov. 3:13 happy is . . the man that *g* understanding
　4:5 *g* wisdom, *g* understanding: forget it not
　4:7 and with all thy *g g* understanding
　19:8 he that *g* wisdom loveth his own soul
　21:6 the *g* of treasures by a lying tongue is a
Eccl. 1:16 have *g* more wisdom than all they that
　3:6 a time to *g*, and a time to lose; a time to
Jer. 17:11 so he that *g* riches, and not by right
Mt. 16:23 (Mk. 8:33) *g* thee behind me, Satan

Gethsemane Mt. 26:36 (Mk. 14:32)

Gezer

Josh. 16:10; 21:21; Judg. 1:29; 1 Kgs. 9:15-17

Ghost *See also* Spirit

Gen. 25:8 then Abraham gave up the *g*, and died
Job 10:18 oh that I had given up the *g*
14:10 yea, man giveth up the *g*, and where is he?
Mt. 27:50 (Mk. 15:37; Lk. 23:46; Jn. 19:30) Jesus . .
cried again with a loud voice, yielded up the *g*
Acts 5:5 and Ananias . . fell down, and gave up the *g*
12:23 he was eaten of worms, and gave up the *g*

Ghost, Holy *See* Holy Ghost

Giant

Gen. 6:4 there were *g* in the earth in those days
Num. 13:33 there we saw the *g*, the sons of Anak
Deut. 2:11 also were accounted *g*, as the Anakim
2:20 a land of *g*: *g* dwelt therein in old time
Josh. 12:4 was of the remnant of the *g*, that dwelt
2 Sam. 21:22 (1 Chr. 20:8) were born to the *g* in Gath
Job 16:14 upon breach; he runneth upon me like a *g*

Gibeah Judg. 19:12-20:43

1 Sam. 10:26 Saul also went home to *G*; and there
Hos. 9:9 corrupted themselves, as in the days of *G*
10:9 thou hast sinned from the days of *G*

Gibeon

Josh. 9:3 inhabitants of *G* heard what Joshua had
10:4 we may smite *G*: for it hath made peace with
10:10 and slew them with a great slaughter at *G*
2 Sam. 2:13 and met together by the pool of *G*
1 Kgs. 3:5 in *G* the LORD appeared to Solomon in a
1 Chr. 16:39 tabernacle of the LORD . . that was at *G*

Gibeonite 2 Sam. 21:1-9

Gideon (Jerubbaal) Judg. 6:11-8:35

Heb. 11:32 time would fail me to tell of *G*, and of

Gift *See also* Contribution, Offering, Present

Gen. 25:6 Abraham gave *g*, and sent them away
Ex. 23:8 (Deut. 16:19) take no *g*: for the *g* blindeth
28:38 Israel shall hallow in all their holy *g*
Num. 8:19 I have given the Levites as a *g* to Aaron
2 Sam. 8:2 (1 Chr. 18:2) so the Moabites . . brought *g*
19:42 the king's cost? or hath he given us any *g*?
2 Chr. 19:7 respect of persons, nor taking of *g*
32:23 many brought *g* unto the LORD to Jerusalem
Ps. 45:12 daughter of Tyre shall be there with a *g*
68:18 (Eph. 4:8) thou hast received *g* for men
72:10 the kings of Sheba and Seba shall offer *g*
Prov. 6:35 rest content, though thou givest many *g*
15:27 but he that hateth *g* shall live
17:8 *g* is as a precious stone in the eyes of him
17:23 wicked man taketh a *g* out of the bosom
18:16 man's *g* maketh room for him, and bringeth
19:6 every man is a friend to him that giveth *g*
21:14 *g* in secret pacifieth anger: and a reward
29:4 but he that receiveth *g* overthroweth it
Eccl. 3:13 of all his labor, it is the *g* of God
5:19 rejoice in his labor; this is the *g* of God
7:7 a wise man mad; and a *g* destroyeth the heart
Is. 1:23 companions of thieves: every one loveth *g*
Ezek. 20:39 pollute . . holy name no more with your *g*
Mt. 2:11 him *g*; gold, and frankincense, and myrrh
5:23 if thou bring thy *g* to the altar, and there
5:24 leave there thy *g* before the altar, and go
7:11 (Lk. 11:13) to give good *g* unto your children
8:4 and offer the *g* that Moses commanded

Mt. 15:5 (Mk. 7:11) father or his mother, It is a *g*
23:18 sweareth by the *g* that is upon it . . guilty
Lk. 21:1 saw the rich men casting their *g* into the
21:5 how it was adorned with goodly stones and *g*
Jn. 4:10 if thou knewest the *g* of God, and who it
Acts 2:38 ye shall receive the *g* of the Holy Ghost
8:20 thought that the *g* of God may be purchased
10:45 on the Gentiles also was poured out the *g*
11:17 God gave them the *g* as he did unto us
Rom. 1:11 I may impart unto you some spiritual *g*
5:15 not as the offense, so also is the free *g*
5:18 by the righteousness of one the free *g* came
6:23 the *g* of God is eternal life through Jesus
11:29 for the *g* and calling of God are without
12:6 *g* differing according to the grace that is
1 Cor. 1:7 so that ye come behind in no *g*
7:7 but every man hath his proper *g* of God
12:4 are diversities of *g*, but the same Spirit
12:31 covet earnestly the best *g*: and yet show I
13:2 and though I have the *g* of prophecy
14:1 follow after charity, and desire spiritual *g*
2 Cor. 1:11 the *g* bestowed upon us by the means of
8:4 we would receive the *g*, and take upon us the
9:15 thanks be unto God for his unspeakable *g*
Eph. 2:8 not of yourselves: it is the *g* of God
3:7 minister, according to the *g* of the grace of
Phil. 4:17 not because I desire a *g*: but I desire
1 Tim. 4:14 neglect not the *g* that is in thee
2 Tim. 1:6 stir up the *g* of God, which is in thee
Heb. 2:4 divers miracles, and *g* of the Holy Ghost
6:4 have tasted of the heavenly *g*, and were made
8:3 priest is ordained to offer *g* and sacrifices
Jas. 1:17 good *g* and every perfect *g* is from above
1 Pet. 4:10 every man hath received the *g*, even so

Gihon Gen. 2:13; 1 Kgs. 1:35, 38, 45

Gilboa 1 Sam. 31:1 (1 Chr. 10:1)

Gilead

Gen. 31:21 and set his face toward the mount *G*
Num. 32:29 then ye shall give them the land of *G*
Deut. 34:1 the LORD showed him all the land of *G*
Josh. 22:9 go unto the country of *G*, to the land
Judg. 7:3 return and depart early from mount *G*
10:17 of Ammon were gathered . . encamped in *G*
11:5 elders of *G* went to fetch Jephthah out of
12:4 men of *G* smote Ephraim, because they said
Ps. 60:7 (108:8) *G* is mine, and Manasseh is mine
Jer. 8:22 no balm in *G* ? is there no physician
46:11 go up into *G*, and take balm, O virgin
Hos. 6:8 *G* is a city of them that work iniquity
12:11 is there iniquity in *G* ? surely they are
Obad. 19 of Samaria: and Benjamin shall possess *G*

Gilgal

Josh. 4:19 and encamped in *G*, in the east border
9:6 they went to Joshua unto the camp at *G*
1 Sam. 10:8 thou shalt go down before me to *G*
11:15 they made Saul king before the LORD in *G*
13:8 but Samuel came not to *G*
2 Kgs. 2:1 that Elijah went with Elisha from *G*
4:38 and Elisha came again to *G*: and there was a

Gird (Girt) *See also* Bind, Clothe

Judg. 3:16 he did *g* it under his raiment upon his
2 Sam. 22:40 (Ps. 18:39) hast *g* me with strength
1 Kgs. 20:11 let not him that *g* on his harness
Ps. 30:11 off my sackcloth, and *g* me with gladness
45:3 *g* thy sword upon thy thigh, O most Mighty
Prov. 31:17 she *g* her loins with strength
Is. 8:9 shall be broken in pieces; *g* yourselves
45:5 is no God besides me: I *g* thee, though thou

Ezek. 16:10 I *g* thee about with fine linen
　44:18 they shall not *g* themselves with any thing
Joel 1:13 *g* yourselves, and lament, ye priests
Lk. 12:37 he shall *g* himself, and make them to sit
　17:8 *g* thyself, and serve me, till I have eaten
Jn. 13:4 and took a towel, and *g* himself
　21:7 it was the Lord, he *g* his fisher's coat
　21:18 when thou wast young, thou *g* thyself
Acts 12:8 angel said unto him, *G* thyself, and bind
1 Pet. 1:13 wherefore *g* up the loins of your mind

Girded (Girt) *See also* Gird

Ex. 12:11 thus shall ye eat it; with your loins *g*
1 Sam. 2:18 Samuel. . a child, *g* with a linen ephod
Ezek. 23:15 *g* with girdles upon their loins
Joel 1:8 lament like a virgin *g* with sackcloth for
Eph. 6:14 having your loins *g* about with truth
Rev. 1:13 *g* about the paps with a golden girdle
　15:6 their breasts *g* with golden girdles

Girdle

Ex. 28:4 a *g*: and they shall make holy garments
Lev. 16:4 shall be girded with a linen *g*, and with
Ps. 109:19 garment which covereth him, and for a *g*
Prov. 31:24 and delivereth *g* unto the merchant
Is. 3:24 and instead of a *g* a rent; and instead of
　5:27 *g* of their loins be loosed, nor the latchet
　11:5 righteousness shall be the *g* of his loins
Jer. 13:1 LORD unto me, Go and get thee a linen *g*
Mt. 3:4 (Mk. 1:6) a leathern *g* about his loins
Acts 21:11 took Paul's *g*, and bound his own hands
Rev. 1:13 and girt about the paps with a golden *g*

Girl *See also* Damsel, Handmaid, Maid, Maiden

Joel 3:3 a boy for a harlot, and sold a *g* for wine
Zech. 8:5 of boys and *g* playing in the streets

Give (Gave, Given) *See also* Bestow, Grant, Offer, Present

Gen. 3:12 she *g* me of the tree, and I did eat
　12:7 (24:7) unto thy seed will I *g* this land
　14:20 (Heb. 7:2) and he *g* him tithes of all
　28:22 *g* me I will surely *g* the tenth unto thee
Ex. 12:25 to the land which the LORD will *g* you
　22:29 firstborn of thy sons shalt thou *g* unto me
　25:2 that *g* it willingly with his heart ye shall
　30:15 rich shall not *g* more, and the poor shall
　33:14 shall go with thee, and I will *g* thee rest
Num. 6:26 countenance upon thee, and *g* thee peace
Deut. 1:35 which I sware to *g* unto your fathers
　8:10 for the good land which he hath *g* thee
　8:18 it is he that *g* thee power to get wealth
　9:11 the LORD *g* me the two tables of stone
　15:10 thou shalt surely *g* him, and thine heart
　16:17 every man shall *g* as he is able, according
Josh. 1:3 shall tread upon, that have I *g* unto you
　15:19 (Judg. 1:15) *g* me a blessing
Judg. 15:18 thou hast *g* this great deliverance
1 Sam. 1:11 child, then I will *g* him unto the LORD
2 Sam. 12:8 I *g* thee thy master's house, and thy
1 Kgs. 3:5 (2 Chr. 1:7) ask what I shall *g* thee
　4:29 God *g* Solomon wisdom and understanding
2 Kgs. 22:8 (2 Chr. 34:18) Hilkiah *g* the book to
1 Chr. 16:18 (Ps. 105:11) unto thee will I *g* the land
　16:28 (Ps. 96:7) *g* unto the LORD glory and strength
　16:34 (Ps. 106:1; 107:1; 118:1; 136:1) O *g* thanks
　　unto the LORD; for he is good
　29:14 and of thine own have we *g* thee
Ezra 2:69 (Neh. 7:71) they *g*. . unto the treasure
　9:9 to *g* us a reviving, to set up the house of

Neh. 9:20 thou *g* also thy good Spirit to instruct
Job 1:21 the LORD *g*, and the LORD hath taken away
　2:4 all that a man hath will he *g* for his life
　10:18 oh that I had *g* up the ghost, and no eye
　33:4 the breath of the Almighty hath *g* me life
　35:10 is God my maker, who *g* songs in the night
　39:13 *g* thou the goodly wings unto the peacocks?
Ps. 2:8 ask of me, and I shall *g* thee the heathen
　6:5 in the grave who shall *g* thee thanks?
　16:7 will bless the LORD, who hath *g* me counsel
　21:2 thou hast *g* him his heart's desire
　28:4 *g* them according to their deeds
　29:2 (96:8) *g* unto the LORD the glory due unto his
　29:11 the LORD will *g* strength unto his people
　37:4 he shall *g* thee the desires of thine heart
　60:4 thou hast *g* a banner to them that fear thee
　78:20 can he *g* bread also? can he provide flesh
　84:11 LORD will *g* grace and glory: no good thing
　85:12 yea, the LORD shall *g* that which is good
　91:11 (Mt. 4:6; Lk. 4:10) shall *g* his angels charge
　112:9 (2 Cor. 9:9) he hath *g* to the poor
　115:16 earth hath he *g* to the children of men
　119:34 *g* me understanding, and I shall keep thy
　119:130 the entrance of thy words *g* light; it *g*
　145:15 and thou *g* them their meat in due season
Prov. 2:6 LORD *g* wisdom: out of his mouth cometh
　3:34 (Jas. 4:6; 1 Pet. 5:5) he *g* grace unto the lowly
　21:26 but the righteous *g* and spareth not
　23:26 my son, *g* me thine heart, and let thine
　25:21 thine enemy be hungry, *g* him bread to eat
　28:27 he that *g* unto the poor shall not lack
　30:8 *g* me neither poverty nor riches; feed me
　30:15 horseleech hath two daughters, crying, *G*
Eccl. 12:7 spirit shall return unto God who *g* it
Is. 7:14 Lord himself shall *g* you a sign; Behold
　9:6 unto us a child is born, unto us a son is *g*
　40:29 he *g* power to the faint; and to them that
　42:8 my glory will I not *g* to another, neither
　42:24 who *g* Jacob for a spoil, and Israel to the
　43:3 Saviour: I *g* Egypt for thy ransom, Ethiopia
　43:20 because I *g* waters in the wilderness
　49:6 will also *g* thee for a light to the Gentiles
　49:8 and *g* thee for a covenant of the people
　55:4 I have *g* him for a witness to the people
　55:10 that it may *g* seed to the sower, and bread
　61:3 in Zion, to *g* unto them beauty for ashes
Jer. 11:5 to *g* them a land flowing with milk and
　17:10 even to *g* every man according to his ways
　24:7 I will *g* them a heart to know me, that I am
　32:12 and I *g* the evidence of the purchase unto
　32:39 I will *g* them one heart, and one way
Ezek. 11:19 (36:26) will *g* them a heart of flesh
　18:7 *g* his bread to the hungry, and hath covered
　20:11 I *g* them my statutes, and showed them my
Dan. 7:22 and judgment was *g* to the saints
　9:22 Daniel, I am now come forth to *g* thee skill
Hos. 11:8 how shall I *g* thee up, Ephraim?
Zech. 8:12 *g* her increase, and the heavens shall *g*
Mt. 4:9 (Lk. 4:6) all these things will I *g* thee, if thou
　5:42 (Lk. 6:30) *g* to him that asketh thee
　6:11 (Lk. 11:3) *g* us this day our daily bread
　7:7 (Lk. 11:9) ask, and it shall be *g* you
　7:9 (Lk. 11:11) son ask bread, will he *g* him a stone?
　7:11 your Father. . *g* good things to them that ask
　10:1 (Mk. 6:7; Lk. 9:1) he *g* them power against
　10:8 freely ye have received, freely *g*
　11:28 and are heavy laden, and I will *g* you rest
　13:11 (Mk. 4:11; Lk. 8:10) it is *g* unto you to know
　13:12 (Mk. 4:25; Lk. 8:18) hath, to him shall be *g*
　14:19 (Mk. 6:41; Lk. 9:16) brake, and *g* the loaves
　15:36 (Mk. 8:6) brake them, and *g* to his disciples
　16:19 I will *g* unto thee the keys of the kingdom
　16:26 (Mk. 8:37) a man *g* in exchange for his soul?

Mt. 19:21 (Mk. 10:21) sell. . and *g* to the poor
20:4 whatsoever is right I will *g* you
20:8 call the laborers, and *g* them their hire
20:23 (Mk. 10:40) *g* to them for whom it is prepared
20:28 (Mk. 10:45) *g* his life a ransom for many
21:23 (Mk. 11:28; Lk. 20:2) *g* thee this authority?
25:15 unto one he *g* five talents, to another two
25:29 (Lk. 19:26) every one that hath shall be *g*
25:35 ahungered, and ye *g* me meat: I was thirsty
26:9 (Mk. 14:5) sold for much, and *g* to the poor
27:34 (Mk. 15:36) they *g* him vinegar to drink
28:18 all power is *g* unto me in heaven and in
Mk. 12:15 shall we *g*, or shall we not *g*? But he
15:45 of the centurion, he *g* the body to Joseph
Lk. 1:77 *g* knowledge of salvation unto his people
1:79 to *g* light to them that sit in darkness and
4:6 and to whomsoever I will, I *g* it
6:38 *g*, and it shall be *g* unto you; good measure
9:1 *g* them power and authority over all devils
11:13 *g* the Holy Spirit to them that ask him?
12:32 your Father's good pleasure to *g* you the
12:48 much is *g*, of him shall be much required
18:12 I fast. . I *g* tithes of all that I possess
22:19 this is my body which is *g* for you
Jn. 1:12 them *g* he power to become the sons of God
3:16 the world, that he *g* his only begotten Son
3:34 God *g* not the Spirit by measure unto him
4:7 water: Jesus saith unto her, *G* me to drink
4:14 water that I shall *g* him shall never thirst
5:27 hath *g* him authority to execute judgment
6:27 life, which the Son of man shall *g* unto you
6:32 my Father *g* you the true bread from heaven
6:37 all that the Father *g* me shall come to me
6:51 which I will *g* for the life of the world
6:65 except it were *g* unto him of my Father
7:39 for the Holy Ghost was not yet *g*
10:11 the good shepherd *g* his life for the sheep
10:28 I *g* unto them eternal life; and they shall
11:22 thou wilt ask of God, God will *g* it thee
13:29 that he should *g* something to the poor
13:34 commandment I *g* unto you, That ye love
14:16 and he shall *g* you another Comforter
14:27 peace I leave with you, my peace I *g* unto
14:31 as the Father *g* me commandment, even so I
15:16 ask of the Father in my name, he may *g* it
17:2 *g* eternal life to as many as thou hast *g* him
17:11 whom thou hast *g* me, that they may be one
17:12 those that thou *g* me I have kept, and none
17:24 whom thou hast *g* me, be with me where I am
Acts 2:4 tongues, as the Spirit *g* them utterance
3:6 have I none; but such as I have *g* I thee
4:12 none other name under heaven *g* among men
6:4 we will *g* ourselves continually to prayer
10:43 to him *g* all the prophets witness
17:16 when he saw the city wholly *g* to idolatry
17:25 seeing he *g* to all life, and breath
20:35 it is more blessed to *g* than to receive
27:24 God hath *g* thee all them that sail with
Rom. 1:28 God *g* them over to a reprobate mind
5:5 hearts by the Holy Ghost which is *g* unto us
8:32 with him also freely *g* us all things?
11:35 or who hath first *g* to him, and it shall
12:8 he that *g*, let him do it with simplicity
12:19 yourselves, but rather *g* place unto wrath
14:12 of us shall *g* account of himself to God
1 Cor. 2:12 things that are freely *g* to us of God
3:6 Apollos watered; but God *g* the increase
7:5 ye may *g* yourselves to fasting and prayer
13:3 though I *g* my body to be burned, and have
15:57 thanks be to God, which *g* us the victory
2 Cor. 1:22 and *g* the earnest of the Spirit in our
5:5 hath *g* unto us the earnest of the Spirit
5:12 but *g* you occasion to glory on our behalf

2 Cor. 8:5 but first *g* their own selves to the Lord
9:7 let him *g*; not grudgingly, or of necessity
Gal. 1:4 who *g* himself for our sins, that he might
2:5 to whom we *g* place by subjection, no, not
2:20 Son of God, who loved me, and *g* himself for
3:21 had been a law *g* which could have *g* life
Eph. 1:17 may *g* unto you the spirit of wisdom and
3:8 least of all saints, is this grace *g*, that I
4:7 unto every one of us is *g* grace according to
4:8 led captivity captive, and *g* gifts unto men
4:27 neither *g* place to the devil
4:28 that he may have to *g* to him that needeth
5:2 *g* himself for us an offering and a sacrifice
5:14 from the dead, and Christ shall *g* thee light
Phil. 1:29 for unto you it is *g* in the behalf of
2:9 and *g* him a name which is above every name
4:15 as concerning *g* and receiving, but ye only
Col. 4:1 *g* unto your servants that which is just
1 Thes. 4:8 hath also *g* unto us his Holy Spirit
2 Thes. 2:16 and hath *g* us everlasting consolation
1 Tim. 2:6 who *g* himself a ransom for all, to be
4:15 upon these things; *g* thyself wholly to them
6:17 God, who *g* us richly all things to enjoy
2 Tim. 3:16 Scripture is *g* by inspiration of God
Heb. 7:2 to whom also Abraham *g* a tenth part of
13:17 as they that must *g* account, that they may
Jas. 1:5 ask of God, that *g* to all men liberally
2:16 notwithstanding ye *g* them not those things
4:6 he *g* more grace. . *g* grace unto the humble
1.Pet. 3:15 and be ready always to *g* an answer to
4:11 let him do it as of the ability which God *g*
2 Pet. 1:3 as his divine power hath *g* unto us all
1 Jn. 3:24 in us, by the Spirit which he hath *g* us
5:11 record, that God hath *g* to us eternal life
5:16 he shall *g* him life for them that sin not
Rev. 2:10 and I will *g* thee a crown of life
14:7 a loud voice, Fear God, and *g* glory to him
20:13 and the sea *g* up the dead which were in it
22:5 Lord God *g* them light: and they shall reign
22:12 *g* every man according as his work shall be

Giver

2 Cor. 9:7 for God loveth a cheerful *g*

Glad *See also* Happy, Joyful, Please

Ex. 4:14 when he seeth thee, he will be *g* in his
1 Kgs. 8:66 (2 Chr. 7:10) unto their tents joyful and *g*
1 Chr. 16:31 (Ps. 96:11) let the heavens be *g*
Job 3:22 and are *g*, when they can find the grave?
22:19 the righteous see it, and are *g*
Ps. 9:2 I will be *g* and rejoice in thee: I will
14:7 (Ps. 53:6) and Israel shall be *g*
16:9 (Acts 2:26) my heart is *g*. . my glory rejoiceth
21:6 made him exceeding *g* with thy countenance
31:7 I will be *g* and rejoice in thy mercy
32:11 be *g* in the LORD, and rejoice, ye righteous
34:2 the humble shall hear thereof, and be *g*
40:16 (70:4) that seek thee rejoice and be *g*
46:4 streams whereof shall make *g* the city of
48:11 rejoice, let the daughters of Judah be *g*
64:10 the righteous shall be *g* in the LORD
67:4 let the nations be *g* and sing for joy
68:3 let the righteous be *g*; let them rejoice
69:32 the humble shall see this, and be *g*
90:15 make us *g* according to the days wherein
92:4 thou, LORD, hast made me *g* through thy work
104:15 wine that maketh *g* the heart of man
104:34 shall be sweet: I will be *g* in the LORD
118:24 hath made; we will rejoice and be *g* in it
119:74 that fear thee will be *g* when they see me
122:1 I was *g* when they said unto me, Let us go
126:3 done great things for us; whereof we are *g*

Prov. 10:1 (15:20) a wise son maketh a *g* father
  12:25 the heart . . a good word maketh it *g*
  17:5 is *g* at calamities shall not be unpunished
  24:17 let not thine heart be *g* when he stumbleth
Song 1:4 we will be *g* and rejoice in thee, we will
Is. 25:9 we will be *g* and rejoice in his salvation
  35:1 and the solitary place shall be *g* for them
  65:18 but be ye *g* and rejoice for ever in that
  66:10 rejoice ye with Jerusalem, and be *g* with
Jer. 50:11 because ye were *g*, because ye rejoiced
Lam. 1:21 trouble; they are *g* that thou hast done
  4:21 rejoice and be *g*, O daughter of Edom
Joel 2:21 fear not, O land; be *g* and rejoice
Jon. 4:6 so Jonah was exceeding *g* of the gourd
Hab. 1:15 therefore they rejoice and are *g*
Zeph. 3:14 Zion; shout, O Israel; be *g* and rejoice
Zech. 10:7 their children shall see it, and be *g*
Mt. 5:12 rejoice, and be exceeding *g*: for great is
Mk. 14:11 (Lk. 22:5) were *g*, and promised . . money
Lk. 1:19 and to show thee these *g* tidings
  8:1 showing the *g* tidings of the kingdom of God
  15:32 meet that we should make merry, and be *g*
  23:8 when Herod saw Jesus, he was exceeding *g*
Jn. 8:56 to see my day: and he saw it, and was *g*
  11:15 I am *g* for your sakes that I was not there
  20:20 the disciples *g*, when they saw the Lord
Acts 11:23 seen the grace of God, was *g*, and exhorted
  13:32 we declare unto you *g* tidings, how that
Rom. 10:15 and bring *g* tidings of good things!
  16:19 I am *g* therefore on your behalf: but yet I
2 Cor. 2:2 sorry, who is he then that maketh me *g*
  13:9 are *g*, when we are weak, and ye are strong
1 Pet. 4:13 ye may be *g* also with exceeding joy
Rev. 19:7 let us be *g* and rejoice, and give honor

Gladly

Mk. 6:20 for Herod feared John . . and heard him *g*
  12:37 and the common people heard him *g*
Lk. 8:40 Jesus was returned, the people *g* received
Acts 2:41 that *g* received his word were baptized
2 Cor. 12:9 most *g* therefore will I rather glory
  12:15 I will very *g* spend and be spent for you

Gladness *See also* Delight, Joy, Pleasure

Num. 10:10 also in the day of your *g*, and in your
Deut. 28:47 thy God with joyfulness, and with *g* of
2 Sam. 6:12 the ark . . into the city of David with *g*
1 Chr. 16:27 strength and *g* are in his place
  29:22 before the LORD on that day with great *g*
2 Chr. 30:21 the feast . . seven days with great *g*
Neh. 8:17 done so. And there was very great *g*
  12:27 Jerusalem, to keep the dedication with *g*
Esth. 8:16 the Jews had light, and *g*, and joy
  9:17 (9:18, 19) made it a day of feasting and *g*
Ps. 4:7 thou hast put *g* in my heart, more than in
  30:11 put off my sackcloth, and girded me with *g*
  45:7 (Heb. 1:9) anointed thee with the oil of *g*
  51:8 make me to hear joy and *g*; that the bones
  97:11 righteous, and *g* for the upright in heart
  100:2 serve the LORD with *g*: come before his
  105:43 people with joy, and his chosen with *g*
Prov. 10:28 hope of the righteous shall be *g*
Is. 16:10 (Jer. 48:33) *g* is taken away, and joy
  30:29 holy solemnity is kept; and *g* of heart, as
  35:10 (51:11) they shall obtain joy and *g*
  51:3 joy and *g* shall be found therein
Jer. 31:7 saith the LORD; Sing with *g* for Jacob
Joel 1:16 yea, joy and *g* from the house of our God?
Mk. 4:16 the word, immediately receive it with *g*
Lk. 1:14 thou shalt have joy and *g*; and many shall
Acts 2:46 did eat their meat with *g* and singleness
  12:14 she opened not the gate for *g*, but ran in
  14:17 seasons, filling our hearts with food and *g*

Glass

1 Cor. 13:12 now we see through a *g*, darkly
2 Cor. 3:18 beholding as in a *g* the glory of the
Jas. 1:23 a man beholding his natural face in a *g*
Rev. 4:6 there was a sea of *g* like unto crystal
  15:2 saw as it were a sea of *g* mingled with fire
  21:18 the city was pure gold, like unto clear *g*

Glean

Lev. 19:10 (Deut. 24:21) shalt not *g* thy vineyard
Ruth 2:7 let me *g* and gather after the reapers
  2:15 saying, Let her *g* even among the sheaves
  2:19 said unto her, Where hast thou *g* today?
Jer. 6:9 shall thoroughly g the remnant of Israel
  49:9 would they not leave some *g* grapes?

Glistering

1 Chr. 29:2 be set, *g* stones, and of divers colors
Lk. 9:29 altered, and his raiment was white and *g*

Glittering

Deut. 32:41 if I whet my *g* sword, and mine hand
Job 20:25 yea, the *g* sword cometh out of his gall
  39:23 against him, the *g* spear and the shield
Nah. 3:3 up both the bright sword and the *g* spear
Hab. 3:11 went, and at the shining of thy *g* spear

Gloominess

Joel 2:2 (Zeph. 1:15) day of darkness and of *g*

Glorify *See also* Exalt, Honor, Praise

Lev. 10:3 and before all the people I will be *g*
Ps. 22:23 seed of Jacob, *g* him; and fear him
  50:15 I will deliver thee, and thou shalt *g* me
  50:23 whoso offereth praise *g* me: and to him
  86:9 (Rev. 15:4) O Lord; and shall *g* thy name
  86:12 and I will *g* thy name for evermore
Is. 24:15 wherefore *g* ye the LORD in the fires
  25:3 therefore shall the strong people *g* thee
  44:23 LORD hath redeemed Jacob, and *g* himself in
  49:3 my servant, O Israel, in whom I will be *g*
  55:5 (60:9) Holy One of Israel; for he hath *g* thee
  60:7 altar, and I will *g* the house of my glory
  66:5 that hated you . . said, Let the LORD be *g*
Jer. 30:19 I will also *g* them, and they shall not
Ezek. 28:22 and I will be *g* in the midst of thee
Dan. 5:23 whose are all thy ways, hast thou not *g*
Hag. 1:8 will take pleasure in it, and I will be *g*
Mt. 5:16 see your good works, and *g* your Father
  9:8 (Mk. 2:12; Lk. 5:26) they marveled, and *g* God
  15:31 blind to see: and they *g* the God of Israel
Lk. 2:20 shepherds returned, *g* and praising God
  4:15 taught in their synagogues, being *g* of all
  7:16 there came a fear on all: and they *g* God
  18:43 received his sight, and followed him, *g* God
Jn. 7:39 because that Jesus was not yet *g*
  11:4 that the Son of God might be *g* thereby
  12:16 but when Jesus was *g*, then remembered they
  12:23 is come, that the Son of man should be *g*
  12:28 *g* thy name . . I have both *g* it, and will *g* it
  13:31 is the Son of man *g*, and God is *g* in him
  13:32 if God be *g* in him, God shall also *g* him
  14:13 I do, that the Father may be *g* in the Son
  15:8 is my Father *g*, that ye bear much fruit
  16:14 shall *g* me: for he shall receive of mine
  17:1 Father, the hour is come; *g* thy Son
  17:4 I have *g* thee on the earth: I have finished
  21:19 signifying by what death he should *g* God
Acts 3:13 God of our fathers, hath *g* his Son Jesus
  4:21 for all men *g* God for that which was done
  13:48 they were glad, and *g* the word of the Lord
Rom. 1:21 knew God, they *g* him not as God, neither
  8:17 with him, that we may be also *g* together

Rom. 8:30 and whom he justified, them he also *g*
  15:6 ye may with one mind and one mouth *g* God
1 Cor. 6:20 *g* God in your body, and in your spirit
2 Thes. 1:10 he shall come to be *g* in his saints
  1:12 Jesus Christ may be *g* in you, and ye in him
  3:1 may have free course, and be *g*, even as it
Heb. 5:5 so also Christ *g* not himself to be made a
1 Pet. 2:12 *g* God in the day of visitation
  4:11 God in all things may be *g* through Jesus
  4:14 is evil spoken of, but on your part he is *g*
  4:16 not be ashamed; but let him *g* God on this
Rev. 15:4 not fear thee, O Lord, and *g* thy name?

Glorious *See also* Excellent, Honorable, Magnificent, Noble

Ex. 15:11 who is like thee, *g* in holiness, fearful
Deut. 28:58 fear this *g* and fearful name, THE LORD
2 Sam. 6:20 how *g* was the king of Israel today
1 Chr. 29:13 we thank thee, and praise thy *g* name
Neh. 9:5 blessed be thy *g* name, which is exalted
Ps. 45:13 the King's daughter is all *g* within
  66:2 the honor of his name: make his praise *g*
  72:19 blessed be his *g* name for ever: and let
  76:4 art more *g* and excellent than the mountains
  87:3 *g* things are spoken of thee, O city of God
  111:3 his work is honorable and *g*
  145:5 I will speak of the *g* honor of thy majesty
  145:12 acts, and the *g* majesty of his kingdom
Is. 11:10 Gentiles seek: and his rest shall be *g*
  22:23 he shall be for a *g* throne to his father's
  28:1 Ephraim, whose *g* beauty is a fading flower
  33:21 there the *g* LORD will be unto us a place
  49:5 yet shall I be *g* in the eyes of the LORD
  60:13 and I will make the place of my feet *g*
  63:1 from Bozrah? this that is *g* in his apparel
  63:14 lead thy people, to make thyself a *g* name
Jer. 17:12 *g* high throne from the beginning is the
Ezek. 27:25 made very *g* in the midst of the seas
Dan. 11:16 stand in the *g* land, which by his hand
  11:41 he shall enter also into the *g* land
  11:45 between the seas in the *g* holy mountain
Lk. 13:17 the people rejoiced for all the *g* things
Rom. 8:21 bondage of corruption into the *g* liberty
2 Cor. 3:7 written and engraven in stones, was *g*
  3:11 was *g*, much more that which remaineth is *g*
  4:4 lest the light of the *g* gospel of Christ
Eph. 5:27 might present it to himself a *g* church
Phil. 3:21 may be fashioned like unto his *g* body
Col. 1:11 with all might, according to his *g* power
1 Tim. 1:11 the *g* gospel of the blessed God
Tit. 2:13 the *g* appearing of the great God and our

Gloriously

Ex. 15:1 unto the LORD, for he hath triumphed *g*
Is. 24:23 in Jerusalem, and before his ancients *g*

Glory *See also* Boast, Honor, Majesty, Praise

Ex. 16:7 then ye shall see the *g* of the LORD
  16:10 *g* of the LORD appeared in the cloud
  24:16 the *g* of the LORD abode upon mount Sinai
  33:18 and he said, I beseech thee, show me thy *g*
  40:34 the *g* of the LORD filled the tabernacle
Lev. 9:23 and the *g* of the LORD appeared unto all
Num. 14:21 the earth shall be filled with the *g* of
1 Sam. 4:21 the *g* is departed from Israel
1 Kgs. 8:11 (2 Chr. 5:14) *g* of the LORD had filled
1 Chr. 16:24 (Ps. 96:3) declare his *g* among . . heathen
  16:27 *g* and honor are in his presence
  16:29 (Ps. 96:8) give unto the LORD the *g* due unto
  22:5 fame and of *g* throughout all countries

1 Chr. 29:11 is the greatness, and the power, and the *g*
Job 19:9 he hath stripped me of my *g*, and taken
  29:20 my *g* was fresh in me, and my bow was
Ps. 8:1 who hast set thy *g* above the heavens
  8:5 (Heb. 2:7) crowned him with *g* and honor
  16:9 my *g* rejoiceth: my flesh also shall rest in
  19:1 the heavens declare the *g* of God; and the
  21:5 his *g* is great in thy salvation: honor and
  24:8 (24:10) who is this King of *g* ?
  29:2 give unto the LORD the *g* due unto his name
  49:16 rich, when the *g* of his house is increased
  62:7 in God is my salvation and my *g*: the rock
  63:2 to see thy power and thy *g*, so as I have
  72:19 let the whole earth be filled with his *g*
  73:24 thy counsel, and afterward receive me to *g*
  84:11 LORD will give grace and *g*: no good thing
  85:9 that fear him; that *g* may dwell in our land
  89:17 for thou art the *g* of their strength
  89:44 thou hast made his *g* to cease, and cast
  90:16 servants, and thy *g* unto their children
  97:6 righteousness, and all the people see his *g*
  104:31 the *g* of the LORD shall endure for ever
  108:1 I will sing and give praise, even with my *g*
  115:1 not unto us, but unto thy name give *g*
  145:11 they shall speak of the *g* of thy kingdom
  148:13 his *g* is above the earth and heaven
Prov. 3:35 wise shall inherit *g*: but shame shall
  16:31 hoary head is a crown of *g*, if it be found
  17:6 and the *g* of children are their fathers
  20:29 the *g* of young men is their strength
  25:2 it is the *g* of God to conceal a thing
  25:27 so for men to search their own *g* is not *g*
Is. 6:3 of hosts: the whole earth is full of his *g*
  10:3 for help? and where will ye leave your *g* ?
  13:19 Babylon, the *g* of kingdoms, the beauty of
  17:3 shall be as the *g* of the children of Israel
  24:16 we heard songs, even *g* to the righteous
  35:2 the *g* of Lebanon shall be given unto it
  40:5 the *g* of the LORD shall be revealed
  41:16 and shalt *g* in the Holy One of Israel
  42:8 my *g* will I not give to another, neither
  43:7 I have created him for my *g*, I have formed
  58:8 the *g* of the LORD shall be thy rearward
  60:1 and the *g* of the LORD is risen upon thee
  60:7 and I will glorify the house of my *g*
  61:6 and in their *g* shall ye boast yourselves
  66:18 and they shall come, and see my *g*
Jer. 2:11 gods? but my people have changed their *g*
  9:24 (1 Cor. 1:31; 2 Cor. 10:17) him that *g g* in this
  13:16 give *g* to the LORD your God, before he
Ezek. 1:28 appearance of the likeness of the *g*
  10:4 the *g* of the LORD went up from the cherub
  20:6 (20:15) milk and honey . . the *g* of all lands
  31:18 to whom art thou thus like in *g* and in
  39:21 I will set my *g* among the heathen, and all
  43:5 behold, the *g* of the LORD filled the house
Dan. 2:37 a kingdom, power, and strength, and *g*
  7:14 given him dominion, and *g*, and a kingdom
Hos. 4:7 therefore will . . change their *g* into shame
Hab. 2:14 with the knowledge of the *g* of the LORD
  3:3 his *g* covered the heavens, and the earth
Hag. 2:7 I will fill this house with *g*, saith the
Zech. 2:5 and will be the *g* in the midst of her
Mt. 4:8 kingdoms of the world, and the *g* of them
  6:2 in the streets, that they may have *g* of men
  6:13 is the kingdom, and the power, and the *g*
  6:29 (Lk. 12:27) even Solomon in all his *g* was not
  16:27 (Mk. 8:38; Lk. 9:26) in the *g* of his Father
  19:28 shall sit in the throne of his *g*, ye also
  24:30 (Mk. 13:26; Lk. 21:27) power and great *g*
Lk. 2:9 the *g* of the Lord shone round about them
  2:14 *g* to God in the highest, and on earth peace
  2:32 Gentiles, and the *g* of thy people Israel

Lk. 4:6 power will I give thee, and the *g* of them
  9:31 who appeared in *g*, and spake of his decease
  17:18 not found that returned to give *g* to God
  19:38 peace in heaven, and *g* in the highest
  24:26 ought not Christ . . to enter into his *g*?
Jn. 1:14 and we beheld his *g*, the *g* as of the only
  2:11 Cana of Galilee, and manifested forth his *g*
  7:18 speaketh of himself seeketh his own *g*
  8:50 I seek not mine own *g*: there is one that
  11:4 is not unto death, but for the *g* of God
  17:5 with the *g* which I had with thee before the
  17:22 *g* which thou gavest me I have given them
  17:24 may behold my *g*, which thou hast given me
Acts 7:2 God of *g* appeared unto our father Abraham
  12:23 smote him, because he gave not God the *g*
  22:11 I could not see for the *g* of that light
Rom. 1:23 changed the *g* of the uncorruptible God
  3:23 have sinned, and come short of the *g* of God
  4:20 but was strong in faith, giving *g* to God
  5:3 not only so, but we *g* in tribulations also
  8:18 are not worthy to be compared with the *g*
  9:23 he might make known the riches of his *g* on
  11:36 (Gal. 1:5; 2 Tim. 4:18; Heb. 13:21; 1 Pet.
    5:11) to whom be *g* for ever
1 Cor. 1:31 he that *g*, let him *g* in the Lord
  2:8 they would not have crucified the Lord of *g*
  3:21 therefore let no man *g* in men: for all
  9:16 I preach the gospel, I have nothing to *g* of
  10:31 whatsoever ye do, do all to the *g* of God
  11:7 forasmuch as he is the image and *g* of God
  11:15 a woman have long hair, it is a *g* to her
  15:40 the *g* of the celestial is one, and the *g*
  15:41 there is one *g* of the sun, and another *g*
  15:43 it is sown in dishonor, it is raised in *g*
2 Cor. 3:7 the *g* of his countenance; which *g* was
  3:18 beholding as in a glass the *g* of the Lord
  4:6 of the *g* of God in the face of Jesus Christ
  4:17 far more exceeding and eternal weight of *g*
  5:12 which *g* in appearance, and not in heart
  10:17 but he that *g*, let him *g* in the Lord
  11:18 that many *g* after the flesh, I will *g* also
  12:9 therefore will I rather *g* in my infirmities
Gal. 6:14 but God forbid that I should *g*, save in
Eph. 1:6 the praise of the *g* of his grace, wherein
  1:12 (1:14) to the praise of his *g*
  1:17 Father of *g*, may give unto you the spirit
  3:21 unto him be *g* in the church by Christ Jesus
Phil. 2:11 Jesus Christ is Lord, to the *g* of God
  3:19 their belly, and whose *g* is in their shame
  4:19 need according to his riches in *g* by Christ
  4:20 now unto God and our Father be *g* for ever
Col. 1:27 is the riches of the *g* of this mystery
  3:4 then shall ye also appear with him in *g*
1 Thes. 2:6 nor of men sought we *g*, neither of you
  2:20 for ye are our *g* and joy
2 Thes. 1:4 we ourselves *g* in you in the churches
  2:14 to the obtaining of the *g* of our Lord
1 Tim. 3:16 in the world, received up into *g*
Heb. 1:3 who being the brightness of his *g*
  2:10 in bringing many sons unto *g*, to make the
  3:3 this man was counted worthy of more *g* than
Jas. 3:14 *g* not, and lie not against the truth
1 Pet. 1:8 with joy unspeakable and full of *g*
  1:11 sufferings of Christ, and the *g* that should
  1:24 and all the *g* of man as the flower of grass
  2:20 what *g* is it, if, when ye be buffeted for
  4:13 that, when his *g* shall be revealed, ye may
  4:14 the Spirit of *g* and of God resteth upon you
  5:1 a partaker of the *g* that shall be revealed
  5:4 shall appear, ye shall receive a crown of *g*
  5:10 hath called us unto his eternal *g* by Christ
2 Pet. 1:3 him that hath called us to *g* and virtue
  1:17 he received from God the Father honor and *g*

Jude 24 faultless before the presence of his *g*
  25 Saviour, be *g* and majesty, dominion and power
Rev. 4:11 thou art worthy, O Lord, to receive *g*
  7:12 saying, Amen: Blessing, and *g*, and wisdom
  14:7 a loud voice, Fear God, and give *g* to him
  18:1 and the earth was lightened with his *g*
  21:23 the *g* of God did lighten it, and the Lamb

Glorying

1 Cor. 5:6 your *g* is not good
  9:15 than that any man should make my *g* void
2 Cor. 7:4 great is my *g* of you
  12:11 am become a fool in *g*; ye have compelled me

Glutton

Deut. 21:20 he will not obey our voice; he is a *g*
Prov. 23:21 and the *g* shall come to poverty

Gluttonous

Mt. 11:19 (Lk. 7:34) behold a man *g* . . a winebibber

Gnash

Job 16:9 (Ps. 37:12) he *g* upon me with his teeth
Ps. 112:10 he shall *g* with his teeth, and melt
Lam. 2:16 against thee: they hiss and *g* the teeth
Mk. 9:18 foameth, and *g* with his teeth, and pineth
Acts 7:54 were cut to the heart, and they *g* on him

Gnashing

Mt. 8:12 (13:42, 50; 22:13; 24:51; 25:30; Lk. 13:28)
  there shall be weeping and *g* of teeth

Gnat

Mt. 23:24 which strain at a *g*, and swallow a camel

Gnaw

Zeph. 3:3 they *g* not the bones till the morrow
Rev. 16:10 they *g* their tongues for pain

Go (Gone) *See also* Depart, Proceed, Went

Gen. 3:14 upon thy belly shalt thou *g*, and dust
  11:3 they said one to another, *G* to, let us make
  28:15 keep thee in all places whither thou *g*
  32:26 he said, Let me *g*, for the day breaketh
  44:34 how shall I *g* up to my father, and the lad
Ex. 4:23 let my son *g*, that he may serve me
  5:1 (7:16; 8:1; 20; 9:1, 13; 10:3) let my people *g*
  14:15 speak unto . . Israel, that they *g* forward
  23:23 mine angel shall *g* before thee, and bring
  32:1 (32:23; Acts 7:40) gods, which shall *g* before us
  33:14 and he said, My presence shall *g* with thee
Deut. 31:6 thy God, he it is that doth *g* with thee
  34:4 but thou shalt not *g* over thither
Josh. 1:9 God is with thee whithersoever thou *g*
  23:14 this day I am *g* the way of all the earth
Ruth 1:16 whither thou *g*, I will *g*; and where thou
  2:2 let me now *g* to the field, and glean
2 Sam. 5:24 (1 Chr. 14:15) the LORD *g* out before thee
  12:23 I shall *g* to him, but he shall not return
2 Chr. 14:11 in thy name we *g* against this multitude
Job 23:8 behold, I *g* forward, but he is not there
  27:6 my righteousness I hold fast . . not let it *g*
Ps. 32:8 teach thee in the way which thou shalt *g*
  39:13 I may recover strength, before I *g* hence
  42:4 for I had *g* with the multitude, I went with
  48:12 walk about Zion, and *g* round about her
  58:3 they *g* astray as soon as they be born
  60:10 (108:11) didst not *g* out with our armies?
  66:13 will *g* into thy house with burnt offerings
  71:16 I will *g* in the strength of the Lord GOD
  84:7 they *g* from strength to strength, every one
  89:14 mercy and truth shall *g* before thy face

Ps. 118:19 the gates of righteousness: I will *g* into
119:176 I have *g* astray like a lost sheep: seek
122:1 let us *g* into the house of the LORD
139:7 whither shall I *g* from thy Spirit?
Prov. 6:6 *g* to the ant, thou sluggard; consider
6:22 when thou *g*, it shall lead thee; when thou
9:6 and live; and *g* in the way of understanding
22:6 train up a child in the way he should *g*
30:29 three things which *g* well, yea, four are
Eccl. 3:20 *g* unto one place; all are of the dust
7:2 better to *g* to the house of mourning, than
Is. 2:3 (Mic. 4:2) let us *g* up to the mountain of
6:8 whom shall I send, and who will *g* for us?
49:9 thou mayest say to the prisoners, *G* forth
52:12 nor *g* by flight: for the LORD will *g* before
53:6 all we like sheep have *g* astray; we have
55:12 ye shall *g* out with joy, and be led forth
Jer. 51:45 my people, *g* ye out of the midst of her
Mt. 5:41 compel thee to *g* a mile, *g* with him twain
7:13 destruction, and there be many which *g* in
8:9 (Lk. 7:8) and I say to this man, *G*, and he *g*
8:19 (Lk. 9:57) follow thee whithersoever thou *g*
9:6 (Mk. 2:11; Lk. 5:24) take up thy bed, and *g* unto
10:6 but *g* rather to the lost sheep of . . Israel
17:21 howbeit this kind *g* not out but by prayer
21:30 answered and said, I *g*, sir; and went not
24:26 (Lk. 17:23) is in the desert; *g* not forth
26:24 (Mk. 14:21; Lk. 22:22) Son . . *g* as it is written
26:46 (Mk. 14:42) let us be *g*: behold, he is at hand
28:19 (Mk. 16:15) *g* ye . . and teach all nations
Mk. 5:19 *g* home to thy friends, and tell them how
5:30 (Lk. 8:46) knowing . . that virtue had *g* out of
Lk. 1:76 thou shalt *g* before the face of the Lord
8:31 not command them to *g* out into the deep
10:37 Jesus unto him, *G*, and do thou likewise
15:18 I will arise and *g* to my father, and will
Jn. 6:67 Jesus unto the twelve, Will ye also *g* away?
6:68 to whom shall we *g* ? thou hast the words of
7:33 with you, and then I *g* unto him that sent me
8:21 I *g* my way . . whither I *g*, ye cannot come
11:44 Jesus saith . . Loose him, and let him *g*
13:36 whither I *g*, thou canst not follow me now
14:2 I *g* to prepare a place for you
14:4 whither I *g* ye know, and the way ye know
14:5 Lord, we know not whither thou *g*; and how
14:12 shall he do; because I *g* unto my Father
18:8 am he: if therefore ye seek me, let these *g*
19:12 thou let this man *g*, thou art not Caesar's
Acts 1:11 manner as ye have seen him *g* into heaven
5:20 *g*, stand and speak in the temple to the
9:6 (22:10) arise, and *g* into the city
9:15 Lord said unto him, *G* thy way
15:33 they were let *g* in peace from the brethren
15:36 let us *g* again and visit our brethren in
16:10 we endeavored to *g* into Macedonia
18:6 from henceforth I will *g* unto the Gentiles
Rom. 10:3 *g* about to establish . . own righteousness
1 Cor. 5:10 then must ye needs *g* out of the world
9:7 who *g* a warfare any time at his own charges?
1 Tim. 5:24 open beforehand, *g* before to judgment
Heb. 6:1 let us *g* on unto perfection; not laying
11:8 Abraham, when he was called to *g* out into a
Jas. 5:1 *g* to now, ye rich men, weep and howl for
Jude 7 to fornication, and *g* after strange flesh
11 for they have *g* in the way of Cain
Rev. 3:12 he shall *g* no more out: and I will write

Goad

1 Sam. 13:21 for the axes, and to sharpen the *g*
Eccl. 12:11 the words of the wise are as *g*, and as

Goat *See also* Kid, Scapegoat, Sheep

Gen. 27:9 two good kids of the *g*: and I will make

Gen. 27:16 skins of the kids of the *g* upon his hands
30:35 removed that day the he *g* . . ring-streaked
Lev. 9:3 take ye a kid of the *g* for a sin offering
16:10 but the *g*, on which the lot fell to be the
16:22 *g* shall bear upon him all their iniquities
Num. 28:22 and one *g* for a sin offering, to make
Deut. 14:5 wild *g*, and the pygarg, and the wild ox
2 Chr. 29:21 seven he *g*, for a sin offering for
Job 39:1 when the wild *g* of the rock bring forth?
Ps. 50:9 of thy house, nor he *g* out of thy folds
50:13 flesh of bulls, or drink the blood of *g* ?
104:18 high hills are a refuge for the wild *g*
Prov. 27:26 and the *g* are the price of the field
30:31 a greyhound; a he *g* also; and a king
Is. 1:11 and I delight not in the blood of . . he *g*
Dan. 8:5 as I was considering, behold, a he *g* came
Mt. 25:32 a shepherd divideth his sheep from the *g*
Heb. 9:12 neither by the blood of *g* and calves
10;4 of bulls and of *g* should take away sins

God *See also* Father, god, LORD

Gen. 1:1 in the beginning *G* created the heaven and
1:27 (5:1) so *G* created man in his own image
5:24 Enoch walked with *G*: and he was not; for *G*
6:9 in his generations, and Noah walked with *G*
16:13 thou *G* seest me: for she said, Have I also
17:1 I am the Almighty *G*; walk before me, and be
17:7 everlasting covenant, to be a *G* unto thee
21:22 *G* is with thee in all that thou doest
28:21 then shall the LORD be my *G*
31:13 am the *G* of Bethel, where thou anointedst
32:30 Peniel: for I have seen *G* face to face
33:11 because *G* hath dealt graciously with me
45:8 it was not you that sent me hither, but *G*
Ex. 2:24 *G* heard their groaning, and *G* remembered
3:6 (Mt. 22:32; Mk. 12:26; Lk. 20:37; Acts 7:32)
    G of Abraham, the *G* of Isaac, and the *G* of Jacob
3:12 ye shall serve *G* upon this mountain
3:14 *G* said unto Moses, I AM THAT I AM
6:7 and ye shall know that I am the LORD your *G*
18:19 that thou mayest bring the causes unto *G*
20:2 (Deut. 5:6; Ps. 81:10) I am the LORD thy *G*
20:5 (Deut. 5:9) I the LORD thy *G* am a jealous *G*
20:7 (Deut. 5:11) name of the LORD thy *G* in vain
20:19 but let not *G* speak with us, lest we die
31:18 (Deut. 9:10) written with the finger of *G*
Lev. 24:15 whosoever curseth his *G* shall bear his
Num. 16:22 O *G*, the *G* of the spirits of all flesh
21:5 people spake against *G*, and against Moses
23:19 *G* is not a man, that he should lie
23:23 Jacob and of Israel, What hath *G* wrought!
Deut. 3:24 what *G* is there in heaven or in earth
4:24 (Heb. 12:29) LORD thy *G* is a consuming fire
4:31 LORD thy *G* is a merciful *G*); he will not
5:24 seen this day that *G* doth talk with man
7:9 is *G*, the faithful *G*, which keepeth covenant
8:19 if thou do at all forget the LORD thy *G*
10:12 to serve the LORD thy *G* with all thy heart
10:17 is *G* of gods, and Lord of lords, a great *G*
32:4 a *G* of truth and without iniquity, just and
33:27 the eternal *G* is thy refuge, and underneath
Josh. 1:9 LORD thy *G* is with thee whithersoever
Ruth 1:16 people shall be my people . . thy *G* my *G*
1 Sam. 2:2 neither is there any rock like our *G*
17:46 earth may know that there is a *G* in Israel
28:15 war against me, and *G* is departed from me
2 Sam. 7:22 (1 Chr. 17:20) neither is there any *G*
22:32 (Ps. 18:31) who is *G*, save the LORD?
22:33 *G* is my strength and power; and he maketh
1 Kgs. 8:23 (2 Chr. 6:14) *G* of Israel . . no *G* like thee
8:27 (2 Chr. 6:18) will *G* indeed dwell on the earth?
18:21 if the LORD be *G*, follow him: but if Baal
18:39 LORD, he is the *G*; the LORD, he is the *G*

2 Chr. 2:5 for great is our *G* above all gods
Ezra 5:5 the eye of their *G* was upon the elders of
  8:22 the hand of our *G* is upon all them for good
Neh. 9:17 thou art a *G* ready to pardon, gracious
Job 2:10 shall we receive good at the hand of *G*
  8:20 *G* will not cast away a perfect man, neither
  9:2 a truth: but how should man be just with *G*?
  11:7 canst thou by searching find out *G*?
  22:13 (Ps. 73:11) how doth *G* know?
Ps. 7:1 LORD my *G*, in thee do I put my trust: save
  14:1 (53:1) fool hath said. . There is no *G*
  19:1 the heavens declare the glory of *G*; and the
  22:1 (Mt. 27:46; Mk. 15:34) my *G*, my *G*, why hast
  31:14 in thee, O LORD: I said, Thou art my *G*
  33:12 blessed is the nation whose *G* is the LORD
  36:1 (Rom. 3:18) no fear of *G* before his eyes
  42:3 (42:10) continually say. . Where is thy *G*?
  42:5 (42:11; 43:5) disquieted in me? hope thou in *G*
  46:1 *G* is our refuge and strength, a very present
  46:10 be still, and know that I am *G*: I will be
  47:7 for *G* is the King of all the earth: sing ye
  48:14 for this *G* is our *G* for ever and ever
  55:16 for me, I will call upon *G*; and the LORD
  57:2 I will cry unto *G* most high; unto *G* that
  60:6 (108:7) *G* hath spoken in his holiness; I will
  67:1 *G* be merciful unto us, and bless us
  68:20 he that is our *G* is the *G* of salvation
  71:19 great things: O *G*, who is like unto thee!
  73:28 but it is good for me to draw near to *G*
  86:10 doest wondrous things: thou art *G* alone
  89:7 *G* is greatly to be feared in the assembly
  89:26 father, my *G*, and the rock of my salvation
  90:2 from everlasting to everlasting, thou art *G*
  91:2 and my fortress: my *G*; in him will I trust
  100:3 know ye that the LORD he is *G*: it is he
  116:5 and righteous; yea, our *G* is merciful
Prov. 26:10 great *G* that formed all things
  30:5 every word of *G* is pure: he is a shield
Eccl. 3:14 whatsoever *G* doeth, it shall be for
  5:2 hasty to utter any thing before *G*: for *G* is
  12:13 the conclusion of the whole matter: Fear *G*
Is. 9:6 The mighty *G*, The everlasting Father
  12:2 behold, *G* is my salvation; I will trust
  26:1 salvation will *G* appoint for walls and
  31:3 now the Egyptians are men and not *G*
  40:28 the everlasting *G*. . fainteth not, neither
  41:10 be not dismayed; for I am thy *G*: I will
  44:8 is there a *G* besides me? yea, there is no *G*
  45:22 (46:9) for I am *G*, and there is none else
  52:7 that saith unto Zion, Thy *G* reigneth!
  53:4 we did esteem him stricken, smitten of *G*
Jer. 10:10 LORD is the true *G*, he is the living *G*
  23:23 am I a *G* at hand. . and not a *G* afar off?
  31:33 (32:38; Heb. 8:10) will be their *G*, and they
  32:27 behold, I am the LORD, the *G* of all flesh
Dan. 2:28 is a *G* in heaven that revealeth secrets
  2:47 a truth it is, that your *G* is a *G* of gods
  3:17 our *G* whom we serve is able to deliver us
  5:23 and the *G* in whose hand thy breath is
  6:20 *G*. . able to deliver thee from the lions?
Hos. 2:23 (Zech. 13:9) they shall say, Thou art my *G*
  6:6 the knowledge of *G* more than burnt offerings
  11:9 to destroy Ephraim: for I am *G*, and not man
Amos 4:12 prepare to meet thy *G*, O Israel
  5:27 the LORD, whose name is The *G* of hosts
Jon. 1:6 call upon thy *G*, if so be that *G* will
  3:10 *G* repented of the evil, that he had said
Mic. 6:8 love mercy, and to walk humbly with thy *G*?
  7:18 who is a *G* like unto thee, that pardoneth
Mal. 2:10 one father? hath not one *G* created us?
  3:8 will a man rob *G*? Yet ye have robbed me
Mt. 1:23 Emmanuel. . being interpreted is, *G* with us
  6:24 (Lk. 16:13) ye cannot serve *G* and mammon

Mt. 16:16 (Jn. 6:69) Christ, the Son of the living *G*
  19:17 (Mk. 10:18; Lk. 18:19) none good but. . *G*
  19:26 (Mk. 10:27; Lk. 18:27) with *G* all. . possible
  22:21 (Mk. 12:17; Lk. 20:25) unto *G*. . that are *G*'s
  22:32 (Mk. 12:26; Lk. 20:37) the *G* of Abraham
  27:46 (Mk. 15:34) my *G*, why hast thou forsaken
Mk. 2:7 (Lk. 5:21) who can forgive sins but *G* only?
  11:22 Jesus. . saith unto them, Have faith in *G*
  12:32 hast said the truth: for there is one *G*
Lk. 7:16 and, That *G* hath visited his people
  8:39 show how great things *G* hath done unto thee
  12:24 and *G* feedeth them: how much more are ye
  16:15 before men; but *G* knoweth your hearts
  18:13 saying, *G* be merciful to me a sinner
Jn. 1:1 the Word was with *G*, and the Word was *G*
  1:13 were born. . nor of the will of man, but of *G*
  1:18 no man hath seen *G* at any time; the only
  3:16 for *G* so loved the world, that he gave his
  3:34 he whom *G* hath sent speaketh the words of *G*
  4:24 *G* is a Spirit: and they that worship him
  5:18 was his Father, making himself equal with *G*
  8:42 I proceeded forth and came from *G*
  10:33 that thou, being a man, makest thyself *G*
  11:22 whatsoever thou wilt ask of *G*, *G* will give
  14:1 believe in *G*, believe also in me
  17:3 that they might know thee the only true *G*
  20:17 and your Father; and to my *G*, and your *G*
  20:28 Thomas answered. . My Lord and my *G*
Acts 2:32 this Jesus hath *G* raised up, whereof we
  5:29 said, We ought to obey *G* rather than men
  5:39 if it be of *G*, ye cannot overthrow it
  10:34 perceive that *G* is no respecter of persons
  10:38 how *G* anointed Jesus of Nazareth with
  15:7 *G* made choice among us, that the Gentiles
  15:8 and *G*, which knoweth the hearts, bare them
  15:18 known unto *G* are all his works from the
  17:23 with this inscription, TO THE UNKNOWN *G*
  20:21 repentance toward *G*, and faith toward our
  26:8 incredible. . that *G* should raise the dead?
Rom. 1:16 for it is the power of *G* unto salvation
  1:21 they knew *G*, they glorified him not as *G*
  2:11 (Gal. 2:6) no respect of persons with *G*
  2:16 when *G* shall judge the secrets of men by
  3:23 sinned, and come short of the glory of *G*
  3:29 is he the *G* of the Jews only? is he not
  5:8 but *G* commendeth his love toward us, in that
  8:31 if *G* be for us, who can be against us?
  9:14 is there unrighteousness with *G*? *G* forbid
  11:2 *G* hath not cast away his people which he
  11:33 both of the wisdom and knowledge of *G*!
  13:1 of *G*: the powers that be are ordained of *G*
  14:11 and every tongue shall confess to *G*
  15:5 *G* of patience and consolation grant you to
1 Cor. 1:9 *G* is faithful, by whom ye were called
  1:24 Christ the power of *G*, and the wisdom of *G*
  1:25 the foolishness of *G* is wiser than men
  2:10 *G* hath revealed them unto us by his Spirit
  3:6 Apollos watered; but *G* gave the increase
  7:17 but as *G* hath distributed to every man
  8:6 but to us there is but one *G*, the Father
  10:13 *G* is faithful, who will not suffer you to
  11:3 is the man; and the head of Christ is *G*
  14:33 for *G* is not the author of confusion
  15:10 but by the grace of *G* I am what I am
  15:28 things under him, that *G* may be all in all
  15:34 for some have not the knowledge of *G*
2 Cor. 1:3 of mercies, and the *G* of all comfort
  3:5 as of ourselves; but our sufficiency is of *G*
  5:19 *G* was in Christ, reconciling the world unto
  9:8 *G* is able to make all grace abound toward
  13:11 the *G* of love and peace shall be with you
Gal. 2:6 matter to me: *G* accepteth no man's person
  4:4 of the time was come, *G* sent forth his Son

Gal. 6:7 be not deceived; *G* is not mocked
Eph. 2:4 *G*, who is rich in mercy, for his great
  2:8 that not of yourselves: it is the gift of *G*
  2:10 which *G* hath before ordained that we should
  2:12 having no hope, and without *G* in the world
  3:19 might be filled with all the fulness of *G*
  4:6 one *G* and Father of all, who is above all
Phil. 2:6 who, being in the form of *G*, thought it
  2:13 for it is *G* which worketh in you both to
  3:19 end is destruction, whose *G* is their belly
  4:7 peace of *G*, which passeth all understanding
  4:19 my *G* shall supply all your need according
Col. 1:15 who is the image of the invisible *G*
1 Thes. 1:9 to serve the living and true *G*
  5:9 for *G* hath not appointed us to wrath, but to
2 Thes. 1:8 vengeance on them that know not *G*
  2:4 so that he as *G* sitteth in the temple of *G*
1 Tim. 2:5 one *G*. . one mediator between *G* and men
  3:16 *G* was manifest in the flesh, justified in
2 Tim. 2:19 foundation of *G* standeth sure
  3:16 all Scripture is given by inspiration of *G*
Tit. 2:13 glorious appearing of the great *G* and
Heb. 1:1 *G*, who at sundry times and in divers
  6:10 *G* is not unrighteous to forget your work
  6:18 in which it was impossible for *G* to lie
  10:31 to fall into the hands of the living *G*
  11:6 he that cometh to *G* must believe that he is
  12:29 for our *G* is a consuming fire
Jas. 1:13 am tempted of *G*: for *G* cannot be tempted
  2:23 Abraham. . was called the Friend of *G*
  4:4 be a friend of the world is the enemy of *G*
  4:8 draw nigh to *G*, and he will draw nigh to you
1 Pet. 1:2 according to the foreknowledge of *G*
2 Pet. 2:4 if *G* spared not the angels that sinned
1 Jn. 1:5 *G* is light, and in him is no darkness
  3:20 condemn us, *G* is greater than our heart
  4:1 but try the spirits whether they are of *G*
  4:8 loveth not, knoweth not *G*; for *G* is love
  4:12 if we love one another, *G* dwelleth in us
  4:16 *G* is love. .dwelleth in love dwelleth in *G*
  5:11 that *G* hath given to us eternal life
  5:20 this is the true *G*, and eternal life
Jude 25 to the only wise *G* our Saviour, be glory
Rev. 4:8 saying, Holy, holy, holy, Lord *G* Almighty
  11:17 Lord *G* Almighty, which art, and wast, and
  14:7 a loud voice, Fear *G*, and give glory to him
  19:6 Alleluia. . the Lord *G* omnipotent reigneth
  21:3 *G* himself shall be with them, and be their *G*
  21:4 *G* shall wipe away all tears from their eyes

god *See also* God, Idol, Image

Gen. 3:5 ye shall be as *g*, knowing good and evil
Ex. 18:11 know that the LORD is greater than all *g*
  20:3 (Deut. 5:7) shalt have no other *g* before me
  20:23 ye shall not make with me *g* of silver
  22:28 shalt not revile the *g*, nor curse the ruler
  32:1 (Acts 7:40) make us *g*, which shall go before
  32:4 (Neh. 9:18) calf: and they said, These be thy *g*
  34:14 for thou shalt worship no other *g*
  34:17 thou shalt make thee no molten *g*
Deut. 8:19 and walk after other *g*, and serve them
  11:16 and ye turn aside, and serve other *g*
  17:3 hath gone and served other *g*, and worshipped
  18:20 or that shall speak in the name of other *g*
1 Kgs. 18:27 cry aloud: for he is a *g*; either he is
2 Kgs. 17:33 feared the LORD, and served their own *g*
2 Chr. 28:23 he sacrificed unto the *g* of Damascus
Ps. 82:1 of the mighty; he judgeth among the *g*
  82:6 (Jn. 10:34) I have said, Ye are *g*
  138:1 before the *g* will I sing praise unto thee
Is. 44:17 the residue thereof he maketh a *g*
Jer. 2:11 changed their *g*, which are yet no *g*?
  16:13 there shall ye serve other *g* day and night

Jer. 16:20 make *g* unto himself, and they are no *g*?
Ezek. 28:2 said, I am a *g*, I sit in the seat of God
Dan. 3:18 O king, that we will not serve thy *g*
Acts 14:11 *g* are come down to us in the likeness
  17:18 seemeth to be a setter forth of strange *g*
  19:26 they be no *g*, which are made with hands
  28:6 changed their minds. . said that he was a *g*
1 Cor. 8:5 for though there be that are called *g*
2 Cor. 4:4 *g* of this world hath blinded the minds
Gal. 4:8 service unto them which by nature are no *g*

Godhead

Acts 17:29 not to think that the *G* is like unto gold
Rom. 1:20 even his eternal power and *G*
Col. 2:9 dwelleth all the fulness of the *G* bodily

Godliness

1 Tim. 2:2 and peaceable life in all *g* and honesty
  2:10 women professing *g* with good works
  3:16 great is the mystery of *g*: God was manifest
  4:7 and exercise thyself rather unto *g*
  4:8 but *g* is profitable unto all things
  6:3 and to the doctrine which is according to *g*
  6:5 that gain is *g*: from such withdraw thyself
  6:6 but *g* with contentment is great gain
  6:11 follow after righteousness, *g*, faith, love
2 Tim. 3:5 having a form of *g*, but denying the power
Tit. 1:1 acknowledging of the truth which is after *g*
2 Pet. 1:3 all things that pertain unto life and *g*
  1:6 to temperance, patience; and to patience, *g*
  3:11 to be in all holy conversation and *g*

Godly

Ps. 4:3 the LORD hath set apart him that is *g* for
  12:1 help, LORD; for the *g* man ceaseth; for the
  32:6 shall every one that is *g* pray unto thee in
Mal. 2:15 that he might seek a *g* seed
2 Cor. 1:12 that in simplicity and *g* sincerity
  7:10 *g* sorrow worketh repentance to salvation
  11:2 for I am jealous over you with *g* jealousy
1 Tim. 1:4 questions, rather than *g* edifying which
2 Tim. 3:12 all that will live *g* in Christ Jesus
Tit. 2:12 should live soberly, righteously, and *g*
Heb. 12:28 acceptably with reverence and *g* fear
2 Pet. 2:9 Lord knoweth how to deliver the *g* out
3 Jn. 6 journey after a *g* sort, thou shalt do well

God-ward

Ex. 18:19 be thou for the people to *G*, that thou
2 Cor. 3:4 such trust have we through Christ to *G*
1 Thes. 1:8 your faith to *G* is spread abroad

Gog

Ezek. 38:2 Son of man, set thy face against *G*
Rev. 20:8 *G* and Magog, to gather them together

Going *See also* Go

2 Sam. 5:24 (1 Chr. 14:15) hearest the sound of a *g*
Job 1:7 (2:2) said, From *g* to and fro in the earth
  34:21 the ways of man, and he seeth all his *g*
Ps. 17:5 hold up my *g* in thy paths, that my
  19:6 his *g* forth is from the end of the heaven
  40:2 my feet upon a rock, and established my *g*
  68:24 seen thy *g*, O God; even the *g* of my God
  121:8 the LORD shall preserve thy *g* out and thy
  140:4 who have purposed to overthrow my *g*
Prov. 5:21 of the LORD, and he pondereth all his *g*
  14:15 but the prudent man looketh well to his *g*
  20:24 man's *g* are of the LORD; how can a man
Mic. 5:2 whose *g* forth have been from of old, from

Gold

Gen. 2:11 whole land of Havilah, where there is *g*

Ex. 20:23 neither shall ye make unto you gods of *g*
  25:17 (37:6) shalt make a mercy seat of pure *g*
  32:24 whosoever hath any *g*, let them break it off
Num. 31:22 only the *g*, and the silver, the brass
Deut. 8:13 and thy silver and thy *g* is multiplied
  17:17 greatly multiply to himself silver and *g*
1 Kgs. 7:48 the altar of *g*, and the table of *g*
  9:28 (2 Chr. 8:18) Ophir, and fetched from thence *g*
  10:2 (2 Chr. 9:1) bare spices, and very much *g*
  20:3 silver and thy *g* is mine; thy wives also
2 Kgs. 18:16 Hezekiah cut off the *g* from the doors
2 Chr. 1:15 king made silver and *g* at Jerusalem
Job 22:24 lay up *g* as dust, and the *g* of Ophir as
  23:10 he hath tried me, I shall come forth as *g*
  28:1 silver, and a place for *g* where they fine
  28:15 it cannot be gotten for *g*, neither shall
  28:17 the *g* and the crystal cannot equal it
  28:19 neither shall it be valued with pure *g*
  31:24 made *g* my hope, or have said to the fine *g*
Ps. 19:10 are they than *g*, yea, than much fine *g*
  21:3 thou settest a crown of pure *g* on his head
  68:13 silver, and her feathers with yellow *g*
  72:15 to him shall be given of the *g* of Sheba
Prov. 11:22 as a jewel of *g* in a swine's snout, so
  16:16 how much better is it to get wisdom than *g!*
  25:11 a word fitly spoken is like apples of *g* in
Is. 13:12 make a man more precious than fine *g*
  46:6 lavish *g* out of the bag, and weigh silver
  60:6 they shall bring *g* and incense; and they
  60:17 for brass I will bring *g*, and for iron I
Lam. 4:1 the *g* become dim! how is the most fine *g*
Dan. 2:38 over them all. Thou art this head of *g*
Zeph. 1:18 nor their *g* shall be able to deliver them
Hag. 2:8 silver is mine, and the *g* is mine, saith
Zech. 4:2 and behold a candlestick all of *g*
  13:9 is refined, and will try them as *g* is tried
Mt. 2:11 him gifts; *g*, and frankincense, and myrrh
  10:9 provide neither *g*, nor silver, nor brass in
  23:16 shall swear by the *g* of the temple, he is
Acts 3:6 Peter said, Silver and *g* have I none
  17:29 the Godhead is like unto *g*, or silver, or
  20:33 I have coveted no man's silver, or *g*, or
1 Cor. 3:12 build upon this foundation *g*, silver
1 Tim. 2:9 (1 Pet. 3:3) not with braided hair, or *g*
2 Tim. 2:20 house there are not only vessels of *g*
Heb. 9:4 and the ark . . overlaid round about with *g*
Jas. 2:2 unto your assembly a man with a *g* ring
  5:3 your *g* and silver is cankered; and the rust
1 Pet. 1:7 being much more precious than of *g* that
  1:18 with corruptible things, as silver and *g*
Rev. 3:18 I counsel thee to buy of me *g* tried in
  17:4 and decked with *g* and precious stones and
  21:18 the city was pure *g*, like unto clear glass
  21:21 the street of the city was pure *g*, as it

Golden

Eccl. 12:6 cord be loosed, or the *g* bowl be broken
Is. 13:12 even a man than the *g* wedge of Ophir
Dan. 3:18 gods, nor worship the *g* image which thou
Rev. 1:12 being turned, I saw seven *g* candlesticks

Goldsmith

Neh. 3:32 gate repaired the *g* and the merchants
Is. 40:19 image, and the *g* spreadeth it over with
  41:7 so the carpenter encouraged the *g*, and he
  46:6 hire a *g*; and he maketh it a god: they fall

Golgotha Mt. 27:33 (Mk. 15:22; Jn. 19:17)

Goliath 1 Sam. 17:4–54; 21:9

Gomer Hos. 1:3

Gomorrah *See also* Sodom

Gen. 13:10 before the LORD destroyed Sodom and *G*
  14:10 kings of Sodom and *G* fled, and fell there
  19:24 rained upon Sodom and upon *G* brimstone
Is. 1:9 (Rom. 9:29) we should have been like unto *G*
Jer. 23:14 Sodom, and the inhabitants thereof as *G*
Amos 4:11 of you, as God overthrew Sodom and *G*
Zeph. 2:9 as Sodom, and the children of Ammon as *G*
Mt. 10:15 (Mk. 6:11) tolerable for . . Sodom and *G*

Gone *See also* Go

Num. 16:46 for there is wrath *g* out from the LORD
Deut. 23:23 which is *g* out of thy lips thou shalt
1 Kgs. 20:40 was busy here and there, he was *g*
Ps. 14:3 are all *g* aside, they are all together
  38:10 light of mine eyes, it also is *g* from me
  73:2 as for me, my feet were almost *g*; my steps
  77:8 is his mercy clean *g* for ever? doth his
  89:34 alter the thing that is *g* out of my lips
  103:16 for the wind passeth over it, and it is *g*
  109:23 I am *g* like the shadow when it declineth
Song 2:11 winter is past, the rain is over and *g*
  6:1 whither is thy beloved *g*, O thou fairest
Is. 1:4 unto anger, they are *g* away backward
  24:11 is darkened, the mirth of the land is *g*
  45:23 word is *g* out of my mouth in righteousness
  51:5 is near; my salvation is *g* forth
Jer. 15:9 her sun is *g* down while it was yet day
Dan. 2:5 to the Chaldeans, The thing is *g* from me
Mt. 12:43 (Lk. 11:24) unclean spirit is *g* out of a man
  25:8 give us of your oil; for our lamps are *g* out
Jn. 6:22 but that his disciples were *g* away alone
  12:19 nothing? behold, the world is *g* after him
Acts 16:19 saw that the hope of their gains was *g*
Rom. 3:12 they are all *g* out of the way, they are
1 Pet. 3:22 who is *g* into heaven, and is on the
2 Pet. 2:15 *g* astray, following the way of Balaam

Good *See also* Better, Best

Gen. 1:4 God saw the light, that it was *g*
  1:31 that he had made, and, behold, it was very *g*
  2:9 the tree of knowledge of *g* and evil
  2:18 it is not *g* that the man should be alone
  3:5 and ye shall be as gods, knowing *g* and evil
  26:29 as we have done unto thee nothing but *g*
  32:12 thou saidst, I will surely do thee *g*
  44:4 wherefore have ye rewarded evil for *g*?
  50:20 evil against me; but God meant it unto *g*
Ex. 3:8 out of that land unto a *g* land and a large
Num. 10:29 do thee *g*: for the LORD hath spoken *g*
  14:7 we passed through . . is an exceeding *g* land
Deut. 1:25 said, It is a *g* land which the LORD our
  6:11 and houses full of all *g* things, which thou
  6:18 right and *g* in the sight of the LORD
  8:10 shalt bless the LORD thy God for the *g* land
  12:28 when thou doest that which is *g* and right
  30:5 and he will do thee *g*, and multiply thee
  30:15 I have set before thee this day life and *g*
Josh. 21:45 (23:14) failed not aught of any *g* thing
1 Sam. 12:23 I will teach you the *g* and the right
1 Kgs. 3:9 that I may discern between *g* and bad
  8:36 (2 Chr. 6:27) that thou teach them the *g* way
  8:56 not failed one word of all his *g* promise
  12:7 (2 Chr. 10:7) speak *g* words to them, then they
  22:8 (2 Chr. 18:7) for he doth not prophesy *g*
2 Kgs. 7:9 this day is a day of *g* tidings, and we
  20:19 (Is. 39:8) *g* is the word of the LORD
2 Chr. 7:3 for he is *g*; for his mercy endureth for
  19:11 and the LORD shall be with the *g*
  30:18 saying, The *g* LORD pardon every one
Ezra 7:9 according to the *g* hand of his God upon
  8:22 hand of our God is upon all them for *g*
Neh. 5:19 think upon me, my God, for *g*, according

Neh. 9:20 thou gavest also thy *g* Spirit to instruct
  13:31 remember me, O my God, for *g*
Job 2:10 shall we receive *g* at the hand of God
  5:27 hear it, and know thou it for thy *g*
  7:7 life is wind: mine eye shall no more see *g*
  21:16 their *g* is not in their hand: the counsel
  22:21 be at peace. . *g* shall come unto thee
  30:26 when I looked for *g*. . evil came unto me
Ps. 4:6 be many that say, Who will show us any *g*?
  14:1 (14:3; 53:1, 3; Rom. 3:12) none that doeth *g*
  25:8 *g* and upright is the LORD: therefore will
  34:8 O taste and see that the LORD is *g*: blessed
  34:10 seek the LORD shall not want any *g* thing
  34:12 and loveth many days, that he may see *g*?
  34:14 (37:27; 1 Pet. 3:11) depart from evil. . do *g*
  37:23 steps of a *g* man are ordered by the LORD
  38:20 render evil for *g* are mine adversaries
  45:1 my heart is inditing a *g* matter: I speak of
  73:28 but it is *g* for me to draw near to God
  84:11 no *g* thing will he withhold from them that
  85:12 yea, the LORD shall give that which is *g*
  86:17 show me a token for *g*; that they which
  92:1 is a *g* thing to give thanks unto the LORD
  100:5 the LORD is *g*; his mercy is everlasting
  103:5 who satisfieth thy mouth with *g* things
  106:5 that I may see the *g* of thy chosen, that I
  112:5 *g* man showeth favor, and lendeth: he will
  119:68 art *g*, and doest *g*: teach me thy statutes
  119:71 it is *g* for me that I have been afflicted
  125:4 do *g*, O LORD, unto those that be *g*
  133:1 how *g* and how pleasant it is for brethren
  145:9 LORD is *g* to all: and his tender mercies
Prov. 2:20 thou mayest walk in the way of *g* men
  3:27 withhold not *g* from them to whom it is due
  11:17 the merciful man doeth *g* to his own soul
  11:23 the desire of the righteous is only *g*
  11:27 that diligently seeketh *g* procureth favor
  12:25 maketh it stoop. . a *g* word maketh it glad
  13:15 *g* understanding giveth favor: but the way
  13:21 but to the righteous *g* shall be repaid
  14:14 a *g* man shall be satisfied from himself
  14:19 the evil bow before the *g*; and the wicked
  15:23 a word spoken in due season, how *g* is it!
  17:13 whoso rewardeth evil for *g*, evil shall not
  17:20 he that hath a froward heart findeth no *g*
  19:2 the soul be without knowledge, it is not *g*
  20:18 by counsel: and with *g* advice make war
  22:1 a *g* name is rather to be chosen than great
  25:25 soul, so is *g* news from a far country
  31:18 she perceiveth that her merchandise is *g*
Eccl. 2:26 giveth to a man that is *g* in his sight
  3:12 no *g* in them, but. . to rejoice, and to do *g*
  6:12 who knoweth what is *g* for man in this life
  7:1 a *g* name is better than precious ointment
  7:20 is not a just man upon earth, that doeth *g*
  9:2 and to the wicked; to the *g* and to the clean
  9:18 but one sinner destroyeth much *g*
Is. 1:19 obedient, ye shall eat the *g* of the land
  5:20 woe unto them that call evil *g*, and *g* evil
  7:15 know to refuse the evil, and choose the *g*
  40:9 O Zion, that bringest *g* tidings, get thee
  52:7 (Nah. 1:15; Rom. 10:15) bringeth *g* tidings
  55:2 eat ye that which is *g*, and let your soul
  61:1 hath anointed me to preach *g* tidings unto
Jer. 4:22 but to do *g* they have no knowledge
  6:16 where is the *g* way, and walk therein
  13:23 may ye also do *g*, that are accustomed
  18:20 shall evil be recompensed for *g*?
  29:10 perform my *g* word toward you, in causing
  32:42 so will I bring upon them all the *g* that I
  42:6 whether it be *g*, or whether it be evil
Lam. 3:25 LORD is *g* unto them that wait for him
  3:26 it is *g* that a man should both hope and

Lam. 3:27 is *g* for a man that he bear the yoke in his
Amos 5:14 seek *g*, and not evil, that ye may live
  5:15 hate the evil, and love the *g*, and establish
Mic. 3:2 who hate the *g*, and love the evil
  6:8 he hath showed thee, O man, what is *g*
Nah. 1:7 the LORD is *g*, a stronghold in the day of
Zeph. 1:12 LORD will not do *g*, neither will he do evil
Zech. 1:13 angel that talked with me with *g* words
Mt. 5:13 salted? it is thenceforth *g* for nothing
  5:16 that they may see your *g* works, and glorify
  5:44 (Lk. 6:27) do *g* to them that hate you
  7:11 (Lk. 11:13) to give *g* gifts unto your children
  7:17 (Lk. 6:43) *g* tree bringeth forth *g* fruit
  11:26 (Lk. 10:21) so it seemed *g* in thy sight
  12:34 how can ye, being evil, speak *g* things?
  12:35 (Lk. 6:45) a *g* man out of the *g* treasure of
  13:8 (Mk. 4:8; Lk. 8:8) other fell into *g* ground
  13:24 likened unto a man which sowed *g* seed in
  13:38 the *g* seed are the children of the kingdom
  13:48 the *g* into vessels, but cast the bad away
  17:4 (Mk. 9:5; Lk. 9:33) *g* for us to be here
  19:10 be so with his wife, it is not *g* to marry
  19:16 (Mk. 10:17; Lk. 18:18) *g* Master, what *g*. . I
  19:17 (Mk. 10:18; Lk. 18:19) is none *g* but. . God
  20:15 is thine eye evil, because I am *g*?
  25:21 (Lk. 19:17) well done. . *g* and faithful servant
  26:10 (Mk. 14:6) she. . wrought a *g* work upon me
  26:24 (Mk. 14:21) *g* for that man if he had not been
Mk. 3:4 (Lk. 6:9) lawful to do *g* on the sabbath
Lk. 2:10 I bring you *g* tidings of great joy
  2:14 and on earth peace, *g* will toward men
  6:33 and if ye do *g* to them which do *g* to you
  6:45 *g* man out of the *g* treasure of his heart
  10:42 needful; and Mary hath chosen that *g* part
  12:32 it is your Father's *g* pleasure to give you
  16:25 in thy lifetime receivedst thy *g* things
  23:50 counselor; and he was a *g* man, and a just
Jn. 1:46 can there any *g* thing come. . of Nazareth?
  2:10 at the beginning doth set forth *g* wine
  5:29 have done *g*, unto the resurrection of life
  7:12 some said, He is a *g* man; others said, Nay
  10:11 (10:14) I am the *g* shepherd
  10:32 many *g* works have I showed you from my
Acts 9:36 Dorcas: this woman was full of *g* works
  10:38 who went about doing *g*, and healing all
  11:24 he was a *g* man, and full of the Holy Ghost
  14:17 he did *g*, and gave us rain from heaven
Rom. 2:10 and peace, to every man that worketh *g*
  3:8 let us do evil, that *g* may come?
  7:12 and the commandment holy, and just, and *g*
  7:16 I consent unto the law that it is *g*
  7:18 for I know that in me. . dwelleth no *g* thing
  7:19 for the *g* that I would, I do not: but the
  8:28 all things work together for *g* to them that
  12:2 ye may prove what is that *g*, and acceptable
  12:9 which is evil; cleave to that which is *g*
  13:3 for rulers are not a terror to *g* works, but
  13:4 for he is the minister of God to thee for *g*
  14:16 let not then your *g* be evil spoken of
  16:19 would have you wise unto that which is *g*
1 Cor. 7:8 it is *g* for them if they abide even as I
  7:26 this is *g* for the present distress
  7:26 I say, that it is *g* for a man so to be
  15:33 evil communications corrupt *g* manners
2 Cor. 5:10 he hath done, whether it be *g* or bad
  9:8 in all things, may abound to every *g* work
Gal. 6:6 unto him that teacheth in all *g* things
  6:10 let us do *g* unto all men, especially unto
Eph. 1:9 of his will, according to his *g* pleasure
  2:10 created in Christ Jesus unto *g* works
  6:7 with *g* will doing service, as to the Lord
Phil. 1:6 he which hath begun a *g* work in you will
  4:8 whatsoever things are of *g* report

Col. 1:10 pleasing, being fruitful in every *g* work
1 Thes. 5:15 but ever follow that which is *g*, both
5:21 prove all things; hold fast that which is *g*
2 Thes. 2:17 stablish you in every *g* word and work
1 Tim. 1:8 the law is *g*, if a man use it lawfully
1:18 that thou by them mightest war a *g* warfare
2:3 this is *g* and acceptable in the sight of God
3:1 the office of a bishop, he desireth a *g* work
3:7 *g* report of them which are without; lest he
4:4 every creature of God is *g*, and nothing to
4:6 thou shalt be a *g* minister of Jesus
5:25 the *g* works of some are manifest
6:12 fight the *g* fight of faith, lay hold on
6:18 they do *g*, that they be rich in *g* works
6:19 up in store for themselves a *g* foundation
2 Tim. 2:3 as a *g* soldier of Jesus Christ
3:3 fierce, despisers of those that are *g*
4:7 I have fought a *g* fight, I have finished my
Tit. 1:16 disobedient . . unto every *g* work reprobate
2:7 showing thyself a pattern of *g* works
3:8 might be careful to maintain *g* works
Heb. 6:5 tasted the *g* word of God, and the powers
11:39 having obtained a *g* report through faith
13:16 but to do *g* and to communicate forget not
13:21 make you perfect in every *g* work to do his
Jas. 1:17 every *g* gift and every perfect gift is
3:13 show out of a *g* conversation his works
3:17 to be entreated, full of mercy and *g* fruits
4:17 knoweth to do *g*, and doeth it not, to him
1 Pet. 2:12 they may by your *g* works . . glorify God
3:11 let him eschew evil, and do *g*; let him seek
3:16 having a *g* conscience; that, whereas they
1 Jn. 3:17 whoso hath this world's *g*, and seeth
3 Jn. 11 which is *g*. He that doeth *g* is of God

Goodliness

Is. 40:6 all the *g* thereof is as the flower of the

Goodly (Goodlier, Goodliest)

Gen. 39:6 Joseph was a *g* person, and well-favored
Ex. 2:2 he was a *g* child, she hid him three months
Num. 24:5 how *g* are thy tents, O Jacob, and thy
Deut. 6:10 to give thee great and *g* cities, which
8:12 eaten and art full, and hast built *g* houses
1 Sam. 8:16 your *g* young men, and your asses, and
9:2 Saul, a choice young man, and a *g*
16:12 a beautiful countenance, and *g* to look to
1 Kgs. 20:3 and thy children, even the *g*, are mine
Ps. 16:6 pleasant places; yea, I have a *g* heritage
Jer. 3:19 a *g* heritage of the hosts of nations?
Ezek. 17:8 bear fruit, that it might be a *g* vine
Zech. 11:13 a *g* price that I was prized at of them
Mt. 13:45 like unto a merchantman, seeking *g* pearls
Lk. 21:5 temple, how it was adorned with *g* stones
Jas. 2:2 a man with a gold ring, in *g* apparel
Rev. 18:14 dainty and *g* are departed from thee

Goodness *See also* Virtue

Ex. 33:19 I will make all my *g* pass before thee
34:6 long-suffering, and abundant in *g* and truth
Num. 10:32 what *g* the LORD shall do unto us
2 Sam. 7:28 (1 Chr. 17:26) promised this *g* unto thy
1 Kgs. 8:66 (2 Chr. 7:10) for all the *g* that the LORD
2 Chr. 6:41 let thy saints rejoice in *g*
Neh. 9:25 and delighted themselves in thy great *g*
9:35 and in thy great *g* that thou gavest them
Ps. 16:2 art my Lord: my *g* extendeth not to thee
21:3 thou preventest him with the blessings of *g*
23:6 surely *g* and mercy shall follow me all the
25:7 thy mercy remember thou me for thy *g*' sake
27:13 unless I had believed to see the *g* of the
31:19 how great is thy *g*, which thou hast laid

Ps. 33:5 the earth is full of the *g* of the LORD
52:1 the *g* of God endureth continually
65:4 shall be satisfied with the *g* of thy house
65:11 thou crownest the year with thy *g*
68:10 O God, hast prepared of thy *g* for the poor
107:8 (107:15, 21, 31) praise the LORD for his *g*
107:9 and filleth the hungry soul with *g*
144:2 my *g*, and my fortress; my high tower
145:7 abundantly utter the memory of thy great *g*
Prov. 20:6 men will proclaim every one his own *g*
Is. 63:7 the great *g* toward the house of Israel
Jer. 2:7 eat the fruit thereof and the *g* thereof
31:12 shall flow together to the *g* of the LORD
31:14 and my people shall be satisfied with my *g*
33:9 they shall fear and tremble for all the *g*
Hos. 3:5 and shall fear the LORD and his *g* in the
6:4 for your *g* is as a morning cloud
10:1 according to the *g* of his land they have
Zech. 9:17 how great is his *g*, and how great is
Rom. 2:4 the *g* of God leadeth thee to repentance?
11:22 behold therefore the *g* and severity of God
15:14 are full of *g*, filled with all knowledge
Gal. 5:22 long-suffering, gentleness, *g*, faith
Eph. 5:9 the fruit of the Spirit is in all *g* and
2 Thes. 1:11 fulfil all the good pleasure of his *g*

Goods *See also* Possession, Wealth

Gen. 14:16 and he brought back all the *g*, and also
14:21 Abram, Give me the persons, and take the *g*
24:10 all the *g* of his master were in his hand
31:18 carried away all his cattle, and all his *g*
Ex. 22:8 have put his hand unto his neighbor's *g*
Deut. 28:11 LORD shall make thee plenteous in *g*
Neh. 9:25 possessed houses full of all *g*, wells
Eccl. 5:11 *g* increase, they are increased that eat
Zeph. 1:13 therefore, their *g* shall become a booty
Mt. 12:29 (Mk. 3:27) man's house, and spoil his *g*
24:47 he shall make him ruler over all his *g*
25:14 servants, and delivered unto them his *g*
Lk. 6:30 that taketh away thy *g* ask them not again
12:19 to my soul, Soul, thou hast much *g* laid up
15:12 give me the portion of *g* that falleth to me
16:1 accused unto him that he had wasted his *g*
19:8 Lord, the half of my *g* I give to the poor
Acts 2:45 sold their possessions and *g*, and parted
1 Cor. 13:3 bestow all my *g* to feed the poor
Heb. 10:34 took joyfully the spoiling of your *g*
Rev. 3:17 sayest, I am rich, and increased with *g*

Goshen

Gen. 45:10 and thou shalt dwell in the land of *G*
46:28 and they came into the land of *G*
47:4 let thy servants dwell in the land of *G*
Ex. 8:22 I will sever in that day the land of *G*
9:26 only in the land of *G*. . was there no hail

Gospel *See also* Promise, Salvation, Tidings, Truth, Word

Mt. 4:23 in their synagogues, and preaching the *g*
9:35 preaching the *g* of the kingdom, and healing
11:5 (Lk. 7:22) poor have the *g* preached to them
24:14 (Mk. 13:10) this *g*. . shall be preached in all
26:13 (Mk. 14:9) wheresoever this *g*. . be preached
Mk. 1:1 the beginning of the *g* of Jesus Christ
1:14 preaching the *g* of the kingdom of God
1:15 is at hand: repent ye, and believe the *g*
8:35 shall lose his life for my sake, and the *g*'s
10:29 hath left house. . for my sake, and the *g*'s
16:15 world, and preach the *g* to every creature
Lk. 4:18 anointed me to preach the *g* to the poor
Acts 8:25 preached the *g* in many villages of the

Acts 20:24 to testify the *g* of the grace of God
Rom. 1:1 an apostle, separated unto the *g* of God
1:16 I am not ashamed of the *g* of Christ: for it
2:16 judge the secrets of men. . according to my *g*
10:15 feet of them that preach the *g* of peace
10:16 they have not all obeyed the *g*. For Esaias
15:19 I have fully preached the *g* of Christ
1 Cor. 1:17 not to baptize, but to preach the *g*
9:12 all things, lest we should hinder the *g*
9:14 which preach the *g* should live of the *g*
9:16 yea, woe is unto me, if I preach not the *g*!
9:17 dispensation of the *g* is committed unto me
9:18 may make the *g* of Christ without charge
15:1 I declare unto you the *g* which I preached
2 Cor. 2:12 I came to Troas to preach Christ's *g*
4:3 *g* be hid, it is hid to them that are lost
4:4 lest the light of the glorious *g* of Christ
11:4 or another *g*, which ye have not accepted
Gal. 1:6 so soon removed from him. . unto another *g*
1:8 preach any other *g* unto you than that which
1:11 *g* which was preached of me is not after man
2:7 *g* of the uncircumcision was committed unto
Eph. 1:13 word of truth, the *g* of your salvation
6:15 shod with the preparation of the *g* of peace
6:19 boldly, to make known the mystery of the *g*
Phil. 1:7 in the defense and confirmation of the *g*
1:12 fallen out. . unto the furtherance of the *g*
1:17 knowing. . I am set for the defense of the *g*
1:27 your conversation be as it becometh the *g*
Col. 1:5 before in the word of the truth of the *g*
1:23 be not moved away from the hope of the *g*
1 Thes. 1:5 our *g* came not unto you in word only
2:4 allowed of God to be put in trust with the *g*
2 Thes. 2:14 whereunto he called you by our *g*
1 Tim. 1:11 according to the glorious *g* of the
2 Tim. 1:10 and immortality to light through the *g*
Heb. 4:2 unto us was the *g* preached, as well as
1 Pet. 1:25 which by the *g* is preached unto you
4:6 the *g* preached also to them that are dead
Rev. 14:6 having the everlasting *g* to preach unto

Gourd

Jon. 4:6 God prepared a *g*. . Jonah. . glad of the *g*

Govern

1 Kgs. 21:7 dost thou now *g* the kingdom of Israel?
Job 34:17 shall even he that hateth right *g*?
Ps. 67:4 righteously, and *g* the nations upon earth

Government

Is. 9:6 *g* shall be upon his shoulder: and his name
22:21 I will commit thy *g* into his hand
1 Cor. 12:28 then gifts of healings, helps, *g*
2 Pet. 2:10 and despise *g*. Presumptuous are they

Governor *See also* King, Ruler

Gen. 42:6 Joseph was the *g* over the land
45:26 Joseph is yet alive, and he is *g* over all
Judg. 5:9 my heart is toward the *g* of Israel
2 Chr. 1:2 judges, and to every *g* in all Israel
Neh. 5:18 required not I the bread of the *g*
Ps. 22:28 LORD's: and he is the *g* among. . nations
Jer. 20:1 also chief *g* in the house of the LORD
40:7 king of Babylon had made Gedaliah. . *g*
Zech. 9:7 he shall be as a *g* in Judah, and Ekron
Mt. 2:6 Juda: for out of thee shall come a *G*
10:18 ye shall be brought before *g* and kings for
28:14 and if this come to the *g*'s ears, we will
Jn. 2:8 draw out now, and bear unto the *g* of the feast
Acts 7:10 made him *g* over Egypt and all his house
23:34 and when the *g* had read the letter
24:1 Tertullus, who informed the *g* against Paul

Gal. 4:2 but is under tutors and *g* until the time
Jas. 3:4 small helm, whithersoever the *g* listeth

Grace *See also* Compassion, Favor, Kindness, Love, Loving-kindness, Mercy

Gen. 6:8 but Noah found *g* in the eyes of the LORD
Ex. 33:17 for thou hast found *g* in my sight
Ruth 2:10 why have I found *g* in thine eyes
Ps. 45:2 *g* is poured into thy lips: therefore God
84:11 LORD will give *g* and glory: no good thing
Prov. 1:9 shall be an ornament of *g* unto thy head
3:22 be life unto thy soul, and *g* to thy neck
3:34 (Jas. 4:6; 1 Pet. 5:5) he giveth *g* unto the lowly
Zech. 4:7 with shoutings, crying, *G*, *g* unto it
12:10 spirit of *g* and of supplications: and they
Lk. 2:40 and the *g* of God was upon him
Jn. 1:14 and dwelt among us. . full of *g* and truth
1:16 fulness have all we received, and *g* for *g*
1:17 but *g* and truth came by Jesus Christ
Acts 4:33 and great *g* was upon them all
13:43 persuaded them to continue in the *g* of God
14:3 which gave testimony unto the word of his *g*
15:11 *g* of the Lord Jesus Christ we shall be saved
18:27 them much which had believed through *g*
20:32 word of his *g*, which is able to build you
Rom. 1:5 whom we have received *g* and apostleship
3:24 being justified freely by his *g* through the
4:4 is the reward not reckoned of *g*, but of debt
4:16 it is of faith, that it might be by *g*
5:2 we have access by faith into this *g* wherein
5:15 much more the *g* of God, and the gift by *g*
5:17 much more they which receive abundance of *g*
5:20 where sin abounded, *g* did much more abound
6:1 shall we continue in sin, that *g* may abound?
6:14 for ye are not under the law, but under *g*
11:5 is a remnant according to the election of *g*
11:6 and if by *g*, then is it no more of works
12:3 for I say, through the *g* given unto me
12:6 gifts differing according to the *g* that is
16:24 *g* of our Lord Jesus Christ be with you all
1 Cor. 15:10 but by the *g* of God I am what I am
2 Cor. 4:15 abundant *g* might. . redound to the glory
6:1 that ye receive not the *g* of God in vain
8:9 ye know the *g* of our Lord Jesus Christ
9:8 God is able to make all *g* abound toward you
12:9 my *g* is sufficient for thee. . my strength
13:14 *g* of the Lord Jesus Christ, and the love
Gal. 1:15 my mother's womb, and called me by his *g*
2:21 I do not frustrate the *g* of God: for if
5:4 justified by the law; ye are fallen from *g*
Eph. 1:7 of sins, according to the riches of his *g*
2:7 he might show the exceeding riches of his *g*
2:8 by *g* are ye saved through faith; and that
3:8 least of all saints, is this *g* given, that I
4:7 unto every one of us is given *g* according to
4:29 that it may minister *g* unto the hearers
6:24 *g* be with all them that love our Lord Jesus
Phil. 1:7 the gospel, ye all are partakers of my *g*
Col. 3:16 singing with *g* in your hearts to. . Lord
4:6 let your speech be always with *g*, seasoned
2 Thes. 2:16 consolation and good hope through *g*
1 Tim. 1:14 *g* of our Lord was exceeding abundant
2 Tim. 2:1 be strong in the *g* that is in Christ
Tit. 2:11 for the *g* of God that bringeth salvation
3:7 being justified by his *g*, we should be made
Heb. 2:9 he by the *g* of God should taste death for
4:16 come boldly unto the throne of *g*, that we
12:15 lest any man fail of the *g* of God
12:28 let us have *g*, whereby we may serve God
13:9 heart be established with *g*; not with meats
1 Pet. 1:13 sober, and hope to the end for the *g*
3:7 and as being heirs together of the *g* of life

1 Pet. 4:10 as good stewards of the manifold *g* of God
    5:12 this is the true *g* of God wherein ye stand
2 Pet. 3:18 but grow in *g*, and in the knowledge of
Jude 4 turning the *g* of. . God into lasciviousness

Gracious *See also* Kind, Merciful

Gen. 43:29 and he said, God be *g* unto thee, my son
Ex. 22:27 crieth unto me. . I will hear; for I am *g*
    33:19 will be *g* to whom I will be *g*, and will
    34:6 LORD God, merciful and *g*, long-suffering
Num. 6:25 face shine upon thee, and be *g* unto thee
2 Sam. 12:22 who can tell whether GOD will be *g* to
2 Kgs. 13:23 and the LORD was *g* unto them, and had
2 Chr. 30:9 LORD your God is *g* and merciful
Neh. 9:17 a God ready to pardon, *g* and merciful
    9:31 for thou art a *g* and merciful God
Ps. 77:9 hath God forgotten to be *g*? hath he in
    103:8 LORD is merciful and *g*, slow to anger, and
    116:5 *g* is the LORD, and righteous; yea, our God
    145:8 the LORD is *g*, and full of compassion
Prov. 11:16 a *g* woman retaineth honor: and strong
Eccl. 10:12 the words of a wise man's mouth are *g*
Is. 30:18 the LORD wait, that he may be *g* unto you
    33:2 LORD, be *g* unto us; we have waited for thee
Jer. 22:23 how *g* shalt thou be when pangs come upon
Joel 2:13 turn unto the LORD your God: for he is *g*
Amos 5:15 God of hosts will be *g* unto the remnant
Jon. 4:2 for I knew that thou art a *g* God
Lk. 4:22 bare him witness. . wondered at the *g* words
1 Pet. 2:3 so be ye have tasted that the Lord is *g*

Graciously

Gen. 33:5 children. . God hath *g* given thy servant
Hos. 14:2 take away all iniquity, and receive us *g*

Graff

Rom. 11:17 a wild olive tree, wert *g* in among them

Grain

Amos 9:9 shall not the least *g* fall upon the earth
1 Cor. 15:37 bare *g*. . wheat, or of some other *g*

Grandmother

2 Tim. 1:5 which dwelt first in thy *g* Lois

Grant *See also* Give

Lev. 25:24 ye shall *g* a redemption for the land
Ruth 1:9 LORD *g* you that ye may find rest, each
1 Sam. 1:17 God of Israel *g* thee thy petition that
1 Chr. 4:10 and God *g* him that which he requested
    21:22 then David said to Ornan, *G* me the place
Job 6:8 God would *g* me the thing that I long for!
Ps. 20:4 *g* thee according to thine own heart
    85:7 thy mercy, O LORD, and *g* us thy salvation
Prov. 10:24 the desire of the righteous shall be *g*
Mt. 20:21 (Mk. 10:37) *g* that. . my two sons may sit
Acts 3:14 and desired a murderer to be *g* unto you
    4:29 their threatenings: and *g* unto thy servants
    11:18 hath God also to the Gentiles *g* repentance
    14:3 and *g* signs and wonders to be done by their
Rom. 15:5 God of patience. . *g* you to be likeminded
Eph. 3:16 he would *g* you, according to the riches
2 Tim. 1:18 Lord *g* unto him that he may find mercy
Rev. 3:21 overcometh will I *g* to sit with me in my
    19:8 to her was *g* that she should be arrayed in

Grape

Gen. 40:10 clusters thereof brought forth ripe *g*
    49:11 in wine, and his clothes in the blood of *g*
Lev. 19:10 neither shalt thou gather every *g* of
    25:5 neither gather the *g* of thy vine undressed
Num. 6:3 drink any liquor of *g*, nor eat moist *g*
    13:23 from thence a branch with one cluster of *g*

Deut. 23:24 eat *g* thy fill at thine own pleasure
    28:30 a vineyard, and shalt not gather the *g*
    32:14 thou didst drink the pure blood of the *g*
    32:32 their *g* are *g* of gall, their clusters *g*
Song 2:13 with the tender *g* give a good smell
    2:15 for our vines have tender *g*
    7:7 palm tree, and thy breasts to clusters of *g*
Is. 5:2 bring forth *g*, and it brought forth wild *g*
    17:6 yet gleaning *g* shall be left in it, as the
    18:5 sour *g* is ripening in the flower, he shall
    24:13 as the gleaning *g* when the vintage is done
Jer. 8:13 shall be no *g* on the vine, nor figs on
    31:29 (Ezek. 18:2) the fathers have eaten a sour *g*
Hos. 9:10 I found Israel like *g* in the wilderness
Amos 9:13 the treader of *g* him that soweth seed
Mt. 7:16 (Lk. 6:44) gather *g* of thorns, or figs of
Rev. 14:18 of the earth; for her *g* are fully ripe

Grass *See also* Herb, Plant

Gen. 1:11 God said, Let the earth bring forth *g*
Num. 22:4 as the ox licketh up the *g* of the field
Deut. 11:15 will send *g* in thy fields for thy cattle
    32:2 herb, and as the showers upon the *g*
2 Sam. 23:4 as the tender *g* springing out of the
1 Kgs. 18:5 peradventure we may find *g* to save the
2 Kgs. 19:26 (Is. 37:27) were as the *g* of the field
Job 5:25 and thine offspring as the *g* of the earth
Ps. 37:2 they shall soon be cut down like the *g*
    72:6 shall come down like rain upon the mown *g*
    72:16 and they of the city shall flourish like *g*
    90:5 morning they are like *g* which groweth up
    92:7 when the wicked spring as the *g*, and when
    103:15 for man, his days are as *g*: as a flower
    129:6 let them be as the *g* upon the housetops
    147:8 who maketh *g* to grow upon the mountains
Prov. 19:12 but his favor is as dew upon the *g*
Is. 40:6 (1 Pet. 1:24) shall I cry? All flesh is *g*
    40:8 (1 Pet. 1:24) *g* withereth, the flower fadeth
Jer. 14:6 eyes did fail, because there was no *g*
    50:11 ye are grown fat as the heifer at *g*
Dan. 4:25 (4:32; 5:21) make thee to eat *g* as oxen
Mic. 5:7 as the showers upon the *g*, that tarrieth
Mt. 6:30 (Lk. 12:28) if God so clothe the *g* of the
    14:19 (Mk. 6:39) the multitude to sit down on the *g*
Jn. 6:10 there was much *g* in the place. So the men
Jas. 1:10 as the flower of the *g* he shall pass
Rev. 8:7 burnt up, and all green *g* was burnt up
    9:4 that they should not hurt the *g* of the earth

Grasshopper

Num. 11:33 we were in our own sight as *g*, and so
Judg. 6:5 they came as *g* for multitude
Job 39:20 canst thou make him afraid as a *g*?
Is. 40:22 the inhabitants thereof are as *g*
Jer. 46:23 more than the *g*, and are innumerable
Amos 7:1 behold, he formed *g* in the beginning of

Grave (adjective) *See also* Sober

1 Tim. 3:8 the deacons be *g*, not double-tongued
    3:11 their wives be *g*, not slanderers, sober
Tit. 2:2 that the aged men be sober, *g*, temperate

Grave (noun) *See also* Death, Hell, Pit, Sepulchre, Tomb

Gen. 35:20 her *g*: that is the pillar of Rachel's *g*
    42:38 down my gray hairs with sorrow to the *g*
Ex. 14:11 Moses, Because there were no *g* in Egypt
1 Sam. 2:6 bringeth down to the *g*, and bringeth up
1 Kgs. 2:6 let not his hoar head go down to the *g*
Job 3:22 and are glad, when they can find the *g*?
    5:26 thou shalt come to thy *g* in a full age
    7:9 goeth down to the *g* shall come up no more

Job 14:13 oh that thou wouldest hide me in the *g*
17:1 my days are extinct, the *g* are ready for me
17:13 I wait, the *g* is mine house: I have made
24:19 so doth the *g* those which have sinned
33:22 yea, his soul draweth near unto the *g*
Ps. 6:5 in the *g* who shall give thee thanks?
30:3 thou hast brought up my soul from the *g*
31:17 ashamed, and let them be silent in the *g*
49:15 redeem my soul from the power of the *g*
88:3 and my life draweth nigh unto the *g*
Prov. 1:12 let us swallow them up alive as the *g*
30:16 the *g*; and the barren womb; the earth
Eccl. 9:10 nor knowledge, nor wisdom, in the *g*
Song 8:6 as death; jealousy is cruel as the *g*
Is. 14:19 out of thy *g* like an abominable branch
38:10 I shall go to the gates of the *g*: I am
38:18 for the *g* cannot praise thee, death cannot
53:9 he made his *g* with the wicked, and with the
Jer. 20:17 or that my mother might have been my *g*
Ezek. 32:23 her company is round about her *g*
37:12 behold, O my people, I will open your *g*
Hos. 13:14 O *g*, I will be thy destruction
Mt. 27:52 *g* were opened; and many bodies of the
Lk. 11:44 Pharisees, hypocrites! for ye are as *g*
Jn. 5:28 that are in the *g* shall hear his voice
11:17 he had lain in the *g* four days already
11:31 saying, She goeth unto the *g* to weep there
1 Cor. 15:55 thy sting? O *g*, where is thy victory?

Grave (Graven) (verb) *See also* Engrave

Ex. 28:9 (39:6) onyx stones, and *g* on them the names
28:36 make a plate of pure gold, and *g* upon it
2 Chr. 2:7 that can skill to *g* with the cunning men
2:14 *g* any manner of graving, and to find out
Job 19:24 they were *g* with an iron pen and lead
Is. 49:16 I have *g* thee upon the palms of my hands
Jer. 17:1 it is *g* upon the table of their heart

Gravel

Prov. 20:17 his mouth shall be filled with *g*
Is. 48:19 the offspring of thy bowels like the *g*
Lam. 3:16 hath also broken my teeth with *g* stones

Graven Image

Ex. 20:4 (Deut. 5:8) shalt not make unto thee any *g i*
Ps. 78:58 moved him to jealousy with their *g i*
Is. 40:19 the workman melteth a *g i*
Jer. 8:19 provoked me to anger with their *g i*
10:14 every founder is confounded by the *g i*
Hos. 11:2 unto Baalim, and burned incense to *g i*
Mic. 5:13 thy *g i* also will I cut off, and thy
Hab. 2:18 what profiteth the *g i* that the maker

Gravity

1 Tim. 3:4 his children in subjection with all *g*
Tit. 2:7 in doctrine showing uncorruptness, *g*

Gray

Prov. 20:29 the beauty of old men is the *g* head
Hos. 7:9 *g* hairs are here and there upon him, yet

Grayheaded

1 Sam. 12:2 I am old and *g*; and, behold, my sons
Job 15:10 with us are both the *g* and very aged men
Ps. 71:18 I am old and *g*, O God, forsake me not

Great (Greater, Greatest)

See also Excellent, Large, Mighty

Gen. 4:13 LORD, My punishment is *g* than I can bear
6:5 GOD saw that the wickedness of man was *g* in
12:2 I will make of thee a *g* nation, and I will
18:18 shall surely become a *g* and mighty nation

Gen. 41:40 only in the throne will I be *g* than thou
46:3 for I will there make of thee a *g* nation
48:19 truly his younger brother shall be *g* than
Ex. 3:3 this *g* sight, why the bush is not burnt
11:3 man Moses was very *g* in the land of Egypt
18:11 I know that the LORD is *g* than all gods
32:30 that Moses said. . Ye have sinned a *g* sin
Num. 14:17 the power of my LORD be *g*, according as
Deut. 1:17 shall hear the small as well as the *g*
4:7 what nation is there so *g*, who hath God so
10:17 a *g* God, a mighty, and a terrible, which
29:24 what meaneth the heat of this *g* anger?
Josh. 23:9 driven out from before you *g* nations
Judg. 16:5 and see wherein his *g* strength lieth
1 Sam. 12:17 see that your wickedness is *g*, which
12:24 consider how *g* things he hath done for you
14:30 a much *g* slaughter among the Philistines?
19:5 LORD wrought a *g* salvation for all Israel
26:25 my son David: thou shalt both do *g* things
2 Sam. 5:10 David went on, and grew *g*
7:22 thou art *g*, O LORD God: for there is none
13:16 this evil in sending me away is *g* than the
22:36 (Ps. 18:35) thy gentleness hath made me *g*
2 Kgs. 5:13 prophet had bid thee do some *g* thing
22:13 (2 Chr. 34:21) for *g* is the wrath of the LORD
1 Chr. 11:9 so David waxed *g* and *g*: for the LORD
16:25 (Ps. 96:4) for *g* is the LORD, and greatly
Neh. 7:4 the city was large and *g*: but the people
9:32 now therefore, our God, the *g*, the mighty
Job 1:3 *g* household; so that this man was the *g* of
5:9 doeth *g* things and unsearchable; marvelous
5:25 shalt know also that they seed shall be *g*
22:5 is not thy wickedness *g*?
32:9 *g* men are not always wise: neither do the
33:12 I will answer thee, that God is *g* than man
36:26 God is *g*, and we know him not, neither can
38:21 or because the number of thy days is *g*?
Ps. 14:5 (53:5) there were they in *g* fear: for God is
19:11 and in keeping of them there is *g* reward
19:13 shall be innocent from the *g* transgression
21:5 his glory is *g* in thy salvation: honor and
25:11 O LORD, pardon mine iniquity; for it is *g*
31:19 oh how *g* is thy goodness, which thou hast
47:2 terrible; he is a *g* King over all the earth
48:1 *g* is the LORD, and greatly to be praised
77:13 who is so *g* a God as our God?
86:10 for thou art *g*, and doest wondrous things
92:5 LORD, how *g* are thy works! and thy thoughts
95:3 the LORD is a *g* God, and a *g* King above all
103:11 so *g* is his mercy toward them that fear
111:2 the works of the LORD are *g*, sought out
119:165 *g* peace have they which love thy law
126:3 LORD hath done *g* things for us; whereof we
138:5 the LORD: for *g* is the glory of the LORD
139:17 unto me, O God! how *g* is the sum of them!
145:8 compassion; slow to anger, and of *g* mercy
147:5 *g* is our Lord, and of *g* power
Prov. 22:1 is rather to be chosen than *g* riches
25:6 and stand not in the place of *g* men
26:10 *g* God that formed all things both rewardeth
Eccl. 2:7 had *g* possessions of *g* and small cattle
2:9 so I was *g*, and increased more than all
2:21 this also is vanity and a *g* evil
Is. 2:9 the mean man boweth. . the *g* man humbleth
9:2 (Mt. 4:16) in darkness have seen a *g* light
12:6 *g* is the Holy One of Israel in the midst of
19:20 he shall send them a saviour, and a *g* one
53:12 will I divide him a portion with the *g*
54:13 and *g* shall be the peace of thy children
Jer. 5:5 I will get me unto the *g* men, and will speak
10:6 O LORD; thou art *g*, and thy name is *g*
30:7 alas! for that day is *g*, so that none is
31:34 (Heb. 8:11) know me, from the least. . the *g*

Jer. 32:19 *g* in counsel, and mighty in work: for thine
33:3 show thee *g* and mighty things, which thou
44:26 I have sworn by my *g* name, saith the LORD
45:5 and seekest thou *g* things for thyself?
Lam. 3:23 new every morning: *g* is thy faithfulness
Ezek. 36:23 I will sanctify my *g* name, which was
Dan. 2:31 thou, O king, sawest, and behold a *g* image
2:48 made Daniel a *g* man . . gave him many *g* gifts
8:4 he did according to his will, and became *g*
9:4 the *g* and dreadful God, keeping the covenant
11:5 his dominion shall be a *g* dominion
Hos. 8:12 written to him the *g* things of my law
Joel 2:20 come up, because he hath done *g* things
2:21 rejoice: for the LORD will do *g* things
Jon. 1:17 prepared a *g* fish to swallow up Jonah
Mic. 5:4 shall he be *g* unto the ends of the earth
Nah. 1:3 the LORD is slow to anger, and *g* in power
Zeph. 1:14 *g* day of the LORD is near, it is near
Hag. 2:9 glory of this latter house shall be *g* than
Zech. 9:17 how *g* is his goodness, and how *g* is his
Mal. 1:11 my name shall be *g* among the Gentiles
Mt. 5:12 (Lk. 6:23) for *g* is your reward in heaven
5:19 the same shall be called *g* in the kingdom
6:23 in thee be darkness, how *g* is that darkness!
7:27 (Lk. 6:49) and it fell: and *g* was the fall
8:10 (Lk. 7:9) found so *g* faith, no, not in Israel
11:11 (Lk. 7:28) not risen a *g* than John the Baptist
12:6 that in this place is one *g* than the temple
12:42 (Lk. 11:31) a *g* than Solomon is here
13:32 (Mk. 4:32) grown, it is the *g* among herbs
13:46 found one pearl of *g* price, went and sold
15:28 O woman, *g* is thy faith: be it unto thee
18:1 Jesus, saying, Who is the *g* in the kingdom
19:22 (Mk. 10:22) sorrowful . . he had *g* possessions
20:26 (Mk. 10:43; Lk. 22:26) will be *g* among you
22:36 which is the *g* commandment in the law?
23:11 that is *g* among you shall be your servant
23:17 for whether is *g*, the gold, or the temple
24:21 then shall be *g* tribulation, such as was
28:2 there was a *g* earthquake: for the angel of
Mk. 3:8 they had heard what *g* things he did, came
5:19 (Lk. 8:39) how *g* things the Lord hath done
9:34 (Lk. 9:46; 22:24) who should be the *g*
Lk. 1:15 he shall be *g* in the sight of the Lord
2:10 behold, I bring you good tidings of *g* joy
10:2 harvest truly is *g*, but the laborers are few
12:18 I will pull down my barns, and build *g*
15:20 he was yet a *g* way off, his father saw him
16:26 between us and you there is a *g* gulf fixed
22:27 whether is *g*, he that sitteth at meat, or
22:44 his sweat was as it were *g* drops of blood
Jn. 1:50 thou shalt see *g* things than these
4:12 art thou *g* than our father Jacob, which
5:20 he will show him *g* works than these
5:36 but I have *g* witness than that of John
8:53 art thou *g* than our father Abraham, which
10:29 Father, which gave them me, is *g* than all
13:16 (15:20) servant is not *g* than his lord
14:12 *g* works than these shall he do; because I
14:28 unto the Father: for my Father is *g* than I
15:13 *g* love hath no man than this, that a man
Acts 8:9 giving out that himself was some *g* one
19:28 (19:34) saying, *G* is Diana of the Ephesians
22:6 shone from heaven a *g* light round about me
26:22 witnessing both to small and *g*, saying
1 Cor. 13:13 three; but the *g* of these is charity
15:6 brethren at once; of whom the *g* part remain
16:9 a *g* door and effectual is opened unto me
2 Cor. 1:10 who delivered us from so *g* a death
7:4 *g* is my boldness of speech toward you, *g* is
Eph. 2:4 mercy, for his *g* love wherewith he loved
5:32 this is a *g* mystery: but I speak concerning
1 Tim. 3:16 *g* is the mystery of godliness: God was

Tit. 2:13 and the glorious appearing of the *g* God
Heb. 2:3 we escape, if we neglect so *g* salvation
4:14 seeing then that we have a *g* high priest
6:13 he could swear by no *g*, he sware by himself
7:4 consider how *g* this man was, unto whom even
9:11 to come, by a *g* and more perfect tabernacle
12:1 about with so *g* a cloud of witnesses
13:20 that *g* shepherd of the sheep, through the
Jas. 3:1 that we shall receive the *g* condemnation
3:5 boasteth *g* things. Behold, how *g* a matter a
1 Pet. 3:4 which is in the sight of God of *g* price
2 Pet. 1:4 exceeding *g* and precious promises
1 Jn. 3:20 condemn us, God is *g* than our heart
4:4 *g* is he that is in you, than he that is
3 Jn. 4 I have no *g* joy than to hear that my
Jude 6 darkness unto the judgment of the *g* day
Rev. 2:22 into *g* tribulation, except they repent
6:17 the *g* day of his wrath is come; and who
7:14 are they which came out of *g* tribulation
8:10 there fell a *g* star from heaven, burning as
11:18 and them that fear thy name, small and *g*
15:3 Lamb, saying, *G* and marvelous are thy works
18:10 (18:16, 19) alas, alas, that *g* city Babylon
20:11 I saw a *g* white throne, and him that sat
20:12 I saw the dead, small and *g*, stand before
21:10 showed me that *g* city, the holy Jerusalem

Greatly

Gen. 3:16 I multiply thy sorrow and thy conception
Ex. 19:18 a furnace, and the whole mount quaked *g*
Num. 11:10 the anger of the LORD was kindled *g*
14:39 Moses told these . . the people mourned *g*
Deut. 15:4 the LORD shall *g* bless thee in the land
Judg. 16:2 Israel was *g* impoverished because of the
2 Sam. 24:10 (1 Chr. 21:8) I have sinned *g* in that
1 Kgs. 18:3 now Obadiah feared the LORD *g*
1 Chr. 16:25 (Ps. 48:1; 96:4; 145:3) *g* to be praised
Ps. 21:1 in thy salvation how *g* shall he rejoice!
28:7 my heart *g* rejoiceth; and with my song will
47:9 the earth belong unto God: he is *g* exalted
62:2 he is my defense; I shall not be *g* moved
89:7 God is *g* to be feared in the assembly of
Is. 61:10 I will *g* rejoice in the LORD, my soul
Jer. 9:19 how are we spoiled! we are *g* confounded
Dan. 10:11 O Daniel, a man *g* beloved, understand
Obad. 2 among the heathen: thou art *g* despised
Zech. 9:9 rejoice *g*, O daughter of Zion; shout
Mt. 27:14 insomuch that the governor marveled *g*
27:54 feared *g*, saying, Truly this was the Son
Mk. 5:23 besought . . *g*, saying, My little daughter
9:15 when they beheld him, were *g* amazed
12:27 God of the living: ye therefore do *g* err
Acts 6:7 disciples multiplied in Jerusalem *g*
Phil. 1:8 how *g* I long after you all in the bowels
2 Tim. 1:4 *g* desiring to see thee, being mindful

Greatness *See also* Majesty, Might, Power

Ex. 15:7 in the *g* of thine excellency thou hast
15:16 by the *g* of thine arm they shall be as
Num. 14:19 according to the *g* of thy mercy
Deut. 3:24 hast begun to show thy servant thy *g*
5:24 our God hath showed us his glory and his *g*
9:26 which thou hast redeemed through thy *g*
11:2 your God, his *g*, his mighty hand, and his
32:3 name of the LORD: ascribe ye *g* unto our God
1 Chr. 17:19 hast thou done all this *g*, in making
17:21 to make thee a name of *g* and terribleness
29:11 thine, O LORD, is the *g*, and the power
Neh. 13:22 spare me according to the *g* of thy mercy
Ps. 66:3 through the *g* of thy power shall thine
71:21 thou shalt increase my *g*, and comfort me

Ps. 79:11 according to the *g* of thy power preserve
145:3 to be praised; and his *g* is unsearchable
145:6 terrible acts: and I will declare thy *g*
150:2 praise him according to his excellent *g*
Is. 40:26 them all by names by the *g* of his might
57:10 thou art wearied in the *g* of thy way
63:1 traveling in the *g* of his strength?
Jer. 13:22 the *g* of thine iniquity are thy skirts
Ezek. 31:2 whom art thou like in thy *g*?
Dan. 7:27 *g* of the kingdom under the whole heaven
Eph. 1:19 what is the exceeding *g* of his power to

Grecia (Greece)

Dan. 8:21 the rough goat is the king of *G*
10:20 gone forth, lo, the prince of *G* shall come
11:2 he shall stir up all against the realm of *G*
Zech. 9:13 O *G*, and made thee as the sword of a
Acts 20:2 them much exhortation, he came into *G*

Grecian *See also* Greek

Joel 3:6 the children . . have ye sold unto the *G*
Acts 6:1 a murmuring of the *G* against the Hebrews
9:29 disputed against the *G*: but they went about
11:20 spake unto the *G*, preaching the Lord Jesus

Greedily

Prov. 21:26 he coveteth *g* all the day long
Ezek. 22:12 thou hast *g* gained of thy neighbors by
Jude 11 ran *g* after the error of Balaam for reward

Greediness

Eph. 4:19 to work all uncleanness with *g*

Greedy

Ps. 17:12 as a lion that is *g* of his prey, and as
Prov. 1:19 the ways of every one that is *g* of gain
15:27 that is *g* of gain troubleth his own house
Is. 56:11 are *g* dogs which can never have enough
1 Tim. 3:3 (3:8) not *g* of filthy lucre

Greek *See also* Grecian

Mk. 7:26 woman was a *G*, a Syrophoenician by nation
Lk. 23:38 (Jn. 19:20) letters of *G* . . Latin . . Hebrew
Jn. 12:20 and there were certain *G* among them that
Acts 14:1 of the Jews and also of the *G* believed
16:1 named Timotheus . . but his father was a *G*
17:4 of the devout *G* a great multitude
18:17 then all the *G* took Sosthenes, the chief
21:37 who said, Canst thou speak *G*?
Rom. 1:14 debtor both to . . *G*, and to the Barbarians
1:16 to the Jew first, and also to the *G*
1 Cor. 1:22 a sign, and the *G* seek after wisdom
1:23 stumblingblock, and unto the *G* foolishness
Gal. 2:3 neither Titus, who was with me, being a *G*
3:28 (Col. 3:11) there is neither Jew nor *G*

Green

Gen. 1:30 I have given every *g* herb for meat
Judg. 16:7 if they bind me with seven *g* withes
Ps. 23:2 he maketh me to lie down in *g* pastures
Lk. 23:31 for if they do these things in a *g* tree

Greeting

Mt. 23:7 (Lk. 11:43; 20:46) and *g* in the markets
Jas. 1:1 to the twelve tribes . . scattered abroad, *g*

Greyhound

Prov. 30:31 a *g* . . against whom there is no rising up

Grief *See also* Affliction, Anguish, Calamity, Distress, Misery, Pain, Sorrow, Suffering, Tribulation, Trouble

Gen. 26:35 a *g* of mind unto Isaac and to Rebekah
1 Sam. 1:16 complaint and *g* have I spoken hitherto
2 Chr. 6:29 shall know his own sore and his own *g*
Job 6:2 oh that my *g* were thoroughly weighed
16:6 though I speak, my *g* is not assuaged
Ps. 6:7 (31:9) mine eye is consumed because of *g*
31:10 my life is spent with *g*, and my years with
Prov. 17:25 foolish son is a *g* to his father
Eccl. 1:18 for in much wisdom is much *g*
Is. 53:3 a man of sorrows, and acquainted with *g*
53:4 hath borne our *g*, and carried our sorrows
53:10 LORD to bruise him; he hath put him to *g*
Jer. 6:7 before me continually is *g* and wounds
10:19 I said, Truly this is a *g*, and I must bear
45:3 LORD hath added *g* to my sorrow; I fainted
Jon. 4:6 over his head, to deliver him from his *g*
Heb. 13:17 they may do it with joy, and not with *g*

Grievance

Hab. 1:3 me iniquity, and cause me to behold *g*?

Grieve *See also* Lament, Mourn, Repent, Sorrow

Gen. 6:6 had made man on the earth, and it *g* him
45:5 be not *g*, nor angry with yourselves
49:23 archers have sorely *g* him, and shot at him
Judg. 10:16 soul was *g* for the misery of Israel
1 Sam. 1:8 why is thy heart *g*? am not I better to
2:33 to consume thine eyes, and to *g* thine heart
15:11 it *g* Samuel; and he cried unto the LORD
1 Chr. 4:10 me from evil, that it may not *g* me!
Ps. 73:21 my heart was *g*, and I was pricked in my
78:40 in the wilderness, and *g* him in the desert!
95:10 (Heb. 3:10) was I *g* with this generation
119:158 I beheld the transgressors, and was *g*
Is. 57:10 of thine hand; therefore thou was not *g*
Dan. 7:15 I Daniel was *g* in my spirit in the midst
Mk. 3:5 being *g* for the hardness of their hearts
10:22 he was sad at that saying, and went away *g*
Jn. 21:17 Peter was *g* because he said unto him
Acts 4:2 being *g* that they taught the people
16:18 Paul, being *g*, turned and said to the spirit
Rom. 14:15 but if thy brother be *g* with thy meat
2 Cor. 2:4 not that ye should be *g*, but that ye
Eph. 4:30 *g* not the Holy Spirit of God, whereby ye

Grievous

Gen. 12:10 to sojourn there; for the famine was *g*
18:20 Sodom and Gomorrah . . their sin is very *g*
21:11 the thing was very *g* in Abraham's sight
41:31 famine following; for it shall be very *g*
50:11 a *g* mourning to the Egyptians: wherefore
Ex. 8:24 came a *g* swarm of flies into the house of
9:3 there shall be a very *g* murrain
9:18 I will cause it to rain a very *g* hail, such
1 Kgs. 12:4 (2 Chr. 10:4) thy father made our yoke *g*
Ps. 10:5 his ways are always *g*; thy judgments are
31:18 speak *g* things proudly and contemptuously
Prov. 15:1 away wrath: but *g* words stir up anger
Eccl. 2:17 wrought under the sun is *g* unto me
Is. 15:4 cry out; his life shall be *g* unto him
21:2 a *g* vision is declared unto me
Jer. 10:19 woe is me for my hurt! my wound is *g*
16:4 they shall die of *g* deaths; they shall not
23:19 is gone forth in fury, even a *g* whirlwind
30:12 bruise is incurable, and thy wound is *g*
Nah. 3:19 no healing of thy bruise; thy wound is *g*
Mt. 23:4 (Lk. 11:46) heavy burdens and *g* to be borne
Acts 20:29 after my departing shall *g* wolves enter
25:7 and laid many and *g* complaints against Paul
Phil. 3:1 to me indeed is not *g*, but for you it is safe
Heb. 12:11 now no chastening . . to be joyous, but *g*
1 Jn. 5:3 and his commandments are not *g*

Grievously

Mt. 8:6 my servant. . sick of the palsy, *g* tormented
15:22 my daughter is *g* vexed with a devil

Grind

Judg. 16:21 and he did *g* in the prison house
Eccl. 12:4 when the sound of the *g* is low
Is. 3:15 to pieces, and *g* the faces of the poor?
Lam. 5:13 they took the young men to *g*
Mt. 21:44 (Lk. 20:18) fall, it will *g* him to powder
24:41 (Lk. 17:35) two women shall be *g* at the mill

Grinder

Eccl. 12:3 and the *g* cease because they are few

Groan

Job 24:12 men *g* from out of the city, and the soul
Jer. 51:52 through all her land. . wounded shall *g*
Ezek. 30:24 break Pharaoh's arms, and he shall *g*
Joel 1:18 how do the beasts *g*! the herds of cattle
Jn. 11:33 he *g* in the spirit, and was troubled
11:38 again *g* in himself cometh to the grave
Rom. 8:22 whole creation *g* and travaileth in pain
8:23 we ourselves *g* within ourselves, waiting
2 Cor. 5:2 in this we *g*, earnestly desiring to be
5:4 are in this tabernacle do *g*, being burdened

Groaning *See also* Groan

Ex. 2:24 God heard their *g*, and God remembered his
Ps. 6:6 I am weary with my *g*; all the night make I
38:9 before thee; and my *g* is not hid from thee
102:20 to hear the *g* of the prisoner; to loose
Ezek. 30:24 with the *g* of a deadly wounded man
Rom. 8:26 maketh intercession for us with *g* which

Grope

Deut. 28:29 *g* at noonday, as the blind *g* in darkness
Job 5:14 and *g* in the noonday as in the night
12:25 they *g* in the dark without light
Is. 59:10 *g* for the wall like the blind, and we *g*

Gross

Is. 60:2 *g* darkness the people: but the LORD shall
Mt. 13:15 for this people's heart is waxed *g*

Ground *See also* Earth, Land

Gen. 2:5 and there was not a man to till the *g*
3:17 not eat of it: cursed is the *g* for thy sake
4:10 brother's blood crieth unto me from the *g*
Ex. 3:5 (Acts 7:33) whereon thou standest is holy *g*
1 Sam. 3:19 let none of his words fall to the *g*
2 Sam. 23:12 but he stood in the midst of the *g*
2 Kgs. 2:19 the water is naught, and the *g* barren
Job 5:6 neither doth trouble spring out of the *g*
Ps. 107:33 he turneth. . the watersprings into dry *g*
Is. 35:7 the parched *g* shall become a pool
Jer. 4:3 (Hos. 10:12) break up your fallow *g*
Ezek. 19:13 the wilderness, in a dry and thirsty *g*
Zech. 8:12 and the *g* shall give her increase
Mk. 4:26 as if a man should cast seed into the *g*
Lk. 12:16 *g* of a certain rich man brought forth
13:7 cut it down; why cumbereth it the *g*?
14:18 have bought a piece of *g*, and I must needs
19:44 shall lay thee even with the *g*, and thy
Jn. 8:6 with his finger wrote on the *g*
12:24 fall into the *g* and die, it abideth alone
Acts 22:7 fell unto the *g*, and heard a voice saying
Eph. 3:17 that ye, being rooted and *g* in love
Col. 1:23 ye continue in the faith *g* and settled
1 Tim. 3:15 house of God. . pillar and *g* of the truth

Grove

Gen. 21:33 Abraham planted a *g* in Beer-sheba
Ex. 34:13 (Deut. 7:5) images, and cut down their *g*
Deut. 16:21 shalt not plant thee a *g* of any trees
1 Kgs. 14:15 they have made their *g*, provoking the
16:33 Ahab made a *g*. . Ahab did more to provoke
2 Kgs. 17:16 made a *g*, and worshipped all the host
2 Chr. 31:1 images in pieces, and cut down the *g*

Grow (Grew, Grown) *See also* Enlarge, Flourish, Increase

Gen. 2:9 God to *g* every tree that is pleasant to
48:16 and let them *g* into a multitude
Judg. 16:22 the hair of his head began to *g* again
2 Sam. 5:10 David went on, and *g* great
23:5 all my desire, although he make it not to *g*
2 Kgs. 19:26 (Is. 37:27) corn blasted before it be *g*
Job 8:19 and out of the earth shall others *g*
Ps. 92:12 he shall *g* like a cedar in Lebanon
Is. 11:1 and a Branch shall *g* out of his roots
17:11 in the day shalt thou make thy plant to *g*
53:2 he shall *g* up before him as a tender plant
Jer. 12:2 they *g*, yea, they bring forth fruit
Hos. 14:5 dew unto Israel: he shall *g* as the lily
Zech. 6:12 BRANCH; and he shall *g* up out of his place
Mal. 4:2 go forth, and *g* up as calves of the stall
Mt. 6:28 (Lk. 12:27) lilies of the field, how they *g*
13:30 let both *g* together until the harvest
21:19 let no fruit *g* on thee henceforward
Mk. 4:27 should spring and *g* up, he knoweth not
Acts 5:24 doubted of them whereunto this would *g*
12:24 but the word of God *g* and multiplied
19:20 mightily *g* the word of God and prevailed
Eph. 2:21 framed together *g* unto a holy temple in
2 Thes. 1:3 because that your faith *g* exceedingly
1 Pet. 2:2 milk of the word, that ye may *g* thereby
2 Pet. 3:18 but *g* in grace, and in the knowledge

Grudge

Lev. 19:18 thou shalt not avenge, nor bear any *g*
Ps. 59:15 for meat, and *g* if they be not satisfied
Jas. 5:9 *g* not one against another, brethren, lest
1 Pet. 4:9 hospitality one to another without *g*

Grudgingly

2 Cor. 9:7 so let him give; not *g*, or of necessity

Guard

Gen. 40:4 the captain of the *g* charged Joseph with
2 Sam. 23:23 (1 Chr. 11:25) David set him over his *g*
2 Kgs. 11:11 and the *g* stood. . round about the king
Neh. 4:22 that in the night they may be a *g* to us
Ezek. 38:7 unto thee, and be thou a *g* unto them
Acts 28:16 prisoners to the captain of the *g*

Guest

Mt. 22:10 and the wedding was furnished with *g*
Mk. 14:14 (Lk. 22:11) where is the *g* chamber, where
Lk. 19:7 gone to be *g* with a man that is a sinner

Guide *See also* Direct, Lead, Order

Ex. 15:13 thou hast *g* them. . unto thy holy habitation
Job 38:32 or canst thou *g* Arcturus with his sons?
Ps. 25:9 meek will he *g* in judgment: and the meek
32:8 thou shalt go: I will *g* thee with mine eye
48:14 he will be our *g* even unto death
55:13 but it was thou, a man mine equal, my *g*
73:24 shalt *g* me with thy counsel, and afterward
112:5 a good man. . *g* his affairs with discretion
Prov. 2:17 which forsaketh the *g* of her youth
6:7 which having no *g*, overseer, or ruler

Prov. 11:3 the integrity of the upright shall *g* them
23:19 and be wise, and *g* thine heart in the way
Is. 58:11 the LORD shall *g* thee continually
Jer. 3:4 my father, thou art the *g* of my youth?
Mt. 23:16 (23:24) woe unto you, ye blind *g*
Lk. 1:79 to *g* our feet into the way of peace
Jn. 16:13 Spirit of truth, is come, he will *g* you
Acts 1:16 Judas . . was *g* to them that took Jesus
8:31 how can I, except some man should *g* me?
Rom. 2:19 a *g* of the blind, a light of them which
1 Tim. 5:14 marry, bear children, *g* the house

Guile *See also* Craft, Deceit, Subtilty

Ex. 21:14 upon his neighbor, to slay him with *g*
Ps. 32:2 blessed . . in whose spirit there is no *g*
34:13 (1 Pet. 3:10) and thy lips from speaking *g*
Jn. 1:47 an Israelite indeed, in whom is no *g*!
2 Cor. 12:16 being crafty, I caught you with *g*
1 Thes. 2:3 deceit, nor of uncleanness, nor in *g*
1 Pet. 2:1 laying aside all malice, and all *g*
2:22 no sin, neither was *g* found in his mouth
Rev. 14:5 in their mouth was found no *g*

Guilt

Deut. 21:9 thou put away the *g* of innocent blood

Guiltless *See also* Faultless, Innocent

Ex. 20:7 (Deut. 5:11) LORD will not hold him *g* that
Num. 5:31 then shall the man be *g* from iniquity
Josh. 2:19 be upon his head, and we will be *g*
1 Sam. 26:9 against the LORD's anointed, and be *g*?
2 Sam. 3:28 I and my kingdom are *g* before the LORD
1 Kgs. 2:9 now therefore hold him not *g*: for thou
Mt. 12:7 ye would not have condemned the *g*

Guilty

Gen. 42:21 we are verily *g* concerning our brother
Ex. 34:7 (Num. 14:18) will by no means clear the *g*
Lev. 5:3 when he knoweth of it, then he shall be *g*
6:4 because he hath sinned, and is *g*, that he
Num. 35:27 kill the slayer; he shall not be *g* of blood
Prov. 30:10 he curse thee, and thou be found *g*
Ezek. 22:4 thou art become *g* in thy blood that thou
Zech. 11:5 slay them, and hold themselves not *g*
Mt. 23:18 sweareth by the gift . . upon it, he is *g*
26:66 (Mk. 14:64) and said, He is *g* of death
Rom. 3:19 all the world may become *g* before God
1 Cor. 11:27 *g* of the body and blood of the Lord
Jas. 2:10 yet offend in one point, he is *g* of all

Gulf

Lk. 16:26 between us and you there is a great *g* fixed

Gush

1 Kgs. 18:28 cut . . till the blood *g* out upon them
Ps. 78:20 he smote the rock, that the waters *g* out
Jer. 9:18 tears, and our eyelids *g* out with waters
Acts 1:18 burst asunder . . and all his bowels *g* out

H

Habakkuk Hab. 1:1–3:19

Habitable

Prov. 8:31 rejoicing in the *h* part of his earth

Habitation *See also* Abode, Dwelling, House

Gen. 49:5 instruments of cruelty are in their *h*
Ex. 15:2 he is my God, and I will prepare him a *h*
15:13 guided them in . . strength unto thy holy *h*

Lev. 13:46 alone; without the camp shall his *h* be
Deut. 26:15 look down from thy holy *h*, from heaven
2 Chr. 6:2 but I have built a house of *h* for thee
Ezra 7:15 God of Israel, whose *h* is in Jerusalem
Job 5:3 taking root: but suddenly I cursed his *h*
5:24 thou shalt visit thy *h*, and shalt not sin
8:6 make the *h* of thy righteousness prosperous
Ps. 26:8 LORD, I have loved the *h* of thy house
33:14 from the place of his *h* he looketh upon
68:5 a judge of the widows, is God in his holy *h*
69:25 (Acts 1:20) let their *h* be desolate
71:3 be thou my strong *h*, whereunto I may
74:20 of the earth are full of the *h* of cruelty
89:14 justice and judgment . . the *h* of thy throne
91:9 is my refuge, even the Most High, thy *h*
107:7 that they might go to a city of *h*
107:36 that they may prepare a city for *h*
132:5 place for the LORD, a *h* for the mighty God
132:13 chosen Zion; he hath desired it for his *h*
Prov. 3:33 but he blesseth the *h* of the just
Is. 32:18 my people shall dwell in a peaceable *h*
33:20 thine eyes shall see Jerusalem a quiet *h*
63:15 and behold from the *h* of thy holiness
Jer. 21:13 or who shall enter into our *h*?
25:30 holy *h*; he shall mightily roar upon his *h*
25:37 the peaceable *h* are cut down because of
31:23 the LORD bless thee, O *h* of justice
50:7 sinned against the LORD, the *h* of justice
50:19 I will bring Israel again to his *h*
Ezek. 29:14 of Pathros, into the land of their *h*
Amos 1:2 and the *h* of the shepherds shall mourn
Lk. 16:9 they may receive you into everlasting *h*
Acts 17:26 appointed, and the bounds of their *h*
Eph. 2:22 builded together for a *h* of God through
Jude 6 their first estate, but left their own *h*
Rev. 18:2 is fallen, and is become the *h* of devils

Hagar (Agar)

Gen. 16:1–16; 21:9–21; Gal. 4:22–31

Haggai Ezra 5:1; 6:14; Hag. 1:1–2:23

Hail

Ex. 9:18 I will cause it to rain a very grievous *h*
Job 38:22 or hast thou seen the treasures of the *h*
Ps. 78:47 he destroyed their vines with *h*
105:32 he gave them *h* for rain, and flaming fire
Is. 28:17 *h* shall sweep away the refuge of lies
Hag. 2:17 with blasting and with mildew and with *h*
Rev. 8:7 followed *h* and fire mingled with blood
11:19 thunderings, and an earthquake, and great *h*
16:21 fell upon men a great *h* out of heaven

Hair

Gen. 42:38 (44:29) bring down my gray *h* with sorrow
Lev. 13:3 when the *h* in the plague is turned white
Num. 6:19 after the *h* of his separation is shaven
Judg. 16:22 the *h* of his head began to grow again
2 Sam. 14:26 *h* was heavy on him . . he weighed the *h*
1 Kgs. 1:52 shall not a *h* of him fall to the earth
Job 4:15 spirit passed . . the *h* of my flesh stood up
Ps. 40:12 (69:4) more than the *h* of mine head
Song 4:1 (6:5) thy *h* is as a flock of goats
Is. 3:24 and instead of well set *h* baldness
46:4 and even to hoar *h* will I carry you
50:6 my cheeks to them that plucked off the *h*
Jer. 7:29 cut off thine *h*, O Jerusalem, and cast
Dan. 4:33 his *h* were grown like eagles' feathers
Hos. 7:9 gray *h* are here and there upon him, yet
Mt. 3:4 (Mk. 1:6) John had his raiment of camel's *h*
5:36 thou canst not make one *h* white or black
10:30 (Lk. 12:7) *h* of your head are all numbered
Lk. 7:38 (Jn. 11:2; 12:3) did wipe them with the *h* of

Lk. 21:18 there shall not a *h* of your head perish
1 Cor. 11:14 if a man have long *h*, it is a shame
    11:15 if a woman have long *h*, it is a glory to
1 Tim. 2:9 not with braided *h*, or gold, or pearls
1 Pet. 3:3 outward adorning of plaiting the *h*
Rev. 1:14 his head and his *h* were white like wool

Hairy

Gen. 25:25 came out red, all over like a *h* garment
    27:11 behold, Esau my brother is a *h* man, and I
2 Kgs. 1:8 was a *h* man . . And he said, It is Elijah

Hale

Lk. 12:58 adversary . . lest he *h* thee to the judge
Acts 8:3 *h* men and women committed them to prison

Half

Ex. 24:6 *h* of the blood . . in basins . . *h* . . on the altar
1 Kgs. 3:25 give *h* to the one, and *h* to the other
Lk. 19:8 the *h* of my goods I give to the poor

Hall

Mt. 27:27 (Mk. 15:16) took Jesus into the common *h*
Lk. 22:55 fire in the midst of the *h*, and were set
Jn. 18:28 led they Jesus . . unto the *h* of judgment

Hallelujah *See* Alleluia

Hallow *See also* Consecrate, Purify,
    Sanctify

Ex. 20:11 LORD blessed the sabbath day, and *h* it
    28:38 Israel shall *h* in all their holy gifts
    29:1 that thou shalt do unto them to *h* them
Lev. 22:32 I will be *h* . . I am the LORD which *h* you
    25:10 ye shall *h* the fiftieth year, and proclaim
1 Kgs. 9:3 *h* this house, which thou hast built
Jer. 17:22 *h* ye the sabbath day, as I commanded
Ezek. 20:20 *h* my sabbaths . . sign between me and you
    44:24 assemblies; and they shall *h* my sabbaths

Hallowed *See also* Hallow, Holy

Lev. 19:8 he hath profaned the *h* thing of the LORD
Num. 5:10 and every man's *h* things shall be his
    16:37 take up the censers . . for they are *h*
1 Sam. 21:4 no common bread . . but there is *h* bread
Mt. 6:9 (Lk. 11:2) *h* be thy name

Halt

Gen. 32:31 rose upon him, and he *h* upon his thigh
1 Kgs. 18:21 how long *h* ye between two opinions?
Ps. 38:17 for I am ready to *h*, and my sorrow is
Jer. 20:10 all my familiars watched for my *h*
Mic. 4:6 (Zeph. 3:19) assemble her that *h*, and I
Mt. 18:8 (Mk. 9:45) better . . to enter into life *h* or
Lk. 14:21 and the maimed, and the *h*, and the blind
Jn. 5:3 blind, *h*, withered, waiting for the moving

Ham Gen. 6:10; 9:22

Haman Esth. 3:1–7:10

Hammer

Judg. 4:21 a nail of the tent, and took a *h* in her
1 Kgs. 6:7 neither *h* nor axe nor any tool of iron
Jer. 23:29 and like a *h* that breaketh the rock in
    50:23 how is the *h* of the whole earth cut asunder

Hanameel Jer. 32:7–12

Hanani the seer 2 Chr. 16:7–10

Hanani the governor Neh. 1:2; 7:2

Hananiah Jer. 28:1–17

Hand

Gen. 9:2 into your *h* are they delivered
    16:12 wild man; his *h* will be against every man
    24:2 put, I pray thee, thy *h* under my thigh
    27:22 Jacob's voice, but the *h* the *h* of Esau
Ex. 3:20 I will stretch out my *h*, and smite Egypt
    4:2 what is that in thine *h*? And he said, A rod
    9:29 I will spread abroad my *h* unto the LORD
    14:8 children of Israel went out with a high *h*
    15:6 thy right *h* . . glorious in power: thy right *h*
    17:12 Moses' *h* were heavy; and they took a stone
    21:24 (Deut. 19:21) tooth for tooth, *h* for *h*
    23:1 put not thine *h* with the wicked to be an
    29:10 (Lev. 8:14) *h* upon the head of the bullock
    33:22 will cover thee with my *h* while I pass by
Lev. 4:24 lay his *h* upon the head of the goat
    9:22 and Aaron lifted up his *h* toward the people
Num. 11:23 Moses, Is the LORD's *h* waxed short?
    21:34 (Deut. 3:2) I have delivered him into thy *h*
Deut. 3:24 servant thy greatness, and thy mighty *h*
    8:17 might of mine *h* hath gotten me this wealth
    15:7 nor shut thine *h* from thy poor brother
    21:6 shall wash their *h* over the heifer that is
    32:27 our *h* is high, and the LORD hath not done
    33:3 all his saints are in thy *h*: and they sat
    34:9 for Moses had laid his *h* upon him
Josh. 8:7 your God will deliver it into your *h*
    9:25 behold, we are in thine *h*: as it seemeth
Judg. 2:15 *h* of the LORD was against them for evil
    7:2 against me, saying, Mine own *h* hath saved me
    14:9 took thereof in his *h*, and went on eating
1 Sam. 5:6 *h* of the LORD was heavy upon them of
    6:9 know that it is not his *h* that smote us
    17:46 day will the LORD deliver thee into mine *h*
    18:17 not mine *h* . . but let the *h* of the Philistines
    23:16 went to David . . strengthened his *h* in God
2 Sam. 2:7 now let your *h* be strengthened
    6:6 (1 Chr. 13:10) Uzzah put forth his *h* to the ark
    24:14 (1 Chr. 21:13) fall now into the *h* of the LORD
1 Kgs. 13:4 and his *h*, which he put forth . . dried up
    18:46 *h* of the LORD was on Elijah
1 Chr. 29:12 *h* is power and might; and in thine *h*
2 Chr. 15:7 let not your *h* be weak: for your work
Ezra 7:9 according to the good *h* of his God upon
    8:22 *h* of our God is upon all them for good that
Neh. 2:8 according to the good *h* of my God upon me
Job 2:10 shall we receive good at the *h* of God
    4:3 and thou hast strengthened the weak *h*
    12:9 that the *h* of the LORD hath wrought this?
    12:10 in whose *h* is the soul of every living
    17:9 hath clean *h* shall be stronger and stronger
    19:21 pity upon me . . *h* of God hath touched me
    33:7 neither shall my *h* be heavy upon thee
    34:19 for they all are the work of his *h*
    40:14 that thine own right *h* can save thee
Ps. 16:8 (Acts 2:25) he is at my right *h*, I shall
    16:11 of joy; at thy right *h* there are pleasures
    20:6 with the saving strength of his right *h*
    22:16 inclosed me: they pierced my *h* and my feet
    24:4 he that hath clean *h*, and a pure heart
    26:6 I will wash mine *h* in innocency
    28:2 when I lift up my *h* toward thy holy oracle
    31:5 (Lk. 23:46) into thine *h* I commit my spirit
    31:15 times are in thy *h*: deliver me from the *h*
    37:24 for the LORD upholdeth him with his *h*
    75:8 in the *h* of the LORD there is a cup
    90:17 establish thou the work of our *h* upon us
    91:7 thy side, and ten thousand at thy right *h*
    91:12 (Mt. 4:6; Lk. 4:11) bear thee up in their *h*
    102:25 (Heb. 1:10) heavens are the work of thy *h*

Ps. 104:28 openest thine *h*, they are filled with good
110:1 (Mt. 22:44; Mk. 12:36; Lk. 20:42; Acts 2:34;
    Heb. 1:13) sit thou at my right *h*, until I make
115:7 they have *h*, but they handle not: feet have
118:15 the right *h* of the LORD doeth valiantly
119:73 thy *h* have made me and fashioned me
134:2 lift up your *h* in the sanctuary, and bless
139:10 *h* lead me, and thy right *h* shall hold me
Prov. 6:1 thou hast stricken thy *h* with a stranger
6:17 lying tongue, and *h* that shed innocent blood
10:4 slack *h*: but the *h* of the diligent maketh rich
11:21 though *h* join in *h*, the wicked shall not
12:24 the *h* of the diligent shall bear rule
16:5 though *h* join in *h*, he shall not be
19:24 (26:15) slothful man hideth his *h* in his bosom
21:25 killeth him; for his *h* refuse to labor
22:26 be not thou one of them that strike *h*
31:20 her *h* to the poor; yea . . her *h* to the needy
Eccl. 2:24 I saw, that it was from the *h* of God
4:6 quietness, than both the *h* full with travail
9:1 wise, and their works, are in the *h* of God
9:10 whatsoever thy *h* findeth to do, do it with
11:6 in the evening withhold not thine *h*
Is. 1:15 I will not hear: your *h* are full of blood
5:25 (9:12, 17, 21; 10:4) but his *h* is stretched out
11:8 child shall put his *h* on the cockatrice' den
13:6 (Joel 1:15; Zeph. 1:7) day of the LORD is at *h*
35:3 strengthen ye the weak *h*, and confirm the
40:2 of the LORD'S *h* double for all her sins
40:12 measured the waters in the hollow of his *h*
41:10 I will uphold thee with the right *h* of my
42:6 will hold thine *h*, and will keep thee
43:13 there is none that can deliver out of my *h*
45:12 even my *h*, have stretched out the heavens
53:10 pleasure of the LORD shall prosper in his *h*
56:2 and keepeth his *h* from doing any evil
59:1 LORD'S *h* is not shortened, that it cannot
64:8 potter; and we all are the work of thy *h*
65:2 (Rom. 10:21) my *h* . . unto a rebellious people
66:14 *h* of the LORD shall be known toward his
Jer. 16:21 I will cause them to know mine *h* and my
18:6 as the clay is in the potter's *h*, so are ye
23:23 am I a God at *h*, saith the LORD, and not a
31:32 (Heb. 8:9) I took them by the *h* to bring
Lam. 2:15 pass by clap their *h* at thee; they hiss
Ezek. 3:14 (3:22; 8:1; 37:1) *h* of the LORD . . upon me
3:18 (33:8) his blood will I require at thine *h*
10:2 fill thine *h* with coals of fire from between
12:23 the days are at *h*, and the effect
13:9 mine *h* shall be upon the prophets that see
Dan. 4:35 and none can stay his *h*, or say unto him
5:23 God in whose *h* thy breath is, and whose are
Hos. 12:7 the balances of deceit are in his *h*
Zech. 8:9 let your *h* be strong, ye that hear in
Mt. 3:2 (4:17; 10:7; Mk. 1:15) kingdom . . is at *h*
3:12 (Lk. 3:17) whose fan is in his *h*
5:30 (18:8; Mk. 9:43) if thy right *h* offend thee
6:3 let not thy left *h* know what thy right *h*
8:3 (Mk. 1:41; Lk. 5:13) Jesus put forth his *h*
12:10 (Mk. 3:1; Lk. 6:6) man . . had his *h* withered
15:20 to eat with unwashen *h* defileth not a man
19:13 children, that he should put his *h* on them
26:18 Master saith, My time is at *h*; I will keep
26:45 (Mk. 14:41) betrayed into the *h* of sinners
26:64 (Mk. 14:62; Lk. 22:69) the right *h* of power
27:24 Pilate . . washed his *h* before the multitude
Mk. 14:58 I will build another made without *h*
16:18 lay *h* on the sick, and they shall recover
16:19 into heaven, and sat on the right *h* of God
Lk. 9:62 no man, having put his *h* to the plow
21:31 ye that the kingdom of God is nigh at *h*
22:21 *h* of him that betrayeth me is with me on
23:46 Father, into thy *h* I commend my spirit

Lk. 24:39 behold my *h* and my feet, that it is I myself
24:50 and he lifted up his *h*, and blessed them
Jn. 3:35 Son, and hath given all things into his *h*
10:28 neither shall any man pluck them out of my *h*
13:3 the Father had given all things into his *h*
20:20 he showed unto them his *h* and his side
20:25 see in his *h* the print . . my *h* into his side
20:27 behold my *h*; and reach hither thy *h*
Acts 2:33 being by the right *h* of God exalted
5:12 by the *h* of the apostles were many signs
6:6 they had prayed, they laid their *h* on them
7:25 how that God by his *h* would deliver them
8:18 that through laying on of the apostles' *h*
9:12 *h* on him, that he might receive his sight
11:21 *h* of the Lord was with them: and a great
13:3 laid their *h* on them, they sent them away
13:11 behold, the *h* of the Lord is upon thee
Rom. 8:34 who is even at the right *h* of God
13:12 night is far spent, the day is at *h*
1 Cor. 12:15 because I am not the *h*, I am not of
16:21 (Col. 4:18; 2 Thes. 3:17) Paul . . mine own *h*
2 Cor. 5:1 a house not made with *h*, eternal in the
Gal. 2:9 me and Barnabas the right *h* of fellowship
Eph. 1:20 him at his own right *h* in the heavenly
Phil. 4:5 be known unto all men. The Lord is at *h*
Col. 2:11 with the circumcision made without *h*
3:1 where Christ sitteth on the right *h* of God
2 Thes. 2:2 as that the day of Christ is at *h*
1 Tim. 2:8 lifting up holy *h*, without wrath and
4:14 the laying on of the *h* of the presbytery
2 Tim. 4:6 and the time of my departure is at *h*
Heb. 1:3 sat down on the right *h* of the Majesty on
9:11 more perfect tabernacle, not made with *h*
10:31 to fall into the *h* of the living God
Jas. 4:8 cleanse your *h*, ye sinners; and purify
1 Pet. 3:22 heaven, and is on the right *h* of God
4:7 end of all things is at *h*: be ye therefore
5:6 humble yourselves . . under the mighty *h* of God
1 Jn. 1:1 our *h* have handled, of the Word of life
Rev. 1:17 he laid his right *h* upon me, saying unto
6:5 sat on him had a pair of balances in his *h*
10:2 he had in his *h* a little book open
14:9 receive his mark in his forehead, or in his *h*

Handbreadth

Ex. 25:25 (37:12) make . . a border of a *h* round about
Ps. 39:5 thou hast made my days as a *h*; and mine

Handful

Gen. 41:47 years the earth brought forth by *h*
Ruth 2:16 let fall also some of the *h* of purpose
1 Kgs. 17:12 I have not a cake, but a *h* of meal in
Ps. 72:16 there shall be a *h* of corn in the earth
Eccl. 4:6 better is a *h* with quietness, than both

Handiwork

Ps. 19:1 glory of God . . the firmament showeth his *h*

Handkerchief

Acts 19:12 were brought unto the sick *h* or aprons

Handle

Gen. 4:21 the father of all such as *h* the harp and
Judg. 5:14 they that *h* the pen of the writer
1 Chr. 12:8 that could *h* shield and buckler, whose
Ps. 115:7 they have hands, but they *h* not: feet
Prov. 16:20 that *h* a matter wisely shall find good
Jer. 2:8 that *h* the law knew me not: the pastors
46:9 that *h* the shield; and the Lydians, that *h*
Lk. 24:39 that it is I myself: *h* me, and see
2 Cor. 4:2 nor *h* the word of God deceitfully
Col. 2:21 touch not; taste not; *h* not
1 Jn. 1:1 our hands have *h*, of the Word of life

Handmaid *See also* Damsel, Girl, Handmaiden, Maid, Maiden

Gen. 16:1 and she had a *h*. . whose name was Hagar
1 Sam. 1:18 let thine *h* find grace in thy sight
   25:28 pray thee, forgive the trespass of thine *h*
2 Sam. 6:20 uncovered himself. . in the eyes of the *h*
Ps. 86:16 thy servant, and save the son of thine *h*
   116:16 son of thine *h*: thou hast loosed my bonds
Prov. 30:23 and a *h* that is heir to her mistress
Joel 2:29 (Acts 2:18) upon the *h*. . pour out my Spirit
Lk. 1:38 Mary said, Behold the *h* of the Lord

Handmaiden *See also* Handmaid

Lk. 1:48 he hath regarded the low estate of his *h*
Acts 2:18 on my servants and on my *h* I will pour

Hang

Gen. 40:22 but he *h* the chief baker: as Joseph had
Deut. 21:23 (Gal. 3:13) that is *h* is accursed of God
Josh. 10:26 Joshua smote. . slew them, and *h* them
2 Sam. 17:23 and put his household in order, and *h*
   18:10 said, Behold, I saw Absalom *h* in an oak
   21:9 they *h* them in the hill . . all seven together
Ezra 6:11 let him be *h* thereon; and let his house
Esth. 7:9 then the king said, *H* him thereon
   9:13 Haman's ten sons be *h* upon the gallows
Job 26:7 empty place. . *h* the earth upon nothing
Ps. 137:2 we *h* our harps upon the willows in the
Is. 22:24 *h* upon him all the glory of his father's
Mt. 18:6 (Mk. 9:42; Lk. 17:2) millstone. . *h* about
   22:40 on these two commandments *h* all the law
   27:5 and departed, and went and *h* himself
Acts 5:30 Jesus, whom ye slew and *h* on a tree
Heb. 12:12 lift up the hands which *h* down

Hannah 1 Sam. 1:2–2:21

Happen *See also* Befall, Chance

1 Sam. 6:9 smote us; it was a chance that *h* to us
   28:10 no punishment *h* to thee for this thing
Prov. 12:21 there shall no evil *h* to the just
Eccl. 2:14 perceived. . that one event *h* to them all
   8:14 *h* according to the work of the wicked
   9:11 but time and chance *h* to them all
Is. 41:22 show us what shall *h*: let them show the
Jer. 44:23 therefore this evil is *h* unto you
Mk. 10:32 tell them what things should *h* unto him
Lk. 24:14 talked. . of all these things which had *h*
Acts 3:10 amazement at that which had *h* unto him
Rom. 11:25 that blindness in part is *h* to Israel
1 Cor. 10:11 things *h* unto them for ensamples
Phil. 1:12 things which *h* unto me have fallen out
1 Pet. 4:12 as though some strange thing *h* unto you
2 Pet. 2:22 but it is *h* unto them according to the

Happy (Happier) *See also* Blessed, Glad, Joyful, Please

Gen. 30:13 Leah said, *H* am I, for the daughters
Deut. 33:29 *h* art thou, O Israel: who is like unto
1 Kgs. 10:8 (2 Chr. 9:7) *h* are thy men, *h* are these
Job 5:17 behold, *h* is the man whom God correcteth
Ps. 127:5 *h* is the man that hath his quiver full
   128:2 labor of thine hands: *h* shalt thou be
   144:15 *h* is that people, whose God is the LORD
   146:5 *h* is he that hath the God of Jacob for his
Prov. 3:13 *h* is the man that findeth wisdom
   14:21 he that hath mercy on the poor, *h* is he
   16:20 and whoso trusteth in the LORD, *h* is he
   28:14 *h* is the man that feareth always: but he
   29:18 but he that keepeth the law, *h* is he
Jer. 12:1 all they *h* that deal very treacherously?

Mal. 3:15 now we call the proud *h*; yea, they that
Jn. 13:17 ye know these things, *h* are ye if ye do
Acts 26:2 I think myself *h*, king Agrippa, because
Rom. 14:22 *h* is he that condemneth not himself in
1 Cor. 7:40 but she is *h* if she so abide, after my
Jas. 5:11 behold, we count them *h* which endure
1 Pet. 3:14 suffer for righteousness' sake, *h* are
   4:14 reproached for the name of Christ, *h* are ye

Haran (Charran)

Gen. 11:31 Canaan; and they came unto *H*, and dwelt
   27:43 arise, flee thou to Laban my brother to *H*
Acts 7:4 and dwelt in *C*: and from thence, when his

Hard (Harder)

Gen. 18:14 is any thing too *h* for the LORD?
   35:16 and Rachel travailed, and she had *h* labor
Ex. 1:14 made their lives bitter with *h* bondage
Deut. 1:17 the cause that is too *h* for you, bring
   17:8 arise a matter too *h* for thee in judgment
1 Kgs. 10:1 (2 Chr. 9:1) prove him with *h* questions
2 Kgs. 2:10 asked a *h* thing: nevertheless, if thou
Job 41:24 as *h* as a piece of the nether millstone
Ps. 60:3 thou hast showed thy people *h* things
   94:4 long shall they utter and speak *h* things?
Prov. 13:15 but the way of transgressors is *h*
   18:19 a brother offended is *h* to be won than a
Jer. 32:17 and there is nothing too *h* for thee
   32:27 all flesh: is there any thing too *h* for me?
Ezek. 3:5 of a strange speech and of a *h* language
   3:9 than flint have I made thy forehead
Dan. 5:12 showing of *h* sentences, and dissolving
Mt. 25:24 Lord, I knew thee that thou art a *h* man
Mk. 10:24 how *h* is it for them that trust in riches
Jn. 6:60 said, This is a *h* saying; who can hear it?
Acts 9:5 (26:14) *h* for thee to kick against the pricks
Heb. 5:11 many things to say, and *h* to be uttered
2 Pet. 3:16 some things *h* to be understood, which

Harden *See also* Rebel, Resist

Ex. 4:21 (7:3; 10:1; 14:4) I will *h* his heart
   7:13 (9:12; 10:20, 27; 11:10; 14:8) he *h* Pharaoh's
   14:17 I will *h* the hearts of the Egyptians
Deut. 15:7 thou shalt not *h* thine heart, nor shut
Josh. 11:20 it was of the LORD to *h* their hearts
1 Sam. 6:6 wherefore then do ye *h* your hearts
2 Kgs. 17:14 would not hear, but *h* their necks
Job 6:10 yea, I would *h* myself in sorrow: let him
   9:4 *h* himself against him, and hath prospered?
   39:16 she is *h* against her young ones, as though
Ps. 95:8 (Heb. 3:8, 15; 4:7) *h* not your heart, as in
Prov. 21:29 wicked man *h* his face: but as for the
   28:14 that *h* his heart shall fall into mischief
   29:1 that being often reproved *h* his neck, shall
Is. 63:17 thy ways, and *h* our heart from thy fear?
Jer. 7:26 nor inclined their ear, but *h* their neck
   19:15 because they have *h* their necks, that they
Dan. 5:20 his mind *h* in pride, he was deposed from
Mk. 6:52 of the loaves; for their heart was *h*
   8:17 why reason ye. . have ye your heart yet *h*?
Jn. 12:40 blinded their eyes, and *h* their heart
Acts 19:9 when divers were *h*, and believed not
Rom. 9:18 will have mercy, and whom he will he *h*
Heb. 3:13 be *h* through the deceitfulness of sin

Hardly

Gen. 16:6 when Sarai dealt *h* with her, she fled
Ex. 13:15 when Pharaoh would *h* let us go, that the
Mt. 19:23 (Mk. 10:23; Lk. 18:24) rich man . . *h* enter

Hardness

Mt. 19:8 (Mk. 10:5) because of the *h* of your hearts
Mk. 3:5 being grieved for the *h* of their hearts

Mk. 16:14 upbraided . . their unbelief and *h* of heart
Rom. 2:5 but, after thy *h* and impenitent heart
2 Tim. 2:3 endure *h*, as a good soldier of Jesus

Harlot *See also* Adulteress, Whore

Gen. 34:31 he deal with our sister as with a *h*?
38:15 Judah saw her, he thought her to be a *h*
Lev. 21:14 widow . . or a *h*, these shall he not take
Josh. 6:17 only Rahab the *h* shall live, she and
Prov. 7:10 met him a woman with the attire of a *h*
Is. 1:21 how is the faithful city become a *h*!
Jer. 2:20 and under every green tree . . playing the *h*
3:1 thou hast played the *h* with many lovers; yet
Ezek. 16:15 playedst the *h* because of thy renown
16:41 cause thee to cease from playing the *h*
23:5 Aholah played the *h* when she was mine
Hos. 2:5 their mother hath played the *h*: she that
4:15 thou, Israel, play the *h*, yet let not Judah
Mt. 21:31 publicans and the *h* go into the kingdom
Lk. 15:30 which hath devoured thy living with *h*
1 Cor. 6:15 and make them the members of a *h*?
Heb. 11:31 by faith the *h* Rahab perished not with
Jas. 2:25 was not Rahab the *h* justified by works
Rev. 17:5 BABYLON THE GREAT, THE MOTHER OF *H*

Harm *See also* Damage, Hurt, Mischief

Gen. 31:52 over this heap and this pillar . . for *h*
Lev. 5:16 he shall make amends for the *h* that he
Num. 35:23 was not his enemy, neither sought his *h*
1 Sam. 26:21 David; for I will no more do thee *h*
2 Kgs. 4:41 may eat. And there was no *h* in the pot
1 Chr. 16:22 (Ps. 105:15) and do my prophets no *h*
Prov. 3:30 strive not . . if he have done thee no *h*
Jer. 39:12 and look well to him, and do him no *h*
Acts 16:28 do thyself no *h*: for we are all here
27:21 Crete, and to have gained this *h* and loss
28:5 and he shook off the beast . . and felt no *h*
1 Pet. 3:13 who is he that will *h* you, if ye be

Harmless *See also* Innocent

Mt. 10:16 be ye . . wise as serpents, and *h* as doves
Phil. 2:15 ye may be blameless and *h*, the sons of
Heb. 7:26 a high priest became us, who is holy, *h*

Harness

Ex. 13:18 Israel went up *h* out of the land of Egypt
1 Kgs. 20:11 girdeth on his *h* boast himself as he
22:34 (2 Chr. 18:33) between the joints of the *h*

Harod Judg. 7:1–7

Harp

Gen. 4:21 father of all such as handle the *h* and
1 Sam. 16:16 seek . . who is a cunning player on a *h*
16:23 upon Saul, that David took a *h*, and played
2 Sam. 6:5 (1 Chr. 13:8) on *h*, and on psalteries
1 Chr. 25:3 Jeduthun, who prophesied with a *h*
Job 21:12 they take the timbrel and *h*, and rejoice
30:31 my *h* also is turned to mourning, and my
Ps. 33:2 praise the LORD with *h*: sing unto him
49:4 I will open my dark saying upon the *h*
57:8 (108:2) my glory; awake, psaltery and *h*
137:2 we hanged our *h* upon the willows in the
Is. 16:11 my bowels shall sound like a *h* for Moab
1 Cor. 14:7 or *h*, except they give a distinction
Rev. 5:8 having every one of them *h*, and golden
14:2 I heard the voice of harpers *h* with their *h*
15:2 on the sea of glass, having the *h* of God

Harrow

2 Sam. 12:31 (1 Chr. 20:3) saws, and under *h* of iron
Job 39:10 or will he *h* the valleys after thee?

Hart

Ps. 42:1 as the *h* panteth after the water brooks
Song 2:9 my beloved is like a roe or a young *h*
Is. 35:6 then shall the lame man leap as a *h*
Lam. 1:6 are become like *h* that find no pasture

Harvest *See also* Firstfruit, Fruit

Gen. 8:22 seedtime and *h*, and cold and heat
45:6 there shall neither be earing nor *h*
Ex. 23:16 feast of *h*, the firstfruits of thy labors
Lev. 23:10 reap the *h* thereof, then ye shall bring
Josh. 3:15 Jordan overfloweth . . all the time of *h*
Ruth 1:22 Bethlehem in the beginning of barley *h*
1 Sam. 6:13 Beth-shemesh were reaping their wheat *h*
12:17 is it not wheat *h* today? I will call unto
Job 5:5 whose *h* the hungry eateth up, and taketh
Prov. 6:8 summer, and gathereth her food in the *h*
10:5 sleepeth in *h* is a son that causeth shame
25:13 as the cold of snow in the time of *h*, so
26:1 as rain in *h*, so honor is not seemly for a
Is. 9:3 joy before thee according to the joy in *h*
16:9 for the shouting . . for thy *h* is fallen
17:11 the *h* shall be a heap in the day of grief
18:4 and like a cloud of dew in the heat of *h*
Jer. 5:17 they shall eat up thine *h* and thy bread
5:24 reserveth unto us . . appointed weeks of the *h*
8:20 the *h* is past, the summer is ended, and we
51:33 little while . . the time of her *h* shall come
Joel 3:13 (Rev. 14:15) the sickle, for the *h* is ripe
Mt. 9:37 (Lk. 10:2) the *h* truly is plenteous
9:38 (Lk. 10:2) pray ye . . the Lord of the *h*
13:30 until the *h*: and in the time of *h* I will
13:39 the devil; the *h* is the end of the world
Mk. 4:29 in the sickle, because the *h* is come
Jn. 4:35 are yet four months, and then cometh *h*?
Rev. 14:15 to reap; for the *h* of the earth is ripe

Haste

Gen. 19:22 *h* thee, escape thither; for I cannot do
Ex. 5:13 taskmasters *h* them, saying, Fulfil your
10:16 Pharaoh called for Moses and Aaron in *h*
12:11 eat it in *h*: it is the LORD's passover
1 Sam. 17:48 David *h* . . to meet the Philistine
21:8 because the king's business required *h*
Job 9:26 ships: as the eagle that *h* to the prey
31:5 with vanity, or if my foot hath *h* to deceit
40:23 behold, he drinketh up a river, and *h* not
Ps. 22:19 O LORD: O my strength, *h* thee to help me
31:22 I said in my *h*, I am cut off from before
38:22 make *h* to help me, O Lord my salvation
40:13 (70:1) deliver me: O LORD, make *h* to help
116:11 I said in my *h*, All men are liars
141:1 LORD, I cry unto thee: make *h* unto me
Prov. 19:2 and he that *h* with his feet sinneth
28:20 maketh *h* to be rich shall not be innocent
28:22 he that *h* to be rich hath an evil eye
Eccl. 1:5 the sun . . *h* to his place where he arose
Is. 52:12 shall not go out with *h*, nor go by flight
Zeph. 1:14 day of the LORD is near . . and *h* greatly
Lk. 2:16 came with *h*, and found Mary and Joseph
19:5 Zaccheus, make *h*, and come down; for today
Acts 20:16 for he . . to be at Jerusalem the day of
2 Pet. 3:12 *h* unto the coming of the day of God

Hasten

1 Kgs. 22:9 an officer, and said, *H* hither Micaiah
Ps. 16:4 be multiplied that *h* after another god
55:8 I would *h* my escape from the windy storm
Eccl. 2:25 or who else can *h* hereunto, more than I?
Is. 60:22 I the LORD will *h* it in his time
Jer. 1:12 for I will *h* my word to perform it

Hastily

Gen. 41:14 they brought him *h* out of the dungeon
1 Sam. 4:14 and the man came in *h*, and told Eli
Prov. 20:21 an inheritance may be gotten *h* at the
25:8 go not forth *h* to strive, lest thou know
Jn. 11:31 Mary, that she rose up *h* and went out

Hasty

Prov. 14:29 he that is *h* of spirit exalteth folly
21:5 but of every one that is *h* only to want
29:20 seest thou a man that is *h* in his words?
Eccl. 5:2 let not thine heart be *h* to utter any
7:9 be not *h* in thy spirit to be angry
Dan. 2:15 why is the decree so *h* from the king?

Hate *See also* Abhor, Contemn, Despise, Detest, Loathe, Scorn

Gen. 24:60 possess the gate of those which *h* them
27:41 and Esau *h* Jacob because of the blessing
37:4 him more than all his brethren, they *h* him
Ex. 20:5 (Deut. 5:9) generation of them that *h* me
23:5 thou see the ass of him that *h* thee lying
Lev. 19:17 shalt not *h* thy brother in thine heart
26:17 they that *h* you shall reign over you
Num. 10:35 (Ps. 68:1) let them that *h* thee flee before
Deut. 16:22 any image; which the LORD thy God *h*
19:11 if any man *h* his neighbor, and lie in wait
32:41 enemies, and will reward them that *h* me
2 Sam. 13:15 then Amnon *h* her exceedingly; so that
13:22 Absalom *h* Amnon, because he had forced
22:41 (Ps. 18:40) might destroy them that *h* me
1 Kgs. 22:8 (2 Chr. 18:7) but I *h* him; for he doth not
2 Chr. 19:2 and love them that *h* the LORD?
Job 8:22 that *h* thee shall be clothed with shame
16:9 he teareth me in his wrath, who *h* me
Ps. 5:5 thy sight: thou *h* all workers of iniquity
26:5 I have *h* the congregation of evildoers
34:21 they that *h* the righteous shall be desolate
35:19 (69:4; Jn. 15:25) that *h* me without a cause
45:7 (Heb. 1:9) righteousness, and *h* wickedness
55:3 iniquity upon me, and in wrath they *h* me
83:2 they that *h* thee have lifted up the head
97:10 that love the LORD, *h* evil: he preserveth
101:3 I *h* the work of them that turn aside
119:104 I get understanding . . I *h* every false way
119:113 I *h* vain thoughts: but thy law do I love
119:163 I *h* and abhor lying: but thy law do I love
139:21 do not I *h* them, O LORD, that *h* thee?
139:22 I *h* them with perfect hatred: I count
Prov. 1:22 their scorning, and fools *h* knowledge?
1:29 that they *h* knowledge, and did not choose
6:16 six things doth the LORD *h*; yea, seven are
8:13 fear of the LORD is to *h* evil: pride, and
13:5 righteous man *h* lying: but a wicked man is
13:24 he that spareth his rod *h* his son: but he
14:20 the poor is *h* even of his own neighbor
15:10 and he that *h* reproof shall die
19:7 all the brethren of the poor do *h* him
28:16 that *h* covetousness shall prolong his days
Eccl. 2:17 therefore I *h* life; because the work
3:8 time to love, and a time to *h*; a time of war
Is. 1:14 moons and your appointed feasts my soul *h*
61:8 I *h* robbery for burnt offering; and I will
Jer. 44:4 do not this abominable thing that I *h*
Amos 5:15 *h* the evil, and love the good
5:21 I *h*, I despise your feast days, and I will
Mic. 3:2 who *h* the good, and love the evil
Zech. 8:17 for all these are things that I *h*
Mal. 1:2, 3 (Rom. 9:13) I loved Jacob, and I *h* Esau
2:16 God of Israel, saith that he *h* putting away

Mt. 5:44 (Lk. 6:27) do good to them that *h* you
6:24 (Lk. 16:13) will *h* the one, and love. the other
10:22 (24:9; Mk. 13:13; Lk. 21:17) shall be *h* of all
24:10 betray. . another, and shall *h* one another
Lk. 6:22 blessed are ye, when men shall *h* you
14:26 any man come to me, and *h* not his father
Jn. 3:20 for every one that doeth evil *h* the light
7:7 the world cannot *h* you; but me it *h*, because
12:25 *h* his life in this world shall keep it
15:18 the world *h* you . . it *h* me before it *h* you
15:23 he that *h* me *h* my Father also
15:24 both seen and *h* both me and my Father
17:14 world hath *h* them, because they are not of
Rom. 7:15 that do I not; but what I *h*, that do I
Eph. 5:29 for no man ever yet *h* his own flesh
1 Jn. 2:9 (2:11) and *h* his brother, is in darkness
3:13 marvel not, my brethren, if the world *h* you
3:15 whosoever *h* his brother is a murderer
4:20 I love God, and *h* his brother, he is a liar
Jude 23 *h* even the garment spotted by the flesh
Rev. 2:6 (2:15) deeds of the Nicolaitans. . I also *h*

Hateful

Ps. 36:2 eyes, until his iniquity be found to be *h*
Tit. 3:3 living in malice and envy, *h*, and hating
Rev. 18:2 and a cage of every unclean and *h* bird

Hatefully

Ezek. 23:29 they shall deal with thee *h*, and shall

Hater

Ps. 81:15 the *h* of the LORD should have submitted
Rom. 1:30 backbiters, *h* of God, despiteful, proud

Hatred

Num. 35:20 if he thrust him of *h*, or hurl at him
Ps. 25:19 are many; and they hate me with cruel *h*
Prov. 15:17 than a stalled ox and *h* therewith
Ezek. 25:15 vengeance. . to destroy it for the old *h*
35:5 because thou hast had a perpetual *h*
Hos. 9:7 multitude of thine iniquity, and the great *h*

Haughtiness *See also* Arrogancy, Conceit, Pride

Is. 2:11 and the *h* of men shall be bowed down
13:11 and will lay low the *h* of the terrible
16:6 (Jer. 48:29) the pride of Moab. . even of his *h*

Haughty *See also* Proud

2 Sam. 22:28 thine eyes are upon the *h*, that thou
Ps. 131:1 my heart is not *h*, nor mine eyes lofty
Prov. 16:18 and a *h* spirit before a fall
18:12 before destruction the heart of man is *h*
21:24 proud and *h* scorner is his name
Is. 3:16 because the daughters of Zion are *h*
10:33 be hewn down, and the *h* shall be humbled
24:4 the *h* people of the earth do languish
Ezek. 16:50 they were *h*, and committed abomination
Zeph. 3:11 thou shalt no more be *h* because of my

Haven

Gen. 49:13 *h* of the sea; and he shall be for a *h*
Ps. 107:30 he bringeth them unto their desired *h*
Acts 27:8 unto a place which is called the Fair *H*

Havoc

Acts 8:3 Saul, he made *h* of the church, entering

Hawk

Lev. 11:16 (Deut. 14:15) and the *h* after his kind
Job 39:26 doth the *h* fly by thy wisdom

Hay

Prov. 27:25 the *h* appeareth, and the tender grass
Is. 15:6 the *h* is withered away, the grass faileth

Hazael 1 Kgs. 19:15; 2 Kgs. 8:8–13:25

Hazard

Acts 15:26 *h* their lives for the name of our Lord

Hazor Josh. 11:10–13

Head

Gen. 2:10 it was parted, and became into four *h*
3:15 shall bruise thy *h*, and thou shalt bruise
Ex. 18:25 and made them *h* over the people, rulers
29:10 (Lev. 8:14) hands upon the *h* of the bullock
Lev. 10:6 uncover not your *h*, neither rend your
Num. 6:5 (Judg. 13:5) shall no razor come upon his *h*
25:4 take all the *h* of the people, and hang them
Josh. 2:19 street, his blood shall be upon his *h*
Judg. 11:9 and Jephthah said. . shall I be your *h*?
1 Sam. 17:51 and slew him, and cut off his *h*
2 Sam. 4:8 brought the *h* of Ish-bosheth unto David
20:21 his *h* shall be thrown to thee over the wall
2 Kgs. 4:19 he said unto his father, My *h*, my *h*!
6:5 the axe *h* fell into the water: and he cried
19:21 (Is. 37:22) hath shaken her *h* at thee
1 Chr. 10:10 fastened his *h* in the temple of Dagon
Esth. 6:8 the crown royal which is set upon his *h*
Ps. 7:16 his mischief shall return upon his own *h*
23:5 thou anointest my *h* with oil; my cup runneth
24:7 (24:9) lift up your *h*, O ye gates
27:6 shall mine *h* be lifted up above mine enemies
38:4 mine iniquities are gone over mine *h*
60:7 (108:8) Ephraim. . is the strength of mine *h*
68:21 but God shall wound the *h* of his enemies
109:25 they looked upon me they shook their *h*
110:6 he shall wound the *h* over many countries
110:7 therefore shall he lift up the *h*
118:22 (Mt. 21:42; Mk. 12:10; Lk. 20:17; Acts 4:11;
1 Pet. 2:7) builders refused is become the *h* stone
140:7 hast covered my *h* in the day of battle
Prov. 10:6 blessings are upon the *h* of the just
16:31 the hoary *h* is a crown of glory, if it be
20:29 and the beauty of old men is the gray *h*
25:22 (Rom. 12:20) heap coals of fire upon his *h*
Eccl. 2:14 the wise man's eyes are in his *h*
Song 7:5 thine *h* upon thee is like Carmel
Is. 1:5 whole *h* is sick, and the whole heart faint
9:14 LORD will cut off from Israel *h* and tail
35:10 songs and everlasting joy upon their *h*
59:17 helmet of salvation upon his *h*; and he put
Jer. 9:1 oh that my *h* were waters, and mine eyes a
14:3 ashamed and confounded, and covered their *h*
18:16 thereby shall be astonished, and wag his *h*
Ezek. 9:10 will recompense their way upon their *h*
33:4 him away, his blood shall be upon his own *h*
Dan. 2:38 over them all. Thou art this *h* of gold
7:6 the beast had also four *h*; and dominion was
Amos 8:10 baldness upon every *h*; and I will make
Mt. 5:36 neither shalt thou swear by thy *h*, because
8:20 (Lk. 9:58) Son. . hath not where to lay his *h*
10:30 (Lk. 12:7) hairs of your *h* are all numbered
14:8 (Mk. 6:25) give me here John Baptist's *h* in a
27:29 (Mk. 15:17; Jn. 19:2) they put it upon his *h*
27:39 (Mk. 15:29) reviled him, wagging their *h*
Lk. 7:38 and did wipe them with the hairs of her *h*
7:46 my *h* with oil thou didst not anoint
21:18 there shall not a hair of your *h* perish
21:28 then look up, and lift up your *h*; for your
Jn. 13:9 my feet only, but also my hands and my *h*
Rom. 12:20 thou shalt heap coals of fire on his *h*
1 Cor. 11:3 *h* of every man is Christ; and the *h* of

1 Cor. 11:4 having his *h* covered, dishonoreth his *h*
11:10 have power on her *h* because of the angels
Eph. 1:22 be the *h* over all things to the church
4:15 in all things, which is the *h*, even Christ
5:23 *h* of the wife, even as Christ is the *h* of
Col. 1:18 he is the *h* of the body, the church
2:10 is the *h* of all principality and power
2:19 not holding the *H*, from which all the body
Rev. 4:4 and they had on their *h* crowns of gold
9:7 on their *h* were as it were crowns like gold
12:3 red dragon, having seven *h* and ten horns
17:9 seven *h* are seven mountains, on which
19:12 and on his *h* were many crowns; and he had

Heal *See also* Cure, Restore, Save

Gen. 20:17 and God *h* Abimelech, and his wife
Ex. 15:26 for I am the LORD that *h* thee
Num. 12:13 Moses cried unto the LORD. . *H* her
Deut. 32:39 I wound, and I *h*: neither is there any
2 Kgs. 2:22 so the waters were *h* unto this day
8:29 (2 Chr. 22:6) went back to be *h* in Jezreel
20:5 I have seen thy tears. . I will *h* thee
2 Chr. 7:14 forgive their sin, and will *h* their land
30:20 LORD hearkened to Hezekiah. . *h* the people
Ps. 6:2 O LORD, *h* me; for my bones are vexed
30:2 God, I cried unto thee, and thou hast *h* me
41:4 *h* my soul; for I have sinned against thee
103:3 thine iniquities; who *h* all thy diseases
107:20 sent his word, and *h* them, and delivered
147:3 he the *h* the broken in heart, and bindeth up
Eccl. 3:3 a time to kill, and a time to *h*
Is. 6:10 (Mt. 13:15; Jn. 12:40; Acts 28:27) understand with their heart, and convert, and be *h*
19:22 shall smite Egypt: he shall smite and *h* it
53:5 (1 Pet. 2:24) and with his stripes we are *h*
57:19 is near, saith the LORD; and I will *h* him
Jer. 3:22 children, and I will *h* your backslidings
6:14 (8:11) have *h* also the hurt of the daughter
17:14 *h* me, O LORD, and I shall be *h*; save me
30:17 restore health unto thee, and I will *h* thee
51:9 we would have *h* Babylon, but she is not *h*
Ezek. 30:21 lo, it shall not be bound up to be *h*
47:8 into the sea, the waters shall be *h*
Hos. 7:1 I would have *h* Israel, then the iniquity
11:3 their arms; but they knew not that I *h* them
14:4 will *h* their backsliding, I will love them
Mt. 4:23 (9:35) *h* all manner of sickness and all
8:8 (Lk. 7:7) word only, and my servant shall be *h*
10:1 (Mk. 3:15) power. . to *h* all manner of sickness
10:8 (Lk. 10:9) *h* the sick, cleanse the lepers
12:10 (Lk. 14:3) lawful to *h* on the sabbath days?
12:15 (14:14) multitudes followed him. . he *h* them
12:22 he *h* them, insomuch that the blind and dumb
15:30 cast them down at Jesus' feet; and he *h* them
Mk. 1:34 he *h* many that were sick of divers diseases
3:2 (Lk. 6:7) would *h* him on the sabbath day
5:23 lay thy hands on her, that she may be *h*
Lk. 4:18 he hath sent me to *h* the broken-hearted
4:23 unto me this proverb, Physician, *h* thyself
5:17 the power of the Lord was present to *h* them
6:17 to hear him, and to be *h* of their diseases
8:2 women, which had been *h* of evil spirits and
8:36 he that was possessed of the devils was *h*
13:14 because that Jesus had *h* on the sabbath day
22:51 he touched his ear, and *h* him
Jn. 4:47 besought him. . come down, and *h* his son
5:13 was *h* wist not who it was: for Jesus
Acts 3:11 lame man which was *h* held Peter and John
4:14 beholding the man which was *h* standing with
4:30 by stretching forth thine hand to *h*
5:16 vexed with unclean spirits: and they were *h*
8:7 with palsies, and that were lame, were *h*
10:38 *h* all that were oppressed of the devil

Acts 14:9 and perceiving that he had faith to be *h*
   28:8 prayed, and laid his hands on him, and *h*
   28:9 had diseases in the island, came, and were *h*
Heb. 12:13 out of the way; but let it rather be *h*
Jas. 5:16 pray one for another, that ye may be *h*
1 Pet. 2:24 by whose stripes ye were *h*
Rev. 13:12 first beast, whose deadly wound was *h*

Healing *See also* Heal

Jer. 14:19 smitten us, and there is no *h* for us?
   30:13 be bound up: thou hast no *h* medicines
Nah. 3:19 there is no *h* of thy bruise; thy wound
Mal. 4:2 Sun of righteousness arise with *h* in his
Lk. 9:11 and healed them that had need of *h*
Acts 4:22 on whom this miracle of *h* was showed
1 Cor. 12:9 Spirit; to another the gifts of *h* by
   12:28 after that miracles, then gifts of *h*
Rev. 22:2 the leaves. . were for the *h* of the nations

Health

Gen. 43:28 thy servant our father is in good *h*
Ps. 42:11 (43:5) who is the *h* of my countenance
   67:2 upon earth, thy saving *h* among all nations
Prov. 3:8 *h* to thy navel, and marrow to thy bones
   4:22 that find them, and *h* to all their flesh
   12:18 a sword: but the tongue of the wise is *h*
   13:17 mischief: but a faithful ambassador is *h*
   16:24 sweet to the soul, and *h* to the bones
Is. 58:8 and thine *h* shall spring forth speedily
Jer. 8:15 and for a time of *h*, and behold trouble!
   8:22 *h* of the daughter of my people recovered?
   30:17 will restore *h* unto thee, and I will heal
Acts 27:34 take some meat; for this is for your *h*
3 Jn. 2 thou mayest prosper and be in *h*, even as

Heap

Gen. 31:46 a *h*: and they did eat there upon the *h*
   31:52 this *h* be witness. . this pillar be witness
Ex. 8:14 they gathered them together upon a *h*
   15:8 floods stood upright as a *h*, and the depths
Deut. 13:16 be a *h* for ever; it shall not be built
   32:23 I will *h* mischiefs upon them; I will spend
Josh. 3:13 and they shall stand upon a *h*
   7:26 they raised over him a great *h* of stones
Judg. 15:16 with the jawbone of an ass, *h* upon *h*
2 Kgs. 19:25 (Is. 37:26) fenced cities into. . *h*
Neh. 4:2 stones out of the *h* of the rubbish
Job 16:4 I could *h* up words against you, and shake
   27:16 though he *h* up silver as the dust
   36:13 hypocrites in heart *h* up wrath: they cry
Ps. 33:7 the waters of the sea together as a *h*
   39:6 he *h* up riches, and knoweth not who shall
   79:1 they defiled; they have laid Jerusalem on *h*
Prov. 25:22 (Rom. 12:20) shalt *h* coals of fire
Is. 17:11 harvest shall be a *h* in the day of grief
   25:2 of a city a *h*; of a defensed city a ruin
Jer. 9:11 make Jerusalem *h*, and a den of dragons
   26:18 (Mic. 3:12) and Jerusalem shall become *h*
   31:21 set thee up waymarks, make thee high *h*
   51:37 Babylon shall become *h*, a dwelling place
Ezek. 24:10 *h* on wood, kindle the fire, consume
Hos. 12:11 their altars are as *h* in the furrows of
Mic. 1:6 I will make Samaria as a *h* of the field
Hab. 1:10 for they shall *h* dust, and take it
   2:5 all nations, and *h* unto him all people
Rom. 12:20 thou shalt *h* coals of fire on his head
2 Tim. 4:3 shall they *h* to themselves teachers
Jas. 5:3 *h* treasure together for the last days

Hear (Heard) *See also* Hearken

Gen. 3:8 they *h* the voice of the LORD God walking
   16:11 because the LORD hath *h* thy affliction
   21:17 God *h* the voice of the lad; and the angel

Gen. 45:2 the Egyptians and the house of Pharaoh *h*
Ex. 2:24 God *h* their groaning, and God remembered
   3:7 (Acts 7:34) *h* their cry by reason of their
   6:12 how then shall Pharaoh *h* me, who am of
Num. 11:1 the LORD *h* it; and his anger was kindled
Deut. 4:10 I will make them *h* my words, that they
   4:12 *h*. . but saw no similitude; only ye *h* a voice
   4:33 did ever people *h* the voice of God. . and live?
   6:4 *h*, O Israel: The LORD our God is one LORD
   30:17 thou wilt not *h*, but shalt be drawn away
   31:12 that they may *h*, and that they may learn
Josh. 6:5 when ye *h* the sound of the trumpet
   24:27 it hath *h* all the words of the LORD which
1 Sam. 3:9 speak, LORD; for thy servant *h*
   7:9 Samuel cried. . for Israel; and the LORD *h* him
   15:14 and the lowing of the oxen which I *h*?
2 Sam. 5:24 (1 Chr. 14:15) thou *h* the sound of a going
   15:3 no man deputed of the king to *h* thee
   22:45 (Ps. 18:44) as soon as they *h*, they shall
1 Kgs. 6:7 axe nor any tool of iron *h* in the house
   8:30 (2 Chr. 6:21) *h* thou in heaven. . when thou *h*
   8:42 they shall *h* of thy great name, and of thy
   9:3 (2 Chr. 7:12) I have *h* thy prayer and thy
   18:26 O Baal, *h* us. But there was no voice
   18:37 *h* me, O LORD, *h* me, that this people may
2 Kgs. 19:16 (Is. 37:17) bow down thine ear, and *h*
   19:25 (Is. 37:26) hast thou not *h* long ago how I
2 Chr. 7:14 will I *h* from heaven, and will forgive
Ezra 3:13 loud shout, and the noise was *h* afar off
Neh. 1:6 thou mayest *h* the prayer of thy servant
   12:43 the joy of Jerusalem was *h* even afar off
Job 15:8 hast thou *h* the secret of God? and dost
   16:2 *h* many such things: miserable comforters
   19:7 behold, I cry out of wrong, but I am not *h*
   26:14 but how little a portion is *h* of him?
   31:35 oh that one would *h* me! behold, my desire
   42:5 have *h* of thee by the hearing of the ear
Ps. 4:1 *h* me when I call, O God of my righteousness
   4:3 the LORD will *h* when I call unto him
   6:9 LORD hath *h* my supplication; the LORD will
   10:17 LORD, thou hast *h* the desire of the humble
   13:3 consider and *h* me, O LORD my God: lighten
   17:1 *h* the right, O LORD, attend unto my cry
   17:6 have called upon thee, for thou wilt *h* me
   20:1 LORD *h* thee in the day of trouble; the name
   27:7 *h*, O LORD, when I cry with my voice
   34:4 sought the LORD, and he *h* me, and delivered
   34:17 the LORD *h*, and delivereth them out of all
   49:1 *h* this, all ye people; give ear, all ye
   51:8 make me to *h* joy and gladness; that the
   59:7 in their lips: for who, say they, doth *h*?
   61:1 *h* my cry, O God; attend unto my prayer
   61:5 for thou, O God, hast *h* my vows: thou hast
   65:2 O thou that *h* prayer, unto thee shall all
   66:18 iniquity in my heart, the Lord will not *h*
   66:19 but verily God hath *h* me; he hath attended
   85:8 I will *h* what God the LORD will speak
   94:9 he that planted the ear, shall he not *h*?
   97:8 Zion *h*, and was glad; and. . Judah rejoiced
   102:20 the groaning of the prisoner; to loose
   116:1 he hath *h* my voice and my supplications
   118:21 I will praise thee: for thou hast *h* me
   119:145 cried with my whole heart; *h* me, O LORD
   143:7 *h* me speedily, O LORD; my spirit faileth
Prov. 1:8 my son, *h* the instruction of thy father
   8:33 *h* instruction, and be wise. . refuse it not
   13:8 are his riches: but the poor *h* not rebuke
   15:29 but he *h* the prayer of the righteous
   18:13 he that answereth a matter before he *h* it
   22:17 thine ear, and *h* the words of the wise
Eccl. 5:1 ready to *h*, than to give the sacrifice
   7:5 better to *h* the rebuke of the wise, than for
   9:17 words of wise men are *h* in quiet more than

Eccl. 12:13 *h* the conclusion of the whole matter
Song 8:13 hearken to thy voice: cause me to *h* it
Is. 1:2 *h*, O heavens, and give ear, O earth
  1:15 when ye make many prayers, I will not *h*
  6:9 (Mt. 13:14; Mk. 4:12; Lk. 8:10; Acts 28:26) *h*
    ye indeed, but understand not; and see ye indeed
  33:13 *h*, ye that are far off, what I have done
  34:1 come near, ye nations, to *h*; and hearken
  40:21 have ye not known? have ye not *h*? hath it
  40:28 hast thou not *h*, that the everlasting God
  52:15 (Rom. 15:21) had not *h* shall they consider
  55:3 come unto me: *h*, and your soul shall live
  64:4 (1 Cor. 2:9) not *h*, nor perceived by the ear
  65:24 and while they are yet speaking, I will *h*
  66:8 who hath *h* such a thing? who hath seen such
Jer. 6:10 speak, and give warning, that they may *h*?
  7:13 speaking, but ye *h* not; and I called you
  7:16 intercession to me: for I will not *h* thee
  8:6 I hearkened and *h*, but they spake not aright
  14:12 when they fast, I will not *h* their cry
  18:2 and there I will cause thee to *h* my words
  20:10 *h* the defaming of many, fear on every side
  31:18 I have surely *h* Ephraim bemoaning himself
Ezek. 3:17 (33:7) *h* the word at my mouth, and give
  3:27 that *h*, let him *h*; and he that forbeareth
  33:5 he *h* the sound of the trumpet, and took not
  33:31 *h* thy words, but they will not do them
Dan. 12:8 I *h*, but I understood not: then said I
Hos. 2:21 I will *h*, saith the LORD, I will *h* the
Jon. 2:2 belly of hell cried I . . thou *h* my voice
Mic. 7:7 I will wait for the God . . my God will *h* me
Hab. 3:16 I *h*, my belly trembled; my lips quivered
Zech. 7:13 not *h*; so they cried, and I would not *h*
  8:23 for we have *h* that God is with you
Mt. 6:7 they think that they shall be *h* for their
  11:4 (Lk. 7:22) show John . . things which ye do *h*
  13:9 (13:43; Mk. 4:9; Lk. 8:8) ears to *h*, let him *h*
  13:17 (Lk. 10:24) and to *h* those things which ye *h*
  14:1 (Mk. 6:14; Lk. 9:7) *h* of the fame of Jesus
  17:5 (Mk. 9:7; Lk. 9:35) beloved Son . . *h* ye him
  18:16 but if he will not *h* thee, then take with
  24:6 (Mk. 13:7; Lk. 21:9) ye shall *h* of wars and
  26:65 (Mk. 14:64; Lk. 22:71) have *h* his blasphemy
Mk. 3:21 when his friends *h* of it, they went out
  4:24 and unto you that *h* shall more be given
  12:37 and the common people *h* him gladly
  16:11 when they had *h* that he was alive, and had
Lk. 1:13 fear not, Zacharias: for thy prayer is *h*
  2:46 the doctors, both *h* them, and asking them
  5:1 people pressed upon him to *h* the word of God
  9:9 but who is this, of whom I *h* such things?
  10:16 he that *h* you *h* me; and he that despiseth
  12:3 spoken in darkness shall be *h* in the light
  15:25 nigh to the house, he *h* music and dancing
  16:31 if they *h* not Moses and the prophets
  18:36 the multitude pass by, he asked what it
Jn. 3:8 listeth, and thou *h* the sound thereof
  4:42 for we have *h* him ourselves, and know that
  5:25 dead shall *h* the voice of the Son of God
  5:37 neither *h* his voice at any time, nor seen
  6:60 this is a hard saying; who can *h* it?
  7:51 doth our law judge any man, before it *h* him
  8:6 wrote on the ground, as though he *h* them not
  8:47 of God *h* God's words: ye therefore *h* . . not
  9:31 God *h* not sinners . . doeth his will, him he *h*
  10:3 porter openeth; and the sheep *h* his voice
  10:27 my sheep *h* my voice, and I know them
  11:41 Father, I thank thee that thou hast *h* me
  11:42 I knew that thou *h* me always: but because
  12:47 if any man *h* my words, and believe not
  18:37 every one that is of the truth *h* my voice
Acts 2:8 and how *h* we every man in our own tongue
  2:37 *h* this, they were pricked in their heart

Acts 3:22 (7:37) him shall ye *h* in all things
  4:4 which *h* the word believed; and the number of
  4:20 speak the things which we have seen and *h*
  8:30 and *h* him read the prophet Esaias
  9:7 speechless, *h* a voice, but seeing no man
  10:44 Holy Ghost fell on all them which *h*
  13:44 whole city together to *h* the word of God
  14:14 when the apostles, Barnabas and Paul, *h* of
  16:25 sang praises unto God: and the prisoners *h*
  17:21 but either to tell or to *h* some new thing
  17:32 when they *h* of the resurrection of the dead
  19:2 not . . *h* whether there be any Holy Ghost
  22:15 unto all men of what thou hast seen and *h*
  24:22 and when Felix *h* these things . . he deferred
Rom. 10:14 not *h*? and how shall they *h* without a
  10:18 but I say, Have they not *h*? Yes verily
  15:21 and they that have not *h* shall understand
1 Cor. 2:9 written, Eye hath not seen, nor ear *h*
  11:18 I *h* that there be divisions among you
2 Cor. 12:4 into paradise, and *h* unspeakable words
Eph. 1:13 also trusted, after that ye *h* the word
  4:21 if so be that ye have *h* him, and have been
Phil. 4:9 have both learned, and received, and *h*
1 Tim. 4:16 both save thyself, and them that *h*
2 Tim. 2:2 the things that thou hast *h* of me among
Phlm. 5 of thy love and faith, which thou hast
Heb. 2:1 heed to the things which we have *h*, lest
  2:3 and was confirmed unto us by them that *h* him
  4:2 not being mixed with faith in them that *h* it
  5:7 offered up prayers . . was *h* in that he feared
Jas. 1:19 every man be swift to *h*, slow to speak
2 Pet. 1:18 this voice which came from heaven we *h*
1 Jn. 1:1 which we have *h*, which we have seen with
  4:5 speak they of the world, and the world *h* them
  4:6 that knoweth God *h* us . . not of God *h* not us
  5:14 ask any thing according to his will, he *h* us
Rev. 1:3 he that readeth, and they that *h* the words
  2:7 (2:11, 17, 29; 3:6, 13, 22) hath an ear, let him *h*
  3:3 how thou hast received and *h*, and hold fast
  3:20 if any man *h* my voice, and open the door
  10:4 about to write: and I *h* a voice from heaven
  13:9 if any man have an ear, let him *h*
  14:2 I *h* the voice of harpers harping with their
  18:4 I *h* another voice from heaven, saying, Come
  22:8 *h* them. And when I had *h* and seen, I fell

Hearer

Rom. 2:13 not the *h* of the law are just before God
Eph. 4:29 that it may minister grace unto the *h*
2 Tim. 2:14 profit, but to the subverting of the *h*
Jas. 1:22 be ye doers of the word, and not *h* only
  1:25 not a forgetful *h*, but a doer of the work

Hearing *See also* Hear

Deut. 31:11 this law before all Israel in their *h*
Eccl. 1:8 with seeing, nor the ear filled with *h*
Is. 11:3 neither reprove after the *h* of his ears
  21:3 bowed down at the *h* of it; I was dismayed
  33:15 that stoppeth his ears from *h* of blood
Amos 8:11 a famine . . of *h* the words of the LORD
Mt. 13:15 heart is waxed gross . . ears are dull of *h*
Acts 25:21 to be reserved unto the *h* of Augustus
Rom. 10:17 faith cometh by *h*, and *h* by the word of
1 Cor. 12:17 where were the *h*? If the whole were *h*
Gal. 3:2 works of the law, or by the *h* of faith?
Heb. 5:11 hard . . uttered, seeing ye are dull of *h*
2 Pet. 2:8 in seeing and *h*, vexed his righteous soul

Hearken *See also* Attend, Hear, Obey

Gen. 4:23 ye wives of Lamech, *h* unto my speech
  23:16 Abraham *h* unto Ephron; and . . weighed
Ex. 6:30 Moses said . . how shall Pharaoh *h* unto me?
Deut. 4:1 *h*, O Israel, unto the statutes and unto

Deut. 7:12 if ye *h* to these judgments, and keep and
  15:5 thou carefully *h* unto the voice of the LORD
  17:12 do presumptuously, and will not *h* unto the
  18:14 these nations . . *h* unto observers of times
  18:15 Prophet . . like unto me; unto him ye shall *h*
  30:10 if thou shalt *h* unto the voice of the LORD
Josh. 1:17 we *h* unto Moses . . so will we *h* unto thee
1 Sam. 15:22 and to *h* than the fat of rams
1 Kgs. 8:30 (2 Chr. 6:21) *h* thou to the supplication
  22:28 and he said, *H*, O people, every one of you
2 Chr. 33:10 to his people: but they would not *h*
Neh. 13:27 shall we then *h* unto you to do . . evil
Job 34:34 tell me, and let a wise man *h* unto me
Ps. 58:5 which will not *h* to the voice of charmers
  81:8 unto thee: O Israel, if thou wilt *h* unto me
  81:11 but my people would not *h* to my voice
  103:20 his angels . . *h* unto the voice of his word
Prov. 1:33 but whoso *h* unto me shall dwell safely
  12:15 but he that *h* unto counsel is wise
  23:22 *h* unto thy father . . despise not thy mother
  29:12 if a ruler *h* to lies, all his servants are
Is. 21:7 a chariot of camels; and he *h* diligently
  51:1 *h* to me, ye that follow after righteousness
  55:2 *h* diligently unto me, and eat ye that which
Jer. 7:24 but they *h* not, nor inclined their ear
  17:24 if ye diligently *h* unto me, saith the LORD
  26:3 if so be they will *h*, and turn every man
Ezek. 3:6 to them, they would have *h* unto thee
Dan. 9:19 O Lord, hear; O Lord, forgive; O Lord, *h*
Mic. 1:2 hear, all ye people; *h*, O earth, and all
Mk. 7:14 *h* unto me every one of you, and understand
Acts 2:14 this known unto you, and *h* to my words
  4:19 to *h* unto you more than unto God, judge ye
  7:2 men, brethren, and fathers, *h*; The God of
  12:13 and as Peter knocked . . a damsel came to *h*

Heart *See also* Conscience, Love, Mind, Soul

Gen. 6:5 thoughts of his *h* was only evil continually
  45:26 Jacob's *h* fainted, for he believed them not
Ex. 7:22 Pharaoh's *h* was hardened, neither did he
  35:5 whosoever is of a willing *h*, let him bring
Lev. 19:17 shalt not hate thy brother in thine *h*
Deut. 4:29 if thou seek him with all thy *h*
  6:5 (Mt. 22:37; Mk. 12:30; Lk. 10:27) shalt love
    the LORD thy God with all thine *h*
  8:14 *h* be lifted up, and thou forget the LORD
  11:13 to serve him with all your *h* and with all
  11:18 shall ye lay up these my words in your *h*
  13:3 know whether ye love . . God with all your *h*
  20:3 against your enemies: let not your *h* faint
  30:14 (Rom. 10:8) the word is . . in thy *h*
  32:46 set your *h* unto all the words which
Josh. 24:23 and incline your *h* unto the LORD God
Judg. 5:16 there were great searchings of *h*
1 Sam. 7:3 prepare your *h* unto the LORD, and serve
  10:9 to go from Samuel, God gave him another *h*
  13:14 (Acts 13:22) sought . . a man after his own *h*
  16:7 appearance, but the LORD looketh on the *h*
  25:37 *h* died within him, and he became as a stone
1 Kgs. 3:9 give . . thy servant an understanding *h* to
  8:23 (2 Chr. 6:14) walk before thee with all their *h*
  8:61 your *h* therefore be perfect with the LORD
  11:4 wives turned away his *h* after other gods
  14:8 who followed me with all his *h*, to do that
  15:3 his *h* was not perfect with the LORD his God
1 Chr. 12:33 keep rank: they were not of double *h*
  28:9 LORD searcheth all *h*, and understandeth
  29:17 I know also, my God, that thou triest the *h*
2 Chr. 11:16 such as set their *h* to seek the LORD God
  31:21 he did it with all his *h*, and prospered
Job 12:24 he taketh away the *h* of the chief of the

Job 23:16 for God maketh my *h* soft
  31:7 if . . mine *h* walked after mine eyes
  33:3 words shall be of the uprightness of my *h*
  38:36 or who hath given understanding to the *h*?
Ps. 4:4 commune with your own *h* upon your bed
  4:7 thou hast put gladness in my *h*, more than in
  10:17 of the humble: thou wilt prepare their *h*
  14:1 (53:1) fool hath said in his *h*, There is no God
  19:8 the statutes . . are right, rejoicing the *h*
  19:14 meditation of my *h*, be acceptable in thy
  20:4 grant thee according to thine own *h*
  24:4 he that hath clean hands, and a pure *h*
  27:3 encamp against me, my *h* shall not fear
  28:7 strength and my shield; my *h* trusted in him
  31:24 courage, and he shall strengthen your *h*
  32:11 for joy, all ye that are upright in *h*
  34:18 nigh unto them that are of a broken *h*
  37:31 law of his God is in his *h*; none of his
  44:21 for he knoweth the secrets of the *h*
  45:1 my *h* is inditing a good matter: I speak of
  51:10 create in me a clean *h*, O God; and renew a
  51:17 a broken and a contrite *h* . . not despise
  55:21 smoother than butter, but war was in his *h*
  57:7 (108:1) my *h* is fixed, O God, my *h* is fixed
  64:6 both the inward thought . . and the *h*, is deep
  66:18 regard iniquity in my *h*, the Lord will not
  69:32 and your *h* shall live that seek God
  78:37 their *h* was not right with him, neither
  84:2 my *h* and my flesh crieth out for the living
  90:12 that we may apply our *h* unto wisdom
  95:8 (Heb. 3:8, 15; 4:7) harden not your *h*, as in
  95:10 (Heb. 3:10) a people that do err in their *h*
  119:11 thy word have I hid in mine *h*, that I
  119:145 I cried with my whole *h*; hear me, O LORD
  139:23 search me, O God, and know my *h*: try me
  147:3 he healeth the broken in *h*, and bindeth up
Prov. 2:2 and apply thine *h* to understanding
  3:5 trust in the LORD with all thine *h*; and lean
  4:23 keep thy *h* with all diligence; for out of
  6:21 bind them continually upon thine *h*, and tie
  8:5 and, ye fools, be ye of an understanding *h*
  13:12 hope deferred maketh the *h* sick: but when
  15:11 much more . . the *h* of the children of men?
  15:13 a merry *h* maketh a cheerful countenance
  16:9 deviseth his way: but the LORD directeth
  17:22 a merry *h* doeth good like a medicine
  18:12 before destruction the *h* of man is haughty
  20:9 who can say, I have made my *h* clean, I am
  21:2 his own eyes: but the LORD pondereth the *h*
  23:7 as he thinketh in his *h*, so is he
  23:26 my son, give me thine *h*, and let thine
  24:12 doth not he that pondereth the *h* consider
  26:23 and a wicked *h* are like a potsherd covered
  27:19 face answereth to face . . *h* of man to man
  28:14 he that hardeneth his *h* shall fall into
  28:26 he that trusteth in his own *h* is a fool
  31:6 and wine unto those that be of heavy *h*
  31:11 *h* of her husband doth safely trust in her
Eccl. 3:11 also he hath set the world in their *h*
  7:4 *h* of the wise is in the house of mourning
  7:7 a wise man mad; and a gift destroyeth the *h*
  8:16 when I applied mine *h* to know wisdom
  9:3 the *h* of the sons of men is full of evil
  10:2 a wise man's *h* is at his right hand; but
Is. 1:5 whole head is sick, and the whole *h* faint
  6:10 (Mt. 13:15; Acts 28:27) *h* of this people fat
  29:13 (Mt. 15:8; Mk. 7:6) their *h* far from me
  35:4 to them that are of a fearful *h*, Be strong
  44:20 a deceived *h* hath turned him aside
  51:7 people in whose *h* is my law; fear ye not
  57:15 and to revive the *h* of the contrite ones
  59:13 and uttering from the *h* words of falsehood
  65:14 my servants shall sing for joy of *h*

Jer. 4:14 Jerusalem, wash thine *h* from wickedness
11:20 triest the reins and the *h*, let me see thy
17:9 the *h* is deceitful above all things
17:10 I the LORD search the *h*, I try the reins
24:7 I will give them a *h* to know me, that I am
29:13 ye shall search for me with all your *h*
30:21 that engaged his *h* to approach unto me?
31:33 (Heb. 8:10; 10:16) and write it in their *h*
42:20 ye dissembled in your *h*, when ye sent me
Ezek. 11:19 (36:26) stony *h* out. . them a *h* of flesh
18:31 (36:26) make you a new *h* and a new spirit
25:15 have taken vengeance with a despiteful *h*
28:2 because thine *h* is lifted up, and thou hast
44:7 my sanctuary strangers, uncircumcised in *h*
Dan. 6:14 and set his *h* on Daniel to deliver him
Hos. 4:11 and wine and new wine take away the *h*
Joel 2:12 turn ye even to me with all your *h*
2:13 and rend your *h*, and not your garments
Zech. 7:12 they made their *h* as an adamant stone
Mal. 4:6 (Lk. 1:17) *h* of the fathers to the children
Mt. 5:8 blessed are the pure in *h*: for they shall
5:28 committed adultery with her already in his *h*
6:21 (Lk. 12:34) treasure is, there will your *h* be
9:4 (Mk. 2:8) wherefore think ye evil in your *h*?
11:29 learn of me; for I am meek and lowly in *h*
12:35 (Lk. 6:45) of the good treasure of the *h*
12:40 days and three nights in the *h* of the earth
13:19 (Mk. 4:15; Lk. 8:12) which was sown in his *h*
15:19 (Mk. 7:21) out of the *h* proceed evil thoughts
18:35 if ye from your *h* forgive not every one
19:8 (Mk. 10:5) because of the hardness of your *h*
Mk. 3:5 being grieved for the hardness of their *h*
6:52 of the loaves; for their *h* was hardened
8:17 understand? have ye your *h* yet hardened?
Lk. 2:51 mother kept all these sayings in her *h*
16:15 before men; but God knoweth your *h*
21:26 men's *h* failing them for fear, and for
24:25 O fools, and slow of *h* to believe all that
24:32 did not our *h* burn within us, while he
Jn. 12:40 blinded their eyes, and hardened their *h*
14:1 let not your *h* be troubled: ye believe in
Acts 2:37 heard this, they were pricked in their *h*
2:46 meat with gladness and singleness of *h*
4:32 that believed were of one *h* and of one soul
5:3 why hath Satan filled thine *h* to lie to the
5:33 (7:54) heard that, they were cut to the *h*
8:37 if thou believest with all thine *h*, thou
16:14 Lydia, a seller of purple. . *h* the Lord opened
Rom. 1:21 vain. . and their foolish *h* was darkened
2:5 thy hardness and impenitent *h*, treasurest up
2:15 show the work of the law written in their *h*
2:29 inwardly; and circumcision is that of the *h*
5:5 love of God is shed abroad in our *h* by the
8:27 he that searcheth the *h* knoweth what is the
10:8 word is nigh thee. . in thy mouth, and in thy *h*
10:9 and shalt believe in thine *h* that God hath
10:10 with the *h* man believeth unto righteousness
1 Cor. 2:9 neither have entered into the *h* of man
2 Cor. 3:2 ye are our epistle written in our *h*
3:3 of stone, but in fleshly tables of the *h*
3:15 Moses is read, the veil is upon their *h*
5:12 which glory in appearance, and not in *h*
7:3 ye are in our *h* to die and live with you
9:7 every man according as he purposeth in his *h*
Gal. 4:6 the Spirit of his Son into your *h*, crying
Eph. 3:17 that Christ may dwell in your *h* by faith
4:18 because of the blindness of their *h*
5:19 (Col. 3:16) singing. . in your *h* to the Lord
6:6 of Christ, doing the will of God from the *h*
Phil. 1:7 think this. . because I have you in my *h*
4:7 keep your *h* and minds through Christ
Col. 3:22 but in singleness of *h*, fearing God
2 Tim. 2:22 that call on the Lord out of a pure *h*

Heb. 4:12 is a discerner of the. . intents of the *h*
10:22 near with a true *h*. . having our *h* sprinkled
Jas. 1:26 deceiveth his own *h*, this man's religion
4:8 sinners; and purify your *h*, ye double-minded
1 Pet. 1:22 that ye love one another with a pure *h*
3:4 let it be the hidden man of the *h*, in that
3:15 but sanctify the Lord God in your *h*
1 Jn. 3:19 and shall assure our *h* before him
3:20 our *h* condemn us, God is greater than our *h*
Rev. 2:23 I am he which searcheth the reins and *h*

Heartily

Col. 3:23 do it *h*, as to the Lord, and not unto men

Heat

Gen. 8:22 cold and *h*, and summer and winter
Deut. 29:24 what meaneth the *h* of this great anger?
32:24 with hunger, and devoured with burning *h*
Ps. 19:6 there is nothing hid from the *h* thereof
Eccl. 4:11 if two lie together, then they have *h*
Is. 4:6 for a shadow in the daytime from the *h*
18:4 my dwelling place like a clear *h* upon herbs
25:4 refuge from the storm, a shadow from the *h*
49:10 (Rev. 7:16) neither shall the *h* nor sun smite
Jer. 51:39 in their *h* I will make their feasts
Ezek. 3:14 in bitterness, in the *h* of my spirit
Dan. 3:19 in the furnace one seven times more than
Mt. 20:12 have borne the burden and *h* of the day
Lk. 12:55 south wind blow, ye say, There will be *h*
Acts 28:3 came a viper out of the *h*, and fastened
Jas. 1:11 sun is no sooner risen with a burning *h*
2 Pet. 3:10 (3:12) elements shall melt with fervent *h*
Rev. 7:16 shall the sun light on them, nor any *h*

Heathen *See also* Gentile, Nation

Lev. 25:44 shall be of the *h* that are round about
26:33 I will scatter you among the *h*, and will
2 Kgs. 16:3 (2 Chr. 28:3) the abominations of the *h*
17:15 and became vain, and went after the *h*
1 Chr. 16:24 (Ps. 96:3) declare his glory among the *h*
2 Chr. 33:9 to err, and to do worse than the *h*
Ps. 2:1 (Acts 4:25) why do the *h* rage
2:8 shall give thee the *h* for thine inheritance
33:10 bringeth the counsel of the *h* to nought
44:14 thou makest us a byword among the *h*
46:6 the *h* raged, the kingdoms were moved
46:10 I am God: I will be exalted among the *h*
47:8 God reigneth over the *h*: God sitteth upon
59:8 thou shalt have all the *h* in derision
79:1 O God, the *h* are come into thine inheritance
96:10 say among the *h* that the LORD reigneth
102:15 so the *h* shall fear the name of the LORD
110:6 he shall judge among the *h*, he shall fill
Jer. 10:2 learn not the way of the *h*, and be not
Ezek. 11:16 I have cast them far off among the *h*
20:41 I will be sanctified in you before the *h*
34:28 and they shall no more be a prey to the *h*
36:23 and the *h* shall know that I am the LORD
36:24 for I will take you from among the *h*
38:16 that the *h* may know me, when I shall be
39:21 glory among the *h*, and all the *h* shall see
Obad. 15 day of the LORD is near upon all the *h*
Zech. 8:13 as ye were a curse among the *h*, O house
Mal. 1:11 for my name shall be great among the *h*
Mt. 6:7 use not vain repetitions, as the *h* do
18:17 him be unto thee as a *h* man and a publican
2 Cor. 11:26 in perils by the *h*, in perils in the
Gal. 1:16 that I might preach him among the *h*
2:9 unto the *h*, and they unto the circumcision
3:8 that God would justify the *h* through faith

Heave

Num. 15:19 shall offer up a *h* offering unto the LORD

Heaven *See also* Kingdom, Paradise

Gen. 1:1 beginning God created the *h* and the earth
1:8 and God called the firmament *H*
2:4 the generations of the *h* and of the earth
7:11 broken up, and the windows of *h* were opened
11:4 tower, whose top may reach unto *h*
22:15 of the LORD called unto Abraham out of *h*
28:17 house of God, and this is the gate of *h*
Ex. 16:4 (Jn. 6:31) I will rain bread from *h* for you
20:4 (Deut. 5:8) likeness of any thing that is in *h*
20:22 seen that I have talked with you from *h*
Deut. 3:24 for what God is there in *h* or in earth
10:14 behold, the *h* and the *h* of *h* is the LORD's
28:12 the *h* to give the rain unto thy land in
30:12 (Rom. 10:6) who shall go up for us to *h*
33:13 for the precious things of *h*, for the dew
Josh. 2:11 is God in *h* above, and in earth beneath
10:13 so the sun stood still in the midst of *h*
2 Sam. 22:8 the foundations of *h* moved and shook
22:10 (Ps. 18:9) he bowed the *h*. . and came down
1 Kgs. 8:27 (2 Chr. 2:6; 6:18) behold, the *h* of *h* cannot contain thee
8:49 (2 Chr. 6:39) supplication in *h* thy dwelling
2 Kgs. 1:10 (Lk. 9:54) let fire come down from *h*
2:11 Elijah went up by a whirlwind into *h*
7:2 (7:19) if the LORD would make windows in *h*
21:3 (2 Chr. 33:3) worshipped all the host of *h*
2 Chr. 7:14 will I hear from *h*, and will forgive
Neh. 9:6 made *h*, the *h* of *h*, with all their host
9:13 mount Sinai, and spakest with them from *h*
Job 14:12 till the *h* be no more, they shall not
15:15 yea, the *h* are not clean in his sight
16:19 witness is in *h*, and my record is on high
20:27 *h* shall reveal his iniquity; and the earth
22:12 is not God in the height of *h*? and behold
22:14 and he walketh in the circuit of *h*
26:11 pillars of *h* tremble, and are astonished
38:33 knowest thou the ordinances of *h*?
Ps. 2:4 he that sitteth in the *h* shall laugh
8:3 I consider thy *h*, the work of thy fingers
11:4 his holy temple, the LORD's throne is in *h*
19:1 the *h* declare the glory of God
20:6 he will hear him from his holy *h* with the
33:6 by the word of the LORD were the *h* made
50:6 and the *h* shall declare his righteousness
68:4 extol him that rideth upon the *h* by his
69:34 let the *h* and earth praise him, the seas
73:25 whom have I in *h* but thee? and there is
89:6 who in the *h* can be compared unto the LORD?
89:37 the moon, and as a faithful witness in *h*
102:19 from *h* did the LORD behold the earth
102:25 (Heb. 1:10) *h* are the work of thy hands
103:11 for as the *h* is high above the earth, so
104:2 (Is. 40:22) stretchest . . the *h* like a curtain
105:40 and satisfied them with the bread of *h*
115:16 the *h*, even the *h*, are the LORD's
119:89 ever, O LORD, thy word is settled in *h*
139:8 if I ascend up into *h*, thou art there
146:6 (Acts 4:24) which made *h*, and earth, the sea
Prov. 8:27 when he prepared the *h*, I was there
30:4 who hath ascended up into *h*, or descended?
Eccl. 5:2 for God is in *h*, and thou upon earth
Is. 14:12 how art thou fallen from *h*, O Lucifer
14:13 said in thine heart, I will ascend into *h*
34:4 the *h* shall be rolled together as a scroll
34:5 for my sword shall be bathed in *h*: behold
40:12 who hath meted out *h* with the span
49:13 sing, O *h*; and be joyful, O earth
51:6 your eyes to the *h*. . for the *h* shall vanish
55:9 as the *h* are higher than the earth, so are
64:1 oh that thou wouldest rend the *h*, that thou
65:17 (2 Pet. 3:13; Rev. 21:1) new *h*. . new earth

Is. 66:1 (Acts 7:49) *h* is my throne, and the earth is
66:22 new *h* and the new earth, which I will make
Jer. 7:18 dough, to make cakes to the queen of *h*
10:2 be not dismayed at the signs of *h*; for the
23:24 do not I fill *h* and earth? saith the LORD
31:37 saith the LORD; If *h* above can be measured
51:15 stretched out the *h* by his understanding
Ezek. 32:7 I will cover the *h*, and make the stars
Dan. 2:28 a God in *h* that revealeth secrets
6:27 he worketh signs and wonders in *h* and in
7:13 the Son of man came with the clouds of *h*
Hag. 1:10 the *h* over you is stayed from dew
Mal. 3:10 if I will not open you the windows of *h*
Mt. 3:16 (Mk. 1:10; Lk. 3:21) *h* were opened unto
5:12 (Lk. 6:23) great is your reward in *h*
5:18 (Lk. 16:17) till *h* and earth pass, one jot or
5:34 swear not at all; neither by *h*; for it is
6:9 (Lk. 11:2) our Father which art in *h*
6:20 (Lk. 12:33) for yourselves treasures in *h*
11:23 (Lk. 10:15) Capernaum . . art exalted unto *h*
11:25 (Lk. 10:21) O Father, Lord of *h* and earth
16:1 (Mk. 8:11; Lk. 11:16) show them a sign from *h*
16:19 (18:18) bind on earth shall be bound in *h*
19:21 (Mk. 10:21; Lk. 18:22) have treasure in *h*
21:25 (Mk. 11:30; Lk. 20:4) from *h*, or of men?
24:29 (Mk. 13:25; Lk. 21:26) powers of the *h* shall
24:30 Son of man in *h*. . coming in the clouds of *h*
24:35 (Mk. 13:31; Lk. 21:33) *h* and earth shall pass
26:64 (Mk. 14:62) and coming in the clouds of *h*
28:18 all power is given unto me in *h* and in
Mk. 16:19 (Lk. 24:51) he was received up into *h*
Lk. 4:25 when the *h* was shut up three years and
10:18 I beheld Satan as lightning fall from *h*
10:20 because your names are written in *h*
15:7 likewise joy shall be in *h* over one sinner
15:18 I have sinned against *h*, and before thee
18:13 not lift up so much as his eyes unto *h*
Jn. 1:32 I saw the Spirit descending from *h* like a
1:51 ye shall see *h* open, and the angels of God
3:13 up to *h*, but he that came down from *h*
3:31 he that cometh from *h* is above all
6:32 my Father giveth you the true bread from *h*
Acts 3:21 whom the *h* must receive until the times
4:12 is none other name under *h* given among men
9:3 (22:6; 26:13) round about him a light from *h*
17:24 Lord of *h* and earth, dwelleth not in
Rom. 1:18 wrath of God is revealed from *h* against
1 Cor. 8:5 called gods, whether in *h* or in earth
2 Cor. 5:1 not made with hands, eternal in the *h*
12:2 a man in Christ . . caught up to the third *h*
Gal. 1:8 an angel from *h*, preach any other gospel
Eph. 1:10 which are in *h*, and which are on earth
3:15 the whole family in *h* and earth is named
4:10 same also that ascended up far above all *h*
6:9 (Col. 4:1) knowing that your Master also is in *h*
Phil. 3:20 our conversation is in *h*; from whence
Col. 1:16 were all things created, that are in *h*
1 Thes. 4:16 the Lord himself shall descend from *h*
2 Thes. 1:7 Lord Jesus shall be revealed from *h*
Heb. 4:14 high priest, that is passed into the *h*
9:23 patterns of things in the *h*. . be purified
9:24 but into *h* itself, now to appear in the
10:34 in *h* a better and an enduring substance
12:23 church of the firstborn . . written in *h*
Jas. 5:12 swear not, neither by *h*, neither by the
1 Pet. 1:4 fadeth not away, reserved in *h* for you
3:22 is gone into *h*, and is on the right hand of
2 Pet. 3:10 *h* shall pass away with a great noise
3:13 his promise, look for new *h* and a new earth
1 Jn. 5:7 three that bear record in *h*, the Father
Rev. 4:1 door was opened in *h*: and the first voice
6:14 *h* departed as a scroll when it is rolled
8:1 seventh seal, there was silence in *h* about

Rev. 11:19 temple of God was opened in *h*, and there
　12:1 there appeared a great wonder in *h*; a woman
　12:7 was war in *h*: Michael and his angels fought
　19:1 I heard a great voice of much people in *h*
　20:11 from whose face the earth and the *h* fled
　21:1 a new *h* and a new earth: for the first *h*
　21:3 and I heard a great voice out of *h* saying

Heavenly

Mt. 6:14 your *h* Father will also forgive you
　6:26 yet your *h* Father feedeth them. Are ye not
　18:35 *h* Father do also unto you, if ye . . forgive not
Lk. 2:13 a multitude of the *h* host praising
　11:13 your *h* Father give the Holy Spirit to them
Jn. 3:12 ye believe, if I tell you of *h* things?
Acts 26:19 I was not disobedient unto the *h* vision
1 Cor. 15:48 as is the *h*, such are they . . that are *h*
　15:49 we shall also bear the image of the *h*
Eph. 1:3 spiritual blessings in *h* places in Christ
　2:6 made us sit together in *h* places in Christ
　3:10 the principalities and powers in *h* places
2 Tim. 4:18 will preserve me unto his *h* kingdom
Heb. 3:1 holy brethren, partakers of the *h* calling
　6:4 enlightened, and have tasted of the *h* gift
　8:5 serve unto the example and shadow of *h* things
　9:23 *h* things themselves with better sacrifices
　11:16 they desire a better country, that is, a *h*
　12:22 city of the living God, the *h* Jerusalem

Heaviness

Ezra 9:5 evening sacrifice I arose up from my *h*
Job 9:27 I will leave off my *h*, and comfort myself
Ps. 69:20 hath broken my heart; and I am full of *h*
　119:28 my soul melteth for *h*: strengthen thou me
Prov. 10:1 a foolish son is the *h* of his mother
　12:25 *h* in the heart of man maketh it stoop
　14:13 sorrowful; and the end of that mirth is *h*
Is. 61:3 the garment of praise for the spirit of *h*
Rom. 9:2 I have great *h* and continual sorrow in my
2 Cor. 2:1 that I would not come again to you in *h*
Phil. 2:26 longed after you all, and was full of *h*
Jas. 4:9 laughter . . to mourning, and your joy to *h*
1 Pet. 1:6 are in *h* through manifold temptations

Heavy (Heavier)

Ex. 17:12 but Moses' hands were *h*; and they took a
　18:18 for this thing is too *h* for thee; thou art
Num. 11:14 bear . . alone, because it is too *h* for me
1 Kgs. 12:4 (2 Chr. 10:4) *h* yoke which he put upon us
　14:6 for I am sent to thee with *h* tidings
Neh. 5:18 the bondage was *h* upon this people
Job 33:7 thee afraid, neither shall my hand be *h*
Ps. 32:4 for day and night thy hand was *h* upon me
Prov. 25:20 is he that singeth songs to a *h* heart
　27:3 a stone is *h* . . but a fool's wrath is *h* than
　31:6 and wine unto those that be of *h* hearts
Is. 6:10 make their ears *h*, and shut their eyes
　30:27 burden thereof is *h*: his lips are full of
　58:6 to undo the *h* burdens . . let the oppressed go
　59:1 neither his ear *h*, that it cannot hear
Lam. 3:7 I cannot get out: he hath made my chain *h*
Mt. 11:28 all ye that labor and are *h* laden
　23:4 for they bind *h* burdens and grievous to be
　26:37 (Mk. 14:33) began to be sorrowful and very *h*
　26:43 (Mk. 14:40) sleep again: for their eyes were *h*

Hebrew *See also* Israelite, Jew

Gen. 39:14 brought in a *H* unto us to mock us
　41:12 a *H*, servant . . interpreted to us our dreams
　43:32 Egyptians might not eat bread with the *H*
Ex. 1:15 the king of Egypt spake to the *H* midwives
　2:7 I go and call to thee a nurse of the *H* women
　2:11 he spied an Egyptian smiting a *H*, one of

Ex. 2:13 two men of the *H* strove together: and he
　21:2 (Deut. 15:12; Jer. 34:14) thou buy a *H* servant
1 Sam. 4:6 this great shout in the camp of the *H*?
　29:3 then said the princes . . What do these *H* here?
Jer. 34:9 being a *H* or a Hebrewess, go free
Lk. 23:38 (Jn. 19:20) letters of Greek . . Latin, and *H*
Acts 6:1 a murmuring of the Grecians against the *H*
　21:40 great silence, he spake unto them in the *H*
　26:14 saying in the *H* tongue, Saul, Saul, why
2 Cor. 11:22 they *H*? so am I. Are they Israelites?
Phil. 3:5 of the tribe of Benjamin, a *H* of the *H*

Hebron

Gen. 13:18 which is in *H*, and built there an altar
Num. 13:22 ascended by the south, and came unto *H*
Josh. 14:13 (15:13; Judg. 1:20) gave unto Caleb . . *H*
2 Sam. 2:1 whither shall I go up? . . he said, Unto *H*
　5:1 (1 Chr. 11:1) came all . . Israel to David unto *H*
　15:10 then ye shall say, Absalom reigneth in *H*

Hedge

Job 1:10 hast not thou made a *h* about him
　3:23 whose way is hid, and whom God hath *h* in?
Ps. 80:12 (89:40) hast thou then broken down her *h*
Prov. 15:19 way of the slothful . . as a *h* of thorns
Eccl. 10:8 breaketh a *h*, a serpent shall bite him
Is. 5:5 do to my vineyard: I will take away the *h*
Jer. 49:3 lament, and run to and fro by the *h*
Lam. 3:7 he hath *h* me about, that I cannot get out
Ezek. 13:5 gaps, neither made up the *h* for . . Israel
　22:30 should make up the *h*, and stand in the gap
Hos. 2:6 behold, I will *h* up thy ways with thorns
Mic. 7:4 most upright is sharper than a thorn *h*
Mt. 21:33 (Mk. 12:1) planted a vineyard . . *h* it round
Lk. 14:23 servant, Go out into the highways and *h*

Heed *See also* Regard, Respect

Deut. 2:4 take ye good *h* unto yourselves therefore
2 Chr. 19:6 said to the judges, Take *h* what ye do
Ps. 119:9 taking *h* thereto according to thy word
Prov. 17:4 wicked doer giveth *h* to false lips
Eccl. 12:9 he gave good *h*, and sought out, and set
Jer. 18:18 let us not give *h* to any of his words
　18:19 give *h* to me, O Lᴏʀᴅ, and hearken to the
Mt. 18:10 take *h* that ye despise not one of these
Mk. 13:33 take ye *h*, watch and pray: for ye know
Lk. 11:35 take *h* therefore, that the light which
Acts 3:5 he gave *h* unto them, expecting to receive
　8:6 gave *h* unto those things which Philip spake
1 Cor. 3:10 let every man take *h* how he buildeth
　8:9 but take *h* lest by any means this liberty of
　10:12 thinketh he standeth take *h* lest he fall
Col. 4:17 say to Archippus, Take *h* to the ministry
1 Tim. 1:4 neither give *h* to fables and endless
　4:1 giving *h* to seducing spirits, and doctrines
Tit. 1:14 not giving *h* to Jewish fables
Heb. 2:1 we ought to give the more earnest *h* to

Heel

Gen. 3:15 thy head, and thou shalt bruise his *h*
　25:26 (Hos. 12:3) his hand took hold on Esau's *h*
Job 18:9 the gin shall take him by the *h*
Ps. 41:9 (Jn. 13:18) hath lifted up his *h* against me
　49:5 iniquity of my *h* shall compass me about?

Heifer *See also* Cow, Kine

Gen. 15:9 take me a *h* of three years old
Num. 19:2 they bring thee a red *h* without spot
Deut. 21:3 the elders of that city shall take a *h*
Judg. 14:18 if ye had not plowed with my *h*, ye had
Jer. 46:20 Egypt is like a very fair *h*
　50:11 because ye are grown fat as the *h* at grass
Hos. 4:16 Israel slideth back as a backsliding *h*

Hos. 10:11 and Ephraim is as a *h* that is taught
Heb. 9:13 the ashes of a *h* sprinkling the unclean

Height

1 Sam. 16:7 look not. . on the *h* of his stature
Job 22:12 God in the *h* of heaven? and behold the *h*
Ps. 102:19 looked down from the *h* of his sanctuary
Prov. 25:3 heaven for *h*, and the earth for depth
Is. 7:11 ask it either in the depth, or in the *h*
Ezek. 31:5 his *h* was exalted above all the trees
31:10 thyself in *h*. . heart is lifted up in his *h*
Amos 2:9 whose *h* was like the *h* of the cedars
Rom. 8:39 nor *h*, nor depth, nor any other creature
Eph. 3:18 breadth, and length, and depth, and *h*

Heir *See also* Offspring, Seed

Gen. 15:3 lo, one born in my house is mine *h*
21:10 (Gal. 4:30) shall not be *h* with my son
2 Sam. 14:7 slew; and we will destroy the *h* also
Prov. 30:23 a handmaid that is *h* to her mistress
Jer. 49:1 hath Israel no sons? hath he no *h*?
49:2 shall Israel be *h* unto them that were his *h*
Mic. 1:15 will I bring an *h* unto thee, O inhabitant
Mt. 21:38 (Mk. 12:7; Lk. 20:14) the *h*. . let us kill him
Rom. 4:13 that he should be the *h* of the world
8:17 if children, then *h*; *h* of God, and joint-*h*
Gal. 3:29 seed, and *h* according to the promise
4:1 the *h*, as long as he is a child, differeth
4:7 if a son, then an *h* of God through Christ
Tit. 3:7 we should be made *h* according to the hope
Heb. 1:2 his Son, whom he hath appointed *h* of all
1:14 for them who shall be *h* of salvation?
6:17 show unto the *h* of promise the immutability
11:7 by faith Noah. . became *h* of the righteousness
Jas. 2:5 rich in faith, and *h* of the kingdom which
1 Pet. 3:7 being *h* together of the grace of life

Hell *See also* Damnation, Death, Fire, Flame, Grave, Pit

Deut. 32:22 fire. . and shall burn unto the lowest *h*
2 Sam. 22:6 (Ps. 18:5) sorrows of *h* compassed me
Job 11:8 deeper than *h*; what canst thou know?
26:6 *h* is naked before him, and destruction hath
Ps. 9:17 wicked shall be turned into *h*, and all
16:10 (Acts 2:27, 31) wilt not leave my soul in *h*
55:15 and let them go down quick into *h*
86:13 hast delivered my soul from the lowest *h*
116:3 the pains of *h* gat hold upon me: I found
139:8 if I make my bed in *h*, behold, thou art
Prov. 5:5 down to death; her steps take hold on *h*
7:27 her house is the way to *h*, going down to
9:18 and that her guests are in the depths of *h*
15:11 *h* and destruction are before the LORD
23:14 the rod, and shalt deliver his soul from *h*
27:20 *h* and destruction are never full
Is. 5:14 *h* hath enlarged herself, and opened her
14:9 *h* from beneath is moved for thee to meet
14:15 yet thou shalt be brought down to *h*
28:15 with death, and with *h* are we at agreement
57:9 and didst debase thyself even unto *h*
Ezek. 31:16 when I cast him down to *h* with them
32:21 shall speak to him out of the midst of *h*
Amos 9:2 though they dig into *h*, thence shall mine
Jon. 2:2 heard me; out of the belly of *h* cried I
Mt. 5:22 thou fool, shall be in danger of *h* fire
5:29 (18:9; Mk. 9:43) body should be cast into *h*
10:28 (Lk. 12:5) to destroy both soul and body in *h*
11:23 (Lk. 10:15) shalt be brought down to *h*
16:18 gates of *h* shall not prevail against it
23:15 ye make him twofold more the child of *h*
23:33 how can ye escape the damnation of *h*?
Lk. 16:23 in *h* he lifted up his eyes. . seeth Abraham

Jas. 3:6 of nature; and it is set on fire of *h*
2 Pet. 2:4 but cast them down to *h*, and delivered
Rev. 1:18 and have the keys of *h* and of death
6:8 sat on him was Death, and *H* followed with
20:13 death and *h* delivered up the dead which
20:14 death and *h* were cast into the lake of fire

Helm

Jas. 3:4 are they turned about with a very small *h*

Helmet

1 Sam. 17:5 he had a *h* of brass upon his head
Is. 59:17 a *h* of salvation upon his head; and he
Eph. 6:17 take the *h* of salvation, and the sword
1 Thes. 5:8 and for a *h*, the hope of salvation

Help (Holpen) *See also* Succor

Gen. 2:18 I will make him a *h* meet for him
Ex. 2:17 Moses stood up and *h* them, and watered
Deut. 22:4 thou shalt surely *h* him to lift them up
33:7 and be thou a *h* to him from his enemies
33:29 saved by the LORD, the shield of thy *h*
Judg. 5:23 they came not to the *h* of the LORD
1 Sam. 7:12 saying, Hitherto hath the LORD *h* us
11:9 that time the sun be hot, ye shall have *h*
1 Chr. 18:5 Syrians of Damascus. . to *h* Hadarezer
2 Chr. 14:11 nothing with thee to *h*. . *h* us, O LORD
18:31 Jehoshaphat cried out, and the LORD *h* him
20:4 Judah gathered. . to ask *h* of the LORD
20:9 in our affliction, then thou wilt hear and *h*
25:8 for God hath power to *h*, and to cast down
28:23 the gods of the kings of Syria *h* them
32:8 but with us is the LORD our God to *h* us
Ezra 5:2 with them were the prophets of God *h* them
Job 6:13 is not my *h* in me? and is wisdom driven
8:20 neither will he *h* the evildoers
Ps. 3:2 there is no *h* for him in God
12:1 *h*, LORD; for the godly man ceaseth
20:2 thee *h* from the sanctuary, and strengthen
27:9 thou hast been my *h*; leave me not, neither
28:7 shield; my heart trusted in him, and I am *h*
33:20 for the LORD: he is our *h* and our shield
37:40 LORD shall *h* them, and deliver them
40:13 to deliver me: O LORD, make haste to *h* me
40:17 (70:5) thou art my *h* and my deliverer
42:5 yet praise him for the *h* of his countenance
46:1 and strength, a very present *h* in trouble
46:5 God shall *h* her, and that right early
60:11 (108:12) give us *h*. . for vain is the *h* of man
63:7 because thou hast been my *h*, therefore in
79:9 *h* us, O God of our salvation. . deliver us
86:17 thou, LORD, hast *h* me, and comforted me
89:19 I have laid *h* upon one that is mighty
94:17 unless the LORD had been my *h*, my soul had
107:12 they fell down, and there was none to *h*
116:6 the simple: I was brought low, and he *h* me
119:173 let thine hand *h* me; for I have chosen
121:1 unto the hills, from whence cometh my *h*
121:2 my *h* cometh from the LORD, which made
124:8 our *h* is in the name of the LORD, who made
146:5 happy is he that hath the God. . for his *h*
Eccl. 4:10 for he hath not another to *h* him up
Is. 10:3 to whom will ye flee for *h*? and where
30:7 Egyptians shall *h* in vain, and to no purpose
31:1 woe to them that go down to Egypt for *h*
31:3 both he that *h* shall fall, and he that is *h*
41:6 they *h* every one his neighbor
41:10 I will *h* thee; yea, I will uphold thee
41:14 Jacob, and ye men of Israel; I will *h* thee
49:8 in a day of salvation have I *h* thee
50:7 (50:9) for the Lord GOD will *h* me
63:5 I looked, and there was none to *h*
Hos. 13:9 destroyed thyself; but in me is thine *h*

Mt. 15:25 and worshipped him, saying, Lord, *h* me
Mk. 9:22 have compassion on us, and *h* us
   9:24 Lord, I believe; *h* thou mine unbelief
Lk. 1:54 hath *h* his servant Israel, in remembrance
   10:40 bid her therefore that she *h* me
Acts 16:9 come over into Macedonia, and *h* us
   26:22 obtained *h* of God, I continue unto this day
   27:17 they used *h*, undergirding the ship
Rom. 8:26 the Spirit also *h* our infirmities
2 Cor. 1:11 ye also *h* together by prayer for us
Heb. 4:16 and find grace to *h* in time of need

Helper

2 Kgs. 14:26 nor any left, nor any *h* for Israel
Ps. 10:14 thou art the *h* of the fatherless
   30:10 have mercy upon me: Lord, be thou my *h*
   54:4 behold, God is mine *h*: the Lord is with them
   72:12 the poor also, and him that hath no *h*
2 Cor. 1:24 over your faith, but are *h* of your joy
Heb. 13:6 Lord is my *h*, and I will not fear what
3 Jn. 8 that we might be fellow *h* to the truth

Hem

Mt. 9:20 behind him . . touched the *h* of his garment
   14:36 they might only touch the *h* of his garment

Hen

Mt. 23:37 (Lk. 13:34) as a *h* gathereth her chickens

Herb *See also* Grass, Plant

Gen. 1:11 bring forth grass, the *h* yielding seed
Ex. 10:15 they did eat every *h* of the land
Job 38:27 cause the bud of the tender *h* to spring
Ps. 37:2 like the grass, and wither as the green *h*
   104:14 the cattle, and *h* for the service of man
   105:35 and did eat up all the *h* in their land
Prov. 15:17 better is a dinner of *h* where love is
Mt. 13:32 (Mk. 4:32) it is the greatest among *h*
Rom. 14:2 eat all . . another, who is weak, eateth *h*
Heb. 6:7 bringeth forth *h* meet for them by whom it

Herd

Lev. 1:3 sacrifice of the *h*, let him offer a male
Prov. 27:23 of thy flocks, and look well to thy *h*
Mt. 8:32 into the *h* of swine . . whole *h* of swine ran

Herdman (Herdmen)

Amos 1:1 the words of Amos, who was among the *h*
   7:14 I was a *h*, and a gatherer of sycamore fruit

Here

Ex. 3:4 said, Moses, Moses. And he said, *H* am I
1 Sam. 3:4 called Samuel: and he answered, *H* am I
Is. 6:8 go for us? Then said I, *H* am I; send me
Mt. 17:4 (Mk. 9:5; Lk. 9:33) it is good for us to be *h*
   28:6 (Mk. 16:6; Lk. 24:6) not *h*: for he is risen
Jn. 11:21 (11:32) been *h*, my brother had not died
Acts 16:28 do thyself no harm: for we are all *h*
Heb. 13:14 *h* have we no continuing city, but we

Heresy

Acts 24:14 the way which they call *h*, so worship I
1 Cor. 11:19 there must be also *h* among you, that
Gal. 5:20 emulations, wrath, strife, seditions, *h*
2 Pet. 2:1 who privily shall bring in damnable *h*

Heretic

Tit. 3:10 a man that is a *h*, after . . admonition, reject

Heritage *See also* Inheritance

Ex. 6:8 I will give it you for a *h*: I am the Lord
Job 20:29 the *h* appointed unto him by God
   27:13 *h* of oppressors, which they shall receive
Ps. 16:6 pleasant places; yea, I have a goodly *h*

Ps. 61:5 given me the *h* of those that fear thy name
   127:3 lo, children are a *h* of the Lord
Is. 54:17 is the *h* of the servants of the Lord
   58:14 feed thee with the *h* of Jacob thy father
Jer. 3:19 land, a goodly *h* of the hosts of nations?
   12:7 forsaken mine house, I have left mine *h*
Joel 2:17 O Lord, and give not thine *h* to reproach
   3:2 for my *h* Israel, whom they have scattered
Mic. 7:14 flock of thine *h*, which dwell solitarily
   7:18 the transgression of the remnant of his *h*?
1 Pet. 5:3 neither as being lords over God's *h*

Hermon Deut. 3:8, 9; Ps. 89:12

Herod the Great Mt. 2:1-19; Lk. 1:5

Herod the tetrarch

Mt. 14:1-11 (Mk. 6:14-28; Lk. 9:7-9)
Lk. 13:31 and depart hence; for *H* will kill thee
   23:8 when *H* saw Jesus, he was exceeding glad

Herod (Agrippa) Acts 12:1-23

Herodian

Mt. 22:16-22 (Mk. 12:13-17); Mk. 3:6

Herodias

Mt. 14:3-11 (Mk. 6:17-28; Lk. 3:19)

Heshbon Num. 21:25-34; Judg. 11:19-26

Hew (Hewn) *See also* Cut

Ex. 34:1 (Deut. 10:1) *h* thee two tables of stone like
1 Sam. 11:7 a yoke of oxen, and *h* them in pieces
   15:33 Samuel *h* Agag in pieces before the Lord
1 Kgs. 5:6 they *h* me cedar trees out of Lebanon
   5:18 builders did *h* them, and the stonesquarers
2 Chr. 2:2 fourscore thousand to *h* in the mountain
Prov. 9:1 wisdom . . hath *h* out her seven pillars
Is. 51:1 look unto the rock whence ye are *h*
Jer. 2:13 and *h* them out cisterns, broken cisterns
Mt. 3:10 (7:19; Lk. 3:9) not forth good fruit is *h* down
   27:60 (Mk. 15:46; Lk. 23:53) tomb . . he had *h* out

Hewer

Josh. 9:21 let them be *h* of wood and drawers of water

Hezekiah 2 Kgs. 18:1-21:3 (2 Chr. 28:27-33:3; Is. 36:1-39:8)

Hid (Hidden) *See also* Hide

Josh. 10:17 the five kings are found *h* in
2 Sam. 18:13 there is no matter *h* from the king
Job 3:21 and dig for it more than for *h* treasures
Ps. 51:6 in the *h* part thou shalt make me to know
Is. 40:27 my way is *h* from the Lord . . my judgment
Mt. 13:44 like unto treasure *h* in a field
1 Cor. 2:7 the wisdom of God . . even the *h* wisdom
2 Cor. 4:2 renounced the *h* things of dishonesty
1 Pet. 3:4 but let it be the *h* man of the heart
Rev. 2:17 to him . . will I give to eat of the *h* manna

Hiddekel Gen. 2:14; Dan. 10:4

Hide (Hid, Hidden) *See also* Conceal

Gen. 3:8 (3:10) Adam and his wife *h* themselves from
   18:17 I *h* from Abraham that thing which I
Ex. 2:2 was a goodly child, she *h* him three months
   3:6 Moses *h* his face; for he was afraid to look
Lev. 5:2 be *h* from him; he also shall be unclean
Deut. 30:11 this commandment . . is not *h* from thee
1 Sam. 3:17 I pray thee *h* it not from me
   23:23 all the lurking places where he *h* himself

1 Kgs. 17:3 *h* thyself by the brook Cherith
18:4 prophets, and *h* them by fifty in a cave
2 Kgs. 4:27 LORD hath *h* it from me, and hath not
11:2 (2 Chr. 22:11) they *h* him. . from Athaliah
2 Chr. 22:9 caught him, (for he was *h* in Samaria,)
Job 3:23 why is light given to a man whose way is *h*
5:21 shalt be *h* from the scourge of the tongue
10:13 these things hast thou *h* in thine heart
13:24 (Ps. 44:24; 88:14) wherefore *h* thou thy face
14:13 oh that thou wouldest *h* me in the grave
15:20 the number of years is *h* to the oppressor
20:26 darkness shall be *h* in his secret places
24:1 seeing times are not *h* from the Almighty
28:21 seeing it is *h* from the eyes of all living
33:17 man from his purpose, and *h* pride from man
34:22 where the workers of iniquity may *h*
34:29 when he *h* his face, who then can behold
40:13 *h* them in the dust together; and bind their
Ps. 10:1 why *h* thou thyself in times of trouble?
10:11 heart, God hath forgotten: he *h* his face
13:1 how long wilt thou *h* thy face from me?
17:8 *h* me under the shadow of thy wings
27:5 time of trouble he shall *h* me in his pavilion
30:7 thou didst *h* thy face, and I was troubled
31:20 shalt *h* them in the secret of thy presence
32:5 unto thee, and mine iniquity have I not *h*
40:10 I have not *h* thy righteousness within my
55:1 and *h* not thyself from my supplication
64:2 *h* me from the secret counsel of the wicked
69:5 foolishness; and my sins are not *h* from thee
89:46 wilt thou *h* thyself for ever?
102:2 *h* not thy face from me in the day when I
104:29 thou *h* thy face, they are troubled
119:11 thy word have I *h* in mine heart, that I
119:19 *h* not thy commandments from me
139:12 darkness *h* not from thee; but the night
139:15 my substance was not *h* from thee when I
140:5 the proud have *h* a snare for me, and cords
143:9 mine enemies: I flee unto thee to *h* me
Prov. 2:1 receive my words . . *h* my commandments
19:24 (26:15) slothful man *h* his hand in his bosom
27:16 whosoever *h* her *h* the wind
28:28 when the wicked rise, men *h* themselves
Is. 1:15 I will *h* mine eyes from you; yea, when ye
2:10 enter into the rock, and *h* thee in the dust
3:9 declare their sin as Sodom, they *h* it not
26:20 *h* thyself as it were for a little moment
28:15 and under falsehood have we *h* ourselves
29:15 seek deep to *h* their counsel from the LORD
45:15 verily thou art a God that *h* thyself
49:2 in the shadow of his hand hath he *h* me
53:3 and we *h* as it were our faces from him
58:7 thou *h* not thyself from thine own flesh?
59:2 your sins have *h* his face from you, that he
Jer. 13:5 so I went, and *h* it by Euphrates
16:17 neither is their iniquity *h* from mine eyes
43:10 his throne upon these stones that I have *h*
Ezek. 28:3 is no secret that they can *h* from thee
31:8 cedars in the garden of God could not *h* him
39:29 neither will I *h* my face any more from
Amos 9:3 they *h* themselves in the top of Carmel
Zeph. 2:3 be *h* in the day of the LORD's anger
Mt. 5:14 a city that is set on a hill cannot be *h*
10:26 (Mk. 4:22; Lk. 8:17; 12:2) that shall not be
revealed; and *h*, that shall not be known
11:25 (Lk. 10:21) *h* these things from the wise
25:18 digged in the earth, and *h* his lord's money
Mk. 7:24 no man know it: but he could not be *h*
Lk. 9:45 (18:34) this saying, and it was *h* from them
19:42 peace! but now they are *h* from thine eyes
Jn. 12:36 Jesus, and departed, and did *h* himself
Acts 26:26 none of these things are *h* from him
2 Cor. 4:3 gospel be *h*, it is *h* to them that are lost

Eph. 3:9 mystery, which. . hath been *h* in God
Col. 1:26 the mystery which hath been *h* from ages
3:3 dead, and your life is *h* with Christ in God
Heb. 11:23 by faith Moses, when he was born, was *h*
Jas. 5:20 and shall *h* a multitude of sins
Rev. 6:16 *h* us from the face of him that sitteth on

Hiding

Ps. 32:7 thou art my *h* place; thou shalt preserve
119:114 thou art my *h* place and my shield
Is. 32:2 a man shall be as a *h* place from the wind
Hab. 3:4 and there was the *h* of his power

High (Higher, Highest) *See also* Lofty

Gen. 14:20 blessed be the most *h* God, which hath
Num. 23:3 I will tell thee. And he went to a *h* place
24:7 king shall be *h* than Agag, and his kingdom
24:16 and knew the knowledge of the Most *H*
Deut. 3:5 these cities were fenced with *h* walls
26:19 to make thee *h* above all nations which he
28:43 stranger . . shall get up above thee very *h*
2 Sam. 1:19 of Israel is slain upon thy *h* places
22:14 (Ps. 18:13) and the Most *H* uttered his voice
1 Kgs. 3:2 only the people sacrificed in *h* places
12:31 and he made a house of *h* places, and made
14:23 (2 Kgs. 17:10) they also built them *h* places
15:14 (2 Chr. 15:17) the *h* places were not removed
2 Kgs. 14:4 *h* places were not taken away: as yet
15:35 howbeit the *h* places were not removed
Job 5:11 to set up on *h* those that be low
11:8 it is as *h* as heaven; what canst thou do?
21:22 seeing he judgeth those that are *h*
22:12 the height of the stars, how *h* they are!
41:34 he beholdeth all *h* things: he is a king
Ps. 18:27 but wilt bring down *h* looks
47:2 LORD most *h* is terrible; he is a great King
62:9 are vanity, and men of *h* degree are a lie
68:18 (Eph. 4:8) thou hast ascended on *h*
83:18 JEHOVAH, art the Most *H* over all the earth
87:5 and the *H* himself shall establish her
89:27 make him my first born, *h* than the kings of
92:1 and to sing praises unto thy name, O Most *H*
101:5 him that hath a *h* look and a proud heart
103:11 as the heaven is *h* above the earth, so
107:41 setteth he the poor on *h* from affliction
131:1 great matters, or in things too *h* for me
138:6 though the LORD be *h*, yet hath he respect
139:6 wonderful for me; it is *h*, I cannot attain
Prov. 21:4 a *h* look, and a proud heart . . is sin
24:7 wisdom is too *h* for a fool: he openeth not
Eccl. 5:8 for he that is *h* than the *h* regardeth
12:5 they shall be afraid of that which is *h*
Is. 6:1 Lord sitting upon a throne, *h* and lifted
14:14 of the clouds; I will be like the Most *H*
32:15 the spirit be poured upon us from on *h*
33:16 he shall dwell on *h*; his place of defense
55:9 are *h* than the earth, so are my ways *h* than
57:15 is Holy; I dwell in the *h* and holy place
Jer. 49:16 make thy nest as *h* as the eagle, I will
Ezek. 16:31 makest thine *h* place in every street
17:3 Lebanon, and took the *h* branch of the cedar
21:26 exalt him that is low . . abase him that is *h*
Dan. 4:17 the Most *H* ruleth in the kingdom of men
8:3 the two horns were *h*; but one was *h* than the
Obad. 3 whose habitation is *h*; that saith in his
Mt. 21:9 (Mk. 11:10) of the Lord; Hosanna in the *h*
Lk. 1:32 and shall be called the Son of the *H*
1:35 the power of the *H* shall overshadow thee
1:76 child, shalt be called the prophet of the *H*
1:78 the dayspring from on *h* hath visited us
2:14 glory to God in the *h*, and on earth peace
6:35 ye shall be the children of the *H*

Lk. 14:8 a wedding, sit not down in the *h* room; lest
20:46 markets, and the *h* seats in the synagogues
24:49 until ye be endued with power from on *h*
Jn. 19:31 for that sabbath day was a *h* day
Acts 7:48 the Most *H* dwelleth not in temples made
Rom. 12:16 mind not *h* things, but condescend to
13:1 let every soul be subject unto the *h* powers
13:11 now it is *h* time to awake out of sleep
2 Cor. 10:5 and every *h* thing that exalteth itself
Eph. 6:12 against spiritual wickedness in *h* places
Phil. 3:14 for the prize of the *h* calling of God

Highly

Lk. 1:28 hail, thou that art *h* favored, the Lord
16:15 for that which is *h* esteemed among men is
Rom. 12:3 not to think of himself more *h* than he
Phil. 2:9 wherefore God also hath *h* exalted him
1 Thes. 5:13 and to esteem them very *h* in love for

High-minded

Rom. 11:20 standest by faith. Be not *h-m*, but fear
1 Tim. 6:17 rich in this world, that they be not *h-m*
2 Tim. 3:4 traitors, heady, *h-m*, lovers of pleasures

High Priest *See also* Chief Priest

Lev. 21:10 he that is the *h p* among his brethren
Num. 35:25 (Josh. 20:6) to the death of the *h p*
Zech. 3:1 and he showed me Joshua the *h p* standing
Mt. 26:3 palace of the *h p*, who was called Caiaphas
26:57 (Mk. 14:53; Lk. 22:54) led him . . to . . the *h p*
26:62 (Mk. 14:60) the *h p* arose, and said unto him
Lk. 3:2 Annas and Caiaphas being the *h p*
Jn. 11:49 Caiaphas, being the *h p* that same year
18:15 that disciple was known unto the *h p*
18:19 the *h p* then asked Jesus of his disciples
18:22 struck . . saying, Answerest thou the *h p* so?
Acts 5:17 then the *h p* rose up, and all they that
7:1 then said the *h p*, Are these things so?
9:1 breathing out threatenings . . went unto the *h p*
23:4 that stood by said, Revilest thou God's *h p*?
Heb. 2:17 he might be a merciful and faithful *h p*
3:1 consider the Apostle and *H P* of our profession
4:14 seeing then that we have a great *h p*, that is
4:15 we have not a *h p* which cannot be touched
5:1 *h p* taken from among men is ordained for men
5:10 (6:20) a *h p* after the order of Melchisedec
7:26 such a *h p* became us, who is holy, harmless
7:28 the law maketh men *h p* which have infirmity
8:1 we have such a *h p*, who is set on the right
8:3 for every *h p* is ordained to offer gifts and
9:7 the second went the *h p* alone once every year
9:11 Christ . . a *h p* of good things to come
9:25 *h p* entereth into the holy place every year
10:21 and having a *h p* over the house of God

Highway *See also* Way

Judg. 5:6 the days of Jael, the *h* were unoccupied
1 Sam. 6:12 went along the *h*, lowing as they went
Prov. 16:17 *h* of the upright is to depart from evil
Is. 11:16 be a *h* for the remnant of his people
19:23 in that day shall there be a *h* out of Egypt
33:8 the *h* lie waste, the wayfaring man ceaseth
35:8 a *h* shall be there, and a way, and it shall
40:3 make straight in the desert a *h* for our God
49:11 mountains a way, and my *h* shall be exalted
62:10 cast up the *h*; gather out the stones; lift
Jer. 31:21 set thine heart toward the *h*, even the
Mt. 22:9 (Lk. 14:23) go ye therefore into the *h*
Mk. 10:46 Bartimeus . . sat by the *h* side begging

Hilkiah the high priest

2 Kgs. 22:4–20 (2 Chr. 34:9–28)

Hill *See also* Mount, Mountain

Gen. 7:19 waters . . upon the earth; and all the high *h*
49:26 unto the utmost bound of the everlasting *h*
Deut. 11:11 ye go to possess it, is a land of *h*
1 Sam. 9:11 and as they went up the *h* to the city
1 Kgs. 20:23 their gods are gods of the *h*
Ps. 2:6 have I set my King upon my holy *h* of Zion
15:1 tabernacle? who shall dwell in thy holy *h*?
18:7 foundations also of the *h* moved and were
24:3 who shall ascend into the *h* of the LORD?
43:3 lead me; let them bring me unto thy holy *h*
50:10 is mine, and the cattle upon a thousand *h*
65:12 and the little *h* rejoice on every side
68:15 *h* of God is as the *h* of Bashan; a high *h*
68:16 why leap ye, ye high *h*? this is the *h* which
95:4 the strength of the *h* is his also
97:5 *h* melted like wax at the presence of the
104:18 high *h* are a refuge for the wild goats
121:1 I will lift up mine eyes unto the *h*
Prov. 8:25 before the *h* was I brought forth
Is. 40:4 (Lk. 3:5) mountain and *h* shall be made low
Nah. 1:5 mountains quake at him, and the *h* melt
Mt. 5:14 a city that is set on a *h* cannot be hid
Lk. 4:29 led him unto the brow of the *h* whereon
9:37 come down from the *h*, much people met him
23:30 mountains, Fall on us; and to the *h*, Cover
Acts 17:22 then Paul stood in the midst of Mars' *h*

Hinder *See also* Let, Restrain

Gen. 24:56 *h* me not . . send me away . . to my master
Neh. 4:8 to fight against Jerusalem, and to *h* it
Job 9:12 behold, he taketh away, who can *h* him?
11:10 or gather together, then who can *h* him?
Is. 8:15 in anger, is persecuted, and none *h*
Lk. 11:52 and them that were entering in ye *h*
Acts 8:36 is water; what doth *h* me to be baptized?
Rom. 15:22 I have been much *h* from coming to you
1 Cor. 9:12 lest we should *h* the gospel of Christ
Gal. 5:7 who did *h* you that ye should not obey
1 Thes. 2:18 we would have come . . but Satan *h* us
1 Pet. 3:7 that your prayers be not *h*

Hinge

Prov. 26:14 as the door turneth upon his *h*, so

Hiram (Huram) king of Tyre

2 Sam. 5:11; 1 Kgs. 5:1–12 (2 Chr. 2:3–12);
1 Kgs. 9:11–28 (2 Chr. 8:1–18)

Hiram (Huram) the artisan

1 Kgs. 7:13–45 (2 Chr. 2:13–4:16)

Hire *See also* Recompense, Reward, Wages

Gen. 30:18 and Leah said, God hath given me my *h*
31:8 said thus, The ring-streaked shall be thy *h*
Ex. 22:15 it be a hired thing, it came for his *h*
Lev. 19:13 wages of him that is *h* shall not abide
Deut. 24:15 at his day thou shalt give him his *h*
1 Kgs. 5:6 unto thee will I give *h* for thy servants
Is. 7:20 the Lord shave with a razor that is *h*
23:18 and her *h* shall be holiness to the LORD
Hos. 8:9 alone by himself: Ephraim hath *h* lovers
8:10 though they have *h* among the nations
Mic. 3:11 and the priests thereof teach for *h*
Mt. 20:1 morning to *h* laborers into his vineyard
20:7 they say unto him, Because no man hath *h* us
Lk. 10:7 for the laborer is worthy of his *h*
Jas. 5:4 behold, the *h* of the laborers who have

Hired *See also* Hire

Lev. 25:40 but as a *h* servant, and as a sojourner
Deut. 15:18 worth a double *h* servant to thee
    24:14 shalt not oppress a *h* servant that is poor
Lk. 15:17 how many *h* servants of my father's have
Acts 28:30 Paul dwelt two. . years in his own *h* house

Hireling

Job 7:1 are not his days also like the days of a *h*?
    7:2 as a *h* looketh for the reward of his work
    14:6 till he shall accomplish, as a *h*, his day
Is. 16:14 within three years, as the years of a *h*
Mal. 3:5 against those that oppress the *h* in his
Jn. 10:12 but he that is a *h*, and not the shepherd
    10:13 *h* fleeth, because he is a *h*, and careth not

Hiss

1 Kgs. 9:8 by it shall be astonished, and shall *h*
Job 27:23 at him, and shall *h* him out of his place
Is. 7:18 that the LORD shall *h* for the fly that is
Jer. 19:8 (49:17; 50:13) shall be astonished and *h*
Ezek. 27:36 merchants among the people shall *h* at
Zech. 10:8 I will *h* for them, and gather them

Hissing

2 Chr. 29:8 to trouble, to astonishment, and to *h*
Jer. 18:16 their land desolate, and a perpetual *h*
    25:9 (25:18; 29:18) them an astonishment, and a *h*

Hitherto

Josh. 17:14 as the LORD hath blessed me *h*?
Judg. 16:13 Samson, *H* thou hast mocked me
1 Sam. 7:12 Eben-ezer. . *H* hath the LORD helped us
2 Sam. 7:18 my house, that thou hast brought me *h*?
Job 38:11 said, *H* shalt thou come, but no further
Jn. 5:17 Jesus answered them, My Father worketh *h*
    16:24 *h* have ye asked nothing in my name: ask
1 Cor. 3:2 meat: for *h* ye were not able to bear it

Hittite

Ex. 3:8 unto the place of the Canaanites, and the *H*
Josh. 1:4 all the land of the *H*. . shall be your coast
Judg. 1:26 into the land of the *H*, and built a city
2 Kgs. 7:6 hath hired against us the kings of the *H*

Hivite Ex. 23:23–28; Josh. 9:7; Judg. 3:3–5

Hoar

Is. 46:4 and even to *h* hairs will I carry you

Hoary

Lev. 19:32 thou shalt rise up before the *h* head
Job 41:32 one would think the deep to be *h*
Prov. 16:31 the *h* head is a crown of glory, if it

Hobab *See also* Jethro
    Num. 10:29–32; Judg. 4:11

Hold (noun)

Judg. 9:49 them to the *h*, and set the *h* on fire
Jer. 51:30 to fight, they have remained in their *h*
Ezek. 19:9 Babylon: they brought him into *h*

Hold (Held, Holden) *See also* Keep

Gen. 21:18 arise, lift up the lad, and *h* him in
Ex. 20:7 (Deut. 5:11) LORD will not *h* him guiltless
2 Kgs. 7:9 day of good tidings, and we *h* our peace
Job 2:3 still he *h* fast his integrity, although
    17:9 the righteous also shall *h* on his way
    26:9 he *h* back the face of his throne
    27:6 my righteousness I *h* fast, and will not let
    33:33 *h* thy peace, and I shall teach thee wisdom
    41:26 sword of him that layeth at him cannot *h*

Ps. 17:5 *h* up my goings in thy paths
    18:35 salvation: and thy right hand hath *h* me up
    71:6 by thee have I been *h* up from the womb
    73:23 with thee: thou hast *h* me by my right hand
    77:4 thou *h* mine eyes waking: I am so troubled
    119:117 *h* thou me up, and I shall be safe
    139:10 lead me, and thy right hand shall *h* me
Prov. 4:13 take fast *h* of instruction; let her not go
    11:12 but a man of understanding *h* his peace
    17:28 fool, when he *h* his peace, is counted wise
Is. 41:13 I the LORD thy God will *h* thy right hand
    62:1 for Zion's sake will I not *h* my peace
Jer. 2:13 broken cisterns, that can *h* no water
    4:19 cannot *h* my peace, because thou hast heard
Amos 6:10 *h* thy tongue. . we may not make mention
Mt. 6:24 (Lk. 16:13) will *h* to the one, and despise
    26:48 I shall kiss, that same is he; *h* him fast
Mk. 1:25 (Lk. 4:35) *h* thy peace, and come out of him
    7:8 ye *h* the tradition of men, as the washing of
Lk. 19:40 these should *h* their peace, the stones
    24:16 but their eyes were *h* that they should not
Acts 18:9 afraid, but speak, and *h* not thy peace
Rom. 1:18 men, who *h* the truth in unrighteousness
    14:4 he shall be *h* up: for God is able to make
1 Cor. 14:30 sitteth by, let the first *h* his peace
Phil. 2:16 *h* forth the word of life; that I may
    2:29 with all gladness; and *h* such in reputation
1 Thes. 5:21 all things; *h* fast that which is good
1 Tim. 1:19 *h* faith, and a good conscience
    3:9 *h* the mystery of the faith in a pure conscience
2 Tim. 1:13 *h* fast the form of sound words
Tit. 1:9 *h* fast the faithful word, as he hath been
Heb. 3:14 if we *h* the beginning of our confidence
    4:14 (10:23) let us *h* fast our profession
Rev. 2:1 that *h* the seven stars in his right hand
    2:25 which ye have already, *h* fast till I come
    3:3 received and heard, and *h* fast, and repent

Hole

Ex. 28:32 (39:23) shall be a *h* in the top of it
1 Sam. 14:11 Hebrews come forth out of the *h* where
Is. 2:19 and they shall go into the *h* of the rocks
    11:8 sucking child shall play on the *h* of the asp
    51:1 to the *h* of the pit whence ye are digged
Jer. 13:4 and hide it there in a *h* of the rock
Ezek. 8:7 when I looked, behold a *h* in the wall
Mic. 7:17 shall move out of their *h* like worms
Nah. 2:12 lionesses, and filled his *h* with prey
Hag. 1:6 earneth wages to put it into a bag with *h*
Mt. 8:20 (Lk. 9:58) foxes have *h*, and the birds

Holily

1 Thes. 2:10 how *h* and justly and unblamably we

Holiness *See also* Purity, Righteousness, Sanctification

Ex. 15:11 who is like thee, glorious in *h*, fearful
    28:36 (39:30) engravings. . signet, *H* TO THE LORD
1 Chr. 16:29 (Ps. 29:2; 96:9) worship the LORD in the beauty of *h*
2 Chr. 31:18 they sanctified themselves in *h*
Ps. 30:4 (97:12) thanks at the remembrance of his *h*
    47:8 God sitteth upon the throne of his *h*
    48:1 city of our God, in the mountain of his *h*
    60:6 (108:7) God hath spoken in his *h*
    93:5 *h* becometh thine house, O LORD, for ever
Is. 23:18 and her hire shall be *h* to the LORD
    35:8 called The way of *h*; the unclean shall not
    62:9 shall drink it in the courts of my *h*
    63:15 behold from the habitation of thy *h* and of
    63:18 the people of thy *h* have possessed it but
Jer. 2:3 Israel was *h* unto the LORD

Jer. 23:9 the LORD, and because of the words of his *h*
  31:23 O habitation of justice, and mountain of *h*
Amos 4:2 GOD hath sworn by his *h*, that, lo, the
Zech. 14:20 bells of the horses, *H* UNTO THE LORD
Mal. 2:11 Judah hath profaned the *h* of the LORD
Lk. 1:75 in *h* and righteousness before him
Acts 3:12 as though by our own power or *h* we had
Rom. 1:4 with power, according to the Spirit of *h*
  6:19 members servants to righteousness unto a *h*
  6:22 servants to God, ye have your fruit unto *h*
2 Cor. 7:1 perfecting *h* in the fear of God
Eph. 4:24 is created in righteousness and true *h*
1 Thes. 3:13 hearts unblamable in *h* before God
  4:7 not called us into uncleanness, but unto *h*
1 Tim. 2:15 continue in faith and charity and *h*
Tit. 2:3 aged women. . be in behavior as becometh *h*
Heb. 12:10 that we might be partakers of his *h*
  12:14 follow peace with all men, and *h*, without

Hollow

Gen. 32:25 the *h* of Jacob's thigh was out of joint
Judg. 15:19 clave a *h* place that was in the jaw
Is. 40:12 measured the waters in the *h* of his hand

Holy (Holier, Holiest) *See also* Chaste, Clean, Hallowed, Pure

Ex. 3:5 (Acts 7:33) whereon thou standest is *h* ground
  16:23 tomorrow is the rest of the *h* sabbath
  19:6 (1 Pet. 2:9) kingdom of priests, and a *h* nation
  20:8 remember the sabbath day, to keep it *h*
  22:31 ye shall be *h* men unto me: neither shall
  26:33 divide. . between the *h* place and the most *h*
  30:10 it is most *h* unto the LORD
Lev. 6:17 my offerings made by fire; it is most *h*
  10:10 ye may put difference between *h* and unholy
  10:17 in the *h* place, seeing it is most *h*
  11:44 (19:2; 20:26; 1 Pet. 1:16) be *h*; for I am *h*
  20:7 sanctify yourselves therefore, and be ye *h*
  21:6 shall be *h* unto their God, and not profane
  22:15 they shall not profane the *h* things of the
  23:7 the first day ye shall have a *h* convocation
  27:9 man giveth of such unto the LORD shall be *h*
  27:32 the tenth shall be *h* unto the LORD
Num. 4:20 see when the *h* things are covered, lest
  6:5 all the days of the vow. . he shall be *h*
  16:3 seeing all the congregation are *h*
  16:5 LORD will show who are his, and who is *h*
  18:9 the most *h* things. . shall be most *h* for thee
Deut. 7:6 (14:2, 21) art a *h* people unto the LORD
  23:14 camp be *h*: that he see no unclean thing in
  26:19 thou mayest be a *h* people unto the LORD
Josh. 5:15 the place whereon thou standest is *h*
  24:19 cannot serve the LORD: for he is a *h* God
1 Sam. 2:2 there is none *h* as the LORD: for there
1 Kgs. 8:4 (2 Chr. 5:5) *h* vessels. . in the tabernacle
2 Kgs. 4:9 I perceive that this is a *h* man of God
  19:22 (Is. 37:23) even against the *H* One of Israel
Ezra 8:28 ye are *h* unto the LORD; the vessels are *h*
Neh. 8:10 for this day is *h*. . neither be ye sorry
  11:1 to dwell in Jerusalem the *h* city
Ps. 16:10 (Acts 2:27; 13:35) suffer thine *H* One to see
  22:3 but thou art *h*, O thou that inhabitest the
  24:3 the LORD? or who shall stand in his *h* place
  86:2 preserve my soul; for I am *h*: O thou my God
  89:18 the *H* One of Israel is our King
  98:1 and his *h* arm, hath gotten him the victory
  99:3 thy great and terrible name; for it is *h*
  103:1 all that is within me, bless his *h* name
  145:17 in all his ways, and *h* in all his works
Prov. 9:10 the knowledge of the *H* is understanding
Is. 5:16 and God that is *h* shall be sanctified in
  6:3 *h*, *h*, *h*, is the LORD of hosts: the whole

Is. 12:6 Zion: for great is the *H* One of Israel
  27:13 shall worship the LORD in the *h* mount at
  41:14 saith the LORD. . thy Redeemer, the *H* One
  57:15 name is *H*; I dwell in the high and *h* place
  58:13 from doing thy pleasure on my *h* day
  62:12 they shall call them, The *h* people
  65:5 come not near to me; for I am *h* than thou
Ezek. 20:39 but pollute ye my *h* name no more with
  22:26 my law, and have profaned mine *h* things
  36:38 as the *h* flock, as the flock of Jerusalem
Dan. 4:8 and in whom is the spirit of the *h* gods
  11:28 his heart shall be against the *h* covenant
Hos. 11:9 not man; the *H* One in the midst of thee
Mt. 4:5 the devil taketh him up into the *h* city
  7:6 give not that which is *h* unto the dogs
  24:15 abomination of desolation. . in the *h* place
  25:31 come in his glory, and all the *h* angels
Mk. 1:24 (Lk. 4:34) who thou art, the *H* One of God
  6:20 knowing that he was a just man and a *h*
Lk. 1:35 that *h* thing which shall be born of thee
  1:70 as he spake by the mouth of his *h* prophets
  2:23 every male. . shall be called *h* to the Lord
Acts 3:14 but ye denied the *H* One and the Just
  4:30 be done by the name of thy *h* child Jesus
Rom. 1:2 afore by his prophets in the *h* Scriptures
  7:12 law is *h*, and the commandment *h*, and just
  11:16 be *h*, the lump is also *h*. . if the root be *h*
  12:1 a living sacrifice, *h*, acceptable unto God
1 Cor. 3:17 temple of God is *h*, which temple ye are
  7:14 your children unclean; but now are they *h*
  7:34 she may be *h* both in body and in spirit
  9:13 minister about *h* things live of the things
Eph. 1:4 we should be *h* and without blame before
  2:21 framed together groweth unto a *h* temple in
  3:5 revealed unto his *h* apostles and prophets by
  5:27 but that it should be *h* and without blemish
Col. 1:22 through death, to present you *h* and
  3:12 put on. . *h* and beloved, bowels of mercies
2 Tim. 1:9 and called us with a *h* calling
  3:15 a child thou hast known the *h* Scriptures
Heb. 3:1 *h* brethren, partakers of the heavenly
  9:3 the tabernacle which is called the *h* of all
  9:8 the way into the *h* of all was not yet made
  9:12 blood he entered in once into the *h* place
  10:19 to enter into the *h* by the blood of Jesus
1 Pet. 1:15 as he. . is *h*, so be ye *h* in all manner
  2:5 built up a spiritual house, a *h* priesthood
2 Pet. 1:18 when we were with him in the *h* mount
  1:21 but *h* men of God spake as they were moved
  3:2 which were spoken before by the *h* prophets
  3:11 to be in all *h* conversation and godliness
1 Jn. 2:20 but ye have an unction from the *H* One
Jude 20 building up yourselves on your most *h* faith
Rev. 3:7 these things saith he that is *h*
  4:8 saying, *H*, *h*, *h*, Lord God Almighty
  6:10 how long, O Lord, *h* and true, dost thou not
  15:4 glorify thy name? for thou only art *h*
  20:6 blessed and *h* is he that hath part in the
  21:2 and I John saw the *h* city, new Jerusalem
  21:10 showed me that great city, the *h* Jerusalem
  22:11 and he that is *h*, let him be *h* still

Holy Ghost *See also* Comforter, Holy Spirit, Spirit

Mt. 1:18 Mary. . was found with child of the *H G*
  3:11 (Mk. 1:8; Lk. 3:16) baptize you with the *H G*
  12:31 (Mk. 3:29; Lk. 12:10) but the blasphemy
    against the *H G* shall not be forgiven
  28:19 Father, and of the Son, and of the *H G*
Mk. 12:36 David himself said by the *H G*, The LORD
  13:11 for it is not ye that speak, but the *H G*
Lk. 1:15 shall be filled with the *H G*, even from

Lk. 1:35 said unto her, The *H G* shall come upon thee
1:41 and Elisabeth was filled with the *H G*
1:67 father Zacharias was filled with the *H G*
3:22 *H G* descended in a bodily shape like a dove
4:1 Jesus being full of the *H G* returned from
12:12 *H G* shall teach you in the same hour what
Jn. 1:33 the same is he which baptizeth with the *H G*
7:39 *H G* was not yet given; because that Jesus
14:26 but the Comforter, which is the *H G*, whom
20:22 and saith unto them, Receive ye the *H G*
Acts 1:2 through the *H G* had given commandments
1:5 (11:16) but ye shall be baptized with the *H G*
1:8 receive power, after that the *H G* is come
2:4 (4:31) and they were all filled with the *H G*
2:33 having . . of the Father the promise of the *H G*
2:38 ye shall receive the gift of the *H G*
4:8 Peter, filled with the *H G*, said unto them
5:3 Satan filled thine heart to lie to the *H G*
5:32 witnesses of these . . and so is also the *H G*
6:3 seven men of honest report, full of the *H G*
7:51 ye do . . resist the *H G*: as your fathers
8:15 prayed for them . . they might receive the *H G*
9:31 fear of the Lord . . in the comfort of the *H G*
10:38 God anointed Jesus of Nazareth with the *H G*
10:44 (11:15) *H G* fell on all them which heard
11:24 good man, and full of the *H G* and of faith
13:2 the *H G* said, Separate me Barnabas and Saul
13:4 they, being sent forth by the *H G*, departed
13:52 were filled with joy, and with the *H G*
15:28 seemed good to the *H G*, and to us, to lay
16:6 forbidden of the *H G* to preach the word in
19:2 have ye received the *H G* since ye believed?
20:28 which the *H G* hath made you overseers
28:25 well spake the *H G* by Esaias the prophet
Rom. 5:5 is shed abroad in our hearts by the *H G*
14:17 righteousness . . peace, and joy in the *H G*
15:13 in hope, through the power of the *H G*
15:16 be acceptable, being sanctified by the *H G*
1 Cor. 2:13 but which the *H G* teacheth
6:19 your body is the temple of the *H G* which
12:3 say that Jesus is the Lord, but by the *H G*
2 Cor. 13:14 communion of the *H G*, be with you all
1 Thes. 1:6 much affliction, with joy of the *H G*
2 Tim. 1:14 committed unto thee keep by the *H G*
Tit. 3:5 of regeneration, and renewing of the *H G*
Heb. 2:4 divers miracles, and gifts of the *H G*
6:4 and were made partakers of the *H G*
10:15 whereof the *H G* also is a witness to us
1 Pet. 1:12 you with the *H G* sent down from heaven
2 Pet. 1:21 spake as they were moved by the *H G*
1 Jn. 5:7 bear record . . Father, the Word . . the *H G*
Jude 20 your most holy faith, praying in the *H G*

Holy Spirit *See also* Holy Ghost, Spirit

Ps. 51:11 and take not thy *H S* from me
Is. 63:10 but they rebelled, and vexed his *H S*
Lk. 11:13 Father give the *H S* to them that ask him
Eph. 1:13 were sealed with that *H S* of promise
4:30 grieve not the *H S* of God, whereby ye are
1 Thes. 4:8 who hath also given unto us his *H S*

Home *See also* Abode, Dwelling, Family, House

Gen. 39:16 garment by her, until his lord came *h*
43:16 bring these men *h*, and slay, and make
Lev. 18:9 whether she be born at *h*, or born abroad
Deut. 24:5 but he shall be free at *h* one year
Josh. 2:18 all thy father's household, *h* unto thee
Ruth 1:21 LORD hath brought me *h* again empty
1 Sam. 10:26 Saul also went *h* to Gibeah; and there
1 Chr. 13:12 shall I bring the ark of God *h* to me?
Ps. 68:12 she that tarried at *h* divided the spoil

Eccl. 12:5 because man goeth to his long *h*
Lam. 1:20 sword bereaveth, at *h* there is as death
Hab. 2:5 he is a proud man, neither keepeth at *h*
Hag. 1:9 when ye brought it *h*, I did blow upon it
Mk. 5:19 go *h* to thy friends, and tell them how
Lk. 9:61 first go bid them farewell, which are at *h*
15:6 cometh *h*, he calleth together his friends
Jn. 19:27 that disciple took her unto his own *h*
20:10 disciples went away again unto their own *h*
1 Cor. 11:34 if any man hunger, let him eat at *h*
14:35 let them ask their husbands at *h*: for it
2 Cor. 5:6 whilst we are at *h* in the body, we are
1 Tim. 5:4 let them learn first to show piety at *h*
Tit. 2:5 be discreet, chaste, keepers at *h*, good

Honest *See also* True, Upright

Lk. 8:15 *h* and good heart, having heard the word
Acts 6:3 look ye . . among you seven men of *h* report
Rom. 12:17 provide things *h* in the sight of all
2 Cor. 8:21 providing for *h* things, not only in
13:7 ye should do that which is *h*, though we be
Phil. 4:8 things are true, whatsoever things are *h*
1 Pet. 2:12 your conversation *h* among the Gentiles

Honestly

Rom. 13:13 let us walk *h*, as in the day; not in
1 Thes. 4:12 that ye may walk *h* toward them that
Heb. 13:18 in all things willing to live *h*

Honesty *See also* Integrity, Uprightness

1 Tim. 2:2 peaceable life in all godliness and *h*

Honey

Gen. 43:11 present, a little balm, and a little *h*
Ex. 3:8 unto a land flowing with milk and *h*
16:31 taste of it was like wafers made with *h*
Lev. 2:11 ye shall burn no leaven, nor any *h*, in
Deut. 8:8 pomegranates; a land of oil olive, and *h*
32:13 he made him to suck *h* out of the rock
Judg. 14:8 bees and *h* in the carcass of the lion
14:18 what is sweeter than *h*? and what is
1 Sam. 14:25 and there was *h* upon the ground
1 Kgs. 14:3 a cruse of *h*, and go to him: he shall
Ps. 19:10 sweeter also than *h* and the honeycomb
81:16 *h* out of the rock should I have satisfied
119:103 taste! yea, sweeter than *h* to my mouth
Prov. 24:13 my son, eat thou *h*, because it is good
25:16 found *h*? eat so much as is sufficient
25:27 it is not good to eat much *h*: so for men
Song 4:11 *h* and milk are under thy tongue
Is. 7:15 butter and *h* shall he eat, that he may
Ezek. 3:3 it was in my mouth as *h* for sweetness
Mt. 3:4 (Mk. 1:6) his meat was locusts and wild *h*
Rev. 10:9 but it shall be in thy mouth sweet as *h*

Honeycomb

Ps. 19:10 sweeter also than honey and the *h*
Prov. 5:3 lips of a strange woman drop as a *h*, and her
Lk. 24:42 a piece of a broiled fish, and of a *h*

Honor *See also* Fame, Glory, Praise

Ex. 14:17 I will get me *h* upon Pharaoh, and upon
20:12 (Deut. 5:16; Mt. 15:4; 19:19; Mk. 7:10; Lk.
18:20; Eph. 6:2) *h* thy father and thy mother
Lev. 19:32 *h* the face of the old man, and fear thy
Num. 22:17 I will promote thee unto very great *h*
Judg. 9:9 wherewith by me they *h* God and man
1 Sam. 2:30 them that *h* me I will *h*, and they that
2 Sam. 6:22 spoken of, of them shall I be had in *h*
1 Kgs. 3:13 (2 Chr. 1:11) not asked, both riches, and *h*
1 Chr. 16:27 (Ps. 96:6) glory and *h* are in his presence
29:12 both riches and *h* come of thee, and thou
Esth. 1:20 the wives shall give to their husbands *h*

Esth. 6:6 the man whom the king delighteth to *h*?
Job 14:21 sons come to *h*, and he knoweth it not
Ps. 7:5 upon the earth, and lay mine *h* in the dust
   8:5 (Heb. 2:7) hast crowned him with glory and *h*
   15:4 contemned; but he *h* them that fear the LORD
   21:5 thy salvation: *h* and majesty hast thou laid
   26:8 house, and the place where thine *h* dwelleth
   49:12 nevertheless man being in *h* abideth not
   66:2 sing forth the *h* of his name: make his
   91:15 in trouble; I will deliver him, and *h* him
   96:6 *h* and majesty are before him: strength and
   104:1 thou art clothed with *h* and majesty
   145:5 speak of the glorious *h* of thy majesty
Prov. 3:9 *h* the LORD with thy substance, and with
   3:16 and in her left hand riches and *h*
   4:8 she shall bring thee to *h*, when thou dost
   12:9 better than he that *h* himself, and lacketh
   13:18 but he that regardeth reproof shall be *h*
   14:28 in the multitude of people is the king's *h*
   15:33 and before *h* is humility
   20:3 it is an *h* for a man to cease from strife
   22:4 fear of the LORD are riches, and *h*, and life
   25:2 the *h* of kings is to search out a matter
   26:1 in harvest, so *h* is not seemly for a fool
   29:23 but *h* shall uphold the humble in spirit
   31:25 strength and *h* are her clothing; and she
Eccl. 6:2 God hath given riches, wealth, and *h*, so
Is. 29:13 (Mt. 15:8; Mk. 7:6) their lips do *h* me, but
   43:23 neither hast thou *h* me with thy sacrifices
Jer. 33:9 a praise and an *h* before all the nations
Dan. 2:6 gifts and rewards and great *h*: therefore
   4:30 of my power, and for the *h* of my majesty?
   4:36 mine *h* and brightness returned unto me
   4:37 praise and extol and *h* the King of heaven
   11:38 in his estate shall he *h* the God of forces
Mal. 1:6 a son *h* his father. . then. . where is mine *h*?
Mt. 13:57 (Mk. 6:4; Jn. 4:44) prophet is not without *h*
   15:8 *h* me with their lips; but their heart is
Jn. 5:23 *h* the Son, even as they *h* the Father
   5:41 I receive not *h* from men
   5:44 *h* one of another, and seek not the *h* that
   8:49 but I *h* my Father, and ye do dishonor me
   8:54 myself, my *h* is nothing. . Father that *h* me
   12:26 if any man serve me, him will my Father *h*
Acts 28:10 who also *h* us with many *h*
Rom. 2:7 in well doing seek for glory and *h* and
   2:10 *h*. . peace, to every man that worketh good
   9:21 make one vessel unto *h*, and another
   12:10 brotherly love; in *h* preferring one another
   13:7 custom; fear to whom fear; *h* to whom *h*
1 Cor. 12:23 upon these we bestow more abundant *h*
2 Cor. 6:8 by *h* and dishonor, by evil report and
Col. 2:23 in any *h* to the satisfying of the flesh
1 Thes. 4:4 possess his vessel in sanctification and *h*
1 Tim. 1:17 only wise God, be *h* and glory for ever
   5:3 *h* widows that are widows indeed
   5:17 the elders. . be counted worthy of double *h*
   6:1 count their own masters worthy of all *h*
   6:16 to whom be *h* and power everlasting
2 Tim. 2:21 a vessel unto *h*, sanctified, and meet
Heb. 3:3 builded the house. . more *h* than the house
   5:4 no man taketh this *h* unto himself, but he
1 Pet. 1:7 *h* and glory at the appearing of Jesus
   2:17 all men. Love the brotherhood. . *H* the king
   3:7 *h* unto the wife, as unto the weaker vessel
Rev. 4:11 worthy, O Lord, to receive glory and *h*
   19:7 give *h* to him: for the marriage of the Lamb
   21:24 kings. . do bring their glory and *h* into it

Honorable *See also* Noble, Worthy

Gen. 34:19 he was more *h* than all the house of his
1 Sam. 9:6 city a man of God, and he is an *h* man
2 Sam. 23:19 (1 Chr. 11:21) he not most *h* of three?

2 Kgs. 5:1 was a great man with his master, and *h*
1 Chr. 4:9 and Jabez was more *h* than his brethren
Ps. 45:9 kings' daughters were among thy *h* women
   111:3 his work is *h* and glorious
Is. 3:3 *h* man, and the counselor, and the cunning
   9:15 the ancient and *h*, he is the head
   42:21 he will magnify the law, and make it *h*
   58:13 holy of the LORD, *h*; and shalt honor him
Mk. 15:43 Joseph of Arimathea, an *h* counselor
Lk. 14:8 lest a more *h* man than thou be bidden
Acts 13:50 Jews stirred up the devout and *h* women
   17:12 many of them believed; also of *h* women
1 Cor. 4:10 ye are *h*, but we are despised
   12:23 to be less *h*, upon these we bestow more
Heb. 13:4 marriage is *h* in all. . the bed undefiled

Hoof

Ex. 10:26 there shall not a *h* be left behind
Lev. 11:3 (Deut. 14:6) whatsoever parteth the *h*
Mic. 4:13 horn iron, and I will make thy *h* brass

Hook

2 Kgs. 19:28 (Is. 37:29) will put my *h* in thy nose
Job 41:1 canst thou draw out leviathan with a *h*?
Is. 2:4 (Joel 3:10; Mic. 4:3) spears into pruning *h*
Mt. 17:27 cast a *h*, and take up the fish that

Hope *See also* Expectation, Trust

Ruth 1:12 a husband. If I should say, I have *h*
Esth. 9:1 enemies of the Jews *h* to have power
Job 5:16 so the poor man *h*, and iniquity stoppeth
   6:11 what is my strength, that I should *h*?
   7:6 a weaver's shuttle, and are spent without *h*
   8:13 and the hypocrite's *h* shall perish
   11:18 thou shalt be secure, because there is *h*
   11:20 *h* shall be as the giving up of the ghost
   14:7 for there is *h* of a tree, if it be cut down
   14:19 and thou destroyest the *h* of man
   17:15 now my *h*? as for my *h*, who shall see it?
   19:10 and mine *h* hath he removed like a tree
   27:8 what is the *h* of the hypocrite, though he
   31:24 if I have made gold my *h*, or have said to
Ps. 16:9 (Acts 2:26) my flesh also shall rest in *h*
   22:9 make me *h* when I was upon my mother's
   31:24 your heart, all ye that *h* in the LORD
   33:18 (147:11) upon them that *h* in his mercy
   33:22 be upon us, according as we *h* in thee
   38:15 in thee, O LORD, do I *h*: thou wilt hear
   39:7 now, Lord, what wait I for? my *h* is in thee
   42:5 (42:11; 43:5) disquieted in me? *h* thou in God
   71:5 for thou art my *h*, O Lord GOD: thou art my
   71:14 I will *h* continually, and will yet praise
   78:7 that they might set their *h* in God, and not
   119:43 my mouth; for I have *h* in thy judgments
   119:74 they see me; because I have *h* in thy word
   119:81 my soul fainteth. . but I *h* in thy word
   119:116 and let me not be ashamed of my *h*
   119:166 I have *h* for thy salvation, and done thy
   130:7 (131:3) let Israel *h* in the LORD
   146:5 his help, whose *h* is in the LORD his God
Prov. 10:28 *h* of the righteous shall be gladness
   13:12 *h* deferred maketh the heart sick: but when
   14:32 but the righteous hath *h* in his death
   19:18 chasten thy son while there is *h*, and let
   26:12 (29:20) more *h* of a fool than of him
Eccl. 9:4 is joined to all the living there is *h*
Is. 38:18 go down into the pit cannot *h* for thy truth
   57:10 yet saidst thou not, There is no *h*
Jer. 2:25 but thou saidst, There is no *h*: no; for I
   3:23 in vain is salvation *h* for from the hills
   14:8 O the *h* of Israel, the Saviour thereof in
   17:7 trusteth in the LORD, and whose *h* the LORD

Jer. 18:12 they said, There is no *h*: but we will walk
  31:17 there is *h* in thine end, saith the LORD
Lam. 3:18 my strength and my *h* is perished from
  3:21 I recall to my mind, therefore have I *h*
  3:26 both *h* and quietly wait for the salvation
Ezek. 13:6 have made others to *h* that they would
  37:11 our bones are dried, and our *h* is lost
Hos. 2:15 and the valley of Achor for a door of *h*
Joel 3:16 but the LORD will be the *h* of his people
Zech. 9:12 to the stronghold, ye prisoners of *h*
Lk. 6:35 do good, and lend, *h* for nothing again
Acts 16:19 saw that the *h* of their gains was gone
  23:6 of the *h* and resurrection of the dead I am
  24:15 have *h* toward God, which they themselves
  24:26 *h* also that money should have been given
  26:6 and am judged for the *h* of the promise made
  27:20 all *h* that we should be saved . . taken away
  28:20 that for the *h* of Israel I am bound with
Rom. 4:18 who against *h* believed in *h*, that he
  5:2 stand, and rejoice in *h* of the glory of God
  5:5 and *h* maketh not ashamed; because the love
  8:24 are saved by *h*: but *h* that is seen is not *h*
  8:25 but if we *h* for that we see not, then do we
  12:12 rejoicing in *h*; patient in tribulation
  15:4 and comfort of the Scriptures might have *h*
  15:13 now the God of *h* fill you with all joy and
1 Cor. 9:10 that he that ploweth should plow in *h*
  13:7 *h* all things, endureth all things
  13:13 now abideth faith, *h*, charity, these three
  15:19 if in this life only we have *h* in Christ
2 Cor. 1:7 and our *h* of you is steadfast, knowing
  3:12 seeing then that we have such *h*, we use
Gal. 5:5 wait for the *h* of righteousness by faith
Eph. 1:18 ye may know what is the *h* of his calling
  2:12 having no *h*, and without God in the world
  4:4 as ye are called in one *h* of your calling
Phil. 2:23 him therefore I *h* to send presently
Col. 1:5 the *h* which is laid up for you in heaven
  1:23 be not moved away from the *h* of the gospel
  1:27 which is Christ in you, the *h* of glory
1 Thes. 1:3 patience of *h* in our Lord Jesus Christ
  2:19 for what is our *h*, or joy, or crown
  4:13 sorrow not, even as others which have no *h*
  5:8 and for a helmet, the *h* of salvation
2 Thes. 2:16 consolation and good *h* through grace
1 Tim. 1:1 and Lord Jesus Christ, which is our *h*
Tit. 1:2 in *h* of eternal life, which God . . promised
  2:13 looking for that blessed *h*, and the glorious
  3:7 heirs according to the *h* of eternal life
Heb. 3:6 the rejoicing of the *h* firm unto the end
  6:11 to the full assurance of *h* unto the end
  6:18 have fled for refuge to lay hold upon the *h*
  6:19 which *h* we have as an anchor of the soul
  7:19 but the bringing in of a better *h* did
  11:1 now faith is the substance of things *h* for
1 Pet. 1:3 hath begotten us again unto a lively *h*
  1:13 be sober, and *h* to the end for the grace
  1:21 that your faith and *h* might be in God
  3:15 asketh you a reason of the *h* that is in you
1 Jn. 3:3 hath this *h* in him purifieth himself

Hor Num. 20:22-28 (33:37-41)

Horeb *See also* Sinai

Ex. 3:1 came to the mountain of God, even to *H*
  17:6 rock in *H*; and thou shalt smite the rock
Deut. 1:6 LORD our God spake unto us in *H*, saying
  4:10 thou stoodest before the LORD thy God in *H*
  18:16 thy God in *H* in the day of the assembly
1 Kgs. 8:9 (2 Chr. 5:10) Moses put there at *H*
  19:8 forty days and forty nights unto *H*
Mal. 4:4 law of Moses . . I commanded unto him in *H*

Horn

Gen. 22:13 a ram caught in a thicket by his *h*
Ex. 29:12 (Lev. 8:15) put it upon the *h* of the altar
Josh. 6:4 before the ark seven trumpets of rams' *h*
1 Sam. 2:1 mine *h* is exalted in the LORD; my mouth
  16:1 fill thine *h* with oil, and go, I will send
2 Sam. 22:3 (Ps. 18:2) and the *h* of my salvation
1 Kgs. 1:50 and caught hold on the *h* of the altar
  22:11 (2 Chr. 18:10) Zedekiah . . made . . *h* of iron
Job 16:15 my skin, and defiled my *h* in the dust
Ps. 75:4 and to the wicked, Lift not up the *h*
  92:10 but my *h* shalt thou exalt like the *h* of a
  132:17 there will I make the *h* of David to bud
Jer. 48:25 *h* of Moab is cut off, and his arm is
Ezek. 29:21 *h* of the house of Israel to bud forth
Dan. 7:7 (7:20) a fourth beast . . and it had ten *h*
  7:8 came up among them another little *h*
  7:24 (Rev. 17:12) and the ten *h* . . are ten kings
  8:3 ram which had two *h*: and the two *h* were high
  8:5 the goat had a notable *h* between his eyes
Mic. 4:13 will make thine *h* iron . . thy hoofs brass
Hab. 3:4 he had *h* coming out of his hand
Zech. 1:18 mine eyes, and saw, and behold four *h*
Lk. 1:69 hath raised up a *h* of salvation for us in
Rev. 5:6 Lamb as it had been slain, having seven *h*
  12:3 red dragon, having seven heads and ten *h*
  13:1 ten *h*, and upon his *h* ten crowns
  17:3 beast . . having seven heads and ten *h*

Horrible *See also* Terrible

Ps. 11:6 rain . . fire and brimstone, and a *h* tempest
  40:2 he brought me up also out of a *h* pit
Jer. 5:30 a wonderful and *h* thing is committed in
  18:13 virgin of Israel hath done a very *h* thing
  23:14 the prophets of Jerusalem a *h* thing
Hos. 6:10 seen a *h* thing in the house of Israel

Horribly

Jer. 2:12 be *h* afraid, be ye very desolate
Ezek. 32:10 their kings shall be *h* afraid for thee

Horror *See also* Dread, Fear, Terror

Gen. 15:12 lo, a *h* of great darkness fell upon him
Ps. 55:5 come upon me, and *h* hath overwhelmed me
  119:53 *h* hath taken hold upon me because of the
Ezek. 7:18 with sackcloth, and *h* shall cover them

Horse *See also* Mule

Gen. 47:17 Joseph gave them bread in exchange for *h*
Ex. 15:1 *h* and his rider hath he thrown into the
Deut. 17:16 but he shall not multiply *h* to himself
1 Kgs. 10:28 (2 Chr. 1:16; 9:25) Solomon had *h*
  18:5 find grass to save the *h* and mules alive
2 Kgs. 6:17 mountain was full of *h* and chariots of
Neh. 3:28 above the *h* gate repaired the priests
Job 39:19 hast thou given the *h* strength?
Ps. 32:9 be ye not as the *h*, or as the mule
  33:17 a *h* is a vain thing for safety
  147:10 he delighteth not in the strength of the *h*
Prov. 21:31 *h* is prepared against the day of battle
Eccl. 10:7 I have seen servants upon *h*, and princes
Is. 30:16 but ye said, No; for we will flee upon *h*
  31:1 stay on *h*, and trust in chariots, because
Jer. 4:13 his *h* are swifter than eagles
  5:8 as fed *h* . . neighed after his neighbor's wife
  8:6 his course, as the *h* rusheth into the battle
  12:5 then how canst thou contend with *h*?
Amos 6:12 shall *h* run upon the rock? will one plow
Zech. 1:8 behold a man riding upon a red *h*
  6:2 in the first chariot were red *h*; and in
Jas. 3:3 we put bits in the *h*' mouths, that they
Rev. 6:2 and I saw, and behold a white *h*

Rev. 6:5 and lo a black *h*; and he that sat on him
6:8 and I looked, and behold a pale *h*
19:11 I saw heaven opened, and behold a white *h*

Horseback

2 Kgs. 9:18 so there went one on *h* to meet him
Esth. 6:11 arrayed Mordecai, and brought him on *h*

Horseleech

Prov. 30:15 the *h* hath two daughters, crying, Give

Horsemen

Gen. 50:9 went up with him both chariots and *h*
Ex. 14:9 his *h*, and his army, and overtook them
2 Kgs. 2:12 (13:14) chariot of Israel, and the *h*
Acts 23:23 to Caesarea, and *h* threescore and ten
Rev. 9:16 the *h* were two hundred thousand thousand

Hosanna

Mt. 21:9 (Mk. 11:9; Jn. 12:13) *H* . . Blessed is he that
21:15 the children crying. . *H* to the Son of David

Hosea (Osee) Hos. 1:1-14:9

Rom. 9:25 he saith also in *O*, I will call them my

Hoshea the king 2 Kgs. 15:30; 17:1-6

Hospitality

Rom. 12:13 to the necessity of saints; given to *h*
1 Tim. 3:2 good behavior, given to *h*, apt to teach
Tit. 1:8 a lover of *h*, a lover of good men, sober
1 Pet. 4:9 use *h* one to another without grudging

Host *See also* Army, Multitude

Gen. 2:1 were finished, and all the *h* of them
32:2 Jacob saw them, he said, This is God's *h*
Ex. 12:41 the *h* of the LORD went out from the land
14:24 LORD looked unto the *h* of the Egyptians
16:13 the morning the dew lay round about the *h*
Num. 4:3 all that enter into the *h*, to do the work
Josh. 1:11 pass through the *h*, and command the
5:14 as captain of the *h* of the LORD am I now
1 Sam. 14:48 and he gathered a *h*, and smote the
2 Sam. 5:24 (1 Chr. 14:15) smite . . *h* of the Philistines
2 Kgs. 21:3 (2 Chr. 33:3) worshipped . . *h* of heaven
25:1 came, he, and all his *h*, against Jerusalem
1 Chr. 12:22 it was a great *h*, like the *h* of God
Ps. 27:3 though a *h* should encamp against me
33:16 is no king saved by the multitude of a *h*
103:21 bless ye the LORD, all ye his *h*
136:15 overthrew Pharaoh and his *h* in the Red sea
148:2 all his angels: praise ye him, all his *h*
Is. 40:26 that bringeth out their *h* by number
Lk. 2:13 multitude of the heavenly *h* praising God
Acts 7:42 gave them up to worship the *h* of heaven

Host

Lk. 10:35 out two pence, and gave them to the *h*
Rom. 16:23 Gaius mine *h*, and of the whole church

Hostage

2 Kgs. 14:14 (2 Chr. 25:24) took . . *h*, and returned

Hot

Ex. 16:21 and when the sun waxed *h*, it melted
Judg. 2:14 (2:20; 3:8; 10:7) anger of the LORD was *h*
Ps. 6:1 (38:1) neither chasten me in thy *h* displeasure
39:3 heart was *h* within me; while I was musing
Prov. 6:28 can one go upon *h* coals, and his feet
1 Tim. 4:2 their conscience seared with a *h* iron
Rev. 3:15 works, that thou art neither cold nor *h*

Hour *See also* Time

Dan. 3:6 (3:15) the same *h* be cast into the midst
4:19 Daniel . . was astonished for one *h*
Mt. 9:22 and the woman was made whole from that *h*
10:19 (Mk. 13:11; Lk. 12:12) given you in that . . *h*
20:12 these last have wrought but one *h*
24:36 (Mk. 13:32) that day and *h* knoweth no man
24:44 (Lk. 12:40) in such an *h* as ye think not
24:50 (Lk. 12:46) in an *h* that he is not aware of
25:13 ye know neither the day nor the *h* wherein
26:40 (Mk. 14:37) could ye not watch . . one *h*?
26:45 (Mk. 14:41) *h* is at hand, and the Son of man
Mk. 14:35 were possible, the *h* might pass from him
Lk. 10:21 in that *h* Jesus rejoiced in spirit
22:53 this is your *h*, and the power of darkness
Jn. 2:4 I to do with thee? mine *h* is not yet come
4:21 woman, believe me, the *h* cometh, when ye
4:52 inquired . . the *h* when he began to amend
5:25 the *h* is coming, and now is, when the dead
7:30 (8:20) because his *h* was not yet come
11:9 are there not twelve *h* in the day?
12:23 *h* is come, that the Son of man should be
12:27 Father, save me from this *h*: but for this
16:32 the *h* cometh . . that ye shall be scattered
17:1 Father, the *h* is come; glorify thy Son
Acts 3:1 at the *h* of prayer, being the ninth *h*
1 Cor. 15:30 and why stand we in jeopardy every *h*?
Gal. 2:5 to whom we gave place . . no, not for an *h*
Rev. 3:3 not know what *h* I will come upon thee
3:10 will keep thee from the *h* of temptation
8:1 there was silence in heaven about . . half an *h*

House *See also* Family, Home, Household

Gen. 7:1 come thou and all thy *h* into the ark
28:17 this is none other but the *h* of God
Ex. 12:3 to the *h* of their fathers, a lamb for a *h*
12:30 was not a *h* where there was not one dead
20:17 (Deut. 5:21) shalt not covet thy neighbor's *h*
Num. 22:18 (24:13) would give me his *h* full of silver
Deut. 8:12 and art full, and hast built goodly *h*
8:14 of the land of Egypt, from the *h* of bondage
Josh. 24:15 as for me and my *h*, we will serve the
Judg. 20:18 up to the *h* of God, and asked counsel
1 Sam. 3:14 by of Eli, that the iniquity of Eli's *h*
2 Sam. 7:6 (1 Chr. 17:5) have not dwelt in any *h*
7:11 (1 Chr. 17:10) the LORD . . will make thee a *h*
7:18 who am I, O . . GOD? and what is my *h*
23:5 although my *h* be not so with God; yet he
1 Kgs. 5:5 I purpose to build a *h* unto the name of
6:2 (2 Chr. 3:1) the *h* which king Solomon built
6:22 (2 Chr. 3:7) whole *h* he overlaid with gold
7:8 Solomon made . . a *h* for Pharaoh's daughter
8:11 (2 Chr. 5:14) glory . . filled the *h* of the LORD
8:29 that thine eyes may be open toward this *h*
8:43 (2 Chr. 6:33) this *h* . . is called by thy name
9:25 (2 Chr. 8:16) so he finished the *h*
2 Kgs. 20:1 (Is. 38:1) set thine *h* in order; for thou
20:15 (Is. 39:4) what have they seen in thine *h*?
22:8 (2 Chr. 34:15) found the book . . in the *h*
23:27 *h* of which I said, My name shall be there
25:9 (Jer. 52:13) he burnt the *h* of the LORD
1 Chr. 22:5 the *h* that is to be builded for the LORD
2 Chr. 7:1 and the glory of the LORD filled the *h*
24:4 that Joash . . repair the *h* of the LORD
29:5 and sanctify the *h* of the LORD God
29:31 thank offerings into the *h* of the LORD
36:23 (Ezra 1:2) me to build him a *h* in Jerusalem
Neh. 13:11 why is the *h* of God forsaken?
Job 21:9 their *h* are safe from fear, neither is
22:18 yet he filled their *h* with good things
30:23 to death . . to the *h* appointed for all living
Ps. 26:8 LORD, I have loved the habitation of thy *h*

Ps. 42:4 multitude, I went with them to the *h* of God
49:11 that their *h* shall continue for ever
65:4 satisfied with the goodness of thy *h*
69:9 (Jn. 2:17) zeal of thine *h* hath eaten me up
84:3 sparrow hath found a *h*, and the swallow a
84:10 rather be a doorkeeper in the *h* of my God
92:13 planted in the *h* of the LORD shall flourish
118:26 have blessed you out of the *h* of the LORD
122:1 unto me, Let us go into the *h* of the LORD
Prov. 2:18 for her *h* inclineth unto death, and her
7:27 her *h* is the way to hell, going down to the
9:1 wisdom hath builded her *h*, she hath hewn out
19:14 and riches are the inheritance of fathers
24:3 through wisdom is a *h* builded
25:17 withdraw thy foot from thy neighbor's *h*
Eccl. 7:2 it is better to go to the *h* of mourning
10:18 through idleness . . the *h* droppeth
Is. 2:3 (Mic. 4:2) let us go up . . to the *h* of the God
3:14 the spoil of the poor is in your *h*
5:8 woe unto them that join *h* to *h*, that lay
6:4 that cried, and the *h* was filled with smoke
13:22 shall cry in their desolate *h*, and dragons
14:17 that opened not the *h* of his prisoners?
37:1 covered himself. . went into the *h* of the LORD
56:7 (Mt. 21:13; Mk. 11:17; Lk. 19:46) mine *h* shall be called a *h* of prayer
60:7 and I will glorify the *h* of my glory
64:11 our holy and our beautiful *h* . . is burned up
66:1 (Acts 7:49) where is the *h* that ye build
Jer. 7:11 is this *h*. . become a den of robbers
16:5 enter not into the *h* of mourning, neither
18:2 arise, and go down to the potter's *h*
29:5 build ye *h*, and dwell in them; and plant
Ezek. 2:5 for they are a rebellious *h*
3:17 (33:7) thee a watchman unto the *h* of Israel
43:5 the glory of the LORD filled the *h*
Hos. 9:15 I will drive them out of mine *h*
Amos 3:15 *h* of ivory shall perish, and the great *h*
Hag. 1:2 the time that the LORD's *h* should be built
1:4 in your ceiled *h*, and this *h* lie waste?
1:9 mine *h* that is waste, and ye. . unto his own *h*
2:7 will fill this *h* with glory, saith the LORD
Zech. 13:6 I was wounded in the *h* of my friends
Mal. 3·10 tithes. . that there may be meat in mine *h*
Mt. 7:24 (Lk. 6:48) built his *h* upon a rock
8:14 (Mk. 1:29; Lk. 4:38) was come into Peter's *h*
9:23 (Mk. 5:38) when Jesus came into the ruler's *h*
10:12 (Mk. 6:10; Lk. 9:4) when ye come into a *h*
12:4 (Mk. 2:26; Lk. 6:4) entered into the *h* of God
12:25 (Mk. 3:25; Lk. 11:17) *h* divided against itself
23:14 (Mk. 12:40; Lk. 20:47) ye devour widows' *h*
23:38 (Lk. 13:35) your *h* is left unto you desolate
24:17 (Mk. 13:15) to take any thing out of his *h*
26:18 keep the passover at thy *h* with my disciples
Mk. 8:26 sent him away to his *h*, saying, Neither
13:35 know not when the master of the *h* cometh
Lk. 7:44 entered into thine *h*, thou gavest me no
10:7 in the same *h* remain. . Go not from *h* to *h*
14:23 them to come in, that my *h* may be filled
15:8 sweep the *h*, and seek diligently till she
18:14 this man went down to his *h* justified
19:5 come down; for today I must abide at thy *h*
19:9 this day is salvation come to this *h*
Jn. 2:16 make not my Father's *h* a *h* of merchandise
4:53 and himself believed, and his whole *h*
12:3 *h* was filled with the odor of the ointment
14:2 in my Father's *h* are many mansions
Acts 2:46 and breaking bread from *h* to *h*
4:34 possessors of lands or *h* sold them
5:42 daily in the temple, and in every *h*, they
10:2 one that feared God with all his *h*
16:31 thou shalt be saved, and thy *h*
16:40 prison, and entered into the *h* of Lydia

Acts 18:8 believed on the Lord with all his *h*
20:20 have taught you publicly, and from *h* to *h*
28:30 dwelt two whole years in his own hired *h*
Rom. 16:5 (1 Cor. 16:19) church that is in their *h*
1 Cor. 11:22 have ye not *h* to eat and to drink in?
2 Cor. 5:1 if our earthly *h* of this tabernacle
5:2 clothed upon with our *h* which is from heaven
1 Tim. 3:4 one that ruleth well his own *h*, having
3:15 oughtest to behave thyself in the *h* of God
5:8 and specially for those of his own *h*
5:14 women marry, bear children, guide the *h*
2 Tim. 3:6 this sort are they which creep into *h*
Tit. 1:11 who subvert whole *h*, teaching things
Heb. 3:3 builded the *h* hath more honor than the *h*
3:6 Christ as a son over his own *h*; whose *h* are
11:7 prepared an ark to the saving of his *h*
1 Pet. 4:17 that judgment must begin at the *h* of God

Household *See also* Family, House

Gen. 18:19 command his children and his *h* after
31:37 what hast thou found of all thy *h* stuff?
47:12 and Joseph nourished. . all his father's *h*
Deut. 6:22 Egypt, upon Pharaoh, and upon all his *h*
1 Sam. 27:3 every man with his *h*, even David with
2 Sam. 6:11 LORD blessed Obed-edom, and all his *h*
6:20 (1 Chr. 16:43) David returned to bless his *h*
17:23 and put his *h* in order, and hanged himself
2 Kgs. 7:9 that we may go and tell the king's *h*
Prov. 31:21 snow for her *h*: for all her *h* are clothed
31:27 she looketh well to the ways of her *h*
Mt. 10:36 a man's foes shall be they of his own *h*
Acts 16:15 when she was baptized, and her *h*
Gal. 6:10 especially unto them. . of the *h* of faith
Eph. 2:19 with the saints, and of the *h* of God
Phil. 4:22 chiefly they that are of Caesar's *h*
2 Tim. 4:19 salute Prisca. . and the *h* of Onesiphorus

Householder

Mt. 13:27 servants of the *h* came and said unto him
13:52 a *h*. . bringeth forth out of his treasure
21:33 a certain *h*, which planted a vineyard

Housetop

Ps. 129:6 let them be as the grass upon the *h*
Prov. 21:9 (25:24) to dwell in a corner of the *h*
Is. 22:1 that thou art wholly gone up to the *h*?
Zeph. 1:5 worship the host of heaven upon the *h*
Mt. 10:27 (Lk. 12:3) that preach ye upon the *h*
24:17 (Mk. 13:15; Lk. 17:31) on the *h* not come
Lk. 5:19 they went upon the *h*, and let him down
Acts 10:9 Peter went up upon the *h* to pray

Howl

Is. 13:6 ye; for the day of the LORD is at hand
Joel 1:13 ye priests: *h*, ye ministers of the altar
Jas. 5:1 ye rich men, weep and *h* for your miseries

Huldah 2 Kgs. 22:14–20 (2 Chr. 34:22–28)

Humble *See also* Abase, Lowly, Meek

Ex. 10:3 thou refuse to *h* thyself before me?
Lev. 26:41 if then their uncircumcised hearts be *h*
Deut. 8:2 forty years in the wilderness, to *h* thee
1 Kgs. 21:29 seest. . how Ahab *h* himself before me?
2 Kgs. 22:19 (2 Chr. 34:27) *h* thyself before the LORD
2 Chr. 7:14 shall *h* themselves, and pray, and seek
30:11 *h* themselves, and came to Jerusalem
Job 22:29 lifting up; and he shall save the *h* person
Ps. 9:12 he forgetteth not the cry of the *h*
10:10 he croucheth, and *h* himself, that the poor
10:12 God, lift up thine hand: forget not the *h*
10:17 LORD, thou hast heard the desire of the *h*
34:2 the *h* shall hear thereof, and be glad

Ps. 35:13 I *h* my soul with fasting; and my prayer
69:32 the *h* shall see this, and be glad
113:6 who *h* himself to behold the things that
Prov. 16:19 better it is to be of an *h* spirit with
29:23 but honor shall uphold the *h* in spirit
Is. 2:9 boweth down, and the great man *h* himself
2:11 the lofty looks of man shall be *h*, and the
5:15 brought down, and the mighty man shall be *h*
10:33 be hewn down, and the haughty shall be *h*
57:15 *h* spirit, to revive the spirit of the *h*
Lam. 3:20 still in remembrance, and is *h* in me
Mt. 18:4 whosoever therefore shall *h* himself as
23:12 (Lk. 14:11; 18:14) *h* himself shall be exalted
2 Cor. 12:21 when I come again, my God will *h* me
Phil. 2:8 found in fashion as a man, he *h* himself
Jas. 4:6 the proud, but giveth grace unto the *h*
4:10 *h* yourselves in the sight of the Lord
1 Pet. 5:6 *h* yourselves therefore under the mighty

Humbleness

Col. 3:12 bowels of mercies, kindness, *h* of mind

Humbly

2 Sam. 16:4 Ziba said, I *h* beseech thee that I may
Mic. 6:8 to love mercy, and to walk *h* with thy God?

Humiliation

Acts 8:33 in his *h* his judgment was taken away

Humility

Prov. 15:33 (18:12) and before honor is *h*
22:4 by *h* and the fear of the LORD are riches
Acts 20:19 serving the Lord with all *h* of mind
Col. 2:18 a voluntary *h* and worshipping of angels
2:23 a show of wisdom in will-worship, and *h*
1 Pet. 5:5 be clothed with *h*: for God resisteth

Hundred

Mt. 18:12 (Lk. 15:4) if a man have a *h* sheep, and one
Mk. 4:8 some thirty, and some sixty, and some a *h*

Hunger

Ex. 16:3 to kill this whole assembly with *h*
Deut. 8:3 he humbled thee, and suffered thee to *h*
28:48 against thee, in *h*, and in thirst, and in
32:24 they shall be burnt with *h*, and devoured
Neh. 9:15 them bread from heaven for their *h*
Ps. 34:10 young lions do lack, and suffer *h*
Prov. 19:15 and an idle soul shall suffer *h*
Is. 49:10 (Rev. 7:16) they shall not *h* nor thirst
Jer. 38:9 and he is like to die for *h* in the place
42:14 sound of the trumpet, nor have *h* of bread
Lam. 2:19 thy young children, that faint for *h* in
Ezek. 34:29 they shall be no more consumed with *h*
Mt. 5:6 blessed are they which do *h* and thirst after
21:18 (Mk. 11:12) returned into the city, he *h*
Lk. 6:21 blessed are ye that *h* now: for ye shall
6:25 woe unto you that are full! for ye shall *h*
15:17 enough and to spare, and I perish with *h*!
Jn. 6:35 he that cometh to me shall never *h*
Rom. 12:20 therefore if thine enemy *h*, feed him
1 Cor. 4:11 even unto this present hour we both *h*
11:34 if any man *h*, let him eat at home; that ye
2 Cor. 11:27 in *h* and thirst, in fastings often
Rev. 6:8 the earth, to kill with sword, and with *h*
7:16 they shall *h* no more, neither thirst any

Hunger-bitten

Job 18:12 his strength shall be *h-b*, and destruction

Hungry

1 Sam. 2:5 and they that were *h* ceased: so that
Job 5:5 whose harvest the *h* eateth up, and taketh

Job 22:7 and thou hast withholden bread from the *h*
24:10 and they take away the sheaf from the *h*
Ps. 50:12 if I were *h*, I would not tell thee
107:5 *h* and thirsty, their soul fainted in them
107:9 and filleth the *h* soul with goodness
146:7 the oppressed: which giveth food to the *h*
Prov. 6:30 steal to satisfy his soul when he is *h*
25:21 if thine enemy be *h*, give him bread to eat
27:7 to the *h* soul every bitter thing is sweet
Is. 8:21 bestead and *h*: and . . when they shall be *h*
9:20 he shall snatch on the right hand, and be *h*
29:8 a *h* man dreameth, and, behold, he eateth
32:6 make empty the soul of the *h*; and he will
58:7 is it not to deal thy bread to the *h*
58:10 if thou draw out thy soul to the *h*
65:13 my servants shall eat, but ye shall be *h*
Ezek. 18:7 hath given his bread to the *h*, and hath
Mk. 11:12 were come from Bethany, he was *h*
Lk. 1:53 he hath filled the *h* with good things
Acts 10:10 he became very *h*, and would have eaten
1 Cor. 11:21 and one is *h*, and another is drunken
Phil. 4:12 instructed both to be full and to be *h*

Hunt

Gen. 27:5 Esau went to the field to *h* for venison
1 Sam. 24:11 yet thou *h* my soul to take it
26:20 a flea, as when one doth *h* a partridge in
Job 10:16 thou *h* me as a fierce lion: and again
38:39 wilt thou *h* the prey for the lion?
Ps. 140:11 evil shall *h* the violent man to
Jer. 16:16 they shall *h* them from every mountain
Lam. 4:18 they *h* our steps, that we cannot go in
Ezek. 13:18 will ye *h* the souls of my people
Mic. 7:2 they *h* every man his brother with a net

Hunter

Gen. 10:9 as Nimrod the mighty *h* before the LORD
25:27 Esau was a cunning *h*, a man of the field
Prov. 6:5 deliver thyself as a roe from . . the *h*
Jer. 16:16 after will I send for many *h*, and they

Huram *See* Hiram

Hurl

Num. 35:20 *h* at him by laying of wait, that he die
1 Chr. 12:2 right hand and the left in *h* stones
Job 27:21 and as a storm *h* him out of his place

Hurt *See also* Bruise, Damage, Harm, Wound

Gen. 4:23 to my wounding, and a young man to my *h*
Ex. 21:22 if men strive, and *h* a woman with child
Num. 16:15 from them, neither have I *h* one of them
Josh. 24:20 gods, then he will turn and do you *h*
Ps. 15:4 sweareth to his own *h*, and changeth not
35:4 (70:2) brought to confusion that devise my *h*
41:7 against me do they devise my *h*
Eccl. 5:13 riches kept for the owners . . to their *h*
8:9 one man ruleth over another to his own *h*
10:9 whoso removeth stones shall be *h* therewith
Is. 11:9 (65:25) shall not *h* nor destroy in all
27:3 lest any *h* it, I will keep it night and day
Jer. 6:14 (8:11) healed . . the *h* of . . my people slightly
8:21 the *h* of the daughter of my people am I *h*
10:19 woe is me for my *h*! my wound is grievous
25:6 go not after other gods . . I will do you no *h*
38:4 not the welfare of this people, but the *h*
Dan. 6:22 lions' mouths, that they have not *h* me
Mk. 16:18 drink any deadly thing, it shall not *h*
Lk. 4:35 the devil . . came out of him, and *h* him not
10:19 and nothing shall by any means *h* you

Acts 18:10 and no man shall set on thee to *h* thee
27:10 I perceive that this voyage will be with *h*
Rev. 2:11 shall not be *h* of the second death
6:6 and see thou *h* not the oil and the wine
7:2 it was given to *h* the earth and the sea
9:4 they should not *h* the grass of the earth
11:5 if any man will *h* them, fire proceedeth out

Hurtful

Ezra 4:15 a rebellious city, and *h* unto kings and
Ps. 144:10 who delivereth David. . from the *h* sword
1 Tim. 6:9 into many foolish and *h* lusts, which

Husband

Gen. 3:6 also unto her *h* with her; and he did eat
3:16 thy desire shall be to thy *h*, and he shall
Ex. 4:25 said, Surely a bloody *h* art thou to me
Deut. 25:5 *h*'s brother. . perform the duty of a *h*'s
Ruth 1:11 sons in my womb, that they may be your *h*
2 Sam. 3:16 *h* went with her along weeping behind
Esth. 1:17 so that they shall despise their *h* in
1:20 all the wives shall give to their *h* honor
Prov. 12:4 virtuous woman is a crown to her *h*
31:11 heart of her *h* doth safely trust in her
31:23 *h* is known in the gates, when he sitteth
31:28 blessed; her *h* also, and he praiseth her
Is. 54:5 thy Maker is thine *h*; The LORD of hosts
Jer. 31:32 they brake, although I was a *h* unto them
Mt. 1:16 Jacob begat Joseph the *h* of Mary, of whom
Jn. 4:16 Jesus saith unto her, Go, call thy *h*
Rom. 7:2 bound by the law to her *h*. . but if the *h*
1 Cor. 7:2 and let every woman have her own *h*
7:3 the *h* render unto the wife due benevolence
7:14 the unbelieving *h* is sanctified by the wife
7:16 O wife, whether thou shalt save thy *h*?
7:34 of the world, how she may please her *h*
14:35 let them ask their *h* at home: for it is a
2 Cor. 11:2 I have espoused you to one *h*, that I
Eph. 5:22 (Col. 3:18) wives, submit. . unto your. . *h*
5:25 (Col. 3:19) *h*, love your wives
5:33 and the wife see that she reverence her *h*
1 Tim. 3:2 (Tit. 1:6) a bishop. . the *h* of one wife
3:12 let the deacons be the *h* of one wife
Tit. 2:4 young women to be sober, to love their *h*
2:5 obedient to their own *h*, that the word of God
1 Pet. 3:1 ye wives, be in subjection to your own *h*
3:7 ye *h*, dwell with them according to knowledge
Rev. 21:2 prepared as a bride adorned for her *h*

Husbandman

Gen. 9:20 and Noah began to be a *h*, and he planted
Jer. 51:23 with thee will I break in pieces the *h*
Joel 1:11 be ye ashamed, O ye *h*; howl, O ye
Amos 5:16 and they shall call the *h* to mourning
Zech. 13:5 he shall say, I am no prophet, I am a *h*
Mt. 21:33 (Mk. 12:1; Lk. 20:9) and let it out to *h*
Jn. 15:1 am the true vine, and my Father is the *h*
2 Tim. 2:6 *h* that laboreth must be first partaker
Jas. 5:7 the *h* waiteth for the precious fruit of

Husbandry

1 Cor. 3:9 ye are God's *h*, ye are God's building

Hushai 2 Sam. 15:32–37; 16:16–19; 17:5–16

Hymeneus 1 Tim. 1:20; 2 Tim. 2:17–18

Hymn

Mt. 26:30 (Mk. 14:26) had sung a *h*, they went out
Eph. 5:19 speaking to yourselves in psalms and *h*
Col. 3:16 admonishing one another in psalms and *h*

Hypocrisy *See also* Deceit, Falsehood, Lie

Is. 32:6 heart will work iniquity, to practise *h*
Mt. 23:28 but within ye are full of *h* and iniquity
Mk. 12:15 but he, knowing their *h*, said unto them
Lk. 12:1 the leaven of the Pharisees, which is *h*
1 Tim. 4:2 speaking lies in *h*; having their
Jas. 3:17 without partiality, and without *h*
1 Pet. 2:1 aside all malice, and all guile, and *h*

Hypocrite

Job 8:13 forget God; and the *h*'s hope shall perish
13:16 for a *h* shall not come before him
15:34 the congregation of *h* shall be desolate
27:8 what is the hope of the *h*, though he hath
34:30 *h* reign not, lest the people be ensnared
36:13 but the *h* in heart heap up wrath: they cry
Prov. 11:9 *h* with his mouth destroyeth his neighbor
Is. 9:17 for every one is a *h* and an evildoer
33:14 afraid; fearfulness hath surprised the *h*
Mt. 6:2 alms, do not sound a trumpet. . as the *h* do
6:5 thou prayest, thou shalt not be as the *h* are
6:16 when ye fast, be not, as the *h*, of a sad
7:5 (Lk. 6:42) thou *h*, first cast out the beam
15:7 (Mk. 7:6) ye *h*, well did Esaias prophesy of you
16:3 (Lk. 12:56) O ye *h*, ye can discern. . the sky
22:18 perceived. . and said, Why tempt ye me, ye *h*
23:13 (Lk. 11:44) woe. . scribes and Pharisees, *h*!
24:51 appoint him his portion with the *h*
Lk. 13:15 *h*, doth not each. . on the sabbath loose

Hypocritical

Ps. 35:16 with *h* mockers in feasts, they gnashed
Is. 10:6 I will send him against a *h* nation

Hyssop

Ex. 12:22 a bunch of *h*, and dip it in the blood
Ps. 51:7 purge me with *h*, and I shall be clean
Jn. 19:29 put it upon *h*, and put it to his mouth
Heb. 9:19 blood. . with water. . scarlet wool, and *h*

I

Ice

Job 6:16 which are blackish by reason of the *i*
Ps. 147:17 he casteth forth his *i* like morsels

Ichabod 1 Sam. 4:21

Iconium Acts 13:51; 2 Tim. 3:11

Idle

Ex. 5:8 (5:17) for they be *i*; therefore they cry
Prov. 19:15 and an *i* soul shall suffer hunger
Mt. 12:36 every *i* word that men shall speak, they
20:3 saw others standing *i* in the market place
Lk. 24:11 their words seemed to them as *i* tales
1 Tim. 5:13 they learn to be *i*, wandering about

Idleness

Prov. 31:27 and eateth not the bread of *i*
Ezek. 16:49 fulness of bread, and abundance of *i*

Idol *See also* god, Image

Lev. 19:4 turn ye not unto *i*, nor make. . molten gods
26:1 ye shall make you no *i* nor graven image
1 Kgs. 15:13 (2 Chr. 15:16) and Asa destroyed her *i*
2 Kgs. 21:11 hath made Judah also to sin with his *i*
1 Chr. 16:26 (Ps. 96:5) the gods of the people are *i*
2 Chr. 15:8 put away the abominable *i* out of all

2 Chr. 34:7 cut down all the *i* throughout all the land
Ps. 115:4 (135:15) their *i* are silver and gold
Is. 2:8 their land also is full of *i*; they worship
  2:18 and the *i* he shall utterly abolish
  31:7 in that day every man shall cast away his *i*
  48:5 lest thou shouldest say, Mine *i* hath done
  57:5 inflaming yourselves with *i* under every
  66:3 that burneth incense, as if he blessed an *i*
Jer. 22:28 is this man Coniah a despised broken *i*?
  50:2 her *i* are confounded, her images are broken
  50:38 images, and they are mad upon their *i*
Ezek. 14:4 that setteth up his *i* in his heart
  14:6 repent, and turn yourselves from your *i*
  20:18 nor defile yourselves with their *i*
  36:25 and from all your *i*, will I cleanse you
Hos. 4:17 Ephraim is joined to *i*: let him alone
  8:4 silver and their gold have they made them *i*
  14:8 say, What have I to do any more with *i*?
Mic. 1:7 and all the *i* thereof will I lay desolate
Zech. 10:2 *i* have spoken vanity, and the diviners
  11:17 woe to the *i* shepherd that leaveth the
  13:2 cut off the names of the *i* out of the land
Acts 15:20 (15:29; 21:25) abstain from pollutions of *i*
Rom. 2:22 thou that abhorrest *i*, dost thou commit
1 Cor. 8:1 now as touching things offered unto *i*
  8:4 we know that an *i* is nothing in the world
  8:7 conscience of the *i* unto this hour eat it as
  8:10 hast knowledge sit at meat in the *i*'s temple
  10:28 in sacrifice unto *i*, eat not for his sake
  12:2 carried away unto these dumb *i*, even as ye
2 Cor. 6:16 agreement hath the temple of God with *i*?
1 Thes. 1:9 how ye turned to God from *i* to serve
1 Jn. 5:21 little children, keep yourselves from *i*
Rev. 2:14 (2:20) to eat things sacrificed unto *i*

Idolater

1 Cor. 6:9 fornicators, nor *i*, nor adulterers, nor
Eph. 5:5 nor covetous man, who is an *i*, hath any
Rev. 21:8 *i*, and all liars, shall have their part

Idolatry *See also* Abomination

1 Sam. 15:23 and stubbornness is an iniquity and *i*
Acts 17:16 when he saw the city wholly given to *i*
1 Cor. 10:14 my dearly beloved, flee from *i*
Gal. 5:20 *i*, witchcraft, hatred, variance
Col. 3:5 and covetousness, which is *i*
1 Pet. 4:3 lusts. . banquetings, and abominable *i*

Ignorance

Lev. 4:2 if a soul shall sin through *i* against any
  4:13 whole congregation of Israel sin through *i*
Num. 15:25 it shall be forgiven them; for it is *i*
Acts 3:17 brethren, I wot that through *i* ye did it
  17:30 the times of this *i* God winked at; but now
Eph. 4:18 alienated. . through the *i* that is in them
1 Pet. 1:14 according to the former lusts in your *i*
  2:15 ye may put to silence the *i* of foolish men

Ignorant

Ps. 73:22 foolish was I, and *i*: I was as a beast
Is. 56:10 his watchmen are blind: they are all *i*
  63:16 art our Father, though Abraham be *i* of us
Acts 4:13 that they were unlearned and *i* men
Rom. 1:13 (1 Cor. 10:1, 12:1; 2 Cor. 1:8; 1 Thes.
  4:13) now I would not have you *i*, brethren
  10:3 for they, being *i* of God's righteousness
  11:25 that ye should be *i* of this mystery, lest
1 Cor. 14:38 but if any man be *i*, let him be *i*
2 Cor. 2:11 Satan. . for we are not *i* of his devices
Heb. 5:2 who can have compassion on the *i*, and on
2 Pet. 3:5 for this they willingly are *i* of
  3:8 beloved, be not *i* of this one thing, that one

Ignorantly

Num. 15:28 atonement for the soul that sinneth *i*
Deut. 19:4 whoso killeth his neighbor *i*, whom he
Acts 17:23 ye *i* worship, him declare I unto you
1 Tim. 1:13 mercy, because I did it *i* in unbelief

Ill

Job 20:26 it shall go *i* with him that is left in
Ps. 106:32 it went *i* with Moses for their sakes
Is. 3:11 woe unto the wicked! it shall be *i* with
Rom. 13:10 love worketh no *i* to his neighbor

Illuminate *See also* Enlighten, Lighten, Shine

Heb. 10:32 ye were *i*, ye endured a great fight of

Illyricum Rom. 15:19

Image *See also* god, Idol, Likeness

Gen. 1:26 and God said, Let us make man in our *i*
  31:19 had stolen the *i* that were her father's
Ex. 20:4 (Deut. 5:8) not make unto thee any graven *i*
  23:24 overthrow them. . quite break down their *i*
Lev. 26:1 graven *i*, neither rear you up a standing *i*
Deut. 4:16 lest ye. . make you a graven *i*
Judg. 17:4 made thereof a graven *i* and a molten *i*
1 Sam. 19:13 took an *i*, and laid it in the bed
2 Kgs. 10:27 and they brake down the *i* of Baal
Ps. 73:20 thou awakest, thou shalt despise their *i*
  78:58 moved him to jealousy with their graven *i*
  97:7 confounded be all they that serve graven *i*
Is. 41:29 their molten *i* are wind and confusion
  42:17 be greatly ashamed, that trust in graven *i*
  44:9 that make a graven *i* are all of them vanity
  48:5 graven *i*. . my molten *i*, hath commanded them
Jer. 10:14 (51:17) for his molten *i* is falsehood
Dan. 2:31 O king, sawest, and behold a great *i*
  3:1 Nebuchadnezzar the king made an *i* of gold
  3:18 not serve thy gods, nor worship the golden *i*
Mic. 5:13 *i* also will I cut off, and thy standing *i*
Hab. 2:18 what profiteth the graven *i* that the
Mt. 22:20 (Mk. 12:16; Lk. 20:24) whose is this *i*
Acts 19:35 of the *i* which fell down from Jupiter?
Rom. 1:23 glory of the uncorruptible God into an *i*
  8:29 to be conformed to the *i* of his Son
  11:4 have not bowed the knee to the *i* of Baal
1 Cor. 11:7 as he is the *i* and glory of God
  15:49 *i* of the earthy, we shall also bear the *i*
2 Cor. 3:18 changed into the same *i* from glory to
  4:4 glorious gospel of Christ, who is the *i* of God
Col. 1:15 who is the *i* of the invisible God
  3:10 knowledge after the *i* of him that created
Heb. 1:3 his glory, and the express *i* of his person
Rev. 14:11 who worship the beast and his *i*

Imagery

Ezek. 8:12 every man in the chambers of his *i*?

Imagination *See also* Device, Invention

Gen. 6:5 every *i* of the thoughts of his heart was
  8:21 the *i* of man's heart is evil from his youth
Deut. 29:19 though I walk in the *i* of mine heart
  31:21 for I know their *i* which they go about
1 Chr. 28:9 understandeth all the *i* of the thoughts
Prov. 6:18 a heart that deviseth wicked *i*
Jer. 23:17 walketh after the *i* of his own heart
Lam. 3:60 vengeance and all their *i* against me
Lk. 1:51 scattered the proud in the *i* of their
Rom. 1:21 but became vain in their *i*, and their
2 Cor. 10:5 casting down *i*, and every high thing

Imagine *See also* Think

Gen. 11:6 be restrained . . which they have *i* to do
Job 6:26 do ye *i* to reprove words, and the speeches
Ps. 2:1 (Acts 4:25) the people *i* a vain thing?
    10:2 be taken in the devices that they have *i*
    21:11 they *i* a mischievous device, which they
    38:12 seek my hurt . . *i* deceits all the day long
    62:3 how long will ye *i* mischief against a man?
    140:2 which *i* mischiefs in their heart
Prov. 12:20 is in the heart of them that *i* evil
Hos. 7:15 yet do they *i* mischief against me
Nah. 1:9 what do ye *i* against the LORD? he will
Zech. 7:10 (8:17) let none of you *i* evil against his

Immanuel *See also* Emmanuel

Is. 7:14 (Mt. 1:23) a son, and shall call his name *I*
    8:8 shall fill the breadth of thy land, O *I*

Immediately

Mt. 8:3 (Mk. 1:42; Lk. 5:13) *i*. . leprosy was cleansed
    20:34 (Mk. 10:52; Lk. 18:43) *i*. . received sight
Mk. 1:31 (Lk. 4:39) *i* the fever left her
    2:12 (Lk. 5:25) *i* he arose, took up the bed
Lk. 1:64 his mouth was opened *i*, and his tongue
    8:47 had touched him, and how she was healed *i*
    13:13 *i* she was made straight, and glorified God
Jn. 6:21 *i* the ship was at the land whither they went
Acts 3:7 and *i* his feet and ankle bones received

Immortal

1 Tim. 1:17 unto the King eternal, *i*, invisible

Immortality *See also* Life

Rom. 2:7 seek for glory and honor and *i*, eternal
1 Cor. 15:53 and this mortal must put on *i*
1 Tim. 6:16 who only hath *i*, dwelling in the light

Immutability

Heb. 6:17 to show . . the *i* of his counsel, confirmed

Immutable

Heb. 6:18 that by two *i* things, in which it was

Impart

Job 39:17 neither hath he *i* to her understanding
Lk. 3:11 coats, let him *i* to him that hath none
Rom. 1:11 I may *i* unto you some spiritual gift
1 Thes. 2:8 we were willing to have *i* unto you

Impediment

Mk. 7:32 was deaf, and had an *i* in his speech

Impenitent

Rom. 2:5 after thy hardness and *i* heart, treasurest

Implacable

Rom. 1:31 without natural affection, *i*, unmerciful

Importunity

Lk. 11:8 yet because of his *i* he will rise and give

Impose

Ezra 7:24 shall not be lawful to *i* toll, tribute
Heb. 9:10 carnal ordinances, *i* on them until

Impossible

Mt. 17:20 and nothing shall be *i* unto you
    19:26 (Mk. 10:27; Lk. 18:27) with men this is *i*
Lk. 1:37 for with God nothing shall be *i*
    17:1 it is *i* but that offenses will come: but woe
Heb. 6:4 is *i* for those who were once enlightened
    6:18 things, in which it was *i* for God to lie
    11:6 without faith it is *i* to please him

Impotent

Jn. 5:3 in these lay a great multitude of *i* folk
    5:7 the *i* man answered him, Sir, I have no man
Acts 4:9 the good deed done to the *i* man, by what
    14:8 sat a certain man at Lystra, *i* in his feet

Impoverish

Judg. 6:6 and Israel was greatly *i* because of the
Is. 40:20 he that is so *i* that he hath no oblation
Jer. 5:17 they shall *i* thy fenced cities, wherein

Imprison

Acts 22:19 know that I *i* and beat in every synagogue

Imprisonment

Ezra 7:26 or to confiscation of goods, or to *i*
2 Cor. 6:5 in stripes, in *i*, in tumults, in labors
Heb. 11:36 scourgings, yea, moreover of bonds and *i*

Impudent

Prov. 7:13 and kissed him, and with an *i* face said
Ezek. 2:4 for they are *i* children and stiffhearted
    3:7 the house of Israel are *i* and hard-hearted

Impute *See also* Count, Reckon

Lev. 7:18 neither shall it be *i* unto him that offereth
    17:4 blood shall be *i* unto that man; he hath shed
1 Sam. 22:15 king *i* any thing unto his servant
2 Sam. 19:19 let not my lord *i* iniquity unto me
Ps. 32:2 (Rom. 4:8) whom the LORD *i* not iniquity
Hab. 1:11 offend, *i* this his power unto his god
Rom. 4:6 whom God *i* righteousness without works
    4:22 (Jas. 2:23) was *i* to him for righteousness
    5:13 but sin is not *i* when there is no law
2 Cor. 5:19 not *i* their trespasses unto them

Incense

Ex. 30:8 he shall burn *i* upon it, a perpetual *i*
    30:9 ye shall offer no strange *i* thereon
Lev. 16:13 *i* upon the fire . . may cover the mercy seat
2 Chr. 26:18 not unto thee, Uzziah, to burn *i*
Ps. 141:2 my prayer be set forth before thee as *i*
Is. 1:13 vain oblations; *i* is an abomination unto me
    60:6 they shall bring gold and *i*; and they shall
Jer. 6:20 to what purpose cometh there to me *i* from
    11:17 provoke me to anger in offering *i* unto Baal
Ezek. 8:11 censer . . and a thick cloud of *i* went up
Mal. 1:11 every place *i* shall be offered unto my
Lk. 1:9 his lot was to burn *i* when he went into
    1:10 people were praying without at the time of *i*
Rev. 8:3 was given unto him much *i*, that he should

Incline *See also* Turn

Josh. 24:23 and *i* your heart unto the LORD God
1 Kgs. 8:58 he may *i* our hearts unto him, to walk
Ps. 40:1 LORD; and he *i* unto me, and heard my cry
    71:2 and cause me to escape: *i* thine ear unto me
    78:1 *i* your ears to the words of my mouth
    116:2 hath *i* his ear unto me, therefore will I
    119:36 *i* my heart unto thy testimonies, and not
    119:112 have *i* mine heart to perform thy statutes
    141:4 *i* not my heart to any evil thing
Prov. 2:2 *i* thine ear unto wisdom, and apply thine
    2:18 her house *i* unto death, and her paths unto
    5:13 nor *i* mine ear to them that instructed me!
Is. 55:3 *i* your ear, and come unto me: hear, and
Jer. 7:24 (7:26; 11:8; 17:23; 34:14) nor *i* their ear

Inclose

Ex. 39:6 onyx stones *i* in ouches of gold, graven
Ps. 17:10 they are *i* in their own fat: with their
    22:16 the assembly of the wicked have *i* me

Lam. 3:9 he hath *i* my ways with hewn stone
Lk. 5:6 they *i* a great multitude of fishes

Incontinency

1 Cor. 7:5 that Satan tempt you not for your *i*

Incontinent

2 Tim. 3:3 false accusers, *i*, fierce, despisers of

Incorruptible *See also* Uncorruptible

1 Cor. 9:25 obtain a corruptible crown; but we an *i*
15:52 dead shall be raised *i*, and we shall be
1 Pet. 1:4 to an inheritance *i*, and undefiled
1:23 born again, not of corruptible seed, but of *i*

Incorruption

1 Cor. 15:42 sown in corruption, it is raised in *i*
15:50 neither doth corruption inherit *i*
15:53 this corruptible must put on *i*, and this

Increase *See also* Enlarge, Flourish. Grow, Multiply

Gen. 7:17 waters *i*, and bare up the ark, and it
47:24 in the *i*, that ye shall give the fifth part
Ex. 1:7 of Israel were fruitful, and *i* abundantly
Lev. 19:25 may yield unto you the *i* thereof
25:16 of years thou shalt *i* the price thereof
25:20 we shall not sow, nor gather in our *i*
25:36 take thou no usury of him, or *i*: but fear
26:4 the land shall yield her *i*, and the trees
Num. 32:14 an *i* of sinful men, to augment yet the
Deut. 7:22 lest the beasts of the field *i* upon thee
14:22 shalt truly tithe all the *i* of thy seed
16:15 thy God shall bless thee in all thine *i*
Judg. 6:4 and destroyed the *i* of the earth, till
1 Sam. 2:33 all the *i* of thine house shall die in
1 Chr. 27:23 he would *i* Israel like to the stars
Job 1:10 and his substance is *i* in the land
8:7 small, thy latter end should greatly *i*
31:12 destruction, and would root out all mine *i*
Ps. 3:1 LORD, how are they *i* that trouble me!
4:7 in the time that their corn and their wine *i*
44:12 and dost not *i* thy wealth by their price
62:10 if riches *i*, set not your heart upon them
67:6 then shall the earth yield her *i*; and God
73:12 who prosper in the world; they *i* in riches
74:23 tumult of those that rise up against thee *i*
115:14 LORD shall *i* you more and more, you and
Prov. 1:5 wise man will hear, and will *i* learning
3:9 honor . . with the firstfruits of all thine *i*
9:9 teach a just man, and he will *i* in learning
11:24 there is that scattereth, and yet *i*
18:20 with the *i* of his lips shall he be filled
28:8 by usury and unjust gain *i* his substance
Eccl. 1:18 and he that *i* knowledge *i* sorrow
5:10 nor he that loveth abundance with *i*
5:11 when goods *i*, they are *i* that eat them
Is. 9:3 multiplied the nation, and not *i* the joy
9:7 of the *i* of his government and peace there
26:15 *i* the nation, O LORD, thou hast *i* the nation
29:19 meek also shall *i* their joy in the LORD
40:29 to them that have no might he *i* strength
Jer. 2:3 Israel was . . the firstfruits of his *i*
23:3 and they shall be fruitful and *i*
Ezek. 18:8 upon usury, neither hath taken any *i*
34:27 earth shall yield her *i*, and they shall be
36:37 I will *i* them with men like a flock
Dan. 12:4 run to and fro, and knowledge shall be *i*
Hos. 4:7 as they were *i*, so they sinned against me
12:1 he daily *i* lies and desolation; and they do
Hab. 2:6 woe to him that *i* that which is not his!
Zech. 10:8 and they shall *i* as they have *i*

Mk. 4:8 and did yield fruit that sprang up and *i*
Lk. 2:52 Jesus *i* in wisdom and stature, and in favor
17:5 apostles said unto the Lord, *I* our faith
Jn. 3:30 he must *i*, but I must decrease
Acts 6:7 the word of God *i*; and the number of the
16:5 in the faith, and *i* in number daily
1 Cor. 3:6 Apollos watered; but God gave the *i*
2 Cor. 9:10 and *i* the fruits of your righteousness
10:15 having hope, when your faith is *i*, that we
Eph. 4:16 maketh *i* of the body unto the edifying
Col. 1:10 good work, and *i* in the knowledge of God
2:19 and knit together, *i* with the *i* of God
1 Thes. 3:12 Lord make you to *i* and abound in love
4:10 we beseech you, brethren, that ye *i* more
2 Tim. 2:16 for they will *i* unto more ungodliness
Rev. 3:17 thou sayest, I am rich, and *i* with goods

Incredible

Acts 26:8 why should it be thought a thing *i* with

Incurable

2 Chr. 21:18 him in his bowels with an *i* disease
Job 34:6 my wound is *i* without transgression
Jer. 15:18 why is my pain perpetual, and my wound *i*
30:12 thy bruise is *i*, and thy wound is grievous
Mic. 1:9 her wound is *i*; for it is come unto Judah

Indebted

Lk. 11:4 we also forgive every one that is *i* to us

India Esth. 1:1 (8:9)

Indignation *See also* Anger, Fury, Wrath

Deut. 29:28 in great *i*, and cast them into another
2 Kgs. 3:27 and there was great *i* against Israel
Ps. 69:24 pour out thine *i* upon them, and let thy
102:10 because of thine *i* and thy wrath
Is. 10:5 and the staff in their hand is mine *i*
26:20 a little moment, until the *i* be overpast
34:2 for the *i* of the LORD is upon all nations
Jer. 10:10 nations shall not be able to abide his *i*
15:17 thy hand: for thou hast filled me with *i*
Dan. 11:30 and have *i* against the holy covenant
Mic. 7:9 I will bear the *i* of the LORD, because I
Nah. 1:6 who can stand before his *i*? and who can
Zech. 1:12 of Judah, against which thou hast had *i*
Mt. 20:24 moved with *i* against the two brethren
26:8 (Mk. 14:4) his disciples saw it, they had *i*
Acts 5:17 high priest rose up, and all . . filled with *i*
Rom. 2:8 but obey unrighteousness, *i* and wrath
2 Cor. 7:11 yea, what *i*, yea, what fear, yea, what
Heb. 10:27 judgment and fiery *i*, which shall devour
Rev. 14:10 without mixture into the cup of his *i*

Indite

Ps. 45:1 my heart is *i* a good matter: I speak of

Industrious

1 Kgs. 11:28 seeing the young man that he was *i*

Inexcusable

Rom. 2:1 thou art *i*, O man, whosoever thou art

Infallible

Acts 1:3 by many *i* proofs, being seen of them

Infamous

Ezek. 22:5 mock thee, which art *i* and much vexed

Infamy

Prov. 25:10 to shame, and thine *i* turn not away

Infant

1 Sam. 15:3 slay both man and woman, *i* and suckling
Job 3:16 had not been; as *i* which never saw light
Is. 65:20 shall be no more thence an *i* of days
Hos. 13:16 their *i* shall be dashed in pieces
Lk. 18:15 they brought unto him also *i*, that he

Inferior

2 Cor. 12:13 wherein ye were *i* to other churches

Infidel

2 Cor. 6:15 what . . hath he that believeth with an *i*?
1 Tim. 5:8 denied the faith, and is worse than an *i*

Infinite

Job 22:5 wickedness great? and thine iniquities *i*?
Ps. 147:5 of great power: his understanding is *i*
Nah. 3:9 and Egypt were her strength, and it was *i*

Infirmity *See also* Disease, Sickness, Weakness

Lev. 12:2 days of the separation for her *i* shall
Ps. 77:10 said, This is my *i*: but I will remember
Prov. 18:14 the spirit of a man will sustain his *i*
Mt. 8:17 saying, Himself took our *i*, and bare our
Lk. 5:15 to hear, and to be healed by him of their *i*
    7:21 he cured many of their *i* and plagues
    13:11 there was a woman which had a spirit of *i*
Jn. 5:5 a certain man was there, which had an *i*
Rom. 6:19 because of the *i* of your flesh
    8:26 Spirit also helpeth our *i*: for we know not
    15:1 strong ought to bear the *i* of the weak
2 Cor. 11:30 glory of the things which concern mine *i*
    12:5 of myself I will not glory, but in mine *i*
    12:10 I take pleasure in *i*, in reproaches
Gal. 4:13 how through *i* of the flesh I preached
1 Tim. 5:23 thy stomach's sake and thine often *i*
Heb. 4:15 be touched with the feeling of our *i*
    5:2 for that he himself also is compassed with *i*

Inflame

Is. 5:11 continue until night, till wine *i* them!
    57:5 *i* yourselves with idols under every green

Inflict

2 Cor. 2:6 is this punishment, which was *i* of many

Influence

Job 38:31 canst thou bind the sweet *i* of Pleiades

Inform

Deut. 17:10 do according to all that they *i* thee
Dan. 9:22 he *i* me, and talked with me, and said
Acts 24:1 Tertullus . . *i* the governor against Paul

Ingathering

Ex. 23:16 (34:22) feast of *i*. . in the end of the year

Inhabit *See also* Abide, Dwell, Live

Lev. 16:22 all their iniquities unto a land not *i*
Ps. 22:3 holy, O thou that *i* the praises of Israel
Prov. 10:30 but the wicked shall not *i* the earth
Is. 13:20 (Jer. 50:39) it shall never be *i*
    44:26 saith to Jerusalem, Thou shalt be *i*
    45:18 created it not in vain, he formed it to be *i*
    57:15 the high and lofty One that *i* eternity
    65:21 they shall build houses, and *i* them
Jer. 6:8 lest I make thee desolate, a land not *i*
    46:26 afterward it shall be *i*, as in the days of
Ezek. 12:20 cities that are *i* shall be laid waste
Amos 9:14 shall build the waste cities, and *i* them

Zeph. 1:13 shall also build houses, but not *i* them
Zech. 2:4 Jerusalem shall be *i* as towns without walls
    12:6 Jerusalem shall be *i* again in her own place

Inhabitant

Gen. 19:25 overthrew those cities. . and all the *i*
Ex. 15:15 all the *i* of Canaan shall melt away
Num. 13:32 is a land that eateth up the *i* thereof
Judg. 5:7 the *i* of the villages ceased, they ceased
    5:23 curse ye bitterly the *i* thereof; because
1 Kgs. 17:1 and Elijah . . who was of the *i* of Gilead
    21:11 who were the *i* in his city, did as Jezebel
Job 28:4 the flood breaketh out from the *i*
Ps. 33:8 let all the *i* of the world stand in awe
    49:1 ye people; give ear, all ye *i* of the world
    75:3 earth and all the *i* thereof are dissolved
Is. 6:11 until the cities be wasted without *i*
    12:6 cry out and shout, thou *i* of Zion: for great
    26:9 the *i* of the world will learn righteousness
    33:24 the *i* shall not say, I am sick: the people
    40:22 the *i* thereof are as grasshoppers
    42:11 let the *i* of the rock sing, let them shout
Jer. 2:15 waste: his cities are burned without *i*
    10:17 gather up thy wares. . O *i* of the fortress
Zech. 8:21 the *i* of one city shall go to another
Rev. 17:2 *i* of the earth have been made drunk with

Inherit *See also* Possess

Gen. 15:7 out of Ur . . to give thee this land to *i* it
    28:4 thou mayest *i* the land wherein thou art a
Ex. 23:30 until thou be increased, and *i* the land
    32:13 I give unto your seed, and they shall *i* it
Lev. 20:24 ye shall *i* their land, and I will give
    25:46 to *i* them for a possession; they shall be
Num. 18:24 tithes. . I have given to the Levites to *i*
    34:13 this is the land which ye shall *i* by lot
Deut. 1:38 for he shall cause Israel to *i* it
    12:10 which the LORD your God giveth you to *i*
    21:16 he maketh his sons to *i* that which he hath
Josh. 14:1 countries which the children of Israel *i*
Judg. 11:2 thou shalt not *i* in our father's house
1 Sam. 2:8 to make them *i* the throne of glory
2 Chr. 20:11 possession, which thou hast given us to *i*
Ps. 25:13 at ease; and his seed shall *i* the earth
    37:9 wait upon the LORD, they shall *i* the earth
    37:11 (Mt. 5:5) the meek shall *i* the earth
    37:22 as be blessed of him shall *i* the earth
    37:29 the righteous shall *i* the land, and dwell
    37:34 and he shall exalt thee to *i* the land
    82:8 judge the earth: for thou shall *i* all nations
    105:44 and they *i* the labor of the people
Prov. 3:35 wise shall *i* glory: but shame shall be
    8:21 may cause those that love me to *i* substance
    14:18 the simple *i* folly: but the prudent are
Is. 49:8 to cause to *i* the desolate heritages
    54:3 thy seed shall *i* the Gentiles, and make the
    57:13 shall possess the land . . *i* my holy mountain
    60:21 righteous: they shall *i* the land for ever
    65:9 and mine elect shall *i* it, and my servants
Jer. 12:14 I have caused my people Israel to *i*
    16:19 shall say, Surely our fathers have *i* lies
Ezek. 33:24 Abraham was one, and he *i* the land
    47:13 be the border, whereby ye shall *i* the land
Zech. 2:12 LORD shall *i* Judah his portion in the
Mt. 5:5 are the meek: for they shall *i* the earth
    19:29 hundredfold, and shall *i* everlasting life
    25:34 *i* the kingdom prepared for you from the
Mk. 10:17 (Lk. 10:25; 18:18) I may *i* eternal life?
1 Cor. 6:9 unrighteous . . not *i* the kingdom of God?
    15:50 flesh and blood cannot *i* . . kingdom of God
Gal. 5:21 do such things shall not *i* the kingdom
Heb. 6:12 through faith and patience *i*. . promises

Heb. 12:17 when he would have *i* the blessing, he was
1 Pet. 3:9 called, that ye should *i* a blessing
Rev. 21:7 he that overcometh shall *i* all things

Inheritance *See also* Heritage, Possession, Riches, Wealth

Gen. 31:14 is there yet any portion or *i* for us in
Ex. 15:17 plant them in the mountain of thine *i*
34:9 pardon. . our sin, and take us for thine *i*
Num. 18:20 shalt have no *i*. . I am thy part and thine *i*
18:21 Levi all the tenth in Israel for an *i*
26:53 land shall be divided for an *i* according
27:8 no son. . cause his *i* to pass unto his daughter
27:11 then ye shall give his *i* unto his kinsman
36:9 neither shall the *i* remove from one tribe
Deut. 4:20 to be unto him a people of *i*, as ye are
4:38 to give thee their land for an *i*, as it is
9:29 yet they are thy people and thine *i*, which
Job 31:2 and what *i* of the Almighty from on high?
Ps. 2:8 I shall give thee the heathen for thine *i*
16:5 LORD is the portion of mine *i* and of my cup
33:12 people whom he hath chosen for his own *i*
37:18 the upright: and their *i* shall be for ever
79:1 O God, the heathen are come into thine *i*
94:14 his people, neither will he forsake his *i*
106:5 thy nation, that I may glory with thine *i*
Prov. 13:22 man leaveth an *i* to his children's
19:14 house and riches are the *i* of fathers
20:21 *i* may be gotten hastily at the beginning
Eccl. 7:11 wisdom is good with an *i*: and by it
Is. 19:25 the work of my hands, and Israel mine *i*
Jer. 12:14 mine evil neighbors, that touch the *i*
Lam. 5:2 our *i* is turned to strangers, our houses
Ezek. 47:14 this land shall fall unto you for *i*
Mt. 21:38 (Mk. 12:7; Lk. 20:14) kill him. . seize. . *i*
Lk. 12:13 my brother, that he divide the *i* with me
Acts 20:32 to give you an *i* among all them which
26:18 receive forgiveness of sins, and *i* among
Gal. 3:18 if the *i* be of the law, it is no more of
Eph. 1:11 in whom also we have obtained an *i*
1:14 the earnest of our *i* until the redemption
1:18 riches of the glory of his *i* in the saints
5:5 hath any *i* in the kingdom of Christ
Col. 1:12 to be partakers of the *i* of the saints
3:24 receive the reward of the *i*: for ye serve
Heb. 1:4 hath by *i* obtained a more excellent name
9:15 might receive the promise of eternal *i*
11:8 which he should after receive for an *i*
1 Pet. 1:4 to an *i* incorruptible, and undefiled

Iniquity *See also* Sin, Transgression, Trespass, Wickedness

Gen. 15:16 the *i* of the Amorites is not yet full
Ex. 20:5 (34:7; Num. 14:18; Deut. 5:9) visiting the *i*
34:7 (Num. 14:18) forgiving *i* and transgression
Lev. 16:22 goat shall bear upon him all their *i*
Num. 23:21 he hath not beheld *i* in Jacob, neither
Deut. 32:4 a God of truth and without *i*, just and
1 Sam. 3:14 *i* of Eli's house shall not be purged
15:23 and stubbornness is as *i* and idolatry
Ezra 9:13 hast punished us less than our *i* deserve
Job 4:8 they that plow *i*, and sow wickedness, reap
6:30 is there *i* in my tongue? cannot my taste
15:16 filthy is man, which drinketh *i* like water?
20:27 heaven shall reveal his *i*; and the earth
22:23 shalt put away *i* far from thy tabernacles
33:9 I am innocent; neither is there *i* in me
34:32 if I have done *i*, I will do no more
36:23 or who can say, Thou hast wrought *i*?
Ps. 6:8 (Mt. 7:23; Lk. 13:27) depart. . workers of *i*

Ps. 7:3 if there be *i* in my hands
7:14 he travaileth with *i*, and hath conceived
25:11 O LORD, pardon mine *i*; for it is great
32:2 the man unto whom the LORD imputeth not *i*
37:1 neither be. . envious against the workers of *i*
38:4 mine *i* are gone over mine head: as a heavy
51:2 wash me thoroughly from mine *i*, and cleanse
51:5 I was shapen in *i*; and in sin did my mother
51:9 face from my sins, and blot out all mine *i*
65:3 *i* prevail against me. . thou shalt purge them
66:18 if I regard *i* in my heart, the Lord will
69:27 add *i* unto their *i*: and let them not come
79:8 O remember not against us former *i*: let thy
90:8 thou hast set our *i* before thee, our secret
92:9 all the workers of *i* shall be scattered
94:20 shall the throne of *i* have fellowship with
103:3 who forgiveth all thine *i*; who healeth all
119:3 they also do no *i*: they walk in his ways
119:133 and let not any *i* have dominion over me
130:3 shouldest mark *i*, O Lord, who shall stand?
130:8 and he shall redeem Israel from all his *i*
Prov. 5:22 his own *i* shall take the wicked himself
16:6 by mercy and truth *i* is purged: and by
22:8 he that soweth *i* shall reap vanity
Is. 5:18 woe unto. . that draw *i* with cords of vanity
6:7 thine *i* is taken away, and thy sin purged
40:2 warfare is accomplished. . her *i* is pardoned
43:24 thy sins, thou hast wearied me with thine *i*
53:5 he was bruised for our *i*: the chastisement
53:6 the LORD hath laid on him the *i* of us all
53:11 justify many; for he shall bear their *i*
59:2 *i* have separated between you and your God
59:3 defiled with blood, and your fingers with *i*
64:9 O LORD, neither remember *i* for ever
65:7 your *i*, and the *i* of your fathers together
Jer. 2:5 what *i* have your fathers found in me
3:13 only acknowledge thine *i*, that thou hast
31:30 every one shall die for his own *i*
31:34 (Heb. 10:17) for I will forgive their *i*
33:8 and I will cleanse them from all their *i*
Ezek. 3:18 same wicked man shall die in his *i*
4:5 have laid upon thee the years of their *i*
16:49 this was the *i* of thy sister Sodom
18:17 he shall not die for the *i* of his father
18:30 repent, and turn. . so *i* shall not be your ruin
28:15 wast perfect. . till *i* was found in thee
36:33 I shall have cleansed you from all your *i*
39:23 of Israel went into captivity for their *i*
Dan. 9:5 we have sinned, and have committed *i*
9:24 to make reconciliation for *i*, and to bring
Hos. 7:1 then the *i* of Ephraim was discovered
14:2 take away all *i*. . receive us graciously
Mic. 2:1 woe to them that devise *i*, and work evil
7:18 a God like unto thee, that pardoneth *i*
Hab. 1:3 why dost thou show me *i*, and cause me
1:13 to behold evil, and canst not look on *i*
Mal. 2:6 mouth, and *i* was not found in his lips
Mt. 7:23 (Lk. 13:27) depart from me, ye that work *i*
23:28 but within ye are full of hypocrisy and *i*
24:12 because *i* shall abound, the love of many
Acts 1:18 purchased a field with the reward of *i*
3:26 in turning away every one of you from his *i*
Rom. 4:7 blessed are they whose *i* are forgiven
6:19 servants to uncleanness and to *i* unto *i*
1 Cor. 13:6 rejoiceth not in *i*, but rejoiceth in
2 Thes. 2:7 for the mystery of *i* doth already work
2 Tim. 2:19 nameth the name of Christ depart from *i*
Tit. 2:14 might redeem us from all *i*, and purify
Heb. 1:9 hast loved righteousness, and hated *i*
8:12 (10:17) and their *i* will I remember no more
Jas. 3:6 the tongue is a fire, a world of *i*
2 Pet. 2:16 but was rebuked for his *i*
Rev. 18:5 unto heaven. . God hath remembered her *i*

Injure

Gal. 4:12 I am as ye are: ye have not *i* me at all

Injurious

1 Tim. 1:13 a persecutor, and *i*: but I obtained

Injustice

Job 16:17 not for any *i* in mine hands: also my

Ink

Jer. 36:18 and I wrote them with *i* in the book
2 Cor. 3:3 written not with *i*, but with the Spirit
2 Jn. 12 I would not write with paper and *i*: but I
3 Jn.13 I will not with *i* and pen write unto thee

Inn

Gen. 42:27 sack to give his ass provender in the *i*
Ex. 4:24 by the way in the *i*. . the LORD met him
Lk. 2:7 there was no room for them in the *i*
   10:34 brought him to an *i*, and took care of him

Inner *See also* Inward

1 Kgs. 6:27 he set the cherubim within the *i* house
Acts 16:24 a charge, thrust them into the *i* prison
Eph. 3:16 with might by his Spirit in the *i* man

Innocency

Gen. 20:5 integrity of my heart and *i* of my hands
Ps. 26:6 I will wash mine hands in *i*: so will I
   73:13 my heart in vain, and washed my hands in *i*
Dan. 6:22 forasmuch as before him *i* was found in me
Hos. 8:5 how long will it be ere they attain to *i*?

Innocent *See also* Guiltless, Harmless

Ex. 23:7 *i* and righteous slay thou not: for I will
Deut. 19:10 that *i* blood be not shed in thy land
   27:25 cursed. . he that taketh reward to slay an *i*
Job 4:7 who ever perished, being *i*? or where were
   9:23 he will laugh at the trial of the *i*
   9:28 I know that thou wilt not hold me *i*
   22:19 are glad: and the *i* laugh them to scorn
   33:9 I am clean without transgression, I am *i*
Ps. 15:5 to usury, nor taketh reward against the *i*
   19:13 I shall be *i* from the great transgression
   106:38 shed *i* blood, even the blood of their sons
Prov. 1:11 let us lurk privily for the *i* without
   6:17 a lying tongue, and hands that shed *i* blood
   28:20 maketh haste to be rich shall not be *i*
Jer. 2:34 blood of the souls of the poor *i*
   2:35 yet thou sayest, Because I am *i*, surely his
   19:4 have filled this place with the blood of *i*
Mt. 27:4 sinned in that I have betrayed the *i* blood
   27:24 I am *i* of the blood of this just person

Innumerable

Job 21:33 draw after him, as there are *i* before him
Ps. 40:12 *i* evils have compassed me about
   104:25 wide sea, wherein are things creeping *i*
Lk. 12:1 gathered. . an *i* multitude of people
Heb. 11:12 as the sand which is by the seashore *i*
   12:22 Jerusalem, and to an *i* company of angels

Inordinate

Ezek. 23:11 more corrupt in her *i* love than she
Col. 3:5 fornication, uncleanness, *i* affection

Inquire *See also* Ask, Question, Seek

Gen. 24:57 we will call the damsel, and *i* at her
Ex. 18:15 the people come unto me to *i* of God
Deut. 12:30 and that thou *i* not after their gods
Judg. 20:27 the children of Israel *i* of the LORD
1 Sam. 9:9 a man went to *i* of God, thus he spake
   23:2 David *i* of the LORD, saying, Shall I go and

2 Sam. 16:23 if a man had *i* at the oracle of God
   21:1 year after year; and David *i* of the LORD
2 Kgs. 1:2 *i* of Baal-zebub the god of Ekron whether
   3:11 a prophet. . that we may *i* of the LORD by him
   16:15 the brazen altar shall be for me to *i* by
   22:13 (2 Chr. 34:21) *i* of the LORD for me, and
1 Chr. 13:3 for we *i* not at it in the days of Saul
   18:10 his son to king David, to *i* of his welfare
Job 8:8 for *i*, I pray thee, of the former age
   10:6 thou *i* after mine iniquity, and searchest
Ps. 27:4 beauty of the LORD, and to *i* in his temple
   78:34 and they returned and *i* early after God
Eccl. 7:10 thou dost not *i* wisely concerning this
Is. 21:12 if ye will *i*, *i* ye: return, come
Ezek. 14:3 should I be *i* of at all by them?
   20:3 come to *i* of me?. . I will not be *i* of by you
   20:31 shall I be *i* of by you. . I will not be *i*
   36:37 I will yet. . be *i* of by the house of Israel
Dan. 1:20 understanding, that the king *i* of them
Zeph. 1:6 have not sought the LORD, nor *i* for him
Mt. 2:7 *i* of them. . what time the star appeared
   10:11 town ye shall enter, *i* who in it is worthy
Lk. 22:23 they began to *i* among themselves, which
Jn. 4:52 then *i* he of them the hour when he began
Acts 9:11 Straight, and *i* in the house of Judas
   19:39 if ye *i* any thing concerning other matters
   23:15 tomorrow, as though ye would *i* something
1 Pet. 1:10 of which salvation the prophets have *i*

Inquiry

Prov. 20:25 it is a snare. . after vows to make *i*
Acts 10:17 the men. . had made *i* for Simon's house

Inquisition

Deut. 19:18 and the judges shall make diligent *i*
Esth. 2:23 when *i* was made of the matter, it was
Ps. 9:12 maketh *i* for blood, he remembereth them

Inscription

Acts 17:23 altar with this *i*, TO THE UNKNOWN GOD

Inspiration

Job 32:8 *i* of the Almighty giveth them understanding
2 Tim. 3:16 all Scripture is given by *i* of God

Instant

Is. 29:5 yea, it shall be at an *i* suddenly
   30:13 whose breaking cometh suddenly at an *i*
Jer. 18:7 at what *i* I shall speak concerning
Lk. 2:38 she coming in that *i* gave thanks likewise
Rom. 12:12 in tribulation; continuing *i* in prayer
2 Tim. 4:2 preach the word; be *i* in season, out of

Instantly

Lk. 7:4 came to Jesus, they besought him *i*, saying
Acts 26:7 our twelve tribes, *i* serving God day and

Instruct *See also* Command, Teach

Deut. 4:36 to hear his voice, that he might *i* thee
   32:10 he led him about, he *i* him, he kept him
Neh. 9:20 gavest also thy good Spirit to *i* them
Job 4:3 hast *i* many, and thou hast strengthened
   40:2 he that contendeth with the Almighty *i* him?
Ps. 2:10 be *i*, ye judges of the earth
   16:7 my reins also *i* me in the night seasons
   32:8 I will *i* thee and teach thee in the way
Prov. 21:11 the wise is *i*, he receiveth knowledge
Is. 28:26 his God doth *i* him to discretion
   40:14 with whom took he counsel, and who *i* him
Jer. 6:8 be thou *i*, O Jerusalem, lest my soul
Mt. 13:52 every scribe which is *i* unto the kingdom
   14:8 being before *i* of her mother, said, Give me
Lk. 1:4 of those things, wherein thou hast been *i*
Acts 18:25 this man was *i* in the way of the Lord

Rom. 2:18 more excellent, being *i* out of the law
1 Cor. 2:16 mind of the Lord, that he may *i* him?
Phil. 4:12 I am *i* both to be full and to be hungry
2 Tim. 2:25 in meekness *i* those that oppose

Instruction *See also* Advice, Counsel

Job 33:16 openeth the ears of men. . sealeth their *i*
Ps. 50:17 thou hatest *i*, and castest my words
Prov. 1:7 but fools despise wisdom and *i*
    1:8 hear the *i* of thy father, and forsake not
    4:1 hear, ye children, the *i* of a father, and
    4:13 take fast hold of *i*; let her not go
    5:12 I hated *i*, and my heart despised reproof
    6:23 and reproofs of *i* are the way of life
    8:10 receive my *i*, and not silver; and knowledge
    8:33 hear *i*, and be wise, and refuse it not
    9:9 give *i* to a wise man, and he will be yet wiser
    10:17 he is in the way of life that keepeth *i*
    12:1 whoso loveth *i* loveth knowledge
    15:32 he that refuseth *i* despiseth his own soul
    19:27 cease. . to hear the *i* that causeth to err
    23:12 apply thine heart unto *i*, and thine ears
    24:32 I looked upon it, and received *i*
Jer. 17:23 that they might not hear, nor receive *i*
Ezek. 5:15 an *i* and an astonishment unto the nations
Zeph. 3:7 thou wilt fear me, thou wilt receive *i*
2 Tim. 3:16 for correction, for *i* in righteousness

Instructor *See also* Master, Rabbi, Teacher

Gen. 4:22 an *i* of every artificer in brass and iron
Rom. 2:20 an *i* of the foolish, a teacher of babes
1 Cor. 4:15 ye have ten thousand *i* in Christ

Instrument *See also* Tool

Gen. 49:5 *i* of cruelty are in their habitations
Num. 3:8 shall keep all the *i* of the tabernacle
    35:16 if he smite him with an *i* of iron, so that
1 Chr. 9:29 to oversee. . all the *i* of the sanctuary
Neh. 12:36 with the musical *i* of David
Ps. 7:13 hath also prepared for him the *i* of death
    87:7 singers as the players on *i* shall be there
    144:9 upon a psaltery and an *i* of ten strings
Eccl. 2:8 as musical *i*, and that of all sorts
Is. 38:20 we will sing my songs to the stringed *i*
    41:15 I will make thee a new sharp threshing *i*
    54:16 and that bringeth forth an *i* for his work
Ezek. 33:32 can play well on an *i*: for they hear
Dan. 6:18 neither were *i* of music brought before
Amos 6:5 and invent to themselves *i* of music
Zech. 11:15 take unto thee. . *i* of a foolish shepherd
Rom. 6:13 your members as *i* of unrighteousness

Insurrection *See also* Rebellion, Sedition

Ezra 4:19 of old time hath made *i* against kings
Ps. 64:2 from the *i* of the workers of iniquity
Mk. 15:7 Barabbas. . committed murder in the *i*
Acts 18:12 Jews made *i* with one accord against Paul

Integrity *See also* Honesty, Righteousness, Uprightness

Gen. 20:5 *i* of my heart and innocency of my hands
1 Kgs. 9:4 David thy father walked, in *i* of heart
Job 2:3 still he holdeth fast his *i*, although thou
    2:9 dost thou still retain thine *i*? curse God
    27:5 till I die I will not remove mine *i* from me
    31:6 in an even balance, that God may know mine *i*
Ps. 7:8 my righteousness, and according to mine *i*
    25:21 let *i* and uprightness preserve me
    26:1 have walked in mine *i*: I have trusted also

Ps. 26:11 as for me, I will walk in mine *i*: redeem me
    41:12 thou upholdest me in mine *i*, and settest
    78:72 fed them according to the *i* of his heart
Prov. 11:3 the *i* of the upright shall guide them
    19:1 better is the poor that walketh in his *i*
    20:7 just man walketh in his *i*: his children are

Intelligence

Dan. 11:30 have *i* with them that forsake the holy

Intend

Ex. 2:14 judge over us? *i* thou to kill me, as thou
Josh. 22:33 did not *i* to go up against them in battle
Lk. 14:28 for which of you, *i* to build a tower
Acts 5:35 what ye *i* to do as thouching these men

Intent

2 Sam. 17:14 to the *i* that the LORD might bring
Jer. 30:24 until he have performed the *i* of his
Jn. 11:15 I was not there, to the *i* ye may believe
1 Cor. 10:6 to the *i* we should not lust after evil
Eph. 3:10 to the *i* that now unto the principalities

Intercession *See also* Meditation, Prayer, Supplication

Is. 53:12 and made *i* for the transgressors
Jer. 7:16 neither make *i* to me: for I will not hear
Rom. 8:26 the Spirit itself maketh *i* for us
    8:34 right hand of God, who also maketh *i* for us
    11:2 Elias? how he maketh *i* to God against Israel
1 Tim. 2:1 *i*, and giving of thanks, be made for all
Heb. 7:25 seeing he ever liveth to make *i* for them

Intercessor

Is. 59:16 no man, and wondered that there was no *i*

Intermeddle

Prov. 14:10 and a stranger doth not *i* with his joy
    18:1 through desire a man. . *i* with all wisdom

Interpret

Gen. 40:22 hanged the chief baker: as Joseph had *i*
    41:8 was none that could *i* them unto Pharaoh
Ezra 4:7 was written. . and *i* in the Syrian tongue
1 Cor. 12:30 do all speak with tongues? do all *i*?
    14:13 in an unknown tongue pray that he may *i*

Interpretation

Gen. 40:5 (41:11) according to the *i* of his dream
    40:8 do not *i* belong to God? tell me them
Judg. 7:15 telling of the dream, and the *i* thereof
Prov. 1:6 to understand a proverb, and the *i*
Eccl. 8:1 and who knoweth the *i* of a thing?
Dan. 2:4 (2:7, 36) the dream, and we will show the *i*
    2:45 dream is certain, and the *i* thereof sure
    4:18 Belteshazzar, declare the *i* thereof,
    4:19 let not the dream, or the *i*. . trouble thee
    5:12 Daniel be called, and he will show the *i*
    5:26 this is the *i* of the thing: MENE; God hath
1 Cor. 12:10 tongues; to another the *i* of tongues
    14:26 hath a tongue, hath a revelation, hath an *i*
Heb. 7:2 first being by *i* King of righteousness
2 Pet. 1:20 of the Scripture is of any private *i*

Intrude

Col. 2:18 *i* into those things which he hath not

Invade

1 Sam. 23:27 for the Philistines have *i* the land
    27:8 David and his men. . *i* the Geshurites

Invasion

1 Sam. 30:14 we made an *i* upon the south of the

Invent *See also* Create, Fashion, Form

2 Chr. 26:15 Jerusalem engines, *i* by cunning men
Amos 6:5 and *i* to themselves instruments of music

Invention *See also* Device, Imagination

Ps. 99:8 though thou tookest vengeance of their *i*
106:29 they provoked him to anger with their *i*
106:39 and went a whoring with their own *i*
Prov. 8:12 and find out knowledge of witty *i*
Eccl. 7:29 but they have sought out many *i*

Inventor

Rom. 1:30 *i* of evil things, disobedient to parents

Invisible

Rom. 1:20 the *i* things of him from the creation of
Col. 1:15 the image of him the *i* God, the firstborn of
· 1:16 visible and *i*, whether they be thrones, or
1 Tim. 1:17 now unto the King eternal, immortal, *i*
Heb. 11:27 for he endured, as seeing him who is *i*

Inward *See also* Inner

Lev. 13:55 it is fret *i*, whether it be bare within
2 Chr. 3:13 on their feet, and their faces were *i*
Job 19:19 all my *i* friends abhorred me
38:36 who hath put wisdom in the *i* parts?
Ps. 5:9 their *i* part is very wickedness
51:6 thou desirest truth in the *i* parts
Prov. 20:27 searching all the *i* parts of the belly
Jer. 31:33 I will put my law in their *i* parts
Lk. 11:39 but your *i* part is full of ravening and
Rom. 7:22 delight in the law of God after the *i* man
2 Cor. 4:16 yet the *i* man is renewed day by day
7:15 his *i* affection is more abundant toward you

Inwardly

Ps. 62:4 bless with their mouth, but they curse *i*
Mt. 7:15 but *i* they are ravening wolves
Rom. 2:29 but he is a Jew, which is one *i*

Iron

Gen. 4:22 of every artificer in brass and *i*
Deut. 8:9 a land whose stones are *i*, and out of
1 Kgs. 6:7 nor any tool of *i* heard in the house
2 Kgs. 6:6 cast it in thither; and the *i* did swim
Job 41:27 esteemeth *i* as straw, and brass as rotten
Ps. 2:9 thou shalt break them with a rod of *i*
107:10 such as sit. . bound in affliction and *i*
Prov. 27:17 *i* sharpeneth *i*; so a man sharpeneth
Eccl. 10:10 if the *i* be blunt, and he do not whet
Is. 45:2 of brass, and cut in sunder the bars of *i*
48:4 thy neck is an *i* sinew, and thy brow brass
60:17 bring gold, and for *i* I will bring silver
Jer. 1:18 have made thee this day. . an *i* pillar
15:12 shall *i* break the northern *i* and the
17:1 the sin of Judah is written with a pen of *i*
28:13 but thou shalt make for them yokes of *i*
Ezek. 4:3 *i* pan, and set it for a wall of *i* between
Dan. 2:33 his legs of *i*, his feet part of *i* and
Acts 12:10 they came unto the *i* gate that leadeth
1 Tim. 4:2 their conscience seared with a hot *i*
Rev. 2:27 (19:15) he shall rule them with a rod of *i*

Isaac

His birth foretold, Gen. 18:1–15; born, Gen. 21:1–7;
offered to God, Gen. 22:1–19; married Rebekah,
Gen. 24; father of twins, Gen. 25:19–26; dwelt in
Gerar, Gen. 26:1–6; Isaac and Abimelech, Gen.
26:7–33; blessed Jacob, Gen. 27:1–40; death and
burial, Gen. 35:29.

Gal. 4:28 as *I* was, are the children of promise
Heb. 11:20 by faith *I* blessed Jacob and Esau

Isaiah (Esaias)

Called, Is. 6; father of two sons, Is. 7:3; 8:3; prophe-
sied during the reign of Uzziah, Jotham, Ahaz,
Hezekiah, Is. 1:1; counseled Ahaz, Is. 7; counseled
Hezekiah, 2 Kgs. 19–20 (Is. 37–39).

Mt. 3:3 (Lk. 3:4) spoken of by the prophet *E*
15:7 (Mk. 7:6) hypocrites, well did *E* prophesy of
Lk. 4:17 delivered unto him. . book of the prophet *E* ·
Jn. 12:41 said *E*, when he saw his glory, and spake
Acts 8:28 sitting in his chariot read *E* the prophet
28:25 well spake the Holy Ghost by *E* the prophet
Rom. 9:27 *E* also crieth concerning Israel
10:20 *E* is very bold, and saith, I was found

Ish-bosheth 2 Sam. 2:8–4:12

Ishi Hos. 2:16

Ishmael son of Abraham

Gen. 16:11 bear a son, and shalt call his name *I*
17:18 God, O that *I* might live before thee!
25:12 these are the generations of *I*, Abraham's

Ishmael son of Nethaniah

2 Kgs. 25:25 (Jer. 41:2)

Ishmaelite Gen. 37:28; Judg. 8:24

Island

Job 22:30 he shall deliver the *i* of the innocent
Is. 11:11 from Hamath, and from the *i* of the sea
34:14 also meet with the wild beasts of the *i*
41:1 keep silence before me, O *i*; and let the
Acts 27:16 and running under a certain *i* which is
27:26 howbeit we must be cast upon a certain *i*
28:1 then they knew that the *i* was called Melita
Rev. 6:14 mountain and *i* were moved out of their

Isle

Gen. 10:5 by these were the *i* of the Gentiles divided
Ps. 72:10 the kings. . of the *i* shall bring presents
Is. 20:6 inhabitant of this *i* shall say in that
40:15 he taketh up the *i* as a very little thing
42:4 the earth: and the *i* shall wait for his law
49:1 listen, O *i*, unto me; and hearken, ye people
51:5 (60:9) the *i* shall wait upon me
Ezek. 27:3 art a merchant of the people for many *i*
Dan. 11:18 shall he turn his face unto the *i*
Acts 13:6 they had gone through the *i* unto Paphos
28:11 ship of Alexandria. . had wintered in the *i*
Rev. 1:9 was in the *i* that is called Patmos

Israel *See also* Jacob

Gen. 32:28 shall be called no more Jacob, but *I*
35:10 *I* shall be thy name; and he called his name *I*
Ex. 4:22 thus saith the LORD, *I* is my son, even my
Deut. 6:4 (Mk. 12:29) hear, O *I*: The LORD our God
1 Kgs. 12:19 (2 Chr. 10:19) *I* rebelled against the
2 Kgs. 17:6 took Samaria. . carried *I*. . into Assyria
17:23 the LORD removed *I* out of his sight
Amos 2:6 for three transgressions of *I*, and for four
Rom. 9:6 for they are not all *I*, which are of *I*
11:26 so all *I* shall be saved: as it is written
Gal. 6:16 peace. . and mercy, and upon the *I* of God

Israelite *See also* Hebrew, Jew

Jn. 1:47 behold an *I* indeed, in whom is no guile!
Rom. 9:4 who are *I*; to whom pertaineth the adoption
11:1 I also am an *I*, of the seed of Abraham

Issachar

Gen. 30:18; 49:14; Deut. 33:18; Josh. 19:17

Issue

Gen. 48:6 thy *i*, which thou begettest after them
Lev. 12:7 be cleansed from the *i* of her blood
  15:2 when any man hath a running *i*. . he is unclean
Josh. 8:22 other *i* out of the city against them
Ps. 68:20 GOD the Lord belong the *i* from death
Prov. 4:23 heart. . for out of it are the *i* of life
Mt. 9:20 (Mk. 5:25; Lk. 8:43) *i* of blood twelve years
  22:25 deceased, and, having no *i*, left his wife
Rev. 9:17 out of their mouths *i* fire and smoke and

Italian Acts 10:1

Italy

Acts 18:2 come from *I*, with his wife Priscilla
  27:1 we should sail into *I*, they delivered Paul
Heb. 13:24 they of I salute you

Itching

2 Tim. 4:3 to themselves teachers, having *i* ears

Ivory

1 Kgs. 10:18 (2 Chr. 9:17) made a great throne of *i*
  22:39 and the *i* house which he made
Ps. 45:8 out of the *i* palaces, whereby they have
Song 5:14 his belly is as bright *i* overlaid with
  7:4 thy neck is as a tower of *i*; thine eyes like
Ezek. 27:6 Ashurites have made thy benches of *i*
Amos 3:15 houses of *i* shall perish, and the great
  6:4 lie upon beds of *i*, and stretch themselves
Rev. 18:12 thyine wood, and all manner vessels of *i*

J

Jabbok Gen. 32:22; Num. 21:24

Jabesh-gilead

Judg. 21:8 there came none to the camp from *J-g*
1 Sam. 11:1 Nashah. . encamped against *J-g*
2 Sam. 2:4 the men of *J-g* were they that buried Saul

Jabez 1 Chr. 4:9–10

Jabin Josh. 11:1; Judg. 4:2, 17, 24; Ps. 83:9

Jacob See also Israel

Born, Gen. 25:19–26; obtained Esau's birthright, Gen. 25:27–34; received Isaac's blessing, Gen. 27:1–29; fled from Esau, Gen. 27:41–28:5; dream at Bethel and his vow, Gen. 28:10–22; served Laban for Rachel and Leah, Gen. 29:1–30; dealings with Laban, Gen. 30:25–43; departure from Padan-aram, Gen. 31; wrestled at Peniel, Gen. 32:24–32; reconciled with Esau, Gen. 33:1–16; blessed by God at Bethel, Gen. 35:1–15; went down to Egypt, Gen. 46–47; blessed Ephraim and Manasseh, Gen. 48; blessed his own sons, Gen. 49:1–27; death and burial, Gen. 49:28–50:14

Num. 24:17 there shall come a Star out of *J*
Hos. 12:12 *J* fled into the country of Syria
Mal. 1:2 (Rom. 9:13) saith the LORD: yet I loved *J*
Mt. 8:11 (Lk. 13:28) sit. . with Abraham. . Isaac. . *J*
Jn. 4:6 now *J*'s well was there. Jesus therefore
  4:12 art thou greater than our father *J*, which
Rom. 9:13 *J* have I loved, but Esau have I hated
Heb. 11:21 by faith, *J*, when he was a dying, blessed

Jael Judg. 4:17–22; 5:24

JAH Ps. 68:4

Jailer

Acts 16:23 charging the *j* to keep them safely

Jair Judg. 10:3–5

Jairus Mk. 5:22 (Lk. 8:41)

James the son of Zebedee

Called, Mt. 4:21 (Mk. 1:19; Lk. 5:10); at Jairus' house, Mk. 5:37 (Lk. 8:51); at transfiguration, Mt. 17:1 (Mk. 9:2; Lk. 9:28); at Gethsemane, Mt. 26:37 (Mk. 14:33); suffered martyrdom, Acts 12:2.

James the son of Alpheus

Mt. 10:3 (Mk. 3:18; Lk. 6:15; Acts 1:13)

James the brother of Jesus

Brother of Jesus, Mt. 13:55 (Mk. 6:3); disapproved Jesus' works, Jn. 7:3–5; saw the risen Christ, 1 Cor 15:7; met in the upper room, Acts 1:14; visited by Paul, Gal. 1:19; 2:9; at the Council of Jerusalem, Acts 15:13–34; received Paul's report, Acts 21:18.

Jangling

1 Tim. 1:6 swerved have turned aside unto vain *j*

Japheth Gen. 5:32; 9:18–10:2

Jason Acts 17:5–9

Jasper

Ex. 28:20 (39:13) row a beryl, and an onyx, and a *j*
Ezek. 28:13 and the *j*, the sapphire, the emerald
Rev. 4:3 he that sat was to look upon like a *j*
  21:18 the building of the wall of it was of *j*

Javelin

Num. 25:7 Phinehas. . took a *j* in his hand
1 Sam. 18:11 Saul cast the *j*; for he said, I will
  19:10 smote the *j* into the wall: and David fled

Jaw

Judg. 15:19 clave a hollow place that was in the *j*
Job 29:17 I brake the *j* of the wicked, and plucked
Ps. 22:15 and my tongue cleaveth to my *j*
Ezek. 29:4 I will put hooks in thy *j*, and I will
Hos. 11:4 as they that take off the yoke on their *j*

Jawbone

Judg. 15:16 with the *j* of an ass, heaps upon heaps

Jealous

Ex. 20:5 (Deut. 5:9) I the LORD thy God am a *j* God
  34:14 for the LORD, whose name is *J*, is a *j* God
Num. 5:14 he be *j* of his wife, and she be defiled
Deut. 4:24 God is a consuming fire, even a *j* God
  6:15 for the LORD thy God is a *j* God among you
1 Kgs. 19:10 (19:14) I have been very *j* for the LORD
Ezek. 39:25 and will be *j* for my holy name
Joel 2:18 then will the LORD be *j* for his land
Nah. 1:2 God is *j*, and the LORD revengeth
Zech. 1:14 I am *j* for Jerusalem and for Zion with
  8:2 I was *j* for Zion with great jealousy
2 Cor. 11:2 I am *j* over you with godly jealousy

Jealousy See also Envy

Num. 5:14 or if the spirit of *j* come upon him
  5:29 this is the law of *j*, when a wife goeth
  25:11 consumed not the children of Israel in my *j*
Deut. 32:16 provoked him to *j* with strange gods
  32:21 (Rom. 10:19) I will move them to *j* with those
1 Kgs. 14:22 they provoked him to *j* with their sins

Ps. 78:58 moved him to *j* with their graven images
79:5 angry for ever? shall thy *j* burn like fire?
Prov. 6:34 *j* is the rage of a man: therefore he
Song 8:6 strong as death; *j* is cruel as the grave
Is. 42:13 he shall stir up *j* like a man of war
Ezek. 8:3 of the image of *j*, which provoketh to *j*
Zech. 1:14 Jerusalem and for Zion with a great *j*
Rom. 11:11 unto the Gentiles. . provoke them to *j*
1 Cor. 10:22 do we provoke the Lord to *j*?
2 Cor. 11:2 for I am jealous over you with godly *j*

Jebusite
Josh. 15:63 (Judg. 1:21); 2 Sam. 5:6 (1 Chr. 11:4)

Jeconiah *See also* Jehoiachin
Esth. 2:6 (Jer. 24:1)

Jehoahaz king of Israel 2 Kgs. 13:1–9

Jehoahaz king of Judah
2 Kgs. 23:30–34 (2 Chr. 36:1–4)

Jehoash (Joash) king of Judah
2 Kgs. 11:2–12:21 (2 Chr. 22:11–24:27)

Jehoash (Joash) king of Israel
2 Kgs. 13:10–14:16

Jehoiachin *See also* Jeconiah
2 Kgs. 24:6–25:30

Jehoiada
2 Kgs. 11:4–12:16 (2 Chr. 22:11–24:16)

Jehoiakim 2 Kgs. 23:34–24:6 (2 Chr. 36:4–8)
Jer. 22:18 thus saith the LORD concerning *J*
26:21 when *J*. . heard his words, the king sought
36:32 the book which *J* king of Judah had burned
Dan. 1:2 Lord gave *J* king of Judah into his hand

Jehoram (Joram) king of Israel
2 Kgs. 3:1–9:26

Jehoram (Joram) king of Judah
2 Kgs. 8:16–24 (2 Chr. 21:1–20)

Jehoshaphat
1 Kgs. 22:2–50 (2 Chr. 17:1–21:1)
Joel 3:2 will bring them down into the valley of *J*

Jehosheba (Jehoshabeath)
2 Kgs. 11:2 (2 Chr. 22:11)

JEHOVAH *See also* God, LORD, Lord
Ex. 6:3 but by my name *J* was I not known to them
Ps. 83:18 whose name alone is *J*, art the Most High
Is. 12:2 *J* is my strength and my song; he also is
26:4 for in the LORD *J* is everlasting strength

Jehovah-jireh Gen. 22:14

Jehovah-nissi Ex. 17:15

Jehovah-shalom Judg. 6:24

Jehu the seer
1 Kgs. 16:1 then the word of the LORD came to *J*
2 Chr. 19:2 and *J*. . the seer went out to meet him
20:34 behold, they are written in the book of *J*

Jehu king of Israel
2 Kgs. 9:2–10:36; 2 Chr. 22:7–9

1 Kgs. 19:16 *J* the son of Nimshi shalt thou anoint
Hos. 1:4 the blood of Jezreel upon the house of *J*

Jeopardy *See also* Danger, Peril
2 Sam. 23:17 (1 Chr. 11:19) went in *j* of their lives?
Lk. 8:23 they were filled with water, and were in *j*
1 Cor. 15:30 and why stand we in *j* every hour?

Jephthah Judg. 11:1–12:7; Heb. 11:32

Jeremiah (Jeremias)
Called, Jer. 1:1–10; vision of almond rod and seething pot, 1:11–19; sign of marred girdle, 13:1–11; sign
of potter's vessel, 18; sign of earthen bottle, 19; put
in stocks, 20:1–6; sign of baskets of figs, 24; his life
threatened, 26; sign of purchase of field, 32:6–44;
prophesied to Rechabites, 35; wrote prophecies, 36;
imprisoned, 32:1–5; 37:11–38:28; released, 39:11–14;
40:1–6; taken into Egypt, 43:1–7.

Mt. 16:14 and others, *J*, or one of the prophets

Jericho
Num. 22:1 Israel set forward, and pitched. . by *J*
Josh. 2:1 go view the land, even *J*. And they went
6:2 Joshua, See, I have given into thine hand *J*
6:26 that riseth up and buildeth this city *J*
2 Sam. 10:5 (1 Chr. 19:5) tarry at *J* until your beards
1 Kgs. 16:34 did Hiel the Bethelite build *J*
2 Kgs. 2:5 the sons of the prophets that were at *J*
Mt. 20:29 (Mk. 10:46; Lk. 18:35) departed from *J*
Lk. 10:30 Jerusalem to *J*, and fell among thieves
18:35 was come nigh unto *J*, a certain blind man
19:1 and Jesus entered and passed through *J*
Heb. 11:30 by faith the walls of *J* fell down

Jeroboam son of Nebat
1 Kgs. 11:26–14:20 (2 Chr. 10:2–13:20)
1 Kgs. 12:20 when all Israel heard that *J* was come
14:16 (15:30; 2 Kgs. 3:3; 13:11; 14:24; 15:18;
17:22) sins of *J*. . who made Israel to sin

Jeroboam son of Joash
2 Kgs. 14:23–29; Hos. 1:1; Amos 7:10

Jerubbaal *See* Gideon

Jerusalem *See also* Salem, Zion
Josh. 15:63 (Judg. 1:21) the Jebusites dwell. . at *J*
Judg. 1:8 Judah had fought against *J*, and had taken
2 Sam. 5:6 (1 Chr. 11:4) the king. . went to *J* unto
16:15 Absalom, and all the people. . came to *J*
20:3 David came to his house at *J*; and the king
24:16 (1 Chr. 21:15) his hand upon *J* to destroy it
1 Kgs. 11:36 may have a light alway before me in *J*
14:25 (2 Chr. 12:2, 9) Shishak. . came up against *J*
2 Kgs. 14:13 (2 Chr. 25:23) brake down the wall of *J*
16:5 (Is. 7:1) Rezin. . Pekah. . came up to *J* to war
18:17 (Is. 36:2) Assyria sent. . great host against *J*
24:10 Nebuchadnezzar. . came up against *J*
25:10 (Jer. 52:14) brake. . the walls of *J*
2 Chr. 36:23 (Ezra 1:2) me to build him a house at *J*
Neh. 2:17 how *J* lieth waste. . build up the wall of *J*
12:27 at the dedication of the wall of *J* they
Ps. 51:18 unto Zion: build thou the walls of *J*
79:1 they defiled; they have laid *J* on heaps
122:6 pray for the peace of *J*; they shall prosper
137:5 if I forget thee, O *J*, let my right hand
Is. 44:26 that saith to *J*, Thou shalt be inhabited
52:1 O Zion; put on thy beautiful garments, O *J*
62:7 and till he make *J* a praise in the earth
Jer. 9:11 will make *J* heaps, and a den of dragons
26:18 (Mic. 3:12) and *J* shall become heaps

Lam. 1:8 *J* hath grievously sinned; therefore she
Ezek. 5:5 this is *J*: I have set it in the midst of
16:2 son of man, cause *J* to know her abominations
Dan. 9:16 thy fury be turned away from thy city *J*
Joel 3:17 then shall *J* be holy, and there shall no
Zech. 2:2 and he said unto me, To measure J
12:6 *J* shall be inhabited again in her own place
14:2 will gather all nations against *J* to battle
Mt. 5:35 by *J*; for it is the city of the great king
20:18 (Mk. 10:32; Lk. 18:31) behold, we go up to *J*
21:1 (Mk. 11:1) drew nigh unto *J* . . then sent Jesus
23:37 (Lk. 13:34) O *J*, *J* . . that killest the prophets
Lk. 2:22 they brought him to *J*, to present him to
2:42 he was twelve years old, they went up to *J*
9:51 he stedfastly set his face to go to *J*
21:24 *J* shall be trodden down of the Gentiles
24:47 be preached in his name . . beginning at *J*
24:49 but tarry ye in the city of *J*, until ye be
Acts 1:8 witnesses unto me both in *J*, and in all Judea
2:5 there were dwelling at *J* Jews, devout men
8:1 great persecution against the church . . at *J*
15:2 should go up to *J* unto the apostles and
21:13 not to be bound only, but also to die at *J*
Gal. 1:18 I went up to *J* to see Peter, and abode
2:1 went up again to *J* with Barnabas, and took
4:26 but *J* which is above is free, which is the
Heb. 12:22 city of the living God, the heavenly *J*
Rev. 21:2 I John saw the holy city, new *J*, coming
21:10 showed me that great city, the holy *J*

Jeshua *See* Joshua

Jesse

1 Sam. 16:1 I will send thee to *J* the Bethlehemite
Is. 11:1 a rod out of the stem of *J*, and a Branch
11:10 (Rom. 15:12) there shall be a root of *J*

Jesus (Joshua) Acts 7:45; Heb. 4:8

Jesus (Justus) Col. 4:11

Jesus *See also* Christ, Christ Jesus, Jesus Christ, Lord, Lord Jesus, Lord Jesus Christ, Messiah, Saviour

His birth foretold, Lk. 1:26–38; born, Mt. 1:18–25; Lk. 2:1–7; circumcised, Lk. 2:21; presented in the temple, Lk. 2:22–38; visited by the wise men, Mt. 2:1–12; fled to Egypt, Mt. 2:13–18; brought to Nazareth, Mt. 2:19–23 (Lk. 2:39); visited Jerusalem, Lk. 2:41–50; his brothers and sisters, Mt. 13:55–56 (Mk. 6:3); baptized, Mt. 3:13–17 (Mk. 1:9–11; Lk. 3:21–23); tempted by the devil, Mt. 4:1–11 (Mk. 1:12–13; Lk. 4:1–13); called his disciples, Mt. 4:18–22; 9:9; Mk. 1:16–20; 2:13–14; Lk. 5:1–11, 27–28; 6:12–16; Jn. 1:35–51; commissioned the twelve, Mt. 10:1–4 (Mk. 3:13–19; Lk. 6:12–16); Sermon on the Mount, Mt. 5–7; sent disciples forth by twos, Mt. 9:35–11:1 (Mk. 6:7–13; Lk. 9:1–6); foretold his death and resurrection, Mt. 16:21–26 (17:22–23; 20:17–28; Mk. 8:31–37; 9:30–32; 10:32–45; Lk. 9:22–25; 9:43–45; 18:31–34); transfigured, Mt. 17:1–8 (Mk. 9:2–8; Lk. 9:28–36); sent forth the seventy, Lk. 10:1–24; triumphal entry into Jerusalem, Mt. 21:1–11 (Mk. 11:1–11; Lk. 19:29–44; Jn. 12:12–19); instituted the Lord's supper, Mt. 26:26–29 (Mk. 14:22–25; Lk. 22:17–20; 1 Cor. 11:23–26); betrayed, arrested, and forsaken, Mt. 26:47–57 (Mk. 14:43–53; Lk. 22:47–54; Jn. 18:2–13); crucified, Mt. 27:31–56 (Mk. 15:20–41; Lk. 23:26–49; Jn. 19:16–30); appeared after his resurrection, Mt. 28:9–20 (Mk. 16:9–18; Lk. 24:13–50; Jn. 20:11–31); Acts 1:3–8; 1 Cor. 15:5–7; ascended to heaven, Mk. 16:19–20 (Lk. 24:50–53; Acts 1:9–12).

Acts 1:1 of all that *J* began both to do and teach
1:11 this same *J*, which is taken up from you
2:22 *J* of Nazareth, a man approved of God among
2:32 this *J* hath God raised up, whereof we all are
2:36 God hath made that same *J*, whom ye have
4:13 knowledge of them, that they had been with *J*
5:30 God of our fathers raised up *J*, whom ye slew
7:55 saw the glory of God, and *J* standing on the
8:35 opened his mouth . . and preached unto him *J*
9:5 (22:8; 26:15) I am *J* whom thou persecutest
10:38 how God anointed *J* of Nazareth with the
13:23 hath God . . raised unto Israel a Saviour, *J*
17:3 this *J*, whom I preach unto you, is Christ
17:18 preached unto them *J*, and the resurrection
18:5 testified to the Jews that *J* was Christ
19:15 the evil spirit . . said, *J* I know, and Paul
Rom. 3:26 justifier of him which believeth in *J*
1 Cor. 12:3 no man can say that *J* is the Lord, but
Phil. 2:10 at the name of *J* every knee should bow
1 Thes. 4:14 we believe that *J* died and rose again
Heb. 2:9 but we see *J*, who was made a little lower
4:14 have a great high priest . . *J* the Son of God
6:20 the forerunner is for us entered, even *J*
12:2 looking unto *J* the author and finisher of
1 Jn. 2:22 but he that denieth that *J* is the Christ?
4:15 shall confess that *J* is the Son of God
5:1 whosoever believeth that *J* is the Christ
Rev. 22:16 I *J* have sent mine angel to testify

Jesus Christ *See also* Christ, Christ Jesus, Jesus, Lord, Lord Jesus, Lord Jesus Christ, Messiah, Saviour

Mt. 1:1 the book of the generation of *J C*, the son
Mk. 1:1 the beginning of the gospel of *J C*, the Son
Jn. 1:17 by Moses, but grace and truth came by *J C*
17:3 know thee . . and *J C*, whom thou hast sent
Acts 3:6 in the name of *J C* of Nazareth rise up
3:20 shall send *J C*, which before was preached
5:42 they ceased not to teach and preach *J C*
8:12 the kingdom of God, and the name of *J C*
8:37 said, I believe that *J C* is the Son of God
10:36 which God sent . . preaching peace by *J C*
Rom. 1:3 his Son *J C* our Lord, which was made
2:16 God shall judge the secrets of men by *J C*
3:22 the righteousness of God . . by faith of *J C*
5:15 gift by grace, which is by one man, *J C*
6:3 so many of us as were baptized into *J C*
15:16 be the minister of *J C* to the Gentiles
1 Cor. 2:2 any thing . . save *J C*, and him crucified
3:11 foundation . . than that is laid, which is *J C*
2 Cor. 4:6 of the glory of God in the face of *J C*
5:18 who hath reconciled us to himself by *J C*
13:5 know ye not . . that *J C* is in you, except ye
Gal. 1:12 taught it, but by the revelation of *J C*
3:1 *J C* hath been evidently set forth, crucified
Eph. 2:20 *J C* himself being the chief corner stone
Phil. 1:6 will perform it until the day of *J C*
2:11 every tongue should confess that *J C* is Lord
2 Tim. 2:8 *J C* of the seed of David was raised
Tit. 2:13 of the great God and our Saviour *J C*
Heb. 13:8 *J C* the same yesterday, and today, and
1 Pet. 1:7 honor and glory at the appearing of *J C*
2 Pet. 3:18 knowledge of our Lord and Saviour *J C*
1 Jn. 1:3 is with the Father, and with his Son *J C*
1:7 the blood of *J C* his Son cleanseth us from
2:1 advocate with the Father, *J C* the righteous
4:2 confesseth that *J C* is come in the flesh
Rev. 1:1 the Revelation of *J C*, which God gave

Jethro *See also* Hobab Ex. 3:1; 4:18; 18:1–12

Jew *See also* Hebrew, Israelite

Ezra 4:12 the *J* which came up from thee to us are
Neh. 1:2 asked. . concerning the *J* that had escaped
Esth. 3:6 Haman sought to destroy all the *J* that
Dan. 3:8 Chaldeans came near, and accused the *J*
Zech. 28:23 take hold of the skirt of him that is a *J*
Mt. 28:15 saying is commonly reported among the *J*
Jn. 1:19 *J* sent priests and Levites from Jerusalem
   3:25 between some of John's disciples and the *J*
   4:9 for the *J* have no dealings with the Samaritans
   4:22 what we worship; for salvation is of the *J*
   5:16 therefore did the *J* persecute Jesus
   18:20 the temple, whither the *J* always resort
   18:35 Pilate answered, Am I a *J*?
Acts 2:5 *J*, devout men, out of every nation under
   10:28 unlawful thing for a. . *J* to keep company
   11:19 preaching. . to none but unto the *J* only
   14:19 came thither certain *J* from Antioch and
   16:20 being *J*, do exceedingly trouble our city
   18:2 Claudius had commanded all *J* to depart
   21:20 how many thousands of *J*. . which believe
   21:39 (22:3) I am a man which am a *J* of Tarsus
Rom. 1:16 to the *J* first, and also to the Greek
   2:9 of the *J* first, and also of the Gentile
   2:17 thou art called a *J*, and restest in the law
   2:28 for he is not a *J*, which is one outwardly
   3:1 what advantage then hath the *J*? or what
   10:12 no difference between the *J* and the Greek
1 Cor. 1:23 unto the *J* a stumblingblock, and unto
   9:20 unto the *J* I became as a *J*, that I might
Gal. 3:28 (Col. 3:11) there is neither *J* nor Greek
Rev. 2:9 of them which say they are *J*, and are not

Jewel

Gen. 24:53 servant brought forth *j* of silver, and *j*
Ex. 3:22 (11:2) borrow. . *j* of silver, and *j* of gold
Prov. 11:22 as a *j* of gold in a swine's snout, so
   20:15 but the lips of knowledge are a precious *j*
Is. 3:21 and the earrings, the rings, and nose *j*
   61:10 as a bride adorneth herself with her *j*
Ezek. 16:12 I put a *j* on thy forehead, and earrings
Mal. 3:17 in that day when I make up my *j*

Jewess Acts 16:1

Jezebel

   1 Kgs. 16:31–21:25; 2 Kgs. 9:7–37; Rev. 2:20

Jezreel

1 Sam. 29:1 Israelites pitched by a fountain. . in *J*
1 Kgs. 18:46 ran before Ahab to the entrance of *J*
   21:1 that Naboth. . had a vineyard, which was in *J*
2 Kgs. 8:29 (2 Chr. 22:6) went back to be healed in *J*
   9:16 so Jehu rode in a chariot, and went to *J*
Hos. 1:4 his name *J*; for. . I will avenge the blood of *J*

Joab

Murdered Abner, 2 Sam. 3:22–30; set Uriah in the
forefront, 2 Sam. 11:6–21; reconciled David and Absalom, 2 Sam. 14:28–33; killed Absalom, 2 Sam. 18:
9–17; pursued Sheba and slew Amasa, 2 Sam. 20:4–
23; put to death by Solomon, 1 Kgs. 2:28–34.

Joash *See* Jehoash

Job Job 1:1–42:17

Ezek. 14:20 though Noah, Daniel, and *J*, were in it
Jas. 5:11 ye have heard of the patience of *J*

Jochebed Ex. 6:20 (Num. 26:59)

Joel Joel 1:1–3:21

John (Mark) *See* Mark

John the Apostle

Called, Mt. 4:21 (Mk. 1:19; Lk. 5:10); sent out with
the twelve, Mt. 10:2 (Mk. 3:17); desire for revenge
rebuked, Lk. 9:51–56; selfish request rejected, Mt.
20:20–24 (Mk. 10:35–41); healed and preached in the
temple, Acts 3:1–4:22.

John the Baptist

Birth foretold, Lk. 1:5–25; born, Lk. 1:57–66;
preached and baptized, Mt. 3:1–12 (Mk. 1:4–11; Lk.
3:1–17); imprisoned, Mt. 3:1–12 (Mk. 6:17–18; Lk.
3:19–20); sent messengers to Jesus, Mt. 11:1–6 (Lk.
7:18–23); commended by Jesus, Mt. 11:7–15 (Lk. 7:
24–35); beheaded and buried, Mt. 14:6–12 (Mk. 6:
17–29).

Acts 1:5 (11:16) *J* truly baptized with water
   18:25 taught. . knowing only the baptism of *J*
   19:4 *J* verily baptized with the baptism of

Join *See also* Cleave

Gen. 14:3 were *j* together in the vale of Siddim
Ezra 4:12 the walls thereof, and *j* the foundations
Prov. 11:21 (16:5) though hand *j* in hand, the wicked
Eccl. 9:4 that is *j* to all the living there is hope
Is. 5:8 woe unto them that *j* house to house
   9:11 against him, and *j* his enemies together
Jer. 50:5 come, and let us *j* ourselves to the LORD
Hos. 4:17 Ephraim is *j* to idols: let him alone
Zech. 2:11 many nations shall be *j* to the LORD
Mt. 19:6 (Mk. 10:9) what. . God hath *j* together
Lk. 15:15 ; himself to a citizen of that country
Acts 5:13 of the rest durst no man *j* himself to
   8:29 go near, and *j* thyself to this chariot
   9:26 Saul. . assayed to *j* himself to the disciples
1 Cor. 1:10 be perfectly *j* together in the same mind
   6:16 that he which is *j* to a harlot is one body?
   6:17 he that is *j* unto the Lord is one spirit
Eph. 4:16 from whom the whole body fitly *j* together
   5:31 and shall be *j* unto his wife, and they two

Joint

Gen. 32:25 hollow of Jacob's thigh was out of *j*
1 Kgs. 22:34 (2 Chr. 18:33) between. . *j* of. . harness
Ps. 22:14 bones are out of *j*: my heart is like wax
Prov. 25:19 like a broken tooth, and a foot out of *j*
Dan. 5:6 so that the *j* of his loins were loosed
Eph. 4:16 compacted by that which every *j* supplieth
Col. 2:19 from which all the body by *j* and bands
Heb. 4:12 of the *j* and marrow, and is a discerner

Joint-heir

Rom. 8:17 heirs of God, and *j-h* with Christ, if so

Jonah (Jonas) Jon. 1:1–4:11

2 Kgs. 14:25 he spake by the hand of his servant *J*
Mt. 12:40 as *J* was three days and three nights in
   16:4 (Lk. 11:29) but the sign of the prophet *J*
Lk. 11:30 as *J* was a sign unto the Ninevites

Jonathan son of Saul

Smote the Philistine garrison, 1 Sam. 13:2–4; 14:1–
15; transgressed Saul's oath, 1 Sam. 14:24–30; rescued the people, 1 Sam. 14:36–46; made a
covenant with David, 1 Sam. 18:1–5; friendship with
David, 1 Sam. 20; killed by the Philistines, 1 Sam.
31:2.

Jonathan son of Abiathar

   2 Sam. 15:27; 17:17

Joppa

2 Chr. 2:16 bring it to thee in floats by sea to *J*
Jon. 1:3 and went down to *J*; and he found a ship
Acts 9:36 at *J* a certain disciple named Tabitha
　10:5 (10:32; 11:13) send men to *J* . . for one Simon
　11:5 I was in the city of *J* praying

Joram *See* Jehoram

Jordan

Gen. 13:11 then Lot chose him all the plain of *J*
　32:10 with my staff I passed over this *J*
Deut. 4:22 I must not go over *J*: but ye shall go
Josh. 1:2 go over this *J*, thou, and all this people
　3:17 stood firm on dry ground in the midst of *J*
2 Sam. 19:15 Judah came . . to conduct . . king over J
2 Kgs. 2:7 view afar off: and they two stood by *J*
　5:10 go and wash in *J* seven times, and thy flesh
　6:4 when they came to *J*, they cut down wood
Job 40:23 that he can draw up *J* into his mouth
Ps. 114:3 sea saw it, and fled: *J* was driven back
Jer. 12:5 how wilt thou do in the swelling of *J*?
　49:19 come up like a lion from the swelling of *J*
Zech. 11:3 lions; for the pride of *J* is spoiled
Mt. 3:6 (Mk. 1:5) baptized of him in *J*, confessing
　3:13 (Mk. 1:9) Jesus . . to *J* . . to be baptized

Joseph son of Jacob

Born, Gen. 30:22–24; incurred jealousy by his dreams,
Gen. 37:5–11; sold into Egypt, Gen. 37:12–28; re-
fused Potiphar's wife, Gen. 39:1–18; imprisoned,
Gen. 39:19–23; interpreted the prisoners' dreams,
Gen. 40; interpreted Pharaoh's dreams, Gen. 41:1–
36; made ruler over Egypt, Gen. 41:37–57; met his
brothers, Gen. 42–44; made himself known to them,
Gen. 45; saw his father again, Gen. 46:28–34; died,
Gen. 50:22–26; buried in Shechem, Josh. 24:32.

Ex. 1:8 (Acts 7:18) a new king . . which knew not *J*
Deut. 33:13 of *J* . . Blessed of the LORD be his land
Ps. 80:1 O Shepherd . . that leadest *J* like a flock
　105:17 he sent a man before them, even *J*, who
Amos 6:6 are not grieved for the affliction of *J*
Jn. 4:5 of ground that Jacob gave to his son *J*
Acts 7:9 patriarchs . . with envy, sold *J* into Egypt
Heb. 11:22 by faith *J*, when he died, made mention

Joseph husband of Mary, mother of Jesus

Betrothed to Mary, Mt. 1:18 (Lk. 1:27); instructed
by an angel, Mt. 1:19–21; went to Bethlehem, Lk.
2:4; fled into Egypt, Mt. 2:13–15; returned to
Nazareth, Mt. 2:19–23.

Lk. 2:16 Mary and *J*, and the babe lying in a manger
　2:33 *J* and his mother marveled at those things
　4:22 (Jn. 6:42) is not this *J*'s son?

Joseph of Arimathea Mt. 27:57–60 (Mk. 15:42–46; Lk. 23:50–53; Jn. 19:38–42)

Joses Mt. 13:55 (Mk. 6:3); Mt. 27:56 (Mk. 15:40)

Joshua

Defeated the Amalekites, Ex. 17:8–13; in charge of
the tabernacle, Ex. 33:11; sent with the spies, Num.
13:1–16; 14:6–9; chosen to succeed Moses, Num.
27:18–23; Deut. 3:28; commissioned by Moses, Deut.
31:23; 34:9; encouraged by the LORD, Josh. 1:1–9;
sent spies to Jericho, Josh. 2; passed over Jordan,
Josh. 3; captured Jericho, Josh. 6; captured Ai,
Josh. 7–8; warred against the kings, Josh. 10–12; al-

lotted the land, Josh. 13:1–22:8; charged the people,
Josh. 23:1–24:24; made a covenant, Josh. 24:25–27;
death and burial, Josh. 24:29–30.

Joshua (Jeshua) the priest

Ezra 3:2 stood up *J*. . and his brethren the priests
　5:2 Zerubbabel . . and *J*. . began to build the house
Hag. 1:1 word of the LORD . . to *J*. . the high priest
Zech. 3:1 he showed me *J* the high priest standing

Josiah

2 Kgs. 21:24–23:30 (2 Chr. 33:25–35:27)

Jot

Mt. 5:18 one *j* or one tittle shall in no wise pass

Jotham son of Gideon Judg. 9:5–21

Jotham king of Judah

2 Kgs. 15:5–38 (2 Chr. 26:21–27:9)

Journey

Gen. 11:2 as they *j* from the east, that they found
　13:3 went on his *j* from the south even to Bethel
Ex. 3:18 three days' *j* into the wilderness, that we
Num. 10:28 thus were the *j* of . . Israel according to
　33:1 these are the *j* of the children of Israel
Deut. 2:24 rise ye up, take your *j*, and pass over
1 Kgs. 18:27 or he is pursuing, or he is in a *j*, or
　19:4 himself went a day's *j* into the wilderness
　19:7 eat; because the *j* is too great for thee
Neh. 2:6 how long shall thy *j* be? and when wilt
Prov. 7:19 is not at home, he is gone a long *j*
Mt. 10:10 (Mk. 6:8; Lk. 9:3) nor scrip for your *j*
Mk. 13:34 Son of man is as a man taking a far *j*
Lk. 11:6 a friend of mine in his *j* is come to me
　15:13 took his *j* into a far country, and there
Jn. 4:6 wearied with his *j*, sat thus on the well
Acts 1:12 which is from Jerusalem a sabbath day's *j*
　9:7 *j* with him stood speechless, hearing a voice
Rom. 1:10 at length I might have a prosperous *j* by
　15:24 whensoever I take my *j* into Spain, I will
2 Cor. 11:26 in *j* often, in perils of waters

Joy *See also* Delight, Gladness, Pleasure, Rejoicing

1 Kgs. 1:40 with pipes, and rejoiced with great *j*
Ezra 3:12 loud voice; and many shouted aloud for *j*
　6:16 the dedication of this house of God with *j*
Neh. 8:10 for the *j* of the LORD is your strength
Esth. 8:16 the Jews had light, and gladness, and *j*
　9:22 turned unto them from sorrow to *j*, and from
Job 20:5 the *j* of the hypocrite but for a moment?
　33:26 he shall see his face with *j*
　41:22 and sorrow is turned into *j* before him
Ps. 16:11 in thy presence is fulness of *j*
　21:1 the king shall *j* in thy strength, O LORD
　30:5 for a night, but *j* cometh in the morning
　32:11 and shout for *j*, all ye that are upright
　43:4 altar of God, unto God my exceeding *j*
　48:2 the *j* of the whole earth, is mount Zion
　51:12 restore unto me the *j* of thy salvation
　67:4 O let the nations be glad and sing for *j*
　126:5 they that sow in tears shall reap in *j*
　132:9 and let thy saints shout for *j*
　137:6 if I prefer not Jerusalem above my chief *j*
Prov. 14:10 stranger doth not intermeddle with his *j*
　15:21 folly is *j* to him that is destitute of wisdom
　15:23 a man hath *j* by the answer of his mouth
　21:15 it is *j* to the just to do judgment
　23:24 begetteth a wise child shall have *j* of him
Eccl. 2:10 I withheld not my heart from any *j*
　9:7 eat thy bread with *j*, and drink thy wine

Is. 9:3 not increased the *j*: they *j* before thee
12:3 therefore with *j* shall ye draw water out of
24:8 rejoice endeth, the *j* of the harp ceaseth
29:19 the meek also shall increase their *j* in
35:10 *j* upon their heads: they shall obtain *j*
51:3 Zion. . *j* and gladness shall be found therein
52:9 break forth into *j*, sing together, ye waste
55:12 ye shall go out with *j*, and be led forth
60:15 I will make thee. . a *j* of many generations
61:3 beauty for ashes, the oil of *j* for mourning
65:14 my servants shall sing for *j* of heart
65:19 rejoice in Jerusalem, and *j* in my people
66:5 he shall appear to your *j*, and they shall
Jer. 15:16 thy word was unto me the *j* and rejoicing
31:13 for I will turn their mourning into *j*
33:9 it shall be to me a name of *j*, a praise and
Lam. 2:15 that men call. . The *j* of the whole earth?
Zeph. 3:17 his love, he will *j* over thee with singing
Mt. 2:10 star, they rejoiced with exceeding great *j*
13:20 (Lk. 8:13) the word. . with *j* receiveth. . it
13:44 and for *j* thereof goeth and selleth all
25:21 (25:23) enter thou into the *j* of thy lord
28:8 from the sepulchre with fear and great *j*
Lk. 1:14 thou shalt have *j* and gladness; and many
1:44 the babe leaped in my womb for *j*
2:10 behold, I bring you good tidings of great *j*
10:17 the seventy returned again with *j*, saying
15:7 *j* shall be in heaven over one sinner that
24:41 they yet believed not for *j*, and wondered
Jn. 3:29 this my *j* therefore is fulfilled
15:11 my *j* might remain in you, and that your *j*
16:20 but your sorrow shall be turned into *j*
16:22 rejoice, and your *j* no man taketh from you
16:24 ye shall receive, that your *j* may be full
17:13 they might have my *j* fulfilled in themselves
Acts 2:28 make me full of *j* with thy countenance
8:8 and there was great *j* in that city
13:52 disciples were filled with *j*, and with the
20:24 so that I might finish my course with *j*
Rom. 5:11 we also *j* in God through our Lord Jesus
14:17 but righteousness, and peace, and *j*
15:13 fill you with all *j* and peace in believing
15:32 come unto you with *j* by the will of God
2 Cor. 1:24 your faith, but are helpers of your *j*
2:3 in you all, that my *j* is the *j* of you all
8:2 abundance of their *j* and their deep poverty
Gal. 5:22 the fruit of the Spirit is love, *j*, peace
Phil. 1:4 for you all making request with *j*
2:2 fulfil ye my *j*, that ye be likeminded
2:17 sacrifice and service of your faith, I *j*
4:1 beloved and longed for, my *j* and crown
1 Thes. 1:6 affliction, with *j* of the Holy Ghost
2:20 for ye are our glory and *j*
3:9 all the *j* wherewith we *j* for your sakes
2 Tim. 1:4 thy tears, that I may be filled with *j*
Heb. 12:2 who for the *j* that was set before him
13:17 they may do it with *j*, and not with grief
Jas. 1:2 count it all *j* when ye fall into divers
4:9 turned to mourning, and your *j* to heaviness
1 Pet. 1:8 ye rejoice with *j* unspeakable and full
4:13 revealed, ye may be glad. . with exceeding *j*
1 Jn. 1:4 write we unto you, that your *j* may be full
2 Jn. 12 speak face to face, that our *j* may be full
3 Jn. 4 no greater *j* than to hear that my children
Jude 24 the presence of his glory with exceeding *j*

Joyful *See also* Glad, Happy, Merry

1 Kgs. 8:66 and went unto their tents *j* and glad
Ezra 6:22 with joy: for the LORD had made them *j*
Ps. 5:11 let them also that love thy name be *j* in
35:9 my soul shall be *j* in the LORD: it shall
63:5 and my mouth shall praise thee with *j* lips
Ps. 66:1 make a *j* noise unto God, all ye lands
89:15 blessed is the people that know the *j* sound
95:1 make a *j* noise to the rock of our salvation
98:4 (100:1) make a *j* noise unto the LORD, all
98:8 floods clap their hands: let the hills be *j*
149:2 let the children of Zion be *j* in their King
149:5 let the saints be *j* in glory: let them sing
Eccl. 7:14 in the day of prosperity be *j*, but in
Is. 49:13 sing, O heavens; and be *j*, O earth
56:7 and make them *j* in my house of prayer
61:10 my soul shall be *j* in my God; for he hath
2 Cor. 7:4 I am exceeding *j* in all our tribulation

Joyfully

Heb. 10:34 and took *j* the spoiling of your goods

Joyfulness

Deut. 28:47 servedst not the LORD thy God with *j*
Col. 1:11 all patience and long-suffering with *j*

Joyous

Heb. 12:11 no chastening for the present. . to be *j*

Jubilee

Lev. 25:11 *j* shall that fiftieth year be unto you
25:50 shall reckon with him. . unto the year of *j*

Judah

Born, Gen. 29:35; saved Joseph's life, Gen. 37:26–28;
Judah and Tamar, Gen. 38; pleaded for Benjamin,
Gen. 44:14–34; blessed by Jacob, Gen. 49:8–12.

Deut. 33:7 this is the blessing of *J*: and he said
Josh. 15:20 is the inheritance of the tribe. . of *J*
Judg. 1:2 the LORD said, *J* shall go up: behold, I
2 Sam. 2:4 men of *J* came, and. . anointed David
19:15 *J* came to Gilgal, to go to meet the king
1 Kgs. 12:20 house of David, but the tribe of *J* only
14:22 *J* did evil in the sight of the LORD
2 Kgs. 25:21 (Jer. 52:27) *J* was carried away out of
Amos 2:4 for three transgressions of *J* and for four,
Heb. 7:14 it is evident that our Lord sprang out of *J*
Rev. 5:5 weep not: behold, the Lion of the tribe of *J*

Judas (Jude) the brother of Jesus

Mt. 13:55 (Mk. 6:3); Jude 1:1

Judas the brother of James

See also Thaddeus Lk. 6:16; Jn. 14:22

Judas of Galilee Acts 5:37

Judas of Damascus Acts 9:11

Judas (Barsabas) Acts 15:22, 27

Judas (Iscariot)

Mt. 10:4 (Mk. 3:19; Lk. 6:16) *J* Iscariot. . betrayed
26:14 (Mk. 14:10) *J* Iscariot, went to the chief
26:47 (Mk. 14:43; Lk. 22:47; Jn. 18:3) while he yet
spake, lo, *J*, one of the twelve, came
27:3 *J*. . saw that he was condemned, repented
Jn. 6:71 he spake of *J* Iscariot the son of Simon
13:26 had dipped the sop, he gave it to *J*
Acts 1:16 Holy Ghost. . spake before concerning *J*
1:25 from which *J* by transgression fell

Judea

Ezra 5:8 that we went into the province of *J*
Jn. 3:22 Jesus and his disciples into the land of *J*
11:7 to his disciples, Let us go into *J* again

Acts 1:8 Jerusalem, and in all *J*, and in Samaria
Gal. 1:22 unknown by face unto the churches of *J*

Judge *See also* Accuse, Condemn

Gen. 15:14 (Acts 7:7) whom they shall serve, will I *j*
16:5 the LORD *j* between me and thee
18:25 shall not the *J* of all the earth do right?
Ex. 2:14 (Acts 7:27) who made thee. . a *j* over us?
18:13 on the morrow. . Moses sat to *j* the people
18:22 let them *j* the people at all seasons
Lev. 19:15 righteousness shalt thou *j* thy neighbor
Num. 35:24 *j* between the slayer and the revenger
Deut. 1:16 I charged your *j*. . *j* righteously between
19:18 and the *j* shall make diligent inquisition
32:36 (Heb. 10:30) the LORD shall *j* his people
Judg. 2:16 LORD raised up *j*, which delivered them
2:18 LORD raised them up *j*. . LORD was with the *j*
11:27 the LORD the *J* be *j* this day between the
1 Sam. 2:25 sin against another, the *j* shall *j* him
7:16 from year to year in circuit. . and *j* Israel
8:5 make us a king to *j* us like all the nations
2 Sam. 15:4 oh that I were made *j* in the land
1 Kgs. 3:9 (2 Chr. 1:10) who is able to *j* this. . people
8:32 (2 Chr. 6:23) *j* thy servants, condemning the
1 Chr. 16:33 (Ps. 96:13; 98:9) he cometh to *j* the earth
2 Chr. 19:6 for ye *j* not for man, but for the LORD
Job 9:15 but I would make supplication to my *j*
22:13 God know? can he *j* through the dark cloud
Ps. 2:10 be instructed, ye *j* of the earth
7:8 the LORD shall *j* the people: *j* me, O LORD
7:11 God *j* the righteous, and God is angry with
9:8 (Acts 17:31) shall *j* the world in righteousness
10:18 to *j* the fatherless and the oppressed
26:1 *j* me. . for I have walked in mine integrity
35:24 *j* me. . according to thy righteousness
37:33 not leave. . nor condemn him when he is *j*
43:1 *j* me, O God, and plead my cause against an
50:6 declare his righteousness: for God is *j*
51:4 (Rom. 3:4) speakest, and be clear when thou *j*
58:11 verily he is a God that *j* in the earth
67:4 for thou shalt *j* the people righteously
68:5 father of the fatherless. . a *j* of the widows
72:2 he shall *j* thy people with righteousness
75:7 but God is the *j*: he putteth down one
82:1 God standeth. . he *j* among the gods
94:2 lift up thyself, thou *j* of the earth
109:7 when he shall be *j*, let him be condemned
110:6 he shall *j* among the heathen, he shall fill
135:14 (Heb. 10:30) the LORD will *j* his people
Eccl. 3:17 God shall *j* the righteous and the wicked
Is. 1:17 relieve the oppressed, *j* the fatherless
2:4 (Mic. 4:3) he shall *j* among the nations
11:3 he shall not *j* after the sight of his eyes
33:22 LORD is our *j*, the LORD is our lawgiver
40:23 he maketh the *j* of the earth as vanity
Jer. 5:28 and the right of the needy do they not *j*
11:20 that *j* righteously, that triest the reins
Ezek. 7:3 (7:8) will *j* thee according to thy ways
18:30 I will *j* you, O house of Israel
33:20 house of Israel, I will *j* you every one
36:19 and according to their doings I *j* them
Joel 3:12 there will I sit to *j* all the heathen
Mt. 5:25 (Lk. 12:58) to the *j*, and the *j* deliver thee to
7:1 (Lk. 6:37) *j* not, that ye be not *j*
7:2 for with what judgment ye *j*, ye shall be *j*
12:27 (Lk. 11:19) therefore they shall be your *j*
19:28 (Lk. 22:30) *j* the twelve tribes of Israel
Lk. 7:43 and he said unto him, Thou hast rightly *j*
12:14 man, who made me a *j* or a divider over you
18:2 there was. . a *j*, which feared not God
18:6 the Lord said, Hear what the unjust *j* saith
19:22 out of thine own mouth will I *j* thee
Jn. 5:22 Father *j* no man, but hath committed all

Jn. 7:24 *j* not according to the appearance, but *j*
7:51 doth our law *j* any man, before it hear him
8:15 ye *j* after the flesh; I *j* no man
8:26 I have many things to say and to *j* of you
12:47 I *j* him not: for I came not to *j* the world
16:11 because the prince of this world is *j*
Acts 7:27 who made thee a ruler and a *j* over us?
10:42 ordained of God to be the *J* of quick
13:20 and after that he gave unto them *j*
17:31 he will *j* the world in righteousness by
23:3 thou whited wall: for sittest thou to *j* me
26:6 I stand and am *j* for the hope of the promise
Rom. 2:1 that *j*: for wherein thou *j* another, thou
2:12 sinned in the law shall be *j* by the law
2:16 God shall *j* the secrets of men by Jesus
3:6 for then how shall God *j* the world?
14:3 not him which eateth not *j* him that eateth
14:13 *j* one another any more: but *j* this rather
1 Cor. 2:15 *j* all things, yet he. . is *j* of no man
4:3 I should be *j* of you. . I *j* not mine own self
4:4 justified: but he that *j* me is the Lord
4:5 *j* nothing before the time, until the Lord
5:3 but present in spirit, have *j* already
5:12 *j* them also that are without? do not ye *j*
6:2 saints shall *j* the world? and if the world
6:3 know ye not that we shall *j* angels? how much
6:5 no, not one. . able to *j* between his brethren?
11:31 would *j* ourselves, we should not be *j*
14:29 speak two or three, and let the other *j*
2 Cor. 5:14 we thus *j*, that if one died for all
Col. 2:16 let no man therefore *j* you in meat
2 Tim. 4:1 who shall *j* the quick and the dead
4:8 the Lord, the righteous *j*, shall give me
Heb. 11:11 she *j* him faithful who had promised
12:23 to God the *J* of all, and to the spirits of
13:4 but whoremongers and adulterers God will *j*
Jas. 2:4 partial. . and are become *j* of evil thoughts?
2:12 they that shall be *j* by the law of liberty
4:11 the law: but if thou *j* the law, thou art
4:12 and to destroy: who art thou that *j* another?
5:9 behold, the *j* standeth before the door
1 Pet. 1:17 without respect of persons *j* according
2:23 committed himself to him that *j* righteously
4:5 that is ready to *j* the quick and the dead
4:6 might be *j* according to men in the flesh
Rev. 6:10 dost thou not *j* and avenge our blood
11:18 time of the dead, that they should be *j*
20:12 book of life: and the dead were *j* out of

Judgment *See also* Condemnation, Equity, Justice, Law, Ordinance

Gen. 18:19 way of the LORD, to do justice and *j*
Ex. 12:12 all the gods of Egypt I will execute *j*
Lev. 18:4 shall do my *j*, and keep mine ordinances
19:15 ye shall do no unrighteousness in *j*
Num. 33:4 upon their gods also the LORD executed *j*
Deut. 1:17 not respect persons in *j*. . the *j* is God's
4:1 hearken. . unto the statutes and unto the *j*
16:19 shalt not wrest *j*; thou shalt not respect
32:4 his work is perfect: for all his ways are *j*
1 Sam. 8:3 lucre, and took bribes, and perverted *j*
1 Chr. 16:14 (Ps. 105:7) his *j* are in all the earth
Neh. 9:13 and gavest them right *j*, and true laws
Job 8:3 doth God pervert *j*? or doth the Almighty
27:2 (34:5) God liveth, who hath taken away my *j*
29:14 clothed me: my *j* was as a robe and a diadem
32:9 neither do the aged understand *j*
34:4 let us choose to us *j*: let us know among
34:12 neither will the Almighty pervert *j*
37:23 he is excellent in power, and in *j*
Ps. 1:5 the ungodly shall not stand in the *j*
7:6 awake for me to the *j*. . thou hast commanded

Ps. 9:8 shall minister *j* to the people in uprightness
9:16 LORD is known by the *j* which he executeth
10:5 thy *j* are far above out of his sight
19:9 the *j* of the LORD are true and righteous
25:9 the meek will he guide in *j*
33:5 he loveth righteousness and *j*: the earth is
36:6 the great mountains; thy *j* are a great deep
37:6 righteousness as the light. . *j* as the noonday
37:28 LORD loveth *j*, and forsaketh not his saints
76:9 when God arose to *j*, to save all the meek
97:2 righteousness and *j* are the habitation of
101:1 I will sing of mercy and *j*: unto thee
106:3 blessed are they that keep *j*, and he that
111:7 the works of his hands are verity and *j*
119:39 reproach which I fear: for thy *j* are good
119:43 out of my mouth; for I have hoped in thy *j*
119:66 teach me good *j* and knowledge: for I have
119:75 I know, O LORD, that thy *j* are right
119:108 of my mouth, O LORD, and teach me thy *j*
119:120 fear of thee; and I am afraid of thy *j*
119:149 O LORD, quicken me according to thy *j*
119:175 shall praise thee; and let thy *j* help me
143:2 enter not into *j* with thy servant
146:7 which executeth *j* for the oppressed
147:20 as for his *j*, they have not known them
Prov. 2:8 keepeth the paths of *j*, and preserveth
19:28 an ungodly witness scorneth *j*
21:3 to do justice and *j* is more acceptable to
21:15 joy to the just to do *j*: but destruction
28:5 evil men understand not *j*: but they that
29:26 but every man's *j* cometh from the LORD
Eccl. 3:16 the place of *j*, that wickedness was there
8:6 to every purpose there is time and *j*
11:9 all these things God will bring thee into *j*
12:14 God shall bring every work into *j*
Is. 1:21 it was full of *j*; righteousness lodged in
1:27 Zion shall be redeemed with *j*
3:14 LORD will enter into *j* with the ancients
5:7 and he looked for *j*, but behold oppression
9:7 and to establish it with *j* and with justice
16:3 take counsel, execute *j*; make thy shadow as
28:6 for a spirit of *j* to him that sitteth in *j*
28:17 *j* also will I lay to the line
30:18 LORD is a God of *j*: blessed are all they
40:14 taught him in the path of *j*, and taught
42:1 (Mt. 12:18) shall bring forth *j* to the Gentiles
42:3 (Mt. 12:20) he shall bring forth *j* unto truth
49:4 in vain: yet surely my *j* is with the LORD
53:8 (Acts 8:33) was taken from prison and from *j*
54:17 rise against thee in *j* thou shalt condemn
56:1 saith the LORD, Keep ye *j*, and do justice
59:11 we look for *j*, but there is none
61:8 I the LORD love *j*, I hate robbery for burnt
Jer. 1:16 and I will utter my *j* against them
5:1 a man, if there be any that executeth *j*
8:7 but my people know not the *j* of the LORD
10:24 correct me, but with *j*; not in thine anger
22:3 execute ye *j* and righteousness, and deliver
23:5 (33:15) Branch. . shall execute *j* and justice
48:47 thus far is the *j* of Moab
51:47 that I will do *j* upon the graven images of
Ezek. 5:15 when I shall execute *j* in thee in anger
14:21 I send my four sore *j* upon Jerusalem
23:10 for they had executed *j* upon her
30:19 thus will I execute *j* in Egypt
34:16 fat and the strong; I will feed them with *j*
39:21 all the heathen shall see my *j* that I have
44:24 stand in *j*. . shall judge it according to my *j*
Dan. 4:37 whose works are truth, and his ways *j*
7:10 the *j* was set, and the books were opened
7:22 was given to the saints of the Most High
Hos. 6:5 thy *j* are as the light that goeth forth
12:6 turn thou to thy God: keep mercy and *j*

Amos 5:15 love the good, and establish *j* in the gate
5:24 *j* run down as waters, and righteousness
Mic. 3:1 of Israel; Is it not for you to know *j*?
Hab. 1:4 law is slacked, and *j* doth never go forth
1:12 O LORD, thou hast ordained them for *j*
Zech. .7:9 saying, Execute true *j*, and show mercy
8:16 execute the *j* of truth and peace in your
Mt. 5:21 shall kill shall be in danger of the *j*
7:2 for with what *j* ye judge, ye shall be judged
10:15 (Mk. 6:11) and Gomorrah in the day of *j*
12:36 shall give account thereof in the day of *j*
12:41 (Lk. 11:32) men of Nineveh shall rise in *j*
23:23 (Lk. 11:42) weightier matters of the law, *j*
Jn. 5:22 but hath committed all *j* unto the Son
5:30 as I hear, I judge: and my *j* is just
7:24 to the appearance, but judge righteous *j*
8:16 yet if I judge, my *j* is true: for I am not
9:39 Jesus said, For *j* I am come into this world
12:31 now is the *j* of this world: now shall the
16:8 world of sin, and of righteousness, and of *j*
16:11 of *j*, because the prince of this world is
18:28 then led they Jesus. . unto the hall of *j*
19:13 Pilate therefore. . sat down in the *j* seat
Acts 8:33 in his humiliation his *j* was taken away
23:35 commanded him to be kept in Herod's *j* hall
24:25 temperance, and *j* to come, Felix trembled
25:15 informed me, desiring to have *j* against him
Rom. 1:32 knowing the *j* of God, that they which
2:2 sure that the *j* of God is according to truth
2:3 that thou shalt escape the *j* of God?
2:5 and revelation of the righteous *j* of God
5:16 for the *j* was by one to condemnation
5:18 by the offense of one *j* came upon all men
11:33 how unsearchable are his *j*, and his ways
14:10 shall all stand before the *j* seat of Christ
1 Cor. 6:4 have *j* of things pertaining to this life
7:25 no commandment of the Lord: yet I give my *j*
2 Cor. 5:10 all appear before the *j* seat of Christ
Phil. 1:9 more and more in knowledge and in all *j*
2 Thes. 1:5 a manifest token of the righteous *j* of
Heb. 6:2 resurrection of the dead, and of eternal *j*
9:27 unto men once to die, but after this the *j*
10:27 but a certain fearful looking for of *j* and
Jas. 2:13 *j* without mercy. . mercy rejoiceth against *j*
1 Pet. 4:17 that *j* must begin at the house of God
2 Pet. 2:3 whose *j* now of a long time lingereth not
2:4 chains of darkness, to be reserved unto *j*
2:9 the unjust unto the day of *j* to be punished
3:7 reserved unto fire against the day of *j* and
1 Jn. 4:17 we may have boldness in the day of *j*
Jude 6 under darkness unto the *j* of the great day
15 execute *j* upon all, and to convince all that
Rev. 14:7 hour of his *j* is come: and worship him
16:7 God Almighty, true and righteous are thy *j*
17:1 show unto thee the *j* of the great whore
20:4 I saw thrones. . and *j* was given unto them

Juniper

1 Kgs. 19:4 and came and sat down under a *j* tree

Jupiter Acts 14:12; 19:35

Jurisdiction

Lk. 23:7 he knew that he belonged unto Herod's *j*

Just *See also* Perfect, Righteous, Upright

Gen. 6:9 Noah was a *j* man and perfect in his
Lev. 19:36 *j* balances, *j* weights, a *j* ephah
Deut. 16:18 shall judge the people with *j* judgment
32:4 a God of truth. . *j* and right is he
2 Sam. 23:3 he that ruleth over men must be *j*
Neh. 9:33 thou art *j* in all that is brought upon
Job 4:17 shall mortal men be more *j* than God?

Job 9:2 but how should man be *j* with God?
Prov. 3:33 but he blesseth the habitation of the *j*
  4:18 the path of the *j* is as the shining light
  9:9 teach a *j* man, and he will increase
  10:6 blessings are upon the head of the *j*
  10:7 memory of the *j* is blessed: but the name of
  11:1 but a *j* weight is his delight
  12:13 but the *j* shall come out of trouble
  12:21 there shall no evil happen to the *j*
  16:11 a *j* weight and balance are the LORD's
  20:7 *j* man walketh in his integrity: his children
Eccl. 7:15 there is a *j* man that perisheth in his
  7:20 there is not a *j* man upon earth, that
  8:14 that there be *j* men, unto whom it happeneth
Is. 26:7 the way of the *j* is uprightness
  45:21 no God else. . a *j* God and a Saviour
Lam. 4:13 that have shed the blood of the *j* in the
Ezek. 18:5 but if a man be *j*, and do that which is
  45:10 ye shall have *j* balances, and a *j* ephah
Hab. 2:4 (Rom. 1:17; Gal. 3:11; Heb. 10:38) the *j*
  shall live by his faith
Zeph. 3:5 the *j* LORD is in the midst thereof
Zech. 9:9 thy King cometh unto thee: he is *j*
Mt. 1:19 Joseph her husband, being a *j* man
  5:45 and sendeth rain on the *j* and on the unjust
  13:49 and sever the wicked from among the *j*
  27:19 have thou nothing to do with that *j* man
  27:24 am innocent of the blood of this *j* person
Lk. 14:14 recompensed at the resurrection of the *j*
  15:7 more than over ninety and nine *j* persons
  23:50 counselor; and he was a good man, and a *j*
Jn. 5:30 as I hear, I judge: and my judgment is *j*
Acts 3:14 but ye denied the Holy One and the *J*
  7:52 showed before of the coming of the *J* One
  22:14 shouldest know his will, and see that *J* One
  24:15 a resurrection of the dead, both of the *j*
Rom. 2:13 not the hearers of the law are *j* before God
  3:26 that he might be *j*, and the justifier of
  7:12 and the commandment holy, and *j*, and good
Phil. 4:8 whatsoever things are *j*, whatsoever
Col. 4:1 give unto your servants that which is *j*
Tit. 1:8 a lover of good men, sober, *j*, holy
Heb. 2:2 and disobedience received a *j* recompense
  12:23 and to the spirits of *j* men made perfect
Jas. 5:6 ye have condemned and killed the *j*
1 Pet. 3:18 suffered for sins, the *j* for the unjust
2 Pet. 2:7 delivered *j* Lot, vexed with the filthy
1 Jn. 1:9 is faithful and *j* to forgive us our sins
Rev. 15:3 *j* and true are thy ways, thou King

Justice *See also* Equity, Judgment, Righteousness

Gen. 18:19 to do *j* and judgment; that the LORD may
2 Sam. 15:4 unto me, and I would do him *j*!
Job 8:3 judgment? or doth the Almighty pervert *j*?
  37:23 power, and in judgment, and in plenty of *j*
Ps. 82:3 do *j* to the afflicted and needy
  89:14 *j* and judgment are the habitation of thy
Prov. 1:3 to receive the instruction of wisdom, *j*
  8:15 by me kings reign, and princes decree *j*
  21:3 to do *j* and judgment is more acceptable to
Is. 9:7 establish it with judgment and with *j* from
  56:1 saith the LORD, Keep ye judgment, and do *j*
  59:4 none calleth for *j*, nor any pleadeth for
  59:9 far from us, neither doth *j* overtake us
  59:14 *j* standeth afar off: for truth is fallen
Jer. 23:5 shall execute judgment and *j* in the earth
  31:23 O habitation of *j*, and mountain of holiness
  50:7 sinned against the LORD, the habitation of *j*
Ezek. 45:9 execute judgment and *j*, take away your

Justification

Rom. 4:25 offenses, and was raised again for our *j*

Rom. 5:16 the free gift is of many offenses unto *j*
  5:18 free gift came upon all men unto *j* of life

Justify

Ex. 23:7 slay thou not: for I will not *j* the wicked
1 Kgs. 8:32 (2 Chr. 6:23) *j* the righteous, to give him
Job 9:20 if I *j* myself, mine own mouth shall condemn
  13:18 ordered my cause; I know that I shall be *j*
  25:4 how then can man be *j* with God? or how can
  32:2 was his wrath kindled, because he *j* himself
  33:32 answer me: speak, for I desire to *j* thee
Ps. 51:4 (Rom. 3:4) mightest be *j* when thou speakest
  143:2 for in thy sight shall no man living be *j*
Prov. 17:15 he that *j* the wicked. . are abomination to
Is. 5:23 which *j* the wicked for reward, and take
  45:25 the LORD shall all the seed of Israel be *j*
  50:8 he is near that *j* me; who will contend
  53:11 shall my righteous servant *j* many
Mt. 11:19 (Lk. 7:35) but wisdom is *j* of her children
  12:37 by thy words thou shalt be *j*, and by thy
Lk. 7:29 that heard him, and the publicans, *j* God
  10:29 he, willing to *j* himself, said unto Jesus
  18:14 this man went down to his house *j* rather
Acts 13:39 that believe are *j*. . not be *j* by the law
Rom. 2:13 but the doers of the law shall be *j*
  3:20 (Gal. 2:16) the law there shall no flesh be *j*
  3:24 *j* freely by his grace through the redemption
  3:28 man is *j* by faith without the deeds of the law
  3:30 God, which shall *j* the circumcision by faith
  4:2 if Abraham were *j* by works, he hath whereof
  4:5 but believeth on him that *j* the ungodly
  5:1 being *j* by faith, we have peace with God
  5:9 being now *j* by his blood, we shall be saved
  8:30 he called, them he also *j*: and whom he *j*
  8:33 the charge of God's elect? It is God that *j*
1 Cor. 4:4 nothing by myself; yet am I not hereby *j*
  6:11 washed, but ye are sanctified, but ye are *j*
Gal. 2:16 not *j* by the works. . be *j* by the faith of
  3:8 that God would *j* the heathen through faith
  3:11 no man is *j* by the law in the sight of God
  3:24 us unto Christ, that we might be *j* by faith
1 Tim. 3:16 manifest in the flesh, *j* in the Spirit
Tit. 3:7 being *j* by his grace, we should be made heirs
Jas. 2:21 was not Abraham our father *j* by works
  2:24 by works a man is *j*, and not by faith only

Justle

Nah. 2:4 *j* one against another in the broad ways

Justly

Mic. 6:8 do *j*, and to love mercy, and to walk humbly
Lk. 23:41 indeed *j*; for we receive the due reward
1 Thes. 2:10 how holily and *j* and unblamably we

K

Kadesh (Kadesh-barnea)

Num. 13:26 to *K*; and brought back word unto them
  20:1 the people abode in *K*; and Miriam died there
  32:8 when I sent them from *K* to see the land

Kedesh Josh. 20:7; Judg. 4:9

Keep (Kept) *See also* Guard, Hold, Obey, Observe, Preserve, Reserve, Retain

Gen. 2:15 garden of Eden to dress it and to *k* it
  3:24 flaming sword. . to *k* the way of the tree of life
  17:9 Abraham, Thou shalt *k* my covenant therefore

Gen. 18:19 they shall *k* the way of the LORD, to do
28:15 behold, I am with thee, and will *k* thee in
42:16 your brother, and ye shall be *k* in prison
Ex. 3:1 now Moses *k* the flock of Jethro his
20:6 (Deut. 5:10) that . . *k* my commandments
20:8 remember the sabbath day, to *k* it holy
23:20 I send an angel before thee, to *k* thee in
31:13 my sabbaths ye shall *k*: for it is a sign
Num. 6:24 the LORD bless thee, and *k* thee
36:7 Israel shall *k* himself to the inheritance
Deut. 4:6 *k* therefore and do them; for this is your
4:9 thy soul diligently, lest thou forget
6:17 (11:22) shall diligently *k* the commandments
7:8 he would *k* the oath which he had sworn unto
7:9 (Neh. 1:5) *k* covenant and mercy with them
17:19 to *k* all the words of this law and these
23:9 then *k* thee from every wicked thing
29:9 *k* therefore the words of this covenant
32:10 he *k* him as the apple of his eye
Josh. 14:10 now, behold, the LORD hath *k* me alive
1 Sam. 2:9 he will *k* the feet of his saints
2 Sam. 22:22 (Ps. 18:21) have *k* the ways of the LORD
22:24 (Ps. 18:23) *k* myself from mine iniquity
1 Kgs. 2:3 *k* the charge of the LORD . . *k* his statutes
6:12 *k* all my commandments to walk in them; then
11:11 thou hast not *k* my covenant and . . statutes
2 Kgs. 23:21 (2 Chr. 35:1) saying, *K* the passover
Job 23:11 his way have I *k*, and not declined
Ps. 12:7 shalt *k* them, O LORD, thou shalt preserve
17:8 *k* me as the apple of the eye; hide me under
19:13 *k* back thy servant . . from presumptuous sins
25:10 such as *k* his covenant and his testimonies
25:20 O *k* my soul, and deliver me: let me not be
31:20 thou shalt *k* them secretly in a pavilion
34:13 *k* thy tongue from evil, and thy lips from
37:34 and *k* his way, and he shall exalt thee to
78:10 *k* not the covenant of God, and refused to
91:11 (Lk. 4:10) angels charge over thee, to *k* thee
103:9 neither will he *k* his anger for ever
105:45 observe his statutes, and *k* his laws
106:3 blessed are they that *k* judgment
119:4 commanded us to *k* thy precepts diligently
119:5 my ways were directed to *k* thy statutes!
119:146 save me, and I shall *k* thy testimonies
121:3 he that *k* thee will not slumber
121:4 he that *k* Israel shall neither slumber
127:1 except the LORD *k* the city, the watchman
141:3 before my mouth; *k* the door of my lips
Prov. 2:8 *k* the paths of judgment, and preserveth
2:11 preserve thee, understanding shall *k* thee
2:20 good men, and *k* the paths of the righteous
3:1 but let thine heart *k* my commandments
3:21 *k* sound wisdom and discretion
4:4 my words: *k* my commandments, and live
4:6 preservê thee: love her, and she shall *k*
4:23 *k* thy heart with all diligence; for out of
6:22 when thou sleepest, it shall *k* thee
8:32 for blessed are they that *k* my ways
13:3 (21:23) he that *k* his mouth *k* his life
19:8 he that *k* understanding shall find good
29:18 but he that *k* the law, happy is he
Eccl. 3:6 a time to *k*, and a time to cast away
12:13 fear God, and *k* his commandments
Is. 26:3 thou wilt *k* him in perfect peace, whose
27:3 I the LORD do *k* it . . I will *k* it night and day
42:6 will hold thine hand, and will *k* thee
43:6 north, Give up; and to the south, *K* not
Jer. 3:12 LORD, and I will not *k* anger for ever
16:11 have forsaken me, and have not *k* my law
31:10 and *k* him, as a shepherd doth his flock
42:4 it unto you; I will *k* nothing back from you
Ezek. 5:7 neither have *k* my judgments
Hos. 12:6 *k* mercy and judgment, and wait on . . God

Hab. 2:20 let all the earth *k* silence before him
Zech. 13:5 man taught me to *k* cattle from my youth
Mal. 2:7 for the priest's lips should *k* knowledge
Mt. 8:33 and they that *k* them fled, and went their
13:35 I will utter things which have been *k* secret
19:17 wilt enter into life, *k* the commandments
19:20 (Lk. 18:21) have I *k* from my youth up
Mk. 7:9 that ye may *k* your own tradition
Lk. 2:8 *k* watch over their flock by night
2:19 Mary *k* all these things, and pondered them
8:15 heard the word, *k* it, and bring forth fruit
9:36 they *k* it close, and told no man in those
11:28 they that hear the word of God, and *k* it
19:20 here is thy pound, which I have *k* laid up
Jn. 8:51 (8:52) *k* my saying, he shall never see death
14:15 if ye love me, *k* my commandments
14:21 he that hath my commandments, and *k* them
14:23 if a man love me, he will *k* my words
15:10 even as I have *k* my Father's commandments
17:6 gavest them me; and they have *k* thy word
17:11 Father, *k* through thine own name those
17:12 those that thou gavest me I have *k*
17:15 that thou shouldest *k* them from the evil
Acts 5:2 *k* back part of the price, his wife also
9:33 Aeneas, which had *k* his bed eight years
12:4 to four quaternions of soldiers to *k* him
15:5 and to command them to *k* the law of Moses
16:4 they delivered them the decrees for to *k*
18:21 *k* this feast that cometh in Jerusalem
20:20 how I *k* back nothing that was profitable
21:25 *k* themselves from things offered to idols
27:43 to save Paul, *k* them from their purpose
Rom. 16:25 mystery, which was *k* secret since the
1 Cor. 9:27 I *k* under my body, and bring it into
11:2 and *k* the ordinances, as I delivered them
Gal. 3:23 before faith came, we were *k* under the
Eph. 4:3 endeavoring to *k* the unity of the Spirit
Phil. 4:7 shall *k* your hearts and minds through
2 Thes. 3:3 stablish you, and *k* you from evil
1 Tim. 5:22 of other men's sins: *k* thyself pure
6:20 *k* that which is committed to thy trust
2 Tim. 1:12 able to *k* that which I have committed
1:14 *k* by the Holy Ghost which dwelleth in us
4:7 have finished my course, I have *k* the faith
Jas. 1:27 to *k* himself unspotted from the world
2:10 *k* the whole law, and yet offend in one
1 Pet. 1:5 are *k* by the power of God through faith
2 Pet. 3:7 are *k* in store, reserved unto fire
1 Jn. 2:3 we know him, if we *k* his commandments
5:2 when we love God, and *k* his commandments
5:21 little children, *k* yourselves from idols
Jude 21 *k* yourselves in the love of God
24 unto him that is able to *k* you from falling
Rev. 1:3 *k* those things which are written therein
2:26 *k* my works unto the end, to him will I give
3:8 hast *k* my word, and hast not denied my name
3:10 *k* the word of my patience, I also will *k*
22:7 blessed is he that *k* the sayings of the
22:9 *k* the sayings of this book: worship God

Keeper

Gen. 4:2 and Abel was a *k* of sheep, but Cain was a
4:9 and he said, I know not: Am I my brother's *k*?
Job 27:18 a moth, and as a booth that the *k* maketh
Ps. 121:5 the LORD is thy *k*: the LORD is thy shade
Eccl. 12:3 when the *k* of the house shall tremble
Song 1:6 they made me the *k* of the vineyards
Mt. 28:4 for fear of him the *k* did shake
Acts 5:23 *k* standing without before the doors
12:6 and the *k* before the door kept the prison
12:19 and found him not, he examined the *k*
16:27 *k* of the prison awaking out of his sleep
Tit. 2:5 to be discreet, chaste, *k* at home, good

Keilah 1 Sam. 23:1–13

Kerchief

Ezek. 13:18 make *k* upon the head of every stature
  13:21 *k* also will I tear, and deliver my people

Keturah Gen. 25:1

Key

Judg. 3:25 therefore they took a *k*, and opened
Is. 22:22 *k* of the house of David will I lay upon
Mt. 16:19 will give unto thee the *k* of the kingdom
Lk. 11:52 ye have taken away the *k* of knowledge
Rev. 1:18 and have the *k* of hell and of death
  3:7 he that hath the *k* of David, he that openeth
  9:1 to him was given the *k* of the bottomless pit
  20:1 an angel . . having the *k* of the bottomless pit

Kick

Deut. 32:15 Jeshurun waxed fat, and *k*: thou art
1 Sam. 2:29 wherefore *k* ye at my sacrifice
Acts 9:5 (26:14) hard for thee to *k* against the pricks

Kid See also Goat, Scapegoat, Sheep

Gen. 27:9 fetch me . . two good *k* of the goats
  37:31 Joseph's coat, and killed a *k* of the goats
Ex. 23:19 (34:26; Deut. 14:21) *k* in his mother's milk
Lev. 4:23 bring his offering, a *k* of the goats
Judg. 6:19 and Gideon went in, and made ready a *k*
  14:6 and he rent him as he would have rent a *k*
1 Sam. 10:3 to Bethel, one carrying three *k*
Song 1:8 feed thy *k* beside the shepherds' tents
Is. 11:6 and the leopard shall lie down with the *k*
Lk. 15:29 and yet thou never gavest me a *k*

Kill See also Murder, Slain, Slaughter, Slay, Smite

Gen. 4:15 Cain, lest any finding him should *k* him
  37:21 Reuben heard it . . and said, Let us not *k*
Ex. 2:14 (Acts 7:28) to *k* me, as thou *k* the Egyptian?
  20:13 (Deut. 5:17; Mt. 5:21; Mk. 10:19; Lk. 18:20; Rom. 13:9; Jas. 2:11) thou shalt not *k*
Num. 11:15 *k* me, I pray thee, out of hand
  16:13 to *k* us in the wilderness, except thou
  31:17 *k* every male . . and *k* every woman that hath
  35:27 revenger of blood *k* the slayer; he shall
Deut. 32:39 no god with me; I *k*, and I make alive
1 Sam. 2:6 LORD *k*, and maketh alive: he bringeth
  19:1 all his servants, that they should *k* David
2 Sam. 12:9 thou hast *k* Uriah the Hittite with the
1 Kgs. 21:19 hast thou *k*, and also taken possession?
2 Kgs. 5:7 said, Am I God, to *k* and to make alive
  7:4 and if they *k* us, we shall but die
  11:15 him that followeth her *k* with the sword
Esth. 3:13 to *k*, and to cause to perish, all Jews
Ps. 44:22 (Rom. 8:36) for thy sake are we *k* all the day
Eccl. 3:3 a time to *k*, and a time to heal
Mt. 10:28 (Lk. 12:4) *k* the body . . not able to *k* the
  16:21 (Mk. 8:31) be *k*, and be raised again
  17:23 (Mk. 9:31) shall *k* him, and the third day
  21:35 (Mk. 12:5) beat one . . *k* another, and stoned
  23:31 the children of them which *k* the prophets
  23:34 some of them ye shall *k* and crucify
  23:37 (Lk. 13:34) Jerusalem . . that *k* the prophets
  26:4 (Lk. 22:2) take Jesus by subtilty, and *k* him
Mk. 3:4 do evil? to save life, or to *k*?
  14:12 unleavened bread, when they *k* the passover
Lk. 15:27 and thy father hath *k* the fatted calf
Jn. 5:18 (7:1) Jews sought the more to *k* him, because
  7:20 hast a devil: who goeth about to *k* thee?
  8:22 then said the Jews, Will he *k* himself?
  10:10 but for to steal, and to *k*, and to destroy

Jn. 16:2 *k* you will think that he doeth God service
Acts 3:15 and *k* the Prince of life, whom God hath
  9:23 (26:21) the Jews took counsel to *k* him
  10:13 a voice to him, Rise, Peter; *k*, and eat
  16:27 would have *k* himself, supposing that the
  23:12 neither eat nor drink till they had *k* Paul
  23:15 we, or ever he come near, are ready to *k* him
Rom. 11:3 they have *k* thy prophets, and digged down
2 Cor. 3:6 letter *k*, but the spirit giveth life
  6:9 behold, we live; as chastened, and not *k*
1 Thes. 2:15 who both *k* the Lord Jesus, and their
Jas. 4:2 ye lust, and have not: ye *k*, and desire
  5:6 ye have condemned and *k* the just
Rev. 13:10 he that *k* with the sword must be *k* with

Kin See also Kindred, Kinsfolk, Kinsman

Lev. 18:6 approach to any that is near of *k* to him
  25:25 if any of his *k* come to redeem it, then
Mk. 6:4 and among his own *k*, and in his own house

Kind (adjective) See also Gentle, Gracious, Merciful

2 Chr. 10:7 thou be *k* to this people, and please
Lk. 6:35 *k* unto the unthankful and to the evil
1 Cor. 13:4 charity suffereth long, and is *k*
Eph. 4:32 be ye *k* one to another, tender-hearted

Kind (noun)

Gen. 1:11 fruit tree yielding fruit after his *k*
  1:24 bring forth the living creature after his *k*
Mt. 13:47 into the sea, and gathered of every *k*
  17:21 (Mk. 9:29) this *k* goeth not out but by prayer
1 Cor. 14:10 so many *k* of voices in the world

Kindle

Gen. 39:19 the words of his wife . . his wrath was *k*
2 Sam. 22:13 (Ps. 18:8) were coals of fire *k*
Job 19:11 he hath also *k* his wrath against me
  32:2 then was *k* the wrath of Elihu the son of
Ps. 2:12 when his wrath is *k* but a little
Prov. 26:21 so is a contentious man to *k* strife
Is. 50:11 that *k* a fire, that compass yourselves
Jer. 33:18 *k* meat offerings, and to do sacrifice
Ezek. 20:48 shall see that I the LORD have *k* it
Hos. 11:8 within me, my repentings are *k* together
Lk. 12:49 and what will I, if it be already *k*?
Jas. 3:5 behold, how great a matter a little fire *k*!

Kindly

Gen. 24:49 ye will deal *k* and truly with my master
  50:21 he comforted them, and spake *k* unto them
Ruth 1:8 LORD deal *k* with you, as ye have dealt
Rom. 12:10 be *k* affectioned one to another

Kindness See also Compassion, Loving-kindness, Mercy, Pity

Gen. 20:13 this is thy *k* which thou shalt show
  24:12 O LORD . . show *k* unto my master Abraham
Josh. 2:12 showed you *k*, that ye will also show *k*
Ruth 3:10 showed more *k* in the latter end than at
1 Sam. 15:6 showed *k* to all the children of Israel
  20:14 while yet I live show me the *k* of the LORD
2 Sam. 2:6 the LORD show *k* and truth unto you
  9:1 that I may show him *k* for Jonathan's sake?
Neh. 9:17 merciful, slow to anger, and of great *k*
Esth. 2:9 pleased him, and she obtained *k* of him
Ps. 31:21 for he hath showed me his marvelous *k* in
  117:2 for his merciful *k* is great toward us
  119:76 thy merciful *k* be for my comfort
  141:5 the righteous smite me; it shall be a *k*
Prov. 19:22 the desire of a man is his *k*

Prov. 31:26 and in her tongue is the law of *k*
Is. 54:8 but with everlasting *k* will I have mercy
54:10 my *k* shall not depart from thee, neither
Jer. 2:2 I remember thee, the *k* of thy youth
Joel 2:13 great *k*, and repenteth him of the evil
Acts 28:2 barbarous people showed us no little *k*
2 Cor. 6:6 longsuffering, by *k*, by the Holy Ghost
Eph. 2:7 riches of his grace, in his *k* toward us
Col. 3:12 bowels of mercies, *k*, humbleness of mind
Tit. 3:4 but after that the *k* and love of God our
2 Pet. 1:7 *k*; and to brotherly *k*, charity

Kindred *See also* Kin, Kinsfolk, Kinsman

Gen. 12:1 (Acts 7:3) of thy country, and from thy *k*
Num. 10:30 depart to mine own land, and to my *k*
Ruth 3:2 and now is not Boaz of our *k*, with whose
Acts 3:25 in thy seed shall all the *k* of the earth
Rev. 1:7 *k* of the earth shall wail because of him
5:9 redeemed us . . out of every *k*, and tongue

Kine *See also* Cow, Heifer

Gen. 41:2 seven well-favored *k* and fat-fleshed
1 Sam. 6:7 take two milch *k* . . tie the *k* to the cart
Amos 4:1 hear this word, ye *k* of Bashan, that are

King *See also* Governor, Lord, Ruler

Gen. 14:18 (Heb. 7:1) Melchizedek *k* of Salem
17:6 nations of thee . . *k* shall come out of thee
36:31 *k* that reigned in the land of Edom, before
Ex. 1:8 (Acts 7:18) *k* over Egypt . . knew not Joseph
2:23 the *k* of Egypt died: and . . Israel sighed
Deut. 17:15 set him *k* over thee, whom the LORD
33:5 he was *k* in Jeshurun, when the heads of the
Josh. 10:16 five *k* fled, and hid themselves in a cave
Judg. 9:8 the trees went . . to anoint a *k* over them
17:6 (18:1; 19:1; 21:25) there was no *k* in Israel
1 Sam. 2:10 and he shall give strength unto his *k*
8:5 make us a *k* to judge us like all the nations
10:24 people shouted, and said, God save the *k*
12:12 *k* shall reign over us: when . . God was your *k*
21:8 because the *k*'s business required haste
24:20 I know well that thou shalt surely be *k*
2 Sam. 5:3 (1 Chr. 11:3) anointed David *k* over Israel
1 Kgs. 1:5 exalted himself, saying, I will be *k*
1:34 hath the prophet anoint him there *k*
2 Kgs. 9:13 blew with trumpets, saying, Jehu is *k*
11:12 (2 Chr. 23:11) and they made him *k*
Neh. 6:7 *k* in Judah . . shall it be reported to the *k*
Job 18:14 it shall bring him to the *k* of terrors
41:34 he is a *k* over all the children of pride
Ps. 2:2 (Acts 4:26) the *k* of the earth set themselves
2:6 have I set my *K* upon my holy hill of Zion
5:2 hearken unto the voice of my cry, my *K*
10:16 LORD is *K* for ever and ever: the heathen
20:9 save, LORD: let the *k* hear us when we call
24:7 (24:9) and the *K* of glory shall come in
24:8 (24:10) who is this *K* of glory? The LORD
29:10 yea, the LORD sitteth *K* for ever
33:16 is no *k* saved by the multitude of a host
44:4 thou art my *K*, O God: command deliverances
45:1 the things which I have made touching the *K*
47:7 for God is the *K* of all the earth: sing ye
72:1 give the *k* thy judgments, O God
74:12 for God is my *K* of old, working salvation
89:18 and the Holy One of Israel is our *K*
102:15 and all the *k* of the earth thy glory
138:4 all the *k* of the earth shall praise thee
144:10 it is he that giveth salvation unto *k*
149:2 the children of Zion be joyful in their *K*
Prov. 8:15 by me *k* reign . . princes decree justice
20:26 wise *k* scattereth the wicked, and bringeth

Prov. 22:29 in his business? he shall stand before *k*
24:21 my son, fear thou the LORD and the *k*
29:14 the *k* that faithfully judgeth the poor
30:31 and a *k*, against whom there is no rising
31:4 *k*, O Lemuel, it is not for *k* to drink wine
Eccl. 2:12 can the man do that cometh after the *k*?
5:9 the *k* himself is served by the field
8:4 where the word of a *k* is, there is power
10:16 woe to thee, O land, when thy *k* is a child
Song 1:4 the *K* hath brought me into his chambers
Is. 6:5 for mine eyes have seen the *K*, the LORD
32:1 *K* shall reign in righteousness, and princes
33:17 thine eyes shall see the *K* in his beauty
33:22 LORD is our lawgiver, the LORD is our *K*
43:15 Holy One, the Creator of Israel, your *K*
62:2 see thy righteousness, and all *k* thy glory
Jer. 10:7 who would not fear thee, O *K* of nations?
10:10 he is the living God, and an everlasting *K*
23:5 a righteous Branch, and a *K* shall reign
30:9 David their *k*, whom I will raise up unto
46:18 (48:15; 51:57) *K*, whose name is The LORD
Dan. 2:4 spake the Chaldeans to the *k* in Syriac
2:37 thou, O *k*, art a *k* of *k*: for the God
2:47 your God is a God of gods, and a Lord of *k*
7:17 great beasts, which are four, are four *k*
7:24 the ten horns out of this kingdom are ten *k*
8:20 having two horns are the *k* of Media and
11:2 there shall stand up yet three *k* in Persia
11:5 and the *k* of the south shall be strong
Hos. 3:5 seek the LORD their God, and David their *k*
13:10 I will be thy *k*: where is any other that
Mic. 2:13 their *k* shall pass before them
Zech. 9:9 (Mt. 21:5; Jn. 12:15) behold, thy *K* cometh
14:9 and the LORD shall be *K* over all the earth
14:16 go up from year to year to worship the *K*
Mal. 1:14 I am a great *K*, saith the LORD of hosts
Mt. 2:2 where is he that is born *K* of the Jews?
5:35 Jerusalem; for it is the city of the great *K*
10:18 (Mk. 13:9; Lk. 21:12) before governors and *k*
18:23 kingdom of heaven likened unto a certain *k*
22:2 like unto a certain *k*, which made a marriage
25:34 shall the *K* say unto them on his right hand
27:11 (Mk. 15:2; Lk. 23:3; Jn. 18:33) *K* of the Jews?
27:29 (Jn. 19:3) saying, Hail, *K* of the Jews!
27:37 (Mk. 15:26; Lk. 23:38; Jn. 19:19) written, THIS IS JESUS THE *K* OF THE JEWS
Lk. 10:24 prophets and *k* have desired to see those
14:31 what *k*, going to make war against another *k*
19:38 (Jn. 12:13) blessed be the *K* that cometh
23:2 saying that he himself is Christ a *k*
Jn. 1:49 the Son of God; thou art the *K* of Israel
6:15 and take him by force, to make him a *k*
19:14 and he saith unto the Jews, Behold your *K*!
Acts 17:7 saying that there is another *k*, one Jesus
1 Tim. 1:17 unto the *K* eternal, immortal, invisible
6:15 Potentate, the *K* of *k*, and Lord of lords
1 Pet. 2:17 fear God. Honor the *k*
Rev. 1:6 hath made us *k* and priests unto God
15:3 just and true are thy ways, thou *K* of saints
16:12 way of the *k* of the east might be prepared
17:12 the ten horns which thou sawest are ten *k*
17:14 he is Lord of lords, and *K* of *k*
17:18 the woman . . reigneth over the *k* of the earth
19:16 a name written, *K* OF *K*, AND LORD OF LORDS

Kingdom *See also* Dominion, Heaven, Reign, Rule

Gen. 10:10 beginning of his *k* was Babel
Ex. 19:6 ye shall be unto me a *k* of priests
1 Sam. 10:25 told the people the manner of the *k*
18:8 what can he have more but the *k*?
2 Sam. 7:12 (1 Chr. 17:11; 28:7) I will establish his *k*

2 Kgs. 19:19 (Is. 37:20) the *k* of the earth may know
1 Chr. 29:11 thine is the *k*, O LORD, and thou art
Ps. 22:28 *k* is the LORD's: and he is the governor
45:6 (Heb. 1:8) sceptre of thy *k* is a right sceptre
46:6 heathen raged, the *k* were moved: he uttered
68:32 sing unto God, ye *k* of the earth; O sing
103:19 in the heavens; and his *k* ruleth over all
145:12 acts, and the glorious majesty of his *k*
145:13 *k* is an everlasting *k*, and thy dominion
Is. 9:7 throne of David, and upon his *k*, to order
14:16 made the earth to tremble, that did shake *k*
23:11 out his hand over the sea, he shook the *k*
Jer. 10:7 in all their *k*, there is none like unto
Dan. 2:37 hath given thee a *k*, power, and strength
4:3 his *k* is an everlasting *k*
4:17 Most High ruleth in the *k* of men, and giveth
4:30 that I have built for the house of the *k*
4:31 it is spoken; The *k* is departed from thee
7:18 take the *k*, and possess the *k* for ever
7:27 *k* and dominion, and the greatness of the *k*
8:22 four *k* shall stand up out of the nation
11:4 when he shall stand up, his *k* shall be broken
Obad. 21 of Esau; and the *k* shall be the LORD's
Hag. 2:22 I will overthrow the throne of *k*
Mt. 3:2 (4:17) repent ye. . the *k* of heaven is at hand
4:8 (Lk. 4:5) showeth him all the *k* of the world
4:23 (9:35) preaching the gospel of the *k*
5:3 (Lk. 6:20) for theirs is the *k* of heaven
5:19 shall be called great in the *k* of heaven
6:10 (Lk. 11:2) thy *k* come. Thy will be done in
6:13 for thine is the *k*, and the power, and the
6:33 (Lk. 12:31) seek ye first the *k* of God
7:21 unto me, Lord, Lord, shall enter into the *k*
8:11 (Lk. 13:28) with . . Jacob, in the *k* of heaven
8:12 but the children of the *k* shall be cast out
10:7 (Lk. 10:9) the *k* of heaven is at hand
11:12 until now the *k* of heaven suffereth violence
12:25 (Mk. 3:24; Lk. 11:17) *k* divided against itself
12:28 cast out devils. . *k* of God is come unto you
13:11 (Mk. 4:11; Lk. 8:10) the mysteries of the *k*
13:19 when any one heareth the word of the *k*
13:38 the good seed are the children of the *k*
16:19 give unto thee the keys of the *k* of heaven
16:28 they see the Son of man coming in his *k*
18:3 children, ye shall not enter into the *k*
19:14 (Mk. 10:14; Lk. 18:16) for of such is the *k* of
19:23 (Mk. 10:23; Lk. 18:24) rich man . . into the *k*
21:43 *k* of God shall be taken from you, and given
24:7 (Mk. 13:8; Lk. 21:10) nation, and *k* against *k*
25:34 inherit the *k* prepared for you from the
26:29 (Mk. 14:25; Lk. 22:18) new . . my Father's *k*
Mk. 11:10 blessed be the *k* of our father David
12:34 thou art not far from the *k* of God
Lk. 1:33 and of his *k* there shall be no end
9:62 plow, and looking back, is fit for the *k* of
11:20 no doubt the *k* of God is come upon you
12:32 Father's good pleasure to give you the *k*
13:29 and shall sit down in the *k* of God
16:16 since that time the *k* of God is preached
17:20 the *k* of God cometh not with observation
17:21 for, behold, the *k* of God is within you
19:12 far country to receive for himself a *k*
21:31 know ye that the *k* of God is nigh at hand
22:29 I appoint unto you a *k*, as my Father hath
23:42 remember me when thou comest into thy *k*
Jn. 3:3 be born again, he cannot see the *k* of God
18:36 my *k* is not of this world: if my *k* were of
Acts 1:3 of the things pertaining to the *k* of God
1:6 at this time restore again the *k* to Israel?
14:22 through much tribulation enter into the *k*
19:8 the things concerning the *k* of God
28:23 he expounded and testified the *k* of God
Rom. 14:17 the *k* of God is not meat and drink

1 Cor. 4:20 *k* of God is not in word, but in power
6:9 unrighteous shall not inherit the *k* of God?
15:24 he shall have delivered up the *k* to God
15:50 that flesh and blood cannot inherit the *k*
Gal. 5:21 do such things shall not inherit the *k*
Eph. 5:5 hath any inheritance in the *k* of Christ
Col. 1:13 translated us into the *k* of his dear Son
1 Thes. 2:12 hath called you unto his *k* and glory
2 Thes. 1:5 may be counted worthy of the *k* of God
Heb. 11:33 who through faith subdued *k*, wrought
12:28 we receiving a *k* which cannot be moved
Jas. 2:5 poor. . rich in faith, and heirs of the *k*
2 Pet. 1:11 into the everlasting *k* of our Lord
Rev. 11:15 *k* of this world are become the *k* of our
12:10 *k* of our God, and the power of his Christ
16:10 the beast; and his *k* was full of darkness
17:17 give their *k* unto the beast, until

Kinsfolk *See also* Kin, Kindred, Kinsman

Job 19:14 *k* have failed, and my familiar friends
Lk. 2:44 sought him among their *k* and acquaintance
21:16 betrayed. . by parents, and brethren, and *k*

Kinsman (Kinsmen) *See also* Kin, Kindred, Kinsfolk

Ruth 2:20 near of kin unto us, one of our next *k*
3:12 near *k*: howbeit there is a *k* nearer than I
3:13 part of a *k*, well; let him do the *k*'s part
Rom. 9:3 my brethren, my *k* according to the flesh

Kirjath-jearim 1 Sam. 7:1

Kish 1 Sam. 9:1

Kiss *See also* Embrace

Gen. 27:26 Isaac said. . Come near now, and *k* me
29:11 Jacob *k* Rachel, and lifted up his voice
31:28 hast not suffered me to *k* my sons and my
33:4 fell on his neck, and *k* him: and they wept
45:15 he *k* all his brethren, and wept upon them
48:10 Israel. . *k* them, and embraced them
50:1 father's face, and wept upon him, and *k* him
Ruth 1:14 Orpah *k* her mother-in-law; but Ruth
1 Sam. 20:41 *k* one another, and wept one with
2 Sam. 14:33 the king: and the king *k* Absalom
15:5 put forth his hand, and took him, and *k* him
1 Kgs. 19:18 and every mouth which hath not *k* him
Job 31:27 enticed, or my mouth hath *k* my hand
Ps. 2:12 *k* the Son, lest he be angry, and ye perish
85:10 righteousness and peace have *k* each other
Prov. 24:26 *k* his lips that giveth a right answer
27:6 but the *k* of an enemy are deceitful
Song 1:2 let him *k* me with the *k* of his mouth
Hos. 13:2 let the men that sacrifice *k* the calves
Mt. 26:48 (Mk. 14:44) I shall *k*, that same is he
Lk. 7:38 and *k* his feet, and anointed them with
7:45 thou gavest me no *k*: but this woman, since
15:20 and ran, and fell on his neck, and *k* him
22:47 Judas. . drew near unto Jesus to *k* him
Acts 20:37 and fell on Paul's neck, and *k* him
Rom. 16:16 (1 Cor. 16:20; 1 Thes. 5:26) with a holy *k*
1 Pet. 5:14 greet ye one another with a *k* of charity

Kittim *See* Chittim

Knead

Gen. 18:6 of fine meal, *k* it, and make cakes upon
Hos. 7:4 he hath *k* the dough, until it be leavened

Kneadingtrough

Ex. 8:3 frogs. . into thine ovens, and into thy *k*
12:34 their *k* being bound up in their clothes

Knee

Gen. 30:3 unto her; and she shall bear upon my *k*
1 Kgs. 19:18 (Rom. 11:4) *k* . . not bowed unto Baal
Ezra 9:5 I fell upon my *k*, and spread out my hands
Job 4:4 and thou hast strengthened the feeble *k*
Is. 35:3 (Heb. 12:12) and confirm the feeble *k*
45:23 (Rom. 14:11) every *k* shall bow, every tongue
Nah. 2:10 heart melteth, and the *k* smite together
Mt. 27:29 (Mk. 15:19) bowed the *k* before him
Eph. 3:14 for this cause I bow my *k* unto the Father
Phil. 2:10 at the name of Jesus every *k* should bow

Kneel

Gen. 24:11 his camels to *k* down without the city
Ps. 95:6 let us *k* before the LORD our maker
Dan. 6:10 he *k* upon his knees three times a day
Mt. 17:14 came to him a certain man, *k* down to him
Lk. 22:41 a stone's cast, and *k* down, and prayed
Acts 7:60 he *k* down, and cried with a loud voice
9:40 Peter put them all forth, and *k* down
21:5 out of the city: and we *k* down on the shore

Knew *See* Know

Knife (Knives)

Gen. 22:10 hand, and took the *k* to slay his son
Josh. 5:2 Joshua, Make thee sharp *k*, and circumcise
Judg. 19:29 took a *k*, and laid hold on his concubine
1 Kgs. 18:28 cut themselves. . with *k* and lancets
Prov. 23:2 and put a *k* to thy throat, if thou be a
Ezek. 5:1 son of man, take thee a sharp *k*

Knit

Judg. 20:11 against the city, *k* together as one man
1 Sam. 18:1 Jonathan was *k* with the soul of David
1 Chr. 12:17 mine heart shall be *k* unto you
Acts 10:11 a great sheet *k* at the four corners
Col. 2:2 comforted, being *k* together in love
2:19 all the body by joints and bands. . *k* together

Knock

Song 5:2 it is the voice of my beloved that *k*, saying
Mt. 7:7 (Lk. 11:9) *k*, and it shall be opened unto you
Lk. 12:36 when he cometh and *k*, they may open
13:25 to *k* at the door, saying, Lord, Lord, open
Acts 12:16 but Peter continued *k*: and when they
Rev. 3:20 behold, I stand at the door, and *k*

Know (Knew, Known) *See also* Comprehend, Discern, Perceive, Understand

Gen. 3:5 God doth *k* . . ye shall be as gods, *k* good
3:7 opened, and they *k* that they were naked
3:22 is become as one of us, to *k* good and evil
18:19 I *k* him, that he will command his children
28:16 the LORD is in this place; and I *k* it not
42:8 Joseph *k* his brethren, but they *k* not him
Ex. 1:8 (Acts 7:18) a new king. . which *k* not Joseph
3:7 of their taskmasters; for I *k* their sorrows
6:3 but by my name JEHOVAH was I not *k* to them
6:7 and ye shall *k* that I am the LORD your God
9:29 mayest *k* how that the earth is the LORD's
9:30 I *k* that ye will not yet fear the LORD God
18:11 I *k* that the LORD is greater than all gods
18:16 I do make them *k* the statutes of God
33:12 yet thou hast said, I *k* thee by name
Num. 24:16 and *k* the knowledge of the Most High
Deut. 4:35 thou mightest *k* that the LORD he is God

Deut. 18:21 how shall we *k* the word which the LORD
34:10 unto Moses, whom the LORD *k* face to face
Josh. 4:22 ye shall let your children *k*, saying
Judg. 2:10 generation after them. . *k* not the LORD
1 Sam. 17:46 may *k* that there is a God in Israel
1 Kgs. 8:43 (2 Chr. 6:33) that all. . may *k* thy name
2 Kgs. 5:15 now I *k* that there is no God in all
19:19 (Is. 37:20) kingdoms of the earth may *k*
19:27 (Is. 37:28) I *k* thy abode, and thy going out
1 Chr. 28:9 my son, *k* thou the God of thy father
2 Chr. 33:13 Manasseh *k* that the LORD he was God
Ezra 7:25 *k* ye them that *k* them not
Esth. 4:14 who *k* whether thou art come. . for such
Job 11:8 do? deeper than hell; what canst thou *k*?
13:23 make me to *k* my transgression and my sin
19:25 for I *k* that my Redeemer liveth, and that
22:13 how doth God *k*? can he judge through the
23:3 oh that I *k* where I might find him!
23:10 but he *k* the way that I take: when he hath
30:23 I *k* that thou wilt bring me to death
36:26 God is great, and we *k* him not, neither
38:33 *k* thou the ordinances of heaven?
42:2 I *k* that thou canst do every thing
Ps. 1:6 the LORD *k* the way of the righteous
9:10 that thy name will put their trust in thee
35:11 they laid to my charge things that I *k* not
36:10 thy loving-kindness unto them that *k* thee
39:4 to *k* mine end. . that I may *k* how frail I am
44:21 for he *k* the secrets of the heart
46:10 be still, and *k* that I am God: I will be
51:6 hidden part thou shalt make me to *k* wisdom
67:2 thy way may be *k* upon earth, thy saving
73:11 how doth God *k*? and is there knowledge in
91:14 set him on high, because he hath *k* my name
94:11 (1 Cor. 3:20) LORD *k* the thoughts of man
95:10 (Heb. 3:10) err . . they have not *k* my ways
100:3 *k* ye that the LORD he is God: it is he
103:14 he *k* our frame; he remembereth that we
139:1 O LORD, thou hast searched me, and *k* me
139:2 thou *k* my downsitting and mine uprising
139:23 search me, O God, and *k* my heart: try me
Prov. 1:2 to *k* wisdom and instruction; to perceive
27:1 for thou *k* not what a day may bring forth
Eccl. 3:14 I *k* that, whatsoever God doeth, it shall
9:5 living *k* that they shall die. . the dead *k* not
9:12 for man also *k* not his time: as the fishes
Is. 1:3 but Israel doth not *k*, my people doth not
7:15 he may *k* to refuse the evil, and choose
19:21 and the LORD shall be *k* to Egypt
40:28 hast thou not *k*? hast thou not heard
45:4 surnamed thee, though thou hast not *k* me
49:26 all flesh shall *k* that I the LORD am thy
52:6 shall *k* my name: therefore they shall *k* in
55:5 thou *k* not, and nations that *k* not thee shall
58:2 seek me daily, and delight to *k* my ways
59:8 (Rom. 3:17) the way of peace they *k* not
66:18 for I *k* their works and their thoughts
Jer. 1:5 before I formed thee in the belly I *k* thee
8:7 but my people *k* not the judgment of the LORD
9:6 through deceit they refuse to *k* me
9:24 understandeth and *k* me, that I am the LORD
17:9 heart. . desperately wicked: who can *k* it?
24:7 I will give them a heart to *k* me, that I
29:11 I *k* the thoughts that I think toward you
31:34 (Heb. 8:11) *k* the LORD: for they shall all *k*
33:3 great and mighty things, which thou *k* not
Ezek. 6:10 they shall *k* that I am the LORD
39:7 and the heathen shall *k* that I am the LORD
Hos. 6:3 shall we *k*, if we follow on to *k* the LORD
11:3 but they *k* not that I healed them
Amos 3:2 you only have I *k* of all the families
Jon. 4:2 for I *k* that thou art a gracious God
Mic. 4:12 but they *k* not the thoughts of the LORD

Nah. 1:7 and he *k* them that trust in him
Zech. 11:11 *k* that it was the word of the LORD
Mt. 6:3 thy left hand *k* what thy right hand doeth
6:8 your Father *k* what things ye have need of
7:16 ye shall *k* them by their fruits
7:23 (Lk. 13:27) profess unto them, I never *k* you
9:6 (Mk. 2:10; Lk. 5:24) may *k* that the Son . . hath
10:26 (Lk. 8:17; 12:2) and hid, that shall not be *k*
11:27 (Lk. 10:22) no man *k* the Son, but the Father
12:25 (Lk. 11:17) Jesus *k* their thoughts
13:11 (Mk. 4:11; Lk. 8:10) you to *k* the mysteries
17:12 Elias is come already, and they *k* him not
22:16 (Mk. 12:14; Lk. 20:21) we *k* . . thou art true
22:29 (Mk. 12:24) ye do err, not *k* the Scriptures
24:36 (Mk. 13:32) of that day and hour *k* no man
24:42 for ye *k* not what hour your Lord doth come
25:12 said, Verily I say unto you, I *k* you not
25:24 I *k* thee that thou art a hard man, reaping
26:70 (Mk. 14:68; Lk. 22:60) I *k* not . . thou sayest
27:18 (Mk. 15:10) he *k* that for envy they had
Mk. 1:24 (Lk. 4:34) I *k* thee who thou art, the Holy
5:43 them straitly that no man should *k* it
13:35 *k* not when the master of the house cometh
15:45 when he *k* it of the centurion, he gave the
Lk. 4:41 to speak: for they *k* that he was Christ
12:47 that servant, which *k* his lord's will
16:15 before men; but God *k* your hearts
22:34 that thou shalt thrice deny that thou *k* me
24:31 and their eyes were opened, and they *k* him
24:35 how he was *k* of them in breaking of bread
Jn. 1:10 was made by him, and the world *k* him not
2:25 testify of man; for he *k* what was in man
3:10 master of Israel, and *k* not these things?
4:10 said unto her, If thou *k* the gift of God
4:22 worship ye *k* not what: we *k* what we worship
4:42 and *k* that this is indeed the Christ
6:64 Jesus *k* from the beginning who they were
7:17 do his will, he shall *k* of the doctrine
7:27 but when Christ cometh, no man *k* whence he
8:19 neither *k* me, nor my Father: if ye had *k* me
8:32 ye shall *k* the truth, and the truth shall
8:55 yet ye have not *k* him; but I *k* him: and if
9:25 sinner or no, I *k* not: one thing I *k*, that
10:4 the sheep follow him: for they *k* his voice
10:14 shepherd, and *k* my sheep, and am *k* of mine
10:15 as the Father *k* me, even so *k* I the Father
13:1 when Jesus *k* that his hour was come that he
13:7 what I do thou *k* not now; but thou shalt *k*
13:35 shall all men *k* that ye are my disciples
14:4 and whither I go ye *k*, and the way ye *k*
14:7 if ye had *k* me, ye should have *k* my Father
14:17 seeth him not, neither *k* him: but ye *k* him
15:21 because they *k* not him that sent me
16:30 now are we sure that thou *k* all things
17:3 that they might *k* thee the only true God
17:25 world hath not *k* thee: but I have *k* thee
18:15 that disciple was *k* unto the high priest
20:9 yet they *k* not the Scripture, that he must
Acts 1:7 not for you to *k* the times or the seasons
1:24 thou, Lord, which *k* the hearts of all men
3:10 they *k* that it was he which sat for alms at
15:8 God, which *k* the hearts, bare them witness
19:15 Jesus I *k*, and Paul I *k*; but who are ye?
Rom. 1:19 that which may be *k* of God is manifest
1:21 they *k* God, they glorified him not as God
7:7 *k* sin, but by the law: for I had not *k* lust
8:26 *k* not what we should pray for as we ought
8:27 *k* what is the mind of the Spirit, because
8:28 we *k* that all things work together for good
11:34 who hath *k* the mind of the Lord? or who
1 Cor. 1:21 world by wisdom *k* not God, it pleased
2:2 I determined not to *k* any thing among you
2:8 princes of this world *k*: for had they *k* it

1 Cor. 2:11 the things of God *k* no man, but the Spirit
2:14 foolishness unto him: neither can he *k* them
3:16 (6:19) *k* ye not that ye are the temple of God
3:20 Lord *k* the thoughts of the wise, that they
4:4 I *k* nothing by myself; yet am I not hereby
8:2 man think that he *k* any thing, he *k* nothing
13:9 for we *k* in part, and we prophesy in part
13:12 *k* in part; but then shall I *k* even as . . I am *k*
2 Cor. 5:16 henceforth *k* we no man after the flesh
5:21 made him to be sin for us, who *k* no sin
8:9 for ye *k* the grace of our Lord Jesus Christ
12:2 I *k* a man in Christ above fourteen years ago
Gal. 4:8 when ye *k* not God, ye did service unto
Eph. 1:18 ye may *k* what is the hope of his calling
3:19 and to *k* the love of Christ, which passeth
Phil. 3:10 that I may *k* him, and the power of his
4:12 I *k* both how to be abased, and I *k* how to
Col. 4:6 ye may *k* how ye ought to answer every man
1 Thes. 4:5 even as the Gentiles which *k* not God
2 Thes. 1:8 vengeance on them that *k* not God
2 Tim. 1:12 for I *k* whom I have believed
2:19 this seal, The Lord *k* them that are his
3:15 from a child thou hast *k* the holy Scriptures
Tit. 1:16 profess that they *k* God; but in works
Heb. 11:8 he went out, not *k* whither he went
Jas. 4:14 ye *k* not what shall be on the morrow
4:17 that *k* to do good, and doeth it not, to him
1 Pet. 1:18 as ye *k* that ye were not redeemed with
2 Pet. 2:9 Lord *k* how to deliver the godly out of
2:21 better for them not to have *k* the way of
1 Jn. 2:3 hereby we do *k* that we *k* him, if we keep
2:5 perfected: hereby *k* we that we are in him
2:20 from the Holy One, and ye *k* all things
3:1 the world *k* us not, because it *k* him not
3:2 but we *k* that, when he shall appear
3:14 that we have passed from death unto life
3:19 hereby we *k* that we are of the truth
3:24 we *k* that he abideth in us, by the Spirit
4:7 that loveth is born of God, and *k* God
4:16 we have *k* and believed the love that God
5:13 that ye may *k* that ye have eternal life
5:15 *k* that he hear us, whatsoever we ask, we *k*
5:19 we *k* that we are of God, and the whole world
3 Jn. 12 and ye *k* that our record is true
Rev. 2:2 (2:19; 3:1, 8, 15) I *k* thy works
2:24 and which have not *k* the depths of Satan
3:3 shalt not *k* what hour I will come upon thee
19:12 name written, that no man *k*, but he himself

Knowledge *See also* Prudence, Understanding, Wisdom

Gen. 2:9 garden, and the tree of *k* of good and evil
Num. 24:16 knew the *k* of the Most High, which saw
Deut. 1:39 had no *k* between good and evil
1 Sam. 2:3 LORD is a God of *k*, and by him actions
2 Chr. 1:10 give me now wisdom and *k*, that I may
30:22 Levites that taught the good *k* of the LORD
Job 21:14 for we desire not the *k* of thy ways
21:22 shall any teach God *k*? seeing he judgeth
35:16 he multiplieth words without *k*
36:4 he that is perfect in *k* is with thee
Ps. 14:4 (53:4) have all the workers of iniquity no *k*?
19:2 and night unto night showeth *k*
73:11 God know? and is there *k* in the Most High?
94:10 he that teacheth man *k*, shall not he know?
119:66 teach me good judgment and *k*: for I have
139:6 such *k* is too wonderful for me; it is high
144:3 what is man, that thou takest *k* of him!
Prov. 1:4 to the young man *k* and discretion
1:7 fear of the LORD is the beginning of *k*
2:3 yea, if thou criest after *k*, and liftest up
2:6 out of his mouth cometh *k* and understanding

Prov. 2:10 thine heart, and *k* is pleasant unto thy soul
8:10 not silver; and *k* rather than choice gold
9:10 and the *k* of the Holy is understanding
10:14 wise men lay up *k*: but the mouth of the
12:1 whoso loveth instruction loveth *k*
15:2 tongue of the wise useth *k* aright
17:27 he that hath *k* spareth his words
18:15 getteth *k* . . the ear of the wise seeketh *k*
22:17 and apply thine heart unto my *k*
24:5 yea, a man of *k* increaseth strength
30:3 learned wisdom, nor have the *k* of the holy
Eccl. 1:18 he that increaseth *k* increaseth sorrow
9:10 nor device, nor *k*, nor wisdom, in the grave
Is. 11:2 spirit of *k* and of the fear of the LORD
11:9 (Hab. 2:14) shall be full of the *k* of the LORD
28:9 whom shall he teach *k*? and whom shall he
33:6 and *k* shall be the stability of thy times
40:14 taught him *k*, and showed to him the way of
53:11 by his *k* shall my righteous servant justify
Jer. 3:15 shall feed you with *k* and understanding
Dan. 1:17 God gave them *k* and skill in all learning
12:4 run to and fro, and *k* shall be increased
Hos. 4:6 my people are destroyed for lack of *k*
6:6 and the *k* of God more than burnt offerings
Lk. 1:77 to give *k* of salvation unto his people by
11:52 for ye have taken away the key of *k*
Acts 4:13 took *k* of them, that they had been with
24:22 more perfect *k* of that way, he deferred
Rom. 1:28 did not like to retain God in their *k*
2:20 teacher of babes, which hast the form of *k*
3:20 for by the law is the *k* of sin
10:2 have a zeal of God, but not according to *k*
11:33 the riches both of the wisdom and *k* of God!
1 Cor. 8:1 we all have *k*. *K* puffeth up, but charity
12:8 to another the word of *k* by the same Spirit
13:2 understand all mysteries, and all *k*
13:8 whether there be *k*, it shall vanish away
15:34 sin not; for some have not the *k* of God
2 Cor. 4:6 to give the light of the *k* of the glory
10:5 that exalteth itself against the *k* of God
Eph. 3:4 understand my *k* in the mystery of Christ
3:19 to know the love of Christ, which passeth *k*
4:13 the *k* of the Son of God, unto a perfect man
Phil. 3:8 for the excellency of the *k* of Christ
Col. 1:9 ye might be filled with the *k* of his will
1:10 good work, and increasing in the *k* of God
2:3 are hid all the treasures of wisdom and *k*
3:10 is renewed in *k* after the image of him that
1 Tim. 2:4 and to come unto the *k* of the truth
2 Tim. 3:7 never able to come to the *k* of the truth
Heb. 10:26 we have received the *k* of the truth
Jas. 3:13 a wise man and endued with *k* among you?
1 Pet. 3:7 husbands, dwell with them according to *k*
2 Pet. 1:3 through the *k* of him that hath called
1:5 add to your faith virtue; and to virtue, *k*
1:8 barren nor unfruitful in the *k* of our Lord
3:18 but grow in grace, and in the *k* of our Lord

Known *See also* Know

Gen. 45:1 (Acts 7:13) Joseph made himself *k* unto his
1 Kgs. 18:36 let it be *k* this day that thou art God in
1 Chr. 16:8 (Ps. 105:1) make *k* his deeds among the
Ps. 9:16 LORD is *k* by the judgment . . he executeth
76:1 in Judah is God *k*: his name is great in
98:2 the LORD hath made *k* his salvation
Prov. 20:11 even a child is *k* by his doings, whether
Mt. 12:16 (Mk. 3:12) they should not make him *k*
12:33 (Lk. 6:44) for the tree is *k* by his fruit
Lk. 2:17 made *k* abroad the saying which was told
Acts 7:13 Joseph was made *k* to his brethren
15:18 *k* unto God are all his works from the
2 Cor. 3:2 written in our hearts, *k* and read of all

Eph. 6:19 to make *k* the mystery of the gospel
Phil. 4:5 let your moderation be *k* unto all men
4:6 let your requests be made *k* unto God

Korah (Core) Num. 16:1; 26:10; Jude 11

L

Laban Gen. 24:29–31:55

Labor *See also* Toil, Work

Gen. 31:42 mine affliction and the *l* of my hands
35:16 Rachel travailed, and she had hard *l*
Ex. 5:9 more work be laid . . that they may *l* therein
20:9 (Deut. 5:13) six days shalt thou *l*, and do all
Deut. 26:7 and looked on our affliction, and our *l*
Josh. 7:3 and make not all the people to *l* thither
24:13 given you a land for which ye did not *l*
Job 9:29 if I be wicked, why then *l* I in vain?
Ps. 90:10 years, yet is their strength *l* and sorrow
104:23 his work and to his *l* until the evening
105:44 and they inherited the *l* of the people
127:1 the house, they *l* in vain that build it
128:2 thou shalt eat the *l* of thine hands
Prov. 10:16 the *l* of the righteous tendeth to life
13:11 but he that gathereth by *l* shall increase
14:23 in all *l* there is profit: but the talk of
16:26 he that *l*, *l* for himself; for his mouth
21:25 killeth him; for his hands refuse to *l*
23:4 *l* not to be rich: cease from thine own
Eccl. 1:3 (2:22) what profit hath a man of all his *l*
1:8 all things are full of *l*; man cannot utter
2:10 my *l*: and this was my portion of all my *l*
2:18 I hated all my *l* which I had taken under
3:13 (5:18) and enjoy the good of all his *l*
4:8 yet is there no end of all his *l*; neither is
5:12 sleep of a *l* man is sweet, whether he eat
5:15 as he came, and shall take nothing of his *l*
5:16 profit hath he that hath *l* for the wind?
6:7 *l* of man is for his mouth . . yet the appetite
Is. 45:14 *l* of Egypt, and merchandise of Ethiopia
55:2 and your *l* for that which satisfieth not?
65:23 they shall not *l* in vain, nor bring forth
Jer. 3:24 shame hath devoured the *l* of our fathers
51:58 and the people shall *l* in vain
Lam. 5:5 under persecution: we *l*, and have no rest
Hab. 2:13 that the people shall *l* in the very fire
3:17 in the vines; the *l* of the olive shall fail
Mt. 11:28 come unto me, all ye that *l* and are heavy
Jn. 4:38 ye bestowed no *l*: other men *l*, and ye are
6:27 *l* not for the meat which perisheth, but for
Acts 20:35 that so *l* ye ought to support the weak
1 Cor. 3:8 his own reward according to his own *l*
4:12 and *l*, working with our own hands
15:10 *l* more abundantly than they all: yet not
15:58 know that your *l* is not in vain in the Lord
2 Cor. 5:9 we *l*, that, whether present or absent, we
6:5 in tumults, in *l*, in watchings, in fastings
10:15 not boasting of things . . of other men's *l*
11:23 I am more; in *l* more abundant, in stripes
Gal. 4:11 lest I have bestowed upon you *l* in vain
Eph. 4:28 steal no more: but rather let him *l*
Phil. 1:22 in the flesh, this is the fruit of my *l*
2:16 I have not run in vain, neither *l* in vain
4:3 those women which *l* with me in the gospel
Col. 1:29 whereunto I also *l*, striving according
4:12 always *l* fervently for you in prayers, that
1 Thes. 1:3 your work of faith, and *l* of love
2:9 (2 Thes. 3:8) and travail: for *l* night and day
3:5 tempter have tempted you, and our *l* be in vain
5:12 brethren, to know them which *l* among you

1 Tim. 4:10 we both *l* and suffer reproach, because
    5:17 honor, especially they who *l* in the word
2 Tim. 2:6 husbandman that *l* must be first partaker
Heb. 4:11 let us *l* therefore to enter into that rest
    6:10 to forget your work and *l* of love, which ye
Rev. 2:2 I know thy works, and thy *l*, and thy
    2:3 name's sake hast *l*, and hast not fainted
    14:13 die in the Lord . . they may rest from their *l*

Laborer *See also* Workman

Mt. 9:37 (Lk. 10:2) is plenteous, but the *l* are few
    20:1 in the morning to hire *l* into his vineyard
Lk. 10:7 the *l* is worthy of his hire
1 Cor. 3:9 for we are *l* together with God
1 Tim. 5:18 and, The *l* is worthy of his reward
Jas. 5:4 hire of the *l* who have reaped down your

Lachish Josh. 10:32; 2 Chr. 32:9; Mic. 1:13

Lack *See also* Need, Want

Gen. 18:28 thou destroy all the city for *l* of five?
Ex. 16:18 (2 Cor. 8:15) that gathered little had no *l*
Deut. 8:9 thou shalt not *l* any thing in it
Job 38:41 cry unto God, they wander for *l* of meat
Ps. 34:10 young lions do *l*, and suffer hunger
Prov. 6:32 adultery with a woman *l* understanding
    28:27 he that giveth unto the poor shall not *l*
Eccl. 9:8 and let thy head *l* no ointment
Hos. 4:6 people are destroyed for *l* of knowledge
Mt. 19:20 I kept from my youth up: what *l* I yet?
Mk. 10:21 (Lk. 18:22) one thing thou *l*: go . . sell
Lk. 8:6 it withered away, because it *l* moisture
    22:35 I sent you without purse . . *l* ye any thing?
Acts 4:34 neither was there any among them that *l*
2 Cor. 11:9 that which was *l* to me the brethren
Phil. 2:30 to supply your *l* of service toward me
    4:10 ye were also careful, but ye *l* opportunity
1 Thes. 4:12 and that ye may have *l* of nothing
Jas. 1:5 if any of you *l* wisdom, let him ask of God
2 Pet. 1:9 he that *l* these things is blind

Lad *See also* Child

Gen. 21:12 grievous in thy sight because of the *l*
    43:8 send the *l* with me, and we will arise and go
    44:34 up to my father, and the *l* be not with me?
    48:16 the angel which redeemed me . . bless the *l*
1 Sam. 20:21 if I expressly say unto the *l*, Behold
2 Sam. 17:18 a *l* saw them, and told Absalom
2 Kgs. 4:19 he said to a *l*, Carry him to his mother
Jn. 6:9 there is a *l* here, which hath five barley

Ladder

Gen. 28:12 a *l* set up on the earth, and the top of

Lade

Neh. 13:15 and bringing in sheaves, and *l* asses
Lk. 11:46 ye lawyers! for ye *l* men with burdens

Laden

Gen. 45:23 asses *l* with the good things of Egypt
Is. 1:4 ah sinful nation, a people *l* with iniquity
Mt. 11:28 all ye that labor and are heavy *l*
2 Tim. 3:6 lead captive silly women *l* with sins

Lady

Judg. 5:29 wise *l* answered her, yea, she returned
Esth. 1:18 shall the *l* of Persia and Media say
Is. 47:5 shalt no more be called, The *l* of kingdoms
2 Jn. 1 elder unto the elect *l* and her children

Laid *See* Lay

Laish *See also* Dan Judg. 18:7, 14, 27, 29

Lake *See also* Sea

Lk. 5:1 to hear the word of God, he stood by the *l*
    8:23 there came down a storm of wind on the *l*
    8:33 a steep place into the *l*, and were choked
Rev. 19:20 both were cast alive into a *l* of fire
    20:10 devil that deceived them was cast into the *l*
    21:8 all liars, shall have their part in the *l*

Lamb *See also* Goat, Sheep

Gen. 22:8 my son, God will provide himself a *l*
Ex. 12:3 take to them every man a *l* . . *l* for a house
    12:5 your *l* shall be without blemish, a male
    29:39 (Num. 28:4) *l* thou shalt offer in the morning
Lev. 4:32 and if he bring a *l* for a sin offering
    14:25 shall kill the *l* of the trespass offering
    23:12 ye wave the sheaf a he *l* without blemish
1 Sam. 7:9 Samuel took a sucking *l*, and offered it
2 Sam. 12:3 man had nothing, save one little ewe *l*
Ps. 114:4 like rams, and the little hills like *l*
Is. 11:6 (65:25) the wolf also shall dwell with the *l*
    40:11 he shall gather the *l* with his arm
    53:7 he is brought as a *l* to the slaughter
Jer. 11:19 I was like a *l* or an ox that is brought
Lk. 10:3 behold, I send you forth as *l* among wolves
Jn. 1:29 (1:36) behold the *L* of God
    21:15 I love thee. He saith unto him, Feed my *l*
Acts 8:32 and like a *l* dumb before his shearer, so
1 Pet. 1:19 of Christ, as of a *l* without blemish
Rev. 5:6 stood a *L* as it had been slain
    5:12 worthy is the *L* that was slain to receive
    6:16 on us, and hide us . . from the wrath of the *L*
    7:10 saying, Salvation to our God . . and unto the *L*
    12:11 they overcame him by the blood of the *L*
    13:8 not written in the book of life of the *L*
    14:1 looked, and, lo, a *L* stood on the mount Sion
    14:4 which follow the *L* whithersoever he goeth
    17:14 war with the *L*, and the *L* shall overcome
    19:7 the marriage of the *L* is come, and his wife
    21:23 and the *L* is the light thereof
    22:3 throne of God and of the *L* shall be in it

Lame

Lev. 21:18 shall not approach: a blind man, or a *l*
2 Sam. 4:4 (9:3) Jonathan . . had a son that was *l*
    5:8 the *l* and the blind . . hated of David's soul
Job 29:15 eyes to the blind . . feet was I to the *l*
Prov. 26:7 the legs of the *l* are not equal: so is
Is. 33:23 great spoil divided; the *l* take the prey
    35:6 then shall the *l* man leap as a hart
Mal. 1:8 ye offer the *l* and sick, is it not evil?
Mt. 11:5 (Lk. 7:22) receive . . sight, and the *l* walk
    15:31 the maimed to be whole, the *l* to walk
    21:14 blind and the *l* came to him in the temple
Lk. 14:13 feast, call the poor, the maimed,.the *l*
Acts 3:2 certain man *l* from his mother's womb was
Heb. 12:13 that which is *l* be turned out of the way

Lamech Gen. 4:19–24; 5:25–31

Lament *See also* Cry, Mourn, Wail, Weep

Judg. 11:40 yearly to *l* the daughter of Jephthah
1 Sam. 7:2 all the house of Israel *l* after the Lord
Is. 19:8 that cast angle into the brooks shall *l*
    32:12 *l* for the teats, for the pleasant fields
Jer. 4:8 gird you with sackcloth, *l* and howl
Joel 1:8 *l* like a virgin girded with sackcloth for
Mt. 11:17 have mourned unto you, and ye have not *l*
Lk. 23:27 of women, which also bewailed and *l* him
Jn. 16:20 ye shall weep and *l*, but the world shall
Rev. 18:9 *l* for her, when they shall see the smoke

Lamentation *See also* Mourning, Wailing, Weeping

Gen. 50:10 mourned with a great and very sore *l*
2 Sam. 1:17 David lamented with this *l* over Saul
2 Chr. 35:25 women spake of Josiah in their *l*
Jer. 6:26 as for an only son, most bitter *l*
   31:15 (Mt. 2:18) in Ramah, *l*, and bitter weeping
Ezek. 19:1 take. . up a *l* for the princes of Israel
   27:2 thou son of man, take up a *l* for Tyrus
   32:2 son of man, take up a *l* for Pharaoh
Amos 5:1 against you, even a *l*, O house of Israel
Acts 8:2 Stephen to his burial, and made great *l*

Lamp *See also* Candle, Light

Gen. 15:17 a smoking furnace, and a burning *l* that
Ex. 25:37 (37:23) make the seven *l*. . shall light the *l*
Judg. 7:16 empty pitchers, and *l* within the pitchers
1 Sam. 3:3 ere the *l* of God went out in the temple
2 Sam. 22:29 thou art my *l*, O LORD
1 Kgs. 15:4 LORD his God give him a *l* in Jerusalem
Job 12:5 to slip with his feet is as a *l* despised
Ps. 119:105 thy word is a *l* unto my feet, and a light
   132:17 I have ordained a *l* for mine anointed
Prov. 6:23 commandment is a *l*; and the law is light
   13:9 but the *l* of the wicked shall be put out
Is. 62:1 the salvation thereof as a *l* that burneth
Dan. 10:6 his eyes as *l* of fire, and his arms and
Zech. 4:2 *l* thereon, and seven pipes to the seven *l*
Mt. 25:8 give us of your oil; for our *l* are gone out
Rev. 4:5 seven *l* of fire burning before the throne
   8:10 star from heaven, burning as it were a *l*

Land *See also* Country, Earth, Ground

Gen. 1:9 and let the dry *l* appear: and it was so
   12:1 (Acts 7:3) unto a *l* that I will show thee
   12:7 (24:7) unto thy seed will I give this *l*
   17:8 *l* of Canaan, for an everlasting possession
   28:15 will bring thee again into this *l*
Ex. 3:8 unto a good *l* and a large, unto a *l* flowing
   6:8 I will bring you in unto the *l*, concerning
   14:21 made the sea dry *l*, and the waters were
   23:10 six years thou shalt sow thy *l*, and shalt
Lev. 18:25 *l* is defiled. . and the *l* itself vomiteth
   25:4 year shall be a sabbath of rest unto the *l*
   25:23 *l* shall be not sold for ever: for the *l* is
   26:20 for your *l* shall not yield her increase
   26:34 then shall the *l* enjoy her sabbaths
   27:30 tithe of the *l*, whether of the seed of the *l*
Num. 13:16 men which Moses sent to spy out the *l*
   14:7 the *l*. . is an exceeding good *l*
   26:53 the *l* shall be divided for an inheritance
   33:53 for I have given you the *l* to possess it
   35:33 blood it defileth the *l*: and the *l* cannot
Deut.1:8 the *l* before you: go in and possess the *l*
   6:3 in the *l* that floweth with milk and honey
   6:10 (11:21) *l* which he sware unto thy fathers
   7:1 thy God shall bring thee into the *l* whither
   8:10 bless the LORD thy God for the good *l* which
   24:4 thou shalt not cause the *l* to sin
   26:9 (26:15) hath given us this *l*, even a *l*
   28:63 ye shall be plucked from off the *l* whither
   32:43 be merciful unto his *l*, and to his people
   34:4 this is the *l* which I sware unto Abraham
Josh. 1:11 over this Jordan, to go in to possess the *l*
   4:22 Israel came over this Jordan on dry *l*
   24:13 given you a *l* for which ye did not labor
1 Kgs. 9:7 (2 Chr. 7:20) cut off Israel out of the *l*
2 Chr. 7:14 forgive their sin, and will heal their *l*
   36:21 until the *l* had enjoyed her sabbaths
Neh. 9:35 in the large and fat *l* which thou gavest
Job 10:21 even to the *l* of darkness and the shadow
Ps. 37:29 righteous shall inherit the *l*, and dwell

Ps. 66:1 (100:1) make a joyful noise unto God, all ye *l*
   68:6 but the rebellious dwell in a dry *l*
   95:5 he made it: and his hands formed the dry *l*
   116:9 walk before the LORD in the *l* of the living
   143:10 lead me into the *l* of uprightness
Prov. 2:21 for the upright shall dwell in the *l*
Eccl. 10:16 woe to thee, O *l*, when thy king is a
Is. 5:30 if one look unto the *l*, behold darkness
   7:24 all the *l* shall become briers and thorns
   35:7 a pool, and the thirsty *l* springs of water
   60:21 righteous: they shall inherit the *l* for ever
   62:4 shall thy *l* any more be termed Desolate
Jer. 4:27 LORD said, The whole *l* shall be desolate
   16:13 I cast you out of this *l* into a *l* that ye
   24:6 I will bring them again to this *l*
   32:41 I will plant them in this *l* assuredly with
Ezek. 15:8 and I will make the *l* desolate, because
   36:24 and will bring you into your own *l*
   36:34 the desolate *l* shall be tilled, whereas it
   38:16 I will bring thee against my *l*
   45:1 unto the LORD, a holy portion of the *l*
Hos. 9:3 they shall not dwell in the LORD's *l*
Joel 2:3 *l* is as the garden of Eden before them
Mal. 3:12 blessed: for ye shall be a delightsome *l*
Mt. 19:29 (Mk. 10:29) children, or *l*, for my. . sake
   27:45 (Mk. 15:33) darkness over all the *l* unto
Acts 4:37 having *l*, sold it, and brought the money
   5:3 and to keep back part of the price of the *l*?
Heb. 11:9 by faith he sojourned in the *l* of promise

Landmark

Deut. 19:14 thou shalt not remove thy neighbor's *l*
   27:17 cursed be he that removeth his neighbor's *l*
Job 24:2 remove the *l*; they violently take away
Prov. 22:28 (23:10) remove not the ancient *l*

Lane

Lk. 14:21 into the streets and *l* of the city

Language *See also* Speech, Tongue

Gen. 11:1 the whole earth was of one *l*, and of one
2 Kgs. 18:28 (Is. 36:13) a loud voice in the Jews'
Neh. 13:24 Jews' *l*, but according to the *l* of each
Ps. 19:3 no speech nor *l*, where their voice is not
   81:5 where I heard a *l* that I understood not
   114:1 house of Jacob from a people of strange *l*
Is. 19:18 the land of Egypt speak the *l* of Canaan
Jer. 5:15 a nation whose *l* thou knowest not
Ezek. 3:5 of a strange speech and of a hard *l*
Dan. 7:14 people, nations, and *l*, should serve him
Zeph. 3:9 then will I turn to the people a pure *l*
Acts 2:6 every man heard them speak in his own *l*

Languish

Ps. 41:3 LORD will strengthen him upon the bed of *l*
Is. 24:4 world *l* and fadeth away, the haughty. . do *l*
Jer. 15:9 she that hath borne seven *l*: she hath
Nah. 1:4 Bashan *l*. . and the flower of Lebanon *l*

Laodicea Col. 2:1; 4:13-16; Rev. 1:11; 3:14

Lap (noun)

Prov. 16:33 lot is cast into the *l*; but the whole

Lap (verb)

Judg. 7:5 *l* of the water with his tongue, as a dog *l*

Large *See also* Great

Gen. 34:21 land, behold, it is *l* enough for them
Ex. 3:8 out of that land unto a good land and a *l*
2 Sam. 22:20 (Ps. 18:19) forth also into a *l* place
Neh. 7:4 city was *l* and great. . the people were few
Ps. 31:8 thou hast set my feet in a *l* room

Hos. 4:16 will feed them as a lamb in a *l* place
Mk. 14:15 (Lk. 22:12) a *l* upper room furnished
Gal. 6:11 how *l* a letter I have written unto you
Rev. 21:16 and the length is as *l* as the breadth

Largeness

1 Kgs. 4:29 God gave Solomon wisdom . . *l* of heart

Lasciviousness

Mk. 7:22 deceit, *l*, an evil eye, blasphemy, pride
2 Cor. 12:21 the uncleanness and fornication and *l*
Gal. 5:19 adultery, fornication, uncleanness, *l*
Eph. 4:19 given themselves unto *l*, to work
1 Pet. 4:3 we walked in *l*, lusts, excess of wine
Jude 4 men, turning the grace of our God into *l*

Last *See also* End

Gen. 49:1 that which shall befall you in the *l* days
Num. 23:10 righteous, and let my *l* end be like his!
Prov. 21:32 at the *l* it biteth like a serpent
Is. 2:2 (Mic. 4:1) shall come to pass in the *l* days
  41:4 the LORD, the first, and with the *l*
  44:6 I am the first, and I am the *l*; and besides
Lam. 1:9 her skirts; she remembereth not her *l* end
Mt. 12:45 (Lk. 11:26) the *l* state of that man is worse
  19:30 (20:16; Mk. 10:31; Lk. 13:30) first shall be *l*;
  and the *l* shall be first
  27:64 the *l* error shall be worse than the first
Mk. 9:35 same shall be *l* of all, and servant of all
Jn. 6:39 (6:40, 44, 54) raise it up again at the *l* day
  11:24 rise again in the resurrection at the *l* day
  12:48 the same shall judge him in the *l* day
1 Cor. 4:9 God hath set forth us the apostles *l*
  15:8 *l* of all he was seen of me also, as of one
2 Tim. 3:1 in the *l* days perilous times shall come
Heb. 1:2 in these *l* days spoken us by his Son
1 Pet. 1:5 salvation ready to be revealed in the *l*
  1:20 but was manifest in these *l* times for you
2 Pet. 3:3 there shall come in the *l* days scoffers
1 Jn. 2:18 little children, it is the *l* time
Rev. 1:11 I am Alpha and Omega, the first and the *l*
  1:17 (22:13) I am the first and the *l*

Latchet

Is. 5:27 loosed, nor the *l* of their shoes be broken
Mk. 1:7 (Lk. 3:16; Jn. 1:27) *l* of . . shoes I am not

Latin

Lk. 23:38 (Jn. 19:20) letters of Greek, and *L*, and

Latter

Ex. 4:8 they will believe the voice of the *l* sign
Deut. 11:14 first rain and the *l* rain, that thou
Job 19:25 shall stand at the *l* day upon the earth
Prov. 19:20 that thou mayest be wise in thy *l* end
Hag. 2:9 glory of this *l* house shall be greater
Zech. 10:1 ask ye . . rain in the time of the *l* rain
1 Tim. 4:1 in the *l* times some shall depart from

Lattice

Judg. 5:28 mother of Sisera . . cried through the *l*
2 Kgs. 1:2 Ahaziah fell down through a *l* in his
Song 2:9 windows, showing himself through the *l*

Laugh *See also* Scorn

Gen. 17:17 then Abraham fell upon his face, and *l*
  18:12 therefore Sarah *l* within herself, saying
  21:6 made me to *l*, so that all that hear will *l*
2 Kgs. 19:21 (Is. 37:22) daughter of Zion . . *l* thee to
2 Chr. 30:10 they *l* them to scorn, and mocked them
Job 5:22 at destruction and famine thou shalt *l*
  8:21 till he fill thy mouth with *l*, and thy lips
  9:23 he will *l* at the trial of the innocent

Job 41:29 as stubble; he *l* at the shaking of a spear
Ps. 2:4 he that sitteth in the heavens shall *l*
  22:7 they that see me *l* me to scorn: they shoot
  37:13 Lord shall *l* at him: for he seeth that his
  52:6 also shall see, and fear, and shall *l* at him
  59:8 but thou, O LORD, shalt *l* at them
Prov. 1:26 I also will *l* at your calamity; I will
Eccl. 3:4 a time to weep, and a time to *l*
Ezek. 23:32 thou shalt be *l* to scorn and had in
Mt. 9:24 (Mk. 5:40; Lk. 8:53) and they *l* him to scorn
Lk. 6:21 blessed are ye that weep . . for ye shall *l*
  6:25 woe unto you that *l* now! for ye shall mourn

Laughter

Ps. 126:2 then was our mouth filled with *l*, and our
Prov. 14:13 even in *l* the heart is sorrowful
Eccl. 2:2 I said of *l*, It is mad: and of mirth
  7:3 sorrow is better than *l*: for by the sadness
  7:6 thorns under a pot, so is the *l* of the fool
Jas. 4:9 and weep: let your *l* be turned to mourning

Launch

Lk. 5:4 Simon, *L* out into the deep, and let down
  8:22 other side of the lake. And they *l* forth

Laver

Ex. 30:18 (38:8) thou shalt also make a *l* of brass
1 Kgs. 7:38 (2 Chr. 4:6) then made he ten *l* of brass

Law *See also* Commandment, Decree, Order, Ordinance, Precept, Statute

Gen. 47:26 and Joseph made it a *l* over the land
Ex. 13:9 that the LORD's *l* may be in thy mouth
  16:4 prove . . whether they will walk in my *l*, or no
  24:12 I will give thee tables of stone, and a *l*
Num. 6:13 this is the *l* of the Nazarite
  15:16 one *l* and one manner shall be for you
Deut. 1:5 began Moses to declare this *l*
  4:8 judgments so righteous as all this *l*
  17:18 shall write him a copy of this *l* in a book
  27:3 shalt write upon them all the words of this *l*
  27:26 (Gal. 3:10) all the words of this *l* to do them
  31:9 Moses wrote this *l*, and delivered it unto
  33:2 from his right hand went a fiery *l* for them
Josh. 1:7 observe to do according to all the *l*
  1:8 this book of the *l* shall not depart out of
  8:34 afterward he read all the words of the *l*
2 Kgs. 10:31 no heed to walk in the *l* of the LORD
  22:8 (2 Chr. 34:15) have found the book of the *l*
1 Chr. 16:17 (Ps. 105:10) the same to Jacob for a *l*
  22:12 thou mayest keep the *l* of the LORD thy God
2 Chr. 12:1 Rehoboam . . forsook the *l* of the LORD
  17:9 and they taught in Judah . . the *l* of the LORD
Ezra 7:10 prepared his heart to seek the *l* of the
Neh. 8:7 caused the people to understand the *l*
  8:8 read in the book in the *l* of God distinctly
  9:13 and gavest them right judgments, and true *l*
  10:29 into an oath, to walk in God's *l*, which
Esth. 1:19 the *l* of the Persians and the Medes
Ps. 1:2 *l* of the LORD; and in his *l* doth he meditate
  19:7 the *l* of the LORD is perfect, converting
  37:31 of his God is in his heart; none of his
  40:8 O my God: yea, thy *l* is within my heart
  81:4 statute for Israel . . a *l* of the God of Jacob
  94:12 O LORD, and teachest him out of thy *l*
  119:1 in the way, who walk in the *l* of the LORD
  119:18 I may behold wondrous things out of thy *l*
  119:34 me understanding, and I shall keep thy *l*
  119:70 as fat as grease: but I delight in thy *l*
  119:72 the *l* of thy mouth is better unto me than
  119:77 that I may live: for thy *l* is my delight
  119:97 O how love I thy *l*! it is my meditation

Ps. 119:142 righteousness, and thy *l* is the truth
   119:165 great peace have they which love thy *l*
Prov. 1:8 (6:20) and forsake not the *l* of thy mother
   6:23 commandment is a lamp; and the *l* is light
   13:14 the *l* of the wise is a fountain of life
   28:7 whoso keepeth the *l* is a wise son
   29:18 but he that keepeth the *l*, happy is he
Is. 2:3 (Mic. 4:2) out of Zion shall go forth the *l*
   5:24 have cast away the *l* of the LORD of hosts
   8:16 testimony, seal the *l* among my disciples
   42:4 and the isles shall wait for his *l*
   42:21 will magnify the *l*, and make it honorable
   51:4 for a *l* shall proceed from me, and I will
   51:7 people in whose heart is my *l*; fear ye not
Jer. 31:33 (Heb. 8:10; 10:16) my *l* in. . inward parts
Ezek. 43:12 behold, this is the *l* of the house
Dan. 6:8 to the *l* of the Medes and Persians
Hos. 4:6 thou hast forgotten the *l* of thy God
   8:12 written to him the great things of my *l*
Amos 2:4 they have despised the *l* of the LORD
Mal. 2:6 *l* of truth was in his mouth, and iniquity
Mt. 5:17 think not that I am come to destroy the *l*
   5:18 (Lk. 16:17) one tittle. . no wise pass from the *l*
   7:12 for this is the *l* and the prophets
   11:13 (Lk. 16:16) the *l* prophesied until John
   22:36 which is the great commandment in the *l*?
   22:40 on these two commandments hang all the *l*
   23:23 have omitted the weightier matters of the *l*
Lk. 2:22 purification according to the *l* of Moses
   10:26 what is written in the *l*? how readest thou?
   24:44 be fulfilled, which were written in the *l*
Jn. 1:17 *l* was given by Moses, but grace and truth
   1:45 found him, of whom Moses in the *l*. . did write
   7:51 doth our *l* judge any man, before it hear him
   12:34 heard out of the *l* that Christ abideth for ever
   19:7 we have a *l*, and by our *l* he ought to die
Acts 5:34 named Gamaliel, a doctor of the *l*
   7:53 received the *l* by the disposition of angels
   13:15 after the reading of the *l* and the prophets
   13:39 could not be justified by the *l* of Moses
   15:5 and to command them to keep the *l* of Moses
   18:15 it be a question of. . your *l*, look ye to it
   21:20 and they are all zealous of the *l*
   22:12 Ananias, a devout man according to the *l*
Rom. 2:12 sinned in the *l* shall be judged by the *l*
   2:13 but the doers of the *l* shall be justified
   2:14 having not the *l*, are a *l* unto themselves
   2:15 the work of the *l* written in their hearts
   3:20 for by the *l* is the knowledge of sin
   3:27 what *l*? of works? Nay; but by the *l* of faith
   3:28 justified by faith without the deeds of the *l*
   3:31 make void the *l*. . yea, we establish the *l*
   4:15 *l* worketh wrath: for where no *l* is, there
   5:13 but sin is not imputed when there is no *l*
   6:14 for ye are not under the *l*, but under grace
   7:4 become dead to the *l* by the body of Christ
   7:7 is the *l* sin?. . not known sin, but by the *l*
   7:12 wherefore the *l* is holy, and the commandment
   7:14 that the *l* is spiritual: but I am carnal
   7:16 I consent unto the *l* that it is good
   7:21 I find then a *l*, that, when I would do good
   7:22 delight in the *l* of God after the inward man
   8:2 *l* of the Spirit. . made me free from the *l* of
   8:3 what the *l* could not do, in that it was weak
   10:4 Christ is the end of the *l* for righteousness
   13:10 therefore love is the fulfilling of the *l*
1 Cor. 6:1 go to *l* before the unjust, and not
   6:6 brother goeth to *l* with brother, and that
   9:21 to them that are without *l*, as without *l*
   15:56 and the strength of sin is the *l*
Gal. 2:16 is not justified by the works of the *l*
   2:19 I through the *l* am dead to the *l*, that I
   3:10 of the works of the *l* are under the curse

Gal. 3:13 hath redeemed us from the curse of the *l*
   3:19 wherefore then serveth the *l*? It was added
   3:24 the *l* was our schoolmaster to bring us unto
   4:4 his Son, made of a woman, made under the *l*
   4:5 redeem them that were under the *l*, that we
   5:4 justified by the *l*; ye are fallen from grace
   5:14 all the *l* is fulfilled in one word, even in
   5:23 against such there is no *l*
   6:2 another's burden. . so fulfil the *l* of Christ
Phil. 3:6 the righteousness. . in the *l*, blameless
1 Tim. 1:8 the *l* is good, if a man use it lawfully
   1:9 *l* is not made for a righteous man, but for
Heb. 7:19 *l* made nothing perfect, but the bringing
   10:1 *l* having a shadow of good things to come
   10:28 that despised Moses' *l* died without mercy
Jas. 1:25 looketh into the perfect *l* of liberty
   2:8 if ye fulfil the royal *l* according to the
   2:10 keep the whole *l*, and yet offend in one
   2:12 that shall be judged by the *l* of liberty
   4:11 speaketh evil of the *l*, and judgeth the *l*
1 Jn. 3:4 for sin is the transgression of the *l*

Lawful *See also* Right

Ezra 7:24 it shall not be *l* to impose toll, tribute
Ezek. 18:5 and do that which is *l* and right
   33:14 turn from his sin, and do that which is *l*
Mt. 12:2 (Mk. 2:24; Lk. 6:2) *l*. . upon the sabbath
   12:10 is it *l* to heal on the sabbath days?
   14:4 (Mk. 6:18) it is not *l* for thee to have her
   19:3 (Mk. 10:2) *l* for a man to put away his wife
   22:17 (Mk. 12:14; Lk. 20:22) is it *l* to give tribute
Jn. 5:10 it is not *l* for thee to carry thy bed
   18:31 it is not *l* for us to put any man to death
Acts 16:21 customs, which are not *l* for us to receive
   19:39 it shall be determined in a *l* assembly
   22:25 *l* for you to scourge a man that is a Roman
1 Cor. 6:12 (10:23) all things are *l* for me, but
2 Cor. 12:4 which it is not *l* for a man to utter

Lawfully

1 Tim. 1:8 that the law is good, if a man use it *l*
2 Tim. 2:5 is he not crowned, except he strive *l*

Lawgiver

Gen. 49:10 nor a *l* from between his feet, until
Num. 21:18 digged it, by the direction of the *l*
Deut. 33:21 in a portion of the *l*, was he seated
Ps. 60:7 (108:8) strength of mine head; Judah is my *l*
Is. 33:22 the LORD is our *l*, the LORD is our King
Jas. 4:12 there is one *l*, who is able to save and

Lawless

1 Tim. 1:9 the law is. . for the *l* and disobedient

Lawyer *See also* Scribe

Mt. 22:35 (Lk. 10:25) a *l*, asked him a question
Lk. 7:30 Pharisees and *l* rejected the counsel of
   11:46 woe unto you also, ye *l*! for ye lade men
   11:52 woe unto you, *l*! for ye have taken away
   14:3 and Jesus answering spake unto the *l* and

Lay (Laid) *See also* Lie

Num. 12:11 I beseech thee, *l* not the sin upon us
Deut. 29:22 sicknesses which the LORD hath *l* upon
Ruth. 3:8 and, behold, a woman *l* at his feet
1 Sam. 6:11 *l* the ark of the LORD upon the cart
   15:2 Amalek did to Israel, how he *l* wait for him
Ps. 3:5 I *l* me down and slept; for the
   35:11 they *l* to my charge things that I knew not
   49:14 like sheep they are *l* in the grave
   62:9 to be *l* in the balance. . lighter than vanity
   142:3 walked have they privily *l* a snare for me
Is. 28:16 (1 Pet. 2:6) I *l* in Zion for a foundation

Mt. 3:10 (Lk. 3:9) axe is *l* unto the root of the trees
6:19 *l* not up for yourselves treasures upon earth
8:20 (Lk. 9:58) Son . . hath not where to *l* his head
26:55 in the temple, and ye *l* no hold on me
28:6 (Mk. 16:6) see the place where the Lord *l*
Lk. 12:21 so is he that *l* up treasure for himself
Jn. 10:15 and I *l* down my life for the sheep
11:34 where have ye *l* him? They say unto him
13:4 and *l* aside his garments; and took a towel
13:37 I will *l* down my life for thy sake
15:13 that a man *l* down his life for his friends
Acts 7:60 Lord, *l* not this sin to their charge
13:3 *l* their hands on them, they sent them away
20:3 Jews *l* wait for him, as he was about to sail
Rom. 8:33 who shall *l* any thing to the charge of
1 Cor. 3:10 I have *l* the foundation, and another
3:11 other foundation can no man *l* than that is *l*
16:2 let every one of you *l* by him in store, as
1 Tim. 4:14 *l* on of the hands of the presbytery
6:12 good fight of faith, *l* hold on eternal life
2 Tim. 4:8 is *l* up for me a crown of righteousness
Heb. 6:18 to *l* hold upon the hope set before us
1 Jn. 3:16 because he *l* down his life for us
Rev. 1:17 he *l* his right hand upon me, saying unto

Lazarus the beggar Lk. 16:20–25

Lazarus of Bethany Jn. 11:1–12:10

Lead (noun)

Ex. 15:10 they sank as *l* in the mighty waters
Zech. 5:7 behold, there was lifted up a talent of *l*

Lead (Led) *See also* Direct, Guide

Gen. 24:27 Lord *l* me to the house of my master's
33:14 and I will *l* on softly, according as the
Ex. 13:18 but God *l* the people about, through the
13:21 in a pillar of a cloud, to *l* them the way
Deut. 4:27 heathen, whither the Lord shall *l* you
8:2 *l* thee these forty years in the wilderness
32:10 wilderness; he *l* him about, he instructed
32:12 the Lord alone did *l* him, and there was no
1 Kgs. 8:48 enemies, which *l* them away captive
2 Chr. 25:11 Amaziah . . *l* forth his people, and went
Ps. 5:8 *i* me, O Lord, in thy righteousness because
23:2 he *l* me beside the still waters
23:3 he *l* me in the paths of righteousness for
25:5 *l* me in thy truth, and teach me: for thou
27:11 *l* me in a plain path, because of mine enemies
31:3 for thy name's sake *l* me, and guide me
43:3 thy light and thy truth: let them *l* me
61:2 *l* me to the rock that is higher than I
68:18 (Eph. 4:8) thou hast *l* captivity captive
77:20 thou *l* thy people like a flock by the
78:14 in the daytime also he *l* them with a cloud
80:1 Shepherd of Israel, thou that *l* Joseph like
107:7 and he *l* them forth by the right way
136:16 to him which *l* his people through the
139:10 even there shall thy hand *l* me, and thy
139:24 way in me, and *l* me in the way everlasting
Prov. 6:22 when thou goest, it shall *l* thee
8:20 I *l* in the way of righteousness
Is. 11:6 and a little child shall *l* them
40:11 shall gently *l* those that are with young
42:16 I will *l* them in paths . . they have not known
48:17 *l* thee by the way that thou shouldest go
49:10 he that hath mercy on them shall *l* them
55:12 go out with joy, and be *l* forth with peace
63:12 that *l* them by the right hand of Moses
63:14 so didst thou *l* thy people
Jer. 2:6 that *l* us through the wilderness
Mt. 4:1 (Lk. 4:1) then was Jesus *l* up of the Spirit
6:13 (Lk. 11:4) *l* us not into temptation, but deliver

Mt. 7:14 narrow is the way, which *l* unto life
15:14 (Lk. 6:39) blind *l* the blind, both shall fall
27:31 (Mk. 15:20; Lk. 23:26) *l* him away to crucify
Mk. 8:23 took the blind . . and *l* him out of the town
Lk. 4:29 and *l* him unto the brow of the hill
24:50 he *l* them out as far as to Bethany
Jn. 10:3 his own sheep by name, and *l* them out
Acts 8:32 he was *l* as a sheep to the slaughter
9:8 (22:11) they *l* him by the hand, and brought
12:10 unto the iron gate that *l* unto the city
13:11 about seeking some to *l* him by the hand
Rom. 2:4 the goodness of God *l* thee to repentance?
8:14 as many as are *l* by the Spirit of God, they
1 Cor. 9:5 have we not power to *l* about a sister
12:2 unto these dumb idols, even as ye were *l*
Gal. 5:18 but if ye be *l* of the Spirit, ye are not
1 Tim. 2:2 we may *l* a quiet and peaceable life in
2 Tim. 3:6 and *l* captive silly women . . *l* away with
2 Pet. 3:17 beware lest ye also, being *l* away with
Rev. 7:17 *l* them unto living fountains of waters

Leader

Is. 9:16 the *l* of this people cause them to err
55:4 a witness to the people, a *l* and commander
Mt. 15:14 them alone: they be blind *l* of the blind

Leaf (Leaves)

Gen. 3:7 were naked; and they sewed fig *l* together
8:11 lo, in her mouth was an olive *l* plucked off
Lev. 26:36 sound of a shaken *l* shall chase them
Job 13:25 wilt thou break a *l* driven to and fro?
Ps. 1:3 in his season; his *l* also shall not wither
Is. 1:30 for ye shall be as an oak whose *l* fadeth
34:4 their host shall fall down, as the *l* falleth
64:6 as filthy rags; and we all do fade as a *l*
Jer. 17:8 heat cometh, but her *l* shall be green
Ezek. 47:12 *l* shall not fade . . *l* thereof for medicine
Mt. 21:19 (Mk. 11:13) found nothing . . but *l* only
24:32 (Mk. 13:28) yet tender, and putteth forth *l*
Rev. 22:2 the *l* of the tree were for the healing

League *See also* Covenant

Josh. 9:6 to Joshua . . therefore make ye a *l* with us
Judg. 2:2 ye shall make no *l* with the inhabitants
2 Sam. 3:12 Abner sent . . saying . . Make thy *l* with
5:3 and king David made a *l* with them in Hebron
1 Kgs. 15:19 (2 Chr. 16:3) a *l* between me and thee
Job 5:23 for thou shalt be in *l* with the stones of

Leah

Gen. 29:16 daughters: the name of the elder was *L*
29:31 when the Lord saw that *L* was hated
49:31 they buried Isaac . . and there I buried *L*

Lean (adjective)

Gen. 41:20 *l* and the ill-favored kine did eat up

Lean (verb)

Judg. 16:26 feel the pillars . . that I may *l* upon
2 Sam. 1:6 Gilboa, behold, Saul *l* upon his spear
Job 8:15 *l* upon his house, but it shall not stand
Prov. 3:5 and *l* not unto thine own understanding
Song 8:5 from the wilderness, *l* upon her beloved?
Amos 5:19 *l* his hand on the wall, and a serpent bit
Mic. 3:11 for money: yet will they *l* upon the Lord
Jn. 13:23 (21:20) *l* on Jesus' bosom one of . . disciples
Heb. 11:21 worshipped, *l* upon the top of his staff

Leanness

Ps. 106:15 but sent *l* into their soul
Is. 10:16 shall the Lord . . send among his fat ones *l*
24:16 my *l*, my *l*, woe unto me! the treacherous

Leap

Gen. 31:10 behold, the rams which *l* upon the cattle
2 Sam. 22:30 (Ps. 18:29) by. . God. . I *l* over a wall
1 Kgs. 18:26 they *l* upon the altar which was made
Ps. 68:16 why *l* ye, ye high hills? this is the hill
Song Is. he cometh *l* upon the mountains, skipping
Is. 35:6 then shall the lame man *l* as a hart
Zeph. 1:9 punish all those that *l* on the threshold
Lk. 1:41 the babe *l* in her womb; and Elisabeth was
Acts 3:8 into the temple, walking, and, *l*, and praising
   14:10 stand upright on thy feet. And he *l* and

Learn

Gen. 30:27 for I have *l* by experience that
Deut. 4:10 (31:13) hear. . that they may *l* to fear
   5:1 that ye may *l* them, and keep and do them
   18:9 shalt not *l* to do after the abominations of
Ps. 119:7 I shall have *l* thy righteous judgments
   119:71 afflicted; that I might *l* thy statutes
Prov. 22:25 lest thou *l* his ways, and get a snare
   30:3 I neither *l* wisdom, nor have the knowledge
Is. 1:17 *l* to do well; seek judgment, relieve the
   2:4 (Mic. 4:3) neither shall they *l* war any more
   26:9 inhabitants of the world will *l* righteousness
   29:24 and they that murmured shall *l* doctrine
Jer. 10:2 *l* not the way of the heathen, and be not
   12:16 will diligently *l* the ways of my people
Mt. 9:13 *l* what that meaneth, I will have mercy
   11:29 take my yoke upon you, and *l* of me
   24:32 (Mk. 13:28) now *l* a parable of the fig tree
Jn. 6:45 and hath *l* of the Father, cometh unto me
   7:15 knoweth this man letters, having never *l*?
Rom. 16:17 contrary to the doctrine. . ye have *l*
1 Cor. 4:6 ye might *l* in us not to think of men
   14:31 that all may *l*, and all may be comforted
Gal. 3:2 this only would I *l* of you, Received ye
Eph. 4:20 but ye have not so *l* Christ
Phil. 4:9 which ye have both *l*, and received, and
   4:11 for I have *l*, in whatsoever state I am
1 Tim. 1:20 that they may *l* not to blaspheme
   2:11 the woman *l* in silence with all subjection
   5:4 let them *l* first to show piety at home
   5:13 withal they *l* to be idle, wandering about
2 Tim. 3:7 ever *l*, and never able to come to the
   3:14 which thou hast *l* and hast been assured of
Tit. 3:14 let ours also *l* to maintain good works
Heb. 5:8 though he were a Son, yet *l* he obedience
Rev. 14:3 no man could *l* that song but the hundred

Learned *See also* Learn

Is. 29:11 book. . which men deliver to one that is *l*
   50:4 Lord GOD hath given me the tongue of the *l*
Acts 7:22 and Moses was *l* in all the wisdom of the

Learning *See also* Learn

Prov. 1:5 wise man will hear, and will increase *l*
   9:9 teach a just man, and he will increase in *l*
   16:21 and the sweetness of the lips increaseth *l*
   16:23 teacheth his mouth, and addeth *l* to his lips
Dan. 1:4 they might teach the *l*. . of the Chaldeans
Acts 26:24 Paul. . much *l* doth make thee mad
Rom. 15:4 written aforetime were written for our *l*

Leasing

Ps. 4:2 long will ye love vanity, and seek after *l*?
   5:6 thou shalt destroy them that speak *l*

Least *See also* Less

Gen. 32:10 not worthy of the *l* of all thy mercies
Judg. 6:15 and I am the *l* in my father's house
Jer. 31:34 (Heb. 8:11) all know me, from the *l*. . unto
Mt. 2:6 art not the *l* among the princes of Juda
   5:19 he shall be called the *l* in the kingdom

Mt. 11:11 (Lk. 7:28) *l* in the kingdom. . is greater than
   13:32 is the *l* of all seeds: but when it is grown
   25:40 unto one of the *l* of these my brethren
Lk. 9:48 *l* among you all, the same shall be great
   12:26 not able to do that thing which is *l*, why
   16:10 in that which is *l* is faithful also in much
1 Cor. 6:4 to judge who are *l* esteemed in the church
   15:9 am the *l* of the apostles, that am not meet
Eph. 3:8 me, who am less than the *l* of all saints

Leave (Left) *See also* Depart, Go

Gen. 2:24 (Mt. 19:5; Mk. 10:7; Eph. 5:31) *l* his father
   11:8 and they *l* off to build the city
   24:27 not *l* destitute my master of his mercy
   28:15 I will not *l* thee, until I have done that
   39:12 and he *l* his garment in her hand, and fled
Ruth 1:16 Ruth said, Entreat me not to *l* thee
1 Sam. 9:24 Samuel said, Behold that which is *l*!
1 Kgs. 19:10 (Rom. 11:3) I only, am *l*; and they seek
2 Kgs. 2:2 (2:4, 6; 4:30) soul liveth, I will not *l* thee
Job 9:27 I will *l* off my heaviness, and comfort
   32:15 they answered no more: they *l* off speaking
Ps. 16:10 (Acts 2:27) wilt not *l* my soul in hell
   27:9 *l* me not, neither forsake me, O God
   36:3 he hath *l* off to be wise, and to do good
   49:10 person perish, and *l* their wealth to others
Prov. 2:13 who *l* the paths of uprightness, to walk
   29:15 a child *l* to himself bringeth his mother to
Is. 10:14 as one gathereth eggs that are *l*, have I
Jer. 12:7 I have *l* mine heritage; I have given the
Ezek. 9:8 while they were slaying them, and I was *l*
Mt. 4:11 devil *l* him. . angels came and ministered
   4:20 straightway *l* their nets, and followed
   5:24 *l* there thy gift before the altar, and go
   15:37 (Mk. 8:8) that was *l* seven baskets full
   18:12 (Lk. 15:4) doth he not *l* the ninety and nine
   23:23 (Lk. 11:42) and not to *l* the other undone
   24:2 (Mk. 13:2; Lk. 21:6) shall not be *l*. . one stone
Mk. 10:28 (Lk. 18:28) we have *l* all, and. . followed
Lk. 5:28 and he *l* all, rose up, and followed him
   10:30 wounded him, and departed, and *l* him half dead
Jn. 8:9 Jesus was *l* alone, and the woman standing
   14:18 I will not *l* you comfortless: I will come
   16:28 again, I *l* the world, and go to the Father
1 Cor. 7:13 pleased to dwell with her, let her not *l* him
2 Tim. 4:13 cloak that I *l* at Troas with Carpus
   4:20 but Trophimus have I *l* at Miletum sick
Heb. 6:1 *l* the principles of the doctrine of Christ
   13:5 I will never *l* thee, nor forsake thee
1 Pet. 2:21 also suffered for us, *l* us an example
Rev. 2:4 because thou hast *l* thy first love

Leaven

Ex. 12:19 seven days shall there be no *l* found in
Lev. 2:11 made with *l*: for ye shall burn no *l*
   10:12 eat it without *l* beside the altar
Hos. 7:4 he hath kneaded the dough, until it be *l*
Amos 4:5 offer a sacrifice of thanksgiving with *l*
Mt. 13:33 (Lk. 13:21) kingdom. . is like unto *l*
   16:6 (16:11; Mk. 8:15; Lk. 12:1) *l* of the Pharisees
1 Cor. 5:6 (Gal. 5:9) a little *l l* the whole lump?
   5:7 purge out therefore the old *l*, that ye may
   5:8 not with old *l*, neither with the *l* of malice

Leavened *See also* Leaven

Ex. 12:15 whosoever eateth *l* bread from the first
Deut. 16:4 shall be no *l* bread seen with thee in

Leaves *See* Leaf

Lebanon

1 Kgs. 5:6 (2 Chr. 2:8) hew me cedar trees out of *L*
Ps. 92:12 righteous. . shall grow like a cedar in *L*

Is. 35:2 the glory of *L* shall be given unto it
  40:16 and *L* is not sufficient to burn
Jer. 18:14 will a man leave the snow of *L* which
Hos. 14:5 as the lily, and cast forth his roots as *L*

Led *See* Lead

Lees

Is. 25:6 a feast of wines on the *l*, of fat things
Jer. 48:11 Moab hath been at ease. . settled on his *l*
Zeph. 1:12 and punish the men. . settled on their *l*

Left (adjective)

Gen. 13:9 the right hand, then I will go to the *l*
1 Chr. 12:2 right hand and the *l* in hurling stones
Prov. 3:16 and in her *l* hand riches and honor
  4:27 turn not to the right hand nor to the *l*
Mt. 6:3 let not thy *l* hand know what thy right
  20:21 (Mk. 10:37) and the other on the *l*
  25:33 sheep on his right hand. . goats on the *l*

Left (verb) *See* Leave

Left-handed

Judg. 3:15 a deliverer, Ehud. . a man *l-h*
  20:16 seven hundred chosen men *l-h*

Leg

Ps. 147:10 taketh not pleasure in the *l* of a man
Prov. 26:7 the *l* of the lame are not equal: so is
Jn. 19:33 was dead already, they brake not his *l*

Legion

Mt. 26:53 give me more than twelve *l* of angels?
Mk. 5:9 (Lk. 8:30) my name is *L*: for we are many

Leisure

Mk. 6:31 and they had no *l* so much as to eat

Lemuel Prov. 31:1

Lend (Lent)

Ex. 12:36 *l* unto them such things as they required
  22:25 *l* money to any of my people that is poor
Lev. 25:37 nor *l* him thy victuals for increase
Deut. 15:6 and thou shalt *l* unto many nations
  15:8 shalt surely *l* him sufficient for his need
  23:19 thou shalt not *l* upon usury to thy brother
  24:10 when thou dost *l* thy brother any thing
  28:44 *l* to thee, and thou shalt not *l* to him
1 Sam. 1:28 I have *l* him to the LORD; as long as
Ps. 37:26 he is ever merciful, and *l*; and his seed
  112:5 a good man showeth favor, and *l*: he will
Prov. 19:17 hath pity upon the poor *l* unto the LORD
Jer. 15:10 neither *l* on usury, nor men have *l* to me
Lk. 6:34 if ye *l* to them of whom ye hope to receive
  6:35 do good, and *l*, hoping for nothing again
  11:5 and say unto him, Friend, *l* me three loaves

Length

Gen. 13:17 walk through the land in the *l* of it
Deut. 30:20 he is thy life, and the *l* of thy days
Ps. 21:4 gavest it him, even *l* of days for ever
Prov. 3:2 for *l* of days, and long life, and peace
  3:16 *l* of days is in her right hand; and in her
Eph. 3:18 breadth, and *l*, and depth, and height
Rev. 21:16 the *l* is as large as the breadth

Lengthen

1 Kgs. 3:14 walk in my ways. . I will *l* thy days
Is. 54:2 *l* thy cords, and strengthen thy stakes
Dan. 4:27 if it may be a *l* of thy tranquillity

Lentil

Gen. 25:34 Jacob gave Esau bread and pottage of *l*
2 Sam. 23:11 where was a piece of ground full of *l*

Leopard

Is. 11:6 and the *l* shall lie down with the kid
Jer. 5:6 a *l* shall watch over their cities
  13:23 Ethiopian change his skin, or. . *l* his spots?
Dan. 7:6 I beheld, and lo another, like a *l*
Hos. 13:7 as a *l* by the way will I observe them
Hab. 1:8 their horses also are swifter than the *l*
Rev. 13:2 the beast which I saw was like unto a *l*

Leper

Lev. 14:2 law of the *l* in the day of his cleansing
Num. 5:2 that they put out of the camp every *l*
2 Kgs. 5:1 a mighty man in valor, but he was a *l*
  7:8 when these *l* came to the uttermost part of
2 Chr. 26:21 Uzziah the king was a *l*
Mt. 8:2 (Mk. 1:40) came a *l* and worshipped him
  10:8 heal the sick, cleanse the *l*, raise the dead
  11:5 (Lk. 7:22) lame walk, the *l* are cleansed
  26:6 (Mk. 14:3) in the house of Simon the *l*
Lk. 4:27 many *l* were in Israel in the time of Eliseus
  17:12 there met him ten men that were *l*

Leprosy

Lev. 13:2 plague of *l*; then he shall be brought
  14:3 if the plague of *l* be healed in the leper
  14:34 and I put the plague of *l* in a house of
Deut. 24:8 take heed in the plague of *l*, that thou
2 Kgs. 5:3 for he would recover him of his *l*
  5:27 the *l*. . of Naaman shall cleave unto thee
Mt. 8:3 (Mk. 1:42; Lk. 5:13) his *l* was cleansed

Leprous

Ex. 4:6 when he took it out. . his hand was *l* as snow
Num. 12:10 behold, Miriam became *l*, white as snow
2 Kgs. 7:3 were four *l* men at the entering in of
2 Chr. 26:20 he was *l* in his forehead, and they

Less (Lesser) *See also* Least

Gen. 1:16 and the *l* light to rule the night
Ex. 16:17 did so, and gathered, some more, some *l*
  30:15 give more, and the poor shall not give *l*
1 Kgs. 8:27 (2 Chr. 6:18) how much *l* this house that I
2 Chr. 32:15 how much *l* shall your God deliver you
Ezra 9:13 punished us *l* than our iniquities
Job 11:6 God exacteth of thee *l* than thine iniquity
  25:6 how much *l* man, that is a worm? and the
Is. 40:17 they are counted to him *l* than nothing
Mk. 4:31 *l* than all the seeds that be in the earth
2 Cor. 12:15 the more. . I love you, the *l* I be loved
Eph. 3:8 who am *l* than the least of all saints
Heb. 7:7 the *l* is blessed of the better

Let

Ex. 3:19 king of Egypt will not *l* you go
  5:4 wherefore. . *l* the people from their works?
Is. 43:13 I will work, and who shall *l* it?
Acts 27:30 when they had *l* down the boat into the
2 Thes. 2:7 only he who now *l* will *l*, until he be

Letter *See also* Epistle

2 Sam. 11:15 wrote in the *l*, saying, Set ye Uriah
1 Kgs. 21:8 she wrote *l* in Ahab's name. . sent the *l*
2 Kgs. 5:6 he brought the *l* to the king of Israel
  10:1 Jehu wrote *l*, and sent to Samaria, unto the
  19:14 (Is. 37:14) Hezekiah received the *l*
Ezra 4:11 *l* that they sent. . unto Artaxerxes the king
  7:11 *l* that the king Artaxerxes gave unto Ezra
Jer. 29:1 the *l* that Jeremiah. . sent from Jerusalem
Lk. 23:38 in *l* of Greek, and Latin, and Hebrew

Jn. 7:15 knoweth this man *l*, having never learned?
Acts 15:23 they wrote *l* by them after this manner
　23:25 and he wrote a *l* after this manner
Rom. 2:29 in the spirit, and not in the *l*
　7:6 of spirit, and not in the oldness of the *l*
2 Cor. 3:1 to you, or *l* of commendation from you?
　3:6 for the *l* killeth, but the spirit giveth life
　7:8 though I made you sorry with a *l*, I do not
　10:10 his *l*, say they, are weighty and powerful
Gal. 6:11 how large a *l* I have written unto you
Heb. 13:22 have written a *l* unto you in few words

Levi son of Jacob

Gen. 29:34 therefore was his name called *L*
　34:25 Simeon and *L*, Dinah's brethren, took each
　49:5 Simeon and *L* are brethren; instruments of
Ex. 32:26 sons of *L* gathered themselves. . unto him
Deut. 10:8 LORD separated the tribe of *L*, to bear the

Levi *See also* Matthew Mk. 2:14 (Lk. 5:27)

Leviathan

Job 41:1 canst thou draw out *l* with a hook?
Ps. 74:14 thou brakest the heads of *l* in pieces
　104:26 is that *l*, whom thou hast made to play
Is. 27:1 punish *l* the piercing serpent, even *l*

Levite *See also* Priest

Ex. 6:25 are the heads of the fathers of the *L*
Num. 1:47 the *L*. . were not numbered among them
　1:50 shalt appoint the *L* over the tabernacle
　3:9 shalt give the *L* unto Aaron and to his sons
　8:14 shalt thou separate the *L*. . *L* shall be mine
　35:2 they give unto the *L*. . cities to dwell in
Deut. 12:19 thou forsake not the *L* as long as thou
　18:1 the *L*. . shall have no part nor inheritance
Judg. 19:1 certain *L*. . who took to him a concubine
2 Chr. 11:14 *L* left their suburbs. . came to Judah
　29:34 *L* were more upright in heart to sanctify
Ezra 6:18 *L* in their courses, for the service of
Lk. 10:32 likewise a *L*, when he was at the place

Levy

1 Kgs. 5:13 Solomon raised a *l* out of all Israel
　9:15 of the *l* which king Solomon raised

Lewdness

Ezek. 23:21 calledst to remembrance. . *l* of thy youth

Liar

Deut. 33:29 enemies shall be found *l* unto thee
Ps. 116:11 I said in my haste, All men are *l*
Prov. 19:22 and a poor man is better than a *l*
Is. 44:25 that frustrateth the tokens of the *l*
Jn. 8:44 for he is a *l*, and the father of it
　8:55 know him not, I shall be a *l* like unto you
Rom. 3:4 let God be true, but every man a *l*
1 Tim. 1:10 for menstealers, for *l*, for perjured
Tit. 1:12 the Cretians are always *l*, evil beasts
1 Jn. 1:10 we have not sinned, we make him a *l*
　2:4 and keepeth not his commandments, is a *l*
　2:22 who is a *l* but he that denieth that Jesus
　4:20 love God, and hateth his brother, he is a *l*
　5:10 he that believeth not God hath made him a *l*
Rev. 2:2 hast tried them. . and hast found them *l*
　21:8 and all *l*, shall have their part in the lake

Liberal

Prov. 11:25 the *l* soul shall be made fat
Is. 32:5 the vile person shall be no more called *l*
　32:8 *l* deviseth *l* things; and by *l* things shall
2 Cor. 9:13 *l* distribution unto them, and unto all men

Liberality

1 Cor. 16:3 I send to bring your *l* unto Jerusalem
2 Cor. 8:2 abounded unto the riches of their *l*

Liberally

Deut. 15:14 shalt furnish him *l* out of thy flock
Jas. 1:5 ask of God, that giveth to all men *l*

Libertine Acts 6:9

Liberty *See also* Deliverance, Freedom

Lev. 25:10 hallow the fiftieth year, and proclaim *l*
Ps. 119:45 will walk at *l*: for I seek thy precepts
Is. 61:1 to proclaim *l* to the captives
Jer. 34:8 at Jerusalem, to proclaim *l* unto them
　34:17 I proclaim a *l* for you, saith the LORD
Ezek. 46:17 then it shall be his to the year of *l*
Lk. 4:18 to set at *l* them that are bruised
Acts 24:23 keep Paul, and to let him have *l*
　26:32 this man might have been set at *l*, if he
　27:3 Paul, and gave him *l* to go unto his friends
Rom. 8:21 the glorious *l* of the children of God
1 Cor. 7:39 be dead, she is at *l* to be married to
　8:9 this *l* of yours become a stumblingblock to
　10:29 is my *l* judged of another man's conscience?
2 Cor. 3:17 the Spirit of the Lord is, there is *l*
Gal. 2:4 to spy out our *l* which we have in Christ
　5:1 in the *l* wherewith Christ hath made us free
　5:13 been called unto *l*; only use not *l* for an
Heb. 13:23 know ye that. . Timothy is set at *l*
Jas. 1:25 whoso looketh into the perfect law of *l*
　2:12 they that shall be judged by the law of *l*
1 Pet. 2:16 free, and not using your *l* for a cloak
2 Pet. 2:19 they promise them *l*, they themselves

Lice

Ex. 8:16 and smite the dust. . that it may become *l*

Lick

1 Kgs. 21:19 place where dogs *l* the blood of Naboth
Lk. 16:21 moreover the dogs came and *l* his sores

Lie (Lay, Lain)

Gen. 4:7 if thou doest not well, sin *l* at the door
　26:10 people might lightly have *l* with thy wife
Ps. 10:9 as a lion. . he *l* in wait to catch the poor
　23:2 he maketh me to *l* down in green pastures
　68:13 though ye have *l* among the pots, yet shall
Song 1:13 he shall *l* all night betwixt my breasts
Is. 11:6 and the leopard shall *l* down with the kid
Mt. 28:6 come, see the place where the Lord *l*
Acts 23:21 *l* in wait for him. . more than forty men

Lie *See also* Deceive, Falsehood, Lying

Lev. 6:2 and *l* unto his neighbor in that which was
　19:11 not steal, neither deal falsely, neither *l*
Num. 23:19 God is not a man, that he should *l*
1 Kgs. 13:18 and drink water. But he *l* unto him
Job 6:28 look upon me; for it is evident. . if I *l*
　13:4 forgers of *l*. . physicians of no value
Ps. 58:3 astray as soon as they be born, speaking *l*
　62:4 they delight in *l*: they bless with their
　62:9 are vanity, and men of high degree are a *l*
　89:35 by my holiness that I will not *l* unto David
　101:7 that telleth *l* shall not tarry in my sight
Prov. 14:5 not *l*: but a false witness will utter *l*
　19:5 and he that speaketh *l* shall not escape
　19:9 he that speaketh *l* shall perish
　29:12 if a ruler hearken to *l*, all his servants
Is. 9:15 prophet that teacheth *l*, he is the tail
　28:15 for we have made *l* our refuge, and under
　63:8 are my people, children that will not *l*

Jer. 9:3 bend their tongues like their bow for *l*
  14:14 the prophets prophesy *l* in my name
  27:10 for they prophesy a *l* unto you, to remove
  28:15 thou makest this people to trust in a *l*
  29:31 and he caused you to trust in a *l*
Ezek. 13:9 prophets that see vanity . . that divine *l*
Hos. 10:13 ye have eaten the fruit of *l*: because
  11:12 Ephraim compasseth me about with *l*
Nah. 3:1 the bloody city! it is all full of *l* and
Hab. 2:3 shall speak, and not *l*: though it tarry
Zech. 13:3 thou speakest *l* in the name of the LORD
Acts 5:3 filled thine heart to the Holy Ghost
  5:4 thou hast not *l* unto men, but unto God
Rom. 1:25 who changed the truth of God into a *l*
Col. 3:9 *l* not one to another, seeing that ye have
2 Thes. 2:11 delusion, that they should believe a *l*
Tit. 1:2 life, which God, that cannot *l*, promised
Heb. 6:18 in which it was impossible for God to *l*
Jas. 3:14 glory not, and *l* not against the truth
1 Jn. 1:6 and walk in darkness, we *l*, and do not
  2:21 ye know it, and that no *l* is of the truth
Rev. 22:15 and whosoever loveth and maketh a *l*

Lier

Judg. 20:29 Israel set *l* in wait round about Gibeah

Life (Lives) *See also* Immortality, Resurrection, Soul, Spirit

Gen. 2:7 breathed into his nostrils the breath of *l*
  2:9 tree of *l* also in the midst of the garden
  9:5 man's brother will I require the *l* of man
  44:30 that his *l* is bound up in the lad's *l*
Ex. 21:23 follow, then thou shalt give *l* for *l*
Lev. 17:11 for the *l* of the flesh is in the blood
Deut. 12:23 blood is the *l*. . mayest not eat the *l*
  28:66 and thy *l* shall hang in doubt before thee
  30:19 before you *l* and death . . therefore choose *l*
  30:20 he is thy *l*, and the length of thy days
1 Sam. 25:29 bound in the bundle of *l* with the LORD
1 Kgs. 3:11 (2 Chr. 1:11) not asked for thyself long *l*
  19:4 it is enough; now, O LORD, take away my *l*
2 Kgs. 8:1 woman, whose son he had restored to *l*
Job 2:4 all that a man hath will he give for his *l*
  2:6 behold, he is in thine hand; but save his *l*
  6:11 what is mine end, that I should prolong my *l*?
  7:7 O remember that my *l* is wind: mine eye shall
  10:1 my soul is weary of my *l*; I will leave my
  24:22 he riseth up, and no man is sure of *l*
  33:4 the breath of the Almighty hath given me *l*
  36:6 he preserveth not the *l* of the wicked
Ps. 16:11 (Acts 2:28) wilt show me the path of *l*
  21:4 he asked *l* of thee, and thou gavest it him
  27:1 LORD is the strength of my *l*; of whom shall
  30:5 in his favor is *l*: weeping may endure for a
  34:12 what man is he that desireth *l*, and loveth
  36:9 for with thee is the fountain of *l*
  63:3 because thy loving-kindness is better than *l*
  64:1 prayer: preserve my *l* from fear of the enemy
  91:16 with long *l* will I satisfy him, and show
  103:4 who redeemeth thy *l* from destruction
  133:3 commanded the blessing . . *l* for evermore
Prov. 3:22 so shall they be *l* unto thy soul
  4:22 for they are *l* unto those that find them
  4:23 thy heart . . for out of it are the issues of *l*
  6:23 reproofs of instruction are the way of *l*
  11:19 as righteousness tendeth to *l*; so he that
  13:3 he that keepeth his mouth keepeth his *l*
  14:27 the fear of the LORD is a fountain of *l*
  14:30 a sound heart is the *l* of the flesh
  19:23 fear of the LORD tendeth to *l*: and he that
Eccl. 2:17 therefore I hated *l*; because the work
  6:12 what is good for man in this *l* . . his vain *l*

Is. 15:4 cry out; his *l* shall be grievous unto him
  57:10 thou hast found the *l* of thine hand
Jer. 8:3 death shall be chosen rather than *l*
  21:8 I set before you the way of *l*, and the way
Lam. 3:58 hast pleaded . . thou hast redeemed my *l*
Ezek. 3:18 warn . . from his wicked way, to save his *l*
Dan. 12:2 shall awake, some to everlasting *l*
Jon. 4:3 LORD, take, I beseech thee, my *l* from me
Mt. 6:25 (Lk. 12:22) take no thought for your *l*
  7:14 and narrow is the way, which leadeth unto *l*
  10:39 (16:25; Mk. 8:35; Lk. 9:24; 17:33) findeth his
    l shall lose it . . loseth his *l* for my sake shall find
  18:8 (Mk. 9:43, 45) it is better . . to enter into *l* halt
  19:16 (Mk. 10:17; Lk. 18:18) I may have eternal *l*?
  19:29 (Mk. 10:30; Lk. 18:30) inherit everlasting *l*
  20:28 (Mk. 10:45) give his *l* a ransom for many
  25:46 but the righteous into *l* eternal
Mk. 3:4 (Lk. 6:9) to save *l*, or to kill?
Lk. 8:14 cares and riches and pleasures of this *l*
  9:56 is not come to destroy men's *l*, but to save
  12:15 man's *l* consisteth not in the abundance of
  14:26 his own *l* also, he cannot be my disciple
Jn. 1:4 in him was *l*; and the *l* was the light of
  3:16 should not perish, but have everlasting *l*
  3:36 that believeth on the Son hath everlasting *l*
  4:14 of water springing up into everlasting *l*
  4:36 wages, and gathereth fruit unto *l* eternal
  5:24 hath everlasting *l*. . passed from death unto *l*
  5:26 Father hath *l* in himself; so hath he given
  5:39 for in them ye think ye have eternal *l*
  5:40 will not come to me, that ye might have *l*
  6:35 I am the bread of *l*: he that cometh to me
  6:47 he that believeth on me hath everlasting *l*
  6:53 and drink his blood, ye have no *l* in you
  6:68 we go? thou hast the words of eternal *l*
  8:12 in darkness, but shall have the light of *l*
  10:10 I am come that they might have *l*, and that
  10:11 good shepherd giveth his *l* for the sheep
  10:15 and I lay down my *l* for the sheep
  10:17 my Father love me, because I lay down my *l*
  10:28 I give unto them eternal *l*; and they shall
  11:25 I am the resurrection, and the *l*
  12:25 hateth his *l*. . shall keep it unto *l* eternal
  13:37 I will lay down my *l* for thy sake
  14:6 I am the way, the truth, and the *l*
  15:13 that a man lay down his *l* for his friends
  17:2 eternal *l* to as many as thou hast given him
  17:3 this is *l* eternal, that they might know thee
  20:31 believing ye might have *l* through his name
Acts 11:18 the Gentiles granted repentance unto *l*
  13:48 many as were ordained to eternal *l* believed
  15:26 hazarded their *l* for the name of our LORD
  17:25 seeing he giveth to all *l*, and breath, and
  20:24 neither count I my *l* dear unto myself
Rom. 5:10 reconciled, we shall be saved by his *l*
  5:17 shall reign in *l* by one, Jesus Christ
  6:4 even so we also should walk in newness of *l*
  6:23 the gift of God is eternal *l* through Jesus
  7:10 ordained to *l*, I found to be unto death
  8:6 but to be spiritually minded is *l* and peace
  8:10 the Spirit is *l* because of righteousness
  8:38 I am persuaded, that neither death, nor *l*
1 Cor. 15:19 in this *l* only we have hope in Christ
2 Cor. 2:16 and to the other the savor of *l* unto *l*
  3:6 the letter killeth, but the spirit giveth *l*
  4:10 the *l* also of Jesus . . manifest in our body
  4:12 so then death worketh in us, but *l* in you
  5:4 that mortality might be swallowed up of *l*
Gal. 2:20 the *l* which I now live in the flesh
  3:21 been a law given which could have given *l*
  6:8 shall of the Spirit reap *l* everlasting
Eph. 4:18 alienated from the *l* of God through the
Phil. 1:20 magnified in my body, whether it be by *l*

Phil. 2:16 holding forth the word of *l*; that I may
 4:3 laborers, whose names are in the book of *l*
Col. 3:3 dead, and your *l* is hid with Christ in God
 3:4 when Christ, who is our *l*, shall appear, then
1 Tim. 2:2 we may lead a quiet and peaceable *l* in
 4:8 *l* that now is, and of that which is to come
 6:12 good fight of faith, lay hold on eternal *l*
2 Tim. 1:1 according to the promise of *l* which is
 1:10 and hath brought *l* and immortality to light
 3:10 known my doctrine, manner of *l*, purpose
Heb. 7:16 but after the power of an endless *l*
 7:16 tried, he shall receive the crown of *l*
 4:14 what is your *l*? It is even a vapor, that
1 Pet. 3:7 being heirs together of the grace of *l*
 3:10 he that will love *l*, and see good days, let
2 Pet. 1:3 things that pertain unto *l* and godliness
1 Jn. 1:2 the *l* was manifested, and we have seen it
 3:14 know that we have passed from death unto *l*
 3:16 his *l* for us: and we ought to lay down our *l*
 5:11 to us eternal *l*, and this *l* is in his Son
 5:12 he that hath the Son hath *l*
 5:13 that ye may know that ye have eternal *l*
 5:16 give him *l* for them that sin not unto death
Rev. 2:7 will I give to eat of the tree of *l*
 3:5 not blot out his name out of the book of *l*
 11:11 Spirit of *l* from God entered into them
 12:11 and they loved not their *l* unto the death
 13:15 he had power to give *l* unto the image
 21:6 of the fountain of the water of *l* freely
 22:1 he showed me a pure river of water of *l*
 22:2 side of the river, was there the tree of *l*
 22:17 let him take the water of *l* freely

Lift *See also* Exalt, Magnify

Ex. 14:16 but *l* thou up thy rod, and stretch out
Num. 6:26 the LORD *l* up his countenance upon thee
1 Sam. 2:7 maketh rich: he bringeth low, and *l* up
2 Chr. 17:6 heart was *l* up in the ways of the LORD
Ps. 4:6 *l* thou up the light of thy countenance
 7:6 arise, O LORD, in thine anger, *l* up thyself
 24:4 who hath not *l* up his soul unto vanity, nor
 24:7 (24:9) *l* up your heads, O ye gates; and be ye *l*
 25:1 (86:4) unto thee, O LORD, do I *l* up my soul
 30:1 will extol thee, O LORD; for thou hast *l* me
 63:4 I live: I will *l* up my hands in thy name
 75:5 *l* not up your horn on high: speak not with
 93:3 floods have *l* up, O LORD, the floods have *l*
 102:10 for thou hast *l* me up, and cast me down
 121:1 I will *l* up mine eyes unto the hills
 123:1 unto thee *l* I up mine eyes, O thou that
 143:8 I should walk; for I *l* up my soul unto thee
 147:6 LORD *l* up the meek: he casteth the wicked
Eccl. 4:10 they fall, the one will *l* up his fellow
Is. 2:4 (Mic. 4:3) shall not *l* up sword against nation
 26:11 when thy hand is *l* up, they will not see
 33:10 will I be exalted; now will I *l* up myself
 37:4 wherefore *l* up thy prayer for the remnant
 42:2 he shall not cry, nor *l* up, nor cause his
 59:19 Spirit of the LORD shall *l* up a standard
Jer. 7:16 (11:14) neither *l* up thy cry nor prayer for them
Lam. 3:41 let us *l* up our heart with our hands unto
Ezek. 28:2 thine heart is *l* up, and thou hast said
Hab. 2:4 soul which is *l* up is not upright in him
Mk. 1:31 her up; and immediately the fever left
 1:31 Jesus took him by the hand, and *l* him up
Lk. 21:28 and *l* up your heads; for your redemption
 24:50 Bethany, and he *l* up his hands, and blessed
Jn. 3:14 as Moses *l* up the serpent in the wilderness
 8:28 when ye have *l* up the Son of man, then shall
 12:32 if I be *l* up from the earth, will draw all
1 Tim. 2:8 men pray every where, *l* up holy hands
 3:6 not a novice, lest being *l* up with pride he
Heb. 12:12 *l* up the hands which hang down

Jas. 4:10 humble yourselves. . and he shall *l* you up
Rev. 10:5 and the angel. . *l* up his hand to heaven

Light (Lighter) (adjective) *See also* Easy, Little, Small

Deut. 27:16 cursed. . that setteth *l* by his father or
1 Sam. 18:23 a *l* thing to be a king's son-in-law
2 Sam. 2:18 Asahel was as *l* of foot as a wild roe
1 Kgs. 12:4 make. . yoke which he put upon us, *l*
2 Kgs. 3:18 but a *l* thing in the sight of the LORD
Ps. 62:9 balance, they are altogether *l* than vanity
Is. 49:6 a *l* thing thou shouldest be my servant
Ezek. 22:7 in thee have they set *l* by father and
Zeph. 3:4 prophets are. *l* and treacherous persons
Mt. 11:30 for my yoke is easy, and my burden is *l*
 22:5 but they made *l* of it, and went their ways
2 Cor. 4:17 for our *l* affliction. . worketh for us a

Light (verb) *See also* Descend, Fall

2 Sam. 17:12 we will *l* upon him as the dew falleth
Is. 9:8 word into Jacob, and it hath *l* upon Israel
Mt. 3:16 descending like a dove, and *l* upon him

Light (noun) *See also* Brightness, Candle, Enlighten, Lamp, Shine

Gen. 1:3 God said, Let there be *l*: and there was *l*
 1:15 *l* in the firmament of the heaven to give *l*
Ex. 10:23 but all. . Israel had *l* in their dwellings
 13:21 night in a pillar of fire, to give them *l*
2 Sam. 23:4 he shall be as the *l* of the morning
1 Kgs. 11:36 have a *l* alway before me in Jerusalem
Esth. 8:16 Jews had *l*, and gladness, and joy
Job 3:23 why is *l* given to a man whose way is hid
 10:22 and where the *l* is as darkness
 12:25 they grope in the dark without *l*
 18:5 yea, the *l* of the wicked shall be put out
 24:13 they are of those that rebel against the *l*
 29:3 and when by his *l* I walked through darkness
 30:26 when I waited for *l*, there came darkness
Ps. 4:6 lift thou up the *l* of thy countenance upon
 27:1 LORD is my *l* and my salvation; whom shall I
 36:9 fountain of life: in thy *l* shall we see *l*
 37:6 shall bring forth thy righteousness as the *l*
 43:3 send out thy *l* and thy truth: let them lead
 49:19 of his fathers; they shall never see *l*
 74:16 thou hast prepared the *l* and the sun
 89:15 walk, O LORD, in the *l* of thy countenance
 97:11 *l* is sown for the righteous, and gladness
 104:2 coverest thyself with *l* as with a garment
 112:4 unto the upright there ariseth *l*
 118:27 God is the LORD, which hath showed us *l*
 119:105 lamp unto my feet, and a *l* unto my path
 119:130 entrance of thy words giveth *l*; it giveth
 139:11 even the night shall be *l* about me
Prov. 4:18 path of the just is as the shining *l*
 6:23 the commandment is a lamp; and the law is *l*
Eccl. 11:7 truly the *l* is sweet, and a pleasant
Is. 2:5 come ye. . let us walk in the *l* of the LORD
 5:20 that put darkness for *l*, and *l* for darkness
 9:2 (Mt. 4:16) in darkness have seen a great *l*
 42:6 covenant of the people. . a *l* of the Gentiles
 45:7 I form the *l*, and create darkness
 49:6 (Acts 13:47) give thee for a *l* to the Gentiles
 51:4 my judgment to rest for a *l* of the people
 58:8 then shall thy *l* break forth as the morning
 60:1 arise, shine; for thy *l* is come
 60:19 LORD shall be unto thee an everlasting *l*
Jer. 13:16 while ye look for *l*, he turn it into
Ezek. 32:8 bright *l* of heaven will I make dark
Hos. 6:5 judgments are as the *l* that goeth forth

Amos 5:18 the day of the LORD is darkness, and not *l*
Mic. 7:8 I sit in darkness, the LORD shall be a *l*
Hab. 3:4 his brightness was as the *l*; he had horns
Zech. 14:7 at evening time it shall be *l*
Mt. 5:14 ye are the *l* of the world. A city that is
  5:16 let your *l* so shine before men, that they
  6:22 (Lk. 11:34) the *l* of the body is the eye
  10:27 tell you in darkness, that speak ye in *l*
  17:2 the sun, and his raiment was white as the *l*
Lk. 1:79 to give *l* to them that sit in darkness
  2:32 a *l* to lighten the Gentiles, and the glory
  8:16 no man, when he hath *l* a candle, covereth it
  11:35 the *l* which is in thee be not darkness
  12:35 loins be girded about, and your *l* burning
  16:8 generation wiser than the children of *l*
Jn. 1:4 was life; and the life was the *l* of men
  1:5 the *l* shineth in darkness; and the darkness
  1:8 not that *L*. . sent to bear witness of that *L*
  1:9 that was the true *L*, which *l* every man
  3:19 *l* is come . . men loved darkness rather than *l*
  5:35 willing for a season to rejoice in his *l*
  8:12 (9:5) I am the *l* of the world
  12:35 *l* with you. Walk while ye have the *l*, lest
  12:46 am come a *l* into the world, that whosoever
Acts 9:3 (22:6; 26:13) about him a *l* from heaven
  13:47 I have set thee to be a *l* of the Gentiles
  20:8 and there were many *l* in the upper chamber
  26:18 to turn them from darkness to *l*, and from
  26:23 and should show *l* unto the people
Rom. 2:19 a guide of the blind, a *l* of them which
  13:12 and let us put on the armor of *l*
1 Cor. 4:5 bring to *l* the hidden things of darkness
2 Cor. 4:4 the *l* of the glorious gospel of Christ
  4:6 who commanded the *l* to shine out of darkness
  6:14 and what communion hath *l* with darkness?
Eph. 5:8 ye *l* in the Lord: walk as children of *l*
  5:13 for whatsoever doth make manifest is *l*
  5:14 arise . . and Christ shall give thee *l*
Phil. 2:15 among whom ye shine as *l* in the world
Col. 1:12 of the inheritance of the saints in *l*
1 Thes. 5:5 ye are all the children of *l*
1 Tim. 6:16 dwelling in the *l*. . no man can approach
2 Tim. 1:10 hath brought life and immortality to *l*
Jas. 1:17 and cometh down from the Father of *l*
1 Pet. 2:9 out of darkness into his marvelous *l*
2 Pet. 1:19 unto a *l* that shineth in a dark place
1 Jn. 1:5 that God is *l*, and in him is no darkness
  1:7 but if we walk in the *l*, as he is in the *l*
  2:8 darkness is past, and the true *l* now shineth
  2:10 he that loveth his brother abideth in the *l*
Rev. 21:23 and the Lamb is the *l* thereof
  22:5 neither *l* of the sun; for . . God giveth them *l*

Lighten *See also* Enlighten

2 Sam. 22:29 art my lamp . . LORD will *l* my darkness
Ezra 9:8 God may *l* our eyes, and give us a little
Ps. 13:3 *l* mine eyes, lest I sleep the sleep of
  34:5 they looked unto him, and were *l*
Lk. 2:32 a light to *l* the Gentiles, and the glory
Acts 27:18 a tempest, the next day they *l* the ship
Rev. 21:23 glory of God did *l* it, and the Lamb is

Lightning *See also* Thundering

Ex. 19:16 were thunders and *l*, and a thick cloud
2 Sam. 22:15 (Ps. 18:14) sent out . . *l*, and discomfited
Job 28:26 decree for the rain, and a way for the *l*
  37:3 heaven, and his *l* unto the ends of the earth
Ps. 77:18 *l* lightened the world: the earth trembled
  135:7 he maketh *l* for the rain; he bringeth the
  144:6 cast forth *l*, and scatter them: shoot out
Ezek. 1:13 bright, and out of the fire went forth *l*
Dan. 10:6 his face as the appearance of *l*

Nah. 2:4 like torches, they shall run like the *l*
Zech. 9:14 and his arrow shall go forth as the *l*
Mt. 24:27 (Lk. 17:24) as the *l* cometh out of the east
  28:3 his countenance was like *l*, and his raiment
Lk. 10:18 I beheld Satan as *l* fall from heaven
  17:24 for as the *l*, that lighteneth out of the
Rev. 4:5 and out of the throne proceeded *l*
  8:5 (11:19; 16:18) voices, and thunderings, and *l*

Like

Ex. 15:11 who is *l* unto thee, O LORD . . who is *l* thee
Is. 46:9 I am God, and there is none *l* me
Hos. 4:9 there shall be, *l* people, *l* priest
Acts 1:11 into heaven, shall so come in *l* manner

Likeminded

Rom. 15:5 grant you to be *l* one toward another
Phil. 2:2 *l*, having the same love, being of one
  2:20 I have no man *l*, who will naturally

Liken *See also* Compare

Ps. 89:6 sons of the mighty can be *l* unto the LORD?
Is. 40:18 whom then will ye *l* God? or what likeness
Jer. 6:2 I have *l* the daughter of Zion to a comely
Mt. 7:24 I will *l* him unto a wise man, which built
  11:16 (Lk. 7:31) whereunto shall I *l* this generation
  13:24 kingdom . . is *l* unto a man which sowed
  18:23 kingdom of heaven *l* unto a certain king
  25:1 the kingdom of heaven be *l* unto ten virgins
Mk. 4:30 whereunto shall we *l* the kingdom of God?

Likeness *See also* Similitude

Gen. 1:26 let us make man in our image, after our *l*
  5:1 God created man, in the *l* of God made he him
Ex. 20:4 (Deut. 5:8) image, or any *l* of any thing
Deut. 4:16 of any figure, the *l* of male or female
Ps. 17:15 be satisfied, when I awake, with thy *l*
Is. 40:18 or what *l* will ye compare unto him?
Acts 14:11 gods are come down to us in the *l* of men
Rom. 6:5 *l* of his death . . the *l* of his resurrection
  8:3 sending his own Son in the *l* of sinful flesh
Phil. 2:7 a servant, and was made in the *l* of men

Likewise

Lk. 6:31 should do to you, do ye also to them *l*
  10:37 said Jesus unto him, Go, and do thou *l*

Lily

Song 2:1 rose of Sharon, and the *l* of the valleys
  2:2 as the *l* among thorns, so is my love among
Hos. 14:5 he shall grow as the *l*, and cast forth
Mt. 6:28 (Lk. 12:27) consider the *l* of the field

Lime

Is. 33:12 the people shall be as the burnings of *l*

Limit

Ps. 78:41 tempted God, and *l* the Holy One of Israel
Ezek. 43:12 the whole *l* thereof . . shall be most holy
Heb. 4:7 again, he *l* a certain day, saying in David

Line

Josh. 2:18 shalt bind this *l* of scarlet thread in
2 Sam. 8:2 smote Moab, and measured them with a *l*
Ps. 16:6 *l* are fallen unto me in pleasant places
  19:4 their *l* is gone out through all the earth
Is. 28:10 precept upon precept; *l* upon *l*, *l* upon *l*
  28:17 judgment also will I lay to the *l*
  34:11 stretch out upon it the *l* of confusion
Zech. 2:1 behold a man with a measuring *l* in his
2 Cor. 10:16 boast in another man's *l* of things

Linen

Gen. 41:42 and arrayed him in vestures of fine *l*
Ex. 25:4 (35:6) and purple, and scarlet, and fine *l*
Lev. 6:10 put on his *l* garment, and his *l* breeches
1 Sam. 2:18 being a child, girded with a *l* ephod
Jer. 13:1 go and get thee a *l* girdle, and put it
Mt. 27:59 (Mk. 15:46; Lk. 23:53) wrapped it in a clean *l* cloth
Lk. 16:19 which was clothed in purple and fine *l*
 24:12 he beheld the *l* clothes laid by themselves
Rev. 15:6 clothed in pure and white *l*, and having
 19:8 the fine *l* is the righteousness of saints

Linger

Gen. 19:16 while he *l*, the men laid hold upon his
 43:10 except we had *l*, surely now we had returned
2 Pet. 2:3 whose judgment now of a long time *l* not

Lintel

Ex. 12:22 strike the *l* and the. . posts with the blood
Amos 9:1 smite the *l* of the door, that the posts

Lion

Gen. 49:9 Judah is a *l* 's whelp. . he couched as a *l*
Num. 24:9 he lay down as a *l*, and as a great *l*
Judg. 14:5 behold, a young *l* roared against him
 14:18 sweeter than honey?. . stronger than a *l*
1 Sam. 17:34 there came a *l*, and a bear, and took
2 Sam. 23:20 (1 Chr. 11:22) slew a *l*. . in time of snow
1 Kgs. 13:24 a *l* met him by the way, and slew him
2 Kgs. 17:25 Lord sent *l* among them, which slew
Job 4:10 and the teeth of the young *l*, are broken
 10:16 thou huntest me as a fierce *l*
 38:39 *l*? or fill the appetite of the young *l*
Ps. 7:2 lest he tear my soul like a *l*, rending it
 10:9 he lieth in wait secretly as a *l* in his den
 17:12 as a *l* that is greedy. . a young *l* lurking
 22:13 they gaped. . as a ravening and a roaring *l*
 22:21 save me from the *l* 's mouth: for thou hast
 34:10 the young *l* do lack, and suffer hunger
 57:4 my soul is among *l*: and I lie even among
 91:13 tread upon the *l* and adder: the young *l*
Prov. 22:13 there is a *l* without, I shall be slain
 26:13 there is a *l* in the way: a *l* is in the
 28:1 but the righteous are bold as a *l*
 30:30 a *l*, which is strongest among beasts
Eccl. 9:4 for a living dog is better than a dead *l*
Is. 11:7 (65:25) the *l* shall eat straw like the ox
 35:9 no *l* shall be there, nor any ravenous beast
Jer. 12:8 heritage is unto me as a *l* in the forest
Lam. 3:10 bear lying in wait, and as a *l* in secret
Ezek. 1:10 (10:14) face of a man, and the face of a *l*
 19:3 one of her whelps: it became a young *l*
Dan. 6:20 thy God. . able to deliver thee from the *l*?
 7:4 the first was like a *l*, and had eagle's wings
Hos. 5:14 *l*, and as a young *l* to the house of Judah
Amos 3:8 the *l* hath roared, who will not fear?
Mic. 5:8 as a *l* among the beasts of the forest
Zeph. 3:3 her princes within her are roaring *l*
2 Tim. 4:17 was delivered out of the mouth of the *l*
Heb. 11:33 stopped the mouths of *l*
1 Pet. 5:8 your adversary the devil, as a roaring *l*
Rev. 4:7 first beast was like a *l*, and the second
 5:5 the *L* of the tribe of Juda, the Root of David

Lip *See also* Mouth, Tongue

Ex. 6:12 hear me, who am of uncircumcised *l*?
1 Sam. 1:13 *l* moved, but her voice was not heard
Job 27:4 my *l* shall not speak wickedness, nor my
 33:3 and my *l* shall utter knowledge clearly
Ps. 12:4 our *l* are our own: who is lord over us?
 34:13 (1 Pet. 3:10) and thy *l* from speaking guile

Ps. 45:2 grace is poured into thy *l*; therefore God
 51:15 O Lord, open thou my *l*; and my mouth shall
 59:7 with their mouth: swords are in their *l*
 63:3 is better than life, my *l* shall praise thee
 89:34 alter the thing that is gone out of my *l*
 119:171 my *l* shall utter praise, when thou hast
 140:3 a serpent; adders' poison is under their *l*
 141:3 before my mouth; keep the door of my *l*
Prov. 5:3 of a strange woman drop as a honeycomb
 8:6 the opening of my *l* shall be right things
 10:19 but he that refraineth his *l* is wise
 10:21 *l* of the righteous feed many: but fools
 10:32 *l* of the righteous know what is acceptable
 12:19 *l* of truth shall be established for ever
 13:3 openeth wide his *l* shall have destruction
 14:3 but the *l* of the wise shall preserve them
 14:7 perceivest not in him the *l* of knowledge
 14:23 the talk of the *l* tendeth only to penury
 15:7 the *l* of the wise disperse knowledge
 16:10 a divine sentence is in the *l* of the king
 16:13 righteous *l* are the delight of kings
 16:21 the sweetness of the *l* increaseth learning
 18:7 and his *l* are the snare of his soul
 20:15 the *l* of knowledge are a precious jewel
 27:2 let another man praise thee. . not thine own *l*
Eccl. 10:12 the *l* of a fool will swallow up himself
Song 4:3 thy *l* are like a thread of scarlet
 7:9 causing the *l* of those. . asleep to speak
Is. 6:5 I am a man of unclean *l*, and I dwell in
 6:7 this hath touched thy *l*; and thine iniquity
 29:13 (Mt. 15:8; Mk. 7:6) with their *l* do honor me
Dan. 10:16 touched my *l*: then I opened my mouth
Hos. 14:2 so will we render the calves of our *l*
Hab. 3:16 trembled; my *l* quivered at the voice
Rom. 3:13 poison of asps is under their *l*
1 Cor. 14:21 with men of other tongues and other *l*
Heb. 13:15 fruit of our *l*, giving thanks to his

Liquor

Num. 6:3 neither shall he drink any *l* of grapes

List

Jn. 3:8 wind bloweth where it *l*, and thou hearest
Jas. 3:4 small helm, whithersoever the governor *l*

Little *See also* Light (adjective), Small

Gen. 19:20 it is a *l* one: O, let me escape thither
 30:30 it was *l* which thou hadst before I came
Ex. 16:18 (2 Cor. 8:15) that gathered *l* had no lack
 23:30 (Deut. 7:22) by *l* and *l* I will drive them out
1 Sam. 15:17 when thou wast *l* in thine own sight
Job 4:12 and mine ear received a *l* thereof
 26:14 but how *l* a portion is heard of him?
Ps. 2:12 when his wrath is kindled but a *l*
 8:5 (Heb. 2:7) made him a *l* lower than the angels
 37:16 a *l* that a righteous man hath is better
Prov. 6:10 (24:33) a *l* sleep, a *l* slumber, a *l* folding
 15:16 better is *l* with the fear of the Lord, than
 16:8 better is a *l* with righteousness, than great
 30:24 four things which are *l* upon the earth
Is. 28:10 line upon line; here a *l*, and there a *l*
 40:15 he taketh up the isles as a very *l* thing
 60:22 *l* one shall become a thousand, and a small
Ezek. 11:16 yet will I be to them as a *l* sanctuary
 16:47 as if that were a very *l* thing, thou wast
Mic. 5:2 thou be *l* among the thousands of Judah
Hag. 1:6 ye have sown much, and bring in *l*
 1:9 ye looked for much, and, lo, it came to *l*
Zech. 1:15 for I was but a *l* displeased, and they
Mt. 6:30 (8:26; 16:8; Lk. 12:28) O ye of *l* faith?
 10:42 one of these *l* ones a cup of cold water
 14:31 thou of *l* faith, wherefore didst thou doubt?
 18:6 (Mk. 9:42; Lk. 17:2) offend one of these *l* ones

Mt. 19:14 (Mk. 10:14; Lk. 18:16) suffer *l* children
Lk. 7:47 to whom *l* is forgiven, the same loveth *l*
  19:3 for the press, because he was *l* of stature
  19:17 because thou hast been faithful in a very *l*
Jn. 7:33 (13:33) yet a *l* while am I with you
  12:35 yet a *l* while is the light with you
  14:19 a *l* while, and the world seeth me no more
2 Cor. 11:16 as a fool. . that I may boast myself a *l*
1 Tim. 4:8 for bodily exercise profiteth *l*
Heb. 2:9 see Jesus. . made a *l* lower than the angels
  10:37 yet a *l* while, and he that shall come will
Jas. 3:5 tongue is a *l* member, and boasteth great
Rev. 10:2 and he had in his hand a *l* book open

Live *See also* Abide, Dwell, Inhabit

Gen. 3:22 tree of life, and eat, and *l* for ever
  12:13 my soul shall *l* because of thee
Ex. 33:20 for there shall no man see me, and *l*
Lev. 18:5 (Rom. 10:5; Gal. 3:12) which if a man do,
  he shall *l* in them
Num. 21:9 when he beheld the serpent of brass, he *l*
  24:23 alas, who shall *l* when God doeth this!
Deut. 5:24 that God doth talk with man, and he *l*
  5:33 your God hath commanded you, that ye may *l*
  8:3 (Mt. 4:4; Lk. 4:4) man doth not *l* by bread only
  16:20 just shalt thou follow, that thou mayest *l*
  30:19 choose life. . both thou and thy seed may *l*
Job 7:16 I loathe it; I would not *l* alway: let me
  14:14 if a man die, shall he *l* again?
  19:25 for I know that my Redeemer *l*, and that he
Ps. 22:26 seek him: your heart shall *l* for ever
  63:4 thus will I bless thee while I *l*
  69:32 be glad. . your heart shall *l* that seek God
  104:33 I will sing unto the LORD as long as I *l*
  118:17 I shall not die, but, *l*, and declare the
  119:17 that I may *l*, and keep thy word
  119:175 let my soul *l*, and it shall praise thee
  146:2 while I *l* will I praise the LORD
Prov. 4:4 my words: keep my commandments, and *l*
  9:6 forsake the foolish, and *l*; and go in the
Eccl. 9:9 *l* joyfully with the wife whom thou lovest
Is. 26:19 thy dead men shall *l*, together with my dead
  38:16 O Lord, by these things men *l*, and in all
  55:3 come unto me: hear, and your soul shall *l*
Jer. 4:2 swear, The LORD *l*, in truth, in judgment
Lam. 4:20 under his shadow we shall *l* among the
Ezek. 3:21 and he doth not sin, he shall surely *l*
  18:9 is just, he shall surely *l*, saith the Lord
  18:23 that he should return from his ways, and *l*?
  18:32 wherefore turn yourselves, and *l* ye
  20:11 which if a man do, he shall even *l* in them
  33:10 pine away in them, how should we then *l*?
  33:11 wicked turn from his way and *l*
  37:3 said unto me, Son of man, can these bones *l*?
Dan. 4:34 I praised and honored him that *l* for ever
Hos. 6:2 raise us up, and we shall *l* in his sight
Amos 5:4 Israel, Seek ye me, and ye shall *l*
  5:14 seek good, and not evil, that ye may *l*
Jon. 4:3 (4:8) better for me to die than to *l*
Hab. 2:4 (Rom. 1:17; Gal. 3:11; Heb. 10:38) the just
  shall *l* by his faith
Mt. 9:18 (Mk. 5:23) thy hand upon her. . she shall *l*
Lk. 10:28 answered right: this do, and thou shalt *l*
  20:38 God. . of the living: for all *l* unto him
Jn. 4:50 go thy way; thy son *l*
  5:25 voice of the Son. . they that hear shall *l*
  6:51 man eat of this bread, he shall *l* for ever
  11:25 in me, though he were dead, yet shall he *l*
  14:19 but ye see me: because I *l*, ye shall *l* also
Acts 17:28 in him we *l*, and move, and have our being
  23:1 brethren, I have *l* in all good conscience
Rom. 6:2 that are dead to sin, *l* any longer therein?

Rom. 6:8 we believe that we shall also *l* with him
  6:10 but in that he *l*, he *l* unto God
  8:13 mortify the deeds of the body, ye shall *l*
  12:18 as lieth in you, *l* peaceably with all men
  14:7 none of us *l* to himself, and no man dieth
  14:8 for whether we *l*, we *l* unto the Lord
1 Cor. 9:14 preach the gospel should *l* of the gospel
2 Cor. 5:15 should not henceforth *l* unto themselves
  6:9 yet well known; as dying, and, behold, we *l*
  13:4 weakness, yet he *l* by the power of God
Gal. 2:20 I *l*; yet not I, but Christ *l* in me
  5:25 if we *l* in the Spirit, let us also walk in
Eph. 6:3 be well with thee, and thou mayest *l* long
Phil. 1:21 to me to *l* is Christ, and to die is gain
1 Thes. 5:10 we should *l* together with him
1 Tim. 5:6 that *l* in pleasure is dead while she *l*
2 Tim. 2:11 dead with him, we shall also *l* with him
  3:12 all that will *l* godly in Christ Jesus shall
Tit. 2:12 we should *l* soberly, righteously
Heb. 7:25 he ever *l* to make intercession for them
  9:17 of no strength at all while the testator *l*
  13:18 in all things willing to *l* honestly
Jas. 4:15 if the Lord will, we shall *l*, and do
1 Pet. 1:23 word of God, which *l* and abideth for
  2:24 dead to sins, should *l* unto righteousness
  4:6 but *l* according to God in the spirit
2 Pet. 2:18 clean escaped from them who *l* in error
1 Jn. 4:9 sent his. . Son. . that we might *l* through
Rev. 1:18 am he that *l*, and was dead; and, behold
  3:1 thou hast a name that thou *l*, and art dead
  15:7 the wrath of God, who *l* for ever and ever
  20:4 they *l* and reigned with Christ a thousand
  20:5 but the rest of the dead *l* not again until

Lively

Ex. 1:19 are *l*, and are delivered ere the midwives
Acts 7:38 received the *l* oracles to give unto us
1 Pet. 1:3 again unto a *l* hope by the resurrection
  2:5 as *l* stones, are built up a spiritual house

Liver

Lev. 3:4 the caul above the *l*, with the kidneys
Prov. 7:23 till a dart strike through his *l*
Lam. 2:11 troubled, my *l* is poured upon the earth
Ezek. 21:21 consulted with images. . looked in the *l*

Living *See also* Alive, Quick

Gen. 1:21 whales, and every *l* creature that moveth
  2:7 the breath of life; and man became a *l* soul
  3:20 Eve; because she was the mother of all *l*
  7:23 every *l* substance was destroyed which was
Num. 16:48 and he stood between the dead and the *l*
Josh. 3:10 shall know that the *l* God is among you
Job 12:10 whose hand is the soul of every *l* thing
  28:13 neither is it found in the land of the *l*
  30:23 to death. . to the house appointed for all *l*
  33:30 to be enlightened with the light of the *l*
Ps. 27:13 goodness of the LORD in the land of the *l*
  42:2 my soul thirsteth for God, for the *l* God
  56:13 may walk before God in the light of the *l*?
  69:28 them be blotted out of the book of the *l*
  116:9 walk before the LORD in the land of the *l*
  143:2 in thy sight shall no man *l* be justified
  145:16 satisfiest the desire of every *l* thing
Eccl. 7:2 and the *l* will lay it to his heart
  9:5 the *l* know that they shall die: but the dead
Is. 38:19 the *l*, the *l*, he shall praise thee
  53:8 for he was cut off out of the land of the *l*
Jer. 2:13 forsaken me the fountain of *l* waters
  10:10 he is the *l* God, and an everlasting King
  11:19 let us cut him off from the land of the *l*
Ezek. 1:5 came the likeness of four *l* creatures
Dan. 6:20 Daniel, servant of the *l* God, is thy God

Zech. 14:8 *l* waters shall go out from Jerusalem
Mt. 22:32 (Mk. 12:27; Lk. 20:38) the God . . of the *l*
Mk. 12:44 (Lk. 21:4) cast in all . . even all her *l*
Lk. 15:13 there wasted his substance with riotous *l*
    24:5 unto them, Why seek ye the *l* among the dead?
Jn. 4:10 him, and he would have given thee *l* water
    6:51 am the *l* bread which came down from heaven
    6:57 as the *l* Father hath sent me, and I live by
    7:38 of his belly shall flow rivers of *l* water
Acts 14:15 turn from these vanities unto the *l* God
Rom. 12:1 ye present your bodies a *l* sacrifice
    14:9 he might be Lord both of the dead and *l*
1 Cor. 15:45 the first man Adam was made a *l* soul
Col. 2:20 why, as though *l* in the world, are ye
1 Thes. 1:9 from idols to serve the *l* and true God
1 Tim. 3:15 is the church of the *l* God, the pillar
Heb. 10:20 new and *l* way, which he hath consecrated
    10:31 to fall into the hands of the *l* God
1 Pet. 2:4 unto a *l* stone, disallowed indeed of men
Rev. 7:17 lead them unto *l* fountains of waters

Load

Ps. 68:19 the Lord, who daily *l* us with benefits

Loaf (Loaves)

Mt. 14:17 (Mk. 6:38; Lk. 9:13; Jn. 6:9) five *l*, and two
    15:34 (Mk. 8:5) how many *l* have ye? . . Seven
Mk. 6:52 they considered not the miracle of the *l*
Lk. 11:5 midnight, and say . . Friend, lend me three *l*
Jn. 6:26 miracles, but because ye did eat of the *l*

Loan

1 Sam. 2:20 give thee seed of this woman for the *l*

Loathe *See also* Abhor, Contemn, Despise, Detest, Hate, Scorn

Num. 21:5 our soul *l* this light bread
Job 7:16 *l* it; I would not live alway
Jer. 14:19 rejected Judah? hath soul *l* Zion?
Ezek. 6:9 they shall *l* themselves for the evils
    20:43 (36:31) shall *l* yourselves in your own sight
Zech. 11:8 my soul *l* them, and their soul also

Loathsome *See also* Abominable, Base, Vile, Wicked

Job 7:5 my skin is broken, and become *l*
Ps. 38:7 for my loins are filled with a *l* disease
Prov. 13:5 a wicked man is *l*, and cometh to shame

Lock (noun)

Judg. 16:19 to shave off the seven *l* of his head
Is. 47:2 uncover thy *l*, make bare the leg, uncover

Locked

Judg. 3:24 behold, the doors of the parlor were *l*

Locust

Ex. 10:4 tomorrow will I bring the *l* into thy
Lev. 11:22 them ye may eat; the *l* after his kind
Deut. 28:38 little in; for the *l* shall consume it
2 Chr. 7:13 if I command the *l* to devour the land
Ps. 105:34 spake, and the *l* came, and caterpillars
Prov. 30:27 the *l* have no king, yet go they forth
Is. 33:4 as the running to and fro of *l* shall he
Joel 2:4 *l* eaten; and that which the *l* hath left
    2:25 restore . . the years that the *l* hath eaten
Nah. 3:15 cankerworm, make thyself many as the *l*
Mt. 3:4 (Mk. 1:6) his meat was *l* and wild honey
Rev. 9:3 came out of the smoke *l* upon the earth

Lodge *See also* Abide, Dwell

Gen. 24:23 room in thy father's house for us to *l*
Judg. 19:15 to go in and to *l* in Gibeah
Ruth 1:16 where thou *l*, I will *l*: thy people shall
Is. 1:8 vineyard, as a *l* in a garden of cucumbers
    1:21 righteousness *l* in it; but now murderers
Mt. 13:32 (Mk. 4:32; Lk. 13:19) birds of the air . . *l*
Acts 10:6 (10:32) he *l* with one Simon a tanner
    28:7 received us, and *l* us three days courteously
1 Tim. 5:10 well reported . . if she have *l* strangers

Lodging *See also* Dwelling

Josh. 4:3 and leave them in the *l* place, where ye
2 Kgs. 19:23 I will enter into the *l* of his borders
Jer. 9:2 the wilderness a *l* place of wayfaring men
Acts 28:23 came many to him into his *l*; to whom he
Phlm. 22 withal prepare me also a *l*: for I trust

Loft

1 Kgs. 17:19 and carried him up into a *l*, where he
Acts 20:9 sleep, and fell down from the third *l*

Loftiness

Is. 2:17 the *l* of man shall be bowed down

Lofty *See also* High

Ps. 131:1 my heart is not haughty, nor mine eyes *l*
Prov. 30:13 a generation, O how *l* are their eyes!
Is. 2:11 the *l* looks of man shall be humbled
    2:12 shall be upon every one that is proud and *l*
    5:15 and the eyes of the *l* shall be humbled
    57:15 high and *l* One that inhabiteth eternity

Loins

Gen. 35:11 and kings shall come out of thy *l*
Ex. 12:11 thus shall ye eat it; with your *l* girded
2 Kgs. 4:29 then he said to Gehazi, Gird up thy *l*
Job 38:3 gird up now thy *l* like a man; for I will
Prov. 31:17 she girdeth her *l* with strength
Is. 11:5 righteousness shall be the girdle of his *l*
Lk. 12:35 your *l* be girded about, and your lights
Eph. 6:14 having your *l* girt about with truth
1 Pet. 1:13 wherefore gird up the *l* of your mind

Lois 2 Tim. 1:5

Long (adjective, adverb)

Ex. 19:13 when the trumpet soundeth *l*, they shall
    20:12 that thy days may be *l* upon the land
1 Kgs. 3:11 (2 Chr. 1:11) not asked for thyself *l* life
Ps. 91:16 with *l* life will I satisfy him, and show
Eccl. 12:5 because man goeth to his *l* home
Mt. 23:14 (Mk. 12:40; Lk. 20:47) make *l* prayers
    25:19 after a *l* time the lord of those servants
Mk. 12:38 (Lk. 20:46) love to go in *l* clothing
Lk. 1:21 marveled . . he tarried so *l* in the temple
Jn. 14:9 have I been so *l* time with you, and yet
Acts 20:9 deep sleep: and as Paul was *l* preaching
1 Cor. 13:4 charity suffereth *l*, and is kind

Long (verb) *See also* Desire, Wish

Gen. 31:30 thou sore *l* after thy father's house
Job 3:21 which *l* for death, but it cometh not
    6:8 God would grant me the thing that I *l* for!
Ps. 84:2 my soul *l* . . for the courts of the LORD
    107:9 he satisfieth the *l* soul, and filleth
    119:174 I have *l* for thy salvation, O LORD
Rom. 1:11 for I *l* to see you, that I may impart
Phil. 1:8 my record, how greatly I *l* after you all
    2:26 *l* after you all, and was full of heaviness

Long-suffering *See also* Patience

Ex. 34:6 the LORD God, merciful and gracious, *l-s*
Rom. 9:22 endured with much *l-s* the vessels of wrath
2 Cor. 6:6 by pureness, by knowledge, by *l-s*
Gal. 5:22 fruit of the Spirit is love, joy, peace, *l-s*
Eph. 4:2 (Col. 3:12) with *l-s*, forbearing one another
Col. 1:11 unto patience and *l-s* with joyfulness
  3:12 kindness, humbleness of mind, meekness, *l-s*
1 Tim. 1:16 in me . . Christ might show forth all *l-s*
2 Tim. 4:2 rebuke, exhort with all *l-s* and doctrine
1 Pet. 3:20 *l-s* of God waited in the days of Noah
2 Pet. 3:9 is *l-s* to us-ward, not willing that any
  3:15 account that the *l-s* of our Lord is salvation

Look *See also* Behold, See

Gen. 6:12 God *l* upon the earth . . it was corrupt
  13:14 *l* from the place where thou art northward
  19:17 escape for thy life; *l* not behind thee
  42:1 Jacob said . . Why do ye *l* one upon another?
Ex. 3:6 Moses hid his face; for he was afraid to *l*
  4:31 that he had *l* upon their affliction
  14:24 the LORD *l* unto the host of the Egyptians
Num. 21:8 is bitten, when he *l* upon it, shall live
Deut. 26:15 *l* down from thy holy habitation
1 Sam. 6:19 smote . . because they had *l* into the ark
  9:16 I have *l* upon my people, because their
  16:7 for man *l* on the outward appearance, but
2 Kgs. 14:8 come, let us *l* one another in the face
Job 6:28 *l* upon me; for it is evident . . if I lie
  13:27 and I narrowly unto all my paths
  30:26 when I *l* for good, then evil came unto me
  33:27 he *l* upon men, and if any say, I have sinned
  35:5 I unto the heavens, and see; and behold the
Ps. 5:3 direct my prayer unto thee, and will *l* up
  14:2 (53:2) the LORD *l* down from heaven upon
  18:27 but wilt bring down high *l*
  34:5 they *l* unto him, and were lightened
  80:14 *l* down from heaven, and . . visit this vine
  84:9 and *l* upon the face of thine anointed
  102:19 *l* down from the height of his sanctuary
Prov. 6:17 proud *l*, a lying tongue, and hands that
  14:15 but the prudent man *l* well to his going
  24:32 I *l* upon it, and received instruction
  31:27 she *l* well to the ways of her household
Song 6:13 return, return, that we may *l* upon thee
Is. 5:7 he *l* for judgment, but behold oppression
  8:22 shall *l* unto the earth; and behold trouble
  17:7 at that day shall a man *l* to his Maker
  33:20 *l* upon Zion, the city of our solemnities
  42:18 hear, ye deaf; and *l*, ye blind, that ye
  45:22 *l* unto me, and be ye saved, all the ends
  51:1 *l* unto the rock whence ye are hewn
  59:11 we *l* for judgment, but there is none
  63:5 and I *l*, and there was none to help
  66:2 but to this man will I *l*, even to him that
Jer. 8:15 we *l* for peace, but no good came
  39:12 I well to him, and do him no harm
Mic. 7:7 therefore I will *l* unto the LORD; I will
Hab. 1:13 behold evil, and canst not *l* on iniquity
Hag. 1:9 ye *l* for much, and, lo, it came to little
Zech. 12:10 (Jn. 19:37) *l* upon me . . they . . pierced
Mt. 5:28 whosoever *l* on a woman to lust after her
  11:3 (Lk. 7:19) or do ye *l* for another?
  14:19 (Mk. 6:41; Lk. 9:16) *l* . . to heaven, he blessed
  24:50 (Lk. 12:46) in a day when he *l* not for him
Mk. 3:5 (Lk. 6:10) *l* round about on them with anger
  7:34 and *l* up to heaven, he sighed, and saith
  8:25 made him *l* up; and he was restored, and saw
Lk. 9:38 Master, I beseech thee, *l* upon my son
  9:62 hand to the plow, and *l* back, is fit for
  10:32 a Levite . . came and *l* on him, and passed by
  21:28 then *l* up, and lift up your heads

Lk. 22:61 the LORD turned, and *l* upon Peter
Jn. 1:36 and *l* upon Jesus as he walked, he saith
  4:35 *l* on the fields; for they are white already
  13:22 disciples *l* one on another, doubting of
Acts 3:4 fastening his eyes . . said, *L* on us
  3:12 or why *l* ye so earnestly on us, as though by
  6:3 *l* ye out among you seven men of honest report
  6:15 sat in the council, *l* steadfastly on him
  7:55 full of the Holy Ghost, *l* up steadfastly
2 Cor. 4:18 we *l* not at the things which are seen
  10:7 ye *l* on things after the outward appearance?
Phil. 2:4 *l* not every man on his own things, but
  3:20 from whence also we *l* for the Saviour
Tit. 2:13 *l* for that blessed hope, and the glorious
Heb. 9:28 unto them that *l* for him shall he appear
  10:27 but a certain fearful *l* for of judgment
  11:10 for he *l* for a city which hath foundations
  12:2 *l* unto Jesus the author and finisher of our
  12:15 *l* diligently lest any man fail of the grace
1 Pet. 1:12 which things the angels desire to *l* into
2 Pet. 3:12 *l* for and hasting unto the coming of
  3:13 *l* for new heavens and a new earth
1 Jn. 1:1 seen with our eyes, which we have *l* upon
2 Jn. 8 *l* to yourselves, that we lose not those
Jude 21 *l* for the mercy of our Lord Jesus Christ

Looking-glass

Ex. 38:8 the laver of brass . . of the *l-g* of the women

Loose

Gen. 49:21 Naphtali is a hind let *l*: he giveth
Deut. 25:9 *l* his shoe from off his foot, and spit
Josh. 5:15 Joshua, *L* thy shoe from off thy foot
Judg. 15:14 and his bands *l* from off his hands
Job 30:11 because he hath *l* my cord, and afflicted
  38:31 of Pleiades, or *l* the bands of Orion?
Ps. 102:20 to *l* those that are appointed to death
  116:16 of thine handmaid: thou hast *l* my bonds
  146:7 the LORD *l* the prisoners
Eccl. 12:6 silver cord be *l*, or the golden bowl be
Is. 45:1 and I will *l* the loins of kings, to open
  51:14 captive exile hasteneth that he may be *l*
Dan. 3:25 I see four men *l*, walking in the midst
Mt. 16:19 (18:18) shalt *l* on earth shall be *l* in heaven
  21:2 (Mk. 11:2; Lk. 19:30) colt . . *l* them, and bring
Lk. 13:12 woman, thou art *l* from thine infirmity
Jn. 11:44 Jesus saith unto them, *L* him . . let him go
Acts 2:24 raised up, having *l* the pains of death
  13:25 shoes of his feet I am not worthy to *l*
Rom. 7:2 she is *l* from the law of her husband
1 Cor. 7:27 bound unto a wife? seek not to be *l*
Rev. 5:2 open the book, and to *l* the seals thereof?
  9:14 the four angels . . bound in the great river
  20:3 after that he must be *l* a little season

LORD *See also* LORD of Hosts, Lord, Lord Jesus, Lord Jesus Christ, lord, God, Jehovah, King, Name of the LORD

Gen. 4:26 began men to call on the name of the *L*
  12:7 and the *L* appeared unto Abram, and said
  18:14 is any thing too hard for the *L*?
  26:2 *L* appeared unto him, and said, Go not
  28:16 the *L* is in this place; and I knew it not
  31:49 the *L* watch between me and thee, when we
Ex. 3:18 the *L* God of the Hebrews hath met with us
  5:2 who is the *L*, that I should obey his voice
  6:7 and ye shall know that I am the *L* your God
  14:4 the Egyptians may know that I am the *L*
  14:14 *L* shall fight for you, and ye shall hold
  15:2 (Is. 12:2) the *L* is my strength and song
  15:11 who is like unto thee, O *L*, among the gods?

Ex. 15:26 for I am the *L* that healeth thee
  18:11 I know that the *L* is greater than all gods
  20:2 (Ps. 81:10) the *L* thy God, which have brought
  23:25 and ye shall serve the *L* your God
  31:13 know that I am the *L* that doth sanctify
  32:26 who is on the *L*'s side? let him come unto
  33:11 *L* spake unto Moses face to face, as a man
  34:6 *L* passed by. . proclaimed, The *L*, The *L* God
Lev. 19:2 be holy: for I the *L* your God am holy
Num. 6:24 the *L* bless thee, and keep thee
  14:9 rebel not ye against the *L*. . *L* is with us
  23:21 the *L* his God is with him, and the shout
Deut. 4:35 thou mightest know that the *L* he is God
  6:4 (Mk. 12:29) O Israel: The *L* our God is one *L*
  10:17 the *L* your God is God of gods, and Lord
  26:17 avouched the *L* this day to be thy God
  29:29 secret things belong unto the *L* our God
  33:2 the *L* came from Sinai . . with ten thousands
Josh. 1:9 dismayed: for the *L* thy God is with thee
  13:33 the *L* God of Israel was their inheritance
  22:24 have ye to do with the *L* God of Israel?
  23:10 *L* your God, he it is that fighteth for you
  24:15 as for me and my house, we will serve the *L*
  24:24 unto Joshua, The *L* our God will we serve
Judg. 2:12 they forsook the *L* God of their fathers
  8:23 the *L* shall rule over you
  11:27 *L* the Judge be judge this day between the
Ruth 2:4 said unto the reapers, The *L* be with you
1 Sam. 2:3 the *L* is a God of knowledge
  3:4 *L* called Samuel: and he answered, Here am I
  3:18 it is the *L*: let him do what seemeth him good
  16:7 appearance, but the *L* looketh on the heart
2 Sam. 22:2 (Ps. 18:2) *L* is my rock, and my fortress
  22:32 (Ps. 18:31) who is God, save the *L*?
1 Kgs. 8:12 (2 Chr. 6:1) *L* said that he would dwell in
  18:21 if the *L* be God, follow him: but if Baal
  18:39 the *L*, he is the God; the *L*, he is the God
  19:11 the *L* passed by. . the *L* was not in the wind
2 Kgs. 5:17 henceforth offer . . unto the *L*
1 Chr. 16:11 seek the *L* and his strength
  16:14 (Ps. 105:7) he is the *L* our God
  16:25 (Ps. 96:4) great is the *L*, and greatly to be
  16:26 are idols: but the *L* made the heavens
  16:29 (Ps. 96:8) give unto the *L* the glory due unto
2 Chr. 13:10 but as for us, the *L* is our God
  30:8 yield yourselves unto the *L*, and enter
  33:13 Manasseh knew that the *L* he was God
Neh. 9:6 thou, even thou, art *L* alone; thou hast
Ps. 8:1 (8:9) O *L* our Lord, how excellent is thy name
  10:16 *L* is King for ever and ever: the heathen
  16:8 (Acts 2:25) I have set the *L* always before me
  20:7 we will remember the name of the *L* our God
  23:1 the *L* is my shepherd; I shall not want
  24:8 *L* strong and mighty, the *L* mighty in battle
  27:1 *L* is my light and my salvation; whom shall
  27:14 wait on the *L*: be of good courage, and he
  29:10 *L* sitteth upon the flood . . *L* sitteth King
  33:12 blessed is the nation whose God is the *L*
  34:1 I will bless the *L* at all times: his praise
  34:3 magnify the *L* with me, and let us exalt his
  34:8 O taste and see that the *L* is good: blessed
  89:6 compared unto the *L*? . . likened unto the *L*?
  89:8 O *L* God of hosts, who is a strong *L* like
  91:2 I will say of the *L*, He is my refuge and my
  93:4 the *L* on high is mightier than the noise of
  95:3 for the *L* is a great God, and a great King
  100:3 know ye that the *L* he is God: it is he
  103:1 (103:2, 22; 104:1) bless the *L*, O my soul
  110:1 (Mt. 22:44; Mk. 12:36; Lk. 20:42; Acts 2:34)
    L said unto my Lord, Sit thou at my right hand
  113:4 *L* is high above all nations, and his glory
  118:8 it is better to trust in the *L* than to put
  118:23 (Mt. 21:42; Mk. 12:11) this is the *L*'s doing

Ps. 118:27 God is the *L*, which hath showed us light
  121:2 my help cometh from the *L*, which made
  121:5 *L* is thy keeper: the *L* is thy shade upon
  126:3 *L* hath done great things for us; whereof
  127:1 except the *L* build the house, they labor
  135:5 the *L* is great. . our Lord is above all gods
  145:17 *L* is righteous in all his ways, and holy
  145:18 *L* is nigh unto all them that call upon him
Is. 2:11 the *L* alone shall be exalted in that day
  26:4 trust ye in the *L* for ever: for in the *L*
  30:18 the *L* is a God of judgment: blessed are
  33:21 *L* will be unto us a place of broad rivers
  42:8 I am the *L*; that is my name: and my glory
  43:3 I am the *L* thy God, the Holy One of Israel
  43:11 I, am the *L*. . beside me there is no saviour
  60:16 I the *L* am thy Saviour and thy Redeemer
Jer. 3:23 truly in the *L* our God is the salvation
  10:10 *L* is the true God, he is the living God
  23:6 he shall be called, THE *L* OUR RIGHTEOUSNESS
  31:34 (Heb. 8:11) know the *L*. . they shall all know
Lam. 3:24 the *L* is my portion, saith my soul
  3:25 the *L* is good unto them that wait for him
Ezek. 6:10 and they shall know that I am the *L*
  20:19 I am the *L* your God; walk in my statutes
  34:24 I the *L* will be their God, and my servant
  48:35 name of the city . . shall be, The *L* is there
Dan. 2:47 your God is a God of gods . . a *L* of kings
Hos. 12:9 the *L* thy God from the land of Egypt
Joel 2:21 rejoice: for the *L* will do great things
  3:16 but the *L* will be the hope of his people
Mic. 1:3 behold, the *L* cometh forth out of his place
  2:13 pass before them, and the *L* on the head
Nah. 1:3 *L* is slow to anger, and great in power
Hab. 3:19 *L* God is my strength, and he will make
Zeph. 3:5 the just *L* is in the midst thereof
  3:17 *L* thy God in the midst of thee is mighty
Zech. 14:9 *L* shall be King. . shall there be one *L*
Mal. 3:6 I am the *L*, I change not; therefore ye
Mt. 22:44 (Mk. 12:36; Lk. 20:42; Acts 2:34) *L* said
  unto my Lord, Sit thou on my right hand

LORD of Hosts

1 Sam. 1:11 she vowed a vow, and said, O *L* of *h*
  17:45 I come to thee in the name of the *L* of *h*
2 Sam. 5:10 (1 Chr. 11:9) *L* God of *h* was with him
  6:2 name is called by the name of the *L* of *h*
  7:26 (1 Chr. 17:24) *L* of *h* is the God over Israel
Ps. 24:10 who is this King of glory? The *L* of *h*
  46:7 (46:11) the *L* of *h* is with us; the God of Jacob
Is. 6:3 holy, holy, holy, is the *L* of *h*: the whole
  8:13 sanctify the *L* of *h* himself; and let him be
  14:27 *L* of *h* hath purposed. . who shall disannul
  47:4 as for our Redeemer, the *L* of *h* is his name
Hab. 2:13 is it not of the *L* of *h* that the people
Hag. 2:4 for I am with you, saith the *L* of *h*
Zech. 1:6 like as the *L* of *h* thought to do unto us
  2:9 ye shall know that the *L* of *h* hath sent me
  8:22 shall come to seek the *L* of *h* in Jerusalem
  14:16 worship the King, the *L* of *h*, and to keep

Lord *See also* LORD, Lord Jesus, Lord Jesus Christ, lord, Master

Deut. 10:17 your God is God of gods, and *L* of *l*
Ps. 16:2 thou art my *L*: my goodness extendeth not
  110:1 (Mt. 22:44; Mk. 12:36; Lk. 20:42; Acts 2:34)
    LORD said unto my *L*, sit thou at my right hand
  136:3 O give thanks to the *L* of *l*: for his mercy
Is. 6:1 I saw also the *L* sitting upon a throne
Amos 9:1 I saw the *L* standing upon the altar
Mt. 4:10 (Lk. 4:8) thou shalt worship the *L* thy God
  7:21 not every one that saith unto me, *L*, *L*
  9:38 (Lk. 10:2) pray ye. . the *L* of the harvest

Mt. 11:25 (Lk. 10:21) Father, *L* of heaven and earth
12:8 (Mk. 2:28; Lk. 6:5) *L* even of the sabbath day
22:37 (Mk. 12:30) love the *L* thy God with all thy
22:44 (Mk. 12:36; Lk. 20:42; Acts 2:34) LORD said
    unto my *L*, Sit thou on my right hand
24:42 for ye know not what hour your *L* doth come
26:22 to say unto him, *L*, is it I?
28:6 come, see the place where the *L* lay
Mk. 5:19 how great things the *L* hath done for thee
16:20 the *L* working with them, and confirming
Lk. 1:46 and Mary said, My soul doth magnify the *L*
2:11 a Saviour, which is Christ the *L*
6:46 why call ye me, *L*, *L*, and do not the things
24:34 *L* is risen indeed, and hath appeared to
Jn. 6:68 *L*, to whom shall we go? thou hast the
13:13 ye call me Master and *L*: and ye say well
20:20 disciples glad, when they saw the *L*
20:28 Thomas . . said unto him, My *L* and my God
21:7 heard that it was the *L*, he girt his . . coat
Acts 2:36 whom ye have crucified, both *L* and Christ
2:47 *L* added to the church daily such as should
4:24 with one accord, and said, *L*, thou art God
9:5 (22:8; 26:15) who art thou, *L*? And the *L* said
11:21 number believed, and turned unto the *L*
17:24 *L* of heaven and earth, dwelleth not in
17:27 seek the *L*, if haply they might feel
Rom. 10:12 the same *L* over all is rich unto all
14:8 the *L*; and whether we die, we die unto the *L*
14:9 he might be *L* both of the dead and living
1 Cor. 1:31 that glorieth, let him glory in the *L*
2:8 they would not have crucified the *L* of glory
6:14 and God hath both raised up the *L*, and will
7:12 but to the rest speak I, not the *L*
7:32 careth for things that belong to the *L*
10:22 do we provoke the *L* to jealousy?
11:20 this is not to eat the *L*'s supper
12:3 no man can say that Jesus is the *L*, but by
15:47 the second man is the *L* from heaven
2 Cor. 3:17 where the Spirit of the *L* is, there is
Eph. 4:5 one *L*, one faith, one baptism
6:7 doing service, as to the *L*, and not to men
Phil. 2:11 should confess that Jesus Christ is *L*
4:5 moderation be known unto all . . *L* is at hand
1 Thes. 4:6 that the *L* is the avenger of all such
4:16 *L* himself shall descend from heaven with a
4:17 to meet the *L* in the air . . ever be with the *L*
2 Thes. 3:3 *L* is faithful, who shall stablish you
3:16 now the *L* of peace himself give you peace
1 Tim. 6:15 Potentate . . King of kings, and *L* of *l*
2 Tim. 2:19 seal, The *L* knoweth them that are his
3:11 but out of them all the *L* delivered me
4:8 the *L*, the righteous judge, shall give me
4:17 the *L* stood with me, and strengthened me
Heb. 13:6 we may boldly say, The *L* is my helper
Jas. 4:15 ye ought to say, If the *L* will, we shall
5:11 the end of the *L*; that the *L* is very pitiful
1 Pet. 2:3 ye have tasted that the *L* is gracious
2 Pet. 2:1 (Jude 4) heresies, even denying the *L*
3:9 the *L* is not slack concerning his promise
Jude 14 *L* cometh with ten thousands of his saints
Rev. 1:10 I was in the Spirit on the *L*'s day
4:11 worthy, O *L*, to receive glory and honor
16:5 thou art righteous, O *L*, which art, and wast
17:14 (19:16) for he is *L* of *l*, and King of kings

Lord Jesus *See also* Christ, Christ Jesus, Jesus, Jesus Christ, Lord, Lord Jesus Christ, Messiah, Saviour

Acts 1:21 that the *L J* went in and out among us
7:59 Stephen . . saying, *L J*, receive my spirit

Acts 9:29 he spake boldly in the name of the *L J*
11:20 spake unto the Grecians, preaching the *L J*
19:5 they were baptized in the name of the *L J*
19:17 and the name of the *L J* was magnified
21:13 but also to die . . for the name of the *L J*
Rom. 10:9 shalt confess with thy mouth the *L J*
1 Cor. 11:23 *L J*, the same night . . he was betrayed
Gal. 6:17 for I bear in my body the marks of the *L J*
Col. 3:17 do all in the name of the *L J*, giving
1 Thes. 2:15 who both killed the *L J*, and their own
2 Thes. 1:7 the *L J* shall be revealed from heaven
Rev. 22:20 I come quickly: Amen. Even so, come, *L J*

Lord Jesus Christ *See also* Christ, Christ Jesus, Jesus, Jesus Christ, Lord, Lord Jesus, Messiah, Saviour

Acts 11:17 did unto us, who believed on the *L J C*
15:11 the grace of the *L J C* we shall be saved
15:26 hazarded . . lives for the name of our *L J C*
16:31 believe on the *L J C*, and thou shalt be
20:21 repentance . . and faith toward our *L J C*
28:31 teaching . . things which concern the *L J C*
Rom. 5:1 we have peace with God through our *L J C*
13:14 but put ye on the *L J C*, and make not
1 Cor. 1:7 waiting for the coming of our *L J C*
5:4 in the name of our *L J C* . . gathered together
15:57 giveth us the victory through our *L J C*
2 Cor. 8:9 ye know the grace of our *L J C*, that
Phil. 3:20 also we look for the Saviour, the *L J C*
1 Thes. 2:19 even ye in the presence of our *L J C*
3:13 the coming of our *L J C* with all his saints
5:9 but to obtain salvation by our *L J C*
2 Thes. 1:12 the name of our *L J C* may be glorified
2:14 to the obtaining of the glory of our *L J C*
1 Tim. 6:14 keep . . until the appearing of our *L J C*
2 Pet. 1:8 unfruitful in the knowledge of our *L J C*
1:16 unto you the power and coming of our *L J C*

lord *See also* Master

Gen. 18:12 shall I have pleasure, my *l* being old
27:29 be *l* over thy brethren . . let thy mother's sons
45:9 God hath made me *l* of all Egypt: come down
2 Kgs. 7:2 then a *l* on whose hand the king leaned
Is. 26:13 *l* besides thee have had dominion over us
Jer. 2:31 wherefore say my people, We are *l*
Dan. 5:1 made a great feast to a thousand of his *l*
Mt. 10:24 (Jn. 13:16; 15:20) nor . . servant above his *l*
18:27 *l* of that servant was moved with compassion
25:21 (25:23) *l* said unto him, Well done, thou good
Lk. 12:36 like unto men that wait for their *l*
14:23 *l* said unto the servant, Go out into the
16:8 *l* commended the unjust steward, because he
Jn. 15:15 the servant knoweth not what his *l* doeth
1 Cor. 8:5 as there be gods many, and *l* many
Gal. 4:1 nothing from a servant, though he be *l* of all
1 Pet. 3:6 as Sarah obeyed Abraham, calling him *l*
5:3 neither as being *l* over God's heritage, but

Lordship

Mk. 10:42 (Lk. 22:25) exercise *l* over them

Lose (Lost)

Judg. 18:25 run upon thee, and thou *l* thy life
Eccl. 3:6 a time to get, and a time to *l*
Is. 49:21 I have *l* my children, and am desolate
Mt. 5:13 (Mk. 9:50; Lk. 14:34) salt have *l* his savor
10:39 (16:25; Mk. 8:35; Lk. 9:24; 17:33) findeth his
    life shall *l* it . . *l* his life for my sake shall find it
16:26 (Mk. 8:36; Lk. 9:25) world . . *l* his own soul?

Lk. 15:4 hundred sheep, if he *l* one of them, doth
  15:8 ten pieces of silver, if she *l* one piece
Jn. 6:12 fragments that remain, that nothing be *l*
  6:39 which he hath given me I should *l* nothing
  18:9 of them which thou gavest me have I *l* none
2 Jn. 8 we *l* not those things which we have wrought

Loss

Gen. 31:39 was torn of beasts. . I bare the *l* of it
1 Cor. 3:15 work shall be burned, he shall suffer *l*
Phil. 3:7 gain to me, those I counted *l* for Christ
  3:8 count all things but *l*. . suffered the *l* of all

Lost *See also* Lose

Ex. 22:9 for any manner of *l* thing, which another
Lev. 6:3 or have found that which was *l*, and lieth
1 Kgs. 20:25 like the army that thou hast *l*
Ps. 119:176 I have gone astray like a *l* sheep
Jer. 50:6 my people hath been *l* sheep
Ezek. 34:16 I will seek that which was *l*, and bring
  37:11 our bones are dried, and our hope is *l*
Mt. 10:6 (15:24) to the *l* sheep of the house of Israel
  18:11 (Lk. 19:10) is come to save that which was *l*
Lk. 15:24 (15:32) is alive again; he was *l*, and is found
Jn. 17:12 none of them is *l*, but the son of perdition
2 Cor. 4:3 be hid, it is hid to them that are *l*

Lot

Accompanied Abram to Canaan, Gen. 11:31; 12:5;
separated from Abram, Gen. 13; rescued by Abram,
Gen. 14:1–16; sheltered angels, Gen. 19:1–11; fled to
Zoar, Gen. 19:15–23; Lot and his daughters, Gen.
19:30–38.

Lk. 17:28 as it was in the days of *L*; they did eat
2 Pet. 2:7 delivered just *L*, vexed with the filthy

Lot *See also* Portion

Lev. 16:8 Aaron shall cast *l* upon the two goats
Num. 26:55 land shall be divided by *l*
  34:13 this is the land which ye shall inherit by *l*
Josh. 13:6 divide thou it by *l* unto the Israelites
1 Sam. 14:42 cast *l* between me and Jonathan my son
1 Chr. 16:18 (Ps. 105:11) the *l* of your inheritance
Ps. 16:5 and of my cup: thou maintainest my *l*
  22:18 (Mt. 27:35; Mk. 15:24; Lk. 23:34; Jn. 19:24)
  and cast *l* upon my vesture
  125:3 shall not rest upon the *l* of the righteous
Prov. 1:14 cast in thy *l* among us; let us all have
  16:33 the *l* is cast into the lap; but the whole
  18:18 *l* causeth contentions to cease, and parteth
Jer. 13:25 is thy *l*, the portion of thy measures
Dan. 12:13 stand in thy *l* at the end of thy days
Joel 3:3 they have cast *l* for my people; and have
Obad. 11 into his gates, and cast *l* upon Jerusalem
Jon. 1:7 so they cast *l*, and the *l* fell upon Jonah
Lk. 1:9 priest's office, his *l* was to burn incense
Acts 1:26 their *l*; and the *l* fell upon Matthias
  8:21 thou hast neither part nor *l* in this matter

Love *See also* Affection, Charity, Compassion, Heart

Gen. 25:28 Isaac *l* Esau, because he did eat. . venison
  29:20 but a few days, for the *l* he had to her
  34:3 soul clave unto Dinah. . and he *l* the damsel
  37:3 Israel *l* Joseph more than all his children
Ex. 20:6 (Deut. 5:10) unto thousands. . that *l* me
Lev. 19:18 (Mt. 5:43; 19:19; 22:39; Mk. 12:31; Lk.
  10:27; Rom. 13:9; Gal. 5:14; Jas. 2:8) thou shalt
  l thy neighbor as thyself
Deut. 6:5 (Mt. 22:37; Mk. 12:30; Lk. 10:27) thou
  shalt *l* the LORD thy God with all thine heart

Deut. 7:7 LORD did not set his *l* upon you, nor
  choose
  10:12 to walk in all his ways, and to *l* him
  10:19 *l* ye. . the stranger: for ye were strangers
  11:1 thou shalt *l* the LORD thy God, and keep his
  11:13 command you. . *l* the LORD your God
  13:3 proveth you, to know whether ye *l* the LORD
  19:9 which I command thee this day, to *l* the LORD
  23:5 unto thee, because the LORD thy God *l* thee
  30:16 *l* the LORD thy God, to walk in his ways
1 Sam. 18:1 (18:3; 20:17) Jonathan *l* him as his own
2 Sam. 1:26 *l* to me was wonderful, passing the *l* of
  13:1 Tamar; and Amnon the son of David *l* her
1 Kgs. 3:3 Solomon *l* the LORD, walking in the
  11:1 but king Solomon *l* many strange women
2 Chr. 2:11 because the LORD hath *l* his people
  19:2 the ungodly, and *l* them that hate the LORD?
Neh. 1:5 covenant and mercy for them that *l* him
Ps. 4:2 will ye *l* vanity, and seek after leasing?
  5:11 them also that *l* thy name be joyful in thee
  18:1 I will *l* thee, O LORD, my strength
  31:23 O *l* the LORD, all ye his saints: for the
  37:28 the LORD *l* judgment, and forsaketh not his
  45:7 (Heb. 1:9) *l* righteousness. . hatest wickedness
  69:36 they that *l* his name shall dwell therein
  91:14 he hath set his *l* upon me, therefore will
  97:10 ye that *l* the LORD, hate evil
  116:1 I *l* the LORD, because he hath heard my voice
  119:97 O how I *l* thy law! it is my meditation
  119:165 great peace have they which I *l* thy law
  122:6 Jerusalem: they shall prosper that *l* thee
  145:20 the LORD preserveth all them that *l* him
Prov. 3:12 (Heb. 12:6) whom. . LORD *l* he correcteth
  4:6 preserve thee: *l* her, and she shall keep thee
  7:18 let us take our fill of *l* until the morning
  8:17 I *l* them that *l* me; and those that seek me
  9:8 rebuke a wise man, and he will *l* thee
  10:12 stirreth up strifes: but *l* covereth all sins
  12:1 whoso *l* instruction *l* knowledge
  15:17 better is a dinner of herbs where *l* is
  17:9 he that covereth a transgression seeketh *l*
  17:17 a friend *l* at all times, and a brother is
  21:17 *l* pleasure shall be a poor man: he that *l*
  22:11 he that *l* pureness of heart, for the grace
  27:5 open rebuke is better than secret *l*
  29:3 whoso *l* wisdom rejoiceth his father
Eccl. 3:8 a time to *l*, and a time to hate
  5:10 *l* silver shall not be satisfied with silver
Song 1:2 his mouth: for thy *l* is better than wine
  1:15 (4:1) thou art fair, my *l*; behold, thou art fair
  2:4 banqueting house. . his banner over me was *l*
  8:6 *l* is strong as death; jealousy is cruel as
  8:7 many waters cannot quench *l*, neither can the
Is. 38:17 thou hast in *l* to my soul delivered it
  48:14 LORD hath *l* him: he will do his pleasure
  61:8 I the LORD *l* judgment, I hate robbery for
  63:9 in his *l* and in his pity he redeemed them
Jer. 31:3 yea, I have *l* thee with an everlasting *l*
Ezek. 23:11 more corrupt in her inordinate *l* than
Hos. 11:4 with cords of a man, with bands of *l*
  14:4 heal their backsliding, I will *l* them freely
Amos 5:15 and *l* the good, and establish judgment
Mic. 6:8 but to do justly, and to *l* mercy
Zeph. 3:17 he will rest in his *l*, he will joy over
Zech. 8:19 cheerful feasts; therefore *l* the truth
Mal. 1:2, 3 (Rom. 9:13) I have *l* you. . I *l* Jacob
Mt. 5:44 (Lk. 6:27, 35) *l* your enemies
  6:24 (Lk. 16:13) will hate the one, and *l* the other
  10:37 is not worthy of me: and he that *l* son or
  24:12 shall abound, the *l* of many shall wax cold
Mk. 10:21 then Jesus beholding him *l* him
Lk. 7:5 for he *l* our nation, and he hath built us
  7:42 therefore, which of them will *l* him most?

Lk. 7:47 whom little is forgiven, the same *l* little
11:42 pass over judgment and the *l* of God
Jn. 3:16 God so *l* the world, that he gave his only
3:19 men *l* darkness rather than light, because
3:35 Father *l* the Son, and hath given all things
5:20 Father *l* the Son, and showeth him all things
5:42 that ye have not the *l* of God in you
8:42 if God were your Father, ye would *l* me
10:17 my Father *l* me, because I lay down my life
11:3 Lord, behold, he whom thou *l* is sick
11:5 Jesus *l* Martha, and her sister, and Lazarus
11:36 then said the Jews, Behold how he *l* him!
12:25 he that *l* his life shall lose it
13:1 having *l* his own. . he *l* them unto the end
13:23 bosom one of his disciples, whom Jesus *l*
13:34 (15:12, 17) *l* one another; as I have *l* you
14:15 if ye *l* me, keep my commandments
14:21 *l* me shall be *l* of my Father, and I will *l*
14:23 if a man *l* me. . my Father will *l* him
15:9 *l* me, so have I *l* you: continue ye in my *l*
15:13 greater *l* hath no man than this, that a
16:27 Father himself *l* you, because ye have *l* me
17:23 sent me, and hast *l* them, as thou hast *l* me
17:24 *l* me before the foundation of the world
17:26 *l* wherewith thou hast *l* me may be in them
21:15 son of Jonas, *l* thou me more than these?
Rom. 5:5 *l* of God is shed abroad in our hearts by
5:8 but God commendeth his *l* toward us, in that
8:28 work together for good to them that *l* God
8:35 who shall separate us from the *l* of Christ?
8:37 more than conquerors through him that *l* us
8:39 be able to separate us from the *l* of God
9:13 Jacob have I *l*, but Esau have I hated
12:9 let *l* be without dissimulation. Abhor that
13:8 *l* one another: for he that *l* another hath
13:10 *l* worketh no ill. . *l* is the fulfilling of
1 Cor. 2:9 God hath prepared for them that *l* him
8:3 if any man *l* God, the same is known of him
16:22 if any man *l* not the LORD Jesus Christ, let
2 Cor. 2:4 know the *l* which I have more abundantly
5:14 *l* of Christ constraineth us; because
6:6 kindness, by the Holy Ghost, by *l* unfeigned
8:8 and to prove the sincerity of your *l*
9:7 or of necessity: for God *l* a cheerful giver
12:15 more abundantly I *l* you, the less I be *l*
13:14 and the *l* of God, and the communion of the
Gal. 2:20 Son of God, who *l* me, and gave himself
5:6 uncircumcision; but faith which worketh by *l*
5:13 to the flesh, but by *l* serve one another
5:22 the fruit of the Spirit is *l*, joy, peace
Eph. 2:4 mercy, for his great *l* wherewith he *l* us
3:17 that ye, being rooted and grounded in *l*
3:19 and to know the *l* of Christ, which passeth
4:2 long-suffering, forbearing one another in *l*
4:15 but speaking the truth in *l*, may grow up
5:2 and walk in *l*, as Christ also hath *l* us
5:25 (Col. 3:19) husbands, *l* your wives
Phil. 1:9 that your *l* may abound yet more and more
1:17 but the other of *l*, knowing that I am set
2:2 ye be likeminded, having the same *l*, being
Col. 1:4 the *l* which ye have to all the saints
2:2 be comforted, being knit together in *l*
1 Thes. 1:3 your work of faith, and labor of *l*
3:12 increase and abound in *l* one toward another
4:9 brotherly *l* ye need not that I write
5:8 putting on the breastplate of faith and *l*
2 Thes. 2:10 they received not the *l* of the truth
2:16 hath *l* us, and hath given us everlasting
1 Tim. 6:10 the *l* of money is the root of all evil
2 Tim. 1:7 spirit of fear; but of power, and of *l*
4:8 unto all them also that *l* his appearing
Tit. 2:4 to *l* their husbands, to *l* their children
3:4 and *l* of God our Saviour toward man appeared

Phlm. 5 hearing of thy *l* and faith, which thou hast
Heb. 6:10 to forget your work and labor of *l*
10:24 consider one another to provoke unto *l*
13:1 let brotherly *l* continue
Jas. 1:12 Lord hath promised to them that *l* him
1 Pet. 1:8 whom having not seen, ye *l*
1:22 *l* one another with a pure heart fervently
2:17 honor all men. *L* the brotherhood. Fear God
1 Jn. 2:5 in him verily is the *l* of God perfected
2:10 he that *l* his brother abideth in the light
2:15 *l* not the world, neither the things that
3:1 what manner of *l* the Father hath bestowed
3:11 the message. . that we should *l* one another
3:14 death unto life, because we *l* the brethren
3:16 hereby perceive we the *l* of God, because he
3:18 let us not *l* in word, neither in tongue
3:23 *l* one another, as he gave us commandment
4:7 let us *l* one another for *l* is of God
4:8 he that *l* not, knoweth not God; for God is *l*
4:10 is *l*, not that we *l* God, but that he *l* us
4:16 God is *l*. . dwelleth in *l* dwelleth in God
4:18 no fear in *l*; but perfect *l* casteth out fear
4:19 we *l* him, because he first *l* us
4:21 that he who *l* God *l* his brother also
5:1 *l* him that begat *l* him also that is begotten
5:2 that we *l* the children of God, when we *l* God
2 Jn. 5 a new commandment. . that we *l* one another
Jude 21 keep yourselves in the *l* of God, looking
Rev. 1:5 unto him that *l* us, and washed us from
2:4 because thou hast left thy first *l*
3:19 as many as I *l*, I rebuke and chasten
12:11 and they *l* not their lives unto the death

Lovely

2 Sam. 1:23 Saul and Jonathan were *l* and pleasant
Song 5:16 is most sweet: yea, he is altogether *l*
Ezek. 33:32 thou art unto them as a very *l* song
Phil. 4:8 pure, whatsoever things are *l*, whatsoever

Lover

1 Kgs. 5:1 for Hiram was ever a *l* of David
Ps. 88:18 *l* and friend hast thou put far from me
Jer. 4:30 thyself fair; thy *l* will despise thee
22:20 pastors, and thy *l* shall go into captivity
30:14 *l* have forgotten thee; they seek thee not
Ezek. 16:33 but thou givest thy gifts to all thy *l*
23:22 behold, I will raise up thy *l* against thee
Hos. 2:5 I will go after my *l*, that give me my
8:9 gone up to Assyria. . Ephraim hath hired *l*
2 Tim. 3:2 for men shall be *l* of their own selves
3:4 *l* of pleasures more than *l* of God
Tit. 1:8 but a *l* of hospitality, a *l* of good men

Loving-kindness *See also* Kindness, Mercy

Ps. 17:7 show thy marvelous *l-k*, O thou that savest
25:6 remember. . thy tender mercies and thy *l-k*
26:3 for thy *l-k* is before mine eyes: and I have
36:7 how excellent is thy *l-k*, O God! therefore
36:10 O continue thy *l-k* unto them that know thee
40:10 I have not concealed thy *l-k* and thy truth
42:8 the LORD will command his *l-k* in the daytime
51:1 mercy upon me, O God, according to thy *l-k*
63:3 because thy *l-k* is better than life, my lips
69:16 hear me, O LORD; for thy *l-k* is good
88:11 shall thy *l-k* be declared in the grave?
89:33 my *l-k* will not utterly take from him
92:2 to show forth thy *l-k* in the morning
103:4 crowneth thee with *l-k* and tender mercies
107:43 they shall understand the *l-k* of the LORD
119:88 quicken me after thy *l-k* so shall I keep
143:8 cause me to hear thy *l-k* in the morning

Is. 63:7 I will mention the *l-k* of the LORD
Jer. 9:24 I am the LORD which exercise *l-k*, judgment
16:5 taken away my peace. . even *l-k* and mercies
31:3 therefore with *l-k* have I drawn thee
32:18 *l-k* unto thousands, not recompensest

Low (Lower, Lowest)

Deut. 28:43 high; and thou shalt come down very *l*
32:22 mine anger, and shall burn unto the *l* hell
1 Sam. 2:7 he bringeth *l*, and lifteth up
1 Kgs. 12:31 made priests of the *l* of the people
Ps. 8:5 (Heb. 2:7) made him a little *l* than the angels
49:2 both *l* and high, rich and poor, together
63:9 shall go into the *l* parts of the earth
86:13 hast delivered my soul from the *l* hell
88:6 thou hast laid me in the *l* pit, in darkness
136:23 who remembered us in our *l* estate
Prov. 29:23 a man's pride shall bring him *l*
Eccl. 12:4 daughters of music shall be brought *l*
Is. 22:9 gathered together the waters of the *l* pool
26:5 lofty city, he layeth it *l*; he layeth it *l*
32:19 and the city shall be *l* in a *l* place
44:23 shout, ye *l* parts of the earth: break forth
Ezek. 17:24 the high tree, have exalted the *l* tree
40:18 pavement by the side. . was the *l* pavement
Lk. 14:9 thou begin with shame to take the *l* room
Rom. 12:16 condescend to men of *l* estate
Eph. 4:9 he also descended first into the *l* parts
Heb. 2:9 see Jesus, who was made a little *l* than
Jas. 1:9 let the brother of *l* degree rejoice in
1:10 but the rich, in that he is made *l*

Low (verb)

1 Sam. 6:12 *l* as they went, and turned not aside
Job 6:5 he hath grass? or *l* the ox over his fodder?

Lowing

1 Sam. 15:14 what meaneth then. . the *l* of the oxen

Lowliness

Eph. 4:2 all *l* and meekness, with long-suffering
Phil. 2:3 but in *l* of mind let each esteem other

Lowly *See also* Humble

Ps. 138:6 be high, yet hath he respect unto the *l*
Prov. 3:34 but he giveth grace unto the *l*
11:2 then cometh shame: but with the *l* is wisdom
16:19 to be of an humble spirit with the *l*, than
Zech. 9:9 he is just. . *l*, and riding upon an ass
Mt. 11:29 learn of me; for I am meek and *l* in heart

Lucifer Is. 14:12

Lucre

1 Sam. 8:3 turned aside after *l*, and took bribes
1 Tim. 3:3 (3:8; Tit. 1:7) not greedy of filthy *l*
Tit. 1:11 which they ought not, for filthy *l*'s sake
1 Pet. 5:2 not for filthy *l*, but of a ready mind

Luke

Col. 4:14 *L*, the beloved physician, and Demas
2 Tim. 4:11 only *L* is with me

Lukewarm

Rev. 3:16 thou art *l*, and neither cold nor hot

Lump

2 Kgs. 20:7 (Is. 38:21) said, Take a *l* of figs
Rom. 9:21 the same *l* to make one vessel unto honor
11:16 the firstfruit be holy, the *l* is also holy
1 Cor. 5:6 (Gal. 5:9) leaven leaveneth the whole *l*

Lunatic

Mt. 4:24 were *l*, and those that had the palsy
17:15 Lord, have mercy on my son; for he is *l*

Lurk

Prov. 1:11 *l* privily for the innocent without cause
1:18 they *l* privily for their own lives

Lust *See also* Desire, Pleasure

Ex. 15:9 spoil; my *l* shall be satisfied upon them
Deut. 12:15 kill and eat. . whatsoever thy soul *l*
Ps. 81:12 I gave them up unto their own hearts' *l*
Prov. 6:25 *l* not after her beauty in thine heart
Mt. 5:28 whosoever looketh on a woman to *l* after
Mk. 4:19 *l* of other things entering in, choke the
Jn. 8:44 and the *l* of your father ye will do
Rom. 1:27 burned in their *l* one toward another
6:12 that ye should obey it in the *l* thereof
7:7 I had not known *l*, except the law had said
13:14 provision for the flesh, to fulfil the *l*
1 Cor. 10:6 not *l* after evil things, as they also *l*
Gal. 5:16 ye shall not fulfil the *l* of the flesh
5:17 flesh *l* against the Spirit, and the Spirit
Eph. 2:3 in times past in the *l* of our flesh
1 Tim. 6:9 foolish and hurtful *l*, which drown men
2 Tim. 2:22 flee also youthful *l*: but follow
Tit. 2:12 denying ungodliness and worldly *l*
3:3 deceived, serving divers *l* and pleasures
Jas. 1:14 is drawn away of his own *l*, and enticed
1:15 when *l* hath conceived, it bringeth forth sin
4:1 even of your *l* that war in your members?
4:2 ye *l*, and have not: ye kill, and desire to
4:5 the spirit that dwelleth in us *l* to envy?
1 Pet. 1:14 according to the former *l* in your
2:11 abstain from fleshly *l*, which war against
4:2 live. . in the flesh to the *l* of men
2 Pet. 1:4 the corruption. . in the world through *l*
2:18 they allure through the *l* of the flesh
1 Jn. 2:16 *l* of the flesh, and the *l* of the eyes
2:17 the world passeth away, and the *l* thereof
Jude 16 complainers, walking after their own *l*
18 who should walk after their own ungodly *l*
Rev. 18:14 fruits that thy soul *l* after are departed

Lydia Acts 16:14, 40

Lying *See also* False, Falsehood, Lie, Wrong

1 Kgs. 22:22 (2 Chr. 18:21) be a *l* spirit in the mouth
Ps. 31:18 let the *l* lips be put to silence
109:2 they have spoken against me with a *l* tongue
119:29 remove from me the way of *l*: and grant me
119:163 I hate and abhor *l*: but thy law do I love
Prov. 6:17 proud look, a *l* tongue, and hands that
12:19 but a *l* tongue is but for a moment
12:22 *l* lips are abomination to the LORD
13:5 a righteous man hateth *l*: but a wicked man
21:6 the getting of treasures by a *l* tongue is a
Is. 30:9 this is a rebellious people, *l* children
59:13 in transgressing and *l* against the LORD
Jer. 7:4 trust ye not in *l* words, saying, The temple
Dan. 2:9 for ye have prepared *l* and corrupt words
Eph. 4:25 putting away *l*, speak every man truth
2 Thes. 2:9 with all power and signs and *l* wonders

Lystra

Acts 14:6 they were ware of it, and fled unto *L*
14:21 taught many, they returned again to *L*
16:1 then came he to Derbe and *L*: and, behold
2 Tim. 3:11 at *L*; what persecutions I endured

M

Macedonia

Acts 16:9 saying, Come over into *M*, and help us
Rom. 15:26 it hath pleased them of *M* and Achaia to
2 Cor. 8:1 the grace . . bestowed on the churches of *M*

Machpelah Gen. 23:9; 50:13

Mad

Deut. 28:34 shalt be *m* for the sight of thine eyes
1 Sam. 21:13 and feigned himself *m* in their hands
Ps. 102:8 are *m* against me are sworn against me
Eccl. 2:2 said of laughter, It is *m*: and of mirth
Jer. 51:7 of her wine; therefore the nations are *m*
Hos. 9:7 prophet is a fool, the spiritual man is *m*
Jn. 10:20 hath a devil, and is *m*; why hear ye him?
Acts 12:15 they said unto her, Thou art *m*. But she
  26:11 exceedingly *m* against them, I persecuted
  26:24 Paul . . much learning doth make thee *m*
1 Cor. 14:23 will they not say that ye are *m*?

Made *See also* Make

Gal. 4:4 his Son, *m* of a woman, *m* under the law

Madness

Deut. 28:28 the LORD shall smite thee with *m*
Eccl. 2:12 I turned myself to behold wisdom, and *m*
  9:3 *m* is in their heart while they live
  10:13 and the end of his talk is mischievous *m*
Zech. 12:4 smite every horse . . and his rider with *m*
Lk. 6:11 and they were filled with *m*; and communed
2 Pet. 2:16 dumb ass . . forbade the *m* of the prophet

Magician *See also* Soothsayer, Sorcerer

Gen. 41:8 called for all the *m* of Egypt, and all
Ex. 7:11 (7:22; 8:7, 18) *m* of Egypt . . in like manner
  9:11 *m* could not stand before Moses because of
Dan. 2:2 then the king commanded to call the *m*

Magistrate

Judg. 18:7 there was no *m* in the land, that might
Lk. 12:11 bring you unto . . synagogues, and unto *m*
  12:58 thou goest with thine adversary to the *m*
Acts 16:22 *m* rent off their clothes, and commanded
Tit. 3:1 to obey *m*, to be ready to every good work

Magnificence

Acts 19:27 despised, and her *m* should be destroyed

Magnificent *See also* Excellent, Noble

1 Chr. 22:5 house . . must be exceeding *m*

Magnify *See also* Exalt, Glorify, Praise

Gen. 19:19 in thy sight, and thou hast *m* thy mercy
Josh. 3:7 Joshua, This day will I begin to *m* thee
2 Sam. 7:26 (1 Chr. 17:24) let thy name be *m* for ever
1 Chr. 29:25 and the LORD *m* Solomon exceedingly
2 Chr. 32:23 he was *m* in the sight of all nations
Job 7:17 what is man, that thou shouldest *m* him?
Ps. 34:3 O *m* the LORD with me, and let us exalt
  35:26 dishonor that *m* themselves against me
  35:27 (40:16; 70:4) say continually . . LORD be *m*
  138:2 thou hast *m* thy word above all thy name
Is. 42:21 he will *m* the law, and make it honorable
Jer. 48:26 for he *m* himself against the LORD
Ezek. 38:23 will I *m* myself, and sanctify myself
Dan. 11:36 *m* himself above every god, and shall
Mal. 1:5 LORD will be *m* from the border of Israel
Lk. 1:46 and Mary said, My soul doth *m* the Lord
Acts 5:13 but the people *m* them
  10:46 heard them speak with tongues, and *m* God

Acts 19:17 and the name of the LORD Jesus was *m*
Rom. 11:13 apostle of the Gentiles, I *m* mine office
Phil. 1:20 so now also Christ shall be *m* in my body

Magog Ezek. 38:2; Rev. 20:8

Maher-shalal-hash-baz Is 8:1

Maid *See also* Damsel, Girl, Handmaid, Maiden

Gen. 16:3 Sarai, Abram's wife, took Hagar her *m*
Ex. 2:5 she saw the ark . . she sent her *m* to fetch it
2 Kgs. 5:2 a little *m*; and she waited on Naaman's
Esth. 2:7 *m* was fair and beautiful; whom Mordecai
Job 31:1 why then should I think upon a *m*?
Prov. 30:19 and the way of a man with a *m*
Amos 2:7 and his father will go in unto the same *m*
Mt. 9:24 the *m* is not dead, but sleepeth
  26:71 (Mk. 14:69; Lk. 22:56) another *m* saw him

Maiden *See also* Damsel, Girl, Handmaid, Maid, Virgin

Ruth 2:8 but abide here fast by my *m*
Ps. 123:2 as the eyes of a *m* unto the hand of her
  148:12 young men, and *m*; old men, and children
Prov. 9:3 she hath sent forth her *m*: she crieth
Lk. 12:45 begin to beat the menservants and *m*

Maidservant

Ex. 20:17 not covet thy neighbor's wife . . nor his *m*
  21:7 if a man sell his daughter to be a *m*, she
2 Sam. 6:22 and of the *m* which thou hast spoken of

Maimed

Mt. 15:31 saw the dumb to speak, the *m* to be whole
  18:8 (Mk. 9:43) better . . to enter into life halt or *m*
Lk. 14:13 makest a feast, call the poor, the *m*
  14:21 bring in hither the poor, and the *m*, and

Maintain

1 Kgs. 8:45 their supplication, and *m* their cause
  8:59 that he *m* the cause of his servant
1 Chr. 26:27 dedicate to *m* the house of the LORD
Job 13:15 but I will *m* mine own ways before him
Ps. 9:4 for thou hast *m* my right and my cause
  16:5 portion of mine inheritance . . thou *m* my lot
Tit. 3:8 might be careful to *m* good works

Maintenance

Ezra 4:14 because we have *m* from the king's palace
Prov. 27:27 thy food . . for the *m* for thy maidens

Majesty *See also* Glory, Greatness

1 Chr. 29:11 thine, O LORD, is . . the victory, and . . *m*
  29:25 bestowed upon him such royal *m* as had not
Job 37:22 out of the north: with God is terrible *m*
  40:10 deck thyself now with *m* and excellency
Ps. 29:4 the voice of the LORD is full of *m*
  93:1 the LORD reigneth, he is clothed with *m*
  96:6 honor and *m* are before him: strength and
  104:1 thou art clothed with honor and *m*
  145:5 will speak of the glorious honor of thy *m*
  145:12 mighty acts . . glorious *m* of his kingdom
Is. 2:10 fear of the LORD, and for the glory of his *m*
Dan. 4:36 and excellent *m* was added unto me
Mic. 5:4 in the *m* of the name of the LORD his God
Heb. 1:3 (8:1) on the right hand of the *M* on high
2 Pet. 1:16 but were eyewitnesses of his *m*
Jude 25 be glory and *m*, dominion and power, both

Make (Made) *See also* Create, Fashion, Form, Invent, Shape

Gen. 1:31 and God saw every thing that he had *m*
Ex. 4:11 who hath *m* man's mouth . . who *m* the dumb
20:11 (31:17) six days the LORD *m* heaven and
32:1 (Acts 7:40) *m* us gods, which shall go before
Deut. 32:6 hath he not *m* thee, and established thee?
Judg. 18:3 and what *m* thou in this place?
Job 10:8 thine hands have *m* me and fashioned me
31:15 did not he that *m* me in the womb *m* him?
Ps. 8:5 (Heb. 2:7) *m* him a little lower than the angels
89:47 wherefore hast thou *m* all men in vain?
95:5 the sea is his, and he *m* it: and his hands
100:3 he that hath *m* us, and not we ourselves
104:24 thy works! in wisdom hast thou *m* them all
118:24 this is the day which the LORD hath *m*
139:14 for I am fearfully and wonderfully *m*
146:6 (Acts 4:24) which *m* heaven, and earth
149:2 let Israel rejoice in him that *m* him
Prov. 16:4 the LORD hath *m* all things for himself
Eccl. 3:11 no man can find out the work that God *m*
7:29 that God hath *m* man upright; but they have
Is. 29:16 work say of him that *m* it, He *m* me not?
44:2 thus saith the LORD that *m* thee, and formed
66:2 (Acts 7:50) all those things hath mine hand *m*
Jn. 1:3 without him was not any thing *m* that was *m*
8:53 the prophets are dead: whom *m* thou thyself?
10:33 because . . thou, being a man, *m* thyself God
19:7 to die, because he *m* himself the Son of God
Acts 17:24 God that *m* the world and all things
17:26 hath *m* of one blood all nations of men
Rom. 1:20 understood by the things that are *m*
9:28 a short work will the Lord *m* upon the earth
1 Cor. 9:22 I am *m* all things to all men, that I
Heb. 1:2 all things, by whom also he *m* the worlds
8:5 thou *m* all things according to the pattern

Maker

Job 4:17 shall a man be more pure than his *M*?
32:22 in so doing my *M* would soon take me away
35:10 none saith, Where is God my *m*, who giveth
36:3 and will ascribe righteousness to my *M*
Ps. 95:6 let us kneel before the LORD our *M*
Prov. 14:31 oppresseth the poor reproacheth his *M*
22:2 rich and poor . . the LORD is the *m* of them
Is. 17:7 at that day shall a man look to his *M*
45:9 woe unto him that striveth with his *M*!
51:13 and forgettest the LORD thy *M*, that hath
54:5 thy *M* is thine husband; The LORD of hosts
Hos. 8:14 for Israel hath forgotten his *M*
Heb. 11:10 for a city . . whose builder and *m* is God

Makkedah Josh. 10:16

Malchus Jn. 18:10

Male

Gen. 1:27 image of God . . *m* and female created he

Malefactor

Lk. 23:32 two . . *m*, led with him to be put to death
Jn. 18:30 if he were not a *m*, we would not have

Malice

1 Cor. 5:8 leaven, neither with the leaven of *m*
14:20 in *m* be ye children, but in understanding
Eph. 4:31 anger . . be put away from you, with all *m*
Col. 3:8 also put off all these; anger, wrath, *m*
Tit. 3:3 living in *m* and envy, hateful, and hating
1 Pet. 2:1 laying aside all *m*, and all guile, and

Malicious

3 Jn. 10 he doeth, prating against us with *m* words

Maliciousness

Rom. 1:29 covetousness, *m*; full of envy, murder
1 Pet. 2:16 not using . . liberty for a cloak of *m*

Mammon *See also* Money, Riches, Wealth

Mt. 6:24 two masters . . Ye cannot serve God and *m*
Lk. 16:9 make . . friends of the *m* of unrighteousness
16:11 have not been faithful in the unrighteous *m*

Mamre Gen. 13:18

Man *See also* Man of God, Adam, Men, Son of Man

Gen. 1:26 God said, Let us make *m* in our image
2:7 LORD God formed *m* of the dust of the ground
3:24 so he drove out the *m*: and he placed at the
Ex. 33:20 for there shall no *m* see me, and live
Num. 23:19 God is not a *m*, that he should lie
Deut. 5:24 God doth talk with *m*, and he liveth
8:3 (Mt. 4:4; Lk. 4:4) *m* doth not live by bread only
Josh. 10:14 LORD hearkened unto the voice of a *m*
1 Sam. 13:14 sought him a *m* after his own heart
15:29 for he is not a *m*, that he should repent
16:7 *m* looketh on the outward appearance, but
2 Sam. 12:7 Nathan said to David, Thou art the *m*
24:14 and let me not fall into the hand of *m*
1 Kgs. 2:2 be thou strong . . and show thyself a *m*
Job 4:17 mortal *m* be more just than God? shall a *m*
5:7 *m* is born unto trouble, as the sparks fly
7:1 an appointed time to *m* upon earth? are not
7:17 what is *m*, that thou shouldest magnify him?
9:2 a truth: but how should *m* be just with God?
9:32 he is not a *m*, as I am, that I should answer
14:1 *m* that is born of a woman is of few days
14:10 *m* dieth, and wasteth away: yea, *m* giveth up
15:16 how much more abominable and filthy is *m*
32:8 there is a spirit in *m*: and the inspiration
33:12 answer thee, that God is greater than *m*
34:15 shall perish . . *m* shall turn again unto dust
Ps. 8:4 what is *m*, that thou art mindful of him?
39:5 *m* at his best state is altogether vanity
49:12 *m* being in honor abideth not: he is like
56:11 (118:6; Heb. 13:6) afraid what *m* can do
60:11 give us help . . for vain is the help of *m*
90:3 thou turnest *m* to destruction; and sayest
103:15 for *m*, his days are as grass: as a flower
144:4 *m* is like to vanity: his days are as a
Prov. 5:21 the ways of *m* are before the eyes of
30:19 way of a ship . . way of a *m* with a maid
Eccl. 3:19 a *m* hath no preeminence above a beast
7:29 I found, that God hath made *m* upright; but
9:12 *m* also knoweth not his time: as the fishes
Is. 2:22 cease ye from *m*, whose breath is in his
4:1 that day seven women shall take hold of one *m*
13:12 will make a *m* more precious than fine gold
45:12 made the earth, and created *m* upon it
Jer. 10:23 the way of *m* is not in himself . . not in *m*
17:5 trusteth in *m*, and maketh flesh his arm
Ezek. 28:2 yet thou art a *m*, and not God, though
Hos. 11:9 for I am God, and not *m*; the Holy One in
Mt. 8:27 what manner of *m* is this, that even the
12:12 how much then is a *m* better than a sheep?
15:18 forth from the heart; and they defile the *m*
19:6 hath joined together, let not *m* put asunder
Mk. 2:27 sabbath was made for *m*, and not *m* for the
Lk. 18:2 which feared not God, neither regarded *m*

Jn. 2:25 testify of *m*; for he knew what was in *m*
7:46 officers answered, Never *m* spake like this *m*
10:33 that thou, being a *m*, makest thyself God
19:5 and Pilate saith unto them, Behold the *m*
Acts 10:26 saying, Stand up; I myself also am a *m*
13:38 through this *m* is preached unto you
17:31 by that *m* whom he hath ordained
Rom. 1:23 into an image made like to corruptible *m*
6:6 our old *m* is crucified with him, that the
7:22 delight in the law of God after the inward *m*
7:24 O wretched *m* that I am! who shall deliver me
1 Cor. 2:11 what *m* knoweth the things of a *m*, save
11:3 and the head of the woman is the *m*
11:8 *m* is not of the woman; but . . woman of the *m*
13:11 became a *m*, I put away childish things
15:21 since by *m* came death, by *m* came also the
15:45 the first *m* Adam was made a living soul
15:47 first *m* is of the earth, earthy . . second *m*
2 Cor. 4:16 outward *m* perish, yet the inward *m* is
Gal. 1:12 I neither received it of *m*, neither was
Eph. 3:16 with might by his Spirit in the inner *m*
4:13 unto a perfect *m*, unto the measure of the
4:24 that ye put on the new *m*, which after God
Phil. 2:8 found in fashion as a *m*, he humbled
Col. 3:9 ye have put off the old *m* with his deeds
2 Thes. 2:3 and that *m* of sin be revealed
1 Tim. 2:5 and one mediator . . the *m* Christ Jesus
Tit. 3:4 love of God our Saviour toward *m* appeared

Man of God *See also* Man

Josh. 14:6 that the LORD said unto Moses the *m* of *G*
Judg. 13:6 a *m* of *G* came unto me . . his countenance
1 Sam. 2:27 there came a *m* of *G* unto Eli, and said
9:6 behold now, there is in this city a *m* of *G*
1 Kgs. 13:1 there came a *m* of *G* out of Judah
17:24 now by this I know that thou art a *m* of *G*
20:28 came a *m* of *G*, and spake unto the king
2 Kgs. 1:10 if I be a *m* of *G* . . let fire come down
4:9 I perceive that this is a holy *m* of *G*
2 Chr. 8:14 for so had David the *m* of *G* commanded
25:7 there came a *m* of *G* to him, saying, O king
1 Tim. 6:11 but thou, O *m* of *G*, flee these things
2 Tim. 3:17 the *m* of *G* may be perfect, thoroughly

Manasseh (Manasses) son of Joseph

Gen. 41:51 Joseph called . . the firstborn *M*: For God
48:20 and as *M*: and he set Ephraim before *M*
Josh. 16:4 *M* and Ephraim, took their inheritance
1 Chr. 12:19 there fell some of *M* to David, when
Ps. 60:7 Gilead is mine, and *M* is mine; Ephraim
Is. 9:21 *M*, Ephraim; and Ephraim, *M* . . they together

Manasseh king of Judah

2 Kgs. 21:1–18 (2 Chr. 33:1–20)
Jer. 15:4 cause them to be removed . . because of *M*

Mandrake

Gen. 30:14 Reuben went . . and found *m* in the field
Song 7:13 the *m* give a smell, and at our gates are

Manger

Lk. 2:7 laid him in a *m*; because there was no room

Manifest *See also* Evident, Show

Eccl. 3:18 sons of men, that God might *m* them
Mk. 4:22 is nothing hid, which shall not be *m*
Jn. 1:31 but that he should be made *m* to Israel
2:11 in Cana of Galilee, and *m* forth his glory
3:21 to the light, that his deeds may be made *m*
9:3 the works of God should be made *m* in him
14:21 I will love him, and will *m* myself to him
14:22 *m* thyself unto us, and not unto the world?

Jn. 17:6 I have *m* thy name unto the men which thou
Acts 4:16 is *m* to all them that dwell in Jerusalem
Rom. 1:19 which may be known of God is *m* in them
3:21 righteousness of God without the law is *m*
16:26 but now is made *m*, and by the Scriptures
1 Cor. 3:13 every man's work shall be made *m*
4:5 and will make *m* the counsels of the hearts
14:25 thus are the secrets of his heart made *m*
15:27 put under him, it is *m* that he is excepted
2 Cor. 2:14 maketh *m* the savor of his knowledge by
4:10 life . . of Jesus might be made *m* in our body
5:11 made *m* unto God . . *m* in your consciences
Gal. 5:19 the works of the flesh are *m*, which are
Eph. 5:13 by the light . . whatsoever doth make *m*
Phil. 1:13 so that my bonds in Christ are *m* in all
Col. 1:26 hid . . but now is made *m* to his saints
4:4 that I may make it *m*, as I ought to speak
2 Thes. 1:5 a *m* token of the righteous judgment of
1 Tim. 3:16 God was *m* in the flesh, justified in
5:25 the good works of some are *m* beforehand
2 Tim. 1:10 is now made *m* by the appearing of our
Heb. 4:13 any creature that is not *m* in his sight
1 Pet. 1:20 but was *m* in these last times for you
1 Jn. 1:2 for the life was *m*, and we have seen it
3:5 ye know that he was *m* to take away our sins
4:9 in this was *m* the love of God toward us

Manifestation

Rom. 8:19 waiteth for the *m* of the sons of God
1 Cor. 12:7 the *m* of the Spirit is given to every

Manifold

Neh. 9:19 thou in thy *m* mercies forsookest them not
Ps. 104:24 O LORD, how *m* are thy works! in wisdom
Amos 5:12 I know your *m* transgressions and your
Lk. 18:30 receive *m* more in this present time, and
Eph. 3:10 known by the church the *m* wisdom of God
1 Pet. 1:6 are in heaviness through *m* temptations
4:10 as good stewards of the *m* grace of God

Mankind

Lev. 18:22 thou shalt not lie with *m*, as with
Job 12:10 living thing, and the breath of all *m*
1 Tim. 1:10 for them that defile themselves with *m*

Manna

Ex. 16:15 it is *m*: for they wist not what it was
16:35 children of Israel did eat *m* forty years
Num. 11:7 *m* was as coriander seed, and the color
Deut. 8:3 suffered thee to hunger . . fed thee with *m*
Josh. 5:12 the *m* ceased on the morrow after they
Neh. 9:20 withheldest not thy *m* from their mouth
Ps. 78:24 and had rained down *m* upon them to eat
Jn. 6:31 our fathers did eat *m* in the desert
6:58 not as your fathers did eat *m*, and are dead
Heb. 9:4 wherein was the golden pot that had *m*
Rev. 2:17 will I give to eat of the hidden *m*

Manner *See also* Behavior

1 Sam. 8:11 will be the *m* of the king that shall reign
10:25 told the people the *m* of the kingdom
2 Sam. 7:19 and is this the *m* of man, O Lord GOD?
Mt. 8:27 what *m* of man is this, that even the winds
Lk. 1:66 saying, What *m* of child shall this be?
9:55 ye know not what *m* of spirit ye are of
Acts 13:18 suffered he their *m* in the wilderness
17:2 Paul, as his *m* was, went in unto them
26:4 my *m* of life from my youth, which was at
1 Cor. 15:33 evil communications corrupt good *m*
Gal. 2:14 a Jew, livest after the *m* of Gentiles
2 Tim. 3:10 hast fully known my doctrine, *m* of life
Heb. 1:1 God, who at sundry times and in divers *m*
Jas. 1:24 straightway forgetteth what *m* of man he

1 Pet. 1:15 so be ye holy in all *m* of conversation
2 Pet. 3:11 what *m* of persons ought ye to be in all
1 Jn. 3:1 what *m* of love the Father hath bestowed

Manoah Judg. 13:2-22

Mansion

Jn. 14:2 in my Father's house are many *m*

Mantle

Judg. 4:18 into the tent, she covered him with a *m*
1 Sam. 28:14 an old man cometh . . covered with a *m*
1 Kgs. 19:19 passed by him, and cast his *m* upon him
2 Kgs. 2:8 and Elijah took his *m*, and wrapped it
   2:13 took up also the *m* of Elijah that fell from
Job 1:20 Job arose, and rent his *m*, and shaved his
Ps. 109:29 with their own confusion, as with a *m*

Mar

Lev. 19:27 neither . . *m* the corners of thy beard
Ruth 4:6 lest I *m* mine own inheritance
1 Sam. 6:5 images of your mice that *m* the land
2 Kgs. 3:19 *m* every good piece of land with stones
Job 30:13 they *m* my path, they set forward my
Is. 52:14 his visage was so *m* more than any man
Jer. 13:7 girdle was *m*, it was profitable for nothing
   18:4 the vessel that he made of clay was *m* in
Mk. 2:22 wine is spilled . . the bottles will be *m*

Marah Ex. 15:23

Maranatha

1 Cor. 16:22 man love not . . let him be Anathema, *M*

Marble

1 Chr. 29:2 precious stones . . *m* stones in abundance
Song 5:15 his legs are as pillars of *m*, set upon
Rev. 18:12 vessels of most precious wood . . and *m*

March

Ex. 14:10 behold, the Egyptians *m* after them
Judg. 5:4 when thou *m* out of the field of Edom
Ps. 68:7 when thou didst *m* through the wilderness
Hab. 3:12 didst *m* through the land in indignation

Marcus See Mark

Mariner

Ezek. 27:8 inhabitants of Zidon and Arvad . . thy *m*
   27:29 *m*, and all the pilots of the sea, shall
Jon. 1:5 then the *m* were afraid, and cried every

Mark (John Mark, Marcus)

Cousin of Barnabas, Col. 4:10; lived in Jerusalem,
Acts 12:12; accompanied Barnabas and Paul to An-
tioch, Acts 12:25; began missionary work, Acts 13:5;
deserted the group at Perga, Acts 13:13; subject of
contention, Acts 15:37-38; went with Barnabas to
Cyprus, Acts 15:39; ministered to Paul in Rome,
Col. 4:10; 2 Tim. 4:11; Phlm. 24; companion of
Peter, 1 Pet. 5:13.

Mark

Gen. 4:15 and the LORD set a *m* upon Cain, lest any
Lev. 19:28 for the dead, nor print any *m* upon you
1 Sam. 1:12 she continued praying . . Eli *m* her mouth
Job 7:20 why hast thou set me as a *m* against thee
   18:2 of words? *m*, and afterward we will speak
Ps. 37:37 *m* the perfect man . . behold the upright
   48:13 *m* ye . . her bulwarks, consider her palaces
   130:3 if thou, LORD, shouldest *m* iniquities
Lam. 3:12 and set me as a *m* for the arrow
Ezek. 9:4 set a *m* upon the foreheads of the men

Lk. 14:7 he *m* how they chose out the chief rooms
Rom. 16:17 brethren, *m* them which cause divisions
Gal. 6:17 for I bear in my body the *m* of the Lord
Phil. 3:14 I press toward the *m* for the prize of
   3:17 *m* them which walk so as ye have us for an
Rev. 13:16 to receive a *m* in their right hand
   14:9 (20:4) and receive his *m* in his forehead

Market

Ezek. 27:13 they traded . . vessels of brass in thy *m*
Mt. 11:16 (Lk. 7:32) like . . children sitting in the *m*
   20:3 and saw others standing idle in the *m* place
   23:7 (Lk. 11:43) greetings in the *m*, and to be
Jn. 5:2 at Jerusalem by the sheep *m* a pool
Acts 16:19 Silas, and drew them into the *m* place
   17:17 disputed he . . in the *m* daily with them

Marriage See also Wedding

Gen. 34:9 make ye *m* with us . . give your daughters
Deut. 7:3 neither shalt thou make *m* with them
Josh. 23:12 among you, and shall make *m* with them
Ps. 78:63 and their maidens were not given to *m*
Mt. 22:2 certain king, which made a *m* for his son
   22:30 neither marry, nor are given in *m*, but are
   25:10 that were ready went in with him to the *m*
Jn. 2:1 third day there was a *m* in Cana of Galilee
1 Cor. 7:38 that giveth her not in *m* doeth better
Heb. 13:4 *m* is honorable in all . . the bed undefiled
Rev. 19:7 the *m* of the Lamb is come, and his wife

Marrow

Ps. 63:5 shall be satisfied as with *m* and fatness
Prov. 3:8 health to thy navel, and *m* to thy bones
Heb. 4:12 soul and spirit, and of the joints and *m*

Marry See also Betroth, Espouse

Gen. 38:8 go in unto thy brother's wife, and *m* her
Num. 12:1 for he had *m* an Ethiopian woman
   36:6 let them *m* to whom they think best; only to
Deut. 24:1 when a man hath taken a wife, and *m* her
   25:5 wife of the dead shall not *m* without unto a
Neh. 13:23 saw I Jews that had *m* wives of Ashdod
Is. 62:5 man *m* a virgin, so shall thy sons *m* thee
Jer. 3:14 saith the LORD; for I am *m* unto you
Mal. 2:11 and hath *m* the daughter of a strange god
Mt. 5:32 *m* her . . divorced committeth adultery
   19:10 be so with his wife, it is not good to *m*
   22:30 in the resurrection they neither *m*, nor
   24:38 *m* and giving in marriage, until the day
Mk. 10:11 shall put away his wife, and *m* another
Lk. 14:20 I have *m* a wife . . therefore I cannot come
Rom. 7:4 that ye should be *m* to another, even to
1 Cor. 7:9 *m*: for it is better to *m* than to burn
   7:28 *m*, thou hast not sinned; and if a virgin *m*
   7:33 but he that is *m* careth for the things that
   7:36 do what he will, he sinneth not: let them *m*
1 Tim. 4:3 forbidding to *m* . . commanding to abstain
   5:11 to wax wanton against Christ, they will *m*
   5:14 I will therefore that the younger women *m*

Mars' Hill Acts 17:22

Martha

Lk. 10:38 certain woman named *M* received him into
Jn. 11:5 Jesus loved *M*, and her sister, and Lazarus
   11:20 *M*, as soon as she heard . . went and met him
   12:2 there they made him a supper; and *M* served

Martyr

Acts 22:20 the blood of thy *m* Stephen was shed
Rev. 2:13 Antipas was my faithful *m*, who was slain
   17:6 drunken . . with the blood of the *m* of Jesus

Marvel *See also* Wonder

Gen. 43:33 they sat before him . . *m* one at another
Ex. 34:10 before all thy people I will do *m*, such
Ps. 48:5 saw it, and so they *m*; they were troubled
Eccl. 5:8 seest the oppression . . *m* not at the matter
Mt. 8:10 when Jesus heard it, he *m*, and said to
9:8 multitudes saw it, they *m*, and glorified God
22:22 heard these words, they *m*, and left him
27:14 (Mk. 15:5) that the governor *m* greatly
Mk. 5:20 Jesus had done for him: and all men did *m*
6:6 he *m* because of their unbelief
Jn. 3:7 *m* not that I said . . Ye must be born again
Acts 2:7 and they were all amazed and *m*, saying
3:12 ye men of Israel, why *m* ye at this?
4:13 saw the boldness of Peter and John . . they *m*
2 Cor. 11:14 no *m*; for Satan . . is transformed
Gal. 1:6 I *m* that ye are so soon removed from him
1 Jn. 3:13 *m* not, my brethren, if the world hate

Marvelous *See also* Wonderful

Job 5:9 and unsearchable; *m* things without number
Ps. 9:1 O LORD . . I will show forth all thy *m* works
17:7 show thy *m* loving-kindness, O thou that
78:12 *m* things did he in the sight of their
98:1 sing . . a new song; for he hath done *m* things
118:23 is the LORD's doing; it is *m* in our eyes
139:14 *m* are thy works; and that my soul knoweth
Is. 29:14 proceed to do a *m* work among this people
Zech. 8:6 be *m* . . should it also be *m* in mine eyes?
Jn. 9:30 why herein is a *m* thing, that ye know not
1 Pet. 2:9 you out of darkness into his *m* light
Rev. 15:3 sing . . saying, Great and *m* are thy works

Mary of Bethany

Listened to the Lord's teaching, Lk. 10:38–42; at the
raising of Lazarus, Jn. 11:1–44; anointed Jesus' feet,
Jn. 12:1–8.

Mary mother of Jesus

Espoused to Joseph, Mt. 1:18 (Lk. 1:27); Jesus' birth
foretold to her, Lk. 1:26–38; visited Elisabeth, Lk. 1:
39–45; "The Magnificat," Lk. 1:46–55; went to Bethlehem, Lk. 2:4; "brought forth her firstborn son," Mt.
1:25 (Lk. 2:7); found Jesus in the temple, Lk. 2:41–
51; attended the marriage at Cana, Jn. 2:1–5; con-
cerned over Jesus' ministry, Mk. 3:31–35; at the
cross, Jn. 19:25–27; in the upper room, Acts 1:14.

Mary mother of James

Mt. 27:56 (Mk. 15:40); Mk. 16:1 (Lk. 24:10)

Mary mother of Mark Acts 12:12

Mary Magdalene

Demons cast out by Jesus, Lk. 8:2; ministered to
Jesus, Lk. 8:3; stood by the cross, Mt. 27:56 (Mk. 15:
40; Jn. 19:25); watched Jesus' burial, Mt. 27:61
(Mk. 15:47); came early to the sepulchre, Mt. 28:1
(Mk. 16:1; Lk. 24:10; Jn. 20:1); saw the risen Lord,
Mt. 28:9 (Mk. 16:9; Jn. 20:11–18).

Mason

2 Sam 5:11 (1 Chr. 14:1) sent . . carpenters, and *m*
1 Chr. 22:2 set *m* to hew wrought stones to build
2 Chr. 24:12 hired *m* and carpenters to repair the

Massah *See also* Meribah

Ex. 17:7; Deut. 6:16; 33:8

Mast

Prov. 23:34 as he that lieth upon the top of a *m*
Ezek. 27:5 taken cedars from Lebanon to make *m* for

Master *See also* Instructor, Lord, Rabbi, Teacher

Gen. 24:35 the LORD hath blessed my *m* greatly
39:3 and his *m* saw that the LORD was with him
Ex. 21:5 I love my *m*, my wife, and my children
1 Sam. 26:16 die, because ye have not kept your *m*
1 Kgs. 22:17 LORD said, These have no *m*: let them
Ps. 123:2 servants look unto the hand of their *m*
Prov. 27:18 that waiteth on his *m* shall be honored
30:10 accuse not a servant unto his *m*, lest he
Is. 24:2 as with the servant, so with his *m*
Mal. 1:6 and if I be a *m*, where is my fear?
Mt. 6:24 no man can serve two *m*: for either he
9:11 eateth your *m* with publicans and sinners?
10:24 the disciple is not above his *m*, nor the
17:24 to Peter . . Doth not your *m* pay tribute?
23:8 for one is your *M*, even Christ; and all ye
23:10 neither be ye called *m*: for one is your *M*
26:18 the *M* saith, My time is at hand; I will
Mk. 5:35 (Lk. 8:49) why troublest thou the *M*
13:35 know not when the *m* of the house cometh
Lk. 13:25 *m* of the house is risen up, and hath shut
Jn. 3:10 art thou a *m* of Israel, and knowest not
11:28 saying, The *M* is come, and calleth for thee
13:13 ye call me *M* and Lord: and ye say well
20:16 saith unto him, Rabboni; which is to say, *M*
Rom. 14:4 to his own *m* he standeth or falleth
Eph. 6:5 be obedient to them that are your *m*
6:9 ye *m* . . knowing that your *M* also is in heaven
Col. 3:22 servants, obey in all things your *m*
1 Tim. 6:1 count their own *m* worthy of all honor
6:2 that have believing *m*, let them not despise
2 Tim. 2:21 sanctified, and meet for the *m*'s use
Tit. 2:9 servants to be obedient unto their own *m*
Jas. 3:1 brethren, be not many *m*, knowing that we
1 Pet. 2:18 be subject to your *m* with all fear

Masterbuilder

1 Cor. 3:10 as a wise *m*, I have laid the foundation

Mastery

1 Cor. 9:25 striveth for the *m* is temperate in all
2 Tim. 2:5 strive for *m*, yet is he not crowned

Matter

Deut. 17:8 if there arise a *m* too hard for thee
Job 19:28 seeing the root of the *m* is found in me?
32:18 for I am full of *m*; the spirit within me
Ps. 35:20 but they devise deceitful *m* against them
45:1 my heart is inditing a good *m*: I speak of
Prov. 16:20 he that handleth a *m* wisely shall find
18:13 answereth a *m* before he heareth it, it is
25:2 but the honor of kings is to search out a *m*
Eccl. 10:20 that which hath wings shall tell the *m*
12:13 let us hear the conclusion of the whole *m*
Dan. 4:17 this *m* is by the decree of the watchers
Mt. 23:23 have omitted the weightier *m* of the law
Acts 17:32 said, We will hear thee again of this *m*
18:14 if it were a *m* of wrong or wicked lewdness
1 Cor. 6:1 having a *m* against another, go to law
Jas. 3:5 how great a *m* a little fire kindleth!
1 Pet. 4:15 or as a busybody in other men's *m*

Matthew *See also* Levi

Mt. 9:9 saw a man, named *M*, sitting at the receipt
10:3 Bartholomew; Thomas, and *M* the publican
Acts 1:13 Philip, and Thomas, Bartholomew, and *M*

Matthias Acts 1:26

Meal

1 Kgs. 17:12 handful of *m* in a barrel, and a little oil

Mean (adjective)

Prov. 22:29 kings; he shall not stand before *m* men
Acts 21:39 a Jew of Tarsus. . a citizen of no *m* city

Mean (Meant)

Gen. 21:29 Abraham, What *m* these seven ewe lambs
  33:8 what *m* thou by all this drove which I met?
  50:20 evil against me; but God *m* it unto good
Ex. 12:26 say unto you, What *m* ye by this service?
Deut. 6:20 *m* the testimonies, and the statutes
Josh. 4:6 children ask. . What *m* ye by these stones?
1 Sam. 15:14 what *m* . . this bleating of the sheep
2 Sam. 16:2 unto Ziba, What *m* thou by these?
Is. 3:15 what *m* ye that ye beat my people to pieces
Ezek. 17:12 know ye not what these things *m*?
  18:2 what *m* ye, that ye use this proverb
Mt. 9:13 (12:7) learn what that *m*, I will have mercy
Mk. 9:10 what the rising from the dead should *m*
Lk. 15:26 servants, and asked what these things *m*
Acts 2:12 doubt, saying one to another, What *m* this?
  10:17 what this vision which he had seen should *m*
  17:20 would know therefore what these things *m*
  21:13 then Paul answered, What *m* ye to weep and
2 Cor. 8:13 I *m* not that other men be eased, and ye

Meaning

Dan. 8:15 seen the vision, and sought for the *m*
1 Cor. 14:11 if I know not the *m* of the voice

Measure *See also* Weight

Num. 35:5 ye shall *m* from without the city on the
Deut. 25:14 shalt not have in thine house divers *m*
Job 11:9 the *m* thereof is longer than the earth
  28:25 the winds; and he weigheth the waters by *m*
Ps. 39:4 me to know mine end, and the *m* of my days
  80:5 and givest them tears to drink in great *m*
Prov. 20:10 divers weights, and divers *m*, both of
Is. 40:12 *m* the waters in the hollow of his hand
  65:7 will I *m* their former work into their bosom
Jer. 30:11 I will correct thee in *m*, and will not
  31:37 saith the LORD; If heaven above can be *m*
  33:22 neither the sand of the sea *m*; so will I
Ezek. 4:11 thou shalt drink also water by *m*
  40:3 line of flax in his hand, and a *m* reed
  40:5 he *m* the breadth of the building, one reed
Zech. 2:2 and he said unto me, To *m* Jerusalem
Mt. 7:2 (Mk. 4:24; Lk. 6:38) *m* ye mete. . *m* to you
  13:33 hid in three of meal, till the whole was
  23:32 fill ye up then the *m* of your fathers
Mk. 6:51 were sore amazed in themselves beyond *m*
Lk. 6:38 good *m*, pressed down, and shaken together
Jn. 3:34 God giveth not the Spirit by *m* unto him
Rom. 12:3 hath dealt to every man the *m* of faith
2 Cor. 1:8 in Asia, that we were pressed out of *m*
  10:12 *m* themselves by themselves. . are not wise
  10:15 not boasting of things without our *m*
  11:23 labors more abundant, in stripes above *m*
  12:7 lest I should be exalted above *m* through
Gal. 1:13 beyond *m* I persecuted the church of God
Eph. 4:7 grace according to the *m* of the gift of
  4:13 *m* of the stature of the fulness of Christ
Rev. 6:6 a *m* of wheat for a penny, and three of *m*
  11:1 rise, and *m* the temple of God, and the altar
  21:15 had a golden reed to *m* the city
  21:17 he *m* the wall. . according to the *m* of a man

Meat *See also* Food

Gen. 1:29 yielding seed; to you it shall be for *m*
  9:3 moving thing that liveth shall be *m* for you

Gen. 27:4 make savory *m*, such as I love, and bring
Lev. 2:1 when any will offer a *m* offering
  6:14 this is the law of the *m* offering
Judg. 14:14 out of the eater came forth *m*, and out
1 Kgs. 19:8 went in the strength of that *m* forty
Job 33:20 abhorreth bread, and his soul dainty *m*
  38:41 cry unto God, they wander for lack of *m*
Ps. 42:3 my tears have been my *m* day and night
  59:15 let them wander up and down for *m*
  69:21 they gave me also gall for my *m*
  78:25 angels' food: he sent them *m* to the full
  107:18 their soul abhorreth all manner of *m*
  145:15 thou givest them their *m* in due season
Prov. 6:8 provideth her *m* in the summer
  23:6 evil eye, neither desire thou his dainty *m*
  30:22 and a fool when he is filled with *m*
  31:15 she riseth. . and giveth *m* to her household
Is. 65:25 and dust shall be the serpent's *m*
Ezek. 4:10 thy *m* . . thou shalt eat shall be by weight
Dan. 1:8 not defile himself with. . the king's *m*
Hab. 3:17 fail, and the fields shall yield no *m*
Mal. 3:10 that there may be *m* in mine house
Mt. 3:4 and his *m* was locusts and wild honey
  6:25 is not the life more than *m*, and the body
  10:10 for the workman is worthy of his *m*
  24:45 household, to give them *m* in due season?
  25:35 I was ahungered, and ye gave me *m*
Mk. 8:8 the broken *m* that was left seven baskets
Lk. 3:11 and he that hath *m*, let him do likewise
  8:55 she arose. . and he commanded to give her *m*
  9:13 we should go and buy *m* for all this people
  24:41 he said unto them, Have ye here any *m*?
Jn. 4:32 he said. . I have *m* to eat that ye know not
  4:34 my *m* is to do the will of him that sent me
  6:27 labor not for the *m* which perisheth, but
  6:55 my flesh is *m* indeed, and my blood is drink
  21:5 then Jesus saith. . Children, have ye any *m*?
Acts 2:46 eat their *m* with gladness and singleness
  15:29 that ye abstain from *m* offered to idols
  27:33 Paul besought them all to take *m*, saying
Rom. 14:15 destroy not him with thy *m*, for whom
  14:17 for the kingdom of God is not *m* and drink
1 Cor. 3:2 have fed you with milk, and not with *m*
  6:13 *m* for the belly, and the belly for *m*
  8:8 but *m* commendeth us not to God: for neither
  8:13 if *m* make my brother to offend, I will eat no
  10:3 and did all eat the same spiritual *m*
Col. 2:16 let no man. . judge you in *m*, or in drink
1 Tim. 4:3 commanding to abstain from *m*, which
Heb. 5:12 have need of milk, and not of strong *m*
  12:16 for one morsel of *m* sold his birthright
  13:9 heart be established with grace; not with *m*

Meddle

Deut. 2:5 *m* not with them; for I will not give you
2 Kgs. 14:10 for why shouldest thou *m* to thy hurt
Prov. 17:14 leave off contention, before it be *m* with
  20:3 cease from strife: but every fool will be *m*
  20:19 *m* not with him that flattereth with his lips
  24:21 *m* not with them that are given to change
  26:17 *m* with strife belonging not to him, is like

Mede *See also* Persian

Is. 13:17 I will stir up the *M* against them
Dan. 5:28 kingdom is divided, and given to the *M*
  6:8 according to the law of the *M* and Persians

Media *See also* Persia Dan. 8:20

Mediator

Gal. 3:19 ordained by angels in the hand of a *m*
  3:20 now a *m* is not a *m* of one, but God is one
1 Tim. 2:5 God, and one *m* between God and men

Heb. 8:6 also he is the *m* of a better covenant
9:15 he is the *m* of the new testament
12:24 to Jesus the *m* of the new covenant

Medicine

Prov. 17:22 a merry heart doeth good like a *m*
Jer. 30:13 be bound up: thou hast no healing *m*
46:11 O virgin . . in vain shalt thou use many *m*
Ezek. 47:12 for meat, and the leaf thereof for *m*

Meditate *See also* Muse, Ponder, Think

Gen. 24:63 and Isaac went out to *m* in the field
Josh. 1:8 but thou shalt *m* therein day and night
Ps. 1:2 and in his law doth he *m* day and night
63:6 and *m* on thee in the night watches
77:12 I will *m* also of all thy work, and talk of
119:15 will *m* in thy precepts, and have respect
119:23 but thy servant did *m* in thy statutes
119:48 I have loved; and I will *m* in thy statutes
119:148 night watches, that I might *m* in thy word
143:5 I *m* on all thy works; I muse on the work
Is. 33:18 thine heart shall *m* terror
Lk. 21:14 not to *m* before what ye shall answer
1 Tim. 4:15 *m* upon these things; give thyself

Meditation *See also* Prayer, Thought

Ps. 5:1 give ear to my words . . consider my *m*
19:14 *m* of my heart, be acceptable in thy sight
49:3 the *m* of my heart shall be of understanding
104:34 my *m* of him shall be sweet: I will be glad
119:97 how love I thy law! it is my *m* all the day
119:99 my teachers: for thy testimonies are my *m*

Meek *See also* Gentle, Humble, Kind

Num. 12:3 Moses was very *m*, above all the men
Ps. 22:26 the *m* shall eat and be satisfied
25:9 *m* will he guide in judgment . . teach his way
37:11 the *m* shall inherit the earth; and shall
76:9 God arose . . to save all the *m* of the earth
147:6 the LORD lifteth up the *m*: he casteth down
149:4 he will beautify the *m* with salvation
Is. 11:4 reprove with equity for the *m* of the earth
29:19 *m* also shall increase their joy in the LORD
61:1 anointed me to preach good tidings unto the *m*
Zeph. 2:3 seek ye the LORD, all ye *m* of the earth
Mt. 5:5 blessed are the *m*: for they shall inherit
11:29 learn of me; for I am *m* and lowly in heart
21:5 thy King cometh unto thee, *m*, and sitting
1 Pet. 3:4 the ornament of a *m* and quiet spirit

Meekness *See also* Gentleness, Kindness

Ps. 45:4 ride prosperously, because of truth and *m*
Zeph. 2:3 seek righteousness, seek *m*: it may be ye
1 Cor. 4:21 with a rod, or . . in the spirit of *m*?
2 Cor. 10:1 by the *m* and gentleness of Christ
Gal. 5:23 *m*, temperance: against such there is no law
6:1 restore such a one in the spirit of *m*
Eph. 4:2 all lowliness and *m*, with long-suffering
Col. 3:12 humbleness of mind, *m*, long-suffering
1 Tim. 6:11 godliness, faith, love, patience, *m*
2 Tim. 2:25 in *m* instructing those that oppose
Tit. 3:2 but gentle, showing all *m* unto all men
Jas. 1:21 receive with *m* the engrafted word
3:13 let him show . . his works with *m* of wisdom
1 Pet. 3:15 to give an answer . . with *m* and fear

Meet (adjective) *See also* Fit, Worthy

Gen. 2:18 I will make him a help *m* for him
Mt. 3:8 bring forth . . fruits *m* for repentance
15:26 not *m* to take the children's bread, and to
Lk. 15:32 it was *m* that we should make merry
Acts 26:20 turn to God . . do works *m* for repentance
Rom. 1:27 recompense of their error which was *m*

1 Cor. 15:9 that am not *m* to be called an apostle
Phil. 1:7 it is *m* for me to think this of you all
Col. 1:12 *m* to be partakers of the inheritance
2 Tim. 2:21 sanctified, and *m* for the master's use
Heb. 6:7 herbs *m* for them by whom it is dressed
2 Pet. 1:13 I think it *m*, as long as I am in this

Meet (Met)

Gen. 19:1 and Lot seeing them rose up to *m* them
32:1 Jacob went on his way . . angels of God *m* him
32:6 brother Esau, and also he cometh to *m* thee
46:29 and Joseph . . went up to *m* Israel his father
Ex. 3:18 LORD God of the Hebrews hath *m* with us
4:27 to Aaron, Go into the wilderness to *m* Moses
25:22 there I will *m* with thee . . I will commune
Num. 23:3 peradventure the LORD will come to *m* me
Judg. 11:34 behold, his daughter came out to *m* him •
1 Sam. 10:5 thou shalt *m* a company of prophets
13:10 Samuel came; and Saul went out to *m* him
30:21 went forth to *m* David, and to *m* the people
2 Sam. 6:20 daughter of Saul came out to *m* David
19:15 Judah came to Gilgal, to go to *m* the king
1 Kgs. 13:24 a lion *m* him by the way, and slew him
18:16 Obadiah went to *m* Ahab . . and Ahab . . to *m*
2 Kgs. 8:8 take a present . . and go, *m* the man of God
Neh. 6:2 come, let us *m* together in some one of
Ps. 85:10 mercy and truth are *m* together
Prov. 17:12 a bear robbed of her whelps *m* a man
22:2 rich and poor *m* together: the LORD is the
29:13 the poor and the deceitful man *m* together
Hos. 13:8 I will *m* them as a bear that is bereaved
Amos 4:12 thee, prepare to *m* thy God, O Israel
Mt. 8:34 the whole city came out to *m* Jesus
25:1 ten virgins . . went forth to *m* the bridegroom
28:9 to tell his disciples, behold, Jesus *m* them
Mk. 14:13 *m* you a man bearing a pitcher of water
Lk. 17:12 there *m* him ten men that were lepers
Jn. 11:20 then Martha . . went and *m* him: but Mary
Acts 10:25 as Peter was coming in, Cornelius *m* him
1 Thes. 4:17 caught up . . to *m* the Lord in the air
Heb. 7:1 Abraham returning from the slaughter

Meeting

Is. 1:13 it is iniquity, even the solemn *m*

Megiddo 2 Kgs. 23:29

Melchizedek (Melchisedec)

Gen. 14:18 *M* king of Salem brought forth bread and
Ps. 110:4 a priest for ever after the order of *M*
Heb. 7:1 this *M*, king of Salem, priest of the most
7:15 similitude of *M* there ariseth another

Melita Acts 28:1

Melody

Is. 23:16 make sweet *m*, sing many songs, that thou
51:3 therein, thanksgiving, and the voice of *m*
Amos 5:23 for I will not hear the *m* of thy viols
Eph. 5:19 and making *m* in your heart to the Lord

Melon

Num. 11:5 the *m*, and the leeks, and the onions

Melt

Ex. 15:15 the inhabitants of Canaan shall *m* away
Josh. 2:11 heard these things, our hearts did *m*
14:8 made the heart of the people *m*: but I
Judg. 5:5 mountains *m* from before the LORD, even
Ps. 22:14 heart . . is *m* in the midst of my bowels
46:6 he uttered his voice, the earth *m*
97:5 hills *m* like wax at the presence of the LORD
107:26 their soul is *m* because of trouble

Ps. 119:28 my soul *m* for heaviness: strengthen thou
147:18 he sendeth out his word, and *m* them
Is. 13:7 be faint, and every man's heart shall *m*
40:19 workman *m* a graven image . . the goldsmith
Jer. 9:7 behold, I will *m* them, and try them
Ezek. 22:22 as silver is *m* . . so shall ye be *m* in
Nah. 1:5 mountains quake at him, and the hills *m*
2 Pet. 3:10 the elements shall *m* with fervent heat

Member

Job 17:7 of sorrow, and all my *m* are as a shadow
Ps. 139:16 and in thy book all my *m* were written
Mt. 5:29 that one of thy *m* should perish, and not
Rom. 6:13 neither yield ye your *m* as instruments
6:19 have yielded your *m* servants to uncleanness
7:23 I see another law in my *m*, warring against
12:4 have many *m* in one body, and all *m* have not
1 Cor. 6:15 that your bodies are the *m* of Christ?
12:12 body is one, and hath many *m* and all the *m*
12:27 ye are the body of Christ . . *m* in particular
Eph. 4:25 for we are *m* one of another
5:30 we are *m* of his body, of his flesh, and of
Col. 3:5 mortify therefore your *m* which are upon
Jas. 3:5 tongue is a little *m*, and boasteth great
4:1 even of your lusts that war in your *m*?

Memorial *See also* Remembrance

Ex. 3:15 and this is my *m* unto all generations
12:14 this day shall be unto you for a *m*
13:9 for a *m* between thine eyes, that the LORD's
17:14 write this for a *m* in a book, and rehearse
28:12 (39:7) of the ephod for stones of *m*
30:16 it may be a *m* unto the children of Israel
Lev. 2:2 priest shall burn the *m* of it upon the
Num. 10:10 may be to you for a *m* before your God
Josh. 4:7 these stones shall be for a *m* unto the
Ps. 9:6 destroyed cities; their *m* is perished with
135:13 thy *m*, O LORD, throughout all generations
Hos. 12:5 the LORD God of hosts; the LORD is his *m*
Zech. 6:14 for a *m* in the temple of the LORD
Mt. 26:13 woman hath done, be told for a *m* of her
Acts 10:4 thine alms are come up for a *m* before God

Memory *See also* Remembrance

Ps. 109:15 cut off the *m* of them from the earth
145:7 utter the *m* of thy great goodness
Prov. 10:7 *m* of the just is blessed: but the name
Eccl. 9:5 dead know not . . *m* of them is forgotten
Is. 26:14 destroyed . . made all their *m* to perish
1 Cor. 15:2 if ye keep in *m* what I preached unto

Memphis Hos. 9:6

Men *See also* Man

Ex 10:11 go now ye that are *m*, and serve the LORD
Judg. 7:6 them that lapped . . were three hundred *m*
1 Sam. 4:9 be strong, and quit yourselves like *m*
2 Chr. 6:18 but will God in very deed dwell with *m*
Ps. 9:20 nations may know themselves to be but *m*
45:2 thou art fairer than the children of *m*
Is. 31:3 now the Egyptians are *m*, and not God
38:16 O Lord, by these things *m* live
Mic. 7:2 there is none upright among *m*: they all
Zeph. 2:11 and *m* shall worship him, every one from
Mt. 4:19 follow me . . I will make you fishers of *m*
5:16 let your light so shine before *m*, that they
6:2 hypocrites do . . that they may have glory of *m*
7:12 would that *m* should do to you, do ye even
10:32 confess me before *m*, him will I confess
16:13 whom do *m* say that I, the Son of man, am?
16:23 that be of God, but those that be of *m*
19:26 with *m* this is impossible; but with God all
21:25 the baptism of John . . from heaven, or of *m*?

Jn. 3:19 *m* loved darkness rather than light
12:43 loved the praise of *m* more than . . of God
Acts 5:29 said, We ought to obey God rather than *m*
5:38 refrain from these *m*, and let them alone
14:11 gods . . come down to us in the likeness of *m*
17:26 made of one blood all nations of *m* for to
Rom. 1:27 *m* with *m* working that which is unseemly
1 Cor. 1:25 the foolishness of God is wiser than *m*
3:3 divisions, are ye not carnal, and walk as *m*?
3:21 let no man glory in *m*: for all things are
9:22 I am made all things to all *m*, that I might
16:13 stand fast in the faith, quit you like *m*
2 Cor. 5:11 the terror of the Lord, we persuade *m*
Gal. 1:10 seek to please *m*? for if I yet pleased *m*
Phil. 2:7 of a servant . . made in the likeness of *m*
1 Thes. 2:4 we speak; not as pleasing *m*, but God
1 Tim. 2:5 one mediator between God and *m*
Heb. 9:27 as it is appointed unto *m* once to die
Rev. 21:3 the tabernacle of God is with *m*

Menahem 2 Kgs. 15:14–22

Mend

2 Chr. 24:12 and brass to *m* the house of the LORD
Mt. 4:21 (Mk. 1:19) two brethren . . *m* their nets

Mene

Dan. 5:25 this is the writing that was written, *M, M*

Menpleaser

Eph. 6:6 not with eyeservice, as *m*; but as the

Mention

Gen. 40:14 *m* of me unto Pharaoh, and bring me out
Ex. 23:13 and make no *m* of the name of other gods
Ps. 71:16 I will make *m* of thy righteousness, even
Is. 26:13 by thee only will we make *m* of thy name
62:6 that make *m* of the LORD, keep not silence
63:7 I will make the loving-kindnesses of the LORD
Ezek. 18:22 all his transgressions . . shall not be *m*
18:24 all his righteousness . . shall not be *m*
Amos 6:10 may not make *m* of the name of the LORD
Rom. 1:9 I make *m* of you always in my prayers
Eph. 1:16 for you, making *m* of you in my prayers
Heb. 11:22 by faith Joseph . . made *m* of the departing

Mephibosheth

Crippled by a fall, 2 Sam. 4:4; dined continually at
the royal table, 2 Sam. 9:1–13; reported to David as
a deserter, 2 Sam. 16:1–4; cleared himself before
David, 2 Sam. 19:24–30.

Merchandise

Deut. 21:14 thou shalt not make *m* of her, because
24:7 and maketh *m* of him, or selleth him
Prov. 3:14 *m* of it is better than the *m* of silver
31:18 she perceiveth that her *m* is good
Is. 23:18 her *m* and her hire shall be holiness to
Ezek. 27:15 many isles were the *m* of thine hand
27:33 the multitude of thy riches and of thy *m*
Mt. 22:5 ways, one to his farm, another to his *m*
Jn. 2:16 make not my Father's house a house of *m*
2 Pet. 2:3 they with feigned words make *m* of you
Rev. 18:11 for no man buyeth their *m* any more

Merchant

Prov. 31:14 is like the *m*' ships; she bringeth
Is. 23:8 whose *m* are princes, whose traffickers are
23:11 given a commandment against the *m* city
Ezek. 17:4 of traffic; he set it in a city of *m*
Hos. 12:7 he is a *m*, the balances of deceit are in
Nah. 3:16 hast multiplied thy *m* above the stars
Rev. 18:3 *m* of the earth are waxed rich through

Merchantman

Gen. 37:28 *m*; and they drew and lifted up Joseph
1 Kgs. 10:15 besides that he had of the *m*
Mt. 13:45 is like unto a *m*, seeking goodly pearls

Merciful *See also* Gentle, Gracious, Kind, Pitiful

Ex. 34:6 LORD God, *m* and gracious, long-suffering
Deut. 4:31 LORD thy God is a *m* God;) he will not
  21:8 be *m*, O LORD, unto thy people Israel, whom
  32:43 will be *m* unto his land, and to his people
2 Sam. 22:26 with the *m* thou wilt show thyself *m*
2 Chr. 30:9 God is gracious and *m*, and will not
Neh. 9:17 a God ready to pardon, gracious and *m*
Ps. 41:4 LORD, be *m* unto me: heal my soul; for I
  67:1 God be *m* unto us, and bless us; and cause
  86:3 be *m* unto me, O Lord: for I cry unto thee
  103:8 the LORD is *m* and gracious, slow to anger
  117:2 for his *m* kindness is great toward us
Prov. 11:17 the *m* man doeth good to his own soul
Is. 57:1 *m* men are taken away, none considering
Jer. 3:12 I am *m*, saith the LORD, and I will not
Jon. 4:2 knew that thou art a gracious God, and *m*
Mt. 5:7 blessed are the *m*: for they shall obtain
Lk. 6:36 be ye therefore *m*, as your Father also is *m*
  18:13 God be *m* to me a sinner
Heb. 2:17 he might be a *m* and faithful high priest
  8:12 I will be *m* to their unrighteousness

Mercurius Acts 14:12

Mercy *See also* Compassion, Grace, Kindness, Loving-kindness, Pity

Gen. 19:19 thou hast magnified thy *m*, which thou
  32:10 I am not worthy of the least of all the *m*
  43:14 God Almighty give you *m* before the man
Ex. 15:13 thou in thy *m* hast led forth the people
  20:6 (Deut. 5:10) showing *m* unto thousands of
  25:17 and thou shalt make a *m* seat of pure gold
  33:19 (Rom. 9:15) *m* on whom I will show *m*
  34:7 keeping *m* for thousands, forgiving iniquity
Lev. 16:2 place within the veil before the *m* seat
Num. 14:18 LORD is long-suffering, and of great *m*
Deut. 7:9 keepeth covenant and *m* with them that
2 Sam. 7:15 my *m* shall not depart away from him
  24:14 the hand of the LORD; for his *m* are great
1 Chr. 16:34 is good; for his *m* endureth for ever
2 Chr. 6:42 remember the *m* of David thy servant
Ezra 3:11 his *m* endureth for ever toward Israel
Neh. 9:27 according to thy manifold *m* thou gavest
  9:31 thy great *m*' sake thou didst not utterly
Ps. 13:5 I have trusted in thy *m*; my heart shall
  18:50 and showeth *m* to his anointed, to David
  23:6 goodness and *m* shall follow me all the days
  25:6 remember, O LORD, thy tender *m* and thy
  25:10 all the paths of the LORD are *m* and truth
  25:16 turn thee unto me, and have *m* upon me
  32:10 trusteth in the LORD, *m* shall compass him
  33:18 fear him, upon them that hope in his *m*
  36:5 thy *m*, O LORD, is in the heavens
  37:21 but the righteous showeth *m*, and giveth
  51:1 I have *m* upon me, O God, according to thy
  52:8 I trust in the *m* of God for ever and ever
  57:10 (108:4) thy *m* is great unto the heavens
  59:16 I will sing aloud of thy *m* in the morning
  85:10 *m* and truth. . met together; righteousness
  86:5 plenteous in *m* unto all them that call upon
  89:1 I will sing of the *m* of the LORD for ever
  89:14 *m* and truth shall go before thy face
  90:14 O satisfy us early with thy *m*; that we may
  94:18 my foot slippeth; thy *m*, O LORD, held me

Ps. 100:5 for the LORD is good; his *m* is everlasting
  103:4 who crowneth thee with. . tender *m*
  103:8 gracious, slow to anger. . plenteous in *m*
  103:17 the *m* of the LORD is from everlasting to
  106:7 they remembered not the multitude of thy *m*
  115:1 glory, for thy *m*, and for thy truth's sake
  118:1 he is good. . his *m* endureth for ever
  119:41 let thy *m* come also unto me, O LORD
  119:64 earth, O LORD, is full of thy *m*: teach me
  119:156 great are thy tender *m*, O LORD: quicken
  123:3 have *m* upon us, O LORD, have *m* upon us
  136:1 give thanks. . for his *m* endureth for ever
  145:9 and his tender *m* are over all his works
Prov. 3:3 let not *m* and truth forsake thee: bind
  14:21 he that hath *m* on the poor, happy is he
  16:6 by *m* and truth iniquity is purged
  21:21 that followeth after righteousness and *m*
Is. 14:1 LORD will have *m* on Jacob, and will yet
  16:5 and in *m* shall the throne be established
  49:13 and will have *m* upon his afflicted
  54:7 but with great *m* will I gather thee
  55:3 (Acts 13:34) even the sure *m* of David
Jer. 6:23 they are cruel, and have no *m*
  13:14 I will not pity, nor spare, nor have *m*
  31:20 will surely have *m* upon him, saith the LORD
  42:12 I will show *m* unto you, that he may have *m*
Lam. 3:22 of the LORD's *m* that we are not consumed
Dan. 9:9 to the Lord. . belong *m* and forgivenesses
Hos. 6:6 (Mt. 9:13; 12:7) desired *m*. . not sacrifice
  12:6 keep *m* and judgment, and wait on thy God
  14:3 for in thee the fatherless findeth *m*
Mic. 6:8 but to do justly, and to love *m*
  7:18 anger for ever, because he delighteth in *m*
Hab. 3:2 revive thy work. . in wrath remember *m*
Zech. 1:16 LORD; I am returned to Jerusalem with *m*
  7:9 true judgment, and show *m* and compassions
Mt. 5:7 are the merciful: for they shall obtain *m*
  9:27 saying, Thou Son of David, have *m* on us
  23:23 weightier matters of the law, judgment, *m*
Lk. 1:50 and his *m* is on them that fear him from
  1:72 to perform the *m* promised to our fathers
  10:37 and he said, He that showed *m* on him
  16:24 Abraham, have *m* on me. . send Lazarus
Rom. 11:30 now obtained *m* through their unbelief
  12:1 I beseech you. . brethren, by the *m* of God
  12:8 he that showeth *m*, with cheerfulness
2 Cor. 1:3 Father of *m*, and the God of all comfort
  4:1 as we have received *m*, we faint not
Eph. 2:4 God, who is rich in *m*, for his great love
Phil. 2:1 if any fellowship. . if any bowels and *m*
Col. 3:12 put on. . as the elect of God. . bowels of *m*
1 Tim. 1:13 obtained *m*, because I did it ignorantly
2 Tim. 1:18 he may find *m* of the Lord in that day
Tit. 3:5 but according to his *m* he saved us
Heb. 4:16 throne of grace, that we may obtain *m*
  9:5 the cherubim of glory shadowing the *m* seat
  10:28 he that despised Moses' law died without *m*
Jas. 2:13 judgment without *m*, that hath showed no *m*
  5:11 the Lord is very pitiful, and of tender *m*
1 Pet. 1:3 which according to his abundant *m* hath
  2:10 had not obtained *m*, but now have obtained *m*
Jude 21 looking for the *m* of our Lord Jesus Christ

Meribah *See also* Massah

Ex. 17:7; Num. 20:13, 24; 27:14

Merodach-baladan
See Berodach-baladan

Merom Josh. 11:5

Merry *See also* Glad, Happy, Joyful

Gen. 43:34 and they drank, and were *m* with him

Judg. 16:25 were *m* . . they said, Call for Samson
1 Kgs. 21:7 eat bread, and let thine heart be *m*
Prov. 15:13 *m* heart maketh a cheerful countenance
    15:15 is of a *m* heart hath a continual feast
    17:22 a *m* heart doeth good like a medicine
Eccl. 8:15 than to eat, and to drink, and to be *m*
    9:7 drink thy wine with a *m* heart; for God now
    10:19 wine maketh *m*: but money answerth all
Lk. 12:19 take thine ease, eat, drink, and be *m*
    15:23 the fatted calf . . and let us eat, and be *m*
Jas. 5:13 is any *m*? let him sing psalms
Rev. 11:10 shall rejoice over them, and make *m*

Meshach Dan. 1:7–3:30

Mesopotamia Gen. 24:10; Acts 7:2

Mess

Gen. 43:34 Benjamin's *m* was five times so much

Message

Judg. 3:20 Ehud said, I have a *m* from God unto
1 Kgs. 20:12 Ben-hadad heard this *m*, as he was
Prov. 26:6 that sendeth a *m* by the hand of a fool
Hag. 1:13 LORD's messenger in the LORD's *m* unto
Lk. 19:14 citizens hated him . . sent a *m* after him
1 Jn. 1:5 this then is the *m* which we have heard
    3:11 is the *m* that ye heard from the beginning

Messenger *See also* Ambassador, Post

Gen. 32:3 Jacob sent *m* before him to Esau
Judg. 11:12 Jephthah sent *m* unto the king of
1 Sam. 19:20 Spirit of God was upon the *m* of Saul
2 Kgs. 1:5 when the *m* turned back unto him
2 Chr. 36:16 mocked the *m* of God, and despised
Prov. 13:17 a wicked *m* falleth into mischief
    16:14 the wrath of a king is as *m* of death
    25:13 so is a faithful *m* to them that send him
Is. 18:2 go, ye swift *m*, to a nation scattered
    42:19 blind, but my servant? or deaf, as my *m*
    44:26 and performeth the counsel of his *m*
    57:9 didst send thy *m* far off, and didst debase
Ezek. 30:9 in that day shall *m* go forth from me
Mal. 2:7 for he is the *m* of the LORD of hosts
    3:1 (Mt. 11:10; Mk. 1:2) behold, I will send my *m*
Lk. 9:52 sent *m* before his face: and they went
2 Cor. 8:23 they are the *m* of the churches
    12:7 thorn in the flesh, the *m* of Satan to
Phil. 2:25 and fellow soldier, but your *m*
Jas. 2:25 by works, when she had received the *m*

Messiah (Messias) *See also* Christ

Dan. 9:25 build Jerusalem, unto the *M* the Prince
    9:26 threescore and two weeks shall *M* be cut off
Jn. 1:41 and saith unto him, We have found the *M*
    4:25 woman saith unto him, I know that *M* cometh

Mete

Ex. 16:18 when they did *m* it with an omer
Is. 40:12 his hand, and *m* out heaven with the span
Mt. 7:2 (Mk. 4:24; Lk. 6:38) what measure ye *m*

Methuselah Gen. 5:21–27

Micah of Ephraim Judg. 17:1–18:31

Micah the prophet Mic. 1:1–7:20; Jer. 26:18

Micaiah 1 Kgs. 22:8–28 (2 Chr. 18:7–27)

Michael

Dan. 10:13 lo, *M*, one of the chief princes, came to
    12:1 at that time shall *M* stand up, the great

Jude 9 yet *M* the archangel, when contending with
Rev. 12:7 *M* and his angels fought against the dragon

Michal

Married to David, 1 Sam. 18:20–30; helped David
escape, 1 Sam. 19:12–17; restored to David, 2 Sam.
3:13–16; rebuked for despising David, 2 Sam. 6:12–
23.

Midian Ex. 2:15; Judg. 7:14

Midianite

Gen. 37:28 passed by *M* merchantmen; and they
Num. 25:17 vex the *M*, and smite them
    31:2 avenge the children of Israel of the *M*
Judg. 6:6 Israel . . impoverished because of the *M*

Midnight

Ex. 11:4 thus saith the LORD, About *m* will I go
Judg. 16:3 Samson lay till *m*, and arose at *m*, and
Ps. 119:62 at *m* I will rise to give thanks unto
Mt. 25:6 at *m* there was a cry . . bridegroom cometh
Mk. 13:35 the master . . cometh, at even, or at *m*
Lk. 11:5 a friend, and shall go unto him at *m*
Acts 16:25 at *m* Paul and Silas prayed, and sang
    20:7 preached . . and continued his speech until *m*

Midst

Ex. 33:3 for I will not go up in the *m* of thee
Ps. 46:5 God is in the *m* of her; she shall not be
Is. 12:6 the Holy One of Israel in the *m* of thee
Jer. 14:9 thou, O LORD, art in the *m* of us, and we
Joel 2:27 shall know that I am in the *m* of Israel
Zeph. 3:15 the King of Israel . . is in the *m* of thee
Mt. 18:2 little child . . and set him in the *m* of them
    18:20 in my name, there am I in the *m* of them
Lk. 24:36 Jesus himself stood in the *m* of them

Midwife (Midwives)

Gen. 35:17 that the *m* said unto her, Fear not
Ex. 1:17 but the *m* feared God, and did not as the

Might *See also* Arm, Authority, Power, Strength

Gen. 49:3 Reuben, thou art my firstborn, my *m*
Num. 14:13 thou broughtest up this people in thy *m*
Deut. 3:24 to thy works, and according to thy *m*?
    6:5 and with all thy soul, and with all thy *m*
    8:17 *m* of mine hand hath gotten me this wealth
Judg. 6:14 go in this thy *m*, and thou shalt save
2 Sam. 6:14 danced before the LORD with all his *m*
1 Chr. 29:12 in thine hand is power and *m*
2 Chr. 20:12 have no *m* against this great company
Ps. 145:6 shall speak of the *m* of thy terrible acts
Eccl. 9:10 hand findeth to do, do it with thy *m*
Is. 40:26 all by names by the greatness of his *m*
    40:29 them that have no *m* he increaseth strength
Jer. 9:23 neither let the mighty man glory in his *m*
    51:30 their *m* hath failed; they became as women
Dan. 2:20 name of God . . for wisdom and *m* are his
Zech. 4:6 not by *m*, nor by power, but by my Spirit
Eph. 3:16 to be strengthened with *m* by his Spirit
    6:10 strong in the Lord . . in the power of his *m*
Col. 1:11 strengthened with all *m*, according to his
Rev. 7:12 honor, and power, and *m*, be unto our God

Mightily

Judg. 14:6 the Spirit of the LORD came *m* upon him
Jon. 3:8 with sackcloth, and cry *m* unto God
Acts 18:28 he *m* convinced the Jews, and . . publicly
    19:20 so *m* grew the word of God and prevailed
Col. 1:29 to his working, which worketh in me *m*

Mighty (Mightier) *See also* Great

Gen. 10:8 Nimrod: he began to be a *m* one in the
18:18 Abraham. . become a great and *m* nation
26:16 go from us; for thou art much *m* than we
Ex. 1:9 children of Israel are more and *m* than we
Lev. 19:15 the poor, nor honor the person of the *m*
Num. 14:12 thee a greater nation and *m* than they
22:6 curse me this people. . they are too *m* for me
Judg. 5:23 to the help of the LORD against the *m*
2 Sam. 1:19 thy high places: how are the *m* fallen!
23:8 be the names of the *m* men whom David had
Job 9:4 he is wise in heart, and *m* in strength
21:7 the wicked live, become old, yea, are *m*
34:20 and the *m* shall be taken away without hand
36:5 behold, God is *m*, and despiseth not any
Ps. 24:8 LORD strong and *m*, the LORD *m* in battle
89:13 thou hast a *m* arm: strong is thy hand
89:19 I have laid help upon one that is *m*
93:4 LORD on high is *m* than the noise of many
112:2 his seed shall be *m* upon earth
145:4 shall praise. . and shall declare thy *m* acts
Prov. 16:32 is slow to anger is better than the *m*
23:11 their Redeemer is *m*; he shall plead their
Eccl. 6:10 he contend with him that is *m* than he
7:19 strengtheneth the wise more than ten *m* men
Is. 1:24 the LORD of hosts, the *M* One of Israel
5:15 down, and the *m* man shall be humbled
5:22 woe unto them that are *m* to drink wine
63:1 I that speak in righteousness, *m* to save
Jer. 32:19 great in counsel, and *m* in work
Ezek. 20:33 with a *m* hand. . will I rule over you
Amos 2:14 neither shall the *m* deliver himself
Zeph. 3:17 LORD thy God in the midst of thee is *m*
Mt. 3:11 but he that cometh after me is *m* than I
11:20 wherein most of his *m* works were done
13:54 (Mk. 6:2) this wisdom, and these *m* works?
14:2 works do show forth themselves in him
Lk. 1:52 he hath put down the *m* from their seats
9:43 they were all amazed at the *m* power of God
24:19 a prophet in deed and word before God
Acts 2:2 sound from heaven as of a rushing *m* wind
7:22 learned. . and was *m* in words and in deeds
18:24 an eloquent man, and *m* in the Scriptures
Rom. 15:19 through *m* signs and wonders
1 Cor. 1:26 not many *m*, not many noble, are called
1:27 weak. . to confound the things which are *m*
2 Cor. 10:4 *m* through God to the pulling down of
13:3 to you-ward is not weak, but is *m* in you
Gal. 2:8 the same was *m* in me toward the Gentiles
Eph. 1:19 according to the working of his *m* power

Milcom 1 Kgs. 11:5

Mile

Mt. 5:41 compel thee to go a *m*, go with him twain

Miletus Acts 20:17

Milk

Gen. 18:8 and he took butter, and *m*, and the calf
49:12 red with wine, and his teeth white with *m*
Ex. 3:8 unto a land flowing with *m* and honey
23:19 shalt not seethe a kid in his mother's *m*
Deut. 26:9 (26:15) land. . floweth with *m* and honey
Judg. 4:19 she opened a bottle of *m*, and gave him
5:25 he asked water, and she gave him *m*
Job 10:10 hast thou not poured me out as *m*
Prov. 27:27 shalt have goats' *m* enough for thy food
30:33 churning of *m* bringeth forth butter
Is. 55:1 buy wine and *m* without money and without
60:16 thou shalt also suck the *m* of the Gentiles
66:11 that ye may *m* out, and be delighted with

Lam. 4:7 purer than snow, they were whiter than *m*
Ezek. 25:4 thy fruit, and they shall drink thy *m*
Joel 3:18 new wine, and the hills shall flow with *m*
1 Cor. 3:2 I have fed you with *m*, and not with meat
9:7 who feedeth a flock, and eateth not of the *m*
Heb. 5:12 become such as have need of *m*, and not
1 Pet. 2:2 babes, desire the sincere *m* of the word

Mill

Ex. 11:5 of the maidservant that is behind the *m*
Num. 11:8 gathered it, and ground it in *m*, or beat
Mt. 24:41 two women shall be grinding at the *m*

Millstone

Deut. 24:6 take the nether or the upper *m* to pledge
Judg. 9:53 cast a piece of a *m* upon Abimelech's
Job 41:24 hard, as hard as a piece of the nether *m*
Jer. 25:10 will take from them. . the sound of the *m*
Mt. 18:6 better for him that a *m* were hanged about
Rev. 18:21 angel took up a stone like a great *m*
18:22 the sound of a *m* shall be heard no more

Mind *See also* Heart, Thought

Lev. 24:12 the *m* of the LORD might be showed them
1 Sam. 2:35 do. . which is in mine heart and in my *m*
1 Chr. 22:7 it was in my *m* to build a house unto
28:9 with a perfect heart and with a willing *m*
Neh. 4:6 built we. . for the people had a *m* to work
Job 23:13 he is in one *m*, and who can turn him?
Prov. 21:27 when he bringeth it with a wicked *m*?
29:11 a fool uttereth all his *m*: but a wise man
Is. 26:3 perfect peace, whose *m* is stayed on thee
Jer. 15:1 yet my *m* could not be toward this people
Ezek. 23:18 then my *m* was alienated from her, like
Dan. 5:20 lifted up, and his *m* hardened in pride
Mt. 22:37 with all thy soul, and with all thy *m*
Mk. 5:15 sitting, and clothed, and in his right *m*
Lk. 12:29 shall drink, neither be ye of doubtful *m*
Acts 17:11 received the word with. . readiness of *m*
20:19 serving the Lord with all humility of *m*
Rom. 1:28 God gave them over to a reprobate *m*
7:23 my members, warring against the law of my *m*
7:25 with the *m* I myself serve the law of God
8:5 after the flesh do *m* the things of the flesh
8:7 because the carnal *m* is enmity against God
8:27 knoweth what is the *m* of the Spirit
11:34 who hath known the *m* of the Lord?
12:2 be ye transformed by the renewing of your *m*
12:16 the same *m* one toward another. *M* not high
14:5 every man be fully persuaded in his own *m*
1 Cor. 2:16 *m* of the Lord. . we have the *m* of Christ
2 Cor. 3:14 but their *m* were blinded: for until
4:4 hath blinded the *m* of them which believe not
8:12 there be first a willing *m*, it is accepted
11:3 his subtilty, so your *m* should be corrupted
13:11 good comfort, be of one *m*, live in peace
Eph. 2:3 desires of the flesh and of the *m*
4:17 as. . Gentiles walk, in the vanity of their *m*
4:23 and be renewed in the spirit of your *m*
Phil. 1:27 one *m* striving together for the faith
2:2 the same love, being of one accord, of one *m*
2:3 lowliness of *m* let each esteem other better
2:5 this *m* be in you, which was also in Christ
3:15 perfect, be thus *m*. . ye be otherwise *m*
3:19 glory. . in their shame, who *m* earthly things
4:2 I beseech. . they be of the same *m* in the Lord
4:7 shall keep your hearts and *m* through Christ
Col. 1:21 and enemies in your *m* by wicked works
2:18 not seen, vainly puffed up by his fleshly *m*
2 Thes. 2:2 that ye be not soon shaken in *m*, or be
2 Tim. 1:7 of power, and of love, and of a sound *m*
3:8 resist the truth: men of corrupt *m*, reprobate
Tit. 1:15 even their *m* and conscience is defiled

Heb. 8:10 will put my laws into their *m*, and write
   12:3 lest ye be wearied and faint in your *m*
1 Pet. 1:13 gird up the loins of your *m*, be sober
   3:8 be ye all of one *m*, having compassion one of
   5:2 not for filthy lucre, but of a ready *m*
2 Pet. 3:1 in both which I stir up your pure *m* by
Rev. 17:9 and here is the *m* which hath wisdom
   17:13 these have one *m*, and shall give their

Mindful

1 Chr. 16:15 be ye *m* always of his covenant
Ps. 8:4 what is man, that thou art *m* of him?
   111:5 fear him: he will ever be *m* of his covenant
   115:12 LORD hath been *m* of us: he will bless us
Is. 17:10 not been *m* of the Rock of thy strength
2 Tim. 1:4 see thee, being *m* of thy tears, that I
Heb. 11:15 if they had been *m* of that country from
2 Pet. 3:2 that ye may be *m* of the words which

Mine

Jn. 17:10 all *m* are thine, and thine are *m*

Mingle

Lk. 13:1 blood Pilate had *m* with their sacrifices

Minister *See also* Servant, Serve, Steward

Ex. 28:1 he may *m* unto me in the priest's office
Deut. 18:5 to stand to *m* in the name of the LORD
   21:5 LORD thy God hath chosen to *m* unto him
1 Sam. 2:11 child did *m* unto the LORD before Eli
   3:1 child Samuel *m* unto the LORD before Eli
1 Chr. 15:2 carry the ark of God, and to *m* unto
Neh. 10:36 priests that *m* in the house of our God
Ps. 103:21 ye his hosts; ye *m* of his, that do his
   104:4 (Heb. 1:7) angels spirits; his *m* a flaming fire
Is. 60:10 and their kings shall *m* unto thee
   61:6 men shall call you The *m* of our God
Ezek. 44:11 yet they shall be *m* in my sanctuary
Dan. 7:10 before him: thousand thousands *m* unto
Joel 1:13 howl, ye *m* of the altar . . ye *m* of my God
Mt. 4:11 devil leaveth . . angels came and *m* unto him
   8:15 fever left her . . she arose, and *m* unto them
   20:26 will be great among you, let him be your *m*
   20:28 Son of man came not to be *m* unto, but to *m*
   25:44 when saw we . . and did not *m* unto thee?
Lk. 1:2 were eye witnesses, and *m* of the word
   4:20 the book, and he gave it again to the *m*
Acts 13:2 as they *m* to the Lord, and fasted
   13:5 they had also John to their *m*
   26:16 make thee a *m* and a witness both of these
Rom. 13:4 for he is the *m* of God to thee for good
   13:6 for they are God's *m*, attending continually
   15:16 I should be the *m* . . to the Gentiles
   15:25 I go unto Jerusalem to *m* unto the saints
1 Cor. 4:1 so account of us, as of the *m* of Christ
   9:13 *m* about holy things live of the things
2 Cor. 3:6 made us able *m* of the new testament
   6:4 approving ourselves as the *m* of God
   8:4 the fellowship of the *m* to the saints
   9:1 for as touching the *m* to the saints
   9:10 he that *m* seed to the sower both *m* bread
   11:15 if his *m* also be transformed as the *m* of
   11:23 are they *m* of Christ? . . I am more
Gal. 2:17 therefore Christ the *m* of sin? God forbid
   3:5 he therefore that *m* to you the Spirit
Eph. 4:29 that it may *m* grace unto the hearers
   6:21 beloved brother and faithful *m* in the Lord
Phil. 2:25 your messenger . . he that *m* to my wants
Col. 1:23 the gospel . . whereof I Paul am made a *m*
1 Tim. 4:6 thou shalt be a good *m* of Jesus Christ
Heb. 1:14 *m* spirits, sent forth to *m* for them who
   6:10 in that ye have *m* to the saints, and do *m*
   8:2 a *m* of the sanctuary . . of the true tabernacle

Heb. 10:11 every priest standeth daily *m* and offering
1 Pet. 4:10 even so *m* the same one to another, as
   4:11 any man *m*, let him do it as of the ability

Ministration *See also* Service

Lk. 1:23 as the days of his *m* were accomplished
Acts 6:1 widows were neglected in the daily *m*
2 Cor. 3:7 if the *m* of death, written and engraven
   3:8 not the *m* of the spirit be rather glorious?
   3:9 *m* of condemnation . . the *m* of righteousness
   9:13 by the experiment of this *m* they glorify God

Ministry

2 Chr. 7:6 when David praised by their *m*
Hos. 12:10 similitudes, by the *m* of the prophets
Acts 1:17 with us, and had obtained part of this *m*
   1:25 he may take part of this *m* and apostleship
   6:4 continually to prayer . . to the *m* of the word
   12:25 returned . . when they had fulfilled their *m*
   20:24 and the *m*, which I have received of the Lord
   21:19 had wrought among the Gentiles by his *m*
Rom. 12:7 or *m*, let us wait on our ministering
1 Cor. 16:15 themselves to the *m* of the saints
2 Cor. 4:1 have this *m*, as we have received mercy
   5:18 hath given to us the *m* of reconciliation
   6:3 giving no offense . . that the *m* be not blamed
Eph. 4:12 for the work of the *m*, for the edifying
Col. 4:17 and say to Archippus, Take heed to the *m*
1 Tim. 1:12 me faithful, putting me into the *m*
2 Tim. 4:5 an evangelist, make full proof of thy *m*
   4:11 take Mark . . he is profitable to me for the *m*
Heb. 8:6 now hath he obtained a more excellent *m*

Minstrel

2 Kgs. 3:15 now bring me a *m* . . when the *m* played
Mt. 9:23 saw the *m* and the people making a noise

Mint

Mt. 23:23 (Lk. 11:42) hypocrites! . . ye pay tithe of *m*

Miracle *See also* Marvel, Sign, Wonder

Ex. 7:9 when Pharaoh shall speak . . Show a *m* for you
Num. 14:22 my glory, and my *m*, which I did in Egypt
Deut. 11:3 his *m*, and his acts, which he did in
Judg. 6:13 where be all his *m* which our fathers
Mk. 6:52 they considered not the *m* of the loaves
   9:39 no man which shall do a *m* in my name, that
Lk. 23:8 he hoped to have seen some *m* done by him
Jn. 2:11 this beginning of *m* did Jesus in Cana
   2:23 believed . . when they saw the *m* which he did
   3:2 for no man can do these *m* that thou doest
   4:54 this is again the second *m* that Jesus did
   6:2 followed him, because they saw his *m* which
   6:26 ye seek me, not because ye saw the *m*, but
   7:31 when Christ cometh, will he do more *m* than
   9:16 how can a man that is a sinner do such *m*?
   10:41 John did no *m*: but all things that John
   11:47 what do we? for this man doeth many *m*
   12:37 though he had done so many *m* before them
Acts 2:22 a man approved of God among you by *m*
   4:16 indeed a notable *m* hath been done by them
   6:8 and Stephen . . did great wonders and *m* among
   8:6 hearing and seeing the *m* which he did
   15:12 Paul, declaring what *m* and wonders God
   19:11 God wrought special *m* by the hands of Paul
1 Cor. 12:10 to another the working of *m*
   12:29 are all teachers? are all workers of *m*?
Gal. 3:5 worketh *m* among you, doeth he it by the
Heb. 2:4 divers *m*, and gifts of the Holy Ghost
Rev. 13:14 deceiveth them . . by the means of those *m*
   16:14 they are the spirits of devils, working *m*
   19:20 false prophet that wrought *m* before him

Mire

Job 30:19 he hath cast me into the *m* . . I am become
Ps. 69:2 sink in deep *m*, where there is no standing
69:14 deliver me out of the *m* . . let me not sink
Jer. 38:6 no water, but *m* . . Jeremiah sunk in the *m*
2 Pet. 2:22 and the sow . . to her wallowing in the *m*

Miriam

Song of Miriam, Ex. 15:20–21; became leprous for
criticizing Moses, Num. 12:1–10; her leprosy healed,
Num. 12:11–16; died in Kadesh, Num. 20:1.

Deut. 24:9 remember what the LORD . . did unto *M*
Mic. 6:4 I sent before thee Moses, Aaron, and *M*

Mirth *See also* Cheer

Gen. 31:27 that I might have sent thee away with *m*
Neh. 8:12 great *m*, because they had understood
Ps. 137:3 and they that wasted us required of us *m*
Prov. 14:13 and the end of that *m* is heaviness
Eccl. 2:1 I will prove thee with *m*; therefore enjoy
7:4 but the heart of fools is in the house of *m*
8:15 I commended *m*, because a man hath no
Is. 24:11 is darkened, the *m* of the land is gone
Jer. 7:34 then will I cause to cease . . the voice of *m*

Miry

Ps. 40:2 out of a horrible pit, out of the *m* clay

Mischief *See also* Damage, Harm, Hurt

Gen. 42:4 he said, Lest peradventure *m* befall him
Ex. 32:22 knowest the people . . they are set on *m*
1 Sam. 23:9 Saul secretly practised *m* against him
Neh. 6:2 Sanballat and Geshem . . to do me *m*
Job 15:35 they conceive *m*, and bring forth vanity
Ps. 7:14 conceived *m*, and brought forth falsehood
7:16 his *m* shall return upon his own head
10:7 under the tongue is *m* and vanity
26:10 in whose hands is *m*, and their right hand
28:3 which speak peace . . but *m* is in their hearts
36:4 deviseth *m* upon his bed; he setteth himself
52:1 why boastest thou . . in *m*, O mighty man?
62:3 how long will ye imagine *m* against a man?
94:20 with thee, which frameth *m* by a law?
Prov. 4:16 they sleep not, except they have done *m*
10:23 it is as sport to a fool to do *m*: but a man
11:27 he that seeketh *m*, it shall come unto him
13:17 a wicked messenger falleth into *m*
24:2 studieth destruction . . their lips talk of *m*
24:16 up again: but the wicked shall fall into *m*
Is. 59:4 they conceive *m*, and bring forth iniquity
Ezek. 7:26 *m* shall come upon *m*, and rumor shall be
Hos. 7:15 yet do they imagine *m* against me
Acts 13:10 O full of all subtilty and all *m*

Miserable

Job 16:2 *m* comforters are ye all
1 Cor. 15:19 we are of all men most *m*
Rev. 3:17 knowest not . . thou art wretched, and *m*

Misery *See also* Anguish, Distress, Grief, Sorrow

Judg. 10:16 soul was grieved for the *m* of Israel
Job 3:20 light given to him that is in *m*, and life
11:16 shalt forget thy *m*, and remember it as
Prov. 31:7 his poverty, and remember his *m* no more
Eccl. 8:6 therefore the *m* of man is great upon him
Lam. 3:19 remembering mine affliction and my *m*
Rom. 3:16 destruction and *m* are in their ways
Jas. 5:1 weep and howl for your *m* that shall come

Mist

Gen. 2:6 went up a *m* from the earth, and watered
Acts 13:11 there fell on him a *m* and a darkness
2 Pet. 2:17 to whom the *m* of darkness is reserved

Mite

Mk. 12:42 poor widow, and she threw in two *m*
Lk. 12:59 till thou hast paid the very last *m*

Mitre

Ex. 28:39 and thou shalt make the *m* of fine linen
Zech. 3:5 set a fair *m* upon his head, and clothed

Mixed

Ex. 12:38 and a *m* multitude went up also with them
Prov. 23:30 the wine; they that go to seek *m* wine
Is. 1:22 thy silver . . dross, thy wine *m* with water
Dan. 2:41 thou sawest the iron *m* with miry clay
Heb. 4:2 not being *m* with faith in them that heard

Mizpah Gen. 31:49

Mizpeh Judg. 20:1; 1 Sam. 7:5

Mnason Acts 21:16

Moab

Gen. 19:37 bare a son, and called his name *M*
Num. 22:3 and *M* was distressed because of . . Israel
24:17 shall smite the corners of *M*, and destroy
Ruth 1:1 went to sojourn in the country of *M*
2 Kgs. 1:1 then *M* rebelled against Israel after
Ps. 60:8 *M* is my washpot; over Edom will I cast
Is. 15:1 the burden of *M* . . Ar of *M* is laid waste
Jer. 48:1 against *M* thus saith the LORD of hosts
Ezek. 25:11 I will execute judgments upon *M*
Amos 2:1 three transgressions of *M*, and for four
Zeph. 2:9 as I live . . Surely *M* shall be as Sodom

Moabite

Deut. 2:9 distress not the *M*, neither contend with
23:3 or *M* shall not enter into the congregation
Judg. 3:28 LORD hath delivered your enemies the *M*
2 Sam. 8:2 (1 Chr. 18:2) *M* became David's servants
2 Kgs. 3:18 will deliver the *M* also into your hand
13:20 the bands of the *M* invaded the land

Mock

Gen. 19:14 but he seemed as one that *m* unto his
21:9 Sarah saw the son of Hagar the Egyptian . . *m*
39:14 hath brought in a Hebrew unto us to *m* us
Num. 22:29 said unto the ass . . thou hast *m* me
Judg. 16:10 thou hast *m* me, and told me lies
1 Kgs. 18:27 Elijah *m* them, and said, Cry aloud
2 Kgs. 2:23 children out of the city, and *m* him
2 Chr. 36:16 but they *m* the messengers of God
Job 12:4 am as one *m* of his neighbor, who calleth
13:9 or as one man *m* another, do ye so *m* him?
Prov. 1:26 I will *m* when your fear cometh
14:9 fools make a *m* at sin: but among the
17:5 whoso *m* the poor reproacheth his Maker
30:17 eye that *m* at his father, and despiseth to
Jer. 20:7 I am in derision daily, every one *m* me
Mt. 2:16 when he saw that he was *m* of the wise men
20:19 (Mk. 10:34; Lk. 18:32) to *m*, and to scourge
27:29 and *m* him, saying, Hail, King of the Jews!
27:41 (Mk. 15:31) also the chief priests *m* him
Lk. 14:29 lest . . all that behold it begin to *m* him
Acts 2:13 others *m* said, These men are full of new
17:32 of the resurrection of the dead, some *m*
Gal. 6:7 be not deceived; God is not *m* . . whatsoever

Mocker

Job 17:2 are there not *m* with me? and doth not
Ps. 35:16 with hypocritical *m* in feasts, they
Prov. 20:1 wine is a *m*, strong drink is raging
Is. 28:22 be ye not *m*, lest your bands be made
Jer. 15:17 I sat not in the assembly of the *m*
Jude 18 there should be *m* in the last time

Moderation

Phil. 4:5 let your *m* be known unto all men

Modest

1 Tim. 2:9 women adorn themselves in *m* apparel

Moisture

Ps. 32:4 my *m* is turned into the drought of summer
Lk. 8:6 it withered away, because it lacked *m*

Mole

Lev. 11:30 the lizard, and the snail, and the *m*
Is. 2:20 cast his idols. . to the *m* and to the bats

Molech (Moloch) *See also* Milcom

Lev. 18:21 of thy seed pass through the fire to *M*
20:2 giveth any of his seed unto *M* . . put to death
Amos 5:26 ye have borne the tabernacle of your *M*

Mollify

Is. 1:6 neither bound up, neither *m* with ointment

Moment

Ex. 33:5 come up into the midst of thee in a *m*
Num. 16:21 separate . . I may consume them in a *m*
Job 7:18 him every morning, and try him every *m*?
21:13 in wealth, and in a *m* go down to the grave
34:20 in a *m* shall they die, and the people
Ps. 30:5 his anger endureth but a *m*; in his favor
73:19 they brought into desolation, as in a *m*!
Prov. 12:19 but a lying tongue is but for a *m*
Is. 26:20 hide thyself as it were for a little *m*
27:3 do keep it; I will water it every *m*: lest
54:7 for a small *m* have I forsaken thee; but
Lk. 4:5 the kingdoms of the world in a *m* of time
1 Cor. 15:52 in a *m*, in the twinkling of an eye
2 Cor. 4:17 light affliction, which is but for a *m*

Money *See also* Mammon, Riches, Wealth

Gen. 42:25 to restore every man's *m* into his sack
47:14 Joseph gathered up all the *m* . . in the land
Ex. 12:44 every man's servant that is bought for *m*
22:25 if thou lend *m* to any of my people that is
30:16 and thou shalt take the atonement *m* of the
Lev. 25:37 shalt not give him thy *m* upon usury
Num. 3:49 Moses took the redemption *m* of them
2 Kgs. 5:26 is it a time to receive *m*
12:10 saw that there was much *m* in the chest
Ps. 15:5 he that putteth not out his *m* to usury
Eccl. 7:12 wisdom is a defense, and *m* is a defense
10:19 maketh merry: but *m* answereth all things
Is. 52:3 and ye shall be redeemed without *m*
55:1 he that hath no *m*; come ye, buy, and eat
55:2 do ye spend *m* for that which is not bread?
Mic. 3:11 the prophets thereof divine for *m*
Mt. 17:27 thou shalt find a piece of *m*: that take
21:12 (Mk. 11:15) tables of the *m* changers
22:19 show me the tribute *m*. And they brought
25:18 digged in the earth, and hid his lord's *m*
28:12 they gave large *m* unto the soldiers
Mk. 6:8 a staff only; no scrip, no bread, no *m*
12:41 how the people cast *m* into the treasury
14:11 were glad, and promised to give him *m*
Jn. 2:15 poured out the changers' *m* and overthrew
Acts 4:37 having land, sold it, and brought the *m*

Acts 8:20 Peter said unto him, Thy *m* perish with thee
24:26 he hoped also that *m* should have been given
1 Tim. 6:10 the love of *m* is the root of all evil

Month *See also* Day, Time, Year

Ex. 12:2 this *m* shall be unto you the beginning of *m*
Num. 11:21 flesh, that they may eat a whole *m*
Job 3:6 let it not come into the number of the *m*
14:5 seeing. . the number of his *m* are with thee
Gal. 4:10 ye observe days, and, *m*, and times

Moon *See also* Sun

Gen. 37:9 *m* and the eleven stars made obeisance to
Josh. 10:13 the sun stood still, and the *m* stayed
1 Sam. 20:5 tomorrow is the new *m*, and I should
Job 31:26 shined, or the *m* walking in brightness
Ps. 8:3 *m* and the stars, which thou hast ordained
72:5 fear thee as long as the sun and *m* endure
72:7 abundance of peace so long as the *m* endureth
89:37 it shall be established for ever as the *m*
104:19 he appointed the *m* for seasons
121:6 not smite thee by day, nor the *m* by night
136:9 the *m* and stars to rule by night
Song 6:10 fair as the *m*, clear as the sun
Is. 1:14 your new *m* and your appointed feasts
3:18 and their round tires like the *m*
13:10 the *m* shall not cause her light to shine
24:23 the *m* shall be confounded, and the sun
30:26 the light of the *m* shall be as . . the sun
60:19 neither. . shall the *m* give light unto thee
Joel 2:31 (Acts 2:20) darkness, and the *m* into blood
Mt. 24:29 and the *m* shall not give her light
1 Cor. 15:41 another glory of the *m*, and another
Col. 2:16 or of the new *m*, or of the sabbath days
Rev. 6:12 became black . . and the *m* became as blood
12:1 clothed with the sun . . the *m* under her feet
21:23 sun, neither of the *m*, to shine in it

Mordecai

Counseled Esther, Esth. 2:5–20; informed Esther of
a conspiracy, Esth. 2:21–23; refused to reverence Haman, Esth. 3:2–6; arrayed in royal apparel, Esth. 6:1–
11; promoted next to the king, Esth. 8:1–2; 10:3; reversed Haman's decree, Esth. 8:3–9:4; decreed feast
of Purim, Esth. 9:20–31.

Moriah Gen. 22:2; 2 Chr. 3:1

Morning

Gen. 1:5 the evening and the *m* were the first day
19:15 the *m* arose, then the angels hastened Lot
Ex. 16:7 in the *m*, then ye shall see the glory
Deut. 28:67 at even. . say, Would God it were *m*!
2 Sam. 23:4 the light of the *m* . . a *m* without clouds
Job 11:17 shalt shine forth, thou shalt be as the *m*
38:12 hast thou commanded the *m* since thy days
Ps. 5:3 hear in the *m*, O LORD; in the *m* will I direct
30:5 endure for a night, but joy cometh in the *m*
90:6 in the *m* it flourisheth, and groweth up
130:6 more than they that watch for the *m*
Is. 21:12 the *m* cometh, and also the night
58:8 then shall thy light break forth as the *m*
Lam. 3:23 new every *m*: great is thy faithfulness
Hos. 6:3 his going forth is prepared as the *m*
Joel 2:2 as the *m* spread upon the mountains
Mk. 13:35 cometh. . at the cockcrowing, or in the *m*
Rev. 2:28 and I will give him the *m* star
22:16 spring of David, and the bright and *m* star

Morrow *See also* Tomorrow

Lev. 23:11 on the *m* after the sabbath the priest
Mt. 6:34 no thought for the *m*: for the *m* shall
Jas. 4:14 ye know not what shall be on the *m*

Morsel

Gen. 18:5 I will fetch a *m* of bread, and comfort
1 Sam. 2:36 for a piece of silver and a *m* of bread
Job 31:17 or have eaten my *m* myself alone
Prov. 17:1 better is a dry *m*, and quietness
Heb. 12:16 for one *m* of meat sold his birthright

Mortal

Job 4:17 shall *m* man be more just than God?
Rom. 6:12 let not sin . . reign in your *m* body
8:11 also quicken your *m* bodies by his Spirit
1 Cor. 15:53 and this *m* must put on immortality
2 Cor. 4:11 might be made manifest in our *m* flesh

Mortality

2 Cor. 5:4 that *m* might be swallowed up of life

Mortar

Gen. 11:3 brick for stone . . slime had they for *m*
Ex. 1:14 with hard bondage, in *m*, and in brick
Prov. 27:22 thou shouldest bray a fool in a *m*
Ezek. 13:10 lo, others daubed it with untempered *m*

Mortgage

Neh. 5:3 have *m* our lands, vineyards, and houses

Mortify

Rom. 8:13 do *m* the deeds of the body, ye shall live
Col. 3:5 *m* therefore your members which are upon

Moses

Born, Ex. 2:1–4; adopted by Pharaoh's daughter, Ex. 2:5–10; trained at the Egyptian court, Acts 7:22; killed the Egyptian, Ex. 2:11–12; fled to Midian, Ex. 2:15–20; married Zipporah, Ex. 2:21–22; called by God, Ex. 3:1–4:17; returned to Egypt, Ex. 4:18–31; interceded with Pharaoh, Ex. 5–11; crossed the Red Sea, Ex. 14; sang for triumph, Ex. 15:1–18; appointed rulers, Ex. 18:13–26; met God on Sinai, Ex. 19:3–13; 24–31; enraged by Israel's idolatry, Ex. 32; talked with the LORD, Ex. 33–34; built the tabernacle, Ex. 35–40; numbered the people, Num. 1; vindicated before Aaron and Miriam, Num. 12; sent twelve spies to Canaan, Num. 13:1–20; consecrated Joshua as his successor, Num. 27:18–23; Deut. 31:23; recounted Israel's history, Deut. 1–3; exhorted Israel to obedience, Deut. 4:1–40; song of Moses, Deut. 32:1–43; viewed Canâan, Deut. 3:23–27; 32:48–52; 34:1–4; blessed the tribes, Deut. 33; death and burial in Moab, Deut. 34:5–7. (*See also* Acts 7:20–44.)

Josh. 1:5 as I was with *M*, so I will be with thee
Ps. 77:20 thou leddest the people . . by the hand of *M*
103:7 he made known his ways unto *M*, his acts
105:26 he sent *M* his servant; and Aaron whom he
106:23 destroy them, had not *M* his chosen stood
Is. 63:12 led them by the right hand of *M* with his
Jer. 15:1 though *M* and Samuel stood before me, yet
Mic. 6:4 I sent before thee *M*, Aaron, and Miriam
Mt. 17:3 appeared unto them *M* and Elias talking
19:8 *M* because of the hardness of your hearts
Lk. 16:29 they have *M* and . . prophets; let them hear
24:27 beginning at *M* and all the prophets, he
Jn. 1:17 law was given by *M*, but grace and truth
3:14 *M* lifted up the serpent in the wilderness
5:46 ye believed *M*, ye would have believed me
6:32 *M* gave you not that bread from heaven
7:19 did not *M* give you the law, and yet none of
9:29 we know that God spake unto *M*: as for this
Acts 3:22 *M* truly said unto the fathers, A Prophet
6:11 speak blasphemous words against *M*

Acts 21:21 thou teachest all the Jews . . to forsake *M*
Rom. 5:14 death reigned from Adam to *M*, even over
10:5 *M* describeth the righteousness which is of
1 Cor. 10:2 were all baptized unto *M* in the cloud
2 Cor. 3:7 could not . . behold the face of *M* for the
3:15 *M* is read, the veil is upon their heart
2 Tim. 3:8 as Jannes and Jambres withstood *M*, so
Heb. 3:2 as also *M* was faithful in all his house
7:14 tribe *M* spake nothing concerning priesthood
9:19 when *M* had spoken every precept to all
11:23 by faith *M*, when he was born, was hid
Jude 9 yet Michael . . disputed about the body of *M*
Rev. 15:3 sing the song of *M* the servant of God

Most High

Ps. 9:2 I will sing praise to thy name, O thou *M H*

Mote

Mt. 7:3 beholdest thou the *m* . . in thy brother's eye

Moth   *See also* Worm

Job 27:18 he buildeth his house as a *m*, and as a
Ps. 39:11 makest his beauty to consume away like a *m*
Is. 50:9 old as a garment; the *m* shall eat them up
Hos. 5:12 therefore will I be unto Ephraim as a *m*
Mt. 6:19 upon earth, where *m* and rust doth corrupt

Moth-eaten

Job 13:28 consumeth, as a garment that is *m-e*
Jas. 5:2 riches are corrupted . . your garments are *m-e*

Mother   *See also* Parent

Gen. 2:24 shall a man leave his father and his *m*
3:20 Eve; because she was the *m* of all living
17:16 bless her, and she shall be a *m* of nations
Ex. 20:12 (Deut. 5:16; Mt. 15:4; Mk. 7:10; Eph. 6:2) honor thy father and thy *m*
Judg. 5:7 I Deborah arose . . I arose a *m* in Israel
1 Sam. 2:19 moreover his *m* made him a little coat
2 Sam. 20:19 to destroy a city and a *m* in Israel
Job 17:14 the worm, Thou art my *m*, and my sister
Ps. 51:5 and in sin did my *m* conceive me
113:9 barren woman . . to be a joyful *m* of children
Prov. 1:8 and forsake not the law of thy *m*
10:1 but a foolish son is the heaviness of his *m*
15:20 but a foolish man despiseth his *m*
23:22 and despise not thy *m* when she is old
Is. 66:13 as one whom his *m* comforteth, so will I
Jer. 15:10 woe is me, my *m*, that thou hast borne
Ezek. 16:44 as is the *m*, so is her daughter
Mic. 7:6 (Mt. 10:35; Lk. 12:53) against her *m*
Mt. 10:37 he that loveth father or *m* more than me
12:48 (Mk. 3:33) who is my *m*? . . my brethren?
Jn. 19:27 saith he to the disciple, Behold thy *m*!
Gal. 4:26 Jerusalem which is above is . . *m* of us all
1 Tim. 5:2 the elder women as *m*; the younger as
2 Tim. 1:5 thy grandmother Lois, and thy *m* Eunice

Mount   (noun)   *See also* Hill, Mountain

Gen. 22:14 in the *m* of the LORD it shall be seen
Ex. 4:27 met him in the *m* of God, and kissed him
18:5 unto Moses . . encamped at the *m* of God
19:2 Sinai . . there Israel camped before the *m*
19:18 smoke thereof ascended . . whole *m* quaked
24:12 come up to me into the *m* . . I will give thee
32:15 Moses turned, and went down from the *m*
Deut. 1:6 ye have dwelt long enough in this *m*
2 Sam. 15:32 David was come to the top of the *m*
1 Kgs. 19:11 and stand upon the *m* before the LORD
Is. 27:13 shall worship . . in the holy *m* at Jerusalem
Heb. 12:18 ye are not come unto the *m* that might
2 Pet. 1:18 when we were with him in the holy *m*

Mount (verb) *See also* Ascend

Job 20:6 though his excellency *m* up to the heavens
39:27 doth the eagle *m* up at thy command
Ps. 107:26 they *m* up to the heaven, they go down
Is. 9:18 shall *m* up like the lifting up of smoke
40:31 they shall *m* up with wings as eagles
Jer. 51:53 though Babylon should *m* up to heaven
Ezek. 10:16 the cherubim. . *m* up from the earth

Mountain *See also* Hill, Mount

Gen. 7:20 waters prevail; and the *m* were covered
19:17 escape to the *m*, lest thou be consumed
Ex. 3:1 Moses. . came to the *m* of God. . to Horeb
3:12 of Egypt, ye shall serve God upon this *m*
15:17 plant them in the *m* of thine inheritance
20:18 the *m* smoking: and when the people saw it
Deut. 2:3 ye have compassed this *m* long enough
Josh. 2:16 get you to the *m*, lest the pursuers meet
14:12 now therefore give me this *m*, whereof
17:18 but the *m* shall be thine; for it is a wood
2 Sam. 1:21 ye *m* of Gilboa, let there be no dew
2 Kgs. 6:17 the *m* was full of horses and chariots
2 Chr. 18:16 see all Israel scattered upon the *m*
Job 9:5 which removeth the *m*, and they know not
28:9 he overturneth the *m* by the roots
Ps. 30:7 by thy favor thou hast made my *m* to stand
46:2 though the *m* be carried into the midst
48:1 city of our God, in the *m* of his holiness
65:6 which by his strength setteth fast the *m*
72:3 the *m* shall bring peace to the people
90:2 before the *m* were brought forth, or ever
114:4 *m* skipped like rams, and the little hills
125:2 as the *m* are round about Jerusalem, so the
Is. 2:2 *m* of the LORD's house. . in the top of the *m*
2:3 come ye. . let us go up to the *m* of the LORD
11:9 shall not hurt nor destroy in all my holy *m*
25:6 in this *m* shall the LORD of hosts make unto
34:3 and the *m* shall be melted with their blood
40:4 (Lk. 3:5) every *m* and hill shall be made low
40:9 get thee up into the high *m*; O Jerusalem
40:12 in a measure, and weighed the *m* in scales
52:7 how beautiful upon the *m* are the feet of
54:10 *m* shall depart, and the hills be removed
55:12 the *m* and the hills shall break forth
57:7 a lofty and high *m* hast thou set thy bed
64:1 that the *m* might flow down at thy presence
Jer. 3:6 she is gone up upon every high *m*
4:24 I beheld the *m*, and, lo, they trembled
17:3 O my *m* in the field, I will give thy
31:23 O habitation of justice, and *m* of holiness
51:25 behold, I am against thee, O destroying *m*
Ezek. 6:3 ye *m* of Israel, hear the word of the Lord
11:23 glory of the LORD. . stood upon the *m*
20:40 mine holy *m*. . the *m* of the height of Israel
28:14 thou wast upon the holy *m* of God
36:1 prophesy unto the *m* of Israel
38:20 and the *m* shall be thrown down
40:2 and set me upon a very high *m*, by which was
Dan. 2:35 the stone. . became a great *m*, and filled
Hos. 10:8 (Lk. 23:30) shall say to the *m*, Cover us
Joel 3:18 that the *m* shall drop down new wine
Amos 4:13 he that formeth the *m*, and createth
Mic. 1:4 and the *m* shall be molten under him
6:2 hear ye, O *m*, the LORD's controversy
Zech. 4:7 who art thou, O great *m*? . . Zerubbabel
8:3 and the *m* of the LORD of hosts, The holy *m*
Mt. 4:8 devil taketh him. . into an exceeding high *m*
5:1 seeing the multitudes, he went up into a *m*
14:23 he went up into a *m* apart to pray
15:29 and went up into a *m*, and sat down there
17:1 and bringeth them up into a high *m* apart
17:20 say unto this *m*, Remove hence to yonder

Mt. 24:16 (Mk. 13:14; Lk. 21:21) Judea flee into
the *m*
28:16 into a *m* where Jesus had appointed them
Jn. 4:20 our fathers worshipped in this *m*
1 Cor. 13:2 all faith, so that I could remove *m*
Rev. 6:14 and every *m* and island were moved out of
6:16 and said to the *m* and rocks, Fall on us
8:8 and as it were a great *m* burning
16:20 island fled away, and the *m* were not found
17:9 the seven heads are seven *m*, on which the
21:10 away in the spirit to a great and high *m*

Mourn *See also* Cry, Grieve, Lament, Weep

Num. 14:39 Moses told these. . the people *m* greatly
1 Sam. 16:1 Samuel, How long wilt thou *m* for Saul
2 Sam. 1:12 *m*, and wept, and fasted until even
13:37 and David *m* for his son every day
Ezra 10:6 for he *m* because of the transgression of
Neh. 8:9 this day is holy. . *m* not, nor weep
Job 2:11 to come to *m* with him, and to comfort him
5:11 that those which *m* may be exalted to safety
Ps. 42:9 why go I *m* because of the oppression of
55:2 I *m* in my complaint, and make a noise
Prov. 5:11 thou *m* at the last, when thy flesh and
29:2 when the wicked beareth rule, the people *m*
Eccl. 3:4 a time to *m*, and a time to dance
Is. 24:4 the earth *m* and fadeth away, the world
59:11 roar all like bears, and *m* sore like doves
61:2 vengeance of our God; to comfort all that *m*
66:10 for joy with her, all ye that *m* for her
Jer. 4:28 for this shall the earth *m*, and the heavens
Ezek. 24:23 ye shall not *m* nor weep; but ye shall
Dan. 10:2 I Daniel was *m* three full weeks
Hos. 4:3 therefore shall the land *m*, and every one
Joel 1:9 the priests, the LORD's ministers, *m*
Amos 9:5 melt, and all that dwell therein shall *m*
Zech. 12:10 *m* for him, as one *m* for his only son
Mt. 5:4 blessed are they that *m*: for they shall be
9:15 can the children of the bridechamber *m*
11:17 we. . *m* unto you, and ye have not lamented
24:30 then shall all the tribes of the earth *m*
Lk. 6:25 that laugh now! for ye shall *m* and weep
Jas. 4:9 be afflicted, and, *m*, and weep: let your
Rev. 18:11 merchants of the earth shall. . *m* over

Mourner

2 Sam. 14:2 feign thyself to be a *m*, and put on
Eccl. 12:5 and the *m* go about the streets
Is. 57:18 restore comforts unto him and to his *m*

Mournfully

Mal. 3:14 that we have walked *m* before the LORD of

Mourning *See also* Grief, Lamentation, Wailing, Weeping

Gen. 50:11 saw the *m*. . said, This is a grievous *m*
Deut. 34:8 so the days of weeping and *m* for Moses
2 Sam. 11:27 when the *m* was past, David sent and
19:2 victory that day was turned into *m* unto all
Esth. 4:3 there was great *m* among the Jews
Job 30:31 harp also is turned to *m*, and my organ
Ps. 30:11 hast turned for me my *m* into dancing
Eccl. 7:2 better to go to the house of *m*, than to
Is. 22:12 GOD of hosts call to weeping, and to *m*
60:20 and the days of thy *m* shall be ended
61:3 beauty for ashes, the oil of joy for *m*
Jer. 6:26 in ashes: make thee *m*, as for an only son
31:13 for I will turn their *m* into joy, and will
Lam. 5:15 is ceased; our dance is turned into *m*
Ezek. 24:17 forbear to cry, make no *m* for the dead

Ezek. 31:15 he went down to the grave I caused a *m*
Amos 5:16 and they shall call the husbandman to *m*
  8:10 your feasts into *m* . . as the *m* of an only son
Zech. 12:11 be a great *m* in Jerusalem, as the *m* of
Mt. 2:18 great *m*, Rachel weeping for her children
2 Cor. 7:7 your *m*, your fervent mind toward me
Jas. 4:9 let your laughter be turned to *m*

Mouse

Lev. 11:29 unclean unto you . . the weasel, and the *m*
Is. 66:17 swine's flesh . . the abomination, and the *m*

Mouth *See also* Lip, Tongue

Gen. 8:11 dove came in . . in her *m* was an olive leaf
Ex. 4:11 who hath made man's *m*? or who maketh the
Deut. 30:14 very nigh unto thee, in thy *m*, and in
2 Kgs. 4:34 upon the child, and put his *m* upon his *m*
Job 9:20 justify myself, mine own *m* shall condemn
  40:4 answer thee? I will lay mine hand upon my *m*
Ps. 8:2 (Mt. 21:16) out of the *m* of babes
  10:7 his *m* is full of cursing . . deceit and fraud
  32:9 whose *m* must be held in with bit and bridle
  35:21 they opened their *m* wide against me
  37:30 the *m* of the righteous speaketh wisdom
  39:1 I will keep my *m* with a bridle, while the
  40:3 he hath put a new song in my *m*, even praise
  49:3 my *m* shall speak of wisdom
  51:15 and my *m* shall show forth thy praise
  63:11 *m* them that speak lies shall be stopped
  103:5 who satisfieth thy *m* with good things
  109:2 *m* of the wicked and the *m* of the deceitful
  115:5 they have *m*, but they speak not
  126:2 then was our *m* filled with laughter
  141:3 set a watch, O LORD, before my *m*
Prov. 4:24 put away from thee a froward *m*
  10:6 but violence covereth the *m* of the wicked
  10:14 the *m* of the foolish is near destruction
  10:31 the *m* of the just bringeth forth wisdom
  12:6 but the *m* of the upright shall deliver them
  13:3 he that keepeth his *m* keepeth his life
  18:7 a fool's *m* is his destruction, and his lips
  19:28 and the *m* of the wicked devoureth iniquity
  21:23 whoso keepeth his *m* and his tongue, keepeth
Eccl. 6:7 the labor of man is for his *m*, and yet
Is. 29:13 (Mt. 15:8) people draw near me with their *m*
Dan. 7:8 (Rev. 13:5) and a *m* speaking great things
Mal. 2:6 law of truth was in his *m*, and iniquity
Mt. 12:34 the abundance of the heart the *m* speaketh
Lk. 1:64 his *m* was opened immediately, and his
  21:15 I will give you a *m* and wisdom, which all
Rom. 3:14 whose *m* is full of cursing and bitterness
  3:19 that every *m* may be stopped
  10:10 and with the *m* confession is made unto
Eph. 4:29 no corrupt communication . . out of your *m*
Tit. 1:11 whose *m* must be stopped, who subvert
Heb. 11:33 through faith . . stopped the *m* of lions
Jas. 3:10 out of the same *m* proceedeth blessing
Jude 16 and their *m* speaketh great swelling words
Rev. 13:5 given unto him a *m* speaking great things

Move

Gen. 1:2 Spirit of God *m* upon the face of the waters
Deut. 32:21 have *m* me to jealousy . . I will *m* them
Judg. 13:25 the Spirit of the LORD began to *m* him
1 Sam. 1:13 lips *m*, but her voice was not heard
2 Sam. 22:8 (Ps. 18:7) foundations of heaven *m* and
Job 2:3 although thou *m* me against him, to destroy
Ps. 10:6 hath said in his heart, I shall not be *m*
  15:5 he that doeth these things shall never be *m*
  16:8 (Acts 2:25) at my right hand, I shall not be *m*
  18:7 foundations . . of the hills *m* and were shaken
  21:7 mercy of the Most High he shall not be *m*
  30:6 in my prosperity I said, I shall never be *m*

Ps. 46:5 she shall not be *m*: God shall help her
  55:22 he shall never suffer the righteous to be *m*
  68:8 Sinai itself was *m* at the presence of God
  112:6 he shall not be *m* for ever: the righteous
  121:3 he will not suffer thy foot to be *m*
Prov. 12:3 root of the righteous shall not be *m*
  23:31 color in the cup, when it *m* itself aright
Is. 7:2 heart was *m* . . as the trees of the wood are *m*
  19:1 idols of Egypt shall be *m* at his presence
Mt. 14:14 and was *m* with compassion toward them
  21:10 come into Jerusalem, all the city was *m*
  23:4 will not *m* them with one of their fingers
Mk. 15:11 but the chief priests *m* the people, that
Acts 17:28 for in him we live, and, *m*, and have our
  20:24 none of these things *m* me, neither count I
  21:30 and all the city was *m*, and the people ran
Col. 1:23 not *m* away from the hope of the gospel
1 Thes. 3:3 no man should be *m* by these afflictions
Heb. 12:28 receiving a kingdom which cannot be *m*
2 Pet. 1:21 spake as they were *m* by the Holy Ghost
Rev. 6:14 and island were *m* out of their places

Much

Ex. 16:18 (2 Cor. 8:15) gathered *m* had nothing over
Num. 16:3 ye take too *m* upon you, seeing all the
Lk. 12:48 *m* is given, of him shall be *m* required
  16:10 faithful in . . least is faithful also in *m*

Mulberry

2 Sam. 5:23 come upon them . . against the *m* trees

Mule *See also* Horse

2 Sam. 18:9 Absalom rode upon a *m*, and the *m* went
1 Kgs. 1:33 Solomon . . to ride upon mine own *m*
Ps. 32:9 be ye not as the horse, or as the *m*, which

Multiply *See also* Flourish, Grow,

Increase

Gen. 1:22 be fruitful, and *m*, and fill the waters
  1:28 be fruitful, and *m*, and replenish the earth
  3:16 will greatly *m* thy sorrow and thy conception
  6:1 when men began to *m* on the face of the earth
  16:10 unto her, I will *m* thy seed exceedingly
  17:2 make my covenant . . will *m* thee exceedingly
  22:17 (Heb. 6:14) in multiplying I will *m* thy seed
  35:11 I am God Almighty: be fruitful and *m*
Ex. 1:12 more they afflicted them, the more they *m*
  7:3 will harden Pharaoh's heart, and *m* my signs
  11:9 my wonders may be *m* in the land of Egypt
Deut. 1:10 LORD your God hath *m* you, and, behold
  8:1 observe to do, that ye may live, and *m*
  8:13 thy gold is *m*, and all that thou hast is *m*
  11:21 that your days may be *m*, and the days of
Josh. 24:3 and *m* his seed, and gave him Isaac
Job 9:17 breaketh me . . *m* my wounds without cause
  34:37 and *m* his words against God
  35:16 in vain; he *m* words without knowledge
Ps. 16:4 their sorrows shall be *m* that hasten after
  107:38 he blesseth them also, so that they are *m*
Prov. 29:16 wicked are *m*, transgression increaseth
Is. 9:3 thou hast *m* the nation, and not increased
  59:12 our transgressions are *m* before thee
Jer. 3:16 when ye be *m* and increased in the land
  33:22 so will I *m* the seed of David my servant
Ezek. 5:7 because ye *m* more than the nations that
  16:7 caused thee to *m* as the bud of the field
  16:51 hast *m* thine abominations more than they
  36:10 I will *m* men upon you, all the house of
  37:26 I will place them, and *m* them, and will
Hos. 8:14 Judah hath *m* fenced cities: but I will
  12:10 and I have *m* visions, and used similitudes

Amos 4:4 at Gilgal *m* transgression; and bring your
Nah. 3:16 hast *m* thy merchants above the stars
Acts 6:1 when the number of the disciples was *m*
9:31 in the comfort of the Holy Ghost, were *m*
12:24 but the word of God grew and *m*
2 Cor. 9:10 and *m* your seed sown, and increase the

Multitude *See also* Host, Nation, People

Gen. 28:3 that thou mayest be a *m* of people
Ex. 23:2 thou shalt not follow a *m* to do evil
Deut. 1:10 ye are . . as the stars of heaven for *m*
Josh. 11:4 as the sand . . upon the seashore in *m*
Ps. 5:7 come into thy house in the *m* of thy mercy
33:16 there is no king saved by the *m* of a host
42:4 I had gone with the *m* . . with a *m* that kept
51:1 according unto the *m* of thy tender mercies
69:13 O God, in the *m* of thy mercy hear me
94:19 in the *m* of my thoughts within me
Prov. 10:19 the *m* of words there wanteth not sin
11:14 but in the *m* of counselors there is safety
Is. 47:13 art wearied in the *m* of thy counsels
Dan. 10:6 voice of his words like the voice of a *m*
Joel 3:14 *m*, *m* in the valley of decision
Mt. 5:1 seeing the *m*, he went up into a mountain
12:15 great *m* followed him, and he healed them
14:14 saw a great *m* . . was moved with compassion
15:32 I have compassion on the *m*, because they
21:8 a very great *m* spread their garments in
26:47 Judas . . came, and with him a great *m*
Mk. 3:9 ship should wait on him because of the *m*
Lk. 2:13 with the angel a *m* of the heavenly host
Acts 2:6 the *m* came together, and were confounded
5:14 more added . . *m* both of men and women
6:5 pleased the whole *m*: and they chose Stephen
21:22 the *m* must needs come together: for they
Jas. 5:20 save a soul . . and shall hide a *m* of sins
1 Pet. 4:8 for charity shall cover the *m* of sins
Rev. 7:9 after this I beheld, and, lo, a great *m*
19:6 I heard as it were the voice of a great *m*

Murder *See also* Kill, Slay

Ps.10:8 the secret places doth he *m* the innocent
94:6 they slay the widow . . and *m* the fatherless
Jer. 7:9 will ye steal, *m*, and commit adultery
Hos. 6:9 company of priests *m* in the way by consent
Mt. 15:19 of the heart proceed evil thoughts, *m*
19:18 which? Jesus said, Thou shalt do no *m*
Mk. 15:7 who had committed *m* in the insurrection
Lk. 23:19 who . . for *m*, was cast into prison
Rom. 1:29 maliciousness; full of envy, *m*, debate
Gal. 5:21 envyings, *m*, drunkenness, revelings
Rev. 9:21 neither repented they of their *m*, nor of

Murderer

Num. 35:16 the *m* shall surely be put to death
Job 24:14 *m* rising with the light killeth the poor
Is. 1:21 righteousness lodged in it; but now *m*
Hos. 9:13 shall bring forth his children to the *m*
Mt. 22:7 destroyed those *m* . . burned up their city
Jn. 8:44 a *m* from the beginning, and abode not in
Acts 3:14 and desired a *m* to be granted unto you
7:52 whom ye have been now the betrayers and *m*
21:38 wilderness four thousand men that were *m*?
28:4 no doubt this man is a *m*, whom, though he
1 Tim. 1:9 for *m* of fathers and *m* of mothers
1 Pet. 4:15 let none of you suffer as a *m*, or as a
1 Jn. 3:15 hateth his brother is a *m* . . no *m* hath
Rev. 21:8 the abominable, and, *m*, and whoremongers

Murmur

Ex. 15:24 the people *m* against Moses, saying, What
16:2 congregation . . *m* against Moses and Aaron
Num. 14:2 all the children of Israel *m* against Moses

Num. 14:27 evil congregation, which *m* against me?
16:11 and what is Aaron, that ye *m* against him?
16:41 Israel *m* against Moses and against Aaron
Deut. 1:27 ye *m* in your tents, and said, Because
Ps. 106:25 but in their tents, and hearkened not
Is. 29:24 and they that *m* shall learn doctrine
Mt. 20:11 they *m* against the goodman of the house
Mk. 14:5 given to the poor. And they *m* against her
Lk. 5:30 and Pharisees *m* against his disciples
15:2 and scribes *m* . . This man receiveth sinners
19:7 all *m*, saying, That he was gone to be guest
Jn. 6:41 Jews then *m* at him, because he said, I am
6:61 when Jesus knew . . that his disciples *m* at it
7:32 the Pharisees heard that the people *m* such
1 Cor. 10:10 neither *m* ye, as some of them also *m*

Murmurer

Jude 16 these are *m*, complainers, walking after

Murmuring

Ex. 16:7 that he heareth your *m* against the LORD
Num. 14:27 I have heard the *m* of the children of
17:5 I will make to cease from me the *m* of the
Jn. 7:12 much *m* among the people concerning him
Acts 6:1 a *m* of the Grecians against the Hebrews
Phil. 2:14 do all things without *m* and disputings

Murrain

Ex. 9:3 there shall be a very grievous *m*

Muse *See also* Meditate, Ponder

Ps. 39:3 while I was *m* the fire burned; then spake
143:5 thy works; I *m* on the work of thy hands
Lk. 3:15 and all men *m* in their hearts of John

Music

1 Chr. 15:16 to be the singers with instruments of *m*
Eccl. 12:4 the daughters of *m* shall be brought low
Lam. 3:63 sitting down . . rising up; I am their *m*
Amos 6:5 and invent to themselves instruments of *m*
Lk. 15:25 nigh . . the house, he heard *m* and dancing

Musician

Rev. 18:22 voice of harpers, and, *m*, and of pipers

Mustard

Mt. 13:31 (Mk. 4:31; Lk. 13:19) *m* seed . . sowed in
17:20 if ye have faith as a grain of *m* seed

Mutter

Is. 8:19 seek . . unto wizards that peep and that *m*

Mutual

Rom. 1:12 be comforted . . with you by the *m* faith

Muzzle

Deut. 25:4 (1 Cor. 9:9; 1 Tim. 5:18) shalt not *m* . . ox

Myrrh

Ex. 30:23 principal spices, of pure *m* five hundred
Ps. 45:8 all thy garments smell of *m*, and aloes
Song 1:13 a bundle of *m* is my well-beloved unto me
Mt. 2:11 him gifts; gold, and frankincense, and *m*
Mk. 15:23 gave him to drink wine mingled with *m*
Jn. 19:39 brought a mixture of *m* and aloes

Myrtle

Is. 55:13 instead of the brier . . come up the *m* tree
Zech. 1:8 he stood among the *m* trees that were in

Mystery *See also* Secret

Mt. 13:11 (Mk. 4:11; Lk. 8:10) the *m* of the kingdom
Rom. 11:25 that ye should be ignorant of this *m*

Rom. 16:25 revelation of the *m*, which was kept secret
1 Cor. 2:7 but we speak the wisdom of God in a *m*
  4:1 ministers of Christ, and stewards of the *m*
  13:2 gift of prophecy, and understand all *m*
  14:2 howbeit in the spirit he speaketh *m*
  15:51 I show you a *m*; We shall not all sleep
Eph. 1:9 made known unto us the *m* of his will
  3:3 by revelation he made known unto me the *m*
  3:4 understand my knowledge in the *m* of Christ
  3:9 all men see what is the fellowship of the *m*
  5:32 this is a great *m*: but I speak concerning
  6:19 boldly, to make known the *m* of the gospel
Col. 1:26 even the *m* which hath been hid from ages
  1:27 what is the riches of the glory of this *m*
  2:2 to the acknowledgment of the *m* of God
  4:3 to speak the *m* of Christ
2 Thes. 2:7 the *m* of iniquity doth already work
1 Tim. 3:9 holding the *m* of the faith in a pure
  3:16 great is the *m* of godliness: God was manifest
Rev. 1:20 *m* of the seven stars which thou sawest
  10:7 to sound, the *m* of God should be finished
  17:5 *M*, BABYLON THE GREAT, THE MOTHER
  17:7 I will tell thee the *m* of the woman

N

Naaman 2 Kgs. 5:1–27; Lk. 4:27

Nabal 1 Sam. 25:3–38

Naboth 1 Kgs. 21:1–14

Nadab son of Aaron Lev. 10:1

Nadab king of Israel 1 Kgs. 15:25–27

Nahash 1 Sam. 11:1–2

Nahor Gen. 11:26–29; 24:10

Nahum Nah. 1:1–3:19

Nail

Judg. 4:21 took a *n*. . smote the *n* into his temples
Ezra 9:8 to give us a *n* in his holy place
Eccl. 12:11 and as *n* fastened by the masters
Is. 22:23 I will fasten him as a *n* in a sure place
Dan. 4:33 Nebuchadnezzar. . his *n* like birds' claws
  7:19 teeth were of iron, and his *n* of brass
Jn. 20:25 put my finger into the print of the *n*
Col. 2:14 took it out of the way, *n* it to his cross

Nain Lk. 7:11

Naked

Gen. 2:25 they were both *n*, the man and his wife
  3:7 eyes. . opened, and they knew that they were *n*
Ex. 32:25 when Moses saw that the people were *n*
Job 1:21 *n* came I out of my mother's womb, and *n*
  26:6 hell is *n* before him, and destruction hath
Eccl. 5:15 *n* shall he return to go as he came
Is. 20:2 and he did so, walking *n* and barefoot
Hos. 2:3 lest I strip her *n*, and set her as in the
Mt. 25:36 *n*, and ye clothed me: I was sick, and ye
Mk. 14:52 left the linen cloth. . fled from them *n*
Jn. 21:7 his fisher's coat unto him, (for he was *n*,)
Acts 19:16 so that they fled out of that house *n*
1 Cor. 4:11 we both hunger, and thirst, and are *n*
2 Cor. 5:3 being clothed we shall not be found *n*
Heb. 4:13 but all things are *n* and opened unto the
Jas. 2:15 brother or sister be *n*, and destitute
Rev. 16:15 keepeth his garments, lest he walk *n*

Nakedness

Gen. 9:22 Ham. . saw the *n* of his father, and told
  42:9 spies; to see the *n* of the land ye are come
Lev. 18:6 near of kin to him, to uncover their *n*
Is. 47:3 thy *n* shall be uncovered, yea, thy shame
Lam. 1:8 despise her, because they have seen her *n*
Ezek. 16:8 my skirt over thee, and covered thy *n*
  16:36 thy *n* discovered through thy whoredoms
Nah. 3:5 I will show the nations thy *n*
Hab. 2:15 that thou mayest look on their *n*!
Rom. 8:35 shall tribulation. . or *n*, or peril, or
2 Cor. 11:27 in hunger and thirst. . in cold and *n*
Rev. 3:18 that the shame of thy *n* do not appear

Name *See also* Name of the LORD

Gen. 2:20 Adam gave *n* to all cattle
  5:2 blessed them, and called their *n* Adam
  11:4 let us make us a *n*, lest we be scattered
  12:2 and I will bless thee, and make thy *n* great
  17:5 thy *n* any more be called Abram, but thy *n*
  32:29 Jacob. . said, Tell me, I pray thee, thy *n*
  35:10 thy *n* is Jacob. . but Israel shall be thy *n*
Ex. 3:13 they shall say to me, What is his *n*?
  6:3 but by my *n* JEHOVAH was I not known to them
  9:16 (Rom. 9:17) my *n* may be declared throughout
  15:3 the LORD is a man of war: the LORD is his *n*
  20:24 in all places where I record my *n* I will
  23:21 and obey his voice. . for my *n* is in him
  33:12 yet thou hast said, I know thee by *n*
  34:14 LORD, whose *n* is Jealous, is a jealous God
Lev. 19:12 and ye shall not swear by my *n* falsely
  21:6 be holy. . and not profane the *n* of their God
Deut. 7:24 shalt destroy their *n* from under heaven
  12:5 out of all your tribes to put his *n* there
  18:20 prophet. . presume to speak a word in my *n*
  28:58 fear this glorious and fearful *n*, THE LORD
  29:20 LORD shall blot out his *n* from under heaven
Josh. 7:9 and what wilt thou do unto thy great *n*?
Judg. 13:17 what is thy *n*, that when thy sayings
1 Sam. 12:22 his people for his great *n*'s sake
2 Sam. 7:13 (1 Kgs. 8:19; 2 Chr. 6:9) house for my *n*
1 Kgs. 8:43 (2 Chr. 6:33) all people. . may know thy *n*
1 Chr. 16:8 call upon his *n*, make known his deeds
  16:29 (Ps. 29:2; 96:8) the glory due unto his *n*
2 Chr. 6:33 all people of the earth may know thy *n*
  7:14 my people, which are called by my *n*, shall
Job 18:17 and he shall have no *n* in the street
Ps. 8:1 how excellent is thy *n* in all the earth!
  9:10 know thy *n* will put their trust in thee
  20:1 the *n* of the God of Jacob defend thee
  20:5 in the *n* of our God we will set up. . banners
  22:22 (Heb. 2:12) declare thy *n* unto my brethren
  23:3 the paths of righteousness for his *n*'s sake
  33:21 because we have trusted in his holy *n*
  34:3 with me, and let us exalt his *n* together
  72:17 his *n* shall endure for ever: his *n* shall
  83:18 know that thou, whose *n* alone is JEHOVAH
  91:14 him on high, because he hath known my *n*
  100:4 be thankful unto him, and bless his *n*
  103:1 all that is within me, bless his holy *n*
  105:1 give thanks unto the LORD; call upon his *n*
  111:9 his covenant. . holy and reverend is his *n*
  115:1 not unto us, but unto thy *n* give glory
  138:2 and praise thy *n* for thy loving-kindness
Prov. 10:7 but the *n* of the wicked shall rot
  22:1 a good *n* is rather to be chosen than great
Eccl. 7:1 good *n* is better than precious ointment
Is. 7:14 bear a son, and shall call his *n* Immanuel
  9:6 his *n* shall be called Wonderful, Counselor
  42:8 I am the LORD; that is my *n*: and my glory
  43:1 I have called thee by thy *n*; thou art mine
  48:2 God of Israel: The LORD of hosts is his *n*

Is. 48.9 for my *n*'s sake will I defer mine anger
52:5 (Rom. 2:24) Lord; and my *n* . . is blasphemed
52:6 my people shall know my *n*: therefore they
55:13 and it shall be to the Lord for a *n*
56:5 I will give them an everlasting *n*
57:15 that inhabiteth eternity, whose *n* is Holy
62:2 new *n*, which the mouth of the Lord shall *n*
63:12 led them. . to make himself an everlasting *n*?
Jer. 7:11 is this house, which is called by my *n*
10:6 art great, and thy *n* is great in might
14:14 prophesy lies in my *n*: I sent them not
15:16 I am called by thy *n*, O Lord God of hosts
20:9 nor speak any more in his *n*. But his word
23:27 to cause my people to forget my *n* by their
44:26 that my *n* shall no more be *n* in the mouth
Ezek. 36:21 but I had pity for mine holy *n*, which
39:25 have mercy. . will be jealous for my holy *n*
Amos 9:12 (Acts 15:17) heathen. . called by my *n*
Zeph. 3:20 I will make you a *n* and a praise among
Zech. 6:12 behold the man whose *n* is The Branch
10:12 and they shall walk up and down in his *n*
14:9 day shall there be one Lord, and his *n* one
Mal. 1:6 O priests, that despise my *n*. And ye say
4:2 but unto you that fear my *n* shall the Sun of
Mt. 1:21 (Lk. 1:31) thou shalt call his *n* Jesus
6:9 (Lk. 11:2) hallowed be thy *n*
7:22 Lord, Lord, have we not prophesied in thy *n*?
10:22 shall be hated of all men for my *n*'s sake
12:21 and in his *n* shall the Gentiles trust
18:5 receive one such little child in my *n*
18:20 two or three are gathered together in my *n*
19:29 forsaken houses. . or lands, for my *n*'s sake
24:5 many shall come in my *n*, saying, I am Christ
28:19 baptizing them in the *n* of the Father
Mk. 6:14 Herod heard of him; (for his *n* was spread
9:39 is no man which shall do a miracle in my *n*
Lk. 1:61 none of thy kindred that is called by this *n*
10:20 because your *n* are written in heaven
Jn. 1:12 even to them that believe on his *n*
5:43 in my Father's *n*, and ye receive me not
10:3 he calleth his own sheep by *n*, and leadeth
12:28 Father, glorify thy *n*. Then came there a
14:13 whatsoever ye shall ask in my *n*, that will
15:16 ask of the Father in my *n*, he may give it
17:11 keep through thine own *n* those whom thou
20:31 believing ye might have life through his *n*
Acts 3:16 faith in his *n* . . made this man strong
4:12 none other *n* under heaven given among men
8:16 were baptized in the *n* of the Lord Jesus
9:15 vessel. . to bear my *n* before the Gentiles
10:43 through his *n* whosoever believeth in him
15:14 to take out of them a people for his *n*
19:17 and the *n* of the Lord Jesus was magnified
Rom. 2:24 *n* of God is blasphemed among. . Gentiles
15:20 preach the gospel, not where Christ was *n*
1 Cor. 1:13 or were ye baptized in the *n* of Paul?
Eph. 1:21 every *n* that is *n*, not only in this world
3:15 the whole family in heaven and earth is *n*
5:3 covetousness, let it not be once *n* among you
Phil. 2:9 and given him a *n* which is above every *n*
4:3 laborers, whose *n* are in the book of life
Col. 3:17 do in word or deed, do all in the *n* of
2 Tim. 2:19 let every one that *n* the *n* of Christ
Heb. 1:4 obtained a more excellent *n* than they
Jas. 2:7 do not they blaspheme that worthy *n* by
1 Pet. 4:14 ye be reproached for the *n* of Christ
1 Jn. 2:12 sins are forgiven you for his *n*'s sake
5:13 you that believe on the *n* of the Son of God
Rev. 2:3 for my *n*'s sake hast labored, and hast
2:13 thou holdest fast my *n*, and hast not denied
2:17 in the stone a new *n* written, which no man
3:5 not blot out his *n* . . but I will confess his *n*
14:1 his Father's *n* written in their foreheads

Rev. 19:13 and his *n* is called The Word of God
22:4 and his *n* shall be in their foreheads

Name of the Lord *See also* Name

Gen. 4:26 began men to call upon the *n* of the L
12:8 an altar. . and called upon the *n* of the L
16:13 called the *n* of the L. . Thou God seest me
26:25 called upon the *n* of the L, and pitched
Ex. 20:7 not take the *n* of the L thy God in vain
34:5 stood. . and proclaimed the *n* of the L
Lev. 24:16 he that blasphemeth the *n* of the L, he
Deut. 18:5 to stand to minister in the *n* of the L
21:5 to minister. . and to bless in the *n* of the L
28:10 see that thou art called by the *n* of the L
32:3 because I will publish the *n* of the L
Josh. 9:9 come, because of the *n* of the L thy God
2 Sam. 6:2 is called by the *n* of the L of hosts
6:18 David. . blessed the people in the *n* of the L
Job 1:21 hath taken away; blessed be the *n* of the L
Ps. 118:26 (Mt. 21:9; 23:39; Mk. 11:9; Lk. 13:35; 19:
38; Jn. 12:13) he that cometh in the *n* of the L
124:8 our help is in the *n* of the L, who made
Prov. 18:10 the *n* of the L is a strong tower
Is. 50:10 let him trust in the *n* of the L, and stay
56:6 to serve him, and to love the *n* of the L
Joel 2:32 (Rom. 10:13) shall call on the *n* of the L
Amos 6:10 may not make mention of the *n* of the L
Mic. 4:5 we will walk in the *n* of the L our God
Zeph. 3:9 they may all call upon the *n* of the L

Naomi Ruth 1:2–4:17

Naphtali

Gen. 30:8 prevailed: and she called his name *N*
49:21 *N* is a hind let loose: he giveth goodly
Deut. 33:23 *N* he said, O *N*, satisfied with favor
2 Kgs. 15:29 of *N*. . carried them captive to Assyria
Is. 9:1 (Mt. 4:15) land of Zebulun, and the land of *N*

Napkin

Lk. 19:20 pound, which I have kept laid up in a *n*
Jn. 11:44 and his face was bound about with a *n*
20:7 the *n*, that was about his head, not lying

Narrow (Narrower)

Num. 22:26 angel of the Lord. . stood in a *n* place
Josh. 17:15 if mount Ephraim be too *n* for thee
Is. 28:20 covering *n* than that he can wrap himself
49:19 now be too *n* by reason of the inhabitants
Mt. 7:14 strait is the gate, and *n* is the way, which

Nathan

Counseled David about the temple, 2 Sam. 7:2–17
(1 Chr. 17:1–15); rebuked David, 2 Sam. 12:1–23;
anointed Solomon as king, 1 Kgs. 1:8–45.

Nathanael Jn. 1:45–51; 21:2

Nation *See also* Country, Gentile,

Heathen, Land, People

Gen. 10:5 divided. . after their families, in their *n*
12:2 I will make of thee a great *n*, and I will
17:5 (Rom. 4:17) father of many *n* have I made
18:18 (Gal. 3:8) all the *n*. . shall be blessed in him
20:4 Lord, wilt thou slay also a righteous *n*?
26:4 and in thy seed shall all the *n* . . be blessed
35:11 a *n* and a company of *n* shall be of thee
46:3 for I will there make of thee a great *n*
48:19 and his seed shall become a multitude of *n*
Ex. 19:6 unto me a kingdom of priests, and a holy *n*
33:13 and consider that this *n* is thy people
34:24 for I will cast out the *n* before thee

Num. 14:12 and will make of thee a greater *n* and
   23:9 people. . shall not be reckoned among the *n*
Deut. 4:7 what *n* is there so great, who hath God
   4:27 LORD shall scatter you among the *n*, and ye
   9:14 will make of thee a *n* mightier and greater
   14:2 to be a peculiar people. . above all the *n*
   26:19 and to make thee high above all *n* which he
   32:8 Most High divided to the *n* their inheritance
   32:43 rejoice, O ye *n*, with his people: for he
1 Sam. 8:5 a king to judge us like all the *n*
2 Sam. 7:23 (1 Chr. 17:21) what one *n*. . is like thy
1 Chr. 16:20 when they went from *n* to *n*, and from
   16:24 his marvelous works among all *n*
2 Chr. 15:6 *n* was destroyed of *n*, and city of city
Job 12:23 he increaseth the *n*, and destroyeth them
Ps. 9:17 into hell, and all the *n* that forget God
   33:12 blessed is the *n* whose God is the LORD
   66:7 his power for ever; his eyes behold the *n*
   67:4 O let the *n* be glad and sing for joy
   72:11 fall down before him: all *n* shall serve
   106:5 I may rejoice in the gladness of thy *n*
   113:4 LORD is high above all *n*, and his glory
   117:1 O praise the LORD, all ye *n*: praise him
   147:20 he hath not dealt so with any *n*
Prov. 14:34 righteousness exalteth a *n*: but sin is
Is. 1:4 ah sinful *n*, a people laden with iniquity
   2:2 above the hills; and all *n* shall flow unto
   2:4 *n* shall not lift up sword against *n*, neither
   9:3 hast multiplied the *n*, and not increased
   26:2 the righteous *n* which keepeth the truth may
   40:15 behold, the *n* are as a drop of a bucket
   40:17 all *n* before him are as nothing; and they
   55:5 shalt call a *n* that thou knowest not, and *n*
   58:2 know my ways, as a *n* that did righteousness
   65:1 unto a *n* that was not called by my name
   66:8 in one day? or shall a *n* be born at once?
Jer. 4:2 and the *n* shall bless themselves in him
   5:15 I will bring a *n* upon you from far, O house
   7:28 a *n* that obeyeth not the voice of the LORD
   27:7 all *n* shall serve him, and his son, and his
   27:8 that *n* will I punish, saith the LORD
   29:14 I will gather you from all the *n*, and from
   30:11 though I make a full end of all *n* whither
Ezek. 37:22 and I will make them one *n* in the land
Dan. 7:14 all people, *n*, and languages, should serve
   8:22 four kingdoms shall stand up out of the *n*
Hos. 9:17 and they shall be wanderers among the *n*
Joel 3:2 I will also gather all *n*, and will bring
Mic. 4:3 many people, and rebuke strong *n* afar off
Hab. 1:17 and not spare continually to slay the *n*?
Hag. 2:7 shake all *n*. . Desire of all *n* shall come
Zech. 2:11 many *n* shall be joined to the LORD
   7:14 I scattered them. . among all the *n* whom they
   8:22 and strong *n* shall come to seek the LORD
   14:2 gather all *n* against Jerusalem to battle
Mal. 3:9 for ye have robbed me, even this whole *n*
   3:12 all *n* shall call you blessed: for ye shall
Mt. 24:7 for *n* shall rise against *n*, and kingdom
   24:9 shall be hated of all *n* for my name's sake
   24:14 witness unto all *n*. . then shall the end come
   25:32 before him shall be gathered all *n*: and he
   28:19 go ye therefore, and teach all *n*, baptizing
Mk. 11:17 be called of all *n* the house of prayer?
Lk. 7:5 he loveth our *n*. . hath built us a synagogue
   12:30 things do the *n* of the world seek after
   21:25 the earth distress of *n*, with perplexity
Jn. 11:50 and that the whole *n* perish not
   18:35 thine own *n* and the chief priests have
Acts 2:5 devout men, out of every *n* under heaven
   10:35 in every *n* he that feareth him, and worketh
   17:26 hath made of one blood all *n* of men for to
Rom. 1:5 for obedience to the faith among all *n*
Phil. 2:15 in the midst of a crooked and perverse *n*

1 Pet. 2:9 a royal priesthood, a holy *n*, a peculiar
Rev. 2:26 to him will I give power over the *n*
   5:9 every kindred, and tongue, and people, and *n*
   7:9 no man could number, of all *n*, and kindreds
   15:4 for all *n* shall come and worship before thee
   21:24 *n* of them which are saved shall walk in
   22:2 the leaves. . were for the healing of the *n*

Natural

Rom. 1:26 even their women did change the *n* use
   1:31 covenant-breakers, without *n* affection
   11:21 for if God spared not the *n* branches. . heed
1 Cor. 2:14 but the *n* man receiveth not the things
   15:44 is sown a *n* body. . raised a spiritual body
   15:46 which is spiritual, but that which is *n*
Jas. 1:23 a man beholding his *n* face in a glass

Naturally

Phil. 2:20 no man. . who will *n* care for your state
Jude 10 but what they know *n*, as brute beasts

Nature

Rom. 1:26 natural use into that which is against *n*
   2:14 do by *n* the things contained in the law
   2:27 shall not uncircumcision which is by *n*, if
   11:24 wild by *n*, and wert graffed contrary to *n*
1 Cor. 11:14 doth not even *n* itself teach you
Gal. 2:15 we who are Jews by *n*, and not sinners
   4:8 did service unto them which by *n* are no gods
Eph. 2:3 were by *n* the children of wrath, even as
Heb. 2:16 he took not on him the *n* of angels
Jas. 3:6 and setteth on fire the course of *n*
2 Pet. 1:4 ye might be partakers of the divine *n*

Naught *See* Nought

Naughtiness

1 Sam. 17:28 thy pride, and the *n* of thine heart
Prov. 11:6 transgressors. . be taken in their own *n*
Jas. 1:21 all filthiness and superfluity of *n*

Naughty

Prov. 6:12 *n* person. . walketh with a froward mouth
   17:4 and a liar giveth ear to a *n* tongue
Jer. 24:2 and the other basket had very *n* figs

Navy

1 Kgs. 9:26 and king Solomon made a *n* of ships
   10:22 at sea a *n* of Tharshish with the *n* of Hiram

Nay

2 Cor. 1:17 with me there should be yea, yea, and *n*, *n*
Jas. 5:12 but let your yea be yea; and your *n*, *n*

Nazarene

Mt. 2:23 by the prophets, He shall be called a *N*
Acts 24:5 and a ringleader of the sect of the *N*

Nazareth

Mt. 2:23 and he came and dwelt in a city called *N*
Lk. 1:26 was sent. . unto a city of Galilee, named *N*
   4:16 he came to *N*, where he had been brought up
Jn. 1:46 can there any good thing come out of *N*?

Nazarite

Num. 6:2 vow a vow of a *N*, to separate themselves
Judg. 13:5 for the child shall be a *N* unto God
Amos 2:12 but ye gave the *N* wine to drink

Near (Nearer) *See also* Nigh

Gen. 19:20 behold now, this city is *n* to flee unto
Judg. 20:34 but they knew not that evil was *n* them
Ps. 22:11 be not far from me; for trouble is *n*
   119:151 thou art *n*, O LORD. . thy commandments

Ps. 148:14 children of Israel, a people *n* unto him
Prov. 27:10 better is a neighbor that is *n* than a
Is. 51:5 righteousness is *n* . . salvation is gone forth
    55:6 be found, call ye upon him while he is *n*
Obad. 15 day of the Lord is *n* upon all the heathen
Zeph. 1:14 the great day of the Lord is *n*, it is *n*
Mt. 24:33 see all these things, know that it is *n*
Mk. 13:28 forth leaves, ye know that summer is *n*
Lk. 21:8 saying, I am Christ . . the time draweth *n*
Rom. 13:11 our salvation *n* than when we believed
Heb. 10:22 let us draw *n* with a true heart in full

Nebo Deut. 34:1

Nebuchadnezzar (Nebuchadrezzar)

Won the battle of Carchemish, 2 Kgs. 24:1–7; Jer. 46:2; conquered Judah, 2 Kgs. 24:10–25:10 (2 Chr. 36:6–19; Jer. 39:1–8; 52:1–14); deported the people, 2 Kgs. 24:14–16; 25:11–21 (2 Chr. 36:20–21; Jer. 39:9–10; 52:15–30); favored Jeremiah, Jer. 39:11–14; revealed his dreams, Dan. 2:1–13; 4:4–18; set up the golden image, Dan. 3:1–7; punished for boasting, Dan. 4:31–33; his reason returned, Dan. 4:34–37.

Nebuzar-adan 2 Kgs. 25:8 (Jer. 52:12)

Necessary

Job 23:12 words of his mouth more than my *n* food
Acts 13:46 was *n* that the word of God should first
    15:28 lay . . no greater burden than these *n* things
    28:10 they laded us with such things as were *n*
1 Cor. 12:22 which seem to be more feeble, are *n*
2 Cor. 9:5 I thought it *n* to exhort the brethren
Phil. 2:25 yet I supposed it *n* to send to you
Tit. 3:14 learn to maintain good works for *n* uses

Necessity *See also* Need

Lk. 23:17 of *n* he must release one . . at the feast
Acts 20:34 these hands have ministered unto my *n*
Rom. 12:13 distributing to the *n* of saints
1 Cor. 9:16 *n* is laid upon me; yea, woe is unto me
2 Cor. 6:4 in afflictions, in *n*, in distresses
    9:7 so let him give; not grudgingly, or of *n*
    12:10 in infirmities, in reproaches, in *n*, in
Phil. 4:16 ye sent once and again unto my *n*
Phlm. 14 not be as it were of *n*, but willingly
Heb. 7:12 is made of *n* a change also of the law
    8:3 is of *n* that this man have somewhat also to
    9:16 must also of *n* be the death of the testator

Necho *See* Pharaoh-necho

Neck *See also* Stiffnecked

Gen. 41:42 Pharaoh . . put a gold chain about his *n*
Deut. 31:27 I know thy rebellion, and thy stiff *n*
Josh. 10:24 your feet upon the *n* of these kings
1 Sam. 4:18 he fell . . and his *n* brake, and he died
2 Sam. 22:41 also given me the *n* of mine enemies
Neh. 9:29 and hardened their *n*, and would not hear
Prov. 3:3 bind them about thy *n*; write them upon
    29:1 being often reproved hardeneth his *n*, shall
Song 1:10 are comely . . thy *n* with chains of gold
Is. 3:16 with stretched forth *n* and wanton eyes
Jer. 30:8 that I will break his yoke from off thy *n*
Mt. 18:6 that a millstone were hanged about his *n*
Lk. 15:20 ran, and fell on his *n*, and kissed him
Acts 15:10 put a yoke upon the *n* of the disciples
    20:37 all wept . . fell on Paul's *n*, and kissed him
Rom. 16:4 have for my life laid down their own *n*

Need *See also* Necessity, Want

Deut. 15:8 surely lend him sufficient for his *n*
1 Sam. 21:15 have I *n* of madmen, that ye have

Prov. 31:11 so that he shall have no *n* of spoil
Mt. 6:8 Father knoweth what things ye have *n* of
    9:12 they that be whole *n* not a physician, but
    14:16 they *n* not depart; give ye them to eat
    21:3 ye shall say, The Lord hath *n* of them
    26:65 (Mk. 14:63) further *n* have we of witnesses?
Lk. 11:8 he will rise and give him as many as he *n*
    15:7 than . . just persons, which *n* no repentance
Jn. 2:25 and *n* not that any should testify of man
    13:29 buy those . . we have *n* of against the feast
Acts 2:45 parted them to all . . as every man had *n*
    4:35 distribution was . . according as he had *n*
    17:25 as though he *n* any thing, seeing he giveth
1 Cor. 12:21 say unto the hand, I have no *n* of thee
2 Cor. 3:1 *n* we . . epistles of commendation to you
Eph. 4:28 that he may have to give to him that *n*
Phil. 4:12 both to abound and to suffer *n*
    4:19 my God shall supply all your *n* according to
1 Thes. 4:9 ye *n* not that I write unto you: for ye
2 Tim. 2:15 a workman that *n* not to be ashamed
Heb. 4:16 and find grace to help in time of *n*
    5:12 ye have *n* that one teach you again which be
    7:11 what further *n* was there that another priest
1 Jn. 3:17 seeth his brother have *n*, and shutteth
Rev. 3:17 increased with goods . . have *n* of nothing
    21:23 city had no *n* of the sun, neither of the

Needful

Ezra 7:20 more shall be *n* for the house of thy God
Lk. 10:42 but one thing is *n*; and Mary hath chosen
Phil. 1:24 to abide in the flesh is more *n* for you
Jas. 2:16 not those things which are *n* to the body
Jude 3 was *n* for me to write unto you, and exhort

Needle

Mt. 19:24 for a camel to go through the eye of a *n*

Needlework

Ex. 26:36 shalt make a hanging . . wrought with *n*
Judg. 5:30 of divers colors of *n* on both sides
Ps. 45:14 be brought unto the King in raiment of *n*

Needy *See also* Afflicted, Destitute, Poor

Deut. 15:11 open thine hand . . to thy *n*, in thy land
Job 24:4 they turn the *n* out of the way
Ps. 9:18 for the *n* shall not always be forgotten
    40:17 (70:5) but I am poor and *n*; yet the Lord
    72:13 and *n*, and shall save the souls of the *n*
    113:7 and lifteth the *n* out of the dunghill
Is. 14:30 the *n* shall lie down in safety
    25:4 strength to the *n* in his distress, a refuge
Amos 8:4 hear this, O ye that swallow up the *n*

Neglect

Mt. 18:17 but if he *n* to hear the church, let him
Acts 6:1 widows were *n* in the daily ministration
Col. 2:23 will-worship . . humility . . *n* of the body
1 Tim. 4:14 *n* not the gift that is in thee
Heb. 2:3 we escape, if we *n* so great salvation

Negligent

2 Chr. 29:11 be not now *n*: for the Lord hath chosen
2 Pet. 1:12 I will not be *n* to put you always in

Nehemiah Neh. 1:1–13:31

Neighbor

Ex. 3:22 but every woman shall borrow of her *n*
    20:16 shalt not bear false witness against thy *n*
    20:17 shalt not covet thy *n*'s house . . *n*'s wife
    21:14 if a man come presumptuously upon his *n*
    32:27 slay every man his brother . . every man his *n*
Lev. 6:2 lie unto his *n* . . or hath deceived his *n*

Lev. 19:13 thou shalt not defraud thy *n*, neither rob
19:18 (Mt. 19:19; 22:39; Mk. 12:31; Lk. 10:27;
Rom. 13:9; Gal. 5:14; Jas. 2:8) love thy *n* as
Deut. 19:4 may live: Whoso killeth his *n* ignorantly
19:11 if any man hate his *n*, and lie in wait for
19:14 thou shalt not remove thy *n*'s landmark
Josh. 9:16 they heard that they were their *n*
1 Kgs. 8:31 (2 Chr. 6:22) man trespass against his *n*
Job 12:4 I am as one mocked of his *n*, who calleth
Ps. 12:2 they speak vanity every one with his *n*
15:3 evil to his *n*, nor . . reproach against his *n*
28:3 which speak peace to their, *n*, but mischief
101:5 privily slandereth his *n*, him will I cut
Prov. 3:29 devise not evil against thy *n*, seeing
11:9 a hypocrite with his mouth destroyeth his *n*
11:12 he that is void of wisdom despiseth his *n*
14:20 the poor is hated even of his own *n*
14:21 he that despiseth his *n* sinneth
16:29 a violent man enticeth his *n*, and leadeth
24:28 not a witness against thy *n* without cause
25:8 thereof, when thy *n* hath put thee to shame
25:18 false witness against his *n* is a maul
27:10 better is a *n* that is near than a brother
29:5 flattereth his *n* spreadeth a net for his
Eccl. 4:4 that for this a man is envied of his *n*
Is. 41:6 they helped every one his *n*; and every
Jer. 9:4 take ye heed every one of his *n*
22:13 that useth his *n*'s service without wages
31:34 (Heb. 8:11) teach no more every man his *n*
34:15 in proclaiming liberty every man to his *n*
Hab. 2:15 woe unto him that giveth his *n* drink
Zech. 3:10 shall ye call every man his *n* under the
8:16 speak ye every man the truth to his *n*
Mt. 5:43 shalt love thy *n*, and hate thine enemy
Lk. 10:29 said unto Jesus, And who is my *n*?
Jn. 9:8 the *n* therefore, and they which before had
Rom. 13:10 love worketh no ill to his *n*
15:2 let every one of us please his *n* for his
Eph. 4:25 speak every man truth with his *n*

Nest

Num. 24:21 and thou puttest thy *n* in a rock
Deut. 22:6 if a bird's *n* chance to be before thee
32:11 an eagle stirreth up her *n*, fluttereth
Job 29:18 then I said, I shall die in my *n*
Ps. 84:3 hath found a house, and the swallow a *n*
Prov. 27:8 as a bird that wandereth from her *n*, so
Is. 10:14 my hand hath found as a *n* the riches of
Jer. 49:16 make thy *n* as high as the eagle, I will
Obad. 4 and though thou set thy *n* among the stars
Hab. 2:9 that he may set his *n* on high, that he
Mt. 8:20 foxes have holes . . birds of the air have *n*

Net

Job 19:6 overthrown me . . compassed me with his *n*
Ps. 25:15 for he shall pluck my feet out of the *n*
35:7 have they hid for me their *n* in a pit
57:6 they have prepared a *n* for my steps
66:11 thou broughtest us into the *n*; thou laidst
140:5 they have spread a *n* by the wayside
141:10 let the wicked fall into their own *n*
Prov. 1:17 in vain the *n* is spread in the sight of
29:5 man that flattereth . . spreadeth a *n* for his
Eccl. 9:12 the fishes that are taken in an evil *n*
Lam. 1:13 he hath spread a *n* for my feet, he hath
Ezek. 12:13 my *n* also will I spread upon him
Mic. 7:2 they hunt every man his brother with a *n*
Hab. 1:16 therefore they sacrifice unto their *n*
Mt. 4:18 and Andrew his brother, casting a *n* into
13:47 kingdom of heaven is like unto a *n*, that
Lk. 5:5 Master . . at thy word I will let down the *n*
Jn. 21:6 cast the *n* on the right side of the ship

New

Ex. 1:8 a *n* king over Egypt, which knew not Joseph
Num. 16:30 but if the LORD make a *n* thing
Deut. 32:17 knew not, to *n* gods that came newly up
Judg. 5:8 they chose *n* gods; then was war in the
Ps. 33:3 sing unto him a *n* song; play skilfully
40:3 hath put a *n* song in my mouth
Eccl. 1:9 and there is no *n* thing under the sun
Is. 42:9 come to pass, and *n* things do I declare
43:19 behold, I will do a *n* thing; now it shall
48:6 I have showed thee *n* things from this time
62:2 thou shalt be called by a *n* name, which the
65:17 behold, I create *n* heavens and a *n* earth
Jer. 31:22 LORD hath created a *n* thing in the earth
31:31 make a *n* covenant with the house of Israel
Lam. 3:23 they are *n* every morning: great is thy
Ezek. 36:26 a *n* heart . . I give you, and a *n* spirit
Mt. 9:16 (Mk. 2:21; Lk. 5:36) *n* cloth unto an old
9:17 (Mk. 2:22; Lk. 5:38) put *n* wine into *n* bottles
13:52 forth out of his treasure things *n* and old
26:29 drink it *n* with you in my Father's kingdom
Mk. 1:27 is this? what *n* doctrine is this? for
16:17 devils; they shall speak with *n* tongues
Jn. 13:34 a *n* commandment I give unto you, That ye
19:41 *n* sepulchre, wherein was never man yet laid
Acts 17:21 either to tell or to hear some *n* thing
2 Cor. 5:17 a *n* creature . . all things are become *n*
Gal. 6:15 nor incircumcision, but a *n* creature
Eph. 2:15 to make in himself of twain one *n* man
4:24 ye put on the *n* man, which after God is
Col. 3:10 the *n* man, which is renewed in knowledge
Heb. 8:13 a *n* covenant, he hath made the first old
9:15 he is the mediator of the *n* testament
10:20 by a *n* and living way, which he hath
2 Pet. 3:13 we . . look for *n* heavens and a *n* earth
1 Jn. 2:8 again, a *n* commandment I write unto you
Rev. 2:17 in the stone a *n* name written, which no
3:12 I will write upon him my *n* name
21:1 I saw a *n* heaven and a *n* earth
21:2 saw the holy city, *n* Jerusalem, coming down
21:5 behold, I make all things *n*

Newness

Rom. 6:4 even so we also should walk in *n* of life
7:6 we should serve in *n* of spirit, and not in

News

Prov. 25:25 so is good *n* from a far country

Nicodemus

Jn. 3:1 Pharisees, named *N*, a ruler of the Jews
7:50 *N* saith unto them, (he that came to Jesus
19:39 and there came also *N*, which at the first

Nicolaitan Rev. 2:6; 2:15

Nicopolis Tit. 3:12

Nigh *See also* Near

Ex. 3:5 draw not *n* hither: put off thy shoes from
Num. 24:17 not now: I shall behold him, but not *n*
Deut. 4:7 who hath God so *n* unto them, as the LORD
30:14 the word is very *n* unto thee, in thy mouth
Ps. 34:18 LORD is *n* unto them . . of a broken heart
85:9 his salvation is *n* them that fear him
91:7 but it shall not come *n* thee
145:18 LORD is *n* unto all them that call upon him
Joel 2:1 day of the LORD cometh . . it is *n* at hand
Mt. 15:8 people draweth *n* unto me with their mouth
21:1 when they drew *n* unto Jerusalem, and were
Lk. 21:28 heads; for your redemption draweth *n*
21:31 know . . that the kingdom of God is *n* at hand

Jn. 6:4 the passover, a feast of the Jews, was *n*
Acts 22:6 was come *n* unto Damascus about noon
Eph. 2:13 ye. . are made *n* by the blood of Christ
    2:17 which were afar off, and to them that were *n*
Phil. 2:27 he was sick *n* unto death: but God had
Heb. 7:19 hope. . by the which we draw *n* unto God
Jas. 4:8 draw *n* to God, and he will draw *n* to you
    5:8 patient. . the coming of the Lord draweth *n*

Night *See also* Darkness

Gen. 1:5 light Day, and the darkness he called *N*
Ex. 12:42 is a *n* to be much observed unto the LORD
    13:21 by *n* in a pillar of fire, to give. . light
Num. 9:16 by day, and the appearance of fire by *n*
Judg. 6:27 because he feared. . that he did it by *n*
1 Sam. 15:11 Samuel. . cried unto the LORD all *n*
Job 5:14 and grope in the noonday as in the *n*
    7:3 vanity, and wearisome *n* are appointed to me
    7:4 I say, When shall I arise, and the *n* be gone?
    17:12 they change the *n* into day: the light is
    35:10 is God my maker, who giveth songs in the *n*
    36:20 desire not the *n*, when people are cut off
Ps. 16:7 my reins. . instruct me in the *n* seasons
    17:3 thou hast visited me in the *n*; thou hast
    19:2 *n* unto *n* showeth knowledge
    30:5 weeping may endure for a *n*, but joy cometh
    42:8 in the *n* his song shall be with me
    74:16 the day is thine, the *n* also is thine
    77:6 I call to remembrance my song in the *n*
    91:5 thou shalt not be afraid for the terror by *n*
    92:2 the morning, and thy faithfulness every *n*
    104:20 thou makest darkness, and it is *n*
    121:6 not smite thee by day, nor the moon by *n*
    136:9 moon and stars to rule by *n*: for his mercy
    139:11 even the *n* shall be light about me
    139:12 but the *n* shineth as the day
Prov. 7:9 in the evening, in the black and dark *n*
Eccl. 2:23 yea, his heart taketh not rest in the *n*
Is. 21:11 what of the *n*? Watchman, what of the *n*?
    26:9 with my soul have I desired thee in the *n*
    27:3 lest any hurt it, I will keep it *n* and day
    59:10 we stumble at noonday as in the *n*
Dan. 2:19 was. . revealed unto Daniel in a *n* vision
    7:2 I saw in my vision by *n*, and, behold
Joel 1:13 lie all *n* in sackcloth, ye ministers of
Amos 5:8 maketh the day dark with *n*: that calleth
Jon. 4:10 came up in a *n*, and perished in a *n*
Mic. 3:6 therefore *n* shall be unto you, that ye
Mt. 26:31 shall be offended because of me this *n*
    27:64 lest his disciples come by *n*, and steal
Lk. 2:8 field, keeping watch over their flock by *n*
    2:37 served. . with fastings and prayers *n* and day
    5:5 toiled all the *n*, and have taken nothing
    6:12 and continued all *n* in prayer to God
    12:20 this *n* thy soul shall be required of thee
    17:34 that *n* there shall be two men in one bed
Jn. 3:2 the same came to Jesus by *n*, and said unto
    9:4 is day: the *n* cometh, when no man can work
    11:10 but if a man walk in the *n*, he stumbleth
    13:30 sop, went immediately out; and it was *n*
    21:3 go a fishing. . and that *n* they caught nothing
Acts 5:19 angel of the LORD by *n* opened the prison
    16:9 a vision appeared to Paul in the *n*
    27:23 there stood by me this *n* the angel of God
Rom. 13:12 the *n* is far spent, the day is at hand
1 Cor. 11:23 the same *n* in which he was betrayed
1 Thes. 2:9 laboring *n* and day, because we would
    5:2 day of the Lord. . cometh as a thief in the *n*
    5:5 day: we are not of the *n*, nor of darkness
1 Tim. 5:5 in supplications and prayers *n* and day
2 Tim. 1:3 remembrance of thee in my prayers *n* and
Rev. 21:25 for there shall be no *n* there

Nimrod Gen. 10:9

Nine

Lk. 17:17 not ten cleansed? but where are the *n*?

Nineveh

Gen. 10:11 went forth Asshur, and builded *N*
2 Kgs. 19:36 Sennacherib. . returned, and dwelt at *N*
Jon. 1:2 go to *N*, that great city, and cry against
    3:4 yet forty days, and *N* shall be overthrown
    4:11 and should not I spare *N*, that great city
Nah. 1:1 the burden of *N*. The book of the vision
    3:7 say, *N* is laid waste: who will bemoan her?
Zeph. 2:13 will make *N* a desolation, and dry like
Mt. 12:41 the men of *N* shall rise in judgment with

Noah (Noe)

Born, Gen. 5:29; walked with God, Gen. 6:9; built
the ark, Gen. 6:11–22; built an altar, Gen. 8:20–22;
covenant with God, Gen. 9:8–17; died, Gen. 9:28–29.

Is. 54:9 for this is as the waters of *N* unto me
Ezek. 14:14 though. . *N*, Daniel, and Job, were in it
Mt. 24:37 as the days of *N* were, so shall also the
Heb. 11:7 by faith *N*, being warned of God of things
1 Pet. 3:20 God waited in the days of *N*, while
2 Pet. 2:5 spared not the old world, but saved *N*

Nob 1 Sam. 21:1

Noble *See also* Excellent, Honorable, Magnificent

Ex. 24:11 upon the *n* of the children of Israel he
Num. 21:18 the well, the *n* of the people digged it
Neh. 3:5 their *n* put not their necks to the work
Job 29:10 the *n* held their peace, and their tongue
Ps. 149:8 chains, and their *n* with fetters of iron
Prov. 8:16 by me princes rule, and *n*, even all the
Eccl. 10:17 blessed. . when thy king is the son of *n*
Is. 43:14 to Babylon. . brought down all their *n*
Jer. 2:21 yet I had planted thee a *n* vine, wholly
    14:3 *n* have sent their little ones to the waters
    30:21 their *n* shall be of themselves, and their
Nah. 3:18 Assyria: thy *n* shall dwell in the dust
Acts 17:11 were more *n* than those in Thessalonica
1 Cor. 1:26 not many mighty, not many *n*, are called

Nobleman

Lk. 19:12 a certain *n* went into a far country to
Jn. 4:46 certain *n*, whose son was sick at Capernaum

Noise *See also* Voice

Ex. 20:18 the lightnings, and the *n* of the trumpet
    32:17 Moses, There is a *n* of war in the camp
2 Kgs. 7:6 hear a *n* of chariots, and a *n* of horses
1 Chr. 15:28 making a *n* with psalteries and harps
Ezra 3:13 the *n* of. . joy from the *n* of the weeping
Ps. 65:7 which stilleth the *n* of the seas, the *n*
    66:1 make a joyful *n* unto God, all ye lands
    93:3 LORD. . is mightier than the *n* of many waters
    98:4 make a joyful *n* unto the LORD, all the earth
Is. 13:4 the *n* of a multitude. . a tumultuous *n* of
    17:12 which make a *n* like the *n* of the seas
Jer. 4:19 I am pained. . my heart maketh a *n* in me
    46:17 Pharaoh king of Egypt is but a *n*; he hath
Lam. 2:7 made a *n* in the house of the LORD, as in
Ezek. 1:24 heard the *n* of their wings, like the *n*
Mt. 9:23 the minstrels and the people making a *n*
Lk. 1:65 these sayings were *n* abroad throughout
Acts 2:6 now when this was *n* abroad, the multitude
2 Pet. 3:10 heavens shall pass away with a great *n*
Rev. 6:1 and I heard, as it were the *n* of thunder

Noon

1 Kgs. 18:26 morning even until *n*, saying, O Baal
Ps. 55:17 evening. . morning, and at *n*, will I pray
Amos 8:9 that I will cause the sun to go down at *n*
Acts 22:6 nigh unto Damascus about *n*, suddenly

Noonday

Deut. 28:29 shalt grope at *n*, as the blind gropeth
Job 11:17 thine age shall be clearer than the *n*
Ps. 37:6 as the light, and thy judgment as the *n*
Is. 58:10 obscurity, and thy darkness be as the *n*
59:10 no eyes: we stumble at *n* as in the night

North

Job 26:7 stretcheth out the *n* over the empty place
Is. 43:6 I will say to the *n*, Give up; and to the
Jer. 3:12 go and proclaim these words toward the *n*
6:22 behold, a people cometh from the *n* country
Dan. 11:6 shall come to the king of the *n* to make
Zeph. 2:13 will stretch out his hand against the *n*
Zech. 6:8 these that go toward the *n* country have
Lk. 13:29 come. . from the *n*, and from the south

Nose

Job 40:24 his *n* pierceth through snares
Ps. 115:6 hear not: *n* have they, but they smell not
Prov. 30:33 wringing of the *n* bringeth forth blood
Is. 3:21 the rings, and *n* jewels
Ezek. 39:11 it shall stop the *n* of the passengers

Nostril

Gen. 2:7 breathed into his *n* the breath of life
7:22 all in whose *n* was the breath of life. . died
Job 27:3 and the spirit of God is in my *n*
39:20 the glory of his *n* is terrible
Is. 2:22 cease ye from man, whose breath is in his *n*

Note

Is. 30:8 write it before them. . *n* it in a book
Dan. 10:21 which is *n* in the Scripture of truth
Rom. 16:7 who are of *n* among the apostles
2 Thes. 3:14 *n* that man, and have no company with

Nothing

Gen. 11:6 and now *n* will be restrained from them
Ex. 16:18 he that gathered much had *n* over
Deut. 2:7 God hath been with thee; thou. . lacked *n*
2 Sam. 24:24 which doth cost me *n*. So David bought
2 Chr. 14:11 said, LORD, it is *n* with thee to help
Neh. 8:10 send portions unto them for whom *n* is
Job 6:18 turned aside; they go to *n*, and perish
6:21 ye are *n*; ye see my casting down, and are
8:9 we are but of yesterday, and know *n*, because
34:9 it profiteth a man *n* that he should delight
Ps. 39:5 and mine age is as *n* before thee: verily
49:17 when he dieth he shall carry *n* away
119:165 love thy law: and *n* shall offend them
Prov. 13:4 the sluggard desireth, and hath *n*
13:7 is that maketh himself rich, yet hath *n*
22:27 if thou hast *n* to pay, why should he take
Eccl. 5:15 take *n* of his labor, which he may carry
Is. 40:17 nations before him are as *n*. . less than *n*
40:23 that bringeth the princes to *n*; he maketh
41:12 they that war against thee shall be as *n*
41:24 ye are of *n*, and your work of nought
41:29 they are all vanity; their works are *n*
Lam. 1:12 is it *n* to you, all ye that pass by?
Dan. 4:35 inhabitants of the earth. . reputed as *n*
Joel 2:3 wilderness; yea, and *n* shall escape them
Hag. 2:3 in your eyes in comparison of it as *n*?
Mt. 5:13 is thenceforth good for *n*, but to be cast
10:26 is *n* covered, that shall not be revealed

Mt. 17:20 if ye have faith. . *n* shall be impossible
21:19 found *n* thereon, but leaves only, and said
26:62 answerest thou *n*? what is it which these
27:19 have thou *n* to do with that just man
Mk. 1:44 see thou say *n* to any man: but go thy way
7:15 *n* from without a man, that. . can defile him
Lk. 1:37 for with God *n* shall be impossible
6:35 and do good, and lend, hoping for *n* again
7:42 when they had *n* to pay, he frankly forgave
Jn. 5:19 the Son can do *n* of himself, but what he
6:63 Spirit that quickeneth; the flesh profiteth *n*
15:5 much fruit; for without me ye can do *n*
Acts 21:24 were informed concerning thee, are *n*
1 Cor. 1:19 will bring to *n* the understanding of
4:4 for I know *n* by myself; yet am I not hereby
4:5 judge *n* before the time, until the Lord come
2 Cor. 6:10 as having *n*. . yet possessing all things
13:8 we can do *n* against the truth, but for the
Gal. 5:2 circumcised, Christ shall profit you *n*
1 Tim. 4:4 *n* to be refused, if it be received with
6:7 brought *n* into this world. . can carry *n* out
Heb. 7:19 law made *n* perfect, but the bringing in
Jas. 1:4 ye may be perfect and entire, wanting *n*
3 Jn. 7 they went forth, taking *n* of the Gentiles

Nought (Naught)

Gen. 29:15 shouldest thou therefore serve me for *n*?
Job 1:9 then Satan. . said, Doth Job fear God for *n*?
Ps. 33:10 bringeth the counsel of the heathen to *n*
44:12 sellest thy people for *n*, and dost not
Prov. 1:25 but ye have set at *n* all my counsel
20:14 it is *n*, it is *n*, saith the buyer: but
Is. 49:4 in vain, I have spent my strength for *n*
52:3 ye have sold yourselves for *n*; and ye shall
Mk. 9:12 must suffer many things, and be set at *n*
Acts 4:11 stone which was set at *n* of you builders
5:38 or this work be of men, it will come to *n*
19:27 our craft is in danger to be set at *n*
Rom. 14:10 or why dost thou set at *n* thy brother?
1 Cor. 1:28 are not, to bring to *n* things that are
Rev. 18:17 one hour so great riches is come to *n*

Nourish

Gen. 45:11 there will I *n* thee; for yet there are
Is. 1:2 I have *n* and brought up children, and they
44:14 he planteth an ash, and the rain doth *n* it
Dan. 1:5 so *n* them three years, that at the end
Acts 12:20 country was *n* by the king's country
Eph. 5:29 his own flesh; but *n* and cherisheth it
1 Tim. 4:6 *n* up in the words of faith and of good
Jas. 5:5 *n* your hearts, as in a day of slaughter
Rev. 12:14 where she is *n* for a time, and times

Nourishment

Col. 2:19 having *n* ministered, and knit together

Novice

1 Tim. 3:6 not a *n*, lest being lifted up with pride

Number

Gen. 13:16 if a man can *n* the dust of the earth
15:5 tell the stars, if thou be able to *n* them
Num. 1:19 as the LORD commanded Moses, so he *n*
2:32 these. . were *n* of the children of Israel
23:10 and the *n* of the fourth part of Israel?
26:51 these were the *n* of the children of Israel
Deut. 4:27 shall be left few in *n* among the heathen
7:7 nor choose you, because ye were more in *n*
Josh. 8:10 and Joshua. . *n* the people, and went up
2 Sam. 24:1 (1 Chr. 21:2) go, *n* Israel and Judah
Job 14:16 thou *n* my steps: dost thou not watch
38:37 who can *n* the clouds in wisdom? or who can
Ps. 40:5 of them, they are more than can be *n*

Ps. 90:12 teach us to *n* our days, that we may apply
139:18 they are more in *n* than the sand
147:4 he telleth the *n* of the stars; he calleth
Eccl. 1:15 and that which is wanting cannot be *n*
Is. 53:12 he was *n* with the transgressors
65:12 therefore will I *n* you to the sword
Dan. 5:26 God hath *n* thy kingdom, and finished it
Hos. 1:10 the *n* of. . Israel shall be as the sand
Mt. 10:30 the very hairs of your head are all *n*
Jn. 6:10 men sat down, in *n* about five thousand
Acts 1:17 he was *n* with us, and had obtained part
6:1 when the *n* of the disciples was multiplied
11:21 great *n* believed, and turned unto the Lord
2 Cor. 10:12 we dare not make ourselves of the *n*
1 Tim. 5:9 let not a widow be taken into the *n*
Rev. 7:4 I heard the *n* of them which were sealed
7:9 a great multitude, which no man could *n*
13:17 name of the beast, or the *n* of his name
13:18 *n* of the beast. . is the *n* of a man . . his *n*

Nurse (Nursing)

Ex. 2:7 a *n* of the Hebrew women, that she may *n*
2 Sam. 4:4 and his *n* took him up, and fled
Is. 49:23 *n* fathers, and their queens thy *n* mothers
60:4 and thy daughters shall be *n* at thy side
1 Thes. 2:7 gentle. . as a *n* cherisheth her children

Nurture

Eph. 6:4 but bring them up in the *n* and admonition

O

Oak

Gen. 35:4 Jacob hid them under the *o* which was by
Judg. 6:11 angel of the LORD, and sat under an *o*
2 Sam. 18:9 under the thick boughs of a great *o*
1 Kgs. 13:14 found him sitting under an *o*
Is. 1:30 for ye shall be as an *o* whose leaf fadeth
Zech. 11:2 howl, O ye *o* of Bashan; for the forest

Oath *See also* Covenant, Pledge, Promise, Swear, Vow

Gen. 24:8 then thou shalt be clear from this my *o*
26:3 and I will perform the *o* which I sware unto
Ex. 22:11 an *o* of the LORD be between them both
Lev. 5:4 be that a man shall pronounce with an *o*
Num. 5:19 priest shall charge her by an *o*, and say
30:2 or swear an *o* to bind his soul with a bond
Deut. 7:8 he would keep the *o* which he had sworn
29:12 into his *o*, which the LORD thy God maketh
Josh. 2:17 we will be blameless of this thine *o*
9:20 because of the *o* which we sware unto
Judg. 21:5 for they had made a great *o* concerning
1 Sam. 14:26 mouth: for the people feared the *o*
2 Sam. 21:7 king spared . . because of the LORD's *o*
1 Kgs. 2:43 hast thou not kept the *o* of the LORD
2 Kgs. 11:4 an *o* of them in the house of the LORD
1 Chr. 16:16 (Ps. 105:9) and of his *o* unto Isaac
2 Chr. 6:22 and the *o* come before thine altar in
Neh. 5:12 called the priests. . took an *o* of them
10:29 entered. . into an *o*, to walk in God's law
Eccl. 8:2 commandment. . in regard of the *o* of God
9:2 he that sweareth, as he that feareth an *o*
Jer. 11:5 I may perform the *o* which I have sworn
Ezek. 16:59 (17:18) despised the *o* in breaking the
Dan. 9:11 curse is poured upon us, and the *o* that
Zech. 8:17 and love no false *o*: for all these are
Mt. 5:33 but shalt perform unto the Lord thine *o*
14:9 (Mk. 6:26) sorry: nevertheless for the *o*'s sake
26:72 he denied with an *o*, I do not know the man

Lk. 1:73 *o* which he sware to our father Abraham
Acts 2:30 knowing that God had sworn with an *o* to
23:21 which have bound themselves with an *o*
Heb. 6:16 *o* for confirmation is to them an end of
6:17 to show. . his counsel, confirmed it by an *o*
7:20 as not without an *o* he was made priest

Obadiah Ahab's governor 1 Kgs. 18:3–16

Obadiah the prophet Obad. 1–21

Obed-edom 2 Sam. 6:10

Obedience *See also* Obeisance, Subjection

Rom. 1:5 for *o* to the faith among all nations
5:19 by the *o* of one shall many be made righteous
6:16 sin unto death, or of *o* unto righteousness?
16:19 your *o* is come abroad unto all men
16:26 known to all nations for the *o* of faith
1 Cor. 14:34 but they are commanded to be under *o*
2 Cor. 7:15 whilst he remembereth the *o* of you all
10:5 captivity every thought to the *o* of Christ
Phlm. 21 having confidence in thy *o* I wrote unto
Heb. 5:8 though he were a Son, yet learned he *o*
1 Pet. 1:2 unto *o* and sprinkling of the blood of

Obedient *See also* Faithful

Ex. 24:7 the LORD hath said will we do, and be *o*
Num. 27:20 the congregation of. . Israel may be *o*
Deut. 4:30 turn to the LORD. . be *o* unto his voice
8:20 shall ye perish; because ye would not be *o*
2 Sam. 22:45 as soon as they hear, they shall be *o*
Prov. 25:12 so is a wise reprover upon an *o* ear
Is. 1:19 if ye be willing and *o*, ye shall eat the
42:23 his ways, neither were they *o* unto his law
Acts 6:7 company of the priests were *o* to the faith
Rom. 15:18 make the Gentiles *o*, by word and deed
2 Cor. 2:9 proof of you, whether ye be *o* in all
Eph. 6:5 be *o* to them that are your masters
Phil. 2:8 became *o* unto death, even the death of
Tit. 2:5 *o* to their own husbands, that the word of
2:9 exhort servants to be *o* unto their. . masters
1 Pet. 1:14 *o* children, not fashioning yourselves

Obeisance *See also* Obedience, Subjection

Gen. 37:7 behold, your sheaves. . made *o* to my sheaf
37:9 the moon and the eleven stars made *o* to me
43:28 they bowed down their heads, and made *o*
Ex. 18:7 to meet his father-in-law, and did *o*
2 Sam. 15:5 any man came nigh to him to do him *o*
1 Kgs. 1:16 Bath-sheba bowed. . did *o* unto the king
2 Chr. 24:17 princes of Judah. . made *o* to the king

Obey *See also* Hearken, Keep, Observe, Serve, Submit

Ex. 19:5 if ye will *o* my voice indeed, and keep my
23:21 beware. . *o* his voice, provoke him not
Deut. 11:27 a blessing, if ye *o* the commandments
13:4 keep his commandments, and *o* his voice
21:18 rebellious son, which will not *o* the voice
27:10 shalt therefore *o* the voice of the LORD
28:62 because thou wouldest not *o* the voice of
30:2 *o* his voice according to all that I command
30:8 shalt return and *o* the voice of the LORD
Josh. 5:6 because they *o* not the voice of the LORD
24:24 God will we serve, and his voice will we *o*
1 Sam. 12:14 *o* his voice, and not rebel against
15:22 behold, to *o* is better than sacrifice

2 Chr. 11:4 they *o* the words of the LORD . . returned
Neh. 9:17 refused to *o*, neither were mindful of
Job 36:11 if they *o* and serve him, they shall spend
Ps. 18:44 as soon as they hear of me, they shall *o*
Prov. 30:17 father, and despiseth to *o* his mother
Is. 50:10 that *o* the voice of his servant
Jer. 7:23 *o* my voice, and I will be your God
  11:3 cursed be the man that *o* not the words of
  11:8 yet they *o* not, nor inclined their ear
  12:17 if they will not *o*, I will utterly pluck
  18:10 evil in my sight, that it *o* not my voice
  26:13 now amend . . your doings, and *o* the voice of
  35:8 thus have we *o* the voice of Jonadab
  42:6 well with us, when we *o* the voice of the LORD
  43:4 so Johanan . . *o* not the voice of the LORD
Dan. 7:27 and all dominions shall serve and *o* him
Zech. 6:15 if ye will diligently *o* the voice of
Mt. 8:27 (Mk. 4:41; Lk. 8:25) winds and the sea *o* him
Mk. 1:27 the unclean spirits, and they do *o* him
Lk. 17:6 planted in the sea; and it should *o* you
Acts 5:29 said, We ought to *o* God rather than men
  5:32 whom God hath given to them that *o* him
  7:39 to whom our fathers would not *o*, but thrust
Rom. 2:8 do not *o* the truth, but *o* unrighteousness
  6:16 to whom ye yield yourselves servants to *o*
  6:17 but ye have *o* from the heart that form of
  10:16 they have not all *o* the gospel
Gal. 3:1 (5:7) that ye should not *o* the truth
Eph. 6:1 (Col. 3:20) children, *o* your parents
Col. 3:22 *o* in all things your masters according
2 Thes. 1:8 and that *o* not the gospel of our Lord
  3:14 if any man *o* not our word by this epistle
Tit. 3:1 *o* magistrates, to be ready to every good
Heb. 5:9 eternal salvation unto all them that *o*
  11:8 by faith Abraham, when he was called . . *o*
  13:17 *o* them that have the rule over you
Jas. 3:3 bits in the horses' mouths, that they may *o*
1 Pet. 1:22 have purified your souls in *o* the truth
  3:6 even as Sara *o* Abraham, calling him lord
  4:17 end be of them that *o* not the gospel

Object

Acts 24:19 and *o*, if they had aught against me

Oblation *See also* Offering, Sacrifice

Lev. 7:38 Israel to offer their *o* unto the LORD
  22:18 will offer his *o* for all his vows, and for
Num. 31:50 have therefore brought an *o* for the LORD
Is. 1:13 no more vain *o*; incense is an abomination
Ezek. 44:30 every *o* of all, of every sort of your *o*
Dan. 2:46 they should offer an *o* and sweet odors
  9:27 shall cause the sacrifice and the *o* to cease

Obscurity

Is. 29:18 the eyes of the blind shall see out of *o*
  58:10 then shall thy light rise in *o*, and thy
  59:9 we wait for light, but behold *o*

Observation

Lk. 17:20 the kingdom of God cometh not with *o*

Observe *See also* Behold, Keep, Obey

See

Gen. 37:11 envied him; but his father *o* the saying
Ex. 12:42 it is a night to be much *o* unto the LORD
  31:16 *o* the sabbath throughout their generations
Lev. 19:26 neither . . use enchantment, nor *o* times
Deut. 5:32 *o* to do . . as the LORD . . hath commanded
Josh. 1:8 *o* to do according to all that is written
2 Sam. 11:16 Joab *o* the city, that he assigned
Ps. 105:45 they might *o* his statutes, and keep his
  107:43 whoso is wise, and will *o* these things

Ps. 119:34 thy law . . I shall *o* it with my whole heart
Prov. 23:26 and let thine eyes *o* my ways
Is. 42:20 seeing many things, but thou *o* not
Ezek. 20:18 neither *o* their judgments, nor defile
Hos. 13:7 as a leopard by the way will I *o* them
  14:8 I have heard him, and *o* him: I am like a
Jon. 2:8 *o* lying vanities forsake their own mercy
Mt. 23:3 they bid you *o*, that *o* and do; but do not
  28:20 teaching them to *o* all things whatsoever I
Mk. 6:20 Herod feared John . . and *o* him; and when
  10:20 Master, all these have I *o* from my youth
Acts 16:21 to receive, neither to *o*, being Romans
Gal. 4:10 ye *o* days, and months, and times
1 Tim. 5:21 thou *o* these things without preferring

Obstinate *See also* Stiffnecked, Stubborn

Deut. 2:30 made his heart *o*, that he might deliver
Is. 48:4 because I knew that thou art *o*, and thy

Occasion *See also* Cause

Gen. 43:18 that he may seek *o* against us, and fall
Deut. 22:14 and give *o* of speech against her
1 Sam. 22:22 I have *o* the death of all the persons
2 Sam. 12:14 hast given great *o* to the enemies of
Job 33:10 he findeth *o* against me, he counteth me
Dan. 6:4 princes sought to find *o* against Daniel
Rom. 7:8 sin, taking *o* by the commandment
  14:13 no man put a stumblingblock or an *o* to fall
2 Cor. 5:12 but give you *o* to glory on our behalf
  8:8 but by *o* of the forwardness of others
  11:12 I may cut off *o* from them which desire *o*
Gal. 5:13 use not liberty for an *o* to the flesh
1 Tim. 5:14 give none *o* to the adversary to speak
1 Jn. 2:10 and there is none *o* of stumbling in him

Occupation

Gen. 46:33 when Pharaoh . . shall say, What is your *o*
Jon. 1:8 what is thine *o*? and whence comest thou?
Acts 18:3 for by their *o* they were tentmakers
  19:25 called together with the workmen of like *o*

Occupy *See also* Trade

Ezek. 27:9 mariners . . in thee to *o* thy merchandise
Lk. 19:13 called . . and said unto them, *O* till I come

Oded 2 Chr. 15:8; 28:9

Odious

1 Chr. 19:6 Ammon . . made themselves *o* to David
Prov. 30:23 for an *o* woman when she is married

Odor

Lev. 26:31 not smell the savor of your sweet *o*
Jer. 34:5 so shall they burn *o* for thee
Jn. 12:3 house was filled with the *o* of the ointment
Phil. 4:18 sent from you, an *o* of a sweet smell
Rev. 5:8 golden vials full of *o* . . prayers of saints

Offend *See also* Hurt, Sin, Transgress, Trespass

2 Chr. 28:13 we have *o* against the LORD already
Job 34:31 borne chastisement, I will not *o* any more
Ps. 73:15 *o* against the generation of thy children
  119:165 love thy law: and nothing shall *o* them
Jer. 2:3 all that devour him shall *o*; evil shall
  37:18 what have I *o* against thee, or against thy
Ezek. 25:12 hath greatly *o*, and revenged himself
Hos. 4:15 play the harlot, yet let not Judah *o*
  13:1 but when he *o* in Baal, he died
Hab. 1:11 he shall pass over, and *o*, imputing this
Mt. 5:29 (18:9; Mk. 9:47) if thy right eye *o* thee
  13:41 gather out of his kingdom all things that *o*

Mt. 18:6 but whoso shall *o* one of these little ones
18:8 (Mk. 9:43) if thy hand . . *o* thee, cut them off
Jn. 6:61 murmured at it, he said . . Doth this *o* you?
Acts 25:8 nor yet against Caesar, have I *o* any
1 Cor. 8:13 if meat make my brother to *o*, I will
Jas. 2:10 keep the whole law, and yet *o* in one
3:2 in many things we *o* all. If any man *o* not in

Offended *See also* Offend

. Prov. 18:19 a brother *o* is harder to be won than
Mt. 11:6 (Lk. 7:23) whosoever shall not be *o* in me
13:21 (Mk. 4:17) persecution . . by and by he is *o*
13:57 (Mk. 6:3) they were *o* in him. But Jesus
24:10 and then shall many be *o*, and shall betray
26:31 (Mk. 14:27) all ye shall be *o* because of me
Jn. 16:1 spoken unto you, that ye should not be *o*
Rom. 14:21 whereby thy brother stumbleth, or is *o*
2 Cor. 11:29 not weak? who is *o*, and I burn not?

Offense *See also* Sin, Transgression, Trespass

Eccl. 10:4 place; for yielding pacifieth great *o*
Is. 8:14 (Rom. 9:33; 1 Pet. 2:8) and for a rock of *o*
Hos. 5:15 till they acknowledge their *o*, and seek
Mt. 16:23 behind me, Satan: thou art an *o*, unto me
18:7 (Lk. 17:1) for it must needs be that *o* come
Acts 24:16 a conscience void of *o* toward God
Rom. 4:25 who was delivered for our *o*, and was
5:15 not as the *o*. . for if through the *o* of one
5:16 free gift is of many *o* unto justification
5:17 for if by one man's *o* death reigned by one
9:33 lay in Sion a stumblingstone and rock of *o*
14:20 it is evil for that man who eateth with *o*
16:17 mark them which cause divisions and *o*
1 Cor. 10:32 give none *o*, neither to the Jews, nor
2 Cor. 6:3 giving no *o* in any thing, that the
Gal. 5:11 then is the *o* of the cross ceased
Phil. 1:10 ye may be sincere and without *o* till
1 Pet. 2:8 rock of *o*, even to them which stumble

Offer *See also* Give, Present, Sacrifice

Gen. 22:2 and *o* him there for a burnt offering
46:1 Israel . . came to Beer-sheba, and *o* sacrifices
Ex. 22:29 not delay to *o* the first of thy ripe
29:36 thou shalt *o* every day a bullock for a sin
30:9 ye shall *o* no strange incense thereon
35:22 *o*, *o* an offering of gold unto the LORD
Lev. 1:3 *o* a male. . *o* it of his own voluntary will
6:21 shalt thou *o* for a sweet savor unto the LORD
7:29 that *o* the sacrifice of his peace offerings
10:1 and *o* strange fire before the LORD
17:7 no more *o* their sacrifices unto devils
19:5 peace offerings. . shall *o* it at your own will
21:8 he *o* the bread of thy God: he shall be holy
22:23 mayest thou *o* for a freewill offering
22:29 when ye will *o* a sacrifice of thanksgiving
Deut. 33:19 shall *o* sacrifices of righteousness
Josh. 8:31 they *o* thereon burnt offerings unto the
Judg. 5:2 when the people willingly *o* themselves
13:16 *o* a burnt offering, thou must *o* it unto
1 Sam. 1:21 *o* unto the LORD the yearly sacrifice
2 Sam. 24:22 and *o* up what seemeth good unto him
1 Kgs. 3:15 and *o* up burnt offerings, and *o* peace
9:25 (2 Chr. 8:12) Solomon *o* burnt offerings
13:2 shall he *o* the priests of the high places
2 Kgs. 10:24 and when they went in to *o* sacrifices
1 Chr. 29:9 *o* willingly . . with perfect heart they *o*
29:17 I have willingly *o* all these things
2 Chr. 17:16 who willingly *o* himself unto the LORD
35:12 to *o* unto the LORD, as it is written
Ezra 1:6 things, besides all that was willingly *o*
2:68 *o* freely for the house of God to set it up

Ezra 3:5 that willingly *o* a freewill offering unto
6:17 *o* at the dedication of this house of God
7:15 king and his counselors have freely *o* unto
Neh. 11:2 *o* themselves to dwell at Jerusalem
12:43 also that day they *o* great sacrifices
Job 1:5 that Job. . *o* burnt offerings according to
42:8 and *o* up for yourselves a burnt offering
Ps. 4:5 *o* the sacrifices of righteousness, and put
27:6 will I *o* in his tabernacle sacrifices of joy
50:14 *o* unto God thanksgiving; and pay thy vows
50:23 whoso *o* praise glorifieth me: and to him
66:15 *o* unto thee burnt sacrifices of fatlings
72:10 the kings of Sheba and Seba shall *o* gifts
116:17 *o* to thee the sacrifice of thanksgiving
Is. 57:7 thither wentest thou up to *o* sacrifice
66:3 *o* an oblation, as if he *o* swine's blood
Jer. 11:12 unto the gods unto whom they *o* incense
32:29 whose roofs they have *o* incense unto Baal
48:35 him that *o* in the high places, and him
Ezek. 20:28 and they *o* there their sacrifices
20:31 when ye *o* your gifts, when ye make your
Dan. 2:46 they should *o* an oblation and sweet odors
Hos. 9:4 shall not *o* wine offerings to the LORD
Amos 4:5 *o* a sacrifice of thanksgiving with leaven
5:22 though ye *o* me burnt offerings and your
5:25 have ye *o* unto me sacrifices and offerings
Jon. 1:16 *o* a sacrifice unto the LORD
Hag. 2:14 and that which they *o* there is unclean
Mal. 1:7 *o* polluted bread upon mine altar
1:11 every place incense shall be *o* unto my name
2:12 and him that *o* an offering unto the LORD
3:3 *o* unto the LORD an offering in righteousness
Mt. 5:24 be reconciled. . then come and *o* thy gift
8:4 (Mk. 1:44; Lk. 5:14) and *o* the gift that Moses
Lk. 2:24 to *o* a sacrifice according to that which
6:29 smiteth thee on. . one cheek *o* also the other
11:12 ask an egg, will he *o* him a scorpion?
Phil. 2:17 if I be *o* upon the sacrifice and service
2 Tim. 4:6 I am now ready to be *o*, and the time of
Heb. 5:1 may *o* both gifts and sacrifices for sins
5:7 when he had *o* up prayers and supplications
7:27 needeth not daily. . to *o* up sacrifice
9:14 *o* himself without spot to God, purge your
9:25 nor yet that he should *o* himself often, as
9:28 Christ was once *o* to bear the sins of many
10:12 he had *o* one sacrifice for sins for ever
11:4 by faith Abel *o*. . a more excellent sacrifice
11:17 *o* up Isaac. . *o* up his only begotten son
13:15 let us *o* the sacrifice of praise to God
Jas. 2:21 he had *o* Isaac his son upon the altar?
1 Pet. 2:5 *o* up spiritual sacrifices, acceptable
Rev. 8:3 *o* it with the prayers of all saints upon

Offering *See also* Gift, Oblation, Sacrifice

Gen. 4:4 LORD had respect unto Abel and to his *o*
Ex. 25:2 they bring me an *o*. . ye shall take my *o*
30:15 an *o* unto the LORD, to make an atonement
35:29 Israel brought a willing *o* unto the LORD
36:3 brought yet unto him free *o* every morning
Lev. 1:2 if any man. . bring an *o* unto the LORD
7:16 sacrifice of his *o* be a vow. . a voluntary *o*
23:38 your vows, and beside all your freewill *o*
Num. 7:3 brought their *o*. . six covered wagons
1 Sam. 2:17 for men abhorred the *o* of the LORD
1 Chr. 16:29 (Ps. 96:8) bring an *o*, and come before
2 Chr. 31:12 brought in the *o* and the tithes
Ezra 1:4 besides the freewill *o* for the house of
3:5 willingly offered a freewill *o* unto the LORD
7:16 Babylon, with the freewill *o* of the people
Ps. 20:3 remember all thy *o*, and accept thy
40:6 (Heb. 10:5) sacrifice and *o* thou didst not

Ps. 119:108 accept. . the freewill *o* of my mouth
Is. 53:10 thou shalt make his soul an *o* for sin
  66:20 they shall bring all your brethren for an *o*
Ezek. 20:28 presented the provocation of their *o*
  20:40 and there will I require your *o*
Amos 4:5 proclaim and publish the free *o*
Mal. 1:10 neither will I accept an *o* at your hand
  1:11 incense shall be offered. . and a pure *o*
  3:3 offer unto the LORD an *o* in righteousness
  3:8 wherein have we robbed thee? In tithes and *o*
Lk. 21:4 of their abundance cast in unto the *o*
Acts 21:26 until that an *o* should be offered for
  24:17 I came to bring alms to my nation, and *o*
Rom. 15:16 *o* up of the Gentiles might be acceptable
Eph. 5:2 given himself for us an *o* and a sacrifice
Heb. 10:10 sanctified through the *o* of the body
  10:14 by one *o* he hath perfected for ever them
  10:18 remission. . is, there is no more *o* for sin

Office

Gen. 41:13 me he restored unto mine *o*, and him he
Ex. 28:1 he may minister unto me in the priest's *o*
  29:9 priest's *o* shall be theirs for a perpetual
Num. 18:7 thou and thy sons. . keep your priest's *o*
1 Sam. 2:36 put me. . into one of the priests' *o*
Neh. 13:13 *o* was to distribute unto their brethren
Ps. 109:8 days be few; and let another take his *o*
Lk. 1:8 while he executed the priest's *o* before God
Rom. 11:13 as I am the apostle. . I magnify mine *o*
  12:4 and all members have not the same *o*
1 Tim. 3:1 if a man desire the *o* of a bishop
  3:10 then let them use the *o* of a deacon
Heb. 7:5 Levi, who receive the *o* of the priesthood

Officer

Gen. 41:34 let Pharaoh. . appoint *o* over the land
Ex. 5:14 *o* of the children of Israel. . were beaten
Is. 60:17 I will also make thy *o* peace, and thine
Jer. 29:26 ye should be *o* in the house of the LORD
Mt. 5:25 (Lk. 12:58) the judge deliver thee to the *o*
Jn. 7:32 and the chief priests sent *o* to take him
  7:46 *o* answered, Never man spake like this man
  18:3 having received a band of men and *o* from

Offscouring

Lam. 3:45 thou hast made us as the *o* and refuse
1 Cor. 4:13 are the *o* of all things unto this day

Offspring *See also* Heir, Posterity, Seed

Job 5:25 and thine *o* as the grass of the earth
  27:14 his *o* shall not be satisfied with bread
  31:8 let another eat. . let my *o* be rooted out
Is. 44:3 thy seed, and my blessing upon thine *o*
Acts 17:28 poets have said, For we are also his *o*
Rev. 22:16 I am the root and the *o* of David

Often

Mt. 23:37 how *o* would I have gathered thy children
1 Cor. 11:26 as *o* as ye eat this bread, and drink
Heb. 9:25 nor yet that he should offer himself *o*

Og Num. 21:33

Oil

Gen. 28:18 pillar, and poured *o* upon the top of it
Ex. 25:6 *o* for the light, spices for anointing *o*
  29:7 (Lev. 8:12) shalt thou take the anointing *o*
  30:25 (37:29) shalt make it an *o* of holy ointment
Deut. 32:13 the rock, and *o* out of the flinty rock
  33:24 brethren, and let him dip his foot in *o*
1 Sam. 10:1 Samuel took a vial of *o*, and poured it
  16:13 Samuel took the horn of *o*, and anointed

1 Kgs. 17:12 a barrel, and a little *o* in a cruse
2 Kgs. 4:2 any thing in the house, save a pot of *o*
  9:1 take this box of *o* in thine hand, and go to
Job 29:6 and the rock poured me out rivers of *o*
Ps. 23:5 thou anointest my head with *o*; my cup
  45:7 (Heb. 1:9) anointed. . with the *o* of gladness
  55:21 his words were softer than *o*, yet were
  89:20 David. . with my holy *o* have I anointed him
  92:10 I shall be anointed with fresh *o*
  104:15 *o* to make his face to shine, and bread
  141:5 him reprove me; it shall be an excellent *o*
Prov. 21:17 loveth wine and *o* shall not be rich
Is. 61:3 beauty for ashes. . *o* of joy for mourning
Mic. 6:7 or with ten thousands of rivers of *o*?
Zech. 4:12 empty the golden *o* out of themselves?
Mt. 25:3 foolish took their lamps, and took no *o*
Mk. 6:13 anointed with *o* many that were sick
Lk. 7:46 my head with *o* thou didst not anoint
  10:34 bound up his wounds, pouring in *o* and wine
Jas. 5:14 anointing him with *o* in the name of the
Rev. 6:6 and see thou hurt not the *o* and the wine

Ointment *See also* Perfume

Ex. 30:25 an oil of holy *o*, an *o* compound after
1 Chr. 9:30 the priests made the *o* of the spices
Job 41:31 he maketh the sea like a pot of *o*
Ps. 133:2 it is like the precious *o* upon the head
Prov. 27:9 *o* and perfume rejoice the heart: so
  27:16 hideth the wind, and the *o* of his right
Eccl. 7:1 a good name is better than precious *o*
  9:8 garments be always white. . head lack no *o*
  10:1 dead flies cause the *o* of the apothecary
Song 1:3 thy name is as *o* poured forth
Is. 1:6 neither bound up, neither mollified with *o*
Amos 6:6 and anoint themselves with the chief *o*
Mt. 26:7 (Mk. 14:3; Lk. 7:37; Jn. 12:3) box of. . *o*
Lk. 23:56 they returned, and prepared spices and *o*
Jn. 12:3 then took Mary a pound of *o* of spikenard

Old

Deut. 8:4 thy raiment waxed not *o* upon thee
Josh. 9:4 took *o* sacks. . and wine bottles, *o*, and rent
1 Kgs. 12:8 (2 Chr. 10:8) forsook the counsel of the *o*
Ps. 37:25 I have been young, and now am *o*
  71:9 cast me not off in the time of *o* age
  71:18 I am *o* and grayheaded. . forsake me not
  92:14 shall still bring forth fruit in *o* age
  102:26 (Is. 50:9; Heb. 1:11) wax *o* like a garment
Prov. 20:29 the beauty of *o* men is the gray head
  22:6 when he is *o*, he will not depart from it
Is. 46:4 even to your *o* age I am he; and even to
  58:12 be of thee shall build the *o* waste places
  65:20 nor an *o* man that hath not filled his days
Jer. 6:16 ask for the *o* paths, where is the good
Joel 2:28 (Acts 2:17) your *o* men shall dream dreams
Zech. 8:4 shall yet *o* men and *o* women dwell in the
Mt. 5:21 heard that it was said by them of *o* time
  9:16 (Mk. 2:21; Lk. 5:36) cloth unto an *o* garment
  9:17 neither do men put new wine into *o* bottles
Lk. 5:39 having drunk *o* wine. . saith, The *o* is better
Jn. 3:4 how can a man be born when he is *o*?
  21:18 but when thou shalt be *o*. . another shall gird
Rom. 6:6 our *o* man is crucified with him
1 Cor. 5:7 purge out therefore the *o* leaven
2 Cor. 5:17 *o* things are passed away; behold, all
Eph. 4:22 ye put off. . the *o* man, which is corrupt
Col. 3:9 ye have put off the *o* man with his deeds
Heb. 8:13 a new covenant, he hath made the first *o*
2 Pet. 2:5 spared not the *o* world, but saved Noah
1 Jn. 2:7 but an *o* commandment which ye had from
Rev. 12:9 *o* serpent, called the Devil, and Satan

Olive

Gen. 8:11 lo, in her mouth was an *o* leaf plucked
Judg. 9:8 unto the *o* tree, Reign thou over us
Ps. 52:8 like a green *o* tree in the house of God
128:3 thy children like *o* plants round about thy
Jer. 11:16 LORD called thy name, A green *o* tree
Hos. 14:6 his beauty shall be as the *o* tree
Hab. 3:17 the labor of the *o* shall fail
Zech. 4:3 two *o* trees by it, one upon the right
Rom. 11:17 thou, being a wild *o* tree, wert graffed
Jas. 3:12 can the fig tree. . bear *o* berries?
Rev. 11:4 these are the two *o* trees, and the two

Olivet (Olives, Mount of)

2 Sam. 15:30 David went up . . mount *O*, and wept
Mt. 21:1 (Mk. 11:1; Lk. 19:29) come . . mount of *O*
24:3 (Mk. 13:3) he sat upon the mount of *O*
26:30 a hymn, they went out into the mount of *O*
Lk. 21:37 went out, and abode in . . the mount of *O*
Jn. 8:1 Jesus went unto the mount of *O*
Acts 1:12 unto Jerusalem from the mount called *O*

Omega

Rev. 1:8 (21:6; 22:13) am Alpha and *O*, the beginning

Omit

Mt. 23:23 have *o* the weightier matters of the law

Omnipotent

Rev. 19:6 Alleluia: for the Lord God *o* reigneth

Omri 1 Kgs. 16:16–28

Mic. 6:16 for the statutes of *O* are kept, and all

Onan Gen. 38:4–10

Once

Gen. 18:32 angry, and I will speak yet but this *o*
Lev. 16:34 atonement . . for all their sins *o* a year
Job 33:14 for God speaketh *o*, yea twice, yet man
Rom. 6:10 in that he died, he died unto sin *o*
Heb. 6:4 for those who were *o* enlightened, and have
7:27 this he did *o*, when he offered up himself
9:26 but now *o* in the end of the world hath he
10:10 offering of the body of Jesus . . *o* for all
1 Pet. 3:18 Christ also hath *o* suffered for sins

One

Gen. 2:24 (Mt. 19:5; Mk. 10:8; 1 Cor. 6:16; Eph.
5:31) his wife: and they shall be *o* flesh
11:6 people is *o*, and they have all *o* language
27:38 hast thou but *o* blessing, my father?
Deut. 6:4 (Mk. 12:29) the LORD our God is *o* LORD
Josh. 23:14 not *o* thing hath failed of all the good
Job 9:3 he cannot answer him *o* of a thousand
Ps. 27:4 *o* thing have I desired of the LORD
Eccl. 4:9 two are better than *o*; because they have
7:27 counting *o* by *o*, to find out the account
Is. 27:12 ye shall be gathered *o* by *o*, O . . Israel
Mt. 5:18 *o* jot or *o* tittle shall in no wise pass
19:17 there is none good but *o*, that is, God
25:24 received the *o* talent came and said, Lord
Mk. 10:21 *o* thing thou lackest: go thy way, sell
Lk. 10:42 *o* thing is needful; and Mary hath chosen
Jn. 9:25 *o* thing I know, that, whereas I was blind
10:30 I and my Father are *o*
17:11 given me, that they may be *o*, as we are
17:21 they all may be *o* . . also may be *o* in us
Acts 4:32 believed were of *o* heart and of *o* soul
17:26 made of *o* blood all nations of men for to

Rom. 12:5 so we, being many, are *o* body in Christ
1 Cor. 8:6 is but *o* God . . and *o* Lord Jesus Christ
Gal. 3:28 neither male nor female . . all *o* in Christ
Eph. 2:15 to make in himself of twain *o* new man
4:5 *o* Lord, *o* faith, *o* baptism
Phil. 3:13 but this *o* thing I do, forgetting those
1 Jn. 5:7 are three that bear record . . three are *o*

Onesimus Col. 4:9; Phlm. 10

Onesiphorus 2 Tim. 1:16

Onion

Num. 11:5 and the leeks, and the *o*, and the garlic

Only

Jn. 3:16 world, that he gave his *o* begotten Son
Heb. 11:17 promises offered up his *o* begotten son
1 Jn. 4:9 God sent his *o* begotten Son into the world

Open

Gen. 3:5 day ye eat thereof, then your eyes shall be *o*
3:7 eyes of them both were *o*, and they knew
Num. 16:30 earth *o* her mouth, and swallow them up
Deut. 15:11 shalt *o* thine hand wide unto thy brother
Job 11:5 God would speak . . *o* his lips against thee
33:16 he *o* the ears of men, and sealeth their
38:17 have the gates of death been *o* unto thee?
Ps. 49:4 I will *o* my dark saying upon the harp
51:15 O Lord, *o* thou my lips; and my mouth shall
78:2 (Mt. 13:35) I will *o* my mouth in a parable
81:10 *o* thy mouth wide, and I will fill it
104:28 *o* thine hand, they are filled with good
118:19 *o* to me the gates of righteousness: I
119:131 I *o* my mouth, and panted: for I longed
119:18 *o* thou mine eyes, that I may behold
Prov. 31:8 *o* thy mouth for the dumb in the cause
Is. 22:22 he shall *o*, and none shall shut
26:2 *o* ye the gates, that the righteous nation
35:5 then the eyes of the blind shall be *o*
42:7 *o* the blind eyes, to bring out the prisoners
50:5 GOD hath *o* mine ear . . I was not rebellious
53:7 (Acts 8:32) afflicted, yet he *o* not his mouth
60:11 therefore thy gates shall be *o* continually
Ezek. 16:63 never *o* thy mouth any more because of
Mal. 3:10 I will not *o* you the windows of heaven
Mt. 3:16 (Mk. 1:10; Lk. 3:21) the heavens were *o*
7:7 (Lk. 11:9) knock, and it shall be *o* unto you
25:11 other virgins, saying, Lord, Lord, *o* to us
27:52 graves were *o*; and many bodies . . arose
Mk. 1:10 he saw the heavens *o*, and the Spirit like
7:34 saith unto him, Ephphatha, that is, Be *o*
Lk. 13:25 to knock . . saying, Lord, Lord, *o* unto us
24:32 heart burn . . while he *o* to us the Scriptures?
24:45 then *o* he their understanding, that they
Acts 5:19 angel of the Lord . . *o* the prison doors
10:11 and saw heaven *o*, and a certain vessel
12:14 knew Peter's voice, she *o* not the gate
14:27 how he had *o* the door of faith unto the
16:14 Lydia . . whose heart the Lord *o*, that she
17:3 *o* and alleging, that Christ must needs have
26:18 to *o* their eyes, and to turn them from
1 Cor. 16:9 great door and effectual is *o* unto me
2 Cor. 2:12 and a door was *o* unto me of the Lord
Eph. 6:19 I may *o* my mouth boldly, to make known
Col. 4:3 God would *o* unto us a door of utterance
1 Tim. 5:24 some men's sins are *o* beforehand
Heb. 4:13 all things are naked and *o* unto the eyes
Rev. 3:7 *o* . . no man shutteth . . shutteth . . no man
5:2 who is worthy to *o* the book, and to loose
6:1 and I saw when the Lamb *o* one of the seals

Openly

Mt. 6:4 seeth in secret himself shall reward thee *o*
Jn. 7:10 went he also up unto the feast, not *o*
  11:54 Jesus therefore walked no more *o* among the

Operation

Ps. 28:5 works of the LORD, nor the *o* of his hands
1 Cor. 12:6 diversities of *o*, but it is the same God
Col. 2:12 through the faith of the *o* of God

Ophir 1 Kgs. 9:28 (2 Chr. 8:18)

Ophrah Judg. 6:11, 24

Opinion

1 Kgs. 18:21 how long halt ye between two *o*?
Job 32:6 was afraid, and durst not show you mine *o*

Opportunity

Mt. 26:16 (Lk. 22:6) time he sought *o* to betray him
Gal. 6:10 as we have. . *o*, let us do good unto all
Phil. 4:10 ye were also careful, but ye lacked *o*

Oppose

Job 30:21 strong hand thou *o* thyself against me
Acts 18:6 when they *o* themselves, and blasphemed
2 Thes. 2:4 who *o* and exalteth himself above all
2 Tim. 2:25 instructing those that *o* themselves

Opposition

1 Tim. 6:20 and *o* of science falsely so called

Oppress See also Afflict, Persecute

Ex. 3:9 oppression wherewith the Egyptians *o* them
  22:21 (23:9) neither vex a stranger, nor *o* him
Lev. 25:17 ye shall not therefore *o* one another
Deut. 23:16 dwell with thee. . thou shalt not *o* him
  24:14 shalt not *o* a hired servant that is poor
1 Sam. 12:3 whom have I defrauded? whom have I *o*?
Job 10:3 is it good unto thee that thou shouldest *o*
  20:19 because he hath *o* and. . forsaken the poor
Ps. 10:18 that the man of the earth may no more *o*
  17:9 from the wicked that *o* me, from my deadly
  119:121 servant for good: let not the proud *o* me
Prov. 14:31 that *o* the poor reproacheth his Maker
  22:16 he that *o* the poor to increase his riches
  22:22 rob not the poor. . neither *o* the afflicted
  28:3 poor man that *o* the poor is like a sweeping
Is. 3:5 the people shall be *o*, every one by another
  53:7 he was *o*, and he was afflicted, yet he
Jer. 7:6 if ye *o* not the stranger, the fatherless
Ezek. 18:12 hath *o* the poor and needy, hath spoiled
Hos. 12:7 deceit are in his hand: he loveth to *o*
Amos 4:1 which *o* the poor, which crush the needy
Mic. 2:2 so they *o* a man and his house, even a man
Zech. 7:10 and *o* not the widow, nor the fatherless
Mal. 3:5 against those that *o* the hireling in his
Acts 10:38 healing all that were *o* of the devil
Jas. 2:6 do not rich men *o* you, and draw you

Oppressed See also Oppress

Job 35:9 make the *o* to cry: they cry out by reason
Ps. 9:9 the LORD also will be a refuge for the *o*
  10:18 to judge the fatherless and the *o*
  74:21 O let not the *o* return ashamed
Is. 58:6 heavy burdens, and to let the *o* go free
Amos 3:9 and behold. . the *o* in the midst thereof

Oppression See also Affliction, Persecution, Tribulation

Ex. 3:9 I have. . seen the *o* wherewith the Egyptians

Deut. 26:7 and looked on our affliction. . and our *o*
2 Kgs. 13:4 he saw the *o* of Israel, because the
Job 35:9 by reason of the multitude of *o* they make
Ps. 12:5 for the *o* of the poor, for the sighing of
  42:9 (43:2) mourning because of the *o* of the enemy
  44:24 and forgettest our affliction and our *o*?
  62:10 trust not in *o*. . become not vain in robbery
  107:39 are minished and brought low through *o*
  119:134 deliver me from the *o* of man: so will I
Eccl. 4:1 considered all the *o*. . done under the sun
  5:8 if thou seest the *o* of the poor, and violent
  7:7 surely *o* maketh a wise man mad; and a gift
Is. 5:7 he looked for judgment, but behold *o*
  30:12 because ye despise this word, and trust in *o*
  33:15 uprightly; he that despiseth the gain of *o*
  54:14 thou shalt be far from *o*; for thou shalt
Jer. 6:6 she is wholly *o* in the midst of her
  22:17 to shed innocent blood, and for *o*, and for
Ezek. 22:7 have they dealt by *o* with the stranger
  22:29 the people of the land have used *o*

Oppressor

Job 3:18 they hear not the voice of the *o*
Ps. 54:3 up against me, and *o* seek after my soul
  72:4 the needy, and shall break in pieces the *o*
  119:121 and justice: leave me not to mine *o*
Prov. 3:31 envy thou not the *o*, and choose none of
  28:16 wanteth understanding is also a great *o*
Eccl. 4:1 on the side of their *o* there was power
Is. 14:4 hath the *o* ceased! the golden city ceased!
  51:13 destroy? and where is the fury of the *o*?
Jer. 25:38 because of the fierceness of the *o*
Zech. 9:8 no *o* shall pass through them any more

Oracle

2 Sam. 16:23 was as if a man had inquired at the *o*
1 Kgs. 8:6 (2 Chr. 5:7) into the *o* of the house
Ps. 28:2 when I lift up my hands toward thy holy *o*
Acts 7:38 received the lively *o* to give unto us
Rom. 3:2 unto them were committed the *o* of God
Heb. 5:12 be the first principles of the *o* of God
1 Pet. 4:11 speak, let him speak as the *o* of God

Oration

Acts 12:21 a set day Herod. . made an *o* unto them

Orator

Is. 3:3 the cunning artificer, and the eloquent *o*
Acts 24:1 certain *o* named Tertullus, who informed

Ordain See also Appoint, Decree

Num. 28:6 offering, which was *o* in mount Sinai for
1 Chr. 9:22 whom David and Samuel the seer did *o*
  17:9 also I will *o* a place for my people Israel
2 Chr. 11:15 he *o* him priests for the high places
Ps. 7:13 he *o* his arrows against the persecutors
  8:2 of babes and sucklings hast thou *o* strength
  8:3 the moon and the stars, which thou hast *o*
  81:5 this he *o* in Joseph for a testimony
  132:17 I have *o* a lamp for mine anointed
Is. 26:12 LORD, thou wilt *o* peace for us: for thou
  30:33 for Tophet is *o* of old; yea, for the king
Jer. 1:5 and I *o* thee a prophet unto the nations
Hab. 1:12 O LORD, thou hast *o* them for judgment
Mk. 3:14 he *o* twelve, that they should be with him
Jn. 15:16 I have chosen you, and *o* you, that ye
Acts 1:22 must one be *o* to be a witness with us
  10:42 of God to be the Judge of quick and dead
  13:48 as many as were *o* to eternal life believed
  14:23 they had *o* them elders in every church
  16:4 that were *o* of the apostles and elders
  17:31 he will judge. . by that man whom he hath *o*
Rom. 7:10 the commandment, which was *o* to life

Rom. 13:1 but of God: the powers that be are *o*
of God
1 Cor. 2:7 hidden wisdom, which God *o* before the
7:17 so let him walk. And so *o* I in all churches
9:14 Lord *o* that they which preach the gospel
Gal. 3:19 *o* by angels in the hand of a mediator
Eph. 2:10 good works, which God hath before *o* that
1 Tim. 2:7 whereunto I am *o* a preacher, and an
Tit. 1:5 *o* elders in every city, as I had appointed
Heb. 5:1 priest taken from among men is *o* for men
8:3 every high priest is *o* to offer gifts and
9:6 when these things were thus *o*, the priests
Jude 4 were before of old *o* to this condemnation

Order *See also* Charge, Command, Decree, Law, Ordinance, Statute

Judg. 13:12 how shall we *o* the child
2 Sam. 17:23 put his household in *o*, and hanged
1 Kgs. 18:33 and he put the wood in *o*, and cut the
20:14 who shall *o* the battle? . . he answered, Thou
2 Kgs. 20:1 (Is. 38:1) set thine house in *o* . . shalt die
2 Chr. 8:14 appointed, according to the *o* of David
Job 10:22 of the shadow of death, without any *o*
23:4 I would *o* my cause before him, and fill my
37:19 cannot *o* our speech by reason of darkness
Ps. 37:23 steps of a good man are *o* by the LORD
50:21 but I will reprove thee, and set them in *o*
50:23 to him that *o* his conversation aright will
110:4 (Heb. 5:6; 5:10; 6:20; 7:11; 7:17; 7:21)
a priest for ever after the *o* of Melchizedek
119:133 *o* my steps in thy word: and let not any
Is. 9:7 to *o* it, and to establish it with judgment
1 Cor. 11:34 the rest will I set in *o* when I come
14:40 all things be done decently and in *o*
15:23 but every man in his own *o*: Christ the
Col. 2:5 in the spirit, joying and beholding your *o*
Tit. 1:5 thou shouldest set in *o* the things that

Ordinance *See also* Commandment, Judgment, Law, Order, Precept, Statute

Ex. 12:14 shall keep it a feast by an *o* for ever
15:25 there he made for them a statute and an *o*
Lev. 18:4 and keep mine *o*, to walk therein
Num. 9:14 one *o*, both for the stranger, and for him
Josh. 24:25 set them a statute and an *o* in Shechem
1 Sam. 30:25 made it a statute and an *o* for Israel
Ezra 3:10 to praise the LORD, after the *o* of David
Neh. 10:32 we made *o* for us, to charge ourselves
Job 38:33 knowest thou the *o* of heaven? canst thou
Ps. 99:7 they kept his testimonies, and the *o* that
119:91 continue this day according to thine *o*
Is. 24:5 have transgressed the laws, changed the *o*
58:2 nation that . . forsook not the *o* of their God
Jer. 31:35 and the *o* of the moon and of the stars
Ezek. 11:20 walk in my statutes, and keep mine *o*
Mal. 3:7 are gone away from mine *o*, and have not
3:14 what profit is it that we have kept his *o*
Lk. 1:6 walking in all the commandments and *o*
Rom. 13:2 resisteth the power, resisteth the *o*
1 Cor. 11:2 keep the *o*, as I delivered them to you
Eph. 2:15 the law of commandments contained in *o*
Col. 2:14 the handwriting of *o* that was against us
2:20 living in the world, are ye subject to *o*
Heb. 9:1 first covenant had . . *o* of divine service
9:10 carnal *o*, imposed on them until the time of
1 Pet. 2:13 submit yourselves to every *o* of man

Oreb Judg. 7:25

Organ

Gen. 4:21 of all such as handle the harp and *o*

Job 21:12 harp, and rejoice at the sound of the *o*
30:31 and my *o* into the voice of them that weep
Ps. 150:4 praise . . with stringed instruments and *o*

Orion

Job 38:31 of Pleiades, or loose the bands of *O*?
Amos 5:8 seek him that maketh the seven stars and *O*

Ornament

Ex. 33:4 mourned: and no man did put on him his *o*
Prov. 1:9 shall be an *o* of grace unto thy head
25:12 an *o* of fine gold, so is a wise reprover
Is. 3:18 take away the bravery of their tinkling *o*
30:22 *o* of thy molten images of gold: thou shalt
49:18 clothe thee with them all, as with an *o*
61:10 as a bridegroom decketh himself with *o*
Jer. 2:32 can a maid forget her *o*, or a bride her
1 Pet. 3:4 even the *o* of a meek and quiet spirit

Ornan *See also* Araunah 1 Chr. 21:15

Orpah Ruth 1:4–15

Orphan

Lam. 5:3 we are *o* and fatherless, our mothers are

Osee *See* Hosea

Ostrich

Job 39:13 gavest . . wings and feathers unto the *o*?
Lam. 4:3 become cruel, like the *o* in the wilderness

Othniel Judg. 3:9–11

Josh. 15:17 (Judg. 1:13) *O* . . took it: and he gave

Ought

Mt. 23:23 (Lk. 11:42) these *o* ye to have done, and
Jas. 3:10 my brethren, these things *o* not so to be
2 Pet. 3:11 what manner of persons *o* ye to be in

Outcast

Ps. 147:2 (Is. 56:8) gathereth together the *o* of Israel
Is. 11:12 and shall assemble the *o* of Israel
16:3 hide the *o*; bewray not him that wandereth
Jer. 30:17 called thee an *O*, saying, This is Zion

Outrageous

Prov. 27:4 wrath is cruel, and anger is *o*

Outrun

Jn. 20:4 the other disciple did *o* Peter, and came

Outstretched

Deut. 26:8 with a mighty hand, and with an *o* arm
Jer. 21:5 will fight against you with an *o* hand
27:5 by my great power and by my *o* arm

Outward

1 Sam. 16:7 man looketh on the *o* appearance, but
Mt. 23:27 appear beautiful *o*, but are within full
Rom. 2:28 circumcision, which is *o* in the flesh
2 Cor. 4:16 but though our *o* man perish, yet the
10:7 do ye look on things after the *o* appearance?

Oven

Ps. 21:9 thou shalt make them as a fiery *o* in the
Hos. 7:6 they have made ready their heart like an *o*
Mal. 4:1 the day cometh, that shall burn as an *o*
Mt. 6:30 (Lk. 12:28) tomorrow is cast into the *o*

Overcharge

Lk. 21:34 lest . . your hearts be *o* with surfeiting
2 Cor. 2:5 but in part: that I may not *o* you all

Overcome (Overcame)

Gen. 49:19 Gad, a troop shall *o* him: but he shall *o*
Num. 13:30 possess it; for we are well able to *o*
    22:11 peradventure I shall be able to *o* them
Jer. 23:9 like a man whom wine hath *o*, because of
Lk. 11:22 when a stronger. . come upon him, and *o*
Jn. 16:33 but be of good cheer; I have *o* the world
Acts 19:16 evil spirit. . leaped on them, and *o* them
Rom. 3:4 and mightest *o* when thou art judged
    12:21 be not *o* of evil, but *o* evil with good
2 Pet. 2:19 of whom a man is *o*, of the same is he
1 Jn. 2:13 (2:14) because ye have *o* the wicked one
    4:4 ye are of God, little children, and have *o*
    5:4 born of God *o* the world. . the victory that *o*
Rev. 2:7 to him that *o* will I give to eat of the
    2:11 that *o* shall not be hurt of the second death
    2:17 *o* will I give to eat of the hidden manna
    2:26 that *o*, and keepeth my works unto the end
    3:5 he that *o*. . shall be clothed in white raiment
    3:12 that *o* will I make a pillar in the temple
    3:21 to him that *o* will I grant to sit with me
    12:11 they *o* him by the blood of the Lamb
    17:14 Lamb shall *o* them: for he is Lord of lords
    21:7 he that *o* shall inherit all things

Overflow (Overflown) *See also*
Abound

Deut. 11:4 Red sea to *o* them as they pursued after
Josh. 3:15 Jordan *o* all his banks all the time of
Ps. 69:15 let not the waterflood *o* me, neither let
    78:20 the waters gushed out, and the streams *o*
Is. 43:2 through the rivers, they shall not *o* thee
Dan. 11:22 with the arms of a flood shall they be *o*
2 Pet. 3:6 the world. . being *o* with water, perished

Overflowing

Job 28:11 he bindeth the floods from *o*
    38:25 divided a watercourse for the *o* of waters
Hab. 3:10 the *o* of the water passed by

Overpass

Jer. 5:28 yea, they *o* the deeds of the wicked

Overpast

Ps. 57:1 my refuge, until these calamities be *o*
Is. 26:20 moment, until the indignation be *o*

Overseer

Gen. 39:4 made him *o* over his house, and all that
2 Chr. 34:13 were *o* of all that wrought the work
Prov. 6:7 which having no guide, *o*, or ruler
Acts 20:28 Holy Ghost hath made you *o*, to feed the

Overshadow

Mt. 17:5 (Mk. 9:7; Lk. 9:34) a bright cloud *o* them
Lk. 1:35 and the power of the Highest shall *o* thee
Acts 5:15 shadow of Peter passing by might *o* some

Oversight

Gen. 43:12 in your hand; peradventure it was an *o*
Num. 4:16 pertaineth. . the *o* of all the tabernacle
2 Kgs. 12:11 had the *o* of the house of the LORD
1 Pet. 5:2 taking the *o* thereof, not by constraint

Overspread

Gen. 9:19 and of them was the whole earth *o*
Dan. 9:27 for the *o* of abominations he shall make

Overtake (Overtook, Overtaken)

Gen. 31:25 Laban *o* Jacob. Now Jacob had pitched
    44:4 follow after the men. when thou dost *o* them

Judg. 20:42 the wilderness; but the battle *o* them
Ps. 18:37 I have pursued mine enemies, and *o* them
Is. 59:9 far from us, neither doth justice *o* us
Jer. 42:16 the sword. . shall *o* you there in. . Egypt
Amos 9:13 that the plowman shall *o* the reaper
Gal. 6:1 brethren, if a man be *o* in a fault, ye
1 Thes. 5:4 that day should *o* you as a thief

Overthrow (Overthrew, Overthrown)

Gen. 19:21 I will not *o* this city, for the which
    19:25 and he *o* those cities, and all the plain
Ex. 14:27 LORD *o* the Egyptians in the midst of the
    15:7 thou hast *o* them that rose up against thee
    23:24 *o* them, and quite break down their images
Deut. 12:3 *o* their altars, and break their pillars
2 Sam. 10:3 (1 Chr. 19:3) spy it out, and to *o* it?
Job 12:19 princes away spoiled, and *o* the mighty
    19:6 God hath *o* me, and hath compassed me with
Ps. 106:26 his hand. . to *o* them in the wilderness
    140:4 wicked. . who have purposed to *o* my goings
    140:11 evil shall hunt the violent man to *o* him
Prov. 11:11 city. . is *o* by the mouth of the wicked
    12:7 wicked are *o*, and are not: but the house of
    13:6 in the way: but wickedness *o* the sinner
    14:11 house of the wicked shall be *o*: but the
    18:5 is not good. . to *o* the righteous in judgment
    21:12 but God *o* the wicked for their wickedness
    22:12 the LORD. . *o* the words of the transgressor
    29:4 the land: but he that receiveth gifts *o* it
Is. 13:19 (Jer. 50:40; Amos 4:11) when God *o* Sodom
Jer. 18:23 but let them be *o* before thee; deal thus
Lam. 4:6 sin of Sodom, that was *o* as in a moment
Dan. 11:41 many countries shall be *o*: but these
Amos 4:11 I have *o* some of you, as God *o* Sodom
Jon. 3:4 yet forty days, and Nineveh shall be *o*
Hag. 2:22 I will *o* the throne of kingdoms, and I
Mt. 21:12 (Mk. 11:15; Jn. 2:15) and *o* the tables of
Acts 5:39 if it be of God, ye cannot *o* it; lest
2 Tim. 2:18 have erred. . and *o* the faith of some

Overturn

Judg. 7:13 smote it that it fell, and *o* it, that
Job 9:5 the mountains. . which *o* them in his anger
    12:15 he sendeth them out, and they *o* the earth
    34:25 their works, and he *o* them in the night
Ezek. 21:27 I will *o*, *o*, *o* it: and it shall be no

Overwhelm

Job 6:27 ye *o* the fatherless, and ye dig a pit for
Ps. 55:5 are come upon me, and horror hath *o* me
    61:2 will I cry unto thee, when my heart is *o*
    77:3 troubled: I complained, and my spirit was *o*
    78:53 feared not: but the sea *o* their enemies
    124:4 then the waters had *o* us, the stream had
    142:3 (143:4) when my spirit was *o* within me, then

Owe

Mt. 18:24 which *o* him ten thousand talents
    18:28 *o* him a hundred pence. . Pay me that thou *o*
Lk. 7:41 one *o* five hundred pence. . the other fifty
    16:5 the first, How much *o* thou unto my lord?
Rom. 13:8 *o* no man any thing, but to love one
Phlm. 18 or *o* thee aught, put that on mine account

Own

1 Chr. 29:14 and of thine *o* have we given thee
Ps. 12:4 our lips are our *o*: who is lord over us?
    67:6 and God, even our *o* God, shall bless us
Mt. 20:15 lawful. . to do what I will with mine *o*?
Jn. 1:11 came unto his *o*. . his *o* received him not
    13:1 having loved his *o* which were in the world

Jn. 15:19 of the world, the world would love his *o*
1 Cor. 6:19 know ye not that. . ye are not your *o*?
   10:24 let no man seek his *o*, but every man
   13:5 seeketh not her *o*, is not easily provoked
Phil. 2:4 look not every man on his *o* things, but
   2:21 for all seek their *o*, not. . Jesus Christ's
1 Tim. 5:8 but if any provide not for his *o*

Owner

Ex. 21:28 stoned. . the *o* of the ox shall be quit
Prov. 1:19 which taketh away the life of the *o*
Eccl. 5:11 and what good is there to the *o* thereof
Is. 1:3 ox knoweth his *o*, and the ass his master's
Lk. 19:33 were loosing the colt, the *o* thereof said

Ox (Oxen)

Ex. 21:28 if an *o* gore a man. . then the *o* shall be
   22:1 steal an *o*. . shall restore five *o* for an *o*
Num. 22:4 as the *o* licketh up the grass of the field
Deut. 25:4 (1 Cor. 9:9; 1 Tim. 5:18) not muzzle the *o*
1 Sam. 11:7 took a yoke of *o*. . hewed them in pieces
1 Kgs. 19:20 he left the *o*, and ran after Elijah
Job 6:5 or loweth the *o* over his fodder?
Ps. 69:31 shall please the LORD better than an *o*
Prov. 14:4 much increase. . by the strength of the *o*
   15:17 than a stalled *o* and hatred therewith
Is. 1:3 the *o* knoweth his owner, and the ass his
   11:7 and the lion shall eat straw like the *o*
Jer. 11:19 an *o* that is brought to the slaughter
Mt. 22:4 prepared. . my *o* and my fatlings are killed
Lk. 14:19 bought five yoke of *o*, and I go to prove
Jn. 2:14 found in the temple those that sold *o* and
1 Cor. 9:9 of the *o*. . Doth God take care for *o*?

P

Pacify

Esth. 7:10 then was the king's wrath *p*
Prov. 16:14 wrath of a king. . a wise man will *p* it
   21:14 a gift in secret *p* anger: and a reward in
Eccl. 10:4 place; for yielding *p* great offenses
Ezek. 16:63 when I am *p* toward thee for all that

Padan-aram Gen. 28:5

Paid *See* Pay

Pain *See also* Affliction, Anguish,
Distress, Grief

Job 14:22 but his flesh upon him shall have *p*
   33:19 chastened also with *p*. . bones with strong *p*
Ps. 25:18 look upon mine affliction and my *p*
   48:6 (Is. 13:8; Jer. 6:24; 22:23) *p*, as. . in travail
   55:4 my heart is sore *p* within me
   116:3 *p* of hell gat hold upon me: I found trouble
Is. 21:3 my loins filled with *p*: pangs have taken
   26:18 we have been with child, we have been in *p*
   66:7 before her *p* came, she was delivered of a
Jer. 4:19 my bowels! I am *p* at my very heart
   30:23 whirlwind: it shall fall with *p* upon the
Acts 2:24 raised up, having loosed the *p* of death
Rom. 8:22 creation groaneth and travaileth in *p*
Rev. 16:10 and they gnawed their tongues for *p*
   21:4 neither shall there be any more *p*

Painful

Ps. 73:16 thought to know this. . was too *p* for me

Painfulness

2 Cor. 11:27 weariness and *p*, in watchings often

Paint

2 Kgs. 9:30 and she *p* her face, and tired her head
Jer. 22:14 ceiled with cedar, and *p* with vermilion
Ezek. 23:40 *p* thy eyes, and deckedst thyself with

Palace

1 Chr. 29:1 the *p* is not for man, but for the LORD
Ezra 4:14 we have maintenance from the king's *p*
Ps. 45:8 of myrrh, and aloes. . out of the ivory *p*
   45:15 they shall enter into the King's *p*
   48:3 God is known in her *p* for a refuge
   48:13 mark ye well her bulwarks, consider her *p*
   122:7 thy walls, and prosperity within thy *p*
   144:12 polished after the similitude of a *p*
Song 8:9 we will build upon her a *p* of silver
Is. 25:2 a ruin: a *p* of strangers to be no city
Ezek. 25:4 shall set their *p* in thee, and make
Amos 6:8 abhor the excellency of Jacob. . hate his *p*
Mt. 26:3 assembled. . unto the *p* of the high priest
   26:58 (Mk. 14:54) unto the high priest's *p*
Lk. 11:21 when a strong man armed keepeth his *p*
Jn. 18:15 with Jesus into the *p* of the high priest
Phil. 1:13 bonds in Christ. . manifest in all the *p*

Pale

Is. 29:22 ashamed, neither shall his face now wax *p*
Rev. 6:8 I looked, and behold a *p* horse

Paleness

Jer. 30:6 do I see. . all faces are turned into *p*?

Palestina (Palestine)
Ex. 15:14; Is. 14:29; Joel 3:4

Palm *See also* Hand

Is. 49:16 have graven thee upon the *p* of my hands
Mt. 26:67 (Mk. 14:65) smote him with the *p* of their
Jn. 18:22 struck Jesus with the *p* of his hand

Palm *See also* Tree

Deut. 34:3 (2 Chr. 28:15) Jericho, the city of *p* trees
Judg. 4:5 she dwelt under the *p* tree of Deborah
Ps. 92:12 righteous shall flourish like the *p* tree
Song 7:7 this thy stature is like to a *p* tree
Jer. 10:5 are upright as the *p* tree, but speak not
Jn. 12:13 took branches of *p* trees, and went forth
Rev. 7:9 with white robes, and *p* in their hands

Palmerworm

Joel 1:4 the *p* hath left hath the locust eaten
   2:25 the caterpillar, and the *p*, my great army
Amos 4:9 *p* devoured them: yet have ye not returned

Palsy

Mt. 4:24 those that had the *p*; and he healed them
   8:6 my servant lieth at home sick of the *p*
   9:2 (Mk. 2:3; Lk. 5:18) brought. . man sick of the *p*
Acts 8:7 with *p*, and that were lame, were healed
   9:33 his bed eight years, and was sick of the *p*

Pamphylia Acts 13:13; 14:24; 15:38

Pang

Is. 13:8 *p* and sorrows shall take hold of them
Mic. 4:9 *p* have taken thee as a woman in travail

Pant

Ps. 38:10 my heart *p*, my strength faileth me
   42:1 as the hart *p* after the water brooks, so *p*
   119:131 I opened my mouth, and *p*: for I longed
Is. 21:4 my heart *p*, fearfulness affrighted me
Amos 2:7 that *p* after the dust of the earth on the

Paphos Acts 13:6, 13

Parable *See also* Byword, Proverb

Num. 23:7 and he took up his *p*, and said, Balak
Job 27:1 (29:1) moreover Job continued his *p*
Ps. 49:4 will incline mine ear to a *p*: I will open
78:2 (Mt. 13:35) I will open my mouth in a *p*
Prov. 26:7 equal: so is a *p* in the mouth of fools
Ezek. 17:2 and speak a *p* unto the house of Israel
20:49 they say of me, Doth he not speak *p*?
24:3 utter a *p* unto the rebellious house, and say
Mic. 2:4 day shall one take up a *p* against you
Hab. 2:6 shall not . . these take up a *p* against him
Mt. 13:3 (Mk. 4:2) spake many things unto them in *p*
13:13 (Mk. 4:11; Lk. 8:10) speak I to them in *p*
13:34 (Mk. 4:34) and without a *p* spake he not
24:32 (Mk. 13:28; Lk. 21:29) learn a *p* of the fig
Mk. 4:13 this *p*? and how then will ye know all *p*?

Paradise *See also* Eden, Heaven

Lk. 23:43 today shalt thou be with me in *p*
2 Cor. 12:4 how that he was caught up into *p*
Rev. 2:7 which is in the midst of the *p* of God

Paran Num. 12:16

Parchment

2 Tim. 4:13 bring . . the books, but especially the *p*

Pardon *See also* Forgive, Remission, Remit

Ex. 23:21 for he will not *p* your transgressions
34:9 *p* our iniquity and our sin, and take us
Num. 14:19 *p*, I beseech thee, the iniquity of this
14:20 LORD said, I have *p* according to thy word
1 Sam. 15:25 I pray thee, *p* my sin, and turn again
2 Kgs. 5:18 in this thing the LORD *p* thy servant
24:4 innocent blood; which the LORD would not *p*
2 Chr. 30:18 saying, The good LORD *p* every one
Neh. 9:17 but thou art a God ready to *p*, gracious
Job 7:21 and why dost thou not *p* my transgression
Ps. 25:11 thy name's sake, O LORD, *p* mine iniquity
Is. 40:2 is accomplished, that her iniquity is *p*
55:7 return . . to our God, for he will abundantly *p*
Jer. 5:1 that seeketh the truth; and I will *p* it
5:7 how shall I *p* . . thy children have forsaken me
33:8 I will *p* all their iniquities, whereby they
50:20 he found: for I will *p* them whom I reserve
Lam. 3:42 transgressed . . rebelled: thou hast not *p*
Mic. 7:18 is a God like unto thee, that *p* iniquity

Parent *See also* Father, Mother

Mt. 10:21 (Mk. 13:12) shall rise up against their *p*
Lk. 2:27 and when the *p* brought in the child Jesus
18:29 no man that hath left house, or *p*, or
21:16 shall be betrayed both by *p*, and brethren
Jn. 9:2 Master, who did sin, this man, or his *p*
Rom. 1:30 despiteful, proud . . disobedient to *p*
2 Cor. 12:14 not to lay up for the *p*, but the *p*
Eph. 6:1 (Col. 3:20) children, obey your *p*
1 Tim. 5:4 piety at home, and to requite their *p*
2 Tim. 3:2 disobedient to *p*, unthankful, unholy
Heb. 11:23 born, was hid three months of his *p*

Parlor

Judg. 3:20 Ehud came . . he was sitting in a summer *p*
1 Sam. 9:22 and Samuel . . brought them into the *p*

Part *See also* Divide, Portion, Separate

Lev. 2:6 thou shalt *p* it in pieces, and pour oil
Num. 18:20 any *p* among them: I am thy *p* and thine
Ruth 1:17 if aught but death *p* thee and me

1 Sam. 30:24 so shall his *p* be that tarrieth by
2 Sam. 19:43 we have ten *p* in the king
20:1 we have no *p* in David, neither have we
2 Kgs. 2:14 the waters, they *p* hither and thither
Ps. 2:8 uttermost *p* of the earth for thy possession
5:9 their inward *p* is very wickedness
22:18 (Mt. 27:35; Mk. 15:24; Lk. 23:34; Jn. 19:24)
p my garments among them, and cast lots
51:6 truth in the inward *p*: and in the hidden *p*
118:7 LORD taketh my *p* with them that help me
139:9 and dwell in the uttermost *p* of the sea
Mk. 9:40 for he that is not against us is on our *p*
Lk. 10:42 and Mary hath chosen that good *p*, which
11:39 but your inward *p* is full of ravening and
24:51 he was *p* from them, and carried up into
Jn. 13:8 if I wash thee not, thou hast no *p* with me
19:23 and made four *p*, to every soldier a *p*
Acts 1:8 and unto the uttermost *p* of the earth
2:45 sold their . . goods, and *p* them to all men
5:2 and kept back *p* of the price, his wife also
8:21 thou hast neither *p* nor lot in this matter
1 Cor. 13:9 for we know in *p*, and we prophesy in *p*
2 Cor. 6:15 or what *p* hath he that believeth with
Heb. 2:14 also himself likewise took *p* of the same
Rev. 20:6 he that hath *p* in the first resurrection
21:8 all liars, shall have their *p* in the lake
22:19 take away his *p* out of the book of life

Partaker

Ps. 50:18 with him, and hast been *p* with adulterers
Mt. 23:30 *p* with them in the blood of the prophets
Rom. 15:27 been made *p* of their spiritual things
1 Cor. 9:10 thresheth in hope . . be *p* of his hope
9:13 wait at the altar are *p* with the altar?
10:17 for we are all *p* of that one bread
10:18 which eat of the sacrifices *p* of the altar?
10:21 ye cannot be *p* of the Lord's table, and of
2 Cor. 1:7 as ye are of the sufferings, so shall
Eph. 3:6 of his promise in Christ by the gospel
5:7 be not ye therefore *p* with them
Phil. 1:7 of the gospel, ye all are *p* of my grace
Col. 1:12 made us meet to be *p* of the inheritance
1 Tim. 5:22 neither be *p* of other men's sins
2 Tim. 1:8 but be thou *p* of the afflictions of the
Heb. 2:14 as the children are *p* of flesh and blood
3:1 holy brethren, *p* of the heavenly calling
3:14 for we are made *p* of Christ, if we hold the
6:4 and were made *p* of the Holy Ghost
12:10 that we might be *p* of his holiness
1 Pet. 4:13 as ye are *p* of Christ's sufferings
5:1 also a *p* of the glory that shall be revealed
2 Pet. 1:4 ye might be *p* of the divine nature
2 Jn. 11 biddeth him God-speed is *p* of his evil
Rev. 18:4 my people, that ye be not *p* of her sins

Parthian Acts 2:9

Partial

Mal. 2:9 not kept my ways . . have been *p* in the law
Jas. 2:4 are ye not then *p* in yourselves, and are

Partiality

1 Tim. 5:21 one before another, doing nothing by *p*
Jas. 3:17 fruits, without *p*, and without hypocrisy

Partition

1 Kgs. 6:21 made a *p* by the chains of gold before
Eph. 2:14 broken down the middle wall of *p* between

Partner

Prov. 29:24 is *p* with a thief hateth his own soul
Lk. 5:7 they beckoned unto their *p*, which were in
2 Cor. 8:23 of Titus, he is my *p* and fellow helper
Phlm. 17 if thou count me . . a *p*, receive him as

Partridge

1 Sam. 26:20 seek a flea, as when one doth hunt a *p*
Jer. 17:11 as the *p* sitteth on eggs, and hatcheth

Pashur Jer. 20:1-6

Pass *See also* Exceed, Past

Ex. 12:13 when I see the blood, I will *p* over you
   12:23 LORD will *p* through to smite the Egyptians
   33:22 while my glory *p* by, that I will put thee
Num. 20:17 let us *p*, I pray thee, through thy country
Josh. 3:4 for ye have not *p* this way heretofore
   3:17 *p* over on dry ground, until all the people
2 Sam. 1:26 thy love to me was wonderful, *p* the
   15:23 people *p* over: the king also himself *p* over
1 Kgs. 19:11 LORD *p* by, and a great and strong wind
2 Chr. 9:22 Solomon *p* all the kings of the earth
Ps. 84:6 who *p* through the valley of Baca make it
Prov. 4:15 *p* not by it, turn from it, and *p* away
Is. 43:2 when thou *p* through the waters, I will be
Jer. 2:6 through a land that no man *p* through
Lam. 1:12 is it nothing to you, all ye that *p* by?
Ezek. 20:37 I will cause you to *p* under the rod
   32:19 whom dost thou *p* in beauty? go down, and
Amos 7:8 I will not again *p* by them any more
Mic. 7:18 *p* by the transgression of the remnant
Zech. 3:4 caused thine iniquity to *p* from thee
Mt. 5:18 one jot or one tittle shall in no wise *p*
   20:30 (Lk. 18:37) when they heard that Jesus *p* by
   24:35 (Mk. 13:31; Lk. 21:33) heaven . . earth shall *p*
   26:39 (Mk. 14:35) possible, let this cup *p* from me
Mk. 5:21 when Jesus was *p* over again by ship unto
   15:21 they compel one Simon a Cyrenian, who *p* by
Lk. 4:30 but he, *p* through the midst of them, went
   10:31 when he saw him, he *p* by on the other side
   16:17 and it is easier for heaven and earth to *p*
   16:26 which would *p* from hence to you cannot
   19:1 and Jesus entered and *p* through Jericho
Jn. 5:24 condemnation; but is *p* from death unto life
Acts 5:15 shadow of Peter *p* by might overshadow
Rom. 5:12 death by sin; and so death *p* upon all men
1 Cor. 7:31 for the fashion of this world *p* away
2 Cor. 5:17 a new creature: old things are *p* away
Eph. 3:19 the love of Christ, which *p* knowledge
Phil. 4:7 peace of God, which *p* all understanding
Heb. 4:14 high priest, that is *p* into the heavens
Jas. 1:10 as the flower of the grass he shall *p*
2 Pet. 3:10 heavens shall *p* away with a great
1 Jn. 2:17 world *p* away, and the lust thereof
   3:14 we know that we have *p* from death unto life
Rev. 21:1 first heaven and . . first earth were *p* away
   21:4 any more pain . . the former things are *p* away

Passage

Num. 20:21 Edom refused to give Israel *p* through
Josh. 22:11 at the *p* of the children of Israel
1 Sam. 14:4 between the *p*, by which Jonathan
Jer. 51:32 that the *p* are stopped, and the reeds

Passenger

Prov. 9:15 to call *p* who go right on their ways
Ezek. 39:11 valley of the *p* on the east of the sea

Passion

Acts 1:3 showed himself alive after his *p* by many
   14:15 we also are men of like *p* with you
Jas. 5:17 Elias was a man subject to like *p* as we

Passover

Ex. 12:11 shall eat it in haste: it is the LORD's *p*
Lev. 23:5 (Num. 28:16) fourteenth . . the LORD's *p*
Num. 9:5 they kept the *p* on the fourteenth day

Deut. 16:1 and keep the *p* unto the LORD thy God
Josh. 5:10 encamped in Gilgal, and kept the *p*
2 Kgs. 23:21 (2 Chr. 35:1) keep the *p* unto the LORD
2 Chr. 30:1 and Hezekiah sent to all . . to keep the *p*
Ezra 6:19 the children of the captivity kept the *p*
Mt. 26:2 (Mk. 14:1; Lk. 22:1) is the feast of the *p*
   26:19 (Mk. 14:16; Lk. 22:13) made ready the *p*
Lk. 22:15 to eat this *p* with you before I suffer
Jn. 2:23 now when he was in Jerusalem at the *p*
   13:1 before the feast of the, *p*, when Jesus knew
   18:39 I should release.unto you one at the *p*
1 Cor. 5:7 even Christ our *p* is sacrificed for us
Heb. 11:28 through faith he kept the *p*

Past *See also* Pass

1 Sam. 15:32 surely the bitterness of death is *p*
Job 17:11 my days are *p*, my purposes are broken off
   29:2 oh that I were as in months *p*, as in the
Ps. 90:4 thousand years . . as yesterday when it is *p*
Eccl. 3:15 and God requireth that which is *p*
Song 2:11 winter is *p*, the rain is over and gone
Jer. 8:20 the harvest is *p*, the summer is ended
Acts 14:16 who in times *p* suffered all nations to
Rom. 3:25 remission of sins that are *p*, through the
   11:33 his judgments, and his ways *p* finding out!
Eph. 2:2 wherein in time *p* ye walked according to
2 Tim. 2:18 that the resurrection is *p* already
Heb. 1:1 spake in time *p* unto the fathers by the
1 Jn. 2:8 darkness is *p* . . the true light now shineth

Pastor *See also* Shepherd

Jer. 2:8 the *p* also transgressed against me
   3:15 I will give you *p* according to mine heart
   10:21 *p* are become brutish, and have not sought
   17:16 not hastened from being a *p* to follow thee
   23:1 woe be unto the *p* that destroy and scatter
Eph. 4:11 evangelists; and some, *p* and teachers

Pasture

Gen. 47:4 thy servants have no *p* for their flocks
Ps. 23:2 he maketh me to lie down in green *p*
   65:13 the *p* are clothed with flocks; the valleys
   74:1 anger smoke against the sheep of thy *p*?
   79:13 we thy people and sheep of thy *p* will give
   95:7 we are the people of his *p*, and the sheep
   100:3 we are his people, and the sheep of his *p*
Is. 49:9 and their *p* shall be in all high places
Jer. 23:1 destroy and scatter the sheep of my *p*!
Lam. 1:6 are become like harts that find no *p*
Ezek. 34:14 I will feed them in a good *p*, and upon
   34:31 ye my flock, the flock of my *p*, are men
Hos. 13:6 according to their *p* . . were they filled
Joel 1:18 are perplexed, because they have no *p*
Jn. 10:9 and shall go in and out, and find *p*

Path *See also* Highway, Way

Num. 22:24 angel . . stood in a *p* of the vineyards
Job 8:13 so are the *p* of all that forget God
   28:7 there is a *p* which no fowl knoweth
Ps. 16:11 thou wilt show me the *p* of life
   17:4 I have kept me from the *p* of the destroyer
   23:3 he leadeth me in the *p* of righteousness for
   25:4 show me thy ways, O LORD; teach me thy *p*
   25:10 all the *p* of the LORD are mercy and truth
   27:11 lead me in a plain *p*, because of mine enemies
   65:11 with thy goodness; and thy *p* drop fatness
   77:19 in the sea, and thy *p* in the great waters
   119:105 lamp unto my feet, and a light unto my *p*
   139:3 thou compassest my *p* and my lying down
Prov. 3:6 acknowledge him, and he shall direct thy *p*
   3:17 ways of pleasantness, and all her *p* are peace
   4:14 enter not into the *p* of the wicked, and
   4:18 the *p* of the just is as the shining light

Is. 2:3 (Mic. 4:2) his ways, and we will walk in his *p*
  26:7 most upright, dost weigh the *p* of the just
  40:14 taught him in the *p* of judgment
  42:16 lead them in *p* that they have not known
  59:8 they have made them crooked *p*; whosoever
Jer. 6:16 ask for the old *p*, where is the good way
  18:15 stumble in their ways from the ancient *p*
Lam. 3:9 inclosed my ways. . made my *p* crooked
Mt. 3:3 (Mk. 1:3; Lk. 3:4) make his *p* straight
Heb. 12:13 and make straight *p* for your feet, lest

Patience *See also* Long-suffering

Mt. 18:26 have *p* with me, and I will pay thee all
Lk. 8:15 keep it, and bring forth fruit with *p*
  21:19 in your *p* possess ye your souls
Rom. 5:3 knowing that tribulation worketh *p*
  8:25 we see not, then do we with *p* wait for it
  15:4 we through *p* and comfort of the Scriptures
  15:5 now the God of *p* and consolation grant you
2 Cor. 6:4 as the ministers of God, in much *p*, in
  12:12 were wrought among you in all *p*, in signs
Col. 1:11 all *p* and long-suffering with joyfulness
1 Thes. 1:3 and *p* of hope in our Lord Jesus Christ
2 Thes. 1:4 *p* and faith in all your persecutions
1 Tim. 6:11 godliness, faith, love, *p*, meekness
Tit. 2:2 sober. . sound in faith, in charity, in *p*
Heb. 6:12 through faith and *p* inherit the promises
  10:36 have need of *p*, that, after ye have done
  12:1 and let us run with *p* the race that is set
Jas. 1:3 that the trying of your faith worketh *p*
  1:4 but let *p* have her perfect work, that ye may
  5:7 husbandman waiteth. . and hath long *p* for it
  5:10 example of suffering affliction, and of *p*
  5:11 have heard of the *p* of Job, and have seen
2 Pet. 1:6 to temperance, *p*; and to *p*, godliness
Rev. 1:9 and in the kingdom and *p* of Jesus Christ
  2:2 (2:19) I know thy works. . thy labor, and thy *p*
  3:10 because thou hast kept the word of my *p*
  13:10 (14:12) here is the *p*. . of the saints

Patient

Eccl. 7:8 the *p* in spirit is better than the proud
Rom. 2:7 them who by *p* continuance in well doing
  12:12 rejoicing in hope; *p* in tribulation
1 Thes. 5:14 support the weak, be *p* toward all men
2 Thes. 3:5 and into the *p* waiting for Christ
1 Tim. 3:3 but *p*, not a brawler, not covetous
2 Tim. 2:24 gentle unto all men, apt to teach, *p*
Jas. 5:7 be *p* therefore, brethren, unto the coming
  5:8 be ye also *p*; stablish your hearts: for the

Patiently

Ps. 37:7 rest in the LORD, and wait *p* for him
  40:1 I waited *p* for the LORD; and he inclined
Heb. 6:15 so, after he had *p* endured, he obtained
1 Pet. 2:20 for your faults, ye shall take it *p*?

Patmos Rev. 1:9

Patriarch

Acts 7:8 begat Jacob; and Jacob begat the twelve *p*

Pattern *See also* Example, Form, Image

Ex. 25:9 after the *p* of the tabernacle, and the *p*
  25:40 (Heb. 8:5) *p*. . showed thee in the mount
Num. 8:4 the *p* which the LORD had showed Moses
1 Chr. 28:11 David gave to Solomon his son the *p*
1 Tim. 1:16 for a *p* to them which should hereafter
Tit. 2:7 in all things showing thyself a *p* of good
Heb. 9:23 *p* of things in. . heavens should be purified

Paul (Saul)

Born in Tarsus, Acts 22:3; educated under Gamaliel,

Acts 22:3; consented to Stephen's death, Acts 7:58;
8:1 (22:20); persecuted the Church, Acts 8:3; 9:1–2
(22:4–5; 26:10–11; 1 Cor. 15:9; Gal. 1:13; Phil. 3:6);
converted near Damascus, Acts 9:3–19 (22:6–16;
26: 12–20); went into Arabia, Gal. 1:17; preached
three years in Damascus, Gal. 1:17; went up to
Jerusalem, Acts 9:26–28; Gal. 1:18–19; abode in
Cilicia, Gal. 1:21–23; missionary work, Acts 13–14;
15:36–18:22; 18:23–21:17; attended the Council of
Jerusalem, Acts 15:1–29; Gal. 2:1–10; arrested in
Jerusalem, Acts 21:27–40; imprisoned in Caesarea,
Acts 23:23–35; defended himself before Felix, Acts
24; appealed unto Caesar, Acts 25:10–12; defended
himself before Agrippa, Acts 26; journeyed to Rome,
Acts 27:1–28:16; preached during imprisonment,
Acts 28:17–31.

1 Cor. 1:13 is Christ divided? was *P* crucified for
  3:4 I am of *P*; and another, I am of Apollos
2 Pet. 3:15 as our beloved brother *P*. . hath written

Paulus Acts 13:7

Pavement

Jn. 19:13 judgment seat in a place. . called the *P*

Pavilion

2 Sam. 22:12 (Ps. 18:11) he made darkness *p* round
Ps. 27:5 time of trouble he shall hide me in his *p*
  31:20 keep them secretly in a *p* from the strife
Jer. 43:10 he shall spread his royal *p* over them

Pay (Paid) *See also* Bestow, Give

Ex. 21:19 only he shall *p* for the loss of his time
  22:7 if the thief be found, let him *p* double
Num. 20:19 drink of thy water, then I will *p* for it
Deut. 23:21 a vow. . thou shalt not slack to *p* it
2 Sam. 15:7 Absalom said. . let me go and *p* my vow
2 Kgs. 4:7 go, sell the oil, and *p* thy debt
2 Chr. 8:8 them did Solomon make to *p* tribute
Ps. 22:25 will *p* my vows before them that fear him
  37:21 the wicked borroweth, and *p* not again
  66:13 with burnt offerings: I will *p* thee my vows
  76:11 vow, and *p* unto the LORD your God: let all
Prov. 19:17 he hath given will he *p* him again
  22:27 if thou hast nothing to *p*, why should he
Eccl. 5:4 vowest a vow unto God, defer not to *p* it
Jon. 1:3 ship going to Tarshish: so he *p* the fare
  2:9 I will *p* that that I have vowed
Mt. 5:26 till thou hast *p* the uttermost farthing
  17:24 and said, Doth not your master *p* tribute?
  18:26 have patience with me, and I will *p* thee
  18:28 by the throat, saying, *P* me that thou owest
  23:23 hypocrites! for ye *p* tithe of mint and anise
Lk. 7:42 they had nothing to *p*, he frankly forgave
  12:59 till thou hast *p* the very last mite
Rom. 13:6 for this cause *p* ye tribute also
Heb. 7:9 Levi also, who receiveth tithes, *p* tithes

Peace *See also* Peace Offering, Quietness, Rest

Gen. 41:16 God shall give Pharaoh an answer of *p*
  43:23 he said, *P* be to you, fear not: your God
Lev. 26:6 and I will give *p* in the land, and ye shall
Num. 6:26 lift up his countenance. . give thee *p*
  25:12 behold, I give unto him my covenant of *p*
Deut. 20:10 to fight against it, then proclaim *p*
  29:19 saying, I shall have *p*, though I walk in
Judg. 6:23 the LORD said unto him, *P* be unto thee
2 Sam. 10:19 (1 Chr. 19:19) made *p* with Israel
1 Kgs. 2:5 he slew, and shed the blood of war in *p*
  2:33 shall there be *p* for ever from the LORD

2 Kgs. 7:9 day of good tidings, and we hold our *p*
  20:19 (Is. 39:8) *p* and truth be in my days?
1 Chr. 22:9 will give *p* and quietness unto Israel
Job 22:21 acquaint now thyself with him . . be at *p*
  25:2 he maketh *p* in his high places
Ps. 4:8 I will both lay me down in *p*, and sleep
  28:3 speak *p* to their neighbors, but mischief is
  29:11 the LORD will bless his people with *p*
  34:14 (1 Pet. 3:11) do good; seek *p*, and pursue it
  35:20 speak not *p*: but they devise deceitful
  37:11 delight themselves in the abundance of *p*
  37:37 the upright: for the end of that man is *p*
  72:3 the mountains shall bring *p* to the people
  85:8 speak *p* unto his people, and to his saints
  85:10 righteousness and *p* have kissed each other
  119:165 great *p* have they which love thy law
  120:7 I am for *p*: but when I speak, they are
  122:6 pray for the *p* of Jerusalem: they shall
  125:5 of iniquity: but *p* shall be upon Israel
Prov. 3:2 long life, and, *p*, shall they add to thee
  3:17 ways of pleasantness, and all her paths are *p*
  11:12 but a man of understanding holdeth his *p*
  12:20 evil: but to the counselors of *p* is joy
Eccl. 3:8 a time of war, and a time of *p*
Is. 9:6 The everlasting Father, The Prince of *P*
  9:7 of his government and *p* there shall be no end
  26:3 thou wilt keep him in perfect *p*, whose mind
  26:12 LORD, thou wilt ordain *p* for us: for thou
  27:5 make *p* with me; and he shall make *p* with me
  32:17 the work of righteousness shall be *p*
  33:7 the ambassadors of *p* shall weep bitterly
  38:17 behold, for *p* I had great bitterness
  45:7 I make *p*, and create evil: I the LORD do all
  48:18 then had thy *p* been as a river, and thy
  48:22 (57:21) no *p*, saith the LORD, unto the wicked
  52:7 (Nah. 1:15) good tidings, that publisheth *p*
  53:5 the chastisement of our *p* was upon him
  54:10 neither shall . . covenant of my *p* be removed
  54:13 and great shall be the *p* of thy children
  55:12 go out with joy, and be led forth with *p*
  57:2 he shall enter into *p*; they shall rest in
  57:19 *p*, *p* to him that is far off, and . . that is near
  59:8 (Rom. 3:17) the way of *p* they know not
  60:17 I will also make thy officers *p*, and thine
  66:12 behold, I will extend *p* to her like a river
Jer. 6:14 (8:11; Ezek. 13:10) *p*, *p*; when there is no *p*
  8:15 (14:19) looked for *p*, but no good came
  14:13 but I will give you assured *p* in this place
  16:5 for I have taken away my *p* from this people
  28:9 the prophet which prophesieth of *p*, when
  29:7 seek the *p* . . for in the *p* . . shall ye have *p*
  29:11 thoughts of *p*, and not of evil, to give you
  33:6 reveal unto them the abundance of *p* and truth
Lam. 3:17 thou hast removed my soul far off from *p*
Ezek. 7:25 shall seek *p*, and there shall be none
  13:16 see visions of *p* for her, and there is no *p*
  34:25 (37:26) I will make with them a covenant of *p*
Obad. 7 that were at *p* with thee have deceived thee
Mic. 3:5 that bite with their teeth, and cry, *P*
  5:5 this man shall be the *p*, when the Assyrian
Hag. 2:9 in this place will I give *p*, saith the LORD
Zech. 8:19 therefore love the truth and *p*
  9:10 he shall speak *p* unto the heathen: and his
Mal. 2:5 my covenant was with him of life and *p*
  2:6 he walked with me in *p* and equity, and did
Mt. 10:13 (Lk. 10:5) worthy, let your *p* come upon it
  10:34 (Lk. 12:51) that I am come to send *p* on earth
Mk. 4:39 wind, and said unto the sea, *P*, be still
  9:50 have salt . . and have *p* one with another
Lk. 1:79 to guide our feet into the way of *p*
  2:14 and on earth *p*, good will toward men
  14:32 ambassage, and desireth conditions of *p*
  19:38 *p* in heaven, and glory in the highest

Lk. 19:42 the things which belong unto thy *p*!
  24:36 (Jn. 20:19) saith unto them, *P* be unto you
Jn. 14:27 *p* I leave with you, my *p* I give unto you
  16:33 spoken unto you, that in me ye might have *p*
Acts 10:36 of Israel, preaching *p* by Jesus Christ
Rom. 1:7 (1 Cor. 1:3; 2 Cor. 1:2; Gal. 1:3; Eph. 1:2;
    Phil. 1:2; Col. 1:2; 1 Thes. 1:1; 2 Thes. 1:2;
    Phlm. 3) grace to you, and *p*
  5:1 being justified by faith, we have *p* with God
  8:6 but to be spiritually minded is life and *p*
  10:15 feet of them that preach the gospel of *p*
  14:17 drink; but righteousness, and *p*, and joy in
  14:19 follow after the things which make for *p*
  15:13 God of hope fill you with all joy and *p* in
  15:33 now the God of *p* be with you all
1 Cor. 7:15 such cases: but God hath called us to *p*
  14:33 God is not . . author of confusion, but of *p*
2 Cor. 13:11 live in *p*; and the God of love and *p*
Gal. 5:22 the fruit of the Spirit is love, joy, *p*
  6:16 walk according to this rule, *p* be on them
Eph. 2:14 for he is our *p*, who hath made both one
  2:15 himself of twain one new man, so making *p*
  2:17 preached *p* to you which were afar off
  6:23 *p* be to the brethren, and love with faith
Phil. 4:7 *p* of God, which passeth all understanding
  4:9 do: and the God of *p* shall be with you
Col. 1:20 made *p* through the blood of his cross
  3:15 let the *p* of God rule in your hearts
1 Thes. 5:3 *p* and safety; then sudden destruction
  5:13 and be at *p* among yourselves
2 Thes. 3:16 LORD of *p* himself give you *p* always
1 Tim. 1:2 (2 Tim. 1:2; Tit. 1:4) grace, mercy, and *p*
2 Tim. 2:22 follow righteousness, faith, charity, *p*
Heb. 12:14 follow *p* with all men, and holiness
  12:11 fruit . . is sown in *p* of them that make *p*
1 Pet. 1:2 (2 Pet. 1:2) grace . . and *p*, be multiplied
  5:14 *p* be with you all that are in Christ Jesus
2 Pet. 3:14 may be found of him in *p*, without spot
Rev. 1:4 grace be unto you, and *p*, from him which
  6:4 power was given to him . . to take *p* from the

Peaceable *See also* Quiet

Gen. 34:21 these men are *p* with us; therefore let
2 Sam. 20:19 am one of them that are *p* and faithful
Is. 32:18 my people shall dwell in a *p* habitation
Jer. 25:37 *p* habitations are cut down because of
1 Tim. 2:2 that we may lead a quiet and *p* life
Heb. 12:11 afterward it yieldeth the *p* fruit of
Jas. 3:17 wisdom . . from above is first pure, then *p*

Peaceably

Gen. 37:4 hated him, and could not speak *p* unto him
1 Sam. 16:4 elders of the town . . said, Comest thou *p*?
1 Kgs. 2:13 she said, Comest thou *p*? And he said, *P*
1 Chr. 12:17 if ye be come *p* unto me to help me
Jer. 9:8 deceit: one speaketh *p* to his neighbor
Dan. 11:21 shall come in *p*, and obtain the kingdom
Rom. 12:18 if it be possible . . live *p* with all men

Peacemaker

Mt. 5:9 blessed are the *p*: for they shall be called

Peace Offering

Lev. 3:1 if his oblation be a sacrifice of *p o*
  7:11 this is the law of the sacrifice of *p o*
  17:5 offer them for *p o* unto the LORD
Deut. 27:7 thou shalt offer *p o*, and shalt eat
Amos 5:22 neither will I regard the *p o* of your fat

Peacock

1 Kgs. 10:22 (2 Chr. 9:21) bringing gold . . apes, and *p*
Job 39:13 gavest thou the goodly wings unto the *p*?

Pearl

Mt. 7:6 neither cast ye your *p* before swine, lest
13:46 found one *p* of great price, went and sold
1 Tim. 2:9 not with braided hair, or gold, or *p*
Rev. 17:4 and decked with . . precious stones and *p*
21:21 twelve *p*; every several gate was of one *p*

Peculiar

Ex. 19:5 then ye shall be a *p* treasure unto me
Deut. 14:2 LORD hath chosen thee to be a *p* people
26:18 avouched thee this day to be his *p* people
Ps. 135:4 hath chosen . . Israel for his *p* treasure
Tit. 2:14 purify unto himself a *p* people, zealous
1 Pet. 2:9 priesthood, a holy nation, a *p* people

Peeled

Is. 18:2 to a nation scattered and *p*, to a people

Peep

Is. 8:19 seek . . unto wizards that *p* and that mutter
10:14 moved the wing, or opened the mouth, or *p*

Pekah 2 Kgs. 15:25–16:5; 2 Chr. 28:6; Is. 7:1

Pekahiah 2 Kgs. 15:22–26

Pelican

Ps. 102:6 I am like a *p* of the wilderness

Pen

Judg. 5:14 they that handle the *p* of the writer
Job 19:24 that they were graven with an iron *p*
Ps. 45:1 my tongue is the *p* of a ready writer
Is. 8:1 great roll, and write in it with a man's *p*
Jer. 8:8 the *p* of the scribes is in vain
17:1 sin of Judah is written with a *p* of iron
3 Jn. 13 but I will not with ink and *p* write unto

Peniel (Penuel) Gen. 32:30; Judg. 8:8

Penknife

Jer. 36:23 cut it with the *p* . . cast it into the fire

Penny (Pence)

Mt. 18:28 his fellow servants . . owed him a hundred *p*
20:2 had agreed with the laborers for a *p* a day
22:19 tribute money . . they brought unto him a *p*
Mk. 12:15 (Lk. 20:24) bring me a *p*, that I may see it
14:5 (Jn. 12:5) sold for more than three hundred *p*
Lk. 7:41 owed five hundred *p*, and the other fifty
10:35 took out two *p*, and gave them to the host
Rev. 6:6 say, A measure of wheat for a *p*

Pennyworth

Mk. 6:37 (Jn. 6:7) go and buy two hundred *p* of bread

Pentecost

Acts 2:1 when the day of *P* was fully come
20:16 he hasted . . to be at Jerusalem the day of *P*
1 Cor. 16:8 but I will tarry at Ephesus until *P*

Penury

Prov. 14:23 the talk of the lips tendeth only to *p*
Lk. 21:4 she of her *p* hath cast in all the living

People *See also* Multitude, Nation

Gen. 11:6 and the LORD said, Behold, the *p* is one
27:29 let *p* serve thee, and nations bow down to
Ex. 3:7 (Acts 7:34) surely seen the affliction of my *p*
5:1 (7:16; 8:1, 20; 9:1, 13; 10:3) let my *p* go
6:7 I will take you to me for a *p*, and I will be
12:27 and the *p* bowed the head and worshipped
14:31 and the *p* feared the LORD, and believed

Ex. 15:13 led forth the *p* which thou hast redeemed
19:5 be a peculiar treasure unto me above all *p*
24:8 (Heb. 9:19) blood, and sprinkled it on the *p*
31:14 that soul shall be cut off from among his *p*
32:9 (Deut. 9:13) seen this *p* . . it is a stiffnecked *p*
33:13 and consider that this nation is thy *p*
33:16 be separated, I and thy *p*, from all the *p*
Lev. 20:24 which have separated you from other *p*
26:12 (2 Cor. 6:16) your God, and ye shall be my *p*
Num. 14:9 neither fear ye the *p* of the land
14:14 have heard that thou LORD art among this *p*
16:41 saying, Ye have killed the *p* of the LORD
22:5 behold, there is a *p* come out from Egypt
23:9 the *p* shall dwell alone, and . . not be reckoned
Deut. 4:6 nation is a wise and understanding *p*
4:20 of Egypt, to be unto him a *p* of inheritance
7:6 thou art a holy *p* . . a special *p* . . above all *p*
9:26 God, destroy not thy *p* and thine inheritance
10:15 he chose their seed . . even you above all *p*
21:8 be merciful, O LORD, unto thy *p* Israel, whom
26:15 and bless thy *p* Israel, and the land which
27:9 this day thou art become the *p* of the LORD
29:13 establish thee today for a *p* unto himself
32:9 LORD's portion is his *p*; Jacob is the lot of
32:36 (Heb. 10:30) for the LORD shall judge his *p*
32:43 (Rom. 15:10) rejoice, O ye nations, with his *p*
33:3 yea, he loved the *p*; all his saints are in
Josh. 1:6 for unto this *p* shalt thou divide for an
8:33 that they should bless the *p* of Israel
Judg. 2:20 this *p* hath transgressed my covenant
Ruth 1:6 LORD . . visited his *p* in giving them bread
1:16 thy *p* shall be my *p*, and thy God my God
1 Sam. 2:24 ye make the LORD's *p* to transgress
8:7 hearken unto the voice of the *p* in all that
9:16 may save my *p* . . for I have looked upon my *p*
12:22 for the LORD will not forsake his *p* for
14:45 the *p* rescued Jonathan, that he died not
15:24 because I feared the *p*, and obeyed their voice
2 Sam. 3:18 by . . my servant David I will save my *p*
5:2 (1 Chr. 11:2) said to thee, Thou shalt feed my *p*
5:12 (1 Chr. 14:2) exalted his kingdom for his *p*
7:7 (1 Chr. 17:6) I commanded to feed my *p* Israel
7:10 (1 Chr. 17:9) appoint a place for my *p* Israel
7:23 (1 Chr. 17:21) what one nation . . is like thy *p*
7:24 (1 Chr. 17:22) thy *p* Israel . . a *p* unto thee for
22:44 (Ps. 18:43) *p* which I knew not shall serve me
1 Kgs. 3:8 thy *p* which thou hast chosen, a great *p*
3:9 (2 Chr. 1:10) to judge this thy so great a *p*?
6:13 I will dwell . . will not forsake my *p* Israel
8:16 (2 Chr. 6:5) brought . . *p* Israel out of Egypt
8:43 (2 Chr. 6:33) that all *p* . . may know thy name
8:51 for they be thy *p*, and thine inheritance
8:56 the LORD, that hath given rest unto his *p*
8:60 all the *p* . . may know that the LORD is God
16:2 hast made my *p* Israel to sin, to provoke me
18:37 this *p* may know that thou art the LORD God
20:42 thy life . . for his life, and thy *p* for his *p*
22:4 (2 Kgs. 3:7; 2 Chr. 18:3) my *p* as thy *p*
2 Kgs. 11:17 (2 Chr. 23:16) should be the LORD's *p*
23:3 and all the *p* stood to the covenant
1 Chr. 16:8 (Ps. 105:1) known his deeds among the *p*
29:17 now have I seen with joy thy *p*, which are
2 Chr. 2:11 because the LORD hath loved his *p*, he
7:14 if my *p*, which are called by my name, shall
36:15 because he had compassion on his *p*
36:16 the wrath of the LORD arose against his *p*
Neh. 1:10 now these are thy servants and thy *p*
8:7 caused the *p* to understand the law: and the *p*
Esth. 2:10 (2:20) Esther had not showed her *p* nor
7:3 my life be given me . . and my *p* at my request
Job 12:2 no doubt but ye are the *p*, and wisdom
Ps. 3:8 unto the LORD: thy blessing is upon thy *p*
9:11 in Zion: declare among the *p* his doings

Ps. 14:7 LORD bringeth back the captivity of his *p*
28:9 save thy *p*, and bless thine inheritance
29:11 his *p*; the LORD will bless his *p* with peace
33:12 and the *p* whom he hath chosen for his own
47:1 O clap your hands, all ye *p*; shout unto God
60:3 thou hast showed thy *p* hard things
67:3 (67:5) the *p* praise thee, O God; let all the *p*
68:22 I will bring my *p* again from the depths of
68:35 that giveth strength and power unto his *p*
77:15 thou hast with thine arm redeemed thy *p*
77:20 thou leddest thy *p* like a flock by the
78:52 but made his own *p* to go forth like sheep
79:13 so we thy *p* and sheep of thy pasture will
81:11 but my *p* would not hearken to my voice
85:6 revive us. . that thy *p* may rejoice in thee?
85:8 he will speak peace unto his *p*, and to his
94:14 LORD will not cast off his *p*, neither will
95:7 we are the *p* of his pasture, and the sheep
95:10 said, It is a *p* that do err in their heart
100:3 we are his *p*, and the sheep of his pasture
105:43 he brought forth his *p* with joy, and his
106:40 wrath of the LORD kindled against his *p*
111:9 he sent redemption unto his *p*: he hath
117:1 (Rom. 15:11) ye nations: praise him, all ye *p*
125:2 Jerusalem, so the LORD is round about his *p*
135:14 (Heb. 10:30) the LORD will judge his *p*
136:16 led his *p* through the wilderness: for his
144:15 happy is that *p*, whose God is the LORD
149:4 the LORD taketh pleasure in his *p*: he will
Is. 1:3 Israel doth not know, my *p* doth not consider
1:4 ah sinful nation, a *p* laden with iniquity
2:6 thou hast forsaken thy *p* the house of Jacob
5:25 the anger of the LORD kindled against his *p*
6:5 I dwell in the midst of a *p* of unclean lips
8:19 should not a *p* seek unto their God?
19:25 blessed be Egypt my *p*, and Assyria the work
24:2 shall be, as with the *p*, so with the priest;
25:8 rebuke of his *p* shall he take away from off
27:11 it is a *p* of no understanding: therefore
28:5 diadem of beauty, unto the residue of his *p*
29:13 (Mt. 15:8; Mk. 7:6) this *p* draw near me with
32:18 my *p* shall dwell in a peaceable habitation
40:1 comfort ye, comfort ye my *p*, saith your God
40:7 LORD bloweth upon it: surely the *p* is grass
43:21 this *p* have I formed for myself; they shall
47:6 I was wroth with my *p*, I have polluted mine
51:4 hearken unto me, my *p*; and give ear unto me
51:7 the *p* in whose heart is my law; fear ye not
51:16 that I may. . say unto Zion, Thou art my *p*
52:6 my *p* shall know my name: therefore they
53:8 the transgression of my *p* was he stricken
56:7 shall be called a house of prayer for all *p*
58:1 and show my *p* their transgression, and the
60:21 thy *p* also shall be all righteous
63:8 they are my *p*, children that will not lie
63:14 so didst thou lead thy *p*, to make thyself
65:19 will rejoice in Jerusalem, and joy in my *p*
Jer. 2:11 but my *p* have changed their glory for
2:13 my *p* have committed two evils; they have
2:32 her attire? yet my *p* have forgotten me
4:10 surely thou hast greatly deceived this *p*
5:23 this *p* hath a revolting and a rebellious
7:12 what I did to it for the wickedness of my *p*
7:16 (11:14; 14:11) pray not thou for this *p*
7:23 (11:4; Ezek. 36:28) God, and ye shall be my *p*
9:15 I will feed them, even this *p*, with wormwood
13:10 this evil *p*, which refuse to hear my words
13:11 they might be unto me for a *p*, and for a
15:1 yet my mind could not be toward this *p*
15:7 I will destroy my *p*, since they return not
18:15 because my *p* hath forgotten me, they have
19:11 even so will I break this *p* and this city

Jer. 23:13 prophesied in Baal. . caused my *p*. . to err
23:27 think to cause my *p* to forget my name by
24:7 (32:38; Zech. 8:8) shall be my *p*, and I will be
29:32 he behold the good that I will do for my *p*
30:22 ye shall be my *p*, and I will be your God
31:7 O LORD, save thy *p*, the remnant of Israel
31:14 my *p* shall be satisfied with my goodness
31:33 (Heb. 8:10) their God, and they shall be my *p*
32:21 and hast brought forth thy *p* Israel out of
35:16 but this *p* hath not hearkened unto me
50:6 my *p* hath been lost sheep: their shepherds
Ezek. 11:20 shall be my *p*, and I will be their God
13:21 and deliver my *p* out of your hand
14:11 they may be my *p*, and I may be their God
34:30 they, even the house of Israel, are my *p*
36:20 these are the *p* of the LORD, and are gone
38:14 when my *p* of Israel dwelleth safely
45:8 and my princes shall no more oppress my *p*
Dan. 7:14 all *p*, nations, and languages, should serve
9:16 Jerusalem and thy *p* are become a reproach
9:19 thy city and thy *p* are called by thy name
9:24 seventy weeks are determined upon thy *p*
10:14 what shall befall thy *p* in the latter days
11:32 *p* that do know their God shall be strong
12:1 and at that time thy *p* shall be delivered
Hos. 1:9 call his name Lo-ammi: for ye are not my *p*
1:10 (Rom. 9:26) said unto them, Ye are not my *p*
2:23 (Rom. 9:25) were not my *p*, Thou art my *p*
4:6 my *p* are destroyed for lack of knowledge
11:7 my *p* are bent to backsliding from me
Joel 2:2 a great *p* and a strong; there hath not
2:18 LORD be jealous for his land, and pity his *p*
2:26 with you: and my *p* shall never be ashamed
3:16 but the LORD will be the hope of his *p*
Amos 7:15 unto me, Go, prophesy unto my *p* Israel
8:2 the end is come upon my *p* of Israel; I will
Mic. 3:5 concerning the prophets that make my *p* err
4:1 exalted above the hills. . *p* shall flow unto it
4:3 and he shall judge among many *p*, and rebuke
6:2 for the LORD hath a controversy with his *p*
Hab. 3:13 wentest forth for the salvation of thy *p*
Zeph. 2:8 they have reproached my *p*, and magnified
2:9 the residue of my *p* shall spoil them
Hag. 1:12 and the *p* did fear before the LORD
Zech. 2:11 many nations. . shall be my *p*: and I will
8:7 I will save my *p* from the east country
8:22 many *p* and strong nations shall come to seek
10:9 I will sow them among the *p*: and they shall
13:9 I will say, It is my *p*: and they shall say
Mt. 1:21 for he shall save his *p* from their sins
2:6 come a Governor, that shall rule my *p* Israel
Lk. 1:17 to make ready a *p* prepared for the Lord
1:68 for he hath visited and redeemed his *p*
1:77 to give knowledge of salvation unto his *p*
2:10 of great joy, which shall be to all *p*
2:32 the Gentiles, and the glory of thy *p* Israel
7:16 among us; and, That God hath visited his *p*
9:18 he asked them. . Whom say the *p* that I am?
Jn. 11:50 (18:14) one man should die for the *p*
Acts 8:6 the *p* with one accord gave heed unto
10:42 and he commanded us to preach unto the *p*
11:24 and much *p* was added unto the Lord
13:17 exalted the *p* when they dwelt as strangers
15:14 to take out of them a *p* for his name
18:10 hurt thee: for I have much *p* in this city
26:23 show light unto the *p*, and to the Gentiles
Rom. 9:25 (1 Pet. 2:10) my *p*, which were not my *p*
10:21 hands unto a disobedient and gainsaying *p*
11:1 hath God cast away his *p*? God forbid
2 Cor. 6:16 be their God, and they shall be my *p*
Tit. 2:14 a peculiar *p*, zealous of good works
Heb. 4:9 remaineth therefore a rest to the *p* of God

Heb. 7:27 first for his own sins, and then for the *p*'s
11:25 suffer affliction with the *p* of God, than
13:12 he might sanctify the *p* with his own blood
1 Pet. 2:9 priesthood, a holy nation, a peculiar *p*
2:10 past were not a *p*, but are now the *p* of God
Jude 5 having saved the *p* out of the land of Egypt
Rev. 5:9 out of every kindred, and tongue, and *p*
7:9 all nations, and kindreds, and *p*, and tongues
18:4 come out of her, my *p*. . be not partakers
21:3 dwell with them, and they shall be his *p*

Peor *See also* Baal-peor

Num. 23:28; 25:18; 31:16; Josh. 22:17

Perceive *See also* Comprehend, Discern, Know, See

Deut. 29:4 LORD hath not given you a heart to *p*
Josh. 22:31 this day we *p* that the LORD is among us
Judg. 6:22 when Gideon *p* that he was an angel of
1 Sam. 3:8 Eli *p* that the LORD had called the child
Neh. 6:12 lo, I *p* that God had not sent him
Job 9:11 he passeth on also, but I *p* him not
23:8 not there; and backward, but I cannot *p* him
33:14 speaketh once, yea twice, yet man *p* it not
38:18 thou *p* the breadth of the earth? declare
Prov. 1:2 to know. . to *p* the words of understanding
Eccl. 3:22 I *p* that there is nothing better, than
Is. 6:9 (Mt. 13:14; Mk. 4:12; Acts 28:26) see. . *p* not
33:19 people of a deeper speech than thou canst *p*
64:4 have not heard, nor *p* by the ear, neither
Mt. 21:45 (Lk. 20:19) they *p* that he spake of them
22:18 (Lk. 20:23) Jesus *p* their wickedness
Mk. 2:8 when Jesus *p* in his spirit that they so
8:17 no bread? *p* ye not yet, neither understand?
12:28 *p* that he had answered them well, asked him
Lk. 5:22 when Jesus *p* their thoughts, he answering
6:41 but *p* not the beam that is in thine own eye?
8:46 for I *p* that virtue is gone out of me
9:45 saying. . hid from them, that they *p* it not
9:47 Jesus, *p* the thought of their heart, took a
Jn. 4:19 woman saith. . I *p* that thou art a prophet
12:19 *p* ye how ye prevail nothing? behold, the
Acts 4:13 *p* that they were unlearned and ignorant
8:23 I *p* that thou art in the gall of bitterness
10:34 I *p* that God is no respecter of persons
14:9 Paul. . *p* that he had faith to be healed
Gal. 2:9 *p* the grace that was given unto me
1 Jn. 3:16 hereby *p* we the love of God, because he

Perdition

Jn. 17:12 none of them is lost, but the son of *p*
Phil. 1:28 to them an evident token of *p*, but to
2 Thes. 2:3 man of sin be revealed, the son of *p*
1 Tim. 6:9 which drown men in destruction and *p*
Heb. 10:39 we are not of them who draw back unto *p*
Rev. 17:8 out of the bottomless pit, and go into *p*

Perfect *See also* Just, Whole

Gen. 6:9 Noah. . a just man and *p* in his generations
17:1 to Abram. . walk before me, and be thou *p*
Lev. 22:21 or sheep, it shall be *p* to be accepted
Deut. 18:13 thou shalt be *p* with the LORD thy God
25:15 a *p* and just weight, a *p* and just measure
32:4 he is the Rock, his work is *p*: for all his
2 Sam. 22:31 (Ps. 18:30) as for God, his way is *p*
22:33 (Ps. 18:32) strength. . he maketh my way *p*
1 Kgs. 11:4 (15:3) heart was not *p* with the LORD
15:14 (2 Chr. 15:17) Asa's heart was *p*
2 Kgs. 20:3 (Is. 38:3) I have walked. . with a *p* heart.
1 Chr. 28:9 and serve him with a *p* heart and with
29:9 because with *p* heart they offered willingly
29:19 give unto Solomon my son a *p* heart, to keep

2 Chr. 16:9 of them whose heart is *p* toward him
Job 1:1 (1:8; 2:3) *p*. . upright. . one that feared God
8:20 God will not cast away a *p* man, neither will
9:20 if I say, I am *p*, it shall also prove me
9:22 I said. . He destroyeth the *p* and the wicked
22:3 gain to him, that thou makest thy ways *p*?
36:4 he that is *p* in knowledge is with thee
Ps. 19:7 law of the LORD is *p*, converting the soul
37:37 mark the *p* man, and behold the upright
101:2 I will walk within my house with a *p* heart
101:6 that walketh in a *p* way, he shall serve me
138:8 the LORD will *p* that which concerneth me
Prov. 2:21 the land, and the *p* shall remain in it
4:18 that shineth more and more unto the *p* day
11:5 righteousness of the *p* shall direct his way
Is. 26:3 thou wilt keep him in *p* peace, whose mind
42:19 who is blind as he that is *p*
Ezek. 28:15 thou wast *p* in thy ways from the day
Mt. 5:48 be ye therefore *p*, even as your Father
19:21 if thou wilt be *p*, go and sell that thou
21:16 of babes and sucklings thou hast *p* praise?
Lk. 6:40 every one that is *p* shall be as his master
13:32 tomorrow, and the third day I shall be *p*
Jn. 17:23 in me, that they may be made *p* in one
Rom. 12:2 good, and acceptable, and *p* will of God
1 Cor. 2:6 we speak wisdom among them that are *p*
13:10 but when that which is *p* is come, then that
2 Cor. 7:1 spirit, *p* holiness in the fear of God
12:9 for my strength is made *p* in weakness
13:11 be *p*, be of good comfort, be of one mind
Gal. 3:3 Spirit, are ye now made *p* by the flesh?
Eph. 4:12 for the *p* of the saints, for the work
4:13 unto a *p* man, unto the measure of the
Phil. 3:12 already attained, either were already *p*
3:15 let us. . as many as be *p*, be thus minded
Col. 1:28 that we may present every man *p* in Christ
4:12 stand *p* and complete in all the will of God
1 Thes. 3:10 *p* that which is lacking in your faith?
2 Tim. 3:17 the man of God may be *p*, thoroughly
Heb. 2:10 to make the captain of their salvation *p*
5:9 being made *p*, he became the author of eternal
7:19 law made nothing *p*, but the bringing in of
9:9 could not make him that did the service *p*
9:11 to come, by a greater and more *p* tabernacle
10:1 law. . never. . make the comers thereunto *p*
10:14 by one offering he hath *p* for ever them
11:40 that they without us should not be made *p*
12:23 and to the spirits of just men made *p*
13:21 make you *p* in every good work to do his
Jas. 1:4 patience have her *p* work, that ye may be *p*
1:17 good gift and every *p* gift is from above
1:25 but whoso looketh into the *p* law of liberty
2:22 his works, and by works was faith made *p*?
3:2 man offend not in word, the same is a *p* man
1 Pet. 5:10 make you *p*, stablish, strengthen
1 Jn. 2:5 word, in him verily is the love of God *p*
4:12 God dwelleth in us, and his love is *p* in us
4:17 herein is our love made *p*, that we may have
4:18 no fear in love; but *p* love casteth out fear
Rev. 3:2 I have not found thy works *p* before God

Perfection

Job 11:7 canst thou find out the Almighty unto *p*?
28:3 end to darkness, and searcheth out all *p*
Ps. 50:2 out of Zion, the *p* of beauty, God. . shined
119:96 I have seen an end of all *p*: but thy
Lam. 2:15 The *p* of beauty, The joy of the whole
2 Cor. 13:9 and this also we wish, even your *p*
Heb. 6:1 doctrine of Christ, let us go on unto *p*
7:11 if. . *p* were by the Levitical priesthood

Perfectly

Jer. 23:20 the latter days ye shall consider it *p*

Acts 18:26 and expounded . . the way of God more *p*
23:15 inquire something more *p* concerning him
1 Cor. 1:10 be *p* joined together in the same mind

Perfectness

Col. 3:14 put on charity, which is the bond of *p*

Perform *See also* Accomplish, Do, Execute, Fulfil, Keep

Gen. 26:3 I will *p* the oath . . I sware unto Abraham
Ex. 18:18 thou art not able to *p* it thyself alone
Deut. 4:13 covenant, which he commanded you to *p*
9:5 that he may *p* the word which the LORD sware
Ruth 3:13 will *p* unto thee the part of a kinsman
1 Kgs. 8:20 (2 Chr. 6:10) the LORD hath *p* his word
Esth. 5:6 to the half of the kingdom it shall be *p*
Job 5:12 their hands cannot *p* their enterprise
23:14 he *p* the thing that is appointed for me
Ps. 57:2 cry . . unto God that *p* all things for me
65:1 in Zion: and unto thee shall the vow be *p*
119:106 I have sworn, and I will *p* it, that I
119:112 inclined mine heart to *p* thy statutes
Is. 9:7 the zeal of the LORD of hosts will *p* this
44:28 my shepherd, and shall *p* all my pleasure
Jer. 29:10 visit you, and *p* my good word toward you
33:14 *p* that good thing which I have promised
51:29 purpose of the LORD . . be *p* against Babylon
Ezek. 12:25 I will say the word, and will *p* it
Mic. 7:20 thou wilt *p* the truth to Jacob
Mt. 5:33 but shalt *p* unto the Lord thine oaths
Lk. 1:20 until the day that these things shall be *p*
1:72 to *p* the mercy promised to our fathers
2:39 and when they had *p* all things according to
Rom. 4:21 he had promised, he was able also to *p*
7:18 but how to *p* that which is good I find not
15:28 when therefore I have *p* this, and have
Phil. 1:6 begun a good work in you will *p* it until

Performance

Lk. 1:45 there shall be a *p* of those things which
2 Cor. 8:11 so there may be a *p* also out of that

Perfume *See also* Ointment

Ex. 30:35 and thou shalt make it a *p*, a confection
Prov. 7:17 I have *p* my bed with myrrh, aloes
27:9 ointment and *p* rejoice the heart: so doth
Song 3:6 *p* with myrrh and frankincense, with all

Perga Acts 13:13; 14:25

Pergamos Rev. 1:11; 2:12

Peril *See also* Danger, Jeopardy

Lam. 5:9 we gat our bread with the *p* of our lives
Rom. 8:35 or famine, or nakedness, or *p*, or sword?
2 Cor. 11:26 in *p* of waters, in *p* of robbers, in *p*

Perilous

2 Tim. 3:1 in the last days *p* times shall come

Perish *See also* Destroy, Die

Gen. 41:36 that the land *p* not through the famine
Ex. 19:21 unto the LORD to gaze, and many of them *p*
Lev. 26:38 ye shall *p* among the heathen
Num. 17:12 Moses . . Behold, we die, we *p*, we all *p*
24:20 his latter end shall be that he *p* for ever
Deut. 4:26 shall soon utterly *p* from off the land
8:19 (30:18) I testify . . that ye shall surely *p*
11:17 (Josh. 23:16) *p* quickly from . . the good land
26:5 a Syrian ready to *p* was my father
Judg. 5:31 so let all thine enemies *p*, O LORD

Esth. 3:13 to kill, and to cause to *p*, all Jews
4:16 will I go in unto the king . . and if I *p*, I *p*
Job 3:3 let the day *p* wherein I was born, and the
4:7 who ever *p*, being innocent? or where were
4:9 by the blast of God they *p*, and by the breath
6:18 are turned aside; they go to nothing, and *p*
8:13 forget God; and the hypocrite's hope shall *p*
31:19 if I have seen any *p* for want of clothing
34:15 all flesh shall *p* together, and man shall
Ps. 1:6 but the way of the ungodly shall *p*
2:12 kiss the Son, lest he be angry, and ye *p*
9:3 they shall fall and *p* at thy presence
9:18 expectation of the poor shall not *p* for ever
37:20 but the wicked shall *p*, and the enemies of
49:12 abideth not: he is like the beasts that *p*
73:27 lo, they that are far from thee shall *p*
92:9 O LORD, for, lo, thine enemies shall *p*
102:26 (Heb. 1:11) they shall *p* . . thou shalt endure
112:10 melt away . . desire of the wicked shall *p*
Prov. 10:28 the expectation of the wicked shall *p*
11:7 expectation shall *p* . . hope of unjust men *p*
19:9 and he that speaketh lies shall *p*
21:28 a false witness shall *p*: but the man that
29:18 where there is no vision, the people *p*
31:6 strong drink unto him that is ready to *p*
Eccl. 5:14 but those riches *p* by evil travail
Is. 29:14 for the wisdom of their wise men shall *p*
41:11 and they that strive with thee shall *p*
57:1 righteous *p*, and no man layeth it to heart
60:12 kingdom that will not serve thee shall *p*
Jer. 7:28 nor receiveth correction: truth is *p*
10:11 even they shall *p* from the earth, and from
40:15 be scattered, and the remnant in Judah *p*
48:36 because the riches . . he hath gotten are *p*
Lam. 3:18 my strength and my hope is *p*
Ezek. 7:26 but the law shall *p* from the priest
Amos 2:14 the flight shall *p* from the swift
3:15 will smite . . and the houses of ivory shall *p*
Jon. 3:9 turn . . from his fierce anger, that we *p* not?
Mic. 7:2 the good man is *p* out of the earth
Mt. 5:29 that one of thy members should *p*, and not
8:25 (Mk. 4:38; Lk. 8:24) Lord, save us: we *p*
9:17 (Lk. 5:37) wine runneth out, and the bottles *p*
18:14 that one of these little ones should *p*
26:52 that take the sword shall *p* with the sword
Lk. 13:3 (13:5) ye repent, ye shall all likewise *p*
15:17 bread enough and to spare . . I *p* with hunger
21:18 but there shall not a hair of your head *p*
Jn. 3:15 (3:16) whosoever believeth in him . . not *p*
6:27 labor not for the meat which *p*, but for the
10:28 them eternal life; and they shall never *p*
11:50 die for the people . . the whole nation *p* not
Acts 8:20 but Peter said . . Thy money *p* with thee
Rom. 2:12 sinned without law shall . . *p* without law
1 Cor. 1:18 cross is to them that *p*, foolishness
8:11 the weak brother *p*, for whom Christ died?
15:18 which are fallen asleep in Christ are *p*
2 Cor. 2:15 in them that are saved . . in them that *p*
4:16 though our outward man *p*, yet the inward
Col. 2:22 which all are to *p* with the using
2 Thes. 2:10 of unrighteousness in them that *p*
Heb. 11:31 by faith the harlot Rahab *p* not with
Jas. 1:11 grace of the fashion of it *p*: so also
1 Pet. 1:7 much more precious than of gold that *p*
2 Pet. 2:12 shall utterly *p* in their own corruption
3:6 whereby the world . . overflowed with water, *p*
3:9 long-suffering . . not willing that any should *p*
Jude 11 for reward, and *p* in the gainsaying of Core

Perizzite Gen. 13:7

Permission

1 Cor. 7:6 I speak this by *p* . . not of commandment

Permit

Acts 26:1 Paul, Thou art *p* to speak for thyself
1 Cor. 14:34 for it is not *p* unto them to speak
  16:7 tarry a while with you, if the Lord *p*
Heb. 6:3 and this will we do, if God *p*

Pernicious

2 Pet. 2:2 and many shall follow their *p* ways

Perpetual

Gen. 9:12 token of the covenant . . for *p* generations
Ex. 31:16 to observe the sabbath . . for a *p* covenant
Lev. 25:34 not be sold . . it is their *p* possession
Ps. 9:6 enemy, destructions are come to a *p* end
  74:3 lift up thy feet unto the *p* desolations
Jer. 5:22 for the bound of the sea by a *p* decree
  8:5 Jerusalem slidden back by a *p* backsliding?
  15:18 why is my pain *p*, and my wound incurable
  23:40 a *p* shame, which shall not be forgotten
  50:5 join ourselves to the LORD in a *p* covenant
Hab. 3:6 mountains were scattered . . *p* hills did bow

Perpetually

1 Kgs. 9:3 (2 Chr. 7:16) mine heart shall be there *p*
Amos 1:11 his anger did tear *p* . . he kept his wrath

Perplexed

Esth. 3:15 but the city Shushan was *p*
Joel 1:18 cattle are *p*, because they have no pasture
Lk. 9:7 Herod the tetrarch heard of all . . he was *p*
  24:4 they were much *p* . . behold, two men stood by
2 Cor. 4:8 distressed; we are *p*, but not in despair

Perplexity

Is. 22:5 day of trouble . . and of *p* by the Lord GOD
Mic. 7:4 visitation cometh; now shall be their *p*
Lk. 21:25 the earth distress of nations, with *p*

Persecute *See also* Afflict, Oppress

Deut. 30:7 and on them that hate thee, which *p* thee
Job 19:22 why do ye *p* me as God, and are not
  19:28 ye should say, Why *p* we him, seeing
Ps. 7:1 my trust: save me from all them that *p* me
  10:2 the wicked in his pride doth *p* the poor
  35:6 let the angel of the LORD *p* them
  69:26 for they *p* him whom thou hast smitten
  71:11 God hath forsaken him: *p* and take him
  83:15 so *p* them with thy tempest, and make them
  109:16 but *p* the poor and needy man, that he
  119:84 thou execute judgment on them that *p* me?
  119:161 princes have *p* me without a cause
  143:3 the enemy hath *p* my soul; he hath smitten
Is. 14:6 he that ruled the nations in anger, is *p*
Jer. 17:18 let them be confounded that *p* me
  29:18 and I will *p* them with the sword
Lam. 3:66 *p* and destroy them in anger from under
Mt. 5:10 they which are *p* for righteousness' sake
  5:11 when men shall revile you, and *p* you
  5:12 rejoice . . for so *p* they the prophets which
  5:44 them which despitefully use you, and *p* you
  10:23 *p* you in this city, flee ye into another
  23:34 (Lk. 11:49) *p* them from city to city
Lk. 21:12 *p* you, delivering you up to the synagogues
Jn. 5:16 the Jews *p* Jesus, and sought to slay him
  15:20 if they have *p* me, they will also *p* you
Acts 7:52 which . . prophets have not your fathers *p*?
  9:4 (22:7; 26:14) Saul, Saul, why *p* thou me?
  9:5 (22:8; 26:15) I am Jesus whom thou *p*
  22:4 I *p* this way unto the death, binding and
  26:11 I *p* them even unto strange cities
Rom. 12:14 bless them which *p* you: bless, and
1 Cor. 4:12 reviled, we bless; being *p*, we suffer

1 Cor. 15:9 (Gal. 1:13) because I *p* the church of God
2 Cor. 4:9 *p*, but not forsaken; cast down, but not
Gal. 1:23 which *p* us in times past now preacheth
  4:29 born after the flesh *p* him that was born
Phil. 3:6 concerning zeal, *p* the church; touching
1 Thes. 2:15 and have *p* us; and they please not God
Rev. 12:13 was cast unto the earth, he *p* the woman

Persecution *See also* Affliction, Oppression, Tribulation

Lam. 5:5 our necks are under *p*: we labor, and have
Mt. 13:21 (Mk. 4:17) tribulation or *p* ariseth because
Mk. 10:30 receive a hundredfold now . . with *p*
Acts 8:1 there was a great *p* against the church
  11:19 abroad upon the *p* that arose about Stephen
  13:50 raised *p* against Paul and Barnabas
Rom. 8:35 shall tribulation, or distress, or *p*
2 Cor. 12:10 in *p*, in distresses for Christ's sake
Gal. 5:11 circumcision, why do I yet suffer *p*?
  6:12 lest they should suffer *p* for the cross
2 Thes. 1:4 your patience and faith in all your *p*
2 Tim. 3:11 *p*, afflictions . . came unto me at Antioch
  3:12 live godly in Christ Jesus shall suffer *p*

Persecutor

Neh. 9:11 and their *p* thou threwest into the deeps
Ps. 7:13 he ordaineth his arrows against the *p*
  142:6 deliver me from my *p*; for they are stronger
Jer. 20:11 my *p* shall stumble . . shall not prevail
1 Tim. 1:13 who was before a blasphemer, and a *p*

Perseverance

Eph. 6:18 and watching thereunto with all *p* and

Persia *See also* Media

2 Chr. 36:20 until the reign of the kingdom of *P*
Esth. 1:3 the power of *P* and Media, the nobles and
Ezek. 38:5 *P*, Ethiopia, and Libya with them
Dan. 10:13 prince of the kingdom of *P* withstood me
  11:2 there shall stand up yet three kings in *P*

Persian

Esth. 1:19 written among the laws of the *P* and the
Dan. 5:28 divided, and given to the Medes and *P*
  6:8 (6:12; 6:15) the law of the Medes and *P*

Person *See also* Man, Soul

Gen. 14:21 Abram, Give me the *p* . . take the goods
Lev. 19:15 the *p* of the poor, nor honor the *p* of
Deut. 1:17 (16:19) not respect *p* in judgment
  10:17 which regardeth not *p*, nor taketh reward
1 Sam. 25:35 hearkened . . and have accepted thy *p*
2 Sam. 14:14 neither doth God respect any *p*
  17:11 and that thou go to battle in thine own *p*
2 Chr. 19:7 nor respect of *p*, nor taking of gifts
Job 13:8 will ye accept his *p*? will ye contend for God
Prov. 18:5 not good to accept the *p* of the wicked
  24:23 (28:21) it is not good to have respect of *p*
Ezek. 16:5 wast cast out . . to the loathing of thy *p*
Mal. 1:8 be pleased with thee, or accept thy *p*?
Mt. 22:16 (Mk. 12:14; Lk. 20:21) regardest not the *p*
Lk. 15:7 more than over ninety and nine just *p*
Acts 10:34 perceive that God is no respecter of *p*
Rom. 2:11 (Eph. 6:9; Col. 3:25) no respect of *p* with
2 Cor. 2:10 sakes forgave I it in the *p* of Christ
Gal. 2:6 no matter to me: God accepteth no man's *p*
Heb. 1:3 his glory, and the express image of his *p*
Jas. 2:1 faith of our Lord . . with respect of *p*
1 Pet. 1:17 without respect of *p* judgeth according
2 Pet. 3:11 manner of *p* ought ye to be in all holy
Jude 16 having men's *p* in admiration because of

Persuade *See also* Plead

1 Kgs. 22:20 LORD said, Who shall *p* Ahab, that he
2 Kgs. 18:32 (Is. 36:18) Hezekiah, when he *p* you
2 Chr. 18:2 *p* him to go up. . to Ramoth-gilead
Prov. 25:15 by long forbearing is a prince *p*
Mt. 27:20 chief priests and elders *p* the multitude
 28:14 come to the governor's ears, we will *p* him
Lk. 16:31 neither will they be *p*, though one rose
Acts 13:43 *p* them to continue in the grace of God
 18:13 *p* men to worship God contrary to the law
 19:8 *p* the things concerning the kingdom of God
 19:26 Paul hath *p* and turned away much people
 26:28 Paul, Almost thou *p* me to be a Christian
 28:23 *p* them concerning Jesus, both out of the
Rom. 4:21 being fully *p*, that what he had promised
 8:38 I am *p*, that neither death, nor life
 14:5 let every man be fully *p* in his own mind
2 Cor. 5:11 knowing. . terror of the Lord, we *p* men
Gal. 1:10 do I now *p* men, or God? or do I seek to
2 Tim. 1:12 and am *p* that he is able to keep that
Heb. 6:9 beloved, we are *p* better things of you
 11:13 seen them afar off, and were *p* them

Persuasion

Gal. 5:8 this *p* cometh not of him that calleth you

Perverse

Num. 22:32 to withstand thee, because thy way is *p*
Deut. 32:5 they are a *p* and crooked generation
Job 6:30 tongue? cannot my taste discern *p* things?
 9:20 say, I am perfect, it shall also prove me *p*
Prov. 4:24 froward mouth. . *p* lips put far from thee
 12:8 he that is of a *p* heart shall be despised
 17:20 that hath a *p* tongue falleth into mischief
 23:33 and thine heart shall utter *p* things
 28:18 that is *p* in his ways shall fall at once
Mt. 17:17 (Lk. 9:41) O faithless and *p* generation
Acts 20:30 speaking *p* things . draw away disciples
Phil. 2:15 in the midst of a crooked and *p* nation
1 Tim. 6:5 *p* disputings of men of corrupt minds

Perversely

1 Kgs. 8:47 we have sinned, and have done *p*
Ps. 119:78 they dealt *p* with me without a cause

Perverseness

Num. 23:21 Jacob, neither hath he seen *p* in Israel
Prov. 15:4 but *p* therein is a breach in the spirit
Is. 59:3 spoken lies, your tongue hath muttered *p*
Ezek. 9:9 full of blood, and the city full of *p*

Pervert *See also* Corrupt, Debase, Wrest

Ex. 23:8 (Deut. 16:19) *p* the words of the righteous
Deut. 24:17 not *p* the judgment of the stranger
Job 8:3 doth God *p* judgment?. . Almighty *p* justice?
Prov. 10:9 but he that *p* his ways shall be known
 19:3 foolishness of man *p* his way: and his heart
Eccl. 5:8 and violent *p* of judgment and justice in
Jer. 3:21 have *p* their way. . have forgotten the LORD
 23:36 for ye have *p* the words of the living God
Mic. 3:9 that abhor judgment, and *p* all equity
Lk. 23:2 saying, We found this fellow *p* the nation
Acts 13:10 wilt thou not cease to *p* the right ways
Gal. 1:7 that trouble you, and would *p* the gospel

Pestilence

Ex. 5:3 our God; lest he fall upon us with *p*
 9:15 that I may smite thee and thy people with *p*
Lev. 26:25 I will send the *p* among you
Num. 14:12 I will smite them with the *p*
Deut. 28:21 LORD shall make the *p* cleave unto thee

2 Sam. 24:15 (1 Chr. 21:14) LORD sent a *p* upon Israel
Ps. 91:3 he shall deliver thee. . from the noisome *p*
 91:6 nor for the *p* that walketh in darkness
Jer. 14:12 (21:9; 24:10; 27:8, 13; 29:17, 18; 32:24, 36;
 38:2; 42:17, 22; 44:13; Ezek. 6:11; 12:16) con-
 sume. . by the sword. . the famine, and by the *p*
Ezek. 5:12 third part of thee shall die with the *p*
 7:15 sword is without. . *p* and the famine within
Amos 4:10 sent among you the *p* after the manner of
Hab. 3:5 before him went the *p*, and burning coals
Mt. 24:7 (Lk. 21:11) famines, and *p*, and earthquakes

Pestilent

Acts 24:5 for we have found this man a *p* fellow

Peter (Cephas, Simon, Simeon)

Called to be a fisher of men, Mt. 4:18–20 (Mk. 1:16–
18; Lk. 5:1–11); "a stone," Jn. 1:40–42; sent out with
the twelve, Mt. 10:2 (Mk. 3:16); walked on the sea,
Mt. 14:28–33; confessed Jesus as the Christ, Mt. 16:
13–20 (Mk. 8:27–30; Lk. 9:18–22); interceded for by
the Lord, Lk. 22:31–32; cut off the servant's ear, Jn.
18:10–11; denied Jesus thrice, Mt. 26:69–75 (Mk. 14:
66–72; Lk. 22:54–62; Jn. 18:15–18); "Feed my
sheep," Jn. 21:15–19; addressed the disciples, Acts
1:15–26; preached at Pentecost, Acts 2:14–42; healed
the lame, Acts 3:1–10; witnessed in Solomon's porch,
Acts 3:11–26; preached to the Council, Acts 4:1–12;
imprisoned and released, Acts 5:17–42; denounced
Simon Magus, Acts 8:14–24; visited Cornelius after
the vision, Acts 10; reported to the Jerusalem
Church, Acts 11:1–18; imprisoned and delivered,
Acts 12:1–19; at the Council of Jerusalem, Acts 15:
6–12; visited by Paul, Gal. 1:18; blamed by Paul,
Gal. 2:11–14; Peter's wife's mother, Mt. 8:14 (Mk. 1:
30; Lk. 4:38); his wife, 1 Cor. 9:5.

Petition *See also* Ask, Beg, Beseech,

Entreat, Request

1 Sam. 1:17 God of Israel grant thee thy *p* that
 1:27 LORD hath given me my *p* which I asked
1 Kgs. 2:20 she said, I desire one small *p* of thee
Esth. 5:6 what is thy *p*? and it shall be granted
Ps. 20:5 up our banners: the LORD fulfill all thy *p*
Dan. 6:7 (6:12) shall ask a *p* of any God or man
 6:13 that Daniel. . maketh his *p* three times a day
1 Jn. 5:15 we ask, we know that we have the *p* that

Pharaoh

Gen. 12:15 of *P* saw her. . commended her before *P*
 41:1 *P* dreamed. . he stood by the river
 45:8 he hath made me a father to *P*, and lord of
 47:2 his brethren. . and presented them unto *P*
Ex. 1:11 and they built for *P* treasure cities
 2:5 daughter of *P* came down to wash herself at
 3:10 I will send thee unto *P*, that thou mayest
 5:6 *P* commanded the same day the taskmasters
 7:3 will harden *P*'s heart, and multiply my signs
 10:24 *P* called unto Moses. . Go. . serve the LORD
 14:8 LORD hardened the heart of *P*. . he pursued
1 Kgs. 3:1 and Solomon made affinity with *P* king
Ps. 136:15 overthrew *P* and his host in the Red sea
Rom. 9:17 Scripture saith unto *P*, Even for this

Pharaoh-hophra Jer. 44:30

Pharaoh-necho (Pharaoh-nechoh)

2 Kgs. 23:29–35 (Jer. 46:2)

Pharez Gen. 38:29

Pharisee *See also* Sadducee, Scribe, Chief Priest

Mt. 3:7 he saw many of the *P* and Sadducees come to
9:11 (Mk. 2:16; Lk. 5:30) *P* saw it, they said
9:14 (Mk. 2:18; Lk. 5:33) why do we and the *P* fast
12:14 (Mk. 3:6) *P* went out, and held a council
15:12 knowest thou that the *P* were offended
16:1 (Mk. 8:11) *P*. . came, and tempting desired
23:13 (23:14, 15, 23, 25, 27, 29; Lk. 11:42, 43, 44) woe unto you, scribes and *P*, hypocrites!
23:26 thou blind *P*, cleanse first that which is
Lk. 5:17 *P* and doctors of the law sitting by
7:30 the *P* and lawyers rejected the counsel of
7:36 into the *P*'s house, and sat down to meat
11:37 a certain *P* besought him to dine with him
14:1 into the house of one of the chief *P* to eat
15:2 *P* and scribes murmured, saying, This man
16:14 *P* also, who were covetous, heard all these
18:10 pray; the one a *P*, and the other a publican
Jn. 1:24 and they which were sent were of the *P*
3:1 there was a man of the *P*, named Nicodemus
7:32 the *P* heard that the people murmured such
7:48 have any of the rulers or of the *P* believed
9:13 they brought to the *P* him that. . was blind
Acts 15:5 rose up certain of the sect of the *P*
23:6 men and brethren, I am a *P*, the son of a *P*
26:5 straitest sect of our religion I lived a *P*
Phil. 3:5 of the Hebrews; as touching the law, a *P*

Pharpar 2 Kgs. 5:12

Philadelphia Rev. 1:11; 3:7

Philemon Phlm. 1

Philip the apostle

Mt. 10:3 (Mk. 3:18; Lk. 6:14; Acts 1:13) *P*, and Bartholomew; Thomas, and Matthew
Jn. 1:43 findeth *P*, and saith unto him, Follow me
6:5 he saith unto *P*, Whence shall we buy bread
12:21 the same came therefore to *P*. . and desired
14:8 *P* saith unto him, Lord, show us the Father

Philip the evangelist

Acts 8:5 then *P* went down to the city of Samaria
8:26 the angel of the Lord spake unto *P*, saying
8:39 the Spirit of the Lord caught away *P*
21:8 entered into the house of *P* the evangelist

Philip the tetrarch

Mt. 14:3 (Mk. 6:17; Lk. 3:19); Lk. 3:1

Philippi Acts 16:12; Phil. 1:1; 1 Thes. 2:2

Philippian Phil. 4:15

Philistine

Gen. 26:15 for all the wells. . the *P* had stopped them
Judg. 13:1 delivered them into the hand of the *P*
14:4 occasion against the *P*. . the *P* had dominion
16:9 (16:12, 14, 20) the *P* be upon thee, Samson
1 Sam. 4:1 Israel went out against the *P* to battle
5:1 *P* took the ark of God, and brought it from
6:1 ark of the LORD was in the country of the *P*
7:10 thunder. . upon the *P*, and discomfited them
13:5 the *P* gathered themselves together to fight
14:4 Jonathan sought to go. . unto the *P*' garrison
17:8 am not I a *P*, and ye servants to Saul?
17:49 slang it, and smote the *P* in his forehead
27:7 that David dwelt in the country of the *P*
31:1 (1 Chr. 10:1) *P* fought against Israel
2 Sam. 5:17 (1 Chr. 14:8) *P* heard. . anointed David

2 Kgs. 18:8 he smote the *P*, even unto Gaza
Jer. 47:1 word of the LORD that came. . against the *P*
Ezek. 25:16 I will stretch out mine hand upon the *P*
Zeph. 2:5 land of the *P*, I will even destroy thee
Zech. 9:6 and I will cut off the pride of the *P*

Philosopher

Acts 17:18 *p* of the Epicureans, and of the Stoics

Philosophy

Col. 2:8 beware lest any man spoil you through *p*

Phinehas son of Eleazar

Num. 25:7; Judg. 20:28

Phinehas son of Eli 1 Sam. 1:3–4:11

Phoebe Rom. 16:1

Phrygia Acts 16:6; 18:23

Phylactery

Mt. 23:5 they make broad their *p*, and enlarge the

Physician

Gen. 50:2 Joseph commanded. . *p* to embalm his
2 Chr. 16:12 sought not to the LORD, but to the *p*
Job 13:4 forgers of lies, ye are all *p* of no value
Jer. 8:22 no balm in Gilead? is there no *p* there?
Mt. 9:12 (Mk. 2:17; Lk. 5:31) be whole need not a *p*
Mk. 5:26 and had suffered many things of many *p*
Lk. 4:23 say unto me this proverb, *P*, heal thyself
8:43 had spent all her living upon *p*, neither
Col. 4:14 Luke, the beloved *p*, and Demas, greet you

Picture

Num. 33:52 destroy all their *p*, and destroy all
Prov. 25:11 is like apples of gold in *p* of silver
Is. 2:16 upon all the ships. . upon all pleasant *p*

Piece *See also* Portion

Gen. 15:10 and laid each *p* one against another
1 Sam. 2:36 come and crouch to him for a *p* of silver
1 Kgs. 11:30 new garment. . and rent it in twelve *p*
Amos 4:7 one *p* was rained upon, and the *p*
Zech. 11:12 (Mt. 26:15; 27:9) price thirty *p* of silver
Mt. 9:16 (Mk. 2:21; Lk. 5:36) a *p* of new cloth unto
17:27 his mouth, thou shalt find a *p* of money
Lk. 14:18 I have bought a *p* of ground, and I must
15:9 for I have found the *p* which I had lost
Acts 27:44 on boards. . some on broken *p* of the ship

Pierce

Num. 24:8 and *p* them through with his arrows
Judg. 5:26 had *p* and stricken through his temples
2 Kgs. 18:21 (Is. 36:6) go into his hand, and *p* it
Job 40:24 with his eyes: his nose *p* through snares
Ps. 22:16 inclosed me: they *p* my hands and my feet
Prov. 12:18 that speaketh like the *p* of a sword
Zech. 12:10 (Jn. 19:37) look upon me. . they have *p*
Lk. 2:35 a sword shall *p* through thy own soul also
Jn. 19:34 of the soldiers with a spear *p* his side
1 Tim. 6:10 *p* themselves through with many sorrows
Heb. 4:12 *p* even to the dividing asunder of soul
Rev. 1:7 shall see him, and they also which *p* him

Piety

1 Tim. 5:4 let them learn first to show *p* at home

Pigeon

Gen. 15:9 a ram. . and a turtledove, and a young *p*
Lev. 5:7 (5:11; 12:8; 14:22; Num. 6:10; Lk. 2:24) or two young *p*

Pi-hahiroth Ex. 14:2

Pilate, Pontius
Governor of Judea, Lk. 3:1; killed Galileans, Lk. 13:
1; sentenced Jesus to be crucified, Mt. 27:1–26 (Mk.
15:1–15; Lk. 23:1–25; Jn. 18:28–19:22). "Suffered
under Pontius Pilate," Acts 3:13; 13:28; 1 Tim. 6:13.

Pilgrim
Heb. 11:13 they were strangers and *p* on the earth
1 Pet. 2:11 I beseech you as strangers and *p*

Pilgrimage
Gen. 47:9 years of my *p* are a hundred and thirty
Ex. 6:4 the land of Canaan, the land of their *p*
Ps. 119:54 have been my songs in the house of my *p*

Pillar *See also* Post
Gen. 19:26 wife looked back . . she became a *p* of salt
28:18 and set it up for a *p*, and poured oil upon
31:51 behold this heap, and behold this *p*, which
35:14 set up a *p* in the place where he talked
Ex. 13:21 (Num. 14:14; Neh. 9:12) *p* of a cloud . . *p* of
33:9 into the tabernacle, the cloudy *p* descended
Judg. 16:25 Samson . . and they set him between the *p*
1 Sam. 2:8 for the *p* of the earth are the LORD's
2 Sam. 18:18 Absalom . . reared up for himself a *p*
1 Kgs. 7:21 (2 Chr. 3:17) set up the *p* . . of the temple
Job 9:6 shaketh the earth . . the *p* thereof tremble
26:11 of heaven tremble, and are astonished
Ps. 75:3 are dissolved: I bear up the *p* of it
99:7 he spake unto them in the cloudy *p*
Prov. 9:1 her house, she hath hewn out her seven *p*
Is. 19:19 a *p* at the border thereof to the LORD
Gal. 2:9 James, Cephas . . John, who seemed to be *p*
1 Tim. 3:15 the *p* and ground of the truth
Rev. 3:12 will I make a *p* in the temple of my God
10:1 face was as . . sun, and his feet as *p* of fire

Pillow
Gen. 28:11 took of the stones . . put them for his *p*
1 Sam. 19:13 put a *p* of goats' hair for his bolster
Ezek. 13:18 the women that sew *p* to all armholes
Mk. 4:38 hinder part of the ship, asleep on a *p*

Pilot
Ezek. 27:8 thy wise men, O Tyrus . . were thy *p*

Pin
Judg. 16:14 she fastened it with the *p*, and said

Pine (adjective)
Neh. 8:15 and fetch olive branches, and *p* branches
Is. 41:19 in the desert the fir tree, and the *p*
60:13 fir tree, the *p* tree, and the box together

Pine (verb)
Lev. 26:39 of you shall *p* away in their iniquity
Lam. 4:9 these *p* away, stricken through for want of
Ezek. 24:23 ye shall p away for your iniquities
33:10 our sins be upon us, and we *p* away in them
Mk. 9:18 and gnasheth with his teeth, and *p* away

Pinnacle
Mt. 4:5 (Lk. 4:9) setteth him on a *p* of the temple

Pipe
1 Kgs. 1:40 the people *p* with *p*, and rejoiced with
Jer. 48:36 mine heart shall sound for Moab like *p*
Zech. 4:12 two golden *p* empty the golden oil out
Mt. 11:17 (Lk. 7:23) *p* unto you . . ye have not danced
1 Cor. 14:7 shall it be known what is *p* or harped?

Pisgah Deut. 3:27 (34:1)

Pison Gen. 2:11

Pit *See also* Death, Grave, Hell
Gen. 37:20 slay him, and cast him into some *p*
Ex. 21:33 shall open a *p*, or if a man shall dig a *p*
Num. 16:33 alive into the *p*, and the earth closed
2 Sam. 23:20 (1 Chr. 11:22) slew a lion in . . a *p*
Job 6:27 fatherless, and ye dig a *p* for your friend
17:16 they shall go down to the bars of the *p*
33:18 he keepeth back his soul from the *p*
33:24 deliver him from going down to the *p*
Ps. 7:15 he made a *p* and digged it, and is fallen
9:15 the heathen are sunk down in the *p* that
28:1 I become like them that go down into the *p*
30:9 profit is there . . when I go down into the *p*?
40:2 he brought me up also out of a horrible *p*
88:4 counted with them that go down into the *p*
119:85 the proud have digged *p* for me, which are
Prov. 22:14 the mouth of strange women is a deep *p*
23:27 ditch; and a strange woman is a narrow *p*
26:27 (Eccl. 10:8) diggeth a *p* shall fall therein
28:10 he shall himself fall into his own *p*
Is. 24:17 (Jer. 48:43) fear, and the *p*, and the snare
38:17 delivered it from the *p* of corruption
51:1 to the hole of the *p* whence ye are digged
Jer. 14:3 they came to the *p*, and found no water
18:20 for they have digged a *p* for my soul
Lam. 4:20 anointed of the LORD . . taken in their *p*
Ezek. 28:8 they shall bring thee down to the *p*
32:18 with them that go down into the *p*
Zech. 9:11 sent forth thy prisoners out of the *p*
Mt. 12:11 (Lk. 14:5) fall into a *p* on the sabbath
Rev. 9:1 him was given the key of the bottomless *p*
9:2 opened the bottomless *p*; and there arose
11:7 (17:8) that ascendeth out of the bottomless *p*
20:3 cast him into the bottomless *p*, and shut him

Pitch *See also* Encamp, Set
Gen. 12:8 on the east of Bethel, and *p* his tent
13:12 and Lot dwelt . . and *p* his tent toward Sodom
Ex. 33:7 the tabernacle, and *p* it without the camp
Num. 2:2 about the tabernacle . . shall they *p*
9:18 at the commandment of the LORD they *p*
Josh. 4:20 twelve stones . . did Joshua *p* in Gilgal
Heb. 8:2 of the true tabernacle, which the Lord *p*

Pitch
Gen. 6:14 and shalt *p* it within and without with *p*
Is. 34:9 streams thereof shall be turned into *p*

Pitcher
Gen. 24:14 to whom I shall say, Let down thy *p*
24:15 Rebekah came out . . with her *p* upon her
Judg. 7:16 with empty *p*, and lamps within the *p*
7:19 and brake the *p* that were in their hands
Eccl. 12:6 or the *p* be broken at the fountain
Lam. 4:2 how are they esteemed as earthen *p*
Mk. 14:13 (Lk. 22:10) man bearing a *p* of water

Pithom Ex. 1:11

Pitiful
Lam. 4:10 *p* women have sodden their own children
Jas. 5:11 the Lord is very *p*, and of tender mercy
1 Pet. 3:8 love as brethren, be *p*, be courteous

Pity *See also* Compassion, Kindness, Mercy
Deut. 7:16 thine eye shall have no *p* upon them
2 Sam. 12:6 he did this thing . . because he had no *p*

Job 6:14 him that is afflicted *p* should be showed
19:21 *p* upon me, have *p* upon me . . my friends
Ps. 69:20 I looked for some to take *p*, but . . none
103:13 as a father *p* his children, so the LORD *p*
Prov. 19:17 he that hath *p* upon the poor lendeth
28:8 gather it for him that will *p* the poor
Is. 13:18 shall have no *p* on the fruit of the womb
63:9 in his love and in his *p* he redeemed them
Jer. 13:14 I will not *p*, nor spare, nor have mercy
15:5 who shall have *p* upon thee, O Jerusalem?
21:7 he shall not spare them, neither have *p*, nor
Ezek. 5:11 (7:4, 9; 8:18; 9:10) neither will I have . . *p*
16:5 none eye *p* thee, to do any of these unto
36:21 but I had *p* for mine holy name, which the
Joel 2:18 be jealous for his land, and *p* his people
Amos 1:11 did pursue his brother . . cast off all *p*
Jon. 4:10 Thou hast had *p* on the gourd
Zech. 11:6 no more *p* the inhabitants of the land
Mt. 18:33 fellow servant, even as I had *p* on thee?

Place

Gen. 3:24 he *p* at the east of the garden of Eden
Ex. 3:5 (Acts 7:33) *p* whereon thou standest is holy
Deut. 11:24 (Josh. 1:3) every *p* . . your feet shall tread
12:5 (12:11, 14, 18, 21, 26; 14:23, 25; 15:20; 16:2, 6, 7, 11, 15, 16; 17:8, 10; 18:6; 23:16; 26:2; 31:11) the *p* which the LORD your God shall choose .
Josh. 5:15 the *p* whereon thou standest is holy
Judg. 18:10 *p* where there is no want of any thing
1 Kgs. 8:29 toward the *p* of which thou hast said
2 Kgs. 5:11 and strike his hand over the *p*
6:1 the *p* where we dwelt with thee is too strait
2 Chr. 30:27 prayer came up to his holy dwelling *p*
Job 7:10 neither shall his *p* know him any more
8:22 dwelling *p* of the wicked shall come to nought
28:23 way thereof, and he knoweth the *p* thereof
Ps. 16:6 lines are fallen unto me in pleasant *p*
24:3 the LORD? or who shall stand in his holy *p*?
26:8 house, and the *p* where thine honor dwelleth
32:7 thou art my hiding *p*; thou shalt preserve
33:14 from the *p* of his habitation he looketh
74:20 for the dark *p* of the earth are full of
90:1 hast been our dwelling *p* in all generations
103:16 and the *p* thereof shall know it no more
119:114 thou art my hiding *p* and my shield
Prov. 14:26 his children shall have a *p* of refuge
15:3 eyes of the LORD are in every *p*, beholding
Eccl. 3:20 all go unto one *p*; all are of the dust
Is. 5:8 that lay field to field, till there be no *p*
54:2 enlarge the *p* of thy tent . . let them stretch
60:13 and I will make the *p* of my feet glorious
66:1 (Acts 7:49) and where is the *p* of my rest?
Jer. 4:26 and, lo, the fruitful *p* was a wilderness
6:3 the shepherds . . shall feed every one in his *p*
Hos. 5:15 I will go and return to my *p*, till they
11:11 will *p* them in their houses, saith the LORD
Amos 4:13 treadeth upon the high *p* of the earth
Mic. 1:3 LORD cometh forth out of his *p*, and will
Mal. 1:11 in every *p* incense shall be offered unto
Mt. 28:6 (Mk. 16:6) see the *p* where the Lord lay
Mk. 6:10 in what *p* soever ye enter into a house
Lk. 14:9 give this man *p*; and thou begin with shame
Jn. 8:37 kill me, because my word hath no *p* in you
14:2 many mansions . . I go to prepare a *p* for you
18:2 Judas also, which betrayed him, knew the *p*
Acts 2:1 they were all with one accord in one *p*
4:31 the *p* was shaken where they were assembled
Rom. 15:23 now having no more *p* in these parts
1 Cor. 11:20 when ye come together . . into one *p*
Eph. 4:27 neither give *p* to the devil
Phil. 1:13 in all the palace, and in all other *p*
Heb. 9:12 he entered in once into the holy *p*
11:8 when he was called to go out into a *p* which

Heb. 12:17 rejected: for he found no *p* of repentance
Rev. 12:6 where she hath a *p* prepared of God
20:11 fled away . . there was found no *p* for them

Plague

Gen. 12:17 *p* Pharaoh and his house with great *p*
Ex. 11:1 yet will I bring one *p* more upon Pharaoh
12:13 pass over you . . the *p* shall not be upon you
32:35 *p* the people, because they made the calf
Num. 11:33 smote the people with a very great *p*
14:37 those men . . died by the *p* before the LORD
16:46 wrath . . out from the LORD; the *p* is begun
25:9 died in the *p* were twenty and four thousand
Deut. 28:59 will make thy *p* wonderful, and the *p*
29:22 when they see the *p* of that land
2 Sam. 24:21 (1 Chr. 21:22) the *p* may be stayed
1 Kgs. 8:38 know every man the *p* of his own heart
Ps. 73:5 neither are they *p* like other men
73:14 for all the day long have I been *p*
89:23 beat down his foes . . *p* them that hate him
91:10 neither shall any *p* come nigh thy dwelling
106:30 executed judgment . . so the *p* was stayed
Hos. 13:14 O death, I will be thy *p*; O grave, I
Zech. 14:12 be the *p* wherewith the LORD will smite
Mk. 3:10 pressed . . to touch him, as many as had *p*
5:29 and she felt . . that she was healed of that *p*
Rev. 11:6 have power . . to smite the earth with all *p*
15:1 seven angels having the seven last *p*
18:4 come out of her . . that ye receive not of her *p*
22:18 shall add unto him the *p* that are written

Plain (adjective, adverb)

Gen. 25:27 Jacob was a *p* man, dwelling in tents
Ps. 27:11 and lead me in a *p* path, because of mine
Prov. 8:9 they are all *p* to him that understandeth
15:19 but the way of the righteous is made *p*
Is. 40:4 be made straight, and the rough places *p*
Hab. 2:2 write the vision, and make it *p* upon tables
Mk. 7:35 of his tongue was loosed, and he spake *p*

Plain (noun)

Gen. 11:2 they found a *p* in the land of Shinar
13:11 then Lot chose him all the *p* of Jordan
1 Kgs. 20:23 let us fight against them in the *p*
Zech. 4:7 before Zerubbabel thou shalt become a *p*
Lk. 6:17 came down with them, and stood in the *p*

Plainly

Deut. 27:8 write . . all the words of this law very *p*
Is. 32:4 the stammerers shall be ready to speak *p*
Jn. 10:24 doubt? If thou be the Christ, tell us *p*
16:25 but I shall show you *p* of the Father
16:29 speakest thou *p*, and speakest no proverb
Heb. 11:14 declare *p* that they seek a country

Plainness

2 Cor. 3:12 such hope, we use great *p* of speech

Plant *See also* Grass, Herb

Gen. 2:5 and every *p* of the field before it was in
2:8 the LORD God *p* a garden eastward in Eden
Ex. 15:17 thou shalt bring them in, and *p* them
2 Sam. 7:10 (1 Chr. 17:9) *p* them, that they may dwell
Ps. 44:2 didst drive out the heathen . . and *p* them
80:15 the vineyard which thy right hand hath *p*
92:13 those that be *p* in the house of the LORD
94:9 he that *p* the ear, shall he not hear?
128:3 thy children like olive *p* round about thy
144:12 that our sons may be as *p* grown up in
Eccl. 3:2 a time to *p*, and a time to pluck up that
Song 4:13 thy *p* are an orchard of pomegranates
Is. 5:7 Israel, and the men of Judah his pleasant *p*
16:8 have broken down the principal *p* thereof

Is. 17:10 therefore shalt thou *p* pleasant *p*
40:24 yea, they shall not be *p*; yea, they shall
41:19 I will *p* in the wilderness the cedar
44:14 he *p* an ash, and the rain doth nourish it
53:2 he shall grow up before him as a tender *p*
61:3 Trees of righteousness, The *p* of the LORD
65:21 they shall *p* vineyards, and eat the fruit
Jer. 2:21 yet I had *p* thee a noble vine, wholly a
11:17 LORD of hosts, that *p* thee, hath pronounced
24:6 I will *p* them, and not pluck them up
29:5 and *p* gardens, and eat the fruit of them
32:41 I will *p* them in this land assuredly
Ezek. 17:10 yea, behold, being *p*, shall it prosper?
34:29 and I will raise up for them a *p* of renown
Mt. 15:13 *p*, which my heavenly Father hath not *p*
Lk. 17:6 be thou *p* in the sea; and it should obey
Rom. 6:5 *p* together in the likeness of his death
1 Cor. 3:6 I have *p*, Apollos watered; but God gave
9:7 who *p* a vineyard, and eateth not of the fruit

Plat (Plait)

Mt. 27:29 (Mk. 15:17; Jn. 19:2) *p* a crown of thorns
1 Pet. 3:3 that outward adorning of *p* the hair

Plate

Ex. 28:36 (39:30) thou shalt make a *p* of pure gold
Num. 16:38 broad *p* for a covering of the altar

Platter

Mt. 23:25 (Lk. 11:39) outside of the cup and of the *p*

Play

Ex. 32:6 (1 Cor. 10:7) to drink, and rose up to *p*
1 Sam. 16:17 provide me now a man that can *p* well
18:7 the women answered one another as they *p*
2 Sam. 2:14 young men now arise, and *p* before us
6:21 therefore will I *p* before the LORD
10:12 let us *p* the men for our people, and for
Job 40:20 where all the beasts of the field *p*
41:5 wilt thou *p* with him as with a bird? or wilt
Ps. 33:3 a new song; *p* skilfully with a loud noise
104:26 leviathan, whom thou hast made to *p*
Is. 11:8 child shall *p* on the hole of the asp
Ezek. 33:32 voice, and can *p* well on an instrument
Zech. 8:5 full of boys and girls *p* in the streets

Player

Ps. 68:25 the *p* on instruments followed after
87:7 as the *p* on instruments shall be there

Plead *See also* Ask, Beg, Beseech, Petition

Judg. 6:31 ye *p* for Baal? . . let him *p* for himself
Job 9:19 of judgment, who shall set me a time to *p*?
13:19 who is he that will *p* with me? for now, if
16:21 oh that one might *p* for a man with God
23:6 will he *p* against me with his great power?
Ps. 35:1 *p* my cause, O LORD, with them that strive
Prov. 31:9 and *p* the cause of the poor and needy
Is. 1:17 judge the fatherless, *p* for the widow
3:13 the LORD standeth up to *p*, and . . to judge
43:26 put me in remembrance: let us *p* together
59:4 nor any *p* for truth: they trust in vanity
66:16 by fire and by his sword will the LORD *p*
Jer. 2:9 with your children's children will I *p*
25:31 he will *p* with all flesh; he will give
Lam. 3:58 Lord, thou hast *p* the causes of my soul
Ezek. 20:36 like as I *p* with your fathers in the
Hos. 2:2 *p* with your mother, *p*; for she is not my
Joel 3:2 and will *p* with them there for my people
Mic. 6:2 with his people, and he will *p* with Israel

Pleasant

Gen. 2:9 to grow every tree that is *p* to the sight

Gen. 3:6 was *p* to the eyes, and a tree to be desired
2 Sam. 1:23 Saul and Jonathan were lovely and *p* in
1:26 Jonathan: very *p* hast thou been unto me
Ps. 16:6 the lines are fallen unto me in *p* places
106:24 despised the *p* land . . believed not his word
133:1 how *p* it is for brethren to dwell together
135:3 sing praises unto his name; for it is *p*
Prov. 2:10 heart, and knowledge is *p* unto thy soul
9:17 are sweet, and bread eaten in secret is *p*
15:26 but the words of the pure are *p* words
16:24 *p* words are as a honeycomb, sweet to the
Eccl. 11:7 *p* thing . . for the eyes to behold the sun
Song 1:16 thou art fair, my beloved, yea, *p*
Is. 32:12 lament for the teats, for the *p* fields
64:11 and all our *p* things are laid waste
Jer. 23:10 *p* places of the wilderness are dried up
31:20 is Ephraim my dear son? is he a *p* child?
Ezek. 33:32 lovely song of one that hath a *p* voice
Dan. 8:9 toward the east, and toward the *p* land
10:3 I ate no *p* bread, neither came flesh nor
Amos 5:11 ye have planted *p* vineyards, but ye shall
Mal. 3:4 offering of Judah and Jerusalem be *p* unto

Pleasantness

Prov. 3:17 her ways are ways of *p*, and all her

Please *See also* Glad

Num. 23:27 peradventure it will *p* God that thou
24:1 when Balaam saw that it *p* the LORD to bless
Deut. 1:23 and the saying *p* me well; and I took
Josh. 22:33 and the thing *p* the children of Israel
Judg. 13:23 if the LORD were *p* to kill us, he would
1 Sam. 12:22 *p* the LORD to make you his people
2 Sam. 7:29 (1 Chr. 17:27) *p* thee to bless the house
1 Kgs. 3:10 *p* the Lord, that Solomon had asked
Esth. 7:3 if it *p* the king, let my life be given
Job 6:9 even that it would *p* God to destroy me
20:10 his children shall seek to *p* the poor
Ps. 51:19 shalt thou be *p* with the sacrifices of
69:31 also shall *p* the LORD better than an ox
115:3 our God . . hath done whatsoever he hath *p*
135:6 whatsoever the LORD *p*, that did he in
Prov. 16:7 when a man's ways *p* the LORD, he maketh
Eccl. 7:26 whoso *p* God shall escape from her
8:3 an evil thing; for he doeth whatsoever *p* him
Song 2:7 (3:5; 8:4) nor awake my love, till he *p*
Is. 2:6 *p* themselves in the children of strangers
42:21 LORD is well *p* for his righteousness' sake
53:10 yet it *p* the LORD to bruise him; he hath
55:11 but it shall accomplish that which I *p*
Jon. 1:14 for thou, O LORD, hast done as it *p* thee
Mic. 6:7 will the LORD be *p* with thousands of rams
Mal. 1:8 will he be *p* with thee, or accept thy
Mt. 3:17 (17:5; Mk. 1:11; Lk. 3:22; 2 Pet. 1:17) this
is my beloved Son, in whom I am well *p*
12:18 my beloved, in whom my soul is well *p*
Jn. 8:29 for I do always those things that *p* him
Acts 6:5 and the saying *p* the whole multitude
12:3 he saw it *p* the Jews, he proceeded further
15:22 then *p* it the apostles and elders
Rom. 8:8 they that are in the flesh cannot *p* God
15:1 infirmities of the weak . . not to *p* ourselves
15:2 *p* his neighbor for his good to edification
15:3 for even Christ *p* not himself; but, as it is
1 Cor. 1:21 *p* God by the foolishness of preaching
7:13 if he be *p* to dwell with her, let her not
7:32 careth for the things . . how he may *p* the Lord
7:34 married careth . . how she may *p* her husband
10:5 but with many of them God was not well *p*
10:33 even as I *p* all men in all things
15:38 but God giveth it a body as it hath *p* him
Gal. 1:10 do I seek to *p* men? for if I yet *p* men
1:15 but when it *p* God, who separated me from

Col. 1:19 it *p* the Father that in him should all
1 Thes. 2:4 not as *p* men, but God, which trieth
   2:15 they *p* not God, and are contrary to all men
   4:1 ye ought to walk and to *p* God, so ye would
2 Tim. 2:4 he may *p* him who hath chosen him to be
Tit. 2:9 masters, and to *p* them well in all things
Heb. 11:5 he had this testimony, that he *p* God
   11:6 but without faith it is impossible to *p* him
   13:16 for with such sacrifices God is well *p*

Pleasing *See also* Please

Hos. 9:4 LORD, neither shall they be *p* unto him
Col. 1:10 might walk worthy of the Lord unto all *p*
1 Jn. 3:22 do those things that are *p* in his sight

Pleasure *See also* Delight, Gladness, Joy

1 Chr. 29:17 the heart, and hast *p* in uprightness
Ezra 10:11 confession unto the LORD . . and do his *p*
Esth. 1:8 they should do according to every man's *p*
Job 21:21 what *p* hath he in his house after him
   22:3 is it any *p* to the Almighty, that thou art
   36:11 days in prosperity, and their years in *p*
Ps. 5:4 art not a God that hath *p* in wickedness
   16:11 at thy right hand there are *p* for evermore
   35:27 hath *p* in the prosperity of his servant
   51:18 do good in thy good *p* unto Zion
   102:14 for thy servants take *p* in her stones
   103:21 ye ministers of his, that do his *p*
   111:2 sought out of all them that have *p* therein
   147:11 the LORD taketh *p* in them that fear him
   149:4 the LORD taketh *p* in his people: he will
Prov. 21:17 he that loveth *p* shall be a poor man
Eccl. 2:1 enjoy *p*: and, behold, this also is vanity
   5:4 defer not to pay it . . he hath no *p* in fools
   12:1 when thou shalt say, I have no *p* in them
Is. 21:4 the night of my *p* hath he turned into
   44:28 is my shepherd, and shall perform all my *p*
   46:10 my counsel shall stand . . I will do all my *p*
   47:8 hear now this, thou that art given to *p*
   48:14 he will do his *p* on Babylon, and his arm
   53:10 *p* of the LORD shall prosper in his hand
   58:3 behold, in the day of your fast ye find *p*
   58:13 from doing thy *p* on my holy day; and call
Jer. 22:28 is he a vessel wherein is no *p*?
Ezek. 16:37 lovers, with whom thou hast taken *p*
   18:23 I any *p* at all that the wicked should die?
   18:32 (33:11) I have no *p* in the death of
Hag. 1:8 build the house; and I will take *p* in it
Mal. 1:10 I have no *p* in you, saith the LORD
Lk. 8:14 choked with cares and riches and *p*
   12:32 Father's good *p* to give you the kingdom
Acts 24:27 to show the Jews a *p*, left Paul bound
   25:9 but Festus, willing to do the Jews a *p*
Rom. 1:32 not only do the same, but have *p* in them
2 Cor. 12:10 therefore I take *p* in infirmities
Eph. 1:5 according to the good *p* of his will
   1:9 his good *p* which he hath purposed in himself
Phil. 2:13 both to will and to do of his good *p*
2 Thes. 1:11 fulfil all the good *p* of his goodness
   2:12 not the truth, but had *p* in unrighteousness
1 Tim. 5:6 liveth in *p* is dead while she liveth
2 Tim. 3:4 lovers of *p* more than lovers of God
Tit. 3:3 serving divers lusts and *p*, living in
Heb. 10:6 sacrifices for sin thou hast had no *p*
   10:38 draw back, my soul shall have no *p* in him
   11:25 than to enjoy the *p* of sin for a season
   12:10 chastened us after their own *p*; but he for
Jas. 5:5 ye have lived in *p* on the earth, and been
2 Pet. 2:13 that count it *p* to riot in the daytime
Rev. 4:11 and for thy *p* they are and were created

Pledge

Gen. 38:17 wilt thou give me a *p*, till thou send

Ex. 22:26 if thou . . take thy neighbor's raiment to *p*
Deut. 24:6 to *p*: for he taketh a man's life to *p*
   24:10 shalt not go into his house to fetch his *p*
1 Sam. 17:18 thy brethren fare, and take their *p*
2 Kgs. 18:23 (Is. 36:8) give *p* to my lord the king
Job 22:6 taken a *p* from thy brother for nought
   24:3 they take the widow's ox for a *p*
Prov. 20:16 (27:13) a *p* of him for a strange woman
Ezek. 18:7 but hath restored to the debtor his *p*
   33:15 if the wicked restore the *p*, give again
Amos 2:8 upon clothes laid to *p* by every altar

Pleiades Job 38:31

Plenteous *See also* Abundant

Gen. 41:34 take up the fifth . . in the seven *p* years
Deut. 28:11 the LORD shall make thee *p* in goods
   30:9 make thee *p* in every work of thine hand
Ps. 86:5 *p* in mercy unto all them that call upon
   103:8 gracious, slow to anger, and *p* in mercy
   130:7 is mercy, and with him is *p* redemption
Hab. 1:16 their portion is fat, and their meat *p*
Mt. 9:37 harvest truly is *p*, but the laborers are

Plenteousness

Gen. 41:53 and the seven years of *p* . . were ended
Prov. 21:5 thoughts of the diligent tend only to *p*

Plentiful

Ps. 68:9 thou, O God didst send a *p* rain, whereby
Is. 16:10 (Jer. 48:33) and joy out of the *p* field
Jer. 2:7 I brought you into a *p* country, to eat

Plentifully

Job 26:3 how hast thou *p* declared the thing as it
Ps. 31:23 faithful, and *p* rewardeth the proud doer
Lk. 12:16 ground of a . . rich man brought forth *p*

Plenty *See also* Abundance, Fulness

Gen. 27:28 fatness of the earth . . *p* of corn and wine
   41:29 behold, there come seven years of great *p*
Job 22:25 defense, and thou shalt have *p* of silver
   37:23 and in *p* of justice: he will not afflict
Prov. 3:10 so shall thy barns be filled with *p*
   28:19 tilleth his land shall have *p* of bread
Joel 2:26 and ye shall eat in *p*, and be satisfied

Plot

Ps. 37:12 wicked *p* against the just, and gnasheth

Plow

Deut. 22:10 thou shalt not *p* with an ox and an ass
1 Kgs. 19:19 Elisha . . was *p* with twelve yoke of oxen
Job 4:8 that *p* iniquity, and sow wickedness, reap
Ps. 129:3 the plowers *p* upon my back: they made
Prov. 20:4 sluggard will not *p* by reason of . . cold
   21:4 proud heart, and the *p* of the wicked, is sin
Is. 28:24 doth the plowman *p* all day to sow?
Jer. 26:18 (Mic. 3:12) Zion shall be *p* like a field
Hos. 10:13 *p* wickedness, ye have reaped iniquity
Amos 6:12 the rock? will one *p* there with oxen?
Lk. 9:62 put his hand to the *p*, and looking back
1 Cor. 9:10 he that *p* should *p* in hope

Plowman (Plowmen)

Is. 28:24 doth the *p* plow all day to sow?
   61:5 sons of the alien shall be your *p* and your
Jer. 14:4 *p* were ashamed, they covered their heads
Amos 9:13 that the *p* shall overtake the reaper

Plowshare

Is. 2:4 (Mic. 4:3) shall beat their swords into *p*
Joel 3:10 beat your *p* into swords, and your pruning

Pluck

Ex. 4:7 and *p* it out of his bosom, and, behold
Num. 33:52 and quite *p* down all their high places
Deut. 23:25 thou mayest *p* the ears with thine hand
Ruth 4:7 confirm all things; a man *p* off his shoe
2 Chr. 7:20 then will I *p* them up by the roots
Job 24:9 they *p* the fatherless from the breast
Ps. 25:15 for he shall *p* my feet out of the net
    52:5 *p* thee out of thy dwelling place, and root
    74:11 even thy right hand? *p* it out of thy bosom
    80:12 all they which pass by the way do *p* her?
Prov. 14:1 the foolish *p* it down with her hands
Eccl. 3:2 and a time to *p* up that which is planted
Is. 50:6 and my cheeks to them that *p* off the hair
Jer. 12:14 *p* them out of their land, and *p* out
    22:24 my right hand, yet would I *p* thee thence
Ezek. 23:34 and *p* off thine own breasts: for I have
Mt. 5:29 (18:9; Mk. 9:47) eye offend thee, *p* it out
    12:1 (Mk. 2:23; Lk. 6:1) *p* the ears of corn
Mk. 5:4 and the chains had been *p* asunder by him
Jn. 10:28 neither shall any . . *p* them out of my hand
Gal. 4:15 ye would have *p* out your own eyes

Plucked *See also* Pluck

Gen. 8:11 lo, in her mouth was an olive leaf *p* off
Amos 4:11 were as a firebrand *p* out of the burning
Lk. 17:6 sycamine tree, Be thou *p* up by the root
Jude 12 twice dead, *p* up by the roots

Plumbline

Amos 7:8 Amos, what seest thou? And I said, A *p*

Plummet

2 Kgs. 21:13 and the *p* of the house of Ahab
Is. 28:17 to the line, and righteousness to the *p*
Zech. 4:10 see the *p* in the hand of Zerubbabel

Poet

Acts 17:28 as certain also of your own *p* have said

Point

Num. 34:7 border . . ye shall *p* out for you mount Hor
Jer. 17:1 with the *p* of a diamond: it is graven
Heb. 4:15 was in all *p* tempted like as we are, yet
Jas. 2:10 yet offend in one *p*, he is guilty of all

Poison

Deut. 32:24 with the *p* of serpents of the dust
Job 6:4 the *p* whereof drinketh up my spirit
Ps. 58:4 their *p* is like the *p* of a serpent
    140:3 (Rom. 3:13) adders' *p* is under their lips
Jas. 3:8 it is an unruly evil, full of deadly *p*

Pole

Num. 21:8 make . . fiery serpent, and set it upon a *p*

Pollute *See also* Corrupt, Defile, Profane

Ex. 20:25 lift up thy tool upon it, thou hast *p* it
Num. 18:32 neither shall ye *p* the holy things
    35:33 so ye shall not *p* the land wherein ye are
2 Chr. 36:14 *p* the house of the Lord which he had
Is. 56:2 that keepeth the sabbath from *p* it
Jer. 3:1 shall not that land be greatly *p*?
    34:16 but ye turned and *p* my name, and caused
Lam. 2:2 he hath *p* the kingdom and the princes
    4:14 they have *p* themselves with blood, so that
Ezek. 7:21 and to the wicked . . and they shall *p* it
    13:19 and will ye *p* me among my people
    16:6 saw thee *p* in thine own blood, I said unto
    20:31 ye *p* yourselves with all your idols
    20:39 but *p* ye my holy name no more with
    39:7 I will not let them *p* my holy name any more
Dan. 11:31 they shall *p* the sanctuary of strength

Hos. 6:8 that work iniquity, and is *p* with blood
Zeph. 3:4 her priests have *p* the sanctuary
Mal. 1:7 ye offer *p* bread . . Wherein have we *p* thee?
Acts 21:28 into the temple . . hath *p* this holy place

Pollution

Ezek. 22:10 humbled her that was set apart for *p*
Acts 15:20 they abstain from *p* of idols, and from
2 Pet. 2:20 escaped the *p* of the world through the

Pomegranate

Ex. 28:33 (39:24) make *p* of blue, and of purple
Num. 13:23 they brought of the *p*, and of the figs
Deut. 8:8 a land of . . vines, and fig trees, and *p*
Song 4:13 orchard of *p*, with pleasant fruits

Pomp

Is. 5:14 and their *p*, and he that rejoiceth, shall
    14:11 thy *p* is brought down to the grave
Ezek. 7:24 also make the *p* of the strong to cease
    30:18 (33:28) the *p* of her strength shall cease
    32:12 they shall spoil the *p* of Egypt, and all
Acts 25:23 when Agrippa was come . . with great *p*

Ponder *See also* Meditate, Muse, Think

Prov. 4:26 *p* the path of thy feet, and let all thy
    5:6 lest thou shouldest *p* the path of life
    5:21 eyes of the Lord, and he *p* all his goings
    21:2 in his own eyes: but the Lord *p* the hearts
    24:12 doth not he that *p* the heart consider it?
Lk. 2:19 Mary kept all . . and *p* them in her heart

Pool

Ex. 7:19 *p* of water, that they may become blood
Is. 35:7 and the parched ground shall become a *p*
    41:18 I will make the wilderness a *p* of water
    42:15 rivers islands, and I will dry up the *p*
Jn. 5:2 is at Jerusalem by the sheep market a *p*
    9:7 said unto him, Go, wash in the *p* of Siloam

Poor *See also* Afflicted, Destitute, Needy

Ex. 22:25 lend money to any of my people that is *p*
    23:3 neither shalt thou countenance a *p* man in
    23:6 thou shalt not wrest the judgment of thy *p*
    23:11 lie still; that the *p* of thy people may eat
    30:15 shall not give more . . *p* shall not give less
Lev. 14:21 and if he be *p*, and cannot get so much
    19:10 (23:22) thou shalt leave them for the *p*
    19:15 thou shalt not respect the person of the *p*
    25:25 if thy brother be waxen *p*, and hath sold
    25:35 if thy brother be waxen *p* . . relieve him
Deut. 15:4 save when there shall be no *p* among you
    15:7 if there be among you a *p* man of one of thy
    15:11 the *p* shall never cease out of the land
    24:12 if the man be *p*, thou shalt not sleep with
Judg. 6:15 I save Israel? behold, my family is *p*
1 Sam. 2:7 the Lord maketh *p*, and maketh rich
    2:8 (Ps. 113:7) raiseth up the *p* out of the dust
2 Sam. 12:1 one city; the one rich, and the other *p*
2 Kgs. 25:12 (Jer. 52:16) the *p* . . to be vinedressers
Job 5:15 but he saveth the *p* from the sword
    20:19 he hath oppressed and hath forsaken the *p*
    24:4 the *p* of the earth hide themselves together
    24:14 the murderer . . killeth the *p* and needy
    29:12 because I delivered the *p* that cried
    29:16 I was a father to the *p*: and the cause which
    30:25 trouble? was not my soul grieved for the *p*?
    31:16 if I have withheld the *p* from their desire
    31:19 want of clothing, or any *p* without covering
    34:19 nor regardeth the rich more than the *p*?
    36:6 of the wicked: but giveth right to the *p*
    36:15 he delivereth the *p* in his affliction
Ps. 9:18 the expectation of the *p* shall not perish

Ps. 10:2 wicked in his pride doth persecute the *p*
10:14 the *p* committeth himself unto thee
34:6 this *p* man cried, and the LORD heard him
35:10 which deliverest the *p* from him that is
40:17 (70:5; 86:1; 109:22) I am *p* and needy
41:1 blessed is he that considereth the *p*
69:29 I am *p* and sorrowful: let thy salvation
69:33 LORD heareth the *p*, and despiseth not his
72:4 he shall judge the *p* of the people, he shall
74:19 forget not the congregation of thy *p*
107:41 setteth he the *p* on high from affliction
112:9 (2 Cor. 9:9) he hath given to the *p*
132:15 provision: I will satisfy her *p* with bread
Prov. 10:4 he becometh *p* that dealeth with a slack
13:7 that maketh himself *p*, yet hath great riches
14:20 the *p* is hated even of his own neighbor
14:21 he that hath mercy on the *p*, happy is he
17:5 whoso mocketh the *p* reproacheth his Maker
19:1 better is the *p* that walketh in his integrity
19:22 and a *p* man is better than a liar
21:17 he that loveth pleasure shall be a *p* man
22:16 oppresseth the *p* to increase his riches
22:22 rob not the *p*, because he is *p*: neither
28:6 better is the *p*. . walketh in his uprightness
29:14 the king that faithfully judgeth the *p*
30:9 or lest I be *p*, and steal, and take the name
31:20 she stretcheth out her hand to the *p*
Eccl. 4:13 better is a *p* and a wise child, than
9:15 yet no man remembered that same *p* man
Is. 10:2 to take away the right from the *p* of my
11:4 but with righteousness shall he judge the *p*
14:32 and the *p* of his people shall trust in it
25:4 for thou hast been a strength to the *p*
29:19 *p* among men shall rejoice in the Holy One
41:17 when the *p* and needy seek water, and there
58:7 bring the *p* that are cast out to thy house?
66:2 to him that is *p* and of a contrite spirit
Jer. 5:4 surely these are *p*; they are foolish
Ezek. 16:49 strengthen the hand of the *p* and needy
18:12 oppressed the *p* and needy, hath spoiled by
Dan. 4:27 by showing mercy to the *p*; if it may
Amos 2:6 for silver, and the *p* for a pair of shoes
4:1 which oppress the *p*, which crush the needy
5:11 therefore as your treading is upon the *p*
8:6 we may buy the *p* for silver, and the needy
Hab. 3:14 their rejoicing was as to devour the *p*
Zeph. 3:12 midst of thee an afflicted and *p* people
Zech. 11:7 I will feed . . even you, O *p* of the flock
Mt. 5:3 (Lk. 6:20) blessed are the *p*
11:5 (Lk. 7:22) *p* have the gospel preached to them
19:21 (Mk. 10:21; Lk. 18:22) sell . . give to the *p*
26:9 (Mk. 14:5; Jn. 12:5) sold . . and given to the *p*
26:11 (Mk. 14:7; Jn. 12:8) the *p* always with you
Mk. 12:43 (Lk. 21:3) this *p* widow hath cast more in
Lk. 4:18 anointed me to preach the gospel to the *p*
14:13 but when thou makest a feast, call the *p*
19:8 Lord, the half of my goods I give to the *p*
Rom. 15:26 a certain contribution for the *p* saints
1 Cor. 13:3 I bestow all my goods to feed the *p*
2 Cor. 6:10 as *p*, yet making many rich; as having
8:9 he was rich, yet for your sakes he became *p*
Gal. 2:10 they would that we should remember the *p*
Jas. 2:2 there come in also a *p* man in vile raiment
2:5 God chosen the *p* of this world rich in faith
2:6 but ye have despised the *p*. Do not rich men
Rev. 3:17 thou art wretched, and miserable, and *p*

Porch

Judg. 3:23 then Ehud went forth through the *p*
1 Kgs. 7:6 and he made a *p* of pillars; the length
Mt. 26:71 when he was gone out into the *p*, another
Jn. 5:2 a pool . . called . . Bethesda, having five *p*

Jn. 10:23 Jesus walked in the temple in Solomon's *p*
Acts 3:11 unto them in the *p* that is called Solomon's

Porter

2 Kgs. 7:10 so they came and called unto the *p*
1 Chr. 23:5 four thousand were *p*; and four thousand
Mk. 13:34 left his house . . commanded the *p* to watch
Jn. 10:3 to him the *p* openeth; and the sheep hear

Portion *See also* Divide, Lot, Part, Piece

Gen. 31:14 is there yet any *p* or inheritance for us
47:22 priests had a *p* assigned them of Pharaoh
48:22 given to thee one *p* above thy brethren
Deut. 32:9 LORD's *p* is his people; Jacob is the
1 Kgs. 12:16 (2 Chr. 10:16) what *p* have we in David?
Neh. 2:20 no *p*, nor right, nor memorial, in Jerusalem
8:10 send *p* unto them for whom nothing is
Job 20:29 this is the *p* of a wicked man from God
26:14 but how little a *p* is heard of him?
31:2 what *p* of God is there from above? and what
Ps. 11:6 tempest: this shall be the *p* of their cup
16:5 LORD is the *p* of mine inheritance and of my
63:10 by the sword: they shall be a *p* for foxes
73:26 God is the strength of my heart, and my *p*
119:57 thou art my *p*, O LORD: I have said that I
142:5 thou art . . my *p* in the land of the living
Prov. 31:15 her household, and a *p* to her maidens
Eccl. 2:10 and this was my *p* of all my labor
3:22 rejoice in his own works; for that is his *p*
5:18 the good of all his labor . . for it is his *p*
9:6 neither have they any more a *p* for ever in
9:9 live joyfully with the wife . . that is thy *p*
11:2 give a *p* to seven, and also to eight
Is. 53:12 will I divide him a *p* with the great
61:7 for confusion they shall rejoice in their *p*
Jer. 10:16 the *p* of Jacob is not like them
12:10 destroyed my vineyard . . have trodden my *p*
52:34 every day a *p* until the day of his death
Lam. 3:24 LORD is my *p*, saith my soul; therefore
Dan. 1:8 not defile . . with the *p* of the king's meat
4:15 let his *p* be with the beasts in the grass
Mic. 2:4 he hath changed the *p* of my people
Zech. 2:12 the LORD shall inherit Judah his *p*
Mt. 24:51 (Lk. 12:46) his *p* with the hypocrites
Lk. 12:42 give them their *p* of meat in due season?
15:12 give me the *p* of goods that falleth to me

Portray

Ezek. 4:1 and *p* upon it the city, even Jerusalem
23:14 saw men *p* upon the wall, the images . . *p*

Possess *See also* Inherit

Gen. 22:17 thy seed shall *p* the gate of his enemies
Lev. 20:24 I will give it unto you to *p* it, a land
Num. 13:30 let us go up at once, and *p* it; for we
14:24 my servant Caleb . . and his seed shall *p* it
33:53 for I have given you the land to *p* it
Deut. 1:8 (4:1; 8:1; 11:8) go in and *p* the land
1:39 there will I give it, and they shall *p* it
3:18 your God hath given you this land to *p* it
4:22 but ye shall go over, and *p* that good land
9:1 go in to *p* nations greater and mightier than
9:4 LORD hath brought me in to *p* this land
15:4 God giveth thee for an inheritance to *p* it
Josh. 1:11 the LORD your God giveth you to *p* it
18:3 how long are ye slack to go to *p* the land
Judg. 11:24 *p* . . Chemosh thy god giveth thee to *p*?
18:9 not slothful to go, and to enter to *p* the land
1 Chr. 28:8 ye may *p* this good land, and leave it
Neh. 9:15 they should go in to *p* the land which
9:25 *p* houses full of all goods, wells digged
Job 7:3 so am I made to *p* months of vanity
13:26 makest me to *p* the iniquities of my youth

Ps. 139:13 thou hast *p* my reins: thou hast covered
Prov. 8:22 LORD *p* me in the beginning of his way
Is. 14:2 Israel shall *p* them in the land of the
　34:17 they shall *p* it for ever, from generation
　57:13 putteth his trust in me shall *p* the land
　61:7 in their land they shall *p* the double
　63:18 the people of thy holiness have *p* it but a
Jer. 30:3 return to the land. . and they shall *p* it
　32:15 vineyards shall be *p* again in this land
　32:23 they came in, and *p* it; but they obeyed not
Ezek. 7:24 heathen, and they shall *p* their houses
　33:26 ye work abomination. . shall ye *p* the land?
　36:12 my people Israel; and they shall *p* thee
Dan. 7:18 shall take the kingdom, and *p* the kingdom
Obad. 17 house of Jacob shall *p* their possessions
Hab. 1:6 the Chaldeans. . to *p* the dwelling places
Zeph. 2:9 the remnant of my people shall *p* them
Zech. 8:12 remnant of this people to *p* all these
Lk. 12:15 the abundance of the things which he *p*
　18:12 I fast twice. . I give tithes of all that I *p*
　21:19 in your patience *p* ye your souls
Acts 4:32 that aught. . which he *p* was his own
1 Cor. 7:30 they that buy, as though they *p* not
2 Cor. 6:10 as having nothing, and yet *p* all things
1 Thes. 4:4 how to *p* his vessel in sanctification

Possessed *See also* Possess

Mt. 4:24 and those which were *p* with devils
　8:28 there met him two *p* with devils, coming out
　9:32 brought to him a dumb man *p* with a devil
　12:22 brought unto him one *p* with a devil, blind
Acts 16:16 damsel *p* with a spirit of divination met

Possession *See also* Goods, Inheritance, Riches, Wealth

Gen. 17:8 the land of Canaan, for an everlasting *p*
　48:4 this land to thy seed. . for an everlasting *p*
Lev. 14:34 Canaan, which I give to you for a *p*
　25:10 and ye shall return every man unto his *p*
　25:34 field of the suburbs. . is their perpetual *p*
Num. 27:4 hath no son? Give unto us therefore a *p*
　32:22 this land shall be your *p* before the LORD
Deut. 32:49 give unto the children of Israel for a *p*
1 Kgs. 21:19 hast thou killed, and also taken *p*?
Neh. 11:3 cities of Judah dwelt every one in his *p*
Ps. 2:8 the uttermost parts of the earth for thy *p*
　69:35 they may dwell there, and have it in *p*
Prov. 28:10 upright shall have good things in *p*
Eccl. 2:7 I had great *p* of great and small cattle
Is. 14:23 I will also make it a *p* for the bittern
Ezek. 36:3 be a *p* unto the residue of the heathen
　36:5 which have appointed my land into their *p*
　44:28 give them no *p* in Israel; I am their *p*
Obad. 17 the house of Jacob shall possess their *p*
Mt. 19:22 (Mk. 10:22) sorrowful: for he had great *p*
Acts 2:45 sold their *p* and goods, and parted them
　5:1 Ananias, with Sapphira his wife, sold a *p*
　7:5 promised that he would give it to him for a *p*
　7:45 in with Jesus into the *p* of the Gentiles
Eph. 1:14 until the redemption of the purchased *p*

Possessor

Gen. 14:19 the most high God, *p* of heaven and earth
Acts 4:34 as many as were *p* of lands or houses sold

Possible

Mt. 19:26 (Mk. 10:27; Lk. 18:27) God all things are *p*
　24:24 (Mk. 13:22) if it were *p*, they shall deceive
　26:39 (Mk. 14:35) if it be *p*, let this cup pass
Mk. 9:23 all things are *p* to him that believeth
　14:36 Abba, Father, all things are *p* unto thee
Acts 2:24 was not *p* that he should be holden of it

Rom. 12:18 if it be *p*. . live peaceably with all men
Heb. 10:4 for it is not *p* that the blood of bulls

Post *See also* Pillar

Ex. 12:7 blood, and strike it on the two side *p*
Deut. 6:9 shalt write them upon the *p* of thy house
Is. 6:4 *p* of the door moved at the voice of him
Amos 9:1 smite the lintel. . that the *p* may shake

Post *See also* Messenger

2 Chr. 30:6 so the *p* went with the letters from
Esth. 3:13 sent by *p* into all the king's provinces
　8:10 sent letters by *p* on horseback, and riders
Job 9:25 my days are swifter than a *p*: they flee
Jer. 51:31 one *p* shall run to meet another

Posterity *See also* Offspring, Seed

Gen. 45:7 to preserve you a *p* in the earth
1 Kgs. 21:21 evil upon thee. . will take away thy *p*
Ps. 49:13 folly: yet their *p* approve their sayings
　109:13 his *p* be cut off. . their name be blotted
Dan. 11:4 kingdom. . shall be divided. . not to his *p*
Amos 4:2 with hooks, and your *p* with fishhooks

Pot

Ex. 16:33 take a *p*, and put an omer full of manna
Lev. 6:28 if it be sodden in a brazen *p*, it shall
2 Kgs. 4:40 man of God, there is death in the *p*
Job 41:31 he maketh the sea like a *p* of ointment
Ps. 68:13 though ye have lain among the *p*, yet
Prov. 17:3 (27:21) fining *p* is for silver. . the furnace
Jer. 1:13 I said, I see a seething *p*; and the face
Ezek. 24:3 set on a *p*, set it on. . pour water into it
Zech. 14:21 every *p* in Jerusalem and in Judah shall
Mk. 7:8 tradition of men, as the washing of *p*
Heb. 9:4 wherein was the golden *p* that had manna

Potentate

1 Tim. 6:15 blessed and only *P*, the King of kings

Potiphar Gen. 37:36; 39:1

Potsherd

Job 2:8 he took him a *p* to scrape himself withal
Ps. 22:15 my strength is dried up like a *p*
Prov. 26:23 are like a *p* covered with silver dross
Is. 45:9 let the *p* strive with the *p* of the earth

Pottage

Gen. 25:29 and Jacob sod *p*: and Esau came from the
2 Kgs. 4:38 seethe *p* for the sons of the prophets

Potter

1 Chr. 4:23 the *p*, and those that dwelt among plants
Ps. 2:9 (Rev. 2:27) them in pieces like a *p*'s vessel
Is. 29:16 shall be esteemed as the *p*'s clay
　30:14 break it as the breaking of the *p*' vessel
　41:25 as upon mortar, and as the *p* treadeth clay
　64:8 we are the clay, and thou our *p*
Jer. 18:2 arise, and go down to the *p*'s house
　18:6 Israel, cannot I do with you as this *p*?
　19:1 go and get a *p*'s earthen bottle, and break
Lam. 4:2 pitchers, the work of the hands of the *p*!
Zech. 11:13 pieces of silver, and cast them to the *p*
Mt. 27:7 bought with them the *p*'s field, to bury
Rom. 9:21 hath not the *p* power over the clay

Pound

Lk. 19:13 ten servants, and delivered them ten *p*
Jn. 12:3 took Mary a *p* of ointment of spikenard
　19:39 myrrh and aloes, about a hundred *p* weight

Pour

Ex. 4:9 take of the water. . *p* it upon the dry land

1 Sam. 1:15 but have *p* out my soul before the LORD
2 Sam. 23:16 (1 Chr. 11:18) not drink . . but *p* it out
Job 10:10 hast thou not *p* me out as milk
  16:20 scorn me: but mine eye *p* out tears unto God
  29:6 and the rock *p* me out rivers of oil
  30:16 now my soul is *p* out upon me; the days of
  36:27 they *p* down rain according to the vapor
Ps. 22:14 I am *p* out like water, and all my bones
  42:4 when I remember . . I *p* out my soul in me
  45:2 grace is *p* into thy lips: therefore God hath
  62:8 *p* out your heart before him: God is a refuge
  79:6 *p* out thy wrath upon the heathen that have
Prov. 1:23 behold, I will *p* out my spirit unto you
  15:28 the mouth of the wicked *p* out evil things
Is. 26:16 they *p* out a prayer when they chastening
  32:15 until the Spirit be *p* upon us from on high
  44:3 *p* water upon him that is thirsty . . *p* my Spirit
  45:8 let the skies *p* down righteousness
  53:12 because he hath *p* out his soul unto death
Jer. 6:11 I will *p* it out upon the children abroad
  7:20 my fury shall be *p* out upon this place
  10:25 *p* out thy fury upon the heathen that know
  18:21 and *p* out their blood by the force of the
Lam. 2:19 *p* out thine heart like water before the
Ezek. 7:8 will I shortly *p* out my fury upon thee
  39:29 *p* out my Spirit upon the house of Israel
Hos. 5:10 therefore I will *p* out my wrath upon them
Joel 2:28 (Acts 2:17) *p* out my Spirit upon all flesh
Amos 5:8 (9:6) *p* them out upon the face of the earth
Mic. 1:6 I will *p* down the stones . . into the valley
Nah. 1:6 of his anger? his fury is *p* out like fire
Zech. 12:10 *p* upon the house of David . . the spirit
Mal. 3:10 windows of heaven . . *p* you out a blessing
Mt. 26:7 (Mk. 14:3) ointment, and *p* it on his head
Jn. 2:15 *p* out the changers' money, and overthrew
  13:5 he *p* water into a basin, and began to wash
Acts 10:45 on the Gentiles also was *p* out the gift
Rev. 14:10 wine of the wrath of God, which is *p* out
  16:1 (16:2, 3, 4, 8, 10, 12, 17) *p* out the vials . . upon

Poverty

Gen. 45:11 lest thou, and thy household . . come to *p*
Prov. 6:11 (24:34) thy *p* come as one that travaleth
  10:15 the destruction of the poor is their *p*
  11:24 is that withholdeth . . but it tendeth to *p*
  13:18 *p* and shame shall be to him that refuseth
  20:13 love not sleep, lest thou come to *p*
  23:21 drunkard and the glutton shall come to *p*
  28:19 followeth after vain persons shall have *p*
  30:8 give me neither *p* nor riches; feed me with
  31:7 let him drink, and forget his *p*
2 Cor. 8:2 their deep *p* abounded unto the riches
  8:9 poor, that ye through his *p* might be rich
Rev. 2:9 I know thy works, and tribulation, and *p*

Powder

Deut. 28:24 make the rain of thy land *p* and dust
2 Kgs. 23:6 stamped it small to *p*, and cast the *p*
Mt. 21:44 (Lk. 20:18) fall, it will grind him to *p*

Power *See also* Authority, Force, Might, Strength

Gen. 32:28 hast thou *p* with God and with men
Ex. 9:16 (Rom. 9:17) to show in thee my *p*
  15:6 thy right hand, O LORD, is . . glorious in *p*
  32:11 brought forth out of . . Egypt with great *p*
Lev. 26:37 have no *p* to stand before your enemies
Num. 14:17 beseech . . let the *p* of my LORD be great
Deut. 4:37 and brought thee out . . with his mighty *p*
  8:17 my *p* and the might of mine hand hath gotten
  8:18 it is he that giveth thee *p* to get wealth
Josh. 17:17 art a great people, and hast great *p*

1 Chr. 29:11 thine . . is the greatness, and the *p*
2 Chr. 25:8 God hath *p* to help, and to cast down
Ezra 8:22 but his *p* and his wrath is against all
Neh. 1:10 whom thou hast redeemed by thy great *p*
Job 1:12 behold, all that he hath is in thy *p*; only
  23:6 will he plead against me with his great *p*?
  26:14 the thunder of his *p* who can understand?
  37:23 he is excellent in *p*, and in judgment
Ps. 21:13 so will we sing and praise thy *p*
  37:35 I have seen the wicked in great *p*
  49:15 will redeem my soul from the *p* of the grave
  59:16 but I will sing of thy *p*; yea, I will sing
  62:11 I heard this; that *p* belongeth unto God
  63:2 to see thy *p* and thy glory, so as I have
  66:3 through the greatness of thy *p* shall thine
  90:11 who knoweth the *p* of thine anger?
  106:8 he might make his mighty *p* to be known
  111:6 hath showed his people the *p* of his works
  147:5 great is our Lord, and of great *p*
Prov. 3:27 when it is in the *p* of thine hand to do it
  18:21 and life are in the *p* of the tongue
Eccl. 8:8 no man that hath *p* over the spirit to
Is. 40:29 he giveth *p* to the faint; and to them
  50:2 cannot redeem? or have I no *p* to deliver?
Jer. 27:5 by my great *p* and by my outstretched arm
Dan. 2:37 God . . hath given thee a kingdom, *p*, and
  8:24 his *p* shall be mighty, but not by his own *p*
  12:7 scatter the *p* of the holy people, all these
Hos. 12:3 and by his strength he had *p* with God
  13:14 I will ransom them from the *p* of the grave
Mic. 3:8 I am full of *p* by the Spirit of the LORD
Nah. 1:3 the LORD is slow to anger, and great in *p*
Hab. 1:11 offend, imputing this his *p* unto his god
  2:9 that he may be delivered from the *p* of evil!
  3:4 his hand: and there was the hiding of his *p*
Zech. 4:6 not by might, nor by *p*, but by my Spirit
Mt. 6:13 for thine is the kingdom, and the *p*
  9:6 (Mk. 2:10; Lk. 5:24) *p* on earth to forgive sins
  10:1 (Mk. 3:15; 6:7; Lk. 9:1) *p* against . . spirits
  22:29 (Mk. 12:24) the Scriptures, nor the *p* of God
  24:29 (Mk. 13:25; Lk. 21:26) *p* . . shall be shaken
  24:30 (Mk. 13:26; Lk. 21:27) coming . . with *p*
  26:64 (Mk. 14:62; Lk. 22:69) on the right hand of *p*
  28:18 all *p* is given unto me in heaven and in
Lk. 1:35 *p* of the Highest shall overshadow thee
  4:6 all this *p* will I give thee, and the glory
  4:14 Jesus returned in the *p* of the Spirit into
  4:32 at his doctrine: for his word was with *p*
  5:17 the *p* of the Lord was present to heal them
  9:43 they were all amazed at the mighty *p* of God
  10:19 I give unto you *p* to tread on serpents
  12:5 fear him, which . . hath *p* to cast into hell
  22:53 this is your hour, and the *p* of darkness
  24:49 until ye be endued with *p* from on high
Jn. 1:12 them gave he *p* to become the sons of God
  10:18 I have *p* to lay it down, and I have *p* to
  17:2 thou hast given him *p* over all flesh, that
  19:11 thou couldest have no *p* at all against me
Acts 1:8 but ye shall receive *p*, after that the
  3:12 on us, as though our own *p* or holiness
  4:7 what *p*, or by what name, have ye done this?
  4:33 with great *p* gave the apostles witness of
  6:8 and Stephen, full of faith and *p*, did great
  8:10 saying, This man is the great *p* of God
  8:19 give me also this *p*, that on whomsoever I
  10:38 anointed . . with the Holy Ghost and with *p*
  26:18 to light, and from the *p* of Satan unto God
Rom. 1:4 and declared to be the Son of God with *p*
  1:16 it is the *p* of God unto salvation to every
  1:20 even his eternal *p* and Godhead
  8:38 nor angels, nor principalities, nor *p*
  9:21 hath not the potter *p* over the clay
  13:1 no *p* but of God: the *p* that be are ordained

Rom. 13:2 resisteth the *p*, resisteth the ordinance of
15:13 in hope, through the *p* of the Holy Ghost
15:19 and wonders, by the *p* of the Spirit of God
16:25 now to him that is of *p* to stablish you
1 Cor. 1:18 us which are saved, it is the *p* of God
1:24 Christ the *p* of God, and the wisdom of God
2:4 but in demonstration of the Spirit and of *p*
2:5 in the wisdom of men, but in the *p* of God
4:20 the kingdom of God is not in word, but in *p*
5:4 and my spirit, with the *p* of our Lord Jesus
6:12 but I will not be brought under the *p* of any
6:14 Lord, and will also raise up us by his own *p*
7:37 no necessity, but hath *p* over his own will
9:12 if others be partakers of this *p* over you
9:18 charge, that I abuse not my *p* in the gospel
11:10 to have *p* on her head because of the angels
15:43 it is sown in weakness, it is raised in *p*
2 Cor. 4:7 the excellency of the *p* may be of God
6:7 by the word of truth, by the *p* of God
12:9 that the *p* of Christ may rest upon me
13:4 weakness, yet he liveth by the *p* of God
Eph. 1:19 what is the exceeding greatness of his *p*
1:21 far above all principality, and *p*, and might
2:2 according to the prince of the *p* of the air
3:7 unto me by the effectual working of his *p*
3:20 think, according to the *p* that worketh in us
6:10 strong in the Lord, and in the *p* of his might
6:12 against principalities, against *p*, against
Phil. 3:10 know him, and the *p* of his resurrection
Col. 1:11 all might, according to his glorious *p*
1:13 hath delivered us from the *p* of darkness
2:10 which is the head of all principality and *p*
1 Thes. 1:5 unto you in word only, but also in *p*
2 Thes. 1:11 goodness, and the work of faith with *p*
2:9 is after the working of Satan with all *p*
1 Tim. 6:16 to whom be honor and *p* everlasting
2 Tim. 1:7 spirit of fear; but of *p*, and of love
3:5 having a form of godliness, but denying the *p*
Heb. 1:3 upholding all things by the word of his *p*
2:14 might destroy him that had the *p* of death
6:5 word of God, and the *p* of the world to come
7:16 who is made . . after the *p* of an endless life
1 Pet. 1:5 are kept by the *p* of God through faith
3:22 authorities and *p* being made subject unto
2 Pet. 1:3 as his divine *p* hath given unto us all
1:16 known unto you the *p* and coming of our Lord
Rev. 2:26 to him will I give *p* over the nations
5:12 worthy is the Lamb . . to receive *p*
11:3 and I will give *p* unto my two witnesses
12:10 and the *p* of his Christ: for the accuser
13:12 exerciseth all the *p* of the first beast
15:8 smoke from the glory of God, and from his *p*
20:6 on such the second death hath no *p*

Powerful

Ps. 29:4 voice of the LORD is *p* . . full of majesty
2 Cor. 10:10 his letters . . are weighty and *p*
Heb. 4:12 word of God is quick, and *p*, and sharper

Praise *See also* Exalt, Extol, Glorify, Honor, Magnify

Gen. 29:35 son; and she said, Now will I *p* the LORD
49:8 Judah, thou art he . . thy brethren shall *p*
Ex. 15:11 thee, glorious in holiness, fearful in *p*
Lev. 19:24 fruit thereof shall be holy to *p* the LORD
Deut. 10:21 he is thy *p*, and he is thy God, that
Judg. 5:2 *p* ye the LORD for the avenging of Israel
16:24 when the people saw him, they *p* their god
2 Sam. 22:4 call on the LORD, who is worthy to be *p*
22:50 (Ps. 18:49) and I will sing *p* unto thy name
1 Chr. 16:25 (Ps. 48:1; 96:4) LORD, and greatly to be *p*
16:35 (Ps. 106:47) thy holy name, and glory in thy *p*

1 Chr. 23:5 thousand *p* the LORD with the instruments
29:13 God, we thank thee, and *p* thy glorious name
2 Chr. 20:21 that should *p* the beauty of holiness
Ezra 3:10 *p* the LORD, after the ordinance of David
Ps. 7:17 *p* the LORD according to his righteousness
9:1 (138:1) I will *p* thee, O LORD, with my whole
9:14 I may show forth all thy *p* in the gates
21:13 exalted . . so will we sing and *p* thy power
22:3 holy, O thou that inhabitest the *p* of Israel
22:22 (Heb. 2:12) midst of the congregation will I *p*
22:23 ye that fear the LORD, *p* him; all ye
28:7 rejoiceth; and with my song will I *p* him
30:9 the dust *p* thee? shall it declare thy truth?
30:12 that my glory may sing *p* to thee
33:1 righteous: for *p* is comely for the upright
33:2 *p* the LORD with harp: sing unto him with
34:1 his *p* shall continually be in my mouth
35:18 in the great congregation: I will *p* thee
42:5 yet *p* him for the help of his countenance
43:4 upon the harp will I *p* thee, O God my God
43:5 hope in God: for I shall yet *p* him, who is
45:17 shall the people *p* thee for ever and ever
47:6 sing *p* to God, sing *p*: sing *p* unto our King
48:10 God, so is thy *p* unto the ends of the earth
49:18 men will *p* thee, when thou doest well to
50:23 whoso offereth *p* glorifieth me: and to him
51:15 lips; and my mouth shall show forth thy *p*
54:6 I will *p* thy name, O LORD; for it is good
56:4 in God I will *p* his word, in God I have put
57:9 (108:3) *p* thee, O Lord, among the people
61:8 will I sing *p* unto thy name for ever, that I
63:3 is better than life, my lips shall *p* thee
65:1 *p* waiteth for thee, O God, in Zion: and unto
66:2 the honor of his name: make his *p* glorious
67:3 *p* thee, O God; let all the people *p* thee
71:6 my *p* shall be continually of thee
71:8 let my mouth be filled with thy *p* and with
71:22 I will also *p* thee with the psaltery
72:15 him continually; and daily shall he be *p*
74:21 let the poor and needy *p* thy name
76:10 surely the wrath of man shall *p* thee
88:10 shall the dead arise and *p* thee?
89:5 and the heavens shall p thy wonders, O LORD
92:1 a good thing to give thanks . . and to sing *p*
99:3 let them *p* thy great and terrible name
100:4 thanksgiving, and into his courts with *p*
102:18 people which shall be created shall *p* the
106:2 of the LORD? who can show forth all his *p*?
107:8 (107:15, 21, 31) that men would *p* the LORD
107:32 and *p* him in the assembly of the elders
111:1 *p* ye the LORD. I will *p* the LORD with my
111:10 his commandments: his *p* endureth for ever
113:1 (135:1) *p* ye the LORD . . *p* the name of the
113:3 from the rising . . LORD's name is to be *p*
115:17 the dead *p* not the LORD, neither any that
117:1 (Rom. 15:11) *p* the LORD . . ye nations: *p*
118:21 I will *p* thee: for thou hast heard me
118:28 thou art my God, and I will *p* thee
119:7 I will *p* thee with uprightness of heart
119:164 seven times a day do I *p* thee, because
119:175 let my soul live, and it shall *p* thee
135:1 *p* ye the LORD. *P* ye the name of the LORD
138:2 and *p* thy name for thy loving-kindness
138:4 all the kings of the earth shall *p* thee
139:14 I will *p* thee; for I am . . wonderfully made
145:2 and I will *p* thy name for ever and ever
145:4 one generation shall *p* thy works to another
145:10 all thy works shall *p* thee, O LORD
146:1 *p* the LORD, *P* the LORD, O my soul
146:2 I live will I *p* the LORD: I will sing *p*
147:1 *p* ye the LORD: for it is good to sing *p*
147:12 the LORD, O Jerusalem; *p* thy God
148:1 *p* ye the LORD from the heavens: *p* him in

Ps. 148:2 *p* ye him, all his angels: *p* ye him, all
148:13 let them *p* the name of the LORD
149:6 let the high *p* of God be in their mouth
150:1 *p* God in his sanctuary: *p* him in the
150:6 let every thing that hath breath *p* the LORD
Prov. 27:2 let another man *p* thee, and not thine
28:4 they that forsake the law *p* the wicked
31:28 blessed; her husband also, and he *p* her
31:30 woman that feareth the LORD, she shall be *p*
31:31 and let her own works *p* her in the gates
Eccl. 4:2 I *p* the dead . . more than the living which
Is. 12:1 O LORD, I will *p* thee: though thou wast
25:1 I will exalt thee, I will *p* thy name
38:18 for the grave cannot *p* thee, death cannot
38:19 the living, he shall *p* thee, as I do this day
42:8 to another, neither my *p* to graven images
42:10 song, and his *p* from the end of the earth
43:21 for myself; they shall show forth my *p*
60:18 call thy walls Salvation, and thy gates *P*
62:7 and till he make Jerusalem a *p* in the earth
Jer. 17:14 and I shall be saved: for thou art my *p*
20:13 *p* ye the LORD: for he hath delivered the
33:11 *p* the LORD of hosts: for the LORD is good
51:41 how is the *p* of the whole earth surprised!
Dan. 2:23 I thank thee, and *p* thee, O thou God of
4:37 now I Nebuchadnezzar *p* and extol and honor
5:4 they drank wine, and *p* the gods of gold
Joel 2:26 be satisfied, and *p* the name of the LORD
Hab. 3:3 heavens, and the earth was full of his *p*
Zeph. 3:20 make you a name and a *p* among all
Mt. 21:16 and sucklings thou hast perfected *p*?
Lk. 1:64 tongue loosed, and he spake, and *p* God
2:13 a multitude of the heavenly host *p* God
2:20 shepherds returned, glorifying and *p* God
18:43 people, when they saw it, gave *p* unto God
19:37 disciples began to rejoice and *p* God with
24:53 in the temple, *p* and blessing God. Amen
Jn. 9:24 give God the *p*: we know that this man is
12:43 loved the *p* of men more than the *p* of God
Acts 2:47 *p* God, and having favor with all the
3:8 the temple, walking, and leaping, and *p* God
16:25 Paul and Silas prayed, and sang *p* unto God
Rom. 2:29 whose *p* is not of men, but of God
13:3 do that which is good, and thou shalt have *p*
1 Cor. 4:5 and then shall every man have *p* of God
11:2 I *p* you, brethren, that ye remember me in
11:22 to you? shall I *p* you in this? I *p* you not
2 Cor. 8:18 whose *p* is in the gospel throughout all
Eph. 1:6 to the *p* of the glory of his grace
1:12 that we should be to the *p* of his glory
Phil. 4:8 if there be any *p*, think on these things
Heb. 13:15 let us offer the sacrifice of *p* to God
1 Pet. 1:7 might be found unto *p* and honor
2:9 ye should show forth the *p* of him who hath
2:14 sent by him . . for the *p* of them that do well
4:11 to whom be *p* and dominion for ever and ever
Rev. 19:5 saying, *P* our God, all ye his servants

Prating

Prov. 10:8 but a *p* fool shall fall
3 Jn. 10 doeth, *p* against us with malicious words

Pray *See also* Entreat

Gen. 20:7 he shall *p* for thee, and thou shalt live
20:17 Abraham *p* . . God healed Abimelech
Num. 11:2 when Moses *p* . . fire was quenched
21:7 serpents from us . . Moses *p* for the people
Deut. 9:26 I *p* . . Lord GOD, destroy not thy people
1 Sam. 1:10 she was in bitterness of soul, and *p*
1:27 for this child I *p*; and the LORD hath given
7:5 to Mizpah, and I will *p* for you unto the LORD
8:6 king to judge us. And Samuel *p* unto the LORD
12:19 Samuel, *P* for thy servants unto the LORD

1 Sam. 12:23 that I should sin . . in ceasing to *p* for
2 Sam. 7:27 (1 Chr. 17:25) found in his heart to *p*
1 Kgs. 8:33 (2 Chr. 6:24) and confess thy name, and *p*
8:35 (2 Chr. 6:26) if they *p* toward this place
8:54 (2 Chr. 7:1) Solomon had made an end of *p*
13:6 *p* for me, that my hand may be restored me
2 Kgs. 6:17 Elisha *p*, and said, LORD . . open his eyes
19:15 (Is. 37:15) Hezekiah *p* before the LORD
20:2 (Is. 38:2) his face to the wall, and *p*
2 Chr. 7:14 humble themselves, and *p*, and seek my
Ezra 6:10 *p* for the life of the king, and of his
10:1 when Ezra had *p*, and when he had confessed
Neh. 1:4 mourned certain days, and fasted, and *p*
1:6 I *p* before thee now, day and night
2:4 make request? So I *p* to the God of heaven
Job 21:15 profit should we have, if we *p* unto him?
33:26 shall *p* unto God, and he will be favorable
42:10 captivity of Job, when he *p* for his friends
Ps. 5:2 my King, and my God: for unto thee will I *p*
32:6 for this shall every one that is godly *p*
55:17 evening, and morning, and at noon, will I *p*
122:6 *p* for the peace of Jerusalem: they shall
Is. 16:12 Moab . . shall come to his sanctuary to *p*
45:20 image, and *p* unto a god that cannot save
Jer. 7:16 (14:11) *p* not thou for this people
11:14 therefore *p* not thou for this people
29:7 *p* unto the LORD for it: for in the peace
29:12 and ye shall go and *p* unto me, and I will
32:16 purchase unto Baruch . . I *p* unto the LORD
37:3 saying, *P* now unto the LORD our God for us
42:2 *p* for us unto the LORD thy God, even for all
Dan. 6:10 he kneeled . . three times a day, and *p*
9:4 I *p* unto the LORD . . and made my confession
Jon. 2:1 then Jonah *p* unto the LORD his God out of
Zech. 7:2 sent . . Regem-melech, and their men, to *p*
8:21 let us go speedily to *p* before the LORD
Mt. 5:44 (Lk. 6:28) *p* for them which despitefully use
6:5 thou *p*, thou shalt not be as the hypocrites
6:6 thy door, *p* to thy Father which is in secret
6:7 when ye *p*, use not vain repetitions, as the
6:9 (Lk. 11:2) after this manner therefore *p* ye
9:38 (Lk. 10:2) *p* ye . . the Lord of the harvest, that
14:23 (Mk. 6:46) up into a mountain apart to *p*
19:13 that he should put his hands on them, and *p*
24:20 (Mk. 13:18) *p* ye that your flight be not in
26:36 (Mk. 14:32) sit ye here, while I go and *p*
26:39 (Mk. 14:35; Lk. 22:41) a little further . . and *p*
26:41 (Mk. 14:38; Lk. 22:40, 46) watch and *p*, that
ye enter not into temptation
26:53 thinkest thou . . I cannot now *p* to my Father
Mk. 1:35 departed into a solitary place, and there *p*
11:24 when ye *p*, believe that ye receive them
11:25 when ye stand *p*, forgive, if ye have aught
13:33 watch and *p*: for ye know not when the time
Lk. 3:21 that Jesus also being baptized, and *p*
9:18 as he was alone *p*, his disciples were with
9:29 as he *p*, the fashion of his countenance was
18:1 that men ought always to *p*, and not to faint
18:11 the Pharisee stood and *p* thus with himself
22:32 I have *p* for thee, that thy faith fail not
Jn. 14:16 I will *p* the Father, and he shall give
16:26 unto you, that I will *p* the Father for you
17:9 I *p* for them: I *p* not for the world, but
17:15 I *p* not that thou shouldest take them out
17:20 neither *p* I for these alone, but for them
Acts 1:24 they *p*, and said . . Lord, which knowest the
4:31 when they had *p*, the place was shaken where
6:6 they had *p*, they laid their hands on them
8:15 *p* for them, that they might receive the Holy
8:22 repent . . of this thy wickedness, and *p* God
8:24 *p* ye to the Lord for me, that none of these
9:11 called Saul, of Tarsus: for, behold, he *p*
9:40 but Peter put them all forth . . and *p*

Acts 10:2 much alms to the people, and *p* to God
  10:9 Peter went up upon the housetop to *p*
  12:12 where many were gathered together *p*
  13:3 when they had fasted and *p*, and laid their
  14:23 had *p* with fasting, they commended them to
  16:9 there stood a man of Macedonia, and *p* him
  16:25 and at midnight Paul and Silas *p*, and sang
  20:36 spoken, he kneeled down, and *p* with them
  21:5 and we kneeled down on the shore, and *p*
  22:17 while I *p* in the temple, I was in a trance
  28:8 to whom Paul entered in, and *p*. . and healed
Rom. 8:26 for we know not what we should *p* for as
1 Cor. 11:5 but every woman that *p* or prophesieth
  11:13 comely that a woman *p* unto God uncovered
  14:13 an unknown tongue *p* that he may interpret
  14:15 I will *p* with the spirit, and I will *p* with
2 Cor. 5:20 we *p* you in Christ's stead, be ye
  13:7 now I *p* to God that ye do no evil; not that
Eph. 6:18 *p* always with all prayer and supplication
Phil. 1:9 I *p*, that your love may abound yet more
Col. 1:3 we give thanks to God. . *p* always for you
  1:9 day we heard it, do not cease to *p* for you
  4:3 *p* also for us, that God would open unto us a
1 Thes. 3:10 night and day *p* exceedingly that we
  5:17 *p* without ceasing
  5:23 I *p* God your whole spirit and soul and body
  5:25 (2 Thes. 3:1) brethren, *p* for us
2 Thes. 1:11 we *p* always for you, that our God
1 Tim. 2:8 I will therefore that men *p* every where
Heb. 13:18 *p* for us: for we trust we have a good
Jas. 5:13 is any among you afflicted? let him *p*
  5:14 elders of the church; and let them *p* over
  5:16 and *p* one for another, that ye may be healed
  5:17 Elias. . *p* earnestly that it might not rain
1 Jn. 5:16 I do not say that he shall *p* for it
Jude 20 building up yourselves. . *p* in the Holy Ghost

Prayer *See also* Intercession, Meditation, Supplication

2 Sam. 7:27 found in his heart to pray this *p* unto
1 Kgs. 8:28 (2 Chr. 6:19) have thou respect unto the *p*
  9:3 (2 Chr. 7:12) LORD said. . I have heard thy *p*
2 Kgs. 19:4 (Is. 37:4) lift up thy *p* for the remnant
  20:5 (Is. 38:5) heard thy *p*, I have seen thy tears
2 Chr. 6:40 and let thine ears be attent unto the *p*
  30:27 their *p* came up to his holy dwelling
Neh. 1:6 thou mayest hear the *p* of thy servant
  4:9 nevertheless we made our *p* unto our God
Job 15:4 thou castest off fear, and restrainest *p*
  16:17 any injustice in mine hands. . my *p* is pure
  22:27 thou shalt make thy *p* unto him, and he shall
Ps. 5:3 in the morning will I direct my *p* unto thee
  6:9 my supplication; the LORD will receive my *p*
  39:12 hear my *p*, O LORD, and give ear unto my cry
  42:8 with me, and my *p* unto the God of my life
  65:2 O thou that hearest *p*, unto thee shall all
  66:19 he hath attended to the voice of my *p*
  66:20 hath not turned away my *p*, nor his mercy
  69:13 but as for me, my *p* is unto thee, O LORD
  72:15 *p* also shall be made for him continually
  72:20 the *p* of David the son of Jesse are ended
  88:13 and in the morning shall my *p* prevent thee
  102:17 he will regard the *p* of the destitute
  109:4 my adversaries: but I give myself unto *p*
  109:7 him be condemned: and let his *p* become sin
  141:2 my *p* be set forth before thee as incense
  143:1 hear my *p*. . give ear to my supplications
Prov. 15:8 but the *p* of the upright is his delight
  15:29 but he heareth the *p* of the righteous
  28:9 the law, even his *p* shall be abomination
Is. 1:15 yea, when ye make many *p*, I will not hear
  26:16 they poured out a *p* when thy chastening

Is. 56:7 (Mt. 21:13; Mk. 11:17; Lk. 19:46) house of *p*
Jer. 7:16 neither lift up cry nor *p* for them
Lam. 3:44 cloud, that our *p* should not pass through
Dan. 9:3 my face unto the Lord God, to seek by *p*
Jon. 2:7 my *p* came in unto thee, into thine holy
Hab. 3:1 *p* of Habakkuk the prophet upon Shigionoth
Mt. 17:21 (Mk. 9:29) this kind goeth not out but by *p*
  21:22 shall ask in *p*, believing, ye shall receive
  23:14 (Mk. 12:40; Lk. 20:47) pretense make long *p*
Lk. 1:13 fear not, Zacharias: for thy *p* is heard
  2:37 served God with fastings and *p* night and day
  5:33 disciples of John fast often, and make *p*
  6:12 and continued all night in *p* to God
  22:45 when he rose up from *p*, and was come to his
Acts 1:14 all continued with one accord in *p* and
  2:42 fellowship. . in breaking of bread, and in *p*
  6:4 but we will give ourselves continually to *p*
  10:4 thy *p* and thine alms are come up for a
  10:31 Cornelius, thy *p* is heard, and thine alms
  12:5 in prison: but *p* was made without ceasing
  16:13 a river side, where *p* was wont to be made
Rom. 1:9 (Eph. 1:16; 1 Thes. 1:2; Phlm. 4) I make
  mention of you always in my *p*
  10:1 my heart's desire and *p* to God for Israel
  12:12 in tribulation; continuing instant in *p*
  15:30 strive together with me in your *p* to God
1 Cor. 7:5 may give yourselves to fasting and *p*
2 Cor. 1:11 ye also helping together by *p* for us
Eph. 6:18 praying always with all *p* and supplication
Phil. 1:4 always in every *p* of mine for you all
  1:19 shall turn to my salvation through your *p*
  4:6 but in every thing by *p* and supplication
Col. 4:2 continue in *p*, and watch in the same with
  4:12 laboring fervently for you in *p*, that ye
1 Tim. 2:1 that, first of all, supplications, *p*
  4:5 for it is sanctified by the word of God and *p*
2 Tim. 1:3 I have remembrance of thee in my *p*
Phlm. 22 through your *p* I shall be given unto you
Heb. 5:7 when he had offered up *p* and supplications
Jas. 5:15 and the *p* of faith shall save the sick
  5:16 the effectual fervent *p* of a righteous man
1 Pet. 3:7 that your *p* be not hindered
  3:12 righteous. . his ears are open unto their *p*
  4:7 be ye therefore sober, and watch unto *p*
Rev. 5:8 full of odors, which are the *p* of all saints
  8:3 he should offer it with the *p* of all saints

Preach *See also* Declare, Proclaim, Prophesy, Publish

Neh. 6:7 also appointed prophets to *p* of thee at
Ps. 40:9 *p* righteousness in the great congregation
Is. 61:1 (Lk. 4:18) anointed me to *p* good tidings
Jon. 3:2 arise, go unto Nineveh. . and *p* unto it
Mt. 3:1 John the Baptist, *p* in the wilderness
  4:17 Jesus began to *p*, and to say, Repent
  4:23 (9:35) *p* the gospel of the kingdom. . healing
  10:7 *p*, saying, The kingdom of heaven is at hand
  10:27 in the ear, that *p* ye upon the housetops
  11:1 departed thence to teach and to *p* in their
  11:5 (Lk. 7:22) poor have the gospel *p* to them
  24:14 shall be *p* in all the world for a witness
  26:13 (Mk. 14:9) wheresoever this gospel shall be *p*
Mk. 1:4 (Lk. 3:3) and *p* the baptism of repentance
  1:38 (Lk. 4:43) into the next towns, that I may *p*
  1:39 (Lk. 4:44) he *p* in their synagogues
  2:2 gathered together. . he *p* the word unto them
  6:12 (Lk. 9:6) they went out, and *p* that men should
  16:15 world, and *p* the gospel to every creature
  16:20 and they went forth, and *p* every where
Lk. 8:1 *p* and showing the glad tidings
  9:2 *p* the kingdom of God, and to heal the sick
  9:60 dead: but go thou and *p* the kingdom of God

Lk. 24:47 remission of sins should be *p* in his name
Acts 3:20 Christ, which before was *p* unto you
 4:2 and *p* through Jesus the resurrection from
 5:42 they ceased not to teach and *p* Jesus Christ
 8:4 scattered abroad went every where *p* the word
 8:5 the city of Samaria, and *p* Christ unto them
 8:25 when they had testified and *p* the word of
 8:35 at the same Scripture, and *p* unto him Jesus
 9:20 he *p* Christ in synagogues, that he is the
 9:27 how he had *p* boldly at Damascus in the name
 10:36 *p* peace by Jesus Christ: (he is Lord of all:)
 10:37 after the baptism which John *p*
 10:42 and he commanded us to *p* unto the people
 11:19 *p* the word to none but unto the Jews only
 13:38 is *p* unto you the forgiveness of sins
 13:42 that these words might be *p* to them
 14:15 *p* unto you that ye should turn from these
 16:6 forbidden of the Holy Ghost to *p* . . in Asia
 16:10 called us for to *p* the gospel unto them
 17:3 this Jesus, whom I *p* unto you, is Christ
 17:18 he *p* unto them Jesus, and the resurrection
 28:31 *p* the kingdom of God, and teaching
Rom. 1:15 I am ready to *p* . . to you that are at Rome
 2:21 *p* a man should not steal, dost thou steal?
 10:8 in thy heart . . the word of faith, which we *p*
 10:15 and how shall they *p*, except they be sent?
 15:19 unto Illyricum, I have fully *p* the gospel
 15:20 yea, so have I strived to *p* the gospel
1 Cor. 1:17 sent me not to baptize, but to *p* the
 1:23 but we *p* Christ crucified, unto the Jews and
 9:14 which *p* the gospel should live of the gospel
 9:16 woe is unto me, if I *p* not the gospel!
 9:27 when I have *p* to others, I myself should
 15:2 saved, if ye keep in memory what I *p* unto
 15:11 were I or they, so we *p*, and so ye believed
 15:12 if Christ be *p* that he rose from the dead
2 Cor. 4:5 we *p* not ourselves, but Christ Jesus
 10:16 the gospel in the regions beyond you
 11:4 cometh *p* another Jesus, whom we have not *p*
Gal. 1:8 *p* any other gospel unto you than that
 1:16 that I might *p* him among the heathen
 1:23 persecuted us in times past now *p* the faith
 3:8 *p* before the gospel unto Abraham, saying
 5:11 if I yet *p* circumcision, why do I yet suffer
Eph. 2:17 and *p* peace to you which were afar off
 3:8 *p* among the Gentiles the unsearchable riches
Phil. 1:15 some indeed *p* Christ even of envy and
Col. 1:28 whom we *p*, warning every man, and
1 Thes. 2:9 chargeable unto any of you, we *p* unto
1 Tim. 3:16 seen of angels, *p* unto the Gentiles
2 Tim. 4:2 *p* the word; be instant in season, out of
Heb. 4:2 unto us was the gospel *p*, as well as unto
1 Pet. 1:12 that have *p* the gospel unto you with
 1:25 the word which by the gospel is *p* unto you
 3:19 he went and *p* unto the spirits in prison
 4:6 for this cause was the gospel *p* also to them
Rev. 14:6 having the everlasting gospel to *p* unto

Preacher

Eccl. 1:1 the words of the *P*, the son of David
 1:12 I the *P* was king over Israel in Jerusalem
 12:9 the *P* was wise, he still taught the people
Rom. 10:14 and how shall they hear without a *p*?
1 Tim. 2:7 (2 Tim. 1:11) ordained a *p*, and an apostle
2 Pet. 2:5 but saved Noah . . a *p* of righteousness

Preaching *See also* Preach

Jon. 3:2 go . . preach unto it the *p* that I bid thee
Mt. 12:41 (Lk. 11:32) they repented at the *p* of Jonas
Rom. 16:25 to my gospel, and the *p* of Jesus Christ
1 Cor. 1:18 *p* of the cross is to them that perish
 1:21 pleased God by the foolishness of *p* to save
 2:4 my *p* was not with enticing words of man's

1 Cor. 15:14 if Christ be not risen, then is our *p* vain
2 Tim. 4:17 that by me the *p* might be fully known
Tit. 1:3 in due times manifested his word through *p*

Precept *See also* Commandment, Law, Statute

Neh. 9:14 commandedst them *p*, statutes, and laws
Ps. 119:4 commanded us to keep thy *p* diligently
 119:15 I will meditate in thy *p*, and have respect
 119:45 I will walk at liberty: for I seek thy *p*
 119:69 but I will keep thy *p* with my whole heart
 119:93 I will never forget thy *p*: for with them
 119:104 through thy *p* I get understanding
 119:128 I esteem all thy *p* concerning all things
 119:159 consider how I love thy *p*: quicken me
Is. 28:10 *p* must be upon *p*, upon *p*; line upon
 29:13 fear toward me is taught by the *p* of men
Jer. 35:18 Jonadab your father, and kept all his *p*
Dan. 9:5 rebelled, even by departing from thy *p*
Mk. 10:5 hardness of your heart he wrote you this *p*
Heb. 9:19 for when Moses had spoken every *p* to all

Precious

Gen. 24:53 to her brother and to her mother *p* things
Deut. 33:13 for the *p* things of heaven, for the
1 Sam. 3:1 word of the LORD was *p* in those days
 26:21 harm, because my soul was *p* in thine eyes
2 Kgs. 1:13 life of these fifty . . be *p* in thy sight
Ps. 49:8 the redemption of their soul is *p*
 72:14 and *p* shall their blood be in his sight
 116:15 *p* in the sight of the LORD is the death
 126:6 goeth forth and weepeth, bearing *p* seed
 139:17 how *p* . . are thy thoughts unto me, O God!
Prov. 3:15 she is more *p* than rubies: and all the
 12:27 but the substance of a diligent man is *p*
Is. 13:12 I will make a man more *p* than fine gold
 28:16 (1 Pet. 2:6) I lay in Zion . . a *p* corner stone
 43:4 since thou wast *p* in my sight, thou hast
Jer. 15:19 if thou take forth the *p* from the vile
Lam. 4:2 *p* sons of Zion, comparable to fine gold
Mt. 26:7 (Mk. 14:3) alabaster box of very *p* ointment
1 Pet. 1:7 trial of your faith, being much more *p*
 1:19 with the *p* blood of Christ, as of a lamb
 2:4 disallowed . . of men, but chosen of God, and *p*
 2:7 unto you therefore which believe he is *p*
2 Pet. 1:1 that have obtained like *p* faith with us
 1:4 given unto us exceeding great and *p* promises

Predestinate *See also* Foreordain

Rom. 8:29 whom he did foreknow, he also did *p* to be
Eph. 1:5 having *p* us unto the adoption of children
 1:11 being *p* according to the purpose of him who

Preeminence

Eccl. 3:19 so that a man hath no *p* above a beast
Col. 1:18 that in all things he might have the *p*
3 Jn. 9 Diotrephes, who loveth to have the *p* among

Prefer

Esth. 2:9 and he *p* her and her maids unto the best
Ps. 137:6 if I *p* not Jerusalem above my chief joy
Dan. 6:3 Daniel was *p* above the presidents
Jn. 1:15 (1:27) that cometh after me is *p* before me
Rom. 12:10 brotherly love; in honor *p* one another
1 Tim. 5:21 observe . . without *p* one before another

Premeditate

Mk. 13:11 what ye shall speak, neither do ye *p*

Preparation

1 Chr. 22:5 I will therefore now make *p* for it
Prov. 16:1 the *p* of the heart . . is from the LORD

Mt. 27:62 next day, that followed the day of the *p*
Mk. 15:42 (Lk. 23:54; Jn. 19:31, 42) it was the *p*
Jn. 19:14 it was the *p* of the passover, and about
Eph. 6:15 shod with the *p* of the gospel of peace

Prepare

Gen. 24:31 I have *p* the house, and room for the
Ex. 15:2 is my God, and I will *p* him a habitation
    23:20 bring thee into the place which I have *p*
Josh. 1:11 *p* you victuals; for. . ye shall pass over
1 Sam. 7:3 *p* your hearts unto the LORD, and serve
    23:22 go, I pray you, *p* yet, and know and see his
1 Chr. 22:5 so David *p* abundantly before his death
    29:18 of thy people, and *p* their heart unto thee
2 Chr. 20:33 yet the people had not *p* their hearts
    30:19 that *p* his heart to seek God, the LORD God
Job 8:8 *p* thyself to the search of their fathers
    11:13 if thou *p* thine heart, and stretch out
Ps. 9:7 the LORD. . hath *p* his throne for judgment
    10:17 humble: thou wilt *p* their heart, thou wilt
    23:5 thou *p* a table before me in the presence of
    61:7 O *p* mercy and truth, which may preserve him
    65:9 thou *p* them corn, when thou hast so provided
    68:10 O God, hast *p* of thy goodness for the poor
    80:9 thou *p* room before it, and didst cause it
    103:19 the LORD hath *p* his throne in the heavens
    107:36 that they may *p* a city for habitation
    147:8 who *p* rain for the earth, who maketh grass
Prov. 8:27 when he *p* the heavens, I was there
    30:25 ants. . yet they *p* their meat in the summer
Is. 21:5 *p* the table, watch in the watchtower, eat
    40:3 (Mt. 3:3; Mk. 1:3; Lk. 3:4) *p* ye the way of the
    62:10 *p* ye the way of the people; cast up, cast
    64:4 (1 Cor. 2:9) what he hath *p* for him that
Hos. 2:8 silver and gold, which they *p* for Baal
Amos 4:12 unto thee, *p* to meet thy God, O Israel
Jon. 1:17 had *p* a great fish to swallow up Jonah
    4:6 God *p* a gourd. . to come up over Jonah
    4:7 God *p* a worm when the morning rose
    4:8 God *p* a vehement east wind; and the sun beat
Zeph. 1:7 LORD hath *p* a sacrifice, he hath bid his
Mal. 3:1 (Mt. 11:10; Mk. 1:2; Lk. 7:27) messenger. .
    he shall *p* the way
Mt. 20:23 (Mk. 10:40) for whom it is *p* of my Father
    26:17 (Mk. 14:12; Lk. 22:8) we *p*. . the passover?
Lk. 1:76 before the face of the Lord to *p* his ways
    2:31 thou hast *p* before the face of all people
    12:47 knew his lord's will, and *p* not himself
Jn. 14:2 have told you. I go to *p* a place for you
Rom. 9:23 vessels of mercy, which he had afore *p*
1 Cor. 2:9 which God hath *p* for them that love him
    14:8 sound, who shall *p* himself to the battle?
Heb. 10:5 wouldest not, but a body hast thou *p* me
    11:7 *p* an ark to the saving of his house
    11:16 their God: for he hath *p* for them a city

Prepared See also Prepare

Lk. 1:17 to make ready a people *p* for the Lord
2 Tim. 2:21 sanctified. . and *p* unto every good work
Rev. 21:2 *p* as a bride adorned for her husband

Presbytery

1 Tim. 4:14 the laying on of the hands of the *p*

Prescribe

Is. 10:1 that write grievousness which they have *p*

Presence

Gen. 3:8 hid themselves from the *p* of the LORD God
    4:16 and Cain went out from the *p* of the LORD
    47:15 give us bread. . why should we die in thy *p*?
Ex. 33:14 my *p* shall go with thee, and I will give
2 Kgs. 24:20 (Jer. 52:3) had cast them out from his *p*

1 Chr. 16:33 trees. . sing out at the *p* of the LORD
Job 1:12 Satan went forth from the *p* of the LORD
Ps. 16:11 path of life: in thy *p* is fulness of joy
    17:2 let my sentence come forth from thy *p*
    23:5 preparest a table. . in the *p* of mine enemies
    31:20 thou shalt hide them in the secret of thy *p*
    51:11 cast me not away from thy *p*; and take not
    95:2 let us come before his *p* with thanksgiving
    97:5 hills melted like wax at the *p* of the LORD
    100:2 come before his *p* with singing
    114:7 tremble, thou earth, at the *p* of the Lord
    116:14 pay my vows. . in the *p* of all his people
    139:7 Spirit? or whither shall I flee from thy *p*?
    140:13 the upright shall dwell in thy *p*
Prov. 14:7 go from the *p* of a foolish man, when
Is. 63:9 was afflicted. . angel of his *p* saved them
    64:1 that the mountains might flow down at thy *p*
    64:2 that the nations may tremble at thy *p*!
Jer. 5:22 will ye not tremble at my *p*, which have
    23:39 will forsake you. . and cast you out of my *p*
Ezek. 38:20 shall shake at my *p*, and the mountains
Jon. 1:3 flee unto Tarshish from the *p* of the LORD
Zeph. 1:7 hold thy peace at the *p* of the Lord GOD
Lk. 1:19 I am Gabriel, that stand in the *p* of God
    13:26 to say, We have eaten and drunk in thy *p*
    15:10 joy in the *p* of the angels of God over one
Acts 3:13 denied him in the *p* of Pilate, when he
    3:19 times of refreshing. . from the *p* of the Lord
1 Cor. 1:29 that no flesh should glory in his *p*
2 Cor. 10:1 who in *p* am base. . being absent am bold
    10:10 but his bodily *p* is weak, and his speech
Phil. 2:12 obeyed, not as in my *p* only, but now
2 Thes. 1:9 destruction from the *p* of the Lord
Heb. 9:24 now to appear in the *p* of God for us
Jude 24 present you faultless before the *p* of his
Rev. 14:10 *p* of the holy angels, and. . *p* of the Lamb

Present (adjective)

Ps. 46:1 and strength, a very *p* help in trouble
Lk. 5:17 the power of the Lord was *p* to heal them
Jn. 14:25 spoken unto you, being yet *p* with you
Acts 10:33 are we all here *p* before God, to hear
Rom. 7:18 to will is *p* with me; but how to perform
    7:21 when I would do good, evil is *p* with me
    8:18 sufferings of this *p* time are not worthy to
1 Cor. 3:22 or things *p*, or things to come; all are
    5:3 absent in body, but *p* in spirit, have judged
    7:26 that this is good for the *p* distress
2 Cor. 5:8 absent from the body. . *p* with the Lord
Gal. 1:4 might deliver us from this *p* evil world
    4:18 always. . and not only when I am *p* with you
    4:20 I desire to be *p* with you now, and to
2 Tim. 4:10 forsaken me, having loved this *p* world
Tit. 2:12 live soberly. . and godly, in this *p* world
Heb. 12:11 no chastening for the *p* seemeth to be

Present (noun) See also Gift

Gen. 32:13 took of that. . a *p* for Esau his brother
    43:11 the best fruits. . and carry down the man a *p*
1 Sam. 10:27 despised him, and brought him no *p*
1 Kgs. 9:16 a *p* unto his daughter, Solomon's wife
    10:25 (2 Chr. 9:24) brought every man his *p*
2 Kgs. 16:8 sent it for a *p* to the king of Assyria
    18:31 (Is. 36:16) make an agreement with me by a *p*
2 Chr. 32:23 gifts unto the LORD. . and *p* to Hezekiah
Ps. 68:29 Jerusalem shall kings bring *p* unto thee
    72:10 kings of Tarshish and. . isles shall bring *p*
Is. 18:7 shall the *p* be brought unto the LORD of hosts
Ezek. 27:15 brought thee for a *p*, horns of ivory

Present (verb) See also Give, Offer

Ex. 34:2 mount Sinai, and *p* thyself there to me
Lev. 14:11 shall *p* the man that is to be made clean

Mt. 2:11 *p* unto him gifts; gold, and frankincense
Lk. 2:22 him to Jerusalem, to *p* him to the Lord
Rom. 12:1 that ye *p* your bodies a living sacrifice
2 Cor. 11:2 may *p* you as a chaste virgin to Christ
Eph. 5:27 might *p* it to himself a glorious church
Col. 1:22 *p* you holy. . unblamable and unreprovable
    1:28 we may *p* every man perfect in Christ Jesus
Jude 24 to *p* you faultless before the presence of

Preserve *See also* Keep

Gen. 32:30 seen God face to face, and my life is *p*
    45:5 for God did send me before you to *p* life
Deut. 6:24 for our good always, that he might *p* us
Josh. 24:17 *p* us in all the way wherein we went
2 Sam. 8:6 (1 Chr. 18:6, 13) the LORD *p* David
Neh. 9:6 all that is therein, and thou *p* them all
Job 29:2 oh that I were. . in the days when God *p* me
Ps. 16:1 *p* me, O God: for in thee do I put my trust
    25:21 let integrity and uprightness *p* me
    31:23 the LORD *p* the faithful, and plentifully
    32:7 hiding place; thou shalt *p* me from trouble
    36:6 a great deep: O LORD, thou *p* man and beast
    41:2 the LORD will *p* him, and keep him alive
    61:7 O prepare mercy and truth, which may *p* him
    64:1 O God. . *p* my life from fear of the enemy
    79:11 *p* thou those that are appointed to die
    97:10 hate evil: he *p* the souls of his saints
    116:6 the LORD *p* the simple: I was brought low
    121:7 *p* thee from all evil: he shall *p* thy soul
    121:8 LORD shall *p* thy going out and thy coming
    145:20 the LORD *p* all them that love him
Prov. 2:8 of judgment, and *p* the way of his saints
    2:11 discretion shall *p* thee, understanding shall
    16:17 he that keepeth his way *p* his soul
    20:28 mercy and truth *p* the king: and his throne
    22:12 the eyes of the LORD *p* knowledge
Is. 49:8 I will *p* thee, and give thee for a covenant
Jer. 49:11 thy fatherless children, I will *p* them
Mt. 9:17 (Lk. 5:38) into new bottles, and both are *p*
Lk. 17:33 whosoever shall lose his life shall *p* it
1 Thes. 5:23 be *p* blameless unto the coming of our
2 Tim. 4:18 will *p* me unto his heavenly kingdom
Jude 1 that are sanctified. . and *p* in Jesus Christ

Preserver

Job 7:20 O thou *p* of men? why hast thou set me as

President

Dan. 6:2 over these three *p*; of whom Daniel was first

Press

Gen. 19:3 he *p* upon them greatly; and they turned
Judg. 16:16 *p* him daily with her words, and urged
Ps. 38:2 stick fast in me, and thy hand *p* me sore
Prov. 3:10 and thy *p* shall burst out with new wine
Joel 3:13 come, get you down; for the *p* is full
Amos 2:13 I am *p* under you, as a cart is *p* that is
Mk. 2:4 (Lk. 8:19) not come nigh unto him for the *p*
    3:10 healed many; insomuch that they *p* upon him
    5:30 Jesus. . turned him about in the *p*, and said
Lk. 6:38 good measure, *p* down, and shaken together
    8:45 Master, the multitude throng thee and *p* thee
    16:16 kingdom. . preached, and every man *p* into it
    19:3 could not for the *p*, because he was little
Acts 18:5 Paul was *p* in the spirit, and testified
2 Cor. 1:8 in Asia, that we were *p* out of measure
Phil. 3:14 I *p* toward the mark for the prize of

Presume

Num. 14:44 but they *p* to go up unto the hilltop
Deut. 18:20 prophet, which shall *p* to speak a word
Esth. 7:5 he, that durst *p* in his heart to do so?

Presumptuous

Ps. 19:13 keep back thy servant also from *p* sins
2 Pet. 2:10 *p* are they, self-willed, they are not

Presumptuously

Ex. 21:14 but if a man come *p* upon his neighbor
Num. 15:30 the soul that doeth aught *p*, whether he
Deut. 17:13 shall hear, and fear, and do no more *p*
    18:22 but the prophet hath spoken it *p*

Pretense

Mt. 23:14 (Mk. 12:40) and for a *p* make long prayer
Phil. 1:18 in *p*, or in truth, Christ is preached

Pretorium Mk. 15:16

Prevail

Gen. 7:18 the waters *p*, and were increased greatly
    32:28 power with God and with men, and hast *p*
Ex. 17:11 Moses held up his hand, that Israel *p*
1 Sam. 2:9 for by strength shall no man *p*
    17:50 David *p* over the Philistine with a sling
    26:25 do great things, and also shalt still *p*
1 Kgs. 22:22 (2 Chr. 18:21) shalt persuade him, and *p*
2 Chr. 14:11 our God; let not man *p* against thee
Esth. 6:13 if Mordecai. . thou shalt not *p* against him
Job 18:9 heel, and the robber shall *p* against him
Ps. 9:19 arise, O LORD; let not man *p*: let the
    12:4 who have said, With our tongue will we *p*
    65:3 iniquities *p* against me. . our transgressions
Eccl. 4:12 one *p* against him, two shall withstand
Is. 16:12 his sanctuary to pray; but he shall not *p*
    42:13 yea, roar; he shall *p* against his enemies
Jer. 1:19 (15:20) but they shall not *p* against thee
    20:7 O LORD. . thou art stronger than I, and hast *p*
    20:11 my persecutors shall stumble. . shall not *p*
Hos. 12:4 yea, he had power over the angel, and *p*
Mt. 16:18 the gates of hell shall not *p* against it
Jn. 12:19 perceive ye how ye *p* nothing? behold
Acts 19:20 so mightily grew the word of God and *p*
Rev. 5:5 Root of David, hath *p* to open the book

Prevent

2 Sam. 22:6 (Ps. 18:5) the snares of death *p* me
Job 3:12 why did the knees *p* me? or why the breasts
    41:11 who hath *p* me, that I should repay him?
Ps. 21:3 thou *p* him with the blessings of goodness
    59:10 God of my mercy shall *p* me: God shall let
    79:8 let thy tender mercies speedily *p* us
    88:13 and in the morning shall my prayer *p* thee
    119:147 I *p* the dawning of the morning, and cried
Amos 9:10 the evil shall not overtake nor *p* us
Mt. 17:25 Jesus *p* him, saying, what thinkest thou
1 Thes. 4:15 shall not *p* them which are asleep

Prey *See also* Spoil

Gen. 49:9 from the *p*, my son, thou art gone up
Num. 14:3 our wives and our children should be a *p*?
Judg. 5:30 not sped? have they not divided the *p*
Job 24:5 rising betimes for a *p*: the wilderness
Ps. 104:21 the young lions roar after their *p*
    124:6 who hath not given us as a *p* to their teeth
Prov. 23:28 she also lieth in wait as for a *p*
Is. 10:2 widows may be their *p*, and that they may
    42:22 they are for a *p*, and none delivereth
    49:24 shall the *p* be taken from the mighty
Jer. 21:9 (38:2) his life shall be unto him for a *p*
    30:16 all that *p* upon thee will I give for a *p*
    45:5 but thy life will I give unto thee for a *p*
Ezek. 34:22 my flock. . they shall no more be a *p*
Amos 3:4 will a lion roar. . when he hath no *p*?

Price

Lev. 25:16 shalt increase the *p* . . diminish the *p*
  25:52 he give him again the *p* of his redemption
Deut. 23:18 *p* of a dog, into the house of the LORD
2 Sam. 24:24 (1 Chr. 21:24) buy it of thee at a *p*
Job 28:13 man knoweth not the *p* thereof; neither
  28:18 for the *p* of wisdom is above rubies
Prov. 17:16 *p* in the hand of a fool to get wisdom
  31:10 virtuous woman . . her *p* is far above rubies
Is. 55:1 wine and milk without money and without *p*
Zech. 11:12 if ye think good, give me my *p*; and if
Mt. 13:46 when he had found one pearl of great *p*
  27:6 the treasury, because it is the *p* of blood
Acts 5:2 kept back part of the *p*, his wife also
1 Cor. 6:20 (7:23) for ye are bought with a *p*
1 Pet. 3:4 which is in the sight of God of great *p*

Prick

Num. 33:55 remain of them shall be *p* in your eyes
Ps. 73:21 was grieved, and I was *p* in my reins
Acts 2:37 heard this, they were *p* in their heart
  9:5 (26:14) hard for thee to kick against the *p*

Pride *See also* Arrogancy, Conceit, Haughtiness

Lev. 26:19 and I will break the *p* of your power
1 Sam. 17:28 I know thy *p*, and the naughtiness of
2 Chr. 32:26 humbled himself for the *p* of his heart
Job 33:17 from his purpose, and hide *p* from man
  35:12 giveth answer, because of the *p* of evil men
Ps. 10:2 wicked in his *p* doth persecute the poor
  10:4 the wicked, through the *p* of his countenance
  31:20 secret of thy presence from the *p* of man
  59:12 let them even be taken in their *p*
  73:6 *p* compasseth them about as a chain; violence
Prov. 8:13 *p*, and arrogancy, and the evil way . . I hate
  11:2 when *p* cometh, then cometh shame: but with
  13:10 only by *p* cometh contention: but with
  14:3 in the mouth of the foolish is a rod of *p*
  16:18 *p* goeth before destruction, and a haughty
  29:23 a man's *p* shall bring him low: but honor
Is. 9:9 that say in the *p* and stoutness of heart
  16:6 (Jer. 48:29) we have heard of the *p* of Moab
  25:11 he shall bring down their *p* together with
Jer. 13:9 I mar the *p* of Judah, and the great *p* of
  13:17 shall weep in secret places for your *p*
  49:16 (Obad. 3) deceived thee, and the *p* of thine
Ezek. 7:10 the rod hath blossomed, *p* hath budded
  30:6 fall; and the *p* of her power shall come down
Dan. 4:37 those that walk in *p* he is able to abase
  5:20 his mind hardened in *p*, he was deposed from
Hos. 5:5 (7:10) *p* of Israel doth testify to his face
Obad. 3 the *p* of thine heart hath deceived thee
Zeph. 2:10 shall they have for their *p*, because
  3:11 I will take away . . them that rejoice in thy *p*
Zech. 11:3 roaring . . for the *p* of Jordan is spoiled
Mk. 7:22 an evil eye, blasphemy, *p*, foolishness
1 Tim. 3:6 lest being lifted up with *p* he fall into
1 Jn. 2:16 the lust of the eyes, and the *p* of life

Priest *See also* Chief Priest, High Priest, Levite

Gen. 14:18 (Heb. 7:1) the *p* of the most high God
  47:22 *p* had a portion assigned them of Pharaoh
Ex. 3:1 Jethro his father-in-law, the *p* of Midian
  19:6 and ye shall be unto me a kingdom of *p*
  31:10 (35:19; 39:41) garments for Aaron the *p*
Lev. 4:3 if the *p* that is anointed do sin according
  4:20 and the *p* shall make an atonement for them
  13:6 *p* shall look . . *p* shall pronounce him clean
  16:32 the *p* whom he shall anoint, and . . consecrate

Lev. 21:1 Moses, Speak unto the *p* the sons of Aaron
Deut. 17:12 and will not hearken unto the *p* that
Josh. 3:8 shalt command the *p* that bear the ark
Judg. 17:10 be unto me a father and a *p*, and I will
  18:19 go with us, and be to us a father and a *p*
1 Sam. 2:35 I will raise me up a faithful *p*
  5:5 therefore neither the *p* of Dagon, nor any
  22:17 turn, and slay the *p* of the LORD
1 Kgs. 8:11 (2 Chr. 5:14) *p* could not stand to minister
  12:31 made *p* of the lowest of the people
2 Kgs. 17:32 lowest of them *p* of the high places
  23:5 and he put down the idolatrous *p*, whom the
  23:20 and he slew all the *p* of the high places
1 Chr. 15:14 so the *p* and the Levites sanctified
2 Chr. 6:41 (Ps. 132:9) let thy *p* . . be clothed with
  13:9 have ye not cast out the *p* of the LORD
  15:3 without the true God . . without a teaching *p*
  26:19 Uzziah . . was wroth with the *p*, the leprosy
  30:21 the *p* praised the LORD day by day, singing
Ezra 2:63 (Neh. 7:65) till there stood up a *p* with
  6:20 *p* and the Levites were purified together
Ps. 78:64 their *p* fell by the sword . . their widows
  110:4 (Heb. 5:6; 7:17, 21) *p* for ever after the order
  132:16 I will also clothe her *p* with salvation
Is. 24:2 as with the people, so with the *p*
  28:7 the *p* and the prophet have erred through
  61:6 but ye shall be named The *p* of the LORD
  66:21 and I will also take of them for *p* and for
Jer. 2:8 the *p* said not, Where is the LORD?
  4:9 the *p* shall be astonished, and the prophets
  6:13 (8:10) from the prophet even unto the *p* every
  18:18 for the law shall not perish from the *p*
  23:11 both prophet and *p* are profane
Lam. 2:20 shall the *p* and the prophet be slain in
Ezek. 7:26 but the law shall perish from the *p*
  22:26 her *p* have violated my law . . have profaned
  44:15 the *p* . . kept the charge of my sanctuary
  44:21 neither shall any *p* drink wine, when they
Hos. 4:4 thy people . . as they that strive with the *p*
  4:6 reject thee, that thou shalt be no *p* to me
  4:9 there shall be, like people, like *p*
  6:9 company of *p* murder in the way by consent
Joel 2:17 the *p*, the ministers of the LORD, weep
Mic. 3:11 reward, and the *p* thereof teach for hire
Zeph. 3:4 her *p* have polluted the sanctuary
Mal. 1:6 O *p*, that despise my name. And ye say
  2:1 and now, O ye *p*, this commandment is for you
  2:7 the *p*'s lips should keep knowledge, and they
Mt. 8:4 (Mk. 1:44; Lk. 5:14) show thyself to the *p*
  12:5 *p* in the temple profane the sabbath
Mk. 2:26 (Lk. 6:4) is not lawful to eat but for the *p*
Lk. 1:8 while he executed the *p*'s office before God
  10:31 there came down a certain *p* that way
  17:14 unto them, Go show yourselves unto the *p*
Jn. 1:19 Jews sent *p* and Levites from Jerusalem
Acts 4:1 as they spake unto the people, the *p*, and
  6:7 company of the *p* were obedient to the faith
  14:13 then the *p* of Jupiter . . brought oxen and
Heb. 7:3 like unto the Son . . abideth a *p* continually
  7:20 as not without an oath he was made *p*
  9:6 the *p* went always into the first tabernacle
  10:11 and every *p* standeth daily ministering and
Rev. 1:6 (5:10) made us kings and *p* unto God
  20:6 but they shall be *p* of God and of Christ

Priesthood

Ex. 40:15 surely be an everlasting *p* throughout
Num. 16:10 Levi with thee: and seek ye the *p* also?
  25:13 even the covenant of an everlasting *p*
Josh. 18:7 the *p* of the LORD is their inheritance
Neh. 13:29 defiled the *p* . . the covenant of the *p*
Heb. 7:11 if . . perfection were by the Levitical *p*
  7:14 which tribe Moses spake nothing concerning *p*

Heb. 7:24 continueth ever, hath an unchangeable *p*
1 Pet. 2:5 are built up a spiritual house, a holy *p*
   2:9 ye are a chosen generation, a royal *p*

Prince *See also* Chief, Noble

Gen. 23:6 my lord: thou art a mighty *p* among us
   32:28 as a *p* hast thou power with God and with
Ex. 2:14 who made thee a *p* and a judge over us?
Num. 7:2 the *p* of Israel. . *p* of the tribes. . offered
   16:13 thou make thyself altogether a *p* over us?
2 Sam. 3:38 a *p* and a great man fallen this day in
Job 12:19 leadeth *p* away spoiled, and overthroweth
   21:28 for ye say, Where is the house of the *p*?
   31:37 my steps; as a *p* would I go near unto him
   34:19 to him that accepteth not the persons of *p*
Ps. 45:16 whom thou mayest make *p* in all the earth
   113:8 may set him with *p*, even with the *p* of his
   118:9 trust in the LORD than to put confidence in *p*
   119:23 *p* also did sit and speak against me
   146:3 put not your trust in *p*, nor in the son of
Prov. 8:15 by me kings reign, and *p* decree justice
   17:26 is not good, nor to strike *p* for equity
   25:15 by long forbearing is a *p* persuaded
   28:16 *p* that wanteth understanding is. . oppressor
   31:4 kings to drink wine; nor for *p* strong drink
Eccl. 10:7 servants upon horses, and *p* walking as
   10:16 king is a child. . thy *p* eat in the morning!
Is. 1:23 thy *p* are rebellious, and companions of
   3:4 I will give children to be their *p*, and babes
   9:6 God, The everlasting Father, The *P* of Peace
   34:12 none shall be there. . her *p* shall be nothing
   40:23 that bringeth the *p* to nothing; he maketh
Jer. 26:10 when the *p* of Judah heard these things
Ezek. 28:2 Son of man, say unto the *p* of Tyrus
   45:9 O *p* of Israel: remove violence and spoil
Mic. 7:3 the *p* asketh, and the judge. . for a reward
Mt. 9:34 (12:24; Mk. 3:22) through the *p* of the devils
   20:25 *p* of the Gentiles exercise dominion over
Jn. 12:31 now shall the *p* of this world be cast out
   14:30 for the *p* of this world cometh, and hath
   16:11 because the *p* of this world is judged
Acts 3:15 and killed the *P* of life, whom God hath
   5:31 hath God exalted. . to be a *P* and a Saviour
1 Cor. 2:6 this world, nor of the *p* of this world
   2:8 which none of the *p* of this world knew
Eph. 2:2 the *p* of the power of the air, the spirit
Rev. 1:5 and the *p* of the kings of the earth

Principal

Lev. 6:5 falsely; he shall even restore it in the *p*
Prov. 4:7 wisdom is the *p* thing; therefore get wisdom
Mic. 5:5 raise. . seven shepherds, and eight *p* men

Principality

Jer. 13:18 sit down: for your *p* shall come down
Rom. 8:38 nor life, nor angels, nor *p*, nor powers
Eph. 1:21 far above all *p*, and power, and might
   3:10 unto the *p* and powers in heavenly places
   6:12 not against flesh and blood, but against *p*
Col. 1:16 *p*, or powers: all. . were created by him
   2:10 in him, which is the head of all *p* and power
   2:15 having spoiled *p* and powers, he made a show
Tit. 3:1 put them in mind to be subject to *p* and

Principle

Heb. 5:12 teach you again. . first *p* of the oracles
   6:1 leaving the *p* of the doctrine of Christ

Print

Lev. 19:28 any cuttings. . nor *p* any marks upon you
Job 13:27 settest a *p* upon the heels of my feet
   19:23 now written! oh that they were *p* in a book!
Jn. 20:25 see in his hands the *p* of the nails

Priscilla Acts 18:2; 18:18; Rom. 16:3

Prison *See also* Dungeon

Gen. 39:20 and Joseph's master. . put him into the *p*
Judg. 16:21 with fetters. . and he did grind in the *p*
1 Kgs. 22:27 (2 Chr. 18:26) put this fellow in the *p*
Ps. 142:7 bring my soul out of *p*, that I may praise
Eccl. 4:14 out of *p* he cometh to reign; whereas
Is. 42:7 to bring out the prisoners from the *p*
   53:8 he was taken from *p* and from judgment
   61:1 the opening of the *p* to them that are bound
Jer. 37:21 commit Jeremiah into the court of the *p*
Mt. 4:12 (Mk. 1:14) that John was cast into *p*
   5:25 (Lk. 12:58) the officer, and thou be cast into *p*
   14:3 (Mk. 6:17) in *p* for Herodias' sake
   18:30 cast him into *p*, till he should pay the debt
   25:36 visited me: I was in *p*, and ye came upon me
Lk. 21:12 persecute you, delivering you up. . into *p*
   22:33 I am ready to go with thee, both into *p*
Jn. 3:24 for John was not yet cast into *p*
Acts 5:18 apostles, and put them in the common *p*
   5:19 but the angel. . by night opened the *p* doors
   8:3 (22:4) haling men. . committed them to *p*
   12:4 he had apprehended him, he put him in *p*
   12:5 Peter therefore was kept in *p*: but prayer
   12:17 how the Lord had brought him out of the *p*
   16:24 a charge, thrust them into the inner *p*
   16:26 that the foundations of the *p* were shaken
   26:10 and many of the saints did I shut up in *p*
2 Cor. 11:23 in *p* more frequent, in deaths oft
1 Pet. 3:19 went and preached unto the spirits in *p*
Rev. 2:10 the devil shall cast some of you into *p*
   20:7 expired, Satan shall be loosed out of his *p*

Prisoner *See also* Captive

Num. 21:1 against Israel, and took some of them *p*
Ps. 69:33 heareth the poor, and despiseth not his *p*
   79:11 let the sighing of the *p* come before thee
   146:7 food to the hungry. The LORD looseth the *p*
Is. 42:7 to bring out the *p* from the prison
   49:9 thou mayest say to the *p*, Go forth; to them
Zech. 9:12 turn you to the stronghold, ye *p* of hope
Mt. 27:16 had then a notable *p*, called Barabbas
Acts 25:27 seemeth to me unreasonable to send a *p*
Eph. 3:1 I Paul, the *p* of Jesus Christ for you
   4:1 I therefore, the *p* of the Lord, beseech you
Phlm. 1 Paul, a *p* of Jesus Christ, and Timothy

Private

2 Pet. 1:20 Scripture is of any *p* interpretation

Privately

Mt. 24:3 (Mk. 13:3) disciples came unto him *p*
Mk. 6:32 (Lk. 9:10) into a desert place by ship *p*
Lk. 10:23 turned him unto his disciples, and said *p*
Gal. 2:2 but *p* to them which were of reputation

Privily

1 Sam. 24:4 and cut off the skirt of Saul's robe *p*
Ps. 11:2 they may *p* shoot at the upright in heart
Mt. 1:19 Joseph. . was minded to put her away *p*
   2:7 Herod, when he had *p* called the wise men
Acts 16:37 now do they thrust us out *p*? nay verily
Gal. 2:4 came in *p* to spy out our liberty which we
2 Pet.2:1 who *p* shall bring in damnable heresies

Prize

1 Cor. 9:24 race run all, but one receiveth the *p*?
Phil. 3:14 the mark for the *p* of the high calling

Proceed *See also* Depart, Go, Went

Gen. 24:50 the thing *p* from the LORD: we cannot
Deut. 8:3 (Mt. 4:4) word that *p* out of the mouth

Is. 51:4 O my nation: for a law shall *p* from me
Mt. 15:18 which *p* out of the mouth come forth from
Jn. 8:42 for I *p* forth and came from God; neither
15:26 Spirit of truth, which *p* from the Father
Eph. 4:29 let no corrupt communication *p* out of
2 Tim. 3:9 they shall *p* no further: for their folly
Rev. 22:1 pure river. . *p* out of the throne of God

Proclaim *See also* Declare, Preach, Publish

Ex. 33:19 I will *p* the name of the LORD before thee
34:5 stood with him. . and *p* the name of the LORD
Lev. 23:2 which ye shall *p* to be holy convocations
25:10 *p* liberty throughout all the land unto all
Judg. 7:3 *p* in the ears of the people, saying
2 Kgs. 10:20 *p* a solemn assembly for Baal. . they *p*
Prov. 12:23 but the heart of fools *p* foolishness
20:6 most men will *p* every one his own goodness
Is. 61:1 to *p* liberty to the captives
61:2 to *p* the acceptable year of the LORD
62:11 the LORD hath *p* unto the end of the world
Jer. 3:12 go and *p* these words toward the north
7:2 gate of the LORD's house. . *p* there this word
34:15 in *p* liberty every man to his neighbor
Joel 3:9 *p* ye this among the Gentiles; Prepare war
Lk. 12:3 in closets shall be *p* upon the housetops
Rev. 5:2 I saw a strong angel *p* with a loud voice

Procure

Prov. 11:27 that diligently seeketh good *p* favor
Jer. 2:17 hast thou not *p* this unto thyself
4:18 thy way and thy doings have *p* these things
26:19 thus might we *p* great evil against our
33:9 and for all the prosperity that I *p* unto it

Prodigal Lk. 15:11–32

Produce *See also* Yield

Is. 41:21 *p* your cause, saith the LORD; bring forth

Profane *See also* Corrupt, Defile, Pollute

Lev. 18:21 (19:12) neither. . *p* the name of thy God
20:3 defile my sanctuary, and to *p* my holy name
21:6 shall be holy. . not *p* the name of their God
Neh. 13:17 this that ye do, and *p* the Sabbath day?
Ps. 89:39 thou hast *p* his crown by casting it to
Is. 43:28 I have *p* the princes of the sanctuary
Jer. 23:11 for both prophet and priest are *p*
Ezek. 22:8 (23:38) and hast *p* my sabbaths
22:26 have *p* mine holy things. . I am *p* among
36:20 whither they went, they *p* my holy name
44:23 teach. . difference between the holy and *p*
Mal. 1:12 ye have *p* it, in that ye say, The table
2:10 by *p* the covenant of our fathers?
2:11 for Judah hath *p* the holiness of the LORD
Mt. 12:5 priests in the temple *p* the sabbath
Acts 24:6 who also hath gone about to *p* the temple
1 Tim. 4:7 but refuse *p* and old wives' fables
6:20 (2 Tim. 2:16) avoiding *p* and vain babblings
Heb. 12:16 be any fornicator, or *p* person, as Esau

Profess

Deut. 26:3 I *p* this day unto the LORD thy God, that
Mt. 7:23 then will I *p* unto them, I never knew you
Rom. 1:22 *p* themselves to be wise, they became
1 Tim. 2:10 but (which becometh women *p* godliness)
6:12 a good profession before many witnesses
6:21 some *p* have erred concerning the faith
Tit. 1:16 they *p* that they know God; but in works

Profession

1 Tim. 6:12 hast professed a good *p* before many

Heb. 3:1 Apostle and High Priest of our *p*, Christ
4:14 seeing then that. . let us hold fast our *p*
10:23 let us hold fast the *p* of our faith without

Profit *See also* Advantage, Gain

Gen. 25:32 what *p* shall this birthright do to me?
37:26 what *p* is it if we slay our brother
1 Sam. 12:21 go after vain things, which cannot *p*
Job 21:15 what *p* should we have, if we pray unto
30:2 whereto might the strength of their hands *p*
33:27 sinned, and perverted. . and it *p* me not
34:9 it *p* a man nothing that he should delight
35:3 what *p* shall I have, if I be cleansed from
35:8 and thy righteousness may *p* the son of man
Ps. 30:9 what *p* is there. . when I go down to the pit
Prov. 10:2 treasures of wickedness *p* nothing
11:4 riches *p* not in the day of wrath
14:23 in all labor there is *p*: but the talk of
Eccl. 1:3 (5:16) what *p* hath a man of all his labor
2:11 was vanity. . there was no *p* under the sun
3:9 what *p* hath he that worketh in that wherein
7:11 by it there is *p* to them that see the sun
Is. 30:5 ashamed of a people that could not *p* them
44:9 and their delectable things shall not *p*
47:12 if so be thou shalt be able to *p*, if so be
48:17 the LORD thy God which teacheth thee to *p*
57:12 and thy works; for they shall not *p* thee
Jer. 2:8 and walked after things that do not *p*
2:11 changed their glory for that which doth not *p*
7:8 behold, ye trust in lying words, that cannot *p*
12:13 put themselves to pain, but shall not *p*
16:19 vanity, and things wherein there is no *p*
23:32 therefore they shall not *p* this people
Hab. 2:18 what *p* the graven image that the maker
Mal. 3:14 and what *p* is it that we have kept his
Mt. 15:5 (Mk. 7:11) whatsoever thou mightest be *p* by
16:26 (Mk. 8:36) what is a man *p*, if he shall gain
Jn. 6:63 Spirit that quickeneth. . flesh *p* nothing
Rom. 2:25 for circumcision. . *p*, if thou keep the law
3:1 the Jew? or what *p* is there of circumcision?
1 Cor. 7:35 this I speak for your own *p*; not that I
10:33 not seeking mine own *p*, but the *p* of many
12:7 of the Spirit is given to every man to *p*
13:3 and have not charity, it *p* me nothing
Gal. 1:14 and *p* in the Jews' religion above many
5:2 ye be circumcised, Christ shall *p* you nothing
1 Tim. 4:8 bodily exercise *p* little: but godliness
4:15 to them, that thy *p* appear to all
2 Tim. 2:14 they strive not about words to no *p*
Heb. 4:2 but the word preached did not *p* them
12:10 after their own pleasure; but he for our *p*
13:9 not with meats, which have not *p* them that
Jas. 2:14 what doth it *p*. . though a man say he hath

Profitable

Job 22:2 *p* unto God, as he that is wise may be *p*
Eccl. 10:10 strength: but wisdom is *p* to direct
Mt. 5:29 *p* for thee that one of thy members should
Acts 20:20 I kept back nothing that was *p* unto you
1 Tim. 4:8 but godliness is *p* unto all things
2 Tim. 3:16 and is *p* for doctrine, for reproof
4:11 take Mark. . he is *p* to me for the ministry
Tit. 3:8 these things are good and *p* unto men
Phlm. 11 unprofitable, but now *p* to thee and to me

Prolong

Deut. 4:26 ye shall not *p* your days upon it
5:16 thy days may be *p*, and that it may go well
30:18 that ye shall not *p* your days upon the land
Job 6:11 what is mine end, that I should *p* my life?
Prov. 10:27 the fear of the LORD *p* days: but the
28:16 that hateth covetousness shall *p* his days
Eccl. 8:13 the wicked, neither shall he *p* his days

Is. 53:10 shall see his seed, he shall *p* his days
Ezek. 12:22 days are *p*, and every vision faileth?
12:25 shall come to pass; it shall be no more *p*
Dan. 7:12 yet their lives were *p* for a season

Promise *See also* Covenant, Pledge, Swear, Vow

Ex. 12:25 will give you, according as he hath *p*
Num. 14:40 up unto the place which the LORD hath *p*
Deut. 1:11 (15:6) LORD . . bless you, as he hath *p* you!
6:3 as the LORD God of thy fathers hath *p* thee
9:28 to bring them into the land which he *p* them
23:23 offering . . which thou hast *p* with thy mouth
Josh. 23:5 as the LORD your God hath *p* unto you
23:10 is that fighteth for you, as he hath *p* you
2 Sam. 7:28 (1 Chr. 17:26) thou hast *p* this goodness
1 Kgs. 5:12 LORD gave Solomon wisdom, as he *p* him
8:20 (2 Chr. 6:10) sit on the throne . . as the LORD *p*
8:56 hath not failed one word of all his good *p*
2 Chr. 1:9 God, let thy *p* unto David my father be
Neh. 5:12 that they should do according to this *p*
9:23 land . . which thou hadst *p* to their fathers
Ps. 77:8 doth his *p* fail for evermore?
105:42 he remembered his holy *p*, and Abraham his
Jer. 32:42 (33:14) all the good that I have *p* them
Ezek. 13:22 the hands of the wicked . . by *p* him life
Mt. 14:7 he *p* . . to give her whatsoever she would ask
Lk. 1:72 to perform the mercy *p* to our fathers, and
24:49 I send the *p* of my Father upon you
Acts 1:4 not depart . . wait for the *p* of the Father
2:33 received of the Father the *p* of . . Holy Ghost
2:39 for the *p* is unto you, and to your children
7:5 *p* that he would give it to him . . a possession
7:17 but when the time of the *p* drew nigh
13:23 according to his *p*, raised unto Israel a
13:32 that the *p* which was made unto the fathers
26:6 I stand and am judged for the hope of the *p*
Rom. 1:2 which he had *p* afore by his prophets in
4:13 the *p* . . was not to Abraham, or to his seed
4:14 is made void, and the *p* made of none effect
4:16 the end the *p* might be sure to all the seed
4:20 he staggered not at the *p* of God through
4:21 what he had *p*, he was able also to perform
9:4 to whom pertaineth the adoption . . and the *p*
9:8 children of the *p* are counted for the seed
15:8 to confirm the *p* made unto the fathers
2 Cor. 1:20 for all the *p* of God in him are yea
7:1 having therefore these *p* . . let us cleanse
Gal. 3:14 receive the *p* of the Spirit through faith
3:16 to Abraham and his seed were the *p* made
3:17 that it should make the *p* of none effect
3:18 inheritance be of the law, it is no more of *p*
3:19 seed should come to whom the *p* was made
3:21 law then against the *p* of God? God forbid
3:22 *p* by faith of Jesus Christ might be given
3:29 Abraham's seed, and heirs according to the *p*
4:23 flesh; but he of the free woman was by *p*
4:28 now we . . as Isaac was, are the children of *p*
Eph. 1:13 ye were sealed with that Holy Spirit of *p*
2:12 strangers from the covenants of *p*, having no
3:6 partakers of his *p* in Christ by the gospel
6:2 which is the first commandment with *p*
1 Tim. 4:8 having *p* of the life that now is
2 Tim. 1:1 according to the *p* of life which is in
Tit. 1:2 that cannot lie, *p* before the world began
Heb. 4:1 lest, a *p* being left us of entering into
6:12 who through faith and patience inherit the *p*
6:13 God made *p* to Abraham . . sware by himself
6:15 he had patiently endured, he obtained the *p*
8:6 a better covenant . . established upon better *p*
9:15 might receive the *p* of eternal inheritance
10:23 without wavering; for he is faithful that *p*

Heb. 10:36 done the will of God . . receive the *p*
11:9 by faith he sojourned in the land of *p*, as
11:11 because she judged him faithful who had *p*
11:13 died in faith, not having received the *p*
11:17 he that had received the *p* offered up his
11:33 through faith . . obtained *p*
11:39 obtained a good report . . received not the *p*
12:26 but now he hath *p*, saying, Yet once more I
Jas. 1:12 the crown of life, which the Lord hath *p*
2:5 kingdom which he hath *p* to them that love him
2 Pet. 1:4 unto us exceeding great and precious *p*
2:19 while they *p* them liberty, they themselves
3:4 where is the *p* of his coming? for since the
3:9 Lord is not slack concerning his *p*, as some
3:13 we, according to his *p*, look for new heavens
1 Jn. 2:25 *p* that he hath *p* us, even eternal life

Promote

Num. 22:17 for I will *p* thee unto very great honor
Judg. 9:9 I leave . . and go to be *p* over the trees?
Prov. 4:8 exalt her, and she shall *p* thee
Dan. 3:30 then the king *p* Shadrach, Meshach, and

Promotion

Ps. 75:6 *p* cometh neither from the east, nor from
Prov. 3:35 but shame shall be the *p* of fools

Pronounce

Lev. 5:4 a man shall *p* with an oath, and it be hid
Judg. 12:6 for he could not frame to *p* it right
Jer. 34:5 for I have *p* the word, saith the LORD

Proof

Acts 1:3 after his passion by many infallible *p*
2 Cor. 2:9 I write, that I might know the *p* of you
8:24 and before the churches, the *p* of your love
13:3 since ye seek a *p* of Christ speaking in me
Phil. 2:22 know the *p* of him, that . . he hath served
2 Tim. 4:5 evangelist, make full *p* of thy ministry

Proper

1 Chr. 29:3 of mine own *p* good, of gold and silver
1 Cor. 7:7 but every man hath his *p* gift of God
Heb. 11:23 because they saw he was a *p* child

Prophecy

Neh. 6:12 but that he pronounced this *p* against me
Prov. 31:1 Lemuel, the *p* that his mother taught him
Ezek. 6:2 mountains of Israel, and *p* against them.
Dan. 9:24 seal up the vision and *p*, and to anoint
Rom. 12:6 the grace that is given to us, whether *p*
1 Cor. 12:10 to another *p*; to another discerning of
13:2 though I have the gift of *p*, and understand
13:8 whether there be *p*, they shall fail
1 Tim. 1:18 according to the *p* which went before
4:14 the gift . . in thee, which was given thee by *p*
2 Pet. 1:19 we have also a more sure word of *p*
1:20 no *p* of the Scripture is of any private
1:21 *p* came not in old time by the will of man
Rev. 1:3 and they that hear the words of this *p*
19:10 the testimony of Jesus is the spirit of *p*
22:7 blessed is he . . keepeth the sayings of the *p*
22:18 heareth the words of the *p* of this book

Prophesy *See also* Declare, Preach, Proclaim

Num. 11:25 when the spirit rested upon them, they *p*
1 Sam. 10:5 a company of prophets . . and they shall *p*
10:10 Spirit of God came upon him, and he *p*
19:20 the messengers of Saul, and they also *p*
1 Kgs. 22:8 (2 Chr. 18:7) not *p* good concerning me
22:10 (2 Chr. 18:9) all the prophets *p* before them

1 Chr. 25:1 should *p* with harps, with psalteries
   25:2 which *p* according to the order of the king
Ezra 6:14 they prospered through the *p* of Haggai
Is. 30:10 *p* not unto us right things. . *p* deceits
Jer. 2:8 the prophets *p* by Baal, and walked after
   5:31 prophets *p* falsely, and the priests bear
   11:21 *p* not in the name of the LORD, that thou
   14:14 prophets *p* lies in my name: I sent them not
   19:14 Tophet, whither the LORD had sent him to *p*
   20:6 all thy friends, to whom thou hast *p* lies
   23:13 *p* in Baal. . caused my people Israel to err
   23:21 I have not spoken to them, yet they *p*
   23:32 I am against them that *p* false dreams
   25:13 Jeremiah hath *p* against all the nations
   25:30 *p* thou against them all these words
   26:9 why hast thou *p* in the name of the LORD
   26:11 to die; for he hath *p* against this city
   26:12 LORD sent me to *p* against this house and
   26:18 Micah the Morasthite *p* in the days of
   26:20 that *p* in the name of the LORD, Urijah the
   27:10 they *p* a lie unto you, to remove you far
   28:6 LORD perform thy words which thou hast *p*
   28:8 *p* both against many countries, and against
   28:9 the prophet which *p* of peace, when the word
   29:9 they *p* falsely unto you in my name
   29:31 because that Shemaiah hath *p* unto you
   32:3 shut him up, saying, Wherefore dost thou *p*
Ezek. 4:7 uncovered, and thou shalt *p* against it
   11:4 therefore *p* against them, *p*, O son of man
   12:27 and he *p* of the times that are far off
   13:2 son of man, *p* against the prophets. . that *p*
   21:2 holy places, and *p* against the land of Israel
   21:28 son of man, *p* and say, Thus saith the Lord
   34:2 *p* against the shepherds of Israel, *p*, and
   37:4 again he said unto me, *P* upon these bones
   38:14 therefore, son of man, *p* and say unto Gog
Joel 2:28 (Acts 2:17) sons and your daughters shall *p*
Amos 2:12 commanded the prophets, saying, *P* not
   3:8 the Lord GOD hath spoken, who can but *p*?
   7:15 said unto me, Go, *p* unto my people Israel
   7:16 thou sayest, *P* not against Israel, and drop
Mic. 2:6 *p* ye not, say they to them that *p*
Zech. 13:3 shall thrust him through when he *p*
Mt. 7:22 Lord, Lord, have we not *p* in thy name?
   11:13 all the prophets and the law *p* until John
   26:68 (Mk. 14:65; Lk. 22:64) *p* unto us. . Who
Lk. 1:67 was filled with the Holy Ghost, and *p*
Jn. 11:51 *p* that Jesus should die for that nation
Acts 19:6 and they spake with tongues, and *p*
   21:9 had four daughters, virgins, which did *p*
Rom. 12:6 *p* according to the proportion of faith
1 Cor. 11:4 every man praying or *p*, having his head
   13:9 for we know in part, and we *p* in part
   14:1 spiritual gifts, but rather that ye may *p*
   14:3 he that *p* speaketh unto men to edification
   14:4 himself; but he that *p* edifieth the church
   14:5 rather that ye *p*: for greater is he that *p*
   14:22 but *p* serveth not for them that believe not
   14:24 if all *p*. . one that believeth not. . convinced
   14:39 covet to *p*, and forbid not to speak with
1 Thes. 5:20 despise not *p*
1 Pet. 1:10 who *p* of the grace that should come
Jude 14 Enoch also. . seventh from Adam, *p* of these
Rev. 10:11 thou must *p* again before many peoples
   11:3 unto my two witnesses, and they shall *p*

Prophet *See also* Apostle, Priest, Seer

Gen. 20:7 restore the man his wife; for he is a *p*
Ex. 7:1 and Aaron thy brother shall be thy *p*
Num. 11:29 that all the LORD's people were *p*
   12:6 if there be a *p* among you, I the LORD will
Deut. 13:1 there arise among you a *p*, or a dreamer
   18:15 (Acts 3:22; 7:37) will raise up unto thee a *P*

Deut. 18:20 but the *p*, which shall presume to speak
   18:22 but the *p* hath spoken it presumptuously
   34:10 not a *p* since in Israel like unto Moses
Judg. 6:8 LORD sent a *p* unto the children of Israel
1 Sam. 3:20 that Samuel was established to be a *p*
   9:9 now called a *P* was beforetime called a Seer
   10:11 (19:24) is Saul also among the *p*?
1 Kgs. 13:11 now there dwelt an old *p* in Bethel
   18:4 when Jezebel cut off the *p* of the LORD
   18:19 and the *p* of Baal. . and the *p* of the groves
   18:22 I only, remain a *p* of the LORD; but Baal's *p*
   19:10 (19:14; Rom. 11:3) altars, and slain thy *p*
   19:16 Elisha. . anoint to be *p* in thy room
   22:7 (2 Chr. 18:6) is there not here a *p* of the LORD
   22:22 (2 Chr. 18:21) lying spirit in the mouth of. . *p*
2 Kgs. 5:8 he shall know that there is a *p* in Israel
1 Chr. 16:22 (Ps. 105:15) and do my *p* no harm
2 Chr. 20:20 believe his *p*, so shall ye prosper
   36:16 and despised his words, and misused his *p*
Neh. 6:7 thou hast also appointed *p* to preach of
   9:26 and slew thy *p* which testified against them
   9:30 against them by thy Spirit in thy *p*
Ps. 74:9 see not our signs: there is no more any *p*
Is. 9:15 the *p* that teacheth lies, he is the tail
   28:7 and the *p* have erred through strong drink
Jer. 1:5 and I ordained thee a *p* unto the nations
   2:8 against me, and the *p* prophesied by Baal
   4:9 shall be astonished, and the *p* shall wonder
   5:13 *p* shall become wind, and the word is not in
   5:31 *p* prophesy falsely, and the priests bear
   6:13 (8:10) from the *p* even unto the priest every
   7:25 even sent unto you all my servants that *p*
   14:18 yea, both the *p* and the priest go about
   23:11 both *p* and priest are profane; yea, in my
   23:13 and I have seen folly in the *p* of Samaria
   23:21 I have not sent these *p*, yet they ran
   23:28 *p* that hath a dream, let him tell a dream
   23:30 behold, I am against the *p*, saith the LORD
   27:9 hearken not ye to your *p*, nor to your
   27:18 if they be *p*, and if the word of the LORD
   28:9 come to pass, then shall the *p* be known
   29:26 man that is mad, and maketh himself a *p*
Lam. 2:9 her *p* also find no vision from the LORD
   2:14 thy *p* have seen vain and foolish things for
   4:13 for the sins of her *p*, and the iniquities
Ezek. 2:5 (33:33) know. . there hath been a *p* among
   13:2 son of man, prophesy against the *p* of Israel
   14:9 I the LORD have deceived that *p*, and I will
   22:25 there is a conspiracy of her *p* in the
Hos. 4:5 *p* also shall fall with thee in the night
   9:7 the *p* is a fool, the spiritual man is mad
   12:10 I have also spoken by the *p*, and I have
   12:13 by a *p*. . brought Israel out of Egypt. . by a *p*
Amos 2:11 I raised up of your sons for *p*
   7:14 I was no *p*, neither was I a *p*'s son
Mic. 2:11 he shall even be the *p* of this people
   3:5 concerning the *p* that make my people err
   3:11 and the *p* thereof divine for money
Zeph. 3:4 her *p* are light and treacherous persons
Zech. 7:7 which the LORD hath cried by the former *p*
   13:5 he shall say, I am no *p*, I am a husbandman
Mt. 5:12 (Lk. 6:23) for so persecuted they the *p*
   5:17 that I am come to destroy the law, or the *p*
   7:12 so to them: for this is the law and the *p*
   7:15 beware of false *p*, which come to you in
   10:41 that receiveth a *p* in the name of a *p* shall
   11:9 (Lk. 7:26) a *p*? yea, I say. . more than a *p*
   11:13 (Lk. 16:16) *p* and the law prophesied until
   13:17 (Lk. 10:24) *p* and righteous men have desired
   13:57 (Mk. 6:4; Jn. 4:44) a *p* is not without honor
   14:5 multitude, because they counted him as a *p*
   16:14 (Mk. 8:28; Lk. 9:19) Jeremias, or one of the *p*
   21:11 this is Jesus the *p* of Nazareth of Galilee

Mt. 21:26 (Mk. 11:32; Lk. 20:6) all hold John as a *p*
22:40 on these two . . hang all the law and the *p*
23:31 are the children of them which killed the *p*
23:37 (Lk. 13:34) Jerusalem, thou that killest the *p*
24:11 (24:24; Mk. 13:22) false *p* shall rise, and shall
Lk. 1:76 shalt be called the *p* of the Highest
4:24 no *p* is accepted in his own country
6:26 for so did their fathers to the false *p*
7:16 saying, That a great *p* is risen up among us
13:33 cannot be that a *p* perish out of Jerusalem
16:31 if they hear not Moses and the *p*, neither
24:19 a *p* mighty in deed and word before God
24:25 slow . . to believe all that the *p* have spoken
24:27 and beginning at Moses and all the *p*, he
24:44 written in the law of Moses, and in the *p*
Jn. 1:21 art thou that *P*? And he answered, No
4:19 woman saith . . I perceive that thou art a *p*
6:14 this is of a truth that *P* that should come
7:40 heard this . . said, Of a truth this is the *P*
9:17 hath opened thine eyes? He said, He is a *p*
Acts 2:30 being a *p*, and knowing that God had
3:18 had showed by the mouth of all his *p*, that
3:21 spoken by . . his holy *p* since the world began
7:52 which . . *p* have not your fathers persecuted?
10:43 to him give all the *p* witness, that through
13:1 that was at Antioch certain *p* and teachers
13:6 found a certain sorcerer, a false *p*, a Jew
13:27 knew him not, nor yet the voices of the *p*
15:15 to this agree the words of the *p*; as it is
24:14 which are written in the law and in the *p*
26:22 which the *p* and Moses did say should come
26:27 king Agrippa, believest thou the *p*? I know
Rom. 1:2 which he had promised afore by his *p* in
1 Cor. 12:28 first apostles, secondarily *p*
12:29 all apostles? are all *p*? are all teachers?
14:32 the spirits of the *p* are subject to the *p*
14:37 if any man think himself to be a *p*
Eph. 2:20 upon the foundation of the apostles and *p*
3:5 is now revealed unto his holy apostles and *p*
4:11 gave some, apostles; and some, *p*; and some
Tit. 1:12 even a *p* of their own, said, The Cretians
Heb. 1:1 spake in time past unto . . fathers by the *p*
11:32 of David also, and Samuel, and of the *p*
Jas. 5:10 take, my brethren, the *p* . . for an example
1 Pet. 1:10 of which salvation the *p* have inquired
2 Pet. 2:1 there were false *p* also among the people
3:2 words which were spoken before by the holy *p*
1 Jn. 4:1 many false *p* gone out into the world
Rev. 11:10 because these two *p* tormented them that
16:6 they have shed the blood of saints and *p*
16:13 beast, and out of the mouth of the false *p*
18:20 rejoice over her . . ye holy apostles and *p*
19:20 with him the false *p* that wrought miracles
20:10 where the beast and the false *p* are

Propitiation *See also* Atonement, Reconciliation, Sacrifice

Rom. 3:25 hath set forth to be a *p* through faith
1 Jn. 2:2 (4:10) and he is the *p* for our sins

Proselyte

Mt. 23:15 ye compass sea and land to make one *p*
Acts 2:10 and strangers of Rome, Jews and *p*
13:43 and religious *p* followed Paul and Barnabas

Prosper

Gen. 24:40 send his angel with thee, and *p* thy way
24:56 hinder me not, seeing the LORD hath *p* my
Num. 14:41 now do ye transgress . . but it shall not *p*
Deut. 28:29 thou shalt not *p* in thy ways
29:9 and do them, that ye may *p* in all that ye do
Josh. 1:7 thou mayest *p* whithersoever thou goest

Judg. 4:24 the hand of the children of Israel *p*
1 Kgs. 2:3 thou mayest *p* in all that thou doest
1 Chr. 22:11 son, the LORD be with thee; and *p* thou
2 Chr. 20:20 believe his prophets, so shall ye *p*
26:5 as he sought the LORD, God made him to *p*
Ezra 5:8 work goeth fast on, and *p* in their hands
Neh. 2:20 God of heaven, he will *p* us; therefore
Job 12:6 the tabernacles of robbers *p*, and they
Ps. 1:3 not wither; and whatsoever he doeth shall *p*
37:7 fret not . . because of him who *p* in his way
73:12 these are the ungodly, who *p* in the world
122:6 of Jerusalem: they shall *p* that love thee
Prov. 17:8 a gift . . whithersoever it turneth, it *p*
28:13 that covereth his sins shall not *p*
Eccl. 11:6 for thou knowest not whether shall *p*
Is. 53:10 pleasure of the LORD shall *p* in his hand
54:17 no weapon . . formed against thee shall *p*
55:11 it shall *p* in the thing whereto I sent it
Jer. 12:1 wherefore doth the way of the wicked *p*?
22:30 shall not *p* . . no man of his seed shall *p*
23:5 a King shall reign and *p*, and shall execute
32:5 fight with the Chaldeans, ye shall not *p*?
Ezek. 16:13 beautiful . . thou didst *p* into a kingdom
17:15 shall he *p*? shall he escape that doeth such
Dan. 6:28 so this Daniel *p* in the reign of Darius
11:27 they shall speak lies . . but it shall not *p*
1 Cor. 16:2 lay by him in store, as God hath *p* him
3 Jn. 2 *p* and be in health, even as thy soul *p*

Prosperity *See also* Success

Deut. 23:6 shalt not seek their peace nor their *p*
1 Sam. 25:6 shall ye say to him that liveth in *p*
1 Kgs. 10:7 thy wisdom and *p* exceedeth the fame
Job 15:21 in *p* the destroyer shall come upon him
36:11 serve him, they shall spend their days in *p*
Ps. 30:6 in my *p* I said, I shall never be moved
35:27 hath pleasure in the *p* of his servant
73:3 was envious . . when I saw the *p* of the wicked
118:25 save . . O LORD, I beseech thee, send now *p*
122:7 within thy walls, and *p* within thy palaces
Prov. 1:32 and the *p* of fools shall destroy them
Eccl. 7:14 in the day of *p* be joyful, but in the
Jer. 22:21 I spake unto thee in thy *p*; but thou
Lam. 3:17 my soul far off from peace: I forgat *p*
Zech. 7:7 when Jerusalem was inhabited and in *p*

Prosperous *See also* Rich, Wealthy

Gen. 24:21 the LORD had made his journey *p* or not
39:2 LORD was with Joseph, and he was a *p* man
Josh. 1:8 then thou shalt make thy way *p*, and then
Judg. 18:5 whether our way which we go shall be *p*
Job 8:6 make the habitation of thy righteousness *p*
Is. 48:15 brought him, and he shall make his way *p*
Zech. 8:12 for the seed shall be *p*; the vine shall
Rom. 1:10 now at length I might have a *p* journey

Prostitute

Lev. 19:29 do not *p* thy daughter, to cause her to

Protection

Deut. 32:38 rise up and help you, and be your *p*

Protest

Gen. 43:3 the man did solemnly *p* unto us, saying
1 Sam. 8:9 yet *p* solemnly unto them, and show
1 Kgs. 2:42 *p* unto thee, saying, Know for a certain
Jer. 11:7 for I earnestly *p* unto your fathers in
Zech. 3:6 angel of the LORD *p* unto Joshua, saying
1 Cor. 15:31 I *p* by your rejoicing which I have in

Proud *See also* Haughty

Job 26:12 understanding he smiteth through the *p*
40:11 behold every one that is *p*, and abase him

Ps. 12:3 cut off. . the tongue that speaketh *p* things
31:23 the LORD. . plentifully rewardeth the *p* doer
40:4 respecteth not the *p*, nor such as turn aside
94:2 judge of the earth: render a reward to the *p*
101:5 high look and a *p* heart will not I suffer
119:21 thou hast rebuked the *p* that are cursed
119:78 let the *p* be ashamed; for they dealt
138:6 the lowly: but the *p* he knoweth afar off
Prov. 6:17 a *p* look, a lying tongue, and hands that
15:25 the LORD will destroy the house of the *p*
16:5 one that is *p* in heart is an abomination to
21:4 a *p* heart. . the plowing of the wicked, is sin
28:25 he that is of a *p* heart stirreth up strife
Eccl. 7:8 patient in spirit is better than the *p*
Is. 2:12 shall be upon every one that is *p*
Jer. 13:15 hear ye, and give ear; be not *p*
43:2 all the *p* men, saying unto Jeremiah
50:29 she hath been *p* against the LORD
50:32 the most *p* shall stumble and fall, and none
Hab. 2:5 he is a *p* man, neither keepeth at home
Mal. 3:15 now we call the *p* happy; yea, they that
4:1 and all the *p*, yea, and all that do wickedly
Lk. 1:51 hath scattered the *p* in the imagination
Rom. 1:30 haters of God, despiteful, *p*, boasters
1 Tim. 6:4 he is *p*, knowing nothing, but doting
Jas. 4:6 (1 Pet. 5:5) God resisteth the *p*, but giveth

Proudly

Ex. 18:11 wherein they dealt *p* he was above them
1 Sam. 2:3 talk no more so exceeding *p*; let not
Neh. 9:16 (9:29) fathers dealt *p*. . and hearkened not
Obad. 12 neither shouldest thou have spoken *p* in

Prove *See also* Examine, Tempt, Try

Gen. 42:15 ye shall be *p*. . ye shall not go. . except
Ex. 15:25 made. . an ordinance, and there he *p* them
16:4 *p* them, whether they will walk in my law
20:20 fear not: for God is come to *p* you
Deut. 8:2 wilderness, to humble thee, and to *p* thee
13:3 *p* you, to know whether ye love the LORD
Judg. 2:22 through them I may *p* Israel, whether
6:39 let me *p*. . but this once with the fleece
1 Sam. 17:39 he assayed to go; for he had not *p* it
1 Kgs. 10:1 (2 Chr. 9:1) to *p* him with hard questions
Ps. 17:3 thou hast *p* mine heart; thou hast visited
26:2 examine me, O LORD, and *p* me; try my reins
66:10 thou, O God, hast *p* us: thou hast tried us
81:7 I *p* thee at the waters of Meribah
95:9 (Heb. 3:9) your fathers tempted me, *p* me
Eccl. 2:1 go to now, I will *p* thee with mirth
Dan. 1:12 *p* thy servants, I beseech thee, ten days
Mal. 3:10 meat in mine house, and *p* me now
Lk. 14:19 five yoke of oxen, and I go to *p* them
Jn. 6:6 this he said to *p* him: for he himself knew
Acts 9:22 at Damascus, *p* that this is very Christ
24:13 neither can they *p* the things whereof
Rom. 3:9 we have before *p* both Jews and Gentiles
12:2 ye may *p* what is that good, and acceptable
2 Cor. 8:8 and to *p* the sincerity of your love
13:5 whether ye be in the faith; *p* your own selves
Gal. 6:4 let every man *p* his own work, and then
1 Thes. 5:21 *p* all things; hold fast that which is
1 Tim. 3:10 let these also first be *p*; then let
Heb. 3:9 when your fathers tempted me, *p* me, and

Proverb *See also* Byword, Parable

Num. 21:27 wherefore they that speak in *p* say
Deut. 28:37 thou shalt become an astonishment, a *p*
1 Sam. 10:12 a *p*, Is Saul also among the prophets?
24:13 as saith the *p* of the ancients, Wickedness
1 Kgs. 4:32 and he spake three thousand *p*
9:7 (2 Chr. 7:20) Israel shall be a *p* and a byword
Ps. 69:11 sackcloth. . my garment; and I became a *p*

Prov. 1:6 understand a *p*, and the interpretation
25:1 are also *p* of Solomon, which the men
Eccl. 12:9 and sought out, and set in order many *p*
Jer. 24:9 a reproach and a *p*, a taunt and a curse
Ezek. 12:22 what is that *p* that ye have in the land
16:44 that useth *p* shall use this *p* against thee
18:2 what mean ye, that ye use this *p* concerning
Hab. 2:6 these take up. . a taunting *p* against him
Lk. 4:23 unto me this *p*, Physician, heal thyself
Jn. 16:25 when I shall no more speak unto you in *p*
16:29 now speakest thou plainly. . speakest no *p*
2 Pet. 2:22 is happened. . according to the true *p*

Provide *See also* Furnish

Gen. 22:8 my son, God will *p* himself a lamb for a
30:30 when shall I *p* for mine own house also?
1 Sam. 16:17 *p* me now a man that can play well
Job 38:41 who *p* for the raven his food?
Ps. 78:20 can he *p* flesh for his people?
Prov. 6:8 *p* her meat in the summer, and gathereth
Mt. 10:9 *p* neither gold, nor silver, nor brass in
Lk. 12:20 shall those things be, which thou hast *p*?
12:33 *p* yourselves bags which wax not old
Rom. 12:17 *p* things honest in the sight of all men
1 Tim. 5:8 if any *p* not for his own, and specially
Heb. 11:40 God having *p* some better thing for us

Providence

Acts 24:2 deeds are done unto this nation by thy *p*

Provision *See also* Food, Victuals

Gen. 42:25 sack, and to give them *p* for the way
Ps. 132:15 I will abundantly bless her *p*
Dan. 1:5 them a daily *p* of the king's meat
Rom. 13:14 make not *p* for the flesh, to fulfill the

Provocation

1 Kgs. 15:30 his *p* wherewith he provoked the LORD
Job 17:2 doth not mine eye continue in their *p*?
Ps. 95:8 (Heb. 3:8, 15) harden not. . as in the *p*
Jer. 32:31 for this city hath been to me as a *p* of
Ezek. 20:28 they presented the *p* of their offering

Provoke *See also* Displease, Vex

Ex. 23:21 *p* him not; for he will not pardon your
Num. 14:11 Moses, How long will this people *p* me?
Deut. 31:20 other gods, and serve them, and *p* me
32:21 have *p* me to anger with their vanities
1 Sam. 1:6 her adversary also *p* her sore
1 Kgs. 14:22 they *p* him to jealousy with their sins
1 Chr. 21:1 Satan stood. . *p* David to number Israel
Ezra 5:12 our fathers had *p* the God of heaven
Job 12:6 prosper, and they that *p* God are secure
Ps. 78:17 sinned. . against him by *p* the Most High
78:40 how oft did they *p* him in the wilderness
78:56 yet they tempted and *p* the most high God
106:7 but *p* him at the sea, even at the Red sea
106:29 they *p* him to anger with their inventions
Prov. 20:2 whoso *p* him to anger sinneth against
Is. 1:4 they have *p* the Holy One of Israel unto
65:3 a people that *p* me to anger continually
Jer. 7:19 *p* me to anger. . do they not *p* themselves
44:8 in that ye *p* me unto wrath with the works
Zech. 8:14 to punish you, when your fathers *p* me
Lk. 11:53 and to *p* him to speak of many things
Rom. 11:11 the Gentiles, for to *p* them to jealousy
1 Cor. 13:5 seeketh not her own, is not easily *p*
2 Cor. 9:2 ready. . and your zeal hath *p* very many
Gal. 5:26 not. . desirous of vainglory, *p* one another
Eph. 6:4 (Col. 3:21) *p* not your children to wrath
Heb. 3:16 for some, when they had heard, did *p*
10:24 let us consider one another to *p* unto love

Prudence *See also* Discretion, Understanding, Wisdom

2 Chr. 2:12 to David . . a wise son, endued with *p*
Prov. 8:12 I wisdom dwell with *p*, and find out
Eph. 1:8 abounded toward us in all wisdom and *p*

Prudent *See also* Wise

1 Sam. 16:18 and *p* in matters, and a comely person
Prov. 12:16 known: but a *p* man covereth shame.
  13:16 every *p* man dealeth with knowledge: but
  14:15 but the *p* man looketh well to his going
  14:18 folly: but the *p* are crowned with knowledge
  16:21 the wise in heart shall be called *p*
  18:15 the heart of the *p* getteth knowledge
  19:14 of fathers: and a *p* wife is from the LORD
  22:3 (27:12) a *p* man forseeth the evil, and hideth
Is. 5:21 their own eyes, and *p* in their own sight!
  29:14 understanding of their *p* men shall be hid
Jer. 49:7 in Teman? is counsel perished from the *p*?
Hos. 14:9 these things? *p*, and he shall know them?
Amos 5:13 the *p* shall keep silence in that time
Mt. 11:25 (Lk. 10:21) hast hid . . from the wise and *p*
Acts 13:7 with the deputy . . Sergius Paulus, a *p* man
1 Cor. 1:19 to nothing the understanding of the *p*

Prudently

Is. 52:13 behold, my servant shall deal *p*, he shall

Prune

Lev. 25:3 six years thou shalt *p* thy vineyard
Is. 5:6 lay it waste: it shall not be *p*, nor digged

Pruning Hook

Is. 2:4 (Mic. 4:3) plowshares . . their spears into *p h*
Joel 3:10 into swords, and your *p h* into spears

Psalm

1 Chr. 16:7 David delivered first this *p* to thank
  16:9 (Ps. 105:2) sing unto him, sing *p* unto him
Ps. 81:2 take a *p*, and bring hither the timbrel
  95:2 let us . . make a joyful noise unto him with *p*
  98:5 sing . . with the harp, and the voice of a *p*
Lk. 24:44 prophets, and in the *p*, concerning me
1 Cor. 14:26 together, every one of you hath a *p*
Eph. 5:19 (Col. 3:16) *p* and hymns and spiritual songs
Jas. 5:13 him pray. Is any merry? let him sing

Psalmist

2 Sam. 23:1 David . . the sweet *p* of Israel, said

Psaltery

1 Sam. 10:5 with a *p*, and a tabret, and a pipe
Ps. 33:2 with harp: sing unto him with the *p* and
  57:8 (108:2) awake, *p* and harp: I myself will awake
  150:3 praise him with the *p* and harp

Public

Mt. 1:19 and not willing to make her a *p* example

Publican

Mt. 5:46 have ye? do not even the *p* the same?
  9:11 (Mk. 2:16; Lk. 5:30) why eateth . . with *p* and
  11:19 (Lk. 7:34) a friend of *p* and sinners
  18:17 him be unto thee as a heathen man and a *p*
  21:31 *p* and the harlots go into the kingdom
Lk. 3:12 then came also *p* to be baptized, and said
  7:29 that heard him, and the *p*, justified God
  15:1 drew near unto him all the *p* and sinners
  18:10 pray; the one a Pharisee, and the other a *p*
  19:2 Zaccheus, which was the chief among the *p*

Publicly

Acts 18:28 mightily convinced the Jews, and that *p*
  20:20 have taught you *p*, and from house to house

Publish *See also* Declare, Preach, Proclaim

Deut. 32:3 because I will *p* the name of the LORD
1 Sam. 31:9 to *p* it in the house of their idols
2 Sam. 1:20 *p* it not in the streets of Askelon
Ps. 26:7 I may *p* with the voice of thanksgiving
  68:11 great was the company of those that *p* it
Is. 52:7 (Nah. 1:15) good tidings, that *p* peace
Jon. 3:7 and *p* through Nineveh by the decree of
Mk. 1:45 but he went out, and began to *p* it much
  5:20 (Lk. 8:39) to *p* in Decapolis how great things
  13:10 gospel must first be *p* among all nations
Acts 13:49 word of the Lord was *p* throughout all

Publius Acts 28:7

Puff

Ps. 10:5 as for all his enemies, he *p* at them
  12:5 set him in safety from him that *p* at him
1 Cor. 4:6 no one of you be *p* up for one against
  4:18 some are *p* up, as though I would not come
  5:2 and ye are *p* up, and have not rather mourned
  8:1 knowledge *p* up, but charity edifieth
  13:4 charity vaunteth not itself, is not *p* up
Col. 2:18 vainly *p* up by his fleshly mind

Pul *See* Tiglath-pileser

Pull

Gen. 8:9 took her . . *p* her in unto him into the ark
1 Kgs. 13:4 dried up, so that he could not *p* it in
Ps. 31:4 *p* me out of the net that they have laid
Is. 22:19 and from thy state shall he *p* thee down
Jer. 1:10 the kingdoms, to root out, and to *p* down
  12:3 *p* them out like sheep for the slaughter
Lam. 3:11 turned aside my ways, and *p* me in pieces
Ezek. 17:9 shall he not *p* up the roots thereof
Amos 9:15 shall no more be *p* up out of their land
Mic. 2:8 ye *p* off the robe with the garment from
Mt. 7:4 (Lk. 6:42) *p* out the mote out of thine eye
Lk. 12:18 I will *p* down my barns, and build greater
  14:5 straightway *p* him out on the sabbath day?
Acts 23:10 lest Paul should have been *p* in pieces
2 Cor. 10:4 mighty. . to the *p* down of strongholds
Jude 23 save with fear, *p* them out of the fire

Pulpit

Neh. 8:4 Ezra the scribe stood upon a *p* of wood

Pulse

Dan. 1:12 give us *p* to eat, and water to drink

Punish *See also* Chasten, Chastise

Ex. 21:22 and hurt a woman . . he shall be surely *p*
Lev. 26:18 *p* you seven times more for your sins
Ezra 9:13 us less than our iniquities deserve
Job 31:11 it is an iniquity to be *p* by the judges
Prov. 17:26 also to *p* the just is not good, nor to
  22:3 (27:12) but the simple pass on, and are *p*
Is. 10:12 I will *p* the fruit of the stout heart
  13:11 and I will *p* the world for their evil
  24:21 the LORD shall *p* the host of the high ones
  26:21 to *p* the inhabitants of the earth for their
Jer. 9:25 I will *p* all them which are circumcised
  13:21 what wilt thou say when he shall *p* thee?
  21:14 I will *p* you according to the fruit of your
  23:34 I will even *p* that man and his house
  25:12 that I will *p* the king of Babylon

Jer. 29:32 behold, I will *p* Shemaiah the Nehelamite
  30:20 before me, and I will *p* all that oppress them
  44:13 *p* them that dwell in the land of Egypt
  50:18 I will *p* the king of Babylon and his land
Hos. 4:9 I will *p* them for their ways, and reward
  12:2 the LORD. . will *p* Jacob according to his ways
Amos 3:2 I will *p* you for all your iniquities
Zeph. 3:7 should not be cut off, howsoever I *p* them
Zech. 8:14 as I thought to *p* you, when your fathers
Acts 4:21 finding nothing how they might *p* them
  26:11 and I *p* them oft in every synagogue
2 Thes. 1:9 shall be *p* with everlasting destruction
2 Pet. 2:9 unjust unto the day of judgment to be *p*

Punishment *See also* Chastening, Chastisement, Correction

Gen. 4:13 LORD, My *p* is greater than I can bear
Lev. 26:41 then accept of the *p* of their iniquity
1 Sam. 28:10 shall no *p* happen to thee for this
Job 31:3 a strange *p* to the workers of iniquity?
Ps. 149:7 upon the heathen, and *p* upon the people
Prov. 19:19 a man of great wrath shall suffer *p*
Lam. 3:39 complain, a man for the *p* of his sins?
  4:6 *p*. . is greater than the *p* of the sin of Sodom
  4:22 the *p* of thine iniquity is accomplished
Ezek. 14:10 of the prophet shall be. . as the *p* of him
Amos 1:3 (1:6, 9, 11, 13; 2:1, 4, 6) not turn away the *p*
Zech. 14:19 the *p* of all nations that come not up
Mt. 25:46 these shall go away into everlasting *p*
2 Cor. 2:6 sufficient to such a man is this *p*
Heb. 10:29 how much sorer *p*. . shall he be thought
1 Pet. 10:24 are sent by him for the *p* of evildoers

Pur (Purim)

Esth. 3:7 (9:24) cast *P*, that is, the lot, before Haman
  9:26 they called these days *P* after the name of *P*

Purchase

Gen. 25:10 the field which Abraham *p* of the sons of
Ex. 15:16 the people pass over, which thou hast *p*
Lev. 25:33 and if a man *p* of the Levites, then the
Ruth 4:10 moreover Ruth. . have I *p* to be my wife
Ps. 74:2 congregation, which thou hast *p* of old
  78:54 this mountain, which his right hand had *p*
Jer. 32:16 had delivered the evidence of the *p* unto
Acts 1:18 *p* a field with the reward of iniquity
  8:20 hast thought that the gift of God may be *p*
  20:28 church. . which he hath *p* with his own blood
1 Tim. 3:13 deacon. . *p* to themselves a good degree

Pure (Purer) *See also* Chaste, Clean, Holy

2 Sam. 22:27 (Ps. 18:26) with the *p*. . show thyself *p*
Job 4:17 shall a man be more *p* than his Maker?
  8:6 if thou wert *p* and upright; surely now he
  11:4 hast said, My doctrine is *p*, and I am clean
  16:17 not for any injustice. . also my prayer is *p*
  25:5 shineth not. . stars are not *p* in his sight
Ps. 12:6 words of the LORD are *p* words: as silver
  19:8 commandment of the LORD is *p*, enlightening
  24:4 he that hath clean hands, and a *p* heart
  119:140 thy word is very *p*. . thy servant loveth it
Prov. 15:26 the words of the *p* are pleasant words
  20:9 made my heart clean, I am *p* from my sin?
  20:11 a child is known. . whether his work be *p*
  21:8 but as for the *p*, his work is right
  30:5 every word of God is *p*: he is a shield unto
  30:12 a generation that are *p* in their own eyes
Lam. 4:7 her Nazarites were *p* than snow, they were
Mic. 6:11 I count them *p* with the wicked balances
Hab. 1:13 thou art of *p* eyes than to behold evil

Zeph. 3:9 will I turn to the people a *p* language
Mal. 1:11 offered unto my name, and a *p* offering
Mt. 5:8 blessed are the *p* in heart: for they shall
Acts 20:26 that I am *p* from the blood of all men
Rom. 14:20 all things indeed are *p*; but it is evil
Phil. 4:8 things are just, whatsoever things are *p*
1 Tim. 1:5 charity out of a *p* heart, and of a good
  3:9 the mystery of the faith in a *p* conscience
  5:22 partaker of other men's sins: keep thyself *p*
2 Tim. 1:3 God, whom I serve. . with *p* conscience
  2:22 them that call on the Lord out of a *p* heart
Tit. 1:15 unto the *p* all things are *p*
Heb. 10:22 and our bodies washed with *p* water
Jas. 1:27 *p* religion and undefiled before God
  3:17 wisdom that is from above is first *p*, then
1 Pet. 1:22 ye love one another with a *p* heart
2 Pet. 3:1 in both which I stir up your *p* minds by
1 Jn. 3:3 in him purifieth himself, even as he is *p*
Rev. 15:6 angels. . clothed in *p* and white linen
  22:1 and he showed me a *p* river of water of life

Pureness

Job 22:30 it is delivered by the *p* of thine hands
Prov. 22:11 he that loveth *p* of heart, for the
2 Cor. 6:6 by *p*, by knowledge, by long-suffering

Purge

1 Sam. 3:14 iniquity of Eli's house shall not be *p*
2 Chr. 34:3 he began to *p* Judah and Jerusalem from
Ps. 51:7 *p* me with hyssop, and I shall be clean
  65:3 our transgressions, thou shalt *p* them away
  79:9 and *p* away our sins, for thy name's sake
Prov. 16:6 by mercy and truth iniquity is *p*
Is. 1:25 *p* away thy dross. . take away all thy tin
  4:4 and shall have *p* the blood of Jerusalem
  6:7 thine iniquity is taken away, and thy sin *p*
  22:14 this iniquity shall not be *p* from you till
  27:9 by this. . shall the iniquity of Jacob be *p*
Ezek. 24:13 I have *p* thee, and thou wast not *p*
Dan. 11:35 try them. . to *p*, and to make them white
Mal. 3:3 sons of Levi, and *p* them as gold
Mt. 3:12 (Lk. 3:17) will thoroughly *p* his floor
Jn. 15:2 every branch that beareth fruit, he *p* it
1 Cor. 5:7 *p* out therefore the old leaven, that ye
2 Tim. 2:21 if a man. . *p* himself from these, he
Heb. 1:3 when he had by himself *p* our sins, sat
  9:14 *p* your conscience from dead works to serve
  9:22 all things are by the law *p* with blood
2 Pet. 1:9 forgotten. . he was *p* from his old sins

Purification

Num. 19:9 a water of separation: it is a *p* for sin
2 Chr. 30:19 according to the *p* of the sanctuary
Esth. 2:12 were the days of their *p* accomplished
Lk. 2:22 when the days of her *p*. . were accomplished
Acts 21:26 accomplishment of the days of *p*, until

Purifier

Mal. 3:3 he shall sit as a refiner and *p* of silver

Purify *See also* Cleanse, Hallow, Sanctify

Lev. 8:15 *p* the altar, and poured the blood at the
Num. 8:21 and the Levites were *p*, and they washed
  19:12 he shall *p* himself with it on the third day
  31:23 it shall be *p* with the water of separation
2 Sam. 11:4 for she was *p* from her uncleanness
Ezra 6:20 priests and the Levites were *p* together
Neh. 12:30 priests. . *p* themselves, and the people
Job 41:25 by reason of breakings they *p* themselves
Ps. 12:6 silver tried in a furnace. . *p* seven times
Is. 66:17 and *p* themselves in the gardens behind
Dan. 12:10 many shall be *p*, and made white
Mal. 3:3 he shall *p* the sons of Levi, and purge

Jn. 11:55 to Jerusalem before the passover, to *p*
Acts 15:9 no difference. . *p* their hearts by faith
  21:24 them take, and *p* thyself with them
Tit. 2:14 and *p* unto himself a peculiar people
Heb. 9:23 patterns of things in the heavens. . be *p*
Jas. 4:8 and *p* your hearts, ye double-minded
1 Pet. 1:22 *p* your souls in obeying the truth
1 Jn. 3:3 man that hath this hope in him *p* himself

Purifying *See also* Purify

Lev. 12:4 shall. . continue in the blood of her *p*
Num. 8:7 sprinkle water of *p* upon them, and let
Jn. 2:6 six waterpots. . after the manner of the *p*
  3:25 of John's disciples and the Jews about *p*
Heb. 9:13 unclean, sanctifieth to the *p* of the flesh

Purim *See* Pur

Purity *See also* Holiness

1 Tim. 4:12 in charity, in spirit, in faith, in *p*
  5:2 as mothers; the younger as sisters, with all *p*

Purloin

Tit. 2:10 not *p*, but showing all good fidelity

Purple

Ex. 25:4 (28:5; 35:6; 39:1) blue, and *p*, and scarlet
Num. 4:13 the altar, and spread a *p* cloth thereon
Prov. 31:22 of tapestry; her clothing is silk and *p*
Mk. 15:17 (Jn. 19:2) clothed him with *p*, and platted
Lk. 16:19 which was clothed in *p* and fine linen
Acts 16:14 certain woman named Lydia, a seller of *p*
Rev. 17:4 woman was arrayed in *p* and scarlet color

Purpose *See also* Desire, End, Will

Gen. 27:42 behold, thy brother Esau. . *p* to kill thee
Job 17:11 my days are past, my *p* are broken off
Ps. 17:3 I am *p* that my mouth shall not transgress
Prov. 20:18 every *p* is established by counsel
Eccl. 3:1 and a time to every *p* under the heaven
Is. 1:11 what *p* is the multitude of your sacrifices
  14:24 surely. . as I have *p*, so shall it stand
  14:26 is the *p* that is *p* upon the whole earth
  14:27 LORD of hosts hath *p*, and who shall
  19:10 and they shall be broken in the *p* thereof
  23:9 LORD of hosts hath *p* it, to stain the pride
  46:11 it to pass; I have *p* it, I will also do it
Jer. 4:28 I have *p* it, and will not repent
  51:29 for every *p* of the LORD shall be performed
Dan. 1:8 Daniel *p* in his heart that he would not
  6:17 the *p* might not be changed concerning Daniel
Mt. 26:8 saw it. . saying, To what *p* is this waste?
Acts 11:23 that with *p* of heart they would cleave
  26:16 for I have appeared unto thee for this *p*
Rom. 8:28 who are the called according to his *p*
  9:11 *p* of God according to election might stand
2 Cor. 1:17 things that I *p*, do I *p* according to
  9:7 as he *p* in his heart, so let him give
Eph. 1:9 good pleasure which he hath *p* in himself
  1:11 predestinated according to the *p* of him who
  3:11 the eternal *p* which he *p* in Christ Jesus
2 Tim. 1:9 but according to his own *p* and grace
1 Jn. 3:8 for this *p* the Son of God was manifested

Purse

Prov. 1:14 thy lot among us; let us all have one *p*
Mt. 10:9 provide neither gold. . nor brass in your *p*
Lk. 10:4 carry neither *p*, nor scrip, nor shoes
  22:36 but now, he that hath a *p*, let him take it

Pursue

Gen. 14:14 his trained servants. . *p* them unto Dan
  31:36 my sin, that thou hast so hotly *p* after me?

Ex. 14:8 Pharaoh. . *p* after the children of Israel
Lev. 26:17 and ye shall flee when none *p* you
Deut. 19:6 (Josh. 20:5) avenger of blood *p* the slayer
  28:22 and they shall *p* thee until thou perish
Judg. 8:4 and the three hundred men. . faint, yet *p*
1 Sam. 30:8 shall I *p*. . And he answered him, *P*
2 Sam. 2:19 *p* after Abner; and in going he turned not
  22:38 (Ps. 18:37) I have *p* mine enemies, and
1 Kgs. 18:27 god; either he is talking, or he is *p*
Job 13:25 and wilt thou *p* the dry stubble?
  30:15 turned upon me: they *p* my soul as the wind
Ps. 34:14 evil, and do good; seek peace, and *p* it
Prov. 11:19 he that *p* evil *p* it to his own death
  13:21 evil *p* sinners: but to the righteous good
  28:1 wicked flee when no man *p*: but the righteous
Amos 1:11 he did *p* his brother with the sword

Push

Ex. 21:29 if the ox were wont to *p* with his horn
1 Kgs. 22:11 (2 Chr. 18:10) shalt thou *p* the Syrians
Job 30:12 they *p* away my feet, and they raise up
Ps. 44:5 through thee will we *p* down our enemies
Dan. 11:40 shall the king of the south *p* at him

Put *See also* Place, Set

Gen. 2:8 in Eden; and there he *p* the man whom he
Ex. 3:5 (Acts 7:33) *p* off thy shoes from off thy feet
  17:14 I will utterly *p* out the remembrance of
  23:1 *p* not thine hand with the wicked to be an
Lev. 1:4 he shall *p* his hand upon the head of the
Num. 23:5 and the LORD *p* a word in Balaam's mouth
Deut. 7:22 LORD thy God will *p* out those nations
Judg. 12:3 I *p* my life in my hands, and passed over
1 Sam. 2:36 *p* me. . into one of the priests' offices
1 Kgs. 9:3 hallowed this house. . to *p* my name there
  11:36 city which I have chosen me to *p* my name
  20:11 harness boast himself as he that *p* it off
2 Chr. 34:10 they *p* it in the hand of the workmen
Neh. 2:12 what my God had *p* in my heart to do at
Job 19:13 he hath *p* my brethren far from me
Ps. 8:6 (Eph. 1:22; Heb. 2:8) hast *p* all things under
Eccl. 10:10 then must he *p* to more strength
Song 2:13 the fig tree *p* forth her green figs
Is. 42:1 (Mt. 12:18) I have *p* my Spirit upon him
  51:9 (52:1) awake, awake, *p* on strength
Ezek. 11:19 (36:26) I will *p* a new spirit within you
Amos 6:3 ye that *p* far away the evil day, and cause
Mt. 6:25 (Lk. 12:22) for your body, what ye shall *p* on
  8:3 (Mk. 1:41; Lk. 5:13) and Jesus *p* forth his hand
  19:6 (Mk. 10:9) joined. . let not man *p* asunder
Mk. 10:16 *p* his hands upon them, and blessed them
Lk. 9:62 no man, having *p* his hand to the plow
Jn. 5:7 sir, I have no man. . to *p* me into the pool
  10:4 he *p* forth his own sheep, he goeth before
  13:2 devil having now *p* into the heart of Judas
Acts 13:46 word of God. . but seeing ye *p* it from you
Rom. 13:14 but *p* ye on the Lord Jesus Christ
1 Cor. 15:24 when he shall have *p* down all rule
  15:25 till he hath *p* all enemies under his feet
Gal. 3:27 baptized into Christ have *p* on Christ
Eph. 4:22 (Col. 3:9) that ye *p* off. . the old man
  4:24 (Col. 3:10) *p* on the new man, which after God
  6:11 *p* on the whole armor of God, that ye may
Col. 3:12 *p* on therefore. . bowels of mercies
  3:14 above all these things *p* on charity
1 Thes. 2:4 be *p* in trust with the gospel, even so
  5:8 be sober, *p* on the breastplate of faith
Phlm. 18 oweth thee aught, *p* that on mine account
Heb. 9:26 to *p* away sin by the sacrifice of himself
2 Pet. 1:14 I must *p* off this my tabernacle
Rev. 2:24 I will *p* upon you none other burden

Q

Quail

Ex. 16:13 the *q* came up, and covered the camp
Num. 11:31 a wind from the LORD, and brought *q*
Ps. 105:40 the people asked, and he brought *q*

Quake *See also* Fear, Tremble

Ex. 19:18 smoke thereof ascended. . whole mount *q*
1 Sam. 14:15 they also trembled, and the earth *q*
Ezek. 12:18 Son of man, eat thy bread with *q*
Dan. 10:7 but a great *q* fell upon them, so that
Joel 2:10 earth shall *q* before them; the heavens
Nah. 1:5 the mountains *q* at him, and the hills melt
Mt. 27:51 and the earth did *q*, and the rocks rent
Heb. 12:21 Moses said, I exceedingly fear and *q*

Quarrel

Lev. 26:25 that shall avenge the *q* of my covenant
2 Kgs. 5:7 and see how he seeketh a *q* against me
Mk. 6:19 therefore Herodias had a *q* against him
Col. 3:13 if any man have a *q* against any

Queen

1 Kgs. 10:1 (2 Chr. 9:1) *q* of Sheba heard of the fame
    15:13 (2 Chr. 15:16) her he removed from being *q*
Esth. 1:11 to bring Vashti the *q* before the king
    2:17 loved Esther. . made her *q* instead of Vashti
Ps. 45:9 upon thy right hand did stand the *q*
Is. 49:23 fathers, and their *q* thy nursing mothers
Jer. 7:18 to make cakes to the *q* of heaven
    44:17 to burn incense unto the *q* of heaven
Dan. 5:10 now the *q*. . came into the banquet house
Mt. 12:42 (Lk. 11:31) *q* of the south shall rise up
Acts 8:27 under Candace *q* of the Ethiopians
Rev. 18:7 she saith in her heart, I sit a *q*, and am

Quench

Num. 11:2 Moses prayed unto the LORD. . fire was *q*
2 Sam. 14:7 so they shall *q* my coal which is left
    21:17 that thou *q* not the light of Israel
Ps. 118:12 they are *q* as the fire of thorns
Song 8:7 many waters cannot *q* love, neither can
Is. 1:31 both burn together, and none shall *q* them
    34:10 is shall not be *q* night nor day; the smoke
    42:3 (Mt. 12:20) the smoking flax shall he not *q*
    43:17 they are extinct, they are *q* as tow
    66:24 shall not die, neither shall their fire be *q*
Jer. 4:4 (21:12) burn that none can *q* it, because of
Ezek. 20:47 flaming flame shall not be *q*, and all
Mk. 9:44 (9:46, 48) dieth not, and the fire is not *q*
Eph. 6:16 ye shall be able to *q* all the fiery darts
1 Thes. 5:19 *q* not the Spirit
Heb. 11:34 *q* the violence of fire, escaped the edge

Question *See also* Ask, Inquire

1 Kgs. 10:1 (2 Chr. 9:1) to prove him with hard *q*
Mt. 22:46 (Mk. 12:34; Lk. 20:40) ask him any more *q*
Mk. 1:27 insomuch that they *q* among themselves
    9:10 *q* one with another what the rising from the
    9:16 he asked the scribes, What *q* ye with them?
    11:29 I will also ask of you one *q*, and answer me
Lk. 2:46 both hearing them, and asking them *q*
Jn. 3:25 a *q* between some of John's disciples and
Acts 18:15 if it be a *q* of words and names, and of
    19:40 to be called in *q* for this day's uproar
1 Cor. 10:25 eat, asking no *q* for conscience' sake
1 Tim. 1:4 minister *q*, rather than godly edifying
    6:4 doting about *q* and strifes of words, whereof
2 Tim. 2:23 (Tit. 3:9) foolish and unlearned *q* avoid

Quick *See also* Alive, Living

Num. 16:30 they go down *q* into the pit
Ps. 124:3 then they had swallowed us up *q*, when
Is. 11:3 and shall make him of *q* understanding in
Acts 10:42 ordained. . to be the Judge of *q* and dead
2 Tim. 4:1 judge the *q* and the dead at his appearing
Heb. 4:12 word of God is *q*. . powerful, and sharper
1 Pet. 4:5 is ready to judge the *q* and the dead

Quicken

Ps. 71:20 shalt *q* me again, and shalt bring me up
    80:18 *q* us, and we will call upon thy name
    119:25 (119:107, 154) *q* thou me according to thy
    119:37 beholding vanity; and *q* thou me in thy way
    119:40 thy precepts: *q* me in thy righteousness
    119:50 this is my comfort. . for thy word hath *q* me
    119:88 *q* me after thy loving-kindness; so shall I
    119:149 (119:156) *q* me according to thy judgment
    143:11 *q* me, O LORD, for thy name's sake
Jn. 5:21 Father raiseth up the dead, and *q* them
    6:63 Spirit that *q*; the flesh profiteth nothing
Rom. 4:17 even God, who *q* the dead, and calleth
    8:11 also *q* your mortal bodies by his Spirit
1 Cor. 15:36 thou sowest is not *q*, except it die
    15:45 living soul. . last Adam was made a *q* spirit
Eph. 2:1 you hath he *q*, who were dead in trespasses
    2:5 (Col. 2:13) dead in sins, hath *q* us together with
1 Tim. 6:13 in the sight of God, who *q* all things
1 Pet. 3:18 death in the flesh, but *q* by the Spirit

Quickly

Gen. 27:20 how is it that thou hast found it so *q*
Ex. 32:8 (Deut. 9:12) turned aside *q* out of the way
Num. 16:46 go *q* unto the congregation, and make an
Josh. 2:5 pursue after them *q*. . ye shall overtake
    10:6 come up to us *q*, and save us, and help us
2 Sam. 17:16 now therefore send *q*, and tell David
Mt. 5:25 agree with thine adversary *q*, while thou
    28:7 go *q*. . tell his disciples that he is risen
Mk. 16:8 went out *q*, and fled from the sepulchre
Jn. 13:27 said Jesus unto him, That thou doest, do *q*
Acts 22:18 haste, and get thee *q* out of Jerusalem
Rev. 2:5 (2:16) or else I will come unto thee *q*
    3:11 (22:7, 12) behold, I come *q*
    22:20 surely I come *q*. . Even so, come, Lord Jesus

Quiet *See also* Peaceable, Still

2 Kgs. 11:20 (2 Chr. 23:21) and the city was in *q*
2 Chr. 14:1 in his days the land was *q* ten years
Job 3:13 now should I have lain still and been *q*
    21:23 full strength, being wholly at ease and *q*
    37:17 when he *q* the earth by the south wind?
Ps. 107:30 then are they glad because they be *q*
    131:2 I have behaved and *q* myself, as a child
Prov. 1:33 safely, and shall be *q* from fear of evil
Eccl. 9:17 words of wise men are heard in *q* more
Is. 7:4 say unto him, Take heed, and be *q*; fear not
    14:7 whole earth is at rest, and is *q*: they break
    32:18 sure dwellings, and in *q* resting places
    33:20 eyes shall see Jerusalem a *q* habitation
Jer. 30:10 return, and shall be in rest, and be *q*
    49:23 there is sorrow on the sea; it cannot be *q*
Ezek. 16:42 I will be *q*, and will be no more angry
Nah. 1:12 though they be *q*, and likewise many
Acts 19:36 ought to be *q*, and to do nothing rashly
1 Thes. 4:11 that ye study to be *q*, and to do your
1 Tim. 2:2 that we may lead a *q* and peaceable life
1 Pet. 3:4 even the ornament of a meek and *q* spirit

Quietness *See also* Peace, Rest

Judg. 8:28 the country was in a *q* forty years in the
1 Chr. 22:9 I will give peace and *q* unto Israel in

Job 34:29 when he giveth *q*, who. . can make trouble
Prov. 17:1 better is a dry morsel, and *q* therewith
Eccl. 4:6 better is a handful with *q*, than both
Is. 30:15 in *q* and in confidence shall be your
32:17 effect of righteousness, *q* and assurance
Acts 24:2 seeing that by thee we enjoy great *q*
2 Thes. 3:12 with *q* they work, and eat their own

Quit

Ex. 21:19 then shall he that smote him be *q*
Josh. 2:20 then we will be *q* of thine oath which
1 Sam. 4:9 be strong, and *q* yourselves like men
1 Cor. 16:13 the faith, *q* you like men, be strong

Quiver

Gen. 27:3 take. . thy weapons, thy *q* and thy bow
Job 39:23 *q* rattleth against him, the glittering
Ps. 127:5 happy is the man that hath his *q* full
Is. 49:2 a polished shaft; in his *q* hath he hid me
Jer. 5:16 their *q* is as an open sepulchre
Lam. 3:13 arrows of his *q* to enter into my reins
Hab. 3:16 my belly trembled; my lips *q* at the voice

R

Raamses (Rameses)

Gen. 47:11; Ex. 1:11; 12:37

Rabbah 2 Sam. 11:1; 12:26

Rabbi *See also* Instructor, Master, Teacher

Mt. 23:7 greetings. . and to be called of men, *R, R*
23:8 but be not ye called *R*: for one is your

Rab-shakeh 2 Kgs. 18:17–19:8 (Is. 36:2–37:8)

Raca

Mt. 5:22 whosoever shall say to his brother, *R*

Race *See also* Run

Ps. 19:5 and rejoiceth as a strong man to run a *r*
Eccl. 9:11 the *r* is not to the swift, nor the battle
1 Cor. 9:24 they which run in a *r* run all, but one
Heb. 12:1 let us run with patience the *r* that is

Rachel Gen. 29:6–31:34; 35:16–19

Ruth 4:11 make the woman. . like *R* and like Leah
Jer. 31:15 (Mt. 2:18) *R* weeping for her children

Rage *See also* Anger, Fury, Indignation, Passion, Wrath

2 Kgs. 5:12 so he turned and went away in a *r*
19:57 (Is. 37:28) but I know. . thy *r* against me
2 Chr. 28:9 in a *r* that reacheth up unto heaven
Job 40:11 cast abroad the *r* of thy wrath
Ps. 2:1 (Acts 4:25) why do the heathen *r*, and the
7:6 lift up. . because of the *r* of mine enemies
46:6 the heathen *r*, the kingdoms were moved
Prov. 6:34 jealousy is the *r* of a man: therefore
14:16 from evil: but the fool *r*, and is confident
29:9 whether he *r* or laugh, there is no rest
Hos. 7:16 shall fall. . for the *r* of their tongue
Nah. 2:4 the chariots shall *r* in the streets

Raging

Ps. 89:9 thou rulest the *r* of the sea: when the
Prov. 20:1 wine is a mocker, strong drink is *r*
Jon. 1:15 and the sea ceased from her *r*

Lk. 8:24 rebuked the wind and the *r* of the water
Jude 13 *r* waves of the sea, foaming out. . shame

Rags

Prov. 23:21 drowsiness shall clothe a man with *r*
Is. 64:6 all our righteousnesses are as filthy *r*
Jer. 38:11 took. . old cast clouts and old rotten *r*

Rahab

Josh. 2:1 came into a harlot's house, named *R*
6:17 only *R* the harlot shall live, she and all
Heb. 11:31 by faith the harlot *R* perished not with
Jas. 2:25 was not *R* the harlot justified by works

Rail

1 Sam. 25:14 to salute our master; and he *r* on them
2 Chr. 32:17 he wrote also letters to *r* on the LORD
Mk. 15:29 they that passed by *r* on him, wagging
Lk. 23:39 one of the malefactors. . *r* on him, saying

Railer

1 Cor. 5:11 or an idolater, or a *r*, or a drunkard

Railing

1 Tim. 6:4 whereof cometh envy, strife, *r*, evil
1 Pet. 3:9 not rendering evil for evil, or *r* for *r*
2 Pet. 2:11 bring not *r* accusation against them
Jude 9 durst not bring against him a *r* accusation

Raiment *See also* Clothes, Clothing, Garment, Robe, Vesture

Gen. 27:15 Rebekah took goodly *r* of her eldest son
28:20 will give me bread to eat, and *r* to put on
Ex. 22:26 at all take thy neighbor's *r* to pledge
Deut. 8:4 thy *r* waxed not old upon thee, neither
22:3 do with his *r*; and with all lost things of
24:13 he may sleep in his own *r*, and bless thee
24:17 nor take a widow's *r* to pledge
2 Kgs. 5:5 and took with him. . ten changes of *r*
Job 27:16 as the dust, and prepare *r* as the clay
Ps. 45:14 brought unto the King in *r* of needlework
Is. 14:19 and as the *r* of those that are slain
63:3 their blood. . and I will stain all my *r*
Zech. 3:4 and I will clothe thee with change of *r*
Mt. 3:4 the same John had his *r* of camel's hair
6:25 (Lk. 12:23) than meat, and the body than *r*?
6:28 and why take ye thought for *r*? Consider the
11:8 (Lk. 7:25) to see? A man clothed in soft *r*?
17:2 transfigured. . his *r* was white as the light
27:31 put his own *r* on him, and led him away to
Mk. 9:3 *r* became shining, exceeding white as snow
Lk. 9:29 altered, and his *r* was white and glistering
10:30 thieves, which stripped him of his *r*
23:34 and they parted his *r*, and cast lots
Acts 22:20 and kept the *r* of them that slew him
1 Tim. 6:8 having food and *r*, let us be. . content
Jas. 2:2 there come in also a poor man in vile *r*
Rev. 3:5 the same shall be clothed in white *r*
3:18 and white *r*, that thou mayest be clothed

Rain *See also* Shower

Gen. 2:5 God had not caused it to *r* upon the earth
7:12 *r* was upon the earth forty days and. . nights
8:2 stopped, and the *r* from heaven was restrained
Ex. 16:4 behold, I will *r* bread from heaven for you
Lev. 26:4 then I will give you *r* in due season
Deut. 11:11 and drinketh water of the *r* of heaven
11:14 give you the *r*. . the first *r* and the latter *r*
28:12 to give the *r* unto thy land in his season
32:2 my doctrine shall drop as the *r*, my speech
2 Sam. 23:4 of the earth by clear shining after *r*
1 Kgs. 8:35 (2 Chr. 6:26) no *r*, because they. . sinned

1 Kgs. 17:1 shall not be dew nor *r* these years
18:41 for there is a sound of abundance of *r*
Ezra 10:13 it is a time of much *r*, and we are not
Job 5:10 who giveth *r* upon the earth, and sendeth
37:6 to the small *r*, and to the great *r* of his
38:28 hath the *r* a father? or who hath begotten
Ps. 11:6 upon the wicked he shall *r* snares, fire
72:6 shall come down like *r* upon the mown grass
78:24 and had *r* down manna upon them to eat
84:6 make it a well; the *r* also filleth the pools
147:8 who prepareth *r* for the earth, who maketh
Prov. 25:14 is like clouds and wind without *r*
25:23 the north wind driveth away *r*: so doth an
26:1 as snow in summer, and as *r* in harvest, so
28:3 is like a sweeping *r* which leaveth no food
Eccl. 11:3 if the clouds be full of *r*, they empty
Song 2:11 winter is past, the *r* is over and gone
Is. 4:6 and for a covert from storm and from *r*
44:14 planteth an ash, and the *r* doth nourish it
55:10 as the *r* cometh down, and the snow from
Jer. 5:24 giveth *r*, both the former and the latter
14:4 is chapped, for there was no *r* in the earth
Ezek. 38:22 I will *r* upon him. . an overflowing *r*
Hos. 6:3 as the *r*, as the latter and former *r* unto
10:12 till he come and *r* righteousness upon you
Joel 2:23 the *r*, the former, and the latter *r* in
Amos 4:7 and also I have withholden the *r* from you
Zech. 10:1 ask ye. . *r* in the time of the latter *r*
14:17 will not come. . even upon them shall be no *r*
Mt. 5:45 sendeth *r* on the just and on the unjust
7:25 (7:27) the *r* descended, and the floods came
Acts 14:17 did good, and gave us *r* from heaven
28:2 and received us. . because of the present *r*
Heb. 6:7 the earth which drinketh in the *r* that
Jas. 5:7 until he receive the early and latter *r*
5:17 he prayed earnestly that it might not *r*
Rev. 11:6 power to shut heaven, that it *r* not

Rainbow *See also* Bow

Rev. 4:3 and there was a *r* round about the throne
10:1 angel come down. . and a *r* was upon his head

Rainy

Prov. 27:15 a continual dropping in a very *r* day

Raise *See also* Rear

Ex. 9:16 (Rom. 9:17) for this cause have I *r* thee up
Deut. 18:15 (Acts 3:22; 7:37) will *r* up. . a Prophet
Josh. 8:29 and *r* thereon a great heap of stones
Judg. 2:16 LORD *r* up judges, which delivered them
1 Sam. 2:8 (Ps. 113:7) *r* up the poor out of the dust
Ezra 1:5 whose spirit God had *r*, to go up to build
Job 14:12 not awake, nor be *r* out of their sleep
Ps. 41:10 be merciful unto me, and *r* me up, that
145:14 LORD. . *r* up all those that be bowed down
Is. 23:13 set up the towers. . *r* up the palaces
44:26 and I will *r* up the decayed places thereof
45:13 I have *r* him up in righteousness
Jer. 23:5 I will *r* unto David a righteous Branch
Hos. 6:2 in the third day he will *r* us up, and we
Joel 3:7 I will *r* them out of the place whither ye
Amos 9:11 in that day will I *r* up the tabernacle
Zech. 2:13 he is *r* up out of his holy habitation
11:16 lo, I will *r* up a shepherd in the land
Mt. 3:9 (Lk. 3:8) of these stones to *r* up children
10:8 cleanse the lepers, *r* the dead, cast out
11:5 (Lk. 7:22) the deaf hear, the dead are *r* up
16:21 (17:23; Lk. 9:22) killed. . be *r* again the third
Lk. 1:69 hath *r* up a horn of salvation for us in
20:37 that the dead are *r*, even Moses showed
Jn. 2:19 temple, and in three days I will *r* it up
5:21 Father *r* up the dead, and quickeneth them
6:40 (6:44, 54) I will *r* him up at the last day

Acts 2:24 whom God hath *r* up, having loosed the
2:30 he would *r* up Christ to sit on his throne
2:32 this Jesus hath God *r* up, whereof we all
3:15 Prince of life, whom God hath *r* from the dead
3:26 God, having *r* up his Son Jesus, sent him
4:10 ye crucified, whom God *r* from the dead
5:30 the God of our fathers *r* up Jesus, whom ye
10:40 him God *r* up the third day, and showed him
13:23 hath God. . *r* unto Israel a Saviour, Jesus
13:30 but God *r* him from the dead
17:31 in that he hath *r* him from the dead
26:8 incredible. . that God should *r* the dead?
Rom. 4:25 and was *r* again for our justification
6:4 like as Christ was *r* up from the dead by the
8:11 but if the Spirit of him that *r* up Jesus
10:9 believe. . that God hath *r* him from the dead
1 Cor. 6:14 *r* up the Lord, and will also *r* up us
15:15 have testified of God that he *r* up Christ
15:35 some man will say, How are the dead *r* up?
15:42 sown in corruption, it is *r* in incorruption
2 Cor. 1:9 ourselves, but in God which *r* the dead
4:14 he which *r* up the Lord Jesus shall *r* up us
Eph. 1:20 in Christ, when he *r* him from the dead
2:6 hath *r* us up together, and made us sit
Col. 2:12 of God, who hath *r* him from the dead
1 Thes. 1:10 whom he *r* from the dead, even Jesus
2 Tim. 2:8 that Jesus Christ. . was *r* from the dead
Heb. 11:19 accounting that God was able to *r* him
11:35 women received their dead *r* to life again
Jas. 5:15 the sick, and the Lord shall *r* him up
1 Pet. 1:21 do believe in God, that *r* him up from the

Ram

Gen. 15:9 a *r* of three years old, and a turtledove
22:13 a *r* caught in a thicket by his horns
31:10 behold, the *r* which leaped upon the cattle
Ex. 25:5 (26:14; 35:7; 36:19; 39:34) *r* skins dyed red
29:15 (Lev. 8:18) their hands upon the head of the *r*
Lev. 5:15 for his trespass. . a *r* without blemish
Ps. 114:4 the mountains skipped like *r*
Is. 1:11 I am full of the burnt offerings of *r*
Dan. 8:3 before the river a *r* which had two horns
Mic. 6:7 the LORD be pleased with thousands of *r*

Ramah (Rama)

1 Sam. 8:4 elders of Israel. . came to Samuel unto *R*
19:18 so David fled. . and came to Samuel to *R*
Jer. 31:15 (Mt. 2:18) a voice was heard in *R*

Rameses *See* Raamses

Ramoth-gilead

1 Kgs. 22:4 (2 Chr. 18:3); 2 Kgs. 9:1

Ran *See* Run

Rank

1 Chr. 12:33 fifty thousand, which could keep *r*
Mk. 6:40 they sat down in *r*, by hundreds, and by

Ransom *See also* Deliver, Redeem, Redemption, Save

Ex. 21:30 give for the *r* of his life whatsoever
30:12 every man a *r* for his soul unto the LORD
Job 33:24 going down to the pit: I have found a *r*
36:18 beware lest. . a great *r* cannot deliver thee
Ps. 49:7 his brother, nor give to God a *r* for him
Prov. 6:35 he will not regard any *r*; neither will
13:8 the *r* of a man's life are his riches
21:18 the wicked shall be a *r* for the righteous

Is. 43:3 I gave Egypt for thy *r*, Ethiopia and Seba
Jer. 31:11 the LORD hath redeemed Jacob, and *r* him
Hos. 13:14 will *r* them from the power of the grave
Mt. 20:28 (Mk. 10:45) to give his life a *r* for many
1 Tim. 2:6 who gave himself a *r* for all

Ransomed *See also* Ransom, Redeemed

Is. 35:10 and the *r* of the LORD shall return
51:10 the sea a way for the *r* to pass over?

Rare

Dan. 2:11 it is a *r* thing that the king requireth

Rase

Ps. 137:7 said, *R* it, *r* it, even to the foundation

Rash

Eccl. 5:2 be not *r* with thy mouth, and let not
Is. 32:4 the heart also of the *r* shall understand

Rashly

Acts 19:36 ought to be quiet, and to do nothing *r*

Raven

Gen. 8:7 he sent forth a *r*, which went forth to
Lev. 11:15 (Deut. 14:14) every *r* after his kind
1 Kgs. 17:6 and the *r* brought him bread and flesh
Job 38:41 who provideth for the *r* his food?
Lk. 12:24 consider the *r*: for they neither sow nor

Ravening

Ps. 22:13 gaped upon me . . as a *r* and a roaring lion
Mt. 7:15 clothing, but inwardly they are *r* wolves
Lk. 11:39 inward part is full of *r* and wickedness

Ravenous

Is. 35:9 lion . . nor any *r* beast shall go up thereon
46:11 calling a *r* bird from the east, the man
Ezek. 39:4 I will give thee unto the *r* birds

Ravish

Prov. 5:19 and be thou *r* always with her love
Song 4:9 hast *r* my heart, my sister, my spouse
Is. 13:16 houses . . spoiled, and their wives *r*
Lam. 5:11 *r* the women in Zion, and the maids
Zech. 14:2 the houses rifled, and the women *r*

Raw

Ex. 12:9 eat not of it *r*, nor sodden at all with
1 Sam. 2:15 not have sodden flesh of thee, but *r*

Razor

Num. 6:5 (Judg. 13:5; 1 Sam. 1:11) no *r* come upon
Ps. 52:2 tongue deviseth mischiefs; like a sharp *r*
Is. 7:20 the Lord shave with a *r* that is hired
Ezek. 5:1 a sharp knife, take thee a barber's *r*

Reach

Prov. 31:20 she *r* forth her hands to the needy
Jn. 20:27 *r* hither thy finger . . *r* hither thy hand
2 Cor. 10:13 to us, a measure to *r* even unto you
Phil. 3:13 *r* . . unto those things which are before

Read

Ex. 24:7 and *r* in the audience of the people
Deut. 17:19 he shall *r* therein all the days of his
31:11 thou shalt *r* this law before all Israel in
Josh. 8:34 afterward he *r* all the words of the law
2 Kgs. 23:2 (2 Chr. 34:30) he *r* in their ears all
Neh. 8:3 he *r* therein . . from . . morning until midday
8:8 *r* in the book in the law of God distinctly
Is. 29:11 *r* this, I pray . . and he saith, I cannot
34:16 seek ye out of the book of the LORD, and *r*
Jer. 36:6 *r* in the roll, which thou hast written

Dan. 5:7 whosoever shall *r* this writing, and show
Hab. 2:2 make it plain . . that he may run that *r* it
Mt. 12:3 (Mk. 2:25; Lk. 6:3) not *r* what David did
24:15 (Mk. 13:14) whoso *r*, let him understand
Lk. 4:16 into the synagogue . . and stood up for to *r*
Jn. 19:20 this title then *r* many of the Jews
Acts 8:28 in his chariot *r* Esaias the prophet
13:15 after the *r* of the law and the prophets
23:34 and when the governor had *r* the letter, he
2 Cor. 1:13 we write none other . . than what ye *r* or
3:2 ye are our epistle . . known and *r* of all men
Col. 4:16 this epistle is *r* . . cause that it be *r* also in
1 Thes. 5:27 this epistle be *r* unto all the holy
1 Tim. 4:13 till I come, give attendance to *r*
Rev. 1:3 blessed is he that *r*, and they that hear
5:4 was found worthy to open and to *r* the book

Readiness

Acts 17:11 received the word with all *r* of mind
2 Cor. 8:11 as there was a *r* to will, so there may
10:6 having in a *r* to revenge all disobedience

Ready

Ex. 34:2 and be *r* in the morning, and come up
Deut. 1:41 ye were *r* to go up into the hill
2 Sam. 18:22 seeing that thou hast no tidings *r*?
Neh. 9:17 but thou art a God *r* to pardon, gracious
Esth. 8:13 the Jews should be *r* against that day
Job 15:23 the day of darkness is *r* at his hand
Ps. 38:17 for I am *r* to halt, and my sorrow is
45:1 King: my tongue is the pen of a *r* writer
86:5 for thou, Lord, art good, and *r* to forgive
88:15 am afflicted and *r* to die from my youth up
Prov. 31:6 drink unto him that is *r* to perish
Eccl. 5:1 be more *r* to hear, than to give the
Is. 27:13 they shall come which were *r* to perish
32:4 the stammerers shall be *r* to speak plainly
38:20 the LORD was *r* to save me: therefore we
Dan. 3:15 now if ye be *r* that at what time ye hear
Mt. 22:4 all things are *r*: come unto the marriage
24:44 (Lk. 12:40) be ye also *r*: for in such an hour
25:10 were *r* went in with him to the marriage
26:19 (Mk. 14:16; Lk. 22:13) made *r* the passover
Mk. 14:38 spirit truly is *r*, but the flesh is weak
Lk. 1:17 to make *r* a people prepared for the Lord
14:17 bidden, Come; for all things are now *r*
22:33 Lord, I am *r* to go with thee, both into
Jn. 7:6 not yet come: but your time is always *r*
Acts 21:13 I am *r* not to be bound only, but also
23:21 now are they, *r*, looking for a promise from
Rom. 1:15 I am *r* to preach the gospel to you that
2 Cor. 8:19 and declaration of your *r* mind
9:2 boast of you . . that Achaia was *r* a year ago
1 Tim. 6:18 be rich in good works, *r* to distribute
2 Tim. 4:6 I am now *r* to be offered, and the time
Tit. 3:1 them in mind . . to be *r* to every good work
Heb. 8:13 decayeth and waxeth old is *r* to vanish
1 Pet. 1:5 faith unto salvation *r* to be revealed
3:15 be *r* always to give an answer to every man
4:5 that is *r* to judge the quick and the dead
5:2 not for filthy lucre, but of a *r* mind
Rev. 3:2 things which remain, that are *r* to die
19:7 is come, and his wife hath made herself *r*

Reap

Lev. 19:9 (23:22) when ye *r* the harvest of your land
Job 4:8 they that . . sow wickedness, *r* the same
24:6 they *r* every one his corn in the field
Ps. 126:5 they that sow in tears shall *r* in joy
Prov. 22:8 he that soweth iniquity shall *r* vanity
Eccl. 11:4 he that regardeth the clouds shall not *r*
Jer. 12:13 they have sown wheat, but shall *r* thorns
Hos. 8:7 have sown the wind . . shall *r* the whirlwind

Hos. 10:12 sow . . in righteousness, *r* in mercy
Mic. 6:15 (Jn. 4:37) shalt sow, but thou shalt not *r*
Mt. 6:26 (Lk. 12:24) they sow not, neither do they *r*
   25:24 (Lk. 19:21) *r* where thou hast not sown
Jn. 4:36 he that *r* receiveth wages, and gathereth
   4:37 saying true, One soweth, and another *r*
   4:38 I sent you to *r* that whereon ye bestowed no
1 Cor. 9:11 if we shall *r* your carnal things?
2 Cor. 9:6 soweth sparingly shall *r* also sparingly
Gal. 6:7 whatsoever a man soweth . . shall he also *r*
   6:9 in due season we shall *r*, if we faint not
Jas. 5:4 cries of them which have *r* are entered
Rev. 14:15 *r*: for the time is come for thee to *r*

Reaper

Ruth 2:3 gleaned in the field after the *r*
2 Kgs. 4:18 he went out to his father to the *r*
Mt. 13:30 I will say to the *r*, Gather ye together
   13:39 end of the world; and the *r* are the angels

Rear *See also* Raise

Ex. 26:30 thou shalt *r* up the tabernacle according to
   40:17 in the second year . . the tabernacle was *r* up
Jn. 2:20 and wilt thou *r* it up in three days?

Rearward

Is. 52:12 and the God of Israel will be your *r*
   58:8 the glory of the LORD shall be thy *r*

Reason *See also* Cause, Think

1 Sam. 12:7 that I may *r* with you before the LORD
Job 9:14 and choose out my words to *r* with him?
   13:3 to the Almighty, and I desire to *r* with God
   15:3 should he *r* with unprofitable talk?
   32:11 I gave ear to your *r*, whilst ye searched
Prov. 26:16 than seven men that can render a *r*
Eccl. 7:25 to seek out wisdom, and the *r* of things
Is. 1:18 come now, and let us *r* together, saith the
   41:21 bring forth your strong *r*, saith the King
Dan. 4:36 at the same time my *r* returned unto me
Mt. 16:8 (Mk. 8:17) why *r* ye among yourselves
   21:25 (Mk. 11:31; Lk. 20:5) they *r* with themselves
Mk. 2:8 (Lk. 5:22) why *r* ye these things in your hearts
Lk. 5:21 the scribes and the Pharisees began to *r*
   24:15 while they communed together and *r*, Jesus
Acts 6:2 it is not *r* that we should leave the word
   17:2 and Paul . . *r* with them out of the Scriptures
   18:4 and he *r* in the synagogue every sabbath
   24:25 as he *r* of righteousness, temperance, and
1 Pet. 3:15 asketh . . a *r* of the hope that is in you

Reasonable

Rom. 12:1 unto God, which is your *r* service

Reasoning

Job 13:6 hear now my *r*, and hearken to the pleadings
Lk. 9:46 arose a *r* . . which of them should be greatest
Acts 28:29 Jews departed, and had great *r* among

Rebekah (Rebecca) Gen. 24:15–27:46

Rom. 9:10 but when *R* also had conceived by one

Rebel *See also* Harden, Resist, Revolt

Num. 14:9 *r* not ye against the LORD, neither fear
   17:10 rod . . to be kept for a token against the *r*
   20:10 hear now, ye *r*; must we fetch you water
   20:24 *r* against my word at the water of Meribah
   27:14 ye *r* against my commandment in the desert
Deut. 1:26 (1:43; 9:23) *r* against the commandment
Josh. 1:18 whosoever he be that doth *r* against thy
   22:16 that ye might *r* this day against the LORD?
1 Sam. 12:14 obey his voice, and not *r* against the
1 Kgs. 12:19 (2 Chr. 10:19) Israel *r* against . . David

2 Kgs. 1:1 (3:5) then Moab *r* against Israel after
   18:7 *r* against the king of Assyria and served
   18:20 (Is. 36:5) trust, that thou *r* against me?
   24:20 (2 Chr. 36:13; Jer. 52:3) Zedekiah *r* against
Neh. 2:19 that ye do? will ye *r* against the king?
   6:6 reported . . that thou and the Jews think to *r*
   9:26 they were disobedient, and *r* against thee
Job 24:13 *r* against the light; they know not the
Ps. 5:10 cast them out . . they have *r* against thee
   105:28 made it dark . . they *r* not against his word
   107:11 because they *r* against the words of God
Is. 1:2 brought up children . . they have *r* against me
   1:20 but if ye refuse and *r*, ye shall be devoured
   63:10 but they *r*, and vexed his Holy Spirit
Lam. 1:18 I have *r* against his commandment
   3:42 we have transgressed and *r*: thou hast
Ezek. 2:3 rebellious nation that hath *r* against me
   20:8 they *r* against me, and would not hearken
   20:13 of Israel *r* against me in the wilderness
   20:38 I will purge out from among you the *r*
Dan. 9:5 have done wickedly, and have *r*, even by
Hos. 7:14 for corn and wine, and they *r* against me
   13:16 desolate; for she hath *r* against her God

Rebellion *See also* Disobedience, Insurrection, Sedition

Deut. 31:27 for I know thy *r*, and thy stiff neck
Josh. 22:22 Israel he shall know; if it be in *r*
1 Sam. 15:23 for *r* is as the sin of witchcraft
Ezra 4:19 *r* and sedition have been made therein
Neh. 9:17 in their *r* appointed a captain to return
Job 34:37 he added *r* unto his sin, he clappeth
Prov. 17:11 an evil man seeketh only *r*: therefore
Jer. 28:16 thou hast taught *r* against the LORD
   29:32 because he hath taught *r* against the LORD

Rebellious *See also* Disobedient

Deut. 9:7 (9:24; 31:27) have been *r* against the LORD
   21:18 if a man have a stubborn and *r* son
Ezra 4:12 building the *r* and the bad city
Ps. 66:7 he ruleth . . let not the *r* exalt themselves
   68:6 with chains: but the *r* dwell in a dry land
   68:18 received gifts for men; yea, for the *r* also
   78:8 a stubborn and *r* generation; a generation
Is. 1:23 thy princes are *r* . . companions of thieves
   30:1 woe to the *r* children, saith the LORD
   30:9 this is a *r* people, lying children
   50:5 GOD hath opened mine ear, and I was not *r*
   65:2 out my hands all the day unto a *r* people
Jer. 4:17 hath been *r* against me, saith the LORD
   5:23 this people hath a revolting and a *r* heart
Ezek. 2:3 to the children of Israel, to a *r* nation
   2:6 (3:9; 12:3) though they be a *r* house
   2:8 be not thou *r* like that *r* house: open thy
   3:26 (3:27; 12:2) for they are a *r* house
   12:25 in your days, O *r* house, will I say the word
   17:12 say now to the *r* house, Know ye not what
   24:3 utter a parable unto the *r* house, and say
   44:6 say to the *r*, even to the house of Israel

Rebuke *See also* Reproach, Reprove

2 Sam. 22:16 (Ps. 18:15) at the *r* of the LORD
2 Kgs. 19:3 (Is. 37:3) a day of trouble, and of *r*
1 Chr. 12:17 the God of our fathers look . . and *r* it
Neh. 5:7 consulted with myself, and I *r* the nobles
Ps. 6:1 (38:1) *r* me not in thine anger, neither chasten
   9:5 thou hast *r* the heathen, thou hast destroyed
   18:15 the foundations . . were discovered at thy *r*
   39:11 thou with *r* dost correct man for iniquity
   80:16 they perish at the *r* of thy countenance
   104:7 at thy *r* they fled; at the voice of thy
   106:9 he *r* the Red sea also, and it was dried up

Ps. 119:21 thou hast *r* the proud that are cursed
Prov. 9:7 *r* a wicked man getteth himself a blot
9:8 *r* a wise man, and he will love thee
13:1 instruction: but a scorner heareth not *r*
13:8 are his riches: but the poor heareth not *r*
27:5 open *r* is better than secret love
28:23 that *r* a man. . shall find more favor than
Eccl. 7:5 better to hear the *r* of the wise, than
Is. 2:4 (Mic. 4:3) shall judge. . shall *r* many people
17:13 nations shall rush. . but God shall *r* them
25:8 and the *r* of his people shall he take away
30:17 one thousand shall flee at the *r* of one
50:2 at my *r* I dry up the sea, I make the rivers
Jer. 15:15 that for thy sake I have suffered *r*
Amos 5:10 they hate him that *r* in the gate
Zech. 3:2 (Jude 9) the LORD *r* thee, O Satan
Mal. 3:11 and I will *r* the devourer for your sakes
Mt. 8:26 (Mk. 4:39; Lk. 8:24) *r* the winds and. . sea
16:22 (Mk. 8:32) Peter took. . and began to *r* him
17:18 (Mk. 9:25; Lk. 9:42) and Jesus *r* the devil
19:13 (Mk. 10:13; Lk. 18:15) the disciples *r* them
Mk. 1:25 (Lk. 4:35) *r* him, saying, Hold thy peace
Lk. 4:39 over her, and *r* the fever; and it left
9:55 *r* them. . what manner of spirit ye are of
17:3 if thy brother trespass against thee, *r* him
19:39 said unto him, Master, *r* thy disciples
23:40 but the other answering *r* him, saying, Dost
Phil. 2:15 harmless, the sons of God, without *r*
1 Tim. 5:1 *r* not an elder, but entreat him as a
5:20 them that sin *r* before all, that others
2 Tim. 4:2 reprove, *r*, exhort with all long-suffering
Tit. 1:13 *r* them sharply, that they may be sound
2:15 speak, and exhort, and *r* with all authority
Heb. 12:5 nor faint when thou art *r* of him
Jude 9 railing accusation, but said, The Lord *r* thee
Rev. 3:19 as many as I love, I *r* and chasten

Rebuker

Hos. 5:2 though I have been a *r* of them all

Recall

Lam. 3:21 I *r* to my mind, therefore have I hope

Receipt

Mt. 9:9 (Mk. 2:14; Lk. 5:27) sitting at the *r* of custom

Receive *See also* Accept

Judg. 19:18 there is no man that *r* me to house
2 Kgs. 5:26 is it a time to *r* money. . to *r* garments
12:7 *r* no more money of your acquaintance
Job 2:10 shall we *r* good. . and shall we not *r* evil?
22:22 *r*, I pray thee, the law from thy mouth
Ps. 6:9 my supplication; the LORD will *r* my prayer
24:5 he shall *r* the blessing from the LORD
49:15 God will redeem my soul. . for he shall *r* me
68:18 thou hast *r* gifts for men; yea, for the
73:24 shalt guide. . and afterward *r* me to glory
Prov. 2:1 my son, if thou wilt *r* my words
10:8 the wise in heart will *r* commandments
29:4 land: but he that *r* gifts overthroweth it
Is. 40:2 for she hath *r* of the LORD's hand double
Jer. 2:30 your children; they *r* no correction
Hos. 14:2 take away all iniquity. . *r* us graciously
Mt. 7:8 (Lk. 11:10) for every one that asketh *r*
10:8 freely ye have *r*, freely give
10:14 (Mk. 6:11; Lk. 9:5; 10:10) shall not *r* you
10:40 he that *r* you *r* me. . *r* me *r* him that sent
10:41 *r* a prophet. . shall *r* a prophet's reward
11:14 if ye will *r* it, this is Elias, which was
13:20 (Mk. 4:16; Lk. 8:13) and anon with joy *r* it
18:5 (Mk. 9:37; Lk. 9:48) *r* one such little child
19:12 he that is able to *r* it, let him *r* it
19:29 (Mk. 10:30; Lk. 18:30) shall *r* a hundredfold

Mt. 20:10 they supposed that they should have *r* more
21:22 (Mk. 11:24) in prayer, believing, ye shall *r*
21:34 (Mk. 12:2) that they might *r* the fruits
23:14 (Mk. 12:40; Lk. 20:47) *r*. . greater damnation
25:16 then he that had *r* the five talents went
25:27 coming I should have *r* mine own with usury
Mk. 9:37 (Lk. 9:48) *r* me, *r* not me, but him that sent
15:23 wine mingled with myrrh: but he *r* it not
16:19 he was *r* up into heaven, and sat on the
Lk. 6:34 if ye lend to them of whom ye hope to *r*
8:40 Jesus was returned, the people gladly *r* him
9:11 *r* them, and spake unto them of the kingdom
9:53 they did not *r* him, because his face
10:8 whatsoever city ye enter, and they *r* you
10:38 woman named Martha *r* him into her house
15:2 this man *r* sinners, and eateth with them
15:27 because he hath *r* him safe and sound
16:4 put out of the stewardship, they may *r* me
16:9 they may *r* you into everlasting habitations
16:25 thou in thy lifetime *r* thy good things
19:6 haste, and came down, and *r* him joyfully
19:12 went into a far country to *r*. . a kingdom
23:41 for we *r* the due reward of our deeds
Jn. 1:11 came unto his own, and his own *r* him not
1:12 as many as *r* him, to them gave he power to
1:16 of his fulness have all we *r*, and grace for
3:11 we have seen; and ye *r* not our witness
3:27 a man can *r* nothing, except it be given
4:45 was come into Galilee, the Galileans *r* him
5:34 I *r* not testimony from man: but these. . I say
5:41 I *r* not honor from men
5:43 come in my Father's name, and ye *r* me not
6:21 then they willingly *r* him into the ship
7:39 Spirit. . they that believe on him should *r*
13:20 *r* whomsoever I send *r* me. . *r* me *r* him that
14:3 I will come again, and *r* you unto myself
14:17 Spirit of truth; whom the world cannot *r*
16:14 he shall glorify me: for he shall *r* of mine
16:24 ask, and ye shall *r*, that your joy may be
20:22 and saith unto them, *R* ye the Holy Ghost
Acts 1:8 ye shall *r* power, after that the Holy Ghost
2:38 and ye shall *r* the gift of the Holy Ghost
3:5 gave heed. . expecting to *r* something of them
3:21 whom the heaven must *r* until the times of
7:59 Stephen. . saying, Lord Jesus, *r* my spirit
8:15 prayed. . that they might *r* the Holy Ghost
17:11 *r* the word with all readiness of mind
18:27 wrote, exhorting the disciples to *r* him
19:2 have ye *r* the Holy Ghost since ye believed?
20:24 ministry, which I have *r* of the Lord Jesus
20:35 it is more blessed to give than to *r*
22:18 they will not *r* thy testimony concerning me
Rom. 5:11 by whom we have now *r* the atonement
5:17 much more they which *r* abundance of grace
13:2 that resist shall *r* to themselves damnation
14:1 him that is weak in the faith *r* ye, but not
14:3 judge him that eateth: for God hath *r* him
15:7 *r* ye one another, as Christ also *r* us
16:2 *r* her in the Lord, as becometh saints
1 Cor. 2:14 natural man *r* not. . things of the Spirit
3:8 *r* his own reward according to his own labor
4:7 not *r*? now if thou didst *r* it, why dost thou
11:23 for I have *r* of the Lord that which also I
15:3 I delivered unto you. . that which I also *r*
2 Cor. 5:10 that every one may *r* the things done
6:1 that ye *r* not the grace of God in vain
7:2 *r* us; we have wronged no man, we have
8:4 with much entreaty that we would *r* the gift
11:4 if ye *r* another spirit, which ye have not *r*
11:16 as a fool *r* me, that I may boast myself
Gal. 1:12 for I neither *r* it of man, neither was I
3:2 *r* ye the Spirit by the works of the law
3:14 that we might *r* the promise of the Spirit

Gal. 4:5 that we might *r* the adoption of sons
    4:14 *r* me as an angel of God, even as Christ
Eph. 6:8 doeth, the same shall he *r* of the Lord
Phil. 2:29 *r* him therefore in the Lord with all
Col. 2:6 as ye have. . *r* Christ Jesus the Lord, so
    3:24 ye shall *r* the reward of the inheritance
    3:25 he that doeth wrong shall *r* for the wrong
    4:10 *r* commandments: if he come unto you, *r* him
1 Thes. 2:13 ye *r* it not as the word of men, but
1 Tim. 3:16 manifest in the flesh. . *r* up into glory
Phlm. 12 thou therefore *r* him, that is, mine own
    17 if thou count me. . a partner, *r* him as myself
Heb. 9:15 *r* the promise of eternal inheritance
    11:13 died in faith, not having *r* the promises
    11:39 obtained a good report. . *r* not the promise
Jas. 1:7 that he shall *r* any thing of the Lord
    1:12 he is tried, he shall *r* the crown of life
    1:21 *r* with meekness the engrafted word
    4:3 ye ask, and *r* not, because ye ask amiss
1 Pet. 5:4 *r* a crown of glory that fadeth not away
2 Pet. 2:13 shall *r* the reward of unrighteousness
1 Jn. 3:22 whatsoever we ask, we *r* of him, because
2 Jn. 10 not this doctrine, *r* him not into your
3 Jn. 8 we therefore ought to *r* such, that we might
    9 wrote unto the church: but Diotrephes. . *r* us not
Rev. 3:3 remember. . how thou hast *r* and heard
    17:12 *r* no kingdom as yet; but *r* power as kings
    18:4 come out. . that ye *r* not of her plagues

Rechab 2 Sam. 4:2–9

Rechabite Jer. 35:2–18

Reckon *See also* Account, Record

Lev. 25:50 he shall *r* with him that bought him
Ps. 40:5 thy thoughts. . cannot be *r* up in order
Is. 38:13 I *r* till morning, that, as a lion, so
Mt. 18:24 when he had begun to *r*, one was brought
    25:19 lord of those servants cometh, and *r* with
Lk. 22:37 and he was *r* among the transgressors
Rom. 4:4 the reward not *r* of grace, but of debt
    4:9 faith was *r* to Abraham for righteousness
    6:11 *r* ye. . yourselves to be dead indeed unto sin
    8:18 I *r* that the sufferings of this present time

Recommend

Acts 14:26 they had been *r* to the grace of God for
    15:40 *r* by the brethren unto the grace of God

Recompense *See also* Avenge, Pay, Render, Reward, Vengeance

Num. 5:7 shall *r* his trespass with the principal
Deut. 32:35 (Heb. 10:30) belongeth vengeance, and *r*
Ruth 2:12 LORD *r* thy work, and a full reward be
2 Sam. 22:25 (Ps. 18:24) LORD hath *r* me according
Job 15:31 trust in vanity. . vanity shall be his *r*
    34:33 he will *r* it, whether thou refuse, or
Prov. 11:31 the righteous shall be *r* in the earth
    12:14 *r* of a man's hands shall be rendered unto
    20:22 say not thou, I will *r* evil; but wait on
Is. 34:8 the year of *r* for the controversy of Zion
    35:4 will come with vengeance, even God with a *r*
    59:18 *r* to his enemies. . islands he will repay *r*
    65:6 but will *r*, even *r* into their bosom
    66:6 of the LORD that rendereth *r* to his enemies
Jer. 16:18 first I will *r* their iniquity and their
    18:20 shall evil be *r* for good? for they have
    25:14 and I will *r* them according to their deeds
    32:18 and *r* the iniquity of the fathers into the
    50:29 *r* her according to her work; according to
    51:6 LORD's vengeance; he will render unto her a *r*
Lam. 3:64 render unto them a *r*, O LORD, according

Ezek. 7:3 will *r* upon thee all thine abominations
    9:10 but I will *r* their way upon their head
    23:49 they shall *r* your lewdness upon you
Hos. 9:7 days of *r* are come; Israel shall know it
    12:2 according to his doings will he *r* him
Joel 3:4 a *r*? and if ye *r* me. . will I return your *r*
Lk. 14:12 also bid thee again, and a *r* be made thee
    14:14 shalt be *r* at the resurrection of the just
Rom. 1:27 that *r* of their error which was meet
    11:9 a trap. . a stumblingblock, and a *r* unto them
    11:35 to him, and it shall be *r* unto him again?
    12:17 *r* to no man evil for evil. Provide things
2 Cor. 6:13 for a *r* in the same. . be ye also enlarged
2 Thes. 1:6 *r* tribulation to them that trouble you
Heb. 2:2 disobedience received a just *r* of reward
    10:35 confidence, which hath great *r* of reward
    11:26 he had respect unto the *r* of the reward

Reconcile

Lev. 6:30 to *r* withal in the holy place, shall be
    16:20 he hath made an end of *r* the holy place
1 Sam. 29:4 should he *r* himself unto his master?
Ezek. 45:20 that erreth. . so shall ye *r* the house
Mt. 5:24 first be *r* to thy brother, and then come
Rom. 5:10 were *r* to God. . being *r*, we shall be saved
    11:15 casting away of them be the *r* of the world
1 Cor. 7:11 unmarried, or be *r* to her husband
2 Cor. 5:18 God, who hath *r* us to himself by Jesus
    5:19 God was in Christ, *r* the world unto himself
    5:20 we pray you in Christ's stead, be ye *r* to God
Eph. 2:16 he might *r* both unto God in one body by
Col. 1:20 by him to *r* all things unto himself
    1:21 were sometime alienated. . yet now hath he *r*

Reconciliation *See also* Atonement, Propitiation, Sacrifice

Lev. 8:15 and sanctified it, to make *r* upon it
2 Chr. 29:24 made *r* with their blood upon the altar
Ezek. 45:17 to make *r* for the house of Israel
Dan. 9:24 end of sins, and to make *r* for iniquity
2 Cor. 5:18 and hath given to us the ministry of *r*
    5:19 and hath committed unto us the word of *r*
Heb. 2:17 to make *r* for the sins of the people

Record *See also* Account, Reckon

Ex. 20:24 in all places where I *r* my name I will
Deut. 30:19 I call heaven and earth to *r* this day
Job 16:19 my witness is in heaven. . my *r* is on high
Jn. 1:19 this is the *r* of John, when the Jews sent
    1:34 saw, and bare *r* that this is the Son of God
    8:13 bearest *r* of thyself; thy *r* is not true
    8:14 though I bear *r* of myself, yet my *r* is true
    19:35 he that saw it bare *r*, and his *r* is true
Acts 20:26 I take you to *r* this day, that I am pure
Rom. 10:2 I bear them *r* that they have a zeal of God
2 Cor. 1:23 I call God for a *r* upon my soul
Phil. 1:8 God is my *r*, how greatly I long after
1 Jn. 5:7 there are three that bear *r* in heaven
    5:10 believeth not the *r* that God gave of his Son
3 Jn. 12 bear *r*; and ye know that our *r* is true
Rev. 1:2 who bare *r* of the word of God, and of the

Recount

Nah. 2:5 shall *r* his worthies: they shall stumble

Recover

Judg. 11:26 did ye not *r* them within that time?
1 Sam. 30:19 they had taken to them: David *r* all
2 Kgs. 5:3 the prophet. . would *r* him of his leprosy
    8:8 saying, Shall I *r* of this disease?
Ps. 39:13 spare me, that I may *r* strength, before
Is. 11:11 again. . to *r* the remnant of his people

Is. 38:21 a plaster upon the boil, and he shall *r*
Jer. 8:22 health of the daughter of my people *r*?
Hos. 2:9 will *r* my wool and my flax given to cover
Mk. 16:18 lay hands on the sick, and they shall *r*
Lk. 4:18 and *r* of sight to the blind, to set at
2 Tim. 2:26 may *r* themselves out of the snare of

Red

Gen. 25:25 the first came out *r*, all over
25:30 feed me. . with that same *r* pottage
49:12 his eyes shall be *r* with wine, and his
2 Kgs. 3:22 Moabites saw the water. . as *r* as blood
Ps. 75:8 in the hand. . is a cup, and the wine is *r*
Prov. 23:31 look not. . upon the wine when it is *r*
Is. 1:18 though they be *r* like crimson, they shall
27:2 sing ye unto her, A vineyard of *r* wine
63:2 wherefore art thou *r* in thine apparel
Nah. 2:3 the shield of his mighty men is made *r*
Zech. 1:8 and behold a man riding upon a *r* horse
Mt. 16:2 will be fair weather: for the sky is *r*
Rev. 6:4 there went out another horse that was *r*

Red Sea

Ex. 10:19 west wind, which. . cast them into the *R s*
13:18 through the way of the wilderness of the *R s* .
Ps. 106:9 rebuked the *R s* also, and it was dried
136:13 to him which divided the *R s* into parts
Heb. 11:29 by faith they passed through the *R s*

Redeem *See also* Deliver, Ransom, Rescue, Save

Gen. 48:16 angel which *r* me from all evil, bless
Ex. 6:6 and I will *r* you with a stretched out arm
13:13 (34:20) the firstborn of man. . shalt thou *r*
15:13 led forth the people which thou hast *r*
21:8 her to himself, then shall he let her be *r*
Lev. 25:25 his kin come to *r* it, then shall he *r*
25:48 be *r* again; one of his brethren may *r* him
27:13 if he will at all *r* it, then he shall add
Num. 18:16 to be *r* from a month old shalt thou *r*
Deut. 7:8 and *r* you out of the house of bondmen
9:26 which thou hast *r* through thy greatness
15:15 thy God *r* thee: therefore I command thee
21:8 unto thy people Israel, whom thou hast *r*
24:18 Egypt, and the LORD thy God *r* thee thence
Ruth 4:4 if thou wilt *r* it, *r* it: but if thou wilt
2 Sam. 4:9 who hath *r* my soul out of all adversity
7:23 (1 Chr. 17:21) God went to *r* for a people
1 Kgs. 1:29 hath *r* my soul out of all distress
Neh. 1:10 whom thou hast *r* by thy great power
5:5 neither is it in our power to *r* them
5:8 our ability, have *r* our brethren the Jews
Job 5:20 in famine he shall *r* thee from death
6:23 or, *R* me from the hand of the mighty?
Ps. 25:22 *r* Israel, O God, out of all his troubles
26:11 integrity: *r* me, and be merciful unto me
31:5 I commit my spirit: thou hast *r* me, O LORD
34:22 LORD *r* the soul of his servants: and none
44:26 our help, and *r* us for thy mercies' sake
49:7 none of them can by any means *r* his brother
49:15 will *r* my soul from the power of the grave
69:18 draw nigh unto my soul, and *r* it: deliver
71:23 sing unto thee. . my soul, which thou hast *r*
72:14 he shall *r* their soul from deceit
77:15 thou hast with thine arm *r* thy people
103:4 who *r* thy life from destruction
106:10 and *r* them from the hand of the enemy
130:8 he shall *r* Israel from all his iniquities
136:24 hath *r* us from our enemies: for his mercy
Is. 1:27 Zion shall be *r* with judgment, and her
29:22 saith the LORD, who *r* Abraham, concerning
43:1 O Israel, Fear not: for I have *r* thee

Is. 44:22 return unto me; for I have *r* thee
48:20 say ye: The LORD hath *r* his servant Jacob
50:2 my hand shortened at all, that it cannot *r*?
52:3 for nought; and ye shall be *r* without money
63:9 in his love and in his pity he *r* them
Jer. 15:21 *r* thee out of the hand of the terrible
31:11 LORD hath *r* Jacob, and ransomed him from
Lam. 3:58 pleaded the causes. . thou hast *r* my life
Hos. 7:13 I have *r* them, yet they have spoken lies
13:14 I will *r* them from death: O death, I will
Mic. 4:10 there the LORD shall *r* thee from the hand
6:4 and *r* thee out of the house of servants
Zech. 10:8 I have *r* them: and they shall increase
Lk. 1:68 for he hath visited and *r* his people
24:21 it had been he which should have *r* Israel
Gal. 3:13 Christ hath *r* us from the curse of the
4:5 to *r* them that were under the law, that we
Eph. 5:16 the time, because the days are evil
Col. 4:5 walk in wisdom toward them. . *r* the time
Tit. 2:14 that he might *r* us from all iniquity
1 Pet. 1:18 ye were not *r* with corruptible things
Rev. 5:9 hast *r* us to God by thy blood out of every
14:3 that song but. . which were *r* from the earth
14:4 were *r* from among men, being the firstfruits

Redeemed *See also* Redeem, Ransomed

Ps. 107:2 let the *r* of the LORD say so, whom he
Is. 35:9 found there; but the *r* shall walk there
51:11 therefore the *r* of the LORD shall return
62:12 the holy people, The *r* of the LORD

Redeemer *See also* Deliverer, Saviour

Job 19:25 for I know that my *R* liveth, and that he
Ps. 19:14 thy sight, O LORD, my strength, and my *r*
78:35 was their rock, and the high God their *r*
Prov. 23:11 for their *R* is mighty; he shall plead
Is. 41:14 (43:14; 48:17; 54:5) thy *R*, the Holy One of
44:6 and his *R* the LORD of hosts; I am the first
44:24 thus saith the LORD, thy *R*. . I am the LORD
47:4 as for our *R*, the LORD of hosts is his name
49:7 the *R* of Israel, and his Holy One, to him
49:26 (60:16) I the LORD am thy Saviour and thy *R*
59:20 the *R* shall come to Zion, and unto them
63:16 thou, O LORD, art our Father, our *R*
Jer. 50:34 their *R* is strong; The LORD of hosts is

Redemption *See also* Deliverance, Ransom, Salvation

Lev. 25:24 ye shall grant a *r* for the land
Num. 3:49 and Moses took the *r* money of them that
Ps. 49:8 for the *r* of their soul is precious
111:9 sent *r* unto his people: he hath commanded
130:7 is mercy, and with him is plenteous *r*
Jer. 32:7 for the right of *r* is thine to buy it
Lk. 2:38 them that looked for the *r* in Jerusalem
21:28 lift up your heads; for your *r* draweth nigh
Rom. 3:24 grace through the *r* that is in Christ
8:23 waiting for the adoption. . the *r* of our body
1 Cor. 1:30 unto us wisdom. . sanctification, and *r*
Eph. 1:7 (Col. 1:14) we have *r* through his blood
1:14 until the *r* of the purchased possession
4:30 whereby ye are sealed unto the day of *r*
Heb. 9:12 having obtained eternal *r* for us
9:15 for the *r* of the transgressions that

Redound

2 Cor. 4:15 thanksgiving of many *r* to the glory of

Reed

1 Kgs. 14:15 Israel, as a *r* is shaken in the water
2 Kgs. 18:21 (Is. 36:6) the staff of this bruised *r*
Is. 19:6 dried up: the *r* and flags shall wither

Is. 42:3 (Mt. 12:20) a bruised *r* shall he not break
Ezek. 40:3 flax in his hand, and a measuring *r*
Mt. 11:7 (Lk. 7:24) see? A *r* shaken with the wind?
　27:29 upon his head, and a *r* in his right hand
Rev. 21:15 had a golden *r* to measure the city

Reel

Ps. 107:27 they *r* to and fro, and stagger like a
Is. 24:20 earth shall *r* to and fro like a drunkard

Refine

Is. 48:10 I have *r* thee, but not with silver
Zech. 13:9 will *r* them as silver is *r*, and will try

Refiner

Mal. 3:2 he appeareth? for he is like a *r*'s fire
　3:3 he shall sit as a *r* and purifier of silver

Reform

Lev. 26:23 if ye will not be *r* by me by these

Reformation

Heb. 9:10 ordinances, imposed . . until the time of *r*

Refrain

Gen. 45:1 Joseph could not *r* himself before all
Job 7:11 I will not *r* my mouth; I will speak in
　29:9 princes *r* talking, and laid their hand on
Ps. 40:9 I have not *r* my lips, O LORD, thou knowest
　119:101 I have *r* my feet from every evil way
Prov. 1:15 my son . . *r* thy foot from their path
　10:19 not sin: but he that *r* his lips is wise
Eccl. 3:5 time to embrace, and a time to *r* from
Is. 64:12 wilt thou *r* thyself for these things
Acts 5:38 *r* from these men, and let them alone
1 Pet. 3:10 let him *r* his tongue from evil

Refresh

Ex. 23:12 and the son . . and the stranger, may be *r*
　31:17 on the seventh day he rested, and was *r*
1 Sam. 16:23 took a harp, and played . . so Saul was *r*
Job 32:20 I will speak, that I may be *r*
Prov. 25:13 for he *r* the soul of his masters
Acts 3:19 when the times of *r* shall come from the
Rom. 15:32 come unto you . . and may with you be *r*
1 Cor. 16:18 for they have *r* my spirit and yours
2 Cor. 7:13 because his spirit was *r* by you all
2 Tim. 1:16 for he oft *r* me, and was not ashamed
Phlm. 7 the bowels of the saints are *r* by thee

Refuge

Num. 35:11 (Josh. 20:2) appoint . . cities of *r* for you
Deut. 33:27 eternal God is thy *r*, and underneath
2 Sam. 22:3 my high tower, and my *r*, my saviour
Ps. 9:9 a *r* for the oppressed, a *r* in times of
　14:6 of the poor, because the LORD is his *r*
　46:1 God is our *r* and strength, a very present
　46:7 (46:11) the God of Jacob is our *r*
　48:3 God is known in her palaces for a *r*
　57:1 in the shadow of thy wings will I make my *r*
　59:16 my defense and *r* in the day of my trouble
　62:7 rock of my strength, and my *r*, is in God
　62:8 trust in him at all times . . God is a *r* for us
　71:7 wonder unto many; but thou art my strong *r*
　91:2 he is my *r* and my fortress: my God; in him
　91:9 thou hast made the LORD, which is my *r*
　94:22 and my God is the rock of my *r*
　142:4 failed me; no man cared for my soul
　142:5 thou art my *r* and my portion in the land
Prov. 14:26 his children shall have a place of *r*
Is. 4:6 a place of *r*, and for a covert from storm
　25:4 a *r* from the storm, a shadow from the heat
　28:15 have made lies our *r*, and under falsehood

Jer. 16:19 fortress . . my *r* in the day of affliction
Heb. 6:18 fled for *r* to lay hold upon the hope set

Refuse (noun)

Lam. 3:45 hast made us as the offscouring and *r*
Amos 8:6 shoes; yea, and sell the *r* of the wheat?

Refuse (verb) *See also* Reject

Gen. 37:35 comfort him; but he *r* to be comforted
　39:8 but he *r*, and said unto his master's wife
Ex. 4:23 (8:2; 9:2; 10:4) if thou *r* to let him go
　7:14 is hardened, he *r* to let the people go
　16:28 how long *r* ye to keep my commandments
Num. 20:21 Edom *r* to give Israel passage through
1 Sam. 16:7 of his stature; because I have *r* him
Neh. 9:17 *r* to obey, neither were mindful of thy
Esth. 1:12 the queen Vashti *r* to come at the king's
Job 6:7 things that my soul *r* to touch are as my
　34:33 he will recompense it, whether thou *r*, or
Ps. 77:2 ceased not: my soul *r* to be comforted
　78:10 kept not the covenant . . *r* to walk in his law
　118:22 the stone which the builders *r* is become
Prov. 1:24 because I have called, and ye *r*; I have
　8:33 hear instruction, and be wise, and *r* it not
　10:17 instruction: but he that *r* reproof erreth
　13:18 shame shall be to him that *r* instruction
　15:32 that *r* instruction despiseth his own soul
　21:25 slothful killeth . . for his hands *r* to labor
Is. 1:20 if ye *r* and rebel, ye shall be devoured
　7:15 may know to *r* the evil, and choose the good
Jer. 5:3 have *r* to receive correction . . *r* to return
　8:5 they hold fast deceit, they *r* to return
　9:6 through deceit they *r* to know me, saith the
　13:10 this evil people, which *r* to hear my words
　25:28 if they *r* to take the cup at thine hand to
　31:15 Rachel . . *r* to be comforted for her children
　50:33 held them fast; they *r* to let them go
Ezek. 5:6 they have *r* my judgments and my statutes
Hos. 11:5 be his king, because they *r* to return
Zech. 7:11 but they *r* to hearken, and pulled away
Acts 7:35 this Moses whom they *r*, saying, Who
1 Tim. 4:4 creature . . is good, and nothing to be *r*
　4:7 but *r* profane and old wives' fables
Heb. 11:24 *r* to be called the son of Pharaoh's
　12:25 see that ye *r* not him that speaketh

Regard *See also* Heed, Respect

Ex. 5:9 may labor . . and let them not *r* vain words
　9:21 he that *r* not the word of the LORD left his
Lev. 19:31 *r* not them that have familiar spirits
Deut. 10:17 a great God . . which *r* not persons, nor
2 Sam. 19:6 thou *r* neither princes nor servants
Job 3:4 be darkness; let not God *r* it from above
　30:20 not hear me: I stand up, and thou *r* me not
　34:19 nor *r* the rich more than the poor?
　35:13 vanity, neither will the Almighty *r* it
　39:7 neither *r* he the crying of the driver
Ps. 28:5 because they *r* not the works of the LORD
　94:7 not see, neither shall the God of Jacob *r* it
　102:17 he will *r* the prayer of the destitute
Prov. 1:24 stretched out my hand, and no man *r*
　6:35 he will not *r* any ransom; neither will he
　12:10 a righteous man *r* the life of his beast
　13:18 but he that *r* reproof shall be honored
Eccl. 5:8 he that is higher than the highest *r*
　11:4 and he that *r* the clouds shall not reap
Is. 5:12 they *r* not the work of the LORD, neither
Dan. 11:37 *r* the God of his fathers . . nor *r* any god
Mt. 22:16 (Mk. 12:14) thou *r* not the person of men
Lk. 1:48 hath *r* the low estate of his handmaiden
　18:4 he said . . Though I fear not God, nor *r* man
Acts 8:11 to him they had *r*, because that of long
Rom. 14:6 he that *r* the day, *r* it unto the Lord

Phil. 2:30 he was nigh unto death, not *r* his life
Heb. 8:9 not in my covenant, and I *r* them not

Regeneration

Mt. 19:28 in the *r* when the Son of man shall sit
Tit. 3:5 he saved us, by the washing of *r*

Region

Acts 13:49 word . . was published throughout all the *r*

Rehearse

Ex. 17:14 a book, and *r* it in the ears of Joshua
Judg. 5:11 they *r* the righteous acts of the LORD
Acts 11:4 Peter *r* the matter from the beginning
  14:27 they *r* all that God had done with them

Rehoboam

1 Kgs. 11:43–14:31 (2 Chr. 9:31–12:16)

Reign *See also* Authority, Dominion, Power, Rule

Gen. 37:8 shalt thou indeed *r* over us? or shalt
Ex. 15:18 the LORD shall *r* for ever and ever
Lev. 26:17 they that hate you shall *r* over you
Deut. 15:6 thou shalt *r* . . they shall not *r* over thee
Judg. 9:8 said unto the olive tree, *R* thou over us
1 Sam. 8:7 rejected me, that I should not *r* over them
  9:17 the man . . this same shall *r* over my people
  11:12 who is he that said, Shall Saul *r* over us
  12:12 nay; but a king shall *r* over us
2 Sam. 15:10 then ye shall say, Absalom *r* in Hebron
  16:8 house of Saul, in whose stead thou hast *r*
1 Kgs. 1:13 Solomon thy son shall *r* after me
1 Chr. 16:31 (Ps. 96:10) let men say . . The LORD *r*
  29:12 thou *r* over all; and in thine hand is
Job 34:30 the hypocrite *r* not, lest the people be
Ps. 47:8 God *r* over the heathen: God sitteth upon
  93:1 the LORD *r*, he is clothed with majesty
  97:1 the LORD *r*; let the earth rejoice; let the
  99:1 LORD *r*; let the people tremble: he sitteth
  146:10 the LORD shall *r* for ever, even thy God
Prov. 8:15 by me kings *r* . . princes decree justice
  30:22 for a servant when he *r*; and a fool when
Eccl. 4:14 out of prison he cometh to *r*
Is. 24:23 the LORD of hosts shall *r* in mount Zion
  32:1 behold, a King shall *r* in righteousness
  52:7 salvation; that saith unto Zion, Thy God *r*!
Jer. 22:15 thou *r*, because thou closest . . in cedar?
  23:5 a righteous Branch, and a King shall *r*
Mic. 4:7 the LORD shall *r* over them in mount Zion
Lk. 1:33 he shall *r* over the house of Jacob for ever
  19:14 we will not have this man to *r* over us
Rom. 5:17 if by one man's offense death *r* by one
  5:21 that as sin hath *r* . . even so might grace *r*
  6:12 let not sin therefore *r* in your mortal body
1 Cor. 4:8 ye have *r* as kings without us
  15:25 he must *r*, till he hath put all enemies
2 Tim. 2:12 if we suffer, we shall also *r* with him
Rev. 5:10 kings and priests: and we shall *r* on the
  11:15 Christ; and he shall *r* for ever and ever
  19:6 Alleluia: for the Lord God omnipotent *r*
  20:4 lived and *r* with Christ a thousand years
  22:5 and they shall *r* for ever and ever

Reins

Job 16:13 he cleaveth my *r* asunder, and doth not
  19:27 though my *r* be consumed within me
Ps. 7:9 the righteous God trieth the hearts and *r*
  16:7 my *r* also instruct me in the night seasons
  26:2 examine me, O LORD . . try my *r* and my heart
  73:21 was grieved, and I was pricked in my *r*
  139:13 for thou hast possessed my *r*: thou hast

Prov. 23:16 my *r* shall rejoice, when thy lips speak
Jer. 11:20 O LORD . . that triest the *r* and the heart
  12:2 near in their mouth, and far from their *r*
Rev. 2:23 I am he which searcheth the *r* and hearts

Reject *See also* Refuse

1 Sam. 8:7 have not *r* thee, but they have *r* me
  10:19 ye have this day *r* your God, who himself
  15:23 thou hast *r* the word . . he hath also *r* thee
  16:1 I have *r* him from reigning over Israel?
2 Kgs. 17:15 they *r* his statutes, and his covenant
Is. 53:3 he is despised and *r* of men; a man of
Jer. 2:37 for the LORD hath *r* thy confidences
  6:19 have not hearkened . . to my law, but *r* it
  7:29 LORD hath *r* . . the generation of his wrath
  8:9 lo, they have *r* the word of the LORD
Lam. 5:22 but thou hast utterly *r* us; thou art
Hos. 4:6 thou hast *r* knowledge, I will also *r* thee
Mt. 21:42 (Mk. 12:10; Lk. 20:17) stone which the
  builders *r*, the same is become the head
Mk. 7:9 ye *r* the commandment of God, that ye may
  8:31 (Lk. 9:22) suffer . . and be *r* of the elders
Lk. 7:30 *r* the counsel of God against themselves
  17:25 but first must he . . be *r* of this generation
Jn. 12:48 he that *r* me, and receiveth not my words
Tit. 3:10 after the first and second admonition, *r*
Heb. 12:17 have inherited the blessing, he was *r*

Rejoice *See also* Cheer, Sing

Lev. 23:40 (Deut. 12:12; 16:11) *r* before the LORD
Deut. 12:7 *r* in all that ye put your hand unto
  16:14 shalt *r* in thy feast, thou, and thy son
  26:11 thou shalt *r* in every good thing which the
  28:63 that as the LORD *r* over you to do you good
  30:9 again *r* over thee for good, as he *r* over
  32:43 (Rom. 15:10) *r*, O ye nations, with his people
1 Sam. 2:1 *r* in the LORD . . I *r* in thy salvation
1 Kgs. 1:40 piped with pipes, and *r* with great joy
1 Chr. 16:10 (Ps. 105:3) them *r* that seek the LORD
  16:31 (Ps. 96:11) be glad, and let the earth *r*
  16:32 let the fields *r*, and all that is therein
2 Chr. 6:41 and let thy saints *r* in goodness
  20:27 LORD had made them to *r* over their enemies
Neh. 12:43 *r*: for God had made them *r* with great joy
Job 3:22 which *r* exceedingly, and are glad, when
  21:12 and harp, and *r* at the sound of the organ
  31:25 if I *r* because of my wealth was great
  39:21 paweth in the valley, and *r* in his strength
Ps. 2:11 serve . . with fear, and *r* with trembling
  5:11 let all those that put their trust in thee *r*
  9:14 all thy praise . . I will *r* in thy salvation
  13:5 mercy; my heart shall *r* in thy salvation
  16:9 (Acts 2:26) heart is glad, and my glory *r*
  19:5 chamber, and *r* as a strong man to run a race
  19:8 statutes of the LORD are right, *r* the heart
  20:5 we will *r* in thy salvation, and in the name
  31:7 I will be glad and *r* in thy mercy: for thou
  33:1 *r* in the LORD, O ye righteous: for praise
  33:21 our heart shall *r* in him, because we have
  35:15 but in mine adversity they *r* and gathered
  35:19 let not . . mine enemies wrongfully *r* over me
  40:16 (70:4) those that seek thee *r* and be glad
  51:8 that the bones which thou hast broken may *r*
  58:10 righteous shall *r* when he seeth . . vengeance
  60:6 (108:7) hath spoken in his holiness; I will *r*
  63:7 my help . . in the shadow of thy wings will I *r*
  68:3 *r* before God: yea, let them exceedingly *r*
  71:23 my lips shall greatly *r* when I sing unto
  85:6 revive us again: that thy people may *r* in
  89:16 in thy name shall they *r* all the day
  89:42 thou hast made all his enemies to *r*
  90:14 satisfy us . . with thy mercy; that we may *r*
  96:11 let the heavens *r*, and . . the earth be glad

Ps. 97:1 the LORD reigneth; let the earth *r*
97:12 *r* in the LORD, ye righteous; and give
104:31 for ever: the LORD shall *r* in his works
107:42 the righteous shall see it, and *r*: and all
118:24 hath made; we will *r* and be glad in it
119:14 I have *r* in the way of thy testimonies
119:162 I *r* at thy word, as one that findeth
149:2 let Israel *r* in him that made him
Prov. 2:14 who *r* to do evil, and delight in the
5:18 blessed: and *r* with the wife of thy youth
8:30 I was daily his delight, *r* always before him
11:10 goeth well with the righteous, the city *r*
15:30 light of the eyes *r* the heart: and a good
23:15 if thine heart be wise, my heart shall *r*
23:24 father of the righteous shall greatly *r*
24:17 *r* not when thine enemy falleth, and let
28:12 righteous men do *r*, there is great glory
29:2 righteous are in authority, the people *r*
31:25 and she shall *r* in time to come
Eccl. 2:10 my heart *r* in all my labor: and this
3:12 for a man to *r*, and to do good in his life
3:22 than that a man should *r* in his own works
5:19 to *r* in his labor; this is the gift of God
11:9 *r*, O young man, in thy youth; and let thy
Song 1:4 we will be glad and *r* in thee, we will
Is. 5:14 and he that *r*, shall descend into it
13:3 my mighty ones . . them that *r* in my highness
14:29 *r* not thou, whole Palestina, because
23:12 shalt no more *r*, O thou oppressed virgin
29:19 the poor among men shall *r* in the Holy One
35:1 the desert shall *r*, and blossom as the rose
41:16 thou shalt *r* in the LORD, and shalt glory
61:10 I will greatly *r* in the LORD, my soul shall
62:5 *r* over the bride, so shall thy God *r* over thee
65:13 my servants shall *r*, but ye shall be ashamed
66:10 *r* ye with Jerusalem . . *r* for joy with her
66:14 and when ye see this, your heart shall *r*
Jer. 11:15 when thou doest evil, then thou *r*
31:13 virgin *r*. . make them *r* from their sorrow
32:41 yea, I will *r* over them to do them good
Lam. 2:17 hath caused thine enemy to *r* over thee
4:21 *r* and be glad, O daughter of Edom, that
Ezek. 7:12 let not the buyer *r*, nor the seller
35:14 whole earth *r*, I will make thee desolate
Hos. 9:1 *r* not, O Israel, for joy, as other people
Joel 2:23 ye children of Zion, and *r* in the LORD
Amos 6:13 ye which *r* in a thing of nought, which
Mic. 7:8 *r* not against me, O mine enemy: when I fall
Hab. 3:18 yet I will *r* in the LORD, I will joy in
Zeph. 3:17 will save, he will *r* over thee with joy
Zech. 9:9 greatly, O daughter of Zion; shout
10:7 *r* as through wine: yea . . shall *r* in the LORD
Mt. 2:10 the star, they *r* with exceeding great joy
5:12 (Lk. 6:23) *r*, and be exceeding glad
18:13 he *r* more of that sheep, than of the ninety
Lk. 1:14 gladness; and many shall *r* at his birth
1:47 and my spirit hath *r* in God my Saviour
10:20 rather *r*, because your names are written
10:21 in that hour Jesus *r* in spirit, and said
13:17 the people *r* for all the glorious things
15:5 found it, he layeth it on his shoulders, *r*
15:9 *r* with me; for I have found the piece which
19:37 began to *r* and praise God with a loud voice
Jn. 3:29 *r* greatly because of the bridegroom's
4:36 soweth and he that reapeth may *r* together
5:35 were willing for a season to *r* in his light
8:56 your father Abraham *r* to see my day: and he
14:28 if ye loved me, ye would *r*, because I said
16:20 that ye shall weep . . but the world shall *r*
16:22 will see you again, and your heart shall *r*
Acts 2:26 did my heart *r*, and my tongue was glad
5:41 *r* that they were counted worthy to suffer
8:39 eunuch saw him no more . . went on his way *r*

Acts 16:34 he set meat before them, and *r*, believing
Rom. 5:2 wherein we . . *r* in hope of the glory of God
12:12 *r* in hope; patient in tribulation
12:15 *r* with them that do *r*, and weep with them
1 Cor. 7:30 and they that *r*, as though they *r* not
12:26 one member be honored, all the members *r*
13:6 *r* not in iniquity, but *r* in the truth
2 Cor. 6:10 as sorrowful, yet alway *r*, as poor
7:9 I *r*, not that ye were made sorry, but that
7:16 I *r* therefore that I have confidence in you
Gal. 4:27 written, *R*, thou barren that bearest not
Phil. 1:18 and I therein do *r*, yea, and will *r*
2:16 that I may *r* in the day of Christ, that I
3:1 finally, my brethren, *r* in the Lord
4:4 *r* in the Lord always: and again I say, *R*
4:10 but I *r* in the Lord greatly, that now at
Col. 1:24 who now *r* in my sufferings for you
1 Thes. 5:16 *r* evermore
Jas. 1:9 let the brother of low degree *r* in that
2:13 and mercy *r* against judgment
4:16 ye *r* in your boastings: all such rejoicing
1 Pet. 1:6 wherein ye greatly *r*, though now for a
1:8 ye *r* with joy unspeakable and full of glory
4:13 *r*, inasmuch as ye are partakers of Christ's
2 Jn. 4 I *r* greatly that I found of thy children
3 Jn. 3 I *r* greatly, when the brethren came
Rev. 12:12 *r*, ye heavens, and ye that dwell in them
19:7 let us be glad and *r*, and give honor to him

Rejoicing *See also* Rejoice, Joy
Job 8:21 thy mouth with laughing . . thy lips with *r*
Ps. 107:22 let them . . declare his works with *r*
118:15 the voice of *r* and salvation is in the
119:111 thy testimonies . . are the *r* of my heart
126:6 come again with *r*, bringing his sheaves
Is. 65:18 behold, I create Jerusalem a *r*
2 Cor. 1:12 for our *r* is this, the testimony of
1:14 we are your *r*, even as ye also are ours
Phil. 1:26 your *r* may be more abundant in Jesus
1 Thes. 2:19 our hope, or joy, or crown of *r*?
Heb. 3:6 if we hold fast . . the *r* of the hope firm
Jas. 4:16 in your boastings: all such *r* is evil

Release
Deut. 15:1 every seven years thou shalt make a *r*
Esth. 2:18 he made a *r* to the provinces, and gave
Mt. 27:15 (Mk. 15:6; Lk. 23:17; Jn. 18:39) wont to *r*
 unto the people a prisoner
27:26 (Mk. 15:15; Lk. 23:25) then *r* he Barabbas
Jn. 19:10 crucify thee, and have power to *r* thee?
19:12 from thenceforth Pilate sought to *r* him

Relief
Acts 11:29 determined to send *r* unto the brethren

Relieve
Lev. 25:35 be waxen poor . . then thou shalt *r* him
Ps. 146:9 the LORD . . *r* the fatherless and widow
Is. 1:17 seek judgment, *r* the oppressed, judge
Lam. 1:11 pleasant things for meat to *r* the soul
1 Tim. 5:10 if she have *r* the afflicted, if she
5:16 that believeth have widows, let them *r* them

Religion
Acts 26:5 after the most straitest sect of our *r*
Gal. 1:13 conversation in time past in the Jews' *r*
Jas. 1:27 pure *r* and undefiled before God and the

Religious
Acts 13:43 Jews and *r* proselytes followed Paul
Jas. 1:26 if any man among you seem to be *r*

Rely

2 Chr. 13:18 *r* upon the LORD God of their fathers
 16:7 *r* on the king of Syria. . not *r* on the LORD

Remain *See also* Abide, Dwell, Sojourn, Stay, Tarry

Gen. 8:22 while the earth *r*, seedtime and harvest
Ex. 12:10 let nothing of it *r* until the morning
Deut. 2:34 utterly destroyed. . we left none to *r*
 21:23 body shall not *r* all night upon the tree
Josh. 1:14 shall *r* in the land which Moses gave
 13:1 there *r* yet very much land to be possessed
1 Sam. 24:3 and David and his men *r* in. . the cave
1 Kgs. 18:22 even I only, *r* a prophet of the LORD
Ps. 55:7 wander far off, and *r* in the wilderness
Eccl. 2:9 I was great. . also my wisdom *r* with me
Jer. 17:25 Jerusalem. . this city shall *r* for ever
 48:11 his taste *r* in him, and his scent is not
 51:30 they have *r* in their holds: their might
Lam. 2:22 of the LORD's anger none escaped nor *r*
 5:19 thou, O LORD, *r* for ever; thy throne
Ezek. 3:15 *r* there astonished among them seven days
Hag. 2:5 so my Spirit *r* among you: fear ye not
Zech. 5:4 and it shall *r* in the midst of his house
Mt. 11:23 in Sodom, it would have *r* until this day
Lk. 10:7 in the same house *r*, eating and drinking
Jn. 1:33 see the Spirit descending, and *r* on him
 9:41 now ye say, We see; therefore your sin *r*
 15:11 my joy might *r* in you, and that your joy
 15:16 forth fruit, and that your fruit should *r*
 19:31 should not *r* upon the cross on the sabbath
Acts 5:4 while it *r*, was it not thine own?
1 Cor. 15:6 the greater part *r* unto this present
1 Thes. 4:15 which are alive and *r* unto the coming
 4:17 we which are alive and *r* shall be caught up
Heb. 1:11 they shall perish, but thou *r*: and they
 4:9 *r* therefore a rest to the people of God
 10:26 there *r* no more sacrifice for sins
1 Jn. 3:9 for his seed *r* in him: and he cannot sin
Rev. 3:2 strengthen the things which *r*, that are

Remedy

2 Chr. 36:16 arose against. . till there was no *r*
Prov. 6:15 suddenly shall he be broken without *r*
 29:1 suddenly be destroyed, and that without *r*

Remember

Gen. 8:1 and God *r* Noah, and every living thing
 9:15 I will *r* my covenant, which is between me
 19:29 that God *r* Abraham, and sent Lot out
 30:22 God *r* Rachel, and God hearkened to her
 41:9 the chief butler. . saying, I do *r* my faults
Ex. 2:24 (6:5) their groaning. . God *r* his covenant
 13:3 *r* this day, in which ye came out from Egypt
 20:8 *r* the sabbath day, to keep it holy
Lev. 26:42 I *r* my covenant with Jacob. . *r* the land
Num. 10:9 ye shall be *r* before the LORD your God
 11:5 we *r* the fish, which we did eat in Egypt
 15:39 *r* all the commandments of the LORD, and do
Deut. 5:15 (15:15; 16:12; 24:18, 22) *r* . . thou wast a
 7:18 *r* what the LORD thy God did unto Pharaoh
 8:2 *r* all the way which the LORD thy God led thee
 8:18 thou shalt *r* the LORD thy God: for it is he
 15:15 shalt *r* that thou wast a bondman in. . Egypt
 16:3 mayest *r* the day when thou camest forth out
 24:9 *r* what the LORD thy God did unto Miriam by
 32:7 *r* the days of old, consider the years of
Josh. 1:13 the word which Moses. . commanded
Judg. 8:34 children of Israel *r* not the LORD their
 16:28 Samson. . said, O Lord GOD, *r* me
2 Sam. 14:11 let the king *r* the LORD thy God, that
2 Kgs. 20:3 (Is. 38:3) *r* now how I have walked

1 Chr. 16:12 (Ps. 105:5) *r* his marvelous works that
2 Chr. 6:42 *r* the mercies of David thy servant
Neh. 4:14 *r* the Lord, which is great and terrible
 13:14 (13:22) *r* me, O my God, concerning this
Esth. 9:28 that these days should be *r* and kept
Job 10:9 *r* . . that thou hast made me as the clay
 14:13 wouldest appoint me a set time, and *r* me!
Ps. 9:12 maketh inquisition for blood, he *r* them
 20:7 but we will *r* the name of the LORD our God
 22:27 all the ends of the world shall *r* and turn
 25:6 *r* . . tender mercies and thy loving-kindnesses
 25:7 *r* not the sins of my youth. . *r* thou me for
 42:6 will I *r* thee from the land of Jordan
 45:17 make thy name to be *r* in all generations
 63:6 when I *r* thee upon my bed, and meditate on
 74:2 *r* thy congregation, which thou hast purchased
 77:3 I *r* God, and was troubled: I complained
 77:11 *r* the works of the LORD. . *r* thy wonders of
 78:35 they *r* that God was their rock
 78:39 he *r* that they were but flesh; a wind that
 79:8 O *r* not against us former iniquities
 89:50 *r*, Lord, the reproach of thy servants
 98:3 he hath *r* his mercy and his truth toward
 103:14 knoweth our frame; he *r* that we are dust
 103:18 those that *r* his commandments to do them
 105:8 he hath *r* his covenant for ever, the word
 105:42 he *r* his holy promise, and Abraham his
 106:7 they *r* not the multitude of thy mercies
 109:16 he *r* not to show mercy, but persecuted
 111:4 he hath made his wonderful works to be *r*
 119:52 I *r* thy judgments of old, O LORD
 136:23 who *r* us in our low estate: for his mercy
 137:1 we sat down, yea, we wept, when we *r* Zion
 137:6 if I do not *r* thee, let my tongue cleave
Eccl. 11:8 yet let him *r* the days of darkness
 12:1 *r* now thy Creator in the days of thy youth
Is. 43:18 *r* ye not the former things, neither
 43:25 thy transgressions. . and will not *r* thy sins
 54:4 shalt not *r* the reproach of thy widowhood
 57:11 thou hast lied, and hast not *r* me, nor laid
 64:9 be not wroth. . neither *r* iniquity for ever
 65:17 former shall not be *r*, nor come into mind
Jer. 2:2 thus saith the LORD; I *r* thee, the kindness
 14:10 *r* their iniquity, and visit their sins
 31:34 (Heb. 8:12; 10:17) I will *r* their sin no more
 44:21 people of the land, did not the LORD *r* them
Lam. 1:7 Jerusalem *r* in the days of her affliction
 1:9 she *r* not her last end; therefore she
 2:1 *r* not his footstool in the day of his anger!
Ezek. 16:22 thou hast not *r* the days of thy youth
 16:60 nevertheless, I will *r* my covenant with
 16:61 then thou shalt *r* thy ways, and be ashamed
 20:43 there shall ye *r* your ways, and all your
 36:31 then shall ye *r* your own evil ways
Hos. 2:17 they shall no more be *r* by their name
 7:2 consider not. . that I *r* all their wickedness
 8:13 now will he *r* their iniquity, and visit
Amos 1:9 to Edom, and *r* not the brotherly covenant
Jon. 2:7 when my soul fainted within me I *r* the LORD
Hab. 3:2 O LORD, revive thy work. . in wrath *r* mercy
Zech. 10:9 and they shall *r* me in far countries
Mal. 4:4 *r* ye the law of Moses my servant
Mt. 5:23 and there *r* that thy brother hath aught
 26:75 (Lk. 22:61) and Peter *r* the word of Jesus
Lk. 1:72 perform the mercy. . to *r* his holy covenant
 16:25 *r* that thou in thy lifetime receivedst thy
 17:32 *r* Lot's wife
 23:42 *r* me when thou comest into thy kingdom
 24:6 is not here, but is risen: *r* how he spake
 24:8 and they *r* his words
Jn. 2:17 disciples *r* that it was written, The zeal
 2:22 disciples *r* that he had said this unto them
 12:16 then *r* they that these things were written

Jn. 16:4 shall come, ye may *r* that I told you of them
Acts 11:16 then *r* I the word of the Lord, how that
20:35 and to *r* the words of the Lord Jesus
Gal. 2:10 they would that we should *r* the poor
Eph. 2:11 *r*, that ye being in time past Gentiles
Col. 4:18 *r* my bonds. Grace be with you
1 Thes. 1:3 *r* without ceasing your work of faith
2 Thes. 2:5 *r* ye not, that, when I was yet with you
2 Tim. 2:8 *r* that Jesus Christ . . was raised from
Heb. 13:3 *r* them that are in bonds, as bound with
13:7 *r* them which have the rule over you
3 Jn. 10 I come, I will *r* his deeds which he doeth
Jude 17 *r* ye the words which were spoken before of
Rev. 3:3 *r* therefore from whence thou art fallen
3:3 *r* therefore how thou hast received and heard
18:5 unto heaven, and God hath *r* her iniquities

Remembrance *See also* Memorial, Memory

Num. 5:15 is an offering . . bringing iniquity to *r*
Deut. 32:26 I would make the *r* of them to cease
1 Kgs. 17:18 art thou come . . to call my sin to *r*
Job 18:17 his *r* shall perish from the earth
Ps. 6:5 for in death there is no *r* of thee
30:4 (97:12) give thanks at the *r* of his holiness
77:6 I call to *r* my song in the night: I commune
102:12 for ever; and thy *r* unto all generations
112:6 the righteous shall be in everlasting *r*
Eccl. 1:11 there is no *r* of former things
2:16 is no *r* of the wise more than of the fool
Is. 26:8 desire of our soul is . . to the *r* of thee
43:26 put me in *r*: let us plead together
57:8 behind the doors . . hast thou set up thy *r*
Lam. 3:20 my soul hath them still in *r*, and is
Ezek. 21:23 he will call to *r* the iniquity that
23:19 in calling to *r* the days of her youth
Mal. 3:16 a book of *r* was written before him for
Lk. 1:54 hath holpen . . Israel, in *r* of his mercy
22:19 (1 Cor. 11:24) this do in *r* of me
Jn. 14:26 teach you . . and bring all things to your *r*
Acts 10:31 alms are had in *r* in the sight of God
Phil. 1:3 I thank my God upon every *r* of you
1 Thes. 3:6 and that ye have good *r* of us always
1 Tim. 4:6 if thou put the brethren in *r* of these
2 Tim. 1:3 *r* of thee in my prayers night and day
2:14 these things put them in *r*, charging them
Heb. 10:3 is a *r* again made of sins every year
10:32 but call to *r* the former days, in which
2 Pet. 1:12 negligent to put you always in *r* of
1:15 be able . . to have these things always in *r*
3:1 which I stir up your pure minds by way of *r*
Jude 5 I will therefore put you in *r*, though ye
Rev. 16:19 and great Babylon came in *r* before God

Remission *See also* Forgiveness, Pardon

Mt. 26:28 blood . . shed for many for the *r* of sins
Mk. 1:4 (Lk. 3:3) baptism . . for the *r* of sins
Lk. 1:77 unto his people by the *r* of their sins
24:47 *r* of sins should be preached in his name
Acts 2:38 be baptized every one . . for the *r* of sins
10:43 believeth in him shall receive *r* of sins
Rom. 3:25 his righteousness for the *r* of sins
Heb. 9:22 and without shedding of blood is no *r*
10:18 now where *r* of these is, there is no more

Remit *See also* Forgive, Pardon

Jn. 20:23 whosesoever sins ye *r*, they are *r* unto

Remnant *See also* Residue

Lev. 5:13 the *r* shall be the priest's, as a meat
1 Kgs. 12:23 speak unto Rehoboam . . and to the *r* of
2 Kgs. 19:4 (Is. 37:4) lift up thy prayer for the *r*

2 Kgs. 19:30 (Is. 37:31) and the *r* that is escaped of
Ezra 9:8 grace . . to leave us a *r* to escape
Is. 1:9 except the LORD . . had left . . a very small *r*
10:21 the *r* shall return, even the *r* of Jacob
10:22 (Rom. 9:27) sea, yet a *r* . . shall return
11:11 second time to recover the *r* of his people
11:16 shall be a highway for the *r* of his people
16:14 and the *r* shall be very small and feeble
Jer. 15:11 verily it shall be well with thy *r*
23:3 I will gather the *r* of my flock out of all
31:7 O LORD, save thy people, the *r* of Israel
40:11 the king of Babylon had left a *r* of Judah
44:12 I will take the *r* of Judah, that have set
44:28 all the *r* of Judah . . shall know whose words
Ezek. 6:8 yet will I leave a *r*, that ye may have
23:25 thy *r* shall fall by the sword: they shall
Joel 2:32 and in the *r* whom the LORD shall call
Mic. 2:12 I will surely gather the *r* of Israel
5:3 then the *r* of his brethren shall return unto
Zeph. 3:13 the *r* of Israel shall not do iniquity
Zech. 8:12 cause the *r* of this people to possess
Rom. 9:27 though the number . . a *r* shall be saved
11:5 is a *r* according to the election of grace
Rev. 11:13 the *r* were affrighted, and gave glory
19:21 and the *r* were slain with the sword of him

Remove

Deut. 19:14 shalt not *r* thy neighbor's landmark
Job 9:5 which *r* the mountains, and they know not
24:2 some *r* the landmarks; they violently take
Ps. 36:11 and let not the hand of the wicked *r* me
39:10 *r* thy stroke away from me: I am consumed
46:2 will not we fear, though the earth be *r*
81:6 I *r* his shoulder from the burden: his hands
103:12 so far hath he *r* our transgressions from
119:22 *r* from me reproach and contempt
125:1 shall be as mount Zion, which cannot be *r*
Prov. 4:27 nor to the left: *r* thy foot from evil
10:30 the righteous shall never be *r*
22:28 *r* not the ancient landmark, which thy
30:8 *r* far from me vanity and lies; give me
Eccl. 10:9 whoso *r* stones shall be hurt therewith
11:10 *r* sorrow from thy heart, and put away evil
Is. 13:13 *r* and the earth shall *r* out of her place
24:20 the earth . . shall be *r* like a cottage
54:10 hills be *r* . . the covenant of my peace be *r*
Jer. 50:3 they shall *r*, they shall depart, both
Ezek. 12:3 for *r*, and *r* by day in their sight
Dan. 2:21 he *r* kings, and setteth up kings
Mt. 17:20 *r* hence to yonder place; and it shall *r*
21:21 (Mk. 11:23) be thou *r*, and . . cast into the sea
Lk. 22:42 if thou be willing, *r* this cup from me
Acts 7:4 *r* him into this land, wherein ye now dwell
1 Cor. 13:2 all faith, so that I could *r* mountains
Gal. 1:6 I marvel that ye are so soon *r* from him
Heb. 12:27 the *r* of those things that are shaken
Rev. 2:5 will *r* thy candlestick out of his place

Rend (Rent) *See also* Tear

Gen. 37:33 Joseph is without doubt *r* in pieces
Lev. 10:6 neither *r* your clothes; lest ye die
Judg. 14:6 and he *r* him as he would have *r* a kid
1 Sam. 15:28 (28:17) the LORD hath *r* the kingdom
1 Kgs. 1:40 the earth *r* with the sound of them
11:11 I will surely *r* the kingdom from thee
13:3 gave a sign . . Behold, the altar shall be *r*
19:11 a great and strong wind *r* the mountains
2 Kgs. 22:19 (2 Chr. 34:27) *r* thy clothes, and wept
Ezra 9:3 I *r* my garment and my mantle, and plucked
Job 1:20 Job arose, and *r* his mantle, and shaved
26:8 waters . . and the cloud is not *r* under them
Ps. 7:2 tear my soul like a lion, *r* it in pieces
Eccl. 3:7 a time to *r*, and a time to sew

Is. 64:1 oh that thou wouldest *r* the heavens
Jer. 36:24 were not afraid, nor *r* their garments
Ezek. 30:16 No shall be *r* asunder, and Noph shall
Hos. 13:8 and will *r* the caul of their heart
Joel 2:13 *r* your heart, and not your garments
Mt. 7:6 trample them . . and turn again and *r* you
27:51 (Mk. 15:38; Lk. 23:45) veil . . was *r* in twain
Mk. 9:26 and the spirit cried, and *r* him some
Lk. 5:36 otherwise, then both the new maketh a *r*
Jn. 19:24 let us not *r* it, but cast lots for it

Render *See also* Recompense

Deut. 32:41 I will *r* vengeance to mine enemies
Judg. 9:57 the evil . . did God *r* upon their heads
1 Sam. 26:23 *r* to every man his righteousness
2 Chr. 6:30 *r* unto every man according unto all
Job 33:26 he will *r* unto man his righteousness
34:11 for the work of a man shall he *r* unto him
Ps. 28:4 of their hands; *r* to them their desert
38:20 that *r* evil for good are mine adversaries
62:12 thou *r* to every man according to his work
79:12 *r* unto our neighbors sevenfold into their
94:2 judge of the earth: *r* a reward to the proud
116:12 what shall I *r* unto the LORD for all his
Prov. 24:12 *r* to every man according to his works?
Hos. 14:2 so will we *r* the calves of our lips
Zech. 9:12 declare that I will *r* double unto thee
Mt. 21:41 shall *r* him the fruits in their seasons
22:21 (Mk. 12:17; Lk. 20:25) *r* . . unto Caesar
Rom. 2:6 will *r* to every man according to his deeds
13:7 *r* therefore to all their dues: tribute to
1 Thes. 3:9 what thanks can we *r* to God again for
5:15 see that none *r* evil for evil unto any man
1 Pet. 3:9 not *r* evil for evil, or railing for

Renew

Ps. 51:10 O God; and *r* a right spirit within me
103:5 so that thy youth is *r* like the eagle's
104:30 created: and thou *r* the face of the earth
Is. 40:31 wait upon the LORD shall *r* their strength
Lam. 5:21 we shall be turned; *r* our days as of old
Rom. 12:2 be ye transformed by the *r* of your mind
2 Cor. 4:16 yet the inward man is *r* day by day
Eph. 4:23 and be *r* in the spirit of your mind
Col. 3:10 the new man, which is *r* in knowledge
Tit. 3:5 of regeneration, and *r* of the Holy Ghost
Heb. 6:6 to *r* them again unto repentance; seeing

Renounce *See also* Deny

2 Cor. 4:2 have *r* the hidden things of dishonesty

Renown

Gen. 6:4 mighty men which were of old, men of *r*
Num. 16:2 two hundred and fifty princes . . men of *r*
Is. 14:20 the seed of evildoers shall never be *r*
Ezek. 14:8 thy *r* went forth among the heathen for
34:29 I will raise up for them a plant of *r*
Dan. 9:15 and hast gotten thee *r*, as at this day

Renowned *See also* Renown

Num. 1:16 these were the *r* of the congregation
Ezek. 23:23 and *r*, all of them riding upon horses
26:17 inhabited of seafaring men, the *r* city

Rent *See also* Rend

Josh. 9:4 wine bottles, old, and *r*, and bound up
Is. 3:24 instead of a girdle a *r*; and instead of
Mt. 9:16 (Mk. 2:21) garment, and the *r* is made worse
Lk. 5:36 otherwise, then both the new maketh a *r*

Repair

2 Kgs. 12:5 let them *r* the breaches of the house
22:5 (2 Chr. 34:8) *r* the breaches of the house

2 Chr. 24:4 Joash was minded to *r* the house of the
24:5 money to *r* the house of your God from
32:5 and *r* Millo in the city of David, and made
34:8 to *r* the house of the LORD his God
Ezra 9:9 to give us a reviving . . to *r* the desolations
Neh. 3:32 unto the sheep gate *r* the goldsmiths and
Is. 61:4 and they shall *r* the waste cities

Repairer

Is. 58:12 shalt be called, The *r* of the breach

Repay

Deut. 7:10 and *r* them that hate him to their face
Job 21:31 and who shall *r* him what he hath done?
41:11 hath prevented me, that I should *r* him?
Prov. 13:21 but to the righteous good shall be *r*
Is. 59:18 their deeds, accordingly he will *r*
Lk. 10:35 more, when I come again, I will *r* thee
Rom. 12:19 written, Vengeance is mine; I will *r*
Phlm. 19 I Paul have written it . . I will *r* it

Repeat

Prov. 17:9 that *r* a matter separateth very friends

Repent *See also* Change, Grieve, Return, Turn

Gen. 6:6 it *r* the LORD that he had made man
Ex. 13:17 lest . . the people *r* when they see war
32:14 LORD *r* of the evil which he thought to do
Num. 23:19 neither the son of man, that he should *r*
Judg. 2:18 it *r* the LORD because of their groanings
21:6 the children of Israel *r* them for Benjamin
1 Sam. 15:11 (15:35) *r* me that I have set up Saul
15:29 he is not a man, that he should *r*
2 Sam. 24:16 (1 Chr. 21:15) LORD *r* him of the evil
1 Kgs. 8:47 whither they were carried captives, and *r*
Job 42:6 I abhor myself, and *r* in dust and ashes
Ps. 90:13 let it *r* thee concerning thy servants
110:4 (Heb. 7:21) LORD hath sworn, and will not *r*
Jer. 8:6 no man *r* him of his wickedness, saying
18:8 I will *r* of the evil that I thought to do
26:3 I may *r* me of the evil, which I purpose to
26:13 obey . . and the LORD will *r* him of the evil
42:10 I *r* me of the evil that I have done unto
Ezek. 14:6 *r*, and turn yourselves from your idols
18:30 *r*, and turn . . from all your transgressions
24:14 neither will I spare, neither will I *r*
Joel 2:14 who knoweth if he will return and *r*
Amos 7:3 (7:6) the LORD *r* for this: It shall be
Jon. 3:9 who can tell if God will turn and *r*
Mt. 3:2 (4:17) *r* ye: for the kingdom of heaven is
11:20 to upbraid the cities . . because they *r* not
11:21 (Lk. 10:13) have *r* long ago in sackcloth
12:41 (Lk. 11:32) they *r* at the preaching of Jonas
21:29 I will not; but afterward he *r*, and went
21:32 ye, when ye had seen it, *r* not afterward
27:3 Judas . . saw that he was condemned, *r*
Mk. 1:15 is fulfilled . . *r* ye, and believe the gospel
6:12 went out, and preached that men should *r*
Lk. 13:3 except ye *r*, ye shall all likewise perish
15:7 joy . . be in heaven over one sinner that *r*
16:30 went unto them from the dead, they will *r*
17:3 rebuke him; and if he *r*, forgive him
Acts 2:38 *r*, and be baptized every one of you in
3:19 *r* ye therefore, and be converted, that your
8:22 *r* therefore of this thy wickedness
17:30 now commandeth all men every where to *r*
26:20 that they should *r* and turn to God, and do
2 Cor. 7:10 repentance to salvation not to be *r* of
12:21 not *r* of the uncleanness and fornication
Rev. 2:5 and *r*, and do the first works; or else I
2:16 *r*; or else I will come unto thee quickly

Rev. 2:21 space to *r* of her fornication; and she *r* not
2:22 tribulation, except they *r* of their deeds
3:3 hast received and heard, and hold fast, and *r*
3:19 and chasten: be zealous therefore, and *r*
9:20 yet *r* not of the works of their hands
9:21 neither *r* they of their murders, nor of
16:9 and they *r* not to give him glory
16:11 and their sores, and *r* not of their deeds

Repentance

Hos. 13:14 *r* shall be hid from mine eyes
Mt. 3:8 (Lk. 3:8) bring forth. . fruits meet for *r*
3:11 I indeed baptize you with water unto *r*
9:13 (Mk. 2:17; Lk. 5:32) to call. . sinners to *r*
Mk. 1:4 (Lk. 3:3) baptism of *r* for the remission
Lk. 15:7 than over. . just persons, which need no *r*
24:47 *r* and remission of sins should be preached
Acts 5:31 to give *r* to Israel, and forgiveness
11:18 also to the Gentiles granted *r* unto life
13:24 baptism of *r* to all the people of Israel
20:21 *r* toward God, and faith toward our Lord
26:20 and turn to God, and do works meet for *r*
Rom. 2:4 the goodness of God leadeth thee to *r*?
11:29 the gifts and calling of God are without *r*
2 Cor. 7:9 made sorry, but that ye sorrowed to *r*
7:10 godly sorrow worketh *r* to salvation not to
2 Tim. 2:25 if God peradventure will give them *r*
Heb. 6:1 not laying again the foundation of *r* from
6:6 shall fall away, to renew them again unto *r*
12:17 he found no place of *r*, though he sought it
2 Pet. 3:9 perish, but that all should come to *r*

Repetition

Mt. 6:7 when ye pray, use not vain *r*, as the heathen

Rephaim 2 Sam. 5:18 (1 Chr. 14:9)

Rephidim Ex. 17:1

Replenish

Gen. 1:28 fruitful, and multiply, and *r* the earth
Is. 2:6 because they be *r* from the east, and are
Jer. 31:25 and I have *r* every sorrowful soul
Ezek. 26:2 I shall be *r*, now she is laid waste

Reply

Rom. 9:20 O man, who art thou that *r* against God?

Report *See also* Rumor

Gen. 37:2 brought unto his father their evil *r*
Ex. 23:1 thou shalt not raise a false *r*
Num. 13:32 they brought up an evil *r* of the land
1 Sam. 2:24 my sons. . it is no good *r* that I hear
Prov. 15:30 and a good *r* maketh the bones fat
Is. 53:1 (Jn. 12:38; Rom. 10:16) hath believed our *r*?
Jer. 20:10 *r*, say they, and we will *r* it
Mt. 28:15 this saying is commonly *r* among the Jews
Acts 6:3 look ye. . among you seven men of honest *r*
16:2 which was well *r* of by the brethren that
22:12 Ananias. . having a good *r* of all the Jews
1 Cor. 14:25 and *r* that God is in you of a truth
2 Cor. 6:8 by evil and good *r*: as deceivers, and yet
Phil. 4:8 whatsoever things are of good *r*
1 Tim. 3:7 moreover he must have a good *r* of them
5:10 well *r* of for good works; if she have
Heb. 11:2 for by it the elders obtained a good *r*
11:39 having obtained a good *r* through faith
3 Jn. 12 Demetrius hath good *r* of all men

Reproach *See also* Disgrace, Dishonor, Rebuke, Reproof, Scorn, Shame

Gen. 30:23 and said, God hath taken away my *r*

Num. 15:30 presumptuously. . the same *r* the LORD
Josh. 5:9 I rolled away the *r* of Egypt from off you
Ruth 2:15 saying, Let her glean. . and *r* her not
1 Sam. 17:26 and taketh away the *r* from Israel?
25:39 hath pleaded the cause of my *r* from. . Nabal
2 Kgs. 19:4 (Is. 37:4) hath sent to *r* the living God
19:22 (Is. 37:23) whom hast thou *r* and blasphemed
Neh. 1:3 the remnant. . are in great affliction and *r*
2:17 wall of Jerusalem, that we be no more a *r*
5:9 because of the *r* of the heathen our enemies?
Job 19:3 ten times have ye *r* me: ye are not ashamed
27:6 my heart shall not *r* me so long as I live
Ps. 15:3 nor taketh up a *r* against his neighbor
22:6 but I am a worm, and no man; a *r* of men
31:11 I was a *r* among all mine enemies
39:8 deliver me. . make me not the *r* of the foolish
42:10 as. . a sword in my bones, mine enemies *r* me
44:13 thou makest us a *r* to our neighbors, a scorn
55:12 for it was not an enemy that *r* me
57:3 from the *r* of him that would swallow me up
69:7 for thy sake I have borne *r*; shame hath
69:9 (Rom. 15:3) *r* of them that *r* thee are fallen
69:19 thou hast known my *r*, and my shame
69:20 *r* hath broken my heart; and I am full of
71:13 let them be covered with *r* and dishonor
74:10 O God, how long shall the adversary *r*?
74:22 remember how the foolish man *r* thee daily
78:66 his enemies. . he put them to a perpetual *r*
79:12 their *r*, wherewith they have *r* thee, O Lord
89:50 *r* of thy servants. . the *r* of all the mighty
89:51 thine enemies have *r*, O LORD. . they have *r*
102:8 mine enemies *r* me all the day
109:25 I became also a *r* unto them: when they
119:22 remove from me *r* and contempt; for I have
119:39 turn away my *r* which I fear: for thy
119:42 I have wherewith to answer him that *r* me
Prov. 6:33 and his *r* shall not be wiped away
14:31 he that oppresseth the poor *r* his Maker
14:34 but sin is a *r* to any people
17:5 whoso mocketh the poor *r* his Maker
18:3 cometh also contempt, and with ignominy *r*
19:26 a son that causeth shame, and bringeth *r*
22:10 shall go out; yea, strife and *r* shall cease
27:11 be wise. . that I may answer him that *r* me
Is. 30:5 nor profit, but a shame, and also a *r*
51:7 fear ye not the *r* of men, neither be ye
Jer. 6:10 the word of the LORD is unto them a *r*
20:8 the word of the LORD was made a *r* unto me
23:40 and I will bring an everlasting *r* upon you
24:9 for their hurt, to be a *r* and a proverb
31:19 because I did bear the *r* of my youth
Lam. 3:61 thou hast heard their *r*, O LORD, and all
Ezek. 5:15 shall be a *r* and a taunt, an instruction
22:4 have I made thee a *r* unto the heathen
36:15 neither shalt thou bear the *r* of the people
Dan. 9:16 Jerusalem and thy people are become a *r*
Hos. 12:14 his *r* shall his Lord return unto him
Joel 2:19 I will no more make you a *r* among the
Mic. 6:16 ye shall bear the *r* of my people
Zeph. 2:8 *r* of Moab. . they have *r* my people
3:18 of thee, to whom the *r* of it was a burden
Lk. 1:25 looked on me, to take away my *r* among men
6:22 shall *r* you, and cast out your name as evil
11:45 Master, thus saying thou *r* us also
Rom. 15:3 the *r* of them that *r* thee fell on me
2 Cor. 12:10 I take pleasure in infirmities, in *r*
1 Tim. 3:7 lest he fall into *r* and the snare of
4:10 we both labor and suffer *r*, because we
Heb. 10:33 a gazingstock both by *r* and afflictions
11:26 esteeming the *r* of Christ greater riches
13:13 unto him without the camp, bearing his *r*
1 Pet. 4:14 if ye be *r* for the name of Christ

Reproachfully

Job 16:10 they have smitten me upon the cheek *r*
1 Tim. 5:14 occasion to the adversary to speak *r*

Reprobate

Jer. 6:30 *r* silver shall men call them, because
Rom. 1:28 God gave them over to a *r* mind, to do
2 Cor. 13:5 Jesus Christ is in you, except ye be *r*?
2 Tim. 3:8 corrupt minds, *r* concerning the faith
Tit. 1:16 disobedient, and unto every good work *r*

Reproof *See also* Rebuke, Reproach

Job 26:11 tremble, and are astonished at his *r*
Prov. 1:23 turn you at my *r*: behold, I will pour
5:12 hated instruction, and my heart despised *r*
6:23 and *r* of instruction are the way of life
15:5 but he that regardeth *r* is prudent
15:31 ear that heareth the *r* of life abideth
17:10 a *r* entereth more into a wise man than a
29:15 the rod and *r* give wisdom: but a child
2 Tim. 3:16 is profitable for doctrine, for *r*, for

Reprove *See also* Admonish, Rebuke, Reproach, Warn

Gen. 20:16 unto Sarah he said . . thus she was *r*
1 Chr. 16:21 (Ps. 105:14) he *r* kings for their sakes
Job 6:25 right words! but what doth your arguing *r*?
13:10 he will surely *r* you, if ye do secretly
22:4 will he *r* thee for fear of thee? will he
40:2 instruct him? he that *r* God, let him answer
Ps. 50:8 I will not *r* thee for thy sacrifices or
141:5 let him *r* me; it shall be an excellent oil
Prov. 9:8 *r* not a scorner, lest he hate thee
19:25 *r* one that hath understanding, and he will
29:1 he, that being often *r* hardeneth his neck
30:6 lest he *r* thee, and thou be found a liar
Is. 11:4 *r* with equity for the meek of the earth
Jer. 2:19 and thy backslidings shall *r* thee
29:27 now therefore why hast thou not *r* Jeremiah
Hos. 4:4 yet let no man strive, nor *r* another
Jn. 3:20 to the light, lest his deeds should be *r*
16:8 when he is come, he will *r* the world of sin
Eph. 5:11 unfruitful works of darkness . . *r* them
5:13 all things that are *r* are made manifest by
2 Tim. 4:2 *r*, rebuke, exhort with all long-suffering

Reprover

Prov. 25:12 so is a wise *r* upon an obedient ear
Ezek. 3:26 be dumb, and shalt not be to them a *r*

Reputation

Eccl. 10:1 him that is in *r* for wisdom and honor
Acts 5:34 Gamaliel, a doctor of the law, had in *r*
Gal. 2:2 but privately to them which were of *r*
Phil. 2:7 made himself of no *r*, and took upon him
2:29 receive him . . and hold such in *r*

Request *See also* Ask, Beseech, Entreat, Petition

Judg. 8:24 Gideon said . . I would desire a *r* of you
Esth. 5:3 (7:2) queen Esther? and what is thy *r*?
Job 6:8 oh that I might have my *r*; and that God
Ps. 21:2 hast not withholden the *r* of his lips
106:15 he gave them their *r*; but sent leanness
Dan. 1:8 he *r* of the prince of the eunuchs that he
2:49 Daniel *r* of the king, and he set Shadrach
Phil. 1:4 prayer . . for you all making *r* with joy
4:6 let your *r* be made known unto God

Require *See also* Demand

Gen. 9:5 surely your blood of your lives will I *r*

Deut. 10:12 what doth the LORD thy God *r* of thee
18:19 shall speak in my name, I will *r* it of him
23:21 the LORD thy God will surely *r* it of thee
Josh. 22:23 thereon, let the LORD himself *r* it
1 Sam. 20:16 let the LORD even *r* it at the hand of
2 Chr. 24:22 said, The LORD look upon it, and *r* it
Ps. 10:13 said in his heart, Thou wilt not *r* it
40:6 burnt offering . . sin offering hast thou not *r*
137:3 *r* of us a song; and . . *r* of us mirth, saying
Prov. 30:7 two things have I *r* of thee; deny me
Eccl. 3:15 already been . . God *r* that which is past
Is. 1:12 who hath *r* this at your hand, to tread my
Ezek. 3:18 (33:8) his blood will I *r* at thine hand
20:40 and there will I *r* your offerings
33:6 his blood will I *r* at the watchman's hand
34:10 I will *r* my flock at their hand, and cause
Mic. 6:8 what doth the LORD *r* of thee, but to do
Lk. 11:50 that the blood . . may be *r* of this generation
12:20 this night thy soul shall be *r* of thee
12:48 much is given, of him shall be much *r*
19:23 coming I might have *r* mine own with usury?
23:23 loud voices, *r* that he might be crucified
1 Cor. 1:22 the Jews *r* a sign, and the Greeks seek
4:2 *r* in stewards, that a man be found faithful

Requite

Gen. 50:15 *r* us all the evil which we did unto him
Deut. 32:6 do ye thus *r* the LORD, O foolish people
Judg. 1:7 cut off . . as I have done, so God hath *r* me
1 Sam. 25:21 and he hath *r* me evil for good
2 Sam. 2:6 I also will *r* you this kindness, because
16:12 will *r* me good for his cursing this day
Ps. 41:10 O LORD . . raise me up, that I may *r* them
Jer. 51:56 LORD God of recompenses shall surely *r*
1 Tim. 5:4 piety at home, and to *r* their parents

Rescue *See also* Deliver, Redeem, Save

Deut. 28:31 and thou shalt have none to *r* them
1 Sam. 14:45 people *r* Jonathan, that he died not
30:18 David recovered all . . and . . *r* his two wives
Ps. 35:17 *r* my soul from their destructions
Hos. 5:14 I will take away, and none shall *r* him
Acts 23:27 then came I with an army, and *r* him

Resemble

Judg. 8:18 each one *r* the children of a king
Lk. 13:18 kingdom of God . . whereunto shall I *r* it?

Reserve *See also* Keep

Gen. 27:36 hast thou not *r* a blessing for me?
Job 21:30 wicked is *r* to the day of destruction?
38:23 which I have *r* against the time of trouble
Jer. 3:5 will he *r* his anger for ever? will he keep
50:20 for I will pardon them whom I *r*
Nah. 1:2 revengeth . . and he *r* wrath for his enemies
Rom. 11:4 I have *r* to myself seven thousand men
1 Pet. 1:4 fadeth not away, *r* in heaven for you
2 Pet. 2:4 into . . darkness, to be *r* unto judgment
2:9 and to *r* the unjust unto the day of judgment
2:17 to whom the mist of darkness is *r* for ever
3:7 *r* unto fire against the day of judgment
Jude 6 hath *r* in everlasting chains under darkness

Residue *See also* Remnant

Is. 28:5 diadem of beauty, unto the *r* of his people
38:10 grave: I am deprived of the *r* of my years
44:17 and the *r* thereof he maketh a god
Jer. 15:9 *r* of them will I deliver to the sword
Ezek. 9:8 wilt thou destroy all the *r* of Israel in
Zech. 8:11 I will not be unto the *r* of this people
Mal. 2:15 make one? Yet had he the *r* of the Spirit
Acts 15:17 the *r* of men might seek after the Lord

Resist *See also* Harden, Rebel, Revolt

Zech. 3:1 Satan standing at his right . . to *r* him
Mt. 5:39 but I say unto you, That ye *r* not evil
Lk. 21:15 shall not be able to gainsay nor *r*
Acts 6:10 not able to *r* the wisdom and the spirit
   7:51 ye do always *r* the Holy Ghost
Rom. 9:19 yet find fault? For who hath *r* his will?
   13:2 *r* the power, *r* the ordinance of God
2 Tim. 3:8 also *r* the truth: men of corrupt minds
Heb. 12:4 ye have not yet *r* unto blood, striving
Jas. 4:6 (1 Pet. 5:5) God *r* the proud, but giveth grace
   4:7 *r* the devil, and he will flee from you
1 Pet. 5:9 whom *r* steadfast in the faith, knowing

Resolved

Lk. 16:4 I am *r* what to do, that, when I am put out

Resort

Neh. 4:20 hear . . the trumpet, *r* ye thither unto us
Ps. 71:3 habitation, whereunto I may continually *r*
Mk. 2:13 the multitude *r* unto him, and he taught
   10:1 of Judea . . and the people *r* unto him again
Jn. 18:2 Jesus ofttimes *r* thither with his disciples
   18:20 in the temple, whither the Jews always *r*

Respect *See also* Esteem, Heed, Regard

Gen. 4:4 LORD had *r* unto Abel and to his offering
Ex. 2:25 children of Israel . . God had *r* unto them
Lev. 19:15 thou shalt not *r* the person of the poor
   26:9 I will have *r* unto you . . make you fruitful
Deut. 1:17 ye shall not *r* persons in judgment
1 Kgs. 8:28 (2 Chr. 6:19) have thou *r* unto the prayer
2 Kgs. 13:23 *r* unto them, because of his covenant
2 Chr. 19:7 nor *r* of persons, nor taking of gifts
Job 37:24 he *r* not any that are wise of heart
Ps. 40:4 *r* not the proud, nor such as turn aside
   74:20 have *r* unto the covenant: for the dark
   119:6 when I have *r* unto all thy commandments
   119:15 thy precepts, and have *r* unto thy ways
   138:6 be high, yet hath he *r* unto the lowly
Prov. 24:23 (28:21) not good to have *r* of persons
Is. 17:7 his eyes shall have *r* to the Holy One of
Rom. 2:11 (Eph. 6:9; Col. 3:25) no *r* of persons with
Heb. 11:26 had *r* unto the recompense of the reward
Jas. 2:1 the faith of our Lord . . with *r* of persons
   2:9 but if ye have *r* to persons, ye commit sin
1 Pet. 1:17 Father, who without *r* of persons judgeth

Respecter

Acts 10:34 I perceive that God is no *r* of persons

Respite

Ex. 8:15 but when Pharaoh saw that there was *r*
1 Sam. 11:3 give us seven days' *r*, that we may

Rest *See also* Peace, Quietness

Gen. 2:2 (Heb. 4:4) God . . *r* on the seventh day
Ex. 16:23 tomorrow is the *r* of the holy sabbath
   16:30 so the people *r* on the seventh day
   20:11 six days the LORD made . . and *r* the seventh
   23:12 (34:21) on the seventh day thou shalt *r*
   31:17 on the seventh day he *r*, and was refreshed
   33:14 shall go with thee, and I will give thee *r*
Lev. 25:5 for it is a year of *r* unto the land
   26:34 shall the land *r*, and enjoy her sabbaths
Deut. 3:20 LORD have given *r* unto your brethren
   12:9 ye are not as yet come to the *r* and to the
   12:10 (25:19) giveth you *r* from all your enemies
Josh. 1:13 the LORD your God hath given you *r*
   11:23 (14:15; Judg. 3:11, 30; 5:31) land *r* from war
   21:44 LORD gave them *r* round about, according to
   23:1 LORD had given *r* unto Israel from all their

Ruth 3:18 will not be in *r*, until he have finished
2 Sam. 7:1 LORD had given him *r* round about from
1 Kgs. 5:4 my God hath given me *r* on every side
2 Kgs. 2:15 the spirit of Elijah doth *r* on Elisha
1 Chr. 22:9 be a man of *r*; and I will give him *r*
   22:18 and hath he not given you *r* on every side?
2 Chr. 14:6 land had *r* . . the LORD had given him *r*
   14:11 help us, O LORD our God; for we *r* on thee
   32:8 the people *r* . . upon the words of Hezekiah
Neh. 9:28 after they had *r*, they did evil again
Esth. 9:22 wherein the Jews *r* from their enemies
Job 3:18 there the prisoners *r* together; they hear
   11:18 be secure . . thou shalt take thy *r* in safety
   17:16 when our *r* together is in the dust
Ps. 16:9 (Acts 2:26) my flesh also shall *r* in hope
   37:7 *r* in the LORD, and wait patiently for him
   38:3 any *r* in my bones because of my sin
   55:6 dove! for then would I fly away, and be at *r*
   94:13 give him *r* from the days of adversity
   95:11 (Heb. 3:11, 18) should not enter into my *r*
   116:7 return unto thy *r*, O my soul; for the LORD
   125:3 rod of the wicked shall not *r* upon the lot
   132:8 arise, O LORD, into thy *r*; thou, and the
   132:14 this is my *r* for ever: here will I dwell
Prov. 29:9 whether he rage or laugh, there is no *r*
   29:17 correct thy son, and he shall give thee *r*
Eccl. 2:23 his heart taketh not *r* in the night
Is. 7:19 *r* all of them in the desolate valleys
   11:2 and the Spirit of the LORD shall *r* upon him
   11:10 Gentiles seek: and his *r* shall be glorious
   14:3 LORD shall give thee *r* from thy sorrow
   23:12 Chittim; there also shalt thou have no *r*
   25:10 this mountain shall the hand of the LORD *r*
   28:12 *r* wherewith ye may cause the weary to *r*
   30:15 in returning and *r* shall ye be saved
   62:1 for Jerusalem's sake I will not *r*, until the
   63:14 the Spirit of the LORD caused him to *r*
   66:1 (Acts 7:49) where is the place of my *r*?
Jer. 6:16 walk therein, and ye shall find *r*
   30:10 (46:27) Jacob shall return, and shall be in *r*
   50:34 he may give *r* to the land, and disquiet
Lam. 1:3 Judah . . findeth no *r*: all her persecutors
   2:18 give thyself no *r*; let not the apple of
   5:5 under persecution: we labor, and have no *r*
Ezek. 16:42 so will I make my fury toward thee to *r*
   38:11 I will go to them that are at *r*, that dwell
Dan. 12:13 for thou shalt *r*, and stand in thy lot
Mic. 2:10 arise ye . . depart; for this is not your *r*
Hab. 3:16 that I might *r* in the day of trouble
Mt. 11:28 are heavy laden, and I will give you *r*
   11:29 and ye shall find *r* unto your souls
   12:43 (Lk. 11:24) through dry places, seeking *r*
   26:45 (Mk. 14:41) sleep on now, and take your *r*
Mk. 6:31 apart into a desert place, and *r* a while
Lk. 23:56 and they returned . . and *r* the sabbath day
Acts 9:31 then had the churches *r* throughout all
Rom. 2:17 thou art called a Jew, and *r* in the law
2 Cor. 7:5 come into Macedonia, our flesh had no *r*
   12:9 that the power of Christ may *r* upon me
2 Thes. 1:7 and to you who are troubled *r* with us
Heb. 4:1 lest, a promise . . of entering into his *r*
   4:3 for we which have believed do enter into *r*
   4:9 there remaineth . . a *r* to the people of God
   4:11 let us labor therefore to enter into that *r*
1 Pet. 4:14 Spirit of glory and of God *r* upon you
Rev. 4:8 they *r* not day and night, saying, Holy
   6:11 they should *r* yet for a little season, until
   14:11 they have no *r* day nor night, who worship
   14:13 that they may *r* from their labors

Resting Place

Num. 10:33 before them . . to search out a *r p* for
2 Chr. 6:41 therefore arise, O LORD God, into thy *r p*

Is. 32:18 and in sure dwellings, and in quiet *r p*
Jer. 50:6 they have gone. . have forgotten their *r p*

Restitution

Ex. 22:3 blood shed for him. . he should make full *r*
22:5 of the best of his own. . shall he make *r*
Job 20:18 according to his substance shall the *r* be
Acts 3:21 must receive until the times of *r* of all

Restore

Gen. 20:7 *r* the man his wife; for he is a prophet
42:25 and to *r* every man's money into his sack
Ex. 22:1 he shall *r* five oxen for an ox, and four
22:4 found in his hand alive. . he shall *r* double
Lev. 6:4 he shall *r* that which he took violently away
25:28 but if he be not able to *r* it to him
Deut. 22:2 seek after it, and thou shalt *r* it to
1 Kgs. 13:6 pray for me, that my hand may be *r* me
2 Kgs. 8:6 officer, saying, *R* all that was hers
Job 20:10 and his hands shall *r* their goods
Ps. 23:3 he *r* my soul: he leadeth me in the paths
51:12 *r* unto me the joy of thy salvation
69:4 then I *r* that which I took not away
Is. 1:26 and I will *r* thy judges as at the first
Jer. 27:22 I bring them up. . *r* them to this place
30:17 will *r* health unto thee, and I will heal
Ezek. 33:15 if the wicked *r* the pledge, give again
Dan. 9:25 commandment to *r* and to build Jerusalem
Joel 2:25 I will *r* to you the years that the locust
Mt. 12:13 (Mk. 3:5; Lk. 6:10) hand. . was *r* whole
17:11 Elias truly shall first come, and *r* all
Mk. 8:25 and he was *r*, and saw every man clearly
Lk. 19:8 if I have taken any. . I *r* him fourfold
Acts 1:6 wilt thou at this time *r* again the kingdom
Gal. 6:1 *r* such a one in the spirit of meekness

Restorer

Ruth 4:15 and he shall be unto thee a *r* of thy life
Is. 58:12 be called. . The *r* of paths to dwell in

Restrain *See also* Hinder, Let, Withhold

Gen. 8:2 stopped, and the rain from heaven was *r*
11:6 now nothing will be *r* from them, which they
Ex. 36:6 so the people were *r* from bringing
1 Sam. 3:13 made themselves vile, and he *r* them not
Job 15:8 and dost thou *r* wisdom to thyself?
Ps. 76:10 the remainder of wrath shalt thou *r*
Is. 63:15 of thy mercies toward me? are they *r*?
Acts 14:18 these sayings scarce *r* they the people

Restraint

1 Sam. 14:6 no *r* to the LORD to save by many or by

Resurrection *See also* Life

Mt. 22:23 (Mk. 12:18; Lk. 20:27; Acts 23:8) Sadducees, which say that there is no *r*
22:28 (Mk. 12:23; Lk. 20:33) in the *r*, whose wife
22:30 in the *r* they neither marry, nor are given
22:31 but as touching the *r* of the dead, have ye
27:53 came out of the graves after his *r*
Lk. 14:14 be recompensed at the *r* of the just
20:36 children of God, being the children of the *r*
Jn. 5:29 unto the *r* of life. . unto the *r* of damnation
11:24 shall rise again in the *r* at the last day
11:25 I am the *r*, and the life: he that believeth
Acts 1:22 ordained to be a witness with us of his *r*
2:31 seeing this before, spake of the *r* of Christ
4:2 preached through Jesus the *r* from the dead
4:33 apostles witness of the *r* of the Lord Jesus
17:18 he preached unto them Jesus, and the *r*
17:32 when they heard of the *r* of the dead, some
23:6 of the hope and *r* of the dead I am called
24:15 there shall be a *r* of the dead, both of

Acts 24:21 touching the *r* of the dead I am called in
Rom. 1:4 declared to be the Son of God by the *r*
6:5 we shall be also in the likeness of his *r*
1 Cor. 15:12 say some among you that there is no *r*
15:21 by man came death, by man came also the *r*
15:42 so also is the *r* of the dead. It is sown
Phil. 3:10 I may know him, and the power of his *r*
3:11 if by any means I might attain unto the *r*
2 Tim. 2:18 have erred, saying that the *r* is past
Heb. 6:2 of *r* of the dead, and of eternal judgment
11:35 that they might obtain a better *r*
1 Pet. 1:3 unto a lively hope by the *r* of Jesus
3:21 also now save us. . by the *r* of Jesus Christ
Rev. 20:5 years were finished. This is the first *r*
20:6 blessed and holy. . hath part in the first *r*

Retain *See also* Keep

Job 2:9 dost thou still *r* thine integrity? curse
Prov. 3:18 and happy is every one that *r* her
4:4 heart *r* my words: keep my commandments
11:16 gracious woman *r* honour. . men *r* riches
Eccl. 8:8 power over the spirit to *r* the spirit
Mic. 7:18 he *r* not his anger for ever, because he
Jn. 20:23 and whosesoever sins ye *r*, they are *r*
Rom. 1:28 did not like to *r* God in their knowledge
Phlm. 13 whom I would have *r* with me, that in thy

Retire

Judg. 20:39 when the men of Israel *r* in the battle
2 Sam. 11:15 of the hottest battle, and *r* ye from him
Jer. 4:6 set up the standard toward Zion: *r*, stay not

Return *See also* Turn

Gen. 3:19 dust thou art, and unto dust shalt thou *r*
Num. 10:36 when it rested, he said, *R*, O LORD, unto
14:4 let us make a captain, and. . *r* into Egypt
32:22 then afterward ye shall *r*, and be guiltless
Deut. 30:2 *r* unto the LORD thy God, and shalt obey
30:8 shalt *r* and obey the voice of the LORD
Josh. 2:16 hide yourselves. . until the pursuers be *r*
Judg. 7:3 afraid, let him *r* and depart early from
Ruth 1:16 entreat me not to leave thee, or to *r*
1 Sam. 7:3 do *r* unto the LORD with all your hearts
2 Sam. 12:23 I shall go to him, but he shall not *r*
2 Chr. 6:24 shall *r* and confess thy name, and pray
30:9 not turn away his face from you, if ye *r*
Job 1:21 naked came I out. . and naked shall I *r*
7:10 he shall *r* no more to his house, neither
10:21 from whence I shall not *r*, even to
15:22 believeth not. . he shall *r* out of darkness
17:10 but as for you all, do ye *r*, and come now
22:23 if thou *r* to the Almighty, thou shalt be
33:25 he shall *r* to the days of his youth
Ps. 73:10 therefore his people *r* hither: and waters
80:14 we beseech thee, O God of hosts: look
90:3 turnest man. . and sayest, *R*, ye children of
116:7 *r* unto thy rest, O my soul; for the LORD
Prov. 2:19 none that go unto her *r* again, neither
26:11 as a dog *r* to his vomit, so a fool *r* to
Eccl. 5:15 naked shall he *r* to go as he came
12:7 dust *r* to the earth. . spirit shall *r* unto God
Song 6:13 *r*, *r*, O Shulamite; *r*, *r*, that we may look
Is. 10:21 the remnant shall *r*, even the remnant
19:22 they shall *r* even to the LORD, and he
21:12 if ye will inquire, inquire ye: *r*, come
30:15 in *r* and rest shall ye be saved
35:10 (51:11) the ransomed of the LORD shall *r*
44:22 *r* unto me; for I have redeemed thee
55:7 let him *r* unto the LORD, and he will have
55:11 not *r* unto me void, but it shall accomplish
Jer. 3:12 go. . and say, *R*, thou backsliding Israel
3:22 *r*, ye backsliding children, and I will
4:1 wilt *r*, O Israel, saith the LORD, *r* unto me

Jer. 15:7 I will destroy my people, since they r not
15:19 if thou r, then will I bring thee again
18:11 (35:15) r ye now every one from his evil way
24:7 they shall r unto me with their whole heart
30:10 (46:27) Jacob shall r, and shall be in rest
32:44 (33:26) I will cause their captivity to r
Ezek. 18:23 he should r from his ways, and live?
Hos. 2:7 I will go and r to my first husband
2:9 therefore will I r, and take away my corn
5:15 I will go and r to my place, till they
6:1 come, and let us r unto the LORD: for he
7:10 they do not r to the LORD their God, nor
7:16 they r, but not to the Most High: they are
Joel 2:14 who knoweth if he will r and repent
Amos 4:6 (4:8, 9, 10, 11) yet have ye not r unto me
Zech. 1:16 I am r to Jerusalem with mercies
Mal. 3:7 r unto me, and I will r unto you, saith
3:18 then shall ye r, and discern between the
Mt. 12:44 (Lk. 11:24) saith, I will r into my house
24:18 (Lk. 17:31) neither let him. . in the field r
Lk. 2:43 as they r, the child Jesus tarried behind
4:14 and Jesus r in the power of the Spirit into
8:39 r to thine own house, and show how great
10:17 the seventy r again with joy, saying, Lord
17:18 r to give glory to God, save this stranger
Heb. 11:15 might have had opportunity to have r
1 Pet. 2:25 astray; but are now r unto the Shepherd

Reuben

Born, Gen. 29:32; found mandrakes for Leah, Gen.
30:14; rescued Joseph, Gen. 37:21–22; blessed by
Jacob, Gen. 49:3–4; his tribe blessed by Moses, Deut.
33:6.

Reveal *See also* Disclose, Manifest, Tell

Deut. 29:29 things which are r belong unto us
1 Sam. 3:7 neither was the word. . yet r unto him
3:21 LORD r himself to Samuel in Shiloh by the
Job 20:27 the heaven shall r his iniquity
Is. 22:14 was r in mine ears by the LORD of hosts
40:5 glory of the LORD shall be r, and all flesh
53:1 (Jn. 12:38) to whom is the arm of the LORD r?
56:1 near to come, and my righteousness to be r
Jer. 11:20 O LORD. . for unto thee have I r my cause
33:6 r unto them the abundance of peace and truth
Dan. 2:22 he r the deep and secret things
2:28 but there is a God in heaven that r secrets
Amos 3:7 but he r his secret unto his servants the
Mt. 10:26 (Lk. 12:2) covered, that shall not be r
11:25 (Lk. 10:21) and hast r them unto babes
11:27 (Lk. 10:22) whomsoever the Son will r him
16:17 flesh and blood hath not r it unto thee
Lk. 2:35 that the thoughts of many hearts may be r
17:30 it be in the day when the Son of man is r
Rom. 1:17 the righteousness of God r from faith to
1:18 wrath of God is r from heaven against all
8:18 be compared with the glory which shall be r
1 Cor. 2:10 God hath r them unto us by his Spirit
3:13 declare it, because it shall be r by fire
Gal. 1:16 to r his Son in me, that I might preach
3:23 unto the faith which should afterward be r
Eph. 3:5 now r unto his holy apostles and prophets
Phil. 3:15 minded, God shall r even this unto you
2 Thes. 1:7 Lord Jesus shall be r from heaven with
2:3 that man of sin be r, the son of perdition
2:8 then shall that Wicked be r, whom the Lord
1 Pet. 1:5 salvation ready to be r in the last time
1:12 unto whom it was r, that not unto
4:13 when his glory shall be r, ye may be glad
5:1 also a partaker of the glory that shall be r

Revealer

Dan. 2:47 and a Lord of kings, and a r of secrets

Revelation *See also* Dream, Trance, Vision

Rom. 2:5 and r of the righteous judgment of God
16:25 according to the r of the mystery
1 Cor. 14:6 I shall speak to you either by r, or
14:26 hath a doctrine, hath a tongue, hath a r
2 Cor. 12:1 will come to visions and r of the Lord
12:7 be exalted. . through the abundance of the r
Gal. 1:12 of man. . but by the r of Jesus Christ
2:2 I went up by r, and communicated unto them
Eph. 1:17 spirit of wisdom and r in the knowledge
3:3 that by r he made known unto me the mystery
1 Pet. 1:13 be brought unto you at the r of Jesus
Rev. 1:1 the R of Jesus Christ, which God gave

Reveling

Gal. 5:21 envyings, murders, drunkenness, r
1 Pet. 4:3 lusts, excess of wine, r, banquetings

Revenge *See also* Avenge, Recompense, Vengeance

Jer. 15:15 and r me of my persecutors; take me not
20:10 be enticed. . and we shall take our r on him
Nah. 1:2 the LORD r; the LORD r, and is furious
2 Cor. 7:11 yea, what zeal, yea, what r!
10:6 having in a readiness to r all disobedience

Revenger *See also* Avenger

Num. 35:19 the r of blood. . shall slay the murderer
2 Sam. 14:11 not suffer the r of blood to destroy
Rom. 13:4 a r to execute wrath upon him that doeth

Revenue

Ezra 4:13 thou shalt endamage the r of the kings
Prov. 8:19 fine gold; and my r than choice silver
15:6 but in the r of the wicked is trouble
16:8 righteousness, than great r without right
Is. 23:3 Sihor, the harvest of the river, is her r
Jer. 12:13 they shall be ashamed of your r because

Reverence *See also* Fear, Honor

Lev. 19:30 (26:2) keep my sabbaths. . r my sanctuary
Esth. 3:2 but Mordecai bowed not, nor did him r
Ps. 89:7 God is. . to be had in r of all them that
Mt. 21:37 (Mk. 12:6; Lk. 20:13) they will r my son
Eph. 5:33 and the wife see that she r her husband
Heb. 12:9 fathers of our flesh. . and we gave them r
12:28 serve God acceptably with r and godly fear

Reverend

Ps. 111:9 sent redemption. . holy and r is his name

Reverse

Num. 23:20 and he hath blessed; and I cannot r it
Esth. 8:5 to r the letters devised by Haman
8:8 sealed with the king's ring, may no man r

Revile

Ex. 22:28 thou shalt not r the gods, nor curse the
Mt. 5:11 blessed are ye, when men shall r you
27:39 that passed by r him, wagging their heads
Mk. 15:32 they that were crucified with him r him
Jn. 9:28 they r him. . said, Thou art his disciple
Acts 23:4 stood by said, R thou God's high priest?
1 Cor. 4:12 being r, we bless; being persecuted
1 Pet. 2:23 who, when he was r, r not again

Revive

Gen. 45:27 the spirit of Jacob their father r
Judg. 15:19 drunk, his spirit came again, and he r
1 Kgs. 17:22 the soul. . came into him again, and he r

2 Kgs. 13:21 touched the bones of Elisha, he *r*
Ezra 9:8 and give us a little *r* in our bondage
Neh. 4:2 will they *r* the stones out of the heaps
Ps. 85:6 wilt thou not *r* us again: that thy people
138:7 in the midst of trouble, thou wilt *r* me
Is. 57:15 to *r* the spirit of the humble, and to *r*
Hos. 6:2 after two days will he *r* us: in the third
14:7 shall *r* as the corn, and grow as the vine
Hab. 3:2 Lord, *r* thy work in the midst of the years
Rom. 7:9 the commandment came, sin *r*, and I died
14:9 Christ both died, and rose, and *r*, that he

Revolt *See also* Harden, Rebel, Resist

2 Kgs. 8:20 (2 Chr. 21:8) in his days Edom *r* from
Is. 1:5 ye will *r* more and more: the whole head is
31:6 from whom . . children of Israel have deeply *r*
59:13 from our God, speaking oppression and *r*
Jer. 5:23 a rebellious heart; they are *r* and gone

Revolter

Jer. 6:28 they are all grievous *r*, walking with
Hos. 5:2 and the *r* are profound to make slaughter
9:15 love them no more: all their princes are *r*

Reward *See also* Hire, Recompense, Wages

Gen. 15:1 am thy shield, and thy exceeding great *r*
44:4 wherefore have ye *r* evil for good?
Num. 18:31 *r* for your service in the tabernacle
Deut. 10:17 regardeth not persons, nor taketh *r*
1 Sam. 24:17 *r* me good, whereas I have *r* thee evil
24:19 wherefore the Lord *r* thee good for that
2 Sam. 3:39 the Lord shall *r* the doer of evil
22:21 (Ps. 18:20) the Lord *r* me according to my
2 Chr. 15:7 hands be weak: for your work shall be *r*
Job 6:22 did I say, Bring unto me? or, Give a *r*
7:2 as a hireling looketh for the *r* of his work
21:19 he *r* him, and he shall know it
Ps. 15:5 usury, nor taketh *r* against the innocent
19:11 and in keeping of them there is great *r*
31:23 faithful, and plentifully *r* the proud doer
35:12 they *r* me evil for good to the spoiling of
58:11 say, Verily there is a *r* for the righteous
91:8 thou behold and see the *r* of the wicked
94:2 judge of the earth: render a *r* to the proud
103:10 nor *r* us according to our iniquities
109:5 *r* me evil for good, and hatred for my love
127:3 a heritage . . the fruit of the womb is his *r*
137:8 happy . . that *r* thee as thou hast served us
Prov. 11:18 soweth righteousness shall be a sure *r*
13:13 he that feareth the commandment shall be *r*
17:13 whoso *r* evil for good, evil shall not depart
24:14 thou hast found it, then there shall be a *r*
25:22 upon his head, and the Lord shall *r* thee
26:10 God . . both the fool, and *r* transgressors
Eccl. 4:9 because they have a good *r* for their labor
9:5 any thing, neither have they any more a *r*
Is. 1:23 every one loveth gifts . . followeth after *r*
3:9 for they have *r* evil unto themselves
5:23 which justify the wicked for *r*, and take
40:10 (62:11) his *r* is with him, and his work
Jer. 31:16 for thy work shall be *r*, saith the Lord
Ezek. 16:34 thou givest a *r*, and no *r* is given
Hos. 4:9 for their ways, and *r* them their doings
9:1 thou hast loved a *r* upon every cornfloor
Obad. 15 thy *r* shall return upon thine own head
Mic. 3:11 the heads thereof judge for *r*, and the
7:3 prince asketh, and the judge asketh for a *r*
Mt. 5:12 (Lk. 6:23) for great is your *r* in heaven
5:46 love them which love you, what *r* have ye?
6:1 alms before men . . ye have no *r* of your Father
6:2 (6:5, 16) I say unto you, They have their *r*

Mt. 6:4 (6:6, 18) and thy Father . . shall *r* thee openly
10:41 receive a prophet's *r* . . a righteous man's *r*
10:42 (Mk. 9:41) he shall in no wise lose his *r*
16:27 shall *r* every man according to his works
Lk. 6:35 *r* shall be great . . ye shall be the children
23:41 we receive the due *r* of our deeds
Rom. 4:4 the *r* not reckoned of grace, but of debt
1 Cor. 3:8 his own *r* according to his own labor
3:14 any man's work abide . . he shall receive a *r*
9:18 what is my *r* then? Verily that, when I preach
Col. 2:18 let no man beguile you of your *r* in a
3:24 ye shall receive the *r* of the inheritance
1 Tim. 5:18 and, The laborer is worthy of his *r*
2 Tim. 4:14 the Lord *r* him according to his works
Heb. 11:26 respect unto the recompense of the *r*
2 Pet. 2:13 shall receive the *r* of unrighteousness
2 Jn. 8 that we lose not . . that we receive a full *r*
Jude 11 greedily after the error of Balaam for *r*
Rev. 18:6 *r* her even as she *r* you, and double unto
22:12 I come quickly; and my *r* is with me

Rewarder

Heb. 11:6 is a *r* of them that diligently seek him

Rezin king of Syria 2 Kgs. 16:5-9 (Is. 7:1)

Rezon 1 Kgs. 11:23

Rhoda Acts 12:13

Rhodes Acts 21:1

Rib

Gen. 2:21 and he slept; and he took one of his *r*
Dan. 7:5 a bear . . and it had three *r* in the mouth

Ribband

Num. 15:38 the fringe of the borders a *r* of blue

Riblah 2 Kgs. 23:33; 25:6 (Jer. 39:5; 52:9)

Rich *See also* Abundant, Wealthy

Gen. 13:2 Abram was very *r* in cattle, in silver
Ex. 30:15 the *r* shall not give more, and the poor
1 Sam. 2:7 the Lord maketh poor, and maketh *r*
2 Sam. 12:1 one city; the one *r*, and the other poor
Job 15:29 he shall not be *r*, neither shall his
27:19 *r* man shall lie down, but he shall not be
34:19 nor regardeth the *r* more than the poor?
Ps. 45:12 the *r* among the people shall entreat thy
49:16 be not thou afraid when one is made *r*
Prov. 10:4 but the hand of the diligent maketh *r*
10:22 blessing of the Lord, it maketh *r*, and he
14:20 own neighbor: but the *r* hath many friends
21:17 he that loveth wine and oil shall not be *r*
22:2 the *r* and poor meet together: the Lord is
22:7 *r* ruleth over the poor, and the borrower is
22:16 giveth to the *r*, shall surely come to want
23:4 labor not to be *r*: cease from thine own
28:11 the *r* man is wise in his own conceit
28:20 maketh haste to be *r* shall not be innocent
28:22 he that hasteth to be *r* hath an evil eye
Eccl. 5:12 abundance of the *r* will not suffer him
10:6 in great dignity, and the *r* sit in low place
10:20 curse not the *r* in thy bedchamber
Is. 53:9 his grave with the wicked, and with the *r*
Jer. 5:27 they are become great, and waxen *r*
9:23 let not the *r* man glory in his riches
Hos. 12:8 Ephraim said, Yet I am become *r*, I have
Mic. 6:12 the *r* men thereof are full of violence
Zech. 11:5 say, Blessed be the Lord; for I am *r*
Mt. 19:23 *r* man shall hardly enter into the kingdom
27:57 came a *r* man of Arimathea, named Joseph
Mk. 12:41 treasury . . many that were *r* cast in much

Lk. 1:53 the *r* he hath sent empty away
6:24 but woe unto you that are *r*! for ye have
12:16 ground of a certain *r* man brought forth
12:21 layeth up treasure. . is not *r* toward God
16:1 was a certain *r* man, which had a steward
16:19 *r* man. . clothed in purple and fine linen
18:23 he was very sorrowful: for he was very *r*
21:1 saw the *r* men casting their gifts into the
Rom. 10:12 the same Lord over all is *r* unto all
1 Cor. 4:8 now ye are full, now ye are *r*, ye have
2 Cor. 6:10 as poor, yet making many *r*; as having
8:9 he was *r*, yet for your sakes he became poor
Eph. 2:4 but God, who is *r* in mercy, for his great
1 Tim. 6:9 they that will be *r* fall into temptation
6:18 they be *r* in good works, ready to distribute
Jas. 1:10 the *r*, in that he is made low: because
1:11 also shall the *r* man fade away in his ways
2:5 God chosen the poor of this world *r* in faith
5:1 ye *r* men, weep and howl for your miseries
Rev. 2:9 I know thy. . poverty, (but thou art *r*)
3:17 sayest, I am *r*, and increased with goods
3:18 to buy of me gold. . that thou mayest be *r*
13:16 *r* and poor, free and bond, to receive a
18:3 merchants of the earth are waxed *r* through

Riches *See also* Mammon, Money, Possession, Wealth

1 Kgs. 3:11 (2 Chr. 1:11) neither. . asked *r* for thyself
10:23 (2 Chr. 9:22) Solomon exceeded all. . for *r*
1 Chr. 29:12 both *r* and honor come of thee, and thou
2 Chr. 32:27 Hezekiah had exceeding much *r* and
Job 20:15 he hath swallowed down *r*. . he shall vomit
36:19 will he esteem thy *r*? no, not gold, nor all
Ps. 37:16 is better than the *r* of many wicked
39:6 he heapeth up *r*, and knoweth not who shall
49:6 boast themselves in the multitude of their *r*
52:7 but trusted in the abundance of his *r*
62:10 if *r* increase, set not your heart upon them
73:12 prosper in the world; they increase in *r*
104:24 made them all: the earth is full of thy *r*
Prov. 3:16 right hand. . in her left hand *r* and honor
8:18 *r* and honor are with me; yea, durable *r* and
11:4 *r* profit not in the day of wrath
11:28 he that trusteth in his *r* shall fall
13:7 that maketh himself poor, yet hath great *r*
14:24 the crown of the wise is their *r*
22:1 good name is rather to be chosen than great *r*
22:4 by humility and the fear of the LORD are *r*
22:16 that oppresseth the poor to increase his *r*
23:5 *r* certainly make themselves wings; they fly
27:24 for *r* are not for ever: and doth the crown
30:8 give me neither poverty nor *r*; feed me with
Eccl. 4:8 neither is his eye satisfied with *r*
5:14 but those *r* perish by evil travail
5:19 to whom God hath given *r* and wealth
9:11 nor yet *r* to men of understanding, nor yet
Is. 45:3 give thee. . and hidden *r* of secret places
61:6 ye shall eat the *r* of the Gentiles
Jer. 17:11 so he that getteth *r*, and not by right
48:36 the *r* that he hath gotten are perished
Ezek. 26:12 and they shall make a spoil of thy *r*
28:4 thine understanding thou hast gotten thee *r*
28:5 thine heart is lifted up because of thy *r*
Mt. 13:22 (Mk. 4:19) deceitfulness of *r*, choke the
Mk. 10:23 (Lk. 18:24) hardly. . they that have *r* enter
Lk. 16:11 who will commit to your trust the true *r*?
Rom. 2:4 or despisest thou the *r* of his goodness
9:23 that he might make known the *r* of his glory
11:12 if the fall of them be the *r* of the world
11:33 O the depth of the *r* both of the wisdom
2 Cor. 8:2 abounded unto the *r* of their liberality
Eph. 1:7 of sins, according to the *r* of his grace

Eph. 1:18 what the *r* of the glory of his inheritance
2:7 he might show the exceeding *r* of his grace
3:8 should preach. . the unsearchable *r* of Christ
3:16 grant you, according to the *r* of his glory
Phil. 4:19 according to his *r* in glory by Christ
Col. 1:27 the *r* of the glory of this mystery among
2:2 all *r* of the full assurance of understanding
1 Tim. 6:17 nor trust in uncertain *r*, but in. . God
Heb. 11:26 the reproach of Christ greater *r* than
Jas. 5:2 your *r* are corrupted, and your garments
Rev. 5:12 worthy. . Lamb. . to receive power, and *r*
18:17 in one hour so great *r* is come to nought

Richly

Col. 3:16 let the word of Christ dwell in you *r*
1 Tim. 6:17 who giveth us *r* all things to enjoy

Rid *See also* Deliver

Gen. 37:22 that he might *r* him out of their hands
Ex. 6:6 I will *r* you out of their bondage
Lev. 26:6 and I will *r* evil beasts out of the land
Ps. 144:7 (144:11) *r* me. . from the hand of strange

Riddance

Lev. 23:22 shalt not make clean *r* of the corners
Zeph. 1:18 he shall make even a speedy *r* of all

Riddle

Judg. 14:12 I will now put forth a *r* unto you
Ezek. 17:2 son of man, put forth a *r*, and speak a

Ride (Rode)

Deut. 33:26 who *r* upon the heaven in thy help
2 Sam. 18:9 Absalom *r* upon a mule, and the mule
22:11 (Ps. 18:10) he *r* upon a cherub, and did fly
Job 30:22 to the wind; thou causest me to *r* upon it
Ps. 45:4 and in thy majesty *r* prosperously, because
66:12 thou hast caused men to *r* over our heads
68:4 extol him that *r* upon the heavens by his
Is. 19:1 behold, the LORD *r* upon a swift cloud
58:14 I will cause thee to *r* upon the high places
Hos. 14:3 we will not *r* upon horses: neither will
Hab. 3:8 thou didst *r* upon thine horses and thy

Rider

Ex. 15:1 (15:21) the horse and his *r* hath he thrown
Job 39:18 on high, she scorneth the horse and his *r*
Jer. 51:21 I break in pieces the horse and his *r*
Zech. 10:5 and the *r* on horses shall be confounded
12:4 with astonishment, and his *r* with madness

Ridge

Ps. 65:10 thou waterest the *r* thereof abundantly

Rifle

Zech. 14:2 the city shall be taken, and the houses *r*

Right *See also* Just, Right Hand, Upright

Gen. 18:25 shall not the Judge of all the earth do *r*?
Ex. 15:26 wilt do that which is *r* in his sight
Deut. 6:18 thou shalt do that which is *r* and good
12:8 every man whatsoever is *r* in his own eyes
12:25 do that which is *r* in the sight of the LORD
13:18 hearken to the voice. . to do that which is *r*
21:9 thou shalt do that which is *r* in the sight
21:17 is the beginning. . *r* of the firstborn is his
Judg. 17:6 (21:25) that which was *r* in his own eyes
Ruth 4:6 redeem thou my *r* to thyself; for I cannot
1 Kgs. 15:5 because David did that which was *r*
15:11 (2 Chr. 14:2) Asa did that which was *r*
22:43 (2 Chr. 20:32) not aside. . doing that. . was *r*

2 Kgs. 10:30 done well in executing that which is *r*
12:2 (2 Chr. 24:2) Jehoash did that which was *r*
14:3 (15:3, 34; 18:3; 22:2; 2 Chr. 24:2; 25:2; 26:4;
27:2; 29:2; 34:2) did that which was *r* in the sight
16:2 Ahaz. . did not that which was *r* in the sight
1 Chr. 13:4 for the thing was *r* in the eyes of all
Neh. 2:20 build: but ye have no portion, nor *r*
9:33 thou hast done *r*, but we have done wickedly
Job 6:25 how forcible are *r* words! but what doth
34:17 shall even he that hateth *r* govern?
34:23 he will not lay upon man more than *r*
36:6 life of the wicked: but giveth *r* to the poor
42:7 ye have not spoken of me the thing that is *r*
Ps. 9:4 for thou hast maintained my *r*. . judging *r*
17:1 hear the *r*, O LORD, attend unto my cry; give
19:8 statutes of the LORD are *r*, rejoicing the heart
33:4 word of the LORD is *r*; and all his works are
45:6 the sceptre of thy kingdom is a *r* sceptre
51:10 O God; and renew a *r* spirit within me
78:37 their heart was not *r* with him, neither
119:75 I know, O LORD, that thy judgments are *r*
119:128 thy precepts concerning all things to be *r*
140:12 the LORD will maintain. . the *r* of the poor
Prov. 4:11 of wisdom; I have led thee in *r* paths
8:6 and the opening of my lips shall be *r* things
8:9 all plain. . and *r* to them that find knowledge
12:5 the thoughts of the righteous are *r*
12:15 way of a fool is *r* in his own eyes: but he
14:12 (16:25) is a way which seemeth *r* unto a man
16:8 righteousness, than great revenues without *r*
16:13 and they love him that speaketh *r*
20:11 whether his work be pure. . whether it be *r*
21:2 every way of a man is *r* in his own eyes
21:8 but as for the pure, his work is *r*
Is. 10:2 and to take away the *r* from the poor
30:10 prophesy not unto us *r* things, speak unto
32:7 to destroy. . even when the needy speaketh *r*
45:19 righteousness, I declare things that are *r*
Jer. 2:21 planted. . a noble vine, wholly a *r* seed
5:28 and the *r* of the needy do they not judge
17:11 so he that getteth riches, and not by *r*
34:15 ye were now turned, and had done *r* in my
Lam. 3:35 to turn aside the *r* of a man before the
Ezek. 21:27 no more, until he come whose *r* it is
Hos. 14:9 the ways of the LORD are *r*, and the just
Amos 3:10 they know not to do *r*, saith the LORD
5:12 turn aside the poor in the gate from their *r*
Mt. 20:4 vineyard, and whatsoever is *r* I will give you
Lk. 10:28 answered *r*: this do, and thou shalt live
12:57 even of yourselves judge ye not what is *r*?
Acts 4:19 whether it be *r* in the sight of God to
8:21 for thy heart is not *r* in the sight of God
Eph. 6:1 obey your parents in the Lord: for this is *r*
Heb. 13:10 an altar, whereof they have no *r* to eat
2 Pet. 2:15 which have forsaken the *r* way, and are
Rev. 22:14 that they may have *r* to the tree of life

Right (Right Hand)

Gen. 13:9 the left hand, then I will go to the *r*
Ex. 15:6 thy *r h*. . glorious in power: thy *r h*. . dashed
Josh. 1:7 turn not from it to the *r h* or to the left
Ps. 16:8 (Acts 2:25) because he is at my *r h*, I shall not
91:7 fall at thy side, and ten thousand at thy *r h*
110:1 (Mt. 22:44; Mk. 12:36; Lk. 20:42; Acts 2:34;
Heb. 1:13) sit thou at my *r h*, until I make
118:16 *r h* of the LORD is exalted: the *r h*. . doeth
Eccl. 10:2 a wise man's heart is at his *r h*
Jon. 4:11 cannot discern between their *r h* and. . left
Mt. 5:39 smite thee on thy *r* cheek, turn to him
6:3 let not thy left hand know what thy *r h* doeth
20:21 (Mk. 10:37) may sit, the one on thy *r h*
25:33 sheep on his *r h*, but the goats on the left
26:64 (Mk. 14:62; Lk. 22:69) on the *r h* of power

Mk. 16:19 into heaven, and sat on the *r h* of God
Acts 2:33 being by the *r h* of God exalted
7:56 Son of man standing on the *r h* of God
Rom. 8:34 risen. . who is even at the *r h* of God
Gal. 2:9 to me and Barnabas the *r h* of fellowship
Eph. 1:20 at his own *r h* in the heavenly places
Col. 3:1 where Christ sitteth on the *r h* of God
Heb. 1:3 sat down on the *r h* of the Majesty on high
10:12 had offered. . sat down on the *r h* of God
1 Pet. 3:22 into heaven, and is on the *r h* of God

Righteous *See also* Just, Upright

Gen. 7:1 into the ark; for thee have I seen *r*
18:23 thou also destroy the *r* with the wicked?
20:4 LORD, wilt thou slay also a *r* nation?
38:26 she hath been more *r* than I; because that
Ex. 9:27 LORD is *r*, and I and my people are wicked
23:7 the innocent and *r* slay thou not: for I will
23:8 (Deut. 16:19) perverteth the words of the *r*
Num. 23:10 let me die the death of the *r*, and let
Deut. 4:8 that hath. . judgments so *r* as all this law
25:1 shall justify the *r*, and condemn the wicked
Judg. 5:11 they rehearse the *r* acts of the LORD
1 Sam. 12:7 reason. . of all the *r* acts of the LORD
2 Sam. 4:11 when wicked men have slain a *r* person
1 Kgs. 8:32 (2 Chr. 6:23) justifying the *r*, to give
2 Chr. 12:6 humbled. . and they said, The LORD is *r*
Ezra 9:15 O LORD God of Israel, thou art *r*; for we
Neh. 9:8 hast performed thy words; for thou art *r*
Job 4:7 or where were the *r* cut off?
9:15 though I were *r*, yet would I not answer
10:15 if I be *r*, yet will I not lift up my head
15:14 is born of a woman, that he should be *r*?
17:9 the *r* also shall hold on his way
22:3 pleasure to the Almighty, that thou art *r*?
22:19 *r* see it, and are glad: and the innocent
32:1 Job, because he was *r* in his own eyes
34:5 Job hath said, I am *r*: and God hath taken
35:7 if thou be *r*, what givest thou him?
36:7 he withdraweth not his eyes from the *r*
40:8 wilt thou condemn me, that thou mayest be *r*?
Ps. 1:5 nor sinners in the congregation of the *r*
1:6 LORD knoweth the way of the *r*: but the way
5:12 for thou, LORD, wilt bless the *r*: with favor
7:11 God judgeth the *r*, and God is angry with the
11:5 the LORD trieth the *r*: but the wicked and
14:5 for God is in the generation of the *r*
19:9 the judgments of the LORD are true and *r*
32:11 be glad in the LORD, and rejoice, ye *r*
33:1 rejoice in the LORD, O ye *r*: for praise is
34:15 (1 Pet. 3:12) eyes of the LORD are upon the *r*
34:17 *r* cry, and the LORD heareth, and delivereth
34:21 and they that hate the *r* shall be desolate
37:16 a little that a *r* man hath is better than
37:17 be broken: but the LORD upholdeth the *r*
37:21 the *r* showeth mercy, and giveth
37:25 yet have I not seen the *r* forsaken
37:29 the *r* shall inherit the land, and dwell
52:6 *r* also shall see, and fear, and shall laugh
55:22 he shall never suffer the *r* to be moved
58:11 verily there is a reward for the *r*
64:10 the *r* shall be glad in the LORD, and shall
72:7 in his days shall the *r* flourish
75:10 but the horns of the *r* shall be exalted
92:12 the *r* shall flourish like the palm tree
97:11 light is sown for the *r*, and gladness for
107:42 the *r* shall see it, and rejoice
112:6 the *r* shall be in everlasting remembrance
118:15 salvation is in the tabernacles of the *r*
118:20 gate of the LORD. . which the *r* shall enter
119:137 *r* art thou, O LORD, and upright are thy
125:3 not rest upon the lot of the *r*; lest the *r*
141:5 let the *r* smite me; it shall be a kindness

Ps. 145:17 LORD is *r* in all his ways, and holy in all
146:8 that are bowed down: the LORD loveth the *r*
Prov. 2:7 he layeth up sound wisdom for the *r*
3:32 to the LORD: but his secret is with the *r*
10:3 will not suffer the soul of the *r* to famish
10:11 mouth of a *r* man is a well of life
10:16 labor of the *r* tendeth to life: the fruit
10:21 lips of the *r* feed many: but fools die for
10:24 but the desire of the *r* shall be granted
10:25 but the *r* is an everlasting foundation
10:30 *r* shall never be removed: but the wicked
11:8 the *r* is delivered out of trouble
11:28 fall: but the *r* shall flourish as a branch
12:10 a *r* man regardeth the life of his beast
13:5 *r* man hateth lying. . wicked man is loathsome
13:21 sinners: but to the *r* good shall be repaid
14:32 wickedness: but the *r* hath hope in his death
18:10 tower: the *r* runneth into it, and is safe
21:18 the wicked shall be a ransom for the *r*
24:24 he that saith unto the wicked, Thou art *r*
28:1 wicked flee. . but the *r* are bold as a lion
28:10 whoso causeth the *r* to go astray in an
29:2 the *r* are in authority, the people rejoice
29:7 the *r* considereth the cause of the poor
Eccl. 3:17 God shall judge the *r* and the wicked
7:16 be not *r* over much, neither make thyself
9:1 the *r*, and the wise. . are in the hand of God
9:2 alike. . one event to the *r*, and to the wicked
Is. 3:10 say ye to the *r*, that it shall be well
24:16 have we heard songs, even glory to the *r*
26:2 *r* nation which keepeth the truth may enter
41:2 who raised up the *r* man from the east
53:11 by his knowledge shall my *r* servant justify
57:1 the *r* perisheth. . the *r* is taken away from
60:21 thy people also shall be all *r*: they shall
Jer. 12:1 *r* art thou, O LORD, when I plead with
23:5 I will raise unto David a *r* Branch
Lam. 1:18 LORD is *r*; for I have rebelled against
Ezek. 3:20 (18:24, 26; 33:18) when a *r* man doth turn
3:21 if thou warn the *r* man, that the *r* sin not
21:3 will cut off from thee the *r* and the wicked
33:13 when I shall say to the *r*, that he shall
Dan. 9:14 God is *r* in all his works which he doeth
Amos 2:6 they sold the *r* for silver, and the poor
Hab. 1:13 devoureth the man that is more *r* than he?
Mal. 3:18 and discern between the *r* and the wicked
Mt. 9:13 (Mk. 2:17; Lk. 5:32) not come to call the *r*
10:41 receiveth a *r* man in the name of a *r* man
13:17 *r* men have desired to see. . which ye see
13:43 then shall the *r* shine forth as the sun
23:28 outwardly appear *r* unto men, but within ye
23:35 that upon you may come all the *r* blood shed
25:37 then shall the *r* answer him, saying, Lord
25:46 punishment: but the *r* into life eternal
Lk. 1:6 they were both *r* before God, walking in
18:9 which trusted in themselves that they were *r*
23:47 saying, Certainly this was a *r* man
Jn. 7:24 to the appearance, but judge *r* judgment
Rom. 3:10 is written, There is none *r*, no, not one
5:7 for scarcely for a *r* man will one die
5:19 by the obedience of one shall many be made *r*
2 Thes. 1:6 it is a *r* thing with God to recompense
1 Tim. 1:9 law is not made for a *r* man, but for
Heb. 11:4 Abel. . obtained witness that he was *r*
Jas. 5:16 fervent prayer of a *r* man availeth much
1 Pet. 4:18 if the *r* scarcely be saved, where shall
2 Pet. 2:8 in seeing and hearing, vexed his *r* soul
1 Jn. 2:1 we have an advocate. . Jesus Christ the *r*
2:29 if ye know that he is *r*, ye know that every
3:7 doeth righteousness is *r*, even as he is *r*
3:12 his own works were evil, and his brother's *r*
Rev. 16:5 thou art *r*, O Lord, which art, and wast
22:11 and he that is *r*, let him be *r* still

Righteously *See also* Uprightly

Deut. 1:16 and judge *r* between every man and his
Ps. 67:4 thou shalt judge the people *r*, and govern
Is. 33:15 he that walketh *r*, and speaketh uprightly
Jer. 11:20 O LORD of hosts, that judgest *r*
Tit. 2:12 we should live soberly, *r*, and godly
1 Pet. 2:23 committeth himself to him that judgeth *r*

Righteousness *See also* Equity, Holiness, Honesty, Integrity, Judgment, Sanctification, Truth, Uprightness

Gen. 15:6 (Rom. 4:3, 22; Gal. 3:6; Jas. 2:23) counted
it to him for *r*
30:33 so shall my *r* answer for me in time to come
Lev. 19:15 but in *r* shalt thou judge thy neighbor
Deut. 6:25 it shall be our *r*, if we observe to do
9:5 not for thy *r*, or for the uprightness of
1 Sam. 26:23 the LORD render to every man his *r*
2 Sam. 22:21 (Ps. 18:20) rewarded. . according to. . *r*
Job 27:6 my *r* I hold fast, and will not let it go
29:14 I put on *r*, and it clothed me: my judgment
33:26 for he will render unto man his *r*
35:2 that thou saidst, My *r* is more than God's?
36:3 from afar, and will ascribe *r* to my Maker
Ps. 5:8 lead me, O LORD, in thy *r* because of mine
9:8 and he shall judge the world in *r*, he shall
11:7 LORD loveth *r*; his countenance doth behold
15:2 he that walketh uprightly, and worketh *r*
22:31 and shall declare his *r* unto a people that
23:3 he leadeth me in the paths of *r* for his
24:5 blessing. . and *r* from the God of his salvation
33:5 he loveth *r* and judgment: the earth is full
35:28 (71:24) my tongue shall speak of thy *r*
36:6 thy *r* is like the great mountains
37:6 he shall bring forth thy *r* as the light
40:9 I have preached *r* in the great congregation
45:7 (Heb. 1:9) lovest *r*, and hatest wickedness
48:10 is thy praise. . thy right hand is full of *r*
50:6 the heavens shall declare his *r*: for God is
58:1 do ye. . speak *r*, O congregation? do ye judge
69:27 and let them not come into thy *r*
71:15 my mouth shall show forth thy *r* and thy
71:19 thy *r* also, O God, is very high, who hast
72:1 thy judgments. . thy *r* unto the king's son
85:10 *r* and peace have kissed each other
85:13 *r* shall go before him; and shall set us in
89:16 and in thy *r* shall they be exalted
94:15 but judgment shall return unto *r*
96:13 (98:9) he shall judge the world with *r*
97:2 *r* and judgment are the habitation of his
97:6 heavens declare his *r*, and all the people
98:2 his *r* hath he openly showed in the sight
103:6 LORD executeth *r* and judgment for all that
103:17 and his *r* unto children's children
106:31 that was counted unto him for *r* unto all
111:3 (112:3, 9; 2 Cor. 9:9) his *r* endureth for ever
119:142 thy *r* is an everlasting *r*, and thy law
119:172 for all thy commandments are *r*
132:9 let thy priests be clothed with *r*; and let
Prov. 2:9 shalt thou understand *r*, and judgment
10:2 (11:4) but *r* delivereth from death
11:5 the *r* of the perfect shall direct his way
11:18 him that soweth *r* shall be a sure reward
11:19 as *r* tendeth to life; so he that pursueth
12:28 the way of *r* is life; and in the pathway
14:34 *r* exalteth a nation: but sin is a reproach
15:9 but he loveth him that followeth after *r*
16:8 better is a little with *r*, than great revenues
16:12 the throne is established by *r*
21:21 followeth after *r* and mercy findeth life, *r*

Is. 1:21 city . . *r* lodged in it; but now murderers
1:26 be called, The city of *r*, the faithful city
5:7 behold oppression; for *r*, but behold a cry
5:23 take away the *r* of the righteous from him!
11:4 with *r* shall he judge the poor, and reprove
11:5 and *r* shall be the girdle of his loins
26:9 the inhabitants of the world will learn *r*
28:17 I lay to the line, and *r* to the plummet
32:1 a King shall reign in *r*, and princes shall
32:17 work of *r* shall be peace; and the effect
42:6 I the LORD have called thee in *r*, and will
45:19 I the LORD speak *r*, I declare things that
45:24 one say, In the LORD have I *r* and strength
46:13 I bring near my *r*; it shall not be far off
51:5 my *r* is near; my salvation is gone forth
51:8 but my *r* shall be for ever, and my salvation
54:14 in *r* shalt thou be established: thou shalt
54:17 and their *r* is of me, saith the LORD
58:8 thy *r* shall go before thee; the glory of
59:17 he put on *r* as a breastplate, and a helmet
60:17 thy officers peace, and thine exactors *r*
61:11 GOD will cause *r* and praise to spring forth
62:2 Gentiles shall see thy *r*, and all kings thy
64:6 all our *r* are as filthy rags; and we all do
Jer. 23:6 (33:16) shall be called, THE LORD OUR *R*
33:15 the Branch of *r* to grow up unto David
Ezek. 3:20 (18:24, 26; 33:18) doth turn from his *r*
14:14 (14:20) deliver but their own souls by their *r*
18:22 in his *r* that he hath done he shall live
33:12 *r* of the righteous shall not deliver him
33:13 trust to his own *r*, and commit iniquity
Dan. 4:27 and break off thy sins by *r*, and thine
9:7 O Lord, *r* belongeth unto thee
9:24 to bring in everlasting *r*, and to seal up
12:3 and they that turn many to *r*, as the stars
Hos. 2:19 I will betroth thee unto me in *r*
10:12 sow to yourselves in *r* . . rain *r* upon you
Amos 5:24 down as waters, and *r* as a mighty stream
Mic. 6:5 that ye may know the *r* of the LORD
7:9 forth to the light, and I shall behold his *r*
Zeph. 2:3 seek *r*, seek meekness: it may be ye shall
Mt. 3:15 for thus it becometh us to fulfill all *r*
5:6 are they which do hunger and thirst after *r*
5:10 persecuted for *r'* sake: for theirs is the
5:20 except your *r* shall exceed the *r* of the
6:33 seek ye first the kingdom of God, and his *r*
21:32 John came unto you in the way of *r*, and ye
Jn. 16:8 he will reprove the world of sin, and of *r*
Acts 10:35 feareth him, and worketh *r*, is accepted
17:31 he will judge the world in *r* by that man
24:25 as he reasoned of *r*, temperance . . judgment
Rom. 1:17 *r* of God revealed from faith to faith
2:26 if the uncircumcision keep the *r* of the law
3:5 if our unrighteousness commend the *r* of God
3:21 the *r* of God without the law is manifested
3:25 to declare his *r* for the remission of sins
4:6 unto whom God imputeth *r* without works
4:11 a seal of the *r* . . that *r* might be imputed
5:18 by the *r* of one the free gift came upon all
5:21 grace reign through *r* unto eternal life by
6:13 your members as instruments of *r* unto God
6:19 now yield your members servants to *r* unto
8:4 the *r* of the law might be fulfilled in us
9:30 followed not after *r*, have attained to *r*
10:3 ignorant of God's *r* . . establish their own *r*
10:4 Christ is the end of the law for *r* to every
14:17 is not meat and drink; but *r*, and peace
1 Cor. 1:30 of God is made unto us wisdom, and *r*
15:34 awake to *r*, and sin not; for some have not
2 Cor. 3:9 the ministration of *r* exceed in glory
5:21 that we might be made the *r* of God in him
6:14 what fellowship hath *r* with unrighteousness?
Gal. 2:21 for if *r* come by the law, then Christ is

Gal. 3:21 verily *r* should have been by the law
Eph. 4:24 new man, which after God is created in *r*
5:9 fruit of the Spirit is in all goodness and *r*
6:14 truth, and having on the breastplate of *r*
Phil. 1:11 filled with the fruits of *r*, which are
3:6 touching the *r* which is in the law, blameless
3:9 not having mine own *r* . . the *r* which is of God
1 Tim. 6:11 (2 Tim. 2:22) and follow after *r*
Tit. 3:5 not by works of *r* which we have done
Heb. 11:7 and became heir of the *r* which is by faith
11:33 through faith subdued kingdoms, wrought *r*
12:11 it yieldeth the peaceable fruit of *r* unto
Jas. 1:20 wrath of man worketh not the *r* of God
3:18 fruit of *r* is sown in peace of them that
1 Pet. 2:24 being dead to sins, should live unto *r*
3:14 and if ye suffer for *r'* sake, happy are ye
2 Pet. 3:13 and a new earth, wherein dwelleth *r*
1 Jn. 2:29 every one that doeth *r* is born of him
3:10 whosoever doeth not *r* is not of God, neither
Rev. 19:8 for the fine linen is the *r* of saints
19:11 True, and in *r* he doth judge and make war

Rightly

Lk. 7:43 and he said unto him, Thou hast *r* judged
20:21 we know that thou sayest and teachest *r*
2 Tim. 2:15 workman . . *r* dividing the word of truth

Rigor

Ex. 1:13 made . . children of Israel to serve with *r*
Lev. 25:43 thou shalt not rule over him with *r*

Rimmon Judg. 20:45; 2 Kgs. 5:18

Ring

Gen. 41:42 Pharaoh took off his *r* from his hand
Ex. 25:12 (37:3) cast four *r* of gold for it
Esth. 3:10 king took his *r* . . and gave it unto Haman
8:8 sealed with the king's *r*, may no man reverse
Lk. 15:22 a *r* on his hand, and shoes on his feet
Jas. 2:2 unto your assembly a man with a gold *r*

Ringleader

Acts 24:5 and a *r* of the sect of the Nazarenes

Ring-streaked

Gen. 30:35 he removed . . the he goats that were *r-s*
31:8 *r-s* shall be thy hire . . bare all the cattle *r-s*

Riot

Tit. 1:6 having faithful children not accused of *r*
1 Pet. 4:4 run not with them to the same excess of *r*
2 Pet. 2:13 count it pleasure to *r* in the daytime

Rioting

Rom. 13:13 walk . . not in *r* and drunkenness

Riotous

Prov. 28:7 companion of *r* men shameth his father
Lk. 15:13 there wasted his substance with *r* living

Ripe

Gen. 40:10 clusters thereof brought forth *r* grapes
Jer. 24:2 good figs . . like the figs that are first *r*
Joel 3:13 put ye in the sickle . . the harvest is *r*
Rev. 14:15 reap; for the harvest of the earth is *r*

Rise (Rose, Risen) *See also* Arise

Num. 10:35 Moses said, *R* up, LORD, and let thine
23:24 the people shall *r* up as a great lion
24:17 a Sceptre shall *r* out of Israel, and shall
Deut. 2:24 *r* ye up, take your journey, and pass over
Josh. 3:16 the waters . . stood and *r* up upon a heap
Job 9:7 which commandeth the sun, and it *r* not

Job 14:12 so man lieth down, and *r* not: till the
  31:14 what then shall I do when God *r* up?
Ps. 35:11 false witnesses did *r* up; they laid to
  124:2 was on our side, when men *r* up against us
  127:2 it is vain for you to *r* up early, to sit
Prov. 24:16 just man falleth seven times, and *r* up
Eccl. 12:4 he shall *r* up at the voice of the bird
Song 2:10 *r* up, my love, my fair one, and come away
Is. 5:11 woe unto them that *r* up early in the
  32:9 *r* up, ye women that are at ease; hear my
  33:10 now will I *r*, saith the LORD; now will I
  58:10 then shall thy light *r* in obscurity
  60:1 and the glory of the LORD is *r* upon thee
Jer. 7:13 *r* up early and speaking, but ye heard not
Mt. 5:45 he maketh his sun to *r* on the evil and on
  10:21 (Mk. 13:12) shall *r* up against their parents
  11:11 hath not *r* a greater than John the Baptist
  12:41 (Lk. 11:32) of Nineveh shall *r* in judgment
  14:2 (Mk. 6:14; Lk. 9:7) John . . is *r* from the dead
  17:9 (Mk. 9:9) no man, until the Son of man be *r*
  20:19 (Mk. 9:31; 10:34; Lk. 18:33; 24:7) third day
    he shall *r* again
  24:7 (Mk. 13:8; Lk. 21:10) nation . . *r* against nation
  24:11 (Mk. 13:22) false prophets shall *r*, and shall
  26:32 (Mk. 14:28) after I am *r* again, I will go
  27:63 yet alive, After three days I will *r* again
  27:64 steal him . . and say . . He is *r* from the dead
  28:6 (Mk. 16:6; Lk. 24:6) not here: for he is *r*
Mk. 3:26 and if Satan *r* up against himself, and be
  8:31 and be killed, and after three days *r* again
Lk. 7:16 that a great prophet is *r* up among us
  16:31 be persuaded, though one *r* from the dead
  24:34 Lord is *r* indeed, and hath appeared to Simon
  24:46 Christ to suffer, and to *r* from the dead
Jn. 11:23 Jesus saith . . Thy brother shall *r* again
  20:9 knew not . . that he must *r* again from the dead
Acts 3:6 in the name of Jesus Christ . . *r* up and walk
  17:3 Christ must needs have suffered, and *r* again
  26:16 but *r*, and stand upon thy feet: for I have
  26:23 be the first that should *r* from the dead
Rom. 8:34 Christ that died, yea rather, that is *r*
  14:9 for to this end Christ both died, and *r*
1 Cor. 15:4 he *r* again the third day according to
  15:13 be no resurrection . . then is Christ not *r*
  15:16 if the dead *r* not, then is not Christ raised
  15:20 now is Christ *r* from the dead, and become
2 Cor. 5:15 him which died for them, and *r* again
Col. 2:12 baptism, wherein also ye are *r* with him
  3:1 if ye then be *r* with Christ, seek those things
1 Thes. 4:16 and the dead in Christ shall *r* first
Rev. 19:3 Alleluia. And her smoke *r* up for ever

Rising *See also* Rise

Lam. 3:63 behold their sitting down, and their *r* up
Mk. 9:10 what the *r* from the dead should mean
Lk. 2:34 set for the fall and *r* again of many

River *See also* Brook, Stream

Gen. 2:10 a *r* went out of Eden to water the garden
  41:1 dreamed: and, behold, he stood by the *r*
Ex. 2:5 came down to wash herself ât the *r*
  7:18 the *r* shall stink; and the Egyptians shall
Judg. 5:21 away, that ancient *r*, the *r* Kishon
2 Kgs. 5:12 *r* of Damascus, better than all the waters
  19:24 (Is. 37:25) I dried up all the *r* of besieged
Job 20:17 he shall not see the *r*, the floods
  28:10 he cutteth out *r* among the rocks; and his
  40:23 behold, he drinketh up a *r*, and hasteth not
Ps. 1:3 be like a tree planted by the *r* of water
  36:8 make them drink of the *r* of thy pleasures
  46:4 there is a *r*, the streams whereof shall make
  65:9 thou greatly enrichest it with the *r* of God
  107:33 he turneth *r* into a wilderness, and the

Ps. 119:136 *r* of waters run down mine eyes, because
  137:1 by the *r* of Babylon, there we sat down
Eccl. 1:7 all the *r* run into the sea; yet the sea
Is. 7:20 razor that is hired . . by them beyond the *r*
  19:5 and the *r* shall be wasted and dried up
  32:2 as *r* of water in a dry place, as the shadow
  41:18 I will open *r* in high places, and fountains
  43:2 through the *r*, they shall not overflow thee
  48:18 then had thy peace been as a *r*, and thy
  50:2 I dry up the sea, I make the *r* a wilderness
  66:12 behold, I will extend peace to her like a *r*
Lam. 2:18 tears run down like a *r* day and night
Ezek. 31:4 her *r* running round about his plants
Dan. 10:4 as I was by the side of the great *r*
Joel 1:20 cry . . for the *r* of water are dried up
Mic. 6:7 pleased . . with ten thousands of *r* of oil?
Jn. 7:38 of his belly shall flow *r* of living water
Acts 16:13 we went out of the city by a *r* side
Rev. 16:4 third angel poured out his vial upon the *r*
  22:1 he showed me a pure *r* of water of life

Rizpah 2 Sam. 3:7; 21:8–11

Road

1 Sam. 27:10 said, Whither have ye made a *r* today?

Roar

1 Chr. 16:32 (Ps. 96:11; 98:7) let the sea *r*
Ps. 38:8 I have *r* by reason of the disquietness
  46:3 though the waters thereof *r* and be troubled
  74:4 enemies *r* in the midst of thy congregations
  104:21 young lions *r* after their prey, and seek
Is. 5:30 and in that day they shall *r* against them
  42:13 he shall cry, yea, *r*; he shall prevail
  59:11 we *r* all like bears . . mourn sore like doves
Jer. 6:23 (50:42) their voice *r* like the sea
  25:30 LORD shall *r* from on high, and utter his
Hos. 11:10 he shall *r* like a lion: when he shall *r*
Joel 3:16 (Amos 1:2) LORD also shall *r* out of Zion
Amos 3:4 will a lion *r* . . when he hath no prey?

Roaring

Job 3:24 and my *r* are poured out like the waters
Ps. 32:3 waxed old through my *r* all the day long
Prov. 19:12 the king's wrath is as the *r* of a lion

Roast

Ex. 12:8 eat the flesh in that night, *r* with fire
Prov. 12:27 slothful man *r* not that which he took
Is. 44:16 eateth flesh; he *r r*, and is satisfied

Rob *See also* Steal

Lev. 19:13 not defraud thy neighbor, neither *r* him
Ps. 119:61 the bands of the wicked have *r* me
Prov. 22:22 *r* not the poor, because he is poor
  28:24 whoso *r* his father or his mother, and saith
Is. 10:2 prey, and that they may *r* the fatherless!
  10:13 and have *r* their treasures, and I have put
  17:14 spoil us, and the lot of them that *r* us
  42:22 but this is a people *r* and spoiled
Mal. 3:8 will a man *r* God? Yet ye have *r* me
2 Cor. 11:8 I *r* other churches, taking wages of

Robber *See also* Thief

Job 5:5 and the *r* swalloweth up their substance
  12:6 the tabernacles of *r* prosper, and they that
  18:9 and the *r* shall prevail against him
Is. 42:24 Jacob for a spoil, and Israel to the *r*?
Jer. 7:11 is called by my name, become a den of *r*
Ezek. 18:10 a son that is a *r*, a shedder of blood
Dan. 11:14 *r* of thy people shall exalt themselves
Jn. 10:1 other way, the same is a thief and a *r*
  10:8 that ever came before me are thieves and *r*

Jn. 18:40 this man, but Barabbas. . Barabbas was a *r*
Acts 19:37 which are neither *r* of churches, nor
2 Cor. 11:26 in perils of waters, in perils of *r*

Robbery

Ps. 62:10 in oppression, and become not vain in *r*
Is. 61:8 I hate *r* for burnt offering; and I will
Amos 3:10 store up violence and *r* in their palaces
Phil. 2:6 thought it not *r* to be equal with God

Robe *See also* Clothes, Clothing, Garment, Raiment

1 Sam. 24:4 cut off the skirt of Saul's *r* privily
Job 29:14 my judgment was as a *r* and a diadem
Is. 61:10 covered me with the *r* of righteousness
Mt. 27:28 (Lk. 23:11; Jn. 19:2) put on him a scarlet *r*
Lk. 15:22 bring forth the best *r*, and put it on him
20:46 the scribes, which desire to walk in long *r*
Rev. 6:11 white *r* were given unto every one of them
7:9 a great multitude. . clothed with white *r*
7:14 have washed their, *r*, and made them white

Rock

Ex. 17:6 *r* in Horeb; and thou shalt smite the *r*
33:21 a place by me, and thou shalt stand upon a *r*
Num. 20:8 speak ye unto the *r*. . water out of the *r*
20:11 smote the *r* twice: and the water came out
Deut. 8:15 who brought thee forth water out of the *r*
32:4 he is the *R*, his work is perfect
32:15 lightly esteemed the *R* of his salvation
32:18 of the *R* that begat thee thou art unmindful
32:31 their *r* is not as our *R*, even our enemies
1 Sam. 2:2 neither is there any *r* like our God
2 Sam. 22:2 (Ps. 18:2) LORD is my *r*, and my fortress
22:32 (Ps. 18:31) and who is a *r*, save our God?
22:47 (Ps. 18:46) LORD liveth. . blessed be my *r*
23:3 the *R* of Israel spake to me, He that ruleth
1 Kgs. 19:11 brake in pieces the *r* before the LORD
Job 14:18 and the *r* is removed out of his place
18:4 and shall the *r* be removed out of his place?
19:24 graven with an iron pen and lead in the *r*
Ps. 27:5 he hide me; he shall set me up upon a *r*
28:1 unto thee will I cry, O LORD my *r*; be not
31:2 be thou my strong *r*, for a house of defense
31:3 (71:3) for thou art my *r* and my fortress
40:2 my feet upon a *r*, and established my goings
61:2 lead me to the *r* that is higher than I
62:2 (62:6) he only is my *r* and my salvation
78:16 he brought streams also out of the *r*
89:26 father, my God, and the *r* of my salvation
92:15 show that the LORD is upright: he is my *r*
95:1 a joyful noise to the *r* of our salvation
105:41 he opened the *r*, and the waters gushed
Is. 2:21 the *r*, and into the tops of the ragged *r*
8:14 (Rom. 9:33; 1 Pet. 2:8) and for a *r* of offense
17:10 not been mindful of the *R* of thy strength
22:16 graveth a habitation for himself in a *r*?
51:1 look unto the *r* whence ye are hewn
Jer. 23:29 a hammer that breaketh the *r* in pieces?
Mt. 7:24 (Lk. 6:48) man. . built his house upon a *r*
16:18 upon this *r* I will build my church
27:51 and the earth did quake, and the *r* rent
Lk. 8:6 and some fell upon a *r*; and as soon as
Acts 27:29 lest we should have fallen upon *r*, they
1 Cor. 10:4 that spiritual *R*. . and that *R* was Christ
Rev. 6:16 said to the mountains and *r*, Fall on us

Rod

Gen. 30:37 Jacob took. . *r*. . and pilled white streaks
Ex. 4:2 what is that in thine hand? And he said, A *r*
4:20 and Moses took the *r* of God in his hand
7:10 and Aaron cast down his *r* before Pharaoh

Num. 17:2 take of every one of them a *r* according
17:8 *r* of Aaron for the house of Levi was budded
2 Sam. 7:14 I will chasten him with the *r* of men
Job 9:34 let him take his *r* away from me
21:9 neither is the *r* of God upon them
Ps. 2:9 thou shalt break them with a *r* of iron
23:4 thy *r* and thy staff they comfort me
74:2 the *r* of thine inheritance, which thou hast
Prov. 10:13 but a *r* is for the back of him that is
13:24 he that spareth his *r* hateth his son
22:15 *r* of correction shall drive it far from him
26:3 bridle for the ass. . a *r* for the fool's back
29:15 the *r* and reproof give wisdom: but a child
Is. 10:5 the *r* of mine anger, and the staff
11:1 come forth a *r* out of the stem of Jesse
Jer. 1:11 and I said, I see a *r* of an almond tree
48:17 strong staff broken. . the beautiful *r*!
51:19 and Israel is the *r* of his inheritance
Ezek. 7:10 the *r* hath blossomed, pride hath budded
19:14 fire is gone out of a *r* of her branches
20:37 and I will cause you to pass under the *r*
Mic. 6:9 hear ye the *r*, and who hath appointed it
1 Cor. 4:21 I come unto you with a *r*, or in love
2 Cor. 11:25 thrice was I beaten with *r*
Heb. 9:4 pot that had manna. . Aaron's *r* that budded
Rev. 2:27 (19:15) he shall rule them with a *r* of iron
12:5 who was to rule all nations with a *r* of iron

Roe

2 Sam. 2:18 Asahel was as light of foot as a wild *r*
Prov. 5:19 be as the loving hind and pleasant *r*
Song 2:9 (2:17; 8:14) is like a *r* or a young hart

Roll

Gen. 29:8 till they *r* the stone from the well's
Josh. 5:9 this day have I *r* away the reproach of me
Job 30:14 in. . desolation they *r* themselves upon me
Is. 8:1 take thee a great *r*, and write in it with
34:4 the heavens shall be *r* together as a scroll
Jer. 36:2 take thee a *r* of a book, and write therein
Ezek. 2:9 and, lo, a *r* of a book was therein
3:1 eat this *r*, and go speak unto the house of
Zech. 5:1 then I. . looked, and behold a flying *r*
Mt. 27:60 (Mk. 15:46) *r* a great stone to the door
28:2 for the angel. . came and *r* back the stone
Mk. 16:3 who shall *r* us away the stone from the
Lk. 24:2 found the stone *r* away from the sepulchre
Rev. 6:14 departed as a scroll when it is *r* together

Roman

Jn. 11:48 the *R* shall come and take away both our
Acts 16:21 to receive, neither to observe, being *R*
16:37 beaten us openly uncondemned, being *R*
22:25 lawful for you to scourge a man that is a *R*
23:27 rescued him. . understood that he was a *R*
25:16 not the manner of the *R* to deliver any man

Rome

Acts 18:2 had commanded all Jews to depart from *R*
19:21 after I have been there, I must also see *R*
23:11 Paul. . so must thou bear witness also at *R*
28:16 when we came to *R*, the centurion delivered
Rom. 1:7 to all that be in *R*, beloved of God, called
1:15 preach the gospel to you that are at *R* also

Roof

Gen. 19:8 came they under the shadow of my *r*
Deut. 22:8 thou shalt make a battlement for thy *r*
Josh. 2:6 but she had brought them up to the *r*
2 Sam. 11:2 from the *r* he saw a woman washing
18:24 the watchman went up to the *r* over
Job 29:10 tongue cleaved to the *r* of their mouth
Mt. 8:8 (Lk. 7:6) thou shouldest come under my *r*

Mk. 2:4 press, they uncovered the *r* where he was

Room

Gen. 24:23 is there *r* in thy father's house for us
  26:22 now the LORD hath made *r* for us
Ps. 80:9 thou preparedst *r* before it, and didst
Prov. 18:16 a man's gift maketh *r* for him
Mal. 3:10 there shall not be *r* enough to receive
Mk. 2:2 that there was no *r* to receive them
  14:15 (Lk. 22:12) he will show you a large upper *r*
Lk. 2:7 because there was no *r* for them in the inn
  12:17 I have no *r* where to bestow my fruits?
  14:7 he marked how they chose out the chief *r*
  14:22 as thou hast commanded, and yet there is *r*
Acts 1:13 come in, they went up into an upper *r*

Root

Deut. 29:18 be among you a *r* that beareth gall
  29:28 the LORD *r* them out of their land in anger
1 Kgs. 14:15 he shall *r* up Israel out of this good
2 Kgs. 19:30 (Is. 37:31) Judah shall yet again take *r*
Job 5:3 seen the foolish taking *r*: but suddenly I
  8:17 his *r* are wrapped about the heap, and seeth
  14:8 though the *r* thereof wax old in the earth
  18:14 confidence shall be *r* out of his tabernacle
  18:16 his *r* shall be dried up beneath, and above
  19:28 seeing the *r* of the matter is found in me?
  29:19 my *r* was spread out by the waters
Ps. 52:5 and *r* thee out of the land of the living
  80:9 didst cause it to take deep *r*, and it filled
Prov. 2:22 and the transgressors shall be *r* out
  12:3 *r* of the righteous shall not be moved
Is. 5:24 their *r* shall be as rottenness, and their
  11:1 Jesse, and a Branch shall grow out of his *r*
  11:10 (Rom. 15:12) there shall be a *r* of Jesse
  27:6 cause them that come of Jacob to take *r*
  37:31 the remnant. . shall again take *r* downward
  53:2 as a *r* out of a dry ground: he hath no form
Jer. 1:10 *r* out, and to pull down, and to destroy
Ezek. 31:7 branches: for his *r* was by great waters
Mal. 4:1 it shall leave them neither *r* nor branch
Mt. 3:10 (Lk. 3:9) axe is laid unto the *r* of the trees
  13:6 (Mk. 4:6; Lk. 8:13) because they had no *r*
  13:29 tares, ye *r* up also the wheat with them
  15:13 Father hath not planted, shall be *r* up
Rom. 11:16 if the *r* be holy, so are the branches
  11:18 thou bearest not the *r*, but the *r* thee
Eph. 3:17 that ye, being *r* and grounded in love
Col. 2:7 *r* and built up in him, and stablished in
1 Tim. 6:10 the love of money is the *r* of all evil
Jude 12 trees. . twice dead, plucked up by the *r*
Rev. 5:5 Lion of the tribe of Juda, the *R* of David
  22:16 I am the *r* and the offspring of David

Rope

Judg. 16:11 if they bind me fast with new *r* that
Is. 5:18 that draw. . sin as it were with a cart *r*
Acts 27:32 the soldiers cut off the *r* of the boat

Rose (noun)

Song 2:1 I am the *r* of Sharon, and the lily of the
Is. 35:1 desert shall rejoice, and blossom as the *r*

Rose (verb) *See* Rise

Rot

Num. 5:21 thy thigh to *r*, and thy belly to swell
Prov. 10:7 but the name of the wicked shall *r*
Is. 40:20 chooseth a tree that will not *r*; he seeketh

Rotten

Job 13:28 he, as a *r* thing, consumeth, as a garment
  41:27 esteemeth iron as straw. . brass as *r* wood

Joel 1:17 seed is *r* under their clods, the garners

Rottenness

Prov. 12:4 maketh ashamed is as *r* in his bones
  14:30 of the flesh: but envy the *r* of the bones
Hos. 5:12 as a moth, and to the house of Judah as *r*

Rough

Is. 40:4 (Lk. 3:5) straight, and the *r* places plain

Row

Jon. 1:13 the men *r* hard to bring it to the land
Mk. 6:48 he saw them toiling in *r*; for the wind
Jn. 6:19 so when they had *r* about five and twenty

Rower

Ezek. 27:26 *r* have brought thee into great waters

Royal

Esth. 5:1 Esther put on her *r* apparel, and stood
Acts 12:21 Herod, arrayed in *r* apparel, sat upon
Jas. 2:8 if ye fulfill the *r* law according to the
1 Pet. 2:9 are a chosen generation, a *r* priesthood

Rubbish

Neh. 4:10 much *r*; so that we are not able to build

Ruby

Job 28:18 for the price of wisdom is above *r*
Prov. 3:15 she is more precious than *r*: and all
  8:11 for wisdom is better than *r*; and all the
  31:10 a virtuous woman. . her price is far above *r*

Ruddy

1 Sam. 16:12 he was *r*, and withal of a beautiful
Song 5:10 my beloved is white and *r*, the chiefest

Rude

2 Cor. 11:6 though I be *r* in speech, yet not in

Rudiment

Col. 2:8 after the *r* of the world, and not after
  2:20 be dead with Christ from the *r* of the world

Rufus Mk. 15:21; Rom. 16:13

Ruin *See also* Desolation, Destruction, Waste

2 Chr. 28:23 were the *r* of him, and of all Israel
Ps. 89:40 thou hast brought his strongholds to *r*
Prov. 24:22 and who knoweth the *r* of them both?
  26:28 and a flattering mouth worketh *r*
Is. 3:6 and let this *r* be under thy hand
  3:8 for Jerusalem is *r*, and Judah is fallen
  25:2 of a city a heap; of a defensed city a *r*
Ezek. 18:30 turn. . so iniquity shall not be your *r*
  21:15 heart may faint, and their *r* be multiplied
Amos 9:11 (Acts 15:16) and I will raise up his *r*
Lk. 6:49 fell; and the *r* of that house was great

Rule *See also* Authority, Dominion, Govern, Reign

Gen. 1:16 to *r* the day. . lesser light to *r* the night
  3:16 be to thy husband, and he shall *r* over thee
Lev. 25:46 shall not *r* one over another with rigor
Judg. 8:23 I will not *r*. . the LORD shall *r* over you
2 Sam. 23:3 *r* over men must be just, *r* in the fear
Esth. 9:1 the Jews had *r* over them that hated them
Ps. 59:13 let them know that God *r* in Jacob unto
  66:7 he *r* by his power for ever; his eyes behold
  89:9 thou *r* the raging of the sea: when the waves

Ps. 103:19 the heavens; and his kingdom *r* over all
106:41 and they that hated them *r* over them
110:2 *r* thou in the midst of thine enemies
Prov. 8:16 by me princes *r*, and nobles, even all
12:24 hand of the diligent shall bear *r*: but
16:32 *r* his spirit than he that taketh a city
22:7 rich *r* over the poor, and the borrower
25:28 that hath no *r* over his own spirit is like
29:2 when the wicked beareth *r*, the people mourn
Eccl. 8:9 one man *r* over another to his own hurt
Is. 3:4 be their princes. . babes shall *r* over them
14:2 and they shall *r* over their oppressors
14:6 that *r* the nations in anger, is persecuted
40:10 strong hand, and his arm shall *r* for him
63:19 we are thine: thou never barest *r* over them
Lam. 5:8 servants have *r* over us: there is none
Ezek. 20:33 with fury poured out, will I *r* over you
29:15 that they shall no more *r* over the nations
34:4 with force and with cruelty have ye *r* them
Dan. 2:39 kingdom of brass, which shall bear *r* over
4:17 (4:25, 32; 5:21) Most High *r* in the kingdom
4:26 thou shalt have known that the heavens do *r*
11:3 a mighty king. . shall *r* with great dominion
Joel 2:17 that the heathen should *r* over them
Zech. 6:13 and shall sit and *r* upon his throne
Mt. 2:6 a Governor, that shall *r* my people Israel
Mk. 10:42 to *r* over the Gentiles exercise lordship
Rom. 12:8 simplicity; he that *r*, with diligence
1 Cor. 15:24 he shall have put down all *r*, and all
2 Cor. 10:13 but according to the measure of the *r*
Gal. 6:16 and as many as walk according to this *r*
Phil. 3:16 let us walk by the same *r*, let us mind
Col. 3:15 let the peace of God *r* in your hearts
1 Tim. 3:4 one that *r* well his own house
5:17 the elders that *r* well be counted worthy of
Heb. 13:7 remember them which have the *r* over you
13:17 obey them that have the *r* over you. . submit
Rev. 2:27 (19:15) he shall *r* them with a rod of iron
12:5 was to *r* all nations with a rod of iron

Ruler *See also* Governor, King, Lord

Gen. 41:43 made him *r* over all the land of Egypt
Ex. 16:22 the *r* of the congregation came and told
18:21 place such over them, to be *r* of thousands
22:28 (Acts 23:5) nor curse the *r* of thy people
Lev. 4:22 when a *r* hath sinned, and done somewhat
1 Sam. 25:30 have appointed thee *r* over Israel
1 Chr. 28:4 for he hath chosen Judah to be the *r*
2 Chr. 7:18 not fail thee a man to be *r* in Israel
Neh. 2:16 *r* knew not whither I went, or what I did
Ps. 2:2 *r* take counsel together, against the LORD
Prov. 23:1 thou sittest to eat with a *r*, consider
28:15 so is a wicked *r* over the poor people
29:12 if a *r* hearken to lies, all his servants
Is. 1:10 hear the word of the LORD, ye *r* of Sodom
22:3 all thy *r* are fled together, they are bound
Dan. 5:29 he should be the third *r* in the kingdom
Mic. 5:2 of thee shall he come. . to be *r* in Israel
Hab. 1:14 as the creeping things, that have no *r*
Mt. 9:18 (Mk. 5:22; Lk. 8:41) there came a certain *r*
24:45 (Lk. 12:42) hath made *r* over his household
25:21 I will make thee *r* over many things
Mk. 5:36 Jesus. . saith unto the *r* of the synagogue
13:9 (Lk. 21:12) brought before *r* and kings for
Jn. 3:1 Pharisees, named Nicodemus, a *r* of the Jews
7:48 any of the *r* or of the Pharisees believed
12:42 among the chief *r* also many believed on him
Acts 4:26 *r* were gathered together against the Lord
7:35 whom they refused. . did God send to be a *r*
23:5 shalt not speak evil of the *r* of thy people
Rom. 13:3 *r* are not a terror to good works, but to
Eph. 6:12 against the *r* of the darkness of this

Rumor *See also* Report, Tidings

2 Kgs. 19:7 (Is. 37:7) shall hear a *r*, and shall return
Jer. 49:14 I have heard a *r* from the LORD
51:46 and ye fear for the *r*. . a *r* shall both come
Ezek. 7:26 *r* shall be upon *r*; then shall they seek
Obad. 1 concerning Edom; We have heard a *r* from
Mt. 24:6 (Mk. 13:7) shall hear of wars and *r* of wars
Lk. 7:17 *r* of him went forth throughout all Judea

Run (Ran) *See also* Race

2 Sam. 22:30 (Ps. 18:29) I have *r* through a troop
1 Kgs. 18:46 Elijah. . *r* before Ahab to the entrance
Ps. 23:5 anointest my head with oil; my cup *r* over
119:32 I will *r* the way of thy commandments
Prov. 1:16 (Is. 59:7) feet *r* to evil, and make haste
Is. 40:31 they shall *r*, and not be weary
55:5 nations that knew not thee shall *r* unto thee
Jer. 5:1 *r* ye to and fro through the streets
12:5 if thou hast *r* with the footmen, and they
Dan. 12:4 many shall *r* to and fro, and knowledge
Hab. 2:2 it plain. . that he may *r* that readeth it
Mt. 9:17 the bottles break, and the wine *r* out
28:8 and did *r* to bring his disciples word
Jn. 20:4 *r* both together. . other disciple did outrun
Rom. 9:16 willeth, nor of him that *r*, but of God
1 Cor. 9:24 in a race *r* all, but one receiveth
Gal. 2:2 lest. . I should *r*, or had *r*, in vain
5:7 ye did *r* well; who did hinder you that ye
Phil. 2:16 I have not *r* in vain, neither labored
Heb. 12:1 let us *r* with patience the race that is
1 Pet. 4:4 ye *r* not with them to the same excess

Rush (noun) *See also* Reed

Job 8:11 can the *r* grow up without mire? can the

Rush (verb)

Is. 17:13 nations shall *r* like the rushing of many
Acts 19:29 they *r* with one accord into the theatre

Rushing

Is. 17:12 *r* of nations, that make a *r* like the *r*
Ezek. 3:12 I heard behind me a voice of a great *r*
Acts 2:2 a sound from heaven as of a *r* mighty wind

Rust

Mt. 6:19 upon earth, where moth and *r* doth corrupt
Jas. 5:3 *r* of them shall be a witness against you

Ruth Ruth. 1:4–4:13

Rye

Ex. 9:32 but the wheat and the *r* were not smitten

S

Sabaoth Rom. 9:29; Jas. 5:4

Sabbath

Ex. 16:26 but on the seventh day, which is the *s*
20:8 remember the *s* day, to keep it holy
20:10 (Deut. 5:14) but the seventh day is the *s*
31:13 verily my *s* ye shall keep: for it is a sign
31:15 (35:2; Lev. 23:3) the seventh is the *s* of rest
Lev. 16:31 it shall be a *s* of rest unto you, and ye
19:30 (26:2) keep my *s*. . reverence my sanctuary
23:24 seventh month, in the first day. . have a *s*
25:4 seventh year. . be a *s* of rest unto the land
25:8 and thou shalt number seven *s* of years unto
Num. 15:32 man that gathered sticks upon the *s* day

Deut. 5:12 keep the *s* day to sanctify it
Neh. 9:14 and madest known unto them thy holy *s*
　10:31 we would not buy it of them on the *s*
　13:17 what evil . . ye do, and profane the *s* day?
Is. 1:13 new moons and *s*, the calling of assemblies
　56:2 that keepeth the *s* from polluting it
　58:13 thy foot from the *s* . . call the *s* a delight
　66:23 from one *s* to another, shall all flesh come
Jer. 17:21 bear no burden on the *s* day, nor bring
Lam. 1:7 adversaries saw her, and did mock at her *s*
Ezek. 20:12 also I gave them my *s*, to be a sign
　20:13 my *s* they greatly polluted: then I said
　22:26 hid their eyes from my *s*, and I am profaned
　44:24 mine assemblies; and they shall hallow my *s*
　46:3 shall worship . . before the LORD in the *s*
Hos. 2:11 cause all her mirth to cease . . and her *s*
Mt. 12:1 (Mk. 2:23; Lk. 6:1) *s* day through the corn
　12:2 (Mk. 2:24; Lk. 6:2) not lawful to do upon the *s*
　12:8 (Mk. 2:28; Lk. 6:5) Lord even of the *s* day
　12:10 (Mk. 3:2; Lk. 6:7) lawful to heal on the *s*
　12:12 wherefore it is lawful to do well on the *s*
　24:20 flight be not in . . winter, neither on the *s*
　28:1 (Mk. 16:1) end of the *s*, as it began to dawn
Mk. 1:21 (Lk. 4:31) *s* day he entered . . the synagogue
　2:27 *s* was made for man, and not man for the *s*
　3:4 (Lk. 6:9) is it lawful to do good on the *s*
Lk. 4:16 he went into the synagogue on the *s* day
　13:16 be loosed from this bond on the *s* day?
　14:1 into the house . . to eat bread on the *s* day
　23:56 rested the *s* day according to the
Jn. 5:18 he not only had broken the *s*, but said
　7:23 if a man on the *s* day receive circumcision
　9:16 is not of God, because he keepeth not the *s*
　19:31 should not remain upon the cross on the *s*
Col. 2:16 or of the new moon, or of the *s* days

Sabean Job 1:15; Ezek. 23:42; Joel 3:8

Sack

Gen. 42:25 Joseph commanded to fill their *s* with
　44:11 *s* to the ground, and opened every man his *s*
Josh. 9:4 wilily . . and took old *s* upon their asses

Sackcloth

Gen. 37:34 Jacob rent his clothes, and put *s* upon
2 Sam. 3:31 gird you with *s*, and mourn before Abner
1 Kgs. 20:32 so they girded *s* on their loins
2 Kgs. 6:30 behold, he had *s* within upon his flesh
　19:1 (Is. 37:1) Hezekiah . . covered himself with *s*
Neh. 9:1 were assembled with fasting, and with *s*
Esth. 4:1 Mordecai rent his clothes, and put on *s*
Ps. 30:11 put off my *s*, and girded me with gladness
　35:13 when they were sick, my clothing was *s*
Is. 20:2 go and loose the *s* from off thy loins
　50:3 with blackness, and I make *s* their covering
Jon. 3:5 and proclaimed a fast, and put on *s*
Rev. 6:12 and the sun became black as *s* of hair

Sacrifice *See also* Atonement, Oblation, Offer, Offering, Propitiation, Reconciliation

Ex. 3:18 now let us go . . that we may *s* to the LORD
　5:17 idle: therefore ye say, Let us go and do *s*
　8:26 we shall . . *s* the abomination of the Egyptians
　12:27 say, It is the *s* of the LORD's passover
　13:15 I *s* to the LORD all that openeth the matrix
　20:24 and shalt *s* thereon thy burnt offerings
　22:20 he that *s* unto any god, save unto the LORD
　29:28 the *s* of their peace offerings, even their
　32:8 molten calf . . have worshipped it, and have *s*
　34:15 *s* unto their gods, and . . thou eat of his *s*

Deut. 15:21 any ill blemish, thou shalt not *s* it
　16:2 thou shalt therefore *s* the passover unto
　32:17 (1 Cor. 10:20) *s* unto devils, not to God
　33:19 there they shall offer *s* of righteousness
Judg. 2:5 Bochim: and they *s* there unto the LORD
1 Sam. 1:21 up to offer unto the LORD the yearly *s*
　2:29 wherefore kick ye at my *s* . . at mine offering
　15:22 to obey is better than *s*, and to hearken
　16:2 take a heifer with thee . . say, I am come to *s*
1 Kgs. 3:2 the people *s* in high places, because
　8:63 (2 Chr. 7:5) and Solomon offered a *s* of
　12:32 Bethel, *s* unto the calves that he had made
　18:38 the fire of the LORD . . consumed the burnt *s*
2 Kgs. 10:19 for I have a great *s* to do to Baal
　17:35 shall not fear other gods . . nor *s* to them
1 Chr. 29:21 *s s* unto the LORD . . and *s* in abundance
2 Chr. 29:31 come . . and bring *s* and thank offerings
　33:17 people did *s* still in the high places
Neh. 4:2 will they fortify themselves? will they *s*?
　12:43 that day they offered great *s*, and rejoiced
Ps. 40:6 (Heb. 10:5) *s* and offering thou didst not
　50:8 I will not reprove thee for thy *s* or thy
　51:16 thou desirest not *s*; else would I give it
　51:17 the *s* of God are a broken spirit
　51:19 thou be pleased with the *s* of righteousness
　54:6 I will freely *s* unto thee: I will praise thy
　106:28 unto Baal-peor, and ate the *s* of the dead
　106:37 *s* their sons and their daughters unto devils
　107:22 and let them *s* the *s* of thanksgiving
Prov. 15:8 (21:27) *s* of the wicked is an abomination
　17:1 morsel . . than a house full of *s* with strife
　21:3 justice . . more acceptable to the LORD than *s*
Eccl. 5:1 to hear, than to give the *s* of fools
　9:2 alike . . to him that *s*, and to him that *s* not
Is. 1:11 what purpose is the multitude of your *s*
　43:23 neither hast thou honored me with thy *s*
　66:3 that *s* a lamb, as if he cut off a dog's neck
Jer. 6:20 not acceptable, nor your *s* sweet unto me
　17:26 *s* of praise, unto the house of the LORD
Ezek. 16:20 hast thou *s* unto them to be devoured
　39:17 *s* that I do *s* for you, even a great *s* upon
Dan. 8:11 by him the daily *s* was taken away
　9:27 shall cause the *s* and the oblation to cease
　11:31 and shall take away the daily *s*, and they
Hos. 3:4 without a prince, and without a *s*
　4:19 they shall be ashamed of their *s*
　6:6 (Mt. 9:13; 12:7) I desired mercy, and not *s*
　8:13 they *s* flesh for the *s* of mine offerings
　9:4 their *s* shall be . . as the bread of mourners
　11:2 they *s* unto Baalim, and burned incense to
Amos 4:4 bring your *s* every morning . . your tithes
　5:25 (Acts 7:42) offered unto me a *s* and offerings
Jon. 2:9 but I will *s* unto thee with . . thanksgiving
Hab. 1:16 they *s* unto their net, and burn incense
Zeph. 1:7 LORD hath prepared a *s*, he hath bid his
Zech. 14:21 all they that *s* shall come and take of
Mal. 1:14 and *s* unto the Lord a corrupt thing
Mk. 9:49 and every *s* shall be salted with salt
　12:33 more than all whole burnt offerings and *s*
Lk. 2:24 to offer a *s* according to that which is
　13:1 whose blood Pilate had mingled with their *s*
Acts 14:13 priest of Jupiter . . would have done *s* with
Rom. 12:1 that ye present your bodies a living *s*
1 Cor. 5:7 even Christ our passover is *s* for us
　8:4 things that are offered in *s* unto idols
　10:19 which is offered in *s* to idols is any thing?
　10:28 this is offered in *s* unto idols, eat not
Eph. 5:2 and a *s* to God for a sweetsmelling savor
Phil. 2:17 if I be offered upon the *s* and service
　4:18 an odor of a sweet smell, a *s* acceptable
Heb. 5:1 he may offer both gifts and *s* for sins
　7:27 needeth not daily . . to offer up *s*, first for
　8:3 high priest is ordained to offer gifts and *s*

Heb. 9:26 to put away sin by the *s* of himself
  10:1 can never with those *s*. . make the comers
  10:3 but in those *s* there is a remembrance again
  10:12 after he had offered one *s* for sins for ever
  10:26 sin wilfully. . remaineth no more *s* for sins
  11:4 Abel offered. . a more excellent *s* than Cain
  13:15 by him . . let us offer the *s* of praise to God
  13:16 do good. . with such *s* God is well pleased
1 Pet. 2:5 to offer up spiritual *s*, acceptable to
Rev. 2:14 (2:20) to eat things *s* unto idols, and to

Sacrilege

Rom. 2:22 that abhorrest idols, dost thou commit *s*?

Sad

Gen. 40:6 Joseph. . looked upon them. . they were *s*
1 Sam. 1:18 eat, and her countenance was no more *s*
1 Kgs. 21:5 why is thy spirit so *s*, that thou
Neh. 2:1 had not been beforetime *s* in his presence
Ezek. 13:22 righteous *s*, whom I have not made *s*
Mt. 6:16 not, as the hypocrites, of a *s* countenance
Mk. 10:22 he was *s* at that saying, and went away
Lk. 24:17 one to another, as ye walk, and are *s*?

Saddle

Gen. 22:3 and Abraham rose up early. . and *s* his ass
2 Sam. 19:26 I will *s* me an ass, that I may ride
1 Kgs. 13:13 sons, *S* me the ass. So they *s* him the

Sadducee *See also* Pharisee, Scribe

Mt. 3:7 Pharisees and *S* come to his baptism
  16:1 Pharisees also with the *S* came, and tempting
  22:23 (Mk. 12:18; Lk. 20:27) came to him the *S*
Acts 4:1 captain of the temple, and the *S*, came
  5:17 were with him, (which is the sect of the *S*,)
  23:6 Paul perceived that the one part were *S*
  23:8 for the *S* say that there is no resurrection

Sadness

Eccl. 7:3 by the *s* of the countenance the heart is

Safe

1 Sam. 12:11 LORD. . delivered you. . and ye dwelt *s*
2 Sam. 18:29 king said, Is the young man Absalom *s*?
Job 21:9 their houses are *s* from fear, neither is
Ps. 119:117 hold thou me up, and I shall be *s*
Prov. 18:10 the righteous runneth into it, and is *s*
  29:25 putteth his trust in the LORD shall be *s*
Ezek. 34:27 shall be *s* in their land, and shall know
Lk. 15:27 because he hath received him *s* and sound
Acts 23:24 set Paul on, and bring him *s* unto Felix
  27:44 to pass, that they escaped all *s* to land
Phil. 3:1 is not grievous, but for you it is *s*

Safeguard

1 Sam. 22:23 but with me thou shalt be in *s*

Safely

Ps. 78:53 led them on *s*, so that they feared not
Prov. 1:33 whoso hearkeneth unto me shall dwell *s*
  3:23 then shalt thou walk in thy way *s*, and thy
Is. 41:3 he pursued them, and passed *s*; even by
Jer. 33:16 Judah be saved. . Jerusalem shall dwell *s*
Hos. 2:18 and will make them to lie down *s*
Acts 16:23 charging the jailer to keep them *s*

Safety

Deut. 33:12 beloved of the LORD shall dwell in *s*
Job 3:26 was not in *s*, neither had I rest, neither
  5:4 his children are far from *s*, and they are
  24:23 though it be given him to be in *s*, whereon
Ps. 4:8 for thou, LORD, only makest me dwell in *s*
  12:5 I will set him in *s* from him that puffeth

Ps. 33:17 horse is a vain thing for *s*: neither shall
Prov. 11:14 (24:6) multitude of counselors there is *s*
  21:31 the day of battle: but *s* is of the LORD
Is. 14:30 feed, and the needy shall lie down in *s*
1 Thes. 5:3 peace and *s*; then sudden destruction

Sail

Is. 33:23 their mast; they could not spread the *s*
Ezek. 27:7 linen. . thou spreadest forth to be thy *s*
Lk. 8:23 as they *s*, he fell asleep: and there came
Acts 18:18 took his leave. . and *s* thence into Syria
  27:17 should fall into the quicksands, struck *s*

Saint *See also* Holy

Deut. 33:2 and he came with ten thousands of *s*
  33:3 loved the people; all his *s* are in thy hand
1 Sam. 2:9 he will keep the feet of his *s*
2 Chr. 6:41 (Ps. 132:9) let thy *s* rejoice in goodness
Job 5:1 and to which of the *s* wilt thou turn?
  15:15 behold, he putteth no trust in his *s*
Ps. 16:3 but to the *s* that are in the earth
  30:4 sing unto the LORD, O ye *s* of his, and give
  31:23 O love the LORD, all ye his *s*: for the LORD
  34:9 O fear the LORD, ye his *s*: for there is no
  37:28 loveth judgment, and forsaketh not his *s*
  50:5 gather my *s* together unto me; those that
  79:2 flesh of thy *s* unto the beasts of the earth
  85:8 speak peace unto his people, and to his *s*
  89:7 greatly to be feared in the assembly of the *s*
  97:10 preserveth the souls of his *s*; he delivereth
  116:15 precious. . is the death of his *s*
  145:10 praise thee. . and thy *s* shall bless thee
  149:9 judgment written: this honor have all his *s*
Prov. 2:8 judgment, and preserveth the way of his *s*
Dan. 7:18 *s* of the Most High shall take the kingdom
  7:21 war with the *s*, and prevailed
  8:13 I heard one *s* speaking, and another *s* said
Hos. 11:12 ruleth with God. . is faithful with the *s*
Zech. 14:5 God shall come, and all the *s* with thee
Mt. 27:52 many bodies of the *s* which slept arose
Acts 9:13 how much evil he hath done to thy *s* at
  26:10 and many of the *s* did I shut up in prison
Rom. 1:7 in Rome, beloved of God, called to be *s*
  8:27 because he maketh intercession for the *s*
  12:13 distributing to the necessity of *s*
  15:25 I go unto Jerusalem to minister unto the *s*
  16:2 ye receive her in the Lord, as becometh *s*
1 Cor. 1:2 sanctified in Christ. . called to be *s*
  6:1 law before the unjust, and not before the *s*?
  6:2 ye not know that the *s* shall judge the world?
  16:1 concerning the collection for the *s*
2 Cor. 8:4 fellowship of the ministering to the *s*
  9:1 as touching the ministering to the *s*, it is
  9:12 not only supplieth the want of the *s*, but is
Eph. 1:15 (Col. 1:4) faith. . and love unto all the *s*
  1:18 of the glory of his inheritance in the *s*
  2:19 foreigners, but fellow citizens with the *s*
  3:8 unto me, who am less than the least of all *s*
  3:18 be able to comprehend with all *s* what is
  4:12 for the perfecting of the *s*, for the work
  5:3 not be once named among you, as becometh *s*
  6:18 all perseverance and supplication for all *s*
Phil. 4:21 salute every *s* in Christ Jesus
Col. 1:12 partakers of the inheritance of the *s*
  1:26 been hid. . but now is made manifest to his *s*
1 Thes. 3:13 the coming of our Lord. . with all his *s*
2 Thes. 1:10 he shall come to be glorified in his *s*
1 Tim. 5:10 if she have washed the *s*' feet
Phlm. 5 toward the Lord Jesus, and toward all *s*
Heb. 6:10 in that ye have ministered to the *s*
  13:24 that have the rule over you, and all the *s*
Jude 3 faith which was once delivered unto the *s*
  14 the Lord cometh with ten thousands of his *s*

Rev. 5:8 full of odors, which are the prayers of *s*
  8:3 he should offer it with the prayers of all *s*
  13:7 it was given unto him to make war with the *s*
  13:10 (14:12) here is the patience . . of the *s*
  16:6 they have shed the blood of *s* and prophets
  17:6 the woman drunken with the blood of the *s*
  18:24 was found the blood of prophets, and of *s*
  20:9 compassed the camp of the *s* about

Salamis Acts 13:5

Salem *See also* Jerusalem
Gen. 14:18; Heb. 7:1–2

Salim Jn. 3:23

Salt
Gen. 19:26 looked back . . she became a pillar of *s*
Lev. 2:13 all thine offerings thou shalt offer *s*
Num. 18:19 it is a covenant of *s* for ever
Judg. 9:45 beat down the city, and sowed it with *s*
2 Kgs. 2:21 spring of the waters, and cast the *s* in
Job 6:6 that which is unsavory be eaten without *s*?
Ezek. 16:4 thou wast not *s* at-all, nor swaddled
Mt. 5:13 ye are the *s* of the earth: but if the *s*
Mk. 9:49 *s* with fire . . sacrifice shall be *s* with *s*
  9:50 (Lk. 14:34) *s* is good: but if the *s* have lost
  9:50 have *s* in yourselves, and have peace one
Col. 4:6 your speech . . with grace, seasoned with *s*
Jas. 3:12 no fountain both yield *s* water and fresh

Salutation
Mk. 12:38 scribes . . and love *s* in the market places
Lk. 1:29 cast in her mind what manner of *s* this
  1:41 that, when Elisabeth heard the *s* of Mary
1 Cor. 16:21 (Col. 4:18; 2 Thes. 3:17) *s* of me Paul

Salute
1 Sam. 10:4 will *s* thee, and give thee two loaves
2 Kgs. 4:29 *s* him not; and if any *s* thee, answer
Mt. 5:47 if ye *s* your brethren only, what do ye
  10:12 and when ye come into a house, *s* it
Mk. 15:18 began to *s* him, Hail, King of the Jews!
Lk. 10:4 scrip, nor shoes: and *s* no man by the way
Acts 21:7 we came to Ptolemais, and *s* the brethren
  21:19 he had *s* them, he declared particularly
Rom. 16:16 *s* one another with a holy kiss
Heb. 13:24 *s* all them that have the rule over you

Salvation *See also* Deliverance, Redemption
Gen. 49:18 I have waited for thy *s*, O LORD
Ex. 14:13 stand still, and see the *s* of the LORD
  15:2 (Ps. 118:14; Is. 12:2) and he is become my *s*
1 Sam. 2:1 because I rejoice in thy *s*
  11:13 today the LORD hath wrought *s* in Israel
  19:5 the LORD wrought a great *s* for all Israel
2 Sam. 22:3 (Ps. 18:2) my shield, and the horn of my *s*
  22:47 (Ps. 18:46) and exalted be the God . . of my *s*
  23:5 for this is all my *s*, and all my desire
1 Chr. 16:23 (Ps. 96:2) show . . from day to day his *s*
2 Chr. 6:41 let thy priests . . be clothed with *s*
  20:17 see the *s* of the LORD with you, O Judah
Job 13:16 he also shall be my *s*: for a hypocrite
Ps. 3:8 *s* belongeth unto the LORD: thy blessing
  13:5 thy mercy; my heart shall rejoice in thy *s*
  14:7 (53:6) oh that the *s* of Israel were come out
  20:5 we will rejoice in thy *s*, and in the name
  25:5 thou art the God of my *s*; on thee do I wait
  27:1 LORD is my light and my *s*: whom shall I fear?
  35:3 persecute me: say unto my soul, I am thy *s*
  37:39 but the *s* of the righteous is of the LORD
  40:10 I have declared thy faithfulness and thy *s*

Ps. 40:16 (70:4) let such as love thy *s* say continually
  62:2 (62:6) he only is my rock and my *s*; he is my
  62:7 in God is my *s* and my glory: the rock of my
  68:20 he that is our God is the God of *s*
  71:15 show forth thy righteousness and thy *s* all
  74:12 King . . working *s* in the midst of the earth
  78:22 believed not in God . . trusted not in his *s*
  85:7 show us thy mercy, O LORD . . grant us thy *s*
  85:9 surely his *s* is nigh them that fear him
  91:16 life will I satisfy him, and show him my *s*
  98:3 ends of the earth have seen the *s* of our God
  116:13 I will take the cup of *s*, and call upon
  119:81 my soul fainteth for thy *s*: but I hope in
  119:123 mine eyes fail for thy *s*, and for the
  119:155 *s* is far from the wicked: for they seek
  132:16 I will also clothe her priests with *s*
  144:10 it is he that giveth *s* unto kings
  149:4 the LORD . . will beautify the meek with *s*
Is. 12:2 behold, God is my *s*; I will trust, and not
  25:9 we will be glad and rejoice in his *s*
  26:1 *s* will God appoint for walls and bulwarks
  33:2 be thou their arm every morning, our *s* also
  45:8 the earth open, and let them bring forth *s*
  45:17 be saved in the LORD with an everlasting *s*
  46:13 my *s* shall not tarry: and I will place *s* in
  49:6 (Acts 13:47) be my *s* unto the end of the earth
  51:6 shall vanish away . . but my *s* shall be for ever
  52:7 good tidings of good, that publisheth *s*
  52:10 all the ends of the earth shall see the *s*
  56:1 my *s* is near to come, and my righteousness
  59:16 therefore his arm brought *s* unto him
  59:17 a breastplate . . a helmet of *s* upon his head
  60:18 shalt call thy walls *S*, and thy gates Praise
  61:10 he hath clothed me with the garments of *s*
  62:11 the daughter of Zion, Behold, thy *s* cometh
  63:5 therefore mine own arm brought *s* unto me
Jer. 3:23 in vain is *s* hoped for from the hills
Lam. 3:26 and quietly wait for the *s* of the LORD
Jon. 2:9 pay . . that I have vowed. *S* is of the LORD
Hab. 3:13 wentest forth for the *s* of thy people
Zech. 9:9 he is just, and having *s*; lowly
Lk. 1:69 hath raised up a horn of *s* for us in the
  1:77 to give knowledge of *s* unto his people by
  2:30 for mine eyes have seen thy *s*
  3:6 and all flesh shall see the *s* of God
  19:9 this day is *s* come to this house, forasmuch
Jn. 4:22 know what we worship; for *s* is of the Jews
Acts 4:12 neither is there *s* in any other
  13:26 feareth God, to you is the word of this *s*
  16:17 high God, which show unto us the way of *s*
  28:28 the *s* of God is sent unto the Gentiles
Rom. 1:16 it is the power of God unto *s* to every
  10:10 with the mouth confession is made unto *s*
  11:11 rather through their fall *s* is come unto
  13:11 now is our *s* nearer than when we believed
2 Cor. 1:6 afflicted, it is for your consolation and *s*
  6:2 accepted time; behold, now is the day of *s*
  7:10 for godly sorrow worketh repentance to *s*
Eph. 1:13 the word of truth, the gospel of your *s*
  6:17 the helmet of *s*, and the sword of the Spirit
Phil. 1:19 shall turn to my *s* through your prayer
  2:12 work out your own *s* with fear and trembling
1 Thes. 5:8 and for a helmet, the hope of *s*
  5:9 but to obtain *s* by our Lord Jesus Christ
2 Thes. 2:13 chosen you to *s* through sanctification
2 Tim. 2:10 they may also obtain the *s* which is in
  3:15 able to make thee wise unto *s* through faith
Tit. 2:11 grace of God that bringeth *s* hath appeared
Heb. 1:14 minister for them who shall be heirs of *s*?
  2:3 how shall we escape, if we neglect so great *s*
  2:10 make the captain of their *s* perfect through
  5:9 author of eternal *s* unto all them that obey
  6:9 better things of you . . things that accompany *s*

Heb. 9:28 appear the second time without sin unto *s*
1 Pet. 1:5 by the power of God through faith unto *s*
1:9 end of your faith, even the *s* of your souls
1:10 of which *s* the prophets have inquired
2 Pet. 3:15 that the long-suffering of our Lord is *s*
Jude 3 diligence to write unto you of the common *s*
Rev. 7:10 saying, *S* to our God which sitteth upon
12:10 now is come *s*. . strength, and the kingdom
19:1 alleluia; *S*, and glory, and honor, and power

Samaria

1 Kgs. 16:24 bought the hill *S*. . built on the hill
20:1 (2 Kgs. 6:24) went up and besieged *S*
2 Kgs. 6:25 and there was a great famine in *S*
17:6 king of Assyria took *S*, and carried
Is. 7:9 head of Ephraim is *S*, and the head of *S* is
10:11 I have done unto *S* and her idols, so do to
Ezek. 16:46 thine elder sister is *S*, she and her
Hos. 13:16 *S* shall become desolate; for she hath
Mic. 1:1 which he saw concerning *S* and Jerusalem
Jn. 4:4 and he must needs go through *S*
Acts 1:8 in Jerusalem, and in all Judea, and in *S*
8:5 Philip went down to. .*S*, and preached Christ

Samaritan

Mt. 10:5 and into any city of the *S* enter ye not
Lk. 9:52 entered into a village of the *S*, to make
10:33 but a certain *S*, as he journeyed, came
17:16 at his feet, giving him thanks. . he was a *S*
Jn. 4:9 for the Jews have no dealings with the *S*
4:39 many of the *S* of that city believed on him
8:48 that thou art a *S*, and hast a devil?

Same

Ps. 102:27 (Heb. 1:12) thou art the *s*, and thy years
Mt. 5:46 have ye? do not even the publicans the *s*?
Acts 1:11 this *s* Jesus, which is taken up from you
Rom. 2:1 for thou that judgest doest the *s* things
10:12 for the *s* Lord over all is rich unto all
12:16 be of the *s* mind one toward another
1 Cor. 10:3 and did all eat the *s* spiritual meat
12:4 are diversities of gifts, but the *s* Spirit
15:39 all flesh is not the *s* flesh: but there is
Eph. 3:6 should be fellow heirs, and of the *s* body
Heb. 13:8 Jesus Christ the *s* yesterday, and today

Samson Judg. 13:24–16:31

Heb. 11:32 tell of Gideon, and of Barak, and of *S*

Samuel

Born, 1 Sam. 1:19–20; dedicated to God, 1 Sam. 1:
21–28; ministered before God, 1 Sam. 2:11, 18–21;
called, 1 Sam. 3:1–18; judged Israel, 1 Sam. 7:3–17;
warned Israel for requesting a king, 1 Sam. 8:10–18;
anointed Saul king, 1 Sam. 10:1–8; reasoned with
Israel, 1 Sam. 12; reproved Saul, 1 Sam. 13:8–15;
15:10–23; hewed Agag in pieces, 1 Sam. 15:33;
anointed David, 1 Sam. 16:1–13; died, 25:1; 28:3.

Ps. 99:6 and *S* among them that call upon his name
Jer. 15:1 though Moses and *S* stood before me, yet
Acts 3:24 prophets from *S* and those that follow
13:20 four hundred and fifty years, until *S* the

Sanballat Neh. 2:10–6:14

Sanctification See also Consecration, Holiness, Righteousness

1 Cor. 1:30 unto us wisdom. . and *s*, and redemption
1 Thes. 4:3 this is the will of God, even your *s*
4:4 should know how to possess his vessel in *s*
2 Thes. 2:13 (1 Pet. 1:2) through *s* of the Spirit

Sanctified See also Sanctify

Is. 13:3 I have commanded my *s* ones, I have also
2 Tim. 2:21 *s*, and meet for the master's use

Sanctify See also Consecrate, Hallow, Purify, Separate

Gen. 2:3 and God blessed the seventh day, and *s* it
Ex. 13:2 *s* unto me all the firstborn, whatsoever
19:10 go unto the people, and *s* them today
28:41 and *s* them, that they may minister unto me
29:37 make an atonement for the altar, and *s* it
29:43 and the tabernacle shall be *s* by my glory
31:13 know that I am the LORD that doth *s* you
Lev. 8:10 tabernacle and all. . therein, and *s* them
10:3 I will be *s* in them that come nigh me
11:44 (20:7) *s* yourselves, and ye shall be holy
21:8 *s* him. . for I the LORD, which *s* you, am holy
27:14 when a man shall *s* his house to be holy
27:22 if a man *s* unto the LORD a field which he
Num. 8:17 all the firstborn. . I *s* them for myself
11:18 *s* yourselves against tomorrow, and ye
20:13 strove with the LORD, and he was *s* in them
Deut. 5:12 keep the sabbath day to *s* it, as the
15:19 firstling males. . thou shalt *s* unto the LORD
32:51 because ye *s* me not in the midst of. . Israel
Josh. 3:5 *s* yourselves: for tomorrow the LORD will
7:13 *s* the people, and say, *S* yourselves against
1 Chr. 15:14 priests and the Levites *s* themselves
2 Chr. 7:16 for now have I chosen and *s* this house
29:15 gathered their brethren, and *s* themselves
29:17 they *s* the house of the LORD in eight days
29:34 Levites were more upright in heart to *s*
30:3 the priests had not *s* themselves sufficiently
31:18 in their set office they *s* themselves
35:6 so kill the passover, and *s* yourselves
Neh. 3:1 they builded the sheep gate; they *s* it
13:22 and keep the gates, to *s* the sabbath day
Job 1:5 that Job sent and *s* them, and rose up early
Is. 5:16 God that is holy shall be *s* in righteousness
8:13 *s* the LORD of hosts himself; and let him be
29:23 they shall *s* my name, and *s* the Holy One
66:17 that *s* themselves, and purify themselves
Jer. 1:5 thou camest forth out of the womb I *s* thee
Ezek. 20:12 know that I am the LORD that *s* them
20:41 and I will be *s* in you before the heathen
36:23 I will *s* my great name, which was profaned
37:28 heathen shall know. . I the LORD do *s* Israel
38:16 know me, when I shall be *s* in thee, O Gog
38:23 thus will I magnify myself, and *s* myself
Joel 1:14 (2:15) *s* ye a fast, call a solemn assembly
Mt. 23:17 the gold, or the temple that *s* the gold?
Jn. 10:36 say ye of him, whom the Father hath *s*
17:17 *s* them through thy truth: thy word is truth
17:19 I *s* myself, that they also might be *s*
Acts 20:32 inheritance among all them which are *s*
26:18 them which are *s* by faith that is in me
Rom. 15:16 acceptable, being *s* by the Holy Ghost
1 Cor. 1:2 to them that are *s* in Christ Jesus
6:11 but ye are washed, but ye are *s*, but ye are
7:14 the unbelieving husband is *s* by the wife
Eph. 5:26 might *s* and cleanse it with the washing
1 Thes. 5:23 the very God of peace *s* you wholly
1 Tim. 4:5 it is *s* by the word of God and prayer
Heb. 2:11 that *s* and they who are *s* are all of one
9:13 if the blood. .*s* to the purifying of the flesh
10:10 *s* through the offering of the body of Jesus
10:14 he hath perfected for ever them that are *s*
10:29 blood of the covenant, wherewith he was *s*
13:12 he might *s* the people with his own blood
1 Pet. 3:15 *s* the Lord God in your hearts
Jude 1 to them that are *s* by God the Father

Sanctuary *See also* Church, Tabernacle, Temple

Ex. 15:17 in the *s*, O LORD, which thy hands have
  25:8 let them make me a *s*; that I may dwell among
  36:1 all manner of work for the service of the *s*
Lev. 12:4 nor come into the *s*, until the days of
  16:33 he shall make an atonement for the holy *s*
  19:30 (26:2) keep my sabbaths, and reverence my *s*
  20:3 given of his seed unto Molech, to defile my *s*
  21:12 shall he go out of the *s*, nor profane the *s*
Num. 8:19 children of Israel come nigh unto the *s*
  19:20 be cut off. . because he hath defiled the *s*
1 Chr. 22:19 build ye the *s* of the LORD God
  28:10 hath chosen thee to build a house for the *s*
2 Chr. 20:8 built thee a *s* therein for thy name
  26:18 go out of the *s*; for thou hast trespassed
  30:8 enter into his *s*, which he hath sanctified
Ps. 63:2 glory, so as I have seen thee in the *s*
  73:17 I went into the *s* of God; then understood I
  74:3 that the enemy hath done wickedly in the *s*
  77:13 thy way, O God, is in the *s*: who is so great
  78:69 and he built his *s* like high places
  96:6 before him: strength and beauty are in his *s*
  102:19 hath looked down from the height of his *s*
  114:2 Judah was his *s*, and Israel his dominion
  134:2 lift up your hands in the *s*, and bless the
  150:1 praise ye the LORD. Praise God in his *s*
Is. 8:14 he shall be for a *s*; but for a stone of
  16:12 shall come to his *s* to pray; but he shall
  60:13 to beautify the place of my *s*; and I will
  63:18 our adversaries have trodden down thy *s*
Jer. 17:12 glorious high throne. . the place of our *s*
  51:51 strangers are come into the *s* of the LORD's
Lam. 1:10 seen that the heathen entered into her *s*
  2:7 cast off his altar, he hath abhorred his *s*
Ezek. 5:11 because thou hast defiled my *s* with all
  8:6 I should go far off from my *s*? but turn thee
  11:16 yet will I be to them as a little *s* in the
  23:38 they have defiled my *s* in the same day
  24:21 I will profane my *s*, the excellency of your
  37:26 set my *s* in the midst of them for evermore
  44:7 in that ye have brought into my *s* strangers
  44:9 uncircumcised in flesh, shall enter into my *s*
  44:16 they shall enter into my *s*, and they shall
  45:3 it shall be the *s* and the most holy place
  45:18 bullock without blemish, and cleanse the *s*
  48:8 and the *s* shall be in the midst of it
Dan. 8:14 hundred days; then shall the *s* be cleansed
  9:17 face to shine upon thy *s* that is desolate
  9:26 shall come shall destroy the city and the *s*
  11:31 they shall pollute the *s* of strength
Zeph. 3:4 her priests have polluted the *s*, they have
Heb. 8:2 a minister of the *s*. . of the true tabernacle
  9:1 ordinances of divine service, and a worldly *s*
  13:11 beasts, whose blood is brought into the *s*

Sand

Gen. 22:17 (Heb. 11:12) multiply thy seed. . as the *s*
Ex. 2:12 slew the Egyptian, and hid him in the *s*
Job 6:3 it would be heavier than the *s* of the sea
Ps. 139:18 they are more in number than the *s*
Prov. 27:3 stone is heavy, and the *s* weighty
Is. 10:22 (Rom. 9:27) as the *s* of the sea. . a remnant
  48:19 thy seed also had been as the *s*
Hos. 1:10 Israel shall be as the *s* of the sea
Mt. 7:26 foolish man. . built his house upon the *s*
Rev. 20:8 number of whom is as the *s* of the sea

Sandal

Mk. 6:9 be shod with *s*; and not put on two coats
Acts 12:8 unto him, Gird thyself, and bind on thy *s*

Sang *See* Sing

Sank *See* Sink

Sapphira Acts 5:1

Sapphire

Ex. 24:10 as it were a paved work of a *s* stone
Is. 54:11 behold, I will. . lay thy foundations with *s*
Ezek. 1:26 throne, as the appearance of a *s* stone
Rev. 21:19 first foundation was jasper. . second, *s*

Sarah (Sarai)

Wife of Abraham, Gen. 11:29; barren, Gen. 11:30; Sarai and Hagar, Gen. 16:1–6; represented as Abraham's sister, Gen. 12:10–20; 20:1–18; name changed to Sarah, Gen. 17:15; laughed at the LORD's promise, Gen. 18:9–15; bare Isaac, Gen. 21:1–8; jealous of Ishmael, Gen. 21:9–11; died at Hebron, Gen. 23:2; buried in Machpelah, Gen. 23:19.

Rom. 4:19 neither yet the deadness of *S*'s womb
  9:9 this time will I come, and *S* shall have a son
Heb. 11:11 through faith also *S* herself received
1 Pet. 3:6 as *S* obeyed Abraham, calling him lord

Sardis Rev. 3:1–6

Sarepta *See* Zarephath

Sargon king of Assyria Is. 20:1

Sat *See* Sit

Satan *See also* Beelzebub, Devil

1 Chr. 21:1 *S* stood up against Israel, and provoked
Job 1:6 (2:1) came. . before the LORD, and *S* came
Ps. 109:6 over him: and let *S* stand at his right hand
Zech. 3:1 standing at his right hand to resist
Mt. 4:10 (Lk. 4:8) get thee hence, *S*: for it is written
  12:26 (Mk. 3:23; Lk. 11:18) if *S* cast out *S*, he is
  16:23 (Mk. 8:33) unto Peter, Get thee behind me, *S*
Mk. 1:13 in the wilderness forty days tempted of *S*
  4:15 *S* cometh immediately, and taketh away the
Lk. 10:18 I beheld *S* as lightning fall from heaven
  13:16 ought not this woman. . whom *S* hath bound
  22:3 then entered *S* into Judas surnamed Iscariot
  22:31 Simon, behold, *S* hath desired to have you
Acts 5:3 why hath *S* filled thine heart to lie to
  26:18 to light, and from the power of *S* unto God
Rom. 16:20 God of peace shall bruise *S* under your
1 Cor. 5:5 to deliver such a one unto *S* for the
  7:5 that *S* tempt you not for your incontinency
2 Cor. 2:11 lest *S* should get an advantage of us
  11:14 for *S* himself is transformed into an angel
  12:7 a thorn in the flesh, the messenger of *S* to
1 Thes. 2:18 would have come. . but *S* hindered us
2 Thes. 2:9 whose coming is after the working of *S*
1 Tim. 1:20 whom I have delivered unto *S*, that they
  5:15 for some are already turned aside after *S*
Rev. 2:9 are not, but are the synagogue of *S*
  2:13 where thou dwellest, even where *S*'s seat is
  2:24 and which have not known the depths of *S*
  3:9 I will make them of the synagogue of *S*
  12:9 that old serpent, called the Devil, and *S*
  20:2 which is the Devil, and *S*, and bound him a
  20:7 thousand years are expired, *S* shall be loosed

Satiate

Jer. 31:14 *s* the soul of the priests with fatness
  31:25 for I have *s* the weary soul, and I have
  46:10 shall be *s* and made drunk with their blood

Satisfaction

Num. 35:31 take no *s* for the life of a murderer

Satisfy *See also* Content

Lev. 26:26 your bread. . ye shall eat, and not be *s*
Deut. 14:29 shall come, and shall eat and be *s*
Job 27:14 his offspring shall not be *s* with bread
   38:27 to *s* the desolate and waste ground
Ps. 17:15 shall be *s*, when I awake, with thy likeness
   22:26 the meek shall eat and be *s*: they shall
   36:8 abundantly *s* with the fatness of thy house
   37:19 and in the days of famine they shall be *s*
   63:5 my soul shall be *s* as with marrow and fatness
   65:4 we shall be *s* with the goodness of thy house
   81:16 honey out of the rock should I have *s* thee
   90:14 O *s* us early with thy mercy; that we may
   91:16 with long life will I *s* him, and show him
   103:5 who *s* thy mouth with good things
   104:13 the earth is *s* with the fruit of thy works
   105:40 and *s* them with the bread of heaven
   107:9 for he *s* the longing soul, and filleth the
   132:15 provision: I will *s* her poor with bread
   145:16 and *s* the desire of every living thing
Prov. 5:19 let her breasts *s* thee at all times
   12:11 that tilleth his land shall be *s* with bread
   13:25 the righteous eateth to the *s* of his soul
   14:14 and a good man shall be *s* from himself
   18:20 shall be *s* with the fruit of his mouth
   19:23 he that hath it shall abide *s*; he shall not
   20:13 open thine eyes. . thou shalt be *s* with bread
   27:20 never full; so the eyes of man are never *s*
   30:15 there are three things that are never *s*
Eccl. 1:8 eye is not *s* with seeing, nor the ear
   4:8 neither is his eye *s* with riches
   5:10 loveth silver shall not be *s* with silver
Is. 9:20 eat on the left hand. . they shall not be *s*
   53:11 of the travail of his soul, and shall be *s*
   55:2 bread? and your labor for that which *s* not?
   58:11 *s* thy soul in drought, and make fat thy bones
Jer. 31:14 my people shall be *s* with my goodness
   50:19 and his soul shall be *s* upon mount Ephraim
Ezek. 7:19 they shall not *s* their souls, neither
   16:28 harlot with them, and yet couldest not be *s*
Joel 2:19 corn, and wine, and oil, and ye shall be *s*
Amos 4:8 to drink water; but they were not *s*
Mic. 6:14 thou shalt eat, but not be *s*; and thy
Mk. 8:4 *s* these men with bread. . in the wilderness?
Col. 2:23 not in any honor to the *s* of the flesh

Satyr

Is. 13:21 shall dwell there, and *s* shall dance there
   34:14 *s* shall cry to his fellow; the screech owl

Saul *See* Paul

Saul king of Israel

Son of Kish, 1 Sam. 9:1–2; met Samuel, 1 Sam. 9:5–24; anointed by Samuel, 1 Sam. 10:1–8; prophesied with the prophets, 1 Sam. 10:9–13; chosen king at Mizpeh, 1 Sam. 10:17–24; defeated the Ammonites, 1 Sam. 11:5–11; made king in Gilgal, 1 Sam. 11:12–15; reproved for his burnt offering, 1 Sam. 13:8–15; built an altar, 1 Sam. 14:35; rejected as king, 1 Sam. 15:11–30; refreshed by David's harp playing, 1 Sam. 16:14–23; became jealous of David, 1 Sam. 18:6–30; sought to kill David, 1 Sam. 19:1–17; killed the priests of Nob, 1 Sam. 22:11–19; spared by David, 1 Sam. 24:1–7; 26:1–12; consulted the woman of Endor, 1 Sam. 28:3–25; died and buried, 1 Sam. 31.

2 Sam. 3:1 the house of *S* waxed weaker and weaker
Acts 13:21 desired a king: and God gave them *S*

Save *See also* Deliver, Redeem, Rescue

Gen. 45:7 to *s* your lives by a great deliverance
   50:20 God meant. . good. . to *s* much people alive
Ex. 1:17 but the midwives. . *s* the men children alive
   14:30 the LORD *s* Israel that day out of the hand
Deut. 20:4 to fight. . against your enemies, to *s* you
   28:29 spoiled evermore, and no man shall *s* thee
Judg. 6:15 O my Lord, wherewith shall I *s* Israel?
   7:2 vaunt themselves. . Mine own hand hath *s* me
   7:7 three hundred men that lapped will I *s* you
1 Sam. 4:3 fetch the ark. . among us, it may *s* us
   10:19 rejected your God, who himself *s* you out
   10:24 people shouted, and said, God *s* the king
   10:27 how shall this man *s* us? And they despised
   14:6 no restraint to the LORD to *s* by many or by
   14:23 the LORD *s* Israel that day: and the battle
   17:47 that the LORD *s* not with sword and spear
2 Sam. 16:16 unto Absalom, God *s* the king, God *s*
   22:4 (Ps. 18:3) so shall I be *s* from mine enemies
   22:28 (Ps. 18:27) afflicted people thou wilt *s*
   22:42 (Ps. 18:41) looked, but there was none to *s*
2 Kgs. 11:12 (2 Chr. 23:11) and said, God *s* the king
   19:19 (Is. 37:20) *s* thou us out of his hand, that
   19:34 (Is. 37:35) I will defend this city, to *s* it
1 Chr. 11:14 the LORD *s* them by a great deliverance
   16:35 (Ps. 106:47) *S* us, O God of our salvation
2 Chr. 32:22 the LORD *s* Hezekiah and. . Jerusalem
Job 2:6 behold, he is in thine hand; but *s* his life
   5:15 he *s* the poor from the sword, from their
   22:29 is lifting up; and he shall *s* the humble
   40:14 that thine own right hand can *s* thee
Ps. 3:7 arise, O LORD; *s* me, O my God: for thou hast
   6:4 deliver my soul. . *s* me for thy mercies' sake
   7:1 *s* me from all them that persecute me
   7:10 my defense is of God, which *s* the upright
   17:7 O thou that *s* by thy right hand them which
   20:6 now know I that the LORD *s* his anointed
   28:9 *s* thy people, and bless thine inheritance
   33:16 is no king *s* by the multitude of a host
   34:6 and the LORD. . *s* him out of all his troubles
   34:18 the LORD. . *s* such as be of a contrite spirit
   44:3 neither did their own arm *s* them: but thy
   44:7 but thou hast *s* us from our enemies
   54:1 *s* me, O God, by thy name, and judge me by
   55:16 I will call upon God. . the LORD shall *s* me
   59:2 workers of iniquity, and *s* me from bloody
   69:1 *s* me, O God; for the waters are come in
   69:35 God will *s* Zion, and will build the cities
   72:4 he shall *s* the children of the needy
   76:9 God arose to judgment, to *s* all the meek
   80:3 (80:7, 19) thy face to shine; and we shall be *s*
   86:2 my God, *s* thy servant that trusteth in thee
   106:8 nevertheless he *s* them for his name's sake
   107:13 and he *s* them out of their distresses
   109:26 my God: O *s* me according to thy mercy
   109:31 to *s* him from those that condemn his soul
   119:94 I am thine, *s* me; for I have sought thy
   138:7 wilt revive me. . thy right hand shall *s* me
   145:19 also will hear their cry, and will *s* them
Prov. 20:22 wait on the LORD, and he shall *s* thee
   28:18 whoso walketh uprightly shall be *s*
Is. 25:9 we have waited for him, and he will *s* us
   30:15 in returning and rest shall ye be *s*
   33:22 the LORD is our King; he will *s* us
   35:4 God with a recompense; he will. . *s* you
   45:17 but Israel shall be *s* in the LORD with an
   45:22 look unto me, and be ye *s*, all the ends
   46:7 he not answer, nor *s* him out of his trouble
   47:15 every one to his quarter; none shall *s* thee
   49:25 contend with him. . and I will *s* thy children
   59:1 LORD's hand is not shortened, that it cannot *s*
   63:1 I that speak in righteousness, mighty to *s*

Is. 63:9 afflicted. . the angel of his presence *s* them
64:5 in those is continuance, and we shall be *s*
Jer. 2:28 if they can *s* thee in the time of thy trouble
4:14 heart from wickedness, that thou mayest be *s*
8:20 past, the summer is ended, and we are not *s*
11:12 but they shall not *s* them at all in the time
14:9 astonished, as a mighty man that cannot *s*?
15:20 am with thee to *s* thee and to deliver thee
17:14 I shall be healed; *s* me, and I shall be *s*
23:6 (33:16) in his days Judah shall be *s*
30:7 time of Jacob's trouble; but he shall be *s*
30:10 (46:27) for, lo, I will *s* thee from afar
31:7 O LORD, *s* thy people, the remnant of Israel
42:11 be not afraid. . for I am with you to *s* you
Lam. 4:17 watched for a nation that could not *s* us
Ezek. 18:27 lawful and right, he shall *s* his soul
34:22 therefore will I *s* my flock, and they shall
36:29 will also *s* you from all your uncleannesses
37:23 but I will *s* them out of all their dwelling
Hos. 1:7 *s* them by. . God. . will not *s* them by bow
13:10 where is any other that may *s* thee in all
14:3 Asshur shall not *s* us; we will not ride upon
Hab. 1:2 how long shall I cry. . and thou wilt not *s*!
Zeph. 3:19 I will *s* her that halteth, and gather
Zech. 8:7 I will *s* my people from the east country
9:16 God shall *s* them in that day as the flock
Mt. 1:21 for he shall *s* his people from their sins
8:25 and awoke him, saying, Lord, *s* us: we perish
10:22 (24:13; Mk. 13:13) endureth. . end shall be *s*
14:30 beginning to sink, he cried. . Lord, *s* me
16:25 (Mk. 8:35; Lk. 9:24) *s* his life shall lose it
18:11 (Lk. 19:10) come to *s* that which was lost
19:25 (Mk. 10:26; Lk. 18:26) who then can be *s*?
24:22 (Mk. 13:20) there should no flesh be *s*
27:40 (Mk. 15:30) *s* thyself. . come down from the
27:42 (Mk. 15:31; Lk. 23:35) he *s* others; himself
Mk. 3:4 (Lk. 6:9) do evil? to *s* life, or to kill?
16:16 that believeth and is baptized shall be *s*
Lk. 7:50 woman, Thy faith hath *s* thee; go in peace
8:12 lest they should believe and be *s*
9:56 not come to destroy men's lives, but to *s*
13:23 Lord, are there few that be *s*? And he said
17:33 whosoever shall seek to *s* his life shall
18:42 receive thy sight: thy faith hath *s* thee
Jn. 3:17 but that the world through him might be *s*
5:34 but these things I say, that ye might be *s*
10:9 by me if any man enter in, he shall be *s*
12:27 Father, *s* me from this hour: but for this
12:47 not to judge the world, but to *s* the world
Acts 2:21 (Rom. 10:13) call on the name. . shall be *s*
2:40 *s* yourselves from this untoward generation
2:47 added to the church daily such as should be *s*
4:12 is none other name. . whereby we must be *s*
15:1 except ye be circumcised. . ye cannot be *s*
15:11 we believe that. . we shall be *s*, even as they
16:30 and said, Sirs, what must I do to be *s*?
16:31 believe on the Lord Jesus. . thou shalt be *s*
27:43 centurion, willing to *s* Paul, kept them
Rom. 5:9 we shall be *s* from wrath through him
5:10 being reconciled, we shall be *s* by his life
8:24 we are *s* by hope: but hope that is seen is
9:27 Israel be as the sand. . a remnant shall be *s*
10:1 prayer. . for Israel is, that they might be *s*
10:9 believe in thine heart. . thou shalt be *s*
11:14 provoke to emulation. . and might *s* some
11:26 so all Israel shall be *s*: as it is written
1 Cor. 1:18 unto us which are *s*, it is the power
1:21 by the foolishness of preaching to *s* them
3:15 shall suffer loss: but he himself shall be *s*
5:5 spirit may be *s* in the day of the Lord Jesus
7:16 shalt *s* thy husband? or. . shalt *s* thy wife?
9:22 to all men, that I might by all means *s* some
10:33 but the profit of many, that they may be *s*

1 Cor. 15:2 by which. . ye are *s*, if ye keep in memory
2 Cor. 2:15 in them that are *s*, and in them that perish
Eph. 2:8 by grace are ye *s* through faith; and that
1 Thes. 2:16 to the Gentiles that they might be *s*
2 Thes. 2:10 love of the truth, that they might be *s*
1 Tim. 1:15 Jesus came into the world to *s* sinners
2:4 who will have all men to be *s*, and to come
2:15 shall be *s* in childbearing, if they continue
4:16 shalt both *s* thyself, and them that hear thee
2 Tim. 1:9 who hath *s* us, and called us with a holy
Tit. 3:5 but according to his mercy he *s* us
Heb. 5:7 unto him that was able to *s* him from death
7:25 he is able also to *s* them to the uttermost
11:7 prepared an ark to the *s* of his house
Jas. 1:21 word, which is able to *s* your souls
2:14 faith, and have not works? can faith *s* him?
4:12 lawgiver, who is able to *s* and to destroy
5:15 and the prayer of faith shall *s* the sick
5:20 shall *s* a soul from death, and shall hide a
1 Pet. 3:20 that is, eight souls were *s* by water
4:18 if the righteous scarcely be *s*, where shall
2 Pet. 2:5 spared not the old world, but *s* Noah
Jude 5 how that the Lord, having *s* the people out
23 others *s* with fear, pulling them out of the
Rev. 21:24 which are *s* shall walk in the light of

Saviour *See also* Deliverer, Redeemer

2 Sam. 22:3 my high tower, and my refuge, my *s*
2 Kgs. 13:5 the LORD gave Israel a *s*, so that they
Neh. 9:27 thy manifold mercies thou gavest them *s*
Ps. 106:21 they forgat God their *s*, which had done
Is. 19:20 he shall send them a *s*, and a great one
43:3 Holy One of Israel, thy *S*: I gave Egypt for
43:11 am the LORD; and beside me there is no *s*
45:21 just God and a *S*; there is none beside me
49:26 that I the LORD am thy *S* and thy Redeemer
60:16 thou shalt know that I the LORD am thy *S*
63:8 surely they are my people. . so he was their *S*
Jer. 14:8 O the hope of Israel, the *S* thereof in
Hos. 13:4 no god but me. . there is no *s* beside me
Obad. 21 *s* shall come up on mount Zion to judge
Lk. 1:47 and my spirit hath rejoiced in God my *S*
2:11 is born this day in the city of David a *S*
Jn. 4:42 is indeed the Christ, the *S* of the world
Acts 5:31 hath God exalted. . to be a Prince and a *S*
13:23 his promise, raised unto Israel a *S*, Jesus
Eph. 5:23 the church: and he is the *s* of the body
Phil. 3:20 whence also we look for the *S*, the Lord
1 Tim. 4:10 who is the *S* of all men, specially of
2 Tim. 1:10 made manifest by the appearing of our *S*
Tit. 2:13 appearing of the great God and our *S*
3:4 and love of God our *S* toward man appeared
2 Pet. 1:1 righteousness of God and our *S* Jesus
1 Jn. 4:14 sent the Son to be the *S* of the world
Jude 25 to the only wise God our *S*, be glory and

Savor

Gen. 8:21 the LORD smelled a sweet *s*
Ex. 5:21 *s* to be abhorred in the eyes of Pharaoh
Lev. 1:9 made by fire, of a sweet *s* unto the LORD
Eccl. 10:1 ointment. . to send forth a stinking *s*
Song 1:3 because of the *s* of thy good ointments
Ezek. 20:41 I will accept you with your sweet *s*
Joel 2:20 his ill *s* shall come up, because he hath
Mt. 5:13 (Lk. 14:34) but if the salt have lost his *s*
16:23 (Mk. 8:33) thou *s* not the things. . of God
2 Cor. 2:14 makest manifest the *s* of his knowledge
2:15 for we are unto God a sweet *s* of Christ
2:16 *s* of death unto death. . *s* of life unto life
Eph. 5:2 a sacrifice to God for a sweetsmelling *s*

Savory

Gen. 27:4 make me *s* meat, such as I love, and bring

Saw *See* See

Saw (Sawn)

1 Kgs. 7:9 stones, sawed with *s*, within and without
Heb. 11:37 they were stoned, they were *s* asunder

Say *See also* Speak

Ex. 3:13 *s* to me, What is his name? what shall I *s*
1 Kgs. 22:14 (2 Chr. 18:13) what the LORD *s*. . I speak
Mt. 16:13 (Mk. 8:27; Lk. 9:18) whom do men *s* that I
23:3 but do not ye after. . for they *s*, and do not
Jn. 16:12 things to *s* unto you, but ye cannot bear

Saying

Gen. 37:11 envied. . but his father observed the *s*
Ps. 49:4 I will open my dark *s* upon the harp
78:2 in a parable: I will utter dark *s* of old
Prov. 1:6 the words of the wise, and their dark *s*
Jon. 4:2 LORD, was not this my *s*, when I was yet
Mt. 19:11 all men cannot receive this *s*, save they
28:15 this *s* is commonly reported among the Jews
Mk. 7:29 for this *s* go thy way; the devil is gone
9:32 (Lk. 9:45) but they understood not that *s*
Lk. 2:50 they understood not the *s* which he spake
2:51 his mother kept all these *s* in her heart
9:44 let these *s* sink down into your ears
Jn. 6:60 said, This is a hard *s*; who can hear it?
8:51 (8:52) keep my *s*, he shall never see death
14:24 he that loveth me not keepeth not my *s*
15:20 if they have kept my *s*, they will keep
21:23 then went this *s* abroad among the brethren
1 Cor. 15:54 then shall be brought to pass the *s*
1 Tim. 1:15 (4:9; Tit. 3:8) this is a faithful *s*
Rev. 22:6 unto me, These *s* are faithful and true
22:7 blessed is he that keepeth the *s* of the

Scale

Lev. 11:9 (Deut. 14:9) whatsoever hath fins and *s*
Job 41:15 his *s* are his pride, shut up together as
Prov. 21:22 a wise man *s* the city of the mighty
Is. 40:12 and weighed the mountains in *s*
Ezek. 29:4 fish of thy rivers to stick unto thy *s*
Acts 9:18 there fell from his eyes as it had been *s*

Scant

Mic. 6:10 and the *s* measure that is abominable?

Scapegoat *See also* Goat, Kid, Sheep

Lev. 16:8 one lot for the LORD. . other lot for the *s*

Scarcely

Rom. 5:7 for *s* for a righteous man will one die
1 Pet. 4:18 if the righteous *s* be saved, where

Scare

Job 7:14 thou *s* me with dreams, and terrifiest me

Scarlet *See also* Purple

Gen. 38:28 midwife. . bound upon his hand a *s* thread
Josh. 2:18 bind this line of *s* thread in the window
2 Sam. 1:24 weep over Saul, who clothed you in *s*
Song 4:3 thy lips are like a thread of *s*
Is. 1:18 though your sins be as *s*, they shall be
Dan. 5:29 they clothed Daniel with *s*, and put
Mt. 27:28 stripped him, and put on him a *s* robe
Rev. 17:3 I saw a woman sit upon a *s*-colored beast

Scatter *See also* Disperse

Gen. 11:4 and let us make us a name, lest we be *s*
11:9 from thence did the LORD *s* them abroad upon
49:7 divide them in Jacob, and *s* them in Israel
Lev. 26:33 I will *s* you among the heathen, and will
Num. 10:35 rise up, LORD. . let thine enemies be *s*

Neh. 1:8 if ye transgress, I will *s* you abroad
Job 18:15 brimstone shall be *s* upon his habitation
37:11 the thick cloud: he *s* his bright cloud
38:24 which *s* the east wind upon the earth?
Ps. 60:1 God, thou hast cast us off, thou hast *s* us
68:1 let God arise, let his enemies be *s*
68:30 *s* thou the people that delight in war
92:9 all the workers of iniquity shall be *s*
147:16 like wool: he *s* the hoar frost like ashes
Prov. 11:24 there is that *s*, and yet increaseth
20:8 in the throne of judgment *s* away all evil
20:26 a wise king *s* the wicked, and bringeth
Is. 41:16 whirlwind shall *s* them: and thou shalt
Jer. 9:16 I will *s* them also among the heathen
10:21 not prosper. . all their flocks shall be *s*
13:24 therefore will I *s* them as the stubble
23:1 the pastors that destroy and *s* the sheep
49:32 I will *s* into all winds them that are in
Ezek. 11:16 I have *s* them among the countries, yet
12:15 when I shall *s* them among the nations
34:6 flock was *s* upon all the face of the earth
Dan. 12:7 to *s* the power of the holy people
Zech. 7:14 I *s* them with a whirlwind among all the
13:7 (Mt. 26:31; Mk. 14:27) the sheep shall be *s*
Mt. 9:36 were *s* abroad, as sheep having no shepherd
12:30 (Lk. 11:23) he that gathereth not with me *s*
Jn. 10:12 the wolf catcheth them, and *s* the sheep
16:32 that ye shall be *s*, every man to his own
Acts 5:36 and all, as many as obeyed him, were *s*
8:1 a great persecution. . they were all *s* abroad
8:4 that were *s* abroad went every where preaching

Scattered *See also* Scatter, Dispersed

1 Kgs. 22:17 (2 Chr. 18:16) I saw all Israel *s* upon
Jer. 50:17 Israel is a *s* sheep; the lions have
Jas. 1:1 to the twelve tribes which are *s* abroad
1 Pet. 1:1 to the strangers *s* throughout Pontus

Scent

Job 14:9 yet through the *s* of water it will bud
Jer. 48:11 taste remained. . and his *s* is not changed
Hos. 14:7 thereof shall be as the wine of Lebanon

Sceptre

Gen. 49:10 the *s* shall not depart from Judah
Num. 24:17 a *S* shall rise out of Israel, and shall
Esth. 5:2 the king held out to Esther the golden *s*
Ps. 45:6 (Heb. 1:8) the *s* of thy kingdom is a right *s*
Is. 14:5 the LORD hath broken. . the *s* of the rulers

Sceva Acts 19:14

Schism

1 Cor. 12:25 that there should be no *s* in the body

Scholar

1 Chr. 25:8 they cast lots. . the teacher as the *s*
Mal. 2:12 that doeth this, the master and the *s*

School

Acts 19:9 disputing daily in the *s* of one Tyrannus

Schoolmaster

Gal. 3:24 the law was our *s* to bring us unto Christ
3:25 faith is come, we are no longer under a *s*

Science

Dan. 1:4 cunning in knowledge, and understanding *s*
1 Tim. 6:20 and oppositions of *s* falsely so called

Scoff

Hab. 1:10 they shall *s* at the kings, and the princes

Scoffer

2 Pet. 3:3 there shall come in the last days *s*

Scorch

Mt. 13:6 (Mk. 4:6) when the sun was up, they were *s*
Rev. 16:8 and power was given unto him to *s* men

Scorn *See also* Contempt, Derision, Laugh, Reproach

2 Kgs. 19:21 (Is. 37:22) despised. . laughed thee to *s*
Esth. 3:6 thought *s* to lay hands on Mordecai alone
Job 16:20 my friends *s* me: but mine eye poureth
Ps. 22:7 all they that see me laugh me to *s*
   44:13 a *s* and a derision to them that are round
Prov. 3:34 surely he *s* the scorners: but he giveth
Hab. 1:10 and the princes shall be a *s* unto them

Scorner

Prov. 1:22 *s* delight in their scorning, and fools
   3:34 he scorneth the *s*: but he giveth grace unto
   9:7 that reproveth a *s* getteth to himself shame
   9:8 reprove not a *s*, lest he hate thee: rebuke a
   13:1 instruction: but a *s* heareth not rebuke
   14:6 a *s* seeketh wisdom, and findeth it not
   15:12 a *s* loveth not one that reproveth him
   19:25 smite a *s*, and the simple will beware
   21:24 proud and haughty *s* is his name, who dealeth
   24:9 is sin: and the *s* is an abomination to men
Is. 29:20 brought to nought, and the *s* is consumed
Hos. 7:5 he stretched out his hand with *s*

Scornful

Ps. 1:1 sinners, nor sitteth in the seat of the *s*
Prov. 29:8 *s* men bring a city into a snare
Is. 28:14 hear the word of the LORD, ye *s* men

Scorpion

Deut. 8:15 wherein were fiery serpents, and *s*
1 Kgs. 12:11 (2 Chr. 10:11) will chastise you with *s*
Ezek. 2:6 thou dost dwell among *s*: be not afraid
Lk. 10:19 unto you power to tread on serpents and *s*
   11:12 he shall ask an egg, will he offer him a *s*?
Rev. 9:3 power, as the *s* of the earth have power

Scourge

Lev. 19:20 nor freedom given her; she shall be *s*
Josh. 23:13 *s* in your sides, and thorns in your eyes
Job 5:21 thou shalt be hid from the *s* of the tongue
   9:23 if the *s* slay suddenly, he will laugh at
Is. 10:26 LORD of hosts shall stir up a *s* for him
   28:15 when the overflowing *s* shall pass through
Mt. 10:17 and they will *s* you in their synagogues
   20:19 (Mk. 10:34; Lk. 18:33) to the Gentiles. . to *s*
   23:34 some of them shall ye *s* in your synagogues
   27:26 (Mk. 15:15; Jn. 19:1) when he had *s* Jesus
Jn. 2:15 made a *s* of small cords, he drove them all
Acts 22:25 is it lawful. . to *s* a man that is a Roman
Heb. 12:6 and *s* every son whom he receiveth

Scribe *See also* Lawyer

Ezra 7:6 Ezra. . was a ready *s* in the law of Moses
Is. 33:18 where is the *s*? where is the receiver?
Jer. 8:8 the pen of the *s* is in vain
Mt. 5:20 shall exceed the righteousness of the *s*
   7:29 (Mk. 1:22) having authority, and not as the *s*
   8:19 a certain *s* came, and said. . Master, I will
   13:52 every *s* which is instructed unto the kingdom
   23:2 the *s* and the Pharisees sit in Moses' seat
   23:13 (Lk. 11:44) woe unto you, *s* and Pharisees
Mk. 9:14 disciples. . and the *s* questioning with them
   12:38 (Lk. 20:46) beware of the *s*, which love to

Lk. 6:7 *s* and Pharisees watched him, whether he
   22:2 priests and *s* sought how they might kill him
Acts 23:9 *s* that were of the Pharisees' part arose
1 Cor. 1:20 where is the wise? where is the *s*?

Scrip

1 Sam. 17:40 in a *s*; and his sling was in his hand
Mt. 10:10 (Mk. 6:8; Lk. 9:3) nor *s* for your journey
Lk. 22:36 let him take it, and likewise his *s*

Scripture

Dan. 10:21 show thee that which is noted in the *S*
Mt. 22:29 (Mk. 12:24) ye do err, not knowing the *S*
Lk. 4:21 this day is this *S* fulfilled in your ears
   24:27 expounded unto them in all the *S* the things
   24:32 our heart burn. . while he opened to us the *S*
   24:45 opened. . that they might understand the *S*
Jn. 2:22 he had said this. . and they believed the *S*
   5:39 search the *S*; for in them ye think ye have
   10:35 and the *S* cannot be broken
   20:9 yet they knew not the *S*, that he must rise
Acts 8:35 began at the same *S*, and preached. . Jesus
   17:11 searched the *S* daily, whether those things
   18:24 an eloquent man, and mighty in the *S*
   18:28 showing by the *S* that Jesus was Christ
Rom. 1:2 promised. . by his prophets in the holy *S*
   15:4 we through patience and comfort of the *S*
1 Cor. 15:3 died for our sins according to the *S*
   15:4 rose again the third day according to the *S*
Gal. 3:8 the *S*, foreseeing that God would justify
   3:22 but the *S* hath concluded all under sin
2 Tim. 3:15 from a child thou hast known the holy *S*
   3:16 all *S* is given by inspiration of God
2 Pet. 1:20 no prophecy of the *S* is of any private
   3:16 unstable wrest, as they do also the other *S*

Scroll

Is. 34:4 heavens shall be rolled together as a *s*
Rev. 6:14 heaven departed as a *s* when it is rolled

Scum

Ezek. 24:6 pot whose *s* is therein, and whose *s* is

Scythian Col. 3:11

Sea *See also* Lake

Gen. 1:10 gathering together of the waters called he *S*
Ex. 14:21 the *s* to go back. . and made the *s* dry land
Deut. 30:13 say, Who shall go over the *s* for us
Job 7:12 am I a *s*, or a whale, that thou settest
   28:14 and the *s* saith, It is not with me
   38:8 or who shut up the *s* with doors
Ps. 66:6 he turned the *s* into dry land: they went
   72:8 (Zech. 9:10) have dominion also from *s* to *s*
   77:19 thy way is in the *s*, and thy path in the
   96:11 (98:7) let the *s* roar, and the fulness thereof
   104:25 so is this great and wide *s*, wherein are
   107:23 they that go down to the *s* in ships
   114:3 *s* saw it, and fled: Jordan was driven back
Prov. 8:29 when he gave to the *s* his decree
Eccl. 1:7 run into the *s*; yet the *s* is not full
Is. 11:9 (Hab. 2:14) be full. . as the waters cover the *s*
   50:2 behold, at my rebuke I dry up the *s*
   57:20 but the wicked are like the troubled *s*
Jon. 1:15 took up Jonah, and cast him forth into the *s*
Mt. 8:26 (Mk. 4:39) and rebuked the winds and the *s*
   8:27 (Mk. 4:41) even the winds and the *s* obey him
   13:47 like unto a net, that was cast into the *s*
   14:26 (Mk. 6:49; Jn. 6:19) saw him walking on the *s*
   23:15 compass *s* and land to make one proselyte
1 Cor. 10:1 our fathers. . all passed through the *s*
Rev. 4:6 before the throne there was a *s* of glass
   15:2 I saw as it were a *s* of glass mingled with

Rev. 16:3 second angel poured out his vial upon the *s*
  21:1 were passed away; and there was no more *s*

Seal *See also* Signet

Esth. 8:8 king's name, and *s* with the king's ring
Song 8:6 set me as a *s* upon thine heart, as a *s*
Is. 29:11 unto you as the words of a book that is *s*
Dan. 12:4 shut up the words, and *s* the book
  12:9 for the words are closed up and *s* till
Mt. 27:66 and made the sepulchre sure, *s* the stone
Jn. 3:33 hath set to his *s* that God is true
  6:27 Son of man . . for him hath God the Father *s*
Rom. 4:11 circumcision, a *s* of the righteousness
1 Cor. 9:2 *s* of mine apostleship are ye in the Lord
2 Cor. 1:22 hath also *s* us, and given the earnest
Eph. 1:13 were *s* with that Holy Spirit of promise
  4:30 whereby ye are *s* unto the day of redemption
2 Tim. 2:19 foundation . . standeth sure, having this *s*
Rev. 5:1 a book written . . *s* with seven *s*
  6:1 I saw when the lamb opened one of the *s*
  7:3 till we have *s* the servants of our God
  8:1 opened the seventh *s*, there was silence
  9:4 only those men which have not the *s* of God
  10:4 *s* up those things which the seven thunders
  20:3 set a *s* upon him, that he should deceive
  22:10 *s* not the sayings of the prophecy of this

Seam

Jn. 19:23 now the coat was without *s*, woven from

Search *See also* Inquire, Seek

Gen. 31:34 Laban *s* all the tent, but found them not
Num. 10:33 before them . . to *s* out a resting place
  13:2 send thou men, that they may *s* the land
1 Chr. 28:9 LORD *s* all hearts, and understandeth
Job 8:8 prepare thyself to the *s* of their fathers
  10:6 after mine iniquity, and *s* after my sin?
  13:9 is it good that he should *s* you out?
  28:3 end to darkness, and *s* out all perfection
  28:27 he prepared it, yea, and *s* it out
  29:16 and the cause which I knew not I *s* out
  32:11 I gave ear . . whilst ye *s* out what to say
  36:26 neither can the number of his years be *s*
  38:16 or hast thou walked in the *s* of the depth?
Ps. 44:21 shall not God *s* this out? for he knoweth
  64:6 *s* out iniquities . . accomplish a diligent *s*
  77:6 I commune . . and my spirit made diligent *s*
  139:1 O LORD, thou hast *s* me, and known me
  139:23 *s* me, O God, and know my heart: try me
Prov. 2:4 if thou . . *s* for her as for hid treasures
  20:27 candle . . *s* all the inward parts of the belly
  25:2 but the honor of kings is to *s* out a matter
  25:27 for men to *s* their own glory is not glory
Eccl. 1:13 *s* out by wisdom concerning all things
Jer. 2:34 I have not found it by secret *s*, but upon
  17:10 I the LORD *s* the heart, I try the reins
  29:13 when ye shall *s* for me with all your heart
  31:37 the foundations of the earth *s* out beneath
Lam. 3:40 let us *s* and try our ways, and turn again
Ezek. 34:6 scattered . . none did *s* or seek after them
  34:11 behold, I, even I, will both *s* my sheep
Amos 9:3 I will *s* and take them out thence
Zeph. 1:12 that I will *s* Jerusalem with candles
Mt. 2:8 go and *s* diligently for the young child
Jn. 5:39 *s* the Scriptures; for in them ye think ye
  7:52 *s* . . for out of Galilee ariseth no prophet
Acts 17:11 *s* the Scriptures daily, whether those
Rom. 8:27 he that *s* the hearts knoweth what is the
1 Cor. 2:10 the Spirit *s* all things, yea, the deep
1 Pet. 1:10 prophets have inquired and *s* diligently
Rev. 2:23 I am he which *s* the reins and hearts

Searching

Judg. 5:16 of Reuben there were great *s* of heart
Job 11:7 canst thou by *s* find out God?
Is. 40:28 there is no *s* of his understanding

Seared

1 Tim. 4:2 their conscience *s* with a hot iron

Season (noun) *See also* Time

Gen. 1:14 let them be for signs, and for *s*
Deut. 28:12 give the rain unto thy land in his *s*
2 Chr. 15:3 for a long *s* Israel hath been without
Job 5:26 like as a shock of corn cometh in in his *s*
Ps. 104:19 he appointed the moon for *s*: the sun
  104:27 thou mayest give them their meat in due *s*
Prov. 15:23 word spoken in due *s*, how good is it!
Eccl. 3:1 to every thing there is a *s*, and a time
Is. 50:4 I should know how to speak a word in *s* to
Jer. 33:20 should not be day and night in their *s*
Dan. 2:21 and he changeth the times and the *s*
  7:12 their lives were prolonged for a *s* and time
Mt. 21:41 shall render him the fruits in their *s*
Jn. 5:4 angel went down at a certain *s* into the pool
  5:35 were willing for a *s* to rejoice in his light
Acts 1:7 is not for you to know the times or the *s*
  14:17 gave us rain from heaven, and fruitful *s*
  20:18 what manner I have been with you at all *s*
  24:25 when I have a convenient *s*, I will call
2 Cor. 7:8 you sorry, though it were but for a *s*
Gal. 6:9 in due *s* we shall reap, if we faint not
1 Thes. 5:1 but of the times and the *s*, brethren
2 Tim. 4:2 preach the word; be instant in *s*, out of *s*
Heb. 11:25 to enjoy the pleasures of sin for a *s*
1 Pet. 1:6 though now for a *s* . . ye are in heaviness
Rev. 6:11 that they should rest yet for a little *s*
  20:3 and after that he must be loosed a little *s*

Season (verb)

Lev. 2:13 thy meat offering shalt thou *s* with salt
Mk. 9:50 (Lk. 14:34) salt . . wherewith will ye *s* it?
Col. 4:6 speech be always with grace, *s* with salt

Seat

Deut. 33:21 in a portion of the lawgiver, was he *s*
1 Sam. 20:18 be missed, because thy *s* will be empty
Job 23:3 find him! that I might come even to his *s*!
  29:7 when I prepared my *s* in the street!
Ezek. 8:3 where was the *s* of the image of jealousy
  28:2 hast said, I am a god, I sit in the *s* of God
Amos 6:3 and cause the *s* of violence to come near
Mt. 21:12 (Mk. 11:15) the *s* of them that sold doves
  23:2 scribes and the Pharisees sit in Moses' *s*
  23:6 (Mk. 12:39; Lk. 11:43; 20:46) love . . chief *s*
Lk. 1:52 he hath put down the mighty from their *s*
Rev. 2:13 thou dwellest, even where Satan's *s* is
  4:4 were four and twenty *s*: and upon the *s* I saw

Second

1 Cor. 15:47 the *s* man is the Lord from heaven
Rev. 2:11 shall not be hurt of the *s* death
  20:14 (21:8) the *s* death . . the *s* death

Secret *See also* Mystery

Gen. 49:6 O my soul, come not thou into their *s*
Deut. 29:29 *s* things belong unto the LORD our God
Judg. 3:19 I have a *s* errand unto thee, O king
  13:18 why askest thou . . my name, seeing it is *s*?
Job 11:6 that he would show thee the *s* of wisdom
  15:8 hast thou heard the *s* of God? and dost thou
  15:11 is there any *s* thing with thee?
  29:4 when the *s* of God was upon my tabernacle
Ps. 10:8 in the *s* places doth he murder the innocent

Ps. 18:11 he made darkness his *s* place; his pavilion
19:12 his errors? cleanse thou me from *s* faults
25:14 *s* of the LORD is with them that fear him
27:5 in the *s* of his tabernacle shall he hide me
31:20 shalt hide them in the *s* of thy presence
44:21 for he knoweth the *s* of the heart
90:8 our *s* sins in the light of thy countenance
91:1 dwelleth in the *s* place of the Most High
Prov. 3:32 but his *s* is with the righteous
9:17 are sweet, and bread eaten in *s* is pleasant
11:13 a talebearer revealeth *s*: but he that is
21:14 a gift in *s* pacifieth anger: and a reward
25:9 and discover not a *s* to another
27:5 open rebuke is better than *s* love
Eccl. 12:14 work into judgment, with every *s* thing
Is. 3:17 and the LORD will discover their *s* parts
45:19 I have not spoken in *s*, in a dark place
48:16 I have not spoken in *s* from the beginning
Jer. 13:17 shall weep in *s* places for your pride
23:24 can any hide himself in *s* places that I
49:10 made Esau bare, I have uncovered his *s*
Lam. 3:10 lying in wait, and as a lion in *s* places
Ezek. 7:22 and they shall pollute my *s* place
28:3 there is no *s* that they can hide from thee
Dan. 2:18 would desire mercies. . concerning this *s*
2:22 he revealeth the deep and *s* things
2:28 there is a God in heaven that revealeth *s*
2:47 a Lord of kings, and a revealer of *s*
Amos 3:7 but he revealeth his *s* unto his servants
Mt. 6:4 thy Father which seeth in *s*. . shall reward
13:35 I will utter things which have been kept *s*
24:26 he is in the *s* chambers; believe it not
Mk. 4:22 (Lk. 8:17) neither was any thing kept *s*
Lk. 11:33 lighted a candle, putteth it in a *s* place
Jn. 7:4 there is no man that doeth any thing in *s*
7:10 the feast, not openly, but as it were in *s*
18:20 spake openly. . and in *s* have I said nothing
Rom. 2:16 shall judge the *s* of men by Jesus Christ
16:25 mystery, which was kept *s* since the world
1 Cor. 14:25 are the *s* of his heart made manifest
Eph. 5:12 those things which are done of them in *s*

Secretly

Jer. 38:16 Zedekiah the king sware *s* unto Jeremiah

Sect

Acts 5:17 which is the *s* of the Sadducees
15:5 rose up certain of the *s* of the Pharisees
24:5 and a ringleader of the *s* of the Nazarenes
26:5 after the most straitest *s* of our religion
28:22 as concerning this *s*, we know that every

Secure

Judg. 8:11 and smote the host: for the host was *s*
18:7 (18:27) manner of the Zidonians, quiet and *s*
Job 11:18 thou shalt be *s*, because there is hope
12:6 prosper, and they that provoke God are *s*
Mt. 28:14 we will persuade him, and *s* you

Sedition *See also* Insurrection, Rebellion

Ezra 4:15 have moved *s* within the same of old time
Lk. 23:19 who for a certain *s* made in the city
Acts 24:5 and a mover of *s* among all the Jews
Gal. 5:20 emulations, wrath, strife, *s*, heresies

Seduce

2 Kgs. 21:9 Manasseh *s* them to do more evil than
Prov. 12:26 but the way of the wicked *s* them
Ezek. 13:10 they have *s* my people, saying, Peace
Mk. 13:22 to *s*, if it were possible, even the elect
1 Tim. 4:1 from the faith, giving heed to *s* spirits
1 Jn. 2:26 have I written. . concerning them that *s*
Rev. 2:20 to *s* my servants to commit fornication

Seducer

2 Tim. 3:13 evil men and *s* shall wax worse and worse

See (Saw, Seen) *See also* Behold, Look, Observe, Watch

Gen. 1:31 and God *s* every thing that he had made
7:1 for thee have I *s* righteous before me
11:5 LORD came down to *s* the city and the tower
16:13 the name of the LORD. . Thou God *s* me
21:16 said, Let me not *s* the death of the child
22:4 Abraham lifted up his eyes, and *s* the place
26:8 Abimelech. . looked out at a window, and *s*
32:30 Peniel: for I have *s* God face to face
45:28 my son is yet alive: I will go and *s* him
Ex. 3:7 (Acts 7:34) I have. . *s* the affliction of my
10:23 they *s* not one another, neither rose any
14:13 ye shall *s* them again no more for ever
24:10 they *s* the God of Israel: and there was
33:20 not *s* my face: for there shall no man *s* me
Num. 14:23 they shall not *s* the land which I sware
24:17 I shall *s* him, but not now: I shall
Deut. 1:36 save Caleb. . he shall *s* it, and to him
3:25 let me go over, and *s* the good land that is
34:4 I have caused thee to *s* it with thine eyes
Judg. 6:22 have *s* an angel of the LORD face to face
13:22 we shall surely die, because we have *s* God
1 Sam. 16:7 LORD *s* not as man *s*; for man looketh on
2 Kgs. 6:17 pray thee, open his eyes, that he may *s*
10:16 come with me, and *s* my zeal for the LORD
20:15 (Is. 39:4) what have they *s* in thine house?
2 Chr. 15:9 when they *s* that the LORD. . was with
25:17 come, let us *s* one another in the face
Neh. 6:16 the heathen that were about us *s* these
Job 7:8 eye of him that hath *s* me shall *s* me no more
9:11 he goeth by me, and I *s* him not: he passeth
13:1 lo, mine eye hath *s* all this, mine ear hath
15:17 hear me. . that which I have *s* I will declare
19:26 this body, yet in my flesh shall I *s* God
22:14 clouds are a covering to him, that he *s* not
28:7 a path. . which the vulture's eye hath not *s*
29:11 when the eye *s* me, it gave witness to me
36:25 every man may *s* it; man may behold it afar
Ps. 10:11 he hideth his face; he will never *s* it
27:13 unless I had believed to *s* the goodness of
34:8 taste and *s* that the LORD is good
37:25 yet have I not *s* the righteous forsaken
40:3 many shall *s* it, and fear, and shall trust
50:18 when thou *s* a thief, then thou consentedst
66:5 come and *s* the works of God: he is terrible
77:16 the waters *s* thee, O God, the waters *s* thee
94:9 he that formed the eye, shall he not *s*?
114:3 sea *s* it, and fled: Jordan was driven back
115:5 (135:16) eyes have they, but they *s* not
Eccl. 1:8 eye is not satisfied with *s*, nor the ear
2:24 also I *s*, that it was from the hand of God
3:22 bring him to *s* what shall be after him?
6:5 he hath not *s* the sun, nor known any thing
6:6 live a thousand years. . yet hath he *s* no good
8:9 all this have I *s*, and applied my heart unto
Is. 6:5 mine eyes have *s* the King, the LORD of hosts
6:9 (Mt. 13:14; Mk. 4:12; Acts 28:26) and *s* ye indeed, but perceive not
6:10 (Mt. 13:15; Acts 28:27) lest they *s* with their
9:2 (Mt. 4:16) in darkness have *s* a great light
29:15 they say, Who *s* us? and who knoweth us?
32:3 the eyes of them that *s* shall not be dim
33:17 thine eyes shall *s* the King in his beauty
40:5 (Lk. 3:6) and all flesh shall *s* it together
52:8 for they shall *s* eye to eye, when the LORD
52:10 the earth shall *s* the salvation of our God
52:15 (Rom. 15:21) been told them shall they *s*

Is. 53:2 and when we shall *s* him, there is no beauty
   53:10 he shall *s* his seed, he shall prolong his
   59:16 he *s* that there was no man, and wondered
   64:4 (1 Cor. 2:9) not heard. . neither hath the eye *s*
   66:8 heard such a thing? who hath *s* such things?
Jer. 5:21 which have eyes, and *s* not; which have
   12:3 thou, O Lord, knowest me: thou hast *s* me
   17:8 shall not *s* when heat cometh, but her leaf
Hab. 3:10 the mountains *s* thee, and they trembled
Zeph. 3:15 thou shalt not *s* evil any more
Hag. 2:3 that *s* this house in her first glory?
Mt. 2:2 born King of the Jews? for we have *s* his star
   5:16 that they may *s* your good works, and glorify
   6:1 do not your alms before men, to be *s* of them
   6:4 Father which *s* in secret. . shall reward thee
   7:5 (Lk. 6:42) then shalt thou *s* clearly to cast
   11:4 (Lk. 7:22) those things which ye do hear and *s*
   11:7 (Lk. 7:24) out into the wilderness to *s*?
   12:38 Master, we would *s* a sign from thee
   13:13 (Lk. 8:10) because they *s s* not; and hearing
   13:14 (Mk. 4:12; Acts 28:26) *s* ye shall *s*
   13:16 (Lk. 10:23) blessed are your eyes, for they *s*
   13:17 (Lk. 10:24) to *s* those things which ye *s*
   15:31 (Lk. 7:22) lame to walk, and the blind to *s*
   16:28 *s* the Son of man coming in his kingdom
   17:8 (Mk. 9:8) they *s* no man, save Jesus only
   22:11 the king came in to *s* the guests, he *s* there
   24:30 (Mk. 13:26; Lk. 21:27) *s* the Son. . coming
   25:37 when *s* we thee ahungered, and fed thee?
   26:64 (Mk. 14:62) shall ye *s* the Son of man sitting
   27:4 they said, What is that to us? *s* thou to that
   28:6 come, *s* the place where the Lord lay
   28:7 (Mk. 16:7) into Galilee: there shall ye *s* him
Mk. 2:5 Jesus *s* their faith, he said unto the sick
   8:18 having eyes, *s* ye not? and having ears, hear
   8:24 looked up. . said, I *s* men as trees, walking
   9:1 (Lk. 9:27) till they have *s* the kingdom of God
   9:9 should tell no man what things they had *s*
   13:29 (Lk. 21:31) when ye shall *s* these things
Lk. 2:26 he should not *s* death, before he had *s*
   2:30 for mine eyes have *s* thy salvation
   5:26 saying, We have *s* strange things today
   8:16 (11:33) they which enter in may *s* the light
   9:9 (23:8) who is this. . And he desired to *s* him
   17:22 when ye shall desire to *s* one of the days
   17:23 say to you, *S* here; or, *s* there: go not
   24:24 as the women said: but him they *s* not
   24:39 that it is I myself: handle me, and *s*
Jn. 1:18 no man hath *s* God at any time; the only
   1:33 upon whom thou shalt *s* the Spirit descending
   1:34 I *s*, and bare record that this is the Son
   1:39 come and *s*. They came and *s* where he dwelt
   1:46 Nazareth? Philip saith unto him, Come and *s*
   1:48 when thou wast under the fig tree, I *s* thee
   1:50 believest thou? thou shalt *s* greater things
   3:3 born again, he cannot *s* the kingdom of God
   3:11 testify that we have *s*; and ye receive not
   3:36 that believeth not the Son shall not *s* life
   5:37 have neither heard his voice. . nor *s* his shape
   6:46 not that any man hath *s* the Father, save he
   7:3 thy disciples also may *s* the works that thou
   8:38 I speak that which I have *s* with my Father
   8:51 man keep my saying, he shall never *s* death
   8:56 Abraham rejoiced to *s* my day: and he *s* it
   9:25 I know, that, whereas I was blind, now I *s*
   9:37 Jesus said unto him, Thou hast both *s* him
   9:39 *s* not might *s*; and that they which *s* might
   12:21 desired him, saying, Sir, we would *s* Jesus
   12:45 and he that *s* me *s* him that sent me
   14:9 he that hath *s* me hath *s* the Father
   14:19 world *s* me no more; but ye *s* me: because I
   15:24 but now have they both *s* and hated both me
   16:16 not *s* me. . a little while, and ye shall *s* me

Jn. 19:35 he that *s* it bare record, and his record
   20:20 were the disciples glad, when they *s* the Lord
   20:25 except I shall *s* in his hands the print of
   20:29 because thou hast *s* me, thou hast believed
Acts 1:11 come in like manner as ye have *s* him go
   4:20 cannot but speak the things which we have *s*
   11:23 came, and had *s* the grace of God, was glad
   16:10 after he had *s* the vision, immediately we
   22:15 witness unto all men of what thou hast *s*
Rom. 8:24 that is *s* is not hope: for what a man *s*
1 Cor. 9:1 have I not *s* Jesus Christ our Lord?
   13:12 now we *s* through a glass, darkly; but then
   15:6 was *s* of above five hundred brethren at once
2 Cor. 4:18 are *s* are temporal. . not *s* are eternal
Gal. 1:18 I went up to Jerusalem to *s* Peter
1 Tim. 6:16 whom no man hath *s*, nor can *s*
Heb. 2:8 now we *s* not yet all things put under him
   2:9 but we *s* Jesus, who was made a little lower
   11:1 things hoped for, the evidence of things not *s*
   12:14 without which no man shall *s* the Lord
1 Pet. 1:8 though now ye *s* him not, yet believing
1 Jn. 1:1 have heard, which we have *s* with our eyes
   3:2 be like him; for we shall *s* him as he is
   4:12 no man hath *s* God at any time. If we love
   4:20 he hath *s*. . love God whom he hath not *s*?
Rev. 1:7 cometh with clouds. . every eye shall *s* him
   1:11 what thou *s*, write in a book, and send it

Seed *See also* Heir, Offspring, Posterity

Gen. 1:11 bring forth grass, the herb yielding *s*
   3:15 will put enmity. . between thy *s* and her *s*
   7:3 keep *s* alive upon the face of all the earth
   12:7 (24:7) unto thy *s* will I give this land
   15:5 (Rom. 4:18) said unto him, So shall thy *s* be
   15:18 unto thy *s* have I given this land, from
   17:7 my covenant between me and thee and thy *s*
   21:12 (Rom. 9:7; Heb. 11:18) in Isaac shall thy *s* be
   22:18 (26:4; 28:14; Acts 3:25) in thy *s*. . the nations
   32:12 do thee good, and make thy *s* as the sand
   38:8 marry her, and raise up *s* to thy brother
   47:19 give us *s*, that we may live, and not die
Ex. 16:31 Manna: and it was like coriander *s*, white
Lev. 19:19 (Deut. 22:9) not sow. . with mingled *s*
   26:16 shall sow your *s* in vain, for your enemies
   27:16 thy estimation shall be according to the *s*
Num. 20:5 no place of *s*, or of figs, or of vines
Deut. 1:8 to give unto them and to their *s* after
   14:22 thou shalt. . tithe all the increase of thy *s*
   28:38 carry much *s* out. . gather but little in
Job 21:8 their *s* is established in their sight
Ps. 22:30 a *s* shall serve him; it shall be accounted
   25:13 at ease; and his *s* shall inherit the earth
   37:25 the righteous forsaken, nor his *s* begging
   89:4 thy *s* will I establish for ever, and build
   112:2 his *s* shall be mighty upon earth
   126:6 bearing precious *s*, shall doubtless come
Eccl. 11:6 morning sow thy *s*, and in the evening
Is. 1:4 laden with iniquity, a *s* of evildoers
   5:10 and the *s* of a homer shall yield an ephah
   6:13 the holy *s* shall be the substance thereof
   17:11 morning shalt thou make thy *s* to flourish
   45:25 shall all the *s* of Israel be justified
   53:10 he shall see his *s*, he shall prolong his
   55:10 (2 Cor. 9:10) *s* to the sower. . bread to the
   57:3 the *s* of the adulterer and the whore
   61:9 their *s* shall be known among the Gentiles
Jer. 2:21 a noble vine, wholly a right *s*: how then
   35:7 neither shall ye build house, nor sow *s*
Joel 1:17 the *s* is rotten under their clods
Hag. 2:19 is the *s* yet in the barn? yea, as yet
Zech. 8:12 the *s* shall be prosperous: the vine shall
Mal. 2:3 I will corrupt your *s*, and spread dung
   2:15 wherefore one? That he might seek a godly *s*

Mt. 13:4 (Lk. 8:5) sowed, some *s* fell by the wayside
13:24 likened unto a man which sowed good *s* in
13:32 (Mk. 4:31) is the least of all *s*: but when
13:38 the good *s* are the children of the kingdom
22:24 (Mk. 12:19; Lk. 20:28) *s* unto his brother
Mk. 4:26 as if a man should cast *s* into the ground
Lk. 8:11 parable is this: The *s* is the word of God
Jn. 7:42 (Rom. 1:3; 2 Tim. 2:8) of the *s* of David
Rom. 9:29 except the Lord . . had left us a *s*, we had
1 Cor. 15:38 God giveth . . to every *s* his own body
Gal. 3:16 not, And to *s*, as of many; but as of one
Heb. 2:16 but he took on him the *s* of Abraham
1 Pet. 1:23 being born again, not of corruptible *s*
1 Jn. 3:9 his *s* remaineth in him . . he cannot sin

Seedtime

Gen. 8:22 *s* and harvest, and cold and heat

Seek (Sought) *See also* Inquire, Search

Gen. 37:15 the man asked him, saying, What *s* thou?
Ex. 4:24 that the LORD met him, and *s* to kill him
Num. 15:39 and that ye *s* not after your own heart
16:10 with thee: and *s* ye the priesthood also?
Deut. 4:29 *s* the LORD thy God, thou shalt find him
12:5 unto his habitation shall ye *s*, and thither
23:6 thou shalt not *s* their peace nor their
Judg. 18:1 Danites *s* them an inheritance to dwell
Ruth 3:1 my daughter, shall I not *s* rest for thee
1 Sam. 9:3 Kish said to Saul . . arise, go *s* the asses
13:14 hath *s* him a man after his own heart
1 Kgs. 19:10 (Rom. 11:3) am left; and they *s* my life
2 Kgs. 2:17 they *s* three days, but found him not
1 Chr. 15:13 that we *s* him not after the due order
16:11 (Ps. 105:4) *s* the LORD and his strength
28:9 if thou *s* him, he will be found of thee
2 Chr. 7:14 humble themselves . . pray, and *s* my face
14:7 have *s* the LORD our God, we have *s* him
15:4 did turn . . and *s* him, he was found of them
15:12 entered into a covenant to *s* the LORD
15:15 *s* him with their whole desire; and he was
16:12 yet in his disease he *s* not to the LORD
19:3 and hast prepared thine heart to *s* God
26:5 as he *s* the LORD, God made him to prosper
34:3 was yet young, he began to *s* after the God
Ezra 4:2 let us build with you: for we *s* your God
7:10 Ezra had prepared his heart to *s* the law
8:22 God is upon all them for good that *s* him
Job 5:8 I would *s* unto God, and unto God would I
7:21 *s* me in the morning, but I shall not be
8:5 if thou wouldest *s* unto God betimes
39:29 she *s* the prey, and her eyes behold afar
Ps. 9:10 thou, LORD, hast not forsaken them that *s*
10:4 the wicked . . will not *s* after God
10:15 *s* out his wickedness till thou find none
14:2 (53:2) any that did understand, and *s* God
24:6 them that *s* him, that *s* thy face, O Jacob
27:4 one thing have I desired . . that will I *s* after
27:8 *s* ye my face . . Thy face, LORD, will I *s*
34:4 I *s* the LORD, and he heard me, and delivered
34:10 they that *s* the LORD shall not want any good
34:14 (1 Pet. 3:11) do good; *s* peace, and pursue it
40:16 (70:4) let all those that *s* thee rejoice
63:1 O God, thou art my God; early will I *s* thee
69:32 and your heart shall live that *s* God
83:16 faces with shame; that they may *s* thy name
119:2 blessed . . that *s* him with the whole heart
119:10 with my whole heart have I *s* thee: O let
119:94 save me; for I have *s* thy precepts
122:9 house of the LORD our God I will *s* thy good
Prov. 1:28 *s* me early, but they shall not find me
8:17 and those that *s* me early shall find me
11:27 good procureth favor: but he that *s*
Eccl. 1:13 I gave my heart to *s* and search out by

Eccl. 7:29 but they have *s* out many inventions
12:10 Preacher *s* to find out acceptable words
Song 3:1 I *s* him whom my soul loveth: I *s* him
Is. 8:19 should not a people *s* unto their God?
11:10 to it shall the Gentiles *s*: and his rest
19:3 shall *s* to the idols, and to the charmers
26:9 with my spirit within me will I *s* thee early
34:16 *s* ye out of the book of the LORD, and read
41:17 poor and needy *s* water, and there is none
45:19 seed of Jacob, *S* ye me in vain: I the LORD
55:6 *s* ye the LORD while he may be found, call ye
58:2 yet they *s* me daily, and delight to know my
65:1 (Rom. 10:20) am found of them that *s* me not
Jer. 5:1 *s* in the broad places thereof, if ye can
10:21 pastors . . brutish, and have not *s* the LORD
29:7 and *s* the peace of the city whither I have
29:13 ye shall *s* me, and find me, when ye shall
30:17 saying, This is Zion, whom no man *s* after
38:4 this man *s* not the welfare of this people
45:5 *s* thou great things for thyself? *s* them not
Lam. 1:19 they *s* their meat to relieve their souls
3:25 the LORD is good . . to the soul that *s* him
Ezek. 7:25 shall *s* peace, and there shall be none
22:30 I *s* for a man among them, that should make
34:4 neither have ye *s* that which was lost
34:12 as a shepherd *s* out his flock . . so will I *s*
34:16 I will *s* that which was lost, and bring
Dan. 9:3 to *s* by prayer and supplications
Hos. 3:5 return, and *s* the LORD their God, and David
5:15 *s* my face . . affliction they will *s* me early
10 :12 it is time to *s* the LORD, till he come
Amos 5:4 house of Israel, *S* ye me, and ye shall live
5:14 *s* good, and not evil, that ye may live
8:12 run to and fro to *s* the word of the LORD
Nah. 3:7 whence shall I *s* comforters for thee?
Zeph. 1:6 that have not *s* the LORD, nor inquired
2:3 *s* ye the LORD . . *s* righteousness, *s* meekness
Mal. 2:7 and they should *s* the law at his mouth
2:15 wherefore one? That he might *s* a godly seed
Mt. 2:20 are dead which *s* the young child's life
6:32 (Lk. 12:30) all these things do the Gentiles *s*
6:33 (Lk. 12:31) but *s* ye first the kingdom of God
7:7 (Lk. 11:9) be given you; *s*, and ye shall find
12:39 (16:4; Mk. 8:12; Lk. 11:29) *s* after a sign
13:45 like unto a merchantman, *s* goodly pearls
18:12 mountains, and *s* that which is gone astray?
26:16 (Lk. 22:6) he *s* opportunity to betray him
26:59 (Mk. 14:55) *s* false witness against Jesus
28:5 (Mk. 16:6) I know that ye *s* Jesus
Mk. 1:37 (Lk. 4:42) said unto him, All men *s* for thee
11:18 (Lk. 19:47) *s* how they might destroy him
14:1 *s* how they might take him by craft, and put
Lk. 2:48 thy father and I have *s* thee sorrowing
11:16 tempting him, *s* of him a sign from heaven
13:7 three years I come *s* fruit on this fig tree
13:24 will *s* to enter in, and shall not be able
15:8 sweep the house, and *s* diligently till she
19:3 he *s* to see Jesus who he was; and could not
19:10 Son of man is come to *s* and to save that
24:5 why *s* ye the living among the dead?
Jn. 1:38 Jesus turned . . and saith . . What *s* ye?
4:23 for the Father *s* such to worship him
5:16 to slay him, because he had done these
5:30 because I *s* not mine own will, but the will
6:26 ye *s* me, not because ye saw the miracles
7:11 then the Jews *s* him at the feast, and said
7:34 ye shall *s* me, and shall not find me
8:21 ye shall *s* me, and shall die in your sins
8:50 I *s* not mine own glory: there is one that *s*
11:8 Master, the Jews of late *s* to stone thee
11:56 then *s* they for Jesus, and spake among
18:4 went forth, and said unto them, Whom *s* ye?
18:8 I am he: if therefore ye *s* me, let these go

Jn. 19:12 Pilate *s* to release him: but the Jews
  20:15 woman, why weepest thou? whom *s* thou?
Acts 10:19 Spirit said . . Behold, three men *s* thee
  15:17 the residue of men might *s* after the Lord
  17:27 they should *s* the Lord, if haply they
Rom. 2:7 *s* for glory and honor and immortality
  3:11 that understandeth . . none that *s* after God
  9:32 wherefore? Because they *s* it not by faith
1 Cor. 1:22 a sign, and the Greeks *s* after wisdom
  10:24 no man *s* his own, but every man another's
  10:33 I please all men . . not *s* mine own profit
  13:5 not behave itself unseemly, *s* not her own
  14:12 *s* that ye may excel to the edifying of the
2 Cor. 12:14 for I *s* not yours, but you
  13:3 since ye *s* a proof of Christ speaking in me
Gal. 1:10 or do I *s* to please men? for if I yet
  2:17 if, while we *s* to be justified by Christ
Phil. 2:21 all *s* their own, not the things which
Col. 3:1 *s* those things which are above
1 Thes. 2:6 nor of men *s* we glory, neither of you
Heb. 11:6 a rewarder of them that diligently *s* him
  11:14 declare plainly that they *s* a country
  12:17 though he *s* it carefully with tears
  13:14 no continuing city, but we *s* one to come
Rev. 9:6 and in those days shall men *s* death

Seem

Gen. 19:14 but he *s* as one that mocked unto his
  29:20 *s* unto him but a few days, for the love
Num. 16:9 *s* it but a small thing unto you
Prov. 14:12 (16:25) a way which *s* right unto a man
1 Cor. 3:18 if any man among you *s* to be wise
  12:22 those members . . which *s* to be more feeble
Gal. 2:6 but of those who *s* to be somewhat
Jas. 1:26 if any man among you *s* to be religious

Seemly

Prov. 19:10 delight is not *s* for a fool; much less
  26:1 in harvest, so honor is not *s* for a fool

Seen *See* See

Seer *See also* Prophet

1 Sam. 9:9 a Prophet was beforetime called a *S*
  9:19 Samuel answered Saul, and said, I am the *s*
2 Sam. 24:11 (1 Chr. 21:9) prophet Gad, David's *s*
2 Chr. 33:19 written among the sayings of the *s*
Is. 30:10 which say to the *s*, See not; and to the
Mic. 3:7 then shall the *s* be ashamed

Seethe (Sod, Sodden)

Gen. 25:29 Jacob *s* pottage: and Esau came from
Ex. 16:23 and *s* that ye will *s*; and that which
  23:19 (34:26; Deut. 14:21) *s* a kid in his mother's
1 Sam. 2:15 will not have *s* flesh of thee, but raw
2 Kgs. 4:38 *s* pottage for the sons of the prophets
2 Chr. 35:13 other holy offerings *s* they in pots
Lam. 4:10 pitiful women have *s* their own children
Ezek. 24:5 and let them *s* the bones of it therein

Seir

Gen. 32:3 to Esau his brother unto the land of *S*
Deut. 2:5 (Josh. 24:4) have given mount *S* unto Esau
Ezek. 35:2 set thy face against mount *S*, and prophesy

Seize

Josh. 8:7 rise up from the ambush . . *s* upon the city
Job 3:6 as for that night, let darkness *s* upon it
Ps. 55:15 let death *s* upon them, and let them go
Jer. 49:24 fear hath *s* on her: anguish and sorrows
Mt. 21:38 kill him, and let us *s* on his inheritance

Seleucia Acts 13:4

Sell (Sold)

Gen. 25:31 Jacob said, *S* me this day thy birthright
  31:15 counted of him strangers? for he hath *s* us
  37:27 let us *s* him to the Ishmaelites, and let
  41:56 Joseph opened all the storehouses, and *s*
  45:4 am Joseph your brother, whom ye *s* into Egypt
Ex. 21:7 if a man *s* his daughter to be a maidservant
Lev. 25:23 the land shall not be *s* for ever
  25:42 my servants . . they shall not be *s* as bondmen
  27:28 no devoted thing . . shall be *s* or redeemed
Deut. 15:12 man, or a Hebrew woman, be *s* unto thee
  32:30 to flight, except their Rock had *s* them
Judg. 2:14 *s* them into the hands of their enemies
2 Kgs. 4:7 *s* the oil, and pay the debt, and live
Neh. 5:8 *s* your brethren? or shall they be *s* unto us?
  10:31 on the sabbath day to *s* . . we would not buy
Esth. 7:4 are *s*, I and my people, to be destroyed
Ps. 44:12 thou *s* thy people for nought, and dost
  105:17 even Joseph, who was *s* for a servant
Prov. 11:26 blessing . . upon the head of him that *s* it
  23:23 buy the truth, and *s* it not; also wisdom
  31:24 she maketh fine linen, and *s* it
Is. 50:1 for your iniquities have ye *s* yourselves
  52:3 ye have *s* yourselves for nought
Joel 3:3 *s* a girl for wine, that they might drink
  3:8 I will *s* your sons and your daughters into
Amos 2:6 because they *s* the righteous for silver
  8:5 the new moon be gone, that we may *s* corn?
Mt. 10:29 are not two sparrows *s* for a farthing?
  13:44 *s* all that he hath, and buyeth that field
  13:46 pearl of great price, went and *s* all that
  18:25 not to pay, his lord commanded him to be *s*
  19:21 (Mk. 10:21; Lk. 18:22) *s* that thou hast
  21:12 (Mk. 11:15; Lk. 19:45) *s* . . in the temple
  26:9 (Mk. 14:5; Jn. 12:5) *s* for much, and given
Lk. 12:33 *s* that ye have, and give alms; provide
  17:28 did eat, they drank, they bought, they *s*
  22:36 no sword, let him *s* his garment, and buy
Acts 2:45 (4:34) *s* their possessions and goods
  4:37 having land, *s* it, and brought the money
  5:1 a certain man named Ananias . . *s* a possession
  7:9 moved with envy, *s* Joseph into Egypt
1 Cor. 10:25 whatsoever is *s* in the shambles . . eat
Heb. 12:16 for one morsel of meat *s* his birthright
Jas. 4:13 there a year, and buy and *s*, and get gain

Seller

Ezek. 7:12 not the buyer rejoice, nor the *s* mourn
Acts 16:14 certain woman named Lydia, a *s* of purple

Senator

Ps. 105:22 to bind his princes . . teach his *s* wisdom

Send (Sent)

Gen. 8:7 he *s* forth a raven, which went forth to
  24:7 he shall *s* his angel before thee
  43:14 that he may *s* away your other brother
  45:5 God did *s* me before you to preserve life
Ex. 3:10 (Acts 7:34) and I will *s* thee unto Pharaoh
  3:14 say unto . . Israel, I AM hath *s* me unto you
  4:13 Lord, *s* . . by the hand of him whom thou wilt *s*
  33:12 hast not let me know whom thou wilt *s* with
Num. 13:2 *s* thou men, that they may search the land
  13:17 Moses *s* them to spy out the land of Canaan
Josh. 2:1 *s* out of Shittim two men to spy secretly
Judg. 6:14 go in this thy might . . have not I *s* thee?
  13:8 let the man of God which thou didst *s* come
Ps. 20:2 *s* thee help from the sanctuary
  43:3 O *s* out thy light and thy truth: let them
  57:3 he shall *s* from heaven, and save me from the
  68:33 he doth *s* out his voice, and that a mighty
  144:7 *s* thine hand from above; rid me . . deliver me

Is. 6:8 whom shall I s. . Then said I, Here am I; s me
  19:20 he shall s them a saviour, and a great one
  48:16 now the Lord GOD, and his Spirit, hath s me
  61:1 (Lk. 4:18) s me to bind up the broken-hearted
Jer. 1:7 thou shalt go to all that I shall s thee
  23:21 have not s these prophets, yet they ran
  26:12 LORD s me to prophesy against this house
Mal. 3:1 (Mt. 11:10; Mk. 1:2; Lk. 7:27) s. . messenger
Mt. 9:38 (Lk. 10:2) will s forth laborers into his
  10:16 (Lk. 10:3) s you forth as sheep in the midst
  10:34 to s peace on earth: I came not to s peace
  10:40 (Lk. 9:48; Jn. 13:20) receiveth him that s me
  11:2 (Lk. 7:19) John. . s two of his disciples
  12:20 till he s forth judgment unto victory
  13:41 the Son of man shall s forth his angels
  15:23 saying, S her away; for she crieth after us
  15:24 s but unto the lost sheep of the house of
  20:2 a penny a day, he s them into his vineyard
  21:1 (Mk. 11:1; Lk. 19:29) then s. . two disciples
  21:3 (Mk. 11:3) and straightway he will s them
  21:34 (Mk. 12:2; Lk. 20:10) he s his servants
Mk. 3:14 and that he might s them forth to preach
  5:12 besought him, saying, S us into the swine
  6:7 and began to s them forth by two and two
  9:37 receiveth not me, but him that s me
  14:13 he s forth two of his disciples, and saith
Lk. 16:24 Abraham, have mercy on me. . s Lazarus
  24:49 I s the promise of my Father upon you
Jn. 5:30 (6:38) will of the Father which hath s me
  5:36 bear witness of me, that the Father hath s me
  6:57 as the living Father hath s me, and I live
  14:26 Holy Ghost, whom the Father will s in my
  15:26 whom I will s unto you from the Father
  16:7 but if I depart, I will s him unto you
  17:3 true God, and Jesus Christ, whom thou hast s
  17:8 and they have believed that thou didst s me
  17:18 as thou hast s me into the world, even so
  17:21 the world may believe that thou hast s me
  20:21 as my Father hath s me, even so s I you
Acts 10:5 (10:32; 11:13) s men to Joppa, and call for
  13:4 being s forth by the Holy Ghost, departed
Rom. 8:3 s his own Son in the likeness of sinful
  10:15 how shall they preach, except they be s?
1 Cor. 1:17 s me not to baptize, but to preach
Gal. 4:4 God s forth his Son, made of a woman
  4:6 God hath s forth the Spirit of his Son into your
2 Thes. 2:11 God shall s them strong delusion
Phlm. 12 whom I have s. . thou therefore receive him
1 Jn. 4:9 s his only begotten Son into the world
  4:14 s the Son to be the Saviour of the world

Sennacherib 2 Kgs. 18:13–19:36 (2 Chr. 32:1–22; Is. 36:1–37:37)

Sense

Heb. 5:14 have their s exercised to discern both

Sensual

Jas. 3:15 from above, but is earthly, s, devilish
Jude 19 separate themselves, s, having not the Spirit

Sentence

Deut. 17:9 they shall show thee the s of judgment
Ps. 17:2 let my s come forth from thy presence
Prov. 16:10 a divine s is in the lips of the king
Eccl. 8:11 s against an evil work is not executed
Jer. 4:12 now also will I give s against them
Dan. 5:12 showing of hard s. . dissolving of doubts
  8:23 and understanding dark s, shall stand up
Lk. 23:24 Pilate gave s that it should be as they
Acts 15:19 my s is, that we trouble not them, which
2 Cor. 1:9 but we had the s of death in ourselves

Separate See also Consecrate, Divide, Part, Portion, Sanctify

Gen. 13:9 whole land before thee? s thyself
Ex. 33:16 so shall we be s, I and thy people
Lev. 15:31 thus shall ye s the children of Israel
  20:24 God, which have s you from other people
  22:2 that they s themselves from the holy things
Num. 6:2 s themselves to vow a vow of a Nazarite
  16:9 hath s you from the congregation of Israel
  16:21 s yourselves from among this congregation
Deut. 10:8 s the tribe of Levi, to bear the ark
  19:2 shalt s three cities for thee in the midst
  29:21 shalt s him unto evil out of all the tribes
  32:8 when he s the sons of Adam, he set the bounds
1 Kgs. 8:53 didst s them from among all the people
1 Chr. 23:13 Aaron was s, that he should sanctify
Ezra 9:1 have not s themselves from the people
  10:11 s yourselves from the people of the land
Neh. 9:2 Israel s themselves from all strangers
  13:3 s from Israel all the mixed multitude
Prov. 16:28 and a whisperer s chief friends
  17:9 he that repeateth a matter s very friends
  18:1 having s himself, seeketh and intermeddleth
  19:4 but the poor is s from his neighbor
Is. 56:3 LORD hath utterly s me from his people
  59:2 iniquities have s between you and your God
Jer. 37:12 then Jeremiah went. . to s himself thence
Ezek. 14:7 for every one. . which s himself from me
Mt. 25:32 and he shall s them one from another
Lk. 6:22 when they shall s you from their company
Acts 13:2 s me Barnabas and Saul for the work
Rom. 1:1 called to be an apostle, s unto the gospel
  8:35 who shall s us from the love of Christ?
  8:39 shall be able to s us from the love of God
2 Cor. 6:17 come out from among them, and be ye s
Gal. 1:15 God, who s me from my mother's womb
  2:12 he withdrew and s himself, fearing them
Heb. 7:26 holy, harmless, undefiled, s from sinners

Separation

Num. 6:4 all the days of his s shall he eat nothing
  6:21 vowed, so he must do after the law of his s
  19:9 a water of s: it is a purification for sin
Ezek. 42:20 to make a s between the sanctuary and

Sepulchre See also Grave, Tomb

Gen. 23:6 in the choice of our s bury thy dead
Deut. 34:6 no man knoweth of his s unto this day
2 Kgs. 13:21 they cast the man into the s of Elisha
  23:17 it is the s of the man of God
Ps. 5:9 (Rom. 3:13) their throat is an open s
Jer. 5:16 their quiver is as an open s, they are
Mt. 23:27 hypocrites! for ye are like unto whited s
  27:60 (Mk. 15:46) great stone to the door of the s
  28:1 (Mk. 16:2; Lk. 24:1; Jn. 20:1) to see the s
Mk. 15:46 (Lk. 23:53; Acts 13:29) laid him in a s
Lk. 11:47 for ye build the s of the prophets
  24:12 (Jn. 20:6) arose Peter, and ran unto the s
Jn. 19:41 a new s, wherein was never man yet laid
  20:11 Mary stood without at the s weeping

Seraphim

Is. 6:2 above it stood the s: each one had six wings
  6:6 flew one of the s unto me, having a live coal

Sergeant

Acts 16:35 the magistrates sent the s, saying, Let

Serpent

Gen. 3:1 now the s was more subtile than any beast
  3:13 woman said, The s beguiled me, and I did eat
  49:17 Dan shall be a s by the way, an adder in

Ex. 4:3 became a *s*; and Moses fled from before it
Num. 21:8 make. . a fiery *s*, and set it upon a pole
2 Kgs. 18:4 brake in pieces the brazen *s* that Moses
Job 26:13 his hand hath formed the crooked *s*
Ps. 58:4 their poison is like the poison of a *s*
   140:3 they have sharpened their tongues like a *s*
Prov. 23:32 it biteth like a *s*, and stingeth like
   30:19 way of a *s* upon a rock; the way of a ship
Eccl. 10:8 breaketh a hedge, a *s* shall bite him
   10:11 the *s* will bite without enchantment
Is. 14:29 and his fruit shall be a fiery flying *s*
   27:1 piercing *s*, even leviathan that crooked *s*
   65:25 dust shall be the *s*'s meat
Jer. 8:17 I will send *s*, cockatrices, among you
Amos 9:3 I command the *s*, and he shall bite them
Mt. 7:10 (Lk. 11:11) a fish, will he give him a *s*?
   10:16 therefore wise as *s*, and harmless as doves
   23:33 ye *s*, ye generation of vipers, how can ye
Mk. 16:18 they shall take up *s*; and if they drink
Lk. 10:19 unto you power to tread on *s* and scorpions
Jn. 3:14 as Moses lifted up the *s* in the wilderness
2 Cor. 11:3 as the *s* beguiled Eve through his
Jas. 3:7 every kind of beasts. . and of *s*. . is tamed
Rev. 12:9 great dragon was cast out, that old *s*
   20:2 and he laid hold on the dragon, that old *s*

Servant *See also* Minister, Slave, Steward

Gen. 9:25 cursed be Canaan; a *s* of *s* shall he be
   26:24 multiply thy seed for my *s* Abraham's sake
   32:10 truth, which thou hast showed unto thy *s*
Ex. 12:45 a foreigner and a hired *s* shall not eat
   14:31 and believed the LORD, and his *s* Moses
   21:2 if thou buy a Hebrew *s*, six years he shall
Lev. 25:55 children of Israel are *s*; they are my *s*
Num. 11:11 wherefore hast thou afflicted thy *s*?
   14:24 my *s* Caleb, because he had another spirit
Deut. 5:15 remember that thou wast a *s* in. . Egypt
   23:15 shalt not deliver unto his master the *s*
   24:14 shalt not oppress a hired *s* that is poor
   32:43 for he will avenge the blood of his *s*
1 Sam. 3:9 (3:10) Speak, LORD; for thy *s* heareth
   17:9 kill me, then will we be your *s*: but if I
2 Sam. 3:18 by the hand of my *s* David I will save
   7:20 for thou, Lord GOD, knowest thy *s*
   15:34 thy *s*, O king; as I have been thy father's *s*
1 Kgs. 3:9 give. . thy *s* an understanding heart
   5:6 (2 Chr. 2:8) and my *s* shall be with thy *s*
   8:23 (2 Chr. 6:14) covenant and mercy with thy *s*
   8:32 (2 Chr. 6:23) then hear thou. . and judge thy *s*
   12:7 (2 Chr. 10:7) be a *s*. . then they will be thy *s*
2 Kgs. 9:7 avenge the blood of my *s* the prophets
   21:10 LORD spake by his *s* the prophets, saying
1 Chr. 16:13 (Ps. 105:6) O ye seed of Israel his *s*
Ezra 5:11 we are the *s* of the God of heaven
Job 1:8 (2:3) Satan, Hast thou considered my *s* Job
   3:19 and the *s* is free from his master
   41:4 wilt thou take him for a *s* for ever?
Ps. 19:11 by them is thy *s* warned; and in keeping
   19:13 keep back thy *s* also from presumptuous sins
   27:9 far from me; put not thy *s* away in anger
   31:16 make thy face to shine upon thy *s*: save me
   34:22 the LORD redeemeth the soul of his *s*
   69:36 the seed also of his *s* shall inherit it
   79:2 dead bodies of thy *s* have they given to be
   86:2 my God, save thy *s* that trusteth in thee
   86:16 give thy strength unto thy *s*, and save
   109:28 let them be ashamed; but let thy *s* rejoice
   113:1 O ye *s* of the LORD, praise the name of the
   116:16 O LORD, truly I am thy *s*; I am thy *s*
   119:17 deal bountifully with thy *s*, that I may
   119:23 but thy *s* did meditate in thy statutes
   119:65 thou hast dealt well with thy *s*, O LORD
   119:122 be surety for thy *s* for good: let not

Ps. 119:125 I am thy *s*; give me understanding
   143:12 them that afflict my soul: for I am thy *s*
Prov. 11:29 fool shall be *s* to the wise of heart
   17:2 a wise *s* shall have rule over a son that
   22:7 and the borrower is *s* to the lender
   29:19 a *s* will not be corrected by words
   30:10 accuse not a *s* unto his master, lest he
Is. 24:2 as with the *s*, so with his master
   41:8 but thou, Israel, art my *s*, Jacob whom I
   42:1 (Mt. 12:18) behold my *s*, whom I uphold
   42:19 who is blind, but my *s*? or deaf, as my
   43:10 my *s* whom I have chosen; that ye may know
   44:1 hear, O Jacob my *s*; and Israel, whom I have
   44:21 my *s*: I have formed thee; thou art my *s*
   48:20 say ye, The LORD hath redeemed his *s* Jacob
   49:3 thou art my *s*, O Israel, in whom I will be
   52:13 behold, my *s* shall deal prudently, he shall
   53:11 shall my righteous *s* justify many
   54:17 this is the heritage of the *s* of the LORD
   65:9 shall inherit it, and my *s* shall dwell there
   66:14 hand of the LORD. . known toward his *s*
Jer. 2:14 is Israel a *s*? is he a homeborn slave?
   7:25 (44:4) I have even sent unto you all my *s*
   25:9 (27:6; 43:10) the king of Babylon, my *s*
   26:5 hearken unto the words of my *s* the prophets
   29:19 I sent unto them by my *s* the prophets
   30:10 (46:27) fear thou not, O my *s* Jacob
   34:11 the *s*. . whom they had let go free, to return
   35:15 sent also unto you all my *s* the prophets
Lam. 5:8 *s* have ruled over us: there is none that
Ezek. 38:17 whom I have spoken in old time by my *s*
Dan. 3:26 ye *s* of the most high God, come forth
   6:20 O Daniel, *s* of the living God, is thy God
Joel 2:29 (Acts 2:18) upon the *s* and. . handmaids
Amos 3:7 but he revealeth his secret unto his *s*
Mic. 6:4 and redeemed thee out of the house of *s*
Zech. 3:8 I will bring forth my *s* the BRANCH
Mt. 8:6 (Lk. 7:2) *s* lieth at home sick of the palsy
   8:8 (Lk. 7:7) word only, and my *s* shall be healed
   10:24 (Jn. 13:16; 15:20) nor the *s* above his lord
   18:23 king, which would take account of his *s*
   18:32 thou wicked *s*, I forgave thee all that debt
   20:27 (Mk. 10:44) will be chief. . let him be your *s*
   21:34 (Mk. 12:2; Lk. 20:10) *s* to the husbandmen
   22:3 sent forth his *s* to call them. . to the wedding
   23:11 that is greatest among you shall be your *s*
   24:45 who then is a faithful and wise *s*, whom his
   24:46 (Lk. 12:43) blessed is that *s*, whom his lord
   25:19 lord of those *s* cometh, and reckoneth with
   25:21 (25:23) well done, thou good and faithful *s*
   26:51 (Mk. 14:47; Lk. 22:50) struck a *s* of the high
Lk. 1:54 hath holpen his *s* Israel, in remembrance
   2:29 now lettest thou thy *s* depart in peace
   14:17 sent his *s* at supper time to say to them
   15:19 make me as one of thy hired *s*
   16:13 no *s* can serve two masters: for either he
   17:10 say, We are unprofitable *s*: we have done
   19:17 thou good *s*: because thou hast been faithful
Jn. 8:34 whosoever committeth sin is the *s* of sin
   12:26 and where I am, there shall also my *s* be
   13:16 (15:20) *s* is not greater than his lord
   15:15 I call you not *s*; for the *s* knoweth not
   18:10 smote the high priest's *s*, and cut off
Acts 16:17 these men are the *s* of the most high God
Rom. 1:1 Paul, a *s* of Jesus Christ, called to be
   6:16 *s* to obey, his *s* ye are to whom ye obey
   6:17 ye were the *s* of sin, but ye have obeyed
   6:18 from sin, ye became the *s* of righteousness
   6:22 made free from sin, and become *s* to God
   14:4 who art thou that judgest another man's *s*?
   16:1 Phoebe our sister, which is a *s* of the church
1 Cor. 7:21 art thou called being a *s*? care not
   7:23 bought with a price; be not ye the *s* of men

1 Cor. 9:19 yet have I made myself *s* unto all, that I
2 Cor. 4:5 and ourselves your *s* for Jesus' sake
Gal. 1:10 pleased men, I should not be the *s* of Christ
    4:1 as he is a child, differeth nothing from a *s*
    4:7 wherefore thou art no more a *s*, but a son
Eph. 6:5 (Col. 3:22) *s*, be obedient to . . your masters.
Phil. 2:7 took upon him the form of a *s*
Col. 4:1 give unto your *s* that which is just
    4:12 Epaphras, who is one of you, a *s* of Christ
1 Tim. 6:1 let as many *s* as are under the yoke
2 Tim. 2:24 the *s* of the Lord must not strive
Tit. 2:9 exhort *s* to be obedient unto their own
Phlm. 16 not now as a *s*, but above a *s*, a brother
Heb. 3:5 Moses . . faithful in all his house as a *s*
Jas. 1:1 James, a *s* of God and of the Lord Jesus
1 Pet. 2:16 of maliciousness, but as the *s* of God
    2:18 *s*, be subject to your masters with all fear
2 Pet. 1:1 Peter, a *s* and an apostle of Jesus Christ
    2:19 they themselves are the *s* of corruption
Jude 1 Jude, the *s* of Jesus Christ, and brother
Rev. 1:1 (22:6) to show unto his *s* things which
    2:20 and to seduce my *s* to commit fornication
    7:3 till we have sealed the *s* of our God in their
    10:7 as he hath declared to his *s* the prophets
    19:2 hath avenged the blood of his *s* at her hand
    22:3 shall be in it; and his *s* shall serve him

Serve *See also* Minister, Obey, Work, Worship

Gen. 15:13 shall *s* them; and they shall afflict them
    25:23 (Rom. 9:12) the elder shall *s* the younger
    27:29 let people *s* thee, and nations bow down to
    29:18 I will *s* thee seven years for Rachel
Ex. 1:13 made the children of Israel to *s* with rigor
    3:12 of Egypt, ye shall *s* God upon this mountain
    4:23 let my son go, that he may *s* me: and if thou
    10:11 go now ye that are men, and *s* the Lord
    14:12 better for us to *s* the Egyptians, than that
    20:5 (Deut. 5:9) not bow down . . to them, nor *s*
    21:2 (Deut. 15:12; Jer. 34:14) six years he shall *s*
    23:24 not bow down to their gods, nor *s* them
    23:25 ye shall *s* the Lord your God, and he shall
    23:33 their gods, it will surely be a snare
Deut. 4:28 there ye shall *s* gods, the work of men's
    6:13 (Mt. 4:10; Lk. 4:8) fear the Lord . . and *s* him
    7:16 neither shalt thou *s* their gods
    10:12 (11:13; Josh. 22:5) to *s* the Lord thy God
    10:20 (13:4) shalt thou *s* . . to him shalt thou cleave
    11:16 turn aside, and *s* other gods, and worship
    28:36 shalt thou *s* other gods, wood and stone
    28:48 therefore shalt thou *s* thine enemies
Josh. 23:7 neither *s* them, nor bow yourselves unto
    24:15 as for me and my house, we will *s* the Lord
    24:18 will we also *s* the Lord; for he is our God
Judg. 3:6 daughters to their sons, and *s* their gods
    10:13 yet ye have forsaken me, and *s* other gods
1 Sam. 7:3 prepare your hearts . . and *s* him only
    12:14 if ye will fear the Lord, and *s* him
    12:20 but *s* the Lord with all your heart
2 Sam. 15:8 to Jerusalem, then I will *s* the Lord
    22:44 (Ps. 18:43) which I knew not shall *s* me
1 Kgs. 9:6 (2 Chr. 7:19) *s* other gods, and worship
    12:4 (2 Chr. 10:4) yoke . . lighter, and we will *s* the
2 Kgs. 17:12 for they *s* idols, whereof the Lord
    17:33 they feared the Lord . . *s* their own gods
1 Chr. 28:9 and *s* him with a perfect heart
2 Chr. 30:8 *s* the Lord your God, that the fierceness
    35:3 *s* now the Lord your God, and his people
Job 21:15 the Almighty, that we should *s* him?
Ps. 2:11 *s* the Lord with fear, and rejoice with
    22:30 a seed shall *s* him; it shall be accounted
    72:11 fall . . before him: all nations shall *s* him

Ps. 97:7 confounded be all they that *s* graven images
    100:2 *s* the Lord with gladness: come before his
    101:6 walketh in a perfect way, he shall *s* me
    106:36 they *s* their idols: which were a snare
Is. 56:6 join themselves to the Lord, to *s* him
    60:12 kingdom that will not *s* thee shall perish
Jer. 5:19 *s* strange gods . . so shall ye *s* strangers
    11:10 and they went after other gods to *s* them
    16:13 there shall ye *s* other gods day and night
    25:11 nations shall *s* the king of Babylon
    27:9 saying, Ye shall not *s* the king of Babylon
    30:9 they shall *s* the Lord their God, and David
    35:15 go not after other gods to *s* them
Ezek. 20:32 be as the heathen . . to *s* wood and stone
Dan. 3:12 not regarded thee: they *s* not thy gods
    3:17 our God whom we *s* is able to deliver us
    3:18 that we will not *s* thy gods, nor worship
    6:20 is thy God, whom thou *s* continually, able
    7:14 people, nations, and languages, should *s* him
    7:27 and all dominions shall *s* and obey him
Zeph. 3:9 the Lord, to *s* him with one consent
Mal. 3:14 ye have said, It is vain to *s* God
    3:18 him that *s* God and him that *s* him not
Mt. 6:24 (Lk. 16:13) no man can *s* two masters
Lk. 2:37 but *s* God with fastings and prayers
    10:40 but Martha was cumbered about much *s*
    15:29 lo, these many years do I *s* thee, neither
    22:26 and he that is chief, as he that doth *s*
    22:27 but I am among you as he that *s*
Jn. 12:26 if any man *s* me, let him follow me
Acts 6:2 should leave the word of God, and *s* tables
    20:19 *s* the Lord with all humility of mind
    26:7 twelve tribes, instantly *s* God day and night
    27:23 the angel of God, whose I am, and whom I *s*
Rom. 1:9 whom I *s* with my spirit in the gospel
    6:6 that henceforth we should not *s* sin
    7:6 we should *s* in newness of spirit, and not in
    7:25 with the mind I myself *s* the law of God
    12:11 in business; fervent in spirit; *s* the Lord
    14:18 that in these things *s* Christ is acceptable
Gal. 3:19 wherefore then *s* the law? It was added
    5:13 to the flesh, but by love *s* one another
Phil. 2:22 as a son . . he hath *s* with me in the gospel
Col. 3:24 the inheritance: for ye *s* the Lord Christ
1 Thes. 1:9 from idols to *s* the living and true God
Tit. 3:3 deceived, *s* divers lusts and pleasures
Heb. 9:14 from dead works to *s* the living God?
    12:28 we may *s* God acceptably with reverence
Rev. 7:15 and *s* him day and night in his temple
    22:3 shall be in it; and his servants shall *s* him

Service *See also* Ministration, Work, Worship

Ex. 1:14 their lives bitter . . in all manner of *s*
    12:25 (13:5) come to the land . . ye shall keep this *s*
    30:16 appoint it for the *s* of the tabernacle
    35:19 (39:41) clothes of *s*, to do *s* in the holy place
    36:5 much more than enough for the *s* of the work
Num. 4:4 this shall be the *s* of the sons of Kohath
    4:19 and appoint them every one to his *s*
    4:30 every one that entereth into the *s*, to do
    8:11 that they may execute the *s* of the Lord
Josh. 22:27 we might do the *s* of the Lord before him
1 Kgs. 12:4 the grievous *s* of thy father . . lighter
1 Chr. 29:5 who then is willing to consecrate his *s*
2 Chr. 12:8 may know my *s* . . the *s* of the kingdoms
Ezra 6:18 Levites in their courses, for the *s* of
    7:19 given thee for the *s* of the house of thy God
Jer. 22:13 useth his neighbor's *s* without wages
Jn. 16:2 killeth you will think that he doeth God *s*
Rom. 9:4 the giving of the law, and the *s* of God
    12:1 living sacrifice . . which is your reasonable *s*

Rom. 15:31 that my *s* which I have for Jerusalem
2 Cor. 11:8 I robbed other churches. . to do you *s*
Gal. 4:8 *s* unto them which by nature are no gods
Eph. 6:7 with good will doing *s*, as to the Lord
Phil. 2:17 upon the sacrifice and *s* of your faith
1 Tim. 6:2 but rather do them *s*, because they are
Heb. 9:1 covenant had also ordinances of divine *s*
9:9 could not make him that did the *s* perfect
Rev. 2:19 I know thy works, and charity, and *s*

Servitude

2 Chr. 10:4 ease thou. . the grievous *s* of thy father

Set *See also* Encamp, Pitch, Place, Put

Gen. 9:13 I do *s* my bow in the cloud, and it shall
Deut. 1:8 behold, I have *s* the land before you
30:15 I have *s* before thee this day life and good
Job 33:5 if thou canst answer me, *s* thy words in order
Ps. 3:6 have *s* themselves against me round about
4:3 the LORD hath *s* apart him that is godly for
8:1 who hast *s* thy glory above the heavens
16:8 I have *s* the LORD always before me
20:5 name of our God we will *s* up our banners
54:3 they have not *s* God before them
75:7 he putteth down one, and *s* up another
85:13 and shall *s* us in the way of his steps
89:42 hast *s* up the right hand of his adversaries
113:8 that he may *s* him with princes, even with
Prov. 8:23 I was *s* up from everlasting, from the
Eccl. 3:11 also hath *s* the world in their heart
7:14 also hath *s* the one over against the other
Jer. 21:8 I *s* before you the way of life, and the way
Dan. 7:10 judgment was *s*. . the books were opened
Acts 13:47 *s* thee to be a light of the Gentiles
1 Cor. 4:9 God hath *s* forth us the apostles last
Eph. 1:20 and *s* him at his own right hand
Heb. 2:7 didst *s* him over the works of thy hands
Rev. 3:8 I have *s* before thee an open door

Seth Gen. 4:25–5:8

Settle *See also* Establish, Found, Stablish

1 Chr. 17:14 *s* him in mine house and in my kingdom
Ps. 65:10 thou *s* the furrows thereof: thou makest
Prov. 8:25 before the mountains were *s*, before the
Jer. 48:11 and he hath *s* on his lees, and hath not
Ezek. 36:11 I will *s* you after your old estates
Lk. 21:14 *s* it therefore in your hearts, not to
1 Pet. 5:10 perfect, stablish, strengthen, *s* you

Seven

Gen. 29:18 I will serve thee *s* years for Rachel
41:27 *s* empty ears. . shall be *s* years of famine
Lev. 26:18 punish you *s* times more for your sins
Num. 23:1 *s* altars, and prepare. . *s* oxen and *s* rams
Josh. 6:4 ye shall compass the city *s* times
Ps. 119:164 *s* times a day do I praise thee, because
Prov. 24:16 a just man falleth *s* times, and riseth
Dan. 9:25 the Messiah the Prince, shall be *s* weeks
Amos 5:8 seek him that maketh the *s* stars and Orion
Zech. 4:2 *s* lamps thereon. . *s* pipes to the *s* lamps
Mt. 18:21 against me, and I forgive him? till *s* times?
22:25 (Mk. 12:20; Lk. 20:29) *s* brethren. . the first
Lk. 17:4 he trespass against thee *s* times in a day
Acts 6:3 look. . among you *s* men of honest report
Rev. 1:4 (1:11) the *s* churches which are in Asia
1:12 being turned, I saw *s* golden candlesticks
1:16 and he had in his right hand *s* stars
1:20 *s* stars are the angels of the *s* churches
3:1 hath the *s* Spirits of God, and the *s* stars
8:2 the *s* angels. . to them were given *s* trumpets
12:3 (13:1; 17:3) having *s* heads and ten horns
15:1 I saw. . *s* angels having the *s* last plagues

Sevenfold

Gen. 4:15 Cain, vengeance shall be taken on him *s*
Prov. 6:31 but if he be found, he shall restore *s*
Is. 30:26 and the light of the sun shall be *s*

Seventh

Gen. 2:2 (Heb. 4:4) rested on the *s* day from all his
Ex. 20:10 (Deut. 5:14) *s* day is. . sabbath of the LORD

Seventy

Gen. 4:24 be avenged sevenfold, truly Lamech *s* and
Ex. 1:5 out of the loins of Jacob were *s* souls
24:1 and *s* of the elders of Israel; and worship
Jer. 25:12 *s* years are accomplished. . I will punish
Dan. 9:2 *s* years in the desolations of Jerusalem
9:24 *s* weeks are determined upon thy people
Mt. 18:22 seven times: but, Until *s* times seven
Lk. 10:1 the Lord appointed other *s* also, and sent

Sever

Ex. 8:22 I will *s* in that day the land of Goshen
9:4 LORD shall *s* between the cattle of Israel and
Lev. 20:26 have *s* you from other people, that ye
Ezek. 39:14 shall *s* out men of continual employment
Mt. 13:49 angels. . *s* the wicked from among the just

Severity

Rom. 11:22 behold. . the goodness and *s* of God

Sew

Gen. 3:7 naked; and they *s* fig leaves together
Job 16:15 I have *s* sackcloth upon my skin
Eccl. 3:7 a time to rend, and a time to *s*
Mk. 2:21 *s* a piece of new cloth on an old garment

Shade

Ps. 121:5 the LORD is thy *s* upon thy right hand

Shadow

Judg. 9:15 then come and put your trust in my *s*
9:36 the *s* of the mountains as if they were men
2 Kgs. 20:10 (Is. 38:8) *s* return backward ten degrees
1 Chr. 29:15 our days on the earth are as a *s*
Job 7:2 as a servant earnestly desireth the *s*
14:2 he fleeth also as a *s*, and continueth not
Ps. 17:8 hide me under the *s* of thy wings
23:4 I walk through the valley of the *s* of death
91:1 shall abide under the *s* of the Almighty
102:11 my days are like a *s* that declineth
109:23 I am gone like the *s* when it declineth
144:4 his days are as a *s* that passeth away
Eccl. 6:12 his vain life which he spendeth as a *s*
Song 2:3 I sat down under his *s* with great delight
2:17 (4:6) until the day break, and the *s* flee away
Is. 4:6 shall be a tabernacle for a *s* in the daytime
25:4 a refuge from the storm, a *s* from the heat
32:2 as the *s* of a great rock in a weary land
49:2 in the *s* of his hand hath he hid me
Jer. 6:4 the *s* of the evening are stretched out
Lam. 4:20 under his *s* we shall live among the heathen
Hos. 14:7 they that dwell under his *s* shall return
Jon. 4:5 a booth, and sat under it in the *s*
Mk. 4:32 fowls of the air may lodge under the *s*
Acts 5:15 *s* of Peter passing by might overshadow
Col. 2:17 which are a *s* of things to come
Heb. 8:5 unto the example and *s* of heavenly things
9:5 cherubim of glory *s* the mercy seat
10:1 the law having a *s* of good things to come
Jas. 1:17 is no variableness, neither *s* of turning

Shadrach Dan. 1:7–3:30

Shaft

Is. 49:2 hath he hid me, and made me a polished *s*

Shake (Shook, Shaken)

Judg. 16:20 as at other times before, and *s* myself
2 Sam. 6:6 his hand to the ark . . for the oxen *s* it
Job 4:14 trembling, which made all my bones to *s*
  9:6 *s* the earth out of her place, and the pillars
Ps. 29:8 the voice of the LORD *s* the wilderness
  44:14 byword among the heathen, a *s* of the head
  46:3 though the mountains *s* with the swelling
  68:8 the earth *s*, the heavens also dropped at
  72:16 the fruit thereof shall *s* like Lebanon
  109:25 when they looked upon me they *s* their heads
Is. 2:19 when he ariseth to *s* terribly the earth
  13:2 *s* the hand, that they may go into the gates
  13:13 (Hag. 2:6) I will *s* the heavens, and the earth
  24:18 and the foundations of the earth do *s*
  52:2 *s* thyself from the dust; arise, and sit
Ezek. 37:7 behold a *s*, and the bones came together
  38:20 shall *s* at my presence, and the mountains
Hag. 2:7 *s* all nations, and the Desire of all nations
Mt. 10:14 (Mk. 6:11; Lk. 9:5) off . . dust of your feet
  24:29 (Mk. 13:25; Lk. 21:26) heavens shall be *s*
  28:4 and for fear of him the keepers did *s*
Lk. 6:48 could not *s* it; for it was founded upon a
Acts 4:31 when they had prayed, the place was *s*
2 Thes. 2:2 that ye be not soon *s* in mind
Heb. 12:26 I *s* not the earth only, but also heaven
  12:27 those things which cannot be *s* may remain

Shallum 2 Kgs. 15:10–15

Shalmaneser 2 Kgs. 17:3; 18:9

Shame *See also* Disgrace, Dishonor,
Reproach

2 Sam. 13:13 I, whither shall I cause my *s* to go?
Job 8:22 that hate thee shall be clothed with *s*
Ps. 4:2 how long will ye turn my glory into *s*?
  14:6 ye have *s* the counsel of the poor, because
  40:15 (70:3) be desolate for a reward of their *s*
  44:7 and hast put them to *s* that hated us
  44:15 and the *s* of my face hath covered me
  53:5 put them to *s*, because God hath despised
  71:24 they are brought unto *s*, that seek my hurt
  89:45 thou hast covered him with *s*
  109:29 let mine adversaries be clothed with *s*
  119:31 thy testimonies: O LORD, put me not to *s*
  132:18 his enemies will I clothe with *s*
Prov. 3:35 but *s* shall be the promotion of fools
  9:7 that reproveth a scorner getteth to himself *s*
  11:2 when pride cometh, then cometh *s*
  12:16 but a prudent man covereth *s*
  13:18 *s* shall be to him that refuseth instruction
  17:2 shall have rule over a son that causeth *s*
  19:26 son that causeth *s*, and bringeth reproach
  25:8 when thy neighbor hath put thee to *s*
Is. 30:3 shall the strength of Pharaoh be your *s*
  47:3 shall be uncovered, yea, thy *s* shall be seen
  50:6 I hid not my face from *s* and spitting
  54:4 for thou shalt forget the *s* of thy youth
  61:7 for your *s* ye shall have double
Jer. 3:25 we lie down in our *s*, and our confusion
  13:26 skirts upon thy face, that thy *s* may appear
  46:12 nations have heard of thy *s*, and thy cry
Ezek. 7:18 *s* shall be upon all faces, and baldness
  16:52 bear thine own *s* for thy sins that thou
  16:54 that thou mayest bear thine own *s*, and
  32:24 yet have they borne their *s* with them that
  44:13 shall bear their *s*, and their abominations
Dan. 12:2 and some to *s* and everlasting contempt

Hos. 4:7 therefore will I change their glory into *s*
  10:6 Ephraim shall receive *s*, and Israel shall
Hab. 2:16 thou art filled with *s* for glory
Zeph. 3:5 faileth not; but the unjust knoweth no *s*
Lk. 14:9 thou begin with *s* to take the lowest room
Acts 5:41 counted worthy to suffer *s* for his name
1 Cor. 4:14 I write not these things to *s* you, but
  6:5 I speak to your *s*. Is it so, that there
  11:6 but if it be a *s* for a woman to be shorn
  11:14 a man have long hair, it is a *s* unto him?
  14:35 it is a *s* for women to speak in the church
  15:34 knowledge of God: I speak this to your *s*
Eph. 5:12 it is a *s* even to speak of those things
Phil. 3:19 and whose glory is in their *s*, who mind
Heb. 6:6 crucify . . afresh, and put him to an open *s*
  12:2 endured the cross, despising the *s*
Jude 13 waves of the sea, foaming out their own *s*
Rev. 3:18 the *s* of thy nakedness do not appear

Shamefully

Hos. 2:5 she that conceived them hath done *s*
Mk. 12:4 (Lk. 20:11) and sent him away *s* handled
1 Thes. 2:2 suffered before, and were *s* entreated

Shamgar Judg. 3:31

Shape (Shapen)

Ps. 51:5 behold, I was *s* in iniquity; and in sin
Lk. 3:22 Holy Ghost descended in a bodily *s* like a
Jn. 5:37 neither heard his voice . . nor seen his *s*
Rev. 9:7 *s* of the locusts were like unto horses

Shaphan 2 Kgs. 22:3–14 (2 Chr. 34:8–20)

Sharon Song 2:1; Is. 33:9; 65:10

Sharp (Sharper)

Josh. 5:2 make thee *s* knives, and circumcise again
1 Sam. 14:4 a *s* rock on the one side, and a *s* rock
Job 41:30 *s* stones are under him: he spreadeth *s*
Ps. 45:5 arrows are *s* in the heart of the King's
  52:2 tongue deviseth mischiefs; like a *s* razor
Prov. 5:4 bitter as wormwood, *s* as a two-edged sword
Is. 41:15 make thee a new *s* threshing instrument
Mic. 7:4 the most upright is *s* than a thorn hedge
Acts 15:39 contention was so *s* between them, that
Heb. 4:12 and *s* than any two-edged sword, piercing
Rev. 1:16 out of his mouth went a *s* two-edged sword
  14:14 a golden crown, and in his hand a *s* sickle

Sharpen

1 Sam. 13:20 *s* every man his share, and his coulter
Job 16:9 his teeth; mine enemy *s* his eyes upon me
Ps. 140:3 they have *s* their tongues like a serpent
Prov. 27:17 iron *s* iron; so a man *s* the countenance
Ezek. 21:9 a sword, a sword is *s*, and also furbished

Sharply

Judg. 8:1 Midianites? And they did chide with him *s*
Tit. 1:13 rebuke them *s*, that they may be sound in

Shave (Shaven)

Gen. 41:14 he *s* himself, and changed his raiment
Lev. 13:33 shall be *s*, but the scall shall he not *s*
Num. 6:9 *s* his head in the day of his cleansing
  6:18 Nazarite shall *s* the head of his separation
Judg. 16:17 if I be *s*, then my strength will go
Job 1:20 then Job . . rent his mantle, and *s* his head
Is. 7:20 shall the Lord *s* with a razor that is hired
Ezek. 44:20 neither shall they *s* their heads
Acts 21:24 at charges . . that they may *s* their heads
1 Cor. 11:5 that is even all one as if she were *s*

Sheaf (Sheaves)

Gen. 37:7 binding *s* in the field, and, lo, my *s* arose
Deut. 24:19 forgot a *s* in the field, thou shalt not
Ruth 2:7 and gather after the reapers among the *s*
  2:15 glean even among the *s*, and reproach her not
Ps. 126:6 with rejoicing, bringing his *s* with him
  129:7 nor he that bindeth *s* his bosom
Amos 2:13 as a cart is pressed that is full of *s*
Mic. 4:12 gather them as the *s* into the floor

Shear (Shorn)

Gen. 31:19 Laban went to *s* his sheep: and Rachel
Acts 18:18 having *s* his head in Cenchrea
1 Cor. 11:6 woman be not covered, let her also be *s*

Shearer

1 Sam. 25:7 now I have heard that thou hast *s*
Is. 53:7 (Acts 8:32) as a sheep before her *s* is dumb

Shear-jashub Is. 7:3

Sheath *See also* Sword

Jn. 18:11 unto Peter, Put up thy sword into the *s*

Sheba queen of 1 Kgs. 10:1-13 (2 Chr. 9:1-12)

Shechem the son of Hamor Gen. 34:2-26

Shechem (Sychem) the city

Gen. 37:12 went to feed their father's flock in *S*
Josh. 21:21 (1 Chr. 6:67) *S*. . a city of refuge
  24:1 gathered all the tribes of Israel to *S*
Judg. 9:1 Abimelech the son of Jerubbaal went to *S*
1 Kgs. 12:1 (2 Chr. 10:1) Rehoboam went to *S*
  12:25 then Jeroboam built *S* in mount Ephraim
Ps. 60:6 (108:7) I will rejoice, I will divide *S*
Acts 7:16 were carried over into *S*, and laid in

Shed

Gen. 9:6 *s* man's blood, by man shall his blood be *s*
Mt. 26:28 (Mk. 14:24; Lk. 22:20) my blood. . *s* for
Acts 2:33 he hath *s* forth this, which ye now see
Rom. 5:5 love of God is *s* abroad in our hearts by
Tit. 3:6 which he *s* on us abundantly through Jesus
Heb. 9:22 and without *s* of blood is no remission

Sheep *See also* Goat, Kid, Lamb,
  Scapegoat

Gen. 4:2 and Abel was a keeper of *s*, but Cain was
Num. 27:17 be not as *s* which have no shepherd
2 Sam. 7:8 (1 Chr. 17:7) sheepcote, from following. . *s*
  24:17 (1 Chr. 21:17) these *s*, what have they done?
1 Kgs. 22:17 (2 Chr. 18:16) *s* that have not a shepherd
Ps. 44:11 hast given us like *s* appointed for meat
  44:22 (Rom. 8:36) counted as *s* for the slaughter
  49:14 like *s* they are laid in the grave
  78:52 made his own people to go forth like *s*
  79:13 so we thy people and *s* of thy pasture will
  95:7 people of his pasture, and the *s* of his hand
  100:3 are his people, and the *s* of his pasture
  119:176 I have gone astray like a lost *s*
Is. 53:6 all we like *s* have gone astray
  53:7 and as a *s* before her shearers is dumb
Jer. 12:3 pull them out like *s* for the slaughter
  23:1 destroy and scatter the *s* of my pasture!
  50:6 my people hath been lost *s*: their shepherds
Ezek. 34:6 my *s* wandered through all the mountains
  34:11 I, will both search my *s*, and seek them out
Zech. 13:7 (Mt. 26:31; Mk. 14:27) *s* shall be scattered
Mt. 7:15 prophets, which come to you in *s*'s clothing
  10:6 (15:24) to the lost *s* of the house of Israel
  10:16 send you forth as *s* in the midst of wolves

Mt. 12:12 how much then is a man better than a *s*?
  18:12 (Lk. 15:4) if a man have a hundred *s*
  25:32 a shepherd divideth his *s* from the goats
Jn. 10:3 *s* hear his voice: and he calleth his own *s*
  10:11 good shepherd giveth his life for the *s*
  10:16 other *s* I have, which are not of this fold
  10:26 ye believe not, because ye are not of my *s*
  10:27 my *s* hear my voice, and I know them
  21:16 I love thee. He saith unto him, Feed my *s*
Acts 8:32 he was led as a *s* to the slaughter
Heb. 13:20 Jesus, that great shepherd of the *s*
1 Pet. 2:25 ye were as *s* going astray; but are now

Sheepfold

Ps. 78:70 he chose David. . and took him from the *s*

Sheet

Judg. 14:12 thirty *s* and thirty change of garments
Acts 10:11 (11:5) a great *s* knit at the four corners

Shekel

Ex. 30:13 half a *s* after the *s* of the sanctuary

Shelter

Job 24:8 and embrace the rock for want of a *s*
Ps. 61:3 thou hast been a *s* for me, and a strong

Shem Gen. 5:32; 6:10

Shemaiah 1 Kgs. 12:22 (2 Chr. 11:2)

Shepherd *See also* Pastor, Sheep

Num. 27:17 be not as sheep which have no *s*
1 Kgs. 22:17 (2 Chr. 18:16) sheep that have not a *s*
Ps. 23:1 the LORD is my *s*; I shall not want
  80:1 give ear, O *S* of Israel, thou that leadest
Is. 40:11 he shall feed his flock like a *s*
  44:28 that saith of Cyrus, He is my *s*, and shall
  56:11 they are *s* that cannot understand
Jer. 23:4 I will set up *s* over them which shall
  25:34 howl, ye *s*, and cry; and wallow yourselves
  31:10 will gather him, and keep him, as a *s* doth
  51:23 also break in pieces. . the *s* and his flock
Ezek. 34:2 prophesy against the *s* of Israel
  34:5 they were scattered, because there is no *s*
  34:8 neither did my *s* search for my flock
  34:12 as a *s* seeketh out his flock in the day
  34:23 I will set up one *s* over them, and he shall
  37:24 they all shall have one *s*: they shall also
Amos 3:12 the *s* taketh out of the mouth of the lion
Zech. 10:2 were troubled, because there was no *s*
  11:16 lo, I will raise up a *s* in the land, which
  11:17 woe to the idol *s* that leaveth the flock!
  13:7 (Mt. 26:31; Mk. 14:27) smite the *s*. . the sheep
Mt. 9:36 (Mk. 6:34) scattered. . as sheep having no *s*
  25:32 as a *s* divideth his sheep from the goats
Lk. 2:8 *s* abiding in the field, keeping watch over
  2:20 the *s* returned, glorifying and praising God
Jn. 10:2 he that entereth in by the door is the *s*
  10:11 I am the good *s*: the good *s* giveth his life
  10:14 I am the good *s*, and know my sheep, and am
  10:16 and there shall be one fold, and one *s*
Heb. 13:20 Lord Jesus, that great *s* of the sheep
1 Pet. 2:25 unto the *S* and Bishop of your souls
  5:4 and when the chief *S* shall appear, ye shall

Shibboleth (Sibboleth)

Judg. 12:6 say now *S*: and he said *S*: for he could

Shield *See also* Buckler, Target

Gen. 15:1 I am thy *s*, and thy exceeding great reward
Deut. 33:29 saved by the LORD, the *s* of thy help
Judg. 5:8 was there a *s* or spear seen among forty

2 Sam. 1:21 *s* of the mighty is vilely cast away
　22:3 he is my *s*, and the horn of my salvation
　22:36 (Ps. 18:35) given me the *s* of thy salvation
1 Kgs. 10:17 (2 Chr. 9:16) made. . *s* of beaten gold
Ps. 3:3 but thou, O LORD, art a *s* for me; my glory
　5:12 with favor wilt thou compass him as with a *s*
　28:7 the LORD is my strength and my *s*; my heart
　33:20 for the LORD: he is our help and our *s*
　47:9 for the *s* of the earth belong unto God
　84:11 LORD God is a sun and *s*: the LORD will give
　91:4 his truth shall be thy *s* and buckler
　115:9 in the LORD: he is their help and their *s*
　119:114 thou art my hiding place and my *s*: I hope
Prov. 30:5 a *s* unto them that put their trust in
Jer. 51:11 make bright the arrows; gather the *s*
Eph. 6:16 taking the *s* of faith, wherewith ye

Shiloah *See also* Siloam Is. 8:6

Shiloh

Gen. 49:10 sceptre shall not depart. . until *S* come
Josh. 18:1 Israel assembled together at *S*, and set
Judg. 21:21 the daughters of *S* come out to dance
1 Sam. 2:14 they did in *S* unto all the Israelites
　4:3 let us fetch the ark. . out of *S* unto us
Ps. 78:60 so that he forsook the tabernacle of *S*
Jer. 7:12 go ye now unto my place which was in *S*

Shimei

2 Sam. 16:5-13; 19:16-23; 1 Kgs. 2:36-44

Shine (Shone) *See also* Enlighten, Illuminate, Lighten

Ex. 34:29 skin of his face *s* while he talked with
Num. 6:25 LORD make his face *s* upon thee, and be
Job 10:3 and *s* upon the counsel of the wicked?
　22:28 and the light shall *s* upon thy ways
　29:3 when his candle *s* upon my head, and when
　36:32 commandeth it not to *s* by the cloud that
Ps. 50:2 Zion, the perfection of beauty, God hath *s*
　67:1 bless us; and cause his face to *s* upon us
　80:1 that dwellest between the cherubim, *s* forth
　80:3 cause thy face to *s*; and we shall be saved
　104:15 and oil to make his face to *s*, and bread
　119:135 make thy face to *s* upon thy servant
　139:12 but the night *s* as the day: the darkness
Prov. 4:18 *s* more and more unto the perfect day
Eccl. 8:1 a man's wisdom maketh his face to *s*
Is. 9:2 of death, upon them hath the light *s*
　60:1 arise, *s*; for thy light is come
Dan. 9:17 cause thy face to *s* upon thy sanctuary
　12:3 they that be wise shall *s* as the brightness
Mt. 5:16 let your light so *s* before men, that they
　13:43 shall the righteous *s* forth as the sun
　17:2 his face did *s* as the sun, and his raiment
Mk. 9:3 his raiment became *s*, exceeding white as
Lk. 2:9 the glory of the Lord *s* round about them
Jn. 1:5 the light *s* in darkness; and the darkness
Acts 9:3 (22:6; 26:13) there *s*. . a light from heaven
2 Cor. 4:4 light of the glorious gospel. . should *s*
　4:6 to *s* out of darkness, hath *s* in our hearts
Phil. 2:15 among whom ye *s* as lights in the world
2 Pet. 1:19 as unto a light that *s* in a dark place
1 Jn. 2:8 darkness is past. . the true light now *s*
Rev. 1:16 his countenance was as the sun *s* in his
　8:12 the day *s* not for a third part of it
　21:23 the sun, neither of the moon, to *s* in it

Ship *See also* Boat

1 Kgs. 22:48 (2 Chr. 20:36) Jehoshaphat made *s* of
Job 9:26 they are passed away as the swift *s*
Ps. 104:26 there go the *s*: there is that leviathan

Ps. 107:23 they that go down to the sea in *s*
Prov. 30:19 the way of a *s* in the midst of the sea
　31:14 she is like the merchants' *s*; she bringeth
Ezek. 27:5 have made all thy *s* boards of fir tree
Jon. 1:3 found a *s* going to Tarshish: so he paid
Mt. 4:22 immediately left the *s* and their father
　14:24 (Mk. 6:47) *s* was now in the midst of the sea
Mk. 4:38 was in the hinder part of the *s*, asleep
Lk. 5:7 filled both the *s*, so that they began to sink
　8:22 that he went into a *s* with his disciples
Jn. 21:6 cast the net on the right side of the *s*
Acts 27:15 when the *s* was caught. . we let her drive
　27:41 two seas met, they ran the *s* aground
Jas. 3:4 also the *s*, which though they be so great
Rev. 18:17 all the company in *s*, and sailors

Shipwreck

2 Cor. 11:25 once was I stoned, thrice I suffered *s*
1 Tim. 1:19 put away, concerning faith have made *s*

Shishak 1 Kgs. 11:40; 14:25 (2 Chr. 12:2)

Shittim

Ex. 25:10 (37:1) they shall make an ark of *s* wood

Shod

Mk. 6:9 be *s* with sandals; and not put on two coats
Eph. 6:15 *s* with the preparation of the gospel

Shoe

Ex. 3:5 (Acts 7:33) put off thy *s* from off thy feet
　12:11 your loins girded, your *s* on your feet
Deut. 25:9 loose his *s* from off his foot, and spit
　33:25 thy *s* shall be iron and brass; and as thy
Josh. 9:13 our garments and our *s* are become old
Ruth 4:8 buy it for thee. So he drew off his *s*
Amos 2:6 for silver, and the poor for a pair of *s*
Mt. 3:11 whose *s* I am not worthy to bear: he shall
　10:10 (Lk. 10:4) neither two coats, neither *s*
Mk. 1:7 (Lk. 3:16) the latchet of whose *s* I am not
Lk. 15:22 put a ring on his hand, and *s* on his feet
　22:35 without purse, and scrip, and *s*, lacked ye
Acts 13:25 *s* of his feet I am not worthy to loose

Shone *See* Shine

Shook *See* Shake

Shoot (Shot)

Ps. 11:2 they may privily *s* at the upright in heart
　18:14 *s* out lightnings, and discomfited them
　22:7 they *s* out the lip, they shake the head
　64:3 bows to *s* their arrows, even bitter words
　64:4 in secret at the perfect: suddenly. . they *s*
　64:7 God shall *s* at them with an arrow; suddenly
Lk. 21:30 when they now *s* forth, ye see and know

Shore

Jn. 21:4 Jesus stood on the *s*; but the disciples
Acts 21:5 and we kneeled down on the *s*, and prayed

Shorn *See* Shear

Short (Shorter)

Num. 11:23 unto Moses, Is the LORD's hand waxed *s*?
Job 17:12 the light is *s* because of darkness
　20:5 the triumphing of the wicked is *s*
Ps. 89:47 remember how *s* my time is: wherefore
Is. 28:20 the bed is *s* than that a man can stretch
Rom. 3:23 sinned, and come *s* of the glory of God
1 Cor. 7:29 but this I say, brethren, the time is *s*
1 Thes. 2:17 being taken from you for a *s* time
Rev. 12:12 he knoweth that he hath but a *s* time

Shorten

Ps. 89:45 days of his youth hast thou *s*: thou hast
Prov. 10:27 but the years of the wicked shall be *s*
Is. 50:2 is my hand *s* . . that it cannot redeem?
59:1 LORD's hand is not *s*, that it cannot save
Mt. 24:22 (Mk. 13:20) except those days should be *s*

Shoulder

Deut. 33:12 and he shall dwell between his *s*
Is. 9:6 and the government shall be upon his *s*
Mt. 23:4 lay them on men's *s*; but they themselves
Lk. 15:5 found it, he layeth it on his *s*, rejoicing

Shout

Num. 23:21 is with him . . *s* of a king is among them
Josh. 6:10 ye shall not *s* . . until the day I bid you *s*
1 Sam. 4:5 all Israel *s* with a great *s*, so that
Ezra 3:11 all the people *s* with a great *s*, when
Ps. 47:1 *s* unto God with the voice of triumph
47:5 God is gone up with a *s*, the LORD with the
Is. 12:6 cry out and *s*, thou inhabitant of Zion
Zeph. 3:14 sing, O daughter of Zion; *s*, O Israel
1 Thes. 4:16 shall descend from heaven with a *s*

Show *See also* Appear, Evident, Manifest

Ex. 33:18 he said, I beseech thee, *s* me thy glory
Deut. 34:1 LORD *s* him . . the land of Gilead unto Dan
2 Kgs. 20:13 (Is. 39:2) Hezekiah . . *s* them . . the house
Ps. 4:6 be many that say, Who will *s* us any good?
25:4 *s* me thy ways, O LORD; teach me thy paths
39:6 surely every man walketh in a vain *s*
50:23 conversation aright will I *s* the salvation
92:15 *s* that the LORD is upright: he is my rock
Is. 60:6 shall *s* forth the praises of the LORD
Jer. 33:3 I will answer thee, and *s* thee great
Joel 2:30 (Acts 2:19) will *s* wonders in the heavens
Mic. 7:15 will I *s* unto him marvelous things
Nah. 3:5 I will *s* the nations thy nakedness
Zech. 1:9 said unto me, I will *s* thee what these be
Mt. 4:8 (Lk. 4:5) *s* him all the kingdoms of the world
8:4 (Mk. 1:44; Lk. 5:14) *s* thyself to the priest
14:2 (Mk. 6:14) therefore mighty works do *s* forth
16:1 him that he would *s* them a sign from heaven
22:19 (Lk. 20:24) *s* me the tribute money
24:24 (Mk. 13:22) shall *s* great signs and wonders
Mk. 14:15 (Lk. 22:12) will *s* you a large upper room
Lk. 8:39 *s* how great things God hath done unto thee
17:14 go *s* yourselves unto the priests
20:47 widows' houses . . for a *s* make long prayers
Jn. 5:20 *s* him all things . . will *s* him greater works
7:4 thou do these things, *s* thyself to the world
14:8 Lord, *s* us the Father, and it sufficeth us
16:13 Spirit of truth . . will *s* you things to come
21:1 Jesus *s* himself . . at the sea of Tiberias
Acts 1:3 he *s* himself alive after his passion
16:17 which *s* unto us the way of salvation
20:35 I have *s* you all things, how that so laboring
23:22 tell no man that thou hast *s* these . . to me
Rom. 1:19 is manifest . . for God hath *s* it unto them
1 Cor. 11:26 ye do *s* the Lord's death till he come
12:31 and yet a I unto you a more excellent way
Col. 2:15 made a *s* of them openly, triumphing over
2:23 have indeed a *s* of wisdom in will-worship
2 Tim. 2:15 study to *s* thyself approved unto God
Jas. 2:18 *s* me thy faith without thy works, and I
1 Jn. 1:2 *s* unto you that eternal life, which was
Rev. 4:1 and I will *s* thee things which must be
17:1 I will *s* unto thee the judgment of the great
21:9 I will *s* thee the bride, the Lamb's wife
21:10 *s* me that great city, the holy Jerusalem
22:1 and he *s* me a pure river of water of life

Showbread

1 Sam. 21:6 for there was no bread there but the *s*
Mt. 12:4 (Mk. 2:26; Lk. 6:4) eat the *s* . . not lawful

Shower *See also* Rain

Deut. 32:2 tender herb, and as the *s* upon the grass
Job 24:8 they are wet with the *s* of the mountains
Ps. 65:10 thou makest it soft with *s*: thou blessest
Jer. 3:3 therefore the *s* have been withholden
14:22 can cause rain? or can the heavens give *s*?
Ezek. 34:26 there shall be *s* of blessing
Mic. 5:7 as the *s* upon the grass, that tarrieth not
Zech. 10:1 make bright clouds, and give them *s*
Lk. 12:54 ye say, There cometh a *s*; and so it is

Shrine

Acts 19:24 a silversmith, which made silver *s* for

Shulamite Song 6:13

Shun

Acts 20:27 I have not *s* to declare unto you all
2 Tim. 2:16 *s* profane and vain babblings: for they

Shunammite 2 Kgs. 4:12–37

Shunem 2 Kgs. 4:8

Shur Gen. 16:7; 20:1; Ex. 15:22; 1 Sam. 15:7

Shushan

Neh. 1:1 it came to pass . . as I was in *S* the palace
Esth. 1:2 throne of his kingdom, which was in *S*
3:15 down to drink; but the city *S* was perplexed
Dan. 8:2 when I saw, that I was at *S* in the palace

Shut *See also* Close

Gen. 7:16 commanded him: and the LORD *s* him in
Deut. 15:7 nor *s* thine hand from thy poor brother
Job 38:8 or who *s* up the sea with doors, when it
Ps. 77:9 hath he in anger *s* up his tender mercies?
88:8 made me . . abomination unto them: I am *s* up
Is. 6:10 *s* their eyes; lest they see with their
22:22 open, and none shall *s*; and he shall *s*, and
60:11 they shall not be *s* day nor night; that men
Jer. 36:5 I am *s* up; I cannot go into the house
Lam. 3:8 when I cry and shout, he *s* out my prayer
Mt. 23:13 hypocrites! for ye *s* up the kingdom
25:10 to the marriage: and the door was *s*
Lk. 3:20 above all, that he *s* up John in prison
4:25 when the heaven was *s* up three years
Jn. 20:26 then came Jesus, the doors being *s*
Acts 26:10 many of the saints did I *s* up in prison
Gal. 3:23 kept under the law, *s* up unto the faith
1 Jn. 3:17 *s* up his bowels of compassion from him
Rev. 3:7 openeth, and no man *s*; and *s*, and no man
3:8 before thee an open door, and no man can *s* it
11:6 these have power to *s* heaven, that it rain
20:3 cast him into the bottomless pit, and *s* him up

Shuttle

Job 7:6 my days are swifter than a weaver's *s*

Sick

1 Sam. 19:14 sent . . to take David, she said, He is *s*
1 Kgs. 17:17 the son of the woman . . fell *s*
2 Kgs. 20:1 (2 Chr. 32:24; Is. 38:1) was Hezekiah *s*
Neh. 2:2 countenance sad, seeing thou art not *s*?
Prov. 13:12 hope deferred maketh the heart *s*
23:35 they have stricken me . . and I was not *s*
Song 2:5 comfort me with apples: for I am *s* of love
5:8 find my beloved . . tell him, that I am *s* of love
Is. 1:5 whole head is *s*, and the whole heart faint

Is. 33:24 and the inhabitant shall not say, I am *s*
Ezek. 34:16 and will strengthen that which was *s*
Hos. 7:5 have made him *s* with bottles of wine
Mic. 6:13 also will I make thee *s* in smiting thee
Mal. 1:8 ye offer the lame and *s*, is it not evil?
Mt. 4:24 and they brought unto him all *s* people
8:6 (Lk. 7:2) servant lieth at home *s* of the palsy
8:14 (Mk. 1:30) wife's mother laid, and *s* of a fever
8:16 (Mk. 1:34; Lk. 4:40) healed all that were *s*
9:12 (Mk. 2:17; Lk. 5:31) but they that are *s*
10:8 (Lk. 9:2; 10:9) heal the *s*
14:14 compassion toward them. . he healed their *s*
25:36 ye clothed me: I was *s*, and ye visited me
Mk. 6:56 laid the *s* in the streets, and besought him
16:18 lay hands on the *s*, and they shall recover
Jn. 4:46 nobleman, whose son was *s* at Capernaum
11:3 Lord, behold, he whom thou lovest is *s*
Acts 5:15 they brought forth the *s* into the streets
19:12 were brought unto the *s* handkerchiefs
28:8 father of Publius lay *s* of a fever and of a
Phil. 2:27 was *s* nigh unto death: but God had mercy
Jas. 5:14 is any *s* among you? let him call for the
5:15 and the prayer of faith shall save the *s*

Sickle

Deut. 23:25 a *s* unto thy neighbor's standing corn
Joel 3:13 (Rev. 14:15) put ye in the *s*. . harvest is ripe
Mk. 4:29 putteth in the *s*, because the harvest is
Rev. 14:14 golden crown, and in his hand a sharp *s*

Sickness *See also* Disease, Infirmity

Ex. 23:25 I will take *s* away from the midst of thee
Deut. 7:15 the LORD will take away from thee all *s*
Ps. 41:3 thou wilt make all his bed in his *s*
Eccl. 5:17 hath much sorrow and wrath with his *s*
Hos. 5:13 when Ephraim saw his *s*, and Judah saw his
Mt. 4:23 healing all manner of *s* and all manner of
8:17 himself took our infirmities, and bare our *s*
10:1 (Mk. 3:15) power. . to heal all manner of *s*
Jn. 11:4 this *s* is not unto death, but for the glory

Side

Ex. 32:26 who is on the LORD's *s*? let him come unto
Ps. 118:6 the LORD is on my *s*; I will not fear
124:1 had not been the LORD who was on our *s*
Jn. 19:34 the soldiers with a spear pierced his *s*
20:27 reach hither thy hand, and thrust it into my *s*
2 Cor. 4:8 troubled on every *s*, yet not distressed

Sidon (Zidon) *See also* Tyre

Ezek. 28:21 set thy face against *Z*, and prophesy
Mt. 11:21 (Lk. 10:13) had been done in Tyre and *S*
Acts 27:3 and the next day we touched at *S*

Siege

Deut. 20:19 not cut them. . to employ them in the *s*
2 Chr. 32:9 but he himself laid *s* against Lachish
32:10 that ye abide in the *s* in Jerusalem?
Ezek. 4:7 set thy face toward the *s* of Jerusalem
Zech. 12:2 shall be in the *s* both against Judah and

Sift

Is. 30:28 *s* the nations with the sieve of vanity
Amos 9:9 I will *s* the house of Israel. . as corn is *s*
Lk. 22:31 to have you, that he may *s* you as wheat

Sigh

Ex. 2:23 king. . died: and the children of Israel *s*
Lam. 1:4 her priests *s*, her virgins are afflicted
1:22 for my *s* are many, and my heart is faint
Ezek. 9:4 mark upon the foreheads of the men that *s*

Sighing

Job 3:24 my *s* cometh before I eat, and my roarings
Ps. 12:5 for the *s* of the needy, now will I arise
31:10 is spent with grief, and my years with *s*
79:11 let the *s* of the prisoner come before thee

Sight

Ex. 3:3 see this great *s*, why the bush is not burnt
Ps. 19:14 acceptable in thy *s*, O LORD, my strength
Eccl. 6:9 better is the *s* of the eyes than the
Mt. 11:5 blind receive their *s*, and the lame walk
20:34 (Mk. 10:52; Lk. 18:43) their eyes received *s*
Lk. 4:18 and recovering of *s* to the blind
18:42 receive thy *s*: thy faith hath saved thee
Acts 9:9 he was three days without *s*, and neither
2 Cor. 5:7 for we walk by faith, not by *s*
Heb. 12:21 so terrible was the *s*, that Moses said
1 Jn. 3:22 those things that are pleasing in his *s*

Sign *See also* Mark, Miracle, Token, Wonder

Gen. 1:14 let them be for *s*, and for seasons
Ex. 4:8 the first *s*. . they will believe. . the latter *s*
7:3 harden Pharaoh's heart, and multiply my *s*
31:13 my sabbaths ye shall keep: for it is a *s*
Num. 16:38 shall be a *s* unto the children of Israel
26:10 when that company died. . they became a *s*
Deut. 6:8 shalt bind them for a *s* upon thine hand
6:22 LORD showed *s* and wonders, great and sore
13:1 or a dreamer of dreams, and giveth thee a *s*
28:46 shall be upon thee for a *s* and for a wonder
Josh. 4:6 this may be a *s* among you, that when
24:17 which did those great *s* in our sight
Judg. 6:17 show me a *s* that thou talkest with me
1 Sam. 2:34 this shall be a *s* unto thee, that shall
1 Kgs. 13:3 and he gave a *s*. . saying, This is the *s*
2 Kgs. 19:29 (Is. 37:30) this shall be a *s* unto thee
20:8 (Is. 38:22) what shall be the *s*. . that I shall
Neh. 9:10 and showedst *s* and wonders upon Pharaoh
Ps. 78:43 how he had wrought his *s* in Egypt
105:27 they showed his *s* among them
Is. 7:11 ask thee a *s* of the LORD thy God; ask it
7:14 shall give you a *s*; Behold, a virgin shall
8:18 for *s* and for wonders in Israel from the
19:20 it shall be for a *s* and for a witness unto
38:7 this shall be a *s* unto thee from the LORD
55:13 an everlasting *s* that shall not be cut off
Jer. 10:2 be not dismayed at the *s* of heaven
44:29 this shall be a *s* unto you, saith the LORD
Ezek. 4:3 this shall be a *s* to the house of Israel
12:6 have set thee for a *s* unto the house
14:8 will make him a *s* and a proverb, and I will
20:12 my sabbaths, to be a *s* between me and them
24:24 thus Ezekiel is unto you a *s*
Dan. 4:3 how great are his *s*! and how mighty are
6:27 he worketh *s* and wonders in heaven and in
Mt. 12:38 Master, we would see a *s* from thee
12:39 (16:4; Lk. 11:29) no *s*. . but the *s* of. . Jonas
16:1 (Mk. 8:11; Lk. 11:16) show. . a *s* from heaven
16:3 but can ye not discern the *s* of the times?
24:3 (Mk. 13:4; Lk. 21:7) be. . *s* of thy coming
24:24 (Mk. 13:22) false prophets. . show great *s*
24:30 (Lk. 21:25) appear the *s* of the Son of man
Mk. 16:17 these *s* shall follow them that believe
16:20 and confirming the word with *s* following
Lk. 2:12 this shall be a *s* unto you; Ye shall find
2:34 and for a *s* which shall be spoken against
Jn. 4:48 ye see *s* and wonders, ye will not believe
6:30 what *s* showest thou then, that we may see
20:30 many other *s*. . did Jesus in the presence
Acts 2:22 among you by miracles and wonders and *s*

Acts 4:30 that *s* and wonders may be done by the
   5:12 *s* and wonders wrought among the people
   14:3 granted *s* and wonders to be done by their
   28:11 a ship. . whose *s* was Castor and Pollux
Rom. 4:11 received the *s* of circumcision, a seal
   15:19 through mighty *s* and wonders, by the power
1 Cor. 1:22 the Jews require a *s*, and the Greeks
   14:22 wherefore tongues are for a *s*, not to them
2 Cor. 12:12 *s* of an apostle were wrought among you
2 Thes. 2:9 with all power and *s* and lying wonders
Heb. 2:4 God also bearing them witness, both with *s*
Rev. 15:1 another *s* in heaven, great and marvelous

Signet *See also* Seal

Gen. 38:18 I give thee? And she said, Thy *s*, and thy
Jer. 22:24 Coniah. . were the *s* upon my right hand
Dan. 6:17 his own *s*, and with the *s* of his lords

Signification

1 Cor. 14:10 voices. . and none of them is without *s*

Signify

Jn. 12:33 this he said, *s* what death he should die
Acts 11:28 Agabus, and *s* by the Spirit that there
   21:26 into the temple, to *s* the accomplishment
   23:15 *s* to the chief captain that he bring him
   25:27 not withal to *s* the crimes laid against
Heb. 9:8 the Holy Ghost this *s*, that the way into
   12:27 this word, Yet once more, *s* the removing
1 Pet. 1:11 the Spirit of Christ. . in them did *s*
Rev. 1:1 *s* it by his angel unto his servant John

Sihon Num. 21:21–34 (Deut. 2:24–32)

Silas (Silvanus)

Acts 15:22, 40; 1 Pet. 5:12

Silence

Job 4:16 there was *s*, and I heard a voice, saying
Ps. 31:18 let the lying lips be put to *s*
   32:3 when I kept *s*, my bones waxed old through
   39:2 I was dumb with *s*, I held my peace
   83:1 keep not thou *s*, O God: hold not thy peace
   94:17 been my help, my soul had almost dwelt in *s*
Eccl. 3:7 a time to keep *s*, and a time to speak
Jer. 8:14 for the LORD our God hath put us to *s*
Amos 5:13 the prudent shall keep *s* in that time
Hab. 2:20 let all the earth keep *s* before him
Mt. 22:34 heard that he had put the Sadducees to *s*
1 Cor. 14:28 there be no interpreter, let him keep *s*
   14:34 let your women keep *s* in the churches
1 Tim. 2:11 the woman learn in *s* with all subjection
1 Pet. 2:15 put to *s* the ignorance of foolish men
Rev. 8:1 *s* in heaven about the space of half an hour

Silent

1 Sam. 2:9 and the wicked shall be *s* in darkness
Ps. 22:2 and in the night season, and am not *s*
   28:1 be not *s* to me: lest, if thou be *s* to me
   30:12 may sing praise to thee, and not be *s*
   31:17 be ashamed, and let them be *s* in the grave
Is. 47:5 sit thou *s*, and get thee into darkness
Jer. 8:14 defensed cities, and let us be *s* there
Zech. 2:13 be *s*, O all flesh, before the LORD

Silk

Prov. 31:22 tapestry; her clothing is *s* and purple
Ezek. 16:10 fine linen, and I covered thee with *s*
Rev. 18:12 linen, and purple, and *s*, and scarlet

Silly

Job 5:2 foolish man, and envy slayeth the *s* one
Hos. 7:11 Ephraim. . is like a *s* dove without heart
2 Tim. 3:6 lead captive *s* women laden with sins

Siloam Lk. 13:4; Jn. 9:7

Silvanus *See* Silas

Silver

Gen. 44:2 and put my cup, the *s* cup, in the sack's
1 Kgs. 10:27 (2 Chr. 1:15) made *s* to be in Jerusalem
2 Kgs. 22:4 that he may sum the *s* which is brought
Job 3:15 had gold, who filled their houses with *s*
   22:25 be thy defense. . thou shalt have plenty of *s*
   27:16 though he heap up *s* as the dust
Ps. 12:6 words of the LORD. . as *s* tried in a furnace
   66:10 proved us: thou hast tried us, as *s* is tried
Prov. 3:14 is better than the merchandise of *s*
   8:10 receive my instruction, and not *s*
   10:20 the tongue of the just is as choice *s*
   16:16 understanding rather to be chosen than *s*!
   17:3 fining pot is for *s*. . the furnace for gold
Eccl. 5:10 loveth *s* shall not be satisfied with *s*
   12:6 or ever the *s* cord be loosed, or the golden
Is. 1:22 thy *s* is become dross, thy wine mixed with
Jer. 6:30 reprobate *s* shall men call them
Amos 2:6 because they sold the righteous for *s*
Hag. 2:8 the *s* is mine, and the gold is mine
Zech. 11:12 (Mt. 26:15; 27:9) price thirty pieces of *s*
Mt. 27:6 chief priests took the *s* pieces, and said
Lk. 15:8 having ten pieces of *s*, if she lose one piece
Acts 3:6 then Peter said, *S* and gold have I none
   19:24 silversmith, which made *s* shrines for Diana

Simeon son of Jacob

Born, Gen. 29:33; detained as a hostage, Gen. 42:24;
his future predicted, Gen. 49:5–7.

Simeon of Jerusalem Lk. 2:25–34

Simeon of Antioch Acts 13:1

Simeon (Peter) Acts 15:14

Similitude *See also* Likeness

Num. 12:8 and the *s* of the LORD shall he behold
Deut. 4:12 but saw no *s*; only ye heard a voice
Ps. 106:20 changed their glory into the *s* of an ox
Hos. 12:10 used *s*, by the ministry of the prophets
Rom. 5:14 that had not sinned after the *s* of Adam's
Heb. 7:15 after the *s* of Melchisedec there ariseth
Jas. 3:9 we men, which are made after the *s* of God

Simon Peter *See* Peter

Simon the Canaanite
Mt. 10:4 (Mk. 3:18; Lk. 6:15)

Simon the brother of Jesus
Mt. 13:55 (Mk. 6:3)

Simon the leper Mt. 26:6 (Mk. 14:3)

Simon of Cyrene
Mt. 27:32 (Mk. 15:21; Lk. 23:26)

Simon the sorcerer Acts 8:9–24

Simon the tanner Acts 9:43–10:32

Simple

Ps. 19:7 of the LORD is sure, making wise the *s*
   116:6 LORD preserveth the *s*: I was brought low
   119:130 it giveth understanding unto the *s*
Prov. 1:4 to give subtilty to the *s*, to the young
   1:22 how long, ye *s* ones, will ye love simplicity?
   1:32 the turning away of the *s* shall slay them

Prov. 8:5 O ye *s*, understand wisdom: and, ye fools
9:4 whoso is *s*, let him turn in hither
14:15 the *s* believeth every word: but the prudent
19:25 smite a scorner, and the *s* will beware
22:3 but the *s* pass on, and are punished
Rom. 16:18 words and fair speeches deceive. . the *s*
16:19 wise unto. . good, and *s* concerning evil

Simplicity

Prov. 1:22 how long, ye simple ones, will ye love *s*?
Rom. 12:8 he that giveth, let him do it with *s*
2 Cor. 1:12 in *s* and godly sincerity, not with
11:3 be corrupted from the *s* that is in Christ

Sin *See also* Iniquity, Offend, Sin Offering, Transgress, Transgression, Trespass, Wickedness

Gen. 4:7 thou doest not well, *s* lieth at the door
18:20 is great. . because their *s* is very grievous
39:9 do this great wickedness, and *s* against God?
Ex. 9:27 I have *s* this time: the LORD is righteous
10:16 I have *s* against the LORD your God
23:33 lest they make thee *s* against me
32:30 said unto the people, Ye have *s* a great *s*
32:32 wilt forgive their *s*—; and if not, blot me
Lev. 4:2 if a soul shall *s* through ignorance
5:5 he shall confess that he hath *s* in that thing
20:20 shall bear their *s*; they shall die childless
24:15 whosoever curseth his God shall bear his *s*
26:28 I will chastise you seven times for your *s*
Num. 5:6 when a man or woman shall commit any *s*
16:22 one man *s*, and wilt thou be wroth with all
16:26 depart. . lest ye be consumed in all their *s*
22:34 and Balaam said unto the angel. . I have *s*
32:23 ye have *s*. . be sure your *s* will find you out
Deut. 9:27 nor to their wickedness, nor to their *s*
21:22 if a man have committed a *s* worthy of death
24:4 thou shalt not cause the land to *s*
24:16 (2 Kgs. 14:6; 2 Chr. 25:4) death for his own *s*
Josh. 7:20 Achan answered Joshua. . Indeed I have *s*
1 Sam. 2:25 if a man *s* against the LORD, who shall
12:23 against the LORD in ceasing to pray
15:23 rebellion is as the *s* of witchcraft
15:24 and Saul said unto Samuel, I have *s*: for I
2 Sam. 12:13 and David said unto Nathan, I have *s*
24:10 (1 Chr. 21:8) David said. . I have *s* greatly
1 Kgs. 8:46 (2 Chr. 6:36) there is no man that *s* not
14:16 Jeroboam, who did *s*, and. . made Israel to *s*
2 Chr. 7:14 hear from heaven, and will forgive their *s*
28:10 not with you. . *s* against the LORD your God?
Neh. 4:5 and let not their *s* be blotted out
9:2 seed of Israel. . stood and confessed their *s*
Job 1:22 in all this Job *s* not, nor charged God
2:10 in all this did not Job *s* with his lips
7:20 I have *s*; what shall I do unto thee, O thou
10:6 mine iniquity, and searchest after my *s*?
13:23 make me to know my transgression and my *s*
14:16 dost thou not watch over my *s*?
20:11 his bones are full of the *s* of his youth
24:19 so doth the grave those which have *s*
33:27 he looketh upon men. . if any say, I have *s*
35:6 if thou *s*, what doest thou against him?
Ps. 4:4 stand in awe, and *s* not: commune with your
19:13 keep. . thy servant also from presumptuous *s*
25:7 remember not the *s* of my youth, nor my
32:1 (Rom. 4:7) forgiven, whose *s* is covered
32:5 I acknowledged my *s* unto thee, and mine
38:18 mine iniquity; I will be sorry for my *s*
39:1 heed to my ways, that I *s* not with my tongue
41:4 heal my soul; for I have *s* against thee
51:2 from mine iniquity, and cleanse me from my *s*

Ps. 51:4 against thee, thee only, have I *s*, and done
51:5 iniquity; and in *s* did my mother conceive me
51:9 hide thy face from my *s*, and blot out all
78:32 for all this they *s* still, and believed not
79:9 and purge away our *s*, for thy name's sake
85:2 thy people; thou hast covered all their *s*
90:8 our secret *s* in the light of thy countenance
103:10 he hath not dealt with us after our *s*
106:6 we have *s* with our fathers, we have
119:11 mine heart, that I might not *s* against thee
Prov. 5:22 shall be holden with the cords of his *s*
8:36 he that *s* against me wrongeth his own soul
10:12 (1 Pet. 4:8) love covereth all *s*
10:16 tendeth to life. . fruit of the wicked to *s*
14:9 fools make a mock at *s*. . among the righteous
14:34 but *s* is a reproach to any people
20:9 made my heart clean, I am pure from my *s*?
24:9 the thought of foolishness is *s*
28:13 he that covereth his *s* shall not prosper
Eccl. 5:6 not thy mouth to cause thy flesh to *s*
7:20 not a just man. . that doeth good, and *s* not
Is. 1:18 though your *s* be as scarlet, they shall
3:9 declare their *s* as Sodom, they hide it not
5:18 that draw. . *s* as it were with a cart rope
6:7 iniquity is taken away, and thy *s* purged
30:1 not of my Spirit, that they may add *s* to *s*
38:17 thou hast cast all my *s* behind thy back
40:2 of the LORD's hand double for all her *s*
43:27 thy first father hath *s*, and thy teachers
53:10 thou shalt make his soul an offering for *s*
53:12 bare the *s* of many, and made intercession
59:2 your *s* have hid his face from you, that he
64:5 thou art wroth; for we have *s*
Jer. 2:35 plead. . because thou sayest, I have not *s*
5:25 your *s* have withholden good things from you
14:7 backslidings are many. . have *s* against thee
17:1 *s* of Judah is written with a pen of iron
31:34 (Heb. 10:17) I will remember their *s* no more
51:5 land was filled with *s* against the Holy One
Lam. 1:8 Jerusalem hath grievously *s*; therefore
5:7 our fathers have *s*, and are not
Ezek. 3:20 he shall die in his *s*. . but his blood
3:21 that the righteous *s* not, and he doth not *s*
18:4 the soul that *s*, it shall die
18:21 (33:14) wicked will turn from all his *s*
18:24 his *s* that he hath *s*, in them shall he die
21:24 so that in all your doings your *s* do appear
Dan. 4:27 and break off thy *s* by righteousness
9:5 we have *s*, and have committed iniquity
9:11 curse is poured upon us. . because we have *s*
9:15 O Lord. . we have *s*, we have done wickedly
9:20 and confessing my *s* and the *s* of my people
9:24 to make an end of *s*. . to make reconciliation
Hos. 4:7 as they were increased, so they *s* against
9:9 their iniquity, he will visit their *s*
10:9 O Israel, thou hast *s* from the days of
13:2 now they *s* more and more, and have made
Mic. 6:7 the fruit of my body for the *s* of my soul?
Zech. 13:1 a fountain. . for *s* and for uncleanness
Mt. 1:21 for he shall save his people from their *s*
9:2 (Mk. 2:5; Lk. 5:20) thy *s* be forgiven thee
12:31 (Mk. 3:28) all manner of *s*. . shall be forgiven
18:21 Lord, how oft shall my brother *s* against me
26:28 is shed for many for the remission of *s*
27:4 have *s* in that I have betrayed the innocent
Mk. 1:4 (Lk. 3:3) repentance for the remission of *s*
4:12 converted, and their *s* should be forgiven
Lk. 11:4 above us our *s*; for we also forgive
15:18 (15:21) father, I have *s* against heaven
Jn. 1:29 which taketh away the *s* of the world!
5:14 thou art made whole: *s* no more, lest a worse
8:7 is without *s* among you, let him first cast
8:11 neither do I condemn thee: go, and *s* no more

Jn. 8:21 (8:24) and ye shall. . die in your *s*
  8:34 whosoever committeth *s* is the servant of *s*
  8:46 which of you convinceth me of *s*?
  9:2 Master, who did *s*, this man, or his parents
  9:34 thou wast altogether born in *s*, and dost
  9:41 if ye were blind, ye should have no *s*
  15:22 if I had not come. . they had not had *s*
  16:8 he is come, he will reprove the world of *s*
  16:9 of *s*, because they believe not on me
  20:23 whosesoever *s* ye remit, they are remitted
Acts 2:38 and be baptized. . for the remission of *s*
  3:19 be converted, that your *s* may be blotted
  7:60 cried. . Lord, lay not this *s* to their charge
  22:16 arise, and be baptized, and wash away thy *s*
Rom. 2:12 as many as have *s* without law shall also
  3:9 Jews and Gentiles, that they are all under *s*
  3:20 for by the law is the knowledge of *s*
  3:23 all have *s*, and come short of the glory
  4:8 the man to whom the Lord will not impute *s*
  5:12 *s* entered into the world, and death by *s*
  5:13 *s* was in the world: but *s* is not imputed
  5:20 where *s* abounded, grace did. . more abound
  5:21 that as *s* hath reigned unto death, even so
  6:1 shall we continue in *s*, that grace may abound?
  6:2 how shall we, that are dead to *s*, live any
  6:6 destroyed. . henceforth we should not serve *s*
  6:7 for he that is dead is freed from *s*
  6:11 be dead indeed unto *s*, but alive unto God
  6:12 let not *s* therefore reign in your mortal
  6:14 *s* shall not have dominion over you
  6:15 shall we *s*, because we are not under the law
  6:20 for when ye were the servants of *s*, ye were
  6:23 the wages of *s* is death; but the gift of God
  7:7 is the law *s*. . Nay, I had not known *s*, but by
  7:13 *s*, that it might appear *s*, working death in
  7:14 is spiritual: but I am carnal, sold under *s*
  7:23 bringing me into captivity to the law of *s*
  7:25 law of God; but with the flesh the law of *s*
  8:2 hath made me free from the law of *s* and death
  8:3 sinful flesh, and for *s*, condemned *s* in the flesh
  8:10 body is dead because of *s*; but the Spirit is
  11:27 my covenant. . when I shall take away their *s*
  14:23 for whatsoever is not of faith is *s*
1 Cor. 6:18 fornication *s* against his own body
  8:12 *s* so against the brethren. . *s* against Christ
  15:3 how that Christ died for our *s* according to
  15:17 your faith is vain; ye are yet in your *s*
  15:34 awake to righteousness, and *s* not; for some
  15:56 sting of death is *s*; and the strength of *s*
2 Cor. 5:21 made him to be *s* for us, who knew no *s*
Gal. 1:4 who gave himself for our *s*, that he might
  2:17 is therefore Christ the minister of *s*?
  3:22 but the Scripture hath concluded all under *s*
Eph. 2:5 when we were dead in *s*, hath quickened us
  4:26 be ye angry, and *s* not: let not the sun go
Col. 2:13 and you, being dead in your *s* and the
2 Thes. 2:3 man of *s* be revealed. . son of perdition
1 Tim. 5:20 them that *s* rebuke before all
  5:22 neither be partaker of other men's *s*
Heb. 1:3 he had by himself purged our *s*, sat down
  2:17 make reconciliation for the *s* of the people
  3:13 be hardened through the deceitfulness of *s*
  4:15 tempted like as we are, yet without *s*
  5:1 he may offer both gifts and sacrifices for *s*
  5:3 people, so also for himself, to offer for *s*
  7:27 sacrifice, first for his own *s*, and then
  8:12 (10:17) their *s* and their iniquities will I
  9:26 to put away *s* by the sacrifice of himself
  9:28 was once offered to bear the *s* of many
  10:3 a remembrance again made of *s* every year
  10:11 sacrifices, which can never take away *s*
  10:18 remission. . there is no more offering for *s*
  10:26 we *s* wilfully after that we have received

Heb. 11:25 to enjoy the pleasures of *s* for a season
  12:1 and the *s* which doth so easily beset us
  12:4 yet resisted unto blood, striving against *s*
  13:11 blood is brought. . by the high priest for *s*
Jas. 1:15 it bringeth forth *s*; and *s*, when it is
  4:17 to do good, and doeth it not, to him it is *s*
  5:20 sown self bare our *s*. . and shall hide a multitude of *s*
1 Pet. 2:22 who did no *s*, neither was guile found
  2:24 his own self bare our *s*. . we, being dead to *s*
  3:18 for Christ also hath once suffered for *s*
  4:1 hath suffered in the flesh hath ceased from *s*
  4:8 for charity shall cover the multitude of *s*
2 Pet. 2:4 for if God spared not the angels that *s*
  2:14 eyes full of adultery. . cannot cease from *s*
1 Jn. 1:7 blood of Jesus. . cleanseth us from all *s*
  1:8 if we say. . we have no *s*, we deceive ourselves
  1:9 if we confess our *s*, he is faithful and just
  1:10 if we say. . we have not *s*, we make him a liar
  2:1 that ye *s* not. And if any man *s*, we have an
  2:2 propitiation for our *s*. . also for the *s* of the
  2:12 your *s* are forgiven you for his name's sake
  3:4 for *s* is the transgression of the law
  3:5 manifested to take away our *s*. . in him is no *s*
  3:6 abideth in him *s* not: whosoever *s* hath not
  3:8 committeth *s* is of the devil; for the devil *s*
  3:9 is born of God doth not commit *s*. . he cannot *s*
  4:10 his Son to be the propitiation for our *s*
  5:16 his brother *s* a *s* which is not unto death
  5:17 all unrighteousness is *s*: and there is a *s*
  5:18 we know that whosoever is born of God *s* not
Rev. 1:5 and washed us from our *s* in his own blood

Sin

Ex. 16:1 Israel came unto the wilderness of *S*

Sinai *See also* Horeb

Ex. 19:1 came they into the wilderness of *S*
Lev. 7:38 the LORD commanded Moses in mount *S*
Num. 1:1 spake unto Moses in the wilderness of *S*
Deut. 33:2 the LORD came from *S*, and rose up from
Judg. 5:5 melted from before the LORD, even that *S*
Ps. 68:8 *S* itself was moved at the presence of God

Sincere

Phil. 1:10 that ye may be *s* and without offense
1 Pet. 2:2 babes, desire the *s* milk of the word

Sincerely

Judg. 9:16 if ye have done truly and *s*, in that ye
Phil. 1:16 preach Christ of contention, not *s*

Sincerity

Josh. 24:14 fear the LORD, and serve him in *s*
1 Cor. 5:8 with the unleavened bread of *s* and truth
2 Cor. 1:12 in simplicity and godly *s*, not with
  2:17 as of *s*, but as of God. . speak we in Christ
  8:8 and to prove the *s* of your love
Eph. 6:24 that love our Lord Jesus Christ in *s*
Tit. 2:7 in doctrine showing uncorruptness. . *s*

Sinew

Gen. 32:32 of Israel eat not of the *s* which shrank
Job 30:17 the night season: and my *s* take no rest
Ezek. 37:6 I will lay *s* upon you, and will bring

Sinful

Num. 32:14 an increase of *s* men, to augment yet
Is. 1:4 ah *s* nation, a people laden with iniquity
Amos 9:8 eyes of the Lord. . are upon the *s* kingdom
Mk. 8:38 in this adulterous and *s* generation
Lk. 5:8 depart from me; for I am a *s* man, O Lord
  24:7 must be delivered into the hands of *s* men

Rom. 7:13 that sin. . might become exceeding *s*
8:3 his own Son in the likeness of *s* flesh

Sing (Sang, Sung) *See also* Rejoice, Song

Ex. 15:1 then *s* Moses and the children of Israel
Num. 21:17 then Israel *s*. . Spring up, O well; *s* ye
Judg. 5:1 then *s* Deborah and Barak. . on that day
1 Sam. 29:5 of whom they *s* one to another in dances
1 Chr. 16:9 (Ps. 105:2) *s* unto him, *s* psalms unto him
    16:23 (Ps. 96:1) *s* unto the LORD, all the earth
Ezra 3:11 they *s* together by course in praising
Job 29:13 I caused the widow's heart to *s* for joy
    38:7 when the morning stars *s* together
Ps. 13:6 I will *s* unto the LORD, because he hath
    30:4 *s* unto the LORD, O ye saints of his
    51:14 tongue shall *s* aloud of thy righteousness
    66:2 *s* forth the honor of his name: make his
    81:1 *s* aloud unto God our strength
    95:1 O come, let us *s* unto the LORD: let us
    98:1 O *s* unto the LORD a new song; for he hath
    101:1 I will *s* of mercy and judgment
    104:33 I will *s* unto the LORD as long as I live
    106:12 believed they his words; they *s* his praise
    137:3 saying, *S* us one of the songs of Zion
    149:5 in glory: let them *s* aloud upon their beds
Prov. 29:6 but the righteous doth *s* and rejoice
Is. 12:5 *S* unto the LORD; for he hath done excellent
    26:1 in that day shall this song be *s* in. . Judah
    26:19 awake and *s*, ye that dwell in dust
    35:6 as a hart, and the tongue of the dumb *s*
    44:23 *s*, O ye heavens; for the LORD hath done it
    52:8 with the voice together shall they *s*
    54:1 *s*, O barren, thou that didst not bear
    65:14 my servants shall *s* for joy of heart
Zech. 2:10 *s* and rejoice, O daughter of Zion
Mt. 26:30 (Mk. 14:26) and when they had *s* a hymn
Acts 16:25 at midnight Paul and Silas prayed, and *s*
1 Cor. 14:15 I will *s* with the spirit, and I will *s*
Eph. 5:19 (Col. 3:16) *s*. . in your heart to the Lord
Jas. 5:13 is any merry? let him *s* psalms
Rev. 5:9 they *s* a new song, saying, Thou art worthy
    14:3 they *s* as it were a new song before the throne
    15:3 they *s* the song of Moses the servant of God

Singer

1 Chr. 15:19 so the *s*, Heman, Asaph, and Ethan
Ps. 68:25 the *s* went before, the players. . followed
    87:7 the *s* as the players on instruments shall be
Eccl. 2:8 I gat me men *s* and women *s*. . the delights
Hab. 3:19 the chief *s* on my stringed instruments

Singing *See also* Sing

Ps. 100:2 come before his presence with *s*
Song 2:12 the time of the *s* of birds is come
Is. 14:7 and is quiet: they break forth into *s*
    51:11 shall return, and come with *s* unto Zion

Single

Mt. 6:22 (Lk. 11:34) if therefore thine eye be *s*

Singleness

Acts 2:46 their meat with gladness and *s* of heart
Eph. 6:5 (Col. 3:22) obedient. . in *s* of your heart

Sinim Is. 49:12

Sink (Sank, Sunk)

Ex. 15:5 they *s* into the bottom as a stone
Ps. 9:15 heathen are *s* down in the pit that they made
    69:2 I *s* in deep mire, where there is no standing
Jer. 38:6 but mire: so Jeremiah *s* in the mire

Jer. 51:64 and thou shalt say, Thus shall Babylon *s*
Mt. 14:30 beginning to *s*, he cried, saying, Lord
Lk. 5:7 filled both the ships, so. . they began to *s*
    9:44 let these sayings *s* down into your ears

Sinner *See also* Evildoer, Transgressor

Gen. 13:13 but the men of Sodom were wicked and *s*
Ps. 1:1 nor standeth in the way of *s*, nor sitteth
    1:5 nor *s* in the congregation of the righteous
    25:8 therefore will he teach *s* in the way
    26:9 gather not my soul with *s*, nor my life with
    51:13 and *s* shall be converted unto thee
    104:35 let the *s* be consumed out of the earth
Prov. 1:10 son, if *s* entice thee, consent thou not
    11:31 recompensed. . more the wicked and the *s*
    13:6 but wickedness overthroweth the *s*
    13:21 evil pursueth *s*: but to the righteous good
    13:22 the wealth of the *s* is laid up for the just
    23:17 let not thine heart envy *s*; but be thou in
Eccl. 2:26 but to the *s* he giveth travail
    8:12 though a *s* do evil a hundred times, and his
    9:2 alike to all. . as is the good, so is the *s*
    9:18 but one *s* destroyeth much good
Is. 13:9 he shall destroy the *s* thereof out of it
    33:14 the *s* in Zion are afraid; fearfulness hath
Amos 9:10 the *s* of my people shall die by the sword
Mt. 9:10 (Mk. 2:15) publicans and *s* sat. . with them
    9:13 (Mk. 2:17; Lk. 5:32) call the righteous, but *s*
    26:45 (Mk. 14:41) betrayed into the hands of *s*
Lk. 6:32 for *s* also love those that love them
    7:37 behold, a woman in the city, which was a *s*
    13:2 suppose ye. . these Galileans were *s* above all
    15:2 this man receiveth *s*, and eateth with them
    15:7 joy. . in heaven over one *s* that repenteth
    18:13 publican. . saying, God be merciful to me a *s*
    19:7 was gone to be guest with a man that is a *s*
Jn. 9:16 can a man that is a *s* do such miracles?
    9:25 be a *s* or no, I know not: one thing I know
Rom. 3:7 his glory; why yet am I also judged as a *s*?
    5:8 that, while we were yet *s*, Christ died for us
    5:19 by one man's disobedience many were made *s*
Gal. 2:17 justified. . we ourselves also are found *s*
1 Tim. 1:9 for the ungodly and for *s*, for unholy
    1:15 Christ Jesus came into the world to save *s*
Heb. 7:26 high priest. . undefiled, separate from *s*
    12:3 endured such contradiction of *s* against
Jas. 4:8 cleanse your hands, ye *s*; and purify your
    5:20 converteth the *s* from the error of his way
1 Pet. 4:18 shall the ungodly and the *s* appear?
Jude 15 hard speeches which ungodly *s* have spoken

Sin Offering

Ex. 29:14 burn with fire without the camp: it is a *s o*
Lev. 4:3 then let him bring for his sin. . a *s o*
    8:14 their hands upon the. . bullock for the *s o*

Sion *See* Zion

Sisera Judg. 4:2–5:30

Sister

Gen. 12:13 say. . thou art my *s*: that it may be well
    20:2 Abraham said of Sarah his wife, She is my *s*
    26:7 he said, She is my *s*: for he feared to say
Prov. 7:4 say unto wisdom, Thou art my *s*; and call
Song 4:9 thou hast ravished my heart, my *s*
    8:8 we have a little *s*, and she hath no breasts
Ezek. 16:48 Sodom thy *s* hath not done. . as thou
Mt. 12:50 (Mk. 3:35) the same is my brother, and *s*
1 Cor. 9:5 have we not power to lead about a *s*
1 Tim. 5:2 the younger as *s*, with all purity
Jas. 2:15 if a brother or *s* be naked, and destitute
2 Jn. 13 the children of thy elect *s* greet thee

Sit (Sat)

Gen. 18:1 LORD appeared. . and he s in the tent door
Ex. 18:14 why s thou thyself alone, and all
Judg. 20:26 s there before the LORD, and fasted
2 Kgs. 7:3 said one to another, Why s we here
Ps. 1:1 nor s in the seat of the scornful
26:4 I have not s with vain persons, neither
29:10 LORD s upon the flood; yea, the LORD s King
47:8 God s upon the throne of his holiness
69:12 they that s in the gate speak against me
107:10 such as s in darkness and in the shadow
110:1 (Mt. 22:44; Mk. 12:36; Lk. 20:42; Acts 2:34;
    Heb. 1:13) LORD said unto my Lord, S thou at
127:2 vain for you to rise up early, to s up late
137:1 by the rivers of Babylon, there we s down
Is. 30:7 have I cried. . Their strength is to s still
40:22 is he that s upon the circle of the earth
47:1 s in the dust, O virgin daughter of Babylon
Jer. 8:14 why do we s still? assemble yourselves
15:17 I s not in the assembly of the mockers
Lam. 3:63 behold their s down, and their rising up
Ezek. 3:15 I s where they s, and remained there
Mic. 4:4 they shall s every man under his vine
Mal. 3:3 he shall s as a refiner and purifier
Mt. 8:11 (Lk. 13:29) shall s down. . in the kingdom
9:10 (Mk. 2:15) Jesus s at meat. . sinners. .s
14:19 (Mk. 6:39; Lk. 9:14; Jn. 6:10) s. . on the grass
19:28 (Lk. 22:30) s upon twelve thrones, judging
20:21 (Mk. 10:37) grant that. . my two sons may s
25:31 shall he s upon the throne of his glory
26:64 (Mk. 14:62; Lk. 22:69) s on the right hand of
28:2 angel. . rolled back the stone. . and s upon it
Mk. 11:2 (Lk. 19:30) colt tied, whereon never man s
16:19 (Heb. 10:12) and s on the right hand of God
Lk. 2:46 found him. . s in the midst of the doctors
7:15 he that was dead s up, and began to speak
8:35 and found the man. . s at the feet of Jesus
10:39 Mary, which also s at Jesus' feet, and heard
22:27 whether is greater, he that s at meat, or
Jn. 4:6 Jesus. . being wearied. . s thus on the well
Acts 2:2 it filled all the house where they were s
Eph. 2:6 made us s together in heavenly places
Col. 3:1 where Christ s on the right hand of God
2 Thes. 2:4 that he as God s in the temple of God
Heb. 1:3 s down on the right hand of the Majesty
Jas. 2:3 s thou here in a good place; and say to
Rev. 3:21 will I grant to s with me in my throne
4:3 he that s was. to look upon like a jasper
17:1 the great whore that s upon many waters

Situation

2 Kgs. 2:19 the s of this city is pleasant
Ps. 48:2 beautiful for s, the joy of the whole earth

Skilful *See also* Cunning, Curious

1 Chr. 28:21 s man, for any manner of service
Dan. 1:4 but well-favored, and s in all wisdom
Amos 5:16 such as are s of lamentation to wailing

Skilfulness

Ps. 78:72 and guided them by the s of his hands

Skill

1 Kgs. 5:6 s to hew timber like unto the Sidonians
2 Chr. 2:7 that can s to grave with the cunning
Eccl. 9:11 nor yet favor to men of s; but time and
Dan. 1:17 God gave them knowledge and s in all
9:22 Daniel, I am now come forth to give thee s

Skin

Gen. 3:21 God make coats of s, and clothed them
27:16 s of the kids of the goats upon his hands

Ex. 34:29 wist not that the s of his face shone
Job 2:4 s for s, yea, all that a man hath will he
19:20 my bone cleaveth to my s and to my flesh
30:30 my s is black upon me, and my bones are
Ps. 102:5 of my groaning my bones cleave to my s
Jer. 13:23 can the Ethiopian change his s
Lam. 5:10 our s was black like an oven, because of
Mk. 1:6 and with a girdle of a s about his loins

Skip

Ps. 29:6 he maketh them also to s like a calf
114:4 mountains s like rams. . hills like lambs
Song 2:8 upon the mountains, s upon the hills
Jer. 48:27 thou spakest of him, thou s for joy

Skirt

Ruth 3:9 spread therefore thy s over thine handmaid
1 Sam. 15:27 he laid hold upon the s of his mantle
24:4 David. . cut off the s of Saul's robe privily
Ps. 133:2 precious ointment. . went down to the s
Jer. 2:34 in thy s is found the blood of. . innocents
Ezek. 16:8 I spread my s over thee, and covered thy
Zech. 8:23 take hold of the s of him that is a Jew

Skull

Judg. 9:53 upon Abimelech's head. . to brake his s
Mt. 27:33 (Mk. 15:22; Jn. 19:17) a place of a s

Sky *See also* Heaven

Job 37:18 hast thou with him spread out the s
Is. 45:8 let the s pour down righteousness
Mt. 16:2 it will be fair weather: for the s is red
16:3 (Lk. 12:56) ye can discern the face of the s

Slack

Deut. 7:10 he will not be s to him that hateth him
23:21 shalt vow a vow. . thou shalt not s to pay it
Josh. 18:3 how long are ye s to go to possess the
Prov. 10:4 becometh poor that dealeth with a s hand
Hab. 1:4 the law is s, and judgment doth never go
Zeph. 3:16 and to Zion, Let not thine hands be s
2 Pet. 3:9 Lord is not s concerning his promise

Slain *See also* Slay, Kill, Slaughter

Deut. 21:1 if one be found s in the land
Is. 22:2 thy s men are not s with the sword
26:21 her blood, and shall no more cover her s
66:16 and the s of the LORD shall be many
Jer. 9:1 I might weep day and night for the s
Ezek. 21:14 the sword of the s: it is the sword of
37:9 breathe upon these s, that they may live
Rev. 13:8 Lamb s from the foundation of the world

Slander

Num. 14:36 murmur. . bringing up a s upon the land
Ps. 31:13 I have heard the s of many: fear was on
50:20 thy brother; thou s thine own mother's son
101:5 whoso privily s his neighbor, him will I
Prov. 10:18 and he that uttereth a s, is a fool
Jer. 9:4 and every neighbor will walk with s

Slanderer

1 Tim. 3:11 must their wives be grave, not s, sober

Slanderously

Rom. 3:8 as we be s reported, and as some affirm

Slaughter *See also* Kill, Murder, Slain, Slay

Gen. 14:17 his return from the s of Chedorlaomer
Ps. 44:22 (Rom. 8:36) counted as sheep for the s
Is. 53:7 (Acts 8:32) is brought as a lamb to the s

Jer. 7:32 but The valley of *s*: for they shall bury
   25:34 days of your *s* and of your dispersions are
   48:15 chosen young men are gone down to the *s*
Ezek. 9:2 and every man a *s* weapon in his hand
Hos. 5:2 and the revolters are profound to make *s*
Acts 9:1 Saul, yet breathing out threatenings and *s*
Jas. 5:5 nourished your hearts, as in a day of *s*

Slave *See also* Servant

Jer. 2:14 is Israel a servant? is he a homeborn *s*?
Rev. 18:13 and chariots, and, *s*, and souls of men

Slay (Slew, Slain) *See also* Kill, Murder, Slaughter

Gen. 4:8 that Cain rose up against Abel . . and *s* him
   4:14 that every one that findeth me shall *s* me
   4:23 I have *s* a man to my wounding, and a young
   18:25 to *s* the righteous with the wicked
   20:4 LORD, wilt thou *s* also a righteous nation?
   20:11 thought . . they will *s* me for my wife's sake
   22:10 and Abraham . . took the knife to *s* his son
   27:41 then will I *s* my brother Jacob
   34:25 upon the city boldly, and *s* all the males
   34:30 they shall gather . . against me, and *s* me
   37:26 what profit is it if we *s* our brother
   49:6 in their anger they *s* a man, and in their
Ex. 2:12 *s* the Egyptian, and hid him in the sand
   4:23 behold, I will *s* thy son, even thy firstborn
   13:15 that the LORD *s* all the firstborn in . . Egypt
   21:14 upon his neighbor, to *s* him with guile
Num. 25:5 *s* ye every one his men that were joined
Judg. 9:54 *s* me, that men say not . . A woman *s* him
   16:30 the dead which he *s* at his death were more
1 Sam. 17:36 servant *s* both the lion and the bear
   18:7 (21:11; 29:5) Saul hath *s* his thousands
   20:33 it was determined of his father to *s* David
   22:21 showed . . that Saul had *s* the LORD's priests
2 Sam. 1:16 saying, I have *s* the LORD's anointed
   13:30 saying, Absalom hath *s* all the king's sons
   23:20 (1 Chr. 11:22) *s* a lion in . . a pit in . . snow
1 Kgs. 20:20 *s* every one his man: and the Syrians fled
2 Kgs. 9:31 had Zimri peace, who *s* his master?
   10:7 the king's sons, and *s* seventy persons
   10:9 my master, and *s* him: but who *s* all these?
   10:25 that Jehu said . . *s* them; let none come forth
   23:29 Pharaoh-nechoh . . *s* him at Megiddo
Neh. 4:11 and *s* them, and cause the work to cease
   9:26 *s* thy prophets which testified against them
Job 9:23 if the scourge *s* suddenly, he will laugh
   13:15 though he *s* me, yet will I trust in him
Ps. 34:21 evil shall *s* the wicked: and they that
   78:31 the wrath of God . . *s* the fattest of them
   139:19 surely thou wilt *s* the wicked, O God
Is. 66:3 he that killeth an ox is as if he *s* a man
Jer. 41:3 Ishmael also *s* all the Jews that were with
Lam. 2:4 *s* all that were pleasant to the eye
   4:9 *s* with the sword . . better than . . *s* with hunger
Ezek. 9:8 while they were *s* them, and I was left
   28:9 yet say before him that *s* thee, I am God?
Dan. 5:19 whom he would he *s* . . whom he would he
Hos. 6:5 I have *s* them by the words of my mouth
Mt. 2:16 *s* all the children that were in Bethlehem
   23:35 whom ye *s* between the temple and the altar
Lk. 9:22 and be *s*, and be raised the third day
   11:49 apostles, and some of them they shall *s*
   19:27 bring hither, and *s* them before me
Jn. 5:16 Jews persecute Jesus, and sought to *s* him
Acts 5:30 raised up Jesus, whom ye *s* and hanged on
   9:29 the Grecians: but they went about to *s* him
   11:7 saying unto me, Arise, Peter; *s* and eat
   22:20 and kept the raiment of them that *s* him

Rom. 7:11 commandment, deceived me . . by it *s* me
Eph. 2:16 by the cross, having *s* the enmity thereby
Heb. 11:37 were tempted, were *s* with the sword
1 Jn. 3:12 *s* his brother. And wherefore *s* he him?
Rev. 5:6 stood a Lamb as it had been *s*, having
   6:9 souls of them that were *s* for the word of God
   9:15 were prepared . . to *s* the third part of men

Slayer

Num. 35:11 be cities of refuge . . that the *s* may flee
Deut. 19:4 this is the case of the *s*, which shall flee
Ezek. 21:11 sword . . give it into the hand of the *s*

Sleep (Slept) *See also* Death, Slumber

Gen. 2:21 God caused a deep *s* to fall upon Adam
   15:12 deep *s* fell upon Abram; and, lo, a horror
   28:11 pillows, and lay down in that place to *s*
Deut. 31:16 Moses . . thou shalt *s* with thy fathers
1 Sam. 3:3 and Samuel was laid down to *s*
   26:7 behold, Saul lay *s* within the trench
   26:12 deep *s* from the LORD was fallen upon them
1 Kgs. 18:27 peradventure he *s*, and must be awaked
   19:5 as he lay and *s* under a juniper tree
Job 3:13 I should have *s*: then had I been at rest
   4:13 visions of the night, when deep *s* falleth
   7:21 shall I *s* in the dust; and thou shalt seek
Ps. 3:5 laid me down and *s*; I awaked; for the LORD
   4:8 I will both lay me down in peace, and *s*
   13:3 lighten mine eyes, lest I *s* the *s* of death
   44:23 why *s* thou, O Lord? arise, cast us not off
   76:5 stout-hearted . . spoiled, they have *s* their *s*
   121:4 keepeth Israel shall neither slumber nor *s*
   127:2 for so he giveth his beloved *s*
   132:4 I will not give *s* to mine eyes, or slumber
Prov. 3:24 shalt lie down, and thy *s* shall be sweet
   4:16 they *s* not, except they have done mischief
   6:4 give not *s* to thine eyes, nor slumber to
   6:9 how long wilt thou *s*, O sluggard? when wilt
   6:10 (24:33) a little folding of the hands to *s*
   6:22 when thou *s*, it shall keep thee
   10:5 *s* in harvest is a son that causeth shame
   20:13 love not *s*, lest thou come to poverty
Eccl. 5:12 *s* of a laboring man is sweet, whether
Song 5:2 I *s*, but my heart waketh: it is the voice
Is. 29:10 poured out upon you the spirit of deep *s*
   56:10 watchmen . . *s*, lying down, loving to slumber
Jer. 51:39 (51:57) *s* a perpetual *s*, and not wake
Dan. 6:18 night fasting . . and his *s* went from him
   8:18 (10:9) I was in a deep *s* on my face toward
   12:2 that *s* in the dust of the earth shall awake
Mt. 9:24 (Mk. 5:39; Lk. 8:52) maid is not dead, but *s*
   13:25 while men *s* . . enemy came and sowed tares
   26:45 (Mk. 14:41) *s* on now, and take your rest
   27:52 many bodies of the saints which *s* arose
   28:13 his disciples . . stole him away while we *s*
Mk. 13:36 lest coming suddenly he find you *s*
   14:37 findeth them *s*, and saith . . Simon, *s* thou?
Lk. 9:32 they that were with him were heavy with *s*
   22:46 why *s* ye? rise and pray, lest ye enter into
Jn. 11:11 Lazarus *s*; but I go, that I may awake him
Acts 12:6 Peter was *s* between two soldiers, bound
   20:9 Eutychus, being fallen into a deep *s*
Rom. 13:11 now it is high time to awake out of *s*
1 Cor. 11:30 weak and sickly among you, and many *s*
   15:20 and become the firstfruits of them that *s*
   15:51 we shall not all *s*, but we shall all be
Eph. 5:14 awake thou that *s*, and arise from the dead
1 Thes. 4:14 which *s* in Jesus will God bring with
   5:6 let us not *s*, as do others; but let us watch
   5:10 wake or *s*, we should live together with him

Sleeper

Jon. 1:6 meanest thou, O *s*? arise, call upon thy God

Sleight

Eph. 4:14 by the *s* of men, and cunning craftiness

Slew *See* Slay

Slide

Deut. 32:35 their foot shall *s* in due time
Ps. 26:1 trusted also in the LORD. . I shall not *s*
37:31 is in his heart; none of his steps shall *s*
Hos. 4:16 Israel *s* back as a backsliding heifer

Slightly

Jer. 6:14 (8:11) healed also the hurt. . of my people *s*

Slime

Gen. 11:3 brick for stone. . *s* had they for mortar

Sling

1 Sam. 17:40 his *s* was in his hand: and he drew
17:50 prevailed over the Philistine with a *s*
25:29 shall he *s* out, as out of the middle of a *s*
Prov. 26:8 as he that bindeth a stone in a *s*, so is
Jer. 10:18 I will *s* out the inhabitants of the land

Slip

Deut. 19:5 axe to cut. . the head *s* from the helve
1 Sam. 19:10 but he *s* away out of Saul's presence
2 Sam. 22:37 (Ps. 18:36) so that my feet did not *s*
Job 12:5 he that is ready to *s* with his feet is as
Ps. 17:5 in thy paths, that my footsteps *s* not
38:16 when my foot *s*, they magnify themselves
73:2 were almost gone; my steps had well-nigh *s*
94:18 my foot *s*; thy mercy, O LORD, held me up
Heb. 2:1 lest at any time we should let them *s*

Slippery

Ps. 35:6 let their way be dark and *s*
73:18 surely thou didst set them in *s* places
Jer. 23:12 their way shall be unto them as *s* ways

Slothful *See also* Sluggard

Judg. 18:9 be not *s* to go, and to enter to possess
Prov. 12:24 but the *s* shall be under tribute
12:27 *s* man roasteth not that. . he took in hunting
18:9 is *s* in his work is brother to. . a great waster
19:24 (26:15) a *s* man hideth his hand in his bosom
21:25 desire of the *s* killeth him; for his hands
26:14 upon his hinges, so doth the *s* upon his bed
Mt. 25:26 thou wicked and *s* servant, thou knewest
Rom. 12:11 not *s* in business; fervent in spirit
Heb. 6:12 ye be not *s*, but followers of them who

Slothfulness

Prov. 19:15 *s* casteth into a deep sleep
Eccl. 10:18 by much *s* the building decayeth

Slow

Ex. 4:10 but I am *s* of speech, and of a *s* tongue
Neh. 9:17 gracious and merciful, *s* to anger
Prov. 14:29 *s* to wrath is of great understanding
16:32 *s* to anger is better than the mighty
Nah. 1:3 LORD is *s* to anger, and great in power
Lk. 24:25 O fools, and *s* of heart to believe all
Jas. 1:19 be swift to hear, *s* to speak, *s* to wrath

Sluggard *See also* Slothful

Prov. 6:6 go to the ant, thou *s*; consider her ways
6:9 how long wilt thou sleep, O *s*? when wilt
10:26 as smoke to the eyes, so is the *s* to them
13:4 soul of the *s* desireth, and hath nothing
20:4 the *s* will not plow by reason of the cold
26:16 *s* is wiser in his own conceit than seven

Sluice

Is. 19:10 be broken in the purposes. . all that make *s*

Slumber *See also* Sleep

Ps. 121:3 he that keepeth thee will not *s*
Prov. 6:10 (24:33) little sleep, a little *s*
Is. 5:27 none shall *s* nor sleep; neither shall he
Nah. 3:18 thy shepherds *s*, O king of Assyria
Mt. 25:5 while the bridegroom tarried, they all *s*
Rom. 11:8 God hath given them the spirit of *s*
2 Pet. 2:3 lingereth not, and their damnation *s* not

Small (Smallest) *See also* Little

Ex. 16:14 a *s* round thing, as *s* as the hoar frost
Num. 16:9 seemeth it but a *s* thing unto you
1 Sam. 9:21 I a Benjamite, of the *s* of the tribes
2 Sam. 7:19 (1 Chr. 17:17) yet a *s* thing in thy sight
1 Kgs. 19:12 and after the fire a still *s* voice
Job 8:7 though thy beginning was *s*, yet thy latter
15:11 are the consolations of God *s* with thee?
Ps. 119:141 am *s* and despised: yet do not I forget
Prov. 24:10 day of adversity, thy strength is *s*
Is. 7:13 is it a *s* thing for you to weary men
16:14 and the remnant shall be very *s* and feeble
60:22 a *s* one a strong nation: I the LORD will
Jer. 30:19 glorify them, and they shall not be *s*
49:15 I will make thee *s* among the heathen
Amos 7:2 by whom shall Jacob arise? for he is *s*
Zech. 4:10 who hath despised the day of *s* things?
1 Cor. 4:3 *s* thing that I should be judged of you
6:2 are ye unworthy to judge the *s* matters?
Jas. 3:4 are they turned about with a very *s* helm

Smart

Prov. 11:15 surety for a stranger shall *s* for it

Smell

Gen. 8:21 LORD *s* a sweet savor; and the LORD said
27:27 he *s* the *s* of his raiment, and blessed him
Job 39:25 he *s* the battle afar off, the thunder of
Ps. 45:8 all thy garments *s* of myrrh, and aloes
115:6 hear not: noses have they, but they *s* not
Song 4:10 the *s* of thine ointments than all spices!
7:13 mandrakes give a *s*, and at our gates are all
Is. 3:24 instead of sweet *s* there shall be stink
Dan. 3:27 nor the *s* of fire had passed on them
Amos 5:21 I will not *s* in your solemn assemblies
1 Cor. 12:17 whole were hearing, where were the *s*?
Phil. 4:18 were sent from you, an odor of a sweet *s*

Smite (Smote, Smitten) *See also* Kill, Strike

Gen. 8:21 neither will I again *s* any more every
Ex. 2:11 and he spied an Egyptian *s* a Hebrew
2:13 did the wrong, Wherefore *s* thou thy fellow?
12:29 at midnight the LORD *s* all the firstborn
21:12 he that *s* a man, so that he die, shall be
Num. 20:11 and with his rod he *s* the rock twice
22:28 that thou hast *s* me these three times?
Deut. 28:25 LORD shall cause thee to be *s* before
1 Sam. 4:3 wherefore hath the LORD *s* us today
17:50 so David prevailed. . and *s* the Philistine
19:10 Saul sought to *s* David even to the wall
24:5 David's heart *s* him, because he had cut off
26:8 then said Abishai to David. . let me *s* him
2 Sam. 2:22 should I *s* thee to the ground? how then
10:15 Syrians saw that they were *s* before Israel
1 Kgs. 22:24 (2 Chr. 18:23) *s* Micaiah on the cheek
2 Kgs. 2:8 and *s* the waters, and they were divided
6:18 *s* this people, I pray thee, with blindness
6:21 my father, shall I *s* them? shall I *s* them?

2 Kgs. 13:19 now thou shalt *s* Syria but thrice
  19:35 (Is. 37:36) the angel. . *s* in the camp of the
Esth. 9:5 thus the Jews *s* all their enemies with
Job 16:10 have *s* me upon the cheek reproachfully
Ps. 3:7 O my God: for thou hast *s* all mine enemies
  78:20 he *s* the rock, that the waters gushed out
  78:66 and he *s* his enemies in the hinder parts
  121:6 the sun shall not *s* thee by day, nor the
  135:10 who *s* great nations, and slew mighty kings
  141:5 the righteous *s* me; it shall be a kindness
  143:3 persecuted my soul; he hath *s* my life down
Prov. 19:25 *s* a scorner, and the simple will beware
Is. 5:25 his hand against them, and hath *s* them
  10:24 the Assyrian: he shall *s* thee with a rod
  27:7 hath he *s* him, as he *s* those that *s* him?
  49:10 neither shall the heat nor sun *s* them
  57:17 of his covetousness was I wroth, and *s* him
  58:4 ye fast. . to *s* with the fist of wickedness
  60:10 for in my wrath I *s* thee, but in my favor
Jer. 2:30 in vain have I *s* your children
  18:18 let us *s* him with the tongue, and let us
  21:6 and I will *s* the inhabitants of this city
  31:19 I was instructed, I *s* upon my thigh
Lam. 3:30 he giveth his cheek to him that *s* him
Ezek. 7:9 ye shall know that I am the Lord that *s*
  21:14 prophesy, and *s* thine hands together
  22:13 I have *s* mine hand at thy dishonest gain
Dan. 2:34 *s* the image upon his feet. . and brake them
  5:6 loosed, and his knees *s* one against another
Hos. 6:1 heal us; he hath *s*, and he will bind us up
Amos 4:9 I have *s* you with blasting and mildew
  9:1 said, *S* the lintel. . that the posts may shake
Hag. 2:17 I *s* you with blasting and with mildew
Zech. 10:11 shall *s* the waves in the sea, and all
  13:7 (Mt. 26:31; Mk. 14:27) *s* the shepherd
Mal. 4:6 lest I come and *s* the earth with a curse
Mt. 5:39 (Lk. 6:29) shall *s* thee on thy right cheek
  24:49 shall begin to *s* his fellow servants
  26:51 (Mk. 14:47; Lk. 22:50; Jn. 18:10) *s* off his ear
  26:68 (Lk. 22:64) prophesy. . Who is he that *s* thee?
  27:30 (Mk. 15:19; Jn. 19:3) and *s* him on the head
Lk. 18:13 the publican. . *s* upon his breast, saying
  22:49 unto him, Lord, shall we *s* with the sword?
  23:48 beholding the things. . *s* their breasts
Jn. 18:23 of the evil: but if well, why *s* thou me?
Acts 12:7 angel of the Lord. . *s* Peter on.the side
  12:23 immediately the angel of the Lord *s* him
  23:3 unto him, God shall *s* thee, thou whited wall
2 Cor. 11:20 ye suffer. . if a man *s* you on the face
Rev. 11:6 power. . to *s* the earth with all plagues

Smith

1 Sam. 13:19 was no *s* found throughout all the land
2 Kgs. 24:14 (Jer. 24:1) captives. . craftsmen and *s*
Is. 44:12 *s* with the tongs doth work in the coals
  54:16 I have created the *s* that bloweth the coals

Smitten *See also* Smite

Ps. 102:4 my heart is *s*, and withered like grass
Is. 53:4 we did esteem him stricken, *s* of God
Hos. 9:16 Ephraim is *s*, their root is dried up

Smoke

Gen. 19:28 the *s*. . went up as the *s* of a furnace
Ex. 19:18 mount Sinai was altogether on a *s*
  20:18 mountain *s*: and when the people saw it
Deut. 29:20 his jealousy shall *s* against that man
Judg. 20:40 up out of the city with a pillar of *s*
2 Sam. 22:9 (Ps. 18:8) went up a *s* out of his nostrils
Ps. 37:20 shall consume; into *s* shall they consume
  68:2 as *s* is driven away, so drive them away
  74:1 anger *s* against the sheep of thy pasture?
  102:3 my days are consumed like *s*, and my bones

Ps. 104:32 he toucheth the hills, and they *s*
  119:83 I am become like a bottle in the *s*
  144:5 touch the mountains, and they shall *s*
Prov. 10:26 as *s* to the eyes, so is the sluggard
Song 3:6 out of the wilderness like pillars of *s*
Is. 6:4 door moved. . and the house was filled with *s*
  34:10 the *s* thereof shall go up for ever
  42:3 (Mt. 12:20) the *s* flax shall he not quench
  51:6 for the heavens shall vanish away like *s*
  65:5 are a *s* in my nose, a fire that burneth all
Hos. 13:3 shall be. . as the *s* out of the chimney
Joel 2:30 (Acts 2:19) and fire, and pillars of *s*
Rev. 8:4 *s* of the incense. . came with the prayers
  9:2 *s* out of the pit, as the *s* of a great furnace
  14:11 *s* of their torment ascendeth up for ever
  15:8 temple was filled with *s* from the glory
  18:9 when they shall see the *s* of her burning
  19:3 said, Alleluia. And her *s* rose up for ever

Smooth (Smoother)

Gen. 27:11 Esau. . is a hairy man, and I am a *s* man
1 Sam. 17:40 and chose him five *s* stones out
Ps. 55:21 words of his mouth were *s* than butter
Prov. 5:3 her mouth is *s* than oil
Is. 30:10 speak unto us *s* things, prophesy deceits
Lk. 3:5 and the rough ways shall be made *s*

Smote *See* Smite

Smyrna Rev. 1:11; 2:8-17

Snail

Ps. 58:8 as a *s* which melteth, let every one of

Snare

Ex. 10:7 how long shall this man be a *s* unto us?
  23:33 (Deut. 7:16) serve their gods, it will. . be a *s*
Deut. 7:25 take it unto thee, lest thou be *s* therein
  12:30 take heed. . thou be not *s* by following them
Josh. 23:13 but they shall be *s* and traps unto you
Judg. 2:3 as thorns. . and their gods shall be a *s*
  8:27 which thing became a *s* unto Gideon
1 Sam. 18:21 give him her, that she may be a *s*
  28:9 wherefore then layest thou a *s* for my life
2 Sam. 22:6 (Ps. 18:5) the *s* of death prevented me
Job 18:8 by his own feet, and he walketh upon a *s*
  22:10 *s* are round about thee, and sudden fear
Ps. 9:16 wicked is *s* in the work of his own hands
  11:6 upon the wicked he shall rain *s*, fire and
  38:12 also that seek after my life lay *s* for me
  64:5 they commune of laying *s* privily; they say
  69:22 (Rom. 11:9) let their table become a *s*
  91:3 shall deliver thee from the *s* of the fowler
  106:36 served their idols: which were a *s*
  124:7 out of the *s* of the fowlers: the *s* is broken
  140:5 the proud have hid a *s* for me, and cords
  141:9 keep me from the *s* which they have laid
  142:3 in the way. . they privily laid a *s* for me
Prov. 6:2 thou art *s* with the words of thy mouth
  7:23 as a bird hasteth to the *s*, and knoweth not
  12:13 wicked is *s* by the transgression of his
  13:14 (14:27) to depart from the *s* of death
  18:7 destruction. . his lips are the *s* of his soul
  22:5 thorns and *s* are in the way of the froward
  29:8 scornful men bring a city into a *s*: but wise
  29:25 the fear of man bringeth a *s*: but whoso
Eccl. 7:26 the woman, whose heart is *s* and nets
  9:12 caught in the *s*; so are the sons of men *s*
Is. 8:15 stumble, and fall, and be broken, and be *s*
  24:17 (Jer. 48:43) pit, and the *s*, are upon thee
  29:21 lay a *s* for him that reproveth in the gate
  42:22 spoiled; they are all of them *s* in holes
Jer. 5:26 as he that setteth *s*; they set a trap

Jer. 18:22 a pit to take me, and hid s for my feet
    50:24 laid a s for thee, and thou art also taken
Lam. 3:47 fear and a s is come upon us, desolation
Ezek. 12:13 (17:20) and he shall be taken in my s
Hos. 9:8 prophet is a s of a fowler in all his ways
Amos 3:5 can a bird fall in a s. . where no gin is
Lk. 21:35 for as a s shall it come on all them that
1 Cor. 7:35 not that I may cast a s upon you
1 Tim. 3:7 fall into reproach and the s of the devil
    6:9 will be rich fall into temptation and a s
2 Tim. 2:26 may recover. . out of the s of the devil

Sneeze

2 Kgs. 4:35 the child s seven times

Snout

Prov. 11:22 as a jewel of gold in a swine's s

Snow

2 Sam. 23:20 and slew a lion in. . a pit in time of s
Job 6:16 by reason of the ice. . wherein the s is hid
    24:19 drought and heat consume the s waters
    37:6 for he saith to the s, Be thou on the earth
    38:22 thou entered into the treasures of the s?
Ps. 51:7 wash me, and I shall be whiter than s
    147:16 he giveth s like wool: he scattereth the
    148:8 s, and vapor; stormy wind fulfilling his
Prov. 25:13 as the cold of s in the time of harvest
    26:1 as s in summer, and as rain in harvest
    31:21 is not afraid of the s for her household
Is. 1:18 as scarlet, they shall be as white as s
    55:10 the rain cometh down, and the s from heaven
Jer. 18:14 will a man leave the s of Lebanon
Lam. 4:7 her Nazarites were purer than s
Dan. 7:9 garment was white as s, and the hair of
Mt. 28:3 (Mk. 9:3) and his raiment white as s

Snuff

Jer. 14:6 wild asses. . s up the wind like dragons
Mal. 1:13 a weariness is it! and ye have s at it

Soak

Is. 34:7 their land shall be s with blood

Soap

Jer. 2:22 take thee much s, yet thine iniquity is
Mal. 3:2 like a refiner's fire, and like fullers' s

Sober See also Grave

2 Cor. 5:13 whether we be s, it is for your cause
1 Thes. 5:6 as do others; but let us watch and be s
    5:8 but let us, who are of the day, be s
1 Tim. 3:2 bishop. . husband of one wife, vigilant, s
    3:11 must their wives be grave, not slanderers, s
Tit. 1:8 lover of good men, s, just, holy, temperate
    2:2 aged men be s, grave, temperate, sound in faith
    2:4 that they may teach the young women to be s
    2:6 young men likewise exhort to be. . s-minded
1 Pet. 1:13 gird up the loins of your mind, be s
    4:7 be ye therefore s, and watch unto prayer
    5:8 be s, be vigilant; because your adversary

Soberly

Rom. 12:3 think s, according as God hath dealt to
Tit. 2:12 we should live s, righteously, and godly

Soberness

Acts 26:25 speak forth the words of truth and s

Sobriety

1 Tim. 2:9 women adorn themselves. . with. . s
    2:15 in faith and charity and holiness with s

Sod (Sodden) See Seethe

Sodom

Gen. 13:13 the men of S were wicked and sinners
    14:12 and they took Lot. . who dwelt in S, and his
    18:20 because the cry of S and Gomorrah is great
    19:1 came two angels to S at even; and Lot sat in
    19:24 rained upon S and. . Gomorrah brimstone
Deut. 29:23 like the overthrow of S and Gomorrah
    32:32 for their vine is of the vine of S
Is. 1:9 (Rom. 9:29) we should have been as S
    13:19 Babylon. . as when God overthrew S
Jer. 23:14 they are all of them unto me as S
Lam. 4:6 greater than the punishment of the sin of S
Ezek. 16:46 younger sister. . is S and her daughters
Amos 4:11 overthrown. . you, as God overthrew S
Zeph. 2:9 Moab shall be as S, and the children of
Mt. 10:15 (11:24; Mk. 6:11; Lk. 10:12) it shall be
    more tolerable for the land of S
Lk. 17:29 that Lot went out of S it rained fire
Rom. 9:29 except. . left us a seed, we had been as S
2 Pet. 2:6 turning the cities of S and Gomorrah
Jude 7 as S and Gomorrah. . giving themselves over
Rev. 11:8 great city, which spiritually is called S

Sodomite

Deut. 23:17 no whore. . nor a s of the sons of Israel
1 Kgs. 14:24 and there were also s in the land
    15:12 and he took away the s out of the land

Soft (Softer)

Job 23:16 God maketh my heart s, and the Almighty
    41:3 unto thee? will he speak s words unto thee?
Ps. 55:21 his words were s than oil, yet were they
    65:10 makest it s with showers: thou blessest
Prov. 15:1 a s answer turneth away wrath
    25:15 and a s tongue breaketh the bone
Mt. 11:8 (Lk. 7:25) see? A man clothed in s raiment?

Softly

Gen. 33:14 will lead on s, according as the cattle
Is. 38:15 shall go s all my years in the bitterness

Soil

Ezek. 17:8 was planted in a good s by great waters

Sojourn See also Abide, Dwell, Remain

Gen. 12:10 Abram went down into Egypt to s there
    19:9 this one fellow came in to s, and he will
    26:3 s in this land, and I will be with thee
    47:4 Pharaoh, For to s in the land are we come
Ex. 12:48 (Num. 9:14) when a stranger. . s with thee
Judg. 17:9 and I go to s where I may find a place
2 Kgs. 8:1 s wheresoever thou canst s: for the LORD
Ps. 105:23 into Egypt. . Jacob s in the land of Ham
    120:5 woe is me, that I s in Mesech, that I dwell
Is. 23:7 her own feet shall carry her afar off to s
    52:4 went down aforetime into Egypt to s there
Jer. 42:15 (44:12) into Egypt, and go to s there
Lam. 4:15 depart, depart. . They shall no more s
Acts 7:6 that his seed should s in a strange land
Heb. 11:9 by faith he s in the land of promise
1 Pet. 1:17 pass the time of your s here in fear

Sojourner See also Alien, Foreigner, Stranger

Lev. 25:40 as a hired servant, and as a s, he shall
    25:47 if a s or stranger wax rich by thee
Ps. 39:12 with thee, and a s, as all my fathers

Solace

Prov. 7:18 let us *s* ourselves with loves

Sold *See* Sell

Soldier *See also* Army, Host

2 Chr. 25:13 *s* of the army which Amaziah sent back
Ezra 8:22 to require of the king a band of *s*
Is. 15:4 the armed *s* of Moab shall cry out
Mt. 8:9 (Lk. 7:8) under authority, having *s* under me
27:27 (Mk. 15:16) *s* of the governor took Jesus into
Lk. 3:14 the *s* likewise demanded of him, saying
Jn. 19:23 then the *s* . . took his garments, and made
Acts 10:7 a devout *s* of them that waited on him
12:6 Peter was sleeping between two *s*, bound with
27:31 Paul said to the centurion and to the *s*
2 Tim. 2:3 endure hardness, as a good *s* of Jesus
2:4 may please him who hath chosen him to be a *s*

Sole *See also* Foot

Gen. 8:9 dove found no rest for the *s* of her foot
Deut. 11:24 (Josh. 1:3) the *s* of your feet shall tread
28:65 neither shall the *s* of thy foot have rest

Solemn

Num. 10:10 day of your gladness, and in your *s* days
Deut. 16:8 seventh day shall be a *s* assembly
Ps. 92:3 psaltery; upon the harp with a *s* sound
Is. 1:13 it is iniquity, even the *s* meeting
Lam. 2:22 thou hast called as in a *s* day my terrors
Hos. 9:5 what will ye do in the *s* day

Solemnity

Deut. 31:10 in the *s* of the year of release
Is. 30:29 as in the night when a holy *s* is kept
33:20 look upon Zion, the city of our *s*
Ezek. 45:17 in all *s* of the house of Israel
46:11 feasts and in the *s* the meat offering shall

Solemnly

Gen. 43:3 the man did *s* protest unto us, saying
1 Sam. 8:9 protest *s* unto them, and show them

Solitary *See also* Desolate

Job 3:7 let that night be *s*; let no joyful voice
30:3 for want and famine they were *s*; fleeing
Ps. 68:6 God setteth the *s* in families: he bringeth
107:4 they wandered in the wilderness in a *s* way
Is. 35:1 wilderness and the *s* place shall be glad
Lam. 1:1 how doth the city sit *s*, that was full
Mk. 1:35 departed into a *s* place, and there prayed

Solomon

Born, 2 Sam. 12:24; anointed king, 1 Kgs. 1:32–40;
established his kingdom, 1 Kgs. 2:12–46; married
Pharaoh's daughter, 1 Kgs. 3:1; asked for wisdom, 1
Kgs. 3:5–15; judged wisely, 1 Kgs. 3:16–28; conferred with Hiram, 1 Kgs. 5; built the temple, 1 Kgs.
6; built his own house, 1 Kgs. 7:1–12; dedicated the
temple, 1 Kgs. 8; the LORD's covenant with Solomon,
1 Kgs. 9:1–9; visited by the queen of Sheba, 1 Kgs.
10:1–13; turned from the LORD, 1 Kgs. 11:1–40; died,
1 Kgs. 11:41–43.

Neh. 13:26 did not *S* king of Israel sin by these
Prov. 1:1 Proverbs of *S* the son of David, king
Song 1:1 the Song of songs, which is *S's*
Mt. 6:29 (Lk. 12:27) *S* in all his glory was not
12:42 (Lk. 11:31) behold, a greater than *S* is here
Jn. 10:23 Jesus walked in the temple in *S* 's porch
Acts 3:11 unto them in the porch that is called *S* 's

Something

Gal. 6:3 think himself to be *s*, when he is nothing

Somewhat

Gal. 2:6 who seemed to be *s*, (whatsoever they were
Rev. 2:4 I have *s* against thee, because thou hast

Son *See also* Son-in-law, Son of God, Son of Man, Child

Gen. 6:2 the *s* of God saw the daughters of men
17:19 (18:10; Rom. 9:9) Sarah. . shall bear thee a *s*
21:2 Sarah conceived, and bare Abraham a *s*
21:10 (Gal. 4:30) *s* of this bondwoman. . not. . heir
22:2 he said, Take now thy *s*, thine only *s* Isaac
22:12 thou hast not withheld thy *s*, thine only *s*
Ex. 1:16 if it be a *s*, then ye shall kill him
1:22 every *s* that is born ye shall cast into
4:22 thus saith the LORD, Israel is my *s*, even
Num. 27:8 if a man die, and have no *s*, then ye
Deut. 4:9 but teach them thy *s*, and thy *s' s*
21:18 if a man have a stubborn and rebellious *s*
2 Sam. 7:14 (Heb. 1:5) father, and he shall be my *s*
18:33 (19:4) O my *s* Absalom. . O Absalom, my *s*
1 Kgs. 17:17 the *s* of the woman. . fell sick
2 Kgs. 4:16 thou shalt embrace a *s*. And she said
6:28 give thy *s* that we may eat him today
16:3 and made his *s* to pass through the fire
21:6 made his *s* pass through the fire, and observed
1 Chr. 28:6 Solomon. . I have chosen him to be my *s*
Job 1:6 (2:1) the *s* of God came to present themselves
Ps. 2:7 (Acts 13:33; Heb. 1:5; 5:5) thou art my *S*
2:12 kiss the *S*, lest he be angry, and ye perish
8:4 (Heb. 2:6) *s* of man, that thou visitest him?
31:19 that trust in thee before the *s* of men!
33:13 from heaven; he beholdeth all the *s* of men
80:17 upon the *s* of man whom thou madest strong
106:37 sacrificed their *s* . . unto devils
144:3 *s* of man, that thou makest account of him!
Prov. 3:12 as a father the *s* in whom he delighteth
10:1 (15:20) a wise *s* maketh a glad father
13:1 a wise *s* heareth his father's instruction
13:24 he that spareth his rod hateth his *s*
17:25 a foolish *s* is a grief to his father
19:18 chasten thy *s* while there is hope
29:17 correct thy *s*, and he shall give thee rest
Eccl. 1:13 travail hath God given to the *s* of man
3:18 concerning the estate of the *s* of men
9:3 also the heart of the *s* of men is full of evil
9:12 so are the *s* of men snared in an evil time
Is. 7:14 (Mt. 1:23) virgin shall conceive, and bear a *s*
9:6 unto us a child is born, unto us a *s* is given
14:12 O Lucifer, *s* of the morning! how art thou
43:6 keep not back: bring my *s* from far, and my
45:11 ask me of things to come concerning my *s*
51:20 thy *s* have fainted, they lie at the head of
60:4 thy *s* shall come from far, and thy daughters
Jer. 7:31 to burn their *s* and their daughters in
16:2 neither shalt thou have *s* nor daughters in
Ezek. 2:1 *s* of man, stand. . and I will speak unto thee
3:17 (33:7) *s* of man, I have made thee a watchman
5:10 eat the *s* . . the *s* shall eat their fathers
18:20 *s* shall not bear the iniquity of the father
20:31 ye make your *s* to pass through the fire
23:47 they shall slay their *s* and their daughters
Hos. 1:10 be said. . Ye are the *s* of the living God
11:1 (Mt. 2:15) and called my *s* out of Egypt
Joel 2:28 (Acts 2:17) *s* . . daughters shall prophesy
Amos 2:11 I raised up of your *s* for prophets
7:14 was no prophet, neither was I a prophet's *s*
Mic. 7:6 for the *s* dishonoreth the father

Mal. 3:17 spare them, as a man spareth his own *s*
Mt. 1:21 (Lk. 1:31) she shall bring forth a *s*
3:17 (Mk. 1:11; Lk. 3:22) saying, This is my. . *S*
7:9 (Lk. 11:11) if his *s* ask bread, will he give
9:27 saying, Thou *S* of David, have mercy on us
10:37 loveth *s* or daughter more than me is not
11:27 (Lk. 10:22) knoweth the *S*, but the Father
12:23 amazed. . said, Is not this the *S* of David?
13:55 (Mk. 6:3; Lk. 4:22) this the carpenter's *s*?
16:16 (Jn. 6:69) Christ, the *S* of the living God
17:5 (Mk. 9:7; Lk. 9:35; 2 Pet. 1:17) my beloved *S*
20:21 grant that these my two *s* may sit, the one
21:9 (21:15) saying, Hosanna to the *S* of David
21:37 (Mk. 12:6; Lk. 20:13) sent unto them his *s*
22:42 what think ye of Christ? whose *s* is he?
22:45 (Mk. 12:37; Lk. 20:44) Lord, how is he his *s*?
28:19 in the name of the Father, and of the *S*
Mk. 5:7 Jesus, thou *S* of the most high God? I adjure
14:61 art thou the Christ, the *S* of the Blessed?
Lk. 1:13 thy wife Elisabeth shall bear thee a *s*
1:32 and shall be called the *S* of the Highest
3:38 was the *s* of Adam, which was the *s* of God
7:12 dead man carried out, the only *s* of his mother
10:6 if the *s* of peace be there, your peace shall
12:53 against the *s*, and the *s* against the father
15:19 (15:21) am no more worthy to be called thy *s*
15:24 for this my *s* was dead, and is alive again
19:9 forasmuch as he also is a *s* of Abraham
Jn. 1:12 them gave he power to become the *s* of God
1:18 only begotten *S*, which is in the bosom
3:16 he gave his only begotten *S*, that whosoever
3:17 God sent not his *S*. . to condemn the world
3:35 the Father loveth the *S*, and hath given all
3:36 believeth on the *S* hath everlasting life
4:50 go thy way; thy *s* liveth. . the man believed
5:20 Father loveth the *S*, and sheweth him all
5:22 but hath committed all judgment unto the *S*
5:23 all men should honor the *S*, even as they
5:26 given to the *S* to have life in himself
6:40 every one which seeth the *S*, and believeth
8:35 servant abideth not. . but the *S* abideth ever
8:36 if the *S* therefore shall make you free
14:13 that the Father may be glorified in the *S*
17:1 glorify thy *S*, that thy *S* also may glorify
17:12 none of them. . lost, but the *s* of perdition
19:26 saith unto his mother, Woman, behold thy *s*
Acts 3:13 God of our fathers, hath glorified his *S*
3:26 having raised up his *S* Jesus, sent him to
Rom. 5:10 reconciled to God by the death of his *S*
8:3 God sending his own *S* in the likeness of
8:14 are led by the Spirit. . they are the *s* of God
8:29 be conformed to the image of his *S*, that he
8:32 he that spared not his own *S*, but delivered
1 Cor. 15:28 *S* also himself be subject unto him
Gal. 1:16 reveal his *S* in me, that I might preach
4:4 God sent forth his *S*, made of a woman
4:5 that we might receive the adoption of *s*
4:6 because ye are *s*, God hath sent. . the Spirit
4:7 a servant, but a *s*; and if a *s*, then an heir
Eph. 3:5 ages was not made known unto the *s* of men
Phil. 2:15 be blameless and harmless, the *s* of God
Col. 1:13 translated. . into the kingdom of his dear *S*
1 Thes. 1:10 to wait for his *S* from heaven, whom he
2 Thes. 2:3 man of sin be revealed, the *s* of perdition
1 Tim. 1:2 (2 Tim. 1:2) Timothy, my own *s* in the faith
Heb. 1:2 in these last days spoken unto us by his *S*
2:10 in bringing many *s* unto glory, to make the
3:6 Christ as a *s* over his own house; whose house
5:8 though he were a *S*, yet learned he obedience
7:28 but the word of the oath. . maketh the *S*
11:17 was tried. . offered up his only begotten *s*
11:24 refused to be called the *s* of Pharaoh's
12:6 and scourgeth every *s* whom he receiveth

Heb. 12:7 God dealeth with you as with *s*; for what *s*
1 Jn. 1:3 fellowship is with the Father, and with his *S*
2:22 antichrist. . denieth the Father and the *S*
3:1 that we should be called the *s* of God
3:2 beloved, now are we the *s* of God, and it doth
3:23 we should believe on the name of his *S* Jesus
4:9 God sent his only begotten *S* into the world
4:10 sent his *S* to be the propitiation for our sins
4:14 sent the *S* to be the Saviour of the world
5:11 eternal life, and this life is in his *S*
5:12 hath the *S* hath life. . he that hath not the *S*
2 Jn. 9 abideth. . he hath both the Father and the *S*
Rev. 21:7 I will be his God, and he shall be my *s*

Son-in-law

1 Sam. 18:22 now therefore be the king's *s-i-l*

Son of God *See also* Christ, Jesus, Lord, Son

Dan. 3:25 form of the fourth is like the *S* of *G*
Mt. 4:3 (Lk. 4:3) if thou be the *S* of *G*, command
8:29 (Mk. 5:7; Lk. 8:28) do with thee. . thou *S* of *G*
14:33 saying, Of a truth thou art the *S* of *G*
26:63 (Lk. 22:70) whether thou be. . the *S* of *G*
27:40 be the *S* of *G*, come down from the cross
27:43 for he said, I am the *S* of *G*
27:54 (Mk. 15:39) saying, Truly this was the *S* of *G*
Mk. 3:11 (Lk. 4:41) cried, saying, Thou art the *S* of *G*
Lk. 1:35 be born of thee shall be called the *S* of *G*
Jn. 1:34 I saw, and bare record. . this is the *S* of *G*
1:49 Nathanael answered. . thou art the *S* of *G*
3:18 not believed in. . the only begotten *S* of *G*
9:35 unto him, Dost thou believe on the *S* of *G*?
10:36 blasphemest; because I said, I am the *S* of *G*
11:4 that the *S* of *G* might be glorified thereby
19:7 to die, because he made himself the *S* of *G*
Acts 9:20 preached Christ. . that he is the *S* of *G*
Rom. 1:4 and declared to be the *S* of *G* with power
2 Cor. 1:19 *S* of *G*, Jesus Christ, who was preached
Eph. 4:13 faith, and of the knowledge of the *S* of *G*
Heb. 4:14 a great high priest. . Jesus the *S* of *G*
6:6 they crucify to themselves the *S* of *G* afresh
7:3 made like unto the *S* of *G*; abideth a priest
10:29 who hath trodden under foot the *S* of *G*
1 Jn. 3:8 for this purpose the *S* of *G* was manifested
4:15 shall confess that Jesus is the *S* of *G*
5:5 he that believeth that Jesus is the *S* of *G*?
5:20 we know that the *S* of *G* is come, and hath
Rev. 2:18 write; These things saith the *S* of *G*

Son of Man *See also* Man, Son

Dan. 7:13 one like the *S* of *m* came with the clouds
Mt. 8:20 (Lk. 9:58) *S* of *m* hath not where to lay
9:6 (Mk. 2:10; Lk. 5:24) *S* of *m*. . power on earth
10:23 cities of Israel, till the *S* of *m* be come
11:19 (Lk. 7:34) *S* of *m* came eating and drinking
12:8 (Mk. 2:28; Lk. 6:5) *S* of *m* is Lord. . sabbath
12:32 (Lk. 12:10) word against. . *S* of *m*. . forgiven
13:37 he that soweth the good seed is the *S* of *m*
16:27 (Mk. 8:38; Lk. 9:26) *S* of *m* shall come in the
17:22 (Mk. 9:31; Lk. 9:44) *S* of *m* shall be betrayed
19:28 when the *S* of *m* shall sit in the throne of
24:30 (Mk. 13:26; Lk. 21:27) *S* of *m* coming in the
25:31 when the *S* of *m* shall come in his glory
26:24 (Lk. 22:22) *S* of *m* goeth as it is written
26:24 (Mk. 14:21) by whom the *S* of *m* is betrayed
Lk. 12:8 him shall the *S* of *m* also confess before
17:24 heaven; so shall the *S* of *m* be in his day
Jn. 3:14 wilderness, even so must the *S* of *m* be lifted
Acts 7:56 *S* of *m* standing on the right hand of God
Rev. 14:14 one sat like unto the *S* of *m*

Song *See also* Sing

Ex. 15:2 (Ps. 118:14; Is. 12:2) is my strength and *s*
Deut. 31:19 write ye this *s* for you, and teach it
Judg. 5:12 awake, Deborah: awake, awake, utter a *s*
1 Kgs. 4:32 and his *s* were a thousand and five
Job 30:9 now am I their *s*, yea, I am their byword
   35:10 is God my maker, who giveth *s* in the night
Ps. 32:7 compass me about with *s* of deliverance
   33:3 sing unto him a new *s*; play skilfully with
   40:3 hath put a new *s* in my mouth, even praise
   42:8 and in the night his *s* shall be with me
   69:12 against me. . I was the *s* of the drunkards
   77:6 I call to remembrance my *s* in the night
   96:1 (98:1; 149:1) O sing unto the LORD a new *s*
   118:14 the LORD is my strength and *s*
   119:54 thy statutes have been my *s* in the house
   137:4 how shall we sing the LORD's *s* in a strange
   144:9 I will sing a new *s* unto thee, O God
Prov. 25:20 is he that singeth *s* to a heavy heart
Song 1:1 the *S* of *s*, which is Solomon's
Is. 5:1 now will I sing to my well-beloved a *s* of
   12:2 the LORD JEHOVAH is my strength and my *s*
   24:9 they shall not drink wine with a *s*
   30:29 ye shall have a *s*, as in the night
   35:10 shall return, and come to Zion with *s*
   42:10 sing unto the LORD a new *s*, and his praise
Lam. 3:14 a derision to all my people; and their *s*
Ezek. 33:32 thou art unto them as a very lovely *s*
Amos 8:3 the *s* of the temple shall be howlings
Eph. 5:19 (Col. 3:16) psalms. . hymns and spiritual *s*
Rev. 5:9 they sung a new *s*, saying, Thou art worthy
   14:3 sung as it were a new *s* before the throne
   15:3 sing the *s* of Moses. . and the *s* of the Lamb

Soothsayer *See also* Magician, Sorcerer

Is. 2:6 and are *s* like the Philistines
Dan. 2:27 the magicians, the *s*, show unto the king
   5:7 bring. . astrologers, the Chaldeans, and the *s*
Mic. 5:12 I will cut off. . thou shalt have no more *s*

Soothsaying

Acts 16:16 which brought her masters much gain by *s*

Sop

Jn. 13:26 he it is, to whom I shall give a *s*

Sorcerer *See also* Magician, Soothsayer

Ex. 7:11 Pharaoh. . called the wise men and the *s*
Jer. 27:9 nor to your enchanters, nor to your *s*
Dan. 2:2 the *s*, and the Chaldeans. . to show the king
Mal. 3:5 I will be a swift witness against the *s*
Acts 13:8 Elymas the *s*. . withstood them, seeking to
Rev. 21:8 *s*, and idolaters, and all liars, shall
   22:15 without are dogs, and *s*, and whoremongers

Sorceress

Is. 57:3 but draw near hither, ye sons of the *s*

Sorcery

Is. 47:9 upon thee. . for the multitude of thy *s*
Acts 8:9 Simon. . used *s*, and bewitched the people
Rev. 9:21 neither repented they. . of their *s*, nor of
   18:23 for by thy *s* were all nations deceived

Sore

Gen. 41:56 the famine waxed *s* in the land of Egypt
2 Chr. 6:28 whatsoever *s*, or whatsoever sickness
Job 5:18 he maketh *s*, and bindeth up: he woundeth
Ps. 38:11 my friends stand aloof from my *s*
   77:2 I sought the Lord: my *s* ran in the night
Lk. 16:20 which was laid at his gate, full of *s*
Rev. 16:2 there fell a noisome and grievous *s* upon

Sorrow *See also* Anguish, Distress, Grief, Misery, Suffering, Tribulation, Trouble

Gen. 3:16 multiply thy *s* and thy conception; in *s*
   3:17 in *s* shalt thou eat of it all the days of
   42:38 bring down my gray hairs with *s* to the grave
Ex. 3:7 and have heard their cry. . I know their *s*
   15:14 *s* shall take hold on the inhabitants of
Lev. 26:16 consume the eyes, and cause *s* of heart
Deut. 28:65 give thee. . failing of eyes, and *s* of mind
1 Sam. 10:2 left the care of the asses, and *s* for you
2 Sam. 22:6 (Ps. 18:5) *s* of hell compassed me about
Neh. 2:2 sick? this is nothing else but *s* of heart
Esth. 9:22 was turned unto them from *s* to joy
Job 6:10 I would harden myself in *s*: let him not
   21:17 upon them! God distributeth *s* in his anger
   41:22 and *s* is turned into joy before him
Ps. 13:2 having *s* in my heart daily? how long
   16:4 their *s* shall be multiplied that hasten
   18:4 (116:3) the *s* of death compassed me
   32:10 many *s* shall be to the wicked: but he that
   38:17 to halt, and my *s* is continually before me
   39:2 I held my peace. . and my *s* was stirred
   55:10 mischief also and *s* are in the midst of it
   90:10 years, yet is their strength labor and *s*
   107:39 and brought low through. . affliction, and *s*
   127:2 vain. . to sit up late, to eat the bread of *s*
Prov. 10:22 maketh rich, and he addeth no *s* with it
   15:13 but by *s* of the heart the spirit is broken
   23:29 woe? who hath *s*? who hath contentions?
Eccl. 1:18 that increaseth knowledge increaseth *s*
   2:23 all his days are *s*, and his travail grief
   7:3 *s* is better than laughter: for by the sadness
   11:10 remove *s* from thy heart, and put away evil
Is. 13:8 pangs and *s* shall take hold of them
   17:11 heap in the day of grief and of desperate *s*
   35:10 (51:11) and *s* and sighing shall flee away
   50:11 have of mine hand; ye shall lie down in *s*
   53:3 a man of *s*, and acquainted with grief
   53:4 hath borne our griefs, and carried our *s*
   65:14 but ye shall cry for *s* of heart
Jer. 8:18 when I would comfort myself against *s*
   13:21 not *s* take thee, as a woman in travail?
   20:18 forth out of the womb to see labor and *s*
   30:15 thy *s* is incurable for. . thine iniquity
   31:12 and they shall not *s* any more at all
   49:23 there is *s* on the sea; it cannot be quiet
   51:29 and the land shall tremble and *s*: for every
Lam. 1:12 and see if there be any *s* like unto my *s*
Ezek. 23:33 shalt be filled with drunkenness and *s*
Hos. 13:13 *s* of a travailing woman shall come upon
Mt. 24:8 (Mk. 13:8) these are the beginning of *s*
Lk. 22:45 disciples, he found them sleeping for *s*
Jn. 16:6 said these things. . *s* hath filled your heart
   16:20 weep. . but your *s* shall be turned into joy
Rom. 9:2 heaviness and continual *s* in my heart
2 Cor. 2:3 lest, when I came, I should have *s* from
   7:10 for godly *s* worketh repentance to salvation
Phil. 2:27 on me also, lest I should have *s* upon *s*
1 Thes. 4:13 ye *s* not. . as others which have no hope
1 Tim. 6:10 pierced themselves through with many *s*
Rev. 21:4 there shall be no more death, neither *s*

Sorrowful

1 Sam. 1:15 no, my lord, I am a woman of a *s* spirit
Job 6:7 my soul refused to touch are as my *s* meat
Ps. 69:29 but I am poor and *s*: let thy salvation
Prov. 14:13 even in laughter the heart is *s*
Jer. 31:25 and I have replenished every *s* soul
Zeph. 3:18 I will gather them that are *s*
Mt. 19:22 (Lk. 18:23) he went away *s*: for he had
   26:22 (Mk. 14:19) they were exceeding *s*, and began

Mt. 26:38 (Mk. 14:34) my soul is exceeding *s*, even
Jn. 16:20 world shall rejoice; and ye shall be *s*
2 Cor. 6:10 as *s*, yet always rejoicing; as poor
Phil. 2:28 rejoice, and that I may be the less *s*

Sorry

1 Sam. 22:8 there is none of you that is *s* for me
Neh. 8:10 for this day is holy . . neither be ye *s*
Ps. 38:18 mine iniquity; I will be *s* for my sin
Is. 51:19 who shall be *s* for thee? desolation, and
Mt. 14:9 (Mk. 6:26) king was *s*: nevertheless for the
  17:23 shall kill him . . And they were exceeding *s*
2 Cor. 2:2 for if I make you *s*, who . . maketh me glad
  7:8 I made you *s* with a letter, I do not repent
  7:9 ye were made *s* after a godly manner, that ye

Sosthenes Acts 18:17; 1 Cor. 1:1

Sottish

Jer. 4:22 have not known me; they are *s* children

Sought *See also* Seek

Ps. 111:2 works of the LORD are great, *s* out of all
Is. 62:12 be called, *S* out, A city not forsaken

Soul *See also* Heart, Person, Spirit

Gen. 2:7 (1 Cor. 15:45) and man became a living *s*
Ex. 30:12 they give every man a ransom for his *s*
Lev. 16:29 ye shall afflict your *s*, and do no work
Num. 11:6 now our *s* is dried away: there is nothing
Deut. 4:29 if thou seek him . . with all thy *s*
  6:5 (Mt. 22:37; Mk. 12:30; Lk. 10:27) love the
    LORD thy God . . with all thy *s*
  10:12 (11:13) serve the LORD . . with all thy *s*
  30:2 shalt obey his voice . . with all thy *s*
1 Sam. 1:15 have poured out my *s* before the LORD
  18:1 *s* of Jonathan was knit with the *s* of David
Job 10:1 my *s* is weary of my life; I will leave
  12:10 in whose hand is the *s* of every living
  27:8 he hath gained, when God taketh away his *s*?
  33:18 he keepeth back his *s* from the pit
Ps. 6:4 return, O LORD, deliver my *s*: oh save me
  16:10 (Acts 2:27, 31) wilt not leave my *s* in hell
  19:7 law of the LORD is perfect, converting the *s*
  23:3 he restoreth my *s*: he leadeth me in the paths
  25:1 (86:4) unto thee, O LORD, do I lift up my *s*
  26:9 gather not my *s* with sinners, nor my life
  30:3 thou hast brought up my *s* from the grave
  33:19 to deliver their *s* from death, and to keep
  34:22 the LORD redeemeth the *s* of his servants
  35:9 my *s* shall be joyful in the LORD: it shall
  41:4 heal my *s*; for I have sinned against thee
  42:1 brooks, so panteth my *s* after thee, O God
  42:2 my *s* thirsteth for God, for the living God
  42:5 (42:11; 43:5) why art thou cast down, O my *s*?
  49:8 for the redemption of their *s* is precious
  55:18 delivered my *s* in peace from the battle
  56:13 for thou hast delivered my *s* from death
  57:4 my *s* is among lions: and I lie even among
  62:1 my *s* waiteth upon God: from him cometh my
  63:1 my *s* thirsteth for thee, my flesh longeth
  66:9 holdeth our *s* in life, and suffereth not
  71:23 rejoice . . my *s*, which thou hast redeemed
  84:2 my *s* longeth, yea, even fainteth for
  86:4 for unto thee, O Lord, do I lift up my *s*
  103:1 (103:2, 22; 104:1, 35) bless the LORD, O my *s*
  107:9 he satisfieth the longing *s*, and filleth
  116:7 return unto thy rest, O my *s*; for the LORD
  119:81 my *s* fainteth for thy salvation
  121:7 from all evil: he shall preserve thy *s*
  124:5 then the proud waters had gone over our *s*
  143:8 for I lift up my *s* unto thee
Prov. 6:32 he that doeth it destroyeth his own *s*

Prov. 11:30 tree of life; and he that winneth *s* is wise
  16:17 he that keepeth his way preserveth his *s*
  19:16 keepeth . . commandment keepeth his own *s*
  23:14 beat him . . shalt deliver his *s* from hell
Is. 26:8 desire of our *s* is to thy name
  38:17 but thou hast in love to my *s* delivered it
  53:10 thou shalt make his *s* an offering for sin
  53:12 he hath poured out his *s* unto death
  55:3 come unto me: hear, and your *s* shall live
  58:10 if thou draw out thy *s* to the hungry
  61:10 my *s* shall be joyful in my God; for he hath
Jer. 6:8 O Jerusalem, lest my *s* depart from thee
  31:12 and their *s* shall be as a watered garden
  38:16 as the LORD liveth, that made us this *s*
Ezek. 3:19 (33:9) but thou hast delivered thy *s*
  13:20 ye there hunt the *s* to make them fly
  18:4 all *s* are mine; as the *s* of the father, so
  33:5 he that taketh warning shall deliver his *s*
Mt. 10:28 the body, but are not able to kill the *s*
  16:26 (Mk. 8:36) gain . . world . . lose his own *s*?
  26:38 (Mk. 14:34) my *s* is exceeding sorrowful
Lk. 1:46 and Mary said, My *s* doth magnify the Lord
  12:19 I will say to my *s*, *S*, thou hast much goods
  21:19 in your patience possess ye your *s*
Jn. 12:27 now is my *s* troubled; and what shall I say?
Acts 2:41 added unto them about three thousand *s*
  4:32 that believed were of one heart and of one *s*
  14:22 confirming the *s* of the disciples
Rom. 2:9 and anguish, upon every *s* . . that doeth evil
  13:1 every *s* be subject unto the higher powers
1 Thes. 5:23 and *s* and body be preserved blameless
Heb. 4:12 to the dividing asunder of *s* and spirit
  6:19 which hope we have as an anchor of the *s*
  10:39 them that believe to the saving of the *s*
  13:17 obey them . . for they watch for your *s*
Jas. 1:21 engrafted word, which is able to save your *s*
  5:20 which converteth . . shall save a *s* from death
1 Pet. 1:9 your faith, even the salvation of your *s*
  1:22 ye have purified your *s* in obeying the truth
  2:11 from fleshly lusts, which war against the *s*
  2:25 unto the Shepherd and Bishop of your *s*
  3:20 few, that is, eight *s* were saved by water
  4:19 the keeping of their *s* to him in well doing
2 Pet. 2:14 beguiling unstable *s*: a heart they have
3 Jn. 2 and be in health, even as thy *s* prospereth
Rev. 6:9 *s* of them that were slain for the word
  16:3 and every living *s* died in the sea
  20:4 I saw the *s* of them that were beheaded for

Sound (adjective)

Ps. 119:80 let my heart be *s* in thy statutes
Prov. 14:30 a *s* heart is the life of the flesh
Lk. 15:27 because he hath received him safe and *s*
1 Tim. 1:10 thing that is contrary to *s* doctrine
2 Tim. 1:7 of power, and of love, and of a *s* mind
  1:13 hold fast the form of *s* words, which thou
Tit. 1:13 rebuke . . that they may be *s* in the faith
  2:2 aged . . be sober, grave, temperate, *s* in faith
  2:8 *s* speech, that cannot be condemned

Sound *See also* Noise, Voice

Ex. 19:19 and when the voice of the trumpet *s* long
  28:35 his *s* shall be heard when he goeth in unto
Lev. 26:36 the *s* of a shaken leaf shall chase them
2 Sam. 5:24 (1 Chr. 14:15) hearest the *s* of a going
1 Kgs. 18:41 for there is a *s* of abundance of rain
2 Kgs. 6:32 the *s* of his master's feet behind him?
Neh. 4:18 and he that *s* the trumpet was by me
Job 15:21 dreadful *s* is in his ears: in prosperity
Ps. 89:15 blessed is the people that know the joyful *s*
Eccl. 12:4 when the *s* of the grinding is low
Is. 16:11 my bowels shall *s* like a harp for Moab
  63:15 *s* of thy bowels and of thy mercies toward

Joel 2:1 *s* an alarm in my holy mountain: let all
Mt. 6:2 thine alms, do not *s* a trumpet before thee
　24:31 send his angels with a great *s* of a trumpet
Jn. 3:8 hearest the *s* thereof, but canst not tell
Acts 2:2 a *s* from heaven as of a rushing mighty wind
Rom. 10:18 verily, their *s* went into all the earth
1 Cor. 13:1 I am become as *s* brass, or a tinkling
　14:7 and even things without life giving *s*
　14:8 for if the trumpet give an uncertain *s*
　15:52 the trumpet shall *s*, and the dead shall be
1 Thes. 1:8 from you *s* out the word of the Lord
Rev. 1:15 and his voice as the *s* of many waters
　8:7 the first angel *s*, and there followed hail
　9:9 *s* of their wings was as the *s* of chariots
　18:22 *s* of a millstone shall be heard no more

Sound (verb)

Acts 27:28 *s*, and found it twenty fathoms . . *s* again

Soundness

Ps. 38:3 no *s* in my flesh because of thine anger
Is. 1:6 foot even unto the head there is no *s* in it
Acts 3:16 given him this perfect *s* in the presence

Sour

Is. 18:5 and the *s* grape is ripening in the flower
Jer. 31:29 (Ezek. 18:2) fathers have eaten a *s* grape
Hos. 4:18 their drink is *s*: they have committed

South

Gen. 12:9 Abram journeyed, going on . . toward the *s*
　13:1 and Abram went up out of Egypt . . into the *s*
Job 37:9 out of the *s* cometh the whirlwind
Is. 43:6 give up; and to the, Keep not back
Ezek. 20:46 son of man, set thy face toward the *s*
Dan. 11:5 and the king of the *s* shall be strong

Sow (Sown)

Gen. 26:12 then Isaac *s* in that land, and received
Lev. 26:5 the vintage shall reach unto the *s* time
Deut. 11:10 where thou *s* thy seed, and wateredst
Job 4:8 that plow iniquity, and *s* wickedness, reap
　31:8 let me *s*, and let another eat; yea, let my
Ps. 97:11 light is *s* for the righteous, and gladness
　107:37 and *s* the fields, and plant vineyards
　126:5 they that *s* in tears shall reap in joy
Prov. 6:14 deviseth mischief continually; he *s* discord
　11:18 that *s* righteousness shall be a sure reward
Eccl. 11:4 he that observeth the wind shall not *s*
　11:6 the morning *s* thy seed, and in the evening
Is. 32:20 blessed are ye that *s* beside all waters
　40:24 not be planted; yea, they shall not be *s*
Jer. 4:3 your fallow ground, and *s* not among thorns
　12:13 they have *s* wheat, but shall reap thorns
　31:27 I will *s* the house of Israel and the house
Hos. 8:7 they have *s* the wind, and they shall reap
　10:12 *s* to yourselves in righteousness, reap in
Mic. 6:15 (Jn. 4:37) shalt *s*, but thou shalt not reap
Nah. 1:14 commandment . . no more of thy name be *s*
Hag. 1:6 ye have *s* much, and bring in little; ye eat
Mt. 6:26 (Lk. 12:24) they *s* not, neither do they reap
　13:3 (Mk. 4:3; Lk. 8:5) a sower went forth to *s*
　13:27 didst not thou *s* good seed in thy field?
　13:37 he that *s* the good seed is the Son of man
Lk. 19:21 and reapest that thou didst not *s*
Jn. 4:36 he that *s* and he that reapeth may rejoice
1 Cor. 9:11 if we have *s* unto you spiritual things
　15:36 which thou *s* is not quickened, except it die
　15:42 is *s* in corruption, it is raised in incorruption
2 Cor. 9:6 *s* sparingly shall reap also sparingly
Gal. 6:7 whatsoever a man *s*, that shall he also reap
Jas. 3:18 fruit of righteousness is *s* in peace

Sower

Is. 55:10 (2 Cor. 9:10) give seed to the *s*, and bread
Jer. 50:16 cut off the *s* from Babylon, and him that
Mt. 13:3 (Mk. 4:3; Lk. 8:5) a *s* went forth to sow
　13:18 hear ye therefore the parable of the *s*

Spain Rom. 15:24

Spake *See* Speak

Span

Is. 48:13 and my right hand hath *s* the heavens

Spare

Gen. 18:24 *s* the place for the fifty righteous
Deut. 29:20 Lord will not *s* him, but then the anger
2 Sam. 21:7 king *s* Mephibosheth . . son of Jonathan
Neh. 13:22 *s* me according to the greatness of thy
Ps. 39:13 O *s* me, that I may recover strength
　72:13 he shall *s* the poor and needy, and shall
Prov. 6:34 he will not *s* in the day of vengeance
　13:24 he that *s* his rod hateth his son: but he
　17:27 he that hath knowledge *s* his words
　19:18 chasten . . let not thy soul *s* for his crying
Is. 54:2 *s* not, lengthen thy cords, and strengthen
　58:1 cry aloud, *s* not, lift up thy voice
Jer. 13:14 I will not pity, nor *s*, nor have mercy
Joel 2:17 and let them say, *S* thy people, O Lord
Jon. 4:11 should not I *s* Nineveh, that great city
Mal. 3:17 I will *s* them, as a man *s* his own son
Lk. 15:17 have bread enough and to *s*, and I perish
Acts 20:29 wolves enter in among you, not *s* the flock
Rom. 8:32 that *s* not his own Son, but delivered him
　11:21 if God *s* not the natural branches, take heed
1 Cor. 7:28 have trouble in the flesh: but I *s* you
2 Cor. 13:2 if I come again, I will not *s*
2 Pet. 2:4 for if God *s* not the angels that sinned
　2:5 and *s* not the old world, but saved Noah

Sparingly

2 Cor. 9:6 he which soweth *s* shall reap also *s*

Spark

Job 5:7 is born unto trouble, as the *s* fly upward
　18:5 be put out . . *s* of his fire shall not shine
Is. 1:31 be as tow, and the maker of it as a *s*
　50:11 that compass yourselves about with *s*

Sparrow

Ps. 84:3 *s* hath found a house . . the swallow a nest
　102:7 and am as a *s* alone upon the housetop
Mt. 10:29 (Lk. 12:6) are not two *s* sold for a farthing?
　10:31 (Lk. 12:7) ye are of more value than many *s*

Spat *See* Spit

Speak (Spake, Spoken) *See also* Talk

Gen. 18:27 I have taken upon me to *s* unto the Lord
　31:11 angel of God *s* unto me in a dream, saying
　35:15 of the place where God *s* with him, Bethel
　46:2 God *s* unto Israel in the visions of the night
Ex. 4:14 thy brother? I know that he can *s* well
　6:2 God *s* unto Moses, and said . . I am the Lord
　7:2 *s* all that I command thee; and Aaron . . shall *s*
　12:1 the Lord *s* unto Moses and Aaron in . . Egypt
　19:8 said, All that the Lord hath *s* we will do
　19:9 that the people may hear when I *s* with thee
　20:1 and God *s* all these words, saying
　20:19 *s* thou with us . . but let not God *s* with us
　33:11 Lord *s* unto Moses face to face, as a man *s*
　34:34 Moses went in before the Lord to *s* with him
Lev. 10:3 this is it that the Lord *s*, saying, I will

Num. 5:4 as the LORD *s* unto Moses, so did . . Israel
  11:25 LORD came down in a cloud, and *s* unto him
  12:8 with him will I *s* mouth to mouth . . apparently
  20:8 *s* ye unto the rock before their eyes
  21:5 the people *s* against God, and against Moses
  22:35 that I shall *s* unto thee, that thou shalt *s*
  23:19 hath he *s*, and shall he not make it good?
  23:26 all that the LORD *s*, that I must do?
  24:13 but what the LORD saith, that will I *s*?
Deut. 1:6 LORD our God *s* unto us in Horeb, saying
  18:18 shall *s* unto them all that I shall command
  18:20 to *s* a word . . not commanded him to *s*
  18:22 LORD hath not *s*, but the prophet hath *s* it
Josh. 1:1 the LORD *s* unto Joshua the son of Nun
Judg. 2:4 when the angel of the LORD *s* these words
1 Sam. 3:9 (3:10) *s*, LORD; for thy servant heareth
  16:4 Samuel did that which the LORD *s*, and came
2 Sam. 23:2 Spirit of the LORD *s* by me, and his
1 Kgs. 13:3 this is the sign which the LORD hath *s*
  18:24 the people answered and said, It is well *s*
  22:14 (2 Chr. 18:13) what the LORD saith . . will I *s*
2 Kgs. 21:10 LORD *s* by his servants the prophets
2 Chr. 32:19 they *s* against the God of Jerusalem
Neh. 9:13 mount Sinai, and *s* with them from heaven
Job 2:13 and none *s* a word unto him: for they saw
  9:35 then would I *s*, and not fear him; but it is
  10:1 I will *s* in the bitterness of my soul
  11:5 but oh that God would *s*, and open his lips
  13:3 I would *s* to the Almighty, and I desire to
  13:7 will ye *s* wickedly for God? and talk
  33:14 for God *s* once . . yet man perceiveth it not
  36:2 show thee . . I have yet to *s* on God's behalf
Ps. 2:5 then shall he *s* unto them in his wrath
  33:9 for he *s*, and it was done; he commanded
  35:28 my tongue shall *s* of thy righteousness
  39:3 while I was musing the fire burned: then *s* I
  50:1 the mighty God, even the LORD, hath *s*
  60:6 (108:7) God hath *s* in his holiness; I will
  78:19 yea, they *s* against God; they said, Can God
  85:8 LORD will *s*: for he will *s* peace unto his
  87:3 glorious things are *s* of thee, O city of God
  89:19 then thou *s* in vision to thy holy one
  99:7 he *s* unto them in the cloudy pillar
  105:31 he *s*, and there came divers sorts of flies
  106:33 so that he *s* unadvisedly with his lips
  115:5 (135:16) they have mouths, but they *s* not
  116:10 (2 Cor. 4:13) I believed, therefore have I *s*
  119:172 my tongue shall *s* of thy word: for all
  139:20 they *s* against thee wickedly, and thine
  145:5 will *s* of the glorious honor of thy majesty
Prov. 8:6 hear; for I will *s* of excellent things
  12:17 he that *s* truth showed forth righteousness
  15:23 a word *s* in due season, how good is it!
  16:13 of kings; and they love him that *s* right
  23:16 shall rejoice, when thy lips *s* right things
Eccl. 3:7 a time to keep silence, and a time to *s*
Is. 1:2 and give ear, O earth: for the LORD hath *s*
  28:11 (1 Cor. 14:21) another tongue will he *s*
  40:2 *s* ye comfortably to Jerusalem, and cry unto
  45:19 I have not *s* in secret, in a dark place
  46:11 I have *s* it, I will also bring it to pass
  50:4 I should know how to *s* a word in season to
  63:1 I that *s* in righteousness, mighty to save
  65:12 when I *s*, ye did not hear; but did evil
  65:24 and while they are yet *s*, I will hear
Jer. 1:6 behold, I cannot *s*: for I am a child
  1:7 and whatsoever I command thee thou shalt *s*
  7:13 (35:14) I *s* unto you, rising up early and *s*
  7:22 I *s* not unto your fathers, nor commanded
  7:27 thou shalt *s* all these words unto them
  10:1 hear ye the word which the LORD *s* unto you
  20:9 I said, I will not . . *s* any more in his name
  23:28 hath my word, let him *s* my word faithfully

Jer. 23:35 answered? and, What hath the LORD *s*?
  30:2 write . . all the words that I have *s* unto thee
  43:2 Jeremiah, Thou *s* falsely . . God hath not sent
Ezek. 2:1 son of man, stand . . and I will *s* unto thee
  2:7 thou shalt *s* my words unto them, whether they
  5:15 in furious rebukes. I the LORD have *s* it
  12:25 I am the LORD: I will *s*, and the word that
  13:7 say, The LORD saith it; albeit I have not *s*?
  22:14 I shall deal with thee? I the LORD have *s*
Hos. 12:10 I have also *s* by the prophets, and I
Amos 3:8 Lord GOD hath *s*, who can but prophesy?
Zech. 8:16 (Eph. 4:25) *s* ye every man the truth
Mal. 3:16 feared the LORD *s* often one to another
Mt. 6:7 that they shall be heard for their much *s*
  9:33 (Lk. 11:14) devil was cast out, the dumb *s*
  10:19 (Mk. 13:11) be given you . . what ye shall *s*
  10:20 (Mk. 13:11) is not ye that *s*, but the Spirit
  10:27 I tell you in darkness, that *s* ye in light
  12:22 that the blind and dumb both *s* and saw
  12:32 (Lk. 12:10) *s* a word against the Son of man
  12:34 (Lk. 6:45) out of the . . heart the mouth *s*
  21:45 (Mk. 12:12; Lk. 20:19) perceived that he *s* of
  22:31 not read that which was *s* unto you by God
Mk. 1:34 (Lk. 4:41) and suffered not the devils to *s*
  9:39 in my name, that can lightly *s* evil of me
  12:26 of Moses, how in the bush God *s* unto him
  14:9 she hath done shall be *s* of for a memorial
Lk. 1:55 as he *s* to our fathers, to Abraham, and to
  1:70 as he *s* by the mouth of his holy prophets
  6:26 woe . . when all men shall *s* well of you!
  22:65 things blasphemously *s* they against him
  24:6 but is risen: remember how he *s* unto you
  24:25 slow . . to believe all that the prophets have *s*
Jn. 3:11 we *s* that we do know, and testify that we
  3:31 of the earth is earthly, and *s* of the earth
  3:34 he whom God hath sent *s* the words of God
  4:26 Jesus saith unto her, I that *s* unto thee am he
  7:17 whether it be of God, or whether I *s* of myself
  7:46 officers answered, Never man *s* like this man
  8:38 I *s* that which I have seen with my Father
  9:29 we know that God *s* unto Moses: as for this
  12:29 thundered: others said, An angel *s* to him
  12:49 for I have not *s* of myself; but the Father
  12:50 even as the Father said unto me, so I *s*
  14:10 words that I *s* unto you I *s* not of myself
  16:13 he hath not *s* of himself; but whatsoever
  16:33 these things I have *s* unto you, that in me
  18:20 Jesus answered him, I *s* openly to the world
Acts 2:4 and began to *s* with other tongues
  2:31 *s* of the resurrection of Christ, that his
  3:21 which God hath *s* by . . all his holy prophets
  4:20 we cannot but *s* the things which we have
  4:31 and they *s* the word of God with boldness
  5:20 go, stand and *s* in the temple to the people
  5:40 that they should not *s* in the name of Jesus
  7:38 the angel which *s* to him in the mount Sina
  8:26 the angel of the Lord *s* unto Philip, saying
  9:29 he *s* boldly in the name of the Lord Jesus
  11:15 I began to *s*, the Holy Ghost fell on them
  13:45 *s* against those things which were *s* by Paul
  14:1 into the synagogue of the Jews, and so *s*
  16:32 and they *s* unto him the word of the Lord
  18:9 *s* the Lord to Paul . . Be not afraid, but *s*
  18:26 and he began to *s* boldly in the synagogue
  19:8 and *s* boldly for the space of three months
  19:36 seeing . . these things cannot be *s* against
  26:25 *s* forth the words of truth and soberness
Rom. 1:8 your faith is *s* of throughout the whole
  6:19 (Gal. 3:15) I *s* after the manner of men
  14:16 let not then your good be evil *s* of
1 Cor. 1:10 that ye all *s* the same thing, and that
  2:6 we *s* wisdom among them that are perfect
  2:13 which things also we *s*, not in the words

1 Cor. 7:6 *s*. . by permission . . not of commandment
  7:12 but to the rest *s* I, not the Lord
  10:30 be a partaker, why am I evil *s* of for that
  13:11 I was a child, I *s* as a child, I understood
  14:2 that *s* in an unknown tongue *s* not unto men
  14:19 rather *s* five words with my understanding
  14:27 if any man *s* in an unknown tongue, let it
  14:35 it is a shame for women to *s* in the church
2 Cor. 7:14 as we *s* all things to you in truth
  11:17 that which I *s*, I *s* it not after the Lord
Eph. 4:15 *s* the truth in love, may grow up into him
  5:19 *s* to yourselves in psalms and hymns
  6:20 that therein I may *s* boldly, as I ought to *s*
Phil. 1:14 more bold to *s* the word without fear
Col. 4:3 door of utterance, to *s* the mystery of Christ
1 Thes. 2:4 even so we *s*; not as pleasing men, but
  2:16 forbidding us to *s* to the Gentiles that they
1 Tim. 4:1 Spirit *s* expressly, that in the latter
Tit. 2:15 these things *s*, and exhort, and rebuke
  3:2 to *s* evil of no man, to be no brawlers
Heb. 1:1 *s* in time past unto the fathers by the
  11:4 of his gifts: and by it he being dead yet *s*
  12:25 see that ye refuse not him that *s*: for if
Jas. 1:19 swift to hear, slow to *s*, slow to wrath
  4:11 *s* not evil one of another . . He that *s* evil
  5:10 prophets, who have *s* in the name of the Lord
1 Pet. 2:12 whereas they *s* against you as evildoers
  4:11 any man *s*, let him *s* as the oracles of God
  4:14 on their part he is evil *s* of, but on your
2 Pet. 1:21 holy men of God *s* as they were moved
  2:2 of whom the way of truth shall be evil *s* of
  2:10 (Jude 8) not afraid to *s* evil of dignities
  2:18 (Jude 16) when they *s* great swelling words
1 Jn. 4:5 therefore *s* they of the world

Spear

Josh. 8:18 LORD said unto Joshua, Stretch out the *s*
1 Sam. 13:22 sword nor *s* found in the hand of any
  17:7 the staff of his *s* was like a weaver's beam
  17:45 comest to me with a sword, and with a *s*
  26:11 take thou now the *s*. . and the cruse of water
Job 41:29 he laugheth at the shaking of a *s*
Ps. 46:9 he breaketh the bow, and cutteth the *s*
  57:4 whose teeth are *s* and arrows, and their
Is. 2:4 (Mic. 4:3) and their *s* into pruning hooks
Joel 3:10 into swords, and your pruning hooks into *s*
Hab. 3:11 and at the shining of thy glittering *s*
Jn. 19:34 one of the soldiers with a *s* pierced his

Spearmen

Ps. 68:30 rebuke the company of *s*, the multitude
Acts 23:23 make ready two hundred soldiers . . and *s*

Special

Deut. 7:6 God hath chosen thee to be a *s* people
Acts 19:11 wrought *s* miracles by the hands of Paul

Speckled

Gen. 30:32 removing from thence all . . *s* and spotted

Spectacle

1 Cor. 4:9 we are made a *s* unto the world

Speech *See also* Language, Tongue

Gen. 11:1 earth was of one language, and of one *s*
Ex. 4:10 but I am slow of *s*, and of a slow tongue
Deut. 32:2 the rain, my *s* shall distil as the dew
1 Kgs. 3:10 the *s* pleased the Lord, that Solomon
Job 6:26 the *s* of one that is desperate . . as wind?
  15:3 or with *s* wherewith he can do no good?
  29:22 spake not again . . my *s* dropped upon them
Ps. 19:2 day unto day uttereth *s*, and night unto
  19:3 no *s* nor language, where their voice is not

Prov. 17:7 excellent *s* becometh not a fool
Song 4:3 and thy *s* is comely: thy temples are like
Is. 33:19 a people of a deeper *s* than thou canst
Ezek. 3:5 art not sent to a people of a strange *s*
Hab. 3:2 O LORD, I have heard thy *s*, and was afraid
Mt. 26:73 (Mk. 14:70) of them; for thy *s* bewrayeth
Mk. 7:32 was deaf, and had an impediment in his *s*
Jn. 8:43 do ye not understand my *s*? even because
Rom. 16:18 fair *s* deceive the hearts of the simple
1 Cor. 2:1 not with excellency of *s* or of wisdom
  4:19 not the *s* of them which are puffed up
2 Cor. 3:12 such hope, we use great plainness of *s*
  10:10 bodily presence is weak . . his *s* contemptible
  11:6 though I be rude in *s*, yet not in knowledge
Col. 4:6 let your *s* be always with grace, seasoned
Tit. 2:8 sound *s*, that cannot be condemned
Jude 15 hard *s* which ungodly sinners have spoken

Speechless *See also* Dumb

Mt. 22:12 having a wedding garment? And he was *s*
Lk. 1:22 for he beckoned unto them, and remained *s*
Acts 9:7 the men which journeyed with him stood *s*

Speed

Gen. 24:12 send me good *s* this day . . show kindness
Acts 17:15 Timotheus for to come to him with all *s*

Speedily

Ezra 6:13 Darius the king had sent, so they did *s*
  7:26 let judgment be executed *s* upon him, whether
Ps. 31:2 deliver me *s*: be thou my strong rock
  79:8 let thy tender mercies *s* prevent us
  102:2 unto me: in the day when I call answer me *s*
  143:7 hear me *s*, O LORD; my spirit faileth
Eccl. 8:11 against an evil work is not executed *s*
Zech. 8:21 let us go *s* to pray before the LORD
Lk. 18:8 I tell you that he will avenge them *s*

Spend (Spent)

Gen. 21:15 water was *s* in the bottle, and she cast
  47:18 we will not hide . . how that our money is *s*
Lev. 26:20 your strength shall be *s* in vain
Deut. 32:23 I will *s* mine arrows upon them
Job 7:6 weaver's shuttle, and are *s* without hope
  21:13 *s* their days in wealth, and in a moment
  36:11 they shall *s* their days in prosperity
Ps. 90:9 we *s* our years as a tale that is told
Prov. 21:20 treasure . . but a foolish man *s* it up
  29:3 company with harlots *s* his substance
Eccl. 6:12 of his vain life which he *s* as a shadow?
Is. 49:4 in vain, I have *s* my strength for nought
  55:2 do ye *s* money for that which is not bread?
Jer. 37:21 until all the bread in the city were *s*
Mk. 5:26 (Lk. 8:43) and had *s* all that she had
  6:35 when the day was now far *s*, his disciples
Lk. 10:35 whatsoever thou *s* more . . I will repay thee
  15:14 he had *s* all, there arose a mighty famine
Acts 17:21 Athenians . . *s* their time in nothing else
Rom. 13:12 the night is far *s*, the day is at hand
2 Cor. 12:15 I will very gladly *s* and be *s* for you

Spew

Lev. 18:28 the land *s* not you out also . . as it *s* out
Hab. 2:16 and shameful *s* shall be on thy glory
Rev. 3:16 neither cold nor hot, I will *s* thee out

Spice

1 Kgs. 10:2 (2 Chr. 9:1) with camels that bare *s*
Song 4:10 the smell of thine ointments than all *s*!
Mk. 16:1 (Lk. 24:1) bought sweet *s*, that they might
Lk. 23:56 returned, and prepared *s* and ointments
Jn. 19:40 and wound it in linen clothes with the *s*

Spider

Job 8:14 and whose trust shall be a *s*'s web
Prov. 30:28 the *s* taketh hold with her hands
Is. 59:5 hatch cockatrice' eggs, and weave the *s*'s web

Spikenard

Song 1:12 my *s* sendeth forth the smell thereof
Mk. 14:3 (Jn. 12:3) alabaster box of ointment of *s*

Spill (Spilt)

2 Sam. 14:14 as water *s* on the ground, which cannot
Mk. 2:22 (Lk. 5:37) burst the bottles . . the wine is *s*

Spin

Ex. 35:25 the women that were wise-hearted did *s*
Mt. 6:28 (Lk. 12:27) toil not, neither do they *s*

Spindle

Prov. 31:19 she layeth her hands to the *s*, and her

Spirit *See also* Spirit of God, Spirit of the LORD, Holy Ghost, Holy Spirit, Soul

Gen. 6:3 my *S* shall not always strive with man
Lev. 19:31 regard not them that have familiar *s*
20:27 that hath a familiar *s* . . be put to death
Num. 11:17 I will take of the *s* which is upon thee
11:25 the *s* rested upon them, they prophesied
14:24 Caleb, because he had another *s* with him
16:22 O God, the God of the *s* of all flesh
27:18 take thee Joshua . . a man in whom is the *s*
Judg. 9:23 God sent an evil *s* between Abimelech
1 Sam. 16:14 (19:9) evil *s* from the LORD troubled him
28:3 Saul had put away those that had familiar *s*
28:7 seek me a woman that hath a familiar *s*
1 Kgs. 22:21 (2 Chr. 18:20) came forth a *s*, and stood
2 Kgs. 2:9 let a double portion of thy *s* be upon me
Ezra 1:5 with all them whose *s* God had raised
Neh. 9:20 thou gavest also thy good *S* to instruct
Job 4:15 then a *s* passed before my face; the hair
15:13 thou turnest thy *s* against God, and lettest
26:4 uttered words? and whose *s* came from thee?
32:8 there is a *s* in man: and the inspiration of
Ps. 31:5 (Lk. 23:46) into thine hand I commit my *s*
32:2 not iniquity, and in whose *s* there is no guile
34:18 and saveth such as be of a contrite *s*
51:10 clean heart . . and renew a right *s* within me
51:12 and uphold me with thy free *S*
51:17 sacrifices of God are a broken *s*: a broken
78:8 whose *s* was not steadfast with God
104:4 (Heb. 1:7) maketh his angels *s*; his ministers
104:30 thou sendest forth thy *s*, they are created
139:7 whither shall I go from thy *S*? or whither
143:10 thou art my God: thy *S* is good; lead me
Prov. 1:23 behold, I will pour out my *s* unto you
16:2 in his own eyes; but the LORD weigheth the *s*
16:32 ruleth his *s* than he that taketh a city
17:27 man of understanding is of an excellent *s*
18:14 the *s* of a man will sustain his infirmity
20:27 the *s* of man is the candle of the LORD
25:28 he that hath no rule over his own *s* is like
Eccl. 3:21 knoweth the *s* of man that goeth upward
8:8 no man . . hath power over the *s* to retain the *s*
11:5 thou knowest not what is the way of the *s*
12:7 and the *s* shall return unto God who gave it
Is. 4:4 purged . . by the *s* of judgment, and by the *s*
11:2 the *s* of wisdom and understanding, the *s* of
28:6 *s* of judgment to him that sitteth in judgment
32:15 until the *S* be poured upon us from on high
42:1 (Mt. 12:18) have put my *S* upon him: he shall
42:5 that giveth breath . . and *s* to them that walk
44:3 will pour my *S* upon thy seed, and my blessing

Is. 57:15 of a contrite and humble *s*, to revive the *s*
Ezek. 1:12 whither the *s* was to go, they went
1:20 (1:21; 10:17) *s* of the living creature was in
3:12 the *s* took me up, and I heard behind me a
8:3 *s* lifted me up between the earth and . . heaven
11:19 (36:26) I will put a new *s* within you
13:3 foolish prophets, that follow their own *s*
18:31 make you a new heart and a new *s*: for why
36:27 (37:14) I will put my *S* within you, and cause
Dan. 4:8 (5:11) in whom is the *s* of the holy gods
Joel 2:28 (Acts 2:17) pour out my *S* upon all flesh
Hag. 2:5 so my *S* remaineth among you: fear ye not
Zech. 4:6 not by might, nor by power, but by my *S*
Mt. 4:1 (Mk. 1:12; Lk. 4:1) Jesus led up of the *S* into
5:3 blessed are the poor in *s*: for theirs is the
8:16 he cast out the *s* with his word, and healed
10:1 (Mk. 6:7) gave them power against unclean *s*
12:43 (Lk. 11:24) when the unclean *s* is gone out
12:45 (Lk. 11:26) seven other *s* more wicked than
14:26 (Mk. 6:49) saying, It is a *s*; and they cried
26:41 (Mk. 14:38) the *s* indeed is willing, but the
Mk. 1:10 (Jn. 1:32) *S* like a dove descending upon
5:2 met . . out of the tombs a man with an unclean *s*
9:26 the *s* cried, and rent him sore, and came out
Lk. 1:47 and my *s* hath rejoiced in God my Saviour
1:80 (2:40) the child grew, and waxed strong in *s*
9:55 ye know not what manner of *s* ye are of
24:37 affrighted . . supposed that they had seen a *s*
24:39 a *s* hath not flesh and bones, as ye see me
Jn. 3:5 except a man be born of water and of the *S*
3:6 and that which is born of the *S* is *s*
3:34 God giveth not the *S* by measure unto him
4:23 shall worship the Father in *s* and in truth
4:24 God is a *S*: and they that worship him must
6:63 *S* that quickeneth . . flesh profiteth nothing
7:39 but this spake he of the *S*, which they that
14:17 *S* of truth; whom the world cannot receive
15:26 the *S* of truth . . proceedeth from the Father
16:13 when he, the *S* of truth, is come, he will
Acts 2:4 other tongues, as the *S* gave them utterance
7:59 Stephen . . saying, Lord Jesus, receive my *s*
8:29 the *S* said unto Philip, Go near, and join
10:19 *S* said unto him, Behold, three men seek
16:7 into Bithynia: but the *S* suffered them not
16:16 damsel possessed with a *s* of divination
20:22 behold, I go bound in the *s* unto Jerusalem
21:4 who said to Paul through the *S*, that he
23:8 is no resurrection, neither angel, nor *s*
Rom. 1:4 Son of God . . according to the *S* of holiness
1:9 I serve with my *s* in the gospel of his Son
2:29 the heart, in the *s*, and not in the letter
7:6 we should serve in newness of *s*, and not in
8:1 (8:4) walk not after the flesh, but after the *S*
8:2 law of the *S* of life in Christ . . made me free
8:5 that are after the *S*, the things of the *S*
8:9 if any man have not the *S* of Christ, he is
8:10 but the *S* is life because of righteousness
8:11 but if the *S* of him that raised up Jesus
8:13 if ye through the *S* do mortify the deeds of
8:15 ye have received the *S* of adoption, whereby
8:16 the *S* itself beareth witness with our *s*
8:26 *S* also helpeth . . *S* itself maketh intercession
8:27 knoweth what is the mind of the *S*, because
1 Cor. 2:4 wisdom, but in demonstration of the *S*
2:10 unto us by his *S*: for the *S* searcheth all
2:12 received, not the *s* of the world, but the *S*
5:3 I verily, as absent in body, but present in *s*
5:5 the *s* may be saved in the day of the Lord
6:20 glorify God in your body, and in your *s*
12:4 are diversities of gifts, but the same *S*
12:10 to another discerning of *s*; to another
12:13 by one *S* are we all baptized into one body
14:14 my *s* prayeth . . understanding is unfruitful

1 Cor. 15:45 the last Adam was made a quickening *s*
2 Cor. 1:22 the earnest of the *S* in our hearts
3:3 not with ink, but with the *S* of the living God
3:6 for the letter killeth, but the *s* giveth life
4:13 we having the same *s* of faith, according as
Gal. 3:2 received ye the *S* by the works of the law
3:14 that we might receive the promise of the *S*
4:6 sent forth the *S* of his Son into your hearts
5:5 through the *S* wait for . . hope of righteousness
5:16 walk in the *S*. . ye shall not fulfil the lust
5:17 the flesh lusteth against the *S*, and the *S*
5:22 but the fruit of the *S* is love, joy, peace
5:25 we live in the *S*, let us also walk in the *S*
6:8 that soweth to the *S* shall of the *S* reap life
Eph. 2:2 the *s* that now worketh in the children of
2:18 we both have access by one *S* unto the Father
2:22 for a habitation of God through the *S*
3:16 to be strengthened with might by his *S* in
4:3 keep the unity of the *S* in the bond of peace
4:4 is one body, and one *S*, even as ye are called
4:23 and be renewed in the *s* of your mind
5:9 the fruit of the *S* is in all goodness and
5:18 and be not drunk . . but be filled with the *S*
6:17 helmet of salvation, and the sword of the *S*
6:18 with all prayer and supplication in the *S*
Phil. 1:27 ye stand fast in one *s*, with one mind
2:1 if any fellowship of the *S*, if any bowels
3:3 the circumcision, which worship God in the *s*
Col. 1:8 also declared unto us your love in the *S*
1 Thes. 5:19 quench not the *S*
5:23 your whole *s* and soul and body be preserved
1 Tim. 3:16 justified in the *S*, seen of angels
4:1 the *S* speaketh expressly, that in the latter
Heb. 1:14 are they not all ministering *s*, sent forth
9:14 who through the eternal *S* offered himself
10:29 and hath done despite unto the *S* of grace?
12:23 and to the *s* of just men made perfect
Jas. 2:26 as the body without the *s* is dead, so
4:5 the *s* that dwelleth in us lusteth to envy?
1 Pet. 3:18 in the flesh, but quickened by the *S*
3:19 he went and preached unto the *s* in prison
4:6 the flesh, but live according to God in the *s*
4:14 the *S* of glory and of God resteth upon you
1 Jn. 3:24 we know that he abideth in us, by the *S*
4:1 believe not every *s*, but try the *s* whether
4:6 know we the *s* of truth, and the *s* of error
4:13 he in us, because he hath given us of his *S*
5:6 *S* that beareth witness, because the *S* is truth
5:8 three that bear witness in earth, the *s*, and
Rev. 1:4 the seven *S* which are before his throne
1:10 I was in the *S* on the Lord's day, and heard
2:7 (2:11, 17, 29; 3:6, 13, 22) what the *S* saith unto
11:11 the *S* of life from God entered into them
16:14 they are the *S* of devils, working miracles
19:10 testimony of Jesus is the *s* of prophecy
21:10 he carried me away in the *s* to a great and
22:17 the *S* and the bride say, Come. And let him

Spirit of God *See also* Spirit, Spirit of the LORD, Holy Ghost, Holy Spirit

Gen. 1:2 *S* of *G* moved upon the face of the waters
41:38 as this is, a man in whom the *S* of *G* is?
Ex. 31:3 (35:31) have filled him with the *s* of *G*
Num. 24:2 Balaam . . and the *S* of *G* came upon him
1 Sam. 10:10 *S* of *G* came upon him . . he prophesied
11:6 *S* of *G* came upon Saul when he heard those
19:20 the *S* of *G* was upon the messengers of Saul
Job 27:3 is in me, and the *s* of *G* is in my nostrils
33:4 the *S* of *G* hath made me, and the breath of
Mt. 3:16 he saw the *S* of *G* descending like a dove
12:28 if I cast out devils by the *S* of *G*, then
Rom. 8:14 as many as are led by the *S* of *G*, they

Rom. 15:19 and wonders, by the power of the *S* of *G*
1 Cor. 2:11 of God knoweth no man, but the *S* of *G*
3:16 temple of God, and . . *S* of *G* dwelleth in you?
7:40 and I think also that I have the *S* of *G*
12:3 no man speaking by the *S* of *G* calleth Jesus
1 Jn. 4:2 hereby know ye the *S* of *G*: Every spirit
Rev. 3:1 saith he that hath the seven *S* of *G*
4:5 lamps of fire . . which are the seven *S* of *G*
5:6 seven *S* of *G* sent forth into all the earth

Spirit of the LORD (Lord) *See also* Spirit, Spirit of God, Holy Ghost, Holy Spirit

Judg. 3:10 *S* of the *L* came upon him, and he judged
11:29 then the *S* of the *L* came upon Jephthah
13:25 *S* of the *L* began to move him at times
14:6 (15:14) *S* of the *L* came mightily upon him
1 Sam. 16:13 *S* of the *L* came upon David from that
16:14 *S* of the *L* departed from Saul, and an evil
2 Sam. 23:2 *S* of the *L* spake by me, and his word
1 Kgs. 18:12 *S* of the *L* shall carry thee whither I
Is. 11:2 *S* of the *L* shall rest upon him, the spirit
40:7 fadeth; because the *s* of the *L* bloweth upon
40:13 who hath directed the *S* of the *L*, or being
61:1 (Lk. 4:18) the *S* of the *L* GOD is upon me
63:14 the *S* of the *L* caused him to rest
Ezek. 11:5 *S* of the *L* fell upon me, and said unto
Mic. 2:7 is the *S* of the *L* straitened?
3:8 truly I am full of power by the *S* of the *L*
Acts 5:9 agreed together to tempt the *S* of the *L*?
8:39 the *S* of the *L* caught away Philip
2 Cor. 3:17 where the *S* of the *L* is, there is liberty

Spiritual

Hos. 9:7 the prophet is a fool, the *s* man is mad
Rom. 1:11 that I may impart unto you some *s* gift
7:14 we know that the law is *s*: but I am carnal
15:27 Gentiles . . made partakers of their *s* things
1 Cor. 2:13 teacheth; comparing *s* things with *s*
2:15 but he that is *s* judgeth all things
3:1 could not speak unto you as unto *s*, but as
9:11 if we have sown unto you *s* things, is it
10:3 and did all eat the same *s* meat
12:1 concerning *s* gifts, brethren, I would not
14:1 follow after charity, and desire *s* gifts
14:12 as ye are zealous of *s* gifts, seek that ye
14:37 any man think himself to be a prophet, or *s*
15:44 sown a natural body, it is raised a *s* body
15:46 howbeit that was not first which is *s*
Gal. 6:1 ye which are *s*, restore such a one in the
Eph. 1:3 who hath blessed us with all *s* blessings
5:19 (Col. 3:16) in psalms and hymns and *s* songs
6:12 world, against *s* wickedness in high places
Col. 1:9 filled . . in all wisdom and *s* understanding
1 Pet. 2:5 up a *s* house . . to offer up *s* sacrifices

Spiritually

Rom. 8:6 but to be *s* minded is life and peace
1 Cor. 2:14 know them, because they are *s* discerned
Rev. 11:8 city, which *s* is called Sodom and Egypt

Spit (Spat)

Mt. 26:67 (Mk. 14:65) they *s* in his face, and buffeted
27:30 (Mk. 15:19) they *s* upon . . and smote him
Mk. 7:33 his ears, and he *s*, and touched his tongue
8:23 when he had *s* on his eyes, and put his hands
10:34 (Lk. 18:32) and shall *s* upon him
Jn. 9:6 he *s* on the ground . . made clay of the spittle

Spitefully

Mt. 22:6 took his servants, and entreated them *s*
Lk. 18:32 and shall be mocked, and *s* entreated

Spittle

Job 7:19 nor let me alone till I swallow down my *s*?
Jn. 9:6 and made clay of the *s*, and he anointed

Spoil *See also* Prey

Gen. 34:27 the sons of Jacob came. . and *s* the city
Ex. 3:22 shall borrow. . and ye shall *s* the Egyptians
Num. 31:53 men of war had taken *s*, every man for
Josh. 7:21 among the *s* a goodly Babylonish garment
1 Sam. 14:32 the people flew upon the *s*, and took
   30:20 and the herds. . and said, This is David's *s*
2 Kgs. 7:16 went out, and *s* the tents of the Syrians
2 Chr. 15:11 they offered unto the LORD. . of the *s*
   20:25 were three days in gathering of the *s*
   28:15 and with the *s* clothed all that were naked
Esth. 9:10 but on the *s* laid they not their hand
Job 29:17 and plucked the *s* out of his teeth
Ps. 35:10 poor and the needy from him that *s* him?
   44:10 and they which hate us *s* for themselves
   68:12 she that tarried at home divided the *s*
   76:5 the stout-hearted are *s*, they have slept
   89:41 all that pass by the way *s* him
   109:11 and let the strangers *s* his labor
   119:162 at thy word, as one that findeth great *s*
Prov. 1:13 find all. . we shall fill our houses with *s*
   16:19 than to divide the *s* with the proud
   22:23 plead. . and *s* the soul of those that *s* them
   24:15 of the righteous; *s* not his resting place
   31:11 in her, so that he shall have no need of *s*
Is. 3:14 the *s* of the poor is in your houses
   9:3 and as men rejoice when they divide the *s*
   17:14 this is the portion of them that *s* us
   33:1 woe to thee that *s*, and thou wast not *s*
   42:24 who gave Jacob for a *s*, and Israel to the
   53:12 and he shall divide the *s* with the strong
Jer. 2:14 is Israel a servant?. . why is he *s*?
   4:30 and when thou art *s*, what wilt thou do?
   5:6 and a wolf of the evenings shall *s* them
   10:20 my tabernacle is *s*. . all my cords are broken
   25:36 howling. . for the LORD hath *s* their pasture
   30:16 they that *s* thee shall be a *s*, and all that
Nah. 2:9 take ye the *s* of silver, take the *s* of gold
Hab. 2:8 because thou hast *s* many nations, all the
Zech. 11:2 howl, fir tree. . because the mighty are *s*
   14:1 thy *s* shall be divided in the midst of thee
Mt. 12:29 (Mk. 3:27) *s* his goods, except he first
Col. 2:8 lest any man *s* you through philosophy
   2:15 having *s* principalities and powers, he made
Heb. 7:4 patriarch Abraham gave the tenth of the *s*
   10:34 took joyfully the *s* of your goods, knowing

Spoken *See* Speak

Spokesman

Ex. 4:16 and he shall be thy *s* unto the people

Sponge

Mt. 27:48 (Mk. 15:36; Jn. 19:29) *s*. . with vinegar

Sport

Gen. 26:8 behold, Isaac was *s* with Rebekah his wife
Judg. 16:25 call for Samson, that he may make us *s*
Prov. 10:23 it is as *s* to a fool to do mischief
   26:19 man that deceiveth. . saith, Am not I in *s*
Is. 57:4 against whom do ye *s* yourselves?
2 Pet. 2:13 *s* themselves with their own deceivings

Spot *See also* Blemish

Lev. 13:38 have in the skin of their flesh bright *s*
Num. 19:2 they bring thee a red heifer without *s*
   28:3 offer. . two lambs of the first year without *s*
Deut. 32:5 their *s* is not the *s* of his children
Job 11:15 shalt thou lift up thy face without *s*

Song 4:7 all fair, my love; there is no *s* in thee
Jer. 13:23 change his skin, or the leopard his *s*?
Eph. 5:27 glorious church, not having *s*, or wrinkle
1 Tim. 6:14 thou keep this commandment without *s*
Heb. 9:14 offered himself without *s* to God
2 Pet. 2:13 *s* they are and blemishes, sporting
   3:14 ye may be found of him in peace, without *s*
Jude 12 these are *s* in your feasts of charity

Spotted

Gen. 30:32 removing. . all the speckled and *s* cattle

Spouse

Song 4:8 come with me from Lebanon, my *s*, with me
Hos. 4:13 and your *s* shall commit adultery

Spread

Deut. 32:11 eagle. . over her young, *s*. . her wings
Judg. 8:25 glorious *s* a garment, and did cast therein
2 Sam. 5:18 (1 Chr. 14:9) Philistines. . *s* themselves
1 Kgs. 8:54 kneeling. . with his hands *s* up to heaven
2 Kgs. 19:14 (Is. 37:14) letter. . *s* it before the LORD
Ezra 9:5 and *s* out my hands unto the LORD my God
Job 9:8 alone *s* out the heavens, and treadeth upon
   29:19 my root was *s* out by the waters, and the dew
   36:30 behold, he *s* his light upon it, and covereth
   37:18 hast thou with him *s* out the sky, which is
   41:30 he *s* sharp pointed things upon the mire
Ps. 140:5 the proud. . have *s* a net by the wayside
Is. 1:15 when ye *s* forth your hands, I will hide
   33:23 tacklings are loosed. . could not *s* the sail
   40:22 and *s* them out as a tent to dwell in
   65:2 I have *s* out my hands all the day unto a
Jer. 8:2 shall *s* them before the sun, and the moon
Lam. 1:17 Zion *s* forth her hands, and there is none
Ezek. 2:10 he *s* it before me; and it was written
Mt. 21:8 (Mk. 11:8; Lk. 19:36) *s* their garments in
Acts 4:17 that it *s* no further among the people
1 Thes. 1:8 your faith to God-ward is *s* abroad

Spring (noun) *See also* Fountain, Well

Josh. 15:19 (Judg. 1:15) the upper *s*, and the nether *s*
Job 38:16 hast thou entered into the *s* of the sea?
Ps. 87:7 all my *s* are in thee
   104:10 he sendeth the *s* into the valleys
Prov. 25:26 a troubled fountain, and a corrupt *s*
Song 4:12 spouse; a *s* shut up, a fountain sealed
Is. 35:7 a pool, and the thirsty land *s* of water
   41:18 the wilderness a pool. . dry land *s* of water
   58:11 like a *s* of water, whose waters fail not
Hos. 13:15 and his *s* shall become dry

Spring (Sprang, Sprung)

Num. 21:17 Israel sang this song, *S* up, O well
Job 5:6 neither doth trouble *s* out of the ground
Ps. 65:10 soft with showers: thou blessest the *s*
   85:11 truth shall *s* out of the earth
   92:7 when the wicked *s* as the grass
Is. 42:9 before they *s* forth I tell you of them
   43:19 I will do a new thing; now it shall *s* forth
   45:8 let righteousness *s* up together; I the LORD
   58:8 thine health shall *s* forth speedily
Joel 2:22 for the pastures of the wilderness do *s*
Mt. 13:5 (Mk. 4:5; Lk. 8:6) upon stony places. . *s* up
Mk. 4:27 seed should *s* and grow up, he knoweth not
Jn. 4:14 well of water *s* up into everlasting life
Heb. 7:14 it is evident that our Lord *s* out of Juda
   11:12 *s* there even of one. . so many as the stars

Sprinkle

Ex. 9:8 let Moses *s* it toward the heaven in the sight
   24:8 Moses took the blood, and *s* it on the people
Lev. 14:7 shall *s* upon him that is to be cleansed
Job 2:12 and *s* dust upon their heads toward heaven

Is. 52:15 shall he *s* many nations; the kings shall
Ezek. 36:25 then will I *s* clean water upon you
Heb. 9:19 and *s* both the book and all the people
   11:28 he kept the passover, and the *s* of blood
1 Pet. 1:2 obedience and *s* of the blood of Jesus

Sprout

Job 14:7 if it be cut down, that it will *s* again

Spy

Gen. 42:9 ye are *s*; to see the . . land ye are come
Ex. 2:11 and he *s* an Egyptian smiting a Hebrew
Num. 13:16 men which Moses sent to *s* out the land
Josh. 2:1 Joshua . . sent out of Shittim two men to *s*
   6:23 that were *s* went in, and brought out Rahab
Judg. 18:2 children of Dan sent . . to *s* out the land
2 Sam. 10:3 (1 Chr. 19:3) to *s* it out, and to overthrow
2 Kgs. 6:13 *s* where he is, that I may . . fetch him
Lk. 20:20 and they watched him, and sent forth *s*
Gal. 2:4 who came in privily to *s* out our liberty
Heb. 11:31 when she had received the *s* with peace

Stability

Is. 33:6 and knowledge shall be the *s* of thy times

Stablish *See also* Establish, Found, Settle

2 Sam. 7:13 (1 Chr. 17:12) I will *s* the throne of his
Ps. 119:38 *s* thy word unto thy servant, who is
Rom. 16:25 now to him that is of power to *s* you
2 Cor. 1:21 now he which *s* us with you in Christ
Col. 2:7 *s* in the faith, as ye have been taught
1 Thes. 3:13 he may *s* your hearts unblamable
2 Thes. 2:17 and *s* you in every good word and work

Staff

Gen. 32:10 for with my *s* I passed over this Jordan
   38:18 thy signet, and thy bracelets, and thy *s*
Num. 13:23 and they bare it between two upon a *s*
Judg. 6:21 the angel . . put forth the end of the *s*
1 Sam. 17:7 *s* of his spear was like a weaver's beam
2 Kgs. 4:29 lay my *s* upon the face of the child
Ps. 23:4 thy rod and thy *s* they comfort me
Is. 9:4 for thou hast broken . . the *s* of his shoulder
   10:5 and the *s* in their hand is mine indignation
   10:15 or as if the *s* should lift up itself
   14:5 the LORD hath broken the *s* of the wicked
Jer. 48:17 strong *s* broken, and the beautiful rod!
Ezek. 29:6 been a *s* of reed to the house of Israel
Zech. 8:4 man with his *s* in his hand for very age
   11:10 I took my *s*, even Beauty, and cut it asunder
Mk. 6:8 save a *s* only; no scrip, no bread, no money
Heb. 11:21 worshipped, leaning upon the top of his *s*

Stagger

Job 12:25 he maketh them to *s* like a drunken man
Ps. 107:27 reel to and fro, and *s* like a drunken man
Is. 19:14 as a drunken man *s* in his vomit
   29:9 with wine; they *s*, but not with strong drink
Rom. 4:20 he *s* not at the promise of God through

Stain

Job 3:5 let darkness and the shadow of death *s* it
Is. 23:9 purposed it, to *s* the pride of all glory
   63:3 my garments, and I will *s* all my raiment

Stairs

1 Kgs. 6:8 with winding *s* into the middle chamber
Neh. 9:4 then stood up upon the *s*, of the Levites
Acts 21:40 Paul stood on the *s*, and beckoned with

Stake

Is. 33:20 not one of the *s*. . shall ever be removed
   54:2 lengthen thy cords, and strengthen thy *s*

Stalk

Gen. 41:5 seven ears of corn came up upon one *s*
Hos. 8:7 it hath no *s*: the bud shall yield no meal

Stall

1 Kgs. 4:26 (2 Chr. 9:25) forty thousand *s* of horses
Amos 6:4 eat . . the calves out of the midst of the *s*
Mal. 4:2 go forth, and grow up as calves of the *s*

Stammerer

Is. 32:4 the *s* shall be ready to speak plainly

Stammering

Is. 28:11 with *s* lips and another tongue will he
   33:19 *s* tongue, that thou canst not understand

Stamp

2 Sam. 22:43 did *s* them as the mire of the street
2 Chr. 15:16 and Asa cut down her idol, and *s* it
Ezek. 6:11 smite with thine hand . . *s* with thy foot
Dan. 8:7 but he cast him down . . and *s* upon him

Stanch

Lk. 8:44 and immediately her issue of blood *s*

Stand (Stood)

Gen. 18:2 three men *s* by him: and . . he ran to meet
   18:22 but Abraham *s* yet before the LORD
Ex. 14:13 fear ye not, *s* still . . see the salvation
   14:19 pillar of the cloud went . . and *s* behind them
   33:21 place by me, and thou shalt *s* upon a rock
Deut. 5:31 but as for thee, *s* thou here by me
   7:24 there shall no man be able to *s* before thee
   29:10 ye *s* this day all of you before the LORD
Josh. 10:13 the sun *s* still, and the moon stayed
1 Sam. 6:20 who is able to *s* before this holy LORD
1 Kgs. 8:11 which *s* continually before thee
   17:1 LORD God of Israel liveth, before whom I *s*
2 Kgs. 23:3 and all the people *s* to the covenant
2 Chr. 34:32 in Jerusalem and Benjamin to *s* to it
Ezra 9:15 cannot *s* before thee because of this
Esth. 8:11 granted the Jews . . to *s* for their life
Job 8:15 lean upon his house, but it shall not *s*
   19:25 he shall *s* at the latter day upon the earth
Ps. 1:1 nor *s* in the way of sinners, nor sitteth
   1:5 the ungodly shall not *s* in the judgment
   5:5 foolish shall not *s* in thy sight: thou hatest
   10:1 why *s* thou afar off, O LORD? why hidest thou
   24:3 the LORD? or who shall *s* in his holy place?
   33:9 it was done; he commanded, and it *s* fast
   33:11 the counsel of the LORD *s* for ever
   35:2 shield and buckler, and *s* up for mine help
   76:7 who may *s* in thy sight when . . thou art angry?
   78:13 he made the waters to *s* as a heap
   94:16 *s* up for me against the workers of iniquity?
   106:23 had not Moses his chosen *s* before him
   109:31 he shall *s* at the right hand of the poor
   111:8 they *s* fast for ever and ever, and are done
   122:2 feet shall *s* within thy gates, O Jerusalem
   130:3 thou . . mark iniquities, O Lord, who shall *s*?
Prov. 12:7 but the house of the righteous shall *s*
   25:6 and *s* not in the place of great men
   27:4 but who is able to *s* before envy?
Eccl. 8:3 *s* not in an evil thing; for he doeth
Is. 7:7 thus saith the Lord GOD, It shall not *s*
   14:24 and as I have purposed, so shall it *s*
   21:8 my lord, I *s* continually upon the watchtower
   28:18 and your agreement with hell shall not *s*
   32:8 the liberal . . by liberal things shall he *s*
   40:8 but the word of our God shall *s* for ever
   46:10 my counsel shall *s*, and I will do all my
   65:5 *s* by thyself, come not near to me; for I am

Jer. 6:16 *s* ye in the ways, and see, and ask for
44:28 know whose words shall *s*, mine, or theirs
Ezek. 2:1 son of man, *s* upon thy feet, and I will
Dan. 2:44 consume all . . and it shall *s* for ever
11:16 none shall *s* before him: and he shall *s* in
12:13 and *s* in thy lot at the end of the days
Mic. 5:4 *s* and feed in the strength of the LORD
Nah. 2:8 *s*, *s*, shall they cry; but none shall look
Mal. 3:2 who shall *s* when he appeareth? for he is
Mt. 12:25 (Mk. 3:25) divided against itself shall not *s*
Lk. 21:36 to escape . . and to *s* before the Son of man
24:36 Jesus himself *s* in the midst of them
Jn. 19:25 there *s* by the cross of Jesus his mother
Acts 4:26 kings of the earth *s* up, and the rulers
7:55 and saw . . Jesus *s* on the right hand of God
23:11 and the night following the LORD *s* by him
Rom. 5:2 by faith into this grace wherein we *s*
11:20 they were broken off, and thou *s* by faith
14:4 he *s* or falleth . . God is able to make him *s*
14:10 we shall all *s* before the judgment seat
1 Cor. 2:5 faith should not *s* in the wisdom of men
10:12 let him that thinketh he *s* take heed lest
16:13 *s* fast in the faith, quit you like men
2 Cor. 1:24 helpers of your joy: for by faith ye *s*
Gal. 5:1 *s* fast therefore in the liberty wherewith
Eph. 6:13 to withstand . . and having done all, to *s*
Phil. 1:27 ye *s* fast in one spirit, with one mind
4:1 so *s* fast in the Lord, my dearly beloved
Col. 4:12 that ye may *s* perfect and complete in all
1 Thes. 3:8 now we live, if ye *s* fast in the Lord
2 Thes. 2:15 *s* fast, and hold the traditions which
2 Tim. 2:19 foundation of God *s* sure, having this
4:16 at my first answer no man *s* with me, but all
Jas. 2:3 say to the poor, *S* thou there, or sit here
5:9 be condemned . . the judge *s* before the door
1 Pet. 5:12 is the true grace of God wherein ye *s*
Rev. 3:20 behold, I *s* at the door, and knock
6:17 wrath is come; and who shall be able to *s*?
7:11 and all the angels *s* round about the throne
20:12 saw the dead, small and great, *s* before God

Standard

Num. 1:52 every man by his own *s*, throughout their
2:2 shall pitch by his own *s* . . about the tabernacle
10:14 in the first place went the *s* of the camp
Is. 49:22 and set up my *s* to the people: and they
59:19 the Spirit . . shall lift up a *s* against him
62:10 prepare ye . . lift up a *s* for the people
Jer. 4:6 set up the *s* toward Zion: retire, stay not
4:21 how long shall I see the *s*, and hear the sound

Standardbearer

Is. 10:18 and they shall be as when a *s* fainteth

Star

Gen. 1:16 light to rule the night: he made the *s* also
15:5 tell the *s*, if thou be able to number
22:17 multiply thy seed as the *s* of the heaven
37:9 moon and the eleven *s* made obeisance to me
Num. 24:17 there shall come a *S* out of Jacob
Judg. 5:20 *s* in their courses fought against Sisera
Job 25:5 shineth not . . *s* are not pure in his sight
38:7 when the morning *s* sang together
Ps. 8:3 moon and the *s*, which thou hast ordained
Is. 13:10 (Mt. 24:29; Mk. 13:25) *s* . . shall not give
Dan. 8:10 (Rev. 12:4) cast . . the *s* to the ground
12 :3 turn many to righteousness, as the *s*
Amos 5:8 him that maketh the seven *s* and Orion
Mt. 2:2 King of the Jews? for we have seen his *s*
Acts 7:43 *s* of your god Remphan, figures which ye
1 Cor. 15:41 and another glory of the *s*; for one *s*
Heb. 11:12 so many as the *s* of the sky in multitude
Jude 13 wandering *s*, to whom is reserved the

Rev. 1:16 and he had in his right hand seven *s*
2:28 and I will give him the morning *s*
6:13 and the *s* of heaven fell unto the earth
8:11 and the name of the *s* is called Wormwood
9:1 and I saw a *s* fall from heaven unto the earth
12:1 a woman . . upon her head a crown of twelve *s*
22:16 offspring of David . . bright and morning *s*

Stargazer

Is. 47:13 let now the astrologers, the *s* . . stand up

State

Gen. 43:7 the man asked us straitly of our *s*
Mt. 12:45 (Lk. 11:26) last *s* of that man is worse
Phil. 2:20 who will naturally care for your *s*
4:11 whatsoever *s* I am, therewith to be content

Stature

Num. 13:32 that we saw in it are men of a great *s*
1 Sam. 16:7 or on the height of his *s*; because I
2 Sam. 21:20 (1 Chr. 20:6) where was a man of great *s*
Song 7:7 this thy *s* is like to a palm tree
Is. 45:14 men of *s*, shall come over unto thee
Mt. 6:27 (Lk. 12:25) can add one cubit unto his *s*?
Lk. 2:52 Jesus increased in wisdom and *s*
Eph. 4:13 measure of the *s* of the fulness of Christ

Statute *See also* Commandment, Decree, Law, Order, Ordinance, Precept

Ex. 15:25 there he made for them a *s* . . an ordinance
18:16 I do make them know the *s* of God, and his
27:21 Aaron and his sons . . a *s* for ever
29:9 priest's office . . be theirs for a perpetual *s*
Lev. 3:17 a perpetual *s* . . eat neither fat nor blood
6:22 offer it: it is a *s* for ever unto the LORD
10:9 do not drink wine . . it shall be a *s* for ever
10:11 may teach the children of Israel all the *s*
16:34 an everlasting *s* . . to make an atonement
26:3 if ye walk in my *s* . . keep my commandments
26:15 if ye shall despise my *s*, or if your soul
Num. 35:29 these things shall be for a *s* of judgment
Deut. 4:8 that hath *s* and judgments so righteous
6:20 what mean the testimonies, and the *s*
6:12 and thou shalt observe and do these *s*
26:16 thy God hath commanded thee to do these *s*
Josh. 24:25 set . . a *s* and an ordinance in Shechem
1 Sam. 30:25 made it a *s* and . . ordinance for Israel
2 Sam. 22:23 (Ps. 18:22) for his *s*, I did not depart
1 Kgs. 2:3 to walk in his ways, to keep his *s*
3:14 if thou wilt walk in my ways, to keep my *s*
6:12 if thou wilt walk in my *s*, and execute my
9:4 (2 Chr. 7:17) commanded . . and wilt keep my *s*
2 Kgs. 17:15 they rejected his *s*, and his covenant
Ps. 19:8 *s* of the LORD are right, rejoicing the heart
50:16 what hast thou to do to declare my *s*
81:4 for this was a *s* for Israel, and a law
89:31 break my *s*, and keep not my commandments
119:5 O that my ways were directed to keep thy *s*!
119:16 I will delight myself in thy *s*: I will not
119:23 but thy servant did meditate in thy *s*
119:48 I have loved; and I will meditate in thy *s*
119:54 thy *s* have been my songs in the house
119:71 been afflicted; that I might learn thy *s*
119:117 will have respect unto thy *s* continually
147:19 his *s* and his judgments unto Israel
Ezek. 11:12 ye have not walked in my *s*, neither
11:20 (36:27) walk in my *s* . . keep mine ordinances
20:11 and I gave them my *s*, and showed them my
20:24 but had despised my *s*, and had polluted my
33:15 if the wicked . . walk in the *s* of life
Mic. 6:16 the *s* of Omri are kept, and all the works

Stave

Ex. 25:13 (37:4) make s of shittim wood, and overlay
1 Sam. 17:43 I a dog, that thou comest to me with s?
1 Kgs. 8:8 (2 Chr. 5:9) drew out the s, that the ends
Zech. 11:7 I took unto me two s; the one I called
Mt. 10:10 (Lk. 9:3) neither two coats . . nor yet s
  26:55 (Mk. 14:48; Lk. 22:52) and s for to take me?

Stay *See also* Abide, Dwell, Lodge, Remain

Gen. 19:17 neither s thou in all the plain; escape
Num. 16:48 he stood between . . and the plague was s
Josh. 10:13 sun stood still, and the moon s, until
1 Sam. 24:7 David s his servants with these words
2 Sam. 22:19 (Ps. 18:18) but the LORD was my s
  24:16 (1 Chr. 21:15) it is enough: s now thine hand
2 Kgs. 4:6 is not a vessel more. And the oil s
Job 37:4 will not s them when his voice is heard
  38:11 and here shall thy proud waves be s?
  38:37 or who can s the bottles of heaven
Prov. 28:17 shall flee to the pit; let no man s him
Song 2:5 s me with flagons, comfort me with apples
Is. 3:1 take away . . from Judah the s and the staff
  19:13 even they that are the s of the tribes
  26:3 in perfect peace, whose mind is s on thee
  27:8 he s his rough wind in the day of the east
  29:9 s yourselves, and wonder; cry ye out
  48:2 and s themselves upon the God of Israel
  50:10 in the name of the LORD, and s upon his God
Jer. 4:6 retire, s not; for I will bring evil from
  20:9 weary with forbearing, and I could not s
Lam. 4:6 as in a moment, and no hands s on her
Dan. 4:35 none can s his hand, or say unto him
Hag. 1:10 the heaven . . is s from dew, and the earth

Stead

Job 16:4 if your soul were in my soul's s, I could
  33:6 I am according to thy wish in God's s
Prov. 11:8 and the wicked cometh in his s
2 Cor. 5:20 pray . . in Christ's s, be ye reconciled

Steadfast

Job 11:15 yea, thou shalt be s, and shalt not fear
Ps. 78:8 and whose spirit was not s with God
  78:37 neither were they s in his covenant
Dan. 6:26 for he is the living God, and s for ever
1 Cor. 15:58 be ye s, unmovable, always abounding
2 Cor. 1:7 our hope of you is s, knowing, that as
Heb. 2:2 for if the word spoken by angels was s
  3:14 we hold the beginning of our confidence s
  6:19 as an anchor of the soul, both sure and s
1 Pet. 5:9 whom resist s in the faith, knowing

Steadfastly

Ruth 1:18 saw that she was s minded to go with her
Acts 2:42 continued s in the apostles' doctrine
  6:15 that sat in the council, looking s on him
  7:55 looked up s into heaven, and saw the glory
2 Cor. 3:13 the children of Israel could not s look

Steadfastness

Col. 2:5 order, and the s of your faith in Christ
2 Pet. 3:17 beware lest ye . . fall from your own s

Steal (Stole, Stolen) *See also* Rob

Gen. 31:19 had s the images that were her father's
  31:20 Jacob s away unawares to Laban the Syrian
  31:30 yet wherefore hast thou s my gods?
  40:15 I was s away out of the land of the Hebrews
  44:8 we s out of thy lord's house silver or gold?
Ex. 20:15 (Deut. 5:19, Mt. 19:18; Mk. 10:19; Lk. 18:
  20; Rom. 13:9) thou shalt not s

Ex. 21:16 he that s a man, and selleth him
  22:7 to keep, and it be s out of the man's house
Deut. 24:7 if a man be found s any of his brethren
2 Sam. 15:6 Absalom s the hearts of the men of Israel
  19:3 as people ashamed s away when they
  19:41 why have our brethren . . of Judah s thee
2 Kgs. 11:2 (2 Chr. 22:11) s him from . . king's sons
Prov. 6:30 not despise a thief, if he s to satisfy
  30:9 or lest I be poor, and s, and take the name
Jer. 7:9 will ye s, murder, and commit adultery
  23:30 I am against the prophets . . that s my words
Obad. 5 would they not have s till they had enough?
Zech. 5:3 for every one that s shall be cut off
Mt. 6:19 and where thieves break through and s
  27:64 come by night, and s him away, and say
  28:13 by night, and s him away while we slept
Jn. 10:10 the thief cometh not, but for to s
Rom. 2:21 preachest a man should not s, dost thou s?
Eph. 4:28 let him that s s no more: but rather let

Steel

2 Sam. 22:35 (Ps. 18:34) bow of s is broken by mine
Job 20:24 the bow of s shall strike him through
Jer. 15:12 iron break the northern iron and the s?

Steep

Ezek. 38:20 s places shall fall, and every wall
Mic. 1:4 the waters that are poured down a s place
Mt. 8:32 (Mk. 5:13; Lk. 8:33) swine . . down a s place

Stem

Is. 11:1 come forth a rod out of the s of Jesse

Step

Ex. 20:26 neither shalt thou go up by s unto mine
1 Sam. 20:3 there is but a s between me and death
2 Sam. 22:37 (Ps. 18:36) hast enlarged my s under me
Job 14:16 thou numberest my s: dost thou not watch
  18:7 the s of his strength shall be straitened
  23:11 my foot hath held his s, his way have I kept
  29:6 when I washed my s with butter, and the rock
  31:4 doth not he see my ways, and count all my s?
Ps. 17:11 they have now compassed us in our s
  37:23 the s of a good man are ordered by the LORD
  37:31 is in his heart; none of his s shall slide
  44:18 neither have our s declined from thy way
  56:6 they mark my s, when they wait for my soul
  73:2 almost gone; my s had well-nigh slipped
  85:13 and shall set us in the way of his s
  119:133 order my s in thy word: and let not any
Prov. 4:12 thou goest, thy s shall not be straitened
  5:5 go down to death; her s take hold on hell
  16:9 deviseth his way: but the LORD directeth his s
Is. 26:6 feet of the poor, and the s of the needy
Jer. 10:23 not in man that walketh to direct his s
Lam. 4:18 they hunt our s, that we cannot go in
Jn. 5:4 whosoever then first . . s in was made whole
Rom. 4:12 but who also walk in the s of that faith
2 Cor. 12:18 walked we not in the same s?
1 Pet. 2:21 example, that ye should follow his s

Stephanas 1 Cor. 1:16

Stephen Acts 6:5–7:59

Acts 11:19 upon the persecution that arose about S
  22:20 when the blood of thy martyr S was shed

Steward *See also* Minister, Servant

Gen. 15:2 and the s of my house is this Eliezer
Mt. 20:8 the lord of the vineyard saith unto his s
Lk. 8:3 and Joanna the wife of Chuza Herod's s
  12:42 who then is that faithful and wise s
  16:8 the lord commended the unjust s, because he

1 Cor. 4:1 ministers . . and *s* of the mysteries of God
  4:2 required in *s*, that a man be found faithful
Tit. 1:7 bishop must be blameless, as the *s* of God
1 Pet. 4:10 as good *s* of the manifold grace of God

Stewardship

Lk. 16:2 give an account of thy *s*; for thou mayest

Stick (noun)

Num. 15:32 a man that gathered *s* upon the sabbath
1 Kgs. 17:12 I am gathering two *s*, that I may go in
2 Kgs. 6:6 he cut down a *s*, and cast it in thither
Ezek. 37:16 son of man, take thee one *s*, and write
Acts 28:3 and when Paul had gathered a bundle of *s*

Stick (Stuck) (verb)

Job 33:21 and his bones that were not seen *s* out
Ps. 38:2 thine arrows *s* fast in me, and thy hand
  119:31 I have *s* unto thy testimonies: O LORD
Prov. 18:24 a friend that *s* closer than a brother
Ezek. 29:4 fish of thy rivers to *s* unto thy scales

Stiff

Deut. 31:27 I know thy rebellion, and thy *s* neck
Ps. 75:5 your horn on high: speak not with a *s* neck
Jer. 17:23 made their neck *s*, that they might not

Stiffen

2 Chr. 36:13 he *s* his neck, and hardened his heart

Stiffhearted

Ezek. 2:4 for they are impudent children and *s*

Stiffnecked *See also* Obstinate, Stubborn

Ex. 32:9 (Deut. 9:13) this people . . it is a *s* people
  33:3 I will not go up . . for thou art a *s* people
Deut. 10:16 circumcise . . your heart . . be no more *s*
2 Chr. 30:8 now be ye not *s*, as your fathers were
Acts 7:51 ye *s* and uncircumcised in heart and ears

Still *See also* Quiet

Ex. 14:13 stand *s*, and see the salvation of the LORD
  15:16 be as *s* as a stone; till thy people pass
Num. 13:30 Caleb *s* the people before Moses
Josh. 10:13 the sun stood *s*, and the moon stayed
Judg. 18:9 are ye *s*? be not slothful to go
1 Kgs. 19:12 and after the fire a *s* small voice
Neh. 8:11 so the Levites *s* all the people, saying
Ps. 4:4 commune with your own heart . . and be *s*
  8:2 thou mightest *s* the enemy and the avenger
  23:2 he leadeth me beside the *s* waters
  46:10 be *s*, and know that I am God: I will be
  65:7 which *s* the noise of the seas, the noise of
  76:8 from heaven; the earth feared, and was *s*
  89:9 when the waves thereof arise, thou *s* them
  107:29 a calm, so that the waves thereof are *s*
Is. 42:14 I have been *s*, and refrained myself
Mk. 4:39 arose . . and said unto the sea, Peace, be *s*

Sting

Prov. 23:32 like a serpent, and *s* like an adder
1 Cor. 15:55 O death, where is thy *s*? O grave
Rev. 9:10 and there were *s* in their tails

Stink

Gen. 34:30 have troubled me to make me to *s* among
Ex. 7:18 the river shall *s*; and the Egyptians shall
  16:24 it did not *s*, neither was there any worm
Ps. 38:5 my wounds *s* and are corrupt because of my
Eccl. 10:1 the ointment . . to send forth a *s* savor
Is. 3:24 instead of sweet smell there shall be a *s*
Joel 2:20 his *s* shall come up, and his ill savor
Amos 4:10 I have made the *s* of your camps to come
Jn. 11:39 he *s*: for he hath been dead four days

Stir

Ex. 35:21 they came, every one whose heart *s* him up
Num. 24:9 and as a great lion: who shall *s* him up?
Deut. 32:11 as an eagle *s* up her nest, fluttereth
1 Sam. 22:8 my son hath *s* up my servant against me
  26:19 if the LORD have *s* thee up against me, let
1 Kgs. 11:14 LORD *s* up an adversary unto Solomon
2 Chr. 36:22 (Ezra 1:1) LORD *s* up the spirit of Cyrus
Job 17:8 shall *s* up himself against the hypocrite
  41:10 none is so fierce that dare *s* him up
Ps. 35:23 *s* up thyself, and awake to my judgment
  39:2 I held my peace . . my sorrow was *s*
  78:38 anger away, and did not *s* up all his wrath
  80:2 *s* up thy strength, and come and save us
Prov. 10:12 hatred *s* up strifes: but love covereth
  15:1 but grievous words *s* up anger
  15:18 a wrathful man *s* up strife: but he that is
  28:25 he that is of a proud heart *s* up strife
Song 2:7 (3:5; 8:4) *s* not up, nor awake my love
Is. 10:26 LORD of hosts shall *s* up a scourge
  14:9 meet thee at thy coming: it *s* up the dead
  22:2 thou that art full of *s*, a tumultuous city
  64:7 that *s* up himself to take hold of thee
Dan. 11:10 but his sons shall be *s* up, and shall
Lk. 23:5 *s* up the people, teaching throughout all
Acts 6:12 they *s* up the people, and the elders
  12:18 there was no small *s* among the soldiers
  13:50 Jews *s* up the devout and honorable women
  14:2 but the unbelieving Jews *s* up the Gentiles
  17:16 his spirit was *s* in him, when he saw
  19:23 there arose no small *s* about that way
2 Tim. 1:6 *s* up the gift of God, which is in thee
2 Pet. 1:13 *s* you up by putting you in remembrance

Stock

Job 13:27 thou puttest my feet also in the *s*
  14:8 wax old in the earth, and the *s* thereof die
Is. 40:24 their *s* shall not take root in the earth
  44:19 shall I fall down to the *s* of a tree?
Jer. 2:27 saying to a *s*, Thou art my father
  20:2 Pashur smote Jeremiah . . and put him in the *s*
Hos. 4:12 my people ask counsel at their *s*
Acts 13:26 brethren, children of the *s* of Abraham
Phil. 3:5 of Israel, of the tribe of Benjamin

Stoic Acts 17:18

Stole *See* Steal

Stolen *See also* Steal

Gen. 30:33 not speckled . . shall be counted *s* with me
  31:39 require it, whether *s* by day, or *s* by night
Prov. 9:17 *s* waters are sweet, and bread eaten in

Stomach

1 Tim. 5:23 but use a little wine for thy *s*'s sake

Stone

Gen. 11:3 had brick for *s*, and slime . . for mortar
  28:18 took the *s* that he had put for his pillows
  31:46 gather *s*; and they took *s*, and made a heap
Num. 15:35 all the congregation shall *s* him with *s*
  35:17 and if he smite him with throwing a *s*
Deut. 8:9 a land whose *s* are iron, and out of whose
  10:1 hew thee two tables of *s* like unto the first
  21:21 all the men of his city shall *s* him with *s*
Josh. 4:6 (4:21) saying, What mean ye by these *s*?
  7:25 all Israel *s* him with *s*, and burned them
  24:27 behold, this *s* shall be a witness unto us
1 Sam. 17:40 chose him five smooth *s* out of the brook
  17:50 prevailed over the Philistine with . . a *s*
  30:6 for the people spake of *s* him, because
2 Sam. 17:13 until there be not one small *s* found

1 Kgs. 7:10 and the foundation was of costly *s*
1 Chr. 22:2 set masons to hew wrought *s* to build
Job 6:12 is my strength the strength of *s*?
  14:19 the waters wear the *s*: thou washest away
  28:3 the *s* of darkness, and the shadow of death
  41:24 his heart is as firm as a *s*; yea, as hard
  41:30 sharp *s* are under him: he spreadeth sharp
Ps. 91:12 (Mt. 4:6; Lk. 4:11) thy foot against a *s*
  118:22 (Mt. 21:42; Mk. 12:10; Lk. 20:17; 1 Pet. 2:7)
    s which the builders refused is become the head *s*
  137:9 and dasheth thy little ones against the *s*
Prov. 27:3 a *s* is heavy, and the sand weighty
Is. 8:14 (1 Pet. 2:8) but for a *s* of stumbling and
  28:16 (1 Pet. 2:6) lay in Zion for a foundation a *s*
  54:11 I will lay thy *s* with fair colors
  57:6 the smooth *s* of the stream is thy portion
  60:17 for wood brass, and for *s* iron: I will also
  62:10 cast up the highway; gather out the *s*
Jer. 2:27 and to a *s*, Thou hast brought me forth
  51:63 this book, that thou shalt bind a *s* to it
Dan. 2:34 (2:45) that a *s* was cut out without hands
Hab. 2:11 *s* shall cry out of the wall, and the beam
Hag. 2:15 before a *s* was laid upon a *s* in the temple
Zech. 7:12 they made their hearts as an adamant *s*
Mt. 3:9 (Lk. 3:8) of these *s* to raise up children
  4:3 (Lk. 4:3) command that these *s* be made bread
  7:9 (Lk. 11:11) ask bread, will he give him a *s*?
  21:44 (Lk. 20:18) fall on this *s* shall be broken
  23:37 (Lk. 13:34) killest the prophets, and *s* them
  24:2 (Mk. 13:2; Lk. 21:6) not be left here one *s*
  27:66 and made the sepulchre sure, sealing the *s*
  28:2 for the angel. . came and rolled back the *s*
Mk. 13:1 see what manner of *s* and what buildings
  16:4 (Lk. 24:2; Jn. 20:1) the *s* was rolled away
Lk. 19:40 hold their peace, the *s* would. . cry out
  19:44 shall not leave in thee one *s* upon another
Jn. 1:42 Cephas, which is by interpretation, A *s*
  8:7 is without sin. . let him first cast a *s* at her
  8:59 took they up *s* to cast at him: but Jesus
  10:31 then the Jews took up *s* again to *s* him
  11:8 Master, the Jews of late sought to *s* thee
  11:39 Jesus said, Take ye away the *s*
Acts 4:11 this is the *s* which was set at nought
  7:58 and cast him out of the city, and *s* him
  14:19 having *s* Paul, drew him out of the city
  17:29 Godhead is like unto gold, or silver, or *s*
2 Cor. 3:3 in tables of *s*, but in fleshly tables
  11:25 once was I *s*, thrice I suffered shipwreck
Eph. 2:20 Christ himself being the chief corner *s*
1 Pet. 2:5 as lively *s*, are built up a spiritual house
Rev. 2:17 give him a white *s*, and in the *s* a new name

Stony

Ps. 141:6 their judges are overthrown in *s* places
Ezek. 11:19 (36:26) and I will take the *s* heart out
Mt. 13:5 (Mk. 4:5) some fell upon *s* places

Stood *See* Stand

Stoop

Job 9:13 the proud helpers do *s* under him
Prov. 12:25 heaviness in the heart. . maketh it *s*
Is. 46:2 they *s*, they bow down together; they could
Mk. 1:7 shoes I am not worthy to *s* down and unloose
Lk. 24:12 *s* down, he beheld the linen clothes laid
Jn. 8:6 Jesus *s* down, and. . wrote on the ground
  20:11 she *s* down, and looked into the sepulchre

Stop

Gen. 8:2 windows of heaven were *s*, and the rain
1 Kgs. 18:44 get thee down, that the rain *s* thee not
2 Kgs. 3:19 and *s* all wells of water, and mar every
2 Chr. 32:3 to *s* the waters of the fountains

Job 5:16 poor hath hope, and iniquity *s* her mouth
Ps. 35:3 *s* the way against them that persecute me
  63:11 mouth of them that speak lies shall be *s*
Prov. 21:13 whoso *s* his ears at the cry of the poor
Is. 33:15 that *s* his ears from hearing of blood
Jer. 51:32 the passages are *s*, and the reeds
Acts 7:57 then they cried out. . and *s* their ears
Rom. 3:19 every mouth may be *s*, and all the world
2 Cor. 11:10 no man shall *s* me of this boasting
Tit. 1:11 whose mouths must be *s*, who subvert whole
Heb. 11:33 obtained promises, *s* the mouths of lions

Store

Gen. 41:36 that food shall be for *s* to the land
Deut. 28:5 blessed shall be thy basket and thy *s*
2 Kgs. 20:17 (Is. 39:6) thy fathers have laid up in *s*
1 Chr. 29:16 this *s* that we have prepared to build
Ps. 144:13 may be full, affording all manner of *s*
Amos 3:10 *s* up violence and robbery in their palaces
Nah. 2:9 for there is none end of the *s* and glory
1 Cor. 16:2 let every one of you lay by him in *s*
1 Tim. 6:19 in *s* for themselves a good foundation
2 Pet. 3:7 kept in *s*, reserved unto fire against

Storehouse

Gen. 41:56 Joseph opened all the *s*, and sold
Mal. 3:10 bring ye all the tithes into the *s*
Lk. 12:24 neither have *s* nor barn; and God feedeth

Stork

Lev. 11:19 (Deut. 14:18) *s*, the heron. . and the bat
Ps. 104:17 for the *s*, the fir trees are her house
Jer. 8:7 the *s* in the heaven knoweth her appointed
Zech. 5:9 for they had wings like the wings of a *s*

Storm *See also* Tempest, Whirlwind, Wind

Job 21:18 and as chaff that the *s* carrieth away
Ps. 55:8 I would hasten my escape from the windy *s*
  107:29 he maketh the *s* a calm, so that the waves
Is. 4:6 a place of refuge, and for a covert from *s*
  25:4 a refuge from the *s*, a shadow from the heat
  29:6 be visited of the LORD. . with *s* and tempest
Ezek. 38:9 thou shalt ascend and come like a *s*
Nah. 1:3 his way in the whirlwind and in the *s*
Mk. 4:37 (Lk. 8:23) there arose a great *s* of wind

Stout

Is. 10:12 I will punish the fruit of the *s* heart
Dan. 7:20 whose look was more *s* than his fellows
Mal. 3:13 your words have been *s* against me

Stout-hearted

Ps. 76:5 the *s-h* are spoiled, they have slept
Is. 46:12 ye *s-h*, that are far from righteousness

Straight

1 Sam. 6:12 kine took the *s* way to. . Beth-shemesh
Ps. 5:8 lead me. . make thy way *s* before my face
Prov. 4:25 let thine eyelids look *s* before thee
Eccl. 1:15 that which is crooked cannot be made *s*
Is. 40:3 make *s* in the desert a highway for our God
  40:4 (Lk. 3:5) the crooked shall be made *s*
  42:16 will make darkness light. . crooked things *s*
  45:2 go before thee, and make the crooked places *s*
Jer. 31:9 walk by the rivers of waters in a *s* way
Ezek. 1:7 their feet were *s* feet; and the sole of
  1:9 (10:22) they went every one *s* forward
Mt. 3:3 (Mk. 1:3; Lk. 3:4; Jn. 1:23) make his paths *s*
Lk. 13:13 she was made *s*, and glorified God
Acts 9:11 and go into the street which is called *S*
Heb. 12:13 make *s* paths for your feet, lest that

Strain

Mt. 23:24 which *s* at a gnat, and swallow a camel

Strait

1 Sam. 13:6 men of Israel saw that they were in a *s*
2 Sam. 24:14 (1 Chr. 21:13) Gad, I am in a great *s*
2 Kgs. 6:1 place where we dwell with thee is too *s*
Job 20:22 of his sufficiency he shall be in *s*
36:16 removed thee out of the *s* into a broad place
Is. 49:20 place is too *s* for me: give place to me
Lam. 1:3 persecutors overtook her between the *s*
Mt. 7:13 (Lk. 13:24) enter ye in at the *s* gate
Phil. 1:23 I am in a *s* betwixt two, having a desire

Straiten

Job 12:23 enlargeth the nations, and *s* them again
18:7 steps of his strength shall be *s*, and his
37:10 and the breadth of the waters is *s*
Prov. 4:12 thou goest, thy steps shall not be *s*
Jer. 19:9 they that seek their lives, shall *s* them
Mic. 2:7 is the Spirit of the LORD *s*? are these his
Lk. 12:50 and how am I *s* till it be accomplished!
2 Cor. 6:12 ye are not *s* in us, but ye are *s* in

Strange

Gen. 42:7 knew them, but made himself *s* unto them
Ex. 30:9 ye shall offer no *s* incense thereon
Lev. 10:1 the sons of Aaron. . offered *s* fire
Ezra 10:11 separate yourselves. . from the *s* wives
Is. 28:21 his work, his *s* work. . his act, his *s* act
Ezek. 3:5 art not sent to a people of a *s* speech
Lk. 5:26 saying, We have seen *s* things today
Acts 26:11 I persecuted them even unto *s* cities
Heb. 11:9 in the land of promise, as in a *s* country
13:9 carried about with divers and *s* doctrines
1 Pet. 4:4 think it *s* that ye run not with them
4:12 as though some *s* thing happened unto you

Stranger *See also* Alien, Foreigner, Sojourner

Gen. 15:13 thy seed shall be a *s* in a land that is
23:4 I am a *s* and a sojourner with you: give me
Ex. 12:19 whether he be a *s*, or born in the land
12:43 the passover: There shall no *s* eat thereof
20:10 (Deut. 5:14) nor thy *s*. . within thy gates
22:21 (23:9) neither vex a *s*. . for ye were *s*
Lev. 19:10 (23:22) shalt leave them for the poor and *s*
19:34 *s*. . shall be unto you as one born among you
25:23 for ye are *s* and sojourners with me
25:35 shalt relieve him: yea, though he be a *s*
Num. 9:14 one ordinance, both for the *s*, and for him
Deut. 10:18 and loveth the *s*, in giving him food
10:19 love ye therefore the *s*: for ye were *s* in
17:15 thou mayest not set a *s* over thee
23:20 unto a *s* thou mayest lend upon usury
24:17 shalt not pervert the judgment of the *s*
27:19 he that perverteth the judgment of the *s*
2 Sam. 22:45 (Ps. 18:44) *s* shall submit themselves
1 Kgs. 8:41 (2 Chr. 6:32) moreover concerning a *s*
1 Chr. 29:15 we are *s* before thee, and sojourners
Neh. 13:30 thus cleansed I them from all *s*
Job 31:32 the *s* did not lodge in the street
Ps. 39:12 hear my prayer. . for I am a *s* with thee
54:3 *s* are risen up against me, and oppressors
69:8 am become a *s* unto my brethren, and an alien
94:6 they slay the widow and the *s*, and murder
119:19 I am a *s* in the earth: hide not thy
146:9 the LORD preserveth the *s*; he relieveth
Prov. 5:10 lest *s* be filled with thy wealth
5:20 strange woman, and embrace the bosom of a *s*
11:15 that is surety for a *s* shall smart for it

Is. 1:7 your land, *s* devour it in your presence
14:1 *s* shall be joined with them, and they shall
60:10 and the sons of *s* shall build up thy walls
61:5 and *s* shall stand and feed your flocks
62:8 the sons of the *s* shall not drink thy wine
Jer. 2:25 I have loved *s*, and after them will I go
5:19 so shall ye serve *s* in a land that is not
7:6 if ye oppress not the *s*, the fatherless
14:8 why shouldest thou be as a *s* in the land
22:3 and do no wrong, do no violence to the *s*
51:51 for *s* are come into the sanctuaries
Lam. 5:2 our inheritance is turned to *s*, our houses
Ezek. 11:9 and deliver you into the hands of *s*
22:7 have they dealt by oppression with the *s*
22:29 yea, they have oppressed the *s* wrongfully
28:7 will bring *s* upon thee, the terrible of
44:7 in that ye have brought into my sanctuary *s*
Hos. 7:9 *s* have devoured his strength, and he
Joel 3:17 shall no *s* pass through her any more
Mal. 3:5 and that turn aside the *s* from his right
Mt. 17:25 tribute? of their own children, or of *s*?
25:35 gave me drink: I was a *s*, and ye took me in
Lk. 24:18 art thou only a *s* in Jerusalem, and hast
Jn. 10:5 a *s* will they not follow, but will flee
Eph. 2:12 *s* from the covenants of promise
2:19 therefore ye are no more *s* and foreigners
1 Tim. 5:10 if she have lodged *s*, if she have
Heb. 11:13 confessed that they were *s* and pilgrims
13:2 be not forgetful to entertain *s*: for thereby
1 Pet. 2:11 beloved, I beseech you as *s* and pilgrims
3 Jn. 5 doest faithfully. . to the brethren, and to *s*

Strangle

Job 7:15 my soul chooseth *s*, and death rather than
Nah. 2:12 for his whelps, and *s* for his lionesses
Acts 15:20 (15:29; 21:25) abstain. . from things *s*

Straw

Ex. 5:7 no more give the people *s* to make brick
Job 41:27 esteemeth iron as *s*, and brass as rotten
Is. 11:7 (65:25) the lion shall eat *s* like the ox

Stream *See also* Brook, River

Ps. 46:4 *s* whereof shall make glad the city of God
124:4 overwhelmed us, the *s* had gone over our soul
Is. 27:12 channel of the river unto the *s* of Egypt
30:28 and his breath, as an overflowing *s*, shall
35:6 shall waters break out, and *s* in the desert
57:6 among. . smooth stones of the *s* is thy portion
66:12 the glory of the Gentiles like a flowing *s*
Dan. 7:10 a fiery *s* issued and came forth from
Amos 5:24 waters, and righteousness as a mighty *s*
Lk. 6:48 the *s* beat vehemently upon that house

Street

Job 31:32 the stranger did not lodge in the *s*
Is. 51:20 thy sons. . lie at the head of all the *s*
Ezek. 11:6 ye have filled the *s*. . with the slain
16:24 and hast made thee a high place in every *s*
Dan. 9:25 the *s* shall be built again, and the wall
Mt. 6:5 the synagogues and in the corners of the *s*
Mk. 6:56 they laid the sick in the *s*, and besought
Lk. 14:21 go out quickly into the *s* and lanes
Acts 9:11 go into the *s* which is called Straight
Rev. 21:21 and the *s* of the city was pure gold
22:2 in the midst of the *s* of it, and on either

Strength *See also* Arm, Might, Power

Ex. 13:3 (13:14) by *s* of hand the LORD brought you
15:2 (Ps. 118:14) LORD is my *s* and song, and he
15:13 thou hast guided them in thy *s* unto thy
Lev. 26:20 your *s* shall be spent in vain
Deut. 33:25 and as thy days, so shall thy *s* be

Judg. 16:6 tell me. . wherein thy great *s* lieth
1 Sam. 2:4 they that stumbled are girded with *s*
2:9 for by *s* shall no man prevail
15:29 the *S* of Israel will not lie nor repent
2 Sam. 22:33 (Ps. 18:32) God is my *s* and power
2 Kgs. 19:3 (Is. 37:3) there is not *s* to bring forth
1 Chr. 16:11 (Ps. 105:4) seek the LORD and his *s*
16:27 (Ps. 96:6) *s* and gladness are in his place
29:12 it is to make great, and to give *s* unto all
Neh. 8:10 for the joy of the LORD is your *s*
Job 6:12 is my *s* the *s* of stones? or is my flesh
9:19 if I speak of *s*, lo, he is strong
12:13 with him is wisdom and *s*, he hath counsel
39:19 hast thou given the horse *s*?
Ps. 8:2 babes and sucklings hast thou ordained *s*
18:1 I will love thee, O LORD, my *s*
19:14 in thy sight, O LORD, my *s*, and my redeemer
20:6 saveth. . with the saving *s* of his right hand
21:1 the king shall joy in thy *s*, O LORD
22:19 O LORD: O my *s*, haste thee to help me
27:1 the LORD is the *s* of my life; of whom shall
28:7 LORD is my *s* and my shield; my heart trusted
29:1 (96:7) give unto the LORD glory and *s*
29:11 the LORD will give *s* unto his people
33:16 a mighty man is not delivered by much *s*
37:39 he is their *s* in the time of trouble
46:1 God is our refuge and *s*, a very present help
52:7 lo, this is the man that made not God his *s*
62:7 the rock of my *s*, and my refuge, is in God
68:34 ascribe ye *s* unto God: his excellency is
71:16 I will go in the *s* of the Lord GOD
73:26 God is the *s* of my heart, and my portion
81:1 sing aloud unto God our *s*: make a joyful
84:5 blessed is the man whose *s* is in thee
84:7 they go from *s* to *s*, every one of them in
89:17 thou art the glory of their *s*: and in thy
93:1 with majesty; the LORD is clothed with *s*
140:7 O GOD the Lord, the *s* of my salvation
Prov. 10:29 the way of the LORD is *s* to the upright
20:29 the glory of young men is their *s*
21:22 and casteth down the *s* of the confidence
24:5 is strong. . a man of knowledge increaseth *s*
31:25 *s* and honor are her clothing; and she shall
Eccl. 9:16 then said I, Wisdom is better than *s*
Is. 10:13 saith, By the *s* of my hand I have done it
12:2 the LORD JEHOVAH is my *s* and my song
25:4 hast been a *s* to the poor, a *s* to the needy
26:4 for in the LORD JEHOVAH is everlasting *s*
30:3 shall the *s* of Pharaoh be your shame
30:15 in quietness. . in confidence shall be your *s*
40:29 to them that have no might he increaseth *s*
40:31 that wait upon the LORD shall renew their *s*
45:24 in the LORD have I righteousness and *s*
49:5 eyes of the LORD, and my God shall be my *s*
51:9 (52:1) awake, put on *s*, O arm of the LORD
63:1 traveling in the greatness of his *s*?
Jer. 16:19 O LORD, my *s*, and my fortress
Lam. 1:14 he hath made my *s* to fall, the Lord hath
Dan. 11:15 neither shall there be any *s* to withstand
Hos. 7:9 strangers have devoured his *s*, and he
12:3 and by his *s* he had power with God
Joel 3:16 hope of his people, and the *s* of. . Israel
Mic. 5:4 shall stand and feed in the *s* of the LORD
Hab. 3:19 God is my *s*, and he will make my feet
Hag. 2:22 I will destroy the *s* of the kingdoms
Mk. 12:30 (Lk. 10:27) all thy mind, and with all thy *s*
Lk. 1:51 he hath showed *s* with his arm
Rom. 5:6 when we were yet without *s*. . Christ died
1 Cor. 15:56 is sin; and the *s* of sin is the law
2 Cor. 12:9 for my *s* is made perfect in weakness
Heb. 9:17 of no *s* at all while the testator liveth
11:11 Sarah herself received *s* to conceive seed
Rev. 3:8 thou hast a little *s*, and hast kept my word

Rev. 5:12 receive power. . riches, and wisdom, and *s*
12:10 is come salvation, and *s*, and the kingdom

Strengthen

Judg. 16:28 and *s* me, I pray thee, only this once
1 Sam. 23:16 went to David. . and *s* his hand in God
2 Sam. 2:7 let your hands be *s*, and be ye valiant
Ezra 7:28 I was *s* as the hand of. . God was upon me
Neh. 6:9 now therefore, O God, *s* my hands
Job 4:3 instructed. . and thou hast *s* the weak hands
15:25 against God. . *s* himself against the Almighty
Ps. 20:2 from the sanctuary, and *s* thee out of Zion
27:14 (31:24) courage, and he shall *s* thine heart
41:3 LORD will *s* him upon the bed of languishing
68:28 *s*, O God, that which thou hast wrought
89:21 be established: mine arm also shall *s* him
119:28 my soul melteth for heaviness: *s* thou me
Eccl. 7:19 wisdom *s* the wise more than ten mighty
Is. 22:21 with thy robe, and *s* him with thy girdle
35:3 *s* ye the weak hands, and confirm the feeble
41:10 I am thy God: I will *s* thee; yea, I will
54:2 lengthen thy cords, and *s* thy stakes
Ezek. 7:13 shall any *s* himself in the iniquity
13:22 *s* the hands of the wicked, that he should
16:49 neither did she *s* the hand of the poor
34:16 and will *s* that which was sick
Dan. 10:18 the appearance of a man, and he *s* me
Zech. 10:6 I will *s* the house of Judah
10:12 *s* them in the LORD; and they shall walk
Lk. 22:32 when thou art converted, *s* thy brethren
22:43 there appeared an angel unto him. . *s* him
Acts 18:23 Galatia and Phrygia. . *s* all the disciples
Eph. 3:16 to be *s* with might by his Spirit in the
Phil. 4:13 do all things through Christ which *s* me
Col. 1:11 *s* with all might, according to his glorious
2 Tim. 4:17 the Lord stood with me, and *s* me
1 Pet. 5:10 you perfect, stablish, *s*, settle you
Rev. 3:2 be watchful, and *s* the things which remain

Stretch

Ex. 8:16 Aaron, *S* out thy rod, and smite the dust
1 Kgs. 17:21 he *s* himself upon the child three times
Ps. 68:31 Ethiopia shall soon *s* out her hands unto
88:9 upon thee, I have *s* out my hands unto thee
104:2 who *s* out the heavens like a curtain
143:6 I *s* forth my hands unto thee: my soul
Prov. 1:24 have *s* out my hand, and no man regarded
Is. 28:20 is shorter than that a man can *s* himself
42:5 he that created the heavens, and *s* them out
54:2 and let them *s* forth the curtains of thine
Jer. 10:12 (51:15) *s* out the heavens by his discretion
Ezek. 16:27 I have *s* out my hand over thee
Amos 6:4 *s* themselves upon their couches, and eat
Mt. 12:13 (Mk. 3:5; Lk. 6:10) *s* forth thine hand
Jn. 21:18 be old, thou shalt *s* forth thy hands
Rom. 10:21 *s* forth my hands unto a disobedient
2 Cor. 10:14 we *s* not ourselves beyond our measure

Strew

Mt. 21:8 (Mk. 11:8) branches. . and *s* them in the way
25:24 sown, and gathering where thou hast not *s*

Stricken *See also* Strike

Is. 1:5 why should ye be *s* any more? ye will revolt
53:4 yet we did esteem him *s*, smitten of God
53:8 for the transgression of my people was he *s*

Strife *See also* Battle, Fight, War

Gen. 13:8 Abram said unto Lot, Let there be no *s*
Deut. 1:12 alone bear. . your burden, and your *s*?
2 Sam. 19:9 the people were at *s* throughout all
Ps. 31:20 in a pavilion from the *s* of tongues
55:9 I have seen violence and *s* in the city

Ps. 80:6 thou makest us a *s* unto our neighbors
  106:32 they angered him also at the waters of *s*
Prov. 10:12 hatred stirreth up *s*: but love covereth
  15:18 a wrathful man stirreth up *s*: but he that
  17:1 than a house full of sacrifices with *s*
  17:14 beginning of *s* is as when one letteth
  17:19 he loveth transgression that loveth *s*
  20:3 it is an honor for a man to cease from *s*
  26:20 where there is no talebearer, the *s* ceaseth
  26:21 so is a contentious man to kindle *s*
  30:33 so the forcing of wrath bringeth forth *s*
Is. 58:4 ye fast for *s* and debate, and to smite
Jer. 15:10 that thou hast borne me a man of *s*
Hab. 1:3 there are that raise up *s* and contention
Lk. 22:24 *s* among them, which . . the greatest
Rom. 13:13 walk honestly . . not in *s* and envying
2 Cor. 12:20 there be debates, envyings, wraths, *s*
Gal. 5:20 variance, emulations, wrath, *s*, seditions
Phil. 1:15 indeed preach Christ even of envy and *s*
  2:3 let nothing be done through *s* or vainglory
1 Tim. 6:4 and *s* of words, whereof cometh envy, *s*
2 Tim. 2:23 avoid, knowing that they do gender *s*
Heb. 6:16 oath for confirmation is . . an end of all *s*
Jas. 3:14 but if ye have bitter envying and *s* in

Strike (Struck, Stricken)

See also Smite

Ex. 12:7 the blood, and *s* it on the two side posts
2 Sam. 12:15 LORD *s* the child . . and it was very sick
Job 17:3 who is he that will *s* hands with me?
Ps. 110:5 *s* through kings in the day of his wrath
Prov. 6:1 if thou hast *s* thy hand with a stranger
  7:23 till a dart *s* through his liver; as a bird
  23:35 they have *s* me, shalt thou say, and I was
Jer. 5:3 thou hast *s* them . . they have not grieved
Mt. 26:51 sword, and *s* a servant of the high priest
Mk. 14:65 (Lk. 22:64; Jn. 18:22) *s* him with the palms

Striker

1 Tim. 3:3 (Tit. 1:7) not given to wine, no *s*

Strip

Num. 20:26 *s* Aaron of his garments, and put them
1 Sam. 31:8 (1 Chr. 10:8) Philistines . . to *s* the slain
Job 19:9 he hath *s* me of my glory, and taken the
Hos. 2:3 lest I *s* her naked, and set her as in

Stripe

Deut. 25:3 forty *s* he may give him, and not exceed
Prov. 17:10 wise man than a hundred *s* into a fool
  19:29 scorners, and *s* for the back of fools
Is. 53:5 (1 Pet. 2:24) and with his *s* we are healed
Lk. 12:47 to his will, shall be beaten with many *s*
2 Cor. 6:5 in *s*, in imprisonments, in tumults
  11:23 in labors more abundant, in *s* above measure

Strive (Strove, Striven)

Gen. 6:3 my Spirit shall not always *s* with man
  26:20 the herdmen of Gerar did *s* with Isaac's
Ex. 2:13 behold, two men of the Hebrews *s* together
  21:18 if men *s* together, and one smite another
Num. 20:13 Meribah; because the children of Israel *s*
Deut. 25:11 when men *s* together one with another
Job 33:13 why dost thou *s* against him?
Ps. 18:43 hast delivered me from the *s* of the people
  35:1 plead my cause . . with them that *s* with me
Prov. 3:30 *s* not with a man without cause
  25:8 go not forth hastily to *s*, lest thou know
Is. 41:11 and they that *s* with thee shall perish
  45:9 *s* with his Maker! Let the potsherd *s* with
Jer. 50:24 because thou hast *s* against the LORD
Hos. 4:4 let no man *s*, nor reprove another

Mt. 12:19 he shall not *s*, nor cry; neither shall
Lk. 13:24 *s* to enter in at the strait gate
Jn. 6:52 Jews therefore *s* among themselves, saying
Acts 23:9 were of the Pharisees' part arose, and *s*
Rom. 15:20 yea, so have I *s* to preach the gospel
  15:30 ye *s* together with me in your prayers
1 Cor. 9:25 that *s* for the mastery is temperate in
Phil. 1:27 *s* together for the faith of the gospel
2 Tim. 2:5 if a man also *s* for masteries, yet is
  2:14 they *s* not about words to no profit
  2:24 and the servant of the Lord must not *s*
Heb. 12:4 yet resisted unto blood, *s* against sin

Stroke

Ps. 39:10 remove thy *s* away from me: I am

Strong (Stronger, Strongest)

Gen. 25:23 one people shall be *s* than the other
  30:41 whensoever the *s* cattle did conceive
Lev. 10:9 do not drink wine nor *s* drink
Num. 13:31 the people; for they are *s* than we
Deut. 1:7 there was not one city too *s* for us
Josh. 1:9 I commanded . . Be *s* and of a good courage
Judg. 14:14 and out of the *s* came forth sweetness
  14:18 sweeter than honey . . what is *s* than a lion?
1 Sam. 4:9 be *s*, and quit yourselves like men
2 Sam. 3:1 David waxed *s* and *s* . . Saul waxed weaker
1 Kgs. 20:23 than we . . we shall be *s* than they
1 Chr. 28:20 David said to Solomon his son, Be *s*
Job 9:19 if I speak of strength, lo, he is *s*
  17:9 he that hath clean hands shall be *s* and *s*
Ps. 19:5 and rejoiceth as a *s* man to run a race
  24:8 this King of glory? The LORD *s* and mighty
  31:2 be thou my *s* rock, for a house of defense
  60:9 (108:10) who will bring me into the *s* city?
  71:3 be thou my *s* habitation, whereunto I may
  89:8 who is a *s* LORD like unto thee? or to thy
  89:13 thou hast a mighty arm: *s* is thy hand
  105:24 and made them *s* than their enemies
  136:12 with a *s* hand . . with a stretched out arm
Prov. 10:15 the rich man's wealth is his *s* city
  11:16 retaineth honor: and *s* men retain riches
  18:10 the name of the LORD is a *s* tower
  24:5 a wise man is *s*; yea, a man of knowledge
  30:30 lion, which is *s* among beasts, and turneth
Eccl. 9:11 to the swift, nor the battle to the *s*
  12:3 tremble, and the *s* men shall bow themselves
Song 8:6 love is *s* as death; jealousy is cruel as
Is. 24:9 *s* drink shall be bitter to them that drink
  26:1 we have a *s* city; salvation will God appoint
  35:4 be *s*, fear not: behold, your God will come
  40:26 for that he is *s* in power; not one faileth
  53:12 and he shall divide the spoil with the *s*
Jer. 20:7 thou art *s* than I, and hast prevailed
Ezek. 34:16 but I will destroy the fat and the *s*
Joel 3:10 let the weak say, I am *s*
Mic. 4:3 many people, and rebuke *s* nations afar
Mt. 12:29 how can one enter into a *s* man's house
Lk. 11:21 when a *s* man armed keepeth his palace
Acts 3:16 faith in his name, hath made this man *s*
Rom. 4:20 but was *s* in faith, giving glory to God
  15:1 *s* ought to bear the infirmities of the weak
1 Cor. 1:25 and the weakness of God is *s* than men
  4:10 we are weak, but ye are *s*; ye are honorable
  10:22 the Lord to jealousy? are we *s* than he?
  16:13 in the faith, quit you like men, be *s*
2 Cor. 12:10 for when I am weak, then am I *s*
Eph. 6:10 be *s* in the Lord, and in the power of his
2 Tim. 2:1 be *s* in the grace that is in Christ Jesus
Heb. 11:34 of weakness were made *s*, waxed valiant
Rev. 5:2 I saw a *s* angel proclaiming with a loud
  18:8 for *s* is the Lord God who judgeth her

Stronghold

Zech. 9:12 turn you to the s, ye prisoners of hope

Strove *See* Strive

Struck *See* Strike

Struggle

Gen. 25:22 and the children s together within her

Stubble

Ex. 5:12 land of Egypt to gather s instead of straw
Job 21:18 they are as s before the wind
Ps. 83:13 like a wheel; as the s before the wind
Is. 33:11 conceive chaff, ye shall bring forth s
    41:2 to his sword, and as driven s to his bow
    47:14 shall be as s; the fire shall burn them
Jer. 13:24 I scatter them as the s that passeth
Nah. 1:10 they shall be devoured as s fully dry
Mal. 4:1 yea, and all that do wickedly, shall be s
1 Cor. 3:12 foundation gold, silver. . wood, hay, s

Stubborn *See also* Obstinate, Stiffnecked

Deut. 21:18 if a man have a s and rebellious son
Judg. 2:19 their own doings, nor from their s way
Ps. 78:8 fathers, a s and rebellious generation
Prov. 7:11 she is loud and s; her feet abide not

Stubbornness

Deut. 9:27 look not unto the s of this people
1 Sam. 15:23 and s is as iniquity and idolatry

Stuck *See* Stick (verb)

Study

Prov. 15:28 the heart of the righteous s to answer
    24:2 their heart s destruction, and their lips
Eccl. 12:12 and much s is a weariness of the flesh
1 Thes. 4:11 ye s to be quiet, and to do your own
2 Tim. 2:15 s to show thyself approved unto God

Stuff

1 Sam. 30:24 shall his part be that tarrieth by the s

Stumble

1 Sam. 2:4 they that s are girded with strength
Prov. 3:23 way safely, and thy foot shall not s
    4:19 as darkness: they know not at what they s
    24:17 and let not thine heart be glad when he s
Is. 5:27 none shall be weary nor s among them
    8:14 (1 Pet. 2:8) stone of s and for a rock of offense
    8:15 many among them shall s, and fall
    28:7 they err in vision, they s in judgment
    59:10 we s at noonday as in the night
    63:13 in the wilderness, that they should not s?
Jer. 13:16 and before your feet s upon the dark
    20:11 my persecutors shall s, and they shall not
    46:6 they shall s, and fall toward the north
    50:32 the most proud shall s and fall, and none
Mal. 2:8 ye have caused many to s at the law
Jn. 11:9 if any man walk in the day, he s not
Rom. 9:32 for they s at that stumblingstone
    11:11 they s that they should fall? God forbid
    14:21 nor any thing whereby thy brother s
1 Jn. 2:10 and there is none occasion of s in him

Stumblingblock

Lev. 19:14 the deaf, nor put a s before the blind
Is. 57:14 take up the s out of the way of my people
Jer. 6:21 behold, I will lay s before this people
Ezek. 7:19 because it is the s of their iniquity
    14:3 put the s of their iniquity before their face
Rom. 11:9 trap, and a s, and a recompense unto them

Rom. 14:13 that no man put a s or an occasion to fall
1 Cor. 1:23 unto the Jews a s, and unto the Greeks
    8:9 this liberty. . become a s to them that are weak
Rev. 2:14 to cast a s before the children of Israel

Stumblingstone

Rom. 9:33 I lay in Sion a s and rock of offense

Stump

1 Sam. 5:4 only the s of Dagon was left to him
Dan. 4:15 (4:23, 26) leave the s of his roots in

Subdue *See also* Conquer

Gen. 1:28 replenish the earth, and s it
Ps. 47:3 he shall s the people under us
    81:14 I should soon have s their enemies
Is. 45:1 to Cyrus. . to s nations before him
Dan. 2:40 as iron breaketh in pieces and s all
Mic. 7:19 he will s our iniquities; and thou wilt
Zech. 9:15 shall devour, and s with sling stones
1 Cor. 15:28 when all things shall be s unto him
Phil. 3:21 able even to s all things unto himself
Heb. 11:33 who through faith s kingdoms

Subject

Lk. 2:51 came to Nazareth, and was s unto them
    10:17 the devils are s unto us through thy name
Rom. 8:7 it is not s to the law of God
    8:20 creature was made s to vanity, not willingly
    13:1 let every soul be s unto the higher powers
1 Cor. 14:32 spirits of the prophets are s to the
    15:28 shall the Son also himself be s unto him
Eph. 5:24 as the church is s unto Christ, so let
Col. 2:20 in the world, are ye s to ordinances
Tit. 3:1 to be s to principalities and powers
Heb. 2:15 were all their lifetime s to bondage
Jas. 5:17 Elias was a man s to like passions as we
1 Pet. 2:18 be s to your masters with all fear
    3:22 authorities and powers being made s unto him
    5:5 yea, all of you be s one to another

Subjection *See also* Obedience, Obeisance

Ps. 106:42 were brought into s under their hand
1 Cor. 9:27 keep under my body, and bring it into s
2 Cor. 9:13 for your professed s unto the gospel
Gal. 2:5 we gave place by s, no, not for an hour
1 Tim. 2:11 the woman learn in silence with all s
    3:4 having his children in s with all gravity
Heb. 2:5 hath he not put in s the world to come
    2:8 thou hast put all things in s under his feet
    12:9 rather be in s unto the Father of spirits
1 Pet. 3:1 ye wives, be in s to your own husbands

Submit *See also* Obey, Yield

Gen. 16:9 return to thy mistress, and s thyself
2 Sam. 22:45 (Ps. 18:44) strangers shall s themselves
Ps. 66:3 thy power shall thine enemies s themselves
    68:30 every one s himself with pieces of silver
Rom. 10:3 not s themselves unto the righteousness
Eph. 5:21 s yourselves one to another in the fear
    5:22 (Col. 3:18) wives, s. . unto your . . husbands
Heb. 13:17 have the rule over you, and s yourselves
Jas. 4:7 s yourselves therefore to God
1 Pet. 2:13 s yourselves to every ordinance of man
    5:5 ye younger, s yourselves unto the elder

Subscribe

Is. 44:5 shall s with his hand unto the LORD
Jer. 32:10 and I s the evidence, and sealed it

Substance

Gen. 13:6 dwell together: for their s was great

Deut. 33:11 bless, LORD, his *s*, and accept the work
Job 22:20 our *s* is not cut down, but the remnant
  30:22 me to ride upon it, and dissolvest my *s*
Ps. 17:14 leave the rest of their *s* to their babes
  139:15 my *s* was not hid from thee when I was
Prov. 1:13 we shall find all precious *s*
  3:9 honor the LORD with thy *s*, and with the
  6:31 shall restore . . give all the *s* of his house
  10:3 but he casteth away the *s* of the wicked
  12:27 but the *s* of a diligent man is precious
  28:8 by usury and unjust gain increaseth his *s*
  29:3 keepeth company with harlots spendeth his *s*
Song 8:7 would give all the *s* of his house for love
Jer. 15:13 thy *s* and thy treasures will I give to
Hos. 12:8 I am become rich, I have found me out *s*
Mic. 4:13 I will consecrate . . their *s* unto the Lord
Lk. 15:13 there wasted his *s* with riotous living
Heb. 10:34 in heaven a better and an enduring *s*
  11:1 now faith is the *s* of things hoped for

Subtile

Gen. 3:1 now the serpent was more *s* than any beast
2 Sam. 13:3 a friend . . and Jonadab was a very *s* man
Prov. 7:10 the attire of a harlot, and *s* of heart

Subtilty *See also* Craft, Deceit, Guile

Gen. 27:35 thy brother came with *s*, and hath taken
Prov. 1:4 to give *s* to the simple, to the young man
Mt. 26:4 consulted that they might take Jesus by *s*
Acts 13:10 O full of all *s* and all mischief
2 Cor. 11:3 the serpent beguiled Eve through his *s*

Subvert

Lam. 3:36 *s* a man in his cause . . Lord approveth not
Acts 15:24 troubled you with words, *s* your souls
2 Tim. 2:14 no profit, but to the *s* of the hearers
Tit. 1:11 who *s* whole houses, teaching things
  3:11 he that is such is *s*, and sinneth

Success *See also* Prosperity

Josh. 1:8 prosperous . . then thou shalt have good *s*

Succor *See also* Help

2 Cor. 6:2 in the day of salvation have I *s* thee
Heb. 2:18 he is able to *s* them that are tempted

Succorer

Rom. 16:2 she hath been a *s* of many, and of myself

Succoth

Gen. 33:17 Jacob journeyed to *S* . . and made booths
Ex. 12:37 Israel journeyed from Rameses to *S*
Judg. 8:5 unto the men of *S*, Give . . loaves of bread
Ps. 60:6 (108:7) and mete out the valley of *S*

Suck

Deut. 32:13 he made him to *s* honey out of the rock
  33:19 they shall *s* of the abundance of the seas
Job 20:16 he shall *s* the poison of asps: the viper's
Is. 60:16 *s* the milk of the Gentiles, and shalt *s*
  66:11 ye may *s*, and be satisfied with the breasts
Ezek. 23:34 thou shalt even drink it and *s* it out
Mt. 24:19 (Mk. 13:17; Lk. 21:23) to them that give *s*
Lk. 11:27 the womb . . and the paps which thou hast *s*
  23:29 never bare, and the paps which never gave *s*

Suckling *See also* Babe

Ps. 8:2 (Mt. 21:16) out of the mouth of babes and *s*
Lam. 2:11 the *s* swoon in the streets of the city

Sue

Mt. 5:40 if any man will *s* thee at the law

Suffer

Mt. 16:21 (Mk. 8:31; Lk. 9:22) and *s* many things
  17:12 (Mk. 9:12) also the Son of man *s* of them
  17:17 (Mk. 9:19; Lk. 9:41) how long shall I *s* you?
  19:14 (Mk. 10:14; Lk. 18:16) *s* little children
  27:19 I have *s* many things this day in a dream
Lk. 17:25 but first must he *s* many things
  24:26 ought not Christ to have *s* these things
  24:46 thus it behooved Christ to *s*, and to rise
Acts 3:18 that Christ should *s*, he hath so fulfilled
  17:3 and alleging, that Christ must needs have *s*
  26:23 Christ should *s*, and . . be the first that
Rom. 8:17 if so be that we *s* with him, that we may
1 Cor. 12:26 one member *s*, all the members *s* with it
  13:4 charity *s* long, and is kind; charity envieth
2 Cor. 11:20 ye *s*, if a man bring you into bondage
Gal. 3:4 have ye *s* so many things in vain?
  6:12 lest they should *s* persecution for the cross
Phil. 1:29 believe on him, but also to *s* for his sake
  3:8 for whom I have *s* the loss of all things
2 Thes. 1:5 kingdom of God, for which ye also *s*
2 Tim. 1:12 the which cause I also *s* these things
  2:12 if we *s*, we shall also reign with him
  3:12 live godly in Christ . . shall *s* persecution
Heb. 2:18 in that he himself hath *s* being tempted
  5:8 learned he obedience by the things which he *s*
  11:25 choosing rather to *s* affliction with the
  13:12 with his own blood, *s* without the gate
1 Pet. 2:20 but if, when ye do well, and *s* for it
  2:21 Christ also *s* for us, leaving us an example
  3:14 if ye *s* for righteousness' sake, happy are ye
  3:17 that ye *s* for well doing, than for evildoing
  3:18 Christ also hath once *s* for sins, the just
  4:1 then as Christ hath *s* for us in the flesh
  4:15 but let none of you *s* as a murderer, or as
  4:16 if any man *s* as a Christian, let him not be
  5:10 ye have *s* a while, make you perfect, stablish
Jude 7 an example, *s* the vengeance of eternal fire
Rev. 2:10 fear none of those things . . thou shalt *s*

Suffering *See also* Adversity, Affliction, Anguish, Calamity, Distress, Grief, Misery, Sorrow, Tribulation, Trouble

Rom. 8:18 I reckon that the *s* of this present time
2 Cor. 1:5 as the *s* of Christ abound in us, so our
  1:6 is effectual in the enduring of the same *s*
  1:7 as ye are partakers of the *s*, so shall ye be
Phil. 3:10 and the fellowship of his *s*, being made
Col. 1:24 who now rejoice in my *s* for you
Heb. 2:10 captain of . . salvation perfect through *s*
1 Pet. 1:11 testified beforehand the *s* of Christ
  4:13 rejoice . . as ye are partakers of Christ's *s*
  5:1 an elder, and a witness of the *s* of Christ

Suffice

Num. 11:22 the herds be slain for them, to *s* them?
Deut. 3:26 let it *s* thee; speak no more unto me of
1 Kgs. 20:10 if the dust of Samaria shall *s* for
Jn. 14:8 Lord, show us the Father, and it *s* us
1 Pet. 4:3 may *s* us to have wrought the will of

Sufficiency

Job 20:22 fulness of his *s* he shall be in straits
2 Cor. 3:5 as of ourselves; but our *s* is of God
  9:8 that ye, always having all *s* in all things

Sufficient *See also* Enough

Deut. 15:8 and shalt surely lend him *s* for his need
Is. 40:16 Lebanon is not *s* to burn, nor the beasts
Mt. 6:34 *s* unto the day is the evil thereof

Lk. 14:28 cost, whether he have *s* to finish it?
Jn. 6:7 two hundred pennyworth of bread is not *s*
2 Cor. 2:16 and who is *s* for these things?
  3:5 not that we are *s* of ourselves to think any
  12:9 my grace is *s* for thee: for my strength is

Sum

Ps. 139:17 O God! how great is the *s* of them!
Acts 22:28 with a great *s* obtained I this freedom
Heb. 8:1 this is the *s*: We have such a high priest

Summer

Gen. 8:22 and cold and heat, and *s* and winter
Ps. 74:17 the earth: thou hast made *s* and winter
Prov. 6:8 provideth her meat in the *s* . . gathereth
  10:5 he that gathereth in *s* is a wise son
  26:1 as snow in *s*, and as rain in harvest, so
Jer. 8:20 the *s* is ended, and we are not saved
Mt. 24:32 (Mk. 13:28; Lk. 21:30) know that *s* is nigh

Sumptuously

Lk. 16:19 clothed in purple. . and fared *s* every day

Sun

Josh. 10:12 *s*, stand thou still upon Gibeon
Judg. 5:31 let them that love him be as the *s* when
2 Sam. 23:4 light of the morning, when the *s* riseth
Job 8:16 he is green before the *s*, and his branch
Ps. 19:4 in them hath he set a tabernacle for the *s*
  84:11 LORD God is a *s* and shield: the LORD will
  104:19 for seasons: the *s* knoweth his going down
  121:6 *s* shall not smite thee by day, nor the moon
  136:8 the *s* to rule by day: for his mercy endureth
Eccl. 1:9 and there is no new thing under the *s*
  11:7 pleasant. . it is for the eyes to behold the *s*
Song 1:6 black, because the *s* hath looked upon me
Is. 13:10 (Mt. 24:29; Mk. 13:24) *s* shall be darkened
  30:26 and the light of the *s* shall be sevenfold
  38:8 *s* dial of Ahaz. . the *s* returned ten degrees
  49:10 (Rev. 7:16) shall the heat nor *s* smite them
  60:19 the *s* shall be no more thy light by day
  60:20 thy *s* shall no more go down; neither shall
Joel 2:10 (3:15) the *s* and the moon shall be dark
  2:31 (Acts 2:20) *s* shall be turned into darkness
Amos 8:9 I will cause the *s* to go down at noon
Mic. 3:6 and the *s* shall go down over the prophets
Hab. 3:11 *s* and moon stood still in their habitation
Mal. 4:2 *S* of righteousness arise with healing
Mt. 5:45 his *s* to rise on the evil and on the good
  13:43 shall the righteous shine forth as the *s*
  17:2 transfigured . . his face did shine as the *s*
  24:29 (Mk. 13:24) shall the *s* be darkened
Lk. 23:45 *s* was darkened, and the veil . . was rent
1 Cor. 15:41 one glory of the *s*, and another glory
Eph. 4:26 let not the *s* go down upon your wrath
Jas. 1:11 *s* is no sooner risen with a burning heat
Rev. 1:16 his countenance was as the *s* shineth
  6:12 and the *s* became black as sackcloth of hair
  8:12 and the third part of the *s* was smitten
  9:2 the *s* and the air were darkened by reason of
  12:1 a woman clothed with the *s*, and the moon
  16:8 fourth angel poured out his vial upon the *s*
  19:17 I saw an angel standing in the *s*
  21:23 the city had no need of the *s*, neither of
  22:5 they need no candle, neither light of the *s*

Sundry

Heb. 1:1 God, who at *s* times and in divers manners

Sung *See* Sing

Sunk *See* Sink

Sup

Hab. 1:9 their faces shall *s* up as the east wind
Lk. 17:8 make ready wherewith I may *s*, and gird
1 Cor. 11:25 when he had *s*, saying, This cup is
Rev. 3:20 will come in to him, and will *s* with him

Superfluity

Jas. 1:21 apart all filthiness and *s* of naughtiness

Superfluous

2 Cor. 9:1 ministering. . it is *s* for me to write

Superscription

Mt. 22:20 (Mk. 12:16; Lk. 20:24) is this image and *s*?
Mk. 15:26 (Lk. 23:38) *s* of his accusation was written

Superstition

Acts 25:19 questions against him of their own *s*

Superstitious

Acts 17:22 perceive that in all things ye are too *s*

Supper *See also* Dinner

Lk. 14:16 a certain man made a great *s*, and bade
  22:20 also the cup after *s*, saying, This cup
Jn. 12:2 there they made him a *s*; and Martha served
  13:2 and *s* being ended, the devil having now put
  21:20 which also leaned on his breast at *s*
1 Cor. 11:20 this is not to eat the Lord's *s*
Rev. 19:9 called unto the marriage *s* of the Lamb
  19:17 gather. . together unto the *s* of the great God

Supplant

Gen. 27:36 Jacob? for he hath *s* me these two times
Jer. 9:4 every brother will utterly *s*

Supplication *See also* Prayer

1 Sam. 13:12 and I have not made *s* unto the LORD
1 Kgs. 8:30 (2 Chr. 6:21) hearken thou to the *s* of thy
  9:3 I have heard thy prayer and thy *s*, that thou
Job 8:5 seek unto God. . make thy *s* to the Almighty
  9:15 not answer, but I would make *s* to my judge
Ps. 6:9 LORD hath heard my *s*; the LORD will receive
  28:2 hear the voice of my *s*, when I cry unto thee
  28:6 because he hath heard the voice of my *s*
  31:22 heardest the voice of my *s* when I cried
  55:1 O God; and hide not thyself from my *s*
  116:1 because he hath heard my voice and my *s*
  119:170 let my *s* come before thee: deliver me
Is. 45:14 make *s* unto thee, saying, Surely God is
Jer. 37:20 let my *s*, I pray thee, be accepted
Dan. 9:3 to seek by prayer and *s*, with fasting
  9:18 for we do not present our *s* before thee
Hos. 12:4 made *s* unto him: he found him in Bethel
Acts 1:14 continued with one accord in prayer and *s*
Phil. 4:6 but in every thing by prayer and *s* with
1 Tim. 2:1 I exhort therefore, that, first of all, *s*
  5:5 and continueth in *s* and prayers night and day

Supply

1 Cor. 16:17 was lacking on your part they have *s*
2 Cor. 8:14 your abundance may be a *s* for their
  9:12 not only *s* the want of the saints, but is
  11:9 to me the brethren. . from Macedonia *s*
Eph. 4:16 compacted by that which every joint *s*
Phil. 1:19 and the *s* of the Spirit of Jesus Christ
  2:30 to *s* your lack of service toward me
  4:19 but my God shall *s* all your need according

Support

Acts 20:35 that so laboring ye ought to *s* the weak
1 Thes. 5:14 *s* the weak, be patient toward all men

Suppose

Mt. 20:10 *s* that they should have received more
Mk. 6:49 upon the sea, they *s* it had been a spirit
Lk. 2:44 they, *s* him to have been in the company
24:37 affrighted . . *s* that they had seen a spirit
Jn. 20:15 she, *s* him to be the gardener, saith
Acts 7:25 he *s* his brethren would have understood
16:27 *s* that the prisoners had been fled
21:29 they *s* that Paul had brought into the temple

Supreme

1 Pet. 2:13 whether it be to the king, as *s*

Sure

1 Sam. 2:35 I will build him a *s* house
2 Sam. 23:5 covenant, ordered in all things, and *s*
Job 24:22 he riseth up, and no man is *s* of life
Ps. 19:7 testimony of the LORD is *s*, making wise
111:7 and judgment; all his commandments are *s*
Prov. 6:3 humble thyself, and make *s* thy friend
Is. 22:23 I will fasten him as a nail in a *s* place
33:16 shall be given him; his waters shall be *s*
Mt. 27:64 sepulchre be made *s* until the third day
Jn. 6:69 we believe and are *s* . . thou art that Christ
Rom. 2:2 but we are *s* that the judgment of God is
2 Tim. 2:19 the foundation of God standeth *s*
Heb. 6:19 anchor of the soul, both *s* and steadfast
2 Pet. 1:10 to make your calling and election *s*
1:19 we have also a more *s* word of prophecy

Surety

Gen. 43:9 I will be *s* for him . . if I bring him not
Ps. 119:122 be *s* for thy servant for good
Prov. 6:1 my son, if thou be *s* for thy friend
11:15 that is *s* for a stranger shall smart for it
Heb. 7:22 was Jesus made a *s* of a better testament

Surfeiting

Lk. 21:34 lest . . your hearts be overcharged with *s*

Surmising

1 Tim. 6:4 cometh envy, strife, railings, evil *s*

Surprise

Is. 33:14 afraid; fearfulness hath *s* the hypocrites
Jer. 48:41 is taken, and the strongholds are *s*
51:41 how is the praise of the whole earth *s*!

Sustain

Gen. 27:37 with corn and wine have I *s* him
1 Kgs. 17:9 commanded a widow . . there to *s* thee
Neh. 9:21 thou *s* them in the wilderness, so that
Ps. 3:5 and slept; for the LORD *s* me
55:22 burden upon the LORD, and he shall *s* thee
Prov. 18:14 spirit of a man will *s* his infirmity
Is. 59:16 and his righteousness, it *s* him

Sustenance

Judg. 6:4 left no *s* for Israel, neither sheep, nor
Acts 7:11 affliction: and our fathers found no *s*

Swaddled

Ezek. 16:4 wast not salted at all, nor *s* at all

Swaddling

Lk. 2:7 wrapped him in *s* clothes, and laid him in

Swallow (noun)

Ps. 84:3 sparrow hath found a house, and the *s* a nest
Prov. 26:2 as the *s* by flying, so the curse causeless
Is. 38:14 like a crane or a *s*, so did I chatter
Jer. 8:7 and the *s* observe the time of their coming

Swallow (verb)

Ex. 7:12 serpents: but Aaron's rod *s* up their rods
Num. 16:30 the earth open her mouth, and *s* them up
Job 5:5 and the robber *s* up their substance
6:3 would be heavier . . therefore my words are *s* up
Ps. 35:25 let them not say, We have *s* him up
56:1 be merciful . . O God: for man would *s* me up
106:17 the earth opened and *s* up Dathan, and
124:3 they had *s* us up quick, when their wrath
Is. 25:8 (1 Cor. 15:54) he will *s* up death in victory
Lam. 2:2 Lord hath *s* up all the habitations of Jacob
Jon. 1:17 LORD . . prepared a great fish to *s* up Jonah
Mt. 23:24 which strain at a gnat, and *s* a camel
2 Cor. 2:7 one should be *s* up with overmuch sorrow
5:4 that mortality might be *s* up of life

Swear (Sware, Sworn) *See also* Covenant, Pledge, Promise, Vow

Gen. 21:31 Beer-sheba; because there they *s* both of
22:16 by myself have I *s*, saith the LORD
24:3 make thee *s* by the LORD, the God of heaven
26:3 will perform the oath which I *s* unto Abraham
Ex. 6:8 which I did *s* to give it to Abraham
13:5 which he *s* unto thy fathers to give thee
32:13 to whom thou *s* by thine own self
Lev. 5:4 if a soul *s*, pronouncing with his lips
6:5 or all that about which he hath *s* falsely
19:12 ye shall not *s* by my name falsely, neither
Deut. 4:21 and *s* that I should not go over Jordan
6:13 and serve him, and shalt *s* by his name
10:11 go in and possess the land, which I *s* unto
34:4 this is the land which I *s* unto Abraham
Josh. 1:6 which I *s* unto their fathers to give them
14:9 Moses *s* on that day, saying, Surely the land
Judg. 21:7 seeing we have *s* by the LORD, that we
1 Sam. 19:6 Saul *s*, As the LORD liveth, he shall not
20:3 and David *s* moreover, and said, Thy father
24:21 *s* now . . thou wilt not cut off my seed
2 Sam. 3:9 as the LORD hath *s* to David, even so I
1 Kgs. 1:17 thou *s* . . Solomon thy son shall reign
2 Chr. 15:14 and they *s* unto the LORD with a loud
Ps. 15:4 that *s* to his own hurt, and changeth not
89:3 my chosen, I have *s* unto David my servant
95:11 (Heb. 3:11; 4:3) I *s* in my wrath that
110:4 (Heb. 7:21) LORD hath *s*, and will not repent
119:106 I have *s*, and I will perform it
132:2 how he *s* unto the LORD, and vowed unto
132:11 (Acts 2:30) LORD hath *s* in truth unto David
Is. 19:18 of Canaan, and *s* to the LORD of hosts
45:23 every knee shall bow, every tongue shall *s*
48:1 of Judah, which *s* by the name of the LORD
62:8 LORD hath *s* by his right hand, and by the arm
65:16 *s* in the earth shall *s* by the God of truth
Jer. 4:2 and thou shalt *s*, The LORD liveth, in truth
5:2 say, The LORD liveth; surely they *s* falsely
5:7 forsaken me, and *s* by them that are no gods
22:5 I *s* by myself, saith the LORD, that this
23:10 for because of *s* the land mourneth
44:26 I have *s* by my great name . . that my name
49:13 have *s* by myself . . that Bozrah shall
Ezek. 16:8 I *s* unto thee . . entered into a covenant
Dan. 12:7 *s* by him that liveth for ever, that it
Hos. 4:2 by *s*, and lying, and killing, and stealing
10:4 spoken words, *s* falsely in making a covenant
Amos 4:2 Lord GOD hath *s* by his holiness, that, lo
Zeph. 1:5 that *s* by the LORD, and that *s* by Malcham
Zech. 5:3 every one that *s* shall be cut off as on
Mt. 5:34 *s* not at all; neither by heaven; for it is
23:16 shall *s* by the temple, it is nothing
23:22 shall *s* by heaven, *s* by the throne of God
26:74 (Mk. 14:71) then began he to curse and to *s*

Mk. 6:23 he *s* unto her, Whatsoever thou shalt ask
Lk. 1:73 the oath which he *s* to our father Abraham
Acts 2:30 knowing that God had *s* with an oath to
   7:17 the promise. .which God had *s* to Abraham
Heb. 3:18 to whom *s* he that they should not enter
   6:13 he could *s* by no greater, he *s* by himself
Jas. 5:12 but above all things, my brethren, *s* not
Rev. 10:6 *s* by him that liveth for ever and ever

Swearer

Mal. 3:5 against the adulterers. .against false *s*

Sweat

Gen. 3:19 in the *s* of thy face shalt thou eat bread
Lk. 22:44 his *s* was as it were great drops of blood

Sweep

Is. 28:17 the hail shall *s* away the refuge of lies
Lk. 15:8 *s* the house, and seek diligently till she

Sweet (Sweeter)

Ex. 15:25 into the waters, the waters were made *s*
Judg. 14:18 what is *s* than honey?
2 Sam. 23:1 and the *s* psalmist of Israel, said
Job 20:12 though wickedness be *s* in his mouth
   38:31 canst thou bind the *s* influences of Pleiades
Ps. 19:10 *s* also than honey and the honeycomb
   55:14 we took *s* counsel together, and walked
   104:34 my meditation of him shall be *s*
   119:103 how *s* are thy words unto my taste! yea, *s*
Prov. 3:24 shalt lie down, and thy sleep shall be *s*
   9:17 stolen waters are *s*, and bread eaten in
   13:19 the desire accomplished is *s* to the soul
   16:24 pleasant words are. .*s* to the soul, and health
   27:7 to the hungry soul every bitter thing is *s*
Eccl. 5:12 the sleep of a laboring man is *s*
   11:7 light is *s*, and a pleasant thing it is for
Song 2:3 delight, and his fruit was *s* to my taste
Is. 5:20 that put bitter for *s*, and *s* for bitter!
   23:16 make *s* melody, sing many songs, that thou
Jas. 3:11 at the same place *s* water and bitter?
Rev. 10:9 but it shall be in thy mouth *s* as honey

Sweetness

Judg. 9:11 should I forsake my *s*, and my good fruit
   14:14 meat, and out of the strong came forth *s*
Prov. 16:21 the *s* of the lips increaseth learning
   27:9 the *s* of a man's friend by hearty counsel

Swell

Num. 5:21 make thy thigh to rot, and thy belly to *s*
Deut. 8:4 neither did thy foot *s*, these forty years
Jer. 12:5 then how wilt thou do in the *s* of Jordan?
2 Pet. 2:18 they speak great *s* words of vanity
Jude 16 and their mouth speaketh great *s* words

Swept

Jer. 46:15 why are thy valiant men *s* away?
Mt. 12:44 (Lk. 11:25) he findeth it empty, *s*

Swift (Swifter)

Job 7:6 my days are *s* than a weaver's shuttle
   9:25 my days are *s* than a post: they flee away
Prov. 6:18 feet that be *s* in running to mischief
Eccl. 9:11 race is not to the *s*, nor the battle to
Rom. 3:15 their feet are *s* to shed blood
Jas. 1:19 *s* to hear, slow to speak, slow to wrath

Swim

2 Kgs. 6:6 cast it in thither; and the iron did *s*
Ps. 6:6 all the night make I my bed to *s*
Is. 25:11 he that *s* spreadeth forth his hands to *s*
Acts 27:42 any of them should *s* out, and escape

Swine

Lev. 11:7 (Deut. 14:8) the *s*. . is unclean to you
Prov. 11:22 as a jewel of gold in a *s*'s snout
Is. 66:17 eating *s*'s flesh, and the abomination
Mt. 7:6 neither cast ye your pearls before *s*, lest
   8:31 (Mk. 5:12; Lk. 8:33) go . .into the herd of *s*
Lk. 15:15 and he sent him into his fields to feed *s*

Swoon

Lam. 2:11 sucklings *s* in the streets of the city

Sword *See also* Sheath

Gen. 3:24 a flaming *s* which turned every way
Deut. 32:25 *s* without, and terror within, shall
   33:29 and who is the *s* of thy excellency!
Josh. 5:13 a man over against him with his *s* drawn
   24:12 but not with thy *s*, nor with thy bow
Judg. 7:20 cried, The *s* of the LORD, and of Gideon
2 Sam. 2:26 shall the *s* devour for ever?
Job 20:25 the glittering *s* cometh out of his gall
Ps. 7:12 if he turn not, he will whet his *s*
   17:13 my soul from the wicked, which is thy *s*
   44:3 not the land in possession by their own *s*
   44:6 trust in my bow, neither shall my *s* save me
   55:21 softer than oil, yet were they drawn *s*
   57:4 and arrows, and their tongue a sharp *s*
   149:6 mouth, and a two-edged *s* in their hand
Is. 2:4 (Mic. 4:3) shall beat their *s* into plowshares
   34:5 for my *s* shall be bathed in heaven
   49:2 and he hath made my mouth like a sharp *s*
   66:16 by fire and by his *s* will the LORD plead
Jer. 9:16 I will send a *s* after them, till I have
   12:12 *s* of the LORD shall devour from the one end
   15:2 such as are for the *s*, to the *s*; and such as
   50:35 a *s* is upon the Chaldeans, saith the LORD
Ezek. 7:15 the *s* is without, and the pestilence
   21:9 a *s*, a *s* is sharpened, and also furbished
   21:28 the *s*, the *s* is drawn: for the slaughter
Hos. 1:7 will not save them by bow, nor by *s*
   2:18 will break the bow and the *s* and the battle
Joel 3:10 beat your plowshares into *s*, and your
Zech. 13:7 awake, O *s*, against my shepherd
Mt. 10:34 I came not to send peace, but a *s*
   26:47 (Mk. 14:43) multitude with a *s* and staves
   26:51 (Mk. 14:47; Jn. 18:10) drew his *s*, and struck
   26:52 that take the *s* shall perish with the *s*
Lk. 2:35 *s* shall pierce through thy own soul also
   22:36 he that hath no *s*, let him sell his garment
   22:38 they said, Lord, behold, here are two *s*
Rom. 8:35 or famine, or nakedness, or peril, or *s*?
   13:4 be afraid; for he beareth not the *s* in vain
Eph. 6:17 *s* of the Spirit, which is the word of God
Heb. 4:12 sharper than any two-edged *s*, piercing
Rev. 1:16 out of his mouth went a sharp two-edged *s*
   13:10 killeth with the *s* must be killed with the *s*
   19:15 out of his mouth goeth a sharp *s*, that with

Sworn *See* Swear

Sycamore

1 Kgs. 10:27 (2 Chr. 1:15) cedars made he. .as the *s*
Amos 7:14 was a herdman, and a gatherer of *s* fruit
Lk. 19:4 and climbed up into a *s* tree to see him

Sychem *See* Shechem

Synagogue *See also* Assembly, Temple

Ps. 74:8 they have burned up all the *s* of God
Mt. 4:23 (9:35; Mk. 1:39; Lk. 4:15) teaching in their *s*
   6:2 the hypocrites do in the *s* and in the streets
   10:17 (Mk. 13:9; Lk. 21:12) scourge you in their *s*
   12:9 (Mk. 3:1; Lk. 6:6) he went into their *s*
   13:54 (Mk. 6:2; Lk. 4:16) he taught them in their *s*

Mt. 23:6 (Mk. 12:39; Lk. 11:43; 20:46) chief seats. . *s*
Mk. 1:21 on the sabbath day he entered into the *s*
5:22 (Lk. 8:41) one of the rulers of the *s*, Jairus
Lk. 7:5 loveth our nation, and he hath built us a *s*
Jn. 9:22 confess. . he should be put out of the *s*
12:42 lest they should be put out of the *s*
16:2 they shall put you out of the *s*
18:20 I ever taught in the *s*, and in the temple
Acts 6:9 *s*, which is called the *s* of the Libertines
9:20 straightway he preached Christ in the *s*
13:5 preached the word of God in the *s* of the Jews
15:21 Moses. . being read in the *s* every sabbath
18:4 and he reasoned in the *s* every sabbath
19:8 and he went into the *s*, and spake boldly
22:19 beat in every *s* them that believed on thee
26:11 punished them oft in every *s*, and compelled
Rev. 2:9 Jews, and are not, but are the *s* of Satan
3:9 behold, I will make them of the *s* of Satan

Syracuse Acts 28:12

Syria

2 Sam. 8:6 (1 Chr. 18:6) David put garrisons in *S*
2 Kgs. 13:17 and the arrow of deliverance from *S*
Is. 7:2 saying, *S* is confederate with Ephraim
7:8 the head of *S* is Damascus, and the head of
Mt. 4:24 his fame went throughout all *S*
Acts 15:41 went through *S* and Cilicia, confirming
18:18 took his leave. . and sailed thence into *S*

Syriac

Dan. 2:4 then spake the Chaldeans to the king in *S*

Syrian

Deut. 26:5 a *S* ready to perish was my father
2 Sam. 10:18 (1 Chr. 19:18) the *S* fled before Israel
1 Kgs. 20:20 the *S* fled; and Israel pursued them
2 Kgs. 6:9 beware. . for thither the *S* are come down
7:4 let us fall unto the host of the *S*
18:26 (Is. 36:11) speak. . in the *S* language
Ezra 4:7 written in the *S*. . and interpreted in the *S*
Is. 9:12 the *S* before, and the Philistines behind

Syrophoenician Mk. 7:26

T

Taberah Num. 11:3; Deut. 9:22

Tabernacle *See also* Church, Temple, Tent

Ex. 25:9 I show thee, after the pattern of the *t*
26:30 shalt rear up the *t* according to the fashion
29:43 and the *t* shall be sanctified by my glory
30:26 shalt anoint the *t* of the congregation
33:7 took the *t*, and pitched it without the camp
40:2 set up the *t* of the tent of the congregation
Lev. 1:1 spake. . out of the *t* of the congregation
15:31 when they defile my *t* that is among them
23:34 (Deut. 16:13) the feast of *t* for seven days
26:11 I will set my *t* among you: and my soul shall
Num. 3:7 before the *t*. . to do the service of the *t*
9:15 the *t* was reared up the cloud covered the *t*
19:13 and purifieth not himself, defileth the *t*
Deut. 31:15 appeared in the *t* in a pillar of a cloud
1 Kgs. 2:28 and Joab fled unto the *t* of the LORD
Job 5:24 shalt know that thy *t* shall be in peace
11:14 and let not wickedness dwell in thy *t*
19:12 against me, and encamp round about my *t*
22:23 thou shalt put away iniquity far from thy *t*

Job 29:4 when the secret of God was upon my *t*
Ps. 15:1 LORD, who shall abide in thy *t*?
19:4 in them hath he set a *t* for the sun
27:5 in the secret of his *t* shall he hide me
43:3 bring me unto thy holy hill, and to thy *t*
46:4 the holy place of the *t* of the Most High
61:4 I will abide in thy *t* for ever: I will trust
78:60 that he forsook the *t* of Shiloh, the tent
84:1 how amiable are thy *t*, O LORD of hosts!
132:7 we will go into his *t*: we will worship at
Prov. 14:11 but the *t* of the upright shall flourish
Is. 4:6 shall be a *t* for a shadow in the daytime
16:5 shall sit upon it in truth in the *t* of David
33:20 a *t* that shall not be taken down
Jer. 10:20 my *t* is spoiled, and all my cords are
Ezek. 37:27 my *t* also shall be with them
Hos. 12:9 will yet make thee to dwell in *t*, as in
Amos 5:26 (Acts 7:43) borne the *t* of your Moloch
9:11 (Acts 15:16) will I raise up the *t* of David
Mt. 17:4 (Mk. 9:5; Lk. 9:33) let us make here three *t*
Jn. 7:2 now the Jews' feast of *t* was at hand
Acts 7:46 desired to find a *t* for the God of Jacob
2 Cor. 5:1 earthly house of this *t* were dissolved
5:4 that are in this *t* do groan, being burdened
Heb. 8:2 minister of the sanctuary. . of the true *t*
9:3 the *t* which is called the holiest of all
9:11 by a greater and more perfect *t*, not made
9:21 he sprinkled likewise with blood both the *t*
11:9 a strange country, dwelling in *t* with Isaac
13:10 have no right to eat which serve the *t*
2 Pet. 1:13 as long as I am in this *t*, to stir you
1:14 shortly I must put off this my *t*, even as
Rev. 15:5 temple of the *t* of the testimony. . opened
21:3 *t* of God is with men, and he will dwell with

Tabitha (Dorcas) Acts 9:36–41

Table

Ex. 24:12 I will give thee *t* of stone, and a law
25:23 (37:10) shalt also make a *t* of shittim wood
31:18 (Deut. 9:10) two *t* of testimony, *t* of stone
32:19 Moses' anger waxed hot, and he cast the *t*
34:1 (Deut. 10:1) hew thee two *t* of stone like
Lev. 24:6 upon the pure *t* before the LORD
Num. 4:7 upon the *t* of showbread they shall spread
Deut. 9:9 the *t* of stone, even the *t* of the covenant
Ps. 23:5 preparest a *t* before me in the presence of
69:22 (Rom. 11:9) *t* become a snare before them
78:19 can God furnish a *t* in the wilderness?
128:3 children like olive plants. . about thy *t*
Prov. 3:3 write them upon the *t* of thine heart
9:2 mingled her wine. . hath also furnished her *t*
Is. 28:8 all *t* are full of vomit and filthiness
Jer. 17:1 is graven upon the *t* of their heart
Ezek. 41:22 this is the *t* that is before the LORD
Dan. 11:27 they shall speak lies at one *t*
Mal. 1:7 ye say, The *t* of the LORD is contemptible
1:12 ye say, The *t* of the LORD is polluted
Mt. 15:27 (Mk. 7:28) crumbs. . from their masters' *t*
21:12 (Mk. 11:15; Jn. 2:15) overthrew the *t* of
Lk. 1:63 and he asked for a writing *t*, and wrote
22:21 him that betrayeth me is with me on the *t*
22:30 ye may eat and drink at my *t* in my kingdom
Jn. 13:28 no man at the *t* knew for what intent he
Acts 6:2 should leave the word of God, and serve *t*
1 Cor. 10:21 the Lord's *t*, and of the *t* of devils
2 Cor. 3:3 not in *t* of stone, but in fleshly *t* of
Heb. 9:4 Aaron's rod. . and the *t* of the covenant

Tabor Judg. 4:6–14

Tabret

1 Sam. 18:6 to meet king Saul, with *t*, with joy

Job 17:6 a byword . . and aforetime I was as a *t*
Is. 5:12 *t* and pipe, and wine, are in their feasts

Tackling

Is. 33:23 thy *t* are loosed; they could not well
Acts 27:19 third day we cast out . . the *t* of the ship

Tahpanhes Jer. 43:8

Tail

Ex. 4:4 put forth thine hand, and take it by the *t*
Judg. 15:4 three hundred foxes . . and turned *t* to *t*
Job 40:17 he moveth his *t* like a cedar: the sinews
Is. 7:4 for the two *t* of these smoking firebrands
    9:14 LORD will cut off from Israel head and *t*
Rev. 9:10 *t* like unto scorpions . . stings in their *t*
    12:4 and his *t* drew the third part of the stars

Take (Took, Taken) *See also* Accept,
    Receive

Ex. 6:7 I will *t* you to me for a people, and I will be
    20:7 (Deut. 5:11) not *t* the name of the LORD
    34:9 and pardon . . and *t* us for thine inheritance
Num. 16:3 ye *t* too much upon you, seeing all the
Job 23:10 but he knoweth the way that I *t*
Ps. 27:10 forsake me, then the LORD will *t* me up
    51:11 thy presence . . *t* not thy Holy Spirit from me
    116:13 I will *t* the cup of salvation, and call
    119:43 *t* not the word of truth . . out of my mouth
Prov. 30:9 steal, and *t* the name of my God in vain
Ezek. 11:19 (36:26) I will *t* the stony heart out of
Hos. 1:6 of Israel; but I will utterly *t* them away
Amos 7:15 the LORD *t* me as I followed the flock
    9:2 into hell, thence shall mine hand *t* them
Mt. 5:40 (Lk. 6:29) *t* away thy coat, let him have
    8:17 *t* our infirmities, and bare our sicknesses
    9:16 (Mk. 2:21) *t* from the garment, and the rent
    9:25 (Mk. 5:41; Lk. 8:54) and *t* her by the hand
    10:38 *t* not his cross, and followeth after me
    11:29 *t* my yoke upon you, and learn of me
    13:12 (25:29; Mk. 4:25; Lk. 8:18; 19:26) from him
        shall be *t* away even that he hath
    16:24 (Mk. 8:34; Lk. 9:23) and *t* up his cross
    20:14 *t* that thine is, and go thy way
    24:40 (Lk. 17:34) one shall be *t* . . the other left
    25:28 *t* therefore the talent from him, and give
    26:26 (Mk. 14:22; 1 Cor. 11:24) *t*, eat; this is my
Mk. 9:36 (Lk. 9:47) he *t* a child, and set him in
Lk. 2:28 then *t* he him up in his arms, and blessed
    19:24 *t* from him the pound, and give it to him
    22:17 *t* the cup . . and said, *T* this, and divide it
    24:30 he *t* bread, and blessed it, and brake
Jn. 1:29 Lamb . . which *t* away the sin of the world!
    10:17 I lay down my life, that I might *t* it again
    16:15 shall *t* of mine, and shall show it unto you
    16:22 shall rejoice, and your joy no man *t* from you
    17:15 not that thou . . *t* them out of the world
    18:12 officers of the Jews *t* Jesus, and bound him
Acts 1:9 while they beheld, he was *t* up; and a cloud
    15:37 Barnabas determined to *t* with them John
1 Cor. 6:7 why do ye not rather *t* wrong?
Phil. 2:7 and *t* upon him the form of a servant
Heb. 2:14 also himself likewise *t* part of the same
1 Pet. 2:20 your faults, ye shall *t* it patiently?
Rev. 3:11 hold that fast . . that no man *t* thy crown
    22:17 let him *t* the water of life freely
    22:19 if any man shall *t* away from the words

Tale

Ps. 90:9 we spend our years as a *t* that is told
Ezek. 22:9 in thee are men that carry *t* to shed blood
Lk. 24:11 and their words seemed to them as idle *t*

Talebearer

Lev. 19:16 thou shalt not go up and down as a *t*
Prov. 11:13 a *t* revealeth secrets: but he that is
    18:8 the words of a *t* are as wounds, and they go
    26:20 so where there is no *t*, the strife ceaseth

Talent

Mt. 18:24 brought . . which owed him ten thousand *t*
    25:15 unto one he gave five *t*, to another two

Talk *See also* Speak, Utter

Gen. 4:8 and Cain *t* with Abel his brother
Ex. 33:9 the tabernacle, and the LORD *t* with Moses
    34:29 skin of his face shone while he *t* with him
Deut. 5:4 LORD *t* with you face to face in the mount
    5:24 have seen this day that God doth *t* with man
    6:7 shalt *t* of them when thou sittest in thine
1 Sam. 2:3 *t* no more so exceeding proudly; let not
1 Kgs. 18:27 either he is *t*, or he is pursuing
2 Kgs. 18:26 *t* not with us in the Jews' language
1 Chr. 16:9 (Ps. 105:2) *t* ye of all his wondrous works
Job 11:2 and should a man full of *t* be justified?
    15:3 should he reason with unprofitable *t*?
Ps. 71:24 my tongue . . shall *t* of thy righteousness
    77:12 meditate . . of all thy work . . *t* of thy doings
    119:27 so shall I *t* of thy wondrous works
    145:11 glory of thy kingdom, and *t* of thy power
Prov. 14:23 *t* of the lips tendeth only to penury
Jer. 12:1 yet let me *t* with thee of thy judgments
Ezek. 33:30 thy people still are *t* against thee
Mt. 12:46 while he yet *t* to the people, behold, his
    22:15 how they might entangle him in his *t*
Lk. 24:14 and they *t* together of all these things
    24:32 heart burn . . while he *t* with us by the way
Jn. 4:27 marveled that he *t* with the woman
    9:37 both seen him, and it is he that *t* with thee
    14:30 hereafter I will not *t* much with you
Rev. 4:1 was as it were of a trumpet *t* with me

Talker

Tit. 1:10 are many unruly and vain *t* and deceivers

Tall (Taller)

Deut. 1:28 the people is greater and *t* than we
    2:10 people great, and many, and *t*, as the Anakim
2 Kgs. 19:23 (Is. 37:24) cut down the *t* cedar trees

Talmai 2 Sam. 13:37

Tamar Judah's daughter-in-law
    Gen. 38:6–26

Tamar Absalom's sister 2 Sam. 13:1–20

Tame

Mk. 5:4 fetters broken . . neither could any man *t* him
Jas. 3:8 tongue can no man *t*; it is an unruly evil

Tammuz Ezek. 8:14

Tanner

Acts 9:43 he tarried . . in Joppa with one Simon a *t*

Tapestry

Prov. 7:16 have decked my bed with coverings of *t*
    31:22 maketh herself coverings of *t*; her clothing

Tare (noun)

Mt. 13:25 enemy came and sowed *t* among the wheat
    13:36 declare unto us the parable of the *t*

Tare (verb) *See* Tear

Target *See also* Shield
1 Kgs. 10:16 made two hundred *t* of beaten gold

Tarry *See also* Remain, Wait
Gen. 19:2 your servant's house, and *t* all night
2 Kgs. 2:2 *t* here, I pray thee; for the LORD hath
  7:9 if we *t* till the morning light
Ps. 68:12 and she that *t* at home divided the spoil
  101:7 that telleth lies shall not *t* in my sight
Prov. 23:30 they that *t* long at the wine
Is. 46:13 not be far off. . my salvation shall not *t*
Jer. 14:8 and as a wayfaring man. . to *t* for a night?
Hab. 2:3 though it *t*, wait for it. . it will not *t*
Mt. 25:5 while the bridegroom *t*, they all slumbered
  26:38 (Mk. 14:34) *t* ye here, and watch
Lk. 24:29 day is far spent. . he went in to *t* with them
  24:49 but *t* ye in the city of Jerusalem, until ye
Jn. 21:22 (21:23) if I will that he *t* till I come
Acts 22:16 now why *t* thou? arise, and be baptized
1 Cor. 11:33 together to eat, *t* one for another
Heb. 10:37 that shall come will come, and will not *t*

Tarshish (Tharshish)
1 Kgs. 10:22 (2 Chr. 9:21) king had at sea a navy of *T*
  22:48 (2 Chr. 20:36) Jehoshaphat made ships of *T*
Jon. 1:3 he found a ship going to *T*: so he paid the

Tarsus
Acts 9:11 called Saul, of *T*: for, behold, he prayeth
  11:25 departed Barnabas to *T*, for to seek Saul
  21:39 (22:3) I am a man which am a Jew of *T*

Taskmaster
Ex. 1:11 they did set over them *t* to afflict them
  3:7 have heard their cry by reason of their *t*
  5:6 Pharaoh commanded the same day the *t* of the

Taste
Num. 11:8 the *t* of it was as the *t* of fresh oil
Job 6:6 or is there any *t* in the white of an egg?
  6:30 cannot my *t* discern perverse things?
  12:11 ear try words? and the mouth *t* his meat?
Ps. 34:8 *t* and see that the LORD is good
  119:103 how sweet are thy words unto my *t*!
Jer. 48:11 therefore his *t* remained in him
Mt. 16:28 (Mk. 9:1; Lk. 9:27) shall not *t* of death, till
  27:34 when he had *t* thereof, he would not drink
Lk. 14:24 that none. . bidden shall *t* of my supper
Jn. 2:9 ruler. . had *t* the water that was made wine
  8:52 keep my saying, he shall never *t* of death
Col. 2:21 touch not; *t* not; handle not
Heb. 2:9 that he. . should *t* death for every man
  6:4 enlightened, and have *t* of the heavenly gift
1 Pet. 2:3 ye have *t* that the Lord is gracious

Tattler
1 Tim. 5:13 not only idle, but *t*. . and busybodies

Taught *See* Teach

Taunt
Jer. 24:9 to be. . a *t* and a curse, in all places
Ezek. 5:15 so it shall be a reproach and a *t*

Tax *See also* Tribute
2 Kgs. 23:35 but he *t* the land to give the money
Dan. 11:20 stand up in his estate a raiser of *t*
Lk. 2:1 a decree. . that all the world should be *t*
Acts 5:37 up Judas of Galilee in the days of the *t*

Teach (Taught) *See also* Doctrine, Instruct
Ex. 4:12 and I will. . *t* thee what thou shalt say
  18:20 and thou shalt *t* them ordinances and laws
Lev. 10:11 ye may *t* the children of Israel all the
Deut. 4:5 I have *t* you statutes and judgments
  4:9 but *t* them thy sons, and thy sons' sons
  6:7 shalt *t* them diligently unto thy children
  11:19 and ye shall *t* them your children
1 Sam. 12:23 I will *t* you the good and the right way
1 Kgs. 8:36 (2 Chr. 6:27) thou *t* them the good way
2 Kgs. 17:27 let him *t* them the manner of the God
  17:28 and *t* them how they should fear the LORD
2 Chr. 17:9 *t* in Judah, and had the book of the law
Job 6:24 *t* me, and I will hold my tongue: and cause
  12:7 ask now the beasts, and they shall *t* thee
  12:8 or speak to the earth, and it shall *t* thee
  21:22 shall any *t* God knowledge?. . he judgeth
  27:11 I will *t* you by the hand of God: that which
  34:32 which I see not *t* thou me: if I have done
Ps. 25:4 show me thy ways, O LORD; *t* me thy paths
  25:8 LORD: therefore will he *t* sinners in the way
  27:11 (86:11) *t* me thy way, O LORD
  34:11 harken. . I will *t* you the fear of the LORD
  51:13 then will I *t* transgressors thy ways
  71:17 O God, thou hast *t* me from my youth
  90:12 *t* us to number our days, that we may apply
  94:10 he that *t* man knowledge, shall not he know?
  94:12 chastenest, O LORD, and *t* him out of thy law
  119:12 (119:26, 64, 68, 124, 135) *t* me thy statutes
  119:33 *t* me, O LORD, the way of thy statutes
  119:66 *t* me good judgment and knowledge
  143:10 *t* me to do thy will; for thou art my God
  144:1 which *t* my hands to war, and my fingers
Prov. 4:11 I have *t* thee in the way of wisdom
  9:9 *t* a just man, and he will increase in learning
Is. 2:3 (Mic. 4:2) he will *t* us of his ways, and we will
  9:15 and the prophet that *t* lies, he is the tail
  28:9 whom shall he *t* knowledge? and whom shall
  29:13 fear toward me is *t* by the precept of men
  40:13 LORD, or being his counselor hath *t* him?
  48:17 am the LORD thy God which *t* thee to profit
  54:13 (Jn. 6:45) thy children shall be *t* of the LORD
Jer. 12:16 as they *t* my people to swear by Baal
  28:16 thou hast *t* rebellion against the LORD
  31:34 (Heb. 8:11) *t* no more every man his neighbor
  32:33 though I *t* them, rising up early and *t* them
Ezek. 44:23 they shall *t* my people the difference
Hos. 11:3 I *t* Ephraim also to go, taking them by
Mic. 3:11 reward, and the priests thereof *t* for hire
Mt. 4:23 (9:35; Lk. 4:15) *t* in their synagogues
  5:2 and he opened his mouth, and *t* them, saying
  5:19 shall *t* men so, he shall be called the least
  7:29 (Mk. 1:22) he *t* them as one having authority
  11:1 he departed thence to *t* and to preach in
  13:54 (Mk. 6:2) he *t* them in their synagogue
  15:9 (Mk. 7:7) *t* for doctrines the commandments
  22:16 (Mk. 12:14; Lk. 20:21) *t* the way of God in
  26:55 (Mk. 14:49) daily with you *t* in the temple
  28:19 go ye therefore, and *t* all nations, baptizing
  28:20 *t* them to observe all things whatsoever
Mk. 4:2 he *t* them many things by parables, and said
  9:31 *t* his disciples. . The Son of man is delivered
Lk. 11:1 Lord, *t* us to pray, as John also *t* his
  12:12 the Holy Ghost shall *t* you in the same hour
  13:10 *t* in one of the synagogues on the sabbath
  19:47 *t* daily in the temple. But the chief priests
Jn. 7:14 Jesus went up into the temple, and *t*
  8:28 but as my Father hath *t* me, I speak these
  9:34 altogether born in sins, and dost thou *t* us?
  14:26 he shall *t* you all things, and bring all

Acts 1:1 of all that Jesus began both to do and *t*
    4:2 grieved that they *t* the people, and preached
    4:18 to speak at all nor *t* in the name of Jesus
    5:28 that ye should not *t* in this name?
    5:42 they ceased not to *t* and preach Jesus Christ
    15:1 which came down from Judea *t* the brethren
    15:35 continued in Antioch, *t* and preaching
    18:25 *t* diligently the things of the Lord, knowing
    21:28 *t* all men every where against the people
    22:3 *t* according to the perfect manner of the law
    28:31 and *t* those things which concern the Lord
Rom. 2:21 which *t* another, *t* thou not thyself?
    12:7 our ministering; or he that *t*, on teaching
1 Cor. 2:13 wisdom *t*, but which the Holy Ghost *t*
    11:14 doth not even nature itself *t* you
    14:19 that by my voice I might *t* others also
Gal. 1:12 neither was I *t* it, but by the revelation
    6:6 is *t* in the word communicate unto him that *t*
Eph. 4:21 have heard him, and have been *t* by him
Col. 1:28 warning every man, and *t* every man in all
    2:7 stablished in the faith, as ye have been *t*
    3:16 *t* and admonishing one another in psalms
1 Thes. 4:9 ye. . are *t* of God to love one another
2 Thes. 2:15 hold the traditions which ye have been *t*
1 Tim. 1:3 charge. . that they *t* no other doctrine
    2:12 but I suffer not a woman to *t*, nor to usurp
    3:2 good behavior, given to hospitality, apt to *t*
    4:11 these things command and *t*
    6:2 these things *t* and exhort
2 Tim. 2:2 to faithful men, who shall be able to *t*
    2:24 be gentle unto all men, apt to *t*, patient
Tit. 1:9 the faithful word as he hath been *t*
    1:11 *t* things which they ought not, for filthy
    2:4 may *t* the young women to be sober, to love
    2:12 *t* us that, denying ungodliness and worldly
Heb. 5:12 ye have need that one *t* you again which
1 Jn. 2:27 *t* you: but as the same anointing *t* you

Teacher *See also* Instructor, Master, Rabbi

Ps. 119:99 I have more understanding than all my *t*
Prov. 5:13 and have not obeyed the voice of my *t*
Is. 30:20 shall not thy *t* be removed into a corner
    43:27 and thy *t* have transgressed against me
Hab. 2:18 the molten image, and a *t* of lies
Jn. 3:2 we know that thou art a *t* come from God
Rom. 2:20 instructor of the foolish, a *t* of babes
1 Cor. 12:29 apostles? are all prophets? are all *t*?
Eph. 4:11 some, evangelists; and some, pastors and *t*
1 Tim. 1:7 be *t* of the law; understanding neither
    2:7 (2 Tim. 1:11) an apostle. . a *t* of the Gentiles
2 Tim. 4:3 heap to themselves *t*, having itching ears
Tit. 2:3 not given to much wine, *t* of good things
Heb. 5:12 the time ye ought to be *t*, ye have need
2 Pet. 2:1 as there shall be false *t* among you

Tear (noun)

2 Kgs. 20:5 (Is. 38:5) thy prayer, I have seen thy *t*
Job 16:20 but mine eye poureth out *t* unto God
Ps. 6:6 bed to swim; I water my couch with my *t*
    39:12 hold not thy peace at my *t*: for I am a
    42:3 my *t* have been my meat day and night, while
    56:8 my wanderings: put thou my *t* into thy bottle
    80:5 the bread of *t*; and givest them *t* to drink
    116:8 my soul from death, mine eyes from *t*
    126:5 they that sow in *t* shall reap in joy
Eccl. 4:1 behold the *t* of such as were oppressed
Is. 16:9 I will water thee with my *t*, O Heshbon
    25:8 (Rev. 7:17; 21:4) GOD will wipe away *t* from
Jer. 9:1 waters, and mine eyes a fountain of *t*
    31:16 voice from weeping, and thine eyes from *t*
Lam. 1:2 she weepeth sore. . her *t* are on her cheeks

Lam. 2:11 mine eyes do fail with *t*, my bowels are
    2:18 let *t* run down like a river day and night
Mk. 9:24 said with *t*, Lord, I believe; help thou
Lk. 7:38 began to wash his feet with *t*, and did wipe
Acts 20:19 all humility of mind, and with many *t*
    20:31 to warn every one night and day with *t*
2 Cor. 2:4 I wrote unto you with many *t*; not that
2 Tim. 1:4 being mindful of thy *t*, that I may be
Heb. 5:7 supplications with strong crying and *t*
    12:17 though he sought it carefully with *t*

Tear (Tare, Tore, Torn) *See also* Rend

Gen. 44:28 he is *t* in pieces; and I saw him not
Judg. 8:7 then I will *t* your flesh with the thorns
2 Sam. 13:31 the king arose, and *t* his garments
2 Kgs. 2:24 two she bears. . *t* forty and two children
Job 16:9 he *t* me in his wrath, who hateth me
    18:4 he *t* himself in his anger: shall the earth
Ps. 7:2 lest he *t* my soul like a lion, rending it
    35:15 the abjects. . they did *t* me, and ceased not
    50:22 now consider this. . lest I *t* you in pieces
Is. 5:25 their carcasses were *t* in the. . streets
Jer. 16:7 neither shall men *t* themselves for them
Ezek. 13:20 and I will *t* them from your arms
Hos. 5:14 I, will *t* and go away; I will take away
    6:1 for he hath *t*, and he will heal us
    13:8 devour them. . the wild beast shall *t* them
Amos 1:11 his anger did *t* perpetually, and he kept
Mic. 5:8 treadeth down, and *t* in pieces, and none
Mal. 1:13 ye brought that which was *t*, and the lame
Mk. 1:26 when the unclean spirit had *t* him, and cried
    9:18 (Lk. 9:39) *t* him. . he foameth, and gnasheth

Teeth *See also* Tooth

Gen. 49:12 red with wine, and his *t* white with milk
Job 13:14 wherefore do I take my flesh in my *t*
    19:20 and I am escaped with the skin of my *t*
    41:14 his face? his *t* are terrible round about
Ps. 3:7 thou hast broken the *t* of the ungodly
    57:4 sons of men, whose *t* are spears and arrows
    58:6 break their *t*, O God. . break out the great *t*
Prov. 10:26 as vinegar to the *t*. . smoke to the eyes
    30:14 is a generation, whose *t* are as swords
Song 4:2 thy *t* are like a flock of sheep that are
Is. 41:15 new sharp threshing instrument having *t*
Jer. 31:29 (Ezek. 18:2) children's *t* are set on edge
Dan. 7:7 (7:19) had great iron *t*: it devoured and
Amos 4:6 I also have given you cleanness of *t* in
Mt. 8:12 (13:42; 22:13; 24:51; 25:30) gnashing of *t*
    27:44 the thieves also. . cast the same in his *t*
Rev. 9:8 and their *t* were as the *t* of lions

Tekoa (Tekoah)

2 Sam. 14:2 to *T*, and fetched thence a wise woman
Amos 1:1 Amos, who was among the herdmen of *T*

Tell (Told) *See also* Declare, Proclaim, Reveal

Gen. 15:5 *t* the stars, if thou be able to number
1 Sam. 9:15 LORD had *t* Samuel in his ear a day before
2 Sam. 1:20 *t* it not in Gath, publish it not in
    12:22 who can *t* whether God will be gracious
1 Kgs. 22:16 I adjure thee that thou *t* me nothing
2 Kgs. 7:9 we may go and *t* the king's household
Job 34:34 let men of understanding *t* me
Ps. 48:12 walk about Zion. . *t* the towers thereof
    48:13 ye may *t* it to the generation following
Eccl. 6:12 (10:14) who can *t* a man what shall be after
Is. 45:21 *t* ye, and bring them near; yea, let them
Jon. 3:9 who can *t* if God will turn and repent
Mt. 8:4 (Lk. 5:14) see thou *t* no man; but go thy way
    8:33 (Mk. 5:16; Lk. 8:36) fled. . into the city, and *t*

Mt. 16:20 (Mk. 8:30; Lk. 9:21) *t* no man . . the Christ
17:9 (Mk. 9:9) *t* the vision to no man, until the Son
18:15 *t* him his fault between thee and him alone
21:5 *t* ye the daughter of Sion, Behold, thy King
21:27 (Mk. 11:33; Lk. 20:7) we cannot *t* . . Neither *t*
24:3 (Mk. 13:4) *t* us, when shall these things be?
26:13 this woman hath done, be *t* for a memorial
26:63 (Lk. 22:67) *t* us whether thou be the Christ
28:7 (Mk. 16:7) *t* his disciples that he is risen
Mk. 5:19 *t* them how great things the Lord hath done
8:26 neither go into the town, nor *t* it to any
16:13 and *t* it unto the residue: neither believed
Lk. 2:18 things which were *t* them by the shepherds
8:56 he charged them that they should *t* no man
13:32 and *t* that fox, Behold, I cast out devils
24:35 they *t* what things were done in the way
Jn. 3:8 canst not *t* whence it cometh, and whither
3:12 if I have *t* you earthly things, and ye
4:25 Christ: when he is come, he will *t* us all
4:29 come, see a man which *t* me all things
8:14 ye cannot *t* whence I come, and whither I go
10:24 if thou be the Christ, *t* us plainly
14:29 now I have *t* you before it come to pass
16:4 these things have I *t* you, that when the time
Acts 16:36 the keeper of the prison *t* this . . to Paul
17:21 either to *t* or to hear some new thing
23:16 Paul's sister's son heard . . he . . *t* Paul
23:22 thou *t* no man that thou hast showed these
2 Cor. 12:2 whether in the body, I cannot *t*
13:2 I *t* you before, and foretell you, as if I

Temper

Ex. 29:2 cakes unleavened *t* with oil, and wafers
Ezek. 46:14 a hin of oil, to *t* with the fine flour
1 Cor. 12:24 God hath *t* the body together, having

Temperance

Acts 24:25 as he reasoned of righteousness, *t*, and
Gal. 5:23 meekness, *t*: against such there is no law
2 Pet. 1:6 to knowledge, *t*; and to *t*, patience

Temperate

1 Cor. 9:25 striveth for the mastery is *t* in all
Tit. 1:8 a lover of good men, sober, just, holy, *t*
2:2 that the aged men be sober, grave, *t*, sound

Tempest *See also* Storm, Whirlwind, Wind

Job 9:17 he breaketh me with a *t*, and multiplieth
Ps. 11:6 shall rain snares, fire . . and a horrible *t*
83:15 persecute them with thy *t*, and make them
Is. 32:2 from the wind, and a covert from the *t*
54:11 O thou afflicted, tossed with *t*, and not
Jon. 1:12 for my sake this great *t* is upon you
Mt. 8:24 behold, there arose a great *t* in the sea
Acts 27:18 we being exceedingly tossed with a *t*
Heb. 12:18 nor unto blackness, and darkness, and *t*
2 Pet. 2:17 clouds that are carried with a *t*

Tempestuous

Ps. 50:3 and it shall be very *t* round about him
Jon. 1:11 for the sea wrought, and was *t*
Acts 27:14 against it a *t* wind, called Euroclydon

Temple *See also* Forehead

Judg. 4:21 smote the nail into his *t*, and fastened
Song 4:3 (6:7) thy *t* are like a piece of a pomegranate

Temple *See also* Sanctuary, Tabernacle

1 Sam. 1:9 Eli the priest sat . . by a post of the *t*
2 Sam. 22:7 (Ps. 18:6) hear my voice out of his *t*
2 Kgs. 23:4 out of the *t* . . all the vessels . . for Baal
2 Chr. 35:20 when Josiah had prepared the *t*, Necho

Ezra 3:6 the foundation of the *t* . . was not yet laid
4:1 children of the captivity builded the *t* unto
5:14 vessels . . Nebuchadnezzar took out of the *t*
6:5 be restored, and brought again unto the *t*
Ps. 5:7 in thy fear will I worship toward thy holy *t*
11:4 the LORD is in his holy *t*, the LORD's throne
27:4 beauty of the LORD, and to inquire in his *t*
48:9 loving-kindness, O God, in the midst of thy *t*
65:4 goodness of thy house, even of thy holy *t*
79:1 thy holy *t* have they defiled; they have laid
138:2 I will worship toward thy holy *t*, and praise
Is. 6:1 and lifted up, and his train filled the *t*
44:28 and to the *t*, Thy foundation shall be laid
66:6 a voice from the *t*, a voice of the LORD that
Jer. 7:4 the *t* of the LORD, The *t* of the LORD, The *t*
Ezek. 41:1 he brought me to the *t*, and measured the
Hos. 8:14 hath forgotten his Maker, and buildeth *t*
Amos 8:3 songs of the *t* shall be howlings in that day
Hab. 2:20 LORD is in his holy *t*: let all the earth
Hag. 2:18 the foundation of the LORD's *t* was laid
Zech. 6:12 BRANCH . . he shall build the *t* of the LORD
8:9 foundation . . was laid, that the *t* might be built
Mal. 3:1 the Lord . . shall suddenly come to his *t*
Mt. 4:5 (Lk. 4:9) setteth him on a pinnacle of the *t*
12:6 that in this place is one greater than the *t*
21:12 (Mk. 11:15; Lk. 19:45; Jn. 2:14) *t* . . and cast
23:16 shall swear by the *t*, it is nothing
24:1 to him for to show him the buildings of the *t*
26:55 (Mk. 14:49; Lk. 22:53) I sat daily . . in the *t*
26:61 (Mk. 14:58) I am able to destroy the *t* of God
27:40 (Mk. 15:29) destroyest the *t*, and buildest it
27:51 (Mk. 15:38; Lk. 23:45) veil of the *t* was rent
Lk. 1:22 that he had seen a vision in the *t*
2:27 he came by the Spirit into the *t*
2:46 after three days they found him in the *t*
18:10 two men went up into the *t* to pray
21:5 as some spake of the *t*, how it was adorned
24:53 continually in the *t*, praising and blessing
Jn. 2:19 destroy this *t*, and in three days I will
2:21 but he spake of the *t* of his body
7:14 feast Jesus went up into the *t*, and taught
Acts 2:46 continuing daily with one accord in the *t*
3:2 whom they laid daily at the gate of the *t*
5:20 stand, and speak in the *t* to the people
7:48 (17:24) dwelleth not in *t* made with hands
19:27 *t* of the great goddess Diana . . be despised
21:28 and further brought Greeks also into the *t*
22:17 while I prayed in the *t*, I was in a trance
24:6 who also hath gone about to profane the *t*
1 Cor. 3:16 know ye not that ye are the *t* of God
3:17 for the *t* of God is holy, which *t* ye are
6:19 that your body is the *t* of the Holy Ghost
8:10 hast knowledge sit at meat in the idol's *t*
2 Cor. 6:16 agreement hath the *t* of God with idols?
Eph. 2:21 framed together groweth unto a holy *t* in
Rev. 3:12 will I make a pillar in the *t* of my God
7:15 God, and serve him day and night in his *t*
11:1 measure the *t* of God, and the altar
11:19 and the *t* of God was opened in heaven
15:8 was filled with smoke from the glory of God
16:1 I heard a great voice out of the *t* saying
21:22 saw no *t* . . the Lord . . and the Lamb are the *t*

Temporal

2 Cor. 4:18 for the things which are seen are *t*

Tempt *See also* Entice, Prove, Try

Gen. 22:1 after these things . . God did *t* Abraham
Ex. 17:2 Moses said . . wherefore do ye *t* the LORD?
Num. 14:22 have *t* me now these ten times, and have
Deut. 6:16 (Mt. 4:7; Lk. 4:12) shall not *t* the LORD
Ps. 78:18 they *t* God in their heart by asking meat
78:41 they turned back and *t* God, and limited the

Ps. 78:56 yet they *t* and provoked the most high God
  95:9 (Heb. 3:9) when your fathers *t* me, proved me
  106:14 in the wilderness, and *t* God in the desert
Is. 7:12 I will not ask, neither will I *t* the LORD
Mal. 3:15 yea, they that *t* God are even delivered
Mt. 4:1 (Mk. 1:13; Lk. 4:2) to be *t* of the devil
  16:1 (Mk. 8:11; Lk. 11:16) *t* desired. . a sign from
  19:3 (Mk. 10:2) Pharisees also came unto him, *t*
  22:18 (Mk. 12:15; Lk. 20:23) said, Why *t* ye me
  22:35 was a lawyer, asked him a question, *t* him
Acts 5:9 ye have agreed together to *t* the Spirit
  15:10 now therefore why *t* ye God, to put a yoke
1 Cor. 7:5 Satan *t* you not for your incontinency
  10:9 neither let us *t* Christ, as some of them . . *t*
  10:13 who will not suffer you to be *t* above that
Gal. 6:1 considering thyself, lest thou also be *t*
1 Thes. 3:5 have *t* you, and our labor be in vain
Heb. 2:18 *t*, he is able to succor them that are *t*
  4:15 but was in all points *t* like as we are
  11:37 they were sawn asunder, were *t*, were slain
Jas. 1:13 no man say when he is *t*, I am *t* of God
  1:14 is *t*, when he is drawn away of his own lust

Temptation *See also* Trial

Deut. 4:34 take him a nation. . by *t*, by signs
  7:19 (29:3) the great *t* which thine eyes saw
Ps. 95:8 (Heb. 3:8) the day of *t* in the wilderness
Mt. 6:13 (Lk. 11:4) lead us not into *t*, but deliver
  26:41 (Mk. 14:38; Lk. 22:40) that ye enter not into *t*
Lk. 4:13 when the devil had ended all the *t*
  8:13 for a while believe, and in time of *t* fall away
  22:28 they which have continued with me in my *t*
Acts 20:19 serving the Lord . . with many tears, and *t*
1 Cor. 10:13 no *t* taken you but such as is common
Gal. 4:14 my *t* which was in my flesh ye despised not
1 Tim. 6:9 they that will be rich fall into *t*
Jas. 1:2 count it all joy when ye fall into divers *t*
  1:12 blessed is the man that endureth *t*: for when
1 Pet. 1:6 ye are in heaviness through manifold *t*
2 Pet. 2:9 to deliver the godly out of *t*
Rev. 3:10 I also will keep thee from the hour of *t*

Tempter

Mt. 4:3 when the *t* came to him, he said, If thou
1 Thes. 3:5 lest by some means the *t* have tempted

Tender *See also* Delicate, Gentle

Gen. 29:17 Leah was *t* eyed; but Rachel was beautiful
Deut. 28:54 so that the man that is *t* among you
2 Kgs. 22:19 (2 Chr. 34:27) because thine heart was *t*
Job 14:7 that the *t* branch thereof will not cease
Prov. 4:3 my father's son, *t* and only beloved in
Is. 47:1 shalt no more be called *t* and delicate
  53:2 he shall grow up before him as a *t* plant
Mt. 24:32 (Mk. 13:28) when his branch is yet *t*

Tender-hearted

2 Chr. 13:7 Rehoboam was young and *t-h*
Eph. 4:32 be ye kind one to another, *t-h*, forgiving

Tent *See also* Tabernacle

Gen. 4:20 he was the father of such as dwell in *t*
  25:27 and Jacob was a plain man, dwelling in *t*
Num. 13:19 dwell in, whether in *t*, or in strongholds
  24:5 goodly are thy *t*, O Jacob, and thy tabernacles
2 Sam. 20:1 every man to his *t*, O Israel
Ps. 84:10 than to dwell in the *t* of wickedness
  120:5 woe is me. . that I dwell in the *t* of Kedar!
Is. 38:12 and is removed from me as a shepherd's *t*
  40:22 and spreadeth them out as a *t* to dwell in
  54:2 enlarge the place of thy *t*, and let them
Jer. 10:20 is none to stretch forth my *t* any more
Zech. 12:7 LORD also shall save the *t* of Judah first

Tenth *See also* Tithe

Gen. 28:22 I will surely give the *t* unto thee
Lev. 27:32 the *t* shall be holy unto the LORD
Num. 18:21 have given the children of Levi all the *t*
1 Sam. 8:15 he will take the *t* of your seed, and of
Is. 6:13 in it shall be a *t*, and it shall return
Heb. 7:2 to whom also Abraham gave a *t* part of all

Tentmaker

Acts 18:3 for by their occupation they were *t*

Terah Gen. 11:24–32

Teraphim *See also* Ephod

Judg. 17:5 the man Micah . . made an ephod, and *t*
Hos. 3:4 days. . without an ephod, and without *t*

Terrestrial

1 Cor. 15:40 bodies *t*. . glory of the *t* is another

Terrible *See also* Fearful, Horrible

Ex. 34:10 it is a *t* thing that I will do with thee
Deut. 1:19 through all that great and *t* wilderness
  7:21 thy God is among you, a mighty God and *t*
  10:21 done for thee these great and *t* things
Judg. 13:6 countenance of an angel of God, very *t*
Job 39:20 the glory of his nostrils is *t*
  41:14 of his face? his teeth are *t* round about
Ps. 45:4 thy right hand shall teach thee *t* things
  47:2 the LORD most high is *t*; he is a great king
  65:5 by *t* things in righteousness wilt thou answer
  66:5 see the works of God: he is *t* in his doing
  68:35 O God, thou art *t* out of thy holy places
  76:12 he is *t* to the kings of the earth
  99:3 let them praise thy great and *t* name
  106:22 land of Ham, and *t* things by the Red sea
  145:6 men shall speak of the might of thy *t* acts
Song 6:4 (6:10) *t* as an army with banners
Is. 13:11 will lay low the haughtiness of the *t*
  18:2 to a people *t* from their beginning hitherto
  64:3 thou didst *t* things which we looked not for
Jer. 15:21 redeem thee out of the hand of the *t*
  20:11 but the LORD is with me as a mighty *t* one
Dan. 7:7 and behold a fourth beast, dreadful and *t*
Joel 2:11 the day of the LORD is great and very *t*
Heb. 12:21 and so *t* was the sight, that Moses said

Terribleness

1 Chr. 17:21 make thee a name of greatness and *t*
Jer. 49:16 thy *t* hath deceived thee, and the pride

Terrify *See also* Affrighted

Deut. 20:3 faint. . neither be ye *t* because of them
Job 3:5 let the blackness of the day *t* it
  7:14 scarest me with dreams. . *t* me through visions
  9:34 rod away from me, and let not his fear *t* me
  31:34 did the contempt of families *t* me, that I
Lk. 21:9 shall hear of wars and commotions, be not *t*
  24:37 they were *t* and affrighted, and supposed
2 Cor. 10:9 not seem as if I would *t* you by letters
Phil. 1:28 and in nothing *t* by your adversaries

Terror *See also* Dread, Fear, Horror

Gen. 35:5 *t* of God was upon the cities that were
Lev. 26:16 I will even appoint over you *t*
Deut. 32:25 sword without. . *t* within, shall destroy
Josh. 2:9 I know. . that your *t* is fallen upon us
Job 18:11 *t* shall make him afraid on every side
  24:17 they are in the *t* of the shadow of death
  27:20 *t* take hold on him as waters, a tempest
  31:23 destruction from God was a *t* to me
  33:7 my *t* shall not make thee afraid, neither

Ps. 55:4 and the *t* of death are fallen upon me
  73:19 a moment! they are utterly consumed with *t*
  91:5 thou shalt not be afraid for the *t* by night
Is. 33:18 thine heart shall meditate *t*
  54:14 and from *t*; for it shall not come near thee
Jer. 17:17 be not a *t* unto me: thou art my hope
  20:4 I will make thee a *t* to thyself, and to all
Ezek. 26:21 I will make thee a *t*, and thou shalt
Rom. 13:3 rulers are not a *t* to good works, but to
2 Cor. 5:11 knowing. . the *t* of the Lord, we persuade
1 Pet. 3:14 be not afraid of their *t*, neither be

Tertius Rom. 16:22

Tertullus Acts 24:1–2

Testament *See also* Covenant, Testimony

Mt. 26:28 (Mk. 14:24) this is my blood of the new *t*
Lk. 22:20 (1 Cor. 11:25) cup is the new *t* in my blood
2 Cor. 3:6 made us able ministers of the new *t*
  3:14 veil untaken away in the reading of the old *t*
Heb. 7:22 was Jesus made a surety of a better *t*
  9:15 the mediator of the new *t*, that by means of
  9:16 where a *t* is, there must also of necessity
  9:17 *t* is of force after men are dead: otherwise
  9:20 the blood of the *t* which God hath enjoined
Rev. 11:19 was seen in his temple the ark of his *t*

Testator

Heb. 9:16 also of necessity be the death of the *t*

Testify *See also* Witness

Num. 35:30 but one witness shall not *t* against any
Deut. 8:19 I *t* against you this day that ye shall
  19:18 witness. . hath *t* falsely against his brother
  31:21 this song shall *t* against them as a witness
  32:46 the words which I *t* among you this day
2 Sam. 1:16 thy mouth hath *t* against thee, saying
2 Kgs. 17:13 yet the Lord *t* against Israel
Neh. 9:26 slew thy prophets which *t* against them
  13:15 I *t* against them in the day wherein they
Job 15:6 yea, thine own lips *t* against thee
Ps. 50:7 Israel, and I will *t* against thee: I am God
Is. 59:12 before thee, and our sins *t* against us
Jer. 14:7 Lord, though our iniquities *t* against us
Hos. 5:5 (7:10) pride of Israel doth *t* to his face
Mic. 6:3 wherein have I wearied thee? *t* against me
Lk. 16:28 I have five brethren. . he may *t* unto them
Jn. 2:25 needed not that any should *t* of man
  3:11 speak that we do know. . *t* that we have seen
  3:32 and what he hath seen and heard, that he *t*
  4:39 the woman, which *t*, He told me all that ever
  4:44 for Jesus himself *t*, that a prophet hath no
  5:39 Scriptures. . and they are they which *t* of me
  7:7 hate you; but me it hateth, because I *t* of it
  13:21 he was troubled in spirit, and *t*, and said
  15:26 even the Spirit of truth. . he shall *t* of me
  21:24 this is the disciple which *t* of these things
Acts 2:40 with many other words did he *t* and exhort
  8:25 they had *t* and preached the word of the Lord
  10:42 *t* that it is he which was ordained of God
  18:5 Paul. . *t* to the Jews that Jesus was Christ
  20:21 *t* both to the Jews, and also to the Greeks
  20:24 to *t* the gospel of the grace of God
  23:11 as thou hast *t* of me in Jerusalem, so must
  28:23 to whom he expounded and *t* the kingdom
1 Cor. 15:15 we have *t* of God that he raised up
Gal. 5:3 I *t* again to every man that is circumcised
Eph. 4:17 this I say therefore, and *t* in the Lord
1 Thes. 4:6 as we also have forewarned you and *t*
1 Tim. 2:6 a ransom for all, to be *t* in due time
Heb. 2:6 in a certain place *t*, saying, What is man
  7:17 for he *t*, Thou art a priest for ever after

Heb. 11:4 Abel. . he was righteous, God *t* of his gifts
1 Pet. 1:11 *t* beforehand the sufferings of Christ
  5:12 exhorting, and *t* that this is the true grace
1 Jn. 4:14 do *t* that the Father sent the Son to be
  5:9 witness of God which he hath *t* of his Son
3 Jn. 3 came and *t* of the truth that is in thee
Rev. 22:16 I Jesus have sent mine angel to *t* unto
  22:20 he which *t* these things saith, Surely I

Testimony *See also* Covenant, Law, Testament, Witness

Ex. 16:34 Aaron laid it up before the *T*, to be kept
  25:16 put into the ark the *t* which I shall give
  26:33 bring in. . within the veil the ark of the *t*
  31:18 and he gave unto Moses. . two tables of *t*
Num. 9:15 covered the tabernacle. . the tent of the *t*
Deut. 4:45 these are the *t*, and the statutes
  6:17 diligently keep. . his *t*, and his statutes
  6:20 what mean the *t*, and the statutes, and
1 Kgs. 2:3 to keep. . his judgments, and his *t*
2 Kgs. 11:12 (2 Chr. 23:11) and gave him the *t*
  23:3 (2 Chr. 34:31) keep his commandments. . his *t*
Ps. 19:7 the *t* of the Lord is sure, making wise
  25:10 unto such as keep his covenant and his *t*
  78:5 he established a *t* in Jacob, and appointed
  78:56 provoked the most high God. . kept not his *t*
  93:5 thy *t* are very sure: holiness becometh thine
  99:7 they kept his *t*, and the ordinance that he
  119:2 blessed are they that keep his *t*, and that
  119:24 thy *t*. . are my delight, and my counselors
  119:36 incline my heart unto thy *t*, and not to
  119:46 I will speak of thy *t* also before kings
  119:99 my teachers: for thy *t* are my meditation
  119:111 thy *t* have I taken as a heritage for ever
  119:125 me understanding, that I may know thy *t*
  119:129 thy *t* are wonderful: therefore doth my
  119:144 the righteousness of thy *t* is everlasting
  119:146 I cried. . save me, and I shall keep thy *t*
  122:4 unto the *t* of Israel, to give thanks unto
  132:12 if thy children. . keep my covenant and my *t*
Is. 8:16 bind up the *t*, seal the law among my disciples
Mt. 8:4 (Mk. 1:44; Lk. 5:14) offer the gift. . for a *t*
  10:18 (Mk. 13:9; Lk. 21:13) kings. . for a *t* against
Mk. 6:11 (Lk. 9:5) shake off the dust. . for a *t* against
Jn. 3:32 he testifieth; and no man receiveth his *t*
  5:34 I receive not *t* from man: but these things
  8:17 in your law, that the *t* of two men is true
  21:24 testifieth. . and we know that his *t* is true
Acts 14:3 which gave *t* unto the word of his grace
  22:18 they will not receive thy *t* concerning me
1 Cor. 1:6 as the *t* of Christ was confirmed in you
  2:1 or of wisdom, declaring unto you the *t* of God
2 Cor. 1:12 rejoicing is this, the *t* of our conscience
2 Thes. 1:10 because our *t* among you was believed
2 Tim. 1:8 be not. . ashamed of the *t* of our Lord
Heb. 11:5 for before his translation he had this *t*
Rev. 1:2 word of God, and of the *t* of Jesus Christ
  6:9 that were slain. . for the *t* which they held
  12:11 they overcame him. . by the word of their *t*
  12:17 keep the commandments. . the *t* of Jesus
  15:5 tabernacle of the *t* in heaven was opened
  19:10 the *t* of Jesus is the spirit of prophecy

Thaddeus *See also* Judas, brother of James

Mt. 10:3 (Mk. 3:18)

Thank *See also* Bless, Praise

2 Sam. 14:22 Joab. . bowed himself, and *t* the king
1 Chr. 16:7 David delivered first this psalm to *t*
  23:30 every morning to *t* and praise the Lord

1 Chr. 29:13 we *t* thee, and praise thy glorious name
2 Chr. 29:31 bring sacrifices and *t* offerings into the
Dan. 2:23 I *t* thee, and praise thee, O thou God
Mt. 11:25 (Lk. 10:21) I *t* thee, O Father. . because
Lk. 6:32 love them which love you, what *t* have ye?
  17:9 doth he *t* that servant because he did the
  18:11 God, I *t* thee, that I am not as other men
Jn. 11:41 Father, I *t* thee that thou hast heard me
Acts 28:15 Paul saw, he *t* God, and took courage
Rom. 1:8 I *t* my God. . for you all, that your faith
  6:17 God be *t*, that ye were the servants of sin
  7:25 I *t* God through Jesus Christ our Lord
1 Cor. 1:4 I *t* my God always on your behalf
Phil. 1:3 I *t* my God upon every remembrance of you
1 Thes. 2:13 also *t* we God without ceasing, because
2 Thes. 1:3 we are bound to *t* God always for you
1 Tim. 1:12 I *t* Christ Jesus. . who hath enabled me
2 Tim. 1:3 I *t* God. . I serve. . with pure conscience

Thankful

Ps. 100:4 praise: be *t* unto him, and bless his name
Rom. 1:21 glorified him not as God, neither were *t*
Col. 3:15 ye are called in one body; and be ye *t*

Thanks *See also* Praise, Thanksgiving

2 Sam. 22:50 (Ps. 18:49) will give *t* unto thee, O LORD
1 Chr. 16:8 (Ps. 105:1) give *t* unto the LORD, call upon
  16:34 (Ps. 106:1) O give *t* unto the LORD; for he is
  25:3 who prophesied with a harp, to give *t*
Ezra 3:11 in praising and giving *t* unto the LORD
Ps. 6:5 in the grave who shall give thee *t*?
  30:12 my God, I will give *t* unto thee for ever
  75:1 O God, do we give *t*, unto thee do we give *t*
  79:13 and sheep of thy pasture will give thee *t*
  92:1 it is a good thing to give *t* unto the LORD
  107:1 (118:1) O give *t* unto the LORD; for he is good
  119:62 at midnight I will rise to give *t* unto thee
  136:2 give *t* unto the God of gods: for his mercy
  140:13 surely the righteous shall give *t* unto
Mt. 15:36 (Mk. 8:6) took the seven loaves. . gave *t*
  26:27 (Mk. 14:23; Lk. 22:17) took the cup. . gave *t*
Lk. 2:38 gave *t* likewise unto the Lord, and spake
  17:16 giving him *t*: and he was a Samaritan
Acts 27:35 thus spoken, he took bread, and gave *t*
Rom. 14:6 eateth to the Lord, for he giveth God *t*
1 Cor. 11:24 when he had given *t*, he brake it
  14:16 the unlearned say Amen at thy giving of *t*
  15:57 *t* be unto God, which giveth us the victory
2 Cor. 2:14 *t* be unto God, which always causeth us
  9:15 *t* be unto God for his unspeakable gift
Eph. 1:16 cease not to give *t* for you, making mention
  5:4 are not convenient: but rather giving of *t*
  5:20 giving *t* always for all things unto God
Col. 3:17 giving *t* to God and the Father by him
1 Thes. 3:9 what *t* can we render to God again for
  5:18 in every thing give *t*: for this is the will
1 Tim. 2:1 and giving of *t*, be made for all men
Heb. 13:15 fruit of our lips, giving *t* to his name
Rev. 4:9 beasts give glory and honor and *t* to him
  11:17 saying, We give thee *t*, O Lord God Almighty

Thanksgiving *See also* Praise, Thanks

Lev. 7:12 if he offer it for a *t*, then he shall
  22:29 ye will offer a sacrifice of *t* unto the LORD
Neh. 11:17 the principal to begin the *t* in prayer
  12:27 dedication with gladness, both with *t*, and
Ps. 26:7 that I may publish with the voice of *t*
  50:14 offer unto God *t*; and pay thy vows unto
  69:30 with a song, and will magnify him with *t*
  95:2 let us come before his presence with *t*
  100:4 enter into his gates with *t*, and into his
  116:17 I will offer to thee the sacrifice of *t*

Ps. 147:7 sing unto the LORD with *t*; sing praise
Is. 51:3 found therein, *t*, and the voice of melody
Amos 4:5 and offer a sacrifice of *t* with leaven
Jon. 2:9 sacrifice unto thee with the voice of *t*
2 Cor. 9:11 which causeth through us *t* to God
  9:12 but is abundant also by many *t* unto God
Phil. 4:6 by prayer and supplication with *t* let your
Col. 4:2 in prayer, and watch in the same with *t*
1 Tim. 4:3 God hath created to be received with *t*
Rev. 7:12 *t*, and honor, and power. . be unto our God

Theatre

Acts 19:29 they rushed with one accord into the *t*

Theft

Ex. 22:3 nothing, then he shall be sold for his *t*
Mt. 15:19 (Mk. 7:22) fornications, *t*, false witness
Rev. 9:21 nor of their fornication, nor of their *t*

Theophilus Lk. 1:3; Acts 1:1

Thessalonica Acts 17:1; Phil. 4:16

Theudas Acts 5:36

Thick (Thicker)

Deut. 32:15 thou art waxen fat, thou art grown *t*
1 Kgs. 7:26 it was a handbreadth *t*, and the brim
  12:10 (2 Chr. 10:10) my little finger shall be *t* than
Ps. 74:5 as he had lifted up axes upon the *t* trees

Thicket

Gen. 22:13 a ram caught in a *t* by his horns
Is. 9:18 wickedness. . kindle in the *t* of the forest
  10:34 and he shall cut down the *t* of the forest
Jer. 4:29 go into *t*, and climb up upon the rocks

Thief (Thieves) *See also* Robber

Ex. 22:2 if a *t* be found breaking up, and be smitten
Deut. 24:7 or selleth him; then that *t* shall die
Ps. 50:18 thou sawest a *t*, then thou consentedst
Prov. 6:30 men do not despise a *t*, if he steal to
  29:24 whoso is partner with a *t* hateth his own
Jer. 2:26 as the *t* is ashamed when he is found, so
Joel 2:9 shall enter in at the windows like a *t*
Mt. 6:19 and where *t* break through and steal
  21:13 (Mk. 11:17; Lk. 19:46) made it a den of *t*
  24:43 (Lk. 12:39) in what watch the *t* would come
  26:55 (Mk. 14:48; Lk. 22:52) come. . as against a *t*
  27:38 (Mk. 15:27) there two *t* crucified with him
Lk. 10:30 Jerusalem to Jericho, and fell among *t*
  12:33 no *t* approacheth, neither moth corrupteth
Jn. 10:1 some other way, the same is a *t* and a robber
  10:8 that ever came before me are *t* and robbers
  10:10 *t* cometh not, but for to steal, and to kill
  12:6 because he was a *t*, and had the bag, and bare
1 Cor. 6:10 nor *t*, nor covetous, nor drunkards
1 Thes. 5:2 (2 Pet. 3:10) day of the Lord. . as a *t*
1 Pet. 4:15 none. . suffer as a murderer, or as a *t*
Rev. 3:3 shalt not watch, I will come on thee as a *t*
  16:15 I come as a *t*. Blessed is he that watcheth

Thigh

Gen. 32:25 hollow of Jacob's *t* was out of joint
Num. 5:21 thy *t* to rot, and thy belly to swell
Judg. 15:8 he smote them hip and *t* with a great
Is. 47:2 uncover the *t*, pass over the rivers
Rev. 19:16 on his *t* a name written, KING OF KINGS

Thin

Gen. 41:6 behold, seven *t* ears and blasted with
  41:27 seven *t* and ill-favored kine that came up
Is. 17:4 that the glory of Jacob shall be made *t*

Thine

Ps. 74:16 the day is *t*, the night also is *t*
 89:11 heavens are *t*, the earth also is *t*
Lk. 22:42 nevertheless, not my will, but *t*, be done
Jn. 17:10 all mine are *t*, and *t* are mine; and I am

Thing

1 Kgs. 12:24 to his house; for this *t* is from me
1 Chr. 29:14 for all *t* come of thee, and of thine
Ps. 126:3 LORD hath done great *t* for us; whereof we
Jn. 16:13 and he will show you *t* to come
Rom. 11:36 and through him, and to him, are all *t*
1 Cor. 2:11 *t* of God knoweth no man, but the Spirit

Think (Thought) *See also* Imagine, Meditate, Reason

Gen. 50:20 ye *t* evil against me; but God meant it
Neh. 5:19 *t* upon me, my God, for good, according to
Ps. 40:17 am poor and needy; yet the Lord *t* upon me
 48:9 we have *t* of thy loving-kindness, O God
 73:16 when I *t* to know this, it was too painful
 119:59 I *t* on my ways, and turned my feet unto
Prov. 23:7 as he *t* in his heart, so is he
 30:32 or if thou hast *t* evil, lay thine hand upon
Eccl. 8:17 though a wise man *t* to know it, yet shall
Is. 10:7 meaneth not so, neither doth his heart *t* so
 14:24 surely as I have *t*, so shall it come to pass
Jer. 18:8 repent of the evil that I *t* to do unto them
 29:11 for I know the thoughts that I *t* toward you
Ezek. 38:10 mind, and thou shalt *t* an evil thought
Jon. 1:6 if so be that God will *t* upon us, that we
Zech. 8:14 as I *t* to punish you, when your fathers
Mal. 3:16 feared the LORD, and that *t* upon his name
Mt. 1:20 but while he *t* on these things, behold
 5:17 *t* not that I am come to destroy the law
 6:7 *t* that they shall be heard for their much
 9:4 said, Wherefore *t* ye evil in your hearts?
 10:34 *t* not that I am come to send peace on earth
 17:25 what *t* thou, Simon? of whom do the kings
 22:42 what *t* ye of Christ? whose son is he?
 24:44 (Lk. 12:40) such an hour as ye *t* not the Son
 26:53 *t* thou that I cannot now pray to my Father
Lk. 7:7 neither *t* I myself worthy to come unto thee
 19:11 *t* that the kingdom. . immediately appear
Jn. 5:39 for in them ye *t* ye have eternal life
 16:2 killeth you will *t* that he doeth God service
Acts 8:20 *t* that the gift of God may be purchased
 12:9 done by the angel; but *t* he saw a vision
 17:29 not to *t* that the Godhead is like unto gold
 26:2 I *t* myself happy, king Agrippa, because I
 26:8 why should it be *t* a thing incredible with
Rom. 12:3 not to *t* of himself more highly than he
1 Cor. 4:6 learn in us not to *t* of men above that
 7:40 and I *t* also that I have the Spirit of God
 8:2 if any man *t* that he knoweth any thing
 10:12 that *t* he standeth take heed lest he fall
 13:5 is not easily provoked, *t* no evil
 13:11 I understood as a child, I *t* as a child
 14:37 if any man *t* himself to be a prophet
2 Cor. 3:5 to *t* any thing as of ourselves; but our
 9:5 I *t* it necessary to exhort the brethren
 12:6 lest any man should *t* of me above that which
Gal. 6:3 if a man *t* himself to be something, when
Eph. 3:20 abundantly above all that we ask or *t*
Phil. 2:6 *t* it not robbery to be equal with God
 3:4 if any other man *t* that he hath whereof he
 4:8 and if there be any praise, *t* on these things
Jas. 1:7 let not that man *t* that he shall receive
1 Pet. 4:4 *t* it strange that ye run not with them
 4:12 *t* it not strange concerning the fiery trial

Thirst

Ex. 17:3 people *t* there for water; and . . murmured
Deut. 29:19 of mine heart, to add drunkenness to *t*
Judg. 15:18 now shall I die for *t*, and fall into
Job 24:11 tread their winepresses, and suffer *t*
Ps. 42:2 my soul *t* for God, for the living God
 63:1 my soul *t* for thee, my flesh longeth for
 69:21 and in my *t* they gave me vinegar to drink
 143:6 my soul *t* after thee, as a thirsty land
Is. 41:17 is none, and their tongue faileth for *t*
 48:21 *t* not when he led them through the desert
 49:10 (Rev. 7:16) shall not hunger nor *t*; neither
 55:1 ho, every one that *t*, come ye to the waters
Hos. 2:3 her like a dry land, and slay her with *t*
Amos 8:11 not a famine of bread, nor a *t* for water
Mt. 5:6 which do hunger and *t* after righteousness
Jn. 4:14 water that I shall give him shall never *t*
 6:35 and he that believeth on me shall never *t*
 7:37 if any man *t*, let him come unto me, and drink
 19:28 the Scripture might be fulfilled, saith, I *t*
Rom. 12:20 hunger, feed him; if he *t*, give him drink
2 Cor. 11:27 in hunger and *t*, in fastings often
Rev. 7:16 shall hunger no more, neither *t* any more

Thirsty

Judg. 4:19 give me . . water to drink; for I am *t*
Ps. 63:1 flesh longeth for thee in a dry and *t* land
 107:5 hungry and *t*, their soul fainted in them
Prov. 25:21 and if he be *t*, give him water to drink
 25:25 as cold waters to a *t* soul . . good news
Is. 21:14 of Tema brought water to him that was *t*
 29:8 or as when a *t* man dreameth, and, behold
 32:6 he will cause the drink of the *t* to fail
 35:7 a pool, and the *t* land springs of water
 44:3 for I will pour water upon him that is *t*
 65:13 my servants shall drink, but ye shall be *t*
Mt. 25:35 I was *t*, and ye gave me drink

Thistle

Gen. 3:18 thorns also and *t* shall it bring forth
2 Kgs. 14:9 (2 Chr. 25:18) *t* that was in Lebanon sent
Job 31:40 let *t* grow instead of wheat, and cockle
Hos. 10:8 and the *t* shall come up on their altars
Mt. 7:16 gather grapes of thorns, or figs of *t*?

Thomas *See also* Didymus

Mt. 10:3 (Mk. 3:18; Lk. 6:15) *T*, and Matthew the
Jn. 11:16 said *T*. . Let us also go, that we may die
 14:5 *T* saith unto him, Lord, we know not whither
 20:28 *T* answered and said . . My Lord and my God

Thorn

Gen. 3:18 *t* also and thistles shall it bring forth
Num. 33:55 pricks in your eyes, and *t* in your sides
Josh. 23:13 *t* in your eyes, until ye perish from off
Judg. 2:3 but they shall be as *t* in your sides
 8:7 tear your flesh with the *t* of the wilderness
Job 41:2 or bore his jaw through with a *t*?
Prov. 15:19 way of the slothful . . is as a hedge of *t*
 24:31 it was all grown over with *t*, and nettles
 26:9 as a *t* goeth up into the hand of a drunkard
Eccl. 7:6 as the crackling of *t* under a pot, so is
Song 2:2 as the lily among *t*, so is my love among
Is. 55:13 instead of the *t* shall come up the fir
Jer. 4:3 your fallow ground, and sow not among *t*
 12:13 they have sown wheat, but shall reap *t*
Hos. 2:6 behold, I will hedge up thy ways with *t*
 10:8 *t* and the thistle shall come up on their
Mic. 7:4 most upright is sharper than a *t* hedge
Mt. 7:16 (Lk. 6:44) do men gather grapes of *t*
 13:7 (Mk. 4:7; Lk. 8:7) fell among *t*. . the *t* sprung
 27:29 (Mk. 15:17; Jn. 19:2) platted a crown of *t*

2 Cor. 12:7 there was given to me a *t* in the flesh
Heb. 6:8 that which beareth *t* and briers is rejected

Thought (verb) *See* Think

Thought (noun) *See also* Device, Imagination

Deut. 15:9 there be not a *t* in thy wicked heart
Job 4:13 in *t* from the visions of the night
  17:11 are broken off, even the *t* of my heart
  21:27 I know your *t*, and the devices which ye
  42:2 and that no *t* can be withholden from thee
Ps. 10:4 seek after God: God is not in all his *t*
  40:5 thy *t* which are to us-ward: they cannot be
  56:5 wrest my words: all their *t* are against me
  92:5 great are thy works! and thy *t* are very deep
  94:11 (1 Cor. 3:20) the LORD knoweth the *t* of man
  119:113 I hate vain *t*: but thy law do I love
  139:2 thou understandest my *t* afar off
  139:17 how precious. . are thy *t* unto me, O God!
  139:23 and know my heart: try me, and know my *t*
  146:4 to his earth; in that very day his *t* perish
Prov. 12:5 the *t* of the righteous are right
  15:26 *t* of the wicked. . abomination to the LORD
  16:3 unto the LORD. . thy *t* shall be established
Is. 55:7 forsake his way. . the unrighteous man his *t*
  55:8 my *t* are not your *t*, neither are your ways
  59:7 feet run to evil. . their *t* are *t* of iniquity
  66:18 I know their works and their *t*: it shall
Jer. 4:14 how long shall thy vain *t* lodge within
  6:19 will bring evil. . even the fruit of their *t*
  29:11 *t* that I think. . *t* of peace, and not of evil
Ezek. 38:10 and thou shalt think an evil *t*
Dan. 2:30 thou mightest know the *t* of thy heart
Amos 4:13 and declareth unto man what is his *t*
Mic. 4:12 but they know not the *t* of the LORD
Mt. 6:25 (Lk. 12:22) take no *t* for your life
  6:34 morrow shall take *t* for the things of itself
  9:4 (Lk. 5:22) and Jesus knowing their *t* said
  10:19 (Mk. 13:11; Lk. 12:11) no *t* how. . ye. . speak
  12:25 (Lk. 11:17) Jesus knew their *t*, and said
  15:19 (Mk. 7:21) out of the heart proceed evil *t*
Lk. 2:35 that the *t* of many hearts may be revealed
  6:8 he knew their *t*, and said to the man. . Rise up
  9:47 Jesus, perceiving the *t* of their heart, took
  24:38 troubled? and why do *t* arise in your hearts?
Acts 8:22 the *t* of thine heart may be forgiven thee
Rom. 2:15 and their *t*. . accusing or else excusing
2 Cor. 10:5 every *t* to the obedience of Christ
Heb. 4:12 discerner of the *t* and intents of the heart
Jas. 2:4 partial. . and are become judges of evil *t*?

Thousand

Ex. 20:6 (Deut. 5:10) showing mercy unto *t* of them
1 Sam. 18:7 (21:11; 29:5) slain his *t*. . David his ten *t*
Ps. 3:6 I will not be afraid of ten *t* of people
  84:10 for a day in thy courts is better than a *t*
  90:4 a *t* years in thy sight are but as yesterday
Eccl. 7:28 one man among a *t* have I found
Is. 60:22 a little one shall become a *t*, and a small
Jer. 32:18 thou showest loving-kindness unto *t*
Dan. 7:10 *t t* ministered before him, and ten *t* times
Mic. 5:2 though thou be little among the *t* of Judah
2 Pet. 3:8 as a *t* years, and a *t* years as one day
Rev. 5:11 number. . was ten *t* times ten *t*, and *t* of *t*
  20:2 which is. . Satan, and bound him a *t* years
  20:4 they lived and reigned with Christ a *t* years

Thread

Gen. 14:23 not take from a *t* even to a shoe-latchet
Josh. 2:18 bind this line of scarlet *t* in the window

Judg. 16:9 brake the withes, as a *t* of tow is broken
Song 4:3 thy lips are like a *t* of scarlet

Threaten

Acts 4:17 spread no further. . let us straitly *t* them
1 Pet. 2:23 he suffered, he *t* not; but committed

Threatening

Acts 4:29 Lord, behold their *t*: and grant unto thy
  9:1 and Saul, yet breathing out *t* and slaughter
Eph. 6:9 forbearing *t*: knowing that your Master

Three *See also* Thrice

Mt. 17:4 (Mk. 9:5; Lk. 9:33) make here *t* tabernacles
  18:20 two or *t* are gathered together in my name
1 Cor. 13:13 abideth faith, hope, charity, these *t*
1 Jn. 5:7 *t* that bear record in heaven. . *t* are one
  5:8 *t* that bear witness in earth. . *t* agree in one

Thresh

Judg. 6:11 his son Gideon *t* wheat by the winepress
Is. 28:27 fitches. . not *t* with a threshing instrument
  41:15 thou shalt *t* the mountains, and beat them
Jer. 51:33 daughter of Babylon. . it is time to *t* her
Amos 1:3 *t* Gilead with threshing instruments of iron
Mic. 4:13 arise and *t*, O daughter of Zion
Hab. 3:12 thou didst *t* the heathen in anger
1 Cor. 9:10 he that *t* in hope should be partaker

Threshing

Lev. 26:5 and your *t* shall reach unto the vintage
2 Kgs. 13:7 and had made them like the dust by *t*
Is. 21:10 O my *t*, and the corn of my floor
  41:15 I will make thee a new sharp *t* instrument

Threshingfloor

Ruth 3:2 he winnoweth barley tonight in the *t*
1 Sam. 23:1 fight against Keilah, and they rob the *t*
2 Sam. 24:18 (1 Chr. 21:18) rear an altar. . in the *t*
Jer. 51:33 the daughter of Babylon is like a *t*
Dan. 2:35 became like the chaff of the summer *t*

Threshold *See also* Door

1 Sam. 5:4 palms of his hands. . cut off upon the *t*
Ezek. 9:3 glory of the God. . was gone up. . to the *t*
  43:8 in their setting of their *t* by my *t*
  47:1 behold, waters issued out from under the *t*
Zeph. 1:9 I punish all those that leap on the *t*
  2:14 desolation shall be in the *t*: for he shall

Threw *See* Throw

Thrice *See also* Three

Ex. 34:23 *t* in the year shall all your men children
Mt. 26:34 (Mk. 14:30; Lk. 22:34; Jn. 13:38) deny me *t*
Acts 10:16 this was done *t*: and the vessel was
2 Cor. 11:25 *t* was I beaten. . *t* I suffered shipwreck
  12:8 for this thing I besought the Lord *t*

Throat

Ps. 5:9 (Rom. 3:13) their *t* is an open sepulchre
  115:7 neither speak they through their *t*
Mt. 18:28 took him by the *t*, saying, Pay me that

Throne

Gen. 41:40 in the *t* will I be greater than thou
1 Sam. 2:8 and to make them inherit the *t* of glory
1 Kgs. 1:13 (1:17, 30) Solomon. . shall sit upon my *t*?
  1:37 make his *t* greater than the *t* of my lord
  10:18 (2 Chr. 9:17) king made a great *t* of ivory
  22:19 (2 Chr. 18:18) I saw the LORD sitting on his *t*
1 Chr. 29:23 then Solomon sat on the *t* of the LORD
Ps. 9:7 he hath prepared his *t* for judgment

Ps. 11:4 the LORD's *t* is in heaven: his eyes behold
45:6 (Heb. 1:8) thy *t*, O God, is for ever
47:8 God sitteth upon the *t* of his holiness
89:14 justice and judgment. . habitation of thy *t*
94:20 shall the *t* of iniquity have fellowship
103:19 LORD hath prepared his *t* in the heavens
122:5 *t* of judgment, the *t* of the house of David
132:11 (Acts 2:30) body will I set upon thy *t*
Prov. 16:12 for the *t* is established by righteousness
20:28 the king: and his *t* is upholden by mercy
25:5 his *t* shall be established in righteousness
Is. 6:1 I saw also the Lord sitting upon a *t*, high
14:13 I will exalt my *t* above the stars of God
66:1 (Acts 7:49) heaven is my *t*, and the earth is
Jer. 3:17 shall call Jerusalem the *t* of the LORD
14:21 do not disgrace the *t* of thy glory
17:12 a glorious high *t* from the beginning is
43:10 and will set his *t* upon these stones
Lam. 5:19 thy *t* from generation to generation
Dan. 7:9 I beheld till the *t* were cast down
Hag. 2:22 I will overthrow the *t* of kingdoms
Mt. 5:34 (23:22) by heaven; for it is God's *t*
19:28 *t* of his glory, ye. . shall sit upon twelve *t*
25:31 then shall he sit upon the *t* of his glory
Lk. 1:32 give unto him the *t* of his father David
22:30 sit on *t* judging the twelve tribes of Israel
Col. 1:16 whether they be *t*, or dominions
Heb. 4:16 let us. . come boldly unto the *t* of grace
8:1 set on the right hand of the *t* of the Majesty
12:2 set down at the right hand of the *t* of God
Rev. 3:21 will I grant to sit with me in my *t*
4:2 a *t* was set in heaven, and one sat on the *t*
7:9 stood before the *t*, and before the Lamb
7:17 Lamb. . in the midst of the *t* shall feed them
12:5 child was caught up unto God, and to his *t*
19:5 a voice came out of the *t*, saying, Praise
20:4 I saw *t*, and they that sat upon them
20:11 I saw a great white *t*, and him that sat on
21:5 he that sat upon the *t* said, Behold, I make
22:1 proceeding out of the *t* of God and of the
22:3 the *t* of God and of the Lamb shall be in it

Throng

Mk. 3:9 of the multitude, lest they should *t* him
5:24 (Lk. 8:42) people followed him, and *t* him

Throw (Threw, Thrown) See also Cast

Ex. 15:1 horse and his rider hath he *t* into the sea
Judg. 2:2 ye shall *t* down their altars: but ye
6:32 Jerubbaal. . because he hath *t* down his altar
Jer. 1:10 and to *t* down, to build, and to plant
Ezek. 16:39 they shall *t* down thine eminent place
Mic. 5:11 thy land, and *t* down all thy strongholds
Mt. 24:2 (Mk. 13:2; Lk. 21:6) that shall not be *t* down
Mk. 12:42 a certain poor widow. . she *t* in two mites
Lk. 4:35 when the devil had *t* him in the midst
9:42 a coming, the devil *t* him down, and tare him
Acts 22:23 they cried out. . and *t* dust into the air
Rev. 18:21 with violence shall. . Babylon be *t* down

Thrust

Deut. 13:10 sought to *t* thee away from the LORD
1 Sam. 11:2 that I may *t* out all your right eyes
Job 32:13 ye should say. . God *t* him down, not man
Ps. 118:13 hast *t* sore at me that I might fall
Joel 2:8 neither shall one *t* another; they shall
Lk. 4:29 rose up, and *t* him out of the city
10:15 exalted to heaven, shalt be *t* down to hell
13:28 in the kingdom. . and you yourselves *t* out
Jn. 20:25 except I shall. . *t* my hand into his side
Acts 16:24 a charge, *t* them into the inner prison
27:39 creek with a shore. . to *t* in the ship
Heb. 12:20 be stoned, or *t* through with a dart
Rev. 14:15 *t* in thy sickle, and reap: for the time

Thummim See also Urim

Ex. 28:30 (Lev. 8:8) breastplate. . the Urim and the *T*
Deut. 33:8 thy *T* and thy Urim be with thy holy one
Ezra 2:63 (Neh. 7:65) a priest with Urim and with *T*

Thunder

Ex. 9:23 the LORD sent *t* and hail, and the fire
1 Sam. 7:10 LORD *t* with a great *t* on that day upon
12:17 will call unto the LORD, and he shall send *t*
2 Sam. 22:14 (Ps. 18:13) the LORD *t* from heaven
Job 26:14 the *t* of his power who can understand?
37:4 he *t* with the voice of his excellency
37:5 God *t* marvelously with his voice
39:19 hast thou clothed his neck with *t*?
40:9 or canst thou *t* with a voice like him?
Ps. 29:3 God of glory *t*. . LORD is upon many waters
77:18 the voice of thy *t* was in the heaven
81:7 I answered thee in the secret place of *t*
104:7 at the voice of thy *t* they hasted away
Is. 29:6 be visited of the LORD of hosts with *t*
Mk. 3:17 Boanerges, which is, The sons of *t*
Jn. 12:29 said that it *t*: others said, An angel spake
Rev. 10:3 had cried, seven *t* uttered their voices
14:2 voice from heaven. . as the voice of a great *t*
16:18 there were voices, and *t*, and lightnings

Thundering See also Lightning

Ex. 9:28 be no more mighty *t* and hail; and I will
20:18 the people saw the *t*, and the lightnings
Rev. 4:5 proceeded lightnings and *t* and voices
8:5 (11:19) there were voices, and *t*, and lightnings
19:6 as the voice of mighty *t*, saying, Alleluia

Thyatira Acts 16:14; Rev. 2:18, 24

Tiberias See also Galilee Jn. 6:1, 23; 21:1

Tiberius Caesar Lk. 3:1

Tidings See also Gospel, Promise, Word

Ex. 33:4 people heard these evil *t*, they mourned
1 Sam. 11:4 to Gibeah of Saul, and told the *t*
2 Sam. 13:30 *t* came to David, saying, Absalom hath
18:19 let me now run, and bear the king *t*
1 Kgs. 14:6 for I am sent to thee with heavy *t*
2 Kgs. 7:9 do not well: this day is a day of good *t*
Ps. 112:7 he shall not be afraid of evil *t*
Is. 40:9 O Zion, that bringest good *t*, get thee up
52:7 (Nah. 1:15) feet of him that bringeth good *t*
61:1 anointed me to preach good *t* unto the meek
Jer. 20:15 cursed. . man who brought *t* to my father
Dan. 11:44 *t* out of the east and out of the north
Nah. 1:15 feet of him that bringeth good *t*
Lk. 1:19 and am sent. . to show thee these glad *t*
2:10 for, behold, I bring you good *t* of great joy
8:1 and showing the glad *t* of the kingdom of God
Acts 11:22 of these things came unto. . the church
13:32 we declare unto you glad *t*, how that the
Rom. 10:15 gospel of peace. . glad *t* of good things!
1 Thes. 3:6 brought us good *t* of your faith

Tied See also Bound

2 Kgs. 7:10 was no man. . but horses *t*, and asses *t*
Mt. 21:2 (Mk. 11:2; Lk. 19:30) shall find an ass *t*

Tiglath-pileser (Pul)

Received tribute from Menaham, 2 Kgs. 15:19–20;
carried the people captive to Assyria, 2 Kgs. 15:29;
paid homage by Ahaz, 2 Kgs. 16:7–10 (2 Chr. 28:20–21); deported the tribes of Israel, 1 Chr. 5:26.

Tile

Ezek. 4:1 take thee a *t*, and lay it before thee
Lk. 5:19 let him down through the *t* with his couch

Till

Gen. 2:5 and there was not a man to *t* the ground
  3:23 sent him forth from the garden of Eden, to *t*
Prov. 12:11 he that *t* his land shall be satisfied
  28:19 that *t* his land shall have plenty of bread
Ezek. 36:9 turn unto you. . ye shall be *t* and sown

Tiller

Gen. 4:2 but Cain was a *t* of the ground

Timber *See also* Wood

1 Kgs. 5:6 skill to hew *t* like unto the Sidonians
  5:18 (2 Chr. 2:9) prepared *t* . . to build the house
Neh. 2:8 king's forest, that he may give me *t*

Timbrel

Ex. 15:20 a *t* in her hand; and all the women. . with *t*
Judg. 11:34 daughter came out to meet him with *t*
Ps. 149:3 sing praises unto him with the *t*
  150:4 praise him with the *t* and dance

Time *See also* Day, Eternity, Generation, Hour, Season

Gen. 21:2 at the set *t* of which God had spoken to
Ex. 9:5 LORD appointed a set *t*, saying, Tomorrow
  21:19 only he shall pay for the loss of his *t*
Lev. 19:26 neither. . use enchantment, nor observe *t*
Deut. 18:10 or an observer of *t*, or an enchanter
2 Kgs. 5:10 go and wash in Jordan seven *t*
  21:6 (2 Chr. 33:6) observed *t* . . used enchantments
1 Chr. 12:32 men that had understanding of the *t*
Esth. 4:14 come to the kingdom for such a *t* as this?
Job 7:1 is there not an appointed *t* to man upon
  14:14 all the days of my appointed *t* will I wait
  24:1 seeing *t* are not hidden from the Almighty
Ps. 31:15 my *t* are in thy hand: deliver me from the
  32:6 godly pray. . in a *t* when thou mayest be found
  34:1 I will bless the LORD at all *t*: his praise
  62:8 trust in him at all *t*; ye people, pour out
  69:13 my prayer is unto thee. . in an acceptable *t*
  89:47 remember how short my *t* is: wherefore hast
  119:126 it is *t* for thee, LORD, to work: for they
Eccl. 3:1 (3:17; 8:6) and a *t* to every purpose
  3:11 he hath made every thing beautiful in his *t*
  3:17 a *t* there for every purpose and for every
  8:6 to every purpose there is *t* and judgment
  9:11 but *t* and chance happeneth to them all
  9:12 man also knoweth not his *t*: as the fishes
Is. 33:6 knowledge shall be the stability of thy *t*
  49:8 (2 Cor. 6:2) in an acceptable *t* have I heard
  60:22 nation: I the LORD will hasten it in his *t*
Jer. 8:7 yea, the stork. . knoweth her appointed *t*
  46:21 upon them, and the *t* of their visitation
  51:33 *t* to thresh. . *t* of her harvest shall come
Ezek. 7:7 the *t* is come, the day of trouble is near
  12:27 he prophesieth of the *t* that are far off
  30:3 cloudy day; it shall be the *t* of the heathen
Dan. 7:25 he shall. . think to change *t* and laws
  8:19 (11:27) at the *t* appointed the end shall be
  11:35 to the *t* of the end. . yet for a *t* appointed
  12:7 it shall be for a *t*, *t*, and a half; and when
Hos. 10:12 it is *t* to seek the LORD, till he come
Amos 5:13 silence in that *t*; for it is an evil *t*
Mt. 8:29 come hither to torment us before the *t*?
  16:3 (Lk. 12:56) not discern the signs of the *t*?
  18:22 until seven *t*: but, Until seventy *t* seven
  26:18 the Master saith, My *t* is at hand
Mk. 1:15 the *t* is fulfilled, and the kingdom of God
  10:30 (Lk. 18:30) receive a hundredfold. . in this *t*
  13:33 watch and pray: for ye know not when the *t*
Lk. 9:51 *t* was come that he should be received up
  19:44 thou knewest not the *t* of thy visitation

Lk. 21:8 saying, I am Christ; and the *t* draweth near
  21:24 until the *t* of the Gentiles be fulfilled
Jn. 1:18 (1 Jn. 4:12) no man hath seen God at any *t*
  7:6 my *t* is not yet come: but your *t* is. . ready
Acts 1:6 Lord, will thou at this *t* restore again
  17:21 spent their *t* in nothing else, but either
  17:26 and hath determined the *t* before appointed
Rom. 5:6 in due *t* Christ died for the ungodly
  13:11 knowing the *t*, that now it is high *t* to
1 Cor. 4:5 judge nothing before the *t*, until the
  7:29 but this I say, brethren, the *t* is short
  15:8 seen of me also, as of one born out of due *t*
2 Cor. 6:2 behold, now is the accepted *t*
Gal. 4:4 when the fulness of the *t* was come, God sent
  4:10 observe days, and months, and *t*, and years
Eph. 1:10 in the dispensation of the fulness of *t*
  5:16 redeeming the *t*, because the days are evil
Col. 4:5 walk in wisdom. . redeeming the *t*
1 Thes. 5:1 but of the *t* and the seasons, brethren
2 Thes. 2:6 that he might be revealed in his *t*
1 Tim. 6:19 good foundation against the *t* to come
2 Tim. 3:1 in the last days perilous *t* shall come
  4:3 for the *t* will come when they will not endure
  4:6 offered, and the *t* of my departure is at hand
Tit. 1:3 hath in due *t* manifested his word through
Heb. 1:1 God, who at sundry *t* and in divers manners
  9:28 shall he appear the second *t* without sin
1 Pet. 1:5 ready to be revealed in the last *t*
  1:20 but was manifest in these last *t* for you
  5:6 humble yourselves. . he may exalt you in due *t*
1 Jn. 2:18 little children, it is the last *t*
  4:12 no man hath seen God at any *t*
Rev. 1:3 keep those things. . for the *t* is at hand
  10:6 therein, that there should be *t* no longer
  12:12 devil. . knoweth that he hath but a short *t*
  12:14 is nourished for a *t*, and *t*, and half a *t*
  14:15 reap: for the *t* is come for thee to reap
  22:10 seal not the sayings. . for the *t* is at hand

Timnath Gen. 38:12; Judg. 14:1

Timothy (Timotheus)

"Beloved son" of Paul, 1 Cor. 4:17; 1 Tim. 1:2, 18; 2 Tim. 1:2; son of a Greek father and a Jewish mother, Acts 16:1; brought up in a devout home, 2 Tim. 1:5; 3:14–15; lived in Lystra (or Derbe), Acts 16:1; circumcised, Acts 16:3; accompanied Paul in the second missionary journey, Acts 16:1–4; 17:14–15; 18:5; 1 Thes. 3:2–6; ordained, 1 Tim. 4:14; 2 Tim. 1:6; sent to the church in Corinth, 1 Cor. 4:17; 16:10; escorted Paul in the third missionary journey, Acts 20:4; in charge of the church in Ephesus, 1 Tim. 1:3; 4:12; urged by Paul to visit him in prison, 2 Tim. 4:9, 13; imprisoned and released, Heb. 13:23.

Tin

Is. 1:25 purge away thy dross. . take away all thy *t*
Ezek. 22:18 become dross: all they are brass, and *t*

Tingle

1 Sam. 3:11 ears of every one that heareth it shall *t*
Jer. 19:3 whosoever heareth, his ears shall *t*

Tinkling

Is. 3:18 of their *t* ornaments about their feet
1 Cor. 13:1 become as sounding brass, or a *t* cymbal

Tire

Is. 3:18 take away. . their round *t* like the moon

Tishbite 1 Kgs. 17:1

Tithe *See also* Offering, Tenth

Gen. 14:20 blessed be. . God. . he gave him *t* of all
Lev. 27:30 all the *t* of the land. . is the LORD'S
   27:31 if a man will at all redeem aught of his *t*
Num. 18:24 but the *t*. . I have given to the Levites
   18:26 heave offering. . even a tenth part of the *t*
Deut. 12:17 mayest not eat within thy gates the *t*
   14:22 shalt truly *t* all the increase of thy seed
   14:28 end of three years. . bring forth all the *t*
   26:12 hast made an end of tithing all the *t*
2 Chr. 31:5 the *t* of all things brought they in
Neh. 10:37 the *t* of our ground unto the Levites
   10:38 Levites shall bring up the *t* of the *t* unto
Amos 4:4 bring. . your *t* after three years
Mal. 3:8 have we robbed thee? In *t* and offerings
   3:10 bring ye all the *t* into the storehouse
Mt. 23:23 (Lk. 11:42) for ye pay *t* of mint and anise
Lk. 18:12 I fast. . I give *t* of all that I possess
Heb. 7:5 have a commandment to take *t* of the people
   7:6 not counted from them received *t* of Abraham
   7:8 here men that die receive *t*; but there he
   7:9 Levi also, who receiveth *t*, paid *t* in Abraham

Title

2 Kgs. 23:17 what *t* is that that I see? And the men
Job 32:21 neither let me give flattering *t* unto man
Jn. 19:19 Pilate wrote a *t*, and put it on the cross

Tittle

Mt. 5:18 (Lk. 16:17) one *t*. . pass from the law

Titus

2 Cor. 2:13 I had no rest. . because I found not *T*
   7:6 comforted us by the coming of *T*
   8:16 earnest care into the heart of *T* for you
   8:23 any do inquire of *T*, he is my partner
   12:18 I desired *T*. . Did *T* make a gain of you?
Gal. 2:1 went up again to Jerusalem. . took *T* with me
Tit. 1:4 to *T*, mine own son after the common faith

Tob Judg. 11:3

Tobiah Neh. 2:10–13:8

Today

Ex. 14:13 salvation. . which he will show to you *t*
2 Kgs. 6:28 give thy son, that we may eat him *t*
Ps. 95:7 (Heb. 3:7, 15; 4:7) *t* if ye will hear his voice
Lk. 13:33 nevertheless I must walk *t*, and tomorrow
   23:43 I say. . *T* shalt thou be with me in paradise
Heb. 3:13 one another daily, while it is called *T*
   5:5 thou art my Son, *t* have I begotten thee
   13:8 Christ the same yesterday, and *t*, and for ever

Toe

Judg. 1:6 and cut off his thumbs and his great *t*
2 Sam. 21:20 six fingers, and on every foot six *t*
Dan. 2:41 *t*, part of potters' clay. . part of iron

Toi king of Hamath 2 Sam. 8:9 (1 Chr. 18:9)

Toil *See also* Labor, Work, Wrought

Gen. 5:29 comfort us concerning our work and *t*
Mt. 6:28 (Lk. 12:27) consider the lilies. . they *t* not,
   neither do they spin
Mk. 6:48 he saw them *t* in rowing; for the wind was
Lk. 5:5 *t* all the night, and have taken nothing

Token *See also* Sign

Gen. 9:12 God said, This is the *t* of the covenant
Ex. 3:12 be a *t* unto thee, that I have sent thee
   12:13 and the blood shall be to you for a *t*
Job 21:29 by the way? and do ye not know their *t*

Ps. 65:8 the uttermost parts are afraid at thy *t*
   86:17 show me a *t* for good; that they which hate
   135:9 sent *t* and wonders into the midst of thee
Mk. 14:44 he that betrayed him had given them a *t*
2 Thes. 1:5 a manifest *t* of the righteous judgment

Told *See* Tell

Tolerable

Mt. 10:15 (Mk. 6:11; Lk. 10:12) more *t* for. . Sodom
   11:22 (Lk. 10:14) more *t* for Tyre and Sidon

Toll *See also* Tribute

Ezra 4:13 walls set up. . then will they not pay *t*
   7:24 it shall not be lawful to impose *t*

Tomb *See also* Grave, Sepulchre

Mt. 8:28 (Mk. 5:2; Lk. 8:27) coming out of the *t*
   23:29 because ye build the *t* of the prophets
   27:60 laid it in his own new *t*, which he had hewn
Mk. 6:29 took up his corpse, and laid it in a *t*

Tomorrow *See also* Morrow

Prov. 27:1 boast not thyself of *t*; for thou knowest
Is. 22:13 (1 Cor. 15:32) and drink. . *t* we shall die

Tongs

Is. 6:6 he had taken with the *t* from of the altar

Tongue *See also* Language, Mouth,
   Speech

Job 5:21 shalt be hid from the scourge of the *t*
   20:12 wickedness. . though he hide it under his *t*
   29:10 their *t* cleaved to the roof of their mouth
Ps. 10:7 fraud: under his *t* is mischief and vanity
   34:13 (1 Pet. 3:10) keep thy *t* from evil
   35:28 my *t* shall speak of thy righteousness
   39:1 heed to my ways, that I sin not with my *t*
   45:1 I speak. . my *t* is the pen of a ready writer
   52:2 thy *t* deviseth mischiefs; like a sharp razor
   55:9 destroy, O Lord, and divide their *t*
   73:9 and their *t* walketh through the earth
   120:3 what shall be done unto thee, thou false *t*?
   137:6 let my *t* cleave to the roof of my mouth
Prov. 10:20 the *t* of the just is as choice silver
   10:31 but the froward *t* shall be cut out
   12:18 a sword: but the *t* of the wise is health
   12:19 for ever: but a lying *t* is but for a moment
   15:4 a wholesome *t* is a tree of life
   18:21 death and life are in the power of the *t*
   25:15 persuaded, and a soft *t* breaketh the bone
   31:26 and in her *t* is the law of kindness
Is. 28:11 (1 Cor. 14:21) stammering lips and another *t*
   30:27 indignation, and his *t* as a devouring fire
   45:23 (Rom. 14:11) shall bow, every *t* shall swear
   50:4 Lord GOD hath given me the *t* of the learned
   54:17 *t* that shall rise against thee in judgment
Jer. 9:8 their *t* is as an arrow shot out
   18:18 come, and let us smite him with the *t*
Mk. 7:35 string of his *t* was loosed, and he spake
   16:17 in my name. . they shall speak with new *t*
Acts 2:4 began to speak with other *t*, as the Spirit
   19:6 Holy Ghost came on them. . they spake with *t*
1 Cor. 12:10 to another divers kinds of *t*; to another
   13:1 I speak with the *t* of men and of angels
   13:8 whether there be *t*, they shall cease
   14:2 for he that speaketh in an unknown *t*
   14:18 I speak with *t* more than ye all
   14:22 *t* are for a sign, not to them that believe
Phil. 2:11 that every *t* should confess that Jesus
Jas. 1:26 to be religious, and bridleth not his *t*
   3:5 the *t* is a little member, and boasteth great

Jas. 3:8 the *t* can no man tame; it is an unruly evil
1 Jn. 3:18 let us not love in word, neither in *t*

Took *See* Take

Tool *See also* Instrument

Ex. 20:25 lift up thy *t* upon it, thou hast polluted
Deut. 27:5 shalt not lift up any iron *t* upon them
1 Kgs. 6:7 nor any *t* of iron heard in the house

Tooth *See also* Teeth

Ex. 21:24 (Lev. 24:20; Deut. 19:21; Mt. 5:38) *t* for *t*
21:27 he shall let him go free for his *t*'s sake
Prov. 25:19 like a broken *t*. . a foot out of joint

Top

Gen. 11:4 a tower, whose *t* may reach unto heaven
28:12 a ladder. . the *t* of it reached to heaven
2 Sam. 5:24 (1 Chr. 14:15) the *t* of the mulberry trees
Is. 2:2 (Mic. 4:1) established in the *t* of the mountains
Ezek. 17:4 he cropped off the *t* of his young twigs

Topaz

Ex. 28:17 (39:10) first row shall be a sardius, a *t*
Job 28:19 the *t* of Ethiopia shall not equal it
Ezek. 28:13 was thy covering, the sardius, *t*
Rev. 21:20 ninth, a *t*; the tenth, a chrysoprasus

Tophet (Topheth)

2 Kgs. 23:10 he defiled *T*. . in the valley of. . Hinnom
Is. 30:33 *T* is ordained of old; yea, for the king
Jer. 7:31 they have built the high places of *T*
7:32 (19:11) bury in *T*, till there be no place

Torch

Nah. 2:3 the chariots shall be with flaming *t* in
Jn. 18:3 cometh. . with lanterns and *t* and weapons

Tore *See* Tear

Torment

Mt. 4:24 were taken v. ith divers diseases and *t*
8:29 (Mk. 5:7; Lk. 8:28) thou come hither to *t* us
Lk. 16:23 in hell. . being in *t*, and seeth Abraham
Heb. 11:37 wandered. . being destitute, afflicted, *t*
1 Jn. 4:18 casteth out fear: because fear hath *t*
Rev. 9:5 be *t* five months: and their *t* was as the *t*
14:10 he shall be *t* with fire and brimstone
14:11 the smoke of their *t* ascendeth up for ever
20:10 devil. . shall be *t* day and night for ever

Torn *See* Tear

Torture

Heb. 11:35 others were *t*, not accepting deliverance

Toss

Job 7:4 I am full of *t* to and fro unto the dawning
Ps. 109:23 am gone. . am *t* up and down as the locust
Is. 22:18 *t* thee like a ball into a large country
Jer. 5:22 though the waves thereof *t* themselves
Acts 27:18 we being exceedingly *t* with a tempest

Tossed

Is. 54:11 O thou afflicted, *t* with tempest, and not
Mt. 14:24 in the midst of the sea, *t* with waves
Eph. 4:14 be no more children, *t* to and fro

Tottering

Ps. 62:3 as a bowing wall. . and as a *t* fence

Touch

Gen. 3:3 shall not eat of it, neither shall ye *t* it

1 Sam. 10:26 a band of men, whose hearts God had *t*
1 Chr. 16:22 (Ps. 105:15) saying, *T* not mine anointed
Job 2:5 *t* his bone and his flesh, and he will curse
5:19 yea, in seven there shall no evil *t* thee
19:21 pity upon me. . the hand of God hath *t* me
Ps. 104:32 trembleth: he *t* the hills, and they smoke
Is. 6:7 this hath *t* thy lips; and thine iniquity is
52:11 (2 Cor. 6:17) go ye out. . *t* no unclean thing
Jer. 1:9 LORD put forth his hand, and *t* my mouth
Zech. 2:8 he that *t* you, *t* the apple of his eye
Mt. 8:3 (Mk. 1:41; Lk. 5:13) *t* him, saying, I will
8:15 and he *t* her hand, and the fever left her
9:21 (Mk. 5:28; Lk. 8:44) if I may but *t* his garment
9:29 (Mk. 6:56) *t* he their eyes, saying, According
14:36 (Mk. 6:56) only *t* the hem of his garment
Mk. 5:30 (Lk. 8:45) Jesus. . said, Who *t* my clothes?
10:13 (Lk. 18:15) children. . that he should *t* them
Lk. 11:46 ye yourselves *t* not the burdens with one
22:51 and he *t* his ear, and healed him
Jn. 20:17 *t* me not; for I am not yet ascended to
Col. 2:21 *t* not; taste not; handle not
Heb. 12:18 not come unto the mount that might be *t*
1 Jn. 5:18 keepeth himself. . wicked one *t* him not

Tow

Judg. 16:9 a thread of *t*. . when it toucheth the fire
Is. 1:31 the strong shall be as *t*, and the maker
43:17 they are extinct, they are quenched as *t*

Towel

Jn. 13:4 and laid aside his garments; and took a *t*

Tower

Gen. 11:4 go to, let us build us a city, and a *t*
Judg. 8:17 he beat down the *t* of Penuel, and slew
9:46 when all the men of the *t* of Shechem heard
2 Sam. 22:3 (Ps. 18:2) of my salvation, my high *t*
22:51 he is the *t* of salvation for his king
Ps. 61:3 shelter for me. . a strong *t* from the enemy
144:2 my goodness, and my fortress; my high *t*
Prov. 18:10 the name of the LORD is a strong *t*
Is. 5:2 choicest vine, and built a *t* in the midst
32:14 the forts and *t* shall be for dens for ever
33:18 receiver? where is he that counted the *t*?
Jer. 6:27 I have set thee for a *t* and a fortress
Mic. 4:8 thou, O *t* of the flock, the stronghold of
Hab. 2:1 set me upon the *t*, and will watch to see
Zeph. 3:6 cut off the nations: their *t* are desolate
Mt. 21:33 (Mk. 12:1) digged a winepress. . built a *t*
Lk. 13:4 eighteen, upon whom the *t* in Siloam fell
14:28 for which of you, intending to build a *t*

Town *See also* City, Village

Mk. 8:26 neither go into the *t*, nor tell. . in the *t*
Lk. 5:17 which were come out of every *t* of Galilee
9:6 departed, and went through the *t*, preaching

Townclerk

Acts 19:35 and when the *t* had appeased the people

Trade

Gen. 46:32 for their *t* hath been to feed cattle
Ezek. 27:17 they *t* in thy market wheat of Minnith
Mt. 25:16 had received the five talents went and *t*
Lk. 19:15 know how much every man had gained by *t*
Rev. 18:17 and as many as *t* by sea, stood afar off

Tradition

Mt. 15:2 (Mk. 7:5) thy disciples transgress the *t*
15:6 (Mk. 7:13) of none effect by your *t*
Mk. 7:8 commandment of God, ye hold the *t* of men
Gal. 1:14 being more exceedingly zealous of the *t*
Col. 2:8 after the *t* of men, after the rudiments

2 Thes. 2:15 hold the *t* which ye have been taught
3:6 and not after the *t* which he received of us
1 Pet. 1:18 your vain conversation received by *t*

Traffic

Gen. 42:34 your brother, and ye shall *t* in the land
Ezek. 28:5 by thy *t* hast thou increased thy riches

Trafficker

Is. 23:8 whose *t* are the honorable of the earth?

Train (noun)

1 Kgs. 10:2 came to Jerusalem with a very great *t*
Is. 6:1 high and lifted up . . his *t* filled the temple

Train (verb)

Prov. 22:6 *t* up a child in the way he should go

Traitor

Lk. 6:16 and Judas Iscariot, which also was the *t*
2 Tim. 3:4 *t*, heady . . lovers of pleasures more than

Trample See also Tread

Ps. 91:13 lion and . . dragon shalt thou *t* under feet
Is. 63:3 in mine anger, and *t* them in my fury
Mt. 7:6 swine, lest they *t* them under their feet

Trance See also Dream, Vision

Num. 24:4 vision of the Almighty, falling into a *t*
Acts 10:10 while they made ready, he fell into a *t*
11:5 city of Joppa praying: and in a *t* I saw
22:17 while I prayed in the temple, I was in a *t*

Tranquillity

Dan. 4:27 if it may be a lengthening of thy *t*

Transfigure

Mt. 17:2 (Mk. 9:2) was *t* before them: and his face

Transform

Rom. 12:2 but be ye *t* by the renewing of your mind
2 Cor. 11:13 *t* themselves into the apostles of Christ
11:14 Satan himself is *t* into an angel of light
11:15 also be *t* as the ministers of righteousness

Transgress See also Offend, Sin, Trespass

Num. 14:41 wherefore . . do ye *t* the commandment
Josh. 7:11 Israel hath sinned . . also *t* my covenant
23:16 when ye have *t* the covenant of the LORD
Judg. 2:20 this people hath *t* my covenant which I
1 Sam. 2:24 sons . . ye make the LORD's people to *t*
14:33 eat with the blood. And he said, Ye have *t*
15:24 for I have *t* the commandment of the LORD
2 Kgs. 18:12 they obeyed not . . but *t* his covenant
1 Chr. 5:25 they *t* against the God of their fathers
2 Chr. 24:20 why *t* ye . . commandments of the LORD
Ezra 10:10 ye have *t*, and have taken strange wives
Neh. 1:8 if ye *t*, I will scatter you abroad among
13:27 *t* against our God in marrying strange wives?
Ps. 17:3 I am purposed that my mouth shall not *t*
25:3 let them be ashamed which *t* without cause
Is. 24:5 have *t* the laws, changed the ordinance
43:27 sinned, and thy teachers have *t* against me
59:13 in *t* and lying against the LORD
66:24 carcasses of the men that have *t* against me
Jer. 2:8 pastors also *t* against me . . the prophets
2:20 thou saidst, I will not *t*; when upon every
2:29 ye plead with me? ye all have *t* against me
34:18 I will give the men that have *t* my covenant
Lam. 3:42 we have *t* and have rebelled: thou hast
Ezek. 2:3 they and their fathers have *t* against me

Dan. 9:11 yea, all Israel have *t* thy law, even by
Hos. 6:7 but they like men have *t* the covenant
7:13 unto them! because they have *t* against me
Amos 4:4 come to Bethel, and *t*; at Gilgal multiply
Zeph. 3:11 doings, wherein thou hast *t* against me
Mt. 15:2 why do thy disciples *t* the tradition
15:3 why do ye also *t* the commandment of God by
Lk. 15:29 neither *t* I at any time thy commandment
Rom. 2:27 by the letter and circumcision dost *t*
1 Jn. 3:4 whosoever committeth sin *t* also the law
2 Jn. 9 whosoever *t*, and abideth not in the doctrine

Transgression See also Iniquity, Offense, Sin, Trespass

Ex. 23:21 he will not pardon your *t*: for my name
Lev. 16:16 make an atonement . . because of their *t*
Josh. 24:19 will not forgive your *t* nor your sins
1 Sam. 24:11 is neither evil nor *t* in mine hand
1 Kgs. 8:50 forgive thy people . . and all their *t*
1 Chr. 9:1 were carried away to Babylon for their *t*
10:13 so Saul died for his *t* which he committed
Ezra 10:6 Ezra . . mourned because of the *t* of them
Job 7:21 why dost thou not pardon my *t*, and take
14:17 my *t* is sealed up in a bag, and thou sewest
31:33 if I covered my *t* as Adam, by hiding mine
33:9 I am clean without *t*, I am innocent
Ps. 5:10 cast them out in the multitude of their *t*
19:13 and I shall be innocent from the great *t*
32:1 blessed is he whose *t* is forgiven, whose sin
32:5 I said, I will confess my *t* unto the LORD
39:8 deliver me from all my *t*: make me not the
51:1 of thy tender mercies blot out my *t*
51:3 for I acknowledge my *t*: and my sin is ever
59:3 mighty are gathered against me; not for my *t*
65:3 as for our *t*, thou shalt purge them away
89:32 then will I visit their *t* with the rod
103:12 so far hath he removed our *t* from us
107:17 fools, because of their *t* . . are afflicted
Prov. 12:13 wicked is snared by the *t* of his lips
17:9 he that covereth a *t* seeketh love
19:11 and it is his glory to pass over a *t*
28:2 for the *t* of a land many are the princes
29:6 in the *t* of an evil man there is a snare
29:16 the wicked are multiplied, *t* increaseth
Is. 24:20 and the *t* thereof shall be heavy upon it
43:25 I, even I, am he that blotteth out thy *t*
44:22 I have blotted out, as a thick cloud, thy *t*
53:5 he was wounded for our *t*, he was bruised for
53:8 for the *t* of my people was he stricken
57:4 are ye not children of *t*, a seed of falsehood
58:1 and show my people their *t*, and the house
59:12 our *t* are multiplied before thee
Jer. 5:6 their *t* are many, and their backslidings
Lam. 1:5 afflicted her for the multitude of her *t*
Ezek. 18:22 all his *t* . . shall not be mentioned unto
18:30 repent, and turn yourselves from all your *t*
33:10 if our *t* and our sins be upon us, and we
33:12 shall not deliver him in the day of his *t*
37:23 detestable things, nor with any of their *t*
39:24 according to their *t* have I done unto them
Dan. 9:24 finish the *t*, and to make an end of sins
Amos 1:3 for three *t* of Damascus, and for four
3:14 in the day . . I shall visit the *t* of Israel
4:4 at Gilgal multiply *t* . . bring your sacrifices
5:12 I know your manifold *t* and your mighty sins
Mic. 1:5 is the *t* of Jacob is all this . . What is the *t*
6:7 shall I give my firstborn for my *t*, the fruit
7:18 and passeth by the *t* of the remnant of his
Acts 1:25 apostleship, from which Judas by *t* fell
Rom. 4:15 for where no law is, there is no *t*
5:14 not sinned after the similitude of Adam's *t*
Gal. 3:19 the law? It was added because of *t*, till

1 Tim. 2:14 the woman being deceived was in the *t*
Heb. 2:2 every *t* and disobedience received a just
  9:15 means of death, for the redemption of the *t*
1 Jn. 3:4 also the law: for sin is the *t* of the law

Transgressor *See also* Evildoer, Sinner

Ps. 51:13 then will I teach *t* thy ways; and sinners
  59:5 Lord God . . be not merciful to any wicked *t*
Prov. 2:22 and the *t* shall be rooted out of it
  13:15 giveth favor: but the way of *t* is hard
  21:18 ransom for the righteous . . *t* for the upright
Is. 1:28 the destruction of the *t* and of the sinners
  48:8 treacherously . . wast called a *t* from the womb
  53:12 (Mk. 15:28; Lk. 22:37) numbered with the *t*
Hos. 14:9 walk in them: but the *t* shall fall therein
Gal. 2:18 things which I destroyed, I make myself a *t*
Jas. 2:11 thou kill, thou art become a *t* of the law

Translate

2 Sam. 3:10 *t* the kingdom from the house of Saul
Col. 1:13 *t* us into the kingdom of his dear Son
Heb. 11:5 Enoch was *t* that he should not see death

Transparent

Rev. 21:21 city was pure gold, as it were *t* glass

Trap *See also* Snare

Ps. 69:22 (Rom. 11:9) table become a snare . . a *t*
Jer. 5:26 they lay wait . . they set a *t*, they catch men

Travail

Num. 20:14 knowest all the *t* that hath befallen us
Job 15:20 the wicked man *t* with pain all his days
Ps. 7:14 he *t* with iniquity, and hath conceived
Eccl. 1:13 *t* hath God given to the sons of man
  2:26 to the sinner he giveth *t*, to gather and to
  4:4 I considered all *t*, and every right work
  5:14 but those riches perish by evil *t*
Is. 13:8 they shall be in pain as a woman that *t*
  53:11 he shall see of the *t* of his soul
  66:7 before she *t*, she brought forth; before her
  66:8 as soon as Zion *t*, she brought forth her
Lam. 3:5 against me . . compassed me with gall and *t*
Jn. 16:21 a woman when she is in *t* hath sorrow
Rom. 8:22 groaneth and *t* in pain together until now
Gal. 4:19 my little children, of whom I *t* in birth
1 Thes. 2:9 (2 Thes. 3:8) labor and *t* . . night and day
  5:3 upon them, as *t* upon a woman with child
Rev. 12:2 she being with child cried, *t* in birth

Travel

Prov. 6:11 so shall thy poverty come as one that *t*
Is. 63:1 *t* in the greatness of his strength?
Mt. 25:14 kingdom . . is as a man *t* into a far country
Acts 19:29 men of Macedonia, Paul's companions in *t*
2 Cor. 8:19 chosen of the churches to *t* with us

Traveler

Judg. 5:6 days of Jael . . the *t* walked through byways
2 Sam. 12:4 and there came a *t* unto the rich man
Job 31:32 but I opened my doors to the *t*

Treacherous

Is. 21:2 (24:16) the *t* dealer dealeth treacherously
Jer. 3:8 yet her *t* sister Judah feared not
  9:2 be all adulterers, an assembly of *t* men
Zeph. 3:4 her prophets are light and *t* persons

Treacherously

Is. 33:1 dealest *t*, and they dealt not *t* with thee!
Jer. 3:20 as a wife *t* departeth from her husband, so
  5:11 for the house . . have dealt very *t* against me
  12:1 are all they happy that deal very *t*?

Lam. 1:2 all her friends have dealt *t* with her
Hos. 5:7 they have dealt *t* against the LORD
  6:7 covenant: there have they dealt *t* against me
Mal. 2:10 why do we deal *t* every man against his
  2:16 take heed to your spirit, that ye deal not *t*

Treachery

2 Kgs. 9:23 said to Ahaziah, There is *t*, O Ahaziah

Tread (Trode, Trodden) *See also* Trample

Deut. 11:24 place . . your feet shall *t* shall be yours
  25:4 (1 Cor. 9:9; 1 Tim. 5:18) ox when he *t* out the
Josh. 14:9 feet have *t* shall be thine inheritance
Judg. 5:21 O my soul, thou hast *t* down strength
  9:27 vineyards, and *t* the grapes, and made merry
2 Kgs. 7:17 *t* upon him in the gate, and he died
  14:9 (2 Chr. 25:18) beast . . and *t* down the thistle
Job 9:8 heavens, and *t* upon the waves of the sea
  22:15 marked the old way which wicked men have *t*
  40:12 proud . . bring him low . . *t* down the wicked
Ps. 7:5 yea, let him *t* down my life upon the earth
  44:5 through thy name will we *t* them under
  60:12 (108:13) he it is that shall *t* down our enemies
  91:13 thou shalt *t* upon the lion and adder
  119:118 hast *t* down all them that err from thy
Is. 1:12 required this at your hand, to *t* my courts?
  10:6 to *t* them down like the mire of the streets
  16:10 the treaders shall *t* out no wine in their
  25:10 even as straw is *t* down for the dunghill
  63:2 thy garments like him that *t* in the winevat?
  63:3 I have *t* the winepress alone . . I will *t* them
Jer. 25:30 give a shout, as they that *t* the grapes
  48:33 wine to fail . . none shall *t* with shouting
Lam. 1:15 Lord hath *t* under foot all my mighty men
Hos. 10:11 as a heifer . . loveth to *t* out the corn
Amos 5:11 as your *t* is upon the poor, and ye take
Mic. 1:3 and *t* upon the high places of the earth
  7:10 shall she be *t* down as the mire of the streets
Zech. 10:5 mighty men, which *t* down their enemies
Mal. 4:3 and ye shall *t* down the wicked; for they
Mt. 5:13 to be cast out, and to be *t* under foot
Lk. 8:5 some fell by the wayside; and it was *t* down
  10:19 I give unto you power to *t* on serpents
  12:1 insomuch that they *t* one upon another
  21:24 Jerusalem shall be *t* down of the Gentiles
Heb. 10:29 who hath *t* under foot the Son of God
Rev. 11:2 the holy city shall they *t* under foot
  19:15 *t* the winepress of the fierceness and wrath

Treason

1 Kgs. 16:20 rest of the acts of Zimri, and his *t*
2 Kgs. 11:14 (2 Chr. 23:13) Athaliah . . cried, *T*, *t*

Treasure

Ex. 19:5 then ye shall be a peculiar *t* unto me
Deut. 28:12 LORD shall open unto thee his good *t*
  33:19 abundance of the seas . . *t* hid in the sand
1 Kgs. 14:26 (2 Chr. 12:9) *t* of the house of the LORD
2 Kgs. 12:18 found in the *t* of the house of the LORD
  20:13 (Is. 39:2) and all that was found in his *t*
  24:13 carried out thence all the *t* of the house
Ezra 7:20 be needful . . bestow it out of the king's *t*
Job 3:21 for death . . dig for it more than for hid *t*
  38:22 the *t* of the snow? or . . the *t* of the hail
Ps. 17:14 whose belly thou fillest with thy hid *t*
  135:4 chosen Jacob . . and Israel for his peculiar *t*
Prov. 2:4 if thou . . searchest for her as for hid *t*
  8:21 inherit substance; and I will fill their *t*
  10:2 *t* of wickedness profit nothing
  15:6 in the house of the righteous is much *t*
  15:16 better is little . . than great *t* and trouble

Prov. 21:6 getting of *t* by a lying tongue is a vanity
   21:20 *t* to be desired . . in the dwelling of the wise
Eccl. 2:8 I gathered me . . the peculiar *t* of kings
Is. 2:7 gold, neither is there any end of their *t*
   33:6 of salvation: the fear of the LORD is his *t*
   45:3 and I will give thee the *t* of darkness
Jer. 10:13 (51:16) bringeth forth the wind out of his *t*
   15:13 thy *t* will I give to the spoil without price
   41:8 slay us not: for we have *t* in the field
   48:7 thou hast trusted in thy works and in thy *t*
   51:13 dwellest upon many waters, abundant in *t*
Ezek. 28:4 hast gotten gold and silver into thy *t*
Dan. 11:43 he shall have power over the *t* of gold
Mic. 6:10 are there yet the *t* of wickedness in the
Mt. 2:11 when they had opened their *t*, they presented
   6:19 lay not up for yourselves *t* upon earth
   6:21 (Lk. 12:34) where your *t* is, there will your
   12:35 (Lk. 6:45) out of the good *t* of the heart
   13:44 the kingdom . . is like unto *t* hid in a field
   13:52 bringeth forth out of his *t* things new and
   19:21 (Mk. 10:21; Lk. 18:22) shalt have *t* in heaven
Lk. 12:21 so is he that layeth up *t* for himself
Rom. 2:5 *t* up unto thyself wrath against the day
2 Cor. 4:7 but we have this *t* in earthen vessels
Col. 2:3 in whom are hid all the *t* of wisdom
Heb. 11:26 greater riches than the *t* in Egypt
Jas. 5:3 have heaped *t* together for the last days

Treasurer

Ezra 7:21 a decree to all the *t* . . beyond the river
Neh. 13:13 and I made *t* over the treasuries
Is. 22:15 get thee unto this *t*, even unto Shebna

Treasury

Josh. 6:19 they shall come into the *t* of the LORD
Ps. 135:7 he bringeth the wind out of his *t*
Jer. 38:11 into the house of the king under the *t*
Mt. 27:6 is not lawful for to put them into the *t*
Mk. 12:41 (Lk. 21:1) the people cast money into the *t*
Jn. 8:20 these words spake Jesus in the *t*

Treatise

Acts 1:1 the former *t* have I made, O Theophilus

Tree *See also* Palm

Gen. 1:11 the fruit *t* yielding fruit after his kind
   2:9 *t* of life . . of knowledge of good and evil
   3:1 ye shall not eat of every *t* of the garden?
   3:6 the woman saw that the *t* was good for food
   3:24 sword . . to keep the way of the *t* of life
Ex. 15:25 a *t*, which when he had cast into the waters
Deut. 20:19 not destroy the *t* . . the *t* . . is man's life
   21:23 body shall not remain all night upon the *t*
Judg. 9:8 *t* went forth on a time to anoint a king
1 Kgs. 4:33 he spake of *t*, from the cedar *t* that is
   19:4 and came and sat down under a juniper *t*
Job 14:7 there is hope of a *t*, if it be cut down
Ps. 1:3 he shall be like a *t* planted by the rivers
   37:35 and spreading himself like a green bay *t*
   104:16 *t* of the LORD are full of sap; the cedars
Prov. 3:18 she is a *t* of life to them that lay hold
   11:30 the fruit of the righteous is a *t* of life
   15:4 a wholesome tongue is a *t* of life
Eccl. 11:3 where the *t* falleth, there it shall be
Is. 55:12 *t* of the field shall clap their hands
   56:3 neither let the eunuch say . . I am a dry *t*
   61:3 that they might be called *T* of righteousness
Jer. 17:8 he shall be as a *t* planted by the waters
Ezek. 15:2 what is the vine *t* more than any *t*
   17:24 brought down the high *t* . . exalted the low *t*
   31:8 not any *t* in the garden of God was like unto
   47:7 at the bank of the river were very many *t*
Dan. 4:10 I saw, and behold a *t* in the midst of the

Mt. 3:10 (Lk. 3:9) axe is laid unto the root of the *t*
   7:17 (Lk. 6:43) good *t* bringeth forth good fruit
   7:19 *t* that bringeth not forth good fruit is hewn
   12:33 (Lk. 6:44) for the *t* is known by his fruit
   13:32 (Lk. 13:19) becometh a *t*, so that the birds
   24:32 (Mk. 13:28; Lk. 21:29) parable of the fig *t*
Mk. 8:24 looked up . . said, I see men as *t*, walking
Lk. 17:6 had faith . . ye might say unto this sycamine *t*
Jn. 1:50 saw thee under the fig *t*, believest thou?
Acts 5:30 Jesus, whom ye slew and hanged on a *t*
Rom. 11:17 thou, being a wild olive *t*, wert graffed
Gal. 3:13 cursed is every one that hangeth on a *t*
1 Pet. 2:24 bare our sins in his own body on the *t*
Jude 12 *t* whose fruit withereth, without fruit
Rev. 2:7 will I give to eat of the *t* of life
   7:3 hurt not the earth, neither the sea, nor the *t*
   22:2 *t* of life, which bare twelve manner of fruits
   22:14 that they may have right to the *t* of life

Tremble *See also* Fear, Quake

Deut. 2:25 shall hear report of thee, and shall *t*
Judg. 5:4 the earth *t*, and the heavens dropped
1 Sam. 4:13 for his heart *t* for the ark of God
2 Sam. 22:8 (Ps. 18:7) then the earth shook and *t*
Ezra 9:4 every one that *t* at the words of the God
Job 9:6 shaketh the earth . . the pillars thereof *t*
   26:11 the pillars of heaven *t*, and are astonished
   37:1 at this also my heart *t*, and is moved
Ps. 60:2 thou hast made the earth to *t*; thou hast
   77:18 lightened the world: the earth *t* and shook
   99:1 LORD reigneth; let the people *t*: he sitteth
   104:32 he looketh on the earth, and it *t*
   114:7 *t*, thou earth, at the presence of the Lord
   119:120 my flesh *t* for fear of thee; and I am
Eccl. 12:3 when the keepers of the house shall *t*
Is. 14:16 is this the man that made the earth to *t*
   32:11 *t*, ye women that are at ease; be troubled
   64:2 that the nations may *t* at thy presence!
   66:5 the word of the LORD, ye that *t* at his word
Jer. 5:22 will ye not *t* at my presence, which have
   10:10 the LORD . . at his wrath the earth shall *t*
   33:9 they shall fear and *t* for all the goodness
Dan. 6:26 men *t* and fear before the God of Daniel
Hos. 11:10 then the children shall *t* from the west
Amos 8:8 shall not the land *t* for this, and every
Mk. 5:33 (Lk. 8:47) the woman fearing and *t*
   16:8 from the sepulchre . . they *t* and were amazed
Acts 7:32 then Moses *t*, and durst not behold
   16:29 came *t*, and fell down before Paul and Silas
   24:25 temperance, and judgment to come, Felix *t*
Jas. 2:19 the devils also believe, and *t*

Trembling *See also* Tremble, Fear

1 Sam. 14:15 there was *t* in the host, in the field
Job 4:14 fear came upon me, and *t*, which made all
   21:6 I am afraid, and *t* taketh hold on my flesh
Ps. 2:11 serve the LORD with fear . . rejoice with *t*
Ezek. 26:16 they shall clothe themselves with *t*
1 Cor. 2:3 in weakness, and in fear, and in much *t*
2 Cor. 7:15 how with fear and *t* ye received him
Eph. 6:5 servants, be obedient . . with fear and *t*
Phil. 2:12 work out your . . salvation with fear and *t*

Trench

1 Sam. 17:20 David . . came to the *t*, as the host was
   26:5 Saul lay in the *t*, and the people pitched
1 Kgs. 18:32 he made a *t* about the altar, as great
Lk. 19:43 thine enemies shall cast a *t* about thee

Trespass *See also* Offend, Offense, Sin, Transgress

Ex. 22:9 for all manner of *t*, whether it be for ox

Lev. 5:6 shall bring his *t* offering unto the LORD
  5:15 soul commit a *t*, and sin through ignorance
  7:1 likewise this is the law of the *t* offering
  26:40 confess. . their *t* which they *t* against me
Num. 5:7 shall recompense his *t* with the principal
Deut. 32:51 *t* against me among the children of Israel
Josh. 7:1 Israel committed a *t* in the accursed thing
  22:16 what *t* is this that ye have committed
1 Kgs. 8:31 if any man *t* against his neighbor
2 Chr. 24:18 Judah and Jerusalem for this their *t*
  28:13 our *t* is great, and there is fierce wrath
  28:22 the time of his distress did he *t* yet more
Ezra 9:6 and our *t* is grown up unto the heavens
  9:13 for our evil deeds, and for our great *t*
  9:15 we are before thee in our *t*; for we cannot
  10:2 said unto Ezra, We have *t* against our God
Ps. 68:21 of such a one as goeth on still in his *t*
Ezek. 15:8 desolate, because they have committed a *t*
  18:24 in his *t* that he hath *t*, and in his sin
  39:23 they *t* against me, therefore hid I my face
Dan. 9:7 of their *t* that they have *t* against thee
Hos. 8:1 transgressed my covenant. . *t* against my law
Mt. 6:14 if ye forgive men their *t*, your heavenly
  18:15 if thy brother shall *t* against thee, go and
  18:35 forgive not every one his brother their *t*
Lk. 17:3 if thy brother *t* against thee, rebuke him
2 Cor. 5:19 not imputing their *t* unto them
Eph. 2:1 quickened, who were dead in *t* and sins
Col. 2:13 he quickened. . having forgiven you all *t*

Trial *See also* Temptation

Job 9:23 he will laugh at the *t* of the innocent
2 Cor. 8:2 how that in a great *t* of affliction
Heb. 11:36 had *t* of cruel mockings and scourgings
1 Pet. 1:7 the *t* of your faith, being much more
  4:12 think it not strange concerning the fiery *t*

Tribe

Num. 36:9 neither. . remove from one *t* to another *t*
Judg. 21:3 should be today one *t* lacking in Israel?
Ps. 105:37 was not one feeble person among their *t*
  122:4 whither the *t* go up, the *t* of the LORD
Is. 19:13 they that are the stay of the *t* thereof
  49:6 be my servant to raise up the *t* of Jacob
  63:17 servants' sake, the *t* of thine inheritance
Hab. 3:9 according to the oaths of the *t*, even thy
Mt. 24:30 then shall all the *t* of the earth mourn
Jas. 1:1 to the twelve *t* which are scattered abroad
Rev. 7:4 of all the *t* of the children of Israel

Tribulation *See also* Affliction, Anguish, Calamity, Distress, Grief, Misery, Oppression, Persecution, Sorrow, Suffering, Trouble

Deut. 4:30 when thou art in *t*, and all these things
Judg. 10:14 them deliver you in the time of your *t*
1 Sam. 10:19 out of all your adversities and your *t*
  26:24 LORD, and let him deliver me out of all *t*
Mt. 13:21 when *t* or persecution ariseth because of
  24:21 for then shall be great *t*, such as was not
  24:29 (Mk. 13:24) after the *t* of those days shall
Jn. 16:33 in the world ye shall have *t*: but be of
Acts 14:22 through much *t* enter into the kingdom
Rom. 5:3 glory in *t* also; knowing that *t* worketh
  8:35 separate us from the love of Christ? shall *t*
  12:12 patient in *t*; continuing instant in prayer
2 Cor. 1:4 who comforteth us in all our *t*, that we
  7:4 I am exceeding joyful in all our *t*
Eph. 3:13 desire that ye faint not at my *t* for you
1 Thes. 3:4 we told you. . that we should suffer *t*
2 Thes. 1:4 faith in all your persecutions and *t*

Rev. 1:9 John. . your brother, and companion in *t*
  2:22 that commit adultery with her into great *t*
  7:14 these are they which came out of great *t*

Tributary

Deut. 20:11 is found therein shall be *t* unto thee
Judg. 1:30 Canaanites dwelt among them. . became *t*
  1:35 of Joseph prevailed, so that they became *t*
Lam. 1:1 she that was great. . how is she become *t*!

Tribute *See also* Tax

Gen. 49:15 to bear, and became a servant unto *t*
Num. 31:28 levy a *t* unto the LORD of the men of war
Deut. 16:10 with a *t* of a freewill offering
1 Kgs. 9:21 (2 Chr. 8:8) those did Solomon levy a *t*
Ezra 7:24 not be lawful to impose toll, *t*, or custom
Prov. 12:24 but the slothful shall be under *t*
Mt. 17:24 and said, Doth not your master pay *t*?
  22:17 (Mk. 12:14; Lk. 20:22) is it lawful to give *t*
Lk. 23:2 forbidding to give *t* to Caesar, saying
Rom. 13:6 pay ye *t* also: for they are God's ministers
  13:7 to all their dues: *t* to whom *t* is due

Trim

2 Sam. 19:24 dressed his feet, nor *t* his beard
Jer. 2:33 why *t* thou thy way to seek love?
Mt. 25:7 all those virgins arose, and *t* their lamps

Triumph *See also* Victory

Ex. 15:1 (15:21) the LORD, for he hath *t* gloriously
2 Sam. 1:20 the daughters of the uncircumcised *t*
Job 20:5 the *t* of the wicked is short, and the joy
Ps. 25:2 ashamed, let not mine enemies *t* over me
  47:1 shout unto God with the voice of *t*
  60:8 (108:9) Philistia, *t* thou because of me
  92:4 I will *t* in the works of thy hands
  94:3 LORD. . how long shall the wicked *t*
  106:47 unto thy holy name, and to *t* in thy praise
2 Cor. 2:14 which always causeth us to *t* in Christ
Col. 2:15 a show of them openly, *t* over them in it

Troas Acts 16:8; 20:5; 2 Cor. 2:12

Trode (Trodden) *See* Tread

Troop

Gen. 30:11 Leah said, A *t* cometh: and she called
2 Sam. 22:30 (Ps. 18:29) I have run through a *t*
Is. 65:11 are they. . that prepare a table for that *t*
Hos. 7:1 and the *t* of robbers spoileth without
Amos 9:6 hath founded his *t* in the earth

Trophimus Acts 21:29; 2 Tim. 4:20

Trouble *See also* Affliction, Anguish, Calamity, Distress, Grief, Misery, Sorrow, Suffering, Tribulation, Vexation

Deut. 31:17 and many evils and *t* shall befall them
Josh. 7:25 why hast thou *t* us? the LORD shall *t* thee
1 Sam. 16:14 an evil spirit from the LORD *t* him
1 Kgs. 18:17 Ahab said. . Art thou he that *t* Israel?
1 Chr. 22:14 in my *t* I have prepared for the house
2 Chr. 15:4 they in their *t* did turn unto the LORD
  29:8 hath delivered them to *t*, to astonishment
Ezra 4:4 the people of the land. . *t* them in building
Neh. 9:27 in the time of their *t*, when they cried
  9:32 let not all the *t* seem little before thee
Job 3:26 I rest, neither was I quiet; yet *t* came
  4:5 faintest; it toucheth thee, and thou art *t*
  5:6 neither doth *t* spring out of the ground
  5:7 man is born unto *t*, as the sparks fly upward

Job 5:19 shall deliver thee in six *t*: yea, in seven
  14:1 born of a woman is of few days, and full of *t*
  15:24 *t* and anguish shall make him afraid
  23:15 therefore am I *t* at his presence
  23:16 maketh my heart soft, and the Almighty *t* me
  34:29 he giveth quietness, who then can make *t*?
Ps. 3:1 LORD, how are they increased that *t* me!
  9:9 for the oppressed, a refuge in times of *t*
  9:13 LORD; consider my *t* which I suffer of them
  13:4 and those that *t* me rejoice when I am moved
  20:1 the LORD hear thee in the day of *t*
  22:11 be not far from me; for *t* is near
  25:22 redeem Israel, O God, out of all his *t*
  27:5 in the time of *t* he shall hide me in his
  31:7 thou hast considered my *t*; thou hast known
  32:7 hiding place; thou shalt preserve me from *t*
  34:6 heard him, and saved him out of all his *t*
  37:39 LORD: he is their strength in the time of *t*
  41:1 the LORD will deliver him in time of *t*
  46:1 God is our refuge . . a very present help in *t*
  50:15 call upon me in the day of *t*: I will deliver
  54:7 for he hath delivered me out of all *t*
  59:16 my defense and refuge in the day of my *t*
  60:11 (108:12) give us help from *t*: for vain is
  66:14 and my mouth hath spoken, when I was in *t*
  73:5 they are not in *t* as other men; neither are
  77:2 in the day of my *t* I sought the Lord
  77:3 I remembered God, and was *t*: I complained
  77:4 I am so *t* that I cannot speak
  81:7 thou calledst in *t*, and I delivered thee
  86:7 in the day of my *t* I will call upon thee
  91:15 I will be with him in *t*; I will deliver him
  102:2 face from me in the day when I am in *t*
  116:3 and the pains of hell . . I found *t* and sorrow
  138:7 though I walk in the midst of *t*, thou wilt
  142:2 my complaint . . I showed before him my *t*
Prov. 11:8 the righteous is delivered out of *t*
  11:17 but he that is cruel *t* his own flesh
  12:13 snared . . but the just shall come out of *t*
  15:16 better is little . . than great treasure and *t*
  15:27 he that is greedy of gain *t* his own house
  21:23 keepeth his mouth . . keepeth his soul from *t*
Is. 1:14 they are a *t* unto me; I am weary to bear
  8:22 look unto the earth . . behold *t* and darkness
  17:14 at eveningtide *t*; and before the morning
  22:5 for it is a day of *t*, and of treading down
  26:16 LORD, in *t* have they visited thee
  30:6 into the land of *t* and anguish, from whence
  32:11 be *t*, ye careless ones: strip you
  33:2 be thou . . our salvation also in the time of *t*
  46:7 can he not answer, nor save him out of his *t*
  65:16 because the former *t* are forgotten
Jer. 2:27 but in the time of their *t* they will say
  8:15 looked . . for a time of health, and behold *t*!
  14:8 hope of Israel, the Saviour . . in time of *t*
  30:7 it is even the time of Jacob's *t*
Dan. 4:5 thoughts . . and the visions of my head *t* me
  12:1 there shall be a time of *t*, such as never
Nah. 1:7 LORD is good, a stronghold in the day of *t*
Zeph. 1:15 that day is a day of wrath, a day of *t*
Zech. 10:2 were *t*, because there was no shepherd
Mt. 2:3 when Herod . . heard these things, he was *t*
  24:6 (Mk. 13:7) wars and rumors of wars . . be not *t*
  26:10 (Mk. 14:6) why *t* ye the woman? for she hath
Mk. 5:35 (Lk. 8:49) why *t* thou the Master any further
  13:8 there shall be famines and *t*
Lk. 7:6 Lord, *t* not thyself; for I am not worthy
  10:41 Martha, thou art careful and *t* about many
  11:7 say, *T* me not: the door is now shut
  18:5 because this widow *t* me, I will avenge her
  24:38 why are ye *t*? and why do thoughts arise
Jn. 5:4 angel went . . into the pool, and *t* the water
  12:27 now is my soul *t*; and what shall I say?

Jn. 13:21 when Jesus had thus said, he was *t* in spirit
  14:1 let not your heart be *t*: ye believe in God
  14:27 let not your heart be *t*, neither . . be afraid
Acts 15:19 my sentence is, that we *t* not them
1 Cor. 7:28 such shall have *t* in the flesh
2 Cor. 1:4 able to comfort them which are in any *t*
  4:8 we are *t* on every side, yet not distressed
  7:5 had no rest, but we were *t* on every side
Gal. 1:7 that *t* you, and would pervert the gospel
  5:10 but he that *t* you shall bear his judgment
  6:17 from henceforth let no man *t* me: for I bear
2 Thes. 1:6 recompense tribulation to them that *t*
  1:7 to you who are *t* rest with us, when the Lord
Heb. 12:15 root of bitterness springing up *t* you
1 Pet. 3:14 not afraid of their terror, neither be *t*

Troublous

Dan. 9:25 the street . . and the wall, even in *t* times

Trucebreaker

2 Tim. 3:3 *t*, false accusers, incontinent, fierce

True *See also* Honest, Upright

Gen. 42:11 we are *t* men; thy servants are no spies
2 Sam. 7:28 thou art that God, and thy words be *t*
1 Kgs. 10:6 (2 Chr. 9:5) it was a *t* report that I heard
  22:16 thou tell me nothing but that which is *t*
2 Chr. 15:3 Israel hath been without the *t* God
Ps. 19:9 judgments of the LORD are *t* and righteous
  119:160 thy word is *t* from the beginning
Prov. 14:25 a *t* witness delivereth souls
Jer. 10:10 LORD is the *t* God, he is the living God
Ezek. 18:8 executed *t* judgment between man and
Zech. 7:9 execute *t* judgment, and show mercy
Mt. 22:16 (Mk. 12:14) we know that thou art *t*
Lk. 16:11 will commit to your trust the *t* riches?
Jn. 1:9 that was the *t* Light, which lighteth every
  3:33 testimony hath set to his seal that God is *t*
  4:23 the *t* worshippers shall worship the Father
  5:31 bear witness of myself, my witness is not *t*
  6:32 my Father giveth you the *t* bread from heaven
  7:18 same is *t*, and no unrighteousness is in him
  7:28 but he that sent me is *t*, whom ye know not
  8:14 I bear record of myself, yet my record is *t*
  8:17 your law, that the testimony of two men is *t*
  8:26 he that sent me is *t*; and I speak to the world
  10:41 things that John spoke of this man were *t*
  15:1 am the *t* vine . . my Father is the husbandman
  17:3 that they might know thee the only *t* God
  19:35 saw it bare record, and his record is *t*
  21:24 testifieth . . we know that his testimony is *t*
Rom. 3:4 yea, let God be *t*, but every man a liar
2 Cor. 1:18 but as God is *t*, our word toward you
  6:8 evil . . and good report: as deceivers, and yet *t*
Phil. 4:8 whatsoever things are *t*, whatsoever things
1 Thes. 1:9 from idols to serve the living and *t* God
Tit. 1:13 this witness is *t*. Wherefore rebuke them
Heb. 8:2 of the sanctuary, and of the *t* tabernacle
  9:24 holy places . . which are the figures of the *t*
  10:22 draw near with a *t* heart in full assurance
1 Jn. 2:8 darkness is past . . the *t* light now shineth
  5:20 this is the *t* God, and eternal life
3 Jn. 12 and ye know that our record is *t*
Rev. 3:7 saith he that is holy, he that is *t*
  3:14 saith the Amen, the faithful and *t* witness
  6:10 how long, O Lord, holy and *t*, dost thou not
  15:3 just and *t* are thy ways, thou King of saints
  16:7 Almighty, *t* and righteous are thy judgments
  19:11 that sat upon him was called Faithful and *T*
  21:5 write: for these words are *t* and faithful

Trump

1 Cor. 15:52 the twinkling of an eye, at the last *t*
1 Thes. 4:16 the archangel, and with the *t* of God

Trumpet *See also* Cornet

Ex. 19:16 and the voice of the *t* exceeding loud
Lev. 23:24 a sabbath, a memorial of blowing of *t*
Num. 10:2 make thee two *t* of silver; of a whole
Josh. 6:4 and the priests shall blow with the *t*
Judg. 7:16 and he put a *t* in every man's hand
2 Chr. 29:27 song of the LORD began also with the *t*
Neh. 4:20 ye hear the sound of the *t*, restore ye
Job 39:25 he saith among the *t*, Ha, ha!
Ps. 81:3 blow up the *t* in the new moon, in the time
    98:6 with *t* and sound of cornet make a joyful
Is. 27:13 that the great *t* shall be blown, and they
    58:1 lift up thy voice like a *t*, and show
Jer. 4:5 blow ye the *t* in the land: cry, gather
Ezek. 33:5 he heard the sound of the *t*, and took
Zech. 9:14 GOD shall blow the *t*, and shall go with
Mt. 6:2 thine alms, do not sound a *t* before thee
    24:31 send his angels with a great sound of a *t*
1 Cor. 14:8 if the *t* give an uncertain sound, who
    15:52 *t* shall sound, and the dead shall be raised
Rev. 1:10 heard behind me a great voice, as of a *t*
    8:2 seven angels. . and to them were given seven *t*

Trust *See also* Believe, Confidence, Faith,
    Hope

Deut. 28:52 fenced walls come down, wherein thou *t*
    32:37 are their gods, their rock in whom they *t*
Ruth 2:12 under whose wings thou art come to *t*
2 Sam. 22:3 (Ps. 18:2) God of my rock; in him will I *t*
    22:31 (Ps. 18:30) buckler to all them that *t* in him
2 Kgs. 18:5 he *t* in the LORD God of Israel
    18:19 (Is. 36:4) what confidence. . wherein thou *t*?
    18:22 (Is. 36:7) but if ye say. . We *t* in the LORD
    19:10 (Is. 37:10) God in whom thou *t* deceive thee
1 Chr. 5:20 helped. . because they put their *t* in him
Job 8:14 and whose *t* shall be a spider's web
    13:15 though he slay me, yet will I *t* in him
    15:15 behold, he putteth no *t* in his saints
    15:31 let not him that is deceived *t* in vanity
    39:11 thou *t* him, because his strength is great?
Ps. 2:12 blessed. . all they that put their *t* in him
    4:5 of righteousness, and put your *t* in the LORD
    5:11 all those that put their *t* in thee rejoice
    7:1 (16:1; 31:1; 71:1) my God, in thee do I put my *t*
    9:10 that know thy name will put their *t* in thee
    11:1 in the LORD put I my *t*: how say ye to my
    13:5 have *t* in thy mercy; my heart shall rejoice
    20:7 some *t* in chariots, and some in horses
    21:7 king *t* in the LORD, and through the mercy
    22:4 our fathers *t* in thee: they *t*, and thou didst
    25:2 my God, I *t* in thee: let me not be ashamed
    26:1 I have *t* also in the LORD. . I shall not slide
    28:7 my heart *t* in him, and I am helped
    31:6 regard lying vanities: but I *t* in the LORD
    31:14 I *t* in thee, O LORD: I said, Thou art my God
    32:10 he that *t* in the LORD, mercy shall compass
    33:21 rejoice. . because we have *t* in his holy name
    34:8 is good: blessed is the man that *t* in him
    34:22 and none. . that *t* in him shall be desolate
    36:7 put their *t* under the shadow of thy wings
    37:3 *t* in the LORD, and do good; so shalt thou
    37:5 commit thy way unto the LORD; *t* also in him
    40:3 see it, and fear, and shall *t* in the LORD
    40:4 blessed. . that man that maketh the LORD his *t*
    41:9 yea, mine own familiar friend, in whom I *t*
    44:6 I will not *t* in my bow, neither shall my
    49:6 that *t* in their wealth, and boast themselves
    52:7 but *t* in the abundance of his riches
    52:8 I *t* in the mercy of God for ever and ever
    55:23 half their days; but I will *t* in thee
    56:4 in God I have put my *t*; I will not fear
    61:4 I will *t* in the covert of thy wings

Ps. 62:8 *t* in him at all times; ye people, pour out
    71:5 O Lord GOD: thou art my *t* from my youth
    78:22 believed not in God. . *t* not in his salvation
    84:12 O LORD. . blessed is the man that *t* in thee
    91:2 my refuge and my fortress. . in him will I *t*
    91:4 and under his wings shalt thou *t*
    112:7 his heart is fixed, *t* in the LORD
    115:9 Israel, *t* thou in the LORD: he is their help
    118:8 it is better to *t* in the LORD than to put
    125:1 that *t* in the LORD shall be as mount Zion
    143:8 in thee do I *t*: cause me to know the way
    146:3 put not your *t* in princes, nor in the son
Prov. 3:5 *t* in the LORD with all thine heart
    11:28 he that *t* in his riches shall fall
    16:20 and whoso *t* in the LORD, happy is he
    22:19 that thy *t* may be in the LORD, I have
    28:25 putteth his *t* in the LORD shall be made fat
    28:26 he that *t* in his own heart is a fool
    29:25 whoso putteth his *t* in the LORD shall be safe
    30:5 a shield unto them that put their *t* in him
    31:11 heart of her husband doth safely *t* in her
Is. 12:2 my salvation; I will *t*, and not be afraid
    26:3 mind is stayed on thee: because he *t* in thee
    30:2 Pharaoh, and to *t* in the shadow of Egypt!
    31:1 stay on horses, and *t* in chariots, because
    42:17 greatly ashamed, that *t* in graven images
    47:10 thou hast *t* in thy wickedness: thou hast
    50:10 let him *t* in the name of the LORD, and stay
    57:13 he that putteth his *t* in me shall possess
    59:4 nor any pleadeth for truth: they *t* in vanity
Jer. 5:17 impoverish. . fenced cities, wherein thou *t*
    7:4 *t* ye not in lying words, saying, The temple
    13:25 thou hast forgotten me, and *t* in falsehood
    17:5 cursed be the man that *t* in man, and maketh
    17:7 blessed is the man that *t* in the LORD
    28:15 but thou makest this people to *t* in a lie
    29:31 I sent him not. . he caused you to *t* in a lie
    48:7 because thou hast *t* in thy works and in thy
    49:4 *t* in her treasures, saying, Who shall come
Ezek. 16:15 but thou didst *t* in thine own beauty
    33:13 if he *t* to his own righteousness, and commit
Hos. 10:13 because thou didst *t* in thy way
Amos 6:1 at ease. . and *t* in the mountain of Samaria
Mic. 7:5 *t* ye not in a friend, put ye not confidence
Nah. 1:7 LORD is good. . knoweth them that *t* in him
Zeph. 3:12 and they shall *t* in the name of the LORD
Mt. 12:21 (Rom. 15:12) in his name. . the Gentiles *t*
    27:43 he *t* in God; let him deliver him now, if he
Mk. 10:24 hard. . for them that *t* in riches to enter
Lk. 16:11 who will commit to your *t* the true riches?
    18:9 *t* in themselves that they were righteous
Jn. 5:45 accuseth you, even Moses, in whom ye *t*
2 Cor. 1:9 should not *t* in ourselves, but in God
    3:4 such *t* have we through Christ to God-ward
    10:7 if any man *t* to himself that he is Christ's
Eph. 1:12 praise of his glory, who first *t* in Christ
Phil. 1:14 whereof he might *t* in the flesh, I more
1 Thes. 2:4 to be put in *t* with the gospel, even so
1 Tim. 1:11 gospel. . which was committed to my *t*
    4:10 reproach, because we *t* in the living God
    6:17 *t* in uncertain riches, but in the living God
    6:20 Timothy, keep that. . committed to thy *t*
Heb. 2:13 and again, I will put my *t* in him
1 Pet. 3:5 holy women also, who *t* in God, adorned

Trusty

Job 12:20 he removeth away the speech of the *t*

Truth *See also* Faithfulness

Gen. 24:27 not left destitute. . of his mercy and his *t*
    32:10 least of all the mercies, and of all the *t*
Ex. 18:21 able men, such as fear God, men of *t*
Deut. 32:4 a God of *t* and without iniquity

Josh. 24:14 and serve him in sincerity and in *t*
1 Sam. 12:24 fear the LORD, and serve him in *t*
2 Sam. 2:6 the LORD show kindness and *t* unto you
1 Kgs. 2:4 to walk before me in *t* with all their
    17:24 the word of the LORD in thy mouth is *t*
2 Kgs. 20:3 (Is. 38:3) I have walked before thee in *t*
    20:19 (Is. 39:8) peace and *t* be in my days?
2 Chr. 31:20 that which was good and right and *t*
Ps. 15:2 worketh righteousness, and speaketh the *t*
    25:5 lead me in thy *t*, and teach me: for thou
    30:9 the dust praise thee? shall it declare thy *t*?
    33:4 is right; and all thy works are done in *t*
    40:11 thy loving-kindness and thy *t*. . preserve me
    43:3 send out thy light and thy *t*: let them lead
    51:6 behold, thou desirest *t* in the inward parts
    57:10 (108:4) heavens, and thy *t* unto the clouds
    60:4 that it may be displayed because of the *t*
    85:10 mercy and *t* are met together; righteousness
    86:11 teach me thy way. . I will walk in thy *t*
    91:4 his *t* shall be thy shield and buckler
    98:3 he hath remembered his mercy and his *t*
    100:5 and his *t* endureth to all generations
    117:2 and the *t* of the LORD endureth for ever
    119:30 I have chosen the way of *t*: thy judgments
    119:142 righteousness, and thy law is the *t*
    119:151 O LORD; and all thy commandments are *t*
    145:18 is nigh unto. . all that call upon him in *t*
    146:6 which made heaven. . keepeth *t* for ever
Prov. 8:7 my mouth shall speak *t*; and wickedness is
    12:17 that speaketh *t* showeth forth righteousness
    12:19 the lip of *t* shall be established for ever
    22:21 know the certainty of the words of *t*
    23:23 buy the *t*, and sell it not; also wisdom
Eccl. 12:10 written was upright, even words of *t*
Is. 25:1 thy counsels of old are faithfulness and *t*
    26:2 nation which keepeth the *t* may enter in
    38:18 go down into the pit cannot hope for thy *t*
    42:3 he shall bring forth judgment unto *t*
    48:1 make mention of the God of Israel, but not in *t*
    59:4 calleth for justice, nor any pleadeth for *t*
    59:14 for *t* is fallen in the street, and equity
    59:15 *t* faileth; and he that departeth from evil
Jer. 4:2 thou shalt swear, The LORD liveth, in *t*
    5:1 that executeth judgment, that seeketh the *t*
    7:28 nor receiveth correction: *t* is perished
    9:3 they are not valiant for the *t* upon the earth
    33:6 reveal unto them the abundance of peace and *t*
Dan. 4:37 the King of heaven, all whose works are *t*
    8:12 and it cast down the *t* to the ground
    9:13 from our iniquities, and understand thy *t*
    11:2 and now will I show thee the *t*
Hos. 4:1 because there is no *t*, nor mercy
Zech. 8:3 Jerusalem shall be called A city of *t*
    8:8 will be their God, in *t* and in righteousness
    8:16 (Eph. 4:25) speak ye every man the *t* to his
    8:19 therefore love the *t* and peace
Mal. 2:6 law of *t* was in his mouth, and iniquity
Mt. 22:16 (Mk. 12:14) teachest the way of God in *t*
Mk. 12:32 well, Master, thou hast said the *t*
Jn. 1:14 and dwelt among us. . full of grace and *t*
    1:17 Moses, but grace and *t* came by Jesus Christ
    3:21 but he that doeth *t* cometh to the light
    4:24 must worship him in spirit and in *t*
    5:33 unto John, and he bare witness unto the *t*
    8:32 know the *t*, and the *t* shall make you free
    8:40 to kill me, a man that hath told you the *t*
    8:44 abode not in the *t*, because there is no *t* in
    8:46 if I say the *t*, why do ye not believe me?
    14:6 I am the way, the *t*, and the life: no man
    14:17 Spirit of *t*; whom the world cannot receive
    15:26 even the Spirit of *t*. . shall testify of me
    16:13 Spirit of *t*. . he will guide you into all *t*
    17:17 sanctify them through thy *t*: thy word is *t*

Jn. 18:37 that I should bear witness unto the *t*
    18:38 Pilate saith unto him, What is *t*?
Acts 26:25 but speak. . the words of *t* and soberness
Rom. 1:18 men, who hold the *t* in unrighteousness
    1:25 who changed the *t* of God into a lie
    2:2 that the judgment of God is according to *t*
    2:8 that are contentious, and do not obey the *t*
    3:7 if the *t* of God. . more abounded through my lie
    9:1 say the *t* in Christ, I lie not, my conscience
    15:8 minister of the circumcision for the *t* of God
1 Cor. 5:8 the unleavened bread of sincerity and *t*
    13:6 not in iniquity, but rejoiceth in the *t*
2 Cor. 4:2 by manifestation of the *t*, commending
    6:7 by the word of *t*, by the power of God
    7:14 even so our boasting. . is found a *t*
    11:10 as the *t* of Christ is in me, no man shall
    12:6 I shall not be a fool; for I will say the *t*
    13:8 can do nothing against the *t*, but for the *t*
Gal. 2:5 *t* of the gospel might continue with you
    3:1 bewitched you, that ye should not obey the *t*
    4:16 become your enemy, because I tell you the *t*?
    5:7 did hinder you that ye should not obey the *t*?
Eph. 1:13 trusted, after that ye heard the word of *t*
    4:15 speaking the *t* in love, may grow up into
    4:21 been taught by him, as the *t* is in Jesus
    5:9 is in all goodness and righteousness and *t*
    6:14 having your loins girt about with *t*
Col. 1:6 ye heard. . and knew the grace of God in *t*
1 Thes. 2:13 but, as it is in *t*, the word of God
2 Thes. 2:10 they received not the love of the *t*
    2:12 all might be damned who believed not the *t*
1 Tim. 2:4 and to come unto the knowledge of the *t*
    3:15 the church. . the pillar and ground of the *t*
    6:5 men of corrupt minds, and destitute of the *t*
2 Tim. 2:15 workman. . rightly dividing the word of *t*
    2:18 who concerning the *t* have erred, saying that
    2:25 repentance to the acknowledging of the *t*
    3:7 never able to come to the knowledge of the *t*
    3:8 withstood Moses, so do these. . resist the *t*
    4:4 they shall turn away their ears from the *t*
Tit. 1:1 acknowledging of the *t*. . after godliness
    1:14 commandments of men, that turn from the *t*
Heb. 10:26 we have received the knowledge of the *t*
Jas. 1:18 his own will begat he us with the word of *t*
    5:19 if any of you do err from the *t*, and one
1 Pet. 1:22 purified your souls in obeying the *t*
2 Pet. 1:12 and be established in the present *t*
    2:2 of whom the way of *t* shall be evil spoken of
1 Jn. 1:6 walk in darkness, we lie, and do not the *t*
    1:8 we deceive ourselves, and the *t* is not in us
    2:4 is a liar, and the *t* is not in him
    2:21 because ye know not the *t*. . no lie is of the *t*
    2:27 anointing teacheth you of all things, and is *t*
    3:18 let us not love in word. . but in deed and in *t*
    3:19 hereby we know that we are of the *t*, and shall
    4:6 know we the spirit of *t*, and the spirit of error
    5:6 that beareth witness, because the Spirit is *t*
2 Jn. 2 for the *t*'s sake, which dwelleth in us
    4 that I found of thy children walking in *t*
3 Jn. 3 came and testified of the *t* that is in thee
    4 joy than to hear that my children walk in *t*
    8 that we might be fellow helpers to the *t*

Try (Tried) *See also* Examine, Prove, Tempt

2 Sam. 22:31 (Ps. 18:30) the word of the LORD is *t*
2 Chr. 32:31 God left him, to *t* him, that he might
Job 23:10 he hath *t* me, I shall come forth as gold
    34:36 desire is that Job may be *t* unto the end
Ps. 7:9 the righteous God *t* the hearts and reins
    11:5 the LORD *t* the righteous
    17:3 thou hast *t* me, and shalt find nothing

Ps. 26:2 examine me. . *t* my reins and my heart
　66:10 proved us: thou hast *t* us, as silver is *t*
　139:23 know my heart: *t* me. . know my thoughts
Jer. 9:7 behold, I will melt them, and *t* them
　12:3 hast seen me, and *t* mine heart toward thee
Lam. 3:40 let us search and *t* our ways, and turn
Dan. 11:35 shall fall, to *t* them, and to purge
Zech. 13:9 will *t* them as gold is *t*: they shall call
1 Cor. 3:13 and the fire shall *t* every man's work
1 Thes. 2:4 pleasing men, but God, which *t* our hearts
Jas. 1:3 that the *t* of your faith worketh patience
　1:12 when he is *t*, he shall receive the crown
1 Pet. 4:12 the fiery trial which is to *t* you
1 Jn. 4:1 but *t* the spirits whether they are of God
Rev. 2:10 some of you into prison, that ye may be *t*
　3:18 counsel thee to buy of me gold *t* in the fire

Tubal-cain Gen. 4:22

Tumble

Judg. 7:13 a cake of barley bread *t* into the host

Tumult

1 Sam. 4:14 said, What meaneth the noise of this *t*?
2 Kgs. 19:28 (Is. 37:29) thy *t* is come. . into mine ears
Ps. 65:7 noise of their waves. . the *t* of the people
　83:2 lo, thine enemies make a *t*: and they that hate
Hos. 10:14 therefore shall a *t* arise among thy people
Mt. 27:24 but that rather a *t* was made, he took water
Acts 21:34 could not know the certainty for the *t*
2 Cor. 12:20 lest there be debates. . swellings, *t*

Tumultuous

Is. 13:4 a great people; a *t* noise of the kingdoms
　22:2 art full of stirs, a *t* city, a joyous city
Jer. 48:45 and the crown of the head of the *t* ones

Turn See also Change, Incline, Repent, Return

Ex. 14:5 heart of Pharaoh. . was *t* against the people
Num. 22:33 ass saw me, and *t* from me. . three times
Deut. 4:30 if thou *t* to the LORD thy God, and shalt
Josh. 7:8 Israel *t* their backs before their enemies!
Ruth 1:11 *t* again, my daughters: why will ye go
1 Kgs. 2:3 prosper. . whithersoever thou *t* thyself
　8:35 (2 Chr. 6:26) confess thy name. . *t* from. . sin
　18:37 that thou hast *t* their heart back again
2 Kgs. 2:24 *t* back, and looked on them, and cursed
　17:13 *t* ye from your evil ways, and keep my
2 Chr. 7:14 *t* from their wicked ways; then will I
Neh. 1:9 ye *t* unto me, and keep my commandments
Job 5:1 and to which of the saints wilt thou *t*?
　23:13 but he is in one mind, and who can *t* him?
Ps. 4:2 how long will ye *t* my glory into shame?
　7:12 if he *t* not, he will whet his sword
　9:17 the wicked shall be *t* into hell, and all
　22:27 ends of the world shall. . *t* unto the LORD
　60:1 hast been displeased; O *t* thyself to us again
　66:6 *t* the sea into dry land: they went through
　66:20 hath not *t* away my prayer, nor his mercy
　80:3 (80:7, 19) *t* us again. . cause thy face to shine
　85:4 *t* us. . cause thine anger toward us to cease
　85:8 but let them not *t* again to folly
　89:43 thou hast also *t* the edge of his sword
　90:3 thou *t* man to destruction; and sayest, Return
　114:8 which *t* the rock into a standing water
　126:1 when the LORD *t* again the captivity of Zion
　146:9 but the way of the wicked he *t* upside down
Prov. 1:23 *t* you at my reproof: behold, I will pour
　4:27 *t* not to the right hand nor to the left
　15:1 a soft answer *t* away wrath: but grievous
Eccl. 3:20 of the dust, and all *t* to dust again

Song 1:7 I be as one that *t* aside by the flocks
Is. 24:1 maketh the earth empty. . *t* it upside down
　53:6 we have *t* every one to his own way
Jer. 18:8 if that nation. . *t* from their evil, I will
　25:5 *t* ye again now every one from his evil way
　26:3 will hearken, and *t* every man from his evil
　31:13 I will *t* their mourning into joy, and will
　31:18 *t* thou me, and I shall be *t*; for thou art
Lam. 1:20 are troubled; mine heart is *t* within me
　3:40 and try our ways, and *t* again to the LORD
　5:21 *t* thou us unto thee, O LORD. . we shall be *t*
Ezek. 3:20 righteous man. . *t* from his righteousness
　14:6 repent, and *t* yourselves from your idols
　18:30 *t* yourselves from all your transgressions
　33:11 wicked *t* from his way and live: *t* ye, *t* ye
Dan. 12:3 *t* many to righteousness, as the stars
Hos. 7:8 among the people; Ephraim is a cake not *t*
　12:6 *t* thou to thy God: keep mercy and judgment
　14:2 take with you words, and *t* to the LORD
　14:4 love them freely: for mine anger is *t* away
Joel 2:12 *t* ye even to me with all your heart
　2:31 (Acts 2:20) the sun shall be *t* into darkness
Amos 5:8 *t* the shadow of death into the morning
Jon. 3:8 let them *t* every one from his evil way
Zech. 1:3 *t* ye unto me. . and I will *t* unto you
　9:12 *t* you to the stronghold, ye prisoners of hope
Mal. 4:6 (Lk. 1:17) shall *t* the heart of the fathers to
Mt. 5:39 on thy right cheek, *t* to him the other also
　9:22 but Jesus *t* him about, and when he saw her
Mk. 13:16 let him that is in the field not *t* back
Lk. 1:16 children of Israel shall he *t* to the Lord
　2:45 they *t* back again to Jerusalem, seeking him
Acts 13:46 everlasting life, lo, we *t* to the Gentiles
　14:15 *t* from these vanities unto the living God
　26:18 to *t* them from darkness to light, and from
1 Tim. 5:15 some are already *t* aside after Satan
2 Tim. 3:5 but denying the power. . from such *t* away
Tit. 1:14 commandments of men, that *t* from the truth

Turning

Prov. 1:32 the *t* away of the simple shall slay them
Acts 3:26 in *t* away every one. . from his iniquities
Jas. 1:17 is no variableness, neither shadow of *t*

Turtle See also Turtledove

Lev. 12:8 shall bring two *t*, or two young pigeons
Song 2:12 the voice of the *t* is heard in our land
Jer. 8:7 the *t* and the crane and the swallow observe

Turtledove See also Turtle

Gen. 15:9 take. . a ram of three years old, and a *t*
Lev. 1:14 then he shall bring his offering of *t*
Lk. 2:24 offer. . a pair of *t*, or two young pigeons

Tutor

Gal. 4:2 is under *t* and governors until the time

Twain See also Two

Is. 6:2 with *t* he covered his face, and with *t* he
Mt. 5:41 compel thee to go a mile, go with him *t*
　19:5 (Mk. 10:8) and they *t* shall be one flesh?
　27:21 whether of the *t* will ye that I release
　27:51 (Mk. 15:38) veil of the temple was rent in *t*
Eph. 2:15 to make in himself of *t* one new man

Twelve

Judg. 19:29 concubine, and divided her. . into *t*
Mt. 26:20 (Mk. 14:17; Lk. 22:14) sat down with the *t*
Mk. 3:14 (Lk. 6:13) ordained *t*, that they should be
　6:7 he called unto him the *t*, and began to send
Lk. 2:42 when he was *t* years old, they went up to
Jn. 6:70 have I not chosen you *t*, and one of you

1 Cor. 15:5 he was seen of Cephas, then of the *t*
Rev. 21:12 had *t* gates, and at the gates *t* angels

Twice

Num. 20:11 and with his rod he smote the rock *t*
Job 42:10 LORD gave Job *t* as much as he had before
Ps. 62:11 God hath spoken once; *t* have I heard this
Mk. 14:30 before the cock crow *t*, thou shalt deny
Lk. 18:12 I fast *t* in the week, I give tithes
Jude 12 trees. . without fruit, *t* dead, plucked up

Twilight

2 Kgs. 7:7 wherefore they arose and fled in the *t*
Job 24:15 eye. . of the adulterer waiteth for the *t*
Prov. 7:9 in the *t*, in the evening, in the. . night

Twin

Gen. 25:24 be delivered. . there were *t* in her womb
38:27 travail, that, behold, *t* were in her womb

Twinkling

1 Cor. 15:52 in the *t* of an eye, at the last trump

Two *See also* Twain

Gen. 7:9 (7:15) went in *t* and *t* unto Noah into the ark
1 Kgs. 3:25 divide the living child in *t*, and give
Eccl. 4:9 *t* are better than one; because they have
Amos 3:3 can *t* walk together, except they be agreed?
Mt. 6:24 (Lk. 16:13) no man can serve *t* masters
18:19 that if *t* of you shall agree on earth as
18:20 where *t* or three are gathered together in
24:40 (Lk. 17:36) *t* be in the field; the one shall
25:17 had received *t*, he also gained other *t*
Mk. 6:7 and began to send them forth by *t* and *t*
12:42 (Lk. 21:2) poor widow. . she threw in *t* mites
16:12 he appeared in another form unto *t* of them
Lk. 3:11 he that hath *t* coats, let him impart to
1 Cor. 6:16 (Eph. 5:31) for *t*. . shall be one flesh

Two-edged

Heb. 4:12 word of God. . sharper than any *t-e* sword
Rev. 1:16 out of his mouth went a sharp *t-e* sword

Tychicus

Eph. 6:21 (Col. 4:7); 2 Tim. 4:12; Tit. 3:12

Tyrannus Acts 19:9

Tyre (Tyrus)

Ps. 45:12 daughter of *T* shall be there with a gift
Is. 23:1 burden of *T*. Howl, ye ships of Tarshish
Ezek. 26:3 behold, I am against thee, O *T*
27:2 son of man, take up a lamentation for *T*
28:2 son of man, say unto the prince of *T*
Joel 3:4 what have ye to do with me, O *T*, and Zidon
Amos 1:9 for three transgressions of *T*, and for four
Mt. 11:21 (Lk. 10:13) had been done in *T* and Sidon
Mk. 7:24 and went into the borders of *T* and Sidon
Acts 12:20 Herod. . displeased with them of *T*
21:3 sailed into Syria, and landed at *T*

U

Ulai Dan. 8:2

Unadvisedly

Ps. 106:33 provoked his spirit, so that he spake *u*

Unawares

Num. 35:11 thither, which killeth any person at *u*
Ps. 35:8 let destruction come upon him at *u*

Lk. 21:34 lest. . that day come upon you *u*
Gal. 2:4 because of false brethren *u* brought in
Heb. 13:2 thereby some have entertained angels *u*
Jude 4 there are certain men crept in *u*, who were

Unbelief *See also* Doubt

Mt. 13:58 mighty works there because of their *u*
17:20 because of your *u*. . If ye have faith
Mk. 6:6 and he marveled because of their *u*
9:24 Lord, I believe; help thou mine *u*
16:14 upbraided them with their *u* and hardness
Rom. 3:3 *u* make the faith of God without effect?
4:20 he staggered not at the promise. . through *u*
11:20 because of *u* they were broken off
11:30 have now obtained mercy through their *u*
11:32 God hath concluded them all in *u*, that he
1 Tim. 1:13 mercy, because I did it ignorantly in *u*
Heb. 3:12 there be in any of you an evil heart of *u*
4:6 and they. . entered not in because of *u*
4:11 any man fall after the same example of *u*

Unbeliever

Lk. 12:46 will appoint him his portion with the *u*
1 Cor. 6:6 law with brother, and that before the *u*
14:23 there come in those that are unlearned, or *u*
2 Cor. 6:14 not unequally yoked together with *u*

Unbelieving

Acts 14:2 but the *u* Jews stirred up the Gentiles
1 Cor. 7:14 the *u* husband is sanctified by the wife
Tit. 1:15 that are defiled and *u* is nothing pure
Rev. 21:8 the fearful, and *u*, and the abominable

Unblamable

Col. 1:22 present you holy and *u* and unreprovable
1 Thes. 3:13 may stablish your hearts *u* in holiness

Unblamably

1 Thes. 2:10 and justly and *u* we behaved ourselves

Uncertain

1 Cor. 14:8 if the trumpet give an *u* sound, who
1 Tim. 6:17 not high-minded, nor trust in *u* riches

Uncertainly

1 Cor. 9:26 I therefore so run, not as *u*; so fight

Unchangeable

Heb. 7:24 he continueth ever, hath an *u* priesthood

Uncircumcised

Ex. 6:12 shall Pharaoh hear me, who am of *u* lips?
12:48 the passover. . no *u* person shall eat thereof
Lev. 19:23 ye shall count the fruit thereof as *u*
Judg. 15:18 die. . and fall into the hand of the *u*?
1 Sam. 31:4 (1 Chr. 10:4) lest these *u*. . abuse me
2 Sam. 1:20 lest the daughters of the *u* triumph
Is. 52:1 there shall be no more come into thee the *u*
Jer. 9:25 all them which are circumcised with the *u*
Ezek. 32:19 go down, and be thou laid with the *u*
44:7 strangers, *u* in heart, and *u* in flesh
Acts 7:51 ye stiffnecked and *u* in heart and ears
11:3 wentest in to men *u*, and didst eat with them
Rom. 4:11 of the faith which he had yet being *u*
1 Cor. 7:18 any. . circumcised? let him not become *u*

Uncircumcision

Rom. 2:25 breaker of the law, thy circumcision is. . *u*
2:26 if the *u* keep the righteousness of the law
3:30 circumcision by faith, and *u* through faith
4:9 the circumcision only, or upon the *u* also?
1 Cor. 7:18 is any called in *u*? let him not be
7:19 circumcision is nothing, and *u* is nothing

Gal. 2:7 the gospel of the *u* were committed unto me
5:6 (6:15) circumcision availeth any thing, nor *u*
Eph. 2:11 Gentiles in the flesh, who are called *U*
Col. 2:13 in your sins and the *u* of your flesh
3:11 neither Greek nor Jew, circumcision nor *u*

Unclean

Lev. 5:2 touch any *u* thing . . he also shall be *u*
10:10 holy and unholy, and between *u* and clean
11:8 (Deut. 14:7) shall . . not eat . . they are *u*
11:47 a difference between the *u* and the clean
12:2 a man child, then she shall be *u* seven days
13:3 priest shall look on him, and pronounce him *u*
13:45 upon his upper lip, and shall cry, *U, u*
15:2 when any man hath a running issue . . he is *u*
Num. 19:11 toucheth the dead . . shall be *u* seven days
Judg. 13:4 nor strong drink, and eat not any *u* thing
Job 14:4 who can bring a clean thing out of an *u*?
36:14 die in youth . . their life is among the *u*
Eccl. 9:2 one event . . to the clean, and to the *u*
Is. 6:5 I am undone; because I am a man of *u* lips
35:8 way of holiness; the *u* shall not pass over
52:1 come into thee the uncircumcised and the *u*
52:11 (2 Cor. 6:17) from thence, touch no *u* thing
64:6 but we are all as an *u* thing, and all our
Ezek. 22:26 difference between the *u* and the clean
44:23 to discern between the *u* and the clean
Hag. 2:14 and that which they offer there is *u*
Zech. 13:2 and the *u* spirit to pass out of the land
Mt. 10:1 (Mk. 6:7) gave them power against *u* spirits
12:43 (Lk. 11:24) the *u* spirit is gone out of a man
Mk. 1:23 (Lk. 4:33) synagogue a man with an *u* spirit
1:27 (Lk. 4:36) commandeth he even the *u* spirits
3:11 *u* spirits, when they saw him, fell down
3:30 because they said, He hath an *u* spirit
5:2 met him out of the tombs a man with an *u* spirit
7:25 woman, whose young daughter had an *u* spirit
Lk. 6:18 vexed with *u* spirits: and they were healed
9:42 rebuked the *u* spirit, and healed the child
Acts 5:16 and them which were vexed with *u* spirits
8:7 *u* spirits, crying with loud voice, came out
10:14 eaten any thing that is common or *u*
10:28 that I should not call any man common or *u*
11:8 for nothing common or *u* hath at any time
Rom. 14:14 nothing *u* of itself: but to him that
1 Cor. 7:14 else were your children *u*; but now are
2 Cor. 6:17 be ye separate . . touch not the *u* thing
Eph. 5:5 know, that no whoremonger, nor *u* person
Heb. 9:13 the ashes of a heifer sprinkling the *u*
Rev. 16:13 I saw three *u* spirits like frogs come out

Uncleanness

Lev. 5:3 if he touch the *u* of man, whatsoever *u* it be
7:20 the soul that eateth . . having his *u* upon him
15:31 from their *u*; that they die not in their *u*
Ezra 9:11 from one end to another with their *u*
Ezek. 36:29 I will also save you from all your *u*
Zech. 13:1 a fountain opened . . for sin and for *u*
Mt. 23:27 full of dead men's bones, and of all *u*
Rom. 1:24 wherefore God also gave them up to *u*
6:19 ye have yielded your members servants to *u*
2 Cor. 12:21 not repented of the *u* and fornication
Gal. 5:19 adultery, fornication, *u*, lasciviousness
Eph. 4:19 unto lasciviousness, to work all *u* with
5:3 *u*, or covetousness, let it not be once named
Col. 3:5 fornication, *u*, inordinate affection, evil
1 Thes. 2:3 exhortation was not of deceit, nor of *u*
4:7 hath not called us unto *u*, but unto holiness
2 Pet. 2:10 walk after the flesh in the lust of *u*

Unclothed

2 Cor. 5:4 not for that we would be *u*, but clothed

Uncomely

1 Cor. 7:36 behaveth himself *u* toward his virgin
12:23 our *u* parts have more abundant comeliness

Uncondemned

Acts 16:37 have beaten us openly *u*, being Romans
22:25 to scourge a man that is a Roman, and *u*?

Uncorruptible *See also* Incorruptible

Rom. 1:23 changed the glory of the *u* God into an

Uncorruptness

Tit. 2:7 in doctrine showing *u*, gravity, sincerity

Uncover

Lev. 10:6 *u* not your heads, neither rend your
18:6 is near of kin to him, to *u* their nakedness
Ruth 3:4 thou shalt go in, and *u* his feet, and lay
2 Sam. 6:20 glorious was the king . . who *u* himself
Is. 47:2 *u* thy locks, make bare the leg, *u* the thigh
Mk. 2:4 for the press, they *u* the roof where he was

Uncovered *See also* Uncover

Gen. 9:21 was drunken; and he was *u* within his tent
1 Cor. 11:5 with her head *u* dishonoreth her head
11:13 is it comely that a woman pray unto God *u*?

Unction

1 Jn. 2:20 ye have an *u* from the Holy One, and ye

Undefiled

Ps. 119:1 blessed are the *u* in the way, who walk
Song 6:9 my dove, my *u* is but one; she is the only
Heb. 7:26 a high priest . . who is holy, harmless, *u*
13:4 marriage is honorable in all, and the bed *u*
Jas. 1:27 pure religion and *u* before God and the
1 Pet. 1:4 to an inheritance incorruptible, and *u*

Understand (Understood) *See also*
Comprehend, Know, Perceive

Gen. 11:7 that they may not *u* one another's speech
41:15 that thou canst *u* a dream to interpret it
Deut. 32:29 that they were wise, that they *u* this
2 Kgs. 18:26 (Is. 36:11) Syrian language; for we *u* it
1 Chr. 28:19 LORD made me *u* in writing by his hand
Neh. 8:7 Levites, caused the people to *u* the law
8:13 unto Ezra . . even to *u* the words of the law
Job 6:24 and cause me to *u* wherein I have erred
23:5 answer me, and *u* what he would say unto me
26:14 but the thunder of his power who can *u*?
28:23 God *u* the way thereof, and he knoweth
32:9 always wise: neither do the aged *u* judgment
42:3 I uttered that I *u* not; things too wonderful
Ps. 14:2 (53:2) to see if there were any that did *u*
19:12 who can *u* his errors? cleanse thou me from
73:17 the sanctuary of God; then *u* I their end
82:5 they know not, neither will they *u*
92:6 man knoweth not; neither doth a fool *u* this
106:7 our fathers *u* not thy wonders in Egypt
107:43 shall *u* the loving-kindness of the LORD
119:27 make me to *u* the way of thy precepts
119:100 I *u* more than the ancients, because I
139:2 thou *u* my thought afar off
Prov. 2:5 then shalt thou *u* the fear of the LORD
8:5 O ye simple, *u* wisdom: and, ye fools, be ye
8:9 they are all plain to him that *u*, and right
14:6 but knowledge is easy unto him that *u*
14:8 the wisdom of the prudent is to *u* his way
20:24 how can a man then *u* his own way?
28:5 evil men *u* not . . they that seek the LORD *u* all

Is. 6:9 (Mt. 13:14; Mk. 4:12; Lk. 8:10; Acts 28:26)
  hear ye indeed, but *u* not
  6:10 (Mt. 13:15; Jn. 12:40; Acts 28:27) lest they. . *u*
  with their heart
  28:9 whom shall he make to *u* doctrine? them that
  32:4 the heart also of the rash shall *u* knowledge
  40:21 have ye not *u* from the foundations of the
  43:10 may know and believe me, and *u* that I am he
  44:18 they have not known nor *u*: for he hath shut
  56:11 they are shepherds that cannot *u*: they all
Jer. 9:12 who is the wise man, that may *u* this?
  9:24 glory in this, that he *u* and knoweth me
Dan. 8:17 but he said unto me, *U*, O son of man
  8:23 fierce countenance, and *u* dark sentences
  8:27 I was astonished at the vision, but none *u*
  9:13 turn from our iniquities, and *u* thy truth
  12:10 none of the wicked shall *u*. . the wise shall *u*
Hos. 4:14 the people that doth not *u* shall fall
  14:9 who is wise, and he shall *u* these things?
Mic. 4:12 they knew not. . neither *u* they his counsel
Mt. 13:19 when any one heareth the word. . *u* it not
  13:51 saith unto them, Have ye *u* all these things?
  15:10 (Mk. 7:14) and said unto them, Hear, and *u*
  16:9 (Mk. 8:17) do ye not yet *u*, neither remember
  24:15 (Mk. 13:14) whoso readeth, let him *u*
Mk. 9:32 (Lk. 9:45) *u* not that saying, and were afraid
Lk. 18:34 they *u* none of these things
  24:45 opened. . that they might *u* the Scriptures
Acts 7:25 his brethren would have *u*. . but they *u* not
  8:30 and Philip. . said, *U* thou what thou readest?
Rom. 1:20 being *u* by the things that are made
  3:11 is none that *u*, there is none that seeketh
  15:21 and they that have not heard shall *u*
1 Cor. 13:2 gift of prophecy, and *u* all mysteries
  13:11 a child, I spake as a child, I *u* as a child
  14:9 ye utter by the tongue words easy to be *u*
Eph. 3:4 *u* my knowledge in the mystery of Christ
  5:17 unwise, but *u* what the will of the Lord is
1 Tim. 1:7 *u* neither what they say, nor whereof
Heb. 11:3 through faith we *u* that the worlds were
2 Pet. 2:12 speak evil of the things. . they *u* not
  3:16 in which are some things hard to be *u*

Understanding *See also* Understand, Knowledge, Prudence, Wisdom

Deut. 32:28 counsel, neither is there any *u* in them
1 Kgs. 3:9 thy servant an *u* heart to judge thy people
  4:29 God gave Solomon wisdom and *u* exceeding
1 Chr. 12:32 men that had *u* of the times, to know
2 Chr. 26:5 who had *u* in the visions of God
Job 12:12 the ancient is wisdom. . in length of days *u*
  17:4 thou hast hid their heart from *u*: therefore
  28:12 (28:20) and where is the place of *u*?
  28:28 is wisdom; and to depart from evil is *u*
  32:8 inspiration of the Almighty giveth them *u*
  38:36 or who hath given *u* to the heart?
Ps. 32:9 horse, or as the mule, which have no *u*
  47:7 God is the King. . sing ye praises with *u*
  49:3 the meditation of my heart shall be of *u*
  111:10 good *u* have all. . do his commandments
  119:34 give me *u*, and I shall keep thy law
  119:99 I have more *u* than all my teachers
  119:104 through thy precepts I get *u*: therefore
  119:125 give me *u*, that I may know thy testimonies
  119:130 giveth light. . giveth *u* unto the simple
  119:144 everlasting: give me *u*, and I shall live
  119:169 O LORD: give me *u* according to thy word
  147:5 great is our Lord. . his *u* is infinite
Prov. 2:2 unto wisdom, and apply thine heart to *u*
  2:11 discretion. . preserve thee, *u* shall keep thee
  3:5 trust in the LORD. . lean not unto thine own *u*

Prov. 3:13 happy is the man that. . getteth *u*
  3:19 by *u* hath he established the heavens
  4:5 get wisdom, get *u*: forget it not
  7:4 thou art my sister; and call *u* thy kinswoman
  8:1 doth not wisdom cry? and *u* put forth her voice
  9:6 forsake. . and live; and go in the way of *u*
  9:10 wisdom: and the knowledge of the Holy is *u*
  10:23 to do mischief: but a man of *u* hath wisdom
  13:15 good *u* giveth favor: but the way of
  14:29 he that is slow to wrath is of great *u*
  15:14 heart of him that hath *u* seeketh knowledge
  15:21 but a man of *u* walketh uprightly
  15:32 but he that heareth reproof getteth *u*
  16:16 to get *u* rather to be chosen than silver!
  16:22 *u* is a wellspring of life unto him that
  17:27 and a man of *u* is of an excellent spirit
  18:2 a fool hath no delight in *u*, but that his
  19:8 he that keepeth *u* shall find good
  24:3 a house builded; and by *u* it is established
  28:16 prince that wanteth *u* is. . a great oppressor
Is. 27:11 for it is a people of no *u*: therefore he
  29:14 (1 Cor. 1:19) *u* of. . prudent men shall be hid
  29:16 say of him that framed it, He had no *u*?
  40:14 knowledge, and showed to him the way of *u*?
  40:28 is weary? there is no searching of his *u*
Jer. 5:21 hear now. . O foolish people, and without *u*
  51:15 and hath stretched out the heaven by his *u*
Dan. 1:17 Daniel had *u* in all visions and dreams
  11:35 some of them of *u* shall fall, to try them
Mt. 15:16 (Mk. 7:18) are ye also yet without *u*?
Mk. 12:33 with all the *u*, and with all the soul
Lk. 2:47 that heard him were astonished at his *u*
  24:45 then opened he their *u*, that they might
Rom. 1:31 without *u*, covenantbreakers, without
1 Cor. 14:15 pray with the *u*. . will sing with the *u*
  14:19 I had rather speak five words with my *u*
  14:20 brethren, be not children in *u*. . in *u* be men
Eph. 1:18 eyes of your *u* being enlightened; that ye
  4:18 having the *u* darkened, being alienated from
Phil. 4:7 peace of God, which passeth all *u*, shall
Col. 1:9 of his will in all wisdom and spiritual *u*
  2:2 unto all riches of the full assurance of *u*
2 Tim. 2:7 and the Lord give thee *u* in all things
1 Jn. 5:20 Son of God is come. . hath given us an *u*

Undertake
Is. 38:14 O LORD, I am oppressed; *u* for me

Undo
Is. 58:6 to *u* the heavy burdens. . to let the oppressed
Zeph. 3:19 that time I will *u* all that afflict thee

Undone
Num. 21:29 woe to thee, Moab! thou art *u*, O people
Josh. 11:15 so did Joshua; he left nothing *u* of all
Is. 6:5 then said I, Woe is me! for I am *u*; because
Mt.23:23 (Lk. 11:42) and not to leave the other *u*

Unequal
Ezek. 18:25 (18:29) my way equal?. . your ways *u*?

Unfaithful
Prov. 25:19 confidence in an *u* man in time of trouble

Unfeigned
2 Cor. 6:6 kindness, by the Holy Ghost, by love *u*
1 Tim. 1:5 of a good conscience, and of faith *u*
2 Tim. 1:5 I call to remembrance the *u* faith that
1 Pet. 1:22 the Spirit unto *u* love of the brethren

Unfruitful
Mt. 13:22 (Mk. 4:19) choke the word. . becometh *u*
1 Cor. 14:14 prayeth, but my understanding is *u*

Eph. 5:11 fellowship with the *u* works of darkness
Tit. 3:14 for necessary uses, that they be not *u*
2 Pet. 1:8 neither be barren nor *u* in the knowledge

Ungird

Gen. 24:32 *u* his camels . . gave straw and provender

Ungodliness

Rom. 1:18 is revealed from heaven against all *u*
11:26 Deliverer, and shall turn away *u* from Jacob
2 Tim. 2:16 for they will increase unto more *u*
Tit. 2:12 denying *u* and worldly lusts, we should

Ungodly *See also* Wicked

2 Sam. 22:5 (Ps. 18:4) floods of *u* men made me afraid
2 Chr. 19:2 Jehoshaphat, Shouldest thou help the *u*
Job 16:11 God hath delivered me to the *u*
34:18 thou art wicked? and to princes, Ye are *u*?
Ps. 1:1 that walketh not in the counsel of the *u*
1:4 the *u* are not so: but are like the chaff which
1:6 but the way of the *u* shall perish
3:7 thou hast broken the teeth of the *u*
43:1 and plead my cause against an *u* nation
73:12 these are the *u*, who prosper in the world
Prov. 16:27 *u* man diggeth up evil: and in his lips
Rom. 4:5 believeth on him that justifieth the *u*
5:6 in due time Christ died for the *u*
1 Tim. 1:9 for the *u* and for sinners, for unholy
1 Pet. 4:18 where shall the *u* and the sinner appear?
2 Pet. 2:5 in the flood upon the world of the *u*
2:6 ensample unto those that after should live *u*
3:7 the day of judgment and perdition of *u* men
Jude 4 *u* men, turning the grace of our God into
15 *u* . . of all their *u* deeds . . they have *u* committed

Unholy

Lev. 10:10 may put difference between holy and *u*
1 Tim. 1:9 for the ungodly and for sinners, for *u*
2 Tim. 3:2 disobedient to parents, unthankful, *u*
Heb. 10:29 hath counted the blood . . an *u* thing

Unicorn

Num. 23:22 (24:8) as it were the strength of a *u*
Job 39:9 will the *u* be willing to serve thee
Ps. 29:6 a calf; Lebanon and Sirion like a young *u*
Is. 34:7 the *u* shall come down with them

Unite

Gen. 49:6 be not thou *u*: for in their anger they
Ps. 86:11 thy truth: *u* my heart to fear thy name

Unity

Ps. 133:1 for brethren to dwell together in *u*!
Eph. 4:3 endeavoring to keep the *u* of the Spirit
4:13 till we all come in the *u* of the faith

Unjust

Ps. 43:1 O deliver me from the deceitful and *u* man
Prov. 11:7 and the hope of *u* men perisheth
28:8 usury and *u* gain increaseth his substance
29:27 an *u* man is an abomination to the just
Zeph. 3:5 faileth not; but the *u* knoweth no shame
Mt. 5:45 and sendeth rain on the just and on the *u*
Lk. 16:8 lord commended the *u* steward, because he
16:10 he that is *u* in the least is *u* also in much
18:6 the Lord said, Hear what the *u* judge saith
18:11 I am not as other men are, extortioners, *u*
Acts 24:15 a resurrection . . both of the just and *u*
1 Cor. 6:1 against another, go to law before the *u*
1 Pet. 3:18 suffered for sins, the just for the *u*
2 Pet. 2:9 reserve the *u* unto the day of judgment
Rev. 22:11 he that is *u*, let him be *u* still

Unjustly

Ps. 82:2 how long will ye judge *u*, and accept the
Is. 26:10 in the land of uprightness will he deal *u*

Unknown

Acts 17:23 with this inscription, TO THE *U* GOD
1 Cor. 14:2 for he that speaketh in an *u* tongue
14:13 let him that speaketh in an *u* tongue pray
14:19 than ten thousand words in an *u* tongue
2 Cor. 6:9 as *u*, and yet well known; as dying, and
Gal. 1:22 was *u* by face unto the churches of Judea

Unlawful

Acts 10:28 *u* thing for a man that is a Jew to keep
2 Pet. 2:8 vexed . . from day to day with their *u* deeds

Unlearned

Acts 4:13 perceived that they were *u* and ignorant
1 Cor. 14:16 occupieth the room of the *u* say Amen
14:23 come in those that are *u*, or unbelievers
2 Tim. 2:23 but foolish and *u* questions avoid
2 Pet. 3:16 that are *u* and unstable wrest, as they

Unleavened

Ex. 12:17 (23:15; 34:18) observe the feast of *u* bread
12:39 they baked *u* cakes of the dough which
Lev. 6:16 with *u* bread shall it be eaten in the
Num. 6:15 basket of *u* bread . . and wafers of *u* bread
Deut. 16:8 six days thou shalt eat *u* bread
Mt. 26:17 (Lk. 22:7) first day of the feast of *u* bread
1 Cor. 5:7 that ye may be a new lump, as ye are *u*
5:8 but with the *u* bread of sincerity and truth

Unloose

Mk. 1:7 (Lk. 3:16; Jn. 1:27) I am not worthy to . . *u*

Unmarried

1 Cor. 7:8 I say therefore to the *u* and widows
7:11 but and if she depart, let her remain *u*
7:32 that is *u* careth . . how he may please the Lord
7:34 *u* woman careth for the things of the Lord

Unmerciful

Rom. 1:31 without natural affection, implacable, *u*

Unmindful

Deut. 32:18 of the Rock that begat thee thou art *u*

Unmoveable

Acts 27:41 the forepart stuck fast, and remained *u*
1 Cor. 15:58 be ye steadfast, *u*, always abounding

Unperfect

Ps. 139:16 eyes did see my substance, yet being *u*

Unprepared

2 Cor. 9:4 of Macedonia come with me . . find you *u*

Unprofitable

Job 15:3 should he reason with *u* talk? or with
Mt. 25:30 cast ye the *u* servant into outer darkness
Lk. 17:10 say, We are *u* servants: we have done that
Rom. 3:12 they are together become *u*; there is none
Tit. 3:9 strivings about the law; for they are *u*
Phlm. 11 which in time past was to thee *u*, but now
Heb. 13:17 not with grief: for that is *u* for you

Unpunished

Prov. 11:21 wicked shall not be *u*: but the seed of
16:5 though hand join in hand, he shall not be *u*
17:5 he that is glad at calamities shall not be *u*
19:5 a false witness shall not be *u*
Jer. 25:29 should ye be utterly *u*? Ye shall not be *u*

Jer. 30:11 and will not leave thee altogether *u*
49:12 go *u*? thou shalt not go *u*, but thou shalt

Unquenchable

Mt. 3:12 (Lk. 3:17) burn up the chaff with *u* fire

Unreasonable

Acts 25:27 it seemeth to me *u* to send a prisoner
2 Thes. 3:2 may be delivered from *u* and wicked men

Unrebukable

1 Tim. 6:14 keep this commandment without spot, *u*

Unreprovable

Col. 1:22 to present you holy and unblamable and *u*

Unrighteous

Ex. 23:1 hand with the wicked to be an *u* witness
Ps. 71:4 out of the hand of the *u* and cruel man
Is. 10:1 woe unto them that decree *u* decrees
55:7 forsake his way, and the *u* man his thoughts
Lk. 16:11 have not been faithful in the *u* mammon
1 Cor. 6:9 *u* shall not inherit the kingdom of God?
Heb. 6:10 God is not *u* to forget your work and labor

Unrighteousness

Lev. 19:15 (19:35) ye shall do no *u* in judgment
Ps. 92:15 he is my rock, and there is no *u* in him
Jer. 22:13 woe unto him that buildeth his house by *u*
Lk. 16:9 make . . friends of the mammon of *u*
Jn. 7:18 the same is true, and no *u* is in him
Rom. 1:18 and *u* of men, who hold the truth in *u*
1:29 filled with all *u*, fornication, wickedness
2:8 not obey the truth, but obey *u*, indignation
3:5 if our *u* commend the righteousness of God
6:13 yield ye your members as instruments of *u*
9:14 what shall we say then? Is there *u* with God?
2 Cor. 6:14 fellowship hath righteousness with *u*?
2 Thes. 2:12 not the truth, but had pleasure in *u*
Heb. 8:12 I will be merciful to their *u*, and their
2 Pet. 2:13 shall receive the reward of *u*, as they
1 Jn. 1:9 our sins, and to cleanse us from all *u*
5:17 all *u* is sin: and there is a sin not unto

Unruly

1 Thes. 5:14 we exhort you . . warn them that are *u*
Tit. 1:6 faithful children not accused of riot or *u*
1:10 for there are many *u* and vain talkers
Jas. 3:8 tongue can no man tame; it is an *u* evil

Unsavory

2 Sam. 22:27 the froward thou wilt show thyself *u*
Job 6:6 can that which is *u* be eaten without salt?

Unsearchable

Job 5:9 which doeth great things and *u*; marvelous
Ps. 145:3 to be praised; and his greatness is *u*
Prov. 25:3 for depth, and the heart of kings is *u*
Rom. 11:33 how *u* are his judgments, and his ways
Eph. 3:8 among the Gentiles the *u* riches of Christ

Unseemly

Rom. 1:27 men with men working that which is *u*
1 Cor. 13:5 doth not behave itself *u*, seeketh not

Unskilful

Heb. 5:13 one that useth milk is *u* in the word

Unspeakable

2 Cor. 9:15 thanks be unto God for his *u* gift
12:4 caught up into paradise, and heard *u* words
1 Pet. 1:8 ye rejoice with joy *u* and full of glory

Unspotted

Jas. 1:27 and to keep himself *u* from the world

Unstable

Gen. 49:4 *u* as water, thou shalt not excel
Jas. 1:8 a double-minded man is *u* in all his ways
2 Pet. 2:14 beguiling *u* souls: a heart they have
3:16 which they that are unlearned and *u* wrest

Unstopped

Is. 35:5 and the ears of the deaf shall be *u*

Unthankful

Lk. 6:35 for he is kind unto the *u* and to the evil
2 Tim. 3:2 blasphemers, disobedient to parents, *u*

Untimely

Job 3:16 or as a hidden *u* birth I had not been
Ps. 58:8 pass away: like the *u* birth of a woman
Eccl. 6:3 I say, that an *u* birth is better than he
Rev. 6:13 even as a fig tree casteth her *u* figs

Untoward

Acts 2:40 save yourselves from this *u* generation

Unwashen

Mt. 15:20 (Mk. 7:2) to eat with *u* hands defileth not

Unwise

Deut. 32:6 O foolish people and *u*? is not he thy
Hos. 13:13 he is an *u* son; for he should not stay
Rom. 1:14 debtor . . both to the wise, and to the *u*
Eph. 5:17 wherefore be ye not *u*, but understanding

Unworthily

1 Cor. 11:27 drink this cup of the Lord, *u*, shall

Unworthy

Acts 13:46 judge yourselves *u* of everlasting life
1 Cor. 6:2 are ye *u* to judge the smallest matters?

Upbraid

Judg. 8:15 Zebah and Zalmunna, with whom ye did *u*
Mt. 11:20 began he to *u* the cities wherein most
Mk. 16:14 *u* them with their unbelief and hardness
Jas. 1:5 giveth to all men liberally, and *u* not

Uphold (Upheld, Upholden)

Job 4:4 thy words have *u* him that was falling
Ps. 37:17 be broken: but the LORD *u* the righteous
37:24 be utterly cast down: for the LORD *u* him
41:12 thou *u* me in mine integrity, and settest me
51:12 thy salvation; and *u* me with thy free Spirit
54:4 helper: the Lord is with them that *u* my soul
63:8 followeth hard after thee: thy right hand *u*
119:116 *u* me according unto thy word, that I may
145:14 the LORD *u* all that fall, and raiseth up
Prov. 20:28 the king: and his throne is *u* by mercy
29:23 but honor shall *u* the humble in spirit
Is. 41:10 I will *u* thee with the right hand of my
42:1 behold my servant, whom I *u*; mine elect
63:5 was none to *u*: therefore . . my fury, it *u* me
Heb. 1:3 and *u* all things by the word of his power

Upper

Mk. 14:15 (Lk. 22:12) will show you a large *u* room
Acts 1:13 were come in, they went up into an *u* room

Uppermost

Mt. 23:6 (Mk. 12:39; Lk. 11:43) love the *u* rooms at

Upright *See also* Correct, Honest, Just, Perfect, Righteous, True

Lev. 26:13 broken . . your yoke, and made you go *u*
1 Sam. 29:6 as the LORD liveth, thou hast been *u*

2 Sam. 22:24 (Ps. 18:23) I was also *u* before him
22:26 (Ps. 18:25) with the *u* man. . show thyself *u*
2 Chr. 29:34 for the Levites were more *u* in heart
Job 1:1 was Job; and that man was perfect and *u*
8:6 if thou wert pure and *u*; surely now he would
17:8 *u* men shall be astonished at their
Ps. 7:10 my defense is of God, which saveth the *u*
11:7 his countenance doth behold the *u*
19:13 then shall I be *u*, and I shall be innocent
25:8 good and *u* is the LORD: therefore will he
32:11 shout for joy, all ye that are *u* in heart
33:1 righteous: for praise is comely for the *u*
36:10 and thy righteousness to the *u* in heart
37:14 and to slay such as be of *u* conversation
37:18 LORD knoweth the days of the *u*: and their
37:37 mark the perfect man, and behold the *u*
49:14 and the *u* shall have dominion over them
64:10 in him; and all the *u* in heart shall glory
92:15 to show that the LORD is *u*: he is my rock
94:15 and all the *u* in heart shall follow it
111:1 my whole heart, in the assembly of the *u*
112:2 the generation of the *u* shall be blessed
112:4 unto the *u*. . ariseth light in the darkness
119:137 art thou, O LORD, and *u* are thy judgments
125:4 do good. . to them that are *u* in their hearts
140:13 the *u* shall dwell in thy presence
Prov. 2:21 for the *u* shall dwell in the land
10:29 the way of the LORD is strength to the *u*
11:3 the integrity of the *u* shall guide them
11:11 by the blessing of the *u* the city is exalted
11:20 such as are *u* in their way are his delight
13:6 righteousness keepeth him that is *u* in the way
14:11 but the tabernacle of the *u* shall flourish
15:8 but the prayer of the *u* is his delight
16:17 the highway of the *u* is to depart from evil
21:29 but as for the *u*, he directeth his way
28:10 the *u* shall have good things in possession
29:27 he that is *u* in the way is abomination
Eccl. 7:29 that God hath made man *u*; but they have
12:10 which was written was *u*, even words of truth
Is. 26:7 most *u*, dost weigh the path of the just
Mic. 7:2 there is none *u* among men: they all lie
Hab. 2:4 soul which is lifted up is not *u* in him

Uprightly *See also* Righteously

Ps. 15:2 that walketh *u*, and worketh righteousness
58:1 do ye judge *u*, O ye sons of men?
84:11 will he withhold from them that walk *u*
Prov. 2:7 he is a buckler to them that walk *u*
10:9 he that walketh *u* walketh surely
28:18 whoso walketh *u* shall be saved
Is. 33:15 that walketh righteously, and speaketh *u*
Amos 5:10 and they abhor him that speaketh *u*
Mic. 2:7 my words do good to him that walketh *u*?
Gal. 2:14 but when I saw that they walked not *u*

Uprightness *See also* Honesty, Integrity, Righteousness

1 Kgs. 3:6 as he walked. . in *u* of heart with thee
1 Chr. 29:17 triest the heart, and hast pleasure in *u*
Job 4:6 confidence, thy hope, and the *u* of thy ways?
33:23 among a thousand, to show unto man his *u*
Ps. 111:8 stand fast. . and are done in truth and *u*
143:10 Spirit is good; lead me into the land of *u*
Prov. 2:13 who leave the paths of *u*, to walk in
14:2 he that walketh in his *u* feareth the LORD
28:6 better is the poor that walketh in his *u*
Is. 26:7 way of the just is *u*: thou, most upright
26:10 in the land of *u* will he deal unjustly
57:2 they shall rest. . each one walking in his *u*

Uprising

Ps. 139:2 thou knowest my downsitting and mine *u*

Uproar

Mt. 26:5 (Mk. 14:2) feast day, lest there be an *u*
Acts 17:5 set all the city on an *u*, and assaulted
19:40 to be called in question for this day's *u*
21:31 tidings. . that all Jerusalem was in an *u*

Upward

Job 5:7 is born unto trouble, as the sparks fly *u*
Eccl. 3:21 knoweth the spirit of man that goeth *u*

Ur Gen. 11:31; 15:7 (Neh. 9:7)

Urge

Gen. 33:11 have enough. And he *u* him, and he took it
Judg. 16:16 when she pressed him daily. . and *u* him
2 Kgs. 2:17 when they *u* him till he was ashamed
Lk. 11:53 the Pharisees began to *u* him vehemently

Urgent

Ex. 12:33 Egyptians were *u* upon the people, that
Dan. 3:22 because the king's commandment was *u*

Uriah 2 Sam. 11:3–26

Urijah the priest 2 Kgs. 16:10–16

Urijah the prophet Jer. 26:20–23

Urim *See also* Thummim

Ex. 28:30 (Lev. 8:8) put in. . the *U* and the Thummim
Num. 27:21 counsel for him after the judgment of *U*
1 Sam. 28:6 answered him not. . by dreams, nor by *U*
Ezra 2:63 (Neh. 7:65) stood up a priest with *U* and

Use

Mt. 5:44 (Lk. 6:28) for them which despitefully *u* you
Acts 14:5 to *u* them despitefully, and to stone them
Rom. 1:26 women did change the natural *u* into that
1 Cor. 7:31 they that *u* this world, as not abusing
9:12 we have not *u* this power; but suffer all
1 Tim. 1:8 the law is good, if a man *u* it lawfully
3:13 for they that have *u* the office of a deacon
2 Tim. 2:21 sanctified, and meet for the master's *u*
Heb. 5:14 by reason of *u* have their senses exercised

Usury

Ex. 22:25 usurer, neither shalt thou lay upon him *u*
Lev. 25:36 take thou no *u* of him, or increase
Deut. 23:20 unto a stranger thou mayest lend upon *u*
Neh. 5:7 ye exact *u*, every one of his brother
Ps. 15:5 he that putteth not out his money to *u*
Prov. 28:8 he that by *u* and unjust gain increaseth
Is. 24:2 taker of *u*, so with the giver of *u* to him
Jer. 15:10 lent on *u*, nor men have lent to me on *u*
Ezek. 18:13 hath given forth upon *u*, and hath taken
22:12 shed blood; thou hast taken *u* and increase
Mt. 25:27 (Lk. 19:23) have received mine own with *u*

Utter *See also* Speak, Talk

2 Sam. 22:14 thundered. . Most High *u* his voice
Job 15:2 should a wise man *u* vain knowledge
33:3 of my heart: and my lips shall *u* knowledge
Ps. 19:2 day unto day *u* speech. . night unto night
78:2 in a parable: I will *u* dark sayings of old
94:4 how long shall they *u* and speak hard things?
106:2 who can *u* the mighty acts of the LORD?
Prov. 23:33 thine heart shall *u* perverse things
29:11 fool *u* all his mind: but a wise man keepeth
Eccl. 1:8 things are full of labor; man cannot *u* it
5:2 let not thine heart be hasty to *u* any thing
Is. 32:6 hypocrisy, and to *u* error against the LORD
48:20 *u* it even to the end of the earth; say ye
Joel 2:11 LORD shall *u* his voice before his army

Hab. 3:10 deep *u* his voice, and lifted up his hands
Mt. 13:35 will *u* things which have been kept secret
Rom. 8:26 for us with groanings which cannot be *u*
1 Cor. 14:9 except ye *u* by the tongue words easy
2 Cor. 12:4 which it is not lawful for a man to *u*
Heb. 5:11 many things to say, and hard to be *u*

Utterance

Acts 2:4 other tongues, as the Spirit gave them *u*
1 Cor. 1:5 ye are enriched by him, in all *u*
2 Cor. 8:7 abound in every thing, in faith, and *u*
Eph. 6:19 that *u* may be given unto me, that I may
Col. 4:3 that God would open unto us a door of *u*

Uttermost

Ps. 2:8 *u* parts of the earth for thy possession
Mk. 13:27 *u* part of the earth to the *u* part of heaven
Acts 1:8 Samaria, and unto the *u* part of the earth
1 Thes. 2:16 the wrath is come upon them to the *u*
Heb. 7:25 able also to save them to the *u* that come

Uz Job 1:1

Uzzah (Uzza) 2 Sam. 6:3–8 (1 Chr. 13:7–11)

Uzziah *See also* Azariah 2 Chr. 26:1–23

Is. 1:1 (Hos. 1:1; Amos 1:1; Zech. 14:5) the days of *U*
6:1 in the year that king *U* died I saw also

V

Vagabond

Gen. 4:12 a fugitive and a *v* shalt thou be in the
Ps. 109:10 his children be continually *v*, and beg
Acts 19:13 then certain of the *v* Jews, exorcists

Vain

Ex. 5:9 may labor . . and let them not regard *v* words
20:7 (Deut. 5:11) name of the LORD thy God in *v*
Deut. 32:47 it is not a *v* thing for you; because
1 Sam. 12:21 for then should ye go after *v* things
2 Sam. 6:20 as one of the *v* fellows shamelessly
2 Chr. 13:7 and there are gathered unto him *v* men
Job 11:11 he knoweth *v* men: he seeth wickedness
16:3 *v* words have an end? or what emboldeneth
27:12 seen it; why then are ye thus altogether *v*?
41:9 behold, the hope of him is in *v*: shall not
Ps. 2:1 (Acts 4:25) the people imagine a *v* thing?
26:4 I have not sat with *v* persons, neither will
33:17 a horse is a *v* thing for safety
39:6 a *v* show: surely they are disquieted in *v*
60:11 (108:12) trouble: for *v* is the help of man
89:47 wherefore hast thou made all men in *v*?
119:113 I hate *v* thoughts: but thy law do I love
127:1 labor in *v* . . the watchman waketh but in *v*
127:2 it is *v* for you to rise up early, to sit up
Prov. 12:11 he that followeth *v* persons is void of
28:19 followeth after *v* persons shall have poverty
31:30 favor is deceitful, and beauty is *v*
Eccl. 6:12 all the days of his *v* life . . as a shadow?
Is. 1:13 bring no more *v* oblations; incense is an
45:18 he created it not in *v*, he formed it to be
45:19 I said not unto . . Jacob, Seek ye me in *v*
49:4 then I said, I have labored in *v*, I have
65:23 they shall not labor in *v*, nor bring forth
Jer. 3:23 in *v* is salvation hoped for from the hills
4:14 how long shall thy *v* thoughts lodge within
10:3 the customs of the people are *v*: for one
23:16 that prophesy unto you; they make you *v*
46:11 in *v* shalt thou use many medicines

Lam. 4:17 our eyes as yet failed for our *v* help
Ezek. 12:24 there shall be no more any *v* vision
Mal. 3:14 ye have said, It is *v* to serve God
Mt. 6:7 but when ye pray, use not *v* repetitions
15:9 (Mk. 7:7) in *v* they do worship me, teaching
Rom. 1:21 but became *v* in their imaginations
13:4 afraid; for he beareth not the sword in *v*
1 Cor. 3:20 thoughts of the wise, that they are *v*
15:2 ye are saved . . unless ye have believed in *v*
15:14 our preaching *v*, and your faith is also *v*
15:58 that your labor is not in *v* in the Lord
2 Cor. 6:1 ye receive not the grace of God in *v*
Gal. 2:2 lest . . I should run, or had run, in *v*
2:21 come by the law, then Christ is dead in *v*
Eph. 5:6 let no man deceive you with *v* words
Phil. 2:16 have not run in *v*, neither labored in *v*
1 Thes. 3:5 have tempted you, and our labor be in *v*
1 Tim. 1:6 some . . have turned aside unto *v* jangling
6:20 (2 Tim. 2:16) avoiding profane . . *v* babblings
Tit. 1:10 many unruly and *v* talkers and deceivers
Jas. 1:26 bridleth not . . this man's religion is *v*
1 Pet. 1:18 from your *v* conversation received by

Vainglory

Gal. 5:26 let us not be desirous of *v*, provoking
Phil. 2:3 let nothing be done through strife or *v*

Valiant (Valiantest) *See also*
Courageous

Judg. 21:10 sent . . twelve thousand men of the *v*
1 Sam. 16:18 and a mighty *v* man, and a man of war
18:17 give thee to wife: only be thou *v* for me
2 Sam. 2:7 your hands be strengthened, and be ye *v*
1 Kgs. 1:42 art a *v* man, and bringest good tidings
Song 3:7 *v* men are about it, of the *v* of Israel
Is. 33:7 behold, their *v* ones shall cry without
Jer. 9:3 they are not *v* for the truth upon the earth
46:15 why are thy *v* men swept away? they stood
Nah. 2:3 *v* men are in scarlet: the chariots shall
Heb. 11:34 waxed *v* in fight, turned to flight the

Valiantly

Num. 24:18 for his enemies; and Israel shall do *v*
1 Chr. 19:13 behave ourselves *v* for our people
Ps. 60:12 (108:13) through God we shall do *v*
118:15 (118:16) the right hand of the LORD doeth *v*

Valley

Deut. 21:4 shall bring down the heifer unto a rough *v*
Josh. 8:13 Joshua went . . into the midst of the *v*
1 Kgs. 20:28 of the hills, but he is not God of the *v*
Ps. 23:4 walk through the *v* of the shadow of death
65:13 the *v* also are covered over with corn
Is. 22:1 the burden of the *v* of vision
28:1 which are on the head of the fat *v* of them
40:4 (Lk. 3:5) every *v* shall be exalted, and every
Jer. 7:32 (19:6) of Hinnom, but The *v* of slaughter
21:13 I am against thee, O inhabitant of the *v*
Ezek. 37:1 midst of the *v* which was full of bones
Hos. 2:15 and the *v* of Achor for a door of hope
Joel 3:14 multitudes, multitudes in the *v* of decision

Valor

Judg. 6:12 LORD is with thee, thou mighty man of *v*
11:1 Jephthah the Gileadite was a mighty man of *v*
1 Kgs. 11:28 Jeroboam was a mighty man of *v*
2 Kgs. 5:1 a mighty man in *v*, but he was a leper

Value *See also* Worth

Lev. 27:8 priest shall *v* him; according to his ability
Job 13:4 ye are forgers of lies . . physicians of no *v*
28:16 it cannot be *v* with the gold of Ophir

Mt. 10:31 (Lk. 12:7) of more *v* than many sparrows
  27:9 thirty pieces. . the price of him that was *v*

Vanish

Job 6:17 what time they wax warm, they *v*: when it
  7:9 as the cloud is consumed and *v* away
Is. 51:6 for the heavens shall *v* away like smoke
Lk. 24:31 knew him; and he *v* out of their sight
1 Cor. 13:8 there be knowledge, it shall *v* away
Heb. 8:13 decayeth and waxeth old is ready to *v*
Jas. 4:14 appeareth for a little time, and then *v*

Vanity

Deut. 32:21 have provoked me to anger with their *v*
1 Kgs. 16:13 in provoking the LORD. . with their *v*
2 Kgs. 17:15 and they followed *v*, and became vain
Job 7:16 let me alone; for my days are *v*
  15:31 let not him that is deceived trust in *v*
  35:13 surely God will not hear *v*, neither will
Ps. 4:2 how long will ye love *v*, and seek after
  10:7 under his tongue is mischief and *v*
  12:2 they speak *v* every one with his neighbor
  24:4 who hath not lifted up his soul unto *v*
  31:6 I have hated them that regard lying *v*
  39:5 every man at his best state is altogether *v*
  39:11 consume. . like a moth: surely every man is *v*
  62:9 men of low degree are *v*. . men of high degree
  78:33 therefore their days did he consume in *v*
  94:11 knoweth the thoughts of man, that they are *v*
  119:37 turn away mine eyes from beholding *v*
  144:4 man is like to *v*: his days are as a shadow
  144:8 whose mouth speaketh *v*, and their right hand
Prov. 13:11 wealth gotten by *v* shall be diminished
  22:8 he that soweth iniquity shall reap *v*
  30:8 remove far from me *v* and lies; give me
Eccl. 1:2 (12:8) *v* of *v*, saith the Preacher. . all is *v*
  1:14 (2:11, 17, 26; 6:9) all is *v* and vexation of spirit
  2:1 (2:15, 19, 23; 4:8; 5:10; 7:6) this also is *v*
  4:7 then I returned, and I saw *v* under the sun
  5:7 there are also divers *v*: but fear thou God
  6:11 seeing there be many things that increase *v*
  11:10 put away evil. . childhood and youth are *v*
Is. 5:18 them that draw iniquity with cords of *v*
  40:17 counted to him less than nothing, and *v*
  41:29 they are all *v*; their works are nothing
  44:9 that make a graven image are all of them *v*
  57:13 shall carry them all away; *v* shall take them
  59:4 trust in *v*, and speak lies; they conceive
Jer. 2:5 gone far from*me, and have walked after *v*
  8:19 with their graven images, and with strange *v*?
  10:15 (51:18) they are *v*, and the work of errors
  16:19 surely our fathers have inherited lies, *v*
Ezek. 13:6 they have seen *v* and lying divination
Hos. 12:11 iniquity in Gilead? surely they are *v*
Hab. 2:13 people shall weary themselves for very *v*?
Zech. 10:2 idols have spoken *v*, and the diviners
Acts 14:15 turn from these *v* unto the living God
Rom. 8:20 for the creature was made subject to *v*
Eph. 4:17 Gentiles walk, in the *v* of their mind
2 Pet. 2:18 they speak great swelling words of *v*

Vapor

Job 36:27 they pour down rain according to the *v*
Ps. 135:7 (Jer. 10:13; 51:16) causeth the *v* to ascend
  148:8 snow, and *v*; stormy wind fulfilling his word
Jas. 4:14 for what is your life? It is even a *v*

Variableness

Jas. 1:17 is no *v*, neither shadow of turning

Variance *See also* Dissension

Mt. 10:35 I am come to set a man at *v* against his
Gal. 5:20 witchcraft, hatred, *v*, emulations, wrath

Vashti Esth. 1:9–2:17

Vaunt *See also* Boast

Judg. 7:2 lest Israel *v* themselves against me
1 Cor. 13:4 charity *v* not itself, is not puffed up

Vehement *See also* Violent

Song 8:6 coals of fire, which hath a most *v* flame
Jon. 4:8 God prepared a *v* east wind; and the sun

Vehemently

Mk. 14:31 but he spake the more *v*, If I should die
Lk. 23:10 chief priests and scribes. . *v* accused him

Veil

Gen. 24:65 she took a *v*, and covered herself
  38:14 covered her with a *v*. . sat in an open place
Ex. 26:31 (36:35) *v* of blue, and purple, and scarlet
  34:33 till Moses had done. . he put a *v* on his face
Lev. 16:2 within the *v* before the mercy seat
  16:15 kill the goat. . bring his blood within the *v*
Num. 4:5 take down the covering *v*, and cover the ark
Ruth 3:15 bring the *v* that thou hast upon thee
Is. 25:7 and the *v* that is spread over all nations
Mt. 27:51 (Mk. 15:38; Lk. 23:45) *v*. . temple was rent
2 Cor. 3:14 the same *v* untaken away in the reading
  3:15 when Moses is read, the *v* is upon their heart
Heb. 6:19 which entereth into that within the *v*
  9:3 after the second *v*, the tabernacle which
  10:20 for us, through the *v*, that is. . his flesh

Vein

Job 28:1 a *v* for the silver, and a place for gold

Vengeance *See also* Avenge, Punishment, Recompense, Revenge

Gen. 4:15 whosoever slayeth Cain, *v* shall be taken
Deut. 32:35 (Heb. 10:30) to me belongeth *v*
  32:41 I will render *v* to mine enemies, and will
Judg. 11:36 as the LORD hath taken *v* for thee of
Ps. 94:1 to whom *v* belongeth; O God, to whom *v*
  149:7 execute *v* upon the heathen. . punishments
Prov. 6:34 he will not spare in the day of *v*
Is. 34:8 is the day of the LORD's *v*, and the year
  35:4 fear not: behold, your God will come with *v*
  47:3 I will take *v*, and I will not meet thee as
  59:17 he put on the garments of *v* for clothing
  61:2 to proclaim. . the day of *v* of our God
  63:4 the day of *v* is in mine heart, and the year
Jer. 11:20 let me see thy *v* on them: for unto thee
  50:15 it is the *v* of the LORD: take *v* upon her
  50:28 declare in Zion the *v* of the LORD our God
  51:6 this is the time of the LORD's *v*; he will
  51:11 is the *v* of the LORD, the *v* of his temple
Ezek. 25:17 and I will execute great *v* upon them
Mic. 5:15 and I will execute *v* in anger and fury
Nah. 1:2 the LORD will take *v* on his adversaries
Lk. 21:22 these be the days of *v*, that all things
Acts 28:4 escaped the sea, yet *v* suffereth not to
Rom. 3:5 is God unrighteous who taketh *v*?
  12:19 *v* is mine; I will repay, saith the Lord
2 Thes. 1:8 taking *v* on them that know not God
Jude 7 example, suffering the *v* of eternal fire

Venison

Gen. 25:28 loved Esau, because he did eat of his *v*
  27:3 and go out to the field, and take me some *v*

Venom

Deut. 32:33 their wine is. . the cruel *v* of asps

Venomous

Acts 28:4 saw the *v* beast hang on his hand

Verify

Gen. 42:20 shall your words be *v*, and ye shall not die
1 Kgs. 8:26 (2 Chr. 6:17) let thy word . . be *v*

Verity

Ps. 111:7 works of his hands are *v* and judgment
1 Tim. 2:7 teacher of the Gentiles in faith and *v*

Vessel *See also* Ware

1 Kgs. 7:48 (2 Chr. 4:19) and Solomon made all the *v*
2 Kgs. 4:3 go, borrow thee *v* abroad . . even empty *v*
25:14 (Jer. 52:18) the *v* of brass . . took they away
2 Chr. 36:7 *v* of the house of the LORD to Babylon
Ezra 1:7 also Cyrus the king brought forth the *v*
Ps. 2:9 shalt dash them in pieces like a potter's *v*
31:12 forgotten as a dead man . . like a broken *v*
Is. 52:11 be ye clean, that bear the *v* of the LORD
65:4 broth of abominable things is in their *v*
Jer. 18:4 *v*. . was marred . . made it again another *v*
19:11 as one breaketh a potter's *v*, that cannot
22:28 is he a *v* wherein is no pleasure?
25:34 and ye shall fall like a pleasant *v*
27:18 the *v* which are left . . go not to Babylon
Dan. 5:2 to bring the golden and silver *v* which
Hos. 8:8 shall they be . . as a *v* wherein is no pleasure
Mt. 13:48 gathered the good into *v*, but cast the bad
25:4 wise took oil in their *v* with their lamps
Mk. 11:16 should carry any *v* through the temple
Jn. 19:29 now there was set a *v* full of vinegar
Acts 9:15 he is a chosen *v* unto me, to bear my name
10:11 (11:5) and a certain *v* descending unto him
Rom. 9:21 the same lump to make one *v* unto honor
9:22 endured with . . long-suffering the *v* of wrath
9:23 the riches of his glory on the *v* of mercy
2 Cor. 4:7 but we have this treasure in earthen *v*
1 Thes. 4:4 how to possess his *v* in sanctification
2 Tim. 2:21 he shall be a *v* unto honor, sanctified
1 Pet. 3:7 honor unto the wife, as unto the weaker *v*
Rev. 2:27 as the *v* of a potter shall they be broken

Vestment

2 Kgs. 10:22 bring forth *v* for all the worshippers

Vesture *See also* Garment, Raiment

Gen. 41:42 arrayed him in *v* of fine linen, and put
Ps. 22:18 (Mt. 27:35; Jn. 19:24) cast lots upon my *v*
102:26 (Heb. 1:12) as a *v* shalt thou change them
Rev. 19:13 he was clothed with a *v* dipped in blood

Vex *See also* Displease, Provoke

Ex. 22:21 (Lev. 19:33) shalt neither *v* a stranger
Num. 25:17 *v* the Midianites, and smite them
33:55 shall *v* you in the land wherein ye dwell
Judg. 16:16 so that his soul was *v* unto death
2 Sam. 12:18 how will he then *v* himself, if we tell
2 Chr. 15:6 for God did *v* them with all adversity
Job 19:2 how long will ye *v* my soul, and break me
Ps. 2:5 wrath, and *v* them in his sore displeasure
6:2 O LORD, heal me; for my bones are *v*
6:3 my soul is also sore *v*
Is. 11:13 not envy Judah . . Judah shall not *v* Ephraim
63:10 but they rebelled, and *v* his Holy Spirit
Ezek. 32:9 I will also *v* the hearts of many people
Hab. 2:7 shall bite thee, and awake that shall *v* thee
Mt. 15:22 my daughter is grievously *v* with a devil
17:15 mercy on my son . . he is lunatic, and sore *v*
Lk. 6:18 and they that were *v* with unclean spirits
Acts 5:16 them which were *v* with unclean spirits
12:1 Herod the king . . to *v* certain of the church
2 Pet. 2:7 just Lot, *v* with the filthy conversation

Vexation *See also* Trouble

Deut. 28:20 LORD shall send upon thee cursing, *v*
Eccl. 1:14 (2:11, 17, 26; 6:9) all is vanity . . *v* of spirit
2:22 the *v* of his heart, wherein he hath labored
4:6 the hands full with travail and *v* of spirit
Is. 9:1 dimness shall not be such as was in her *v*
28:19 shall be a *v* only to understand the report
65:14 cry for sorrow . . shall howl for *v* of spirit

Vial *See also* Bowl

1 Sam. 10:1 Samuel took a *v* of oil, and poured it
Rev. 5:8 having . . harps, and golden *v* full of odors
15:7 seven golden *v* full of the wrath of God
16:1 pour out the *v* of the wrath of God upon the
21:9 the seven *v* full of the seven last plagues

Victory *See also* Triumph

2 Sam. 19:2 *v* that day was turned into mourning
23:10 and the LORD wrought a great *v* that day
1 Chr. 29:11 the glory, and the *v*, and the majesty
Ps. 98:1 and his holy arm, hath gotten him the *v*
Is. 25:8 (1 Cor. 15:54) will swallow up death in *v*
Mt. 12:20 till he send forth judgment unto *v*
1 Cor. 15:55 is thy sting? O grave, where is thy *v*?
15:57 thanks be to God, which giveth us the *v*
1 Jn. 5:4 this is the *v* that overcometh the world
Rev. 15:2 them that had gotten the *v* over the beast

Victuals *See also* Food, Provision

Ex. 12:39 had they prepared for themselves any *v*
Josh. 1:11 prepare you *v*; for within three days
9:14 men took of their *v*, and asked not counsel
1 Sam. 22:10 gave him *v*, and gave him the sword of
Neh. 10:31 bring ware or any *v* on the sabbath day
Mt. 14:15 (Lk. 9:12) may go . . and buy themselves *v*

View

Josh. 2:1 to spy secretly, saying, Go *v* the land
7:2 *v* the country. And the men went up and *v* Ai
2 Kgs. 2:7 prophets went, and stood to *v* afar off
Neh. 2:13 I went out . . and *v* the walls of Jerusalem

Vigilant

1 Tim. 3:2 husband of one wife, *v*, sober, of good
1 Pet. 5:8 be sober, be *v*; because your adversary

Vile (Viler, Vilest)

See also Abominable, Base, Wicked

Deut. 25:3 then thy brother should seem *v* unto thee
Judg. 19:24 but unto this man do not so *v* a thing
1 Sam. 3:13 because his sons made themselves *v*
2 Sam. 6:22 and I will yet be more *v* than thus
Job 18:3 as beasts, and reputed *v* in your sight?
30:8 children of fools . . they were *v* than the earth
40:4 I am *v*; what shall I answer thee? I will lay
Ps. 12:8 on every side, when the *v* men are exalted
15:4 in whose eyes a *v* person is contemned
Is. 32:5 *v* person shall be no more called liberal
Jer. 15:19 thou take forth the precious from the *v*
Lam. 1:11 O LORD, and consider; for I am become *v*
Dan. 11:21 in his estate shall stand up a *v* person
Nah. 1:14 I will make thy grave; for thou art *v*
3:6 abominable filth upon thee, and make thee *v*
Rom. 1:26 God gave them up unto *v* affections
Phil. 3:21 who shall change our *v* body, that it may
Jas. 2:2 there come in also a poor man in *v* raiment

Village *See also* City, Town

Mt. 14:15 (Mk. 6:36) they may go into the *v*, and buy
21:2 (Mk. 11:2; Lk. 19:30) into the *v* over against
Mk. 6:6 and he went round about the *v*, teaching
Lk. 24:13 two of them went that same day to a *v*

Vine

Gen. 40:9 in my dream, behold, a *v* was before me
49:11 binding his foal unto the *v*, and his ass's
Deut. 8:8 a land of wheat, and barley, and *v*
32:32 for their *v* is of the *v* of Sodom
Judg. 9:12 the trees unto the *v*, Come thou, and reign
13:14 not eat of any thing that cometh of the *v*
1 Kgs. 4:25 dwelt safely, every man under his *v*
2 Kgs. 18:31 (Is. 36:16) eat ye every man of his own *v*
Ps. 80:8 thou hast brought a *v* out of Egypt
128:3 thy wife shall be as a fruitful *v* by the
Song 2:15 spoil the *v*: for our *v* have tender grapes
Is. 5:2 planted it with the choicest *v*, and built
24:7 the new wine mourneth, the *v* languisheth
Jer. 2:21 yet I had planted thee a noble *v*
Ezek. 15:2 what is the *v* tree more than any tree
17:6 and became a spreading *v* of low stature
19:10 thy mother is like a *v* in thy blood
Hos. 10:1 Israel is an empty *v*, he bringeth forth
Joel 1:7 laid my *v* waste, and barked my fig tree
Mic. 4:4 shall sit every man under his *v* and under
Hab. 3:17 blossom, neither shall fruit be in the *v*
Zech. 3:10 call every man his neighbor under the *v*
Mal. 3:11 neither shall your *v* cast her fruit before
Mt. 26:29 (Mk. 14:25; Lk. 22:18) of this fruit of the *v*
Jn. 15:1 I am the true *v*, and my Father is the
15:5 I am the *v*, ye are the branches
Jas. 3:12 bear olive berries? either a *v*, figs?
Rev. 14:19 gathered the *v* of the earth, and cast

Vinegar

Num. 6:3 drink no *v* of wine, or *v* of strong drink
Ruth 2:14 the bread, and dip thy morsel in the *v*
Ps. 69:21 and in my thirst they gave me *v* to drink
Prov. 10:26 as *v* to the teeth. . as smoke to the eyes
25:20 and as *v* upon nitre, so is he that singeth
Mt. 27:34 (Lk. 23:36) they gave him *v* to drink
27:48 (Mk. 15:36; Jn. 19:29) a sponge. . with *v*

Vineyard

Gen. 9:20 Noah. . a husbandman, and he planted a *v*
Lev. 19:10 thou shalt not glean thy *v*, neither
Deut. 20:6 what man is he that hath planted a *v*
23:24 when thou comest into thy neighbor's *v*
Judg. 14:5 came to the *v* of Timnath: and, behold
1 Kgs. 21:2 Ahab. . unto Naboth. . Give me thy *v*
Ps. 80:15 the *v* which thy right hand hath planted
Prov. 24:30 the *v* of the man void of understanding
Song 1:6 of the *v*; but mine own *v* have I not kept
Is. 5:1 sing. . a song of my beloved touching his *v*
5:7 *v* of the LORD of hosts is the house of Israel
27:2 that day sing ye unto her, A *v* of red wine
65:21 shall plant *v*, and eat the fruit of them
Amos 9:14 shall plant *v*, and drink the wine thereof
Mt. 20:1 in the morning to hire laborers into his *v*
21:28 and said, Son, go work today in my *v*
21:33 (Mk. 12:1; Lk. 20:9) planted a *v*, and hedged
Lk. 13:6 man had a fig tree planted in his *v*
1 Cor. 9:7 planteth a *v*, and eateth not of the fruit

Vintage

Lev. 26:5 reach unto the *v*, and the *v* shall reach
Job 24:6 and they gather the *v* of the wicked
Is. 16:10 I have made their *v* shouting to cease
Zech. 11:2 for the forest of the *v* is come down

Viol

Is. 5:12 the harp and the *v*. . are in their feasts
Amos 5:23 for I will not hear the melody of thy *v*
6:5 that chant to the sound of the *v*, and invent

Violence

Gen. 6:11 corrupt. . and the earth was filled with *v*

2 Sam. 22:3 my saviour; thou savest me from *v*
Ps. 11:5 and him that loveth *v* his soul hateth
55:9 for I have seen *v* and strife in the city
58:2 ye weigh the *v* of your hands in the earth
72:14 shall redeem their soul from deceit and *v*
73:6 as a chain; *v* covereth them as a garment
Prov. 4:17 of wickedness, and drink the wine of *v*
10:6 but *v* covereth the mouth of the wicked
28:17 that doeth *v* to the blood of any person
Is. 53:9 he had done no *v*, neither was any deceit
60:18 *v* shall no more be heard in thy land
Jer. 22:3 do no *v* to the stranger, the fatherless
22:17 and for oppression, and for *v*, to do it
51:46 and *v* in the land, ruler against ruler
Ezek. 7:11 *v* is risen up into a rod of wickedness
8:17 they have filled the land with *v*, and have
28:16 they have filled the midst of thee with *v*
Amos 3:10 store up *v* and robbery in their palaces
6:3 and cause the seat of *v* to come near
Obad. 10 for thy *v* against thy brother Jacob
Jon. 3:8 turn. . from the *v* that is in their hands
Mic. 2:2 and they covet fields, and take them by *v*
6:12 for the rich men thereof are full of *v*
Hab. 1:3 for spoiling and *v* are before me
2:17 *v* of Lebanon shall cover thee, and the spoil
Mal. 2:16 for one covereth *v* with his garment
Mt. 11:12 until now. . kingdom of heaven suffereth *v*
Lk. 3:14 do *v* to no man, neither accuse any falsely
Acts 5:26 the officers, and brought them without *v*
Heb. 11:34 quenched the *v* of fire, escaped the edge
Rev. 18:21 with *v* shall. . Babylon be thrown down

Violent *See also* Vehement

2 Sam. 22:49 (Ps. 18:48) delivered me from the *v* man
Ps. 7:16 his *v* dealing shall come down upon his own
86:14 assemblies of *v* men have sought after my
140:1 the evil man: preserve me from the *v* man
140:11 evil shall hunt the *v* man to overthrow him
Prov. 16:29 a *v* man enticeth his neighbor
Mt. 11:12 violence, and the *v* take it by force

Violently

Gen. 21:25 Abimelech's servants had *v* taken way
Is. 22:18 he will surely *v* turn and toss thee
Mt. 8:32 (Mk. 5:13; Lk. 8:33) ran *v* down a steep

Viper

Job 20:16 of asps: the *v*'s tongue shall slay him
Mt. 3:7 (Lk. 3:7) O generation of *v*, who hath warned
12:34 O generation of *v*, how can ye, being evil
23:33 ye generation of *v*, how can ye escape
Acts 28:3 came a *v* out of the heat, and fastened

Virgin *See also* Damsel, Maiden

Lev. 21:14 shall take a *v* of his own people to wife
Esth. 2:2 there be fair young *v* sought for the king
Song 1:3 as ointment. . therefore do the *v* love thee
Is. 7:14 (Mt. 1:23) a *v* shall conceive, and bear a son
23:12 shalt no more rejoice, O thou oppressed *v*
47:1 sit in the dust, O *v* daughter of Babylon
62:5 as a young man marrieth a *v*, so shall thy
Jer. 14:17 the *v* daughter of my people is broken
Lam. 2:13 may comfort thee, O *v* daughter of Zion?
Joel 1:8 lament like a *v* girded with sackcloth for
Amos 5:2 *v* of Israel is fallen; she shall no more
Mt. 25:1 kingdom of heaven be likened unto ten *v*
Lk. 1:27 to a *v* espoused to a man whose name was
1 Cor. 7:25 concerning *v* I have no commandment
7:36 behaveth himself uncomely toward his *v*
2 Cor. 11:2 present you as a chaste *v* to Christ
Rev. 14:4 not defiled with women; for they are *v*

Virginity

Lev. 21:13 and he shall take a wife in her *v*
Deut. 22:15 bring. . the tokens of the damsel's *v*
Judg. 11:37 upon the mountains, and bewail my *v*

Virtue *See also* Goodness

Mk. 5:30 (Lk. 8:46) knowing. . *v* had gone out of him
Lk. 6:19 there went *v* out of him, and healed them all
Phil. 4:8 there be any *v*, and if there be any praise
2 Pet. 1:3 him that hath called us to glory and *v*
    1:5 add to your faith *v*; and to *v*, knowledge

Virtuous *See also* Chaste

Ruth 3:11 people doth know that thou art a *v* woman
Prov. 12:4 a *v* woman is a crown to her husband
    31:10 who can find a *v* woman? for her price is

Visage *See also* Face

Is. 52:14 his *v* was so marred more than any man
Lam. 4:8 their *v* is blacker than a coal; they are
Dan. 3:19 his *v* was changed against Shadrach

Visible

Col. 1:16 *v* and invisible, whether they be thrones

Vision *See also* Dream, Revelation, Trance

Gen. 15:1 word of the Lord came unto Abram in a *v*
    46:2 God spake unto Israel in the *v* of the night
Num. 12:6 will make myself known unto him in a *v*
    24:4 saw the *v* of the Almighty, falling into a
1 Sam. 3:1 in those days; there was no open *v*
    3:15 and Samuel feared to show Eli the *v*
2 Sam. 7:17 (1 Chr. 17:15) according to all this *v*
2 Chr. 26:5 who had understanding in the *v* of God
Job 4:13 in thoughts from the *v* of the night
    7:14 with dreams, and terrifiest me through *v*
    20:8 he shall be chased away as a *v* of the night
    33:15 in a dream, in a *v* of the night, when deep
Ps. 89:19 then thou spakest in *v* to thy holy one
Prov. 29:18 where there is no *v*, the people perish
Is. 1:1 *v* of Isaiah the son of Amoz, which he saw
    22:1 the burden of the valley of *v*
    28:7 they err in *v*, they stumble in judgment
    29:11 *v* of all is become unto you as the words
Jer. 14:14 they prophesy unto you a false *v*
    23:16 they speak a *v* of their own heart, and not
Lam. 2:9 her prophets also find no *v* from the Lord
Ezek. 1:1 heavens were opened, and I saw *v* of God
    7:26 then shall they seek a *v* of the prophet
    8:3 and brought me in the *v* of God to Jerusalem
    11:24 brought me in a *v*. . into Chaldea
    12:22 the days are prolonged, and every *v* faileth?
    12:24 for there shall be no more any vain *v*
    13:7 have ye not seen a vain *v*, and have ye not
    40:2 in the *v* of God brought he me into the
    43:3 *v* were like the *v* that I saw by the river
Dan. 1:17 and Daniel had understanding in all *v*
    2:19 secret revealed unto Daniel in a night *v*
    4:5 thoughts. . and the *v* of my head troubled me
    7:2 I saw in my *v* by night, and, behold, the four
    8:1 a *v* appeared unto me, even unto me Daniel
    8:16 Gabriel, make this man to understand the *v*
    8:26 the *v* of the evening and the morning. . is true
    9:24 to seal up the *v* and prophecy, and to anoint
    10:1 the thing, and had understanding of the *v*
    10:7 I Daniel alone saw the *v*: for the men
Hos. 12:10 have multiplied *v*, and used similitudes
Joel 2:28 (Acts 2:17) your young men shall see *v*
Obad. 1 the *v* of Obadiah. Thus saith the Lord God
Mic. 3:6 that ye shall not have a *v*; and it shall

Nah. 1:1 the book of the *v* of Nahum the Elkoshite
Hab. 2:2 said, Write the *v*, and make it plain upon
    2:3 the *v* is yet for an appointed time
Zech. 13:4 prophets. . be ashamed every one of his *v*
Mt. 17:9 tell the *v* to no man, until the Son of man
Lk. 1:22 they perceived that he had seen a *v*
    24:23 they had also seen a *v* of angels, which said
Acts 9:10 and to him said the Lord in a *v*, Ananias
    10:3 saw in a *v* evidently, about the ninth hour
    10:17 Peter doubted. . what this *v*. . should mean
    11:5 and in a trance I saw a *v*, A certain vessel
    12:9 that it was true. . but thought he saw a *v*
    16:9 a *v* appeared to Paul. . a man of Macedonia
    18:9 spake the Lord to Paul in the night by a *v*
    26:19 I was not disobedient unto the heavenly *v*
2 Cor. 12:1 I will come to *v* and revelations
Rev. 9:17 and thus I saw the horses in the *v*

Visit

Gen. 21:1 and the Lord *v* Sarah as he had said
    50:25 (Ex. 13:19) God will surely *v* you, and ye
Ex. 20:5 (34:7; Num. 14:18; Deut. 5:9) *v* the iniquity
    32:34 day when I *v*, I will *v* their sin upon them
Lev. 18:25 therefore I do *v* the iniquity thereof
Ruth 1:6 Lord had *v* his people in giving them bread
Job 5:24 shalt *v* thy habitation, and shalt not sin
    7:18 thou shouldest *v* him every morning, and try
    31:14 and when he *v*, what shall I answer him?
    35:15 hath *v* in his anger; yet he knoweth it not
Ps. 8:4 (Heb. 2:6) the son of man, that thou *v* him?
    59:5 God of Israel, awake to *v* all the heathen
    65:9 *v* the earth, and waterest it: thou greatly
    80:14 from heaven, and behold, and *v* this vine
    106:4 unto thy people: O *v* me with thy salvation
Prov. 19:23 satisfied; he shall not be *v* with evil
Jer. 5:9 (5:29; 9:9) shall I not *v* for these things?
    23:2 have not *v* them: behold, I will *v* upon you
    29:10 be accomplished at Babylon I will *v* you
Lam. 4:22 will *v* thine iniquity, O daughter of Edom
Ezek. 38:8 after many days thou shalt be *v*
Hos. 2:13 and I will *v* upon her the days of Baalim
    8:13 (9:9) remember their iniquity. . *v* their sins
Amos 3:14 I shall *v* the transgressions of Israel
Zeph. 2:7 God shall *v* them, and turn away their
Zech. 11:16 which shall not *v* those that be cut off
Mt. 25:36 I was sick, and ye *v* me: I was in prison
Lk. 1:68 for he hath *v* and redeemed his people
    1:78 whereby the dayspring from on high hath *v* us
    7:16 prophet is risen up. . God hath *v* his people
Acts 7:23 it came into his heart to *v* his brethren
    15:14 how God at the first did *v* the Gentiles
    15:36 let us go again and *v* our brethren in every
Jas. 1:27 is this, To *v* the fatherless and widows

Visitation

Num. 16:29 they be visited after the *v* of all men
Job 10:12 and thy *v* hath preserved my spirit
Is. 10:3 what will ye do in the day of *v*, and in
Jer. 8:12 time of their *v* they shall be cast down
    10:15 (51:18) time of their *v* they shall perish
    11:23 men of Anathoth, even the year of their *v*
    48:44 even upon Moab, the year of their *v*
Hos. 9:7 days of *v* are come, the days of recompense
Mic. 7:4 the day of thy watchmen and thy *v* cometh
1 Pet. 2:12 behold, glorify God in the day of *v*

Vocation

Eph. 4:1 worthy of the *v* wherewith ye are called

Voice *See also* Noise, Sound

Gen. 3:8 they heard the *v* of the Lord God walking
    4:10 the *v* of thy brother's blood crieth unto me

Gen. 27:22 the *v* is Jacob's *v*, but the hands are
Ex. 5:2 who is the LORD, that I should obey his *v*
  15:26 diligently hearken to the *v* of the LORD
  23:21 beware of him . . obey his *v*, provoke him not
  24:3 all the people answered with one *v*, and said
Num. 7:89 heard the *v* of one . . from . . mercy seat
  14:22 tempted me . . have not hearkened to my *v*
  21:3 the LORD hearkened to the *v* of Israel
Deut. 4:12 but saw no similitude; only ye heard a *v*
  4:33 did ever people hear the *v* of God speaking
  8:20 would not be obedient unto the *v* of the LORD
  28:45 hearkenedst not unto the *v* of the LORD
  30:2 return unto the LORD . . and shalt obey his *v*
Josh. 5:6 because they obeyed not the *v* of the LORD
  10:14 the LORD hearkened unto the *v* of a man
  24:24 God will we serve, and his *v* will we obey
Judg. 2:2 but ye have not obeyed my *v*; why have ye
1 Sam. 12:14 and obey his *v*, and not rebel against
  15:19 then didst thou not obey the *v* of the LORD
  24:16 (26:17) said, Is this thy *v*, my son David?
2 Sam. 22:14 (Ps. 18:13) the Most High uttered his *v*
1 Kgs. 19:12 and after the fire a still small *v*
  20:36 thou hast not obeyed the *v* of the LORD
2 Kgs. 4:31 but there was neither *v*, nor hearing
  18:12 because they obeyed not the *v* of the LORD
Job 30:31 my organ into the *v* of them that weep
  37:4 he thundereth with the *v* of his excellency
Ps. 5:3 my *v* shalt thou hear in the morning, O LORD
  29:3 the *v* of the LORD is upon the waters
  31:22 thou heardest the *v* of my supplications
  42:4 to the house of God, with the *v* of joy
  46:6 he uttered his *v*, the earth melted
  68:33 he doth send out his *v*, and that a mighty *v*
  95:7 (Heb. 3:7, 15; 4:7) today if ye will hear his *v*
  103:20 angels . . hearkening unto the *v* of his word
  106:25 and hearkened not unto the *v* of the LORD
Prov. 1:20 wisdom . . uttereth her *v* in the streets
  8:1 wisdom cry? and understanding put forth her *v*
Eccl. 5:3 a fool's *v* is known by multitude of words
  10:20 for a bird of the air shall carry the *v*
  12:4 and he shall rise up at the *v* of the bird
Song 2:8 the *v* of my beloved! behold, he cometh
  2:12 the *v* of the turtle is heard in our land
  2:14 let me hear thy *v*; for sweet is thy *v*
  5:2 it is the *v* of my beloved that knocketh
Is. 6:4 the posts of the door moved at the *v* of him
  6:8 I heard the *v* of the Lord, saying, Whom shall
  13:2 exalt the *v* unto them, shake the hand
  30:30 LORD shall cause his glorious *v* to be heard
  40:3 (Mt. 3:3; Mk. 1:3; Lk. 3:4; Jn. 1:23) *v* of him
    that crieth in the wilderness, Prepare
  40:9 lift up thy *v* with strength; lift it up
  42:2 (Mt. 12:19) his *v* to be heard in the street
  48:20 with a *v* of singing declare ye, tell this
  52:8 thy watchmen shall lift up the *v*; with the *v*
  58:4 not fast . . to make your *v* to be heard on high
  65:19 *v* of weeping shall be no more heard in her
  66:6 a *v* from the temple, a *v* of the LORD that
Jer. 3:21 *v* was heard upon the high places, weeping
  7:23 saying, Obey my *v*, and I will be your God
  7:34 (16:9; 25:10) *v* of mirth, and the *v* of gladness
  26:13 amend your ways . . obey the *v* of the LORD
  30:19 thanksgiving . . *v* of them that make merry
  31:15 (Mt. 2:18) *v* was heard in Ramah . . weeping
  42:6 we will obey the *v* of the LORD our God
  50:28 the *v* of them that flee and escape out of
  51:55 and destroyed out of her the great *v*
Ezek. 1:24 the *v* of the Almighty, the *v* of speech
  10:5 the *v* of the Almighty God when he speaketh
  23:42 *v* of a multitude being at ease was with her
  33:32 lovely song of one that hath a pleasant *v*
  43:2 (Rev. 1:15) *v* was like a noise of many waters
Dan. 4:31 there fell a *v* from heaven, saying, O king

Dan. 7:11 *v* of the great words which the horn spake
  9:10 neither have we obeyed the *v* of the LORD
  10:6 *v* of his words like the *v* of a multitude
Joel 3:16 (Amos 1:2) and utter his *v* from Jerusalem
Mic. 6:9 LORD's *v* crieth unto the city, and the man
Nah. 2:7 maids shall lead her as with the *v* of doves
Zeph. 1:14 near . . even the *v* of the day of the LORD
Mt. 3:17 (Mk. 1:11; Lk. 3:22) a *v* from heaven, saying
  17:5 (Mk. 9:7; Lk. 9:35) a *v* out of the cloud
Lk. 23:23 *v* of them and of the chief priests prevailed
Jn. 3:29 rejoiceth . . because of the bridegroom's *v*
  5:25 the dead shall hear the *v* of the Son of God
  5:37 ye have neither heard his *v* at any time
  10:3 porter openeth; and the sheep hear his *v*
  10:4 the sheep follow him: for they know his *v*
  10:16 shall hear my *v*; and there shall be one fold
  10:27 my sheep hear my *v*, and I know them
  12:28 then came there a *v* from heaven, saying
  12:30 *v* came not because of me, but for your
  18:37 one that is of the truth heareth my *v*
Acts 4:24 lifted up their *v* to God with one accord
  7:31 near to behold it, the *v* of the Lord came
  9:7 speechless, hearing a *v*, but seeing no man
  10:13 (11:7) came a *v* to him, Rise, Peter; kill
  12:22 it is the *v* of a god, and not of a man
  22:7 (26:14) a *v* saying unto me, Saul, Saul, why
  22:14 and shouldest hear the *v* of his mouth
  26:10 were put to death, I gave my *v* against them
1 Cor. 14:10 so many kinds of *v* in the world
  14:19 that by my *v* I might teach others also
Gal. 4:20 present with you now, and to change my *v*
1 Thes. 4:16 a shout, with the *v* of the archangel
Heb. 12:19 which *v* they that heard entreated
  12:26 whose *v* then shook the earth: but now
2 Pet. 1:17 a *v* to him from the excellent glory
  2:16 the dumb ass speaking with man's *v* forbade
Rev. 1:10 Lord's day, and heard behind me a great *v*
  3:20 if any man hear my *v*, and open the door
  10:4 I heard a *v* from heaven saying unto me, Seal
  11:15 were great *v* in heaven, saying, The kingdoms
  12:10 I heard a loud *v* saying in heaven, Now is
  14:2 a *v* from heaven, as the *v* of many waters
  19:1 I heard a great *v* of much people in heaven
  19:5 a *v* came out of the throne, saying, Praise
  21:3 a great *v* out of heaven saying, Behold

Void *See also* Empty

Gen. 1:2 and the earth was without form, and *v*
Num. 30:12 if her husband hath utterly made them *v*
Deut. 32:28 for they are a nation *v* of counsel
Ps. 89:39 hast made *v* the covenant of thy servant
  119:126 for they have made *v* thy law
Prov. 11:12 he that is *v* of wisdom despiseth his
Is. 55:11 shall not return unto me *v*, but it shall
Jer. 19:7 make *v* the counsel of Judah and Jerusalem
Acts 24:16 a conscience *v* of offense toward God
Rom. 3:31 do we then make *v* the law through faith?
  4:14 if they . . of the law be heirs, faith is made *v*
1 Cor. 9:15 that any man should make my glorying *v*

Volume

Ps. 40:7 (Heb. 10:7) I come: in the *v* of the book

Voluntary

Lev. 1:3 offer it of his own *v* will at the door
  7:16 offering be a vow, or a *v* offering, it shall
Ezek. 46:12 prince shall prepare a *v* burnt offering
Col. 2:18 reward in a *v* humility and worshipping

Vomit

Lev. 18:25 the land itself *v* out her inhabitants
Job 20:15 swallowed . . riches, and he shall *v* them up
Prov. 23:8 which thou hast eaten shalt thou *v* up

Prov. 25:16 lest thou be filled therewith, and *v* it
  26:11 as a dog returneth to his *v*, so a fool
Is. 19:14 as a drunken man staggereth in his *v*
  28:8 for all tables are full of *v* and filthiness
Jon. 2:10 spake unto the fish, and it *v* out Jonah
2 Pet. 2:22 the dog is turned to his own *v* again

Vow *See also* Covenant, Pledge, Promise, Swear

Gen. 28:20 Jacob *v* a *v*, saying, If God will be with
  31:13 God of Bethel. . where thou *v* a *v* unto me
Lev. 7:16 if the sacrifice of his offering be a *v*
  22:18 that will offer his oblation for all his *v*
  27:2 a man shall make a singular *v*, the persons
Num. 6:2 *v* a *v* of a Nazarite, to separate themselves
  30:2 if a man *v* a *v* unto *t*he LORD, or swear
  30:3 if a woman also *v* a *v* unto the LORD
Deut. 12:6 and your *v*, and your freewill offerings
  23:21 when thou shalt *v* a *v*. . thou shalt not slack
Judg. 11:30 Jephthah *v* a *v* unto the LORD, and said
  11:39 with her according to his *v* which he had *v*
1 Sam. 1:11 she *v* a *v*, and said, O LORD of hosts
  1:21 offer. . the yearly sacrifice, and his *v*
2 Sam. 15:7 pay my *v*, which I have *v* unto the LORD
Job 22:27 hear thee, and thou shalt pay thy *v*
Ps. 22:25 will pay my *v* before them that fear him
  50:14 and pay thy *v* unto the Most High
  56:12 thy *v* are upon me, O God: I will render
  61:5 for thou, O God, hast heard my *v*: thou hast
  61:8 sing praise. . that I may daily perform my *v*
  65:1 O God. . unto thee shall the *v* be performed
  76:11 *v*, and pay unto the LORD your God: let all
  116:14 (116:18) I will pay my *v* unto the LORD now
Prov. 7:14 peace offerings. . this day have I paid my *v*
  20:25 which is holy, and after *v* to make inquiry
  31:2 son of my womb? and what, the son of my *v*?
Eccl. 5:4 when thou *v* a *v* unto God, defer not to pay
  5:5 not *v*, than that thou shouldest *v* and not pay
Is. 19:21 shall *v* a *v* unto the LORD, and perform it
Jer. 44:25 will surely perform our *v* that we have *v*
Jon. 1:16 a sacrifice unto the LORD, and made *y*
  2:9 thanksgiving; I will pay that that I have *v*
Nah. 1:15 keep thy solemn feasts, perform thy *v*
Acts 18:18 shorn his head in Cenchrea. . he had a *v*
  21:23 we have four men which have a *v* on them

Voyage

Acts 27:10 I perceive that this *v* will be with hurt

Vulture

Lev. 11:14 (Deut. 14:13) and the *v*, and the kite
Job 28:7 is a path. . which the *v*'s eye hath not seen
Is. 34:15 there shall the *v* also be gathered

W

Wafer

Ex. 16:31 taste of it was like *w* made with honey
Lev. 2:4 (7:12) or unleavened *w* anointed with oil

Wag

Jer. 18:16 shall be astonished, and *w* his head
Lam. 2:15 *w* their head at the daughter of Jerusalem
Zeph. 2:15 passeth by her shall hiss, and *w* his hand
Mt. 27:39 (Mk. 15:29) reviled him, *w* their heads

Wages *See also* Hire, Recompense, Reward

Gen. 29:15 tell me, what shall thy *w* be?

Gen. 30:28 said, Appoint me thy *w*, and I will give it
  31:7 hath deceived me. . changed my *w* ten times
  31:8 speckled shall be thy *w*; then all the cattle
Ex. 2:9 nurse it for me, and I will give thee thy *w*
Lev. 19:13 *w* of him that is hired shall not abide
Jer. 22:13 useth his neighbor's service without *w*
Hag. 1:6 earneth *w* to put it into a bag with holes
Mal. 3:5 those that oppress the hireling in his *w*
Lk. 3:14 accuse any falsely. . be content with your *w*
Jn. 4:36 that reapeth receiveth *w*, and gathereth
Rom. 6:23 the *w* of sin is death; but the gift of God
2 Cor. 11:8 taking *w* of them, to do you service
2 Pet. 2:15 who loved the *w* of unrighteousness

Wagon

Gen. 45:19 take you *w* out of the land of Egypt for
Num. 7:3 offering before the LORD, six covered *w*
Ezek. 23:24 against thee with chariots, *w*, and wheels

Wail *See also* Cry, Lament, Mourn, Weep

Ezek. 32:18 *w* for the multitude of Egypt, and cast
Mic. 1:8 I will *w* and howl, I will go stripped
Mk. 5:38 tumult, and them that wept and *w* greatly
Rev. 1:7 all kindreds of the earth shall *w* because

Wailing *See also* Lamentation, Mourning, Weeping

Jer. 9:19 for a voice of *w* is heard out of Zion
Ezek. 27:31 with bitterness of heart and bitter *w*
Amos 5:16 saith thus; *W* shall be in all streets
Mt. 13:42 (13:50) shall be *w* and gnashing of teeth

Wait *See also* Attend, Tarry

Gen. 49:18 I have *w* for thy salvation, O LORD
1 Sam. 15:2 did to Israel, how he laid *w* for him
2 Kgs. 6:33 should I *w* for the LORD any longer?
Job 14:14 the days of my appointed time will I *w*
  17:13 if I *w*, the grave is mine house
  29:23 and they *w* for me as for the rain
Ps. 10:9 lieth in *w* secretly. . lieth in *w* to catch
  25:3 let none that *w* on thee be ashamed
  25:5 my salvation; on thee do I *w* all the day
  27:14 *w* on the LORD: be of good courage, and he
  33:20 our soul *w* for the LORD: he is our help
  37:7 rest in the LORD, and *w* patiently for him
  37:9 that *w* upon the LORD, they shall inherit
  37:34 *w* on the LORD, and keep his way, and he
  39:7 now, Lord, what *w* I for? my hope is in thee
  40:1 I *w* patiently for the LORD; and he inclined
  52:9 I will *w* on thy name; for it is good before
  56:6 they mark my steps, when they *w* for my soul
  62:1 truly my soul *w* upon God: from him cometh
  62:5 *w* thou only upon God; for my expectation is
  69:3 mine eyes fail while I *w* for my God
  104:27 these *w* all upon thee; that thou mayest
  106:13 forgat his works; they *w* not for his counsel
  123:2 so our eyes *w* upon the LORD our God, until
  130:5 I *w* for the LORD, my soul doth *w*
  145:15 eyes of all *w* upon thee; and thou givest
Prov. 8:34 at my gates, *w* at the posts of my doors
  20:22 but *w* on the LORD, and he shall save thee
  27:18 he that *w* on his master shall be honored
Is. 8:17 I will *w* upon the LORD, that hideth his face
  25:9 lo, this is our God; we have *w* for him
  26:8 in the way of thy judgments. . we *w* for thee
  30:18 will the LORD *w*, that he may be gracious
  40:31 *w* upon the LORD shall renew their strength
  42:4 not fail. . and the isles shall *w* for his law
  49:23 they shall not be ashamed that *w* for me
  59:9 we *w* for light, but behold obscurity
  64:4 he hath prepared for him that *w* for him
Jer. 9:8 his mouth, but in heart he layeth his *w*

Jer. 14:22 we will *w* upon thee: for thou hast made all
Lam. 3:25 the LORD is good unto them that *w* for him
   3:26 and quietly *w* for the salvation of the LORD
Dan. 12:12 blessed is he that *w*, and cometh to the
Hos. 12:6 keep mercy and judgment . . *w* on thy God
Mic. 7:7 I will *w* for the God of my salvation
Hab. 2:3 though it tarry, *w* for it; because it will
Zeph. 3:8 *w* ye upon me, saith the LORD, until the
Zech. 11:11 poor of the flock that *w* upon me knew
Mk. 15:43 (Lk. 23:51) also *w* for the kingdom of God
Lk. 2:25 devout, *w* for the consolation of Israel
   12:36 like unto men that *w* for their lord
Acts 1:4 but *w* for the promise of the Father
   20:3 Jews laid *w* for him, as he was about to sail
   25:3 to Jerusalem, laying *w* in the way to kill
Rom. 8:23 we ourselves groan . . *w* for the adoption
   8:25 see not, then do we with patience *w* for it
   12:7 or ministry, let us *w* on our ministering
1 Cor. 1:7 *w* for the coming of our Lord Jesus
   9:13 *w* at the altar are partakers with the altar?
Gal. 5:5 *w* for the hope of righteousness by faith
1 Thes. 1:10 to *w* for his Son from heaven, whom he
2 Thes. 3:5 and into the patient *w* for Christ
Jas. 5:7 husbandman *w* for the precious fruit of the
1 Pet. 3:20 *w* in the days of Noah, while the ark

Wake *See also* Awake

Ps. 77:4 thou holdest mine eyes *w*: I am so troubled
   127:1 keep the city, the watchman *w* but in vain
Song 5:2 I sleep, but my heart *w*: it is the voice
Jer. 51:39 and sleep a perpetual sleep, and not *w*
Joel 3:9 prepare war, *w* up the mighty men, let all
Zech. 4:1 and the angel . . came again, and *w* me
1 Thes. 5:10 whether we *w* or sleep, we should live

Waken

Is. 50:4 he *w* morning by morning, he *w* mine ear to
Joel 3:12 let the heathen be *w*, and come up to the

Walk *See also* Behave, Live, Path, Way

Gen. 3:8 the voice of the LORD God *w* in the garden
   5:24 Enoch *w* with God: and he was not; for God
   6:9 a just man and perfect . . and Noah *w* with God
   17:1 to Abram . . *w* before me, and be thou perfect
   24:40 LORD, before whom I *w*, will send his angel
Ex. 16:4 prove them, whether they will *w* in my law
   18:20 show them the way wherein they must *w*
Lev. 18:3 neither shall ye *w* in their ordinances
   20:23 shall not *w* in the manners of the nation
   26:12 (2 Cor. 6:16) *w* among you . . be your God
Deut. 5:33 shall *w* in all the ways which the LORD
   8:6 thy God, to *w* in his ways, and to fear him
   10:12 but to fear the LORD . . to *w* in all his ways
   13:4 ye shall *w* after the LORD your God, and fear
   23:14 the LORD thy God in the midst of thy camp
Josh. 5:6 Israel *w* forty years in the wilderness
   22:5 and to *w* in all his ways, and to keep his
2 Sam. 7:7 (1 Chr. 17:6) I have *w* with all . . Israel
1 Kgs. 3:14 *w* in my ways . . as thy father David did *w*
   8:25 (2 Chr. 6:16) they *w* before me as thou hast *w*
   8:36 (2 Chr. 6:27) good way wherein they should *w*
   9:4 (2 Chr. 7:17) *w* before me, as David thy father *w*
   11:33 not *w* in my ways, to do that which is right
2 Kgs. 10:31 but Jehu took no heed to *w* in the law
   17:22 Israel *w* in all the sins of Jeroboam
Neh. 5:9 ought ye not to *w* in the fear of our God
Job 1:7 (2:2) earth, and from *w* up and down in it
   18:8 net by his own feet, and he *w* upon a snare
   22:14 and he *w* in the circuit of heaven
Ps. 1:1 blessed is the man that *w* not in the counsel
   12:8 the wicked *w* on every side, when the vilest
   23:4 though I *w* through the valley of the shadow
   26:3 before mine eyes: and I have *w* in thy truth

Ps. 26:11 but as for me, I will *w* in mine integrity
   48:12 *w* about Zion, and go round about her: tell
   55:14 and *w* unto the house of God in company
   56:13 may *w* before God in the light of the living?
   81:13 oh that . . Israel had *w* in my ways!
   82:5 will they understand; they *w* on in darkness
   84:11 will he withhold from them that *w* uprightly
   86:11 teach me thy way . . I will *w* in thy truth
   89:15 shall *w* . . in the light of thy countenance
   115:7 feet have they, but they *w* not
   116:9 *w* before the LORD in the land of the living
   119:1 the undefiled . . who *w* in the law of the LORD
   119:45 will *w* at liberty: for I seek thy precepts
   128:1 that feareth the LORD; that *w* in his ways
   138:7 *w* in the midst of trouble, thou wilt revive
Prov. 1:15 my son, *w* not thou in the way with them
   2:7 he is a buckler to them that *w* uprightly
   2:20 that thou mayest *w* in the way of good men
   10:9 he that *w* uprightly *w* surely: but he that
   28:18 whoso *w* uprightly shall be saved
Eccl. 2:14 in his head; but the fool *w* in darkness
   10:7 and princes *w* as servants upon the earth
Is. 2:3 (Mic. 4:2) his ways, and we will *w* in his paths
   2:5 come ye . . let us *w* in the light of the LORD
   8:11 I should not *w* in the way of this people
   9:2 that *w* in darkness have seen a great light
   30:21 this is the way, *w* ye in it, when ye turn
   35:9 found there; but the redeemed shall *w* there
   40:31 not be weary . . they shall *w*, and not faint
   43:2 when thou *w* through the fire, thou shalt not
   50:10 that *w* in darkness, and hath no light?
   50:11 *w* in the light of your fire, and in the
   57:2 shall rest . . each one *w* in his uprightness
Jer. 2:8 and *w* after things that do not profit
   6:16 paths, where is the good way, and *w* therein
   7:23 *w* ye in all the ways that I have commanded
   10:23 is not in man that *w* to direct his steps
   42:3 God may show us the way wherein we may *w*
   44:10 neither have they feared, nor *w* in my law
Ezek. 5:7 (11:12) and have not *w* in my statutes
   11:20 (36:27) that they may *w* in my statutes
   20:19 I am the LORD your God; *w* in my statutes
   28:14 thou hast *w* up and down in the midst of
   37:24 shall also *w* in my judgments, and observe
Dan. 3:25 four men loose, *w* in the midst of the fire
   4:37 those that *w* in pride he is able to abase
Hos. 11:10 they shall *w* after the LORD: he shall
   14:9 are right, and the just shall *w* in them
Amos 3:3 can two *w* together, except they be agreed?
Mic. 4:5 we will *w* in the name of the LORD our God
   6:8 to love mercy, and to *w* humbly with thy God?
Hab. 3:15 thou didst *w* through the sea with thine
Zeph. 1:17 they shall *w* like blind men, because
Zech. 1:10 sent to *w* to and fro through the earth
   3:7 if thou wilt *w* in my ways, and if thou wilt
   10:12 and they shall *w* up and down in his name
Mt. 9:5 (Mk. 2:9; Lk. 5:23) or to say, Arise, and *w*?
   11:5 (Lk. 7:22) the lame *w*, the lepers are cleansed
   12:43 (Lk. 11:24) *w* through dry places, seeking
   14:26 (Mk. 6:49; Jn. 6:19) saw him *w* on the sea
   14:29 the ship, he *w* on the water, to go to Jesus
   15:31 the lame to *w*, and the blind to see
Mk. 7:5 why *w* not thy disciples according to the
   8:24 looked up, and said, I see men as trees, *w*
   16:12 as they *w*, and went into the country
Lk. 13:33 I must *w* today, and tomorrow, and the day
   24:17 have one to another, as ye *w*, and are sad?
Jn. 5:8 (5:11, 12) take up thy bed, and *w*
   7:1 Jesus *w* in Galilee . . he would not *w* in Jewry
   8:12 that followeth me shall not *w* in darkness
   11:9 if any man *w* in the day, he stumbleth not
   12:35 *w* while ye have the light, lest darkness
   21:18 girdedst thyself . . *w* whither thou wouldest

Acts 3:6 in the name of Jesus Christ . . rise up and *w*
  3:8 leaping up stood, and, *w*, and entered with them
  9:31 *w* in the fear of the Lord . . were multiplied
Rom. 4:12 who also *w* in the steps of that faith
  6:4 even so we also should *w* in newness of life
  8:1 *w* not after the flesh, but after the Spirit
  13:13 let us *w* honestly, as in the day; not in
  14:15 *w* be grieved . . now *w* thou not charitably
1 Cor. 3:3 divisions, are ye not carnal, and *w* as men?
  7:17 Lord hath called every one, so let him *w*
2 Cor. 5:7 for we *w* by faith, not by sight
  10:2 think of us as if we *w* according to the flesh
Gal. 5:16 *w* in the Spirit, and ye shall not fulfil
  5:25 live in the Spirit . . also *w* in the Spirit
  6:16 as many as *w* according to this rule, peace
Eph. 2:2 *w* according to the course of this world
  2:10 before ordained that we should *w* in them
  4:1 beseech you that ye *w* worthy of the vocation
  4:17 *w* not as other Gentiles *w*, in the vanity of
  5:2 and *w* in love, as Christ also hath loved us
  5:8 light in the Lord: *w* as children of light
  5:15 *w* circumspectly, not as fools, but as wise
Phil. 3:16 let us *w* by the same rule, let us mind
  3:17 mark them which *w* so as ye have us for an
Col. 1:10 *w* worthy of the Lord unto all pleasing
  2:6 as ye have . . received Christ . . so *w* ye in him
  4:5 *w* in wisdom toward them that are without
1 Thes. 2:12 *w* worthy of God, who hath called you
  4:1 how ye ought to *w* and to please God, so ye
  4:12 may *w* honestly toward them that are without
2 Thes. 3:6 from every brother that *w* disorderly
1 Pet. 4:3 time past . . when we *w* in lasciviousness
  5:8 devil, as a roaring lion, *w* about, seeking
2 Pet. 2:10 chiefly them that *w* after the flesh
1 Jn. 1:6 fellowship with him, and *w* in darkness
  1:7 if we *w* in the light, as he is in the light
  2:6 abideth in him ought . . so to *w*, even as he *w*
2 Jn. 6 this is love . . we *w* after his commandments
3 Jn. 4 than to hear that my children *w* in truth
Jude 18 who should *w* after their own ungodly lusts
Rev. 3:4 they shall *w* with me in white: for they
  21:24 which are saved shall *w* in the light of it

Wall

Ex. 14:22 waters were a *w* unto them on their right
Num. 22:24 a *w* being on this side, and a *w* on that
Deut. 3:5 cities . . fenced with high *w*, gates, and bars
Josh. 6:20 a great shout, that the *w* fell down flat
1 Sam. 25:16 a *w* unto us both by night and day
2 Sam. 22:30 (Ps. 18:29) have I leaped over a *w*
1 Kgs. 4:33 the hyssop that springeth out of the *w*
  21:23 dogs shall eat Jezebel by the *w* of Jezreel
2 Kgs. 20:2 (Is. 38:2) his face to the *w*, and prayed
Ezra 5:3 build this house, and to make up this *w*?
Neh. 2:13 went out . . and viewed the *w* of Jerusalem
  3:8 they fortified Jerusalem unto the broad *w*
  4:3 go up, he shall even break down their stone *w*
  4:6 so built we the *w*; and all the *w* was joined
  6:15 so the *w* was finished in the twenty and
  12:27 at the dedication of the *w* of Jerusalem
Ps. 51:18 unto Zion: build thou the *w* of Jerusalem
  62:3 as a bowing *w* . . and as a tottering fence
  122:7 peace be within thy *w*, and prosperity within
Prov. 18:11 and as a high *w* in his own conceit
  24:31 and the stone *w* thereof was broken down
Song 8:9 if she be a *w*, we will build upon her a
Is. 5:5 break down the *w* . . it shall be trodden down
  26:1 salvation will God appoint for *w* and bulwarks
  49:16 thy *w* are continually before me
  59:10 we grope for the *w* like the blind
  60:18 call thy *w* Salvation, and thy gates Praise
  62:6 I have set watchmen upon thy *w*, O Jerusalem
Jer. 15:20 and I will make thee . . a fenced brazen *w*

Ezek. 8:7 when I looked, behold a hole in the *w*
Dan. 5:5 hand, and wrote . . upon the plaster of the *w*
Joel 2:7 they shall climb the *w* like men of war
Amos 5:19 leaned his hand on the *w*, and a serpent
  7:7 the Lord stood upon a *w* made by a plumbline
Hab. 2:11 for the stone shall cry out of the *w*
Zech. 2:5 will be unto her a *w* of fire round about
Acts 9:25 (2 Cor. 11:33) down by the *w* in a basket
  23:3 God shall smite thee, thou whited *w*
Eph. 2:14 broken down the middle *w* of partition
Heb. 11:30 by faith the *w* of Jericho fell down
Rev. 21:14 *w* of the city had twelve foundations

Wallow

2 Sam. 20:12 *w* in blood in the midst of the highway
Jer. 6:26 with sackcloth, and *w* thyself in ashes
Ezek. 27:30 they shall *w* themselves in the ashes
Mk. 9:20 and he fell on the ground, and *w* foaming
2 Pet. 2:22 sow that was washed to her *w* in the mire

Wander *See also* Astray

Gen. 20:13 caused me to *w* from my father's house
Num. 14:33 your children shall *w* in the wilderness
  32:13 made them *w* in the wilderness forty years
Deut. 27:18 maketh the blind to *w* out of the way
Job 12:24 *w* in a wilderness where there is no way
  15:23 *w* abroad for bread, saying, Where is it?
Ps. 55:7 lo, then would I *w* far off, and remain in
  59:15 let them *w* up and down for meat, and grudge
  107:4 they *w* in the wilderness in a solitary way
  119:10 O let me not *w* from thy commandments
Prov. 21:16 that *w* out of the way of understanding
  27:8 a bird . . *w* from her nest, so is a man that *w*
Is. 16:3 hide the outcasts; bewray not him that *w*
  47:15 they shall *w* every one to his quarter
Jer. 14:10 this people, Thus have they loved to *w*
Lam. 4:14 they have *w* as blind men in the streets
Ezek. 34:6 my sheep *w* through all the mountains
Amos 4:8 so two or three cities *w* unto one city
  8:12 they shall *w* from sea to sea, and from the
1 Tim. 5:13 idle, *w* about from house to house
Heb. 11:37 *w* about in sheepskins and goatskins

Wanderer

Jer. 48:12 that I will send unto him *w*, that shall
Hos. 9:17 and they shall be *w* among the nations

Wandering *See also* Wander

Ps. 56:8 thou tellest my *w*: put thou my tears into
Prov. 26:2 as the bird by *w*, as the swallow by flying
Eccl. 6:9 sight of the eyes than the *w* of the desire
Jude 13 *w* stars, to whom is reserved the blackness

Want *See also* Lack, Need

Deut. 28:48 in nakedness, and in *w* of all things
Judg. 18:10 place where there is no *w* of any thing
  19:20 let all thy *w* lie upon me; only lodge not
Job 30:3 for *w* and famine they were solitary
  31:19 if I have seen any perish for *w* of clothing
Ps. 23:1 the Lord is my shepherd; I shall not *w*
  34:9 for there is no *w* to them that fear him
  34:10 seek the Lord shall not *w* any good thing
Prov. 6:11 (24:34) and thy *w* as an armed man
  9:4 as for him that *w* understanding, she saith
  10:21 but fools die for *w* of wisdom
  13:25 but the belly of the wicked shall *w*
  22:16 giveth to the rich, shall surely come to *w*
Eccl. 6:2 he *w* nothing . . of all that he desireth
Jer. 44:18 offerings unto her, we have *w* all things
Ezek. 4:17 that they may *w* bread and water, and be
Dan. 5:27 weighed in the balances, and art found *w*
Amos 4:6 cities, and *w* of bread in all your places
Mk. 12:44 she of her *w* did cast in all that she had
Lk. 15:14 famine in that land . . he began to be in *w*

Jn. 2:3 and when they *w* wine, the mother of Jesus
2 Cor. 8:14 abundance may be a supply for their *w*
  9:12 not only supplieth the *w* of the saints, but
  11:9 when I was present with you, and *w*, I was
Phil. 2:25 Epaphroditus. . that ministered to my *w*
  4:11 not that I speak in respect of *w*
Tit. 1:5 set in order the things that are *w*
Jas. 1:4 ye may be perfect and entire, *w* nothing

Wanton

Is. 3:16 walk with stretched forth necks and *w* eyes
1 Tim. 5:11 wax *w* against Christ, they will marry
Jas. 5:5 lived in pleasure on the earth, and been *w*

Wantonness

Rom. 13:13 not in chambering and *w*, not in strife
2 Pet. 2:18 the lusts of the flesh, through much *w*

War *See also* Battle, Fight, Strife

Ex. 15:3 LORD is a man of *w*: the LORD is his name
  32:17 Moses, There is a noise of *w* in the camp
Num. 21:14 said in the book of the *w* of the LORD
  31:7 *w* against the Midianites. . slew all the males
  32:20 if ye will go armed before the LORD to *w*
Deut. 24:5 a new wife, he shall not go out to *w*
Josh. 11:23 whole land. . And the land rested from *w*
Judg. 5:8 chose new gods; then was *w* in the gates
  11:4 children of Ammon made *w* against Israel
1 Sam. 14:52 was sore *w* against the Philistines
  19:8 was *w* again: and David went out, and fought
2 Sam. 22:35 (Ps. 18:34) he teacheth my hands to *w*
1 Kgs. 14:30 (15:6; 2 Chr. 12:15) *w*. . Rehoboam and
2 Kgs. 16:5 (Is. 7:1) came up to Jerusalem to *w*
  18:20 (Is. 36:5) have counsel and strength for the *w*
1 Chr. 5:22 many slain, because the *w* was of God
2 Chr. 6:34 if thy people go out to *w* against their
  13:2 there was *w* between Abijah and Jeroboam
  16:9 from henceforth thou shalt have *w*
Job 10:17 upon me; changes and *w* are against me
Ps. 27:3 though *w* should rise against me, in this
  46:9 maketh *w* to cease unto the end of the earth
  55:21 smoother than butter, but *w* was in his heart
  68:30 scatter thou the people that delight in *w*
  120:7 but when I speak, they are for *w*
  144:1 teacheth my hands to *w*. . my fingers to fight
Prov. 20:18 counsel: and with good advice make *w*
  24:6 for by wise counsel thou shalt make thy *w*
Eccl. 3:8 a time of *w*, and a time of peace
Is. 2:4 (Mic. 4:3) neither shall they learn *w* any
  21:15 for they fled. . from the grievousness of *w*
  41:12 that *w* against thee shall be as nothing
Jer. 6:23 set in array as men for *w* against thee
  42:14 go into. . Egypt, where we shall see no *w*
Dan. 7:21 (Rev. 13:7) *w* with the saints and prevailed
Mic. 2:8 pass by securely as men averse from *w*
Mt. 24:6 (Mk. 13:7; Lk. 21:9) of *w* and rumors of *w*
Lk. 14:31 or what king, going to make *w* against
Rom. 7:23 another law. . *w* against the law of my
2 Cor. 10:3 the flesh, we do not *w* after the flesh
1 Tim. 1:18 thou by them mightest *w* a good warfare
2 Tim. 2:4 no man that *w* entangleth himself with
Jas. 4:1 whence come *w* and fightings among you?
1 Pet. 2:11 fleshly lusts, which *w* against the soul
Rev. 12:7 there was *w* in heaven: Michael and his
  12:17 went to make *w* with the remnant of her seed
  13:7 given unto him to make *w* with the saints
  17:14 these shall make *w* with the Lamb
  19:19 gathered together to make *w* against him

Ware (adjective) *See also* Aware

Acts 14:6 they were *w* of it, and fled unto Lystra
2 Tim. 4:15 of whom be thou *w* also; for he hath

Ware (noun) *See also* Vessel

Neh. 10:31 bring *w* or any victuals on the sabbath
Jer. 10:17 gather up thy *w* out of the land
Ezek. 27:16 the multitude of the *w* of thy making
Jon. 1:5 cast forth the *w* that were in the ship

Warfare

Is. 40:2 cry unto her, that her *w* is accomplished
1 Cor. 9:7 who goeth a *w*. . at his own charges?
2 Cor. 10:4 the weapons of our *w* are not carnal
1 Tim. 1:18 that thou by them mightest war a good *w*

Warm

2 Kgs. 4:34 and the flesh of the child waxed *w*
Job 37:17 how thy garments are *w*, when he quieteth
  39:14 eggs in the earth, and *w* them in the dust
Eccl. 4:11 have heat: but how can one be *w* alone?
Is. 44:16 yea, he *w* himself, and saith, Aha, I am *w*
  47:14 shall not be a coal to *w* at, nor fire to
Hag. 1:6 ye clothe you, but there is none *w*
Mk. 14:54 (Jn. 18:18) Peter. . *w* himself at the fire
Jas. 2:16 depart in peace, be ye *w* and filled

Warn *See also* Admonish, Enjoin, Rebuke, Reprove

2 Kgs. 6:10 the man of God told him and *w* him
Ps. 19:11 by them is thy servant *w*: and in keeping
Ezek. 3:18 (33:8) nor speakest to *w* the wicked from
  33:3 he blow the trumpet, and *w* the people
Mt. 2:12 and being *w* of God in a dream that they
  3:7 (Lk. 3:7) who hath *w* you to flee from the wrath
Acts 10:22 was *w* from God by a holy angel to send
  20:31 I ceased not to *w* every one night and day
1 Cor. 4:14 but as my beloved sons I *w* you
Col. 1:28 whom we preach, *w* every man. . teaching
1 Thes. 5:14 *w* them that are unruly, comfort the
Heb. 11:7 by faith Noah, being *w* of God of things

Warning *See also* Warn

Jer. 6:10 to whom shall I speak, and give *w*, that
Ezek. 3:17 hear the word. . and give them *w* from me
  33:5 heard the sound of the trumpet. . took not *w*

Wash

Ex. 2:5 daughter of Pharaoh came down to *w* herself
  29:4 (40:12) Aaron and his sons thou. . shalt *w*
Lev. 8:6 brought Aaron and his sons, and *w*
Deut. 21:6 *w* their hands over the heifer that is
2 Sam. 11:2 from the roof he saw a woman *w* herself
2 Kgs. 5:10 saying, Go and *w* in Jordan seven times
Job 9:30 if I *w* myself with snow water, and make
  29:6 when I *w* my steps with butter, and the rock
Ps. 26:6 I will *w* mine hands in innocency: so will
  51:2 *w* me thoroughly from mine iniquity
  51:7 *w* me, and I shall be whiter than snow
  58:10 shall *w* his feet in the blood of the wicked
  73:13 heart in vain, and *w* my hands in innocency
Prov. 30:12 and yet is not *w* from their filthiness
Is. 1:16 *w* ye, make you clean; put away the evil
  4:4 when the Lord shall have *w* away the filth of
Jer. 2:22 though thou *w* thee with nitre, and take
  4:14 O Jerusalem, *w* thine heart from wickedness
Ezek. 16:4 neither wast thou *w* in water to supple
  23:40 for whom thou didst *w* thyself, paintedst
Mt. 6:17 fastest, anoint thine head, and *w* thy face
  15:2 they *w* not their hands when they eat bread
  27:24 Pilate. . *w* his hands before the multitude
Mk. 7:3 except they *w* their hands oft, eat not
Lk. 7:38 began to *w* his feet with tears, and did
  11:38 that he had not first *w* before dinner
Jn. 9:7 said unto him, Go, *w* in the pool of Siloam

Jn. 9:11 and *w*: and I went and *w*, and I received sight
  13:5 a basin, and began to *w* the disciples' feet
  13:10 that is *w* needeth not save to *w* his feet
  13:14 ye also ought to *w* one another's feet
Acts 16:33 and *w* their stripes; and was baptized
  22:16 arise, and be baptized, and *w* away thy sins
1 Cor. 6:11 but ye are *w*, but ye are sanctified
Eph. 5:26 cleanse it with the *w* of water by the word
1 Tim. 5:10 if she have *w* the saints' feet, if she
Tit. 3:5 by the *w* of regeneration, and renewing of
Heb. 9:10 only in meats and drinks, and divers *w*
  10:22 sprinkled . . and our bodies *w* with pure water
2 Pet. 2:22 and the sow that was *w* to her wallowing
Rev. 1:5 and *w* us from our sins in his own blood
  7:14 have *w* their robes, and made them white

Waste *See also* Desolate, Desolation, Ruin

1 Kgs. 17:14 barrel of meal shall not *w*, neither
Neh. 2:17 ye see the distress . . how Jerusalem lieth *w*
Job 14:10 man dieth, and *w* away: yea, man giveth
Ps. 80:13 the boar out of the wood doth *w* it
  91:6 nor for the destruction that *w* at noonday
  137:3 and they that *w* us required of us mirth
Prov. 19:26 he that *w* his father, and chaseth away
Is. 6:11 until the cities be *w* without inhabitant
  24:1 Lord maketh the earth empty . . maketh it *w*
  34:10 generation to generation it shall lie *w*
  42:15 I will make *w* mountains and hills, and dry
  51:3 comfort Zion . . will comfort all her *w* places
  60:12 yea, those nations shall be utterly *w*
  61:4 they shall build the old *w*, they shall raise
  64:11 and all our pleasant things are laid *w*
Jer. 27:17 wherefore should this city be laid *w*?
Ezek. 12:20 cities that are inhabited shall be laid *w*
  36:10 inhabited, and the *w* shall be builded
Joel 1:10 field is *w*, the land mourneth; for the corn
Mt. 26:8 (Mk. 14:4) to what purpose is this *w*?
Lk. 15:13 there *w* his substance with riotous living
Gal. 1:13 I persecuted the church of God, and *w* it

Waster

Prov. 18:9 is brother to him that is a great *w*
Is. 54:16 and I have created the *w* to destroy

Watch *See also* Look, See

Gen. 31:49 Lord *w* between me and thee, when we
Neh. 4:9 and set a *w* against them day and night
  7:3 appoint *w* of the inhabitants of Jerusalem
Job 7:12 a whale, that thou settest a *w* over me?
  14:16 my steps: dost thou not *w* over my sin?
Ps. 37:32 the wicked *w* the righteous, and seeketh
  90:4 for a thousand years . . as a *w* in the night
  102:7 I *w* . . as a sparrow alone upon the housetop
  130:6 more than they that *w* for the morning
  141:3 set a *w*, O Lord, before my mouth
Is. 21:5 prepare the table, *w* in the watchtower
  29:20 and all that *w* for iniquity are cut off
Jer. 20:10 my familiars *w* for my halting, saying
  31:28 like as I have *w* over them, to pluck up
  44:27 I will *w* over them for evil . . not for good
  51:12 walls of Babylon, make the *w* strong, set up
Ezek. 7:6 is come, the end is come: it *w* for thee
Hab. 2:1 I will stand upon my *w* . . and will *w* to see
Mt. 24:42 (25:13; Mk. 13:35; Lk. 21:36) *w* therefore
  24:43 *w* the thief would come, he would have *w*
  26:38 (Mk. 14:34) tarry ye here, and *w* with me
  26:40 (Mk. 14:37) could ye not *w* with me one hour
  26:41 (Mk. 14:38) *w* and pray, that ye enter not
  27:65 Pilate said unto them, Ye have a *w*: go your
Mk. 3:2 (Lk. 6:7) they *w* him, whether he would heal
  13:33 take ye heed, *w* and pray: for ye know not

Mk. 13:37 and what I say unto you I say unto all, *W*
Lk. 2:8 field, keeping *w* over their flock by night
  12:37 whom the lord when he cometh shall find *w*
  12:38 come in the second *w*, or . . in the third *w*
  20:20 they *w* him, and sent forth spies
1 Cor. 16:13 *w* ye, stand fast in the faith, quit
Eph. 6:18 and *w* thereunto with all perseverance
Col. 4:2 continue in prayer, and *w* in the same
1 Thes. 5:6 not sleep, as do others; but let us *w*
2 Tim. 4:5 *w* thou in all things, endure afflictions
Heb. 13:17 they *w* for your souls, as they that must
1 Pet. 4:7 be ye therefore sober, and *w* unto prayer
Rev. 16:15 I come as a thief. Blessed is he that *w*

Watchful

Rev. 3:2 be *w*. . strengthen the things which remain

Watchman (Watchmen)

2 Sam. 18:25 and the *w* cried, and told the king
Ps. 127:1 keep the city, the *w* waketh but in vain
Is. 21:11 *W*, what of the night? *W*, what of the night?
  52:8 thy *w* shall lift up the voice
  56:10 his *w* are blind: they are all ignorant
  62:6 I have set *w* upon thy walls, O Jerusalem
Jer. 6:17 also I set *w* over you, saying, Hearken
  31:6 *w* upon the mount Ephraim shall cry, Arise
Ezek. 3:17 (33:7) son of man, I have made thee a *w*
  33:6 if the *w* see the sword come, and blow not
Hos. 9:8 the *w* of Ephraim was with my God
Mic. 7:4 the day of thy *w* and thy visitation cometh

Water *See also* Flood

Gen. 1:2 Spirit of God moved upon the face of the *w*
  9:15 the *w* shall no more become a flood to destroy
  13:10 all the plain of Jordan, that it was well *w*
  21:19 and she went, and filled the bottle with *w*
  26:20 of Gerar did strive . . saying, The *w* is ours
  29:10 Jacob went near . . and *w* the flock of Laban
  49:4 unstable as *w*, thou shalt not excel
Ex. 2:10 Moses . . Because I drew him out of the *w*
  7:20 the *w* . . in the river were turned to blood
  15:22 three days in the wilderness, and found no *w*
  15:23 could not drink of the *w* of Marah, for they
  17:1 and there was no *w* for the people to drink
  17:6 smite the rock, and there shall come *w* out
Num. 5:17 shall take holy *w* in an earthen vessel
  19:9 for a *w* of separation: it is a purification
  20:2 and there was no *w* for the congregation
  20:8 shalt bring forth to them *w* out of the rock
Deut. 8:15 who brought thee forth *w* out of the rock
Josh. 7:5 hearts of the people melted . . became as *w*
1 Sam. 26:12 took . . the cruse of *w* from Saul's bolster
2 Sam. 14:14 die, and are as *w* spilt on the ground
  22:17 (Ps. 18:16) he drew me out of many *w*
1 Kgs. 22:27 (2 Chr. 18:26) feed . . with *w* of affliction
2 Kgs. 2:8 Elijah took his mantle . . and smote the *w*
  2:21 saith the Lord, I have healed these *w*
  3:11 which poured *w* on the hands of Elijah
  3:17 yet that valley shall be filled with *w*
  6:5 the axe head fell into the *w*: and he cried
  20:20 and a conduit, and brought *w* into the city
Job 8:11 without mire? can the flag grow without *w*?
  12:15 he withholdeth the *w*, and they dry up
  14:19 the *w* wear the stones: thou washest away
  22:7 thou hast not given *w* to the weary to drink
  26:8 he bindeth up the *w* in his thick clouds
Ps. 6:6 my bed to swim; I *w* my couch with my tears
  22:14 I am poured out like *w*, and all my bones
  23:2 pastures: he leadeth me beside the still *w*
  33:7 he gathereth the *w* of the sea . . as a heap
  46:3 though the *w* thereof roar and be troubled
  58:7 them melt away as *w* which run continually
  63:1 in a dry and thirsty land, where no *w* is

Ps. 65:9 thou visitest the earth, and *w* it
66:12 we went through fire and through *w*
69:1 save me . . for the *w* are come in unto my soul
73:10 and *w* of a full cup are wrung out to them
77:16 the *w* saw thee, O God, the *w* saw thee
78:20 he smote the rock, that the *w* gushed out
79:3 their blood have they shed like *w* round
81:7 thunder: I proved thee at the *w* of Meribah
104:13 he *w* the hills from his chambers: the earth
114:8 standing *w*, the flint into a fountain of *w*
124:4 then the *w* had overwhelmed us, the stream
Prov. 5:15 drink *w* out of thine own cistern
9:17 stolen *w* are sweet . . bread eaten in secret
11:25 and he that *w* shall be *w* also himself
20:5 counsel in the heart of man is like deep *w*
25:25 as cold *w* to a thirsty soul, so is good news
27:19 in *w* face answereth to face, so the heart
30:4 who hath bound the *w* in a garment?
Eccl. 11:1 cast thy bread upon the *w*: for thou shalt
Song 8:7 many *w* cannot quench love, neither can
Is. 1:22 is become dross, thy wine mixed with *w*
3:1 whole stay of bread, and the whole stay of *w*
11:9 (Hab. 2:14) be full . . as the *w* cover the sea
12:3 shall ye draw *w* out of the wells of salvation
16:9 I will *w* thee with my tears, O Heshbon
19:5 *w* shall fail from the sea, and the river
27:3 LORD do keep it; I will *w* it every moment
28:17 and the *w* shall overflow the hiding place
32:20 blessed are ye that sow beside all *w*
33:16 bread shall be given him; his *w* shall be sure
35:6 for in the wilderness shall *w* break out
41:17 poor and needy seek *w*, and there is none
43:2 when thou passest through the *w*, I will be
43:20 I give *w* in the wilderness, and rivers in
44:3 for I will pour *w* upon him that is thirsty
48:21 he caused the *w* to flow out of the rock
54:9 this is as the *w* of Noah unto me
55:1 every one that thirsteth, come ye to the *w*
55:10 and returneth not hither, but *w* the earth
58:11 and like a spring of *w*, whose *w* fail not
Jer. 2:13 have forsaken me the fountain of living *w*
8:14 and given us *w* of gall to drink, because we
9:1 that my head were *w*, and mine eyes a fountain
10:13 (51:16) is a multitude of *w* in the heavens
14:3 they came to the pits, and found no *w*
47:2 behold, *w* rise up out of the north, and shall
Ezek. 32:6 I will also *w* with thy blood the land
36:25 then will I sprinkle clean *w* upon you
47:1 *w* issued out from under the threshold
Amos 5:24 but let judgment run down as *w*
8:11 not a famine of bread, nor a thirst for *w*
Jon. 2:5 *w* compassed me about, even to the soul
Zech. 14:8 living *w* shall go out from Jerusalem
Mt. 3:11 (Mk. 1:8; Lk. 3:16; Jn. 1:26) I indeed
     baptize you with *w* unto repentance
10:42 (Mk. 9:41) give to drink . . a cup of cold *w*
14:28 be thou, bid me come unto thee on the *w*
27:24 he took *w*, and washed his hands before the
Lk. 7:44 thou gavest me no *w* for my feet: but she
8:23 were filled with *w*, and were in jeopardy
16:24 that he may dip the tip of his finger in *w*
Jn. 2:7 Jesus saith . . Fill the waterpots with *w*
3:5 except a man be born of *w* and of the Spirit
3:23 baptizing . . because there was much *w* there
4:10 asked . . and he would have given thee living *w*
4:14 *w* that I shall give him shall never thirst
5:3 blind, halt . . waiting for the moving of the *w*
7:38 of his belly shall flow rivers of living *w*
19:34 and forthwith came there out blood and *w*
Acts 1:5 (11:16) John truly baptized with *w*; but ye
8:36 eunuch said, See, here is *w*; what doth hinder
10:47 can any man forbid *w*, that these should not
1 Cor. 3:6 I have planted, Apollos *w*; but God gave

2 Cor. 11:26 in journeyings often, in perils of *w*
Heb. 10:22 and our bodies washed with pure *w*
Jas. 3:11 at the same place sweet *w* and bitter?
1 Pet. 3:20 wherein . . eight souls were saved by *w*
2 Pet. 2:17 these are wells without *w*, clouds that
3:5 the earth standing out of the *w* and in the *w*
1 Jn. 5:6 came . . not by *w* only, but by *w* and blood
Jude 12 clouds they are without *w*, carried about
Rev. 7:17 shall lead them unto living fountains of *w*
8:11 *w* became wormwood . . men died of the *w*
17:15 *w* which thou sawest, where the whore sitteth
21:6 of the fountain of the *w* of life freely
22:1 and he showed me a pure river of *w* of life
22:17 whosoever will, let him take the *w* of life

Watercourse

Job 38:25 who hath divided a *w* for the overflowing

Waterpot

Jn. 2:6 and there were set there six *w* of stone
4:28 the woman then left her *w*, and went her way

Waterspring

Ps. 107:33 a wilderness, and the *w* into dry ground

Wave

Ex. 29:24 (Lev. 8:27) shalt *w* them for a *w* offering
Lev. 7:30 the breast may be *w* for a *w* offering
23:11 he shall *w* the sheaf . . the priest shall *w* it
Job 38:11 and here shall thy proud *w* be stayed?
Ps. 42:7 thy *w* and thy billows are gone over me
65:7 the noise of the seas, the noise of their *w*
89:9 when the *w* thereof arise, thou stillest them
93:3 up their voice; the floods lift up their *w*
107:29 a calm, so that the *w* thereof are still
Is. 48:18 thy righteousness as the *w* of the sea
Jer. 5:22 though the *w* thereof toss themselves, yet
51:42 she is covered with the multitude of the *w*
Jon. 2:3 all thy billows and thy *w* passed over me
Zech. 10:11 shall smite the *w* in the sea, and all
Mt. 8:24 (Mk. 4:37) ship was covered with the *w*
Acts 27:41 was broken with the violence of the *w*
Jas. 1:6 he that wavereth is like a *w* of the sea
Jude 13 raging *w* of the sea, foaming out . . shame

Wavering

Heb. 10:23 the profession of our faith without *w*
Jas. 1:6 let him ask in faith, nothing *w*

Wax

Ps. 22:14 my heart is like *w*; it is melted in the
68:2 as *w* melteth before the fire, so let the
Mic. 1:4 as *w* before the fire, and as the waters

Way *See also* Highway, Path, Walk

Gen. 3:24 sword . . to keep the *w* of the tree of life
6:12 all flesh had corrupted his *w* upon the earth
18:19 shall keep the *w* of the LORD, to do justice
24:56 hinder me not . . LORD hath prospered my *w*
Ex. 13:21 a pillar of a cloud, to lead them the *w*
18:20 show them the *w* wherein they must walk
Num. 22:32 withstand . . because thy *w* is perverse
Deut. 8:2 remember all the *w* which . . thy God led
8:6 thy God, to walk in his *w*, and to fear him
26:17 to be thy God, and to walk in his *w*
32:4 for all his *w* are judgment: a God of truth
Josh. 1:8 then thou shalt make thy *w* prosperous
23:14 this day I am going the *w* of all the earth
Judg. 2:22 whether they will keep the *w* of the LORD
1 Sam. 9:8 give to the man of God, to tell us our *w*
12:23 I will teach you the good and the right *w*
2 Sam. 22:22 (Ps. 18:21) I . . kept the *w* of the LORD
22:31 (Ps. 18:30) as for God, his *w* is perfect

2 Sam. 22:33 (Ps. 18:32) and he maketh my *w* perfect
1 Kgs. 2:3 to walk in his *w*, to keep his statutes
8:36 (2 Chr. 6:27) teach them the good *w* wherein
15:34 (16:19; 22:52) walked in the *w* of Jeroboam
20:38 the prophet. . waited for the king by the *w*
2 Kgs. 7:15 the *w* was full of garments and vessels
Job 3:23 why is light given to a man whose *w* is hid
16:22 I shall go the *w* whence I shall not return
19:8 he hath fenced up my *w* that I cannot pass
22:15 hast thou marked the old *w* which wicked
23:10 but he knoweth the *w* that I take
24:23 he resteth; yet his eyes are upon their *w*
28:23 God understandeth the *w* thereof
31:4 doth not he see my *w*, and count all my steps?
38:19 where is the *w* where light dwelleth?
Ps. 25:9 and the meek will he teach his *w*
27:11 (86:11) teach me thy *w*, O LORD
37:5 commit thy *w* unto the LORD; trust also in him
37:34 wait on the LORD, and keep his *w*, and he
49:13 their *w* is their folly: yet their posterity
51:13 then will I teach transgressors thy *w*
67:2 thy *w* may be known upon earth, thy saving
77:19 thy *w* is in the sea, and thy path in the
78:50 he made a *w* to his anger; he spared not
84:5 in thee, in whose heart are the *w* of them
95:10 (Heb. 3:10) and they have not known my *w*
103:7 he made known his *w* unto Moses, his acts
119:5 my *w* were directed to keep thy statutes!
119:168 testimonies: for all my *w* are before thee
143:8 cause me to know the *w* wherein I should
Prov. 3:6 in all thy *w* acknowledge him, and he
3:17 her *w* are *w* of pleasantness, and all her
4:26 ponder. . and let all thy *w* be established
6:6 go to the ant. . consider her *w*, and be wise
6:23 reproofs of instruction are the *w* of life
10:29 *w* of the LORD is strength to the upright
13:15 favor: but the *w* of transgressors is hard
14:12 (16:25) there is a *w* which seemeth right
15:19 *w* of the slothful. . is as a hedge of thorns
15:24 *w* of life is above to the wise, that he may
21:8 the *w* of man is froward and strange
22:6 train up a child in the *w* he should go
23:26 my son. . let thine eyes observe my *w*
30:19 *w* of a ship. . the *w* of a man with a maid
Is. 2:3 (Mic. 4:2) and he will teach us of his *w*
30:21 this is the *w*, walk ye in it, when ye turn
35:8 a *w*, and it shall be called The *w* of holiness
40:3 (Mt. 3:3; Mk. 1:3; Lk. 3:4; Jn. 1:23) prepare
ye the *w* of the LORD
40:27 my *w* is hid from the LORD, and my judgment
43:16 maketh a *w* in the sea, and a path in the
45:13 I will direct all his *w*: he shall build my
51:10 the sea a *w* for the ransomed to pass over?
53:6 we have turned every one to his own *w*
55:7 the wicked forsake his *w*, and the unrighteous
55:8 not your thoughts, neither are your *w* my *w*
55:9 the earth, so are my *w* higher than your *w*
58:2 they seek me daily, and delight to know my *w*
59:8 (Rom. 3:17) the *w* of peace they know not
62:10 prepare ye the *w* of the people; cast up
Jer. 5:4 they know not the *w* of the LORD
6:16 where is the good *w*, and walk therein
7:3 amend your *w* and your doings, and I will
10:23 I know that the *w* of man is not in himself
16:17 mine eyes are upon all their *w*
17:10 even to give every man according to his *w*
23:12 their *w* shall be unto them as slippery *w*
32:19 are open upon all the *w* of the sons of men
32:39 and I will give them one heart, and one *w*
42:3 God may show us the *w* wherein we may walk
50:5 they shall ask the *w* to Zion with their
Lam. 1:4 the *w* of Zion do mourn, because none
Ezek. 7:3 and will judge thee according to thy *w*

Ezek. 18:25 (33:17) the *w* of the Lord is not equal
Dan. 4:37 whose works are truth, and his *w* judgment
Hos. 14:9 the *w* of the LORD are right, and the just
Nah. 1:3 hath his *w* in the whirlwind and in the storm
Hab. 3:6 hills did bow: his *w* are everlasting
Mal. 3:1 (Mt. 11:10; Mk. 1:2; Lk. 7:27) prepare the *w*
Mt. 7:13 for wide is the gate, and broad is the *w*
21:8 (Mk. 11:8; Lk. 19:36) their garments in the *w*
22:16 (Mk. 12:14; Lk. 20:21) teachest the *w* of God
Lk. 1:76 shalt go before. . the Lord to prepare his *w*
Jn. 8:21 I go my *w*, and ye shall seek me, and cannot
10:1 climbeth up some other *w*, the same is a thief
14:4 and whither I go ye know, and the *w* ye know
14:6 I am the *w*, the truth, and the life: no man
Acts 9:2 synagogues, that if he found any of this *w*
9:27 declared. . how he had seen the Lord in the *w*
16:17 these men. . show unto us the *w* of salvation
18:26 expounded. . the *w* of God more perfectly
19:9 spake evil of that *w* before the multitude
19:23 there arose no small stir about that *w*
22:4 I persecuted this *w* unto the death, binding
24:14 that after the *w* which they call heresy
24:22 having more perfect knowledge of that *w*
Rom. 3:12 they are all gone out of the *w*
11:33 his judgments, and his *w* past finding out!
1 Cor. 10:13 with. . temptation. . make a *w* to escape
12:31 and yet show I unto you a more excellent *w*
Heb. 9:8 the *w* into the holiest of all was not yet
10:20 by a new and living *w*. . he hath consecrated
Jas. 1:8 double-minded man is unstable in all his *w*
2 Pet. 2:2 many shall follow their pernicious *w*
2:15 are gone astray, following the *w* of Balaam
Jude 11 for they have gone in the *w* of Cain
Rev. 15:3 just and true are thy *w*, thou King
16:12 *w* of the kings of the east might be prepared

Wayfaring

Judg. 19:17 saw a *w* man in the street of the city
2 Sam. 12:4 to dress for the *w* man that was come
Is. 33:8 the highways lie waste, the *w* man ceaseth
35:8 *w* men, though fools, shall not err therein
Jer. 14:8 as a *w* man that turneth aside to tarry

Wayside

Mt. 13:4 (Mk. 4:4; Lk. 8:5) some seeds fell by the *w*

Weak (Weaker) *See also* Feeble

Judg. 16:7 (16:11, 17) shall I be *w*. . as another man
2 Sam. 3:1 the house of Saul waxed *w* and *w*
3:39 and I am this day *w*, though anointed king
2 Chr. 15:7 let not your hands be *w*: for your work
Job 4:3 and thou hast strengthened the *w* hands
Ps. 6:2 have mercy upon me, O LORD; for I am *w*
Is. 14:10 art thou also become *w* as we? art thou
35:3 strengthen ye the *w* hands, and confirm the
Ezek. 7:17 and all knees shall be *w* as water
16:30 how is thine heart, saith the Lord GOD
Joel 3:10 into spears: let the *w* say, I am strong
Mt. 26:41 (Mk. 14:38) willing, but the flesh is *w*
Acts 20:35 so laboring ye ought to support the *w*
Rom. 4:19 being not *w* in faith, he considered not
8:3 law could not do. . it was *w* through the flesh
14:1 him that is *w* in the faith receive ye
15:1 strong ought to bear the infirmities of the *w*
1 Cor. 1:27 hath chosen the *w* things of the world
4:10 we are *w*, but ye are strong; ye are honorable
8:7 and their conscience being *w* is defiled
8:9 liberty. . a stumblingblock to them that are *w*
8:11 through thy knowledge. . the *w* brother perish
9:22 to the *w* became I as *w*, that I might gain the *w*
11:30 for this cause many are *w* and sickly among
2 Cor. 10:10 powerful; but his bodily presence is *w*
11:29 who is *w*, and I am not *w*?

2 Cor. 13:3 which to you-ward is not *w*, but is mighty
  13:4 for we also are *w* in him, but we shall live
  13:9 are glad, when we are *w*, and ye are strong
Gal. 4:9 turn ye again to the *w* and beggarly elements
1 Thes. 5:14 support the *w*, be patient toward all
1 Pet. 3:7 honor unto the wife, as unto the *w* vessel

Weaken

Neh. 6:9 their hands shall be *w* from the work
Job 12:21 princes, and *w* the strength of the mighty
Ps. 102:23 *w* my strength in the way; he shortened
Is. 14:12 O Lucifer. . which didst *w* the nations!
Jer. 38:4 thus he *w* the hands of the men of war

Weakness *See also* Infirmity

1 Cor. 1:25 and the *w* of God is stronger than men
  2:3 was with you in *w*, and in fear, and in much
  15:43 it is sown in *w*, it is raised in power
2 Cor. 12:9 for my strength is made perfect in *w*
  13:4 though he was crucified through *w*, yet he
Heb. 7:18 for the *w* and unprofitableness thereof
  11:34 out of *w* were made strong, waxed valiant

Wealth *See also* Goods, Inheritance, Mammon, Possession, Riches

Deut. 8:17 might of mine hand hath gotten me this *w*
  8:18 it is he that giveth thee power to get *w*
Ruth 2:1 mighty man of *w*. . and his name was Boaz
1 Sam. 2:32 all the *w* which God shall give Israel
Esth. 10:3 Mordecai. . seeking the *w* of his people
Job 21:13 spend their days in *w*, and in a moment
  31:25 if I rejoiced because my *w* was great
Ps. 44:12 dost not increase thy *w* by their price
  49:6 that trust in their *w*, and boast themselves
  49:10 perish, and leave their *w* to others
  112:3 *w* and riches shall be in his house
Prov. 5:10 lest strangers be filled with thy *w*
  10:15 (18:11) the rich man's *w* is his strong city
  13:11 *w* gotten by vanity shall be diminished
  13:22 the *w* of the sinner is laid up for the just
  19:4 *w* maketh many friends; but the poor is
Eccl. 6:2 a man to whom God hath given riches, *w*
Acts 19:25 know that by this craft we have our *w*
1 Cor. 10:24 his own, but every man another's *w*

Wealthy *See also* Prosperous, Rich

Ps. 66:12 thou broughtest us out into a *w* place
Jer. 49:31 arise, get you up into the *w* nation

Wean

1 Sam. 1:22 I will not go up until the child be *w*
Ps. 131:2 as a child that is *w* of his mother
Is. 28:9 doctrine? them that are *w* from the milk

Weapon

Deut. 23:13 thou shalt have a paddle upon thy *w*
2 Sam. 1:27 mighty fallen. . the *w* of war perished!
Neh. 4:17 work, and with the other hand held a *w*
Job 20:24 shall flee from the iron *w*, and the bow
Eccl. 9:18 wisdom is better than *w* of war
Is. 13:5 and the *w* of his indignation, to destroy
  54:17 no *w*. . formed against thee shall prosper
Jer. 21:4 behold, I will turn back the *w* of war
  51:20 thou art my battle-axe and *w* of war
Ezek. 9:1 every man with his destroying *w* in his
  32:27 are gone down to hell with their *w* of war
2 Cor. 10:4 the *w* of our warfare are not carnal

Wear

Deut. 22:5 woman shall not *w* that which pertaineth
Job 14:19 waters *w* the stones: thou washest away
Is. 4:1 eat our own bread, and *w* our own apparel

Zech. 13:4 neither shall they *w* a rough garment to
Mt. 11:8 that *w* soft clothing are in kings' houses
1 Pet. 3:3 of plaiting the hair, and of *w* of gold

Weariness

Eccl. 12:12 and much study is a *w* of the flesh
Mal. 1:13 ye said also, Behold, what a *w* is it!
2 Cor. 11:27 in *w* and painfulness, in watchings

Weary

Gen. 27:46 Rebekah said to Isaac, I am *w* of my life
2 Sam. 23:10 arose, and smote. . until his hand was *w*
Job 3:17 the wicked cease. . there the *w* be at rest
  10:1 my soul is *w* of my life; I will leave my
  16:7 but now he hath made me *w*: thou hast made
  22:7 thou hast not given water to the *w* to drink
  37:11 also by watering he *w* the thick cloud
Ps. 6:6 I am *w* with my groaning; all the night
Prov. 3:11 neither be *w* of his correction
  25:17 lest he be *w* of thee, and so hate thee
Eccl. 10:15 the labor of the foolish *w* every one
Is. 1:14 a trouble unto me; I am *w* to bear them
  5:27 none shall be *w* nor stumble among them
  7:13 for you to *w* men, but will ye *w* my God also?
  28:12 rest wherewith ye may cause the *w* to rest
  32:2 as the shadow of a great rock in a *w* land
  40:28 the Creator. . fainteth not, neither is *w*?
  40:31 they shall run, and not be *w*
  43:22 but thou hast been *w* of me, O Israel
  43:24 thou hast *w* me with thine iniquities
  46:1 your carriages. . are a burden to the *w* beast
  47:13 thou art *w* in the multitude of thy counsels
  50:4 to speak a word in season to him that is *w*
  57:10 thou art *w* in the greatness of thy way
Jer. 6:11 fury of the LORD; I am *w* with holding in
  9:5 speak lies, and *w* themselves to commit iniquity
  12:5 run with the footmen, and they have *w* thee
  15:6 and destroy thee; I am *w* with repenting
  20:9 was *w* with forbearing, and I could not stay
  31:25 for I have satiated the *w* soul, and I have
Ezek. 24:12 she hath *w* herself with lies, and her
Mic. 6:3 wherein have I *w* thee? testify against me
Hab. 2:13 people shall *w* themselves for very vanity?
Mal. 2:17 ye have *w* the LORD with your words
Lk. 18:5 lest by her continual coming she *w* me
Jn. 4:6 Jesus. . being *w* with his journey, sat thus
Gal. 6:9 (2 Thes. 3:13) not be *w* in well doing
Heb. 12:3 lest ye be *w* and faint in your minds

Weasel

Lev. 11:29 the *w*, and the mouse, and the tortoise

Weather

Job 37:22 fair *w* cometh out of the north
Prov. 25:20 that taketh away a garment in cold *w*
Mt. 16:2 say, It will be fair *w*: for the sky is red

Weave

Judg. 16:13 if thou *w* the seven locks of my head
Is. 19:9 they that *w* networks, shall be confounded
  59:5 cockatrice' eggs, and *w* the spider's web

Weaver

Ex. 35:35 of the *w*, even of them that do any work
1 Sam. 17:7 staff of his spear was like a *w*'s beam
Job 7:6 my days are swifter than a *w*'s shuttle
Is. 38:12 I have cut off like a *w* my life

Web

Judg. 16:13 the seven locks of my head with the *w*
Job 8:14 and whose trust shall be a spider's *w*
Is. 59:5 cockatrice' eggs, and weave the spider's *w*

Wedding *See also* Marriage

Mt. 22:3 to call them that were bidden to the *w*
22:11 he saw . . man which had not on a *w* garment
Lk. 12:36 their lord, when he will return from the *w*
14:8 when thou art bidden of any man to a *w*

Wedge

Josh. 7:21 saw . . a *w* of gold of fifty shekels weight
Is. 13:12 even a man than the golden *w* of Ophir

Wedlock

Ezek. 16:38 will judge thee, as women that break *w*

Weed

Jon. 2:5 the *w* were wrapped about my head

Week

Gen. 29:27 fulfil her *w*, and we will give thee this
Ex. 34:22 (Deut. 16:10) observe the feast of *w*
Jer. 5:24 unto us the appointed *w* of the harvest
Dan. 9:24 seventy *w* are determined upon thy people
9:25 shall be seven *w*, and threescore and two *w*
9:27 for one *w*: and in the midst of the *w* he
Lk. 18:12 I fast twice in the *w*, I give tithes

Weep (Wept) *See also* Cry, Lament, Mourn, Wail

Gen. 21:16 she sat . . and lifted up her voice, and *w*
27:38 and Esau lifted up his voice, and *w*
33:4 Esau ran to meet him . . kissed him . . they *w*
37:35 my son mourning. Thus his father *w* for him
43:30 Joseph . . entered into his chamber, and *w*
45:2 and he *w* aloud: and the Egyptians . . heard
45:14 fell upon his brother Benjamin's neck, and *w*
46:29 went up to meet Israel . . and *w* on his neck
50:17 and Joseph *w* when they spake unto him
Ex. 2:6 she saw the child: and, behold, the babe *w*
Num. 11:4 children of Israel also *w* again, and said
25:6 who were *w* before the door of the tabernacle
Deut. 1:45 and ye returned and *w* before the LORD
34:8 children of Israel *w* for Moses in the plains
Judg. 2:4 the people lifted up their voice, and *w*
20:23 went up and *w* before the LORD until even
1 Sam. 1:8 her husband to her, Hannah, why *w* thou?
11:5 Saul said, What aileth the people that they *w*?
20:41 *w* one with another, until David exceeded
24:16 and Saul lifted up his voice, and *w*
30:4 and *w*, until they had no more power to *w*
2 Sam. 1:24 ye daughters of Israel, *w* over Saul
12:21 thou didst fast and *w* for the child, while
15:30 David went up . . mount Olivet, and *w* as he
19:1 behold, the king *w* and mourneth for Absalom
2 Kgs. 8:11 he was ashamed: and the man of God *w*
13:14 *w* over his face, and said, O my father
20:3 (Is. 38:3) and Hezekiah *w* sore
Ezra 3:12 seen the first house . . *w* with a loud voice
10:1 *w* and casting himself down before the house
Neh. 1:4 I heard these words, that I sat down and *w*
8:9 mourn not, nor *w*. For all the people *w*
Job 27:15 in death: and his widows shall not *w*
30:25 did not I *w* for him that was in trouble?
Ps. 69:10 I *w*, and chastened my soul with fasting
126:6 goeth forth and *w*, bearing precious seed
137:1 sat down, yea, we *w*, when we remembered
Eccl. 3:4 a time to *w*, and a time to laugh
Is. 15:2 he is gone up to . . the high places, to *w*
22:4 I will *w* bitterly, labor not to comfort me
30:19 shalt *w* no more: he will be very gracious
33:7 the ambassadors of peace shall *w* bitterly
Jer. 9:1 I might *w* day and night for the slain
13:17 *w* in secret places for your pride . . *w* sore

Jer. 22:10 *w* ye not for the dead . . but *w* sore for him
31:15 (Mt. 2:18) Rachel *w* for her children refused
Lam. 1:2 she *w* sore in the night, and her tears are
1:16 for these things I *w*; mine eye, mine eye
Ezek. 8:14 behold, there sat women *w* for Tammuz
27:31 shall *w* for thee with bitterness of heart
Joel 1:5 awake, ye drunkards, and *w*; and howl, all
2:17 priests . . *w* between the porch and the altar
Mt. 26:75 (Mk. 14:72; Lk. 22:62) Peter . . *w*
Mk. 5:39 (Lk. 8:52) and *w*? the damsel is not dead
Lk. 6:21 blessed are ye that *w* now: for ye shall
7:13 compassion on her, and said unto her, *W* not
7:32 we have mourned to you, and ye have not *w*
7:38 stood at his feet behind him *w*, and began
19:41 he beheld the city, and *w* over it
23:28 *w* not for me, but *w* for yourselves
Jn. 11:31 saying, She goeth unto the grave to *w*
11:35 Jesus *w*
16:20 ye shall *w* and lament, but the world shall
20:11 but Mary stood without at the sepulchre *w*
20:15 Jesus saith unto her, Woman, why *w* thou?
Acts 9:39 the widows stood by him *w*, and showing
21:13 what mean ye to *w* and to break mine heart?
Rom. 12:15 that do rejoice, and *w* with them that *w*
1 Cor. 7:30 and they that *w*, as though they *w* not
Phil. 3:18 told you often, and now tell you even *w*
Jas. 4:9 be afflicted, and mourn, and *w*: let your
5:1 rich men, *w* and howl for your miseries that
Rev. 5:4 *w* much, because no man was found worthy

Weeping *See also* Weep, Lamentation, Mourning, Wailing

Ezra 3:13 the shout of joy from the noise of the *w*
Esth. 4:3 among the Jews, and fasting, and *w*
Job 16:16 my face is foul with *w*, and on my eyelids
Ps. 6:8 for the LORD hath heard the voice of my *w*
30:5 *w* may endure for a night, but joy cometh in
102:9 eaten ashes . . and mingled my drink with *w*
Is. 16:9 (Jer. 48:32) I will bewail with the *w* of Jazer
22:12 did the Lord . . call to *w*, and to mourning
65:19 voice of *w* shall be no more heard in her
Jer. 9:10 for the mountains will I take up a *w*
31:9 they shall come with *w* . . with supplications
31:15 (Mt. 2:18) Ramah, lamentation, and bitter *w*
31:16 saith the LORD; Refrain thy voice from *w*
Joel 2:12 turn ye . . with fasting, and with *w*
Mal. 2:13 covering the altar . . with tears, with *w*
Mt. 8:12 (22:13; 24:51; 25:30) *w* . . gnashing of teeth

Weigh

2 Sam. 14:26 *w* the hair of his head at two hundred
Job 6:2 oh that my grief were thoroughly *w*
28:25 the winds; and he *w* the waters by measure
31:6 let me be *w* in an even balance, that God may
Ps. 58:2 *w* the violence of your hands in the earth
Prov. 16:2 his own eyes; but the LORD *w* the spirits
Is. 26:7 most upright, dost *w* the path of the just
40:12 *w* the mountains in scales, and the hills
Dan. 5:27 *w* in the balances, and art found wanting
Zech. 11:12 *w* for my price thirty pieces of silver

Weight *See also* Measure

Lev. 26:26 shall deliver you your bread again by *w*
Deut. 25:13 shalt not have in thy bag divers *w*
Job 28:25 to make the *w* for the winds . . he weigheth
Prov. 11:1 abomination . . but a just *w* is his delight
16:11 a just *w* and balance are the LORD's
20:10 divers *w*, and divers measures, both of them
Ezek. 4:10 meat which thou shalt eat shall be by *w*
Mic. 6:11 balances, and with the bag of deceitful *w*?
2 Cor. 4:17 more exceeding and eternal *w* of glory
Heb. 12:1 let us lay aside every *w*, and the sin

Weighty (Weightier)

Prov. 27:3 sand *w*; but a fool's wrath is heavier
Mt. 23:23 have omitted the *w* matters of the law
2 Cor. 10:10 for his letters . . are *w* and powerful

Welfare

Gen. 43:27 and he asked them of their *w*, and said
1 Chr. 18:10 to king David, to inquire of his *w*
Neh. 2:10 to seek the *w* of the children of Israel
Job 30:15 and my *w* passeth away as a cloud
Ps. 69:22 been for their *w*, let it become a trap
Jer. 38:4 seeketh not the *w* of this people

Well (adjective, adverb) *See also* Better, Best, Well-beloved, Well-pleasing

Gen. 4:7 thou doest *w*, shalt thou not be accepted?
12:13 that it may be *w* with me for thy sake
29:6 unto them, Is he *w*? And they said, He is *w*
40:14 think on me when it shall be *w* with thee
Ex. 4:14 thy brother? I know that he can speak *w*
Num. 11:18 to eat? for it was *w* with us in Egypt
Deut. 4:40 go *w* with thee, and with thy children
5:16 (Eph. 6:3) that it may go *w* with thee
1 Sam. 20:7 if he say thus, It is *w*; thy servant
2 Kgs. 4:26 *w* with thee? is it *w* with thy husband?
2 Chr. 12:12 and also in Judah things went *w*
Ps. 49:18 men will praise thee, when thou doest *w*
Prov. 11:10 when it goeth *w* with the righteous
30:29 be three things which go *w*, yea, four are
Eccl. 8:12 it shall be *w* with them that fear God
Is. 3:10 the righteous, that it shall be *w* with him
Jer. 7:23 commanded you, that it may be *w* unto you
15:11 verily it shall be *w* with thy remnant
Jon. 4:4 said the LORD, Doest thou *w* to be angry?
Mt. 12:12 it is lawful to do *w* on the sabbath days
25:21 (Lk. 19:17) *w* done, thou good and faithful
Mk. 7:37 he hath done all things *w*: he maketh both
Lk. 6:26 woe . . when all men shall speak *w* of you!
20:39 answering said, Master, thou hast *w* said
Jn. 11:12 said . . Lord, if he sleep, he shall do *w*
Gal. 4:17 they zealously affect you, but not *w*
5:7 ye did run *w*; who did hinder you that ye
6:9 (2 Thes. 3:13) not be weary in *w* doing
1 Tim. 5:17 elders that rule *w* be counted worthy
1 Pet. 3:17 suffer for *w* doing, than for evildoing

Well (noun) *See also* Fountain, Spring

Gen. 21:19 God opened her eyes, and she saw a *w*
21:25 Abraham reproved Abimelech because of a *w*
24:11 camels to kneel . . without the city by a *w*
26:15 the *w* which his father's servants had digged
29:2 and he looked, and behold a *w* in the field
Ex. 15:27 they came to Elim, where were twelve *w*
Num. 21:17 Israel sang this song, Spring up, O *w*
Deut. 6:11 and *w* digged, which thou diggedst not
2 Sam. 17:18 man's house . . had a *w* in his court
23:15 (1 Chr. 11:17) water of the *w* of Bethlehem
2 Kgs. 3:19 and stop all *w* of water, and mar every
2 Chr. 26:10 he built towers . . and digged many *w*
Ps. 84:6 through the valley of Baca make it a *w*
Prov. 5:15 and running waters out of thine own *w*
10:11 mouth of a righteous man is a *w* of life
Song 4:15 fountain of gardens, a *w* of living waters
Is. 12:3 ye draw water out of the *w* of salvation
Jn. 4:6 Jacob's *w* was there. Jesus . . sat thus on the *w*
4:14 a *w* of water springing up into everlasting
2 Pet. 2:17 these are *w* without water, clouds that

Well-beloved

Song 1:13 a bundle of myrrh is my *w-b* unto me
Is. 5:1 will I sing to my *w-b* a song of my beloved
Mk. 12:6 having yet therefore one son, his *w-b*

Well-pleasing

Phil. 4:18 a sacrifice acceptable, *w-p* to God
Col. 3:20 obey . . parents . . this is *w-p* unto the LORD
Heb. 13:21 working in you that which is *w-p* in his

Wellspring

Prov. 16:22 understanding is a *w* of life unto him
18:4 and the *w* of wisdom as a flowing brook

Went *See also* Depart, Go, Proceed

Gen. 4:16 Cain *w* out from the presence of the LORD
7:9 (7:15) *w* in two and two unto Noah into the ark
11:31 *w* forth with them from Ur of the Chaldees
12:10 Abram *w* down into Egypt to sojourn there
42:3 Joseph's ten brethren *w* down to buy corn
Ex. 7:10 and Moses and Aaron *w* in unto Pharaoh
12:41 all the hosts of the LORD *w* out from . . Egypt
14:22 *w* into the midst of the sea upon the dry
19:3 Moses *w* up unto God, and the LORD called
Num. 10:33 ark of the covenant of the LORD *w* before
20:15 how our fathers *w* down into Egypt, and we
Josh. 6:9 armed men *w* before the priests that blew
1 Sam. 1:22 but Hannah *w* not up; for she said unto
1 Kgs. 13:14 *w* after the man of God, and found him
19:8 *w* in the strength of that meat forty days
2 Kgs. 2:1 that Elijah *w* with Elisha from Gilgal
2:8 divided . . that they two *w* over on dry ground
2:11 and Elijah *w* up by a whirlwind into heaven
5:11 but Naaman *w* wroth, and *w* away, and said
23:2 (2 Chr. 34:30) *w* up into the house of the LORD
1 Chr. 16:20 (Ps. 105:13) *w* from nation to nation
Ezra 2:1 (Neh. 7:6) that *w* up out of the captivity
Neh. 9:11 they *w* through . . the sea on the dry land
Job 1:12 (2:7) so Satan *w* forth from the presence
Ps. 42:4 I *w* with them to the house of God
66:6 sea into dry land: they *w* through the flood
73:17 until I *w* into the sanctuary of God
Jon. 1:3 and *w* down to Joppa; and he found a ship
Mt. 4:23 Jesus *w* about all Galilee, teaching in
5:1 seeing the multitudes, he *w* up into a mountain
9:35 Jesus *w* about all the cities and villages
11:7 (Lk. 7:24) what *w* ye out into the wilderness
19:22 (Mk. 10:22) heard that . . *w* away sorrowful
21:29 will not; but afterward he repented, and *w*
21:33 (Mk. 12:1; Lk. 20:9) *w* into a far country
26:39 (Mk. 14:35) he *w* a little further, and fell
27:53 *w* into the holy city, and appeared unto
Mk. 2:26 (Lk. 6:4) how he *w* into the house of God
Lk. 8:1 that he *w* throughout every city and village
16:30 if one *w* unto them from the dead, they will
19:12 a certain nobleman *w* into a far country to
Jn. 6:66 that time many of his disciples *w* back
8:9 *w* out one by one, beginning at the eldest
13:3 that he was come from God, and *w* to God
13:30 having received the sop, *w* immediately out
18:15 disciple . . *w* in with Jesus into the palace
20:5 saw the linen clothes lying; yet *w* he not in
Acts 3:1 now Peter and John *w* up . . into the temple
8:5 then Philip *w* down to the city of Samaria
10:9 Peter *w* up upon the housetop to pray
10:38 who *w* about doing good, and healing all
13:14 *w* into the synagogue on the sabbath day
15:38 departed . . and *w* not with them to the work
17:2 and Paul, as his manner was, *w* in unto them
24:11 since I *w* up to Jerusalem for to worship
26:12 as I *w* to Damascus with authority
Gal. 1:17 but I *w* into Arabia, and returned again
1:18 I *w* up to Jerusalem to see Peter, and abode
2:1 I *w* up again to Jerusalem with Barnabas
Heb. 11:8 and he *w* out, not knowing whither he *w*
1 Jn. 2:19 *w* out from us, but they were not of us
Rev. 20:9 they *w* up on the breadth of the earth

Wept *See* Weep

West

Ps. 103:12 as far as the east is from the *w*, so far
Mt. 8:11 (Lk. 13:29) shall come from the east and *w*
24:27 of the east, and shineth even unto the *w*
Lk. 12:54 when ye see a cloud rise out of the *w*

Wet

Job 24:8 are *w* with the showers of the mountains
Dan. 4:15 and let it be *w* with the dew of heaven

Whale

Gen. 1:21 God created great *w*, and every living
Job 7:12 am I a sea, or a *w*, that thou settest a
Ezek. 32:2 thou art as a *w* in the seas
Mt. 12:40 as Jonas was three days . . in the *w*'s belly

Wheat *See also* Barley, Corn

Deut. 8:8 a land of *w*, and barley, and vines, and fig
1 Sam. 12:17 is it not *w* harvest today? I will call
Job 31:40 let thistles grow instead of *w*, and cockle
Ps. 81:16 fed them also with the finest of the *w*
147:14 and fillest thee with the finest of the *w*
Jer. 12:13 they have sown *w*, but shall reap thorns
23:28 what is the chaff to the *w*? saith the LORD
Joel 2:24 floors shall be full of *w*, and the vats
Amos 8:5 and the sabbath, that we may set forth *w*
8:6 buy the poor . . and sell the refuse of the *w*?
Mt. 3:12 (Lk. 3:17) gather his *w* into the garner
13:25 enemy came and sowed tares among the *w*
Lk. 22:31 to have you, that he may sift you as *w*
Jn. 12:24 except a corn of *w* fall into the ground
1 Cor. 15:37 bare grain, it may chance of *w*, or of
Rev. 6:6 a measure of *w* for a penny, and three

Wheel

Ex. 14:25 took off their chariot *w*, that they drave
Ps. 83:13 make them like a *w*; as the stubble before
Prov. 20:26 wicked, and bringeth the *w* over them
Eccl. 12:6 or the *w* broken at the cistern
Is. 28:28 nor break it with the *w* of his cart
Ezek. 1:16 was as it were a *w* in the middle of a *w*
10:2 go in between the *w*, even under the cherub
10:9 four *w* by the cherubim, one *w* by one cherub

Whelp

2 Sam. 17:8 as a bear robbed of her *w* in the field
Job 28:8 the lion's *w* have not trodden it
Prov. 17:12 let a bear robbed of her *w* meet a man

Where

Gen. 3:9 LORD God called unto Adam . . *W* art thou?
Job 14:10 man giveth up the ghost, and *w* is he?
35:10 none saith, *W* is God my maker, who giveth
Ps. 42:3 (42:10) say unto me, *W* is thy God?
79:10 (115:2) the heathen say, *W* is their God?
Jer. 2:6 neither said they, *W* is the LORD that
Jn. 17:24 be with me *w* I am; that they may behold

Whet

Deut. 32:41 if I *w* my glittering sword, and mine
Ps. 7:12 if he turn not, he will *w* his sword
64:3 who *w* their tongue like a sword, and bend
Eccl. 10:10 iron be blunt, and he do not *w* the edge

Whip

1 Kgs. 12:11 (2 Chr. 10:11, 14) chastised you with *w*
Prov. 26:3 a *w* for the horse, a bridle for the ass
Nah. 3:2 noise of a *w*, and the noise of the rattling

Whirlwind *See also* Wind

2 Kgs. 2:11 and Elijah went up by a *w* into heaven

Job 37:9 out of the south cometh the *w*: and cold
38:1 LORD answered Job out of the *w*, and said
Ps. 58:9 he shall take them away as with a *w*, both
Prov. 10:25 as the *w* passeth, so is the wicked
Is. 40:24 the *w* shall take them away as stubble
66:15 with fire, and with his chariots like a *w*
Jer. 23:19 a *w* of the LORD is gone forth in fury
25:32 great *w* shall be raised up from the coasts
Ezek. 1:4 and behold, a *w* came out of the north
Hos. 8:7 sown the wind, and they shall reap the *w*
Nah. 1:3 LORD hath his way in the *w*. . in the storm
Hab. 3:14 they came out as a *w* to scatter me
Zech. 9:14 Lord GOD . . shall go with *w* of the south

Whisper

2 Sam. 12:19 when David saw that his servants *w*
Ps. 41:7 all that hate me *w* together against me
Is. 29:4 and thy speech shall *w* out of the dust

Whisperer

Prov. 16:28 and a *w* separateth chief friends
Rom. 1:29 murder, debate, deceit, malignity; *w*

White (Whiter)

Gen. 40:16 behold, I had three *w* baskets on my head
49:12 red with wine, and his teeth *w* with milk
Lev. 13:10 if the rising be *w* in the skin . . hair *w*
Num. 12:10 Miriam became leprous, *w* as snow
Job 6:6 or is there any taste in the *w* of an egg?
Ps. 51:7 wash me, and I shall be *w* than snow
Eccl. 9:8 let thy garments be always *w*
Song 5:10 my beloved is *w* and ruddy, the chiefest
Is. 1:18 be as scarlet, they shall be as *w* as snow
Lam. 4:7 purer than snow, they were *w* than milk
Dan. 11:35 to purge, and to make them *w*, even to
Mt. 5:36 thou canst not make one hair *w* or black
17:2 (Mk. 9:3; Lk. 9:29) raiment was *w* as the light
28:3 like lightning, and his raiment *w* as snow
Mk. 9:3 *w* as snow; so as no fuller on earth can *w*
16:5 a young man . . clothed in a long *w* garment
Jn. 4:35 fields; for they are *w* already to harvest
20:12 seeth two angels in *w* sitting, the one at
Acts 1:10 two men stood by them in *w* apparel
Rev. 2:17 will give him a *w* stone, and in the stone
3:4 shall walk with me in *w*: for they are worthy
3:5 overcometh . . shall be clothed in *w* raiment
4:4 I saw . . elders sitting, clothed in *w* raiment
6:2 and I saw, and behold a *w* horse: and he
7:9 lo, a great multitude . . clothed with *w* robes
19:11 I saw heaven opened, and behold a *w* horse
20:11 I saw a great *w* throne, and him that sat

Whited

Mt. 23:27 hypocrites! for ye are like . . *w* sepulchres
Acts 23:3 God shall smite thee, thou *w* wall

Whole *See also* Complete, Just, Perfect, Well

Job 5:18 bindeth up . . woundeth . . his hands make *w*
Ps. 9:1 will praise thee, O LORD, with my *w* heart
48:2 the joy of the *w* earth, is mount Zion
72:19 let the *w* earth be filled with his glory
111:1 I will praise the LORD with my *w* heart
119:2 blessed . . that seek him with the *w* heart
Is. 1:5 the *w* head is sick, and the *w* heart faint
Jer. 19:11 vessel, that cannot be made *w* again
Ezek. 15:5 when it was *w*, it was meet for no work
Mt. 5:29 not . . thy *w* body should be cast into hell
6:22 (Lk. 11:34) thy *w* body shall be full of light
9:12 (Mk. 2:17; Lk. 5:31) *w* need not a physician
9:21 (Mk. 5:28) touch his garment, I shall be *w*
9:22 (Mk. 5:34; Lk. 8:48) faith hath made thee *w*

Mt. 13:33 (Lk. 13:21) meal, till the *w* was leavened
14:36 (Mk. 6:56) as touched were made perfectly *w*
Jn. 5:6 he saith unto him, Wilt thou be made *w*?
Acts 9:34 Aeneas, Jesus Christ maketh thee *w*
Rom. 8:22 the *w* creation groaneth and travaileth
1 Cor. 5:6 (Gal. 5:9) little leaven leaveneth. . *w* lump
12:17 if the *w* body were an eye, where were the
Gal. 5:3 circumcised. . is a debtor to do the *w* law
1 Thes. 5:23 *w* spirit. . soul and body be preserved
Jas. 2:10 keep the *w* law. . yet offend in one point
1 Jn. 2:2 but also for the sins of the *w* world

Wholesome

Prov. 15:4 a *w* tongue is a tree of life
1 Tim. 6:3 teach otherwise. . consent not to *w* words

Wholly *See also* Fully

Deut. 1:36 (Josh. 14:8) *w* followed the LORD
Jer. 2:21 planted thee a noble vine, *w* a right seed
1 Thes. 5:23 the very God of peace sanctify you *w*
1 Tim. 4:15 meditate upon. . give thyself *w* to them

Whore *See also* Adulteress, Harlot

Deut. 23:17 shall be no *w* of the daughters of Israel
Prov. 23:27 *w* is a deep ditch; and a strange woman
Ezek. 16:28 played the *w* also with the Assyrians
Rev. 17:1 show unto thee the judgment of the great *w*
19:2 for he hath judged the great *w*, which did

Whoredom

Jer. 3:2 thou hast polluted the land with thy *w*
Ezek. 16:20 is this of thy *w* a small matter
43:9 now let them put away their *w*
Hos. 1:2 Hosea, Go, take unto thee a wife of *w*
2:2 let her. . put away her *w* out of her sight
4:11 *w* and wine and new wine take away the heart
4:12 for the spirit of *w* hath caused them to err
5:3 O Ephraim, thou committest *w*, and Israel is
Nah. 3:4 because of the multitude of the *w* of the

Whoremonger

Eph. 5:5 ye know, that no *w*, nor unclean person
1 Tim. 1:10 for *w*, for them that defile themselves
Heb. 13:4 but *w* and adulterers God will judge
Rev. 21:8 *w*, and sorcerers, and idolaters, and all
22:15 for without are dogs, and sorcerers, and *w*

Wicked *See also* Bad, Evil, Ungodly, Vile

Gen. 13:13 the men of Sodom were *w* and sinners
18:23 also destroy the righteous with the *w*?
Ex. 9:27 LORD is righteous. . I and my people are *w*
23:7 slay thou not: for I will not justify the *w*
Deut. 15:9 be not a thought in thy *w* heart, saying
23:9 enemies, then keep thee from every *w* thing
25:1 justify the righteous, and condemn the *w*
1 Sam. 2:9 and the *w* shall be silent in darkness
24:13 wickedness proceedeth from the *w*
2 Kgs. 17:11 wrought *w* things to provoke the LORD
2 Chr. 7:14 turn from their *w* ways; then will I
Neh. 9:35 neither turned they from their *w* works
Job 3:17 there the *w* cease from troubling
8:22 the dwelling. . of the *w* shall come to nought
9:22 I said. . He destroyeth the perfect and the *w*
9:24 the earth is given into the hand of the *w*
9:29 if I be *w*, why then labor I in vain?
11:20 eyes of the *w* shall fail, and they shall
15:20 *w* man travaileth with pain all his days
18:5 yea, the light of the *w* shall be put out
18:21 such are the dwellings of the *w*, and this
20:5 triumphing of the *w* is short, and the joy
21:7 wherefore do the *w* live, become old, yea
21:30 *w* is reserved to the day of destruction?

Job 27:13 this is the portion of a *w* man with God
31:3 is not destruction to the *w*? and a strange
34:18 is it fit to say to a king, Thou art *w*?
36:6 he preserveth not the life of the *w*
40:12 and tread down the *w* in their place
Ps. 7:11 and God is angry with the *w* every day
9:16 *w* is snared in the work of his own hands
10:4 the *w*. . will not seek after God: God is not
10:13 wherefore doth the *w* contemn God?
11:6 upon the *w* he shall rain snares, fire and
12:8 the *w* walk on every side, when the vilest
26:5 of evildoers; and will not sit with the *w*
27:2 the *w*, even mine enemies and my foes, came
28:3 draw me not away with the *w*, and with the
31:17 let the *w* be ashamed. . let them be silent
32:10 many sorrows shall be to the *w*: but he that
34:21 evil shall slay the *w*: and they that hate
37:10 yet a little while, and the *w* shall not be
37:12 *w* plotteth against the just, and gnasheth
37:20 but the *w* shall perish, and the enemies
37:28 but the seed of the *w* shall be cut off
37:35 seen the *w* in great power, and spreading
58:3 the *w* are estranged from the womb: they go
68:2 so let the *w* perish at the presence of God
73:3 foolish, when I saw the prosperity of the *w*
92:7 when the *w* spring as the grass, and when
94:3 shall the *w*, how long shall they triumph?
101:4 depart from me: I will not know a *w* person
112:10 *w* shall see. . desire of the *w* shall perish
119:119 thou puttest away all the *w* of the earth
119:155 salvation is far from the *w*: for they
125:3 rod of the *w* shall not rest upon the lot
139:24 see if there be any *w* way in me, and lead
140:4 keep me, O LORD, from the hands of the *w*
145:20 love him: but all the *w* will he destroy
146:9 the way of the *w* he turneth upside down
Prov. 4:19 way of the *w* is as darkness: they know
6:12 a *w* man, walketh with a froward mouth
6:18 a heart that deviseth *w* imaginations
10:6 violence covereth the mouth of the *w*
10:25 the whirlwind passeth, so is the *w* no more
10:30 but the *w* shall not inhabit the earth
11:5 but the *w* shall fall by his own wickedness
11:21 join in hand, the *w* shall not be unpunished
12:7 the *w* are overthrown, and are not
14:17 foolishly: and a man of *w* devices is hated
14:32 the *w* is driven away in his wickedness
15:29 the LORD is far from the *w*: but he heareth
17:4 a *w* doer giveth heed to false lips
17:15 that justifieth the *w*. . condemneth the just
21:12 God overthroweth the *w* for their wickedness
24:16 riseth. . but the *w* shall fall into mischief
28:1 the *w* flee when no man pursueth
28:28 when the *w* rise, men hide themselves
29:2 when the *w* beareth rule, the people mourn
Eccl. 7:15 there is a *w* man that prolongeth his life
7:17 be not over much *w*, neither be. . foolish
8:10 I saw the *w* buried, who had come and gone
9:2 one event to the righteous, and to the *w*
Is. 3:11 woe unto the *w*! it shall be ill with him
5:23 justify the *w* for reward, and take away
26:10 let favor be showed to the *w*, yet will he
48:22 (57:21) no peace, saith the LORD, unto the *w*
53:9 made his grave with the *w*, and with the rich
55:7 let the *w* forsake his way. . the unrighteous
57:20 the *w* are like the troubled sea, when it
Jer. 2:33 thou also taught the *w* ones thy ways
12:1 wherefore doth the way of the *w* prosper?
17:9 the heart is deceitful. . and desperately *w*
Ezek. 3:18 (33:8) to warn the *w* from his *w* way
11:2 that devise mischief, and give *w* counsel
18:21 but if the *w* will turn from all his sins
18:23 have I any pleasure. . that the *w* should die?

Ezek. 20:44 not according to your *w* ways, nor
   21:3 cut off from thee the righteous and the *w*
   33:11 death of the *w*; but that the *w* turn from
   33:15 if the *w* restore the pledge, give again
   33:19 but if the *w* turn from his wickedness
Dan. 12:10 *w* shall do wickedly: and none of the *w*
Nah. 1:3 the LORD . . will not at all acquit the *w*
Mal. 3:18 discern between the righteous and the *w*
Mt. 12:45 (Lk. 11:26) spirits more *w* than himself
   13:19 then cometh the *w* one, and catcheth away
   13:38 but the tares are the children of the *w* one
   13:49 the angels . . sever the *w* from among the just
   16:4 a *w* and adulterous generation seeketh after
   18:32 *w* servant, I forgave thee all that debt
   21:41 he will miserably destroy those *w* men
   25:26 (Lk. 19:22) thou *w* and slothful servant
Acts 2:23 and by *w* hands have crucified and slain
1 Cor. 5:13 put away from . . yourselves that *w* person
Eph. 6:16 to quench all the fiery darts of the *w*
Col. 1:21 enemies in your mind by *w* works, yet now
2 Thes. 2:8 shall that *W* be revealed, whom the Lord
   3:2 may be delivered from unreasonable and *w* men
2 Pet. 2:7 vexed with the filthy conversation of the *w*
   3:17 led away with the error of the *w*, fall from
1 Jn. 2:13 (2:14) because ye have overcome the *w* one
   3:12 not as Cain, who was of that *w* one, and slew
   5:18 himself, and that *w* one toucheth him not

Wickedly

Gen. 19:7 said, I pray you, brethren, ut not so
Deut. 9:18 in doing *w* in the sight of the LORD
Judg. 19:23 brethren, nay, I pray you, do not so *w*
2 Sam. 24:17 lo, I have sinned, and I have done *w*
Neh. 9:33 thou hast done right, but we have done *w*
Job 13:7 ye speak *w* for God? and talk deceitfully
   34:12 surely God will not do *w*, neither will the
Ps. 73:8 corrupt . . speak *w* concerning oppression
   74:3 that the enemy hath done *w* in the sanctuary
Dan. 11:32 such as do *w* against the covenant shall
Mal. 4:1 yea, and all that do *w*, shall be stubble

Wickedness *See also* Evil, Iniquity, Sin

Gen. 6:5 GOD saw that the *w* of man was great
   39:9 his wife: how then can I do this great *w*
Deut. 9:4 for the *w* of these nations the LORD doth
   28:20 thou perish . . because of the *w* of thy doings
Judg. 20:3 of Israel, Tell us, how was this *w*?
1 Sam. 12:17 perceive and see that your *w* is great
   24:13 proverb . . *W* proceedeth from the wicked
1 Kgs. 1:52 *w* shall be found in him, he shall die
   8:47 have done perversely, we have committed *w*
   21:25 Ahab, which did sell himself to work *w*
Job 4:8 plow iniquity, and sow *w*, reap the same
   11:11 for he knoweth vain men: he seeth *w* also
   11:14 and let not *w* dwell in thy tabernacles
   20:12 though *w* be sweet in his mouth, though he
   22:5 is not thy *w* great? and thine iniquities
   24:20 no more remembered; and *w* shall be broken
   27:4 my lips shall not speak *w*, nor my tongue
   34:10 far be it from God, that he should do *w*
   35:8 thy *w* may hurt a man as thou art
Ps. 5:4 thou art not a God that hath pleasure in *w*
   7:9 oh let the *w* of the wicked come to an end
   45:7 thou lovest righteousness, and hatest *w*
   55:11 *w* is in the midst thereof: deceit and guile
   55:15 *w* is in their dwellings, and among them
   58:2 in heart ye work *w*; ye weigh the violence
   84:10 of my God, than to dwell in the tents of *w*
   94:23 and shall cut them off in their own *w*
Prov. 4:17 for they eat the bread of *w*, and drink
   8:7 and *w* is an abomination to my lips
   10:2 treasures of *w* profit nothing . . righteousness
   12:3 man shall not be established by *w*

Prov. 13:6 keepeth him . . *w* overthroweth the sinner
   26:26 his *w* shall be showed before . . congregation
   30:20 adulterous woman . . saith, I have done no *w*
Eccl. 3:16 the place of judgment, that *w* was there
   7:15 wicked man that prolongeth his life in his *w*
   7:25 to know the *w* of folly, even of foolishness
   8:8 neither shall *w* deliver those that are given
Is. 9:18 *w* burneth as the fire: it shall devour
   47:10 thou hast trusted in thy *w*: thou hast said
   58:4 and debate, and to smite with the fist of *w*
Jer. 2:19 thine own *w* shall correct thee
   6:7 so she casteth out her *w*: violence and spoil
   8:6 not aright: no man repented him of his *w*
   14:20 we acknowledge, O LORD, our *w*
   23:14 that none doth return from his *w*
   33:5 for all whose *w* I have hid my face from this
Ezek. 3:19 he turn not from his *w*, nor from his
   18:27 (33:19) wicked man turneth away from his *w*
   31:11 I have driven him out for his *w*
Hos. 7:2 consider not . . that I remember all their *w*
   10:13 ye have plowed *w*, ye have reaped iniquity
Jon. 1:2 and cry . . for their *w* is come up before me
Mal. 1:4 and they shall call them, The border of *w*
   3:15 they that work *w* are set up
Mt. 22:18 but Jesus perceived their *w*, and said
Mk. 7:22 covetousness, *w*, deceit, lasciviousness
Lk. 11:39 inward part is full of ravening and *w*
Acts 8:22 repent therefore of this thy *w*, and pray
Rom. 1:29 with all unrighteousness, fornication, *w*
1 Cor. 5:8 neither with the leaven of malice and *w*
Eph. 6:12 against spiritual *w* in high places

Wide

Prov. 21:9 (25:24) a brawling woman in a *w* house
Jer. 22:14 that saith, I will build me a *w* house
Mt. 7:13 for *w* is the gate, and broad is the way

Widow

Gen. 38:11 Tamar . . Remain a *w* at thy father's house
Ex. 22:22 ye shall not afflict any *w*, or fatherless
Deut. 10:18 the judgment of the fatherless and *w*
2 Sam. 14:5 am indeed a *w* woman, and mine husband
1 Kgs. 17:9 I have commanded a *w* . . to sustain thee
Job 22:9 thou hast sent *w* away empty, and the arms
   24:3 they take the *w*'s ox for a pledge
   29:13 and I caused the *w*'s heart to sing for joy
   31:16 or have caused the eyes of the *w* to fail
Ps. 68:5 father of the fatherless . . judge of the *w*
   94:6 they slay the *w* and the stranger, and murder
   109:9 children be fatherless, and his wife a *w*
Prov. 15:25 he will establish the border of the *w*
Is. 1:17 judge the fatherless, plead for the *w*
Jer. 49:11 preserve them . . and let thy *w* trust in me
Lam. 1:1 how is she become as a *w*! she that was
Zech. 7:10 oppress not the *w*, nor the fatherless
Mt. 23:14 (Mk. 12:40; Lk. 20:47) devour *w*' houses
Mk. 12:42 (Lk. 21:2) poor *w*, and she threw in two
Lk. 2:37 was a *w* of about fourscore and four years
   4:26 city of Sidon, unto a woman that was a *w*
   7:12 the only son of his mother, and she was a *w*
   18:3 was a *w* in that city; and she came unto him
Acts 6:1 murmuring . . because their *w* were neglected
1 Tim. 5:3 honor *w* that are indeed
Jas. 1:27 to visit the fatherless and *w* in their
Rev. 18:7 I sit a queen, and am no *w*, and shall

Widowhood

Is. 47:9 come to thee . . the loss of children, and *w*
   54:4 not remember the reproach of thy *w* any more

Wife (Wives)

Gen. 2:24 (Mt. 19:5; Mk. 10:7; Eph. 5:31) leave his
   father and his mother, and . . cleave unto his *w*

Gen. 24:4 kindred, and take a *w* unto my son Isaac
  26:9 of a surety she is thy *w*: and how saidst thou
  39:7 his master's *w* cast her eyes upon Joseph
Ex. 20:17 (Deut. 5:21) not covet thy neighbor's *w*
  22:16 (Deut. 22:29) surely endow her to be his *w*
Num. 5:12 if any man's *w* go aside, and commit a
Deut. 24:5 man hath taken a new *w*, he shall not go
Judg. 14:3 *w* of the uncircumcised Philistines?
  21:7 we will not give them of our daughters to *w*?
Ruth 4:13 so Boaz took Ruth, and she was his *w*
1 Sam. 25:39 communed with Abigail, to take. . to *w*
  30:5 David's two *w* were taken captives
2 Sam. 12:9 taken his *w* to be thy *w*, and hast slain
1 Kgs. 11:3 and he had seven hundred *w*, princesses
Ezra 10:2 we have trespassed. . have taken strange *w*
Esth. 1:20 the *w* shall give to their husbands honor
Ps. 128:3 thy *w* shall be as a fruitful vine by the
Prov. 5:18 and rejoice with the *w* of thy youth
  6:29 in to his neighbor's *w*;. . shall not be innocent
  18:22 whoso findeth a *w* findeth a good thing
  19:14 and a prudent *w* is from the LORD
Eccl. 9:9 live joyfully with the *w* whom thou lovest
Is. 54:6 and a *w* of youth, when thou wast refused
Jer. 3:1 if a man put away his *w*, and she go from
  3:20 as a *w* treacherously departeth from her
Ezek. 24:18 in the morning: and at even my *w* died
Hos. 1:2 go, take unto thee a *w* of whoredoms
  12:12 served for a *w*, and for a *w* he kept sheep
Mal. 2:15 treacherously against the *w* of his youth
Mt. 5:31 (Mk. 10:11; Lk. 16:18) shall put away his *w*
  19:3 (Mk. 10:2) lawful for a man to put away his *w*
  19:5((Mk. 10:7) and shall cleave to his *w*
  22:25 (Mk. 12:20; Lk. 20:28) married a *w*, deceased
Lk. 14:20 said, I have married a *w*. . I cannot come
  17:32 remember Lot's *w*
1 Cor. 7:2 let every man have his own *w*
  7:4 *w* hath not power of her own body, but the
  7:14 unbelieving husband is sanctified by the *w*
  7:27 art thou loosed from a *w*? seek not a *w*
  7:29 they that have *w* be as though they had none
  7:39 *w* is bound by the law as long as her
  9:5 have we not power to lead about a. . *w*
Eph. 5:22 (Col. 3:18) *w*, submit yourselves unto
  5:23 husband is the head of the *w*, even as Christ
  5:25 (Col. 3:19) husbands, love your *w*, even as
  5:28 ought men to love their *w* as their own bodies
  5:33 and the *w* see that she reverence her husband
1 Tim. 3:2 must be blameless, the husband of one *w*
  3:11 so must their *w* be grave, not slanderers
  5:9 widow be taken. . having been. . *w* of one man
1 Pet. 3:1 *w*, be in subjection to your own husbands
  3:7 honor unto the *w*, as unto the weaker vessel
Rev. 19:7 is come, and his *w* hath made herself ready
  21:9 I will show thee the bride, the Lamb's *w*

Wild

Gen. 16:12 and he will be a *w* man; his hand will be
Rom. 11:24 of the olive tree which is *w* by nature

Wilderness *See also* Desert

Gen. 16:7 found her by a fountain of water in the *w*
  21:20 and dwelt in the *w*, and became an archer
Ex. 14:11 hast thou taken us away to die in the *w*?
  16:2 murmured against Moses and Aaron in the *w*
  19:2 desert of Sinai, and had pitched in the *w*
Num. 14:29 your carcasses shall fall in this *w*
Deut. 1:19 through all that great and terrible *w*
  8:2 thy God led thee these forty years in the *w*
  29:5 and I have led you forty years in the *w*
  32:10 in the waste howling *w*; he led him about
1 Kgs. 19:4 himself went a day's journey into the *w*
Neh. 9:19 yet thou. . forsookest them not in the *w*
Job 12:24 and causeth them to wander in a *w* where

Job 24:5 *w* yieldeth food for them. . for their children
Ps. 78:40 how oft did they provoke him in the *w*
  95:8 (Heb. 3:8) in the day of temptation in the *w*
  107:33 turneth rivers into a *w*. . the watersprings
  136:16 to him which led his people through the *w*
Song 3:6 who is this that cometh out of the *w*
Is. 14:17 that made the world as a *w*, and destroyed
  33:9 Sharon is like a *w*; and Bashan and Carmel
  35:1 the *w* and the solitary place shall be glad
  35:6 in the *w* shall waters break out, and streams
  40:3 (Mt. 3:3; Mk. 1:3; Lk. 3:4; Jn. 1:23) voice of
    him that crieth in the *w*, Prepare ye the way
  41:18 I will make the *w* a pool of water
  42:11 let the *w* and the cities thereof lift up
  51:3 will make her *w* like Eden, and her desert
  64:10 thy holy cities are a *w*, Zion is a *w*
Jer. 2:2 when thou wentest after me in the *w*
  2:31 been a *w* unto Israel? a land of darkness?
  9:2 oh that I had in the *w* a lodging place
  22:6 yet surely I will make thee a *w*, and cities
Hos. 2:3 make her as a *w*. . set her like a dry land
Mt. 4:1 (Mk. 1:12; Lk. 4:1) was Jesus led. . into the *w*
  11:7 (Lk. 7:24) what went ye out into the *w* to see?
  15:33 (Mk. 8:4) so much bread in the *w*, as to fill
Lk. 5:16 withdrew himself into the *w*, and prayed
Jn. 3:14 as Moses lifted up the serpent in the *w*
1 Cor. 10:5 for they were overthrown in the *w*

Wile

Num. 25:18 they vex you with their *w*, wherewith
Eph. 6:11 able to stand against the *w* of the devil

Wilfully

Heb. 10:26 if we sin *w* after that we have received

Will *See also* Desire, Purpose

Ps. 40:8 (Heb. 10:7, 9) delight to do thy *w*, O my God
  143:10 teach me to do thy *w*; for thou art my God
Dan. 4:17 and giveth it to whomsoever he *w*
  4:35 according to his *w* in the army of heaven
  8:4 he did according to his *w*, and became great
  11:3 great dominion, and do according to his *w*
Mt. 6:10 (Lk. 11:2) thy *w* be done in earth, as it is
  7:21 enter. . but he that doeth the *w* of my Father
  8:3 (Mk. 1:41; Lk. 5:13) I *w*; be thou clean
  12:50 (Mk. 3:35) whosoever shall do the *w* of my
  18:14 not the *w* of your Father. . that one of these
  20:15 is it not lawful for me to do what I *w* with
  21:31 whether of them twain did the *w* of his father
  26:39 (Mk. 14:36; Lk. 22:42) not as I *w*, but as
  26:42 this cup. . except I drink it, thy *w* be done
Lk. 2:14 and on earth peace, good *w* toward men
  12:47 which knew his lord's *w*, and prepared not
Jn. 1:13 of the *w* of the flesh, nor of the *w* of man
  4:34 my meat is to do the *w* of him that sent me
  5:21 even so the Son quickeneth whom he *w*
  5:30 seek not mine own *w*, but the *w* of the Father
  6:38 not to do mine own *w*, but the *w* of him that
  6:39 this is the Father's *w* which hath sent me
  7:17 if any man *w* do his *w*, he shall know of the
  15:7 ask what ye *w*, and it shall be done unto you
  17:24 Father, I *w* that they. . be with me where I
  21:22 (21:23) if I *w* that he tarry till I come, what is
Acts 13:22 found David. . which shall fulfil all my *w*
  13:36 served his own generation by the *w* of God
  21:14 ceased, saying, The *w* of the Lord be done
  22:14 chosen thee, that thou shouldest know his *w*
Rom. 1:10 journey by the *w* of God to come unto you
  2:18 knowest his *w*, and approvest the things
  7:18 to *w* is present with me; but how to perform
  8:27 maketh intercession. . according to the *w* of
  9:16 so then it is not of him that *w*, nor of him
  9:19 find fault? For who hath resisted his *w*?

Rom. 12:2 good. . acceptable, and perfect *w* of God
15:32 may come unto you with joy by the *w* of God
1 Cor. 4:19 will come to you shortly, if the Lord *w*
7:37 no necessity, but hath power over his own *w*
9:17 if against my *w*, a dispensation of the gospel
16:12 his *w* was not at all to come at this time
2 Cor. 8:5 to the Lord, and unto us by the *w* of God
Gal. 1:4 deliver us. . according to the *w* of God
Eph. 1:9 made known unto us the mystery of his *w*
1:11 all things after the counsel of his own *w*
5:17 but understanding what the *w* of the Lord is
6:6 servants. . doing the *w* of God from the heart
Phil. 2:13 God which worketh in you both to *w*
Col. 4:12 perfect and complete in all the *w* of God
1 Thes. 4:3 the *w* of God, even your sanctification
5:18 thanks: for this is the *w* of God in Christ
2 Tim. 2:26 who are taken captive by him at his *w*
Heb. 2:4 of the Holy Ghost, according to his own *w*?
10:36 after ye have done the *w* of God, ye might
13:21 you perfect in every good work to do his *w*
Jas. 1:18 of his own *w* begat he us with the word
4:15 ought to say, If the Lord *w*, we shall live
1 Pet. 2:15 the *w* of God, that with well doing
3:17 it is better, if the *w* of God be so, that ye
4:2 to the lusts of men, but to the *w* of God
4:3 us to have wrought the *w* of the Gentiles
4:19 them that suffer according to the *w* of God
2 Pet. 1:21 the prophecy came not. . by the *w* of man
1 Jn. 2:17 that doeth the *w* of God abideth for ever
5:14 if we ask any thing according to his *w*
Rev. 17:17 hath put in their hearts to fulfil his *w*
22:17 whosoever *w*, let him take the water of life

Willing

Ex. 35:5 whosoever is of a *w* heart, let him bring
1 Chr. 28:9 with a perfect heart and with a *w* mind
29:5 and who then is *w* to consecrate his service
Ps. 110:3 thy people shall be *w* in the day of thy
Is. 1:19 if ye be *w* and obedient, ye shall eat the
Mt. 26:41 spirit indeed is *w*, but the flesh is weak
Lk. 22:42 if thou be *w*, remove this cup from me
Jn. 5:35 ye were *w* for a season to rejoice in his
2 Cor. 5:8 and *w* rather to be absent from the body
8:3 beyond their power they were *w* of themselves
8:12 if there be first a *w* mind, it is accepted
1 Tim. 6:18 ready to distribute, *w* to communicate
2 Pet. 3:9 not *w* that any should perish, but that

Willingly

Judg. 5:2 when the people *w* offered themselves
1 Chr. 29:6 rulers of the king's work, offered *w*
29:17 I have *w* offered all these things: and now
2 Chr. 35:8 and his princes gave *w* unto the people
Ezra 1:6 things, besides all that was *w* offered
3:5 every one that *w* offered a freewill offering
Prov. 31:13 she. . worketh *w* with her hands
Rom. 8:20 made subject to vanity, not *w*, but by
1 Cor. 9:17 if I do this thing *w*, I have a reward
Phlm. -14 not be as it were of necessity, but *w*
1 Pet. 5:2 not by constraint, but *w*; not for filthy
2 Pet. 3:5 this they *w* are ignorant of, that by

Willow

Lev. 23:40 and *w* of the brook; and ye shall rejoice
Job 40:22 the *w* of the brook compass him about
Is. 44:4 shall spring up. . as *w* by the watercourses
Ezek. 17:5 by great waters, and set it as a *w* tree

Will-worship

Col. 2:23 a show of wisdom in *w-w*, and humility

Win (Won)

2 Chr. 32:1 and thought to *w* them for himself

Prov. 11:30 tree of life; and he that *w* souls is wise
Phil. 3:8 count them but dung, that I may *w* Christ
1 Pet. 3:1 be *w* by the conversation of the wives

Wind *See also* Storm, Tempest, Whirlwind

Gen. 8:1 and God made a *w* to pass over the earth
Ex. 15:10 didst blow with thy *w*, the sea covered
Num. 11:31 and there went forth a *w* from the LORD
1 Kgs. 19:11 great and strong *w* rent the mountains
Job 1:19 there came a great *w* from the wilderness
6:26 speeches of one. . desperate, which are as *w*?
7:7 O remember that my life is *w*: mine eye shall
28:25 make the weight for the *w*; and he weigheth
37:21 but the *w* passeth, and cleanseth them
Ps. 103:16 the *w* passeth over it, and it is gone
135:7 he bringeth the *w* out of his treasuries
147:18 causeth his *w* to blow, and the waters flow
Prov. 11:29 troubleth his. . house shall inherit the *w*
25:23 the north *w* driveth away rain: so doth an
27:16 whosoever hideth her hideth the *w*
30:4 who hath gathered the *w* in his fists?
Eccl. 5:16 profit hath he that hath labored for the *w*?
11:4 that observeth the *w* shall not sow
Song 4:16 awake, O north *w*; and come, thou south
Is. 27:8 stayeth his rough *w* in the day of the east *w*
32:2 a man shall be as a hiding place from the *w*
41:16 fan them, and the *w* shall carry them away
Jer. 4:11 a dry *w* of the high places in the wilderness
5:13 prophets shall become *w*, and the word is not
10:13 (51:16) bringeth. . the *w* out of his treasures
Ezek. 37:9 prophesy unto the *w*. . and say to the *w*
Hos. 8:7 they have sown the *w*, and they shall reap
12:1 feedeth on *w*, and followeth after the east *w*
13:15 east *w* shall come, the *w* of the LORD shall
Amos 4:13 formeth the mountains, and createth the *w*
Jon. 1:4 the LORD sent out a great *w* into the sea
Mt. 7:25 the floods came, and the *w* blew, and beat
8:26 (Mk. 4:39; Lk. 8:24) rebuked the *w* and the sea
14:24 (Mk. 6:48) waves: for the *w* was contrary
Jn. 3:8 the *w* bloweth where it listeth
Acts 2:2 sound from heaven as of a rushing mighty *w*
Eph. 4:14 carried about with every *w* of doctrine

Window

Gen. 6:16 a *w* shalt thou make to the ark
7:11 broken up, and the *w* of heaven were opened
Josh. 2:15 let them down by a cord through the *w*
Eccl. 12:3 those that look out of the *w* be darkened
Song 2:9 looketh forth at the *w*, showing himself
Is. 54:12 and I will make thy *w* of agates
60:8 fly as a cloud, and as the doves to their *w*?
Jer. 9:21 for death is come up into our *w*
Dan. 6:10 his *w* being open in his chamber toward
Mal. 3:10 if I will not open you the *w* of heaven
Acts 20:9 and there sat in a *w* a certain young man
2 Cor. 11:33 through a *w* in a basket was I let down

Wine

Gen. 9:21 and he drank of the *w*, and was drunken
Lev. 10:9 do not drink *w* nor strong drink
Num. 6:3 separate himself from *w* and strong drink
Judg. 9:13 should I leave my *w*, which cheereth God
13:4 drink not *w* nor strong drink, and eat not
Ps. 104:15 and *w* that maketh glad the heart of man
Prov. 20:1 *w* is a mocker, strong drink is raging
21:17 he that loveth *w* and oil shall not be rich
23:30 that tarry long at the *w*. . to seek mixed *w*
23:31 look not thou upon the *w* when it is red
31:6 give. . *w* unto those that be of heavy hearts
Eccl. 10:19 *w* maketh merry: but money answereth all
Song 1:2 for thy love is better than *w*

Is. 1:22 is become dross, thy *w* mixed with water
5:11 continue until night, till *w* inflame them!
24:9 they shall not drink *w* with a song
28:7 have erred through *w*. . are swallowed up of *w*
29:9 they are drunken, but not with *w*; they stagger
55:1 yea, come, buy *w* and milk without money
Jer. 35:5 set before. . the Rechabites pots full of *w*
35:6 but they said, We will drink no *w*
Ezek. 44:21 neither shall any priest drink *w*, when
Dan. 1:8 king's meat, nor with the *w* which he drank
Hos. 3:1 look to other gods, and love flagons of *w*
4:11 whoredom. . *w* and new *w* take away the heart
9:4 they shall not offer *w* offerings to the LORD
14:7 scent thereof shall be as the *w* of Lebanon
Joel 3:18 that the mountains shall drop down new *w*
Mic. 6:15 and sweet *w*, but shalt not drink *w*
Hab. 2:5 yea also, because he transgresseth by *w*
Mt. 9:17 (Mk. 2:22; Lk. 5:37) new *w* into old bottles
Mk. 15:23 gave him to drink *w* mingled with myrrh
Lk. 10:34 bound up his wounds, pouring in oil and *w*
Jn. 2:3 they wanted *w*, the mother of Jesus saith
Acts 2:13 mocking said, These men are full of new *w*
Rom. 14:21 neither to eat flesh, nor to drink *w*
Eph. 5:18 be not drunk with *w*, wherein is excess
1 Tim. 3:3 (Tit. 1:7) not given to *w*, no striker
5:23 but use a little *w* for thy stomach's sake
Tit. 2:3 not false accusers, not given to much *w*
1 Pet. 4:3 in lasciviousness, lusts, excess of *w*
Rev. 16:19 of the of the fierceness of his wrath

Winebibber

Prov. 23:20 be not among *w*; among riotous eaters
Mt. 11:19 (Lk. 7:34) a *w*, a friend of publicans

Winecup

Jer. 25:15 take the *w* of this fury at my hand

Winepress

Neh. 13:15 in Judah some treading *w* on the sabbath
Is. 63:3 I have trodden the *w* alone
Mt. 21:33 digged a *w* in it, and built a tower
Rev. 14:19 into the great *w* of the wrath of God
19:15 treadeth the *w* of the fierceness and wrath

Wing

Deut. 32:11 as an eagle. . spreadeth abroad her *w*
Ruth 2:12 under whose *w* thou art come to trust
2 Sam. 22:11 (Ps. 18:10) fly. . upon the *w* of the wind
Ps. 17:8 hide me under the shadow of thy *w*
36:7 put their trust under the shadow of thy *w*
55:6 oh that I had *w* like a dove! for then would
57:1 in the shadow of thy *w* will I make my refuge
61:4 I will trust in the covert of thy *w*
91:4 and under his *w* shalt thou trust: his truth
139:9 if I take the *w* of the morning, and dwell
Prov. 23:5 for riches certainly make themselves *w*
Is. 6:2 stood the seraphim: each one had six *w*
40:31 they shall mount up with *w* as eagles
Ezek. 1:6 had four faces, and every one had four *w*
Hos. 4:19 the wind hath bound her up in her *w*
Mal. 4:2 shall the Sun. . arise with healing in his *w*
Mt. 23:37 (Lk. 13:34) her chickens under her *w*

Wink

Job 15:12 carry thee away? and what do thy eyes *w* at
Ps. 35:19 neither let them *w* with the eye that hate
Prov. 6:13 *w* with his eyes. . speaketh with his feet
10:10 he that *w* with the eye causeth sorrow
Acts 17:30 the times of this ignorance God *w* at

Winnow

Ruth 3:2 he *w* barley tonight in the threshingfloor

Winter

Gen. 8:22 cold and heat, and summer and *w*, and day
Ps. 74:17 the earth: thou hast made summer and *w*
Song 2:11 the *w* is past, the rain is over and gone
Is. 18:6 the beasts of the earth shall *w* upon them
Mt. 24:20 (Mk. 13:18) that your flight be not in the *w*
Jn. 10:22 the feast of the dedication, and it was *w*
Acts 27:12 the haven was not commodious to *w* in
28:11 ship of Alexandria, which had *w* in the isle
1 Cor. 16:6 that I will abide, yea, and *w* with you
2 Tim. 4:21 do thy diligence to come before *w*
Tit. 3:12 Nicopolis. . I have determined there to *w*

Wipe

2 Kgs. 21:13 I will *w* Jerusalem as a man *w* a dish
Neh. 13:14 *w* not out my good deeds that I have done
Is. 25:8 GOD will *w* away tears from off all faces
Lk. 7:38 (Jn. 11:2; 12:3) did *w* them with the hairs
Jn. 13:5 wash the disciples' feet, and to *w* them
Rev. 7:17 (21:4) God shall *w* away all tears from their

Wisdom *See also* Knowledge, Prudence, Understanding

Deut. 4:6 this is your *w* and your understanding
34:9 and Joshua. . was full of the spirit of *w*
1 Kgs. 3:28 the *w* of God was in him to do judgment
4:29 and God gave Solomon *w* and understanding
10:4 (2 Chr. 9:3) queen. . had seen all Solomon's *w*
10:23 (2 Chr. 9:22) Solomon exceeded all. . for *w*
2 Chr. 1:10 give me now *w* and knowledge, that I may
Job 6:13 help in me? and is *w* driven quite from me?
12:2 ye are the people, and *w* shall die with you
12:12 with the ancient is *w*. . and in length of days
12:13 with him is *w* and strength, he hath counsel
13:5 hold your peace! and it should be your *w*
15:8 and dost thou restrain *w* to thyself?
28:12 but where shall *w* be found? and where is
28:28 fear of the Lord, that is *w*; and to depart
32:7 speak, and multitude of years should teach *w*
38:36 who hath put *w* in the inward parts?
Ps. 37:30 the mouth of the righteous speaketh *w*
49:3 mouth shall speak of *w*; and the meditation
51:6 the hidden part thou shalt make me to know *w*
90:12 days, that we may apply our hearts unto *w*
111:10 (Prov. 9:10) fear. . LORD. . beginning of *w*
136:5 to him that by *w* made the heavens
Prov. 1:2 to know *w* and instruction; to perceive
1:20 *w* crieth without; she uttereth her voice
2:6 the LORD giveth *w*: out of his mouth cometh
3:13 happy is the man that findeth *w*, and the man
4:7 *w* is the principal thing; therefore get *w*
5:1 my son, attend unto my *w*, and bow thine ear
7:4 say unto *w*, Thou art my sister; and call
8:1 doth not *w* cry? and understanding put forth
8:11 for *w* is better than rubies; and all the
9:1 *w* hath builded her house, she hath hewn out
10:31 the mouth of the just bringeth forth *w*
11:2 then cometh shame: but with the lowly is *w*
11:12 he that is void of *w* despiseth his neighbor
14:6 a scorner seeketh *w*, and findeth it not
16:16 how much better is it to get *w* than gold!
19:8 he that getteth *w* loveth his own soul
21:30 no *w* nor understanding. . against the LORD
24:3 through *w* is a house builded
24:7 *w* is too high for a fool: he openeth not
29:3 whoso loveth *w* rejoiceth his father
29:15 rod and reproof give *w*: but a child left-
Eccl. 1:18 in much *w* is much grief: and he that
2:9 so I was great. . also my *w* remained with me
7:12 for *w* is a defense. . *w* giveth life to them
8:1 a man's *w* maketh his face to shine

Eccl. 9:16 *w* is better than strength: nevertheless
 9:18 *w* is better than weapons of war
 10:10 but *w* is profitable to direct
Is. 11:2 upon him, the spirit of *w* and understanding
 29:14 (1 Cor. 1:19) *w* of their wise . . shall perish
 33:6 *w* and knowledge shall be the stability of
 47:10 thy *w* and thy knowledge . . hath perverted
Jer. 49:7 is *w* no more in Teman? . . their *w* vanished?
 51:15 he hath established the world by his *w*
Dan. 1:20 in all matters of *w* and understanding
 2:21 he giveth *w* unto the wise, and knowledge to
 5:11 *w*, like the *w* of the gods, was found in him
Mt. 11:19 (Lk. 7:35) *w* is justified of her children
 12:42 (Lk. 11:31) came . . to hear the *w* of Solomon
 13:54 (Mk. 6:2) whence hath this man this *w*
Lk. 1:17 and the disobedient to the *w* of the just
 2:40 and waxed strong in spirit, filled with *w*
 2:52 Jesus increased in *w* and stature
 21:15 I will give you a mouth and *w*, which all
Acts 6:3 seven men . . full of the Holy Ghost and *w*
 6:10 were not able to resist the *w* and the spirit
 7:22 was learned in all the *w* of the Egyptians
Rom. 11:33 riches . . of the *w* and knowledge of God!
1 Cor. 1:17 preach the gospel: not with *w* of words
 1:19 is written, I will destroy the *w* of the wise
 1:20 hath not God made foolish the *w* of this world
 1:21 in the *w* of God the world by *w* knew not God
 1:22 Jews require a sign . . the Greeks seek after *w*
 1:24 Christ the power of God, and the *w* of God
 2:1 came not with excellency of speech or of *w*
 2:6 we speak *w* . . yet not the *w* of this world
 2:7 the *w* of God in a mystery, even the hidden *w*
 3:19 the *w* of this world is foolishness with God
 12:8 to one is given by the Spirit the word of *w*
2 Cor. 1:12 not with fleshly *w*, but by the grace
Eph. 1:8 abounded toward us in all *w* and prudence
 1:17 give unto you the spirit of *w* and revelation
 3:10 known by the church the manifold *w* of God
Col. 1:9 with the knowledge of his will in all *w*
 1:28 teaching every man in all *w*; that we may
 3:16 word of Christ dwell in you richly in all *w*
 4:5 walk in *w* toward them that are without
Jas. 1:5 if any of you lack *w*, let him ask of God
 3:17 but the *w* that is from above is first pure
Rev. 5:12 to receive power, and riches, and *w*
 13:18 here is *w*. Let him that hath understanding

Wise (Wiser) *See also* Prudent

Gen. 3:6 and a tree to be desired to make one *w*
 41:33 let Pharaoh look out a man discreet and *w*
Ex. 7:11 also called the *w* men and the sorcerers
 23:8 (Deut. 16:19) for the gift blindeth the *w*
Deut. 4:6 nation is a *w* and understanding people
 32:29 O that they were *w*, that they understood
1 Kgs. 3:12 given thee a *w* and an understanding heart
 4:31 for he was *w* than all men; than Ethan
Job 5:13 (1 Cor. 3:19) the *w* in their own craftiness
 9:4 he is *w* in heart, and mighty in strength
 11:12 vain man would be *w*, though man be born
 17:10 for I cannot find one *w* man among you
 32:9 great men are not always *w*: neither do
 35:11 and maketh us *w* than the fowls of heaven?
 37:24 he respecteth not any that are *w* of heart
Ps. 2:10 be *w* . . therefore, O ye kings: be instructed
 19:7 the testimony . . is sure, making the simple
 94:8 ye brutish . . and ye fools, when will ye be *w*?
 119:98 made me *w* than mine enemies: for they are
Prov. 1:5 *w* man will hear . . attain unto *w* counsels
 3:7 be not *w* in thine own eyes: fear the LORD
 3:35 the *w* shall inherit glory: but shame shall
 6:6 thou sluggard; consider her ways, and be *w*
 9:9 instruction to a *w* man, and he will be yet *w*
 9:12 if thou be *w*, thou shalt be *w* for thyself

Prov. 10:1 (15:20) a *w* son maketh a glad father
 10:14 *w* men lay up knowledge: but the mouth
 10:19 but he that refraineth his lips is *w*
 11:30 a tree of life . . he that winneth souls is *w*
 12:15 but he that hearkeneth unto counsel is *w*
 13:1 a *w* son heareth his father's instruction
 13:20 he that walketh with *w* men shall be *w*
 14:1 Every *w* woman buildeth her house: but
 15:24 way of life is above to the *w*, that he may
 17:28 when he holdeth his peace, is counted *w*
 19:20 that thou mayest be *w* in thy latter end
 21:11 scorner is punished, the simple is made *w*
 26:5 his folly, lest he be *w* in his own conceit
 26:12 seest thou a man *w* in his own conceit?
 30:24 which are little . . but they are exceeding *w*
Eccl. 2:15 even to me; and why was I then more *w*?
 4:13 better is a poor and a *w* child, than an old
 6:8 for what hath the *w* more than the fool?
 7:4 the heart of the *w* is in the house of mourning
 7:16 neither make thyself over *w*: why shouldest
 9:15 a poor *w* man, and he by his wisdom
 12:9 because the Preacher was *w*, he still taught
 12:11 words of the *w* are as goads, and as nails
Is. 5:21 woe unto them that are *w* in their own eyes
 19:12 where are they? where are thy *w* men?
Jer. 4:22 they are *w* to do evil, but to do good they
 8:8 do ye say, We are *w*, and the law of the LORD
Ezek. 28:3 thou art *w* than Daniel; there is no
Dan. 2:12 to destroy all the *w* men of Babylon
 12:3 they that be *w* shall shine as the brightness
Hos. 14:9 who is *w*, and he shall understand these
Mt. 2:1 there came *w* men from the east to Jerusalem
 7:24 *w* man, which built his house upon a rock
 10:16 be ye . . *w* as serpents, and harmless as doves
 11:25 (Lk. 10:21) hid these things from the *w*
 24:45 (Lk. 12:42) a faithful and *w* servant, whom
 25:2 five of them were *w*, and five were foolish
Lk. 16:8 of this world are in their generation *w*
Rom. 1:14 debtor . . both to the *w*, and to the unwise
 1:22 professing themselves to be *w* . . became fools
 11:25 lest ye should be *w* in your own conceits
 12:16 be not *w* in your own conceits
 16:19 I would have you *w* unto that which is good
 16:27 to God only *w*, be glory through Jesus Christ
1 Cor. 1:20 where is the *w*? where is the scribe?
 1:25 because the foolishness of God is *w* than men
 1:27 the foolish things . . to confound the *w*
 3:18 let him become a fool, that he may be *w*
 3:20 the Lord knoweth the thoughts of the *w*
 4:10 but ye are *w* in Christ; we are weak, but ye
2 Cor. 10:12 comparing themselves . . are not *w*
 11:19 suffer fools . . seeing ye yourselves are *w*
Eph. 5:15 circumspectly, not as fools, but as *w*
1 Tim. 1:17 immortal, invisible, the only *w* God
2 Tim. 3:15 are able to make thee *w* unto salvation
Jas. 3:13 who is a *w* man and endued with knowledge

Wisely

Ex. 1:10 let us deal *w* with them; lest they multiply
1 Sam. 18:5 David went out . . and behaved himself *w*
Ps. 101:2 I will behave myself *w* in a perfect way
Prov. 16:20 that handleth a matter *w* shall find good
Lk. 16:8 the unjust steward, because he had done *w*

Wish *See also* Desire, Long

Job 33:6 I am according to thy *w* in God's stead
Ps. 73:7 they have more than heart could *w*
Jon. 4:8 Jonah . . fainted, and *w* in himself to die
Rom. 9:3 I could *w* that myself were accursed from
2 Cor. 13:9 this also we *w*, even your perfection
3 Jn. 2 I *w* above all things . . thou mayest prosper

Wist *See* Wot

Wit

Ps. 107:27 like a drunken man. . are at their w's end

Witch

Ex. 22:18 thou shalt not suffer a w to live
Deut. 18:10 observer of times. . enchanter, or a w

Witchcraft *See also* Enchantment

1 Sam. 15:23 for rebellion is as the sin of w
2 Kgs. 9:22 mother Jezebel and her w are so many?
Mic. 5:12 and I will cut off w out of thine hand
Nah. 3:4 the mistress of w, that selleth nations
Gal. 5:20 w, hatred, variance, emulations, wrath

Withdraw (Withdrew, Withdrawn)

Job 9:13 if God will not w his anger, the proud
13:21 w thine hand far from me: and let not thy
Ps. 74:11 why w thou thy hand, even thy right hand?
Prov. 25:17 w thy foot from thy neighbor's house
Ezek. 20:22 nevertheless I w mine hand, and wrought
Hos. 5:6 not find him; he hath w himself from them
Mt. 12:15 Jesus knew it, he w himself from thence
Mk. 3:7 Jesus w himself with his disciples to the sea
Lk. 5:16 w himself into the wilderness, and prayed
Gal. 2:12 when they were come, he w and separated
2 Thes. 3:6 w yourselves from every brother that
1 Tim. 6:5 gain is godliness: from such w thyself

Withe

Judg. 16:7 bind me with seven green w

Wither

Ps. 1:3 in his season; his leaf also shall not w
37:2 cut down like the grass. . w as the green herb
90:6 in the evening it is cut down, and w
102:4 my heart is smitten, and w like grass
129:6 as the grass. . which w afore it groweth up
Is. 19:6 and dried up: the reeds and flags shall w
40:7 (1 Pet. 1:24) the grass w, the flower fadeth
Ezek. 17:9 that it w? it shall w in all the leaves
Joel 1:12 the trees. . are w: because joy is w away
Mt. 12:10 (Mk. 3:1; Lk. 6:6) which had his hand w
13:6 (Mk. 4:6; Lk. 8:6) had no root, they w away
21:20 (Mk. 11:21) how soon is the fig tree w away!
Jn. 15:6 he is cast forth as a branch, and is w
Jas. 1:11 with a burning heat, but it w the grass
Jude 12 trees whose fruit w, without fruit, twice

Withhold (Withheld, Withholden)

See also Hinder, Restrain

Gen. 20:6 I also w thee from sinning against me
22:12 hast not w thy son, thine only son, from me
1 Sam. 25:26 hath w thee from coming to shed blood
Job 4:2 but who can w himself from speaking?
22:7 and thou hast w bread from the hungry
31:16 if I have w the poor from their desire
42:2 and that no thought can be w from thee
Ps. 40:11 w not thou thy tender mercies from me
84:11 no good thing will he w from them that
Prov. 3:27 w not good from them to whom it is due
11:24 there is that w more than is meet, but it
Eccl. 11:6 and in the evening w not thine hand
Jer. 5:25 your sins have w good things from you
Amos 4:7 I have w the rain from you, when there
2 Thes. 2:6 know what w that he might be revealed

Withstand (Withstood)

Num. 22:32 I went out to w thee, because thy way
Eccl. 4:12 one prevail against him, two shall w him
Dan. 10:13 prince of the kingdom of Persia w me
Acts 11:17 what was I, that I could w God?

Acts 13:8 Elymas the sorcerer. . w them, seeking to
Gal. 2:11 when Peter was come to Antioch, I w him
Eph. 6:13 that ye may be able to w in the evil day
2 Tim. 3:8 as Jannes and Jambres w Moses, so do
4:15 be thou ware. . he hath greatly w our words

Witness *See also* Evidence, Testify,
Testimony

Gen. 21:30 may be a w unto me, that I have digged
31:48 said, This heap is a w between me and thee
31:50 with us; see, God is w betwixt me and thee
Ex. 20:16 (Deut. 5:20; Mt. 19:18; Mk. 10:19; Lk.
18:20; Rom. 13:9) thou shalt not bear false w
23:1 put not thine hand. . to be an unrighteous w
Num. 35:30 mouth of w: but one w shall not testify
Deut. 4:26 call heaven and earth to w against you
17:6 (19:15; Mt. 18:16; 2 Cor. 13:1) two w, or three
19:18 if the w be a false w, and hath testified
31:19 that this song may be a w for me against
31:26 this book of the law. . may be there for a w
Josh. 22:27 that it may be a w between us, and you
24:27 behold, this stone shall be a w unto us
Judg. 11:10 LORD be w between us, if we do not so
1 Sam. 12:3 here I am: w against me before the LORD
1 Kgs. 21:10 sons of Belial. . to bear w against him
Job 16:19 my w is in heaven. . my record is on high
29:11 and when the eye saw me, it gave w to me
Ps. 35:11 false w did rise up; they laid to my charge
89:37 be established. . as a faithful w in heaven
Prov. 14:5 a faithful w will not lie: but a false w
24:28 be not a w against thy neighbor without
Is. 3:9 show of their countenance doth w against
43:10 ye are my w, said the LORD, and my servant
44:8 ye are even my w. Is there a God besides me?
55:4 I have given him for a w to the people
Jer. 42:5 LORD be a true and faithful w between us
Mic. 1:2 and let the Lord GOD be w against you
Mal. 2:14 because the LORD hath been w between
3:5 I will be a swift w against the sorcerers
Mt. 24:14 be preached. . for a w unto all nations
26:59 (Mk. 14:55) sought false w against Jesus
26:65 (Mk. 14:63; Lk. 22:71) need have we of w?
27:13 (Mk. 15:4) many things they w against thee?
Lk. 24:48 and ye are w of these things
Jn. 1:7 same came for a w, to bear w of the Light
3:11 that we have seen; and ye receive not our w
3:26 to whom thou barest w. . the same baptizeth
5:31 if I bear w of myself, my w is not true
5:33 ye sent unto John. . he bare w unto the truth
5:36 greater w than that of John: for the works
5:37 the Father himself. . hath borne w of me
15:27 ye also shall bear w, because ye have been
18:37 that I should bear w unto the truth
Acts 1:8 ye shall be w unto me both in Jerusalem
1:22 to be a w with us of his resurrection
2:32 hath God raised up, whereof we all are w
3:15 hath raised from the dead; whereof we are w
4:33 gave the apostles w of the resurrection
5:32 we are his w of these things; and so is also
10:39 and we are w of all things which he did
10:41 not to all the people, but unto w chosen
10:43 to him give all the prophets w, that through
14:17 nevertheless he left not himself without w
20:23 save that the Holy Ghost w in every city
22:15 thou shalt be his w unto all men of what
26:16 to make thee a minister and a w both of
26:22 unto this day, w both to small and great
Rom. 2:15 their conscience also bearing w
3:21 being w by the law and the prophets
8:16 the Spirit itself beareth w with our spirit
1 Cor. 15:15 yea, and we are found false w of God
1 Thes. 2:5 nor a cloak of covetousness; God is w

1 Tim. 5:19 accusation, but before two or three *w*
 6:13 before Pontius Pilate *w* a good confession
2 Tim. 2:2 that thou hast heard of me among many *w*
Heb. 2:4 God also bearing them *w*, both with signs
 10:15 whereof the Holy Ghost also is a *w* to us
 10:28 died without mercy under two or three *w*
 11:4 by which he obtained *w* that he was righteous
 12:1 compassed about with so great a cloud of *w*
Jas. 5:3 the rust of them shall be a *w* against you
1 Pet. 5:1 *w* of the sufferings of Christ, and also
1 Jn. 1:2 we have seen it, and bear *w*, and show
 5:8 there are three that bear *w* in earth
 5:9 receive the *w* of men, the *w* of God is greater
 5:10 that believeth on the Son of God hath the *w*
Rev. 1:5 from Jesus Christ, who is the faithful *w*
 3:14 saith the Amen, the faithful and true *w*
 11:3 I will give power unto my two *w*, and they

Wives *See* Wife

Wizard

Lev. 19:31 neither seek after *w*, to be defiled
 20:27 that is a *w*, shall surely be put to death
Is. 8:19 seek. . unto *w* that peep and that mutter

Woe

Eccl. 4:10 *w* to him that is alone when he falleth
Is. 5:8 *w* unto them that join house to house
 5:11 *w* unto them that rise up early in the morning
 5:20 *w* unto them that call evil good, and good evil
 5:21 *w* unto them that are wise in their own eyes
 5:22 *w* unto them that are mighty to drink wine
 6:5 *w* is me! for I am undone; because I am a man
 10:1 *w* unto them that decree unrighteous decrees
 28:1 *w* to the crown of pride, to the drunkards
 29:1 *w* to Ariel. . the city where David dwelt!
 30:1 *w* to the rebellious children, saith the LORD
 31:1 *w* to them that go down to Egypt for help
 45:9 *w* unto him that striveth with his Maker!
Jer. 22:13 *w* unto him that buildeth his house by
 23:1 *w* be unto the pastors that destroy
Amos 6:1 *w* to them that are at ease in Zion
Mic. 2:1 *w* to them that devise iniquity, and work
Nah. 3:1 *w* to the bloody city! it is all full of lies
Hab. 2:6 *w* to him that increaseth that which is not
 2:15 *w* unto him that giveth his neighbor drink
Zech. 11:17 *w* to the idol shepherd that leaveth
Mt. 11:21 (Lk. 10:13) *w* unto thee, Chorazin! *w* unto
 18:7 (Lk. 17:1) *w* to that man by whom the offense
 23:13 (Lk. 11:44) *w* unto you, scribes and Pharisees
 26:24 (Mk. 14:21; Lk. 22:22) but *w* unto that man
Lk. 6:24 but *w* unto you that are rich! for ye have
1 Cor. 9:16 *w* is unto me, if I preach not the gospel!
Jude 11 *w* unto them! for they have gone in the way
Rev. 8:13 *w*, *w*, *w*, to the inhabiters of the earth
 9:12 one *w* is past; and, behold, there come two *w*
 11:14 second *w* is past. . the third *w* cometh quickly

Wolf (Wolves)

Gen. 49:27 Benjamin shall raven as a *w*
Is. 11:6 the *w* also shall dwell with the lamb
 65:25 the *w* and the lamb shall feed together
Zeph. 3:3 roaring lions; her judges are evening *w*
Mt. 7:15 but inwardly they are ravening *w*
 10:16 (Lk. 10:3) send. . as sheep in the midst of *w*
Jn. 10:12 seeth the *w* coming, and leaveth the sheep
Acts 20:29 shall grievous *w* enter in among you

Woman (Women) *See also* Female

Gen. 2:23 flesh of my flesh: she shall be called *W*
 3:12 *w* whom thou gavest to be with me, she gave
 3:15 I will put enmity between thee and the *w*
Deut. 22:5 *w* shall not wear that which pertaineth
Judg. 5:24 blessed above *w* shall Jael the wife of

Judg. 9:53 *w* cast. . a millstone upon Abimelech's
1 Sam. 18:7 *w* answered one another as they played
1 Kgs. 3:16 two *w*, that were harlots, unto the king
 11:1 but king Solomon loved many strange *w*
Job 14:1 man that is born of a *w* is of few days
Ps. 45:9 kings' daughters. . among thy honorable *w*
Prov. 2:16 to deliver thee from the strange *w*
 9:13 a foolish *w* is clamorous: she is simple
 14:1 every wise *w* buildeth her house
 31:3 give not thy strength unto *w*, nor thy ways
 31:10 who can find a virtuous *w*? for her price
 31:30 *w* that feareth the LORD. . shall be praised
Eccl. 7:26 than death the *w*, whose heart is snares
 7:28 but a *w* among all those have I not found
Is. 3:12 their oppressors, and *w* rule over them
 4:1 that day seven *w* shall take hold of one man
 19:16 in that day shall Egypt be like unto *w*
 32:9 rise up, ye *w* that are at ease; hear my
 49:15 can a *w* forget her sucking child, that she
 54:6 the LORD hath called thee as a *w* forsaken
Jer. 31:22 a new thing. . A *w* shall compass a man
Lam. 4:10 pitiful *w* have sodden their own children
Zech. 5:7 a *w* that sitteth in the midst of the ephah
Mt. 5:28 whosoever looketh on a *w* to lust after her
 9:20 (Mk. 5:25; Lk. 8:43) *w*. . with. . issue of blood
 11:11 (Lk. 7:28) born of *w*. . hath not risen a greater
 15:28 O *w*, great is thy faith: be it unto thee
 24:41 (Mk. 13:35) two *w* shall be grinding at the mill
 26:7 (Mk. 14:3; Lk. 7:37) *w* having an alabaster box
 27:55 (Mk. 15:40; Lk. 23:49) *w* were. . beholding
Mk. 7:26 the *w* was a Greek, a Syrophenician
Jn. 2:4 *W*, what have I to do with thee? mine hour
 4:9 askest drink of me, which am a *w* of Samaria?
 8:3 brought unto him a *w* taken in adultery; and
 19:26 saith unto his mother, *W*, behold thy son!
Acts 17:4 believed. . and of the chief *w* not a few
Rom. 1:27 men, leaving the natural use of the *w*
1 Cor. 7:1 it is good for a man not to touch a *w*
 11:7 but the *w* is the glory of the man
 11:8 man is not of the *w*; but the *w* of the man
 11:15 if a *w* have long hair, it is a glory
 14:34 let your *w* keep silence in the churches
Gal. 4:4 God sent forth his Son, made of a *w*
1 Tim. 2:11 let the *w* learn in silence with all
 2:12 but I suffer not a *w* to teach, nor to usurp
 2:14 the *w* being deceived was in the transgression
 5:14 I will therefore that the younger *w* marry
2 Tim. 3:6 lead captive silly *w* laden with sins
Tit. 2:3 aged *w* likewise, that they be in behavior
Heb. 11:35 *w* received their dead raised to life
Rev. 12:1 a *w* clothed with the sun, and the moon
 17:3 I saw a *w* sit upon a scarlet-colored beast

Womb

Gen. 25:23 said unto her, Two nations are in thy *w*
 49:25 blessings of the breast, and of the *w*
1 Sam. 1:5 Hannah: but the LORD had shut up her *w*
Ps. 22:9 but thou art he that took me out of the *w*
 139:13 thou hast covered me in my mother's *w*
Eccl. 11:5 nor how the bones do grow in the *w*
Is. 44:2 made thee, and formed thee from the *w*
 48:8 and wast called a transgressor from the *w*
 49:1 the LORD hath called me from the *w*
 66:9 I cause to bring forth, and shut the *w*?
Jer. 1:5 before thou camest forth out of the *w*
 20:17 because he slew me not from the *w*
Hos. 9:14 give them a miscarrying *w* and dry breasts
Lk. 1:42 and said. . blessed is the fruit of thy *w*
 11:27 blessed is the *w* that bare thee
Jn. 3:4 enter the second time into his mother's *w*
Gal. 1:15 God. . separated me from my mother's *w*

Women *See* Woman

Won *See* Win

Wonder *See also* Amazement, Astonishment, Marvel, Miracle, Sign

Ex. 3:20 smite Egypt with all my *w* which I will do
15:11 in holiness, fearful in praises, doing *w*?
Job 9:10 past finding out; yea, and *w* without number
Ps. 71:7 I am as a *w* unto many; but thou art my
77:14 thou art the God that doest *w*
88:10 wilt thou show a *w* to the dead?
96:3 among the heathen, his *w* among all people
107:24 works of the LORD, and his *w* in the deep
136:4 to him who alone doeth great *w*
Is. 29:9 stay yourselves, and *w*; cry ye out
29:14 will proceed to do. . marvelous work and a *w*
59:16 no man, and *w* that there was no intercessor
63:5 and I *w* that there was none to uphold
Jer. 4:9 be astonished, and the prophets shall *w*
Dan. 12:6 how long shall it be to the end of these *w*?
Joel 2:30 (Acts 2:19) I will show *w* in the heavens
Hab. 1:5 (Acts 13:41) and *w*. .for I will work a work
Lk. 2:18 all they that heard it *w* at those things
4:22 bare him witness. .*w* at the gracious words
24:41 while they yet believed not for joy, and *w*
Acts 3:10 they were filled with *w* and amazement
7:31 when Moses saw it, he *w* at the sight
7:36 had showed *w* and signs in the land of Egypt
8:13 and *w*, beholding the miracles and signs
Rev. 12:1 and there appeared a great *w* in heaven
13:3 healed: and all the world *w* after the beast
13:13 he doeth great *w*, so that he maketh fire
17:6 when I saw her, I *w* with great admiration
17:8 and they that dwell on the earth shall *w*

Wonderful *See also* Marvelous

2 Sam. 1:26 thy love to me was *w*, passing the love
Job 42:3 things too *w* for me, which I knew not
Ps. 111:4 hath made his *w* works to be remembered
119:129 thy testimonies are *w*: therefore doth my
139:6 such knowledge is too *w* for me; it is high
Prov. 30:18 be three things which are too *w* for me
Is. 9:6 and his name shall be called *W*, Counselor
25:1 thou hast done *w* things; thy counsels of old
28:29 is *w* in counsel, and excellent in working
Jer. 5:30 a *w* and horrible thing is committed in
Mt. 7:22 and in thy name done many *w* works?
21:15 and scribes saw the *w* things that he did
Acts 2:11 speak in our tongues the *w* works of God

Wonderfully

Ps. 139:14 for I am fearfully and *w* made

Wondrous

1 Chr. 16:9 (Ps. 105:2) talk ye of all his *w* works
Job 37:14 stand still. .consider the *w* works of God
Ps. 26:7 thanksgiving, and tell of all thy *w* works
72:18 the God of Israel, who only doeth *w* things
75:1 that thy name is near thy *w* works declare
86:10 for thou art great, and doest *w* things
106:22 *w* works in the land of Ham, and terrible
119:18 that I may behold *w* things out of thy law
119:27 precepts: so shall I talk of thy *w* works
145:5 honor of thy majesty, and of thy *w* works
Jer. 21:2 deal with us according to all his *w* works

Wondrously

Judg. 13:19 the angel did *w*; and Manoah and his wife
Joel 2:26 your God, that hath dealt *w* with you

Wood *See also* Timber

Gen. 22:7 behold the fire and the *w*: but where is
2 Sam. 18:6 and the battle was in the *w* of Ephraim

Job 41:27 iron as straw, and brass as rotten *w*
Ps. 83:14 as the fire burneth a *w*, and as the flame
141:7 as when one cutteth and cleaveth *w* upon
Prov. 26:20 where no *w* is, there the fire goeth out
Jer. 28:13 thou hast broken the yokes of *w*
Hag. 1:8 bring *w*, and build the house; and I will
1 Cor. 3:12 gold, silver, precious stones, *w*, hay
2 Tim. 2:20 of silver, but also of *w* and of earth

Wool

Ps. 147:16 he giveth snow like *w*: he scattereth
Prov. 31:13 she seeketh *w*, and flax, and worketh
Is. 1:18 be red like crimson, they shall be as *w*
Dan. 7:9 and the hair of his head like the pure *w*
Rev. 1:14 his head and his hairs were white like *w*

Word *See also* Word of God, Word of the LORD

Deut. 4:2 not add unto the *w* which I command you
8:3 (Mt. 4:4; Lk. 4:4) bread only, but by every *w*
11:18 lay up these my *w* in your heart
18:18 a Prophet. .and will put my *w* in his mouth
30:14 (Rom. 10:8) the *w* is very nigh unto thee
1 Chr. 15:15 (Ps. 105:8) the *w* which he commanded
Job 6:10 have not concealed the *w* of the Holy One
6:25 how forcible are right *w*! but what doth
35:16 in vain; he multiplieth *w* without knowledge
Ps. 12:6 *w* of the LORD are pure *w*: as silver tried
19:14 let the *w* of my mouth, and the meditation
55:21 *w* of his mouth were smoother than butter
56:10 in God will I praise his *w*
68:11 LORD gave the *w*: great was the company of
105:28 and they rebelled not against his *w*
107:20 sent his *w*, and healed them, and delivered
119:9 by taking heed thereto according to thy *w*
119:11 thy *w* have I hid in mine heart, that I
119:38 stablish thy *w* unto thy servant, who is
119:57 I have said that I would keep thy *w*
119:82 mine eyes fail for thy *w*, saying, When
119:89 for ever, O LORD, thy *w* is settled in heaven
119:105 thy *w* is a lamp unto my feet, and a light
119:140 thy *w* is very pure: therefore thy servant
119:160 thy *w* is true from the beginning
119:162 I rejoice at thy *w*, as one that findeth
130:5 my soul doth wait, and in his *w* do I hope
Prov. 15:23 a *w* spoken in due season, how good is it!
17:27 he that hath knowledge spareth his *w*
25:11 a *w* fitly spoken is like apples of gold in
Is. 5:24 despised the *w* of the Holy One of Israel
40:8 but the *w* of our God shall stand for ever
45:23 *w* is gone out of my mouth in righteousness
55:11 so shall my *w* be that goeth forth out
Jer. 5:13 become wind, and the *w* is not in them
15:16 thy *w* were found, and I did eat them
18:18 from the wise, nor the *w* from the prophet
20:9 his *w* was in mine heart as a burning fire
36:2 write therein all the *w* that I have spoken
44:28 know whose *w* shall stand, mine, or theirs
Hos. 14:2 take with you *w*, and turn to the LORD
Mt. 2:13 and be thou there until I bring thee *w*
8:8 (Lk. 7:7) speak the *w* only, and my servant
12:36 that every idle *w* that men shall speak
13:19 when any one heareth the *w* of the kingdom
24:35 (Mk. 13:31; Lk. 21:33) my *w* shall not pass
Mk. 4:14 the sower soweth the *w*
8:38 (Lk. 9:26) shall be ashamed of me and of my *w*
16:20 and confirming the *w* with signs following
Lk. 4:36 what a *w* is this! for with authority
24:19 a prophet mighty in deed and *w* before God
Jn. 1:1 and the *W* was with God, and the *W* was God
1:14 the *W* was made flesh, and dwelt among us
5:24 he that heareth my *w*, and believeth on him

Jn. 5:38 ye have not his *w* abiding in you
6:68 shall we go? thou hast the *w* of eternal life
8:31 continue in my *w*, then are ye my disciples
8:37 kill me, because my *w* hath no place in you
12:47 and if any man hear my *w*, and believe not
14:24 and the *w* which ye hear is not mine
15:3 are clean through the *w* which I have spoken
15:7 if ye abide in me, and my *w* abide in you
17:6 gavest them me; and they have kept thy *w*
17:8 have given unto them the *w* which thou gavest
Acts 2:41 that gladly received his *w* were baptized
5:20 speak. . to the people all the *w* of this life
10:36 *w* which God sent unto the children of Israel
17:11 received the *w* with all readiness of mind
Rom. 15:18 make. . Gentiles obedient, by *w* and deed
1 Cor. 4:20 kingdom of God is not in *w*, but in power
14:19 rather speak five *w* with my understanding
2 Cor. 1:18 our *w* toward you was not yea and nay
5:19 committed unto us the *w* of reconciliation
Gal. 6:6 him that is taught in the *w* communicate
Phil. 1:14 more bold to speak the *w* without fear
2:16 holding forth the *w* of life; that I may
Col. 1:5 in the *w* of the truth of the gospel
3:16 let the *w* of Christ dwell in you richly
1 Thes. 1:5 our gospel came not unto you in *w* only
1 Tim. 5:17 they who labor in the *w* and doctrine .
6:3 not to wholesome *w*, even the *w* of our Lord
2 Tim. 2:17 and their *w* will eat as doth a canker
4:2 preach the *w*; be instant in season, out of
Tit. 1:9 holding fast the faithful *w* as he hath
Heb. 2:2 if the *w* spoken by angels was steadfast
4:2 but the *w* preached did not profit them
5:13 is unskilful in the *w* of righteousness
Jas. 1:21 receive with meekness the engrafted *w*
1:22 be ye doers of the *w*, and not hearers only
3:2 offend not in *w*, the same is a perfect man
1 Pet. 2:2 babes, desire the sincere milk of the *w*
3:1 that, if any obey not the *w*, they also may
2 Pet. 1:19 we have also a more sure *w* of prophecy
3:2 ye may be mindful of the *w* which were spoken
1 Jn. 1:1 our hands have handled, of the *W* of life
1:10 we make him a liar, and his *w* is not in us
2:5 but whoso keepeth his *w*, in him verily is
3:18 let us not love in *w*, neither in tongue
5:7 bear record in heaven, the Father, the *W*, and
Rev. 3:8 kept my *w*, and hast not denied my name
22:19 and if any man shall take away from the *w*

Word of God *See also* Word, Word of the LORD

1 Sam. 9:27 a while, that I may show thee the *w* of G
1 Kgs. 12:22 but the *w* of G came unto Shemaiah
1 Chr. 17:3 that the *w* of G came to Nathan, saying
Prov. 30:5 every *w* of G is pure: he is a shield
Mk. 7:13 making the *w* of G of none effect through
Lk. 3:2 the *w* of G came unto John. . in the wilderness
5:1 people pressed upon him to hear the *w* of G
8:11 the parable is this: The seed is the *w* of G
8:21 my brethren are these which hear the *w* of G
11:28 blessed are they that hear the *w* of G
Acts 4:31 and they spake the *w* of G with boldness
6:2 we should leave the *w* of G, and serve tables
6:7 and the *w* of G increased; and the number of
8:14 heard that Samaria had received the *w* of G
11:1 the Gentiles had also received the *w* of G
12:24 but the *w* of G grew and multiplied
13:7 Sergius Paulus. . desired to hear the *w* of G
13:44 the whole city together to hear the *w* of G
13:46 *w* of G should first have been spoken to you
19:20 so mightily grew the *w* of G and prevailed
Rom. 9:6 as though the *w* of G hath taken none effect
10:17 cometh by hearing, and hearing by the *w* of G

1 Cor. 14:36 what! came the *w* of G out from you?
2 Cor. 2:17 not as many, which corrupt the *w* of G
4:2 nor handling the *w* of G deceitfully
Eph. 6:17 sword of the Spirit, which is the *w* of G
Col. 1:25 given to me for you, to fulfil the *w* of G
1 Thes. 2:13 because, when ye received the *w* of G
1 Tim. 4:5 is sanctified by the *w* of G and prayer
2 Tim. 2:9 unto bonds; but the *w* of G is not bound
Tit. 2:5 that the *w* of G be not blasphemed
Heb. 4:12 for the *w* of G is quick, and powerful
6:5 have tasted the good *w* of G, and the powers
11:3 that the worlds were framed by the *w* of G
13:7 who have spoken unto you the *w* of G
1 Pet. 1:23 by the *w* of G, which liveth and abideth
2 Pet. 3:5 by the *w* of G the heavens were of old
1 Jn. 2:14 the *w* of G abideth in you, and ye have
Rev. 1:2 who bare record of the *w* of G, and of the
1:9 isle that is called Patmos, for the *w* of G
6:9 souls of them that were slain for the *w* of G
19:13 and his name is called The *W* of G
20:4 for the witness of Jesus, and for the *w* of G

Word of the Lord *See also* Word, Word of God

Gen. 15:1 *w* of the *L* came unto Abram in a vision
Ex. 9:20 he that feared the *w* of the *L* among the
Num. 15:31 because he hath despised the *w* of the *L*
1 Sam. 3:1 *w* of the *L* was precious in those days
2 Kgs. 20:19 (Is. 39:8) good is the *w* of the *L*
Ps. 33:4 *w* of the *L* is right; and all his works
Is. 1:10 hear the *w* of the *L*, ye rulers of Sodom
2:3 (Mic. 4:2) and the *w* of the *L* from Jerusalem
38:4 then came the *w* of the *L* to Isaiah, saying
66:5 hear the *w* of the *L*, ye that tremble at his
Jer. 1:2 to whom the *w* of the *L* came in the days
6:10 the *w* of the *L* is unto them a reproach
8:9 they have rejected the *w* of the *L*
17:15 where is the *w* of the *L*? let it come now
20:8 the *w* of the *L* was made a reproach unto me
42:7 ten days. . *w* of the *L* came unto Jeremiah
Dan. 9:2 whereof the *w* of the *L* came to Jeremiah
Hos. 1:1 *w* of the *L* that came unto Hosea
Joel 1:1 *w* of the *L* that came to Joel
Amos 8:12 run to and fro to seek the *w* of the *L*
Jon. 1:1 (3:1) the *w* of the *L* came unto Jonah
Mic. 1:1 *w* of the *L*. . came to Micah the Morasthite
Zeph. 1:1 *w* of the *L* which came unto Zephaniah
2:5 *w* of the *L* is against you; O Canaan, the land
Hag. 2:1 came the *w* of the *L* by the prophet Haggai
Zech. 1:1 came the *w* of the *L* unto Zechariah
Mal. 1:1 of the *w* of the *L* to Israel by Malachi
Acts 11:16 then remembered I the *w* of the *L*, how
13:48 were glad, and glorified the *w* of the *L*
16:32 and they spake unto him the *w* of the *L*
19:10 which dwelt in Asia heard the *w* of the *L*
1 Thes. 1:8 from you sounded out the *w* of the *L*
4:15 for this we say unto you by the *w* of the *L*
2 Thes. 3:1 the *w* of the *L* may have free course
1 Pet. 1:25 but the *w* of the *L* endureth for ever

Work *See also* Labor, Serve, Service, Toil, Wrought

Gen. 2:2 (Heb. 4:4) the seventh day from all his *w*
Ex. 20:9 (Deut. 5:13) six days shalt thou. . do all thy *w*
23:12 (34:21) six days thou shalt do thy *w*
35:2 (Lev. 23:3) six days shall *w* be done
Deut. 4:28 serve gods, the *w* of men's hands
1 Sam. 14:6 it may be that the LORD will *w* for us
1 Chr. 29:1 and the *w* is great: for the palace is
2 Chr. 31:21 every *w* that he began in the service
34:12 and the men did the *w* faithfully

Ezra 6:7 let the *w* of this house of God alone
Neh. 4:6 for the people had a mind to *w*
4:19 the *w* is great and large, and we was wrought of our God
6:16 perceived that this *w* was wrought of our God
Job 1:10 thou hast blessed the *w* of his hands
10:3 thou shouldest despise the *w* of thine hands
33:29 all these things *w* God oftentimes with man
34:11 the *w* of a man shall he render unto him
37:7 of every man; that all men may know his *w*
37:14 still, and consider the wondrous *w* of God
Ps. 8:3 consider thy heavens, the *w* of thy fingers
33:4 is right; and all his *w* are done in truth
40:5 many, O LORD my God, are thy wonderful *w*
44:1 have told us, what *w* thou didst in their days
62:12 renderest to every man according to his *w*
77:11 I will remember the *w* of the LORD
78:11 forgat his *w*, and his wonders that he had
90:17 establish thou the *w* of our hands upon us
102:25 (Heb. 1:10) heavens are the *w* of thy hands
104:23 man goeth forth unto his *w* and to his labor
104:24 LORD, how manifold are thy *w*! in wisdom
111:2 *w* of the LORD are great, sought out of all
111:7 the *w* of his hands are verity and judgment
119:126 it is time for thee, LORD, to *w*: for they
143:5 on all thy *w*; I muse on the *w* of thy hands
145:10 all thy *w* shall praise thee, O LORD
Prov. 16:3 commit thy *w* unto the LORD
20:11 whether his *w* be pure. . whether it be right
24:12 render to every man according to his *w*?
31:13 and flax, and *w* willingly with her hands
31:31 and let her own *w* praise her in the gates
Eccl. 2:17 the *w* that is wrought under the sun is
3:9 what profit hath he that *w* in that wherein
3:11 so that no man can find out the *w* that God
3:17 is a time. . for every purpose and for every *w*
4:4 I considered all travail, and every right *w*
7:13 consider the *w* of God: for who can make
8:9 applied my heart unto every *w* that is done
8:17 *w* of God, that a man cannot find out the *w*
9:10 there is no *w*, nor device, nor knowledge
11:5 even so thou knowest not the *w* of God who
12:14 for God shall bring every *w* into judgment
Is. 2:8 they worship the *w* of their own hands
5:19 let him make speed, and hasten his *w*, that
10:12 when the LORD hath performed his whole *w*
28:21 he may do his *w*, his strange *w*; and bring
29:16 for shall the *w* say of him that made it
32:17 and the *w* of righteousness shall be peace
40:10 (62:11) reward is with him. . his *w* before
43:13 I will *w*, and who shall let it?
49:4 is with the LORD, and my *w* with my God
64:8 our potter; and we all are the *w* of thy hand
65:7 I measure their former *w* into their bosom
66:18 I know their *w* and their thoughts
Jer. 48:7 for because thou hast trusted in thy *w*
50:25 for this is the *w* of the Lord GOD of hosts
Hab. 1:5 (Acts 13:41) for I will *w* a *w* in your days
3:2 LORD, revive thy *w* in the midst of the years
Hag. 2:4 be strong. . and *w*: for I am with you
Mt. 5:16 before men, that they may see your good *w*
13:58 (Mk. 6:5) he did not many mighty *w* there
16:27 shall reward every man according to his *w*
21:28 and said, Son, go *w* today in my vineyard
23:5 all their *w* they do for to be seen of men
Mk. 16:20 Lord *w* with them. . confirming the word
Lk. 13:14 there are six days in which men ought to *w*
Jn. 5:17 answered. . My Father *w* hitherto, and I *w*
5:36 which the Father hath given me to finish
6:28 shall we do, that we might *w* the *w* of God?
6:29 this is the *w* of God, that ye believe on him
7:7 I testify of it, that the *w* thereof are evil
7:21 I have done one *w*, and ye all marvel
9:3 the *w* of God should be made manifest in him

Jn. 9:4 I must *w* the *w* of him that sent me, while it
10:25 *w* that I do in my Father's name, they bear
10:38 though ye believe not me, believe the *w*
14:10 Father that dwelleth in me, he doeth the *w*
14:12 *w* that I do shall he do also; and greater *w*
17:4 I have finished the *w* which thou gavest me
Acts 5:38 for if this counsel or this *w* be of men
Rom. 2:15 the *w* of the law written in their hearts
3:27 what law? of *w*? Nay; but by the law of faith
4:4 him that *w* is the reward not reckoned of grace
4:6 God imputeth righteousness without *w*
8:28 all things *w* together for good to them that
9:11 election. . not of *w*, but of him that calleth
9:28 because a short *w* will the Lord make upon
11:6 and if by grace, then it is no more of *w*
13:12 let us therefore cast off the *w* of darkness
14:20 for meat destroy not the *w* of God
1 Cor. 3:13 every man's *w* shall be made manifest
3:14 if any man's *w* abide which he hath built
9:1 not an apostle?. . are not ye my *w* in the Lord?
9:6 Barnabas, have not we power to forbear *w*?
12:6 but it is the same God which *w* all in all
15:58 always abounding in the *w* of the Lord
2 Cor. 4:12 so then death *w* in us, but life in you
4:17 *w* for us a far more exceeding and eternal
Gal. 2:16 man is not justified by the *w* of the law
5:6 nor uncircumcision; but faith which *w* by love
5:19 now the *w* of the flesh are manifest
6:4 but let every man prove his own *w*, and then
Eph. 1:11 who *w* all things after the counsel of
2:2 that now *w* in the children of disobedience
2:9 not of *w*, lest any man should boast
3:20 according to the power that *w* in us
4:12 for the *w* of the ministry, for the edifying
5:11 fellowship with the unfruitful *w* of darkness
Phil. 1:6 he which hath begun a good *w* in you will
2:12 *w* out your own salvation with fear and
2:13 it is God which *w* in you both to will and to
Col. 1:29 striving according to his *w*, which *w* in me
1 Thes. 4:11 and to *w* with your own hands, as we
5:13 to esteem them. . in love for their *w*'s sake
2 Thes. 2:7 the mystery of iniquity doth already *w*
2:17 and stablish you in every good word and *w*
3:10 if any would not *w*, neither should he eat
2 Tim. 1:9 a holy calling, not according to our *w*
Tit. 1:16 they know God; but in *w* they deny him
Heb. 9:14 purge your conscience from dead *w* to
13:21 *w* in you that which is well-pleasing in his
Jas. 1:4 let patience have her perfect *w*, that ye
1:20 wrath of man *w* not the righteousness of God
2:14 a man say he hath faith, and have not *w*?
2:17 even so faith, if it hath not *w*, is dead
2:22 with his *w*, and by *w* was faith made perfect?
1 Pet. 1:17 judgeth according to every man's *w*
2 Pet. 3:10 *w* that are therein shall be burned up
1 Jn. 3:8 that he might destroy the *w* of the devil
Rev. 2:2 (2:9, 13, 19; 3:1, 8, 15) I know thy *w*
2:23 unto every one of you. . according to your *w*
2:26 overcometh, and keepeth my *w* unto the end
3:2 I have not found thy *w* perfect before God
14:13 their labors; and their *w* do follow them
22:12 give every man according as his *w* shall be

Worker

2 Cor. 6:1 we then, as *w* together with him, beseech

Workman *See also* Laborer

Hos. 8:6 the *w* made it; therefore it is not God
Mt. 10:10 for the *w* is worthy of his meat
2 Tim. 2:15 a *w* that needeth not to be ashamed

Workmanship

Eph. 2:10 we are his *w*, created in Christ Jesus

World *See also* Earth

1 Sam. 2:8 LORD's, and he hath set the *w* upon them
1 Chr. 16:30 (Ps. 96:10) the *w* also shall be stable
Job 34:13 or who hath disposed the whole *w*?
Ps. 9:8 (Acts 17:31) judge the *w* in righteousness
  19:4 (Rom. 10:18) their words to the end of the *w*
  22:27 ends of the *w* shall remember and turn unto
  50:12 for the *w* is mine, and the fulness thereof
  93:1 (96:10) *w* also is stablished. . cannot be moved
Eccl. 3:11 also he hath set the *w* in their heart
Is. 13:11 and I will punish the *w* for their evil
  24:4 *w* languisheth and fadeth away, the haughty
Mt. 5:14 ye are the light of the *w*. A city that is
  12:32 neither in this *w*, neither in the *w* to come
  13:22 (Mk. 4:19) care of this *w*. . choke the word
  13:38 the field is the *w*; the good seed are the
  13:40 so shall it be in the end of this *w*
  16:26 (Mk. 8:36; Lk. 9:25) shall gain the whole *w*
  18:7 woe unto the *w* because of offenses!
  24:14 shall be preached in all the *w* for a witness
Mk. 10:30 (Lk. 18:30) in the *w* to come eternal life
  14:9 preached throughout the whole *w*, this also
  16:15 go ye into all the *w*, and preach the gospel
Lk. 2:1 a decree. . that all the *w* should be taxed
  16:8 children of this *w* are in their generation
  20:35 shall be accounted worthy to obtain that *w*
Jn. 1:10 he was in the *w*, and the *w* was made by him
  1:29 Lamb of God. . taketh away the sin of the *w*!
  3:16 God so loved the *w*, that he gave his only
  4:42 is indeed the Christ, the Saviour of the *w*
  6:33 from heaven, and giveth life unto the *w*
  7:4 thou do these things, show thyself to the *w*
  7:7 *w* cannot hate you; but me it hateth, because
  8:12 (9:5) I am the light of the *w*
  8:23 ye are of this *w*; I am not of this *w*
  9:39 for judgment I am come into this *w*
  12:19 nothing? behold, the *w* is gone after him
  12:25 he that hateth his life in this *w* shall
  12:31 now is the judgment of this *w*: now shall
  12:47 came not to judge the *w*, but to save the *w*
  13:1 having loved his own which were in the *w*
  14:17 Spirit of truth; whom the *w* cannot receive
  14:27 peace I give unto you: not as the *w* giveth
  14:31 that the *w* may know that I love the Father
  15:18 if the *w* hate you, ye know that it hated me
  15:19 because ye are not of the *w*. . the *w* hateth
  16:33 in the *w* ye shall have tribulation
  17:9 I pray for them: I pray not for the *w*
  17:14 are not of the *w*, even as I am not of the *w*
  17:15 that thou shouldest take them out of the *w*
  17:21 the *w* may believe that thou hast sent me
  18:36 my kingdom is not of this *w*: if my kingdom
  21:25 the *w* itself could not contain the books
Acts 17:6 these that have turned the *w* upside down
  17:24 God that made the *w* and all things therein
Rom. 3:19 all the *w* may become guilty before God
  5:12 as by one man sin entered into the *w*
  11:12 if the fall of them be the riches of the *w*
  12:2 and be not conformed to this *w*: but be ye
1 Cor. 1:21 the *w* by wisdom knew not God
  2:6 not the wisdom of this *w*, nor of the princes
  2:12 not the spirit of the *w*, but the Spirit
  3:18 seemeth to be wise in this *w*, let him become
  4:9 for we are made a spectacle unto the *w*
  5:10 altogether with the fornicators of this *w*
  7:31 and they that use this *w*, as not abusing it
2 Cor. 5:19 in Christ, reconciling the *w* unto himself
Gal. 1:4 might deliver us from this present evil *w*
  6:14 the *w* is crucified unto me, and I unto the *w*
Eph. 1:21 is named, not only in this *w*, but also
  2:2 ye walked according to the course of this *w*
  6:12 against the rulers of the darkness of this *w*

2 Tim. 4:10 forsaken me, having loved this present *w*
Heb. 1:2 by his Son. . by whom also he made the *w*
  6:5 word of God, and the powers of the *w* to come
  11:3 that the *w* were framed by the word of God
  11:38 of whom the *w* was not worthy
Jas. 1:27 and to keep himself unspotted from the *w*
  4:4 the friendship of the *w* is enmity with God?
2 Pet. 2:5 spared not the old *w*, but saved Noah
1 Jn. 2:15 love not the *w*, neither the things that
  2:16 all that is in the *w*, the lust of the flesh
  3:1 the *w* knoweth us not, because it knew him not
  3:13 marvel not, my brethren, if the *w* hate you
  4:1 many false prophets are gone out into the *w*
  4:5 they are of the *w*. . and the *w* heareth them
  5:19 know that. . the whole *w* lieth in wickedness
Rev. 3:10 which shall come upon all the *w*, to try
  11:15 kingdoms of this *w* are become the kingdoms
  13:3 and all the *w* wondered after the beast

Worm *See also* Moth

Job 7:5 flesh is clothed with *w* and clods of dust
  17:14 to the *w*, Thou art my mother, and my sister
  19:26 though after my skin *w* destroy this body
  21:26 in the dust, and the *w* shall cover them
  24:20 *w* shall feed sweetly on him; he shall be
  25:6 is a *w*? and the son of man, which is a *w*?
Ps. 22:6 I am a *w*, and no man; a reproach of men
Is. 14:11 *w* is spread under thee. . the *w* cover thee
  51:8 and the *w* shall eat them like wool
  66:24 (Mk. 9:44) their *w* shall not die, neither
Jon. 4:7 God prepared a *w* when the morning rose
Acts 12:23 he was eaten of *w*, and gave up the ghost

Wormwood

Jer. 9:15 will feed them, even this people, with *w*
Amos 5:7 ye who turn judgment to *w*, and leave off
Rev. 8:11 and the name of the star is called *W*

Worse *See also* Bad

Gen. 19:9 now will we deal *w* with thee than with
Jer. 7:26 hardened. . they did *w* than their fathers
  16:12 and ye have done *w* than your fathers
Mt. 9:16 (Mk. 2:21) garment, and the rent is made *w*
  12:45 (Lk. 11:26) the last state of that man is *w*
Mk. 5:26 was nothing bettered, but rather grew *w*
Jn. 2:10 men have well drunk, then that which is *w*
  5:14 sin no more, lest a *w* thing come unto thee
1 Cor. 8:8 neither, if we eat not, are we the *w*
  11:17 ye come. . not for the better, but for the *w*
1 Tim. 5:8 denied the faith, and is *w* than an infidel
2 Tim. 3:13 evil men and seducers shall wax *w* and *w*
2 Pet. 2:20 end is *w* with them than the beginning

Worship *See also* Serve, Service

Gen. 22:5 I and the lad will go yonder and *w*
  24:26 man bowed down his head, and *w* the LORD
Ex. 24:1 seventy of the elders. . and *w* ye afar off
  32:8 have made them a molten calf, and have *w* it
  34:8 and bowed his head toward the earth, and *w*
  34:14 thou shalt *w* no other god: for the LORD
Deut. 4:19 shouldest be driven to *w* them, and serve
  17:3 hath gone and served other gods, and *w* them
1 Sam. 1:3 went up. . yearly to *w* and to sacrifice
2 Kgs. 17:16 (21:3; 2 Chr. 33:3) *w*. . host of heaven
  18:22 (Is. 36:7) ye shall *w* before this altar
1 Chr. 16:29 (Ps. 29:2; 96:9) *w* the LORD in the beauty
Neh. 9:6 and the host of heaven *w* thee
Ps. 5:7 (138:2) will I *w* toward thy holy temple
  22:27 kindreds of the nations shall *w* before thee
  66:4 all the earth shall *w* thee, and shall sing
  81:9 neither shalt thou *w* any strange god
  86:9 (Rev. 15:4) shall come and *w* before thee
  95:6 O come, let us *w* and bow down: let us kneel

Ps. 99:5 exalt ye the Lord . . and *w* at his footstool
106:19 a calf in Horeb, and *w* the molten image
132:7 his tabernacles: we will *w* at his footstool
Is. 2:8 idols; they *w* the work of their own hands
27:13 *w* the Lord in the holy mount at Jerusalem
44:15 yea, he maketh a god, and *w* it
66:23 shall all flesh come to *w* before me
Jer. 7:2 that enter in at these gates to *w* the Lord
Ezek. 46:2 he shall *w* at the threshold of the gate
Dan. 3:5 (3:7, 10, 15) fall down and *w* the golden
3:18 nor *w* the golden image which thou hast set
Zeph. 1:5 *w* the host of heaven upon the housetops
2:11 men shall *w* him, every one from his place
Zech. 14:17 unto Jerusalem to *w* the King, the Lord
Mt. 2:2 his star in the east, and are come to *w* him
4:9 (Lk. 4:7) if thou wilt fall down and *w* me
4:10 (Lk. 4:8) *w* the Lord thy God, and him only
15:9 (Mk. 7:7) but in vain they do *w* me, teaching
28:17 they saw him, they *w* him . . some doubted
Lk. 14:10 then shalt thou have *w* in the presence of
Jn. 4:20 our fathers *w* in this mountain; and ye say
4:22 ye *w* ye know not what: we know what we *w*
4:24 that *w* him must *w* him in spirit and in truth
9:38 and he said, Lord, I believe. And he *w* him
12:20 certain Greeks . . came up to *w* at the feast
Acts 7:42 and gave them up to *w* the host of heaven
8:27 a eunuch . . had come to Jerusalem for to *w*
10:25 and fell down at his feet, and *w* him
16:14 woman named Lydia . . which *w* God, heard
17:23 ye ignorantly *w*, him declare I unto you
18:13 persuadeth men to *w* God contrary to the law
19:27 be destroyed, whom all Asia and the world *w*
24:11 since I went up to Jerusalem for to *w*
24:14 call heresy, so *w* I the God of my fathers
Rom. 1:25 and *w* and served the creature more than
1 Cor. 14:25 falling down on his face he will *w* God
Phil. 3:3 circumcision, which *w* God in the spirit
Heb. 1:6 saith, And let all the angels of God *w* him
Rev. 5:14 make them to come and *w* before thy feet
4:10 and *w* him that liveth for ever and ever
5:14 four and twenty elders fell down and *w* him
11:1 measure . . the altar, and them that *w* therein
13:4 and they *w* the dragon . . and they *w* the beast
13:8 all that dwell upon the earth shall *w* him
14:7 *w* him that made heaven, and earth
14:9 if any man *w* the beast and his image
19:4 and the four beasts fell down and *w* God
19:10 (22:8) I fell at his feet to *w* him
20:4 which had not *w* the beast, neither his image

Worshipper

2 Kgs. 10:21 all Israel: and all the *w* of Baal came

Worshipping

Col. 2:18 in a voluntary humility and *w* of angels

Worth *See also* Value

2 Sam. 18:3 but now thou art *w* ten thousand of us
Job 24:25 me a liar, and make my speech nothing *w*?
Prov. 10:20 the heart of the wicked is little *w*
Ezek. 30:2 saith the Lord . . Howl ye, Woe *w* the day!

Worthy *See also* Fit, Honorable, Meet, Noble

Gen. 32:10 am not *w* of the least of all the mercies
1 Sam. 1:5 unto Hannah he gave a *w* portion
2 Sam. 22:4 (Ps. 18:3) Lord, who is *w* to be praised
1 Kgs. 1:52 if he will show himself a *w* man, there
Mt. 3:11 mightier . . whose shoes I am not *w* to bear
8:8 (Lk. 7:6) I am not *w* that thou shouldest come
10:10 for the workman is *w* of his meat
10:37 loveth father . . more than me is not *w* of me

Mt. 22:8 but they which were bidden were not *w*
Mk. 1:7 (Lk. 3:16; Jn. 1:27; Acts 13:25) whose shoes
I am not *w* to stoop down and unloose
Lk. 3:8 bring forth . . fruits *w* of repentance
10:7 (1 Tim. 5:18) the laborer is *w* of his hire
12:48 knew not . . did commit things *w* of stripes
15:19 (15:21) am no more *w* to be called thy son
20:35 shall be accounted *w* to obtain that world
21:36 be accounted *w* to escape all these things
Acts 24:2 very *w* deeds are done unto this nation
Rom. 8:18 are not *w* to be compared with the glory
Eph. 4:1 beseech you that ye walk *w* of the vocation
Col. 1:10 walk *w* of the Lord unto all pleasing
1 Thes. 2:12 that ye would walk *w* of God, who hath
2 Thes. 1:5 may be counted *w* of the kingdom of God
1:11 our God would count you *w* of this calling
1 Tim. 1:15 (4:9) saying, and *w* of all acceptation
Heb. 10:29 sorer punishment . . shall he be thought *w*
11:38 of whom the world was not *w*
Jas. 2:7 they blaspheme that *w* name by the which
Rev. 3:4 walk with me in white: for they are *w*
4:11 thou art *w*, O Lord, to receive glory
5:2 who is *w* to open the book, and to loose

Wot (Wist)

Gen. 21:26 Abimelech said, I *w* not who hath done
39:8 my master *w* not what is with me in the house
Ex. 16:15 it is manna: for they *w* not what it was
32:1 (Acts 7:40) we *w* not what is become of him
34:29 Moses *w* not that the skin of his face shone
Josh. 2:4 two men . . but I *w* not whence they were
Judg. 16:20 and he *w* not that the Lord was departed
Mk. 9:6 he *w* not what to say: for they were . . afraid
Lk. 2:49 *w* ye not that I must be about my Father's
Acts 3:17 I *w* that through ignorance ye did it
Rom. 11:2 *w* ye not what the Scripture saith of Elias?
Phil. 1:22 yet what I shall choose I *w* not

Wound *See also* Bruise, Hurt

Gen. 4:23 I have slain a man to my *w*
Ex. 21:25 burning for burning, *w* for *w*, stripe for
Deut. 32:39 I kill . . I make alive; I *w*, and I heal
1 Kgs. 22:34 (2 Chr. 18:33) carry me out . . for I am *w*
2 Kgs. 8:29 (9:15; 2 Chr. 22:6) to be healed of the *w*
Job 5:18 bindeth up: he *w*, and his hands make whole
34:6 my *w* is incurable without transgression
Ps. 64:7 with an arrow; suddenly shall they be *w*
68:21 but God shall *w* the head of his enemies
109:22 needy, and my heart is *w* within me
110:6 he shall *w* the heads over many countries
147:3 the broken in heart, and bindeth up their *w*
Prov. 6:33 a *w* and dishonor shall he get
18:8 words of a talebearer are as *w*, and they go
23:29 who hath *w* without cause? who hath redness
27:6 faithful are the *w* of a friend
Is. 1:6 is no soundness in it; but *w*, and bruises
51:9 that hath cut Rahab, and *w* the dragon?
53:5 but he was *w* for our transgressions
Jer. 10:19 woe is me for my hurt! my *w* is grievous
15:18 why is my pain perpetual . . my *w* incurable
30:12 thy bruise is incurable . . thy *w* is grievous
30:17 I will heal thee of thy *w*, saith the Lord
Mic. 1:9 her *w* is incurable; for it is come unto
Hab. 3:13 thou *w* the head out of the house of the
Zech. 13:6 I was *w* in the house of my friends
Mk. 12:4 (Lk. 20:12) *w* him in the head, and sent
Lk. 10:30 stripped him of his raiment, and *w* him
10:34 went to him, and bound up his *w*, pouring
1 Cor. 8:12 and *w* their weak conscience, ye sin
Rev. 13:3 were *w* to death . . his deadly *w* was healed

Wounded *See also* Wound

Job 24:12 men groan . . the soul of the *w* crieth out

Prov. 7:26 for she hath cast down many *w*: yea, many
Jer. 37:10 there remained but *w* men among them
Acts 19:16 they fled out of that house naked and *w*

Wrap

Is. 28:20 covering narrower than . . he can *w* himself
Mic. 7:3 his mischievous desire: so they *w* it up
Mt. 27:59 (Mk. 15:46; Lk. 23:53) *w* it in a . . linen
Lk. 2:7 *w* him in swaddling clothes, and laid him

Wrapped

Jn. 20:7 napkin . . *w* together in a place by itself

Wrath *See also* Anger, Fury, Indignation, Rage

Gen. 49:7 cursed be . . their *w*, for it was cruel
Num. 1:53 that there be no *w* upon the congregation
  16:46 is *w* gone out from the LORD; the plague is
Deut. 9:7 thou provokedst the LORD thy God to *w*
2 Kgs. 22:13 (2 Chr. 34:21) great is the *w* of the LORD
2 Chr. 28:11 the fierce *w* of the LORD is upon you
  30:8 fierceness of his *w* may turn away from you
Ezra 8:22 his *w* is against all them that forsake him
  10:14 *w* of our God for this matter be turned
Esth. 3:5 bowed not . . then was Haman full of *w*
Job 5:2 *w* killeth the foolish man, and envy slayeth
  21:20 he shall drink of the *w* of the Almighty
  36:18 because there is *w*, beware lest he take
Ps. 2:5 then shall he speak unto them in his *w*
  2:12 perish . . when his *w* is kindled but a little
  58:9 take them away . . both living, and in his *w*
  76:10 *w* of man shall praise thee . . remainder of *w*
  78:31 the *w* of God came upon them, and slew
  88:16 thy fierce *w* goeth over me; thy terrors
  90:7 thine anger, and by thy *w* are we troubled
  95:11 (Heb. 3:11) sware in my *w* that they should
  110:5 strike through kings in the day of his *w*
Prov. 11:23 but the expectation of the wicked is *w*
  12:16 fool's *w* is presently known: but a prudent
  14:29 that is slow to *w* is of great understanding
  15:1 a soft answer turneth away *w*: but grievous
  16:14 the *w* of a king is as messengers of death
  19:12 the king's *w* is as the roaring of a lion
  19:19 a man of great *w* shall suffer punishment
  27:3 but a fool's *w* is heavier than them both
  27:4 *w* is cruel, and anger is outrageous; but who
  29:8 city into a snare: but wise men turn away *w*
Eccl. 5:17 much sorrow and *w* with his sickness
Is. 9:19 through the *w* of the LORD of hosts is the
  10:6 against the people of my *w* will I give
  13:9 day of the LORD cometh, cruel both with *w*
  54:8 in a little *w* I hid my face . . for a moment
  60:10 for in my *w* I smote thee, but in my favor
Jer. 10:10 at his *w* the earth shall tremble
Hos. 5:10 I will pour out my *w* upon them like water
Nah. 1:2 and he reserveth *w* for his enemies
Hab. 3:2 revive thy work . . in *w* remember mercy
Zeph. 1:15 that day is a day of *w*, a day of trouble
Zech. 7:12 came a great *w* from the LORD of hosts
Mt. 3:7 (Lk. 3:7) warned you to flee . . the *w* to come?
Lk. 4:28 heard these things, were filled with *w*
Jn. 3:36 believeth not . . the *w* of God abideth on him
Acts 19:28 they were full of *w*, and cried out, saying
Rom. 1:18 *w* of God is revealed from heaven against
  2:5 treasurest up . . *w* against the day of *w*
  4:15 because the law worketh *w*: for where no law
  5:9 we shall be saved from *w* through him
  9:22 willing to show his *w* . . endured . . vessels of *w*
  12:19 avenge not . . but rather give place unto *w*
  13:5 needs be subject, not only for *w*, but also
Gal. 5:20 hatred, variance, emulations, *w*, strife
Eph. 2:3 by nature the children of *w*, even as others

Eph. 4:26 let not the sun go down upon your *w*
  5:6 the *w* of God upon the children of disobedience
  6:4 ye fathers, provoke not your children to *w*
Col. 3:6 the *w* of God cometh on the children of
1 Thes. 1:10 which delivered us from the *w* to come
  2:16 the *w* is come upon them to the uttermost
  5:9 God hath not appointed us to *w*, but to obtain
1 Tim. 2:8 pray . . lifting up holy hands, without *w*
Heb. 11:27 Egypt, not fearing the *w* of the king
Jas. 1:19 swift to hear, slow to speak, slow to *w*
  1:20 *w* of man worketh not . . righteousness of God
Rev. 6:16 and hide us . . from the *w* of the Lamb
  11:18 the nations were angry, and thy *w* is come
  14:10 same shall drink of the wine of the *w* of God
  15:1 plagues . . in them is filled up the *w* of God
  16:1 and pour out the vials of the *w* of God
  16:19 cup of the wine of the fierceness of his *w*

Wrathful

Prov. 15:18 *w* man stirreth up strife: but he that

Wrest *See also* Pervert

Ex. 23:2 cause to decline after many to *w* judgment
Deut. 16:19 thou shalt not *w* judgment
Ps. 56:5 every day they *w* my words
2 Pet. 3:16 they that are unlearned and unstable *w*

Wrestle

Gen. 30:8 great wrestlings have I *w* with my sister
  32:24 Jacob . . alone; and there *w* a man with him
Eph. 6:12 for we *w* not against flesh and blood

Wretched

Rom. 7:24 O *w* man that I am! who shall deliver me
Rev. 3:17 knowest not that thou art *w*, and miserable

Wretchedness

Num. 11:15 favor in thy sight . . let me not see my *w*

Wring (Wrung)

Judg. 6:38 *w* the dew out of the fleece, a bowlful
Ps. 73:10 waters of a full cup are *w* out to them
  75:8 the wicked of the earth shall *w* them out
Prov. 30:33 *w* of the nose bringeth forth blood

Wrinkle

Job 16:8 and thou hast filled me with *w*, which is
Eph. 5:27 a glorious church, not having spot, or *w*

Write (Wrote, Written)

Ex. 24:4 Moses *w* all the words of the LORD
  31:18 (Deut. 9:10) *w* with the finger of God
  34:1 (Deut. 10:2) *w* upon these tables the words
  34:27 LORD said unto Moses, *W* thou these words
Deut. 4:13 and he *w* them upon two tables of stone
  6:9 (11:20) *w* them upon the posts of thy house
  31:9 Moses *w* this law, and delivered it unto the
  31:19 *w* ye this song for you, and teach it
Job 13:26 for thou *w* bitter things against me
  19:23 oh that my words were now *w*! oh that thou
Ps. 40:7 (Heb. 10:7) volume of the book it is *w* of me
  69:28 blotted out . . not be *w* with the righteous
  102:18 shall be *w* for the generation to come
Prov. 3:3 (7:3) *w* them upon the table of thine heart
  22:20 have not I *w* to thee excellent things in
Eccl. 12:10 was *w* was upright, even words of truth
Is. 10:1 *w* grievousness which they have prescribed
Jer. 17:1 the sin of Judah is *w* with a pen of iron
  22:30 saith the LORD, *W* ye this man childless
  30:2 *w* thee all the words that I have spoken unto
  31:33 (Heb. 8:10; 10:16) law . . *w* it in their hearts
  36:2 *w* therein are the words that I have spoken
Ezek. 2:10 *w* within and without: and there was *w*
Dan. 5:5 *w* over against the candlestick upon the

Dan. 5:24 hand sent from him; and this writing was *w*
Hos. 8:12 have *w* to him the great things of my law
Hab. 2:2 *w* the vision, and make it plain upon tables
Lk. 10:20 rejoice, because. . names are *w* in heaven
  18:31 and all things that are *w* by the prophets
  24:46 thus it is *w*, and thus it behooved Christ
Jn. 5:46 ye would have believed me: for he *w* of me
  8:6 but Jesus. . with his finger *w* on the ground
  19:19 Pilate *w* a title, and put it on the cross
  19:22 Pilate answered, What I have *w* I have *w*
  20:31 these are *w*, that ye might believe
  21:25 if they should be *w* every one, I suppose
1 Cor. 4:14 I *w* not these things to shame you
  10:11 ensamples. . they are *w* for our admonition
2 Cor. 3:3 *w* not with ink, but with the Spirit of
1 Thes. 5:1 ye have no need that I *w* unto you
Heb. 12:23 of the firstborn, which are *w* in heaven
1 Jn. 2:7 I *w* no new commandment unto you
  5:13 these things have I *w* unto you that believe
2 Jn. 5 not as though I *w* a new commandment unto
Rev. 1:19 *w* the things which thou hast seen
  3:12 I will *w* upon him the name of my God
  14:13 saying unto me, *W*, Blessed are the dead
  19:9 he saith unto me, *W*, Blessed are they which
  21:5 *w*: for these words are true and faithful

Writer

Ps. 45:1 my tongue is the pen of a ready *w*

Writing

Ex. 32:16 the *w* was the *w* of God, graven upon
Dan. 5:25 and this is the *w* that was written, MENE
Jn. 5:47 but if ye believe not his *w*, how shall ye

Written *See* Write

Wrong *See also* False, Lying

Ex. 2:13 he said to him that did the *w*, Wherefore
1 Chr. 12:17 seeing there is no *w* in mine hands
  16:21 (Ps. 105:14) suffered no man to do them *w*
Job 19:7 behold, I cry out of *w*, but I am not heard
Prov. 8:36 that sinneth against me *w* his own soul
Jer. 22:3 do no *w*, do no violence to the stranger
  22:13 by unrighteousness, and his chambers by *w*
Lam. 3:59 thou hast seen my *w*: judge thou my cause
Mt. 20:13 friend, I do thee no *w*: didst not thou
Acts 7:24 seeing one of them suffer *w*, he defended
  18:14 if it were a matter of *w* or wicked lewdness
  25:10 be judged: to the Jews have I done no *w*
1 Cor. 6:7 why do ye not rather take *w*?
2 Cor. 7:2 receive us; we have *w* no man
  12:13 not burdensome to you? forgive me this *w*
Col. 3:25 he that doeth *w* shall receive for the *w*
Phlm. 18 if he hath *w* thee, or oweth thee aught

Wrote *See* Write

Wroth *See also* Angry

Gen. 4:5 Cain was very *w*, and his countenance fell
  4:6 the LORD said unto Cain, Why are thou *w*?
Ex. 16:20 hearkened not. . and Moses was *w* with
Num. 16:22 one man sin, and wilt thou be *w* with all
Deut. 1:34 the LORD heard. . your words, and was *w*
  3:26 but the LORD was *w* with me for your sakes
2 Sam. 22:8 (Ps. 18:7) and shook, because he was *w*
2 Kgs. 5:11 Naaman was *w*, and went away, and said
  13:19 the man of God was *w* with him, and said
Ps. 78:21 therefore the LORD heard this, and was *w*
  89:38 thou hast been *w* with thine anointed
Is. 47:6 I was *w* with my people, I have polluted
  54:9 I would not be *w* with thee, nor rebuke thee
  57:16 contend for ever, neither will I be always *w*
  57:17 for the iniquity of his covetousness was I *w*
  64:9 be not *w* very sore, O LORD, neither remember

Lam. 5:22 rejected us; thou art very *w* against us
Mt. 18:34 his lord was *w*, and delivered him to the
  22:7 but when the king heard thereof, he was *w*

Wrought *See also* Labor, Toil, Work

Num. 23:23 of Jacob and of Israel, What hath God *w*!
1 Sam. 6:6 when he had *w* wonderfully among them
  11:13 today the LORD hath *w* salvation in Israel
  14:45 who hath *w* this great salvation in Israel?
2 Sam. 23:10 the LORD *w* a great victory that day
Neh. 4:17 with one of his hands *w* in the work
Job 12:9 that the hand of the LORD hath *w* this?
  36:23 or who can say, Thou hast *w* iniquity?
Ps. 31:19 thou hast *w* for them that trust in thee
  68:28 strengthen. . that which thou hast *w* for us
  139:15 curiously *w* in the lowest parts of the earth
Eccl. 2:11 on all the works that my hands had *w*
Is. 26:12 for thou also hast *w* all our works in us
  26:18 we have not *w* any deliverance in the earth
  41:4 who hath *w* and done it. . I the LORD, the first
Jer. 18:3 and, behold, he *w* a work on the wheels
Ezek. 20:9 (20:14, 22, 44) but I *w* for my name's sake
Dan. 4:2 wonders. . the high God hath *w* toward me
Zeph. 2:3 all ye meek. . which have *w* his judgment
Mt. 20:12 saying, These last have *w* but one hour
  26:10 (Mk. 14:6) she hath *w* a good work upon me
Jn. 3:21 be made manifest, that they are *w* in God
Acts 15:12 wonders God had *w* among the Gentiles
  18:3 the same craft, he abode with them, and *w*
  19:11 God *w* special miracles by the hands of Paul
Rom. 7:8 sin. . *w* in me all manner of concupiscence
  15:18 those things which Christ hath not *w* by me
2 Cor. 5:5 that hath *w* us for the selfsame thing
  12:12 the signs of an apostle were *w* among you
Gal. 2:8 for he that *w* effectually in Peter to the
Eph. 1:20 which he *w* in Christ, when he raised him
2 Thes. 3:8 *w* with labor and travail night and day
Heb. 11:33 faith subdued kingdoms, *w* righteousness
1 Pet. 4:3 to have *w* the will of the Gentiles
2 Jn. 8 we lose not those things which we have *w*

Y

Yea

Mt. 5:37 let your communication be, *Y, y*; Nay, nay
2 Cor. 1:17 with me there should be *y, y*. . nay, nay?
  1:18 true, our word toward you was not *y* and nay
  1:19 Christ. . was not *y* and nay, but in him was *y*
  1:20 for all the promises of God in him are *y*
Jas. 5:12 but let your *y* be *y*; and your nay, nay

Year *See also* Day, Month, Time

Gen. 1:14 them be. . for seasons, and for days, and *y*
Ex. 12:2 shall be the first month of the *y* to you
  23:17 (34:23; Deut. 16:16) times in the *y*. . appear
Lev. 16:34 atonement. . for all their sins once a *y*
  25:4 in the seventh *y* shall be a sabbath of rest
  25:10 hallow the fiftieth *y*, and proclaim liberty
  25:50 he was sold to him unto the *y* of jubilee
Num. 14:33 shall wander in the wilderness forty *y*
Deut. 14:22 that the field bringeth forth *y* by *y*
  15:9 the seventh *y*, the *y* of release, is at hand
  26:12 the third *y*, which is the *y* of tithing
1 Sam. 7:16 went from *y* to *y* in circuit to Bethel
Job 10:5 the days of man? are thy *y* as man's days
  15:20 the number of *y* is hidden to the oppressor

Job 32:7 and multitude of *y* should teach wisdom
  36:26 neither can the number of his *y* be searched
Ps. 65:11 thou crownest the *y* with thy goodness
  77:10 the *y* of the right hand of the Most High
  90:4 thousand *y* in thy sight are but as yesterday
  90:9 we spend our *y* as a tale that is told
  90:10 the days of our *y* are threescore *y* and ten
  102:24 thy *y* are throughout all generations
  102:27 (Heb. 1:12) and thy *y* shall have no end
Prov. 4:10 and the *y* of thy life shall be many
  5:9 honor unto others, and thy *y* unto the cruel
  10:27 but the *y* of the wicked shall be shortened
Is. 29:1 add ye *y* to *y*; let them kill sacrifices
  61:2 (Lk. 4:19) the acceptable *y* of the LORD
  63:4 day of vengeance . . *y* of my redeemed is come
Jer. 28:16 this *y* thou shalt die, because thou
Ezek. 4:5 laid upon thee the *y* of their iniquity
  46:17 gift . . it shall be his to the *y* of liberty
Dan. 11:6 the end of *y* they shall join themselves
Zech. 14:16 go up from *y* to *y* to worship the King
Gal. 4:10 observe days . . months, and times, and *y*
Heb. 9:25 priest entereth into the holy place every *y*
  10:1 sacrifices . . they offer *y* by *y* continually
2 Pet. 3:8 thousand *y*, and a thousand *y* as one day
Rev. 20:2 and Satan, and bound him a thousand *y*
  20:4 lived and reigned with Christ a thousand *y*

Yearn

Gen. 43:30 for his bowels did *y* upon his brother

Yesterday

Job 8:9 we are but of *y*, and know nothing, because
Ps. 90:4 thousand years . . but as *y* when it is past
Heb. 13:8 Jesus Christ the same *y*, and today, and

Yield *See also* Produce, Submit

Gen. 4:12 not henceforth *y* unto thee her strength
  49:33 Jacob . . *y* up the ghost, and was gathered
Lev. 19:25 that it may *y* unto you the increase
  26:4 the land shall *y* her increase, and the trees
Num. 17:8 buds . . bloomed blossoms, and *y* almonds
2 Chr. 30:8 *y* yourselves unto the LORD, and enter
Ps. 67:6 then shall the earth *y* her increase
  85:12 and our land shall *y* her increase
Prov. 7:21 much fair speech she caused him to *y*
  12:12 but the root of the righteous *y* fruit
Eccl. 10:4 for *y* pacifieth great offenses
Mt. 27:50 cried . . with a loud voice, *y* up the ghost
Acts 5:10 fell . . at his feet, and *y* up the ghost
  23:21 but do not thou *y* unto them: for there lie
Rom. 6:13 unto sin: but *y* yourselves unto God
  6:16 to whom ye *y* yourselves servants to obey
  6:19 your members servants to righteousness
Heb. 12:11 *y* the peaceable fruit of righteousness
Jas. 3:12 no fountain both *y* salt water and fresh
Rev. 22:2 tree of life . . *y* her fruit every month

Yoke *See also* Bond, Bondage

Gen. 27:40 shalt break his *y* from off thy neck
Lev. 26:13 and I have broken the bands of your *y*
Num. 19:2 no blemish, and upon which never came *y*
Deut. 28:48 he shall put a *y* of iron upon thy neck
1 Sam. 6:7 milch kine, on which . . hath come no *y*
1 Kgs. 12:4 (2 Chr. 10:4) father made our *y* grievous
  12:11 (2 Chr. 10:11) a heavy *y*, I will add to your *y*
Is. 9:4 for thou hast broken the *y* of his burden
  10:27 his *y* from off thy neck, and the *y* shall
  14:25 then shall his *y* depart from off them
  58:6 oppressed go free, and that ye break every *y*?
Jer. 2:20 for of old time I have broken thy *y*
  27:2 make thee bonds and *y*, and put them upon
  28:2 I have broken the *y* of the king of Babylon

Jer. 28:10 took the *y* from off the prophet Jeremiah's
  28:13 *y* of wood; but thou shalt make . . *y* of iron
  30:8 that I will break his *y* from off thy neck
Lam. 1:14 *y* of my transgressions is bound by his
  3:27 for a man that he bear the *y* in his youth
Ezek. 30:18 when I shall break there the *y* of Egypt
Hos. 11:4 as they that take off the *y* on their jaws
Nah. 1:13 for now will I break his *y* from off thee
Mt. 11:29 take my *y* upon you, and learn of me
Acts 15:10 put a *y* upon the neck of the disciples
2 Cor. 6:14 be ye not unequally *y* together with
Gal. 5:1 not entangled again with the *y* of bondage
1 Tim. 6:1 let as many servants as are under the *y*

Yokefellow

Phil. 4:3 I entreat thee also, true *y*, help those

Young (Younger, Youngest)

Gen. 19:31 firstborn said unto the *y*, Our father
  25:23 (Rom. 9:12) the elder shall serve the *y*
  29:26 must not . . give the *y* before the firstborn
  42:13 the *y* is this day with our father, and one
  44:2 put my cup . . in the sack's mouth of the *y*
  48:19 but truly his *y* brother shall be greater
Lev. 22:28 not kill it and her *y* both in one day
Deut. 22:6 thou shalt not take the dam with the *y*
  32:11 stirreth up her nest, fluttereth over her *y*
Josh. 6:26 (1 Kgs. 16:34) in his *y* son shall he set up
1 Sam. 17:14 David was the *y*: and the three eldest
1 Kgs. 12:8 (2 Chr. 10:8) consulted with the *y* men
1 Chr. 22:5 (29:1) Solomon my son is *y* and tender
2 Chr. 34:3 while he was yet *y*, he began to seek
Job 30:1 they that are *y* than I have me in derision
  38:41 when his *y* ones cry unto God, they wander
  39:16 is hardened against her *y* ones, as though
Ps. 37:25 I have been *y*, and now am old; yet have
  84:3 the swallow a nest . . where she may lay her *y*
Is. 11:7 their *y* ones shall lie down together
  40:11 shall gently lead those that are with *y*
Joel 2:28 (Acts 2:17) your *y* men shall see visions
Mk. 14:51 and there followed him a certain *y* man
  16:5 they saw a *y* man sitting on the right side
Lk. 15:12 the *y* of them said . . Father, give me
  22:26 greatest among you, let him be as the *y*
Jn. 21:18 when thou wast *y*, thou girdedst thyself
1 Tim. 5:1 as a father; and the *y* men as brethren
  5:11 but the *y* widows refuse: for when they have
Tit. 2:4 they may teach the *y* women to be sober
1 Pet. 5:5 ye *y*, submit yourselves unto the elder

Youth

Gen. 8:21 imagination of man's heart is evil from . . *y*
1 Sam. 17:33 thou art but a *y*, and he a man of war
  17:42 he disdained him: for he was but a *y*
1 Kgs. 18:12 I thy servant fear the LORD from my *y*
Job 36:14 they die in *y*, and their life is among
Ps. 25:7 remember not the sins of my *y*
  71:5 O Lord GOD: thou art my trust from my *y*
  71:17 O God, thou hast taught me from my *y*
  103:5 so that thy *y* is renewed like the eagle's
  129:1 many a time have they afflicted me from . . *y*
Prov. 2:17 which forsaketh the guide of her *y*
  5:18 and rejoice with the wife of thy *y*
  7:7 I discerned among the *y*, a young man void of
Eccl. 11:9 rejoice, O young man, in thy *y*
  12:1 remember . . thy Creator in the days of thy *y*
Is. 40:30 even the *y* shall faint and be weary
Jer. 2:2 I remember thee, the kindness of thy *y*
  22:21 this hath been thy manner from thy *y*
Lam. 3:27 for a man that he bear the yoke in his *y*
Mt. 19:20 (Mk. 10:20; Lk. 18:21) kept from my *y* up
Acts 26:4 my manner of life from my *y* . . know all
1 Tim. 4:12 let no man despise thy *y*; but be thou

Z

Zabulon *See* Zebulun the region

Zaccheus Lk. 19:2

Zachariah 2 Kgs. 15:8–11

Zacharias *See also* Zechariah

Lk. 1:5 priest named *Z*, of the course of Abia
1:13 fear not, *Z*: for thy prayer is heard
1:67 his father *Z* was filled with the Holy Ghost

Zadok 2 Sam. 15:24–35; 1 Kgs. 1:8–45

Zalmunna Judg. 8:5

Zarephath (Sarepta)
1 Kgs. 17:9 (Lk. 4:26)

Zeal

2 Kgs. 10:16 come with me. . see my *z* for the LORD
19:31 (Is. 37:32) the *z* of the LORD . . shall do this
Ps. 69:9 (Jn. 2:17) *z* of thine house hath eaten me
119:139 my *z* hath consumed me, because mine
Is. 9:7 of the LORD of hosts will perform this
59:17 clothing, and was clad with *z* as a cloak
63:15 thy glory: where is thy *z* and thy strength
Ezek. 5:13 that I the LORD have spoken it in my *z*
Rom. 10:2 they have a *z* of God, but not according
2 Cor. 7:11 yea, what vehement desire, yea, what *z*
9:2 and your *z* hath provoked very many
Phil. 3:6 concerning *z*, persecuting the church
Col. 4:13 that he hath a great *z* for you, and them

Zealous

Num. 25:13 because he was *z* for his God, and made
Acts 21:20 believe; and they are all *z* of the law
22:3 was *z* toward God, as ye all are this day
1 Cor. 14:12 as ye are *z* of spiritual gifts, seek
Gal. 1:14 more exceedingly *z* of the traditions of
Tit. 2:14 a peculiar people, *z* of good works
Rev. 3:19 and chasten: be *z* therefore, and repent

Zealously

Gal. 4:17 they *z* affect you, but not well

Zebah Judg. 8:5

Zebedee Mt. 4:21 (Mk. 1:20)

Zeboim Deut. 29:23; Hos. 11:8

Zebul Judg. 9:28

Zebulun son of Jacob

Gen. 30:20; Deut. 33:18

Zebulun (Zabulon) the region
Is. 9:1 (Mt. 4:15)

Zechariah (Zacharias) the priest
2 Chr. 24:20; Mt. 23:35 (Lk. 11:51)

Zechariah the prophet
Ezra 5:1; Zech. 1:1 (7:1)

Zedekiah the king 2 Kgs. 24:17–25:7
(2 Chr. 36:11–13; Jer. 52:1–11)

Jer. 21:3 then said Jeremiah. . Thus shall ye say to *Z*
24:8 so will I give *Z* the king of Judah, and his
27:12 also to *Z* . . according to all these words
32:3 *Z* king of Judah had shut him up, saying
34:2 go and speak to *Z* king of Judah, and tell

Jer. 37:3 *Z* the king sent. . to the prophet Jeremiah
38:14 then *Z* the king sent, and took Jeremiah

Zedekiah the prophet
1 Kgs. 22:11 (2 Chr. 18:10)

Zeeb Judg. 7:25; 8:3; Ps. 83:11

Zelophehad Num. 26:33; 36:2

Zelotes *See* Simon Zelotes

Zenas Tit. 3:13

Zephaniah the priest
2 Kgs. 25:18 (Jer. 52:24); Jer. 29:29

Zephaniah the prophet Zeph. 1:1

Zerah 2 Chr. 14:9

Zered Deut. 2:13

Zeresh Esth. 5:10; 6:13

Zerubbabel

Ezra 2:2 (Neh. 7:7) came with *Z*: Jeshua, Nehemiah
3:8 began *Z* . . to set forward the work of the house
Neh. 12:47 Israel in the days of *Z* . . gave the portions
Hag. 1:1 word of the Lord . . unto *Z* . . governor
2:2 speak now to *Z* the son of Shealtiel
2:23 in that day . . will I take thee, O *Z*, my servant
Zech. 4:6 this is the word of the LORD unto *Z*

Ziba 2 Sam. 9:2; 16:1

Zidon *See* Sidon

Ziklag 1 Sam. 27:6; 30:1; 1 Chr. 12:1

Zilpah Gen. 29:24–30:12

Zimri 1 Kgs. 16:15–20

Zin Num. 13:21; 27:14

Zion (Sion) *See also* Jerusalem

2 Sam. 5:7 (1 Chr. 11:5) David took. . stronghold of *Z*
Ps. 2:6 have I set my King upon my holy hill of *Z*
9:11 praises to the LORD, which dwelleth in *Z*
14:7 (53:6) salvation of Israel. . come out of *Z*!
48:2 joy of the whole earth, is mount *Z*
48:12 walk about *Z*, and go round about her: tell
50:2 out of *Z*, the perfection of beauty, God hath
69:35 God will save *Z*, and will build the cities
76:2 his tabernacle, and his dwelling place in *Z*
87:2 LORD loveth the gates of *Z* more than all
97:8 *Z* heard, and was glad; and the daughters of
102:16 the LORD shall build up *Z*, he shall appear
125:1 that trust in the LORD shall be as mount *Z*
132:13 the LORD hath chosen *Z*; he hath desired it
137:1 sat down. . we wept, when we remembered *Z*
Is. 1:27 *Z* shall be redeemed with judgment
2:3 (Mic. 4:2) for out of *Z* shall go forth the law
14:32 LORD hath founded *Z*, and the poor of his
24:23 the LORD of hosts shall reign in mount *Z*
28:16 (Rom. 9:33; 1 Pet. 2:6) behold, I lay in *Z*
33:20 look upon *Z*, the city of our solemnities
40:9 O *Z*, that bringest good tidings, get thee
46:13 and I will place salvation in *Z* for Israel
51:3 the LORD shall comfort *Z*: he will comfort all
52:1 awake, awake, put on thy strength, O *Z*
59:20 and the Redeemer shall come to *Z*

Is. 60:14 the city of the LORD, The *Z* of the Holy One
   64:10 *Z* is a wilderness, Jerusalem a desolation
   66:8 as soon as *Z* travailed, she brought forth
Jer. 8:19 is not the LORD in *Z*? is not her king in
   9:19 voice of wailing is heard out of *Z*, How are
   26:18 (Mic. 3:12) *Z* shall be plowed like a field
   30:17 saying, This is *Z*, whom no man seeketh
   31:6 arise ye . . let us go up to *Z* unto the LORD
Lam. 1:17 *Z* spreadeth forth her hands, and there is
Joel 2:32 for in mount *Z* and in Jerusalem shall be
Obad. 17 but upon mount *Z* shall be deliverance

Mic. 3:10 they build up *Z* with blood, and Jerusalem
Zech. 8:2 I was jealous for *Z* with great jealousy
Rom. 11:26 there shall come out of *S* the Deliverer
Heb. 12:22 but ye are come unto mount *S*, and unto
Rev. 14:1 lo, a Lamb stood on the mount *S*, and with

Ziph 1 Sam. 23:14; 26:2

Zipporah Ex. 2:21; 4:25; 18:2

Zoar Gen. 19:22–30

Zophar Job 2:11; 11:1; 20:1; 42:9